The Thomas Guide®

Los Angeles County

street guide

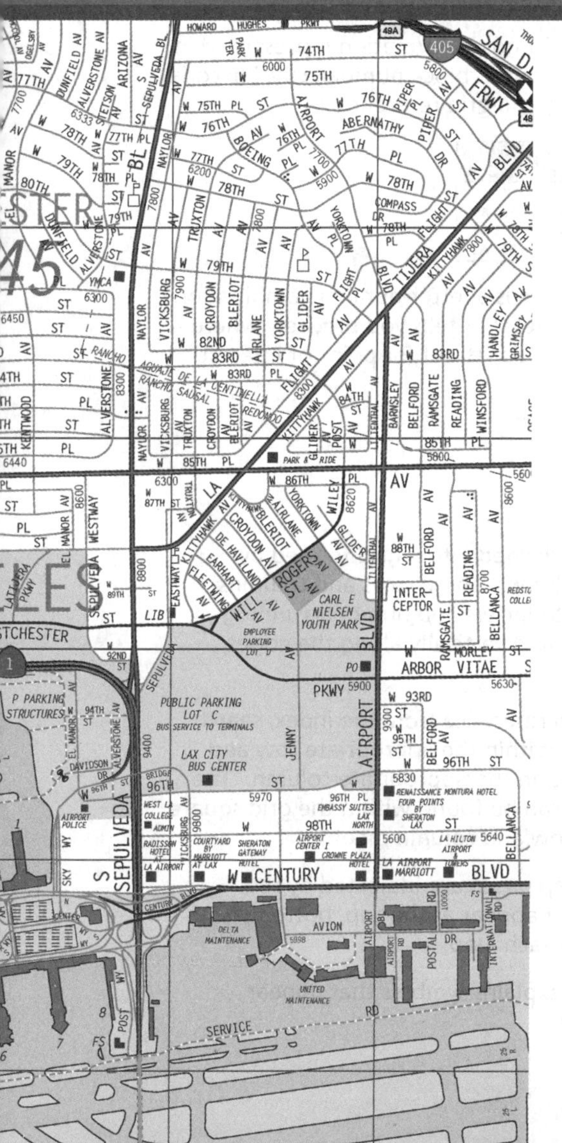

Contents

Introduction

Legend	Inside front cover
Using Your Street Guide	B
PageFinder™ Map	D
Transit Information	M

Maps

Downtown Map	C
Freeway Access Map	H
Airport Map	L
Street Guide Detail Maps	480-5923

Lists and Indexes

Cities & Communities Index	5924
List of Abbreviations	5926
Street Index and Points of Interest Index	5927
Comment Card	Last page

RAND McNALLY
Rand McNally Consumer Affairs
P.O. Box 7600
Chicago, IL 60680-9915
randmcnally.com
For comments or suggestions, please call
(800) 777-MAPS (-6277)
or email us at:
consumeraffairs@randmcnally.com

Using Your Street Guide

PageFinder™ Map

The PageFinder™ Map

> Turn to the PageFinder™ Map. Each of the small squares outlined on this map represents a different map page in the Street Guide.

> Locate the specific part of the Street Guide coverage area that you're interested in.

> Note the appropriate map page number.

> Turn to that map page.

missing pages?

Please note that map pages in this book are numbered according to the PageFinder™ Map. For this reason, your book may look as though it is missing pages. For example, one page might contain map number 15 while the following page contains map number 25.

Use the PageFinder™ Map for fast and easy navigation through your Street Guide.

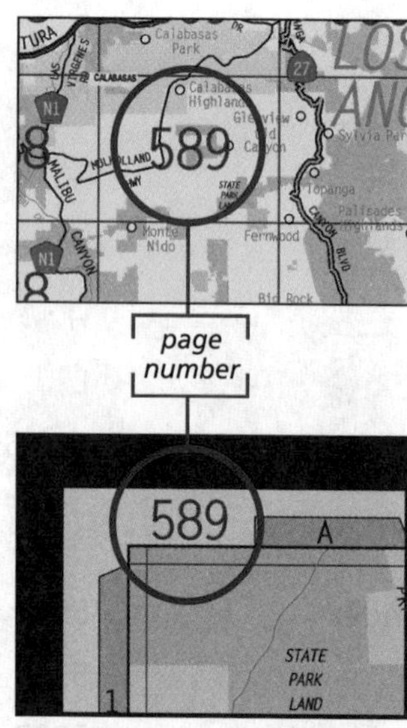

The Index

> The Street Guide includes separate indexes for streets, schools, parks, shopping centers, golf courses, and other points of interest.

> In the street listings, information is presented in the following order: block number, city, ZIP code, page number, and grid reference

STREET Block	City	ZIP	Pg-Grid
BROADWAY DR			
4400	SCH	60646	533-B6
6200	PLA	61644	532-D2
7800	WCH	60656	532-A3

> A grid reference is a letter-number combination (B6 for example) that tells you precisely where to find a particular street (or point of interest) on a map.

The Maps

> Each map is divided into a grid formed by rows and columns. These rows and columns correspond to letters and numbers running horizontally and vertically along the edges of each map.

> To use a grid reference from the index, search horizontally within the appropriate row and vertically within the appropriate column. The destination can be found within the grid square where the row and column meet.

> Adjacent map pages are indicated by red numbers that appear at the top, bottom, and sides of each map.

> The legend explains symbols that appear on the maps.

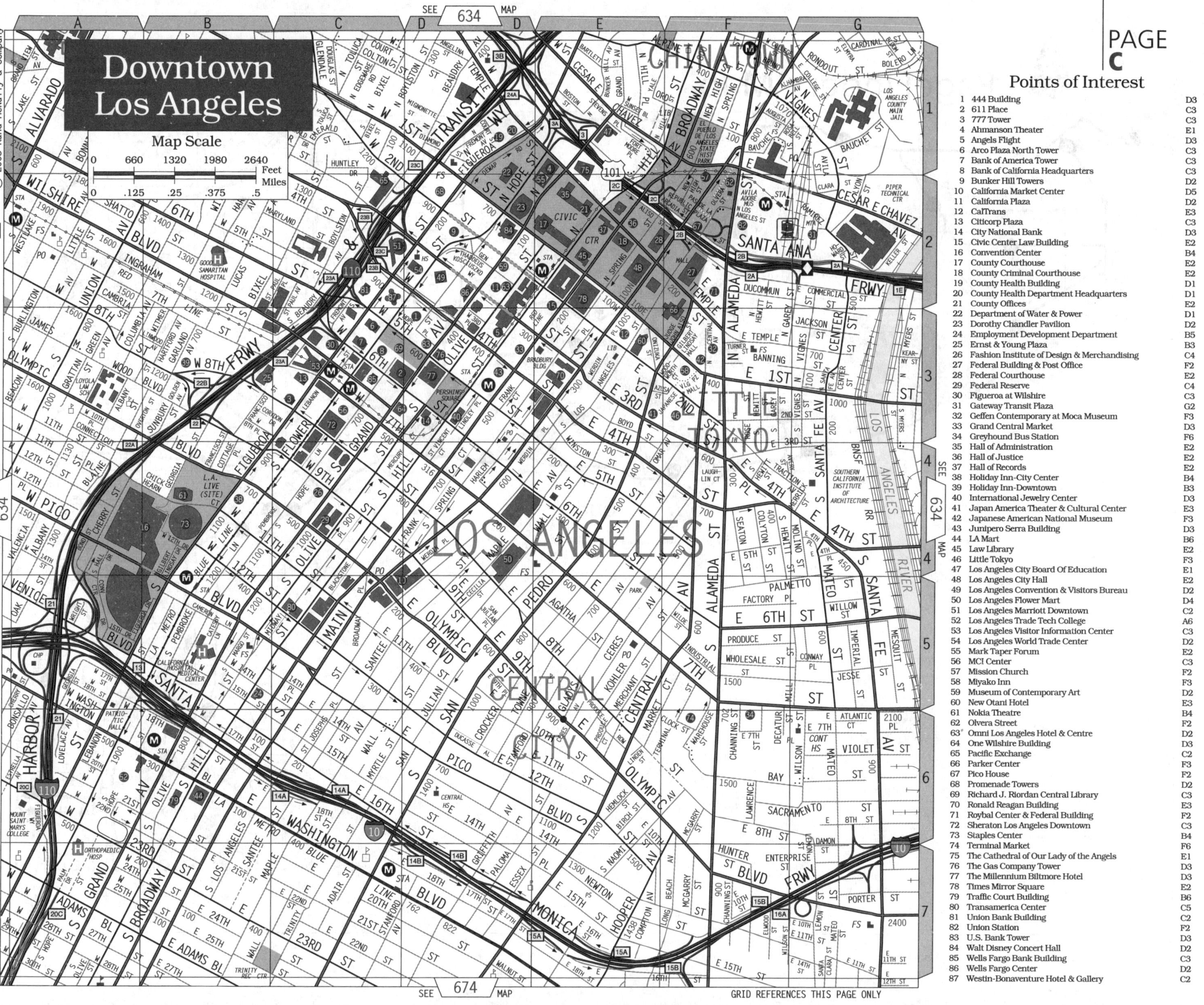

Downtown Los Angeles
Map Scale
0 660 1320 1980 2640 Feet
0 .125 .25 .375 .5 Miles
© 2008 Rand McNally & Company
SEE 634 MAP
SEE 674 MAP
GRID REFERENCES THIS PAGE ONLY
CHINATOWN
CIVIC CTR
LITTLE TOKYO
LOS ANGELES
CENTRAL CITY
LOS ANGELES RIVER
PAGE C
LOS ANGELES CO.
Points of Interest
1 444 Building D3
2 611 Place C3
3 777 Tower C3
4 Ahmanson Theater E1
5 Angels Flight D3
6 Arco Plaza North Tower C3
7 Bank of America Tower C3
8 Bank of California Headquarters C3
9 Bunker Hill Towers D2
10 California Market Center D5
11 California Plaza D2
12 CalTrans E3
13 Citicorp Plaza C3
14 City National Bank D3
15 Civic Center Law Building E2
16 Convention Center B4
17 County Courthouse E2
18 County Criminal Courthouse E2
19 County Health Building D1
20 County Health Department Headquarters D1
21 County Offices E2
22 Department of Water & Power D1
23 Dorothy Chandler Pavilion D2
24 Employment Development Department B5
25 Ernst & Young Plaza B3
26 Fashion Institute of Design & Merchandising C4
27 Federal Building & Post Office F2
28 Federal Courthouse E2
29 Federal Reserve C4
30 Figueroa at Wilshire C3
31 Gateway Transit Plaza G2
32 Geffen Contemporary at Moca Museum F3
33 Grand Central Market D3
34 Greyhound Bus Station F6
35 Hall of Administration E2
36 Hall of Justice E2
37 Hall of Records E2
38 Holiday Inn-City Center B4
39 Holiday Inn-Downtown B3
40 International Jewelry Center D3
41 Japan America Theater & Cultural Center E3
42 Japanese American National Museum F3
43 Junipero Serra Building D3
44 LA Mart B6
45 Law Library E2
46 Little Tokyo F3
47 Los Angeles City Board Of Education E1
48 Los Angeles City Hall E2
49 Los Angeles Convention & Visitors Bureau D2
50 Los Angeles Flower Mart D4
51 Los Angeles Marriott Downtown C2
52 Los Angeles Trade Tech College A6
53 Los Angeles Visitor Information Center C3
54 Los Angeles World Trade Center D2
55 Mark Taper Forum E2
56 MCI Center C3
57 Mission Church F2
58 Miyako Inn F3
59 Museum of Contemporary Art D2
60 New Otani Hotel E3
61 Nokia Theatre B4
62 Olvera Street F2
63 Omni Los Angeles Hotel & Centre D2
64 One Wilshire Building D3
65 Pacific Exchange C2
66 Parker Center F3
67 Pico House F2
68 Promenade Towers D2
69 Richard J. Riordan Central Library C3
70 Ronald Reagan Building E3
71 Roybal Center & Federal Building F2
72 Sheraton Los Angeles Downtown C3
73 Staples Center B4
74 Terminal Market F6
75 The Cathedral of Our Lady of the Angels E1
76 The Gas Company Tower D3
77 The Millennium Biltmore Hotel D3
78 Times Mirror Square E2
79 Traffic Court Building B6
80 Transamerica Center C5
81 Union Bank Building C2
82 Union Station F2
83 U.S. Bank Tower D3
84 Walt Disney Concert Hall D2
85 Wells Fargo Bank Building C3
86 Wells Fargo Center D2
87 Westin-Bonaventure Hotel & Gallery C2

PageFinder™ Map

PageFinder™ Map
U.S. Patent No. 5,419,586
Canadian Patent No. 2,116,425
Patente Mexicana No. 188186

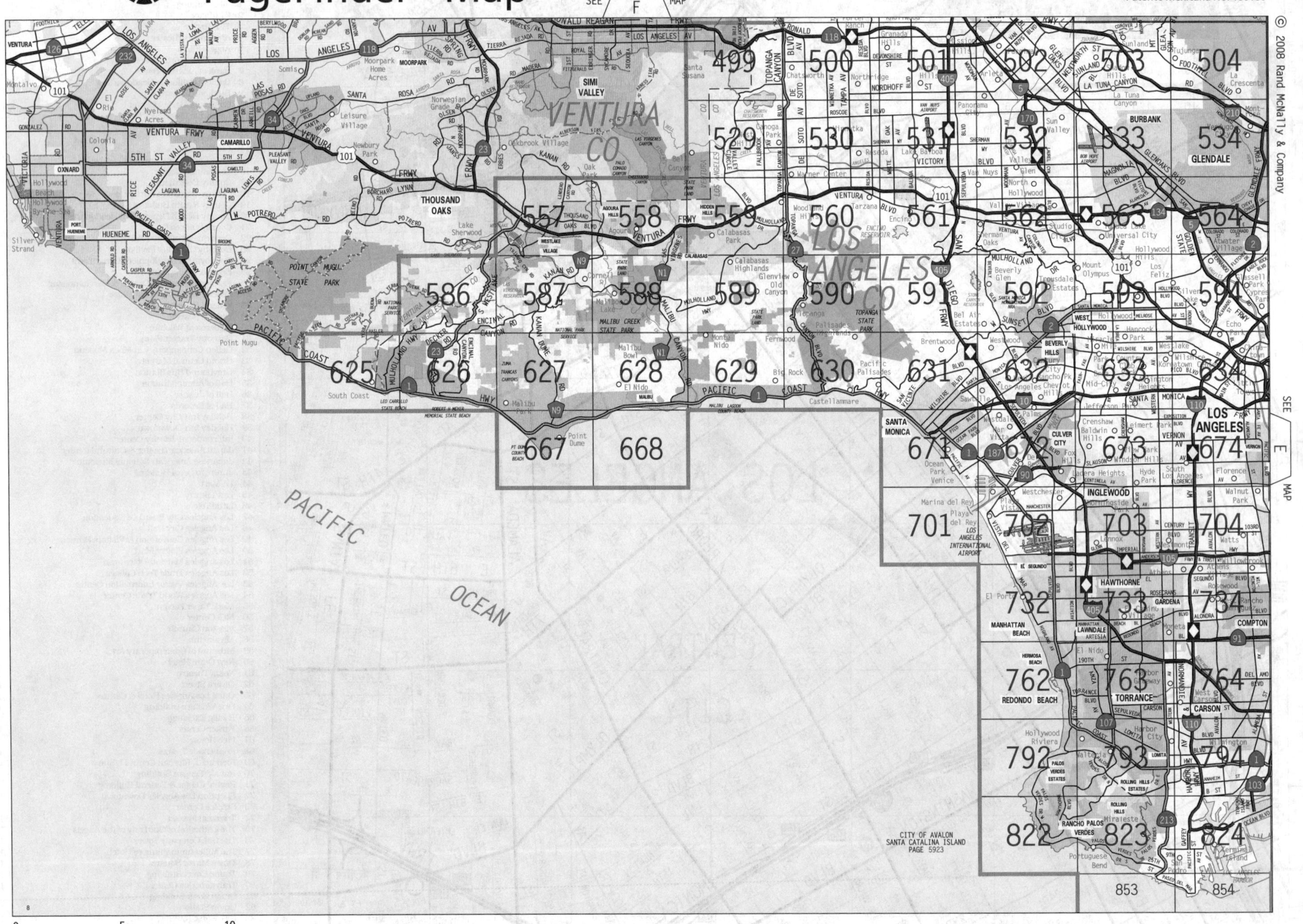

0 5 10 miles 1 in. = 6 mi.

PageFinder™ Map
U.S. Patent No. 5,419,586
Canadian Patent No. 2,116,425
Patente Mexicana No. 188186

SEE G MAP

SEE D MAP

0 5 10 miles 1 in. = 6 mi.

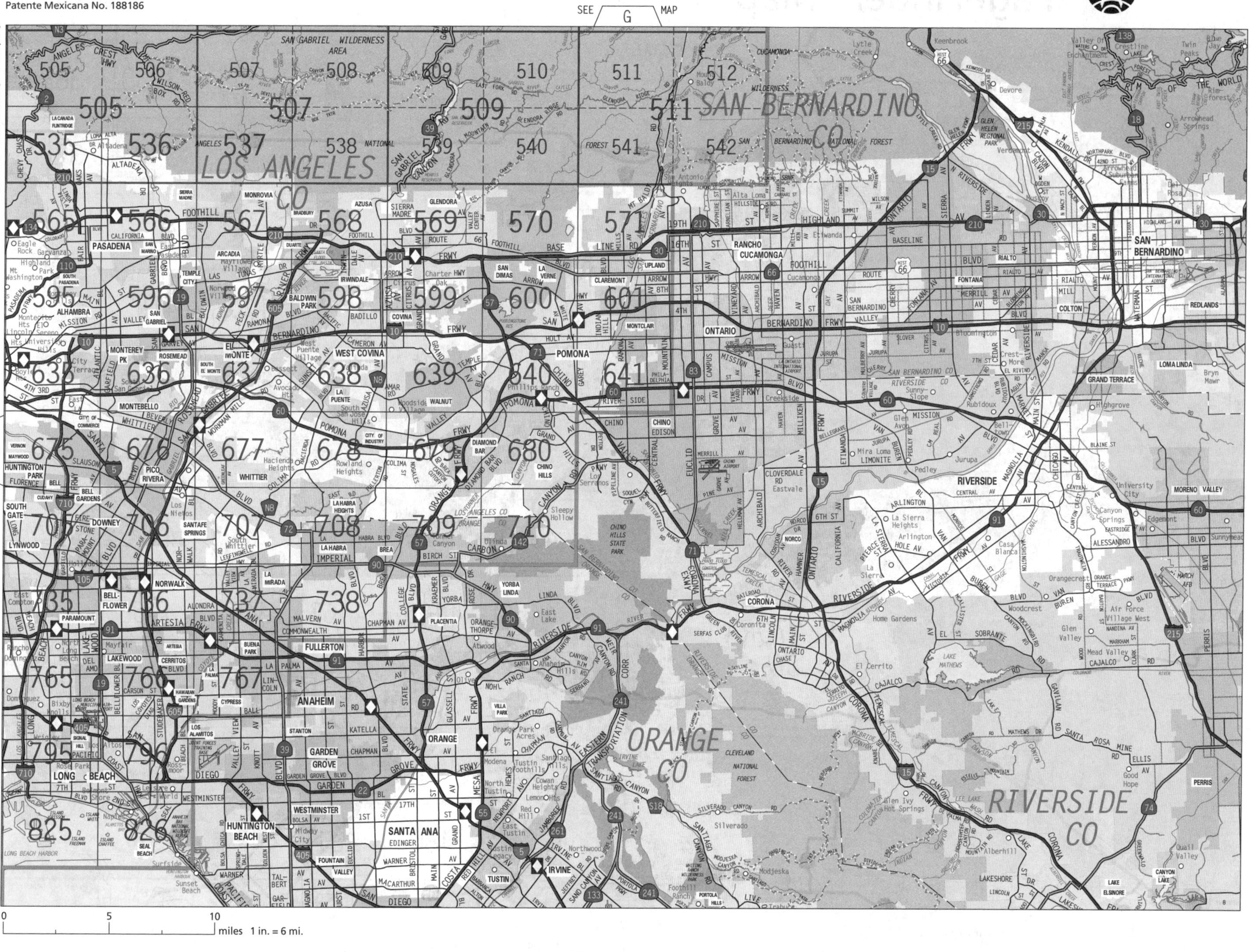

PageFinder™ Map

PageFinder™ Map
U.S. Patent No. 5,419,586
Canadian Patent No. 2,116,425
Patente Mexicana No. 188186

KERN CO

LOS ANGELES CO

VENTURA CO

3833 3834
3923 3924
4013 4014
4101 4102 4103 4104
4192 4193 4194
4279 4280 4281 4282 4283 4284
4279 4281 4283
4369 4370 4371 4372 4373 4374
4459 4460 4461 4462 4463 4464
4464
4549 4550 4551 4552 4553 4554
4640 4641 4642 4643 4644
4643
480 481 482 4723 4724

SEE G MAP

SEE D MAP

0 5 10 miles 1 in. = 6 mi.

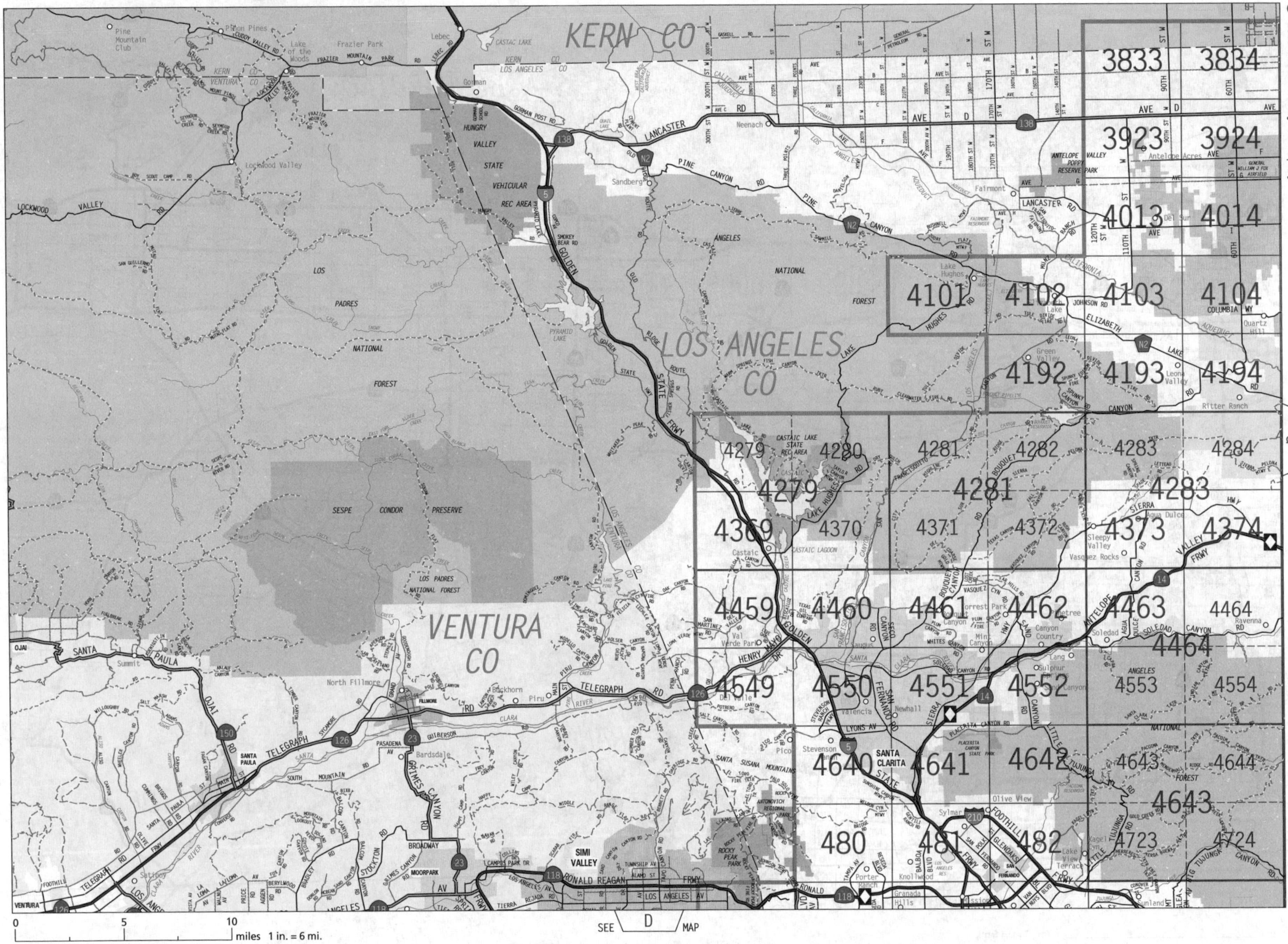

PageFinder™ Map
U.S. Patent No. 5,419,586
Canadian Patent No. 2,116,425
Patente Mexicana No. 188186

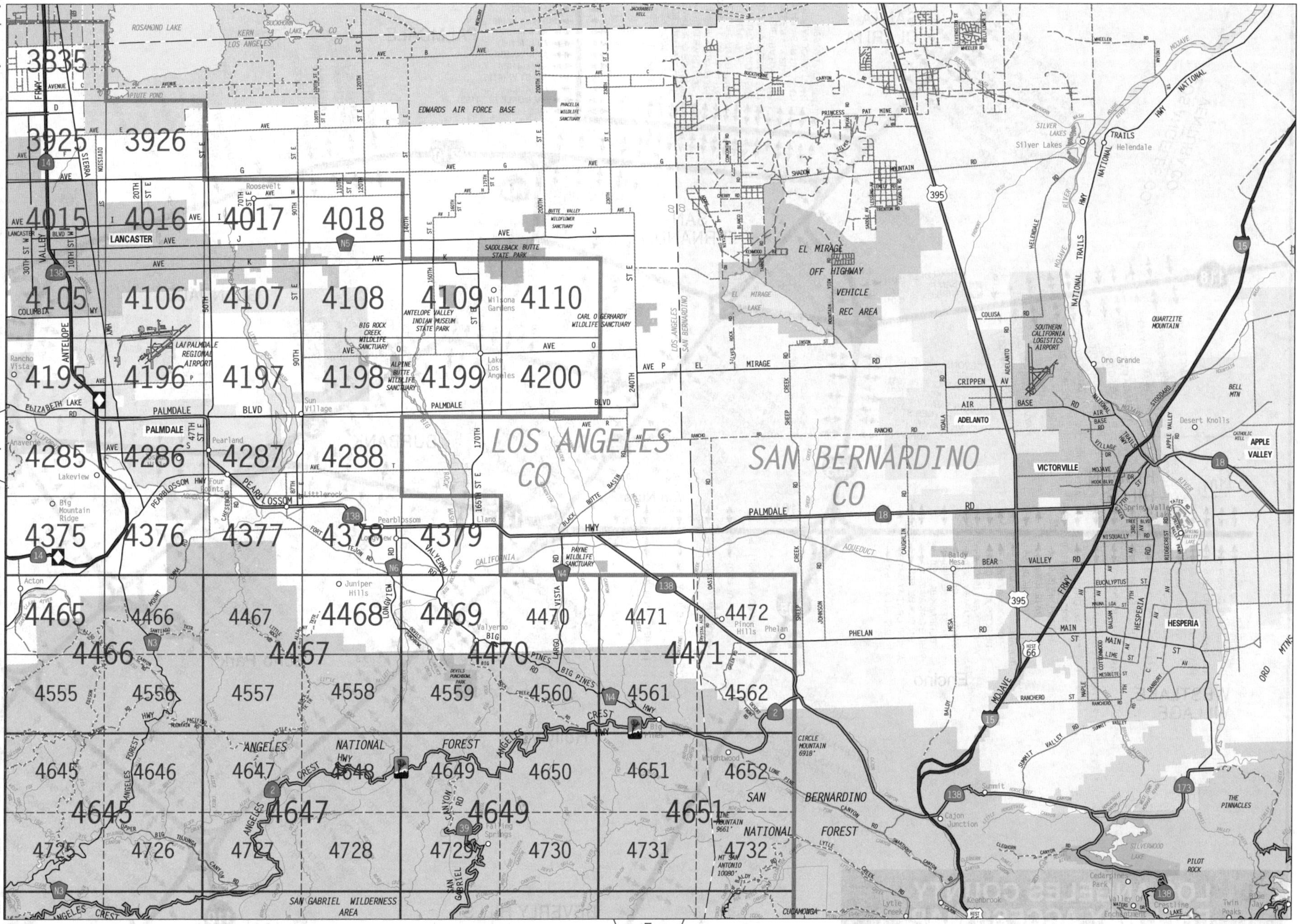

3835

3925 3926

4015 4016 4017 4018

4105 4106 4107 4108 4109 4110

4195 4196 4197 4198 4199 4200

4285 4286 4287 4288

4375 4376 4377 4378 4379

4465 4466 4467 4468 4469 4470 4471 4472

4466 4467 4470 4471

4555 4556 4557 4558 4559 4560 4561 4562

4645 4646 4647 4648 4649 4650 4651 4652

4645 4647 4649 4651

4725 4726 4727 4728 4729 4730 4731 4732

ROSAMOND LAKE
KERN CO
LOS ANGELES CO
EDWARDS AIR FORCE BASE
LANCASTER
PALMDALE
LA/PALMDALE REGIONAL AIRPORT
SADDLEBACK BUTTE STATE PARK
ANTELOPE VALLEY INDIAN MUSEUM STATE PARK
BIG ROCK CREEK WILDLIFE SANCTUARY
ALPINE BUTTE WILDLIFE SANCTUARY
CARL O GERHARDY WILDLIFE SANCTUARY
Wilsona Gardens
Lake Los Angeles
Sun Village
Pearland
Four Points
Littlerock
Pearblossom
Llano
Lakeview
Big Mountain Ridge
Acton
Juniper Hills
Valyermo
Rancho Vista
Anaverde
PAYNE WILDLIFE SANCTUARY
LOS ANGELES CO
SAN BERNARDINO CO
EL MIRAGE OFF HIGHWAY VEHICLE REC AREA
EL MIRAGE LAKE
ADELANTO
VICTORVILLE
APPLE VALLEY
HESPERIA
Silver Lakes
Helendale
Oro Grande
QUARTZITE MOUNTAIN
BELL MTN
Desert Knolls
SOUTHERN CALIFORNIA LOGISTICS AIRPORT
Baldy Mesa
Spring Valley Lake
Pinon Hills
Phelan
Wrightwood
Big Pines
ANGELES NATIONAL FOREST
SAN BERNARDINO NATIONAL FOREST
CIRCLE MOUNTAIN 6918'
PINE MOUNTAIN 9661'
MT SAN ANTONIO 10080'
Cajon Junction
Summit
SILVERWOOD LAKE
Cedarpines Park
PILOT ROCK
THE PINNACLES
Keenbrook
Lytle Creek
Crestline
Twin Peaks
Valyermo Falling Springs
SAN GABRIEL WILDERNESS AREA
ORD MTNS

SEE F MAP
SEE E MAP

0 5 10 miles 1 in. = 6 mi.

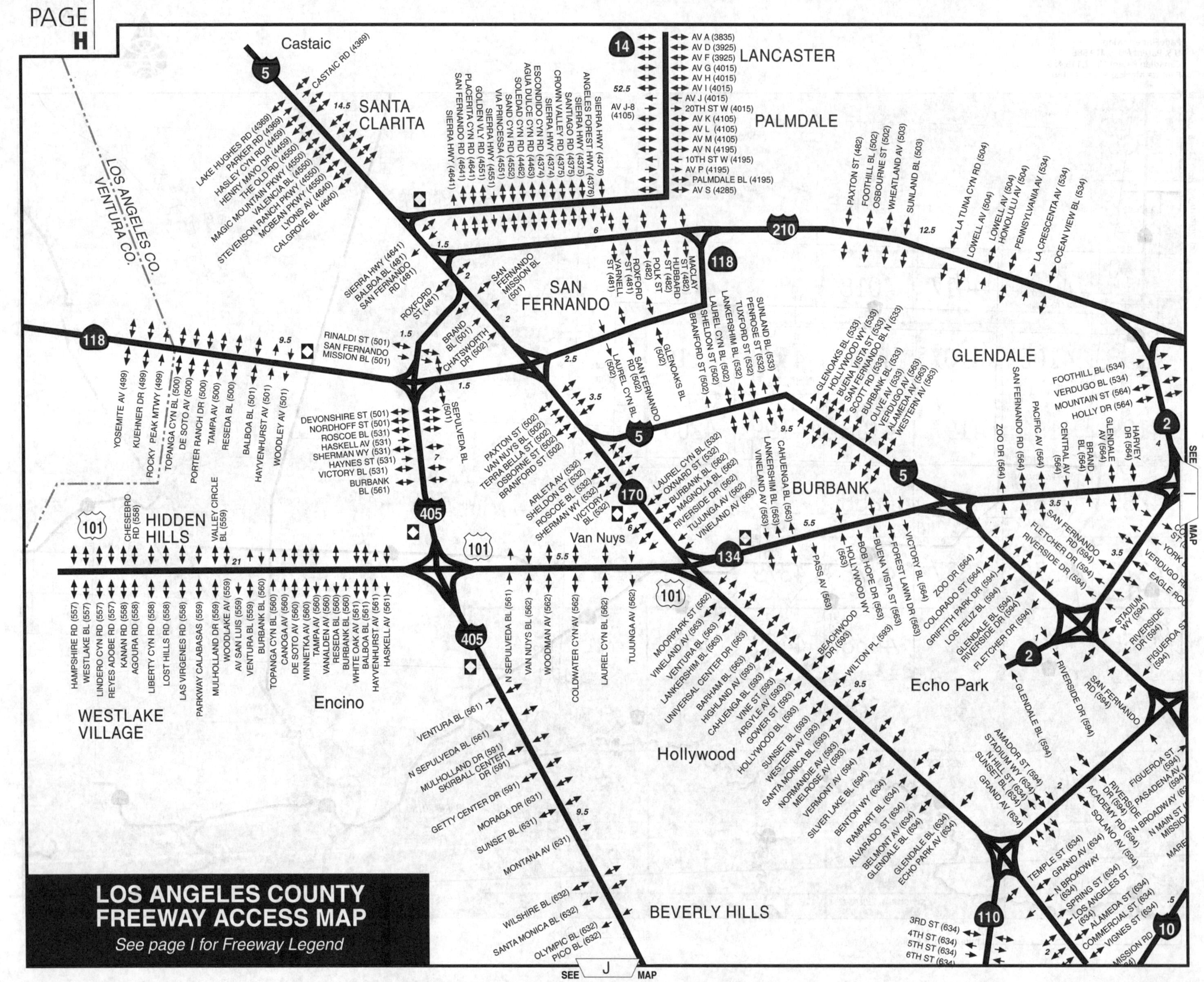
LOS ANGELES COUNTY
FREEWAY ACCESS MAP
See page I for Freeway Legend
Castaic
CASTAIC RD (4369)
SANTA
CLARITA
LANCASTER
PALMDALE
LOS ANGELES CO.
VENTURA CO.
AV A (3835)
AV D (3925)
AV F (3925)
AV G (4015)
AV H (4015)
AV I (4015)
AV J (4015)
AV J-8 (4105)
20TH ST W (4015)
AV K (4105)
AV L (4105)
AV M (4105)
AV N (4195)
10TH ST W (4195)
AV P (4195)
PALMDALE BL (4195)
AV S (4285)
SIERRA HWY (4376)
ANGELES FOREST HWY (4376)
SIERRA HWY (4375)
SANTIAGO RD (4375)
CROWN VALLEY RD (4374)
SIERRA HWY (4374)
ESCONDIDO CYN RD (4463)
AGUA DULCE CYN RD (4463)
SOLEDAD CYN RD (4462)
SAND CYN RD (4552)
VIA PRINCESSA (4551)
SIERRA HWY (4551)
GOLDEN VLY RD (4551)
PLACERITA CYN RD (4641)
SAN FERNANDO RD (4641)
SIERRA HWY (4641)
LAKE HUGHES RD (4369)
PARKER RD (4369)
HASLEY CYN RD (4459)
HENRY MAYO DR (4459)
THE OLD RD (4550)
MAGIC MOUNTAIN PKWY (4550)
VALENCIA BL (4550)
STEVENSON RANCH PKWY (4550)
MCBEAN PKWY (4550)
LYONS AV (4640)
CALGROVE BL (4640)
SAN FERNANDO
GLENDALE
BURBANK
HIDDEN HILLS
Van Nuys
Encino
WESTLAKE VILLAGE
Hollywood
Echo Park
BEVERLY HILLS
PAXTON ST (482)
FOOTHILL BL (502)
OSBOURNE ST (502)
WHEATLAND AV (503)
SUNLAND BL (503)
LA TUNA CYN RD (504)
LOWELL AV (504)
LOWELL AV (504)
HONOLULU AV (504)
PENNSYLVANIA AV (534)
LA CRESCENTA AV (534)
OCEAN VIEW BL (534)
SIERRA HWY (4641)
BALBOA BL (481)
SAN FERNANDO RD (481)
ROXFORD ST (481)
SAN FERNANDO MISSION BL (501)
MACLAY ST (482)
HUBBARD ST (482)
POLK ST (482)
ROXFORD ST (481)
YARNELL ST (481)
RINALDI ST (501)
SAN FERNANDO MISSION BL (501)
BRAND BL (501)
CHATSWORTH DR (502)
SUNLAND BL (533)
PENROSE ST (532)
TUXFORD ST (532)
LANKERSHIM BL (532)
LAUREL CYN BL (502)
SHELDON ST (502)
BRANFORD ST (502)
GLENOAKS BL
SAN FERNANDO RD (502)
LAUREL CYN BL (502)
GLENOAKS BL (502)
YOSEMITE AV (499)
KUEHNER DR (499)
ROCKY PEAK MTWY (499)
TOPANGA CYN BL (500)
DE SOTO AV (500)
PORTER RANCH DR (500)
TAMPA AV (500)
RESEDA BL (500)
BALBOA BL (501)
HAYVENHURST AV (501)
WOODLEY AV (501)
DEVONSHIRE ST (501)
NORDHOFF ST (501)
ROSCOE BL (531)
HASKELL AV (531)
SHERMAN WY (531)
HAYNES ST (531)
VICTORY BL (531)
BURBANK BL (561)
SEPULVEDA BL (501)
PAXTON ST (502)
VAN NUYS BL (502)
TERRA BELLA ST (502)
OSBORNE ST (502)
BRANFORD ST (502)
ARLETA AV (532)
SHELDON ST (532)
ROSCOE BL (532)
SHERMAN WY (532)
VICTORY BL (532)
GLENOAKS BL (533)
HOLLYWOOD WY (533)
BUENA VISTA ST (533)
SAN FERNANDO BL N (533)
SCOTT RD (533)
BURBANK BL (533)
OLIVE AV (533)
VERDUGO AV (563)
ALAMEDA AV (563)
WESTERN AV (563)
FOOTHILL BL (534)
VERDUGO BL (534)
MOUNTAIN ST (564)
HOLLY DR (564)
SAN FERNANDO RD (564)
ZOO DR (564)
PACIFIC AV (564)
CENTRAL AV (564)
BRAND BL (564)
GLENDALE AV (564)
HARVEY DR (564)
LAUREL CYN BL (532)
OXNARD ST (532)
BURBANK BL (562)
MAGNOLIA BL (562)
RIVERSIDE DR (562)
TUJUNGA AV (562)
VINELAND AV (563)
LANKERSHIM BL (563)
VINELAND AV (563)
CAHUENGA BL (563)
CHESEBRO RD (558)
VALLEY CIRCLE BL (559)
HAMPSHIRE RD (557)
WESTLAKE BL (557)
LINDERO CYN RD (557)
REYES ADOBE RD (557)
KANAN RD (558)
AGOURA RD (558)
LIBERTY CYN RD (558)
LOST HILLS RD (558)
LAS VIRGENES RD (558)
PARKWAY CALABASAS (559)
MULHOLLAND DR (559)
WOODLAKE AV (559)
AV SAN LUIS (559)
VENTURA BL (559)
BURBANK BL (560)
TOPANGA CYN BL (560)
CANOGA AV (560)
DE SOTO AV (560)
WINNETKA AV (560)
TAMPA AV (560)
VANALDEN AV (560)
RESEDA BL (560)
BURBANK BL (560)
WHITE OAK AV (561)
BALBOA BL (561)
HAYVENHURST AV (561)
HASKELL AV (561)
N SEPULVEDA BL (561)
VAN NUYS BL (562)
WOODMAN AV (562)
COLDWATER CYN AV (562)
LAUREL CYN BL (562)
TUJUNGA AV (562)
PASS AV (563)
HOLLYWOOD WY (563)
BOB HOPE DR (563)
BUENA VISTA ST (563)
FOREST LAWN DR (563)
VICTORY BL (564)
ZOO DR (564)
COLORADO ST (564)
GRIFFITH PARK DR (594)
LOS FELIZ BL (594)
GLENDALE BL (594)
RIVERSIDE DR (594)
FLETCHER DR (594)
SAN FERNANDO RD (594)
FLETCHER DR (594)
RIVERSIDE DR (594)
STADIUM WY (594)
RIVERSIDE DR (594)
FIGUEROA ST (594)
YORK BL
VERDUGO RD
EAGLE ROCK
MOORPARK ST (562)
VINELAND AV (563)
VENTURA BL (563)
LANKERSHIM BL (563)
UNIVERSAL CENTER DR (563)
BARHAM BL (563)
HIGHLAND AV (593)
CAHUENGA BL (593)
VINE ST (593)
ARGYLE AV (593)
GOWER ST (593)
HOLLYWOOD BL (593)
SUNSET BL (593)
WESTERN AV (593)
SANTA MONICA BL (593)
NORMANDIE AV (593)
MELROSE AV (593)
VERMONT AV (594)
SILVER LAKE BL (594)
BEACHWOOD DR (593)
WILTON PL (593)
GLENDALE BL (594)
RIVERSIDE DR (594)
SAN FERNANDO RD (594)
BENTON WY (634)
RAMPART BL (634)
ALVARADO ST (634)
BELMONT AV (634)
GLENDALE BL (634)
GLENDALE BL (634)
ECHO PARK AV (634)
AMADOR ST (594)
STADIUM WY (634)
N HILL ST (634)
SUNSET BL (634)
GRAND AV (634)
RIVERSIDE DR (594)
ACADEMY RD (594)
SOLANO AV (594)
FIGUEROA ST (594)
PASADENA AV (594)
N BROADWAY (634)
N MAIN ST
MISSION
TEMPLE ST (634)
GRAND AV (634)
N BROADWAY (634)
SPRING ST (634)
LOS ANGELES ST (634)
ALAMEDA ST (634)
COMMERCIAL ST (634)
VIGNES ST (634)
MISSION RD
3RD ST (634)
4TH ST (634)
5TH ST (634)
6TH ST (634)
VENTURA BL (561)
N SEPULVEDA BL (561)
MULHOLLAND DR (591)
SKIRBALL CENTER DR (591)
GETTY CENTER DR (591)
MORAGA DR (631)
SUNSET BL (631)
MONTANA AV (631)
WILSHIRE BL (632)
SANTA MONICA BL (632)
OLYMPIC BL (632)
PICO BL (632)
SEE J MAP
SEE I MAP
5
14
210
118
405
101
170
134
2
110
10

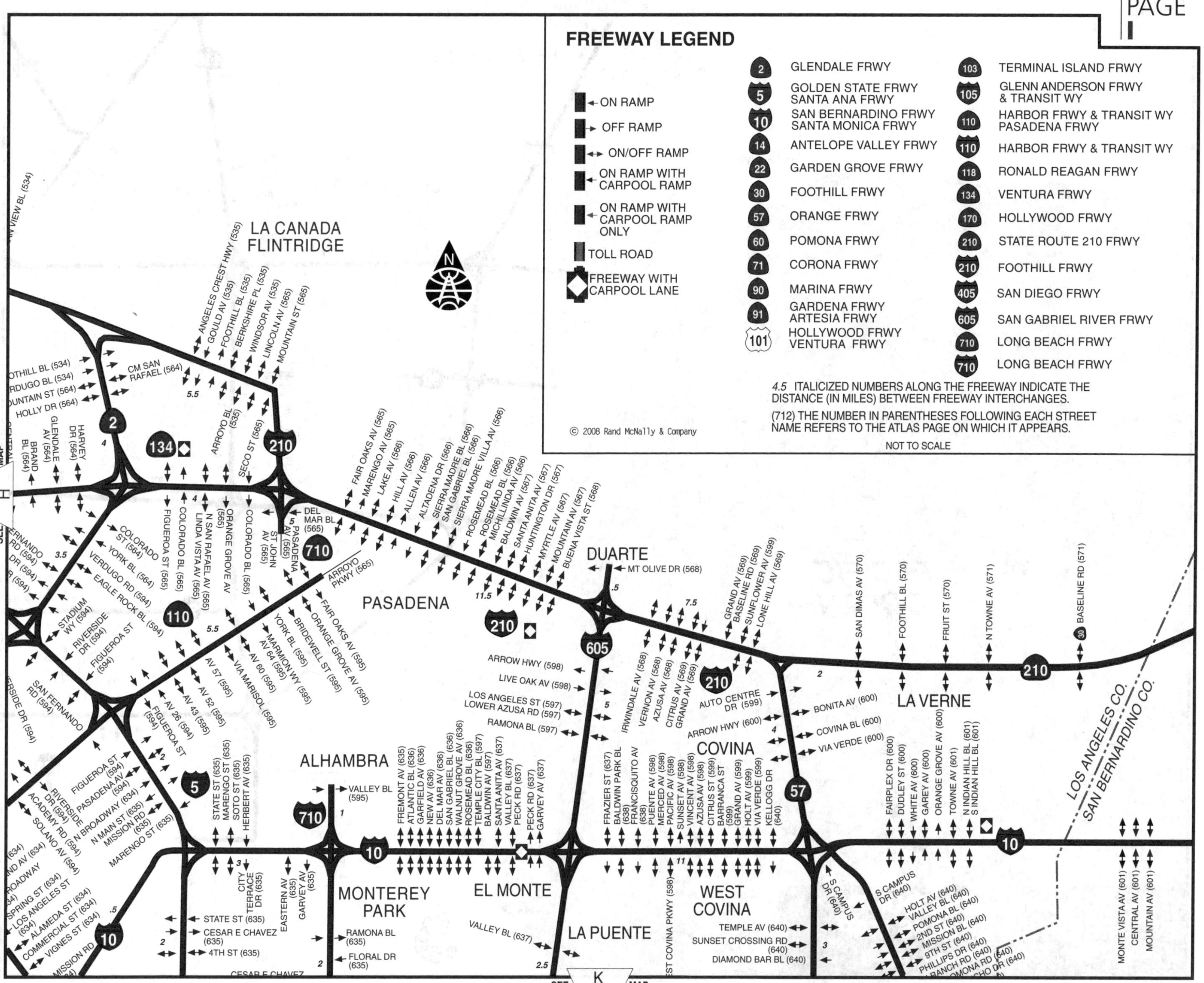
FREEWAY LEGEND
ON RAMP
OFF RAMP
ON/OFF RAMP
ON RAMP WITH CARPOOL RAMP
ON RAMP WITH CARPOOL RAMP ONLY
TOLL ROAD
FREEWAY WITH CARPOOL LANE
2 GLENDALE FRWY
5 GOLDEN STATE FRWY SANTA ANA FRWY
10 SAN BERNARDINO FRWY SANTA MONICA FRWY
14 ANTELOPE VALLEY FRWY
22 GARDEN GROVE FRWY
30 FOOTHILL FRWY
57 ORANGE FRWY
60 POMONA FRWY
71 CORONA FRWY
90 MARINA FRWY
91 GARDENA FRWY ARTESIA FRWY
101 HOLLYWOOD FRWY VENTURA FRWY
103 TERMINAL ISLAND FRWY
105 GLENN ANDERSON FRWY & TRANSIT WY
110 HARBOR FRWY & TRANSIT WY PASADENA FRWY
110 HARBOR FRWY & TRANSIT WY
118 RONALD REAGAN FRWY
134 VENTURA FRWY
170 HOLLYWOOD FRWY
210 STATE ROUTE 210 FRWY
210 FOOTHILL FRWY
405 SAN DIEGO FRWY
605 SAN GABRIEL RIVER FRWY
710 LONG BEACH FRWY
710 LONG BEACH FRWY
4.5 ITALICIZED NUMBERS ALONG THE FREEWAY INDICATE THE DISTANCE (IN MILES) BETWEEN FREEWAY INTERCHANGES.
(712) THE NUMBER IN PARENTHESES FOLLOWING EACH STREET NAME REFERS TO THE ATLAS PAGE ON WHICH IT APPEARS.
NOT TO SCALE
© 2008 Rand McNally & Company
N
LA CANADA FLINTRIDGE
PASADENA
DUARTE
LA VERNE
COVINA
ALHAMBRA
MONTEREY PARK
EL MONTE
WEST COVINA
LA PUENTE
LOS ANGELES CO.
SAN BERNARDINO CO.
SEE H MAP
SEE K MAP
ANGELES CREST HWY (535)
GOULD AV (535)
FOOTHILL BL (535)
BERKSHIRE PL (535)
WINDSOR AV (565)
LINCOLN AV (565)
MOUNTAIN ST (565)
CM SAN RAFAEL (564)
HOLLY DR (564)
ARROYO BL (535)
SECO ST (565)
BRAND BL (564)
GLENDALE AV (564)
HARVEY DR (564)
FIGUEROA ST (565)
COLORADO BL (565)
N SAN RAFAEL AV (565)
LINDA VISTA AV (565)
ORANGE GROVE AV
COLORADO BL (565)
ST JOHN AV (565)
PASADENA AV (565)
DEL MAR BL (565)
ARROYO PKWY (565)
COLORADO ST (564)
YORK BL (564)
VERDUGO RD (594)
EAGLE ROCK BL (594)
STADIUM WY (594)
RIVERSIDE DR (594)
FIGUEROA ST (594)
SAN FERNANDO RD (594)
FAIR OAKS AV (565)
MARENGO AV (565)
LAKE AV (566)
HILL AV (566)
ALLEN AV (566)
ALTADENA DR (566)
SIERRA MADRE BL (566)
SAN GABRIEL BL (566)
SIERRA MADRE VILLA AV (566)
ROSEMEAD BL (566)
MICHILLINDA AV (566)
BALDWIN AV (567)
SANTA ANITA AV (567)
HUNTINGTON DR (567)
MYRTLE AV (567)
MOUNTAIN AV (567)
BUENA VISTA ST (568)
MT OLIVE DR (568)
FAIR OAKS AV (595)
ORANGE GROVE AV (595)
BRIDEWELL ST (595)
YORK BL (595)
MARMION WY (595)
AV 64 (595)
AV 60 (595)
VIA MARISOL (595)
AV 57 (595)
AV 52 (595)
AV 43 (595)
AV 26 (594)
FIGUEROA ST
GRAND AV (569)
BASELINE RD (569)
SUNFLOWER AV (599)
LONE HILL AV (569)
SAN DIMAS AV (570)
FOOTHILL BL (570)
FRUIT ST (570)
N TOWNE AV (571)
BASELINE RD (571)
ARROW HWY (598)
LIVE OAK AV (598)
LOS ANGELES ST (597)
LOWER AZUSA RD (597)
RAMONA BL (597)
IRWINDALE AV (568)
VERNON AV (568)
AZUSA AV (568)
CITRUS AV (569)
GRAND AV (569)
AUTO CENTRE DR (599)
ARROW HWY (600)
BONITA AV (600)
COVINA BL (600)
VIA VERDE (600)
FIGUEROA ST (594)
PASADENA AV (594)
N BROADWAY (634)
N MAIN ST (635)
MISSION RD (635)
MARENGO ST (635)
STATE ST (635)
MARENGO ST (635)
SOTO ST (635)
HERBERT AV (635)
VALLEY BL (595)
FREMONT AV (635)
ATLANTIC BL (636)
GARFIELD AV (636)
NEW AV (636)
DEL MAR AV (636)
SAN GABRIEL BL (636)
WALNUT GROVE AV (636)
ROSEMEAD BL (636)
TEMPLE CITY BL (597)
BALDWIN AV (597)
SANTA ANITA AV (637)
VALLEY BL (637)
PECK RD (637)
PECK RD (637)
GARVEY AV (637)
FRAZIER ST (637)
BALDWIN PARK BL (638)
FRANCISQUITO AV (638)
PUENTE AV (598)
MERCED AV (598)
PACIFIC AV (598)
SUNSET AV (598)
VINCENT AV (598)
AZUSA AV (598)
CITRUS ST (599)
BARRANCA ST (599)
GRAND AV (599)
HOLT AV (599)
VIA VERDE (599)
KELLOGG DR (640)
FAIRPLEX DR (600)
DUDLEY ST (600)
WHITE AV (600)
GAREY AV (600)
ORANGE GROVE AV (600)
TOWNE AV (601)
N INDIAN HILL BL (601)
S INDIAN HILL BL (601)
CITY TERRACE DR (635)
EASTERN AV (635)
GARVEY AV (635)
STATE ST (635)
CESAR E CHAVEZ (635)
4TH ST (635)
RAMONA BL (635)
FLORAL DR (635)
VALLEY BL (637)
TEMPLE AV (640)
SUNSET CROSSING RD (640)
DIAMOND BAR BL (640)
S CAMPUS DR (640)
HOLT AV (640)
VALLEY BL (640)
POMONA BL (640)
2ND ST (640)
MISSION BL (640)
9TH ST (640)
PHILLIPS DR (640)
MONTE VISTA AV (601)
CENTRAL AV (601)
MOUNTAIN AV (601)
ALAMEDA ST (634)
COMMERCIAL ST (634)
VIGNES ST (634)
LOS ANGELES ST
SPRING ST (634)
ACADEMY RD (594)
SOLANO AV (594)
RIVERSIDE DR (594)

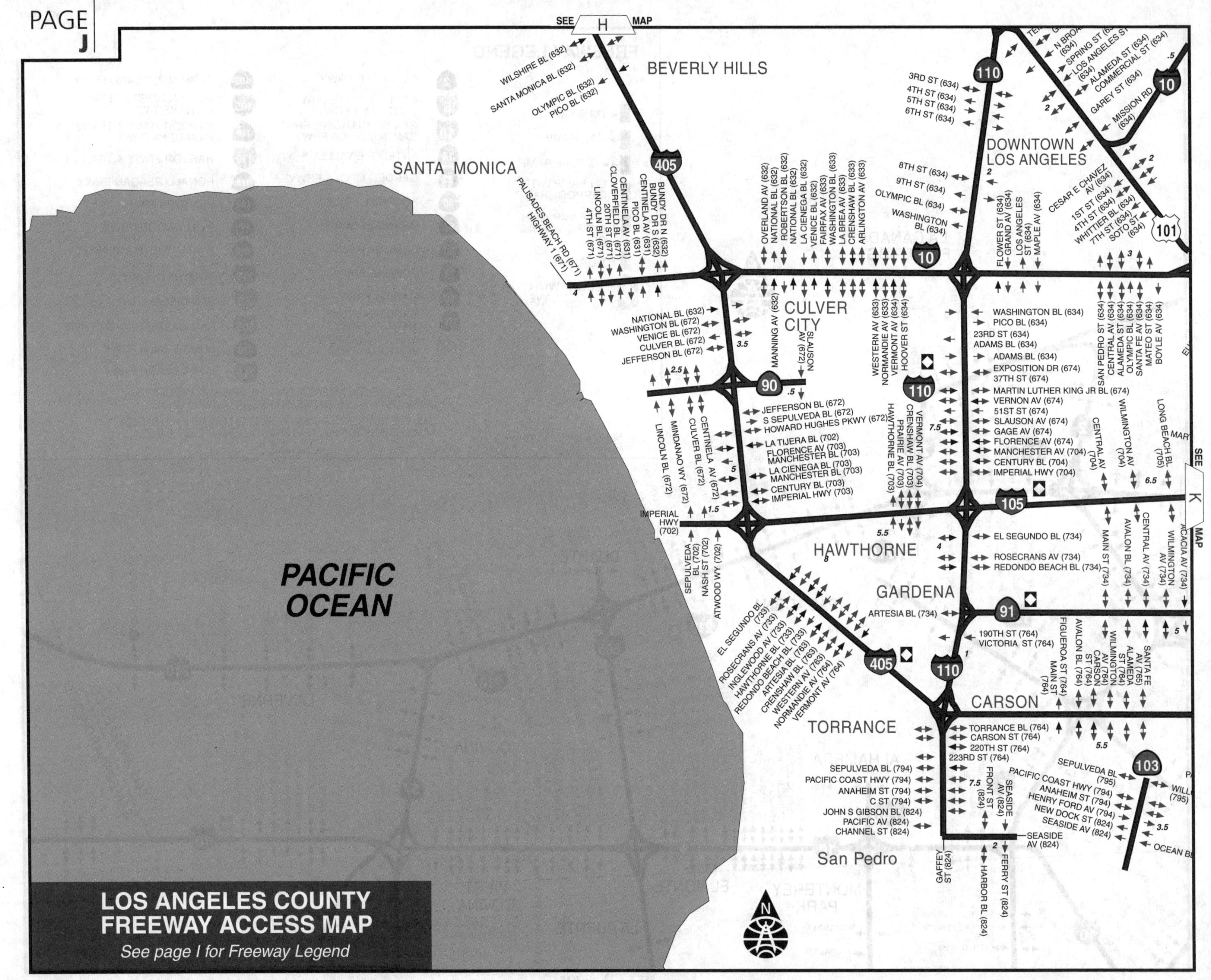
SEE H MAP
BEVERLY HILLS
SANTA MONICA
WILSHIRE BL (632)
SANTA MONICA BL (632)
OLYMPIC BL (632)
PICO BL (632)
PALISADES BEACH RD (671)
HIGHWAY 1 (671)
4TH ST (671)
LINCOLN BL (671)
20TH ST (671)
CLOVERFIELD BL (671)
CENTINELA AV (631)
PICO BL (631)
CENTINELA AV (632)
BUNDY DR S (632)
BUNDY DR N (632)
OVERLAND AV (632)
NATIONAL BL (632)
ROBERTSON BL (632)
NATIONAL BL (632)
LA CIENEGA BL (632)
VENICE BL (632)
FAIRFAX AV (633)
WASHINGTON BL (633)
LA BREA AV (633)
CRENSHAW BL (633)
ARLINGTON AV (633)
3RD ST (634)
4TH ST (634)
5TH ST (634)
6TH ST (634)
8TH ST (634)
9TH ST (634)
OLYMPIC BL (634)
WASHINGTON BL (634)
DOWNTOWN LOS ANGELES
N BROADWAY (634)
SPRING ST (634)
LOS ANGELES ST (634)
ALAMEDA ST (634)
COMMERCIAL ST (634)
GAREY ST (634)
MISSION RD (634)
CESAR E CHAVEZ AV (634)
1ST ST (634)
4TH ST (634)
WHITTIER BL (634)
7TH ST (634)
SOTO ST (634)
FLOWER ST (634)
GRAND AV (634)
LOS ANGELES ST (634)
MAPLE AV (634)
CULVER CITY
NATIONAL BL (632)
WASHINGTON BL (672)
VENICE BL (672)
CULVER BL (672)
JEFFERSON BL (672)
MANNING AV (632)
SLAUSON AV (672)
WESTERN AV (633)
NORMANDIE AV (633)
VERMONT AV (634)
HOOVER ST (634)
WASHINGTON BL (634)
PICO BL (634)
23RD ST (634)
ADAMS BL (634)
ADAMS BL (634)
EXPOSITION DR (674)
37TH ST (674)
MARTIN LUTHER KING JR BL (674)
VERNON AV (674)
51ST ST (674)
SLAUSON AV (674)
GAGE AV (674)
FLORENCE AV (674)
MANCHESTER AV (704)
CENTURY BL (704)
IMPERIAL HWY (704)
SAN PEDRO ST (634)
CENTRAL AV (634)
ALAMEDA ST (634)
OLYMPIC BL (634)
SANTA FE AV (634)
MATEO ST (634)
BOYLE AV (634)
LINCOLN BL (672)
MINDANAO WY (672)
CULVER BL (672)
CENTINELA AV (672)
JEFFERSON BL (672)
S SEPULVEDA BL (672)
HOWARD HUGHES PKWY (672)
LA TIJERA BL (702)
FLORENCE AV (703)
MANCHESTER BL (703)
LA CIENEGA BL (703)
MANCHESTER BL (703)
CENTURY BL (703)
IMPERIAL HWY (703)
VERMONT AV (704)
CRENSHAW BL (703)
PRAIRIE AV (703)
HAWTHORNE BL (703)
CENTRAL AV (704)
WILMINGTON AV (704)
LONG BEACH BL (705)
IMPERIAL HWY (702)
SEPULVEDA BL (702)
NASH ST (702)
ATWOOD WY (702)
PACIFIC OCEAN
HAWTHORNE
GARDENA
EL SEGUNDO BL (734)
ROSECRANS AV (734)
REDONDO BEACH BL (734)
MAIN ST (734)
AVALON BL (734)
CENTRAL AV (734)
WILMINGTON AV (734)
ACACIA AV (734)
SEE K MAP
ARTESIA BL (734)
190TH ST (764)
VICTORIA ST (764)
EL SEGUNDO BL (733)
ROSECRANS AV (733)
INGLEWOOD AV (733)
HAWTHORNE BL (733)
REDONDO BEACH BL (733)
ARTESIA BL (733)
CRENSHAW BL (763)
WESTERN AV (763)
NORMANDIE AV (764)
VERMONT AV (764)
FIGUEROA ST (764)
MAIN ST (764)
AVALON BL (764)
CARSON ST (764)
WILMINGTON AV (764)
ALAMEDA ST (764)
SANTA FE AV (765)
CARSON
TORRANCE
TORRANCE BL (764)
CARSON ST (764)
220TH ST (764)
223RD ST (764)
SEPULVEDA BL (794)
PACIFIC COAST HWY (794)
ANAHEIM ST (794)
C ST (794)
JOHN S GIBSON BL (824)
PACIFIC AV (824)
CHANNEL ST (824)
FRONT ST (824)
SEASIDE AV (824)
SEPULVEDA BL (795)
PACIFIC COAST HWY (794)
ANAHEIM ST (794)
HENRY FORD AV (794)
NEW DOCK ST (824)
SEASIDE AV (824)
OCEAN BL
SEASIDE AV (824)
San Pedro
GAFFEY ST (824)
HARBOR BL (824)
FERRY ST (824)
N
LOS ANGELES COUNTY FREEWAY ACCESS MAP
See page I for Freeway Legend

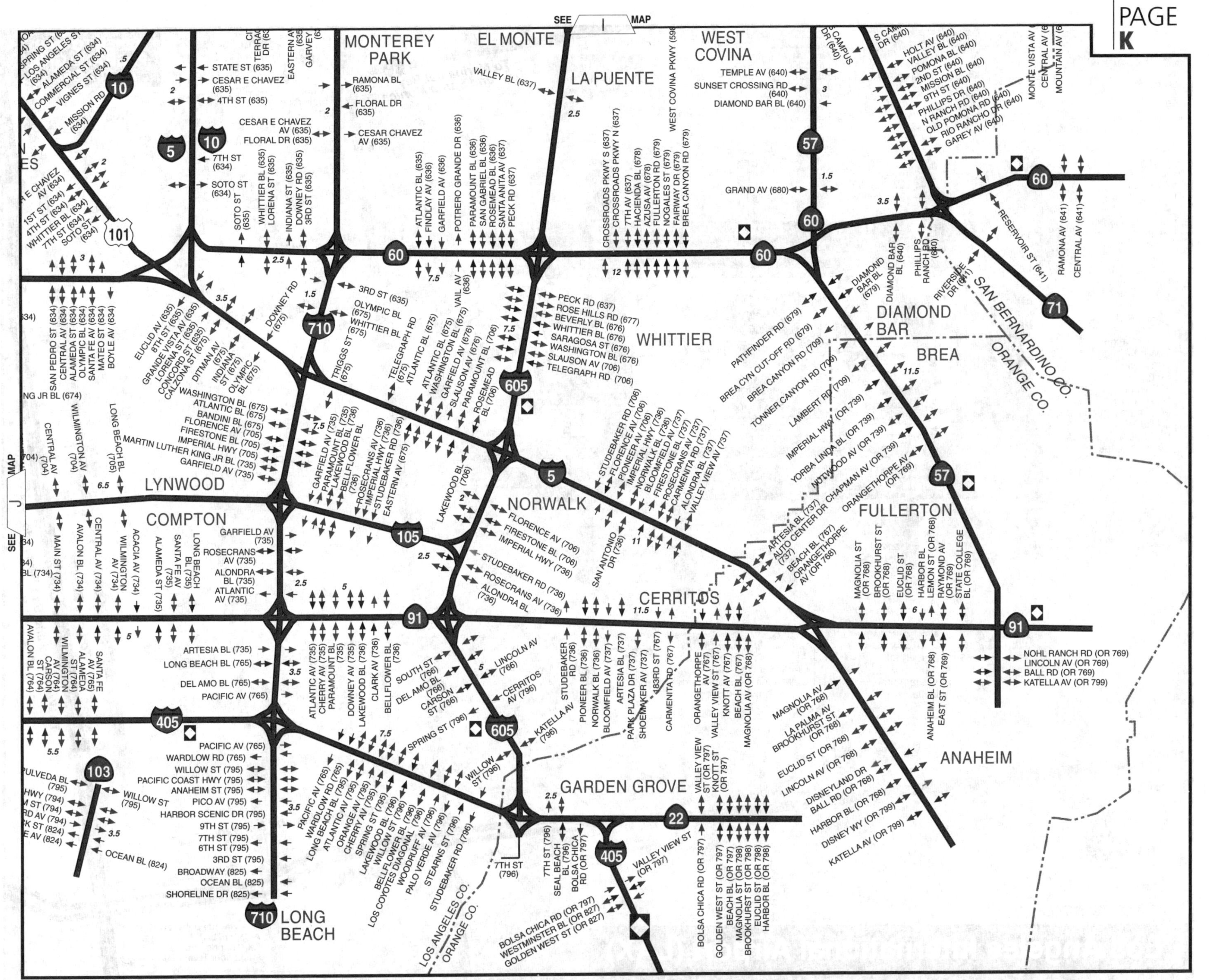
SEE I MAP
SEE J MAP
MONTEREY PARK
EL MONTE
LA PUENTE
WEST COVINA
DIAMOND BAR
BREA
WHITTIER
LYNWOOD
COMPTON
NORWALK
FULLERTON
CERRITOS
ANAHEIM
GARDEN GROVE
LONG BEACH
SAN BERNARDINO CO.
ORANGE CO.
LOS ANGELES CO.
10
5
101
60
57
71
710
605
105
91
405
103
22
STATE ST (635)
CESAR E CHAVEZ (635)
4TH ST (635)
RAMONA BL (635)
FLORAL DR (635)
CESAR CHAVEZ AV (635)
VALLEY BL (637)
TEMPLE AV (640)
SUNSET CROSSING RD (640)
DIAMOND BAR BL (640)
GRAND AV (680)
3RD ST (635)
OLYMPIC BL (675)
WHITTIER BL (675)
PECK RD (637)
ROSE HILLS RD (677)
BEVERLY BL (676)
WHITTIER BL (676)
SARAGOSA ST (676)
WASHINGTON BL (676)
SLAUSON AV (706)
TELEGRAPH RD (706)
WASHINGTON BL (675)
ATLANTIC BL (675)
BANDINI BL (675)
FLORENCE AV (705)
FIRESTONE BL (705)
IMPERIAL HWY (705)
MARTIN LUTHER KING JR BL (735)
GARFIELD AV (735)
FLORENCE AV (706)
FIRESTONE BL (706)
IMPERIAL HWY (736)
STUDEBAKER RD (736)
ROSECRANS AV (736)
ALONDRA BL (736)
GARFIELD AV (735)
ROSECRANS AV (735)
ALONDRA BL (735)
ATLANTIC AV (735)
ARTESIA BL (735)
LONG BEACH BL (765)
DEL AMO BL (765)
PACIFIC AV (765)
PACIFIC AV (765)
WARDLOW RD (765)
WILLOW ST (795)
PACIFIC COAST HWY (795)
ANAHEIM ST (795)
PICO AV (795)
HARBOR SCENIC DR (795)
9TH ST (795)
7TH ST (795)
6TH ST (795)
3RD ST (795)
BROADWAY (825)
OCEAN BL (825)
SHORELINE DR (825)
WILLOW ST (795)
OCEAN BL (824)
NOHL RANCH RD (OR 769)
LINCOLN AV (OR 769)
BALL RD (OR 769)
KATELLA AV (OR 799)
BOLSA CHICA RD (OR 797)
WESTMINSTER BL (OR 827)
GOLDEN WEST ST (OR 827)
VALLEY VIEW ST (OR 797)
7TH ST (796)

Los Angeles International Airport (LAX)

LOS ANGELES COUNTY TRANSIT INFORMATION

Regional Bus, Train, and Metrolink

MAJOR BUS AND TRAIN STATION LOCATIONS

For the location of major bus and Metro stations, see the "Transportation" heading in the Points of Interest index of this guide.

MAJOR PARK/RIDE LOTS

For the location of major park/ride lots, see the "Park/Ride" heading in the Points of Interest index of this guide.

M Metro

METRO BUS AND METRO RAIL SYSTEM

Metro, the popular name for the transit system operated by the Los Angeles County Transportation Authority (MTA), is one of the nation's largest public transportation organizations with more than 2,000 buses operating on nearly 200 routes and 225 trains on four lines in the Metro Rail system. Metro has created a system designed to get you where you want to go without your car and at a fraction of the cost. Metro Rail's Red Line subway provides service between downtown Los Angeles and Mid-Wilshire, Hollywood, Universal City and North Hollywood. The Metro Blue Line, providing service between downtown Los Angeles and Long Beach, connects to the Red Line. Also connecting to the Red Line is the Metro Gold Line, stretching between Union Station and Pasadena with a stop in Chinatown. The Metro Green Line, running between Norwalk and Redondo Beach, connects with free shuttle buses directly into Los Angeles International Airport (LAX). Metro Buses service special venues such as the Sports Arena, Los Angeles Memorial Coliseum, Getty Museum, Great Western Forum, Hollywood Bowl and racetracks as well as theme parks such as the Disney Resort, Knott's Berry Farm and Universal Studios. In addition, there are local buses operated by several municipal operators throughout Los Angeles County.

TRIP PLANNING

For route and schedule information on Metro and other transit operators, go to **metro.net** and use the convenient Trip Planner feature which in just a few moments will give you instructions which you can print out on how to get from Point A to Point B. Or call the regional transit information phone number, **1-800-COMMUTE**. Metro has a system map showing all of Los Angeles County's public transportation routes. For a free copy, write to Metro Customer Relations, One Gateway Plaza, Los Angeles, CA 90012-2952 or call **1-800-COMMUTE**. The map is also available at metro.net and can be downloaded.

FARES AND TRANSFERS

Metro's local base fare is $1.25 which includes Metro Rail and Metro Bus. Freeway express buses have additional charges. A Day Pass, available for $3 on board buses and from rail ticket vending machines, is good for unlimited riding on all Metro trains and local buses. Other Metro passes available include monthly, semimonthly and weekly as well as the EZ Transit Pass good on Metro and 17 other municipal transit operators; these passes and discount tokens are available at hundreds of retail outlets throughout Los Angeles County. Fares for senior citizens or disabled patrons are 45¢; Day Pass is $1.50. Fares for municipal operators vary. Transfers are available only for transferring between Metro trains/buses and municipal buses; a Day Pass or other Metro pass is required when transferring to/from Metro trains or buses. The Metro Rail system is a "barrier-free" operation; patrons must have proof of fare with them at all times for random checking by uniformed fare inspectors or risk a substantial fine.

METRO COMMUTE SERVICES - CARPOOLING OR VANPOOLING ASSISTANCE

It's easy to carpool with two or more people or vanpool with 7 to 15 from convenient park/ride locations. Just call **1-800-COMMUTE**, select either the "RIDESHARING" or **ridematch.info** options to obtain a RideGuide listing all your commute options including a list of potential pooling partners. This service is FREE OF CHARGE. Then you may call your potential partners and agree upon a convenient time and place to meet in order to park and ride to work.

For carpool/vanpool, transit, express bus, telecommuting and bicycle information as well as access to highway conditions call **1-800-COMMUTE** from most locations in the greater Los Angeles area; in Orange County call 714-636-7433.

ACCESSIBLE SERVICE

Metro's bus and rail lines are 100% wheelchair-accessible. For information, please call **1-800-621-7828**. Hearing-impaired (TTY) **1-800-252-9040**

COMMUTER AND LONG-DISTANCE TRAIN

Metrolink is operated by the Southern California Regional Rail Authority and serves Los Angeles, Orange, Riverside, San Bernardino, Ventura and North San Diego Counties. Metrolink trains travel to 54 stations in Southern California, carrying thousands of commuters to centers of employment such as Burbank, Glendale, Irvine and Downtown Los Angeles. Trains are also popular with group travelers, taking students on field trips and families to recreational destinations throughout the region. Metrolink trains feature clean, comfortable, climate controlled interiors as well as restrooms and bicycle racks. All trains, stations, and other facilities are accessible to persons with disabilities.

Metrolink trains operate Monday through Friday on all lines, on Saturdays for the Antelope Valley and San Bernardino lines only and on Sundays for the San Bernardino line only. Trains do not operate on the following holidays: New Year's Day, Memorial Day, Independence Day, Thanksgiving Day and Christmas Day. Trains operate at a reduced service on the following days: Thanksgiving Friday, Martin Luther King Day and Presidents' Day.

For schedule and fare information, call (800) 371-LINK or visit www.metrolinktrains.com. Speech and hearing impaired commuters call (800) 698-4TDD.

AMTRAK®

The Amtrak Pacific Surfliner® corridor extends 347 miles between San Luis Obispo and San Diego, with service to 36 destinations. There are 11 trains daily from Los Angeles to San Diego and five daily to Santa Barbara.

Pacific Surfliner trains feature bi-level cars with panoramic windows, wide, comfortable seats, and a Cafe Car. Accommodations include unreserved coach and reserved Pacific Business Class with additional legroom, video program monitors, laptop outlets, complimentary beverages, light snacks and newspapers. Checked baggage service is available at select stations. Bicycles are allowed.

Amtrak long-distance trains serving Los Angeles include the Coast Starlight® with daily service to the Bay Area, Portland and Seattle. The Southwest Chief℠ provides daily service to Flagstaff, Albuquerque and Chicago and the Sunset Limited℠ with service to San Antonio, New Orleans and Orlando. Amtrak long-distance trains feature coach and sleeping car accommodations, Sightseer Lounges and dining cars with sit-down dining.

Amtrak provides intercity passenger rail service to more than 500 destinations in 46 states on a 22,000-mile route system. For schedules, fares and information call 1-800-USA-RAIL or visit amtrak.com.

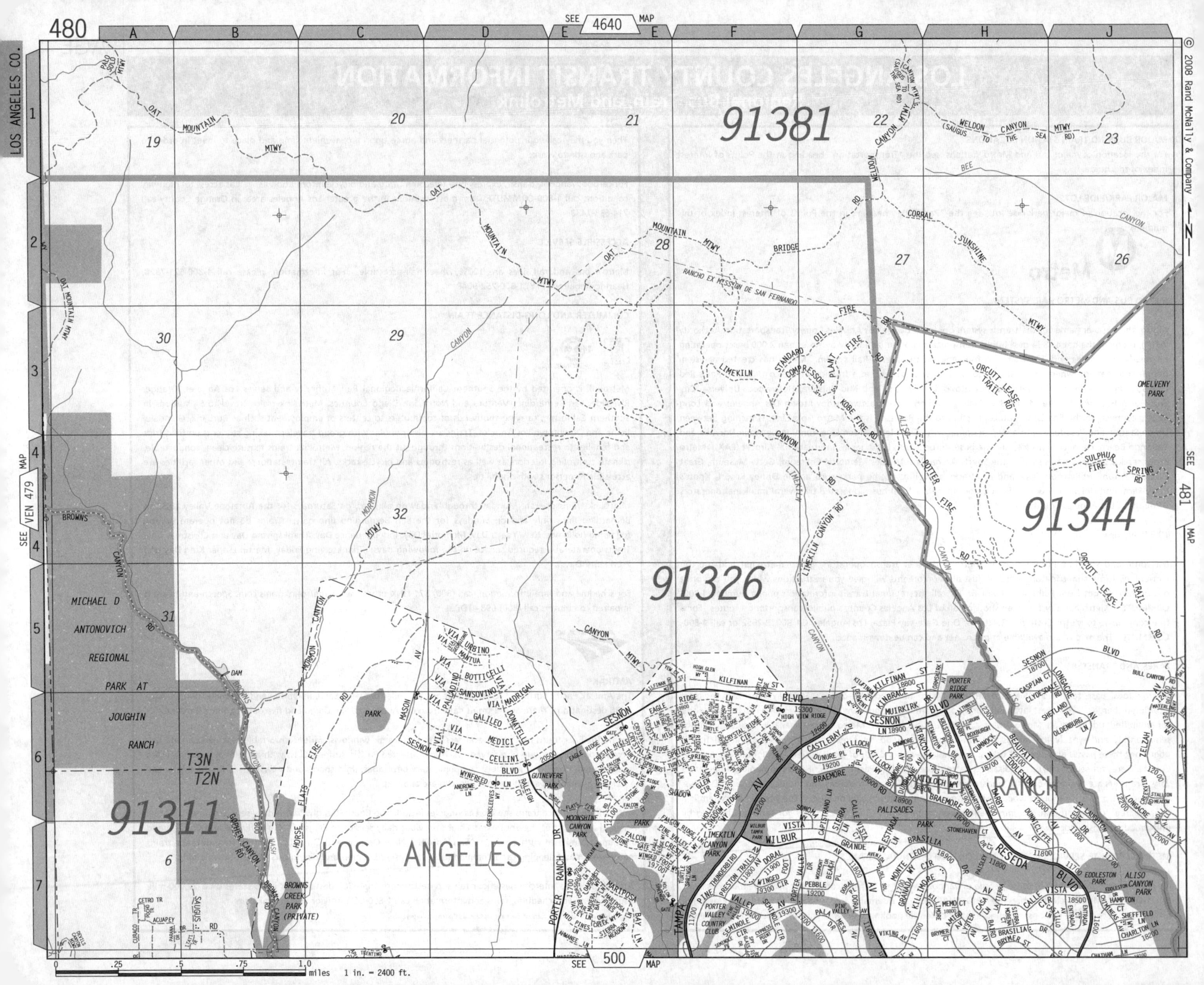

480
SEE 4640 MAP
SEE 500 MAP
SEE VEN 479 MAP
SEE 481 MAP
LOS ANGELES CO.
© 2008 Rand McNally & Company
91381
91344
91326
91311
LOS ANGELES
PORTER RANCH
MICHAEL D ANTONOVICH REGIONAL PARK AT JOUGHIN RANCH
OMELVENY PARK
PORTER RIDGE PARK
MOONSHINE CANYON PARK
LIMEKILN CANYON PARK
PORTER VALLEY COUNTRY CLUB
BROWNS CREEK PARK (PRIVATE)
EDDLESTON PARK
ALISO CANYON PARK
GUINEVERE PARK
WILBUR TAMPA PARK
PARK
OAT MOUNTAIN MTWY
WELDON CANYON (SAUGUS TO THE SEA RD)
RANCHO EX MISSION DE SAN FERNANDO
LIMEKILN CANYON RD
SESNON BLVD
PORTER RANCH DR
RESEDA BLVD
TAMPA AV
WILBUR AV
BROWNS CANYON RD
MORMON CANYON
SULPHUR SPRING FIRE RD
ORCUTT LEASE TRAIL RD
ALISO CANYON
T3N
T2N
0 .25 .5 .75 1.0 miles 1 in. = 2400 ft.

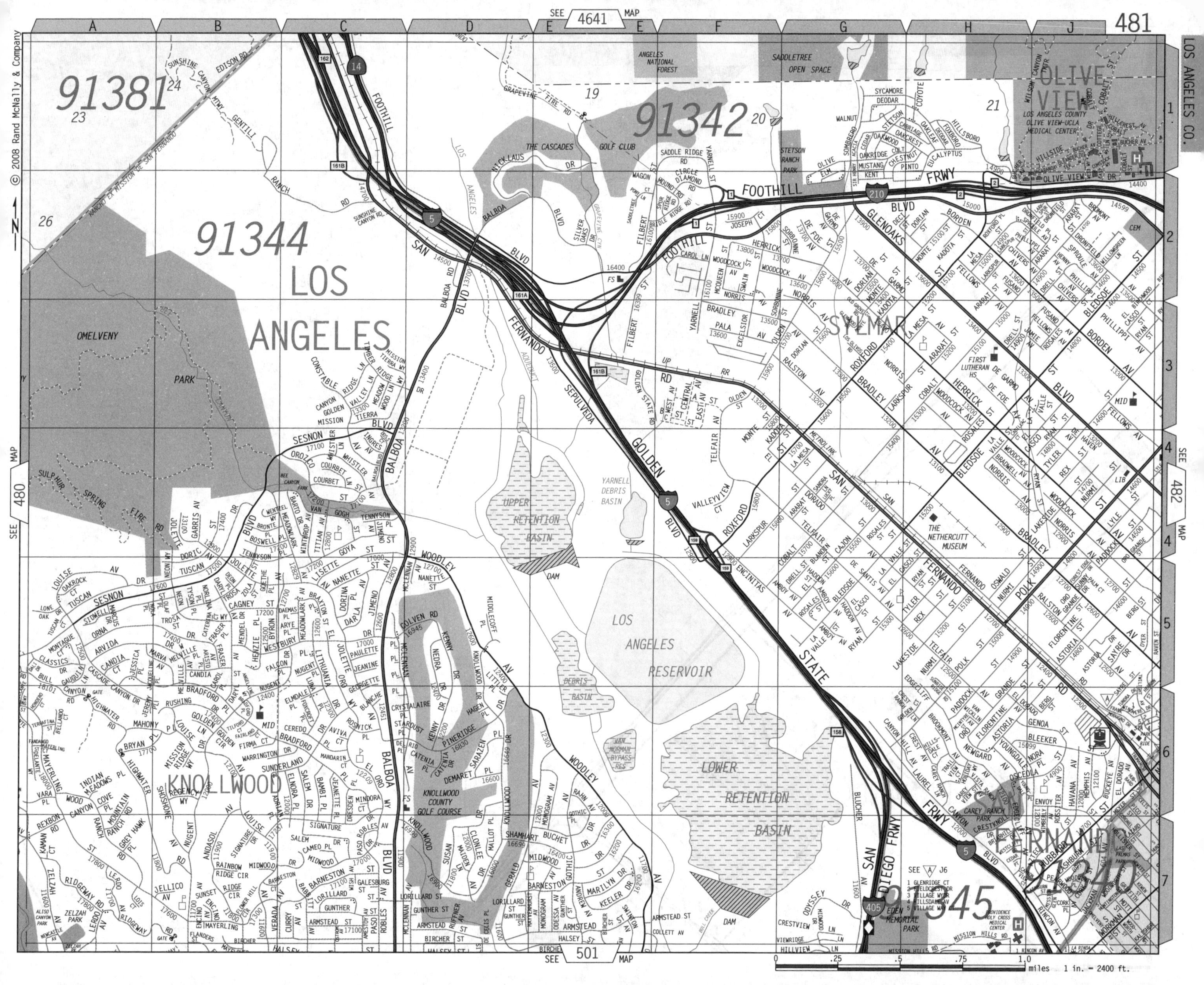

SEE 4641 MAP
SEE 480 MAP
SEE 482 MAP
SEE 501 MAP
LOS ANGELES CO.
© 2008 Rand McNally & Company
91381
91342
91344
91345
91340
LOS ANGELES
ANGELES NATIONAL FOREST
SADDLETREE OPEN SPACE
OLIVE VIEW
LOS ANGELES COUNTY OLIVE VIEW-UCLA MEDICAL CENTER
THE CASCADES GOLF CLUB
STETSON RANCH PARK
OMELVENY PARK
SYLMAR
FIRST LUTHERAN HS
THE NETHERCUTT MUSEUM
UPPER RETENTION BASIN
YARNELL DEBRIS BASIN
LOS ANGELES RESERVOIR
DEBRIS BASIN
VAN NORMAN BYPASS RES
LOWER RETENTION BASIN
KNOLLWOOD
KNOLLWOOD COUNTY GOLF COURSE
EDEN MEMORIAL PARK
PROVIDENCE HOLY CROSS MEDICAL CENTER
CAREY RANCH PARK
SAN FERNANDO
FOOTHILL FRWY
GOLDEN STATE FRWY
SAN DIEGO FRWY
SAN FERNANDO RD
SEPULVEDA BLVD
BALBOA BLVD
WOODLEY AV
GLENOAKS BLVD
FOOTHILL BLVD
SESNON BLVD
RINCON AV
ZELZAH PARK
ALISO CANYON PARK
BEE CANYON PARK
SEE A J6
1 GLENRIDGE CT
2 FIELDCREST DR
3 VILLAGE WY
4 HILLSDALE CT
5 VILLAGE WAY
miles 1 in. = 2400 ft.
0 .25 .5 .75 1.0

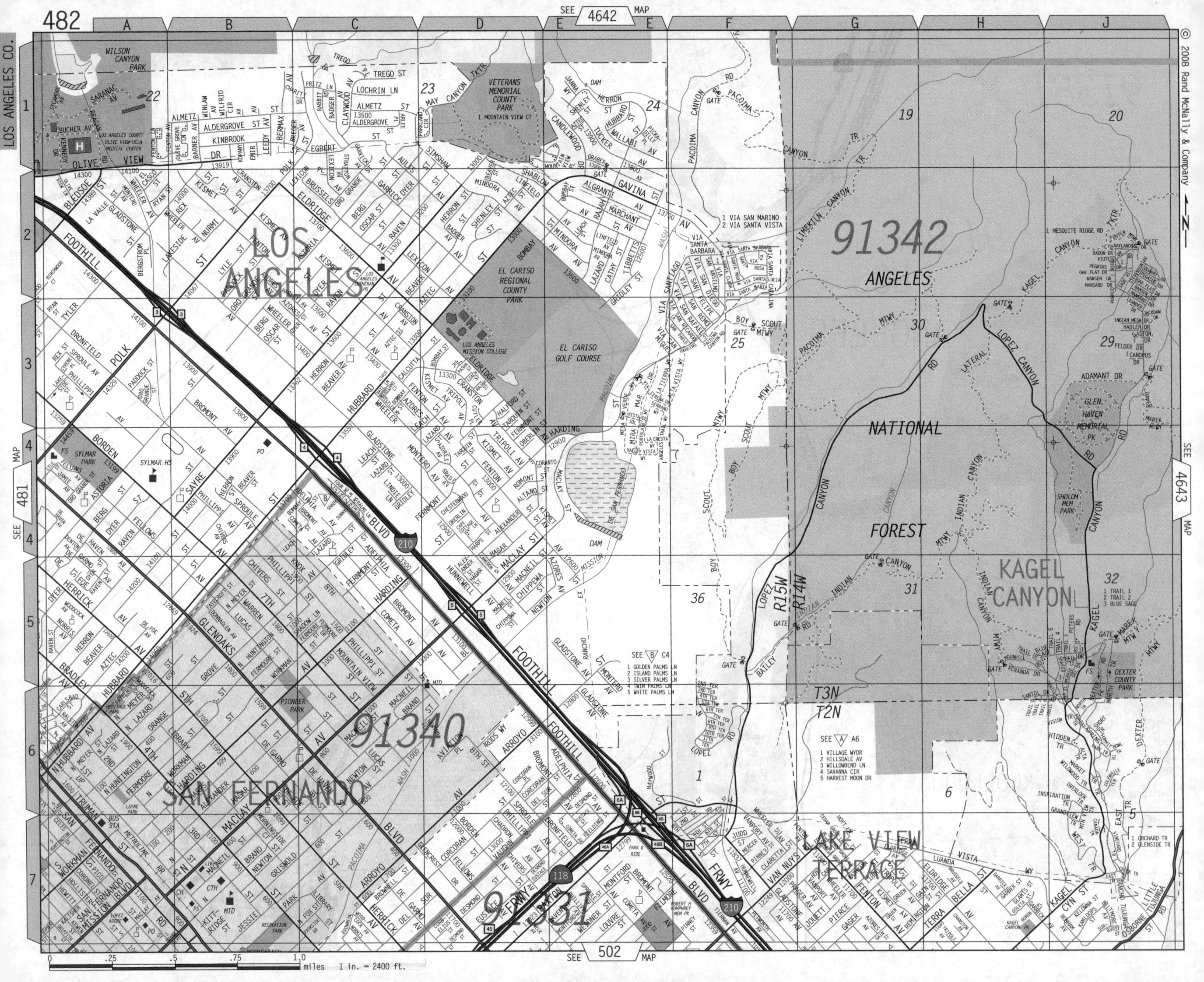
LOS ANGELES CO.
SEE 4642 MAP
SEE 4643 MAP
SEE 481 MAP
SEE 502 MAP
A
B
C
D
E
F
G
H
J
1
2
3
4
5
6
7
WILSON CANYON PARK
VETERANS MEMORIAL COUNTY PARK
LOS ANGELES COUNTY OLIVE VIEW-UCLA MEDICAL CENTER
LOS ANGELES
ANGELES
NATIONAL
FOREST
91342
91340
91331
SAN FERNANDO
LAKE VIEW TERRACE
KAGEL CANYON
EL CARISO REGIONAL COUNTY PARK
EL CARISO GOLF COURSE
LOS ANGELES MISSION COLLEGE
SYLMAR PARK
SYLMAR HS
PIONEER PARK
GLEN HAVEN MEMORIAL PK
SHOLOM MEM PARK
DEXTER COUNTY PARK
LAYNE PARK
RECREATION PARK
KAGEL CANYON PK
HUBERT H HUMPHREY MEM PK
FOOTHILL BLVD
FOOTHILL FRWY
SAN FERNANDO MISSION BLVD
GLENOAKS BLVD
MACLAY AV
POLK ST
HUBBARD AV
ELDRIDGE AV
BORDEN AV
HARDING AV
VAN NUYS BLVD
OSBORNE ST
LITTLE TUJUNGA CANYON RD
LOPEZ CANYON RD
PACOIMA CANYON RD
KAGEL CANYON RD
LIMEKILN CANYON TR
BOY SCOUT MTWY
INDIAN CANYON MTWY
GAVINA AV
OLIVE VIEW DR
R15W
R14W
T3N
T2N
1 VIA SAN MARINO
2 VIA SANTA VISTA
1 MESQUITE RIDGE RD
SEE B C4
1 GOLDEN PALMS LN
2 ISLAND PALMS LN
3 SILVER PALMS LN
4 TWIN PALMS LN
5 WHITE PALMS LN
SEE A A6
1 VILLAGE WYDR
2 HILLSDALE AV
3 WILLOWBEND LN
4 SAVANNA CIR
5 HARVEST MOON DR
1 TRAIL 1
2 TRAIL 2
3 BLUE SAGE
1 ORCHARD TR
2 GLENSIDE TR
0 .25 .5 .75 1.0 miles 1 in. = 2400 ft.

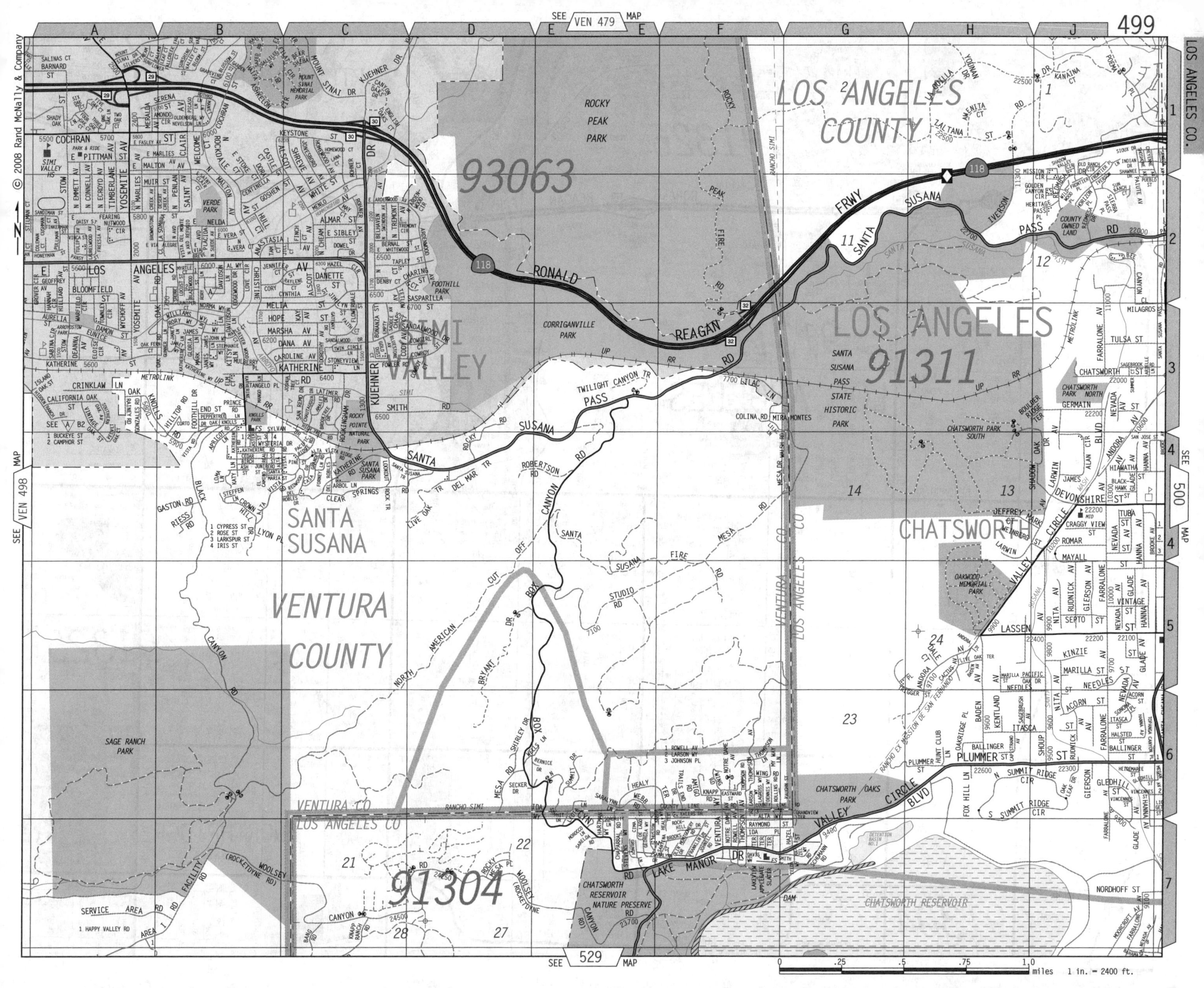
SEE VEN 479 MAP
LOS ANGELES CO.
LOS ANGELES COUNTY
ROCKY PEAK PARK
93063
SIMI VALLEY
RONALD REAGAN FRWY
SANTA SUSANA PASS RD
LOS ANGELES 91311
SANTA SUSANA PASS STATE HISTORIC PARK
CORRIGANVILLE PARK
SANTA SUSANA
VENTURA COUNTY
CHATSWORTH
OAKWOOD MEMORIAL PARK
SAGE RANCH PARK
CHATSWORTH OAKS PARK
CHATSWORTH RESERVOIR NATURE PRESERVE
CHATSWORTH RESERVOIR
91304
VENTURA CO
LOS ANGELES CO
SEE VEN 498 MAP
SEE 500 MAP
SEE 529 MAP
miles 1 in. = 2400 ft.
© 2008 Rand McNally & Company

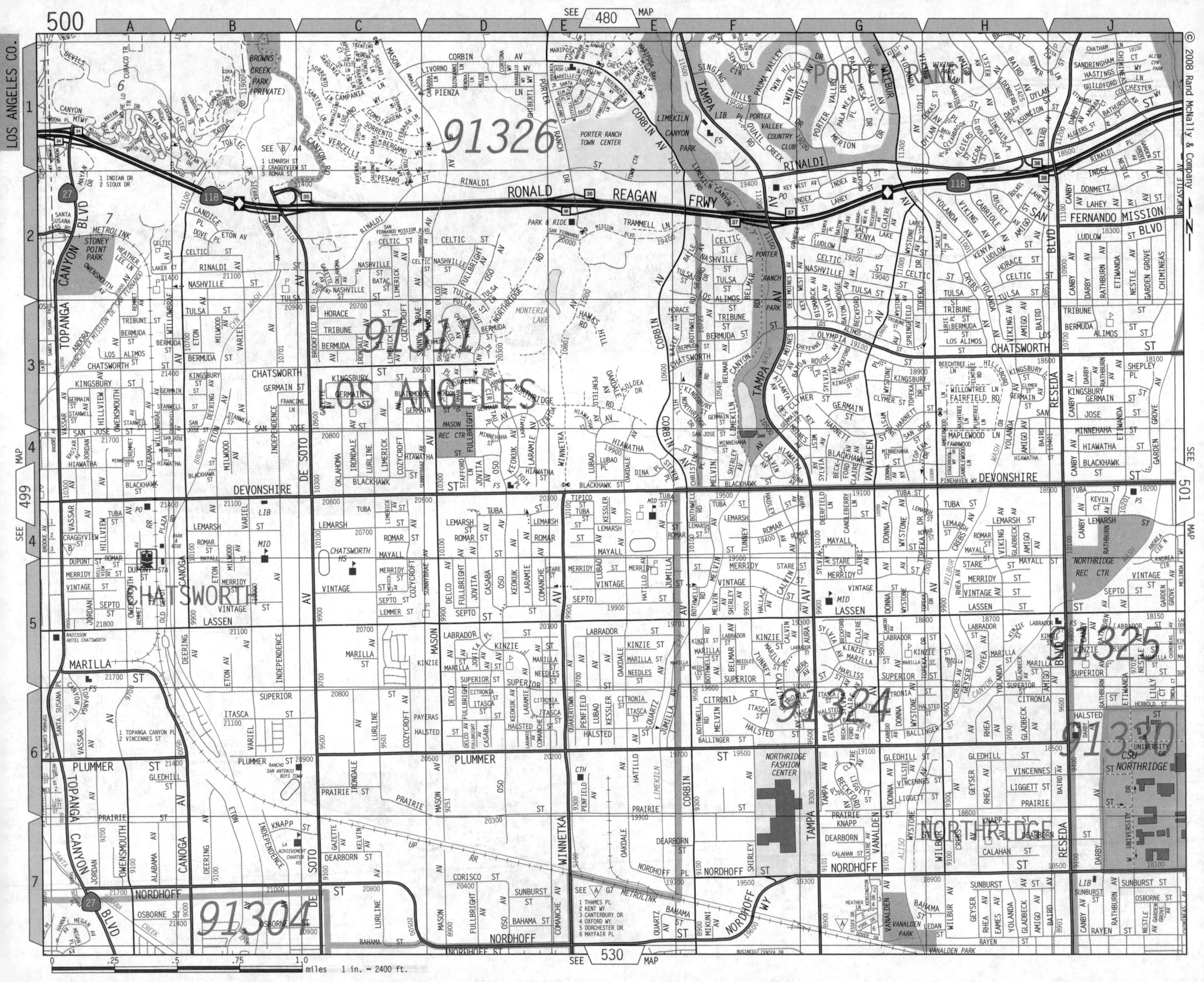
A
B
C
D
E
F
G
H
J
1
2
3
4
5
6
7
LOS ANGELES CO.
SEE 480 MAP
SEE 499 MAP
SEE 501 MAP
SEE 530 MAP
91326
91311
91324
91325
91330
91304
LOS ANGELES
CHATSWORTH
PORTER RANCH
NORTHRIDGE
RONALD REAGAN FRWY
118
27
TOPANGA CANYON BLVD
DEVONSHIRE
PLUMMER
NORDHOFF
RINALDI
CHATSWORTH
DE SOTO AV
WINNETKA AV
CORBIN AV
TAMPA AV
RESEDA BLVD
CANOGA AV
MASON AV
BROWNS CREEK PARK (PRIVATE)
STONEY POINT PARK
PORTER RANCH TOWN CENTER
LIMEKILN CANYON PARK
PORTER VALLEY COUNTRY CLUB
MONTERIA LAKE
MASON REC CTR
CHATSWORTH HS
NORTHRIDGE FASHION CENTER
NORTHRIDGE REC CTR
CSU NORTHRIDGE
VANALDEN PARK
RADISSON HOTEL CHATSWORTH
LA ACHIEVEMENT CHARTER HS
RANCHO SAN ANTONIO BOYS TOWN
METROLINK
0 .25 .5 .75 1.0 miles 1 in. = 2400 ft.

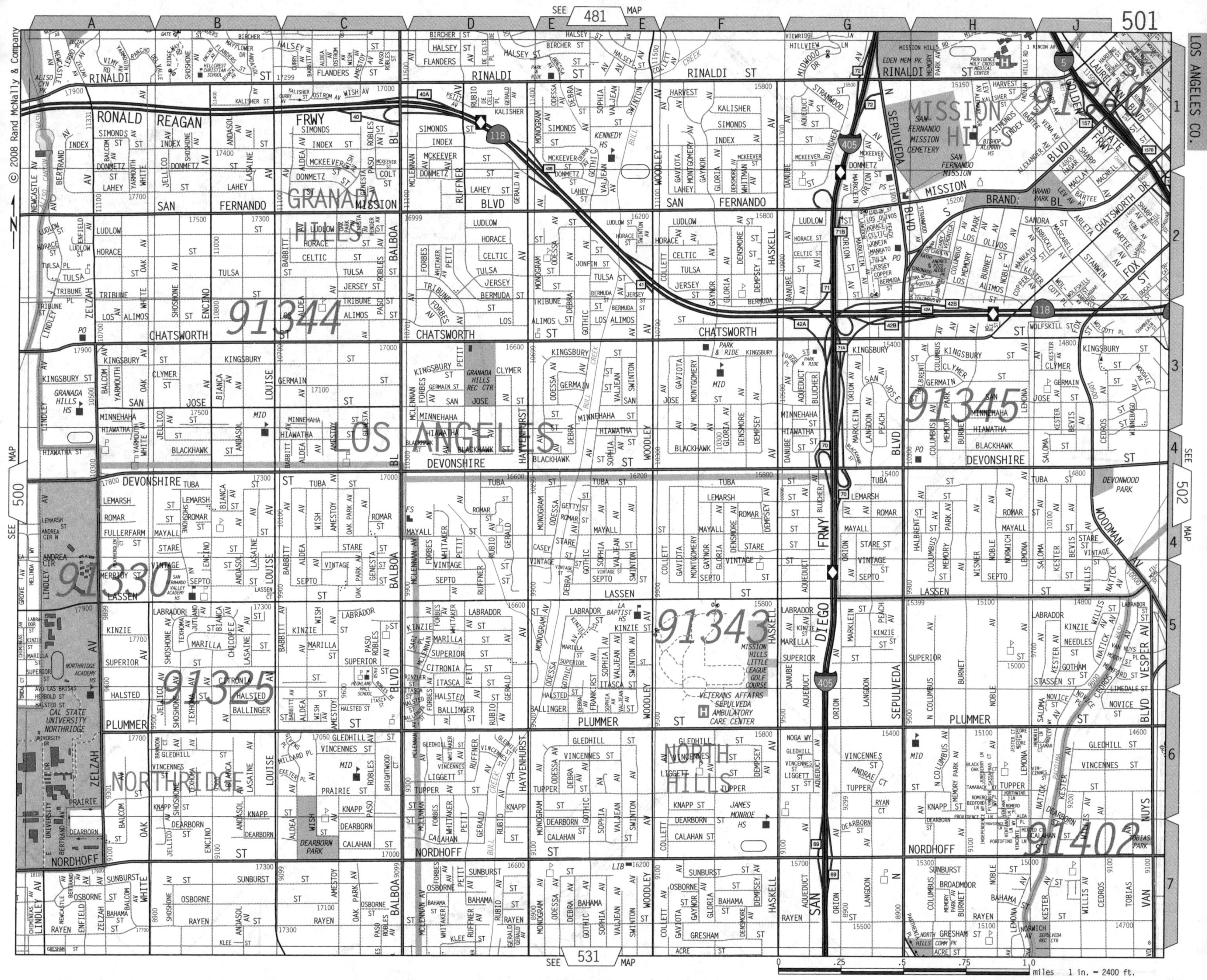

SEE 481 MAP
SEE 500 MAP
SEE 502 MAP
SEE 531 MAP
LOS ANGELES CO.
A
B
C
D
E
F
G
H
J
1
2
3
4
5
6
7
LOS ANGELES
GRANADA HILLS
MISSION HILLS
NORTH HILLS
NORTHRIDGE
91344
91345
91343
91330
91325
91340
91402
RONALD REAGAN FRWY
SAN DIEGO FRWY
GOLDEN STATE FRWY
RINALDI ST
SAN FERNANDO MISSION BLVD
CHATSWORTH ST
DEVONSHIRE ST
LASSEN ST
PLUMMER ST
NORDHOFF ST
SEPULVEDA BLVD
BALBOA BLVD
ZELZAH AV
WOODLEY AV
HAYVENHURST AV
HASKELL AV
WOODMAN AV
VESPER AV
NUYS BLVD
BRAND BL
SAN FERNANDO MISSION CEMETERY
SAN FERNANDO MISSION
EDEN MEM PK
GRANADA HILLS REC CTR
GRANADA HILLS HS
KENNEDY HS
MISSION HILLS LITTLE LEAGUE GOLF COURSE
VETERANS AFFAIRS SEPULVEDA AMBULATORY CARE CENTER
CAL STATE UNIVERSITY NORTHRIDGE
NORTHRIDGE ACADEMY HS
JAMES MONROE HS
DEARBORN PARK
DEVONWOOD PARK
SEPULVEDA REC CTR
NORTH HILLS COMM PK
TOBIAS PARK
LA BAPTIST HS
BISHOP ALEMANY HS
PROVIDENCE HOLY CROSS MEDICAL CENTER
SAN FERNANDO VALLEY ACADEMY HS
HILLCREST CHRISTIAN SCHOOL
HIGHLAND HALL SCHOOL
PARK & RIDE
MID
PO
LIB
0 .25 .5 .75 1.0 miles 1 in. = 2400 ft.

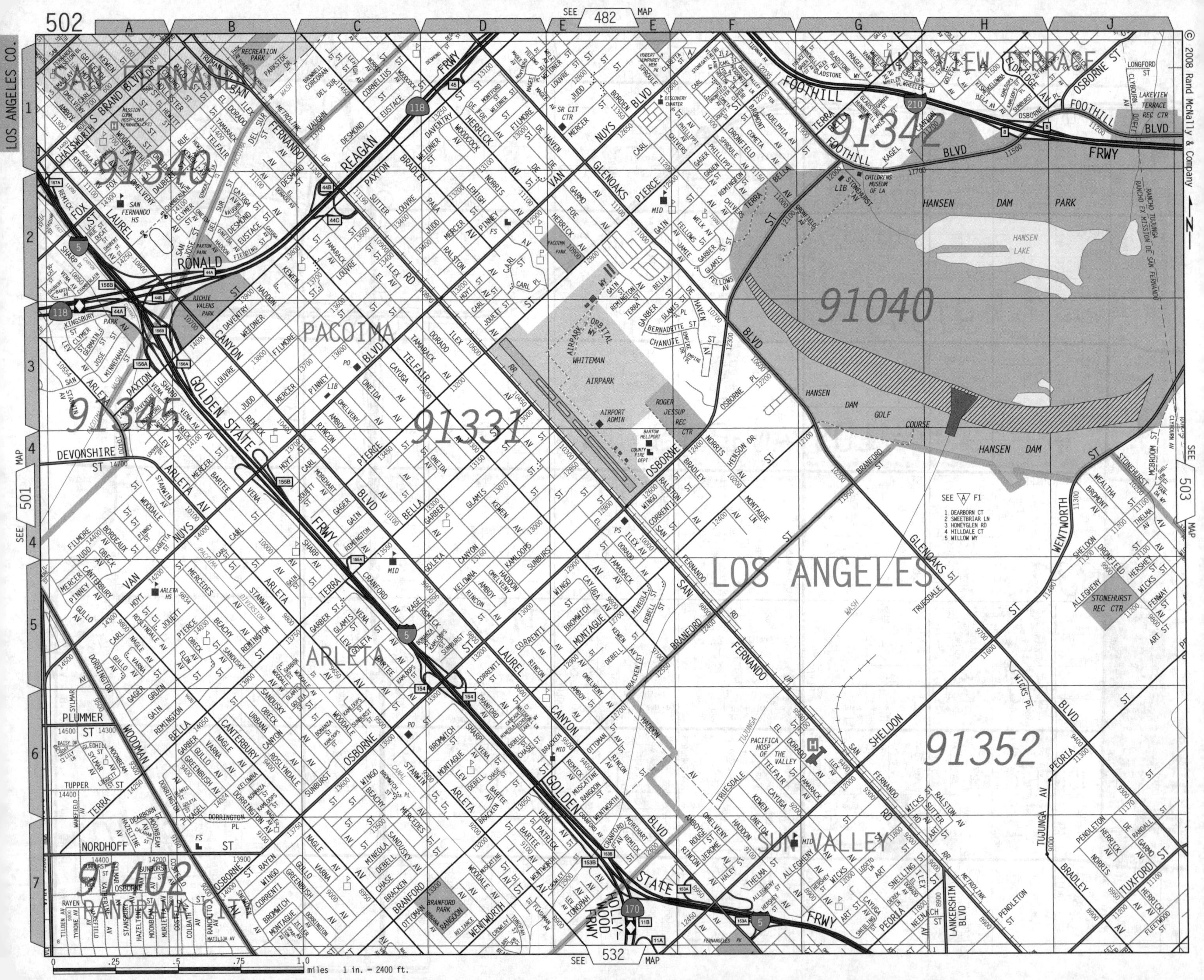
SEE 482 MAP
A
B
C
D
E
F
G
H
J
1
2
3
4
5
6
7
LOS ANGELES CO.
SAN FERNANDO
LAKE VIEW TERRACE
PACOIMA
ARLETA
LOS ANGELES
SUN VALLEY
PANORAMA CITY
91340
91342
91040
91331
91345
91352
91402
RECREATION PARK
MISSION COMM HOSP-SAN FERNANDO
SAN FERNANDO HS
RICHIE VALENS PARK
PACOIMA PARK
WHITEMAN AIRPARK
AIRPORT ADMIN
ROGER JESSUP REC CTR
BARTON HELIPORT
COUNTY FIRE DEPT
CHILDRENS MUSEUM OF LA
HANSEN DAM PARK
HANSEN LAKE
HANSEN DAM GOLF COURSE
HANSEN DAM
LAKEVIEW TERRACE REC CTR
STONEHURST REC CTR
PACIFICA HOSP OF THE VALLEY
ARLETA HS
BRANFORD PARK
GOLDEN STATE FRWY
FOOTHILL FRWY
REAGAN FRWY
HOLLYWOOD FRWY
SAN FERNANDO RD
GLENOAKS BLVD
FOOTHILL BLVD
VAN NUYS BLVD
LAUREL CANYON BLVD
DEVONSHIRE ST
PLUMMER ST
NORDHOFF ST
ROSCOE BLVD
SHELDON ST
LANKERSHIM BLVD
TUJUNGA AV
WENTWORTH ST
OSBORNE ST
SEE A F1
1 DEARBORN CT
2 SWEETBRIAR LN
3 HONEYGLEN RD
4 HILLDALE CT
5 WILLOW WY
SEE 501 MAP
SEE 503 MAP
SEE 532 MAP
0 .25 .5 .75 1.0 miles 1 in. = 2400 ft.
© 2008 Rand McNally & Company

SEE 4643 MAP
LOS ANGELES CO.
ANGELES NATIONAL FOREST
91342
LAKE VIEW TERRACE
HANSEN DAM PARK
ORCAS PARK
ANGELES NATIONAL GOLF CLUB
SUNLAND
SHADOW HILLS
91040
LOS ANGELES
91042
91352
LA TUNA CANYON
VERDUGO MOUNTAIN PARK
LA TUNA CANYON PARK
SUNLAND PARK & REC CTR
VERDUGO HILLS HS
MCGROARTY CULTURAL CENTER PARK
PASKO PARK
GREEN VERDUGO RES
VILLAGE CHRISTIAN HS
HELIPORT
DAM
FOOTHILL FRWY
FOOTHILL BLVD
SUNLAND BLVD
LA TUNA CANYON RD
TUJUNGA CANYON BLVD
BIG TUJUNGA CANYON RD
WENTWORTH ST
SEE 502 MAP
SEE 504 MAP
SEE 533 MAP
miles 1 in. = 2400 ft.

SEE 4643 MAP
A
B
C
D
E
F
G
H
J
LOS ANGELES CO.
© 2008 Rand McNally & Company
ANGELES
NATIONAL
FOREST
91042
DEUKMEJIAN
WILDERNESS
PARK
91214
TUJUNGA
LOS ANGELES
GLENDALE
LA CRESCENTA
LA CANADA FLINTRIDGE
91011
91352
ROADS END CAMPGROUND
MOUNT LUKENS TKTR
HAINES CANYON MTWY
GRAVEYARD TKTR
HAINES DEBRIS BASIN
BLANCHARD DEBRIS BASIN
DUNSMORE DEBRIS BASIN
LITTLE LANDERS PARK
HAINES CANYON PARK
FEHLHABER HOUK PARK
VERDUGO HILLS GOLF COURSE
LA TUNA CANYON PARK
TWO STRIKE COUNTY PARK
DUNSMORE PARK
FOOTHILL BLVD
FOOTHILL FRWY
LA TUNA CANYON RD
TUJUNGA CANYON BL
HONOLULU AV
LA CRESCENTA AV
PENNSYLVANIA AV
ROSEMONT AV
BRIGGS AV
OCEAN VIEW BLVD
CANYONSIDE RD
PICKENS CANYON
HOSTETTER FIRE RD
210
SEE 503 MAP
SEE 505 MAP
SEE 534 MAP
0 .25 .5 .75 1.0 miles 1 in. = 2400 ft.

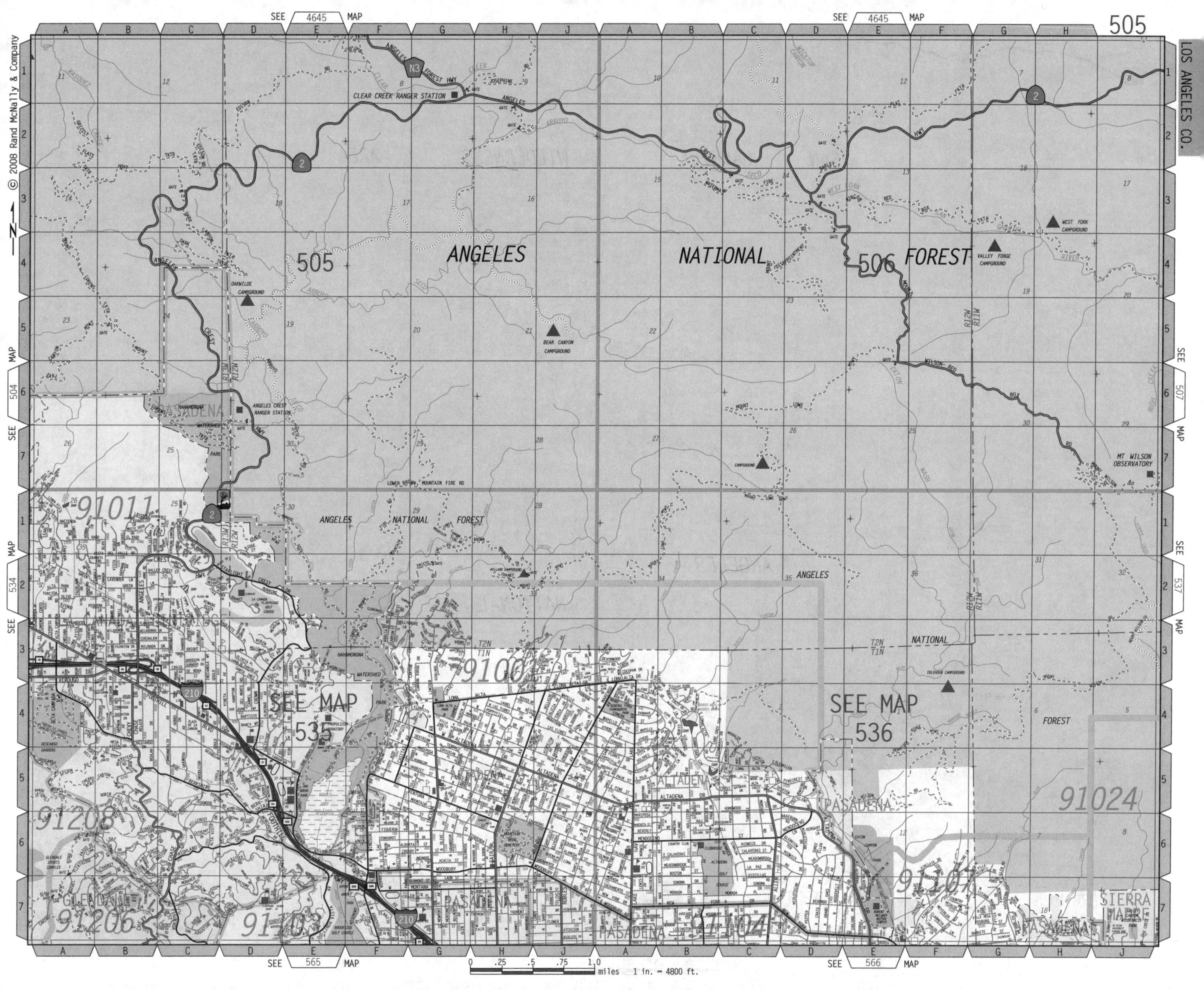

LOS ANGELES CO.
SEE 4645 MAP
SEE 504 MAP
SEE 507 MAP
SEE 534 MAP
SEE 537 MAP
SEE 565 MAP
SEE 566 MAP
SEE MAP 535
SEE MAP 536
ANGELES NATIONAL FOREST
505
506
CLEAR CREEK RANGER STATION
ANGELES FOREST HWY
ANGELES CREST HWY
OAKWILDE CAMPGROUND
BEAR CANYON CAMPGROUND
WEST FORK CAMPGROUND
VALLEY FORGE CAMPGROUND
MT WILSON OBSERVATORY
ANGELES CREST RANGER STATION
HAHAMONGNA WATERSHED PARK
LOWER BROWN MOUNTAIN FIRE RD
MT WILSON RED BOX RD
IDLEHOUR CAMPGROUND
PASADENA
ALTADENA
LA CANADA FLINTRIDGE
GLENDALE
SIERRA MADRE
91011
91001
91024
91208
91206
91103
91104
91107
R13W R12W
R12W R11W
T2N T1N
0 .25 .5 .75 1.0 miles 1 in. = 4800 ft.

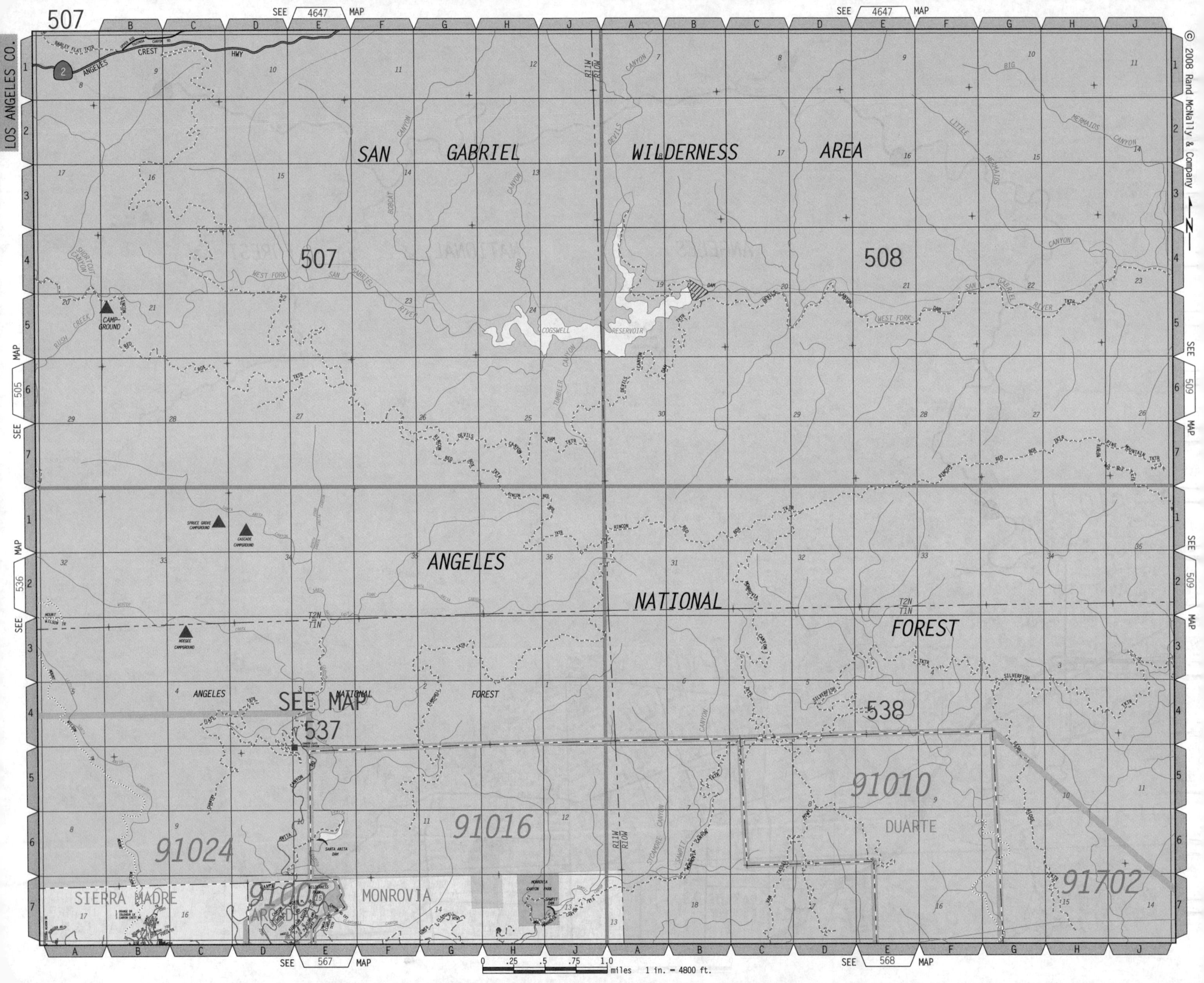
LOS ANGELES CO.
SEE 4647 MAP
SEE 4647 MAP
ANGELES CREST HWY
SAN GABRIEL WILDERNESS AREA
507
508
WEST FORK SAN GABRIEL RIVER
COGSWELL RESERVOIR
DAM
CAMP-GROUND
SHORTCUT CANYON
RUSH CREEK
BOBCAT CANYON
LOBO CANYON
DEVILS CANYON
TUMBLER CANYON
LITTLE MERMAIDS
MERMAIDS CANYON
BIG
CANYON
R11W R10W
RINCON RED BOX TKTR
PINE MOUNTAIN TKTR
SEE 505 MAP
SEE 509 MAP
SEE 536 MAP
SEE 509 MAP
SPRUCE GROVE CAMPGROUND
CASCADE CAMPGROUND
HOEGEES CAMPGROUND
ANGELES NATIONAL FOREST
T2N T1N
SEE MAP 537
538
ANGELES NATIONAL FOREST
SILVERFISH
MONROVIA CANYON
SANTA ANITA DAM
SYCAMORE CANYON
SAWPIT CANYON
91024
91016
91010
91702
91006
DUARTE
SIERRA MADRE
MONROVIA
ARCADIA
MONROVIA CANYON PARK
SAWPIT DAM
SEE 567 MAP
SEE 568 MAP
0 .25 .5 .75 1.0 miles 1 in. = 4800 ft.

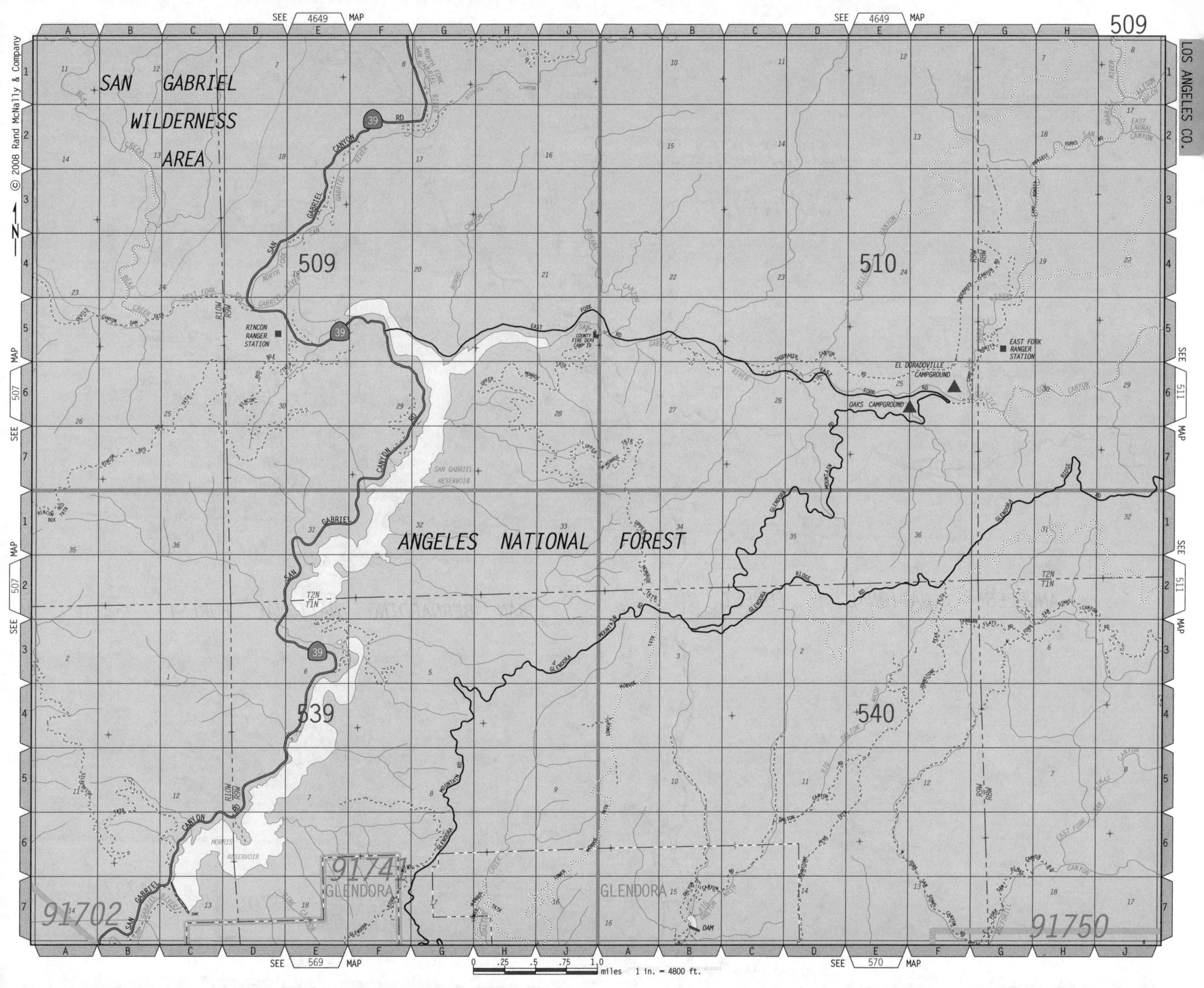
SAN GABRIEL WILDERNESS AREA
ANGELES NATIONAL FOREST
509
510
539
540
LOS ANGELES CO.
SEE 4649 MAP
SEE 507 MAP
SEE 511 MAP
SEE 569 MAP
SEE 570 MAP
RINCON RANGER STATION
EAST FORK RANGER STATION
EL DORADOVILLE CAMPGROUND
OAKS CAMPGROUND
COUNTY FIRE DEPT CAMP 19
SAN GABRIEL RESERVOIR
MORRIS RESERVOIR
GLENDORA
91741
91702
91750
SAN GABRIEL CANYON RD
GLENDORA MOUNTAIN RD
GLENDORA RIDGE RD
EAST FORK RD
T2N
T1N
R10W
R9W
DAM
0 .25 .5 .75 1.0 miles 1 in. = 4800 ft.

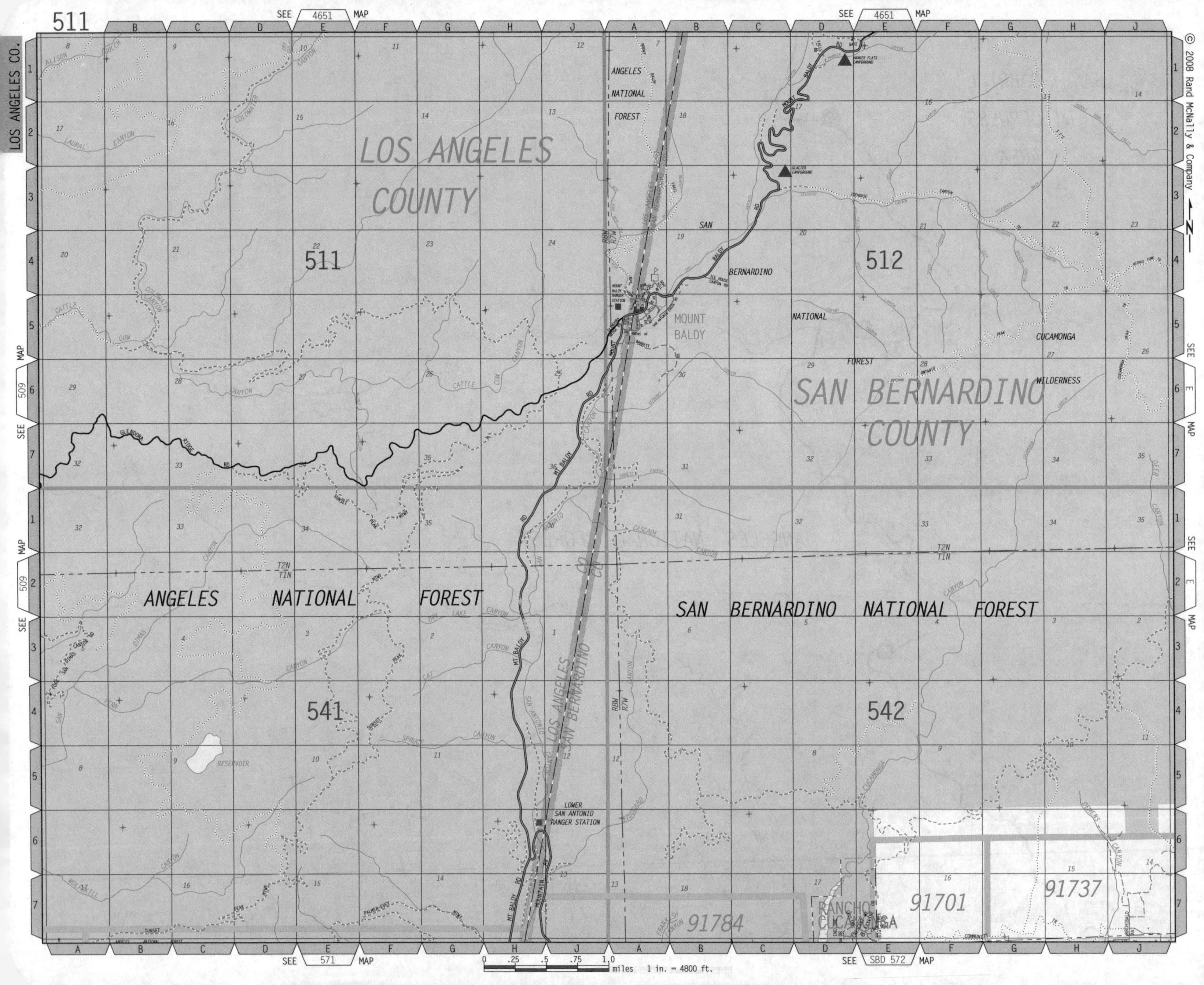

LOS ANGELES CO.
SEE 4651 MAP
SEE 4651 MAP
LOS ANGELES COUNTY
511
512
541
542
ANGELES NATIONAL FOREST
SAN BERNARDINO NATIONAL FOREST
SAN BERNARDINO COUNTY
CUCAMONGA WILDERNESS
MOUNT BALDY
MT BALDY RD
GLENDORA RIDGE RD
MOUNT BALDY RANGER STATION
LOWER SAN ANTONIO RANGER STATION
MANKER FLATS CAMPGROUND
GLACIER CAMPGROUND
LOS ANGELES
SAN BERNARDINO
T2N
T1N
R8W
R7W
RESERVOIR
MOUNTAIN AV
91784
91701
91737
RANCHO CUCAMONGA
SEE 509 MAP
SEE 509 MAP
SEE E MAP
SEE E MAP
SEE 571 MAP
SEE SBD 572 MAP
miles 1 in. = 4800 ft.

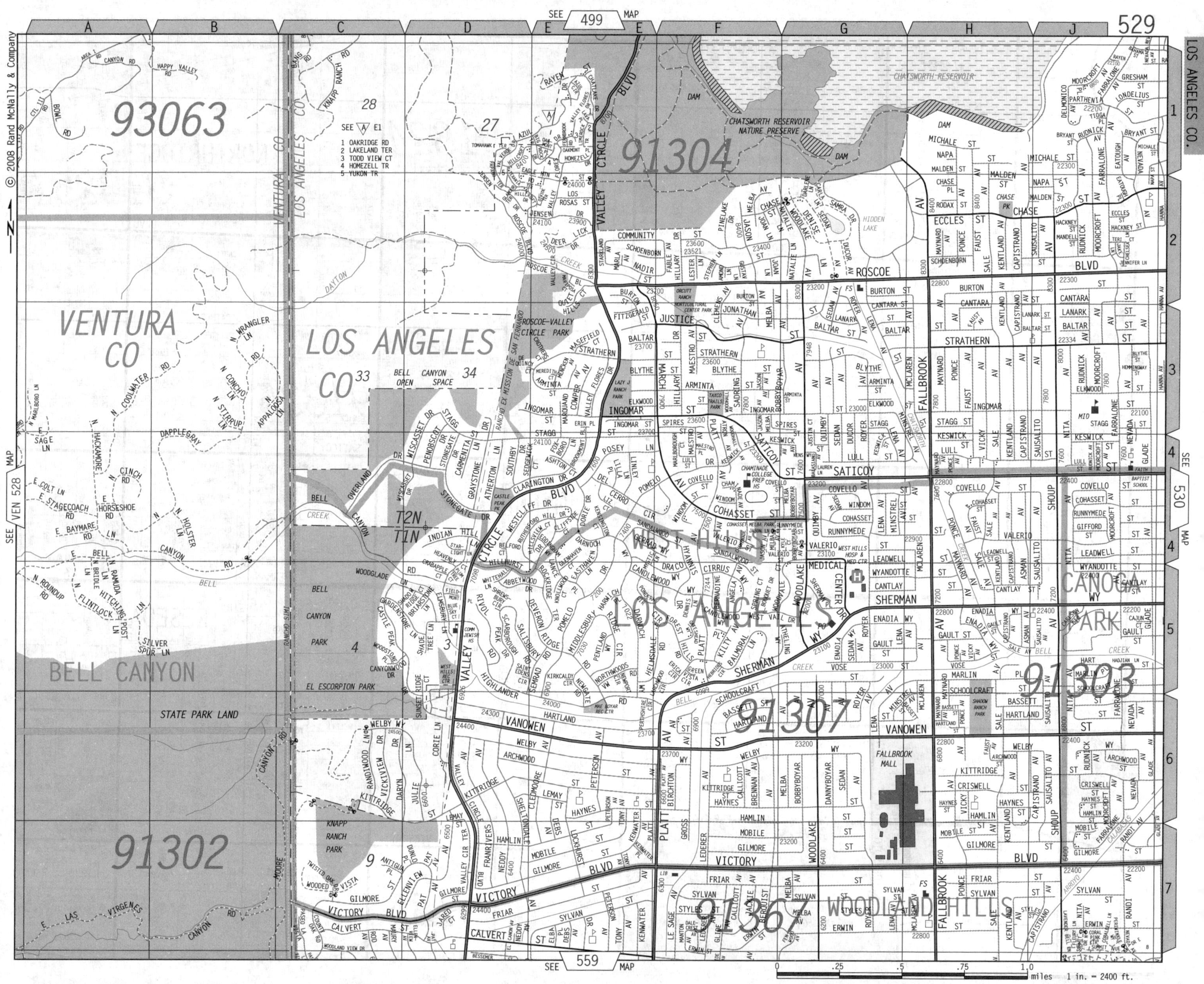
SEE 499 MAP
LOS ANGELES CO.
© 2008 Rand McNally & Company
93063
91304
VENTURA CO
LOS ANGELES CO
BELL CANYON
91302
WEST HILLS
LOS ANGELES
91307
91303
CANOGA PARK
91367
WOODLAND HILLS
CHATSWORTH RESERVOIR
CHATSWORTH RESERVOIR NATURE PRESERVE
STATE PARK LAND
EL ESCORPION PARK
KNAPP RANCH PARK
FALLBROOK MALL
SEE VEN 528 MAP
SEE 530 MAP
SEE 559 MAP
miles 1 in. = 2400 ft.

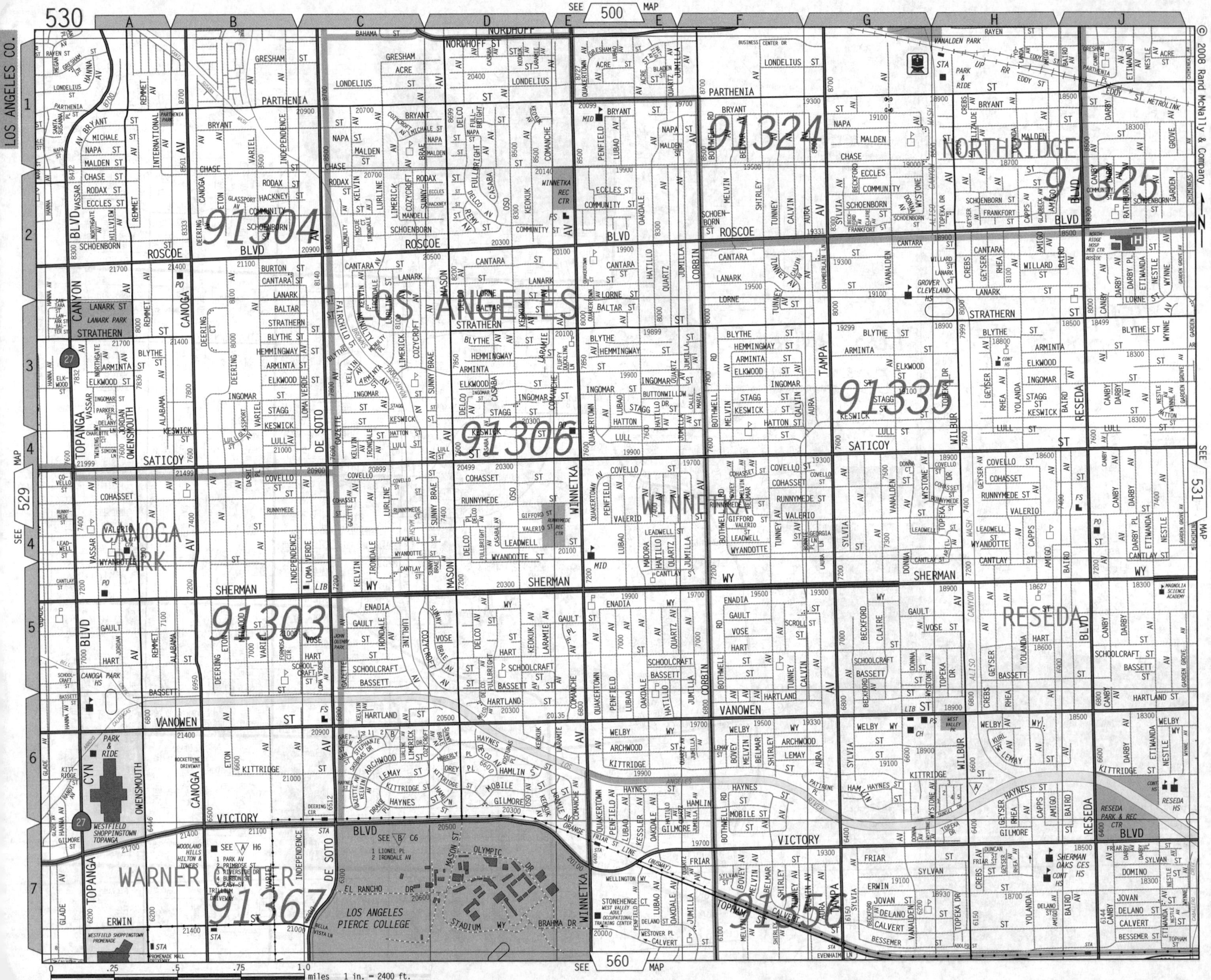
SEE 500 MAP
LOS ANGELES CO.
A
B
C
D
E
F
G
H
J
1
2
3
4
5
6
7
NORTHRIDGE
LOS ANGELES
CANOGA PARK
WINNETKA
RESEDA
WARNER CENTER
91324
91325
91304
91306
91335
91303
91367
91356
NORDHOFF
PARTHENIA
ROSCOE BLVD
SATICOY
SHERMAN WY
VANOWEN
VICTORY BLVD
TOPANGA CANYON BLVD
CANOGA AV
DE SOTO AV
WINNETKA AV
CORBIN AV
TAMPA AV
WILBUR AV
RESEDA BLVD
LOS ANGELES PIERCE COLLEGE
WESTFIELD SHOPPINGTOWN TOPANGA
WINNETKA REC CTR
RESEDA PARK & REC CTR
GROVER CLEVELAND HS
CANOGA PARK HS
RESEDA HS
SEE 529 MAP
SEE 531 MAP
SEE 560 MAP
miles 1 in. = 2400 ft.

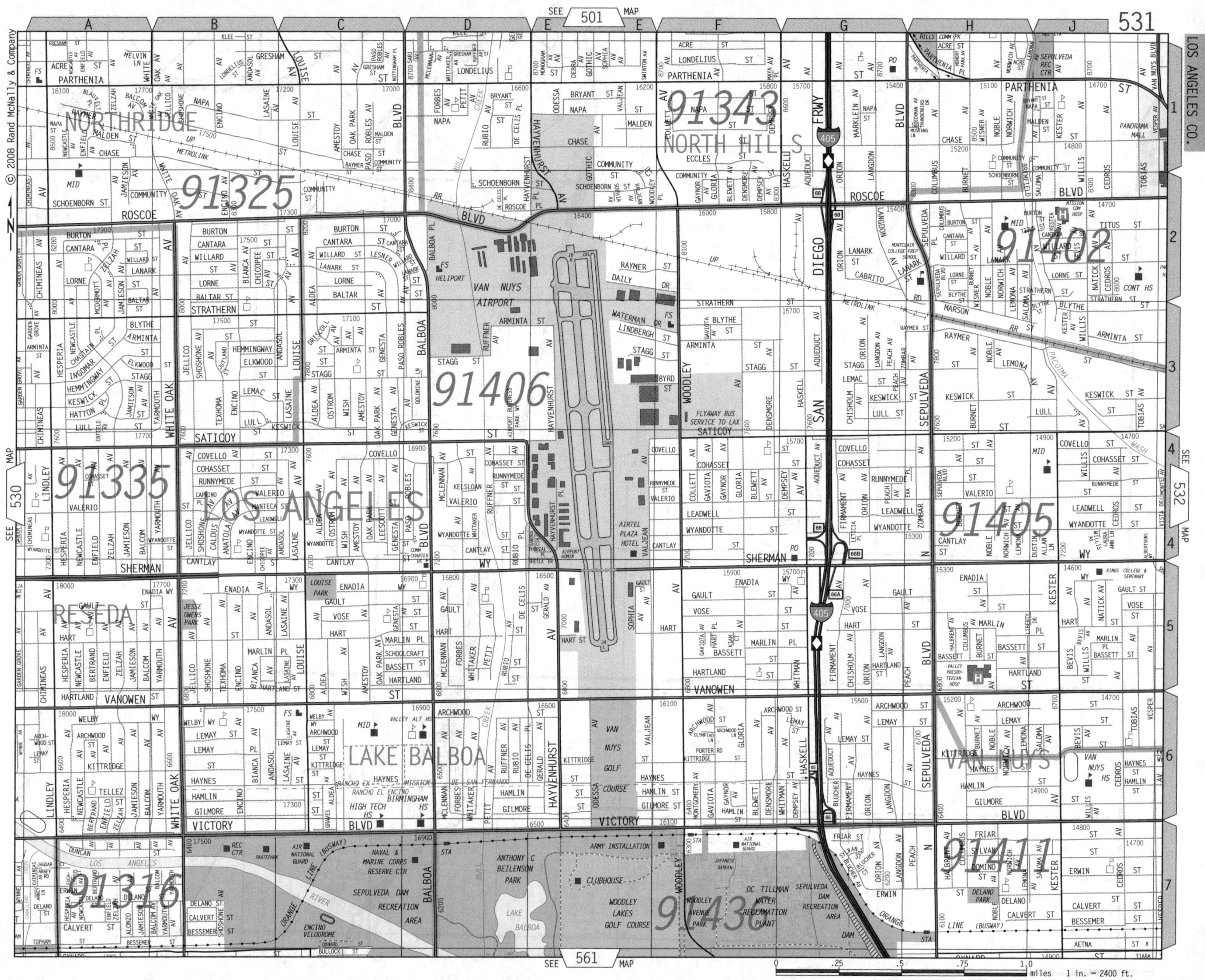
SEE 501 MAP
SEE 561 MAP
SEE 530 MAP
SEE 532 MAP
LOS ANGELES CO.
© 2008 Rand McNally & Company
A B C D E F G H J
1 2 3 4 5 6 7
NORTHRIDGE
NORTH HILLS
LOS ANGELES
RESEDA
LAKE BALBOA
VAN NUYS
91325
91343
91402
91406
91335
91405
91316
91436
91411
VAN NUYS AIRPORT
HELIPORT
AIRTEL PLAZA HOTEL
FLYAWAY BUS SERVICE TO LAX
SAN DIEGO FRWY
PANORAMA MALL
SEPULVEDA REC CTR
MISSION COM HOSP
CONT HS
MONTCLAIR COLLEGE PREP SCHOOL
KINGS COLLEGE & SEMINARY
VALLEY PRESBYTERIAN HOSP
VAN NUYS HS
DELANO PARK
JESSE OWENS PARK
LOUISE PARK
BIRMINGHAM HS
HIGH TECH HS
VALLEY ALT HS
RANCHO EL ENCINO
VAN NUYS GOLF COURSE
ARMY INSTALLATION
AIR NATIONAL GUARD
NAVAL & MARINE CORPS RESERVE CTR
ANTHONY C BEILENSON PARK
SEPULVEDA DAM RECREATION AREA
LAKE BALBOA
WOODLEY LAKES GOLF COURSE
WOODLEY AVENUE PARK
JAPANESE GARDEN
DC TILLMAN WATER RECLAMATION PLANT
ENCINO VELODROME
LOS ANGELES RIVER
ORANGE LINE (BUSWAY)
METROLINK
ROSCOE BLVD
SHERMAN WY
VANOWEN ST
VICTORY BLVD
PARTHENIA ST
SATICOY ST
miles 1 in. = 2400 ft.
0 .25 .5 .75 1.0

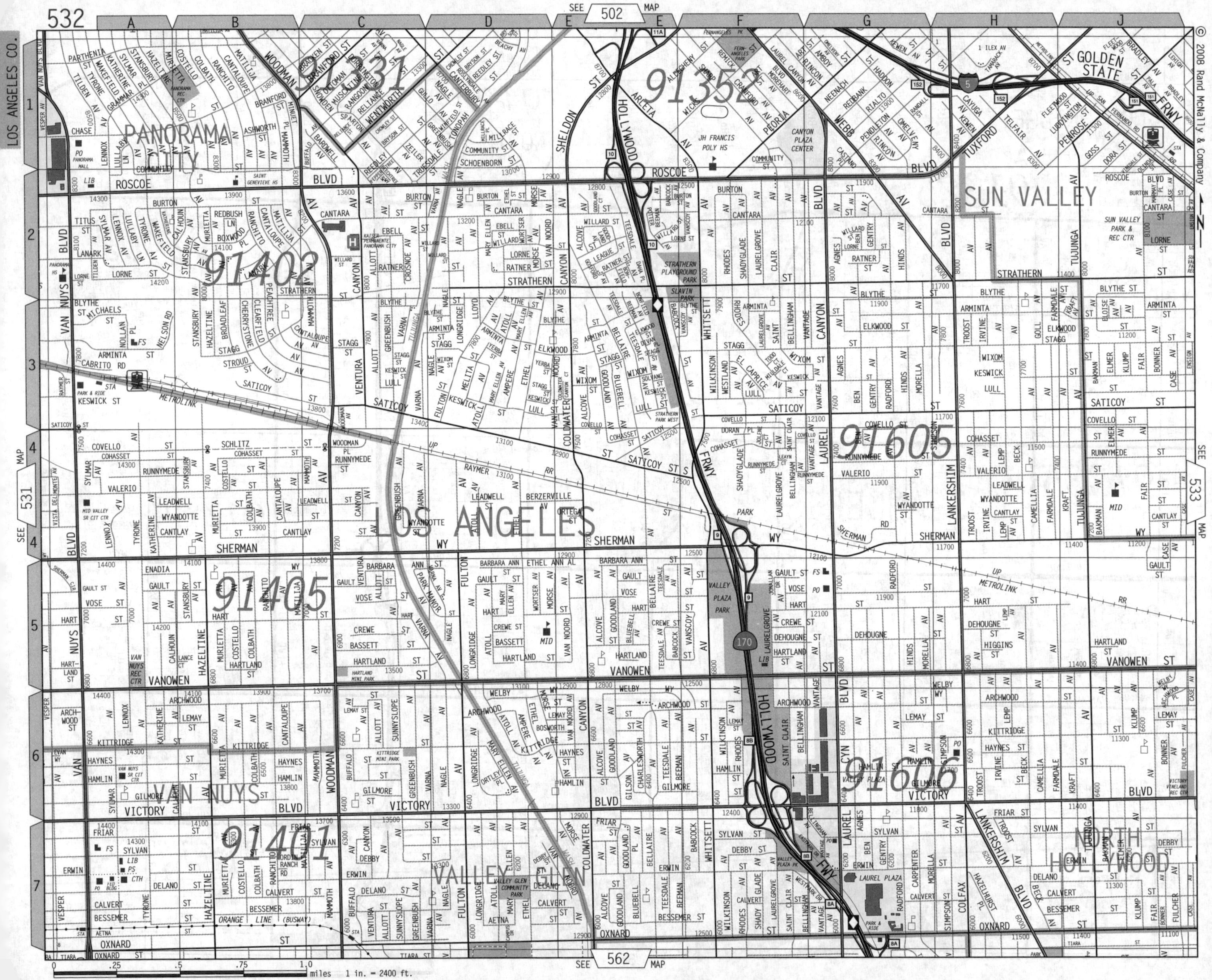

LOS ANGELES CO.
SEE 502 MAP
SEE 531 MAP
SEE 533 MAP
SEE 562 MAP
A
B
C
D
E
F
G
H
J
1
2
3
4
5
6
7
PANORAMA CITY
SUN VALLEY
LOS ANGELES
VAN NUYS
VALLEY GLEN
NORTH HOLLYWOOD
91331
91352
91402
91605
91405
91606
91401
ROSCOE BLVD
SATICOY ST
SHERMAN WY
VANOWEN ST
VICTORY BLVD
OXNARD ST
HOLLYWOOD FRWY
GOLDEN STATE FRWY
VAN NUYS BLVD
WOODMAN AV
LAUREL CANYON BLVD
LANKERSHIM BLVD
TUJUNGA AV
COLDWATER CANYON AV
SHELDON ST
TUXFORD ST
STRATHERN ST
METROLINK
ORANGE LINE (BUSWAY)
PANORAMA MALL
JH FRANCIS POLY HS
CANYON PLAZA CENTER
SUN VALLEY PARK & REC CTR
STRATHERN PLAYGROUND PARK
SLAVIN PARK
VALLEY PLAZA PARK
VALLEY GLEN COMMUNITY PARK
LAUREL PLAZA
VAN NUYS REC CTR
MID VALLEY SR CIT CTR
KAISER PERMANENTE PANORAMA CITY
miles 1 in. = 2400 ft.
0 .25 .5 .75 1.0
© 2008 Rand McNally & Company

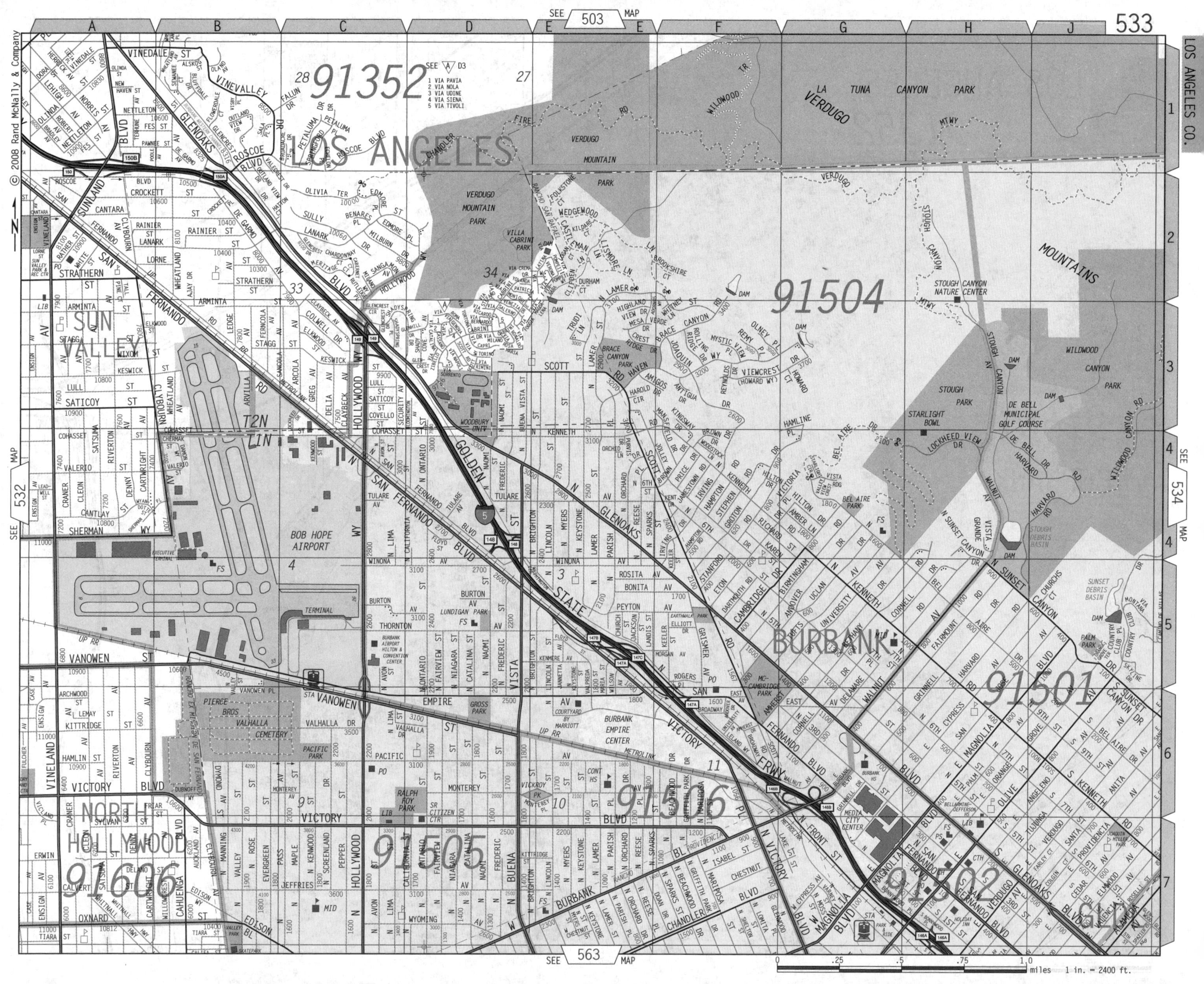

SEE 503 MAP
A
B
C
D
E
F
G
H
J
LOS ANGELES CO.
© 2008 Rand McNally & Company
91352
SEE D3
1 VIA PAVIA
2 VIA NOLA
3 VIA UDINE
4 VIA SIENA
5 VIA TIVOLI
LOS ANGELES
LA TUNA CANYON PARK
VERDUGO MOUNTAIN PARK
VILLA CABRINI PARK
91504
VERDUGO MOUNTAINS
STOUGH CANYON NATURE CENTER
BRACE CANYON PARK
STOUGH PARK
STARLIGHT BOWL
DE BELL MUNICIPAL GOLF COURSE
BEL AIRE PARK
STOUGH DEBRIS BASIN
SUNSET DEBRIS BASIN
WILDWOOD CANYON PARK
SUN VALLEY
SUN VALLEY PARK & REC CTR
T2N
WOODBURY UNIV
BOB HOPE AIRPORT
EXECUTIVE TERMINAL
TERMINAL
BURBANK AIRPORT HILTON & CONVENTION CENTER
LUNDIGAN PARK
BURBANK
91501
91502
91505
91506
91606
NORTH HOLLYWOOD
PIERCE BROS VALHALLA CEMETERY
PACIFIC PARK
GROSS PARK
COURTYARD BY MARRIOTT
BURBANK EMPIRE CENTER
MC-CAMBRIDGE PARK
RALPH FOY PARK
SR CITIZEN CTR
MEDIA CITY CENTER
BURBANK HS
GOLDEN STATE FRWY
SAN FERNANDO BLVD
VICTORY BLVD
GLENOAKS BLVD
HOLLYWOOD WY
VANOWEN ST
ROSCOE BLVD
SUNSET CANYON DR
GLDL
SEE 532 MAP
SEE 534 MAP
SEE 563 MAP
0 .25 .5 .75 1.0 miles 1 in. = 2400 ft.

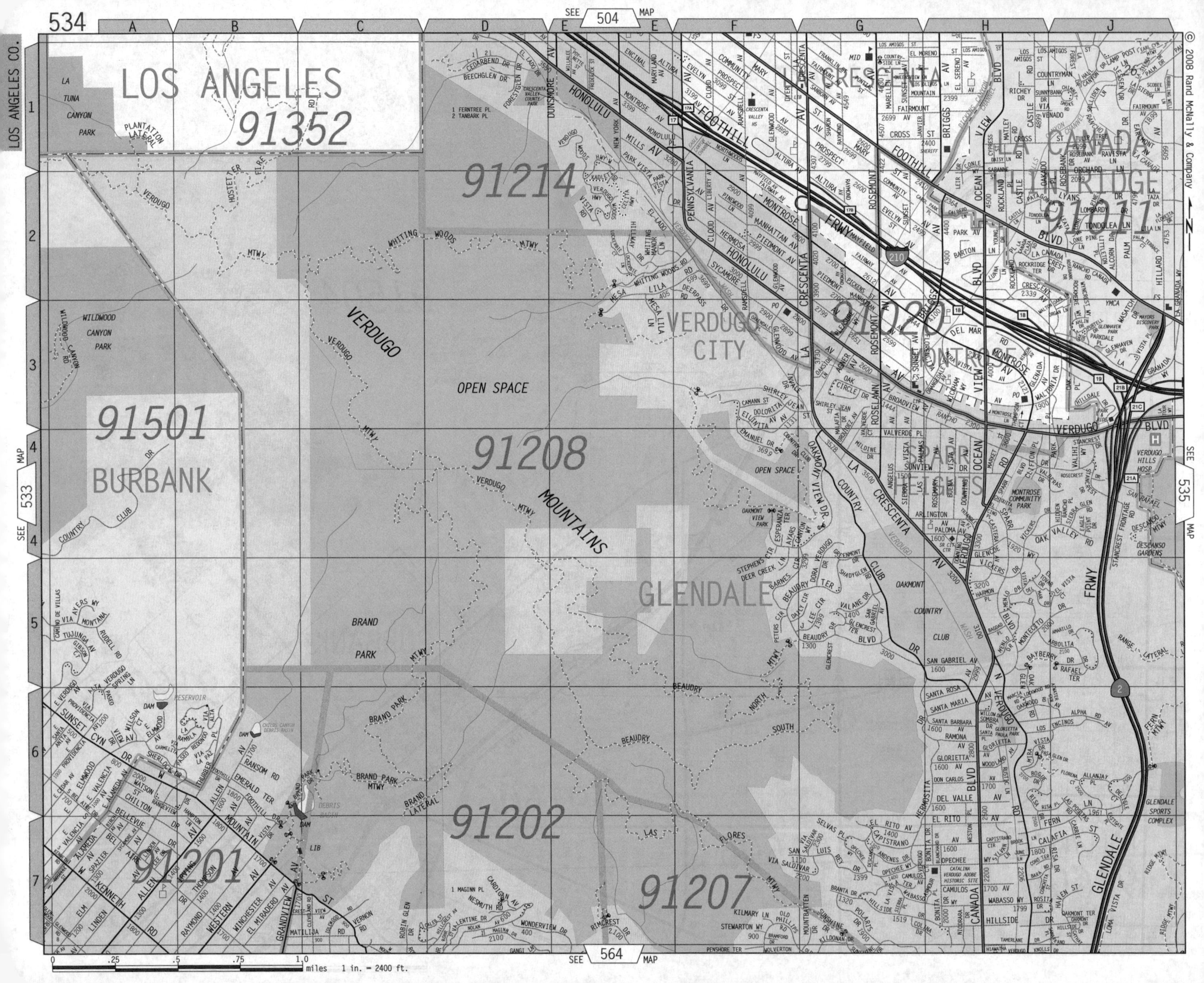
534
SEE 504 MAP
SEE 564 MAP
SEE 533 MAP
SEE 535 MAP
LOS ANGELES CO.
© 2008 Rand McNally & Company
LOS ANGELES
91352
91214
91501
BURBANK
91208
VERDUGO MOUNTAINS
OPEN SPACE
BRAND PARK
91202
91201
91207
GLENDALE
VERDUGO CITY
91020
MONTROSE
LA CRESCENTA
LA CANADA FLINTRIDGE
91011
SPARR HEIGHTS
LA TUNA CANYON PARK
WILDWOOD CANYON PARK
VERDUGO HILLS HOSP
DESCANSO GARDENS
GLENDALE SPORTS COMPLEX
MONTROSE COMMUNITY PARK
OAKMONT VIEW PARK
OAKMONT COUNTRY CLUB
FOOTHILL FRWY
GLENDALE FRWY
HONOLULU AV
MONTROSE AV
LA CRESCENTA AV
VERDUGO BLVD
CANADA BLVD
MOUNTAIN ST
0 .25 .5 .75 1.0 miles 1 in. = 2400 ft.

SEE 505 MAP

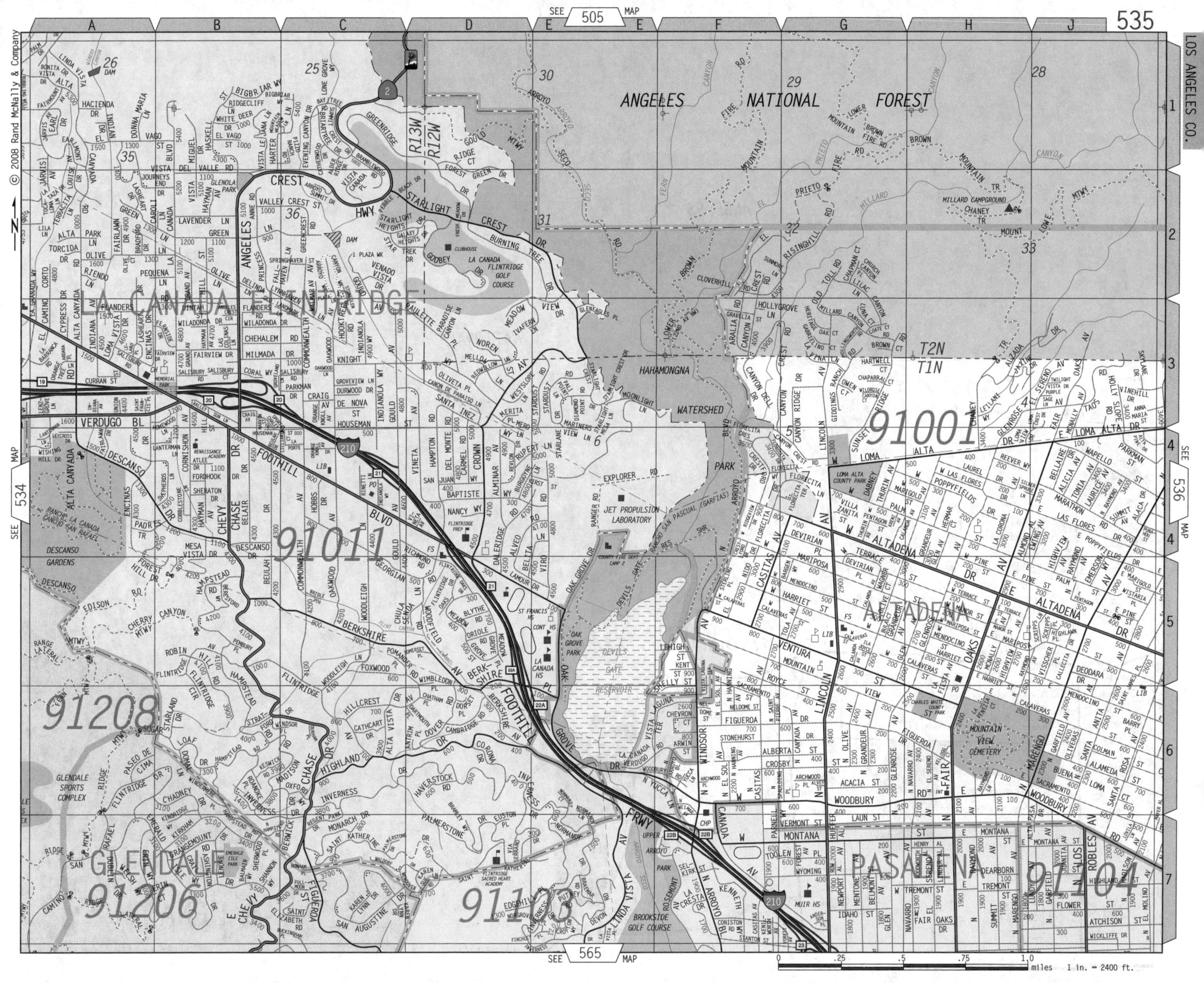

SEE 565 MAP

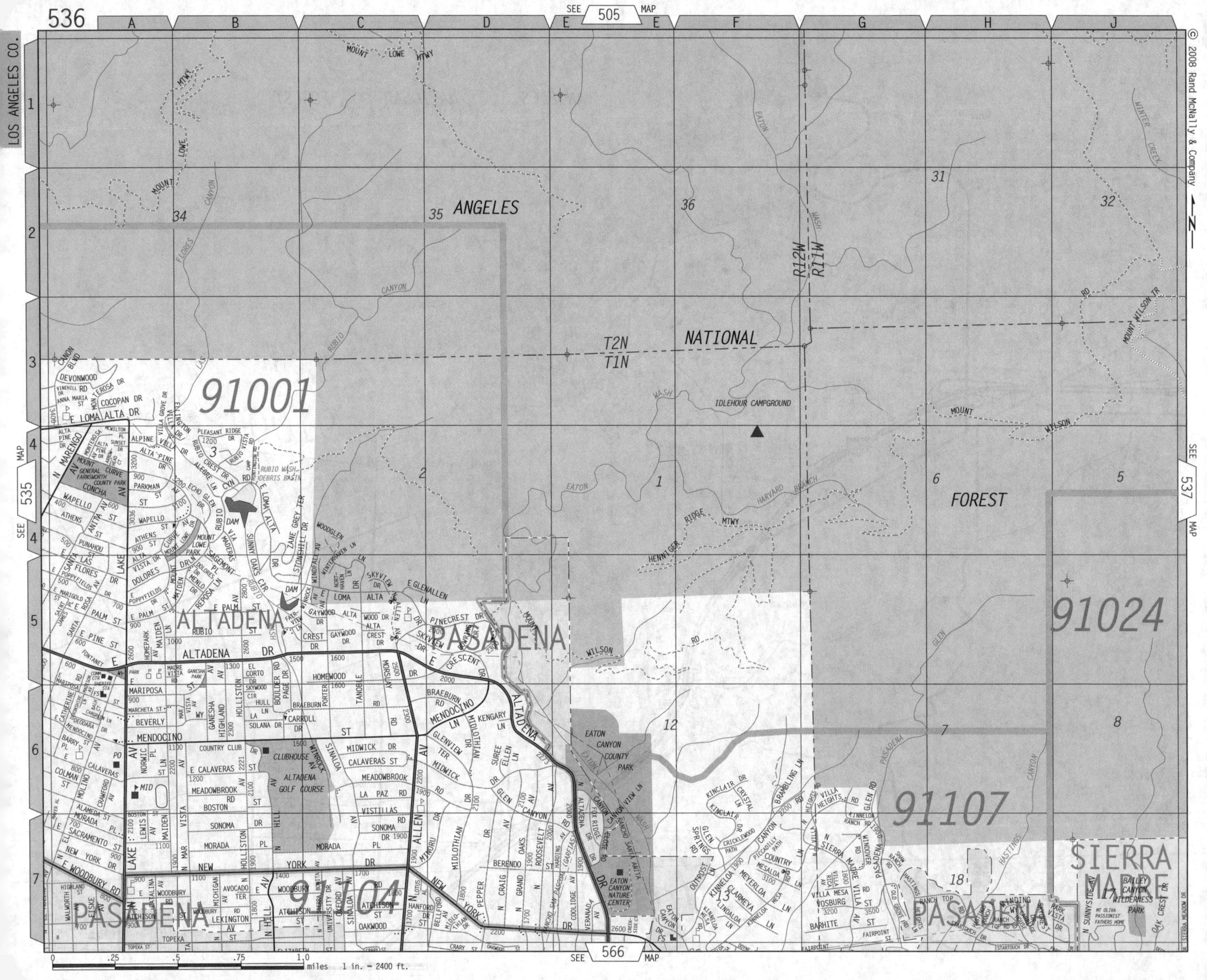
LOS ANGELES CO.
SEE 505 MAP
SEE 535 MAP
SEE 537 MAP
SEE 566 MAP
ANGELES
NATIONAL
FOREST
T2N
T1N
R12W
R11W
91001
91024
91107
91104
ALTADENA
PASADENA
SIERRA MADRE
IDLEHOUR CAMPGROUND
MOUNT LOWE MTWY
MOUNT WILSON
MOUNT WILSON TR
HARVARD BRANCH
HENNIGER RIDGE MTWY
RUBIO WASH DEBRIS BASIN
ALTADENA GOLF COURSE
CLUBHOUSE
EATON CANYON COUNTY PARK
EATON CANYON NATURE CENTER
MOUNT CURVE GENERAL FARNSWORTH COUNTY PARK
BAILEY CANYON WILDERNESS PARK
MT OLIVA PASSIONIST FATHERS HOME
E LOMA ALTA DR
ALTADENA DR
NEW YORK DR
E WOODBURY RD
MENDOCINO
LAKE AV
ALLEN AV
SIERRA MADRE VILLA
0 .25 .5 .75 1.0 miles 1 in. = 2400 ft.

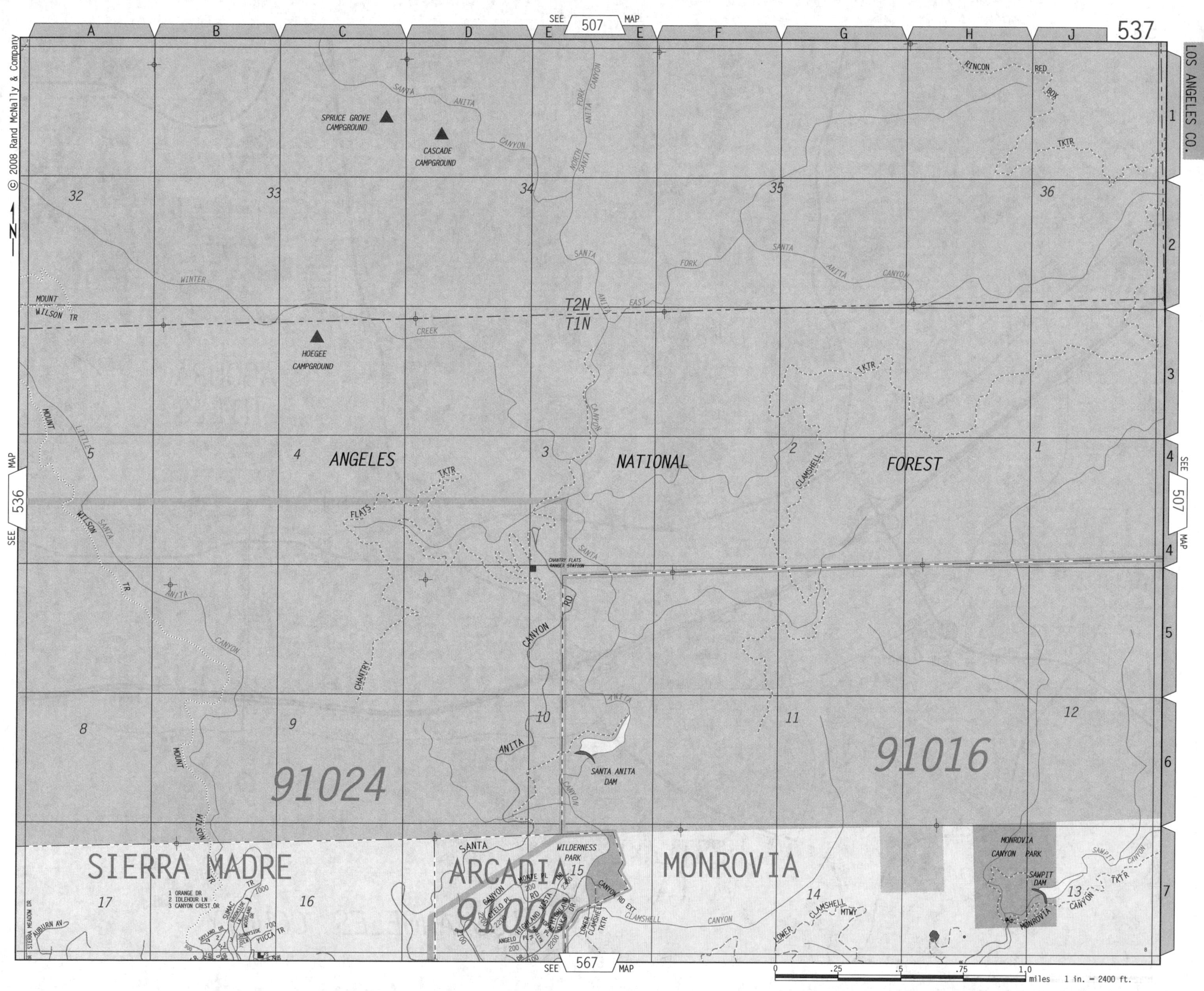
SEE 507 MAP
LOS ANGELES CO.
SPRUCE GROVE CAMPGROUND
CASCADE CAMPGROUND
HOEGEE CAMPGROUND
SANTA ANITA CANYON
NORTH FORK SANTA ANITA CANYON
RINCON RED BOX TKTR
MOUNT WILSON TR
WINTER CREEK
EAST FORK SANTA ANITA CANYON
T2N
T1N
ANGELES NATIONAL FOREST
CHANTRY FLATS RANGER STATION
FLATS TKTR
CLAMSHELL
CHANTRY
SANTA ANITA CANYON RD
SANTA ANITA DAM
91024
91016
91006
SIERRA MADRE
ARCADIA
MONROVIA
WILDERNESS PARK
MONROVIA CANYON PARK
SAWPIT DAM
SAWPIT CANYON
1 ORANGE DR
2 IDLEHOUR LN
3 CANYON CREST DR
AUBURN AV
SIERRA MEADOW DR
SKYLAND DR
SUNNYSIDE
YUCCA TR
CANYON RD EXT
CLAMSHELL CANYON
LOWER CLAMSHELL TKTR
LOWER CLAMSHELL MTWY
HIGHLAND VISTA DR
ANGELO DR
SEE 536 MAP
SEE 567 MAP
miles 1 in. = 2400 ft.

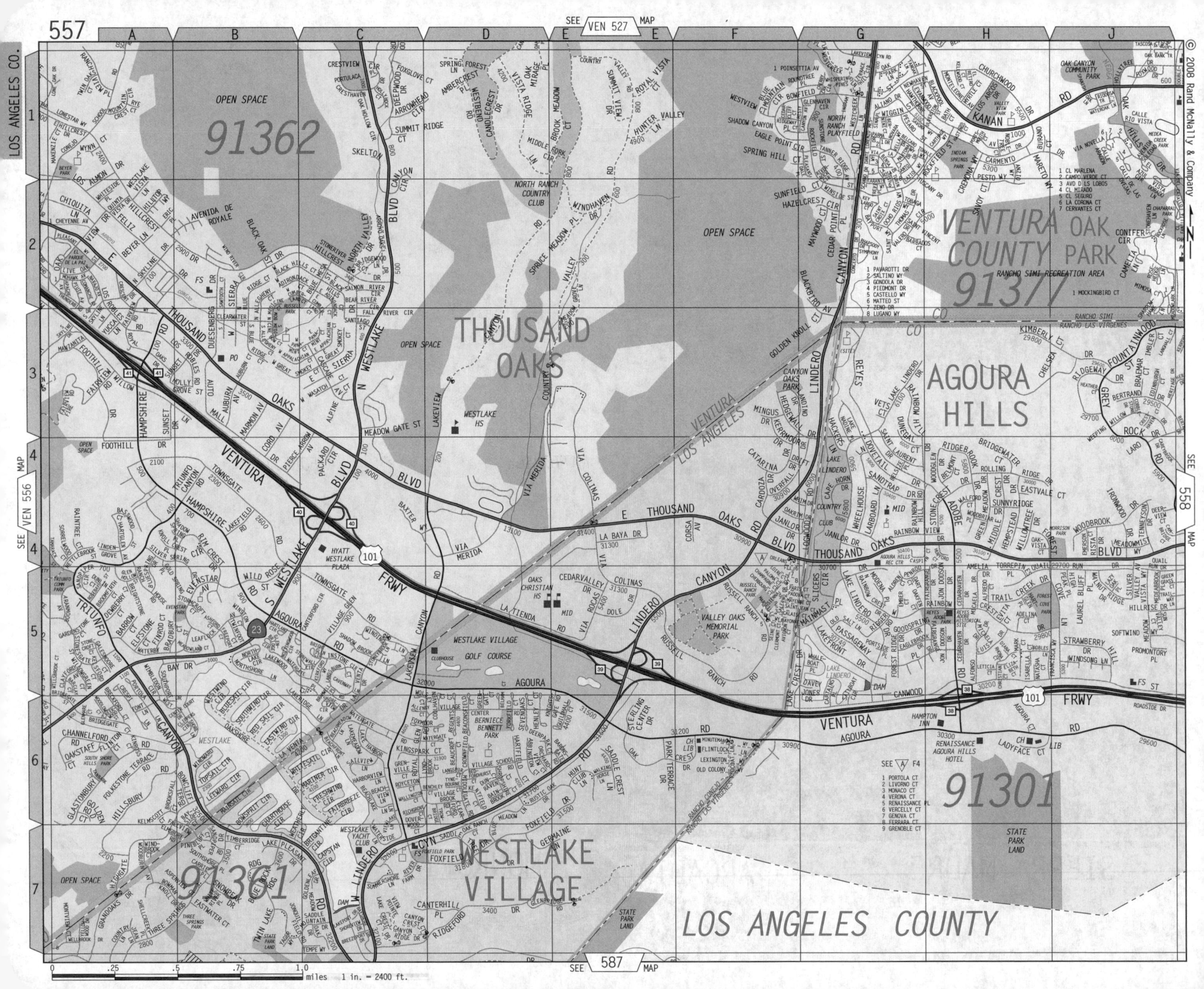

557
SEE VEN 527 MAP
A
B
C
D
E
F
G
H
J
LOS ANGELES CO.
© 2008 Rand McNally & Company
OPEN SPACE
91362
THOUSAND OAKS
NORTH RANCH COUNTRY CLUB
WESTLAKE HS
AGOURA HILLS
VENTURA COUNTY
OAK CANYON COMMUNITY PARK
OAK COUNTY PARK
91377
RANCHO SIMI RECREATION AREA
1 CL MARLENA
2 CAMPO VERDE CT
3 AVD D LS LOBOS
4 CL MIRADO
5 CL SEGURO
6 LA CORONA CT
7 CERVANTES CT
1 PAVAROTTI DR
2 SALTINO WY
3 GONDOLA DR
4 PIEDMONT DR
5 CASTELLO WY
6 MATTEO ST
7 ZENO DR
8 LUGANO WY
1 MOCKINGBIRD CT
RANCHO SIMI
RANCHO LAS VIRGENES
VENTURA
LOS ANGELES
VENTURA FRWY
THOUSAND OAKS BLVD
HYATT WESTLAKE PLAZA
OAKS CHRISTIAN HS
VALLEY OAKS MEMORIAL PARK
WESTLAKE VILLAGE GOLF COURSE
BERNIECE BENNETT PARK
HAMPTON INN
RENAISSANCE AGOURA HILLS HOTEL
SEE A F4
1 PORTOLA CT
2 LIVORNO CT
3 MONACO CT
4 VERONA CT
5 RENAISSANCE PL
6 VERCELLY CT
7 GENOVA CT
8 FERRARA CT
9 GRENOBLE CT
91301
STATE PARK LAND
WESTLAKE VILLAGE
WESTLAKE YACHT CLUB
91361
LOS ANGELES COUNTY
SEE VEN 556 MAP
SEE 558 MAP
SEE 587 MAP
0 .25 .5 .75 1.0 miles 1 in. = 2400 ft.

SEE VEN 528 MAP
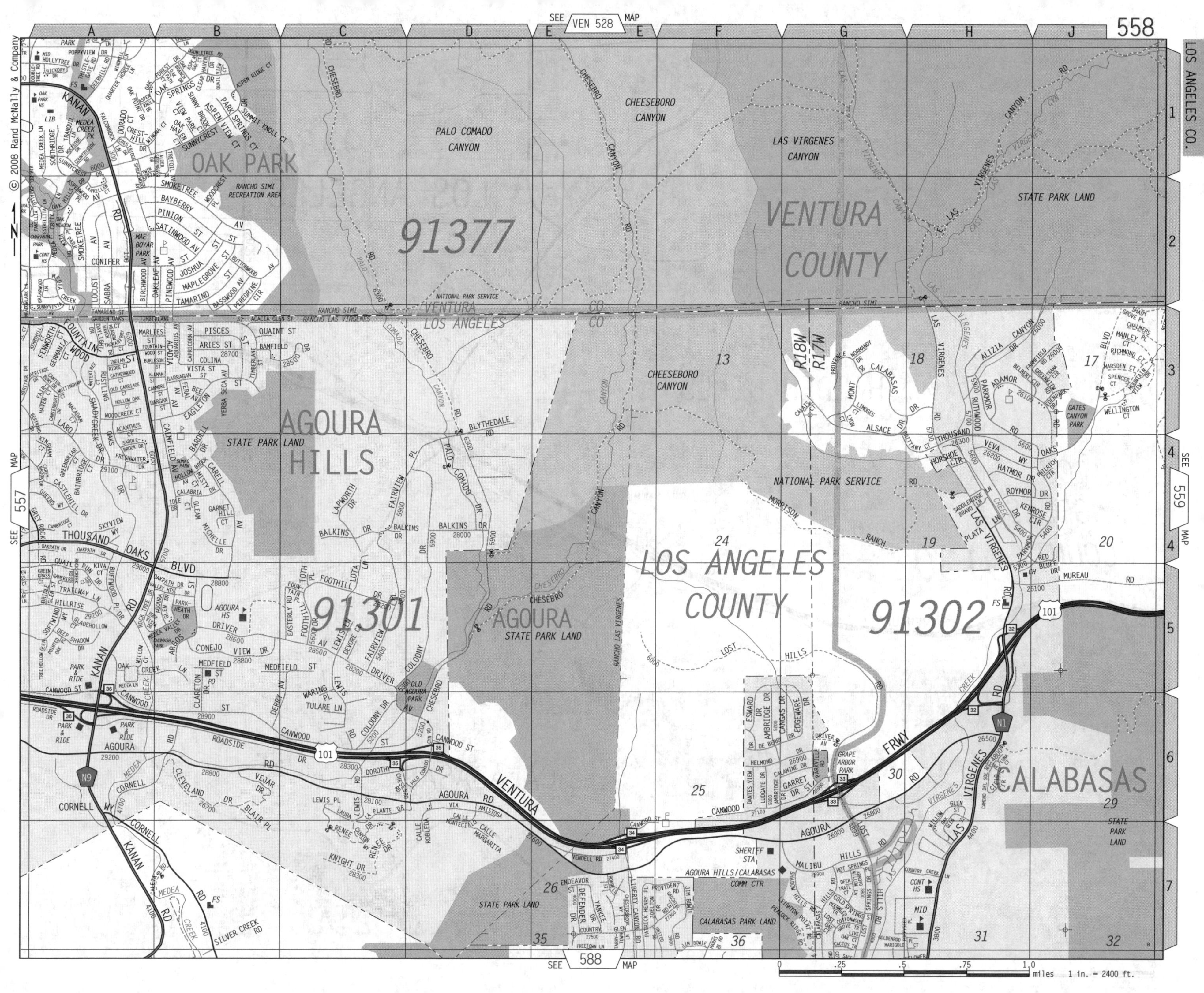

SEE 557 MAP
SEE 559 MAP
SEE 588 MAP
0 .25 .5 .75 1.0 miles 1 in. = 2400 ft.

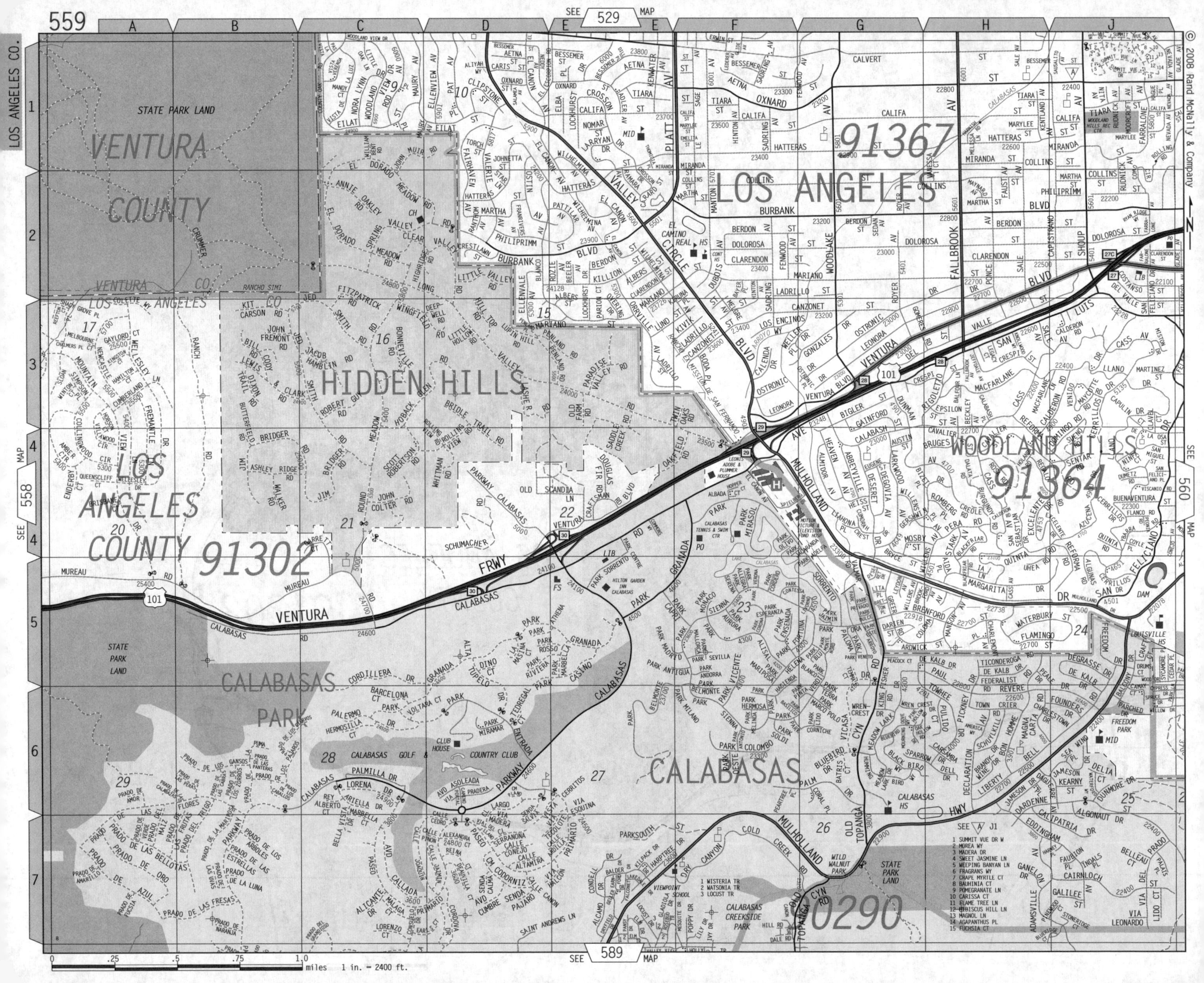
559
SEE 529 MAP
A
B
C
D
E
F
G
H
J
LOS ANGELES CO.
© 2008 Rand McNally & Company
STATE PARK LAND
VENTURA COUNTY
LOS ANGELES COUNTY
HIDDEN HILLS
91302
91367
LOS ANGELES
WOODLAND HILLS
91364
CALABASAS
CALABASAS PARK
CALABASAS GOLF & COUNTRY CLUB
STATE PARK LAND
90290
VENTURA FRWY
101
VENTURA BLVD
MULHOLLAND DR
MULHOLLAND HWY
CALABASAS PARKWAY
OLD TOPANGA CYN RD
TOPANGA CYN RD
LAS VIRGENES
BURBANK BLVD
VALLEY CIRCLE BLVD
CALABASAS HS
FREEDOM PARK
LOUISVILLE HS
CALABASAS CREEKSIDE PARK
WILD WALNUT PARK
VIEWPOINT SCHOOL
SEE 558 MAP
SEE 560 MAP
SEE A J1
1 SUMMIT VUE DR W
2 MOREA WY
3 MADERA DR
4 SWEET JASMINE LN
5 WEEPING BANYAN LN
6 FRAGRANS WY
7 CHAPL MYRTLE CT
8 BAUHINIA CT
9 POMEGRANATE LN
10 CARISSA CT
11 FLAME TREE LN
12 HIBISCUS HILL LN
13 MAGNOL LN
14 AGAPANTHUS PL
15 FUCHSIA CT
1 WISTERIA TR
2 WATSONIA TR
3 LOCUST TR
SEE 589 MAP
0 .25 .5 .75 1.0 miles 1 in. = 2400 ft.

SEE 530 MAP

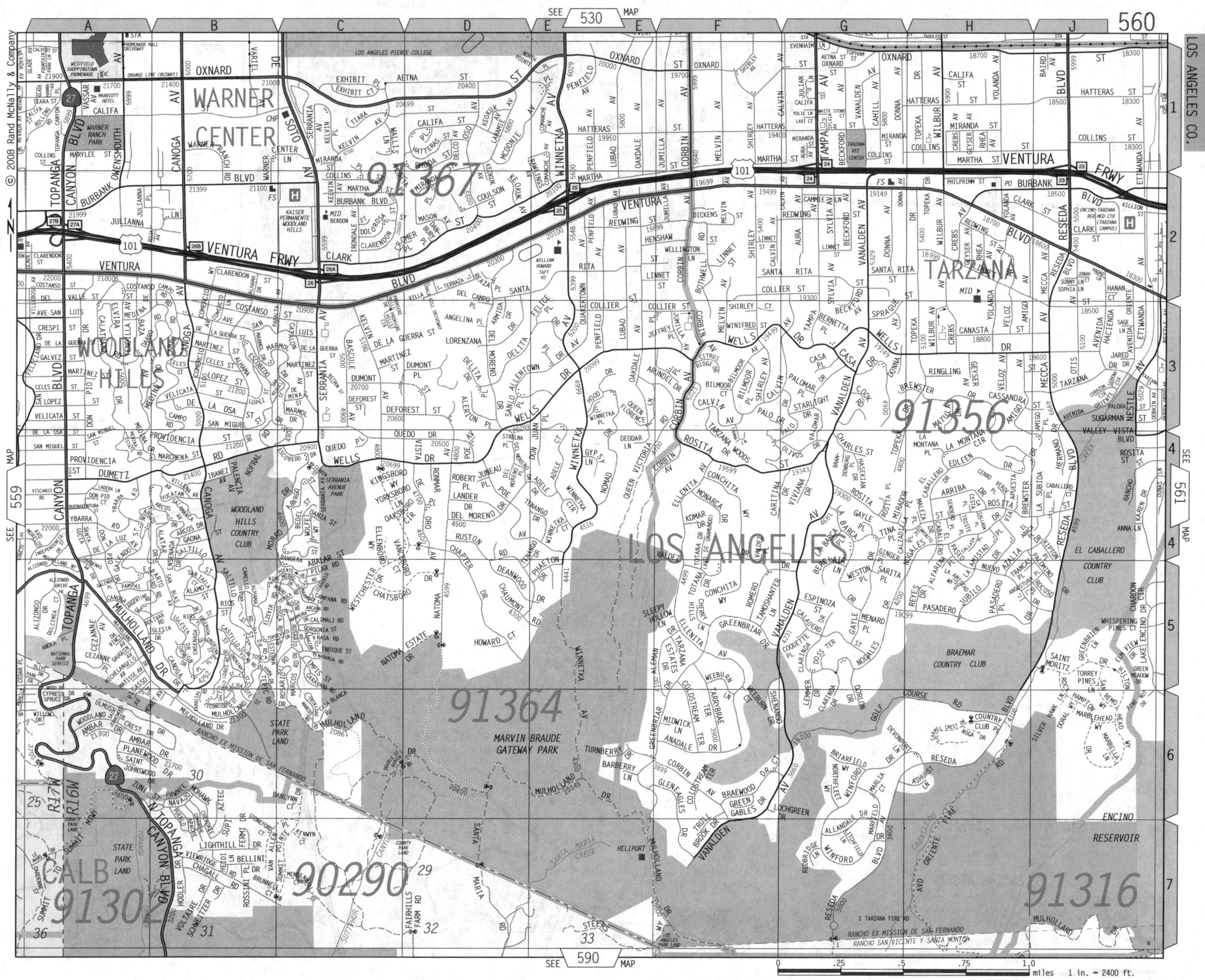

SEE 559 MAP
SEE 561 MAP
SEE 590 MAP

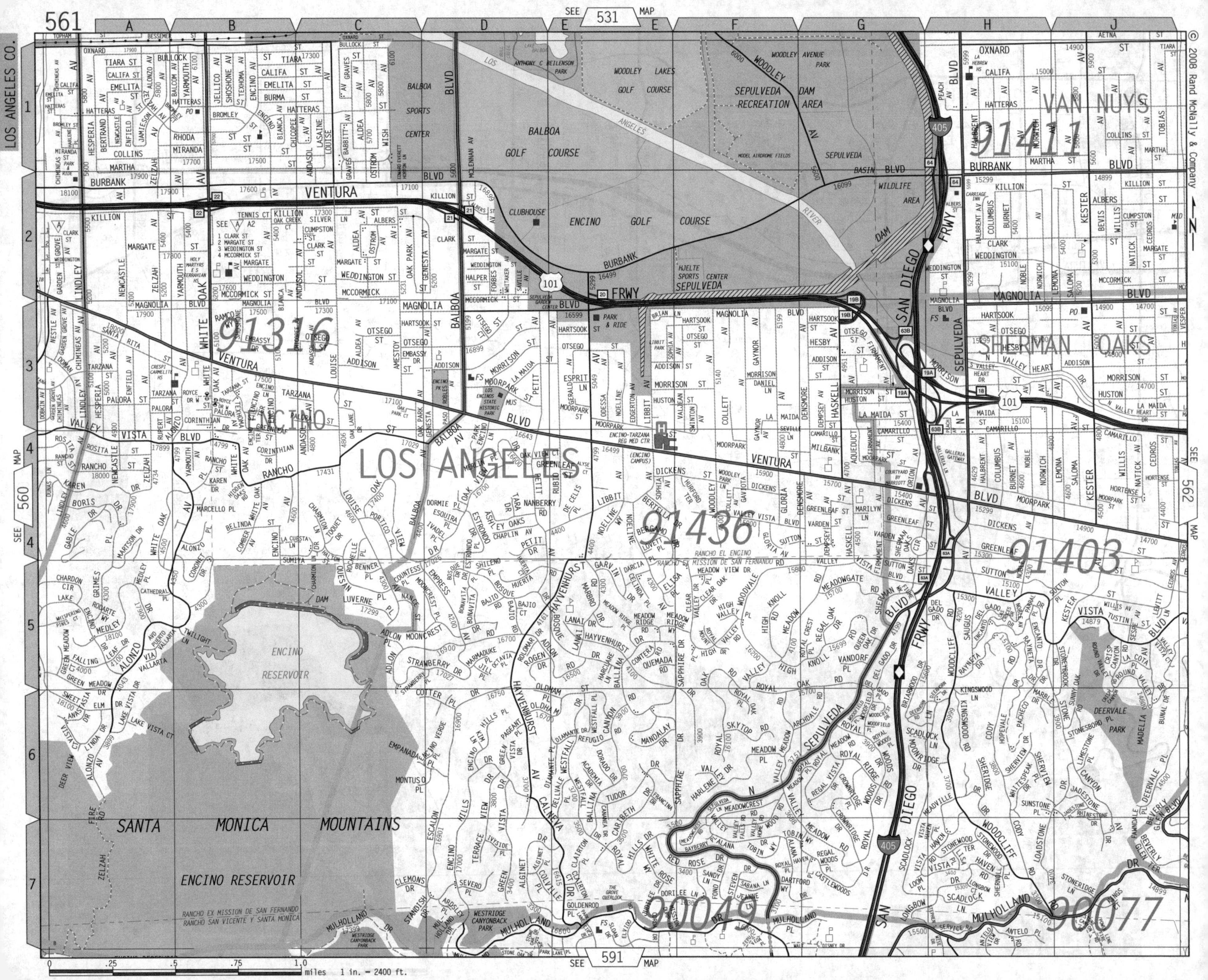
LOS ANGELES CO.
SEE 531 MAP
SEE 560 MAP
SEE 562 MAP
SEE 591 MAP
A
B
C
D
E
F
G
H
J
1
2
3
4
5
6
7
VAN NUYS
91411
91316
SHERMAN OAKS
ENCINO
LOS ANGELES
91436
91403
90049
90077
VENTURA BLVD
VENTURA FRWY
SAN DIEGO FRWY
BALBOA BLVD
BURBANK BLVD
MAGNOLIA BLVD
MULHOLLAND DR
SEPULVEDA BLVD
SEPULVEDA DAM RECREATION AREA
SEPULVEDA BASIN WILDLIFE AREA
WOODLEY LAKES GOLF COURSE
BALBOA GOLF COURSE
ENCINO GOLF COURSE
BALBOA SPORTS CENTER
HJELTE SPORTS CENTER
LOS ANGELES RIVER
ANTHONY C BEILENSON PARK
WOODLEY AVENUE PARK
ENCINO-TARZANA REG MED CTR
LOS ENCINOS STATE HISTORIC PARK
ENCINO RESERVOIR
SANTA MONICA MOUNTAINS
DEERVALE PARK
WESTRIDGE CANYONBACK PARK
RANCHO EL ENCINO
RANCHO EX MISSION DE SAN FERNANDO
RANCHO SAN VICENTE Y SANTA MONICA
0 .25 .5 .75 1.0 miles 1 in. = 2400 ft.

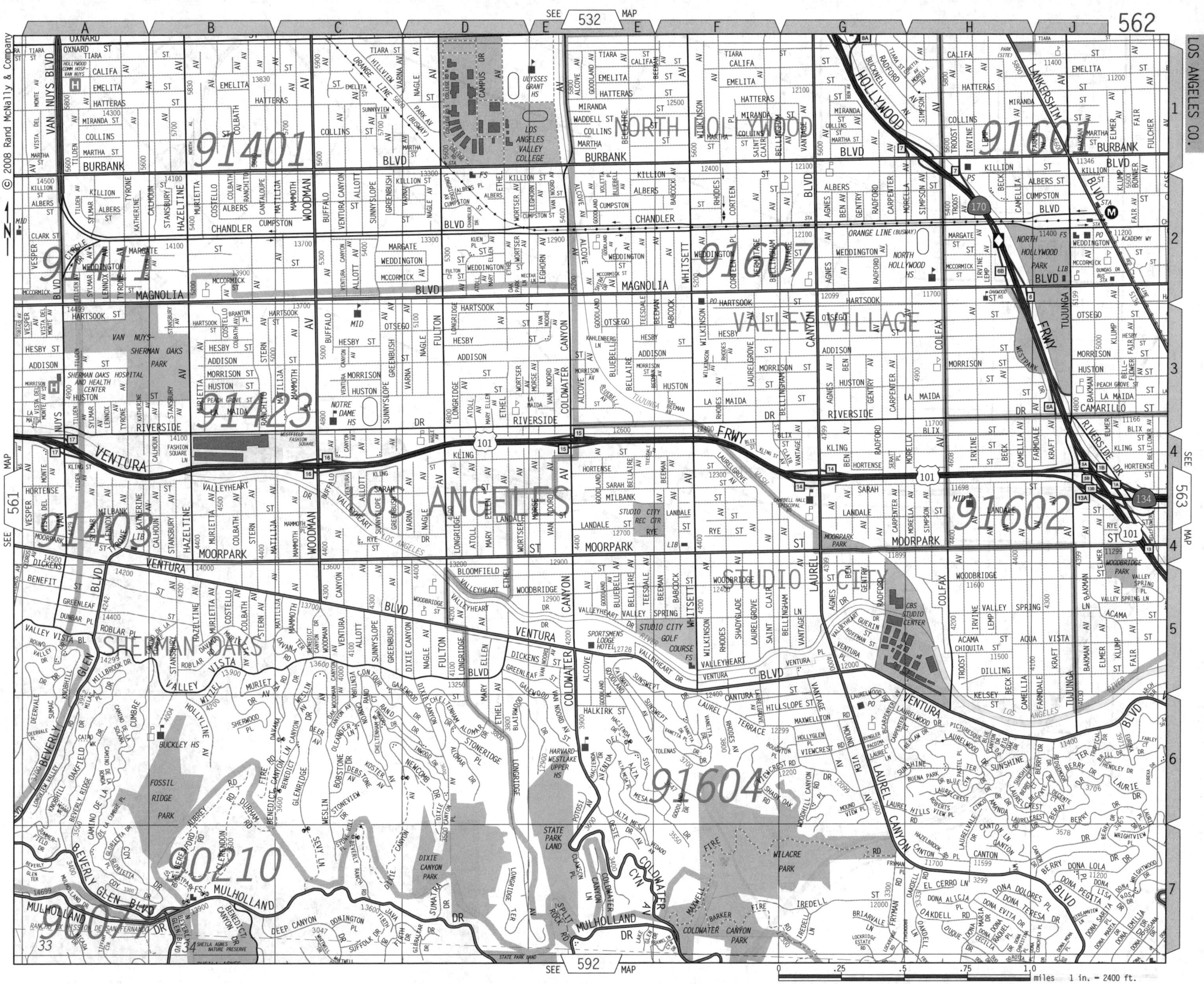

562
SEE 532 MAP
SEE 592 MAP
SEE 561 MAP
SEE 563 MAP
LOS ANGELES CO.
© 2008 Rand McNally & Company
NORTH HOLLYWOOD
VALLEY VILLAGE
STUDIO CITY
LOS ANGELES
SHERMAN OAKS
91401
91411
91423
91403
91607
91601
91602
91604
90210
90077
VENTURA FRWY
HOLLYWOOD FRWY
VENTURA BLVD
BURBANK BLVD
MAGNOLIA BLVD
MOORPARK ST
RIVERSIDE DR
MULHOLLAND DR
LAUREL CANYON BLVD
COLDWATER CANYON AV
BEVERLY GLEN BLVD
VAN NUYS BLVD
LANKERSHIM BLVD
LOS ANGELES VALLEY COLLEGE
NORTH HOLLYWOOD PARK
CBS STUDIO CENTER
STUDIO CITY GOLF COURSE
FOSSIL RIDGE PARK
DIXIE CANYON PARK
WILACRE PARK
COLDWATER CANYON PARK
STATE PARK LAND
VAN NUYS-SHERMAN OAKS PARK
HARVARD-WESTLAKE UPPER HS
NOTRE DAME HS
NORTH HOLLYWOOD HS
ULYSSES GRANT HS
BUCKLEY HS
WESTFIELD FASHION SQUARE
SHEILA AGNES NATURE PRESERVE
SHERMAN OAKS HOSPITAL AND HEALTH CENTER
0 .25 .5 .75 1.0 miles 1 in. = 2400 ft.

LOS ANGELES CO.
SEE 533 MAP
SEE 562 MAP
SEE 564 MAP
SEE 593 MAP
© 2008 Rand McNally & Company
A
B
C
D
E
F
G
H
J
1
2
3
4
5
6
7
BURBANK
NORTH HOLLYWOOD
TOLUCA WOODS
WEST TOLUCA LAKE
TOLUCA LAKE
UNIVERSAL CITY
CAHUENGA PASS
GLENDALE
LOS ANGELES
GRIFFITH PARK
91601
91502
91505
91506
91201
91521
91523
91602
91522
91604
91608
90068
90027
VENTURA FRWY
134
101
5
GOLDEN STATE FRWY
HOLLYWOOD FRWY
LOS ANGELES RIVER
LAKESIDE COUNTRY CLUB
WARNER BROS STUDIOS
WARNER BROS RANCH
DISNEY STUDIOS
NBC STUDIOS
UNIVERSAL STUDIOS
GIBSON AMPHITHEATRE AT UNIVERSAL CITYWALK
FOREST LAWN MEMORIAL PARK HOLLYWOOD HILLS
LOS ANGELES EQUESTRIAN CENTER
TRAVELTOWN MUSEUM
LA LIVE STEAMERS
MOUNT SINAI MEMORIAL PARK
HOLLYWOOD SIGN
HOLLYWOODLAND CAMP
UPPER HOLLYWOOD RESERVOIR
RANCHO PROVIDENCIA
BURBANK BLVD
MAGNOLIA BLVD
VERDUGO AV
OLIVE AV
ALAMEDA AV
RIVERSIDE DR
VENTURA BLVD
CAHUENGA BLVD
BARHAM BLVD
FOREST LAWN DR
MULHOLLAND DR
LANKERSHIM BLVD
VINELAND AV
VICTORY BLVD
ZOO DR
GRIFFITH PARK DR
MT HOLLYWOOD DR
25
34
35
0
.25
.5
.75
1.0
miles 1 in. = 2400 ft.

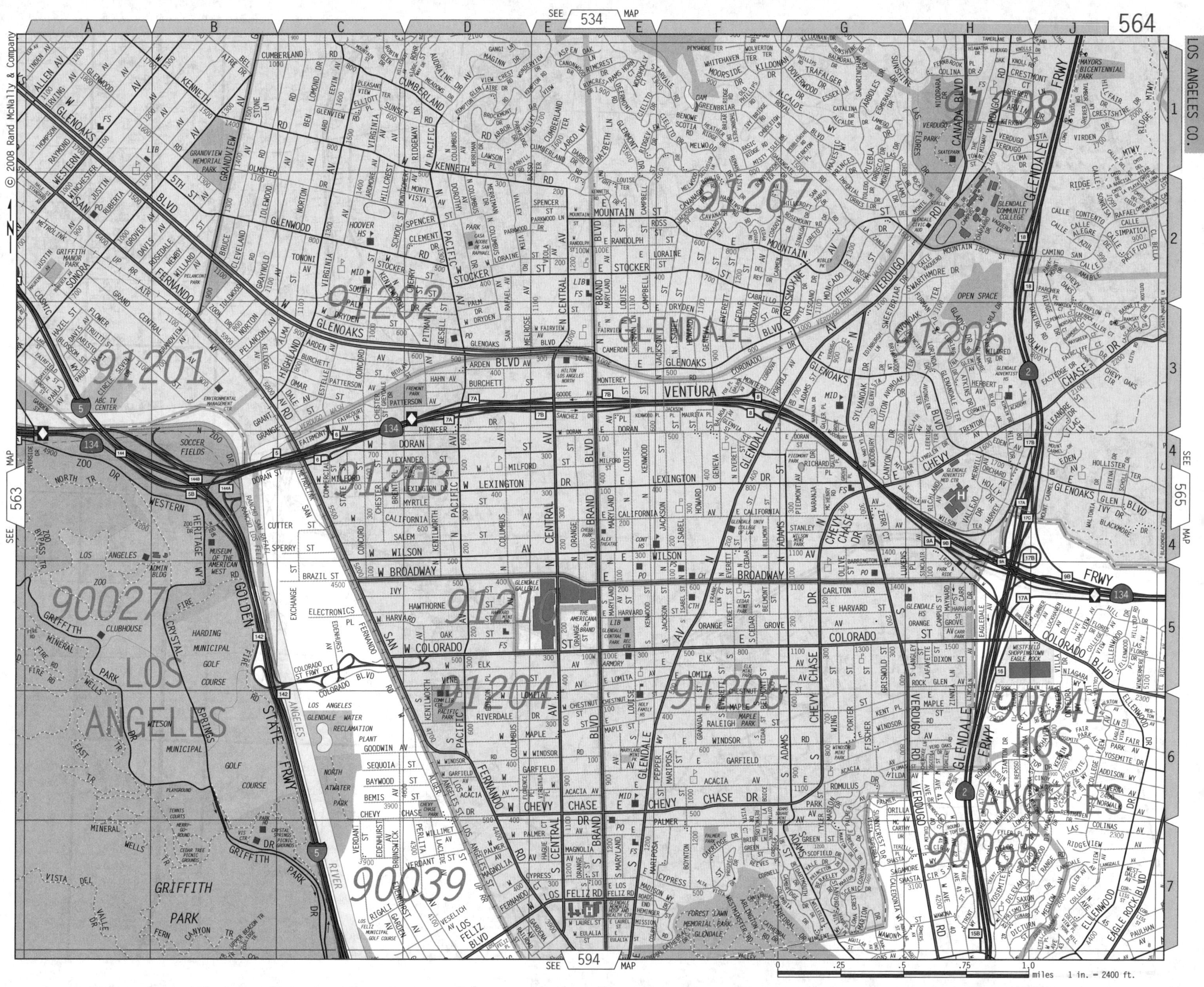

SEE 534 MAP
SEE 594 MAP
SEE 563 MAP
SEE 565 MAP
LOS ANGELES CO.
A
B
C
D
E
F
G
H
J
1
2
3
4
5
6
7
GLENDALE
LOS ANGELES
91201
91202
91203
91204
91205
91206
91207
91208
91210
90027
90039
90041
90065
GRIFFITH PARK
GOLDEN STATE FRWY
GLENDALE FRWY
VENTURA FRWY
GLENOAKS BLVD
BRAND BLVD
COLORADO BLVD
COLORADO ST
BROADWAY
CHEVY CHASE DR
LOS FELIZ RD
MOUNTAIN ST
VERDUGO RD
SAN FERNANDO RD
GLENDALE AV
CENTRAL AV
PACIFIC AV
GRANDVIEW MEMORIAL PARK
GLENDALE COMMUNITY COLLEGE
GLENDALE GALLERIA
THE AMERICANA AT BRAND
WESTFIELD SHOPPINGTOWN EAGLE ROCK
FOREST LAWN MEMORIAL PARK
HARDING MUNICIPAL GOLF COURSE
WILSON MUNICIPAL GOLF COURSE
MUSEUM OF THE AMERICAN WEST
LOS ANGELES ZOO
OPEN SPACE
MAYORS BICENTENNIAL PARK
LOS ANGELES RIVER
miles 1 in. = 2400 ft.
0 .25 .5 .75 1.0

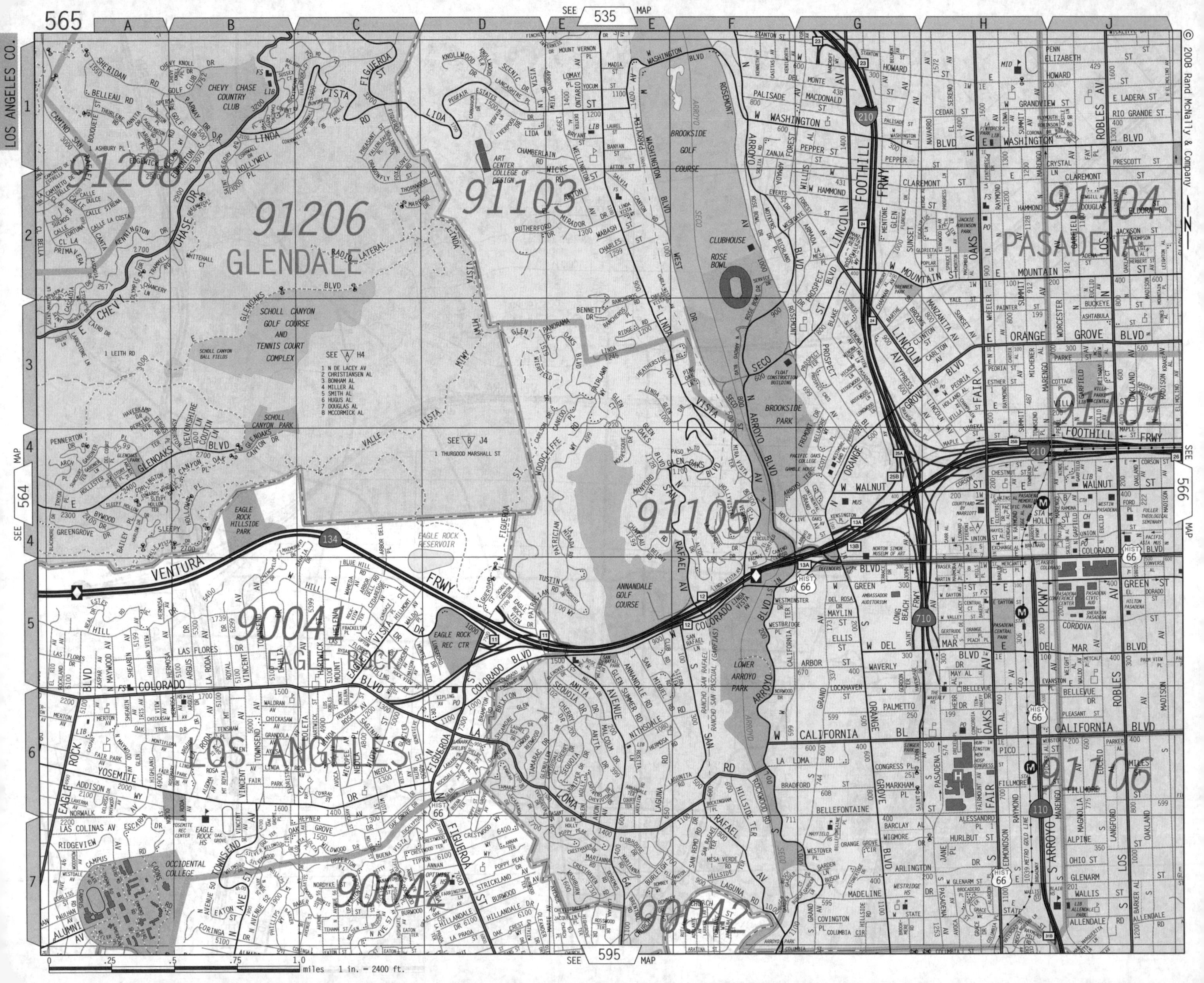
LOS ANGELES CO.
SEE 535 MAP
SEE 595 MAP
SEE 564 MAP
SEE 566 MAP
© 2008 Rand McNally & Company
91208
91206
GLENDALE
91103
91104
PASADENA
91101
91105
91106
90041
EAGLE ROCK
LOS ANGELES
90042
CHEVY CHASE COUNTRY CLUB
SCHOLL CANYON GOLF COURSE AND TENNIS COURT COMPLEX
SCHOLL CANYON BALL FIELDS
SCHOLL CANYON PARK
EAGLE ROCK HILLSIDE PARK
EAGLE ROCK RESERVOIR
EAGLE ROCK REC CTR
ART CENTER COLLEGE OF DESIGN
BROOKSIDE GOLF COURSE
ROSE BOWL
CLUBHOUSE
BROOKSIDE PARK
FLOAT CONSTRUCTION BUILDING
ANNANDALE GOLF COURSE
LOWER ARROYO PARK
PACIFIC OAKS COLLEGE
NORTON SIMON MUSEUM OF ART
AMBASSADOR AUDITORIUM
PASADENA CONFERENCE CENTER
PASADENA CIVIC AUD
PASADENA CENTRAL PARK
FULLER THEOLOGICAL SEMINARY
PACIFIC ASIA MUS
JACKIE ROBINSON PARK
OCCIDENTAL COLLEGE
EAGLE ROCK HS
VENTURA FRWY
FOOTHILL FRWY
LONG BEACH FRWY
ARROYO PKWY
SEE A H4
1 N DE LACEY AV
2 CHRISTIANSEN AL
3 BONHAM AL
4 MILLER AL
5 SMITH AL
6 HUGUS AL
7 DOUGLAS AL
8 MCCORMICK AL
SEE B J4
1 THURGOOD MARSHALL ST
0 .25 .5 .75 1.0 miles 1 in. = 2400 ft.

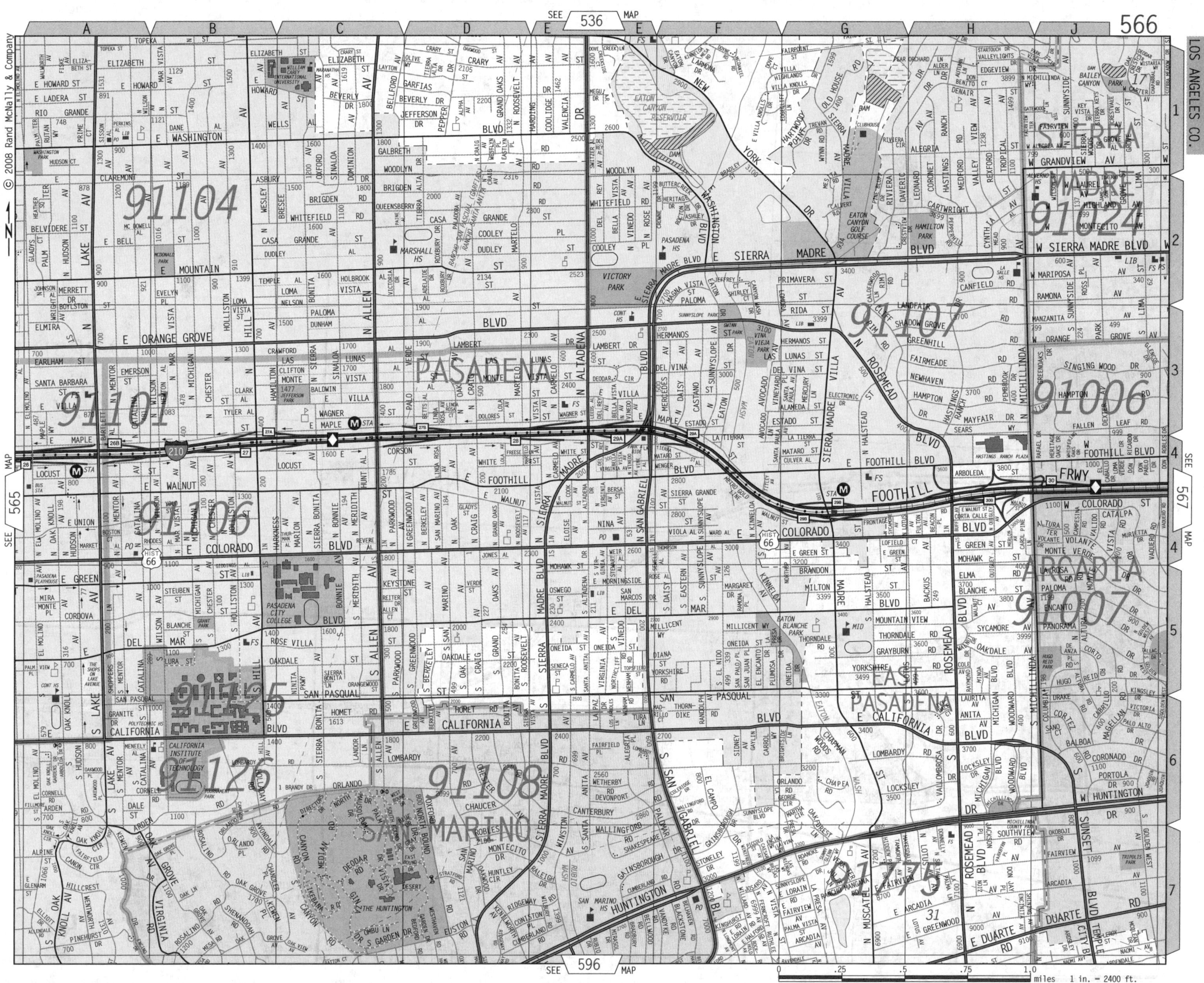
SEE 536 MAP
SEE 596 MAP
SEE 565 MAP
SEE 567 MAP
LOS ANGELES CO.
A
B
C
D
E
F
G
H
J
1
2
3
4
5
6
7
91104
91101
91106
91125
91126
91108
91107
91024
91006
91007
91775
PASADENA
SAN MARINO
EAST PASADENA
SIERRA MADRE
ARCADIA
E ORANGE GROVE BLVD
E COLORADO BLVD
E WALNUT ST
E CALIFORNIA BLVD
E FOOTHILL BLVD
FOOTHILL FRWY
E SIERRA MADRE BLVD
W SIERRA MADRE BLVD
HUNTINGTON DR
E WASHINGTON BLVD
N LAKE AV
N ALLEN AV
N ALTADENA DR
S SAN GABRIEL BLVD
N ROSEMEAD BLVD
N MICHILLINDA AV
N SIERRA MADRE VILLA AV
NEW YORK DR
EATON CANYON RESERVOIR
EATON CANYON GOLF COURSE
VICTORY PARK
PASADENA CITY COLLEGE
CALIFORNIA INSTITUTE OF TECHNOLOGY
WILLIAM CAREY INTERNATIONAL UNIVERSITY
MARSHALL HS
THE HUNTINGTON
HASTINGS RANCH PLAZA
SAN MARINO HS
EATON BLANCHE PARK
210
HIST 66
miles 1 in. = 2400 ft.

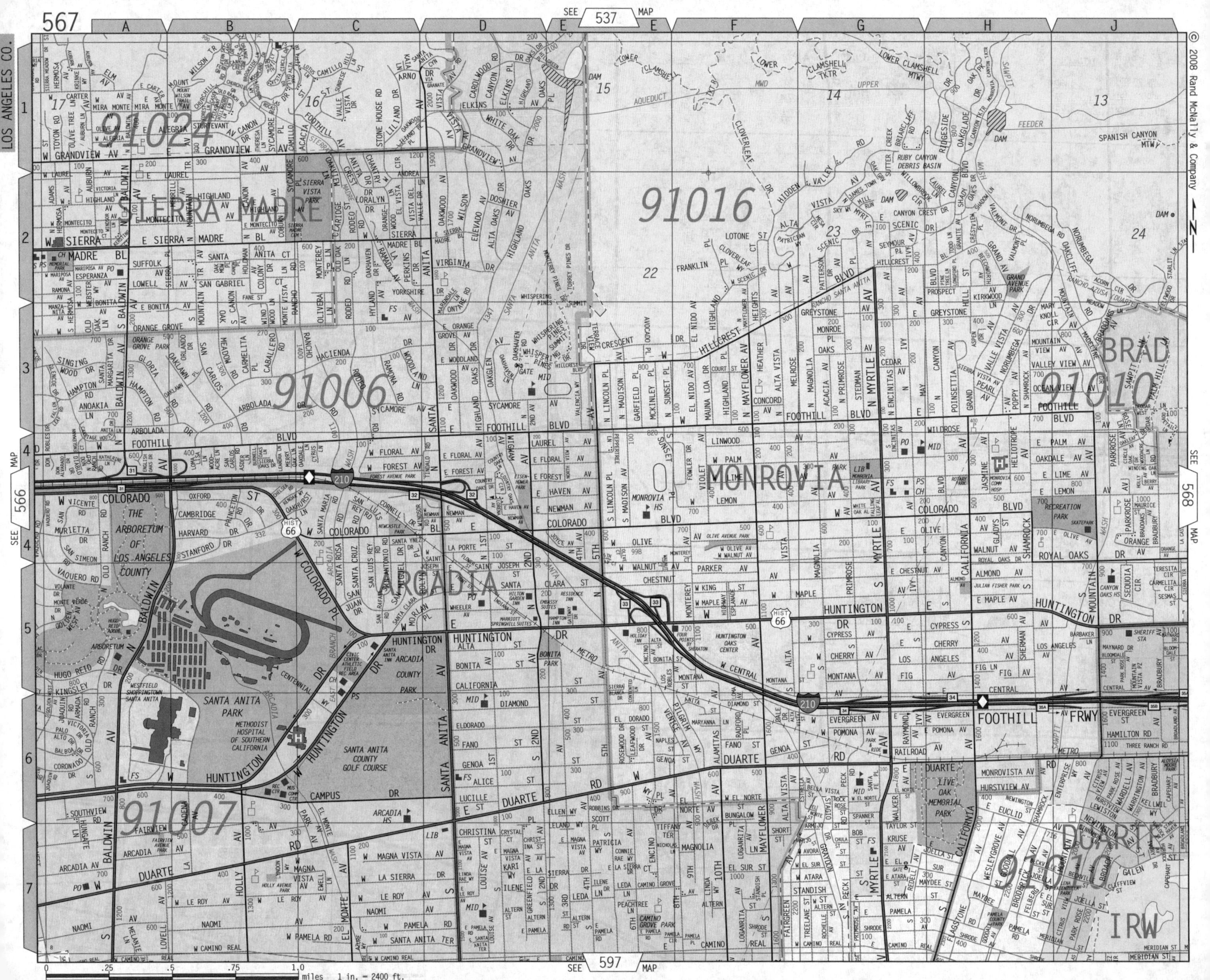

567
LOS ANGELES CO.
A
B
C
D
E
F
G
H
J
SEE 537 MAP
SEE 566 MAP
SEE 568 MAP
SEE 597 MAP
1
2
3
4
5
6
7
© 2008 Rand McNally & Company
SIERRA MADRE
91024
91016
91006
91010
91007
MONROVIA
ARCADIA
BRAD
DUARTE
IRW
THE ARBORETUM OF LOS ANGELES COUNTY
SANTA ANITA PARK
WESTFIELD SHOPPINGTOWN SANTA ANITA
METHODIST HOSPITAL OF SOUTHERN CALIFORNIA
SANTA ANITA COUNTY GOLF COURSE
ARCADIA COUNTY PARK
LIVE OAK MEMORIAL PARK
RECREATION PARK
MONROVIA HS
ARCADIA HS
GRAND AVENUE PARK
RUBY CANYON DEBRIS BASIN
SPANISH CANYON MTWY
LOWER CLAMSHELL MTWY
UPPER AQUEDUCT
FEEDER
FOOTHILL FRWY
FOOTHILL BLVD
HUNTINGTON DR
COLORADO BLVD
DUARTE RD
GRANDVIEW AV
E SIERRA MADRE BL
ORANGE GROVE
BALDWIN AV
SANTA ANITA AV
MYRTLE AV
MOUNTAIN AV
210
66
0
.25
.5
.75
1.0
miles 1 in. = 2400 ft.

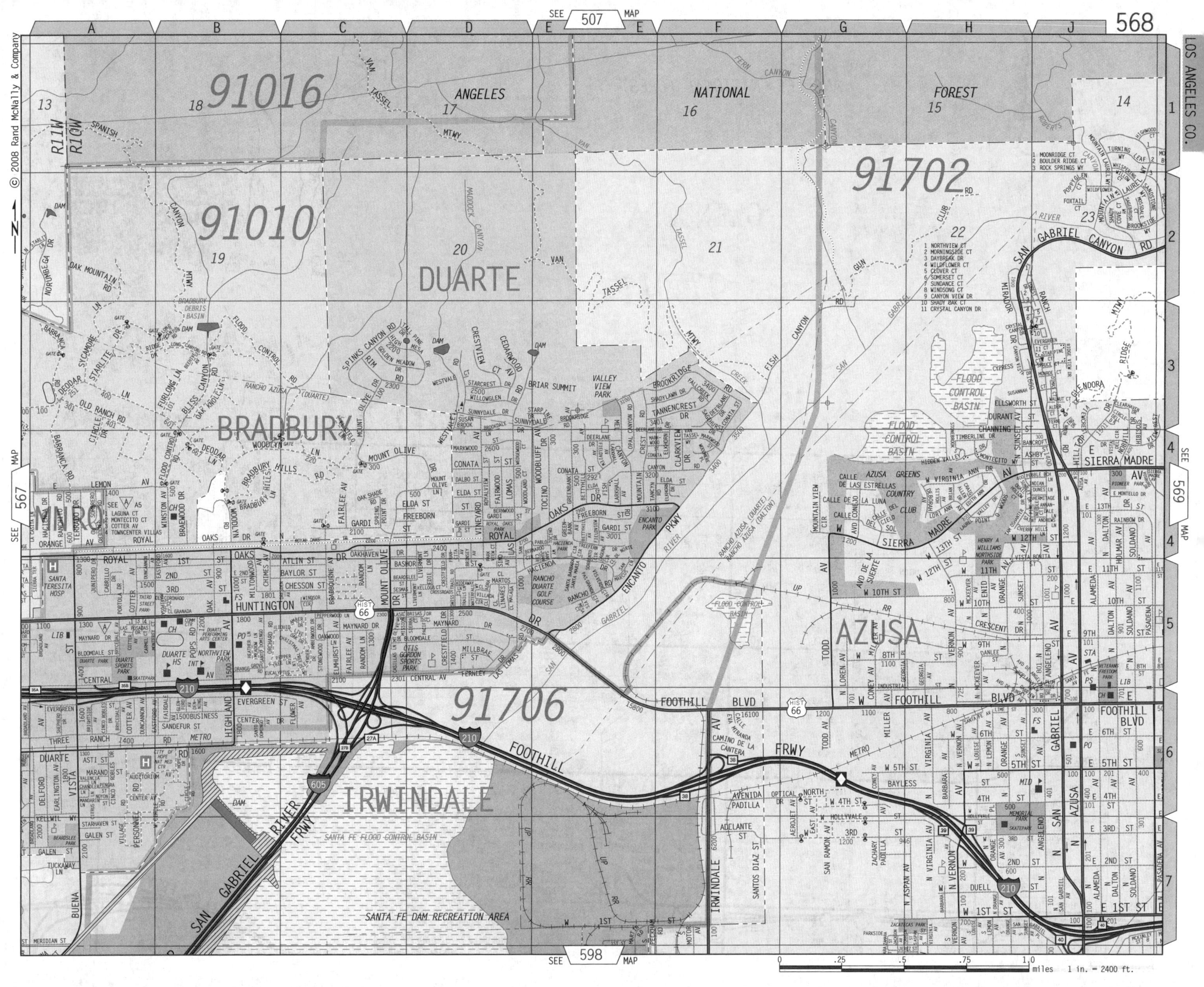
A
B
C
D
E
F
G
H
J
SEE 507 MAP
SEE 598 MAP
SEE 567 MAP
SEE 569 MAP
1
2
3
4
5
6
7
91016
91010
91702
91706
ANGELES
NATIONAL
FOREST
DUARTE
BRADBURY
AZUSA
IRWINDALE
R11W
R10W
SAN GABRIEL CANYON RD
FOOTHILL BLVD
FOOTHILL FRWY
SAN GABRIEL RIVER FRWY
HUNTINGTON DR
ROYAL OAKS DR
MOUNT OLIVE DR
SIERRA MADRE AV
FLOOD CONTROL BASIN
SANTA FE FLOOD CONTROL BASIN
SANTA FE DAM RECREATION AREA
AZUSA GREENS COUNTRY CLUB
RANCHO DUARTE GOLF COURSE
BRADBURY DEBRIS BASIN
VALLEY VIEW PARK
ENCANTO PARK
HENRY A WILLIAMS NORTHSIDE PARK
MEMORIAL PARK
SANTA TERESITA HOSP
DUARTE SPORTS PARK
OTIS GORDON SPORTS PARK
1 MOONRIDGE CT
2 BOULDER RIDGE CT
3 ROCK SPRINGS WY
1 NORTHVIEW CT
2 MORNINGSIDE CT
3 DAYBREAK DR
4 WILDFLOWER CT
5 CLOVER CT
6 SOMERSET CT
7 SUNDANCE CT
8 WINDSONG CT
9 CANYON VIEW DR
10 SHADY OAK CT
11 CRYSTAL CANYON DR
1 LAGUNA CT
2 MONTECITO CT
3 COTTER AV
4 TOWNCENTER VILLAS
0 .25 .5 .75 1.0 miles 1 in. = 2400 ft.

569
SEE 509 MAP
SEE 599 MAP
SEE 568 MAP
SEE 570 MAP
LOS ANGELES CO.
© 2008 Rand McNally & Company
ANGELES NATIONAL FOREST
GLENDORA
AZUSA
91741
91702
91740
GLENDORA WILDERNESS PARK
BIG DALTON CAMPGROUND
LITTLE DALTON PICNIC GROUND
DEBRIS BASIN
DALTON RANGER STA
CARLYLE E LINDER EQUESTRIAN PARK
GLENDORA MOUNTAIN RD
GLENDORA RIDGE MTWY
SAN GABRIEL CANYON RD
SIERRA MADRE AV
FOOTHILL BLVD
ROUTE 66
ALOSTA AV
FOOTHILL FRWY
CITRUS COLLEGE
AZUSA PACIFIC UNIVERSITY
SANDBURG SCHOOL PARK
ST LUCYS HS
GLENDORA HS
AZUSA HS
GLENDORA COUNTRY CLUB
SOUTH HILLS PARK
LOUIE POMPEI SPORTS PARK
PARK & RIDE
R10W R9W
T1N T1S
RANCHO SAN JOSE ADDITION
0 .25 .5 .75 1.0 miles 1 in. = 2400 ft.

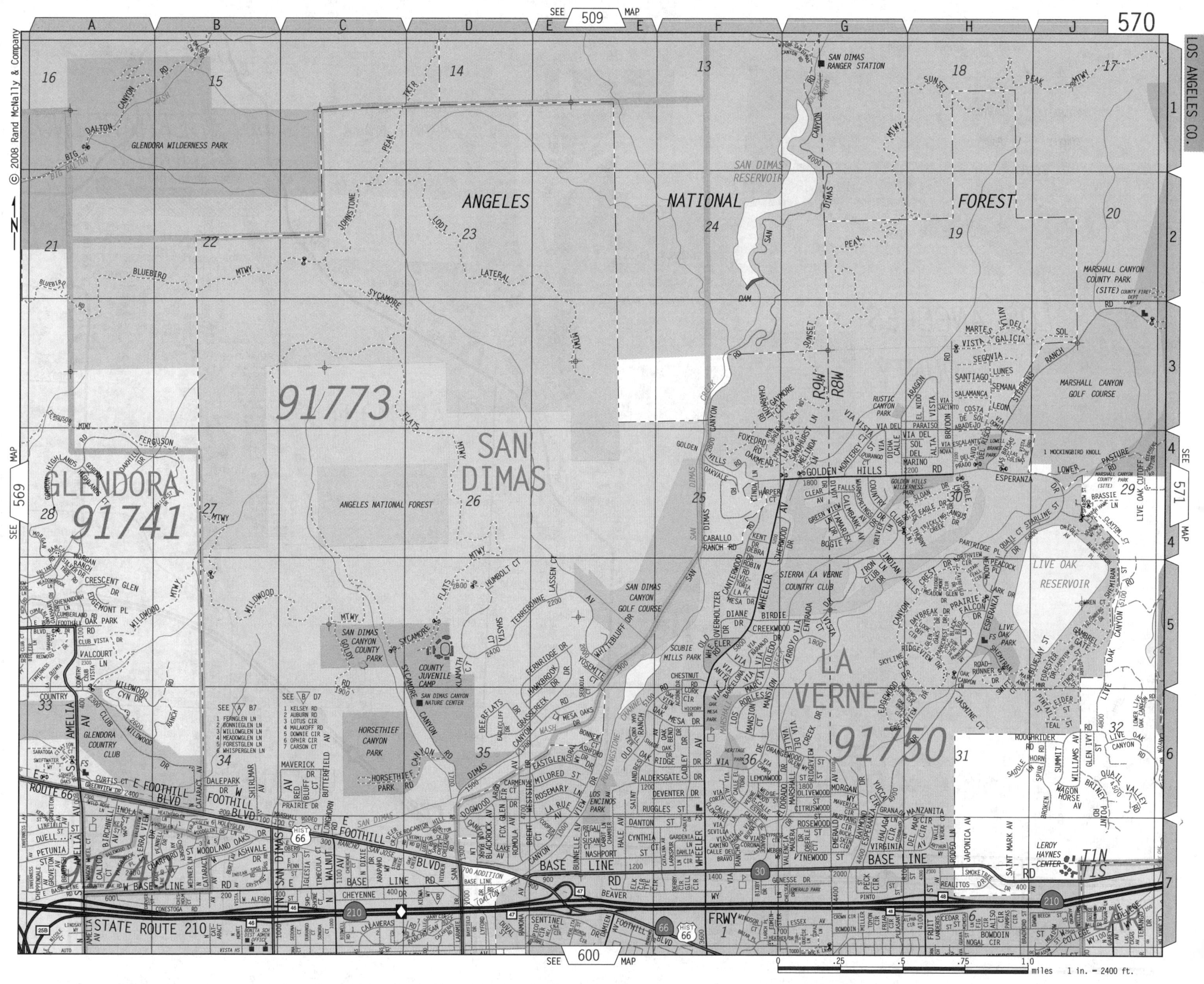

SEE 509 MAP
LOS ANGELES CO.
© 2008 Rand McNally & Company
ANGELES NATIONAL FOREST
SAN DIMAS RESERVOIR
SAN DIMAS RANGER STATION
GLENDORA WILDERNESS PARK
91773
SAN DIMAS
ANGELES NATIONAL FOREST
GLENDORA 91741
MARSHALL CANYON COUNTY PARK (SITE)
MARSHALL CANYON GOLF COURSE
R9W R8W
RUSTIC CANYON PARK
GOLDEN HILLS WILDERNESS PARK
SIERRA LA VERNE COUNTRY CLUB
SAN DIMAS CANYON GOLF COURSE
SAN DIMAS CANYON COUNTY PARK
COUNTY JUVENILE CAMP
SAN DIMAS CANYON NATURE CENTER
HORSETHIEF CANYON PARK
HORSETHIEF PARK
SCUBIE MILLS PARK
LIVE OAK RESERVOIR
LIVE OAK PARK
LA VERNE 91750
GLENDORA COUNTRY CLUB
LOS ENCINOS PARK
LEROY HAYNES CENTER
T1N T1S
SEE 569 MAP
SEE 571 MAP
SEE 600 MAP
STATE ROUTE 210
FOOTHILL FRWY
BASE LINE RD
ROUTE 66
miles 1 in. = 2400 ft.

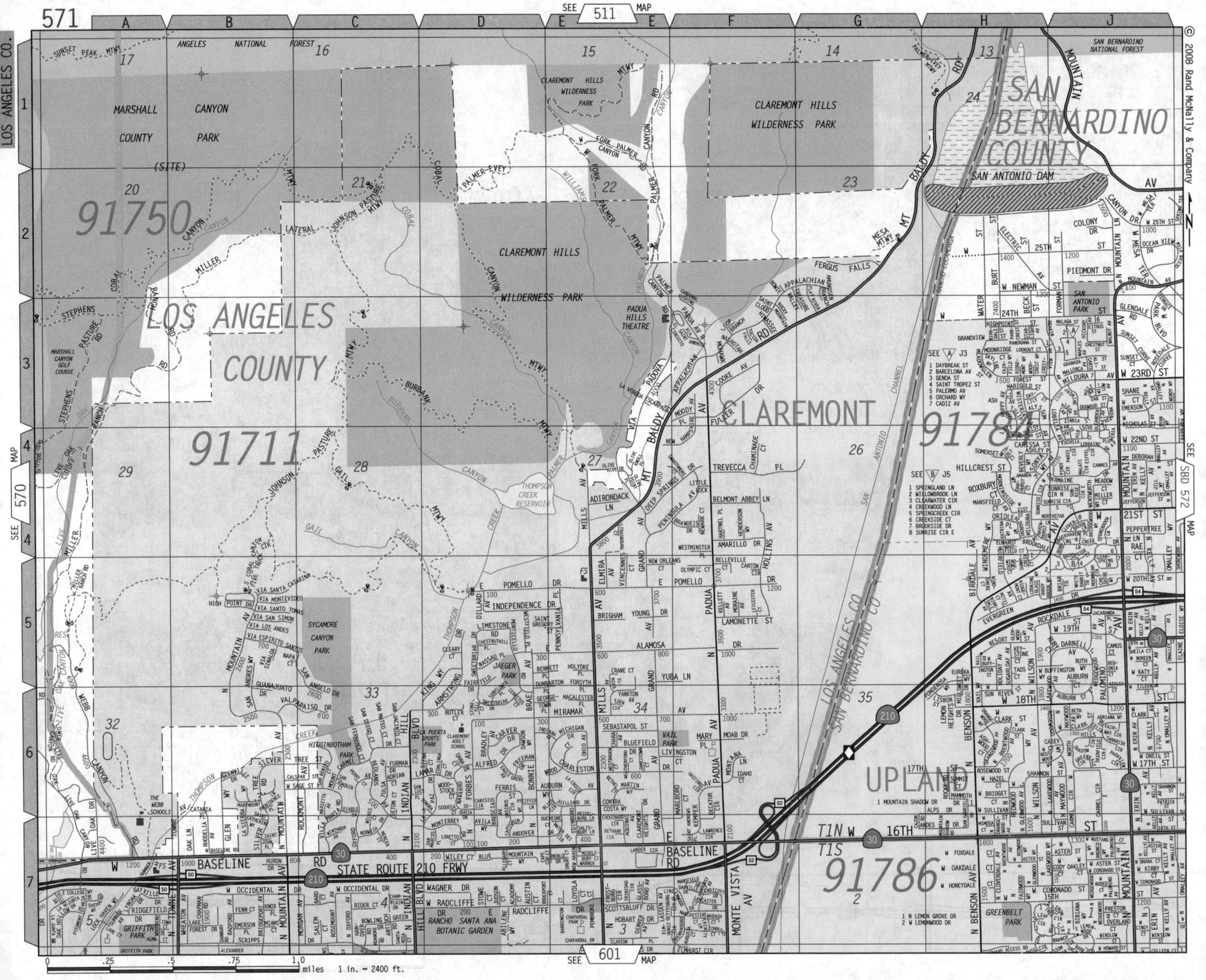

SEE 511 MAP
LOS ANGELES CO.
ANGELES NATIONAL FOREST
SAN BERNARDINO NATIONAL FOREST
MARSHALL CANYON COUNTY PARK (SITE)
CLAREMONT HILLS WILDERNESS PARK
SAN BERNARDINO COUNTY
SAN ANTONIO DAM
91750
LOS ANGELES COUNTY
91711
CLAREMONT
91784
PADUA HILLS THEATRE
THOMPSON CREEK RESERVOIR
MARSHALL CANYON GOLF COURSE
SYCAMORE CANYON PARK
JAEGER PARK
LA PUERTA SPORTS PARK
CLAREMONT ADULT SCHOOL
HIGGINBOTHAM PARK
VAIL PARK
SAN ANTONIO PARK
THE WEBB SCHOOLS
UPLAND
91786
GRIFFITH PARK
RANCHO SANTA ANA BOTANIC GARDEN
GREENBELT PARK
CHAPARRAL PARK
LOS ANGELES CO
SAN BERNARDINO CO
SAN ANTONIO CHANNEL
BASELINE RD
STATE ROUTE 210 FRWY
MT BALDY RD
MILLS AV
PADUA AV
INDIAN HILL BLVD
MOUNTAIN AV
W 16TH ST
FOOTHILL BLVD
T1N
T1S
SEE 570 MAP
SEE SBD 572 MAP
SEE 601 MAP
SEE A J3
1 DAYBREAK ST
2 BARCELONA AV
3 GENOA ST
4 SAINT TROPEZ ST
5 PALERMO AV
6 ORCHARD WY
7 CADIZ AV
SEE B J5
1 SPRINGLAND LN
2 WILLOWBROOK LN
3 CLEARWATER CIR
4 CREEKWOOD LN
5 SPRINGCREEK CIR
6 CREEKSIDE CT
7 BROOKSIDE DR
8 SUNRISE CIR E
1 MOUNTAIN SHADOW DR
1 N LEMON GROVE DR
2 N LEMONWOOD DR
0 .25 .5 .75 1.0 miles 1 in. = 2400 ft.

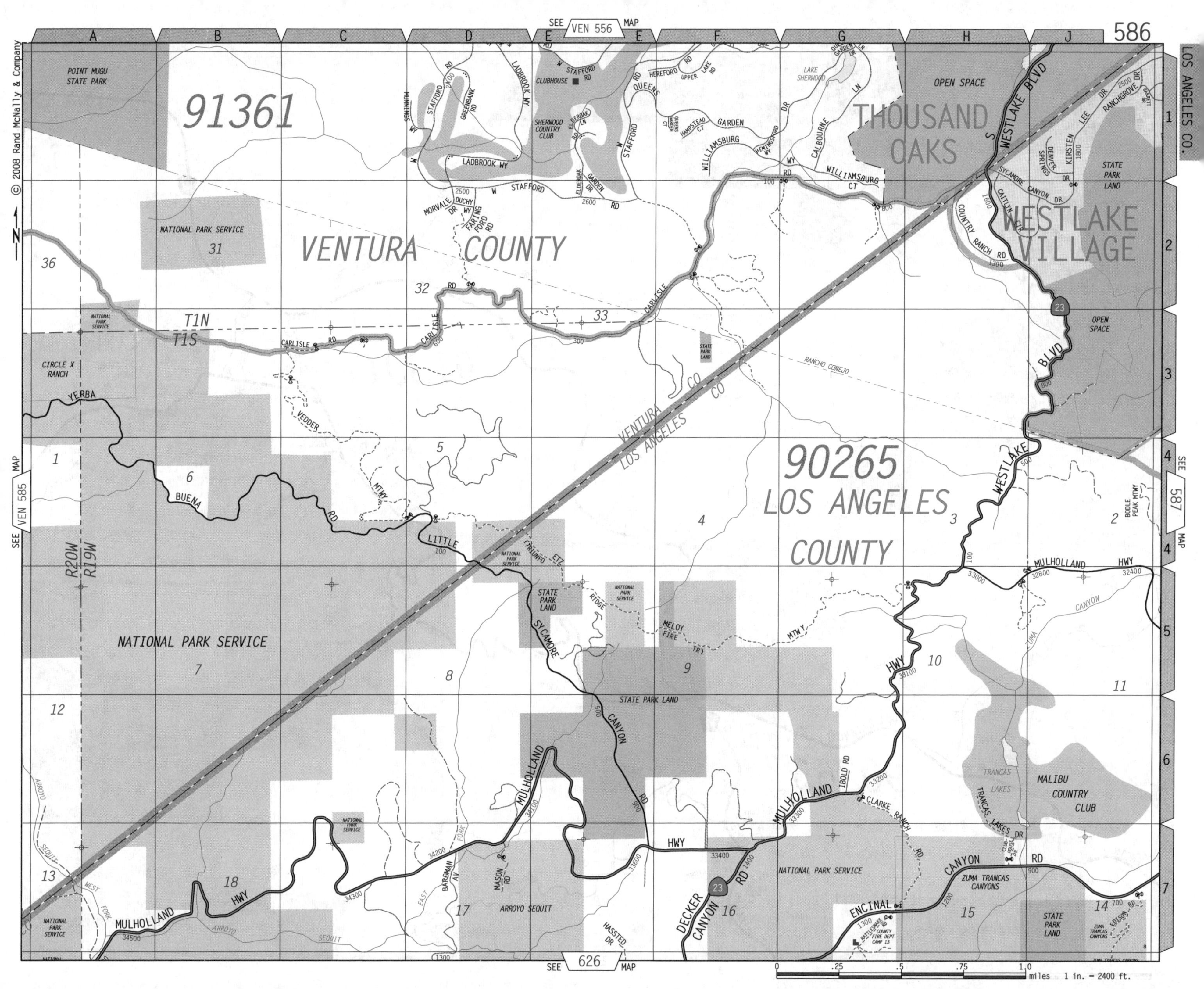

SEE VEN 556 MAP
A B C D E E F G H J
LOS ANGELES CO.
© 2008 Rand McNally & Company
POINT MUGU STATE PARK
91361
VENTURA COUNTY
NATIONAL PARK SERVICE
THOUSAND OAKS
OPEN SPACE
STATE PARK LAND
WESTLAKE VILLAGE
SHERWOOD COUNTRY CLUB
CLUBHOUSE
LAKE SHERWOOD
W STAFFORD RD
LADBROOK WY
CARLISLE RD
T1N
T1S
CIRCLE X RANCH
YERBA BUENA RD
VEDDER MTWY
LITTLE SYCAMORE CANYON RD
RANCHO CONEJO
VENTURA CO
LOS ANGELES CO
90265
LOS ANGELES COUNTY
S WESTLAKE BLVD
MULHOLLAND HWY
TRIUNFO RIDGE ETZ
MELOY FIRE TR
R20W
R19W
SEE VEN 585 MAP
SEE 587 MAP
BODLE PEAK MTWY
ZUMA CANYON
TRANCAS LAKES
MALIBU COUNTRY CLUB
ENCINAL CANYON RD
ZUMA TRANCAS CANYONS
DECKER CANYON RD
CLARKE RANCH RD
IBOLD RD
ARROYO SEQUIT
MASON RD
BARDMAN AV
HASSTED DR
COUNTY FIRE DEPT CAMP 13
SEE 626 MAP
0 .25 .5 .75 1.0 miles 1 in. = 2400 ft.

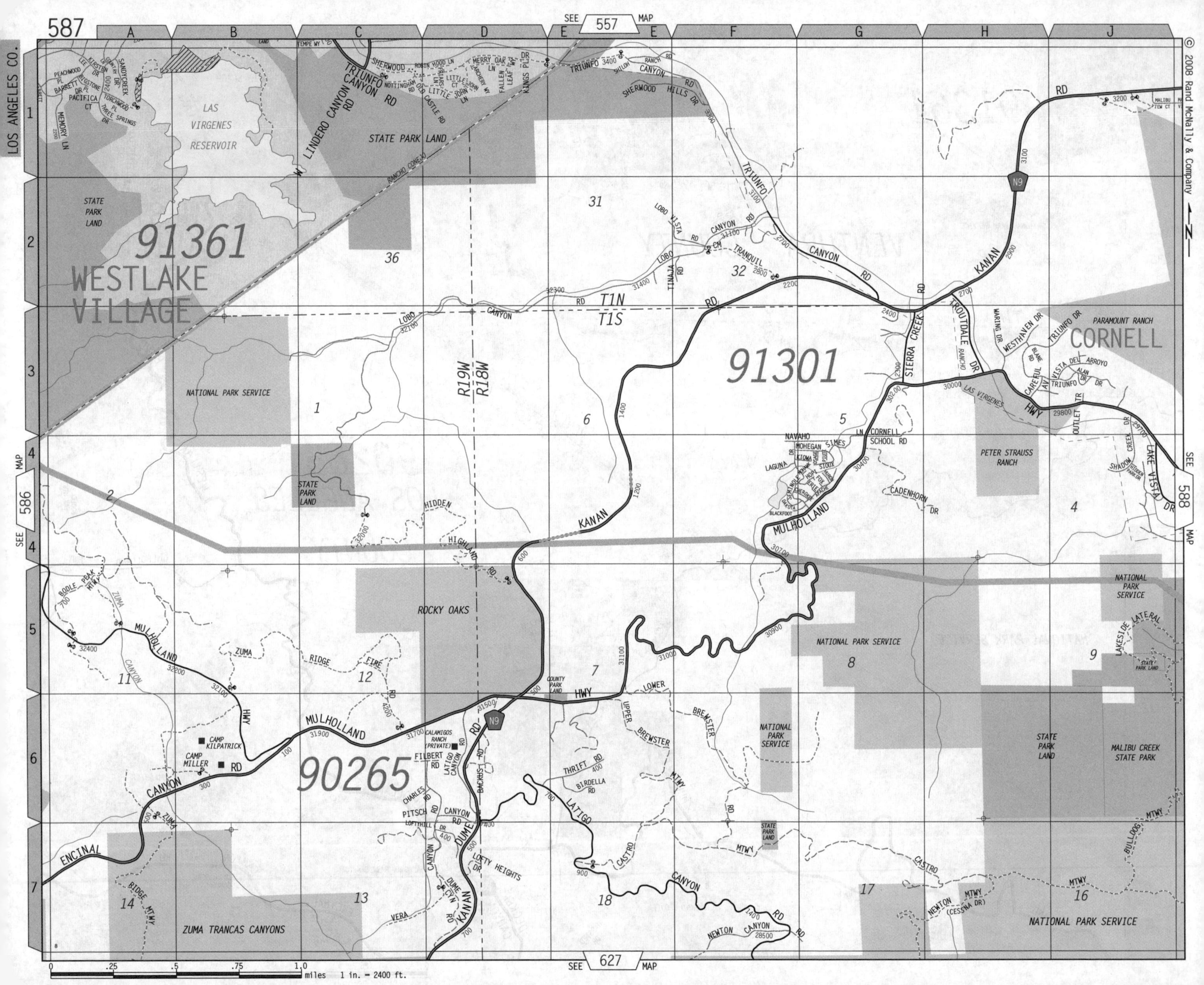
LOS ANGELES CO.
SEE 557 MAP
SEE 586 MAP
SEE 588 MAP
SEE 627 MAP
91361
WESTLAKE VILLAGE
91301
CORNELL
90265
LAS VIRGENES RESERVOIR
STATE PARK LAND
NATIONAL PARK SERVICE
ROCKY OAKS
PETER STRAUSS RANCH
PARAMOUNT RANCH
MALIBU CREEK STATE PARK
ZUMA TRANCAS CANYONS
CAMP KILPATRICK
CAMP MILLER
CALAMIGOS RANCH (PRIVATE)
COUNTY PARK LAND
KANAN RD
MULHOLLAND HWY
TRIUNFO CANYON RD
LOBO CANYON RD
W LINDERO CANYON RD
SIERRA CREEK RD
TROUTDALE DR
LAS VIRGENES RD
LATIGO CANYON RD
ENCINAL CANYON RD
NEWTON CANYON RD
KANAN DUME RD
T1N
T1S
R19W
R18W
miles 1 in. = 2400 ft.
© 2008 Rand McNally & Company

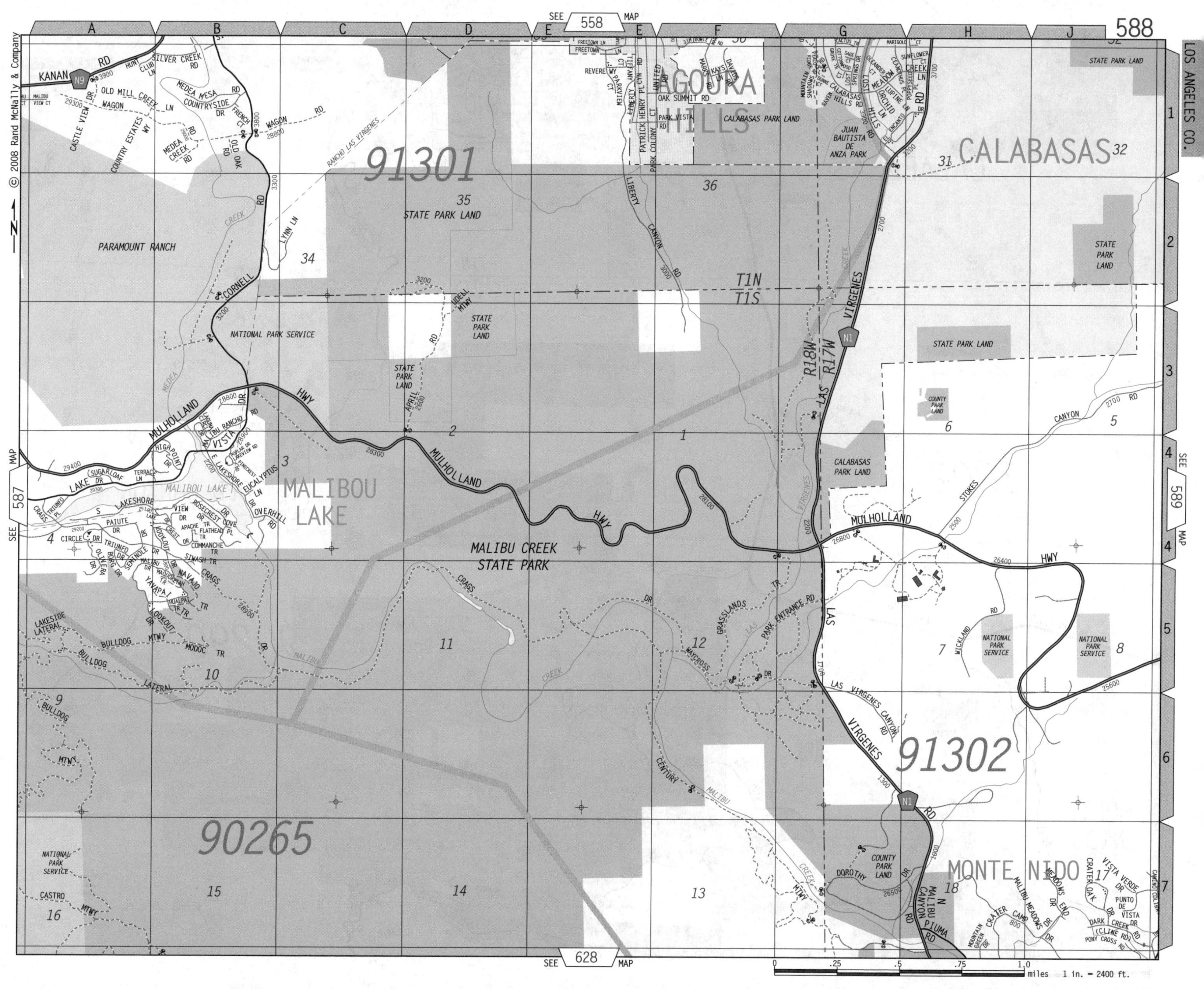

SEE 558 MAP
A
B
C
D
E
F
G
H
J
LOS ANGELES CO.
SEE 587 MAP
SEE 589 MAP
SEE 628 MAP
1
2
3
4
5
6
7
91301
91302
90265
AGOURA HILLS
CALABASAS
MALIBOU LAKE
MONTE NIDO
MALIBU CREEK STATE PARK
PARAMOUNT RANCH
NATIONAL PARK SERVICE
STATE PARK LAND
CALABASAS PARK LAND
COUNTY PARK LAND
JUAN BAUTISTA DE ANZA PARK
T1N
T1S
R18W
R17W
KANAN RD
SILVER CREEK RD
OLD MILL CREEK LN
WAGON
MEDEA MESA
COUNTRYSIDE DR
COUNTRY ESTATES WY
CASTLE VIEW DR
MEDEA CREEK RD
OLD OAK RD
CORNELL RD
LYNN LN
MULHOLLAND HWY
LAKE VISTA DR
HIGHPOINT DR
SUGARLOAF
LAKESHORE
EUCALYPTUS LN
OVERHILL DR
PAIUTE
TRIUNFO
CRAGS DR
BULLDOG MTWY
LAKESIDE LATERAL
MODOC TR
CRAGS
UDELL MTWY
APRIL RD
LIBERTY CANYON RD
OAK SUMMIT RD
PARK VISTA
FREETOWN LN
REVERE WY
LAS VIRGENES RD
LAS VIRGENES CANYON RD
MULHOLLAND HWY
STOKES CANYON RD
WICKLAND RD
PARK ENTRANCE RD
GRASSLANDS TR
MAYCROSS
CENTURY
MALIBU CREEK
DOROTHY DR
MALIBU CANYON RD
PIUMA RD
CRATER CAMP DR
MALIBU MEADOWS DR
MEADOWS END
VISTA VERDE DR
CRATER OAK DR
PUNTO DE VISTA DR
DARK CREEK RD
CLINE RD
PONY CROSS RD
CASTRO MTWY
N1
N9
0 .25 .5 .75 1.0 miles 1 in. = 2400 ft.

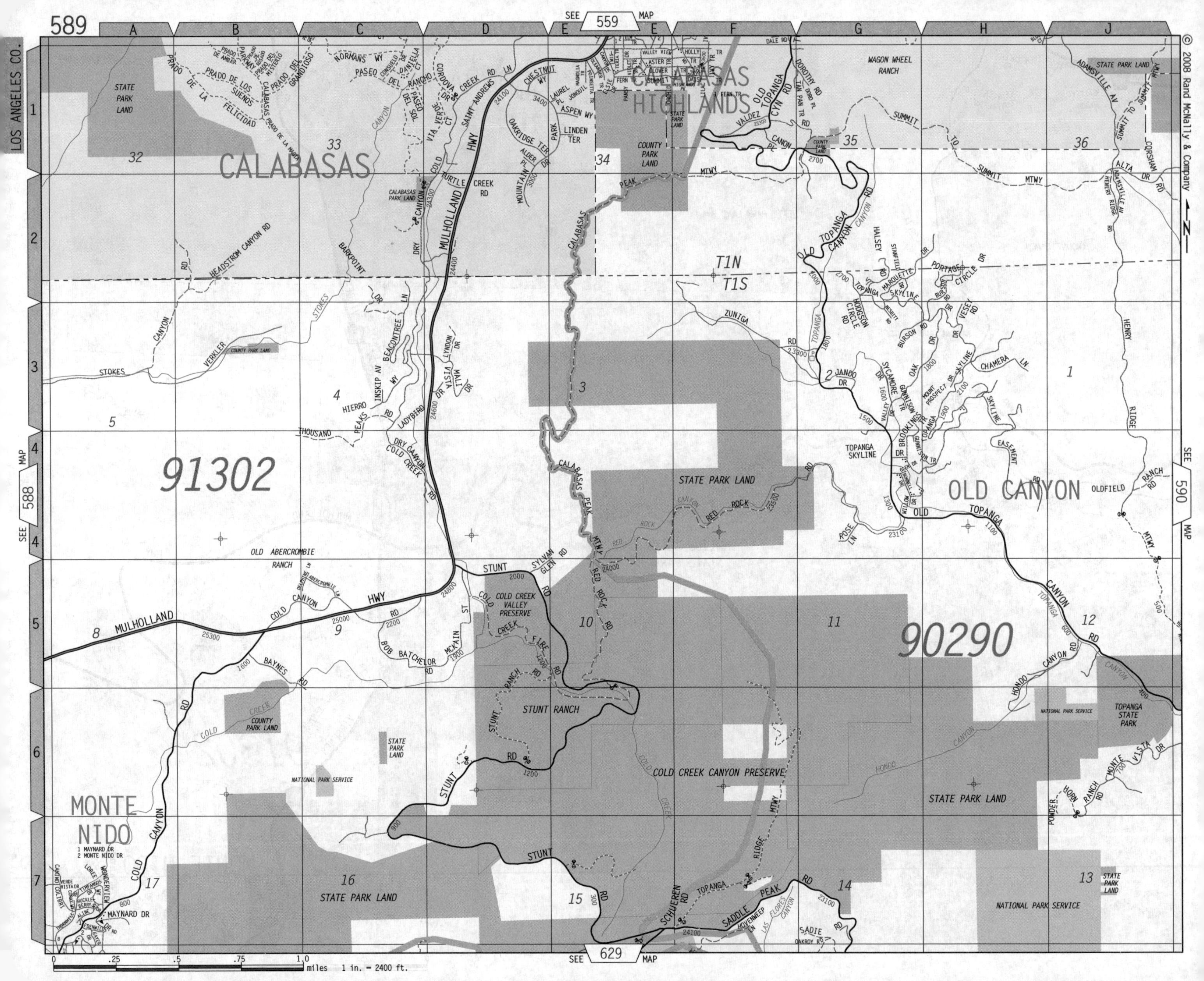

SEE 559 MAP
SEE 629 MAP
SEE 588 MAP
SEE 590 MAP
LOS ANGELES CO.
A
B
C
D
E
F
G
H
J
1
2
3
4
5
6
7
CALABASAS
CALABASAS HIGHLANDS
OLD CANYON
MONTE NIDO
1 MAYNARD DR
2 MONTE NIDO DR
91302
90290
T1N
T1S
STATE PARK LAND
COUNTY PARK LAND
CALABASAS PARK LAND
WAGON WHEEL RANCH
OLD ABERCROMBIE RANCH
COLD CREEK VALLEY PRESERVE
COLD CREEK CANYON PRESERVE
STUNT RANCH
TOPANGA SKYLINE
TOPANGA STATE PARK
NATIONAL PARK SERVICE
MULHOLLAND HWY
OLD TOPANGA CANYON RD
TOPANGA CANYON RD
CALABASAS PEAK MTWY
STUNT RD
COLD CANYON RD
SADDLE PEAK RD
SUMMIT TO SUMMIT MTWY
HENRY RIDGE MTWY
RED ROCK RD
STOKES CANYON RD
HEADSTROM CANYON RD
DRY CANYON COLD CREEK RD
BAYNES RD
BOB BATCHELOR RD
SCHUEREN RD
HONDO CANYON RD
MONTE VISTA DR
ZUNIGA RD
JANDO DR
OLDFIELD
0
.25
.5
.75
1.0
miles 1 in. = 2400 ft.

SEE 560 MAP

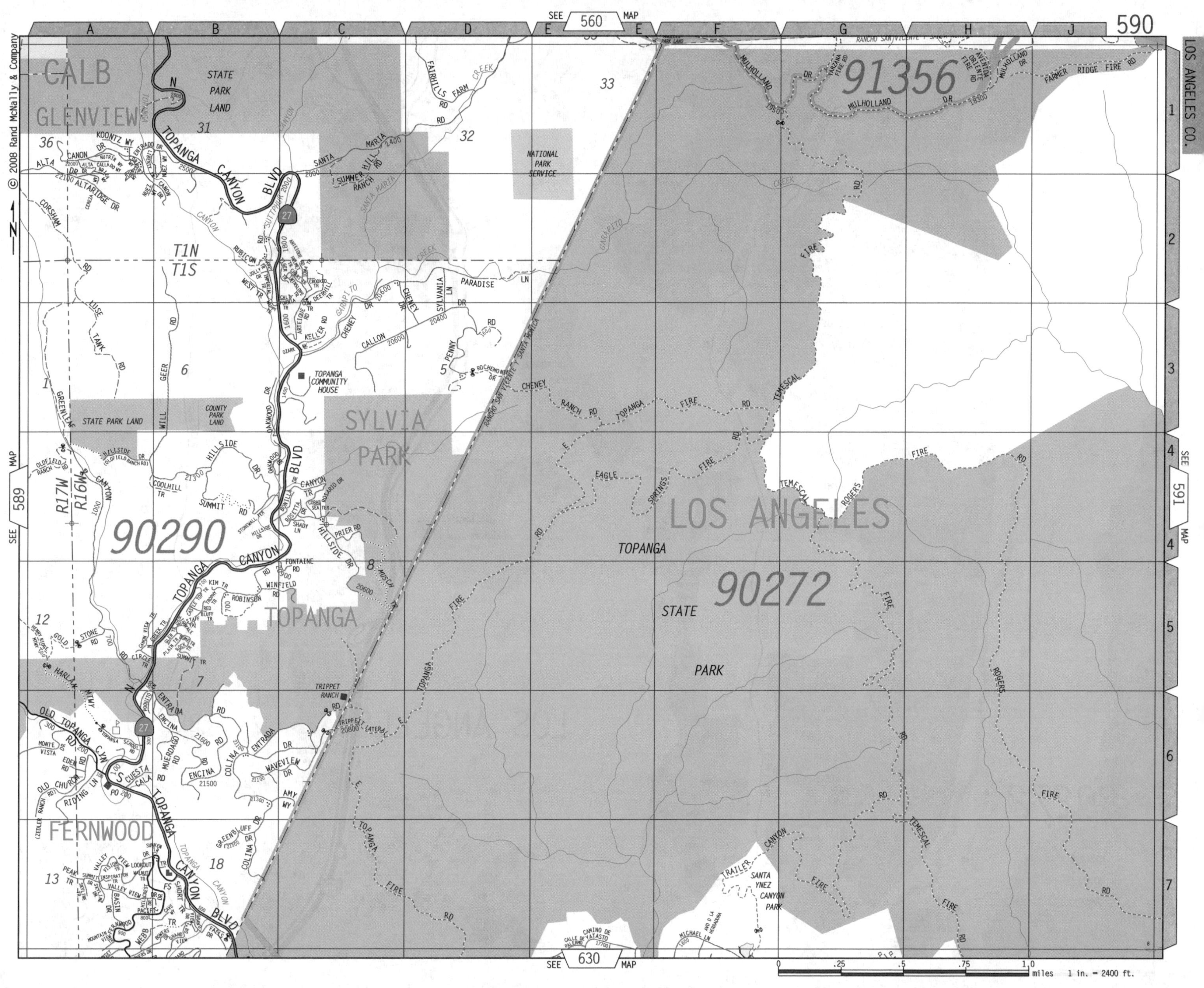

SEE 589 MAP
SEE 591 MAP
SEE 630 MAP

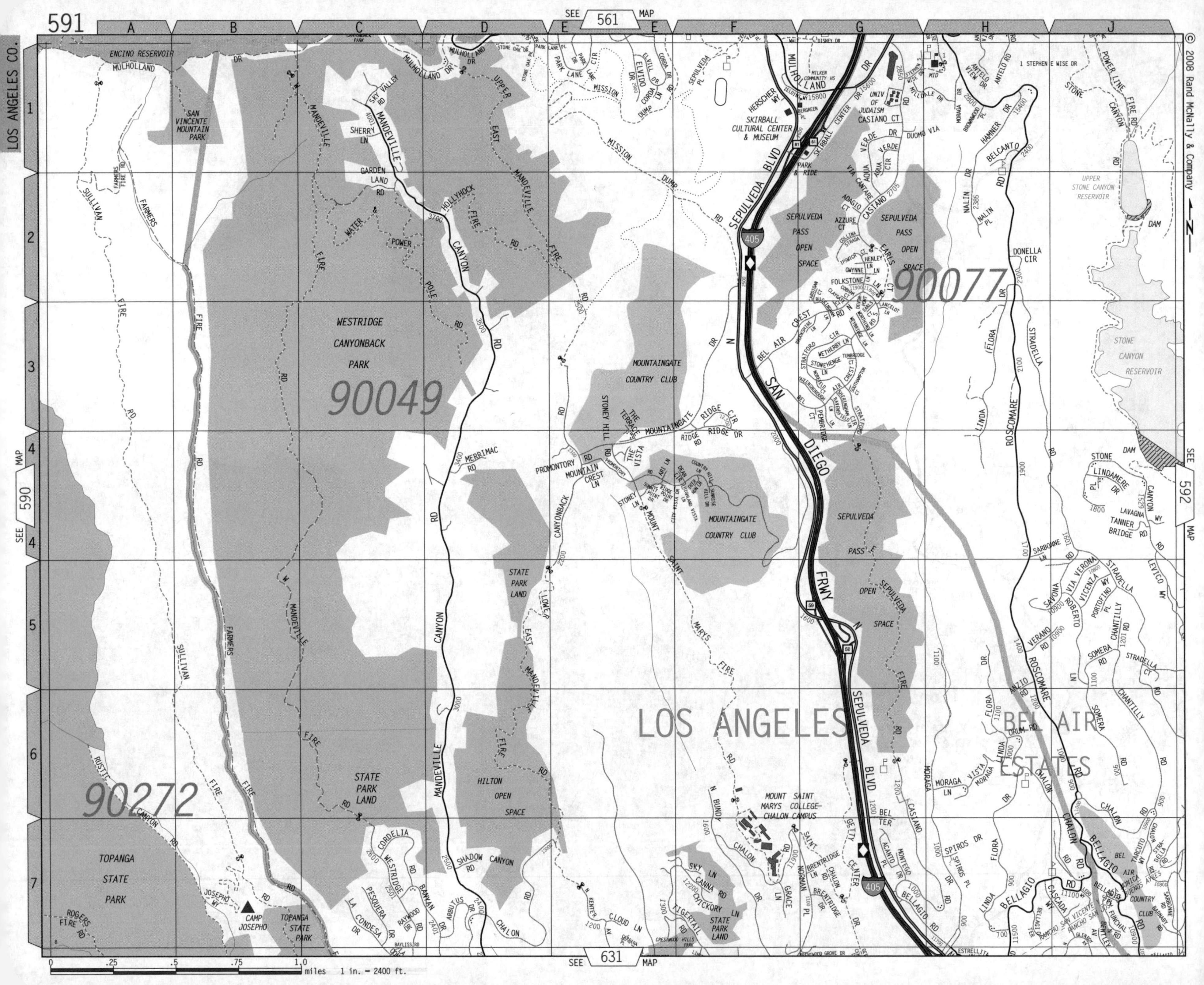

LOS ANGELES CO.
A
B
C
D
E
F
G
H
J
1
2
3
4
5
6
7
SEE 561 MAP
SEE 590 MAP
SEE 592 MAP
SEE 631 MAP
© 2008 Rand McNally & Company
ENCINO RESERVOIR
MULHOLLAND
SAN VINCENTE MOUNTAIN PARK
SULLIVAN
FARMERS
FIRE RD
WESTRIDGE CANYONBACK PARK
90049
MANDEVILLE
CANYON
RD
MULHOLLAND DR
UPPER EAST MANDEVILLE FIRE RD
SKY VALLEY RD
SHERRY LN
GARDEN LAND RD
HOLLYHOCK
WATER & POWER
POLE RD
MISSION
DUMP
SEPULVEDA BLVD
SAN DIEGO FRWY
405
SKIRBALL CULTURAL CENTER & MUSEUM
UNIV OF JUDAISM
SEPULVEDA PASS OPEN SPACE
90077
MOUNTAINGATE COUNTRY CLUB
STONEY HILL RD
MOUNTAINGATE DR
RIDGE CIR
PROMONTORY RD
MOUNTAIN CREST LN
MERRIMAC RD
CANYONBACK RD
STATE PARK LAND
LOWER EAST MANDEVILLE FIRE RD
MOUNT SAINT MARYS FIRE RD
HILTON OPEN SPACE
LOS ANGELES
BEL AIR ESTATES
ROSCOMARE RD
STRADELLA RD
LINDA FLORA DR
MORAGA DR
CHALON RD
BELLAGIO RD
STONE CANYON RESERVOIR
UPPER STONE CANYON RESERVOIR
DAM
STONE CANYON RD
90272
RUSTIC CANYON RD
TOPANGA STATE PARK
CAMP JOSEPHO
JOSEPHO WY
ROGERS FIRE RD
CORDELIA
WESTRIDGE RD
BANYAN
PESQUERA DR
LA CONDESA DR
SHADOW CANYON
MOUNT SAINT MARYS COLLEGE CHALON CAMPUS
N BUNDY DR
SKY CANNA CHICKORY LN
TIGERTAIL RD
STATE PARK LAND
GETTY CENTER DR
CASIANO RD
BEL TER
ESTRELLITA
0 .25 .5 .75 1.0 miles 1 in. = 2400 ft.

SEE 562 MAP

SEE 591 MAP

SEE 593 MAP

SEE 632 MAP

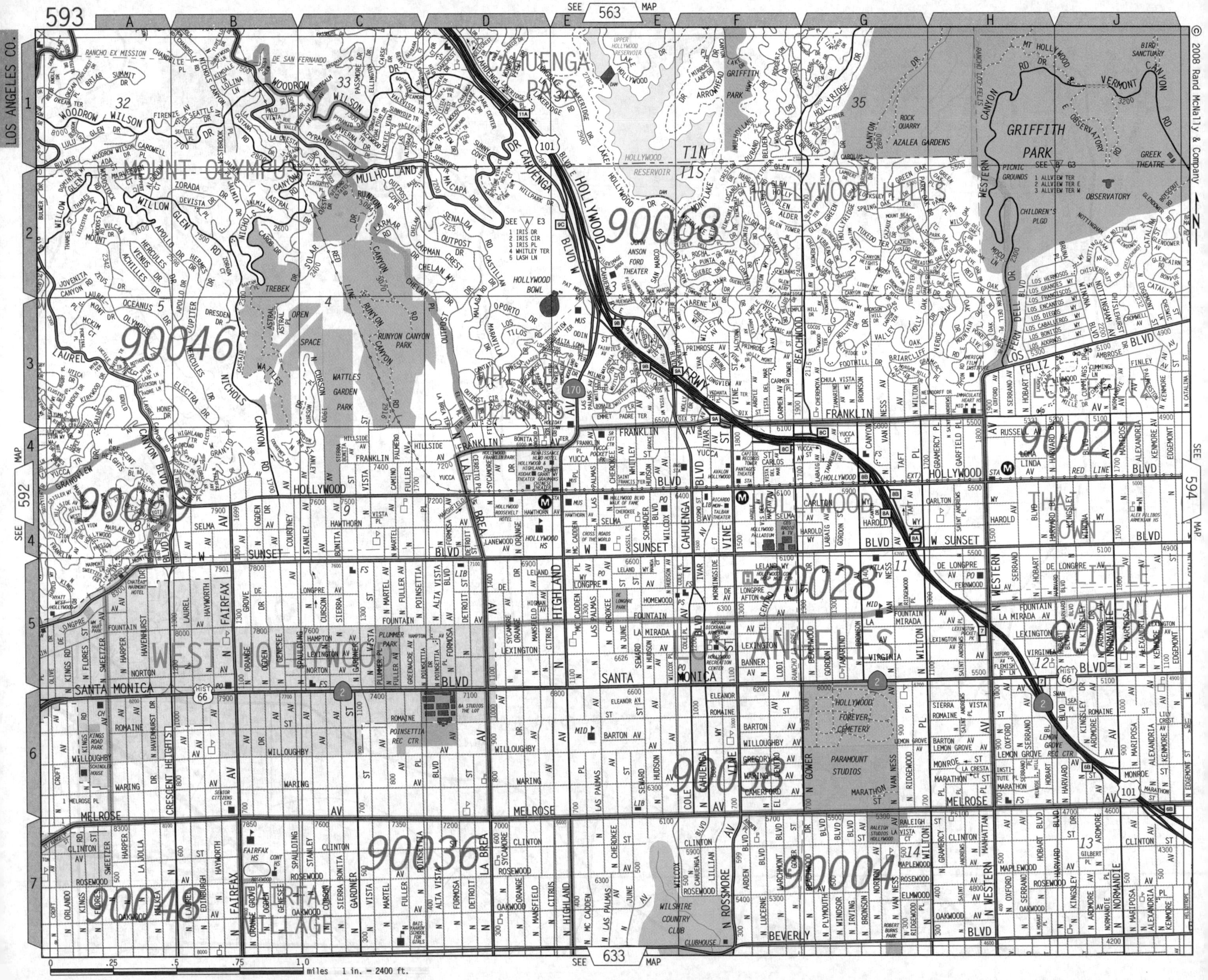
LOS ANGELES CO.
SEE 563 MAP
SEE 592 MAP
SEE 594 MAP
SEE 633 MAP
CAHUENGA PASS
MOUNT OLYMPUS
HOLLYWOOD HILLS
GRIFFITH PARK
HOLLYWOOD
WEST HOLLYWOOD
LOS ANGELES
LOS FELIZ
THAI TOWN
LITTLE ARMENIA
FAIRFAX VILLAGE
WHITLEY HEIGHTS
90046
90068
90069
90028
90027
90029
90038
90036
90048
90004
HOLLYWOOD RESERVOIR
HOLLYWOOD BOWL
JOHN ANSON FORD THEATER
RUNYON CANYON PARK
WATTLES GARDEN PARK
TREBEK OPEN SPACE
OBSERVATORY
GREEK THEATRE
BIRD SANCTUARY
PICNIC GROUNDS
CHILDREN'S PLGD
ROCK QUARRY
AZALEA GARDENS
HOLLYWOOD FOREVER CEMETERY
PARAMOUNT STUDIOS
WILSHIRE COUNTRY CLUB
PLUMMER PARK
POINSETTIA REC CTR
KINGS ROAD PARK
SCHINDLER HOUSE
FAIRFAX HS
HOLLYWOOD HS
HOLLYWOOD PALLADIUM
HOLLYWOOD RECREATION CENTER
CHATEAU MARMONT HOTEL
HOLLYWOOD BLVD
SUNSET BLVD
SANTA MONICA BLVD
MELROSE AV
BEVERLY BLVD
FRANKLIN AV
FOUNTAIN AV
HOLLYWOOD FRWY
MULHOLLAND DR
LAUREL CANYON BLVD
LA BREA AV
HIGHLAND AV
FAIRFAX AV
VINE ST
WESTERN AV
LOS FELIZ BLVD
WOODROW WILSON DR
0 .25 .5 .75 1.0 miles 1 in. = 2400 ft.
© 2008 Rand McNally & Company

SEE 564 MAP

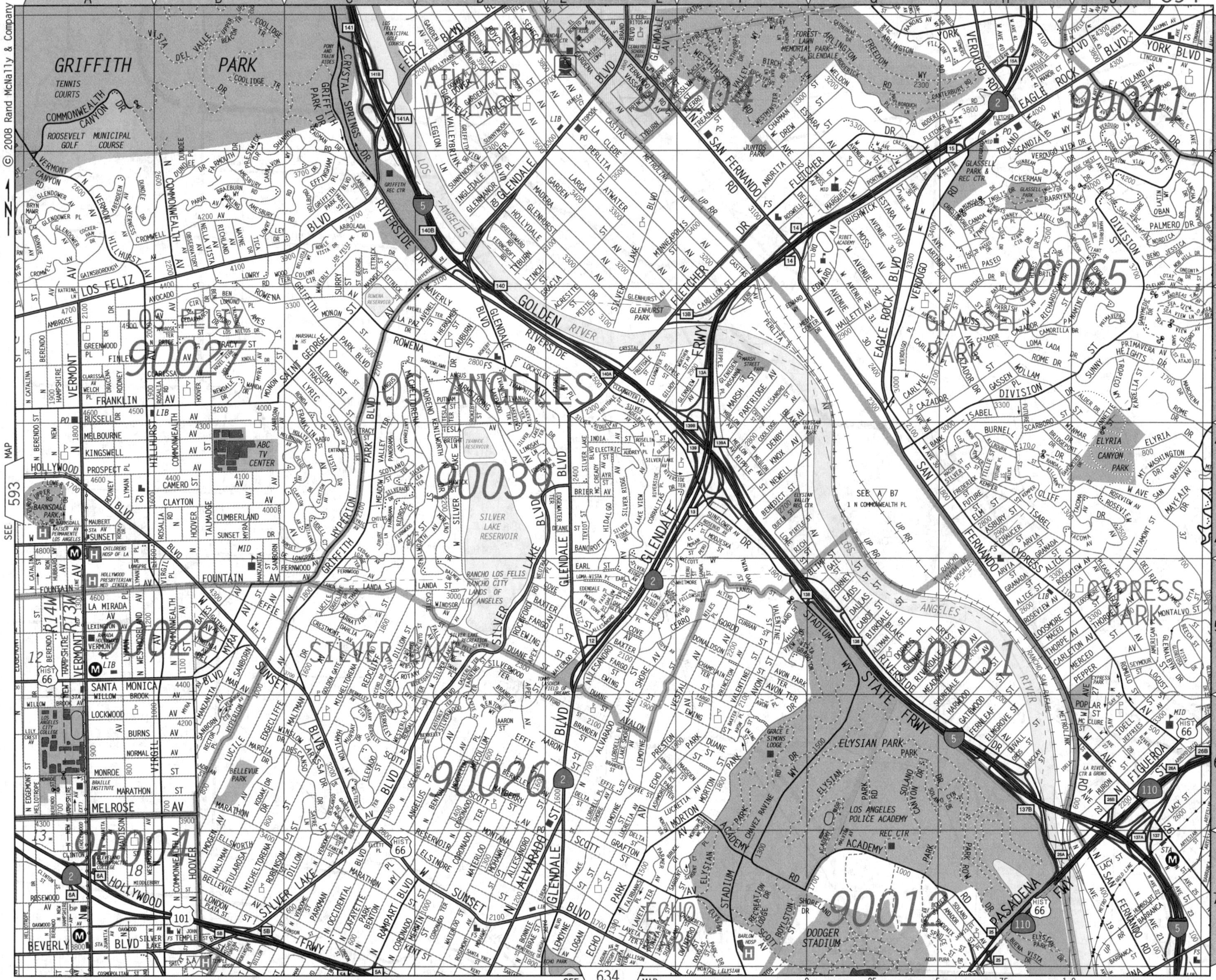

A B C D E F G H J

1 2 3 4 5 6 7

LOS ANGELES CO.

GRIFFITH PARK

ATWATER VILLAGE

GLENDALE

91204

90041

90065

GLASSELL PARK

LOS FELIZ

90027

LOS ANGELES

90039

SILVER LAKE RESERVOIR

ABC TV CENTER

90029

SILVER LAKE

90026

CYPRESS PARK

90031

ELYSIAN PARK

90004

ECHO PARK

DODGER STADIUM

90012

GOLDEN STATE FRWY

PASADENA FWY

HOLLYWOOD FRWY

LOS ANGELES RIVER

SEE 593 MAP

SEE 595 MAP

SEE 634 MAP

0 .25 .5 .75 1.0 miles 1 in. = 2400 ft.

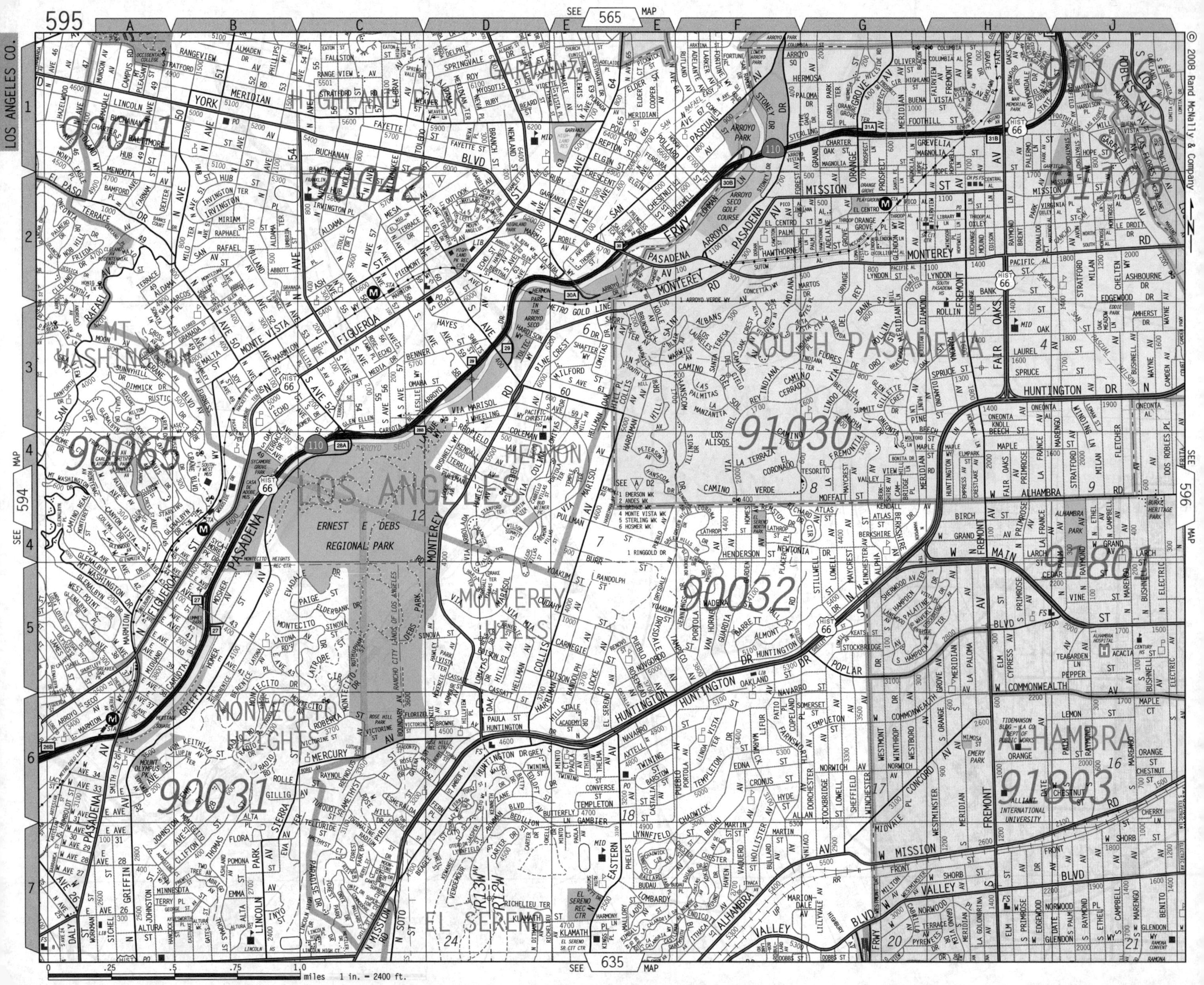
SEE 565 MAP
SEE 594 MAP
SEE 596 MAP
SEE 635 MAP
A
B
C
D
E
F
G
H
J
1
2
3
4
5
6
7
HIGHLAND PARK
GARVANZA
MT WASHINGTON
SOUTH PASADENA
HERMON
LOS ANGELES
MONTEREY HILLS
MONTECITO HEIGHTS
EL SERENO
ALHAMBRA
90041
90042
90065
91030
90032
90031
91801
91803
ERNEST E DEBS REGIONAL PARK
ARROYO SECO GOLF COURSE
ARROYO PARK
ALLIANT INTERNATIONAL UNIVERSITY
YORK BLVD
FIGUEROA ST
PASADENA AV
MONTEREY RD
HUNTINGTON DR
MISSION RD
VALLEY BLVD
W MAIN ST
FREMONT AV
FAIR OAKS AV
METRO GOLD LINE
PASADENA FRWY
110
HIST 66
R13W
R12W
0
.25
.5
.75
1.0
miles 1 in. = 2400 ft.

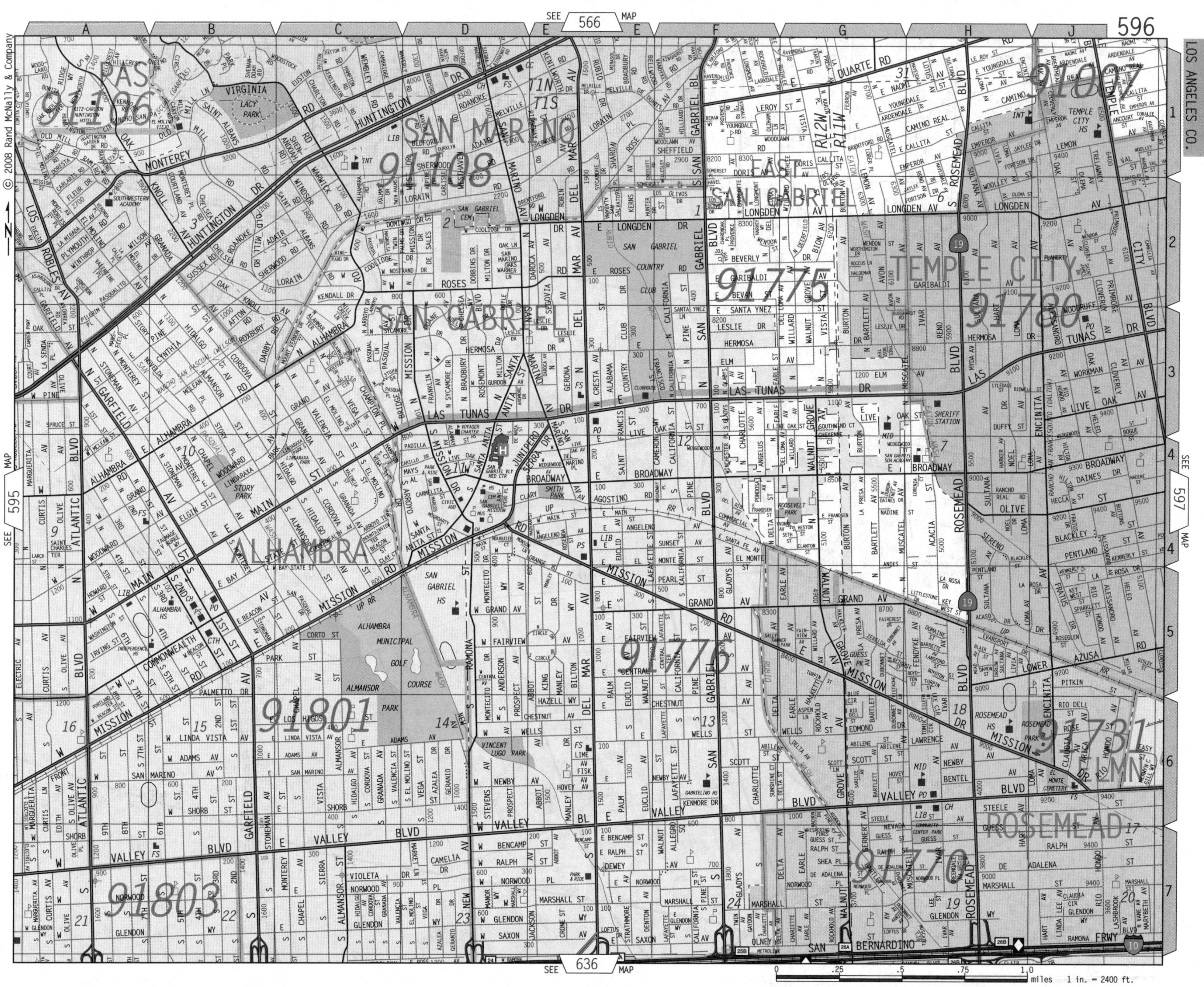
SEE 566 MAP
LOS ANGELES CO.
© 2008 Rand McNally & Company
SAN MARINO
91108
PAS
91106
VIRGINIA
LACY PARK
SAN GABRIEL
EAST SAN GABRIEL
91775
TEMPLE CITY
91780
91007
ALHAMBRA
91801
91803
91776
91770
91731
ROSEMEAD
ELMN
HUNTINGTON DR
LAS TUNAS DR
MISSION RD
VALLEY BLVD
SAN GABRIEL BLVD
ROSEMEAD BLVD
BROADWAY
MAIN ST
GARFIELD AV
ATLANTIC BLVD
LONGDEN AV
DUARTE RD
SAN GABRIEL COUNTRY CLUB
ALHAMBRA MUNICIPAL GOLF COURSE
ALMANSOR PARK
VINCENT LUGO PARK
SMITH PARK
STORY PARK
ROOSEVELT PARK
SAN GABRIEL HS
ALHAMBRA HS
ROSEMEAD HS
GABRIELINO HS
TEMPLE CITY HS
SAN BERNARDINO FRWY
RAMONA FRWY
SEE 595 MAP
SEE 597 MAP
SEE 636 MAP
0 .25 .5 .75 1.0 miles 1 in. = 2400 ft.

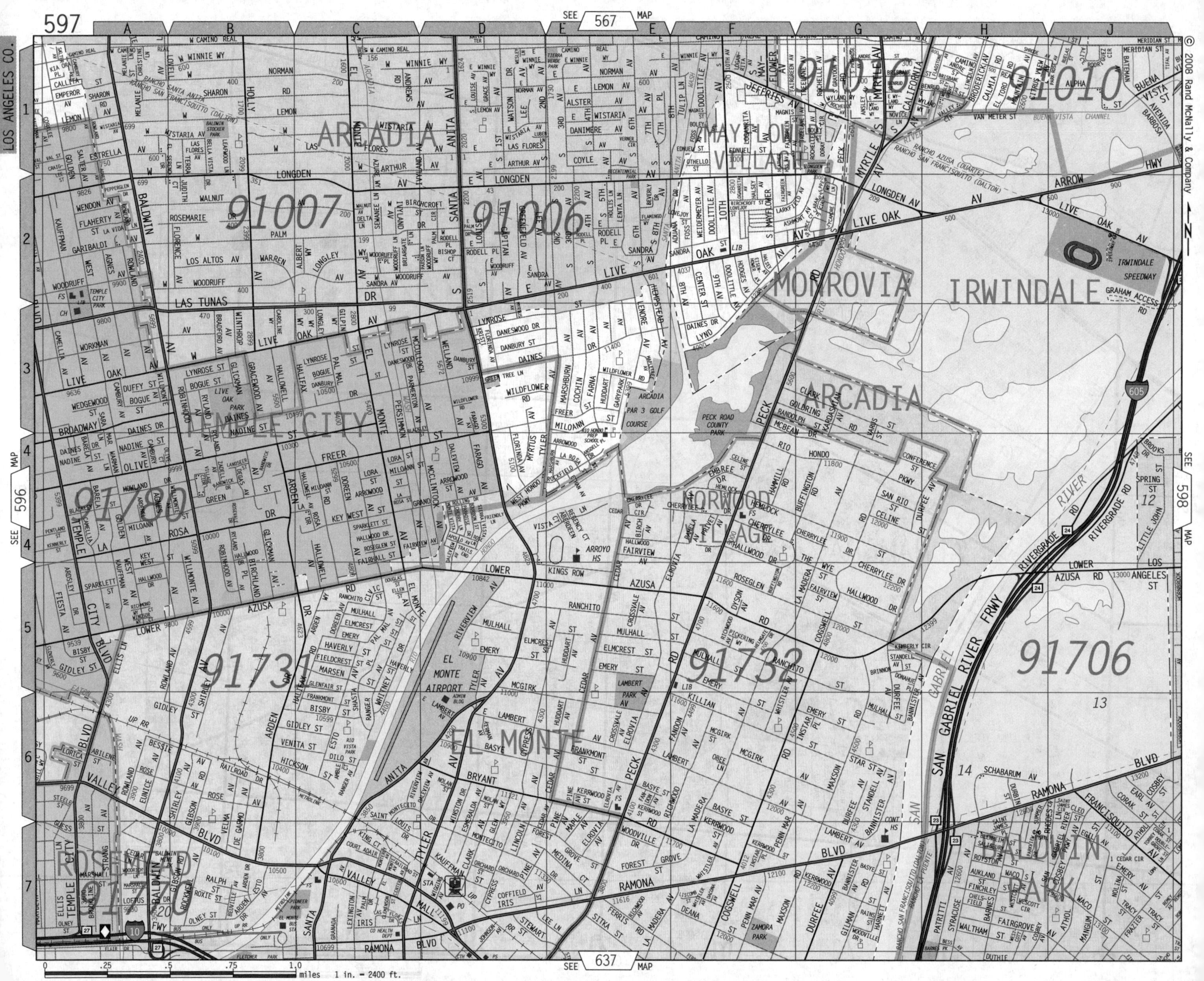

LOS ANGELES CO.
SEE 567 MAP
SEE 637 MAP
SEE 596 MAP
SEE 598 MAP
A
B
C
D
E
F
G
H
J
1
2
3
4
5
6
7
ARCADIA
91007
91006
91016
91010
MAYFLOWER VILLAGE
MONROVIA
IRWINDALE
IRWINDALE SPEEDWAY
TEMPLE CITY
91780
ARCADIA PAR 3 GOLF COURSE
PECK ROAD COUNTY PARK
NORWOOD VILLAGE
91731
91732
91706
EL MONTE
EL MONTE AIRPORT
ROSEMEAD
91770
BALDWIN PARK
SAN GABRIEL RIVER FRWY
LIVE OAK AV
LAS TUNAS DR
LONGDEN AV
ARROW HWY
LOWER AZUSA RD
RAMONA BLVD
VALLEY BLVD
BALDWIN AV
SANTA ANITA AV
PECK RD
MYRTLE AV
ROSEMEAD BLVD
TEMPLE CITY BLVD
ARROYO HS
LAMBERT PARK
ZAMORA PARK
PIONEER PARK
RIO HONDO
SAN GABRIEL RIVER
605
10
0 .25 .5 .75 1.0 miles 1 in. = 2400 ft.
© 2008 Rand McNally & Company

598
SEE 568 MAP
SEE 638 MAP
SEE 597 MAP
SEE 599 MAP
LOS ANGELES CO.
© 2008 Rand McNally & Company
A
B
C
D
E
F
G
H
J
1
2
3
4
5
6
7
91010
91702
AZUSA
IRWINDALE
91706
91722
BALDWIN PARK
COVINA
WEST COVINA
91790
91791
SANTA FE FLOOD CONTROL BASIN
SANTA FE DAM RECREATION AREA
SAN GABRIEL RIVER FRWY
ARROW HWY
SAN BERNARDINO FRWY
VALLEYDALE COUNTY PARK
GLADSTONE HS
NORTHVIEW HS
NORTH PARK HS
BALDWIN PARK HS
SIERRA VISTA HS
MORGAN PARK
PALM VIEW PARK
DEL NORTE PARK
DOCTORS HOSP OF WEST COVINA
WESTFIELD SHOPPINGTOWN WEST COVINA
0
.25
.5
.75
1.0
miles
1 in. = 2400 ft.

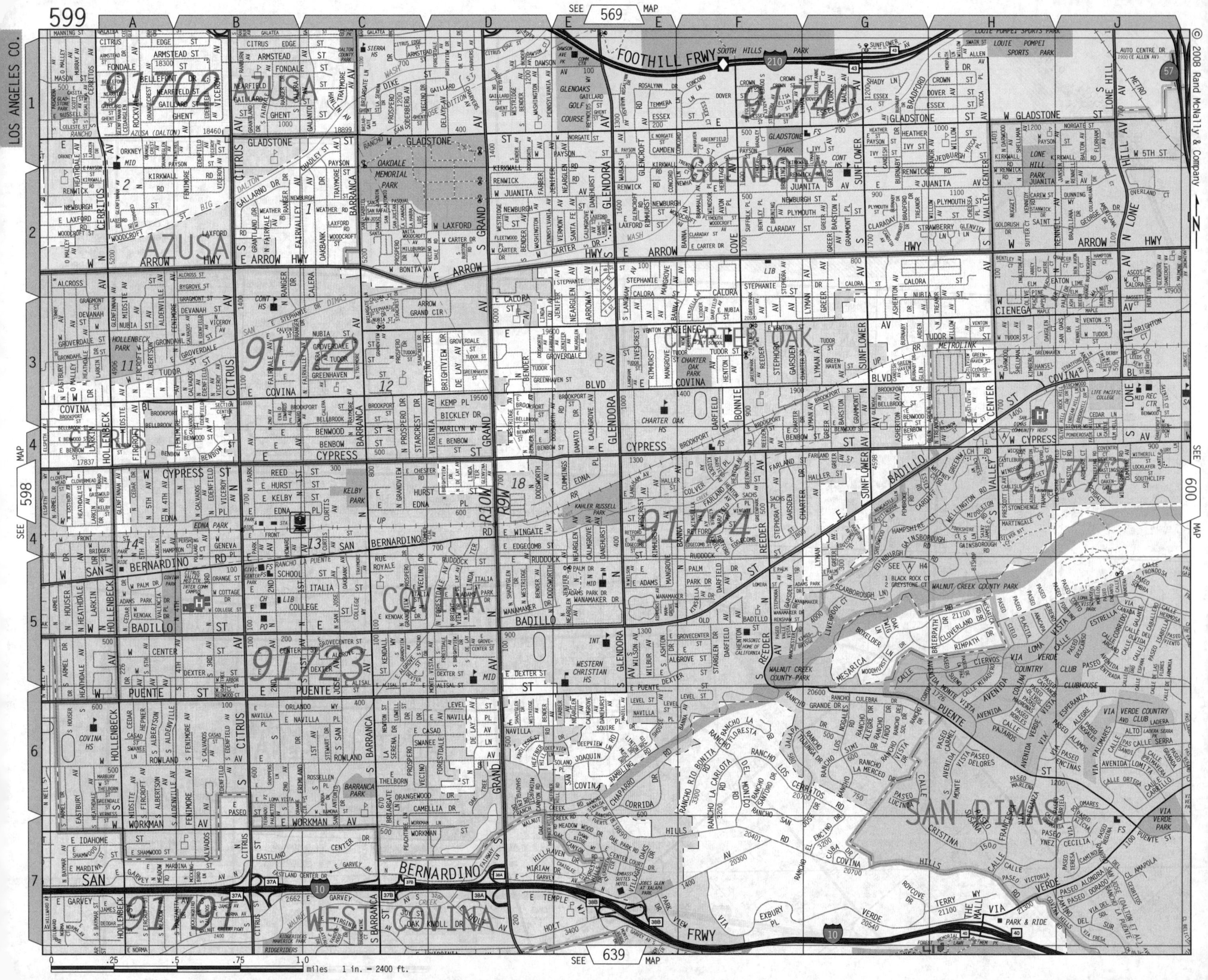

SEE 569 MAP
LOS ANGELES CO.
FOOTHILL FRWY
AZUSA
91702
91740
GLENDORA
91722
CHARTER OAK
91724
COVINA
91723
91773
SAN DIMAS
91791
WEST COVINA
OAKDALE MEMORIAL PARK
GLENOAKS GOLF COURSE
LOUIE POMPEI SPORTS PARK
GLADSTONE PARK
LONE HILL PARK
HOLLENBECK PARK
CHARTER OAK PARK
KAHLER RUSSELL PARK
KELBY PARK
EDNA PARK
BARRANCA PARK
WALNUT CREEK COUNTY PARK
VIA VERDE COUNTRY CLUB
VIA VERDE PARK
COVINA HS
CHARTER OAK HS
WESTERN CHRISTIAN HS
SIERRA HS
LIFE PACIFIC COLLEGE
SAN DIMAS COMMUNITY HOSP
INTER COMM CAMPUS
MASONIC HOME OF CALIFORNIA
METROLINK
E ARROW HWY
ARROW HWY
W GLADSTONE ST
CIENEGA AV
COVINA BLVD
CYPRESS ST
SAN BERNARDINO RD
BADILLO ST
PUENTE ST
WORKMAN AV
SAN BERNARDINO FRWY
CITRUS AV
BARRANCA AV
GRAND AV
GLENDORA AV
SUNFLOWER AV
LONE HILL AV
VALLEY CENTER AV
SEE 598 MAP
SEE 600 MAP
SEE 639 MAP
0 .25 .5 .75 1.0 miles 1 in. = 2400 ft.

SEE 570 MAP

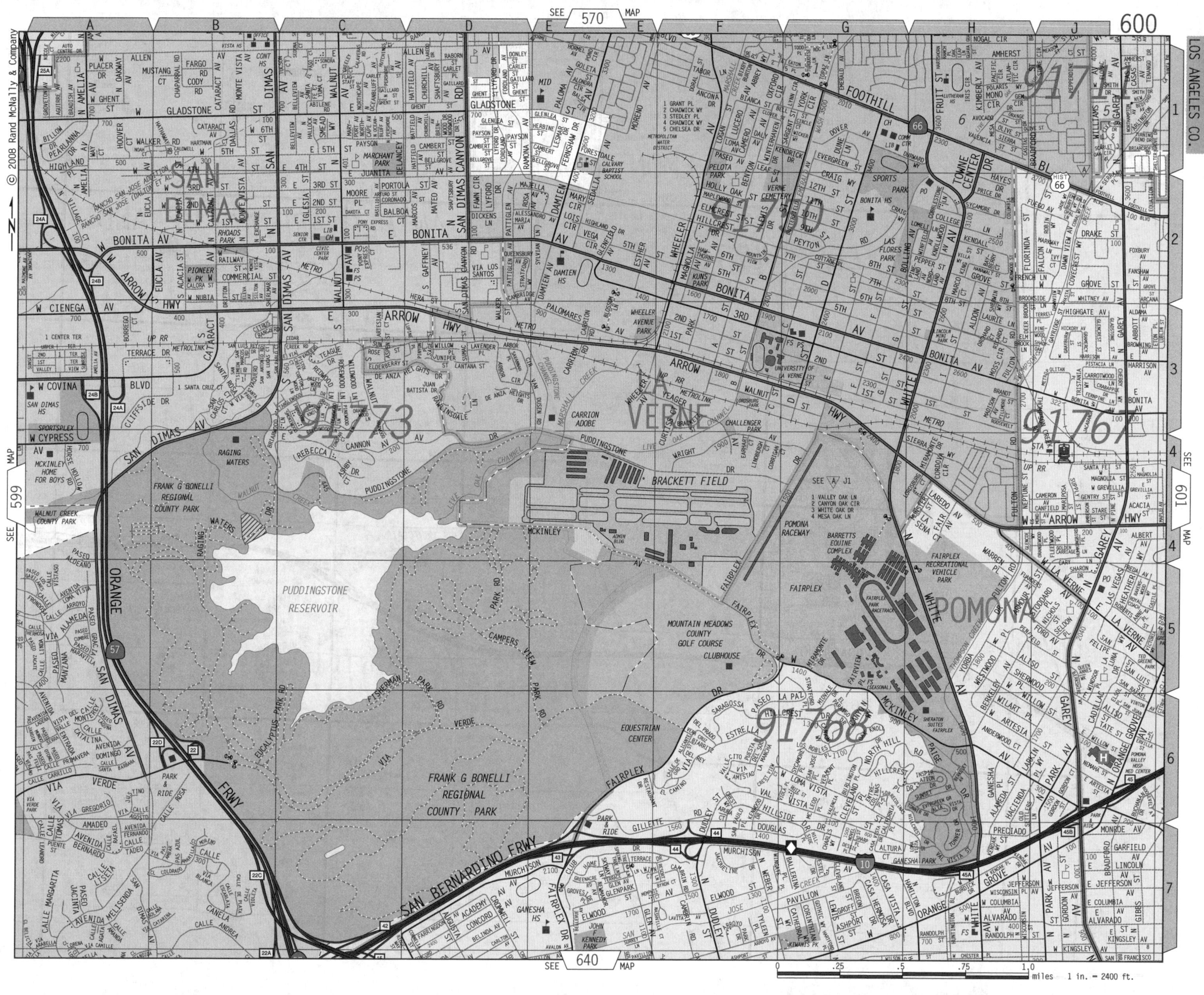

SEE 640 MAP

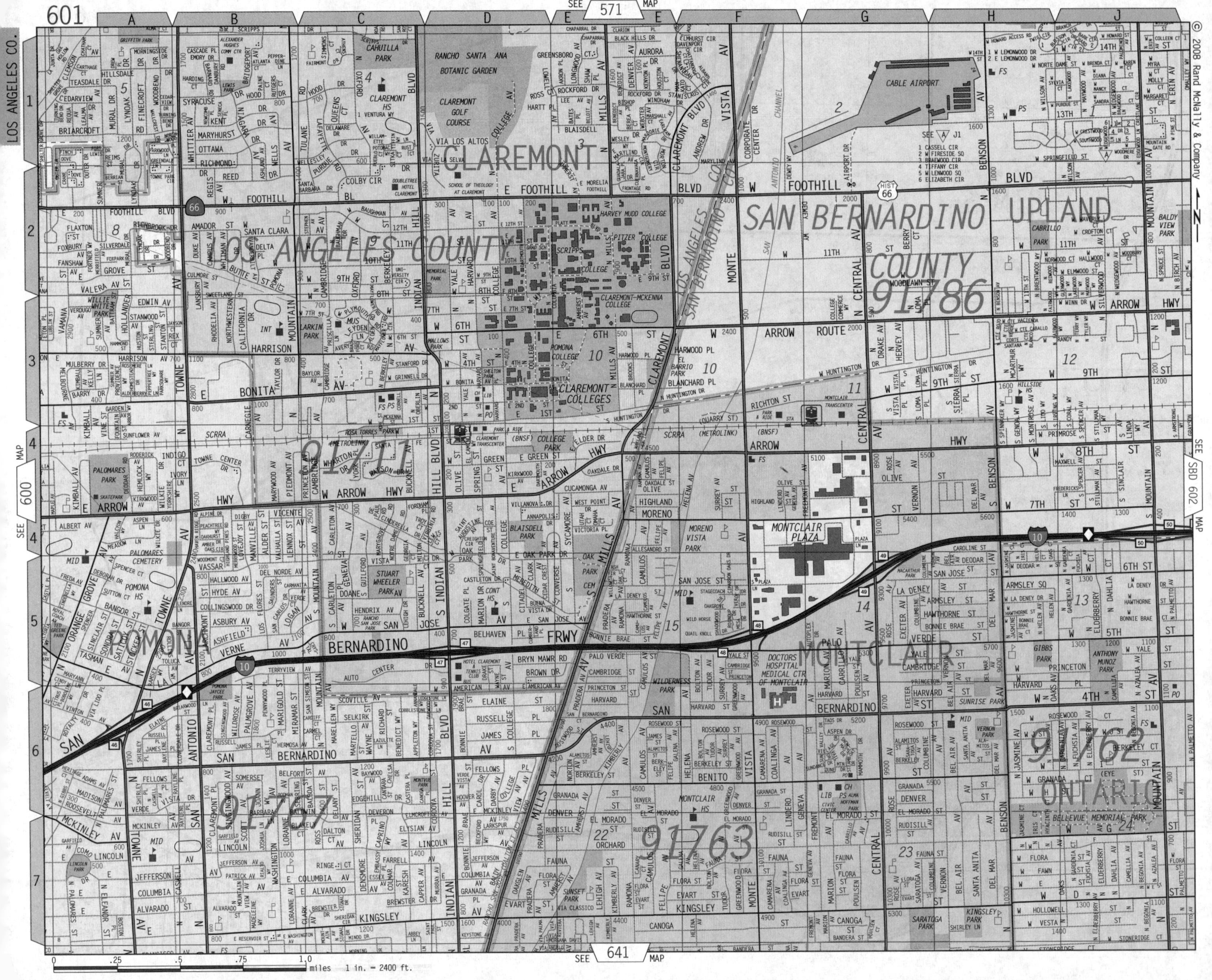
SEE 571 MAP
LOS ANGELES CO.
CLAREMONT
LOS ANGELES COUNTY
SAN BERNARDINO UPLAND
COUNTY
91786
91711
POMONA
MONTCLAIR
ONTARIO
91767
91763
91762
RANCHO SANTA ANA BOTANIC GARDEN
CLAREMONT GOLF COURSE
CABLE AIRPORT
HARVEY MUDD COLLEGE
PITZER COLLEGE
SCRIPPS COLLEGE
CLAREMONT-MCKENNA COLLEGE
POMONA COLLEGE
CLAREMONT COLLEGES
MONTCLAIR PLAZA
DOCTORS HOSPITAL MEDICAL CTR OF MONTCLAIR
PALOMARES CEMETERY
PALOMARES PARK
BELLEVUE MEMORIAL PARK
FOOTHILL BLVD
ARROW HWY
ARROW ROUTE
SAN BERNARDINO FRWY
SEE 600 MAP
SEE SBD 602 MAP
SEE 641 MAP
miles 1 in. = 2400 ft.

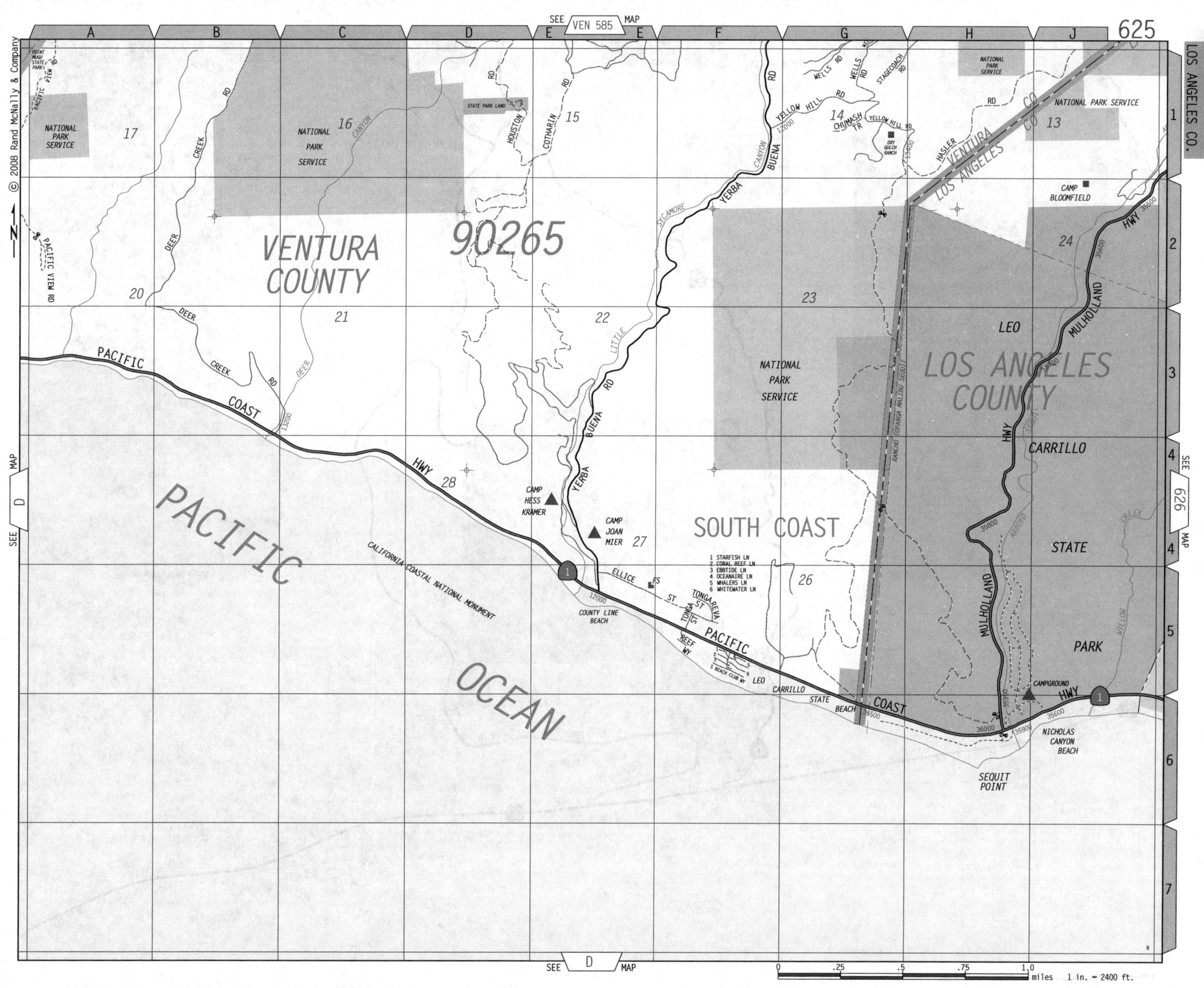
SEE VEN 585 MAP
A B C D E F G H J
1 2 3 4 5 6 7
LOS ANGELES CO.
© 2008 Rand McNally & Company
VENTURA COUNTY
90265
LOS ANGELES COUNTY
PACIFIC OCEAN
SOUTH COAST
LEO CARRILLO STATE PARK
PACIFIC COAST HWY
NATIONAL PARK SERVICE
STATE PARK LAND
CAMP HESS KRAMER
CAMP JOAN MIER
CAMP BLOOMFIELD
DRY GULCH RANCH
COUNTY LINE BEACH
LEO CARRILLO STATE BEACH
NICHOLAS CANYON BEACH
SEQUIT POINT
CAMPGROUND
CALIFORNIA COASTAL NATIONAL MONUMENT
RANCHO TOPANGA MALIBU SEQUIT
YERBA BUENA RD
DEER CREEK RD
MULHOLLAND HWY
ELLICE ST
TONGA ST
TONGA REVA
REEF WY
YELLOW HILL RD
CHUMASH TR
WELLS RD
STAGECOACH RD
HASLER RD
HOUSTON RD
COTHARIN RD
PACIFIC VIEW RD
POINT MUGU STATE PARK
1 STARFISH LN
2 CORAL REEF LN
3 EBBTIDE LN
4 OCEANAIRE LN
5 WHALERS LN
6 WHITEWATER LN
5 BEACH CLUB WY
SEE 626 MAP
SEE D MAP
0 .25 .5 .75 1.0 miles 1 in. = 2400 ft.

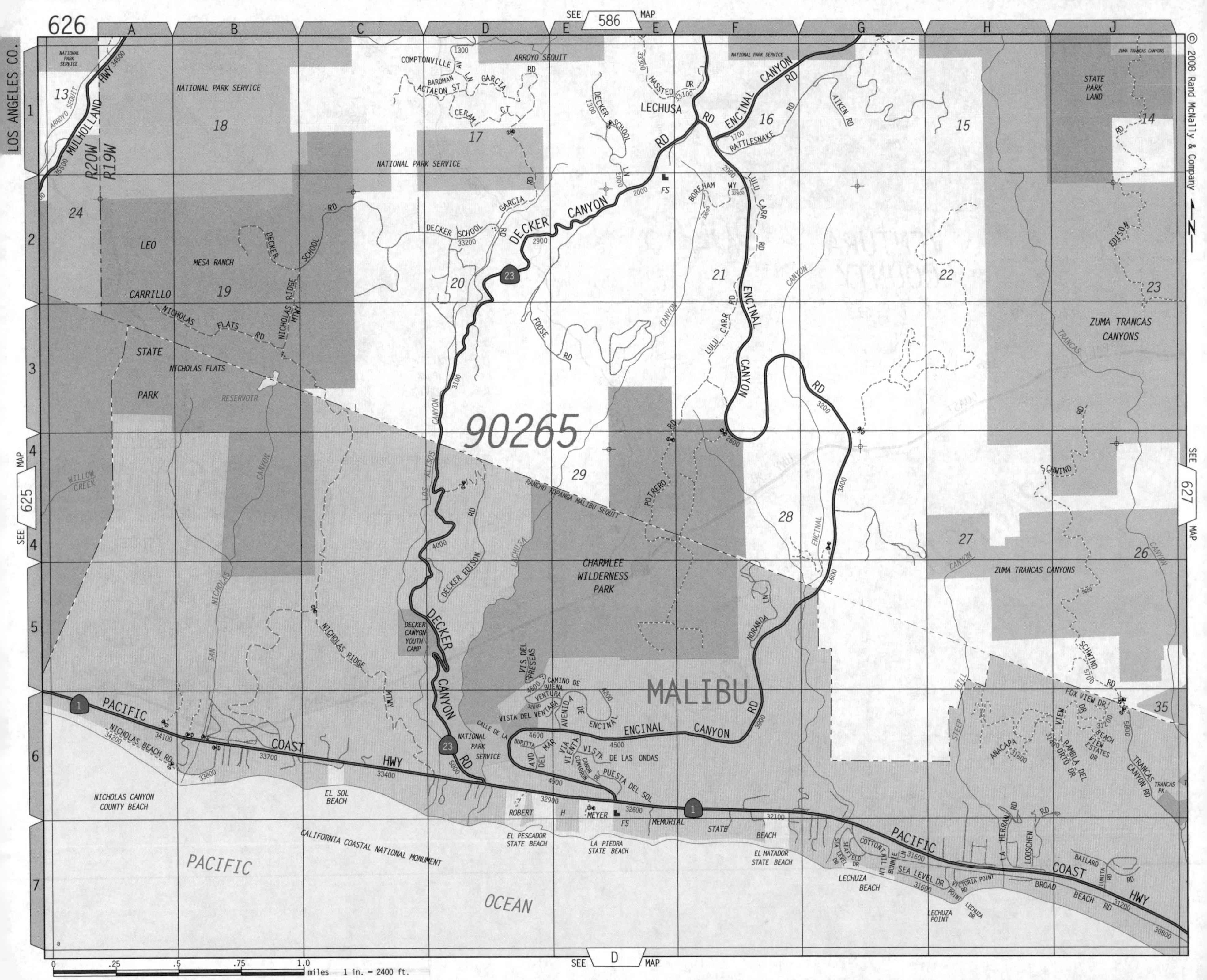
SEE 586 MAP
LOS ANGELES CO.
SEE 625 MAP
SEE 627 MAP
SEE D MAP
90265
MALIBU
LECHUSA
DECKER CANYON RD
ENCINAL CANYON RD
PACIFIC COAST HWY
MULHOLLAND HWY
NATIONAL PARK SERVICE
ARROYO SEQUIT
COMPTONVILLE
LEO CARRILLO STATE PARK
MESA RANCH
NICHOLAS FLATS
NICHOLAS FLATS RD
RESERVOIR
CHARMLEE WILDERNESS PARK
DECKER CANYON YOUTH CAMP
ZUMA TRANCAS CANYONS
STATE PARK LAND
RANCHO TOPANGA MALIBU SEQUIT
NICHOLAS CANYON COUNTY BEACH
EL SOL BEACH
EL PESCADOR STATE BEACH
LA PIEDRA STATE BEACH
ROBERT H MEYER MEMORIAL STATE BEACH
EL MATADOR STATE BEACH
LECHUZA BEACH
LECHUZA POINT
CALIFORNIA COASTAL NATIONAL MONUMENT
PACIFIC OCEAN
R20W R19W
© 2008 Rand McNally & Company
miles 1 in. = 2400 ft.

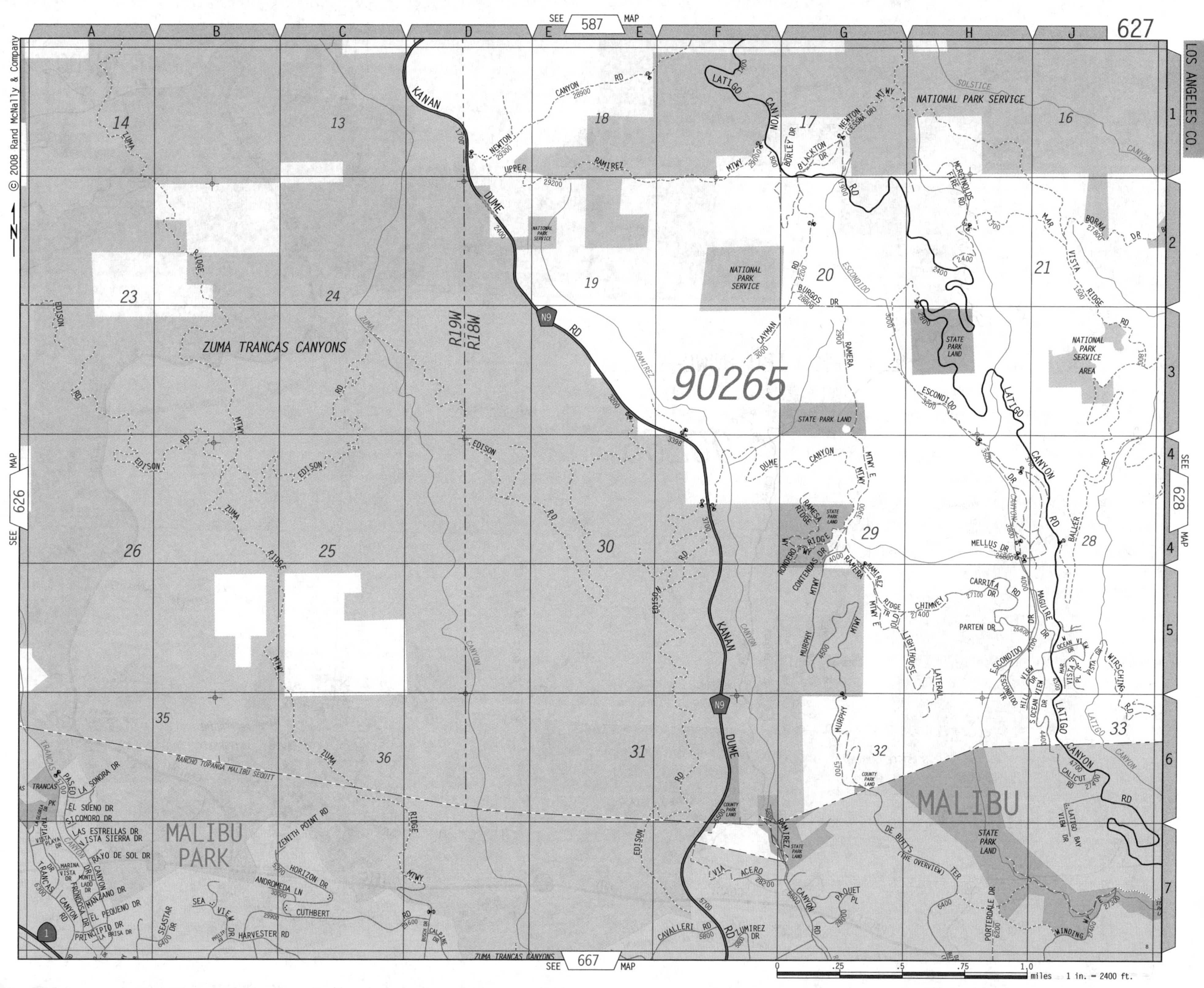
SEE 587 MAP
LOS ANGELES CO.
ZUMA TRANCAS CANYONS
90265
NATIONAL PARK SERVICE
STATE PARK LAND
MALIBU
MALIBU PARK
KANAN DUME RD
LATIGO CANYON RD
SEE 626 MAP
SEE 628 MAP
SEE 667 MAP
RANCHO TOPANGA MALIBU SEQUIT
1 in. = 2400 ft.

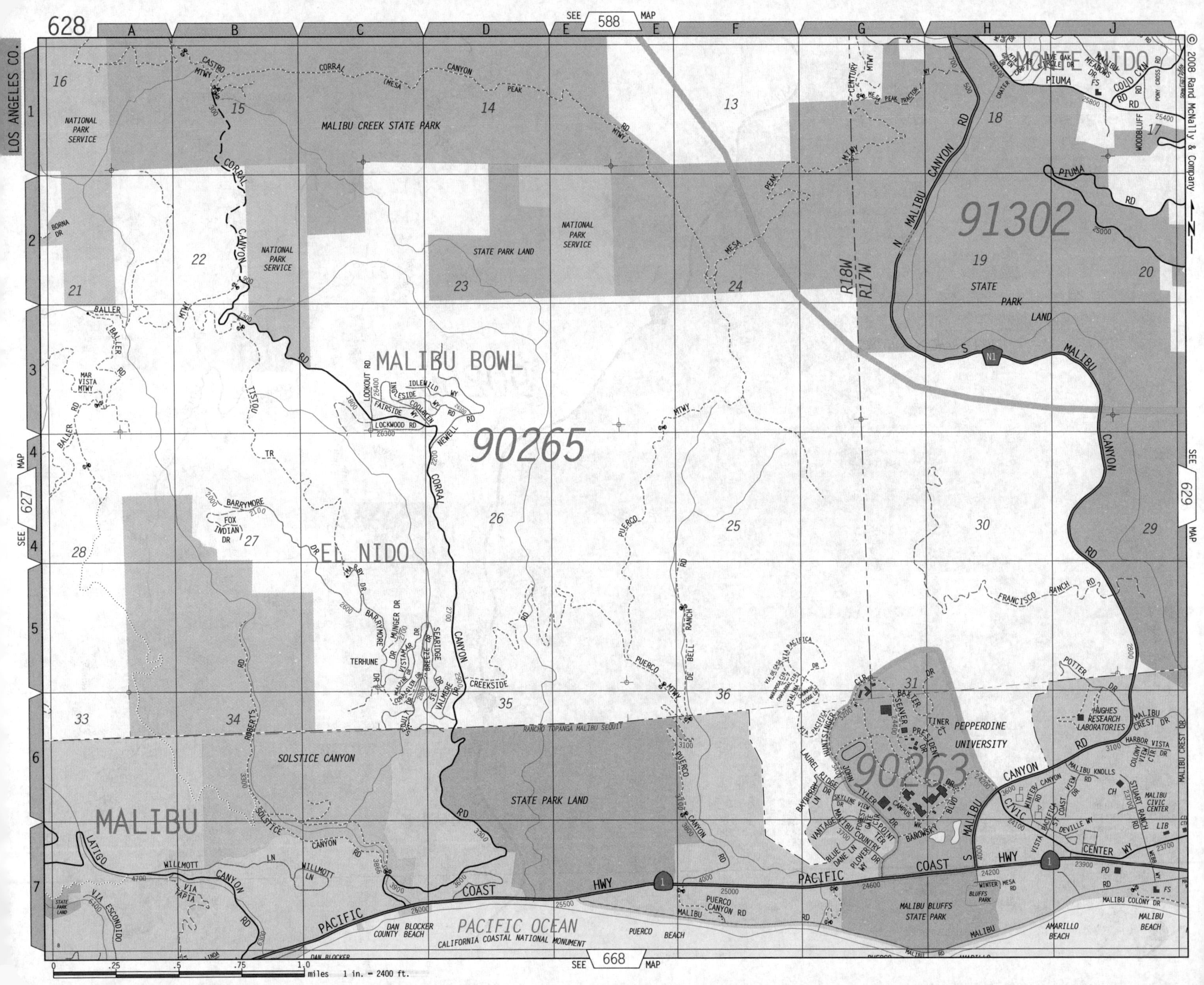

SEE 588 MAP
LOS ANGELES CO.
MONTE NIDO
MALIBU CREEK STATE PARK
NATIONAL PARK SERVICE
STATE PARK LAND
MALIBU BOWL
90265
91302
EL NIDO
MALIBU
90263
PEPPERDINE UNIVERSITY
SOLSTICE CANYON
HUGHES RESEARCH LABORATORIES
MALIBU CIVIC CENTER
MALIBU BLUFFS STATE PARK
PACIFIC OCEAN
CALIFORNIA COASTAL NATIONAL MONUMENT
DAN BLOCKER COUNTY BEACH
PUERCO BEACH
AMARILLO BEACH
MALIBU BEACH
PACIFIC COAST HWY
MALIBU CANYON RD
CORRAL CANYON RD
RANCHO TOPANGA MALIBU SEQUIT
R18W R17W
SEE 627 MAP
SEE 629 MAP
SEE 668 MAP
miles 1 in. = 2400 ft.

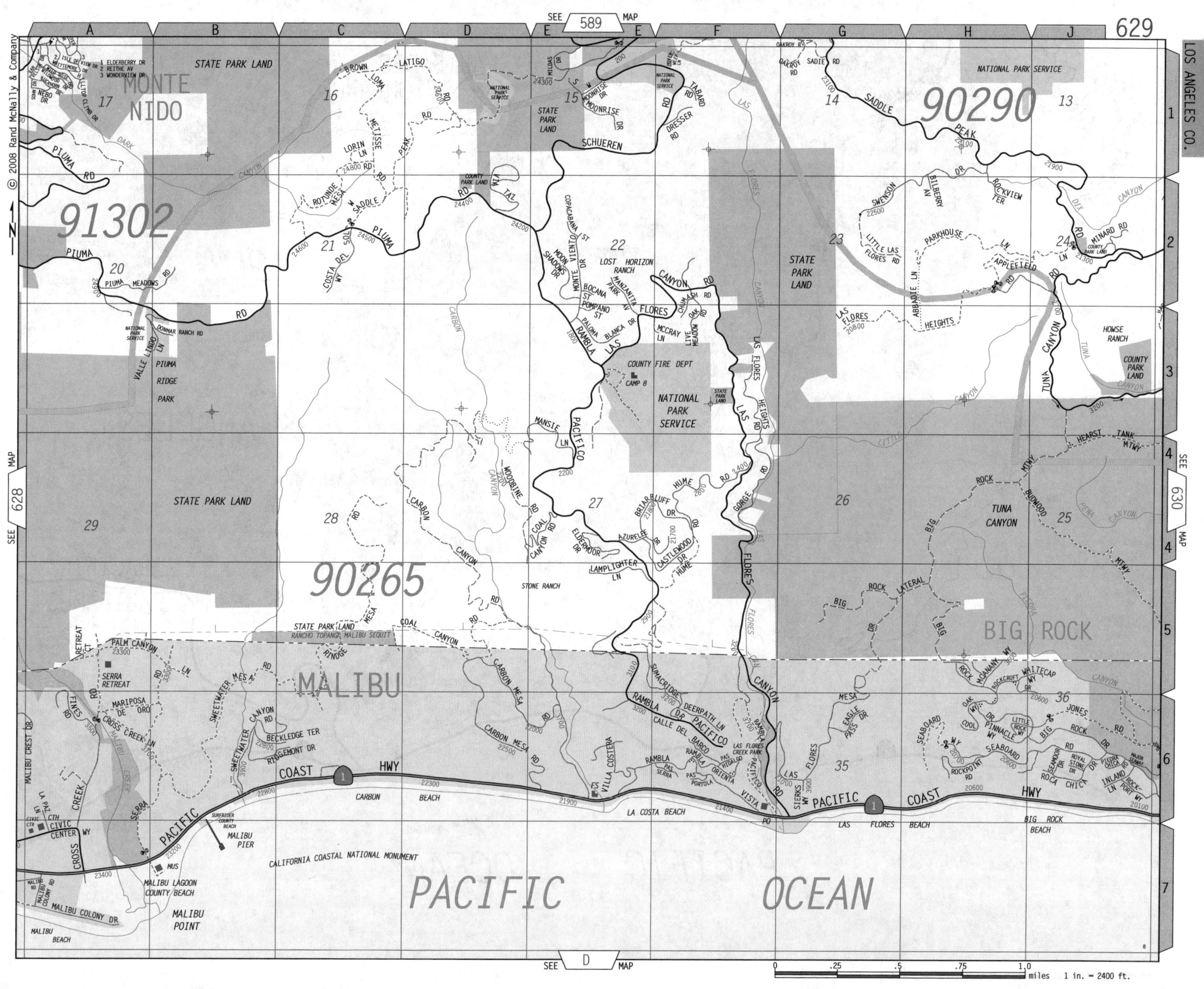
SEE 589 MAP
A
B
C
D
E
F
G
H
J
LOS ANGELES CO.
© 2008 Rand McNally & Company
MONTE NIDO
STATE PARK LAND
1 ELDERBERRY DR
2 REITHE AV
3 WONDERVIEW DR
91302
90290
90265
NATIONAL PARK SERVICE
PIUMA RD
PIUMA MEADOWS RD
VALLE LINDO
DONMAR RANCH RD
PIUMA RIDGE PARK
BROWN
LATIGO
LOMA METISSE
PEAK
LORIN LN
ROTUNDE MESA
W SADDLE
COSTA DEL SOL WY
COUNTY PARK LAND
VIA TAZ
SCHUEREN
MOONRISE DR
STATE PARK LAND
DRESSER RD
TABARD
SADDLE PEAK
SWENSON
BILBERRY AV
ROCKVIEW TER
LITTLE LAS FLORES RD
PARKHOUSE LN
APPLEFIELD
ABBADIE LN
HEIGHTS
MINARD RD
DIX CANYON
TUNA CANYON RD
HOWSE RANCH
COUNTY PARK LAND
COPACABANA ST
MONTE VIENTO DR
MOON SHADOWS DR
LOST HORIZON RANCH
MANZANITA PARK AV
BOCANA ST
POMPANO ST
PALOMA
BLANCA DR
RAMBLA LAS FLORES
CANYON RD
CHUMASH RD
MCCRAY LN
LIVE OAK MEADOW RD
COUNTY FIRE DEPT
CAMP 8
NATIONAL PARK SERVICE
LAS FLORES HEIGHTS RD
MANSIE LN
RAMBLA PACIFICO
HUME RD
GORGE RD
BRIARBLUFF DR
AZURELEE DR
CASTLEWOOD DR
HUME DR
ELDERMOOR DR
LAMPLIGHTER LN
STONE RANCH
COAL CANYON RD
WOODBINE DR
CARBON CANYON RD
CARBON MESA RD
STATE PARK LAND
RANCHO TOPANGA MALIBU SEQUIT
RINDGE
COAL CANYON
HEARST TANK MTWY
ROCK BUDWOOD
TUNA CANYON
BIG ROCK MTWY
BIG ROCK LATERAL
BIG ROCK DR
BIG ROCK
PENA CANYON
SEE 630 MAP
SEE 628 MAP
MALIBU
RETREAT CT
PALM CANYON LN
SERRA RETREAT
SWEETWATER MESA RD
SWEETWATER CANYON RD
BECKLEDGE TER
RIDGEMONT DR
MARIPOSA DE ORO
FINES RD
CROSS CREEK LN
MALIBU CREEK
MALIBU CREST DR
LA PAZ LN
CIVIC CENTER WY
CROSS CREEK RD
SERRA RD
SUMACRIDGE DR
DEERPATH LN
RAMBLA PACIFICO
CALLE DEL BARCO
RAMBLA PAS SERRA
PAS PORTOLA
RAMBLA ORIENTA
PAS HIGUERA
LAS FLORES CREEK PARK
VISTA
VILLA COSTERA
LAS FLORES MESA DR
EAGLE PASS DR
SIERKS WY
ROCK MCCANANY WY
ROCKCROFT WY
WHITECAP DR
OAK
CDOL
PINNACLE WY
LITTLE ROCK WY
JONES
BIG ROCK DR
SEABOARD RD
ROCKPOINT RD
SEAMOOR DR
ROYAL STONE DR
ROCA CHICA
PIEDRA CHICA
INLAND LN
ROCKPORT WY
MAJOR KENWAY
PACIFIC COAST HWY
CARBON BEACH
LA COSTA BEACH
LAS FLORES BEACH
BIG ROCK BEACH
SURFRIDER COUNTY BEACH
MALIBU PIER
MUS
MALIBU LAGOON COUNTY BEACH
CALIFORNIA COASTAL NATIONAL MONUMENT
MALIBU ROAD
MALIBU COLONY RD
MALIBU COLONY DR
MALIBU POINT
MALIBU BEACH
PACIFIC OCEAN
SEE D MAP
0 .25 .5 .75 1.0 miles 1 in. = 2400 ft.

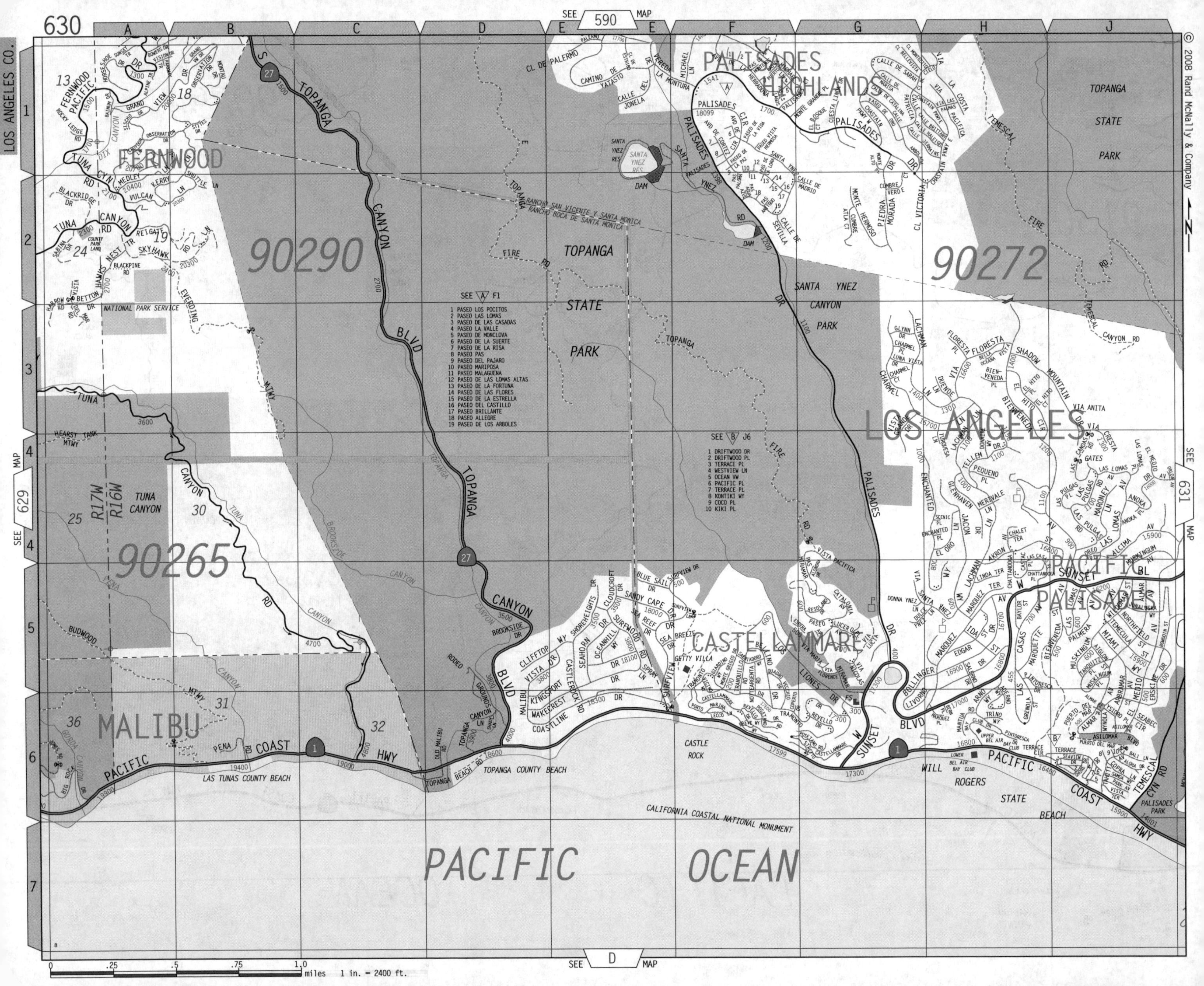

SEE 590 MAP
LOS ANGELES CO.
© 2008 Rand McNally & Company
FERNWOOD
PALISADES HIGHLANDS
TOPANGA STATE PARK
90290
90272
90265
TOPANGA CANYON BLVD
TUNA CANYON RD
SANTA YNEZ CANYON PARK
LOS ANGELES
PACIFIC PALISADES
CASTELLAMMARE
MALIBU
NATIONAL PARK SERVICE
TUNA CANYON
R17W
R16W
SEE A F1
1 PASEO LOS POCITOS
2 PASEO LAS LOMAS
3 PASEO DE LAS CASADAS
4 PASEO LA VALLE
5 PASEO DE MONCLOVA
6 PASEO DE LA SUERTE
7 PASEO DE LA RISA
8 PASEO PAS
9 PASEO DEL PAJARO
10 PASEO MARIPOSA
11 PASEO MALAGUENA
12 PASEO DE LAS LOMAS ALTAS
13 PASEO DE LA FORTUNA
14 PASEO DE LAS FLORES
15 PASEO DE LA ESTRELLA
16 PASEO DEL CASTILLO
17 PASEO BRILLANTE
18 PASEO ALLEGRE
19 PASEO DE LOS ARBOLES
SEE B J6
1 DRIFTWOOD DR
2 DRIFTWOOD PL
3 TERRACE PL
4 WESTVIEW LN
5 OCEAN VW
6 PACIFIC PL
7 TERRACE PL
8 KONTIKI WY
9 COCO PL
10 KIKI PL
SEE 629 MAP
SEE 631 MAP
PACIFIC COAST HWY
SUNSET BLVD
LAS TUNAS COUNTY BEACH
TOPANGA COUNTY BEACH
TOPANGA BEACH
CASTLE ROCK
WILL ROGERS STATE BEACH
PALISADES PARK
GETTY VILLA
CALIFORNIA COASTAL NATIONAL MONUMENT
PACIFIC OCEAN
SEE D MAP
0 .25 .5 .75 1.0 miles 1 in. = 2400 ft.

SEE 591 MAP

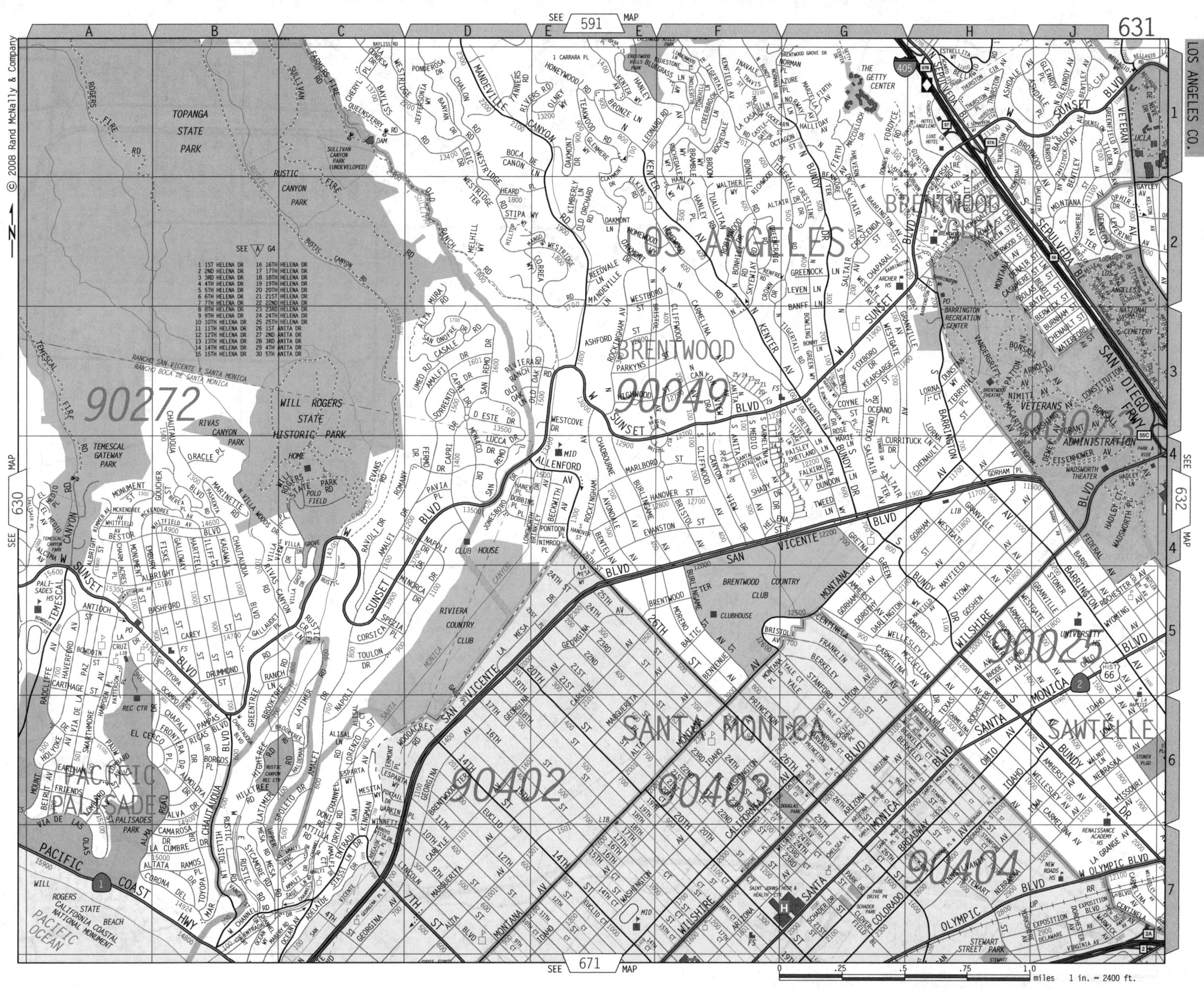

SEE 671 MAP

SEE 592 MAP

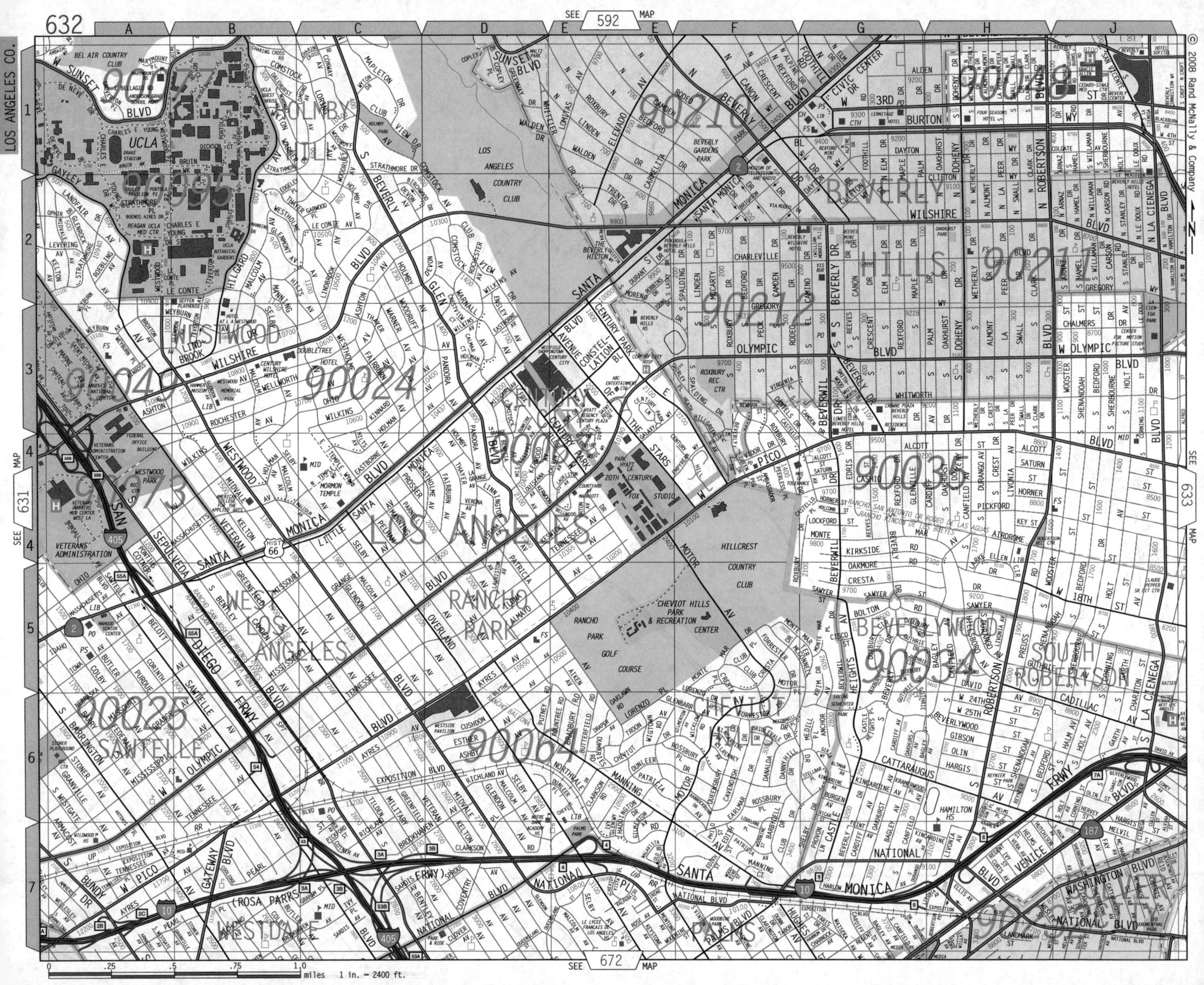

SEE 631 MAP
SEE 633 MAP
SEE 672 MAP

0 .25 .5 .75 1.0 miles 1 in. = 2400 ft.

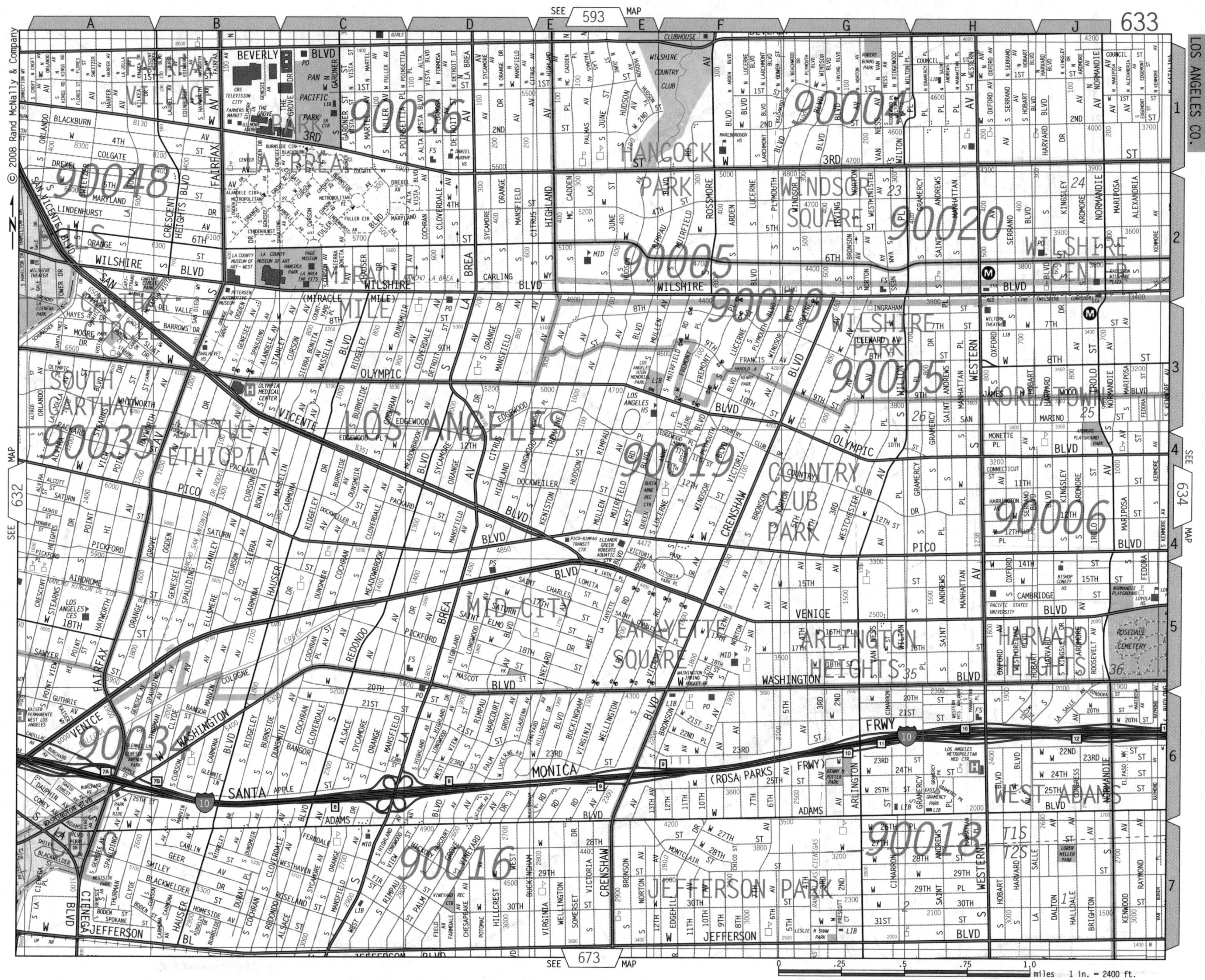

SEE 593 MAP
SEE 632 MAP
SEE 634 MAP
SEE 673 MAP
LOS ANGELES CO.
A
B
C
D
E
F
G
H
J
1
2
3
4
5
6
7
FAIRFAX VILLAGE
BEVERLY
LA BREA
CBS TELEVISION CITY
FARMERS MARKET
THE GROVE
PAN PACIFIC PARK
90036
90048
90004
HANCOCK PARK
WILSHIRE COUNTRY CLUB
WINDSOR SQUARE
90020
90005
90010
WILSHIRE CENTER
MIRACLE MILE
LA COUNTY MUSEUM OF ART
PAGE MUSEUM
LA BREA TAR PITS
PETERSEN AUTOMOTIVE MUSEUM
CARTHAY CIRCLE
SOUTH CARTHAY
90035
LITTLE ETHIOPIA
LOS ANGELES
OLYMPIA MEDICAL CENTER
WILSHIRE PARK
KOREATOWN
90019
COUNTRY CLUB PARK
90006
MID CITY
LAFAYETTE SQUARE
ARLINGTON HEIGHTS
HARVARD HEIGHTS
ROSEDALE CEMETERY
90034
90016
90018
JEFFERSON PARK
WEST ADAMS
LOS ANGELES METROPOLITAN MED CTR
SANTA MONICA FRWY
(ROSA PARKS FRWY)
10
WILSHIRE BLVD
OLYMPIC BLVD
PICO BLVD
VENICE BLVD
WASHINGTON BLVD
ADAMS BLVD
JEFFERSON BLVD
LA CIENEGA BLVD
FAIRFAX AV
LA BREA AV
CRENSHAW BLVD
WESTERN AV
NORMANDIE AV
SAN VICENTE BLVD
3RD ST
BEVERLY BLVD
0 .25 .5 .75 1.0 miles 1 in. = 2400 ft.

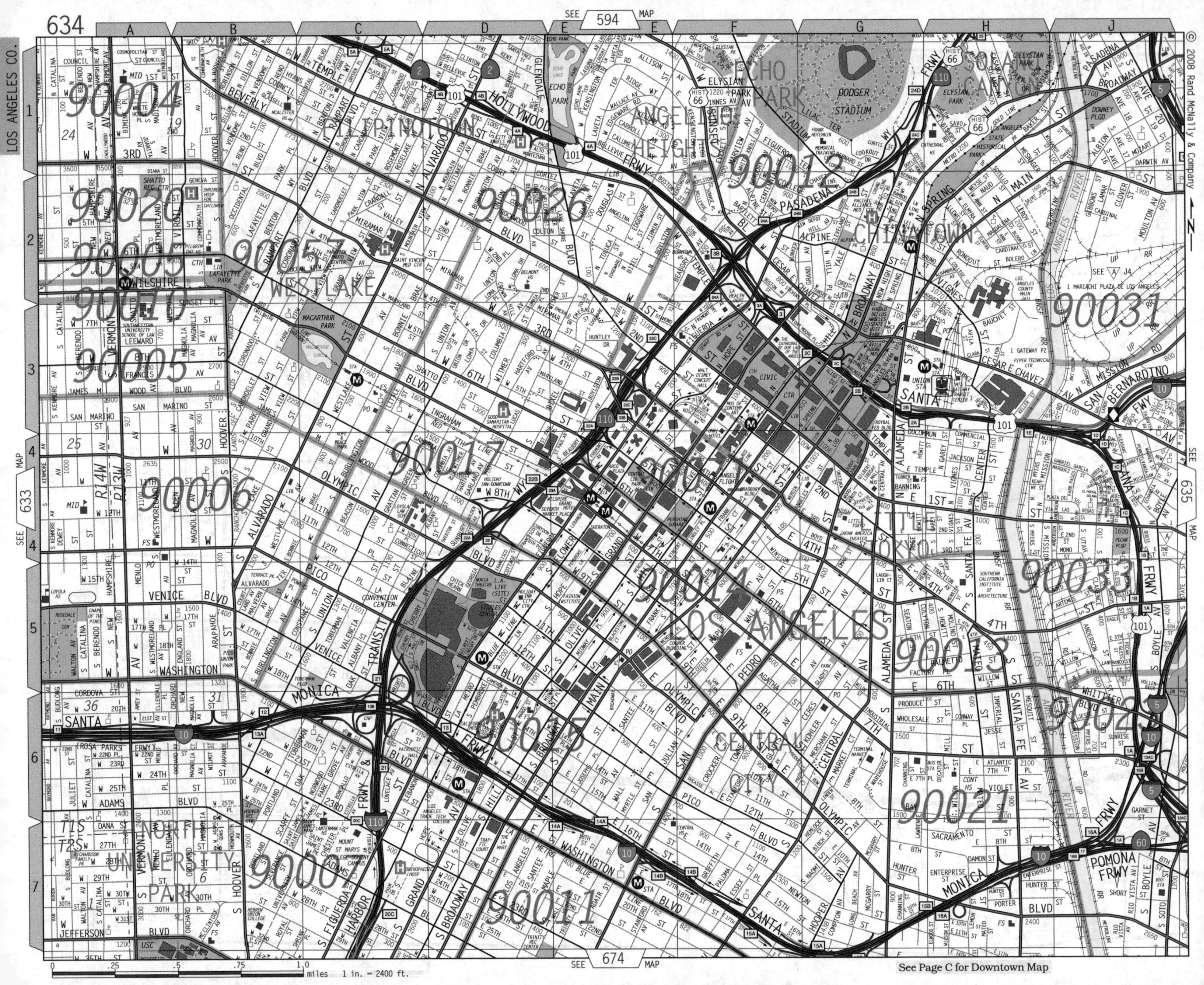
634
LOS ANGELES CO.
SEE 594 MAP
SEE 633 MAP
SEE 635 MAP
SEE 674 MAP
A
B
C
D
E
F
G
H
J
1
2
3
4
5
6
7
© 2008 Rand McNally & Company
90004
90020
90005
90010
90006
90057
90026
90012
90031
90017
90071
90014
90013
90033
90021
90015
90007
90011
90023
ECHO PARK
DODGER STADIUM
ANGELINO HEIGHTS
FILIPINOTOWN
WESTLAKE
MACARTHUR PARK
CHINATOWN
LITTLE TOKYO
LOS ANGELES
CENTRAL CITY
NORTH UNIVERSITY PARK
SOLANO CANYON
ELYSIAN PARK
HOLLYWOOD FRWY
HARBOR FRWY
SANTA MONICA FRWY
SANTA ANA FRWY
POMONA FRWY
SAN BERNARDINO FRWY
PASADENA FRWY
LOS ANGELES RIVER
WILSHIRE
OLYMPIC BLVD
VENICE BLVD
PICO BLVD
WASHINGTON BLVD
JEFFERSON BLVD
TEMPLE ST
BEVERLY BLVD
SUNSET BLVD
ALAMEDA ST
CESAR E CHAVEZ AV
USC
0 .25 .5 .75 1.0 miles 1 in. = 2400 ft.
See Page C for Downtown Map

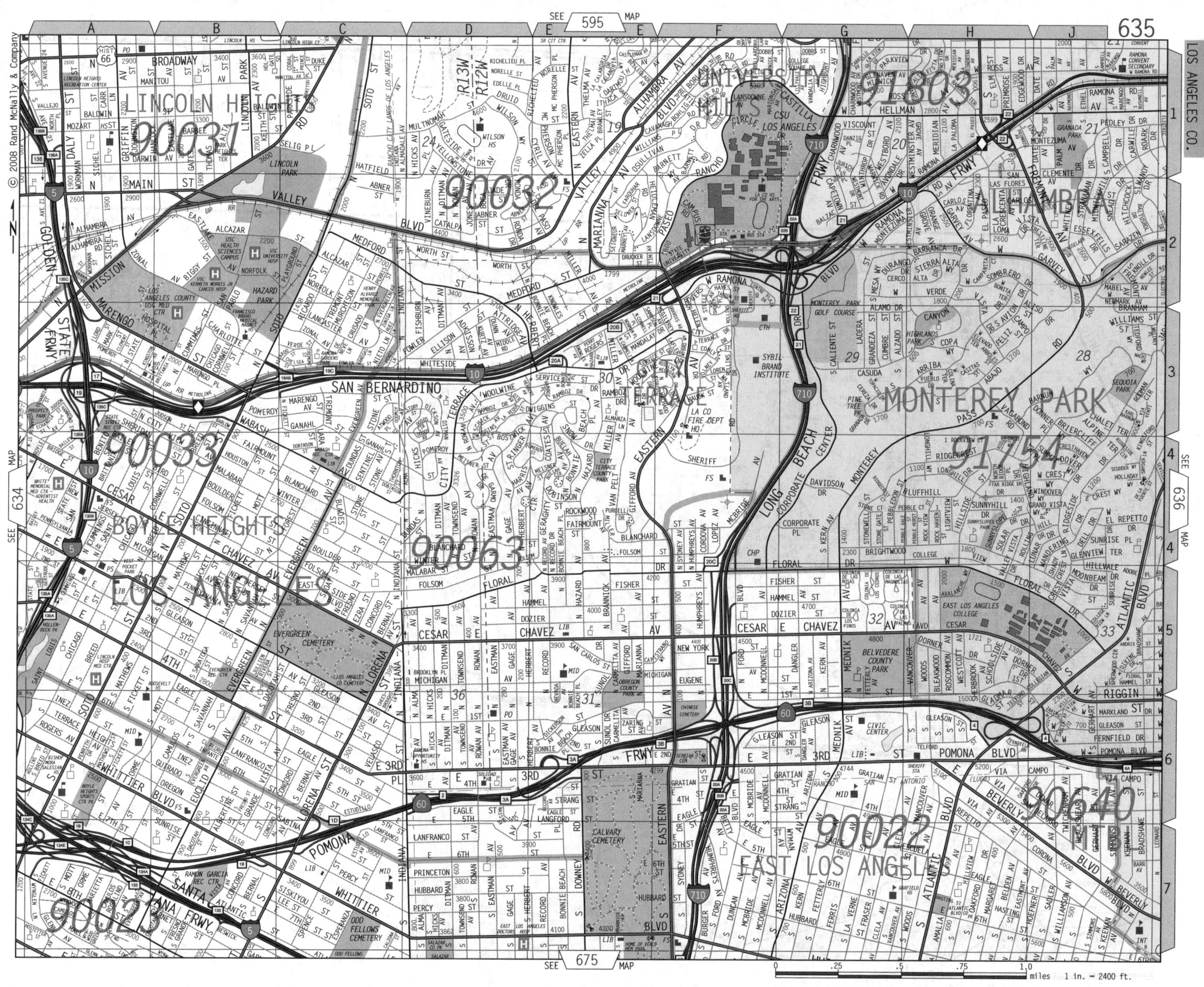
SEE 595 MAP
A
B
C
D
E
F
G
H
J
LOS ANGELES CO.
LINCOLN HEIGHTS
90031
LINCOLN PARK
90032
UNIVERSITY HILLS
CSU LOS ANGELES
91803
ALHAMBRA
GOLDEN STATE FRWY
SAN BERNARDINO FRWY
LOS ANGELES COUNTY USC MED CTR
90033
BOYLE HEIGHTS
LOS ANGELES
CITY TERRACE
SYBIL BRAND INSTITUTE
MONTEREY PARK
91754
LONG BEACH FRWY
90063
EVERGREEN CEMETERY
EAST LOS ANGELES COLLEGE
BELVEDERE COUNTY PARK
CALVARY CEMETERY
90022
EAST LOS ANGELES
90640
90023
SANTA ANA FRWY
POMONA FRWY
ODD FELLOWS CEMETERY
SEE 634 MAP
SEE 636 MAP
SEE 675 MAP
0 .25 .5 .75 1.0 miles 1 in. = 2400 ft.

SEE 596 MAP
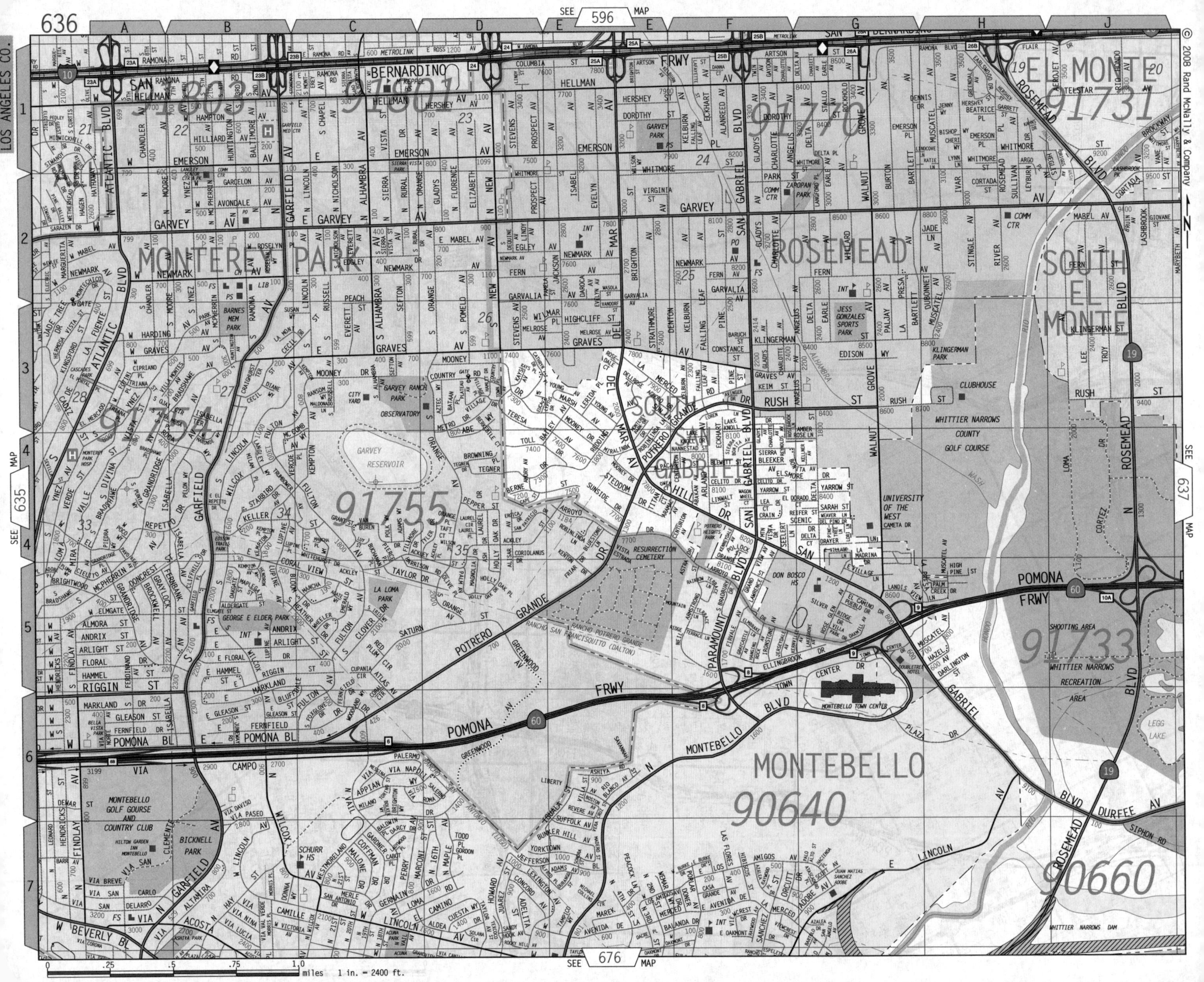

SEE 676 MAP

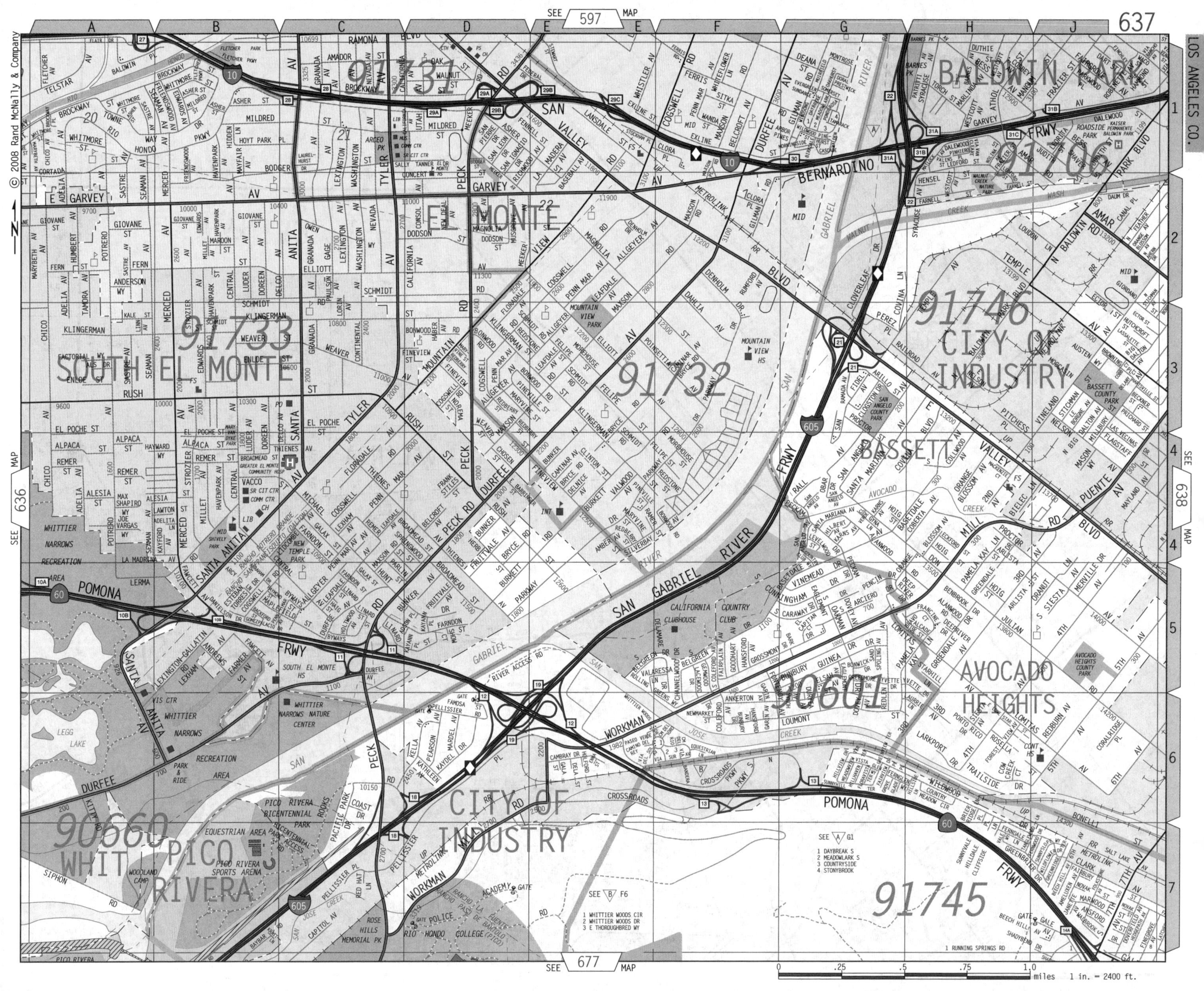
SEE 597 MAP
SEE 677 MAP
SEE 636 MAP
SEE 638 MAP
LOS ANGELES CO.
BALDWIN PARK
91706
91731
EL MONTE
91733
SOUTH EL MONTE
91732
91746
CITY OF INDUSTRY
BASSETT
AVOCADO HEIGHTS
90601
91745
90660
WHIT
PICO RIVERA
CITY OF INDUSTRY
SAN BERNARDINO FRWY
POMONA FRWY
SAN GABRIEL RIVER FRWY
SAN GABRIEL RIVER
WHITTIER NARROWS RECREATION AREA
LEGG LAKE
CALIFORNIA COUNTRY CLUB
MOUNTAIN VIEW PARK
SAN ANGELO COUNTY PARK
BASSETT COUNTY PARK
AVOCADO HEIGHTS COUNTY PARK
PICO RIVERA BICENTENNIAL PARK
PICO RIVERA SPORTS ARENA
ROSE HILLS MEMORIAL PK
RIO HONDO COLLEGE
SEE A G1
1 DAYBREAK S
2 MEADOWLARK S
3 COUNTRYSIDE
4 STONYBROOK
SEE B F6
1 WHITTIER WOODS CIR
2 WHITTIER WOODS DR
3 E THOROUGHBRED WY
1 RUNNING SPRINGS RD
0 .25 .5 .75 1.0 miles 1 in. = 2400 ft.

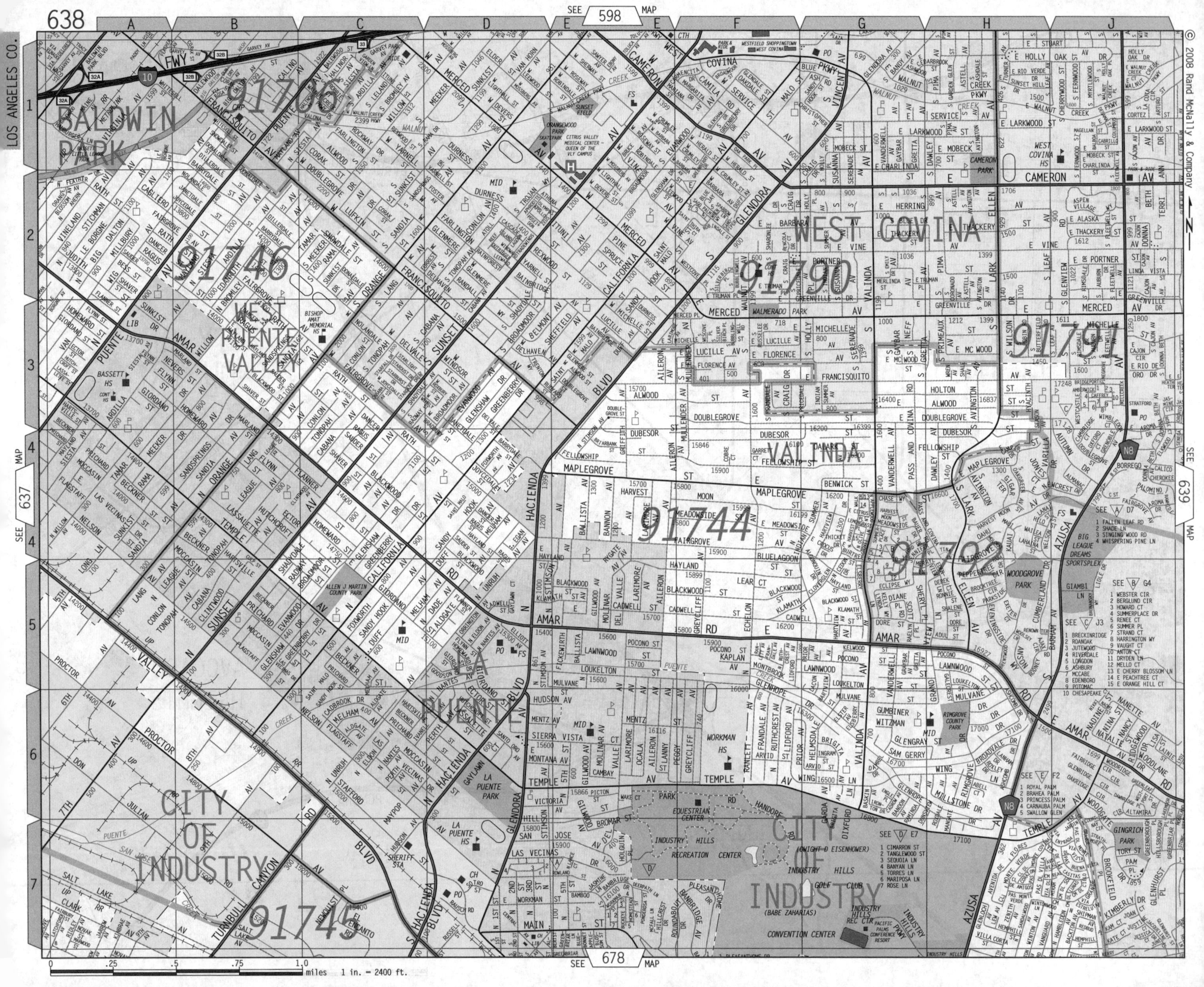
LOS ANGELES CO.
SEE 598 MAP
SEE 637 MAP
SEE 639 MAP
SEE 678 MAP
A
B
C
D
E
F
G
H
J
BALDWIN PARK
WEST PUENTE VALLEY
WEST COVINA
VALINDA
LA PUENTE
CITY OF INDUSTRY
91706
91746
91790
91791
91744
91792
91745
FWY
10
CAMERON AV
GLENDORA AV
FRANCISQUITO AV
SUNSET AV
ORANGE AV
PUENTE AV
AMAR RD
TEMPLE AV
VALLEY BLVD
HACIENDA BLVD
MERCED AV
MAPLEGROVE ST
AZUSA AV
TURNBULL CANYON RD
WESTFIELD SHOPPINGTOWN WEST COVINA
ORANGEWOOD PARK
CITRUS VALLEY MEDICAL CENTER - QUEEN OF THE VLY CAMPUS
BISHOP AMAT MEMORIAL HS
BASSETT HS
WEST COVINA HS
CAMERON PARK
WALMERADO PARK
ALLEN J MARTIN COUNTY PARK
WOODGROVE PARK
BIG LEAGUE DREAMS SPORTSPLEX
WORKMAN HS
LA PUENTE PARK
LA PUENTE HS
RIMGROVE COUNTY PARK
GINGRICH PARK
EQUESTRIAN CENTER
INDUSTRY HILLS RECREATION CENTER
(DWIGHT D EISENHOWER)
INDUSTRY HILLS GOLF CLUB
(BABE ZAHARIAS)
INDUSTRY HILLS REC CTR
PACIFIC PALMS CONFERENCE RESORT
CONVENTION CENTER
SHERIFF STA
SEE A D7
1 FALLEN LEAF RD
2 SHADE LN
3 SINGING WOOD RD
4 WHISPERING PINE LN
SEE B G4
1 WEBSTER CIR
2 BERGLUND CIR
3 HOWARD CT
4 SUMMERPLACE DR
5 RENEE CT
6 SUMMER PL
7 STRAND CT
8 HARRINGTON WY
9 VAUGHT CT
10 ANTON CT
11 DRYDEN LN
12 MELLO CT
13 E CHERRY BLOSSOM LN
14 E PEACHTREE CT
15 E ORANGE HILL CT
SEE C J3
1 BRECKINRIDGE
2 ROANOAK
3 JUTEWOOD
4 RIVERDALE
5 LONGDON
6 ASHBURY
7 MCCABE
8 EDENBORO
9 POTOMAC
10 CHESAPEAKE
SEE D E7
1 CIMARRON ST
2 TANGLEWOOD ST
3 SEQUOIA LN
4 BANYAN LN
5 TORRES LN
6 MARIPOSA LN
7 ROSE LN
SEE E F2
1 ROYAL PALM
2 BRAHEA PALM
3 PRINCESS PALM
4 CARNAUBA PALM
5 SWALLOW GLEN
0 .25 .5 .75 1.0 miles 1 in. = 2400 ft.

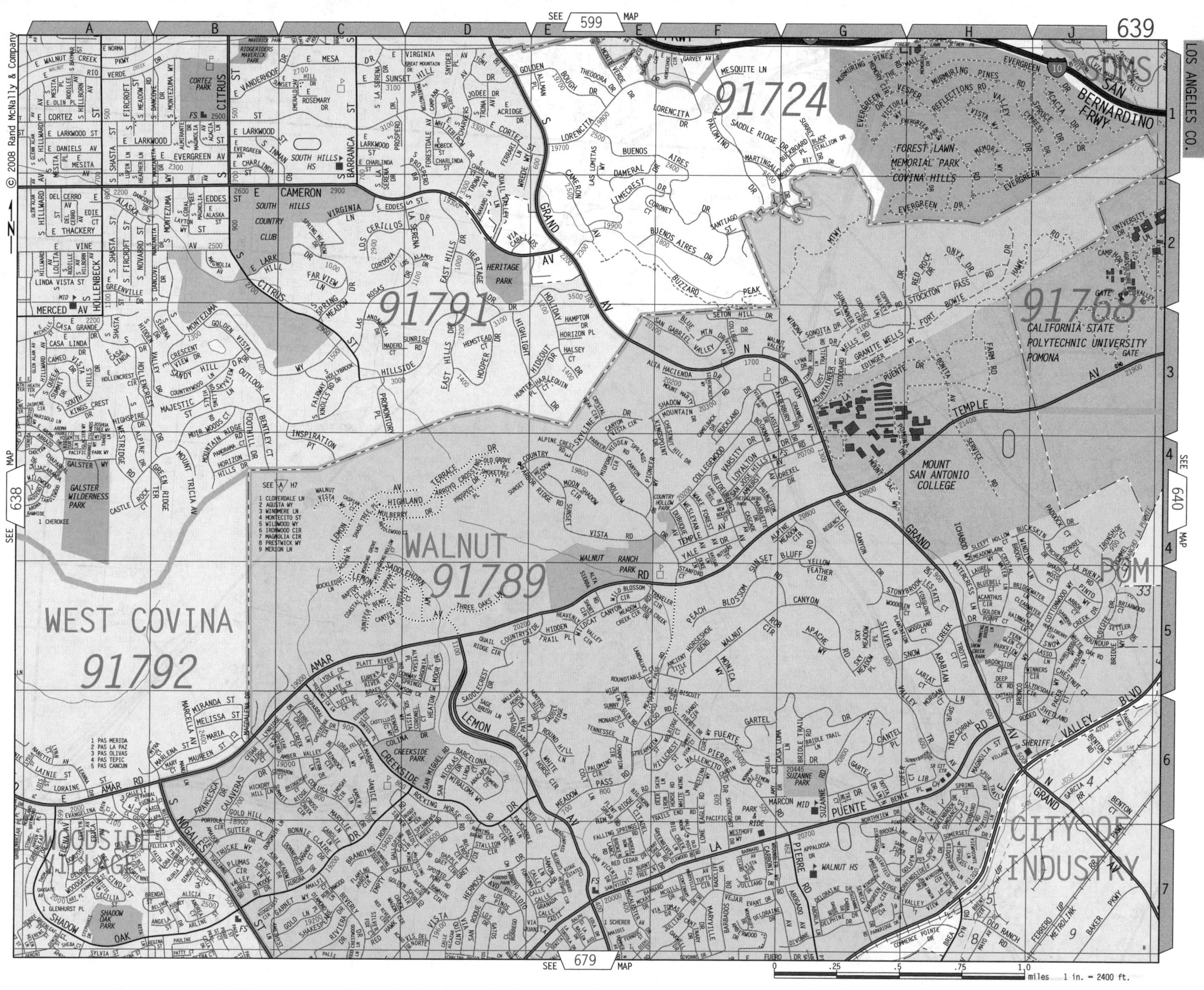
SEE 599 MAP
SEE 679 MAP
SEE 638 MAP
SEE 640 MAP
A
B
C
D
E
F
G
H
J
1
2
3
4
5
6
7
LOS ANGELES CO.
91724
91791
91768
WALNUT
91789
WEST COVINA
91792
CITY OF INDUSTRY
WOODSIDE VILLAGE
POM
SDMS
SAN BERNARDINO FRWY
FOREST LAWN MEMORIAL PARK COVINA HILLS
CALIFORNIA STATE POLYTECHNIC UNIVERSITY POMONA
MOUNT SAN ANTONIO COLLEGE
SOUTH HILLS COUNTRY CLUB
HERITAGE PARK
CORTEZ PARK
SOUTH HILLS HS
GALSTER WILDERNESS PARK
WALNUT RANCH PARK
CREEKSIDE PARK
SUZANNE PARK
SHADOW OAK PARK
WALNUT HS
RIDGERIDERS MAVERICK PARK
GRAND AV
TEMPLE AV
AMAR RD
VALLEY BLVD
LA PUENTE RD
NOGALES ST
CITRUS ST
AZUSA AV
CAMERON AV
LEMON AV
SEE H7
1 CLOVERDALE LN
2 AGUSTA WY
3 WINGMERE LN
4 MONTECITO ST
5 WILLOWOOD WY
6 IRONWOOD CIR
7 MAGNOLIA CIR
8 PRESTWICK WY
9 MERION LN
1 PAS MERIDA
2 PAS LA PAZ
3 PAS OLIVAS
4 PAS TEPIC
5 PAS CANCUN
1 CHEROKEE
1 GLENHURST PL
1 SCHERER
0 .25 .5 .75 1.0 miles 1 in. = 2400 ft.

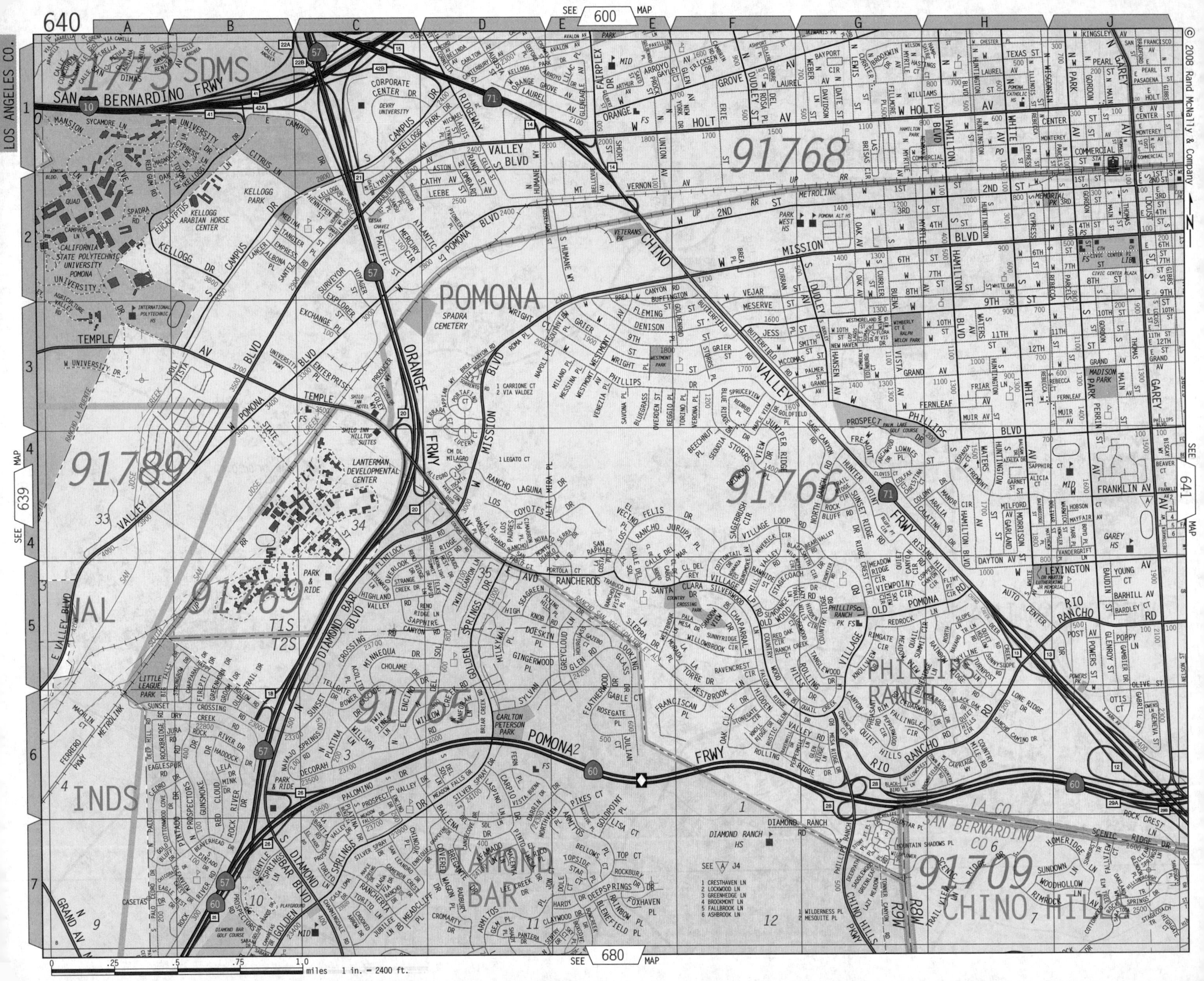

SEE 600 MAP
LOS ANGELES CO.
91773
SDMS
SAN BERNARDINO FRWY
91768
CALIFORNIA STATE POLYTECHNIC UNIVERSITY POMONA
KELLOGG PARK
KELLOGG ARABIAN HORSE CENTER
POMONA
SPADRA CEMETERY
ORANGE FRWY
CHINO VALLEY FRWY
91789
LANTERMAN DEVELOPMENTAL CENTER
SEE 639 MAP
SEE 641 MAP
91769
91766
91765
PHILLIPS RANCH
POMONA FRWY
DIAMOND BAR
91709
CHINO HILLS
INDS
DIAMOND RANCH HS
GAREY HS
CARLTON PETERSON PARK
PROSPECT PARK
MADISON PARK
LA CO
SAN BERNARDINO CO
SEE 680 MAP
miles 1 in. = 2400 ft.
© 2008 Rand McNally & Company

SEE 601 MAP

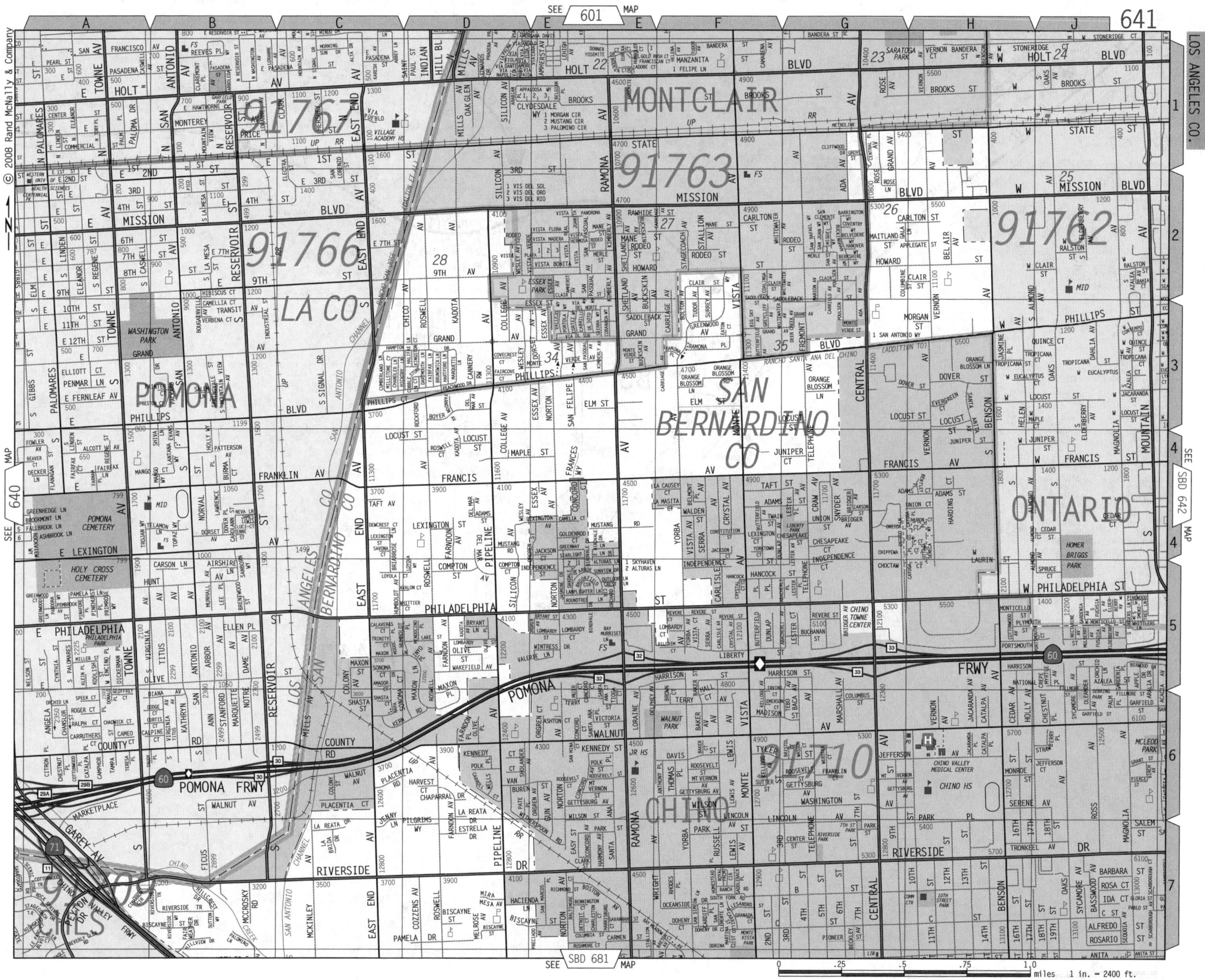

SEE SBD 681 MAP

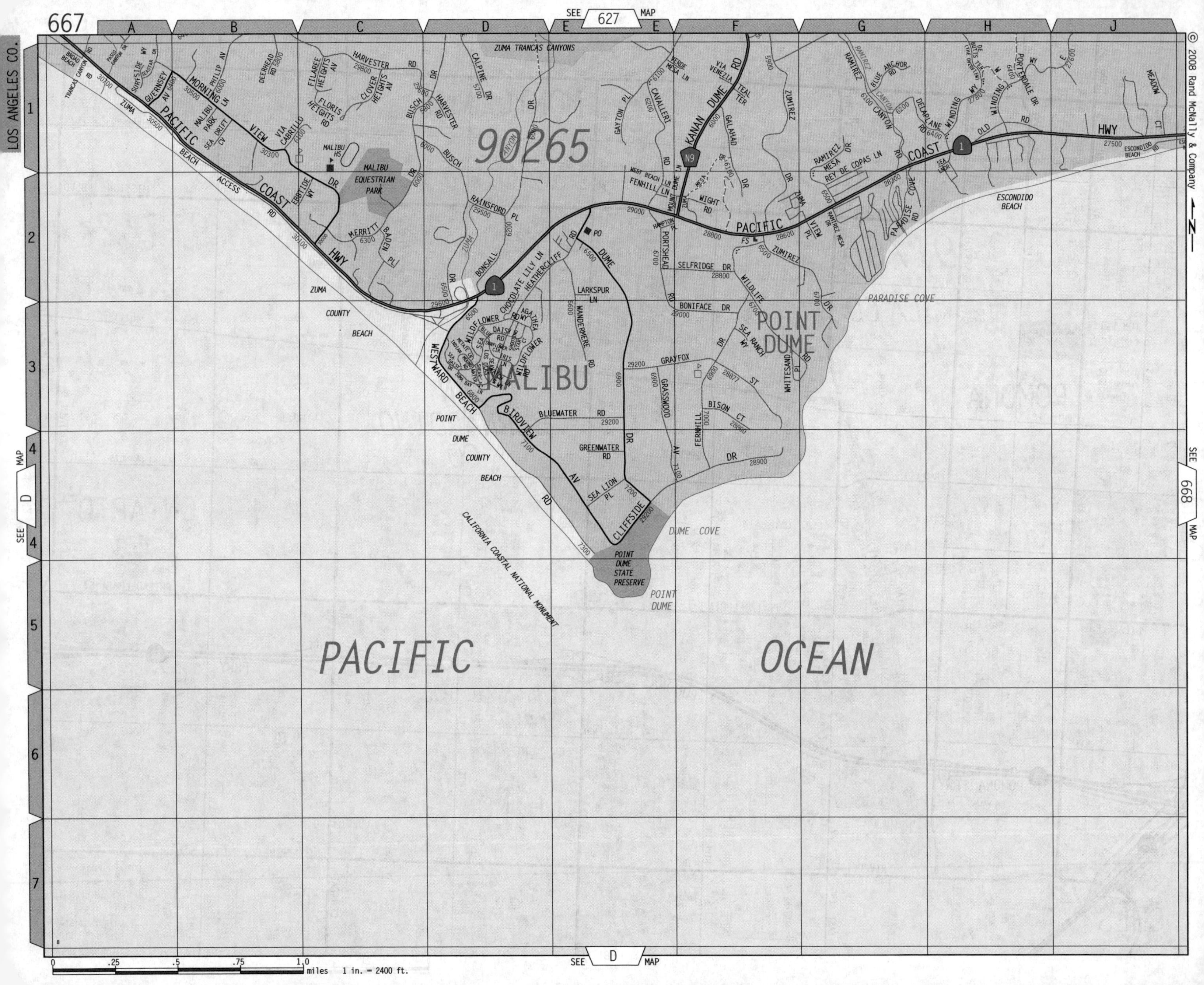
LOS ANGELES CO.
SEE 627 MAP
SEE 668 MAP
SEE D MAP
90265
MALIBU
POINT DUME
PACIFIC OCEAN
ZUMA TRANCAS CANYONS
MALIBU EQUESTRIAN PARK
MALIBU HS
ZUMA COUNTY BEACH
POINT DUME COUNTY BEACH
POINT DUME STATE PRESERVE
DUME COVE
PARADISE COVE
ESCONDIDO BEACH
CALIFORNIA COASTAL NATIONAL MONUMENT
PACIFIC COAST HWY
KANAN DUME RD
DUME DR
CLIFFSIDE DR
BIRDVIEW AV
WESTWARD BEACH RD
ZUMIREZ DR
0 .25 .5 .75 1.0 miles 1 in. = 2400 ft.

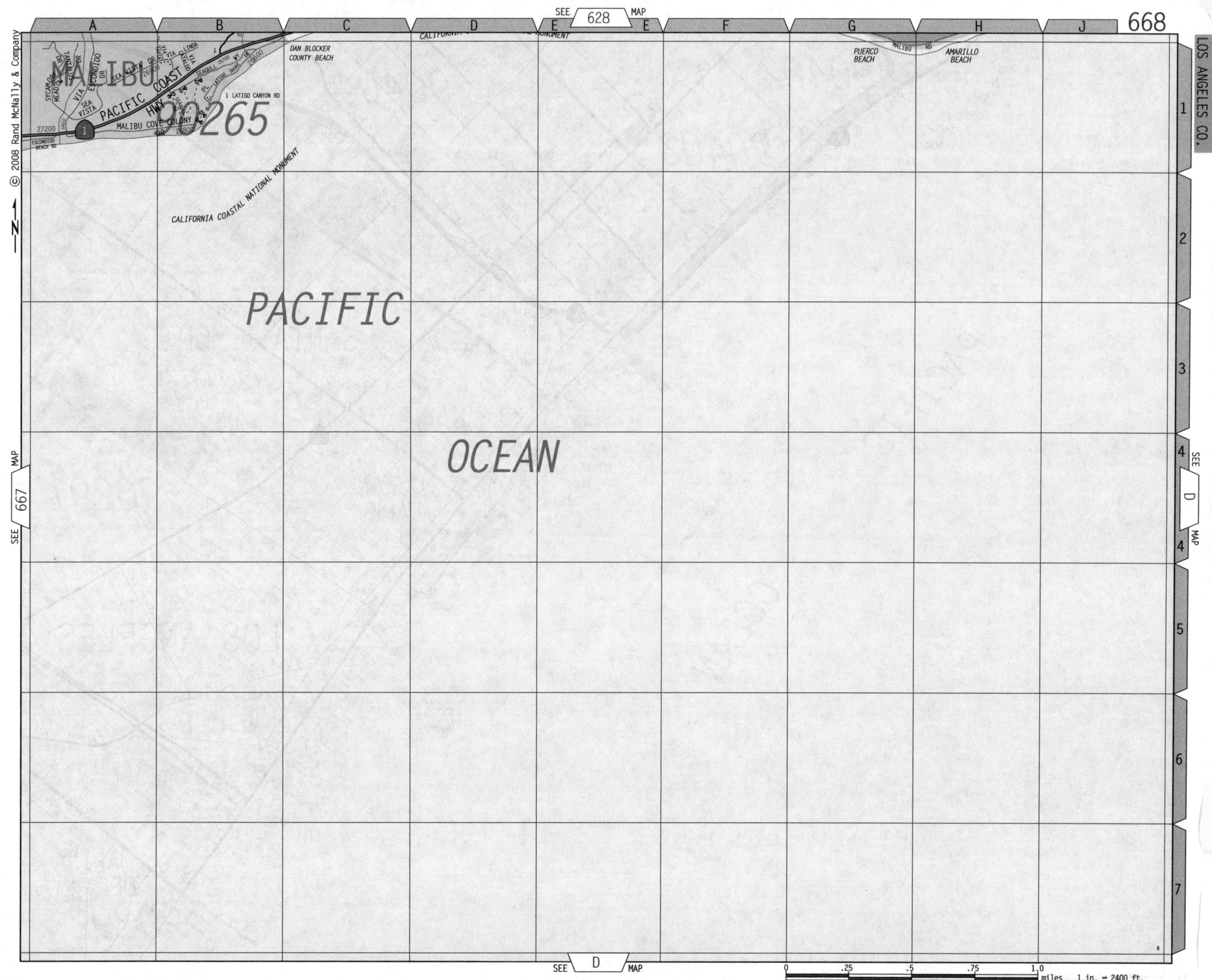
SEE 628 MAP
A
B
C
D
E
F
G
H
J
LOS ANGELES CO.
MALIBU
90265
PACIFIC COAST HWY
DAN BLOCKER
COUNTY BEACH
1 LATIGO CANYON RD
MALIBU COVE COLONY DR
ESCONDIDO BEACH RD
SEA VISTA DR
VIA ESCONDIDO DR
SEAGULL
LATIGO SHORE DR
27200
26800
26600
PUERCO BEACH
MALIBU RD
AMARILLO BEACH
CALIFORNIA COASTAL NATIONAL MONUMENT
PACIFIC
OCEAN
SEE 667 MAP
SEE D MAP
SEE D MAP
1
2
3
4
5
6
7
0 .25 .5 .75 1.0 miles 1 in. = 2400 ft.

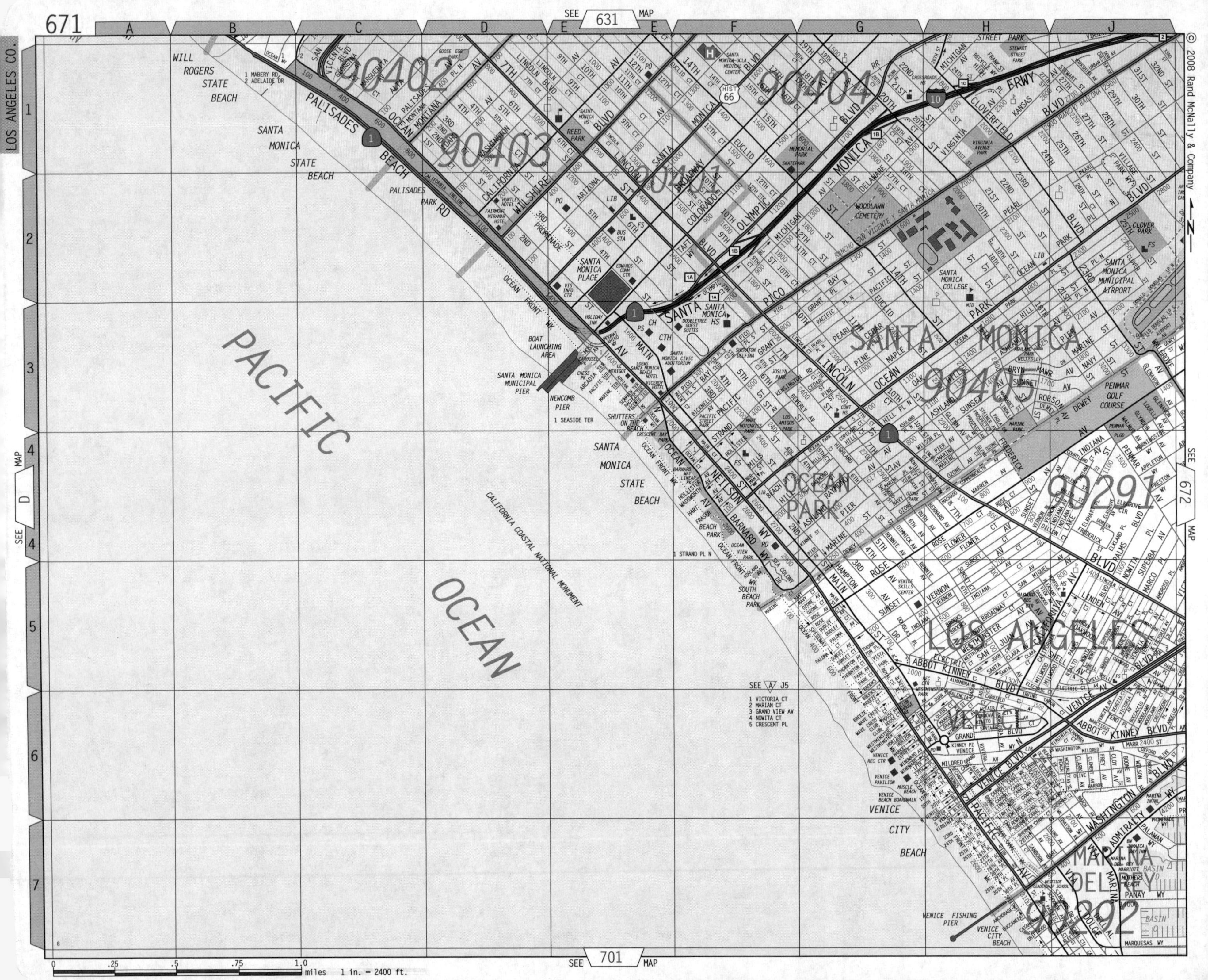
LOS ANGELES CO.
SEE 631 MAP
SEE 672 MAP
SEE 701 MAP
SEE D 4 MAP
A
B
C
D
E
F
G
H
J
1
2
3
4
5
6
7
WILL ROGERS STATE BEACH
SANTA MONICA STATE BEACH
PALISADES PARK
PACIFIC
OCEAN
CALIFORNIA COASTAL NATIONAL MONUMENT
SANTA MONICA MUNICIPAL PIER
NEWCOMB PIER
BOAT LAUNCHING AREA
SANTA MONICA
OCEAN PARK
LOS ANGELES
VENICE
MARINA DEL REY
VENICE CITY BEACH
VENICE FISHING PIER
SOUTH BEACH PARK
CROSSROADS HS
SANTA MONICA COLLEGE
SANTA MONICA MUNICIPAL AIRPORT
PENMAR GOLF COURSE
CLOVER PARK
WOODLAWN CEMETERY
VIRGINIA AVENUE PARK
MEMORIAL PARK
REED PARK
SANTA MONICA PLACE
SANTA MONICA-UCLA MEDICAL CENTER
SANTA MONICA HS
SANTA MONICA CIVIC AUDITORIUM
90402
90403
90401
90404
90405
90291
90292
SEE J5
1 VICTORIA CT
2 MARIAN CT
3 GRAND VIEW AV
4 NOWITA CT
5 CRESCENT PL
1 MABERY RD
2 ADELAIDE DR
1 SEASIDE TER
1 STRAND PL N
© 2008 Rand McNally & Company
0 .25 .5 .75 1.0 miles 1 in. = 2400 ft.

SEE 632 MAP

A B C D E F G H J

LOS ANGELES CO.

SEE 671 MAP

SEE 673 MAP

1 2 3 4 5 6 7

SANTA MONICA 90405

90064

WESTDALE

PALMS

90034

90232

90016

LA

MAR VISTA

90066

LOS ANGELES

CULVER CITY

BALDWIN HILLS

WEST LOS ANGELES COLLEGE

90291

90230

90292

DEL REY

MARINA DEL REY

90094

90045

FOX HILLS

LADERA HEIGHTS

90056

SEE H3
1 SALEM VILLAGE DR
2 SALEM VILLAGE PL
3 SALEM VILLAGE CT
4 TIMBER LAKE TER
5 WILDERNESS LN
6 HUCKFINN LN
7 COPPERFIELD LN
8 GASLIGHT LN
9 SHOWBOAT LN
10 RAINBOWS END
11 SHOWBOAT PL

1 AGUSTIN LN
2 LANTANA LN
3 HERITAGE PL

1 CORPORATE POINTE

1 PROMENADE PZ
2 ENTERTAINMENT WY

SEE 702 MAP

0 .25 .5 .75 1.0 miles 1 in. = 2400 ft.

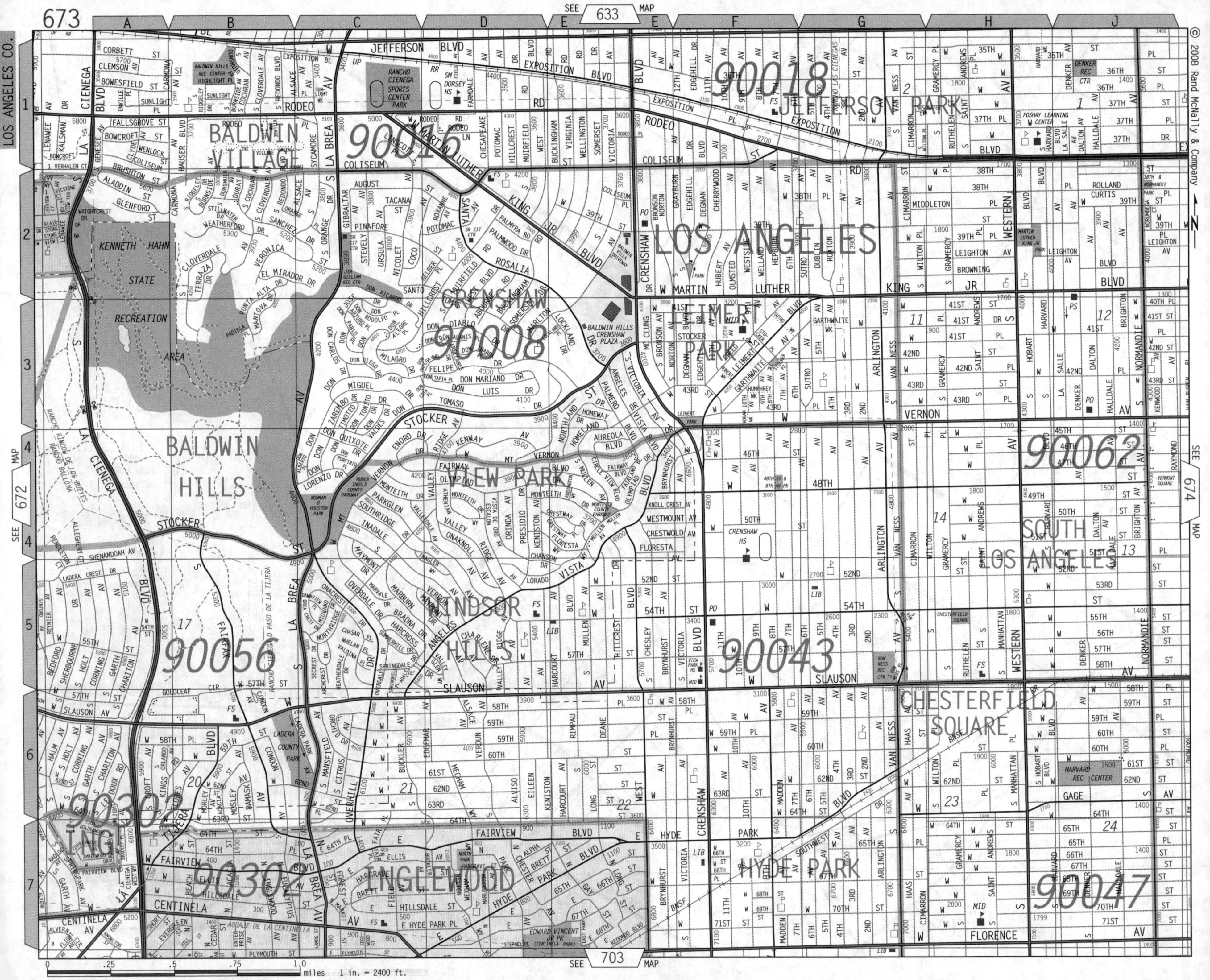

673
LOS ANGELES CO.
SEE 633 MAP
SEE 703 MAP
SEE 672 MAP
SEE 674 MAP
© 2008 Rand McNally & Company
BALDWIN VILLAGE
KENNETH HAHN STATE RECREATION AREA
BALDWIN HILLS
CRENSHAW
LEIMERT PARK
LOS ANGELES
JEFFERSON PARK
VIEW PARK
WINDSOR HILLS
SOUTH LOS ANGELES
CHESTERFIELD SQUARE
HYDE PARK
INGLEWOOD
90018
90016
90008
90062
90056
90043
90302
90047
JEFFERSON BLVD
EXPOSITION BLVD
RODEO RD
COLISEUM ST
MARTIN LUTHER KING JR BLVD
VERNON AV
SLAUSON AV
FLORENCE AV
CENTINELA AV
LA CIENEGA BLVD
LA BREA AV
CRENSHAW BLVD
WESTERN AV
NORMANDIE AV
BALDWIN HILLS CRENSHAW PLAZA
CRENSHAW HS
LADERA COUNTY PARK
EDWARD VINCENT JR PK (CENTINELA PARK)
HARVARD REC CENTER
RANCHO CIENEGA SPORTS CENTER PARK
0 .25 .5 .75 1.0 miles 1 in. = 2400 ft.

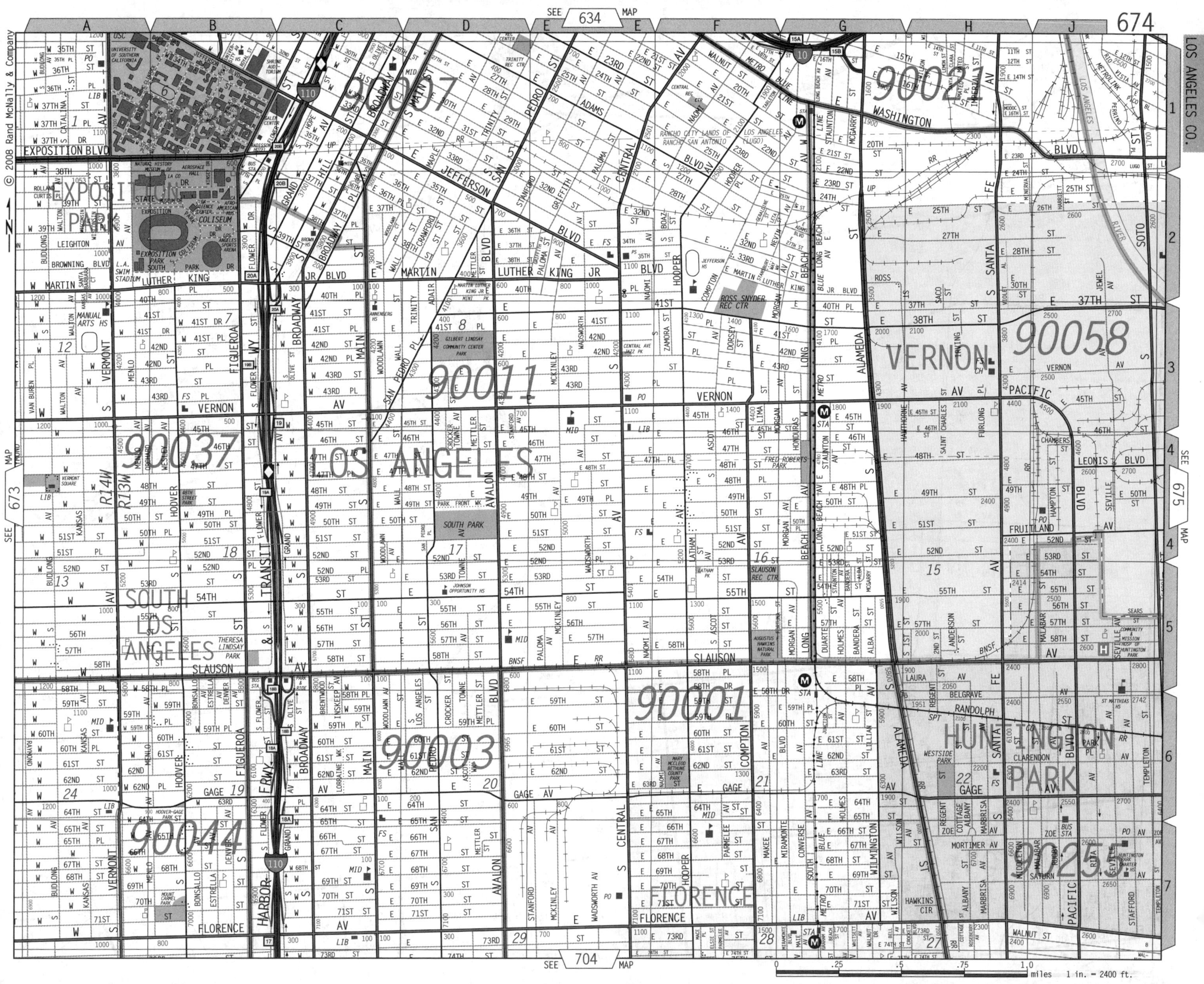

674
LOS ANGELES CO.
SEE 634 MAP
SEE 704 MAP
SEE 673 MAP
SEE 675 MAP
© 2008 Rand McNally & Company
UNIVERSITY OF SOUTHERN CALIFORNIA
EXPOSITION PARK
EXPOSITION BLVD
MARTIN LUTHER KING JR BLVD
JEFFERSON BLVD
WASHINGTON BLVD
VERNON AV
SLAUSON AV
GAGE AV
FLORENCE AV
HARBOR TRANSIT WY
HARBOR FRWY
VERMONT AV
FIGUEROA ST
BROADWAY
MAIN ST
SAN PEDRO ST
AVALON BLVD
CENTRAL AV
HOOPER AV
COMPTON AV
ALAMEDA ST
SANTA FE AV
PACIFIC BLVD
SOTO ST
90007
90021
90011
90037
90058
90001
90003
90044
90255
LOS ANGELES
SOUTH LOS ANGELES
VERNON
HUNTINGTON PARK
FLORENCE
LOS ANGELES RIVER
ROSS SNYDER REC CTR
SOUTH PARK
SLAUSON REC CTR
GILBERT LINDSAY COMMUNITY CENTER PARK
MANUAL ARTS HS
JEFFERSON HS
0 .25 .5 .75 1.0 miles 1 in. = 2400 ft.

SEE 635 MAP

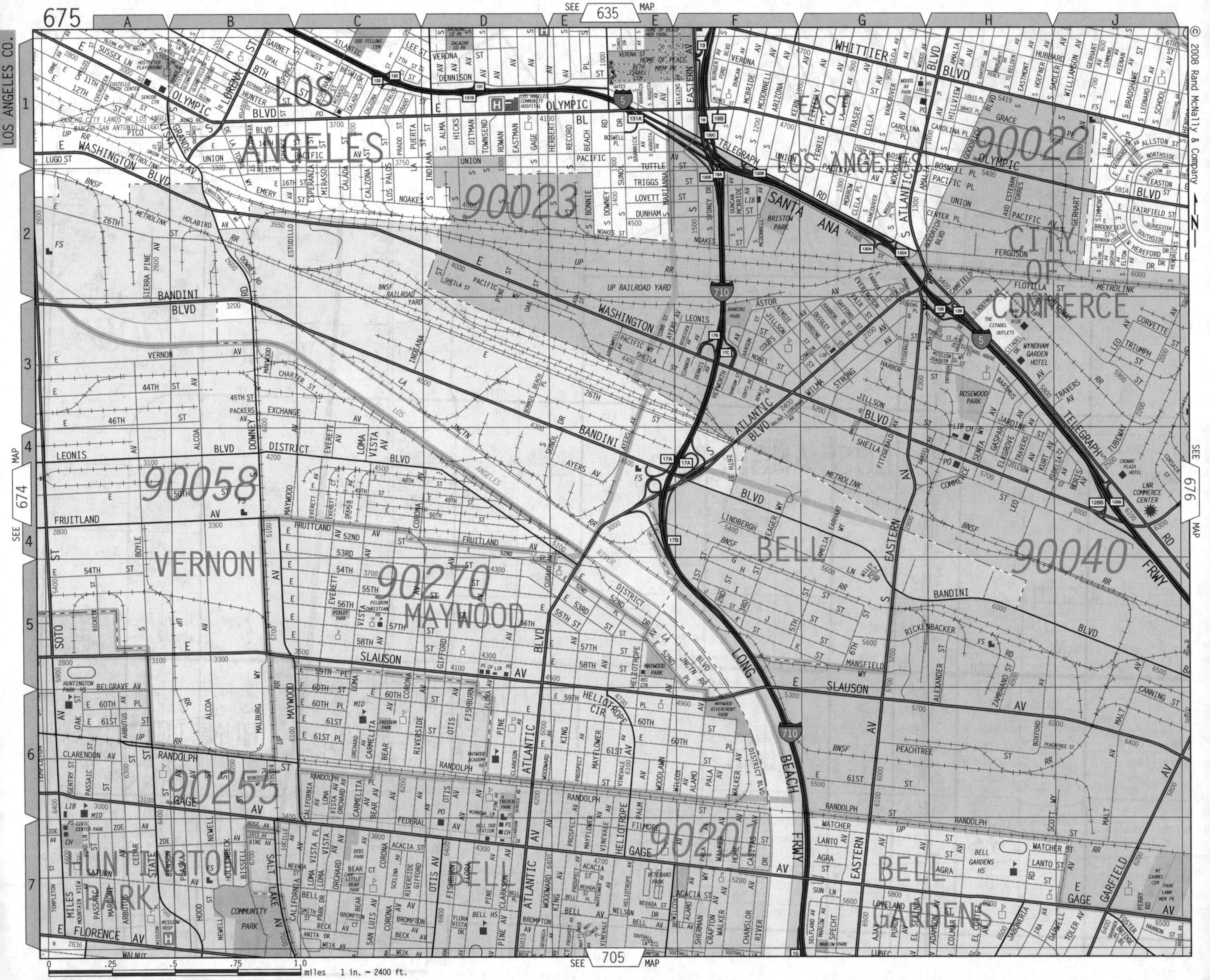

SEE 674 MAP
SEE 676 MAP
SEE 705 MAP

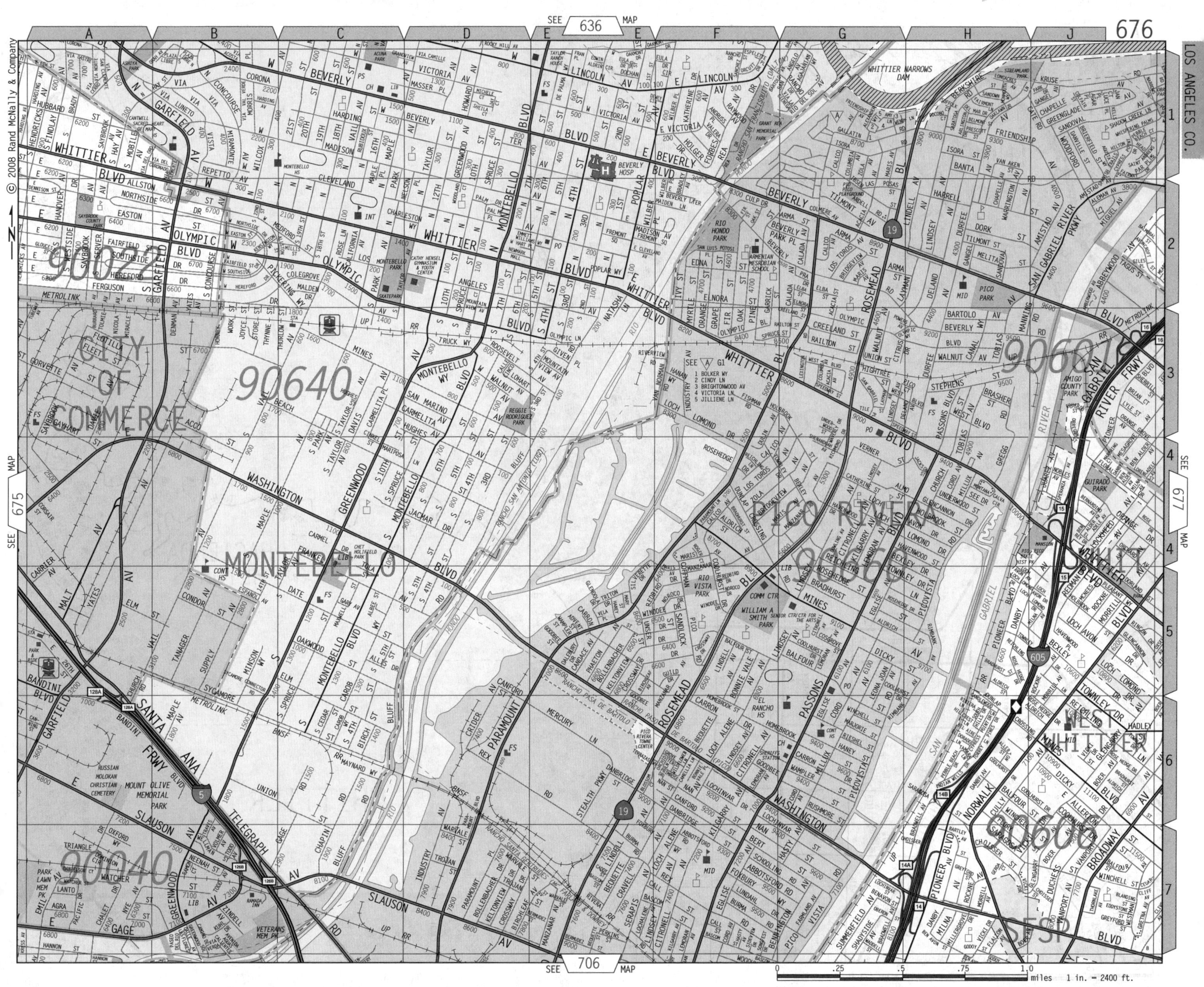
676
SEE 636 MAP
SEE 706 MAP
SEE 675 MAP
SEE 677 MAP
LOS ANGELES CO.
© 2008 Rand McNally & Company
A
B
C
D
E
F
G
H
J
1
2
3
4
5
6
7
90022
90640
90660
90601
90606
90040
CITY OF COMMERCE
MONTEBELLO
PICO RIVERA
WEST WHITTIER
SFSP
WHITTIER NARROWS DAM
WHITTIER BLVD
BEVERLY BLVD
OLYMPIC BLVD
WASHINGTON BLVD
SLAUSON AV
SANTA ANA FRWY
TELEGRAPH RD
GARFIELD AV
MONTEBELLO BLVD
GREENWOOD AV
PARAMOUNT BLVD
ROSEMEAD BLVD
PASSONS BLVD
SAN GABRIEL RIVER PKWY
SAN GABRIEL RIVER FRWY
NORWALK BLVD
PIONEER BLVD
LINCOLN AV
MONTEBELLO HS
BEVERLY HOSP
RIO HONDO PARK
RIO VISTA PARK
WILLIAM A SMITH PARK
REGGIE RODRIGUEZ PARK
PICO PARK
AMIGO COUNTY PARK
GUIRADO PARK
SAYBROOK COUNTY PARK
MONTEBELLO PARK
ACUNA PARK
EL RANCHO HS
RUSSIAN MOLOKAN CHRISTIAN CEMETERY
MOUNT OLIVE MEMORIAL PARK
VETERANS MEM PK
PICO RIVERA TOWNE CENTER
METROLINK
RIO HONDO
SAN GABRIEL RIVER
SEE G1
1 BOLKER WY
2 CINDY LN
3 BRIGHTONWOOD AV
4 VICTORIA LN
5 JILLIENE LN
0 .25 .5 .75 1.0 miles 1 in. = 2400 ft.

SEE 637 MAP
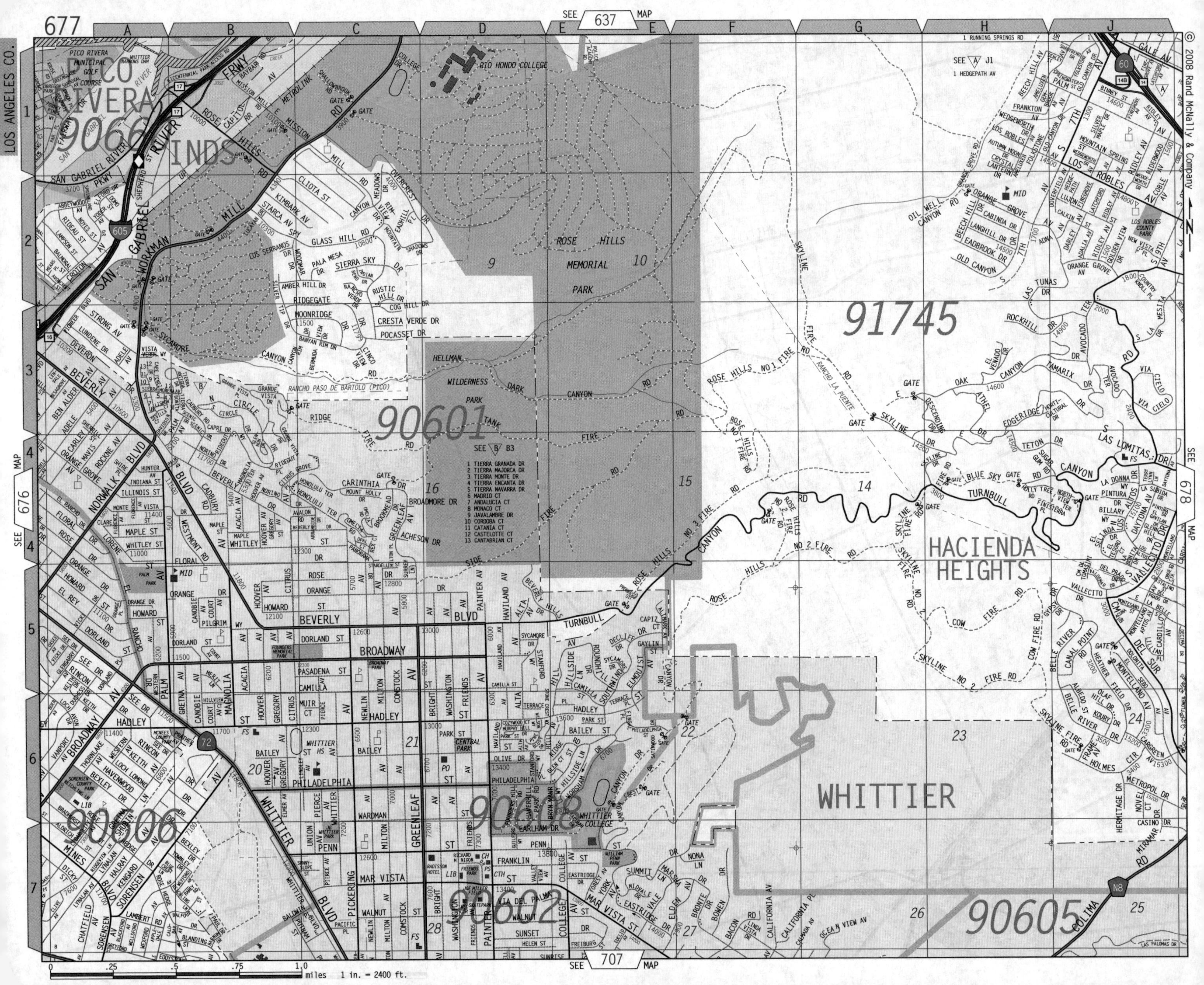

SEE 707 MAP

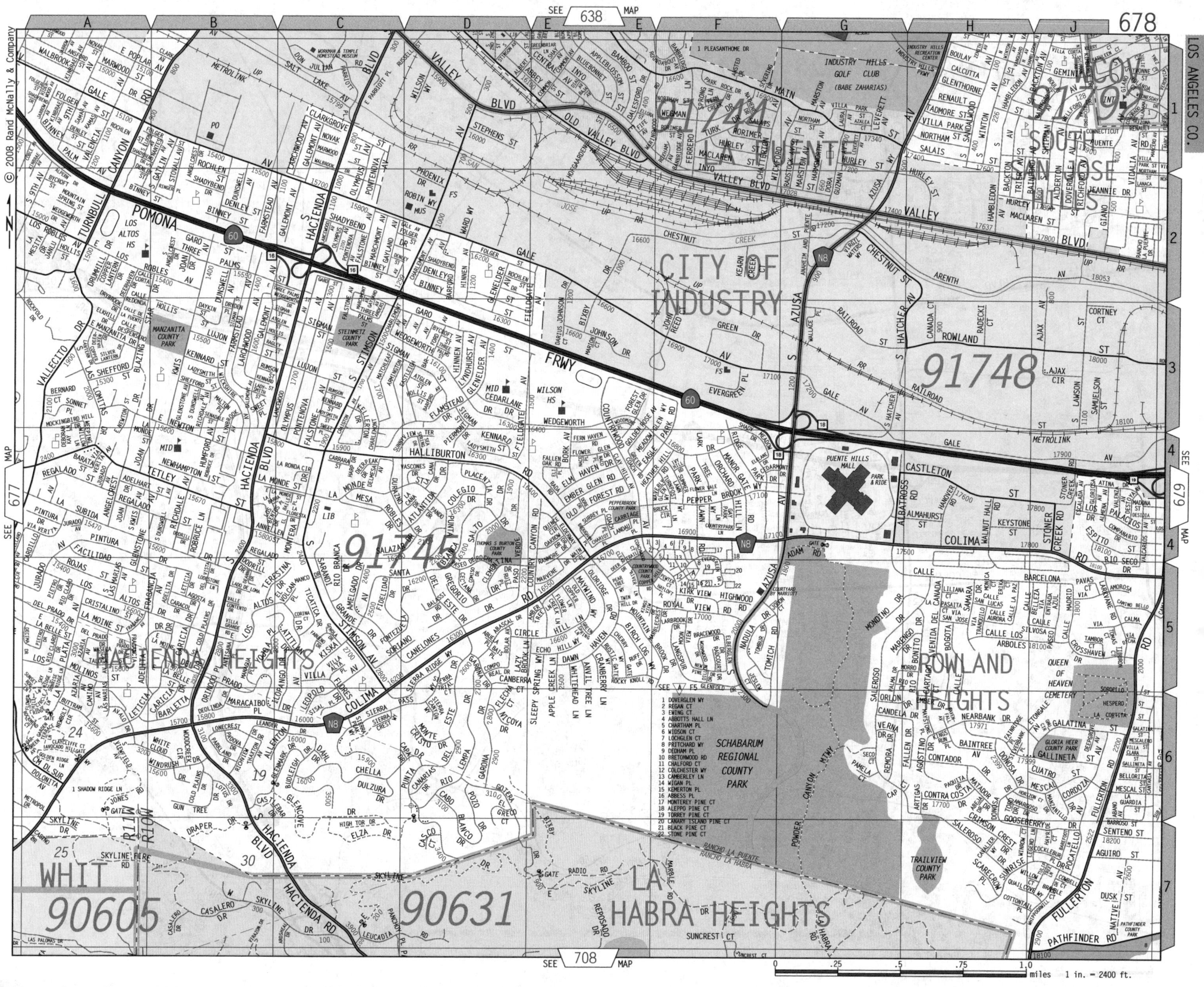
SEE 638 MAP
SEE 708 MAP
SEE 677 MAP
SEE 679 MAP
A
B
C
D
E
F
G
H
J
1
2
3
4
5
6
7
CITY OF INDUSTRY
91744
LA PUENTE
91792
SOUTH SAN JOSE HILLS
WCOV
91748
91745
HACIENDA HEIGHTS
ROWLAND HEIGHTS
LA HABRA HEIGHTS
90631
WHIT
90605
POMONA FRWY
VALLEY BLVD
HACIENDA BLVD
AZUSA AV
COLIMA RD
FULLERTON RD
GALE AV
METROLINK
INDUSTRY HILLS GOLF CLUB (BABE ZAHARIAS)
INDUSTRY HILLS RECREATION CENTER
WORKMAN & TEMPLE HOMESTEAD MUSEUM
LOS ALTOS HS
MANZANITA COUNTY PARK
STEINMETZ COUNTY PARK
WILSON HS
PUENTE HILLS MALL
PARK & RIDE
THOMAS S BURTON COUNTY PARK
COUNTRYWOOD COUNTY PARK
SCHABARUM REGIONAL COUNTY PARK
TRAILVIEW COUNTY PARK
QUEEN OF HEAVEN CEMETERY
GLORIA HEER COUNTY PARK
PEPPERBROOK COUNTY PARK
1 DOVERGLEN WY
2 REGAN CT
3 EWING CT
4 ABBOTTS HALL LN
5 CHARTHAM PL
6 WIDSON CT
7 LOCHGLEN CT
8 PRITCHARD WY
9 DEDHAM PL
10 BRETONWOOD RD
11 CHALFORD CT
12 COLCHESTER WY
13 CAMBERLEY LN
14 WIGAN PL
15 KEMERTON PL
16 ABBESS PL
17 MONTEREY PINE CT
18 ALEPPO PINE CT
19 TORREY PINE CT
20 CANARY ISLAND PINE CT
21 BLACK PINE CT
22 STONE PINE CT
RANCHO LA PUENTE
RANCHO LA HABRA
R11W
R10W
0 .25 .5 .75 1.0 miles 1 in. = 2400 ft.

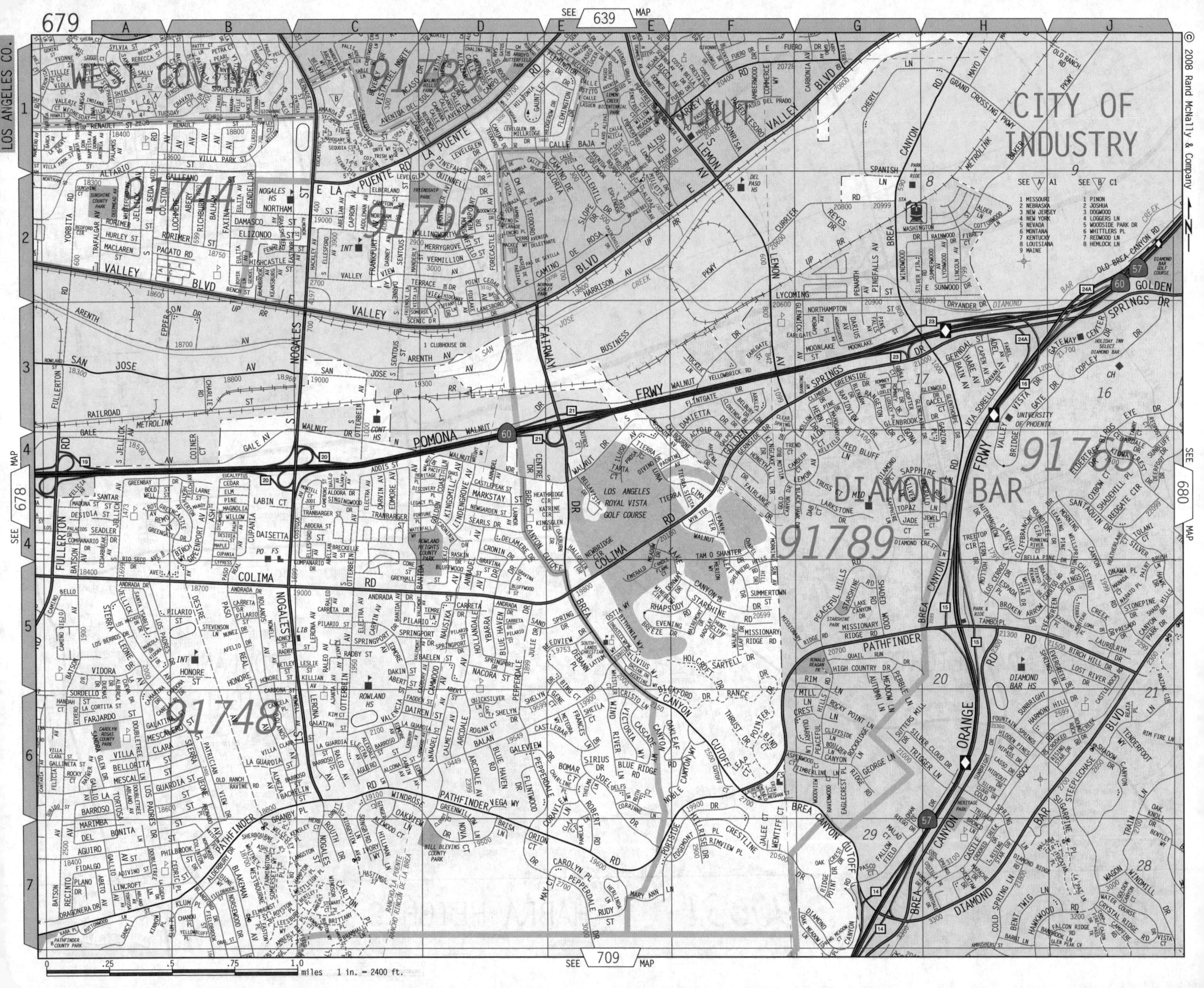

LOS ANGELES CO.
SEE 639 MAP
SEE 678 MAP
SEE 680 MAP
SEE 709 MAP
A
B
C
D
E
F
G
H
J
1
2
3
4
5
6
7
WEST COVINA
91789
91744
91792
WALNUT
CITY OF INDUSTRY
DIAMOND BAR
91765
91789
91748
LOS ANGELES ROYAL VISTA GOLF COURSE
SUNSHINE COUNTY PARK
ROWLAND HEIGHTS COUNTY PARK
CAROLYN ROSAS COUNTY PARK
BILL BLEVINS COUNTY PARK
PATHFINDER COUNTY PARK
RONALD REAGAN PK
FRIENDSHIP PARK
NOGALES HS
DEL PASO HS
CONT HS
ROWLAND HS
DIAMOND BAR HS
UNIVERSITY OF PHOENIX
HOLIDAY INN SELECT DIAMOND BAR
DIAMOND BAR GOLF COURSE
VALLEY BLVD
POMONA FRWY
COLIMA RD
PATHFINDER RD
NOGALES ST
FULLERTON RD
FAIRWAY DR
BREA CANYON RD
ORANGE FRWY
GOLDEN SPRINGS DR
DIAMOND BAR BLVD
GRAND CROSSING PKWY
LA PUENTE RD
AZUSA AV
LEMON AV
SEE A A1
1 MISSOURI
2 NEBRASKA
3 NEW JERSEY
4 NEW YORK
5 NEVADA
6 MONTANA
7 KENTUCKY
8 LOUISIANA
9 MAINE
SEE B C1
1 PINON
2 JOSHUA
3 DOGWOOD
4 LOGGERS LN
5 WOODSIDE PARK DR
6 WHITTLERS PL
7 REDWOOD LN
8 HEMLOCK LN
0 .25 .5 .75 1.0 miles 1 in. = 2400 ft.

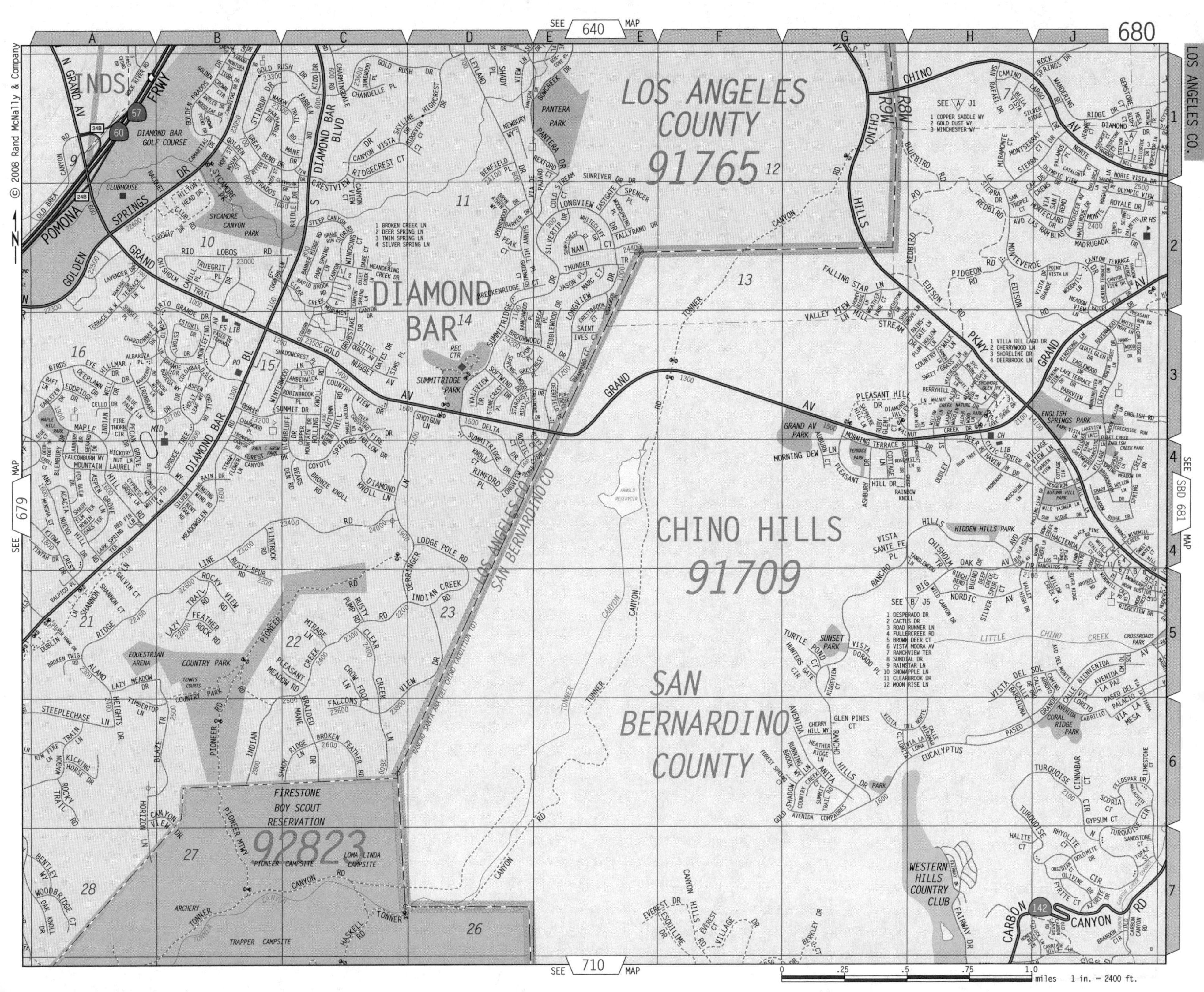
SEE 640 MAP
LOS ANGELES CO.
LOS ANGELES COUNTY
91765
DIAMOND BAR
CHINO HILLS
91709
SAN BERNARDINO COUNTY
92823
FIRESTONE BOY SCOUT RESERVATION
DIAMOND BAR GOLF COURSE
SYCAMORE CANYON PARK
PANTERA PARK
SUMMITRIDGE PARK
GRAND AV PARK
ENGLISH SPRINGS PARK
HIDDEN HILLS PARK
SUNSET PARK
CORAL RIDGE PARK
COUNTRY PARK
EQUESTRIAN ARENA
WESTERN HILLS COUNTRY CLUB
ARNOLD RESERVOIR
PIONEER CAMPSITE
LOMA LINDA CAMPSITE
TRAPPER CAMPSITE
GRAND AV
DIAMOND BAR BLVD
CHINO HILLS PKWY
CARBON CANYON RD
POMONA FRWY
SEE 679 MAP
SEE SBD 681 MAP
SEE 710 MAP
1 in. = 2400 ft.

LOS ANGELES CO.
SEE 671 MAP
SEE 702 MAP
SEE D MAP
A
B
C
D
E
F
G
H
J
1
2
3
4
5
6
7
PACIFIC
OCEAN
LOS
ANGELES
VENICE
CITY
BEACH
90292
MARINA
DEL
REY
CALIFORNIA COASTAL NATIONAL MONUMENT
BREAKWATER
BALLONA CREEK
DOCKWEILER
STATE
BEACH
1 PACIFIC CT
2 W ESPLANADE
MARQUESAS WY
VIA MARINA
TAHITI WY
SPINNAKER
TOPSAIL
UNION JACK
VOYAGE
WESTWIND
YAWL
QUARTERDECK
PRIVATEER
OUTRIGGER
NORTHSTAR
MAST
REEF
HURRICANE
INDEPENDENCE
GALLEON
FLEET
BASIN B
0
.25
.5
.75
1.0
miles 1 in. = 2400 ft.

SEE 672 MAP

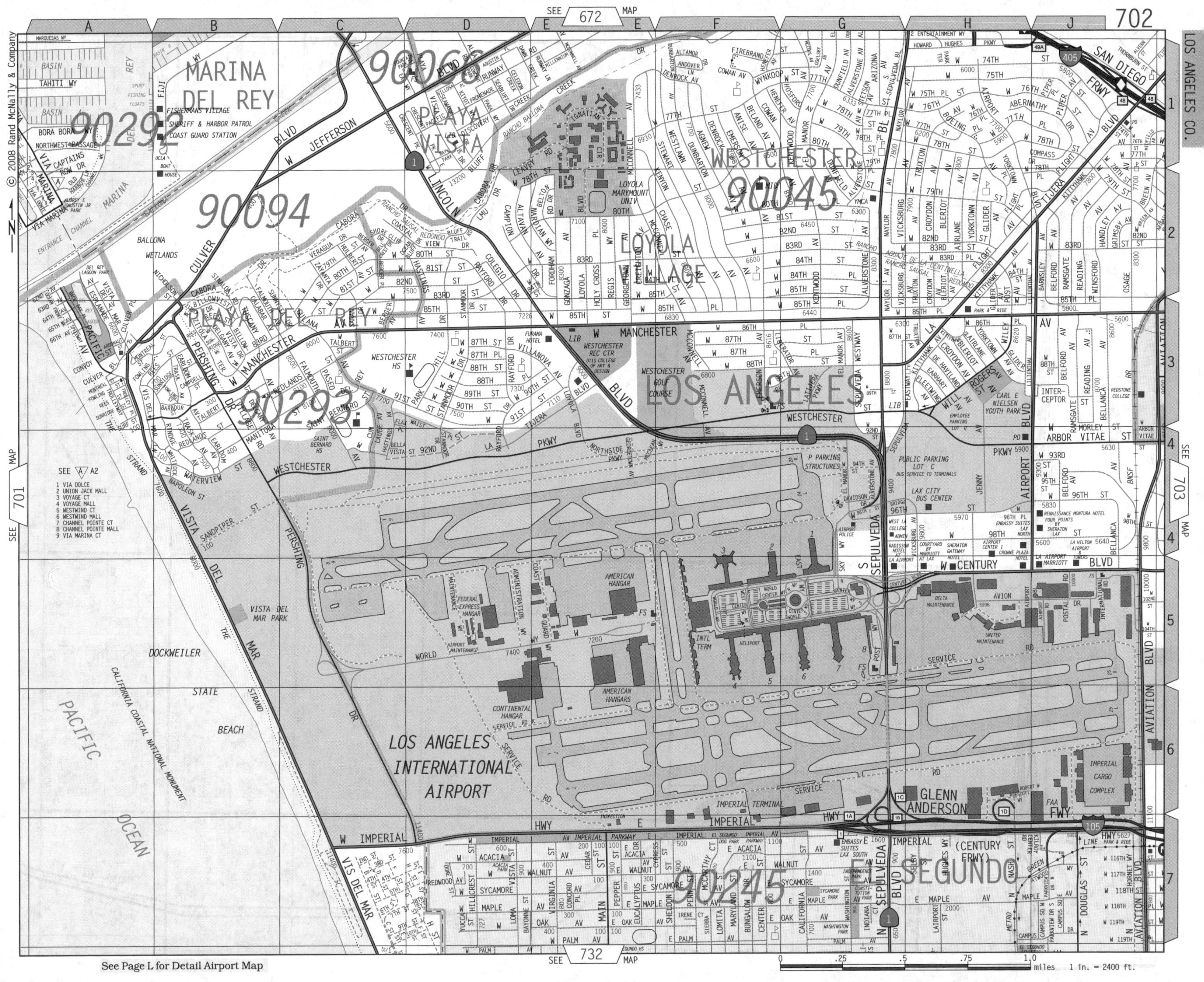

SEE 701 MAP
SEE 703 MAP
SEE 732 MAP
See Page L for Detail Airport Map

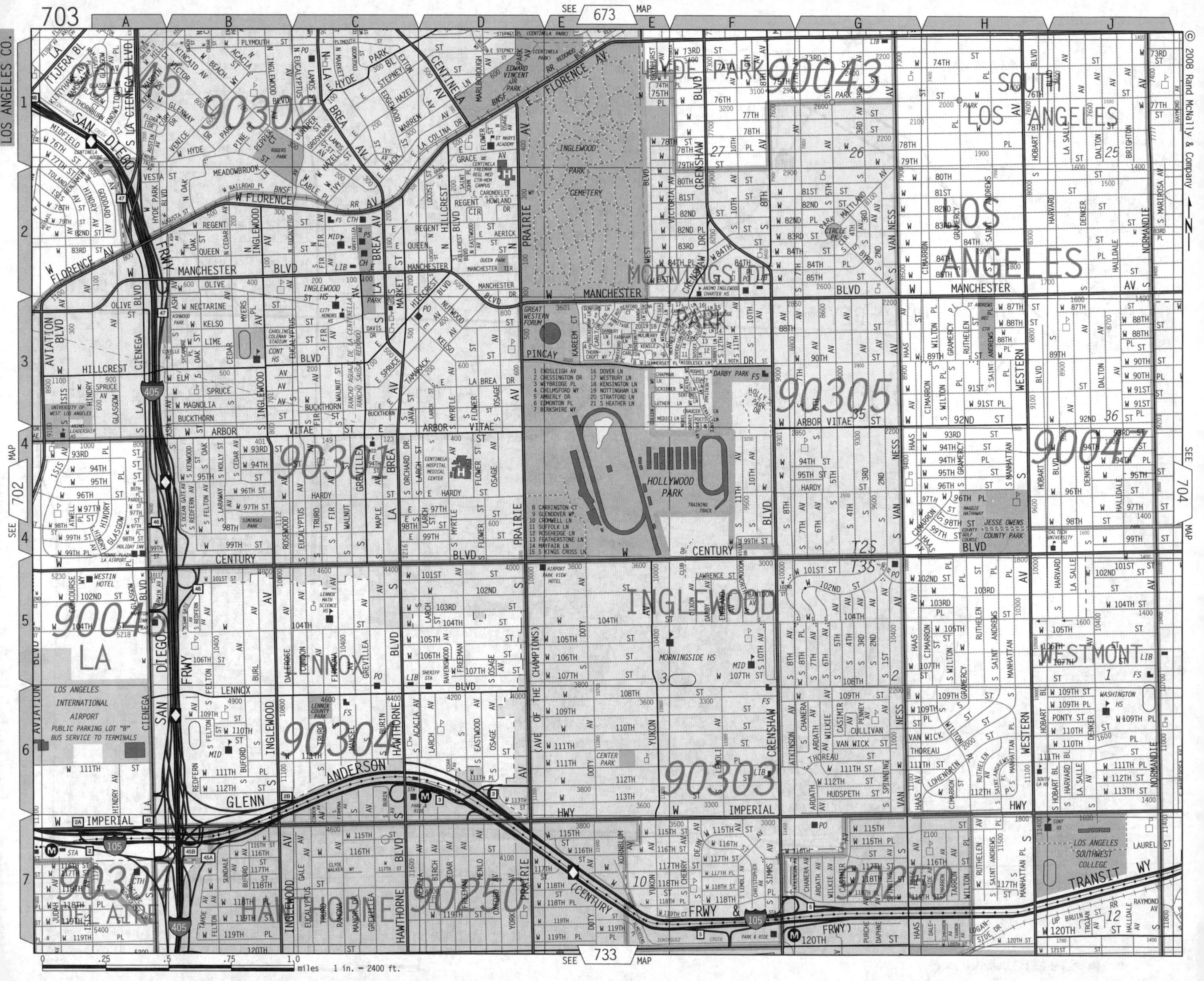

703
LOS ANGELES CO.
SEE 673 MAP
SEE 702 MAP
SEE 704 MAP
SEE 733 MAP
© 2008 Rand McNally & Company
90045
90302
90043
90301
90305
90047
90304
90303
90250
INGLEWOOD
LENNOX
LA
SOUTH LOS ANGELES
LOS ANGELES
WESTMONT
HAWTHORNE
DEL AIRE
MORNINGSIDE PARK
HYDE PARK
HOLLYWOOD PARK
INGLEWOOD PARK CEMETERY
EDWARD VINCENT JR PARK
GREAT WESTERN FORUM
PINCAY
DARBY PARK
CENTER PARK
LENNOX COUNTY PARK
JESSE OWENS COUNTY PARK
LOS ANGELES SOUTHWEST COLLEGE
LOS ANGELES INTERNATIONAL AIRPORT
PUBLIC PARKING LOT "B" BUS SERVICE TO TERMINALS
MORNINGSIDE HS
CENTINELA HOSPITAL MEDICAL CENTER
SAN DIEGO FRWY
CENTURY FRWY
GLENN ANDERSON
W FLORENCE AV
MANCHESTER BLVD
ARBOR VITAE ST
CENTURY BLVD
IMPERIAL HWY
W 120TH ST
AVIATION BLVD
LA CIENEGA BLVD
INGLEWOOD AV
HAWTHORNE BLVD
LA BREA AV
PRAIRIE AV
CRENSHAW BLVD
VAN NESS AV
WESTERN AV
NORMANDIE AV
TRANSIT WY
0 .25 .5 .75 1.0 miles 1 in. = 2400 ft.

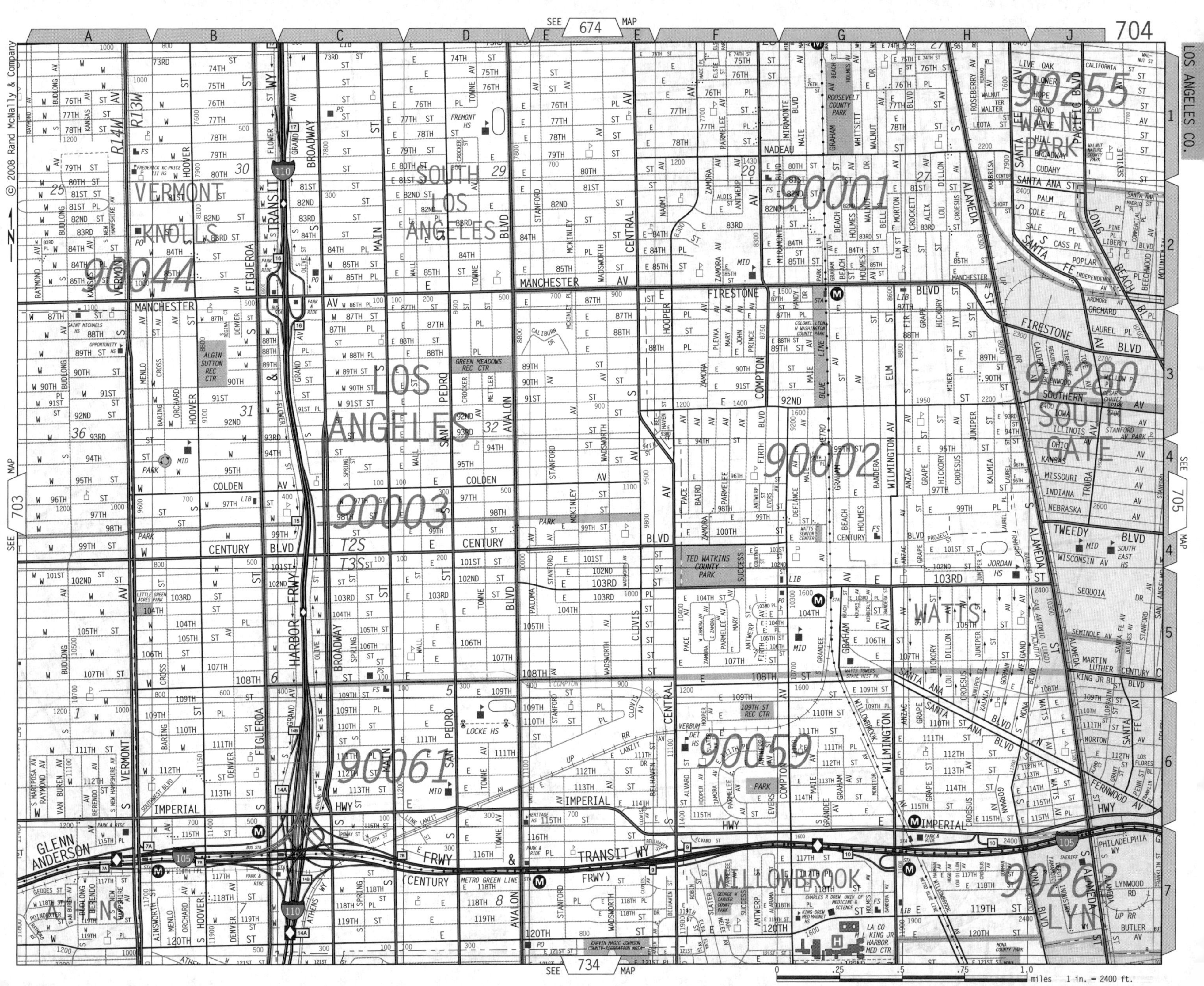

704
SEE 674 MAP
SEE 734 MAP
SEE 703 MAP
SEE 705 MAP
LOS ANGELES CO.
© 2008 Rand McNally & Company
A
B
C
D
E
F
G
H
J
1
2
3
4
5
6
7
VERMONT KNOLLS
SOUTH LOS ANGELES
LOS ANGELES
WALNUT PARK
SOUTH GATE
WATTS
WILLOWBROOK
ATHENS
LYN
90044
90001
90255
90280
90002
90003
90061
90059
90262
MANCHESTER AV
FIRESTONE BLVD
CENTURY BLVD
IMPERIAL HWY
GLENN ANDERSON FRWY (CENTURY FRWY)
TRANSIT WY
HARBOR FRWY
FIGUEROA ST
VERMONT AV
BROADWAY
MAIN ST
SAN PEDRO ST
AVALON BLVD
CENTRAL AV
COMPTON AV
WILMINGTON AV
ALAMEDA ST
SANTA ANA ST
SANTA FE AV
LONG BEACH BL
TWEEDY BLVD
FERNWOOD AV
MARTIN LUTHER KING JR BL
ROOSEVELT COUNTY PARK
TED WATKINS COUNTY PARK
ALGIN SUTTON REC CTR
GREEN MEADOWS REC CTR
109TH ST REC CTR
EARVIN MAGIC JOHNSON COUNTY RECREATION AREA
MONA COUNTY PARK
LA CO M L KING JR HARBOR MED CTR
WATTS TOWERS STATE HIST PK
FREMONT HS
LOCKE HS
JORDAN HS
SOUTH EAST HS
METRO GREEN LINE
METRO BLUE LINE
T2S
T3S
R14W
R13W
0 .25 .5 .75 1.0 miles 1 in. = 2400 ft.

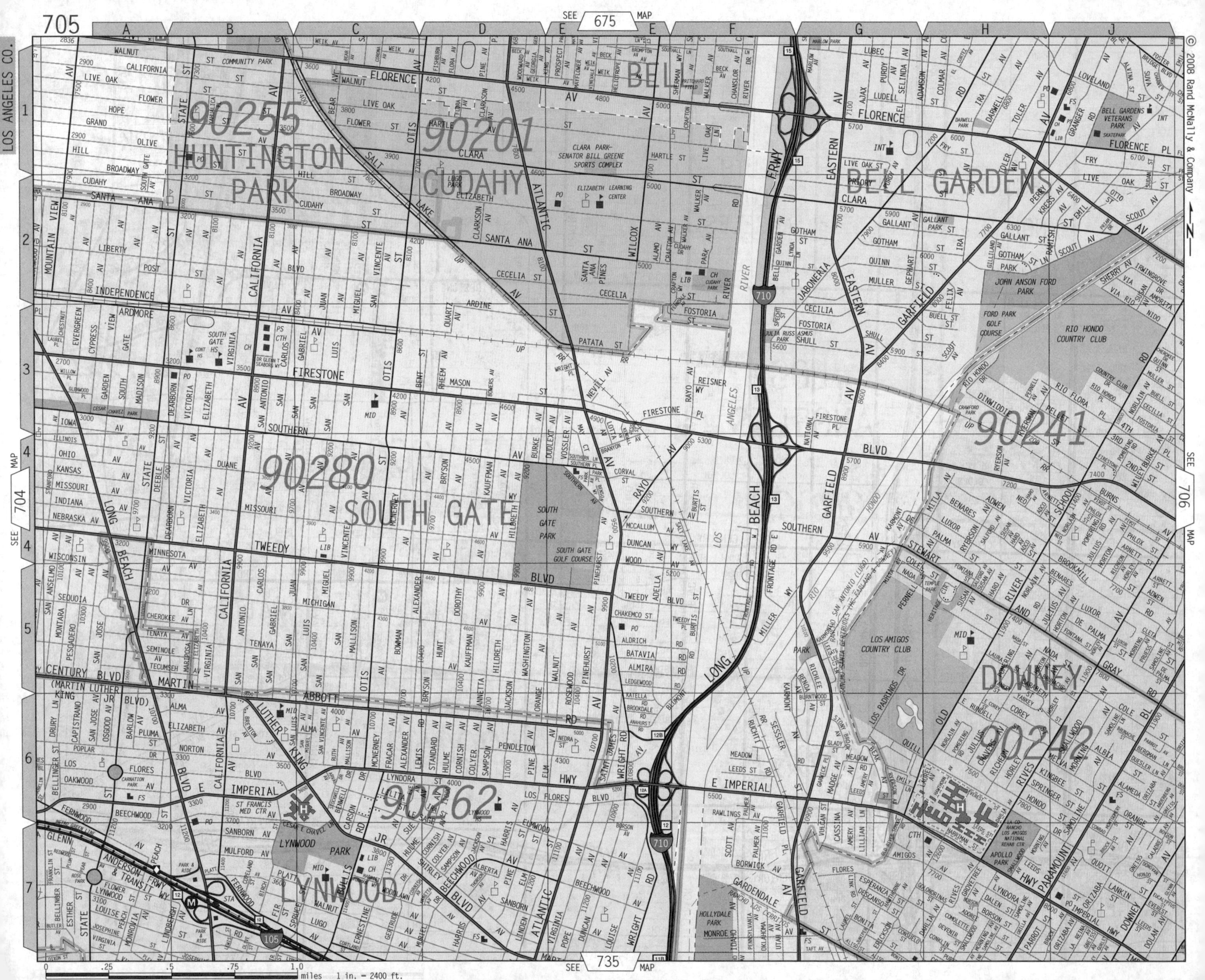
LOS ANGELES CO.
SEE 675 MAP
SEE 704 MAP
SEE 706 MAP
SEE 735 MAP
A
B
C
D
E
F
G
H
J
1
2
3
4
5
6
7
90255
HUNTINGTON PARK
90201
CUDAHY
BELL
BELL GARDENS
90280
SOUTH GATE
90241
DOWNEY
90242
90262
LYNWOOD
CLARA PARK-SENATOR BILL GREENE SPORTS COMPLEX
ELIZABETH LEARNING CENTER
JOHN ANSON FORD PARK
FORD PARK GOLF COURSE
RIO HONDO COUNTRY CLUB
BELL GARDENS VETERANS PARK
SOUTH GATE PARK
SOUTH GATE GOLF COURSE
LOS AMIGOS COUNTRY CLUB
RANCHO LOS AMIGOS NATIONAL REHAB CTR
APOLLO PARK
LYNWOOD PARK
ST FRANCIS MED CTR
HOLLYDALE PARK
LOS ANGELES RIVER
RIO HONDO
FLORENCE AV
FIRESTONE BLVD
SOUTHERN AV
TWEEDY BLVD
CENTURY BLVD
MARTIN LUTHER KING JR BLVD
ABBOTT RD
IMPERIAL HWY
LONG BEACH FRWY
LONG BEACH BLVD
ATLANTIC AV
GARFIELD AV
PARAMOUNT BLVD
STATE ST
CALIFORNIA AV
SANTA ANA ST
SALT LAKE AV
CLARA ST
GLENN ANDERSON FRWY & TRANSIT WY
miles 1 in. = 2400 ft.
0 .25 .5 .75 1.0

SEE 676 MAP

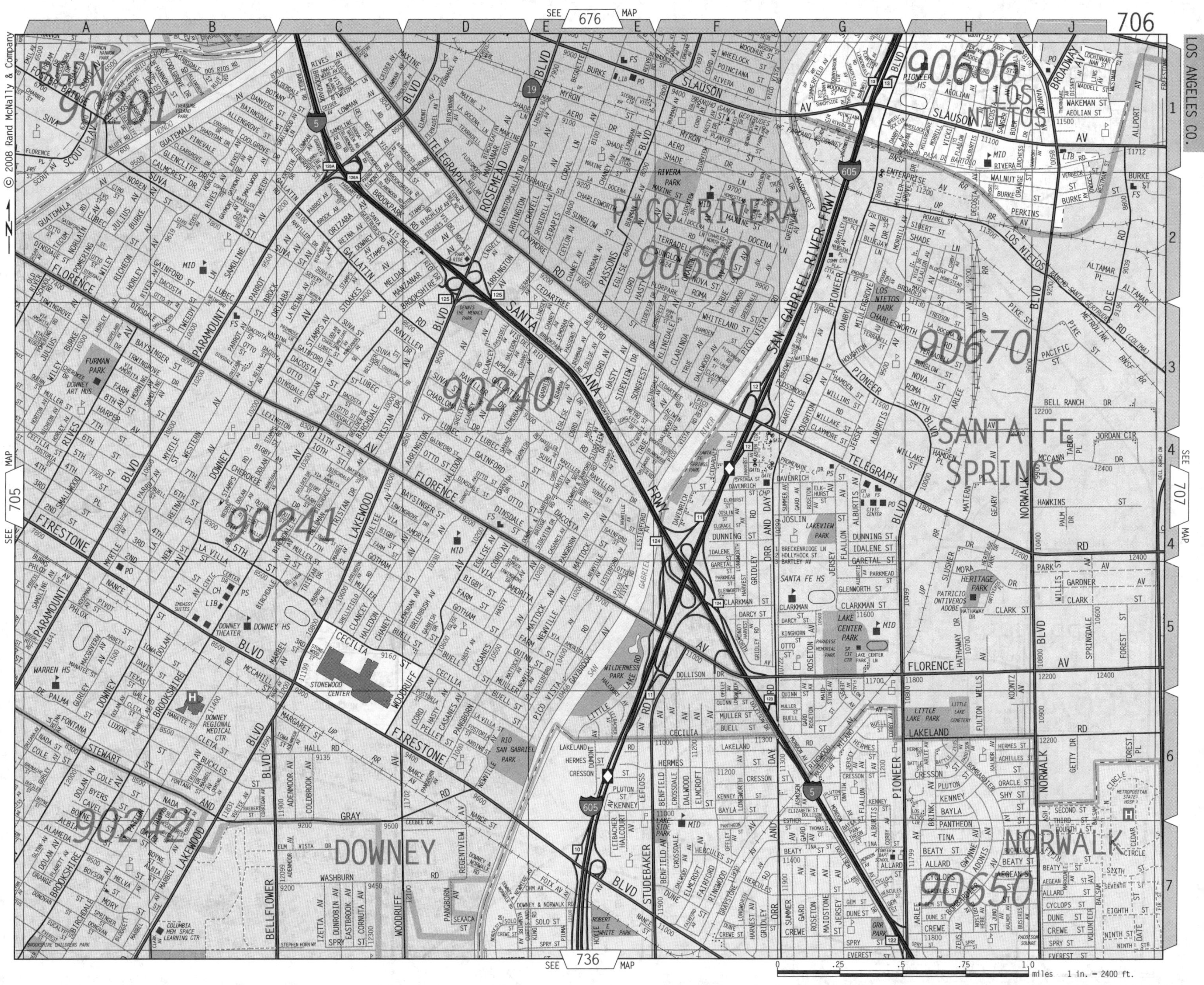

SEE 705 MAP
SEE 707 MAP
SEE 736 MAP

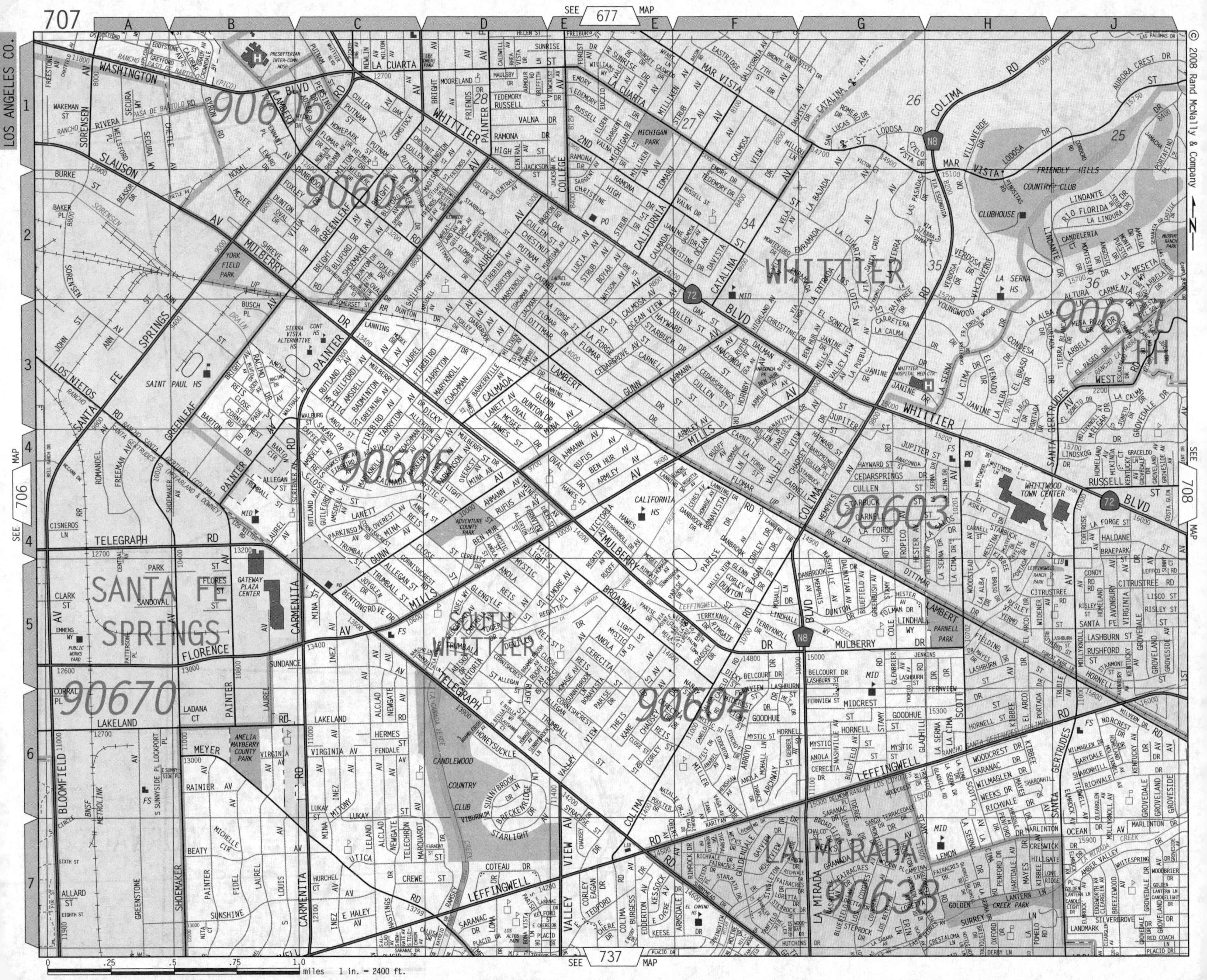

707
LOS ANGELES CO.
SEE 677 MAP
SEE 706 MAP
SEE 708 MAP
SEE 737 MAP
A
B
C
D
E
F
G
H
J
1
2
3
4
5
6
7
© 2008 Rand McNally & Company
WHITTIER
SANTA FE SPRINGS
SOUTH WHITTIER
LA MIRADA
90605
90602
90603
90604
90670
90638
90631
WASHINGTON
WHITTIER BLVD
SLAUSON AV
MULBERRY
TELEGRAPH RD
FLORENCE AV
LAKELAND
LEFFINGWELL RD
COLIMA RD
MAR VISTA
LA CUARTA
PAINTER AV
CARMENITA RD
BLOOMFIELD AV
SHOEMAKER
VALLEY VIEW AV
SANTA GERTRUDES AV
LA MIRADA BLVD
GREENLEAF AV
LAMBERT RD
MILLS AV
BROADWAY
IMPERIAL
LOS NIETOS RD
SANTA FE SPRINGS RD
PRESBYTERIAN INTER-COMM HOSP
MICHIGAN PARK
YORK FIELD PARK
SAINT PAUL HS
SIERRA VISTA ALTERNATIVE HS
ADVENTURE COUNTY PARK
CALIFORNIA HS
GATEWAY PLAZA CENTER
AMELIA MAYBERRY COUNTY PARK
PUBLIC WORKS YARD
CANDLEWOOD COUNTRY CLUB
FRIENDLY HILLS COUNTRY CLUB
CLUBHOUSE
LA SERNA HS
WHITTIER HOSPITAL MED CTR
WHITTWOOD TOWN CENTER
PARNELL PARK
CREEK PARK
EL CAMINO HS
LA CANADA VERDE CREEK
26
27
28
34
35
36
25
72
N8
0
.25
.5
.75
1.0
miles 1 in. = 2400 ft.

SEE 678 MAP

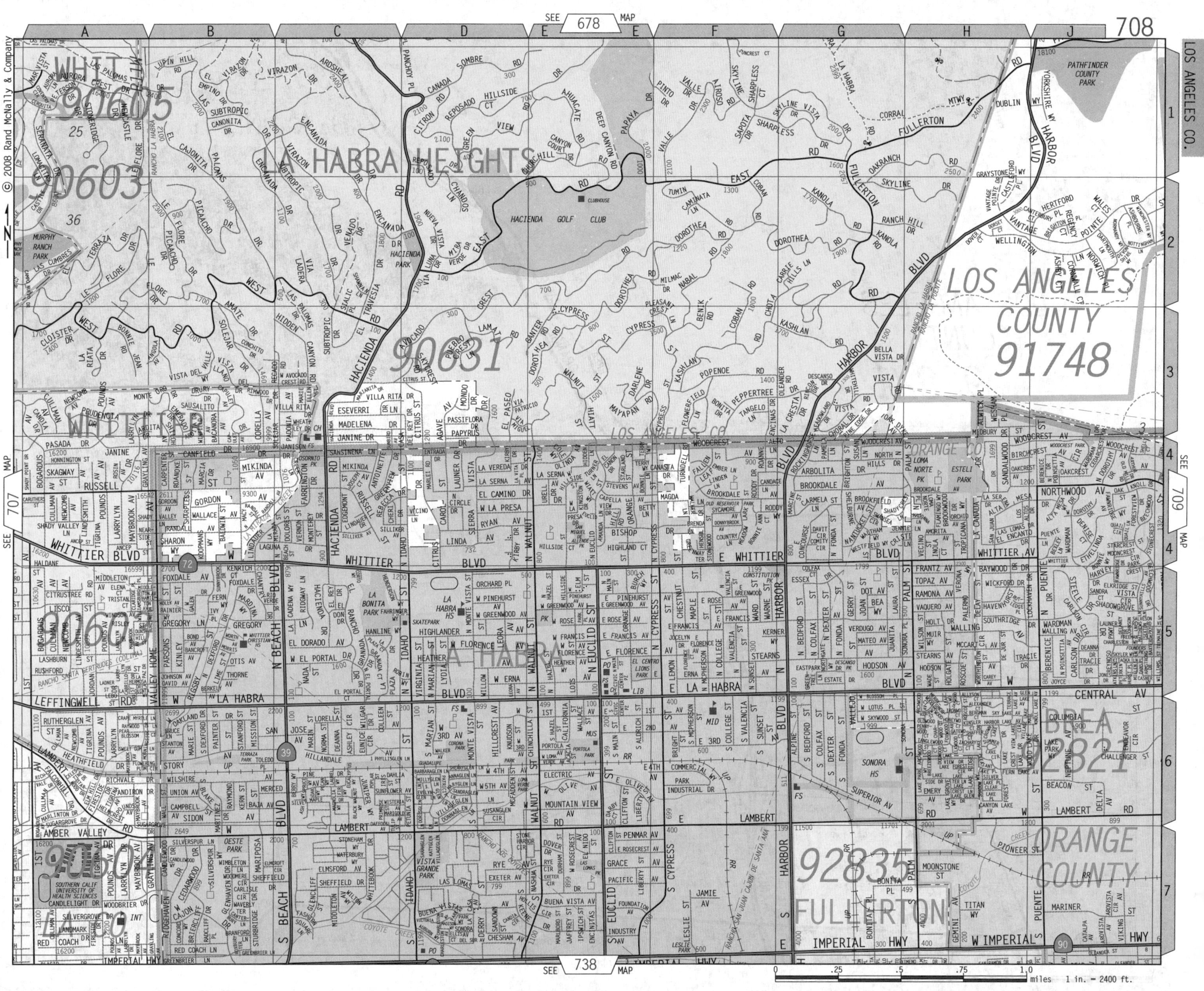

SEE 707 MAP
SEE 709 MAP
SEE 738 MAP

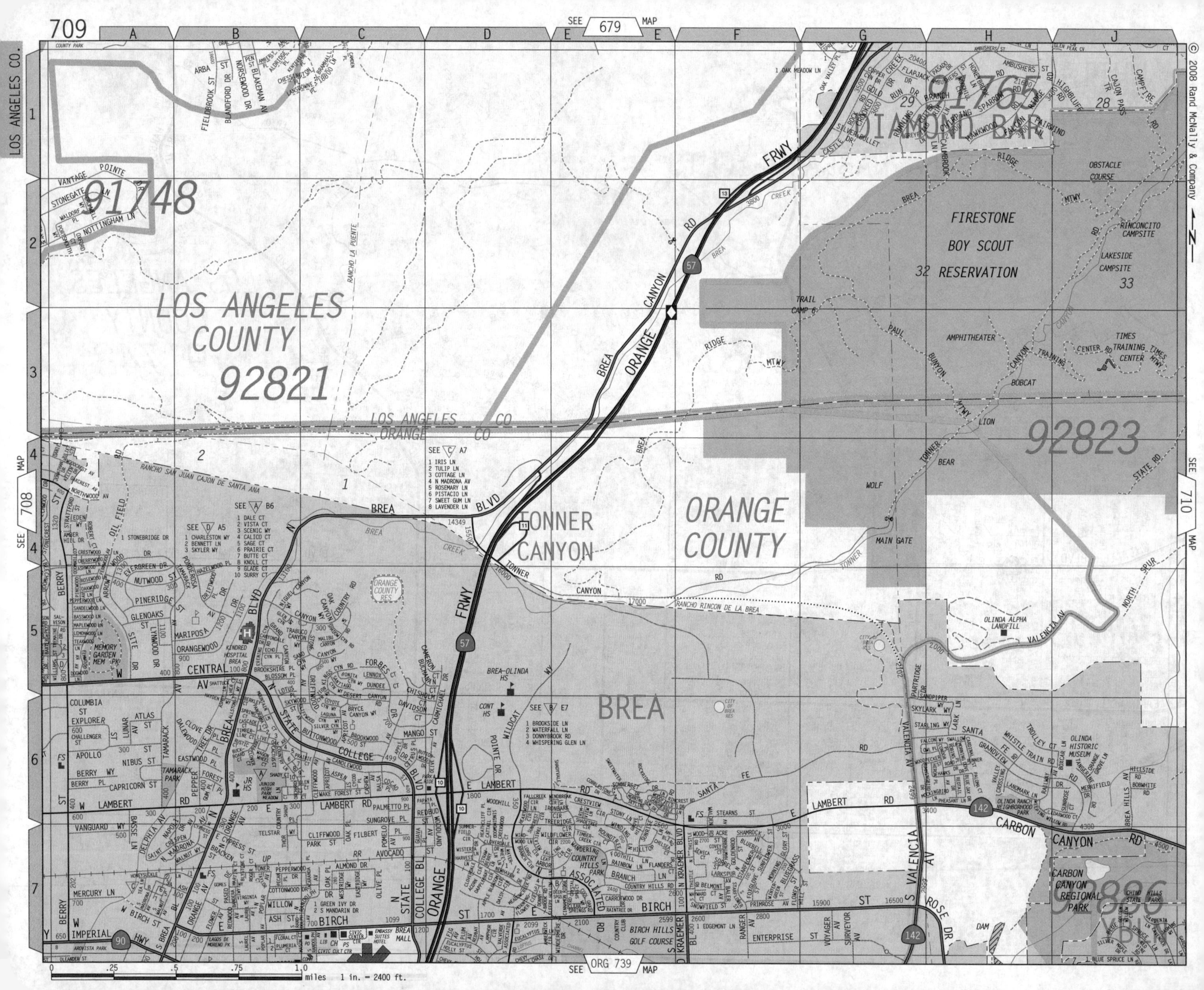
SEE 679 MAP
LOS ANGELES CO.
LOS ANGELES COUNTY
92821
91748
91765
DIAMOND BAR
FIRESTONE BOY SCOUT RESERVATION
92823
ORANGE COUNTY
TONNER CANYON
BREA
ORANGE FRWY
BREA CANYON RD
CARBON CANYON REGIONAL PARK
OLINDA ALPHA LANDFILL
OLINDA HISTORIC MUSEUM
BIRCH HILLS GOLF COURSE
SEE 708 MAP
SEE 710 MAP
SEE ORG 739 MAP
miles 1 in. = 2400 ft.

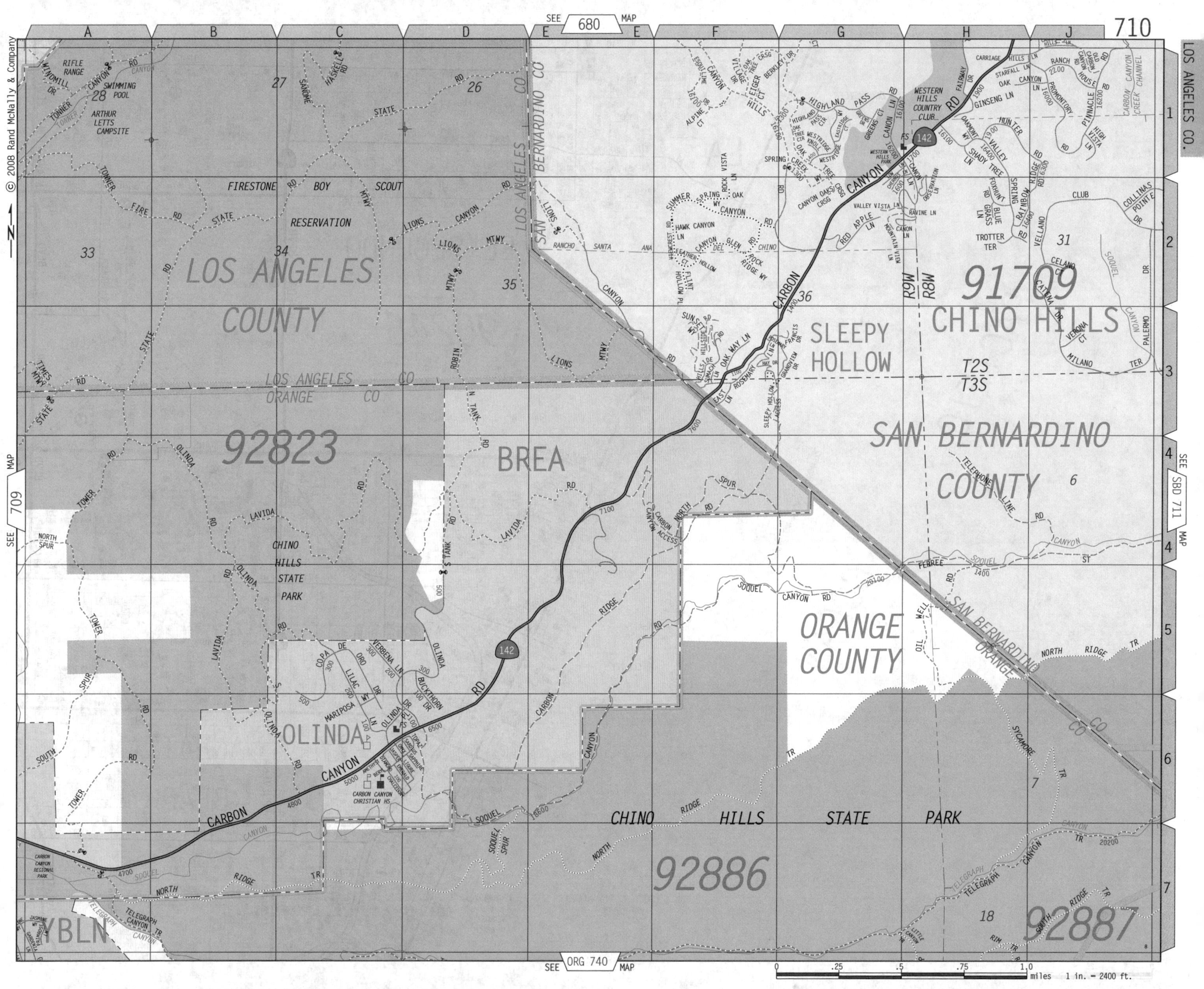
SEE 680 MAP
LOS ANGELES CO.
LOS ANGELES COUNTY
92823
BREA
CHINO HILLS STATE PARK
OLINDA
CARBON CANYON RD
FIRESTONE BOY SCOUT RESERVATION
ARTHUR LETTS CAMPSITE
RIFLE RANGE
SWIMMING POOL
WESTERN HILLS COUNTRY CLUB
SLEEPY HOLLOW
91709
CHINO HILLS
SAN BERNARDINO COUNTY
ORANGE COUNTY
92886
92887
CARBON CANYON CHRISTIAN HS
CARBON CANYON REGIONAL PARK
YBLN
T2S
T3S
R9W
R8W
SEE 709 MAP
SEE SBD 711 MAP
SEE ORG 740 MAP
miles 1 in. = 2400 ft.

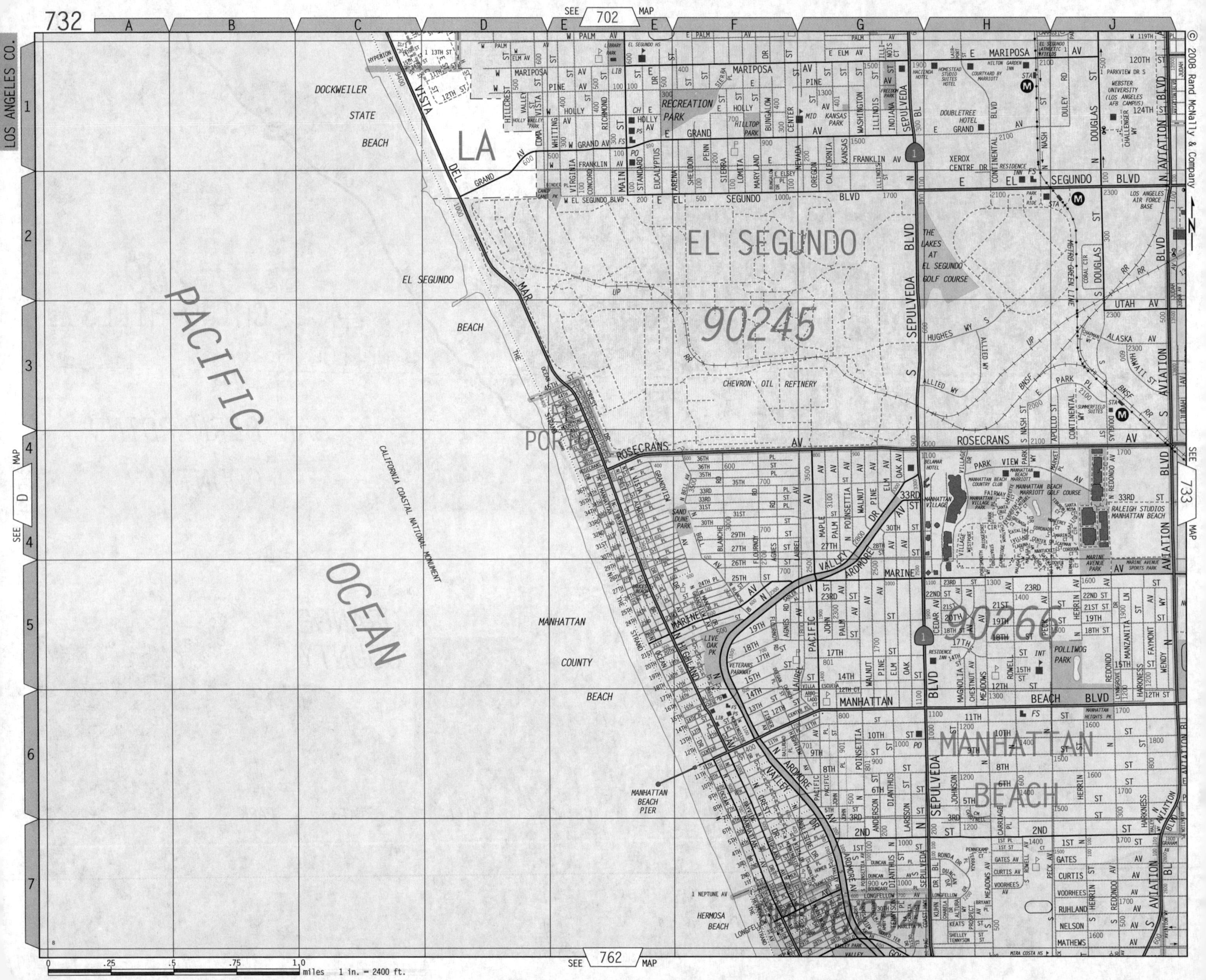
LOS ANGELES CO.
SEE 702 MAP
SEE 733 MAP
SEE D 4 MAP
SEE 762 MAP
A
B
C
D
E
F
G
H
J
1
2
3
4
5
6
7
© 2008 Rand McNally & Company
PACIFIC
OCEAN
DOCKWEILER
STATE
BEACH
EL SEGUNDO
BEACH
CALIFORNIA COASTAL NATIONAL MONUMENT
MANHATTAN
COUNTY
BEACH
MANHATTAN
BEACH
PIER
HERMOSA
BEACH
LA
EL SEGUNDO
90245
90266
MANHATTAN
BEACH
CHEVRON OIL REFINERY
RECREATION
PARK
HILLTOP
PARK
KANSAS
PARK
SAND
DUNE
PARK
LIVE
OAK
PK
POLLIWOG
PARK
MARINE AVENUE
PARK
THE
LAKES
AT
EL SEGUNDO
GOLF COURSE
LOS ANGELES
AIR FORCE
BASE
WEBSTER
UNIVERSITY
(LOS ANGELES
AFB CAMPUS)
DOUBLETREE
HOTEL
XEROX
CENTRE DR
MANHATTAN BEACH
COUNTRY CLUB
MANHATTAN BEACH
MARRIOTT GOLF COURSE
RALEIGH STUDIOS
MANHATTAN BEACH
MANHATTAN
VILLAGE
SEPULVEDA BLVD
AVIATION BLVD
ROSECRANS AV
MARINE AV
MANHATTAN BEACH BLVD
EL SEGUNDO BLVD
MARIPOSA AV
GRAND AV
VISTA DEL MAR
HIGHLAND AV
HUGHES WY
UTAH AV
ALASKA AV
METRO GREEN LINE
BNSF
UP
RR
0
.25
.5
.75
1.0
miles 1 in. = 2400 ft.

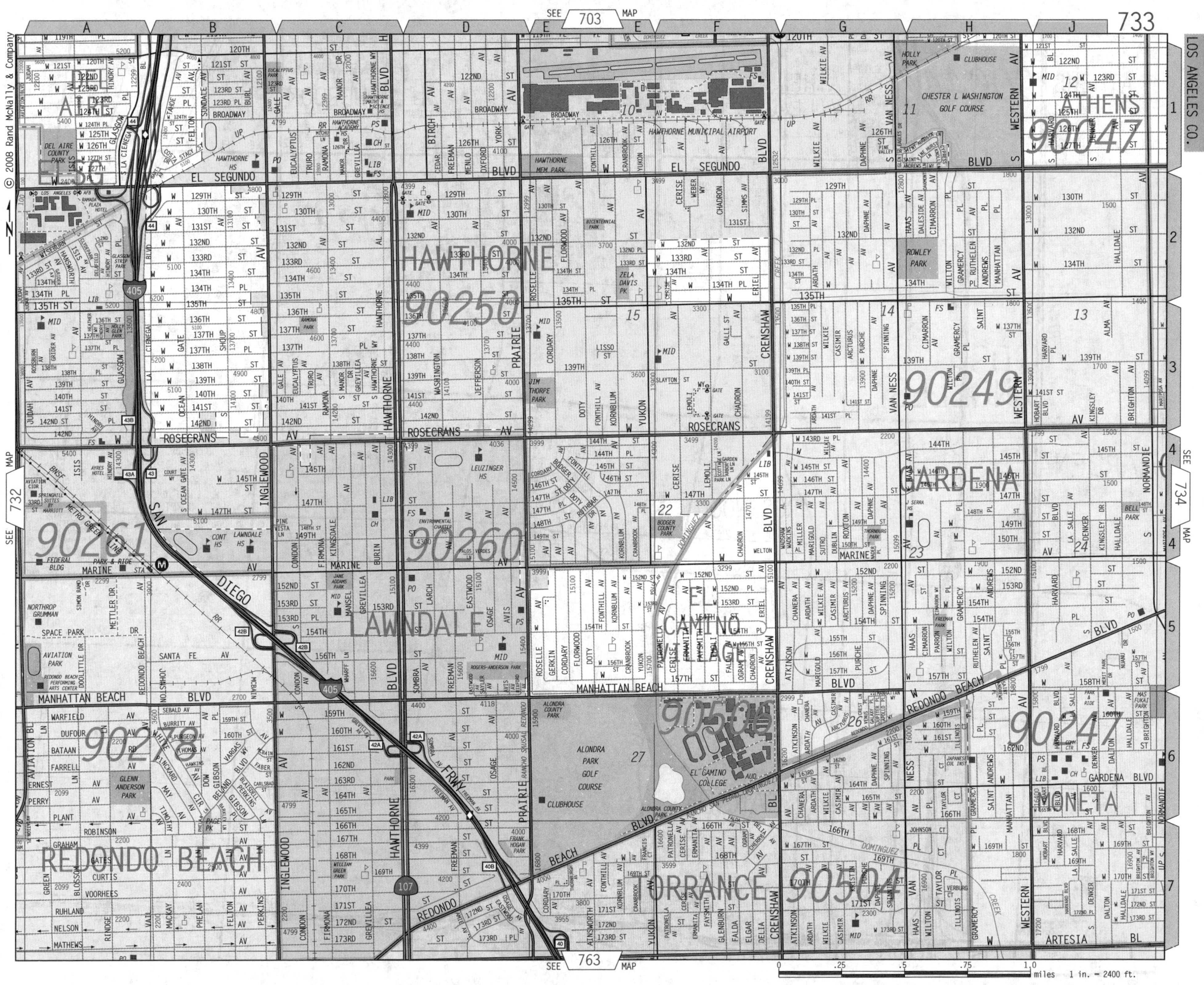

733
SEE 703 MAP
SEE 763 MAP
SEE 732 MAP
SEE 734 MAP
LOS ANGELES CO.
© 2008 Rand McNally & Company
A
B
C
D
E
F
G
H
J
1
2
3
4
5
6
7
DEL AIRE
90250
HAWTHORNE
90260
LAWNDALE
90261
90278
REDONDO BEACH
ATHENS
90047
GARDENA
90249
90247
MONETA
EL CAMINO VILLAGE
TORRANCE
90504
HAWTHORNE MUNICIPAL AIRPORT
CHESTER L WASHINGTON GOLF COURSE
HOLLY PARK
HAWTHORNE MEM PARK
ROWLEY PARK
ZELA DAVIS PK
JIM THORPE PARK
BODGER COUNTY PARK
ALONDRA PARK GOLF COURSE
ALONDRA COUNTY PARK
EL CAMINO COLLEGE
NORTHROP GRUMMAN
SPACE PARK
AVIATION PARK
GLENN ANDERSON PARK
ROGERS-ANDERSON PARK
LEUZINGER HS
HAWTHORNE HS
LAWNDALE HS
EL SEGUNDO BLVD
ROSECRANS AV
MARINE AV
MANHATTAN BEACH BLVD
REDONDO BEACH BLVD
ARTESIA BL
GARDENA BLVD
SAN DIEGO FRWY
HAWTHORNE BLVD
INGLEWOOD AV
PRAIRIE AV
CRENSHAW BLVD
VAN NESS AV
WESTERN AV
NORMANDIE AV
AVIATION BL
BROADWAY
405
107
miles 1 in. = 2400 ft.
0 .25 .5 .75 1.0

SEE 704 MAP

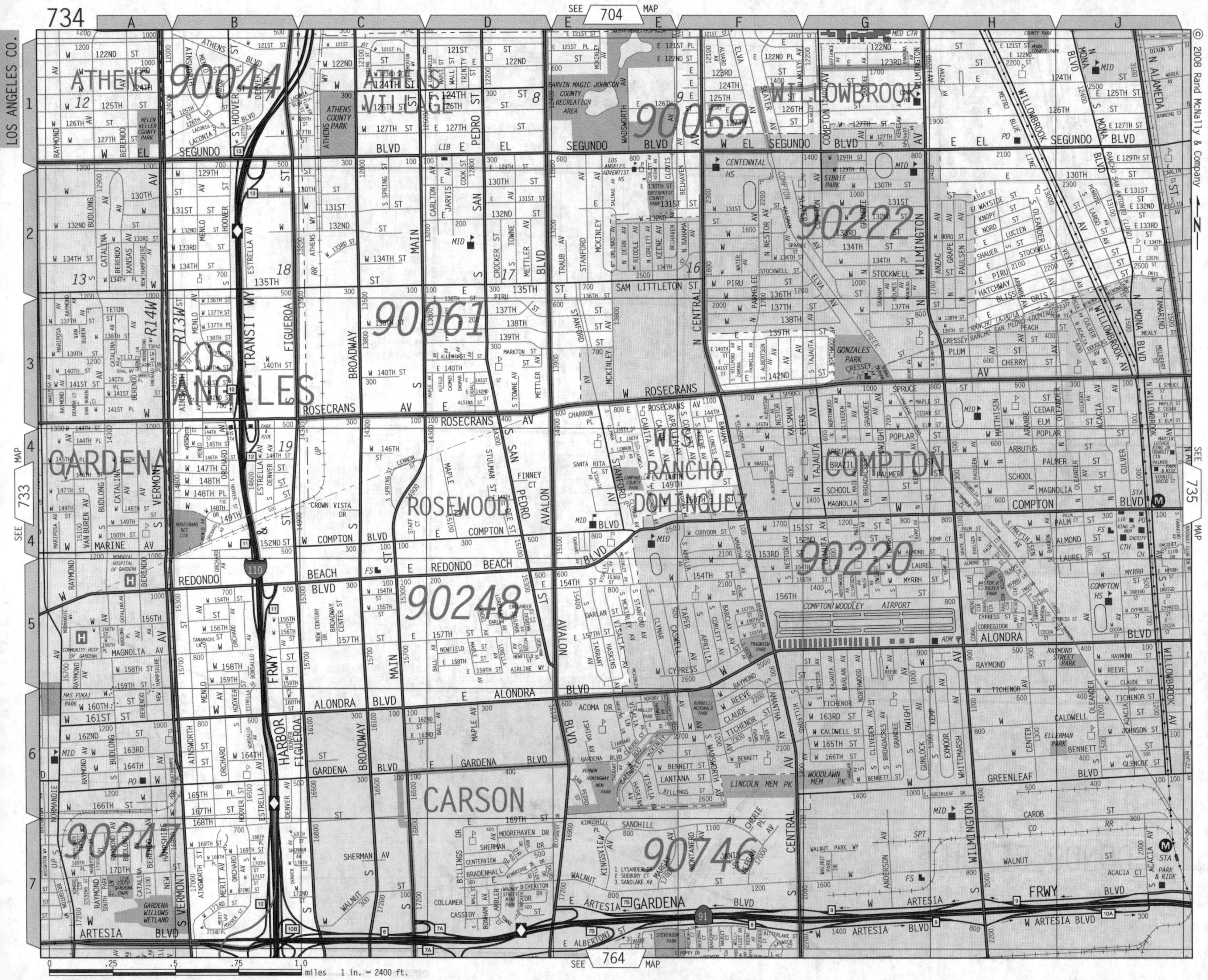

SEE 733 MAP

SEE 735 MAP

SEE 764 MAP

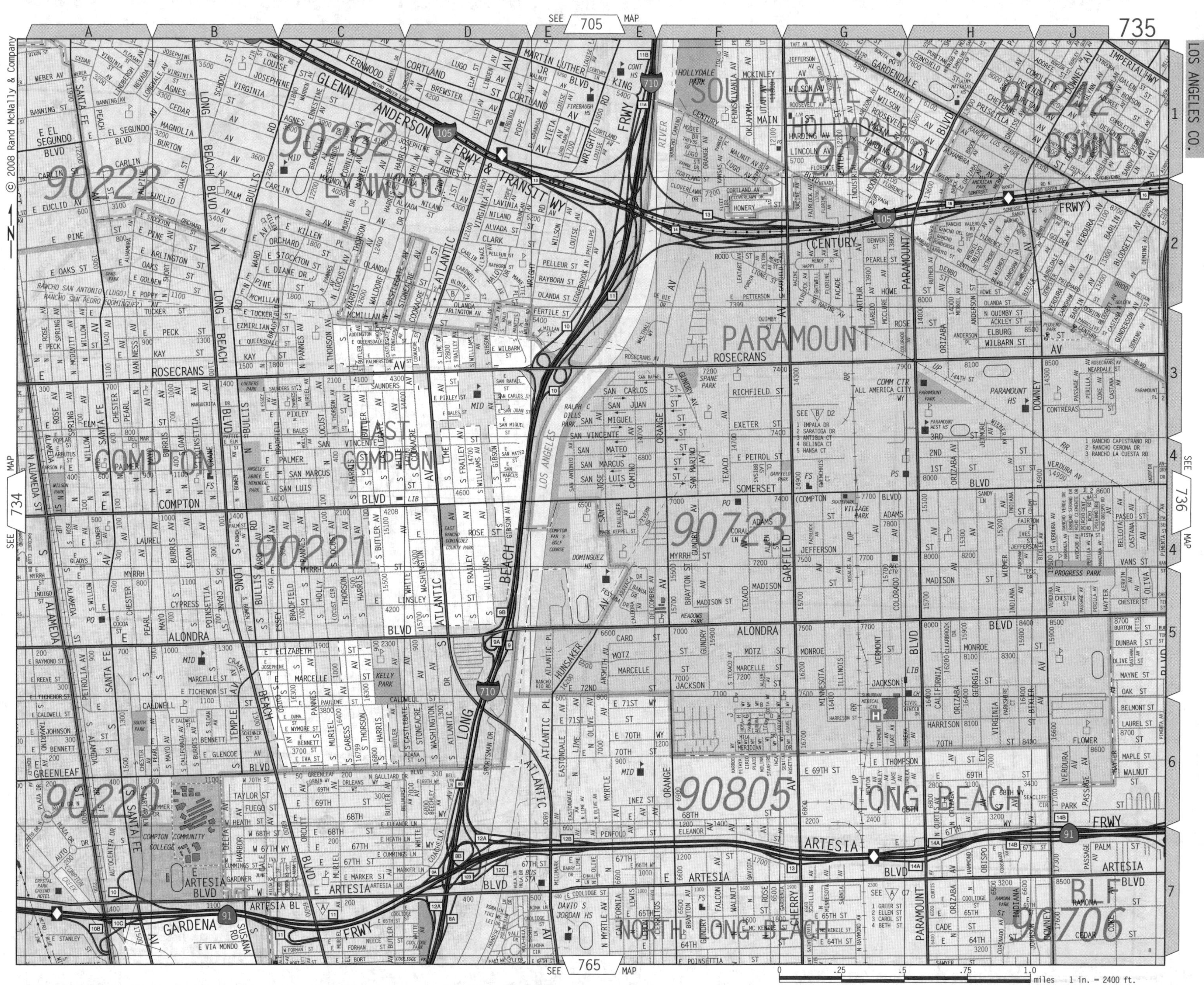
SEE 705 MAP
A
B
C
D
E
F
G
H
J
LOS ANGELES CO.
SOUTH GATE
HOLLYDALE
LYNWOOD
DOWNEY
PARAMOUNT
EAST COMPTON
COMPTON
LONG BEACH
NORTH LONG BEACH
GARDENA
BLF
90262
90280
90242
90222
90221
90723
90220
90805
90706
GLENN ANDERSON FRWY & TRANSIT WY
ROSECRANS
ALONDRA
ARTESIA
ATLANTIC
LONG BEACH BLVD
LOS ANGELES RIVER
COMPTON COMMUNITY COLLEGE
HOLLYDALE PARK
DOMINGUEZ HS
PARAMOUNT HS
DAVID S JORDAN HS
SEE 734 MAP
SEE 736 MAP
SEE 765 MAP
1
2
3
4
5
6
7
miles 1 in. = 2400 ft.
0 .25 .5 .75 1.0

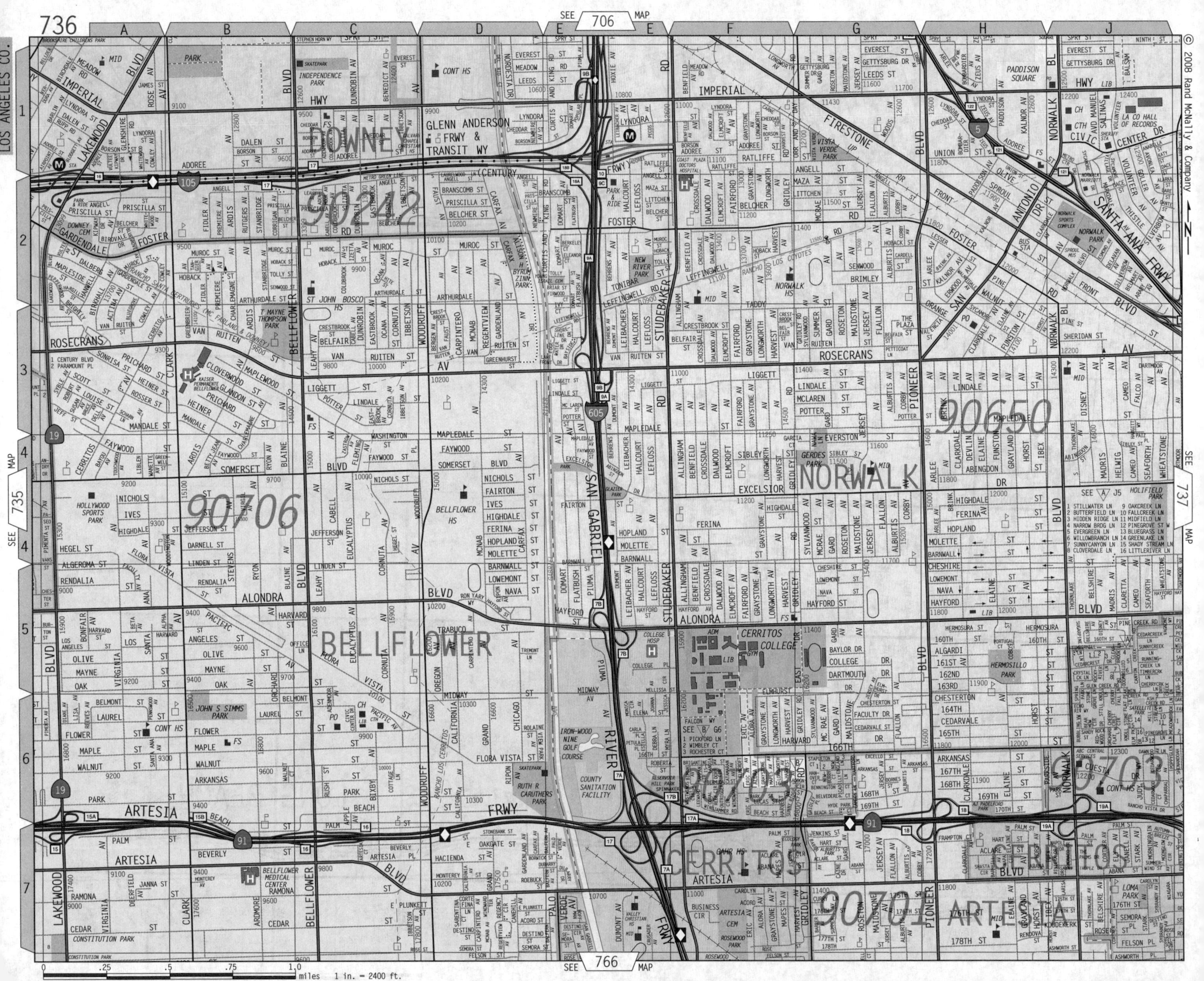
LOS ANGELES CO.
SEE 706 MAP
SEE 735 MAP
SEE 737 MAP
SEE 766 MAP
© 2008 Rand McNally & Company
DOWNEY
90242
GLENN ANDERSON FRWY & TRANSIT WY
IMPERIAL HWY
FIRESTONE BLVD
SANTA ANA FRWY
90706
BELLFLOWER
90650
NORWALK
CERRITOS
90703
90701
ARTESIA
SAN GABRIEL RIVER FRWY
ROSECRANS AV
ALONDRA BLVD
ARTESIA FRWY
LAKEWOOD BLVD
BELLFLOWER BLVD
WOODRUFF AV
STUDEBAKER RD
PIONEER BLVD
NORWALK BLVD
CERRITOS COLLEGE
BELLFLOWER HS
NORWALK HS
HOLLYWOOD SPORTS PARK
IRON-WOOD NINE GOLF COURSE
COUNTY SANITATION FACILITY
CONSTITUTION PARK
1 in. = 2400 ft.
miles

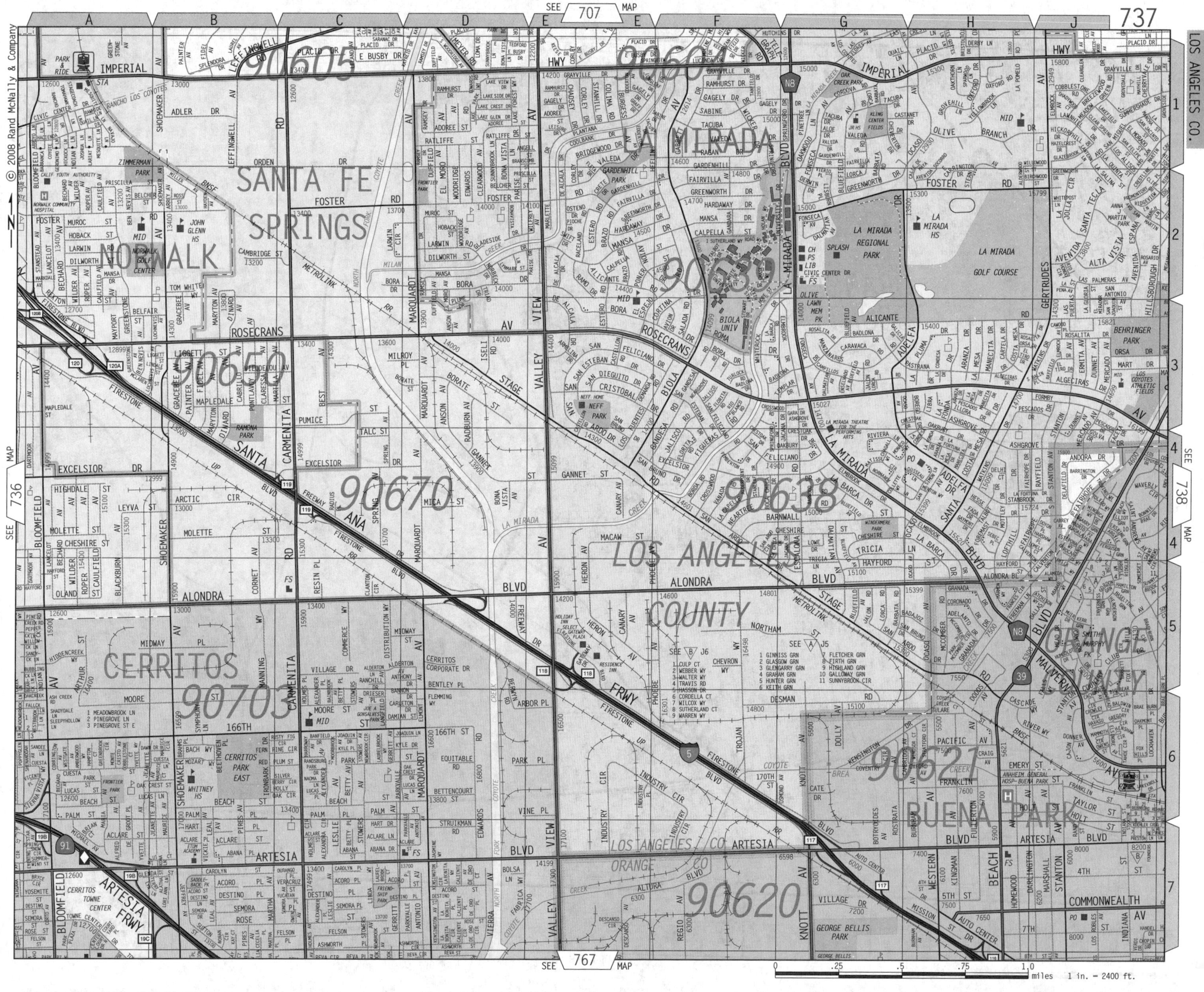
SEE 707 MAP
SEE 736 MAP
SEE 738 MAP
SEE 767 MAP
SANTA FE SPRINGS
NORWALK
LA MIRADA
LOS ANGELES COUNTY
CERRITOS
BUENA PARK
ORANGE COUNTY
90605
90604
90650
90670
90639
90638
90703
90621
90620
IMPERIAL HWY
ROSECRANS AV
ALONDRA BLVD
ARTESIA BLVD
SANTA ANA FRWY
ARTESIA FRWY
FIRESTONE BLVD
VALLEY VIEW AV
LA MIRADA BLVD
LA MIRADA REGIONAL PARK
LA MIRADA GOLF COURSE
BIOLA UNIV
NORWALK GOLF CENTER
CERRITOS PARK EAST
CERRITOS TOWNE CENTER
GEORGE BELLIS PARK
1 MEADOWBROOK LN
2 PINEGROVE LN
3 PINEGROVE ST E
1 CULP CT
2 WEBBER WY
3 WALTER WY
4 TRAVIS RD
5 HASSON DR
6 CORDELLA CT
7 WILCOX WY
8 SUTHERLAND CT
9 WARREN WY
1 GINNISS GRN
2 GLASGOW GRN
3 GLENGARRY GRN
4 GRAHAM GRN
5 HUNTER GRN
6 KEITH GRN
7 FLETCHER GRN
8 FIRTH GRN
9 HIGHLAND GRN
10 GALLOWAY GRN
11 SUNNYBROOK CIR
0 .25 .5 .75 1.0 miles 1 in. = 2400 ft.

SEE 708 MAP

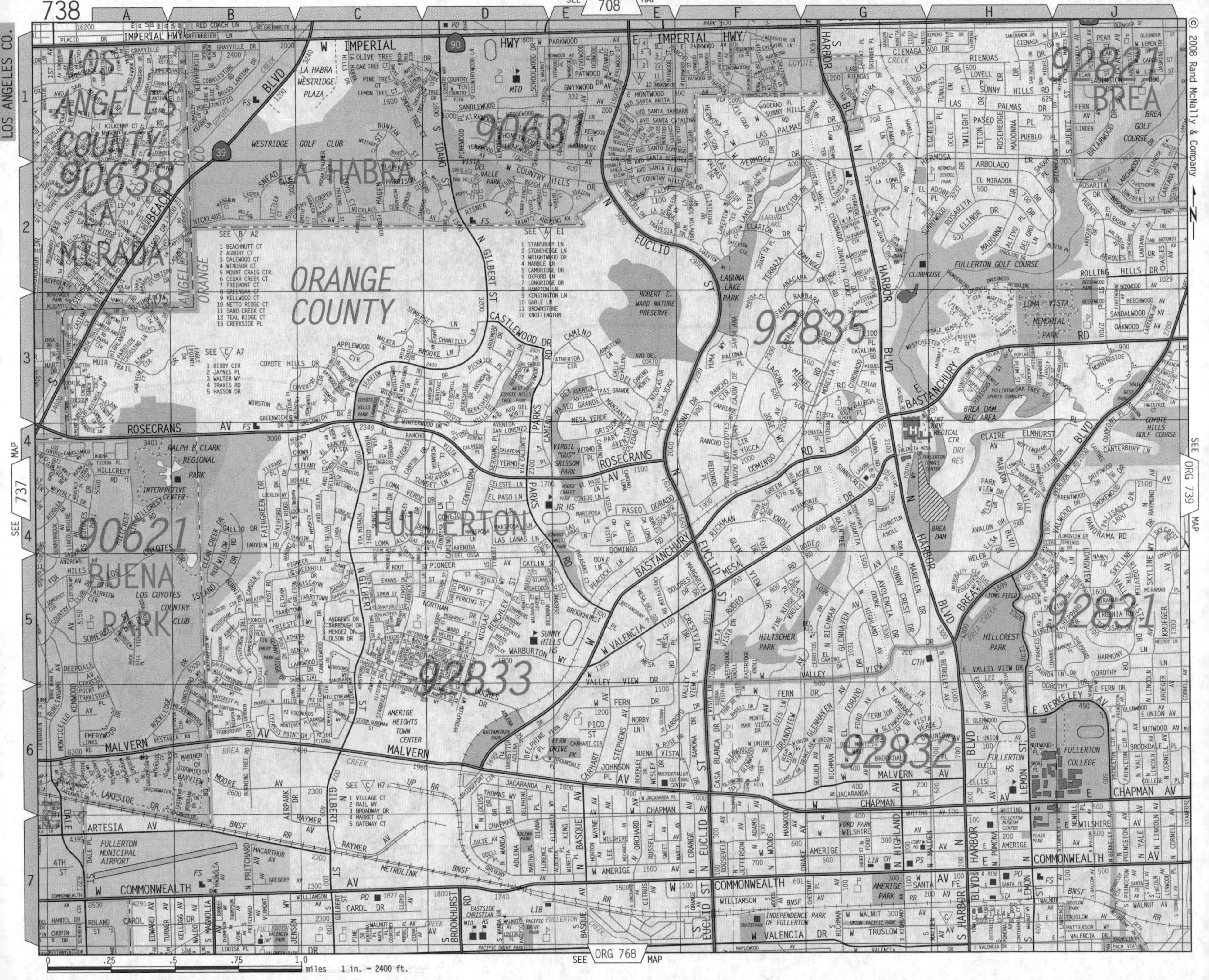

SEE 737 MAP
SEE ORG 739 MAP
SEE ORG 768 MAP

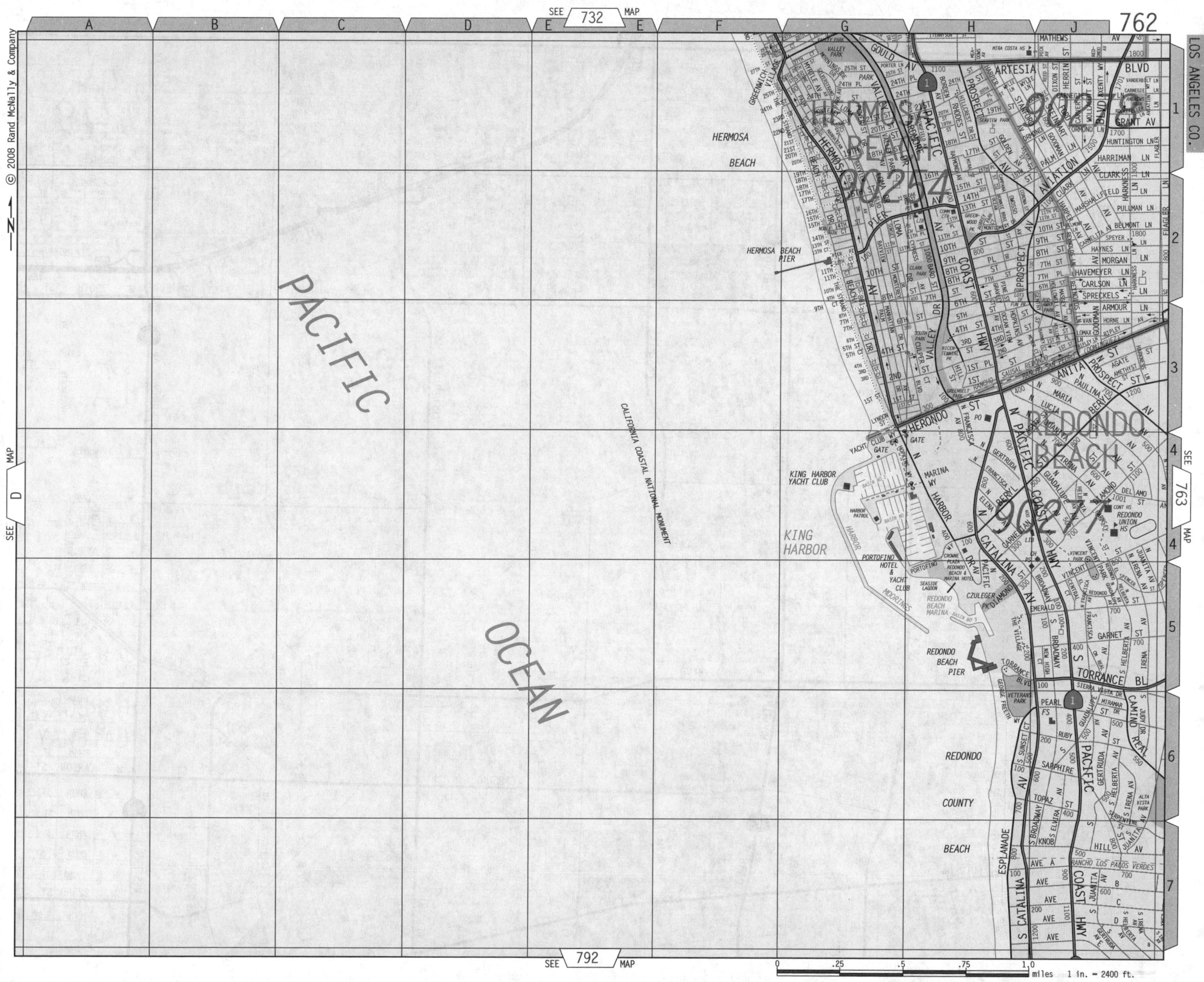

SEE 732 MAP
LOS ANGELES CO.
HERMOSA BEACH
HERMOSA BEACH PIER
PACIFIC
OCEAN
CALIFORNIA COASTAL NATIONAL MONUMENT
KING HARBOR YACHT CLUB
KING HARBOR
PORTOFINO HOTEL & YACHT CLUB
REDONDO BEACH MARINA
REDONDO BEACH PIER
REDONDO
COUNTY
BEACH
HERMOSA BEACH 90254
REDONDO BEACH 90277
90278
SEE 763 MAP
SEE D MAP
SEE 792 MAP
miles 1 in. = 2400 ft.

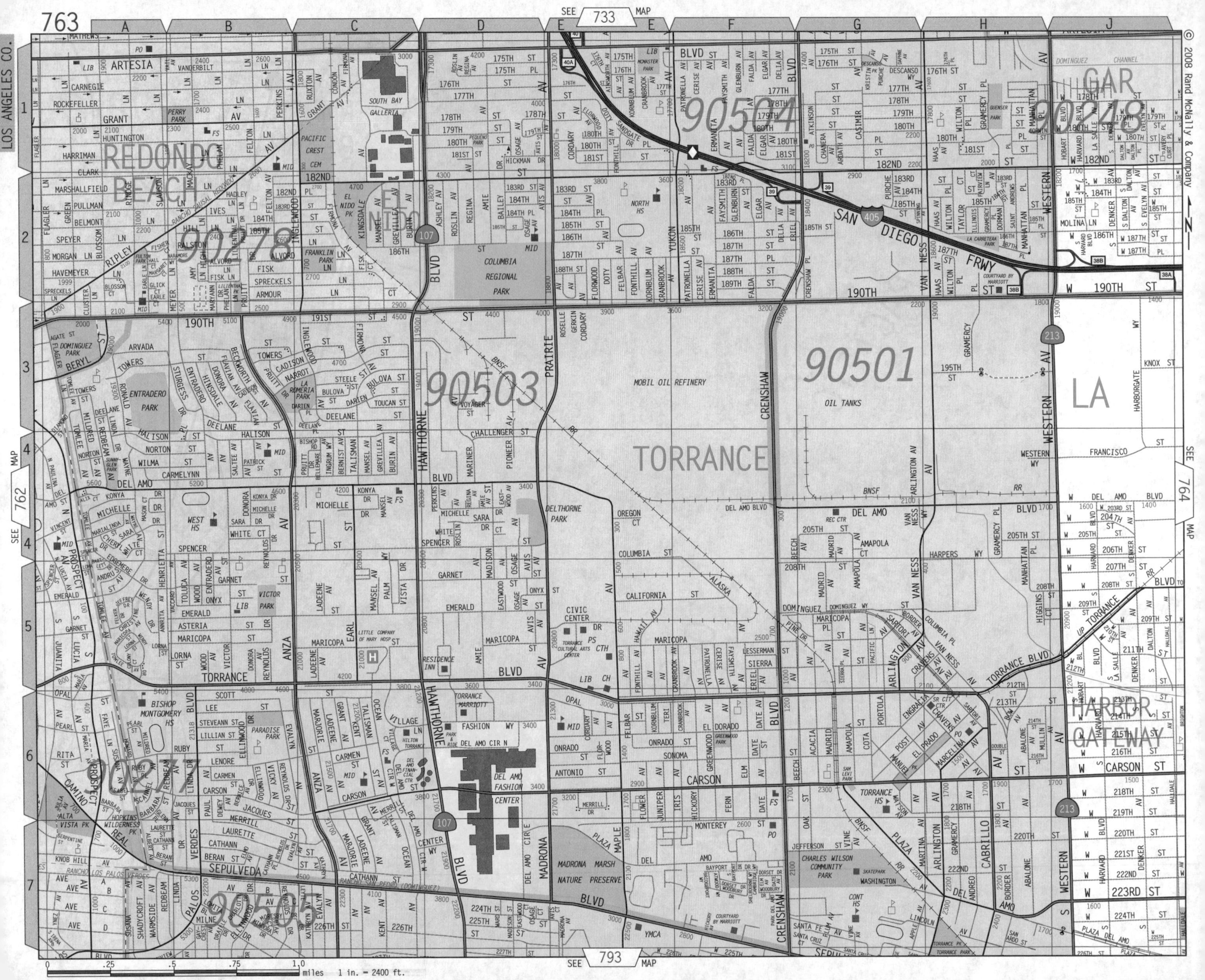
SEE 733 MAP
SEE 762 MAP
SEE 764 MAP
SEE 793 MAP
LOS ANGELES CO.
REDONDO BEACH
TORRANCE
GAR
LA
HARBOR GATEWAY
90504
90248
90278
90503
90501
90277
90505
MOBIL OIL REFINERY
OIL TANKS
SOUTH BAY GALLERIA
COLUMBIA REGIONAL PARK
DEL AMO FASHION CENTER
MADRONA MARSH NATURE PRESERVE
CHARLES WILSON COMMUNITY PARK
SAN DIEGO FRWY
miles 1 in. = 2400 ft.

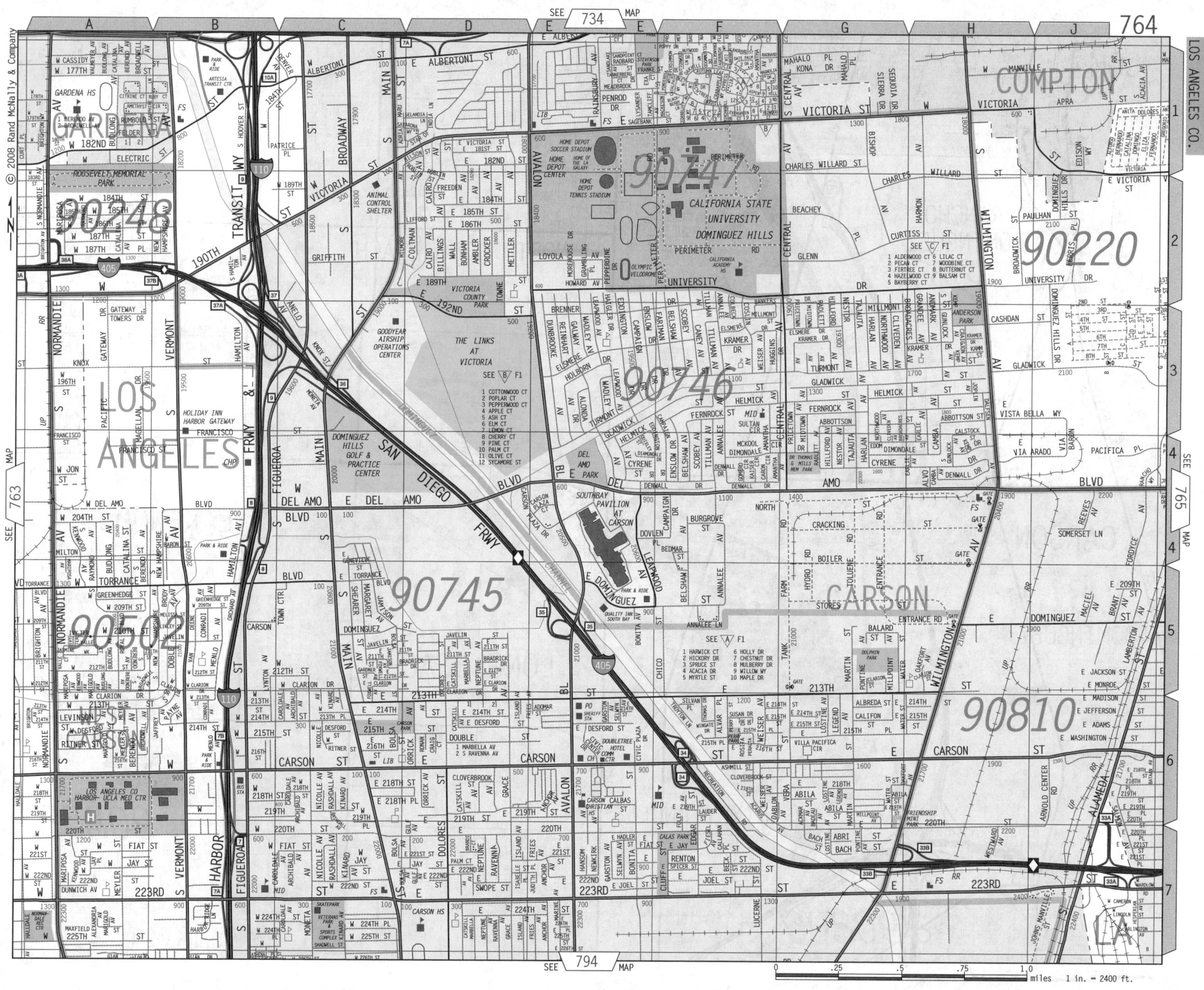
SEE 734 MAP
SEE 765 MAP
SEE 763 MAP
SEE 794 MAP
LOS ANGELES CO.
COMPTON
GARDENA
LOS ANGELES
CARSON
WEST CARSON
LA
90248
90747
90220
90746
90745
90502
90810
CALIFORNIA STATE UNIVERSITY DOMINGUEZ HILLS
HOME DEPOT CENTER
HOME DEPOT SOCCER STADIUM
HOME DEPOT TENNIS STADIUM
OLYMPIC VELODROME
CALIFORNIA ACADEMY HS
ROOSEVELT MEMORIAL PARK
GARDENA HS
ARTESIA TRANSIT CTR
ANIMAL CONTROL SHELTER
VICTORIA COUNTY PARK
GOODYEAR AIRSHIP OPERATIONS CENTER
THE LINKS AT VICTORIA
DOMINGUEZ HILLS GOLF & PRACTICE CENTER
HOLIDAY INN HARBOR GATEWAY
DEL AMO PARK
SOUTHBAY PAVILION AT CARSON
ANDERSON PARK
DOLPHIN PARK
FRIENDSHIP MINI PARK
LOS ANGELES CO HARBOR - UCLA MED CTR
CARSON HS
VETERANS PARK & SPORTS COMPLEX
SKATEPARK
CARSON PARK
DOUBLETREE HOTEL
QUALITY INN SOUTH BAY
CARSON CALBAS CHRISTIAN HS
CALAS PARK
DR THOMAS G MILLS MEM PARK
SAN DIEGO FRWY
HARBOR FRWY
TRANSIT WY
DOMINGUEZ CHANNEL
VICTORIA ST
ALBERTONI ST
190TH ST
UNIVERSITY DR
DEL AMO BLVD
TORRANCE BLVD
CARSON ST
223RD ST
DOMINGUEZ ST
WILMINGTON AV
AVALON BL
MAIN ST
FIGUEROA ST
VERMONT AV
NORMANDIE AV
ALAMEDA ST
CENTRAL AV
SEE B F1
1 COTTONWOOD CT
2 POPLAR CT
3 PEPPERWOOD CT
4 APPLE CT
5 ASH CT
6 ELM CT
7 LEMON CT
8 CHERRY CT
9 PINE CT
10 PALM CT
11 OLIVE CT
12 SYCAMORE ST
SEE C F1
1 ALDERWOOD CT
2 PECAN CT
3 FIRTREE CT
4 HAZELWOOD CT
5 BAYBERRY CT
6 LILAC CT
7 WOODBINE CT
8 BUTTERNUT CT
9 BALSAM CT
SEE A F1
1 HARWICK CT
2 HICKORY DR
3 SPRUCE ST
4 ACACIA DR
5 MYRTLE ST
6 HOLLY DR
7 CHESTNUT DR
8 MULBERRY DR
9 WILLOW WY
10 MAPLE DR
1 MARBELLA AV
2 S RAVENNA AV
0 .25 .5 .75 1.0 miles 1 in. = 2400 ft.

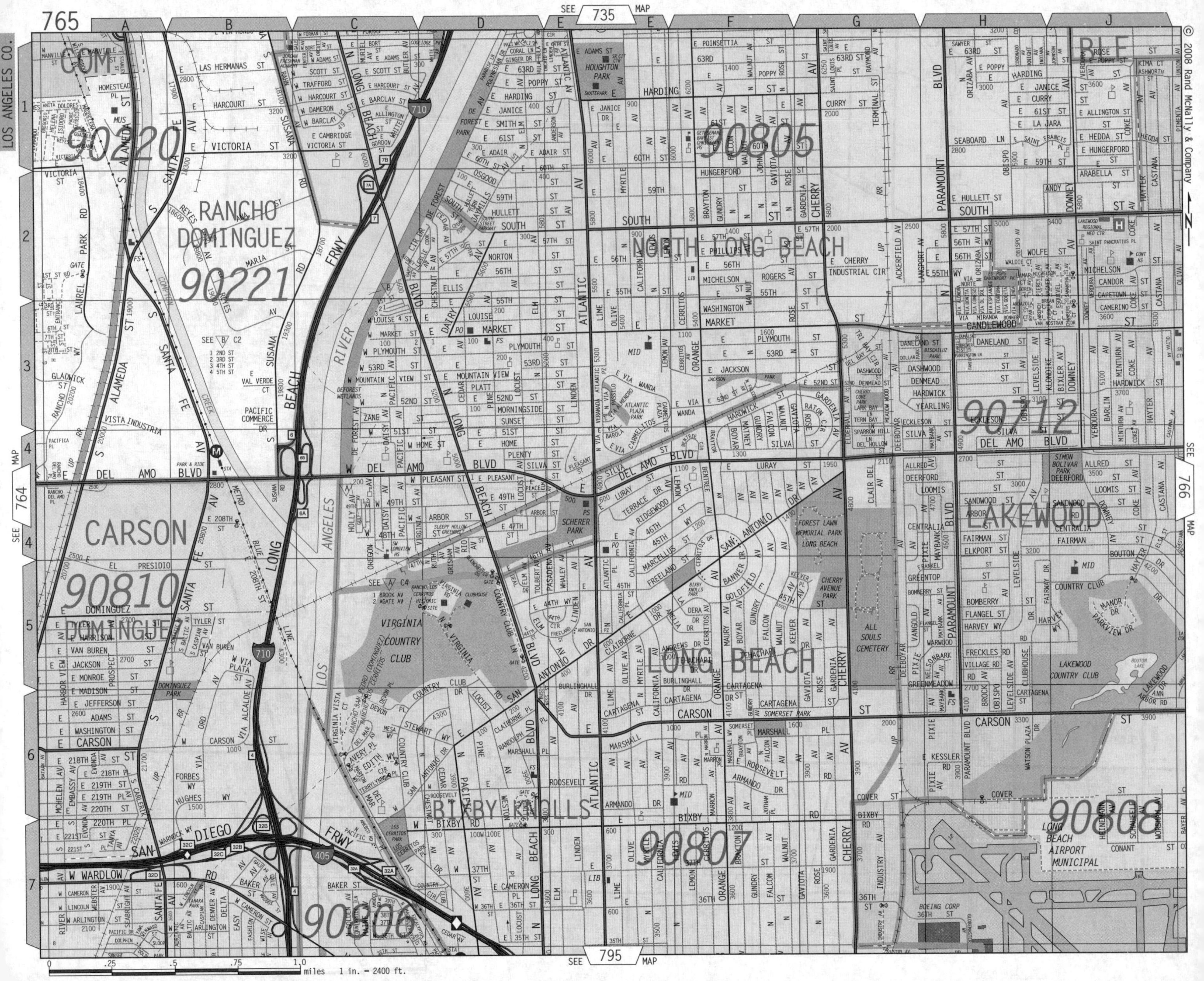
LOS ANGELES CO.
SEE 735 MAP
SEE 764 MAP
SEE 766 MAP
SEE 795 MAP
A
B
C
D
E
F
G
H
J
RANCHO DOMINGUEZ
90221
90220
CARSON
90810
DOMINGUEZ
NORTH LONG BEACH
90805
LONG BEACH
90807
90806
BIXBY KNOLLS
LAKEWOOD
90712
90808
LONG BEACH AIRPORT MUNICIPAL
VIRGINIA COUNTRY CLUB
LAKEWOOD COUNTRY CLUB
ALL SOULS CEMETERY
FOREST LAWN MEMORIAL PARK LONG BEACH
HOUGHTON PARK
SCHERER PARK
DEL AMO BLVD
CARSON ST
SAN DIEGO FRWY
LONG BEACH FRWY
W WARDLOW RD
0 .25 .5 .75 1.0 miles 1 in. = 2400 ft.

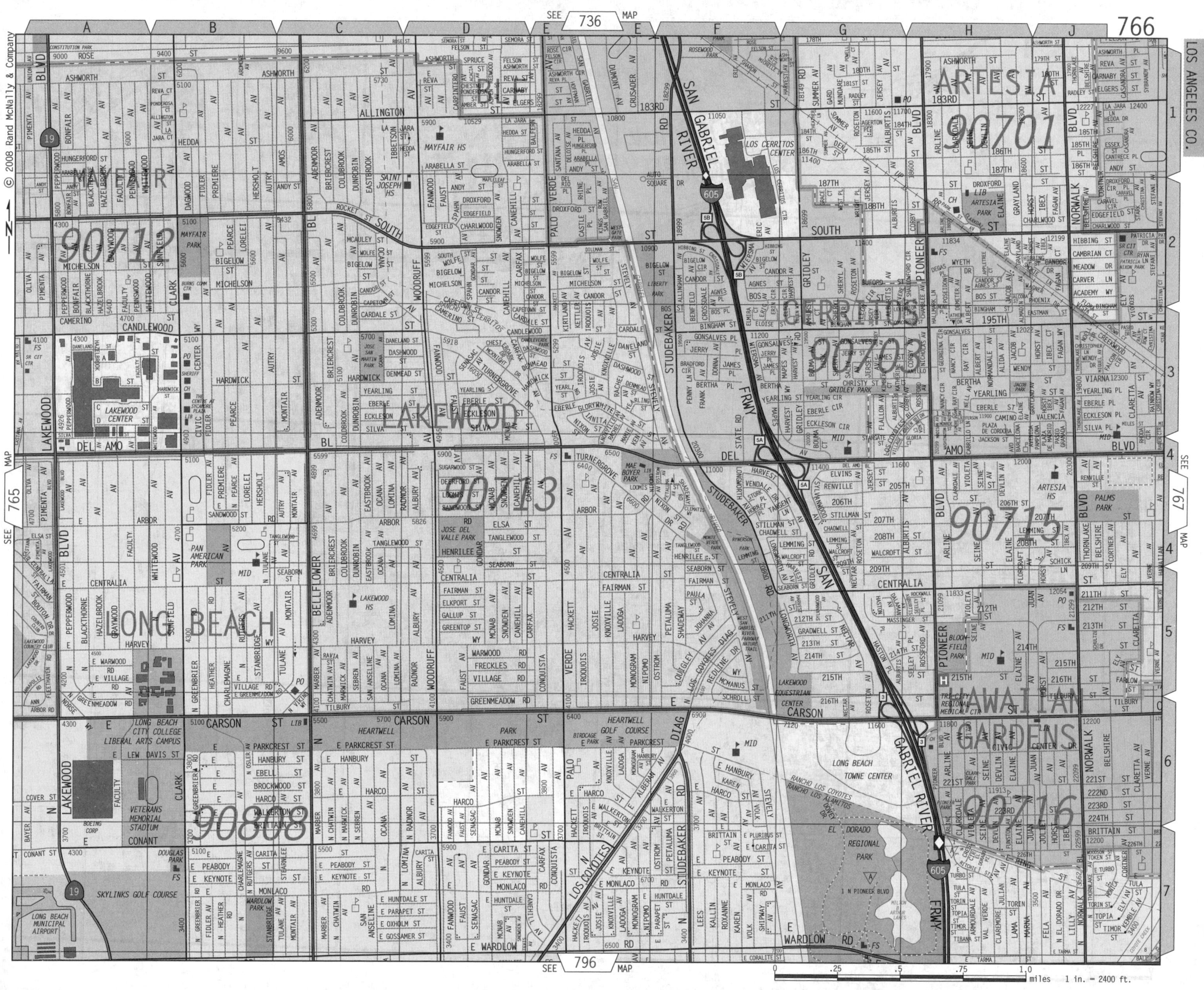

766
SEE 736 MAP
SEE 765 MAP
SEE 767 MAP
SEE 796 MAP
LOS ANGELES CO.
© 2008 Rand McNally & Company
ARTESIA
90701
MAYFAIR
90712
CERRITOS
90703
LAKEWOOD
90713
90715
LONG BEACH
HAWAIIAN GARDENS
90716
90808
LOS CERRITOS CENTER
SAN GABRIEL RIVER FRWY
LAKEWOOD CENTER
LONG BEACH CITY COLLEGE LIBERAL ARTS CAMPUS
VETERANS MEMORIAL STADIUM
SKYLINKS GOLF COURSE
LONG BEACH MUNICIPAL AIRPORT
HEARTWELL PARK
HEARTWELL GOLF COURSE
LONG BEACH TOWNE CENTER
EL DORADO REGIONAL PARK
TRI-CITY REGIONAL MEDICAL CTR
DEL AMO BLVD
CARSON ST
SOUTH ST
WARDLOW RD
LAKEWOOD BLVD
BELLFLOWER BLVD
STUDEBAKER RD
PIONEER BLVD
NORWALK BLVD
0 .25 .5 .75 1.0 miles 1 in. = 2400 ft.

SEE 737 MAP

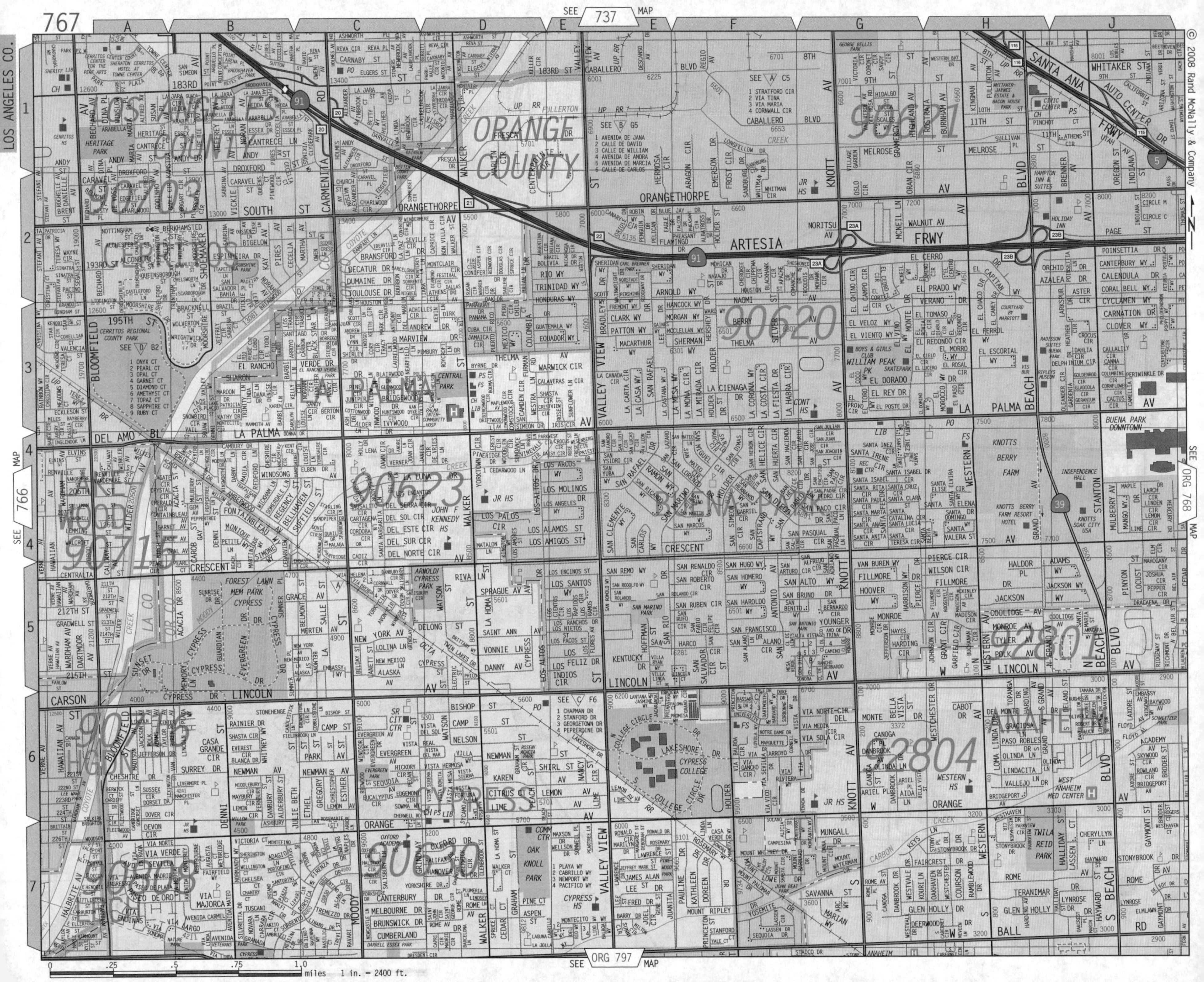
LOS ANGELES CO.
A
B
C
D
E
F
G
H
J
1
2
3
4
5
6
7
LOS ANGELES COUNTY
ORANGE COUNTY
CERRITOS
LA PALMA
BUENA PARK
CYPRESS
LAKEWOOD
HAWAIIAN GARDENS
ANAHEIM
90703
90621
90620
90623
90715
90716
90630
92801
92804
ARTESIA FRWY
SANTA ANA FRWY
91
5
39
ORANGETHORPE
ARTESIA
DEL AMO
LA PALMA
CRESCENT
LINCOLN
ORANGE
BALL
BLOOMFIELD
CARMENITA RD
WALKER
VALLEY VIEW
KNOTT AV
BEACH BLVD
WESTERN AV
MOODY
DENNI
CERRITOS REGIONAL COUNTY PARK
HERITAGE PARK
FOREST LAWN MEM PARK CYPRESS
CENTRAL PARK
ARNOLD/ CYPRESS PARK
OAK KNOLL PARK
TWILA REID PARK
KNOTTS BERRY FARM
INDEPENDENCE HALL
KNOTTS BERRY FARM RESORT HOTEL
KNOTTS SOAK CITY USA
BUENA PARK DOWNTOWN
CYPRESS COLLEGE
LAKESHORE
COLLEGE CIRCLE
JOHN F KENNEDY HS
CYPRESS HS
WESTERN HS
WEST ANAHEIM MED CENTER
LA PALMA INTER-COMMUNITY HOSP
COYOTE CREEK
CARBON CREEK
FULLERTON
SEE 766 MAP
SEE ORG 768 MAP
SEE ORG 797 MAP
0 .25 .5 .75 1.0 miles 1 in. = 2400 ft.

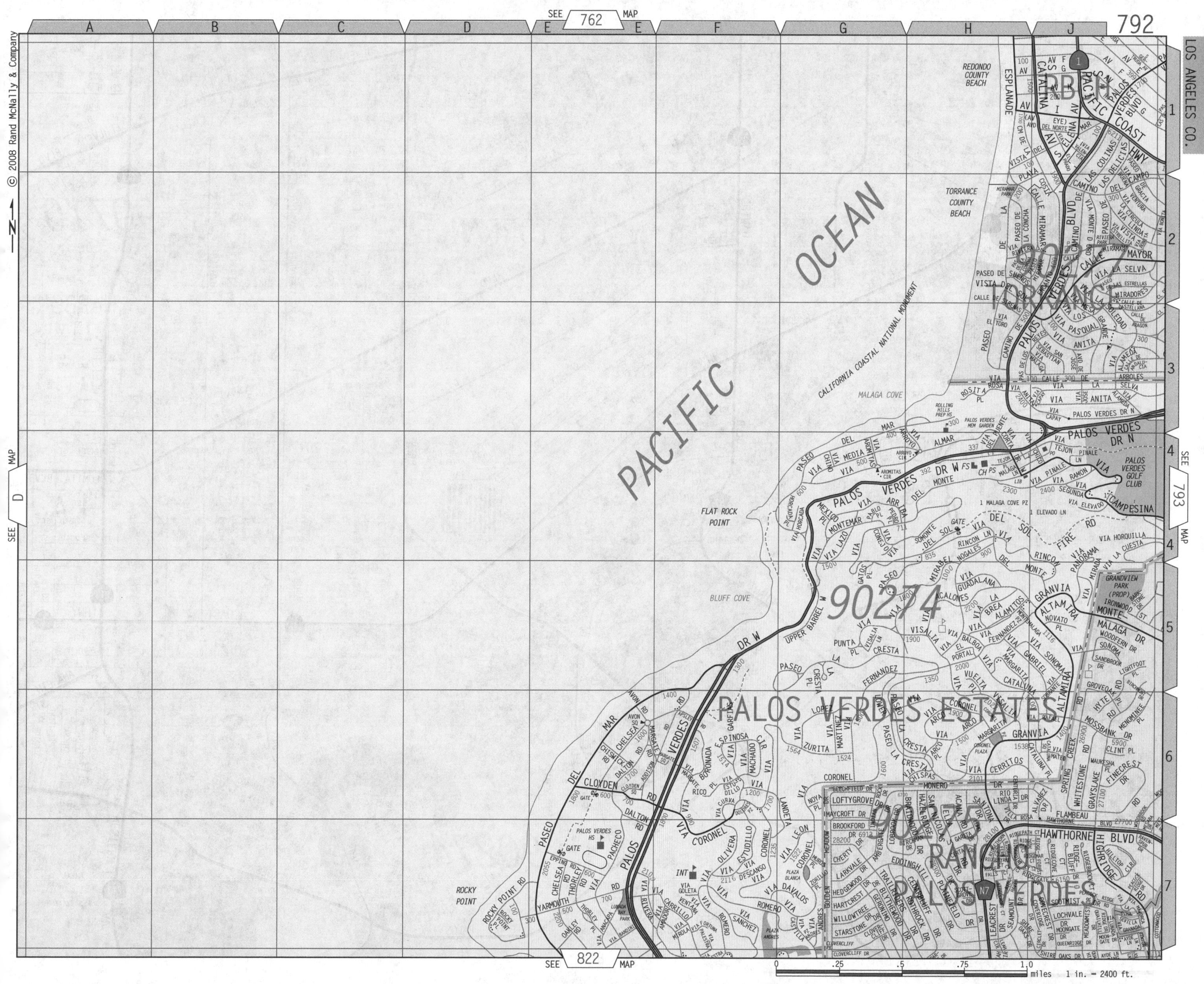

LOS ANGELES CO.
PACIFIC OCEAN
PALOS VERDES ESTATES
RANCHO PALOS VERDES
REDONDO BEACH
TORRANCE
90274
90275
REDONDO COUNTY BEACH
TORRANCE COUNTY BEACH
CALIFORNIA COASTAL NATIONAL MONUMENT
MALAGA COVE
FLAT ROCK POINT
BLUFF COVE
ROCKY POINT
PALOS VERDES GOLF CLUB
GRANDVIEW PARK (PROP)
PALOS VERDES HS
PACIFIC COAST HWY
PALOS VERDES DR N
PALOS VERDES DR W
HAWTHORNE BLVD
SEE 762 MAP
SEE 793 MAP
SEE 822 MAP
SEE D MAP

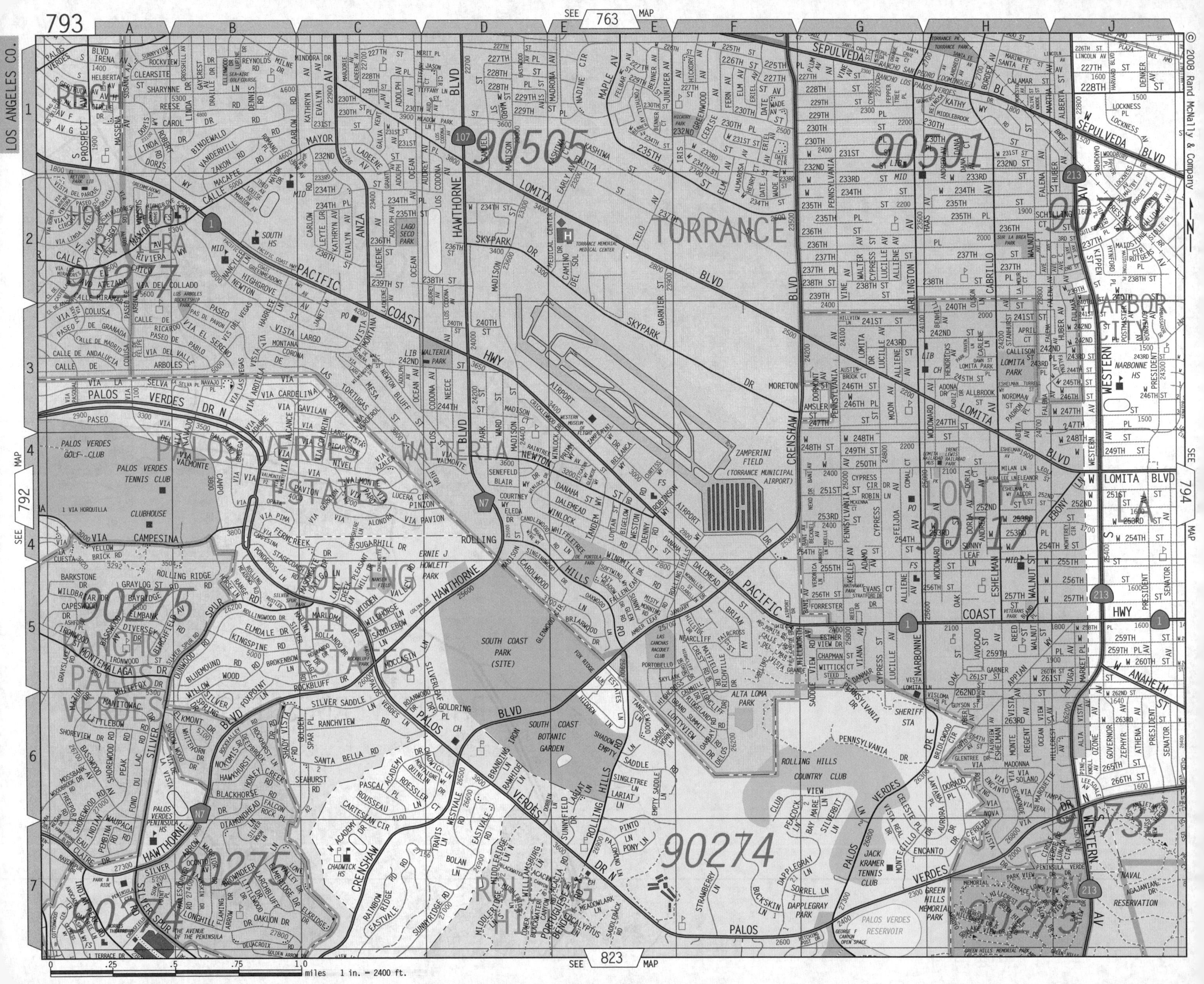

793
LOS ANGELES CO.
SEE 763 MAP
SEE 823 MAP
SEE 792 MAP
SEE 794 MAP
A B C D E F G H J
© 2008 Rand McNally & Company
90505
90501
90710
90277
90275
90717
90274
90732
TORRANCE
HOLLYWOOD RIVIERA
PALOS VERDES ESTATES
WALTERIA
ROLLING HILLS ESTATES
RANCHO PALOS VERDES
ROLLING HILLS
LOMITA
HARBOR CITY
LA
SEPULVEDA BLVD
PACIFIC COAST HWY
HAWTHORNE BLVD
CRENSHAW BLVD
LOMITA BLVD
PALOS VERDES DR N
WESTERN AV
NARBONNE AV
ANAHEIM ST
ZAMPERINI FIELD (TORRANCE MUNICIPAL AIRPORT)
TORRANCE MEMORIAL MEDICAL CENTER
PALOS VERDES GOLF CLUB
PALOS VERDES TENNIS CLUB
CLUBHOUSE
SOUTH COAST PARK (SITE)
SOUTH COAST BOTANIC GARDEN
ROLLING HILLS COUNTRY CLUB
ALTA LOMA PARK
ERNIE J HOWLETT PARK
WALTERIA PARK
LAGO SECO PARK
LOMITA PARK
SHERIFF STA
JACK KRAMER TENNIS CLUB
GREEN HILLS MEMORIAL PARK
PALOS VERDES RESERVOIR
NAVAL AGAJANIAN RESERVATION
DAPPLEGRAY PARK
PALOS VERDES PENINSULA HS
CHADWICK HS
SOUTH HS
NARBONNE HS
0 .25 .5 .75 1.0 miles 1 in. = 2400 ft.

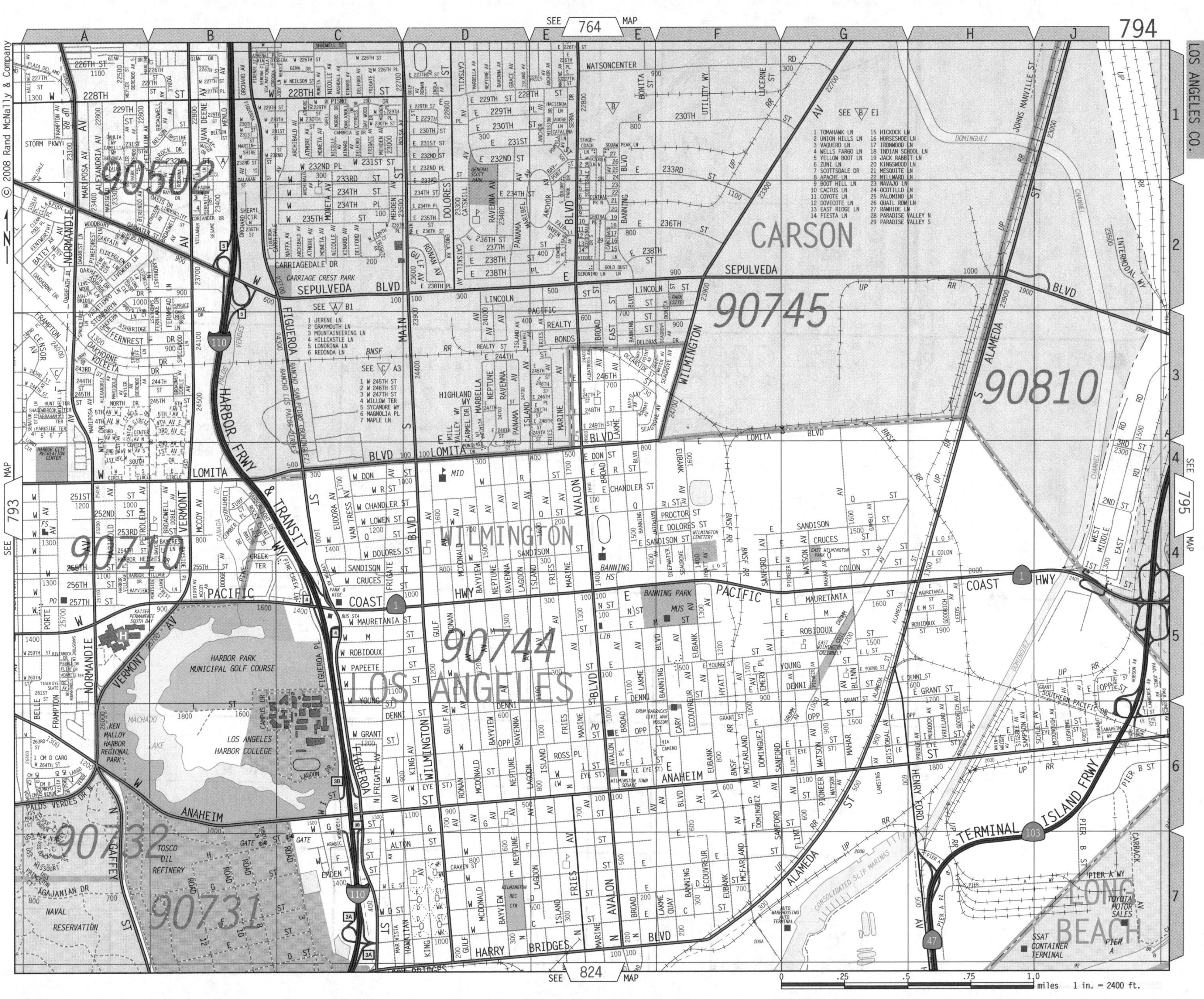
SEE 764 MAP
SEE 793 MAP
SEE 795 MAP
SEE 824 MAP
A
B
C
D
E
F
G
H
J
1
2
3
4
5
6
7
CARSON
WILMINGTON
LOS ANGELES
LONG BEACH
90502
90745
90810
90710
90744
90732
90731
HARBOR FRWY
HARBOR FRWY & TRANSIT WY
SEPULVEDA BLVD
LOMITA BLVD
PACIFIC COAST HWY
ANAHEIM
HARRY BRIDGES BLVD
TERMINAL ISLAND FRWY
ALAMEDA ST
FIGUEROA
NORMANDIE AV
VERMONT AV
WILMINGTON
AVALON BLVD
MAIN ST
GAFFEY ST
HENRY FORD AV
228TH ST
BANNING PARK
HARBOR PARK MUNICIPAL GOLF COURSE
LOS ANGELES HARBOR COLLEGE
KEN MALLOY HARBOR REGIONAL PARK
MACHADO LAKE
TOSCO OIL REFINERY
NAVAL RESERVATION
CARRIAGE CREST PARK
HARBOR CITY RECREATION CENTER
WILMINGTON REC CTR
DRUM BARRACKS CIVIL WAR MUSEUM
WILMINGTON CEMETERY
EAST WILMINGTON PARK
EAST WILMINGTON GREENBELT
CONSOLIDATED SLIP MARINAS
AUTO WAREHOUSING AUTO TERMINAL
TOYOTA MOTOR SALES
SSAT CONTAINER TERMINAL
KAISER PERMANENTE SOUTH BAY
DOMINGUEZ CHANNEL
0 .25 .5 .75 1.0 miles 1 in. = 2400 ft.

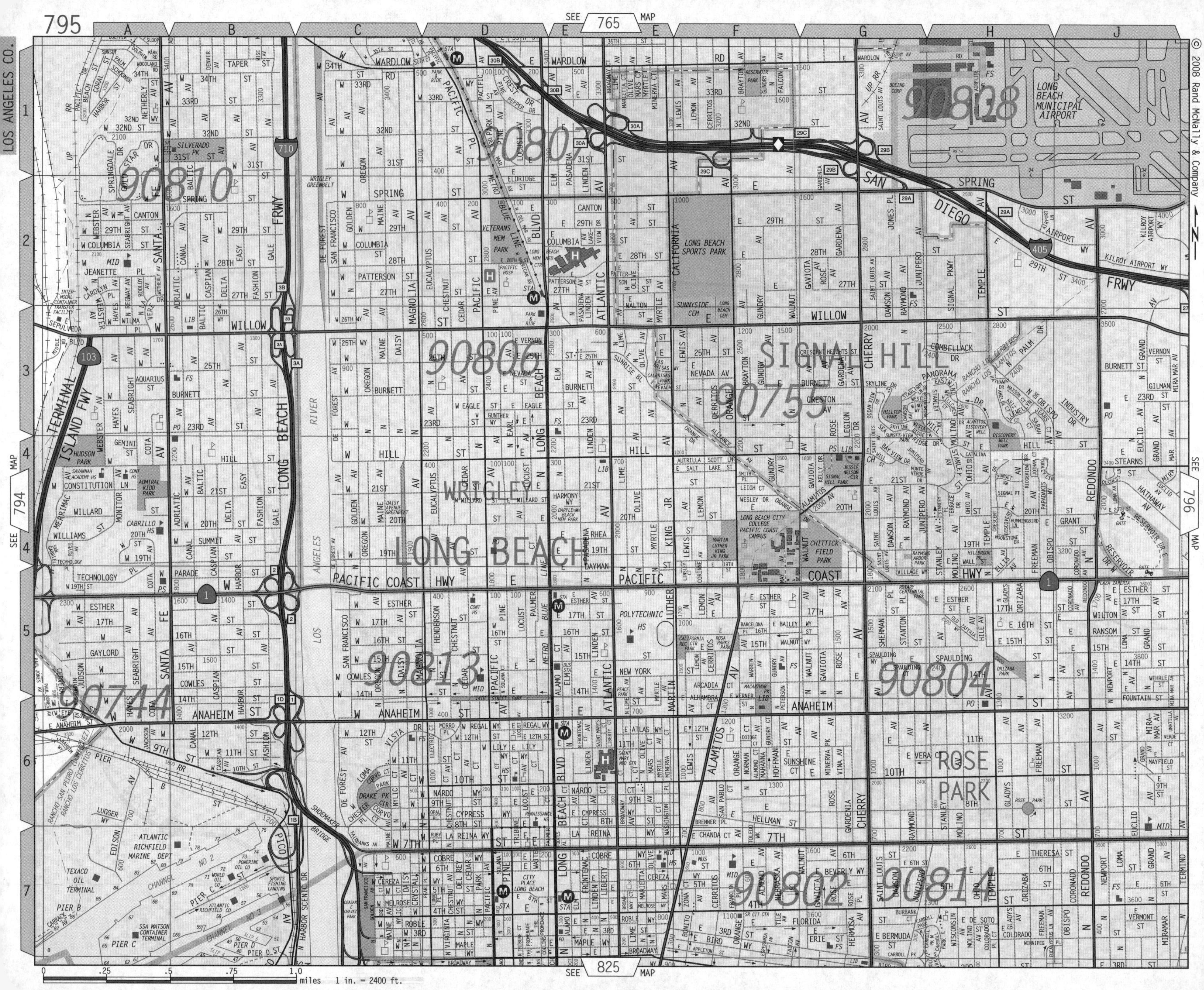

LOS ANGELES CO.
SEE 765 MAP
SEE 825 MAP
SEE 794 MAP
SEE 796 MAP
A
B
C
D
E
F
G
H
J
1
2
3
4
5
6
7
LONG BEACH
SIGNAL HILL
WRIGLEY
ROSE PARK
90810
90807
90808
90806
90755
90813
90744
90804
90802
90814
LONG BEACH MUNICIPAL AIRPORT
LONG BEACH SPORTS PARK
SUNNYSIDE CEM
LONG BEACH CITY COLLEGE PACIFIC COAST CAMPUS
CHITTICK FIELD PARK
HUDSON PARK
ADMIRAL KIDD PARK
SILVERADO PK
VETERANS MEM PARK
POLYTECHNIC HS
CABRILLO HS
WRIGLEY GREENBELT
DRAKE PK
CITY PLACE LONG BEACH
ATLANTIC RICHFIELD MARINE DEPT
TEXACO OIL TERMINAL
SSA MATSON CONTAINER TERMINAL
PIER B
PIER C
PIER D
CHANNEL NO 2
CHANNEL NO 3
SHOEMAKER BRIDGE
LONG BEACH FRWY
SAN DIEGO FRWY
TERMINAL ISLAND FWY
PACIFIC COAST HWY
WILLOW
WARDLOW
SPRING
ANAHEIM
ATLANTIC
CHERRY
REDONDO
LOS ANGELES RIVER
0 .25 .5 .75 1.0 miles 1 in. = 2400 ft.

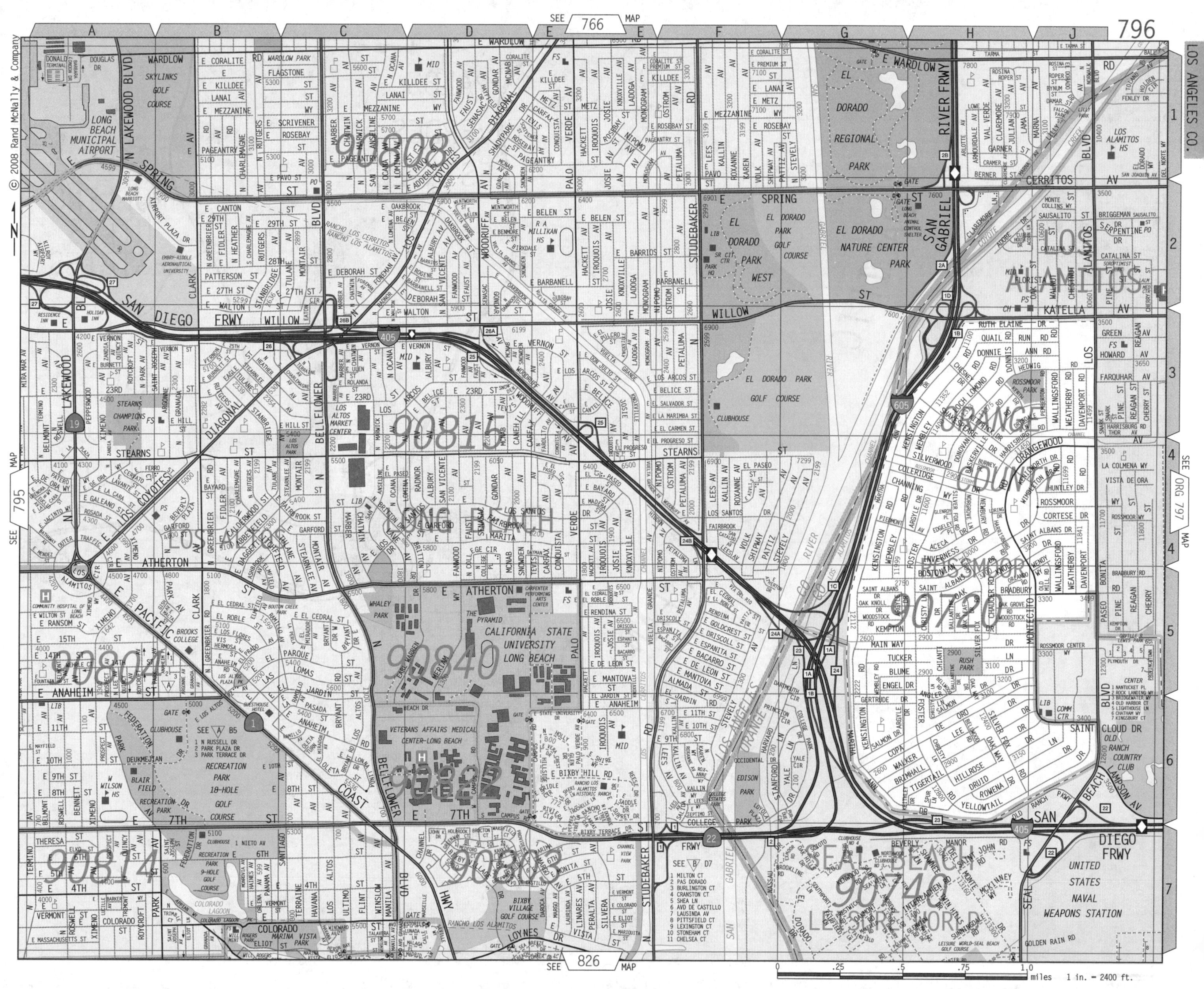

SEE 766 MAP
796
LOS ANGELES CO.
© 2008 Rand McNally & Company
A
B
C
D
E
F
G
H
J
1
2
3
4
5
6
7
LONG BEACH MUNICIPAL AIRPORT
SKYLINKS GOLF COURSE
N LAKEWOOD BLVD
WARDLOW
E WARDLOW
E WARDLOW RD
SPRING
E SPRING
CERRITOS AV
SAN DIEGO FRWY
WILLOW
WILLOW ST
KATELLA AV
90808
90815
90840
90804
90814
90803
90720
90740
EL DORADO REGIONAL PARK
EL DORADO NATURE CENTER PARK
EL DORADO PARK WEST
EL DORADO PARK GOLF COURSE
EL DORADO PARK GOLF COURSE
CLUBHOUSE
RIVER FRWY
SAN GABRIEL
SAN GABRIEL RIVER
LOS ALAMITOS
LOS ALAMITOS HS
ORANGE COUNTY
ROSSMOOR
ROSSMOOR PARK
RUSH PARK
STEARNS
STEARNS CHAMPIONS PARK
LONG BEACH
LOS ALTOS
LOS ALTOS MARKET CENTER
BELLFLOWER
ATHERTON
WHALEY PARK
CALIFORNIA STATE UNIVERSITY LONG BEACH
THE PYRAMID
CARPENTER PERFORMING ARTS CENTER
VETERANS AFFAIRS MEDICAL CENTER-LONG BEACH
COMMUNITY HOSPITAL OF LONG BEACH
BROOKS COLLEGE
PACIFIC COAST HWY
FEDERATION
RECREATION PARK 18-HOLE GOLF COURSE
RECREATION PARK 9-HOLE GOLF COURSE
BLAIR FIELD
W WILSON HS
RANCHO LOS ALAMITOS HISTORIC RANCH
BIXBY HILL RD
BIXBY VILLAGE GOLF COURSE
COLORADO LAGOON
MARINA VISTA PARK
EDISON PARK
STUDEBAKER RD
COLLEGE PARK
SEAL BEACH
LEISURE WORLD
LEISURE WORLD-SEAL BEACH GOLF COURSE
UNITED STATES NAVAL WEAPONS STATION
SEAL BEACH BLVD
DIEGO FRWY
OLD RANCH COUNTRY CLUB
LAMPSON AV
SEE 795 MAP
SEE ORG 797 MAP
SEE 826 MAP
miles 1 in. = 2400 ft.

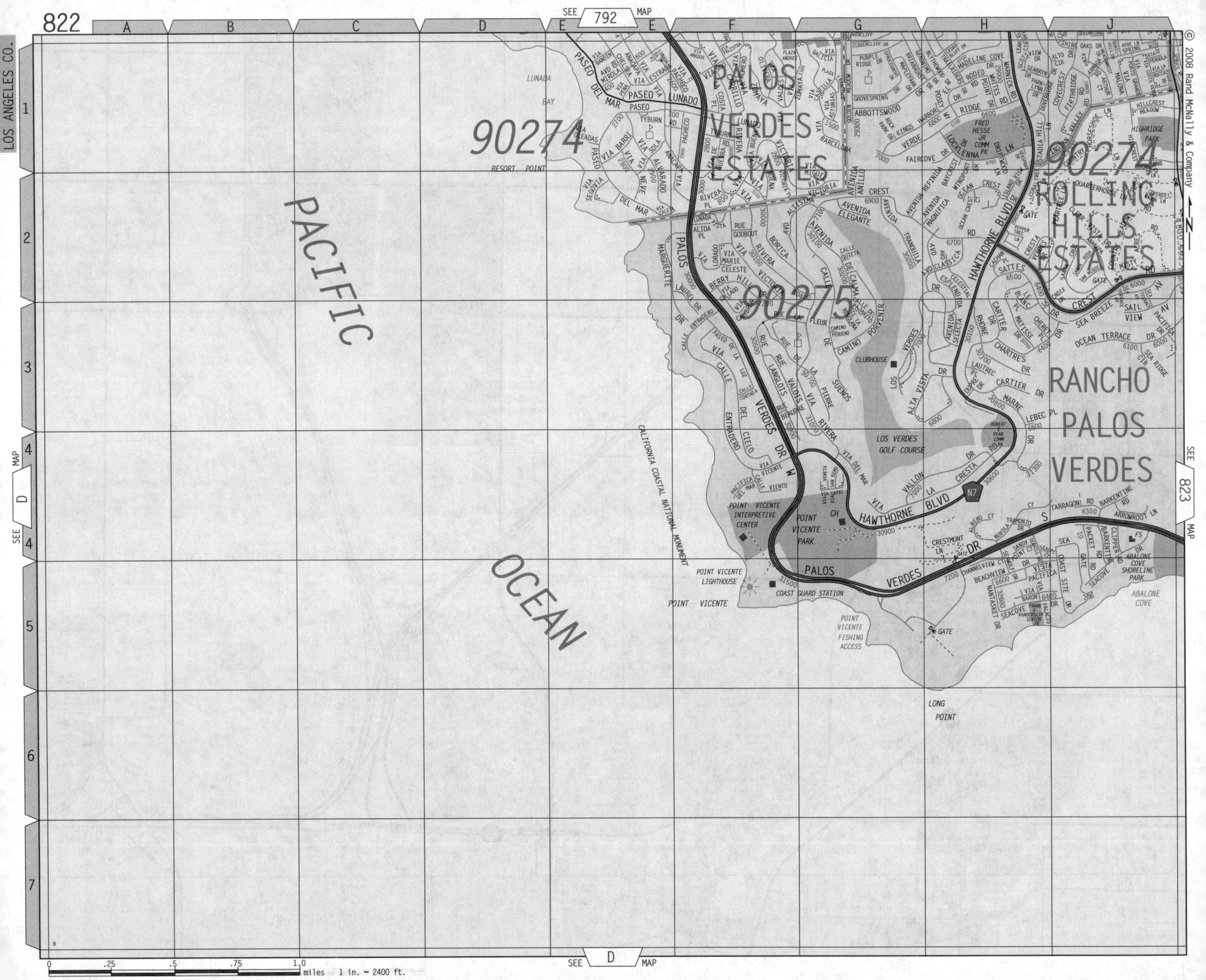

LOS ANGELES CO.
SEE 792 MAP
SEE 823 MAP
SEE D MAP
PACIFIC
OCEAN
90274
90275
PALOS VERDES ESTATES
ROLLING HILLS ESTATES
RANCHO PALOS VERDES
LUNADA BAY
RESORT POINT
PASEO DEL MAR
PASEO LUNADO
PALOS VERDES DR W
PALOS VERDES DR S
HAWTHORNE BLVD
CREST RD
LOS VERDES GOLF COURSE
CLUBHOUSE
FRED HESSE JR COMM PK
ROBERT RYAN COMM PK
HIGHRIDGE PARK
POINT VICENTE INTERPRETIVE CENTER
POINT VICENTE PARK
POINT VICENTE LIGHTHOUSE
COAST GUARD STATION
POINT VICENTE
POINT VICENTE FISHING ACCESS
CALIFORNIA COASTAL NATIONAL MONUMENT
ABALONE COVE SHORELINE PARK
ABALONE COVE
LONG POINT
GATE
N7
© 2008 Rand McNally & Company
0 .25 .5 .75 1.0 miles 1 in. = 2400 ft.

SEE D MAP

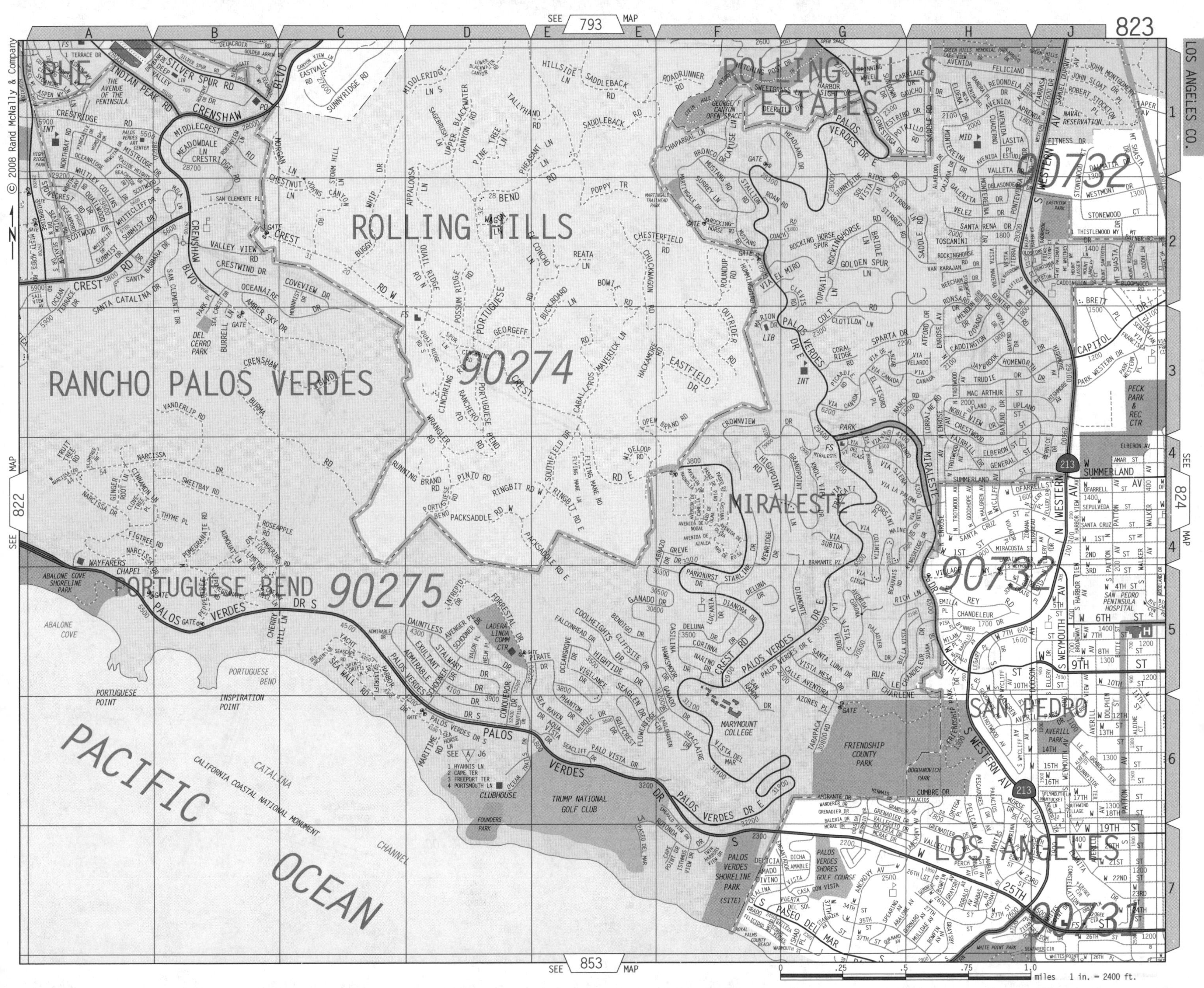
SEE 793 MAP
A
B
C
D
E
F
G
H
J
LOS ANGELES CO.
RHE
ROLLING HILLS ESTATES
ROLLING HILLS
RANCHO PALOS VERDES
90274
MIRALESTE
90732
PORTUGUESE BEND
90275
SAN PEDRO
LOS ANGELES
90731
PACIFIC OCEAN
CATALINA CHANNEL
CALIFORNIA COASTAL NATIONAL MONUMENT
ABALONE COVE
ABALONE COVE SHORELINE PARK
PORTUGUESE POINT
INSPIRATION POINT
PORTUGUESE BEND
WAYFARERS CHAPEL
DEL CERRO PARK
LADERA LINDA COMM CTR
TRUMP NATIONAL GOLF CLUB
FOUNDERS PARK
CLUBHOUSE
MARYMOUNT COLLEGE
FRIENDSHIP COUNTY PARK
BOGDANOVICH PARK
PALOS VERDES SHORELINE PARK (SITE)
PALOS VERDES SHORES GOLF COURSE
ROYAL PALMS COUNTY BEACH
WHITE POINT PARK
PECK PARK & REC CTR
SAN PEDRO PENINSULA HOSPITAL
AVERILL PARK
EASTVIEW PARK
NAVAL RESERVATION
GEORGE F CANYON OPEN SPACE
THE AVENUE OF THE PENINSULA
PALOS VERDES ART CENTER
CRENSHAW BLVD
CREST RD
SILVER SPUR RD
INDIAN PEAK RD
HAWTHORNE BLVD
PALOS VERDES DR S
PALOS VERDES DR E
PALOS VERDES DR N
MIRALESTE DR
S WESTERN AV
N WESTERN AV
PARK WESTERN DR
W 25TH ST
W SUMMERLAND AV
213
SEE 822 MAP
SEE 824 MAP
1
2
3
4
5
6
7
SEE 853 MAP
0 .25 .5 .75 1.0 miles 1 in. = 2400 ft.

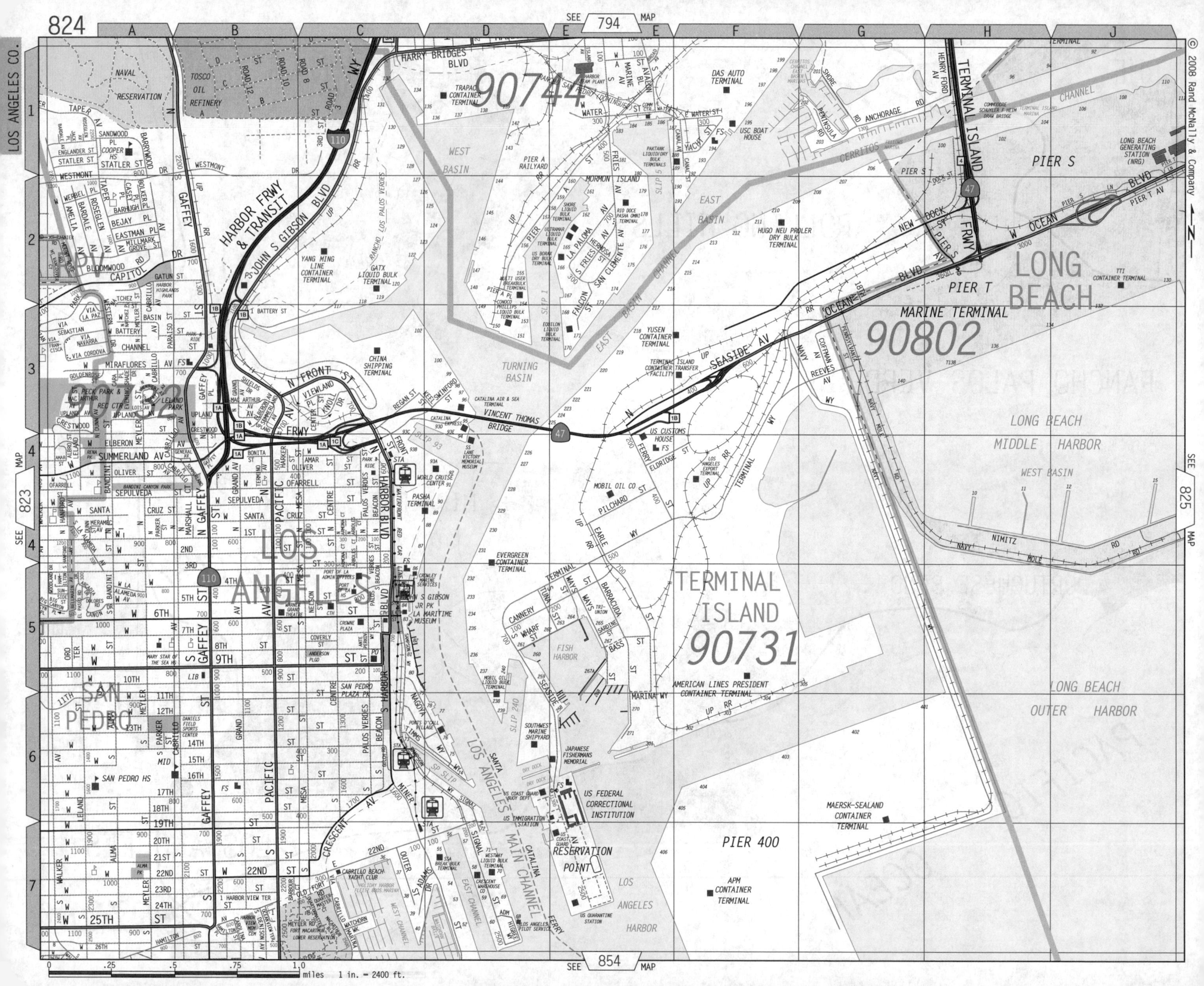

LOS ANGELES CO.
SEE 794 MAP
SEE 823 MAP
SEE 825 MAP
SEE 854 MAP
90744
90731
90802
90732
LOS ANGELES
SAN PEDRO
LONG BEACH
TERMINAL ISLAND
NAVAL RESERVATION
TOSCO OIL REFINERY
HARBOR FRWY & TRANSIT
JOHN S GIBSON BLVD
HARRY BRIDGES BLVD
TRAPAC CONTAINER TERMINAL
WEST BASIN
EAST BASIN
TURNING BASIN
PIER A RAILYARD
MORMON ISLAND
DAS AUTO TERMINAL
USC BOAT HOUSE
YANG MING LINE CONTAINER TERMINAL
GATX LIQUID BULK TERMINAL
CHINA SHIPPING TERMINAL
VINCENT THOMAS BRIDGE
CATALINA AIR & SEA TERMINAL
US CUSTOMS HOUSE
YUSEN CONTAINER TERMINAL
TERMINAL ISLAND CONTAINER TRANSFER FACILITY
HUGO NEU PROLER DRY BULK TERMINAL
MARINE TERMINAL
LONG BEACH GENERATING STATION (NRG)
PIER S
PIER T
TTI CONTAINER TERMINAL
LONG BEACH MIDDLE HARBOR
WEST BASIN
NIMITZ RD
NAVY MOLE RD
MOBIL OIL CO
WORLD CRUISE CENTER
PASHA TERMINAL
EVERGREEN CONTAINER TERMINAL
FISH HARBOR
AMERICAN LINES PRESIDENT CONTAINER TERMINAL
LONG BEACH OUTER HARBOR
LA MARITIME MUSEUM
PORTS O'CALL VILLAGE
SOUTHWEST MARINE SHIPYARD
JAPANESE FISHERMANS MEMORIAL
US FEDERAL CORRECTIONAL INSTITUTION
RESERVATION POINT
LOS ANGELES MAIN CHANNEL
EAST CHANNEL
WEST CHANNEL
LOS ANGELES HARBOR
PIER 400
MAERSK-SEALAND CONTAINER TERMINAL
APM CONTAINER TERMINAL
CABRILLO BEACH YACHT CLUB
SAN PEDRO HS
MARY STAR OF THE SEA HS
DANIELS FIELD SPORTS CENTER
SAN PEDRO PLAZA PK
JOHN S GIBSON JR PK
PECK PARK & REC CTR
GAFFEY ST
PACIFIC AV
HARBOR BLVD
SEASIDE AV
OCEAN BLVD
TERMINAL ISLAND FRWY
0 .25 .5 .75 1.0 miles 1 in. = 2400 ft.

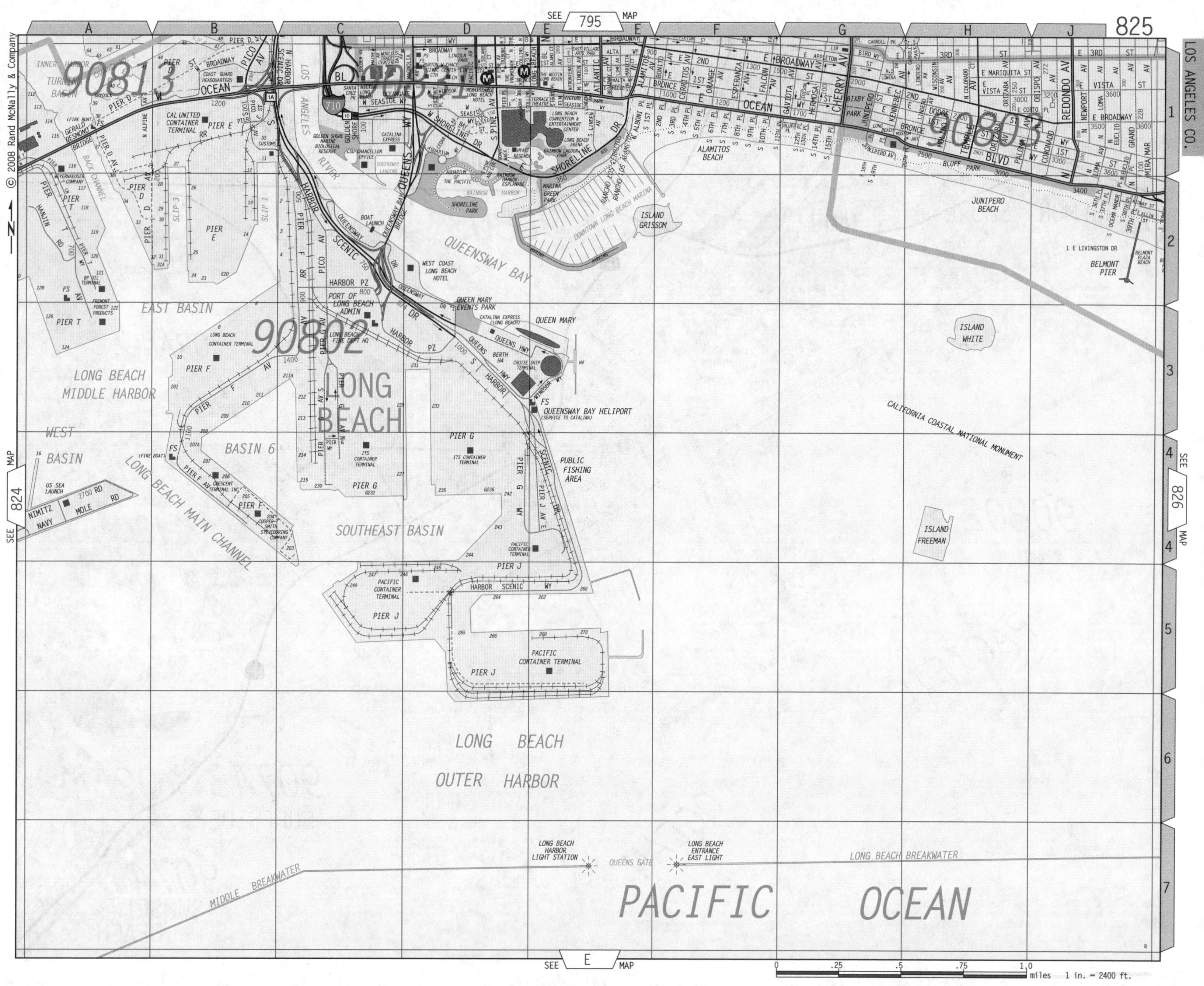

SEE 795 MAP
LOS ANGELES CO.
SEE 824 MAP
SEE 826 MAP
SEE E MAP
90813
90831
90802
90803
LONG BEACH
INNER HARBOR TURNING BASIN
OCEAN
BROADWAY
COAST GUARD HEADQUARTERS
GERALD DESMOND BRIDGE
CAL UNITED CONTAINER TERMINAL
PIER E
PIER D
PIER T
HANJIN
BACK CHANNEL
WEYERHAEUSER COMPANY
BP OIL TERMINAL
FREMONT FOREST PRODUCTS
EAST BASIN
LONG BEACH CONTAINER TERMINAL
PIER F
LONG BEACH MIDDLE HARBOR
WEST BASIN
US SEA LAUNCH
NIMITZ RD
NAVY MOLE RD
LONG BEACH MAIN CHANNEL
BASIN 6
CRESCENT TERMINAL INC.
COOPER-SMITH STEVEDORING COMPANY
SOUTHEAST BASIN
PIER G
ITS CONTAINER TERMINAL
PIER J
PACIFIC CONTAINER TERMINAL
HARBOR SCENIC WY
LOS ANGELES RIVER
GOLDEN SHORE MARINE BIOLOGICAL RESERVE
CSU CHANCELLOR OFFICE
CATALINA EXPRESS
AQUARIUM OF THE PACIFIC
SHORELINE PARK
RAINBOW HARBOR
LONG BEACH CONVENTION & ENTERTAINMENT CENTER
RENAISSANCE LONG BEACH HOTEL
HYATT REGENCY
WEST COAST LONG BEACH HOTEL
PORT OF LONG BEACH ADMIN
LONG BEACH FIRE DEPT HQ
QUEEN MARY EVENTS PARK
QUEEN MARY
CRUISE SHIP TERMINAL
QUEENSWAY BAY
QUEENSWAY BAY HELIPORT (SERVICE TO CATALINA)
PUBLIC FISHING AREA
MARINA GREEN PARK
DOWNTOWN LONG BEACH MARINA
ISLAND GRISSOM
ALAMITOS BEACH
SHORELINE DR
E BROADWAY
E OCEAN BLVD
CHERRY AV
JUNIPERO BEACH
BLUFF PARK
BELMONT PIER
1 E LIVINGSTON DR
ISLAND WHITE
ISLAND FREEMAN
CALIFORNIA COASTAL NATIONAL MONUMENT
LONG BEACH OUTER HARBOR
LONG BEACH HARBOR LIGHT STATION
QUEENS GATE
LONG BEACH ENTRANCE EAST LIGHT
LONG BEACH BREAKWATER
MIDDLE BREAKWATER
PACIFIC OCEAN
0 .25 .5 .75 1.0 miles 1 in. = 2400 ft.

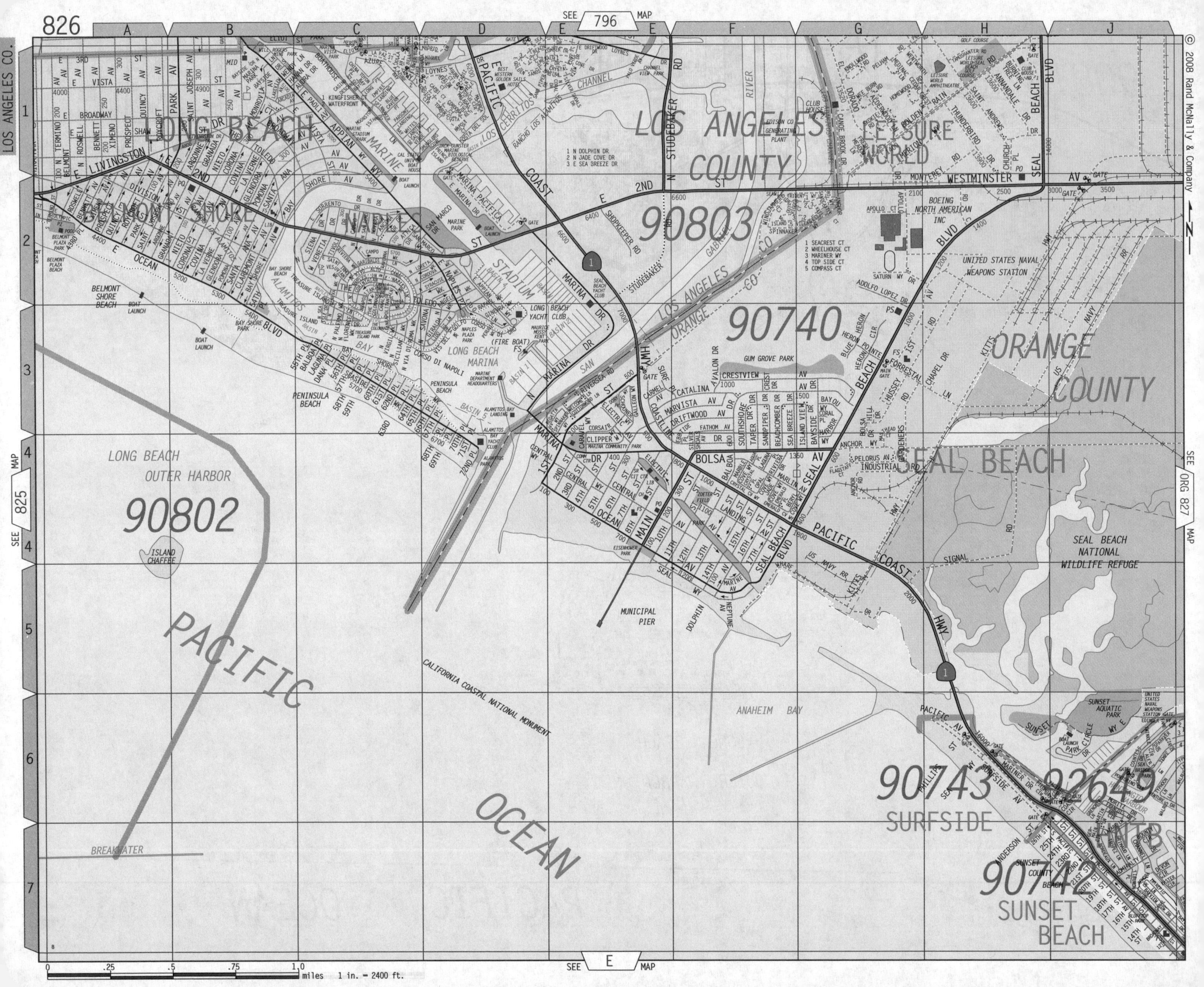

SEE 796 MAP
LOS ANGELES CO.
LONG BEACH
BELMONT SHORE
NAPLES
LOS ANGELES COUNTY
LEISURE WORLD
90803
90740
ORANGE COUNTY
SEAL BEACH
90802
LONG BEACH OUTER HARBOR
ISLAND CHAFFEE
PACIFIC OCEAN
SEAL BEACH NATIONAL WILDLIFE REFUGE
UNITED STATES NAVAL WEAPONS STATION
BOEING NORTH AMERICAN INC
GUM GROVE PARK
LONG BEACH MARINA
MUNICIPAL PIER
ANAHEIM BAY
CALIFORNIA COASTAL NATIONAL MONUMENT
SUNSET AQUATIC PARK
90743 SURFSIDE
92649
90742 SUNSET BEACH
BREAKWATER
SEE 825 MAP
SEE ORG 827 MAP
SEE E MAP
0 .25 .5 .75 1.0 miles 1 in. = 2400 ft.

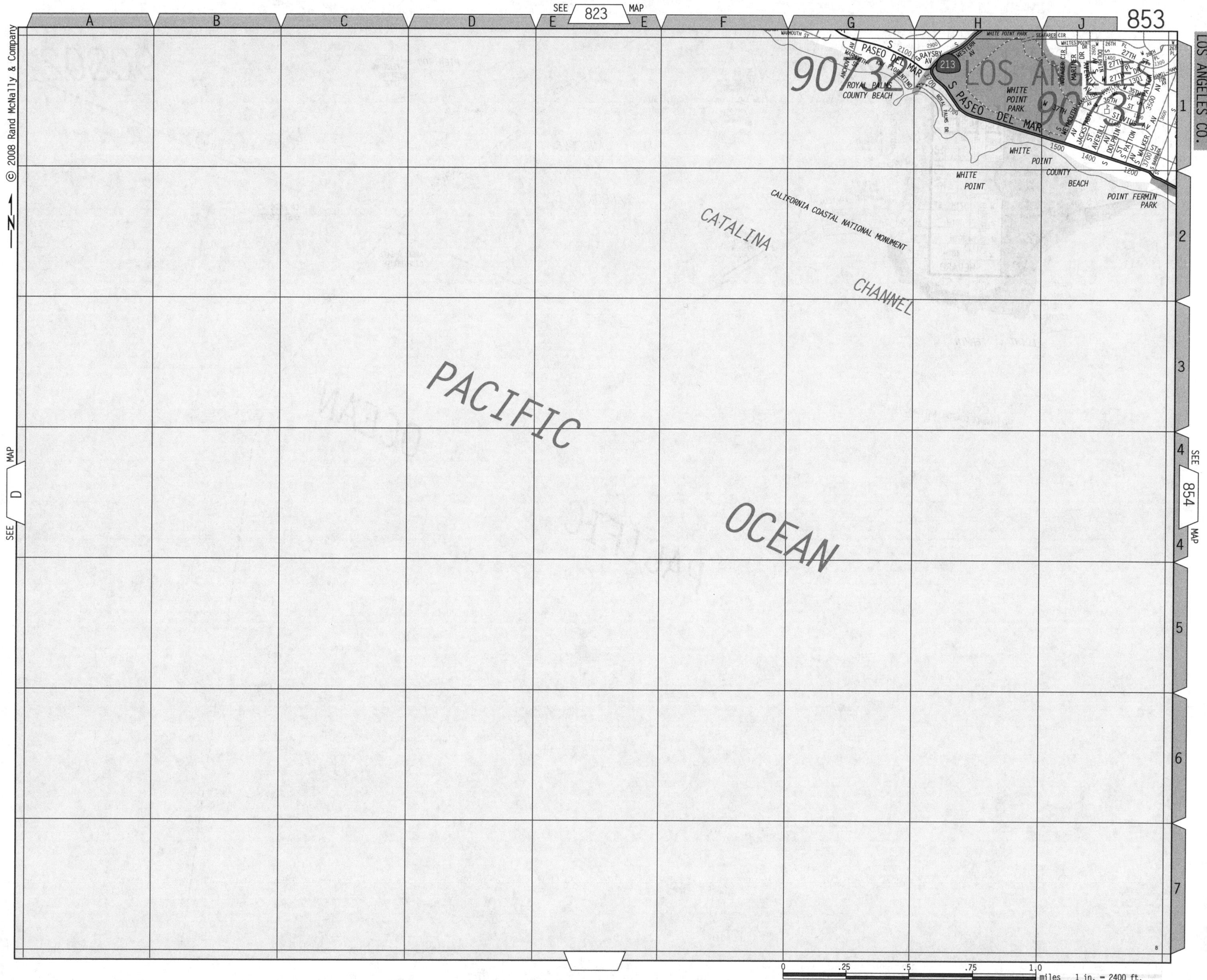
SEE 823 MAP
A
B
C
D
E
F
G
H
J
LOS ANGELES CO.
PASEO DEL MAR
S PASEO DEL MAR
ROYAL PALMS COUNTY BEACH
90732
LOS ANGELES
90731
WHITE POINT PARK
WHITE POINT
WHITE POINT COUNTY BEACH
POINT FERMIN PARK
CALIFORNIA COASTAL NATIONAL MONUMENT
CATALINA
CHANNEL
PACIFIC
OCEAN
SEE D MAP
SEE 854 MAP
1
2
3
4
5
6
7
miles 1 in. = 2400 ft.

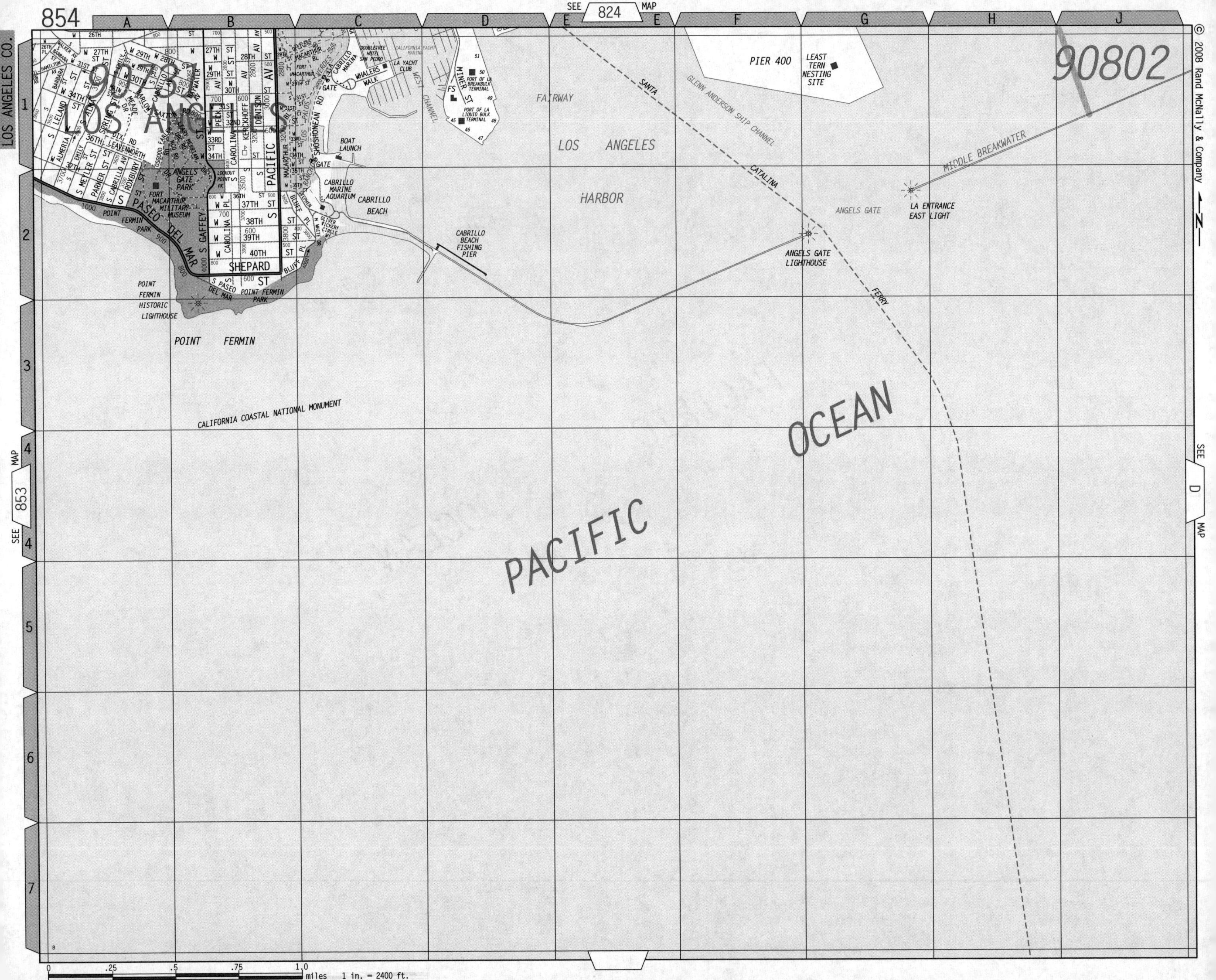
LOS ANGELES CO.
SEE 824 MAP
A
B
C
D
E
F
G
H
J
1
2
3
4
5
6
7
90802
90731
LOS ANGELES
ANGELS GATE PARK
FORT MACARTHUR MILITARY MUSEUM
POINT FERMIN PARK
PASEO DEL MAR
S GAFFEY
SHEPARD
PACIFIC AV
POINT FERMIN HISTORIC LIGHTHOUSE
POINT FERMIN
CABRILLO MARINE AQUARIUM
CABRILLO BEACH
BOAT LAUNCH
CABRILLO BEACH FISHING PIER
DOUBLETREE HOTEL SAN PEDRO
LA YACHT CLUB
WHALERS WALK
CABRILLO MARINA
WEST CHANNEL
MINER ST
PORT OF LA BREAKBULK TERMINAL
PORT OF LA LIQUID BULK TERMINAL
FAIRWAY
LOS ANGELES HARBOR
PIER 400
LEAST TERN NESTING SITE
GLENN ANDERSON SHIP CHANNEL
SANTA CATALINA FERRY
MIDDLE BREAKWATER
ANGELS GATE
ANGELS GATE LIGHTHOUSE
LA ENTRANCE EAST LIGHT
CALIFORNIA COASTAL NATIONAL MONUMENT
PACIFIC OCEAN
SEE 853 MAP
SEE D MAP
0 .25 .5 .75 1.0 miles 1 in. = 2400 ft.

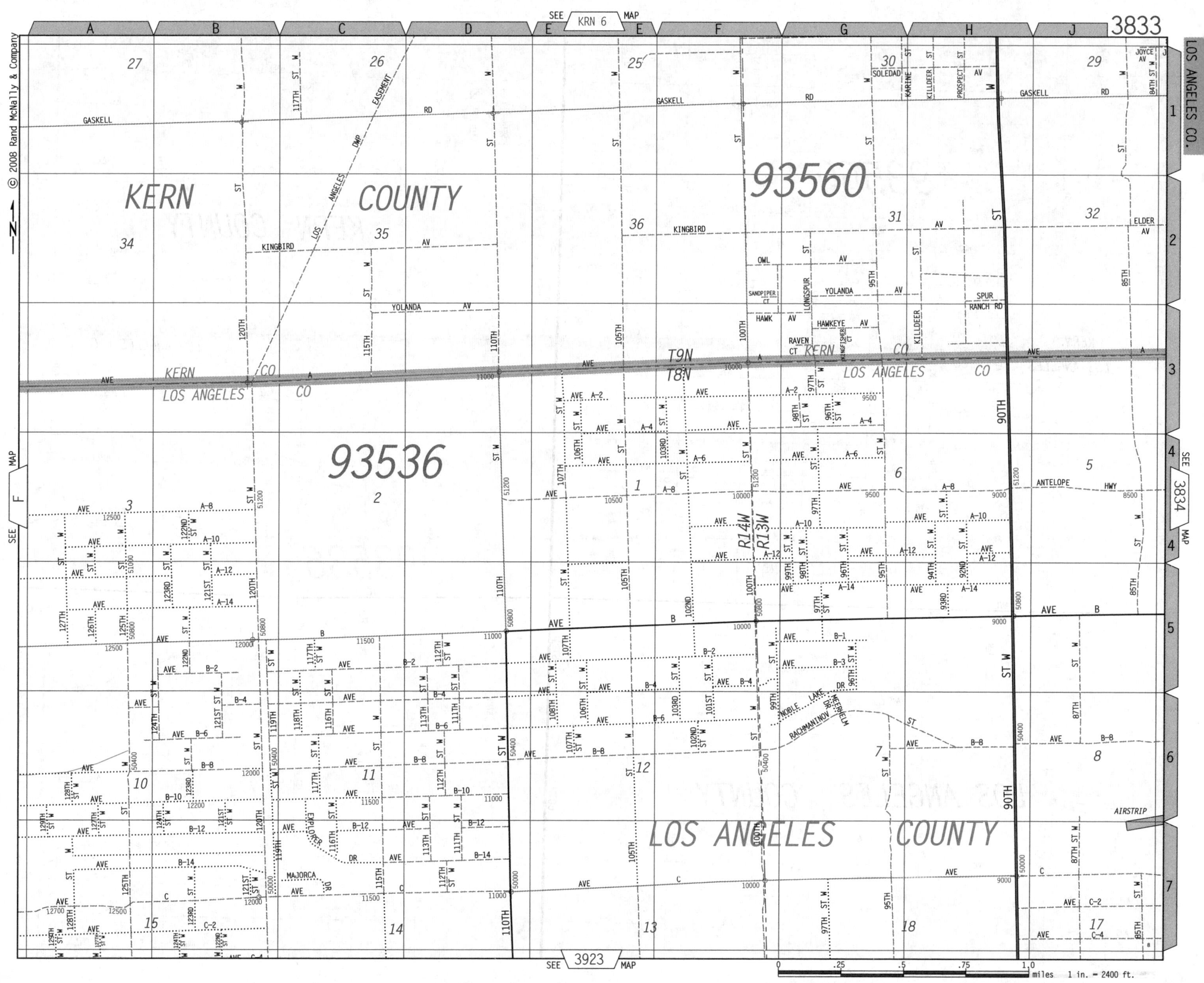
SEE KRN 6 MAP
KERN COUNTY
93560
93536
KERN CO
LOS ANGELES CO
LOS ANGELES COUNTY
LOS ANGELES CO.
T9N
T8N
R14W
R13W
GASKELL RD
KINGBIRD AV
YOLANDA AV
ANTELOPE HWY
AVE A
AVE B
AVE C
LOS ANGELES DWP EASEMENT
110TH ST W
100TH ST W
90TH ST W
AIRSTRIP
SEE F MAP
SEE 3834 MAP
SEE 3923 MAP
miles 1 in. = 2400 ft.

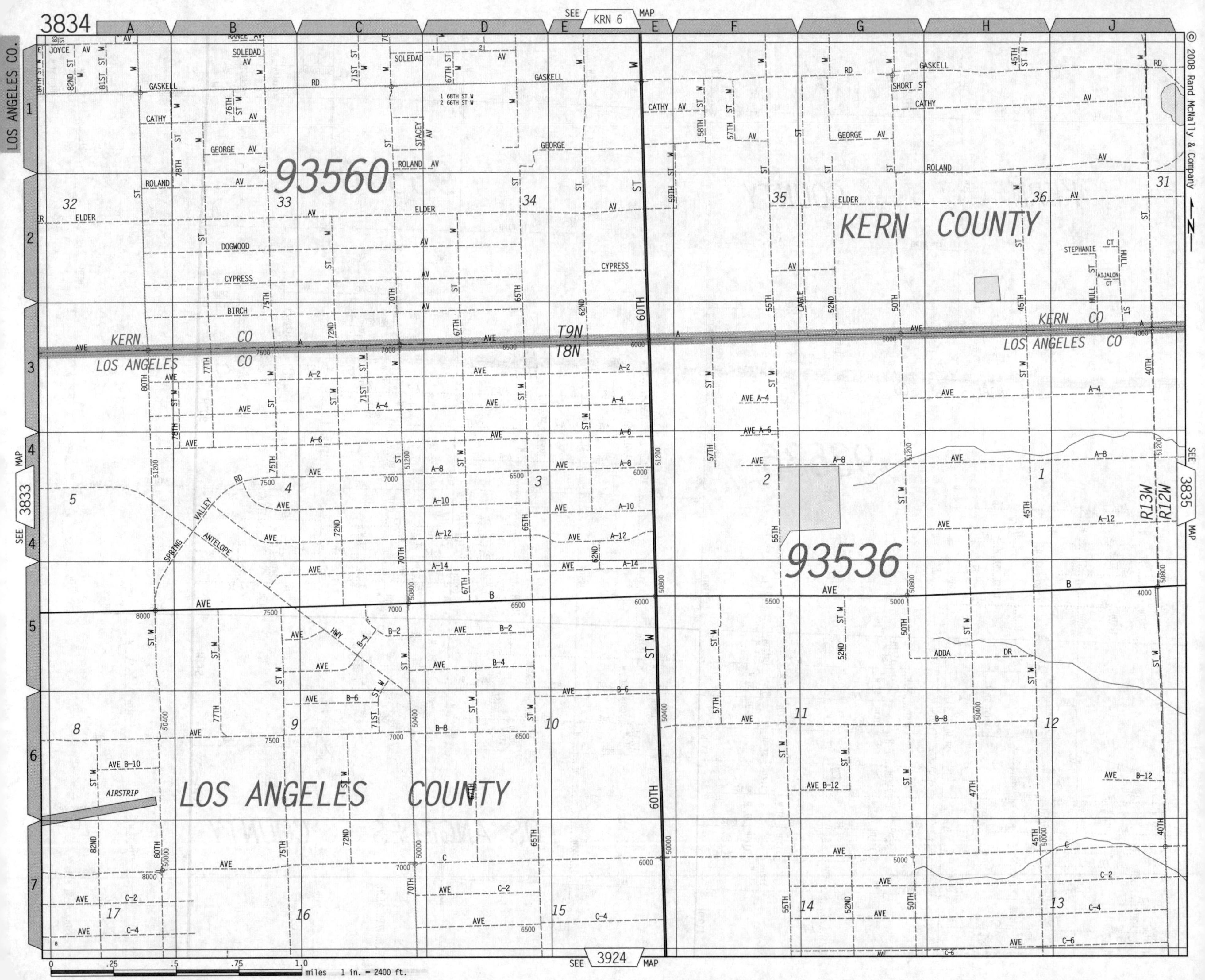

SEE KRN 6 MAP
LOS ANGELES CO.
93560
93536
KERN COUNTY
LOS ANGELES COUNTY
KERN CO
LOS ANGELES CO
T9N
T8N
R13W
R12W
SEE 3833 MAP
SEE 3835 MAP
SEE 3924 MAP
60TH ST W
GASKELL RD
CATHY AV
GEORGE AV
ROLAND AV
ELDER AV
DOGWOOD
CYPRESS
BIRCH
SOLEDAD AV
JOYCE AV
STACEY AV
SHORT ST
STEPHANIE CT
AIJALON CT
HULL ST
SPRING VALLEY RD
ANTELOPE HWY
ADDA DR
AIRSTRIP
AVE A
AVE B
AVE C
miles 1 in. = 2400 ft.

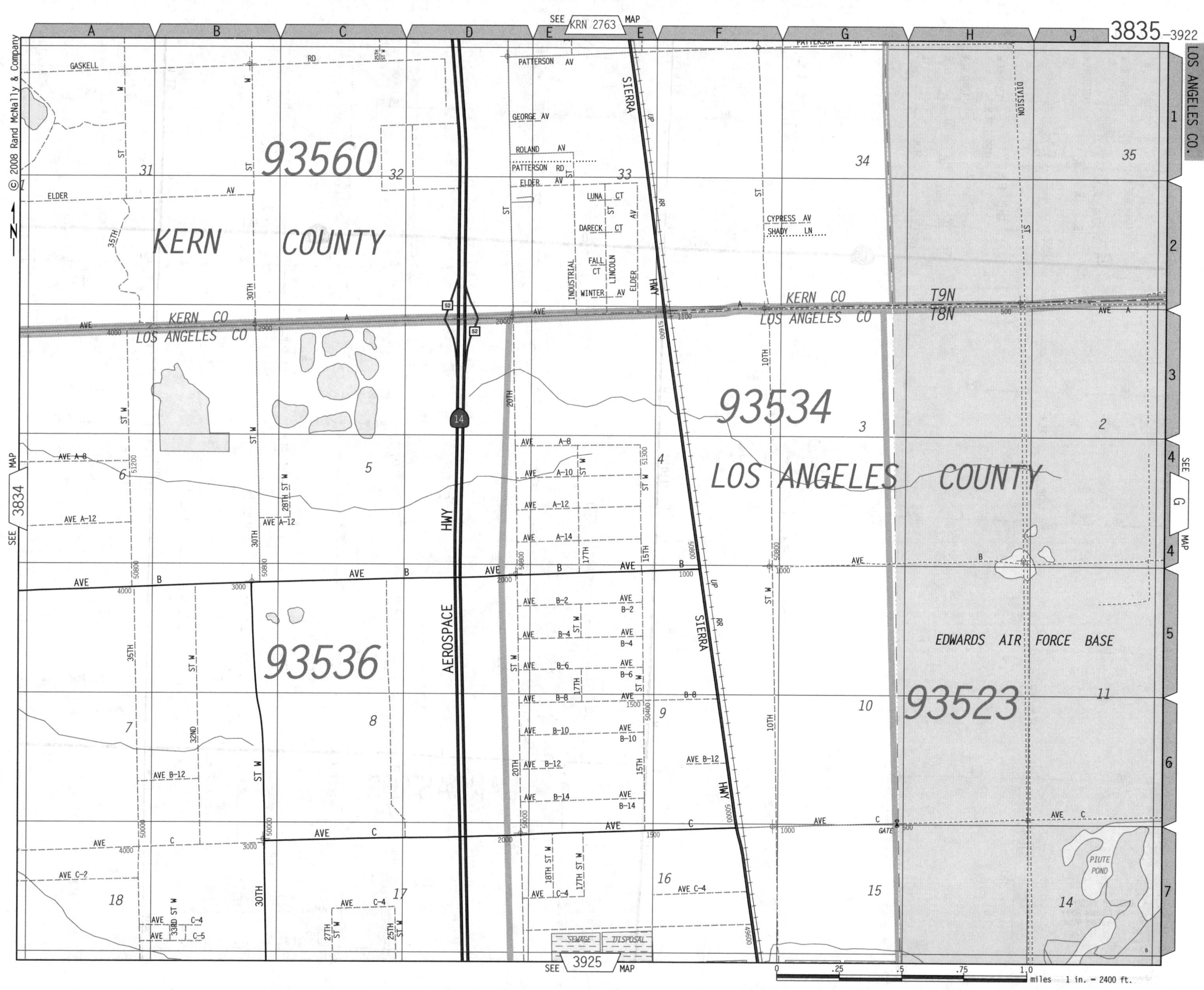

SEE KRN 2763 MAP
SEE 3834 MAP
SEE G MAP
SEE 3925 MAP
LOS ANGELES CO.
© 2008 Rand McNally & Company
KERN COUNTY
LOS ANGELES COUNTY
KERN CO
LOS ANGELES CO
T9N
T8N
93560
93534
93536
93523
EDWARDS AIR FORCE BASE
PIUTE POND
SEWAGE DISPOSAL
GASKELL RD
PATTERSON AV
GEORGE AV
ROLAND AV
PATTERSON RD
ELDER AV
LUNA CT
DARECK CT
FALL CT
WINTER AV
CYPRESS AV
SHADY LN
INDUSTRIAL
LINCOLN
ELDER
DIVISION ST
SIERRA HWY
UP RR
AEROSPACE HWY
AVE A
AVE A-8
AVE A-10
AVE A-12
AVE A-14
AVE B
AVE B-2
AVE B-4
AVE B-6
AVE B-8
AVE B-10
AVE B-12
AVE B-14
AVE C
AVE C-2
AVE C-4
AVE C-5
35TH ST W
30TH ST W
28TH ST W
32ND ST W
33RD ST W
27TH ST W
25TH ST W
20TH ST W
18TH ST W
17TH ST W
15TH ST W
10TH ST W
GATE
0 .25 .5 .75 1.0 miles 1 in. = 2400 ft.

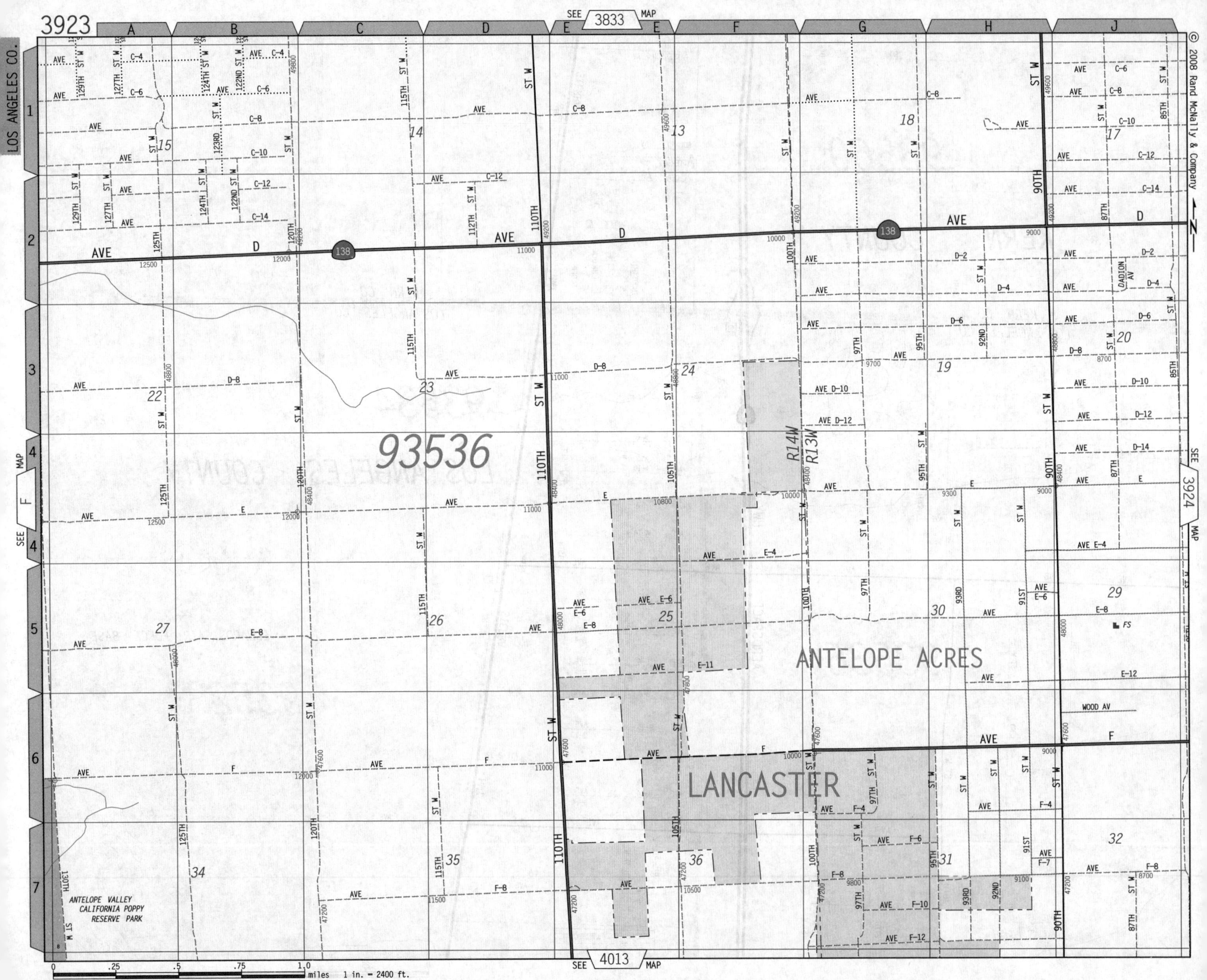

LOS ANGELES CO.
SEE 3833 MAP
SEE 3924 MAP
SEE F MAP
SEE 4013 MAP
93536
ANTELOPE ACRES
LANCASTER
ANTELOPE VALLEY CALIFORNIA POPPY RESERVE PARK
AVE D
AVE E
AVE F
110TH ST W
90TH ST W
R14W
R13W
1 in. = 2400 ft.

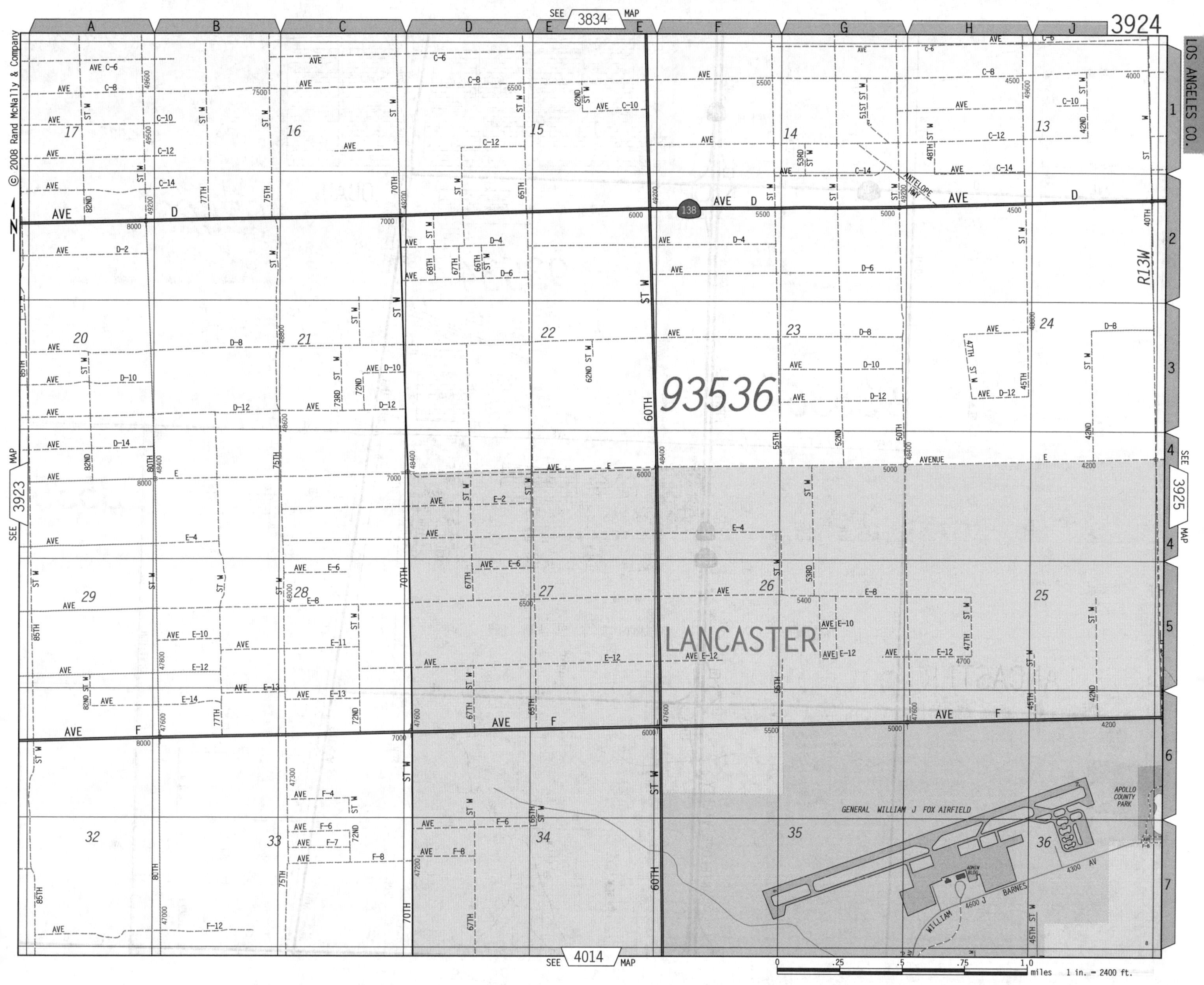
SEE 3834 MAP
SEE 4014 MAP
SEE 3923 MAP
SEE 3925 MAP
LOS ANGELES CO.
© 2008 Rand McNally & Company
93536
LANCASTER
GENERAL WILLIAM J FOX AIRFIELD
APOLLO COUNTY PARK
ADMIN BLDG
ANTELOPE HWY
AVE D
AVE E
AVENUE E
AVE F
60TH ST W
70TH ST W
80TH ST W
50TH ST W
45TH ST W
55TH ST W
40TH ST W
R13W
WILLIAM J BARNES AV
4300 AV
4600 J
0 .25 .5 .75 1.0 miles 1 in. = 2400 ft.

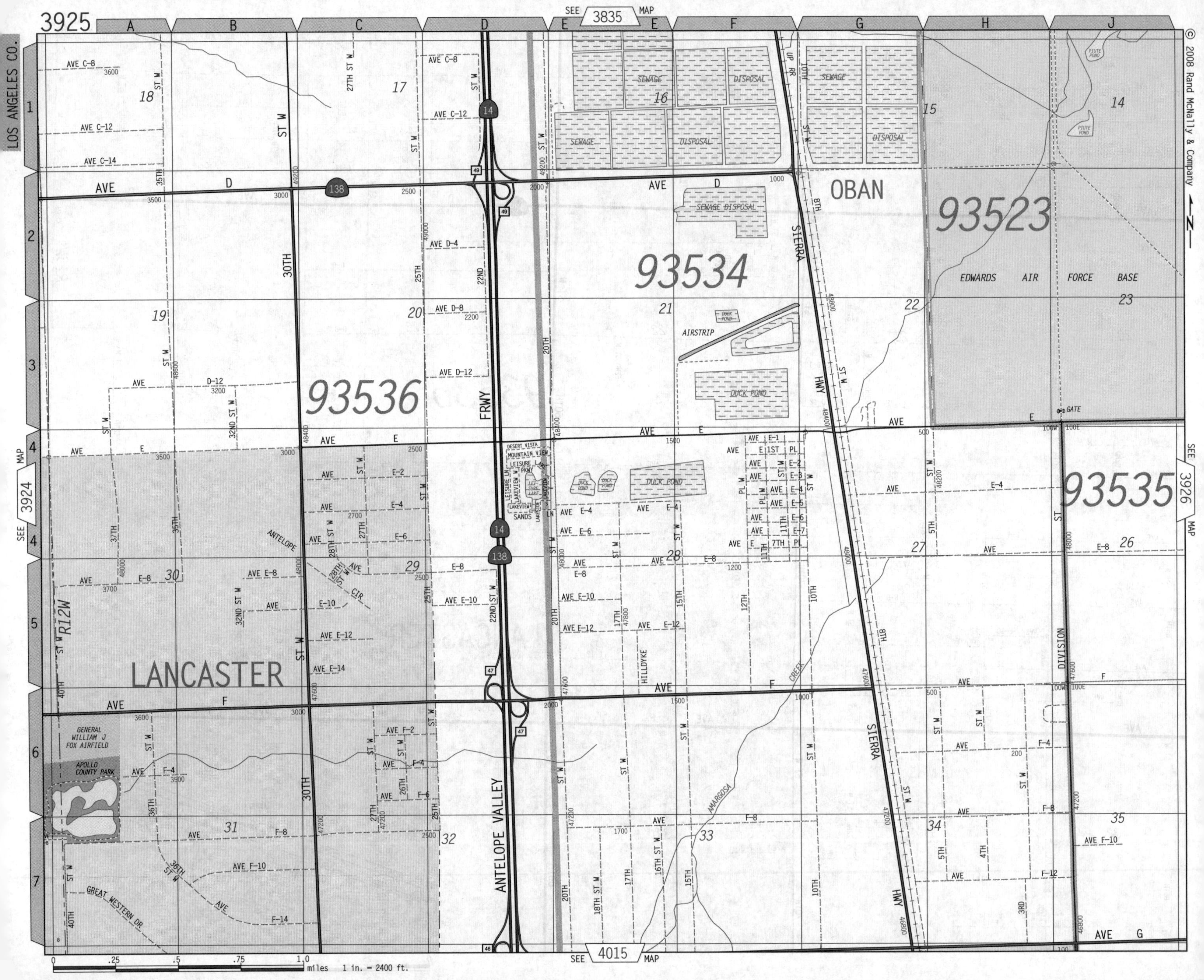

SEE 3835 MAP
LOS ANGELES CO.
93523
93534
93536
93535
OBAN
LANCASTER
EDWARDS AIR FORCE BASE
SEE 3924 MAP
SEE 3926 MAP
ANTELOPE VALLEY FRWY
SIERRA HWY
AVE D
AVE E
AVE F
AVE G
SEWAGE DISPOSAL
DUCK POND
AIRSTRIP
GENERAL WILLIAM J FOX AIRFIELD
APOLLO COUNTY PARK
GREAT WESTERN DR
AMARGOSA CREEK
DIVISION ST
R12W
SEE 4015 MAP
miles 1 in. = 2400 ft.

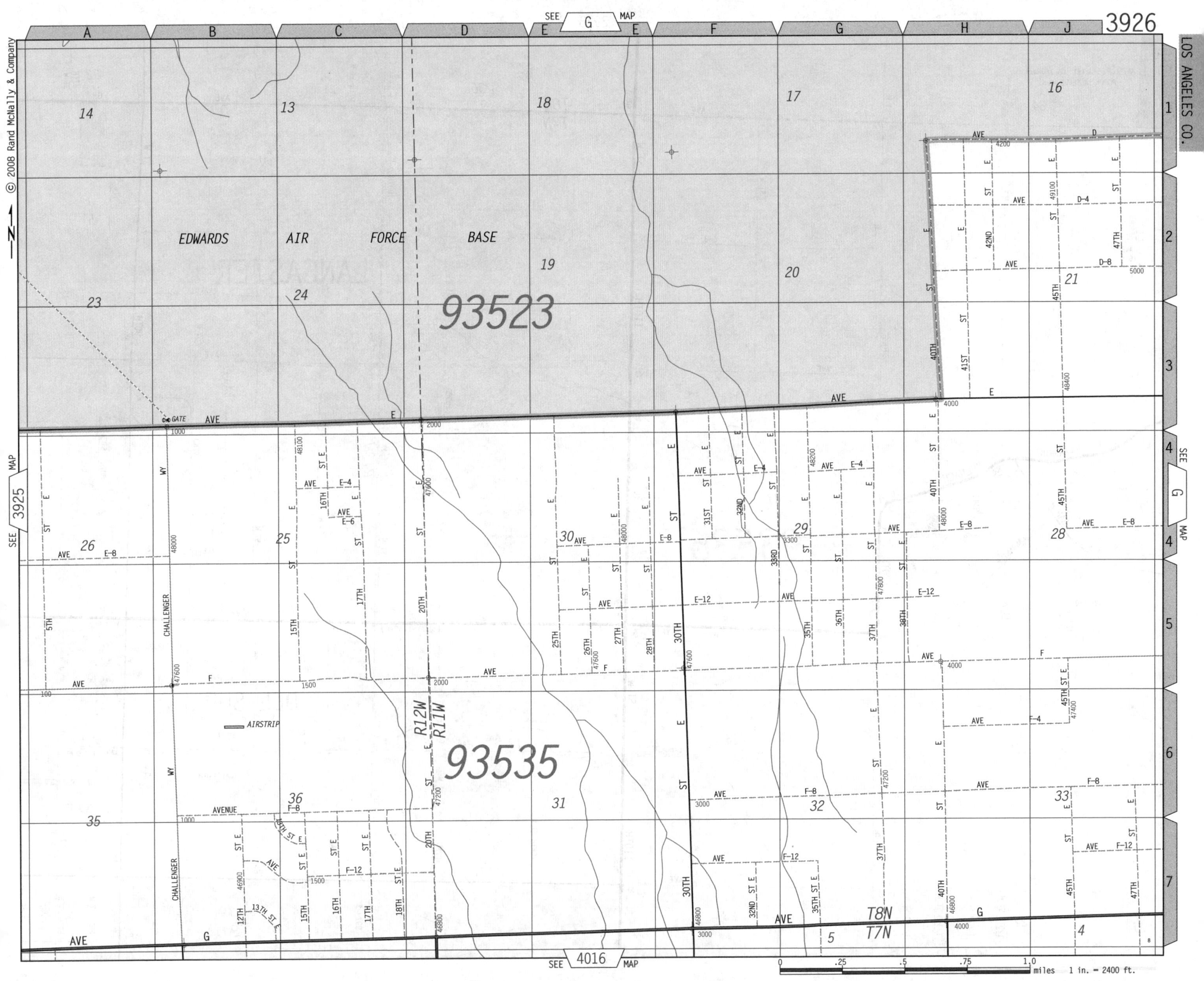

LOS ANGELES CO.
SEE G MAP
SEE 3925 MAP
SEE 4016 MAP
EDWARDS AIR FORCE BASE
93523
93535
R12W
R11W
T8N
T7N
AIRSTRIP
GATE
CHALLENGER WY
AVE E
AVE F
AVE G
AVE D
AVE D-4
AVE D-8
AVE E-4
AVE E-6
AVE E-8
AVE E-12
AVE F-4
AVE F-8
AVE F-12
AVENUE F-8
5TH ST E
12TH ST E
13TH ST E
15TH ST E
16TH ST E
17TH ST E
18TH ST E
20TH ST E
25TH ST E
26TH ST E
27TH ST E
28TH ST E
30TH ST E
31ST ST E
32ND ST E
35TH ST E
36TH ST E
37TH ST E
38TH ST E
38RD ST
40TH ST E
41ST ST E
42ND ST E
45TH ST E
47TH ST E
miles 1 in. = 2400 ft.

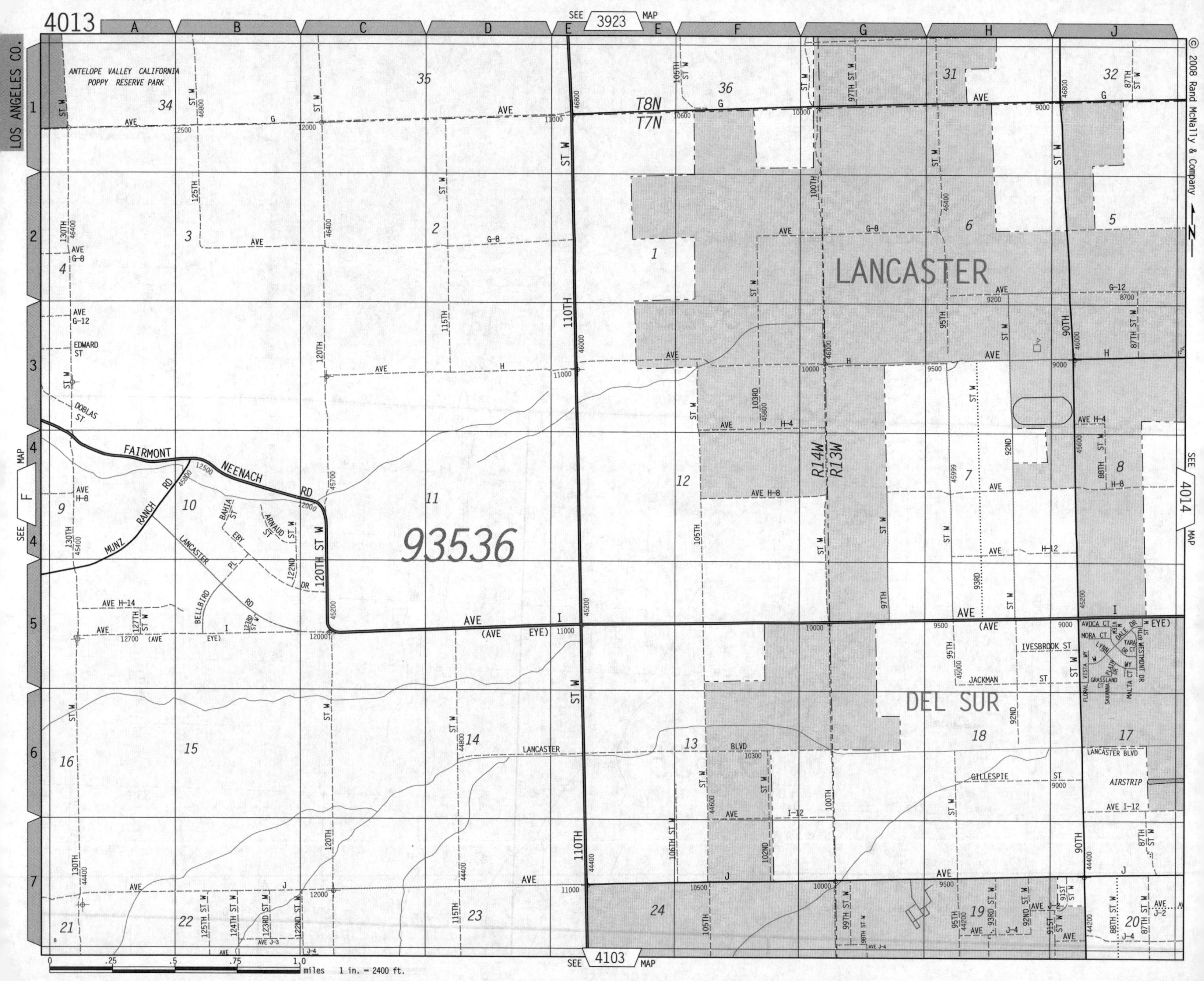

LOS ANGELES CO.
SEE 3923 MAP
ANTELOPE VALLEY CALIFORNIA POPPY RESERVE PARK
LANCASTER
DEL SUR
93536
T8N
T7N
R14W
R13W
FAIRMONT
NEENACH RD
MUNZ RANCH RD
LANCASTER RD
BELLBIRD
EDWARD ST
DOBLAS ST
BAHIA ST
ARNAUD ST
EBY
LANCASTER BLVD
GILLESPIE ST
IVESBROOK ST
JACKMAN ST
AIRSTRIP
AVE G
AVE G-8
AVE G-12
AVE H
AVE H-4
AVE H-8
AVE H-12
AVE H-14
AVE I (AVE EYE)
AVE I-12
AVE J
AVE J-2
AVE J-3
AVE J-4
110TH ST W
120TH ST W
90TH ST W
AVOCA CT
MORA CT
DALE DR
TARA CT
LYNN DR
WESTMONT DR
FLORAL VISTA WY
GRASSLAND CT
SAVANNA PLAIN DR
MALTA CT
SEE 4014 MAP
SEE F MAP
SEE 4103 MAP
© 2008 Rand McNally & Company
miles 1 in. = 2400 ft.

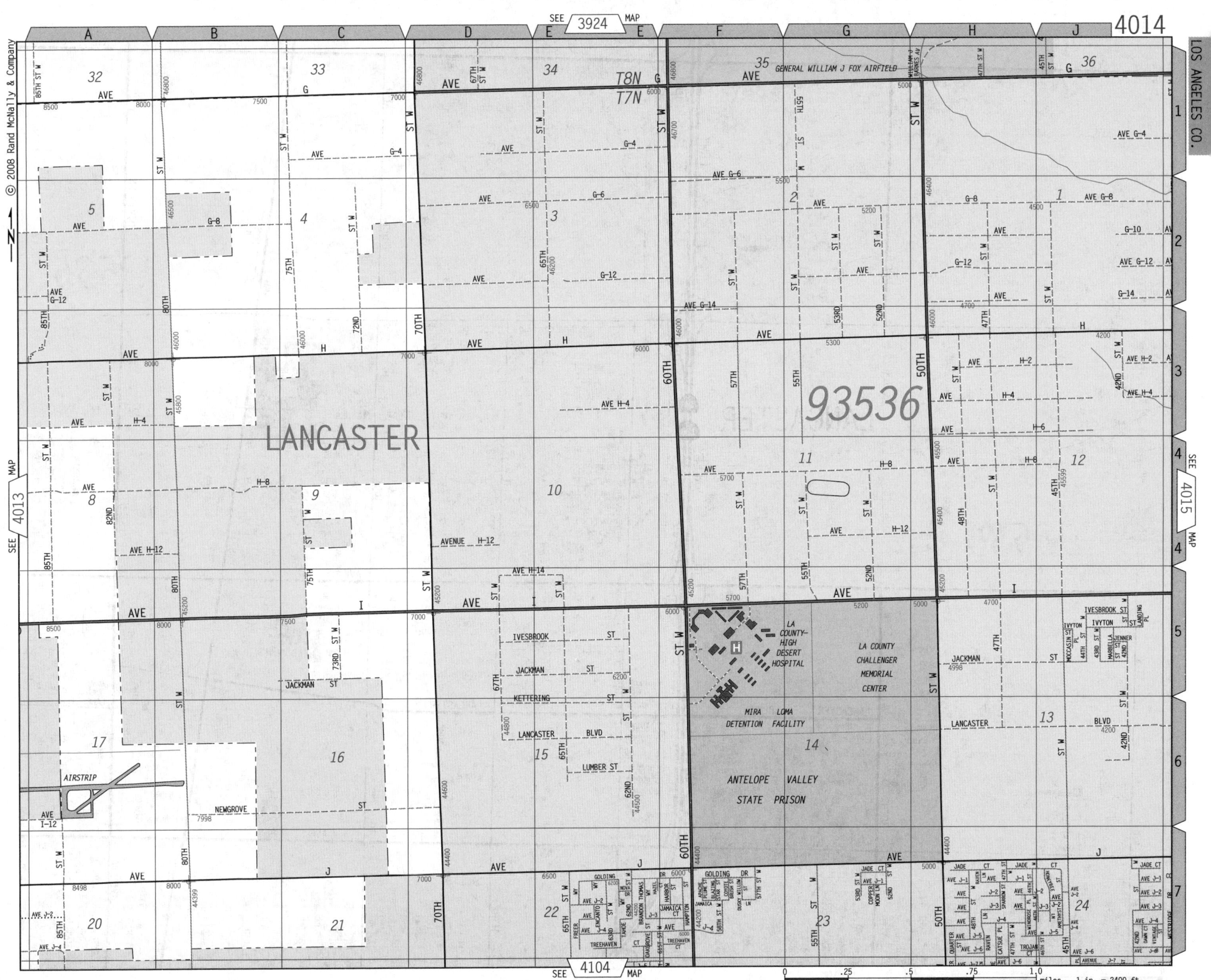

SEE 3924 MAP
LOS ANGELES CO.
© 2008 Rand McNally & Company
GENERAL WILLIAM J FOX AIRFIELD
T8N
T7N
LANCASTER
93536
LA COUNTY HIGH DESERT HOSPITAL
LA COUNTY CHALLENGER MEMORIAL CENTER
MIRA LOMA DETENTION FACILITY
ANTELOPE VALLEY STATE PRISON
AIRSTRIP
AVE G
AVE H
AVE I
AVE J
LANCASTER BLVD
JACKMAN ST
IVESBROOK ST
KETTERING ST
LUMBER ST
NEWGROVE ST
70TH ST W
60TH ST W
50TH ST W
80TH ST W
85TH ST W
SEE 4013 MAP
SEE 4015 MAP
SEE 4104 MAP
miles 1 in. = 2400 ft.

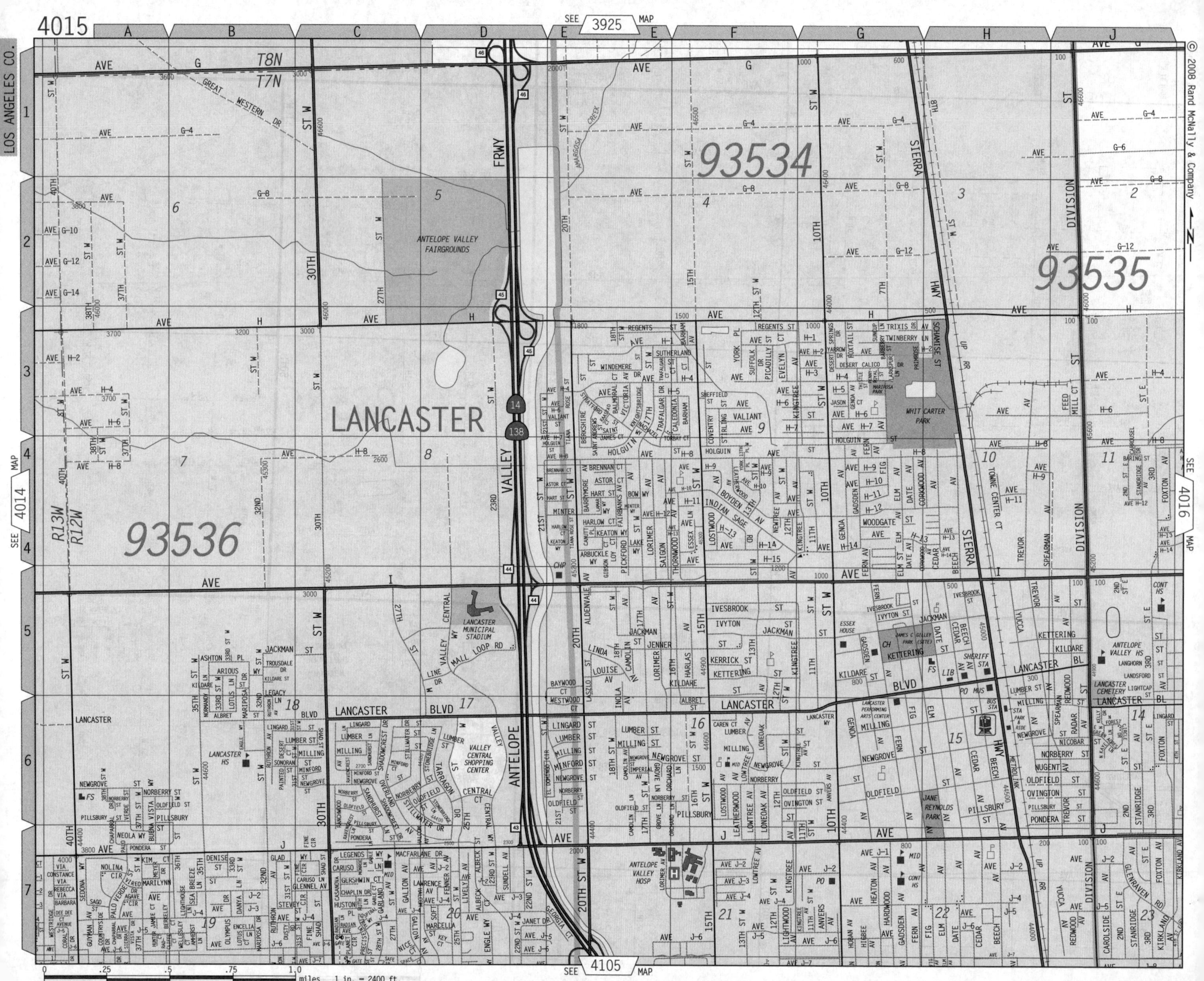

SEE 3925 MAP
LOS ANGELES CO.
SEE 4014 MAP
SEE 4016 MAP
SEE 4105 MAP
LANCASTER
93534
93535
93536
T8N
T7N
R13W
R12W
ANTELOPE VALLEY FAIRGROUNDS
WHIT CARTER PARK
LANCASTER MUNICIPAL STADIUM
VALLEY CENTRAL SHOPPING CENTER
ANTELOPE VALLEY HOSP
ANTELOPE VALLEY HS
LANCASTER HS
LANCASTER CEMETERY
JANE REYNOLDS PARK
JAMES C GILLEY PARK (SITE)
LANCASTER PERFORMING ARTS CENTER
ESSEX HOUSE
ANTELOPE VALLEY FRWY
SIERRA HWY
LANCASTER BLVD
AVE G
AVE H
AVE I
AVE J
DIVISION ST
GREAT WESTERN DR
AMARGOSA CREEK
METROLINK
UP RR
0 .25 .5 .75 1.0 miles 1 in. = 2400 ft.

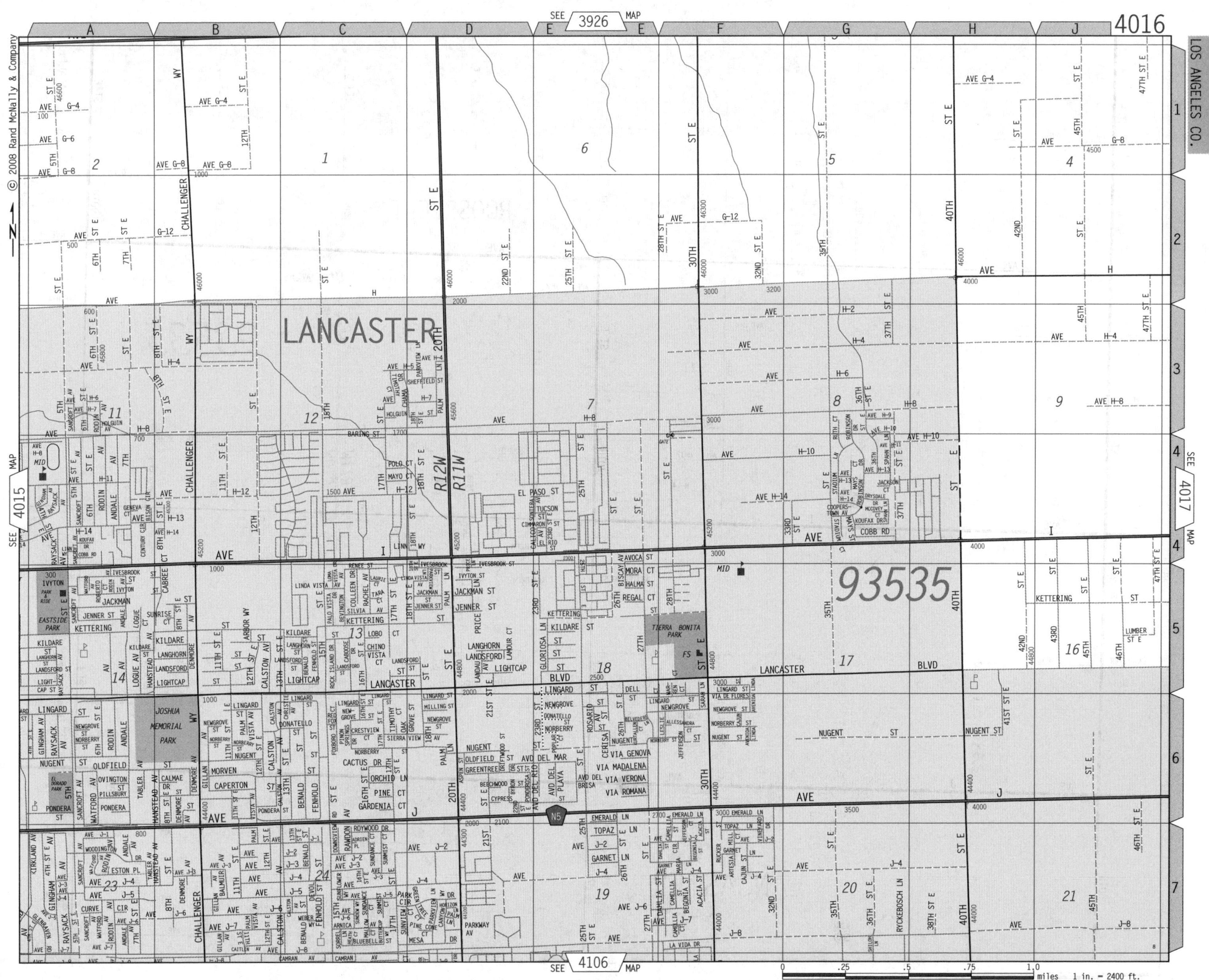
SEE 3926 MAP
LOS ANGELES CO.
LANCASTER
93535
SEE 4015 MAP
SEE 4017 MAP
SEE 4106 MAP
R12W
R11W
LANCASTER BLVD
CHALLENGER WY
EASTSIDE PARK
JOSHUA MEMORIAL PARK
TIERRA BONITA PARK
EL DORADO PARK
IVYTON PARK & RIDE
N5
miles 1 in. = 2400 ft.

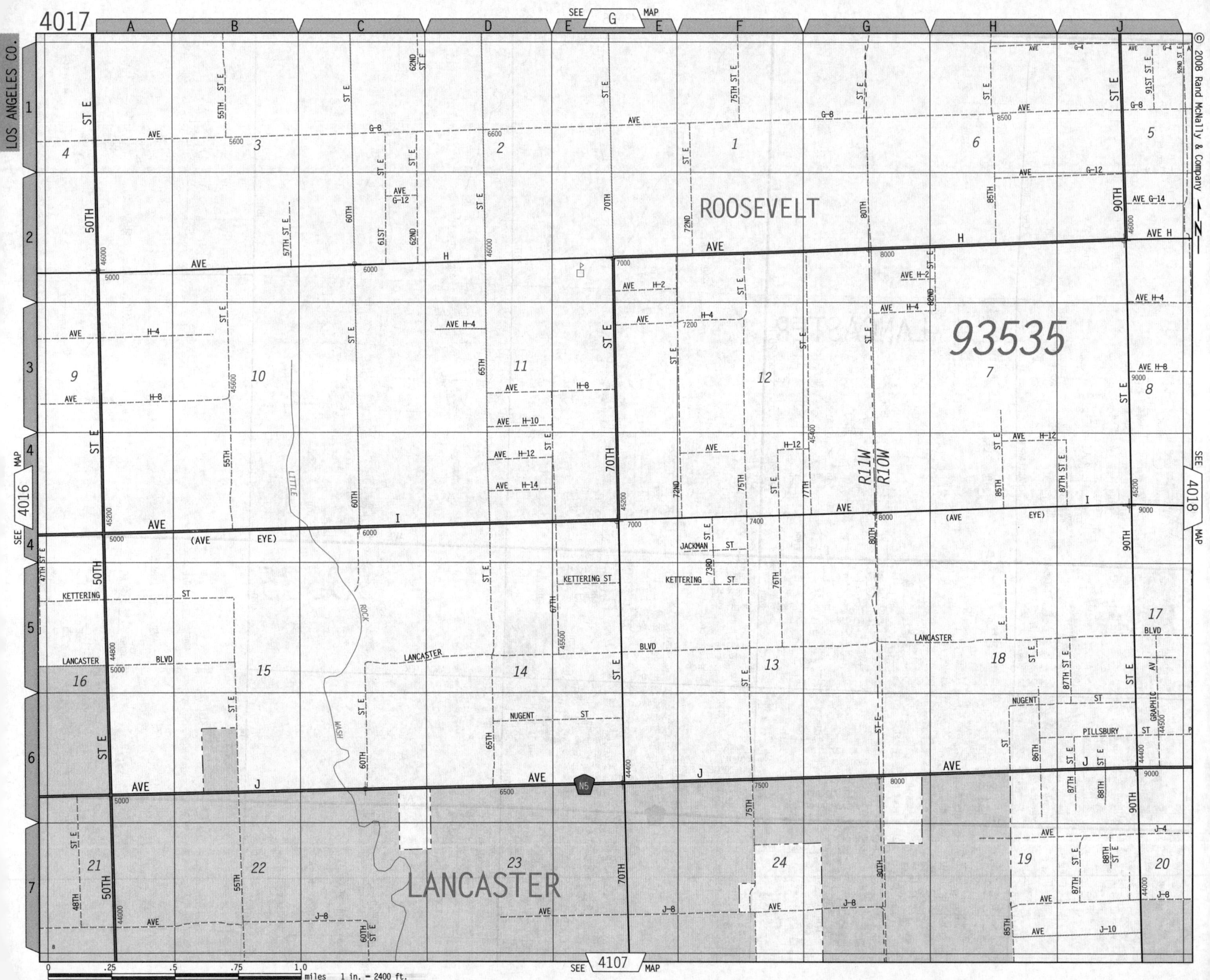

LOS ANGELES CO.
SEE MAP 4016
SEE MAP 4018
SEE MAP 4107
ROOSEVELT
93535
LANCASTER
AVE H
AVE I
(AVE EYE)
AVE J
LANCASTER BLVD
KETTERING ST
JACKMAN ST
NUGENT ST
PILLSBURY ST
50TH ST E
70TH ST E
90TH ST E
80TH ST E
LITTLE ROCK WASH
R11W
R10W
© 2008 Rand McNally & Company
miles 1 in. = 2400 ft.

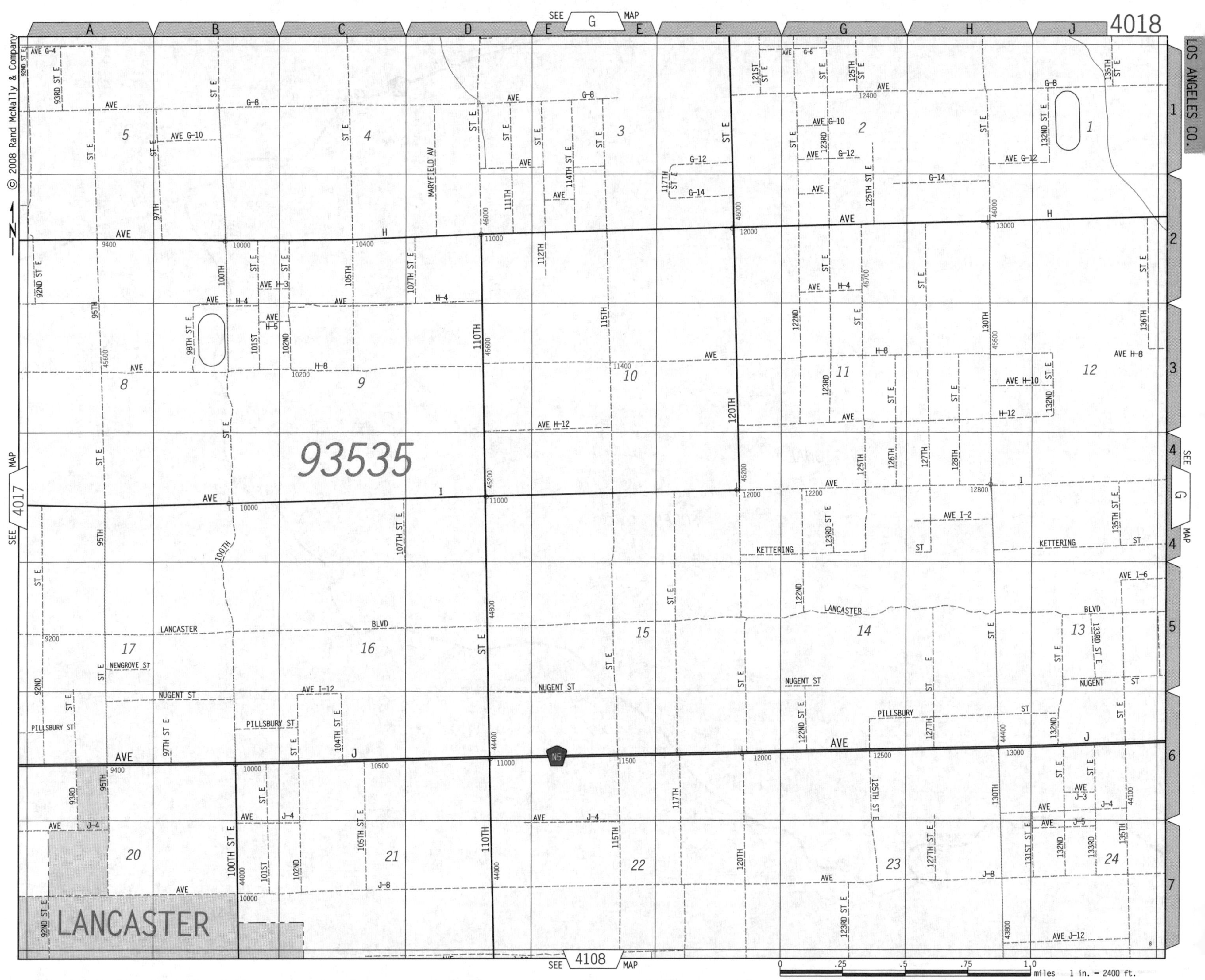

SEE G MAP
LOS ANGELES CO.
93535
LANCASTER
AVE H
AVE I
AVE J
LANCASTER BLVD
KETTERING ST
NUGENT ST
PILLSBURY ST
NEWGROVE ST
MARYFIELD AV
110TH ST E
120TH ST E
100TH ST E
95TH ST E
130TH ST E
N5
SEE MAP 4017
SEE G MAP
SEE 4108 MAP
miles 1 in. = 2400 ft.

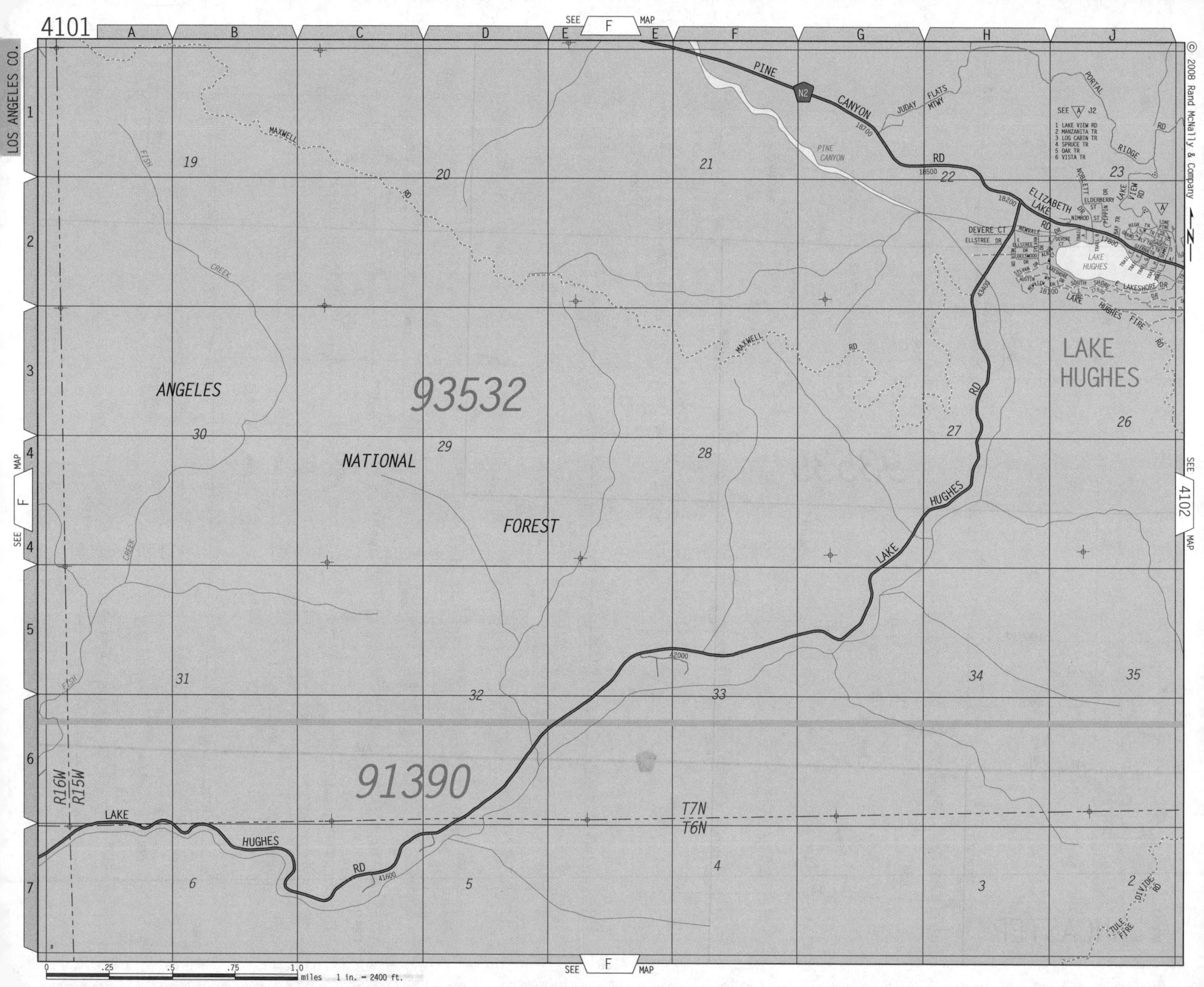
LOS ANGELES CO.
SEE F MAP
PINE CANYON RD
N2
JUDAY FLATS MTWY
PORTAL RIDGE RD
SEE A J2
1 LAKE VIEW RD
2 MANZANITA TR
3 LOG CABIN TR
4 SPRUCE TR
5 OAK TR
6 VISTA TR
MAXWELL RD
FISH CREEK
ELIZABETH LAKE RD
LAKE VIEW RD
DEVERE CT
ELLSTREE DR
LAKE HUGHES
SOUTH SHORE DR
LAKESHORE DR
LAKE HUGHES FIRE RD
LAKE HUGHES RD
ANGELES
NATIONAL
FOREST
93532
91390
R16W
R15W
T7N
T6N
TULE FIRE DIVIDE RD
SEE 4102 MAP
© 2008 Rand McNally & Company
miles 1 in. = 2400 ft.

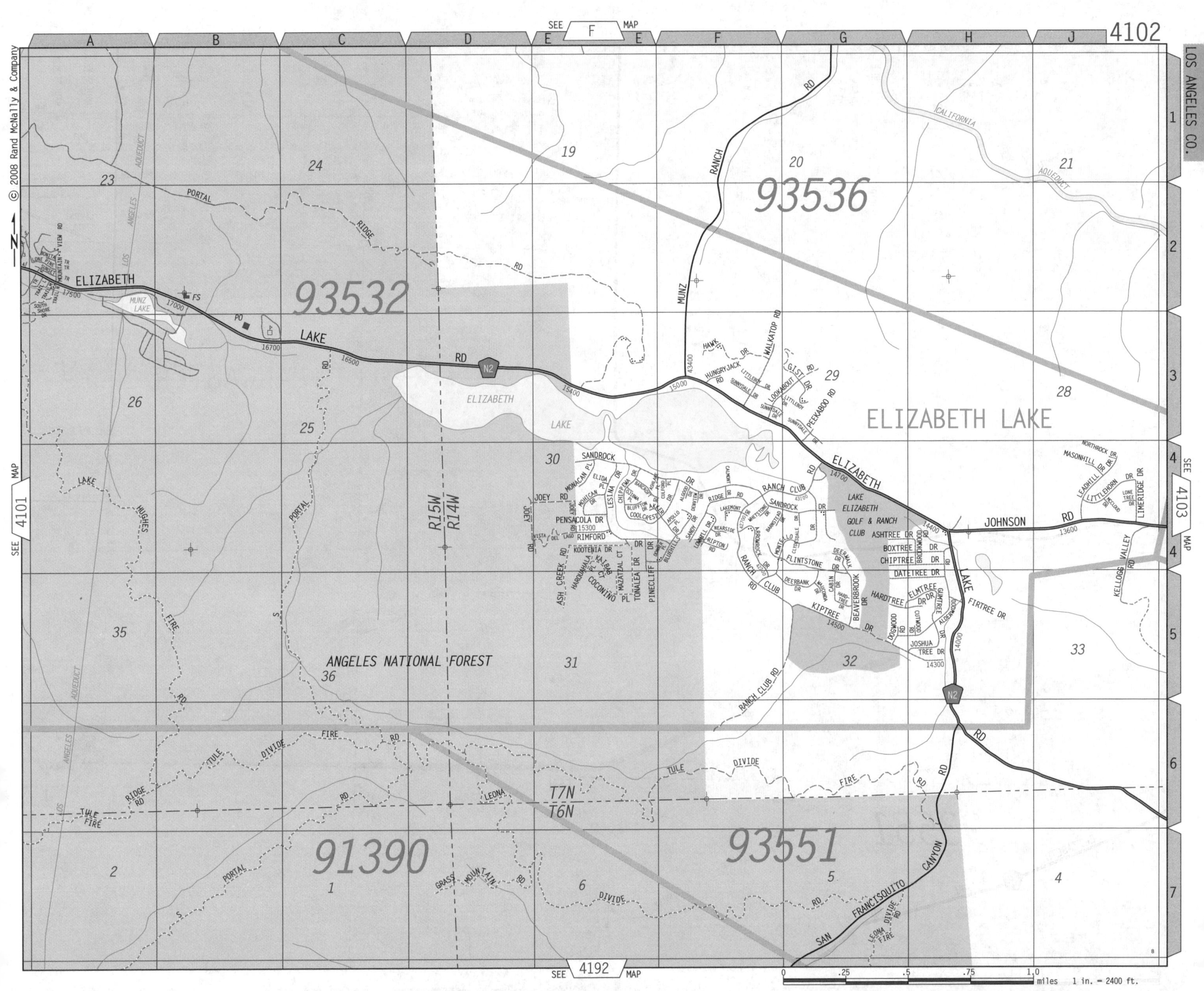
LOS ANGELES CO.
SEE F MAP
SEE 4101 MAP
SEE 4103 MAP
SEE 4192 MAP
93536
93532
91390
93551
ELIZABETH LAKE
ANGELES NATIONAL FOREST
LAKE ELIZABETH GOLF & RANCH CLUB
ELIZABETH LAKE RD
MUNZ RANCH RD
JOHNSON RD
SAN FRANCISQUITO CANYON RD
CALIFORNIA AQUEDUCT
LOS ANGELES AQUEDUCT
PORTAL RIDGE RD
MUNZ LAKE
ELIZABETH LAKE
R15W R14W
T7N T6N
miles 1 in. = 2400 ft.

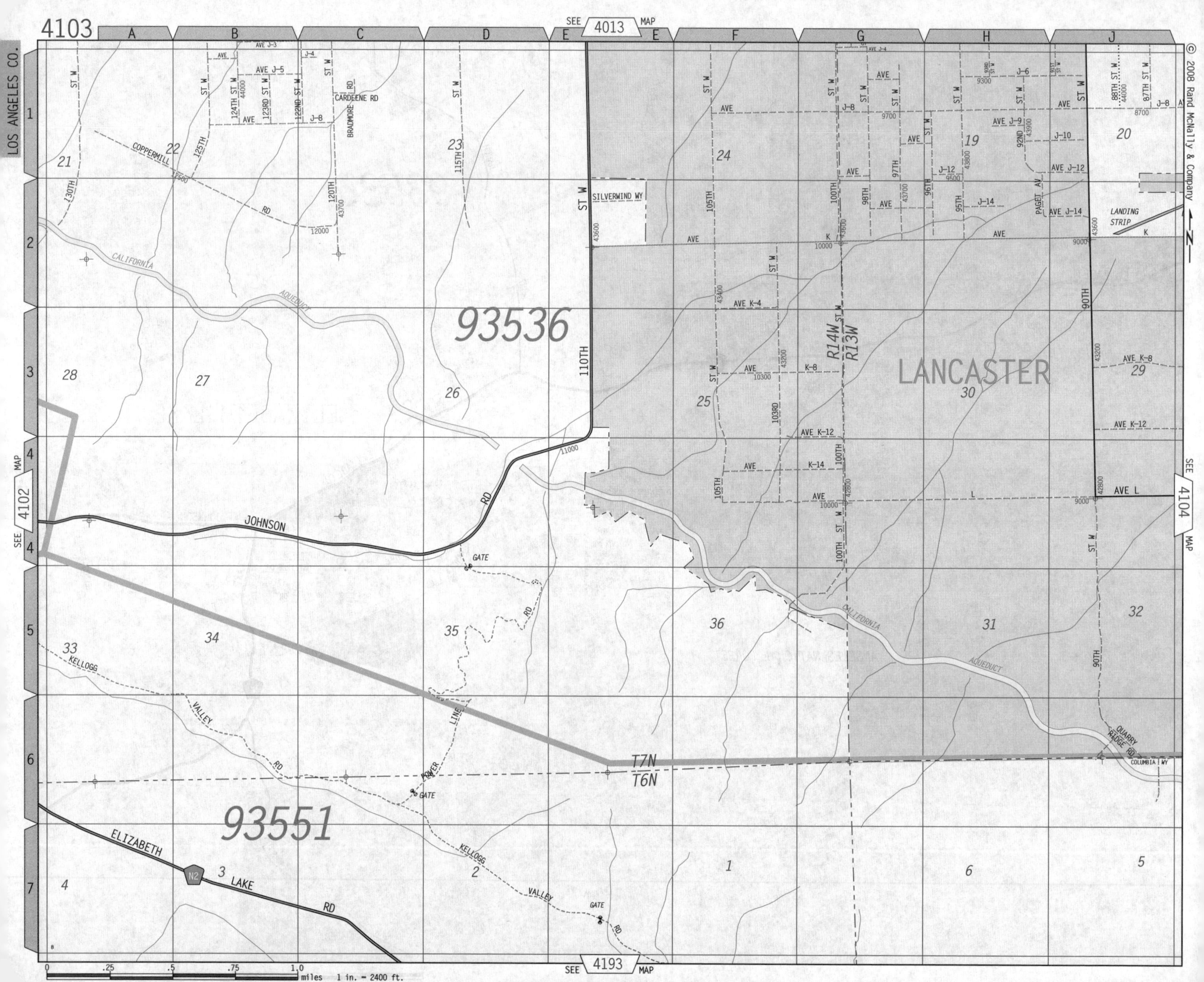

4103
LOS ANGELES CO.
SEE 4013 MAP
SEE 4102 MAP
SEE 4104 MAP
SEE 4193 MAP
© 2008 Rand McNally & Company
93536
93551
LANCASTER
R14W
R13W
T7N
T6N
COPPERMILL RD
CALIFORNIA AQUEDUCT
JOHNSON RD
KELLOGG VALLEY RD
POWER LINE RD
ELIZABETH LAKE RD
N2
CARDEENE RD
BRADMORE RD
SILVERWIND WY
LANDING STRIP
PAGET AV
QUARRY RIDGE RD
COLUMBIA WY
AVE K
AVE L
AVE J-8
AVE K-4
AVE K-8
AVE K-12
AVE K-14
AVE J-14
AVE J-12
110TH ST W
100TH ST W
90TH ST W
105TH ST W
GATE
0 .25 .5 .75 1.0 miles 1 in. = 2400 ft.

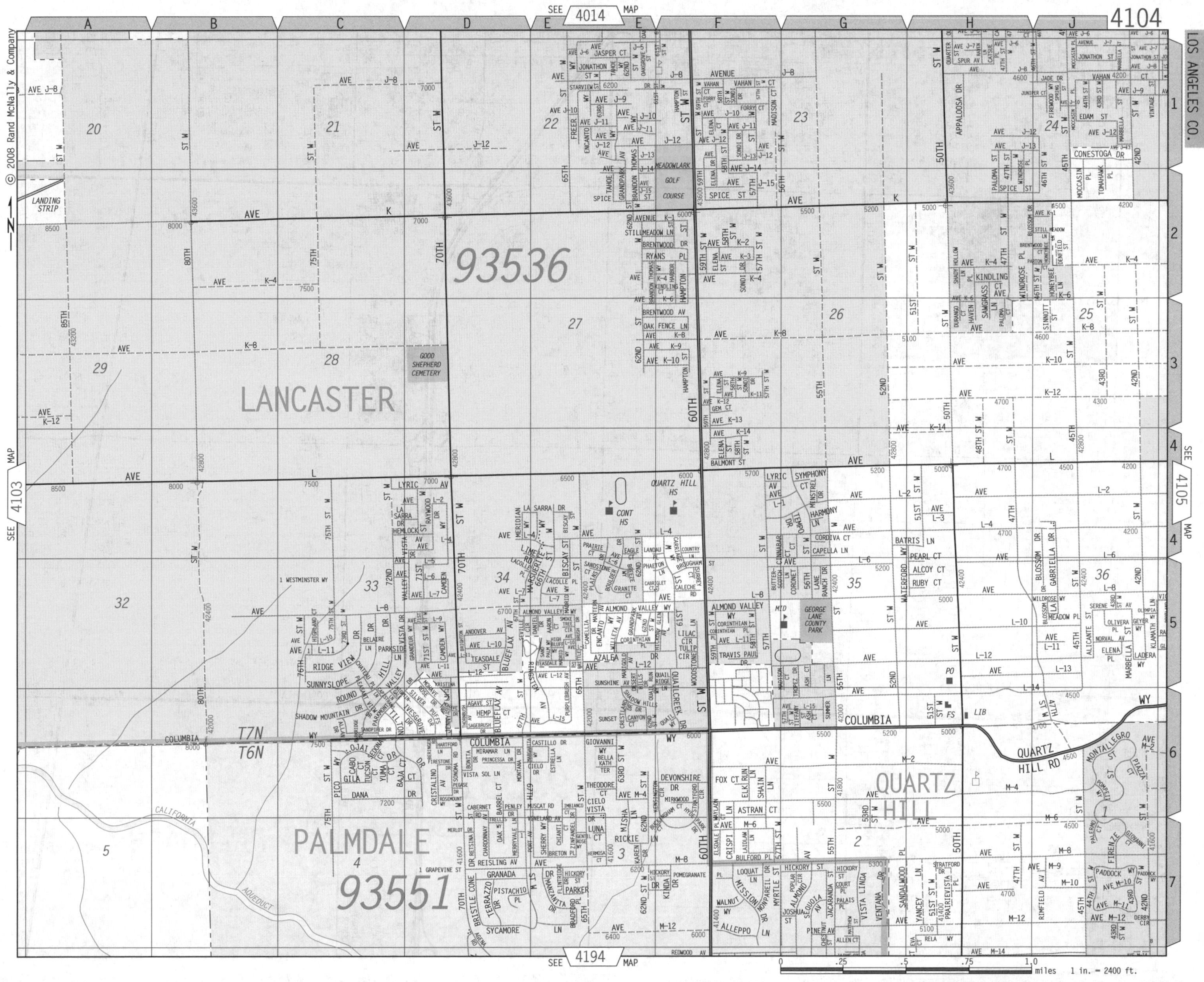
SEE 4014 MAP
A
B
C
D
E
F
G
H
J
LOS ANGELES CO.
© 2008 Rand McNally & Company
LANDING STRIP
AVE J-8
AVE K
AVE K-4
AVE K-8
AVE K-12
AVE L
AVE M-2
AVE M-4
AVE M-6
AVE M-8
AVE M-12
AVENUE J-8
93536
LANCASTER
GOOD SHEPHERD CEMETERY
MEADOWLARK GOLF COURSE
QUARTZ HILL HS
CONT HS
GEORGE LANE COUNTY PARK
MID
PO
FS
LIB
COLUMBIA WY
QUARTZ HILL RD
T7N
T6N
CALIFORNIA AQUEDUCT
PALMDALE
93551
QUARTZ HILL
80TH ST W
75TH ST W
70TH ST W
65TH ST W
60TH ST W
55TH ST W
50TH ST W
45TH ST W
42ND ST W
SEE 4103 MAP
SEE 4105 MAP
SEE 4194 MAP
miles 1 in. = 2400 ft.
0 .25 .5 .75 1.0

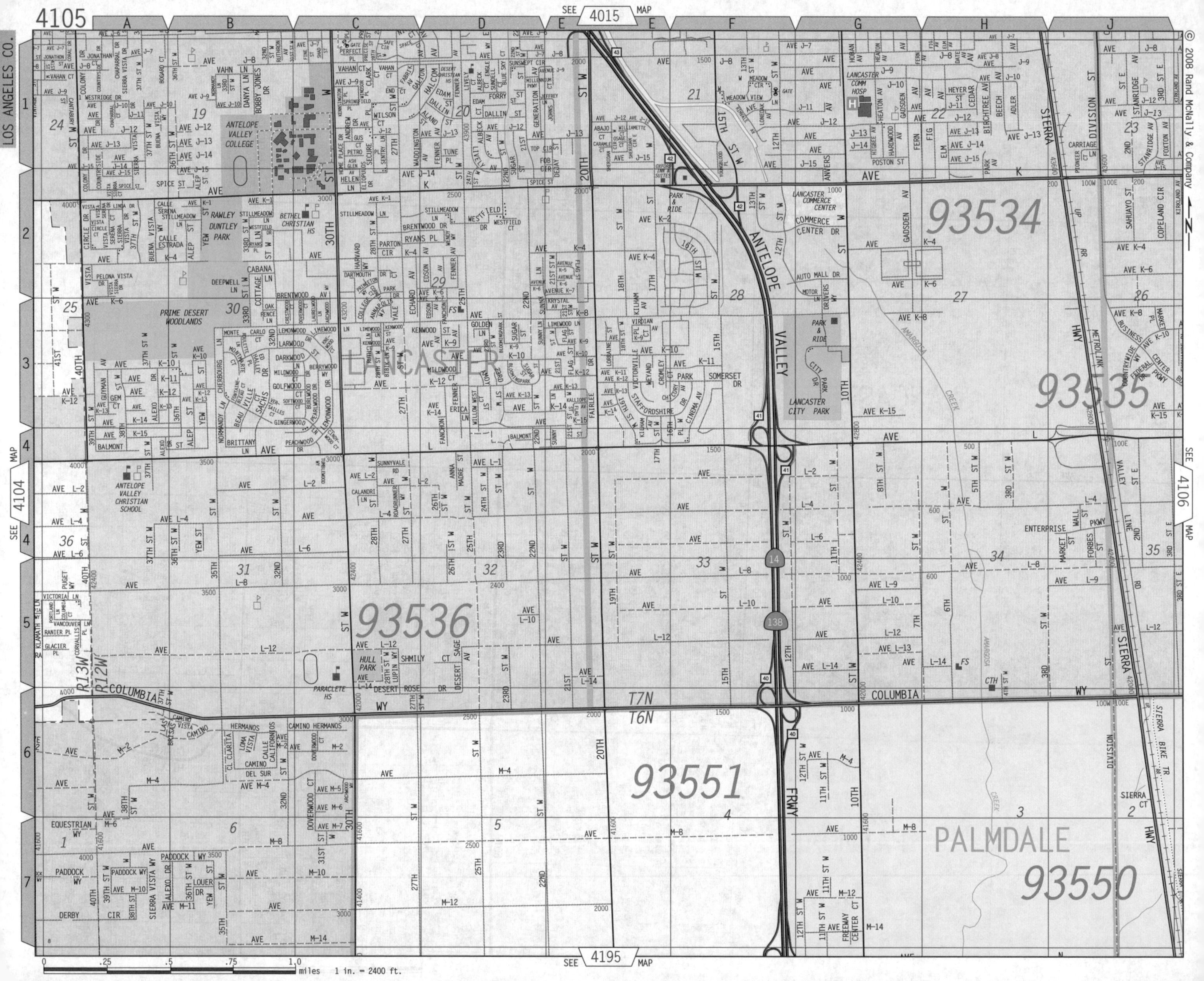

SEE 4015 MAP
LOS ANGELES CO.
LANCASTER
PALMDALE
93534
93535
93536
93551
93550
ANTELOPE VALLEY COLLEGE
RAWLEY DUNTLEY PARK
BETHEL CHRISTIAN HS
PRIME DESERT WOODLANDS
LANCASTER COMM HOSP
LANCASTER COMMERCE CENTER
PARK & RIDE
LANCASTER CITY PARK
ANTELOPE VALLEY CHRISTIAN SCHOOL
HULL PARK
PARACLETE HS
ANTELOPE VALLEY FRWY
SIERRA HWY
COLUMBIA WY
DIVISION ST
METROLINK
AMARGOSA CREEK
T7N
T6N
R13W
R12W
SEE 4104 MAP
SEE 4106 MAP
SEE 4195 MAP
0 .25 .5 .75 1.0 miles 1 in. = 2400 ft.

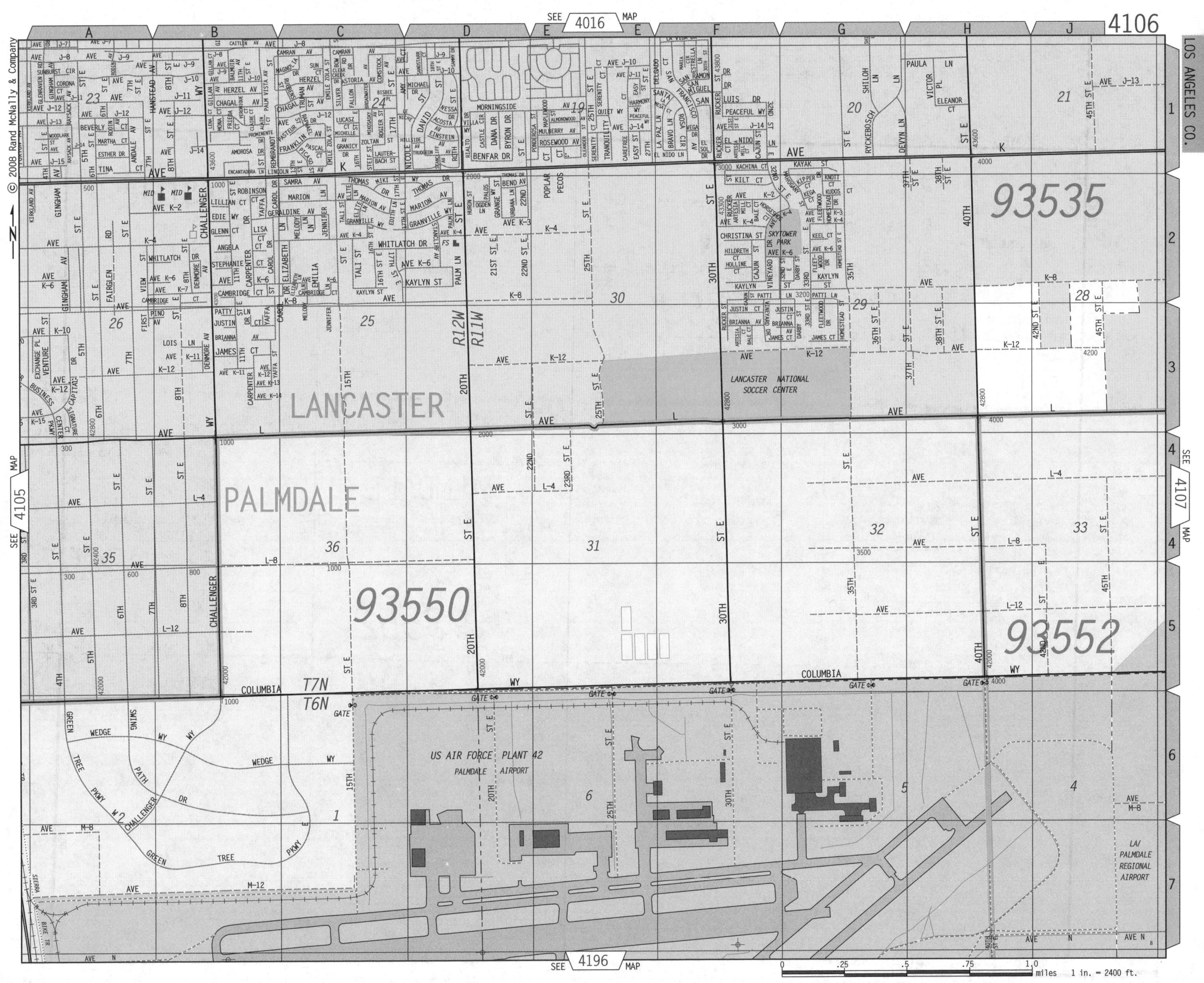
SEE 4016 MAP
LOS ANGELES CO.
LANCASTER
PALMDALE
93535
93550
93552
LANCASTER NATIONAL SOCCER CENTER
SKYTOWER PARK
US AIR FORCE PLANT 42
PALMDALE AIRPORT
LA/ PALMDALE REGIONAL AIRPORT
COLUMBIA WY
AVE K
AVE L
AVE N
R12W
R11W
T7N
T6N
SEE 4105 MAP
SEE 4107 MAP
SEE 4196 MAP
miles 1 in. = 2400 ft.

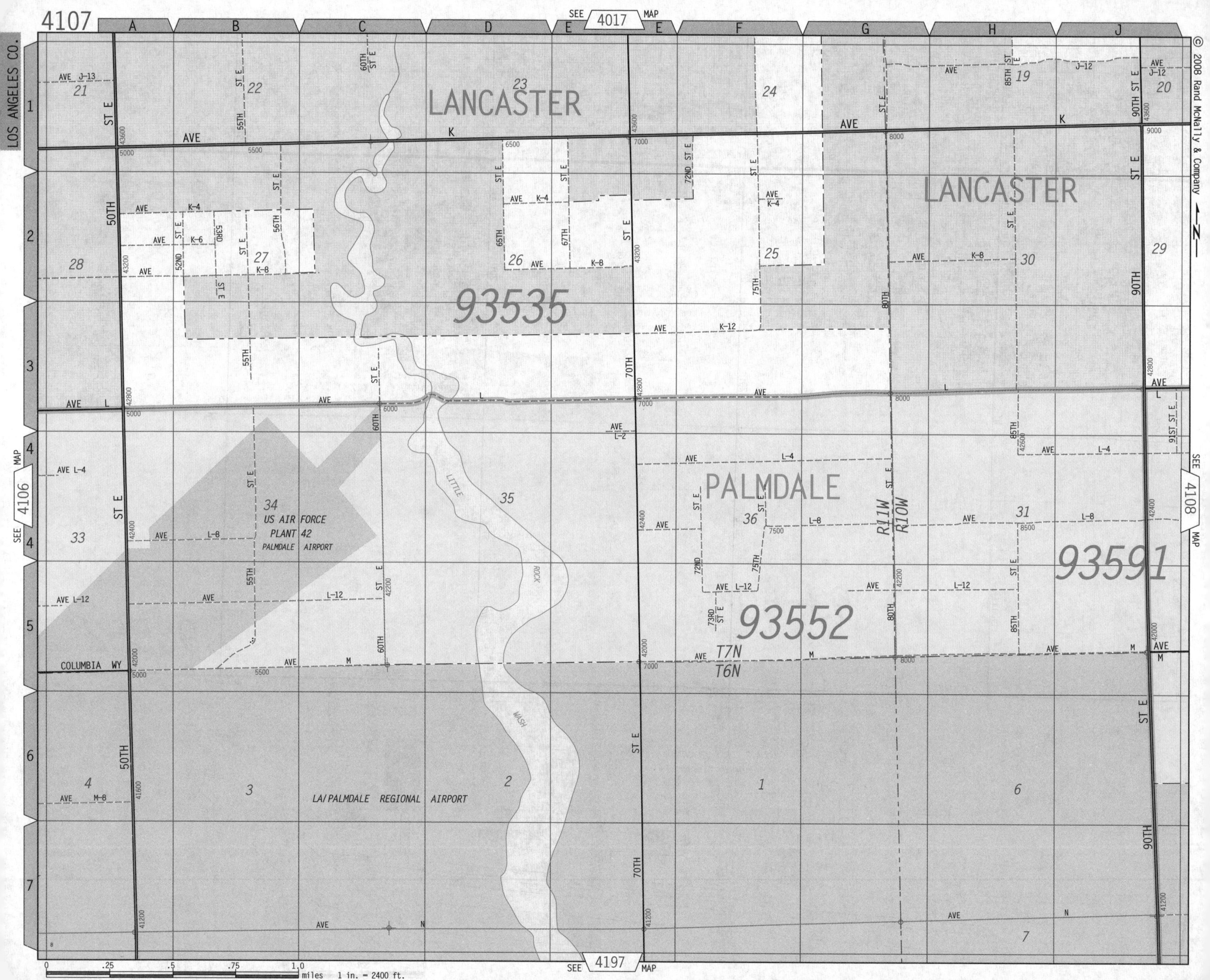
LOS ANGELES CO.
SEE 4017 MAP
SEE 4106 MAP
SEE 4108 MAP
SEE 4197 MAP
LANCASTER
PALMDALE
93535
93552
93591
US AIR FORCE
PLANT 42
PALMDALE AIRPORT
LA/PALMDALE REGIONAL AIRPORT
LITTLE ROCK WASH
AVE K
AVE L
AVE M
AVE N
AVE J-13
AVE J-12
AVE K-4
AVE K-6
AVE K-8
AVE K-12
AVE L-2
AVE L-4
AVE L-8
AVE L-12
AVE M-8
COLUMBIA WY
50TH ST E
52ND ST E
53RD ST E
55TH ST E
56TH ST E
60TH ST E
65TH ST E
67TH ST E
70TH ST E
72ND ST E
72ND ST E
73RD ST E
75TH ST E
80TH ST E
85TH ST E
90TH ST E
91ST ST E
T7N
T6N
R11W
R10W
0 .25 .5 .75 1.0 miles 1 in. = 2400 ft.

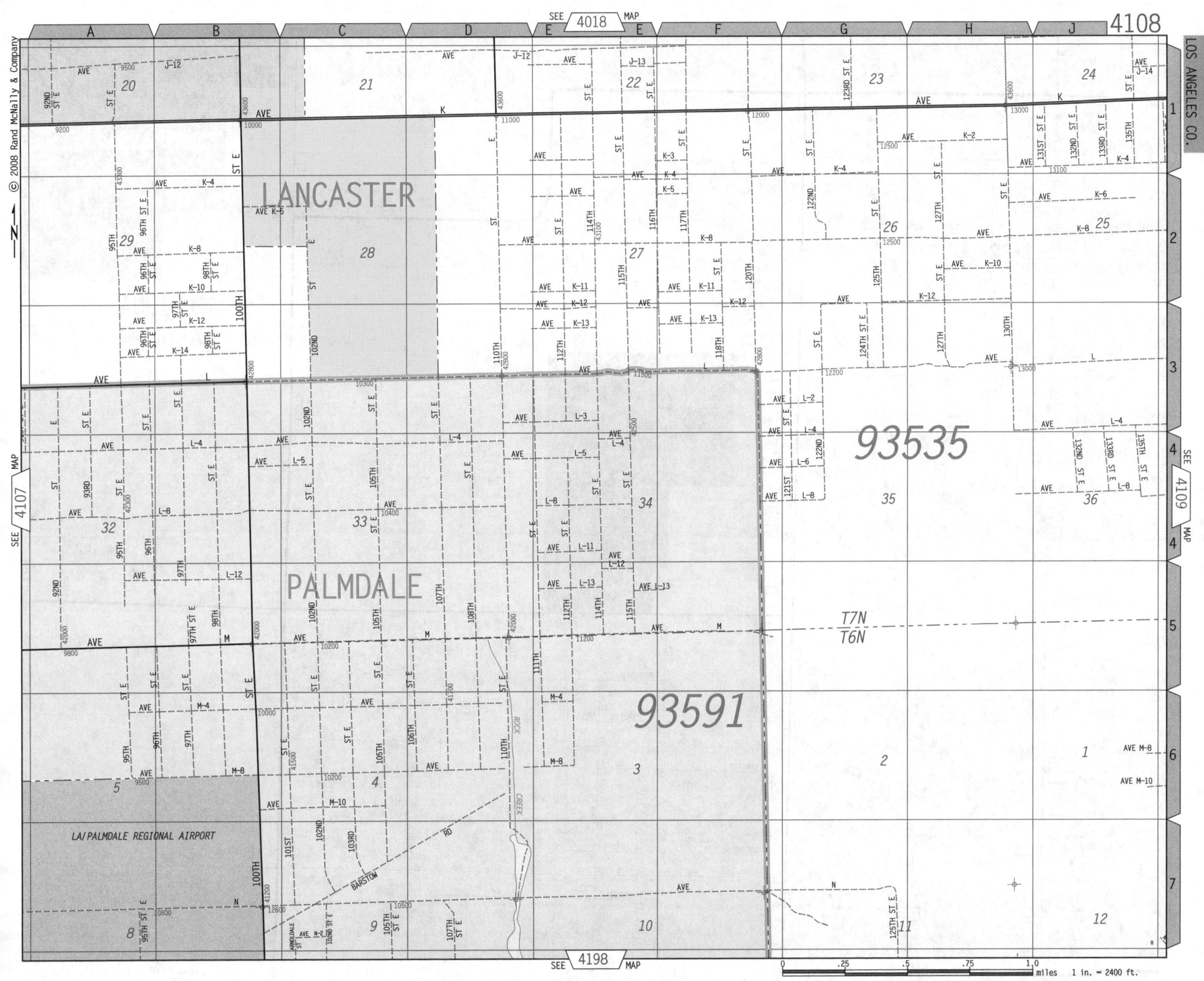

SEE 4018 MAP
SEE 4198 MAP
SEE 4107 MAP
SEE 4109 MAP
LOS ANGELES CO.
LANCASTER
PALMDALE
93535
93591
T7N
T6N
LA/PALMDALE REGIONAL AIRPORT
AVE J-12
AVE K
AVE K-4
AVE K-8
AVE L
AVE L-4
AVE L-8
AVE M
AVE M-4
AVE M-8
AVE M-10
AVE N
BARSTOW RD
ROCK CREEK
100TH ST E
110TH ST E
120TH ST E
130TH ST E
miles 1 in. = 2400 ft.

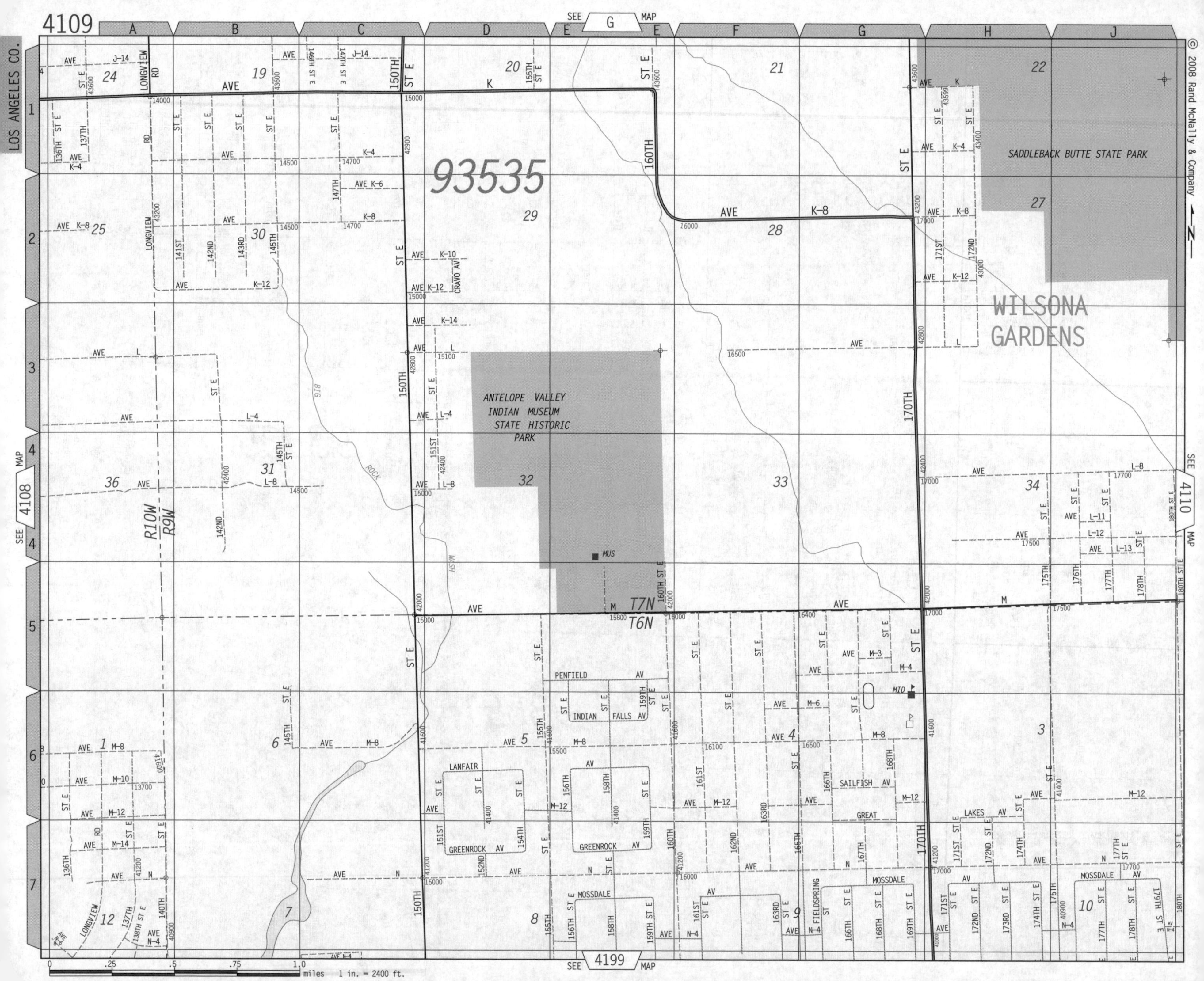
LOS ANGELES CO.
SEE G MAP
A
B
C
D
E
F
G
H
J
1
2
3
4
5
6
7
93535
SADDLEBACK BUTTE STATE PARK
WILSONA GARDENS
ANTELOPE VALLEY INDIAN MUSEUM STATE HISTORIC PARK
MUS
MID
AVE K
AVE K-4
AVE K-6
AVE K-8
AVE K-10
AVE K-12
AVE K-14
AVE J-14
AVE L
AVE L-4
AVE L-8
AVE L-11
AVE L-12
AVE L-13
AVE M
AVE M-3
AVE M-4
AVE M-6
AVE M-8
AVE M-10
AVE M-12
AVE M-14
AVE N
AVE N-4
LONGVIEW RD
150TH ST E
160TH ST E
170TH ST E
180TH ST E
CRAVO AV
PENFIELD AV
INDIAN FALLS AV
LANFAIR AV
GREENROCK AV
SAILFISH AV
GREAT LAKES AV
MOSSDALE AV
FIELDSPRING ST
BIG ROCK WASH
R10W
R9W
T7N
T6N
SEE 4108 MAP
SEE 4110 MAP
SEE 4199 MAP
© 2008 Rand McNally & Company
0 .25 .5 .75 1.0 miles 1 in. = 2400 ft.

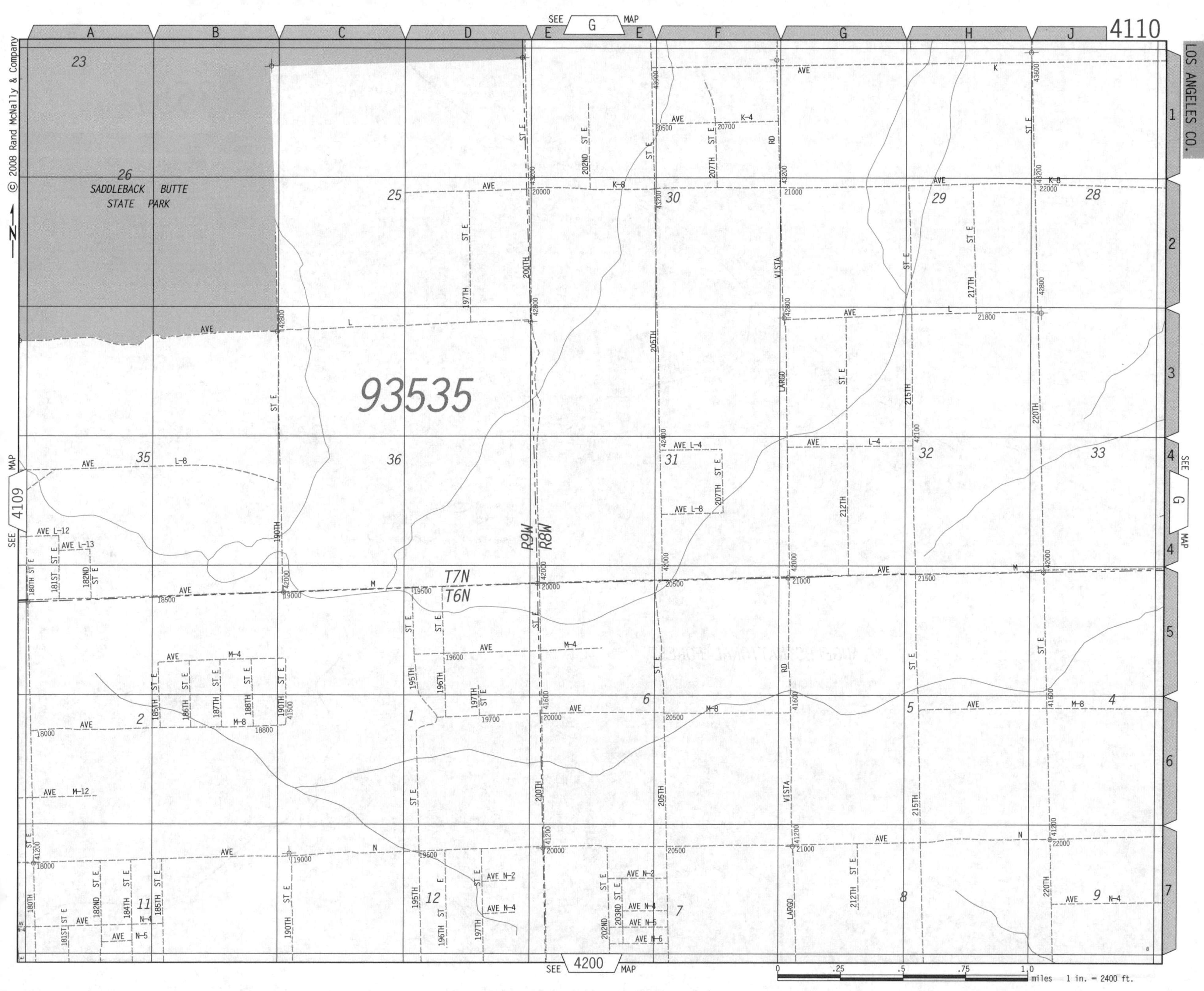
SEE G MAP
LOS ANGELES CO.
SADDLEBACK BUTTE STATE PARK
93535
R9W R8W
T7N T6N
AVE K
AVE K-4
AVE K-8
AVE L
AVE L-4
AVE L-8
AVE L-12
AVE L-13
AVE M
AVE M-4
AVE M-8
AVE M-12
AVE N
AVE N-2
AVE N-4
AVE N-5
AVE N-6
180TH ST E
181ST ST E
182ND ST E
184TH ST E
185TH ST E
186TH ST E
187TH ST E
188TH ST E
190TH ST E
195TH ST E
196TH ST E
197TH ST E
200TH ST E
202ND ST E
203RD ST E
205TH ST E
207TH ST E
212TH ST E
215TH ST E
217TH ST E
220TH ST E
VISTA LARGO RD
SEE 4109 MAP
SEE G MAP
SEE 4200 MAP
0 .25 .5 .75 1.0 miles 1 in. = 2400 ft.

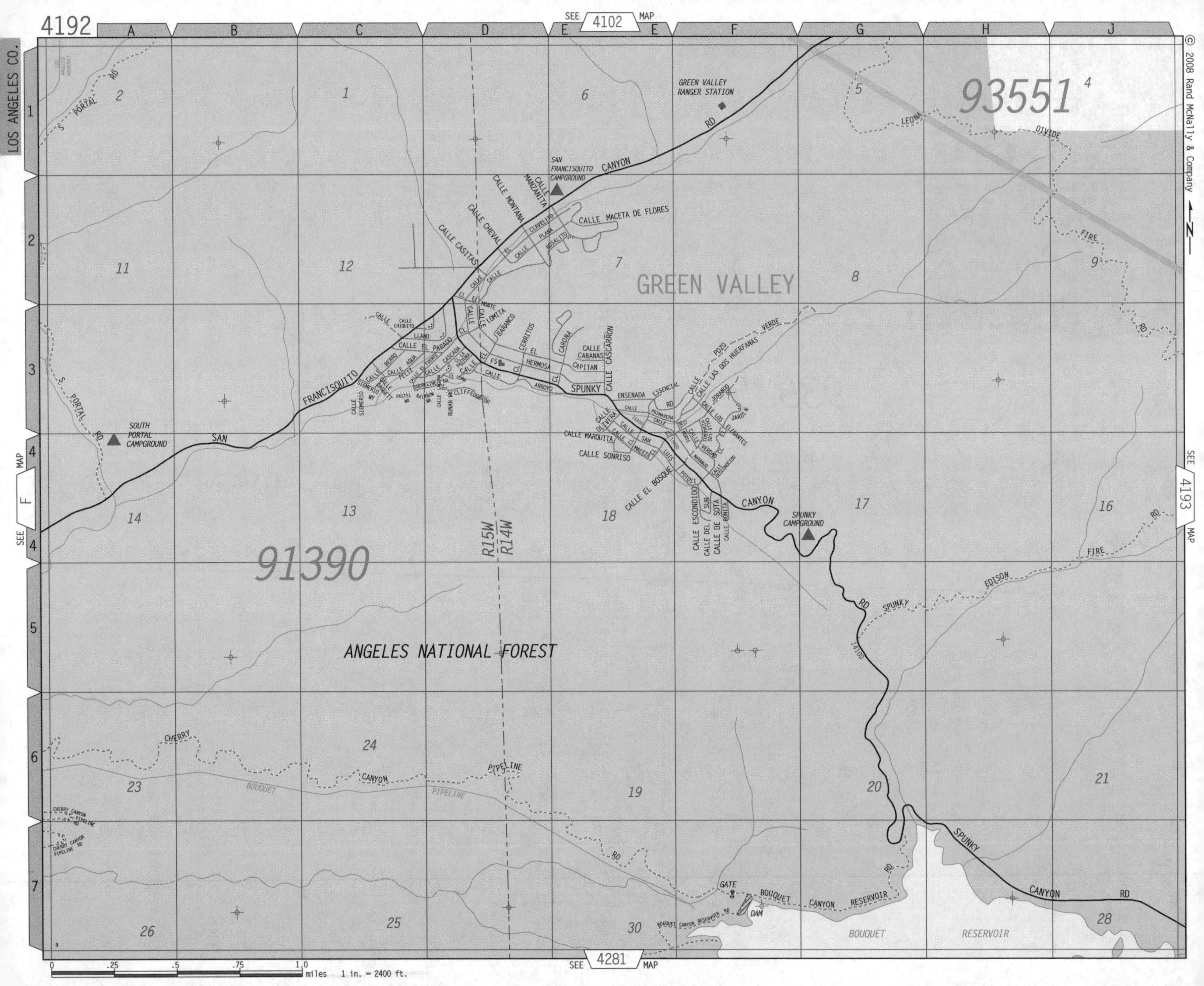

LOS ANGELES CO.
SEE 4102 MAP
SEE F MAP
SEE 4193 MAP
SEE 4281 MAP
93551
91390
GREEN VALLEY
ANGELES NATIONAL FOREST
GREEN VALLEY RANGER STATION
SAN FRANCISQUITO CAMPGROUND
SOUTH PORTAL CAMPGROUND
SPUNKY CAMPGROUND
SAN FRANCISQUITO CANYON RD
SPUNKY CANYON RD
S PORTAL RD
LEONA DIVIDE FIRE RD
POZO VERDE
EDISON FIRE RD
CHERRY CANYON PIPELINE RD
BOUQUET PIPELINE
BOUQUET CANYON RESERVOIR RD
BOUQUET RESERVOIR
GATE
DAM
R15W
R14W
CALLE MACETA DE FLORES
CALLE CASITAS
CALLE CHEVAL
CALLE MONTANA
CALLE MANZANITA
CALLE EL PARADO
CALLE CABANAS
CALLE CASCARRON
CALLE MARQUITA
CALLE SONRISO
CALLE EL BOSQUE
CALLE ESCONDIDO
CALLE DE SOTA
CALLE LOS ELEGANTES
CALLE LAS DOS HUERFANAS
CALLE CHIQUITO
CALLE SIEMERIO
CLIFFEDGE DR
ENSENADA
ESSENCIAL
PRIMAVERA
OLIVERA
CAPITAN
HERMOSA
CERRITOS
CARONA
BARANCO
LOMITA
ARROYO
14100
15400
© 2008 Rand McNally & Company
0 .25 .5 .75 1.0 miles 1 in. = 2400 ft.

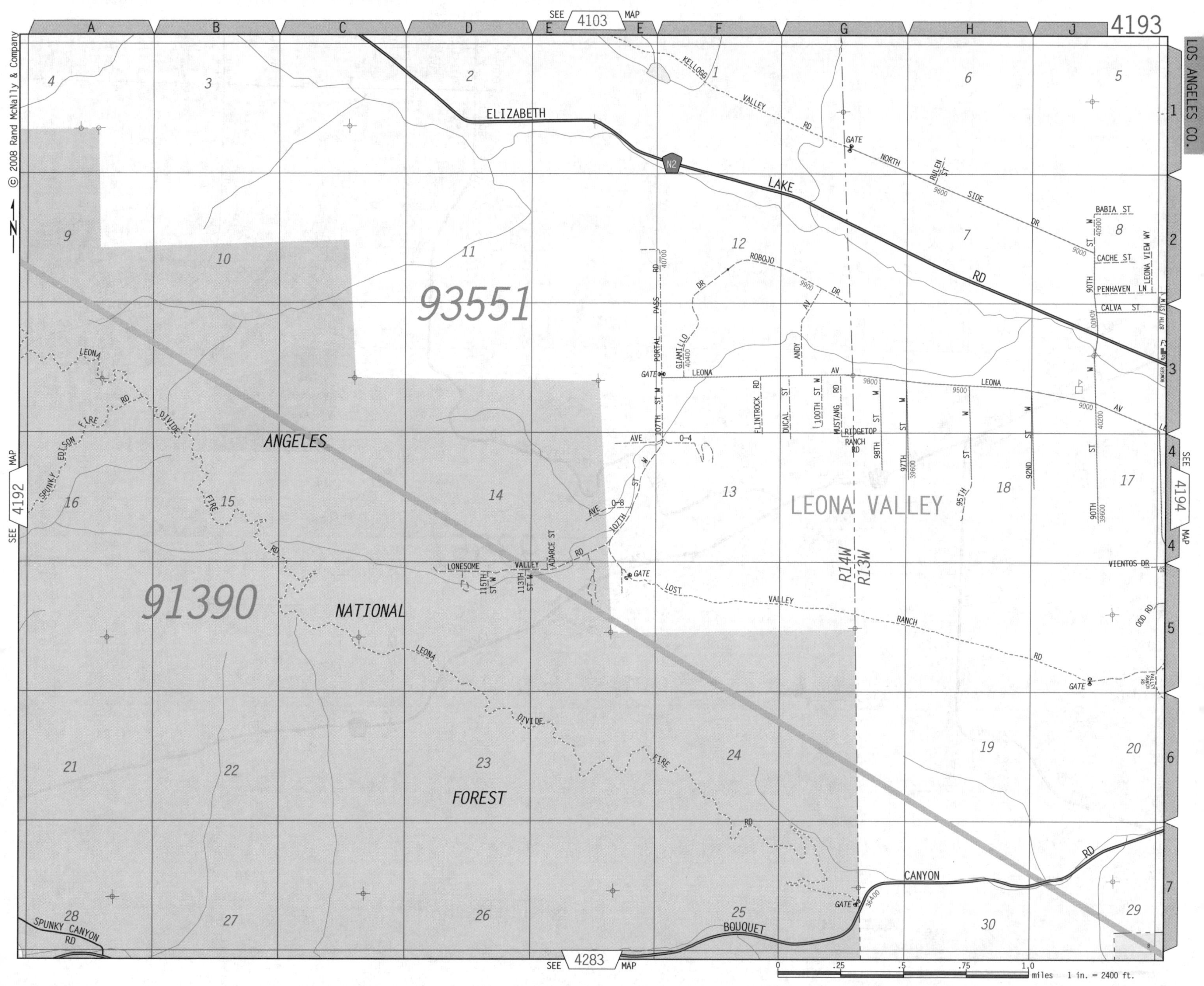

SEE 4103 MAP
LOS ANGELES CO.
© 2008 Rand McNally & Company
93551
91390
ANGELES NATIONAL FOREST
LEONA VALLEY
ELIZABETH LAKE RD
N2
KELLOGG VALLEY RD
NORTH SIDE DR
RULEN ST
BABIA ST
CACHE ST
PENHAVEN LN
CALVA ST
LEONA VIEW WY
90TH ST W
87TH ST W
BOWSER RD
ROBOJO DR
GIAMILLO DR
ANDY AV
PORTAL PASS RD
LEONA AV
107TH ST W
FLINTROCK RD
DUCAL ST
100TH ST W
MUSTANG RD
RIDGETOP RANCH RD
98TH ST
97TH ST
95TH ST
92ND ST
AVE O-4
AVE O-8
LONESOME VALLEY RD
115TH ST W
113TH ST W
ADARCE ST
LEONA DIVIDE FIRE RD
SPUNKY EDISON FIRE RD
LOST VALLEY RANCH RD
VIENTOS DR
ODD RD
GATE
R14W
R13W
BOUQUET CANYON RD
SPUNKY CANYON RD
SEE 4192 MAP
SEE 4194 MAP
SEE 4283 MAP
miles 1 in. = 2400 ft.

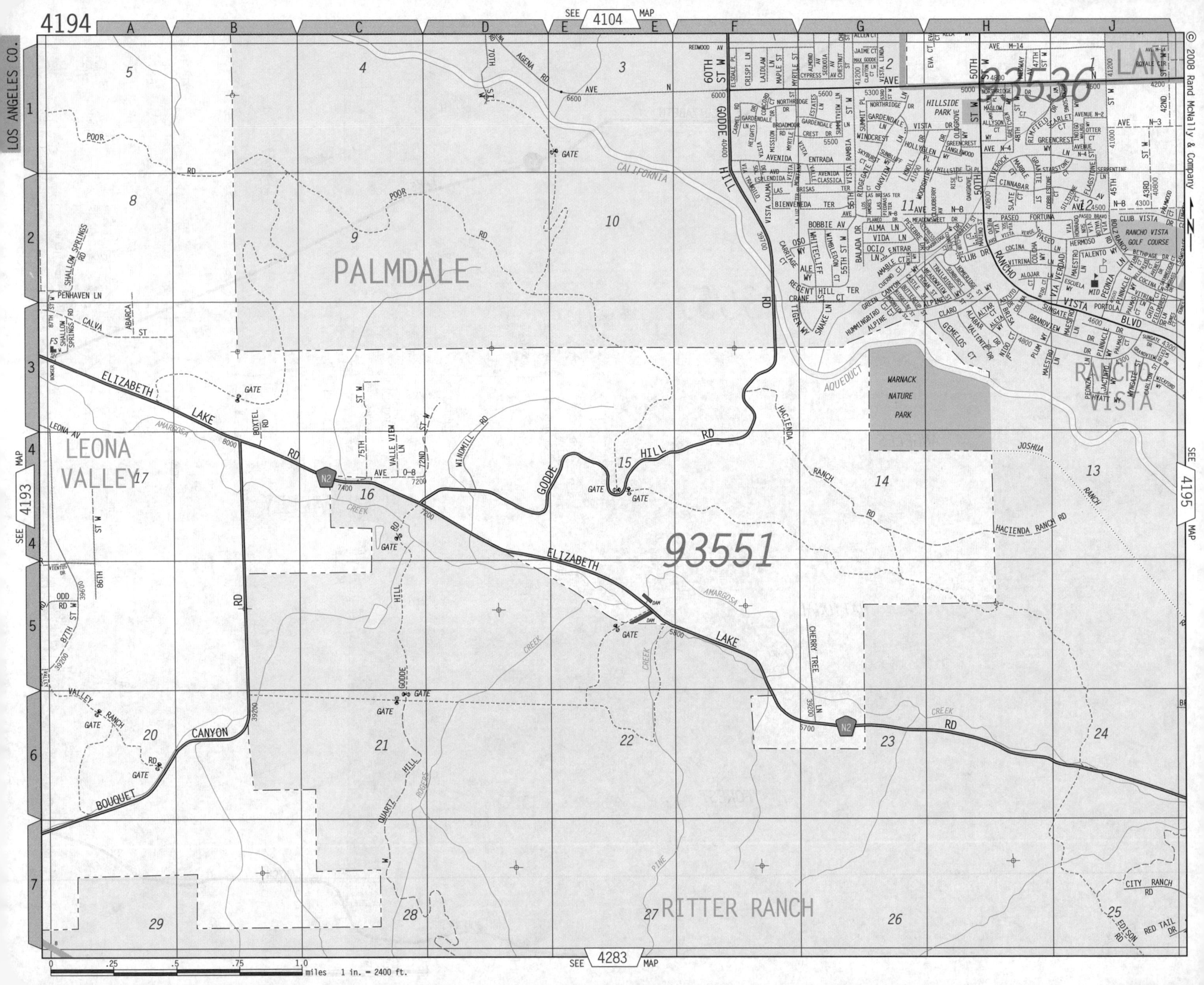

4194
SEE 4104 MAP
SEE 4283 MAP
SEE 4193 MAP
SEE 4195 MAP
LOS ANGELES CO.
© 2008 Rand McNally & Company
PALMDALE
LEONA VALLEY
RITTER RANCH
RANCHO VISTA
93551
93536
WARNACK NATURE PARK
HILLSIDE PARK
RANCHO VISTA GOLF COURSE
ELIZABETH LAKE RD
GODDE HILL RD
BOUQUET CANYON RD
HACIENDA RANCH RD
RANCHO VISTA BLVD
JOSHUA RANCH
CALIFORNIA AQUEDUCT
AMARGOSA CREEK
CITY RANCH RD
EDISON RD
RED TAIL DR
CHERRY TREE LN
QUARTZ HILL
VALLEY RANCH
SHALLOW SPRINGS RD
PENHAVEN LN
CALVA ST
ABARCA
LEONA AV
BOXTEL RD
WINDMILL RD
VALLE VIEW LN
AVE O-8
AVE N
AVE N-8
AVE M-14
60TH ST W
50TH ST W
POOR RD
AGENA RD
70TH ST
GATE
DAM
PINE
ROGERS
N2
0 .25 .5 .75 1.0 miles 1 in. = 2400 ft.

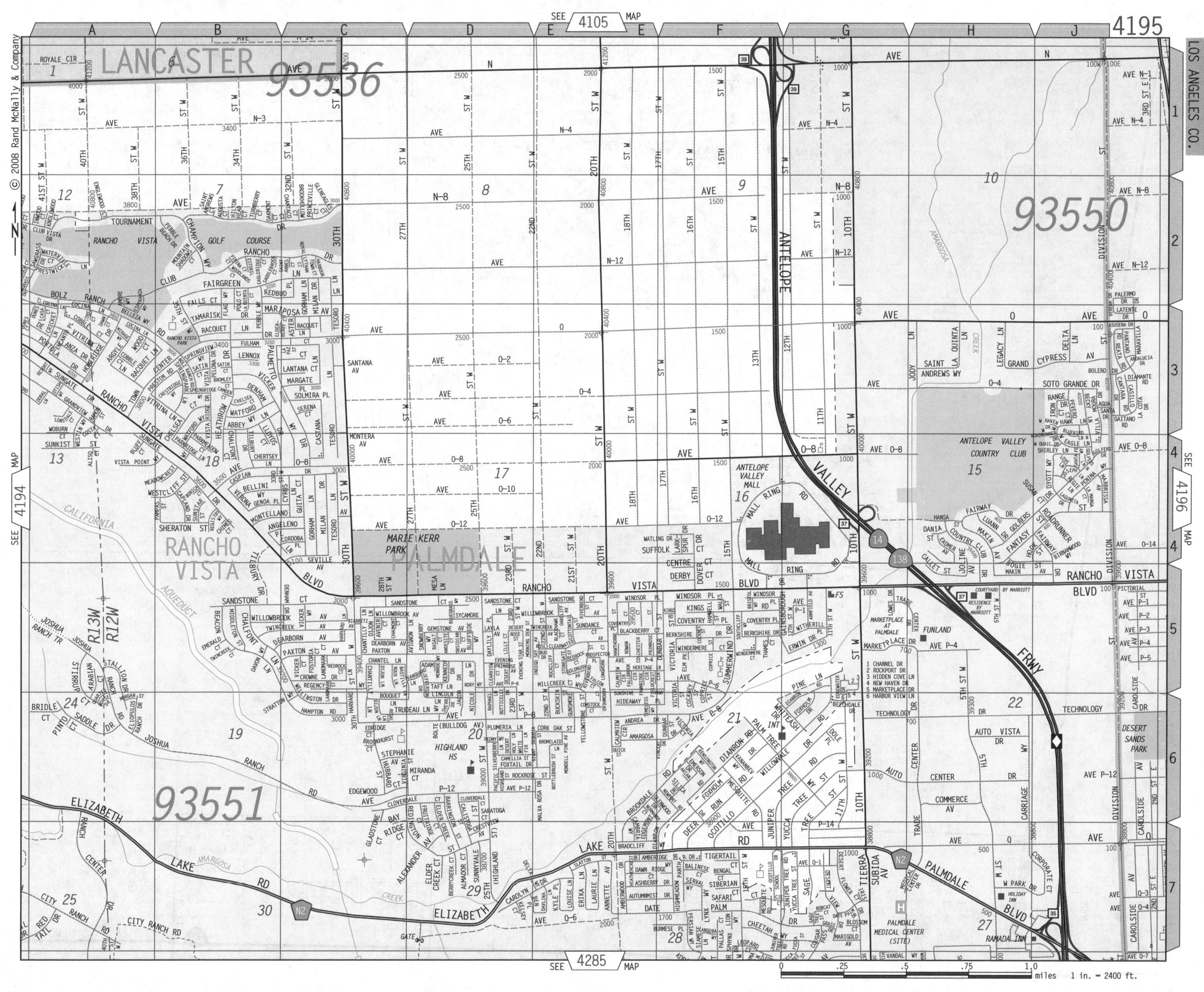
SEE 4105 MAP
SEE 4285 MAP
SEE 4194 MAP
SEE 4196 MAP
LOS ANGELES CO.
© 2008 Rand McNally & Company
A
B
C
D
E
F
G
H
J
1
2
3
4
5
6
7
LANCASTER
PALMDALE
RANCHO VISTA
93536
93550
93551
RANCHO VISTA GOLF COURSE
TOURNAMENT
FAIRGREEN
ANTELOPE VALLEY COUNTRY CLUB
ANTELOPE VALLEY MALL
MALL RING RD
MARIE KERR PARK
HIGHLAND HS
DESERT SANDS PARK
PALMDALE MEDICAL CENTER (SITE)
MARKETPLACE AT PALMDALE
RESIDENCE BY MARRIOTT
COURTYARD BY MARRIOTT
HOLIDAY INN
RAMADA INN
FUNLAND
ANTELOPE VALLEY FRWY
RANCHO VISTA BLVD
ELIZABETH LAKE RD
PALMDALE BLVD
CALIFORNIA AQUEDUCT
AMARGOSA CREEK
CITY RANCH RD
JOSHUA RANCH RD
AVE N
AVE N-4
AVE N-8
AVE N-12
AVE O
AVE O-4
AVE O-8
AVE O-12
AVE P-4
AVE P-12
AVE Q
TECHNOLOGY DR
AUTO CENTER DR
COMMERCE AV
AUTO VISTA DR
TRADE CENTER DR
DIVISION ST
10TH ST W
20TH ST W
30TH ST W
R13W
R12W
1 CHANNEL DR
2 ROCKPORT DR
3 HIDDEN COVE LN
4 NEW HAVEN DR
5 MARKETPLACE DR
6 HARBOR VIEW LN
0 .25 .5 .75 1.0 miles 1 in. = 2400 ft.

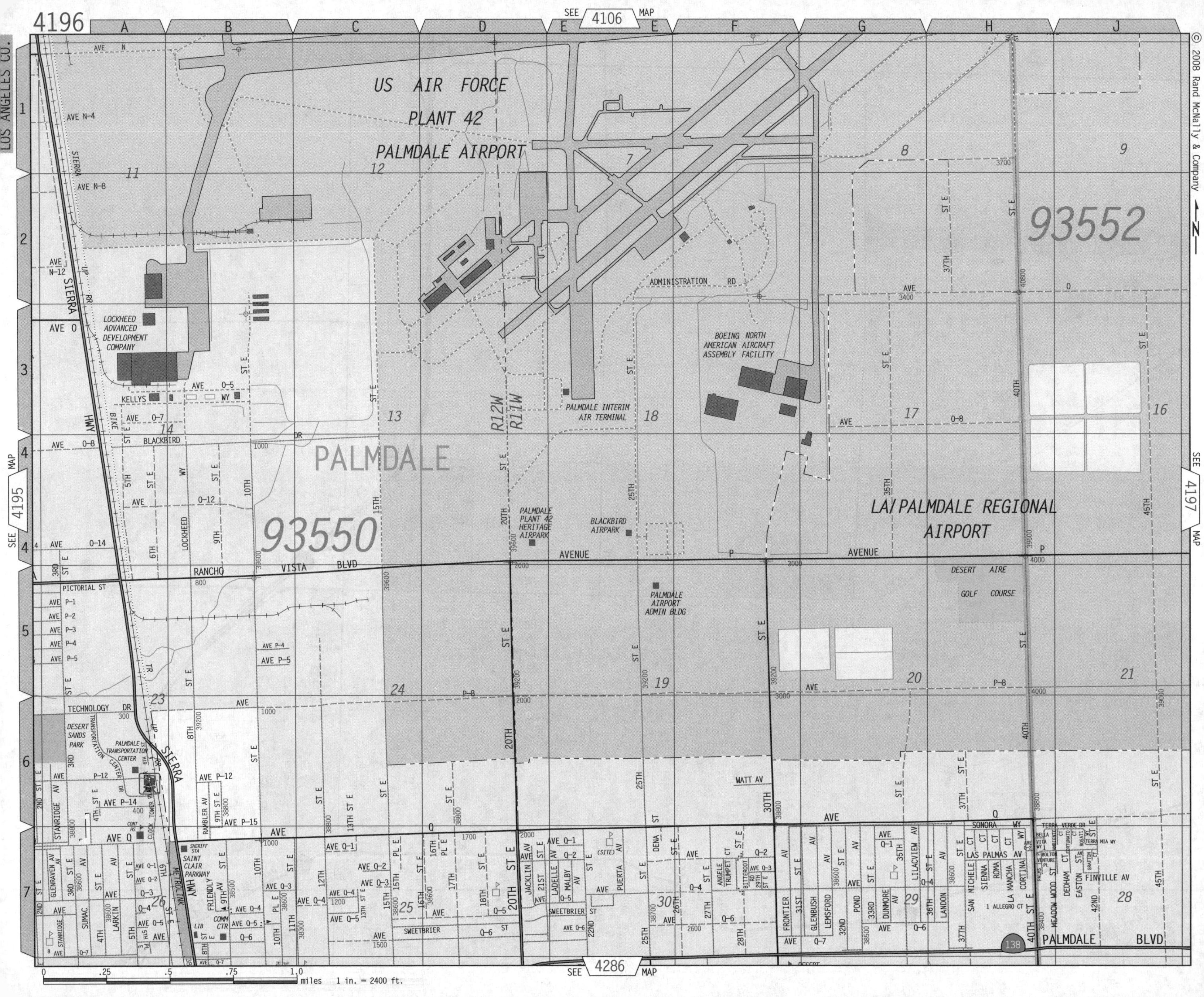

SEE 4106 MAP
LOS ANGELES CO.
US AIR FORCE
PLANT 42
PALMDALE AIRPORT
93552
LOCKHEED ADVANCED DEVELOPMENT COMPANY
ADMINISTRATION RD
BOEING NORTH AMERICAN AIRCRAFT ASSEMBLY FACILITY
PALMDALE INTERIM AIR TERMINAL
PALMDALE
93550
PALMDALE PLANT 42 HERITAGE AIRPARK
BLACKBIRD AIRPARK
LA/PALMDALE REGIONAL AIRPORT
RANCHO VISTA BLVD
AVENUE P
DESERT AIRE GOLF COURSE
PALMDALE AIRPORT ADMIN BLDG
TECHNOLOGY DR
DESERT SANDS PARK
PALMDALE TRANSPORTATION CENTER
SIERRA HWY
SAINT CLAIR PARKWAY
METROLINK
WATT AV
AVE Q
PALMDALE BLVD
SEE 4195 MAP
SEE 4197 MAP
SEE 4286 MAP
0 .25 .5 .75 1.0 miles 1 in. = 2400 ft.

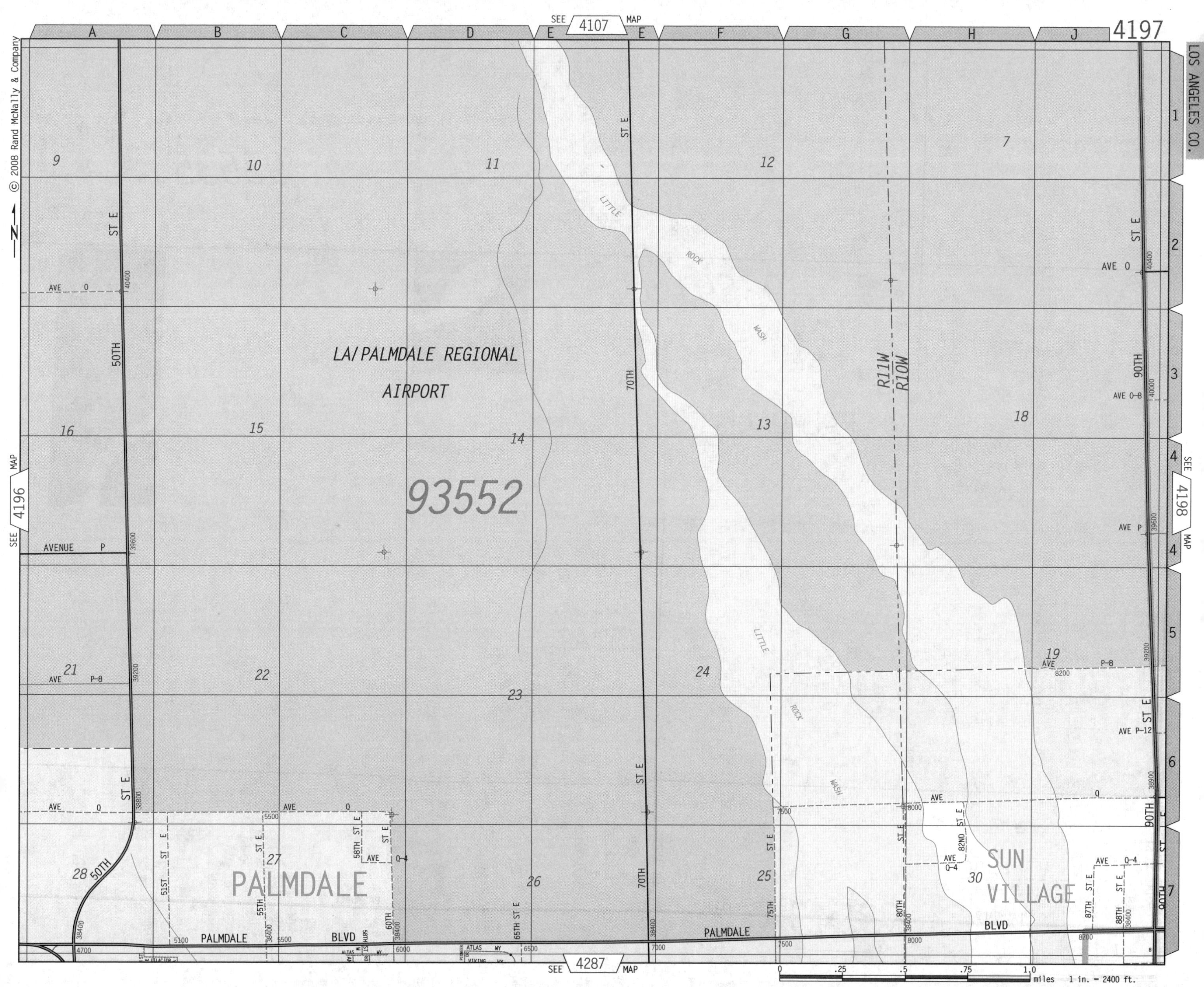
SEE 4107 MAP
LOS ANGELES CO.
© 2008 Rand McNally & Company
LA/PALMDALE REGIONAL
AIRPORT
93552
PALMDALE
SUN
VILLAGE
LITTLE ROCK WASH
R11W
R10W
50TH ST E
70TH ST E
90TH ST E
AVE O
AVENUE P
AVE P
AVE P-8
AVE O-8
AVE P-12
AVE Q
AVE Q-4
PALMDALE BLVD
51ST ST E
55TH ST E
58TH ST E
60TH ST E
65TH ST E
75TH ST E
80TH ST E
82ND ST E
87TH ST E
88TH ST E
SEE 4196 MAP
SEE 4198 MAP
SEE 4287 MAP
miles 1 in. = 2400 ft.

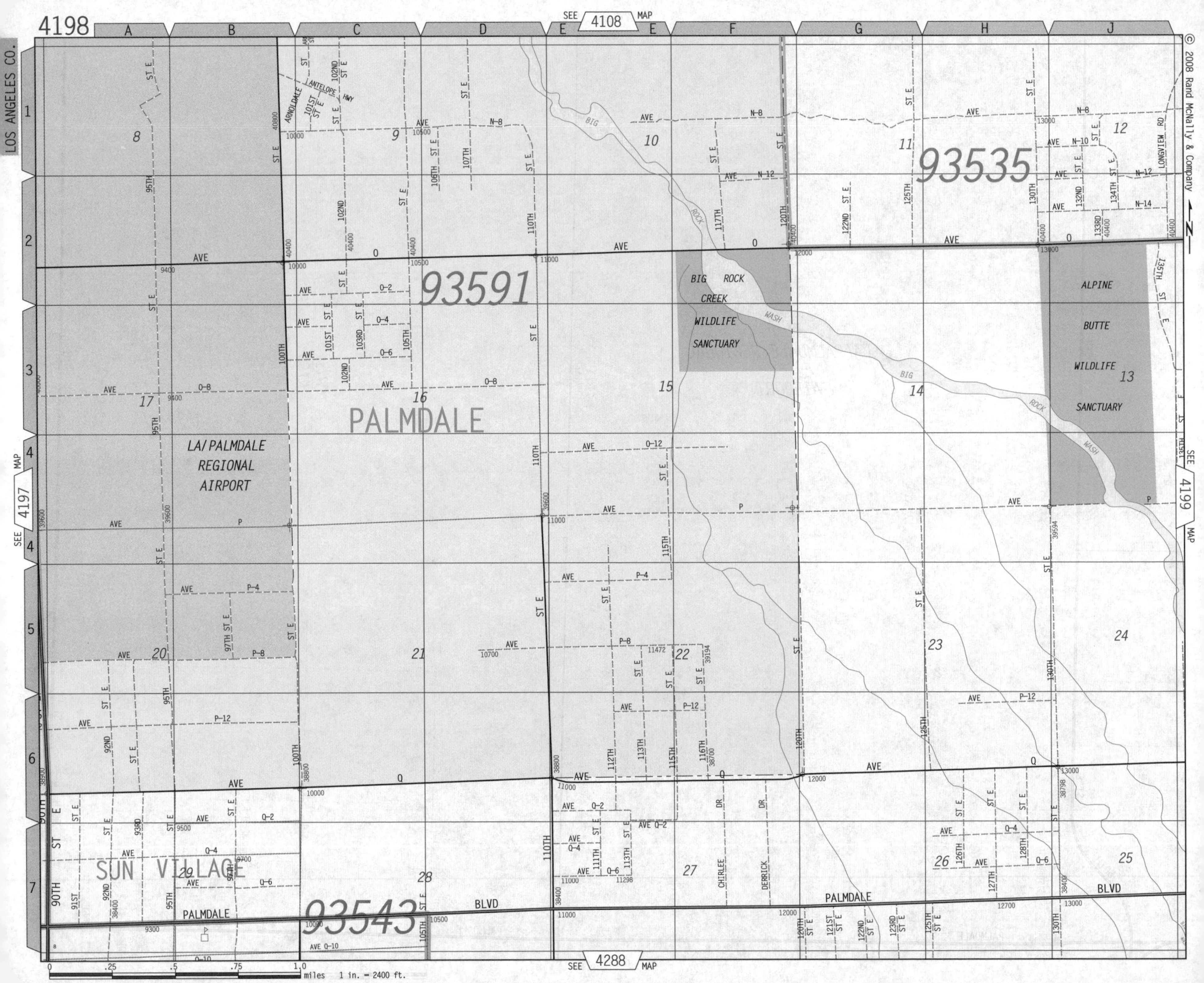
4198
LOS ANGELES CO.
SEE 4108 MAP
SEE 4197 MAP
SEE 4199 MAP
SEE 4288 MAP
PALMDALE
93591
93535
93543
SUN VILLAGE
LA/PALMDALE
REGIONAL
AIRPORT
BIG ROCK
CREEK
WILDLIFE
SANCTUARY
ALPINE
BUTTE
WILDLIFE
SANCTUARY
BIG ROCK WASH
PALMDALE BLVD
AVE O
AVE P
AVE Q
AVE N-8
AVE O-8
AVE P-8
AVE P-12
ANTELOPE HWY
ARNOLDALE
LONGVIEW RD
CHIRLEE DR
DERRICK DR
90TH ST E
100TH ST E
110TH ST E
120TH ST E
130TH ST E
0 .25 .5 .75 1.0 miles 1 in. = 2400 ft.
© 2008 Rand McNally & Company

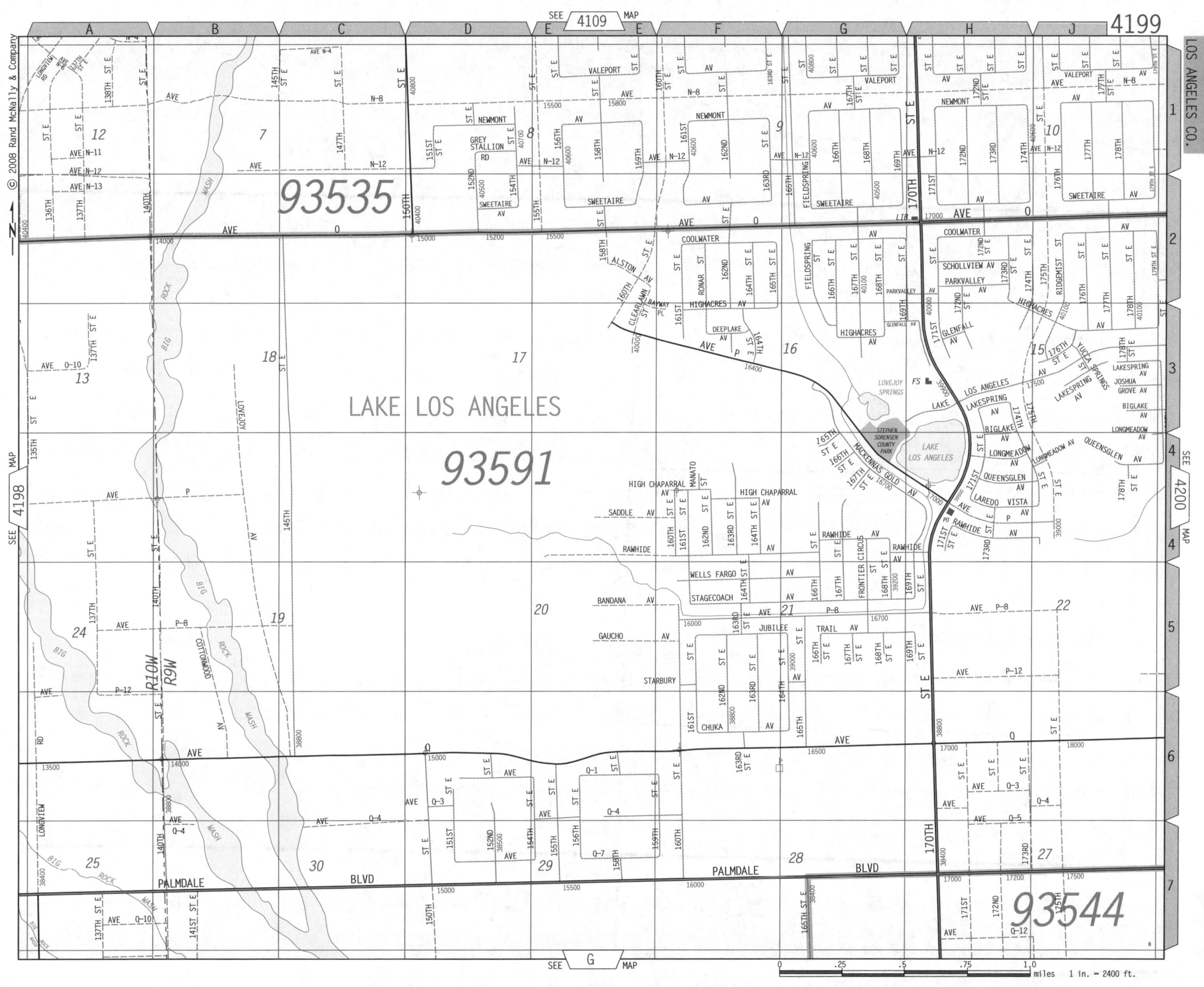

LOS ANGELES CO.
SEE 4109 MAP
SEE 4198 MAP
SEE 4200 MAP
SEE G MAP
93535
93591
93544
LAKE LOS ANGELES
LOVEJOY SPRINGS
STEPHEN SORENSEN COUNTY PARK
LAKE LOS ANGELES
BIG ROCK WASH
R10W
R9W
AVE O
AVE P
AVE Q
PALMDALE BLVD
170TH ST E
150TH ST E
140TH ST E
145TH ST E
VALEPORT AV
NEWMONT AV
GREY STALLION RD
SWEETAIRE AV
COOLWATER AV
ALSTON AV
CLEARLAWN ST
BAYWAY PL
HIGHACRES AV
DEEPLAKE AV
FIELDSPRING ST
SCHOLLVIEW AV
PARKVALLEY AV
GLENFALL AV
RIDGEMIST ST
LAKE LOS ANGELES AV
LAKESPRING AV
YUCCA SPRINGS
JOSHUA GROVE AV
BIGLAKE AV
LONGMEADOW AV
QUEENSGLEN AV
LAREDO VISTA
RAWHIDE ST
MACKENNAS GOLD AV
HIGH CHAPARRAL AV
MANATO ST
SADDLE AV
RAWHIDE AV
WELLS FARGO AV
STAGECOACH AV
FRONTIER CIRCUS ST
BANDANA AV
GAUCHO AV
JUBILEE AV
TRAIL AV
STARBURY AV
CHUKA AV
LOVEJOY AV
COTTONWOOD AV
LONGVIEW RD
FS
LIB
0 .25 .5 .75 1.0 miles 1 in. = 2400 ft.

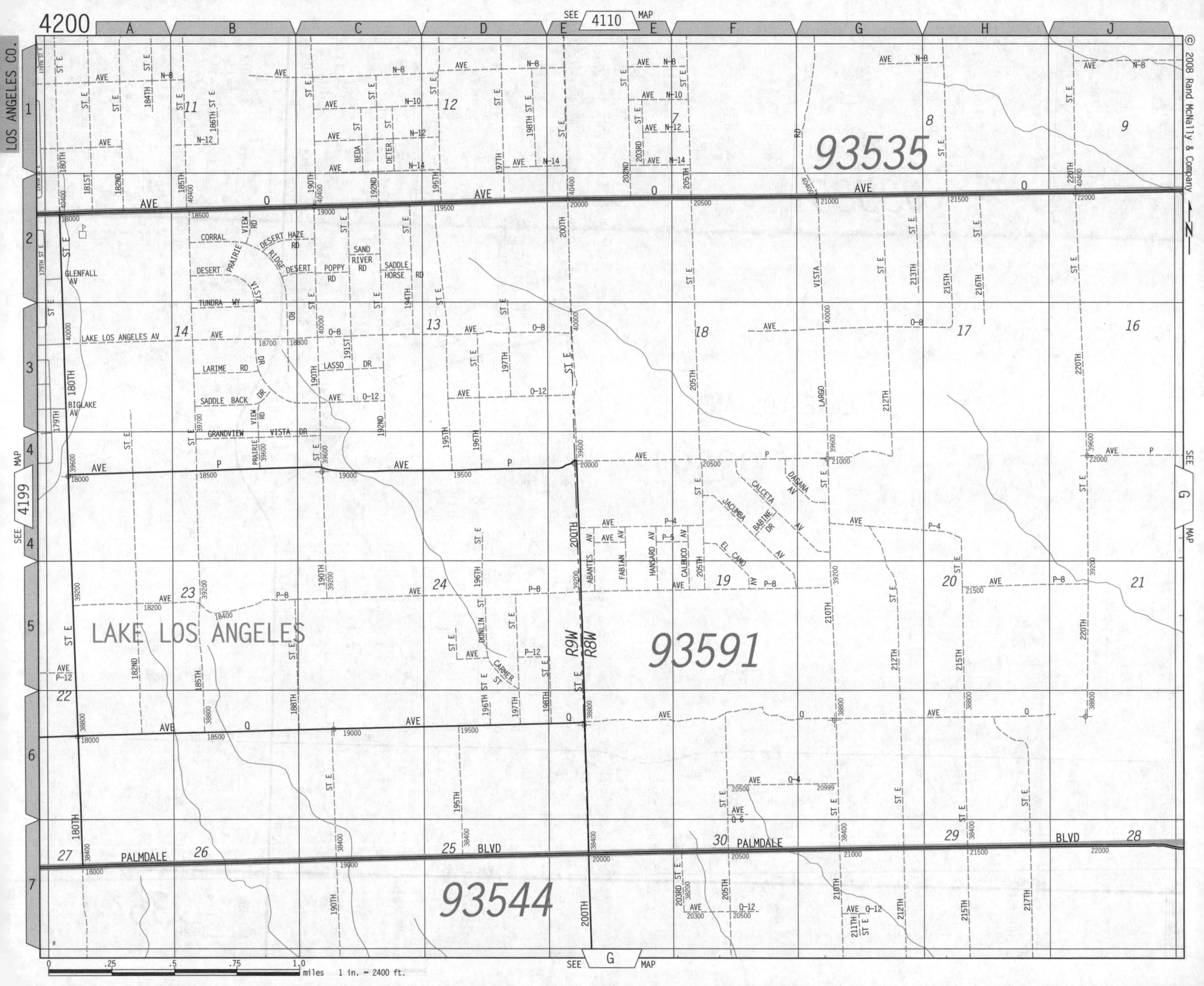

4200
SEE 4110 MAP
A B C D E E F G H J
LOS ANGELES CO.
© 2008 Rand McNally & Company
93535
93591
93544
LAKE LOS ANGELES
AVE O
AVE P
AVE Q
PALMDALE BLVD
AVE N-8
AVE N-10
AVE N-12
AVE N-14
AVE O-8
AVE O-12
AVE P-4
AVE P-5
AVE P-8
AVE P-12
AVE Q-4
AVE Q-6
AVE Q-12
LAKE LOS ANGELES AV
GLENFALL AV
BIGLAKE AV
CORRAL
DESERT HAZE RD
PRAIRIE VIEW RD
RIDGE DESERT RD
DESERT
PRAIRIE VISTA DR
TUNDRA WY
LARIME RD
SADDLE BACK
VIEW RD
GRANDVIEW VISTA DR
POPPY RD
SAND RIVER RD
SADDLE HORSE RD
LASSO DR
BEDA ST
DETER ST
DUNLIN ST
CARMER ST
VISTA LARGO
DAGANA AV
CALCETA AV
JACUMBA
BABINE DR
EL CAMO AV
ABANTES AV
FABIAN
HANSARD AV
CALBUCO AV
170TH ST E
179TH ST E
180TH ST E
181ST ST E
182ND ST E
184TH ST E
185TH ST E
186TH ST E
188TH ST E
190TH ST E
191ST ST E
192ND ST E
194TH ST E
195TH ST E
196TH ST E
197TH ST E
198TH ST E
200TH ST E
202ND ST E
203RD ST E
205TH ST E
210TH ST E
211TH ST E
212TH ST E
213TH ST E
215TH ST E
216TH ST E
217TH ST E
220TH ST E
R9W
R8W
SEE 4199 MAP
SEE G MAP
0 .25 .5 .75 1.0 miles 1 in. = 2400 ft.

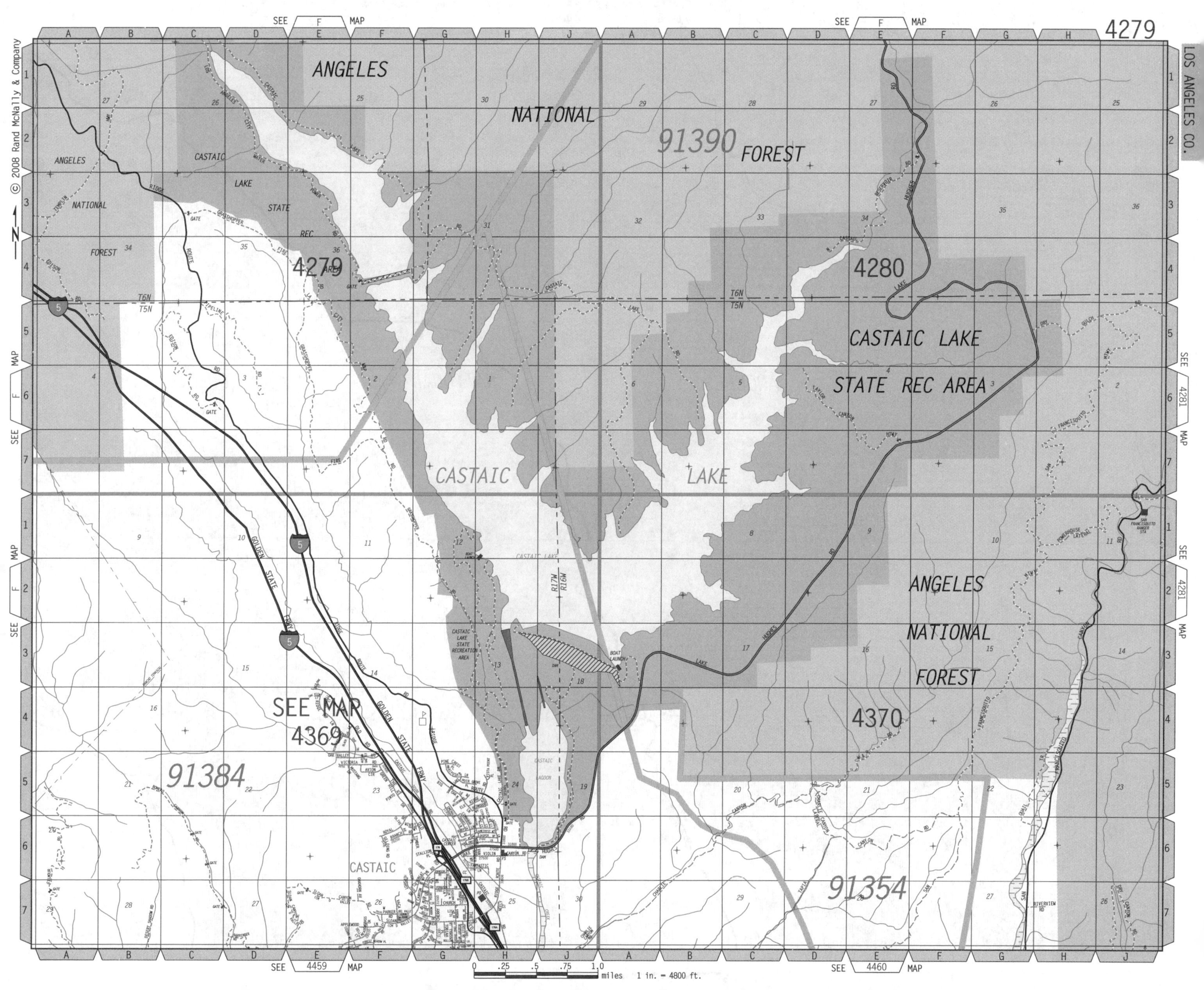

LOS ANGELES CO.
ANGELES NATIONAL FOREST
91390
CASTAIC LAKE STATE REC AREA
CASTAIC LAKE
4279
4280
4370
SEE MAP 4369
91384
91354
CASTAIC
T6N
T5N
R17W
R16W
SEE F MAP
SEE 4281 MAP
SEE 4459 MAP
SEE 4460 MAP
miles 1 in. = 4800 ft.

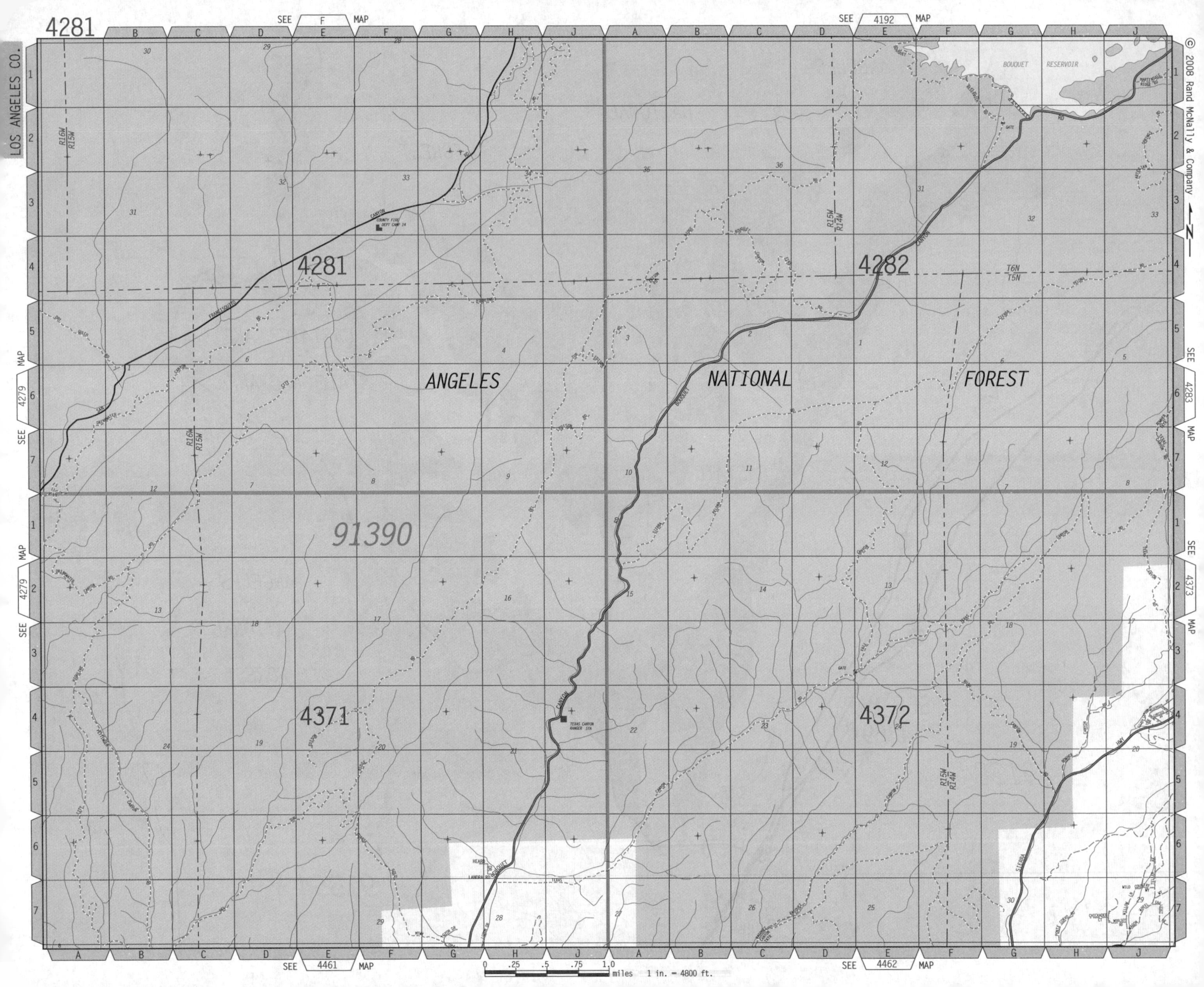
LOS ANGELES CO.
SEE F MAP
SEE 4192 MAP
SEE 4279 MAP
SEE 4283 MAP
SEE 4373 MAP
SEE 4461 MAP
SEE 4462 MAP
4281
4282
4371
4372
91390
ANGELES
NATIONAL
FOREST
BOUQUET RESERVOIR
COUNTY FIRE DEPT CAMP 14
TEXAS CANYON RANGER STA
BOUQUET CANYON RD
SIERRA HWY
T6N
T5N
R16W
R15W
R14W
GATE
0 .25 .5 .75 1.0 miles 1 in. = 4800 ft.

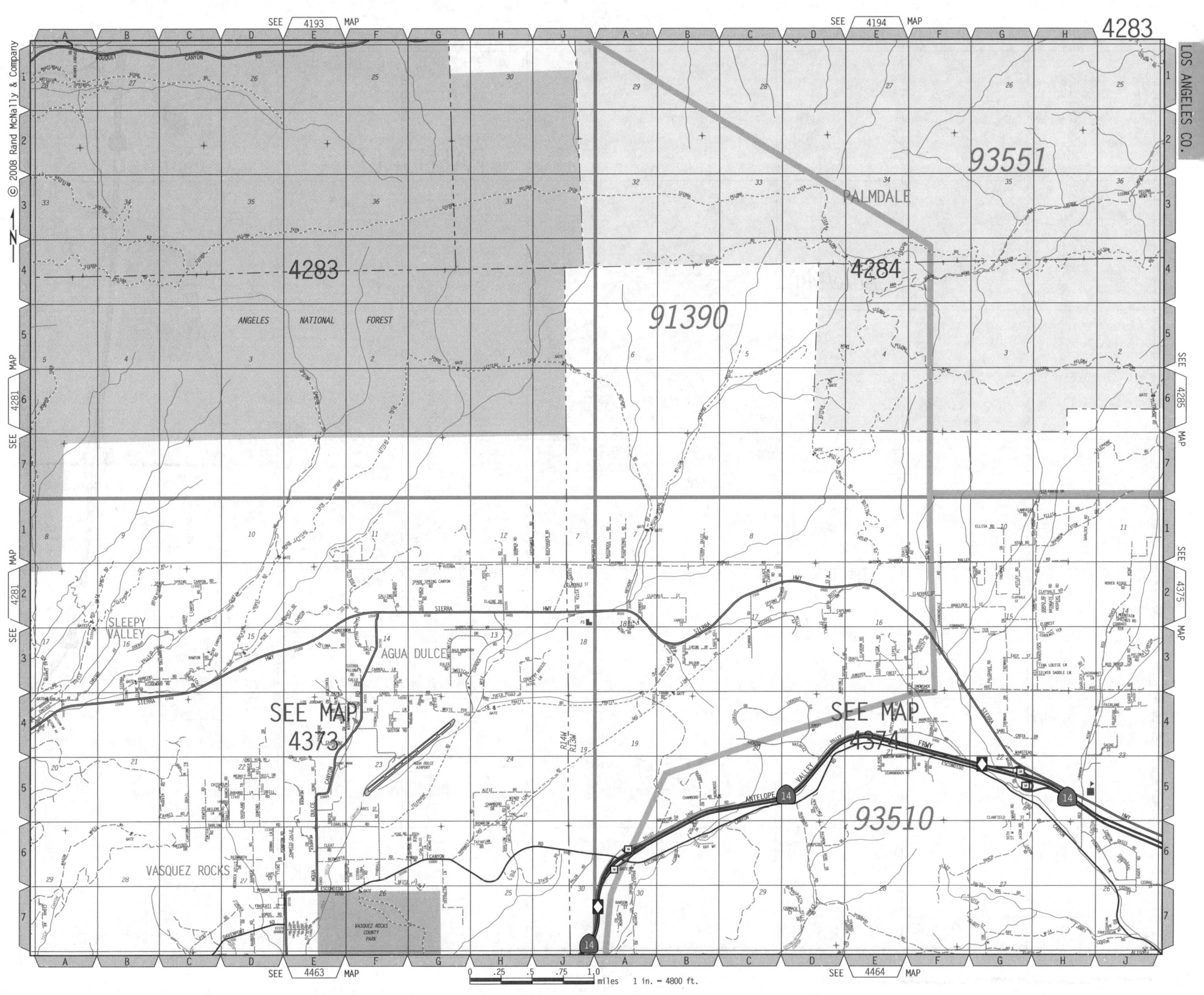
SEE 4193 MAP
SEE 4194 MAP
LOS ANGELES CO.
© 2008 Rand McNally & Company
BOUQUET CANYON RD
93551
PALMDALE
4283
4284
ANGELES NATIONAL FOREST
91390
SEE 4281 MAP
SEE 4285 MAP
SEE 4375 MAP
SLEEPY VALLEY
AGUA DULCE
SIERRA HWY
SEE MAP 4373
SEE MAP 4374
AGUA DULCE AIRPORT
ANTELOPE VALLEY FRWY
93510
VASQUEZ ROCKS
VASQUEZ ROCKS COUNTY PARK
ESCONDIDO
R14W R13W
SEE 4463 MAP
SEE 4464 MAP
0 .25 .5 .75 1.0 miles 1 in. = 4800 ft.

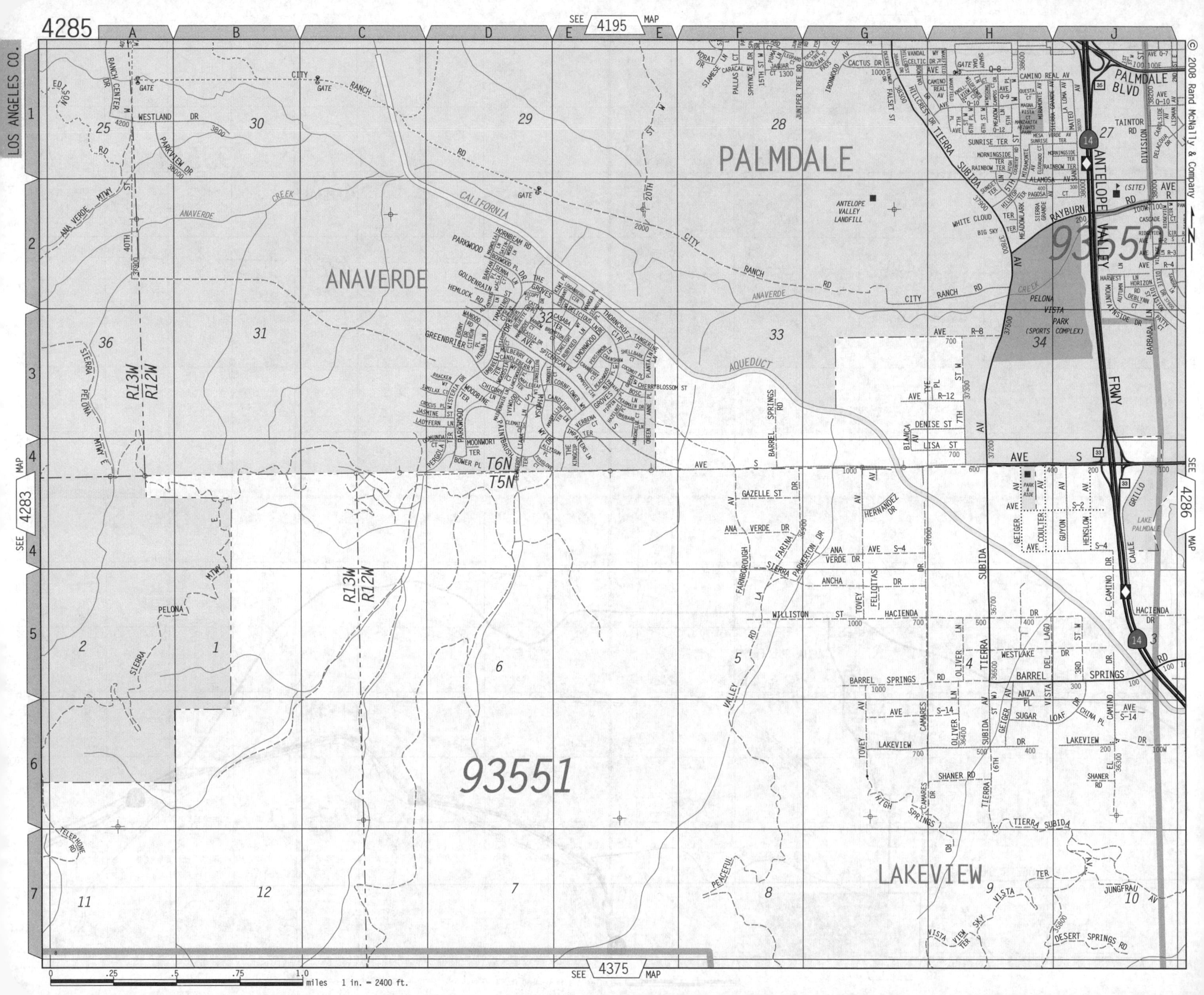

SEE 4195 MAP
SEE 4283 MAP
SEE 4286 MAP
SEE 4375 MAP

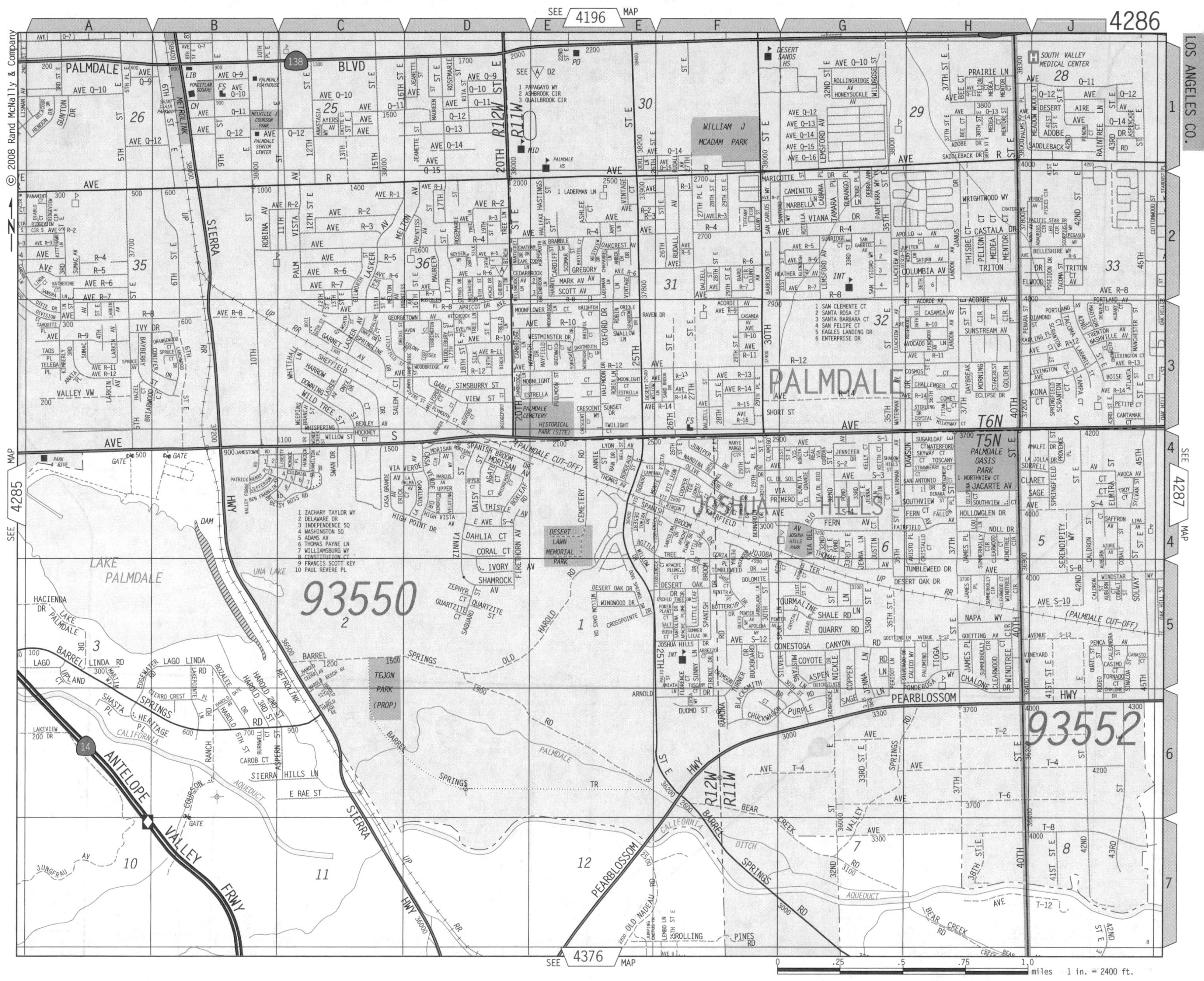

4286
SEE 4196 MAP
SEE 4376 MAP
SEE 4285 MAP
SEE 4287 MAP
LOS ANGELES CO.
© 2008 Rand McNally & Company
PALMDALE
JOSHUA HILLS
93550
93552
PALMDALE BLVD
SIERRA HWY
ANTELOPE VALLEY FRWY
PEARBLOSSOM HWY
BARREL SPRINGS RD
CALIFORNIA AQUEDUCT
LAKE PALMDALE
UNA LAKE
WILLIAM J MCADAM PARK
PALMDALE OASIS PARK
DESERT LAWN MEMORIAL PARK
PALMDALE CEMETERY
HISTORICAL PARK (SITE)
TEJON PARK (PROP)
JOSHUA HILLS PARK
MELVILLE J COURSON PARK
SOUTH VALLEY MEDICAL CENTER
PALMDALE PLAYHOUSE
PALMDALE SENIOR CENTER
PONCITLAN SQUARE
DESERT SANDS HS
PALMDALE HS
METROLINK
(PALMDALE CUT-OFF)
BEAR CREEK
T6N
T5N
R12W
R11W
1 ZACHARY TAYLOR WY
2 DELAWARE DR
3 INDEPENDENCE SQ
4 WASHINGTON SQ
5 ADAMS AV
6 THOMAS PAYNE LN
7 WILLIAMSBURG WY
8 CONSTITUTION CT
9 FRANCIS SCOTT KEY
10 PAUL REVERE PL
1 SAN CLEMENTE CT
2 SANTA ROSA CT
3 SANTA BARBARA CT
4 SAN FELIPE CT
5 EAGLES LANDING DR
6 ENTERPRISE DR
1 PAPAGAYO WY
2 ASHBROOK CIR
3 QUAILBROOK CIR
miles 1 in. = 2400 ft.

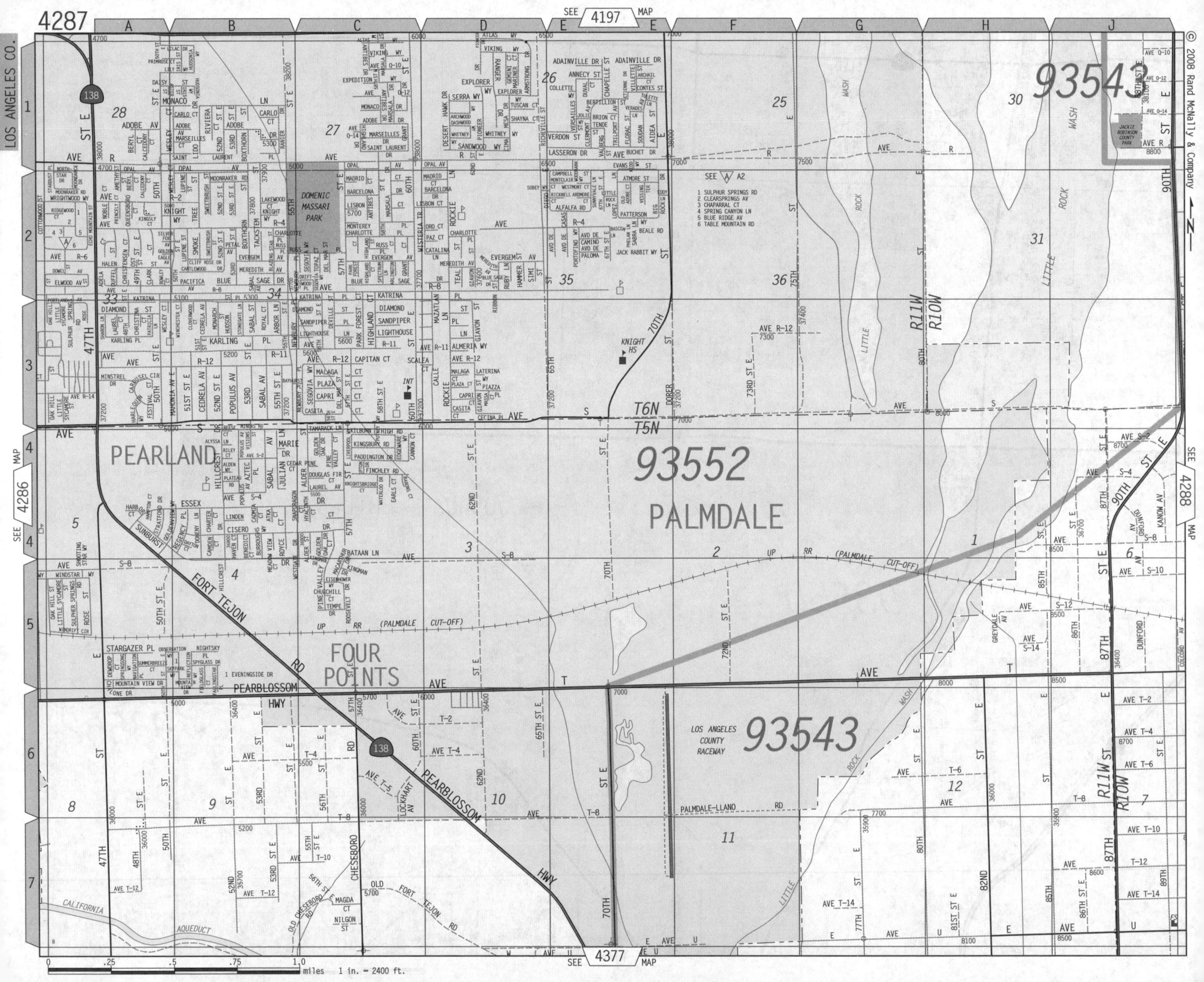

LOS ANGELES CO.
SEE 4197 MAP
SEE 4286 MAP
SEE 4288 MAP
SEE 4377 MAP
A
B
C
D
E
F
G
H
J
1
2
3
4
5
6
7
93543
93552
93543
PEARLAND
PALMDALE
FOUR POINTS
DOMENIC MASSARI PARK
KNIGHT HS
JACKIE ROBINSON COUNTY PARK
LOS ANGELES COUNTY RACEWAY
PEARBLOSSOM HWY
FORT TEJON RD
PEARBLOSSOM AVE
PALMDALE-LLANO RD
OLD FORT TEJON RD
CALIFORNIA AQUEDUCT
UP RR (PALMDALE CUT-OFF)
LITTLE ROCK WASH
T6N
T5N
R11W
R10W
138
SEE A A2
1 SULPHUR SPRINGS RD
2 CLEARSPRINGS AV
3 CHAPARRAL CT
4 SPRING CANYON LN
5 BLUE RIDGE AV
6 TABLE MOUNTAIN RD
1 EVENINGSIDE DR
0 .25 .5 .75 1.0 miles 1 in. = 2400 ft.

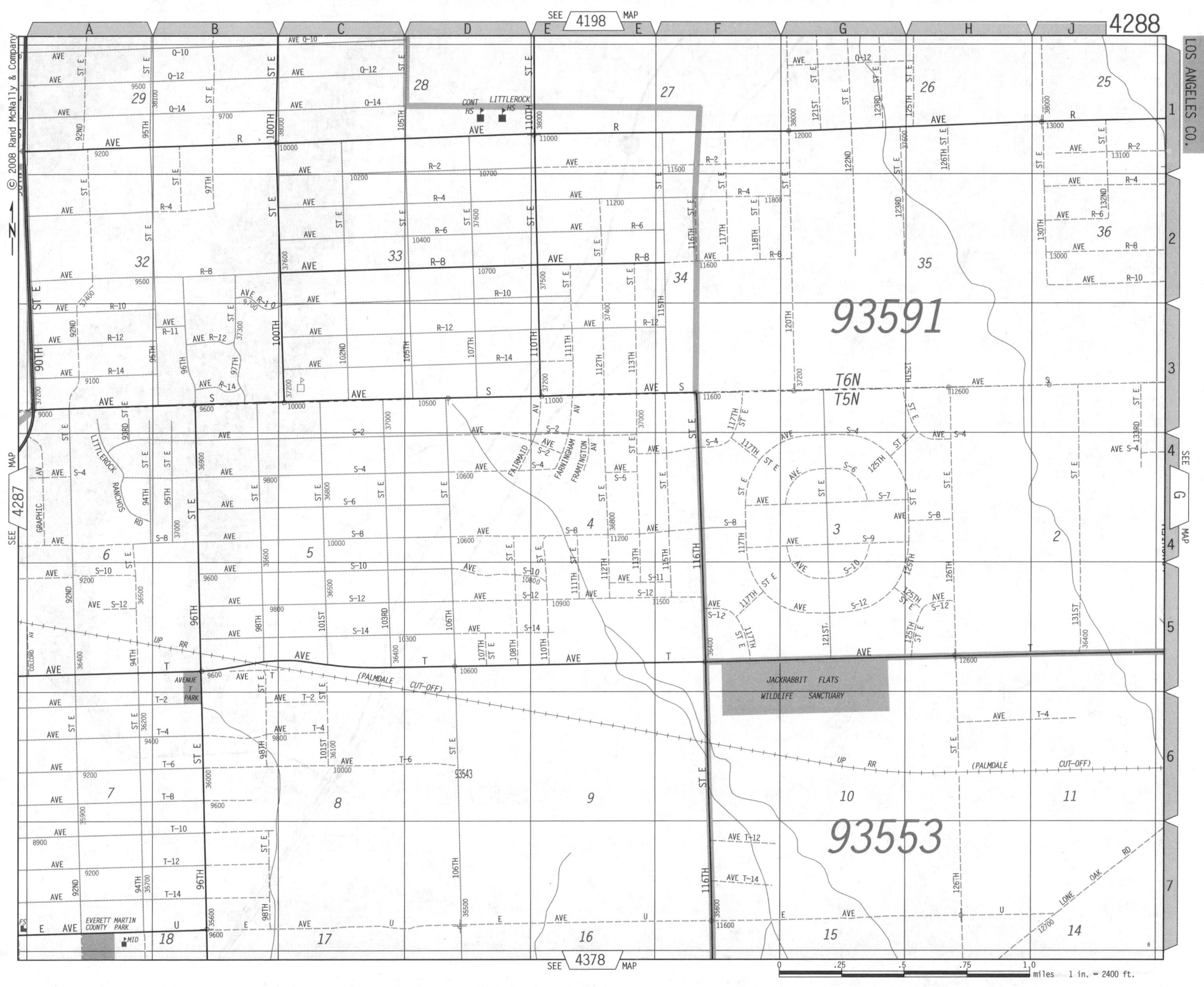

4288
SEE 4198 MAP
SEE 4378 MAP
SEE 4287 MAP
SEE G MAP
LOS ANGELES CO.
© 2008 Rand McNally & Company
93591
93553
93543
T6N
T5N
AVE R
AVE S
AVE T
AVE U
90TH
96TH
100TH
110TH
116TH
ST E
CONT HS
LITTLEROCK HS
LITTLEROCK RANCHOS RD
FAIRMAID
FARNINGHAM
FRAMINGTON AV
GRAPHIC AV
COLCORD AV
AVENUE T PARK
UP RR
(PALMDALE CUT-OFF)
JACKRABBIT FLATS WILDLIFE SANCTUARY
EVERETT MARTIN COUNTY PARK
MID
LONE OAK RD
0 .25 .5 .75 1.0 miles 1 in. = 2400 ft.

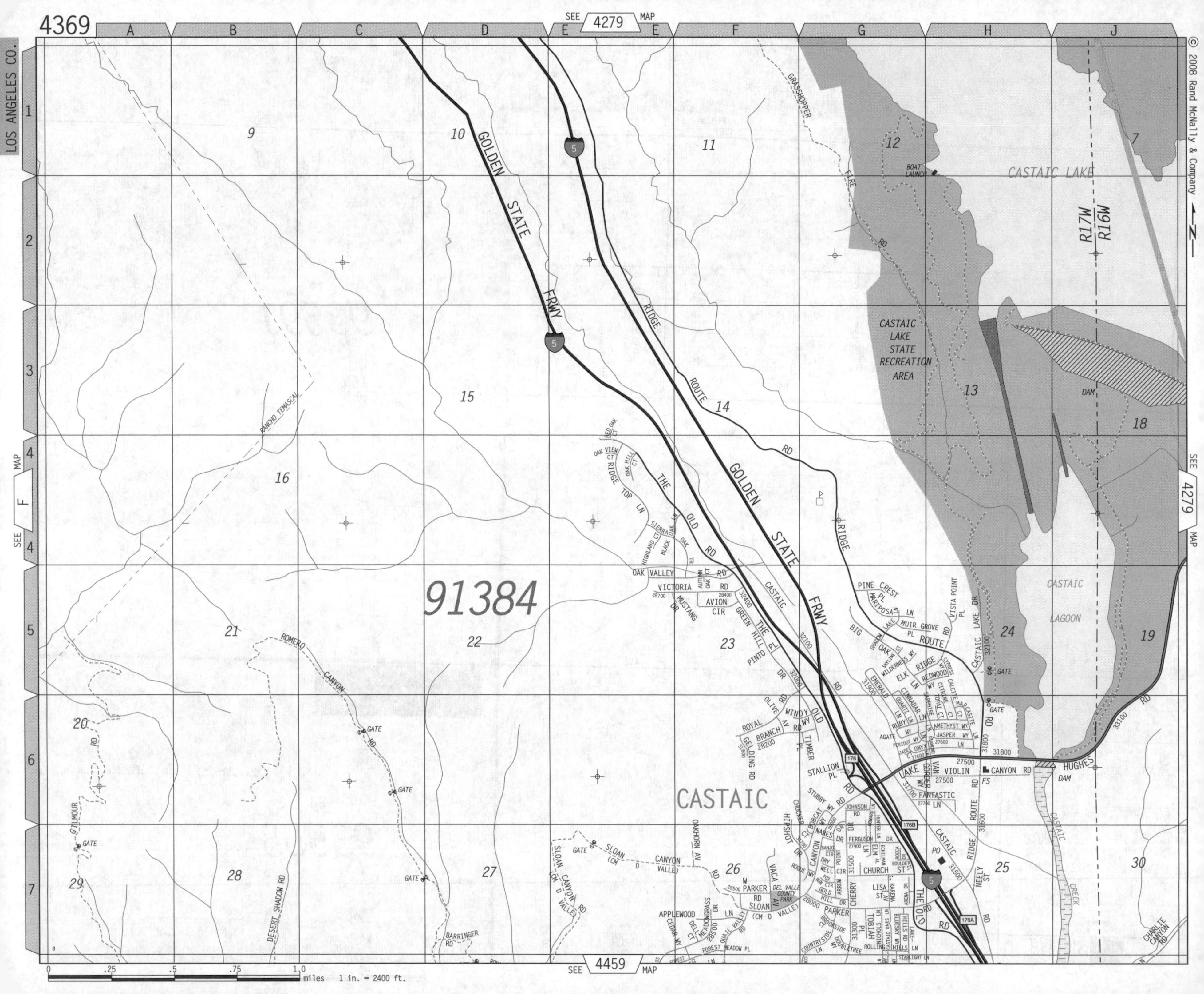
SEE 4279 MAP
SEE 4459 MAP
SEE F 4 MAP
SEE 4279 MAP
LOS ANGELES CO.
A
B
C
D
E
F
G
H
J
1
2
3
4
5
6
7
91384
CASTAIC
CASTAIC LAKE
CASTAIC LAKE STATE RECREATION AREA
CASTAIC LAGOON
BOAT LAUNCH
DAM
R17W
R16W
GOLDEN STATE FRWY
GOLDEN STATE FRWY
RIDGE ROUTE RD
THE OLD RD
GRASSHOPPER FIRE RD
RANCHO TEMASCAL
ROMERO CANYON RD
GILMOUR RD
DESERT SHADOW RD
SLOAN CANYON (CM D VALLE) RD
SLOAN (CM D VALLE)
BARRINGER RD
OAKHORN AV
LAKE HUGHES RD
CASTAIC CREEK
CHARLIE CANYON RD
OAK VALLEY RD
VICTORIA RD
AVION CIR
MUSTANG DR
GREEN HILL PL
PINTO DR
CASTAIC
RIDGE TOP LN
SIERRA
HIGHLAND CT
BLACK OAK TR
RED OAK CT
OAK VIEW CT
OAK HILL CT
PINE CREST PL
MARIPOSA LN
MUIR GROVE PL
VISTA POINT PL
CASTAIC LAKE DR
BIG OAK
ELK RIDGE
REDWOOD WY
EMERALD
CINNABAR
JASPER WY
AGATE
ONYX
VIOLIN CANYON RD
VAN GORDER
FANTASTIC LN
ROUTE RIDGE
NEELY ST
PO
FS
ROYAL BRANCH
GELDING RD
OLIVE AV
WINDY RD
TIMBER
STALLION PL
STUBBY
BOBCAT
CRICKET
HIPSHOT DR
CANYON
JOHNSON RD
FERGUSON DR
CHURCH ST
CHERRY
PARKER
W PARKER RD
VACA AV
DEL VALLE COUNTY PARK
APPLEWOOD
MEADOWGRASS
QUAIL VALLEY
CEDAR WY
FOREST MEADOW PL
COUNTRYSIDE LN
DOUBLETREE
ROLLING HILLS
STARLIGHT LN
LISA ST
TOBIAH PL
GATE
5
176
176A
176B
9
10
11
12
13
14
15
16
18
19
20
21
22
23
24
25
26
27
28
29
30
7
0
.25
.5
.75
1.0
miles 1 in. = 2400 ft.

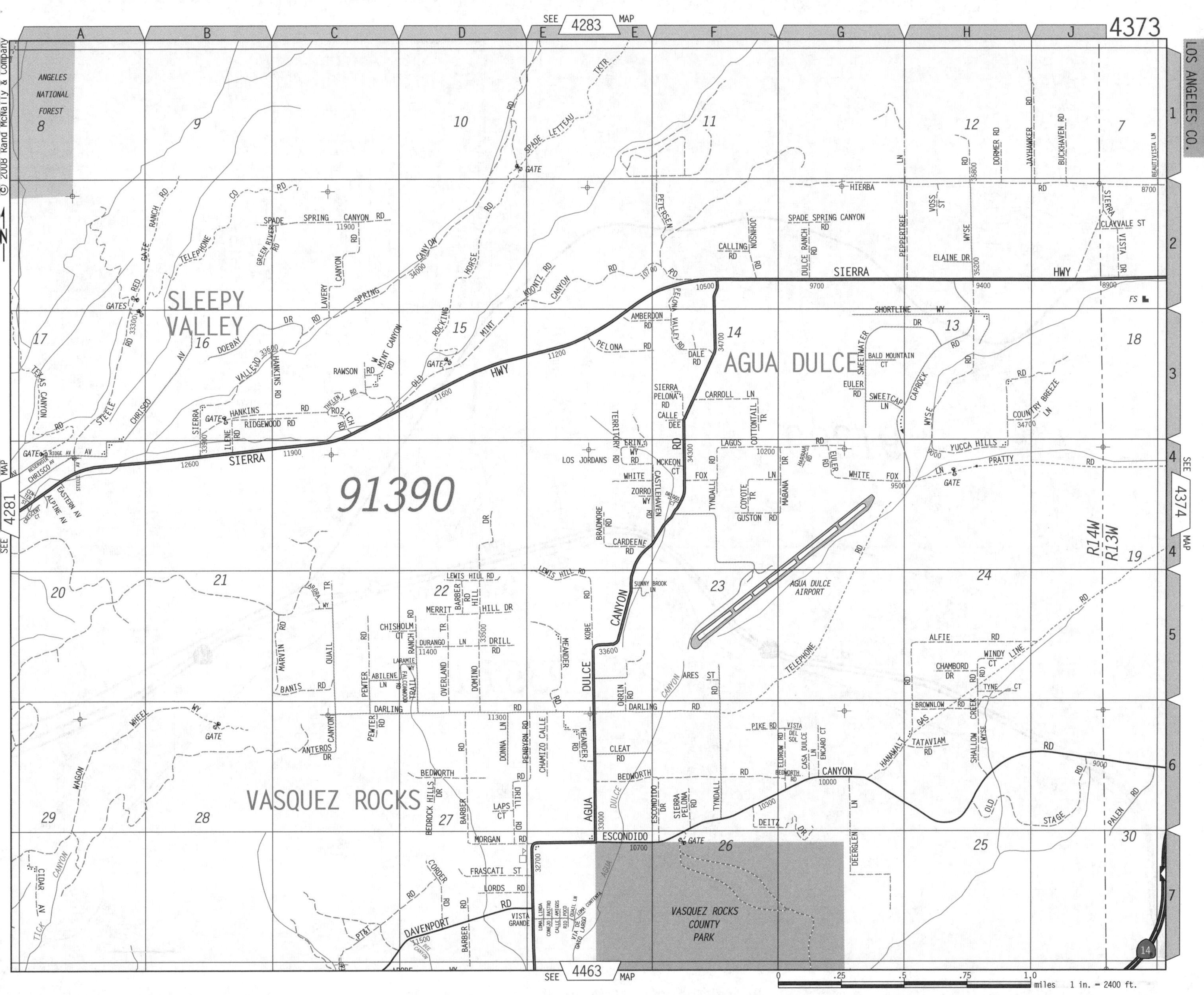

SEE 4283 MAP
SEE 4463 MAP
SEE 4281 MAP
SEE 4374 MAP
LOS ANGELES CO.
ANGELES NATIONAL FOREST
SLEEPY VALLEY
AGUA DULCE
VASQUEZ ROCKS
91390
AGUA DULCE AIRPORT
VASQUEZ ROCKS COUNTY PARK
SIERRA HWY
AGUA DULCE CANYON RD
ESCONDIDO CANYON RD
DAVENPORT RD
SPADE SPRING CANYON RD
SPRING CANYON RD
MINT CANYON RD
PETERSEN RD
JOHNSON RD
DARLING RD
BEDWORTH RD
TELEPHONE RD
R14W
R13W
miles 1 in. = 2400 ft.

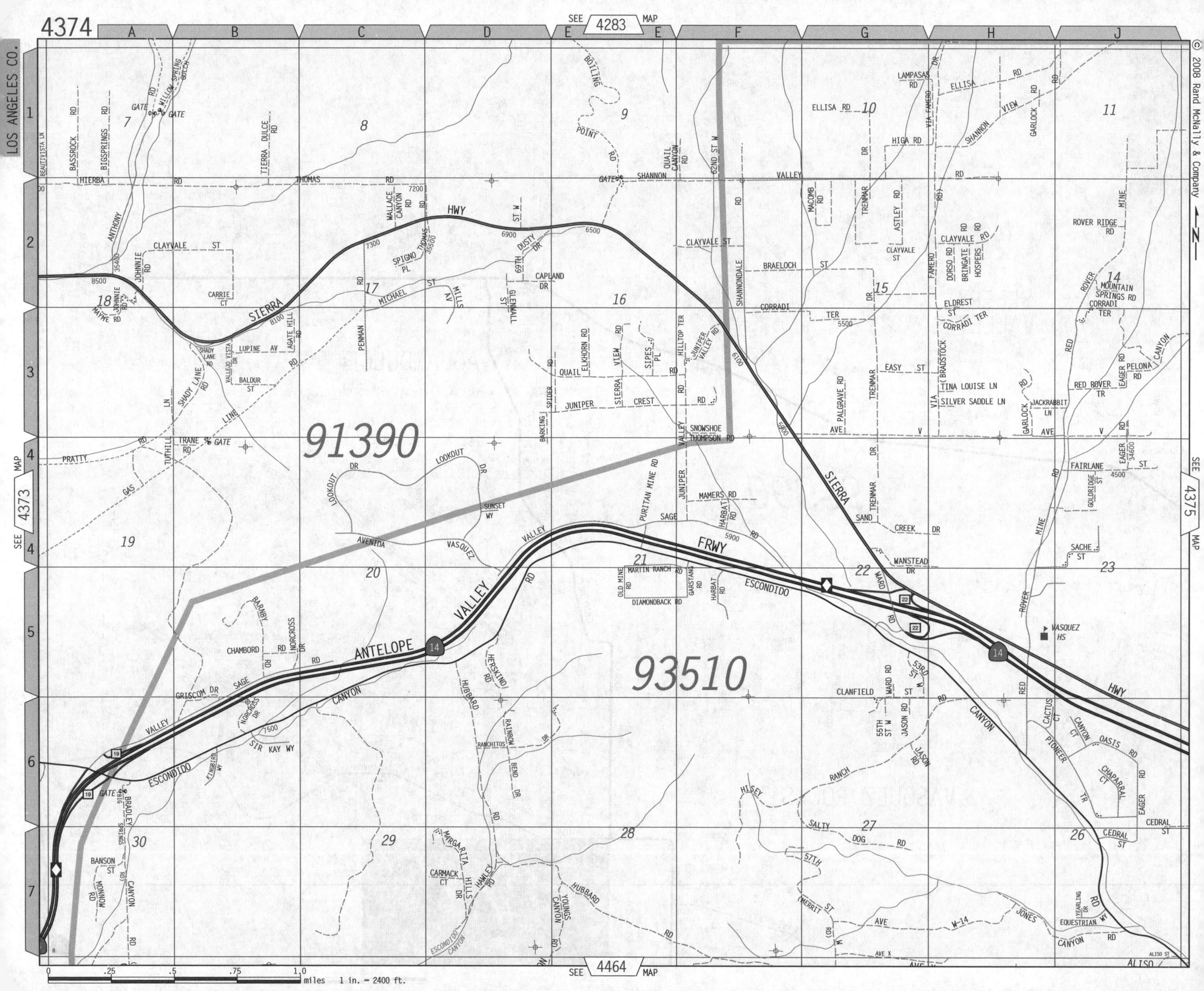

SEE 4283 MAP
LOS ANGELES CO.
SEE 4373 MAP
SEE 4375 MAP
SEE 4464 MAP
91390
93510
SIERRA HWY
ANTELOPE VALLEY FRWY
ESCONDIDO CANYON RD
VASQUEZ HS
0 .25 .5 .75 1.0 miles 1 in. = 2400 ft.

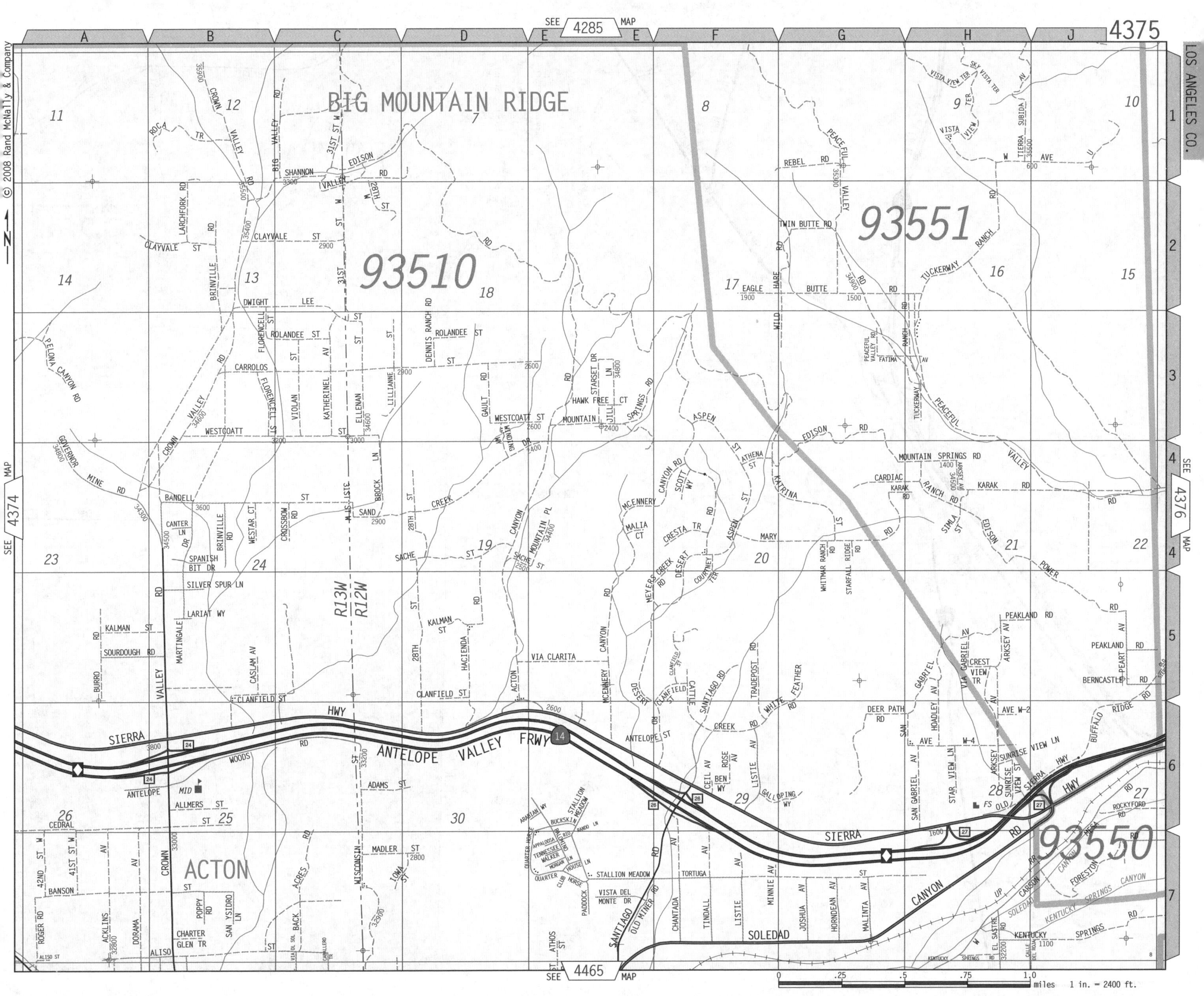

SEE 4285 MAP
LOS ANGELES CO.
BIG MOUNTAIN RIDGE
93510
93551
93550
ACTON
ANTELOPE VALLEY FRWY
SIERRA HWY
SOLEDAD CANYON RD
R13W
R12W
SEE 4374 MAP
SEE 4376 MAP
SEE 4465 MAP
miles 1 in. = 2400 ft.

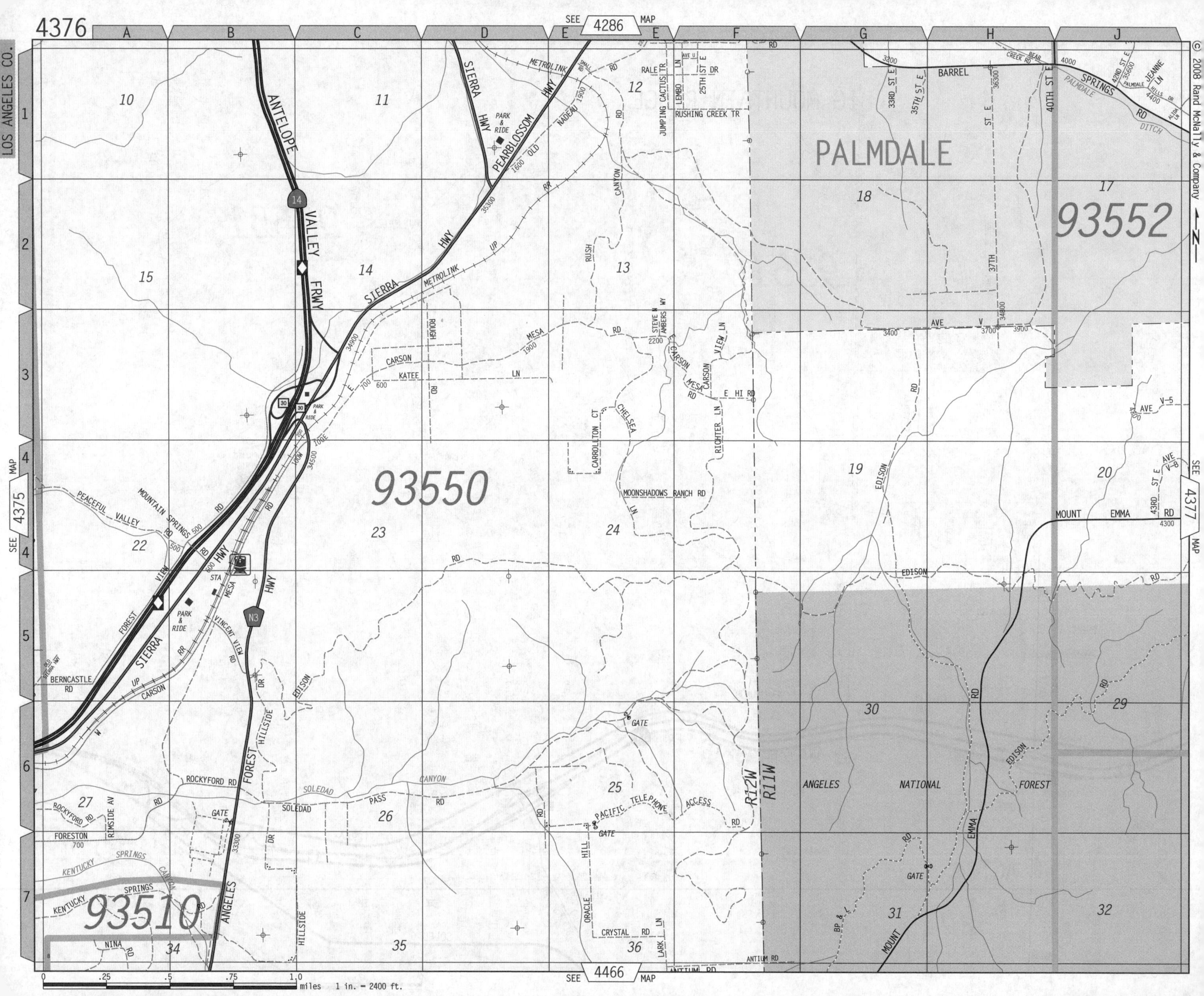

4376
LOS ANGELES CO.
SEE 4286 MAP
SEE 4466 MAP
SEE 4375 MAP
SEE 4377 MAP
© 2008 Rand McNally & Company
PALMDALE
93552
93550
93510
ANTELOPE VALLEY FRWY
SIERRA HWY
PEARBLOSSOM HWY
METROLINK
PARK & RIDE
OLD NADEAU RD
CANYON RD
RUSH CANYON
JUMPING CACTUS TR
LEMBO LN
25TH ST E
RALE DR
RUSHING CREEK TR
33RD ST E
35TH ST E
37TH ST E
40TH ST E
BARREL SPRINGS RD
PALMDALE DITCH
BEAR CREEK RD
42ND ST E
JEANNE LN
AVE V
MESA RD
CARSON MESA RD
KATEE LN
ROUGH RD
STEVE N AMBERS WY
VIEW LN
E HI RD
RICHTER LN
CARROLLTON CT
CHELSEA LN
MOONSHADOWS RANCH RD
EDISON RD
AVE V-5
AVE V-8
43RD ST E
MOUNT EMMA RD
PEACEFUL VALLEY RD
MOUNTAIN SPRINGS RD
FOREST VIEW RD
VINCENT VIEW RD
STA
UP RR
BERNCASTLE RD
ANGELES FOREST HWY
HILLSIDE DR
GATE
ROCKYFORD RD
SOLEDAD CANYON RD
SOLEDAD PASS RD
PACIFIC TELEPHONE ACCESS RD
HILL RD
ORACLE HILL RD
CRYSTAL RD
LARK LN
ANTIUM RD
RIMSIDE AV
FORESTON
KENTUCKY SPRINGS CANYON
NINA RD
R12W
R11W
ANGELES NATIONAL FOREST
BP & L
10
11
12
13
14
15
17
18
19
20
22
23
24
25
26
27
29
30
31
32
34
35
36
0 .25 .5 .75 1.0 miles 1 in. = 2400 ft.

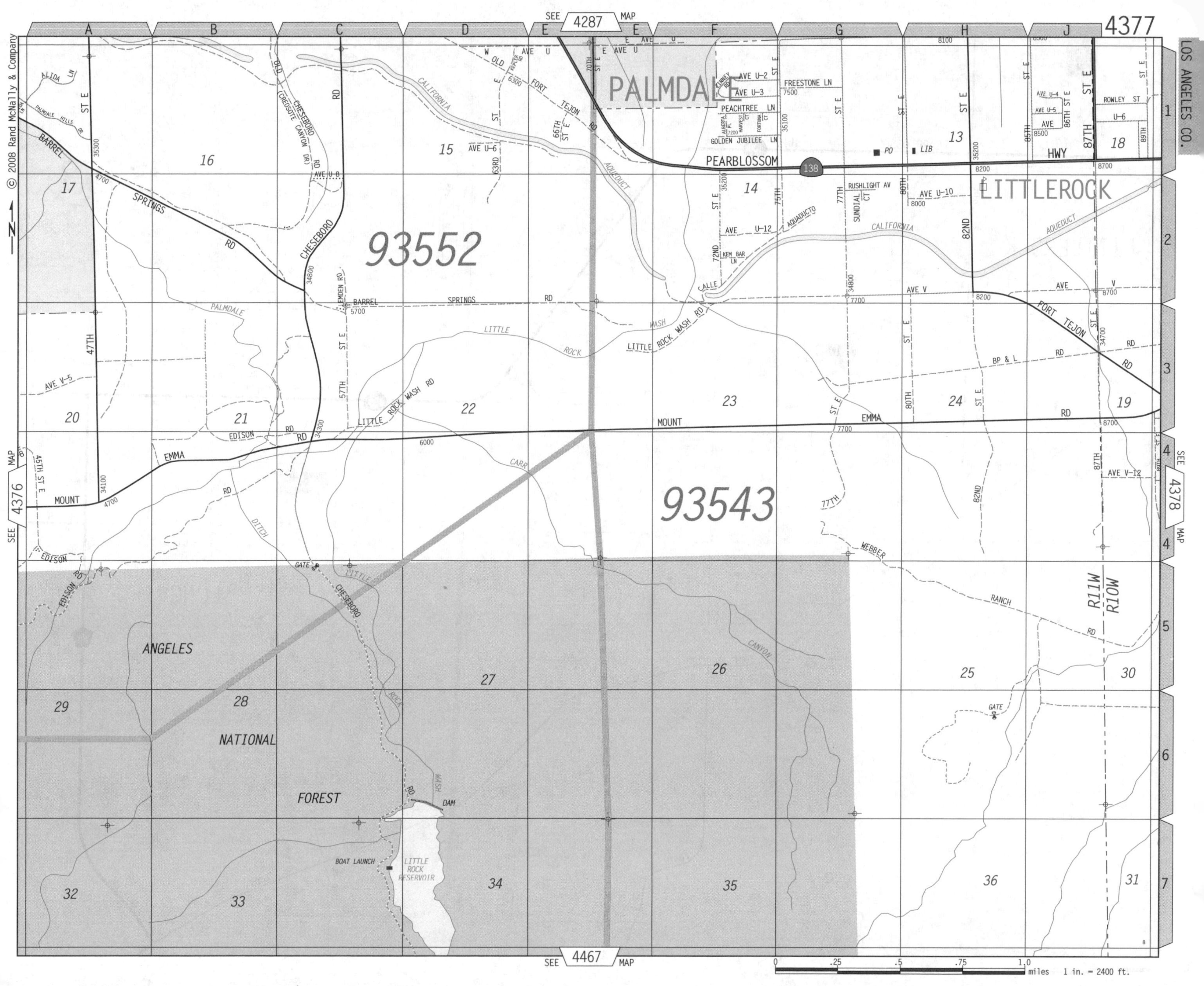

SEE 4287 MAP
LOS ANGELES CO.
PALMDALE
LITTLEROCK
93552
93543
PEARBLOSSOM
HWY
138
BARREL SPRINGS RD
CHESEBORO RD
MOUNT EMMA RD
FORT TEJON RD
CALIFORNIA AQUEDUCT
LITTLE ROCK WASH RD
ANGELES NATIONAL FOREST
LITTLE ROCK RESERVOIR
BOAT LAUNCH
DAM
GATE
WEBBER RANCH RD
R11W R10W
SEE 4376 MAP
SEE 4378 MAP
SEE 4467 MAP

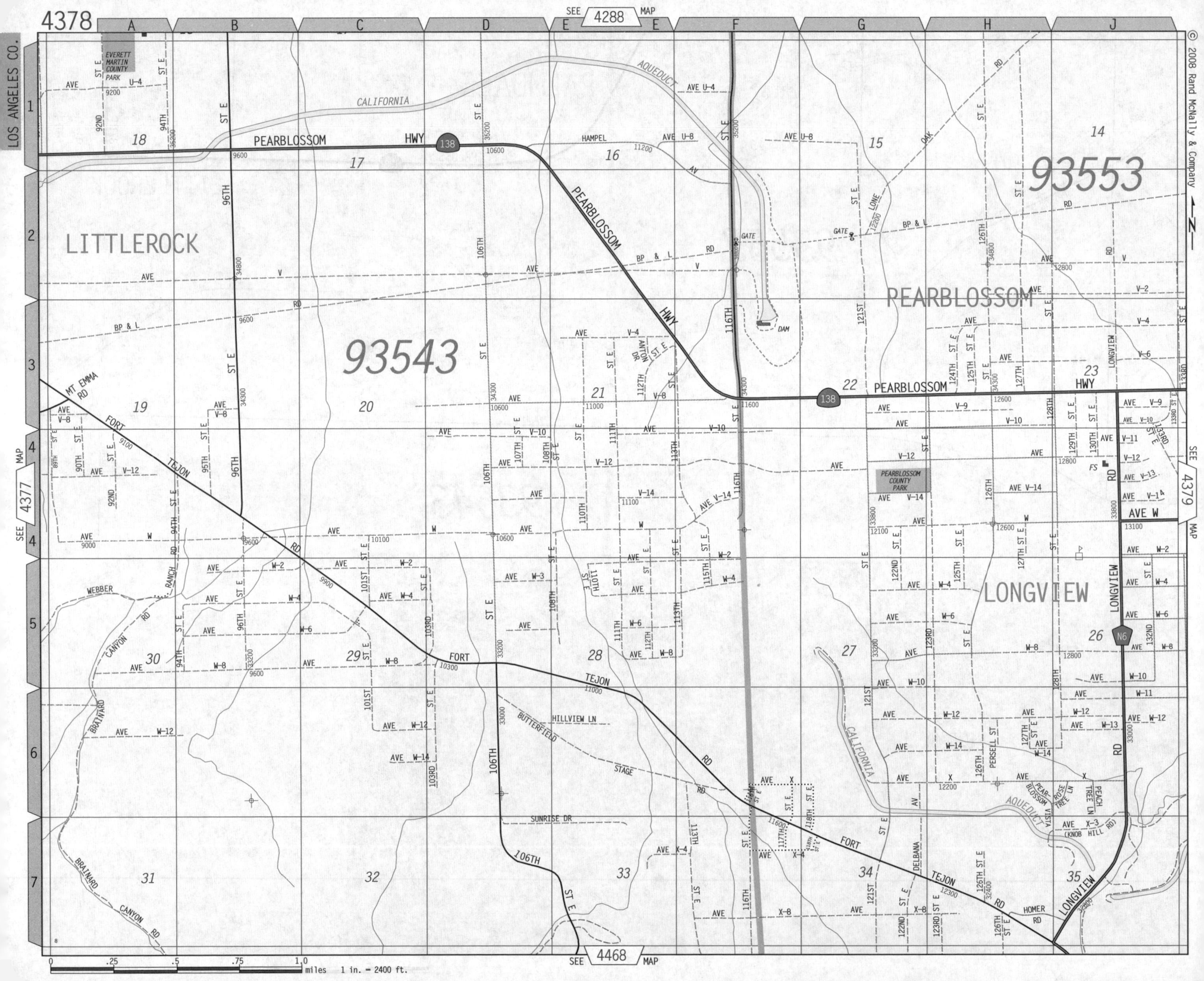

SEE 4288 MAP
LOS ANGELES CO.
© 2008 Rand McNally & Company
LITTLEROCK
PEARBLOSSOM
LONGVIEW
93543
93553
EVERETT MARTIN COUNTY PARK
PEARBLOSSOM COUNTY PARK
CALIFORNIA AQUEDUCT
PEARBLOSSOM HWY
138
N6
FORT TEJON RD
MT EMMA RD
WEBBER CANYON RD
BRAINARD CANYON RD
RANCH RD
BUTTERFIELD STAGE RD
HILLVIEW LN
SUNRISE DR
OAK RD
LONE RD
HAMPEL AV
BP & L RD
LONGVIEW RD
HOMER RD
PEAR BLOSSOM VISTA
ROSE TREE LN
PEACH TREE LN
KNOB HILL RD
ANTON DR
DELBANA AV
PERSELL ST
AVE W
GATE
DAM
FS
96TH ST E
106TH ST E
116TH ST E
126TH ST E
SEE 4377 MAP
SEE 4379 MAP
SEE 4468 MAP
miles 1 in. = 2400 ft.

SEE G MAP
LOS ANGELES CO.
93591
93544
93553
PEARBLOSSOM
LONGVIEW
LLANO
PEARBLOSSOM HWY
VALYERMO RD
WILDLIFE SANCTUARY
LONGVIEW PARK (PROP)
BIG ROCK WASH
CALIFORNIA AQUEDUCT
LANDING STRIP
CRYSTALAIRE COUNTRY CLUB
BOBS GAP RD
FORT TEJON RD
165TH ST E
R10W R9W
SEE 4378 MAP
SEE 4469 MAP
miles 1 in. = 2400 ft.

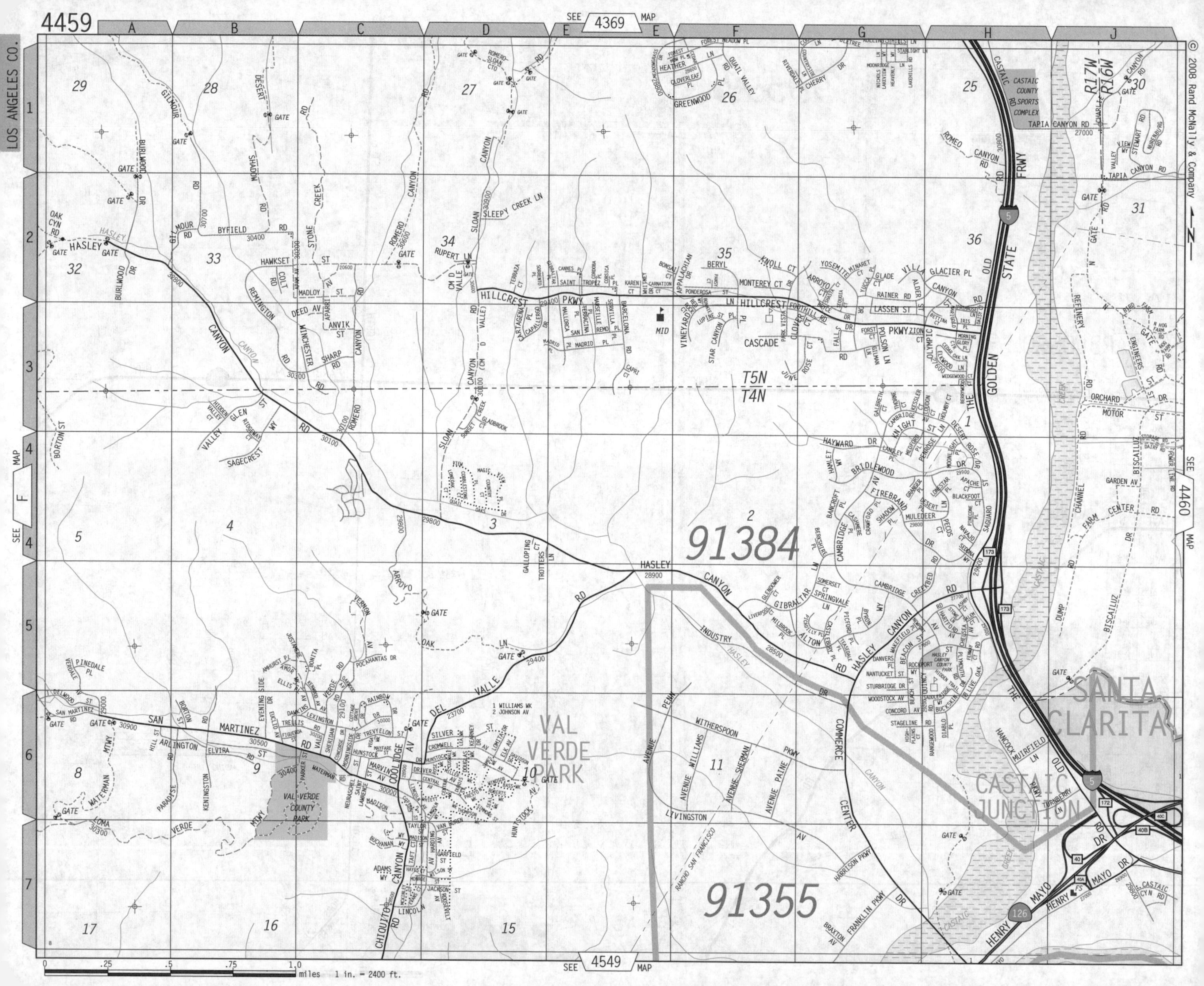

4459
LOS ANGELES CO.
SEE 4369 MAP
SEE 4460 MAP
SEE 4549 MAP
SEE F MAP
A
B
C
D
E
F
G
H
J
1
2
3
4
5
6
7
91384
91355
VAL VERDE PARK
SANTA CLARITA
CASTAIC JUNCTION
CASCADE
T5N
T4N
R17W
R16W
CASTAIC COUNTY SPORTS COMPLEX
VAL VERDE COUNTY PARK
HASLEY CANYON COUNTY PARK
GOLDEN STATE FRWY
THE OLD RD
HASLEY CANYON RD
HILLCREST PKWY
SAN MARTINEZ RD
DEL VALLE RD
COOLIDGE AV
CHIQUITO CANYON RD
COMMERCE CENTER DR
INDUSTRY DR
HENRY MAYO DR
TAPIA CANYON RD
ROMERO CANYON RD
SLOAN CANYON RD
BISCAILUZ DR
ORCHARD DR
MOTOR ST
WITHERSPOON PKWY
LIVINGSTON AV
FRANKLIN PKWY
HARRISON PKWY
MID
GATE
FS
© 2008 Rand McNally & Company
0 .25 .5 .75 1.0 miles 1 in. = 2400 ft.

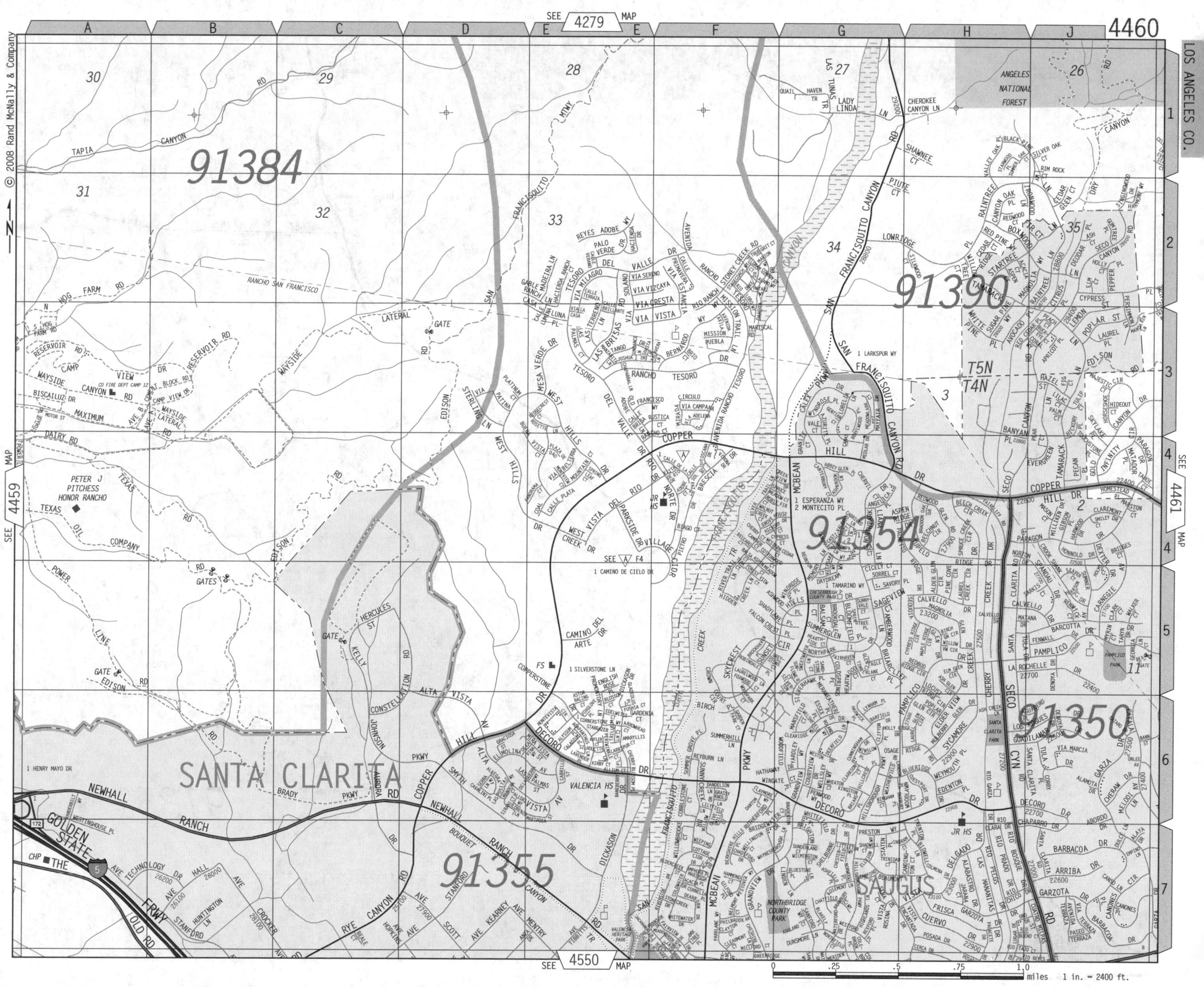

SEE 4279 MAP
SEE 4459 MAP
SEE 4461 MAP
SEE 4550 MAP
LOS ANGELES CO.
A
B
C
D
E
F
G
H
J
1
2
3
4
5
6
7
91384
91390
91354
91350
91355
SANTA CLARITA
SAUGUS
ANGELES NATIONAL FOREST
PETER J PITCHESS HONOR RANCHO
NORTHBRIDGE COUNTY PARK
CHESEBROUGH COUNTY PARK
SANTA CLARITA PARK
PAMPLICO PARK
VALENCIA HERITAGE PARK
VALENCIA HS
JR HS
FS
CHP
CO FIRE DEPT CAMP 12
T5N
T4N
TAPIA CANYON RD
HOG FARM RD
RANCHO SAN FRANCISCO
WAYSIDE CANYON RD
RESERVOIR RD
DAIRY RD
TEXAS OIL COMPANY RD
POWER LINE RD
EDISON RD
SAN FRANCISQUITO CANYON RD
COPPER HILL DR
DECORO DR
MCBEAN PKWY
NEWHALL RANCH RD
BOUQUET CANYON RD
SECO CANYON RD
RYE CANYON RD
GOLDEN STATE FRWY
THE OLD RD
TESORO DEL VALLE DR
RANCHO TESORO
AVENIDA RANCHO TESORO
1 HENRY MAYO DR
1 LARKSPUR WY
1 ESPERANZA WY
2 MONTECITO PL
1 TAMARIND WY
1 CAMINO DE CIELO DR
1 SILVERSTONE LN
0 .25 .5 .75 1.0 miles 1 in. = 2400 ft.

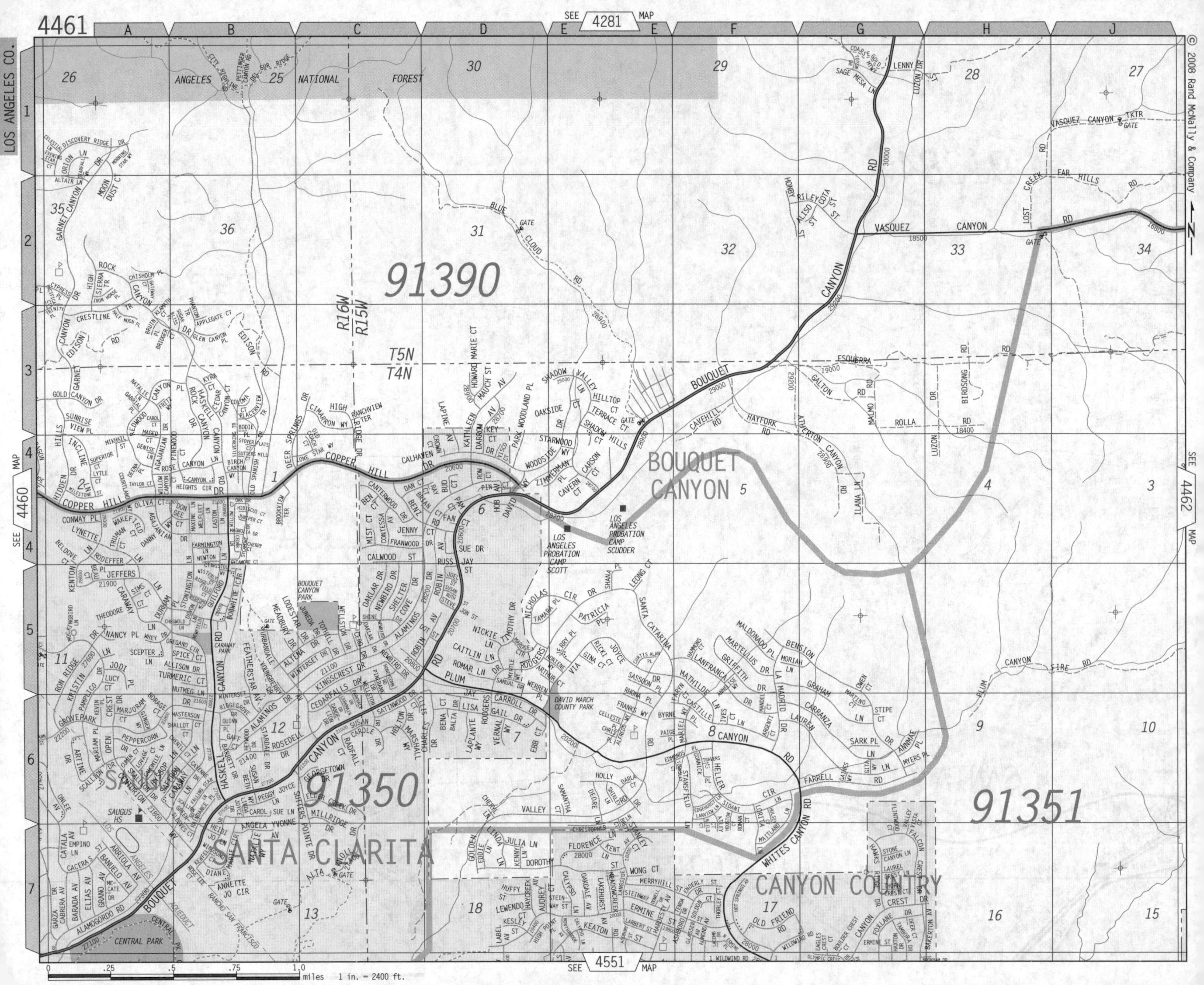

LOS ANGELES CO.
SEE 4281 MAP
SEE 4460 MAP
SEE 4462 MAP
SEE 4551 MAP
ANGELES NATIONAL FOREST
91390
91350
91351
BOUQUET CANYON
SANTA CLARITA
CANYON COUNTRY
SAUGUS
R16W
R15W
T5N
T4N
COPPER HILL DR
BOUQUET CANYON RD
VASQUEZ CANYON RD
ESQUERRA RD
PLUM CANYON RD
WHITES CANYON RD
BLUE CLOUD RD
HASKELL CANYON RD
LOS ANGELES PROBATION CAMP SCOTT
LOS ANGELES PROBATION CAMP SCUDDER
BOUQUET CANYON PARK
CARAWAY PARK
DAVID MARCH COUNTY PARK
CENTRAL PARK
SAUGUS HS
0 .25 .5 .75 1.0 miles 1 in. = 2400 ft.

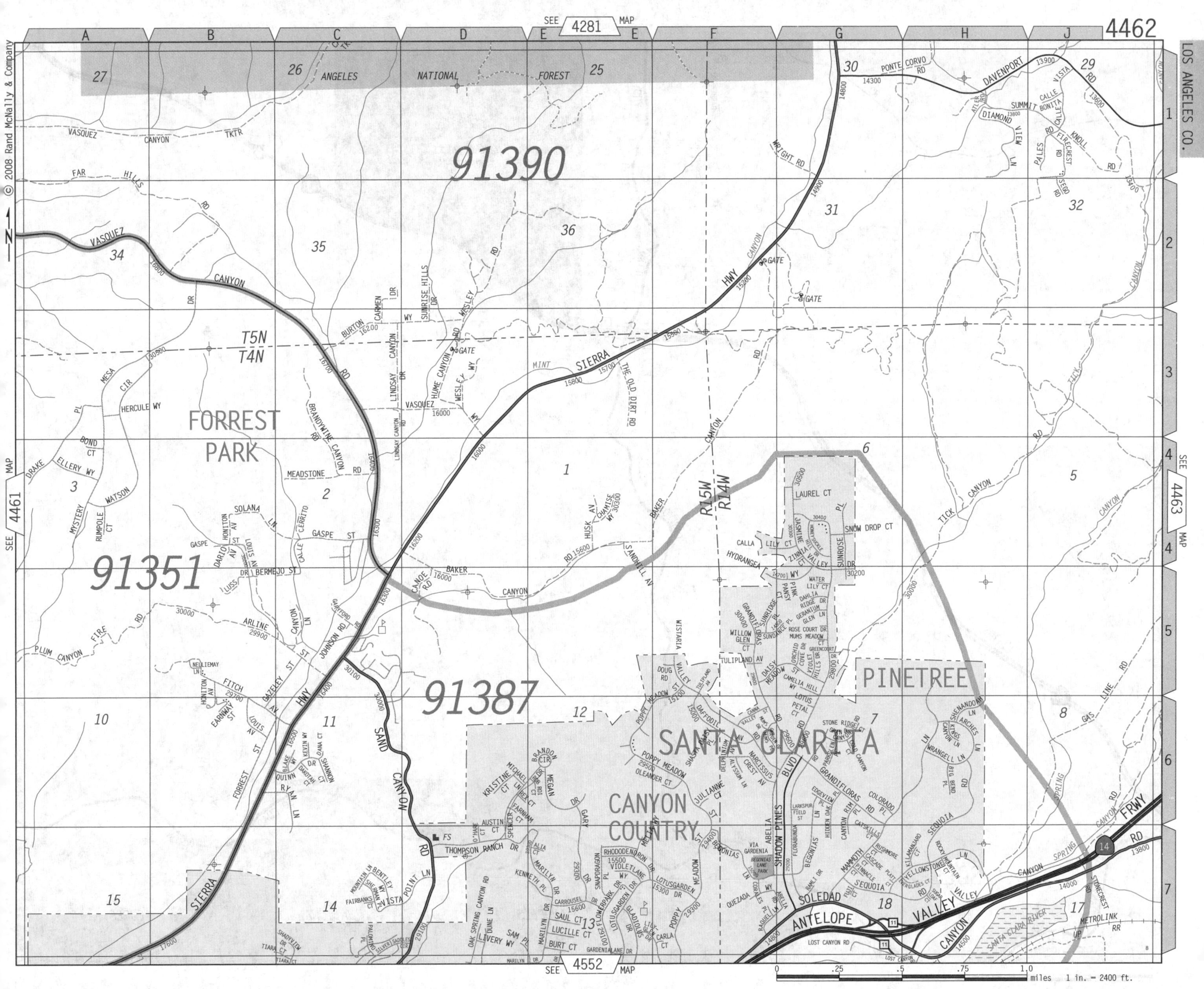

SEE 4281 MAP
SEE 4461 MAP
SEE 4463 MAP
SEE 4552 MAP
LOS ANGELES CO.
ANGELES NATIONAL FOREST
91390
91351
91387
FORREST PARK
SANTA CLARITA
CANYON COUNTRY
PINETREE
T5N
T4N
R15W
R14W
VASQUEZ CANYON RD
SIERRA HWY
ANTELOPE VALLEY FRWY
SAND CANYON RD
SOLEDAD CANYON RD
SHADOW PINES BLVD
BAKER CANYON RD
TICK CANYON RD
SANTA CLARA RIVER
METROLINK RR
miles 1 in. = 2400 ft.

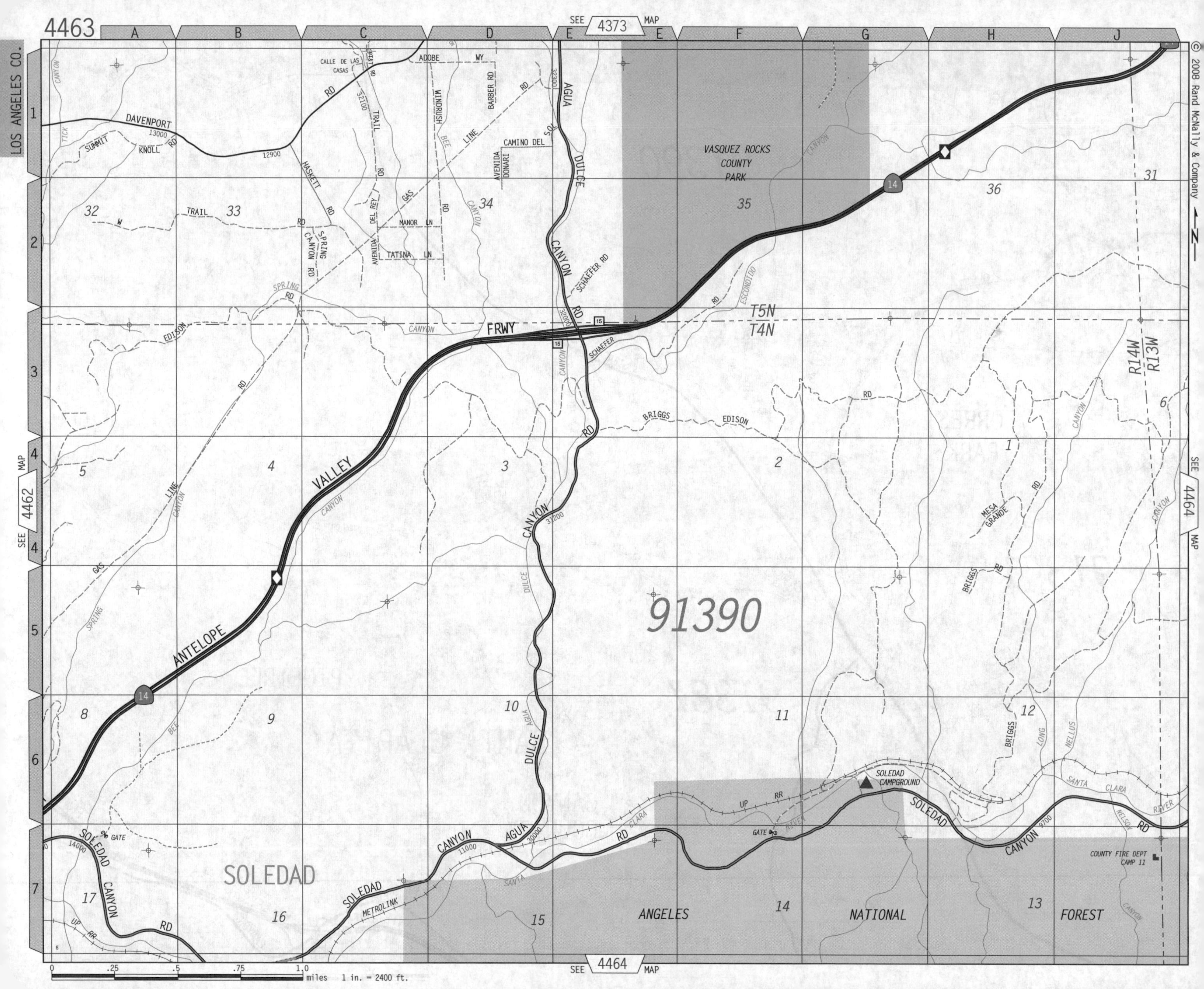

SEE 4373 MAP
LOS ANGELES CO.
ADOBE WY
CALLE DE LAS CASAS
DAVENPORT RD
SUMMIT KNOLL RD
HASKETT RD
WINDRUSH RD
BARBER RD
CAMINO DEL SOL
AVENIDA DONARI
AGUA DULCE CANYON RD
VASQUEZ ROCKS COUNTY PARK
SPRING CANYON RD
MANOR LN
TATINA LN
AVENIDA DEL REY
SCHAEFER RD
ANTELOPE VALLEY FRWY
T5N
T4N
BRIGGS EDISON RD
R14W
R13W
MESA GRANDE RD
BRIGGS RD
91390
SOLEDAD CAMPGROUND
SANTA CLARA RIVER
SOLEDAD CANYON RD
COUNTY FIRE DEPT CAMP 11
SOLEDAD
ANGELES NATIONAL FOREST
METROLINK
UP RR
SEE 4462 MAP
SEE 4464 MAP
© 2008 Rand McNally & Company
miles 1 in. = 2400 ft.

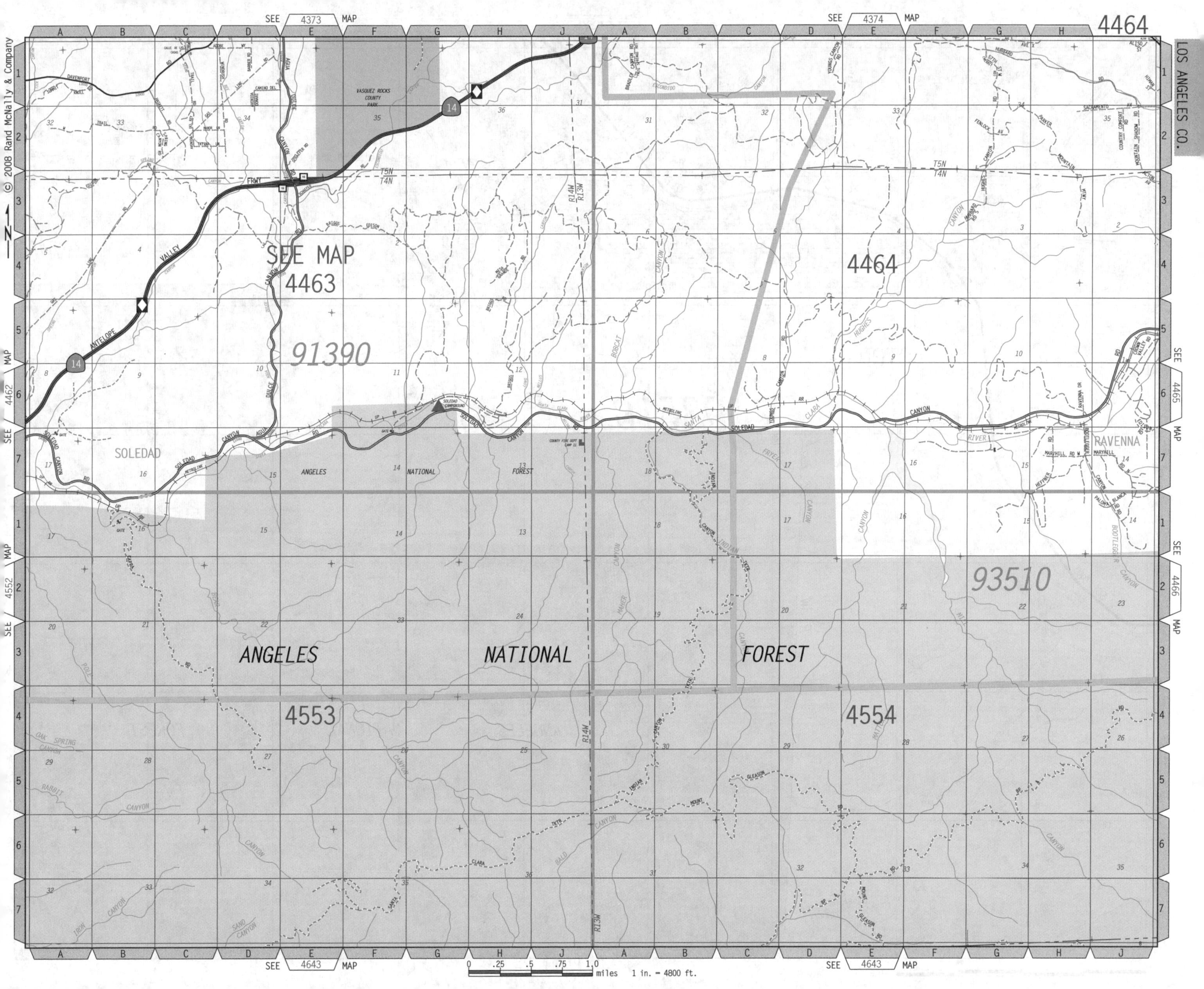
SEE 4373 MAP
SEE 4374 MAP
LOS ANGELES CO.
SEE MAP 4463
4464
91390
93510
SOLEDAD
RAVENNA
VASQUEZ ROCKS COUNTY PARK
ANGELES NATIONAL FOREST
4553
4554
SEE 4462 MAP
SEE 4552 MAP
SEE 4465 MAP
SEE 4466 MAP
SEE 4643 MAP
SEE 4643 MAP
T5N
T4N
R14W
R13W
ANTELOPE VALLEY FRWY
SOLEDAD CANYON RD
AGUA DULCE CANYON RD
SANTA CLARA RIVER
METROLINK
COUNTY FIRE DEPT CAMP 11
SOLEDAD CAMPGROUND
BOBCAT CANYON
INDIAN CANYON
MAHER CANYON
FRYER CANYON
BOOTLEGGER CANYON
HUGHES CANYON
OAK SPRING CANYON
RABBIT CANYON
IRON CANYON
SAND CANYON
BALD CANYON
MOUNT GLEASON RD
SANTA CLARA
DAVENPORT RD
SACRAMENTO AV
PARKER MOUNTAIN RD
MARYHILL RD W
MARYHILL
0 .25 .5 .75 1.0 miles 1 in. = 4800 ft.

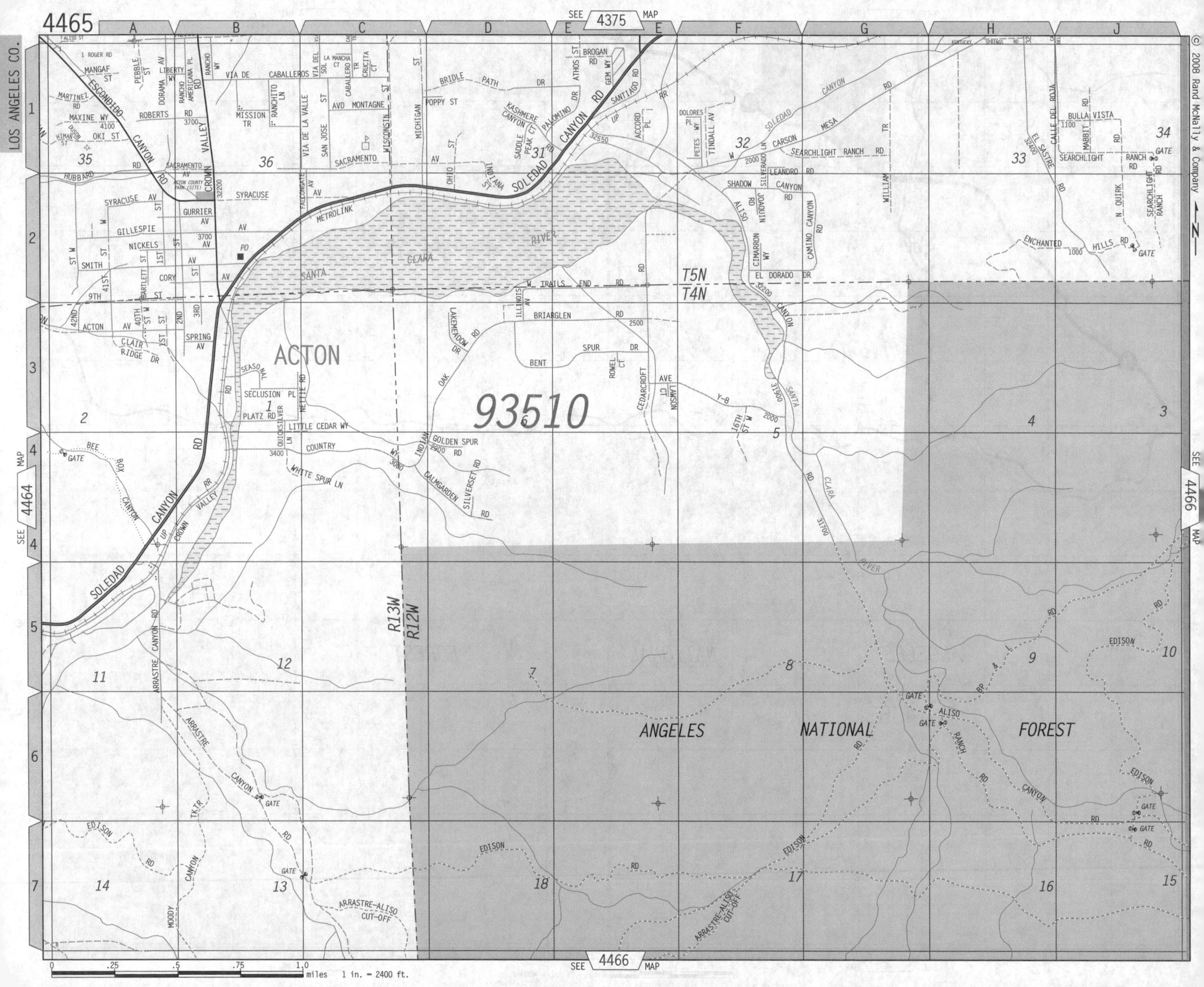

SEE 4375 MAP
LOS ANGELES CO.
ACTON
93510
ANGELES NATIONAL FOREST
SOLEDAD CANYON RD
CROWN VALLEY RD
ESCONDIDO CANYON RD
SANTA CLARA RIVER
METROLINK
T5N
T4N
R13W
R12W
SEE 4464 MAP
SEE 4466 MAP
ARRASTRE CANYON RD
EDISON RD
ARRASTRE-ALISO CUT-OFF
ALISO CANYON RD
SEARCHLIGHT RANCH RD
miles 1 in. = 2400 ft.

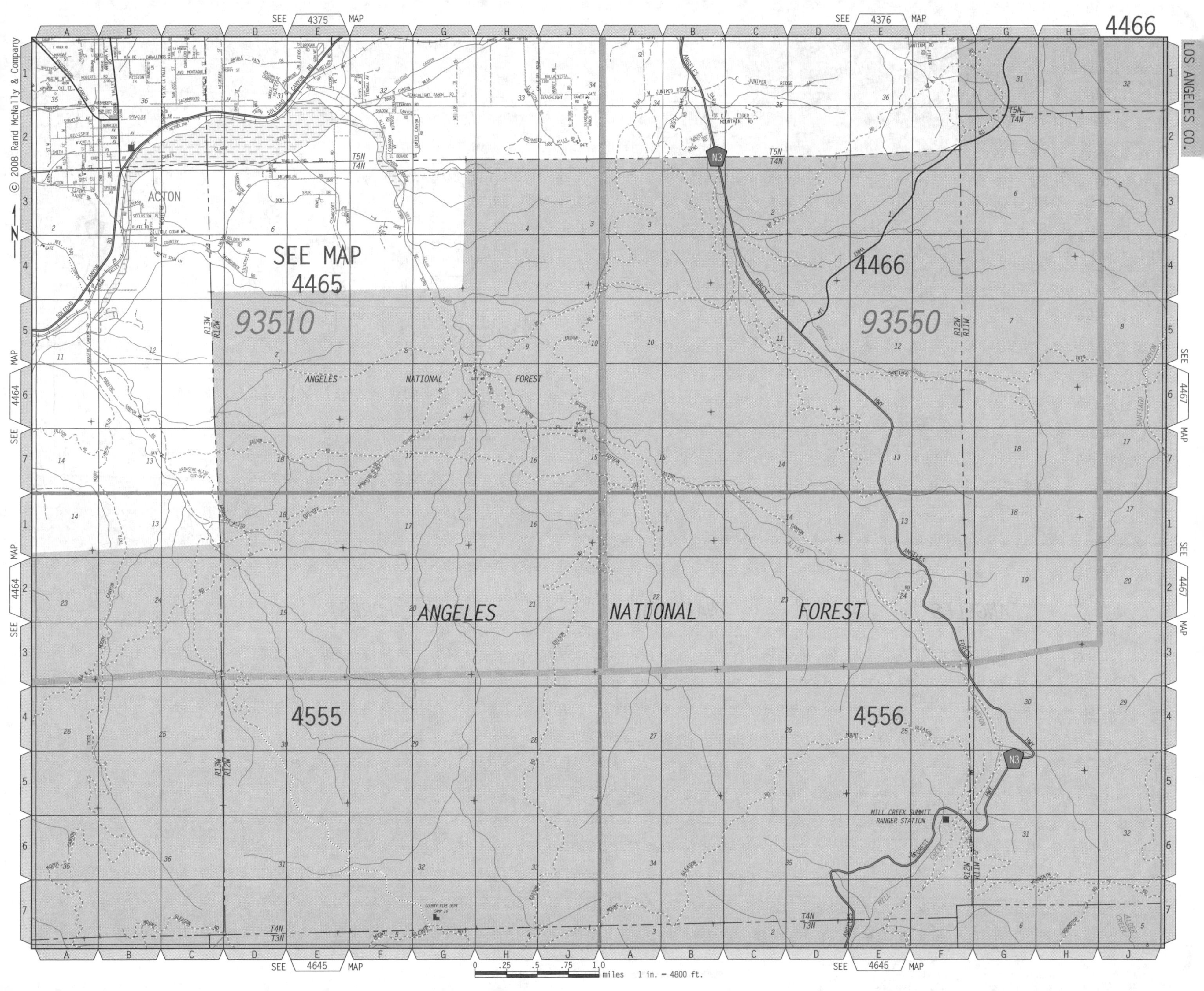

LOS ANGELES CO.
SEE 4375 MAP
SEE 4376 MAP
SEE 4645 MAP
SEE 4464 MAP
SEE 4467 MAP
SEE MAP 4465
4466
4555
4556
ACTON
93510
93550
ANGELES NATIONAL FOREST
MILL CREEK SUMMIT RANGER STATION
COUNTY FIRE DEPT CAMP 16
T5N
T4N
T3N
R13W
R12W
R11W
miles 1 in. = 4800 ft.

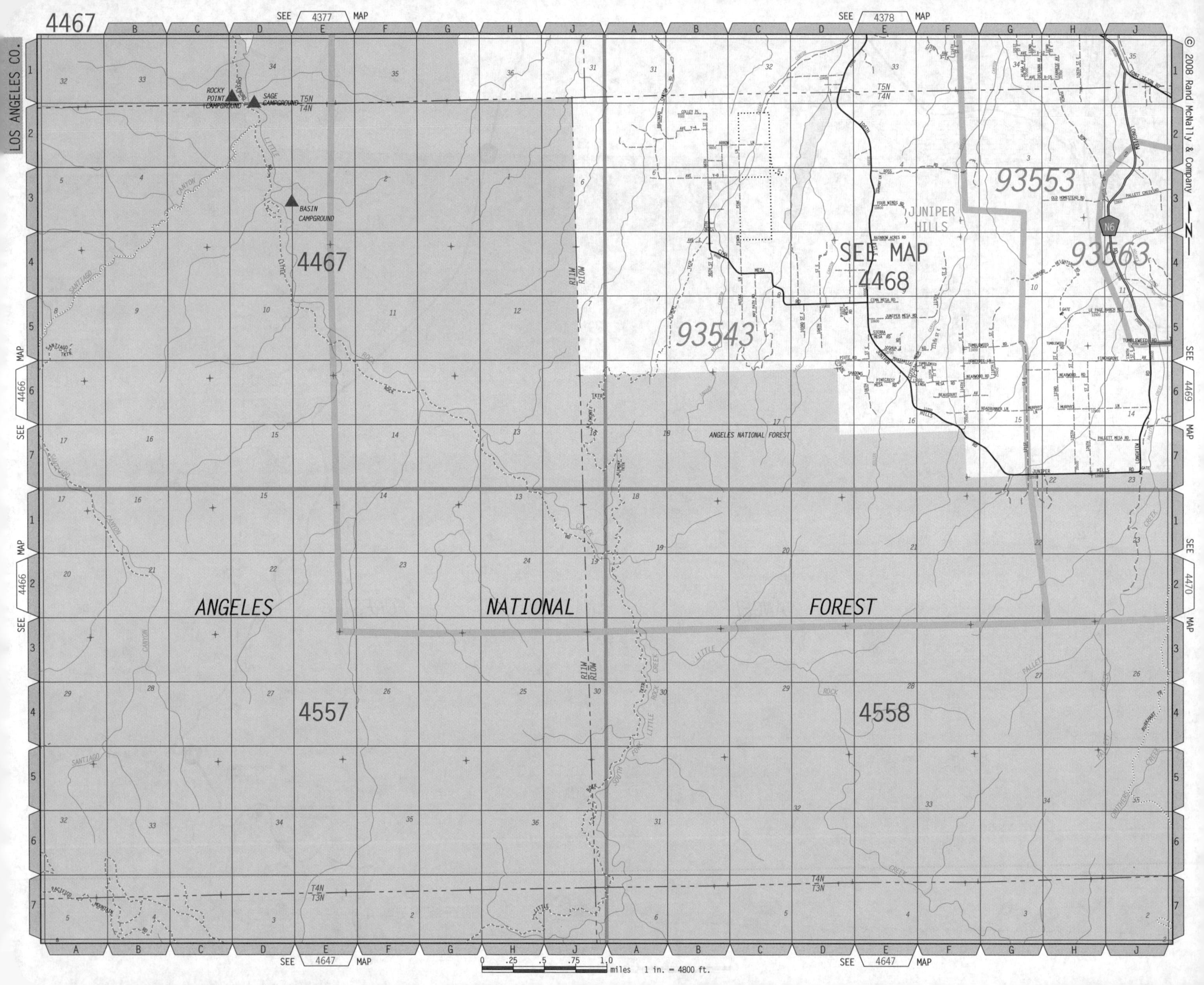
LOS ANGELES CO.
SEE 4377 MAP
SEE 4378 MAP
ROCKY POINT CAMPGROUND
SAGE CAMPGROUND
BASIN CAMPGROUND
T5N
T4N
4467
SEE MAP 4468
JUNIPER HILLS
93553
93563
93543
N6
R11W R10W
ANGELES NATIONAL FOREST
ANGELES
NATIONAL
FOREST
4557
4558
T4N
T3N
SEE 4466 MAP
SEE 4469 MAP
SEE 4470 MAP
SEE 4647 MAP
SANTIAGO
CANYON
LITTLE ROCK CREEK
SOUTH FORK LITTLE ROCK CREEK
PALLETT CREEK
CRUTHERS CREEK
PACIFICO MOUNTAIN
LONGVIEW RD
PALLETT CREEK RD
OLD HOMESTEAD RD
FOUR WINDS RD
RAINBOW ACRES RD
CIMA MESA RD
JUNIPER MESA RD
TUMBLEWEED RD
LE PAGE RANCH RD
PALLETT MESA RD
JUNIPER HILLS RD
BOSS RD
0 .25 .5 .75 1.0 miles 1 in. = 4800 ft.

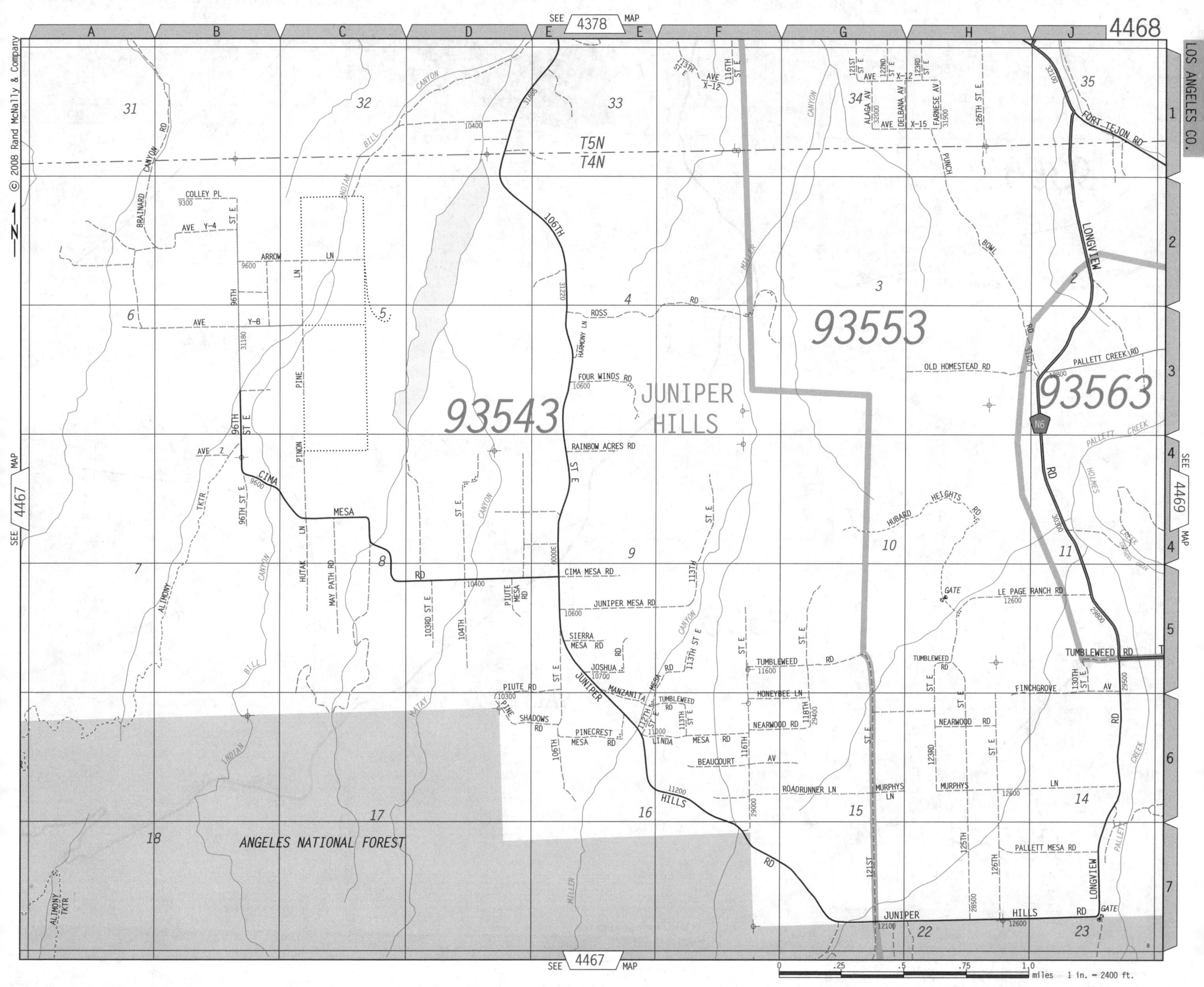

SEE 4378 MAP
SEE 4467 MAP
SEE 4469 MAP
LOS ANGELES CO.
JUNIPER HILLS
93543
93553
93563
T5N
T4N
ANGELES NATIONAL FOREST
106TH ST E
96TH ST E
CIMA MESA RD
JUNIPER HILLS RD
LONGVIEW RD
FORT TEJON RD
PALLETT CREEK RD
OLD HOMESTEAD RD
ROSS RD
FOUR WINDS RD
RAINBOW ACRES RD
JUNIPER MESA RD
SIERRA MESA RD
HUBARD HEIGHTS RD
LE PAGE RANCH RD
TUMBLEWEED RD
FINCHGROVE AV
NEARWOOD RD
MURPHYS LN
ROADRUNNER LN
BEAUCOURT AV
PALLETT MESA RD
HONEYBEE LN
PIUTE RD
PINECREST MESA RD
SHADOWS RD
LINDA MESA RD
MANZANITA MESA RD
JOSHUA RD
AVE Y-4
AVE Y-8
AVE Z
COLLEY PL
ARROW LN
PINE LN
PINON LN
HUTAK LN
MAY PATH RD
PIUTE MESA RD
HARMONY LN
ALIMONY TKTR
BRAINARD CANYON RD
BILL CANYON
INDIAN CANYON
MILLER CANYON
PUNCH BOWL
PALLETT CREEK
HOLMES CREEK
AVE X-12
AVE X-15
ALAGA AV
DELBANA AV
FARNESE AV
N6
GATE
miles 1 in. = 2400 ft.

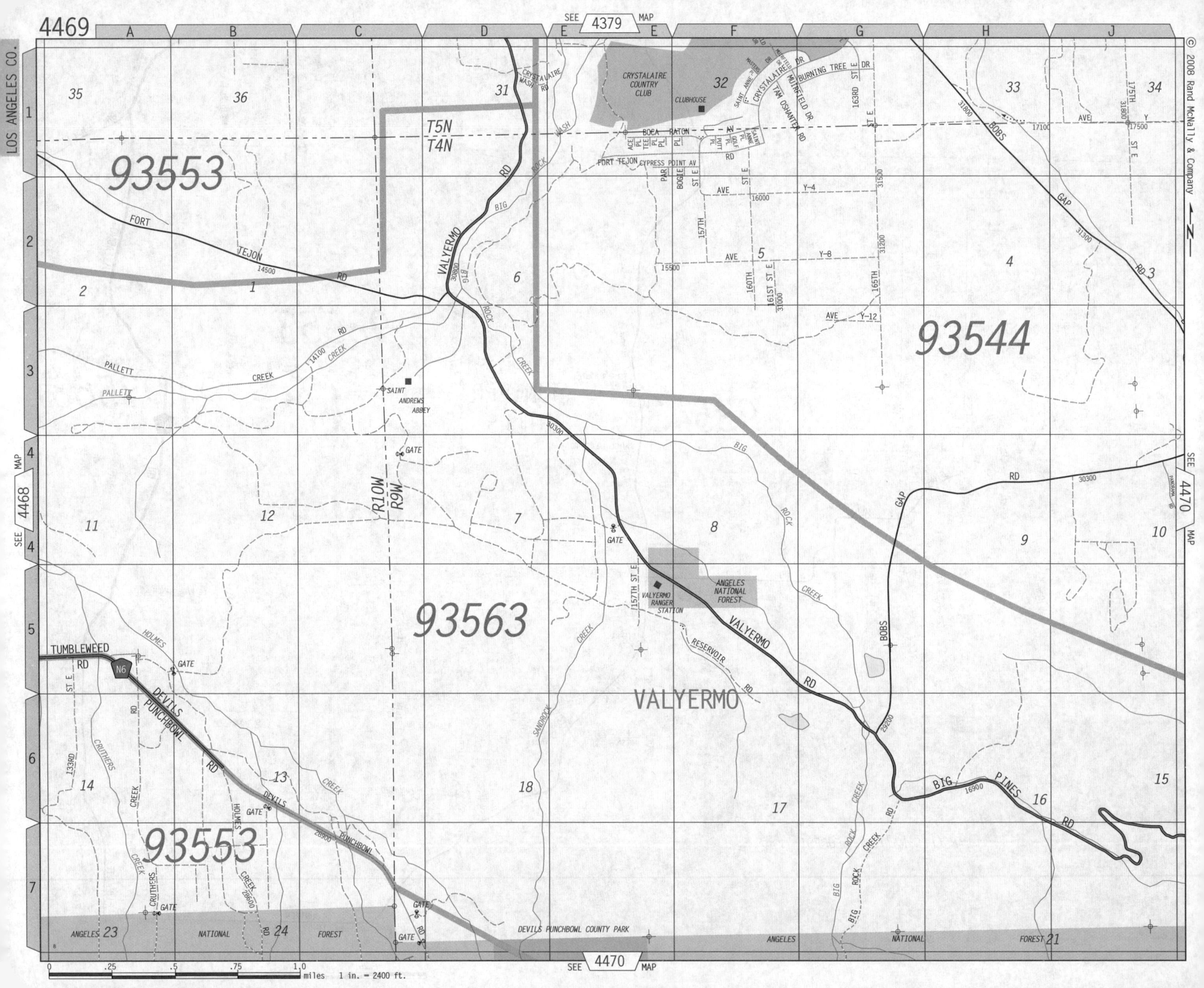
SEE 4379 MAP
LOS ANGELES CO.
CRYSTALAIRE COUNTRY CLUB
CLUBHOUSE
T5N
T4N
93553
93544
93563
93553
FORT TEJON RD
VALYERMO RD
BIG ROCK CREEK
PALLETT CREEK
SAINT ANDREWS ABBEY
R10W
R9W
VALYERMO RANGER STATION
ANGELES NATIONAL FOREST
VALYERMO
BOBS GAP RD
BIG PINES RD
DEVILS PUNCHBOWL RD
TUMBLEWEED RD
N6
DEVILS PUNCHBOWL COUNTY PARK
ANGELES NATIONAL FOREST
SEE 4468 MAP
SEE 4470 MAP
SEE 4470 MAP
miles 1 in. = 2400 ft.

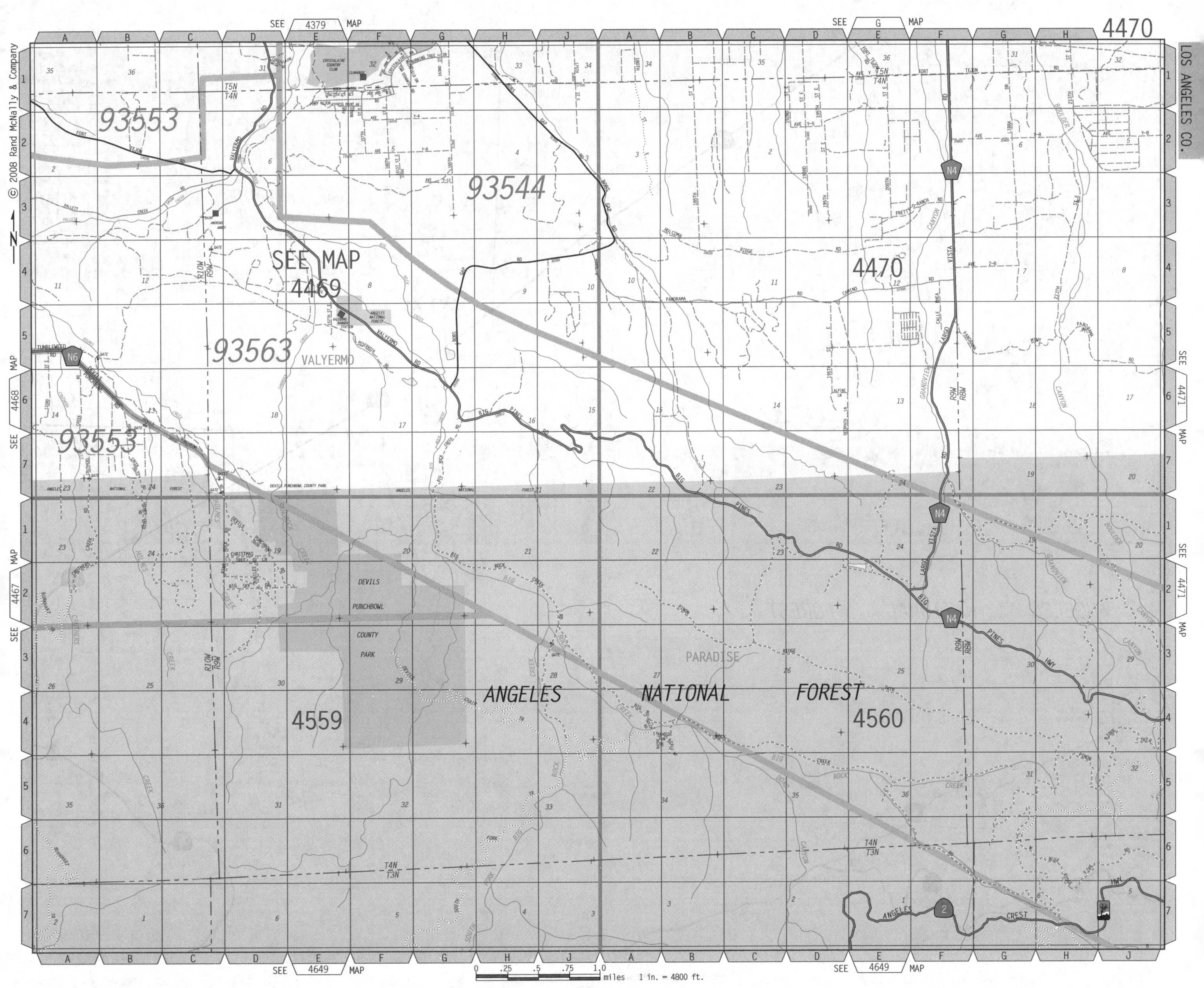
SEE 4379 MAP
SEE G MAP
SEE MAP 4469
4470
93553
93544
93563
VALYERMO
ANGELES NATIONAL FOREST
DEVILS PUNCHBOWL COUNTY PARK
PARADISE
4559
4560
SEE 4468 MAP
SEE 4467 MAP
SEE 4471 MAP
SEE 4649 MAP
CRYSTALAIRE COUNTRY CLUB
FORT TEJON RD
VALYERMO RD
BIG PINES HWY
ANGELES CREST HWY
PALLETT CREEK
HOLCOMB RIDGE RD
PANORAMA RD
BIG ROCK CREEK
T5N
T4N
T4N
T3N
R10W
R9W
R8W
miles 1 in. = 4800 ft.

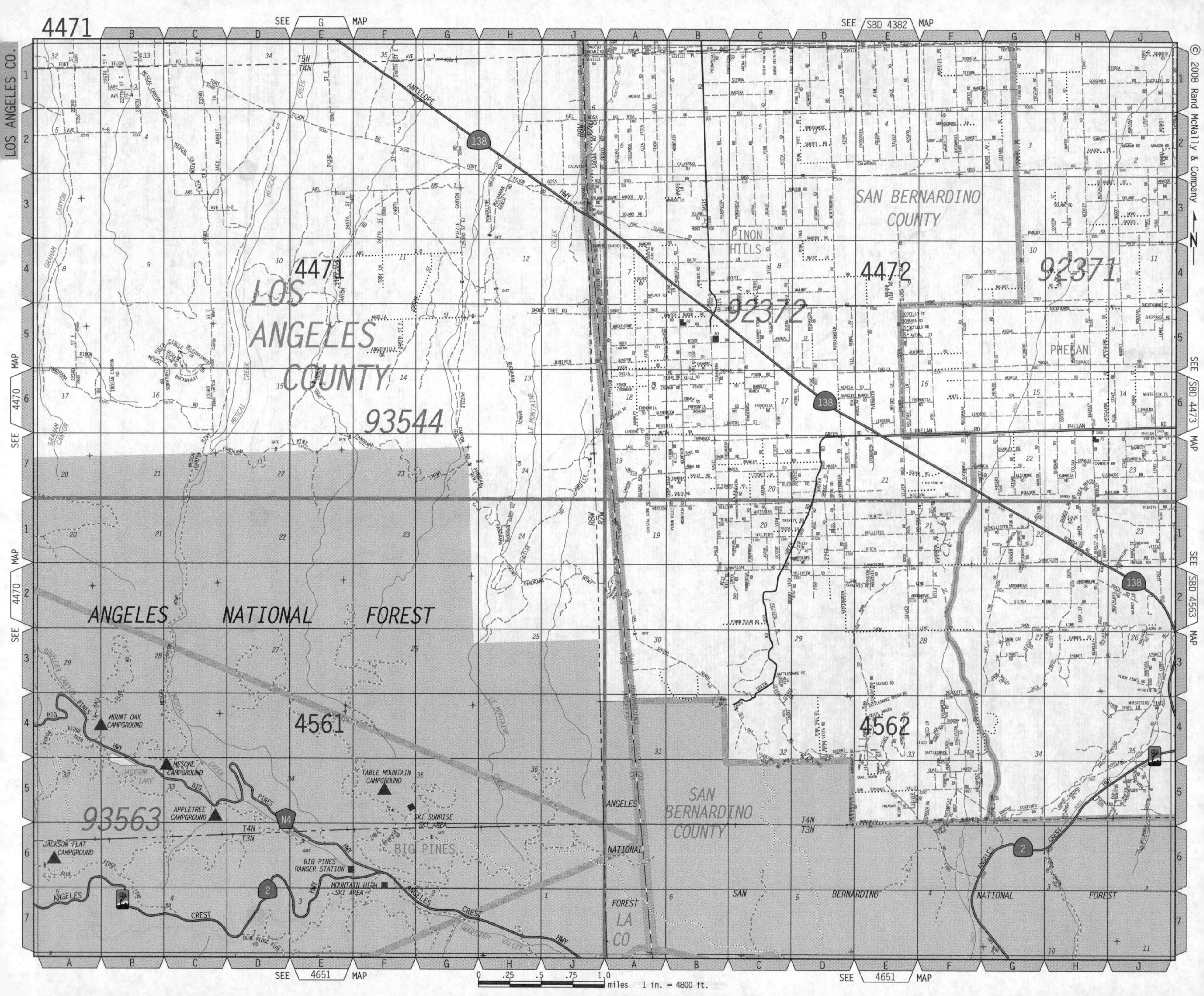

SEE G MAP
SEE SBD 4382 MAP
LOS ANGELES CO.
4471
LOS ANGELES COUNTY
93544
ANTELOPE
HWY
138
PINON HILLS
92372
4472
SAN BERNARDINO COUNTY
92371
PHELAN
ANGELES NATIONAL FOREST
4561
4562
93563
MOUNT OAK CAMPGROUND
MESCAL CAMPGROUND
JACKSON LAKE
APPLETREE CAMPGROUND
JACKSON FLAT CAMPGROUND
TABLE MOUNTAIN CAMPGROUND
SKI SUNRISE SKI AREA
BIG PINES
BIG PINES RANGER STATION
MOUNTAIN HIGH SKI AREA
SAN BERNARDINO COUNTY
SAN BERNARDINO NATIONAL FOREST
LA CO
SEE 4470 MAP
SEE SBD 4473 MAP
SEE SBD 4563 MAP
SEE 4651 MAP
miles 1 in. = 4800 ft.

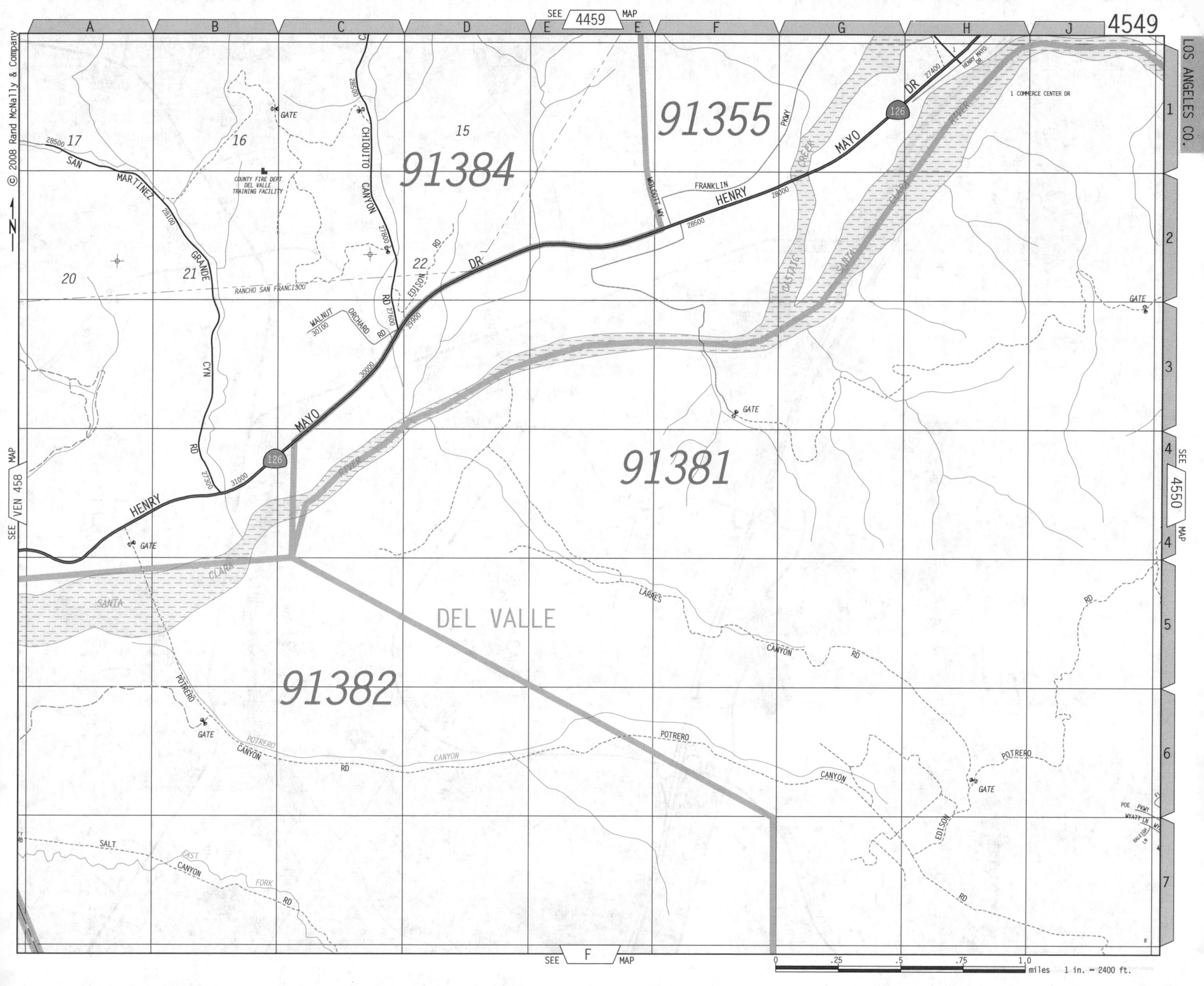

SEE 4459 MAP
LOS ANGELES CO.
91355
91384
91381
91382
DEL VALLE
HENRY MAYO DR
SAN MARTINEZ GRANDE CYN RD
CHIQUITO CANYON RD
COUNTY FIRE DEPT DEL VALLE TRAINING FACILITY
RANCHO SAN FRANCISCO
WALNUT
ORCHARD RD
EDISON RD
WOLCOTT WY
FRANKLIN
PKWY
CASTAIC CREEK
SANTA CLARA RIVER
1 COMMERCE CENTER DR
LARRES CANYON RD
POTRERO CANYON RD
SALT CANYON RD
EAST FORK
GATE
SEE VEN 458 MAP
SEE 4550 MAP
SEE F MAP
miles 1 in. = 2400 ft.

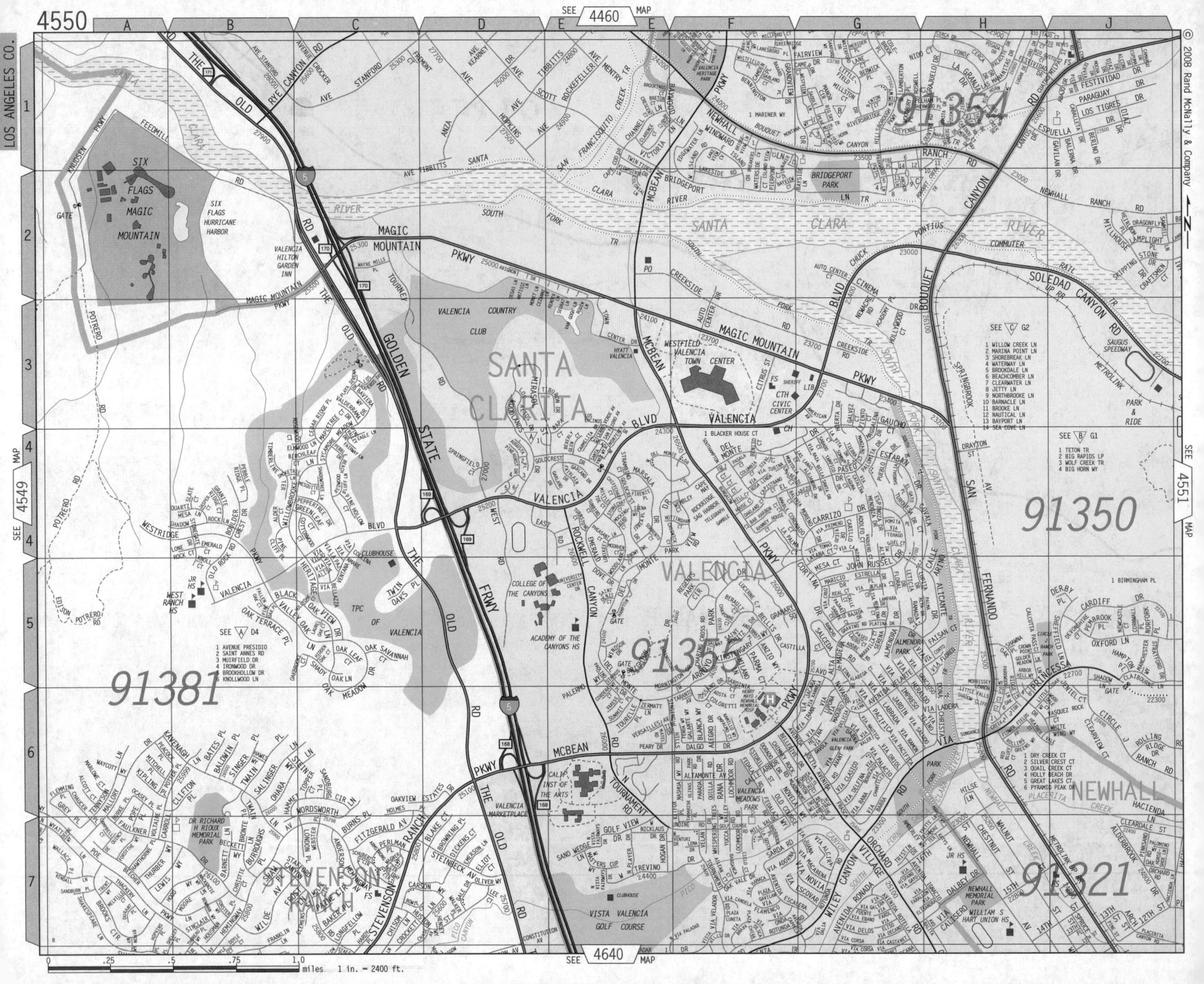

4550
SEE 4460 MAP
SEE 4549 MAP
SEE 4551 MAP
SEE 4640 MAP
LOS ANGELES CO.
© 2008 Rand McNally & Company
SIX FLAGS MAGIC MOUNTAIN
SIX FLAGS HURRICANE HARBOR
VALENCIA HILTON GARDEN INN
SANTA CLARITA
VALENCIA
VALENCIA COUNTRY CLUB
WESTFIELD VALENCIA TOWN CENTER
CIVIC CENTER
COLLEGE OF THE CANYONS
ACADEMY OF THE CANYONS HS
TPC OF VALENCIA
WEST RANCH HS
CALIF INST OF THE ARTS
VALENCIA MARKETPLACE
VISTA VALENCIA GOLF COURSE
STEVENSON RANCH
DR RICHARD H RIOUX MEMORIAL PARK
NEWHALL
NEWHALL MEMORIAL PARK
WILLIAM S HART UNION HS
BRIDGEPORT PARK
SAUGUS SPEEDWAY
PARK & RIDE
SANTA CLARA RIVER
GOLDEN STATE FRWY
MAGIC MOUNTAIN PKWY
MCBEAN PKWY
VALENCIA BLVD
SAN FERNANDO RD
SOLEDAD CANYON RD
NEWHALL RANCH RD
91354
91350
91355
91381
91321
SEE A D4
1 AVENUE PRESIDIO
2 SAINT ANNES RD
3 MUIRFIELD DR
4 IRONWOOD DR
5 BROOKHOLLOW DR
6 KNOLLWOOD LN
SEE C G2
1 WILLOW CREEK LN
2 MARINA POINT LN
3 SHOREBREAK LN
4 WATERWAY LN
5 BROOKDALE LN
6 BEACHCOMBER LN
7 CLEARWATER LN
8 JETTY LN
9 NORTHBROOKE LN
10 BARNACLE LN
11 BROOKE LN
12 NAUTICAL LN
13 BAYPORT LN
14 SEA COVE LN
SEE B G1
1 TETON TR
2 BIG RAPIDS LP
3 WOLF CREEK TR
4 BIG HORN WY
1 BIRMINGHAM PL
1 DRY CREEK CT
2 SILVER CREST CT
3 QUAIL CREEK CT
4 HOLLY BEACH DR
5 GREAT LAKES CT
6 PYRAMID PEAK DR
0 .25 .5 .75 1.0 miles 1 in. = 2400 ft.

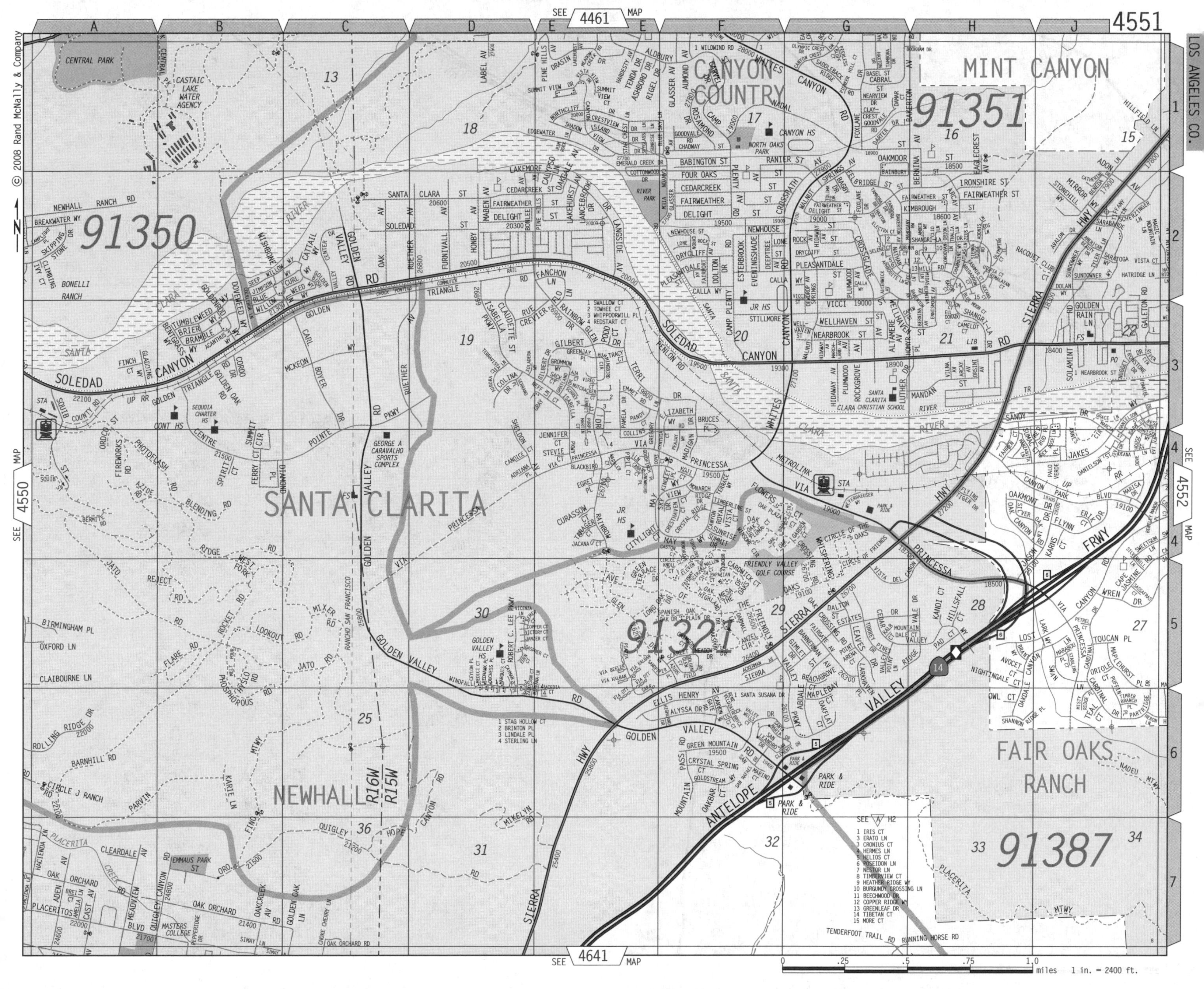

SEE 4461 MAP
SEE 4641 MAP
SEE 4550 MAP
SEE 4552 MAP
LOS ANGELES CO.
A B C D E F G H J
1 2 3 4 5 6 7
MINT CANYON
CANYON COUNTRY
91351
91350
SANTA CLARITA
91321
FAIR OAKS RANCH
91387
NEWHALL
CENTRAL PARK
CASTAIC LAKE WATER AGENCY
BONELLI RANCH
CANYON HS
NORTH OAKS PARK
RIVER PARK
JR HS
SANTA CLARITA CHRISTIAN SCHOOL
SEQUOIA CHARTER HS
CONT HS
GEORGE A CARAVALHO SPORTS COMPLEX
GOLDEN VALLEY HS
FRIENDLY VALLEY GOLF COURSE
EMMAUS PARK
MASTERS COLLEGE
CIRCLE J RANCH
PARK & RIDE
SOLEDAD CANYON RD
GOLDEN VALLEY RD
SIERRA HWY
ANTELOPE VALLEY FRWY
WHITES CANYON RD
VIA PRINCESSA
NEWHALL RANCH RD
SANTA CLARA RIVER
PLACERITA CREEK
R16W R15W
SEE H2
1 IRIS CT
2 ERATO LN
3 CRONIUS CT
4 HERMES LN
5 HELIOS CT
6 POSEIDON LN
7 NESTOR LN
8 TIMBERVIEW CT
9 HEATHER RIDGE WY
10 BURGUNDY CROSSING LN
11 BEECHWOOD DR
12 COPPER RIDGE WY
13 GREENLEAF DR
14 TIBETAN CT
15 MORE CT
1 STAG HOLLOW CT
2 BRINTON PL
3 LINDALE PL
4 STERLING LN
1 SWALLOW CT
2 TOWHEE CT
3 WHIPPOORWILL PL
4 REDSTART CT
0 .25 .5 .75 1.0 miles 1 in. = 2400 ft.

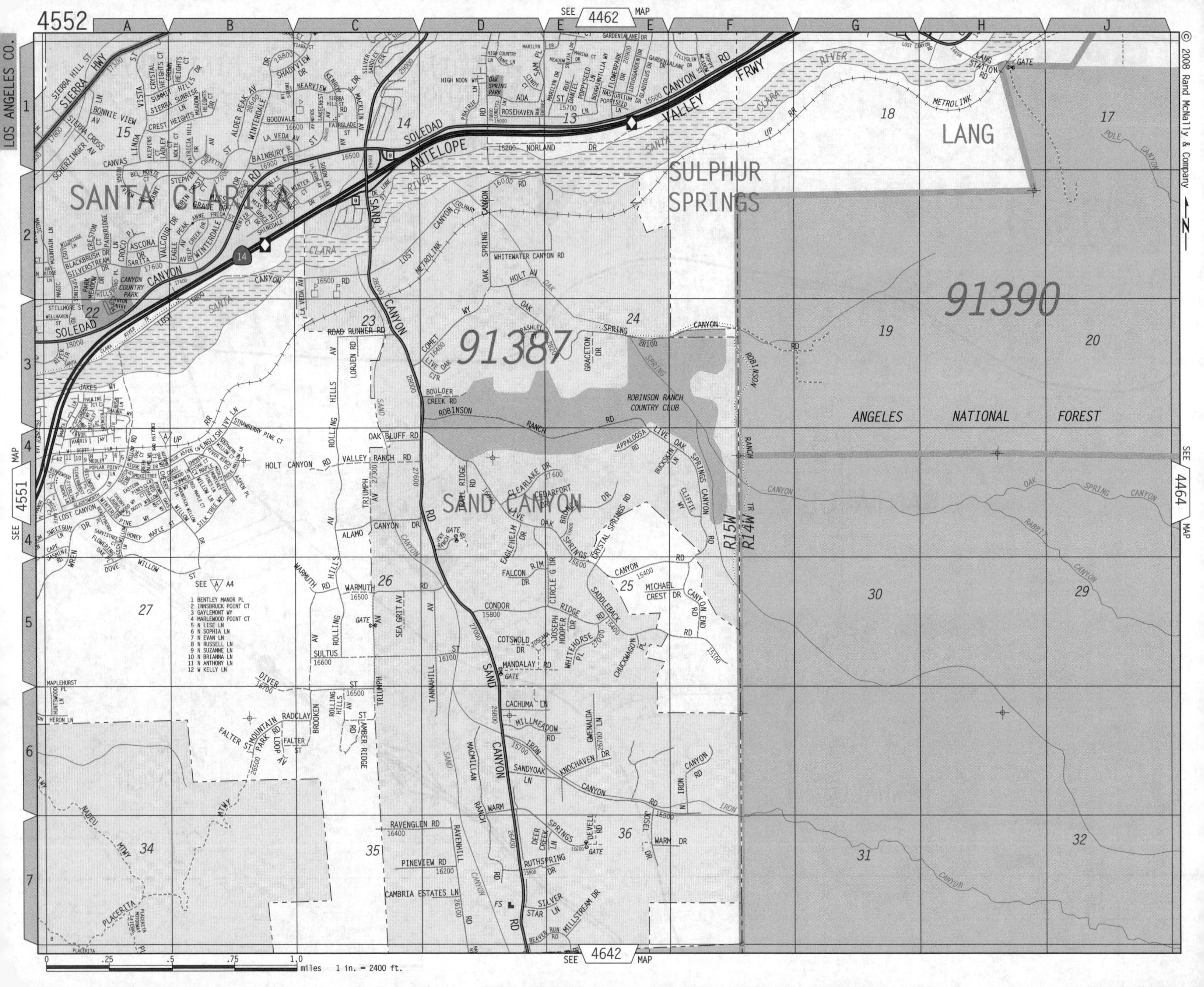
LOS ANGELES CO.
SEE 4462 MAP
SEE 4551 MAP
SEE 4464 MAP
SEE 4642 MAP
A
B
C
D
E
F
G
H
J
SANTA CLARITA
SULPHUR SPRINGS
LANG
SAND CANYON
91387
91390
ANGELES NATIONAL FOREST
ANTELOPE VALLEY FRWY
SOLEDAD CANYON RD
SIERRA HWY
SAND CANYON RD
LOST CANYON RD
OAK SPRING CANYON
ROBINSON RANCH RD
ROBINSON RANCH COUNTRY CLUB
CANYON COUNTRY PARK
SANTA CLARA RIVER
METROLINK
UP RR
LANG STATION RD
PLACERITA CANYON
R15W
R14W
SEE A4
1 BENTLEY MANOR PL
2 INNSBRUCK POINT CT
3 GAYLEMONT WY
4 MARLEWOOD POINT CT
5 N LISE LN
6 N SOPHIA LN
7 N EVAN LN
8 N RUSSELL LN
9 N SUZANNE LN
10 N BRIANNA LN
11 N ANTHONY LN
12 W KELLY LN
0 .25 .5 .75 1.0 miles 1 in. = 2400 ft.

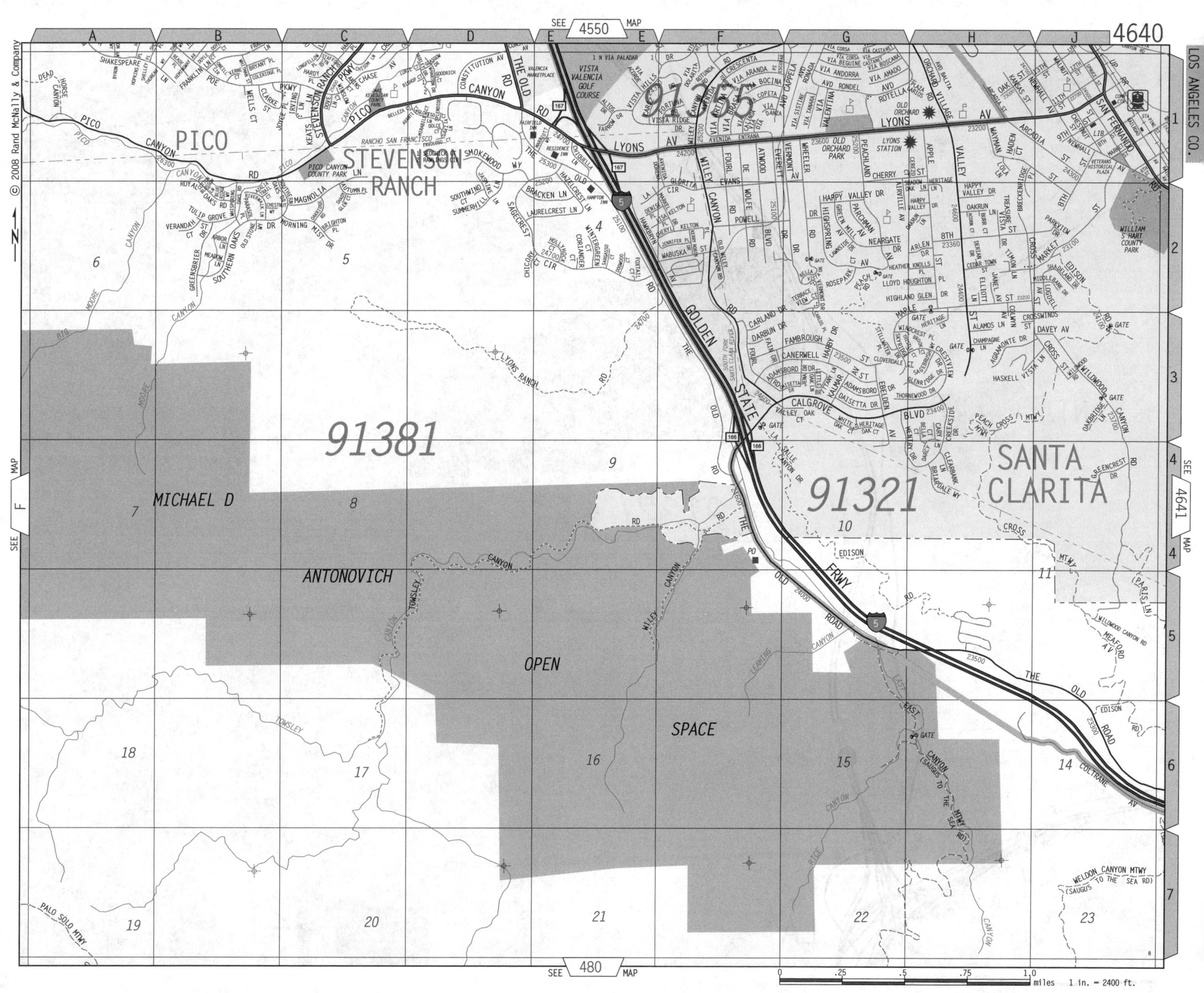

SEE 4550 MAP
LOS ANGELES CO.
PICO
STEVENSON RANCH
SANTA CLARITA
91381
91355
91321
MICHAEL D ANTONOVICH OPEN SPACE
GOLDEN STATE FRWY
THE OLD RD
LYONS AV
PICO CANYON RD
WILEY CANYON RD
CALGROVE BLVD
VALLEY ST
ORCHARD VILLAGE RD
SAN FERNANDO RD
MAGNOLIA LN
SOUTHERN OAKS DR
MARKET ST
ARCADIA ST
NEWHALL AV
WILLIAM S HART COUNTY PARK
VISTA VALENCIA GOLF COURSE
PICO CANYON COUNTY PARK
OLD ORCHARD PARK
LYONS STATION
LYONS RANCH RD
TOWSLEY CANYON
WILDWOOD CANYON
EAST CANYON (SAUGUS TO THE SEA RD) MTWY
WELDON CANYON MTWY (SAUGUS TO THE SEA RD)
PALO SOLO MTWY
COLTRANE AV
EDISON
SEE 4641 MAP
SEE F MAP
SEE 480 MAP
miles 1 in. = 2400 ft.

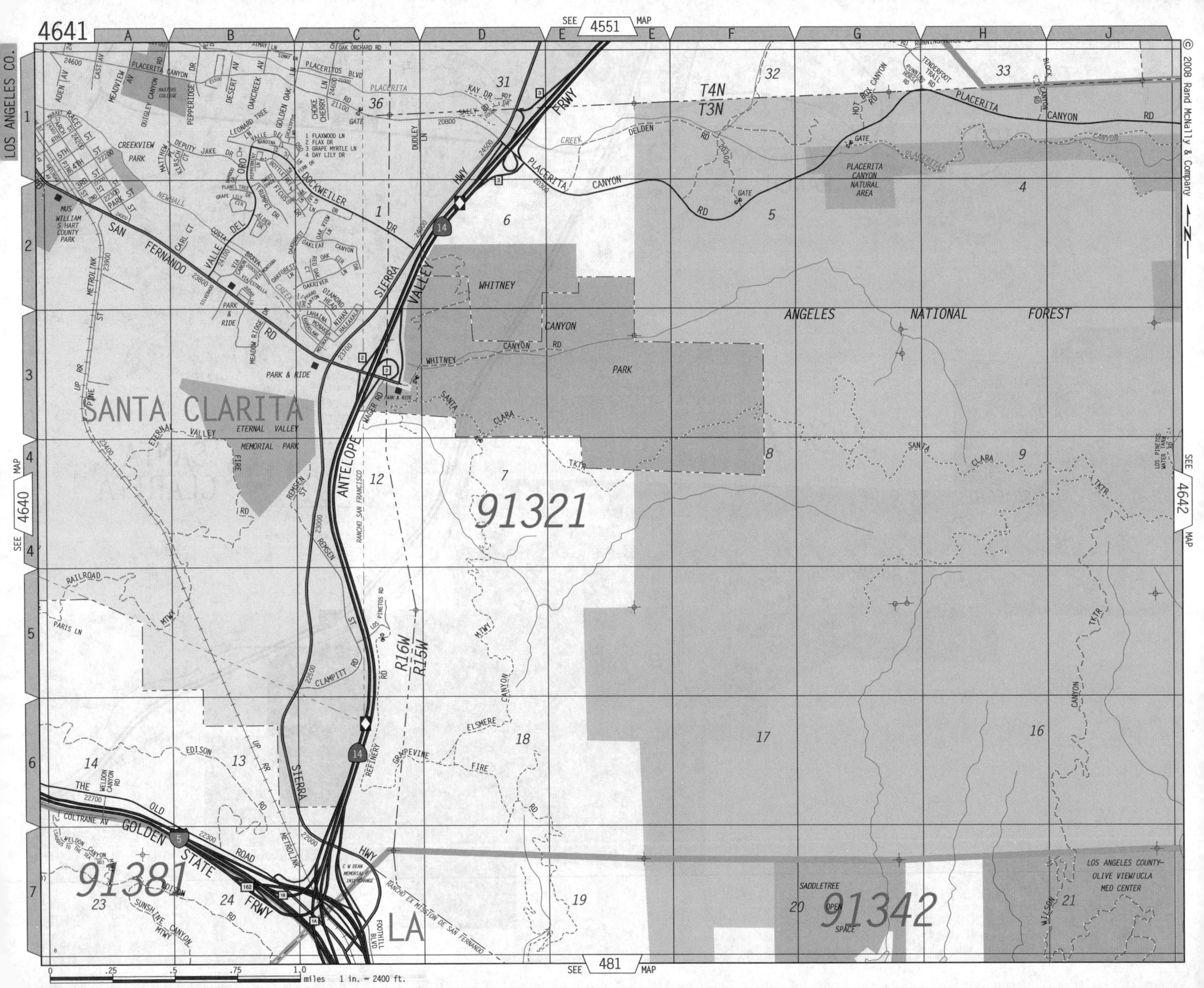
SEE 4551 MAP
LOS ANGELES CO.
SANTA CLARITA
91321
91381
91342
LA
ANGELES NATIONAL FOREST
WHITNEY CANYON PARK
PLACERITA CANYON NATURAL AREA
ETERNAL VALLEY MEMORIAL PARK
MUS WILLIAM S HART COUNTY PARK
MASTERS COLLEGE
CREEKVIEW PARK
SADDLETREE OPEN SPACE
LOS ANGELES COUNTY-OLIVE VIEW/UCLA MED CENTER
C W DEAN MEMORIAL INTERCHANGE
PARK & RIDE
ANTELOPE VALLEY FRWY
GOLDEN STATE FRWY
SAN FERNANDO RD
SIERRA HWY
PLACERITA CANYON RD
DOCKWEILER DR
T4N
T3N
R16W
R15W
RANCHO SAN FRANCISCO
RANCHO EX MISSION DE SAN FERNANDO
1 FLAXWOOD LN
2 FLAX DR
3 GRAPE MYRTLE LN
4 DAY LILY DR
SEE 4640 MAP
SEE 4642 MAP
SEE 481 MAP
miles 1 in. = 2400 ft.

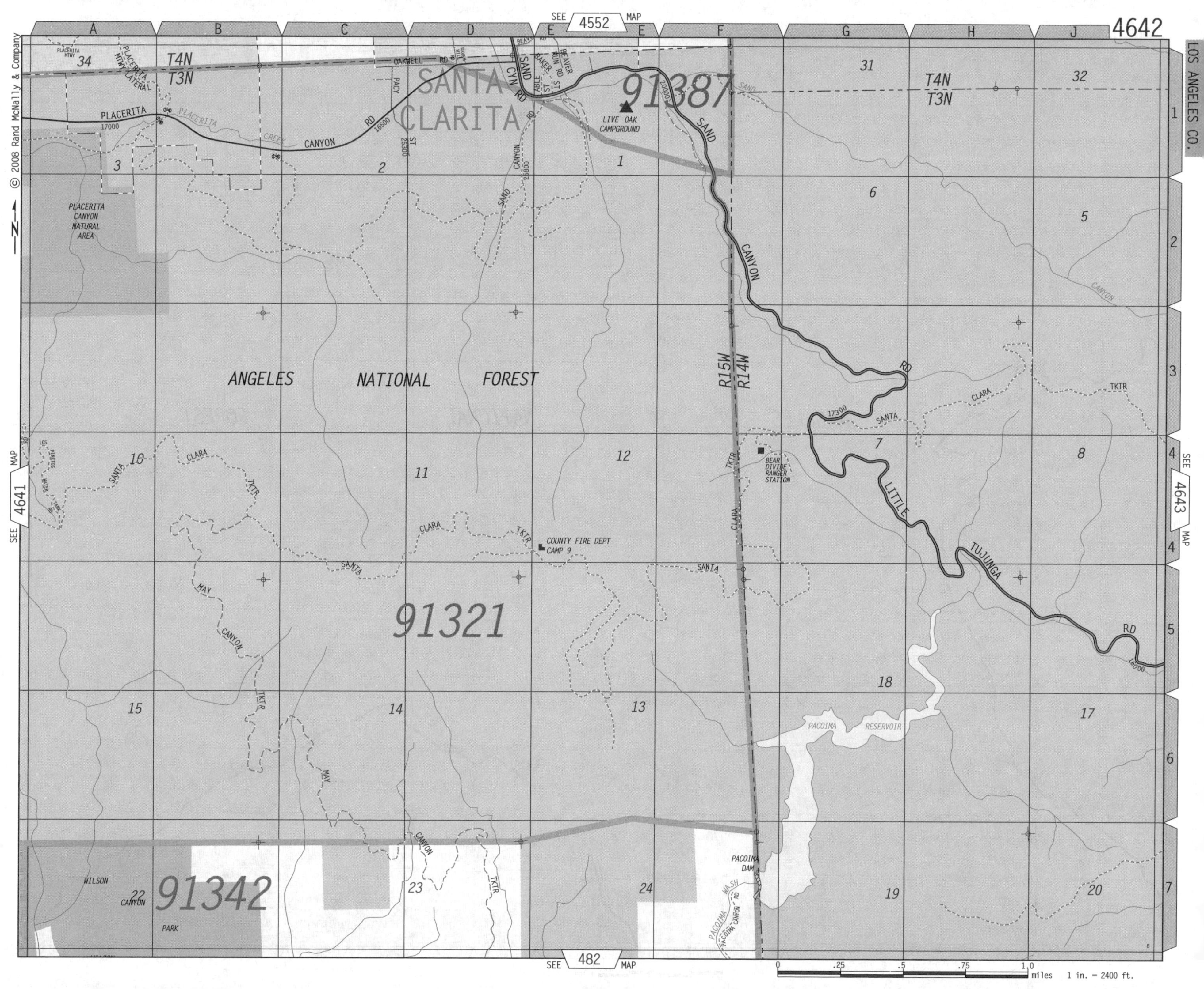
SEE 4552 MAP
LOS ANGELES CO.
SANTA CLARITA
91387
91321
91342
T4N
T3N
R15W
R14W
PLACERITA CANYON NATURAL AREA
PLACERITA CANYON RD
OAKWELL RD
SAND CANYON RD
LIVE OAK CAMPGROUND
ANGELES NATIONAL FOREST
LITTLE TUJUNGA RD
BEAR DIVIDE RANGER STATION
COUNTY FIRE DEPT CAMP 9
SANTA CLARA TKTR
MAY CANYON TKTR
PACOIMA RESERVOIR
PACOIMA DAM
PACOIMA WASH
PACOIMA CANYON RD
WILSON CANYON PARK
SEE 4641 MAP
SEE 4643 MAP
SEE 482 MAP
miles 1 in. = 2400 ft.

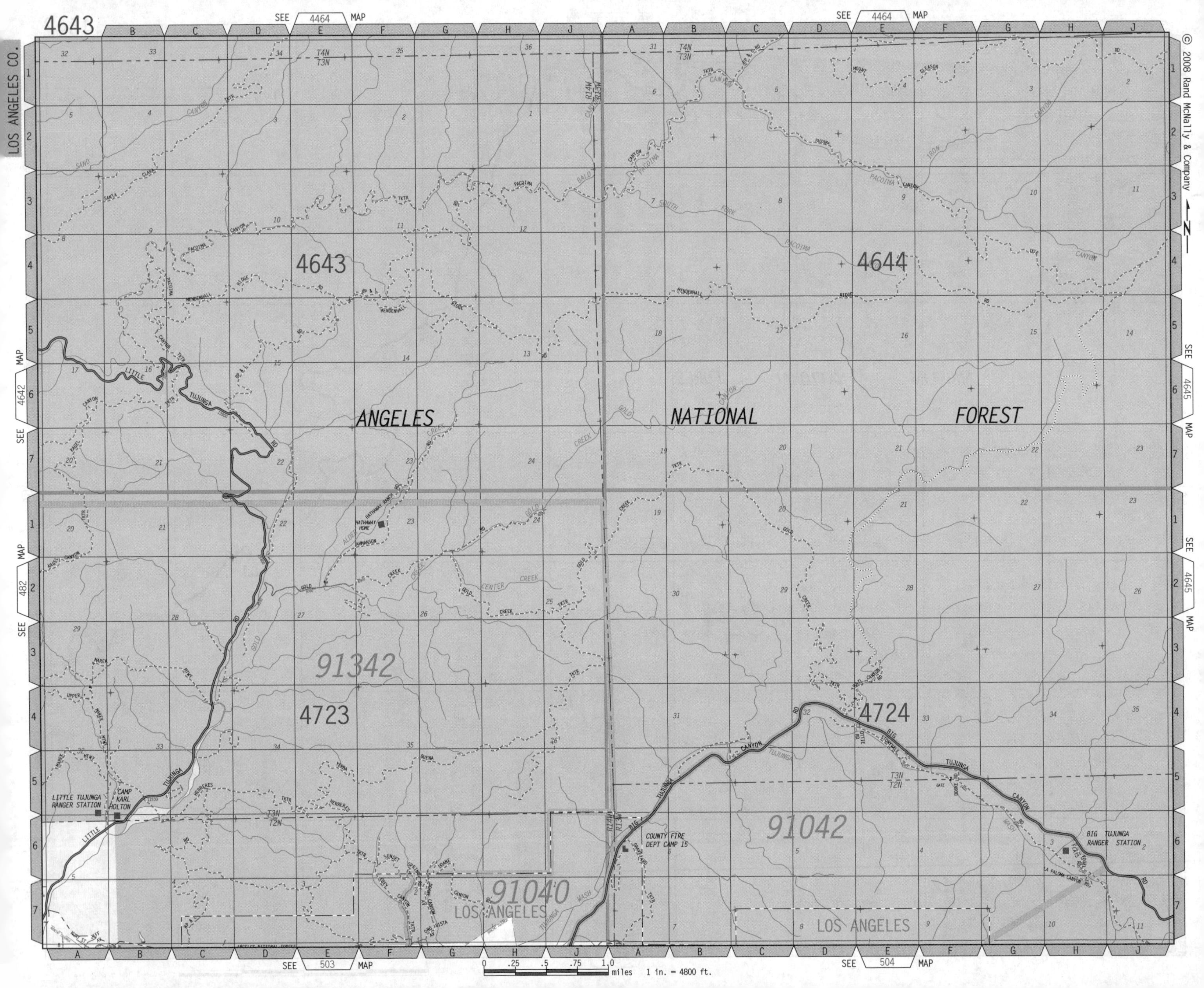

SEE 4464 MAP
SEE 4464 MAP
LOS ANGELES CO.
© 2008 Rand McNally & Company
SEE 4642 MAP
SEE 4645 MAP
SEE 482 MAP
SEE 4645 MAP
4643
4644
4723
4724
ANGELES
NATIONAL
FOREST
91342
91042
91040
LOS ANGELES
LOS ANGELES
LITTLE TUJUNGA RANGER STATION
CAMP KARL HOLTON
HATHAWAY HOME
COUNTY FIRE DEPT CAMP 15
BIG TUJUNGA RANGER STATION
LITTLE TUJUNGA
BIG TUJUNGA CANYON RD
PACOIMA CANYON
MENDENHALL RIDGE RD
T4N T3N
T3N T2N
R14W R13W
SEE 503 MAP
SEE 504 MAP
miles 1 in. = 4800 ft.

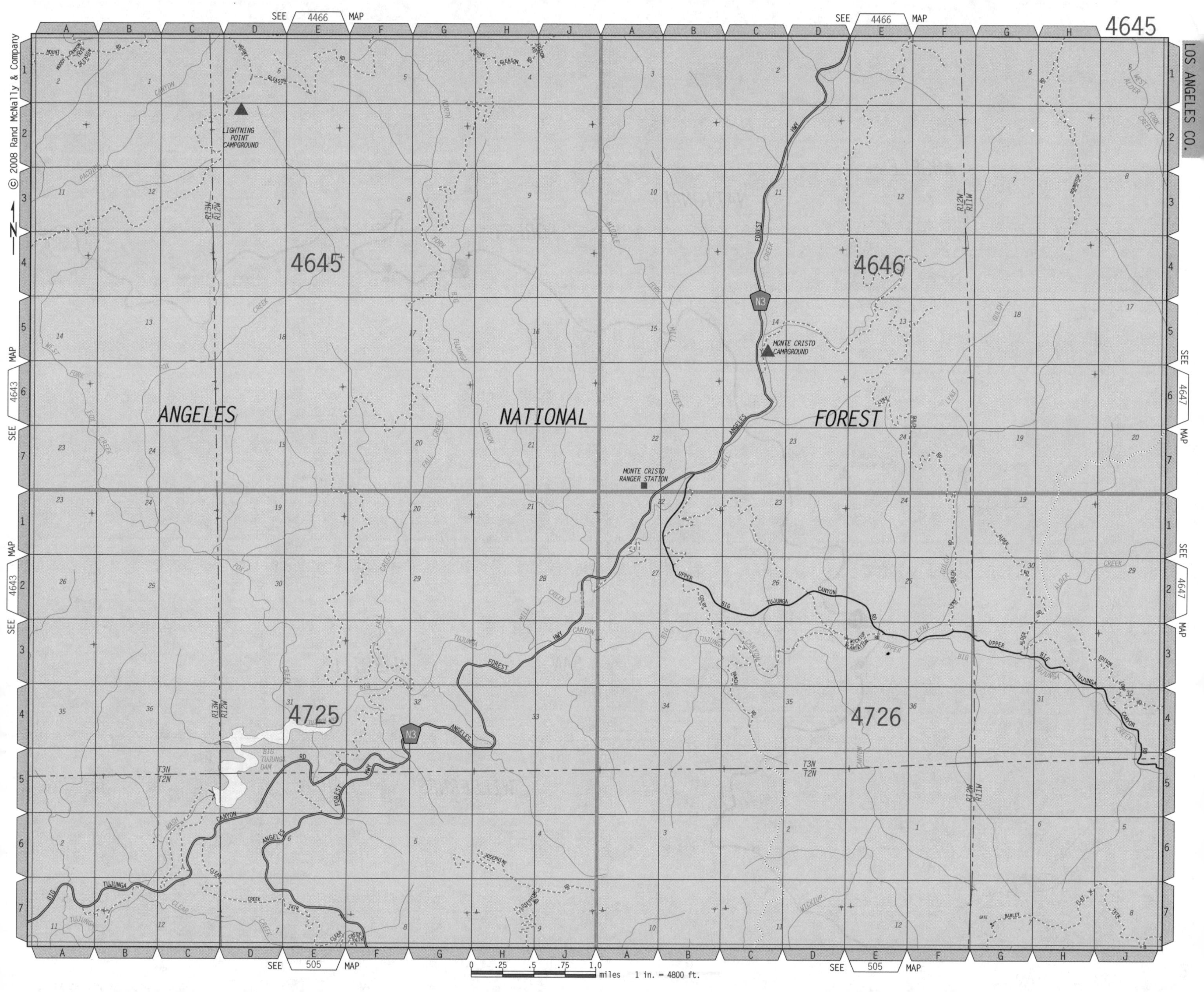
LOS ANGELES CO.
SEE 4466 MAP
SEE 505 MAP
SEE 4643 MAP
SEE 4647 MAP
4645
4646
4725
4726
ANGELES
NATIONAL
FOREST
LIGHTNING POINT CAMPGROUND
MONTE CRISTO CAMPGROUND
MONTE CRISTO RANGER STATION
BIG TUJUNGA DAM
ANGELES FOREST HWY
UPPER BIG TUJUNGA CANYON RD
BIG TUJUNGA CANYON RD
N3
R13W
R12W
R11W
T3N
T2N
miles 1 in. = 4800 ft.
0 .25 .5 .75 1.0

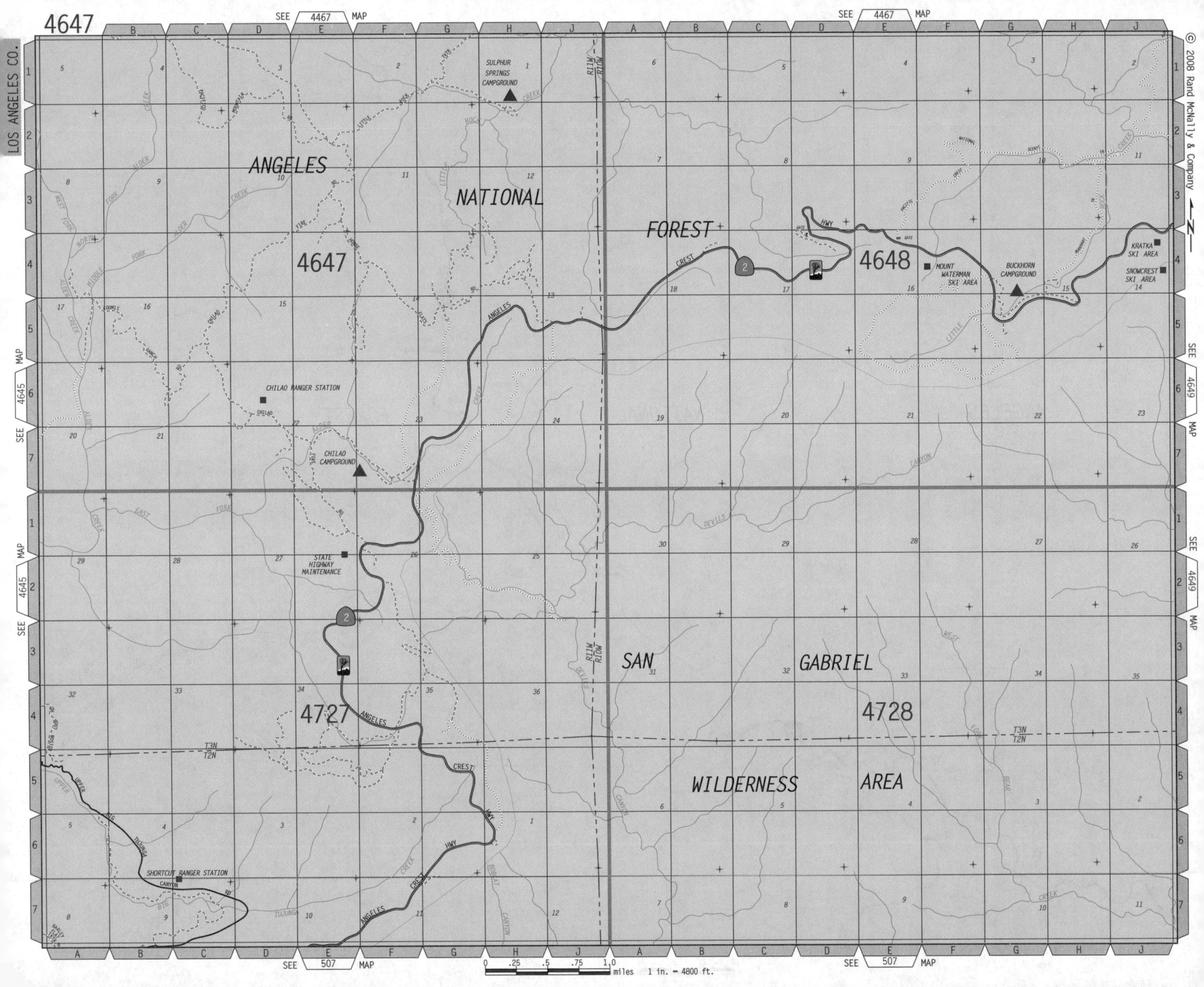

LOS ANGELES CO.
SEE 4467 MAP
SULPHUR SPRINGS CAMPGROUND
ANGELES
NATIONAL
FOREST
4647
4648
MOUNT WATERMAN SKI AREA
BUCKHORN CAMPGROUND
KRATKA SKI AREA
SNOWCREST SKI AREA
CHILAO RANGER STATION
CHILAO CAMPGROUND
STATE HIGHWAY MAINTENANCE
SAN
GABRIEL
WILDERNESS
AREA
4727
4728
SHORTCUT RANGER STATION
R11W R10W
T3N T2N
SEE 4645 MAP
SEE 4649 MAP
SEE 507 MAP
0 .25 .5 .75 1.0 miles 1 in. = 4800 ft.

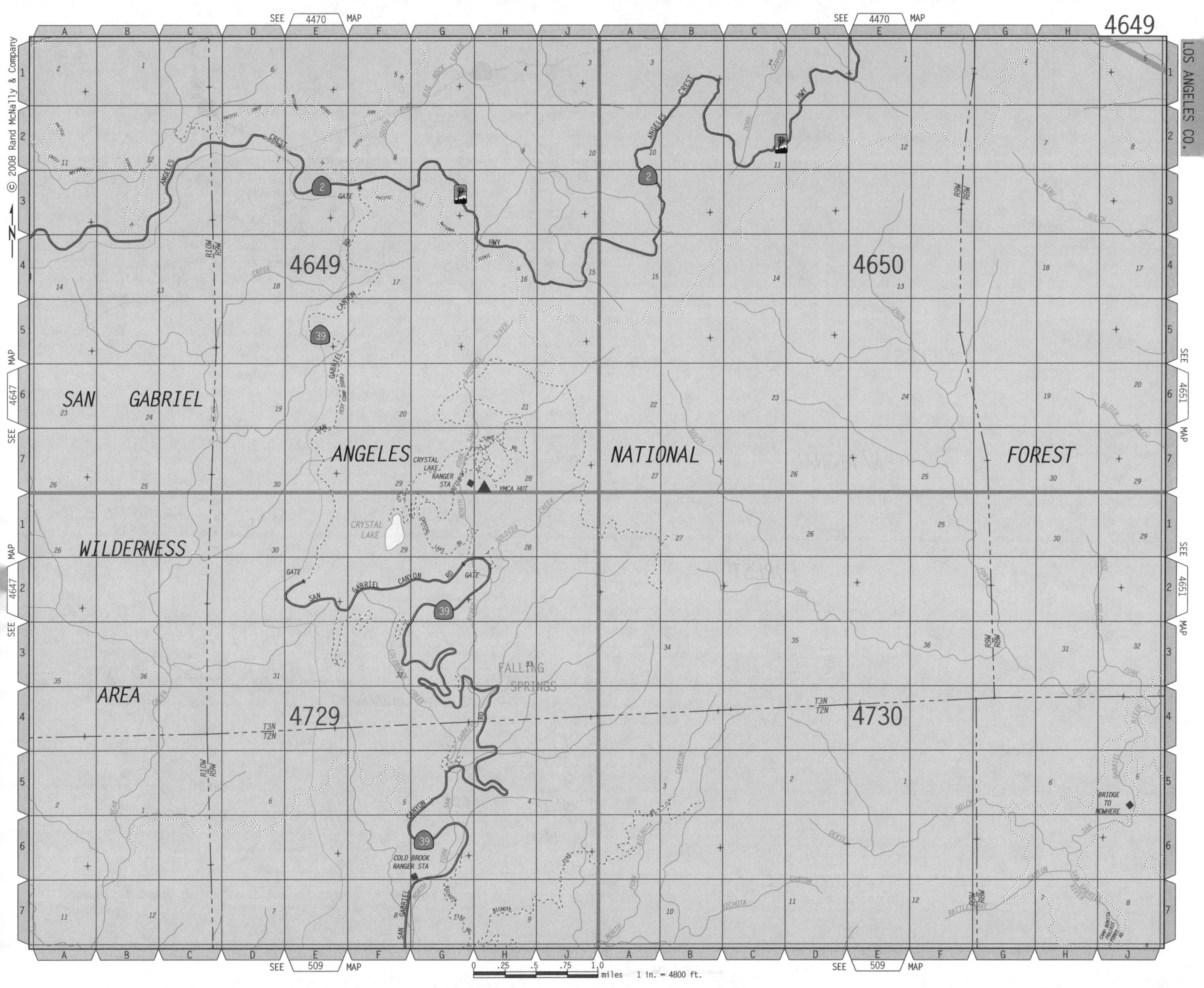
SEE 4470 MAP
SEE 4470 MAP
LOS ANGELES CO.
ANGELES CREST HWY
SAN GABRIEL
ANGELES
NATIONAL
FOREST
WILDERNESS
AREA
4649
4650
4729
4730
CRYSTAL LAKE RANGER STA
YMCA HUT
CRYSTAL LAKE
SAN GABRIEL CANYON RD
GATE
FALLING SPRINGS
COLD BROOK RANGER STA
BRIDGE TO NOWHERE
T3N
T2N
R10W
R9W
R8W
SEE 4647 MAP
SEE 4651 MAP
SEE 509 MAP
SEE 509 MAP
miles 1 in. = 4800 ft.

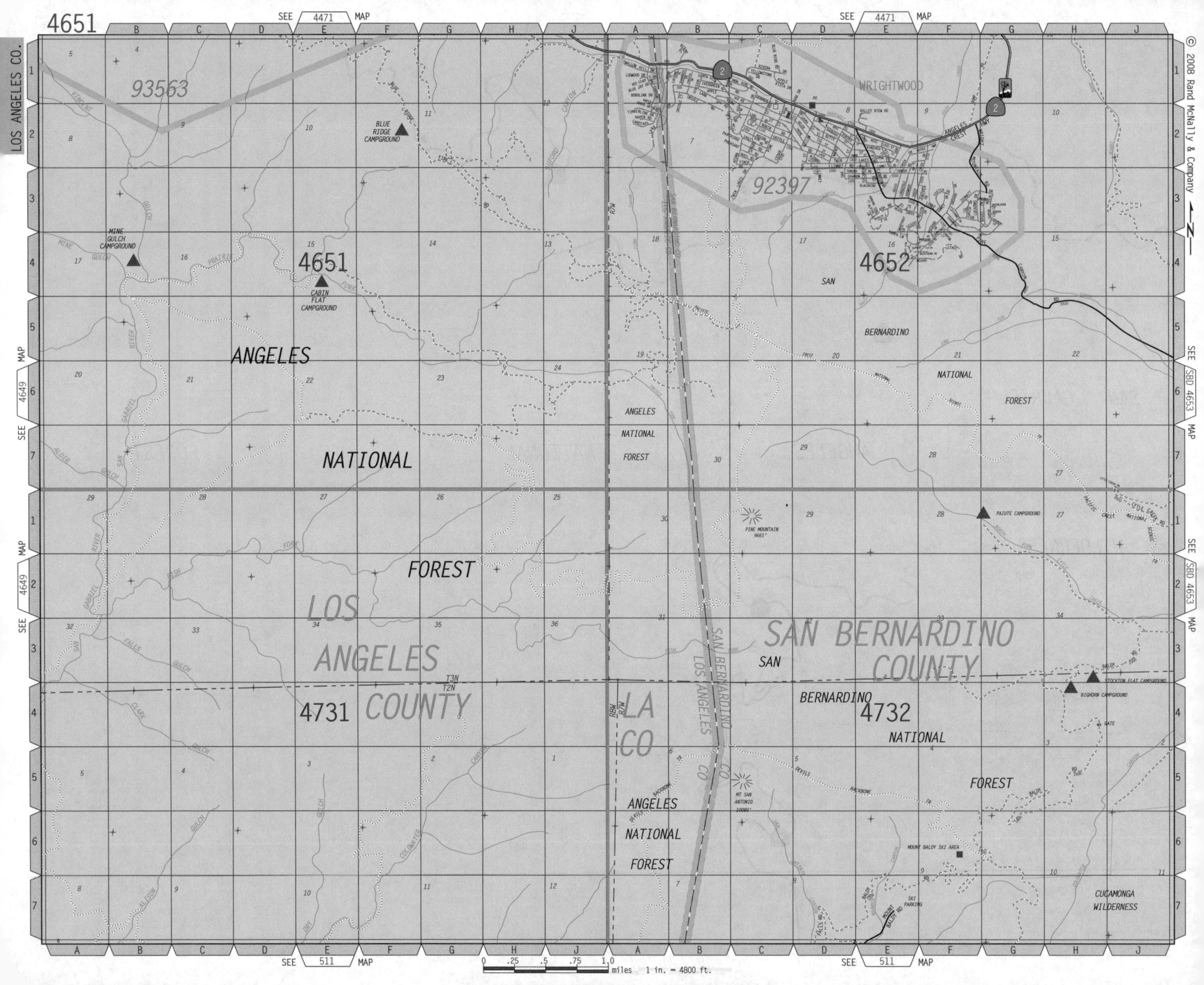
LOS ANGELES CO.
SEE 4471 MAP
SEE 4471 MAP
93563
92397
WRIGHTWOOD
BLUE RIDGE CAMPGROUND
MINE GULCH CAMPGROUND
CABIN FLAT CAMPGROUND
4651
4652
4731
4732
ANGELES
NATIONAL
FOREST
SAN
BERNARDINO
NATIONAL
FOREST
ANGELES NATIONAL FOREST
LOS ANGELES COUNTY
SAN BERNARDINO COUNTY
LA CO
SAN BERNARDINO CO
LOS ANGELES CO
PINE MOUNTAIN 9661'
MT SAN ANTONIO 10080'
PAIUTE CAMPGROUND
STOCKTON FLAT CAMPGROUND
BIGHORN CAMPGROUND
GATE
MOUNT BALDY SKI AREA
SKI PARKING
CUCAMONGA WILDERNESS
ANGELES CREST HWY
T3N
T2N
R8W
R7W
SEE 4649 MAP
SEE 4649 MAP
SEE SBD 4653 MAP
SEE SBD 4653 MAP
SEE 511 MAP
SEE 511 MAP
0 .25 .5 .75 1.0 miles 1 in. = 4800 ft.

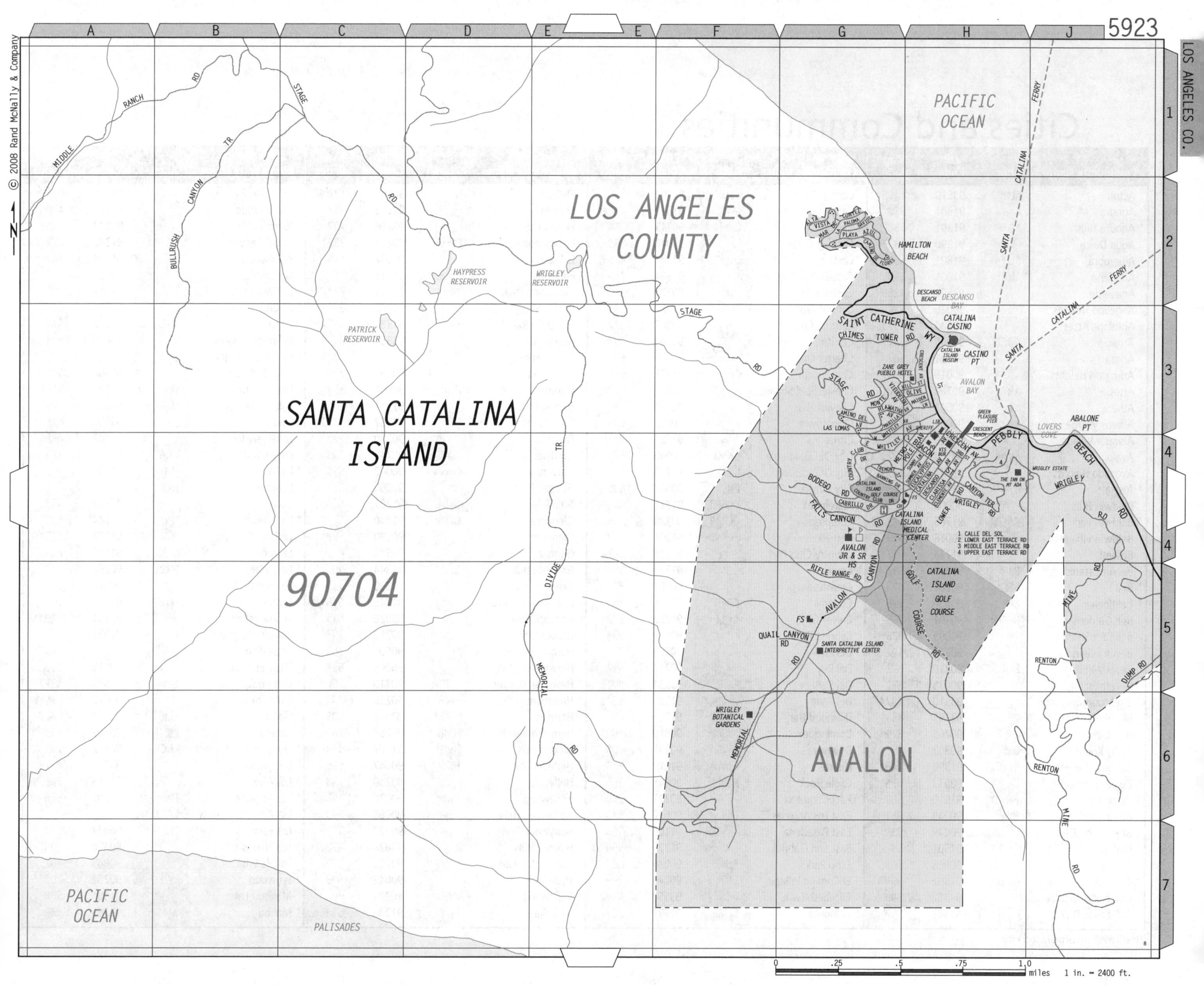

A
B
C
D
E
F
G
H
J
LOS ANGELES CO.
© 2008 Rand McNally & Company
PACIFIC OCEAN
LOS ANGELES COUNTY
SANTA CATALINA ISLAND
90704
AVALON
HAYPRESS RESERVOIR
WRIGLEY RESERVOIR
PATRICK RESERVOIR
HAMILTON BEACH
DESCANSO BEACH
DESCANSO BAY
CATALINA CASINO
CATALINA ISLAND MUSEUM
CASINO PT
AVALON BAY
GREEN PLEASURE PIER
CRESCENT BEACH
LOVERS COVE
ABALONE PT
ZANE GREY PUEBLO HOTEL
THE INN ON MT ADA
WRIGLEY ESTATE
CATALINA ISLAND GOLF COURSE
CATALINA ISLAND MEDICAL CENTER
AVALON JR & SR HS
SANTA CATALINA ISLAND INTERPRETIVE CENTER
WRIGLEY BOTANICAL GARDENS
PALISADES
SANTA CATALINA FERRY
1 CALLE DEL SOL
2 LOWER EAST TERRACE RD
3 MIDDLE EAST TERRACE RD
4 UPPER EAST TERRACE RD
0 .25 .5 .75 1.0 miles 1 in. = 2400 ft.

Cities and Communities

Community Name	Abbr.	ZIP Code	Map Page
Acton	Actn	93510	4465
Agoura	Ago	91301	558
* Agoura Hills	AGRH	91301	558
Agua Dulce		91390	4373
* Alhambra	ALH	91801	596
Altadena	Alta	91001	535
Anaverde		93551	4285
Angelino Heights		90026	634
Antelope Acres		93534	3923
* Arcadia	ARCD	91006	567
Arleta		91331	502
Arlington Heights		90019	633
* Artesia	ART	90701	766
Athens		90044	734
Athens Village		90061	734
Atwater Village		90039	594
* Avalon	AVA	90704	5923
Avocado Heights		91746	637
* Azusa	AZU	91702	568
Baldwin Hills		90008	673
* Baldwin Park	BALD	91706	598
Baldwin Village		90016	673
Bassett		91746	637
Bel Air Estates	BelA	90077	592
* Bell	BELL	90201	675
* Bellflower	BLF	90706	736
* Bell Gardens	BGDN	90201	705
Belmont Shore		90803	826
Beverly Glen		90210	592
* Beverly Hills	BHLS	90210	632
Beverlywood		90035	632
Big Mountain Ridge		93510	4374
Big Pines		92397	4561
Big Rock		90265	629
Bixby Knolls	Bxby	90807	765
Bouquet Canyon	BqtC	91390	4461
Boyle Heights	Boyl	90033	635
* Bradbury	BRAD	91010	568
Brentwood	Brwd	90049	631
Brentwood Glen		90049	631
* Burbank	BURB	91501	533
Cahuenga Pass		90068	563
* Calabasas	CALB	91302	559
Calabasas Highlands		91302	589
Calabasas Park		91302	559
Canoga Park	CanP	91303	530
Canyon Country	CynC	91351	4462
* Carson	CRSN	90745	764
Carthay Circle		90048	633
Castaic	Cstc	91384	4369
Castaic Junction		91384	4459
Castellammare		90272	630
Central City		90021	634
Century City	CenC	90067	632
* Cerritos	CRTS	90703	767
Charter Oak	Char	91724	599
Chatsworth	Chat	91311	500
Chesterfield Square		90047	673
Cheviot Hills		90064	632
Chinatown		90012	634
Citrus		91722	599
* City Of Commerce	CMRC	90040	675
* City Of Industry	INDS	91746	678
City Terrace	City	90063	635
* Claremont	CLAR	91711	601
* Compton	COMP	90220	734
Cornell		91301	587
Country Club Park		90019	633
* Covina	COV	91722	599
Crenshaw		90008	673
* Cudahy	CDHY	90201	705
* Culver City	CULC	90230	672
Cypress Park		90065	594
Del Aire		90250	733
Del Rey		90292	672
Del Sur		93534	4013
Del Valle		91381	4549
* Diamond Bar	DBAR	91765	680
Dominguez		90810	765
* Downey	DWNY	90241	706
* Duarte	DUAR	91010	568
Eagle Rock	Eagl	90041	565
East Compton		90221	735
East Los Angeles	ELA	90022	635
East Pasadena		91106	566
East San Gabriel		91775	596
Echo Park	Echo	90026	634
El Camino Village		90249	733
Elizabeth Lake		93550	4102
* El Monte	ELMN	91731	637
El Nido		90265	628
El Nido		90278	763
El Porto		90266	732
* El Segundo	ELSG	90245	732
El Sereno		90032	595
Encino	Enc	91316	561
Exposition Park		90037	674
Fairfax Village		90048	633
Fair Oaks Ranch		91387	4551
Fairmont		93534	F
Falling Springs			4729
Fernwood		90290	590
Florence	Flor	90001	674
Forrest Park		91351	4462
Four Points		93552	4287
Fox Hills		90230	672
* Gardena	GAR	90247	733
Garvanza	Garv	90042	595
Glassell Park		90065	594
* Glendale	GLDL	91201	564
* Glendora	GLDR	91740	569
Glenview		90290	590
Gorman		93534	F
Granada Hills	GrnH	91344	501
Green Valley		91390	4192
Hacienda Heights	HacH	91745	678
Hancock Park		90020	633
Harbor City	Hrbr	90710	793
Harbor Gateway		90501	763
Harvard Heights		90006	633
* Hawaiian Gardens	HGDN	90716	766
* Hawthorne	HAW	90250	733
Hermon		90042	595
* Hermosa Beach	HMB	90254	762
* Hidden Hills	HIDH	91302	559
Highland Park	HiPk	90042	595
Hollydale		90280	735
Hollywood	Hlwd	90028	593
Hollywood Hills	HHls	90068	593
Hollywood Riviera		90277	793
Holmby Hills		90024	632
* Huntington Park	HNTP	90255	675
Hyde Park		90043	673
* Inglewood	ING	90301	703
* Irwindale	IRW	91706	598
Jefferson Park		90018	633
Joshua Hills		93550	4286
Juniper Hills		93543	4468
Kagel Canyon		91342	482
Knollwood		91344	481
Koreatown		90006	633
* La Canada Flintridge	LCF	91011	535
La Crescenta	LaCr	91214	504
Ladera Heights	LadH	90056	672
Lafayette Square		90019	633
* La Habra Heights	LHH	90631	708
Lake Balboa		91406	531
Lake Hughes	LkHu	93532	4101
Lake Los Angeles	Llan	93550	4199
Lakeview		93550	4285
Lakeview Terrace		91342	482
* Lakewood	LKWD	90712	766
* La Mirada	LMRD	90638	737
* Lancaster	LAN	93534	4015
Lang		91387	4552
* La Puente	LPUE	91744	638
La Tuna Canyon		91352	503
* La Verne	LVRN	91750	600
* Lawndale	LNDL	90260	733
Leimert Park		90008	673
Lennox	Lenx	90304	703
Leona Valley		93551	4194
Lincoln Heights	LinH	90031	635
Little Armenia		90027	593
Little Ethiopia		90019	633
Littlerock	Litl	93543	4377
Little Tokyo		90012	634
Llano	Llan	93544	4379
* Lomita	LMTA	90717	793
* Long Beach	LBCH	90802	795
Longview		93553	4378
Los Altos		90815	796
* Los Angeles	LA	90001	634
-- Los Angeles County	LACo		
Los Feliz	LFlz	90027	593
Los Nietos		90670	706
Loyola Village		90045	702
* Lynwood	LYN	90262	705
Malibou Lake		91301	588
* Malibu	MAL	90265	629

*Indicates incorporated city

Cities and Communities

Community Name	Abbr.	ZIP Code	Map Page
Malibu Bowl		90265	628
Malibu Park		90265	627
* Manhattan Beach	MANB	90266	732
Marina Del Rey	MdlR	90292	672
Mar Vista		90066	672
Mayfair		90712	766
Mayflower Village		91006	597
* Maywood	MYWD	90270	675
Mid-City		90016	633
Mint Canyon		91351	4551
Miracle Mile		90036	633
Miraleste		90274	823
Mission Hills	MsnH	91345	501
Moneta		90247	733
* Monrovia	MNRO	91016	567
* Montebello	MTBL	90640	676
Montecito Heights		90031	595
Monte Nido		91302	629
Monterey Hills		90032	595
* Monterey Park	MONP	91754	636
Montrose	Mont	91020	534
Morningside Park		90305	703
Mount Olympus		90046	593
Mount Washington		90065	595
Naples		90803	826
Neenach		93534	F
Newhall	Nwhl	91350	4551
North Hills		91343	501
North Hollywood	NHol	91601	562
North Long Beach	NLB	90805	765
Northridge	Nor	91324	500
North University Pk		90007	634
* Norwalk	NRWK	90650	736
Norwood Village		91732	597
Oban		93534	3925
Ocean Park		90405	671
Old Canyon		90290	589
Olive View		91342	481
Pacific Palisades	PacP	90272	631
Pacoima	Pcma	91331	502
Palisades Highlands		90272	630
* Palmdale	PMDL	93550	4286
Palms		90034	672
* Palos Verdes Estates	PVE	90274	792
Panorama City	PanC	91402	502
Paradise			4560
* Paramount	PRM	90723	735
Park La Brea		90036	633
* Pasadena	PAS	91101	565
Pearblossom	Pear	93553	4378
Pearland		93550	4287
Phillips Ranch		91766	640
Pico		91381	4640
* Pico Rivera	PRV	90660	676
Pinetree		91387	4462
Playa Del Rey	PdlR	90293	702
Playa Vista		90066	702
Point Dume		90265	667
* Pomona	POM	91766	640
Porter Ranch		91326	480
Portuguese Bend		90274	823
Quartz Hill		93536	4104
Rancho Dominguez	RDom	90221	765
* Rancho Palos Verdes	RPV	90275	822
Rancho Park		90064	632
Rancho Vista		93551	4194
Ravenna		93510	4464
* Redondo Beach	RBCH	90277	762
Reseda	Res	91335	530
Ritter Ranch		93551	4194
* Rolling Hills	RHLS	90274	823
* Rolling Hills Estates	RHE	90274	793
Roosevelt		93535	4017
Rose Park		90804	795
* Rosemead	RSMD	91770	596
Rosewood		90222	734
Rowland Heights	RowH	91748	678
Sandberg		93532	F
Sand Canyon		91387	4552
* San Dimas	SDMS	91773	600
* San Fernando	SFER	91340	482
* San Gabriel	SGBL	91776	596
* San Marino	SMRO	91108	596
San Pedro	SPed	90731	824
* Santa Clarita	SCTA	91355	4550
* Santa Fe Springs	SFSP	90670	706
* Santa Monica	SMCA	90402	671
Saugus	Saug	91350	4461
Sawtelle		90025	632
Shadow Hills		91040	503
Sherman Oaks	Shrm	91403	562
* Sierra Madre	SMAD	91024	567
* Signal Hill	SIGH	90755	795
Silver Lake	Silv	90026	594
Sleepy Valley		91390	4373
Solano Canyon		90012	634
Soledad		91390	4463
South Carthay		90035	633
* South El Monte	SELM	91733	637
* South Gate	SGAT	90280	705
South Los Angeles		90037	674
* South Pasadena	SPAS	91030	595
South Robertson		90034	632
South San Gabriel		91770	636
South San Jose Hills		91744	678
South Whittier		90604	707
Sparr Heights		91208	534
Stevenson Ranch	StvR	91381	4640
Studio City		91604	562
Sulphur Springs		91387	4552
Sunland	Sunl	91040	503
Sun Valley	SunV	91352	532
Sun Village		93552	4197
Sylmar		91342	481
Sylvia Park		90290	590
Tarzana	Tarz	91356	560
* Temple City	TEML	91780	597
Terminal Island		90731	824
Thai Town		90027	593
Toluca Lake		91602	563
Toluca Woods		91601	563
Topanga	Top	90290	590
* Torrance	TOR	90505	763
Trousdale Estates		90210	592
Tujunga	Tuj	91042	504
Universal City	Univ	91608	563
University Hills		90032	635
Valencia	Valc	91355	4550
Valinda		91744	638
Valley Glen		91401	532
Valley Village		91607	562
Val Verde Park		91384	4459
Valyermo	Valy	93563	4469
Van Nuys	VanN	91401	532
Vasquez Rocks		91390	4373
Venice	Ven	90291	671
Verdugo City		91208	534
Vermont Knolls		90044	704
* Vernon	VER	90058	674
View Park		90043	673
* Walnut	WAL	91789	639
Walnut Park		90255	704
Walteria		90505	793
Warner Center		91367	560
Watts	Wats	90002	704
West Adams		90018	633
Westchester	Wch	90045	702
West Carson		90502	764
* West Covina	WCOV	91790	598
Westdale		90064	672
West Hills	WHil	91307	529
* West Hollywood	WHWD	90069	592
Westlake		90057	634
* Westlake Village	WLKV	91361	557
West Los Angeles	WLA	90025	632
Westmont		90047	703
West Puente Valley		91746	638
West Whittier		90606	676
W Rcho Dominguez		90248	734
West Toluca Lake		91601	563
Westwood	Wwd	90024	632
Whitley Heights		90068	593
* Whittier	WHIT	90601	707
Willowbrook	Wbrk	90222	734
Wilmington	Wilm	90744	794
Wilshire Center		90010	633
Wilshire Park		90005	633
Wilsona Gardens		93535	4109
Windsor Hills		90043	673
Windsor Square		90020	633
Winnetka	Win	91306	530
Woodland Hills	WdHl	91364	559
Woodside Village		91792	639
Wrigley		90806	795

*Indicates incorporated city

List of Abbreviations

PREFIXES & SUFFIXES

AL	ALLEY
ARC	ARCADE
AV,AVE	AVENUE
AVCT	AVENUE COURT
AVD	AVENIDA
AVD D LA	AVENIDA DE LA
AVD D LOS	AVENIDA DE LOS
AVD DE	AVENIDA DE
AVD DE LAS	AVENIDA DE LAS
AVD DEL	AVENIDA DEL
AVDR	AVENUE DRIVE
AVEX	AVENUE EXTENSION
AV OF	AVENUE OF
AV OF THE	AVENUE OF THE
AVPL	AVENUE PLACE
BAY	BAY
BEND	BEND
BL, BLVD	BOULEVARD
BLCT	BOULEVARD COURT
BLEX	BOULEVARD EXTENSION
BRCH	BRANCH
BRDG	BRIDGE
BYPS	BYPASS
BYWY	BYWAY
CIDR	CIRCLE DRIVE
CIR	CIRCLE
CL	CALLE
CL DE	CALLE DE
CL DL	CALLE DEL
CL D LA	CALLE DE LA
CL D LAS	CALLE DE LAS
CL D LOS	CALLE DE LOS
CL EL	CALLE EL
CLJ	CALLEJON
CL LA	CALLE LA
CL LAS	CALLE LAS
CL LOS	CALLE LOS
CLTR	CLUSTER
CM	CAMINO
CM D	CAMINO DE
CM DL	CAMINO DEL
CM D LA	CAMINO DE LA
CM D LAS	CAMINO DE LAS
CM D LOS	CAMINO DE LOS
CMTO	CAMINITO
CMTO DEL	CAMINITO DEL
CMTO D LA	CAMINITO DE LA
CMTO D LAS	CAMINITO DE LAS
CMTO D LOS	CAMINITO DE LOS
CNDR	CENTER DRIVE
COM	COMMON
COMS	COMMONS
CORR	CORRIDOR
CRES	CRESCENT
CRLO	CIRCULO
CRSG	CROSSING
CST	CIRCLE STREET
CSWY	CAUSEWAY
CT	COURT
CTAV	COURT AVENUE
CTE	CORTE
CTE D	CORTE DE
CTE DEL	CORTE DEL
CTE D LAS	CORTE DE LAS
CTO	CUT OFF
CTR	CENTER
CTST	COURT STREET
CUR	CURVE
CV	COVE
DE	DE
DIAG	DIAGONAL
DR	DRIVE
DRAV	DRIVE AVENUE
DRCT	DRIVE COURT
DRLP	DRIVE LOOP
DVDR	DIVISION DR
EXAV	EXTENSION AVENUE
EXBL	EXTENSION BOULEVARD
EXRD	EXTENSION ROAD
EXST	EXTENSION STREET
EXT	EXTENSION
EXWY	EXPRESSWAY
FOREST RT	FOREST ROUTE
FRWY	FREEWAY
FRY	FERRY
GDNS	GARDENS
GN, GLN	GLEN
GRN	GREEN
GRV	GROVE
HTS	HEIGHTS
HWY	HIGHWAY
ISL	ISLE
JCT	JUNCTION
LN	LANE
LNCR	LANE CIRCLE
LNDG	LANDING
LNDR	LAND DRIVE
LNLP	LANE LOOP
LP	LOOP
MNR	MANOR
MT	MOUNT
MTWY	MOTORWAY
MWCR	MEWS COURT
MWLN	MEWS LANE
NFD	NAT'L FOREST DEV
NK	NOOK
OH	OUTER HIGHWAY
OVL	OVAL
OVLK	OVERLOOK
OVPS	OVERPASS
PAS	PASEO
PAS DE	PASEO DE
PAS DE LA	PASEO DE LA
PAS DE LAS	PASEO DE LAS
PAS DE LOS	PASEO DE LOS
PAS DL	PASEO DEL
PASG	PASSAGE
PAS LA	PASEO LA
PAS LOS	PASEO LOS
PASS	PASS
PIKE	PIKE
PK	PARK
PKDR	PARK DRIVE
PKWY, PKY	PARKWAY
PL	PLACE
PLWY	PLACE WAY
PLZ, PZ	PLAZA
PT	POINT
PTAV	POINT AVENUE
PTH	PATH
PZ DE	PLAZA DE
PZ DEL	PLAZA DEL
PZ D LA	PLAZA DE LA
PZ D LAS	PLAZA DE LAS
PZWY	PLAZA WAY
RAMP	RAMP
RD	ROAD
RDAV	ROAD AVENUE
RDBP	ROAD BYPASS
RDCT	ROAD COURT
RDEX	ROAD EXTENSION
RDG	RIDGE
RDSP	ROAD SPUR
RDWY	ROAD WAY
RR	RAILROAD
RUE	RUE
RUE D	RUE D
RW	ROW
RY	RAILWAY
SKWY	SKYWAY
SQ	SQUARE
ST	STREET
STAV	STREET AVENUE
STCT	STREET COURT
STDR	STREET DRIVE
STEX	STREET EXTENSION
STLN	STREET LANE
STLP	STREET LOOP
ST OF	STREET OF
ST OF THE	STREET OF THE
STOV	STREET OVERPASS
STPL	STREET PLACE
STPM	STREET PROMENADE
STWY	STREET WAY
STXP	STREET EXPRESSWAY
TER	TERRACE
TFWY	TRAFFICWAY
THWY	THROUGHWAY
TKTR	TRUCK TRAIL
TPKE	TURNPIKE
TRC	TRACE
TRCT	TERRACE COURT
TR, TRL	TRAIL
TRWY	TRAIL WAY
TTSP	TRUCK TRAIL SPUR
TUN	TUNNEL
UNPS	UNDERPASS
VIA D	VIA DE
VIA DL	VIA DEL
VIA D LA	VIA DE LA
VIA D LAS	VIA DE LAS
VIA D LOS	VIA DE LOS
VIA LA	VIA LA
VW	VIEW
VWY	VIEW WAY
VIS	VISTA
VIS D	VISTA DE
VIS D L	VISTA DE LA
VIS D LAS	VISTA DE LAS
VIS DEL	VISTA DEL
WK	WALK
WY	WAY
WYCR	WAY CIRCLE
WYDR	WAY DRIVE
WYLN	WAY LANE
WYPL	WAY PLACE

DIRECTIONS

E	EAST
KPN	KEY PENINSULA NORTH
KPS	KEY PENINSULA SOUTH
N	NORTH
NE	NORTHEAST
NW	NORTHWEST
S	SOUTH
SE	SOUTHEAST
SW	SOUTHWEST
W	WEST

BUILDINGS

CH	CITY HALL
CHP	CALIFORNIA HIGHWAY PATROL
COMM CTR	COMMUNITY CENTER
CON CTR	CONVENTION CENTER
CONT HS	CONTINUATION HIGH SCHOOL
CTH	COURT HOUSE
FAA	FEDERAL AVIATION ADMIN
FS	FIRE STATION
HOSP	HOSPITAL
HS	HIGH SCHOOL
INT	INTERMEDIATE SCHOOL
JR HS	JUNIOR HIGH SCHOOL
LIB	LIBRARY
MID	MIDDLE SCHOOL
MUS	MUSEUM
PO	POST OFFICE
PS	POLICE STATION
SR CIT CTR	SENIOR CITIZENS CENTER
STA	STATION
THTR	THEATER
VIS BUR	VISITORS BUREAU

OTHER ABBREVIATIONS

BCH	BEACH
BLDG	BUILDING
CEM	CEMETERY
CK	CREEK
CO	COUNTY
COMM	COMMUNITY
CTR	CENTER
EST	ESTATE
HIST	HISTORIC
HTS	HEIGHTS
LK	LAKE
MDW	MEADOW
MED	MEDICAL
MEM	MEMORIAL
MHP	MOBILE HOME PARK
MT	MOUNT
MTN	MOUNTAIN
NATL	NATIONAL
PKG	PARKING
PLGD	PLAYGROUND
RCH	RANCH
RCHO	RANCHO
REC	RECREATION
RES	RESERVOIR
RIV	RIVER
RR	RAILROAD
SPG	SPRING
STA	SANTA
VLG	VILLAGE
VLY	VALLEY
VW	VIEW

STREET
Block City ZIP Pg-Grid

A

A
600 LACo 91744 679-A2
A ST
- CULC 90232 672-G1
- LACo 90220 764-J3
- LACo 91724 599-E2
- LKWD 90712 766-A3
- SPed 90731 824-B1
- WCOV 91791 638-J4
1700 LVRN 91750 600-F2
10600 LACo 90230 672-H4
13300 LA 91342 481-F3
W A ST
100 Wilm 90744 824-E1
AARON CT
42300 LAN 93536 4104-E5
AARON ST
2100 Echo 90026 594-D6
ABACHERLI AV
12100 CHNO 91710 641-G5
ABACHERLI PL
12000 CHNO 91710 641-G5
ABADEJO
- LVRN 91750 570-H3
ABAJO CT
1800 LAN 93534 4105-E1
ABAJO DR
26600 SCTA 91350 4550-J1
S ABAJO DR
1200 MONP 91754 635-H3
ABAKAN AV
1500 LACo 91770 636-F4
ABALAR ST
20900 WdHl 91364 560-C5
ABALONE AV
1400 TOR 90501 763-H6
3400 LA 90732 823-G7
ABANA DR
13600 CRTS 90703 737-C7
ABANA PL
13100 CRTS 90703 737-B7
ABANA ST
11300 CRTS 90703 736-F7
11500 ART 90701 736-G7
13500 CRTS 90703 737-C7
ABANO AV
2400 RowH 91748 678-J6
ABANTES AV
39100 LACo 93591 4200-E5
ABARAN WY
5000 BPK 90621 737-J5
ABARCA
40400 LACo 93551 4194-A3
ABARGO ST
4600 WdHl 91364 560-C4
ABASCAL DR
16400 HacH 91745 678-D5
ABBESS PL
- HacH 91745 678-F6
ABBEY CT
100 SDMS 91773 599-H2
ABBEY LN
1400 POM 91767 601-C7
1400 POM 91767 641-C1
3200 PMDL 93551 4195-B3
ABBEY PL
4500 LA 90019 633-F4
ABBEY RD
18100 Res 91335 531-A7
ABBEY ST
16000 LPUE 91744 678-D1
ABBEY WY
3800 LVRN 91750 600-F1
E ABBEYFIELD ST
5200 LBCH 90815 796-B4
ABBEY GLEN PL
- SCTA 91354 4460-G4
ABBEYVILLE AV
4700 WdHl 91364 559-G4
ABBEYWOOD AV
3700 LACo 90601 677-A2
3800 LACo 90601 676-J2
4400 PRV 90660 676-J2
ABBEYWOOD DR
23900 CanP 91307 529-D5
ABBINGTON CT
4200 WLKV 91361 557-D6
ABBOT AV
600 SGBL 91776 596-E6
ABBOT KINNEY BLVD
900 Ven 90291 671-G5
2500 Ven 90291 672-A6
ABBOTSFORD RD
9200 PRV 90660 676-F7
10900 LACo 90606 706-H1
ABBOTT PL
5100 HiPk 90042 595-B2
ABBOTT RD
3600 LYN 90262 705-C6
5100 SGAT 90280 705-C6
ABBOTT ST
2900 POM 91767 600-J3
ABBOTTS HALL LN
- HacH 91745 678-F6
ABBOTTSON ST
1400 CRSN 90746 764-G3
ABBOTTSWOOD DR
6600 RPV 90275 792-H7
6600 RPV 90275 822-G1

ABDALE ST
19200 SCTA 91321 4551-G6
ABDERA ST
19000 RowH 91748 679-C4
ABE WY
700 MONP 91755 636-D4
ABEJA DR
17800 RowH 91748 678-H6
ABELIA RD
29100 SCTA 91387 4462-F7
ABELIAN AV
400 LACo 91792 679-C2
1500 RowH 91748 679-C5
ABELL CT
- LACo 91744 638-H6
ABELLA ST
3100 LaCr 91214 504-F7
3900 GLDL 91214 504-D6
ABERCROMBIE LN
- LACo 91302 589-C5
ABERDEEN AV
2500 LFlz 90027 594-A2
ABERDEEN CT
4900 ELMN 91731 597-E4
ABERNATHY DR
5800 Wch 90045 702-H1
ABERT ST
19300 RowH 91748 679-C5
ABERY AV
300 LACo 91744 679-B2
ABETO AV
2600 RowH 91748 679-A7
ABIGAIL PL
7900 Wch 90045 702-J2
7900 Wch 90045 703-A2
ABILA ST
1400 CRSN 90745 764-G6
ABILENE LN
11800 LACo 91390 4373-C5
ABILENE RD
700 SDMS 91773 600-C1
ABILENE ST
900 SGBL 91776 596-F6
8600 RSMD 91770 596-G6
9700 RSMD 91770 597-A6
ABILENE WY
1800 CLAR 91711 571-D7
1800 CLAR 91711 601-D1
ABINGDON ST
11800 NRWK 90650 736-E4
ABINGTON DR
3000 LA 90210 592-C1
ABISKO DR
10600 LACo 90604 707-D5
ABITA AV
1900 LMTA 90717 793-H4
ABLANO AV
2400 RowH 91748 679-A6
ABLE ST
26500 SCTA 91387 4642-E1
ABNER ST
4100 LA 90032 635-C2
ABOGADO AV
100 WAL 91789 639-G7
100 WAL 91789 679-G1
ABONADO PL
2500 RowH 91748 679-B6
ABORDO DR
22400 SCTA 91350 4460-J7
ABORLA LN
200 WAL 91789 639-G7
ABOURNE RD
4000 LA 90008 673-D3
ABRAHAM DR
10900 SELM 91733 637-B5
ABRAHAM TER
- Hrbr 90710 794-A3
ABRAZO
2000 WCOV 91791 638-J4
2000 WCOV 91791 639-A4
ABRAZO DR
30300 RPV 90275 823-F4
ABRI ST
1500 CRSN 90745 764-G7
ABRIGO AV
2600 LA 90031 595-B7
ABUELA PL
2500 HacH 91745 678-D5
ACACIA
14700 LA 91342 481-G1
ACACIA AV
100 MNRO 91016 567-G3
600 TOR 90501 763-G6
1700 COMP 90222 734-J2
4000 PRV 90660 676-G2
5400 WHIT 90601 677-B4
11300 HAW 90304 703-D7
11400 HAW 90250 703-D7
11900 HAW 90250 733-D1
17900 BLF 90706 766-D1
E ACACIA AV
100 GLDL 91205 564-F6
200 ELSG 90245 702-E7
N ACACIA AV
100 COMP 90220 734-J3
1100 COMP 90222 734-J3
S ACACIA AV
100 COMP 90220 734-J6
2400 COMP 90220 764-J1
10800 Lenx 90304 703-C6
W ACACIA AV
100 GLDL 91204 564-D6
200 ELSG 90245 702-D7

ACACIA CIR
4300 CYP 90630 767-A4
ACACIA CT
- PMDL 93551 4285-D2
2000 COMP 90220 734-J7
22800 SCTA 91390 4460-H2
ACACIA DR
- CRSN 90746 764-F5
- LACo 91724 639-J1
- SCTA 91354 4460-F7
8500 CYP 90630 767-B5
ACACIA LN
- LA 90065 594-F1
- RHLS 90274 793-D7
S ACACIA LN
600 WCOV 91791 639-B1
ACACIA RD
- RHLS 90274 793-E7
1700 SBdC 92372 (4472-D6 See Page 4471)
2400 SBdC 92371 (4472-G6 See Page 4471)
ACACIA ST
200 Alta 91001 535-G6
200 POM 91767 600-J4
200 POM 91767 601-A4
300 LHB 90631 708-E6
300 SMAD 91024 567-C1
1500 ALH 91801 595-J5
4000 BELL 90201 675-C7
4600 PRV 90660 676-G3
4900 LACo 91776 596-H4
6000 LadH 90056 673-B6
6200 LA 90056 673-B6
8000 CYP 90630 767-B4
44100 LAN 93535 4016-F7
N ACACIA ST
100 SDMS 91773 600-B2
1000 ING 90302 673-B7
1400 LA 90056 673-B7
S ACACIA ST
100 SDMS 91773 600-B2
W ACACIA ST
400 BREA 92821 738-J1
800 ING 90302 703-B1
ACACIA GLEN ST
28600 AGRH 91301 558-B3
ACACIA HILL RD
1600 DBAR 91765 680-A4
ACADEMIA DR
16500 Enc 91436 561-E6
ACADEMY AV
2200 POM 91768 600-D7
2300 POM 91768 640-D1
W ACADEMY AV
2900 ANA 92804 767-J6
ACADEMY CT
1900 CLAR 91711 571-D7
ACADEMY DR
1200 Echo 90026 594-G7
1200 LA 90012 594-G7
26400 LACo 90274 793-C6
26400 RHE 90274 793-C6
W ACADEMY DR
26700 LACo 90274 793-C7
ACADEMY PL
- SCTA 91355 4550-G3
1900 GLDL 91206 564-H3
ACADEMY RD
600 LA 90012 594-G7
1200 Echo 90026 594-F6
ACADEMY ST
4700 LA 90032 595-E6
ACADEMY WY
600 NHol 91601 562-J2
12200 ART 90701 766-J2
ACADIA AV
600 AGRH 91301 558-B3
ACALA AV
11200 LA 91340 502-A1
11300 LA 91340 501-J1
ACAMA ST
10700 LA 91602 563-A5
11000 LA 91602 562-J5
11500 LA 91604 562-H5
ACAMPO AV
4300 GLDL 91214 504-D5
ACANA RD
28000 RPV 90275 792-H6
ACANTHUS CIR
21600 WAL 91789 639-H5
ACANTHUS CT
29000 AGRH 91301 558-A3
ACANTHUS WY
21400 SCTA 91350 4551-B3
ACANTO PL
1000 Brwd 90049 591-G7
ACANTO ST
600 Brwd 90049 631-H1
ACAPULCO DR
13400 LACo 90605 707-C4
ACARI DR
100 Brwd 90049 631-H2
ACARUS AV
21700 CRSN 90745 764-F6
ACASO DR
300 WAL 91789 639-C7
300 WAL 91789 679-C1
9000 TEML 91780 596-H5
ACCO ST
6800 CMRC 90040 676-B3
6800 MTBL 90640 676-B3

ACCORD PL
32500 Actn 93510 4465-E1
ACCRA ST
18700 Nor 91326 500-H1
ACE PL
31700 Llan 93544 4469-E1
ACECA DR
2800 OrCo 90720 796-H4
ACEDIA CT
- SCTA 91350 4551-E6
ACERA CT
1800 GLDR 91740 569-J7
ACFOLD DR
20300 DBAR 91789 679-F4
ACHESON DR
12800 WHIT 90601 677-C4
ACHILLES CIR
5200 LPMA 90623 767-C3
ACHILLES DR
2400 LA 90046 593-A2
ACHILLES ST
12100 NRWK 90650 706-H6
ACKERFIELD AV
5500 NLB 90805 765-G2
ACKERMAN AV
- SCTA 91321 4551-F5
ACKERMAN DR
3700 LA 90065 594-H2
ACKLEY PL
1800 MONP 91755 636-D4
ACKLEY ST
400 MONP 91755 636-C4
8200 PRM 90723 735-H3
ACKLINS AV
32900 Actn 93510 4375-A7
ACKMAR AV
21900 CRSN 90745 764-G6
ACLARE CIR
11300 CRTS 90703 736-F7
ACLARE LN
13600 CRTS 90703 737-C7
ACLARE PL
13000 CRTS 90703 737-B7
ACLARE ST
11400 ART 90701 736-G7
11900 CRTS 90703 736-H7
12800 CRTS 90703 737-A7
ACOLITO PL
600 DBAR 91765 640-C5
ACOMA DR
700 CRSN 90746 734-E6
ACORDE AV
2900 PMDL 93550 4286-F3
ACORN CIR
100 BREA 92821 709-D7
900 MNRO 91016 567-J2
ACORN CT
24500 SCTA 91321 4640-H2
36800 PMDL 93550 4286-F5
ACORN DR
4300 LVRN 91750 570-F6
5700 SBdC 92397 (4652-C2 See Page 4651)
ACORN LN
1600 GLDR 91741 569-H5
10600 LALM 90720 796-H2
ACORN PL
- GLDL 91206 564-J3
- WAL 91789 639-C5
ACORN RD
9900 SBdC 92372 (4472-D6 See Page 4471)
ACORN ST
22100 Chat 91311 499-J6
ACORO PL
13100 CRTS 90703 737-B7
ACORO ST
10500 BLF 90706 736-D7
11200 CRTS 90703 736-F7
13000 CRTS 90703 737-B7
ACOSTA AV
1800 LAN 93535 4106-D1
ACRE ST
15000 LA 91343 531-F1
17900 Nor 91325 531-A1
18100 Nor 91325 530-J1
19800 Nor 91324 530-E1
20100 Win 91306 530-C1
ACRESITE ST
2900 LA 90039 594-E3
E ACRIDGE DR
3400 WCOV 91791 639-D1
ACTAEON ST
- LACo 90265 626-C1
ACTINA AV
13700 BLF 90706 736-A3
ACTON AV
- Actn 93510 4464-J3
3800 Actn 93510 4465-A3
ACTON CANYON RD
33900 Actn 93510 4375-D5
ACUPEY DR
- Chat 91311 480-A7
ACUNA DR
3000 HacH 91745 677-J5
ADA AV
- MTCL 91762 641-G3
10700 MTCL 91763 641-G2
10700 SBdC 91763 641-G2
E ADA AV
100 GLDR 91741 569-F6
W ADA AV
100 GLDR 91741 569-D6

ADA ST
2600 LA 90046 593-A1
15600 SCTA 91387 4552-D1
ADAGIO CT
15500 BelA 90077 591-G2
ADAGIO LN
4600 CYP 90630 767-B7
ADAINVILLE DR
- PMDL 93552 4287-E1
ADAIR ST
1100 SMRO 91108 596-D1
1900 LA 90011 634-E7
3600 LA 90011 674-D2
E ADAIR ST
100 NLB 90805 765-D1
ADALE PL
5600 LACo 90043 673-C5
ADALIA AV
1600 HacH 91745 677-J2
ADAM LN
- PMDL 93551 4195-D5
ADAM RD
17200 RowH 91748 678-G4
ADAMANT DR
- LACo 91342 482-J3
ADAMITE TER
- Hrbr 90710 794-A5
ADAMO AV
25400 LMTA 90717 793-G5
ADAMOR RD
26000 CALB 91302 558-H3
ADAMS AV
- CRTS 90703 766-H3
- PMDL 93550 4286-C4
300 POM 91767 601-A6
900 MTBL 90640 636-E7
4200 CYP 90630 767-A6
E ADAMS AV
- ALH 91801 596-C6
N ADAMS AV
300 FUL 92832 738-F7
W ADAMS AV
200 ALH 91801 596-B6
ADAMS BLVD
5800 CULC 90232 633-A7
E ADAMS BLVD
100 LA 90011 634-D7
100 LA 90011 674-E1
W ADAMS BLVD
100 LA 90007 634-A6
4400 LA 90016 633-E6
ADAMS CT
5400 CHNO 91710 641-G4
ADAMS DR
1800 WCOV 91790 598-D5
2400 SPed 90731 824-C7
15200 BALD 91706 598-D5
W ADAMS GDNS
2600 LA 90007 634-B7
ADAMS ST
- Actn 93510 4375-C6
- SBdC 91710 641-D4
100 SMAD 91024 567-A2
2800 LaCr 91214 504-F6
4900 CHNO 91710 641-F4
7300 PRM 90723 735-F4
E ADAMS ST
100 NLB 90805 765-C1
2500 CRSN 90810 764-J6
2500 CRSN 90810 765-A6
N ADAMS ST
100 GLDL 91206 564-G3
S ADAMS ST
100 GLDL 91205 564-G6
W ADAMS ST
- NLB 90805 765-C1
ADAMS WY
- Cstc 91384 4459-C7
1700 MONP 91755 636-C4
7700 BPK 90620 767-J5
ADAMSBORO DR
23500 SCTA 91321 4640-F3
ADAMSGROVE AV
800 DBAR 91789 679-G3
ADAMSON AV
6500 BGDN 90201 675-H7
6500 BGDN 90201 705-H1
ADAMS PARK DR
700 COV 91722 598-J5
1100 COV 91724 599-E5
E ADAMS PARK DR
700 COV 91723 599-D5
1300 COV 91724 599-E5
1900 LACo 91724 599-F5
W ADAMS PARK DR
400 COV 91723 599-A5
ADAMSVILLE AV
1500 Top 90290 589-J1
3500 CALB 90290 559-H7
3500 CALB 90290 589-J1
3500 CALB 91302 559-H7
ADANA ST
2400 COMP 90221 735-D6
ADARCE ST
37700 LACo 93551 4193-E5
ADCO AV
11500 DWNY 90241 705-H4
ADDA DR
4500 LACo 93536 3834-H5
E ADDERLEY DR
5800 LBCH 90808 796-D2
ADDINGTON ST
13200 WHIT 90602 707-C2

E ADDINGTON ST
4200 RDom 90221 735-C3
ADDINGTON WY
4600 LACo 90043 673-E4
ADDIS ST
19200 RowH 91748 679-C4
ADDISON RD
- PVE 90274 792-E6
ADDISON ST
10400 NHol 91601 563-A3
11500 NHol 91601 562-G3
11700 LA 91607 562-E3
12800 Shrm 91423 562-B3
14400 Shrm 91403 562-A3
14500 Shrm 91403 561-J3
15700 Enc 91436 561-E3
16900 Enc 91316 561-C3
ADDISON WY
1900 Eagl 90041 565-A6
2200 Eagl 90041 564-J6
ADDLEMAN AV
300 LACo 91792 679-C2
ADEL AV
1000 DBAR 91789 679-H3
ADEL WY
10400 LACo 90604 707-D5
ADELA CT
37600 PMDL 93552 4287-A2
ADELAIDE DR
100 LA 90402 631-C7
100 LA 90402 671-B1
100 SMCA 90402 631-C7
100 SMCA 90402 671-B1
800 PAS 91104 566-D2
ADELAIDE PL
700 SMCA 90402 631-C7
6300 HiPk 90042 595-E1
ADELAINE AL
600 SPAS 91030 595-G2
ADELAINE AV
700 SPAS 91030 595-G2
ADELANTE AV
900 HiPk 90042 595-F1
1000 HiPk 90042 565-F7
ADELANTE ST
16000 IRW 91702 568-F7
16100 AZU 91702 568-F7
ADELANTO DR
7500 BPK 90621 737-H5
ADELBERT AV
2500 LA 90039 594-E3
ADELE AV
5100 LACo 90601 677-A3
5300 WHIT 90601 677-A3
5600 WHIT 90601 676-J4
5800 WHIT 90606 676-J4
ADELE CT
4700 WdHl 91364 560-E4
ADELE DR
20100 WdHl 91364 560-E4
ADELFA DR
13500 LMRD 90638 737-G3
13700 SFSP 90670 737-G3
ADELHART ST
15500 HacH 91745 678-A4
ADELIA AV
1400 SELM 91733 637-A2
3000 ELMN 91733 637-A2
ADELINA CT
5500 AGRH 91301 557-H5
ADELITA DR
2600 HacH 91745 678-A5
ADELITA LN
9900 SELM 91733 637-B4
ADELITA ST
800 MTBL 90640 636-D7
2100 LMTA 90717 793-H3
ADELLA AV
9500 SGAT 90280 705-E5
ADELPHIA AV
11200 Pcma 91331 502-F1
11900 Pcma 91331 482-E6
12000 LA 91340 482-C4
12900 LA 91342 482-C4
W ADELYN DR
400 SGBL 91775 596-D3
ADEN AV
24500 SCTA 91321 4641-A1
24600 SCTA 91321 4551-A7
ADENA ST
300 PAS 91104 565-J2
ADENMOOR AV
4300 LKWD 90713 766-C2
11400 DWNY 90241 706-C6
11900 DWNY 90242 706-C7
12600 DWNY 90242 736-C1
16500 BLF 90706 736-C6
ADERNO WY
200 PacP 90272 630-H6
ADGER DR
14000 LACo 90604 707-D5
ADINA DR
3300 LA 90068 563-C7
E ADIRONDACK CT
3300 THO 91362 557-C2
W ADIRONDACK CT
3000 THO 91362 557-B2
ADIRONDACK LN
- CLAR 91711 571-E4
ADIVINO ST
18500 RowH 91748 679-A7
ADKINS AV
2600 LA 90032 595-F7

ADKISSON AV
1400 City 90063 635-D3
ADLENA DR
200 FUL 92833 738-D6
ADLENA PL
1800 FUL 92833 738-D6
ADLER AV
5900 WdHl 91367 559-E1
43700 LAN 93534 4105-H1
44000 LAN 93534 4015-H7
ADLER DR
- SFSP 90670 737-B1
12500 WHIT 90606 707-C1
ADLER RD
- LMRD 90638 738-A2
ADLON PL
4100 Enc 91436 561-C5
ADLON RD
16500 Enc 91436 561-C5
ADMINISTRATION RD
- PMDL 93550 4196-E2
ADMINISTRATION WY
- Wch 90045 702-D5
ADMIRABLE DR
3900 RPV 90275 823-C5
ADMIRAL AV
12500 LA 90066 672-C6
13200 LA 90292 672-C7
ADMIRAL HIGBEE WY
2500 SPed 90731 824-D7
ADMIRALTY DR
3100 HNTB 92649 826-J7
ADMIRALTY WY
4100 MdlR 90292 671-J7
4200 MdlR 90292 672-A6
ADNA AV
1600 HacH 91745 677-H2
ADNEY ST
18900 RowH 91748 679-B5
ADOBE
- AZU 91702 598-H1
ADOBE AV
800 MTBL 90640 636-G7
4800 PMDL 93552 4287-A1
ADOBE CT
- BqtC 91354 4460-F4
4500 MTCL 91763 641-E1
ADOBE DR
- LALM 90720 796-H2
- PMDL 93550 4286-H1
4000 PMDL 93552 4286-J1
5200 PMDL 93552 4287-B1
ADOBE LN
- CRSN 90745 794-E1
ADOBE PL
700 MONP 91754 636-A5
700 MONP 91754 635-J5
ADOBE ST
900 LA 90012 634-G2
ADOBE WY
11600 LACo 91390 4463-C1
ADOLFO CT
25900 SCTA 91355 4550-G4
ADOLFO ST
- Res 91335 530-H7
ADOLFO LOPEZ DR
900 SLB 90740 826-G2
ADOLPH AV
22800 TOR 90505 793-C1
ADOMAR ST
600 CRSN 90745 764-E6
ADON AV
27900 SCTA 91387 4551-J1
28000 SCTA 91351 4551-J1
ADONA DR
2100 LMTA 90717 793-H3
ADONIS AV
11300 NRWK 90650 706-H7
ADONIS LN
- SCTA 91351 4551-H2
ADOREE ST
7800 DWNY 90242 705-H7
8000 DWNY 90242 735-J1
8700 DWNY 90242 736-A1
10800 NRWK 90650 736-E1
13800 LMRD 90638 737-D1
ADORNOS WY
3000 BURB 91504 533-E3
ADOUE PL
14400 BALD 91706 598-C6
ADRIA MARU LN
17900 CRSN 90746 764-C1
ADRIAN CT
400 CLAR 91711 571-C6
ADRIAN PL
12000 GmH 91344 481-B6
ADRIAN ST
3900 LA 90029 594-B6
ADRIANA PL
- SCTA 91351 4551-D4
ADRIANA WY
1700 UPL 91784 571-J6
ADRIATIC AV
2000 LBCH 90810 795-B4
3400 LBCH 90810 765-B7
S ADRIATIC AV
2600 LBCH 90810 795-B2
21100 CRSN 90810 765-B5
ADRIEN PL
1600 LAN 93535 4016-C7
ADRIENE WY
- Saug 91350 4461-D5

ADRIENNE DR
2900 WCOV 91792 639-A7
ADSON PL
1500 SELM 91733 637-D5
ADUL ST
1200 WCOV 91792 638-H5
ADVENT ST
8300 PRV 90660 676-E5
ADWEN ST
7100 DWNY 90241 705-H4
7800 DWNY 90241 706-A5
AEGEAN ST
12100 NRWK 90650 706-H7
AEOLIAN ST
10900 LACo 90606 706-H1
E AERICK ST
600 ING 90301 703-D2
AERO DR
9000 PRV 90660 706-E1
AEROJET AV
300 AZU 91702 568-G7
3300 ELMN 91731 636-J1
AEROSPACE HWY
Rt#-14
- KeCo 93560 3835-D5
- LACo 93536 3835-D5
- LACo 93536 3925-D1
AETNA ST
12900 VanN 91401 532-A7
14500 VanN 91411 532-A7
14600 VanN 91411 531-J7
19200 Tarz 91356 560-G1
20200 WdHl 91367 560-C1
23200 WdHl 91367 559-D1
AFAMADO LN
24100 DBAR 91765 640-D7
AFELIO DR
18900 RowH 91748 679-B5
AFTON PL
6100 Hlwd 90028 593-F5
AFTON RD
900 SMRO 91108 596-B3
AFTON ST
100 PAS 91103 565-E2
AGAJANIAN DR
- LACo 91390 4461-A4
700 SPed 90731 794-A7
700 SPed 90731 793-J7
21600 SCTA 91350 4461-A4
AGAJANIAN WY
700 MTBL 90640 676-G1
AGAPANTHUS LN
- BqtC 91354 4460-E6
AGAPANTHUS PL
6000 WdHl 91367 559-H7
AGAR PL
9300 PRV 90660 676-J1
AGATE AV
4800 NLB 90805 765-C5
AGATE CIR
4200 CYP 90630 767-A4
AGATE CT
- GAR 90247 734-A3
37100 PMDL 93550 4286-D4
AGATE ST
400 RBCH 90277 762-J3
1300 RBCH 90277 763-A3
AGATE WY
300 MONP 91755 636-C5
3800 WCOV 91792 679-C1
27600 Cstc 91384 4369-G6
AGATE HILL RD
34900 LACo 91390 4374-B3
AGATHA ST
600 LA 90021 634-F5
AGATHEA WY
29500 MAL 90265 667-D3
AGAVE AV
1500 LACo 90631 708-D3
AGAVE CIR
3700 LAN 93536 4015-A7
AGAVE ST
6800 LACo 93536 4104-D6
AGAVE WY
16600 PRM 90723 735-G6
AGENA RD
6600 PMDL 93551 4104-D7
6600 PMDL 93551 4194-D1
AGERTON PL
11600 ART 90701 766-G1
AGNER AV
3700 GLDL 91020 534-G3
AGNES AV
4200 LA 91604 562-G5
4400 LA 91607 562-G2
4800 ELMN 91780 597-A4
4800 TEML 91780 597-A2
6100 NHol 91606 532-G7
6300 ARCD 91007 597-A1
6800 NHol 91605 532-G2
AGNES PL
11100 CRTS 90703 766-F2
AGNES RD
1800 MANB 90266 732-F4
AGNES ST
1400 SBdC 92397 (4652-D2 See Page 4651)
3300 LYN 90262 735-B1
11200 CRTS 90703 766-F2
AGNEW AV
7400 Wch 90045 702-F1
AGNOLO DR
2000 LACo 91770 636-E3

AGOSTA DR
15700 HacH 91745 678-B5
AGOSTINO DR
2300 RowH 91748 678-H6
AGOSTINO RD
100 SGBL 91776 596-E4
AGOURA CT
29900 AGRH 91301 557-H6
AGOURA RD
2600 THO 91361 557-B5
2900 WLKV 91361 557-D5
26400 CALB 91302 558-G7
26600 LACo 91302 558-G7
26800 CALB 91301 558-G7
27000 Ago 91301 558-D6
27400 AGRH 91301 558-A6
29200 AGRH 91301 557-G6
AGOURA GLEN DR
5500 AGRH 91301 558-B5
AGRA ST
5500 BGDN 90201 675-G7
6700 CMRC 90040 676-A7
AGRAMONTE DR
23200 SCTA 91321 4640-H3
AGRICULTURE VALLEY RD
- LACo 91768 639-J2
- LACo 91768 640-A2
AGUA PL
500 SLB 90740 826-F4
AGUADERO PL
22600 SCTA 91350 4460-H6
AGUA DULCE CANYON RD
30000 LACo 91390 4463-E1
32300 LACo 91390 4373-E6
AGUA SANTA DR
100 PMDL 93551 4195-J3
AGUILAR ST
3700 LA 90065 564-G7
3700 LA 90065 594-G1
AGUILAR WY
4100 LA 90065 564-G7
4100 LA 90065 594-H1
AGUIRO ST
18200 RowH 91748 678-J7
18300 RowH 91748 679-C6
AGUIRRE AV
700 SDMS 91773 600-A1
AGUSTA WY
- PRV 90660 676-J1
21200 WAL 91789 639-B4
AGUSTIN LN
- CULC 90230 672-G5
AGUSTIN PL
- LA 90094 702-D1
AHERN DR
3400 BALD 91706 598-C6
N AHERN DR
800 LACo 91746 637-J2
800 LACo 91746 638-A2
AHLIN DR
2000 LCF 91011 534-J3
AHMANN AV
8900 WHIT 90603 707-F3
9500 LACo 90604 707-E4
9800 LACo 90605 707-D4
AHMANSON RD
- LACo - 4643-G6
- LACo - (4723-F1 See Page 4643)
- LACo 91342 (4723-F1 See Page 4643)
AHTENA DR
1200 DBAR 91789 679-F4
AHUACATE RD
2000 LHH 90631 708-E1
AHWANEE LN
19800 Nor 91326 480-E7
19800 Nor 91326 500-E1
W AIDA LN
3300 ANA 92804 767-G6
AIDA PL
4500 WdHl 91364 559-H5
AIDEA ST
- PMDL 93552 4287-E1
AIGLON ST
16000 PacP 90272 630-J5
AIJALON CT
4100 KeCo 93560 3834-J2
AIKEN AV
2500 LA 90064 632-E5
AIKEN RD
- LACo 90265 626-G1
AILEAN CT
25600 SCTA 91355 4550-F7
AILERON AV
600 LPUE 91744 638-E5
900 INDS 91744 638-E5
900 LPUE 91744 638-E3
AINSWORTH AV
16700 TOR 90504 733-E7
17300 TOR 90504 763-E1
AINSWORTH LN
8000 LPMA 90623 767-B4
AINSWORTH ST
11800 LA 90044 704-B7
12000 LA 90044 734-B1
13500 LA 90247 734-B3
AINTREE LN
3100 LA 90023 675-A1
AIR WY
900 GLDL 91201 564-A2

AIRDROME ST
5500 LA 90019 633-A5
5800 LA 90035 633-A5
6000 LA 90035 632-H4
AIREDALE CT
900 SDMS 91773 599-H4
AIRFLITE WY
3300 Bxby 90807 795-H1
3300 LBCH 90808 795-H1
AIRLANE AV
7800 Wch 90045 702-H2
AIRLIE DR
7600 Tuj 91042 503-J1
AIRLINE WY
400 LACo 90248 734-D5
AIROLE WY
900 BelA 90077 592-A6
AIROSO RD
1200 LHH 90631 708-F1
AIRPARK DR
500 FUL 92833 738-B7
AIRPARK WY
- Pcma 91331 502-E3
AIRPOINT AV
12800 DWNY 90242 736-A1
13000 DWNY 90242 735-J2
AIRPORT AV
2300 LA 90066 671-J3
2300 SMCA 90405 671-J3
2300 SMCA 90405 672-A3
2800 LA 90066 672-A3
AIRPORT BLVD
7300 Wch 90045 702-H1
AIRPORT DR
1000 UPL 91786 601-G2
2600 TOR 90505 793-E3
AIRPORT LN
2900 LBCH 90808 795-H2
AIRPORT RD
- Wch 90045 702-J5
AIRPORT WY
3000 LBCH 90808 795-H2
AIRPORT BUSINESS PARK WY
- VanN 91406 531-D4
AIRPORT PLAZA DR
4500 LBCH 90815 796-A2
AIRSHIRE LN
1000 POM 91766 641-B5
AIRVILLE AV
24700 SCTA 91321 4640-G2
E AIVLIS ST
7000 LBCH 90815 796-F4
AJA CT
- SCTA 91351 4551-E3
AJANTA AV
1300 RowH 91748 679-C4
AJAX AV
900 INDS 91748 678-J3
6200 BGDN 90201 675-G7
6500 BGDN 90201 705-G1
AJAX CIR
1000 INDS 91748 678-J3
2100 WCOV 91792 638-H5
AJAY DR
7900 SunV 91352 533-B2
AJUGA AV
1300 UPL 91784 571-J3
AKELEY DR
100 GLDR 91741 569-G4
AKINS CT
- StvR 91381 4640-C1
AKKER DR
15100 LACo 93532 4102-E4
AKRON PL
1600 CLAR 91711 601-E1
AKRON ST
16300 PacP 90272 630-H5
AL WY
6000 SIMI 93063 499-B2
ALABAMA
3600 WCOV 91792 678-J1
ALABAMA AV
6800 CanP 91303 530-B5
7500 LA 91304 530-A3
9000 Chat 91311 500-A4
ALABAMA ST
100 SGBL 91775 596-E2
100 SGBL 91776 596-E3
1500 Wbrk 90059 704-F7
2700 LaCr 91214 504-F7
3200 GLDL 91214 504-E6
ALABAR DR
40300 PMDL 93551 4194-H3
ALABASTRO DR
27000 SCTA 91354 4460-H7
ALABEGA CT
23600 SCTA 91355 4550-G5
ALACA DR
3100 Alta 91001 535-J4
ALADA DR
23600 DBAR 91765 640-C7
ALADDIN ST
5600 LA 90008 673-A2
5700 LA 90016 673-A2
ALAFLORA DR
27900 RPV 90275 823-H2
ALAGA AV
32000 Pear 93553 4468-G1
ALAHMAR ST
400 ALH 91801 596-C3
N ALAHMAR TER
300 SGBL 91775 596-C3

LOS ANGELES CO.

STREET Block	City	ZIP	Pg-Grid
ALAIN CT			
43700	LAN	93535	4106-B1
ALAMANOR CT			
19100	WAL	91789	639-C7
ALAMEDA AV			
500	AZU	91702	598-J2
1100	GLDL	91201	533-J7
1100	GLDL	91201	563-J1
1200	GLDL	91201	534-A7
E ALAMEDA AV			
100	BURB	91502	563-J1
900	GLDL	91201	563-J1
1400	GLDL	91201	534-A6
1400	BURB	91501	534-A6
N ALAMEDA AV			
100	AZU	91702	568-J5
W ALAMEDA AV			
-	BURB	91502	563-H2
300	BURB	91506	563-H2
2100	BURB	91521	563-E3
2500	BURB	91505	563-E3
2900	BURB	91523	563-E3
ALAMEDA ST			
200	Wilm	90744	794-G5
200	Alta	91001	535-J6
700	Alta	91001	536-A6
1400	POM	91768	600-H6
3100	PAS	91107	566-G3
8000	DWNY	90242	705-J6
8200	DWNY	90242	706-A7
N ALAMEDA ST			
100	COMP	90221	735-A4
100	LA	90012	634-G4
100	COMP	90220	735-A4
1000	COMP	90221	734-J1
1100	COMP	90222	734-J1
1100	COMP	90222	735-A4
12400	Wbrk	90222	734-J1
S ALAMEDA ST			
100	COMP	90221	735-A5
100	LA	90012	634-G5
100	COMP	90220	735-A5
300	LA	90013	634-G5
600	LA	90021	634-G5
1400	LA	90021	674-G3
1900	HNTP	90255	674-G6
1900	LA	90058	674-G3
2500	VER	90058	674-G3
5800	HNTP	90001	674-G6
7200	LACo	90255	674-G6
7200	LACo	90255	704-H2
7200	Flor	90001	674-G6
7200	Flor	90001	704-H2
7900	LACo	90280	704-H2
8600	Wats	90002	704-J4
9200	SGAT	90280	704-H2
10300	LYN	90262	704-J5
10300	LYN	90280	704-J5
10300	Wats	90002	704-J5
10700	LYN	90059	704-J5
10800	Wbrk	90059	704-J5
11900	COMP	90222	704-J7
11900	COMP	90222	734-J1
16800	COMP	90221	765-A1
16800	COMP	90220	765-A1
17800	RDom	90221	765-A3
17800	LACo	90220	765-A1
20400	CRSN	90810	765-A3
21000	CRSN	90810	764-J6
21800	LA	90810	764-J6
22400	CRSN	90810	794-H3
ALAMEDA WY			
5000	BPK	90621	737-J5
ALAMINOS DR			
20500	SCTA	91350	4461-C5
ALAMITAS AV			
1400	MNRO	91016	567-F6
ALAMITOS AV			
200	LBCH	90802	795-F6
700	LBCH	90813	795-F6
1900	LBCH	90806	795-G4
1900	SIGH	90755	795-G4
N ALAMITOS AV			
-	LBCH	90802	825-E1
200	LBCH	90802	795-E7
ALAMITOS ST			
4300	MTCL	91763	601-E6
ALAMO AV			
5800	MYWD	90040	675-F6
5800	VER	90040	675-F6
5800	MYWD	90270	675-F6
6200	BELL	90201	675-F7
8000	CDHY	90201	705-E2
ALAMO CT			
100	LBCH	90802	795-E7
100	LBCH	90802	825-E1
700	LBCH	90813	795-E5
11100	LYN	90262	704-J6
ALAMO DR			
1600	GLDL	91207	564-G2
2000	MONP	91754	635-G3
ALAMO LN			
3000	LBCH	90814	825-J1
ALAMO ST			
21400	WdHl	91364	560-B5
ALAMO WY			
-	BqtC	91354	4460-F2
ALAMO CANYON DR			
-	LACo	91387	4552-C4
-	SCTA	91387	4552-C4
ALAMOGORDO RD			
21800	SCTA	91350	4461-A7
ALAMO HEIGHTS DR			
2300	DBAR	91765	680-A5
ALAMOS LN			
23300	SCTA	91321	4640-H3
ALAMOSA AV			
300	PMDL	93551	4285-H2
E ALAMOSA DR			
200	CLAR	91711	571-E5
ALAMOTA DR			
22400	SCTA	91350	4460-J6
ALAN DR			
-	Ago	91301	587-J3
ALANA DR			
3300	Shrm	91403	561-F7
ALAND ST			
2600	LAN	93536	4105-D1
ALANDA PL			
9100	LA	90210	592-G3
ALANDELE AV			
400	LA	90036	633-B2
ALANDELE CIR			
400	LA	90036	633-B2
ALANMAY AV			
100	SGBL	91776	596-D3
ALANREED AV			
3200	RSMD	91770	636-F1
ALANWOOD RD			
13200	LACo	91746	637-G4
ALARCON PL			
1000	PAS	91105	565-H7
ALARKA ST			
12500	NRWK	90650	736-J2
ALASKA AV			
400	TOR	90503	763-F5
2300	ELSG	90245	732-J3
4700	CYP	90630	767-B5
E ALASKA ST			
1600	WCOV	91791	638-J2
2100	WCOV	91791	639-A2
ALATAR DR			
4800	WdHl	91364	560-B4
ALATHA ST			
17400	CRTS	90703	737-B7
ALAYA DR			
22100	SCTA	91350	4460-J7
ALBA ST			
5200	LA	90058	674-G5
ALBADA CT			
23300	CALB	91302	559-F4
ALBANY CT			
1500	CLAR	91711	601-F1
37500	PMDL	93552	4286-J3
ALBANY ST			
800	LA	90017	634-D4
900	LA	90015	634-D4
5900	HNTP	90255	674-H7
ALBARIZA PL			
1200	DBAR	91765	680-A3
ALBATA ST			
11300	Brwd	90049	631-H3
ALBATROSS AV			
24400	Wilm	90744	794-E3
ALBATROSS DR			
7000	BPK	90620	767-F2
ALBATROSS RD			
1300	INDS	91748	678-H4
ALBECK AV			
43700	LAN	93536	4105-D1
ALBECK CT			
43800	LAN	93536	4105-D1
44200	LAN	93536	4015-D7
ALBECK ST			
44300	LAN	93536	4015-D7
ALBEDO ST			
3300	HacH	91745	677-J5
ALBEE ST			
700	MTBL	90640	676-C5
E ALBERAN AV			
3800	LBCH	90808	766-E6
ALBERCA DR			
2000	RowH	91748	679-A5
ALBERNI AV			
11400	LA	91342	503-B1
ALBERO CT			
-	RPV	90275	822-H4
ALBERS PL			
13200	VanN	91401	562-D2
ALBERS ST			
11400	NHol	91601	562-J2
11700	LA	91607	562-E2
12900	VanN	91401	562-A2
14500	VanN	91411	562-A2
14600	VanN	91411	561-H2
16800	Enc	91436	561-D2
17000	Enc	91316	561-C2
23700	WdHl	91367	559-E2
ALBERT AV			
300	POM	91767	601-A4
1100	POM	91767	600-J4
19100	CRTS	90703	766-H3
22100	TOR	90503	763-A7
ALBERT ST			
100	LPUE	91744	638-D7
100	LPUE	91744	678-D1
ALBERT WY			
2400	ARCD	91007	597-C2
ALBERTA AV			
2000	Ven	90291	671-H6
4000	LYN	90262	705-D7
ALBERTA DR			
12000	LA	90230	672-E6
ALBERTA PL			
100	FUL	92833	738-E7
ALBERTA PL			
35300	Litl	93543	4377-F1
ALBERTA ST			
400	Alta	91001	535-F6
1400	LA	90732	823-J6
2800	TOR	90501	793-J1
ALBERTINE ST			
800	LA	90023	635-B7
ALBERTO CT			
26100	SCTA	91355	4550-F4
E ALBERTONI ST			
100	CRSN	90746	764-D1
600	CRSN	90746	734-E7
W ALBERTONI ST			
100	CRSN	90248	764-C1
N ALBERTSON AV			
400	COMP	90220	734-F3
1200	COV	91722	599-A3
4800	LACo	91722	599-A3
S ALBERTSON AV			
300	COV	91723	599-A6
13900	Wbrk	90222	734-F3
ALBERTSONS WY			
-	VanN	91405	531-J4
ALBIA ST			
7800	DWNY	90242	705-J6
8300	DWNY	90242	706-A7
ALBION ST			
1700	LA	90031	634-J1
ALBONA PL			
600	POM	91768	640-B2
N ALBONI PL			
-	LBCH	90802	825-E1
ALBREDA ST			
1600	CRSN	90745	764-G6
ALBRET ST			
-	LAN	93536	4015-B6
1500	LAN	93534	4015-F6
ALBRIGHT AV			
3800	CULC	90066	672-E3
3900	LA	90066	672-E3
ALBRIGHT ST			
14600	PacP	90272	631-A4
ALBRO ST			
500	LA	90732	824-A4
ALBURTIS AV			
8300	LACo	90606	706-H1
9000	SFSP	90670	706-G4
11000	NRWK	90650	706-G7
13200	NRWK	90650	736-G2
16600	ART	90701	736-G6
17800	ART	90701	766-G1
19300	CRTS	90703	766-G3
19900	LKWD	90715	766-G3
ALBURY AV			
2000	LBCH	90815	796-D2
3600	LBCH	90808	766-D7
4300	LKWD	90713	766-D4
ALBYN CT			
18000	LACo	93532	4101-H2
ALCADE ST			
13600	LACo	91746	637-H5
ALCALDE DR			
1000	GLDL	91207	564-G1
ALCALDE WY			
900	GLDL	91207	564-F1
ALCAMO DR			
3500	CALB	91302	559-E7
ALCAMO LN			
4800	CYP	90630	767-C7
ALCAZAR ST			
1500	Boyl	90033	635-B2
ALCHESTER ST			
-	CRTS	90703	767-A2
ALCIMA AV			
15900	PacP	90272	630-J4
15900	PacP	90272	631-A4
ALCLAD AV			
10700	LACo	90605	707-C6
S ALCLAD AV			
12300	LACo	90605	707-C7
ALCOA AV			
4300	VER	90058	675-B4
ALCOBA ST			
12000	CRTS	90703	766-H2
ALCON DR			
26800	SCTA	91350	4550-J1
ALCONA ST			
19300	RowH	91748	679-C6
ALCONBURY ST			
-	CRTS	90703	767-A2
ALCOR ST			
1900	LMTA	90717	793-H4
ALCORN DR			
4500	LCF	91011	534-J2
ALCOTT AV			
600	POM	91766	641-A4
ALCOTT CT			
-	StvR	91381	4550-A6
ALCOTT ST			
6000	LA	90035	633-A4
6100	LA	90035	632-G4
ALCOVE AV			
3900	LA	91604	562-E5
4800	LA	91607	562-E1
6000	NHol	91606	532-E6
6800	NHol	91605	532-E2
ALCOY CT			
5100	LACo	93536	4104-H5
ALCROSS ST			
200	COV	91722	599-A2
16800	LACo	91722	598-H2
ALCYONA DR			
2100	LA	90068	593-F3
ALDA CT			
20600	DBAR	91789	679-G4
ALDA PL			
15000	LA	91343	501-H6
ALDAMA AV			
200	POM	91767	600-J3
200	POM	91767	601-A3
ALDAMA ST			
4800	HiPk	90042	595-D1
ALDAMA TER			
600	HiPk	90042	595-B2
ALDBURY CT			
9700	LA	90210	592-C2
ALDBURY ST			
19500	SCTA	91351	4551-E1
19800	SCTA	91351	4461-E7
ALDEA AV			
5000	Enc	91316	561-C1
6000	Enc	91316	531-C6
6400	VanN	91406	531-C3
9100	Nor	91325	501-C5
10300	GrnH	91344	501-C1
ALDEA DR			
1300	MTBL	90640	636-D7
ALDEN DR			
8700	LA	90048	632-G1
9100	BHLS	90210	632-G1
ALDEN RD			
600	CLAR	91711	601-C3
ALDEN WY			
-	PMDL	93552	4287-B4
ALDENVALE AV			
45000	LAN	93534	4015-E5
N ALDENVILLE AV			
1200	COV	91722	599-A3
4800	LACo	91722	599-A3
S ALDENVILLE AV			
300	COV	91723	599-A6
ALDER			
3500	WCOV	91792	679-C1
ALDER CT			
-	StvR	91381	4550-B4
200	AZU	91702	568-J3
ALDER DR			
-	SCTA	91321	4641-B2
1800	LA	90065	594-J3
ALDER LN			
3600	PAS	91107	566-H1
5000	LPMA	90623	767-C3
21200	DBAR	91789	679-H2
ALDER PL			
21300	CALB	91302	589-D1
ALDER RD			
-	LACo	-	(4726-G1 See Page 4645)
ALDER ST			
2400	POM	91767	601-B4
27800	Cstc	91384	4459-G2
36800	PMDL	93552	4287-C4
ALDERBERRY LN			
-	POM	91767	601-A3
ALDERBROOK DR			
24600	SCTA	91321	4550-J7
ALDERBURY DR			
18600	RowH	91748	679-B7
ALDERBURY ST			
9300	CYP	90630	767-B6
ALDERCREEK ST			
-	SCTA	91354	4460-F7
ALDERDALE ST			
7700	DWNY	90240	706-C1
ALDERGATE ST			
200	MONP	91755	636-B5
ALDER GLEN CIR			
27800	SCTA	91354	4460-H5
ALDERGROVE ST			
13300	LA	91342	482-B1
ALDER OAK RD			
-	LACo	-	(512-A5 See Page 511)
ALDER PEAK AV			
28400	SCTA	91387	4552-B1
ALDERPOINT DR			
15100	LMRD	90638	737-F4
ALDER RIDGE DR			
5700	LCF	91011	535-C2
ALDERSGATE DR			
1100	LVRN	91750	570-E6
ALDERSON AV			
4100	BALD	91706	598-D3
4100	IRW	91706	598-D3
ALDER SPRINGS DR			
300	VeCo	91377	558-B1
ALDERTON AV			
300	LACo	91744	678-J2
13700	CRTS	90703	737-C5
ALDERTON LN			
13600	CRTS	90703	737-C5
ALDERWOOD CT			
-	CRSN	90746	764-G2
ALDER WOOD LN			
14200	CHLS	91709	680-H3
ALDERWOOD LN			
13600	SLB	90740	826-G1
ALDERWOOD RD			
14200	LACo	93532	4102-H5
ALDERWOOD ST			
13200	LMRD	90638	737-H2
ALDGATE AV			
300	LPUE	91744	638-C6
700	LACo	91744	638-D5
ALDINE CT			
1100	SPed	90731	823-J6
ALDIS ST			
500	POM	91768	640-D1
1400	Flor	90001	704-F2
ALDON AV			
2600	LVRN	91750	600-H3
ALDORA DR			
19100	RowH	91748	679-C4
ALDREN CT			
5500	AGRH	91301	557-G5
ALDRICH RD			
5200	SGAT	90280	705-E5
ALDRICH ST			
100	LHB	90631	708-E6
8700	PRV	90660	676-F4
10300	LACo	90606	676-H5
11400	LACo	90606	677-A7
ALDRIDGE PL			
2900	RowH	91748	679-B7
2900	RowH	91748	709-B1
ALE WY			
5700	PMDL	93551	4194-G2
ALEGRE LN			
3200	Alta	91001	536-B4
ALEGRE PL			
900	LA	90065	594-J2
E ALEGRIA AV			
-	SMAD	91024	567-A1
W ALEGRIA AV			
-	SMAD	91024	567-A1
500	SMAD	91024	566-H1
ALEGRIA PL			
600	SMRO	91108	566-E6
ALEGRIA ST			
3500	PAS	91107	566-H1
ALEGRO DR			
25800	SCTA	91355	4550-F6
ALEJANDRO DR			
26000	SCTA	91355	4550-G4
ALEMAN AV			
3800	PRV	90660	676-J2
ALEMAN DR			
4100	Tarz	91356	560-F5
ALEMANY DR			
-	MsnH	91345	501-H1
ALENE DR			
9600	Tuj	91042	504-A5
ALENE WK			
9800	Tuj	91042	504-A5
ALEP ST			
42800	LAN	93536	4105-B2
ALEPPO PINE CT			
-	HacH	91745	678-F6
ALERION PL			
20300	WdHl	91364	560-D3
ALERT LN			
16100	HNTB	92649	826-J6
ALESIA ST			
9700	SELM	91733	637-A4
ALESNA DR			
25500	SCTA	91355	4550-G5
ALESSANDRO AV			
800	LVRN	91750	600-D2
4800	TEML	91780	596-J3
ALESSANDRO PL			
-	PAS	91105	565-H7
ALETA WY			
4900	PMDL	93551	4194-H3
ALETHEA DR			
11300	Sunl	91040	503-H1
ALETTA AV			
10900	CULC	90232	672-F3
ALEX CT			
-	LA	91342	502-G1
ALEXANDER AV			
-	SBdC	-	(512-A5 See Page 511)
2600	PMDL	93551	4195-C7
8900	SGAT	90280	705-C5
10600	LYN	90262	705-C6
16700	CRTS	90703	737-C6
18300	CRTS	90703	767-C1
ALEXANDER CIR			
18700	CRTS	90703	767-C1
ALEXANDER CT			
1500	BREA	92821	708-H6
ALEXANDER PL			
16400	CRTS	90703	737-C6
ALEXANDER ST			
100	SFER	91340	482-B6
500	GLDL	91203	564-C4
4900	CMRC	90040	675-H6
12900	LA	91342	482-D4
14600	LA	91340	501-H2
14700	MsnH	91345	501-H2
ALEXANDER WY			
-	PRV	90660	676-G1
ALEXANDRA CIR			
17100	CRTS	90703	737-C7
ALEXANDRA CT			
24800	CALB	91302	559-D7
ALEXANDRIA AV			
22300	LACo	90502	764-A7
22800	LACo	90502	794-A2
24300	Hrbr	90710	794-A3
N ALEXANDRIA AV			
100	LA	90004	633-J1
200	LA	90004	593-J7
700	LA	90029	593-J5
1300	LFlz	90027	593-J4
S ALEXANDRIA AV			
100	LA	90004	633-J2
S ALEXANDRIA AV			
300	LA	90020	633-J2
600	LA	90005	633-J2
600	LA	90010	633-J2
ALEXANDRIA PL			
4200	LA	90004	593-J7
ALEXDALE LN			
2100	RowH	91748	679-C6
ALEXIS PL			
1500	BHLS	90210	592-G4
ALEXO DR			
42800	LAN	93536	4105-A3
ALFALFA RD			
-	PMDL	93552	4287-E2
ALFARENA PL			
4400	Tarz	91356	560-H5
ALFELD AV			
13900	LACo	90061	734-D3
ALFIE RD			
33800	LACo	91390	4373-H5
ALFONSO			
18000	LACo	90220	764-J1
ALFONSO DR			
5300	AGRH	91301	557-H5
ALFORD ST			
900	AZU	91702	569-B7
18000	LACo	91702	569-A7
19000	GLDR	91740	569-C7
W ALFORD ST			
100	SDMS	91773	570-B7
ALFRED AV			
17000	CRTS	90703	737-A7
18300	CRTS	90703	767-A1
ALFRED DR			
100	CLAR	91711	571-D6
ALFRED PL			
900	MTBL	90640	636-D7
N ALFRED ST			
300	LA	90048	632-J1
300	LA	90048	592-J7
500	WHWD	90048	592-J7
700	LA	90069	592-J7
1000	WHWD	90069	592-J7
S ALFRED ST			
1000	LA	90035	633-A3
1200	LA	90035	632-J4
ALFREDO CT			
5500	AGRH	91301	557-H5
ALFREDO ST			
5900	CHNO	91710	641-J7
ALFREDS WY			
-	Saug	91350	4461-E6
ALGARDI ST			
11800	NRWK	90650	736-H5
ALGECIRAS DR			
14500	LMRD	90638	737-H3
ALGER ST			
4300	LA	90039	564-D6
ALGEROMA ST			
9000	BLF	90706	736-A5
ALGIERS ST			
18300	Nor	91326	500-H1
ALGINET DR			
3200	Enc	91436	561-D7
ALGINET PL			
16700	Enc	91436	561-D7
ALGODON CT			
2600	LA	90046	593-A2
ALGOMA AV			
4800	Eagl	90041	565-B6
ALGONAUT DR			
3800	CALB	91302	559-J7
ALGONQUIN DR			
1100	LACo	91744	638-G4
ALGOOD DR			
42900	LACo	93532	4102-F4
ALGRANTI AV			
13600	LA	91342	482-E2
E ALGROVE ST			
300	COV	91723	599-C5
1400	COV	91724	599-E5
ALGUNAS RD			
22300	WdHl	91364	559-J5
ALHAMA DR			
4100	WdHl	91364	560-B3
5400	WdHl	91367	560-B2
ALHAMBRA AV			
800	LA	90012	634-H2
1700	COMP	90221	735-A2
2100	LA	90031	635-A2
5000	LA	90032	635-E1
5200	LA	90032	595-F7
8000	PRM	90723	735-H1
8000	SGAT	90280	735-H1
N ALHAMBRA AV			
100	MONP	91755	636-C2
S ALHAMBRA AV			
100	MONP	91755	636-C3
ALHAMBRA CT			
1100	Ven	90291	671-H5
E ALHAMBRA CT			
1100	LBCH	90813	795-F6
ALHAMBRA RD			
900	ALH	91801	596-C2
1100	SGBL	91775	596-C2
1400	SMRO	91108	596-C2
1700	LA	90031	635-A2
E ALHAMBRA RD			
-	ALH	91801	596-B4
N ALHAMBRA RD			
300	SGBL	91775	596-C3
W ALHAMBRA RD			
-	ALH	91801	596-A4
W ALHAMBRA RD			
1200	ALH	91801	595-H4
1200	SPAS	91030	595-H4
ALHOHA CIR			
300	NLB	90805	735-E7
ALIA CT			
-	SCTA	91387	4462-E7
ALIANO DR			
4800	VeCo	91377	557-G1
ALIANTHUS LN			
-	PMDL	93551	4285-D3
ALICANTE AV			
2300	UPL	91784	571-J3
ALICANTE DR			
24900	CALB	91302	559-C7
25500	SCTA	91355	4550-H5
ALICANTE RD			
14300	LMRD	90638	737-E2
16000	LMRD	90638	738-A3
ALICANTE ST			
1700	POM	91768	600-F6
42200	LACo	93536	4104-J5
ALICE ST			
-	ARCD	91006	567-D6
2600	LA	90065	594-H5
ALICE RODRIGUEZ CIR			
-	IRW	91010	597-J1
ALICIA AV			
3200	Alta	91001	535-J4
ALICIA CT			
800	POM	91766	640-H4
ALICIA ST			
2400	WCOV	91792	639-B7
ALICIA WY			
600	ANA	90620	767-F7
ALIDA AV			
19500	CRTS	90703	766-H3
ALIDA LN			
35400	LACo	93552	4376-J1
35400	LACo	93552	4377-A1
ALIDA PL			
-	RPV	90275	822-F2
ALIMONY TKTR			
-	Litl	93543	4467-J7
-	Litl	93543	4468-B5
-	Litl	93543	(4558-A1 See Page 4467)
ALINE WY			
25600	LACo	91302	589-A7
ALISAL CT			
800	LA	90402	631-C6
ALISAL LN			
14100	LA	90402	631-C6
E ALISAL ST			
400	COV	91723	599-C6
W ALISAL ST			
1600	WCOV	91790	598-E6
ALISAR AV			
1600	MONP	91755	636-D5
ALISO CIR			
4100	LVRN	91750	570-H7
ALISO CT			
-	PMDL	93551	4195-A4
14200	CHLS	91709	680-H3
ALISO ST			
-	Actn	93510	4374-J7
-	Actn	93510	4464-J1
-	LACo	91390	4461-G2
100	LA	90012	634-G3
300	MONP	91754	635-H3
3100	Actn	93510	4375-A7
7400	DWNY	90242	705-G7
7500	DWNY	90242	735-G1
E ALISO ST			
100	LA	90012	634-H4
100	POM	91767	600-J6
1100	Boyl	90033	634-H4
W ALISO ST			
100	POM	91768	600-H5
ALISO CANYON RD			
-	Actn	93510	4466-B7
-	PMDL	93550	4466-B7
-	PMDL	93550	(4556-C1 See Page 4466)
31200	Actn	93510	4465-F2
ALISON DR			
-	BLF	90706	736-D2
ALISU CT			
20200	WAL	91789	679-E1
ALIWIN ST			
9700	DWNY	90240	706-F3
ALIX AV			
7900	Flor	90001	704-H2
ALIX CT			
-	TOR	90503	763-A4
ALIYAH WY			
24400	WdHl	91367	559-D1
ALIZIA CANYON DR			
26000	CALB	91302	558-H3
26000	VeCo	91302	558-H3
ALIZONDO DR			
22000	WdHl	91364	560-A5
ALLA RD			
3900	LA	90066	672-B5
3900	CULC	90066	672-B5
4300	LA	90292	672-C6
5400	LA	90066	702-D1
ALL AMERICA CITY WY			
7800	PRM	90723	735-G3
ALLAN AV			
3500	BURB	91505	563-B1
ALLAN DR			
42000	LAN	93536	4104-C6
ALLAN ST			
5300	LA	90032	595-F6
ALLANDALE DR			
19100	Tarz	91356	560-G7
ALLANJAY PL			
2400	GLDL	91208	534-J6
ALLARD ST			
11600	NRWK	90650	706-G7
12600	SFSP	90670	707-A7
ALLASEBA DR			
11800	LA	90066	672-B2
ALLBROOK ST			
2000	LMTA	90717	793-H3
ALLEGAN ST			
13300	LACo	90605	707-C5
14100	LACo	90604	707-D5
ALLEGANY CT			
2000	CLAR	91711	571-D7
ALLEGHANY CIR			
400	SDMS	91773	570-D7
ALLEGHENY CT			
5000	LadH	90056	673-A4
N ALLEGHENY CT			
200	THO	91362	557-B3
S ALLEGHENY CT			
100	THO	91362	557-B3
ALLEGHENY ST			
9900	Sunl	91040	502-J5
9900	Sunl	91040	503-A4
11000	SunV	91352	502-J5
12400	SunV	91352	532-E1
ALLEGRA WY			
-	SCTA	91355	4460-D6
ALLEGRO CT			
-	PMDL	93552	4196-H7
ALLEGRO LN			
-	POM	91766	640-D4
ALLEGRO SQ			
1600	SGBL	91776	596-F7
ALLEN AV			
100	GLDL	91201	563-H2
1000	GLDL	91201	564-A1
1200	GLDL	91201	534-B6
16300	PRM	90723	735-F5
E ALLEN AV			
100	SDMS	91773	600-D1
600	SDMS	91750	600-D1
700	LACo	91750	600-D1
700	LVRN	91750	600-D1
1100	GLDR	91740	599-H1
N ALLEN AV			
-	PAS	91106	566-C3
-	PAS	91107	566-C3
600	PAS	91104	566-C3
1300	LACo	91104	566-C3
1500	LACo	91104	536-C7
1800	Alta	91001	536-C5
S ALLEN AV			
-	PAS	91106	566-C5
-	PAS	91107	566-C5
500	SMRO	91108	566-C6
W ALLEN AV			
100	SDMS	91773	600-A1
ALLEN CT			
-	PMDL	93551	4104-G7
S ALLEN CT			
1800	PAS	91107	566-C5
ALLEN DR			
4900	IRW	91706	598-G3
ALLEN ST			
15300	PRM	90723	735-F4
ALLENBY CT			
32000	WLKV	91361	557-C6
ALLENDALE RD			
200	PAS	91106	565-J7
500	PAS	91106	566-A7
ALLENFORD AV			
1300	Brwd	90049	631-E4
1300	SMCA	90402	631-E4
1400	PacP	90272	631-E4
ALLENGROVE ST			
7300	DWNY	90240	706-B1
ALLENHURST ST			
100	LACo	90061	734-D3
ALLENTON AV			
2600	HacH	91745	678-B6
ALLENTOWN DR			
20100	WdHl	91364	560-D3
ALLENTOWN PL			
5100	WdHl	91364	560-E3
ALLENWICK AV			
27400	SCTA	91351	4551-G2
ALLENWOOD RD			
8400	LA	90046	592-H2
ALLEPPO LN			
5700	PMDL	93551	4104-F7
ALLER CT			
-	GLDL	91206	564-J3
ALLERTON ST			
10700	LACo	90606	676-H6
13600	LACo	90605	707-C3
E ALLERTON ST			
11100	LACo	90606	676-J6
ALLESANDRO ST			
1300	Echo	90026	594-D7
1900	LA	90039	594-F3
4500	MTCL	91763	601-E4
4800	CHNO	91710	641-F7
ALLESANDRO WY			
2200	LA	90039	594-E5
ALLESSANDRA CT			
-	LAN	93535	4016-F6
ALLGEYER AV			
1200	SELM	91733	637-C5
2200	ELMN	91732	637-E2
ALLIANCE AV			
1100	SIGH	90755	795-F3
ALLIED WY			
600	ELSG	90245	732-G3
ALLIENE AV			
23700	TOR	90501	793-G2
24100	LMTA	90717	793-G3
ALLIN ST			
11700	LA	90230	672-F5
12400	LA	90066	672-D6
E ALLIN ST			
3900	LBCH	90803	825-J2
3900	LBCH	90803	826-A2
ALLINGHAM AV			
13700	NRWK	90650	736-F3
19000	CRTS	90703	766-F2
ALLINGTON ST			
5000	LKWD	90712	766-B1
5500	LKWD	90713	766-C1
10300	BLF	90706	766-C1
E ALLINGTON ST			
100	NLB	90805	765-C1
ALLIS DR			
400	MTBL	90640	676-C5
ALLISON AV			
1300	Echo	90026	634-E1
1400	Echo	90026	594-E7
ALLISON DR			
21600	SCTA	91350	4461-A5
ALLISON LN			
-	CYP	90630	767-D6
ALLIUM CT			
-	BqtC	91354	4460-E6
ALLMAN PL			
2700	LACo	91724	639-E1
ALLMAN ST			
28900	AGRH	91301	558-A3
ALLMERS ST			
-	Actn	93510	4375-B6
ALLORI WY			
-	SCTA	91355	4460-D6
ALLOTT AV			
4100	Shrm	91423	562-C4
5200	VanN	91401	562-C2
6000	VanN	91401	532-C6
7100	VanN	91405	532-C5
7700	PanC	91402	532-C2
ALLPORT AV			
8000	SFSP	90606	706-J1
8000	SFSP	90670	706-J1
ALLRED ST			
2400	LKWD	90712	765-G4
E ALLSTON ST			
1000	ELA	90022	675-J1
1900	MTBL	90640	676-C2
5700	ELA	90022	676-A2
6600	MTBL	90022	676-A2
ALLSTON WY			
-	BREA	92821	709-B6
ALLVIEW TER			
2300	LA	90068	593-H2
ALLVIEW TER E			
2300	LA	90068	593-H2
ALLVIEW TER W			
2300	LA	90068	593-H2
ALLWOOD CT			
19100	RowH	91748	679-C7
ALLYSON CT			
-	PMDL	93551	4194-H1
1500	BREA	92821	708-H6
ALLYSSUM PL			
-	PMDL	93551	4285-D4
ALMA AV			
3300	LYN	90262	705-B6
13500	GAR	90249	733-J3
N ALMA AV			
100	City	90063	635-D4
1100	LA	90063	635-D4
2200	MANB	90266	732-E4
S ALMA AV			
100	City	90063	635-D7
100	LA	90063	635-D7
800	LACo	90023	635-D7
900	LACo	90023	675-D1
ALMA CT			
1100	CLAR	91711	571-A7
ALMA LN			
5300	PMDL	93551	4194-G2
ALMA ST			
-	NLB	90805	735-C7
700	GLDL	91202	564-C3
S ALMA ST			
700	SPed	90731	824-A6
2600	SPed	90731	854-A1
ALMADA ST			
1200	LBCH	90815	796-F5
N ALMADALE AV			
2000	LA	90032	635-C1
ALMADEN CT			
2500	BelA	90077	592-A2
ALMADEN DR			
4900	HiPk	90042	595-B1
ALMADIN AV			
19200	CRTS	90703	766-H3
ALMADOR CT			
38700	PMDL	93551	4195-D7
ALMAHURST ST			
17600	INDS	91748	678-H4
ALMANAC DR			
17300	WCOV	91791	638-J4
N ALMANSOR ST			
-	ALH	91801	596-B3
S ALMANSOR ST			
-	ALH	91801	596-C4
500	ALH	91801	636-C1
S ALMANSOR ST OVPS			
-	ALH	91801	596-C7
400	ALH	91801	636-C1
E ALMANZA LN			
4000	City	90063	635-E3
ALMAR AV			
400	PacP	90272	630-J5
ALMAR PZ			
16000	PacP	90272	630-J6
ALMAR ST			
6300	SIMI	93063	499-C2
ALMA REAL DR			
200	PacP	90272	631-A7
ALMAROSA AV			
23200	TOR	90505	793-F2
ALMAYO AV			
10200	LA	90064	632-D5
ALMAZAN RD			
20900	WdHl	91364	560-C5
ALMENA AV			
1400	RowH	91748	678-J4
ALMENDRA DR			
25500	SCTA	91355	4550-G5
ALMERIA ST			
3100	SPed	90731	854-A1
ALMERIA WY			
6200	PMDL	93552	4287-D3
ALMERTENS PL			
11900	HAW	90303	703-E7
ALMETZ ST			
13300	LA	91342	482-B1
ALMEZA AV			
2300	RowH	91748	679-B6
ALMIDOR AV			
4700	WdHl	91364	559-G4
ALMINAR AV			
4700	LCF	91011	535-D4
ALMIRA RD			
5200	SGAT	90280	705-E5
S ALMIRANTE DR			
600	WCOV	91791	639-B1
ALMO ST			
9200	PRV	90660	676-G4
ALMOLOYA DR			
500	PacP	90272	631-B6
ALMON DR			
200	THO	91362	557-A2
ALMOND AL			
3000	Alta	91001	535-H4
ALMOND AV			
-	ONT	91762	641-J4
300	MNRO	91016	567-H5
400	LBCH	90802	795-F7
41200	PMDL	93551	4194-G1
41200	PMDL	93551	4104-G7
S ALMOND AV			
1200	ONT	91762	641-J3
ALMOND CT			
-	ONT	91762	641-J4
4900	RCUC	91737	(542-J7 See Page 511)
N ALMOND CT			
1000	LBCH	90813	795-F6
ALMOND DR			
800	BREA	92821	709-C7
ALMOND ST			
500	COMP	90220	734-H5
4100	LVRN	91750	570-J7
W ALMOND ST			
300	COMP	90220	734-G4
ALMOND VALLEY WY			
5800	LAN	93536	4104-D5
6100	LACo	93536	4104-E5
ALMONDWOOD AV			
2300	LAN	93535	4106-E1
ALMONDWOOD ST			
-	FUL	92835	738-H3
900	LHB	90631	738-D1
ALMONOR ST			
600	LACo	91792	679-C2
N ALMONT DR			
100	BHLS	90211	632-H2
100	LA	90048	632-H1
100	WHWD	90048	592-H7
100	WHWD	90048	632-H1
600	WHWD	90069	592-H7
S ALMONT DR			
100	BHLS	90211	632-H3
100	LA	90048	632-H1
ALMONT ST			
5100	LA	90032	595-F5
W ALMORA ST			
200	MONP	91754	636-A5
500	MONP	91754	635-J5
ALOE DR			
15100	LMRD	90638	737-G1
ALOHA DR			
15900	PacP	90272	630-J6
ALOHA ST			
3700	LFlz	90027	594-C3
ALOJAR LN			
4600	PMDL	93551	4194-H2
ALOMAR DR			
3700	Shrm	91423	562-D6
ALONDA DR			
19700	CRSN	90746	764-E3
ALONDRA BLVD			
6200	PRM	90723	735-F5

STREET
Block City ZIP Pg-Grid

ALONDRA BLVD
6200 PRM 90221 735-F5
6400 COMP 90221 735-F5
7500 BPK 90621 737-H5
7800 LMRD 90638 737-F5
8700 BLF 90706 735-F5
8800 BLF 90706 736-B5
8800 PRM 90723 736-B5
10500 NRWK 90650 736-F5
10500 NRWK 90703 736-F5
10800 CRTS 90703 736-F5
11000 CRTS 90650 736-F5
12400 NRWK 90650 737-B5
12400 CRTS 90703 737-B5
12600 NRWK 90703 737-B5
13000 SFSP 90670 737-B5
E ALONDRA BLVD
100 COMP 90220 734-D6
100 COMP 90220 735-B5
100 CRSN 90248 734-D6
100 LACo 90248 734-D6
300 COMP 90221 735-B5
600 CRSN 90746 734-D6
600 LACo 90220 734-D6
2000 RDom 90221 735-B5
6200 COMP 90723 735-B5
6200 PRM 90723 735-B5
6200 PRM 90221 735-B5
W ALONDRA BLVD
100 COMP 90220 734-H5
100 CRSN 90248 734-C6
100 LACo 90248 734-C6
500 LA 90248 734-C6
600 LA 90247 734-C6
2600 CRSN 90746 734-C6
2800 COMP 90746 734-C6
2900 LACo 90220 734-C6
ALONDRA CIR
1000 LVRN 91750 600-E1
ALONDRA DR
800 PacP 90272 630-G5
ALONZO AV
3700 Enc 91316 561-A1
6100 Enc 91316 531-A7
ALONZO PL
17700 Enc 91316 561-B4
ALORA AV
16300 NRWK 90650 736-F6
16300 NRWK 90703 736-F6
16600 LACo 90703 736-F6
17400 CRTS 90703 736-F7
E ALOSTA AV
800 AZU 91702 569-C6
ALPACA ST
7700 LACo 91770 636-E4
9600 SELM 91733 637-A4
ALPERN DR
14900 HacH 91745 678-A2
ALPHA AV
1300 LACo 91104 566-D1
1800 SPAS 91030 595-G3
15900 BLF 90706 736-A5
ALPHA CIR
2100 LVRN 91750 570-H7
ALPHA RD
1800 GLDL 91208 534-J6
ALPHA ST
700 IRW 91010 597-J1
900 ING 90302 673-D7
4300 LA 90032 595-G5
ALPHINGTON AV
- CRTS 90703 767-A2
ALPINE AV
12100 LYN 90262 735-A2
13000 LACo 91390 4373-A4
N ALPINE AV
- LBCH 90802 825-A1
ALPINE CT
1000 CHLS 91709 710-F1
2800 THO 91362 557-C3
5800 PMDL 93551 4194-G3
ALPINE DR
800 POM 91767 601-B4
1800 SMRO 91108 596-D2
N ALPINE DR
300 BHLS 90210 632-F1
500 BHLS 90210 592-F6
S ALPINE DR
1400 WCOV 91791 639-A4
ALPINE LN
- Llan 93544 4470-D6
- SBdC 92397 (4652-E3
See Page 4651)
ALPINE PL
16100 LMRD 90638 738-A2
ALPINE ST
100 LA 90012 634-F2
100 LHB 90631 708-G6
200 PAS 91106 565-J7
600 PAS 91106 566-A7
ALPINE TER
1000 MONP 91754 635-J3
ALPINE TR
1200 Top 90290 630-A1
ALPINE WY
5000 PMDL 93551 4194-H3
7300 Tuj 91042 503-J1
7300 Tuj 91042 504-A1
ALPINE CREST RD
19700 WAL 91789 639-E4
ALPINE MEADOW CIR
20600 WAL 91789 639-F4

ALPINE VILLA DR
900 Alta 91001 536-A4
ALPS DR
- UPL 91784 571-H6
ALS DR
9700 SELM 91733 637-A3
ALSACE AV
1800 LA 90019 633-C6
2100 LA 90016 633-C6
3000 LA 90016 673-C1
3800 LA 90008 673-C2
5800 LA 90043 673-D6
ALSACE DR
- Ago 91301 558-G3
- LACo 91302 558-G3
ALSCOT AV
1800 SIMI 93063 499-B1
ALSINA ST
200 LACo 90061 734-D3
ALSKOG ST
10500 SunV 91352 533-B1
ALSTER AV
200 ARCD 91006 597-E1
ALSTON AV
- LACo 93591 4199-E2
ALTA AV
100 SMCA 90402 671-C1
400 SMCA 90402 631-E6
5800 WHIT 90601 677-D5
ALTA DR
600 POM 91767 641-C1
600 POM 91767 601-C7
21900 Top 90290 590-A1
22000 Top 90290 589-J1
25700 SCTA 91355 4550-G4
N ALTA DR
500 BHLS 90210 592-G6
ALTA PL
3400 LA 90031 595-B6
ALTA ST
- ARCD 91006 567-D5
800 MNRO 91016 567-E5
1900 LA 90031 635-B1
2400 LA 90031 595-B7
ALTA TER
2800 LaCr 91214 504-F6
ALTA TR
12200 LACo 91342 482-J6
ALTA WY
23200 Chat 91311 499-F6
E ALTA WY
400 LBCH 90802 825-E1
ALTA CANYADA RD
4300 LCF 91011 535-A1
5400 LCF 91011 505-A7
ALTA CREST DR
1700 Alta 91001 536-C5
E ALTADENA DR
- Alta 91001 535-J5
500 Alta 91001 536-B5
N ALTADENA DR
- PAS 91107 566-E3
600 PAS 91104 566-E3
1200 LACo 91104 566-E3
1300 LACo 91107 566-E3
1500 LACo 91107 536-E6
1500 LACo 91104 536-E6
1600 Alta 91001 536-D6
1600 PAS 91107 536-E6
2100 PAS - 536-D6
S ALTADENA DR
- PAS 91107 566-E5
W ALTADENA DR
- Alta 91001 535-G4
600 PAS 91001 535-G4
ALTAGRACIA DR
6400 Tuj 91042 504-C5
ALTA HACIENDA DR
20200 WAL 91789 639-E3
ALTAIR DR
12200 Brwd 90049 631-F2
ALTAIR LN
- LACo 91390 4461-A2
ALTAIR PL
400 Ven 90291 671-H6
ALTA KNOLL DR
27400 SCTA 91350 4461-C7
ALTALAKE AV
4300 BALD 91706 598-C5
ALTA LOMA RD
1100 WHWD 90069 592-J5
ALTA LOMA TER
6700 LA 90068 593-E3
ALTA MADERA DR
23300 SCTA 91355 4550-G5
ALTAMAR PL
11900 SFSP 90670 706-J2
ALTAMERE AV
27300 SCTA 91351 4551-G3
ALTA MESA DR
1100 BREA 92821 708-H4
3500 LA 91604 562-E6
ALTA MESA PL
3700 LA 91604 562-E6
S ALTA MESA PL
700 MONP 91754 636-A3
ALTA MESA WY
1400 BREA 92821 708-J4
ALTAMIRA CIR
2700 WCOV 91792 638-J6
ALTAMIRA DR
2600 WCOV 91792 638-J6

ALTA MIRA PL
- POM 91766 640-E4
ALTAMONT ST
3500 LA 90065 594-J4
ALTAMONTE AV
24000 SCTA 91355 4550-F6
ALTAMOR DR
6700 Wch 90045 702-F1
ALTA MURA RD
1600 PacP 90272 631-D3
ALTANO ST
12900 LA 91342 482-D4
ALTA OAKS DR
1600 ARCD 91006 567-D2
ALTA PARK LN
1500 LCF 91011 535-A2
ALTA PASA DR
2000 Alta 91001 535-J7
2000 PAS 91104 535-J7
ALTA PASEO
1200 BURB 91501 534-A6
ALTA PINE DR
300 Alta 91001 535-J4
300 Alta 91001 536-A4
ALTAR CT
4900 PMDL 93551 4194-H3
ALTARIDGE DR
21800 Top 90290 590-A2
ALTARIO ST
18300 LACo 91744 679-A2
ALTAS WY
- PMDL 93552 4287-C1
ALTA SIERRA RD
1000 WAL 91789 639-E5
ALTATA DR
14900 PacP 90272 631-A7
ALTA TUPELO DR
4400 CALB 91302 559-D5
ALTAVAN AV
7800 Wch 90045 702-D2
ALTA VIEW DR
10800 LA 91604 563-A7
ALTA VISTA
- AVA 90704 5923-G2
5700 LVRN 91750 570-H4
6700 BPK 90620 767-F5
ALTA VISTA AV
- BqtC 91354 4460-D6
- SCTA 91355 4460-D6
300 SPAS 91030 595-F3
400 MNRO 91016 567-F6
900 ARCD 91006 567-F6
26200 Hrbr 90710 793-J6
26300 Hrbr 90710 793-J6
N ALTA VISTA AV
100 MNRO 91016 567-F2
2000 LA 90046 592-H3
S ALTA VISTA AV
100 MNRO 91016 567-F5
N ALTA VISTA BLVD
100 LA 90036 633-D1
300 LA 90036 593-D7
700 LA 90046 593-D5
S ALTA VISTA BLVD
100 LA 90036 633-D1
ALTA VISTA CIR
500 SPAS 91030 595-F3
ALTA VISTA DR
- POM 91768 600-H6
500 SMAD 91024 567-B1
600 GLDL 91205 564-F7
900 Alta 91001 536-A5
1100 FUL 92835 738-F5
1700 ALH 91803 635-H1
3900 LCF 91011 535-C6
6900 RPV 90275 822-G3
15900 LMRD 90638 737-J2
ALTA VISTA RD
600 VeCo 93063 499-B4
11400 SBdC 92372 (4472-A2
See Page 4471)
S ALTA VISTA ST
1500 MNRO 91016 567-F6
ALTA VISTA WY
- LA 91342 482-F3
ALTA VISTA RIDGE RD
6300 VeCo 93063 499-C4
ALTA WOOD DR
1700 Alta 91001 536-C5
ALTENA DR
21100 SCTA 91350 4461-B5
ALTERN ST
100 ARCD 91006 567-D7
E ALTERN ST
200 LACo 91016 567-G7
W ALTERN ST
100 LACo 91016 567-G7
100 MNRO 91016 567-G7
ALTIVO PL
2800 FUL 92835 738-H2
ALTIVO WY
1500 Echo 90026 594-F5
ALTMAN AV
9700 LA 90034 632-G6
ALTMAN ST
2300 LA 90031 594-G5
ALTMARK AV
6000 WHIT 90601 677-E5
6100 WHIT 91745 677-E5
ALTO CIR
6300 RPV 90275 822-J1
ALTO LN
1100 LHB 90631 708-F4

ALTO CEDRO DR
8900 LA 90210 592-G2
ALTON ST
1000 Wilm 90744 794-C7
ALTON WY
- Cstc 91384 4459-G5
ALTO OAK DR
2300 LA 90068 593-G2
ALTOS DR
25400 SCTA 91355 4640-E1
ALTRIDGE DR
1400 LA 90210 592-D5
ALTURA AV
2400 Mont 91020 534-G2
2600 LaCr 91214 534-F1
3200 GLDL 91214 534-E1
3300 GLDL 91214 504-D6
4000 LA 91214 504-C6
ALTURA BLVD
6300 BPK 90620 737-E7
ALTURA CT
700 POM 91768 600-G7
ALTURA DR
200 FUL 92835 738-G1
ALTURA LN
9100 WHIT 90603 707-J2
N ALTURA RD
- ARCD 91007 566-J5
S ALTURA RD
- ARCD 91007 566-J5
ALTURA ST
2800 LA 90031 595-A7
ALTURA TER
1100 ARCD 91007 566-J4
ALTURA WK
3200 LA 90031 595-B7
ALTURA WY
400 MANB 90266 732-H7
ALTURAS LN
4300 CHNO 91710 641-E5
ALUMNI AV
4400 Eagl 90041 594-J1
4500 Eagl 90041 564-J7
4600 Eagl 90041 565-A7
ALVA DR
14900 PacP 90272 631-B6
ALVADA ST
4200 LYN 90262 735-D2
ALVAR PL
21300 CRSN 90745 764-F6
E ALVARADO AV
1000 POM 91767 601-C7
ALVARADO CIR
200 FUL 92835 738-G2
ALVARADO ST
800 POM 91767 601-B7
E ALVARADO ST
100 POM 91767 600-J7
300 POM 91767 601-A7
N ALVARADO ST
100 Echo 90026 634-D2
100 LA 90057 634-D2
1600 Echo 90026 594-E6
1900 LA 90039 594-E5
N ALVARADO ST Rt#-2
- Echo 90026 594-D7
- Echo 90026 634-D1
S ALVARADO ST
100 LA 90057 634-B4
900 LA 90006 634-B4
W ALVARADO ST
100 POM 91768 600-H7
ALVARADO TER
1300 LA 90006 634-B5
ALVAREZ DR
27900 RPV 90275 792-J6
ALVARO AV
12100 Wbrk 90059 704-F7
12100 Wbrk 90059 734-F1
ALVARO ST
11200 LA 90059 704-F6
11500 Wbrk 90059 704-F7
ALVEO RD
4500 LCF 91011 535-D4
ALVERN CIR
5400 Wch 90045 673-A7
5400 Wch 90045 703-A1
ALVERN ST
6600 LadH 90056 672-J7
6700 Wch 90045 672-J7
6700 Wch 90045 673-A7
7000 Wch 90045 702-J1
ALVERSTONE AV
7000 Wch 90045 672-G7
7100 Wch 90045 702-G1
ALVESTA PL
27600 RPV 90275 823-H1
ALVEY ST
400 Alta 91001 535-G6
ALVINA ST
6700 BGDN 90201 705-J1
ALVINE LN
14900 BALD 91706 598-D6
ALVIRA ST
1000 LA 90035 633-A4
1600 LA 90035 632-J7
2600 LA 90034 632-J7
ALVISO AV
1400 ING 90302 673-D6
5400 LACo 90043 673-D6
5700 LA 90043 673-D6
ALVO AV
19800 CRSN 90746 764-H4

ALVORD LN
2400 RBCH 90278 763-B2
ALWICK PL
1600 BREA 92821 708-H3
ALWOOD ST
2200 WCOV 91790 638-C1
15600 LACo 91744 638-E3
E ALWOOD ST
600 WCOV 91790 638-H3
16400 LACo 91744 638-H3
17000 LACo 91791 638-H3
W ALWOOD ST
900 LPUE 91744 638-E3
900 WCOV 91790 638-E3
ALYESKA PL
1000 WAL 91789 639-D5
ALYSE CT
- Enc 91436 561-E4
ALYSSA DR
- SCTA 91321 4551-F6
ALYSSA LN
- PMDL 93552 4287-B4
ALYSSUM AV
2200 UPL 91784 571-H3
ALYSSUM LN
- SCTA 91387 4462-F6
ALYSSUM PL
- BqtC 91354 4460-E6
ALZADA DR
3700 Alta 91001 535-H3
S ALZADO ST
400 MONP 91754 635-G3
AMABEL ST
200 LA 90065 595-A5
AMABLE
2300 LA 90732 823-G7
AMABLE CT
5300 PMDL 93551 4194-G2
26000 SCTA 91355 4550-F4
AMADO
2400 LA 90732 823-F7
AMADOR CIR
700 WAL 91789 639-B7
AMADOR CT
3700 CHNO 91710 641-C5
AMADOR LN
600 SBdC 92372 (4472-B3
See Page 4471)
AMADOR PL
1800 LA 90012 594-H7
AMADOR RD
300 SBdC 92372 (4472-A3
See Page 4471)
3700 SBdC 92371 (4472-J3
See Page 4471)
AMADOR ST
500 LA 90012 634-H1
500 LA 90012 594-H7
1100 CLAR 91711 601-B2
10600 ELMN 91731 637-C1
AMALFI CT
14900 LA 90402 631-C7
19200 WAL 91789 639-C7
AMALFI DR
200 LA 90402 631-C7
400 PacP 90272 631-D3
1300 SIMI 93063 499-C3
4100 PMDL 93552 4286-J4
AMALFI ST
4600 CYP 90630 767-B7
AMALFI WY
- Nor 91326 500-C1
AMALIA AV
300 ELA 90022 635-H7
600 ELA 90022 675-H1
AMANDA DR
11400 LA 91604 562-H6
AMANDA LN
900 LHB 90631 708-E4
AMANDA PL
2100 UPL 91784 571-H4
AMANDA ST
2700 WCOV 91792 679-C1
AMANITA AV
9600 Tuj 91042 504-C5
AMANTHA AV
17500 CRSN 90746 734-F7
17500 CRSN 90746 764-F1
S AMANTHA AV
100 COMP 90220 734-F4
AMAPOLA AV
300 TOR 90501 763-G6
AMAPOLA CT
2200 TOR 90501 763-G4
AMAPOLA LN
400 BelA 90077 592-B7
AMAR RD
800 LPUE 91746 638-B3
1200 BALD 91706 637-H1
1400 WCOV 91792 638-D5
2500 WAL 91789 639-C5
2500 WCOV 91792 639-C5
13000 LACo 91706 637-J2
13200 INDS 91746 637-J2
13300 LACo 91746 637-J2
13400 LACo 91746 638-B3
14300 LPUE 91744 638-D5
14300 LACo 91744 638-B3
15800 INDS 91744 638-D5
E AMAR RD
1500 WCOV 91792 638-G5
1900 WCOV 91792 639-A6
16100 LACo 91744 638-G5

AMAR ST
1100 LA 90732 824-A4
1200 LA 90732 823-J4
W AMAR ST
200 SPed 90731 824-C4
AMARGOSA DR
- PMDL 93551 4195-E6
AMARGOSO DR
18000 RowH 91748 678-H6
AMARILLO DR
1000 CLAR 91711 571-F4
2000 GLDL 91208 534-J5
AMARILLO RD
11500 SBdC 92372 (4472-F1
See Page 4471)
AMARYLLIS CT
- BqtC 91354 4460-E6
AMARYLLIS TER
- PMDL 93551 4285-D3
AMATE DR
1500 LHH 90631 708-B3
AMBAR DR
21600 WdHl 91364 560-A6
AMBASSADOR AV
1700 BHLS 90210 592-D6
AMBASSADOR DR
24200 Hrbr 90710 793-J3
AMBASSADOR ST
1400 LA 90035 632-F4
AMBAZAC WY
10800 BelA 90077 592-A7
10800 BelA 90077 632-A1
AMBECO RD
3900 LBCH 90806 765-C7
AMBER AV
2100 ELMN 91733 637-E4
2200 ELMN 91732 637-E4
AMBER CIR
5400 LACo 91302 559-A4
AMBER LN
1800 BURB 91504 533-G4
37700 PMDL 93550 4286-E2
AMBER PL
- GAR 90247 734-A3
4500 LA 90032 595-D6
AMBER ST
10300 BLF 90706 766-D1
AMBER WY
- SCTA 91351 4551-H2
AMBERCREST PL
4000 THO 91362 557-D1
AMBERDON RD
10700 LACo 91390 4373-E3
AMBERGATE DR
6700 RPV 90275 792-G7
AMBER HILL DR
500 BREA 92821 709-A4
11700 LACo 90601 677-B2
AMBERIDGE WY
1700 PMDL 93551 4195-E7
AMBER LEAF RD
25600 TOR 90505 793-E5
AMBERLEAF ST
- FUL 92835 738-H3
AMBERLEY WY
23300 SCTA 91355 4550-G7
AMBERLY DR
3800 ING 90305 703-D3
AMBERLY PL
- RowH 91748 679-B7
- RowH 91748 709-B1
AMBER LYNN CT
- Hrbr 90710 794-A2
AMBER OAKS CIR
800 POM 91767 601-B4
AMBER OAKS LN
100 GLDR 91741 569-B5
AMBER RIDGE LN
200 WAL 91789 639-G7
AMBER RIDGE RD
27500 LACo 91387 4552-C6
AMBER ROSE LN
8300 RSMD 91770 636-G4
AMBER SKY DR
- RPV 90275 823-B2
AMBERSON ST
2300 POM 91767 600-J4
AMBER TREE LN
16500 HacH 91745 678-E5
AMBER VALLEY DR
15900 LACo 90604 707-J7
16100 LACo 90604 708-A7
18900 WAL 91789 639-C6
AMBERWICK
1600 WCOV 91791 638-J3
AMBERWICK CIR
200 BREA 92821 709-D7
9600 CYP 90630 767-D7
AMBERWICK PL
1300 DBAR 91765 680-C3
AMBERWOOD AV
4400 PRV 90660 676-J2
4500 LPMA 90623 767-B4
AMBERWOOD DR
100 WAL 91789 679-F1
100 WAL 91789 639-F7
1200 DUAR 91010 568-C5
1600 SPAS 91030 595-H1
5200 ING 90302 673-A7
38700 PMDL 93551 4195-E7
AMBERWOOD LN
- SCTA 91354 4460-G5
10500 Nor 91326 500-H4

AMBERWOOD WY
16600 CRTS 90703 737-A6
AMBIENTE CT
- PMDL 93552 4196-J7
AMBLE CT
4200 ELMN 91731 597-C6
AMBLER AV
16900 CRSN 90746 734-D7
18200 CRSN 90746 764-D2
AMBLESIDE WY
100 GLDR 91741 569-C5
AMBLING DR
100 BREA 92821 709-E7
AMBOY AV
8300 SunV 91352 532-G1
8800 SunV 91352 502-F7
9400 Pcma 91331 502-C3
11100 LA 91340 502-A1
11400 LA 91340 501-J1
11500 LA 91340 481-G5
12500 LA 91342 481-G5
AMBRIDGE DR
5000 CALB 91301 558-F6
AMBROSE AV
4300 LFlz 90027 594-A3
4800 LFlz 90027 593-J3
AMBROSE TER
4400 LFlz 90027 594-B3
AMBRUZZI DR
4600 CYP 90630 767-B7
AMBUSHERS ST
20400 DBAR 91765 709-H1
21400 DBAR 91765 679-H7
AMBY PL
2800 HMB 90254 732-G7
AMC PL
- WdHl 91367 560-A1
AMEBCO RD
3700 LBCH 90806 765-C7
AMELGA DR
9300 WHIT 90603 707-J2
AMELGADO DR
2400 HacH 91745 678-C5
AMELIA AV
700 SDMS 91773 600-A3
1400 LA 90732 824-A2
1400 SPed 90731 824-A2
1400 RPV 90275 824-A2
1400 RPV 90732 824-A2
2200 SPed 90731 823-J1
N AMELIA AV
300 SDMS 91773 600-A1
900 SDMS 91773 570-A7
1000 GLDR 91740 570-A7
1200 GLDR 91740 600-A1
S AMELIA AV
100 GLDR 91741 570-A6
700 GLDR 91740 570-A7
1000 SDMS 91773 570-A6
1100 SDMS 91740 570-A7
AMELIA CT
- SIGH 90755 795-H3
AMELIA DR
1000 Bxby 90807 765-E5
30100 AGRH 91301 557-H5
AMELIA LN
- SCTA 91321 4551-A7
AMELIA EARHART WY
- BELL 90201 675-G4
AMELUXEN AV
900 HacH 91745 637-J7
1100 HacH 91745 677-H1
AMERICA WY
22700 CALB 91302 559-H6
AMERICAN AV
- SCTA 91355 4550-G3
E AMERICAN AV
100 CLAR 91711 601-D6
1800 POM 91767 601-D6
1800 POM 91711 601-D6
W AMERICAN AV
100 CLAR 91711 601-D6
1600 POM 91767 601-D6
2700 LBCH 90806 795-D2
AMERICAN PL
- Eagl 90041 565-A7
- Eagl 90041 595-A1
600 LA 90065 594-J5
AMERICANA DR
200 SDMS 91773 599-J2
AMERICAN BEAUTY DR
18100 SCTA 91387 4551-J2
E AMERIGE AV
100 FUL 92832 738-H7
W AMERIGE AV
100 FUL 92832 738-G7
1100 FUL 92833 738-E7
AMERY AV
5800 SGAT 90280 705-G6
AMES ST
2000 LFlz 90027 594-B3
AMESBURY RD
3400 LFlz 90027 594-B2
AMESTOY AV
5000 Enc 91316 561-C3
6800 VanN 91406 531-C3
8200 Nor 91325 531-C1
8800 Nor 91325 501-C4
10300 GrnH 91344 501-C1
11600 GrnH 91344 481-C7
AMETHYST
- BREA 92823 710-C6

AMETHYST CIR
- GAR 90248 764-A1
AMETHYST CT
- CRTS 90703 767-A3
4000 LA 90032 595-C7
AMETHYST LN
500 WAL 91789 639-B7
500 WAL 91789 679-C1
AMETHYST ST
- LAN 93536 4014-J7
1200 RBCH 90277 762-J3
1300 RBCH 90277 763-A3
2900 LA 90032 595-C6
37800 PMDL 93552 4287-A2
AMETHYST WY
27500 Cstc 91384 4369-H6
AMEY ST
2000 LA 90007 634-A6
AMHERST AV
100 CLAR 91711 601-E2
800 Brwd 90049 631-G5
1200 WLA 90025 631-J6
2200 LA 90064 632-A7
2400 LA 90064 672-A1
9700 MTCL 91763 601-E6
10300 MTCL 91763 641-E1
AMHERST DR
100 BURB 91504 533-F6
2000 SPAS 91030 595-J3
AMHERST LN
44100 LAN 93536 4015-B7
AMHERST ST
100 CLAR 91711 600-J1
2500 LVRN 91750 600-H1
AMHURST AV
20400 WAL 91789 639-F4
AMHURST CT
19400 CRTS 90703 766-G3
AMHURST PL
30200 Cstc 91384 4459-B5
AMIATA LN
- PMDL 93550 4286-F5
AMIDON PL
10800 Tuj 91042 504-A2
AMIE AV
17100 TOR 90504 733-D7
17400 TOR 90504 763-D2
20300 TOR 90503 763-D4
AMIENS AV
- Brwd 90049 631-J2
AMIGO
3800 LA 90732 823-F7
AMIGO AV
4700 Tarz 91356 560-H3
6200 Res 91335 530-H2
8200 Nor 91324 530-H1
8800 Nor 91324 500-H4
10400 Nor 91326 500-H1
11400 Nor 91326 480-H7
AMIGO PL
4700 Tarz 91356 560-J3
AMIGO RD
100 Chat 91311 499-F6
AMIGOS AV
7500 DWNY 90242 705-G7
AMIGOS DR
3000 BURB 91504 533-E3
AMIGOS RD
14600 CHLS 91709 680-J5
AMIRANTE DR
2200 LA 90732 823-G6
AMISTAD AV
3900 PRV 90660 676-J2
AMOND LN
8300 LA 91304 529-F2
AMONDO CIR
5900 SIMI 93063 499-A1
AMOR RD
8100 LA 90046 592-J1
AMOR WK
29100 Cstc 91384 4459-B5
AMORE WY
- PMDL 93551 4195-A2
AMORET DR
9500 Tuj 91042 504-A5
AMORITA AV
2000 LHB 90631 708-H4
AMORITA PL
5600 WdHl 91367 560-C1
AMOROSA DR
1100 LAN 93535 4106-B1
AMOROSO CT
700 Ven 90291 671-J5
AMOROSO PL
700 Ven 90291 671-J5
1000 Ven 90291 672-A5
AMORY AV
1600 LACo 91770 636-D4
AMOS AV
5900 LKWD 90712 766-C1
AMOY ST
42900 LAN 93536 4105-D3
AMPERE AV
6600 NHol 91606 532-D6
7600 NHol 91605 532-D3
AMPHORA PL
- SCTA 91354 4460-F7
AMSDELL AV
8600 WHIT 90605 707-D2
9200 LACo 90605 707-C3
AMSLER ST
2400 TOR 90505 793-G3

AMUNDSEN BRANCH
- CLAR 91711 571-G2
AMY CT
43800 LAN 93535 4106-D1
AMY DR
600 WAL 91789 639-F6
AMY LN
- PRV 90660 676-G1
700 RBCH 90278 763-B2
38800 PMDL 93550 4286-E2
AMY WY
200 Top 90290 590-C6
AMY LYNN PL
- PMDL 93551 4194-H1
E ANA ST
2800 RDom 90221 765-B2
ANABAS AV
2300 LA 90732 823-H7
ANABEL AV
11200 LACo 90604 707-F6
ANABELLA ST
12500 NRWK 90650 736-J1
ANACAPA
- RHE 90274 822-J2
ANACAPA LN
- SCTA 91354 4460-G4
ANACAPA PL
800 WAL 91789 639-D6
2800 FUL 92835 738-F2
ANACAPA WY
- ANA 92801 767-J5
ANACAPA VIEW DR
31100 LACo 90265 626-H6
31100 MAL 90265 626-H6
ANACONDA ST
14400 WHIT 90603 707-F3
ANADA ST
4800 BALD 91706 598-B3
ANADALE DR
19500 Tarz 91356 560-F6
ANAHEIM PL
1400 LBCH 90804 796-B5
E ANAHEIM RD
5100 LBCH 90815 796-B5
E ANAHEIM ST
100 LBCH 90813 795-F6
100 Wilm 90744 794-F6
2000 LBCH 90804 795-F6
3000 Wilm 90744 795-A6
3900 LBCH 90804 796-A6
W ANAHEIM ST
100 LBCH 90813 795-B6
100 Wilm 90744 794-B6
1000 SPed 90731 794-B6
1200 Hrbr 90710 794-B6
1500 Hrbr 90710 793-J5
ANAHEIM WY
2800 Wilm 90744 794-J6
3000 Wilm 90744 795-A6
ANAHEIM AND PUENTE RD
700 INDS 91745 678-G2
ANAHURST RD
5200 SGAT 90280 705-E6
ANASTASIA AV
6200 SIMI 93063 499-B2
ANASTASIA DR
3900 Enc 91316 561-A6
ANASTASIA WY
- PMDL 93550 4286-C1
ANATA PL
37300 PMDL 93550 4286-A3
ANATOLA AV
7200 VanN 91406 531-B4
ANA VERDE DR
1000 LACo 93551 4285-F4
ANA VERDE MTWY
- PMDL 91390 (4284-E4
See Page 4283)
- PMDL 93551 (4284-G3
See Page 4283)
- PMDL 93551 4285-A2
ANCEP ST
16300 WHIT 90603 708-A4
ANCHOR AV
600 CRSN 90745 764-E6
2600 LA 90064 632-G6
22400 CRSN 90745 794-E1
ANCHOR LN
- SCTA 91355 4550-G2
ANCHOR RD
- SLB 90740 826-G4
ANCHOR WY
1800 SLB 90740 826-G4
7100 LBCH 90803 826-G2
ANCHORAGE RD
1200 Wilm 90744 824-G1
ANCHORAGE ST
- LA 90292 671-H7
ANCHOVY AV
1700 LA 90732 823-G7
3700 LA 90732 853-G1
ANCIENT TITLE CT
900 WAL 91789 639-F5
ANCONA DR
1300 LVRN 91750 600-F1
N ANCONA DR
200 LBCH 90803 826-C2
ANCOURT ST
9600 LACo 91007 596-J1
ANDALE AV
43600 LAN 93535 4106-A1
44000 LAN 93535 4016-A4

ANDALUCIA CT
5200 WHIT 90601 677-D4
ANDALUCIA DR
100 PMDL 93550 4195-J3
1400 WCOV 91791 639-C3
ANDALUSIA AV
600 LA 90065 594-J5
600 LA 90065 595-A5
1200 Ven 90291 671-H6
ANDASOL AV
4800 Enc 91316 561-C2
6500 VanN 91406 531-C4
7800 Nor 91325 531-B1
8800 Nor 91325 501-B5
10300 GrnH 91344 501-B1
11600 GrnH 91344 481-B7
ANDAZOLA CT
3100 LKWD 90712 765-H3
ANDENES DR
1300 GLDL 91208 534-G7
ANDERBERG AV
12100 DWNY 90242 705-J6
ANDERMATT PL
25900 SCTA 91355 4550-F5
ANDERMOTT DR
- SBdC 92397 (4652-F3
See Page 4651)
ANDERS AV
1200 HacH 91745 678-C3
ANDERSON AV
1600 COMP 90220 734-G7
3600 GLDL 91214 504-D7
6100 NLB 90805 765-E1
6200 LA 91214 504-C7
ANDERSON LN
25800 StvR 91381 4550-C7
ANDERSON PL
400 PAS 91103 535-G7
8100 PRM 90723 735-H3
ANDERSON ST
200 MANB 90266 732-G7
5700 VER 90058 674-H5
13900 PRM 90723 735-H3
16300 Surf 90743 826-H7
16300 SLB 90743 826-H7
N ANDERSON ST
100 Boyl 90033 634-J4
S ANDERSON ST
100 Boyl 90033 634-J4
600 LA 90023 634-J5
ANDERSON WY
9800 ELMN 91733 637-A2
S ANDERSON WY
400 SGBL 91776 596-D5
ANDERWOOD CT
400 POM 91768 600-H6
ANDES DR
- UPL 91784 571-G7
ANDES ST
8700 LACo 91776 596-G5
ANDES WK
6100 HiPk 90042 595-E4
ANDESITE CT
39400 PMDL 93551 4195-D5
ANDIRON DR
16400 LACo 90604 708-A6
ANDMARK AV
19000 CRSN 90746 764-H2
ANDORA AV
9600 Chat 91311 499-J4
10600 Chat 91311 500-A3
ANDORA DR
8000 OrCo 90638 737-J4
ANDORA PL
9800 Chat 91311 499-H5
ANDOVER AV
500 SDMS 91773 599-J3
6700 LAN 93536 4104-D5
ANDOVER DR
100 BURB 91504 533-G5
100 CLAR 91711 571-D7
ANDOVER LN
6700 Wch 90045 702-F1
ANDRADA DR
18500 RowH 91748 679-A5
ANDRAE CT
15500 LA 91343 501-G6
ANDRE LN
8000 LPMA 90623 767-C4
ANDREA CIR
18100 Nor 91325 501-A5
18100 Nor 91325 500-J5
ANDREA CIR N
18100 Nor 91325 500-J4
18100 Nor 91325 501-A4
ANDREA CT
3200 WCOV 91792 639-B7
ANDREA DR
- PMDL 93551 4195-E6
W ANDREA LN
- ARCD 91006 567-C2
ANDREO AV
1700 TOR 90501 763-H7
2700 TOR 90501 793-H1
25000 LMTA 90717 793-H4
ANDREW AV
11700 GrnH 91344 481-E7
ANDREW DR
1300 CLAR 91711 601-F1
5000 LPMA 90623 767-C3
43700 LAN 93536 4105-C1
ANDREWS DR
- FUL 92833 738-C5

STREET
Block City ZIP Pg-Grid

ANDREWS DR
1000 Bxby 90807 765-E5
ANDREWS RD
1600 ARCD 91007 597-C1
ANDREWS ST
11000 LACo 91733 637-B5
11000 SELM 91733 637-B5
11000 LACo 90660 637-B5
11000 SELM 90660 637-B5
ANDRITA ST
3000 LA 90065 594-F2
E ANDRIX ST
100 MONP 91755 636-B5
W ANDRIX ST
200 MONP 91754 636-A5
500 MONP 91754 635-J5
ANDROMEDA LN
30000 MAL 90265 627-B7
ANDROWE LN
- Nor 91326 480-D6
ANDRUS AV
5600 TOR 90503 763-A5
ANDRUSS PL
400 MTBL 90640 676-F1
ANDRY DR
14900 PRM 90723 735-J4
14900 PRM 90723 736-A4
ANDY AV
40400 LACo 93551 4193-G3
ANDY DR
12900 CRTS 90703 767-B1
ANDY ST
3200 NLB 90805 765-J2
4200 LKWD 90712 765-J2
4200 LKWD 90712 766-A2
6000 LKWD 90713 766-D2
10700 CRTS 90703 766-E1
12400 CRTS 90703 767-A1
ANELO AV
19000 CRSN 90248 764-C3
ANETA ST
11800 LA 90230 672-F6
12400 LACo 90066 672-F6
ANGELA AV
7200 CanP 91307 529-F5
ANGELA CT
1000 LAN 93535 4106-B2
ANGELA ST
2200 POM 91766 641-A6
2400 WCOV 91792 639-B7
ANGELAINE WY
17300 GrnH 91344 481-B5
ANGELA YVONNE AV
21400 SCTA 91350 4461-B7
ANGELCREST DR
1100 HacH 91745 678-A4
S ANGELCREST DR
1400 HacH 91745 678-B2
E ANGELENO AV
- BURB 91502 533-J6
100 SGBL 91776 596-E4
400 BURB 91501 533-J6
N ANGELENO AV
100 AZU 91702 568-J5
S ANGELENO AV
100 AZU 91702 568-J7
100 AZU 91702 598-J1
W ANGELENO AV
100 SGBL 91776 596-E4
900 BURB 91506 563-G1
ANGELENO PL
3100 PMDL 93551 4195-B4
ANGELES CREST CIR
1000 LCF 91011 535-B3
ANGELES CREST HWY Rt#-2
- LACo - (506-J1 See Page 505)
- LACo - 507-A1
- LACo - 4647-H5
- LACo - (4648-D3 See Page 4647)
- LACo - 4649-C3
- LACo - (4650-A2 See Page 4649)
- LACo - 4651-J1
- LACo - (4652-F2 See Page 4651)
- LACo - (4727-F4 See Page 4647)
- LACo 91011 505-B4
- LACo 92397 (4652-F2 See Page 4651)
4100 SBdC 92371 (4562-G6 See Page 4471)
4500 LCF 91011 535-B2
5800 LACo - 505-H1
5800 PAS 91011 505-B4
5800 PAS 91011 535-B2
7200 SBdC - (4562-G6 See Page 4471)
13700 SBdC - (4652-F2 See Page 4651)
17900 SBdC 92397 (4652-F2 See Page 4651)
21600 LACo - (4560-E7 See Page 4470)
21600 Valy 93563 (4560-E7 See Page 4470)
21600 Valy 93563 (4561-A7 See Page 4471)
24900 LACo - (4561-F7 See Page 4471)
ANGELES FOREST HWY Rt#-N3
- LACo - 505-F1
- PMDL 93550 (4556-E1 See Page 4466)
800 LACo - (4646-C7 See Page 4645)
800 LACo - (4725-G4 See Page 4645)
800 LACo - (4726-A1 See Page 4645)
1000 LACo - (4556-E7 See Page 4466)
31800 PMDL 93550 4466-B1
33100 Actn 93510 4376-B7
33100 PMDL 93550 4376-B7
ANGELES TRAIL WY
- LA 91342 482-E4
ANGELES VISTA BLVD
4100 LACo 90008 673-E3
4400 LACo 90043 673-D5
5600 LA 90043 673-D5
ANGELE TRUMPET CT
38600 PMDL 93550 4196-F7
ANGELICA PL
- SCTA 91354 4460-G4
ANGELINA PL
20300 WdHl 91364 560-D3
ANGELINA ST
1100 LA 90012 634-E2
1300 Echo 90026 634-E2
ANGELL ST
9000 DWNY 90242 736-A2
10500 NRWK 90650 736-G1
14100 LMRD 90638 737-D1
ANGELO CIR
10100 BelA 90077 592-C6
ANGELO DR
1000 BelA 90077 592-A2
1000 LA 90210 592-C6
1200 BHLS 90210 592-C6
2500 BelA 90077 592-B2
ANGELO PL
200 ARCD 91006 537-D7
N ANGELO WK
- LBCH 90803 826-D3
ANGELO VIEW DR
10100 LA 90210 592-C5
ANGELUS AV
1300 Echo 90026 594-C6
2100 RSMD 91770 636-G3
3400 GLDL 91208 534-G4
5500 LACo 91776 596-F4
5500 SGBL 91776 596-F4
ANGELUS PL
600 Ven 90291 671-J6
600 Ven 90291 672-A6
ANGLER LN
2900 OrCo 90720 796-H6
ANGLIA ST
24500 Llan 93544 4471-F5
ANGOLA AV
1200 LHH 90631 708-B3
ANGORA WY
- PMDL 93551 4195-F7
ANGOSTO DR
9300 WHIT 90603 707-J2
ANGOSTURA PL
4300 Tarz 91356 560-H5
ANGUS DR
2300 LVRN 91750 570-H4
ANGUS ST
2700 LA 90039 594-C3
ANGUSVILLE DR
24500 Llan 93544 4471-F5
ANILLO ST
11700 CRTS 90703 766-H3
ANISE AV
7700 Wch 90045 702-F1
ANITA
2400 LACo 90220 764-J1
2400 LACo 90220 765-A1
ANITA AV
3700 LACo 91107 566-H6
N ANITA AV
100 Brwd 90049 631-F3
S ANITA AV
100 Brwd 90049 631-F4
ANITA DR
- PAS 91105 565-E6
3600 BELL 90201 675-C7
ANITA LN
- ARCD 91006 567-A3
ANITA ST
300 RBCH 90277 762-J3
300 RBCH 90278 762-J3
600 MNRO 91016 567-F6
800 RBCH 90277 763-A3
800 RBCH 90278 763-A3
ANITA CREST DR
1800 ARCD 91006 567-C1
ANKARA CT
18200 Nor 91326 500-J1
ANKERTON ST
13200 LACo 90601 637-F6
ANN ST
9400 SFSP 90670 707-A3
E ANN ST
100 LA 90012 634-H2
W ANN ST
100 LA 90012 634-H2
ANNA LN
18200 Tarz 91356 560-J4
ANNA RD
700 SBdC 92372 (4472-B7 See Page 4471)
ANNADEL AV
1200 RowH 91748 679-D4
ANNAGLEN LN
900 LHB 90631 708-D6
ANNALEE AV
19000 CRSN 90746 764-F2
ANNALEE LN
20900 CRSN 90746 764-F5
ANNA MADRE ST
42600 LAN 93536 4105-D4
ANNA MARIA ST
300 Alta 91001 535-J3
300 Alta 91001 536-A3
ANNAN TER
800 HiPk 90042 565-C7
ANNAN WY
5900 HiPk 90042 565-D7
ANNANDALE DR
13600 SLB 90740 826-H1
ANNANDALE LN
300 AZU 91702 568-J4
ANNANDALE RD
- PAS 91105 565-E5
ANNANDALE TER
1300 PAS 91105 565-E6
ANNANDALE WY
- POM 91767 601-C6
ANNAPOLIS DR
100 CLAR 91711 601-D4
ANNAPOLIS RD
4100 LKWD 90712 766-A6
ANNAPOLIS WY
2700 LAN 93536 4105-C3
ANN ARBOR AV
2100 POM 91766 641-B6
ANN ARBOR RD
3900 LKWD 90712 765-J6
3900 LKWD 90712 766-A6
ANNE CIR
3100 HNTB 92649 826-J6
ANNE PL
2100 POM 91767 600-J5
ANNECY ST
- PMDL 93552 4287-E1
ANNE FREDA ST
17100 SCTA 91387 4552-B2
ANNELISE WY
- Saug 91350 4461-F6
ANNELLEN ST
15800 HacH 91745 678-B4
ANNES CIR
- LACo 91387 4551-J3
ANNETTA AV
8900 SGAT 90280 705-D6
10600 LYN 90262 705-D7
ANNETTE AV
- PMDL 93551 4195-E7
ANNETTE ST
3500 LA 90065 594-J4
ANNETTE JO CIR
27400 SCTA 91350 4461-B7
ANNEY LN
6200 Res 91335 531-A7
ANNHURST AV
1800 CLAR 91711 571-F7
ANNIE ST
37100 PMDL 93550 4286-E4
ANNIE OAKLEY RD
- HIDH 91302 559-C2
ANNISTON AV
4800 BALD 91706 598-E3
ANNITA DR
3000 GLDL 91206 565-A1
ANNMAE PL
- Saug 91350 4461-G6
ANNRITA AV
20600 TOR 90503 763-A5
ANOAKIA LN
700 ARCD 91006 567-A3
ANOCHECER AV
2200 CHLS 91709 680-J2
ANOKA DR
16000 PacP 90272 630-J4
ANOKA PL
1000 PacP 90272 630-J4
22000 WdHl 91364 560-A5
ANOLA ST
13000 LACo 90605 707-B3
14000 LACo 90604 707-D5
ANO NUEVO DR
1600 DBAR 91765 680-A4
ANSFORD ST
14500 HacH 91745 637-J7
14800 HacH 91745 638-A7
14800 HacH 91745 678-A1
ANSMITH AV
7100 PRM 90723 735-E5
7100 NLB 90805 735-E5
ANSON AV
14200 SFSP 90670 737-D3
ANSON WY
2100 WCOV 91792 638-H5
ANSTED DR
100 LPUE 91744 678-F1
ANTELO PL
15200 BelA 90077 561-H7
ANTELO RD
3100 BelA 90077 561-H7
3100 BelA 90077 591-H1
ANTELOPE CIR
2700 LAN 93536 3925-B4
ANTELOPE HWY
4800 LACo 93536 3924-H2
7000 LACo 93536 3834-B4
8000 LACo 93536 3833-J4
10000 PMDL 93591 4198-C1
ANTELOPE HWY Rt#-138
100 Llan 93544 4471-F1
100 SBdC 92372 4471-F1
200 SBdC 92372 (4472-A3 See Page 4471)
ANTELOPE RD
9700 LA 90210 592-D2
ANTELOPE ST
- Actn 93510 4375-E6
ANTELOPE VALLEY FRWY Rt#-14
- Actn - 4374-C5
- Actn - 4375-C6
- GrnH - 481-C1
- GrnH - 4641-C4
- LA - 481-C1
- LA - 4641-C4
- LACo - 3925-D7
- LACo - 4015-D6
- LACo - 4105-F2
- LACo - 4195-F2
- LACo - 4285-J1
- LACo - 4373-J7
- LACo - 4374-C5
- LACo - 4375-C6
- LACo - 4376-B1
- LACo - 4462-G7
- LACo - 4463-B5
- LACo - 4551-F7
- LACo - 4552-D1
- LACo - 4641-C4
- LAN - 4015-D6
- Nwhl - 4551-F7
- Nwhl - 4641-C4
- PMDL - 4105-F2
- PMDL - 4195-F2
- PMDL - 4285-J1
- PMDL - 4286-A6
- PMDL - 4376-B1
- SCTA - 4462-G7
- SCTA - 4551-F7
- SCTA - 4552-D1
- SCTA - 4641-C4
- StvR - 4641-C4
ANTELOPE WOODS RD
3000 Actn 93510 4375-A6
ANTELO VIEW DR
2900 BelA 90077 561-H7
2900 BelA 90077 591-H1
ANTE PERKOV WY
700 SPed 90731 824-C5
ANTEROS DR
12000 LACo 91390 4373-C6
ANTHONY CIR
7500 LPMA 90623 767-C3
8200 LA 90046 593-A3
ANTHONY DR
13700 CRTS 90703 737-C5
N ANTHONY LN
- LACo 91387 4552-B5
ANTHONY PL
9900 LA 90210 592-C4
12500 CHNO 91710 641-F6
ANTHONY RD
35100 LACo 91390 4374-A2
35400 LACo 91390 (4284-A6 See Page 4283)
35700 LACo 91390 4283-J5
ANTIBES CT
37800 PMDL 93552 4287-C2
ANTIBES DR
- PMDL 93552 4287-C1
ANTIETAM AV
- Brwd 90049 631-J2
- Brwd 90049 632-A3
ANTIGUA CT
4300 LYN 90262 735-G4
ANTIGUA DR
2800 BURB 91504 533-F3
ANTIGUA PL
6400 CanP 91307 529-C7
ANTIOCH RD
1800 CLAR 91711 571-C7
1800 CLAR 91711 601-C1
ANTIOCH ST
15200 PacP 90272 631-A5
ANTISANA PL
2800 HacH 91745 678-B5
ANTIUM RD
- PMDL 93550 4376-F7
- PMDL 93550 4466-F1
ANTLER DR
23200 DBAR 91765 680-B1
ANTOINETTE DR
1200 LHB 90631 708-C4
1200 LACo 90631 708-C4
ANTON CT
1900 WCOV 91792 638-J5
ANTON DR
34400 Litl 93543 4378-E3
ANTONIO AV
17100 CRTS 90703 737-D7
17900 CRTS 90703 767-D1
ANTONIO ST
3000 TOR 90503 763-E6
ANTRIM PL
600 LCF 91011 535-D6
ANTWERP AV
7900 Flor 90001 704-F2
ANTWERP ST
1500 Wbrk 90059 704-F7
9600 Wats 90002 704-F4
11100 LA 90059 704-F6
ANVERS AV
43600 LAN 93534 4105-G2
44100 LAN 93534 4015-G6
ANVIK ST
30000 Cstc 91384 4459-C3
ANVIL TREE LN
2500 HacH 91745 678-E5
ANZA AV
4400 TOR 90503 763-B5
22100 TOR 90505 763-C6
22600 TOR 90505 793-C2
ANZA DR
24800 SCTA 91355 4460-D7
24800 SCTA 91355 4550-D1
ANZA PL
500 LACo 93551 4285-H5
ANZAC AV
1600 COMP 90222 734-H2
9200 Wats 90002 704-H4
10700 LA 90059 704-H6
12300 Wbrk 90222 734-H1
ANZAC CIR
500 COMP 90220 734-H5
ANZEL CIR
19300 SCTA 91321 4551-F5
ANZIO CT
9500 CYP 90630 767-B7
ANZIO RD
11000 BelA 90077 591-H6
ANZIO WY
600 VeCo 91377 557-H1
25800 SCTA 91355 4550-F5
AOSTA CT
25900 SCTA 91355 4550-F6
APACHE
- Ago 91301 587-G4
3300 Top 90290 560-B7
APACHE AV
- THO 91362 557-A2
APACHE CT
27600 Cstc 91384 4459-H4
APACHE DR
7300 BPK 90620 767-F2
APACHE LN
- CRSN 90745 794-G1
APACHE TR
21400 Chat 91311 500-A1
28900 Ago 91301 588-B4
APACHE WY
20800 WAL 91789 639-G5
APACHE PLUME CT
2500 PMDL 93550 4286-F5
APACHE PLUME DR
36600 PMDL 93550 4286-F4
APACHE PLUME ST
- LAN 93536 4014-F7
APAM AV
- Cstc 91384 4459-C2
APARRI AV
30400 Cstc 91384 4459-C3
APEX AV
1700 Echo 90026 594-D5
1900 LA 90039 594-D5
APHRODITE
1300 WCOV 91790 638-D2
APHRODITE LN
- SCTA 91351 4551-G2
APOGEE CIR
- LA 90732 823-J7
APOLENA WY
- PMDL 93550 4286-F5
APOLLO
1400 WCOV 91790 638-D2
APOLLO AV
3500 PMDL 93550 4286-G2
10700 ELMN 91731 597-D4
APOLLO CT
- SLB 90740 826-G2
APOLLO DR
- SLB 90740 826-G2
2100 LA 90046 593-A2
APOLLO PL
15700 GAR 90249 733-G6
42800 LACo 93532 4102-F4
APOLLO ST
400 BREA 92821 709-A6
800 ELSG 90245 732-J4
APPALACHIAN
- CLAR 91711 571-F2
E APPALACHIAN CT
2800 THO 91362 557-C3
W APPALACHIAN CT
2700 THO 91362 557-B3
APPALACHIAN DR
- Cstc 91384 4459-F2
APPALOOSA
- Actn 93510 4375-E7
APPALOOSA DR
20600 WAL 91789 639-G7
43800 LAN 93536 4104-H1
APPALOOSA LN
- RHLS 90274 823-D2
N APPALOOSA LN
- VeCo 91307 529-B3
APPALOOSA RD
- SCTA 91387 4552-E4
APPALOOSA WY
- MTCL 91763 641-D1
9600 Sunl 91040 503-D4
APPERSON ST
6700 Tuj 91042 504-A4
7300 Tuj 91042 503-G4
7800 Sunl 91040 503-G4
APPIAN WY
- POM 91766 640-D3
1400 MTBL 90640 636-C6
1600 SMCA 90401 671-E3
8500 LA 90046 592-J3
25800 LMTA 90717 793-H5
E APPIAN WY
300 LBCH 90803 826-C1
4800 LBCH 90814 796-B7
4900 LBCH 90803 796-B7
APPLE
300 SDMS 91773 599-H3
APPLE AV
700 SBdC 92397 (4652-B1 See Page 4651)
2300 TOR 90501 763-G7
2500 TOR 90501 793-G1
17100 BLF 90706 736-C6
APPLE CT
- CRSN 90746 764-D3
APPLE DR
800 BREA 92821 709-C6
12300 CHNO 91710 641-J5
APPLE ST
5100 LA 90016 633-C6
24400 SCTA 91321 4640-H1
APPLE BLOSSOM CIR
100 BREA 92821 709-D7
APPLEBLOSSOM ST
16100 LPUE 91744 638-E7
16100 LPUE 91744 678-E1
APPLEBY ST
700 Ven 90291 671-J4
9100 DWNY 90240 706-D3
APPLE CREEK LN
2500 HacH 91745 678-E6
APPLECROSS AV
5500 LACo 91702 598-F1
APPLEDALE AV
7600 LACo 90606 677-A7
7800 LACo 90606 707-A1
APPLEFIELD LN
2400 Top 90290 629-H2
2600 LACo 90265 629-H2
APPLEGATE CT
- LACo 91390 4461-B3
APPLEGATE LN
14100 CHLS 91709 680-H3
APPLEGATE ST
- SBdC 91762 641-G2
APPLEGATE TER
9200 Chat 91311 499-F7
APPLE GROVE LN
- LA 91342 482-G7
APPLETON ST
3300 LA 90039 594-D1
E APPLETON ST
900 LBCH 90802 795-F7
1100 LBCH 90802 825-G1
2000 LBCH 90803 825-G1
APPLETON WY
1200 Ven 90291 671-J4
1300 Ven 90291 672-A4
1700 POM 91767 601-C6
12400 LA 90066 672-A3
APPLETREE CT
19100 CRTS 90703 766-H2
APPLE VISTA DR
6200 SBdC 92397 (4652-C1 See Page 4651)
APPLEWOOD CIR
2300 FUL 92833 738-C3
APPLEWOOD LN
28400 Cstc 91384 4369-E7
N APPLEWOOD LN
- LACo 91744 638-G4
APPOMATOX DR
- Brwd 90049 631-J3
- Brwd 90049 632-A3
APRA ST
100 COMP 90220 764-J1
2400 LACo 90220 764-J1
APRICOT AV
400 BREA 92821 709-C6
APRICOT DR
1700 PMDL 93550 4286-D3
APRICOT LN
9700 LA 90210 592-D3
23600 VeCo 93063 499-B4
APRICOT PL
28600 SCTA 91390 4460-J3
APRICOT WY
- CRSN 90746 764-E1
APRIL CT
1900 LMTA 90717 793-H3
APRIL LN
11500 Tuj 91042 503-J1
APRIL RD
2600 Ago 91301 588-D3
APRIL WY
3100 WCOV 91792 639-A7
3100 WCOV 91792 679-A1
APRILIA AV
1000 LACo 90220 734-E3
S APRILIA AV
100 COMP 90220 734-F4
APSLEY RD
700 PVE 90274 792-F6
APTOS AV
3000 HacH 91745 677-J5
APULIA CT
- Nor 91326 500-C1
AQAURIUS CIR
- PMDL 93552 4286-J2
AQUA PURA DR
600 LA 90012 594-G7
600 LA 90012 634-H1
AQUARIUM WY
100 LBCH 90802 825-D1
AQUARIUS AV
6300 AGRH 91301 558-B3
AQUARIUS ST
1700 LBCH 90810 795-A3
AQUA VERDE CIR
2700 BelA 90077 591-G2
AQUA VERDE DR
15500 BelA 90077 591-G2
AQUA VISTA DR
3400 RPV 90275 823-E6
AQUA VISTA ST
10700 LA 91602 563-A5
11000 LA 91602 562-H5
11400 LA 91604 562-H5
AQUEDUCT AV
4700 Enc 91436 561-G4
4800 Shrm 91403 561-G4
6400 VanN 91406 531-G3
8400 LA 91343 531-G2
8700 LA 91343 501-G5
10200 GrnH 91344 501-G1
AQUINAS AV
2100 CLAR 91711 571-E7
ARABELLA DR
13100 CRTS 90703 767-B1
ARABELLA LN
13000 CRTS 90703 767-B1
ARABELLA PL
10700 CRTS 90703 766-E1
12900 CRTS 90703 767-B1
ARABELLA ST
4300 LKWD 90712 766-A2
5900 LKWD 90713 766-D1
12600 CRTS 90703 767-A1
E ARABELLA ST
3500 NLB 90805 765-J2
ARABIAN CT
- PMDL 93551 4195-A5
ARABIAN LN
600 WAL 91789 639-H5
ARABIAN PL
- MTCL 91763 641-D1
ARABIAN WY
- Actn 93510 4375-D6
ARABIC ST
1300 Wilm 90744 794-C7
ARABY AV
13800 NRWK 90650 736-J2
ARAGON AV
700 LA 90065 594-J5
ARAGON CIR
6900 BPK 90620 767-F2
ARAGON CT
300 Ven 90291 671-H6
ARAGON PL
3900 FUL 92835 738-G1
ARAGON RD
3300 SBdC 92371 (4472-H2 See Page 4471)
ARALIA DR
1700 POM 91766 640-H4
12300 CHNO 91710 641-J6
ARALIA RD
4100 Alta 91001 535-F3
ARAMA AV
6900 Tuj 91042 504-A6
ARAMAC AV
1500 LACo 91770 636-E4
ARANBE AV
500 COMP 90220 734-H5
13000 Wbrk 90222 734-H5
N ARANBE AV
100 COMP 90220 734-H4
1100 COMP 90222 734-H4
1600 Wbrk 90222 734-H4
S ARANBE AV
500 COMP 90220 734-H2
13100 Wbrk 90222 734-H2
ARANMOOR AV
900 THO 91361 557-A5
ARANZA DR
14300 LMRD 90638 737-H3
ARAPAHO AV
2300 THO 91362 557-A2
ARAPAHO WY
1000 SDMS 91773 570-C7
ARAPAHOE ST
900 LA 90006 634-B5
1900 LA 90007 634-B6
ARAPAHOE TR
21400 Chat 91311 500-A1
ARARAT ST
14700 LA 91342 481-J2
ARATINA ST
900 HiPk 90042 595-F1
1000 HiPk 90042 565-F7
ARAVACA DR
15600 PRM 90723 735-E5
ARBA ST
18600 RowH 91748 709-B1
ARBELA DR
15700 LHH 90631 707-J3
15700 WHIT 90603 707-J2
ARBOL DR
3000 FUL 92835 738-G2
ARBOL LN
6400 VeCo 93063 499-C4
ARBOL ST
800 LA 90065 595-A3
ARBOLADA DR
200 ARCD 91006 567-B3
ARBOLADA LN
- PMDL 93550 4286-F5
ARBOLADA RD
3600 LFlz 90027 594-C2
ARBOLADO CT
- MANB 90266 732-G6
ARBOLADO DR
500 FUL 92835 738-H2
ARBOLEDA DR
- PAS 91106 566-A6
ARBOLEDA ST
3700 LACo 91107 566-H4
ARBOLEDA WY
500 POM 91767 641-B1
N ARBOLES CT
100 SPed 90731 824-C4
S ARBOLES CT
100 SPed 90731 824-C5
ARBOLES DR
1500 GLDL 91207 564-G1
ARBOLES ST
500 MONP 91754 635-H3
ARBOLITA DR
1000 LHB 90631 708-G4
ARBOR CIR
800 LVRN 91750 600-D3
2000 BREA 92821 709-D7
12000 CHNO 91710 641-E5
ARBOR CT
21800 WAL 91789 639-J5
W ARBOR CT
- COV 91723 599-B5
ARBOR DR
1600 GLDL 91202 564-D1
ARBOR LN
- HAW 90250 733-F4
- StvR 91381 4640-B2
9400 CYP 90630 767-C7
37400 PMDL 93552 4287-B3
ARBOR PL
- SCTA 91354 4460-E7
12200 LA 90044 734-B1
14100 CRTS 90703 737-D6
ARBOR RD
2700 LKWD 90712 765-H4
3900 LKWD 90712 766-C4
4700 LKWD 90713 766-C4
E ARBOR RD
4300 LBCH 90808 766-A4
ARBOR ST
400 PAS 91105 565-G5
E ARBOR ST
300 NLB 90805 765-D4
W ARBOR ST
- NLB 90805 765-D4
ARBOR WY
- POM 91767 601-A3
44900 LAN 93535 4016-B5
ARBOR DELL PL
1200 Eagl 90041 565-C4
ARBOR DELL RD
1100 Eagl 90041 565-C5
ARBOR HILL WY
- SCTA 91350 4550-H5
ARBOR PINES
12400 ELMN 91732 637-F1
ARBOR RIDGE RD
19700 WAL 91789 639-D4
E ARBOR VITAE ST
100 ING 90301 703-D4
W ARBOR VITAE ST
100 ING 90301 703-B4
1200 ING 90301 702-J4
2200 ING 90305 703-G3
5200 Wch 90045 703-B4
5500 Wch 90045 702-J4
ARBRAMAR AV
400 PacP 90272 630-J6
ARBUCKLE AV
10800 MsnH 91345 501-J2
ARBUCKLE WY
1800 LAN 93534 4015-E4
ARBURY DR
1500 DBAR 91765 680-A4
ARBUTUS AV
6000 HNTP 90255 675-A6
ARBUTUS DR
2400 Brwd 90049 591-D7
E ARBUTUS ST
200 COMP 90220 734-J4
200 COMP 90220 735-A4
300 COMP 90221 735-A4
W ARBUTUS ST
300 COMP 90220 734-G4
ARBY DR
9500 LA 90210 592-C1
S ARC WY
800 ANA 92804 767-G7
ARCADE PL
400 GLDL 91206 565-A4
ARCADIA AV
300 LBCH 90803 826-B1
500 ARCD 91007 567-A7
700 ARCD 91007 566-J7
1100 LACo 91775 566-G7
E ARCADIA AV
1100 LACo 91775 566-H7
ARCADIA CT
1300 LBCH 90813 795-F5
ARCADIA DR
300 SPed 90731 824-A5
ARCADIA ST
100 LA 90012 634-G3
24300 SCTA 91321 4640-H1
24500 SCTA 91355 4640-H1
ARCADIA TER
- SMCA 90401 671-E3
ARCADIA WY
400 WAL 91789 679-C1
ARCANA CT
100 POM 91767 600-J2
ARCANA RD
20900 WdHl 91364 560-C5
ARCAY AV
27500 SCTA 91351 4551-H2
ARCDALE AV
1700 RowH 91748 679-D6
ARCH DR
4000 LA 91604 562-J5
4000 LA 91604 563-A5
ARCH PL
500 GLDL 91206 565-A4
ARCH ST
23900 SCTA 91321 4641-A1
24600 SCTA 91321 4550-J7
ARCHAIL CT
- PMDL 93552 4287-E1
ARCHCREST DR
5500 LACo 90043 673-C6
ARCHDALE RD
3900 Enc 91436 561-F6
ARCHERY WY
- WLKV 91361 587-D1
ARCHES LN
- SCTA 91387 4462-H6
ARCHIBALD AV
4800 RCUC 91737 (542-J7 See Page 511)
4800 SBdC 91737 (542-J7 See Page 511)
21200 CRSN 90745 764-C6
22900 CRSN 90745 794-C1
ARCHWAY DR
10800 LACo 90604 707-F6
ARCHWOOD AV
500 BREA 92821 708-H6
ARCHWOOD CT
500 BREA 92821 708-H6
ARCHWOOD DR
1300 POM 91766 640-G4
ARCHWOOD LN
- VanN 91406 531-F6
ARCHWOOD PL
400 Alta 91001 535-F6
11100 NHol 91606 532-J6
11100 NHol 91606 533-A5
ARCHWOOD ST
10900 NHol 91606 533-A6
11100 NHol 91606 532-E6
13200 VanN 91401 532-D6
13700 VanN 91405 532-A6
14500 VanN 91405 531-H6
15300 VanN 91406 531-C6
17900 Res 91335 531-A6
18900 Res 91335 530-F6
19700 Win 91306 530-C6
22100 CanP 91303 529-J6
22600 CanP 91307 529-D6
ARCHWOOD WY
- PMDL 93552 4287-D1
43200 LAN 93536 4105-C3
S ARCIERO DR
600 LACo 90601 637-G5
600 LACo 91746 637-G5
ARCO PL
1400 PVE 90274 792-H6
ARCOLA AV
4200 LA 91602 563-C3
4800 NHol 91601 563-C3
7600 SunV 91352 533-C3
ARCOS DR
21400 WdHl 91364 560-A4
ARCTIC CIR
13000 SFSP 90670 737-B4
ARCTURUS AV
12900 GAR 90249 733-G3
16000 GAR 90247 733-G6
ARCY LN
10900 SELM 91733 637-B5
ARDARA PL
4400 LCF 91011 535-A3
ARDATH AV
10900 ING 90303 703-G6
11600 HAW 90250 703-G7
11600 HAW 90303 703-G7
12900 GAR 90249 733-G2
16000 GAR 90247 733-G6
16200 TOR 90247 733-G6
16200 TOR 90504 733-G6
17300 TOR 90504 763-G1
ARD EEVIN AV
1500 GLDL 91202 564-C1
1700 GLDL 91202 534-C7
ARDELL RD
8900 PRV 90660 676-G2
ARDEMORE DR
2200 FUL 92833 738-D3
ARDEN AV
100 GLDL 91203 564-D3
600 GLDL 91202 564-C3
5000 LACo 91724 599-G3
N ARDEN BLVD
100 LA 90004 593-F7
100 LA 90004 633-F1
S ARDEN BLVD
100 LA 90004 633-F2
300 LA 90020 633-F2
600 LA 90005 633-F2
600 LA 90010 633-F2
ARDEN DR
3700 ELMN 91731 597-B6
4800 ELMN 91780 597-B4
4800 TEML 91780 597-B4
N ARDEN DR
500 BHLS 90210 592-G7
ARDEN PL
600 LA 90004 593-F7
ARDEN RD
600 PAS 91106 566-A6
1100 PAS 91125 566-A6
1100 PAS 91126 566-A6
ARDEN WY
4600 ELMN 91731 597-C5
ARDENDALE AV
9400 LACo 91007 596-J1
E ARDENDALE AV
8600 LACo 91775 596-G1
ARDENEL AV
5100 TEML 91780 597-A4
ARDENWOOD AV
1800 SIMI 93063 499-D2
E ARDENWOOD AV
6500 SIMI 93063 499-C2
N ARDENWOOD CIR
6600 SIMI 93063 499-D2
ARDILLA AV
300 LPUE 91746 638-A3
900 LACo 91746 638-B2
3400 BALD 91706 598-D6
N ARDILLA AV
100 WCOV 91790 598-D7
100 BALD 91706 598-D7
S ARDILLA AV
1200 WCOV 91790 638-C1
ARDINE ST
4400 SGAT 90280 705-D3
4600 CDHY 90201 705-D3
9500 DWNY 90241 706-D6
ARDIS AV
12600 DWNY 90242 736-B2
13400 BLF 90706 736-B3
ARDITA DR
16500 WHIT 90603 708-A3
ARDMORE AV
- HMB 90254 762-G1
1400 GLDL 91202 564-C2
2500 HMB 90254 732-G7
2700 SGAT 90280 704-J2
2800 SGAT 90280 705-A3
16100 BLF 90706 736-B7
17800 BLF 90706 766-B1
N ARDMORE AV
100 LA 90004 633-J1
100 MANB 90266 732-G5
200 LA 90004 593-J7
700 LA 90029 593-J5
S ARDMORE AV
100 LA 90004 633-J2
100 MANB 90266 732-G7
300 LA 90020 633-J2
600 LA 90005 633-J2
600 LA 90010 633-J2
900 LA 90006 633-J4
ARDMORE CT
- PMDL 93552 4287-E2
800 SDMS 91773 599-J4
ARDMORE DR
100 SGBL 91775 596-D3
100 SGBL 91776 596-D3
ARDMORE RD
2700 PAS 91108 596-A1
2700 SMRO 91108 596-A1
ARDSHEAL DR
2100 LHH 90631 708-C1
2600 LHH 90631 678-C7
ARDSLEY DR
4800 TEML 91780 597-A5
6800 LACo 91007 566-J7
6800 LACo 91007 596-J1
ARDSLEY PL
3400 Enc 91436 561-D7
ARDWICK ST
22800 WdHl 91364 559-G5
AREA I RD
23600 VeCo 93063 499-A7
23600 VeCo 93063 529-A1
ARENA DR
- Cstc 91384 4369-G7
ARENA RD
8900 SBdC 92372 (4562-C1 See Page 4471)
9300 SBdC 92372 (4472-C1 See Page 4471)
ARENA ST
100 ELSG 90245 732-F2

STREET — Block City ZIP Pg-Grid

ARENTH AV
17100 INDS 91745 678-H2
17200 INDS 91748 678-H2
17200 INDS 91748 679-A3
19300 RowH 91748 679-C3
ARES ST
10500 LACo 91390 4373-F5
ARGAN AV
11200 LA 90230 672-F4
ARGENTI CT
- Saug 91350 4461-F6
ARGENTINA CIR
7200 BPK 90620 767-D2
ARGENTINE RD
4500 WdHl 91364 560-A5
ARGO CIR
4700 LVRN 91750 570-D6
ARGO PL
9000 RSMD 91770 636-H1
ARGONAUT ST
100 PdlR 90293 702-A3
ARGONIA PL
1000 WAL 91789 639-D5
ARGONNE AV
- Brwd 90049 631-J3
- LBCH 90803 826-B1
300 LBCH 90814 826-B1
300 LBCH 90814 796-B5
1300 LBCH 90804 796-B5
2200 LBCH 90815 796-B3
ARGOS ST
5300 AGRH 91301 558-B5
ARGOSY WY
2400 LA 90068 593-G2
ARGUS DR
4800 Eagl 90041 565-B5
ARGYLE
40300 PMDL 93551 4195-A3
ARGYLE AV
2100 LA 90068 593-F3
N ARGYLE AV
1500 Hlwd 90028 593-F4
1900 LA 90068 593-F3
ARGYLE DR
4600 BPK 90621 737-J4
11600 OrCo 90720 796-H4
ARGYLE WY
4900 BPK 90621 737-J5
ARI LN
2000 Brwd 90049 591-E4
ARIAN
38800 PMDL 93551 4195-F6
ARICA AV
4100 RSMD 91770 596-J6
ARIEL AV
7200 Res 91335 530-H4
W ARIEL PL
3300 ANA 92804 767-G6
ARIELLA DR
24800 CALB 91302 559-C6
ARIELLE LN
- Chat 91311 499-J3
ARIES ST
28700 AGRH 91301 558-B3
ARILLO ST
13000 LACo 91746 637-G3
ARIMO LN
1400 BelA 90077 592-B5
ARIOUS WY
- LAN 93536 4015-B5
ARISTO PL
- PMDL 93550 4286-H5
12500 GrnH 91344 481-B5
ARISTO ST
1300 GLDL 91201 564-A3
ARIZONA
1800 WCOV 91792 678-J1
ARIZONA AV
100 SMCA 90401 671-E2
1200 SMCA 90404 671-E2
1600 SMCA 90404 631-G6
6500 Wch 90045 672-G7
6900 Wch 90045 702-G1
10800 CULC 90232 672-F2
11700 SGAT 90280 735-G1
N ARIZONA AV
100 ELA 90022 635-G5
S ARIZONA AV
100 ELA 90022 635-G6
800 ELA 90022 675-F1
ARIZONA CIR
6300 Wch 90045 672-G7
ARIZONA PL
6300 Wch 90045 672-G7
ARIZONA PL N
2900 SMCA 90404 631-G6
ARIZONA PL S
2600 SMCA 90404 631-G6
ARIZONA ST
6500 BPK 90621 767-J1
ARKANSAS ST
9400 BLF 90706 736-B6
11600 ART 90701 736-G6
ARKELL DR
500 BHLS 90210 592-G3
ARKLEY DR
1100 DBAR 91789 679-F3
ARKSEY AV
33500 Actn 93510 4375-H6
34500 LACo 93551 4375-H4
ARLAND AV
1500 LACo 91770 636-F4

ARLEE AV
9100 SFSP 90670 706-H3
11000 NRWK 90650 706-H6
12300 NRWK 90650 736-H1
ARLEE PL
13300 LA 91342 482-C1
ARLEN DR
23500 SCTA 91321 4640-H2
ARLENE TER
8700 LA 90046 592-H2
ARLETA AV
8300 SunV 91352 532-E1
8800 SunV 91352 502-D6
8800 Pcma 91331 502-A4
10400 MsnH 91345 502-A3
10600 MsnH 91345 501-J2
E ARLIGHT ST
100 MONP 91755 636-B5
W ARLIGHT ST
200 MONP 91754 636-A5
500 MONP 91754 635-J5
ARLINE AV
17900 ART 90701 766-H1
18800 CRTS 90703 766-H2
20300 LKWD 90715 766-H4
21700 HGDN 90716 766-H6
ARLINE ST
2400 WCOV 91792 639-B7
29700 CynC 91351 4462-B5
ARLINGTON AV
800 TOR 90501 763-G4
1000 LA 90019 633-G6
1500 GLDL 91208 534-G4
1900 LA 90018 633-G6
2500 TOR 90501 793-G3
2900 FUL 92835 738-J2
3400 LA 90018 673-G3
3800 LA 90008 673-G3
4400 LA 90043 673-G5
4500 LYN 90262 735-D3
23900 LMTA 90717 793-G3
W ARLINGTON AV
1400 LBCH 90810 765-B7
2300 LBCH 90810 764-J7
ARLINGTON CT
37600 PMDL 93552 4287-C2
ARLINGTON DR
- PAS 91105 565-G7
100 CLAR 91711 600-J1
3800 PRV 90660 676-H1
ARLINGTON RD
- GLDL 91205 564-F7
- LA 90065 564-F7
3700 LA 90065 594-G1
ARLINGTON ST
30300 Cstc 91384 4459-A6
E ARLINGTON ST
900 COMP 90221 735-B2
W ARLINGTON ST
1700 LBCH 90810 765-A7
ARLISTA ST
300 LACo 91746 637-H4
ARLOTTE AV
3000 LBCH 90808 796-H1
ARMA ST
8500 PRV 90660 676-G2
ARMACOST AV
1200 WLA 90025 631-H5
2000 WLA 90025 632-A7
2400 LA 90064 632-A7
2500 LA 90064 672-B1
ARMADA DR
1000 PAS 91103 565-F1
ARMADA RD
300 ARCD 91007 567-A6
ARMADALE AV
1300 HiPk 90042 595-A1
ARMAGA SPRING RD
5900 RPV 90275 822-J1
ARMANDO DR
600 Bxby 90807 765-E6
N ARMEL DR
100 COV 91722 599-A3
4800 LACo 91722 599-A3
S ARMEL DR
100 COV 91722 599-A5
500 COV 91723 599-A6
500 WCOV 91791 599-A6
ARMELINA DR
14300 LMRD 90638 737-E3
ARMFIELD AV
39500 PMDL 93551 4195-G5
ARMIDA DR
5200 WdHl 91364 560-D3
ARMIJO ST
- FUL 92833 738-D5
200 LACo 91016 567-G7
W ARMIJO ST
100 LACo 91016 567-F7
ARMINGTON AV
1400 HacH 91745 678-C3
ARMINTA ST
10100 SunV 91352 533-A3
11000 SunV 91352 532-J3
11400 NHol 91605 532-D3
14500 PanC 91402 532-A3
14500 PanC 91402 531-J3
15700 VanN 91406 531-C3
17400 Nor 91325 531-A3
17700 Res 91335 531-A3
18100 Res 91335 530-F3
19700 Win 91306 530-C3
20900 LA 91304 530-A3

ARMINTA ST
22900 LA 91304 529-E3
ARMITAGE AV
3700 ING 90305 703-E3
ARMITAGE ST
1600 Echo 90026 594-E6
ARMITOS PL
300 DBAR 91765 640-D7
600 DBAR 91765 680-D1
ARMLEY AV
9100 WHIT 90603 707-F3
9600 LACo 90604 707-E4
N ARMONA CT
100 SPed 90731 824-C4
S ARMONA CT
100 SPed 90731 824-C5
ARMOUR AV
3600 LA 90032 595-D6
ARMOUR CT
- LHB 90631 738-C2
ARMOUR LN
1400 RBCH 90278 762-J3
1800 RBCH 90278 763-B2
ARMOUR PL
2100 GLDL 91208 534-H7
ARMOUR RD
8000 WHIT 90602 707-D1
ARMOUR ST
2000 POM 91768 600-H5
ARMOURDALE AV
3000 LBCH 90808 796-H1
3400 LBCH 90808 766-H7
ARMSDALE AV
11700 LMRD 90638 707-F7
11900 LACo 90604 707-F7
ARMSLEY SQ
1300 ONT 91762 601-H5
ARMSLEY ST
5400 MTCL 91763 601-G5
ARMSTEAD LN
1300 FUL 92833 738-E3
ARMSTEAD ST
600 GLDR 91740 599-C1
900 AZU 91702 599-B1
16000 GrnH 91344 481-C7
18000 LACo 91702 599-A1
ARMSTRONG AV
2400 LA 90039 594-D3
ARMSTRONG CIR
25700 StvR 91381 4550-C7
ARMSTRONG DR
- BREA 92821 708-J5
- FUL 92833 738-C6
- PMDL 93552 4287-D1
2400 CLAR 91711 571-D6
S ARMSTRONG WY
- UPL 91786 601-J4
ARNAUD ST
12100 LACo 93536 4013-B4
N ARNAZ DR
100 BHLS 90211 632-J2
S ARNAZ DR
100 BHLS 90211 632-J2
300 LA 90048 632-J1
ARNEL PL
10600 Chat 91311 500-D3
ARNELL PL
3800 GLDL 91214 504-D4
ARNETT ST
7300 DWNY 90241 705-H4
7800 DWNY 90241 706-A5
ARNICA AV
1500 LAN 93535 4016-C7
ARNIE AV
8700 RSMD 91770 596-G7
ARNO DR
1100 SMAD 91024 567-C1
ARNO WY
200 PacP 90272 630-H6
ARNOLD AV
- LACo 90073 631-H3
ARNOLD DR
2500 PMDL 93550 4286-E6
ARNOLD WY
- FUL 92833 738-D6
6200 BPK 90620 767-E2
ARNOLDALE ST
- PMDL 93591 4108-C7
- PMDL 93591 4198-B1
ARNOLD CENTER RD
21700 CRSN 90810 764-J6
ARNWOOD RD
10200 LA 91342 503-B1
AROMA DR
1600 WCOV 91791 639-A4
1900 WCOV 91791 638-J4
E AROMA DR
1800 WCOV 91791 638-J4
2000 WCOV 91791 639-A3
AROMITAS CIR
500 PVE 90274 792-G4
ARORA WY
12100 LACo 91390 4373-C5
AROVISTA AV
200 BREA 92821 708-J7
300 BREA 92821 738-J1
AROVISTA CIR
200 BREA 92821 708-J7
ARRAMBIDE DR
5400 WHIT 90601 677-C4
ARRASTRE-ALISO CUT-OFF
- Actn 93510 4465-C7

ARRASTRE-ALISO CUT-OFF
- Actn 93510 (4555-C1 See Page 4466)
ARRASTRE CANYON RD
30000 Actn 93510 4465-A5
ARREY AV
13200 NRWK 90650 737-B2
ARREZZO CT
- PMDL 93550 4286-F5
ARRIBA DR
4600 Tarz 91356 560-H4
22500 SCTA 91350 4460-J7
S ARRIBA DR
1400 MONP 91754 635-H3
ARRINGTON AV
8100 PRV 90660 706-D2
8800 DWNY 90240 706-D2
10500 DWNY 90241 706-C5
ARRIOLA AV
27300 SCTA 91350 4461-A7
ARROUES DR
700 FUL 92835 738-J2
ARROW HWY
- LACo 91702 598-F2
400 POM 91767 600-F3
400 POM 91768 600-F3
500 IRW 91706 597-J2
900 IRW 91706 598-A1
1300 LVRN 91750 600-F3
4500 CLAR 91711 601-F4
4500 MTCL 91763 601-F4
14000 BALD 91706 598-A1
E ARROW HWY
- AZU 91722 599-B2
100 CLAR 91711 601-D4
100 POM 91767 600-C3
100 POM 91767 601-A4
100 SDMS 91773 600-C3
100 GLDR 91740 599-D2
100 COV 91722 599-B2
400 LVRN 91750 600-C3
900 COV 91724 599-D2
16500 LACo 91722 598-G2
16500 AZU 91702 598-G2
16600 LACo 91702 598-G2
17100 COV 91722 598-G2
18800 LACo 91722 599-B2
19600 LACo 91724 599-D2
W ARROW HWY
- AZU 91702 598-J2
- LACo 91702 598-J2
100 CLAR 91711 601-C4
100 POM 91767 600-J4
100 SDMS 91773 600-A2
100 COV 91722 599-A2
500 AZU 91702 599-A2
700 COV 91722 598-J2
900 SDMS 91773 599-J2
900 POM 91767 601-C4
1000 UPL 91786 601-J3
ARROW LN
- Litl 93543 4468-B2
ARROWAY AV
5000 LACo 91724 599-E3
ARROW GRAND CIR
600 COV 91722 599-C3
ARROWHEAD AV
5400 BPK 90621 737-J5
ARROWHEAD CIR
3900 THO 91362 557-C1
ARROWHEAD CT
- BqtC 91354 4460-E6
3200 Alta 91001 536-A4
39300 PMDL 93551 4195-E5
ARROWHEAD DR
2100 SBdC 92372 (4562-E2 See Page 4471)
2500 SBdC 92371 (4562-G2 See Page 4471)
3000 LA 90068 593-F1
3100 LA 90068 563-F7
ARROWHEAD LN
- RHE 90274 822-J1
ARROWHEAD PL
6300 LA 90068 593-F1
ARROWMILL AV
2400 CMRC 90023 675-E3
ARROWOOD DR
9600 LA 90210 592-F3
ARROWOOD ST
10600 TEML 91780 597-C4
ARROW POINT DR
31400 Cstc 91384 4369-G7
ARROWROCK DR
42200 LACo 93532 4102-F4
ARROWROOT LN
6100 RPV 90275 822-J4
W ARROW ROUTE
1600 UPL 91786 601-F3
2400 CLAR 91711 601-F3
ARROW WOOD DR
1000 BREA 92821 709-A5
ARROYO AV
600 SFER 91340 482-C7
1300 POM 91768 600-F7
1400 POM 91768 640-E1
ARROYO BLVD
600 PAS 91105 565-F1
800 PAS 91103 565-F1
N ARROYO BLVD
- PAS 91105 565-F3
100 PAS 91103 565-F3

N ARROYO BLVD
1500 PAS 91103 535-F7
2100 Alta 91001 535-F6
2800 PAS 91011 535-F4
S ARROYO BLVD
- PAS 91105 565-F6
1200 PAS 91105 595-F1
ARROYO CIR
- PVE 90274 792-G4
7600 LPMA 90623 767-B3
ARROYO CT
- Cstc 91384 4459-G2
ARROYO DR
- RPV 90275 793-H7
- RPV 90275 823-H1
- PAS 91105 565-G4
100 LACo 91770 636-F5
100 MTBL 90640 636-E4
100 PAS 91103 565-G4
200 SPAS 91030 595-F2
1000 FUL 92833 738-E6
1100 MONP 91755 636-E4
2100 POM 91768 640-D1
5500 HiPk 90042 595-E2
8000 MTBL 91770 636-F5
8200 RSMD 91770 636-F5
10800 LACo 90604 707-F6
11600 LMRD 90638 707-F6
N ARROYO DR
300 SGBL 91775 596-C3
S ARROYO DR
200 SGBL 91776 596-D4
ARROYO LN
- SGBL 91775 596-C3
12800 NRWK 90650 737-A1
N ARROYO PKWY
- PAS 91103 565-H4
S ARROYO PKWY Rt#-110
- PAS 91105 565-J7
ARROYO PL
800 FUL 92833 738-E6
ARROYO SQ
500 SPAS 91030 595-F1
ARROYO ST
12700 LA 91342 482-D6
12900 LA 91340 482-D6
12900 SFER 91340 482-D6
ARROYO TER
100 PAS 91103 565-F4
900 ALH 91801 596-C4
ARROYO WK
- LCF 91011 535-C2
ARROYO CROSSING DR
- WAL 91789 639-D4
ARROYO GLEN ST
6200 HiPk 90042 595-D2
ARROYO OAK LN
29000 Cstc 91384 4459-C5
ARROYO OAKS DR
500 THO 91362 557-C2
ARROYO PARK DR
1000 POM 91768 600-F7
23800 SCTA 91355 4550-F5
ARROYO SECO
3200 LA 90065 594-J6
3200 LA 90065 595-A6
ARROYO SECO AV
3400 LA 90065 595-A6
ARROYO SECO RD
- LACo - 505-D6
- LACo - 535-D1
3900 PAS 91011 535-D1
ARROYO SUMMIT DR
5400 LCF 91011 535-C2
ARROYO VERDE RD
1000 SPAS 91030 595-E2
ARROYO VERDE WY
1000 SPAS 91030 595-F3
ARROYO VIEW DR
1400 PAS 91103 565-E1
ARROYO VISTA DR
100 SMCA 90402 631-C7
ARROYO VISTA PL
400 SPAS 91030 595-F1
ARROYO WILLOW LN
4100 CALB 91301 558-G7
ART PL
2100 WCOV 91792 639-A7
ART ST
10500 Sunl 91040 503-A5
10900 SunV 91352 502-J5
10900 SunV 91352 503-A5
12100 SunV 91352 532-F1
ART CENTER DR
- GLDR 91741 569-B6
ARTEIQUE RD
1600 Top 90290 590-C2
ARTEMIS PL
2200 LA 90064 632-A6
ARTEMUS ST
1300 Boyl 90033 634-J5
ARTESIA AV
2300 FUL 92833 738-A7
8400 BPK 90621 738-A7
ARTESIA BLVD
- TOR 90278 763-A1
900 RBCH 90278 762-H1
1100 HMB 90254 762-H1
1100 HMB 90266 762-H1
1100 MANB 90266 762-H1
1900 RBCH 90278 763-A1
2200 TOR 90504 733-H7

ARTESIA BLVD
2200 TOR 90504 763-A1
4500 LNDL 90260 763-A1
6000 BPK 90620 737-F7
7000 BPK 90621 737-H7
8200 BPK 90621 738-A7
8500 BLF 90706 735-J7
8700 BLF 90706 736-A7
10600 CRTS 90703 736-F7
11400 ART 90701 736-F7
11500 LMRD 90638 737-F7
12500 CRTS 90703 737-B7
E ARTESIA BLVD
100 COMP 90220 735-B7
100 NLB 90805 735-C7
300 COMP 90221 735-B7
600 CRSN 90746 734-E7
W ARTESIA BLVD
- LA 90247 734-A7
- LA 90248 734-A7
100 COMP 90220 735-B7
100 NLB 90805 735-B7
100 COMP 90220 734-G7
200 COMP 90221 735-B7
1000 GAR 90247 734-A7
1000 GAR 90248 734-A7
1300 GAR 90248 733-J7
1300 GAR 90247 733-J7
1800 TOR 90504 733-J7
2700 TOR 90504 763-G1
ARTESIA CT
- LAN 93535 4106-F3
17300 BLF 90706 736-C7
ARTESIA FRWY Rt#-91
- ART - 736-A6
- BLF - 735-G7
- BLF - 736-A6
- BPK - 767-F2
- CRTS - 736-A6
- CRTS - 737-A7
- CRTS - 767-F2
- LPMA - 767-F2
- NLB - 735-G7
ARTESIA LN
300 NLB 90805 735-C7
ARTESIA PL
10000 BLF 90706 736-C7
E ARTESIA ST
100 POM 91767 600-J6
W ARTESIA ST
100 POM 91768 600-H6
ARTESIA MILL CT
- LAN 93535 4016-F7
- LAN 93535 4106-F1
ARTESIAN CT
300 SDMS 91773 600-C3
ARTESIAN PL
- LA 90031 595-A7
2600 LA 90031 594-J7
ARTESIAN ST
2600 LA 90031 594-J7
2600 LA 90031 595-A6
ARTESIAN SPRINGS RD
- LACo 91390 (4282-J3 See Page 4281)
- LACo 91390 4283-A1
ARTHUR AV
700 POM 91768 640-E1
13800 PRM 90723 735-G2
E ARTHUR AV
- ARCD 91006 597-D1
S ARTHUR AV
300 AZU 91702 598-J1
W ARTHUR AV
- ARCD 91007 597-C1
ARTHUR CT
- Saug 91350 4461-D5
ARTHUR DR
1600 BREA 92821 708-J4
ARTHUR ST
2300 LA 90065 594-G2
16000 CRTS 90703 737-A6
ARTHUR WY
2300 LVRN 91750 570-H7
ARTHURDALE ST
9500 BLF 90706 736-B2
ARTIGAS DR
2500 RowH 91748 678-H6
ARTINE DR
27500 SCTA 91350 4461-A6
ARTISANS WY
- LA 90094 672-F6
- Wch 90045 672-F6
ARTRUDE ST
10600 Sunl 91040 503-A5
ARTSON ST
7800 RSMD 91770 636-E1
ARTURO ST
300 SDMS 91773 600-C2
S ARTURO ST
400 WCOV 91791 638-J1
ARUBA CT
1400 POM 91768 600-F6
ARUNDEL DR
5000 WdHl 91364 560-E3
ARUNDEL PL
1500 GLDL 91206 565-A1
19700 WdHl 91364 560-F3
ARVADA ST
4900 TOR 90503 763-A3
ARVAL AV
11000 LYN 90262 705-C6

ARVEE ST
4100 CULC 90232 672-E3
ARVIA ST
2600 LA 90065 594-H4
ARVID ST
16400 LACo 91744 638-F6
ARVIDA DR
17800 GrnH 91344 481-A5
ARVILLA AV
7600 LA 91505 533-B3
7600 SunV 91352 533-B3
ARVIN DR
1800 GLDL 91208 564-H1
ARWIN ST
800 Alta 91001 535-F6
800 PAS 91001 535-F6
800 PAS 91103 535-F6
ARYE PL
17200 GrnH 91344 481-C5
ASBURY AV
800 POM 91767 601-B5
ASBURY CT
900 LMRD 90638 738-B2
ASBURY DR
1400 PAS 91104 566-B2
ASBURY ST
2900 LA 90065 594-H4
ASCENSION RD
- LA 90068 563-F4
ASCONA DR
17400 SCTA 91387 4552-A2
S ASCOT AV
4100 LA 90011 674-F4
5800 Flor 90001 674-F5
ASCOT CT
1000 SDMS 91773 599-J2
ASCOT WK
6100 LA 90003 674-D6
ASDER LN
1000 ARCD 91006 567-B4
ASH
300 SDMS 91773 599-J3
1300 RowH 91748 679-B4
11400 NRWK 90650 706-J6
ASH AV
100 BURB 91502 563-H1
2200 UPL 91784 571-H3
N ASH AV
100 ING 90301 703-B2
S ASH AV
100 ING 90301 703-B3
ASH CT
- CRSN 90746 764-D3
4400 MTCL 91763 601-E5
22500 SCTA 91390 4460-J2
42000 LAN 93536 4104-G5
ASH DR
- PMDL 93550 4286-F4
1700 MONP 91755 636-D4
7900 LPMA 90623 767-C3
ASH LN
- Nor 91326 500-E1
ASH RD
1800 SBdC 92397 (4652-E3 See Page 4651)
9700 SBdC 92371 (4472-F6 See Page 4471)
ASH ST
- VeCo 93063 499-B4
2400 CMRC 90023 675-E3
5400 HiPk 90042 595-C2
E ASH ST
200 BREA 92821 709-B7
W ASH ST
100 BREA 92821 709-B7
ASH WY
500 LHB 90631 708-C6
ASHBERRY DR
1700 PMDL 93551 4195-E7
ASHBORO DR
19700 SCTA 91351 4461-F7
27900 SCTA 91351 4551-E1
ASHBOURNE DR
2000 SPAS 91030 595-J2
2100 SMRO 91108 596-A2
ASHBOURNE PL
- RowH 91748 708-J2
ASHBRIDGE DR
1100 Hrbr 90710 794-A2
ASHBRIDGE LN
900 Hrbr 90710 794-A3
ASHBROOK AV
1800 LBCH 90815 796-B5
ASHBROOK CIR
2000 PMDL 93550 4286-D1
ASHBROOK LN
- POM 91766 640-F7
- POM 91766 641-A4
- SCTA 91354 4460-G4
ASHBURN TER
900 FUL 92831 738-J3
ASHBURTON PL
400 GLDL 91206 565-B3
ASHBURY
1500 WCOV 91791 638-J5
ASHBURY AV
4600 CYP 90630 767-B7
ASHBURY DR
14300 CHLS 91709 680-G4
ASHBURY PL
2900 GLDL 91206 565-A1
ASHBY AV
10600 LA 90064 632-D6

ASHBY CT
- RowH 91748 708-J2
900 SDMS 91773 600-C4
27600 Cstc 91384 4459-H5
ASHBY LN
- BREA 92821 709-B6
ASHBY ST
300 AZU 91702 568-H4
ASHCOMB DR
600 LACo 91744 638-H6
ASH CREEK LN
27400 SCTA 91354 4460-H6
ASH CREEK RD
- LACo 93532 4102-E5
12400 CRTS 90703 736-J6
12500 CRTS 90703 737-A6
ASHCROFT AV
8600 WHWD 90048 592-H7
ASHCROFT CT
13200 CHLS 91709 680-J1
ASHDALE AV
100 Brwd 90049 631-H1
ASHDALE LN
11900 LA 91604 592-G1
ASHDALE PL
100 Brwd 90049 631-H1
200 Brwd 90049 591-J7
S ASHDALE ST
100 WCOV 91790 598-H7
200 WCOV 91790 638-H1
ASHER ST
9800 ELMN 91733 637-A1
10600 ELMN 91731 637-B1
11400 ELMN 91732 637-D1
ASHERTON AV
4600 COV 91724 599-G4
4600 LACo 91724 599-G3
ASHFIELD AV
800 POM 91767 601-B5
ASHFIELD PL
27200 SCTA 91354 4460-G7
ASHFORD CT
900 THO 91361 557-B5
ASHFORD DR
1000 LVRN 91750 570-E6
ASHFORD ST
12700 Brwd 90049 631-E3
ASHFORK PL
26400 RPV 90275 793-A5
ASH GLEN AV
2800 LAN 93536 4105-C1
ASH GLEN CIR
23000 SCTA 91354 4460-H5
ASHGROVE DR
8000 OrCo 90638 737-H4
13400 LMRD 90638 737-G3
ASHINGTON DR
1900 GLDL 91206 535-B7
ASHIYA RD
800 MTBL 90640 636-E6
ASHKELON CIR
- SIMI 93063 499-B1
ASHLAKE PL
42900 LACo 93532 4102-E4
ASHLAND AV
- SMCA 90405 671-H3
1400 CLAR 91711 601-B2
2800 LA 90031 595-B7
ASHLAND CT
23600 SCTA 91354 4460-G7
ASHLAND PL N
900 SMCA 90405 671-G3
ASHLEE CT
37800 PMDL 93550 4286-E2
ASHLEY AV
18200 TOR 90504 763-D2
ASHLEY CIR
300 LHB 90631 708-C6
ASHLEY CT
- WHIT 90603 707-H4
ASHLEY DR
2800 PAS 91107 566-F2
ASHLEY PL
2100 UPL 91784 571-H4
18800 RowH 91748 679-B7
ASHLEY OAKS
16600 Enc 91436 561-D4
ASHLEY RIDGE RD
25000 HIDH 91302 559-B4
ASH MEADOW DR
600 WAL 91789 639-B7
ASHMILL ST
1200 CRSN 90745 764-F6
ASHMORE PL
1700 Echo 90026 594-E6
ASHPARK LN
1000 Hrbr 90710 794-A2
ASHPORT ST
900 POM 91768 600-G7
1300 POM 91768 640-F1
ASHTABULA ST
300 PAS 91104 565-J3
600 PAS 91104 566-A3
ASHTON AV
10300 Wwd 90024 632-A3
ASHTON CT
- CHNO 91710 641-E6
7500 LA 91304 529-E4
S ASHTON DR
100 COV 91724 599-E5
ASHTON PL
- LAN 93536 4015-B5
900 FUL 92833 738-B6

ASHTREE DR
14400 LACo 93532 4102-G4
ASHURST LN
19000 Tarz 91356 560-H6
W ASHVALE DR
100 SDMS 91773 570-B7
ASHWIN DR
3000 LaCr 91214 504-F7
ASHWOOD AV
3400 LA 90066 672-A4
ASHWOOD CT
1500 UPL 91784 571-H6
36800 PMDL 93550 4286-G5
ASHWOOD LN
500 BREA 92821 709-A5
ASHWOOD PL
- SCTA 91354 4460-F5
E ASHWOOD ST
1100 WCOV 91790 638-G1
ASHWORTH CIR
10700 CRTS 90703 766-E1
13700 CRTS 90703 737-D7
ASHWORTH PL
900 GLDR 91741 569-C5
12300 CRTS 90703 766-J1
13400 CRTS 90703 737-C7
ASHWORTH ST
3700 LKWD 90712 765-J1
3700 NLB 90805 765-J1
4100 LKWD 90712 766-A1
5500 LKWD 90713 766-D1
6000 BLF 90706 766-D1
11300 CRTS 90703 766-G1
11800 ART 90701 766-H1
12000 ART 90701 736-J7
13300 CRTS 90703 737-D7
13800 PanC 91402 532-B1
ASILOMAR BLVD
15800 PacP 90272 630-J6
ASMAN AV
7100 CanP 91307 529-H5
ASMUSEN AV
11400 NRWK 90650 706-G6
ASPAN AV
4400 LACo 91722 598-H3
5500 LACo 91702 598-H1
N ASPAN AV
100 AZU 91702 568-H7
S ASPAN AV
- AZU 91702 568-H7
300 AZU 91702 598-H1
ASPEN AV
10800 BLF 90706 766-D1
ASPEN CIR
7300 LPMA 90623 767-D2
9900 SFSP 90670 706-F4
ASPEN CT
22800 SCTA 91390 4460-H2
ASPEN DR
200 MNRO 91016 567-H3
2400 LA 90068 593-G2
5100 MTCL 91763 601-G6
ASPEN LN
600 POM 91767 601-A4
3000 PMDL 93550 4286-G5
8400 RSMD 91770 596-G6
ASPEN PL
- LACo 91387 4552-B4
ASPEN ST
- Actn 93510 4375-F3
500 BREA 92821 709-C6
2000 LVRN 91750 600-C3
5500 CYP 90630 767-D7
44500 LAN 93535 4016-D6
ASPEN WY
- RHE 90274 822-J1
- RHE 90274 823-A1
100 RHE 90274 793-A7
23900 CALB 91302 589-E1
ASPENCADE CT
38000 PMDL 93552 4286-J1
ASPENDALE CT
- AZU 91702 569-A2
ASPEN GROVE LN
1600 DBAR 91765 680-A4
ASPEN HILL RD
- CRSN 90746 764-F1
ASPEN KNOLL DR
6100 VeCo 91377 558-A1
22900 DBAR 91765 680-B3
ASPEN MEADOW CT
- SCTA 91354 4460-F4
ASPEN OAK CT
700 VeCo 91377 558-B1
ASPEN OAK LN
100 GLDL 91202 564-E1
100 GLDL 91207 564-E1
ASPEN RIDGE CT
500 VeCo 91377 558-B1
ASPEN RIDGE DR
23200 SCTA 91354 4460-G4
ASPEN VIEW CT
500 VeCo 91377 558-B1
ASPENVIEW CT
32500 WLKV 91361 557-A7
ASPEN VILLAGE WY
1600 WCOV 91791 638-J2
ASPENWOOD CT
20600 DBAR 91789 679-F6
ASPENWOOD PL
5900 VeCo 91377 558-A2
ASPERN ST
- PMDL 93550 4286-C6

N ASSOCIATED RD
100 BREA 92821 709-E7
S ASSOCIATED RD
200 BREA 92821 709-D7
ASTAIRE AV
4000 CULC 90232 672-F2
ASTELL AV
5500 LACo 91702 598-H1
N ASTELL AV
300 WCOV 91790 598-H6
S ASTELL AV
100 WCOV 91790 598-H7
200 WCOV 91790 638-H1
ASTER CIR
7800 BPK 90620 767-J2
ASTER PL
40400 PMDL 93551 4195-C3
ASTER ST
- PMDL 93552 4287-B1
1200 VeCo 93063 499-B4
W ASTER ST
1000 UPL 91786 571-H7
ASTER TR
23500 CALB 91302 589-E1
ASTERIA ST
4700 TOR 90503 763-B5
ASTI ST
1300 DUAR 91010 568-A6
ASTLEY RD
35300 Actn 93510 4374-G2
ASTON AV
2500 POM 91768 640-D2
ASTOR AV
4800 CMRC 90040 675-F3
ASTOR CT
- LAN 93536 4015-D4
1800 LAN 93534 4015-E4
ASTORIA AV
1500 LAN 93535 4106-C1
ASTORIA DR
- LA 91342 481-J5
ASTORIA ST
13300 LA 91342 482-C2
14300 LA 91342 481-J5
ASTOR RACING CT
- BqtC 91354 4460-E6
ASTRA DR
1200 LACo 91770 636-F5
ASTRAL DR
2100 LA 90046 593-B2
ASTRAL PL
2200 LA 90046 593-B3
ASTRAN CT
5700 LACo 93536 4104-F6
ASTUTO DR
4800 PMDL 93551 4194-H3
ASUNCION ST
18400 Nor 91326 500-H1
ASUSENA DR
100 PMDL 93550 4195-J3
E ATARA ST
100 MNRO 91016 567-G7
W ATARA ST
200 LACo 91016 567-G7
ATASCADERO PL
900 MTBL 90640 636-G7
ATCHISON ST
200 PAS 91104 535-J7
600 PAS 91104 536-A7
1000 LACo 91104 536-B7
ATCHISON WY
- BPK 90621 737-J5
ATFORD DR
28700 RPV 90275 823-H3
ATGLEN ST
15700 HacH 91745 678-B3
ATHEL DR
2800 HacH 91745 677-H3
ATHELING WY
7100 CanP 91307 529-G5
ATHENA
1400 WCOV 91790 638-D2
ATHENA AV
26200 Hrbr 90710 793-J6
ATHENA PL
- CRSN 90745 794-B1
2600 FUL 92833 738-B5
ATHENA ST
- Actn 93510 4375-F4
ATHENE DR
11800 CRTS 90703 766-H3
ATHENIAN WY
4000 LACo 90043 673-D4
ATHENS BLVD
400 LACo 90061 734-B1
500 LA 90044 734-B1
800 LA 90044 704-B7
ATHENS CIR
5300 LPMA 90623 767-D2
6700 BPK 90621 767-J1
ATHENS CT
1700 CLAR 91711 601-C1
ATHENS ST
400 Alta 91001 535-J4
400 Alta 91001 536-A4
ATHENS WY
400 LACo 90061 734-C1
11300 LA 90061 704-C6
12000 LACo 90061 704-C7
ATHERTON CIR
1400 FUL 92833 738-E3
E ATHERTON DR
7100 LBCH 90815 796-F5

STREET Block City ZIP Pg-Grid

ATHERTON LN
7400 LA 91304 529-D4
E ATHERTON ST
1700 LBCH 90815 796-A5
5400 LBCH 90840 796-D5
ATHERTON CANYON RD
28800 LACo 91390 4461-F3
ATHOL ST
3000 BALD 91706 637-H1
3100 BALD 91706 597-J7
3800 BALD 91706 598-A6
ATHOS ST
- Actn 93510 4375-E7
- Actn 93510 4465-E1
ATINA DR
18000 RowH 91748 678-J4
ATITLAN DR
15900 HacH 91745 678-C5
ATKA CT
36900 PMDL 93552 4287-B4
ATKINS DR
600 GLDL 91206 564-H3
ATKINS LN
- BREA 92821 708-J5
ATKINSON AV
10900 ING 90303 703-F6
11600 HAW 90250 703-G7
11600 HAW 90303 703-G7
15100 GAR 90249 733-G5
15900 GAR 90247 733-G6
16200 TOR 90247 733-G6
16200 TOR 90504 733-G7
17300 TOR 90504 763-G1
ATLANTA AV
10600 Nor 91326 500-F3
ATLANTA CT
800 CLAR 91711 601-B1
ATLANTA ST
37300 PMDL 93552 4286-J3
ATLANTIC AV
- LBCH 90802 825-E1
100 LBCH 90802 795-E6
500 NLB 90805 735-D6
700 LBCH 90813 795-E6
1400 COMP 90221 735-D6
1400 NLB 90805 735-D6
1800 LBCH 90806 795-E3
3000 Bxby 90807 795-E3
3400 Bxby 90807 765-E6
4400 BELL 90201 675-D7
4700 NLB 90805 765-E1
5000 LYN 90262 705-D7
6800 BELL 90201 705-D2
7100 PRM 90723 735-D6
7200 CDHY 90201 705-D2
8600 SGAT 90280 705-D2
11300 LYN 90262 735-D2
11800 CULC 90066 672-D4
11800 LA 90066 672-D4
S ATLANTIC AV
1400 COMP 90221 735-D5
12800 RDom 90221 735-D5
ATLANTIC BLVD
- CMRC 90040 675-D6
2600 VER 90040 675-D6
2900 VER 90201 675-D6
5200 MYWD 90270 675-D6
N ATLANTIC BLVD
- ALH 91801 596-A4
100 MONP 91754 636-A2
1800 SPAS 91030 596-A4
S ATLANTIC BLVD
- ALH 91801 596-A6
100 MONP 91754 636-A3
200 MONP 90022 635-H7
200 ELA 90022 635-H7
300 ALH 91803 596-A6
600 ELA 90022 675-G2
800 ALH 91803 636-A3
900 MONP 91754 635-J5
1500 CMRC 90022 675-G2
1600 CMRC 90040 675-F4
2600 VER 90040 675-F4
2800 VER 90201 675-F4
5000 VER 90023 675-F4
5100 MYWD 90270 675-F4
ATLANTIC CIR
4100 LVRN 91750 600-H1
E ATLANTIC CT
2000 LA 90021 634-H6
S ATLANTIC DR
1000 COMP 90221 735-D6
ATLANTIC PL
6900 NLB 90805 735-E6
16200 PRM 90723 735-E5
N ATLANTIC PL
4400 Bxby 90807 765-E5
ATLANTIC PZ
600 NLB 90805 765-E3
ATLANTIC ST
100 POM 91768 640-C2
3000 LA 90023 635-B7
3500 LA 90023 675-C1
ATLANTIDA DR
1900 HacH 91745 678-D4
ATLAS AV
500 MONP 91755 636-C5
ATLAS DR
- SPed 90731 823-H7
ATLAS LN
- SCTA 91351 4551-H2
ATLAS ST
400 BREA 92821 709-A6
5300 LA 90032 595-G4
ATLAS WY
- PMDL 93552 4197-D7
- PMDL 93552 4287-D1
E ATLAS WY
500 LBCH 90813 795-E6
ATLEE DR
1000 LCF 91011 535-B4
ATLER RD
- LACo 91390 4462-H1
ATLEY CT
- Saug 91350 4461-F6
ATLIN ST
1900 DUAR 91010 568-C5
ATMORE AV
22800 CRSN 90745 794-C1
ATMORE ST
- PMDL 93552 4287-E2
ATOLL
1400 WCOV 91790 638-D2
ATOLL AV
4400 Shrm 91423 562-D3
5200 VanN 91401 562-D2
6000 VanN 91401 532-D7
6600 NHol 91606 532-D6
6700 NHol 91605 532-D3
ATRON AV
7600 LA 91304 529-F3
ATTERBURY DR
1400 WAL 91789 639-F3
N ATTICA DR
200 LBCH 90803 826-C2
ATTILLA RD
14100 LA 90402 631-C7
ATTRIDGE AV
1400 City 90063 635-D3
ATWATER AV
3000 LA 90039 594-E2
ATWATER CANYON RD
2900 GLDL 91208 534-J5
ATWELL PL
9700 Wch 90045 703-A4
ATWOOD BLVD
25000 SCTA 91321 4640-F1
ATWOOD PL
1200 LA 90063 635-C3
ATWOOD ST
1200 LA 90063 635-C3
ATWOOD WY
- ELSG 90245 702-J7
2100 TOR 90503 763-F7
AUBREY LN
25400 LMTA 90717 793-G5
AUBREY PL
2700 FUL 92833 738-B5
AUBREY RD
13900 LA 90210 562-B6
AUBREY PARK CT
1200 HMB 90254 762-H2
AUBURN AV
- SMAD 91024 567-A1
- THO 91362 557-B3
700 SMAD 91024 537-A7
AUBURN CT
- SCTA 91351 4551-G2
- THO 91362 557-B3
1800 UPL 91784 571-J5
14300 CHLS 91709 680-G3
36700 PMDL 93552 4286-J5
S AUBURN DR
1000 WCOV 91791 638-J2
AUBURN LN
300 SMAD 91024 567-A1
AUBURN RD
900 SDMS 91773 570-C6
AUBURN ST
1300 UPL 91784 571-J6
2700 LA 90039 594-D3
AUBURN WY
300 CLAR 91711 571-D6
900 LHB 90631 708-D7
AUCAS DR
21200 Chat 91311 500-A1
AUCKLAND AV
4400 LA 91602 563-B4
4900 NHol 91601 563-B3
5900 NHol 91601 533-B7
6100 NHol 91606 533-B7
AUCTION AV
4200 BALD 91706 598-D5
AUDITORIUM AV
1400 DUAR 91010 568-A6
AUDITORIUM DR
- GLDR 91741 569-B6
AUDRA DR
400 LBCH 90803 826-C1
AUDRAINE DR
400 GLDL 91202 564-D1
AUDREY AV
22900 TOR 90505 793-D1
AUDREY CT
27800 SCTA 91351 4461-D7
AUDREY LN
2400 WCOV 91792 639-B7
AUDREY PL
2100 LA 90039 594-E4
AUDUBON WY
400 SMAD 91024 567-B1
AUGUST ST
4500 LA 90008 673-C2
S AUGUSTA AV
1100 LACo 90023 675-E1
AUGUSTA CT
- PMDL 93551 4195-B2
400 FUL 92835 738-H3
1800 CLAR 91711 571-F7
2000 LHB 90631 738-D2
9500 CYP 90630 767-B7
AUGUSTA PL
- SCTA 91355 4550-D4
AUGUSTA ST
100 LA 90012 634-H2
1100 POM 91768 640-D1
1200 POM 91768 600-D7
W AUGUSTA ST
600 ING 90302 703-A2
AUGUSTINE CT
2700 LA 90031 595-A7
AUKLAND ST
12700 BALD 91706 597-H7
AULTS AV
13700 LA 91342 482-C1
AUMOND AV
28000 SCTA 91351 4461-F7
28000 SCTA 91351 4551-F1
AURA AV
5300 Tarz 91356 560-G1
6100 Res 91335 530-G3
8300 Nor 91324 530-G2
9700 Nor 91324 500-G4
10300 Nor 91326 500-F4
AURELIA ST
5400 SIMI 93063 499-A3
AUREOLA BLVD
3600 LACo 90008 673-E4
AURORA AV
200 BREA 92821 709-D7
AURORA DR
- SCTA 91355 4460-C6
- RHE 90274 793-H7
500 CLAR 91711 601-E1
19100 WAL 91789 639-C7
AURORA LN
- SCTA 91351 4551-D3
8000 WHIT 90605 708-A1
AURORA ST
300 LA 90012 634-J1
AURORA TER
2500 ALH 91803 635-H1
AURORA WY
16600 PRM 90723 735-F6
AURORA CREST DR
15700 WHIT 90605 707-J1
15700 WHIT 90605 708-A1
AUSTEN WY
13400 LACo 91746 637-J3
N AUSTIN AV
800 ING 90302 703-A1
AUSTIN CT
- SCTA 91387 4462-D6
1900 CLAR 91711 571-D7
AUSTIN ST
22900 WdHl 91364 559-G4
AUSTIN TER
4300 HiPk 90042 595-D4
AUSTIN WY
18000 LACo 93532 4101-H2
AUSTINBROOK CT
2300 LMTA 90717 793-G3
AUTO DR N
200 COMP 90220 735-A6
AUTO DR S
200 COMP 90220 735-A7
300 COMP 90221 735-A7
AUTO CENTER CT
- SCTA 91355 4550-G2
AUTO CENTER DR
- POM 91766 640-H5
300 PMDL 93551 4195-G6
400 CLAR 91711 601-C5
6000 BPK 90621 737-G7
6300 BPK 90621 767-J1
26600 SCTA 91355 4550-F3
AUTOCENTER DR
2000 COMP 90221 735-A7
AUTO CENTRE DR
- SDMS 91773 599-J1
1900 GLDR 91740 599-J1
2100 GLDR 91740 600-A1
2200 SDMS 91773 600-A1
AUTO MALL DR
1000 LAN 93534 4105-G2
3000 THO 91362 557-B3
AUTOPLEX DR
9400 MTCL 91763 601-G5
AUTO SQUARE DR
10800 CRTS 90703 766-E2
AUTO VISTA DR
300 PMDL 93551 4195-H6
AUTRILLA SCOTT LN
- LBCH 90806 795-F4
AUTRY AV
4700 LBCH 90808 766-C4
4900 LKWD 90712 766-B2
AUTUMN DR
17100 WCOV 91791 638-J4
AUTUMN LN
1500 PAS 91107 566-H1
2200 DBAR 91789 679-G5
37700 PMDL 93550 4285-J2
AUTUMN PL
- StvR 91381 4640-C2
AUTUMN BREEZE ST
17100 CRTS 90703 736-J7
17100 CRTS 90703 737-A7
AUTUMN GLEN CT
- Nor 91326 500-E1
AUTUMNGLOW DR
1600 DBAR 91765 679-H4
AUTUMN HILL LN
14300 CHLS 91709 680-J4
AUTUMN HILL RD
1500 DBAR 91765 680-C3
AUTUMN LEAF CIR
10200 BelA 90077 592-A1
AUTUMN LEAF CT
- CRSN 90746 764-F1
AUTUMNMIST DR
1700 PMDL 93551 4195-E7
AUTUMN MOON DR
14400 HacH 91745 677-H1
AUTUMN OAK CT
- Cstc 91384 4369-F5
AUTUMN OAK WY
- LACo 91387 4552-A4
AUTUMN OAKS LN
100 GLDR 91741 569-B5
AVA AV
1800 HMB 90254 762-G1
AVALANCHE WY
- MONP 91754 635-H5
AVALO DR
3100 HacH 91745 678-A6
AVALON AV
2100 POM 91768 600-E7
2100 POM 91768 640-E1
AVALON BLVD
300 LA 90059 704-D3
300 LA 90061 704-D7
1600 Wilm 90744 794-E4
3400 LA 90011 674-D4
5800 LA 90001 674-D4
5800 LA 90003 674-D7
7300 LA 90001 704-D3
7300 LA 90003 704-D3
8600 Wats 90002 704-D3
12000 Wbrk 90059 704-D7
12000 LACo 90061 704-D7
12100 Wbrk 90059 734-D4
12100 LACo 90061 734-D4
14300 LACo 90220 734-E5
14300 LACo 90248 734-D4
16100 CRSN 90746 734-E5
16100 CRSN 90248 734-E5
17400 CRSN 90746 764-E1
18000 CRSN 90747 764-E1
20800 CRSN 90745 764-E6
22600 CRSN 90745 794-E4
N AVALON BLVD
100 Wilm 90744 794-E7
100 Wilm 90744 824-E1
S AVALON BLVD
100 Wilm 90744 824-E1
AVALON CT
- SBdC 91710 641-C5
6100 LBCH 90803 826-D1
AVALON DR
- RPV 90275 793-H7
- SCTA 91351 4551-J2
100 FUL 92835 738-H4
800 SLB 90740 826-F3
AVALON PL
800 Wilm 90744 794-E6
AVALON RD
9100 SBdC 92371 (4562-G1
See Page 4471)
9200 SBdC 92371 (4472-G7
See Page 4471)
12300 WHIT 90601 677-B4
AVALON ST
1500 Echo 90026 594-E6
1900 LA 90039 594-E6
AVALON CANYON RD
- AVA 90704 5923-G5
AVANTI CT
- StvR 91381 4640-C1
AVENAL ST
100 SBdC 92372 (4472-A5
See Page 4471)
2100 SBdC 92371 (4472-E5
See Page 4471)
AVENEL DR
- PMDL 93551 4194-J2
AVENEL ST
2800 LA 90039 594-D3
AVENEL TER
2900 LA 90039 594-C3
AVENGER PL
32200 RPV 90275 823-D5
AVENIDA AGUAS CALIENTES
- CMRC 90040 676-B7
- CMRC 90040 706-B1
N AVENIDA ALIPAZ
100 WAL 91789 679-E1
S AVENIDA ALIPAZ
300 WAL 91789 679-E2
AVENIDA ALTISIMA
7100 RPV 90275 822-F2
AVENIDA AMAIDIS
19900 WAL 91789 639-E7
19900 WAL 91789 679-E1
AVENIDA ANILLO
29900 RPV 90275 822-G2
AVENIDA ANITA
15200 CHLS 91709 680-G6
AVENIDA ANTIGUA
1400 FUL 92833 738-E3
AVENIDA APRENDA
1800 LA 90732 823-H1
1800 RPV 90275 823-H1
AVENIDA ASOLEADA
24700 CALB 91302 559-D6
AVENIDA ATEZADA
200 TOR 90277 793-A2
AVENIDA AVILA
- BqtC 91354 4460-F3
AVENIDA BALITA
24900 SCTA 91355 4550-H7
24900 SCTA 91355 4640-H1
AVENIDA BARBOSA
- IRW 91010 597-J1
- IRW 91010 598-A1
- IRW 91706 598-A1
AVENIDA BARCELONA
20100 CRTS 90703 766-H4
AVENIDA BERNARDO
600 SDMS 91773 600-A7
AVENIDA BONITA
- TOR 90505 793-F5
AVENIDA CABRILLO
2300 CHLS 91709 680-J6
AVENIDA CALLADA
3600 CALB 91302 559-C7
AVENIDA CAPPELA
25300 SCTA 91355 4640-G1
25400 SCTA 91355 4550-F7
AVENIDA CARMEL
4300 CYP 90630 767-B7
AVENIDA CELESTIAL
30000 RPV 90275 822-H2
AVENIDA CESAR CHAVEZ
1100 MONP 91754 635-H5
AVENIDA CLASSICA
5500 PMDL 93551 4194-G2
30000 RPV 90275 822-H2
AVENIDA COLINA
1300 SDMS 91773 599-H6
AVENIDA COMPADRES
1300 CHLS 91709 680-G6
AVENIDA CONEJO
1100 AZU 91702 568-G4
AVENIDA CORONA
- RPV 90275 823-G5
AVENIDA CRESCENTA
23000 SCTA 91355 4640-F1
AVENIDA CUADERNO
27800 RPV 90275 823-H1
AVENIDA CUMBRE
3600 CALB 91302 559-D7
AVENIDA DE ANDRA
6800 BPK 90620 767-E1
AVENIDA DE ANGELENO DR
700 AZU 91702 568-J5
AVENIDA DE AZALEA
29900 RPV 90275 823-F4
AVENIDA DE CALMA
30100 RPV 90275 822-G2
AVENIDA DE CAMELIA
29800 RPV 90275 823-F4
AVENIDA DE CAMINO
6600 PMDL 93552 4287-E2
AVENIDA DE CASAS
37700 PMDL 93552 4287-E2
AVENIDA DE CASTILLO
6000 LBCH 90803 796-D7
AVENIDA DE CORTEZ
1300 PacP 90272 630-F1
AVENIDA DE DIEGO
37700 PMDL 93552 4287-E2
AVENIDA DE ENCINAL
4200 MAL 90265 626-E6
AVENIDA DE FLORES
200 LACo 91744 638-H7
AVENIDA DE JANA
6700 BPK 90620 767-E1
AVENIDA DE JOSE
400 TOR 90277 792-J3
AVENIDA DE LA HERRADURA
17000 PacP 90272 630-F1
17200 PacP 90272 590-F7
E AVENIDA DE LA MERCED
200 MTBL 90640 636-F7
W AVENIDA DE LA MERCED
100 MTBL 90640 636-E7
AVENIDA DE LA RAMBLA
300 WAL 91789 679-D2
AVENIDA DE LA SUERTE
1100 AZU 91702 568-G5
AVENIDA DEL BRISA
2400 LAN 93535 4016-E6
AVENIDA DEL CAMPO
19400 WAL 91789 679-D1
AVENIDA DEL CANADA
1700 RowH 91748 678-H5
AVENIDA DEL CORTO
1100 FUL 92833 738-E3
AVENIDA DELEITANTE
19700 WAL 91789 679-D2
AVENIDA DEL MAR
2300 LAN 93535 4016-E6
4700 MAL 90265 626-D6
AVENIDA DEL MESA
27600 RPV 90275 823-H1
AVENIDA DEL MONTE
15000 CHLS 91709 680-J5
AVENIDA DEL NORTE
200 RBCH 90277 792-J1
1800 FUL 92833 738-D3
AVENIDA DE LOS LOBOS
700 VeCo 91377 557-J2
AVENIDA DEL OSSA
1900 FUL 92833 738-D5
AVENIDA DE LOS WHITTIER BLVD
600 LHB 90631 708-D5
AVENIDA DEL PLAYA
44400 LAN 93535 4016-E6
AVENIDA DEL REY
31900 LACo 91390 4463-C2
AVENIDA DEL RIO
44400 LAN 93535 4016-E6
AVENIDA DEL RISCO
- LVRN 91750 570-H4
AVENIDA DEL SOL
3500 LA 91604 562-E6
19300 WAL 91789 679-D1
44400 LAN 93535 4016-E6
E AVENIDA DEL SOL
11700 Nor 91326 480-G7
AVENIDA DE MAGNOLIA
29700 RPV 90275 823-F4
AVENIDA DE MARCIA
6700 BPK 90620 767-E1
AVENIDA DE NOGAL
3700 RPV 90275 823-F4
AVENIDA DE OLIVA
- RPV 90275 823-F4
AVENIDA DE OLMA
30000 RPV 90275 823-F4
AVENIDA DE PALOMA
6600 PMDL 93552 4287-E2
AVENIDA DE ROSA
3400 RPV 90275 823-F4
AVENIDA DE ROYALE
200 THO 91362 557-B2
AVENIDA DE SANTA YNEZ
16700 PacP 90272 630-F1
AVENIDA DESEO
19800 WAL 91789 679-E1
AVENIDA DE SUNSET AV
700 AZU 91702 568-H6
AVENIDA DE TRINA
6800 BPK 90620 767-G5
AVENIDA DE UNAMUNDO
4500 Tarz 91356 560-F4
AVENIDA DOMINGO
500 SDMS 91773 600-A6
AVENIDA DONARI
32000 LACo 91390 4463-D1
AVENIDA DORENA
25200 SCTA 91321 4640-E1
AVENIDA ELEGANTE
30000 RPV 90275 822-G2
AVENIDA ENTRADA
1400 SDMS 91773 599-J5
1500 SDMS 91773 600-A6
5500 PMDL 93551 4194-G1
AVENIDA ENTRANA
23900 SCTA 91355 4640-F1
AVENIDA ESCALERA
25400 SCTA 91355 4550-F7
AVENIDA ESPANA
13600 LMRD 90638 737-J2
AVENIDA ESPLENDIDA
5700 PMDL 93551 4194-F2
29900 RPV 90275 822-H2
AVENIDA ESPLENDOR
300 WAL 91789 679-E1
AVENIDA ESTEBAN TORRES
1200 CMRC 90022 675-H2
AVENIDA ESTORIL
5700 LBCH 90814 796-D7
AVENIDA ESTUDIANTE
1800 RPV 90275 823-H1
AVENIDA FELICIANO
1800 RPV 90275 823-H1
AVENIDA FERNANDO
100 SDMS 91773 600-A7
AVENIDA FRASCA
25400 SCTA 91355 4550-G6
AVENIDA GRANADA
200 LBCH 90803 826-D1
200 LBCH 90814 826-D1
300 LBCH 90814 796-C7
4400 CYP 90630 767-B7
AVENIDA GRULLA
100 WAL 91789 679-E1
AVENIDA HACIENDA
2000 CHLS 91709 680-J4
5000 Tarz 91356 560-J3
AVENIDA IGNACIO
25100 SCTA 91355 4550-H7
AVENIDA JOLITA
25600 SCTA 91355 4550-G6
AVENIDA LADERA
800 SDMS 91773 600-A6
900 SDMS 91773 599-J6
AVENIDA LA PAZ
2200 CHLS 91709 680-J5
AVENIDA LAS BRISAS
18100 Nor 91325 500-J5
18100 Nor 91325 501-A6
AVENIDA LAS RAMBLAS
2100 CHLS 91709 680-H2
AVENIDA LINDA
- LAN 93535 4016-F5
AVENIDA LOMA VISTA
800 SDMS 91773 600-A5
900 SDMS 91773 599-H5
AVENIDA LOMITA
1000 SDMS 91773 599-J6
AVENIDA LOS PALOS
1100 SDMS 91773 639-J1
AVENIDA MADRID
4100 CYP 90630 767-A7
AVENIDA MAGNIFICA
29900 RPV 90275 822-H2
AVENIDA MANUEL SALINAS
12600 NRWK 90650 736-J1
AVENIDA MATEO
9800 CYP 90630 767-B7
AVENIDA MELISENDA
100 SDMS 91773 600-A7
AVENIDA MIROLA
400 PVE 90274 822-E1
700 PVE 90274 792-F7
AVENIDA MONTAGNE
- Actn 93510 4465-C1
AVENIDA MONTEREY
9500 CYP 90630 767-B7
AVENIDA MONTE VISTA
1700 SDMS 91773 599-H6
S AVENIDA MONTE VISTA
1800 SDMS 91773 599-H6
AVENIDA MORELOS
22100 WdHl 91364 559-J4
22100 WdHl 91364 560-A4
AVENIDA NAVARRE
23700 SCTA 91355 4550-G6
AVENIDA ORIENTE
5000 Tarz 91356 560-J3
AVENIDA ORIENTE FIRE RD
- Enc 91316 590-H1
- PacP 90272 590-H1
- Tarz 91356 560-H7
- Tarz 91356 590-H1
AVENIDA PADILLA
16000 IRW 91702 568-F6
AVENIDA PAMPLONA
20100 CRTS 90703 766-J4
AVENIDA PLACIDA
2000 SIMI 93063 499-B2
AVENIDA PRESIDIO
400 WAL 91789 639-D7
AVENIDA PUERTO VALLARTA
17800 Enc 91316 561-A5
E AVENIDA RANCHEROS
- POM 91766 640-E5
24000 DBAR 91765 640-E5
AVENIDA RANCHO TESORO
- BqtC 91354 4460-F2
AVENIDA REAL
17600 LACo 91744 638-H7
AVENIDA REFINIDA
29900 RPV 90275 822-G2
N AVENIDA REFUGIO
2000 SIMI 93063 499-B2
AVENIDA RONADA
25300 SCTA 91355 4640-G1
25300 SCTA 91355 4550-G7
AVENIDA RONDEL
25100 SCTA 91355 4640-G1
AVENIDA ROTELLA
25000 SCTA 91355 4640-G1
25100 SCTA 91355 4550-G7
AVENIDA SAN LORENZO
1700 FUL 92833 738-D4
AVENIDA SAN MARTIN
- LMRD 90638 737-J1
- LMRD 90638 738-A2
AVENIDA SAN MIGUEL
15900 LMRD 90638 737-J1
16100 LMRD 90638 738-A1
AVENIDA SANTA ANITA
100 LHB 90631 738-E1
AVENIDA SANTA BARBARA
100 LHB 90631 738-E1
AVENIDA SANTA CATALINA
100 LHB 90631 738-E1
AVENIDA SANTA DOROTEA
200 LHB 90631 738-E2
AVENIDA SANTA ELENA
200 LHB 90631 738-E2
AVENIDA SANTA TECLA
13400 LMRD 90638 737-J2
AVENIDA SANTO DOMINGO
200 LHB 90631 738-E1
AVENIDA SELECTA
30200 RPV 90275 822-H3
AVENIDA SELVA
1500 FUL 92833 738-C4
AVENIDA SEVILLA
4000 CYP 90630 767-A7
AVENIDA SOCORRO
15300 LMRD 90638 737-H1
AVENIDA SOLEDAD
700 VeCo 91377 557-J1
2100 FUL 92833 738-E4
AVENIDA TERRAZA
26700 SCTA 91350 4460-J7
AVENIDA TRANQUILA
30000 RPV 90275 822-G2
AVENIDA VASQUEZ
- Actn 93510 4374-D4
- LACo 91390 4374-D4
AVENIDA VELARTE
23200 SCTA 91355 4550-G6
AVENIDA VERDE VISTA
1500 SDMS 91773 599-H6
N AVENIDA VISTA DEL MONTE
2000 SIMI 93063 499-B2
AVENIDA VISTA VERDE
4700 PMDL 93551 4194-H2
AVENIR CT
39500 PMDL 93551 4195-C5
AVENTINE WY
2000 LACo 91789 679-E5
S AVENUE 16
300 LA 90031 634-J1
S AVENUE 17
200 LA 90031 634-J1
N AVENUE 18
100 LA 90031 594-J7
100 LA 90031 634-J1
S AVENUE 18
100 LA 90031 634-J1
N AVENUE 19
100 LA 90031 594-J7
100 LA 90031 634-J1
S AVENUE 19
100 LA 90031 634-J1
S AVENUE 20
100 LA 90031 634-J1
N AVENUE 21
100 LA 90031 594-J7
S AVENUE 21
200 LA 90031 634-J1
300 LA 90031 635-A1
N AVENUE 22
300 LA 90031 594-J7
500 LA 90065 594-J6
S AVENUE 22
100 LA 90031 594-J7
100 LA 90031 634-J1
200 LA 90031 635-A1
N AVENUE 23
100 LA 90031 594-J7
100 LA 90031 595-A7
S AVENUE 23
100 LA 90031 595-A7
S AVENUE 24
100 LA 90031 595-A7
100 LA 90031 635-A1
N AVENUE 25
100 LA 90031 594-J7
100 LA 90031 595-A7
E AVENUE 26
100 LA 90031 595-A7
W AVENUE 26
100 LA 90031 595-A7
200 LA 90031 594-J7
400 LA 90065 594-J7
W AVENUE 27
100 LA 90031 595-A7
600 LA 90065 594-J5
E AVENUE 28
100 LA 90031 595-B6
W AVENUE 28
100 LA 90031 595-A7
500 LA 90065 594-J6
W AVENUE 29
100 LA 90031 595-A7
W AVENUE 30
1900 LA 90065 594-G3
3000 LA 90031 595-A7
E AVENUE 31
100 LA 90031 595-A7
W AVENUE 31
100 LA 90031 595-A6
2100 LA 90065 594-G3
E AVENUE 32
100 LA 90031 595-A6
W AVENUE 32
2400 LA 90065 594-F2
E AVENUE 33
100 LA 90031 595-A6
W AVENUE 33
100 LA 90031 595-A6
2000 LA 90065 594-G2
W AVENUE 34
100 LA 90031 595-A6
2500 LA 90065 594-G1
E AVENUE 35
100 LA 90031 595-A6
W AVENUE 35
2500 LA 90065 594-G2
E AVENUE 36
100 LA 90031 595-A6
W AVENUE 36
2900 LA 90065 594-G2
E AVENUE 37
100 LA 90031 595-A6
W AVENUE 37
100 LA 90065 595-A5
600 LA 90065 594-H2
E AVENUE 38
100 LA 90031 595-A6
W AVENUE 38
300 LA 90065 595-A5
3000 LA 90065 594-H1
E AVENUE 39
100 LA 90031 595-A5
E AVENUE 40
100 LA 90031 595-B5
W AVENUE 40
3700 LA 90065 594-H1
4100 LA 90065 564-H7
E AVENUE 41
100 LA 90031 595-B5
W AVENUE 41
100 LA 90065 595-A5
3800 LA 90065 594-H1
4100 LA 90065 564-H6
E AVENUE 42
100 LA 90031 595-A5
W AVENUE 42
100 LA 90065 595-A5
3500 LA 90065 594-H1
4000 LA 90065 564-H7
E AVENUE 43
100 LA 90031 595-B5
W AVENUE 43
100 LA 90065 595-A5
3600 LA 90065 594-J1
3800 Eagl 90041 594-J1
3900 Eagl 90041 564-J7
E AVENUE 44
100 LA 90031 595-B5
N AVENUE 44
1400 Eagl 90041 594-J1
W AVENUE 44
100 LA 90065 595-A4
E AVENUE 45
100 LA 90031 595-B5
N AVENUE 45
1200 Eagl 90041 594-J1
1500 Eagl 90041 564-J7
W AVENUE 45
100 LA 90065 595-A4
N AVENUE 46
1300 Eagl 90041 595-A1
1500 Eagl 90041 565-A7
W AVENUE 46
400 LA 90065 595-A4
N AVENUE 47
1400 HiPk 90042 595-A1
1400 Eagl 90041 595-A1
1500 HiPk 90042 565-A7
1500 Eagl 90041 565-A7
N AVENUE 48
600 HiPk 90042 595-A3
N AVENUE 49
200 HiPk 90042 595-A1
1400 Eagl 90041 595-A1
S AVENUE 49
100 HiPk 90042 595-B4
N AVENUE 50
100 HiPk 90042 595-B1
1800 HiPk 90042 565-B7
S AVENUE 50
100 HiPk 90042 595-B4
N AVENUE 51
100 HiPk 90042 595-B1
1700 HiPk 90042 565-B7
1900 Eagl 90041 565-B7
S AVENUE 51
200 HiPk 90042 595-C3
N AVENUE 52
100 HiPk 90042 595-B1
1800 HiPk 90042 565-B7
2000 Eagl 90041 565-B7
S AVENUE 52
100 HiPk 90042 595-C3
N AVENUE 53
100 HiPk 90042 595-B1
1800 HiPk 90042 565-C7
S AVENUE 53
100 HiPk 90042 595-C3
N AVENUE 54
100 HiPk 90042 595-C1
S AVENUE 54
100 HiPk 90042 595-C3
N AVENUE 55
100 HiPk 90042 595-C1
1800 HiPk 90042 565-C7
S AVENUE 55
100 HiPk 90042 595-C3
N AVENUE 56
100 HiPk 90042 595-C1
1600 HiPk 90042 565-C7
S AVENUE 56
100 HiPk 90042 595-C3
N AVENUE 57
100 HiPk 90042 595-C1
1300 HiPk 90042 565-C7
S AVENUE 57
100 HiPk 90042 595-C3
N AVENUE 58
100 HiPk 90042 595-C2
S AVENUE 58
100 HiPk 90042 595-D3
N AVENUE 59
100 HiPk 90042 595-C2
S AVENUE 59
100 HiPk 90042 595-D3
N AVENUE 60
100 HiPk 90042 595-D2
S AVENUE 60
100 HiPk 90042 595-E3
N AVENUE 61
100 HiPk 90042 595-D2
S AVENUE 61
100 HiPk 90042 595-D2
N AVENUE 62
200 HiPk 90042 595-D2
AVENUE 63
1000 HiPk 90042 565-E7
1000 HiPk 90042 595-E1
1100 HiPk 90042 565-E7
1100 PAS 91105 565-E7
N AVENUE 63
100 HiPk 90042 595-E1
S AVENUE 63
100 HiPk 90042 595-D2
AVENUE 64
- PAS 91105 565-E7
1100 HiPk 90042 565-E7
N AVENUE 64
100 HiPk 90042 595-E1
1000 PAS 91105 565-E7
1000 PAS 91105 595-E1
1000 HiPk 90042 565-E7
S AVENUE 64
100 HiPk 90042 595-D2
N AVENUE 65
100 HiPk 90042 595-E1
900 PAS 91105 565-E7
900 PAS 91105 595-E1
N AVENUE 66
100 HiPk 90042 595-E1
S AVENUE 66
100 HiPk 90042 595-E2
N AVENUE 67
500 HiPk 90042 595-F1
AVENUE A
- Cstc 91384 4460-B3
100 RBCH 90277 762-J7
500 LACo 93523 3835-J3
500 LACo 93534 3835-F2
500 KeCo 93523 3835-F2
500 KeCo 93560 3835-C3
700 RBCH 90277 763-A7
2000 LACo 93536 3835-C3
3500 KeCo 93560 3834-B3
3500 LACo 93536 3834-B3
5600 TOR 90505 763-A7
8000 LACo 93536 3833-C3
8000 KeCo 93560 3833-C3
18500 RowH 91748 679-B5
23700 TOR 90501 793-J2
AVENUE A-2
6000 LACo 93536 3834-C3
9500 LACo 93536 3833-E3
AVENUE A-4
4000 LACo 93536 3834-C3
9500 LACo 93536 3833-E3
AVENUE A-6
5500 LACo 93536 3834-C4
9500 LACo 93536 3833-F4
AVENUE A-8
1500 LACo 93534 3835-E4
3500 LACo 93536 3834-D4
3500 LACo 93536 3835-A4
9000 LACo 93536 3833-B4
AVENUE A-10
1500 LACo 93534 3835-E4
6000 LACo 93536 3834-D4
9000 LACo 93536 3833-B4
AVENUE A-12
1500 LACo 93534 3835-E4
2900 LACo 93536 3835-A4
3500 LACo 93536 3834-D4
9000 LACo 93536 3833-F4
AVENUE A-14
1500 LACo 93534 3835-E4
6000 LACo 93536 3834-D5
9000 LACo 93536 3833-B5
AVENUE B
- Cstc 91384 4460-A3
- TOR 90501 793-J2
100 RBCH 90277 762-J7
500 LACo 93523 3835-H4
500 LACo 93534 3835-E5
600 RBCH 90277 763-A7
2000 LACo 93536 3835-B5
3400 LACo 93536 3834-D5
4700 TOR 90505 763-B7
8000 LACo 93536 3833-C5
18600 RowH 91748 679-A4
AVENUE B-1
9500 LACo 93536 3833-G5
AVENUE B-2
1500 LACo 93534 3835-E5
6500 LACo 93536 3834-C5
10000 LACo 93536 3833-B5
AVENUE B-3
9600 LACo 93536 3833-G5
AVENUE B-4
1500 LACo 93534 3835-E5
6500 LACo 93536 3834-C5
9900 LACo 93536 3833-E5
AVENUE B-6
1500 LACo 93534 3835-E5
6000 LACo 93536 3834-C6
10000 LACo 93536 3833-B6
AVENUE B-8
1000 LACo 93534 3835-E6
4500 LACo 93536 3834-D6
8200 LACo 93536 3833-B6
AVENUE B-10
1500 LACo 93534 3835-E6
8000 LACo 93536 3834-A6

STREET Block	City	ZIP	Pg-Grid
AVENUE B-10			
11000	LACo	93536	3833-B6
AVENUE B-12			
1000	LACo	93534	3835-E6
3200	LACo	93536	3835-B6
4000	LACo	93536	3834-G6
11000	LACo	93536	3833-B7
AVENUE B-14			
1500	LACo	93534	3835-E6
11000	LACo	93536	3833-B7
AVENUE C			
-	TOR	90501	793-J2
100	RBCH	90277	762-J7
400	RBCH	90277	763-A7
500	LACo	93523	3835-J6
500	LACo	93534	3835-G6
2000	LACo	93536	3835-B7
3500	LACo	93536	3834-D7
4600	TOR	90505	763-B7
8200	LACo	93536	3833-B7
AVENUE C-2			
3500	LACo	93536	3834-A7
3500	LACo	93536	3835-A7
8200	LACo	93536	3833-B7
AVENUE C-4			
-	LACo	93536	3833-J7
1000	LACo	93534	3835-E7
2500	LACo	93536	3835-B7
4000	LACo	93536	3834-A7
12000	LACo	93536	3923-A1
AVENUE C-5			
3200	LACo	93536	3835-B7
AVENUE C-6			
4000	LACo	93536	3834-J7
4500	LACo	93536	3924-A1
12000	LACo	93536	3923-A1
AVENUE C-8			
2200	LACo	93536	3925-A1
3600	LACo	93536	3924-A1
8200	LACo	93536	3923-B1
AVENUE C-10			
4200	LACo	93536	3924-B1
8300	LACo	93536	3923-B1
AVENUE C-12			
2200	LACo	93536	3925-A1
3500	LACo	93536	3924-B1
11000	LACo	93536	3923-J1
AVENUE C-14			
3500	LACo	93536	3924-H1
3500	LACo	93536	3925-A1
12000	LACo	93536	3923-B2
AVENUE CROCKER			
28000	SCTA	91355	4460-B7
28000	SCTA	91355	4550-C1
AVENUE D			
-	TOR	90501	793-J2
100	RBCH	90277	762-J7
600	RBCH	90277	763-A7
1000	LACo	93534	3925-F2
2000	LACo	93536	3925-F2
4100	LACo	93535	3926-J1
4100	LACo	93523	3926-J1
4400	LACo	93536	3924-J2
AVENUE D Rt#-138			
1300	LACo	93536	3925-B2
3500	LACo	93536	3924-B2
8200	LACo	93536	3923-B2
AVENUE D-2			
8000	LACo	93536	3923-H2
8000	LACo	93536	3924-A2
AVENUE D-4			
2200	LACo	93536	3925-D2
4000	LACo	93535	3926-J2
5500	LACo	93536	3924-D2
8500	LACo	93536	3923-H2
AVENUE D-6			
5000	LACo	93536	3924-D2
8500	LACo	93536	3923-H3
AVENUE D-8			
2200	LACo	93536	3925-D3
4000	LACo	93536	3924-B3
4000	LACo	93535	3926-J2
8200	LACo	93536	3923-B3
AVENUE D-10			
5000	LACo	93536	3924-A3
8200	LACo	93536	3923-G3
AVENUE D-12			
2200	LACo	93536	3925-B3
4500	LACo	93536	3924-B3
8200	LACo	93536	3923-G3
AVENUE D-14			
8000	LACo	93536	3924-A4
8500	LACo	93536	3923-J4
AVENUE E			
-	TOR	90501	793-H2
100	LACo	93534	3925-F4
100	LACo	93535	3925-H3
100	LACo	93535	3926-H3
100	RBCH	90277	762-J7
100	LACo	93523	3925-H3
100	LACo	93523	3926-C3
300	RBCH	90277	792-J1
400	RBCH	90277	793-A1
2000	LACo	93536	3925-A4
2500	LAN	93536	3925-A4
4000	LAN	93536	3924-E4
4000	LACo	93536	3924-B4
8500	LACo	93536	3923-B4
10000	LAN	93536	3923-E4
AVENUE E-1			
1000	LACo	93534	3925-F4
AVENUE E-2			
1000	LACo	93534	3925-F4
2500	LAN	93536	3925-C4
6500	LAN	93536	3924-D4
7000	LACo	93536	3924-D4
AVENUE E-3			
1000	LACo	93534	3925-F4
AVENUE E-4			
100	LACo	93534	3925-E4
1500	LACo	93535	3926-C4
2500	LAN	93536	3925-C4
5500	LAN	93536	3924-F4
7000	LACo	93536	3924-B4
8500	LACo	93536	3923-F4
10000	LAN	93536	3923-F4
AVENUE E-5			
1000	LACo	93534	3925-F4
AVENUE E-6			
1500	LACo	93534	3925-E4
2500	LAN	93536	3925-C4
6500	LAN	93536	3924-D5
7200	LACo	93536	3924-C5
9000	LACo	93536	3923-E5
10500	LAN	93536	3923-E5
48100	LACo	93535	3926-C4
AVENUE E-7			
1000	LACo	93534	3925-F4
AVENUE E-8			
100	LACo	93534	3925-E5
100	LACo	93535	3925-J4
100	LACo	93535	3926-A4
2200	LACo	93536	3925-D5
2500	LAN	93536	3925-A5
4700	LAN	93536	3924-G5
7000	LACo	93536	3924-C5
8500	LACo	93536	3923-B5
10000	LAN	93536	3923-E5
AVENUE E-10			
1700	LACo	93534	3925-E5
2200	LACo	93536	3925-D5
2200	LAN	93536	3925-C5
5300	LAN	93536	3924-G5
7700	LACo	93536	3924-B5
AVENUE E-11			
7200	LACo	93536	3924-C5
10500	LAN	93536	3923-F5
10500	LACo	93536	3923-F5
AVENUE E-12			
1500	LACo	93534	3925-E5
2500	LACo	93535	3926-F5
2700	LAN	93536	3925-C5
4700	LAN	93536	3924-E5
7000	LACo	93536	3924-B5
8500	LACo	93536	3923-J5
AVENUE E-13			
7200	LACo	93536	3924-B6
AVENUE E-14			
2800	LAN	93536	3925-C5
7700	LACo	93536	3924-B6
AVENUE E 1ST PL			
1000	LACo	93534	3925-F4
AVENUE E 7TH PL			
1000	LACo	93534	3925-F4
AVENUE EYE			
100	RBCH	90277	792-J1
300	TOR	90277	792-J1
5000	LACo	93535	4017-B4
9000	LACo	93536	4013-B5
9700	LAN	93536	4013-J5
AVENUE F			
100	LACo	93534	3925-F6
100	LACo	93535	3925-J5
100	LACo	93535	3926-B5
100	RBCH	90277	792-J1
400	RBCH	90277	793-A1
2000	LACo	93536	3925-F6
2500	LAN	93536	3925-B6
4000	LAN	93536	3924-E6
7000	LACo	93536	3924-A6
8500	LACo	93536	3923-B6
9500	LAN	93536	3923-F6
23700	TOR	90501	793-H2
AVENUE F-2			
2500	LAN	93536	3925-C6
AVENUE F-4			
100	LACo	93534	3925-H6
2500	LAN	93536	3925-A6
4000	LACo	93535	3926-J6
7200	LACo	93536	3924-C6
9000	LACo	93536	3923-H6
9600	LAN	93536	3923-G6
AVENUE F-6			
2500	LAN	93536	3925-C6
6500	LAN	93536	3924-D7
7200	LACo	93536	3924-C7
9500	LAN	93536	3923-G7
AVENUE F-7			
7200	LACo	93536	3924-C7
9000	LACo	93536	3923-H7
AVENUE F-8			
100	LACo	93534	3925-H6
1000	LACo	93535	3926-C6
2500	LACo	93536	3925-F7
2500	LAN	93536	3925-B7
4000	LAN	93536	3924-D7
7000	LACo	93536	3924-C7
8500	LACo	93536	3923-D7
9100	LAN	93536	3923-G7
AVENUE F-10			
100	LACo	93535	3925-J7
3000	LAN	93536	3925-B7
9500	LAN	93536	3923-G7
AVENUE F-12			
100	LACo	93534	3925-H7
1200	LACo	93535	3926-C7
7600	LACo	93536	3924-B7
9000	LACo	93536	3923-G7
9200	LAN	93536	3923-G7
AVENUE F-14			
3000	LAN	93536	3925-B7
AVENUE G			
-	TOR	90501	793-H2
100	LACo	93535	3925-J7
100	LACo	93535	3926-B7
100	LACo	93535	4015-F1
100	LAN	93534	4015-F1
100	RBCH	90277	792-J1
100	LACo	93534	4015-F1
500	RBCH	90277	793-A1
2000	LAN	93536	4015-B1
2000	LACo	93536	4015-B1
4000	LAN	93536	4014-E1
7000	LACo	93536	4014-C1
8500	LACo	93536	4013-B1
8700	LAN	93536	4013-F1
AVENUE G-4			
100	LACo	93535	4015-J1
100	LACo	93535	4016-A1
500	LAN	93534	4015-F1
3300	LAN	93536	4015-B1
4000	LAN	93536	4014-E1
7000	LACo	93536	4014-C1
8400	LACo	93535	4017-J1
9200	LACo	93535	4018-A1
AVENUE G-6			
100	LACo	93535	4015-J1
100	LACo	93535	4016-A1
100	LAN	93534	4015-J1
5500	LAN	93536	4014-E2
12100	LACo	93535	4018-G1
AVENUE G-8			
100	LACo	93535	4015-J2
100	LACo	93535	4016-B1
500	LAN	93534	4015-F2
3000	LAN	93536	4015-B2
4000	LAN	93536	4014-B2
4500	LACo	93535	4017-C1
7500	LACo	93536	4014-B2
8500	LAN	93536	4013-G2
8500	LACo	93536	4013-A2
9100	LACo	93535	4018-B1
AVENUE G-10			
4000	LAN	93536	4014-J2
4000	LAN	93536	4015-A2
9800	LACo	93535	4018-B1
AVENUE G-12			
100	LACo	93535	4015-J2
100	LACo	93535	4016-B2
100	LAN	93534	4015-G2
4000	LAN	93536	4014-A2
4000	LAN	93536	4015-A2
6100	LACo	93535	4017-C2
8500	LAN	93536	4013-J2
11000	LACo	93535	4018-F1
13000	LACo	93536	4013-A3
AVENUE G-14			
4000	LAN	93536	4014-J2
4000	LAN	93536	4015-A2
8900	LACo	93535	4017-J2
8900	LACo	93535	4018-F2
AVENUE H			
100	LACo	93535	4015-J3
100	LAN	93534	4015-G3
100	LAN	93535	4015-J3
100	RBCH	90277	792-J1
300	LAN	93535	4016-C2
300	LACo	93535	4016-C2
1000	LAN	93536	4015-B3
1000	RBCH	90277	793-A1
1000	TOR	90505	793-A1
4000	LAN	93536	4014-E3
4700	LACo	93535	4017-D2
7000	LACo	93536	4014-C3
8500	LAN	93536	4013-G3
9000	LACo	93535	4018-C2
9200	LACo	93536	4013-D3
AVENUE H-1			
1000	LAN	93534	4015-E3
AVENUE H-2			
500	LAN	93534	4015-G3
3000	LAN	93535	4016-G3
4000	LAN	93536	4014-H3
4000	LAN	93536	4015-A3
7000	LACo	93535	4017-E2
AVENUE H-3			
1000	LAN	93534	4015-G3
10000	LACo	93535	4018-B2
AVENUE H-4			
100	LAN	93535	4015-J3
300	LAN	93535	4016-B3
700	LAN	93534	4015-E3
3700	LAN	93536	4015-A3
4000	LACo	93535	4016-J3
4000	LAN	93536	4014-A3
4800	LACo	93535	4017-J2
8200	LACo	93536	4014-A3
8800	LAN	93536	4013-F3
8900	LACo	93535	4018-D2
AVENUE H-5			
-	LAN	93535	4016-C3
900	LAN	93534	4015-F3
10000	LACo	93535	4018-B3
AVENUE H-6			
100	LAN	93534	4015-F3
100	LAN	93535	4015-J3
3000	LAN	93535	4016-A3
3700	LAN	93536	4015-A3
4300	LAN	93536	4014-J3
AVENUE H-7			
-	LAN	93535	4016-A3
-	LAN	93536	4015-E4
700	LAN	93534	4015-F3
AVENUE H-8			
-	LAN	93534	4015-F4
100	LAN	93535	4015-J4
300	LAN	93535	4016-A3
2000	LAN	93536	4015-A4
4500	LAN	93536	4014-B4
4500	LACo	93535	4016-J3
4500	LACo	93535	4017-A3
8200	LACo	93536	4014-B4
8500	LACo	93536	4013-A4
8500	LAN	93536	4013-F4
9000	LACo	93535	4018-C3
AVENUE H-9			
-	LAN	93535	4016-G3
700	LAN	93534	4015-F4
AVENUE H-10			
700	LAN	93534	4015-F4
3000	LAN	93535	4016-G3
3700	LACo	93535	4016-H4
6500	LACo	93535	4017-D3
13000	LACo	93535	4018-H3
AVENUE H-11			
300	LAN	93535	4015-H4
300	LAN	93535	4016-A4
700	LAN	93534	4015-F4
AVENUE H-12			
-	LAN	93535	4015-J4
500	LAN	93534	4015-E4
700	LAN	93535	4016-B4
5000	LAN	93536	4014-A4
6500	LACo	93535	4017-D4
8000	LACo	93536	4014-A4
9000	LACo	93536	4013-H4
11000	LACo	93535	4018-E3
AVENUE H-13			
300	LAN	93535	4015-J4
300	LAN	93535	4016-B4
500	LAN	93534	4015-E4
AVENUE H-14			
300	LAN	93535	4015-J4
300	LAN	93535	4016-A4
500	LAN	93534	4015-F4
6500	LACo	93535	4017-D4
6500	LAN	93536	4014-D5
12500	LACo	93536	4013-A5
AVENUE H-15			
1200	LAN	93534	4015-F4
AVENUE HALL			
26000	SCTA	91355	4460-B7
AVENUE HOPKINS			
27400	SCTA	91355	4550-D1
27700	SCTA	91355	4460-C7
AVENUE I			
100	LAN	93534	4015-H5
100	LAN	93535	4015-H5
100	RBCH	90277	792-J1
300	TOR	90277	792-J1
300	LAN	93535	4016-C4
2000	LAN	93536	4015-C5
3900	LACo	93535	4016-J4
4000	LAN	93536	4014-D5
4700	LACo	93535	4017-C4
7000	LACo	93536	4014-C5
8500	LAN	93536	4013-J5
8500	LACo	93536	4013-B5
9000	LACo	93535	4018-D4
AVENUE I-2			
12700	LACo	93535	4018-H4
AVENUE I-6			
13400	LACo	93535	4018-J5
AVENUE I-12			
8500	LACo	93536	4013-F6
8500	LACo	93536	4014-A6
8500	LAN	93536	4013-F6
8500	LAN	93536	4014-A6
10200	LACo	93535	4018-C6
AVENUE J			
100	LAN	93534	4015-F7
100	LAN	93535	4015-J7
300	LAN	93535	4016-D6
2000	LAN	93536	4015-B7
4100	LAN	93536	4014-C7
7000	LACo	93536	4014-C7
8500	LACo	93536	4013-B7
9000	LAN	93536	4013-F7
AVENUE J Rt#-N5			
700	LAN	93535	4016-H6
4500	LAN	93535	4017-B6
4800	LACo	93535	4017-B6
9000	LACo	93535	4018-C6
9300	LAN	93535	4018-C6
AVENUE J-1			
-	LAN	93536	4014-G7
500	LAN	93535	4016-A7
800	LAN	93534	4015-G7
AVENUE J-2			
100	LAN	93535	4015-J7
300	LAN	93534	4015-F7
1200	LAN	93535	4016-C7
2300	LAN	93536	4015-B7
6300	LAN	93536	4014-E7
8500	LACo	93536	4013-J7
8500	LACo	93536	4014-A7
9000	LAN	93536	4013-H7
AVENUE J-3			
900	LAN	93535	4016-A7
1300	LAN	93534	4015-F7
2200	LAN	93536	4015-B7
6000	LAN	93536	4014-E7
12100	LACo	93536	4013-B7
13200	LACo	93535	4018-J6
AVENUE J-4			
300	LAN	93534	4015-F7
400	LAN	93535	4016-A7
2100	LAN	93536	4015-B7
6000	LAN	93536	4014-E7
7500	LACo	93535	4017-J7
7500	LAN	93535	4017-J7
8500	LACo	93536	4013-J7
8500	LACo	93536	4014-A7
9000	LACo	93535	4018-J6
9000	LAN	93535	4018-A7
9000	LAN	93536	4013-G7
12000	LACo	93536	4103-C1
AVENUE J-5			
-	LAN	93536	4014-H7
100	LAN	93534	4015-F7
100	LAN	93535	4015-J7
500	LAN	93535	4016-A7
3500	LAN	93536	4015-A7
6100	LAN	93536	4104-E1
12100	LACo	93536	4103-B1
13100	LACo	93535	4018-J7
AVENUE J-6			
-	LAN	93536	4014-H7
500	LAN	93534	4015-F7
600	LAN	93535	4016-A7
3000	LAN	93536	4015-A7
6400	LAN	93536	4104-E1
9000	LAN	93536	4103-H1
AVENUE J-7			
-	LAN	93536	4104-H1
100	LAN	93535	4105-F1
200	LAN	93535	4015-H7
300	LAN	93534	4015-H7
300	LAN	93534	4105-F1
300	LAN	93535	4016-A7
3000	LAN	93536	4105-A1
AVENUE J-8			
100	LAN	93535	4105-J1
300	LAN	93534	4105-F1
300	LAN	93535	4106-A1
1300	LAN	93535	4016-C7
2000	LAN	93536	4105-A1
4200	LAN	93536	4104-C1
4500	LAN	93535	4017-C7
7000	LACo	93535	4017-J7
8500	LACo	93536	4103-C1
8500	LACo	93536	4104-A1
9000	LAN	93535	4018-C7
9000	LAN	93536	4103-G1
9000	LACo	93535	4018-C7
AVENUE J-9			
-	LAN	93536	4104-E1
300	LAN	93534	4105-G1
500	LAN	93535	4106-A1
2800	LAN	93536	4105-A1
9200	LAN	93536	4103-H1
AVENUE J-10			
-	LAN	93536	4104-E1
300	LAN	93534	4105-G1
500	LAN	93535	4106-B1
3600	LAN	93536	4105-A1
8500	LACo	93535	4017-J7
9000	LAN	93536	4103-J1
AVENUE J-11			
-	LAN	93536	4104-E1
-	LAN	93536	4105-A1
400	LAN	93535	4106-A1
500	LAN	93534	4105-G1
AVENUE J-12			
-	LAN	93535	4016-F7
200	LAN	93535	4105-J1
300	LAN	93535	4106-A1
400	LAN	93534	4105-E1
2100	LAN	93536	4105-A1
6000	LAN	93536	4104-D1
8000	LAN	93535	4107-J1
8400	LACo	93535	4107-J1
9000	LAN	93535	4108-B1
9000	LAN	93536	4103-H1
10500	LACo	93535	4108-D1
13000	LACo	93535	4018-J7
AVENUE J-13			
-	LAN	93536	4104-E1
200	LAN	93534	4105-G1
200	LAN	93535	4105-J1
300	LAN	93535	4106-A1
2000	LAN	93536	4105-A1
4500	LAN	93535	4107-A1
11100	LACo	93535	4108-E1
AVENUE J-14			
-	LAN	93536	4104-E2
300	LAN	93534	4105-G1
400	LAN	93535	4106-A1
2500	LAN	93536	4105-B1
9000	LAN	93536	4103-H2
13500	LACo	93535	4108-J1
13500	LACo	93535	4109-A1
AVENUE J-15			
-	LAN	93536	4104-E2
200	LAN	93535	4105-J2
300	LAN	93534	4105-E1
300	LAN	93535	4106-A1
3500	LAN	93536	4105-A2
AVENUE K			
100	LAN	93534	4105-H2
100	LAN	93535	4105-H2
200	LAN	93535	4106-C1
2000	LAN	93536	4105-D2
4000	LACo	93536	4104-C2
4000	LACo	93536	4105-D2
4000	LAN	93536	4104-C2
4500	LAN	93535	4107-D1
6400	LACo	93535	4107-D1
8500	LAN	93536	4103-G2
8500	LACo	93536	4103-J2
9000	LACo	93535	4108-D1
9000	LAN	93535	4108-D1
13500	LACo	93535	4109-D1
20500	LACo	93535	4110-H1
AVENUE K-1			
-	LAN	93536	4104-F2
2700	LAN	93536	4105-B2
AVENUE K-2			
-	LAN	93536	4104-F2
700	LAN	93535	4106-B2
1500	LAN	93534	4105-E2
12500	LACo	93535	4108-H1
AVENUE K-3			
-	LAN	93536	4104-F2
2100	LAN	93535	4106-D2
11100	LACo	93535	4108-F1
AVENUE K-4			
100	LAN	93535	4105-J2
200	LAN	93535	4106-A2
500	LAN	93534	4105-E2
2000	LAN	93536	4105-B2
4000	LACo	93536	4105-B2
4100	LACo	93536	4104-J2
4500	LAN	93536	4104-B2
5000	LACo	93535	4107-D2
5000	LAN	93535	4107-B2
9500	LACo	93535	4108-G1
10300	LAN	93536	4103-F2
13400	LACo	93535	4109-A1
20500	LACo	93535	4110-F1
AVENUE K-5			
-	LAN	93536	4105-E2
10000	LAN	93535	4108-B2
11100	LACo	93535	4108-F2
AVENUE K-6			
100	LAN	93535	4105-J2
200	LAN	93535	4106-A2
500	LAN	93534	4105-H2
2500	LAN	93536	4105-D2
4500	LACo	93536	4104-J2
4500	LAN	93536	4104-F3
5000	LACo	93535	4107-B2
13000	LACo	93535	4108-J2
14700	LACo	93535	4109-C2
AVENUE K-7			
-	LAN	93536	4105-E2
700	LAN	93535	4106-B2
AVENUE K-8			
100	LAN	93535	4105-J3
200	LAN	93535	4106-C2
500	LAN	93534	4105-G3
2000	LAN	93536	4105-E3
4000	LACo	93535	4106-J2
4000	LACo	93536	4105-E3
4100	LACo	93536	4104-J3
4500	LAN	93535	4107-H2
4500	LAN	93536	4104-B3
5000	LACo	93535	4107-B2
8500	LAN	93536	4103-G3
9500	LACo	93535	4108-B2
13000	LACo	93535	4109-A2
19500	LACo	93535	4110-E2
AVENUE K-9			
-	LAN	93536	4104-F3
1700	LAN	93534	4105-E3
2100	LAN	93536	4105-C3
AVENUE K-10			
-	LAN	93536	4104-F3
200	LAN	93535	4105-J3
300	LAN	93535	4106-A3
1500	LAN	93534	4105-E3
2000	LAN	93536	4105-A3
4100	LACo	93536	4104-J3
4100	LACo	93536	4105-A3
9500	LACo	93535	4108-B2
15000	LACo	93535	4109-D2
AVENUE K-11			
-	LAN	93536	4104-F3
800	LAN	93535	4106-B3
1500	LAN	93534	4105-E3
3600	LAN	93536	4105-A3
11100	LACo	93535	4108-E2
AVENUE K-12			
400	LAN	93535	4106-A3
1700	LAN	93534	4105-E3
2000	LAN	93536	4105-A3
4000	LACo	93535	4106-H3
4000	LACo	93536	4105-A3
4100	LAN	93536	4104-A3
4100	LACo	93536	4104-J3
7000	LACo	93535	4107-F3
7400	LAN	93535	4107-F3
8500	LAN	93536	4103-G3
9500	LACo	93535	4108-H2
14000	LACo	93535	4109-B2
AVENUE K-13			
-	LAN	93535	4106-B3
-	LAN	93536	4104-F3
1900	LAN	93534	4105-E3
2100	LAN	93536	4105-A3
11100	LACo	93535	4108-E3
AVENUE K-14			
-	LAN	93535	4106-B3
-	LAN	93536	4104-F4
1900	LAN	93534	4105-E3
2100	LAN	93536	4105-A3
5000	LACo	93536	4104-H4
9500	LACo	93535	4108-B3
10000	LAN	93536	4103-G4
15000	LACo	93535	4109-D3
AVENUE K-15			
100	LAN	93535	4105-J3
100	LAN	93535	4106-A3
800	LAN	93534	4105-G3
2100	LAN	93536	4105-E3
AVENUE KEARNEY			
24900	SCTA	91355	4460-D7
24900	SCTA	91355	4550-D1
AVENUE L			
100	LAN	93534	4105-H4
100	LAN	93535	4105-H4
200	LAN	93535	4106-B3
1000	PMDL	93550	4106-B3
2000	LAN	93536	4105-D4
4000	LACo	93535	4106-J3
4000	LACo	93536	4104-J4
4000	LACo	93536	4105-D4
4000	LAN	93535	4107-A3
4000	LAN	93536	4104-C4
4000	PMDL	93552	4106-J3
4000	PMDL	93552	4107-A3
5000	LACo	93535	4107-D3
8500	LAN	93536	4103-H4
9000	PMDL	93591	4107-J3
9100	LACo	93535	4108-B3
9100	PMDL	93591	4108-B3
10200	LAN	93535	4108-B3
13000	LACo	93535	4109-A3
18000	LACo	93535	4110-C3
AVENUE L-1			
2300	LAN	93536	4105-D4
5600	LAN	93536	4104-F4
AVENUE L-2			
1000	LAN	93534	4105-G4
2600	LAN	93536	4105-C4
4000	LACo	93536	4104-G4
4000	LACo	93536	4105-A4
5500	LAN	93536	4104-D4
6500	PMDL	93552	4107-E4
12000	LACo	93535	4108-G3
AVENUE L-3			
5000	LACo	93536	4104-H4
11000	PMDL	93591	4108-E3
AVENUE L-4			
100	LAN	93534	4105-G4
100	LAN	93535	4105-J4
200	LAN	93535	4106-B4
2000	LAN	93536	4105-A4
2000	PMDL	93550	4106-E4
4000	LACo	93536	4104-H4
4000	LACo	93536	4105-A4
4000	PMDL	93552	4106-J4
4500	PMDL	93552	4107-A4
5500	LAN	93536	4104-D4
9000	PMDL	93591	4107-J4
9100	PMDL	93591	4108-B4
12000	LACo	93535	4108-J3
13400	LACo	93535	4109-B3
20500	LACo	93535	4110-F4
AVENUE L-5			
-	LAN	93536	4104-D5
9900	PMDL	93591	4108-C4
AVENUE L-6			
1000	LAN	93534	4105-G4
2500	LAN	93536	4105-C4
4000	LACo	93536	4104-G5
4000	LACo	93536	4105-A4
5500	LAN	93536	4104-D5
12000	LACo	93535	4108-G4
AVENUE L-7			
6500	LAN	93536	4104-D5
AVENUE L-8			
100	LAN	93535	4105-H5
100	LAN	93535	4106-B4
100	LAN	93534	4105-F5
1000	PMDL	93550	4106-B4
2000	LAN	93536	4105-B5
4000	LACo	93536	4105-B5
4000	PMDL	93552	4106-H4
4100	LACo	93536	4104-J5
5000	PMDL	93552	4107-B4
5500	LAN	93536	4104-C5
9000	PMDL	93591	4107-J4
9000	PMDL	93591	4108-B4
12000	LACo	93535	4108-J4
13500	PMDL	93591	4109-B4
17900	LACo	93535	4110-B4
AVENUE L-9			
100	LAN	93534	4105-G5
7000	LAN	93536	4104-D5
AVENUE L-10			
700	LAN	93534	4105-F5
2200	LAN	93536	4105-D5
4500	LACo	93536	4104-H5
6500	LAN	93536	4104-C5
AVENUE L-11			
4500	LACo	93536	4104-J5
5800	LAN	93536	4104-C5
11100	PMDL	93591	4108-E4
17600	LACo	93535	4109-J4
AVENUE L-12			
100	LAN	93535	4105-J5
100	LAN	93535	4106-B5
700	LAN	93534	4105-E5
2000	LAN	93536	4105-B5
3300	PMDL	93550	4106-B5
3500	LACo	93536	4105-B5
4000	PMDL	93552	4106-H5
4400	LACo	93536	4104-D5
4500	PMDL	93552	4107-A5
5500	LAN	93536	4104-E5
9500	PMDL	93591	4108-B5
17300	LACo	93535	4109-J4
17900	LACo	93535	4110-A4
AVENUE L-13			
700	LAN	93534	4105-G5
4500	LACo	93536	4104-J5
11100	PMDL	93591	4108-E5
17600	LACo	93535	4109-J4
18100	LACo	93535	4110-A4
AVENUE L-14			
600	LAN	93534	4105-G5
2000	LAN	93536	4105-E5
4500	LACo	93536	4104-H6
5500	LAN	93536	4104-H6
AVENUE L-15			
5500	LAN	93536	4104-G6
6600	LACo	93536	4104-E6
AVENUE M			
5000	PMDL	93552	4107-C5
5000	LACo	93552	4107-C5
9000	PMDL	93591	4107-J5
9000	PMDL	93591	4108-B5
15000	LACo	93535	4109-E5
17800	LACo	93535	4110-C5
18100	LACo	93535	4108-F5
AVENUE M-2			
3200	LAN	93536	4105-A6
4000	LAN	93536	4104-J6
5000	LACo	93536	4104-H6
5800	LACo	93551	4104-H6
AVENUE M-3			
16700	LACo	93535	4109-G5
AVENUE M-4			
1000	PMDL	93551	4105-G6
2000	LACo	93551	4105-D6
2700	LACo	93536	4105-D6
3200	LAN	93536	4105-A6
4000	LAN	93536	4104-H6
4500	LACo	93536	4104-H6
5900	LACo	93551	4104-E6
6300	PMDL	93551	4104-E6
9500	PMDL	93591	4108-B6
16500	LACo	93535	4109-G5
18500	LACo	93535	4110-B5
AVENUE M-5			
-	LAN	93536	4105-C6
AVENUE M-6			
3800	LAN	93536	4105-C6
4500	LACo	93536	4104-F7
16300	LACo	93535	4109-G6
AVENUE M-7			
-	LAN	93536	4105-C7
AVENUE M-8			
200	PMDL	93550	4105-G7
200	PMDL	93550	4106-A7
700	PMDL	93551	4105-G7
1200	LACo	93551	4105-F7
3000	LAN	93536	4105-B7
3000	LAN	93551	4105-B7
4000	LAN	93536	4104-J7
4500	LACo	93536	4104-J7
4500	LACo	93552	4106-J6
4500	LACo	93552	4107-A6
5200	PMDL	93536	4104-F7
5500	PMDL	93551	4104-F7
5500	LACo	93551	4104-F7
9500	PMDL	93591	4108-B6
9500	LACo	93591	4108-B6
13500	LACo	93535	4108-J6
13500	LACo	93535	4109-A6
18000	LACo	93535	4110-B6
AVENUE M-9			
4600	LACo	93536	4104-J7
AVENUE M-10			
-	LAN	93536	4104-J7
3000	LAN	93536	4105-A7
3000	LAN	93551	4105-C7
4500	LACo	93536	4104-J7
10000	PMDL	93591	4108-C6
13500	LACo	93535	4108-J6
13500	LACo	93535	4109-A6
AVENUE M-11			
-	LAN	93536	4104-J7
-	LAN	93536	4105-B7
AVENUE M-12			
-	LAN	93536	4104-J7
200	PMDL	93550	4106-B7
1000	PMDL	93551	4105-G7
2000	LACo	93551	4105-D7
3000	LAN	93536	4105-D7
3000	LAN	93551	4105-D7
4500	LACo	93536	4104-H7
5100	PMDL	93536	4104-H7
5400	PMDL	93551	4104-F7
13600	LACo	93535	4109-A6
17500	LACo	93535	4110-A6
AVENUE M-14			
1000	PMDL	93551	4105-G7
3000	LAN	93536	4105-C7
3000	LAN	93551	4105-C7
4500	LACo	93536	4194-H1
13600	LACo	93535	4109-A7
AVENUE M-14 ST W			
-	LAN	93536	4194-J1
AVENUE MENTRY			
27500	SCTA	91355	4550-E1
27600	SCTA	91355	4460-E7
AVENUE N			
300	PMDL	93550	4195-J1
300	PMDL	93550	4196-A1
400	PMDL	93551	4195-J1
1300	LACo	93551	4195-D1
3000	LACo	93536	4195-D1
3000	LAN	93536	4195-D1
3000	LAN	93551	4195-D1
4000	LACo	93536	4194-J1
4000	LACo	93552	4106-J7
4000	PMDL	93552	4106-J7
4000	LAN	93536	4194-J1
4500	LACo	93552	4107-D7
4500	PMDL	93536	4194-J1
5000	PMDL	93551	4194-E1
9000	LACo	93591	4107-J7
9000	LACo	93591	4108-B7
12000	LACo	93535	4108-G7
12000	PMDL	93591	4108-B7
13600	LACo	93535	4109-A7
17700	LACo	93535	4110-C7
AVENUE N-1			
200	PMDL	93550	4195-J1
AVENUE N-2			
-	PMDL	93551	4194-J1
10000	PMDL	93591	4108-C7
19700	LACo	93535	4110-D7
AVENUE N-3			
3000	LACo	93551	4195-B1
4100	LACo	93551	4194-J1
AVENUE N-4			
100	PMDL	93550	4195-J1
300	PMDL	93550	4196-A1
1000	PMDL	93551	4195-G1
1200	LACo	93551	4195-E1
4500	PMDL	93551	4194-H1
13700	LACo	93535	4109-A7
14500	LACo	93535	4199-C1
17900	LACo	93535	4110-A7
AVENUE N-5			
18200	LACo	93535	4110-A7
AVENUE N-6			
13500	LACo	93535	4109-A7
13500	LACo	93535	4199-A1
20200	LACo	93535	4110-E7
AVENUE N-8			
900	PMDL	93550	4195-J2
900	PMDL	93550	4196-A2
1000	LACo	93551	4195-D2
1000	PMDL	93551	4195-G2
3700	PMDL	93550	4196-A2
4100	PMDL	93551	4194-G2
4100	LACo	93551	4194-J2
10000	PMDL	93591	4198-D1
12000	LACo	93535	4198-J1
13500	LACo	93535	4199-C1
17700	LACo	93535	4200-A1
AVENUE N-10			
13000	LACo	93535	4198-J1
19000	LACo	93535	4200-C1
AVENUE N-11			
13600	LACo	93535	4199-A1
AVENUE N-12			
100	PMDL	93550	4195-J2
100	PMDL	93550	4196-A2
1000	LACo	93551	4195-E2
1000	PMDL	93551	4195-G2
11700	PMDL	93591	4198-F2
13000	LACo	93535	4198-J2
13500	LACo	93535	4199-A1
17900	LACo	93535	4200-B1
AVENUE N-13			
13600	LACo	93535	4199-A2
AVENUE N-14			
13000	LACo	93535	4198-J2
19000	LACo	93535	4200-C1
AVENUE O			
100	PMDL	93550	4195-J3
100	PMDL	93551	4195-H3
100	PMDL	93550	4196-A3
1000	LACo	93551	4195-E3
3100	PMDL	93550	4196-J2
4000	LACo	93552	4196-J2
4500	LACo	93552	4197-A2
9000	LACo	93591	4197-J2
9000	LACo	93591	4198-C2
9900	PMDL	93591	4198-C2
12000	LACo	93535	4198-J2
13300	LACo	93591	4199-C2
13300	LACo	93535	4199-C2
17700	LACo	93535	4200-B2
17700	LACo	93591	4200-B2
AVENUE O-2			
2100	LACo	93551	4195-D3
10000	PMDL	93591	4198-C2
AVENUE O-4			
300	PMDL	93551	4195-H3
900	LACo	93551	4195-E3
10000	PMDL	93591	4198-C3
10800	LACo	93551	4193-F4
AVENUE O-5			
500	PMDL	93550	4196-B3
AVENUE O-6			
2000	LACo	93551	4195-D3
10000	PMDL	93591	4198-C3
AVENUE O-7			
500	PMDL	93550	4196-A3
AVENUE O-8			
-	PMDL	93550	4195-J4
-	PMDL	93550	4196-A4
1000	PMDL	93551	4195-C4
1000	LACo	93551	4195-D4
3500	PMDL	93550	4196-H3
7200	LACo	93551	4194-C4
7200	PMDL	93551	4194-C4
9000	LACo	93591	4197-J3
9000	LACo	93591	4198-B3
10000	PMDL	93591	4198-D3
10900	LACo	93551	4193-E4
18500	LACo	93591	4200-C3
AVENUE O-10			
2200	LACo	93551	4195-D4
39900	LACo	93591	4199-A3
AVENUE O-12			
500	PMDL	93550	4196-B4
1500	PMDL	93551	4195-D4
1500	LACo	93551	4195-D4
11000	PMDL	93591	4198-E4
19000	LACo	93591	4200-C3
AVENUE O-14			
-	PMDL	93550	4195-J4
-	PMDL	93550	4196-A4
AVENUE OF THE CHAMPIONS			
600	ING	90301	703-D6
AVENUE OF THE OAKS			
19000	SCTA	91321	4551-G5
AVENUE OF THE STARS			
1800	CenC	90067	632-E4
2200	LA	90035	632-E4
AVENUE P			
1500	LACo	93591	4199-F3
1500	PMDL	93550	4196-F4
1500	PMDL	93550	4196-F4
4000	LACo	93552	4196-H4
4500	LACo	93552	4197-A4
9000	LACo	93591	4197-J4
9000	LACo	93591	4198-B4
9400	PMDL	93591	4198-F4
18000	LACo	93591	4200-B4
AVENUE P-1			
100	PMDL	93550	4195-J5
100	PMDL	93550	4196-A5
1200	PMDL	93551	4195-G5
AVENUE P-2			
100	PMDL	93550	4195-J5
100	PMDL	93550	4196-A5
AVENUE P-3			
100	PMDL	93550	4195-J5
100	PMDL	93550	4196-A5
AVENUE P-4			
100	PMDL	93550	4195-J5
100	PMDL	93550	4196-A5
400	PMDL	93551	4195-E5
9400	LACo	93591	4198-B5
11000	PMDL	93591	4198-E5
20000	LACo	93591	4200-E4
AVENUE P-5			
100	PMDL	93550	4195-J5
100	PMDL	93550	4196-A5
20000	LACo	93591	4200-E4
AVENUE P-6			
2300	PMDL	93551	4195-D5
AVENUE P-8			
700	PMDL	93550	4196-D6
800	PMDL	93550	4196-H5
2000	PMDL	93551	4195-D6
4000	LACo	93552	4196-H5
4500	LACo	93552	4197-A5
8200	PMDL	93552	4197-J5
9000	LACo	93591	4197-J5
9000	LACo	93591	4198-B5
9000	PMDL	93591	4197-J5
9000	PMDL	93591	4198-E5
13700	LACo	93591	4199-B5
18000	LACo	93591	4200-B5
AVENUE P-12			
100	PMDL	93550	4195-J6
100	PMDL	93550	4196-A6
800	PMDL	93550	4196-B6
2500	PMDL	93551	4195-D6
9000	PMDL	93591	4197-J6
9000	PMDL	93591	4198-B6
12600	LACo	93591	4198-H6
13700	LACo	93591	4199-H5
19500	LACo	93591	4200-A5
AVENUE P-14			
400	PMDL	93550	4196-A6
1000	LACo	93551	4195-G7
AVENUE P-15			
800	PMDL	93550	4196-B6
AVENUE PAINE			
25500	Valc	91355	4459-F6
AVENUE PENN			
-	Cstc	91384	4459-E6
-	Valc	91355	4459-E6
AVENUE PRESIDIO			
-	SCTA	91355	4550-B5
AVENUE Q			
100	PMDL	93550	4195-J7
100	PMDL	93551	4195-H7
100	PMDL	93550	4196-H6
300	PMDL	93550	4196-A7
4200	PMDL	93552	4196-H6
4500	PMDL	93552	4197-A6
8000	LACo	93552	4197-C6
9000	PMDL	93591	4198-C6
9000	LACo	93591	4198-F6
12900	LACo	93591	4199-D6
17400	LACo	93591	4200-B6
AVENUE Q-1			
500	PMDL	93550	4196-A7
1000	LACo	93551	4195-G7

STREET Block City ZIP Pg-Grid

AVENUE Q-1
1000 PMDL 93551 4195-G7
15100 LACo 93591 4199-E6
AVENUE Q-2
500 PMDL 93550 4196-A7
9500 LACo 93591 4198-B6
AVENUE Q-3
100 PMDL 93550 4195-J7
100 PMDL 93550 4196-A7
15000 LACo 93591 4199-D6
AVENUE Q-4
- PMDL 93552 4197-C7
100 PMDL 93550 4195-J7
100 PMDL 93550 4196-A7
8000 LACo 93552 4197-H7
9000 LACo 93591 4197-J7
9000 LACo 93591 4198-B7
13900 LACo 93591 4199-E6
20500 LACo 93591 4200-F6
AVENUE Q-5
500 PMDL 93550 4196-A7
17100 LACo 93591 4199-H7
AVENUE Q-6
500 PMDL 93550 4196-B7
2000 PMDL 93551 4195-E7
9500 LACo 93591 4198-B7
20500 LACo 93591 4200-F7
AVENUE Q-7
100 PMDL 93550 4285-J1
100 PMDL 93550 4196-A7
100 PMDL 93550 4286-B1
15100 LACo 93591 4199-E7
AVENUE Q-8
500 PMDL 93551 4285-H1
AVENUE Q-9
500 PMDL 93550 4286-A1
500 PMDL 93551 4285-H1
AVENUE Q-10
- PMDL 93552 4287-C1
100 PMDL 93550 4285-J1
100 PMDL 93550 4286-A1
500 PMDL 93551 4285-H1
9000 Litl 93543 4287-J1
9000 Litl 93543 4288-B1
10000 Litl 93543 4198-C7
13700 LACo 93591 4199-A7
AVENUE Q-11
800 PMDL 93550 4286-B1
4000 PMDL 93552 4286-J1
AVENUE Q-12
- PMDL 93552 4287-C1
500 PMDL 93550 4286-A1
500 PMDL 93551 4285-H1
4000 PMDL 93552 4286-J1
8800 Litl 93543 4287-J1
9000 Litl 93543 4288-B1
12000 LACo 93591 4288-G1
17000 Llan 93544 4199-H7
20300 Llan 93544 4200-F7
AVENUE Q-13
1200 PMDL 93550 4286-D1
AVENUE Q-14
- PMDL 93552 4287-C1
1700 PMDL 93550 4286-D1
4000 PMDL 93552 4286-H1
8700 Litl 93543 4287-J1
9000 Litl 93543 4288-B1
AVENUE Q-15
1600 PMDL 93550 4286-G1
AVENUE Q-16
3100 PMDL 93550 4286-G1
AVENUE R
100 PMDL 93550 4285-J2
100 PMDL 93550 4286-H1
4000 PMDL 93552 4286-J1
4500 PMDL 93552 4287-A1
8000 LACo 93552 4287-H1
8700 Litl 93543 4287-J1
9000 Litl 93543 4288-B1
11600 LACo 93591 4288-J1
AVENUE R-1
1500 PMDL 93550 4286-C2
AVENUE R-2
100 PMDL 93550 4285-J2
100 PMDL 93550 4286-A2
4700 PMDL 93552 4287-B2
10000 Litl 93543 4288-D1
11500 LACo 93591 4288-F1
AVENUE R-3
100 PMDL 93550 4285-J2
100 PMDL 93550 4286-A2
AVENUE R-4
100 PMDL 93550 4285-J2
100 PMDL 93550 4286-A2
4700 PMDL 93552 4287-B2
9000 Litl 93543 4287-E2
9000 Litl 93543 4288-B2
11500 LACo 93591 4288-F2
AVENUE R-5
100 PMDL 93550 4285-J2
100 PMDL 93550 4286-A2
AVENUE R-6
300 PMDL 93550 4286-A2
4000 PMDL 93552 4286-J2
4500 PMDL 93552 4287-A2
10000 Litl 93543 4288-D2
13000 LACo 93591 4288-J2
AVENUE R-7
300 PMDL 93550 4286-C2
AVENUE R-8
200 PMDL 93550 4286-G2
700 PMDL 93551 4285-H3
700 LACo 93551 4285-H3

AVENUE R-8
4000 PMDL 93552 4286-J2
4500 PMDL 93552 4287-B2
9000 Litl 93543 4288-B2
11600 LACo 93591 4288-F2
AVENUE R-9
200 PMDL 93550 4286-A3
AVENUE R-10
1700 PMDL 93550 4286-D3
9000 Litl 93543 4288-B2
13000 LACo 93591 4288-J2
AVENUE R-11
300 PMDL 93550 4286-A3
4700 PMDL 93552 4287-B3
9500 Litl 93543 4288-B3
AVENUE R-12
300 PMDL 93550 4286-A3
700 LACo 93551 4285-H3
4000 PMDL 93552 4286-J3
4700 PMDL 93552 4287-B3
9000 Litl 93543 4288-A3
AVENUE R-13
2500 PMDL 93550 4286-F3
4000 PMDL 93552 4286-J3
AVENUE R-14
2500 PMDL 93550 4286-E3
4300 PMDL 93552 4286-J3
4500 PMDL 93552 4287-A3
9000 Litl 93543 4288-A3
AVENUE R-15
2700 PMDL 93550 4286-F3
AVENUE R-16
2800 PMDL 93550 4286-F3
AVENUE ROCKEFELLER
24600 SCTA 91355 4550-E1
AVENUE S
100 LACo 93551 4285-F4
100 PMDL 93550 4285-J4
100 PMDL 93550 4286-C4
100 PMDL 93551 4285-E3
4000 PMDL 93552 4286-J3
4500 PMDL 93552 4287-A3
8000 LACo 93552 4287-H3
8700 LACo 93552 4288-B3
9000 Litl 93543 4288-B3
11600 LACo 93591 4288-J3
AVENUE S-1
3000 PMDL 93550 4286-G4
AVENUE S-2
- LACo 93551 4285-J4
3000 PMDL 93550 4286-G4
5200 PMDL 93552 4287-B4
8700 LACo 93552 4287-J4
8700 Litl 93543 4287-J4
9200 Litl 93543 4288-C4
AVENUE S-3
3200 PMDL 93550 4286-G4
AVENUE S-4
100 LACo 93551 4285-G4
3000 PMDL 93550 4286-G4
4000 PMDL 93552 4286-J4
5200 PMDL 93552 4287-B4
8600 LACo 93552 4287-E1
8600 Litl 93543 4287-J4
9100 Litl 93543 4288-A4
11600 LACo 93591 4288-F4
E AVENUE S-4
1700 PMDL 93550 4286-D4
AVENUE S-5
11200 Litl 93543 4288-E4
AVENUE S-6
- LACo 93591 4288-G4
9600 Litl 93543 4288-D4
AVENUE S-7
11700 LACo 93591 4288-G4
AVENUE S-8
- LACo 93591 4288-F4
3700 PMDL 93550 4286-J5
4000 PMDL 93552 4286-J5
4500 PMDL 93552 4287-A5
8200 Litl 93543 4287-F1
8900 Litl 93543 4288-B4
AVENUE S-9
11700 LACo 93591 4288-G4
AVENUE S-10
4000 PMDL 93552 4286-J5
8700 Litl 93543 4287-F1
8800 Litl 93543 4288-A5
11800 LACo 93591 4288-G5
AVENUE S-11
11200 Litl 93543 4288-E5
AVENUE S-12
2800 PMDL 93550 4286-F5
4000 PMDL 93552 4286-J5
8500 Litl 93543 4287-J5
9300 Litl 93543 4288-A5
11600 LACo 93591 4288-F5
AVENUE S-14
100 LACo 93551 4285-H6
8200 Litl 93543 4287-H5
9600 Litl 93543 4288-C5
AVENUE SAN LUIS
20900 WdHl 91364 560-A3
22100 WdHl 91364 559-H3
AVENUE SCOTT
27500 SCTA 91355 4550-D1
27700 SCTA 91355 4470-D7
AVENUE SHERMAN
- Valc 91355 4459-F6
AVENUE STANFORD
24900 SCTA 91355 4460-B7
25200 SCTA 91355 4550-B1

AVENUE T
5600 PMDL 93552 4287-E5
7000 Litl 93543 4287-E5
8200 Litl 93543 4287-H5
8800 Litl 93543 4288-B5
11600 Pear 93553 4288-F5
11600 LACo 93591 4288-J5
AVENUE T-2
3200 PMDL 93550 4286-H6
4000 PMDL 93552 4286-H6
5800 PMDL 93552 4287-D6
8700 Litl 93543 4287-J6
8900 Litl 93543 4288-B6
AVENUE T-4
3400 PMDL 93550 4286-G6
4000 PMDL 93552 4286-J6
5200 LACo 93552 4287-C6
6000 PMDL 93552 4287-D6
8700 Litl 93543 4287-J6
8900 Litl 93543 4288-B6
12600 Pear 93553 4288-J6
AVENUE T-5
5700 PMDL 93552 4287-C6
AVENUE T-6
3200 PMDL 93550 4286-H6
4000 PMDL 93552 4286-J6
7800 Litl 93543 4287-H6
8900 Litl 93543 4288-B6
AVENUE T-8
3200 PMDL 93550 4286-J7
4000 PMDL 93552 4286-J7
4300 PMDL 93552 4286-J7
4300 LACo 93552 4287-C7
5700 PMDL 93552 4287-E6
7600 Litl 93543 4287-J6
8900 Litl 93543 4288-B6
AVENUE T-10
5300 LACo 93552 4287-C7
8700 Litl 93543 4287-J7
8900 Litl 93543 4288-B7
AVENUE T-12
3800 PMDL 93550 4286-J7
4000 LACo 93552 4286-J7
4700 LACo 93552 4287-A7
8500 Litl 93543 4287-J7
8900 Litl 93543 4288-B7
11600 Pear 93553 4288-F7
AVENUE T-14
7500 Litl 93543 4287-G7
8900 Litl 93543 4288-B7
11600 Pear 93553 4288-F7
AVENUE TIBBITTS
24600 SCTA 91355 4460-E7
24600 SCTA 91355 4550-D1
E AVENUE U
- PMDL 93550 4376-F1
7000 Litl 93543 4287-F7
7000 Litl 93543 4377-E1
7500 Litl 93543 4287-H7
8900 Litl 93543 4288-B7
11600 Pear 93553 4288-H7
W AVENUE U
500 LACo 93551 4375-J1
6200 LACo 93552 4377-E1
AVENUE U-2
7400 Litl 93543 4377-F1
AVENUE U-3
7500 Litl 93543 4377-F1
AVENUE U-4
8500 Litl 93543 4377-J1
8900 Litl 93543 4378-A1
13600 Pear 93553 4379-B1
15500 LACo 93591 4379-F1
AVENUE U-5
8500 Litl 93543 4377-J1
AVENUE U-6
6200 LACo 93552 4377-D1
8500 Litl 93543 4377-J1
AVENUE U-8
5500 LACo 93552 4377-C2
11300 Litl 93543 4378-F1
11600 Pear 93553 4378-F1
13600 Pear 93553 4379-B1
AVENUE U-10
8000 Litl 93543 4377-H2
AVENUE U-12
7500 Litl 93543 4377-F2
13600 Pear 93553 4379-B2
AVENUE V
3700 PMDL 93550 4376-H3
4300 Actn 93510 4374-G3
4300 PMDL 93550 4376-J3
7700 Litl 93543 4377-H2
8100 Litl 93543 4378-B2
12600 Pear 93553 4378-J2
13300 Pear 93553 4379-B2
16500 Llan 93544 4379-H2
AVENUE V-2
12600 Pear 93553 4378-J2
13300 Pear 93553 4379-A2
AVENUE V-4
10800 Litl 93543 4378-E3
12300 Pear 93553 4378-J3
13100 Pear 93553 4379-A3
AVENUE V-5
4200 LACo 93552 4376-J3
4200 LACo 93552 4377-A3
AVENUE V-6
9200 Litl 93543 4378-B3
12600 Pear 93553 4378-J3
13100 Pear 93553 4379-A3
AVENUE V-8
4300 LACo 93552 4376-J4
4300 LACo 93552 4377-A4
8900 Litl 93543 4378-A3

AVENUE V-8
17500 Llan 93544 4379-J3
AVENUE V-9
12100 Pear 93553 4378-H3
AVENUE V-10
10300 Litl 93543 4378-D4
11500 Pear 93553 4378-H3
13300 Pear 93553 4379-A4
AVENUE V-11
13100 Pear 93553 4378-J4
AVENUE V-12
8700 Litl 93543 4377-J4
8700 Litl 93543 4378-A4
11500 Pear 93553 4378-G4
13300 Pear 93553 4379-A4
AVENUE V-13
13100 Pear 93553 4378-J4
AVENUE V-14
10600 Litl 93543 4378-E4
12100 Pear 93553 4378-G4
16200 Llan 93544 4379-G4
AVENUE W
9300 Litl 93543 4378-A4
12100 Pear 93553 4378-H4
13100 Pear 93553 4379-A4
16100 Llan 93544 4379-G4
AVENUE W-1
17200 Llan 93544 4379-J4
AVENUE W-2
- LACo 93551 4375-H6
9400 Litl 93543 4378-B5
13100 Pear 93553 4378-J4
13200 Pear 93553 4379-A4
17000 Llan 93544 4379-H4
AVENUE W-3
10600 Litl 93543 4378-D5
AVENUE W-4
- Actn 93510 4375-H6
- LACo 93551 4375-H6
9400 Litl 93543 4378-B5
12100 Pear 93553 4378-H5
13200 Pear 93553 4379-A5
16000 Llan 93544 4379-G5
AVENUE W-6
9400 Litl 93543 4378-C5
12100 Pear 93553 4378-H5
13200 Pear 93553 4379-A5
AVENUE W-8
9000 Litl 93543 4378-B5
12100 Pear 93553 4378-H5
13200 Pear 93553 4379-A5
16000 Llan 93544 4379-G5
AVENUE W-10
12100 Pear 93553 4378-G5
16700 Llan 93544 4379-H5
AVENUE W-11
12800 Pear 93553 4378-J6
13100 Pear 93553 4379-A6
AVENUE W-12
9000 Litl 93543 4378-A6
11600 Pear 93553 4378-H6
16000 Llan 93544 4379-G6
AVENUE W-13
12800 Pear 93553 4378-J6
AVENUE W-14
5400 Actn 93510 4374-H7
10100 Litl 93543 4378-C6
12100 Pear 93553 4378-H6
13400 Pear 93553 4379-B6
16500 Llan 93544 4379-H6
AVENUE WILLIAMS
- Valc 91355 4459-F6
AVENUE X
- Litl 93543 4378-F6
5200 Actn 93510 4374-G7
5200 Actn 93510 4464-H1
12000 Pear 93553 4378-F6
13600 Pear 93553 4379-C6
15500 Llan 93544 4379-G6
AVENUE X-3
12800 Pear 93553 4378-J7
AVENUE X-4
- Pear 93553 4378-F7
AVENUE X-8
11000 Litl 93543 4378-F7
11400 Litl 93543 4378-F7
11600 Pear 93553 4378-F7
AVENUE X-12
12100 Pear 93553 4468-G1
32100 Litl 93543 4468-F1
AVENUE X-15
12100 Pear 93553 4468-H1
AVENUE Y
16800 Llan 93544 4469-J1
17500 Llan 93544 4470-E1
24800 Llan 93544 4471-G1
AVENUE Y-3
22600 Llan 93544 4471-B1
AVENUE Y-4
9300 Litl 93543 4468-B2
15700 Llan 93544 4469-G2
22700 Llan 93544 4471-B1
AVENUE Y-5
19200 Llan 93544 4470-D2
AVENUE Y-8
2000 Actn 93510 4465-F3
9200 Litl 93543 4468-B3
15500 Llan 93544 4469-G2
20500 Llan 93544 4470-H2
21800 Llan 93544 4471-B2
AVENUE Y-12
16200 Llan 93544 4469-G3

AVENUE Z
9300 Litl 93543 4468-B4
23000 Llan 93544 4471-C3
AVENUE Z-2
23300 Llan 93544 4471-D3
AVENUE Z-8
20400 Llan 93544 4470-G4
24300 Llan 93544 4471-G4
AVERILL AV
700 LA 90732 823-J5
2600 SPed 90731 823-J7
2600 SPed 90731 853-J1
AVERILL PARK DR
1500 LA 90732 823-H6
AVERY CIR
20100 CRTS 90703 767-A4
AVERY PL
600 Bxby 90807 765-C6
17900 GAR 90248 763-J1
AVERY RD
600 CLAR 91711 601-C3
AVERY ST
100 LA 90013 634-H5
AVIATION BLVD
800 HMB 90254 762-J2
1200 RBCH 90278 762-J2
8600 ING 90301 703-A3
9200 Wch 90045 703-A3
9300 Wch 90045 702-J6
N AVIATION BLVD
100 ELSG 90245 732-J1
100 LACo 90250 732-J1
100 RBCH 90278 732-J5
100 MANB 90266 732-J5
400 MANB 90266 733-A6
3100 RBCH 90278 733-A6
11400 Wch 90045 702-J7
11600 Lenx 90304 702-J7
11600 ELSG 90245 702-J7
11900 Lenx 90304 732-J1
14300 HAW 90260 732-J5
14700 HAW 90261 732-J5
S AVIATION BLVD
100 HAW 90245 732-J3
100 ELSG 90245 732-J3
100 MANB 90266 732-J7
400 HAW 90250 732-J3
400 RBCH 90278 732-J7
1200 MANB 90266 762-J1
AVIATION CIDR
- HAW 90260 732-J4
- HAW 90260 733-A4
AVIATION PL
200 MANB 90266 733-A6
300 MANB 90266 732-J6
AVIATION WY
500 MANB 90266 732-J7
700 MANB 90266 762-J1
1700 RBCH 90278 762-J1
2000 RBCH 90278 732-J7
AVIGNON CT
5400 WLKV 91362 557-F5
AVIGNON DR
- SCTA 91355 4550-D2
AVIGNON LN
39400 PMDL 93551 4195-D5
AVILA
- LVRN 91750 570-H3
AVILA ST
900 LA 90012 634-H3
AVILA WY
100 CLAR 91711 571-D7
4900 BPK 90621 737-J5
AVINGER DR
8100 RSMD 91770 636-F3
8100 LACo 91770 636-F3
S AVINGTON AV
800 WCOV 91790 638-H2
1700 LACo 91744 638-H3
1700 WCOV 91792 638-H4
S AVINGTON ST
500 WCOV 91790 638-H1
AVION CIR
28400 Cstc 91384 4369-F5
AVION DR
5600 Wch 90045 702-H5
13600 LMRD 90638 737-E2
S AVION DR
1300 MONP 91754 635-H3
AVIS AV
17800 TOR 90504 763-D1
20500 TOR 90503 763-D5
AVIS CT
- SIGH 90755 795-H3
22300 TOR 90505 763-E7
AVIS ST
22800 TOR 90505 793-D1
AVISTON PL
2600 RowH 91748 679-B7
AVIVA CT
17100 GrnH 91344 481-C6
AVOCA AV
1000 PAS 91105 565-H7
1100 PAS 91105 595-H1
4300 PMDL 93552 4286-J4
AVOCA CT
- LAN 93536 4013-J5
AVOCA ST
2600 LAN 93535 4016-E4
4700 Eagl 90041 565-C6

AVOCADO AV
400 PAS 91107 566-F3
15300 PRM 90723 735-J4
AVOCADO LN
- SCTA 91354 4460-F7
- SCTA 91354 4550-F1
- RHE 90274 793-A7
300 PAS 91107 566-F3
3500 PMDL 93550 4286-H3
AVOCADO PL
200 MNRO 91016 567-E3
28500 SCTA 91390 4460-H3
AVOCADO ST
- FUL 92835 738-H3
800 BREA 92821 709-C7
2500 LVRN 91750 600-H1
4200 LFlz 90027 594-A3
25800 LMTA 90717 793-H5
AVOCADO TER
1200 LACo 91104 536-B7
2000 HacH 91745 677-J3
AVOCADO CREST RD
100 LACo 90631 708-D3
100 LHH 90631 708-D3
W AVOCADO CREST RD
300 LHH 90631 708-C3
17000 WHIT 90603 708-C3
AVOCADO HILL WY
3300 HacH 91745 678-A6
AVOCET CT
- LACo 91387 4551-H5
AVOLENCIA DR
1300 FUL 92835 738-G5
AVON AV
400 PAS 91105 565-E6
6000 TEML 91775 596-G2
6300 LACo 91775 596-G2
AVON CIR
8600 LPMA 90623 767-C5
AVON CT
1500 PMDL 93550 4286-D3
AVON PL
1000 SPAS 91030 595-J2
1400 Echo 90026 594-F6
1600 GLDR 91740 599-F2
AVON RD
600 PVE 90274 792-E6
AVON SQ
1600 PVE 90274 792-E6
AVON ST
1900 Echo 90026 594-F5
N AVON ST
100 BURB 91505 563-C1
1400 BURB 91505 533-C7
2400 BURB 91504 533-C4
S AVON ST
100 BURB 91505 563-E4
AVON TER
1400 Echo 90026 594-F5
AVON WY
11700 LA 90066 672-E5
AVONBURY AV
10600 WHIT 90603 707-J5
AVONCROFT ST
9900 LACo 90601 676-J2
10000 LACo 90601 677-A2
AVONDALE AV
200 Brwd 90049 631-E4
W AVONDALE AV
100 MONP 91754 636-B2
AVONDALE DR
2200 ALH 91803 635-G2
2200 FUL 92833 738-D3
AVONDALE RD
900 SMRO 91108 566-B7
AVONGLEN TER
700 GLDL 91206 564-H3
AVONLEA AV
12900 NRWK 90650 736-J1
AVONOAK TER
800 GLDL 91206 564-G3
AVON PARK TER
1400 Echo 90026 594-F5
AVONREA RD
1300 SMRO 91108 596-A3
W AVORA ST
100 LACo 91016 567-G7
AWENITA CT
11400 Chat 91311 499-H1
AWLSBURY CIR
1500 FUL 92833 738-B5
AXENTY
17700 RBCH 90278 762-J1
AXTELL ST
4800 LA 90032 595-E6
AYALA AV
5600 IRW 91706 568-E7
5600 IRW 91706 598-E1
AYARS CANYON WY
3300 GLDL 91208 534-F4
AYDE LN
- RHE 90275 792-J7
- RPV 90275 792-J7
- RPV 90275 822-J1
AYERS AV
- PMDL 93550 4286-C1
2200 CMRC 90040 675-E3
2600 VER 90040 675-E3
2600 VER 90023 675-E4
AYERS WY
1300 BURB 91501 534-A5
AYLESWORTH PL
3100 LA 90031 595-A7

AYON AV
600 AZU 91706 598-G2
600 IRW 91706 598-G2
AYR ST
2200 LA 90039 594-E4
AYRES AV
10500 LA 90064 632-D5
AYRSHIRE RD
11900 Brwd 90049 631-H2
N AZALEA AV
400 ONT 91762 601-J7
S AZALEA AV
1100 ONT 91762 641-J2
AZALEA CT
1200 UPL 91784 571-J6
17200 LPUE 91744 678-G1
AZALEA DR
500 MTBL 90640 636-F7
900 POM 91766 640-H4
1000 ALH 91801 596-D6
1800 ALH 91801 596-F7
6100 LAN 93536 4104-E5
6300 LACo 93536 4104-E5
7700 BPK 90620 767-H2
AZALEA ST
6000 CHNO 91710 641-J5
AZALEA WY
1100 LACo 90502 794-A1
AZALIA DR
4400 Tarz 91356 560-H5
AZALIA TRAIL CT
- StvR 91381 4640-B2
AZARIA AV
3000 HacH 91745 678-A5
AZIDE RD
- SCTA 91350 4551-A4
AZORES AV
11600 LA 91342 482-B2
AZORES PL
2700 RPV 90275 823-G6
AZTEC
3300 Top 90290 560-B6
AZTEC DR
11400 Chat 91311 500-B1
AZTEC PL
37000 PMDL 93552 4287-B4
AZTEC ST
12700 LA 91342 482-E1
14800 LA 91342 481-J7
AZTEC WY
800 MONP 91755 636-D3
2000 ALH 91801 636-C1
AZUCENA DR
4700 WdHl 91364 559-J4
AZUL CIR
8800 LA 91304 529-E1
AZUL DR
8700 WHil 91304 529-D1
8700 LA 91304 529-D1
AZURE AV
4300 PMDL 93552 4286-J4
AZURE BAY
5600 LBCH 90803 826-C1
AZURE PL
11900 Brwd 90049 631-G1
AZURE WY
1500 ARCD 91007 567-C7
1500 ARCD 91007 597-C1
5500 LBCH 90803 826-C1
AZURE FIELD DR
19700 SCTA 91321 4551-F5
AZURELEE DR
21700 LACo 90265 629-E4
AZURE VIEW RD
11400 SBdC 92372 (4472-D2
See Page 4471)
AZURITE DR
15600 CHLS 91709 680-J7
AZURITE PL
- SCTA 91354 4460-G3
AZUSA AV Rt#-N8
100 LACo 91744 638-H7
100 INDS 91744 638-H7
400 WCOV 91792 638-H7
800 WCOV 91791 638-H7
N AZUSA AV
100 AZU 91702 568-J4
N AZUSA AV Rt#-39
100 COV 91722 598-J6
100 WCOV 91791 598-J6
S AZUSA AV
- INDS 91744 678-F5
100 AZU 91702 568-J7
100 LACo 91744 678-F5
100 AZU 91702 598-J1
500 LACo 91702 598-J1
1700 RowH 91748 678-F5
1700 HacH 91745 678-F5
S AZUSA AV Rt#-N8
100 INDS 91744 638-J4
100 INDS 91744 678-G3
100 WCOV 91791 598-J7
100 LPUE 91744 678-G3
200 WCOV 91791 638-J4
700 INDS 91748 678-G3
700 INDS 91745 678-G3
1400 HacH 91745 678-G3
1700 WCOV 91792 638-J4
S AZUSA AV Rt#-39
100 WCOV 91791 598-J5
700 COV 91722 598-J5
E AZUSA LN
100 AZU 91702 598-J1

AZUSA ST
300 LA 90012 634-G4
1200 Boyl 90033 634-H5
AZUSA WY
500 INDS 91744 678-G2
500 LPUE 91744 678-G2
N AZUSA CANYON RD
1100 WCOV 91790 598-E4
4400 IRW 91706 598-E4
4800 BALD 91706 598-E4
AZUSA VETERANS WY
- AZU 91702 569-A5
AZZURE CT
15500 BelA 90077 591-G2

B

B
- PRM 90723 735-F6
18600 LACo 91744 679-B2
B ST
- LA 90245 732-C1
- LACo 90220 764-J3
- LACo 91724 599-E2
- LKWD 90712 766-A3
- PdlR 90293 702-C7
- PdlR 90293 732-C1
- SPed 90731 824-B1
- WCOV 91790 638-J4
1900 LVRN 91750 600-F2
4000 LACo 90230 672-H4
4900 CHNO 91710 641-G7
13400 LA 91342 481-F3
BABBITT AV
5600 Enc 91316 561-C1
9500 Nor 91325 501-C5
10300 GrnH 91344 501-C1
11500 GrnH 91344 481-C7
BABCOCK AV
4200 LA 91604 562-F5
5100 LA 91607 562-F2
6200 NHol 91606 532-F7
6700 NHol 91605 532-E2
BABER AV
17000 ART 90701 736-G7
BABETTE AV
5100 LA 90066 672-E6
BABIA ST
8700 LACo 93551 4193-J2
BABINE DR
- LACo 93591 4200-F4
BABINGTON ST
19500 SCTA 91351 4551-F1
BABY LAND
- LA 90065 594-F1
BACA AV
4800 IRW 91706 598-F3
12300 CHNO 91710 641-G6
BACA CT
- BALD 91706 598-D3
BACANORA AV
9900 WHIT 90603 708-B4
E BACARRO ST
6500 LBCH 90815 796-E5
BACH PL
11300 Nor 91326 500-H1
BACH ST
1400 CRSN 90745 764-G7
BACH WY
13000 CRTS 90703 737-B6
BACHELIN ST
18900 RowH 91748 679-B6
BACHRY PL
8900 Sunl 91040 503-F2
BACK ACRES RD
32800 Actn 93510 4375-C7
BACK BAY CT
- SCTA 91355 4550-E1
BACK BAY PL
6200 PdlR 90293 702-A2
BACKFORD ST
11000 SELM 91733 637-B5
BACKTON AV
100 LACo 91744 678-J1
100 LACo 91744 638-J7
BACKUS AV
100 LACo 91107 566-H5
BACKUS RD
200 LACo 90265 587-D6
BACON CT
18600 SCTA 91351 4551-H2
BACON RD
7700 WHIT 90602 677-F7
7800 WHIT 90602 707-F1
BADAJOZ DR
7500 BPK 90621 737-H5
15300 LMRD 90638 737-H5
BADEAU AV
21900 CRSN 90745 764-G6
BADEN AV
9500 Chat 91311 499-H5
BADEN PL
29800 MAL 90265 667-C2
BADER CIR
20100 CRTS 90703 767-A4
BADGER
3300 SBdC 92371 (4472-J3
See Page 4471)
BADGER AV
13600 LA 91342 482-C1
BADILLO CIR
4000 BALD 91706 598-D5

BADILLO ST
14700 BALD 91706 598-E5
15300 BALD 91790 598-E5
15300 WCOV 91790 598-E5
E BADILLO ST
100 COV 91723 599-D5
900 COV 91724 599-G4
1000 WCOV 91790 598-G5
1000 COV 91722 598-G5
1400 SDMS 91773 599-G4
1500 LACo 91773 599-G4
1700 LACo 91724 599-G4
2200 COV 91773 599-G4
21000 SDMS 91724 599-G4
W BADILLO ST
100 COV 91723 599-A5
500 COV 91722 599-A5
700 WCOV 91791 598-H5
700 WCOV 91791 599-A5
700 COV 91722 598-H5
1700 LACo 91722 598-H5
1700 WCOV 91790 598-H5
BADLONA DR
14800 LMRD 90638 737-F3
BADMINTON AV
9200 LACo 90605 707-C3
BAELEN ST
19300 RowH 91748 679-D5
BAER RD
- Eagl 90041 565-A7
BAFT LN
1300 DBAR 91765 680-A3
BAGBY DR
19000 SCTA 91351 4551-G2
BAGDAD PL
1800 GLDL 91208 534-H5
BAGLEY AV
1700 LA 90035 632-H5
2000 LA 90034 632-H5
3700 LA 90034 672-G1
3700 LA 90232 672-G1
BAGNALL ST
19000 GLDR 91740 569-C6
E BAGNALL ST
700 AZU 91702 569-A6
BAHAMA AV
14400 LACo 90220 734-F3
N BAHAMA AV
1800 COMP 90059 734-F2
BAHAMA ST
15000 LA 91343 501-D7
17800 Nor 91325 501-A7
18900 Nor 91324 500-E7
20100 Chat 91311 500-C7
20500 Win 91306 500-C7
20500 Win 91306 530-C1
20500 Chat 91311 530-C1
22000 LA 91304 530-A1
22000 LA 91304 529-J1
BAHIA CT
1100 ONT 91762 641-J2
BAHIA DR
13000 CRTS 90703 767-B2
BAHIA ST
45600 LACo 93536 4013-B4
BAILARD RD
31200 MAL 90265 626-J7
BAILE AV
10700 Chat 91311 500-F2
BAILEY AV
1800 LACo 91770 636-D4
BAILEY DR
17800 TOR 90504 763-D2
BAILEY PL
100 GLDL 91206 565-A4
BAILEY RD
12000 LACo 91342 482-F5
BAILEY ST
100 Boyl 90033 634-J4
100 Boyl 90033 635-A4
12000 WHIT 90601 677-B6
E BAILEY WY
1500 LBCH 90813 795-F5
BAIN AV
11100 DBAR 91789 679-H3
BAINBRIDGE AV
900 WCOV 91790 638-D2
10400 Wwd 90024 592-B7
BAINBRIDGE CT
5900 AGRH 91301 558-A4
BAINBRIDGE ST
1700 POM 91766 640-H4
BAINBROOK AV
16400 CRTS 90703 737-C6
BAINBROOK CT
18400 CRTS 90703 767-C1
31700 WLKV 91361 557-D6
BAINBURY ST
16700 SCTA 91351 4552-B1
18600 SCTA 91351 4551-G2
BAINFORD AV
100 LACo 91744 678-J1
BAINTREE AV
17800 RowH 91748 678-H6
BAINUM DR
1500 Top 90290 630-A1
BAIRD AV
6000 Tarz 91356 560-J1
6200 Res 91335 530-J2
8700 Nor 91324 530-J1
8800 Nor 91324 500-J6
9200 Wats 90002 704-F4
10400 Nor 91326 500-H1

BAIRD AV
11600 Nor 91326 480-H7
BAIRD RD
1900 LA 90046 593-A3
BAIRNSDALE ST
7200 DWNY 90240 706-B1
BAIS PL
2600 HacH 91745 678-D5
BAJA AV
300 LPUE 91744 678-E1
2000 LHB 90631 708-B6
BAJA CT
41800 PMDL 93551 4104-C6
BAJADA DR
23600 SCTA 91355 4550-G5
BAJIO CT
16700 Enc 91436 561-D5
BAJIO RD
16700 Enc 91436 561-D5
BAKER AL
100 PAS 91105 565-H5
BAKER AV
12400 CHNO 91710 641-F6
BAKER CT
12500 CHNO 91710 641-F6
S BAKER DR
100 ANA 92804 767-J6
BAKER PKWY
- INDS 91789 639-J7
- INDS 91789 679-H1
BAKER PL
11900 SFSP 90670 707-A2
25500 StvR 91381 4550-C7
BAKER RD
700 SBdC 92372 (4472-B5
See Page 4471)
BAKER ST
600 LBCH 90806 765-C7
1200 LBCH 90810 765-B7
1700 LA 90012 634-H1
12300 CHNO 91710 641-F6
26500 SCTA 91387 4642-E1
BAKER CANYON RD
15500 LACo 91390 4462-F4
BAKERTON AV
27300 SCTA 91351 4551-G2
28200 SCTA 91351 4461-H7
BAKMAN AV
4000 LA 91602 562-J5
4800 NHol 91601 562-J1
6200 NHol 91606 532-J7
7200 SunV 91352 532-J3
BALADA DR
40600 PMDL 93551 4194-G2
BALAN RD
19300 RowH 91748 679-D6
BALANDA DR
100 MTBL 90640 636-E7
BALARD ST
1600 CRSN 90745 764-G5
BALASIANO AV
- LA 91304 529-G4
BALASSI RD
16300 HacH 91745 678-D5
BALBOA
10800 MsnH 91345 501-H2
BALBOA AV
600 GLDL 91206 564-F3
4400 Enc 91436 561-D4
4400 Enc 91316 561-C4
BALBOA BLVD
4900 Enc 91436 561-D3
4900 Enc 91316 561-D3
6000 Enc 91436 531-D7
6000 Enc 91316 531-D7
6300 VanN 91406 531-D3
8300 Nor 91325 531-B3
8700 Nor 91325 501-C5
10100 GrnH 91344 501-C2
10100 LA 91343 501-C2
11600 GrnH 91344 481-C4
16500 LA 91342 481-D2
BALBOA CT
400 SDMS 91773 600-C2
BALBOA DR
400 SLB 90740 826-F4
700 ARCD 91007 567-A6
800 ARCD 91007 566-J6
BALBOA PL
- LBCH 90803 826-C3
200 FUL 92835 738-G3
8100 VanN 91406 531-D2
BALBOA RD
- GrnH 91344 481-D3
2200 FUL 92835 738-G3
BALBOA ST
600 WCOV 91790 638-J1
1400 POM 91767 601-C6
BALBOA WY
9700 CYP 90630 767-E7
BALCOM AV
500 FUL 92801 738-J7
500 FUL 92832 738-J7
5800 Enc 91316 561-B1
6100 Enc 91316 531-B7
6400 Res 91335 531-A4
8600 Nor 91325 531-A2
8900 Nor 91325 501-A7
10500 GrnH 91344 501-A1
N BALCOM AV
100 FUL 92832 738-J7
S BALCOM AV
100 FUL 92832 738-J7

STREET
Block City ZIP Pg-Grid

BALCONY DR
4000 CALB 91302 559-J6
BALDER DR
23700 CALB 91302 559-E7
BALD MOUNTAIN CT
9700 LACo 91390 4373-G3
BALDUR ST
7700 LACo 91390 4374-B3
BALDWIN AL
1500 PAS 91106 566-C3
1800 PAS 91107 566-C3
BALDWIN AV
- ELMN 91731 637-A1
1000 POM 91767 601-B7
1400 ARCD 91007 597-A2
2500 TEML 91780 597-A2
3500 ELMN 91731 597-A7
4100 CULC 90232 672-G2
14400 BALD 91706 598-C3
N BALDWIN AV
- ARCD 91007 567-A5
- SMAD 91024 567-A1
1000 ARCD 91006 567-A3
S BALDWIN AV
- ARCD 91007 567-A7
- SMAD 91024 567-A3
1400 ARCD 91007 597-A1
BALDWIN CIR
8200 BPK 90621 737-J6
BALDWIN PL
1700 MTBL 90640 636-C7
7600 WHIT 90602 677-B7
7600 WHIT 90606 677-B7
9700 ELMN 91731 597-A7
9700 ELMN 91731 637-A1
26000 StvR 91381 4550-B6
BALDWIN ST
1200 OrCo 90631 708-B4
2700 LA 90031 635-A1
BALDWIN PARK BLVD
3000 BALD 91706 638-A1
3100 BALD 91706 598-B4
N BALDWIN PARK BLVD
100 INDS 91746 637-J2
900 LACo 91746 637-J2
900 LACo 91706 637-J2
900 INDS 91706 637-J2
900 BALD 91706 637-J2
1200 BALD 91706 638-A1
BALDWIN PARK TOWNE CTR
14500 BALD 91706 598-C7
BALDWIN VILLA DRIVEWAY
- LA 90008 673-E2
BALDY RD
900 SBdC - (512-D1 See Page 511)
900 SBdC - (4732-H3 See Page 4651)
BALDY VIEW AV
900 POM 91767 601-D7
N BALDY VISTA AV
7200 GLDR 91741 569-B5
7200 LACo 91741 569-B5
BALE CT
- LAN 93535 4106-F2
BALEGH PL
3100 GLDL 91206 565-B1
BALER AV
100 BREA 92821 709-F7
BALERIA CT
26000 SCTA 91355 4550-F4
BALERIA DR
2100 LA 90732 823-G6
BALERNA DR
26600 SCTA 91350 4550-J1
E BALES ST
1800 COMP 90221 735-C3
2100 RDom 90221 735-D3
BALFERN AV
6000 LKWD 90713 766-E1
17200 BLF 90706 736-E7
17800 BLF 90706 766-E1
BALFOUR LN
5000 WdHl 91364 559-H3
BALFOUR ST
6200 PRV 90660 676-F5
10700 LACo 90606 676-H6
12000 LACo 90606 677-A7
BALH CT
2400 Alta 91001 536-A6
BALHAM AV
300 LACo 91744 679-B2
BALI DR
3200 WCOV 91792 679-D2
BALI LN
15900 PacP 90272 630-J6
BALI WY
13300 MdlR 90292 672-B7
S BALIN PL
14600 LMRD 90638 737-J3
BALINESE CT
- PMDL 93551 4195-F7
BALKINS DR
28000 AGRH 91301 558-C4
BALL AV
15700 LACo 90248 734-D5
16100 CRSN 90248 734-D6
BALL DR
100 CLAR 91711 570-J7
BALL RD
3700 ANA 92804 767-F7
3800 LBCH 90808 796-J1
3800 LALM 90720 796-J1
6500 BPK 90620 767-F7
W BALL RD
2900 ANA 92804 767-H7
3500 BPK 90620 767-H7
BALLANTINE DR
12100 OrCo 90720 796-H5
BALLARD ST
2700 LA 90032 595-E7
BALLENA DR
200 DBAR 91765 640-D6
BALLENTINE PL
4300 BALD 91706 598-B5
15900 LACo 91722 598-F4
BALLER MTWY
- LACo 90265 628-A3
BALLER RD
- LACo 90265 627-J4
- LACo 90265 628-A3
BALLERINA PL
1300 POM 91768 600-G7
BALLESTROS AV
13100 CHNO 91710 641-E7
BALL FLAT RD
26100 Valy 93563 (4561-A4 See Page 4471)
BALLINA DR
3900 Enc 91436 561-E5
BALLINA CANYON RD
3500 Enc 91436 561-E6
BALLINGER ST
16200 LA 91343 501-D6
16900 Nor 91325 501-B6
18800 Nor 91324 500-F6
22000 Chat 91311 499-H6
BALLISTA AV
800 LPUE 91744 638-E4
1200 LACo 91744 638-E4
BALLONA LN
- CULC 90230 672-G4
BALMAIN WY
2100 GLDL 91206 535-B7
BALMER DR
2000 LA 90039 594-D5
BALMONT ST
- LAN 93536 4104-F4
2100 LAN 93536 4105-A4
BALMORAL CT
45700 LAN 93534 4015-E3
BALMORAL DR
1000 GLDL 91207 564-G1
BALMORAL LN
23300 CanP 91307 529-F5
BALMORAL ST
9900 LACo 90601 676-J2
9900 LACo 90601 677-A2
BALMUIR AV
43900 LAN 93535 4106-B1
44200 LAN 93535 4016-B7
BALSA AV
500 BREA 92821 709-C6
BALSA CIR
1000 LVRN 91750 600-E1
BALSA CT
- SCTA 91354 4460-F4
BALSAM
11600 NRWK 90650 706-J7
12200 NRWK 90650 736-J1
BALSAM AV
2100 WLA 90025 632-D4
2100 LA 90064 632-D4
BALSAM CT
- CRSN 90746 764-H2
- SCTA 91354 4460-G5
BALSAM DR
1500 POM 91766 640-H4
BALTA DR
28100 SCTA 91350 4461-D6
BALTAR ST
16900 VanN 91406 531-C2
17500 Nor 91325 531-B3
17700 Res 91335 531-A3
19900 Win 91306 530-D3
20800 LA 91304 530-A3
22100 LA 91304 529-E3
BALTIC AV
2000 LBCH 90810 795-B2
3400 LBCH 90810 765-B7
S BALTIC AV
21000 CRSN 90810 765-B5
BALTIC ST
12900 Brwd 90049 631-F5
N BALTIMORE AV
100 MONP 91754 636-B1
BALTIMORE CT
12900 CHNO 91710 641-E7
BALTIMORE ST
4700 HiPk 90042 595-A1
BALTON AV
500 SDMS 91773 599-J1
BALTUSROL DR
2400 ALH 91803 635-J2
BALZAC ST
3200 ALH 91803 635-G2
BAMBI PL
12000 GrnH 91344 481-C6
BAMBOO DR
24200 SCTA 91321 4641-B2
BAMBOO LN
400 LA 90012 634-G2
BAMBOO ST
16000 LPUE 91744 638-E7
16200 LPUE 91744 678-E1
BAMFIELD DR
28500 AGRH 91301 558-B3
BAMFORD PL
4800 HiPk 90042 595-A2
BANBRIDGE AV
100 LPUE 91744 638-F7
100 LPUE 91744 678-F1
BANBRIDGE DR
16100 LPUE 91744 638-E7
BANBROOK LN
21600 DBAR 91765 679-H7
BANBURY AL
800 PAS 91103 565-G2
BANBURY CIR
5100 LPMA 90623 767-C5
BANBURY PL
2600 Eagl 90041 564-J7
2600 LA 90065 564-J7
BANCROFT AV
2200 LA 90039 594-E4
2400 LHB 90631 708-B5
BANCROFT PL
- Cstc 91384 4459-G4
BANCROFT ST
300 AZU 91702 568-H4
BANCROFT WY
1500 PAS 91103 565-G1
BANDA DR
6700 PRM 90723 735-E5
BANDANA AV
15700 LACo 93591 4199-E5
BANDANA DR
21000 DBAR 91765 679-G7
BANDELL ST
3500 Actn 93510 4375-B4
BANDERA AV
1700 COMP 90222 734-G2
8800 Wats 90002 704-G4
11700 Wbrk 90059 704-G7
12200 Wbrk 90059 734-G1
BANDERA ST
4200 MTCL 91763 641-F1
5000 MTCL 91763 601-G7
5100 LA 90058 674-G5
8600 Wats 90002 704-G5
9200 Wats 90002 704-G5
20900 WdHl 91364 560-C4
BANDERA WY
100 BREA 92821 709-B7
BANDINI BLVD
2700 VER 90058 674-J3
2700 VER 90058 675-A3
2800 VER 90023 675-A3
3200 LACo 90023 675-A3
4500 VER 90040 675-E4
4700 BELL 90201 675-E4
4700 VER 90201 675-E4
5600 CMRC 90040 675-H5
5600 BELL 90040 675-H5
6500 CMRC 90040 676-A5
N BANDINI ST
100 SPed 90731 824-A4
S BANDINI ST
100 SPed 90731 824-A5
BANDIT CIR
3300 HNTB 92649 826-J6
BANDON AV
400 LACo 91744 638-G6
BANDRA PL
27600 RPV 90275 823-H1
S BANDY AV
100 WCOV 91790 598-H7
100 WCOV 91790 638-G1
BANEBERRY PL
- BqtC 91354 4460-E6
BANEWELL AV
4900 LACo 91722 598-H3
5200 LACo 91702 598-H2
BANFF LN
12100 Brwd 90049 631-G3
BANFIELD DR
13400 CRTS 90703 737-C6
BANG RD
- WHil 91304 499-C7
- WHil 91304 529-C1
BANGLE RD
7700 DWNY 90240 706-C1
BANGOR ST
200 POM 91767 601-A5
5000 LA 90016 633-B6
BANI AV
24900 LMTA 90717 793-G4
S BANICK DR
100 ANA 92804 767-J6
BANIDA AV
1300 RowH 91748 679-C5
BANIS RD
- LACo 91390 4373-C5
BANJO CIR
28000 Cstc 91384 4369-G7
BANK ST
800 SPAS 91030 595-H2
2900 LA 90065 594-G4
BANKERS DR
1200 CRSN 90746 764-F3
BANKFIELD AV
5700 CULC 90230 672-G6
BANKS COURT DR
800 HiPk 90042 595-A2
BANLYNN CT
21200 Top 90290 560-B6
BANN ST
22100 SCTA 91350 4460-J6
BANNA AV
400 COV 91724 599-F6
1600 GLDR 91740 599-F2
5000 LACo 91724 599-E3
N BANNA AV
100 COV 91724 599-F4
700 GLDR 91741 569-E4
BANNER AV
6200 LA 90038 593-F5
BANNER DR
4400 Bxby 90807 765-F5
BANNERMAN AV
26500 SCTA 91321 4551-G5
BANNER RIDGE RD
900 DBAR 91765 680-C2
BANNING AV
3100 LYN 90262 735-A1
BANNING BLVD
300 Wilm 90744 794-E4
23000 CRSN 90745 794-E2
BANNING DR
- AVA 90704 5923-G4
BANNING ST
300 COMP 90222 734-J1
400 COMP 90222 735-A1
500 LA 90012 634-G4
BANNING WY
1000 DBAR 91789 679-G3
1600 PAS 91108 596-A1
1700 SMRO 91108 596-A1
BANNISTER AV
4100 ELMN 91732 597-G6
BANNOCKBURN DR
10200 LA 90064 632-F6
BANNON AV
1200 LACo 91744 638-E4
1200 LPUE 91744 638-E4
BANNON DR
13700 CRTS 90703 737-C6
BANOWSKY BLVD
- LACo 90263 628-G7
BANSON ST
- Actn 93510 4374-A7
3600 Actn 93510 4375-A7
BANTA RD
9200 PRV 90660 676-H1
BANTAM PL
1900 LA 90046 593-B2
BANUELO AV
27200 SCTA 91350 4461-A7
BANYAN DR
2100 Brwd 90049 631-D1
2300 Brwd 90049 591-C7
BANYAN LN
16200 LPUE 91744 638-G7
BANYAN PL
- PMDL 93551 4285-D2
22800 SCTA 91390 4460-H3
BANYAN ST
1100 PAS 91103 565-E1
BANYAN RIM DR
4700 LACo 90601 677-C3
BAPTISTE WY
200 LCF 91011 535-D4
BARA RD
1800 GLDL 91208 534-H7
BARADA AV
27100 SCTA 91350 4461-A7
BARATA ST
15400 HacH 91745 678-A4
BARBACOA DR
22100 SCTA 91350 4460-J7
22100 SCTA 91350 4461-A7
BARBACOA PL
26900 SCTA 91350 4460-J7
BARBADOS CT
4900 VeCo 91377 557-G2
BARBADOS DR
200 WAL 91789 639-F7
BARBAKER LN
800 MNRO 91016 567-J5
E BARBANELL ST
5800 LBCH 90815 796-C2
BARBARA AV
100 AZU 91702 568-H6
12400 LA 90066 672-C4
E BARBARA AV
600 WCOV 91790 638-F2
W BARBARA AV
800 WCOV 91790 638-E1
BARBARA BLVD
100 FUL 92835 738-H4
BARBARA CT
3100 LA 90068 593-C1
3100 LA 90068 563-C7
BARBARA LN
900 POM 91767 601-B7
37600 PMDL 93550 4285-J3
37600 PMDL 93551 4285-J3
BARBARA ST
1000 RBCH 90277 763-A6
1400 SBdC 92397 (4652-D2 See Page 4651)
2700 SPed 90731 854-A1
6000 CHNO 91710 641-J7
21700 TOR 90503 763-A6
S BARBARA ST
3100 SPed 90731 854-A1
3500 SPed 90731 853-J1
BARBARA ANN ST
12500 NHol 91605 532-D5
13500 VanN 91405 532-C5
BARBARAGLEN LN
1000 LHB 90631 708-D6
BARBARA LONDON DR
- LBCH 90808 796-A1
BARBATA RD
12700 LMRD 90638 737-G1
BARBEE ST
3200 LA 90031 635-B1
BARBER AV
17600 ART 90701 736-G7
BARBER RD
32400 LACo 91390 4373-D5
32400 LACo 91390 4463-D1
BARBERRY DR
1300 DBAR 91765 680-A3
BARBERRY LN
20000 Tarz 91356 560-E6
BARBERRY ST
45800 LAN 93534 4015-G3
BARBI LN
7500 LPMA 90623 767-B3
21500 DBAR 91765 679-H7
BARBOUR CT
2200 SPed 90731 824-B7
BARBOUR ST
200 PdlR 90293 702-B3
BARBYDELL DR
3100 LA 90064 632-F7
BARCA AV
300 LACo 91744 679-A1
BARCELONA AV
2300 UPL 91784 571-H3
BARCELONA CIR
200 FUL 92835 738-G2
5200 LPMA 90623 767-C2
BARCELONA CT
24500 CALB 91302 559-C6
BARCELONA DR
2000 LA 90046 592-J3
5700 PMDL 93552 4287-C2
BARCELONA LN
9900 CYP 90630 767-D7
BARCELONA PL
800 WAL 91789 639-D6
1200 LBCH 90813 795-F5
BARCELONA RD
- Cstc 91384 4459-E2
BARCLAY AL
200 PAS 91105 565-G7
BARCLAY AV
500 COMP 90220 734-F5
BARCLAY CT
1900 THO 91361 557-A5
BARCLAY ST
2000 LA 90031 594-H6
E BARCLAY ST
100 NLB 90805 765-C1
W BARCLAY ST
- NLB 90805 765-C1
BARCOTTA DR
22300 SCTA 91350 4460-J5
BARCROFT DR
15100 LACo 93532 4102-E4
BARD CT
1900 CLAR 91711 571-C7
BARD ST
800 HMB 90254 762-H2
2400 Echo 90026 594-F5
BARDALE AV
1600 SPed 90731 824-A1
BARDELL DR
28900 AGRH 91301 558-B4
BARDLEY CT
300 POM 91766 640-J5
BARDMAN AV
1300 LACo 90265 586-D7
1300 LACo 90265 626-D1
BARDWELL AV
8300 PanC 91402 532-C1
BAREFOOT LN
2500 RowH 91748 678-J7
BARELA AV
5100 TEML 91780 597-A4
6300 TEML 91780 596-J1
6600 LACo 91007 596-J1
BARFIELD DR
23400 SCTA 91354 4460-G6
BARFORD AV
1100 HacH 91745 678-D2
BARGANCA CT
25600 SCTA 91355 4550-F7
BARGELLO WY
- Nor 91326 500-D1
BARGEN WY
2900 Alta 91001 535-G5
BARHAM AV
2100 WCOV 91792 638-J5
45900 LAN 93534 4015-F3
BARHAM BLVD
3200 LA 90068 563-D6
3800 BURB 91522 563-D6
3800 BURB 91505 563-D6
BARHAM CT
45600 LAN 93534 4015-F3
BAR HARBOR CT
23900 SCTA 91355 4550-F4
BARHILL AV
300 POM 91766 640-J5
BARHITE ST
3100 LACo 91107 536-G7
BARHUGH PL
800 SPed 90731 824-A2
BARI WY
300 Ven 90291 671-H7
BARING ST
- LAN 93535 4015-J4
1600 LAN 93535 4016-C4
BARING CROSS AV
8600 LA 90044 704-B3
BARING CROSS ST
800 LA 90044 704-B6
BARJUD AV
100 POM 91768 640-C2
BARK CIR
1300 UPL 91786 601-J1
BARK DR
800 LACo 90601 637-G5
BARKENTINE RD
- RPV 90275 822-J4
BARKER AL
1000 PAS 91106 565-J7
BARKER DR
5200 HiPk 90042 565-B7
24200 DBAR 91765 680-D2
E BARKER WY
4400 LBCH 90814 796-A7
BARKER FIRE RD
- LA 90210 592-G1
- LA 91604 592-G1
3200 LA 90210 562-F7
3200 LA 91604 562-F7
BARKERVILLE AV
9300 LACo 90605 707-D3
BARKING SPIDER RD
34900 LACo 91390 4374-D4
BARKLEY LN
2800 RBCH 90278 733-B6
BARKLEY RANCH RD
1100 SBdC 92372 (4472-C6 See Page 4471)
BARKPOINT DR
23900 LACo 91302 589-C2
BARKSTONE DR
26100 RPV 90275 793-A5
26200 RPV 90275 792-J5
BARLETTA DR
15700 HacH 91745 678-B6
BARLEY FLAT TKTR
- LACo - (506-D3 See Page 505)
- LACo - 507-A1
- LACo - (4726-G7 See Page 4645)
- LACo - (4727-A7 See Page 4647)
BARLIN AV
4900 LKWD 90712 765-J3
12600 DWNY 90242 736-A1
12800 DWNY 90242 735-J2
BARLING ST
9900 Sunl 91040 503-C4
BARLOCK AV
100 Brwd 90049 631-J1
BARLOW AV
10700 LYN 90262 705-A6
BARLOW ST
2200 Boyl 90033 635-B3
BARLOW SAXTON RD
800 SPed 90731 854-A1
BARMAN AV
10700 CULC 90230 672-F3
11300 LA 90230 672-E4
BARMORE CT
- GLDL 91206 564-J3
BARNABY RD
500 BelA 90077 591-J7
500 BelA 90077 592-A7
BARNACLE LN
- SCTA 91355 4550-H3
BARNARD AV
20100 WAL 91789 639-E7
BARNARD RD
1600 CLAR 91711 601-B1
BARNARD ST
5400 SIMI 93063 499-A1
BARNARD WY
2400 SMCA 90405 671-F4
BARNBY RD
33900 Actn 93510 4374-B5
BARNER AV
13900 LA 91342 482-B1
BARNES AV
3300 BALD 91706 637-H1
3300 BALD 91706 597-H7
BARNES CIR
3200 GLDL 91208 534-F5
BARNES LN
1600 LA 90046 592-J4
1600 LA 90046 593-A4
BARNESTON CT
17200 GrnH 91344 481-B7
BARNESTON ST
16200 GrnH 91344 481-C7
BARNETT DR
2300 GLDL 91206 564-J3
2400 GLDL 91206 565-A2
BARNETT LN
25700 StvR 91381 4550-B7
BARNETT RD
2000 LA 90032 635-F1
BARNETT WY
1900 LA 90032 635-F1
BARNEY CT
100 HMB 90254 762-J3
BARNEY ST
5200 CMRC 90040 675-G2
BARNHART AL
1100 PAS 91104 565-J2
BARNHILL AV
17300 CRTS 90703 736-H7
BARNHILL RD
25000 SCTA 91350 4551-A6
BARNOWL WY
- LVRN 91750 570-J4
E BARNSDALL AV
4700 LFlz 90027 594-A4
BARNSLEY AV
8100 Wch 90045 702-J2
BARNSTEAD DR
42800 LACo 93532 4102-F4
BARNUM DR
7800 LACo 90606 677-B7
7800 WHIT 90606 677-B7
BARNUM WY
400 MONP 91754 635-J3
BARNWALL ST
10400 BLF 90706 736-D5
10600 NRWK 90650 736-E4
14800 LMRD 90638 737-F4
BARO CIR
37600 PMDL 93550 4286-F2
BARODA DR
100 BelA 90077 592-C7
W BARON ST
800 LACo 90502 764-B4
BARONET PL
1500 FUL 92833 738-B4
BARONS CT
- PMDL 93552 4287-C4
BARONSGATE RD
4200 WLKV 91361 557-E6
BARR AV
3200 MTBL 90640 636-A7
3400 MTBL 90640 635-J7
BARRACUDA ST
600 SPed 90731 824-E5
BARRAGAN ST
28800 AGRH 91301 558-B3
BARRANCA AV
100 COV 91723 599-C2
100 WCOV 91791 599-C2
1000 LACo 91702 569-C7
1000 GLDR 91740 569-C7
5200 GLDR 91740 599-C2
5200 LACo 91722 599-C2
5600 LACo 91702 599-C2
6000 LACo 91740 569-C7
6300 AZU 91702 569-C7
N BARRANCA AV
100 COV 91723 599-C4
100 GLDR 91741 569-C5
100 WCOV 91791 599-C4
500 LACo 91741 569-C5
900 COV 91722 599-C4
1300 LACo 91722 599-C4
S BARRANCA AV
100 COV 91723 599-C6
100 GLDR 91741 569-C6
600 AZU 91702 569-C6
6300 GLDR 91740 569-C6
BARRANCA DR
100 MONP 91754 635-H2
BARRANCA LN
12800 NRWK 90650 737-A2
BARRANCA RD
- BRAD 91010 568-A3
BARRANCA ST
1800 LA 90031 594-J7
2500 LA 90031 595-A7
S BARRANCA ST
100 WCOV 91791 599-C7
300 WCOV 91791 639-C1
BARREL SPRINGS RD
- LACo 93551 4285-F4
- PMDL 93550 4285-H5
100 PMDL 93550 4286-A5
1200 PMDL 93550 4286-C5
3000 PMDL 93550 4376-H1
4000 LACo 93552 4376-H1
4000 PMDL 93552 4376-H1
4200 LACo 93552 4377-C3
4200 PMDL 93552 4377-A1
6700 Litl 93543 4377-C3
BARRETT CIR
5300 BPK 90621 737-J5
BARRETT DR
27700 SCTA 91350 4461-B6
32700 WLKV 91361 587-A1
32700 WLKV 91361 586-J1
BARRETT RD
- LACo - (512-A5 See Page 511)
- SBdC - (512-A5 See Page 511)
3900 LA 90032 595-F5
BARRETTE AV
8800 RSMD 91770 596-H5
BARRIE DR
400 BHLS 90210 592-G4
BARRINGER RD
30000 Cstc 91384 4369-D7
E BARRINGER ST
12100 SELM 91733 637-D4
N BARRINGTON AV
100 Brwd 90049 631-G2
S BARRINGTON AV
- LACo 90073 631-H3
100 Brwd 90049 631-H3
1200 WLA 90025 631-J5
1700 WLA 90025 632-A6
2200 LA 90064 632-A6
2500 LA 90064 672-B1
3000 LA 90066 672-B1
BARRINGTON CT
1900 CLAR 91711 571-E7
11600 Brwd 90049 631-H3
BARRINGTON DR
8000 OrCo 90638 737-J4
S BARRINGTON PL
100 Brwd 90049 631-G2
100 LACo 90073 631-G2
BARRINGTON ST
38800 PMDL 93551 4195-D6
BARRINGTON WK
100 Brwd 90049 631-H2
BARRINGTON WY
1300 GLDL 91206 564-G5
5200 MTCL 91763 641-G2
BARRINSON ST
37600 PMDL 93550 4286-F2
E BARRIOS ST
5800 LBCH 90815 796-D2
BARRIS DR
700 FUL 92832 738-F6
S BARRON AV
100 COMP 90220 734-H4
S BARRON ST
500 COMP 90220 734-H5
BARROSO ST
18200 RowH 91748 678-J7
18400 RowH 91748 679-A6
BARROW CT
1000 THO 91361 557-A5
BARROWS DR
6100 LA 90048 633-B3
BARRY AV
1100 Brwd 90049 631-J4
1200 WLA 90025 631-J4
1600 WLA 90025 632-A6
2200 LA 90064 632-A6
2600 LA 90064 672-B1
3100 LA 90066 672-C1
BARRY DR
300 POM 91767 601-A3
600 NLB 90805 735-E7
6000 CYP 90630 767-E7
BARRY PL
600 Alta 91001 535-J6
600 Alta 91001 536-A6
BARRYDALE ST
13800 LACo 91746 638-B1
15200 LACo 91744 638-D4
BARRYKNOLL DR
3700 LA 90065 594-H2
BARRYMORE AV
45400 LAN 93534 4015-E4
BARRYMORE DR
2000 LACo 90265 628-B4
BARRYWOOD AV
1500 SPed 90731 824-A1
BARSTON AV
400 COV 91724 599-G3
BARSTON PL
1600 GLDR 91740 599-G2
BARSTOW RD
10000 PMDL 93591 4108-C7
BARSTOW ST
4900 LA 90032 595-E6
BART AV
12700 LACo 90250 733-B2
BARTDON AV
3200 ING 90303 703-F5
BARTEE AV
8900 Pcma 91331 502-B4
10700 MsnH 91345 502-A2
10800 MsnH 91345 501-H1
BARTHE DR
200 PAS 91103 565-G3
BARTLETT AL
300 PAS 91106 566-A4
BARTLETT AV
2400 RSMD 91770 636-G2
3500 RSMD 91770 596-G6
N BARTLETT AV
5000 LACo 91776 596-G4
5900 TEML 91775 596-G3
BARTLETT DR
5600 TOR 90503 763-A5
BARTLETT ST
700 LA 90012 634-F2
32000 Actn 93510 4465-A2
BARTLEY AV
7600 LACo 90606 676-H7
9100 SFSP 90670 706-G2
BARTMUS ST
5700 CMRC 90040 675-H3
BARTO DR
12900 GrnH 91344 481-C4
BARTOLO AV
700 MTBL 90640 636-G7
700 MTBL 90640 676-F1
9300 PRV 90660 676-H3
BARTON AV
5000 LA 90038 593-E6
BARTON CIR
13200 SFSP 90605 707-B4
BARTON LN
2200 Mont 91020 534-H2
BARTON RD
8500 WHIT 90605 707-D2
12900 SFSP 90605 707-B3
12900 LACo 90605 707-B3
BARUCH ST
8100 RSMD 91770 636-F3
BARWOOD DR
15000 LMRD 90638 737-G4
BASALT CT
39400 PMDL 93551 4195-D5
BASCOM LN
- PMDL 93552 4287-E2
BASCOM ST
9000 PRV 90660 676-E7
9600 PRV 90660 706-F1
BASCULE AV
4900 WdHl 91364 560-C3
BASEBALL AV
3100 ELMN 91732 637-E2
BASEL DR
5200 SBdC 92397 (4652-G3 See Page 4651)
BASEL ST
18900 SCTA 91351 4551-G1
BASE LINE RD
700 LACo 91750 570-D7
BASE LINE RD Rt#-30
400 LACo 91750 570-G7
600 LVRN 91750 570-E7
E BASE LINE RD
100 SDMS 91773 570-C7
600 AZU 91702 569-A7
2100 GLDR 91740 569-B7
2100 GLDR 91740 570-A7
18500 LACo 91702 569-B7
E BASELINE RD Rt#-30
100 CLAR 91711 571-F7
W BASE LINE RD
100 GLDR 91740 569-C7
100 SDMS 91773 570-A7
300 SDMS 91740 570-A7
19000 LACo 91740 569-C7
W BASELINE RD
1000 LACo 91711 571-B7
W BASELINE RD Rt#-30
- CLAR 91711 570-J7
- LACo 91750 570-J7
100 CLAR 91711 571-B7
600 LACo 91711 571-B7
1300 LACo 91750 571-B7
BASELINE TR
2800 LA 90068 593-C2
BASETDALE AV
100 LACo 91746 637-G4
600 LACo 90601 637-G5
BASHFORD ST
14600 PacP 90272 631-B5
BASHOR ST
2300 DUAR 91010 568-C5
BASIL LN
2500 BelA 90077 592-A1
BASILICA CT
8900 CYP 90630 767-C7
BASILIO AV
200 SDMS 91773 600-C2
BASIN DR
700 Top 90290 590-A7
W BASIN ST
700 SPed 90731 824-A3
BASINGSTOKE LN
26000 SCTA 91355 4550-E5
BASKERVILLE RD
11300 OrCo 90720 796-H4
BASKIN AV
400 LACo 91744 638-G6
BASKIN ROBBINS PL
1500 GLDL 91201 563-J3
N BASQUE AV
100 FUL 92833 738-E7
S BASQUE AV
100 FUL 92833 738-E7
BASS ST
300 SPed 90731 824-E5
BASS WK
- Cstc 91384 4459-D6
BASSE LN
200 BREA 92821 709-A6
BASSETT CT
1000 SDMS 91773 599-J3
BASSETT ST
12700 NHol 91605 532-D5
13400 VanN 91405 532-C5
14600 VanN 91405 531-H5
15700 VanN 91406 531-C5
18300 Res 91335 530-G5
19700 Win 91306 530-C5
20800 CanP 91303 530-A6
22000 CanP 91303 529-H6
22400 CanP 91307 529-F6
BASSO TER
1500 GLDL 91202 564-E2
BASSROCK RD
35500 LACo 91390 4374-A1
BASSWOOD AV
- VeCo 91377 558-B3
12900 CHNO 91710 641-J7
26100 RPV 90275 793-A5
BASSWOOD CT
2100 THO 91361 557-A4
BASSWOOD LN
500 BREA 92821 709-A5
BASTANCHURY PL
1200 FUL 92833 738-E5
E BASTANCHURY RD
100 FUL 92835 738-G3
1100 FUL 92831 738-G3
W BASTANCHURY RD
100 FUL 92835 738-E5
900 FUL 92833 738-E5
BASTILLE LN
- PMDL 93551 4195-C5
BASYE ST
10900 ELMN 91731 597-D6
11300 ELMN 91732 597-E6
BATAAN AV
21700 CRSN 90810 764-J6
BATAAN LN
5600 PMDL 93552 4287-C4
BATAAN PL
800 MONP 91755 636-D3
BATAAN RD
1900 RBCH 90278 733-A6
BATAC ST
20600 Chat 91311 500-C2
BATAVIA RD
5200 SGAT 90280 705-E5
BATEMAN AV
- IRW 91010 567-J7
- IRW 91010 597-J1
BATES AV
1000 LA 90029 594-B5
1300 LFlz 90027 594-B5
BATES PL
1500 CLAR 91711 601-E1
26000 StvR 91381 4550-B6
BATEY AV
23400 Hrbr 90710 794-A2
BATEY PL
1300 Hrbr 90710 794-A2
BATH CT
5000 VeCo 91377 557-H1
BATHURST ST
18200 Nor 91326 500-J1
BATON ROUGE AV
10600 Nor 91326 500-G2
BATON ROUGE PL
10600 Nor 91326 500-G3
BATRIS CT
4000 CALB 91302 559-G6
BATRIS LN
5100 LACo 93536 4104-G4
BATSON AV
1400 RowH 91748 679-A5
BATTERY ST
600 SPed 90731 824-B3
W BATTERY ST
700 SPed 90731 824-A3
BATTLE ST
11800 NRWK 90650 706-H6
BATTRAM ST
500 POM 91767 601-A3
BAUCHARD CT
17400 CRSN 90746 734-F7
17400 CRSN 90746 764-F1
BAUCHET ST
100 LA 90012 634-G3
BAUDIN ST
1900 POM 91766 640-J5
BAUER DR
1800 WCOV 91792 638-G4
W BAUGHMAN AV
400 CLAR 91711 601-C2
N BAUGHMAN DR
1100 CLAR 91711 601-C2
BAUHINIA CT
22100 WdHl 91367 559-H7
BAVIERA WY
- StvR 91381 4550-C3
BAXARD PL
27100 SCTA 91354 4550-F1
BAXTER DR
1100 GLDR 91741 569-G4
24200 LACo 90263 628-G6
BAXTER PKWY
- BREA 92821 708-J5
BAXTER PL
1500 Echo 90026 594-F6
BAXTER ST
1500 Echo 90026 594-E5
1900 LA 90039 594-D5
BAXTER WY
4200 THO 91362 557-C4
BAY DR
2200 THO 91361 557-A5
BAY LN
- LA 90065 594-F1
BAY ST
- LBCH 90802 825-D1
100 SMCA 90405 671-G2
1500 LA 90021 634-G6
BAY TR
43800 LACo 93532 4101-J2
E BAYARD ST
2000 LBCH 90815 796-B4
BAYBAR RD
3900 PRV 90601 637-B7
3900 PRV 90601 677-B1
3900 INDS 90601 677-B1
BAYBERRY CIR
12500 CRTS 90703 767-A3
BAYBERRY CT
- CRSN 90746 764-G2
2900 LVRN 91750 600-H2

LOS ANGELES CO.

STREET
Block City ZIP Pg-Grid

BAYBERRY DR
1900 GLDL 91208 534-H5
BAYBERRY LN
3500 MAL 90265 628-G6
BAYBERRY PL
16100 Shrm 91403 561-F7
BAYBERRY ST
500 PMDL 93550 4286-A3
6300 VeCo 91377 558-B2
BAYBERRY WY
2700 FUL 92833 738-B6
BAY CLUB DR
100 PacP 90272 630-H6
BAYCREST CT
25300 Hrbr 90710 794-B4
BAYCREST DR
29500 RPV 90275 822-H2
BAYCREST LN
25300 Hrbr 90710 794-B4
BAYCREST PL
2700 FUL 92833 738-B6
BAYEND DR
29000 RPV 90275 823-H3
BAYER AV
- LBCH 90808 766-A7
BAYER PL
5300 WdHl 91367 559-F2
BAYFIELD DR
900 SDMS 91750 570-D7
900 SDMS 91750 600-D1
BAYHURST PL
5500 PMDL 93552 4287-B3
BAYLA ST
11200 NRWK 90650 706-F6
BAYLESS ST
500 AZU 91702 568-G6
BAYLISS CT
37000 PMDL 93550 4286-F4
BAYLISS RD
13400 Brwd 90049 631-C1
13700 Brwd 90049 591-C7
BAYLOR AV
700 CLAR 91711 601-C3
BAYLOR DR
11500 NRWK 90650 736-G5
BAYLOR ST
600 PacP 90272 630-H5
1900 DUAR 91010 568-C5
N BAYMAR AV
100 WCOV 91791 599-A7
S BAYMAR ST
100 WCOV 91791 599-A7
200 WCOV 91791 639-A1
BAY MARE LN
- RHE 90274 793-G7
E BAYMARE RD
- VeCo 91307 529-A4
BAY MEADOW AV
13100 CHNO 91710 641-F7
BAY MEADOW CT
13100 CHNO 91710 641-E7
BAYNE DR
25000 LACo - (4560-A4 See Page 4470)
BAYNES RD
25200 LACo 91302 589-B5
BAYONNE CT
30800 WLKV 91362 557-F5
BAYONNE ST
700 ELSG 90245 702-D7
700 ELSG 90245 732-D1
BAYOU AV
14900 BLF 90706 736-A4
BAYOU WY
1700 SLB 90740 826-G3
BAY PARK DR
- LA 90094 702-D1
BAYPOINT AV
1400 Wilm 90744 794-E3
BAYPORT CIR
1200 POM 91768 640-G1
BAYPORT DR
2600 TOR 90503 763-F7
S BAYPORT DR
2100 TOR 90503 763-F7
BAYPORT LN
- SCTA 91355 4550-H3
BAYPORT ST
500 CRSN 90745 794-E1
BAYPORT WY
300 VeCo 91377 557-G2
BAY RIDGE CT
2700 PMDL 93551 4195-C6
BAYRIDGE RD
5300 RPV 90275 793-A5
BAY SHORE AV
- LBCH 90803 826-B2
BAYSHORE DR
32000 WLKV 91361 557-C7
BAY SHORE WK
5500 LBCH 90803 826-C3
BAYSIDE CT
2300 THO 91361 557-B6
BAYSIDE DR
600 SLB 90740 826-G4
13900 NRWK 90650 736-E3
BAYSIDE DR N
400 LBCH 90803 826-B1
BAYSIDE DR S
400 LBCH 90803 826-B1
BAYSIDE LN
- SCTA 91355 4550-G2
BAYSIDE PL
25300 Hrbr 90710 794-B4
BAYSIDE WY
- BPK 90621 738-A6
BAYSINGER ST
7800 DWNY 90241 706-A3
E BAY STATE ST
- ALH 91801 596-B5
W BAY STATE ST
- ALH 91801 596-C5
BAY TREE RD
700 LCF 91011 535-C1
BAYVIEW AV
200 Wilm 90744 794-D5
BAYVIEW CT
- SCTA 91355 4550-F2
BAY VIEW DR
- RPV 90275 793-J7
- RPV 90275 823-J1
- SIGH 90755 795-G4
BAYVIEW DR
- BPK 90621 738-B6
100 HMB 90254 762-G1
16600 OrCo 92649 826-J7
N BAYVIEW DR
- MANB 90266 732-E4
200 HMB 90254 732-F6
BAYVIEW LN
25600 Hrbr 90710 794-A5
BAYWATER AV
2800 SPed 90731 854-B1
BAYWAY PL
- LACo 93591 4199-E3
BAYWOOD AV
1400 POM 91767 601-C6
W BAYWOOD AV
2900 ANA 92804 767-J6
BAYWOOD CT
2000 LAN 93534 4015-E5
2000 LAN 93536 4015-E5
10100 BelA 90077 592-B2
10100 LA 90210 592-B2
BAY WOOD DR
100 CRSN 90745 794-C1
BAYWOOD DR
1200 BREA 92821 708-H5
2100 FUL 92833 738-C3
BAYWOOD LN
- SCTA 91354 4550-E1
- SCTA 91355 4550-E1
BAYWOOD ST
3900 LA 90039 564-C6
BAZA AV
5100 WdHl 91364 560-A3
BEA CT
27600 SCTA 91350 4460-J5
BEA WY
1800 LHB 90631 708-G5
BEACH AV
2300 Ven 90291 671-H6
13300 LA 90292 672-B6
E BEACH AV
100 ING 90302 703-C2
W BEACH AV
100 ING 90302 703-B1
BEACH BLVD Rt#-39
4600 BPK 90621 737-H7
6300 BPK 90621 767-H3
7000 BPK 90620 767-H3
8600 ANA 92801 767-H3
14900 LMRD 90638 737-H7
N BEACH BLVD Rt#-39
100 ANA 92801 767-J5
100 LHB 90631 708-C5
S BEACH BLVD Rt#-39
100 ANA 92804 767-J7
100 LHB 90631 708-C7
1000 LHB 90631 738-A2
1400 LMRD 90638 738-A2
13900 FUL 92833 738-A2
13900 FUL 90638 738-A2
14200 LMRD 90638 737-J3
BEACH CIR
8400 CYP 90630 767-B5
BEACH CT
2300 Ven 90291 671-J6
BEACH DR
- HMB 90254 762-G1
5700 LBCH 90822 796-D6
5700 LBCH 90840 796-D6
BEACH ST
100 MTBL 90640 676-C3
200 SMCA 90405 671-F4
3200 LBCH 90810 795-A1
7200 Flor 90001 674-G7
7200 Flor 90001 704-G1
8600 Wats 90002 704-G2
9200 Wats 90002 704-G4
9400 BLF 90706 736-B6
11200 CRTS 90703 736-F6
11400 ART 90701 736-G6
12600 CRTS 90703 737-A6
29100 Cstc 91384 4459-G6
N BEACH ST
800 LHB 90631 708-C4
900 ING 90302 673-B7
900 ING 90302 703-B1
BEACH WY
4600 BPK 90621 737-J4
S BEACH CLUB WY
11800 VeCo 90265 625-F5
BEACHCOMBER DR
600 SLB 90740 826-F4
E BEACH COMBER DR
6200 LBCH 90803 826-D1
BEACHCOMBER LN
- SCTA 91355 4550-H3
BEACHEY PL
1300 CRSN 90746 764-G2
1300 CRSN 90747 764-G2
BEACHFRONT LN
32100 WLKV 91361 557-C6
BEACHGROVE CT
19200 SCTA 91321 4551-G5
BEACHLAKE LN
32100 WLKV 91361 557-C6
BEACHMEADOW LN
4100 WLKV 91361 557-C6
BEACHNUTT CT
- LMRD 90638 738-B2
BEACHSIDE DR
29200 RPV 90275 823-A1
BEACHVIEW DR
6400 RPV 90275 822-H5
BEACHVIEW LN
32100 WLKV 91361 557-C6
BEACH VIEW ESTATES DR
31200 MAL 90265 626-J6
N BEACHWOOD DR
100 BURB 91506 563-F1
100 LA 90004 593-G7
100 LA 90004 633-G1
500 BURB 91506 533-F6
1100 LA 90038 593-G5
1300 Hlwd 90028 593-G5
1900 LA 90068 593-F3
3100 LA 90068 563-G7
S BEACHWOOD DR
- BURB 91506 563-G2
100 LA 90004 633-F1
BEACHWOOD TER
2100 LA 90068 593-G3
BEACHY AV
8600 Pcma 91331 532-B1
8700 Pcma 91331 502-B5
BEACON AV
200 SPAS 91030 595-G1
700 LA 90017 634-C4
900 LA 90015 634-C4
BEACON LN
39200 PMDL 93551 4195-B5
BEACON PL
- LACo 91107 566-H4
BEACON ST
- ALH 91801 596-C4
200 AVA 90704 5923-H4
900 BREA 92821 708-J6
27800 Cstc 91384 4459-G5
E BEACON ST
- ALH 91801 596-B5
N BEACON ST
100 SPed 90731 824-C4
S BEACON ST
100 SPed 90731 824-C5
W BEACON ST
200 ALH 91801 596-B5
BEACONSFIELD CT
42500 LACo 93532 4102-G5
BEACONTREE LN
2600 LACo 91302 589-C3
BEAGLE ST
4300 LA 90032 595-C7
BEAK AV
10600 SGAT 90280 705-G6
10700 SGAT 90242 705-G6
BEALE CT
- SCTA 91355 4460-C7
BEALE RD
- PMDL 93552 4287-E2
BEAR AV
6000 HNTP 90255 675-C6
6200 BELL 90201 675-C6
7000 BELL 90201 705-C1
7200 CDHY 90201 705-C1
7200 HNTP 90255 705-C1
BEAR CT
3700 BELL 90201 675-C7
BEAR CANYON RD
6600 LACo - (512-A4 See Page 511)
6600 SBdC - (512-A4 See Page 511)
BEARCREEK LN
16200 CRTS 90703 737-A6
BEAR CREEK RD
- PMDL 93550 4286-F6
- PMDL 93550 4286-H7
- PMDL 93550 4376-H1
BEARD ST
6200 HiPk 90042 595-D1
BEARDSLEE ST
2300 DUAR 91010 568-C5
BEARHAVEN CT
28500 RPV 90275 823-H2
BEAR MEADOW CIR
16400 CRTS 90703 736-J6
BEAR RIVER CIR
3400 THO 91362 557-C2
BEARS DEN RD
1600 DBAR 91765 680-C4
BEAR VALLEY LN
- Nor 91326 480-E7
BEAR VALLEY RD
- POM 91766 640-G4
500 SBdC 92372 (4472-A1 See Page 4471)
BEASOR DR
- SFSP 90670 707-A2
BEATIE PL
2200 LA 90032 635-F1
BEATRICE PL
8900 RSMD 91770 636-H1
BEATRICE ST
1700 CULC 90230 672-F6
11800 LA 90230 672-F6
12400 LACo 90066 672-F6
12500 LA 90066 672-E7
BEATY AV
13000 LACo 90605 707-B7
BEATY ST
11400 NRWK 90650 706-G7
BEAU CT
28000 SCTA 91350 4461-A5
BEAUCOURT AV
11200 Litl 93543 4468-F6
BEAUCROFT CT
4200 WLKV 91361 557-D6
BEAUDINE AV
8800 SGAT 90280 704-J3
N BEAUDRY AV
100 LA 90012 634-F2
S BEAUDRY AV
100 LA 90012 634-E4
300 LA 90017 634-E4
BEAUDRY BLVD
1300 GLDL 91208 534-G5
BEAUDRY TER
3100 GLDL 91208 534-F5
BEAUDRY NORTH MTWY
- GLDL 91208 534-F6
BEAUDRY SOUTH
- GLDL 91208 534-E6
BEAUFAIT AV
11800 Nor 91326 480-H6
BEAUMONT ST
23200 SCTA 91354 4460-G7
BEAUTIVISTA LN
35600 LACo 91390 4373-J1
BEAUTYBERRY PL
- LACo 91387 4552-A4
BEAUVAIS AV
4400 LA 90065 595-A4
BEAUVAIS RD
4600 RPV 90275 823-G5
BEAU VILLE CT
42800 LAN 93536 4105-B3
BEAVER CT
100 POM 91766 640-J4
200 POM 91766 641-A4
BEAVER ST
13000 LA 91342 482-C2
BEAVER TR
- SBdC 92371 (4562-J5 See Page 4471)
BEAVER WY
1000 LVRN 91750 570-E7
BEAVERBROOK DR
42500 LACo 93532 4102-G5
BEAVERBROOK LN
4400 WLKV 91361 557-D6
BEAVERHEAD DR
22600 DBAR 91765 640-B7
BEAVER RUN RD
15700 SCTA 91387 4552-D7
15700 SCTA 91387 4642-E1
BEAZLEY CT
- FUL 92833 738-D5
BECHARD AV
13200 NRWK 90650 737-A2
16900 CRTS 90703 737-A6
18300 CRTS 90703 767-A1
BECK AV
3500 BELL 90201 675-C7
4000 LA 91604 562-H5
4400 LA 91602 562-H4
4500 BELL 90201 705-D1
4800 NHol 91601 562-H2
6000 NHol 91606 532-H6
6800 NHol 91605 532-H4
BECK ST
2400 SBdC 91784 571-H3
22100 CRSN 90745 764-F7
BECKENHAM LN
- StvR 91381 4550-A7
BECKETT ST
6800 Tuj 91042 504-B4
7600 Tuj 91040 503-H4
7800 Sunl 91040 503-H4
BECKETT WY
26100 StvR 91381 4550-B7
BECKFORD AV
5200 Tarz 91356 560-G1
6100 Res 91335 530-G5
8300 Nor 91324 530-G2
9300 Nor 91324 500-G5
10300 Nor 91326 500-G2
BECKFORD PL
19200 Nor 91324 500-G6
BECKFORD WY
1200 POM 91767 601-D7
BECKLEDGE TER
22800 MAL 90265 629-B6
BECKLEE RD
1000 GLDR 91741 569-G3
BECKLEY AV
5000 WdHl 91364 559-H3
13100 CHNO 91710 641-G7
BECKMAN CT
- FUL 92833 738-D5
BECKMAN RD
2900 LA 90068 593-C1
BECKNEL AV
25300 LMTA 90717 793-G4
BECKNER ST
13600 LACo 91746 637-J3
13700 LPUE 91746 638-A3
14300 LPUE 91744 638-B4
BECKVILLE ST
800 DUAR 91010 567-J7
E BECKVILLE ST
700 LACo 91010 567-H7
BECKWITH AV
1300 Brwd 90049 631-E4
BECKWORTH AV
19200 TOR 90503 763-B3
BECKY LN
39900 PMDL 93551 4195-J3
BEDA ST
40500 LACo 93535 4200-C1
BEDEL ST
4600 WdHl 91364 560-C4
BEDESSEN AV
2300 CMRC 90040 675-F3
BEDFORD AV
5100 LadH 90056 673-A5
5800 LadH 90056 672-J6
BEDFORD CIR
18300 LACo 91744 679-A2
BEDFORD CT
37200 PMDL 93550 4286-D3
N BEDFORD DR
300 BHLS 90210 632-E1
800 BHLS 90210 592-E7
S BEDFORD DR
100 BHLS 90212 632-F2
400 LA 90035 632-F2
BEDFORD LN
15100 LA 91343 501-H6
BEDFORD RD
1300 SMRO 91108 566-D7
1300 SMRO 91108 596-D1
N BEDFORD ST
300 LHB 90631 708-G5
S BEDFORD ST
100 LHB 90631 708-G6
800 LA 90035 632-J3
1900 LA 90034 632-H6
BEDFORD WY
21600 SCTA 91350 4461-B5
BEDFORDHURST CT
31700 WLKV 91361 557-D6
BEDILION ST
- LA 90032 595-D6
BEDMAR ST
1000 CRSN 90746 764-F4
BEDROCK HILLS DR
33100 LACo 91390 4373-D6
BEDWORTH RD
10400 LACo 91390 4373-D6
BEE AV
6200 AGRH 91301 558-B3
BEE CT
38100 PMDL 93550 4286-H1
BEE CANYON
10800 Chat 91311 499-J2
BEECH
300 SDMS 91773 599-J3
BEECH AV
300 TOR 90501 763-G6
43700 LAN 93534 4105-H1
44000 LAN 93534 4015-H5
BEECH ST
400 LA 90065 594-J5
400 LA 90065 595-G4
1100 SPAS 91030 595-G4
2700 LVRN 91750 570-J7
BEECHAM DR
2000 RPV 90275 823-H2
BEECH CREEK CIR
22900 SCTA 91354 4460-H4
BEECHDALE DR
1000 LACo 93551 4195-G6
1000 PMDL 93551 4195-G6
BEECHER LN
- StvR 91381 4550-A7
BEECHFIELD DR
6900 RPV 90275 792-G6
BEECHGATE DR
27900 RPV 90275 793-B7
27900 RPV 90275 823-B1
28000 RHE 90274 823-B1
BEECHGLEN DR
3700 GLDL 91214 534-D1
BEECH HILL AV
900 HacH 91745 637-J7
1200 HacH 91745 677-H1
BEECH HILL DR
1700 HacH 91745 677-H2
BEECH KNOLL RD
2000 LA 90046 592-J3
BEECHLEY AV
17000 NLB 90805 735-D6
BEECHNUT CIR
27900 SCTA 91354 4460-H4
BEECHNUT PL
1200 POM 91766 640-F4
BEECHTREE LN
18800 Nor 91326 500-H3
BEECHTREE WY
- PanC 91402 532-C2
BEECH WILLOW LN
- LACo 91387 4552-A4
BEECHWOOD AV
700 FUL 92835 738-J3
2900 LYN 90262 705-A6
8100 SGAT 90280 704-J2
8100 SGAT 90280 705-A6
BEECHWOOD DR
- SCTA 91351 4551-G7
- SCTA 91354 4460-F4
1000 BREA 92821 709-A5
1100 BREA 92821 708-J4
BEECHWOOD LN
100 SDMS 91773 600-C4
BEECHWOOD ST
2100 LAN 93535 4016-D6
BEECHWORTH AV
300 MNRO 91016 567-H2
BEEHIVE AV
- BRAD 91010 568-B3
BEEKLEY LN
8900 SBdC 92371 (4562-H1 See Page 4471)
BEEKLEY RD
8200 SBdC 92371 (4562-H1 See Page 4471)
9100 SBdC 92371 (4472-H3 See Page 4471)
BEELER AV
5400 WdHl 91367 559-E2
BEEMAN AV
4200 LA 91604 562-F4
4800 LA 91607 562-F1
5900 LA 91607 532-E7
6000 NHol 91606 532-E6
7600 NHol 91605 532-E2
BEER SHEBA
- SIMI 93063 499-C1
BEESON DR
9800 LA 90210 592-D3
BEETHOVEN DR
8300 BPK 90621 767-J1
BEETHOVEN PL
16600 CRTS 90703 737-B6
BEETHOVEN ST
3300 LA 90066 672-A3
3900 CULC 90066 672-C5
BEGONIA AV
1600 HiPk 90042 565-C7
N BEGONIA AV
200 ONT 91762 601-J6
BEGONIA CT
1200 UPL 91784 571-J5
BEGONIA ST
44100 LAN 93535 4016-F7
BEGONIA WY
1100 LACo 90502 794-A1
BEGONIAS LN
14800 SCTA 91387 4462-F7
BEGOVICH ST
- FUL 92833 738-D6
BEHAN WY
8200 LACo 91775 596-F1
BEHRENS AV
13400 NRWK 90650 736-E2
BEIRUT AV
300 PacP 90272 631-A6
BEJAY PL
800 SPed 90731 824-A2
BEL TER
11800 Brwd 90049 591-G6
BELA ST
- PMDL 93550 4286-E4
BEL AIR AV
9200 MTCL 91763 601-H5
11000 SBdC 91762 641-H2
BEL AIR CT
1000 BelA 90077 592-A5
BEL AIR DR
19100 WAL 91789 679-C1
BELAIR DR
4300 LCF 91011 535-B4
BEL AIR PL
1100 BelA 90077 592-A5
BEL AIR RD
100 BelA 90077 592-A4
N BEL AIR ST
100 ANA 92801 767-J5
8500 BPK 90620 767-J5
BEL AIR TER
10400 BelA 90077 592-A5
BEL AIR CREST RD N
11800 BelA 90077 591-F3
12100 Brwd 90049 591-F3
BEL AIR CREST RD S
11800 BelA 90077 591-G3
BEL AIRE DR
1500 GLDL 91201 564-B1
1600 GLDL 91201 534-A7
1800 BURB 91504 533-G4
N BEL AIRE DR
100 BURB 91501 533-H5
1000 BURB 91504 533-H5
S BEL AIRE DR
100 BURB 91501 533-J6
600 BURB 91501 534-A6
900 GLDL 91201 534-A6
900 BURB 91201 534-A6
BEL AIRE LN
- LACo 90606 676-H6
BELAIRE LN
7300 LAN 93536 4104-C5
BELAND AV
7700 Wch 90045 702-F1
BELAND BLVD
2900 RBCH 90278 733-B6
BELBERT CIR
5800 CALB 91302 558-H3
BELBURY DR
1100 DBAR 91789 679-F3
BELCANTO
400 BelA 90077 591-H1
BELCARO CT
- SCTA 91354 4460-F4
BELCARO WY
500 VeCo 91377 557-G1
BELCHER ST
9200 DWNY 90242 736-A2
10900 NRWK 90650 736-E2
12900 NRWK 90650 737-A2
14000 LMRD 90638 737-D2
BELCOURT DR
14800 LACo 90604 707-F5
BELCROFT AV
1800 SELM 91733 637-D4
3400 ELMN 91732 637-F1
BELDAY RD
100 PAS 91105 565-E4
BELDAY ST
8700 CYP 90630 767-C5
S BELDEN AV
400 ELA 90022 635-H7
600 ELA 90022 675-H1
BELDEN DR
2700 LA 90068 593-F1
BELDOVE CT
22100 SCTA 91350 4461-A4
E BELEN ST
5700 LBCH 90815 796-C2
BELFAIR ST
9800 BLF 90706 736-C3
11000 NRWK 90650 736-F3
12800 NRWK 90650 737-A3
BELFAST DR
1300 LA 90069 592-J5
BELFORD AV
8100 Wch 90045 702-J2
BELFORD CT
24000 LA 91304 529-D4
BELFOREST DR
16900 CRSN 90746 734-E7
BELFORT AV
1000 POM 91767 601-B6
BELGATE ST
4400 BALD 91706 598-A4
BELGIAN PL
- MTCL 91763 641-E1
BELGRAVE AV
1900 HNTP 90255 674-H6
2800 HNTP 90255 675-A6
S BELGREEN DR
1100 LACo 90601 637-E5
BELHAM CT
4500 WLKV 91361 557-D6
BELHAVEN AV
1900 COMP 90059 734-E2
11900 LA 90059 704-E7
12000 Wbrk 90059 704-E7
12700 Wbrk 90059 734-F2
N BELHAVEN AV
1800 SIMI 93063 499-C2
BELHAVEN PL
100 CLAR 91711 601-D5
BELHAVEN RD
1200 SMRO 91108 566-F7
1400 SMRO 91108 596-F1
BELHAVEN ST
9200 Wats 90002 704-F3
11100 LA 90059 704-F6
BELHURST AV
6800 NLB 90805 735-D6
E BELICE ST
5800 LBCH 90815 796-D3
BELINDA AV
2200 POM 91768 600-D7
2200 POM 91768 640-D1
BELINDA CT
12500 LYN 90262 735-G4
BELINDA ST
2400 WCOV 91792 639-B7
4500 Enc 91316 561-B4
BELITA LN
4500 LCF 91011 535-D5
BELL AV
3400 BELL 90201 675-C7
7200 Flor 90001 674-G7
7400 Flor 90001 704-G2
N BELL AV
500 MANB 90266 732-F4
BELL PL
4400 BELL 90201 675-D7
BELL ST
1700 LVRN 91750 600-F1
E BELL ST
800 PAS 91104 566-A2
BELLA CT
- LACo 90604 707-E5
24200 SCTA 91321 4640-H3
BELLA DR
1400 LA 90210 592-C5
BELLAGIO DR
- LA 90095 631-J1
BELLAGIO PL
11000 BelA 90077 591-J7
BELLAGIO RD
10400 BelA 90077 592-A7
10800 BelA 90077 632-A1
10800 BelA 90077 631-J1
10900 BelA 90077 591-J7
11100 Brwd 90049 591-G7
11500 Brwd 90049 631-H1
BELLAGIO TER
400 Brwd 90049 591-H7
BELLAGIO WY
100 BelA 90077 631-J1
400 WAL 91789 679-C1
BELLAIRE AV
4100 LA 91604 562-E4
4800 LA 91607 562-E1
5900 LA 91607 532-E7
6000 NHol 91606 532-E7
6700 NHol 91605 532-E3
BELLAIRE DR
3200 Alta 91001 535-J4
BELLA KATH TER
6300 PMDL 93551 4104-E6
BELLANCA AV
8600 Wch 90045 702-J3
BELLANCA WY
25300 TOR 90505 793-E4
BELLANDO CT
- GmH 91344 481-A6
BELLA OCEANA VISTA
1300 PacP 90272 630-H3
BELLA PINE DR
21300 DBAR 91765 679-H5
BELLA SANTA DR
26000 SCTA 91355 4550-G4
BELLA VISTA
2200 RPV 90275 823-G5
BELLA VISTA AV
200 PAS 91107 566-E2
BELLA VISTA CT
13100 CHLS 91709 680-H1
BELLA VISTA DR
1400 LHH 90631 708-G3
1900 ARCD 91007 597-B1
4300 CALB 91302 559-C7
24900 SCTA 91321 4640-G2
BELLAVISTA DR
- LACo 91789 679-E4
BELLA VISTA LN
- WdHl 91367 530-C7
BELLA VISTA ST
300 MNRO 91016 567-G6
7600 Wch 90045 702-C4
S BELLA VISTA ST
100 ANA 92804 767-G6
BELLA VISTA WY
6500 LA 90068 593-E3
BELLA VITA WY
- PMDL 93552 4196-H7
BELLBIRD PL
45200 LACo 93536 4013-B5
BELLBROOK ST
2100 COV 91724 599-G3
13700 BALD 91706 598-A4
16400 LACo 91722 598-C4
17700 LACo 91722 599-A4
21100 LACo 91724 599-G3
E BELLBROOK ST
200 COV 91722 599-C3
1100 COV 91722 598-G4
16200 LACo 91722 598-G4
19600 LACo 91724 599-D3
BELL CANYON RD
- CanP 91307 529-C4
- VeCo 91307 529-C4
E BELL CANYON RD
- VeCo 91307 529-A4
BELLCLAIRE ST
6900 Tuj 91042 504-B3
BELL CREST DR
- Wch 90045 702-C2
BELLDER DR
9700 DWNY 90240 706-C3
10300 DWNY 90241 706-C4
12500 DWNY 90242 706-C4
12500 DWNY 90242 736-A1
BELLE DR
2100 LA 90210 592-B3
BELLEAU CT
22200 CALB 91302 559-J7
BELLEAU RD
1400 GLDL 91206 565-A1
BELLEAU WOOD DR
- Brwd 90049 631-J2
BELLECHASSE AV
4200 LACo 91722 598-F5
BELLEFONT DR
18000 LACo 91702 599-A1
BELLEFONTAINE PL
800 PAS 91105 565-G7
BELLEFONTAINE ST
- PAS 91105 565-G6
BELLEGLADE AV
2300 LA 90032 635-E1
2400 LA 90032 595-E7
BELLEMARE AV
19900 TOR 90503 763-C4
BELLE PORTE AV
25000 Hrbr 90710 794-A6
BELLERIVE CT
- PMDL 93551 4194-J2
BELLERIVE DR
25600 SCTA 91355 4550-F6
BELLE RIVER DR
3000 HacH 91745 677-J5
BELLESHIRE WY
- PMDL 93552 4286-J2
BELLEVIEW AV
500 SDMS 91773 600-C1
BELLEVILLE CT
3700 CLAR 91711 571-F5
BELLEVUE AV
600 Echo 90026 594-B7
1100 LA 90012 634-F2
1200 Echo 90026 634-D1
1200 POM 91768 600-E7
BELLEVUE DR
1900 GLDL 91201 534-A6
E BELLEVUE DR
200 PAS 91101 565-J6
W BELLEVUE DR
- PAS 91105 565-H6
BELLEZA
2300 LA 90732 823-F7
BELLEZA CT
- StvR 91381 4640-C1
BELLEZA WY
- PMDL 93551 4195-A3
BELLFIELD WY
3600 LA 91604 563-A7
BELLFLOWER AV
4400 LA 91602 562-J4
4800 NHol 91601 562-J3
BELLFLOWER BLVD
4900 LKWD 90713 766-C2
4900 LKWD 90712 766-C2
11500 DWNY 90241 706-B7
11900 DWNY 90242 706-B7
12300 DWNY 90242 736-C3
13400 BLF 90706 736-C3
17800 BLF 90706 766-C2
N BELLFLOWER BLVD
100 LBCH 90814 826-C1
200 LBCH 90814 826-C1
300 LBCH 90803 796-C6
400 LBCH 90803 796-C6
600 LBCH 90804 796-C6
700 LBCH 90822 796-C6
700 LBCH 90815 796-C4
1300 LBCH 90840 796-C4
3000 LBCH 90808 796-C4
3400 LBCH 90808 766-C5
4100 LKWD 90713 766-C5
BELLFORD AV
1300 LACo 91104 566-C1
1300 PAS 91104 566-C1
1600 LACo 91104 536-D7
BELL GARDEN AV
7800 BGDN 90201 705-F2
BELLGAVE PL
8200 LA 90069 593-A4
BELLGREEN ST
4000 BALD 91706 598-A5
BELLGROVE ST
500 SDMS 91773 600-D1
700 LACo 91750 600-D1
BELLHAVEN ST
8100 LPMA 90623 767-B4
11600 LA 90059 704-E7
BELLINGER ST
11000 LYN 90262 705-A6
BELLINGHAM AV
4100 LA 91604 562-G5
4800 LA 91607 562-G1
6000 NHol 91606 532-F6
6800 NHol 91605 532-F3
8300 SunV 91352 532-F3
BELLINI DR
21100 Top 90290 560-B7
BELLINI WY
3200 PMDL 93551 4195-B4
BELLINO DR
200 PacP 90272 630-F5
BELLIS DR
25800 SCTA 91355 4550-F5
BELL LYN LN
300 NLB 90805 735-D6
BELLMAN AV
10200 DWNY 90241 706-C4
BELLMARIN DR
300 SPed 90731 824-A5
500 LACo 90732 824-A5
BELLMORE WY
400 PAS 91103 565-G4
BELLORITA ST
18200 RowH 91748 678-J6
18500 RowH 91748 679-A6
BELLOTA AV
15100 PRM 90723 735-J4
BELLOTA WY
3300 LFlz 90027 594-C2
BELLOWS CT
500 DBAR 91765 640-E7
BELL RANCH DR
9700 SFSP 90670 706-J3
9700 SFSP 90670 707-A4
BELLWOOD AV
10300 LA 90064 632-E4
BELLWOOD RD
1300 SMRO 91108 566-E7
1300 SMRO 91108 596-E1
12300 OrCo 90720 796-H5
BELMAR AV
6200 Res 91335 530-F4
8500 Nor 91324 530-F1
9700 Nor 91324 500-F5
10700 Nor 91326 500-F2
BELMART AV
13700 NRWK 90650 736-J2
BELMONT AV
- LBCH 90803 826-A1
100 Echo 90026 634-D1
700 LBCH 90804 796-A5
1400 WCOV 91790 638-D3
1600 PAS 91103 535-G7
1600 PAS 91103 565-G1
2200 LBCH 90815 796-A4
BELMONT CT
2700 BREA 92821 709-F7
27300 AGRH 91301 557-H4
27300 SCTA 91354 4460-F7
BELMONT LN
1400 RBCH 90278 762-J2
1800 RBCH 90278 763-A2
BELMONT PL
4700 CHNO 91710 641-F4
12600 CRTS 90703 767-A2
BELMONT ST
500 MTBL 90640 636-G3
500 MTBL 90640 676-H1
8500 CYP 90630 767-C5
8700 BLF 90706 735-J6
8700 BLF 90706 736-A6
9200 PRV 90660 676-H1
N BELMONT ST
100 GLDL 91206 564-F4
S BELMONT ST
100 GLDL 91205 564-F5
BELMONT ABBEY LN
1000 CLAR 91711 571-F4
BEL MONTE CT
28200 SCTA 91387 4552-A2
BELOIT AV
100 Brwd 90049 631-H2
700 LACo 90073 631-J2
1500 CLAR 91711 601-E1
1500 WLA 90025 632-A5
2200 LA 90064 632-A5
4700 LA 90230 672-F4
BELRIDGE CT
900 WAL 91789 639-F6
BELSHAW AV
19000 CRSN 90746 764-F3
BELSHIRE AV
12200 LKWD 90715 766-J4
15500 NRWK 90650 736-J5
17300 CRTS 90703 736-J7
17400 ART 90701 736-J7
17800 ART 90701 766-J1
18800 CRTS 90703 766-J2
21400 HGDN 90716 766-J6
BELSIZE PL
5800 AGRH 91301 557-G4
BELSON ST
800 LACo 90502 794-B1
BELTON DR
7900 Wch 90045 702-E2
BELVEDERE CT
11500 CRTS 90703 736-G6
BELVEDERE LN
- LAN 93535 4016-E6
BELVEDERE WY
5200 MTCL 91763 641-G2
BELVIDERE ST
600 PAS 91104 566-A2
BELVOIR AV
9300 LA 91214 504-C6
BEMIS ST
3900 LA 90039 564-C6
BEN AV
4200 LA 91604 562-G5
4400 LA 91607 562-G1
6200 NHol 91606 532-G7
6800 NHol 91605 532-G2
BEN CT
20900 SCTA 91350 4461-C4
BEN PL
- PMDL 93551 4195-D7
BEN WY
- Actn 93510 4375-F6
BENA CT
28000 SCTA 91350 4461-D6
BENALD ST
43400 LAN 93535 4016-C5
BEN ALDER AV
5300 WHIT 90601 677-A3
5400 WHIT 90601 676-J4
5700 LACo 90606 676-J4
5800 WHIT 90606 676-J4
BENARES PL
10000 SunV 91352 533-C2
BENARES ST
7100 DWNY 90241 705-H4
BEN AVON CT
100 SDMS 91773 599-J2
BEN AVON ST
10800 LACo 90606 676-H7
10900 LACo 90606 706-H1
BENAVON ST
10500 LACo 90606 676-G7
BENBOW ST
13300 BALD 91706 598-A4
E BENBOW ST
100 COV 91722 599-C4
1000 COV 91724 599-C4
1100 COV 91722 598-G4

STREET Block City ZIP Pg-Grid

E BENBOW ST
1600 SDMS 91773 599-H3
1800 LACo 91773 599-H3
16200 LACo 91722 598-G4
17700 LACo 91722 599-A4
21100 LACo 91724 599-G4
W BENBOW ST
900 COV 91722 598-J4
900 SDMS 91773 599-J4
BENBROOK DR
13700 LACo 91746 637-H5
E BENCAMP ST
100 SGBL 91776 596-E7
W BENCAMP ST
200 SGBL 91776 596-D7
BENCH ST
18800 LACo 91744 679-B2
18800 LACo 91792 679-B2
BENCHLEY CT
30900 WLKV 91361 557-C6
BENCHLEY ST
- FUL 92833 738-D5
BENCOLA CT
900 WCOV 91790 638-F2
BEND AV
2400 LAN 93535 4106-D2
BEND DR
4500 LA 90065 594-J2
BENDA PL
3200 LA 90068 563-D7
BENDA ST
3100 LA 90068 563-D7
BENDER AV
200 COV 91724 599-D5
3600 LACo 91724 599-D6
N BENDER AV
300 GLDR 91741 569-D4
900 COV 91724 599-D4
4800 LACo 91724 599-D3
S BENDER AV
700 GLDR 91740 569-D7
1100 GLDR 91740 599-D1
BENDIGO DR
3500 RPV 90275 823-E5
BENECIA AV
1800 WLA 90025 632-D4
2200 LA 90064 632-D4
BENEDA LN
17800 SCTA 91351 4551-J2
BENEDICT AV
1500 CLAR 91711 601-E1
12300 DWNY 90242 736-C1
BENEDICT CT
36800 PMDL 93552 4287-B4
BENEDICT ST
2600 LA 90039 594-F4
BENEDICT WY
1700 POM 91767 601-C6
3300 HNTP 90255 675-B6
BENEDICT CANYON DR
900 BHLS 90210 592-D6
1200 LA 90210 592-B1
2900 LA 90210 562-B7
3700 Shrm 91423 562-C5
BENEDICT CANYON LN
3600 Shrm 91423 562-B6
BENEFIT ST
14300 Shrm 91403 562-A5
14300 Shrm 91423 562-A5
14500 Shrm 91403 561-J5
BENFAR DR
- LAN 93535 4106-D1
BENFIELD AV
10800 DWNY 90241 706-F6
11200 NRWK 90650 706-F6
12400 NRWK 90650 736-F1
19100 CRTS 90703 766-F3
BENFIELD PL
24100 DBAR 91765 680-D1
BEN FRANKLIN DR
- PMDL 93550 4286-B4
BENGAL CT
1500 LACo 93551 4195-F7
1500 PMDL 93551 4195-F7
BENHAM AV
4000 BALD 91706 598-B3
BENHILL AV
23900 LMTA 90717 793-H3
BEN HUR AV
8800 WHIT 90605 707-G3
9100 WHIT 90603 707-F3
9600 LACo 90604 707-E4
10000 LACo 90605 707-D4
BENICIA RD
200 DBAR 91765 640-C6
BENIK PL
- WAL 91789 639-G6
BENIK RD
1500 LHH 90631 708-F3
BENITO AV
900 ALH 91803 595-J7
BENITO CT
26200 SCTA 91355 4550-F4
BENITO ST
4200 MTCL 91763 601-F6
5600 MTCL 91762 601-F6
BENJAMIN AV
7500 Wch 90045 703-A2
BEN LOMOND AV
7600 LACo 91741 569-C3
BEN LOMOND DR
1500 GLDL 91202 564-C1
1700 GLDL 91202 534-C7

BEN LOMOND DR
2200 LFlz 90027 594-B3
BEN LOMOND PL
3400 LFlz 90027 594-B3
E BENMORE ST
6000 LBCH 90815 796-D2
BENMORE TER
12000 Brwd 90049 631-G2
BENNER AV
22600 TOR 90505 793-E1
BENNER CT
23000 TOR 90505 793-E1
BENNER PL
17200 Enc 91316 561-C5
BENNER ST
5700 HiPk 90042 595-C3
BENNETT AV
- LBCH 90803 826-A1
700 LBCH 90804 796-A6
1400 GLDR 91741 569-H5
E BENNETT AV
100 GLDR 91741 569-F5
W BENNETT AV
100 GLDR 91741 569-D5
BENNETT DR
1200 PAS 91103 565-E3
3200 LA 90068 563-C7
3200 LA 90068 593-C1
BENNETT LN
- BREA 92821 709-B4
BENNETT PL
300 CLAR 91711 571-D5
E BENNETT ST
100 COMP 90220 734-J6
100 COMP 90220 735-A6
300 COMP 90221 735-B6
3600 RDom 90221 735-C6
W BENNETT ST
100 COMP 90220 734-E6
BEN NEVIS AV
13200 NRWK 90650 737-A2
BENNINGTON AV
7100 PRV 90660 676-F7
7300 PRV 90660 706-F1
BENNINGTON CT
4300 CHNO 91710 641-E7
11400 CRTS 90703 736-G6
BENNINGTON DR
23700 SCTA 91354 4550-F1
BENOWE SCOTIA RD
600 GLDL 91207 564-F1
BENRUD ST
300 MNRO 91016 597-H1
BENSION DR
- Saug 91350 4461-F5
BENSON AV
12100 CHNO 91710 641-H7
N BENSON AV
- UPL 91786 601-H2
100 ONT 91763 641-H1
100 MTCL 91762 601-H2
100 MTCL 91762 641-H1
200 ONT 91762 601-H2
1400 UPL 91786 571-H7
1600 UPL 91784 571-H6
9200 MTCL 91763 601-H7
10400 ONT 91762 641-H1
10400 MTCL 91763 641-H1
S BENSON AV
- MTCL 91763 601-H4
100 ONT 91763 641-H1
300 MTCL 91786 601-H4
400 ONT 91762 641-H3
2000 CHNO 91710 641-H3
2100 MTCL 91763 641-H3
8800 UPL 91763 601-H4
8800 UPL 91786 601-H4
10700 SBdC 91762 641-H3
BENSON ST
6200 HNTP 90255 675-A7
7000 HNTP 90255 705-B1
BENSON WY
9300 SGAT 90280 705-E4
BENT ST
8600 SGAT 90280 705-D3
BENTEL AV
300 Brwd 90049 631-E4
8900 RSMD 91770 596-H6
BENTGRASS WY
26400 SCTA 91350 4551-B3
BENTLEY AV
1500 COMP 90220 735-A6
3800 CULC 90232 672-E2
N BENTLEY AV
100 Brwd 90049 631-J1
200 Brwd 90049 591-J7
S BENTLEY AV
100 Brwd 90049 631-J2
1400 WLA 90025 632-B5
2200 LA 90064 632-C7
3000 LA 90034 632-C7
3100 LA 90034 672-D1
BENTLEY CIR
200 Brwd 90049 631-J1
BENTLEY CT
- WCOV 91791 639-B3
1400 SDMS 91773 599-H2
3000 SMCA 90405 671-G4
BENTLEY PL
- RowH 91748 679-C7
1600 GLDR 91740 599-F2
11700 CHNO 91710 641-H4
13800 CRTS 90703 737-D5

BENTLEY WY
- LACo 91387 4462-C7
2800 DBAR 91765 679-J7
2800 DBAR 91765 680-A7
BENTLEY MANOR PL
- LACo 91387 4551-J4
- LACo 91387 4552-B5
BENT OAK RD
23100 DBAR 91765 680-B4
BENTON AV
2900 LVRN 91750 600-F2
BENTON CT
- INDS 91789 639-J6
27000 SCTA 91354 4550-G1
BENTON RD
300 INDS 91789 639-J6
300 LACo 91789 639-J6
N BENTON WY
100 Echo 90026 634-C1
500 Echo 90026 594-D6
S BENTON WY
100 LA 90057 634-B2
BENTONGROVE DR
13600 LACo 90605 707-C5
14100 LACo 90604 707-D6
BENTREE AV
4700 Bxby 90807 765-F4
BENTREE CIR
5000 Bxby 90807 765-F4
BENT SPUR DR
2400 Actn 93510 4465-D3
BENT TREE DR
14400 CHLS 91709 680-H4
BENT TWIG LN
3200 DBAR 91765 679-H7
BENVENUE ST
12900 Brwd 90049 631-F5
BENWELL DR
11000 LYN 90262 705-C6
BENWICK ST
16200 LACo 91744 638-G4
BENWOOD ST
13600 BALD 91706 598-A4
E BENWOOD ST
100 COV 91722 599-C4
1900 COV 91724 599-G4
16200 LACo 91722 598-G4
17700 LACo 91722 599-A4
19600 LACo 91724 599-G3
W BENWOOD ST
900 COV 91722 598-J4
900 SDMS 91773 599-J3
BENZ RD
20600 SCTA 91350 4461-C4
BEQUETTE AV
6300 PRV 90660 676-F6
BEQUETTE ST
7600 PRV 90660 676-E7
7700 PRV 90660 706-E1
BERAN ST
5000 TOR 90503 763-A7
5300 TOR 90505 763-B7
BERAULT CT
26000 SCTA 91355 4550-F5
BERCLAIR LN
19200 Tarz 91356 560-G5
BERDON ST
20700 WdHl 91367 560-C2
22400 WdHl 91367 559-E2
BEREA CT
1500 CLAR 91711 601-E1
BEREA PL
1300 PacP 90272 631-B4
BERENDO AV
12100 LACo 90044 734-A1
12900 GAR 90247 734-A2
17500 GAR 90248 764-A1
21300 LACo 90502 764-A6
22800 LACo 90502 794-A1
24300 Hrbr 90710 794-A3
S BERENDO AV
11100 LACo 90044 704-A7
12000 LACo 90044 734-A1
20400 LACo 90502 764-A5
BERENDO AV S
22500 LACo 90502 794-A1
BERENDO ST
2200 Alta 91001 536-D7
N BERENDO ST
100 LA 90004 634-A1
200 LA 90004 594-A7
1400 LA 90029 594-A4
1700 LFlz 90027 594-A3
S BERENDO ST
100 LA 90004 634-A3
300 LA 90020 634-A3
600 LA 90005 634-A3
900 LA 90006 634-A5
11200 LACo 90044 704-A6
BERENICE AV
3800 LA 90031 595-B6
BERENICE DR
800 BREA 92821 708-J4
BERENICE PL
4100 LA 90031 595-B6
BERESFORD RD
14100 LA 90210 562-B7
BERESFORD WY
4200 LCF 91011 535-B5
BERG ST
13300 LA 91342 482-C2
14500 LA 91342 481-J5

BERGAMO DR
4300 Enc 91436 561-E4
BERGAMO WY
- Nor 91326 500-C1
BERGEN AV
13800 BLF 90706 736-D3
BERGER AV
7800 PdlR 90293 702-C2
7900 Wch 90045 702-C2
BERGER PL
8000 Wch 90045 702-C2
8000 PdlR 90293 702-C2
BERGLUND CIR
1800 WCOV 91792 638-J5
BERGMAN CT
1500 BREA 92821 708-H6
BERGMAN LN
8000 DWNY 90242 705-J6
BERGREEN PL
- Brwd 90049 591-G1
BERGSTROM PL
14100 LA 91342 482-A2
BERINGER RD
- PMDL 93536 4104-D6
- PMDL 93551 4104-D6
BERINGER WY
- Nor 91326 500-E1
BERINO DR
26600 SCTA 91350 4550-J1
BERKEBILE CT
900 MONP 91755 636-D3
BERKELEY AV
500 LACo 91107 566-D6
500 SMRO 91108 566-D6
1500 POM 91768 600-H6
1800 Echo 90026 594-C5
E BERKELEY AV
100 FUL 92832 738-H6
300 FUL 92831 738-H6
N BERKELEY AV
- PAS 91107 566-D4
100 FUL 92832 738-J7
100 FUL 92832 738-H5
300 CLAR 91711 601-C2
S BERKELEY AV
- PAS 91107 566-D5
200 LACo 91107 566-D5
BERKELEY CIR
200 FUL 92831 738-J7
200 FUL 92832 738-J7
3000 Echo 90026 594-C6
BERKELEY CT
1200 SMCA 90404 631-G6
10600 NRWK 90650 736-E2
44100 LAN 93536 4015-A7
W BERKELEY CT
1100 ONT 91762 601-J6
BERKELEY DR
900 LA 90292 672-A6
1100 GLDL 91205 564-G7
BERKELEY ST
800 SMCA 90403 631-G5
1200 SMCA 90404 631-G6
4300 MTCL 91763 601-E6
BERKELY AV
2300 LHB 90631 708-B5
BERKHAMSTED ST
- CRTS 90703 767-A2
BERKLEY CT
- BREA 92821 709-B6
1300 CHLS 91709 680-G7
BERKLEY DR
1200 CHLS 91709 680-G7
1200 CHLS 91709 710-F1
BERKSHIRE AV
200 LCF 91011 535-C5
2000 SPAS 91030 595-G4
4300 LA 90032 595-G4
BERKSHIRE CT
900 SDMS 91773 599-J4
BERKSHIRE DR
1200 PMDL 93551 4195-F5
1700 FUL 92833 738-D3
5500 LA 90032 595-G4
BERKSHIRE LN
600 LHB 90631 738-F1
BERKSHIRE PL
- Cstc 91384 4459-G4
- LCF 91011 535-D5
BERKSHIRE RD
3600 PRV 90660 676-H1
BERKSHIRE ST
45600 LAN 93534 4015-E4
BERKSHIRE WY
1900 POM 91767 600-J5
5200 MTCL 91763 641-G2
8800 ING 90305 703-D3
BERKSHIRE HILLS PL
- SCTA 91354 4460-F7
BERLO WY
25000 LACo - (4560-B4 See Page 4470)
BERMAX AV
13900 LA 91342 482-B1
BERMEJO ST
16500 CynC 91351 4462-B5
BERMITE RD
- SCTA 91350 4551-A4
BERMUDA CT
- MANB 90266 732-J5
BERMUDA ST
11000 CRTS 90703 736-F6
15400 MsnH 91345 501-G2

BERMUDA ST
15600 GmH 91344 501-D2
18200 Nor 91326 500-F3
19600 Chat 91311 500-A3
E BERMUDA ST
1800 LBCH 90802 795-G7
2000 LBCH 90814 795-G7
BERMUDA VIEW DR
4700 LACo 90601 677-C3
BERMUDEZ ST
8800 PRV 90660 676-E7
9100 PRV 90660 706-E1
BERN PL
300 PacP 90272 630-H6
BERNADETTE ST
3400 WCOV 91792 679-C1
12400 Pcma 91331 502-E3
BERNADINE AV
7200 CanP 91307 529-F5
7400 LA 91304 529-F5
N BERNAL AV
400 LA 90063 635-C5
S BERNAL AV
200 LA 90063 635-C6
700 LA 90023 635-B7
BERNAL ST
6500 SIMI 93063 499-C2
BERNARD AV
200 Ven 90291 671-H4
BERNARD CT
- HacH 91745 678-A3
BERNARD DR
800 FUL 92835 738-J2
BERNARD ST
400 LA 90012 634-G1
BERNARDIN DR
37000 PMDL 93550 4286-F4
BERNARDINO AV
10200 LACo 90606 676-J4
BERNARDO
18000 LACo 90220 764-J1
BERNARDO CIR
2600 DUAR 91010 568-D4
BERNARDO RD
10800 CULC 90230 672-H5
BERNARDO WY
- BqtC 91354 4460-F3
BERNCASTLE RD
800 LACo 93551 4375-J5
800 LACo 93551 4376-A5
800 PMDL 93550 4376-A5
BERNE PL
6200 SBdC 92397 (4652-B1 See Page 4651)
BERNE ST
7200 LACo 91770 636-D4
BERNER ST
7800 LBCH 90808 796-H1
BERNETTA PL
19200 Tarz 91356 560-G3
BERNICE AV
21600 TOR 90503 763-B6
BERNICE DR
23600 WHil 91304 499-E6
29500 RPV 90275 823-J4
BERNINA AV
20800 SCTA 91351 4551-H2
BERNINI CT
600 VeCo 91377 557-G1
BERNIST AV
19900 TOR 90503 763-C4
BERNWOOD ST
2600 DUAR 91010 568-D4
BERQUIST AV
6200 WdHl 91367 529-F7
6400 CanP 91307 529-F7
BERRIAN ST
300 POM 91767 601-A2
1200 CLAR 91711 601-A2
BERRY AV
1000 MNRO 91016 567-J4
6500 BPK 90620 767-F3
BERRY CT
- UPL 91786 601-G2
3800 LA 91604 562-H6
BERRY DR
3200 LA 91604 562-J6
BERRY PL
300 BREA 92821 709-A6
BERRY ST
100 BREA 92821 709-A7
N BERRY ST
200 BREA 92821 709-A5
BERRY WY
300 BREA 92821 709-A6
500 LHB 90631 708-C6
BERRYCREEK CT
38700 PMDL 93551 4195-D7
BERRY HILL DR
7200 RPV 90275 822-F2
BERRYHILL DR
1800 CHLS 91709 680-H3
BERRYMAN AV
3600 LA 90066 672-D2
4000 CULC 90066 672-D3
4400 LA 90230 672-E4
5100 CULC 90230 672-F5
BERRYWOOD CT
- Cstc 91384 4459-H3
BERRYWOOD WY
3000 LAN 93536 4105-C3
BERSA ST
2500 PAS 91107 566-E4

BERT ST
9400 PRV 90660 676-F7
BERTELLA DR
16200 Enc 91436 561-E4
BERTHA PL
11000 CRTS 90703 766-F3
BERTHA ST
6200 HiPk 90042 595-D2
11200 CRTS 90703 766-F3
BERTILLION ST
- PMDL 93552 4287-E1
BERTON CIR
4900 LPMA 90623 767-C3
BERTRAND AV
5700 Enc 91316 561-A1
6300 Enc 91316 531-A7
6400 Res 91335 531-A5
9000 Nor 91325 501-A7
9200 Nor 91330 501-A7
11100 GmH 91344 501-A2
BERTRAND DR
29400 AGRH 91301 557-J3
29400 AGRH 91301 558-A3
BERWICK CT
4000 CYP 90630 767-A6
BERWICK DR
3600 GLDL 91206 535-C7
3600 LCF 91011 535-C7
BERWICK PL
23400 SCTA 91354 4550-G1
BERWICK ST
11300 Brwd 90049 631-J3
BERWYN RD
16400 CRTS 90703 737-D5
BERYL
100 BREA 92823 710-C6
BERYL CT
37800 PMDL 93552 4287-A1
BERYL PL
- Cstc 91384 4459-F2
BERYL ST
- RBCH 90277 762-J3
1300 RBCH 90277 763-A3
2800 LA 90032 595-D6
19000 TOR 90277 763-A3
19000 TOR 90503 763-A3
BERYL COVE WY
400 SLB 90740 826-F4
BERYLWOOD PL
- SCTA 91354 4460-G4
BERZERVILLE AV
12900 NHol 91605 532-D4
BESS AV
12600 BALD 91706 597-H7
12700 BALD 91706 637-H1
BESS ST
13700 LACo 91746 638-A2
BESSEMER ST
11300 NHol 91606 532-E7
13300 VanN 91401 532-A7
14500 VanN 91411 532-A7
14600 VanN 91411 531-J7
17500 Enc 91316 531-E7
18300 Res 91335 530-G7
22400 WdHl 91367 559-D1
BESSIE AV
9900 ELMN 91731 597-A6
BEST AV
14300 NRWK 90650 737-C3
14300 SFSP 90670 737-C3
BESTOR BLVD
14600 PacP 90272 631-A4
BESWICK ST
3300 LA 90023 635-B7
3400 LA 90023 675-C1
BETA AV
15900 BLF 90706 736-A5
BETH PL
4200 GLDL 91214 504-D7
9700 LA 90210 592-D3
BETH ST
- NLB 90805 735-G7
BETH WY
1300 UPL 91784 571-J6
BETHANIE ST
- RSMD 91770 596-G5
BETHANY CIR
600 CLAR 91711 571-E7
BETHANY RD
200 BURB 91504 533-G5
BETHEL CT
2200 CLAR 91711 571-E6
BETHPAGE DR
- PMDL 93551 4194-J2
- PMDL 93551 4195-A2
BETLEY ST
18900 RowH 91748 679-B5
BETRON ST
20800 WdHl 91364 560-C3
BETSY ST
3000 WCOV 91792 639-A7
BETSY ROSS RD
- PMDL 93550 4286-B4
BETTENCOURT ST
13800 CRTS 90703 737-D6
BETTINA CT
27700 Cstc 91384 4459-H3
BETTON DR
20500 Top 90290 630-A2
BETTS AL
400 PAS 91107 566-D3
BETTY AV
400 ELA 90022 635-F6

BETTY AV
16800 CRTS 90703 737-C6
BETTY DR
3200 LA 90032 595-D6
BETTY LN
300 LHB 90631 708-E4
2200 LA 90210 592-F2
BETTY PL
5700 HiPk 90042 565-C7
16400 CRTS 90703 737-C6
BETTY ST
1300 SBdC 92397 (4652-D2 See Page 4651)
BETTY WY
8800 WHWD 90069 592-H6
18400 CRTS 90703 767-C1
BETTYHILL AV
200 DUAR 91010 568-E4
BETTY JEAN AV
14700 BLF 90706 736-B4
BETTY LOU LN
10100 Tuj 91042 503-J2
BEULAH DR
4200 LCF 91011 535-B4
BEULAH ST
600 GLDL 91202 564-C3
BEUVILLE AV
3600 ELMN 91731 597-B7
E BEVAN ST
8200 LACo 91775 596-F2
BEVERLEY DR
600 FUL 92833 738-E6
BEVERLY AV
2400 SMCA 90405 671-F3
BEVERLY BLVD
- WHIT 90660 676-F2
100 Echo 90026 634-B1
1800 LA 90057 634-B1
3300 LA 90004 634-B1
3600 LA 90004 594-A7
4000 LA 90004 593-F7
5300 LA 90004 633-B1
5300 PRV 90660 676-F2
6600 LA 90036 633-B1
7900 LA 90048 633-B1
8400 LA 90048 632-J1
8600 WHWD 90048 632-J1
8700 WHWD 90048 592-H7
9100 BHLS 90210 592-H7
10100 WHIT 90601 676-F2
10200 WHIT 90601 677-A3
E BEVERLY BLVD
100 MTBL 90640 676-F1
5100 ELA 90022 635-H6
8300 PRV 90660 676-F1
W BEVERLY BLVD
100 MTBL 90640 676-C1
2800 MTBL 90640 636-A7
3300 MTBL 90640 635-J7
4400 ELA 90022 635-J7
BEVERLY CT
100 Brwd 90049 631-H2
600 LAN 93535 4106-A1
BEVERLY DR
300 WAL 91789 679-C1
400 WAL 91789 639-C7
600 ARCD 91006 597-E2
1600 LACo 91104 566-C1
2900 LA 90034 632-G6
3000 LA 90210 592-E1
8200 LACo 91775 596-F2
10800 WHIT 90601 677-B4
N BEVERLY DR
100 BHLS 90210 632-F1
200 BHLS 90212 632-F1
700 BHLS 90210 592-E6
1200 LA 90210 592-D3
S BEVERLY DR
100 BHLS 90212 632-G2
400 LA 90035 632-G4
1900 LA 90034 632-G4
BEVERLY PK
1600 LA 90210 592-D1
BEVERLY PL
1900 LA 90210 592-D4
8500 LA 90048 632-J1
8500 WHWD 90048 632-J1
BEVERLY PZ
2000 LBCH 90815 796-B4
BEVERLY RD
8200 PRV 90660 676-F2
BEVERLY ST
9400 BLF 90706 736-B7
E BEVERLY TER
200 MTBL 90640 676-F2
W BEVERLY TER
800 MTBL 90640 676-D1
BEVERLY WY
900 Alta 91001 536-A6
2100 UPL 91784 571-H4
E BEVERLY WY
1800 LBCH 90802 795-G7
BEVERLY CONNECTION WY
- LA 90048 632-J1
BEVERLYCREST DR
9300 LA 90210 592-F4
BEVERLY ESTATE DR
1200 LA 90210 592-C5
BEVERLY ESTATE TER
1200 LA 90210 592-C5
BEVERLY GLEN BLVD
3200 Shrm 91423 562-A6

BEVERLY GLEN BLVD
3500 Shrm 91423 561-J7
N BEVERLY GLEN BLVD
100 BelA 90077 592-A2
3000 BelA 90077 562-B7
S BEVERLY GLEN BLVD
100 Wwd 90024 592-C7
200 Wwd 90024 632-C2
1700 WLA 90025 632-C2
2200 LA 90064 632-C3
BEVERLY GLEN CIR
2900 BelA 90077 592-A1
BEVERLY GLEN CT
- SCTA 91355 4550-E4
BEVERLY GLEN PL
2100 BelA 90077 592-A3
BEVERLY GLEN RD
2600 CHLS 91709 641-A7
BEVERLY GLEN TER
3500 Shrm 91423 562-A7
3600 Shrm 91423 561-J7
BEVERLY GREEN DR
1200 LA 90212 632-F3
1200 BHLS 90212 632-F3
1200 LA 90035 632-F3
BEVERLY GROVE DR
9800 LA 90210 592-C5
BEVERLY GROVE LN
1300 LA 90210 592-C5
BEVERLY GROVE PL
1300 LA 90210 592-D5
BEVERLY HILLS DR
10400 LACo 90604 707-D6
BEVERLY MANOR RD
5800 WHIT 90601 677-D5
2300 SLB 90740 796-G7
BEVERLY PARK CIR
1100 LA 90210 592-D2
BEVERLY PARK CT
1200 LA 90210 592-D1
BEVERLY PARK DR
1800 LA 90210 592-D3
BEVERLY PARK LN
2600 LA 90210 592-E1
BEVERLY PARK PL
8500 PRV 90660 676-F2
BEVERLY PARK ST
2000 LA 90210 592-D3
BEVERLY PARK TER
1000 LA 90210 592-D2
BEVERLY PARK WY
9300 LA 90210 592-D2
BEVERLY RANCH RD
3300 LA 90210 562-C7
BEVERLY RIDGE DR
3500 Shrm 91423 562-A6
BEVERLY RIDGE TER
- LA 90210 592-F2
BEVERLY VIEW DR
1200 LA 90210 592-C5
BEVERLY VIEW PL
9800 LA 90210 592-C5
BEVERLYWOOD ST
8500 LA 90034 632-H6
9700 LA 90064 632-H6
BEVERWIL DR
400 BHLS 90212 632-G3
600 LA 90035 632-G3
2100 LA 90034 632-G5
2100 LA 90064 632-G5
BEVINGTON AV
45000 LAN 93535 4016-C5
BEVIS AV
5300 VanN 91411 561-J2
6600 VanN 91405 531-J5
8100 PanC 91402 531-J2
9900 MsnH 91345 501-J3
BEVON PL
9500 Tuj 91042 504-B6
BEWLEY AV
2400 CMRC 90040 675-F3
BEXLEY AV
1200 PMDL 93550 4286-C3
BEXLEY DR
8800 PRV 90660 676-G4
10400 LACo 90606 676-J5
11400 LACo 90606 677-A6
BEXLEY LN
1300 BREA 92821 708-J4
BEYER LN
200 THO 91362 557-A2
BIAGO CT
- BqtC 91354 4460-F4
BIAK CT
22500 TOR 90505 763-B7
BIANCA AV
5200 Enc 91316 561-B1
6500 VanN 91406 531-B5
8100 Nor 91325 531-B2
9300 Nor 91325 501-B4
10500 GmH 91344 501-B1
37200 LACo 93551 4285-G4
BIANCA ST
1500 LVRN 91750 600-F1
BIARRITZ
1700 POM 91768 600-F6
BIARRITZ AV
2900 PMDL 93551 4195-C5
N BIBIANA WY
1400 UPL 91786 571-J7
BIBIK LN
43100 LAN 93536 4105-C3

BICENTENNIAL PARK ACCESS RD
- PRV 90601 637-B7
- PRV 90601 677-B1
9900 PRV 90660 677-B1
BICHOTA FIRE RD
- LACo - 509-G1
- LACo - (4729-G7 See Page 4649)
- LACo - (4730-A5 See Page 4649)
BICKETT ST
5400 VER 90058 675-A5
5800 HNTP 90255 675-A5
BICKFORD DR
20300 LACo 91789 679-E6
BICKLEY DR
700 COV 91722 599-D3
BICKNELL AV
- SMCA 90405 671-F3
BICKNELL CT
- PMDL 93552 4287-E2
BIDWELL LN
23300 SCTA 91354 4460-H7
BIDWELL RD
300 SDMS 91773 570-C7
BIDWELL ST
9100 TEML 91780 596-H3
BIELEC LN
100 INDS 91746 637-H4
E BIELLA WY
10400 LACo 90604 707-D6
S BIELLA WY
10900 LACo 90604 707-D6
BIENVENEDA AV
500 PacP 90272 630-H3
BIENVENEDA PL
16600 PacP 90272 630-H3
BIENVENIDA TER
5700 PMDL 93551 4194-F2
BIG BEAR CIR
8200 BPK 90621 737-J6
BIG BEND AV
10700 Sunl 91040 503-G2
BIG BEND PL
- SCTA 91387 4462-H6
BIGBRIAR WY
800 LCF 91011 535-B1
BIGBY AV
8400 DWNY 90241 706-B4
BIGBY ST
8500 DWNY 90241 706-C4
BIG CANYON PL
1200 LA 90732 823-J5
1200 LA 90732 824-A5
1200 LACo 90732 823-J5
1200 LACo 90732 824-A5
BIG CREEK LN
600 WAL 91789 639-F7
BIG DALTON AV
1600 BALD 91706 638-B1
3000 BALD 91706 598-D6
N BIG DALTON AV
300 LACo 91746 637-J3
600 LACo 91746 638-A2
BIG DALTON CANYON RD
1800 GLDR - 570-A1
1800 GLDR 91741 569-H2
1800 GLDR 91741 570-A1
1800 LACo 91741 569-H2
BIGELOW CIR
11000 CRTS 90703 766-F2
BIGELOW RD
25200 TOR 90505 793-E4
BIGELOW ST
5200 LKWD 90712 766-B2
5700 LKWD 90713 766-C2
11000 CRTS 90703 766-F2
13000 CRTS 90703 767-B2
BIG FALLS DR
600 DBAR 91765 640-A6
BIG FIR LN
100 GLDR 91741 570-A5
BIGGY ST
1300 Boyl 90033 635-B2
BIG HORN LN
700 WAL 91789 639-E6
BIG HORN WK
- SCTA 91354 4550-G1
BIG HORN WY
- SCTA 91354 4550-H1
BIGLAKE AV
17100 LACo 93591 4199-H3
17100 LACo 93591 4200-A3
BIGLER ST
23000 WdHl 91364 559-G3
BIG OAK AV
1700 CHLS 91709 680-H4
BIG OAK DR
3900 LA 91604 562-H6
BIG OAK LN
- Cstc 91384 4369-G5
BIG PINES HWY Rt#-N4
20400 Valy 93563 (4561-A4 See Page 4471)
20500 Valy 93563 (4560-F2 See Page 4470)
BIG PINES RD
16500 Valy 93563 4469-H6
16900 Valy 93563 4470-B7

BIG PINES RD
18800 Valy 93563 (4560-B1 See Page 4470)
BIG RAPIDS LP
- SCTA 91354 4550-J4
BIG ROCK DR
- PMDL 93552 4287-E2
19900 MAL 90265 630-A6
20100 MAL 90265 629-J6
21000 LACo 90265 629-H5
BIG ROCK MTWY
3400 LACo 90265 629-H4
3400 Top 90290 629-H4
BIG ROCK TR
8500 LA 91304 529-E1
8500 WHil 91304 529-E1
BIG ROCK CREEK RD
25800 Valy 93563 (4560-A4 See Page 4470)
27200 LACo - (4559-G1 See Page 4470)
27200 LACo - (4560-A4 See Page 4470)
27200 Valy 93563 (4559-G1 See Page 4470)
27400 Valy 93563 4469-G7
BIG ROCK LATERAL
20700 LACo 90265 629-G5
BIG SKY AV
11200 MTCL 91763 641-F3
BIG SKY DR
14600 Pear 93553 (4559-D2 See Page 4470)
BIG SKY TER
500 PMDL 93551 4285-H2
BIG SKY WK
- SCTA 91354 4550-G1
BIG SPRINGS RD
32700 Actn 93510 4374-A6
32900 Actn 93510 4464-A1
BIGSPRINGS RD
35500 LACo 91390 4374-A1
BIGSTONE PL
32700 WLKV 91361 587-A1
BIG SUR DR
- SCTA 91354 4550-H1
BIG SUR LN
- WCOV 91791 639-A4
BIG TREE RD
- RCUC 91701 (542-E7 See Page 511)
BIG TUJUNGA CANYON RD
- Sunl 91040 503-G1
- Sunl 91040 (4723-J7 See Page 4643)
- Sunl 91040 (4724-A6 See Page 4643)
- Tuj 91042 503-G1
- Tuj 91042 (4723-J7 See Page 4643)
800 LACo - (4724-E4 See Page 4643)
800 LACo - (4725-A7 See Page 4645)
800 Tuj 91042 (4724-E4 See Page 4643)
4100 LA - (4724-A6 See Page 4643)
4100 Tuj 91042 (4724-A6 See Page 4643)
BIG VALLEY RD
35500 Actn 93510 4375-C1
BILBERRY AV
2100 Top 90290 629-H2
BILLARY WY
- HacH 91745 677-J4
BILL CODY RD
5500 HIDH 91302 559-B3
BILLINGS AV
18400 CRSN 90746 764-D2
BILLINGS DR
16900 CRSN 90746 734-D7
BILLINGS ST
2600 COMP 90220 734-E6
BILLOW DR
500 SDMS 91773 600-A1
BILLOWVISTA DR
8100 PdlR 90293 702-B3
BILMOOR AV
4900 Tarz 91356 560-F3
BILMOOR CT
- Tarz 91356 560-F3
BILMOOR PL
19400 Tarz 91356 560-F3
BILOXI AV
4500 LA 91602 563-B4
4800 NHol 91601 563-B3
BILSON ST
100 CRSN 90746 764-D1
BILTMORE AV
11600 LA 91342 482-J7
BILTON WY
700 SGBL 91776 596-E5
BIMINI AV
16600 CRTS 90703 736-F6
BIMINI PL
100 LA 90004 634-A1
BINA CT
1300 SPAS 91030 595-F3
BIND CT
20500 LACo 91789 679-F6

STREET Block City ZIP Pg-Grid

BINDER PL
500 ELSG 90245 732-E2
BINDEWALD RD
4600 TOR 90505 793-B1
BING CT
2000 RowH 91748 679-E5
BINGHAM CT
23400 SCTA 91354 4460-G6
BINGHAM ST
11000 CRTS 90703 766-F3
12200 ART 90701 766-J3
12400 CRTS 90703 767-A3
BINNEY ST
14600 HacH 91745 677-J1
14900 HacH 91745 678-A2
BINTON LN
- RHE 90275 792-J7
- RPV 90275 792-J7
- RPV 90275 822-J1
BIOLA AV
12600 LMRD 90638 737-F3
13600 LMRD 90639 737-F3
BION AV
6200 LACo 91775 596-G2
BIONA DR
11300 LA 90066 672-D3
BIRCH
300 SDMS 91773 599-J3
BIRCH AV
1400 GLDL 91201 534-A7
5000 ELMN 91732 597-E4
6500 KeCo 93560 3834-B3
11400 HAW 90250 703-D7
11900 HAW 90250 733-D1
12600 CHNO 91710 641-J6
N BIRCH AV
500 UPL 91786 601-J2
BIRCH LN
- LA 90065 594-F1
100 PAS 91103 565-H2
BIRCH PL
- SCTA 91354 4460-F6
BIRCH ST
900 LA 90021 634-G7
1400 MTBL 90640 676-C6
2400 ALH 91801 595-H4
6000 VeCo 93063 499-B4
8300 CYP 90630 767-A4
11100 LYN 90262 705-B7
E BIRCH ST
100 BREA 92821 709-E7
W BIRCH ST
100 BREA 92821 709-A7
BIRCH WY
18700 RowH 91748 679-B4
BIRCHBARK AV
8200 PRV 90660 706-D1
8600 DWNY 90240 706-C2
BIRCH BEND CT
1900 CHLS 91709 680-H5
BIRCH CANYON WY
- LACo 91390 4461-B4
BIRCHCREST AV
900 BREA 92821 708-H4
BIRCHCREST CIR
1500 BREA 92821 708-J4
BIRCHCREST RD
7800 DWNY 90240 706-C1
W BIRCHCROFT ST
- ARCD 91007 597-C2
BIRCHDALE AV
8600 DWNY 90241 706-C4
9600 DWNY 90240 706-C4
12200 DWNY 90242 706-A7
12500 DWNY 90242 736-A1
BIRCHER ST
16200 GrnH 91344 501-E1
16200 GrnH 91344 481-B7
BIRCHFIELD AV
26100 RPV 90275 793-A5
BIRCH GLEN CIR
23000 SCTA 91354 4460-H5
BIRCH GROVE LN
- LA 91342 482-G7
BIRCH HILL DR
21500 DBAR 91765 679-J5
BIRCHKNOLL DR
- CRSN 90746 764-F1
BIRCHLAND PL
4800 TEML 91780 597-B4
BIRCHLEAF AV
6600 PRV 90660 676-E5
8300 PRV 90660 706-D1
8800 DWNY 90240 706-D2
BIRCHLEAF CT
- StvR 91381 4550-B4
BIRCHLEAF ST
7600 PRV 90660 676-D7
BIRCH LOG WY
2300 HacH 91745 678-E5
BIRCHMAN DR
6700 RPV 90275 792-H7
BIRCHMONT DR
5900 RPV 90275 792-J5
BIRCHNELL AV
1300 SDMS 91773 570-A7
BIRCHTON AV
6600 CanP 91307 529-F6
BIRCHTREE AV
43700 LAN 93534 4105-H1
BIRCH TREE CIR
1300 LHB 90631 738-C1
BIRCH TREE LN
1900 PMDL 93550 4286-D2
BIRCHWOOD AV
- VeCo 91377 558-A2
BIRCHWOOD CIR
7800 LPMA 90623 767-D3
BIRCHWOOD CT
- LA 91342 481-J3
- LA 91342 482-A2
BIRCHWOOD DR
800 Wwd 90024 632-C2
BIRCHWOOD LN
1200 SDMS 91773 599-J3
BIRCHWOOD ST
15700 LMRD 90638 737-H2
BIRD RD
1400 Eagl 90041 565-A7
1400 Eagl 90041 595-A1
BIRD ST
2100 Boyl 90033 635-B4
BIRD WY
900 LBCH 90802 795-F7
1500 LBCH 90802 825-G1
2000 LBCH 90803 825-G1
BIRDELLA RD
31300 LACo 90265 587-E6
BIRD FARM
- Cstc 91384 4459-J3
BIRDIE DR
1500 LVRN 91750 570-F5
BIRDS EYE DR
21900 DBAR 91765 679-J4
22100 DBAR 91765 680-A3
BIRDSONG LN
14000 CHLS 91709 680-J3
BIRDSONG RD
29400 LACo 91390 4461-H3
BIRDVALE DR
9100 DWNY 90242 736-A2
11900 CHNO 91710 641-E5
E BIRDVALE DR
11900 CHNO 91710 641-E4
BIRDVIEW AV
6800 MAL 90265 667-D3
BIRGE AL
- PAS 91103 565-H2
BIRKDALE
3400 ELMN 91732 637-G1
BIRKDALE AV
1900 UPL 91784 571-H5
BIRKDALE ST
2300 LA 90031 594-G5
2300 UPL 91784 571-H3
E BIRKDALE ST
6100 LBCH 90815 796-D2
BIRKEWOOD CT
- LACo 91387 4552-A4
BIRKHALL AV
13600 BLF 90706 736-A3
BIRMINGHAM PL
22200 SCTA 91350 4550-J5
22200 SCTA 91350 4551-A5
BIRMINGHAM RD
300 BURB 91504 533-G5
BIRNAMWOOD WY
- PMDL 93551 4195-J4
BISBEE PL
1600 LAN 93535 4106-C1
BISBY ST
9500 TEML 91780 597-A5
10400 ELMN 91731 597-C6
BISCAILUZ DR
- Cstc 91384 4459-J4
- Cstc 91384 4460-A3
- SCTA 91384 4459-J5
BISCAY AV
45000 LAN 93535 4016-E5
BISCAY ST
42500 LAN 93536 4104-E4
BISCAY WY
1500 POM 91766 640-J4
BISCAYNE PL
2500 FUL 92833 738-C5
BISCAYNE ST
3000 SBdC 91710 641-D7
4200 CHNO 91710 641-D7
BISHOP AV
18000 CRSN 90746 764-G1
BISHOP CT
- StvR 91381 4640-C1
8800 ARCD 91007 597-D2
BISHOP DR
100 LHB 90631 708-E4
BISHOP LN
1000 SDMS 91773 599-H5
BISHOP PL
500 CLAR 91711 601-E1
BISHOP RD
4800 TOR 90503 763-C4
BISHOP ST
4800 CYP 90630 767-C6
BISHOP WY
8800 RSMD 91770 636-H1
BISHOPS RD
1200 LA 90012 634-H1
BISMARCK AV
10800 Nor 91326 500-G3
BISON CIR
45300 LAN 93535 4016-A4
BISON CT
28800 MAL 90265 667-F3
BISSELL PL
6200 HNTP 90255 675-B6
BISSELL ST
6200 HNTP 90255 675-B7
6500 BELL 90201 675-B7
6900 HNTP 90255 705-B1
BITHYNIA WY
1900 LACo 91789 679-E5
BITTERLAKE ST
800 CRSN 90746 734-F7
BITTEROOT RD
38600 PMDL 93550 4196-F7
BIXBY
- HacH 91745 678-E7
- LHH 90631 678-E7
BIXBY AV
16800 BLF 90706 736-C6
25600 Hrbr 90710 794-B5
N BIXBY AV
200 WCOV 91790 598-G7
BIXBY CIR
- BPK 90621 738-B3
BIXBY DR
800 INDS 91745 678-E3
3800 LVRN 91750 600-F1
3800 LVRN 91750 570-F7
BIXBY RD
2000 LKWD 90712 765-G7
E BIXBY RD
100 Bxby 90807 765-F7
W BIXBY RD
100 Bxby 90807 765-D7
E BIXBY HILL RD
6200 LBCH 90815 796-E6
BIXBY TERRACE DR
6400 LBCH 90803 796-E7
6400 LBCH 90815 796-E7
BIXBY VILLAGE DR
5700 LBCH 90803 796-D7
N BIXEL ST
200 Echo 90026 634-E2
S BIXEL ST
100 Echo 90026 634-E3
300 LA 90017 634-E3
900 LA 90015 634-E3
BIXLER AV
5100 LKWD 90712 765-J3
13300 DWNY 90242 735-H2
15300 PRM 90723 735-J4
BIZET PL
4700 WdHl 91364 559-G4
BLACKBERRY CT
1700 PMDL 93551 4195-E5
BLACKBERRY LN
- CRSN 90746 764-F1
BLACKBIRD AV
100 THO 91362 557-G2
BLACKBIRD DR
500 PMDL 93550 4196-A4
BLACKBIRD LN
- POM 91766 640-G6
5700 LVRN 91750 570-H5
19800 SCTA 91351 4551-E4
BLACKBIRD RD
1800 SBdC 92397 (4652-E3 See Page 4651)
BLACK BIRD WY
3900 CALB 91302 559-G6
BLACKBRUSH DR
17700 SCTA 91387 4552-A2
BLACKBURN AV
6100 LA 90036 633-C1
7900 LA 90048 633-A1
8400 LA 90048 632-J1
15300 NRWK 90650 737-A5
BLACKBURN DR
16500 LMRD 90638 738-A1
BLACK CANYON RD
- VeCo 93063 499-B4
BLACKER HOUSE CT
24000 SCTA 91355 4550-F4
BLACKFOOT
- Ago 91301 587-F4
BLACKFOOT CT
27600 Cstc 91384 4459-H4
BLACKFORD AV
7800 LACo 90606 677-A7
BLACKFRIAR RD
4500 WdHl 91364 559-H4
BLACKHAWK CIR
7300 BPK 90620 767-F2
BLACKHAWK CT
39400 PMDL 93551 4195-E5
BLACK HAWK DR
1500 DBAR 91789 679-G4
BLACKHAWK ST
- Chat 91311 499-J4
10100 Nor 91326 500-F4
14700 MsnH 91345 501-G4
15600 GrnH 91344 501-B4
19900 Chat 91311 500-A4
E BLACK HILLS CT
3300 THO 91362 557-C2
W BLACK HILLS CT
3000 THO 91362 557-B2
BLACK HILLS DR
500 CLAR 91711 601-E1
BLACKHORSE RD
- RHE 90274 793-B6
- RPV 90275 793-B6
BLACKLEY ST
5300 TEML 91780 597-C3
9100 TEML 91780 596-H4
BLACKMORE DR
2200 GLDL 91206 564-J4
2200 GLDL 91206 565-A4
BLACK OAK CT
- LA 91343 501-H6
BLACK OAK DR
- StvR 91381 4550-B5
- POM 91766 640-H6
5400 LA 90068 593-H3
BLACK OAK LN
- Cstc 91384 4369-E4
BLACK OAK ST
2800 THO 91362 557-B2
BLACK PINE CT
- HacH 91745 678-F7
BLACK PINE RD
2200 CHLS 91709 680-J4
BLACK PINE WY
- LACo 91390 4460-H1
BLACKPOOL AV
800 VeCo 91377 557-H1
BLACKRIDGE DR
2100 Top 90290 630-A2
BLACKROCK AV
4600 LVRN 91750 570-D7
BLACK ROCK CT
700 SDMS 91773 599-G5
BLACKSHEAR AV
200 ELA 90022 635-J7
BLACKSMITH CIR
- POM 91766 640-F4
BLACKSMITH DR
36300 PMDL 93550 4286-F6
BLACK STALLION DR
20300 LACo 91724 639-G1
BLACK STAR LN
7500 LPMA 90623 767-C3
BLACKSTONE CT
900 LA 90015 634-E5
BLACKSTONE RD
1200 SMRO 91108 566-F7
1200 SMRO 91108 596-F1
BLACKTHORNE AV
5400 LKWD 90712 766-A2
N BLACKTHORNE AV
4200 LBCH 90808 766-A5
BLACKTON DR
1700 LACo 90265 627-G1
BLACK WALNUT TR
6200 Tuj 91042 504-C4
BLACK WALNUT WY
500 LHB 90631 708-C6
BLACKWATER CANYON RD
- RHLS 90274 793-D7
BLACKWELDER ST
5100 LA 90016 633-A7
5800 CULC 90232 633-A7
BLACKWOOD ST
14200 LACo 91746 638-B3
14500 LACo 91744 638-C4
15500 LPUE 91744 638-E5
BLADEN ST
19800 Nor 91324 530-E1
BLADES ST
700 LA 90063 635-C4
BLAINE AV
14500 BLF 90706 736-B4
BLAINE ST
900 LA 90015 634-C5
BLAIR AV
1200 SPAS 91030 595-E3
BLAIR CRES
3300 LA 90068 563-C7
BLAIR DR
3200 LA 90068 563-D7
3400 Univ 91608 563-D7
BLAIR LN
14600 WHIT 90603 707-F3
BLAIR PL
4800 AGRH 91301 558-B6
BLAIR ST
9000 RSMD 91770 596-H5
BLAIR WY
3600 TOR 90505 793-D4
BLAIRMOORE ST
20500 Chat 91311 500-C3
BLAIRSTONE DR
5900 CULC 90232 672-J2
5900 CULC 90232 673-A2
BLAIRWOOD DR
5100 LPMA 90623 767-C3
12900 LA 91604 562-D6
BLAISDELL AV
2900 RBCH 90278 733-B6
BLAISDELL DR
200 CLAR 91711 601-E1
BLAKE AV
1000 LA 90031 594-G5
1800 LA 90039 594-F3
BLAKE CT
25800 StvR 91381 4550-D7
BLAKE ST
400 PAS 91103 565-G3
S BLAKE ST
500 LHB 90631 708-B6
BLAKE WY
- LACo 91387 4462-C6
BLAKELY CT
1000 POM 91767 601-B7
BLAKELY PL
27200 SCTA 91354 4460-G7
BLAKEMAN AV
2700 RowH 91748 679-B7
2900 RowH 91748 709-B1
BLAKESLEE AV
5200 NHol 91601 563-A2
BLAKLEY AV
12100 Wbrk 90059 704-G7
12100 Wbrk 90059 734-G1
12500 Wbrk 90222 734-G1
S BLAKLEY AV
12600 Wbrk 90222 734-G1
BLANCA DR
4500 CYP 90630 767-B6
BLANCA WY
25800 SCTA 91355 4550-F6
BLANCHARD DR
2300 GLDL 91208 534-H7
BLANCHARD PL
500 CLAR 91711 601-E3
700 UPL 91786 601-E3
BLANCHARD ST
2700 Boyl 90033 635-C4
3000 LA 90063 635-C4
3200 City 90063 635-D4
4300 ELA 90022 635-E4
BLANCHARD CANYON RD
6200 Tuj 91042 504-C4
BLANCHE PL
16900 GrnH 91344 481-C6
BLANCHE RD
2500 MANB 90266 732-F4
N BLANCHE RD
2100 MANB 90266 732-F5
BLANCHE ST
1000 PAS 91106 566-B5
3700 LACo 91107 566-H5
BLANCO AV
5300 WdHl 91367 559-D2
BLANCO WY
5300 CULC 90230 672-G5
BLAND PL
25700 LMTA 90717 793-H5
BLANDFORD DR
2500 RowH 91748 679-B7
3000 RowH 91748 709-B1
BLANDIN ST
15600 LA 91342 481-G5
BLANDING ST
11500 LACo 90606 676-J7
12000 LACo 90606 677-B7
BLANDWOOD RD
7800 DWNY 90240 706-C1
BLANDWOOD ST
9700 DWNY 90240 706-E4
BLANE RD
2300 Ago 91301 587-H3
BLANTYRE DR
9700 LA 90210 592-D1
BLARNEY STONE RD
10200 SBdC 92372 (4472-C5 See Page 4471)
BLAUVELT PL
8600 Nor 91325 531-A1
BLAZE TR
2400 DBAR 91765 680-B6
BLAZEWOOD ST
- SIMI 93063 499-B2
BLAZING STAR DR
1500 HacH 91745 678-A3
BLAZING STAR ST
- LAN 93536 4014-F7
37600 PMDL 93552 4287-B2
S BLEAKWOOD AV
100 ELA 90022 635-H5
2000 MONP 91754 635-H5
BLEDSOE AV
3800 CULC 90066 672-D3
3800 LA 90066 672-D3
BLEDSOE ST
14200 LA 91342 482-A2
14400 LA 91342 481-J3
BLEECKER ST
4800 BALD 91706 598-D3
BLEEKER AV
8200 LACo 91770 636-F4
BLEEKER ST
14700 LA 91342 481-J6
BLENARM DR
1200 DBAR 91789 679-G3
BLENBURY DR
1400 DBAR 91765 680-A4
BLENDING RD
- SCTA 91350 4551-B4
BLENEFIELD PL
600 DBAR 91765 640-E7
BLENHEIM ST
3600 BALD 91706 597-H7
BLERIOT AV
7800 Wch 90045 702-H2
BLEWETT AV
6400 VanN 91406 531-F4
8300 LA 91343 531-F2
BLEWETT ST
8100 LACo 91770 636-F4
BLIMP ST
2600 LA 90031 594-G5
2600 LA 90039 594-G5
BLINN AV
1000 Wilm 90744 794-G5
BLISS CIR
2200 CLAR 91711 571-D6
BLISS ST
1900 COMP 90222 734-H3
1900 Wbrk 90222 734-H3
BLISS CANYON RD
- BRAD 91010 568-B3
E BLITHEDALE ST
8300 LBCH 90808 767-A7
BLIX ST
10600 LA 91602 563-A3
11000 LA 91602 562-J3
11700 LA 91607 562-F4
BLOCK PL
2300 LA 90032 635-F1
BLOCK CANYON RD
- LACo 91387 4641-H1
- Nwhl 91321 4641-H1
BLODGETT AV
12200 DWNY 90242 706-A7
12700 DWNY 90242 736-A1
13000 DWNY 90242 735-J2
BLOOM DR
100 CLAR 91711 570-J7
200 MONP 91755 636-B5
BLOOM ST
- SIMI 93063 499-B1
100 LA 90012 634-H2
BLOOMDALE ST
900 DUAR 91010 567-J5
1100 DUAR 91010 568-A5
BLOOMFIELD AV
10400 SFSP 90670 707-A6
11000 NRWK 90650 707-A6
11900 SFSP 90670 737-A2
11900 NRWK 90650 737-A2
15900 CRTS 90703 737-A7
15900 NRWK 90703 737-A4
17900 CRTS 90703 767-A3
20300 LKWD 90715 767-A3
21500 HGDN 90716 767-A3
21500 CYP 90630 767-A3
BLOOMFIELD CT
- SCTA 91354 4460-G5
BLOOMFIELD ST
5600 SIMI 93063 499-A2
9000 CYP 90630 767-A6
9100 HGDN 90716 767-A6
9500 LBCH 90716 767-A6
9500 LBCH 90808 767-A6
9800 LALM 90720 767-A6
10400 LA 91602 563-A5
12700 LA 91604 562-D5
13100 Shrm 91423 562-D5
BLOOMINGPARK ST
43000 LAN 93536 4105-D3
BLOOMINGTON AV
7500 LA 91504 533-D3
BLOOMWOOD RD
800 SPed 90731 824-A2
1100 RPV 90275 824-A2
1200 RPV 90275 823-J2
BLOSSOM CIR
1400 UPL 91786 601-H1
BLOSSOM CT
- BqtC 91354 4460-E6
1000 PMDL 93551 4195-G7
2100 RBCH 90278 763-A2
7100 PRV 90660 676-E6
BLOSSOM DR
- LAN 93536 4104-H2
42300 LACo 93536 4104-J5
BLOSSOM LN
500 RBCH 90278 763-A2
2000 RBCH 90278 733-A7
2100 LVRN 91750 600-E3
BLOSSOM PL
200 BREA 92821 709-B5
1800 BREA 92821 708-G6
BLOSSOM ST
- SIMI 93063 499-B1
1300 GLDL 91201 564-A3
BLOUNT PL
4500 LYN 90262 735-D2
BLUCHER AV
6200 VanN 91411 531-G7
6400 VanN 91406 531-G6
10200 LA 91343 501-G4
10200 GrnH 91344 501-G1
11500 GrnH 91344 481-G6
BLUCHER CT
15400 VanN 91411 531-G7
BLUE CIR
8600 RSMD 91770 596-G6
BLUE DR
- SMRO 91108 566-D6
S BLUE DR
900 WCOV 91790 638-G2
BLUE ANCHOR RD
- MAL 90265 667-G1
BLUE ASH RD
800 WCOV 91790 638-G1
BLUE ASPEN LN
- LACo 91387 4552-B4
BLUEBELL AV
2900 BREA 92821 709-F7
4200 LA 91604 562-E5
4800 LA 91607 562-E2
6000 NHol 91606 532-E7
6900 NHol 91605 532-E3
BLUEBELL CT
21600 WAL 91789 639-H5
BLUE BELL LN
- LA 90068 563-G5
BLUEBELL ST
1500 LAN 93535 4016-C7
BLUEBIRD AV
1400 LA 90069 592-G5
BLUEBIRD DR
22900 CALB 91302 559-G6
BLUEBIRD LN
8000 LPMA 90623 767-B4
BLUEBIRD LN N
100 PMDL 93551 4195-J3
BLUEBIRD MTWY
- GLDR 91773 570-A2
- SDMS 91773 570-A2
BLUE BIRD RD
6300 SBdC 92397 (4652-C1 See Page 4651)
BLUEBIRD RD
- CHLS 91709 680-G1
- DBAR 91765 680-G1
- GLDR 91741 570-A2
- GLDR 91773 570-A2
- LACo 91741 569-J3
1600 GLDR 91741 569-J3
BLUEBONNET ST
16100 LPUE 91744 638-E7
16100 LPUE 91744 678-E1
BLUE CANYON DR
3700 LA 91604 562-H6
BLUE CAVERN PT
300 LBCH 90803 826-C1
BLUE CLOUD RD
- LACo 91390 4461-D2
BLUE CREST LN
11800 LACo 90606 677-A7
BLUE CURL WY
21200 SCTA 91351 4551-B3
BLUE DANE LN
24600 MAL 90265 628-G7
BLUEFIELD AV
10400 LACo 90604 707-G5
11900 LMRD 90638 707-G7
12700 LMRD 90638 737-G2
BLUEFIELD DR
500 CLAR 91711 571-E6
BLUEFLAX AV
42000 LACo 93536 4104-D6
42200 LAN 93536 4104-D5
BLUE GRASS LN
16300 CHLS 91709 710-H2
BLUEGRASS LN
900 Brwd 90049 631-E1
16500 CRTS 90703 736-J4
BLUEGRASS PL
900 POM 91766 640-E3
BLUEGRASS ST
100 BREA 92821 709-F7
BLUEGRASS WY
900 Brwd 90049 631-F1
39500 PMDL 93551 4195-D5
BLUEGROVE AV
13300 DWNY 90242 736-A2
13400 BLF 90706 736-A3
BLUE GUM LN
- Tuj 91042 504-B4
BLUE GUM CANYON RD
10200 Tuj 91042 504-B4
BLUE HAVEN DR
1500 RowH 91748 679-D5
BLUE HEIGHTS DR
1800 LA 90046 592-J4
1800 LA 90069 592-J4
BLUE HERON
- SLB 90740 826-G3
BLUE HERON PL
- LVRN 91750 570-J4
BLUE HILL RD
1200 Eagl 90041 565-C5
BLUEHILLS DR
42700 LACo 93532 4102-F4
BLUE IRIS LN
6800 MAL 90265 667-D3
BLUE JAY
900 WCOV 91790 638-F2
BLUE JAY DR
- BREA 92823 709-H6
- LACo 92397 (4652-A1 See Page 4651)
- SBdC 92397 (4652-A1 See Page 4651)
6300 BPK 90620 767-E2
BLUEJAY LN
11000 SFSP 90670 706-G2
BLUEJAY ST
5000 LVRN 91750 570-J5
BLUE JAY WY
1400 LA 90069 592-H4
BLUELAGOON ST
16100 LACo 91744 638-F5
BLUE MEADOW LN
31600 WLKV 91361 557-D7
BLUE MESA ST
2900 THO 91362 557-C2
BLUE MOON CT
18500 SCTA 91351 4551-H2
BLUEMOUND RD
5100 RHE 90274 793-B5
BLUE MOUNTAIN CIR
700 THO 91362 557-F1
BLUE MOUNTAIN DR
20400 WAL 91789 639-F3
BLUE MOUNTAIN WY
100 CLAR 91711 571-D7
BLUE PALM LN
22600 DBAR 91765 680-A3
BLUE RIDGE AV
4600 PMDL 93552 4287-F2
BLUERIDGE CT
22500 CALB 90290 559-H7
22500 CALB 90290 589-H1
N BLUE RIDGE CT
200 THO 91362 557-B2
S BLUE RIDGE CT
100 THO 91362 557-B3
BLUE RIDGE DR
1100 POM 91766 640-F3
BLUERIDGE DR
1400 LA 90210 592-D5
22900 SCTA 91354 4460-H6
BLUERIDGE LN
- POM 91766 640-G6
BLUE RIDGE RD
- RowH 91748 679-E6
BLUE RIDGE WY
- StvR 91381 4640-B2
E BLUE RIDGE FIRE RD
- LACo - 4651-F1
- Valy 93563 (4561-D7 See Page 4471)
- Valy 93563 4651-F1
W BLUE RIDGE FIRE RD
- Valy 93563 (4560-H6 See Page 4470)
- Valy 93563 (4561-A6 See Page 4471)
BLUE ROCK RDG
32300 WLKV 91361 557-B7
BLUE SAGE
12500 LACo 91342 482-J5
BLUE SAGE DR
5100 PMDL 93552 4287-B2
11100 LACo 91342 482-H5
BLUESAIL CIR
1300 THO 91361 557-B6
BLUESAIL CV
- BPK 90621 738-A6
BLUE SAIL DR
18000 PacP 90272 630-E5
BLUE SKY CT
24400 CanP 91307 529-D5
43900 LAN 93536 4105-D1
BLUE SKY LN
27800 SCTA 91351 4551-F1
BLUE SKY RD
14500 HacH 91745 677-H4
BLUESKY WY
31200 Cstc 91384 4369-G7
BLUESPRING DR
800 THO 91361 557-A5
BLUE SPRUCE LN
- YBLN 92886 709-J7
BLUE SPRUCE PL
- SCTA 91354 4460-F7
- SCTA 91354 4550-F1
BLUE STAKE RD
9200 SBdC 92371 (4472-J6 See Page 4471)
BLUESTONE AV
1600 SIMI 93063 499-C3
BLUESTONE LN
1700 MONP 91755 636-E4
BLUESTONE PL
23700 SCTA 91354 4460-G7
BLUESTONE TR
700 Brwd 90049 631-F1
BLUETTE LN
- PMDL 93551 4285-D3
BLUE WATER LN
500 FUL 92831 738-H5
BLUEWATER RD
29200 MAL 90265 667-D3
BLUFF CT
- PMDL 93551 4195-A4
1500 DBAR 91765 680-D3
BLUFF PL
1500 LBCH 90802 825-G1
3600 SPed 90731 854-B2
BLUFF RD
100 MTBL 90640 676-D4
7300 DWNY 90240 706-A1
BLUFF ST
3800 TOR 90505 793-C3
BLUFF CREEK DR
- LA 90094 672-F7
- Wch 90045 672-F7
12600 LA 90094 702-D2
12600 Wch 90045 702-D2
BLUFFDALE DR
8500 SunV 91352 533-B1
8800 SunV 91352 503-B7
BLUFFDALE ST
300 MONP 91755 636-B6
BLUFFHILL DR
1600 MONP 91754 635-H4
BLUFF POINT CIR
- POM 91766 640-G4
BLUFFSIDE DR
10600 LA 91604 563-A6
BLUFFSIDE WY
39400 PMDL 93551 4195-D5
BLUFFTON DR
15100 LACo 93532 4102-E4
BLUFF TRAIL RD
- Wch 90045 702-D2
BLUFFWOOD ST
19400 RowH 91748 679-D5
BLUFORD AV
8600 WHIT 90602 707-C2
9500 LACo 90605 707-B3
BLUME DR
2600 OrCo 90720 796-G5
BLUMONT RD
10200 SGAT 90280 705-F6
BLYSTONE CT
100 BREA 92821 709-B7
BLYTHE AV
10500 LA 90064 632-D6
BLYTHE RD
300 LCF 91011 535-D5
BLYTHE ST
11200 SunV 91352 532-J2
11400 NHol 91605 532-H2
13400 PanC 91402 532-A3
14500 PanC 91402 531-H2
15900 VanN 91406 531-F3
17400 Nor 91325 531-A3
17700 Res 91335 531-A3
18200 Res 91335 530-F3
19700 Win 91306 530-C3
20900 LA 91304 530-A3
22100 LA 91304 529-E3
BLYTHEDALE RD
27800 AGRH 91301 558-D3
BLYTHEWOOD DR
28500 RPV 90275 792-G7
28500 RPV 90275 822-H1
BOARDWALK
- LBCH 90802 825-D1
BOATHOUSE LN
5400 LBCH 90803 796-C7
5400 LBCH 90803 826-C1
BOAZ ST
3200 LA 90011 674-F2
BOB ST
100 MNRO 91016 567-G7
BOB BATCHELOR RD
24800 LACo 91302 589-C5
BOBBIE AV
5500 PMDL 93551 4194-G2
BOBBIE ST
1100 COV 91722 598-H4
BOBBYBOYAR AV
6400 CanP 91307 529-G4
7500 LA 91304 529-G3
BOBBY JONES DR
43800 LAN 93536 4105-B1
BOBBY PARHAM AV
1100 COMP 90222 734-G3
BOBCAT CT
1100 PMDL 93551 4195-G7
BOBCAT WY
28100 Cstc 91384 4369-G7
BOB HOPE DR
200 BURB 91505 563-E3
200 BURB 91523 563-E3
BOBOLINK DR
- LACo 92397 (4652-A1 See Page 4651)
- SBdC 92397 (4652-A1 See Page 4651)
BOBOLINK PL
1300 LA 90069 592-G5
BOBOLINK WY
1900 POM 91767 601-A6
BOBS GAP RD
29200 Llan 93544 4469-H1
29200 Valy 93563 4469-G5
30600 Llan 93544 4470-A3
31900 Llan 93544 4379-G7
BOBSTONE DR
3700 Shrm 91423 562-C6
BOBWHITE CIR
- SCTA 91350 4461-B5
BOBWHITE RD
- BREA 92823 709-J6
BOCA AV
1700 LA 90063 635-D2
1800 LA 90032 635-D2
BOCA CHICA DR
15100 LMRD 90638 737-F4
BOCA DE CANON LN
13100 Brwd 90049 631-D1
BOCANA ST
23300 LACo 90265 629-E2
BOCA RATON AV
15200 Llan 93544 4469-E1
BOCCACCIO AV
500 Ven 90291 671-J6
BOCKDALE AV
28200 SCTA 91387 4552-B2
BODA PL
5000 WdHl 91367 559-F3
BODEGA CT
- Boyl 90033 634-J4
10400 MTCL 91763 641-E1
BODEGA WY
1400 DBAR 91765 680-B3
BODEGO RD
- AVA 90704 5923-G4
BODEN ST
5500 LA 90016 633-A7
BODGER AV
14400 HAW 90250 733-E4
BODGER ST
10000 ELMN 91733 637-B1
10600 ELMN 91731 637-D1
11300 ELMN 91732 637-D1
BODIE PL
- LACo 91390 4461-B3
BODIE ST
100 Boyl 90033 634-J4
BODLE PEAK MTWY
600 LACo 90265 586-J4
600 LACo 90265 587-A5
BOECKMAN AV
- LA 91343 531-H1
BOEING AV
7600 Wch 90045 702-H1
BOEING PL
6000 Wch 90045 702-H1
BOER AV
6700 LACo 90606 676-J6
6700 LACo 90606 677-A6
8000 SFSP 90606 676-H7
8300 LACo 90606 706-H1
BOGAN LN
4100 CLAR 91711 570-J7
BOGARD CT
44000 LAN 93536 4015-A7
44000 LAN 93536 4105-A1
BOGARDUS AV
9800 WHIT 90603 708-A4
11700 LACo 90604 708-A7
12600 LMRD 90638 738-A1
BOGART AV
4100 BALD 91706 598-C3
BOGART CIR
18900 CRTS 90703 767-B2
BOGIE DR
1800 LVRN 91750 570-G4
BOGIE PL
31600 Llan 93544 4469-F2
BOGIE ST
400 PMDL 93551 4195-H5
BOGUE DR
2600 GLDL 91208 534-H6
BOGUE ST
9500 TEML 91780 596-J3
9900 TEML 91780 597-A3
BOHLIG RD
500 GLDL 91207 564-F2
5000 LA 90032 635-F1
BOILER ST
- CRSN 90746 764-G4
BOILING POINT RD
- LACo 91390 (4284-D7 See Page 4283)
35300 LACo 91390 4374-E1
BOISE AV
3600 LA 90066 672-B3
4000 CULC 90066 672-C4
BOISE CT
4200 PMDL 93552 4286-J3
4500 PMDL 93552 4287-A3
BOISE LN
4100 CLAR 91711 570-J7
BOLAN LN
26900 LACo 90274 793-D7
BOLANOS AV
1700 RowH 91748 679-B5
BOLAR AV
2500 HacH 91745 678-D5
BOLAS ST
11300 Brwd 90049 631-H2
BOLD ST
18600 RowH 91748 679-A4
BOLERO DR
40200 PMDL 93550 4195-J3
BOLERO LN
1300 LA 90012 634-H2
BOLEY ST
900 ARCD 91006 597-F1
1200 MNRO 91016 597-G1
BOLIVAR RD
4300 WdHl 91364 560-A5
BOLIVAR ST
1700 POM 91766 640-H4
BOLIVIA DR
5700 BPK 90620 767-D2
BOLKER PL
1800 SPed 90731 824-A2
BOLKER WY
900 MTBL 90640 636-C6
900 PRV 90660 676-F3
BOLLENBACHER DR
6400 PRV 90660 676-E5
BOLLING AV
2800 LVRN 91750 600-G2
BOLLINGER DR
16700 PacP 90272 630-G6
BOLSA AV
900 SLB 90740 826-F4
22000 CRSN 90745 764-C7
22800 CRSN 90745 794-D1
BOLSA DR
- SLB 90740 826-G3
BOLSA LN
14000 CRTS 90703 737-D7
BOLSA ST
21000 CRSN 90745 764-C5
BOLTE WY
- PMDL 93551 4195-D6
BOLTON AV
4000 PMDL 93552 4196-H7
9500 MTCL 91763 601-F6
11100 SBdC 91710 641-F3
BOLTON RD
9300 LA 90034 632-G5
BOLZ RANCH RD
3600 PMDL 93551 4195-A2
4000 PMDL 93551 4194-J2

STREET Block City ZIP Pg-Grid

BOMAR CT
19600 RowH 91748 679-E6
BOMBARDIER AV
11000 NRWK 90650 706-H6
12200 NRWK 90650 736-H1
BOMBAY AV
24700 Wilm 90744 794-E3
BOMBAY ST
12700 LA 91342 482-D2
13600 LA 91340 482-B4
BOMBERRY ST
2500 LKWD 90712 765-G5
BOMER DR
5100 HiPk 90042 595-C3
BONAIR PL
6600 LA 90068 593-E3
BONANZA CT
- POM 91766 640-F5
BONANZA RD
2100 SBdC 92371 (4472-E5 See Page 4471)
BONANZA ST
1700 SIMI 93063 499-C3
13300 Pcma 91331 502-C5
BONAPARTE AV
12600 LA 90066 672-C6
BONA VISTA AV
15100 SFSP 90670 737-D4
BONA VISTA LN
12000 LACo 90604 707-D7
12000 LACo 90604 737-D1
13000 LMRD 90638 737-D2
BONAVISTA LN
9200 WHIT 90603 707-F4
9900 LACo 90604 707-F4
13400 LMRD 90638 737-D2
BONAVITA DR
4200 Enc 91436 561-D5
BONAVITA PL
4200 Enc 91436 561-D5
BOND AV
2400 LHB 90631 708-B5
BOND CT
- CynC 91351 4462-A4
BOND ST
1300 LA 90015 634-C5
E BONDS ST
500 CRSN 90745 794-E3
BONELLI ST
14200 INDS 91745 637-J6
14200 INDS 91746 637-J6
BONFAIR AV
4400 LKWD 90712 766-A1
15900 BLF 90706 736-A5
BONFIELD AV
7900 NHol 91605 532-E2
BONHAM AL
- PAS 91103 565-C3
BONHAM AV
11500 LA 91342 482-J7
11500 LA 91342 502-J1
17200 CRSN 90746 734-D7
18200 CRSN 90746 764-D2
BONHILL RD
600 Brwd 90049 631-F1
N BONHILL RD
200 Brwd 90049 631-F2
BON HOMME RD
3900 CALB 91302 559-H6
4200 WdHl 91364 559-H6
BONIFACE DR
28800 MAL 90265 667-F3
BONILLA DR
1100 Top 90290 590-C4
BONINO DR
38200 PMDL 93551 4285-G1
BONITA AV
200 LACo 91107 566-D5
200 PAS 91107 566-D5
500 SMRO 91108 566-D6
1100 WAL 91789 639-H3
1200 LVRN 91750 600-F2
1700 BURB 91504 533-E5
20900 CRSN 90746 764-E5
E BONITA AV
- SMAD 91024 567-A3
100 POM 91767 600-J3
100 SDMS 91773 600-D2
100 POM 91767 601-B3
400 CLAR 91711 601-D3
700 LVRN 91750 600-D2
W BONITA AV
- SMAD 91024 567-A3
100 CLAR 91711 601-D3
100 POM 91767 600-J3
100 SDMS 91773 600-A2
700 GLDR 91740 599-C2
BONITA DR
- PMDL 93551 4104-D6
600 PAS 91106 596-A1
700 SPAS 91030 595-G4
1700 LHH 90631 708-F3
1900 GLDL 91208 534-H7
1900 GLDL 91208 564-H1
BONITA PL
300 FUL 92835 708-G7
3900 FUL 92835 738-G1
29200 Cstc 91384 4459-C5
BONITA ST
- ARCD 91006 567-D5
500 SPed 90731 824-B4
700 MNRO 91016 567-E5
7400 DWNY 90242 705-G7

BONITA ST
7600 DWNY 90242 735-G1
21700 CRSN 90745 764-E7
22500 CRSN 90745 794-E1
BONITA TER
6800 LA 90068 593-D4
W BONITA TER
1400 MONP 91754 635-H2
BONITA TR
16500 LACo 93532 4102-A2
BONITA CANYON WY
500 BREA 92821 709-C5
BONITA VISTA DR
1700 LCF 91011 534-J1
1700 LCF 91011 535-A1
BONITO AV
- LBCH 90802 825-F1
200 LBCH 90802 795-F7
BONLEE AV
27100 SCTA 91351 4551-D2
BONNELL DR
1300 Top 90290 589-G4
BONNER AV
5500 NHol 91601 562-J2
6000 NHol 91606 532-J6
7700 SunV 91352 532-J3
BONNER CT
1000 LVRN 91750 570-E6
3100 LKWD 90712 765-H3
BONNER DR
8700 WHWD 90048 592-J7
BONNEVILLE RD
5500 HIDH 91302 559-C3
N BONNIE AV
- PAS 91106 566-C4
S BONNIE AV
- PAS 91106 566-C5
BONNIE LN
300 LHB 90631 708-E4
BONNIE PL
7300 Res 91335 530-G4
BONNIE WY
- Cstc 91384 4459-F2
900 BREA 92821 708-J5
BONNIE ANN CT
1000 LHB 90631 708-F4
N BONNIE BEACH PL
100 City 90063 635-E2
S BONNIE BEACH PL
100 City 90063 635-E6
600 LACo 90023 635-E7
1000 LACo 90023 675-E2
1300 CMRC 90023 675-E2
2600 VER 90023 675-D3
N BONNIE BRAE AV
200 CLAR 91711 571-D6
W BONNIE BRAE CT
900 ONT 91762 601-H5
BONNIE BRAE DR
8300 BPK 90621 737-J4
8300 BPK 90621 738-A4
BONNIE BRAE ST
1000 POM 91767 601-D6
1200 HMB 90254 762-H2
4400 MTCL 91763 601-E5
N BONNIE BRAE ST
100 Echo 90026 634-D1
100 LA 90057 634-D2
900 Echo 90026 594-D7
S BONNIE BRAE ST
100 LA 90057 634-C3
900 LA 90006 634-B4
BONNIE CLAIRE DR
600 WAL 91789 639-C7
BONNIE COVE AV
1200 GLDR 91740 599-F3
4600 COV 91724 599-F3
4600 LACo 91724 599-F3
BONNIEGLEN LN
1200 SDMS 91740 570-B6
BONNIE HILL DR
3200 LA 90068 563-B7
BONNIE JEAN RD
1400 LHH 90631 708-A3
BONNIE VALE AV
6300 PRV 90660 676-F5
BONNIE VALE PL
7000 PRV 90660 676-F6
BONNIE VIEW AV
28300 SCTA 91387 4552-A1
BONNY LN
12100 Brwd 90049 631-G3
BONNYBROOK TER
900 GLDL 91207 564-F2
N BONNYWOOD PL
100 BURB 91502 533-G7
S BONNYWOOD PL
100 BURB 91502 533-H7
500 BURB 91502 563-H1
BONSAI CT
- Cstc 91384 4459-E2
BONSALL AV
- LACo 90073 631-H3
- LACo 90073 632-A4
- WLA 90025 631-J3
BONSALL DR
5700 MAL 90265 627-D7
5700 MAL 90265 667-D2
BONSALLO AV
1900 LA 90007 634-C6
5800 LA 90044 674-B6
15400 LA 90247 734-B5

BON VILLA CIR
7100 LPMA 90623 767-D2
BONVUE AV
4700 LFlz 90027 593-J2
4700 LFlz 90027 594-A2
BONWICK DR
13500 LACo 90601 637-G5
BONWOOD RD
11100 ELMN 91733 637-D3
11900 ELMN 91732 637-D3
BOOKHAM DR
18700 SCTA 91351 4551-G1
BOOKMAN AV
1300 WAL 91789 639-F3
BOONE AV
2300 Ven 90291 671-J6
BOOTH CT
- FUL 92833 738-D5
BOOT HILL LN
- CRSN 90745 794-G2
BOOTLEGGER CANYON RD
- Actn 93510 (4554-J1 See Page 4464)
25900 Actn 93510 4464-H7
BORA DR
13600 SFSP 90670 737-C2
13800 LMRD 90638 737-D2
BORA BORA WY
300 LA 90292 701-J1
13800 MdlR 90292 701-J1
13800 MdlR 90292 702-A1
BORAGE CT
27700 SCTA 91350 4461-A6
BORATE ST
13700 SFSP 90670 737-C3
BORDA RD
15200 LMRD 90638 737-F4
BORDEAUX AV
9900 Pcma 91331 502-A4
BORDEAUX LN
16400 HNTB 92649 826-J7
BORDEAUX ST
37000 PMDL 93550 4286-E4
BORDEN AV
2100 HMB 90254 762-H1
9200 SunV 91352 503-A6
11000 Pcma 91331 502-E1
11500 Pcma 91331 482-D7
11800 LA 91340 482-D7
11900 SFER 91340 482-D7
12400 LA 91342 482-A4
13200 LA 91342 481-H2
BORDER AV
600 TOR 90501 763-G5
2400 TOR 90501 793-H1
BOREGO DR
14700 LMRD 90638 737-H3
BOREHAM WY
32800 LACo 90265 626-F2
BOREL ST
3700 LA 90031 595-C6
4800 BALD 91706 598-D3
BORG DR
29100 Ago 91301 588-A4
BORGOS PL
14800 PacP 90272 631-B6
BORICA CT
- PMDL 93551 4195-B4
BORIS AV
42400 LAN 93536 4104-E5
BORIS DR
17900 Enc 91316 561-A4
BORK AV
1600 HacH 91745 678-E4
BORLAND RD
5000 LA 90032 635-F1
5300 LA 90032 595-F7
BORLEY DR
1700 LACo 90265 627-G1
BORNA DR
27800 LACo 90265 627-J2
27800 LACo 90265 628-A2
BOROS CT
- LHB 90631 738-C1
BORREGO
1800 WCOV 91791 638-J4
BORREGO CT
400 SDMS 91773 600-A3
BORREGO DR
4900 LPMA 90623 767-C3
BORSON AV
5200 LYN 90262 705-E7
BORSON ST
7800 DWNY 90242 705-H7
8100 DWNY 90242 735-J1
9000 DWNY 90242 736-A1
10500 NRWK 90650 736-D1
E BORT ST
100 NLB 90805 765-C1
W BORT ST
- NLB 90805 765-C1
100 COMP 90221 765-C1
BORTON ST
29100 Cstc 91384 4459-A4
BORWICK AV
5500 SGAT 90280 705-F7
BORWICK ST
10500 BLF 90706 736-D7
BOS PL
11100 CRTS 90703 766-F3
BOS ST
11000 CRTS 90703 766-F2

BOSC LN
- PMDL 93551 4285-E3
BOSQUE DR
16400 Enc 91436 561-D5
BOSTON AV
800 MTBL 90640 636-E6
3900 GLDL 91214 504-D5
12900 CHNO 91710 641-E7
BOSTON CT
800 PAS 91101 566-A4
800 PAS 91106 566-A4
BOSTON LN
19400 CRTS 90703 766-H3
BOSTON PL
800 POM 91767 601-A7
BOSTON ST
800 LA 90012 634-F2
900 Alta 91001 536-B6
1200 Echo 90026 634-E2
BOSTONIAN DR
2600 OrCo 90720 796-H5
BOSTWICK ST
3700 City 90063 635-D4
BOSWELL PL
4300 LACo 90023 675-E1
5100 ELA 90022 675-E1
17200 GrnH 91344 481-B4
BOSWORTH ST
12700 NHol 91606 532-D6
BOTANY ST
7700 DWNY 90240 706-B1
BOTHWELL RD
5200 Tarz 91356 560-F2
6300 Res 91335 530-F3
8500 Nor 91324 530-F1
9500 Nor 91324 500-F4
10600 Chat 91311 500-F3
10800 Nor 91326 500-F3
BOTRYOIDES AV
6000 BPK 90621 737-G7
BOTTICELLI DR
39200 PMDL 93551 4195-D6
BOTTLEBRUSH
3500 WCOV 91792 679-C1
BOTTLEBRUSH DR
2700 BelA 90077 592-A1
BOTTLEBRUSH ST
- PMDL 93551 4195-E6
BOTTLE TREE DR
2500 PMDL 93550 4286-E4
BOTTLETREE LN
21200 SCTA 91321 4641-B1
BOUETT ST
1800 LA 90012 594-G7
BOUGAINVILLA AV
- POM 91766 641-B3
BOUGAINVILLEA LN
- GLDR 91741 569-E5
BOUGAINVILLEA ST
- AZU 91702 569-A4
BOUGAINVILLIA WY
28800 SCTA 91387 4552-E1
BOUGHTON PL
12100 LA 91604 562-F6
BOULAY ST
17400 LACo 91744 678-H1
BOULDER
- AZU 91702 598-H1
BOULDER DR
42400 LAN 93536 4104-E5
BOULDER LN
20800 DBAR 91789 679-G6
BOULDER RD
2400 Alta 91001 536-B6
BOULDER ST
- Cstc 91384 4369-G7
2400 Boyl 90033 635-B4
3000 LA 90063 635-C4
BOULDER CREEK RD
16000 SCTA 91387 4552-D3
BOULDER CREST CT
- SCTA 91351 4461-G7
- SCTA 91351 4551-G1
BOULDER CREST DR
- StvR 91381 4550-B4
BOULDER RIDGE CT
- AZU 91702 568-J1
- AZU 91702 569-A1
BOULDER RIDGE TER
10500 Chat 91311 499-H3
BOULDER SPRINGS DR
1300 GLDR 91741 569-H3
BOUMA AV
19500 CRTS 90703 766-G3
BOUMA CIR
7700 LPMA 90623 767-D3
BOUMA CT
20100 CRTS 90703 766-G4
BOUNDARY AV
3500 LA 90032 595-C6
BOUNDARY PL
600 HMB 90254 732-G7
800 MANB 90266 732-G7
BOUNTY CIR
3200 HNTB 92649 826-J7
BOUNTY LN
5100 CULC 90230 672-H3
BOUQUET DR
7200 CanP 91307 529-F5
BOUQUET LN
- PMDL 93551 4195-C6
BOUQUET CANYON RD
20300 SCTA 91350 4461-A7

BOUQUET CANYON RD
20300 Saug 91350 4461-F3
25900 SCTA 91350 4550-H3
25900 SCTA 91355 4550-H3
26500 SCTA 91354 4550-H3
26900 SCTA 91350 4551-A1
28700 LACo 91390 4461-F3
28700 SCTA 91390 4461-F3
31200 LACo 91390 (4371-H6 See Page 4281)
33000 LACo 91390 (4372-A1 See Page 4281)
33200 LACo 91390 (4282-B6 See Page 4281)
35800 LACo 91390 4283-B1
36100 LACo 91390 4193-F7
37600 LACo 91390 4193-F7
37600 LACo 93551 4194-A6
38400 PMDL 93551 4194-A6
BOUQUET CANYON FIRE RD
- LACo 91390 (4282-C6 See Page 4281)
BOUQUET CANYON RESERVOIR RD
- LACo 91390 4192-E7
BOUQUETE ST
3900 GLDL 91206 565-A1
BOUQUET RESERVOIR RD
- LACo 91390 4192-E7
- LACo 91390 (4282-E1 See Page 4281)
BOURBON LN
7200 LPMA 90623 767-C2
BOURBON ST
4900 ELMN 91731 597-D4
4900 ELMN 91780 597-D4
BOURDET AV
300 WAL 91789 679-E1
BOUTON DR
3600 LKWD 90712 765-J5
3900 LKWD 90712 766-A5
BOVEY AV
6300 Res 91335 530-F4
BOW AV
1100 TOR 90501 763-H6
BOW WY
1700 LAN 93534 4015-E4
BOWCLIFF TER
1600 THO 91361 557-B6
BOWCREEK DR
600 DBAR 91765 640-E7
600 DBAR 91765 680-E1
BOWCREEK LN
14500 CHLS 91709 680-J4
BOWCROFT ST
5600 LA 90016 673-A1
5900 LA 90016 672-J1
BOWDOIN ST
2000 LVRN 91750 570-G7
15300 PacP 90272 631-A5
15700 PacP 90272 630-J5
N BOWEN AV
100 COMP 90221 735-B4
S BOWEN AV
100 COMP 90221 735-B4
BOWEN DR
7600 WHIT 90602 677-F7
BOWER PL
- PMDL 93551 4285-D4
BOWER CASCADE PL
23600 DBAR 91765 640-C6
BOWERS AV
8600 SGAT 90280 705-D3
BOWERS DR
19500 Top 90290 590-B7
19500 Top 90290 630-A1
BOWESFIELD ST
5600 LA 90016 673-A1
BOWFIELD ST
4800 THO 91362 557-F1
4900 VeCo 91362 557-F1
5000 VeCo 91377 557-F1
BOWFIN AV
2500 LA 90732 823-H7
BOWIE
- CLAR 91711 571-F2
BOWIE CT
25300 StvR 91381 4550-C7
BOWIE RD
- RHLS 90274 823-E2
BOWL RD
23600 VeCo 93063 529-A1
BOWL TR
- LACo 91342 482-J6
BOWLING GREEN DR
400 CLAR 91711 571-C7
N BOWLING GREEN WY
100 Brwd 90049 631-G3
S BOWLING GREEN WY
100 Brwd 90049 631-G3
BOWMAN AV
8900 SGAT 90280 705-C5
10600 LYN 90262 705-C5
BOWMAN BLVD
4300 LA 90032 595-D7
BOWMAN WY
- StvR 91381 4550-B7
BOWMAN KNOLL DR
32500 WLKV 91361 557-A7
BOWMONT DR
2200 LA 90210 592-G2

BOWMORE AV
12000 Nor 91326 480-G6
BOWMORE PL
18900 Nor 91326 480-G6
BOWRING DR
2600 Alta 91001 536-D5
BOWSER RD W
40000 LACo 93551 4194-A3
BOWSPRIT CIR
3800 WLKV 91361 557-B6
BOX CANYON RD
1000 VeCo 93063 499-E5
1000 WHil 91304 499-E5
23600 Chat 91311 499-E6
23700 LA 91304 499-E6
23700 WHil 91304 499-E6
BOXCAR LN
- BREA 92823 709-J6
BOXCOVE PL
600 DBAR 91765 640-E7
600 DBAR 91765 680-E1
BOXELDER LN
3800 LACo 91724 599-G5
BOXFORD AV
3300 CMRC 90040 675-H6
BOXLEAF RD
37000 PMDL 93550 4286-D4
BOXTEL RD
40000 LACo 93551 4194-B3
BOXTHORN ST
37700 PMDL 93552 4287-B1
BOXTREE DR
14300 LACo 93532 4102-G4
BOXWOOD AV
900 FUL 92835 738-J2
BOXWOOD CT
36800 PMDL 93550 4286-F5
BOXWOOD LN
- LACo 91390 4460-H2
6100 CHNO 91710 641-J5
22600 SCTA 91390 4460-H2
BOXWOOD PL
- PMDL 93551 4285-D2
13900 PanC 91402 532-B2
BOYAR AV
4100 Bxby 90807 765-F4
8700 WHIT 90605 707-E2
BOYCE AV
3600 LA 90039 594-D1
BOYD PL
1800 POM 91766 640-J4
BOYD ST
200 LA 90013 634-G4
1300 Boyl 90033 634-J5
BOYDEN AV
1200 LAN 93534 4015-F4
BOYDTON ST
8800 RSMD 91770 596-H5
BOYER LN
600 LACo 91744 679-B2
BOYER ST
3900 SBdC 91710 641-D3
N BOYLE AV
100 Boyl 90033 634-J4
300 Boyl 90033 635-A4
S BOYLE AV
100 Boyl 90033 634-J5
500 LA 90023 634-J7
4300 VER 90058 675-A4
5500 HNTP 90255 675-A4
BOYLSTON ST
700 PAS 91104 566-A3
1300 LA 90012 594-F7
1300 LA 90012 634-F1
1300 Echo 90026 594-F7
N BOYLSTON ST
200 Echo 90026 634-E2
300 LA 90012 634-F2
S BOYLSTON ST
100 LA 90012 634-E3
100 Echo 90026 634-E3
300 LA 90017 634-E3
BOYNE ST
1400 LA 90023 675-B2
8200 DWNY 90242 706-A6
BOYNTON ST
1000 GLDL 91205 564-F7
BOY SCOUT MTWY
- LA 91342 482-F3
- LACo 91342 482-F3
BOY SCOUT RD
10300 SBdC 92372 4471-J4
10300 SBdC 92372 (4472-A5 See Page 4471)
BOYSCOUT RD
4600 LFlz 90027 594-A2
4700 LFlz 90027 593-J2
BOYSENBERRY WY
1700 PMDL 93550 4286-D2
BOYSON ST
8200 DWNY 90242 705-J7
8500 DWNY 90242 706-A7
BP & L RD
- Actn 93510 4465-H5
- Actn 93510 4466-C3
- Actn 93510 (4555-A3 See Page 4466)
- LA 91342 503-C1
- LA 91342 (4723-C7 See Page 4643)
- LACo (4554-G5 See Page 4464)

BP & L RD
- LACo (4555-A3 See Page 4466)
- LACo 4643-F4
- LACo (4644-C1 See Page 4643)
- LACo 91342 (4723-C7 See Page 4643)
- PMDL 93550 4376-G7
- PMDL 93550 4466-F1
7000 Litl 93543 4377-H3
8700 Litl 93543 4378-E2
11600 Pear 93553 4378-G2
13000 Pear 93553 4379-C1
15300 Llan 93544 4379-G1
15500 LACo 93591 4379-G1
BRACE CANYON RD
2900 BURB 91504 533-F3
BRACEWOOD DR
17000 HacH 91745 678-F5
BRACKEN LN
24700 StvR 91381 4640-D2
BRACKEN ST
100 BREA 92821 709-B7
12600 Pcma 91331 502-D6
13500 Pcma 91331 532-C1
BRACKEN WY
- PMDL 93551 4285-D3
BRACKETT ST
- LVRN 91750 600-F3
BRACKNELL ST
- CRTS 90703 767-B3
BRADBOURNE AV
800 DUAR 91010 568-C5
BRADBURY AV
1100 DUAR 91010 567-J5
BRADBURY CT
1000 THO 91361 557-A5
N BRADBURY DR
100 SGBL 91775 596-D3
100 SGBL 91776 596-D3
S BRADBURY DR
1700 MTBL 90640 636-F5
BRADBURY RD
300 BRAD 91010 567-J4
300 MNRO 91016 567-J4
1200 SMRO 91108 566-E7
1300 SMRO 91108 596-E1
3100 OrCo 90720 796-H5
3300 LALM 90720 796-J5
3400 SLB 90740 796-J5
10500 LA 90064 632-E6
W BRADBURY ST
1200 WCOV 91790 638-D3
BRADBURY HILLS LN
- BRAD 91010 568-B4
BRADBURY HILLS RD
- BRAD 91010 568-B4
BRADCLIFF WY
1700 PMDL 93551 4195-E7
BRADDOCK DR
4200 CULC 90232 672-G2
10700 CULC 90230 672-F3
11200 LA 90230 672-E5
12400 LA 90066 672-D6
BRADDON OAK DR
28000 SCTA 91354 4460-H4
BRADENHALL DR
300 CRSN 90746 734-D7
BRADENTON CT
27500 SCTA 91354 4460-G6
BRADFIELD AV
12000 LYN 90262 735-C1
N BRADFIELD AV
100 COMP 90221 735-B3
S BRADFIELD AV
100 COMP 90221 735-C5
900 RDom 90221 735-C5
BRADFORD AV
900 POM 91767 600-J7
2700 ARCD 91007 597-B3
BRADFORD CIR
11000 CRTS 90703 766-F3
BRADFORD CT
500 CLAR 91711 601-C3
BRADFORD DR
1000 GLDL 91740 599-G1
4800 LCF 91011 535-A2
BRADFORD PL
12000 GrnH 91344 481-B6
41400 PMDL 93551 4104-E7
BRADFORD ST
400 PAS 91105 565-F6
700 POM 91767 640-J1
800 POM 91767 600-J1
3600 LVRN 91750 600-J1
4200 LVRN 91750 570-H7
BRADGATE DR
9500 PRV 90660 677-A1
BRADHURST ST
8700 PRV 90660 676-F4
10300 LACo 90606 676-J6
11400 LACo 90606 677-A6
BRADISH AV
700 SDMS 91773 600-A1
800 GLDR 91740 570-A7
BRADLEY AV
400 MTBL 90640 676-F2
2300 CLAR 91711 571-D6
8400 SunV 91352 533-A1
8600 SunV 91352 532-J1
8800 SunV 91352 502-J7
10000 Pcma 91331 502-C1

BRADLEY AV
11400 LA 91340 502-C1
11500 SFER 91340 502-C1
12200 LA 91342 482-A5
12200 SFER 91340 482-A5
12400 LA 91342 481-F3
BRADLEY CT
1300 GLDR 91740 599-F1
BRADLEY DR
7300 BPK 90620 767-E3
BRADLEY PL
6300 LA 90056 673-A7
BRADLEY ST
2900 PAS 91107 566-F2
BRADLEY CANYON RD
32700 Actn 93510 4374-A6
32900 Actn 93510 4464-A1
BRADMORE RD
33900 LACo 91390 4373-E4
44100 LACo 93536 4103-C1
BRADNA DR
5400 LACo 90043 673-C5
BRADNER PL
11100 Nor 91326 500-G2
BRADOAKS AV
200 MNRO 91016 567-J3
BRADRICK DR
100 CRSN 90745 764-D5
S BRADSHAWE AV
600 MONP 91754 636-B3
1900 MONP 91754 635-J5
BRADSHAWE PL
900 MONP 91754 636-A4
N BRADSHAWE ST
500 MTBL 90640 635-J7
S BRADSHAWE ST
500 ELA 90022 635-J5
500 ELA 90022 675-J1
BRADSON PL
11500 LA 90230 672-F5
BRADSTOCK RD
34800 Actn 93510 4374-H3
35800 Actn 93510 (4284-H7 See Page 4283)
35800 LACo 93551 (4284-H7 See Page 4283)
BRADWELL AV
7500 LACo 90606 676-G7
8200 LACo 90606 706-G1
9400 SFSP 90670 706-G3
13000 LA 91342 481-H4
S BRADY AV
600 ELA 90022 676-A1
600 MTBL 90640 676-A1
BRADY PKWY
- SCTA 91355 4460-B6
BRAE BURN CIR
5100 BPK 90621 737-J5
BRAE BURN PL
5300 BPK 90621 737-J6
5300 BPK 90621 738-A6
BRAEBURN RD
1400 Alta 91001 536-B6
BRAEBURN WY
4000 LFlz 90027 594-B2
BRAEHOLM PL
600 HMB 90254 732-G7
BRAELOCH ST
5500 Actn 93510 4374-F2
BRAEMAR CT
6100 AGRH 91301 557-J3
BRAEMAR RD
1800 PAS 91103 535-E7
BRAEMORE PL
12100 Nor 91326 480-G6
BRAEMORE RD
18700 Nor 91326 480-G6
BRAEPARK ST
15900 WHIT 90603 707-J4
BRAERIDGE DR
1300 LA 90210 592-D5
BRAES RIVER DR
19300 WAL 91789 639-C6
BRAEWOOD CIR
1200 UPL 91786 601-G2
BRAEWOOD CT
1500 SPAS 91030 595-G3
3800 Tarz 91356 560-F6
BRAEWOOD DR
700 BRAD 91010 568-B4
19400 Tarz 91356 560-F6
N BRAEWOOD LN
1200 UPL 91786 601-J1
BRAHEA PALM
- WCOV 91790 638-H6
BRAHMA DR
20100 WdHl 91367 530-D7
BRAHMS PL
16600 CRTS 90703 737-B6
BRAIDED MANE DR
2500 DBAR 91765 680-C6
BRAIDWOOD DR
28000 RPV 90275 792-H6
BRAINARD AL
100 PAS 91103 565-H4
200 PAS 91101 565-H4
BRAINARD AV
11300 LA 91342 503-A1
BRAINARD CANYON RD
31200 Litl 93543 4468-A2
31300 Litl 93543 4378-A6
BRALEY CT
- PAS 91105 565-H5

BRAMANTE PZ
6500 RPV 90275 823-G4
BRAMBLE CT
18100 RowH 91748 678-J7
BRAMBLE LN
2100 PMDL 93550 4286-E2
BRAMBLE WY
- FUL 92833 738-C6
800 Brwd 90049 631-F1
21400 SCTA 91350 4551-B3
BRAMBLEBUSH AV
10600 LACo 90604 707-D5
S BRAMBLEBUSH AV
11100 LACo 90604 707-D6
BRAMBLEWOOD RD
5600 LCF 91011 535-C1
BRAMBLING LN
2100 LACo 91107 536-F6
BRAMFORD CT
1100 DBAR 91765 680-E3
BRAMFORD DR
1000 GLDL 91207 534-F7
BRAMHALL AV
1600 GLDR 91740 599-F2
BRAMHALL LN
18800 LACo 92821 679-C7
18800 LACo 92821 709-C1
18900 RowH 91748 679-C7
BRAMPTON RD
1300 Eagl 90041 565-D6
BRAMWELL PL
1200 THO 91361 557-C6
BRANBURY CT
23500 SCTA 91354 4460-G7
BRANCH CIR
1300 UPL 91786 571-J7
BRANCH LN
2300 BREA 92821 709-E7
BRANCH RD
28000 Cstc 91384 4369-F6
BRANCH ST
200 HiPk 90042 595-D1
BRANCH OAK CT
100 GLDR 91741 569-J5
BRANCH OAK DR
1700 GLDR 91741 569-H5
N BRAND BLVD
- SFER 91340 482-C6
100 GLDL 91206 564-E2
100 GLDL 91203 564-E4
900 GLDL 91207 564-E2
900 GLDL 91202 564-E2
13100 LA 91340 482-C6
S BRAND BLVD
- SFER 91340 482-D7
100 GLDL 91205 564-E7
100 GLDL 91204 564-E7
100 GLDL 91210 564-E7
300 SFER 91340 502-A1
800 LA 91340 502-A1
1600 GLDL 91205 594-E1
1600 GLDL 91204 594-E1
14500 LA 91340 501-H2
14500 MsnH 91345 501-H2
BRANDEIS DR
800 CLAR 91711 571-F4
BRANDEN ST
1900 Echo 90026 594-D5
BRANDENBURG PL
4800 Tarz 91356 560-G4
BRANDI CT
300 CRSN 90745 764-D7
BRANDING IRON LN
- RHE 90274 793-D6
BRANDING IRON RD
19300 WAL 91789 639-C7
BRAND LATERAL
- GLDL 91202 534-C6
BRANDO ST
12500 CRTS 90703 767-A3
BRANDON CIR
- SCTA 91387 4462-E6
2300 CHLS 91709 680-J7
BRANDON CT
9400 Nor 91325 501-B6
BRANDON ST
3100 PAS 91107 566-G5
3100 LACo 91107 566-G5
BRANDON THOMAS WY
- LAN 93536 4104-E2
44200 LAN 93536 4014-E7
BRAND PARK DR
- GLDL 91201 534-B6
- GLDL 91202 534-B6
BRAND PARK MTWY
- GLDL 91202 534-C6
- GLDL 91208 534-C6
BRANDT ST
2900 LVRN 91750 600-H3
BRANDY DR
- SMRO 91108 566-C6
BRANDYWINE CT
300 WCOV 91791 599-C7
BRANDYWINE DR
22700 CALB 91302 559-H6
BRANDY WINE WY
3300 TOR 90505 793-D4
BRANDYWINE CANYON RD
30400 CynC 91351 4462-C3
BRANFORD LN
2200 LHB 90631 708-B7

BRANFORD ST
11800 SunV 91352 502-G4
11800 Sunl 91040 502-G4
11900 Pcma 91331 502-F5
13500 Pcma 91331 532-C1
13800 PanC 91402 532-B1
BRANHAM ST
1100 MONP 91754 635-J3
1100 MONP 91754 636-A3
N BRANNICK AV
400 City 90063 635-E5
S BRANNICK AV
900 LACo 90023 635-E7
900 LACo 90023 675-E1
BRANSCOMB ST
10200 DWNY 90242 736-D2
10500 NRWK 90650 736-D2
14100 LMRD 90638 737-D1
BRANSFORD DR
5000 LPMA 90623 767-C2
BRANT AV
20900 CRSN 90810 764-J5
BRANTA DR
1300 GLDL 91208 534-G7
BRANTFELL PL
900 GLDR 91741 569-C5
BRANTON PL
13900 Shrm 91423 562-B3
BRANYON AV
4900 SGAT 90280 705-E4
BRASHER ST
9500 PRV 90660 676-H3
BRASILIA DR
18500 Nor 91326 500-J1
18500 Nor 91326 480-G7
BRASSIE LN
- LACo 91750 570-J4
- LVRN 91750 570-J4
BRASS LANTERN DR
1200 LHB 90631 738-B1
16500 LMRD 90638 738-A1
BRAVO DR
700 LACo 91746 637-H5
BRAVO LN
8000 LPMA 90623 767-D4
26300 CALB 91302 558-H4
43600 LAN 93535 4106-F1
BRAWLEY RD
900 SBdC 92372 (4472-C7 See Page 4471)
2700 SBdC 92371 (4472-G7 See Page 4471)
BRAWLEY ST
2100 LA 90032 635-E1
BRAXTON AV
28600 Valc 91355 4459-G7
BRAXTON PL
12600 GrnH 91344 481-C5
BRAXTON ST
17100 GrnH 91344 481-C5
BRAY ST
11800 LA 90230 672-F6
BRAYTON AV
2400 SIGH 90755 795-F1
3300 Bxby 90807 795-F1
3400 Bxby 90807 765-F4
5200 NLB 90805 765-F2
6400 NLB 90805 735-F7
BRAYTON PL
4800 Eagl 90041 565-D6
BRAYTON ST
15500 PRM 90723 735-F5
BRAZIL DR
5700 BPK 90620 767-D2
BRAZIL ST
- GLDL 91203 564-C5
- GLDL 91204 564-C5
800 COMP 90220 734-G4
4500 LA 90039 564-C5
13000 CRTS 90703 767-B3
W BRAZIL ST
1600 COMP 90220 734-F4
BRAZILIANA DR
200 SDMS 91773 599-J2
BRAZO RD
13400 LMRD 90638 737-E2
BRAZOS PL
1900 DBAR 91765 679-H5
BREA BLVD
1300 FUL 92832 738-H5
1300 FUL 92835 738-H5
1600 FUL 92831 738-H5
N BREA BLVD
100 BREA 92821 709-C4
13100 OrCo 92821 709-C4
S BREA BLVD
100 BREA 92821 709-A7
BREA PL
500 POM 91766 640-F2
BREA CANYON CTO
1200 LACo 91789 679-D4
1200 RowH 91748 679-D4
2700 DBAR 91765 679-G6
2700 DBAR 91789 679-G6
2700 LACo 91765 679-G6
BREA CANYON RD
- OrCo 92821 709-E3
- POM 91766 640-D3
100 INDS 91789 639-H7
100 LACo 91789 639-H7
200 INDS 91789 679-G2
200 LACo 91789 679-G2
600 DBAR 91789 679-G2

STREET Block City ZIP Pg-Grid

BREA CANYON RD
1400 DBAR 91765 679-H5
3300 DBAR 91765 709-E3
3800 LACo 91765 709-E3
W BREA CANYON RD
1800 POM 91766 640-E3
BREA CREST DR
5100 LACo 90043 673-C5
BREA HILLS AV
- BREA 92823 709-J6
BREAKERS CV
- SCTA 91355 4550-F2
BREAKWATER WY
- SCTA 91350 4550-J2
- SCTA 91350 4551-A2
BREAN ST
3300 LKWD 90712 765-H3
BREA RIDGE MTWY
- LACo 91765 709-G2
- LACo 92823 709-G2
- OrCo 92821 709-E4
BRECKELLE ST
- RowH 91748 679-C4
BRECKENRIDGE CT
24200 DBAR 91765 680-D2
BRECKENRIDGE DR
11400 LACo 90604 707-D7
BRECKENRIDGE LN
- SFSP 90670 706-G4
BRECKENRIDGE PL
24500 SCTA 91321 4640-H2
BRECKFORD CT
1300 THO 91361 557-A5
BRECKINRIDGE
1400 WCOV 91791 638-J5
BREED ST
1000 LA 90023 635-B4
2200 Boyl 90033 635-B4
N BREED ST
100 Boyl 90033 635-B4
S BREED ST
100 Boyl 90033 635-A5
600 LA 90023 635-A6
BREEN AV
7700 Wch 90045 702-J2
7700 Wch 90045 703-A1
BREEZE AV
- Ven 90291 671-G6
BREEZE CT
- Ven 90291 671-G6
BREEZE WY
42400 LAN 93536 4104-E5
BREEZEPORT DR
3300 WLKV 91361 557-C7
BREEZEWOOD AV
12000 LACo 90604 707-J7
12200 LACo 90604 737-J1
BREEZEWOOD CT
500 BREA 92821 708-H6
BREEZEWOOD DR
12700 LMRD 90638 737-J1
BREEZIE LN
10300 Tuj 91042 504-B4
BREGANTE DR
400 DBAR 91765 640-D7
BREGER AV
13900 LA 91342 482-C1
BREI CT
- SCTA 91321 4551-A7
BREIDT AV
10000 Tuj 91042 504-C4
BREMERTON WY
12100 LACo 90061 734-C1
BRENDA CT
20000 LKWD 90715 766-H3
W BRENDA CT
1300 UPL 91786 601-J1
BRENDA LN
11100 OrCo 90631 708-F4
BRENDA ST
2400 WCOV 91792 639-B7
BRENDLE WY
19500 SCTA 91321 4551-F4
BRENFORD ST
22700 WdHl 91364 559-G5
23000 LA 91302 559-G5
23000 CALB 91302 559-G5
BRENNAN AV
6600 CanP 91307 529-F6
BRENNAN CT
- LAN 93536 4015-D4
1800 LAN 93534 4015-E4
BRENNER AV
6800 BPK 90621 767-J2
BRENNER DR
600 CRSN 90746 764-E3
BRENNER PL
1000 LBCH 90813 795-F6
BRENT AV
600 SPAS 91030 595-H2
BRENT CIR
100 INDS 91789 639-H7
BRENT CT
4600 LVRN 91750 570-E7
BRENT PL
300 GLDL 91203 564-C4
BRENT ST
18900 CRTS 90703 767-A2
BRENTA PL
2200 Ven 90291 672-A5
BRENTFORD RD
2200 SMRO 91108 596-D2
6500 LACo 91775 596-G1

BRENTMEAD AV
6700 LACo 91007 596-J1
6800 LACo 91007 566-J7
BRENTNAL RD
900 PAS 91105 565-E7
BRENTON AV
3500 LYN 90262 705-B6
BRENTRIDGE DR
11900 Brwd 90049 591-G7
BRENTRIDGE LN
11900 Brwd 90049 591-G7
BRENTWOOD AV
- LAN 93536 4104-E3
3000 LAN 93536 4105-B2
N BRENTWOOD AV
1500 UPL 91786 571-H7
1700 UPL 91784 571-H6
BRENTWOOD CT
- LAN 93536 4104-H2
BRENTWOOD DR
- LAN 93536 4104-E2
1900 FUL 92831 738-J4
2000 WCOV 91792 638-H5
2500 LAN 93536 4105-C2
BRENTWOOD ST
2000 POM 91766 641-B5
5800 LA 90003 674-C6
BRENTWOOD TER
1200 SMCA 90402 631-D6
12900 Brwd 90049 631-E5
N BRENTWOOD WY
500 UPL 91786 601-H2
BRENTWOOD GROVE DR
11900 Brwd 90049 591-G7
11900 Brwd 90049 631-G1
BREON ST
1000 POM 91768 600-G7
BRESCIA AV
2100 CLAR 91711 571-D7
BRESCIA DR
- BqtC 91354 4460-F4
BRESEE AV
1000 PAS 91104 566-C2
3700 BALD 91706 598-B3
BRESEE PL
14200 BALD 91706 598-B7
BRETON AV
13100 CHNO 91710 641-F7
BRETON CT
- SCTA 91355 4550-E1
BRETON PL
- PMDL 93551 4104-E7
BRETONWOOD RD
- HacH 91745 678-F6
BRETT CT
- Saug 91350 4461-E6
BRETT PL
1300 LA 90732 823-J2
1500 RPV 90275 823-J2
1500 RPV 90732 823-J2
E BRETT ST
200 ING 90302 673-C7
BRETTON PL
23000 WdHl 91364 559-G5
BREVE WY
17700 PacP 90272 630-F6
BREVIS ST
5400 HiPk 90042 565-C7
BREWER ST
- LKWD 90712 765-H3
BREWSTER AV
4200 LYN 90262 735-D1
BREWSTER DR
1000 POM 91767 601-C7
4600 Tarz 91356 560-H3
BRIAN AV
1300 AZU 91702 568-H4
2500 TOR 90505 793-F5
BRIAN CT
10200 WHIT 90601 676-J3
12700 CRTS 90703 737-A7
28400 SCTA 91350 4461-C4
BRIAN LN
5100 Enc 91436 561-E3
7300 LPMA 90623 767-D2
BRIANNA AV
1000 LAN 93535 4106-B3
N BRIANNA LN
- LACo 91387 4552-B5
BRIAR PL
1500 LVRN 91750 570-F7
BRIAR ST
10600 NRWK 90650 736-E2
BRIAR TR
1900 UPL 91784 571-J5
BRIARBANK ST
15500 LACo 91744 638-E4
BRIARBLUFF DR
21700 LACo 90265 629-E4
BRIARCLIFF LN
11200 LA 91604 592-H1
BRIARCLIFF PL
- SCTA 91354 4460-G5
BRIARCLIFF RD
1100 MNRO 91016 567-G1
2100 LA 90068 593-G3
BRIAR CREEK RD
200 DBAR 91765 640-D6
BRIARCREST LN
9000 LA 90210 592-G2
11300 LA 91604 592-G2
BRIARCREST RD
2400 LA 90210 592-G2

BRIARCROFT RD
100 CLAR 91711 600-J1
1100 CLAR 91711 601-A1
BRIARDALE WY
24000 SCTA 91321 4640-H4
BRIARFIELD WY
19100 Tarz 91356 560-G6
BRIARGATE LN
700 COV 91723 599-C7
1300 COV 91722 599-C3
1300 GLDR 91740 599-C1
2400 ARCD 91007 597-C2
6000 GLDR 91740 569-C7
6000 LACo 91740 569-C7
BRIARGLEN RD
2400 Actn 93510 4465-D3
BRIARHILL DR
15000 LA 91342 481-H7
BRIARHURST DR
28800 RPV 90275 792-G7
28800 RPV 90275 822-G1
BRIAR KNOLL DR
2900 LA 90046 592-J1
2900 LA 90046 593-A1
BRIAR RIDGE RD
1700 GLDL 91207 564-F1
BRIARROSE LN
- SBdC 91710 641-C5
BRIARS PL
- SCTA 91354 4460-G6
BRIARSTONE LN
7100 CanP 91307 529-D5
BRIAR SUMMIT
2700 DUAR 91010 568-E3
BRIAR SUMMIT DR
7800 LA 90046 593-A1
8000 LA 90046 592-J1
BRIARTREE DR
5700 LCF 91011 535-C1
BRIARVALE LN
11900 LA 91604 562-G7
BRIARWOOD CT
22100 WAL 91789 639-J5
37300 PMDL 93550 4286-A3
BRIARWOOD DR
500 BREA 92821 738-J1
2900 TOR 90505 793-E5
10200 BelA 90077 592-A2
15400 Shrm 91403 561-G6
BRIARWOOD LN
- ING 90305 703-F3
- VeCo 91377 558-A2
600 SDMS 91773 600-B4
800 POM 91767 601-A6
900 GLDL 91206 564-G3
BRIARWOOD ST
13000 CRTS 90703 767-B3
BRIDEWELL ST
100 HiPk 90042 595-E2
BRIDGE RD
- Nor 91326 480-F2
- StvR 91381 480-F2
BRIDGE ST
100 SGBL 91775 596-D3
100 SGBL 91776 596-D3
1400 Boyl 90033 634-J3
1500 Boyl 90033 635-A4
BRIDGEGATE CT
2000 THO 91361 557-A6
BRIDGE GATE DR
1200 DBAR 91765 679-H4
BRIDGEGATE ST
1800 THO 91361 557-A5
BRIDGEPORT
- MANB 90266 732-H4
1600 WCOV 91791 638-J3
BRIDGEPORT AV
1700 CLAR 91711 601-B1
1700 CLAR 91711 571-B7
W BRIDGEPORT AV
500 ANA 92804 767-H6
BRIDGEPORT CIR
600 FUL 92833 738-D6
BRIDGEPORT CT
19000 WAL 91789 639-C6
37000 PMDL 93550 4286-D3
BRIDGEPORT DR
- BPK 90621 738-A6
1600 LA 90065 594-H4
BRIDGEPORT LN
- SCTA 91355 4550-E2
BRIDGEPORT WY
2100 TOR 90503 763-F7
BRIDGER AV
12100 CHNO 91710 641-G4
BRIDGER CT
- LACo 91390 4461-A3
E BRIDGER ST
1100 COV 91722 598-H4
16000 LACo 91722 598-G5
W BRIDGER ST
500 COV 91722 599-A4
BRIDGES CT
22400 SCTA 91350 4460-J4
W BRIDGET CT
1500 UPL 91784 571-H6
BRIDGEVIEW AV
4500 PRV 90660 676-G2
BRIDGEVIEW LN
- SCTA 91355 4550-F1
BRIDGEWATER CT
5900 AGRH 91301 557-H4

BRIDGEWATER DR
27400 SCTA 91354 4460-F7
BRIDGEWATER LN
800 WAL 91789 639-H5
BRIDGEWATER WY
- SLB 90740 796-J6
BRIDGEWOOD DR
5100 LPMA 90623 767-C3
14300 LMRD 90638 737-E1
BRIDGEWOOD LN
3400 THO 91362 557-C2
BRIDGEWOOD WY
1300 UPL 91784 571-J4
E BRIDLE CIR
6200 LBCH 90815 796-E6
BRIDLE CT
- PMDL 93551 4194-J6
- PMDL 93551 4195-A6
BRIDLE DR
800 DBAR 91765 680-C2
BRIDLE LN
- RPV 90275 823-G2
1000 BHLS 90210 592-D7
N BRIDLE LN
- VeCo 91307 529-A5
BRIDLE PTH
- LCF 91011 535-C5
BRIDLE WY
700 WAL 91789 639-J5
BRIDLE GLEN ST
5500 AGRH 91301 558-A5
BRIDLE PATH DR
2600 Actn 93510 4465-D1
BRIDLE PATH LN
900 WAL 91789 639-D6
BRIDLE RIDGE RD
14000 LA 91342 481-E2
BRIDLE TRAIL LN
20700 WAL 91789 639-G6
BRIDLE TRAIL RD
700 WAL 91789 639-G6
24200 HIDH 91302 559-D3
BRIDLEVALE DR
10100 LA 90064 632-F6
BRIDLEWOOD CIR
26300 RHE 90274 793-H6
BRIDLEWOOD CT
- WAL 91789 639-C4
BRIDLEWOOD DR
29900 Cstc 91384 4459-G4
BRIDWELL ST
700 GLDR 91741 569-C6
BRIER AV
2200 LA 90039 594-E4
BRIER DR
8400 LA 90046 592-J4
8400 LA 90046 593-A4
BRIER LN
900 GLDL 91205 564-F7
BRIER WY
21400 SCTA 91350 4551-B3
BRIERBUSH AV
10500 DWNY 90241 706-D5
BRIERCLIFF DR
900 LHB 90631 708-B7
1100 LHB 90631 738-B1
BRIERCLIFF WY
1000 MONP 91754 635-J3
BRIERCREST AV
4300 LKWD 90713 766-C2
BRIERFIELD ST
9500 PRV 90660 676-J1
BRIERHAVEN DR
2700 LaCr 91214 504-G6
BRIERPATH DR
3800 LACo 91724 599-H5
BRIER RIDGE LN
- HacH 91745 637-H6
BRIGADOON CT
18600 SCTA 91351 4551-H2
BRIGANTINE CIR
3700 WLKV 91361 557-C7
BRIGANTINE ST
11000 CRTS 90703 736-F6
BRIGDEN RD
1500 PAS 91104 566-C2
BRIGGEMAN DR
3500 LALM 90720 796-J2
BRIGGS AV
4100 Mont 91020 534-H3
4400 LCF 91011 534-H1
4500 LaCr 91214 534-H1
4900 LaCr 91214 504-H7
BRIGGS RD
30900 LACo 91390 4463-H5
BRIGGS EDISON RD
30900 LACo 91390 4463-E3
BRIGHAM YOUNG DR
600 CLAR 91711 571-E5
BRIGHT AV
5800 WHIT 90601 677-D6
7000 WHIT 90602 677-D7
7700 WHIT 90602 707-D1
9500 LACo 90605 707-B3
BRIGHT LN
2800 LA 90039 594-D4
BRIGHT ST
300 LHB 90631 708-F6
BRIGHT GLEN CIR
2800 THO 91361 557-C5
BRIGHTLY ST
9100 BLF 90706 736-A3

BRIGHTON AV
2600 LA 90018 633-J7
3900 LA 90062 673-J3
7200 LA 90047 673-J4
7200 LA 90047 703-J1
13900 GAR 90249 733-J3
15700 GAR 90247 733-J6
18700 LA 90248 764-A2
21300 LA 90501 764-A6
S BRIGHTON AV
20800 LA 90501 764-A5
BRIGHTON CIR
4000 CYP 90630 767-A7
BRIGHTON CT
1000 SDMS 91773 599-J3
2200 PMDL 93550 4286-E3
BRIGHTON DR
24600 SCTA 91355 4550-E5
BRIGHTON LN
27300 SCTA 91354 4460-G7
BRIGHTON PL
- StvR 91381 4640-C2
2700 FUL 92833 738-B6
3500 RowH 91748 708-J2
BRIGHTON ST
800 LHB 90631 708-G4
1400 LACo 90631 708-G4
1900 SGBL 91776 596-E7
2000 RSMD 91776 636-E1
2000 SGBL 91776 636-E1
3000 RSMD 91770 636-E1
42200 LAN 93536 4104-D5
N BRIGHTON ST
100 BURB 91506 563-E1
900 BURB 91506 533-E7
2000 BURB 91504 533-E4
S BRIGHTON ST
100 BURB 91506 563-F3
BRIGHTON WY
900 MTBL 90640 636-C6
9300 BHLS 90210 632-F2
16900 GAR 90247 733-J7
17000 GAR 90247 734-A7
17900 GAR 90248 764-A1
BRIGHTONWOOD AV
8900 PRV 90660 676-F3
BRIGHTSIDE AV
1600 DUAR 91010 568-A6
BRIGHTSIDE LN
600 PAS 91107 566-G6
BRIGHTSTONE CT
900 THO 91361 557-A5
BRIGHTVIEW DR
1000 GLDR 91740 569-D7
1000 GLDR 91740 599-D1
4800 LACo 91722 599-D3
6500 GLDR 91741 569-D6
N BRIGHTVIEW DR
100 COV 91723 599-D5
4500 LACo 91723 599-D4
S BRIGHTVIEW DR
100 COV 91723 599-D5
BRIGHTWATER PL
23300 Hrbr 90710 793-J2
BRIGHTWELL AV
13900 PRM 90723 735-G2
BRIGHTWOOD CT
9300 Nor 91325 501-C6
BRIGHTWOOD ST
400 MONP 91754 636-A5
600 MONP 91754 635-G4
BRIGITA AV
400 LACo 91744 638-G6
BRILL DR
11300 LA 91604 562-J6
BRILLIANT DR
3700 LA 90065 594-H2
BRILLIANT PL
3700 LA 90065 594-H2
BRILLIANT WY
3900 LA 90065 594-J2
BRIMFIELD AV
7900 PanC 91402 531-H1
BRIMHALL DR
2600 OrCo 90720 796-G6
BRIMLEY ST
11500 NRWK 90650 736-G2
BRINEY POINT RD
4600 LACo 91750 570-J6
BRINGATE RD
35100 Actn 93510 4374-H2
BRINGHAM AV
- LACo 90073 631-H4
800 Brwd 90049 631-H4
BRINK AV
11000 NRWK 90650 706-H7
12300 NRWK 90650 736-H1
BRINKLEY AV
1300 Brwd 90049 631-E4
BRINNON ST
12300 ELMN 91732 597-G5
BRINSEY AV
800 DUAR 91010 568-D5
BRINTON PL
- SCTA 91350 4551-D6
BRINVILLE RD
34300 Actn 93510 4375-B2
BRINWOOD DR
600 SDMS 91773 600-D1
BRIO CT
- BqtC 91354 4460-F3
BRION CT
- PMDL 93552 4287-E1

BRISA DR
4800 PMDL 93551 4194-H3
BRISA LN
2400 RowH 91748 679-D7
BRISBANE CT
25600 LACo 91302 559-A4
BRISBANE ST
100 MNRO 91016 597-G1
BRISTLE CONE DR
41400 PMDL 93551 4104-D7
BRISTOL AV
700 Brwd 90049 631-F5
N BRISTOL AV
100 Brwd 90049 631-E3
S BRISTOL AV
100 Brwd 90049 631-F4
N BRISTOL CIR
12700 Brwd 90049 631-E3
S BRISTOL CIR
12700 Brwd 90049 631-E4
BRISTOL CT
12500 CHNO 91710 641-G6
37700 PMDL 93550 4286-E2
BRISTOL DR
15500 LMRD 90638 707-H7
15500 LMRD 90638 737-H1
BRISTOL PKWY
5900 CULC 90230 672-H6
BRISTOL RD
800 SDMS 91773 599-J4
BRISTOL WY
21600 SCTA 91350 4461-B5
39300 PMDL 93551 4195-F5
BRISTOW DR
2100 LCF 91011 504-H6
BRITTAIN ST
12200 HGDN 90716 766-J7
12400 HGDN 90716 767-A7
E BRITTAIN ST
5100 LBCH 90808 766-B7
BRITTANIA ST
500 Boyl 90033 635-B3
BRITTANY CT
- LACo 91302 558-G4
BRITTANY LN
- SCTA 91321 4640-G3
3300 LAN 93536 4105-B4
24600 GLDL 91214 504-D4
BRITTANY PL
18800 LACo 92821 679-C7
18800 RowH 91748 679-C7
BRITTANY WY
5400 CYP 90630 767-D5
BRITTLE BRUSH DR
42200 LAN 93536 4104-E5
E BRITTON DR
5500 LBCH 90815 796-D4
N BRITTON DR
1900 LBCH 90815 796-C4
BRIXTON RD
1300 Eagl 90041 565-D6
1300 PAS 91105 565-D6
BRIZA WY
21900 Top 90290 590-A1
BROACH AV
1900 DUAR 91010 567-J7
1900 DUAR 91010 568-A6
BROAD AV
100 Wilm 90744 794-E4
100 Wilm 90744 824-E1
BROAD ST
23900 CRSN 90745 794-E3
24300 Wilm 90744 794-E3
BROADACRE DR
8300 SunV 91352 533-C1
BROADACRE PL
10200 SunV 91352 533-C1
BROADACRES AV
19000 CRSN 90746 764-G2
N BROADACRES AV
200 COMP 90220 734-G4
S BROADACRES AV
1200 COMP 90220 734-G6
BROAD BEACH RD
30800 MAL 90265 626-H7
30800 MAL 90265 627-A7
30800 MAL 90265 667-A1
BROADED ST
11000 SFSP 90670 706-G2
BROADFIELD DR
11700 LMRD 90638 707-G7
BROADLAND AV
1300 DUAR 91010 568-A5
1400 DUAR 91010 567-J6
BROADLAWN DR
3700 LA 90068 563-B7
BROADLEAF AV
7800 PanC 91402 532-B3
BROADMEAD ST
10300 SELM 91733 637-B4
BROADMOOR AV
400 LPUE 91744 638-C5
600 LACo 91744 638-C5
N BROADMOOR AV
200 WCOV 91790 598-F7
700 LACo 91722 598-F4
S BROADMOOR AV
700 WCOV 91790 638-E2
BROADMOOR RD
5700 PMDL 93551 4194-F1
BROADMOOR ST
600 WCOV 91790 638-F1
14400 PanC 91402 502-A7

BROADMOOR ST
14800 PanC 91402 501-H7
15000 LA 91343 501-H7
BROADMORE DR
12800 WHIT 90601 677-C4
BROADVALE DR
17000 LACo 91744 638-H6
BROADVIEW DR
2300 GLDL 91208 534-G3
BROADVIEW TER
2100 LA 90068 593-D3
BROADWATER AV
43800 LAN 93535 4106-C1
BROADWAY
100 SMCA 90401 671-F2
900 SGBL 91776 596-J4
900 LACo 91776 596-J4
1000 PAS 91105 565-H7
1200 BURB 91504 533-F6
1200 SMCA 90404 671-F2
2000 SMCA 90404 631-H7
2400 LACo 90255 704-J1
2700 LACo 90255 705-A1
3100 HNTP 90255 705-C2
4000 HAW 90250 733-B1
4900 LACo 90250 733-B1
5200 LBCH 90803 826-B1
8800 TEML 91776 596-J4
8800 TEML 91780 596-J4
9500 TEML 91780 597-A4
11400 WHIT 90606 677-C5
11400 WHIT 90601 677-C5
14100 LACo 90604 707-E5
16600 OrCo 92649 826-J7
16800 SunB 90742 826-J7
E BROADWAY
100 GLDL 91205 564-F5
100 LBCH 90802 825-G1
100 SGBL 91776 596-E4
100 GLDL 91206 564-F5
300 LBCH 90802 795-E7
1000 LACo 91776 596-H4
1600 LA 91205 564-F5
2000 LBCH 90803 825-J1
3900 LBCH 90803 826-A1
N BROADWAY
100 LA 90012 634-G3
100 RBCH 90277 762-J5
1600 LA 90031 634-J1
2200 LA 90031 635-B1
S BROADWAY
100 RBCH 90277 762-J7
1900 LA 90007 634-D7
2600 LA 90007 674-C1
3800 LA 90037 674-C3
5800 LA 90003 674-C6
7200 LA 90003 704-C1
10800 LA 90061 704-C5
12000 LA 90061 734-C3
12000 LACo 90061 704-C5
12000 LACo 90061 734-C3
14300 LACo 90248 734-C3
16100 CRSN 90248 734-C6
17500 CRSN 90248 764-C1
W BROADWAY
- GLDL 91203 564-C5
- GLDL 91210 564-C5
100 LBCH 90802 825-B1
100 SGBL 91776 596-E4
400 GLDL 91204 564-C5
500 LBCH 90831 825-D1
2700 Eagl 90041 564-H5
BROADWAY AV
- HAW 90250 733-E1
200 Ven 90291 671-H5
600 LACo 90732 823-J5
6300 LACo 90606 677-A6
7000 LACo 90606 676-J7
8000 LACo 90606 706-J1
8000 SFSP 90606 676-J7
8000 SFSP 90606 706-J1
BROADWAY CT
- LBCH 90802 825-E1
200 LBCH 90802 795-E7
400 Ven 90291 671-H5
700 LBCH 90813 795-E6
3300 Bxby 90807 795-E1
3300 SIGH 90755 795-E1
BROADWAY DR
- FUL 92832 738-C6
BROADWAY PL
300 SGBL 91776 596-F4
1000 LA 90015 634-E6
3500 LA 90007 674-C2
3800 LA 90037 674-C2
BROADWAY CENTER ST
15400 LACo 90248 734-C5
BROADWELL AV
17500 GAR 90248 764-A1
21300 LACo 90502 764-A6
22800 LACo 90502 794-B1
24300 Hrbr 90710 794-B3
25000 Hrbr 90710 794-B4
S BROADWELL AV
21100 LACo 90502 764-A5
BROADWICK ST
18200 COMP 90220 764-H2
18200 LACo 90220 764-H2
BROCADERO PL
- PAS 91105 565-H7
BROCK AV
4100 LKWD 90712 765-H6
8900 DWNY 90240 706-C2

BROCK AV
12300 DWNY 90242 705-H7
12700 DWNY 90242 735-H1
13100 PRM 90723 735-H1
BROCK LN
34300 Actn 93510 4375-C4
BROCKMONT DR
300 GLDL 91202 564-D1
BROCKPORT CT
1900 CLAR 91711 571-D7
BROCKTON AV
1200 WLA 90025 631-H5
E BROCKWAY PL
- ELMN 91733 637-A1
BROCKWAY ST
9500 ELMN 91733 636-J1
9500 ELMN 91733 637-A1
10600 ELMN 91731 637-C1
BROCKWELL AV
1800 MONP 91754 636-A5
E BROCKWOOD ST
5100 LBCH 90808 766-B6
BROCTON CT
500 LBCH 90803 796-D7
S BRODER ST
300 ANA 92804 767-J6
BRODERICK AV
2400 LACo 91010 567-H7
S BRODERICK AV
2000 LACo 91010 567-H7
BRODY AV
20800 LACo 90502 764-B5
BROGAN RD
- Actn 93510 4465-E1
BROKEN ARROW DR
21300 DBAR 91765 679-H5
BROKEN BIT DR
20200 LACo 91724 639-G2
BROKEN BOW LN
600 WAL 91789 639-E7
BROKENBOW LN
- RHE 90274 793-B5
BROKEN CREEK LN
1000 DBAR 91765 680-C2
BROKEN FEATHER RD
2600 DBAR 91765 680-C6
BROKEN LANCE RD
600 WAL 91789 639-E7
BROKEN SPUR RD
300 LACo 91750 570-J6
8900 SBdC 92371 (4562-G1 See Page 4471)
BROKEN TWIG RD
22300 DBAR 91765 680-A5
BROMAR ST
15900 LPUE 91744 638-E7
BROMELAID LN
- PMDL 93551 4195-E6
N BROMLEY AV
200 WCOV 91790 598-D7
1000 LACo 91746 638-B3
S BROMLEY AV
1200 WCOV 91790 638-C1
BROMLEY CT
3400 PMDL 93551 4195-B3
17800 Enc 91316 561-A1
BROMLEY LN
- ING 90305 703-F3
BROMLEY RD
9800 SBdC 92372 (4472-A6 See Page 4471)
BROMLEY ST
17500 Enc 91316 561-B1
18100 Tarz 91356 561-A1
BROMONT AV
10000 SunV 91352 502-J4
11200 Pcma 91331 502-F1
11500 Pcma 91331 482-E7
12000 LA 91340 482-C4
13000 LA 91342 482-B3
13800 LA 91342 481-J2
BROMPTON AV
4000 BELL 90201 675-C7
4800 BELL 90201 705-E1
BROMPTON CT
- PMDL 93551 4285-D3
3700 BELL 90201 675-C7
BROMWICH PL
13400 Pcma 91331 502-C6
BROMWICH ST
12400 Pcma 91331 502-E5
BRONCE WY
200 LBCH 90802 825-D1
2100 LBCH 90803 825-G1
BRONCO DR
2700 RPV 90275 823-F1
15500 SCTA 91387 4552-E4
BRONCO LN
21200 DBAR 91765 679-H7
BRONCO WY
600 WAL 91789 639-H6
N BRONCO WY
1500 UPL 91786 571-J7
BRONHOLLY DR
2600 LA 90068 593-G2
BRONSON AV
1100 LA 90019 633-F4
N BRONSON AV
300 LA 90004 593-G7
1100 LA 90038 593-G5
1300 Hlwd 90028 593-G3
1900 LA 90068 593-G3

S BRONSON AV
500 LA 90020 633-G2
600 LA 90005 633-G2
600 LA 90010 633-G2
900 LA 90019 633-G2
1900 LA 90018 633-F6
3400 LA 90018 673-E2
3700 LA 90008 673-E2
BRONSON HILL DR
5800 LA 90068 593-G2
BRONTE DR
14000 WHIT 90602 677-F7
14200 WHIT 90602 707-F1
BRONTE LN
25700 StvR 91381 4550-B7
BRONTE PL
17200 GrnH 91344 481-B4
BRONWOOD AV
100 Brwd 90049 631-H1
BRONZE LN
800 Brwd 90049 631-E1
BRONZE KNOLL RD
1600 DBAR 91765 680-C4
BROOK AV
4800 NLB 90805 765-C5
BROOK CT
24300 SCTA 91321 4640-H3
BROOK LN
1700 GLDL 91208 534-H7
BROOKDALE AV
600 LHB 90631 708-F4
BROOKDALE CT
- SCTA 91354 4460-G5
BROOKDALE DR
1200 UPL 91784 571-H4
BROOKDALE LN
- SCTA 91355 4550-H3
2600 DUAR 91010 568-D3
11700 LA 91604 592-H1
E BROOKDALE PL
100 FUL 92832 738-J6
600 FUL 92831 738-J6
W BROOKDALE PL
100 FUL 92832 738-G6
1600 FUL 92833 738-D6
BROOKDALE RD
3000 LA 91604 592-G1
3000 LA 91604 562-G7
5200 SGAT 90280 705-E6
38800 PMDL 93551 4195-E6
BROOKE AV
10100 Chat 91311 499-J4
10400 Chat 91311 500-A4
BROOKE LN
- SCTA 91355 4550-H3
1800 FUL 92833 738-C3
BROOKEN AV
26600 LACo 91387 4552-C6
BROOKFIELD AV
1700 LHB 90631 708-G4
BROOKFIELD CIR
12000 CHNO 91710 641-E5
BROOKFIELD PL
- GLDR 91741 569-B5
2700 WCOV 91792 638-J7
BROOKFIELD RD
10700 Chat 91311 500-C3
E BROOKFIELD ST
5800 ELA 90022 675-J2
BROOKFORD AV
4400 WdHl 91364 559-G5
BROOKFORD DR
6900 RPV 90275 792-G7
BROOKGREEN RD
8000 DWNY 90240 706-C1
BROOKGREEN ST
9700 DWNY 90240 706-E4
BROOKHAVEN AV
10800 LA 90064 632-B7
11500 LA 90064 672-B1
BROOKHAVEN DR
2300 CHLS 91709 680-J4
BROOKHAVEN PL
- SCTA 91354 4460-F5
1300 UPL 91784 571-J4
BROOKHAVEN ST
13100 CRTS 90703 767-B1
BROOKHILL AV
2700 LaCr 91214 504-G7
BROOKHILL DR
600 SDMS 91773 599-J3
BROOKHILL ST
3000 LaCr 91214 504-E6
3200 GLDL 91214 504-E5
BROOKHILL TER
3600 GLDL 91214 504-D5
BROOKHOLLOW CT
- PMDL 93551 4195-C2
BROOKHOLLOW DR
- SCTA 91355 4550-B5
BROOK HOLLOW LN
14200 CHLS 91709 680-J3
BROOKHURST CT
2800 PMDL 93551 4195-C6
BROOKHURST PL
1300 FUL 92833 738-E5
S BROOKHURST RD
100 FUL 92833 738-D7
BROOKINGS CT
- SCTA 91355 4550-E1
BROOKINGS TR
1400 Top 90290 589-G4

BROOKLAKE ST
12400 LA 90066 672-A3
BROOKLAWN DR
1000 BelA 90077 592-C6
1000 LA 90210 592-C6
BROOKLINE AV
3500 RSMD 91770 597-A7
BROOKLINE CT
600 FUL 92835 738-H2
BROOKLINE DR
20900 WAL 91789 639-G7
BROOKLINE PL
500 FUL 92835 738-H3
BROOKLINE RD
1000 SLB 90740 796-G7
BROOKLYN PL
- LA 90063 635-D5
BROOKMEAD DR
5400 WHIT 90601 677-C4
BROOK MEADOW CT
800 THO 91362 557-E1
BROOKMERE RD
1100 PAS 91105 565-G7
1100 PAS 91105 595-G1
BROOKMILL RD
7400 DWNY 90241 705-J4
7900 DWNY 90241 706-A5
BROOKMONT AV
12200 LA 91342 481-H6
BROOKMONT LN
- POM 91766 640-F7
- POM 91766 641-A4
BROOKMONT PL
7600 LA 91304 529-E4
BROOKPARK RD
7900 DWNY 90240 706-C1
BROOKPORT ST
1100 COV 91722 598-J3
1600 COV 91724 599-G3
4600 BALD 91706 598-B4
17600 LACo 91722 598-J3
17700 LACo 91722 599-A3
21100 LACo 91724 599-G3
21100 LACo 91773 599-G3
21100 SDMS 91773 599-G3
E BROOKPORT ST
200 COV 91722 599-B3
1000 COV 91724 599-E3
16500 LACo 91722 598-G3
17000 COV 91722 598-G3
19600 LACo 91724 599-D3
BROOKRIDGE RD
3100 DUAR 91010 568-E3
BROOKS AV
- Ven 90291 671-H5
100 CLAR 91711 601-E3
700 PAS 91103 565-G3
1800 LA 90012 594-G7
BROOKS CIR
- StvR 91381 4550-A7
BROOKS CT
- Ven 90291 671-H5
BROOKS DR
13300 BALD 91706 597-J4
13400 BALD 91706 598-A4
BROOKS RD
23400 Chat 91311 499-F7
BROOKS ST
4300 MTCL 91763 641-E1
W BROOKS ST
200 ONT 91762 641-J1
1200 ONT 91763 641-J1
BROOKSFALL CT
1700 THO 91361 557-A6
BROOKSHIRE AV
9100 DWNY 90240 706-D3
10100 DWNY 90241 706-B6
11900 DWNY 90242 706-A7
12500 DWNY 90242 705-J7
12500 DWNY 90242 735-J1
BROOKSHIRE CT
2300 BURB 91504 533-F2
BROOKSHIRE LN
2200 BelA 90077 591-G3
BROOKSHIRE PL
200 BREA 92821 709-B5
BROOKSIDE CT
- Cstc 91384 4369-G7
1300 UPL 91784 571-J5
21600 WAL 91789 639-H5
BROOKSIDE DR
- SCTA 91354 4460-E7
- SCTA 91354 4550-F1
1200 UPL 91784 571-G4
3300 LACo 90265 630-D5
BROOKSIDE LN
100 BREA 92821 709-D6
400 POM 91767 600-H2
500 SMAD 91024 537-B7
500 SMAD 91024 567-B1
BROOKSIDE WY
- AZU 91702 568-J2
- AZU 91702 569-A2
BROOKSONG WY
- PMDL 93536 4194-J1
- PMDL 93551 4194-J1
BROOKSTONE CIR
13400 LMRD 90638 738-A2
BROOKTREE CIR
1300 WCOV 91792 638-H5
BROOKTREE DR
1300 SIMI 93063 499-C3

STREET Block City ZIP Pg-Grid

BROOKTREE RD
500 LA 90402 631-C6
600 PacP 90272 631-B6
BROOKVIEW DR
10600 LA 91602 563-A5
BROOKVIEW TER
- Saug 91350 4461-B4
BROOKWIN DR
1000 POM 91768 640-G1
BROOKWOOD DR
1000 LHB 90631 708-H4
24200 DBAR 91765 680-D3
BROOKWOOD RD
14400 LACo 93532 4102-H4
BROOKWOOD ST
500 BREA 92821 709-C6
BROOM WY
800 Brwd 90049 631-F1
BROOMFIRTH CT
2000 THO 91361 557-A5
BROUGHAM PL
2100 HacH 91745 678-E4
BROUGHAM ST
6000 LACo 93536 4104-F5
BROWN CT
- Alta 91001 535-G3
12300 CHNO 91710 641-F6
BROWN DR
100 CLAR 91711 601-D5
600 BURB 91504 533-F4
BROWN DEER CT
2300 CHLS 91709 680-G5
BROWNDEER LN
4600 RPV 90275 793-B7
BROWNE AV
4500 LA 90032 595-D6
BROWNELL ST
13300 LA 91340 482-C7
13500 SFER 91340 482-C7
13600 LA 91340 502-C1
BROWNFIELD LN
- POM 91766 640-G6
BROWNING AV
100 POM 91767 600-J3
200 POM 91767 601-A3
BROWNING BLVD
1000 LA 90037 674-A2
1100 LA 90037 673-H2
1400 LA 90062 673-H2
BROWNING PL
700 MONP 91755 636-D4
13400 LACo 91746 637-J3
25800 StvR 91381 4550-D7
BROWN LATIGO RD
24600 LACo 90265 629-C1
24800 LACo 91302 629-C1
BROWNLOW RD
9500 LACo 91390 4373-H6
BROWN MOUNTAIN TR
- LACo - 535-H1
BROWN OAKS WY
- LACo 91387 4552-A4
BROWNSAGE DR
700 GLDR 91741 569-D3
BROWNS CANYON RD
2500 Nor 91326 480-A4
2500 Nor 91326 480-B7
2500 Chat 91311 480-A4
2500 Chat 91311 480-B7
8300 Chat 91311 500-C1
8300 Nor 91326 500-C1
BROWNSTONE
200 LHB 90631 738-D3
BROWNSTONE CIR
9000 CYP 90630 767-C6
BROWNSTONE ST
7900 Sunl 91040 503-G2
BROWNSTONE CREEK AV
2100 SIMI 93063 499-A2
BROWNWOOD PL
15400 BelA 90077 591-H1
BROXBOURNE TER
5200 LaCr 91214 504-F5
BROXTON AV
900 Wwd 90024 632-A3
BRUCE AV
800 WCOV 91790 638-E1
1100 GLDL 91202 564-B2
14700 BLF 90706 736-A3
BRUCE CT
1600 Echo 90026 594-E7
BRUCE LN
1000 BURB 91502 563-H2
2500 LHB 90631 708-B6
BRUCES PL
19600 SCTA 91351 4551-F3
BRUCK CIR
16800 HacH 91745 678-F4
BRUGES AV
4800 WdHl 91364 559-H4
BRUIN AV
2700 SELM 91733 636-J2
BRUIN PL
- LACo 91390 4461-A3
BRUIN ST
1600 LACo 90047 703-J7
BRUIN WK
- LA 90095 632-A1
BRUNA PL
2200 LFlz 90027 593-J2
BRUNACHE ST
7500 DWNY 90242 705-H5
8200 DWNY 90242 706-A6
BRUNANSKY WY
- WCOV 91792 638-J5
BRUNING AV
1300 GLDR 91740 599-F1
BRUNNELL CT
21100 Top 90290 560-B7
BRUNO ST
100 LA 90012 634-G2
BRUNSWICK AV
1200 SPAS 91030 595-E3
3600 LA 90039 594-D1
4000 LA 90039 564-C7
BRUNSWICK DR
5000 CYP 90630 767-C7
BRUNSWICK LN
11300 SBdC 91766 641-D3
BRUSHTON ST
5600 LA 90008 673-A2
5600 LA 90016 673-A2
BRUSSELS AV
11400 LA 91342 502-H1
11700 LA 91342 482-C2
BRYAN AV
2300 Ven 90291 671-J6
BRYAN CIR
21000 WAL 91789 639-G7
BRYAN PL
17600 GrnH 91344 481-A6
BRYANT CIR
900 GLDR 91740 569-D7
BRYANT DR
500 WHil 91304 499-D5
BRYANT DR E
1400 LBCH 90815 796-C5
BRYANT DR W
1400 LBCH 90815 796-C5
BRYANT LN
4000 CHNO 91710 641-D5
BRYANT PL
- StvR 91381 4640-B1
1200 MANB 90266 732-H7
BRYANT RD
900 LBCH 90815 796-C6
10800 ELMN 91731 597-D6
11300 ELMN 91732 597-D6
BRYANT ST
- CHNO 91710 641-E5
1200 PAS 91103 565-E1
14900 PanC 91402 531-H1
15800 LA 91343 531-D1
18400 Nor 91324 530-F1
18400 Nor 91325 530-H1
19700 Win 91306 530-C1
20800 LA 91304 530-A1
22100 LA 91304 529-J1
BRYANT WY
- LACo 91387 4551-H5
BRYCE CIR
12500 CRTS 90703 736-J7
12500 CRTS 90703 737-A7
BRYCE DR
- Cstc 91384 4459-G3
BRYCE RD
- SCTA 91354 4550-H1
1900 LACo 91733 637-D4
2200 ELMN 91732 637-E3
BRYCE ST
23000 WdHl 91364 559-G4
BRYCE CANYON WY
500 BREA 92821 709-C6
BRYCEDALE AV
1200 DUAR 91010 568-A5
BRYDON RD
7100 LVRN 91750 570-H4
BRYMER CT
18800 Nor 91326 480-H7
BRYMER LN
11500 Nor 91326 500-J1
BRYMER ST
18500 Nor 91326 500-H1
18500 Nor 91326 480-H7
BRYN ATHYN WY
24200 DBAR 91765 680-D2
BRYNHURST AV
3400 LA 90043 673-E5
3400 LACo 90043 673-E4
7100 LA 90043 703-E1
BRYN MAWR AV
1600 SMCA 90405 671-H3
BRYN MAWR CT
2300 LA 90068 593-F3
BRYN MAWR DR
6300 LA 90068 593-F2
BRYN MAWR RD
100 CLAR 91711 601-D5
4700 LFlz 90027 593-J2
4700 LFlz 90027 594-A2
BRYN MAWR WY
7000 WHIT 90601 677-E6
7000 WHIT 90608 677-E6
BRYNWOOD PL
2600 WCOV 91792 639-A7
BRYSON AV
8700 SGAT 90280 705-D4
10600 LYN 90262 705-D6
13400 PanC 91402 532-C1
BRYSON ST
13000 Pcma 91331 502-D7
13000 Pcma 91331 532-D1
BUBBLING CREEK LN
12500 CRTS 90703 736-J5
12500 CRTS 90703 737-A5
BUBBLING VIEW CIR
16400 CRTS 90703 736-J6
BUBBLING WELL DR
700 GLDR 91741 569-D3
BUBBLING WELL LN
5200 LCF 91011 534-J1
S BUBBLINGWELL RD
1000 WCOV 91790 638-F2
BUCCANEER ST
- LA 90292 671-H7
BUCHANAN CIR
8800 BPK 90620 767-H5
BUCHANAN CT
800 BREA 92821 709-C5
BUCHANAN DR
1600 POM 91767 600-J6
1700 POM 91767 601-A6
BUCHANAN PL
1800 MONP 91755 636-C4
BUCHANAN ST
400 HiPk 90042 595-A1
5000 CHNO 91710 641-G5
BUCHANAN WY
29800 Cstc 91384 4459-C7
BUCHANAN RANCH RD
27900 Llan 93544 4471-H3
27900 Llan 93544 (4561-H1 See Page 4471)
BUCHER AV
- LA 91342 481-J1
- LA 91342 482-A1
BUCHET DR
- PMDL 93552 4287-E1
16300 GrnH 91344 481-E7
BUCHI LN
- FUL 92833 738-C5
BUCK RD
7300 SBdC - (4562-F5 See Page 4471)
7300 SBdC 92372 (4562-F5 See Page 4471)
BUCKBOARD CIR
100 WCOV 91791 639-E1
BUCKBOARD CT
600 BREA 92821 709-B6
36500 PMDL 93550 4286-F5
BUCKBOARD LN
- RHLS 90274 823-E3
500 GLDR 91741 569-G4
BUCKBOARD PL
20200 LACo 91724 639-G1
BUCKEYE AV
12000 LA 91342 481-J6
BUCKEYE CT
22700 SCTA 91390 4460-J3
BUCKEYE ST
- SIMI 93063 499-A4
100 LPUE 91744 638-E7
300 PAS 91104 565-J3
600 PAS 91104 566-A3
BUCKEYE MEADOW LN
19700 Nor 91326 500-E1
BUCKHAVEN RD
35600 LACo 91390 4373-J1
BUCK HILL AV
5200 BPK 90621 738-A5
BUCK HILL PL
5300 BPK 90621 738-A5
BUCKHORN DR
25600 LACo 91302 629-A1
BUCKINGHAM AV
100 SDMS 91773 599-J2
BUCKINGHAM CT
6000 PMDL 93551 4104-E7
BUCKINGHAM LN
2300 BelA 90077 591-G2
BUCKINGHAM PKWY
5600 CULC 90230 672-J5
BUCKINGHAM PL
2000 GLDL 91206 535-B7
2000 GLDL 91206 565-B6
2500 LA 90016 633-E6
BUCKINGHAM RD
1600 LA 90019 633-E6
3000 GLDL 91206 565-B1
3400 LA 90016 673-E1
3700 LA 90008 673-D3
BUCKINGHAM WY
10900 MTCL 91763 641-G2
BUCKLAND DR
20500 WAL 91789 639-F3
BUCKLER AV
5800 LA 90043 673-C6
N BUCKLER AV
1200 ING 90302 673-C7
BUCKLES ST
8600 DWNY 90241 706-B6
BUCKNELL AV
100 CLAR 91711 601-C4
5700 LA 91607 562-G1
BUCKSKIN
- Actn 93510 4375-E6
BUCKSKIN AV
11100 MTCL 91763 641-E2
11300 MTCL 91710 641-E3
BUCKSKIN CIR
500 WAL 91789 639-D7
2000 LVRN 91750 570-G7
BUCKSKIN DR
21700 WAL 91789 639-H4
27600 Cstc 91384 4459-H6
BUCKSKIN LN
- SCTA 91387 4552-E4
- RHE 90274 793-F7
BUCKSKIN ST
39200 PMDL 93551 4195-E6
BUCKTHORN DR
100 BREA 92823 710-D5
BUCKTHORN RD
1900 SBdC 92397 (4652-F4 See Page 4651)
E BUCKTHORN ST
100 ING 90301 703-C3
W BUCKTHORN ST
100 ING 90301 703-B3
BUCKTHORNE RD
100 SBdC 92372 (4472-A5 See Page 4471)
BUCKTHORNE ST
2900 SBdC 92371 (4472-H5 See Page 4471)
BUCKWHEAT DR
23000 Llan 93544 4471-C6
BUCKWHEAT RD
7300 SBdC - (4562-F5 See Page 4471)
7300 SBdC 92372 (4562-F5 See Page 4471)
7700 SBdC 92371 (4562-F5 See Page 4471)
9300 SBdC 92372 (4472-F2 See Page 4471)
9700 SBdC 92371 (4472-F6 See Page 4471)
BUD CIR
1400 UPL 91786 571-J7
BUD CT
28500 SCTA 91350 4461-D4
BUDAU AV
2600 LA 90032 595-E7
BUDAU PL
5000 LA 90032 595-E7
BUDDY HOLLY DR
3200 LA 90068 563-C7
3300 Univ 91608 563-C7
BUDLEIGH DR
3200 HacH 91745 678-C6
BUDLONG AV
17500 GAR 90248 764-A1
17900 LA 90248 764-A1
20400 LACo 90502 764-A5
S BUDLONG AV
1900 LA 90007 634-A6
3400 LA 90007 674-A1
3700 LA 90037 674-A2
5800 LA 90044 674-A7
7200 LA 90044 704-A1
8600 LACo 90044 704-A3
12000 LACo 90044 734-A2
12800 GAR 90247 734-A2
BUDWOOD MTWY
3600 LACo 90265 629-H4
3600 LACo 90265 630-A5
3600 MAL 90265 630-A5
BUELAH AV
1100 City 90063 635-E4
BUELAH CIR
1000 City 90063 635-E4
BUELL ST
6000 BGDN 90201 705-H3
7400 DWNY 90241 705-J3
7400 DWNY 90241 706-B4
11400 SFSP 90670 706-G6
11700 NRWK 90650 706-G6
BUENA LOMA CT
300 Alta 91001 535-J6
BUENA PARK DR
3600 LA 91604 562-H6
BUENA TIERRA CIR
8500 BPK 90621 738-A4
BUENA TIERRA PL
8500 BPK 90621 738-A4
BUENAVENTURA ST
21900 WdHl 91364 560-A4
22000 WdHl 91364 559-J4
BUENA VISTA AV
- Brwd 90049 631-J2
100 LHB 90631 708-D7
100 LHB 90631 738-D1
3400 GLDL 91208 534-H4
S BUENA VISTA AV
100 POM 91766 640-G2
BUENA VISTA CT
- BqtC 91354 4460-D3
BUENA VISTA DR
100 CLAR 91711 601-D5
100 FUL 92833 738-E6
100 LA 90012 594-H7
100 LA 90012 634-H1
BUENA VISTA LN
- SPAS 91030 595-H1
BUENA VISTA RD
7600 SBdC 92372 (4562-D4 See Page 4471)
9400 SBdC 92372 (4472-C1 See Page 4471)
BUENA VISTA ST
400 SMRO 91108 595-J1
700 DUAR 91010 568-A7
700 MNRO 91016 568-A7
900 SPAS 91030 595-G1
2100 IRW 91010 568-A7
2300 IRW 91010 597-J1
2300 IRW 91010 598-A1
N BUENA VISTA ST
100 BURB 91506 563-E1
100 BURB 91505 563-E1
1000 BURB 91506 533-D7
1000 BURB 91505 533-D7
1800 BURB 91504 533-D3
S BUENA VISTA ST
100 BURB 91506 563-F3
100 BURB 91505 563-F3
300 BURB 91521 563-F3
BUENA VISTA TER
5700 HiPk 90042 565-D6
BUENA VISTA WY
- LAN 93536 4015-A7
43400 LAN 93536 4105-A1
BUENO DR
14600 CHLS 91709 680-H5
BUENOS AIRES DR
- LA 90095 632-A2
1800 LACo 91724 639-E1
BUFF AV
- LACo 91107 566-H4
BUFFALO AV
4600 Shrm 91423 562-C3
5200 VanN 91401 562-C2
5900 VanN 91401 532-C6
8300 PanC 91402 532-C1
BUFFALO TR
1200 GLDR 91740 569-G7
BUFFALO RIDGE RD
- LACo 93551 4375-J6
BUFFINGTON RD
4900 ELMN 91732 597-G4
W BUFFINGTON ST
1000 UPL 91784 571-H5
1700 POM 91766 640-E3
W BUFFINGTON WY
1300 UPL 91784 571-H5
BUFFWOOD PL
5500 AGRH 91301 558-A5
BUFORD AV
11500 HAW 90250 703-B7
S BUFORD AV
10000 ING 90304 703-B6
10000 Lenx 90304 703-B6
BUFORD ST
11600 CRTS 90703 766-G2
BUGGY WHIP CIR
19500 WAL 91789 639-D6
BUGGY WHIP DR
- RHLS 90274 823-C2
BUHMAN AV
7900 PRV 90660 706-F1
9000 DWNY 90240 706-E3
BULA CT
2700 Alta 91001 535-G5
BULFORD PL
5700 LACo 93536 4104-F7
BULLARD AV
2300 LA 90032 595-F7
2300 LA 90032 635-F1
BULLA VISTA
1000 Actn 93510 4465-J1
BULL CANYON RD
17600 GrnH 91344 481-A5
18100 GrnH 91344 480-J5
BULLDOG AV
2000 PMDL 93551 4195-D6
BULLDOG MTWY
- Ago 91301 588-A5
- LACo 90265 587-J7
- LACo 90265 588-A6
BULLDOG LATERAL
- Ago 91301 588-A5
- LACo 90265 588-A5
BULL FROG CIR
600 WAL 91789 639-D7
BULLIS RD
11000 LYN 90262 705-C7
11500 LYN 90262 735-B2
N BULLIS RD
100 COMP 90221 735-B3
12400 LYN 90262 735-B3
S BULLIS RD
100 COMP 90221 735-B5
900 RDom 90221 735-B5
BULLOCK ST
17100 Enc 91316 561-A1
BULLRUSH CANYON TR
- LACo 90704 5923-B2
BULOVA ST
4500 TOR 90503 763-C3
BULWER DR
8000 LA 90046 592-J2
8000 LA 90046 593-A1
BUNAL DR
3900 Shrm 91403 561-J6
BUNBURY DR
800 LACo 90601 637-G5
N BUNDY DR
100 Brwd 90049 631-F1
800 Brwd 90049 591-F6
S BUNDY DR
100 Brwd 90049 631-G3
1200 WLA 90025 631-J6
2000 WLA 90025 632-A7
2100 LA 90064 632-A7
2400 LA 90064 672-A1
3000 LA 90066 672-A1
BUNGALOW CT
26100 SCTA 91355 4550-F4
BUNGALOW DR
100 ELSG 90245 732-F1
600 ELSG 90245 702-F7
BUNGALOW PL
1000 ARCD 91006 567-F6
BUNKER AV
1500 SELM 91733 637-D5
1900 LACo 91733 637-D4
2200 ELMN 91732 637-E4
BUNKER CT
37200 PMDL 93550 4286-D4
BUNKER HILL AV
800 MTBL 90640 636-D7
N BUNKER HILL AV
500 LA 90012 634-F2
BUNNELLE AV
4600 LVRN 91750 570-E7
BUNNIE LN
4900 MAL 90265 626-G7
BURANO CT
700 VeCo 91377 557-H1
BURBANK BLVD
10400 NHol 91601 563-A1
11000 NHol 91601 562-J1
11200 NHol 91601 562-J1
11700 LA 91607 562-E1
12800 VanN 91401 562-A1
14500 VanN 91411 562-A1
14600 VanN 91411 561-H2
15400 Enc 91436 561-E2
17000 Enc 91316 561-A2
18100 Tarz 91356 561-A2
18200 Tarz 91356 560-H2
20700 WdHl 91367 560-A2
22100 WdHl 91367 559-D2
E BURBANK BLVD
100 BURB 91502 533-G6
100 BURB 91504 533-G6
W BURBANK BLVD
- BURB 91504 533-E7
- BURB 91502 533-E7
900 BURB 91506 533-E7
2500 BURB 91505 533-E7
2600 BURB 91505 563-C1
BURBANK CT
2200 LBCH 90814 795-G7
BURBANK MTWY
- CLAR 91711 571-C3
BURBANK RD
9300 SBdC 92371 (4472-H7 See Page 4471)
BURBON ST
6500 Res 91335 530-B7
BURCH WY
700 LHB 90631 708-E5
BURCHARD AV
5800 LA 90034 633-A6
5800 CULC 90232 633-A6
BURCHETT ST
100 GLDL 91203 564-D3
600 GLDL 91202 564-C3
W BURDICK DR
500 POM 91768 600-H7
BURDORF CT
- FUL 92833 738-D5
BURGEN AV
9800 LA 90034 632-G6
BURGER AV
500 ELA 90022 635-F7
S BURGER AV
900 ELA 90022 635-F7
900 ELA 90022 675-F1
BURGESS AV
11600 LACo 90604 707-E7
12200 LACo 90604 737-E1
12600 LMRD 90638 737-E1
BURGHARDT RD
8700 TEML 91775 596-G3
BURGOS DR
28700 LACo 90265 627-G2
BURGOYNE LN
4800 LCF 91011 535-D4
BURGROVE ST
1000 CRSN 90746 764-F4
BURGUNDY RD
4600 WdHl 91364 559-H4
BURGUNDY CROSSING LN
- SCTA 91351 4551-G7
BURIN AV
14300 LNDL 90260 733-C4
18200 TOR 90278 763-C2
19900 TOR 90503 763-C4
S BURIN AV
10000 ING 90304 703-C6
10400 Lenx 90304 703-C6
11100 HAW 90304 703-C6
BURK PL
600 BHLS 90210 592-G3
BURKE AV
8700 SGAT 90280 705-D4
E BURKE DR
200 MTBL 90640 636-F7
W BURKE DR
100 MTBL 90640 636-F7
BURKE PL
- StvR 91381 4550-A7
BURKE ST
9000 PRV 90660 706-E1
11400 LACo 90606 706-H2
11700 SFSP 90670 706-J2
11700 SFSP 90670 706-J2
11800 SFSP 90670 707-A2
BURKETT RD
1500 SELM 91733 637-D5
1800 LACo 91733 637-D5
2000 ELMN 91733 637-E4
2000 ELMN 91732 637-E4
BURKSHIRE AV
2700 LA 90064 672-B1
BURL AV
12100 HAW 90250 733-B1
S BURL AV
10000 ING 90304 703-B5
10000 Lenx 90304 703-B5
BURLAND AV
10800 Tuj 91042 504-A2
BURLEIGH DR
600 PAS 91105 565-E7
BURLESON ST
28900 AGRH 91301 558-A3
BURLINGAME AV
100 Brwd 90049 631-E4
5200 BPK 90621 738-A6
S BURLINGAME AV
700 Brwd 90049 631-F5
BURLINGHALL DR
500 Bxby 90807 765-E5
N BURLINGTON AV
100 Echo 90026 634-D2
S BURLINGTON AV
100 Echo 90026 634-C4
100 LA 90057 634-C4
300 LA 90017 634-C4
800 LA 90015 634-C4
900 LA 90006 634-C4
2000 LA 90007 634-B5
BURLINGTON CT
400 LBCH 90803 796-C7
BURLINGTON PL
1600 POM 91768 600-G6
10600 WHIT 90603 708-B5
BURLWOOD DR
30800 Cstc 91384 4459-A1
42900 LAN 93536 4105-C3
BURMA CT
1600 POM 91766 641-B4
BURMA RD
- RPV 90275 823-B3
9000 PRV 90660 676-E7
BURMA ST
17300 Enc 91316 561-B1
BURMESE PL
- PMDL 93551 4195-E7
N BURNABY AV
400 GLDR 91741 569-G4
BURNABY DR
1300 GLDR 91740 599-G1
4800 LACo 91724 599-G3
N BURNABY DR
100 GLDR 91741 569-G5
S BURNABY DR
100 GLDR 91741 569-G6
BURNELL DR
1600 LA 90065 594-H4
BURNELL OAKS LN
1000 ARCD 91006 567-B4
BURNET AV
4600 Shrm 91403 561-H4
5400 VanN 91411 561-H2
6800 VanN 91405 531-H3
7900 PanC 91402 531-H2
8800 LA 91343 531-H2
8800 LA 91343 501-H5
9900 MsnH 91345 501-H2
BURNETT ST
3500 LBCH 90815 795-J3
E BURNETT ST
100 LBCH 90806 795-E3
900 SIGH 90755 795-G3
4500 LBCH 90815 796-A3
W BURNETT ST
100 LBCH 90806 795-C3
1200 LBCH 90810 795-B3
BURNEY PL
3000 OrCo 90720 796-H4
BURNHAM AV
5600 BPK 90621 737-H7
6200 BPK 90621 767-H1
BURNHAM ST
11300 Brwd 90049 631-J3
BURNING TREE DR
5400 LCF 91011 535-D2
16100 Llan 93544 4469-G1
BURNING TREE LN
- SLB 90740 796-H7
13600 SLB 90740 826-H1
BURNING TREE RD
600 FUL 92833 738-B5
BURNLEY PL
9700 LA 90210 592-G2
BURNS AV
4200 LA 90029 594-A6
7400 DWNY 90241 705-J4
7800 DWNY 90241 706-A4
BURNS PL
25400 StvR 91381 4550-C7
S BURNSIDE AV
300 LA 90036 633-C2
1200 LA 90019 633-C3
2000 LA 90016 633-B6
3500 LA 90016 673-B1
3800 LA 90008 673-B2
BURNSIDE CIR
300 LA 90036 633-B1
BURNT TREE LN
20200 WAL 91789 639-E7
BURNTWOOD ST
5700 SGAT 90280 705-G6
BURNWELL CT
36300 PMDL 93550 4286-B6
BURR CT
24500 SCTA 91321 4640-H2
BURR ST
900 LA 90032 595-E5
BURRARD AV
1500 CMRC 90022 676-A3
BURRELL LN
- RPV 90275 823-B3
BURRELL PL
800 LA 90292 672-A6
BURRELL ST
800 LA 90292 672-A6
N BURRIS AV
100 COMP 90221 735-B4
S BURRIS AV
100 COMP 90221 735-B4
BURRITT AV
2400 RBCH 90278 733-B6
BURRITT WY
3300 GLDL 91214 504-D5
BURRO RD
- Actn 93510 4375-A5
BURROUGHS PL
25700 StvR 91381 4550-B7
BURROUGHS RD
9000 LA 90046 592-G2
BURROUGHS WY
36800 PMDL 93552 4287-B4
BURSON RD
2300 Top 90290 589-H2
BURT AV
1200 SDMS 91773 570-B7
BURT CT
15600 SCTA 91387 4462-E7
BURT ST
2400 SBdC 91784 571-H2
BURTIS ST
9200 SGAT 90280 705-F4
BURTON AV
2700 BURB 91504 533-C5
3000 RSMD 91770 636-G2
3200 LYN 90262 735-B1
5000 LACo 91776 596-G4
5000 SGBL 91776 596-G4
5700 SGBL 91775 596-G3
5900 TEML 91775 596-G2
6300 LACo 91775 596-G2
BURTON PL
3800 LVRN 91750 600-F1
8200 Res 91335 531-A2
S BURTON RD
1700 GLDR 91740 599-D2
BURTON ST
8700 BLF 90706 735-J5
8800 BLF 90706 736-A5
11000 SunV 91352 532-J2
11000 SunV 91352 533-A2
11900 NHol 91605 532-D2
13300 PanC 91402 532-A2
14900 PanC 91402 531-H2
17000 VanN 91406 531-C2
17300 Nor 91325 531-B2
17700 Res 91335 531-A2
20900 LA 91304 530-B2
22100 LA 91304 529-E2
BURTON WY
2800 RowH 91748 679-C7
8500 LA 90048 632-G1
8800 BHLS 90211 632-G1
9100 BHLS 90210 632-G1
16200 LACo 91390 4462-C3
E BURTREE ST
16400 LACo 91744 638-G4
BURWOOD AV
5000 LACo 91722 598-G3
5800 HiPk 90042 565-C7
N BURWOOD AV
300 WCOV 91790 598-G7
BURWOOD ST
1200 LHB 90631 738-E1
1500 FUL 92835 738-E1
BURWOOD TER
600 HiPk 90042 565-D7
E BUSBY DR
13600 LACo 90605 737-C1
14100 LACo 90604 737-D1
14300 LACo 90604 707-E7
BUSCH DR
5500 MAL 90265 627-D7
5600 MAL 90265 667-C1
BUSCH PL
500 PAS 91105 565-G7
12900 SFSP 90670 707-B3
BUSCH GARDEN CT
1000 PAS 91105 565-F7
BUSCH GARDEN DR
600 PAS 91105 565-F7
BUSCH GARDEN LN
600 PAS 91105 565-F7
BUSH WY
5600 CULC 90230 672-G5
BUSHNELL AV
1600 SPAS 91030 595-J3
N BUSHNELL AV
- ALH 91801 595-J5
S BUSHNELL AV
100 ALH 91801 595-J5
1900 ALH 91803 635-J1
BUSHNELL WY
5400 HiPk 90042 595-D4
BUSHROD LN
2400 BelA 90077 592-A3
BUSHWICK ST
3200 LA 90065 594-G2
BUSINESS CIR
11000 CRTS 90703 736-F7
BUSINESS PKWY
19700 INDS 91789 679-E3
BUSINESS ST
4100 Bxby 90807 765-D6
BUSINESS CENTER DR
1500 DUAR 91010 568-B6
15800 IRW 91706 598-F2
19300 Nor 91324 530-F1
BUSINESS CENTER PKWY
42800 LAN 93535 4106-A3
42800 LAN 93535 4105-J3
BUSIRIS AV
12000 NRWK 90650 706-H7
BUTLER AV
300 NLB 90805 735-C6
1400 WLA 90025 631-J5
1400 WLA 90025 632-A5
1600 COMP 90221 735-C6
2200 LA 90064 632-B7
2700 LA 90064 672-C1
2700 LYN 90262 704-J7
2700 LYN 90262 705-A7
3000 LA 90066 672-C1
6200 NLB 90805 765-C1
S BUTLER AV
1300 COMP 90221 735-C6
12800 RDom 90221 735-C3
BUTLER CT
100 CLAR 91711 571-D6
BUTTE CT
500 BREA 92821 709-B4
BUTTE ST
600 LACo 90732 823-J5
800 CLAR 91711 601-B2
BUTTERCREEK DR
2700 PAS 91107 566-F2
BUTTERCUP DR
2700 PMDL 93550 4286-F5
BUTTERCUP ST
40400 PMDL 93551 4194-G2
BUTTERCUP WY
44000 LAN 93535 4016-C7
BUTTERFIELD AV
1400 SDMS 91773 570-C6
2800 LVRN 91750 600-G2
11300 MTCL 91763 641-F3
11700 CHNO 91710 641-F4
BUTTERFIELD CT
5000 CULC 90230 672-H3
BUTTERFIELD LN
16000 CRTS 90703 736-J4
BUTTERFIELD PL
12000 CHNO 91710 641-F5
BUTTERFIELD RD
- HIDH 91302 559-B3
500 POM 91766 640-F3
1200 LA 90064 632-E6
N BUTTERFIELD RD
500 WCOV 91791 598-H6
S BUTTERFIELD RD
100 WCOV 91791 598-H7
200 WCOV 91791 638-H3
BUTTERFIELD STAGE RD
10600 Litl 93543 4378-D6
BUTTERFLY LN
4600 LA 90032 595-D6
BUTTERNUT CT
- CRSN 90746 764-H2
BUTTERNUT LN
- PMDL 93551 4285-D3
BUTTERNUT WY
1600 DBAR 91765 680-A4
BUTTERSCOTCH LN
42400 LAN 93536 4104-F5
BUTTONS AV
5300 TEML 91780 596-J4
BUTTONWILLOW DR
19800 Win 91306 530-E3
BUTTONWOOD AV
6600 VeCo 91377 558-B2
BUTTONWOOD DR
200 BREA 92821 709-C6
BUTTONWOOD LN
18400 RowH 91748 679-A7
BUTTRAM ST
15500 HacH 91745 678-A6
BUZZARD PEAK MTWY
19900 LACo 91724 639-F2
20000 WAL 91789 639-F2
BYCROFT ST
15000 HacH 91745 678-A2
BYERS ST
8400 DWNY 90242 706-A6
BYERTON CT
1700 RPV 90275 823-J2
BYFIELD RD
30200 Cstc 91384 4459-B2
BYGROVE ST
200 COV 91722 599-B2
16600 LACo 91722 598-G3
BYNNER DR
400 LA 90732 823-H5
BYNUM ST
8000 LBCH 90808 796-J1
S BYRD AV
8300 ING 90305 703-G2
BYRD ST
16300 VanN 91406 531-F3
BYRNE DR
5500 LPMA 90623 767-D3
BYRNE PL
- Saug 91350 4461-E6
BYRON AV
12500 GrnH 91344 481-B5
BYRON CT
1500 POM 91768 600-F7
BYRON DR
- LAN 93535 4016-D6
43700 LAN 93535 4106-D1
BYRON PL
- Cstc 91384 4459-G5
2600 LA 90046 592-H2
BYRON RD
8100 WHIT 90606 707-B1
BYRON WY
43600 StvR 91381 4550-A7
43600 StvR 91381 4640-A1
BYWAYS ST
11000 SELM 91733 637-C5
BYWOOD DR
2400 GLDL 91206 565-A4

C

C
- PRM 90723 735-G6
18600 LACo 91744 679-B2
C ST
- LA 90245 732-D1
- LACo 90220 764-J3
- LACo 91724 599-E2
- LKWD 90712 766-A3
- PdlR 90293 702-C7
- PdlR 90293 732-D1
- SPed 90731 824-B1
- WCOV 91791 638-J4
1800 LVRN 91750 600-F3
4800 CHNO 91710 641-G7
10600 LACo 90230 672-H4
13300 LA 91342 481-F3
E C ST
100 Wilm 90744 794-F7
W C ST
100 Wilm 90744 794-E7
C WK
1000 Wilm 90744 794-D7
CABALLERO BLVD
6000 BPK 90620 767-E1
CABALLERO CT
- Tarz 91356 560-J4
CABALLERO RD
1400 ARCD 91006 567-B3
CABALLERO TR
- Actn 93510 4375-C7
- Actn 93510 4465-C1
CABALLEROS RD
- RHLS 90274 823-E3
CABALLETA DR
26600 SCTA 91350 4550-J1
CABALLO AV
1100 GLDR 91740 569-J7
CABALLO RANCH RD
1400 SDMS 91750 570-F4
CABANA AV
300 LPUE 91744 638-B5
900 LACo 91744 638-C4
1400 WCOV 91790 638-D3
S CABANA AV
1700 WCOV 91790 638-C3
CABANA LN
3200 LAN 93536 4105-B2
CABANA PL
37800 PMDL 93550 4286-G2
CABANAS AV
9600 Tuj 91042 504-C5
CABELL AV
13200 DWNY 90242 736-C2
14000 BLF 90706 736-C3
S CABERNET CIR
- ANA 92804 767-H7
CABERNET CT
- SunV 91352 533-C2
CABERNET RD
- PMDL 93551 4104-D6
CABEZO CT
23700 SCTA 91355 4550-G4
CABIN DR
42600 LACo 93532 4102-G5
CABINDA DR
14400 HacH 91745 677-H2
W CABLE PL
200 ING 90302 703-C2
CABO CT
41800 PMDL 93551 4104-C6
CABO DR
- WHIT 90603 708-A6
CABO BLANCO DR
3100 HacH 91745 678-D6
CABOOSE DR
44800 LAN 93535 4016-C5
CABORA DR
7500 PdlR 90293 702-B2
7500 Wch 90045 702-D2
W CABOT DR
3200 ANA 92804 767-H6

STREET Block City ZIP Pg-Grid

CABOT LN
4700 LVRN 91750 570-E7
CABOT PL
1700 MTBL 90640 636-C7
CABOT ST
2300 LA 90031 594-G5
CABRA DR
200 WAL 91789 639-G7
CABRAL ST
18800 SCTA 91351 4551-G1
CABREE CT
45000 LAN 93535 4016-B5
CABRERA AV
27100 SCTA 91350 4461-A7
CABRILLO AV
1100 Ven 90291 671-H6
1200 TOR 90501 763-H7
1400 ALH 91803 595-G7
1700 ALH 91803 635-G1
2500 TOR 90501 793-H2
14300 NRWK 90650 737-B3
23800 LMTA 90717 793-H2
N CABRILLO AV
100 SPed 90731 824-A3
S CABRILLO AV
100 SPed 90731 824-B6
2600 SPed 90731 854-A1
CABRILLO BLVD
3200 LA 90066 672-A3
CABRILLO CIR
200 FUL 92835 738-G2
CABRILLO DR
- AVA 90704 5923-G4
900 DUAR 91010 568-A5
900 GLDL 91207 564-F2
1100 BHLS 90210 592-F5
CABRILLO LN
- SCTA 91354 4460-G4
20000 CRTS 90703 766-H4
CABRILLO RD
- ARCD 91007 566-J6
CABRILLO ST
- SCTA 91355 4460-E6
1700 WCOV 91791 638-J1
11000 WHIT 90603 708-A5
CABRILLO WY
9700 CYP 90630 767-E7
11200 MTCL 91763 641-E3
CABRILLO VILLAS ST
4600 HiPk 90042 595-D4
CABRINI DR
9700 LA 91504 533-D3
CABRINI DR E
9600 LA 91504 533-D3
CABRINI DR W
- LA 91504 533-D2
CABRIOLE AV
11100 Nor 91326 500-H1
CABRIOLET CT
6100 LACo 93536 4104-E5
CABRITO RD
8000 VanN 91406 531-G2
14000 PanC 91402 532-A3
CACERAS ST
22000 SCTA 91350 4461-A7
CACHALOTE ST
4100 WdHl 91364 560-B6
CACHAN PL
30000 RPV 90275 822-H2
CACHE ST
8700 LACo 93551 4193-J2
CACHUMA CIR
8100 BPK 90621 737-J6
CACHUMA LN
15700 SCTA 91387 4552-D6
CACILLEY RD
3700 SBdC 92371 (4472-J1 See Page 4471)
CACTI CT
- PanC 91402 502-A6
CACTUS AV
9600 Chat 91311 499-H5
CACTUS CIR
8000 BPK 90620 767-J3
CACTUS CT
- Actn 93510 4374-H6
600 BREA 92821 709-B6
CACTUS DR
1000 PMDL 93551 4285-G1
1600 LAN 93535 4016-C6
5100 LVRN 91750 570-G4
14500 CHLS 91709 680-G5
CACTUS LN
- CRSN 90745 794-G2
CACTUS TR
26800 CALB 91301 558-G7
26800 CALB 91301 588-G1
CADBROOK DR
300 LPUE 91744 638-C6
CADBURY RD
5200 WHIT 90601 677-B3
CADDINGTON DR
1400 RPV 90275 823-J2
CADDY ST
9000 PRV 90660 676-E7
CADE ST
2800 NLB 90805 735-H7
CADENHORN DR
- Ago 91301 587-G4
CADET CT
3100 LA 90068 593-C1
CADILLAC AV
2300 LA 90034 632-J6
6000 LA 90034 633-A6
CADILLAC CT
- LA 91342 481-H4
CADILLAC DR
1800 POM 91767 600-J6
CADISON ST
4500 TOR 90503 763-B3
CADIZ AV
2300 UPL 91784 571-H3
CADIZ CIR
5000 LPMA 90623 767-C4
CADIZ CT
300 Ven 90291 671-H6
CADIZ DR
24500 LMTA 90717 793-H3
CADIZ LN
6100 LBCH 90803 826-D1
CADIZ ST
900 MONP 91754 636-A3
CADLEY DR
3900 LVRN 91750 570-F6
CADMAN DR
3600 LFlz 90027 594-C1
CADMAN LN
- FUL 92833 738-C5
CADMIA CT
36900 PMDL 93552 4287-B4
CADMUS AV
13900 LACo 90061 734-D3
CADROW AV
400 LACo 91744 638-G6
CADWELL ST
15200 LPUE 91744 638-D5
15800 LACo 91744 638-E5
CAERN AV
11400 Tuj 91042 503-J1
CAESAR AV
1100 LACo 91107 566-F7
CAFFEL WY
13300 LACo 90605 707-C4
CAFFREY
1600 WCOV 91791 638-J3
CAGLE ST
- KeCo 93560 3834-G3
CAGLIERO ST
13700 LACo 91746 638-A2
CAGNEY ST
17200 GmH 91344 481-B5
CAHILL AV
5600 Tarz 91356 560-G1
CAHILL PL
1100 DBAR 91765 680-B2
CAHITA AV
14300 LACo 90220 734-E3
CAHUENGA BLVD
4100 LA 91604 563-B4
4100 LA 91602 563-B4
4800 NHol 91601 563-B4
5900 NHol 91601 533-B7
6000 NHol 91606 533-B7
6100 LA 91505 533-B7
N CAHUENGA BLVD
500 LA 90004 593-F7
700 LA 90038 593-F6
1300 Hlwd 90028 593-F4
1900 LA 90068 593-E3
CAHUENGA BLVD E
2400 LA 90068 593-D1
3000 LA 90068 563-D7
CAHUENGA BLVD W
2500 LA 90068 593-D1
3100 LA 90068 563-B6
3600 LA 91604 563-B6
CAHUENGA TER
6500 LA 90068 593-E3
CAHUENGA PARK TR
6800 LA 90068 593-D1
CAINE DR
17300 ART 90701 736-G7
CAIRN AV
14300 LACo 90220 734-E3
CAIRNGROVE AV
7700 LACo 91741 569-C3
CAIRNLOCH ST
22100 CALB 91302 559-J7
CAIRO AV
18000 CRSN 90746 764-D2
CAIRO WK
14300 Shrm 91423 562-A6
CAITHNESS ST
18700 Nor 91326 480-H6
CAITLIN AV
1100 LAN 93535 4016-B7
CAITLIN LN
20100 SCTA 91350 4461-D5
CAITLYN CIR
- WLKV 91361 586-H2
CAJON AV
800 WCOV 91791 638-J2
5400 BPK 90621 737-J6
S CAJON AV
600 WCOV 91791 638-J1
E CAJON CIR
1800 WCOV 91791 638-J3
CAJON DR
1300 LHB 90631 708-B7
1300 LHB 90631 738-B1
CAJON RD
- UPL 91784 571-G7
CAJON PASS TR
3100 DBAR 91765 679-J7
3100 DBAR 91765 709-J1
CAJUN CT
- CanP 91303 529-J5
CAJUN ST
- LAN 93535 4016-F6
43200 LAN 93535 4106-F1
CALABAR AV
15700 PRM 90723 735-E5
CALABASAS AV
8100 PdlR 90293 702-B3
CALABASAS RD
23400 WdHl 91364 559-D5
23400 LA 91302 559-D5
23500 CALB 91302 559-B5
CALABASAS HILLS RD
- CALB 91301 558-G7
- CALB 91301 588-G1
CALABASAS PEAK MTWY
23300 CALB 91302 589-E2
23300 LACo 91302 589-E2
23300 Top 90290 589-E4
23300 CALB 90290 589-E2
CALABASH PL
5000 WdHl 91364 559-H3
CALABASH ST
22700 WdHl 91364 559-G4
CALABRIA
28800 AGRH 91301 558-B4
CALABRIA DR
700 GLDR 91741 569-F3
CALADA AV
4400 PRV 90660 676-G2
CALADA ST
1100 LA 90023 675-C1
CALADERO ST
19100 Tarz 91356 560-G5
CALADIUM PL
- BqtC 91354 4460-E6
CALADRE AV
12200 DWNY 90242 705-J7
CALAFIA ST
1800 GLDL 91208 534-H7
CALAHAN ST
14200 PanC 91402 502-A7
14800 PanC 91402 501-J7
16000 LA 91343 501-D7
16900 Nor 91325 501-C7
18600 Nor 91324 500-G7
CALAIS CT
- Ago 91301 558-G3
CALAIS ST
13800 BALD 91706 598-A3
CALAISE CT
30800 WLKV 91362 557-F5
CALAMAR ST
1700 TOR 90501 793-H1
CALAMINE DR
26900 CALB 91301 558-F6
CALANDA AV
2600 Alta 91001 535-G4
CALANDRI LN
2800 LAN 93536 4105-C4
CALATINA DR
1600 POM 91766 640-G4
CALATRANA DR
5000 WdHl 91364 560-A3
CALAVERA PL
1700 FUL 92833 738-D4
CALAVERAS CIR
5600 LPMA 90623 767-D3
CALAVERAS CT
3700 CHNO 91710 641-C5
CALAVERAS DR
700 WAL 91789 639-B6
CALAVERAS RD
200 SBdC 92372 4471-J2
200 SBdC 92372 (4472-B2 See Page 4471)
300 SDMS 91773 570-C7
300 SDMS 91773 600-C1
600 SDMS 91750 570-D7
CALAVERAS ST
200 LA 90065 595-A5
E CALAVERAS ST
- Alta 91001 535-H6
500 Alta 91001 536-A6
W CALAVERAS ST
- Alta 91001 535-F5
CALBAS ST
800 CRSN 90745 764-E6
CALBOURNE DR
1100 DBAR 91789 679-E3
CALBOURNE LN
- VeCo 91361 586-G1
CALBUCO AV
39100 LACo 93591 4200-F5
CALCEDONY CT
37800 PMDL 93552 4287-A1
CALCETA AV
- LACo 93591 4200-F4
CALCITE CT
31900 Cstc 91384 4369-H5
CALCUTTA ST
13200 LA 91342 482-C3
17400 LACo 91744 678-H1
CALCUTTA PASS LN
- SCTA 91350 4550-H5
CALDEN AV
8800 SGAT 90280 704-J3
CALDER DR
6800 GLDR 91741 569-D5
CALDERO LN
2300 LCF 91011 534-H2
2300 Mont 91020 534-H2
CALDERON RD
4300 WdHl 91364 559-H3
CALDERWOOD LN
700 PAS 91107 566-G2
E CALDERWOOD ST
5100 LBCH 90815 796-B4
CALDORA AV
15700 PRM 90723 735-E5
CALDRON ST
36700 PMDL 93552 4286-J4
CALDUS AV
7100 VanN 91406 531-B4
CALDWELL AV
7900 WHIT 90602 677-D7
7900 WHIT 90602 707-D1
CALDWELL CT
400 SDMS 91773 600-B1
CALDWELL ST
2300 COMP 90221 735-C6
2300 RDom 90221 735-C6
E CALDWELL ST
100 COMP 90220 734-J6
100 COMP 90220 735-A6
300 COMP 90221 735-A6
W CALDWELL ST
100 COMP 90220 734-E6
CALEANDRA ST
36500 PMDL 93552 4286-J5
CALEB ST
500 GLDL 91202 534-D7
CALECHE RD
6000 LACo 93536 4104-F5
CALEDONIA CT
45700 LAN 93534 4015-F3
CALEDONIA WY
4200 LA 90065 564-G7
CALENDA DR
5100 WdHl 91367 559-F3
CALENDULA DR
8000 BPK 90620 767-J2
CALERA AV
1000 COV 91722 599-C2
5200 LACo 91722 599-C2
6000 LACo 91722 569-B7
6200 AZU 91702 569-B7
N CALERA AV
6300 AZU 91702 569-B5
7000 GLDR 91741 569-B4
S CALERA AV
300 AZU 91702 599-B1
CALETA RD
4300 Ago 91301 558-B7
CALEX DR
- SCTA 91354 4460-G3
CALGARY LN
1900 BelA 90077 592-A4
CALGROVE BLVD
23300 SCTA 91321 4640-G3
23900 Nwhl 91321 4640-G3
23900 StvR 91381 4640-G3
CALHAVEN DR
20300 LACo 91390 4461-C4
20400 SCTA 91390 4461-C4
CALHOUN AV
4300 Shrm 91423 562-B4
5300 VanN 91401 562-B2
5900 VanN 91401 532-A6
6700 VanN 91405 532-A5
8100 PanC 91402 532-B2
CALIBURN DR
600 Wats 90002 704-E3
CALICO
1900 WCOV 91791 638-J4
CALICO AV
3900 PRV 90660 676-G1
45200 LAN 93535 4016-E4
CALICO CT
300 BREA 92821 709-B4
1100 SDMS 91740 570-A7
CALICO WY
36500 PMDL 93550 4286-H5
CALICUT RD
27400 MAL 90265 627-J6
CALIENTE AV
17400 CRTS 90703 737-D7
CALIENTE CIR
17800 CRTS 90703 737-D7
CALIENTE PL
17600 CRTS 90703 737-D7
S CALIENTE ST
500 MONP 91754 635-G3
CALIFA PL
5700 WdHl 91367 560-D1
CALIFA ST
5800 WdHl 91367 559-E1
10400 NHol 91601 563-A1
11000 NHol 91601 562-H1
11700 LA 91607 562-E1
13500 VanN 91401 562-A1
14700 VanN 91411 561-H1
17300 Enc 91316 561-A1
18100 Tarz 91356 561-A1
18800 Tarz 91356 560-G1
20200 WdHl 91367 560-A1
CALIFON ST
1600 CRSN 90745 764-G6
CALIFORNIA AV
100 INDS 91744 638-E2
100 MTBL 90640 676-C2
100 SMCA 90403 671-D2
100 WCOV 91790 598-G7
200 WCOV 91790 638-E2
500 Ven 90291 671-H5
1300 SMCA 90403 631-F7
1500 LPUE 91744 638-E2
1500 LACo 91744 638-E2
2300 LBCH 90806 795-F2
2300 SIGH 90755 795-F2
2600 Bxby 90807 795-F2
2600 ELMN 91733 637-D2
3200 ELMN 91731 637-D1
3400 Bxby 90807 765-E5
3400 ELMN 91731 597-D7
5400 NLB 90805 765-E2
6200 BELL 90201 675-C6
6300 NLB 90805 735-E7
6800 GLDR 91741 569-C5
7000 BELL 90201 705-B2
7200 HNTP 90255 675-B7
7200 HNTP 90255 705-B2
7800 WHIT 90602 677-F7
7900 WHIT 90602 707-F1
8100 SGAT 90280 705-B2
8300 WHIT 90605 707-E2
10400 LYN 90262 705-B6
14400 BALD 91706 598-C3
15100 PRM 90723 735-H6
16200 BLF 90706 736-D6
E CALIFORNIA AV
100 GLDL 91206 564-F4
N CALIFORNIA AV
300 LPUE 91744 638-C5
600 LACo 91744 638-C5
S CALIFORNIA AV
100 MNRO 91016 567-H5
1300 COMP 90221 735-B6
1900 LACo 91010 567-H5
2000 LACo 91016 567-H7
2500 MNRO 91016 597-G1
2600 IRW 91706 597-G1
W CALIFORNIA AV
100 GLDL 91203 564-C4
E CALIFORNIA BLVD
- PAS 91105 565-J6
200 PAS 91106 565-J6
200 PAS 91101 565-J6
500 PAS 91106 566-A6
500 PAS 91101 566-A6
1000 PAS 91125 566-A6
1000 PAS 91126 566-A6
1600 SMRO 91108 566-D6
2700 PAS 91107 566-D6
3100 LACo 91107 566-G6
W CALIFORNIA BLVD
- PAS 91105 565-G6
CALIFORNIA CT
600 Ven 90291 671-H5
CALIFORNIA DR
500 CLAR 91711 601-B3
CALIFORNIA PL
1500 POM 91768 600-G7
2900 SMCA 90403 631-G6
4400 Bxby 90807 765-E5
14400 WHIT 90602 677-F7
CALIFORNIA PL S
2200 SMCA 90403 631-G6
CALIFORNIA ST
- ARCD 91006 567-D5
100 LHB 90631 708-E6
200 ELSG 90245 732-G2
600 ELSG 90245 702-G7
2400 LACo 90255 704-J1
2600 TOR 90503 763-E5
2700 LACo 90255 705-A1
2900 HNTP 90255 705-A1
8100 BPK 90621 767-J1
N CALIFORNIA ST
100 BURB 91505 563-D2
100 SGBL 91775 596-F3
100 SGBL 91776 596-F3
1400 BURB 91505 533-D7
2700 BURB 91504 533-D4
S CALIFORNIA ST
100 SGBL 91776 596-F4
200 BURB 91523 563-E4
200 BURB 91505 563-E4
300 BURB 91522 563-E4
2000 SGBL 91776 636-F1
W CALIFORNIA TER
100 PAS 91105 565-F5
CALIFORNIA TR
1700 Top 90290 590-C2
CALIFORNIA INCLINE
900 SMCA 90403 671-D2
CALIFORNIA OAK ST
- SIMI 93063 499-A3
CALIMALI RD
20900 WdHl 91364 560-C5
CALINO AV
1800 BALD 91706 638-B1
CALIPATRIA DR
22400 CALB 91302 559-H7
CALISTOGA ST
38800 PMDL 93551 4195-D6
CALKIN ST
14700 HacH 91745 677-J2
CALL ST
9200 PRV 90660 676-E7
CALLA WY
19000 SCTA 91351 4551-F2
CALLADA PL
4400 Tarz 91356 560-H4
CALLADO WY
21800 Top 90290 590-A1
CALLAHAN PL
22000 CRSN 90745 764-F7
CALLALILY CIR
8000 BPK 90620 767-J3
CALLA LILY CT
14700 SCTA 91387 4462-F4
CALLAWAY AV
20300 LKWD 90715 767-A4
CALLE CT
25700 SCTA 91355 4550-G5
CALLE RD
- TOR 90505 793-F5
CALLE ADRA
1000 DUAR 91010 568-D5
CALLE ADRIANA
2300 SDMS 91773 640-A1
CALLE AGATA
2300 SDMS 91773 600-A7
CALLE AGOSTO
100 SDMS 91773 600-A6
CALLE AGUA FELIZ
39200 LACo 91390 4192-C3
CALLE ALCAZAR
300 WAL 91789 679-D1
400 WAL 91789 639-D7
CALLE ALEGRE
1000 GLDL 91208 564-J2
CALLE ALEGRIA
1900 FUL 92833 738-C4
CALLE ALICIA
19900 WAL 91789 679-E1
CALLE ALTAMIRA
24700 CALB 91302 559-D7
CALLE ALTO
1700 SDMS 91773 599-J6
CALLE AMABLE
900 GLDL 91208 564-J2
CALLE AMANDA
2300 SDMS 91773 600-A7
CALLE AMAPOLA
1100 SDMS 91773 599-J7
CALLE AMIGO
37100 PMDL 93550 4286-F4
CALLE AMIGOS
- LACo 91390 4373-E7
CALLE ANDREA
100 SDMS 91773 600-B7
100 SDMS 91773 640-B1
CALLE AQUADUCTO
7100 Litl 93543 4377-G2
CALLE ARAGON
600 VeCo 91377 557-J1
5700 LVRN 91750 570-H3
CALLE ARBOLADA
16600 PacP 90272 630-G1
CALLE ARBOR
23800 SCTA 91355 4550-F6
CALLE ARCANO
1100 SDMS 91773 599-J5
CALLE ARDILLA
24600 CALB 91302 559-E7
CALLE ARINO
23300 SCTA 91355 4550-H5
CALLE ARROYO
800 SDMS 91773 600-A5
15900 LACo 91390 4192-D3
CALLE AURORA
17800 RowH 91748 678-H5
CALLE AVENTURA
2600 RPV 90275 823-G5
CALLE AZUL
1000 GLDL 91208 564-J2
CALLE BAJA
3200 WCOV 91792 679-E1
6800 WAL 91789 679-E1
CALLE BANDERA
1200 SDMS 91773 599-J5
CALLE BARCELONA
15100 CHLS 91709 680-H5
17600 RowH 91748 678-F5
CALLE BECERRA
200 WAL 91789 679-E1
CALLE BELICIA
2200 SDMS 91773 600-A7
CALLE BELLA
900 GLDL 91208 564-J2
CALLE BELLEVISTA
16600 PacP 90272 630-G1
CALLE BELLEZA
1800 RowH 91748 678-J5
CALLE BERRO
39300 LACo 91390 4192-C3
CALLE BIENVENIDA
2200 CHLS 91709 680-J5
CALLE BOGOTA
1900 RowH 91748 678-H5
CALLE BONITA
13800 LACo 91390 4462-J1
37000 PMDL 93550 4286-G4
39100 LACo 91390 4192-F4
CALLE BORREGO
400 WAL 91789 639-D7
400 WAL 91789 679-D1
CALLE BRECEDA
- IRW 91706 598-F3
CALLE BRILLANTE
- BqtC 91354 4460-E3
CALLE BRISA
- BqtC 91354 4460-E3
CALLE BRITTANY
16600 PacP 90272 630-H1
CALLE BURROLA
15700 IRW 91706 598-E4
CALLE CABALLERO
1300 SDMS 91773 599-J5
CALLE CABALLEROS
300 WAL 91789 679-D1
CALLE CABANAS
- LACo 91390 4192-E3
CALLE CABRILLO
100 TOR 90277 793-A2
CALLE CADIZ
19800 WAL 91789 639-E7
CALLE CALIFORNIOS
41800 LAN 93536 4105-B6
CALLE CAMPANA
200 WAL 91789 679-D1
CALLE CANDELA
1900 FUL 92833 738-C4
CALLE CANDIDA
100 SDMS 91773 640-A1
CALLE CANELA
300 SDMS 91773 600-B7
CALLE CANON
3600 CALB 91302 559-D7
CALLE CANTA
800 GLDL 91208 565-A2
CALLE CARONA
15600 LACo 91390 4192-E3
CALLE CARRILLO
700 SDMS 91773 600-A6
800 SDMS 91773 599-J6
CALLE CASCADA
39400 LACo 91390 4192-D3
CALLE CASCARRON
39700 LACo 91390 4192-E3
CALLE CASITAS
- LACo 91390 4192-D2
CALLE CATALINA
1700 SDMS 91773 600-A6
CALLE CECILIA
1200 SDMS 91773 599-J7
CALLE CEDRO
24800 CALB 91302 559-D7
CALLE CERRITO
30200 CynC 91351 4462-C4
CALLE CERRITOS
- LACo 91390 4192-D3
CALLE CHEVAL
15900 LACo 91390 4192-D2
CALLE CHIQUITO
39600 LACo 91390 4192-C3
CALLE CIERVOS
1500 SDMS 91773 599-H5
CALLE CINCO
400 MTBL 90640 676-D3
CALLECITA DR
2600 Alta 91001 535-J5
CALLE CLARITA
41800 LAN 93536 4105-B6
CALLE CLEMENTE
1400 LVRN 91750 570-F6
CALLE COLIMA
2600 WCOV 91792 639-A6
CALLE COLORADO
100 SDMS 91773 600-B7
CALLE CONCORDIA
200 SDMS 91773 640-A1
CALLE CONEJO
24700 CALB 91302 559-D7
CALLE CONTENTO
1000 GLDL 91208 564-J2
CALLE CORONADO
1500 DUAR 91010 568-B5
CALLE CORTA
15300 HacH 91745 678-A2
CALLE CORTADA
- RPV 90275 822-F3
CALLE CRISTINA
1500 SDMS 91773 599-H7
CALLE DAGGETT
15100 CHLS 91709 680-H5
CALLE DE AMIGOS
17500 LACo 91744 638-H7
CALLE DE ANDALUCIA
100 TOR 90277 792-J3
100 TOR 90277 793-A3
CALLE DE ARAGON
400 TOR 90277 792-J3
400 TOR 90277 793-A3
CALLE DE ARBOLES
100 TOR 90277 792-J3
600 TOR 90277 793-A3
4900 TOR 90505 793-A3
CALLE DE ARMONIA
1600 SDMS 91773 599-J5
1600 SDMS 91773 600-A6
CALLE DE CABOS
- POM 91766 640-E5
CALLE DE CAMINO
2100 BPK 90620 767-G5
CALLE DE CARLOS
8900 BPK 90620 767-E2
CALLE DE CASTELLANA
400 TOR 90277 792-J3
400 TOR 90277 793-A2
CALLE DE CATALINA
16600 PacP 90272 630-G1
CALLE DE DAVID
8800 BPK 90620 767-E1
CALLE DEE
10600 LACo 91390 4373-F3
CALLE DE ESTRIBO
1500 PacP 90272 590-E7
1500 PacP 90272 630-E1
CALLE DE FELIPE
5300 TOR 90505 793-A3
CALLE DE GRANDE
4600 LVRN 91750 570-F7
CALLE DE HOWARD
8800 BPK 90620 767-G5
CALLE DE LA BURITTA
32900 MAL 90265 626-D6
CALLE DE LA FUENTE
15300 HacH 91745 678-A3
CALLE DE LA LUNA
1000 AZU 91702 568-G4
CALLE DE LA PAZ DR
- BqtC 91354 4460-F4
CALLE DE LAS CASAS
37700 LACo 91390 4463-C1
CALLE DE LAS ESTRELLAS
1000 AZU 91702 568-G4
CALLE DE LAS FLORES
1400 SDMS 91773 599-J5
CALLE DE LAS OVEJAS
500 VeCo 91377 557-J2
CALLE DEL BARCO
21400 MAL 90265 629-F6
CALLE DEL BRAVO
1400 LVRN 91750 570-F7
CALLE DEL CIELO
900 AZU 91702 568-G4
1700 PacP 90272 630-H1
CALLE DEL CORAZON
300 LACo 91744 638-H7
CALLE DE LEWIS
8800 BPK 90620 767-F5
CALLE DEL JONELA
1400 PacP 90272 630-E1
CALLE DEL MAR
- POM 91766 640-F4
CALLE DEL NORTE
- LACo 91390 4192-F4
800 DUAR 91010 568-E4
16000 IRW 91706 598-F3
CALLE DEL OLVIDA
1000 SDMS 91773 599-J5
CALLE DEL PACIFICO
900 GLDL 91208 564-J2
CALLE DEL PAJARITO
7000 RPV 90275 822-G3
CALLE DEL REPOSO
19600 WAL 91789 679-D1
CALLE DEL REY
- POM 91766 640-F5
CALLE DEL RIO
8800 BPK 90620 767-G5
CALLE DEL ROJA
32600 Actn 93510 4375-J7
32600 Actn 93510 4465-J1
CALLE DEL SOL
- GLDL 91208 564-J2
- GLDL 91208 565-A2
- POM 91766 640-E5
200 AVA 90704 5923-H4
900 AZU 91702 568-G4
3000 PMDL 93550 4286-F4
CALLE DEL SUR
- IRW 91706 598-F3
39100 LACo 91390 4192-F4
CALLE DE MADRID
200 TOR 90277 793-A3
1200 PacP 90272 630-G2
CALLE DE MARISA
16600 PacP 90272 630-G1
CALLE DE MAYA
13100 LMRD 90638 737-H2
CALLE DE ORO
1400 SDMS 91773 599-J5
1700 POM 91768 600-F6
15100 CHLS 91709 680-H5
CALLE DE PALERMO
17700 PacP 90272 590-E7
17700 PacP 90272 630-D1
CALLE DE PASEO
16000 IRW 91706 598-F3
CALLE DE PLATA
100 TOR 90277 793-A3
CALLE DE PRIMERA
2000 SDMS 91773 600-B7
4100 TOR 90505 793-C3
CALLE DE RICARDO
5100 TOR 90505 793-A3
CALLE DE RODEO
- POM 91766 640-E5
CALLE DE SARAH
16600 PacP 90272 630-G1
CALLE DESCANSO
200 WAL 91789 679-D1
CALLE DESCONOCIDO
39300 LACo 91390 4192-F4
CALLE DE SEVILLA
1200 PacP 90272 630-F2
CALLE DE SIRENAS
100 TOR 90277 792-H2
CALLE DE SOL DR
- BqtC 91354 4460-F4
CALLE DE SOTA
39100 LACo 91390 4192-F4
CALLE DESPENSERO
15300 HacH 91745 678-A3
CALLE DE SUENOS
30100 RPV 90275 822-G3
CALLE DE WILLIAM
8800 BPK 90620 767-E1
E CALLE DON GUILLERMO
1500 LHB 90631 738-E2
CALLE DON JUAN
1400 LHB 90631 738-F1
CALLE DULCE
1900 GLDL 91208 565-A2
CALLE EL BARANCO
39400 LACo 91390 4192-D3
CALLE EL BOSQUE
- LACo 91390 4192-E4
CALLE EL CAPITAN
15500 LACo 91390 4192-E3
CALLE EL CLAVELITO
39800 LACo 91390 4192-D2
CALLE EL FUENTE
39400 LACo 91390 4192-D3
CALLE EL JARDIN
- LACo 91390 4192-F4
CALLE EL JORANDO
39100 LACo 91390 4192-F3
CALLE EL MONTE
- LACo 91390 4192-D3
CALLE EL PARADO
39400 LACo 91390 4192-D3
CALLE EL TORO
4800 LVRN 91750 570-F6
CALLE ENTRADERO
- RPV 90275 822-F3
CALLE ESCARLATA
2000 SDMS 91773 600-B7
CALLE ESCONDIDO
15000 LACo 91390 4192-F4
CALLE ESPANA
1400 SDMS 91773 599-J5
CALLE ESSENCIAL
15400 LACo 91390 4192-E3
CALLE ESTITO
19700 WAL 91789 679-E1
CALLE ESTRADA
3600 LAN 93536 4105-A2
4800 LVRN 91750 570-F6
CALLE ESTRELLA
1100 SDMS 91773 599-J5
CALLE EVA MIRANDA
6600 IRW 91702 568-F6
CALLE FAMILLIA
200 VeCo 91377 558-A2
CALLE FORTUNA
500 WAL 91789 639-D7
1900 GLDL 91208 565-A2
CALLE FRANCESCA
1400 SDMS 91773 599-H7
CALLE FRONDOSA
900 SDMS 91773 600-A5
900 SDMS 91773 599-J5
CALLE GALANTE
1300 SDMS 91773 599-J5
CALLE GRANADA
- DUAR 91010 568-B5
19800 WAL 91789 639-E7
CALLE GRANDE
37000 PMDL 93550 4286-G4
CALLE GRILLO
36800 LACo 93551 4285-J4
36800 PMDL 93551 4285-J4
CALLE HALEIGH
16600 PacP 90272 630-H1
CALLE HERMOSA
900 SDMS 91773 600-A5
900 SDMS 91773 599-J5
15500 LACo 91390 4192-D3
CALLE JALAPA
2200 WCOV 91792 639-B7
CALLE JAZMIN
3600 CALB 91302 559-D7
CALLE JERMAINE
16600 PacP 90272 630-H1
CALLE JOAQUIN
3600 CALB 91302 559-C7
CALLE JON CABRILLO
19600 WAL 91789 679-D2
CALLE JUCA DR
1000 LHH 90631 707-J3
CALLE JUELA DR
9100 LA 90210 592-G2
CALLE LA COSTA
1900 GLDL 91208 565-A2
CALLE LAGO
19800 WAL 91789 639-E7
CALLE LAGUNA
- LACo 91390 4192-D3
CALLE LA PASTURA
- LACo 91390 4192-D3
CALLE LA PAZ
1800 RowH 91748 678-H5
CALLE LA PRIMAVERA
800 GLDL 91208 565-A2
900 GLDL 91208 564-J2
CALLE LA RESOLANA
30400 RPV 90275 822-G3
CALLE LARGO
24600 CALB 91302 559-D6
CALLE LAS BRISAS
14900 PRM 90723 735-F4
CALLE LAS DOS HUERFANAS
15300 HacH 91745 678-A3
CALLE LAS FLORES
- BGDN 90040 676-B7
CALLE LA SOMBRA
2000 SIMI 93063 499-B2
CALLE LASUEN
19700 WAL 91789 679-E1
CALLE LEANDRO
2000 SDMS 91773 600-A7
CALLE LEON
2200 WCOV 91792 639-A7
CALLE LINARES
1000 DUAR 91010 568-D5
CALLE LINDA
1300 SDMS 91773 600-A5
CALLE LISETA
2200 SDMS 91773 600-A7
CALLE LLANO
39500 LACo 91390 4192-C3
CALLE LOMA
16200 LACo 91390 4192-D3
CALLE LOMITA
15200 CHLS 91709 680-G6
39700 LACo 91390 4192-D3
CALLE LORENA
100 SDMS 91773 600-A7
100 SDMS 91773 640-A1
CALLE LOS ARBOLES
17700 RowH 91748 678-H5
CALLE LOS ELEGANTES
15100 LACo 91390 4192-F3
CALLE LOS HIDALGOS
15200 LACo 91390 4192-F3
CALLE LUMINA
- BqtC 91354 4460-E3
CALLE LUNA
200 WAL 91789 679-D1
CALLE MACETA DE FLORES
40300 LACo 91390 4192-E2
CALLE MADRID
1800 RowH 91748 678-J5
14900 CHLS 91709 680-J5
CALLE MALAGA
1000 DUAR 91010 568-D5
CALLE MALEZA
15300 LACo 91390 4192-E4
CALLE MANZANITA
15800 LACo 91390 4192-D2
CALLE MARGARITA
2200 SDMS 91773 600-A7
27800 AGRH 91301 558-D7
CALLE MARIA
1600 Win 91306 530-F3
CALLE MARIPOSA
1100 DUAR 91010 568-B5
CALLE MARISMA
19800 WAL 91789 639-E7
19800 WAL 91789 679-E1
CALLE MARLENA
600 VeCo 91377 557-J1
CALLE MARQUITA
- LACo 91390 4192-E4
CALLE MARSEILLE
300 LBCH 90814 796-D7
300 LBCH 90803 796-D7
CALLE MARTOS
2600 DUAR 91010 568-D5
CALLE MAYOR
- TOR 90277 792-J2
400 TOR 90277 793-A2
4200 TOR 90505 793-C1
CALLE MAZATLAN
37200 PMDL 93552 4287-D3
CALLE MELENO
2300 FUL 92833 738-E3
CALLE MILAGROS
22000 Chat 91311 499-J3
22000 Chat 91311 500-A3
CALLE MIRADERO
1500 SDMS 91773 599-H5
CALLE MIRADO
600 VeCo 91377 557-J2
CALLE MIRAMAR
200 RBCH 90277 792-J2
200 TOR 90277 792-J2
15200 CHLS 91709 680-H6
S CALLE MIRAMAR
700 TOR 90277 792-J2
700 TOR 90277 793-A2
CALLE MIRANDA
2000 FUL 92833 738-D4
CALLE MONTANA
15800 LACo 91390 4192-D2
CALLE MONTECILLO
4900 AGRH 91301 558-D7
CALLE MONTECITO
16600 PacP 90272 630-G1
CALLE MONTEREY
500 SDMS 91773 600-A6
CALLE MONTE VERDE
200 LACo 91744 638-H7
CALLE MORENO
200 SDMS 91773 600-B7
CALLE NARANJO
15000 LACo 91390 4192-F4
CALLE OLIVERA
39200 LACo 91390 4192-E3
CALLE ORTEGA
1000 SDMS 91773 599-J6
CALLE PAJAROS
1400 SDMS 91773 599-H6
CALLE PALMA LOMA
14600 LACo 90604 707-F5
CALLE PARRAL
2200 WCOV 91792 639-A6
CALLE PATRICIA
1400 PacP 90272 630-G1

STREET Block City ZIP Pg-Grid

CALLE PEDRO INFANTE
2900 LA 90063 635-B6
CALLE PETULA
2300 SDMS 91773 640-A1
CALLE PINON
24800 CALB 91302 559-C7
CALLE PLANA
40000 LACo 91390 4192-D2
CALLE PLATA
- BqtC 91354 4460-E4
CALLE POZO VERDE
39500 LACo 91390 4192-F3
CALLE PRIMAVERA
- BqtC 91354 4460-F2
800 SDMS 91773 600-A6
800 SDMS 91773 599-J6
15300 LACo 91390 4192-E3
CALLE PUEBLA
2200 WCOV 91792 639-A6
CALLE QUIETA
30500 RPV 90275 822-G2
CALLE RAFAEL
2000 SDMS 91773 600-A7
CALLE REAL
37000 PMDL 93550 4286-G4
CALLE REDONDA
200 WAL 91789 679-D1
15300 HacH 91745 678-A3
CALLE RENATA
100 SDMS 91773 640-A1
CALLE RHEA
29700 Llan 93544 4470-F4
CALLE RIO VISTA
5600 VeCo 91377 557-J1
CALLE ROBLEDA
4900 AGRH 91301 558-D7
CALLE ROSA
100 SDMS 91773 600-B6
CALLE ROSALITO
40300 LACo 91390 4192-E2
CALLE ROSAMARIA
1300 SDMS 91773 599-H7
CALLE RUIZ
2600 WCOV 91792 639-B6
CALLE SABINA
2300 SDMS 91773 640-A1
CALLE SAN LUCAS
7700 RowH 91748 678-H5
CALLE SAN LUIS POTOSI
15100 LACo 91390 4192-E4
CALLE SANTA BARBARA
500 SDMS 91773 600-A6
CALLE SEGURO
600 VeCo 91377 557-J2
CALLE SENITA
19800 WAL 91789 639-E7
19800 WAL 91789 679-E1
CALLE SERENA
2000 FUL 92833 738-D4
3600 LAN 93536 4105-A2
CALLE SERRA
800 SDMS 91773 600-A6
800 SDMS 91773 599-J6
CALLE SERRANONA
24700 CALB 91302 559-D7
CALLE SIEMERIO
- LACo 91390 4192-C3
CALLE SILVOSA
17900 RowH 91748 678-H5
CALLE SIMPATICA
900 GLDL 91208 564-J2
CALLE SIRENA
1900 GLDL 91208 565-A2
CALLE SOLANA
200 SDMS 91773 600-B7
CALLE SOLIS
19900 WAL 91789 679-E1
CALLE SONRISA
1000 GLDL 91208 564-J2
CALLE SONRISO
- LACo 91390 4192-E4
CALLE SUENOS
- GLDL 91208 565-A2
CALLET ST
700 PMDL 93551 4195-H4
CALLE TADEO
100 SDMS 91773 600-A7
CALLE TAXCO
2200 WCOV 91792 639-A6
CALLE TERRAZA
- BqtC 91354 4460-E2
CALLE TOMAS
2000 SDMS 91773 600-A7
CALLE TRELLA
2300 SDMS 91773 640-A1
CALLE ULTIMO
2200 FUL 92833 738-D4
CALLE VAQUERO
1200 GLDL 91206 564-H2
CALLE VERANO DR
- BqtC 91354 4460-E2
CALLE VERDAD
15100 LACo 91390 4192-F4
CALLE VERDE
- LACo 91746 637-G4
CALLE VICTORIA
1300 PacP 90272 630-G2
CALLE VIENTO
- RPV 90275 822-F4
CALLE VILLADA CIR
2400 DUAR 91010 568-D5
CALLE VIOLETA
2000 SDMS 91773 600-B7
CALLE VISTA
300 WAL 91789 679-E1
13600 LACo 91390 4462-J1
CALLE VISTA CIR
11500 Nor 91326 480-H7
11500 Nor 91326 500-H1
CALLE VISTA CT
11900 Nor 91326 480-G6
CALLE VISTA DR
1100 BHLS 90210 592-F5
CALLE VISTASO
1200 SDMS 91773 600-A5
CALLICOTT AV
6200 WdHl 91367 529-F7
6600 CanP 91307 529-F6
CALLING RD
10300 LACo 91390 4373-F2
CALLISON ST
1900 LMTA 90717 793-H3
CALLITA PL
300 SMRO 91108 596-A2
CALLITA ST
700 ARCD 91007 597-A1
8500 LACo 91775 596-G1
9000 TEML 91775 596-H1
9600 LACo 91007 596-J1
E CALLITA ST
8800 LACo 91775 596-H1
8800 TEML 91775 596-H1
CALLON DR
20200 Top 90290 590-C3
CALLWAY AV
20900 LKWD 90715 767-A5
CALMADA AV
7900 WHIT 90602 677-F7
7900 WHIT 90602 707-E2
8500 WHIT 90605 707-E2
9200 LACo 90605 707-D3
CALMAE DR
700 LAN 93535 4016-B6
CALMAR CT
1500 Wwd 90024 632-D3
CALMBANK AV
5000 LVRN 91750 570-G4
CALMBROOK LN
3600 DBAR 91765 709-H1
CALMCREST DR
7500 DWNY 90240 706-B1
CALMETTE AV
2100 RowH 91748 679-D6
CALMFIELD AV
5800 AGRH 91301 558-B3
CALMGARDEN RD
2800 Actn 93510 4465-C4
CALMGROVE AV
3600 LACo 91724 599-E6
N CALMGROVE AV
400 COV 91724 599-E4
S CALMGROVE AV
800 GLDR 91740 569-E7
1700 GLDR 91740 599-E2
CALMHILL DR
2700 TOR 90505 793-F6
CALMONT DR
- LACo 93532 4102-F4
CALMOSA AV
7900 WHIT 90602 707-F1
8500 WHIT 90605 707-F2
CALMVIEW AV
4800 BALD 91706 598-D3
CALMVIEW CIR
39300 PMDL 93551 4195-E5
CALNEVA DR
16500 Enc 91436 561-D6
CALOBAR AV
7800 LACo 90606 677-A7
7800 LACo 90606 707-B1
CALORA ST
500 COV 91722 599-C3
20000 LACo 91724 599-F2
E CALORA ST
900 COV 91724 599-D3
19500 LACo 91724 599-D3
W CALORA ST
300 SDMS 91773 600-B2
900 SDMS 91773 599-J2
CALPELLA ST
14400 LMRD 90638 737-E2
CALPET DR
20400 DBAR 91789 679-F4
CALPINE CT
800 POM 91766 641-A6
CALPINE DR
5600 MAL 90265 627-D7
5600 MAL 90265 667-D1
CALSPAR ST
700 LACo 91711 571-B6
CALSTOCK ST
1800 CRSN 90746 764-H3
CALSTON AV
4500 LAN 93535 4016-B5
44100 LAN 93535 4106-C1
CALUMET AV
1300 Echo 90026 634-E1
CALUSA DR
13700 LACo 90605 707-C7
CALVA ST
8200 LACo 93551 4193-J3
8300 LACo 93551 4194-A3
CALVADOS AV
600 COV 91723 599-B4
4600 LACo 91722 599-B4
N CALVADOS AV
100 AZU 91702 569-B7
700 COV 91723 599-B4
800 WCOV 91791 599-B7
1100 COV 91722 599-B3
S CALVADOS AV
100 WCOV 91791 599-B7
500 COV 91723 599-B6
CALVELLO DR
22600 SCTA 91350 4460-H5
22700 SCTA 91354 4460-H5
CALVERT RD
3300 PAS 91107 566-G2
CALVERT ST
6100 Enc 91316 531-A7
10700 NHol 91606 533-A7
11000 NHol 91606 532-F7
12900 VanN 91401 532-A7
14500 VanN 91411 532-A7
14600 VanN 91411 531-H7
18100 Res 91335 531-A7
18100 Res 91335 530-F7
19700 WdHl 91367 530-E7
22000 WdHl 91367 560-A1
22100 WdHl 91367 559-G1
23800 WdHl 91367 529-C7
S CALVERTON DR
15400 LMRD 90638 737-J5
CALVERTON PL
15500 LMRD 90638 737-H4
CALVIN AV
4900 Tarz 91356 560-G1
6000 Tarz 91356 530-G7
6200 Res 91335 530-F2
8300 Nor 91324 530-F2
9500 Nor 91324 500-F5
10200 WLA 90025 632-E4
10300 Nor 91326 500-F4
CALVIN ST
200 COV 91722 599-B3
CALVIN WY
- ING 90305 703-F3
CALWOOD ST
20700 SCTA 91350 4461-C4
CALYPSO LN
27200 SCTA 91351 4551-E2
27700 SCTA 91351 4461-E7
CALZADA DR
28000 RPV 90275 823-H2
CALZADILLA PL
4500 Tarz 91356 560-G4
CALZONA ST
900 LA 90023 635-C7
900 LA 90023 675-C1
CAMALOA AV
11300 LA 91342 503-A1
CAMANN ST
1000 GLDL 91208 534-F3
CAMARENA AV
9700 MTCL 91763 601-F6
10400 MTCL 91763 641-F1
CAMARES DR
36200 LACo 93551 4285-G6
CAMARGO DR
26800 SCTA 91350 4550-J1
CAMARILLO PL
10100 LA 91602 563-C3
CAMARILLO ST
10100 LA 91602 563-B3
10100 NHol 91601 563-C3
11000 LA 91602 562-J3
11000 NHol 91601 562-J3
14600 Shrm 91403 561-G4
15700 Enc 91436 561-G4
CAMARINA DR
2100 RowH 91748 679-A6
CAMARITAS DR
400 DBAR 91765 640-B7
400 DBAR 91765 680-B1
CAMAROSA DR
14900 PacP 90272 631-B7
CAMAS CT
- SCTA 91354 4460-G4
CAMAY CT
22200 CALB 91302 559-J6
CAMBA AV
19700 CRSN 90746 764-H4
CAMBAY ST
15900 LPUE 91744 638-E6
CAMBERLEY LN
1800 HacH 91745 678-F6
CAMBERT ST
500 SDMS 91773 600-D1
700 LACo 91750 600-D1
CAMBON AV
800 DBAR 91789 679-G3
CAMBRAY DR
12800 LACo 90601 637-E6
CAMBRIA CT
- SBdC 92371 (4472-J7 See Page 4471)
CAMBRIA DR
23100 CRSN 90745 794-C1
CAMBRIA RD
500 SBdC 92372 (4472-B7 See Page 4471)
2500 SBdC 92371 (4472-F7 See Page 4471)
CAMBRIA ST
1500 LA 90017 634-C4
CAMBRIA WY
38800 PMDL 93551 4195-E6
CAMBRIA ESTATES LN
16200 SCTA 91387 4552-C7
CAMBRIAN CT
12200 ART 90701 766-J2
CAMBRIDGE
- MANB 90266 732-H5
CAMBRIDGE AV
800 LVRN 91750 600-D2
5600 BPK 90621 737-H6
29500 Cstc 91384 4459-G3
N CAMBRIDGE AV
100 CLAR 91711 601-C2
S CAMBRIDGE AV
100 CLAR 91711 601-C4
CAMBRIDGE CT
700 LAN 93535 4106-A2
1500 WCOV 91791 638-J4
29300 AGRH 91301 558-A4
29400 AGRH 91301 557-J4
CAMBRIDGE DR
100 LHB 90631 738-D2
300 ARCD 91007 567-B4
400 BURB 91504 533-F5
1300 GLDL 91205 564-G7
CAMBRIDGE LN
37300 PMDL 93550 4286-D3
CAMBRIDGE PL
2000 SPAS 91030 595-G4
CAMBRIDGE RD
1300 SMRO 91108 566-C7
1300 SMRO 91108 596-C1
4100 LCF 91011 535-D6
CAMBRIDGE ST
2000 LA 90006 633-H5
4300 MTCL 91763 601-E5
9300 CYP 90630 767-A7
13200 SFSP 90670 737-B2
E CAMBRIDGE ST
100 NLB 90805 765-C1
CAMBRIDGE WY
2100 TOR 90503 763-F7
5600 CULC 90230 672-J6
CAMBRIN RD
1000 POM 91768 600-F7
1000 POM 91768 640-F1
CAMBURY AV
1500 ARCD 91007 597-A1
5400 TEML 91780 597-A3
CAMBURY DR
4500 LPMA 90623 767-B4
CAMDEN AV
1400 WLA 90025 632-B5
1600 SPAS 91030 595-J3
1600 SPAS 91030 596-A3
2200 LA 90064 632-B5
CAMDEN CIR
7800 LPMA 90623 767-D3
CAMDEN CT
3400 PMDL 93551 4195-B3
36800 PMDL 93552 4287-B4
N CAMDEN DR
300 BHLS 90210 632-E1
800 BHLS 90210 592-E7
S CAMDEN DR
100 BHLS 90212 632-F2
1100 LA 90035 632-G3
CAMDEN LN
16700 CRTS 90703 736-G6
CAMDEN PKWY
1500 SPAS 91030 595-J3
1500 SPAS 91030 596-A3
CAMDEN PL
- LACo 92821 679-C7
- LACo 92821 709-C1
1500 FUL 92833 738-B5
27200 SCTA 91354 4550-F1
CAMDEN ST
300 GLDR 91740 599-E1
CAMDEN WY
42200 LAN 93536 4104-D5
CAMELBACK AV
- CRSN 90745 794-E2
CAMELBACK DR
20500 WAL 91789 639-F4
CAMELIA CT
4300 CHNO 91710 641-E4
CAMELIA DR
600 ALH 91801 596-D7
CAMELIA LN
200 VeCo 91377 557-J2
CAMELIA HILL WY
14600 SCTA 91387 4462-G5
CAMELLIA AV
4000 LA 91604 562-H6
4400 LA 91602 562-H4
4800 TEML 91780 597-A3
5400 NHol 91601 562-H2
6000 TEML 91780 596-J2
6200 NHol 91606 532-H6
7200 NHol 91605 532-H4
N CAMELLIA AV
300 ONT 91762 601-J6
CAMELLIA CT
700 POM 91766 641-B3
CAMELLIA DR
600 COV 91723 599-C6
7200 BPK 90620 767-J3
42200 LACo 93536 4104-E5
CAMELLIA LN
2100 FUL 92833 738-A3
7000 PRV 90660 676-F6
CAMELLIA ST
- PMDL 93551 4195-D6
44000 LAN 93535 4016-F7
CAMELLIA WY
1100 LACo 90502 794-A1
CAMELLO RD
4300 WdHl 91364 560-B5
CAMELOT CT
18600 SCTA 91351 4551-H3
CAMEO AV
14300 NRWK 90650 736-J3
CAMEO CT
700 POM 91766 641-A6
CAMEO PL
11900 GrnH 91344 481-C7
CAMEO VISTA DR
2000 WCOV 91791 639-A3
CAMERFORD AV
5700 LA 90038 593-F6
CAMERINO ST
3600 LKWD 90712 765-J3
4000 LKWD 90712 766-A3
5900 LKWD 90713 766-D3
CAMERO AV
3300 LVRN 91750 600-F1
4000 LFlz 90027 594-B4
CAMERON AV
- LA 91342 482-D5
200 POM 91767 600-J4
2300 LACo 91724 639-E2
E CAMERON AV
700 WCOV 91790 638-H2
1400 WCOV 91791 638-H2
1900 WCOV 91791 639-C2
19300 LACo 91791 639-C2
19600 LACo 91724 639-C2
N CAMERON AV
100 WCOV 91790 598-E7
W CAMERON AV
800 WCOV 91790 638-E1
1600 WCOV 91790 598-E7
CAMERON CT
800 BREA 92821 709-C5
23700 SCTA 91354 4550-G1
CAMERON DR
800 PAS 91106 566-B6
800 SMRO 91108 566-B6
5100 BPK 90621 737-J5
CAMERON LN
400 LA 90015 634-D5
CAMERON PL
300 GLDL 91207 564-E3
E CAMERON PL
100 Bxby 90807 765-D7
W CAMERON ST
1200 LBCH 90810 765-A7
2300 LBCH 90810 764-J7
CAMERON WY
200 SGBL 91776 596-F4
CAMERON CREST DR
400 DBAR 91765 640-C7
CAMERONS ST
1300 RowH 91748 679-C4
CAMETA DR
8600 LACo 91770 636-G4
CAMFIELD AV
2000 CMRC 90040 675-H2
CAMFORD PL
- SCTA 91354 4460-G7
CAMILA RD
1100 WCOV 91790 638-F1
CAMILLA ST
6400 WHIT 90601 677-C5
CAMILLO ST
300 SMAD 91024 567-C1
CAMINAR AV
2200 ELMN 91732 637-F3
CAMINATA LN
1300 LHH 90631 708-F2
CAMINITO LN
3000 PMDL 93550 4286-G2
4800 LaCr 91214 504-G7
CAMINITO PL
4500 Tarz 91356 560-H4
CAMINITO DE LA ESTRELLA
1900 GLDL 91208 564-J2
1900 GLDL 91208 565-A1
CAMINITO DE LA LUNA
1900 GLDL 91208 564-J1
CAMINITO DE LA MONTANA
1800 GLDL 91208 564-J2
1800 GLDL 91208 565-A2
CAMINITO DE LA NARCISA
1800 GLDL 91208 564-J2
CAMINITO DE LA PLAYA
1800 GLDL 91208 564-J2
CAMINITO DE LA VALLE
1900 GLDL 91208 565-A2
CAMINITO DEL CIELO
1800 GLDL 91208 564-J2
CAMINITO DEL PILAR
1900 GLDL 91208 564-J1
CAMINO AV
3100 HacH 91745 678-A6
CAMINO RD
19600 Llan 93544 4470-D4
CAMINO ALTO
1500 FUL 92833 738-E4
CAMINO ARROYO
15100 CHLS 91709 680-J5
19700 WAL 91789 679-D1
19700 WAL 91789 639-D7
CAMINO BELLO
18100 RowH 91748 678-J5
18300 RowH 91748 679-A5
CAMINO CANYON RD
- Actn 93510 4465-G2
CAMINO CARDINELL
- MANB 90266 732-H6
CAMINO CENTROLOMA
1500 FUL 92833 738-D4
CAMINO CERRADO
600 SPAS 91030 595-F3
CAMINO CODORNIZ
3700 CALB 91302 559-D7
CAMINO COLIBRI
800 LACo 91302 589-A7
800 LACo 91302 588-J7
CAMINO DE BUENA VENTURA
32800 MAL 90265 626-D5
CAMINO DE CARO
- Hrbr 90710 794-A6
CAMINO DE CIELO DR
- BqtC 91354 4460-E5
CAMINO DE ENCANTO
400 TOR 90277 792-J2
CAMINO DE FLORES
- AVA 90704 5923-G2
CAMINO DE GLORIA
300 WAL 91789 679-E2
3500 WCOV 91792 679-E2
CAMINO DE LA CANTERA
16000 IRW 91702 568-F6
S CAMINO DE LA COSTA
1700 RBCH 90277 792-J2
CAMINO DE LA CUMBRE
3300 Shrm 91423 562-B5
CAMINO DE LA RONDA
3600 Shrm 91423 562-A6
CAMINO DEL ARROYO DR
5400 LaCr 91214 504-H6
CAMINO DEL ARTE DR
- BqtC 91354 4460-E5
CAMINO DE LAS COLINAS AV
100 TOR 90277 792-J1
CAMINO DE LA SOLANA
3800 Shrm 91423 562-A6
CAMINO DEL CAMPO
200 TOR 90277 792-J2
500 TOR 90277 793-A2
CAMINO DEL CERRITOS
1100 SDMS 91773 599-J7
CAMINO DEL CIELO
200 LACo 91744 638-J7
300 SPAS 91030 595-F3
CAMINO DEL LUNAS
200 LACo 91744 638-J7
CAMINO DEL MILAGRO
- POM 91766 640-D4
CAMINO DEL MONTE
- AVA 90704 5923-G3
CAMINO DEL ORO
13000 LACo 90601 637-F6
CAMINO DEL REY
13000 LACo 90601 637-E6
CAMINO DEL RIO
1800 LACo 90601 637-F6
CAMINO DEL SOL
- CALB 91302 558-H6
- CMRC 90040 676-B7
- CMRC 90040 706-B1
- LACo 91390 4463-D1
200 LACo 91744 638-J7
200 SPAS 91030 595-F3
1500 FUL 92833 738-E3
15000 CHLS 91709 680-J5
23700 TOR 90505 793-E2
CAMINO DEL SUR
1100 SDMS 91773 639-J1
1100 SDMS 91773 599-J7
2900 HacH 91745 677-J5
3100 HacH 91745 678-A6
3200 LAN 93536 4105-B6
CAMINO DEL TOMASINI
2900 HacH 91745 677-J5
CAMINO DE MARIPOSA
1900 FUL 92833 738-D4
CAMINO DE MAYO
- Hrbr 90710 794-A6
CAMINO DE ORO
- Hrbr 90710 794-A6
CAMINO DE ROSA
3200 WAL 91789 679-E2
3200 WCOV 91792 679-E2
CAMINO DE TEODORO
300 WAL 91789 679-D2
3500 WCOV 91792 679-D1
CAMINO DE VALLE
27800 Cstc 91384 4369-E7
29700 Cstc 91384 4459-D2
CAMINO DE VILLAS
1200 BURB 91501 534-A5
CAMINO DE YATASTO
17400 PacP 90272 630-E1
17400 PacP 90272 590-E7
CAMINO ESCONDIDO
2300 FUL 92833 738-C4
CAMINO GRANDE
200 LACo 91744 638-J7
CAMINO GROVE AV
800 ARCD 91006 567-F7
E CAMINO GROVE AV
600 ARCD 91006 567-E7
CAMINO HERMANOS
3200 LAN 93536 4105-B6
CAMINO LARGO
1200 Hrbr 90710 794-A6
CAMINO LARGO DR
2300 CHLS 91709 680-H1
CAMINO LA VISTA
1500 FUL 92833 738-E4
CAMINO LINDO
1500 SPAS 91030 595-G3
CAMINO LOMA
1500 FUL 92833 738-E4
CAMINO LOS ROBLES
1500 FUL 92833 738-E4
CAMINO MONTE
2300 FUL 92833 738-E3
CAMINO PALMERO
1700 LA 90046 593-C4
CAMINO PEQUENO
7100 RPV 90275 822-G3
CAMINO PLANO
4000 CALB 91302 559-D6
CAMINO PORTAL
- CALB 91302 559-D6
CAMINO PORVENIR
30300 RPV 90275 822-G3
CAMINO RASO
- Hrbr 90710 794-A6
CAMINO REAL
100 LACo 91016 567-G7
100 MNRO 91016 567-G7
200 RBCH 90277 762-J5
300 ARCD 91006 567-G7
600 RBCH 90277 763-A7
800 ARCD 91007 597-A1
1000 TOR 90505 763-A7
4000 LA 90065 595-A4
8800 LACo 91775 596-H1
9000 TEML 91775 596-J1
9400 TEML 91007 596-J1
9400 TEML 91780 596-J1
9400 LACo 91007 596-J1
9400 LACo 91780 596-J1
17600 LACo 91744 638-J7
E CAMINO REAL
- ARCD 91006 597-E1
100 LACo 91016 567-G7
100 MNRO 91016 567-G7
500 ARCD 91006 567-F7
W CAMINO REAL
- ARCD 91007 597-A1
200 ARCD 91007 567-B7
CAMINO REAL AV
300 PMDL 93551 4285-H1
CAMINO RECONDITO
2300 FUL 92833 738-C4
CAMINO REY
2100 FUL 92833 738-E3
CAMINO SAN RAFAEL
1900 GLDL 91208 564-J2
2200 GLDL 91208 565-A1
2200 GLDL 91206 565-A1
2500 GLDL 91208 534-J7
2500 GLDL 91208 535-A7
2700 GLDL 91206 535-A7
CAMINO SILVOSO
700 PAS 91105 565-F5
CAMINO TRANQUIL
2800 Ago 91301 587-F2
CAMINO VALENCIA
12000 CRTS 90703 766-J3
CAMINO VEGA
- Hrbr 90710 794-A6
CAMINO VERDE
300 SPAS 91030 595-F4
1400 Hrbr 90710 794-A6
CAMINO VIEJO
1800 RowH 91748 679-A5
CAMINO VISTA
- Hrbr 90710 794-A6
3500 LAN 93536 4105-B6
CAMMIE LN
- Tarz 91356 560-G2
CAMOLIN AV
44800 LAN 93534 4015-E5
CAMOLIN LN
- LAN 93534 4015-E7
CAMOMILE LN
27500 SCTA 91350 4461-A6
CAMORILLA DR
2100 LA 90065 594-H3
CAMP ST
4800 CYP 90630 767-C6
CAMPAIGN DR
19000 CRSN 90746 764-E3
CAMPANA RD
20900 WdHl 91364 560-C5
CAMPANA ST
1400 HMB 90254 762-H2
CAMPANA FLORES DR
- WCOV 91791 639-D1
CAMPANIA LN
- Nor 91326 500-C1
CAMPANITA CT
100 MONP 91754 635-H2
CAMPBELL AV
2400 LHB 90631 708-B6
N CAMPBELL AV
400 ALH 91801 595-J4
S CAMPBELL AV
1000 ALH 91803 595-J7
1700 ALH 91803 635-J1
CAMPBELL CT
- StvR 91381 4550-A7
CAMPBELL DR
4200 CULC 90066 672-D5
4200 LA 90066 672-D5
4700 LA 90230 672-E5
CAMPBELL ST
- PMDL 93552 4287-E2
1100 GLDL 91207 564-E2
CAMP BONITA
- LACo - (510-F6 See Page 509)
CAMPDELL ST
400 PdlR 90293 702-B3
E CAMPER DR
1400 WCOV 91792 638-H4
CAMPERS VIEW PARK RD
1400 SDMS 91773 600-D5
CAMPESINA DR
3900 ANA 90620 767-F7
3900 BPK 90620 767-F7
CAMPESINA RD
500 ARCD 91007 566-J4
CAMPFIRE DR
3000 DBAR 91765 679-J7
CAMPFIRE RD
- LACo 92823 709-J1
3000 DBAR 91765 679-J7
3000 DBAR 91765 709-J1
CAMPHOR CIR
200 BREA 92821 709-D7
CAMPHOR CT
- SCTA 91354 4460-F4
CAMPHOR LN
- LACo 91768 639-J2
- LACo 91768 640-A2
CAMPHOR PL
2300 POM 91766 641-A6
CAMPHOR ST
- SIMI 93063 499-A4
CAMP HUNTINGTON RD
3300 Alta 91001 536-B4
CAMPILLOS RD
15000 LMRD 90638 737-G3
CAMPINA LN
15200 LMRD 90638 707-G7
CAMPION DR
7800 Wch 90045 702-D2
N CAMPO DR
100 LBCH 90803 826-C2
CAMPO RD
4900 WdHl 91364 560-B2
CAMPO ST
400 MONP 91754 635-H3
E CAMPO WK
5500 LBCH 90803 826-C2
CAMPO DE CAHUENGA WY
- LA 91604 563-A6
CAMPO NUEVO DR
16200 WHIT 90603 708-A2
CAMPOS DR
38200 PMDL 93551 4285-H1
CAMPO VERDE CT
600 VeCo 91377 557-J2
CAMP PLENTY RD
27200 SCTA 91351 4551-F1
CAMPTON ST
19200 LACo 91792 679-C2
CAMPUS AV
3300 CLAR 91711 601-B2
CAMPUS DR
- ELSG 90245 702-H7
- GLDR 91741 569-B6
- Wilm 90744 794-B6
- ARCD 91007 567-C6
5800 VanN 91401 562-D1
5900 VanN 91401 532-D7
E CAMPUS DR
- LACo 91768 640-B1
- POM 91768 640-B1
S CAMPUS DR
2400 POM 91768 640-C1
2800 LACo 91768 640-C1
CAMPUS LN
- AZU 91702 569-B6
CAMPUS RD
1400 HiPk 90042 595-A1
1400 Eagl 90041 595-A1
1500 City 90063 635-F2
1500 HiPk 90042 565-A7
1500 Eagl 90041 565-A7
1600 LA 90032 635-F2
4300 LACo 90032 635-F2
E CAMPUS RD
700 LBCH 90803 796-E6
700 LBCH 90815 796-E6
700 LBCH 90840 796-E6
S CAMPUS RD
6100 LBCH 90803 796-D6
6100 LBCH 90840 796-D6
W CAMPUS RD
- LBCH 90803 796-D6
700 LBCH 90840 796-D6
700 LBCH 90822 796-D6
CAMPUS SQ E
- ELSG 90245 702-J7
CAMPUS SQ W
- ELSG 90245 702-J7
CAMPUS ST
200 GLDL 91205 564-H5
CAMPUS WK
- LACo 90263 628-G6
CAMPUS WY
- GLDL 91208 564-H2
CAMPUS CENTER DR
- LA 90094 672-F7
CAMP VIEW DR
- Cstc 91384 4460-A3
CAMRAN AV
1200 LAN 93535 4106-C1
CAMROSE DR
6800 LA 90068 593-D3
CAMULOS AV
1500 GLDL 91208 534-G7
8900 MTCL 91763 601-E4
CAMULOS PL
2700 LA 90023 635-A7
CAMULOS ST
400 Boyl 90033 635-B6
600 LA 90023 635-B6
1300 LA 90023 675-A1
CAMUS CT
1200 UPL 91784 571-J5
CAMWOOD AV
1900 RowH 91748 679-C6
CANADA AV
400 PAS 91103 535-F6
2000 Alta 91001 535-F6
CANADA BLVD
1500 GLDL 91208 564-H1
1900 GLDL 91208 534-H7
CANADA CT
- INDS 91748 678-H3
CANADA DR
- HGDN 90716 767-A6
CANADA ST
3500 LA 90065 594-H2
CANADA TR
11800 LACo 91342 482-J7
CANADA SOMBRE RD
100 LHH 90631 708-D1
CANAL AV
300 Wilm 90744 824-F1
900 LBCH 90813 795-B6
1800 LBCH 90810 795-B2
CANAL CT
3500 LA 90292 671-J7
3800 LA 90292 701-J1
CANAL PL
800 INDS 91746 637-J2
CANAL ST
400 Wilm 90744 824-F1
1900 Ven 90291 671-H6
CANAL WY
- OrCo 92649 826-J7
4500 PRV 90660 676-H3
CANALDA DR
2200 LCF 91011 504-H7
CANAL POINT RD
3100 HacH 91745 677-J5
CANANEA DR
3600 Enc 91436 561-E6
CANARIAS DR
16400 HacH 91745 678-D6
CANARY AV
15100 LMRD 90638 737-E4
CANARY CIR
6100 BPK 90620 767-E2
CANARY CT
4500 MTCL 91763 601-E7
20000 SCTA 91351 4551-E4
CANARY ISLAND PINE CT
- HacH 91745 678-F7
CANASTA DR
400 OrCo 90631 708-F4
11000 LHB 90631 708-F4
CANASTA ST
18600 Tarz 91356 560-H3
CANASTO CT
4300 PMDL 93552 4286-J5
CANBERRA CT
16400 HacH 91745 678-D5
CANBY AV
6100 Res 91335 530-J3
8400 Nor 91325 530-J1
8800 Nor 91325 500-J4
10300 Nor 91326 500-J2
CANCELA PL
18900 RowH 91748 679-B6
CANCHO DR
900 LHH 90631 707-J3
CANCION CT
- Boyl 90033 634-J4
CANDACE AV
6500 PRV 90660 676-E5
CANDACE LN
1000 LHB 90631 708-F4
CANDACE PL
5300 Eagl 90041 565-C5
CANDELA DR
17600 RowH 91748 678-G6
CANDELERIA CT
15700 WHIT 90603 707-J2
15700 WHIT 90605 707-J2
CANDIA CIR
600 LHB 90631 708-D7
CANDIA CT
17700 GrnH 91344 481-A5
CANDIA DR
9900 WHIT 90603 708-A3
CANDIA ST
17400 GrnH 91344 481-B5
CANDICE CT
25800 SCTA 91351 4551-D4
CANDICE PL
21300 Chat 91311 500-B2
CANDINGTON CT
- SCTA 91354 4460-H7
CANDISH AV
1300 GLDR 91740 599-G1
4800 LACo 91724 599-G3
CANDLEBERRY LN
10200 Nor 91324 500-G4
CANDLEBERRY WY
- PMDL 93551 4285-D3
CANDLECREST DR
600 THO 91362 557-D1
CANDLE FLAME CT
20100 LACo 91789 679-E5
CANDLELIGHT DR
15800 LACo 90604 707-J7
16100 LACo 90604 708-A7
CANDLER CT
20500 DBAR 91789 679-F4
CANDLESTICK LN
9000 CYP 90630 767-B6
CANDLEWICKE CT
1000 GLDR 91740 569-F6
CANDLEWOOD DR
700 LHB 90631 708-B7
1300 FUL 92833 738-C5
13800 LA 91342 482-E1
CANDLEWOOD LN
- LACo 90606 676-H6
CANDLEWOOD RD
3200 TOR 90505 793-D4
CANDLEWOOD ST
400 BREA 92821 709-C6
2200 LKWD 90712 765-H3
2200 NLB 90805 765-H3
3900 LKWD 90712 766-A3
5500 LKWD 90713 766-D3
CANDLEWOOD WY
- BPK 90621 738-A4
700 LHB 90631 708-B7
23400 CanP 91307 529-E5
CANDOR DR
12100 CRTS 90703 766-J2
CANDOR ST
3600 LKWD 90712 765-J2
5700 LKWD 90713 766-C2
11000 CRTS 90703 766-F2
CANDY
10900 MsnH 91345 501-H2
CANDYTUFT LN
- PMDL 93551 4285-D3
CANEDO AV
9500 Nor 91324 500-G5
CANEDO PL
1200 PAS 91105 565-E3
CANEHILL AV
2200 LBCH 90815 796-D4
3400 LBCH 90808 766-E7
3700 LACo 90808 766-D7
4300 LKWD 90713 766-D2
17600 BLF 90706 736-D7
17800 BLF 90706 766-D2
CANELA PL
18600 RowH 91748 679-A6
CANELO RD
10800 LACo 90604 707-F6
CANELONES DR
16200 HacH 91745 678-D5
CANERWELL ST
23500 SCTA 91321 4640-G3
CANEY AV
19000 CRSN 90746 764-F3
CANFIELD AV
200 POM 91767 600-J4
S CANFIELD AV
1400 LA 90035 632-H4
2000 LA 90034 632-H5
3700 LA 90034 672-G1
3700 LA 90232 632-G7
3700 LA 90232 672-G1
3800 CULC 90232 672-G1
CANFIELD DR
2300 LHB 90631 708-B4
9300 OrCo 90631 708-B4
CANFIELD RD
3700 PAS 91107 566-H2
CANFORD ST
8300 PRV 90660 676-D5
CANGAS DR
5200 CALB 91301 558-G6
CANISIUS CIR
100 CLAR 91711 571-D6
CANMORE ST
28900 AGRH 91301 558-A3
CANNA CIR
8000 BPK 90620 767-J3
CANNA RD
12200 Brwd 90049 591-F7
CANNA VALLEY ST
14800 SCTA 91387 4462-F6
CANNERY RW
11300 SBdC 91766 641-D3
CANNERY ST
100 SPed 90731 824-D5

STREET
Block City ZIP Pg-Grid

CANNES AV
1200 UPL 91784 571-J4
CANNES PL
- Cstc 91384 4459-E2
CANNING ST
6400 CMRC 90040 675-J6
6400 CMRC 90040 676-A6
E CANNON AV
100 SDMS 91773 600-C4
CANNON CT
- PMDL 93552 4287-C4
CANNON LN
300 FUL 92831 738-H5
300 FUL 92832 738-H5
CANOBIE AV
5800 WHIT 90601 677-B5
CANOE RD
29800 LACo 91387 4462-D5
29800 LACo 91390 4462-D5
CANOE BROOK DR
1200 SLB 90740 826-G1
CANOECOVE DR
300 DBAR 91765 640-D7
CANOGA AV
- Chat 91311 500-B5
4100 WdHl 91364 560-B3
5400 WdHl 91367 560-B1
6000 WdHl 91367 530-B6
6500 CanP 91303 530-B6
7500 LA 91304 530-B2
8800 LA 91304 500-B7
9000 Chat 91311 500-B5
CANOGA DR
4200 WdHl 91364 560-A5
CANOGA PL
1500 POM 91767 601-C6
S CANOGA PL
200 ANA 92804 767-G6
CANOGA ST
4500 MTCL 91763 601-E7
S CANOGA ST
400 ANA 92804 767-G6
N CANON AV
- SMAD 91024 567-B2
S CANON AV
100 SMAD 91024 567-B3
CANON BLVD
3400 Alta 91001 536-A3
CANON DR
300 SMAD 91024 567-B1
700 PAS 91106 566-A7
1000 SMRO 91108 566-A7
1000 SPed 90731 824-A5
3500 CALB 90290 559-F7
21600 Top 90290 590-A1
N CANON DR
100 BHLS 90210 632-F1
100 BHLS 90212 632-F1
600 BHLS 90210 592-E7
S CANON DR
100 BHLS 90212 632-G2
CANON LN
16100 CHLS 91709 710-G1
CANON PL
- SMAD 91024 567-B2
3200 CALB 90290 589-F1
CANON CREST ST
300 LA 90065 595-A4
CANON DE CIMARRON
- MAL 90265 626-E6
CANON DE PARAISO LN
300 LCF 91011 535-D3
CANONES CIR
22100 SCTA 91350 4460-J7
22100 SCTA 91350 4461-A7
CANONES PL
27100 SCTA 91350 4460-J7
CANONITA DR
2200 LHH 90631 708-B1
CANON VIEW TR
- Top 90290 590-A5
CANONWOOD DR
100 GLDL 91202 564-E1
CANOPUS DR
11200 LACo 91342 482-J3
CANSO LN
22200 SCTA 91350 4460-J7
CANTABRIAN CT
5100 WHIT 90601 677-D4
CANTABURY ST
- LAN 93536 4105-A1
CANTADA DR
- SCTA 91355 4550-E4
CANTALOUPE AV
5500 VanN 91401 562-B2
5900 VanN 91401 532-B6
6600 VanN 91405 532-B4
7800 PanC 91402 532-B1
CANTAMAR CT
4300 PMDL 93552 4286-J3
CANTARA DR
40100 PMDL 93550 4195-J3
CANTARA ST
1400 POM 91767 601-C6
10400 SunV 91352 533-A2
11000 SunV 91352 532-J2
11600 NHol 91605 532-D2
13300 PanC 91402 532-C2
14800 PanC 91402 531-H2
17000 VanN 91406 531-C2
17300 Nor 91325 531-B2
17800 Res 91335 531-A2
18100 Res 91335 530-F2

CANTARA ST
19900 Win 91306 530-C2
20800 LA 91304 530-B2
22100 LA 91304 529-J2
CANTARIA AV
2100 RowH 91748 678-J6
2100 RowH 91748 679-A6
CANTATA DR
2000 LA 90068 593-D3
CANTEL PL
21000 WAL 91789 639-G6
E CANTEL ST
2200 LBCH 90815 796-E3
CANTER LN
- SunV 91352 503-C7
- WAL 91789 639-C5
3600 Actn 93510 4375-B4
CANTERBURY AV
2200 POM 91768 600-D7
2200 POM 91768 640-D1
8200 NHol 91605 532-D1
8300 SunV 91352 532-D1
8600 Pcma 91331 532-D1
8600 PanC 91402 532-D1
8800 Pcma 91331 502-A5
CANTERBURY CT
- SCTA 91354 4460-G4
18100 RowH 91748 708-H2
CANTERBURY DR
5000 CYP 90630 767-C7
5600 CULC 90230 672-J6
6000 AGRH 91301 558-A3
8900 Nor 91324 500-E7
CANTERBURY LN
- SDMS 91773 599-J4
- SDMS 91773 600-A4
800 LHB 90631 708-B7
800 FUL 92831 738-J4
2000 GLDR 91741 569-J5
CANTERBURY RD
600 SMRO 91108 566-E6
3800 LA 90065 594-G1
CANTERBURY ST
- GLDL 91205 564-F7
CANTERBURY WY
8000 BPK 90620 767-J2
CANTERFORD CIR
1100 THO 91361 557-C5
CANTERHILL PL
32000 WLKV 91361 557-C7
CANTERWOOD DR
20700 SCTA 91350 4461-C4
CANTERWOOD RD
4700 LVRN 91750 570-F5
CANTLAY ST
10700 SunV 91352 533-A4
11000 SunV 91352 532-J4
11500 NHol 91605 532-H4
13500 VanN 91405 532-A4
15200 VanN 91405 531-H4
15900 VanN 91406 531-D4
18200 Res 91335 530-G5
19700 Win 91306 530-C5
22000 CanP 91303 529-J5
22000 CanP 91303 530-A5
22400 CanP 91307 529-G5
CANTLEWOOD DR
5000 PMDL 93552 4287-B2
CANTO DR
4100 LA 90032 595-C7
CANTON CIR
1100 CLAR 91711 571-F5
CANTON DR
11200 LA 91604 562-H7
CANTON LN
3300 LA 91604 562-H7
CANTON PL
11600 LA 91604 562-H7
E CANTON ST
100 LBCH 90806 795-E2
600 SIGH 90755 795-E2
5100 LBCH 90815 796-B2
W CANTON ST
1400 LBCH 90810 795-A2
CANTON WY
3200 LA 91604 562-H7
CANTOS DR
26600 SCTA 91350 4550-H1
CANTRECE LN
13000 CRTS 90703 767-B1
CANTRECE PL
12300 CRTS 90703 766-J1
CANTRECE ST
12800 CRTS 90703 767-A1
CANTRELL AV
10500 LACo 90604 707-D5
CANTURA ST
12100 LA 91604 562-F6
CANUTT PL
45300 LAN 93534 4015-E4
CANVAS ST
16900 SCTA 91387 4552-A1
CANWOOD ST
26800 Ago 91301 558-F6
26800 CALB 91301 558-F6
28000 AGRH 91301 558-A6
29300 AGRH 91301 557-G6
N CANYADA AV
2200 Alta 91001 535-G6
N CANYON BLVD
100 MNRO 91016 567-H1
S CANYON BLVD
100 MNRO 91016 567-H4

CANYON CT
- Actn 93510 4374-J6
CANYON CV
5900 LA 90068 593-G2
CANYON DR
- WHIT 90601 677-E6
- WHIT 91745 677-E5
400 GLDL 91206 564-G4
1100 SBdC 91784 571-J2
1500 FUL 92833 738-D3
1500 Hlwd 90028 593-G4
1900 LA 90068 593-G1
3000 LA 90068 563-H7
3000 LFlz 90027 563-H7
7200 WHIT 90602 677-E5
7200 WHIT 90608 677-E6
23700 CALB 91302 589-E1
E CANYON DR
2200 SBdC 92397 (4652-G3 See Page 4651)
CANYON LN
16500 CynC 91351 4462-C5
CANYON MTWY
- Nor 91326 480-E5
E CANYON MTWY
- StvR 91381 480-G1
- StvR 91381 4640-H6
CANYON RD
- SMRO 91108 566-C7
2000 ARCD 91006 567-D1
2100 ARCD 91006 537-D7
8600 AZU 91702 569-A1
8600 LACo 91702 569-A1
9100 Llan 93544 (4562-A1 See Page 4471)
9100 SBdC 92372 (4472-A7 See Page 4471)
9100 SBdC 92372 (4562-A1 See Page 4471)
23600 VeCo 93063 529-A1
S CANYON RD
- SMRO 91108 566-C7
CANYON RDEX
- ARCD 91006 537-E7
CANYON TER
- AVA 90704 5923-H4
2200 LA 90068 593-G3
CANYON TR
20900 Top 90290 590-C4
CANYON WK
5100 LCF 91011 535-C2
CANYON WY
1200 POM 91768 600-G6
4800 AGRH 91301 558-C7
44000 LAN 93535 4016-D7
CANYONBACK RD
2200 Brwd 90049 591-E4
CANYON CLOSE RD
1800 PAS 91107 536-E6
CANYON COUNTRY PK
- SCTA 91387 4552-A3
CANYON COUNTRY RD
200 BREA 92821 709-B5
CANYON COURT DR
2000 LHH 90631 708-E1
CANYON COVE PL
- GrnH 91344 481-A7
CANYON CREEK RD
15900 CRTS 90703 736-J5
CANYON CREST CT
32100 WLKV 91361 557-C7
CANYON CREST DR
- LVRN 91750 570-G5
- SCTA 91351 4461-G7
- SCTA 91351 4551-G1
200 MNRO 91016 567-G2
600 SMAD 91024 567-B1
600 SMAD 91024 537-B7
7200 WHIT 90602 677-E6
CANYON CREST RD
3300 Alta 91001 535-F3
3400 PAS 91001 535-F4
CANYONDALE DR
- BREA 92821 709-B5
CANYON DELL DR
3800 Alta 91001 535-F3
CANYON END RD
27000 LACo 91387 4552-F5
CANYON GATE RD
- SCTA 91321 4551-F6
CANYON GLEN RD
1000 CHLS 91709 710-F2
CANYON HEIGHTS CIR
- LACo 91390 4461-B4
CANYON HEIGHTS LN
5900 LA 90068 593-G2
CANYON HILL AV
- LA 91342 481-G6
CANYON HILL RD
500 SDMS 91773 570-D7
CANYON HILLS RD
15600 CHLS 91709 680-F7
15700 CHLS 91709 710-F1
CANYON LAKE AV
1500 BREA 92821 708-H6
CANYON LAKE DR
3100 LA 90068 563-F7
3100 LA 90068 593-F1
CANYON MEADOWS DR
11000 LACo 90601 677-C2
CANYON MEADOWS LN
1600 GLDR 91740 569-H7

CANYON OAK CIR
100 POM 91767 600-G4
CANYON OAK DR
2400 LA 90068 593-G2
CANYON OAK PL
- GLDL 91206 565-B4
- LACo 91390 4460-H2
CANYON OAKS CRSG
16200 CHLS 91709 710-G2
CANYON OAKS DR
6500 SIMI 93063 499-C1
CANYON PARK BLVD
19000 LACo 91387 4551-H4
CANYON PARK DR
2300 DBAR 91765 679-J5
CANYON PARK LN
4600 LVRN 91750 570-D7
4600 SDMS 91750 570-D7
CANYON QUAIL TR
12000 LACo 91390 4373-C6
CANYON RIDGE DR
3300 Alta 91001 535-G4
32100 WLKV 91361 557-C7
CANYON RIDGE LN
13300 GrnH 91344 481-C3
CANYON RIDGE RD
20600 DBAR 91789 679-G6
CANYON RIM DR
4700 LACo 90601 677-B3
CANYON RIM PL
29300 SCTA 91387 4462-G7
CANYON RIM RD
- POM 91766 640-G6
CANYONSIDE RD
5500 LaCr 91214 504-H5
CANYON SPRING LN
1000 DBAR 91765 680-C2
CANYON SPRINGS DR
1300 GLDR 91741 569-H3
CANYON TERRACE DR
2400 CHLS 91709 680-J2
CANYON TERRACE WY
- SCTA 91351 4551-F4
CANYON VIEW CT
- DBAR 91765 680-C2
11800 LA 91342 481-H7
CANYON VIEW DR
- DBAR 91765 680-A6
800 LVRN 91750 570-E7
1800 AZU 91702 568-H2
2400 CHLS 91709 680-J2
19700 SCTA 91351 4551-E1
N CANYON VIEW DR
100 Brwd 90049 631-F3
S CANYON VIEW DR
100 Brwd 90049 631-F4
CANYON VIEW LN
- LACo 90274 823-C1
2400 PAS 91107 536-E7
CANYON VISTA CIR
1600 WAL 91789 639-E3
CANYON VISTA CT
- DBAR 91765 680-C1
CANYON VISTA DR
- AZU 91702 568-H3
300 LA 90065 595-A4
CANYON WASH DR
700 PAS 91107 566-F2
CANYONWOOD DR
24600 CanP 91307 529-C5
CANZONET ST
23000 WdHl 91367 559-F3
CAP CT
2400 RowH 91748 678-G6
CAPA DR
3100 HacH 91745 678-D6
CAPALLERGO DR
- Cstc 91384 4459-D3
CAP DE CREWS
13400 CHLS 91709 680-H2
CAPE ST
7300 LACo 91770 636-D4
CAPE TER
- LA 90732 823-D6
CAPE COD CT
2000 CLAR 91711 571-D7
CAPE COD DR
- SCTA 91355 4550-E2
CAPE COD LN
2000 PMDL 93550 4286-D2
CAPE COTTAGE LN
12800 LA 91342 482-D4
CAPEHART AV
1800 DUAR 91010 567-J6
1800 DUAR 91010 568-A6
CAPE HORN DR
5800 AGRH 91301 557-G4
CAPE JASMINE RD
- LACo 91387 4551-J5
- LACo 91387 4552-A4
CAPELLA AV
200 LHB 90631 708-E4
CAPELLA LN
5500 LAN 93536 4104-G4
CAPELLO WY
10600 BelA 90077 592-A6
CAPE MAY CT
24000 SCTA 91355 4550-F4
CAPEN AV
1000 DBAR 91789 679-H3
CAPE POINT DR
- RPV 90275 823-F7

CAPERTON ST
1000 LAN 93535 4016-B6
CAPESWOOD DR
5700 RPV 90275 792-J5
5700 RPV 90275 793-A5
CAPE TENEZ DR
5000 WHIT 90601 677-A3
CAPETOWN AV
1900 ALH 91803 635-G2
CAPETOWN ST
3600 LKWD 90712 765-J3
5700 LKWD 90713 766-D2
CAPEW ST
18800 SCTA 91351 4551-G3
CAPINERO DR
1400 PAS 91105 565-E6
CAPISTRANO AV
1300 GLDL 91208 534-G7
5400 WdHl 91367 559-J2
6100 WdHl 91367 529-J7
6500 CanP 91307 529-H5
7600 LA 91304 529-H2
9500 Chat 91311 499-H6
9900 LYN 90262 705-A6
9900 SGAT 90280 705-A6
CAPISTRANO CIR
200 FUL 92835 738-G3
1700 GLDL 91208 534-H7
CAPISTRANO CT
23900 SCTA 91355 4550-F4
CAPISTRANO LN
11900 Nor 91326 480-G7
42100 LAN 93536 4104-C6
CAPISTRANO RD
- LMRD 90638 738-B2
CAPISTRANO WY
700 LA 90048 633-A2
4200 City 90063 635-E5
CAPITAL DR
42900 LAN 93535 4106-A3
CAPITAN CT
5700 PMDL 93552 4287-C3
CAPITOL AV
3700 INDS 90601 637-C7
3700 INDS 90601 677-B1
CAPITOL DR
700 SPed 90731 824-A2
900 LA 90732 824-A2
1000 LA 90732 823-J3
1100 RPV 90732 823-J3
CAPIZ CT
13700 WHIT 90601 677-E5
CAPLAND DR
- PMDL 93551 4195-B4
6600 LACo 91390 4374-D2
CAPPER AV
900 POM 91767 601-C7
CAPPS AV
6400 Res 91335 530-H4
8300 Nor 91324 530-H2
CAPRA RD
- LACo - (4553-B2 See Page 4464)
- LACo 91390 (4553-B2 See Page 4464)
CAPRI CIR
9900 CYP 90630 767-D7
CAPRI CT
- Cstc 91384 4459-E3
5500 PMDL 93552 4287-C3
6100 LBCH 90803 826-D1
CAPRI DR
- WHIT 90601 677-B3
1200 Brwd 90049 631-D4
1200 PacP 90272 631-D3
CAPRICE CIR
7100 LPMA 90623 767-D2
CAPRICORN AV
6300 AGRH 91301 558-B3
CAPRICORN ST
400 BREA 92821 709-A6
CAPRINO PL
17600 VanN 91406 531-B4
CAPRINO WY
1200 POM 91767 601-C7
CAPROCK CT
- GLDL 91206 564-J3
CAPROCK RD
34100 LACo 91390 4373-H3
CAPRON AV
300 LACo 91792 679-C2
CAPSTAN CIR
3700 WLKV 91361 557-C7
CAPTAINS PL
5300 AGRH 91301 557-G6
CAPTAINS ROW DR
14000 MdlR 90292 702-A1
CAPUCHIN WY
2100 CLAR 91711 571-D7
CAPULET AV
9800 WHIT 90603 708-B3
CAPULIN CT
22200 WdHl 91364 559-J3
CARA PL
900 SPed 90731 824-A3
CARACAL WY
- PMDL 93551 4285-F1
CARACAS ST
2300 LaCr 91214 504-H7
CARACOL DR
15700 HacH 91745 678-B5
CARAMLE CT
1800 LAN 93534 4105-E1

CARARD ST
23700 WdHl 91367 559-E2
CARARRA LN
- Nor 91326 500-D1
CARAVACA RD
15100 LMRD 90638 737-G3
CARAVANA RD
4000 WdHl 91364 560-C5
CARAVEL CIR
12300 CRTS 90703 766-J2
CARAVEL PL
12300 CRTS 90703 766-J2
12500 CRTS 90703 767-C2
CARAVEL ST
12600 CRTS 90703 767-A2
CARAVEL WY
700 SLB 90740 826-E4
S CARAWAY DR
700 LACo 90601 637-G5
CARAWAY LN
27500 SCTA 91350 4461-A5
CARBON CIR
7600 LPMA 90623 767-C3
CARBON CANYON RD
2000 LACo 90265 629-D4
3500 MAL 90265 629-D4
CARBON CANYON RD Rt#-142
1000 BREA 92823 710-B7
1000 CHLS 91709 710-G2
1900 CHLS 91709 680-H7
3400 OrCo 92823 709-H7
3400 BREA 92823 709-H7
CARBON CANYON ACCESS
- BREA 92823 710-F4
- BREA 92886 710-F4
- OrCo 92886 710-F4
CARBONIA AV
100 WAL 91789 679-G1
100 WAL 91789 639-F7
CARBON MESA RD
3700 MAL 90265 629-D5
CARBON RIDGE RD
- BREA 92823 710-E6
- BREA 92886 710-E6
- CHLS 91709 710-E6
- OrCo 92823 710-E6
- OrCo 92886 710-E6
E CARBURTON ST
8200 LBCH 90808 767-A7
CARCASSONNE RD
600 BelA 90077 592-A7
CARDALE ST
5700 LKWD 90713 766-C3
CARDAMINE CT
7400 Tuj 91042 503-J2
CARDAMINE DR
10900 Tuj 91042 503-J1
CARDAMINE PL
10900 Tuj 91042 503-J2
CARDEENE RD
10700 LACo 91390 4373-E4
11000 LACo 93536 4103-C1
CARDELL ST
11700 NRWK 90650 736-G2
CARDENAS AV
4700 WdHl 91364 560-A5
CARDIAC RANCH RD
- LACo 93551 4375-G4
CARDIFF AV
1100 LA 90035 632-H4
2600 LA 90034 632-G6
3700 LA 90034 672-G1
3700 LA 90232 672-G1
3800 CULC 90232 672-G1
CARDIFF CT
1100 POM 91767 601-C6
CARDIFF DR
4000 CYP 90630 767-A6
22300 SCTA 91350 4550-J5
CARDIFF PL
12900 CHNO 91710 641-F7
CARDIFF RD
1600 SDMS 91773 599-G4
CARDIFF ST
37600 PMDL 93550 4286-E2
CARDIGAN AV
300 GLDL 91202 534-D7
CARDIGAN CT
2500 BelA 90077 591-G2
CARDIGAN PL
9800 LA 90210 592-C1
CARDILLO AV
2500 HacH 91745 678-A5
3000 HacH 91745 677-J5
CARDIN ST
20500 WAL 91789 639-F6
CARDINAL DR
- LACo 91387 4551-J5
CARDINAL RD
6000 LACo 92397 (4652-A2 See Page 4651)
6000 SBdC 92397 (4652-A2 See Page 4651)
CARDINAL ST
- BREA 92823 709-H6
1300 LA 90012 634-H2
1700 LA 90031 634-J2
CARDINAL CUSHING
- CLAR 91711 571-F2
CARDONA DR
18700 RowH 91748 679-B6

CARDONA ST
18900 RowH 91748 679-B6
CARDOZA DR
5800 WLKV 91362 557-F4
CARDWELL PL
2700 LA 90046 593-A1
CARDWELL ST
4500 LYN 90262 735-D2
CARDWICK CT
26500 SCTA 91321 4551-F5
CAREFREE CT
43600 LAN 93535 4106-E1
CAREFUL AV
2200 Ago 91301 587-H3
CARELL AV
5700 AGRH 91301 558-B4
CAREN CT
1300 LAN 93534 4015-F6
S CARESS AV
15900 RDom 90221 735-C6
16400 COMP 90221 735-C6
CAREW ST
1300 SDMS 91773 599-H2
CAREY AV
1400 BREA 92821 708-H5
CAREY ST
14600 PacP 90272 631-B5
CAREYBROOK DR
5900 AGRH 91301 558-A4
5900 AGRH 91301 557-J4
CAREY RANCH LN
- LA 91342 481-H6
CAREY VIEW ST
- LA 91342 481-H6
CARFAX AV
1600 LBCH 90840 796-E5
1700 LBCH 90815 796-E4
3000 LBCH 90808 796-E1
3400 LBCH 90808 766-E7
3800 LACo 90808 766-E5
4100 LKWD 90713 766-D2
13000 DWNY 90242 736-D2
13500 BLF 90706 736-D2
CARGREEN AV
15200 HacH 91745 677-J6
15300 HacH 91745 678-A6
CARGREEN LN
700 Alta 91001 536-A6
CARHART AV
700 FUL 92833 738-E6
CARHART CIR
- FUL 92833 738-E6
CARIBETH DR
3400 Enc 91436 561-E7
CARIBOU CT
- SCTA 91354 4550-H1
CARIBOU LN
10300 BelA 90077 592-A4
CARICIA DR
2700 HacH 91745 678-B5
CARILLO DR
800 SGBL 91776 596-D4
25900 SCTA 91355 4550-G4
CARILLON ST
2700 LA 90039 594-F3
CARINTHIA DR
12500 WHIT 90601 677-C4
CARIS ST
24200 WdHl 91367 559-D1
CARISSA CT
- WdHl 91367 559-H7
CARISSA ST
1500 UPL 91784 571-H4
E CARITA ST
5100 LBCH 90808 766-B7
CARITINA DR
4600 Tarz 91356 560-F4
CARIZ DR
25300 SCTA 91355 4640-E1
CARL CT
- SCTA 91321 4641-B2
CARL PL
12800 Pcma 91331 502-D2
CARL ST
11900 LA 91342 482-G7
12300 Pcma 91331 502-E1
CARLA CT
15200 SCTA 91387 4462-F7
CARLA DR
1700 GLDL 91206 564-H3
CARLA LN
1300 BHLS 90210 592-G5
8400 LA 91304 529-G2
CARLA PL
10800 CRTS 90703 736-E6
CARLA RDG
1400 BHLS 90210 592-G3
CARLAND DR
23900 SCTA 91321 4640-F3
CARLARIS RD
2700 SMRO 91108 596-A2
CARL BOYER DR
- SCTA 91350 4551-C3
CARLEEN CT
11100 Tuj 91042 503-H2
CARLENE LN
24300 LMTA 90717 793-H3
S CARLERIK AV
21800 CRSN 90810 765-A6
CARLET PL
600 SDMS 91773 600-D1
CARLET ST
400 SDMS 91773 600-C1

CARLET ST
800 LACo 91750 600-D1
CARLETON AV
2600 LA 90065 594-H5
S CARLETON AV
300 CLAR 91711 601-C4
CARLETON DR
13700 CRTS 90703 737-C6
S CARLETON PL
500 CLAR 91711 601-C5
CARLETON WY
1200 FUL 92833 738-B5
CARLEY AV
5300 WHIT 90601 677-A4
CARLIN AV
3100 LYN 90262 735-A1
4200 COMP 90221 735-D3
CARLIN ST
300 COMP 90222 735-A2
600 COMP 90222 734-J2
5300 LA 90016 633-B7
E CARLIN ST
300 COMP 90222 734-J2
CARLING WY
5000 LA 90036 633-D2
CARLISLE AV
11700 CHNO 91710 641-F5
CARLISLE CIR
2200 LHB 90631 708-B7
CARLISLE CT
1400 SDMS 91773 599-H4
CARLISLE DR
1800 SMRO 91108 596-D2
CARLISLE RD
100 VeCo 90265 586-C3
100 VeCo 91361 586-C3
600 THO 90265 586-E3
600 THO 91361 586-E3
CARLISLE ST
400 SFER 91340 502-A1
CARLO CT
5000 PMDL 93552 4287-B1
CARLOS AV
2700 ALH 91803 635-H2
5900 Hlwd 90028 593-F4
CARLOS PL
24800 SCTA 91321 4640-G3
CARLOS ST
1700 ALH 91803 635-H2
CARLOTA BLVD
3500 LA 90031 595-A5
5500 HiPk 90042 595-C4
CARLOW RD
22900 TOR 90505 793-C1
CARLSBAD ST
2800 RBCH 90278 733-B6
14400 LA 91342 482-A6
CARLSON CIR
900 BREA 92821 708-J5
22200 CanP 91303 529-J5
22200 CanP 91307 529-J5
CARLSON DR
400 PAS 91105 565-D4
800 BREA 92821 708-J5
CARLSON LN
1400 RBCH 90278 762-J2
CARLTON AV
100 PAS 91103 565-H3
2200 POM 91768 600-D7
2200 POM 91768 640-D1
12800 LACo 90061 734-D2
E CARLTON AV
1000 WCOV 91790 598-G6
W CARLTON AV
1200 WCOV 91790 598-F6
CARLTON DR
1200 GLDL 91205 564-G5
3800 ING 90305 703-E3
CARLTON PL
19100 RowH 91748 679-C7
19200 LACo 92821 679-C7
19200 LACo 92821 709-C1
CARLTON ST
- PMDL 93551 4194-J3
4900 MTCL 91763 641-F2
5500 SBdC 91762 641-G2
CARLTON WY
1200 Ven 90291 672-A4
5400 LFlz 90027 593-H4
5500 Hlwd 90028 593-G4
8400 LA 90069 592-J5
CARLY CT
2100 RowH 91748 679-D6
CARLYLE AV
900 SMCA 90402 631-E6
CARLYLE PL
2200 LA 90065 594-G3
CARLYLE ST
3000 LA 90065 594-G3
CARLYNN PL
9400 Tuj 91042 504-C6
CARMACK CT
7500 Actn 93510 4374-D7
CARMAN CREST DR
2500 LA 90068 593-C2
CARMANITA AV
1100 POM 91767 601-B5
CARMAR DR
2600 LA 90046 592-J1
CARMAR PL
8300 LA 90046 592-J1
CARMEL AV
700 SLB 90740 826-E3

CARMEL CIR
900 FUL 92833 738-C6
CARMEL CIR E
1600 UPL 91784 571-J6
CARMEL CIR W
1600 UPL 91784 571-J7
CARMEL CT
1100 POM 91767 601-C6
1200 DUAR 91010 568-A5
CARMEL DR
800 MTBL 90640 676-C4
24700 CRSN 90745 794-D3
CARMEL RD
4800 LCF 91011 535-D4
41000 PMDL 93551 4194-F1
CARMEL ST
3000 GLDL 91204 594-E1
3000 LA 90065 594-E1
CARMEL WY
800 LA 90048 633-A3
CARMELA LN
1200 LHB 90631 708-G4
CARMEL CREST DR
- Tarz 91356 560-H6
N CARMELINA AV
100 Brwd 90049 631-F3
S CARMELINA AV
100 Brwd 90049 631-F3
1300 WLA 90025 631-H6
2200 LA 90064 631-J7
2200 LA 90064 632-A7
CARMELITA AV
800 MTBL 90640 676-D3
1300 RBCH 90278 762-J2
5100 MYWD 90270 675-C6
5900 HNTP 90255 675-C6
6100 BELL 90201 675-C6
9100 BHLS 90210 592-G7
9300 BHLS 90210 632-E2
N CARMELITA AV
300 City 90063 635-E3
S CARMELITA AV
100 City 90063 635-E6
CARMELITA CIR
1100 MNRO 91016 567-J5
1100 MNRO 91016 568-A5
CARMELITA DR
- SCTA 91355 4550-E4
CARMELITA PL
600 MTBL 90640 676-C3
1400 ARCD 91006 567-B3
9100 BHLS 90210 592-H7
CARMELITA ST
700 SGBL 91776 596-D4
CARMELITOS PZ
5100 NLB 90805 765-E3
N CARMELO AV
200 PAS 91107 566-E3
600 PAS 91104 566-E3
S CARMELO AV
300 LACo 91107 566-E5
CARMELYNN ST
4500 TOR 90503 763-A4
CARMEN AV
1900 LA 90068 593-F3
CARMEN CT
800 LVRN 91750 570-D6
CARMEN DR
- LACo 91390 4462-C3
1200 GLDL 91207 564-F2
CARMEN LN
1800 CHLS 91709 680-H3
CARMEN PL
6100 LA 90068 593-F3
CARMEN ST
2000 WCOV 91792 639-A7
4100 TOR 90503 763-B6
4400 CHNO 91710 641-E7
CARMENCITA DR
700 WCOV 91790 638-F1
CARMENIA DR
8900 WHIT 90603 707-J2
CARMENITA LN
7500 LA 91304 529-D4
CARMENITA RD
9600 LACo 90605 707-C7
9700 SFSP 90605 707-C5
10500 SFSP 90670 707-C5
12100 LACo 90605 737-C4
12600 SFSP 90670 737-C4
13300 NRWK 90650 737-C4
15700 CRTS 90703 737-C6
17900 CRTS 90703 767-C2
19000 LPMA 90623 767-C2
CARMENTO DR
5300 VeCo 91377 557-H1
CARMER ST
- LACo 93591 4200-D5
CARMICHAEL DR
700 BREA 92821 709-D6
CARMONA AV
1000 LA 90019 633-C4
1800 LA 90016 633-B6
3400 LA 90016 673-B1
3800 LA 90008 673-B2
CARNABY ST
10500 BLF 90706 766-D1
10700 CRTS 90703 766-J1
13400 CRTS 90703 767-C1
CARNARVON DR
1300 PAS 91103 565-D1
CARNATION AV
3400 Echo 90026 594-C5

CARNATION CT
- Cstc 91384 4459-E2
CARNATION DR
8000 BPK 90620 767-J3
CARNAUBA PALM
- WCOV 91790 638-H6
CARNAVON WY
3800 LFlz 90027 594-B2
CARNE ST
11300 NRWK 90650 736-F1
CARNEGIE AV
100 CLAR 91711 601-B4
2700 POM 91767 601-B4
27600 SCTA 91350 4460-J5
CARNEGIE LN
900 RBCH 90278 762-H1
1900 RBCH 90278 763-A1
CARNEGIE ST
3800 LA 90032 595-D5
CARNELIAN PL
- GAR 90247 734-A3
CARNELIAN ST
200 RBCH 90277 762-H4
CARNELL ST
13500 WHIT 90605 707-D2
14300 WHIT 90603 707-F4
CARO ST
6600 PRM 90723 735-E5
CAROB CT
800 PMDL 93550 4286-B6
CAROB DR
2500 LA 90046 593-B2
CAROB ST
100 COMP 90220 734-H6
8100 CYP 90630 767-B4
W CAROB ST
800 BREA 92821 738-J1
CAROB WY
900 MTBL 90640 676-C6
CAROL CT
- LACo 91390 4461-A3
3900 CULC 90232 672-J2
CAROL DR
1000 WHWD 90069 592-H6
1400 POM 91767 601-D6
1800 FUL 92833 738-C7
4100 BPK 90621 738-A7
5100 TOR 90505 793-A1
43300 LAN 93535 4106-B2
CAROL LN
- LA 91342 481-F2
CAROL PL
12400 GrnH 91344 481-B5
CAROL ST
- NLB 90805 735-G7
1000 LHB 90631 708-D4
1500 LACo 90631 708-D4
CAROLANN ST
1800 POM 91766 641-B4
CAROLDALE AV
21200 CRSN 90745 764-C6
22800 CRSN 90745 794-C2
CAROLFORD WY
1000 BHLS 90210 592-D6
CAROLI LN
5100 LCF 91011 535-B2
CAROLIE LN
600 WAL 91789 639-C7
CAROLINA PL
5100 ELA 90022 675-G1
S CAROLINA PL
3600 SPed 90731 854-B2
CAROLINA ST
2400 SPed 90731 824-B7
2600 SPed 90731 854-B1
CAROLINE AV
3300 CULC 90232 632-J7
6200 SIMI 93063 499-B3
CAROLINE ST
5500 MTCL 91763 601-H4
N CAROLINE ST
700 WCOV 91791 598-J6
CAROLINE WY
2700 ARCD 91007 597-B3
CAROL PARK PL
2400 Mont 91020 534-G2
CAROL PINE LN
- LACo 91107 566-H4
CAROLSIDE AV
38100 PMDL 93550 4285-J1
38400 PMDL 93550 4195-J6
44000 LAN 93535 4015-J7
44000 LAN 93535 4105-J1
CAROL SUE LN
21400 SCTA 91350 4461-B6
CAROLUS DR
5800 LA 90068 593-G1
CAROLWOOD DR
200 ARCD 91006 567-D1
N CAROLWOOD DR
100 BelA 90077 592-C6
CAROLWOOD LN
2900 TOR 90505 793-D5
CAROLYN
15300 MsnH 91345 501-H2
CAROLYN CIR
7900 LPMA 90623 767-B3
CAROLYN DR
- PMDL 93551 4195-D7
CAROLYN PL
11200 CRTS 90703 736-F7
13500 CRTS 90703 737-C7
19700 RowH 91748 679-E7

STREET
Block City ZIP Pg-Grid

W CAROLYN PL
2000 LBCH 90810 795-A2
CAROLYN ST
13000 CRTS 90703 737-B7
17400 CRTS 90703 736-J7
CAROLYN WY
1000 BHLS 90210 592-D6
5000 GLDL 91214 504-D5
CARON CIR
20300 CRSN 90746 764-F4
N CARONDELET ST
100 Echo 90026 634-C1
S CARONDELET ST
100 LA 90057 634-C2
900 LA 90006 634-B3
E CARONDELET WY
500 ING 90301 703-D2
CAROUSEL CIR
37200 PMDL 93552 4287-A3
CARPENTER AV
3800 LA 91604 562-G6
4400 LA 91607 562-G2
5900 LA 91607 532-G7
6000 NHol 91606 532-G7
CARPENTER CT
- FUL 92833 738-D5
3900 LA 91604 562-G6
CARPENTER DR
43300 LAN 93535 4106-B2
CARPENTER ST
1300 LHB 90631 708-B4
CARPINTERO AV
6100 LKWD 90713 766-D1
6200 BLF 90706 766-D1
13600 BLF 90706 736-D3
CARPIO DR
300 DBAR 91765 640-D6
CARR AL
- PAS 91103 565-H4
CARR DR
100 GLDL 91205 564-H5
CARR LN
2200 LA 90031 635-A1
CARRACK AV
1100 LBCH 90813 794-J7
1100 LBCH 90813 795-A7
1100 Wilm 90744 794-J7
CARRANZA LN
- Saug 91350 4461-G6
CARRARA CIR
9700 CYP 90630 767-B7
CARRARA PL
1000 Brwd 90049 591-E7
1000 Brwd 90049 631-E1
CARRARA ST
16000 HacH 91745 678-C4
CARRETA DR
18800 RowH 91748 679-B5
CARRETERA DR
15100 WHIT 90605 707-G3
CARREY AV
8000 OrCo 90638 737-J4
CARREY RD
20200 WAL 91789 679-F1
CARRIAGE
- LA 91342 481-G1
CARRIAGE AV
11100 MTCL 91763 641-F2
11300 SBdC 91710 641-F3
11300 MTCL 91710 641-F3
CARRIAGE CT
40700 PMDL 93551 4194-F2
CARRIAGE DR
- RHE 90274 823-G1
CARRIAGE LN
100 LAN 93534 4105-J1
900 WAL 91789 639-D6
CARRIAGE PL
200 MANB 90266 732-H7
800 FUL 92835 738-F3
16400 HacH 91745 678-E4
CARRIAGE WY
- POM 91766 640-H6
38800 PMDL 93551 4195-H6
42500 LACo 93536 4104-F4
CARRIAGEDALE DR
200 CRSN 90745 794-C2
CARRIAGE HILLS LN
2000 CHLS 91709 710-H1
2100 CHLS 91709 680-J7
CARRIAGE HOUSE DR
- ARCD 91006 567-A3
CARRIAGE HOUSE RD
1500 PAS 91107 536-H7
1500 PAS 91107 566-H1
CARRIE CT
8000 LACo 91390 4374-B2
CARRIE LN
2400 GLDL 91208 534-J7
CARRIE PL
32500 WLKV 91361 557-B7
CARRIE HILLS LN
1700 LHH 90631 708-G2
CARRIER AV
2700 CMRC 90040 676-A5
CARRILLO AV
- MTCL 91763 641-G3
9400 MTCL 91763 601-G5
CARRILLO DR
900 LA 90048 633-A3
CARRILLO ST
13000 CHNO 91710 641-F7
CARRINGTON CT
3700 ING 90305 703-D4
E CARRINGTON DR
15500 LMRD 90638 737-H2
CARRION RD
1800 LVRN 91750 600-E3
CARRIONE CT
300 POM 91766 640-D3
CARRISO RD
21300 DBAR 91765 679-H5
CARRITA DR
27100 LACo 90265 627-H5
CARRIZAL RD
4100 WdHl 91364 560-B6
CARRIZO DR
23400 SCTA 91355 4550-G4
CARROL WY
600 PAS 91107 566-F6
CARROLL AV
400 Ven 90291 671-H6
1300 Echo 90026 634-E1
19000 GLDR 91741 569-C6
E CARROLL AV
100 GLDR 91741 569-G5
W CARROLL AV
100 GLDR 91741 569-D5
CARROLL CT
4000 CHNO 91710 641-D6
CARROLL DR
1400 Alta 91001 536-B6
CARROLL LN
10300 LACo 91390 4373-F3
25900 StvR 91381 4550-A7
CARROLL PK E
300 LBCH 90814 825-H1
300 LBCH 90814 795-H7
CARROLL PK N
2300 LBCH 90814 795-G7
CARROLL PK S
2300 LBCH 90814 795-G7
2300 LBCH 90814 825-G1
CARROLL PK W
300 LBCH 90814 825-H1
300 LBCH 90814 795-H7
CARROLL CANAL CT
200 Ven 90291 671-H6
CARROLL CANAL WK
200 Ven 90291 671-H6
CARROLLTON CT
- PMDL 93550 4376-E4
CARROLOS ST
2600 Actn 93510 4375-B3
CARRON DR
6500 PRV 90660 676-E5
CARROTWOOD DR
2200 BREA 92821 709-E7
CARROTWOOD LN
- POM 91767 600-J3
CARROUSEL DR
- LAN 93535 4015-J4
15500 SCTA 91387 4462-E7
CARRUTHERS CT
500 POM 91766 641-A6
CARSAMBA DR
22700 CALB 91302 559-H6
CARSE DR
3100 LA 90068 593-C1
3200 LA 90068 563-C7
CARSON CT
900 SDMS 91773 570-C6
20000 LACo 91390 4461-E4
CARSON DR
11000 LYN 90262 705-C7
CARSON LN
900 POM 91766 641-B5
CARSON PL
200 COMP 90220 735-A4
N CARSON RD
100 BHLS 90211 632-J2
S CARSON RD
100 BHLS 90211 632-J2
CARSON ST
- CHNO 91710 641-G4
1800 TOR 90501 763-F6
2500 TOR 90503 763-B6
4100 CYP 90630 767-A6
8800 CULC 90232 632-H7
8800 CULC 90232 672-H1
11800 HGDN 90716 766-G6
12400 HGDN 90716 767-A6
E CARSON ST
100 CRSN 90745 764-D6
300 Bxby 90807 765-F6
1900 CRSN 90810 764-H6
2300 LKWD 90712 765-H6
2500 CRSN 90810 765-A6
3300 LBCH 90808 765-H6
3900 LKWD 90712 766-B6
5500 LKWD 90713 766-D6
7100 LKWD 90808 766-D6
11300 LBCH 90713 766-D6
11300 LBCH 90715 766-D6
11300 LKWD 90715 766-D6
W CARSON ST
100 CRSN 90745 764-C6
600 LACo 90745 764-C6
700 LACo 90502 764-C6
900 LBCH 90810 765-B6
1300 LA 90501 763-J6
1300 LA 90501 764-C6
1700 TOR 90501 763-J6
CARSON WY
25200 StvR 91381 4550-C7
E CARSON MESA RD
300 PMDL 93550 4376-C3
W CARSON MESA RD
200 PMDL 93550 4376-A5
500 PMDL 93550 4375-H7
1300 Actn 93510 4375-H7
1500 Actn 93510 4465-F1
CARSON PLAZA CT
500 CRSN 90746 764-E4
CARSON PLAZA DR
2300 CRSN 90746 764-D4
CARSON TOWN CTR
- CRSN 90745 764-B5
CARSON VIEW LN
34600 PMDL 93550 4376-F3
CARTAGENA CIR
5000 LPMA 90623 767-C4
CARTAGENA DR
800 Bxby 90807 765-E6
CARTAGENA PL
- Cstc 91384 4459-D3
CARTAGENA ST
600 Bxby 90807 765-E6
3200 LKWD 90712 765-H6
CARTAGO CT
2100 RowH 91748 678-H5
CARTELA DR
14300 LMRD 90638 737-H3
CARTER AL
600 PAS 91103 565-H3
CARTER AV
2900 LA 90292 672-A6
E CARTER AV
- SMAD 91024 567-A1
W CARTER AV
- SMAD 91024 567-A1
200 SMAD 91024 566-J1
CARTER DR
4500 LA 90032 595-D7
E CARTER DR
300 GLDR 91740 599-F2
W CARTER DR
100 GLDR 91740 599-D2
CARTESIAN CIR
4200 LACo 90274 793-C6
CARTHAGE CT
1300 CLAR 91711 601-A1
CARTHAGE ST
15300 PacP 90272 631-A5
CARTHAGE WY
4900 VeCo 91377 557-H1
CARTIER DR
30000 RPV 90275 822-H3
CARTWRIGHT AV
4000 LA 91604 563-B6
4300 LA 91602 563-B4
4800 NHol 91601 563-B1
5900 NHol 91601 533-A7
6000 NHol 91606 533-A7
7200 SunV 91352 533-A4
CARTWRIGHT ST
3500 PAS 91107 566-H2
CARUSO LN
2700 LAN 93536 4015-C7
CARUTHERS ST
10300 WHIT 90603 708-A4
CARVEL DR
27900 SCTA 91351 4551-F1
CARVER DR
200 CLAR 91711 571-D6
CARVER LN
12200 ART 90701 766-J2
CARVER ST
7700 BPK 90621 737-H6
CARVIN AV
12400 GrnH 91344 481-A5
CASABA AV
7300 Win 91306 530-D1
9500 Chat 91311 500-D5
CASABA TER
- PMDL 93551 4285-E3
CASA BLANCA DR
600 FUL 92832 738-F6
CASA BLANCA RD
4000 WdHl 91364 560-C6
CASA CON VISTA
2300 LA 90732 823-G7
E CASAD AV
600 COV 91723 599-C6
1000 WCOV 91790 598-G6
19300 LACo 91723 599-C6
W CASAD AV
1000 WCOV 91790 598-F6
CASAD ST
100 COV 91723 599-A6
CASA DEL REY DR
1200 LACo 90631 708-D4
CASA DULCE LN
33200 LACo 91390 4373-G6
CASA GRANDE AV
200 MTBL 90640 636-F7
37000 PMDL 93550 4286-C4
CASA GRANDE CIR
4400 CYP 90630 767-B6
E CASA GRANDE DR
2000 WCOV 91791 639-A3
CASA GRANDE RD
1000 VeCo 93063 499-C4
CASA GRANDE ST
1400 PAS 91104 566-B2
CASA HERMOSA DR
900 POM 91768 600-G7
CASALE RD
1500 PacP 90272 631-D3
CASALERO DR
2600 LHH 90631 678-B7
E CASA LINDA DR
2000 WCOV 91791 639-A3
CASA LOMA DR
23500 DBAR 91765 640-C7
CASA LOMA LN
700 WAL 91789 639-G6
CASA LUNA PL
- BqtC 91354 4460-D2
CASAMIA AV
2900 PMDL 93550 4286-F3
CASANDRA AV
17800 CRTS 90703 736-J7
17800 CRTS 90703 766-J1
CASANES AV
9500 DWNY 90240 706-E4
10200 DWNY 90241 706-D5
CASANOVA DR
- LAN 93536 4015-C7
CASANOVA ST
400 LA 90012 634-H1
400 LA 90012 594-H7
CASA VERDE DR
6300 CYP 90630 767-F7
36900 PMDL 93550 4286-D4
CASA VISTA DR
700 POM 91768 600-G7
CASCADA WY
400 Brwd 90049 591-H7
CASCADE
1400 WCOV 91790 638-D2
12500 ELMN 91732 637-G1
CASCADE AV
100 THO 91362 557-C3
1200 WAL 91789 639-F4
CASCADE CIR
10400 LACo 90606 706-G1
CASCADE CT
- Pcma 91331 502-D6
- SCTA 91387 4462-G7
100 BREA 92821 709-B6
100 PMDL 93550 4285-J2
100 PMDL 93550 4286-A2
5000 CULC 90230 672-H3
CASCADE PL
1000 CLAR 91711 601-B1
CASCADE RD
- Cstc 91384 4459-F3
CASCADE WY
- RowH 91748 679-E6
7700 BPK 90621 737-H6
CASCADE CANYON DR
12400 GrnH 91344 481-A5
CASCADIA DR
2300 GLDL 91206 564-J3
2400 GLDL 91206 565-A3
CASCO CT
3400 HacH 91745 678-D7
CASE AV
5500 NHol 91601 563-A2
6000 NHol 91606 533-A6
7100 NHol 91605 532-J4
7200 SunV 91352 532-J2
CASETAS DR
22700 DBAR 91765 640-A7
CASEY CT
1300 UPL 91784 571-H6
CASEY PL
1800 SPed 90731 824-A2
CASEY ST
- SMAD 91024 567-B1
16400 LA 91343 501-E4
CASHDAN ST
1800 CRSN 90746 764-H3
1900 LACo 90220 764-H3
CASHEW AV
400 BREA 92821 709-C6
CASHIO ST
6000 LA 90035 633-A4
9500 LA 90035 632-G4
CASHMERE PL
- Cstc 91384 4459-G4
CASHMERE ST
11000 Brwd 90049 631-J1
CASHMERE TER
500 Brwd 90049 631-J2
CASIANO CT
15500 BelA 90077 591-G1
CASIANO RD
900 Brwd 90049 591-G6
2500 BelA 90077 591-G2
2800 BelA 90077 561-G7
CASILINA DR
30700 RPV 90275 823-F5
CASILLAS LN
1300 DUAR 91010 568-C5
CASILLO RD
40100 PMDL 93550 4195-J3
CASIMIR AV
10900 ING 90303 703-G6
11400 HAW 90250 703-G7
12900 GAR 90249 733-G3
16300 TOR 90504 733-G6
17300 TOR 90504 763-G1
CASIMO CT
4200 PMDL 93552 4286-J5
CASINO DR
15200 HacH 91745 677-J7
15200 HacH 91745 678-A7
CASINO PT
- LBCH 90803 826-C1
CASITA CT
5500 PMDL 93552 4287-C3
E CASITA ST
500 AZU 91702 599-A1
CASITAS AV
1500 PAS 91103 535-F7
1500 PAS 91103 565-F1
2000 LACo 91103 535-F7
2900 LA 90039 594-E1
6200 BELL 90201 675-F7
N CASITAS AV
2100 Alta 91001 535-F5
CASITAS DR
3600 LVRN 91750 600-H1
W CASITAS ST
500 MONP 91754 635-H3
CASLAM AV
33800 Actn 93510 4375-B5
CASNER WY
- BREA 92821 708-J5
- BREA 92821 709-A5
CASPAR AV
5000 Eagl 90041 565-A5
CASPER CT
- LHB 90631 738-B2
CASPIAN AV
1000 LBCH 90813 795-B5
1800 LBCH 90810 795-B5
3400 LBCH 90810 765-B7
S CASPIAN AV
2600 LBCH 90810 795-B2
21100 CRSN 90810 765-B5
CASPIAN CT
- AGRH 91301 557-G4
- GrnH 91344 480-H6
- WAL 91789 639-C4
CASPIAN DR
3000 PMDL 93551 4195-B4
CASS AV
22200 WdHl 91364 559-H3
CASS PL
2400 LACo 90255 704-J2
2400 SGAT 90280 704-J2
CASSANDRA DR
6500 BGDN 90201 676-A7
6500 BGDN 90201 706-A1
CASSANDRA ST
18600 Tarz 91356 560-H3
CASSARA AV
11400 LA 91342 503-B1
CASSATT ST
4500 LA 90032 595-D5
CASSELL CIR
- UPL 91786 601-G1
CASSIA CT
20100 CRTS 90703 767-A4
CASSIA DR
- PMDL 93551 4285-D3
CASSIDY ST
300 CRSN 90746 734-D7
W CASSIDY ST
1000 GAR 90248 764-A1
CASSIL PL
1500 Hlwd 90028 593-E4
CASSINA AV
10600 SGAT 90280 705-G7
CAST AV
24600 SCTA 91321 4551-A7
24600 SCTA 91321 4641-A1
CASTAC PL
800 PacP 90272 630-H5
CASTAIC RD
31000 Cstc 91384 4369-F5
31000 Cstc 91384 4459-H1
CASTAIC CANYON RD
28700 Valc 91355 4459-J7
28700 Valc 91355 4460-A7
CASTAIC LAKE DR
32000 Cstc 91384 4369-H5
CASTAIC LAKE RD
- Cstc 91384 4279-J4
- LACo 4279-D1
- LACo 91390 4279-J4
- LACo 91390 (4280-A4 See Page 4279)
CASTAIC OAKS LN
- Cstc 91384 4369-G7
N CASTAIC RESERVOIR RD
36200 LACo 91390 (4280-D4 See Page 4279)
CASTAIR DR
2000 LA 90046 593-B3
CASTALA DR
3700 PMDL 93550 4286-H2
CASTALIA AV
3200 LA 90032 595-E5
CASTANA AV
4600 LKWD 90712 766-A4
4700 LKWD 90712 765-J2
13300 DWNY 90242 735-J3
13500 PRM 90723 735-J3
16200 BLF 90706 735-J5
CASTANA LN
40000 PMDL 93551 4195-C4
CASTANET DR
15300 LMRD 90638 737-G1
CASTANO AV
300 PAS 91107 566-F3
CASTANO PL
8300 SunV 91352 532-G1
CASTAWAY CV
- FUL 90638 738-A3
- LMRD 90638 738-A3
CASTELLAMMARE DR
17300 PacP 90272 630-F6
S CASTELLO AV
1100 BHLS 90212 632-F3
1100 LA 90035 632-F3
CASTELLO PL
9800 LA 90035 632-G4
CASTELLO WY
4800 VeCo 91377 557-G2
CASTELLON RD
14300 LMRD 90638 737-E3
CASTELOTTE CT
5100 WHIT 90601 677-D4
CASTERA AV
3200 GLDL 91208 534-H4
CASTERA PL
1500 POM 91767 601-C6
CASTILE DR
16100 WHIT 90603 707-J2
16100 WHIT 90603 708-A2
CASTILIAN DR
2000 LA 90068 593-D2
CASTILLA CT
23800 SCTA 91355 4550-F5
CASTILLE LN
- Saug 91350 4461-F6
CASTILLO CT
19300 WAL 91789 639-C6
CASTILLO DR
- PMDL 93551 4104-E6
CASTILLO LN
- SCTA 91354 4460-G4
11700 Nor 91326 480-H7
CASTILLO ST
21300 WdHl 91364 560-B5
CASTLE
700 SDMS 91773 599-J4
CASTLE CIR
43700 LAN 93535 4106-D1
CASTLE CT
2200 SIMI 93063 499-B1
CASTLE LN
1300 PAS 91104 565-J1
4500 LCF 91011 534-H2
CASTLE PL
400 BHLS 90210 592-G3
2100 POM 91767 600-J5
18800 CRTS 90703 766-E2
CASTLE RD
4500 LCF 91011 534-H1
5100 LCF 91011 504-H7
CASTLE ST
3000 Echo 90026 594-D5
3000 LA 90039 594-D5
40400 PMDL 93551 4194-G2
CASTLEBAR DR
15900 HacH 91745 678-B6
19500 RowH 91748 679-D6
CASTLEBAY LN
18900 Nor 91326 480-G6
CASTLEBAY PL
12200 Nor 91326 480-G6
CASTLEBURY CT
800 SDMS 91773 599-H4
CASTLEBURY PL
- Cstc 91384 4459-G5
CASTLE CREST DR
4500 Eagl 90041 564-J6
CASTLEFORD LN
- CRTS 90703 767-A2
CASTLEFORD PL
3400 RowH 91748 708-H2
N CASTLEGATE AV
1600 COMP 90221 735-C2
S CASTLEGATE AV
900 COMP 90221 735-D6
12800 RDom 90221 735-C4
CASTLEGATE DR
12200 Brwd 90049 631-F1
CASTLEHAVEN RD
33900 LACo 91390 4373-F4
CASTLE HEIGHTS AV
2000 LA 90034 632-G7
CASTLE HEIGHTS PL
2600 LA 90034 632-G6
CASTLEHILL DR
300 WAL 91789 679-E1
29300 AGRH 91301 558-A4
29300 AGRH 91301 557-J4
CASTLE KNOLL RD
5400 LCF 91011 504-J7
CASTLEMAN AV
2300 LA 90032 595-E7
2300 LA 90032 635-E1
CASTLEMAN LN
- BURB 91504 533-E2
CASTLE PEAK DR
6900 CanP 91307 529-C5
CASTLEPEAK ST
19500 RowH 91748 679-D4
CASTLE ROCK CT
- WCOV 91791 639-A4
CASTLE ROCK RD
2400 DBAR 91765 679-J6
3400 DBAR 91765 709-G1
CASTLEROCK RD
3700 LACo 90265 630-E5
CASTLETON DR
100 CLAR 91711 601-D5
CASTLETON ST
17600 INDS 91748 678-H4
CASTLE TOP TR
600 Top 90290 590-B5
CASTLEVIEW AV
4600 LACo 91723 599-H3
4900 LACo 91724 599-H3
CASTLE VIEW DR
3800 Ago 91301 588-A1
CASTLEWOOD DR
2600 FUL 92833 738-D3
21700 LACo 90265 629-F5
CASTLEWOODS DR
15600 Shrm 91403 561-G7
CASTLEWOODS PL
3400 Shrm 91403 561-G7
CASTON CT
- SCTA 91321 4551-F4
CASTRO MTWY
- LACo 90265 587-E7
- LACo 90265 588-A7
- LACo 90265 628-B1
CASUDA CANYON DR
100 MONP 91754 635-G3
CASWELL AV
400 COMP 90220 734-E5
12400 LA 90066 672-B4
14600 LACo 90220 734-E4
N CASWELL AV
500 POM 91767 641-A1
700 POM 91767 601-A6
S CASWELL ST
200 POM 91766 641-A2
CASWOOD DR
14000 WHIT 90602 707-E1
CATALA AV
27200 SCTA 91350 4461-A7
27300 SCTA 91350 4460-J6
CATALINA
18000 LACo 90220 764-J1
CATALINA AV
200 AVA 90704 5923-H4
700 SLB 90740 826-F3
4500 LVRN 91750 570-F7
8100 WHIT 90602 707-G1
8100 WHIT 90605 707-F2
12800 GAR 90247 734-A2
17500 GAR 90248 764-A1
18400 LA 90248 764-A2
N CATALINA AV
- PAS 91106 566-A3
200 RBCH 90277 762-H4
500 PAS 91104 566-A3
1600 PAS 91104 536-A7
1700 LACo 91104 536-A7
S CATALINA AV
- PAS 91106 566-A5
100 RBCH 90277 762-H7
200 PAS 91125 566-A5
1400 RBCH 90277 792-J1
CATALINA CT
- MANB 90266 732-H4
CATALINA DR
- LACo 90265 628-F6
- SIGH 90755 795-H4
1000 GLDL 91207 564-G1
CATALINA LN
- CRSN 90745 794-E1
6000 PMDL 93552 4287-D2
CATALINA RD
200 FUL 92835 738-F3
CATALINA ST
3200 LALM 90720 796-J2
20400 LACo 90502 764-A5
N CATALINA ST
100 BURB 91505 563-D2
100 LA 90004 634-A1
200 LA 90004 594-A5
1300 BURB 91505 533-D7
1300 LFlz 90027 594-A3
2200 BURB 91504 533-D5
2200 LFlz 90027 593-J2
S CATALINA ST
100 LA 90004 634-A3
300 LA 90020 634-A3
600 LA 90005 634-A3
600 LA 90010 634-A3
900 LA 90006 634-A5
2200 LA 90007 634-A6
S CATALINA ST
3400 LA 90007 674-A1
CATALINA TER
4200 LA 90032 595-D5
CATALINA VISTA
2500 LA 90732 823-F7
CATALON AV
5000 WdHl 91364 560-C3
CATALONIA AV
500 PacP 90272 630-G5
CATALONIA CT
13300 CHLS 91709 680-J1
CATALPA AV
300 BREA 92821 708-J7
300 BREA 92821 738-J1
12400 CHNO 91710 641-H6
CATALPA PL
2500 POM 91766 641-A6
12500 CHNO 91710 641-H6
CATALPA RD
400 ARCD 91007 566-J4
CATALPA ST
4300 LA 90032 635-D2
CATALPA WY
- CRSN 90746 764-F1
CATALUNA PL
1600 PVE 90274 792-J6
CATALUNA SQ
1500 PVE 90274 792-J6
CATAMARAN AV
16600 CRTS 90703 736-F6
CATAMARAN ST
- LA 90292 671-H7
CATANIA CT
10600 WHIT 90601 677-D4
CATANIA LN
- Nor 91326 500-C1
CATANIA PL
800 LACo 91711 571-B6
N CATARACT AV
100 SDMS 91773 600-B1
900 SDMS 91773 570-B7
1100 SDMS 91740 570-B7
1200 GLDR 91741 570-B6
S CATARACT AV
100 SDMS 91773 600-B2
CATARINA DR
30800 WLKV 91362 557-F4
CATARO DR
22300 SCTA 91350 4460-J6
CATE DR
7000 BPK 90621 737-G6
CATE RD
9300 PRV 90660 676-H1
CATENA DR
- CHLS 91709 710-J2
CATENIA DR
12200 GrnH 91344 481-D6
CATENIA PL
16800 GrnH 91344 481-D6
CATERINA CT
12600 GrnH 91344 481-B5
CATESBY LN
3000 LA 90015 634-D6
CATHANN PL
22100 TOR 90503 763-B7
CATHANN ST
3900 TOR 90503 763-A7
CATHAY ST
1800 GLDL 91208 534-J7
1800 GLDL 91208 564-J1
CATHCART DR
700 LCF 91011 535-C6
CATHEDRAL DR
- GLDL 91205 564-F7
- GLDL 91205 594-E1
- LA 90065 564-F7
- LA 90065 594-F1
- LA 91205 594-F1
CATHEDRAL PL
17800 Enc 91316 561-A5
CATHEDRAL WY
1000 POM 91768 600-G7
CATHERINE DR
- SCTA 91351 4551-J2
CATHERINE LN
1200 LA 90069 592-H5
CATHERINE RD
2300 Alta 91001 536-A6
CATHERINE ST
5200 PRV 90660 676-G4
CATHERINE PARK DR
100 GLDR 91741 569-H5
CATHERWOOD CT
29000 AGRH 91301 558-A3
CATHERWOOD DR
5700 LCF 91011 535-C2
CATHRYN DR
2100 LACo 91770 636-D3
CATHRYN PL
2200 LACo 91770 636-D3
CATHWELL LN
9200 Tuj 91042 504-B6
CATHY AV
2500 POM 91768 640-D2
5800 KeCo 93560 3834-A1
CATHY ST
12500 LA 91342 482-E2
CATLIN ST
- FUL 92833 738-D5
CATO ST
4400 LA 90032 595-D7
CATO WY
4500 LA 90032 595-D6
CATSKILL AV
21000 CRSN 90745 764-D5
22400 CRSN 90745 794-D1
CATSKILL RD
9700 Sunl 91040 503-C4
CATSKILLS CT
- SCTA 91387 4462-G7
CATSUE PL
- LAN 93536 4014-H7
- LAN 93536 4104-H1
CATTAIL CIR
200 BREA 92821 709-D7
CATTAIL CT
21600 WAL 91789 639-H6
CATTAIL PL
- PMDL 93551 4285-D2
CATTAIL WY
26600 SCTA 91351 4551-C2
CATTARAUGUS AV
3200 CULC 90232 632-J7
3200 LA 90034 632-G6
CATTLE CREEK RD
2200 Actn 93510 4375-F5
CAULFIELD AV
13200 NRWK 90650 737-A2
CAVALIER ST
22600 WdHl 91364 559-H4
CAVALIER WY
2600 RowH 91748 678-H7
CAVALINI PL
- SCTA 91355 4460-D6
CAVALLERI RD
5800 MAL 90265 627-F7
5800 MAL 90265 667-E1
CAVAN LN
700 GLDR 91741 569-F3
CAVANAGH CIR
2200 LA 90032 635-F1
CAVANAGH RD
500 GLDL 91207 564-F2
5000 LA 90032 635-E1
CAVE WY
19500 Top 90290 590-B7
CAVEHILL RD
- LACo 91390 4461-F3
CAVEL ST
8300 DWNY 90242 706-A6
CAVELL PL
14300 BALD 91706 598-C4
CAVENDISH DR
2900 LA 90064 632-F6
CAVENWAY LN
3000 THO 91361 557-C5
CAVERN CT
20100 LACo 91390 4461-E4
CAVERNA DR
7200 LA 90068 593-C1
CAVETTE PL
14400 BALD 91706 598-C4
CAWOOD PL
15800 LMRD 90638 737-J3
CAWSTON ST
1000 SPAS 91030 595-F2
CAYENNE DR
27700 SCTA 91350 4461-B6
CAYMAN CT
- MANB 90266 732-J4
CAYMAN PL
- SCTA 91350 4551-D5
CAYMAN RD
2100 LACo 90265 627-F3
CAYUGA AV
8500 SunV 91352 532-H1
8900 SunV 91352 502-F6
9800 Pcma 91331 502-B2
25800 LMTA 90717 793-J6
CAYUGA PL
- CHNO 91710 641-H4
CAYUSE LN
28300 RPV 90275 823-F1
CAZADERO PL
21500 DBAR 91765 679-J5
CAZADOR CT
3300 LA 90065 594-H3
CAZADOR DR
2200 LA 90065 594-H3
CAZADOR ST
2900 LA 90065 594-J2
CAZAUX DR
5800 LA 90068 593-G2
CAZAUX PL
5700 LA 90068 593-G2
CBS LN
2300 SBdC 92372 (4562-F1 See Page 4471)
CEANOTHUS PL
3900 CALB 91302 558-G7
3900 CALB 91302 588-G1
CECELIA CT
18700 CRTS 90703 767-B1
CECELIA PL
17800 CRTS 90703 737-B7
17800 CRTS 90703 767-B1
CECELIA ST
200 LA 90014 634-F5
4500 CDHY 90201 705-D2
4700 CDHY 90201 705-E2
5000 SGAT 90280 705-E2
CECELIA WY
18300 CRTS 90703 767-B1
CECIANA DR
2200 HacH 91745 678-D5
CECIL ST
500 MONP 91755 636-B3
CECILIA ST
3000 WCOV 91792 639-A7
5500 BGDN 90201 705-G3
7400 DWNY 90241 705-J3
7600 DWNY 90241 706-A4
10600 NRWK 90650 706-F6
11400 SFSP 90670 706-F6
CECILVILLE AV
4800 LaCr 91214 504-G7
CECINA PL
- PMDL 93552 4287-D3
CECINA WY
900 BelA 90077 592-A6
CEDAR
11300 NRWK 90650 706-J7
14700 LA 91342 481-G1
18800 RowH 91748 679-B4
CEDAR AV
- LBCH 90802 825-D1
100 MNRO 91016 567-G3
200 FUL 92833 738-C7
700 LBCH 90813 795-D5
1800 LBCH 90806 795-D3
1800 MANB 90266 732-H5
3100 LYN 90262 735-A1
3400 Bxby 90807 765-D6
3400 Bxby 90807 795-D3
3900 ELMN 91731 597-E5
4100 ELMN 91732 597-E5
5000 NLB 90805 765-D2
11100 Lenx 90304 703-D6
11100 HAW 90304 703-D6
11400 HAW 90250 703-D7
11900 HAW 90250 733-D1
12300 CHNO 91710 641-H6
43700 LAN 93534 4105-H1
44000 LAN 93534 4015-H4
E CEDAR AV
- BURB 91502 563-H1
200 BURB 91502 533-J7
400 BURB 91501 533-A7
800 BURB 91501 534-A6
N CEDAR AV
100 ING 90301 703-B2
200 LBCH 90802 795-D7
200 LBCH 90802 825-D1
300 ING 90302 703-B2
S CEDAR AV
100 ING 90301 703-B3
W CEDAR AV
200 BURB 91502 563-G2
300 BURB 91506 563-G2
CEDAR CIR
3700 BALD 91706 597-J7
11300 ELMN 91732 597-E4
CEDAR CT
200 MTBL 90640 676-D3
1200 ONT 91762 641-J4
9700 CYP 90630 767-D7
W CEDAR CT
1000 UPL 91786 601-J2
CEDAR DR
300 COV 91723 599-A6
N CEDAR DR
100 COV 91723 599-A4
CEDAR LN
- Saug 91350 4461-B4
1100 SDMS 91773 599-J3
2500 ELMN 91731 597-A7
CEDAR PL
- SCTA 91354 4460-E7
4100 WdHl 91364 559-J5
CEDAR PT
14900 LA 91342 481-H7
CEDAR ST
- ONT 91762 641-J4
- PAS 91103 565-H1
400 LA 90065 595-A5
700 SMCA 90405 671-G3
900 ELSG 90245 702-E7
1700 ALH 91801 595-H5
2400 LVRN 91750 570-H7
5700 SBdC 92397 (4652-C2 See Page 4651)
6000 VeCo 93063 499-B4
6100 HNTP 90255 675-A7
8500 BLF 90706 735-J7
8700 BLF 90706 736-A7
E CEDAR ST
100 COMP 90220 734-J3
200 COMP 90220 735-A3
N CEDAR ST
100 GLDL 91206 564-F5
900 GLDL 91207 564-F3
900 ING 90302 673-B7
900 ING 90302 703-B1
S CEDAR ST
100 GLDL 91205 564-F5
1400 MTBL 90640 676-C6
W CEDAR ST
100 COMP 90220 734-G3
CEDAR WY
31200 Cstc 91384 4369-E7
31200 Cstc 91384 4459-F1
CEDARBEND DR
3700 GLDL 91214 534-D1
CEDARBLUFF DR
28400 RPV 90275 792-H7
28400 RPV 90275 822-H1

STREET Block City ZIP Pg-Grid

CEDARBLUFF WY
- CRSN 90746 764-F1
CEDARBREAK AV
1500 RowH 91748 679-A5
CEDARBROOK AV
2000 PMDL 93550 4286-D2
CEDARBROOK DR
9500 LA 90210 592-F3
E CEDARBROOK ST
1100 WCOV 91790 638-G1
CEDAR CANYON CT
- LACo 91390 4461-B3
CEDARCLIFF AV
7200 LACo 90606 677-A7
7600 LACo 90606 676-J7
CEDARCLIFF CT
600 THO 91362 557-F1
CEDAR COURT RD
1300 GLDL 91207 564-F2
CEDAR CREEK CT
100 LMRD 90638 738-B2
CEDARCREEK LN
12400 CRTS 90703 736-J5
CEDAR CREEK RD
100 SDMS 91773 600-C3
CEDARCREEK ST
19300 SCTA 91351 4551-D2
CEDAR CREST AV
400 CLAR 91711 601-D5
CEDARCREST AV
100 SPAS 91030 565-H7
100 SPAS 91030 595-H1
CEDARCREST DR
1500 BREA 92821 708-J4
12200 CRTS 90703 736-J5
CEDAR CREST LN
13500 SLB 90740 826-G1
CEDARCROFT RD
31800 Actn 93510 4465-E3
CEDARDALE DR
9900 SFSP 90670 706-F4
22000 DBAR 91765 679-J4
CEDAREDGE AV
1200 Eagl 90041 565-C5
CEDAREDGE CT
1200 Eagl 90041 565-C5
CEDARFALLS DR
20900 SCTA 91350 4461-C6
CEDARFORT DR
15800 SCTA 91387 4552-D4
CEDAR GLEN CT
- LACo 91390 4460-J2
CEDARGLEN DR
600 AZU 91702 569-A6
5300 LACo 91702 599-A1
5800 LACo 91702 569-A7
CEDARGROVE AV
9100 WHIT 90605 707-E3
CEDAR GROVE LN
- LA 91342 482-G7
CEDARHAVEN DR
5300 AGRH 91301 557-H5
CEDARHILL RD
1500 GLDL 91202 564-D2
CEDARHURST CIR
4300 LFlz 90027 594-B3
CEDARHURST DR
2100 LFlz 90027 594-B3
CEDARLANE DR
16200 HacH 91745 678-D3
CEDAR LODGE TER
1900 LA 90039 594-C4
CEDARMONT DR
1500 HacH 91745 678-F4
CEDAR OAK LN
- Cstc 91384 4459-H3
CEDAR PINE CT
5500 PMDL 93552 4287-B4
CEDAR POINT PL
300 THO 91362 557-G2
CEDAR RIDGE CT
- LACo 91390 4460-H2
18900 WAL 91789 639-B6
CEDAR RIDGE PL
- StvR 91381 4550-C4
CEDARSPRINGS DR
14400 WHIT 90603 707-F3
CEDAR TOWN ST
23200 SCTA 91321 4640-H2
CEDARTREE RD
8400 DWNY 90240 706-D2
CEDAR TURN
100 NLB 90805 765-D2
CEDARVALE RD
9500 Tuj 91042 504-A5
CEDARVALE ST
11600 NRWK 90650 736-G6
CEDARVALLEY DR
31200 WLKV 91362 557-E5
CEDAR VALLEY WY
- SCTA 91387 4551-G5
18600 SCTA 91321 4551-G5
CEDARVIEW
8400 CYP 90630 767-B5
CEDARVIEW DR
1100 CLAR 91711 601-A1
CEDARWOOD AV
- DUAR 91010 568-D3
100 GLDR 91741 569-G5
16600 CRTS 90703 736-J6
CEDARWOOD CIR
16700 CRTS 90703 736-J6

CEDARWOOD CT
- BREA 92823 709-H6
16900 CRTS 90703 736-J6
CEDARWOOD DR
- POM 91766 640-G6
800 LHB 90631 708-B7
CEDARWOOD LN
7900 LPMA 90623 767-D4
CEDARWOOD ST
2300 WCOV 91790 598-C7
14200 BALD 91706 598-C6
N CEDON DR
1200 LACo 91744 638-G5
CEDRAL ST
3800 Actn 93510 4374-J6
3800 Actn 93510 4375-A6
CEDRELA AV
37200 PMDL 93552 4287-B3
CEDRIC PL
2600 RowH 91748 679-B7
CEDROS AV
4200 Shrm 91403 561-J4
4300 Shrm 91403 562-A5
5200 VanN 91411 561-J2
6000 VanN 91411 531-J6
6600 VanN 91405 531-J4
8000 PanC 91402 531-J2
8700 PanC 91402 501-J6
10300 MsnH 91345 501-J4
CEEBEE DR
9500 DWNY 90241 706-D7
CEIL AV
- Actn 93510 4375-F6
CEILHUNT AV
2700 LA 90064 632-B7
2700 LA 90064 672-B1
CELANO CT
- CHLS 91709 710-J2
CELEDON CREEK
- LA 90094 702-D1
CELES ST
21200 WdHl 91364 560-A3
CELESTE LN
1700 FUL 92833 738-D4
CELESTE PL
- RHE 90274 793-G6
CELESTE ST
400 AZU 91702 599-A1
CELESTIAL DR
- LA 90068 563-F5
CELESTIAL LN
- LACo 91390 4461-A1
CELESTINE DR
11500 LACo 90604 708-A6
CELIA CT
1200 UPL 91784 571-J6
CELIA ST
2400 POM 91768 640-D1
CELINDA PL
16300 Enc 91436 561-E5
CELINE ST
11500 ELMN 91732 597-F4
CELIS ST
600 SFER 91340 502-B1
800 SFER 91340 482-A7
1600 SFER 91340 481-J6
CELITA HWY
- GLDL 91214 534-E2
CELITO DR
8100 LACo 91770 636-F4
CELLESTE PL
- Saug 91350 4461-E6
CELLO DR
22500 DBAR 91765 680-A3
CELTIC
15400 MsnH 91345 501-G2
CELTIC CT
21400 Chat 91311 500-A2
CELTIC DR
- PMDL 93551 4285-G1
CELTIC ST
15600 GmH 91344 501-C2
18500 Nor 91326 500-F2
20100 Chat 91311 500-B2
CELTIC WY
11900 Nor 91326 480-J6
CEMENT BLOCK RD
- Cstc 91384 4460-A3
CEMETERY RD
36900 PMDL 93550 4286-E4
CENSOR AV
24100 Hrbr 90710 794-A3
CENTENNIAL LN
- AZU 91702 569-A5
CENTENNIAL ST
800 LA 90012 634-F2
CENTENNIAL WY
- ARCD 91007 567-B5
CENTER AV
300 COMP 90220 734-H5
700 GLDR 91740 569-F7
1400 DUAR 91010 568-A6
3600 ELMN 91731 597-C7
CENTER AV N
- Hrbr 90710 794-A3
CENTER AV S
- Hrbr 90710 794-A4
CENTER CT
- Ven 90291 671-H7
CENTER DR
- Wch 90045 702-H1
6200 Wch 90045 672-H7

CENTER DR W
6200 Wch 90045 672-H7
CENTER PL
100 MANB 90266 732-F6
5300 ELA 90022 675-H2
CENTER ST
100 AZU 91702 598-J2
100 ELSG 90245 732-F1
100 LA 90012 634-H4
600 ELSG 90245 702-F7
700 SPed 90731 824-C3
2200 LACo 90255 704-H1
3900 BALD 91706 598-A5
4100 CULC 90232 672-E3
5000 CHNO 91710 641-G7
11500 SGAT 90280 705-G7
11600 SGAT 90280 735-G1
33300 LACo 91390 (4372-J4
See Page 4281)
33300 LACo 91390 4373-A4
E CENTER ST
100 COV 91723 599-B5
100 POM 91767 640-J1
200 POM 91767 641-A1
W CENTER ST
100 COV 91723 599-A5
100 POM 91768 640-H1
CENTER TER
700 SDMS 91773 600-A3
CENTER WY
200 Wch 90045 702-F5
3800 TOR 90503 763-C7
CENTER WY N
- Wch 90045 702-F5
CENTER WY S
- Wch 90045 702-G5
CENTER CIRCLE DR
- Hrbr 90710 794-A3
CENTER COURT DR
2300 THO 91361 557-A6
E CENTER COURT DR
1200 COV 91724 599-E7
CENTER COURT DR N
17700 CRTS 90703 737-A7
17700 CRTS 90703 767-A1
CENTER COURT DR S
12700 CRTS 90703 767-A1
CENTERPOINTE DR
- LPMA 90623 767-D2
CENTERSTONE CIR
- BPK 90620 767-J3
CENTERVIEW DR
300 CRSN 90746 734-D7
CENTINARY DR
100 WAL 91789 679-F1
200 WAL 91789 639-F7
CENTINELA AV
300 ING 90302 703-D1
700 ING 90302 673-A7
800 SMCA 90403 631-G5
1200 WLA 90025 631-H6
1200 SMCA 90404 631-H6
1900 LA 90064 631-J7
2200 SMCA 90404 632-A7
2300 LA 90064 632-A7
6700 Wch 90045 673-A7
6700 LA 90056 673-A7
S CENTINELA AV
2400 LA 90064 632-A7
2400 SMCA 90405 632-A7
2400 LA 90064 672-A1
2400 SMCA 90405 672-A1
3200 LA 90066 672-B2
3900 CULC 90066 672-D5
4300 LA 90066 672-D5
4500 LA 90230 672-G6
5200 LACo 90066 672-D5
5600 LA 90094 672-G6
5800 Wch 90045 672-G6
W CENTINELA AV
5200 Wch 90045 673-A7
5200 LA 90056 673-A7
5300 Wch 90045 672-J7
5300 LadH 90056 672-J7
5300 LadH 90056 673-A6
5800 CULC 90230 672-J7
CENTINELLA ST
6100 SIMI 93063 499-B2
CENTRAL AL
- SPAS 91030 595-H2
CENTRAL AV
- SFSP 90670 707-A5
- WHIT 90605 707-D2
100 SLB 90740 826-E4
900 DUAR 91010 567-J5
900 SBdC - (512-A5
See Page 511)
900 LACo - (512-A5
See Page 511)
1100 DUAR 91010 568-A5
1400 SELM 91733 637-B2
2100 IRW 91706 568-D5
2600 ELMN 91733 637-B2
8200 WHIT 90602 707-D1
8700 MTCL 91763 601-G4
8700 UPL 91786 601-G4
10400 MTCL 91763 641-G3
10600 MTCL 91762 641-G3
10700 SBdC 91762 641-G3
11100 SBdC 91710 641-G3
11300 CHNO 91710 641-G3
14500 BALD 91706 598-C5
15900 LA 91342 481-F3
15900 LPUE 91744 638-D7

CENTRAL AV
15900 LPUE 91744 678-E1
18000 CRSN 90746 764-G2
18000 CRSN 90747 764-G2
29700 Cstc 91384 4459-D6
E CENTRAL AV
100 MNRO 91016 567-H6
100 SGBL 91776 596-E5
N CENTRAL AV
100 COMP 90220 734-F5
100 GLDL 91203 564-E4
100 LA 90012 634-G4
200 UPL 91786 601-G3
900 GLDL 91202 564-E3
1100 COMP 90222 734-F3
1200 Wbrk 90222 734-F3
1300 COMP 90059 734-F3
2200 Wbrk 90059 734-F3
7400 MTCL 91763 601-G3
7400 UPL 91763 601-G3
14300 LACo 90220 734-F3
S CENTRAL AV
- COMP 90059 734-F7
- Wbrk 90222 734-F7
100 COMP 90220 734-F7
100 GLDL 91204 564-E7
100 GLDL 91210 564-E7
100 LA 90012 634-G6
300 LA 90013 634-G6
600 LA 90021 634-G6
1100 Wbrk 90059 704-F6
1100 Wbrk 90059 734-F7
1600 GLDL 91204 594-E1
1600 CRSN 90220 764-G1
1900 LA 90011 634-G6
1900 LA 90011 674-E2
2200 COMP 90220 764-G1
2200 CRSN 90746 734-F7
5800 Flor 90001 674-E7
5800 LA 90001 674-E7
7300 Flor 90001 704-E2
7300 LA 90001 704-E2
8600 Wats 90002 704-E2
10700 LA 90059 704-F6
13900 COMP 90222 734-F7
17500 CRSN 90746 764-G1
17800 CRSN 90220 764-G1
W CENTRAL AV
100 BREA 92821 709-B5
100 MNRO 91016 567-F5
500 SGBL 91776 596-D5
600 BREA 92821 708-J6
1600 LHB 90631 708-J6
CENTRAL CT
- PAS 91105 565-H5
100 RBCH 90277 762-J5
2300 LAN 93536 4015-D6
CENTRAL PK
- SCTA 91350 4461-A7
- SCTA 91350 4551-B1
CENTRAL PK N
- CRSN 90745 794-E2
CENTRAL PK S
- CRSN 90745 794-E2
CENTRAL PL
10700 SBdC 91762 641-G1
CENTRAL ST
16000 IRW 91706 598-F3
CENTRAL TER
400 SGBL 91776 596-F5
CENTRAL WK
- Cstc 91384 4459-D6
CENTRAL WY
100 SLB 90740 826-E4
CENTRALIA ST
2500 LKWD 90712 765-G4
3900 LKWD 90712 766-A5
4400 LKWD 90712 766-D5
11300 LKWD 90715 766-G5
11300 HGDN 90716 766-G5
12400 LKWD 90715 767-A5
12700 LACo 90630 767-A5
E CENTRALIA ST
4300 LBCH 90808 766-A5
CENTRE CT
1600 PMDL 93551 4195-F5
CENTRE DR
1100 INDS 91789 679-D4
N CENTRE ST
100 SPed 90731 824-C4
S CENTRE ST
100 SPed 90731 824-C6
CENTRE PLAZA DR
1500 MONP 91754 635-F2
CENTRE POINTE PKWY
21400 SCTA 91350 4551-B4
CENTURIA DR
27900 RPV 90275 792-H6
CENTURION AV
1300 LACo 91770 636-F4
CENTURION WY
21700 SCTA 91350 4461-A6
CENTURY BLVD
300 LA 90003 704-J5
2700 LYN 90262 704-J5
2700 SGAT 90280 704-J5
2900 LYN 90262 705-A5
2900 SGAT 90280 705-A5
5400 SGAT 90280 735-F1
5400 PRM 90723 735-H2
5600 Wch 90045 702-G5
8400 DWNY 90242 735-J3
8800 PRM 90723 736-A3

CENTURY BLVD
9900 Wats 90002 704-J5
E CENTURY BLVD
100 LA 90003 704-D4
600 Wats 90002 704-G4
1200 Wats 90002 704-G4
W CENTURY BLVD
100 LA 90003 704-B4
500 LA 90044 704-B4
1000 LACo 90044 704-B4
1200 LACo 90044 703-F4
1400 LA 90047 703-F4
1500 LA 90047 703-F4
2200 ING 90303 703-F4
2200 ING 90305 703-F4
3400 ING 90301 703-B5
4000 ING 90304 703-B5
5100 Lenx 90304 703-B5
5200 Wch 90045 703-B5
5400 Wch 90045 702-H5
CENTURY CIR
45300 LAN 93535 4016-A4
CENTURY FRWY I-105
- DWNY - 735-G2
- DWNY - 736-D2
- ELSG - 702-H7
- HAW - 703-E7
- ING - 703-E7
- LA - 704-C7
- LACo - 703-E7
- LACo - 704-C7
- Lenx - 703-E7
- LYN - 704-C7
- LYN - 705-A6
- LYN - 735-G2
- NRWK - 736-D2
- PRM - 735-G2
- SGAT - 735-G2
- Wbrk - 704-C7
- Wch - 702-H7
- Wch - 703-E7
CENTURY LN
5300 LYN 90262 735-E1
CENTURY MTWY
- LACo 91302 588-F6
- LACo 91302 628-G1
CENTURY PK E
1800 CenC 90067 632-E3
2200 LA 90035 632-E3
CENTURY PK W
1800 WLA 90025 632-E3
CENTURY HILL
- CenC 90067 632-E4
- LA 90035 632-E4
CENTURY PARK LN
2100 CenC 90067 632-E3
CENTURY WOODS DR
10200 CenC 90067 632-E4
10200 WLA 90025 632-E4
CENTURY WOODS WY
2100 CenC 90067 632-E4
2100 WLA 90025 632-E4
CERAM CT
- LACo 90265 626-D1
CERCA DR
22900 SCTA 91354 4550-H1
23000 SCTA 91354 4460-H7
CERCO ALTA DR
1800 MONP 91754 635-G2
CERECITA DR
13900 LACo 90605 707-D4
14300 LACo 90604 707-E5
CEREDO PL
17100 GmH 91344 481-C6
CERES AV
500 LA 90013 634-G6
600 LA 90021 634-F6
9900 LACo 90604 707-F4
10900 LACo 90604 707-D6
CEREZA DR
700 MONP 91754 635-G3
CEREZA WY
21900 Top 90290 590-A2
E CEREZA WY
400 LBCH 90802 795-E7
W CEREZA WY
200 LBCH 90802 795-C7
CEREZO CT
23400 SCTA 91321 4640-H1
CERISA ST
44500 LAN 93535 4016-E6
CERISE AV
800 TOR 90503 763-F5
12500 HAW 90250 733-F2
13400 LACo 90250 733-F2
15200 LACo 90249 733-F5
16500 TOR 90504 733-F7
17500 TOR 90504 763-F1
22500 TOR 90505 793-F1
CERO DR
28000 SCTA 91350 4461-C5
CERQUITA DR
16000 WHIT 90603 708-A1
16000 WHIT 90605 708-A1
CERRILLOS DR
4600 WdHl 91364 559-J4
CERRITO PL
- RHE 90274 793-H7
CERRITOS AV
- LBCH 90802 825-F1
200 LBCH 90802 795-F7
700 LBCH 90813 795-F5
1800 LBCH 90806 795-F3

CERRITOS AV
2200 SIGH 90755 795-F1
3200 LALM 90720 796-J2
3200 LALM 90815 796-J2
3300 Bxby 90807 795-F1
3400 Bxby 90807 765-F5
5200 NLB 90805 765-F3
6300 NLB 90805 735-F7
14000 BLF 90706 736-A3
E CERRITOS AV
100 GLDL 91205 594-E1
N CERRITOS AV
100 AZU 91702 569-A7
5200 AZU 91702 599-A2
S CERRITOS AV
- LACo 91702 569-A7
- LACo 91702 599-A1
300 AZU 91702 599-A1
500 AZU 91702 569-A7
W CERRITOS AV
100 GLDL 91204 594-E1
CERRITOS CT
200 CLAR 91711 571-D6
CERRITOS DR
1000 FUL 92835 738-G5
4400 Bxby 90807 765-F5
CERRITOS PL
6500 LA 90068 593-E3
CERRITOS CORPORATE DR
13800 CRTS 90703 737-D5
CERRO WY
19600 WAL 91789 679-D2
CERROCREST DR
1200 LA 90210 592-F5
CERRO GORDO ST
1400 Echo 90026 594-F5
1900 LA 90039 594-F5
CERRO VERDE AV
- SCTA 91355 4550-E4
CERRO VERDE PL
4600 Tarz 91356 560-H4
CERRO VISTA DR
9400 Tuj 91042 504-C6
CERTA DR
6500 RPV 90275 792-H7
CERVANTES CT
600 VeCo 91377 557-J2
CERVANTES PL
7400 LA 90046 593-C2
CERVATO ST
4500 LBCH 90815 796-A4
CERVERA AV
800 Wilm 90744 795-A5
900 LBCH 90813 795-A5
900 Wilm 90744 795-A5
CESAR E CHAVEZ AV
3400 City 90063 635-D5
4300 ELA 90022 635-F5
5000 MONP 91754 635-F5
E CESAR E CHAVEZ AV
100 LA 90012 634-H3
400 Boyl 90033 635-A4
500 Boyl 90033 634-H3
3000 LA 90063 635-A4
W CESAR E CHAVEZ AV
100 LA 90012 634-F2
CESAR E CHAVEZ DR
4100 BALD 91706 598-C5
CESAR E CHAVEZ LN
3700 LYN 90262 705-B7
CESSNA DR
- LACo 90265 587-H7
- LACo 90265 627-G1
CETRO TR
- Chat 91311 480-A7
CEYLON AV
8500 PRV 90660 706-E2
CEYLON PL
- SCTA 91350 4551-D5
CEZANNE AV
4300 WdHl 91364 560-A5
CEZANNE LN
- SCTA 91355 4550-D3
CEZANNE PL
21600 WdHl 91364 560-A5
CHABELA DR
400 MANB 90266 732-H7
CHADBOURNE AV
200 Brwd 90049 631-E4
CHADLEY ST
18700 LACo 91722 599-C2
CHADMONT ST
16500 LACo 91722 598-G3
CHADNEY DR
3000 GLDL 91206 535-B6
CHADRON AV
11800 Pcma 91331 482-D7
11900 LA 91340 482-D7
12500 HAW 90250 733-F2
14500 LACo 90249 733-F4
CHADSEY DR
9800 WHIT 90603 707-F4
10800 LACo 90604 707-F5
12700 LMRD 90638 737-E1
CHADSFORD DR
23800 SCTA 91354 4460-F7
CHADWAY ST
19500 SCTA 91351 4551-F1
CHADWELL ST
11300 LKWD 90715 766-F4
12500 LKWD 90715 767-A4

CHADWICK CIR
2700 LA 90032 595-E7
CHADWICK CT
700 POM 91766 641-A6
CHADWICK DR
2900 LA 90032 595-F7
CHADWICK LN
4000 LACo 90274 793-C6
4000 RHE 90274 793-C6
CHADWICK TER
4200 HiPk 90042 595-D4
CHADWICK WY
1500 LVRN 91750 600-F1
CHAFFEE DR
- FUL 92833 738-C5
CHAFFEE ST
6400 Tuj 91042 504-C4
CHAGAL AV
1000 LAN 93535 4106-C1
CHAGALL RD
21240 Top 90290 560-B7
CHAGALL WY
- LMRD 90638 737-G4
CHAKEMCO ST
5100 SGAT 90280 705-E5
N CHALBURN AV
200 WCOV 91790 598-E6
CHALCEDONY
100 BREA 92823 710-C6
CHALCO ST
15000 LMRD 90638 707-G7
CHALET DR
6200 CMRC 90040 676-A7
6400 BGDN 90201 676-A7
6500 BGDN 90201 706-A1
CHALET TER
1000 MONP 91754 635-J3
16500 PacP 90272 630-H4
CHALETTE DR
500 BHLS 90210 592-G3
CHALFONT CT
40000 PMDL 93551 4195-B4
CHALFONT LN
39200 PMDL 93551 4195-B5
CHALFORD CT
16900 HacH 91745 678-F6
CHALINA DR
19600 WAL 91789 679-D1
CHALK HILL DRIVEWAY
- WdHl 91364 560-D2
CHALLENGER CT
3500 PMDL 93550 4286-H3
CHALLENGER ST
- BREA 92821 708-J6
- BREA 92821 709-A6
3400 TOR 90503 763-D4
CHALLENGER WY
- ELSG 90245 732-J1
42000 LAN 93535 4106-B2
42000 PMDL 93535 4106-A7
44000 LAN 93535 4016-B4
46000 LACo 93535 4016-B2
46500 LACo 93535 3926-B5
CHALMERS DR
8500 LA 90035 632-J3
CHALMERS PL
25800 LACo 91302 558-J3
25800 LACo 91302 559-A3
CHALMETTE LN
25900 RHE 90274 793-C5
CHALON RD
10600 BelA 90077 592-A7
10700 BelA 90077 591-J6
11000 Brwd 90049 591-H6
13100 Brwd 90049 631-D1
CHALONE DR
- PMDL 93552 4287-A5
3700 PMDL 93550 4286-H5
4200 PMDL 93552 4286-J6
CHAMA DR
- LAN 93535 4016-D3
CHAMBER AV
4700 LVRN 91750 570-E7
CHAMBERLAIN LN
- Res 91335 530-G2
CHAMBERLAIN RD
1300 PAS 91103 565-D1
CHAMBERLAIN ST
14000 LA 91340 502-A2
14300 MsnH 91345 502-A2
14600 MsnH 91345 501-J3
CHAMBERS CT
- FUL 92833 738-D5
5300 LKWD 90712 765-J3
CHAMBERS ST
2500 VER 90058 674-J4
CHAMBLEE AV
19300 CRTS 90703 766-H3
CHAMBORD DR
- LACo 91390 4373-H5
CHAMBORD RD
7700 Actn 93510 4374-B5
CHAMERA LN
22700 Top 90290 589-H3
CHAMINADE AV
7400 LA 91304 529-F4
CHAMINADE CT
- CLAR 91711 571-F4
CHAMISE WY
30300 LACo 91390 4462-E4
CHAMIZO CALLE
33300 LACo 91390 4373-E6

CHAMPAGNE CT
30800 WLKV 91362 557-F5
CHAMPAGNE LN
23300 SCTA 91321 4640-H3
CHAMPION CIR
800 WAL 91789 639-E6
CHAMPION PL
- ALH 91801 596-C3
CHAMPION WY
- PMDL 93551 4195-B2
CHAMPLAIN AV
400 PAS 91103 565-H3
CHAMPLAIN DR
400 CLAR 91711 571-C7
CHAMPLAIN TER
1600 Echo 90026 594-F5
CHANCE ST
3400 WCOV 91792 679-B1
CHANCERY LN
2500 GLDL 91206 565-A2
E CHANDA CT
1000 LBCH 90813 795-F7
CHANDELEUR DR
1700 LA 90732 823-H5
2000 RPV 90275 823-H5
CHANDELLE PL
7700 LA 90046 593-A1
23600 DBAR 91765 680-C1
CHANDELLE RD
3000 LA 90046 593-B1
3000 LA 90046 563-B7
N CHANDLER AV
100 MONP 91754 636-A1
S CHANDLER AV
100 MONP 91754 636-A3
CHANDLER BLVD
900 BURB 91506 533-F7
1800 BURB 91506 563-C1
2500 BURB 91505 563-C1
10400 NHol 91601 563-A2
11100 NHol 91601 562-E2
11700 LA 91607 562-E2
12800 VanN 91401 562-B2
CHANDLER DR
5400 VanN 91401 562-D2
CHANDLER LN
- DUAR 91010 568-A6
11300 SBdC 91766 641-C3
CHANDLER PL
- SMRO 91108 566-B7
E CHANDLER ST
100 Wilm 90744 794-E4
W CHANDLER ST
1000 Wilm 90744 794-C4
CHANDLER FIRE RD
- SunV 91352 533-D1
CHANDOS LN
1900 LHH 90631 708-D2
CHANDU PL
18600 RowH 91748 679-B7
CHANERA AV
11600 HAW 90250 703-G7
11600 HAW 90303 703-G7
15200 GAR 90249 733-G5
16400 TOR 90504 733-G6
18000 TOR 90504 763-G1
S CHANERA AV
10900 ING 90303 703-G6
CHANEY AV
8100 PRV 90660 706-E2
9000 DWNY 90240 706-D3
10200 DWNY 90241 706-C5
CHANEY TR
3400 Alta 91001 535-H3
3700 LACo - 535-H2
CHANNEL DR
- PMDL 93551 4195-G5
600 LBCH 90803 796-D7
CHANNEL LN
- SCTA 91355 4550-E1
14800 LA 90402 631-B7
16500 HNTB 92649 826-J7
CHANNEL RD
- Cstc 91384 4459-J4
E CHANNEL RD
400 LA 90402 631-C6
W CHANNEL RD
100 LA 90402 631-B7
CHANNEL ST
600 SPed 90731 824-A3
CHANNEL WK
4500 MdlR 90292 702-A2
CHANNELFORD RD
1900 THO 91361 557-A6
CHANNEL ISLANDS WY
- WCOV 91791 639-A4
CHANNEL POINTE CT
200 LA 90292 702-A4
CHANNEL POINTE MALL
200 LA 90292 702-A4
CHANNELVIEW CT
6600 RPV 90275 822-H5
CHANNELWOOD DR
1500 LACo 90601 637-F6
CHANNELWOOD WY
16400 LMRD 90638 738-A2
CHANNING ST
200 LA 90021 634-G6
300 AZU 91702 568-H4
2200 WCOV 91790 598-C6
3400 BALD 91706 598-C6
CHANNING WY
2600 OrCo 90720 796-G4

CHANRUSS PL
1200 BHLS 90210 592-E6
CHANSLOR AV
6400 BELL 90201 675-F7
6400 BELL 90201 705-F1
CHANSLOR ST
2300 POM 91766 641-A6
CHANSON DR
3800 LACo 90043 673-D5
CHANTACO CT
- PMDL 93551 4195-C2
CHANTADA AV
32200 Actn 93510 4375-F7
CHANTECLAIR CT
- Tuj 91042 503-J2
CHANTEL LN
- PMDL 93551 4195-C5
CHANTILLY LN
- Tuj 91042 503-J1
1700 FUL 92833 738-D3
39400 PMDL 93551 4195-C5
CHANTILLY RD
900 BelA 90077 591-J5
CHANTO DR
9000 WHIT 90603 707-J3
CHANTRY CT
4500 CYP 90630 767-B7
CHANTRY DR
600 LHB 90631 708-B5
1800 ARCD 91006 567-C1
CHANTRY FLATS TKTR
- LACo - 537-C5
- LACo 91024 537-C5
CHANUTE ST
12400 Pcma 91331 502-E3
CHAPALA DR
400 PacP 90272 631-B6
CHAPARAL ST
11700 Brwd 90049 631-G2
CHAPARRAL
2000 WCOV 91791 639-A4
CHAPARRAL AV
16600 CRTS 90703 736-J6
CHAPARRAL CIR
- LACo 90265 628-F6
CHAPARRAL CT
- Actn 93510 4374-J6
- Alta 91001 535-G3
- LAN 93536 4105-A1
37700 PMDL 93552 4287-F2
CHAPARRAL DR
- POM 91766 640-F5
900 WAL 91789 639-C6
1700 CLAR 91711 571-E7
1700 CLAR 91711 601-E1
3900 SBdC 91710 641-D6
44000 LAN 93536 4015-A7
44000 LAN 93536 4105-A1
CHAPARRAL LN
- BqtC 91354 4460-E3
2800 RPV 90275 823-F1
CHAPARRAL RD
500 GLDR 91741 569-F4
500 SDMS 91773 600-B1
600 SMAD 91024 566-J1
9200 Chat 91311 499-E7
9200 LA 91304 499-E7
9200 WHil 91304 499-E7
CHAPARRAL WY
17900 CRTS 90703 737-A7
17900 CRTS 90703 767-A1
CHAPARREL LN
37700 PMDL 93550 4286-E2
CHAPARRO DR
1300 GLDL 91208 564-H2
22500 SCTA 91350 4460-H7
CHAPARRO RD
500 COV 91724 599-E6
500 LACo 91724 599-E6
CHAPEA RD
800 LACo 91107 566-G6
N CHAPEL AV
- ALH 91801 596-B4
S CHAPEL AV
600 ALH 91801 596-C6
1800 ALH 91801 636-C1
CHAPEL DR
- RPV 90275 793-H7
- SLB 90740 826-H3
CHAPEL HILL DR
1600 LACo 91789 679-F4
CHAPELLE AV
3400 PRV 90660 676-J1
CHAPELLE ST
- PMDL 93552 4287-E1
CHAPIN LN
8200 SunI 91040 503-G4
CHAPIN RD
1500 MTBL 90640 676-C7
CHAPIN TR
8200 SunI 91040 503-G4
CHAPIN WY
10000 SunI 91040 503-G4
CHAPLIN AV
16600 Enc 91436 561-D4
CHAPLIN DR
2800 LAN 93536 4015-C7
CHAPMAN AV
800 PAS 91103 565-G3
2000 FUL 92833 738-D7
E CHAPMAN AV
100 FUL 92832 738-J6
600 FUL 92831 738-J6

W CHAPMAN AV
100 FUL 92832 738-G6
1000 FUL 92833 738-E7
CHAPMAN CT
- Alta 91001 535-G2
CHAPMAN DR
- BPK 90620 767-E6
CHAPMAN LN
- ING 90305 703-E3
CHAPMAN RD
1900 CLAR 91711 571-B7
2300 LaCr 91214 504-H7
CHAPMAN ST
2400 LMTA 90717 793-G5
3100 LA 90065 594-F1
N CHAPMAN ST
300 WCOV 91790 598-G6
CHAPMAN WY
2200 ELSG 90245 732-J3
CHAPMAN WOODS RD
600 LACo 91107 566-G6
CHAPPARAL DR
600 DBAR 91765 640-B6
CHAPS CT
1700 SIMI 93063 499-C3
CHAPTER DR
19900 WdHl 91364 560-D4
CHARA AV
2300 CLAR 91711 571-E6
CHARDON CIR
18100 Enc 91316 560-J5
18100 Enc 91316 561-A5
CHARDONNAY AV
- PMDL 93551 4104-D7
CHARDONNAY CT
- SunV 91352 533-C2
CHARDONNAY DR
22600 DBAR 91765 680-A3
CHARFORD ST
2300 SDMS 91740 570-B7
CHARIETTE AV
3400 RSMD 91770 636-G1
3600 RSMD 91770 596-G7
CHARING CT
1800 SIMI 93063 499-D2
CHARING ST
6500 SIMI 93063 499-C2
CHARING CROSS PL
3100 GLDL 91206 565-B1
CHARING CROSS RD
3100 GLDL 91206 565-B1
10200 Wwd 90024 592-C7
10200 Wwd 90024 632-B1
26000 SCTA 91355 4550-F5
CHARIOT PL
16400 HacH 91745 678-E4
S CHARITON AV
5100 LadH 90056 673-A5
CHARITON ST
1900 LA 90034 632-J6
CHARITY DR
13600 LA 91342 482-B1
CHARITY LN
700 NLB 90805 735-E7
CHARL LN
8500 LA 90046 592-H2
CHARL PL
2600 LA 90046 592-H2
CHARLEMAGNE AV
4100 LBCH 90808 766-B6
13400 BLF 90706 736-B3
N CHARLEMAGNE AV
2000 LBCH 90815 796-B2
3000 LBCH 90808 796-B1
3400 LBCH 90808 766-B7
CHARLEMONT AV
1100 HacH 91745 678-D2
4300 WdHl 91364 559-H5
CHARLEMONT PL
22700 WdHl 91364 559-H5
CHARLENE DR
4000 LACo 90043 673-D5
CHARLES AV
2900 FUL 92835 738-J2
4000 CULC 90232 672-F2
CHARLES DR
27900 SCTA 91350 4461-D6
CHARLES RD
300 LACo 90265 587-C6
CHARLES ST
1000 PAS 91103 565-E2
19100 Tarz 91356 560-G4
CHARLES WY
1400 POM 91768 600-G7
CHARLES E YOUNG DR E
- LA 90095 632-B1
CHARLES E YOUNG DR N
- LA 90095 632-A1
CHARLES E YOUNG DR S
- LA 90095 632-A2
CHARLES E YOUNG DR W
- LA 90095 632-A1
CHARLESTON AV
- LHB 90631 708-D7
CHARLESTON CT
13000 CHNO 91710 641-E7
CHARLESTON DR
300 CLAR 91711 571-E6

STREET
Block City ZIP Pg-Grid

CHARLESTON WY
- BREA 92821 708-J5
- BREA 92821 709-B4
1300 MTBL 90640 676-C2
3300 LA 90068 563-D7
CHARLESTOWN DR
22500 CALB 91302 559-H6
CHARLES WILLARD ST
- LACo 90220 764-G2
- LACo 90746 764-G2
1300 CRSN 90746 764-G1
1300 CRSN 90747 764-G1
CHARLESWORTH AV
6400 NHol 91606 532-E6
CHARLESWORTH RD
9200 PRV 90660 706-E2
11000 SFSP 90670 706-G3
CHARLEVILLE BLVD
8500 BHLS 90211 632-F2
9100 BHLS 90212 632-F2
CHARLIE RD
900 INDS 91748 679-B3
CHARLIE CANYON RD
- Cstc 91384 4369-J7
- Cstc 91384 4459-J1
31000 BqtC 91354 (4370-A7 See Page 4279)
31000 Cstc 91384 (4370-A7 See Page 4279)
CHARLIE CANYON LATERAL
- BqtC 91354 (4370-D5 See Page 4279)
CHARLINDA ST
3200 WCOV 91791 639-D1
E CHARLINDA ST
1000 WCOV 91790 638-G2
1600 WCOV 91791 638-J1
2600 WCOV 91791 639-B1
CHARLINE PL
19600 RowH 91748 679-E6
CHARLOMA DR
8300 DWNY 90240 706-C3
CHARLOTTE AV
1800 LACo 91770 636-F4
2200 RSMD 91770 636-F1
N CHARLOTTE AV
100 SGBL 91776 596-F2
100 SGBL 91775 596-F2
5400 LACo 91776 596-F2
5700 LACo 91775 596-F2
S CHARLOTTE AV
100 SGBL 91776 596-F6
200 LACo 91776 596-F4
1800 RSMD 91770 596-F6
3700 RSMD 91776 596-F7
CHARLOTTE CT
- LA 91304 530-A4
CHARLOTTE DR
22300 TOR 90505 763-B7
CHARLOTTE PL
5300 PMDL 93552 4287-B2
CHARLOTTE ST
2000 Boyl 90033 635-B3
CHARLTON LN
18200 Nor 91326 480-J7
CHARLTON RD
1400 SMRO 91108 596-C1
CHARLWOOD CIR
13500 CRTS 90703 767-C2
CHARLWOOD ST
6000 LKWD 90713 766-D2
12000 ART 90701 766-H2
12300 CRTS 90703 766-J2
12700 CRTS 90703 767-A2
CHARM ACRES PL
1100 PacP 90272 631-A4
CHARMAINE DR
1200 UPL 91784 571-H4
CHARMAINE WY
27400 SCTA 91351 4551-H2
CHARMEL CT
1400 PacP 90272 630-G3
CHARMEL LN
16600 PacP 90272 630-G3
CHARMEL PL
1300 PacP 90272 630-G3
CHARMINGDALE RD
400 DBAR 91765 640-C7
500 DBAR 91765 680-C1
CHARMION LN
4500 Enc 91316 561-C4
CHARMONT RD
5900 LVRN 91750 570-F3
CHARNER ST
6600 BGDN 90201 705-J1
6700 BGDN 90201 706-A1
CHARNOCK AV
9700 LA 90034 632-G7
CHARNOCK RD
10700 LA 90034 672-E2
11200 LA 90066 672-D2
CHARNWOOD AV
1900 ALH 91803 635-G1
CHARONNE CT
26000 SCTA 91355 4550-F5
CHARONOAK PL
6200 LACo 91775 596-F2
CHARRICK DR
9300 Tuj 91042 504-A6
CHARRICK PL
7000 Tuj 91042 504-A6

CHARRO CT
400 SDMS 91773 599-J1
CHARRON PL
700 LACo 90220 734-E3
CHART TR
1700 Top 90290 590-C2
CHARTER CT
36900 PMDL 93552 4287-B4
CHARTER DR
600 COV 91724 599-G3
CHARTER ST
4200 VER 90058 675-B3
4300 LACo 90058 675-B3
CHARTER WY
10500 IRW 91706 598-F3
CHARTER GLEN TR
- Actn 93510 4375-B7
CHARTER OAK LN
10000 LA 90210 592-B3
CHARTER OAK ST
600 SPAS 91030 595-G1
CHARTERS AV
4700 HiPk 90042 595-A1
CHARTHAM PL
16900 HacH 91745 678-F6
CHARTHOUSE CIR
3800 WLKV 91361 557-B6
CHARTHOUSE CV
- BPK 90621 738-A6
CHARTRES DR
6300 RPV 90275 822-H3
CHARTRES LN
7400 LPMA 90623 767-C3
CHARVERS AV
1000 GLDR 91740 569-D7
1000 GLDR 91740 599-D1
S CHARVERS AV
300 WCOV 91791 639-D1
CHARWOOD CT
500 BREA 92821 708-H6
CHARWOOD PL
23200 DBAR 91765 680-B3
CHASAR PL
4500 LACo 90043 673-C5
CHASE AV
- StvR 91381 4550-C7
- StvR 91381 4640-C1
4100 CULC 90066 672-C5
4100 LA 90066 672-C5
7900 Wch 90045 702-F2
CHASE PL
22700 LA 91304 529-H2
CHASE ST
8400 LA 91304 529-F2
13000 Pcma 91331 502-D6
13700 Pcma 91331 532-A1
13800 PanC 91402 532-A1
14500 PanC 91402 531-H1
15000 LA 91343 531-E1
17000 Nor 91325 531-A1
18100 Nor 91325 530-G1
18400 Nor 91324 530-G1
19700 Win 91306 530-C2
20800 LA 91304 530-A2
CHASE WY
- LMRD 90639 737-F2
1000 WCOV 91792 638-G4
CHASTAIN AV
7800 Res 91335 531-A3
CHASTAIN PKWY E
1200 PacP 90272 630-G1
CHASTAIN PKWY W
1300 PacP 90272 630-G1
CHASTAIN PL
7900 Res 91335 531-A3
CHATEAU PL
42100 LAN 93536 4104-C5
CHATEAU RD
1000 PAS 91105 565-E4
CHATEAU THIERRY AV
- Brwd 90049 631-J3
- Brwd 90049 632-A3
CHATFIELD AV
7700 LACo 90606 677-A7
7700 LACo 90606 707-A1
CHATFIELD WY
23500 SCTA 91354 4460-G7
CHATHAM
- MANB 90266 732-H4
CHATHAM CT
1700 CLAR 91711 601-A1
CHATHAM DR
2000 PMDL 93550 4286-D2
CHATHAM LN
18100 Nor 91326 500-J1
CHATHAM PL
600 LCF 91011 535-D6
CHATHAM WY
- SLB 90740 796-J6
CHATLAKE DR
8700 LA 91304 529-E1
CHATSBORO DR
20500 WdHl 91364 560-C5
CHATSWORTH DR
200 SFER 91340 502-A1
800 LA 91340 502-A1
14500 LA 91340 501-J2
14500 MsnH 91345 501-J2
CHATSWORTH ST
14600 MsnH 91345 501-F3
14600 MsnH 91345 502-A3
15600 GrnH 91344 501-A3
18100 Nor 91326 500-H3

CHATSWORTH ST
18100 Nor 91326 501-A3
18100 GrnH 91344 500-H3
19600 Chat 91311 500-A3
22000 Chat 91311 499-J3
CHATTANOOGA AV
700 PacP 90272 630-H5
CHATTANOOGA CT
700 CLAR 91711 601-F1
CHATTANOOGA PL
16500 PacP 90272 630-H5
CHATTERTON AV
400 LPUE 91744 678-F2
CHATWIN AV
1800 LBCH 90815 796-C4
4100 LKWD 90713 766-C6
N CHATWIN AV
2300 LBCH 90815 796-C2
3000 LBCH 90808 796-C1
3400 LBCH 90808 766-C7
CHAUCER CT
1200 SDMS 91773 599-H2
CHAUCER LN
- ING 90305 703-F3
CHAUCER PL
- StvR 91381 4550-A6
CHAUCER RD
600 SMRO 91108 566-D6
12000 OrCo 90720 796-H5
CHAUCER ST
3000 LA 90065 594-H4
CHAUMONT CT
39500 PMDL 93551 4195-C5
CHAUMONT DR
5200 SBdC 92397 (4652-F3 See Page 4651)
CHAUMONT LN
- SBdC 92397 (4652-G3 See Page 4651)
CHAUMONT RD
4200 WdHl 91364 560-D5
CHAUNCEY DR
- CRTS 90703 767-A2
CHAUTAUGUA DR
1300 SIMI 93063 499-C3
CHAUTAUQUA BLVD
500 PacP 90272 631-B3
3100 LA 90402 631-B7
W CHAUTAUQUA BLVD
14700 PacP 90272 631-B6
CHAVERS AV
12200 DWNY 90242 705-H6
CHAVEZ ST
1000 BURB 91506 563-H2
1200 GLDL 91201 563-H2
1700 LA 90012 634-J1
CHAVEZ RAVINE PL
900 LA 90012 634-G2
CHAVEZ RAVINE RD
1300 Echo 90026 594-F7
CHAYOTE ST
11600 Brwd 90049 631-H2
N CHEAM AV
2000 SIMI 93063 499-C2
CHEDDAR ST
9600 DWNY 90242 736-C1
10500 NRWK 90650 736-D1
CHEESBROUGHS LN
100 LA 90063 635-C6
CHEETAH WY
1100 PMDL 93551 4195-F7
CHEHALEM RD
800 LCF 91011 535-B3
CHELAN DR
2200 LA 90068 593-C2
CHELAN PL
2200 LA 90068 593-D3
CHELAN WY
7000 LA 90068 593-C2
CHELLA DR
16000 HacH 91745 678-C6
CHELMSFORD WY
8800 ING 90305 703-D3
CHELSA DR
1300 POM 91767 601-C6
CHELSEA AV
- CRTS 90703 767-A2
1000 SMCA 90403 631-F6
1200 SMCA 90404 631-F6
29500 Cstc 91384 4459-H5
CHELSEA CT
500 LBCH 90803 796-F7
1200 SMCA 90404 631-G7
2500 BREA 92821 709-E7
3300 PMDL 93551 4195-B3
4500 CYP 90630 767-B7
6300 AGRH 91301 557-H3
CHELSEA DR
3600 LVRN 91750 600-F1
3700 LVRN 91750 570-G7
CHELSEA LN
- ING 90305 703-E3
- LA 91304 529-J2
34500 PMDL 93550 4376-E3
CHELSEA PL
1600 GLDR 91740 599-H2
2400 SMCA 90404 631-G7
CHELSEA RD
300 ARCD 91007 567-B4
1400 PVE 90274 792-E6
1400 SMRO 91108 596-B2
2300 PVE 90274 822-E1

CHELSEA ST
2400 Boyl 90033 635-C3
CHELSEA WY
- LACo 91387 4551-J4
400 SGBL 91775 596-D3
CHELSFIELD ST
12700 BALD 91706 597-H7
CHELSWORTH LN
- CRTS 90703 767-B2
CHELTEN WY
1200 SPAS 91030 595-J2
CHELTENHAM DR
13100 Shrm 91423 562-C6
CHELTENHAM LN
1200 LHB 90631 738-F1
CHENAULT ST
11300 Brwd 90049 631-J3
CHENEY DR
20500 Top 90290 590-C2
CHENEY RANCH RD
- PacP 90272 590-D3
CHENIL CT
21700 SCTA 91350 4461-A6
CHERAW DR
22300 SCTA 91350 4460-J6
CHERBOURG CT
30800 WLKV 91362 557-F5
CHERBOURG LN
3200 LAN 93536 4105-B3
E CHERE DR
14100 LACo 90604 707-D7
CHEREMOYA AV
1900 LA 90068 593-G2
CHERET PL
30200 RPV 90275 822-H3
CHERI DR
1100 LHB 90631 708-C4
CHERI WY
8800 RSMD 91770 636-H1
CHERIE PL
16900 CRSN 90746 734-F7
CHERITON DR
500 CRSN 90746 734-D7
CHERMAK ST
4500 BURB 91505 533-B4
CHERNUS LN
1600 CHLS 91709 710-G2
CHEROKEE
- Ago 91301 587-F4
1900 WCOV 91791 638-J4
2000 WCOV 91791 639-A4
3300 Top 90290 560-B6
CHEROKEE AV
3100 LYN 90262 705-A5
3100 SGAT 90280 705-A5
N CHEROKEE AV
500 LA 90004 593-E7
700 LA 90038 593-E5
1300 Hlwd 90028 593-E4
CHEROKEE CIR
7200 BPK 90620 767-F2
CHEROKEE CT
300 SDMS 91773 570-C7
6600 Hlwd 90028 593-E4
CHEROKEE DR
7400 DWNY 90241 705-J3
7400 DWNY 90241 706-A3
CHEROKEE LN
800 GLDL 91205 564-H6
9300 BHLS 90210 592-F3
9300 LA 90210 592-F3
CHEROKEE TR
11400 Chat 91311 500-B1
CHEROKEE CANYON LN
23000 LACo 91390 4460-H1
CHERRY AV
- LBCH 90802 825-G1
- LBCH 90803 825-G1
200 LBCH 90803 795-G6
200 LBCH 90802 795-G6
300 LBCH 90814 795-G6
700 LBCH 90804 795-G6
700 LBCH 90813 795-G6
1800 LBCH 90806 795-G3
1800 SIGH 90755 795-G3
3000 Bxby 90807 795-G3
3400 LKWD 90712 765-G2
3400 LKWD 90712 795-G3
3400 Bxby 90807 765-G5
5200 NLB 90805 765-G2
6300 NLB 90805 735-G7
6900 PRM 90723 735-G7
16600 TOR 90504 733-F7
E CHERRY AV
100 MNRO 91016 567-H5
S CHERRY AV
11400 ING 90303 703-F7
W CHERRY AV
100 MNRO 91016 567-G5
CHERRY CT
- CRSN 90746 764-D4
- Saug 91350 4461-B4
- SCTA 91354 4460-F4
CHERRY DR
- Cstc 91384 4459-G1
200 PAS 91105 565-E6
31300 Cstc 91384 4369-G7
37600 PMDL 93550 4286-D2
CHERRY LN
1600 ALH 91803 595-J6
4900 ELMN 91731 597-D4
4900 ELMN 91780 597-D4

CHERRY ST
1100 GLDL 91202 564-D2
1100 LA 90015 634-C5
10700 LALM 90720 796-J3
23400 SCTA 91321 4640-G1
W CHERRY ST
300 COMP 90222 734-H3
CHERRY WY
- POM 91767 600-J3
E CHERRY BLOSSOM LN
- LACo 91744 638-J5
CHERRY BLOSSOM PL
- BqtC 91354 4460-E6
CHERRYBLOSSOM ST
- PMDL 93551 4285-E3
CHERRY CANYON MTWY
3600 GLDL 91208 535-A5
3600 LCF 91011 535-A5
CHERRY CANYON PIPELINE RD
- LACo 91390 4192-A6
CHERRY CREEK CIR
800 THO 91362 557-G1
CHERRY CREEK DR
27400 SCTA 91354 4460-H5
CHERRYCREEK LN
12400 CRTS 90703 736-J5
CHERRY CREST CIR
16400 CRTS 90703 736-J6
CHERRYDALE DR
3100 DBAR 91765 679-H7
CHERRY FALL LN
16200 CRTS 90703 736-J6
CHERRY GATE WY
2300 HacH 91745 678-E5
CHERRY HILL LN
- RPV 90275 823-B5
CHERRY HILL WY
1300 CHLS 91709 680-G6
CHERRY HILLS LN
300 AZU 91702 568-H4
4300 Tarz 91356 560-F5
E CHERRY INDUSTRIAL CIR
2000 NLB 90805 765-G2
CHERRY LAUREL PL
- LACo 91387 4552-A4
CHERRYLEE DR
11300 ELMN 91732 597-E4
CHERRYSTONE AV
7700 PanC 91402 532-B3
CHERRY TREE CT
1300 LHB 90631 738-C1
CHERRY TREE LN
39100 LACo 93551 4194-G5
CHERRYVALE DR
12600 LMRD 90638 737-J1
CHERRY WILLOW DR
- LACo 91387 4552-A4
CHERRYWOOD AV
3700 LA 90018 673-F2
3700 LA 90008 673-F2
CHERRYWOOD LN
- BREA 92821 709-A4
14100 CHLS 91709 680-H3
CHERRYWOOD ST
1700 LHB 90631 738-D2
S CHERRYWOOD ST
100 WCOV 91791 598-J7
200 WCOV 91791 638-J1
CHERTSEY LN
3200 PMDL 93551 4195-B4
CHERTY DR
6900 RPV 90275 792-G7
CHERVIL CT
- SCTA 91354 4460-G4
CHERWELL CT
- CYP 90630 767-C7
CHERWELL LN
- CYP 90630 767-C7
CHERWELL RD
- CYP 90630 767-C6
CHERYL AV
4700 GLDL 91214 504-E5
CHERYL DR
20400 TOR 90503 763-A4
CHERYL LN
- Saug 91350 4461-D6
400 INDS 91789 679-G1
CHERYL PL
2300 Brwd 90049 631-C1
CHERYL KELTON PL
24200 SCTA 91321 4640-F2
W CHERYLLYN LN
3000 ANA 92804 767-J7
CHESAPEAKE
1400 WCOV 91791 638-J6
CHESAPEAKE AV
2800 LA 90016 633-D7
3000 LA 90016 673-D1
CHESAPEAKE CT
5000 CHNO 91710 641-G4
CHESEBORO RD
- LACo - 4377-C5
- LACo - 4467-D1
34200 LACo 93552 4377-C2
35500 LACo 93552 4287-C7
36000 PMDL 93552 4287-C7
CHESEBRO RD
5000 AGRH 91301 558-D3
5300 Ago 91301 558-D3
6300 VeCo 91377 558-D3

CHESEBRO CANYON RD
- VeCo 91377 558-E1
5800 Ago 91301 558-E5
CHESHAM AV
500 LHB 90631 708-D7
CHESHIRE CIR
8000 LPMA 90623 767-B4
CHESHIRE DR
4000 CYP 90630 767-A6
CHESHIRE LN
- SCTA 91354 4460-F7
- SCTA 91354 4550-F1
700 LHB 90631 738-F1
CHESHIRE ST
11200 NRWK 90650 736-G5
12500 NRWK 90650 737-A4
14800 LMRD 90638 737-G4
CHESHIRE WY
1900 UPL 91784 571-J5
CHESLEY AV
4900 LACo 90043 673-E5
5100 LA 90043 673-E5
CHESNEY AV
1200 SDMS 91740 570-B7
CHESNEY DR
2900 OrCo 90720 796-H3
CHESSINGTON DR
8700 ING 90305 703-D3
CHESSINGTON PL
- LACo 92821 709-B1
- RowH 91748 709-B1
CHESSON ST
1800 DUAR 91010 568-C5
CHESTER AV
600 SMRO 91108 566-D6
N CHESTER AV
- PAS 91106 566-B3
100 COMP 90221 735-A3
400 PAS 91104 566-B3
900 ING 90302 673-D7
S CHESTER AV
- PAS 91106 566-B5
100 COMP 90221 735-A5
CHESTER PL
2300 LA 90007 634-C7
W CHESTER PL
300 POM 91768 640-H1
800 LBCH 90813 795-C6
E CHESTER RD
600 COV 91723 599-C4
W CHESTER RD
700 COV 91722 598-J4
CHESTER ST
200 GLDL 91203 564-C3
2900 LA 90032 595-F7
8700 PRM 90723 735-J5
8800 PRM 90723 736-A5
CHESTERFIELD DR
- SCTA 91354 4460-G7
CHESTERFIELD RD
- RHLS 90274 823-E2
CHESTEROARK DR
6000 LKWD 90713 766-D3
CHESTERTON ST
11600 NRWK 90650 736-G6
CHESTERWOOD ST
13100 LA 91342 482-D4
CHESTNUT
- LA 91342 481-G1
CHESTNUT AV
200 HiPk 90042 595-E2
200 LBCH 90802 795-D7
200 LBCH 90802 825-D1
900 BREA 92821 738-J2
1100 MANB 90266 732-H6
3700 Bxby 90807 765-D3
5500 NLB 90805 765-D3
8100 SGAT 90280 705-A3
E CHESTNUT AV
100 MNRO 91016 567-G5
100 SGBL 91776 596-F6
N CHESTNUT AV
700 LBCH 90813 795-D5
1800 LBCH 90806 795-D3
3800 Bxby 90807 765-C6
W CHESTNUT AV
100 MNRO 91016 567-E5
100 SGBL 91776 596-E6
CHESTNUT CT
21800 WAL 91789 639-J5
CHESTNUT DR
- CRSN 90746 764-F5
CHESTNUT LN
- RHLS 90274 823-B2
CHESTNUT PL
100 FUL 92832 738-G7
2500 POM 91766 641-A6
12400 CHNO 91710 641-J6
S CHESTNUT PL
- LBCH 90802 825-D1
CHESTNUT RD
1300 LVRN 91750 570-F5
CHESTNUT ST
- BURB 91502 533-F7
- PAS 91103 565-H4
500 LHB 90631 708-F5
800 OrCo 90631 708-F5
900 BURB 91506 533-F7
1200 UPL 91784 571-J3
1500 ALH 91803 595-J6
10300 BLF 90706 766-D1
10500 LALM 90720 796-J2
13000 WHIT 90602 707-C1

CHESTNUT ST
13600 WHIT 90605 707-D2
16700 INDS 91745 678-F2
17300 INDS 91748 678-G2
24300 SCTA 91321 4640-J1
24700 SCTA 91321 4550-H7
41200 PMDL 93551 4194-G1
41200 PMDL 93551 4104-G7
E CHESTNUT ST
100 GLDL 91205 564-E6
W CHESTNUT ST
100 GLDL 91204 564-E6
2000 ALH 91803 595-J6
2100 BURB 91506 533-E7
CHESTNUT WY
- StvR 91381 4640-B2
24000 CALB 91302 589-D1
CHESTNUT CREEK DR
1900 DBAR 91765 679-J5
CHESTNUT HILL DR
1600 WAL 91789 639-F3
CHESTNUTHILL PL
100 CLAR 91711 571-D5
CHESTRIDGE CIR
19200 WAL 91789 639-C6
CHESWIC LN
2200 LFlz 90027 593-J3
CHESWOLD LN
21700 SCTA 91350 4461-A5
CHETLE AV
8300 WHIT 90670 707-A1
8300 SFSP 90670 707-A1
CHETNEY DR
15000 BALD 91706 598-D6
W CHETNEY DR
1600 WCOV 91790 598-E6
CHETWOOD DR
7200 Tuj 91042 504-A2
CHEVALIER AV
14500 BALD 91706 598-C6
CHEVERTON DR
12800 LMRD 90638 737-G1
CHEVIOT DR
10000 LA 90064 632-E6
CHEVIOTDALE DR
1300 PAS 91105 565-E6
CHEVIOTDALE PL
600 HiPk 90042 565-E7
1500 PAS 91105 565-E6
CHEVIOT VISTA PL
3200 LA 90034 632-E7
CHEVRON CT
800 Alta 91001 535-F6
800 PAS 91001 535-F6
800 PAS 91103 535-F6
CHEVRON WY
- LMRD 90638 737-F5
CHEVY CHASE DR
1000 BHLS 90210 592-D7
3700 LCF 91011 535-B4
3900 LA 90039 564-C6
E CHEVY CHASE DR
100 GLDL 91205 564-F6
1400 GLDL 91206 564-H4
2300 GLDL 91206 565-A3
3400 GLDL 91206 535-B7
3600 LCF 91011 535-B7
N CHEVY CHASE DR
100 GLDL 91206 564-G4
S CHEVY CHASE DR
100 GLDL 91205 564-G6
W CHEVY CHASE DR
100 GLDL 91204 564-E6
CHEVY KNOLL DR
1700 GLDL 91206 565-A1
CHEVY KNOLL PL
1600 GLDL 91206 565-B1
CHEVY OAKS CIR
2200 GLDL 91206 564-J3
CHEVY OAKS DR
- GLDL 91206 564-J2
CHEYENNE AV
- THO 91362 557-A2
8000 DWNY 90242 735-H1
11200 Chat 91311 499-J1
CHEYENNE CT
8500 LACo 91776 596-G4
CHEYENNE DR
- SCTA 91354 4550-G1
300 SDMS 91773 570-C7
CHEYENNE ST
8300 DWNY 90242 735-J1
8800 DWNY 90242 736-A1
19200 Nor 91326 500-G3
CHEYENNE WY
2100 FUL 92833 738-A3
CHEYENNE WELLS CIR
19400 WAL 91789 639-C6
CHIANTI CT
- PMDL 93551 4104-E7
CHIANTI DR
12000 OrCo 90720 796-H5
CHICAGO AV
16200 BLF 90706 736-D6
N CHICAGO ST
100 Boyl 90033 635-B3
S CHICAGO ST
100 Boyl 90033 635-A5
600 LA 90023 635-A5
700 LA 90023 634-J6
CHICKADEE CT
13700 LACo 91390 (4372-H7 See Page 4281)

CHICKASAW AV
1500 Eagl 90041 565-A6
CHICKASAW TR
11400 Chat 91311 500-A1
CHICK HEARN CT
700 LA 90015 634-D5
CHICKORY LN
1200 Brwd 90049 591-F7
CHICO AV
1400 LACo 91733 637-A4
1400 SELM 91733 637-A3
3100 ELMN 91733 637-A1
11100 SBdC 91766 641-D3
CHICO ST
2800 LA 90018 633-F7
20900 CRSN 90745 764-F5
20900 CRSN 90746 764-F5
CHICOPEE AV
5000 Enc 91316 561-C3
7200 VanN 91406 531-B5
8100 Nor 91325 531-B2
9700 Nor 91325 501-B5
CHICORA DR
22700 DBAR 91765 640-A7
CHICORY AV
42900 LAN 93534 4105-E3
CHICORY CT
24900 StvR 91381 4640-D2
CHICORY LN
- PMDL 93551 4285-D3
CHIFFCHAFF CT
26500 SCTA 91355 4550-E4
CHILAO FIRE RD
- LACo - 4647-C5
- LACo - (4727-E1 See Page 4647)
CHILCOT ST
13800 BALD 91706 598-A3
CHILDS CT
3300 LA 90039 594-C4
CHILDS WY
600 LA 90089 674-B1
CHILE CT
7500 BPK 90620 767-D3
CHILE ST
4000 LA 90032 595-C7
CHILTON CT
- FUL 92833 738-D5
CHILTON DR
1900 GLDL 91201 534-A6
CHIMES AV
800 DUAR 91010 568-B5
CHIMES CT
- PMDL 93551 4195-B4
CHIMES TOWER RD
- AVA 90704 5923-G3
CHIMINEAS AV
4900 Tarz 91356 561-A1
6200 Res 91335 531-A2
8200 Nor 91325 531-A1
8800 Nor 91325 501-A7
9700 Nor 91325 500-J5
10800 Nor 91326 500-J1
11500 Nor 91326 480-J7
CHIMNEY ROCK RD
25600 SCTA 91355 4550-F6
CHIMNEYSMOKE RD
2000 LCF 91011 534-J1
CHINA PL
36500 LACo 93551 4285-J6
CHINA PT
5200 LBCH 90803 826-C1
CHINCHILLA ST
200 LHB 90631 708-E6
CHINO AV
2200 CHLS 91709 680-G1
2200 DBAR 91765 680-G1
CHINO HILLS PKWY
500 DBAR 91765 640-G7
500 DBAR 91765 680-G1
500 POM 91766 640-G7
13700 CHLS 91709 680-G1
CHINOOK PL
23800 DBAR 91765 640-C7
CHINO VALLEY FRWY Rt#-71
- CHLS - 641-A7
- POM - 600-C7
- POM - 640-E2
- POM - 641-A7
- SDMS - 600-B7
1100 POM - 640-E2
CHINO VISTA CT
1600 LAN 93535 4016-C5
CHIP CT
40500 PMDL 93551 4194-J3
CHIPPENDALE AV
900 GLDR 91740 570-A7
CHIPPEWA CIR
7200 BPK 90620 767-F2
CHIPPEWA CT
- CHNO 91710 641-G4
CHIPPEWA DR
42300 LACo 93532 4102-E4
CHIPPEWA ST
12800 LA 91342 482-D5
CHIPTREE DR
14300 LACo 93532 4102-G4
CHIQUELLA LN
24900 StvR 91381 4640-E1
CHIQUITA LN
2200 THO 91362 557-A2

CHIQUITA PL
1800 GLDL 91208 534-H4
CHIQUITA ST
10600 LA 91602 563-B5
11500 LA 91604 562-H5
CHIQUITO CANYON RD
27600 Cstc 91384 4549-C1
28200 Cstc 91384 4459-C7
CHIRLEE DR
38400 LACo 93591 4198-F7
CHIRPING SPARROW RD
21000 DBAR 91765 709-H1
CHISHOLM AV
6800 VanN 91406 531-G3
CHISHOLM CT
800 BREA 92821 709-C5
1000 SDMS 91773 570-B7
11700 LACo 91390 4373-C5
CHISHOLM PL
- LACo 91390 4461-A2
CHISHOLM TR
14600 CHLS 91709 680-H4
CHISHOLM TRAIL DR
1100 DBAR 91765 680-B2
CHISLEHURST DR
2200 LFlz 90027 593-J2
CHISLEHURST PL
2500 LFlz 90027 593-J2
CHISOLM WY
3100 FUL 92833 738-A3
CHISOM LN
25500 StvR 91381 4550-C7
25500 StvR 91381 4640-C1
CHISWICK CT
26200 SCTA 91355 4550-E4
CHISWICK RD
500 PVE 90274 792-E6
CHIVERS AV
9400 SunV 91352 503-A6
11000 Pcma 91331 502-E1
11700 Pcma 91331 482-D7
12800 LA 91342 482-B4
13400 LA 91342 481-H2
CHIVERS ST
1900 LA 91342 482-B5
1900 SFER 91340 482-B5
CHOCKTAW DR
21200 DBAR 91765 679-H7
CHOCOLATE LILY LN
29400 MAL 90265 667-D3
CHOCTAW
1900 WCOV 91791 638-J4
1900 WCOV 91791 639-A4
CHOCTAW CT
- CHNO 91710 641-G5
CHOISSER ST
10500 LACo 90606 676-H7
CHOKE CHERRY LN
24500 SCTA 91321 4641-C1
24700 SCTA 91321 4551-C7
CHOLAME DR
23800 DBAR 91765 640-C5
CHOLLA RD
100 SBdC 92372 (4472-A6 See Page 4471)
2100 SBdC 92371 (4472-E6 See Page 4471)
CHOPIN DR
8300 BPK 90621 737-J7
8300 BPK 90621 738-A7
CHORAL DR
2100 LHH 90631 708-G3
CHOSEN ST
12200 ELMN 91733 637-D4
CHOTA RD
1700 LHH 90631 708-F3
CHOUINARD CIR
600 CLAR 91711 571-E7
CHRIS PL
- Saug 91350 4461-E6
400 BHLS 90210 592-G4
CHRISCO AV
13100 LACo 91390 (4372-J4 See Page 4281)
13100 LACo 91390 4373-A3
CHRISTENSEN CT
37600 PMDL 93552 4287-A2
CHRISTIAN CT
5300 AGRH 91301 557-H5
CHRISTIANSEN AL
- PAS 91103 565-C3
CHRISTIE AV
44700 LAN 93535 4016-C6
CHRISTIE CT
25600 StvR 91381 4550-B7
CHRISTIE LN
2900 WCOV 91792 639-A7
CHRISTIE ST
- FUL 92833 738-D5
CHRISTINA AV
18700 CRTS 90703 766-J2
18700 CRTS 90703 767-A2
CHRISTINA CIR
19900 CRTS 90703 767-A3
CHRISTINA CT
1200 POM 91766 640-G4
19300 CRTS 90703 766-J2
19300 CRTS 90703 767-A3
37500 PMDL 93552 4287-A3
CHRISTINA ST
- ARCD 91006 567-D7
3000 LAN 93535 4106-F2

CHRISTINA WY
19500 CRTS 90703 766-J3
CHRISTINE AV
1400 SIMI 93063 499-B2
20600 TOR 90503 763-A5
CHRISTINE DR
13800 WHIT 90605 707-E2
CHRISTINE LN
1500 ARCD 91007 597-A1
CHRISTINE PL
10300 Chat 91311 500-F4
CHRISTINE WY
10900 Tuj 91042 503-J2
CHRISTMAS TREE LN
1400 DUAR 91010 568-C5
14600 Pear 93553 (4559-D1 See Page 4470)
CHRISTOPHER AV
11600 ING 90303 703-F7
CHRISTOPHER LN
- Saug 91350 4461-E7
12200 CRTS 90703 766-J3
CHRISTOPHER ST
600 WCOV 91790 638-G1
9100 CYP 90630 767-C6
CHRISTY AV
11100 LA 91342 503-B1
CHRISTY LN
12000 OrCo 90720 796-H5
CHRISTY ST
11500 CRTS 90703 766-G3
CHRYSANTHEMUM LN
10200 BelA 90077 592-A4
CHUCKER CT
28100 Cstc 91384 4369-F6
CHUCK WAGON CIR
500 WAL 91789 639-C7
CHUCKWAGON PL
26800 SCTA 91387 4552-E5
CHUCKWAGON RD
- RHLS 90274 823-E2
2700 PMDL 93550 4286-F6
CHUDLEIGH LN
900 GLDL 91207 564-F1
CHUKA AV
16100 LACo 93591 4199-F6
CHULA ST
100 LACo 91016 567-G7
CHULA SENDA LN
4200 LCF 91011 535-C5
CHULA VISTA AV
800 PAS 91103 565-E2
CHULA VISTA PL
1000 PAS 91103 565-E3
CHULA VISTA WY
5900 LA 90068 593-G3
CHUMASH RD
2300 LACo 90265 629-F3
CHUMASH TR
23600 VeCo 90265 625-G1
CHUMASH RIDGE LN
- LACo 90265 628-F6
CHUNG KING CT
400 LA 90012 634-G2
CHUNG KING RD
900 LA 90012 634-G2
CHURCH LN
100 Brwd 90049 631-H2
700 LA 90073 631-H2
N CHURCH LN
100 Brwd 90049 631-H1
CHURCH PL
6200 HiPk 90042 565-E7
6200 HiPk 90042 595-E1
13800 SLB 90740 826-H1
CHURCH RD
3100 MTBL 90640 676-A5
3100 CMRC 90040 676-A5
CHURCH ST
1100 HiPk 90042 565-F7
1100 PAS 91105 565-E7
1300 MANB 90266 732-F5
1800 BURB 91504 533-E5
4800 PRV 90660 676-H4
6200 HiPk 90042 595-E1
13400 CRTS 90703 767-C2
27700 Cstc 91384 4369-G7
CHURCH CANYON PL
- Alta 91001 535-G2
CHURCHILL AV
600 SDMS 91773 600-D1
10500 Chat 91311 500-A4
CHURCHILL CT
5500 PMDL 93552 4287-C5
CHURCHILL GN
200 SMAD 91024 567-B1
CHURCHILL RD
200 SMAD 91024 567-B1
500 LHH 90631 708-E1
CHURCHS CT
1100 BURB 91501 533-J5
CHURCHWOOD DR
5100 VeCo 91377 557-H1
CICELY CT
23200 SCTA 91354 4460-G5
CICERO DR
1600 Echo 90026 594-C6
CIDAR AV
32500 LACo 91390 4373-A7
CIE CT
1300 LACo 93551 4195-F7
CIELITO AV
1800 MONP 91754 636-A5

STREET Block City ZIP Pg-Grid

CIELITO DR
1600 GLDL 91207 564-E1
CIELO CIR
- CALB 91302 558-H6
CIELO CT
25600 SCTA 91355 4550-F7
CIELO DR
- PMDL 93551 4104-D6
10000 LA 90210 592-C5
CIELO PL
2200 ARCD 91006 537-D7
3900 FUL 92835 738-G1
CIELO VISTA DR
8100 WHIT 90605 707-G1
41500 PMDL 93551 4104-E6
CIENAGA DR
200 FUL 92835 738-G1
E CIENEGA AV
500 COV 91722 599-F3
1300 COV 91724 599-F3
1300 LACo 91724 599-F3
19100 LACo 91722 599-F3
W CIENEGA AV
600 SDMS 91773 600-A3
700 SDMS 91773 599-H3
CIERRO CREST PL
500 PMDL 93550 4286-A6
CIMA DE LAGO ST
9200 Chat 91311 499-E7
CIMA MESA DR
- PMDL 93552 4287-D1
CIMA MESA RD
9600 Litl 93543 4468-B4
CIMARRON AV
11500 HAW 90250 703-H7
12800 GAR 90249 733-H2
CIMARRON CIR
12900 SBdC 91710 641-A7
CIMARRON LN
5100 CULC 90230 672-H3
CIMARRON PL
- POM 91766 640-D4
CIMARRON ST
100 LPUE 91744 638-G7
1400 LA 90019 633-G6
1800 LA 90018 673-G1
1900 LA 90018 633-G6
3700 LA 90062 673-G2
5800 LA 90047 673-G7
7200 LA 90047 703-H2
10400 LACo 90047 703-H5
15100 GAR 90249 733-H5
CIMARRON WY
- Actn 93510 4465-F2
- LACo 93510 4461-C3
15400 GAR 90249 733-H5
CIMARRON OAKS DR
9300 MTCL 91763 601-F5
CIMMARON CT
19100 WAL 91789 639-C6
CIMMARON ST
22000 LAN 93535 4016-D4
CIMMERON TR
200 GLDR 91741 569-J6
N CINCH RD
- VeCo 91307 529-A4
CINCHRING RD
- RHLS 90274 823-D3
CINCINNATI ST
2300 Boyl 90033 635-B4
CINCO DR
11500 LA 91604 562-H6
CINCO CASITAS LN
2400 LaCr 91214 504-H7
CINCO ROBLES DR
1600 DUAR 91010 568-A6
CINCO VIEW DR
4800 LACo 90601 677-C3
CINDERELLA DR
400 CLAR 91711 601-C4
CINDERELLA WY
2100 POM 91767 601-A5
CINDY CT
300 POM 91767 601-A5
15800 SCTA 91387 4552-D1
W CINDY CT
1100 UPL 91786 571-J7
CINDY LN
- PRV 90660 676-F3
2700 Eagl 90041 564-J6
2700 LA 90065 564-J6
CINDY ST
3000 WCOV 91792 639-A7
CINDY LOU CT
100 AZU 91702 598-J2
CINDYWOOD CT
3000 LAN 93536 4105-C4
CINEMA AV
42800 LAN 93534 4105-F3
CINEMA DR
- SCTA 91355 4550-G2
CINKEL ST
600 MTBL 90640 676-C3
CINNABAR AV
4500 PMDL 93551 4194-H2
CINNABAR CT
15200 CHLS 91709 680-J6
42500 LAN 93536 4104-G5
CINNABAR LN
31800 Cstc 91384 4369-G5
CINNAMON LN
- RPV 90275 823-A4
800 DUAR 91010 567-J7

CINNAMON RIDGE RD
100 BREA 92821 709-E7
CINTHIA ST
700 BHLS 90210 592-G6
W CIPRIANO PL
700 MONP 91754 636-A3
CIR DR
5600 NLB 90805 765-C2
E CIRCLE
- Hrbr 90710 794-B4
N CIRCLE
- NRWK 90650 706-J6
- NRWK 90650 707-A6
S CIRCLE
- Hrbr 90710 794-A4
- NRWK 90650 706-J7
- NRWK 90650 707-A7
W CIRCLE
- Hrbr 90710 794-A4
CIRCLE CT
200 HMB 90254 762-G1
1800 LVRN 91750 600-G1
CIRCLE DR
- Hrbr 90710 794-A3
- BRAD 91010 568-A4
800 LHB 90631 708-D4
1000 RBCH 90277 793-A1
1300 SMRO 91108 566-B7
1300 SMRO 91108 596-B1
1500 GLDL 91208 564-H2
2000 HMB 90254 762-G1
4400 LA 90032 635-F1
5300 VanN 91401 562-A2
29200 Ago 91301 588-A4
N CIRCLE DR
100 SGBL 91776 596-E5
11600 WHIT 90601 677-B3
S CIRCLE DR
200 SGBL 91776 596-E5
11700 WHIT 90601 677-B3
E CIRCLE RD
- DUAR 91010 568-B6
- IRW 91706 568-B6
W CIRCLE RD
- DUAR 91010 568-B6
CIRCLE TR
21600 Top 90290 590-A5
CIRCLE C
8100 BPK 90621 767-J2
CIRCLEDELL DR
200 AZU 91702 568-J3
CIRCLE DIAMOND RD
16000 LA 91342 481-F2
CIRCLE G DR
27100 SCTA 91387 4552-E5
CIRCLE HILL LN
16500 HacH 91745 678-D5
CIRCLE J RANCH RD
22100 SCTA 91350 4550-J6
22100 SCTA 91350 4551-A6
CIRCLE KNOLL CT
26400 SCTA 91321 4551-F5
CIRCLE M
8100 BPK 90621 767-J2
CIRCLE OAK DR
300 MNRO 91016 567-J4
CIRCLE OF FRIENDS
18900 SCTA 91321 4551-G5
CIRCLE OF THE OAKS
18900 SCTA 91321 4551-G4
CIRCLE RIDGE LN
15400 HacH 91745 678-A6
CIRCLE SEVEN DR
500 GLDL 91201 564-A3
CIRCLET DR
28700 RPV 90275 792-J7
28700 RPV 90275 822-J1
CIRCLE VERDE DR
26900 RPV 90275 793-H7
CIRCLE VIEW BLVD
4400 LACo 90043 673-E4
CIRCLE VISTA AV
5100 LaCr 91214 504-G7
CIRIO WY
16700 PRM 90723 735-F6
CIRO ST
7400 DWNY 90240 706-A2
CIRRUS WY
7200 CanP 91307 529-F5
CISCO ST
9700 LA 90034 632-G5
CISERO DR
5000 PMDL 93552 4287-B4
CISNEROS LN
12600 SFSP 90670 707-A4
CITADEL AV
100 CLAR 91711 601-D5
CITADEL DR
100 CMRC 90040 675-H3
400 WAL 91789 639-E6
CITATION CT
2200 GLDR 91741 570-A6
CITICOURT LN
13300 WHIT 90602 707-D2
CITIGATE DR
8500 WHIT 90602 707-D2
CITRINE CT
- GAR 90248 764-A1
31900 Cstc 91384 4369-H5
CITRON PL
- PMDL 93551 4285-D3
2500 POM 91766 641-A6

CITRON RD
2100 LHH 90631 708-D1
CITRONELL AV
5200 PRV 90660 676-G4
7500 PRV 90660 706-F1
CITRONIA ST
16600 LA 91343 501-D5
16900 Nor 91325 501-B5
18300 Nor 91325 500-H6
18500 Nor 91324 500-F6
19800 Chat 91311 500-D6
CITRUS AV
- GLDR 91741 569-B5
100 FUL 92833 738-E7
5400 WHIT 90601 677-B5
N CITRUS AV
- LACo 91702 599-B3
100 AZU 91702 569-B6
100 COV 91723 599-B3
100 LA 90036 633-E1
100 LACo 91702 569-B6
100 POM 91766 640-J2
100 WCOV 91791 599-B3
300 LA 90036 593-D7
500 GLDR 91741 569-B6
700 LA 90038 593-D5
900 COV 91722 599-B3
1300 Hlwd 90028 593-D5
5200 AZU 91702 599-B3
5200 LACo 91702 599-B3
5200 AZU 91702 599-B3
S CITRUS AV
100 AZU 91702 569-B7
100 COV 91723 599-B6
100 LA 90036 633-E2
200 AZU 91702 599-B2
200 LACo 91702 599-B2
500 AZU 91722 599-B2
500 LACo 91722 599-B2
600 WCOV 91791 599-B6
1000 LA 90019 633-D4
5800 LACo 90043 673-C6
CITRUS CT
5500 CYP 90630 767-D6
CITRUS DR
800 LHB 90631 708-D4
900 OrCo 90631 708-D4
4700 PRV 90660 676-G3
37600 PMDL 93550 4286-D2
CITRUS LN
- DUAR 91010 568-A7
800 LACo 91768 640-B1
800 POM 91768 640-B1
13400 LMRD 90638 738-A2
CITRUS PL
- POM 91767 600-J6
- POM 91767 601-A6
500 BREA 92821 709-C6
28700 SCTA 91390 4460-J2
E CITRUS PL
- LACo 91744 638-G4
CITRUS ST
- SCTA 91355 4550-F3
1200 LACo 90631 708-D3
1200 LHB 90631 708-D3
1200 OrCo 90631 708-D3
1200 UPL 91784 571-J3
1300 LHH 90631 708-D3
N CITRUS ST
100 WCOV 91791 599-B7
S CITRUS ST
100 WCOV 91791 599-B7
400 WCOV 91791 639-B1
CITRUS EDGE ST
300 GLDR 91740 569-D7
400 GLDR 91740 599-C1
900 AZU 91702 599-B1
18000 LACo 91702 599-A1
CITRUS GROVE PL
5400 WHIT 90601 677-B4
CITRUS RANCH RD
- SDMS 91773 600-B3
CITRUS RIDGE DR
- Tarz 91356 560-F3
CITRUSTREE RD
15600 WHIT 90603 707-H5
16100 WHIT 90603 708-A5
CITRUS VIEW AV
1800 DUAR 91010 567-J6
2400 IRW 91010 567-J7
2400 IRW 91010 597-H1
CITRUSWOOD ST
1800 LVRN 91750 570-G6
CITTADIN DR
- FUL 92833 738-C6
CITY HIGHLINE RD
- LACo 91390 4281-D6
- LACo 91390 (4371-A5 See Page 4281)
- LACo 91390 4461-B1
CITYLIGHT CT
- SCTA 91351 4551-E4
CITY PARK DR
1000 LAN 93534 4105-G3
CITY RANCH RD
600 PMDL 93551 4285-B1
3100 PMDL 93551 4195-A7
4200 PMDL 93551 4194-J7
CITY TERRACE DR
3100 City 90063 635-F3
3100 LA 90063 635-D4
CITY VIEW AV
1900 Boyl 90033 635-A3

CITY VISTA DR
1900 Brwd 90049 591-F4
CIVIC ST
10600 ELMN 91731 597-C5
CIVIC CENTER CIR
- BREA 92821 709-C7
CIVIC CENTER DR
- LMRD 90638 737-G2
- PRM 90723 735-H6
300 BHLS 90210 632-G1
2000 CHLS 91709 680-H4
3000 TOR 90503 763-E5
9200 BHLS 90210 592-G7
10900 DWNY 90241 706-B5
11800 HGDN 90716 766-H6
12200 NRWK 90650 736-J1
12500 NRWK 90650 737-A1
16600 BLF 90706 736-C6
21400 CRSN 90745 764-E6
CIVIC CENTER PZ
100 POM 91766 640-J2
N CIVIC CENTER PZ
100 LHB 90631 708-E5
S CIVIC CENTER PZ
100 LHB 90631 708-E6
CIVIC CENTER WY
4900 LKWD 90712 766-B4
23400 MAL 90265 629-A7
23500 MAL 90265 628-H6
CIVIC PLAZA DR
- CRSN 90745 764-E6
CLAIBORNE DR
600 Bxby 90807 765-E5
CLAIBORNE PL
200 Bxby 90807 765-D6
CLAIBOURNE LN
22200 SCTA 91350 4550-J5
22200 SCTA 91350 4551-A5
CLAIR ST
4300 MTCL 91763 641-E2
4700 SBdC 91710 641-F2
5400 SBdC 91762 641-H2
W CLAIR ST
1400 ONT 91762 641-J2
CLAIRCREST DR
9300 LA 90210 592-F4
CLAIR DEL AV
4700 Bxby 90807 765-G4
5000 LKWD 90712 765-G4
CLAIRE AV
200 FUL 92835 738-H4
6800 Res 91335 530-G5
8300 Nor 91324 530-G2
9100 Nor 91324 500-G5
10300 Nor 91326 500-G2
CLAIRE CT
43700 LAN 93535 4106-B1
CLAIRE PL
900 POM 91768 640-F1
CLAIR RIDGE DR
- Actn 93510 4465-A3
CLAIRTON CT
3400 Enc 91436 561-E7
CLAIRTON PL
3400 Enc 91436 561-E7
CLAMPITT RD
22600 SCTA 91321 4641-C5
CLAMSHELL TKTR
- LACo 537-G4
- LACo (538-A1 See Page 507)
- MNRO 91016 537-G4
CLANCEY AV
9000 DWNY 90240 706-D3
10200 DWNY 90241 706-C5
CLANFIELD ST
2200 Actn 93510 4375-D5
5400 Actn 93510 4374-G5
CLANTON CIR
15600 SFSP 90670 737-C5
CLANTON ST
8400 LACo 91776 596-G4
CLARA ST
500 LA 90012 634-H3
3900 CDHY 90201 705-D1
5400 BELL 90201 705-G2
5500 BGDN 90201 705-G2
CLARADAY ST
300 GLDR 91740 599-F2
CLARAY DR
2500 BelA 90077 592-A2
CLARE ST
10800 WHIT 90601 677-A4
CLARELLEN ST
2600 TOR 90505 793-F5
CLAREMONT AV
- LBCH 90803 826-B2
2300 LFlz 90027 594-C3
CLAREMONT BLVD
100 CLAR 91711 601-E3
CLAREMONT DR
22400 SCTA 91350 4460-J4
CLAREMONT PL
500 POM 91767 641-B1
800 POM 91767 601-B6
E CLAREMONT ST
- PAS 91103 565-J2
1100 PAS 91104 566-A2
1100 PAS 91104 565-J2
W CLAREMONT ST
- PAS 91103 565-G2

CLAREMONT HEIGHTS DR
2900 CLAR 91711 571-E7
CLAREMORE AV
3000 LBCH 90808 796-H1
3400 LBCH 90808 766-H7
CLAREMORE LN
- LALM 90815 796-H2
3000 LBCH 90815 796-H2
CLARENCE CT
- SCTA 91355 4550-E1
S CLARENCE ST
100 Boyl 90033 634-J5
600 LA 90023 634-J5
CLARENDON AV
2000 HNTP 90255 674-H6
2800 HNTP 90255 675-A6
CLARENDON ST
20600 WdHl 91367 560-A2
22100 WdHl 91367 559-E2
E CLARENDON ST
5800 ELA 90022 675-J2
CLARESSA AV
14300 NRWK 90650 737-B3
CLARET CT
4000 PMDL 93552 4286-H4
CLARETON DR
5100 AGRH 91301 558-B6
CLARETTA AV
12400 LKWD 90715 766-J3
15500 NRWK 90650 736-J5
19800 CRTS 90703 766-J3
21100 HGDN 90716 766-J5
21200 HGDN 90715 766-J5
CLARETTA ST
12000 LA 91342 482-F7
12400 Pcma 91331 502-E1
CLARIDGE DR
1300 LA 90210 592-D5
CLARIDGE PL
10600 WHIT 90603 708-A5
CLARIDGE ST
1700 ARCD 91006 567-C2
CLARIN ST
20900 WdHl 91364 560-C4
CLARINDA AV
8000 PRV 90660 706-F2
CLARINDA DR
4000 Tarz 91356 560-G5
CLARINGTON AV
3400 LA 90034 632-F7
3600 LA 90034 672-F1
3700 LA 90232 672-F1
3800 CULC 90232 672-F1
CLARINGTON DR
23900 LA 91304 529-D4
CLARION DR
700 LACo 90502 764-B5
800 FUL 92835 738-F2
E CLARION DR
100 CRSN 90745 764-C5
W CLARION DR
100 CRSN 90745 764-C5
900 LACo 90502 764-B5
CLARION PL
500 CLAR 91711 571-E7
CLARION ST
1600 CRSN 90745 764-G5
CLARISSA AV
100 AVA 90704 5923-H4
4300 LFlz 90027 594-A3
CLARK AL
1200 PAS 91106 566-B3
CLARK AV
200 POM 91767 641-C1
500 CLAR 91711 601-D5
600 POM 91767 601-C7
900 BURB 91506 563-F1
1300 LBCH 90804 796-B5
1400 LBCH 90815 796-B2
2300 Ven 90291 671-J6
2500 BURB 91505 563-C3
3000 LBCH 90808 796-B2
3400 LBCH 90808 766-B6
3600 ELMN 91731 597-D7
4500 NHol 91601 563-C3
4900 LKWD 90712 766-B2
6200 BLF 90706 766-B2
12300 DWNY 90242 706-B7
12300 DWNY 90242 736-B3
13400 BLF 90706 736-B3
14400 HacH 91745 637-J7
14400 INDS 91745 637-J7
14600 HacH 91745 638-A7
14600 INDS 91745 638-A7
15000 HacH 91745 678-B1
15000 INDS 91745 678-B1
CLARK CT
27700 SCTA 91350 4460-J5
37600 PMDL 93552 4287-A2
43900 LAN 93536 4105-C1
CLARK DR
- FUL 92833 738-C5
N CLARK DR
100 BHLS 90211 632-H1
100 LA 90048 632-H1
100 WHWD 90048 592-H7
100 WHWD 90048 632-H1
S CLARK DR
100 BHLS 90211 632-H2
100 LA 90048 632-H1
1100 LA 90035 632-H3

CLARK LN
1300 RBCH 90278 762-J2
1900 RBCH 90278 763-A2
CLARK PL
1800 SPAS 91030 595-J1
CLARK ST
1100 WHWD 90069 592-H5
1200 LA 90069 592-H5
4300 CHNO 91710 641-E7
5100 LA 90262 735-D2
11600 ARCD 91006 597-G3
12000 ELMN 91732 597-G3
12000 SFSP 90670 706-H5
12500 SFSP 90670 707-A5
14000 BALD 91706 598-A5
14500 VanN 91411 562-A2
14700 VanN 91411 561-H2
16800 Enc 91436 561-D2
17300 Enc 91316 561-C2
18100 Tarz 91356 561-A2
18200 Tarz 91356 560-H2
20100 WdHl 91367 560-C2
W CLARK ST
1100 UPL 91784 571-H6
CLARK WY
6000 BPK 90620 767-E3
CLARKDALE AV
13200 NRWK 90650 736-H2
16600 ART 90701 736-H6
17200 CRTS 90703 736-H7
17900 ART 90701 766-H1
20300 LKWD 90715 766-H4
21700 HGDN 90716 766-H7
CLARKE ST
25300 StvR 91381 4640-B1
CLARKE RANCH RD
- LACo 90265 586-G6
CLARKGROVE ST
15600 HacH 91745 678-C1
CLARKMAN ST
11200 SFSP 90670 706-F5
CLARKSON AV
6000 MYWD 90270 675-D6
6400 BELL 90201 675-D7
7300 CDHY 90201 705-D1
CLARKSON CT
- SCTA 91354 4460-G6
CLARKSON RD
10500 LA 90064 632-E6
11400 LA 90064 672-B1
CLARKSON SERVICE RD
6200 BELL 90201 675-D7
CLARKVIEW DR
300 DUAR 91010 568-F4
CLARMEYA LN
2800 LACo 91107 536-F7
CLARMON PL
10700 CULC 90230 672-H4
CLARO DR
400 WAL 91789 639-F7
CLARO WY
5000 PMDL 93551 4194-H3
CLARY AV
100 SGBL 91776 596-D4
CLASSICS DR
12600 GrnH 91344 481-A5
CLAUDE ST
800 CRSN 90746 734-E6
W CLAUDE ST
100 COMP 90220 734-J5
2700 CRSN 90746 734-F6
CLAUDETTE ST
26600 SCTA 91351 4551-D3
CLAUDIA AV
4100 RSMD 91770 596-J6
CLAUDIA CIR
4100 RSMD 91770 596-J7
S CLAUDINA AV
1900 LA 90016 633-D6
CLAVEL CT
5000 WdHl 91364 559-J3
CLAWSON PL
3300 LA 91604 562-E7
CLAY CT
900 ALH 91801 596-C4
2400 RowH 91748 679-E7
CLAYBECK AV
7500 BURB 91505 533-C3
7500 LA 91505 533-C3
7500 SunV 91352 533-C3
8900 SunV 91352 503-A7
CLAYCLIFFE CT
3400 HacH 91745 678-A6
CLAYCREST
18900 SCTA 91351 4551-G1
CLAYFORD AV
1100 THO 91361 557-A5
CLAYGATE CT
2400 BelA 90077 591-G2
CLAY HILL AV
1600 HacH 91745 678-E4
CLAYHORN DR
23400 DBAR 91765 680-B1
CLAYMONT DR
700 Brwd 90049 631-E2
CLAYMORE ST
9100 PRV 90660 706-D2
11500 SFSP 90670 706-G3
CLAYMORE WY
23800 SCTA 91354 4460-F6
CLAYTON AV
3700 LFlz 90027 594-B4

CLAYTON CT
- LACo 91750 570-J4
- PMDL 93551 4194-G1
23800 SCTA 91354 4460-F7
CLAYVALE RD
5000 Actn 93510 4374-H2
CLAYVALE ST
2900 Actn 93510 4375-A2
5100 Actn 93510 4374-G2
6000 LACo 91390 4374-A2
8800 LACo 91390 4373-J2
CLAYWOOD AV
13900 LA 91342 482-C1
CLAYWOOD DR
24300 DBAR 91765 640-D7
CLEARBANK LN
24100 SCTA 91321 4640-H4
CLEARBROOK DR
2300 CHLS 91709 680-G5
15900 PRM 90723 735-H5
CLEARBROOK LN
16000 CRTS 90703 736-J5
CLEARBROOK PL
11200 Nor 91326 500-H1
CLEARBROOK ST
18700 Nor 91326 500-H1
CLEAR CREEK DR
1500 LAN 93535 4106-C1
1600 FUL 92833 738-B5
CLEAR CREEK LN
2400 DBAR 91765 680-C5
CLEAR CREEK TKTR
- LACo 505-E1
- LACo (4725-C6 See Page 4645)
CLEAR CREEK CANYON DR
700 DBAR 91765 680-C2
CLEARCREST DR
13800 BALD 91706 598-B3
CLEARDALE ST
21500 SCTA 91321 4551-A7
22200 SCTA 91321 4550-J7
CLEAR FALLS AV
1700 LVRN 91750 570-G4
CLEARFIELD AV
7700 PanC 91402 532-B3
CLEARFORD CT
3900 WLKV 91361 557-D6
CLEARGLEN AV
11700 LACo 90604 707-J6
12300 LACo 90604 737-J1
CLEARGROVE DR
7200 DWNY 90240 706-A1
CLEAR HAVEN DR
700 VeCo 91377 558-B1
CLEARHAVEN DR
300 AZU 91702 568-J3
CLEARIDGE DR
23600 SCTA 91354 4460-G6
CLEARLAKE DR
27400 SCTA 91387 4552-D4
CLEAR LAKE PL
1500 BREA 92821 708-H6
CLEARLAWN ST
40000 LACo 93591 4199-E3
CLEARMONT CT
23800 SCTA 91354 4460-F7
CLEAR OAK DR
16100 Enc 91436 561-F5
CLEARPOOL PL
23200 Hrbr 90710 794-A2
23400 Hrbr 90710 793-J2
CLEAR RIVER LN
1700 HacH 91745 678-E4
CLEARSITE ST
5200 TOR 90505 793-A1
CLEAR SPRING CT
20500 DBAR 91789 679-F3
CLEAR SPRING DR
15900 LMRD 90638 737-J1
CLEARSPRING DR
1200 UPL 91784 571-J5
CLEARSPRINGS AV
4500 PMDL 93552 4286-J2
4500 PMDL 93552 4287-F2
CLEAR SPRINGS DR
1600 FUL 92831 738-H4
CLEAR SPRINGS LN
11000 CHLS 91709 640-J7
CLEAR SPRINGS RD
2100 BREA 92821 709-E7
6400 VeCo 93063 499-C4
CLEAR VALLEY DR
4100 Enc 91436 561-F5
CLEAR VALLEY PL
16100 Enc 91436 561-F5
CLEAR VALLEY RD
5800 HIDH 91302 559-C2
CLEARVIEW CT
- PMDL 93551 4195-D5
22500 SCTA 91350 4550-J6
CLEAR VIEW DR
1500 LA 90210 592-C4
CLEARVIEW CREST DR
100 DBAR 91765 640-A7
CLEAR VISTA DR
- RHE 90274 822-J2
CLEARWATER AV
2000 PMDL 93551 4195-E5
CLEARWATER CIR
2000 UPL 91784 571-G4

CLEARWATER CT
800 WAL 91789 639-H5
CLEARWATER CV
- BPK 90621 738-A6
CLEARWATER DR
13300 LMRD 90638 738-A2
CLEARWATER LN
- SCTA 91355 4550-H3
CLEARWATER ST
2500 THO 91362 557-B3
2600 LA 90039 594-E3
CLEARWOOD AV
12900 LMRD 90638 737-D2
CLEARWOOD CT
10400 BelA 90077 592-A1
36400 PMDL 93550 4286-H5
CLEARY CT
200 CLAR 91711 571-D5
CLEARY DR
15000 BALD 91706 598-D6
CLEAT RD
10700 LACo 91390 4373-E6
CLEE CT
5500 AGRH 91301 558-A5
CLEGHORN DR
1200 DBAR 91765 680-C3
CLELA AV
300 ELA 90022 635-G7
700 ELA 90022 675-G1
CLELAND AV
4500 LA 90065 594-J3
4600 LA 90065 595-A2
4800 HiPk 90042 595-A2
CLELAND PL
800 HiPk 90042 595-A2
800 LA 90065 595-A2
CLEMATIS CT
- PMDL 93551 4285-D3
10200 BelA 90077 592-A1
CLEMATIS WY
6900 LKWD 90713 766-F4
CLEMENS AV
8000 LA 91304 529-F3
CLEMENS CT
25400 StvR 91381 4550-C7
CLEMENT AV
2300 Ven 90291 671-J6
CLEMENT DR
500 GLDL 91202 564-D2
CLEMENT ST
1000 Boyl 90033 635-A3
CLEMENTE AV
300 AVA 90704 5923-H4
CLEMENTINA DR
2100 HacH 91745 678-D5
CLEMINSON ST
3500 ELMN 91731 597-C7
CLEMMER DR
800 COMP 90221 735-B6
CLEMONS DR
17100 Enc 91436 561-C7
CLEMSON AV
1300 CLAR 91711 601-A1
CLEMSON ST
5500 LA 90016 673-A1
CLEO ST
12900 BALD 91706 597-J6
CLEOMOORE AV
6500 CanP 91307 529-E6
CLEON AV
4800 NHol 91601 563-A2
5900 NHol 91601 533-A7
6000 NHol 91606 533-A7
6700 NHol 91605 533-A4
7200 SunV 91352 533-A4
CLERENDON RD
3300 LA 90210 562-B7
CLERMONT AV
- PMDL 93552 4287-E1
CLERMONT CT
5400 WLKV 91362 557-F5
CLERMONT ST
4500 LA 90065 595-A4
CLETA ST
7800 DWNY 90241 705-J5
7900 DWNY 90241 706-A6
E CLEVELAND AV
100 MTBL 90640 676-E2
W CLEVELAND AV
100 MTBL 90640 676-C2
CLEVELAND DR
28600 AGRH 91301 558-B6
CLEVELAND PL
1600 POM 91768 600-G6
CLEVELAND RD
800 GLDL 91202 564-B2
1700 GLDL 91202 534-C7
CLEVELAND ST
700 LA 90012 634-G2
1100 POM 91768 600-G6
CLEVIS RD
29000 RPV 90275 823-G2
CLIFDEN LN
- BURB 91504 533-E2
CLIFF DR
- LMRD 90638 737-J2
300 PAS 91107 566-G3
1200 LA 90065 594-H4
CLIFFBRANCH DR
1600 DBAR 91765 679-H4
CLIFFEDGE DR
16000 LACo 91390 4192-D3

CLIFFHILL DR
1800 MONP 91754 636-B5
CLIFFIE WY
- SCTA 91387 4552-F4
CLIFFORD ST
2100 Echo 90026 594-D6
CLIFF ROSE DR
5100 PMDL 93552 4287-B2
CLIFFSIDE CT
- LA 91304 529-E4
CLIFFSIDE DR
600 SDMS 91773 600-A3
28800 MAL 90265 667-E4
CLIFFSIDE LN
- HacH 91745 637-H7
20800 DBAR 91789 679-G6
CLIFFSITE DR
3600 RPV 90275 823-E5
CLIFFTOP WY
18300 LACo 90265 630-D5
CLIFFVIEW ST
800 DUAR 91010 567-J7
800 IRW 91010 567-J7
CLIFFWOOD AV
400 BREA 92821 709-B6
N CLIFFWOOD AV
100 Brwd 90049 631-F3
S CLIFFWOOD AV
100 Brwd 90049 631-F4
CLIFFWOOD DR
- MTCL 91763 641-G1
CLIFFWOOD PARK ST
300 BREA 92821 709-C7
CLIFTON AL
1400 PAS 91106 566-C3
1800 PAS 91107 566-C3
CLIFTON PL
- SCTA 91354 4460-G6
3500 GLDL 91208 534-H4
3600 GLDL 91020 534-H4
25900 StvR 91381 4550-B6
CLIFTON ST
400 LA 90031 595-B7
500 LHB 90631 708-E6
CLIFTON WY
5000 BPK 90621 738-A5
8400 BHLS 90211 632-H2
8500 LA 90048 632-H2
9100 BHLS 90210 632-G2
CLIMBER DR
20700 DBAR 91789 679-G3
CLIMBING IVY CT
- SCTA 91350 4551-A2
CLINE RD
25700 LACo 91302 588-J7
25700 LACo 91302 589-A7
CLINT PL
5900 RPV 90275 792-J6
CLINTON AV
8300 WHWD 90048 593-A7
8400 WHWD 90048 592-J7
8400 LA 90048 592-J7
8400 LA 90048 593-A7
CLINTON PL
600 BHLS 90210 592-G3
CLINTON ST
100 PAS 91103 565-G3
1700 Echo 90026 634-D1
3800 LA 90004 594-A7
4200 LA 90004 593-F7
6600 LA 90036 593-C7
7900 LA 90048 593-C7
12300 ELMN 91732 637-E4
CLINTWOOD AV
300 LPUE 91744 638-B4
900 LACo 91744 638-B4
CLIO LN
- SCTA 91351 4551-H2
CLIOTA ST
10300 LACo 90601 677-C2
CLIPPER RD
- RPV 90275 822-J4
CLIPPER WY
200 SLB 90740 826-E4
CLIPPERS CIR
2300 THO 91361 557-B6
CLIPSTONE ST
24300 WdHl 91367 559-D1
CLIVE AV
7700 LACo 90606 676-J7
7700 LACo 90606 677-A7
CLIVEDEN AV
19000 CRSN 90746 764-G3
N CLIVEDEN AV
600 COMP 90220 734-G3
S CLIVEDEN AV
400 COMP 90220 734-G5
CLOCK TOWER PLAZA DR
38800 PMDL 93550 4196-A7
CLOGSTON DR
100 LACo 91746 637-G3
CLOISTER DR
1400 LHH 90631 708-A3
CLONLEE AV
11700 GrnH 91344 481-D7
CLORA PL
12000 ELMN 91732 637-F1
12300 INDS 91732 637-F2
CLORINDA DR
1100 DBAR 91789 679-F3
CLOSE CT
13000 LACo 90605 707-C4

CLOSE ST
14100 LACo 90604 707-D5
CLOTILDA LN
- RPV 90275 823-G3
CLOUD AV
3700 GLDL 91214 534-F2
4200 LaCr 91214 534-F1
4400 LaCr 91214 504-F7
CLOUD LN
12500 Brwd 90049 591-E7
CLOUDBERRY AV
- PMDL 93551 4194-H2
CLOUDCREST RD
2900 LaCr 91214 504-F5
CLOUDCROFT DR
3400 LACo 90265 630-E5
CLOUDSDALE AV
4800 GLDL 91214 504-E6
CLOUDS REST DR
1100 DBAR 91765 640-D4
CLOUDY CT
2400 RowH 91748 679-D7
CLOVE PL
100 BREA 92821 709-B6
CLOVER AV
11000 LA 90034 632-D7
11100 LA 90034 672-C1
11200 LA 90066 672-C1
CLOVER CT
- Cstc 91384 4459-F3
200 AZU 91702 568-H2
600 BREA 92821 709-B6
S CLOVER DR
1900 MONP 91755 636-C5
CLOVER RD
12200 Pcma 91331 502-F1
CLOVER ST
600 LA 90031 634-J2
1700 LVRN 91750 600-F1
2900 SMCA 90405 671-J2
CLOVER TR
23500 CALB 91302 589-E1
CLOVER WY
8000 BPK 90620 767-J3
CLOVERBROOK LN
1300 UPL 91784 571-J4
CLOVERBROOK ST
400 CRSN 90745 764-D6
CLOVERCLIFF DR
6800 RPV 90275 792-G7
6900 RPV 90275 822-G1
CLOVERDALE AV
3800 LA 90008 673-B2
N CLOVERDALE AV
1500 UPL 91786 571-H7
S CLOVERDALE AV
300 LA 90036 633-D2
1000 LA 90019 633-C4
2100 LA 90016 633-C6
2900 LA 90016 673-B1
CLOVERDALE CT
2500 PMDL 93551 4195-C6
23400 SCTA 91321 4640-G3
CLOVERDALE DR
700 POM 91767 601-B6
1700 BREA 92821 709-D7
CLOVERDALE LN
400 WAL 91789 639-B4
16100 CRTS 90703 736-J4
CLOVERFIELD BLVD
1400 SMCA 90404 631-G7
1600 SMCA 90404 671-H1
2200 SMCA 90405 671-H1
CLOVERGLEN DR
1100 LACo 91744 638-G5
CLOVER HEIGHTS AV
5800 MAL 90265 667-C1
CLOVERHILL RD
1000 Alta 91001 535-F2
CLOVERHURST PL
- LACo 91387 4552-A4
CLOVERLAND DR
21000 LACo 91724 599-H5
CLOVERLAWN DR
7100 PRM 90723 735-F2
7300 SGAT 90280 735-F2
CLOVERLEAF DR
200 BALD 91746 637-G3
400 MNRO 91016 567-F1
400 BALD 91706 637-G3
CLOVERLEAF PL
28600 Cstc 91384 4459-F1
CLOVERLEAF WY
400 MNRO 91016 567-F2
CLOVERLY AV
4500 TEML 91780 597-A5
4600 TEML 91780 596-J2
6600 TEML 91007 596-J1
CLOVERMEAD ST
16100 LACo 91722 598-G4
E CLOVERMEAD ST
16600 LACo 91722 598-G4
17800 COV 91722 599-A4
17800 LACo 91722 599-A4
W CLOVERMEAD ST
600 COV 91722 599-A4
CLOVERSIDE ST
14200 BALD 91706 598-C6
CLOVERTON ST
21300 LACo 91773 599-H3
CLOVERVIEW DR
800 GLDR 91741 569-D3

STREET
Block City ZIP Pg-Grid

CLOVERWOOD CT
37400 PMDL 93552 4287-B3
CLOVERWOOD ST
9500 BLF 90706 736-B3
CLOVETREE PL
- RPV 90275 823-A4
CLOVIS AV
9100 Wats 90002 704-E5
10700 LA 90059 704-E6
12300 Wbrk 90059 734-E2
CLOVIS CT
1300 POM 91766 640-G4
CLOY AV
2300 Ven 90291 671-J6
CLOYDEN RD
500 PVE 90274 792-E6
CLOYDEN SQ
700 PVE 90274 792-E6
CLUB CT
40600 PMDL 93551 4194-H2
CLUB DR
1500 POM 91768 600-E7
2700 LA 90064 632-F5
3000 LA 90034 632-F5
5000 PMDL 93551 4194-H2
10000 ING 90303 703-F5
CLUB PL
10200 LA 90064 632-F5
CLUB RD
- PAS 91105 565-E5
CLUB HOUSE AV
- Ven 90291 671-G6
CLUB HOUSE CT
- Ven 90291 671-G6
CLUB HOUSE DR
- LALM 90720 796-H2
CLUBHOUSE DR
- LACo 90265 586-H7
1200 PAS 91105 565-E7
4100 LKWD 90712 765-H5
4100 WCOV 91792 679-D3
CLUB HOUSE LN
- Actn 93510 4375-E7
CLUB RANCHO DR
- PMDL 93551 4195-B2
CLUB VIEW DR
400 Wwd 90024 632-C1
CLUB VIEW LN
- RHE 90274 793-F6
CLUB VISTA DR
- PMDL 93551 4194-J2
- PMDL 93551 4195-A2
2300 GLDR 91741 570-A5
CLUFF ST
22100 CRSN 90745 764-F7
CLUNE AV
2800 Ven 90291 671-H7
CLUNY AV
37600 PMDL 93550 4286-F2
CLUNY ST
37800 PMDL 93550 4286-F2
CLUSTER LN
500 RBCH 90278 763-A3
CLUSTERBERRY CT
10300 BelA 90077 592-A1
CLYBOURN AV
300 BURB 91505 563-B1
900 NHol 91601 563-B1
1600 BURB 91505 533-B3
4200 BURB 91602 563-C4
4200 LA 91602 563-C2
5900 NHol 91601 533-B7
6000 NHol 91606 533-A6
6400 LA 91505 533-A6
6600 NHol 91605 533-A6
7200 SunV 91352 533-A2
9500 SunV 91352 503-A5
9900 Sunl 91040 503-A4
10300 Sunl 91040 502-J3
11300 LA 91342 502-J1
CLYDE AV
1800 LA 90019 633-B6
2000 LA 90016 633-B6
3400 LA 90016 673-A1
CLYDEBANK AV
4800 LACo 91722 598-G3
5200 LACo 91702 598-G2
5400 AZU 91702 598-G2
CLYDEPARK AV
18500 CRTS 90703 767-C1
S CLYDEPARK AV
13200 HAW 90250 733-A2
CLYDESDALE CIR
21700 WAL 91789 639-J5
CLYDESDALE DR
42700 LACo 93532 4102-G4
CLYDESDALE RD
- GrnH 91344 480-H6
CLYDESDALE WY
- MTCL 91763 641-D1
CLYDE WALKER WY
4500 HAW 90250 703-C7
CLYDEWOOD AV
14500 BALD 91706 598-C6
W CLYDEWOOD AV
2200 WCOV 91790 598-D7
S CLYMAR AV
400 COMP 90220 734-E5
14300 LACo 90220 734-E3
CLYMER ST
14000 LA 91340 502-B2
14400 MsnH 91345 502-A3
14600 MsnH 91345 501-H3

CLYMER ST
16300 GrnH 91344 501-B3
18500 Nor 91326 500-F3
COACH PL
2100 HacH 91745 678-E4
COACH RD
2800 RPV 90275 823-F2
COACHELLA AV
6700 NLB 90805 735-D7
COACHMAN AV
8800 WHIT 90605 707-D3
9200 LACo 90605 707-D3
COACHWOOD AV
12700 LMRD 90638 738-A1
COACHWOOD CT
1700 HacH 91745 678-E4
COACHWOOD ST
1500 LHB 90631 738-E1
COAL CANYON RD
- Sunl 91040 503-A3
2500 LACo 90265 629-E5
21900 MAL 90265 629-D5
COALINGA AV
- MTCL 91763 641-F2
9700 MTCL 91763 601-F6
COALINGA CT
2300 CLAR 91711 571-D6
COAL MOUNTAIN CT
- BqtC 91354 4460-E4
COARSE GOLD MTWY
- LACo 91390 (4371-E5 See Page 4281)
- LACo 91390 4461-G1
COAST CIR
2800 HNTB 92649 826-J6
COAST DR
12200 LACo 90601 637-C6
COASTAL SAGE PL
- WAL 91789 639-C5
COASTAL VIEW DR
- Wch 90045 702-C2
COAST GUARD WY
- Wch 90045 702-E5
COASTLINE DR
100 SLB 90740 826-E3
18000 LACo 90265 630-D6
COAST REDWOOD LN
- LACo 91387 4552-B4
COAST SITE DR
32600 RPV 90275 822-J5
COAST VIEW DR
3400 MAL 90265 628-J6
COATE CT
- Alta 91001 535-G3
COATES AV
1100 City 90063 635-E4
COBAL CANYON MTWY
- CLAR 91711 571-D1
- LACo 91711 571-D1
- LACo 91750 571-A2
S COBAL CANYON FIRE TRUCK CIR
- CLAR 91711 571-B5
COBALT ST
- LACo 91342 481-J1
14600 LA 91342 481-J1
36700 PMDL 93552 4286-J5
COBALT WY
- LA 91342 481-J1
COBAN RD
1500 LHH 90631 708-F2
COBB CT
500 LACo 91746 637-J3
COBB RD
3600 LAN 93535 4016-A4
COBB ST
2400 CMRC 90040 675-E3
COBBLE CT
3700 PMDL 93551 4195-A3
COBBLEFIELD WY
1900 GLDR 91740 569-J7
COBBLESTONE CT
- SCTA 91354 4460-F6
3800 SBdC 91766 641-D3
16600 CRTS 90703 737-A6
29800 Cstc 91384 4459-D4
40800 PMDL 93551 4194-J2
COBBLESTONE DR
2200 BREA 92821 709-E6
6000 AGRH 91301 557-J3
COBBLESTONE LN
- POM 91767 601-C6
100 LVRN 91750 600-H2
4300 LCF 91011 535-B4
9000 CYP 90630 767-C6
COBBLESTONE RD
1200 LHB 90631 738-B1
15800 LMRD 90638 737-J1
16500 LMRD 90638 738-A1
S COBERTA AV
300 LACo 91746 637-H4
COBHAM CT
2400 BelA 90077 591-G2
COBLE AV
1300 HacH 91745 677-J2
1300 HacH 91745 678-A1
COBOS ST
15900 NRWK 90650 736-H5
COBRE CT
800 POM 91768 640-F1
1500 LACo 91744 638-F4
E COBRE WY
100 LBCH 90802 795-E7

W COBRE WY
100 LBCH 90802 795-D7
COBURN AV
- SMAD 91024 567-B2
COCAO PL
800 BREA 92821 709-C6
COCHISE CIR
1800 WAL 91789 639-G2
COCHISE WY
19000 CRSN 90746 764-F2
COCHITI PL
3100 FUL 92833 738-A3
S COCHRAN AV
300 LA 90036 633-D2
1000 LA 90019 633-C3
2100 LA 90016 633-C6
2900 LA 90016 673-B1
3800 LA 90008 673-B2
COCHRAN PL
1800 LA 90019 633-C5
COCHRAN ST
5400 SIMI 93063 499-A1
COCINA LN
3600 PMDL 93551 4195-A3
4300 PMDL 93551 4194-H2
COCKERHAM DR
4500 LFlz 90027 594-A2
COCKLEBUR LN
26500 SCTA 91351 4551-B2
COCKLEBUR PL
18000 RowH 91748 678-J7
COCKNEY ST
39400 PMDL 93551 4195-E5
COCO AV
3800 LA 90008 673-C2
COCO PL
16000 PacP 90272 630-F4
COCOA ST
400 COMP 90220 734-H5
E COCOA ST
100 COMP 90220 734-J5
100 COMP 90220 735-A5
700 COMP 90221 735-A5
W COCOA ST
100 COMP 90220 734-J5
COCONINO PL
- LACo 93532 4102-E5
COCONUT PL
- PMDL 93551 4285-E3
COCOPAN DR
500 Alta 91001 536-A3
COCOS DR
6000 LA 90068 593-G3
CODY AV
1600 SIMI 93063 499-C3
W CODY CT
1300 UPL 91786 571-J7
CODY DR
5000 ELA 90022 675-G1
CODY RD
300 SDMS 91773 600-B1
3400 Shrm 91403 561-H6
COE ST
100 CLAR 91711 601-D4
COEUR D ALENE AV
600 Ven 90291 672-A6
COFER CT
- WAL 91789 639-H6
COFFIELD AV
11300 ELMN 91731 597-D7
COFFMAN AV
- LBCH 90802 824-G3
- SPed 90731 824-G3
COFFMAN DR
800 MTBL 90640 636-C7
COFFMAN PICO RD
8600 PRV 90660 676-F5
COGBURN LN
900 DBAR 91765 680-B2
COG HILL DR
11800 LACo 90601 677-C3
COGSWELL RD
1200 SELM 91733 637-C4
2100 ELMN 91733 637-D3
2200 ELMN 91732 637-F1
3600 ELMN 91732 597-G5
5400 ARCD 91006 597-G5
COHASSET ST
2700 BURB 91504 533-C4
2700 LA 91504 533-C4
3500 BURB 91505 533-B4
7500 VanN 91405 531-J4
8800 VanN 91406 531-B4
10100 LA 91505 533-A4
10500 SunV 91352 533-A4
11000 SunV 91352 532-H4
11400 NHol 91605 532-E4
13700 VanN 91405 532-A4
17900 Res 91335 531-A4
18100 Res 91335 530-F4
20100 Win 91306 530-D4
20800 CanP 91303 530-A4
22000 CanP 91303 529-J4
22600 CanP 91307 529-G4
23200 LA 91304 529-F4
COIL AV
1100 Wilm 90744 794-G5
COINER CT
1100 INDS 91748 679-B4
COKE AV
4700 LKWD 90712 765-J2
5900 NLB 90805 765-J1
6200 BLF 90706 765-J1
14400 PRM 90723 735-J3
17400 BLF 90706 735-J7

COLBATH AV
4100 Shrm 91423 562-B3
5500 VanN 91401 562-B1
6100 VanN 91401 532-B6
6600 VanN 91405 532-B4
8300 PanC 91402 532-B1
8700 PanC 91402 502-B7
COLBECK AV
19000 CRSN 90746 764-F2
COLBERT AV
3300 LA 90066 672-C2
COLBY AV
1000 WLA 90025 631-J5
1500 WLA 90025 632-A5
2200 LA 90064 632-B7
2700 LA 90064 672-C1
3100 LA 90066 672-C1
COLBY CIDR
400 CLAR 91711 601-C2
COLBY DR
1400 GLDL 91205 564-F7
COLBY MTWY
- GLDR 91741 569-G3
- LACo 91741 569-G3
COLBY RANCH RD
- LACo - (4726-B2 See Page 4645)
COLCHA WY
40600 PMDL 93551 4194-H2
COLCHESTER CT
39400 PMDL 93551 4195-E5
COLCHESTER WY
16900 HacH 91745 678-F6
18100 Nor 91326 500-J1
COLCORD AV
36400 Litl 93543 4288-A5
COLDBROOK AV
4500 LKWD 90713 766-C2
9500 DWNY 90242 736-C1
11600 DWNY 90241 706-C6
13400 BLF 90706 736-C2
COLD CANYON CT
29700 SCTA 91387 4462-G6
COLD CANYON RD
400 LACo 91302 628-J1
500 LACo 91302 629-A1
1000 LACo 91302 589-B5
COLD CREEK FIRE RD
1200 LACo 91302 589-D5
E COLDEN AV
100 LA 90003 704-D4
600 Wats 90002 704-D4
W COLDEN AV
100 LA 90003 704-B4
500 LA 90044 704-B4
9500 LACo 90044 704-B4
COLD PLAINS DR
2700 HacH 91745 678-B5
COLD SPRING LN
2500 DBAR 91765 679-H6
22100 DBAR 91765 709-H1
COLDSPRINGS PL
- SCTA 91354 4460-G5
COLD SPRINGS ST
26800 CALB 91301 558-G7
COLD STREAM CT
800 DBAR 91765 680-E2
COLDSTREAM TER
3700 Tarz 91356 560-F5
COLDWATER DR
- SCTA 91354 4460-F7
COLDWATER CANYON AV
3100 LA 90210 562-E7
3100 LA 91604 562-E6
4700 Shrm 91423 562-E3
5200 VanN 91401 562-E3
5600 LA 91607 562-E3
5900 LA 91607 532-E7
5900 VanN 91401 532-E7
6000 NHol 91606 532-E7
6600 NHol 91605 532-E3
COLDWATER CANYON CT
- NHol 91605 532-E3
COLDWATER CANYON DR
1000 BHLS 90210 592-E5
1700 LA 90210 592-F4
COLDWATER CANYON LN
3100 LA 90210 562-E7
COLE AV
700 LA 90038 593-F6
1300 Hlwd 90028 593-F6
3700 LACo 91107 566-H5
COLE PL
600 BHLS 90210 592-G3
1200 LA 90038 593-F5
1400 Hlwd 90028 593-F5
2400 LACo 90255 704-J2
2400 SGAT 90280 704-J2
COLE RD
9800 WHIT 90603 707-G5
10300 LACo 90604 707-G5
COLE ST
7000 DWNY 90242 705-G4
8100 DWNY 90242 706-A6
COLE WY
1500 LHB 90631 708-E4
COLEBROOK PL
27100 SCTA 91354 4460-G7
27100 SCTA 91354 4550-G1
COLEBROOK ST
10500 Sunl 91040 503-A4
COLE CREST DR
8400 LA 90046 592-J4

COLE CREST DR
8400 LA 90069 592-J4
COLEFORD AV
1400 LACo 90601 637-F6
S COLEFORD AV
1200 LACo 90601 637-F5
COLEGIO DR
8100 Wch 90045 702-D2
16300 HacH 91745 678-D4
COLEGROVE AV
1300 MTBL 90640 676-C2
COLEMAN AV
500 HiPk 90042 595-D4
900 LA 90032 595-D4
COLEMAN CT
2000 SIMI 93063 499-A2
COLERIDGE DR
2600 OrCo 90720 796-G4
2900 LACo 91107 566-F6
COLERIDGE PL
25800 StvR 91381 4640-B1
COLETTE WY
25400 LACo 91302 559-A3
COLFAIR ST
9300 PRV 90660 676-J1
COLFAX AV
4000 LA 91604 562-H5
4400 LA 91602 562-H3
4400 LA 91607 562-H3
4800 NHol 91601 562-H3
5900 NHol 91601 532-H7
5900 LA 91607 532-H7
6000 NHol 91606 532-H7
COLFAX CT
1200 POM 91766 640-G4
1300 LHB 90631 708-G5
COLFAX RD
9400 SBdC 92371 (4472-H7 See Page 4471)
N COLFAX ST
300 LHB 90631 708-G5
S COLFAX ST
100 LHB 90631 708-G6
COLGATE AV
5900 LA 90036 633-C2
6300 LA 90048 633-A1
6700 LA 90048 632-J1
COLGATE PL
600 CLAR 91711 601-D5
COLGIN CT
400 BURB 91501 533-J7
COLHARY CT
- SCTA 91387 4552-D2
COLIMA AL
400 LA 90065 595-A4
COLIMA RD
9900 WHIT 90603 707-E7
10400 LACo 90604 707-E7
12100 LACo 90604 737-E1
12700 LMRD 90638 737-E1
16500 HacH 91745 678-H4
17200 RowH 91748 678-H4
17200 INDS 91748 678-H4
18100 RowH 91748 679-B5
19800 LACo 91789 679-E5
20300 DBAR 91789 679-E5
COLIMA RD Rt#-N8
3100 HacH 91745 678-C6
4000 WHIT 90605 677-J7
4000 WHIT 90605 707-H1
4000 WHIT 91745 677-J7
4000 WHIT 91745 678-C6
9800 WHIT 90603 707-G4
10200 LACo 90604 707-G4
COLINA CT
40400 PMDL 93551 4194-H3
COLINA DR
- PacP 90272 590-B7
- SCTA 91351 4551-D3
1400 GLDL 91208 534-G7
1500 GLDL 91208 564-H1
10900 Top 90290 590-B6
19300 WAL 91789 639-C6
COLINA LN
25500 RHE 90274 793-C5
COLINA RD
23600 VeCo 93063 499-B3
W COLINA TER
500 MONP 91754 635-H3
COLINA WY
10400 BelA 90077 592-A1
COLINA VISTA ST
28700 AGRH 91301 558-B3
COLINTON DR
2600 RowH 91748 679-B7
S COLISEUM DR
500 LA 90037 674-B2
COLISEUM PL
3600 LA 90008 673-E2
COLISEUM ST
2700 LA 90018 673-E1
2900 LA 90008 673-E1
3500 LA 90016 673-A1
COLLAMER DR
300 CRSN 90746 734-D7
W COLLEEN CT
1100 UPL 91786 601-J1
COLLEEN DR
45100 LAN 93535 4016-C5
COLLEEN ST
100 LHB 90631 708-C6
COLLEGE AV
1400 POM 91767 601-D6

COLLEGE AV
3800 CULC 90232 672-E2
7200 WHIT 90602 677-E7
7800 WHIT 90602 707-E2
8000 WHIT 90605 707-E2
10900 DWNY 90241 706-A4
11100 MTCL 91763 641-D3
11100 SBdC 91766 641-D3
11600 SBdC 91710 641-D4
N COLLEGE AV
100 CLAR 91711 601-D1
S COLLEGE AV
100 CLAR 91711 601-D4
N COLLEGE CIR
1800 LBCH 90815 796-D5
COLLEGE DR
- GLDL 91208 564-H2
- GLDR 91741 569-B6
- LACo 90601 677-C1
7700 WHIT 90602 677-C1
11500 NRWK 90650 736-G5
COLLEGE LN
2400 LVRN 91750 600-H2
COLLEGE PL
400 FUL 92831 738-J6
10800 CRTS 90703 736-E5
N COLLEGE PL
1800 LBCH 90815 796-D5
COLLEGE RD
- VanN 91401 562-D1
COLLEGE RD N
- VanN 91401 532-D7
- VanN 91401 562-D1
COLLEGE RD S
- VanN 91401 562-D1
E COLLEGE ST
100 COV 91723 599-B5
100 LA 90012 634-H2
N COLLEGE ST
100 LHB 90631 708-F5
S COLLEGE ST
100 LHB 90631 708-F6
W COLLEGE ST
100 COV 91723 599-B5
100 LA 90012 634-F2
COLLEGE WY
100 COV 91723 599-C5
E COLLEGE WY
100 CLAR 91711 570-J7
200 CLAR 91711 571-A7
N COLLEGE WY
300 CLAR 91711 601-D3
W COLLEGE WY
100 CLAR 91711 570-J7
N COLLEGE CIRCLE DR
- CYP 90630 767-E6
S COLLEGE CIRCLE DR
- CYP 90630 767-E6
COLLEGE COMMERCE WY
- UPL 91786 601-G3
COLLEGE CREST DR
4000 LA 90065 594-H2
COLLEGE PARK DR
- LBCH 90815 796-F7
- SLB 90740 796-G6
2700 LAN 93536 4105-C3
COLLEGE SQUARE DR
5400 LA 90032 635-G1
COLLEGE VIEW AV
4400 Eagl 90041 564-J5
COLLEGE VIEW DR
1000 MONP 91754 635-H4
COLLEGE VIEW LN
900 MONP 91754 635-J5
COLLEGE VIEW PL
1700 Eagl 90041 564-J7
COLLEGE VISTA AV
1800 WAL 91789 639-F3
COLLEGEWOOD DR
20200 WAL 91789 639-F4
COLLEGIAN AV
2100 MONP 91754 635-J5
COLLETT AV
4500 Enc 91436 561-F3
7400 VanN 91406 531-F4
8500 LA 91343 531-F1
8800 LA 91343 501-F5
10300 GrnH 91344 501-E1
11500 GrnH 91344 481-F7
COLLETTE WY
- LMRD 90638 737-G4
- PMDL 93552 4287-E1
COLLEY PL
9300 Litl 93543 4468-B2
COLLIER AL
- SPAS 91030 595-G2
COLLIER PL
5200 WdHl 91364 560-E3
COLLIER ST
19300 Tarz 91356 560-F2
19700 WdHl 91364 560-E3
COLLINAS POINTE
- CHLS 91709 710-J2
COLLINA STRADA
15500 BelA 90077 591-G2
COLLINGSWOOD DR
800 POM 91767 601-B5
COLLINGWOOD CIR
5300 LACo 91302 559-A3
COLLINGWOOD DR
8800 LA 90069 592-H5
COLLINGWOOD PL
1300 LA 90069 592-H5

COLLINS LN
7900 LPMA 90623 767-D3
COLLINS PL
5600 WdHl 91367 560-C1
COLLINS RD
19700 SCTA 91351 4551-E4
COLLINS ST
10500 NHol 91601 563-A1
11300 NHol 91601 562-H1
11700 LA 91607 562-E1
13400 VanN 91401 562-A1
14700 VanN 91411 561-J1
17100 Enc 91316 561-A1
18300 Tarz 91356 560-G1
20700 WdHl 91367 560-A1
22300 WdHl 91367 559-F2
N COLLINS WY
- LBCH 90802 825-D1
200 LBCH 90802 795-D7
S COLLINS WY
- LBCH 90802 825-D1
COLLIS AV
3400 LA 90032 595-D5
4900 SPAS 91030 595-E3
S COLLWOOD AV
100 LACo 91746 637-H4
COLMAN ST
400 Alta 91001 535-J6
600 Alta 91001 536-A6
COLMAR AV
6200 BGDN 90201 675-H7
6500 BGDN 90201 705-H1
COLMAR ST
900 POM 91767 601-C7
COLMENA DR
27100 SCTA 91354 4460-H7
COLMENA ST
2200 LCF 91011 504-H7
COLMERE AV
4400 PRV 90660 676-G2
COLODNY DR
5200 AGRH 91301 558-D5
COLOGNE ST
5100 LA 90019 633-B5
5500 LA 90016 633-B5
COLOMA AV
4200 WdHl 91364 559-G5
COLOMA CT
- LACo 91390 4461-B3
COLOMBARD LN
- DBAR 91765 680-B3
COLOMBIA DR
7200 BPK 90620 767-D3
E COLON ST
900 Wilm 90744 794-H4
N COLONIA DE LAS MAGNOLIAS
500 ELA 90022 635-G5
COLONIA DE LAS PALMAS
400 ELA 90022 635-G5
COLONIA DE LAS ROSAS
4800 ELA 90022 635-G5
COLONIA DE LOS CEDROS
500 ELA 90022 635-G5
COLONIA DE LOS PINOS
4800 ELA 90022 635-G5
COLONIAL AV
3200 LA 90066 672-B2
4000 CULC 90066 672-C4
COLONIAL CIR
400 FUL 92835 738-H3
COLONIAL DR
- PMDL 93550 4286-C4
COLONIAL LN
- SCTA 91355 4550-E2
COLONY AV
12200 CHNO 91710 641-C6
COLONY CIR
3200 LFlz 90027 594-C2
COLONY CT
15100 PRM 90723 735-H4
21000 TOR 90503 763-A5
37400 PMDL 93550 4286-D3
COLONY DR
100 SMAD 91024 567-B2
1100 POM 91766 640-G4
1200 SBdC 91784 571-J2
43600 LAN 93536 4105-A1
44000 LAN 93536 4015-A7
COLONY ST
12600 CHNO 91710 641-C6
S COLONY PARK DR
- CRSN 90745 794-E2
COLONY VIEW CIR
3200 MAL 90265 628-J6
COLORADO
1800 WCOV 91792 678-J1
COLORADO AL
1400 Eagl 90041 565-D5
1400 PAS 91105 565-D5
COLORADO AV
- SMCA 90401 671-F2
1200 SMCA 90404 671-F2
2000 SMCA 90404 631-G7
14100 PRM 90723 735-G3
E COLORADO AV
100 GLDR 91740 569-E6
W COLORADO AV
100 GLDR 91740 569-E7

COLORADO BLVD
400 PAS 91105 565-D6
700 Eagl 90041 565-A6
1600 Eagl 90041 564-J5
1600 GLDL 91205 564-J5
4500 LA 90039 564-C6
E COLORADO BLVD
- ARCD 91006 567-E4
- PAS 91103 565-J4
- PAS 91105 565-J4
100 MNRO 91016 567-E4
200 PAS 91101 565-J4
500 PAS 91101 566-B4
800 PAS 91106 566-B4
1800 PAS 91107 566-G4
3200 LACo 91107 566-G4
W COLORADO BLVD
- ARCD 91007 567-C4
- PAS 91103 565-F5
- PAS 91105 565-F5
100 MNRO 91016 567-G4
700 Eagl 90041 565-F5
COLORADO CT
300 LACo 91744 679-A2
N COLORADO CT
200 LBCH 90803 825-H1
COLORADO PL
- SCTA 91387 4462-G6
300 LBCH 90814 795-H7
300 LBCH 90814 825-H1
W COLORADO PL
100 ARCD 91007 567-C4
COLORADO PL N
2800 SMCA 90404 631-H7
COLORADO PL S
3000 SMCA 90404 631-H7
E COLORADO ST
100 GLDL 91205 564-G5
300 LBCH 90814 795-H7
3900 LBCH 90814 796-A7
5200 LBCH 90803 796-B7
W COLORADO ST
100 GLDL 91204 564-D5
200 ARCD 91007 567-A4
300 GLDL 91210 564-D5
900 ARCD 91007 566-J4
COLORETTI CT
25900 SCTA 91355 4550-F6
COLSTON AV
300 LACo 91744 679-A2
COLT
- LA 91342 481-G1
COLT LN
700 WAL 91789 639-E6
E COLT LN
- VeCo 91307 529-A4
COLT RD
2300 RPV 90275 823-G3
30600 Cstc 91384 4459-B2
COLT ST
17000 GrnH 91344 501-C2
COLT WY
3000 FUL 92833 738-A3
COLTMAN AV
18100 CRSN 90746 764-D2
COLTON ST
1200 Echo 90026 634-D2
COLTRANE AV
22600 Nwhl 91321 4641-A6
22600 StvR 91381 4641-A6
22800 Nwhl 91321 4640-J6
22800 StvR 91381 4640-J6
COLUMBIA AL
1100 SPAS 91030 595-H1
COLUMBIA AV
200 Echo 90026 634-D3
300 LA 90017 634-D3
3500 PMDL 93550 4286-H2
4100 PRV 90660 676-G1
E COLUMBIA AV
100 POM 91767 600-J7
300 POM 91767 601-A7
N COLUMBIA AV
800 CLAR 91711 601-E3
W COLUMBIA AV
400 POM 91768 600-H7
COLUMBIA CIR
400 PAS 91105 565-G7
COLUMBIA CT
- LACo 93536 4105-A5
23900 SCTA 91355 4550-F4
COLUMBIA DR
1300 GLDL 91205 564-F7
3400 LVRN 91750 600-H2
COLUMBIA PL
200 Echo 90026 634-D3
700 TOR 90501 763-H5
1200 PAS 91105 565-H7
1200 PAS 91105 595-H1
COLUMBIA RD
100 ARCD 91007 566-J6
COLUMBIA ST
- PAS 91105 595-F1
500 SPAS 91030 595-H1
600 BREA 92821 708-J6
600 BREA 92821 709-A6
1100 RSMD 91770 636-D1
2600 TOR 90503 763-E4
4300 CHNO 91710 641-E7
E COLUMBIA ST
200 LBCH 90806 795-E2
600 SIGH 90755 795-E2

W COLUMBIA ST
700 LBCH 90806 795-C2
1700 LBCH 90810 795-A2
COLUMBIA WY
- LACo 93551 4103-J6
- LAN 93551 4103-J6
100 LAN 93535 4105-G6
100 PMDL 93551 4105-G6
100 LAN 93534 4105-G6
100 PMDL 93550 4105-G6
100 PMDL 93550 4106-G5
100 LAN 93535 4106-B5
1000 PMDL 93534 4105-G6
1000 LAN 93551 4105-G6
1200 LACo 93551 4105-G6
1500 LACo 93534 4105-G6
2000 LACo 93536 4105-A6
2000 LAN 93536 4105-A6
3900 PMDL 93552 4106-G5
4000 LACo 93536 4104-G6
4400 LAN 93536 4104-B6
4500 PMDL 93552 4107-A5
4500 LACo 93552 4106-G5
4500 LACo 93552 4107-A5
6100 PMDL 93536 4104-D6
6300 PMDL 93551 4104-D6
6300 LAN 93551 4104-B6
7000 LACo 93551 4104-B6
COLUMBIANA DR
300 SDMS 91773 599-J2
COLUMBINE AV
9200 MTCL 91763 601-G5
COLUMBINE CIR
8000 BPK 90620 767-J3
COLUMBINE ST
11100 SBdC 91762 641-G2
COLUMBUS AV
4500 Shrm 91403 561-H4
5400 VanN 91411 561-H2
6200 VanN 91411 531-H7
6600 VanN 91405 531-H5
8200 PanC 91402 531-H2
8300 LA 91343 531-H2
8700 LA 91343 501-H7
9900 MsnH 91345 501-H2
N COLUMBUS AV
100 GLDL 91203 564-D4
1000 GLDL 91202 564-D1
9100 LA 91343 501-H6
S COLUMBUS AV
100 GLDL 91210 564-D6
100 GLDL 91204 564-D6
COLUMBUS ST
600 WCOV 91791 638-J1
5200 CHNO 91710 641-G6
COLUMBUS WY
15300 MsnH 91345 501-H3
COLUSA DR
700 WAL 91789 639-C6
COLVEN RD
16800 GrnH 91344 481-D5
E COLVER PL
1300 COV 91724 599-F4
COLVILLE PL
3400 Enc 91436 561-D7
COLWELL DR
10000 SunV 91352 533-C3
COLWYN AV
24200 SCTA 91321 4640-H2
COLYEAR SPRINGS LN
900 WAL 91789 639-C6
COLYER AV
10700 LYN 90262 705-D6
COLYTON ST
400 LA 90013 634-G5
COMAL CT
25000 LMTA 90717 793-G4
COMANCHE
3300 Top 90290 560-B6
COMANCHE AV
2700 THO 91362 557-A2
5600 WdHl 91367 560-E1
6500 Win 91306 530-D1
8900 Chat 91311 500-D5
COMANCHE CIR
- POM 91766 640-G6
COMANCHE DR
7400 BPK 90620 767-F2
COMANCHE PL
20100 Win 91306 530-E5
COMANCHE TR
11400 Chat 91311 500-B1
COMBELLACK DR
2400 SIGH 90755 795-H3
COMBER AV
4500 Enc 91316 561-B4
COMBER PL
800 Hrbr 90710 794-B4
COMERCIO AV
5100 WdHl 91364 560-B3
COMERCIO LN
5300 WdHl 91364 560-B3
COMERCIO WY
5300 WdHl 91364 560-B3
5400 WdHl 91367 560-B3
COMET CT
3600 PMDL 93550 4286-H3
COMET ST
6700 HiPk 90042 595-F1
COMET WY
16000 SCTA 91387 4552-D3
COMETA AV
11100 Pcma 91331 502-F1

COMETA AV
11700 Pcma 91331 482-E7
12500 LA 91340 482-B4
COMEY AV
5900 CULC 90232 633-A6
5900 LA 90034 633-A6
6000 LA 90034 632-J6
COMIDA WY
21700 Top 90290 590-A2
COMISO DR
2200 HacH 91745 678-D5
COMITY CIR
1300 LHB 90631 708-G4
COMLY ST
4300 City 90063 635-F3
COMMANCHE TR
28900 Ago 91301 588-B4
COMMERCE AV
500 PMDL 93551 4195-H6
9700 Tuj 91042 504-A4
COMMERCE CIR
13700 BALD 91706 598-A3
COMMERCE DR
5100 BALD 91706 598-A3
5100 IRW 91706 598-A3
COMMERCE WY
100 WAL 91789 679-F1
2300 CMRC 90040 675-H4
15900 CRTS 90703 737-C5
COMMERCE CENTER DR
- Valc 91355 4549-H1
1000 LAN 93534 4105-G2
29200 Cstc 91384 4459-G6
29200 Valc 91355 4459-G6
COMMERCE POINTE DR
20900 LACo 91789 639-G7
COMMERCIAL AV
700 COV 91723 599-C4
800 SGBL 91776 596-F4
COMMERCIAL PL
8100 SGAT 90280 704-J2
COMMERCIAL ST
500 GLDL 91203 564-C4
E COMMERCIAL ST
100 POM 91767 640-J1
300 POM 91767 641-A1
400 LA 90012 634-H4
W COMMERCIAL ST
100 POM 91768 640-G1
100 SDMS 91773 600-B2
COMMERCIAL WY
400 LHB 90631 708-F6
COMMODORE ST
2500 LA 90032 595-C7
COMMODORE SLOAT DR
6200 LA 90048 633-A2
COMMON AV
100 LPUE 91744 638-E7
100 LPUE 91744 678-E1
COMMON ST
200 LPUE 91744 678-E1
COMMONS WY
- CALB 91302 559-E4
COMMONWEALTH AV
800 Ven 90291 671-H4
4100 CULC 90232 672-E3
4100 LCF 91011 535-C3
4400 CULC 90230 672-E3
6200 BPK 90621 737-J7
8200 BPK 90621 738-A7
8400 FUL 92833 738-A7
E COMMONWEALTH AV
- ALH 91801 596-C4
500 FUL 92832 738-J7
N COMMONWEALTH AV
100 LA 90004 634-B1
300 LA 90004 594-B7
1100 LA 90029 594-B5
1500 LFlz 90027 594-B2
S COMMONWEALTH AV
100 LA 90004 634-B2
300 LA 90020 634-B2
600 LA 90005 634-B2
600 LA 90010 634-B2
W COMMONWEALTH AV
- ALH 91801 596-A5
1100 ALH 91803 596-A5
1400 ALH 91803 595-G6
1400 ALH 91801 595-H5
1500 FUL 92833 738-E7
COMMONWEALTH CIR
4500 CULC 90230 672-F4
N COMMONWEALTH PL
200 LA 90004 594-G4
200 LA 90004 634-B1
COMMONWEALTH CANYON DR
2700 LFlz 90027 594-A1
COMMUNITY AV
2400 Mont 91020 534-G2
2700 LaCr 91214 534-F1
3100 LaCr 91214 504-E7
3200 GLDL 91214 504-D6
COMMUNITY CT
16200 LA 91343 531-E2
COMMUNITY ST
12200 SunV 91352 532-D1
13600 PanC 91402 532-A2
14800 PanC 91402 531-J1
15000 LA 91343 531-E1
17000 Nor 91325 531-C1
18400 Nor 91325 530-J2
18500 Nor 91324 530-G2

STREET Block City ZIP Pg-Grid

COMMUNITY ST
19900 Win 91306 530-D2
20800 LA 91304 530-B2
23200 LA 91304 529-E2
COMO CIR
- WdHl 91367 559-J2
COMO DR
400 POM 91767 601-A7
COMO LN
- Nor 91326 500-C1
COMO ST
5200 CMRC 90040 675-G2
COMOLETTE AV
8000 DWNY 90242 735-H1
COMOLETTE ST
7800 DWNY 90242 705-H7
7900 DWNY 90242 735-J1
COMPANARIO DR
18100 RowH 91748 678-J4
18200 RowH 91748 679-A4
COMPASS CT
- LBCH 90803 826-G2
COMPASS DR
5800 Wch 90045 702-J1
COMPO REAL DR
16400 HacH 91745 678-D5
COMPOTE CIR
- PMDL 93551 4285-E3
COMPRESSOR PLANT FIRE RD
- GmH 91344 480-F3
- Nor 91326 480-F3
- StvR 91381 480-F3
COMPROMISE LINE RD
1600 GLDR 91741 569-H6
COMPTON AV
1200 LA 90021 634-G7
1500 LA 90021 674-F2
1900 COMP 90222 734-G1
1900 LA 90011 674-F2
2700 Wbrk 90222 734-G1
5800 Flor 90001 674-F6
7300 Flor 90001 704-F3
8600 Wats 90002 704-F3
9100 Wats 90002 704-F3
10700 LA 90059 704-G6
11600 Wbrk 90059 704-G6
12100 Wbrk 90059 734-G1
COMPTON BLVD
- PRM 90221 735-G4
6400 PRM 90723 735-G4
6400 COMP 90221 735-G4
8800 PRM 90723 736-A4
E COMPTON BLVD
100 COMP 90220 734-D4
100 LACo 90248 734-D4
200 COMP 90220 735-B4
200 COMP 90221 735-B4
600 LACo 90220 734-D4
4100 RDom 90221 735-B4
W COMPTON BLVD
100 COMP 90220 734-H4
100 LACo 90248 734-C4
COMPTON CT
4100 SBdC 91710 641-D5
COMPTON ST
3900 SBdC 91710 641-D5
COMPTONVILLE LN
33600 LACo 90265 626-C1
COMSTOCK AV
200 Wwd 90024 632-B1
1100 GLDR 91741 569-G4
1800 WLA 90025 632-D3
5800 WHIT 90601 677-C6
7700 WHIT 90602 677-C7
7700 WHIT 90602 707-C1
43900 LAN 93535 4106-C1
E COMSTOCK AV
500 GLDR 91741 569-E4
W COMSTOCK AV
500 GLDR 91741 569-D4
COMSTOCK CIR
7800 LPMA 90623 767-D3
COMSTOCK CT
2000 PMDL 93551 4195-E6
COMSTOCK WY
- LA 91342 481-J1
CONANT ST
- LBCH 90808 765-J7
- LBCH 90808 766-A7
E CONANT ST
3600 LBCH 90808 766-A7
5900 LACo 90808 766-A7
CONATA ST
2500 DUAR 91010 568-F3
CONCERT ST
11000 ELMN 91731 637-D2
CONCERTO DR
200 VeCo 91377 557-G2
CONCERT PARK DR
- LA 90094 702-D1
CONCETTA WY
1200 SPAS 91030 595-F2
CONCHA ST
400 Alta 91001 536-A4
CONCHITA ST
2100 GLDL 91208 534-H7
CONCHITA WY
4400 Tarz 91356 560-F4
CONCHITO DR
1500 LHB 90631 708-B3
N CONCHO LN
- VeCo 91307 529-B3

CONCORD AL
600 LA 90023 635-B7
CONCORD AV
400 MNRO 91016 567-F3
900 MTBL 90640 636-D7
2200 POM 91768 600-D7
2300 POM 91768 640-D1
2600 ALH 91803 595-G6
3200 LA 90032 595-G6
12500 CHNO 91710 641-E6
27900 Cstc 91384 4459-G6
CONCORD CT
11700 CHNO 91710 641-E4
41000 PMDL 93551 4194-F1
CONCORD LN
1200 GLDR 91740 599-F1
CONCORD PL
800 ELSG 90245 702-E7
CONCORD ST
100 ELSG 90245 732-E2
100 GLDL 91203 564-C4
600 GLDL 91202 564-C3
11700 CRTS 90703 766-G3
N CONCORD ST
400 LA 90063 635-C5
S CONCORD ST
100 LA 90063 635-C6
600 LA 90023 635-B7
1100 LA 90023 675-B1
CONCORD WY
1000 LHB 90631 708-B7
CONCORDIA CT
500 PAS 91105 565-H6
CONCORSE DR
29000 Cstc 91384 4459-C6
N CONCOURSE AV
100 MTBL 90640 676-B1
500 MTBL 90640 636-B7
S CONCOURSE AV
100 MTBL 90640 676-B2
100 MTBL 90022 676-B2
900 ELA 90022 676-B2
1500 CMRC 90022 676-B2
CONCOURSE ST
800 LHB 90631 708-G4
CONCOURSE WY
10000 Wch 90045 703-A5
CONDE DR
23000 SCTA 91354 4550-H1
CONDELL DR
3500 CALB 91302 559-E7
CONDESA DR
15400 WHIT 90603 707-H3
CONDON AV
1900 RBCH 90278 763-C1
5700 LadH 90056 673-B6
6200 ING 90302 673-B6
6200 LA 90056 673-B6
10000 ING 90304 703-C5
10000 Lenx 90304 703-C5
11100 HAW 90304 703-C7
16200 LNDL 90260 733-C7
17300 LNDL 90260 763-C1
S CONDON AV
14300 HAW 90250 733-C5
14300 LNDL 90260 733-C5
CONDOR AV
- BREA 92823 709-H6
CONDOR ST
7100 CMRC 90040 676-B5
CONDOR RIDGE RD
15500 SCTA 91387 4552-D5
CONE ST
19200 RowH 91748 679-C5
CONEJO AV
4700 WdHl 91364 559-J4
CONEJO LN
1500 FUL 92833 738-C4
CONEJO RASTRO
- LACo 91390 4373-E7
CONEJO SCHOOL RD
200 THO 91362 557-A1
CONEJO VIEW DR
28500 AGRH 91301 558-B5
CONESTOGA DR
- RHE 90274 823-G1
4200 LACo 93536 4104-J1
4400 LAN 93536 4104-J1
CONESTOGA RD
300 SDMS 91773 570-B7
CONESTOGA CANYON RD
3200 PMDL 93550 4286-G5
CONEY AV
400 AZU 91702 568-G6
4400 LACo 91722 598-G3
CONEY RD
5200 LA 90032 635-F1
CONFERENCE ST
12000 ELMN 91732 597-G4
CONGRESS AV
2000 LA 90018 633-J6
CONGRESS PL
200 PAS 91105 565-G6
CONGRESS ST
- PAS 91105 565-H6
CONIFER CIR
5600 VeCo 91377 557-J2
CONIFER DR
5500 LPMA 90623 767-D2
6200 SBdC 92397 (4652-B1 See Page 4651)
37400 PMDL 93550 4286-B3

CONIFER RD
400 GLDR 91741 569-E3
CONIFER ST
5700 VeCo 91377 557-J2
5700 VeCo 91377 558-A2
CONISTON PL
2300 SMRO 91108 566-D7
CONISTON RD
600 PAS 91103 535-F7
CONKLIN ST
7800 DWNY 90242 705-H7
7800 DWNY 90242 735-J1
CONLE WY
2300 LCF 91011 534-H1
CONLON AV
300 LPUE 91744 638-A5
900 LACo 91744 638-C3
1600 WCOV 91790 598-E5
1700 WCOV 91790 638-C3
4000 LACo 91722 598-E5
N CONLON AV
100 WCOV 91790 598-E6
3900 LACo 91722 598-E6
S CONLON AV
1400 WCOV 91790 638-D2
CONNECTICUT
1800 WCOV 91792 678-J1
1800 WCOV 91792 679-A1
CONNECTICUT ST
1300 LA 90015 634-C4
3200 LA 90006 633-H4
N CONNELL AV
2100 SIMI 93063 499-A2
N CONNELL PL
1500 City 90063 635-E3
CONNICK PL
- Saug 91350 4461-F6
CONNIE CT
28300 SCTA 91387 4552-B2
CONNIE RAE WY
500 ARCD 91006 567-E7
CONNOR AV
2300 CMRC 90040 675-F3
CONNORS CT
5400 LACo 91702 598-J2
CONOVER ST
9400 LA 91342 503-D1
CONOVER FIRE RD
8600 LA 91342 503-E1
8600 Sunl 91040 503-E1
CONOY RD
15800 WHIT 90603 707-J5
CONQUEROR DR
32300 RPV 90275 823-D6
CONQUISTA AV
1800 LBCH 90815 796-E4
3000 LBCH 90808 796-E1
3500 LBCH 90808 766-E7
3700 LACo 90808 766-E5
4100 LKWD 90713 766-E5
CONRAD ST
1400 Eagl 90041 565-C6
8000 DWNY 90242 705-J7
CONRADI AV
20800 LACo 90502 764-B5
CONSOL AV
2800 ELMN 91733 637-D2
3000 ELMN 91731 637-D2
CONSTABLE AV
13100 GmH 91344 481-C3
CONSTANCE ST
1300 LA 90015 634-B5
8100 RSMD 91770 636-F3
CONSTELLATION BLVD
10000 CenC 90067 632-E3
10200 WLA 90025 632-E3
CONSTELLATION RD
- SCTA 91355 4460-C6
CONSTELLATION WY
2200 LA 90732 823-J7
CONSTITUTION AV
- Brwd 90049 631-J3
- Brwd 90049 632-A3
- LACo 90073 631-J3
24800 StvR 91381 4550-D7
24800 StvR 91381 4640-D1
CONSTITUTION CT
- PMDL 93550 4286-C5
W CONSTITUTION LN
2000 LBCH 90810 795-A4
CONSTITUTION ST
4800 CHNO 91710 641-F4
CONSUELO DR
3400 CALB 91302 559-C7
3400 CALB 91302 589-C1
CONSUELO RD
4400 WdHl 91364 560-C5
CONSUELO ST
7500 DWNY 90242 705-G7
7700 DWNY 90242 735-H1
CONTADOR DR
17600 RowH 91748 678-H6
CONTEMPO CT
1000 ONT 91762 641-J3
W CONTEMPO CT
1100 ONT 91762 641-J3
CONTENDAS DR
28300 LACo 90265 627-G5
CONTENTED LN
1300 MNRO 91016 567-E6
CONTERA RD
4000 Enc 91436 561-E5

CONTES ST
- PMDL 93552 4287-E1
CONTESSA AV
28300 SCTA 91350 4461-C4
CONTINENTAL AV
2200 SELM 91733 637-C3
2400 ELMN 91733 637-C3
CONTINENTAL BLVD
100 ELSG 90245 732-H2
CONTINENTAL CT
- FUL 92832 738-H7
100 PAS 91103 565-G4
CONTINENTAL WY
700 ELSG 90245 732-J4
CONTOUR DR
3900 Shrm 91423 562-C5
CONTRA COSTA DR
17700 RowH 91748 678-H6
CONTRA COSTA WY
500 CLAR 91711 571-E6
CONTRERAS ST
8500 PRM 90723 735-J3
CONVENTION CENTER DR
600 LA 90015 634-C5
CONVERSE AL
400 PAS 91101 565-J5
CONVERSE AV
400 CLAR 91711 601-E5
5800 Flor 90001 674-G7
CONVERSE ST
4700 LA 90032 595-E6
CONVOY ST
100 PdlR 90293 702-A3
CONWAY AV
200 Wwd 90024 592-C7
200 Wwd 90024 632-C1
CONWAY PL
1800 LA 90021 634-H6
22000 SCTA 91350 4461-A4
CONWAY SPRINGS LN
19400 WAL 91789 639-D5
CONWELL AV
5400 LACo 91702 598-J2
N CONWELL AV
1100 COV 91722 598-J4
COOGAN CIR
9400 LA 91342 503-D1
COOK AV
100 PAS 91107 566-E4
5700 NLB 90805 765-D2
COOK RD
19100 Tarz 91356 560-G3
COOK ST
12800 LACo 90061 734-D2
S COOKACRE AV
14300 COMP 90221 735-D4
14300 RDom 90221 735-D4
COOKACRE ST
12400 LYN 90262 735-D3
12800 COMP 90221 735-D3
12800 RDom 90221 735-D3
COOKE AV
- CLAR 91711 571-F3
COOK PENCER
7300 SBdC (4562-G5 See Page 4471)
7300 SBdC 92372 (4562-G5 See Page 4471)
COOLBANK DR
14200 LMRD 90638 737-E1
COOLCREST DR
42600 LACo 93532 4102-E4
COOLEY PL
1900 PAS 91104 566-D2
2500 PAS 91107 566-E2
COOLFIELD DR
1100 COV 91722 598-H4
17000 LACo 91722 598-H4
COOLGLEN WY
26200 LACo 90265 628-C3
COOLGROVE DR
7200 DWNY 90240 706-B1
COOLHAVEN CT
4500 WLKV 91361 557-D6
COOLHEIGHTS DR
3400 RPV 90275 823-E5
COOLHILL TR
- Top 90290 590-A4
COOLHURST DR
6100 PRV 90660 676-F4
10700 LACo 90606 676-H6
COOLIDGE AV
1300 PAS 91104 566-E1
1300 LACo 91104 566-E1
1600 Alta 91001 536-E7
2400 LA 90064 632-B7
2700 LA 90064 672-B1
3100 LA 90066 672-C1
4000 CULC 90066 672-D3
4600 LA 90230 672-F5
5100 CULC 90230 672-G5
28900 Cstc 91384 4459-C6
N COOLIDGE AV
2700 LA 90039 594-F4
W COOLIDGE AV
2800 ANA 92801 767-H5
W COOLIDGE DR
400 SGBL 91775 596-C2
COOLIDGE PL
11500 LA 90066 672-C1
COOLIDGE ST
500 NLB 90805 735-D7

E COOLIDGE ST
300 NLB 90805 735-C7
COOLIDGE TR
- LFlz 90027 564-B7
- LFlz 90027 594-B1
S COOLIDGE WY
5800 ELA 90022 675-J2
COOL OAK WY
100 BREA 92821 709-E7
20700 MAL 90265 629-H6
COOL SPRINGS DR
21200 DBAR 91765 679-H7
COOLWATER AV
16100 LACo 93591 4199-F2
N COOLWATER RD
- VeCo 91307 529-A3
COOMBS AV
4200 CULC 90230 672-F3
COONS RD
1400 Eagl 90041 565-A7
1400 Eagl 90041 595-A1
COOPER AV
800 HiPk 90042 595-E1
COOPER CT
- LHB 90631 738-C2
4600 LVRN 91750 570-E7
COOPER TER
37000 PMDL 93550 4286-F4
COOPERGROVE AV
8100 PRV 90660 706-F2
COOPERSTOWN AV
3500 LAN 93535 4016-G4
COORSGOLD LN
- Nor 91326 480-E7
S COPA WY
1600 MONP 91754 635-H3
COPACABANA ST
23400 LACo 90265 629-E2
COPA DE ORO DR
100 BREA 92823 710-C5
2600 OrCo 90720 796-G6
COPA DE ORO RD
100 BelA 90077 592-B7
COPASS ST
9200 DWNY 90240 706-B2
COPELAND CIR
43400 LAN 93535 4105-J2
COPELAND CT
700 SMCA 90405 671-G4
COPELAND PL
3500 LA 90032 595-F6
COPELAND ST
11400 LYN 90262 705-B7
COPERTO DR
200 PacP 90272 630-F6
COPLEY DR
9000 BHLS 90210 592-D7
9000 BHLS 90210 632-D1
9000 Wwd 90024 592-D7
9000 Wwd 90024 632-D1
21600 DBAR 91765 679-J3
COPLEY PL
100 BHLS 90210 632-D1
COPPER
15400 MsnH 91345 501-G2
COPPER CT
- SCTA 91350 4551-D5
COPPER LN
36400 PMDL 93550 4286-G5
COPPER ST
14800 MsnH 91345 501-H2
COPPER CANYON CIR
- POM 91766 640-G5
COPPER CANYON DR
20800 DBAR 91765 709-G1
COPPERFIELD LN
5100 CULC 90230 672-J3
COPPER HILL DR
- BqtC 91354 4460-F4
- SCTA 91354 4460-F4
- SCTA 91355 4460-D6
20200 LACo 91390 4461-A4
20300 Saug 91350 4461-A4
20300 SCTA 91350 4461-A4
20300 SCTA 91390 4461-C4
22200 Saug 91350 4460-J4
22200 SCTA 91350 4460-J4
22200 LACo 91390 4460-J4
22500 SCTA 91390 4460-J4
COPPER HILL RD
2000 HacH 91745 678-E5
COPPER KETTLE WY
16500 LMRD 90638 738-A1
COPPER LANTERN DR
1500 HacH 91745 678-A2
COPPERMILL RD
12000 LACo 93536 4103-A1
COPPER MOON LN
- LAN 93536 4014-G7
COPPER MOUNTAIN DR
1400 DBAR 91765 680-C4
COPPER RIDGE WY
- SCTA 91351 4551-G7
COPPER SADDLE WY
2400 CHLS 91709 680-H1
COPPERSTONE DR
- BqtC 91354 4460-D5
COPPER VALLEY LN
1800 WAL 91789 639-G2
COPPERWOOD AV
6300 ING 90302 673-A7
COPRA LN
15900 PacP 90272 630-J6

COPRICE ST
39300 PMDL 93551 4195-F5
COQUETTE PL
4300 Tarz 91356 560-G5
CORA ST
7800 Sunl 91040 503-G4
CORAK ST
1900 WCOV 91790 638-C1
13100 BALD 91706 597-J6
13300 BALD 91706 598-A7
13900 BALD 91706 638-B1
CORAL AV
400 COMP 90220 734-H5
CORAL CIR
- MONP 91755 636-C6
200 ELSG 90245 732-J2
CORAL CT
1800 PMDL 93550 4286-D4
CORAL DR
- LAN 93536 4015-A7
- LAN 93536 4105-A1
3500 Univ 91608 563-B6
3500 LA 90068 563-B6
N CORAL DR
300 LBCH 90803 826-E1
CORAL LN
300 NLB 90805 765-D1
7200 PRM 90723 735-F4
8100 PRV 90660 706-E2
CORAL PL
1700 SLB 90740 826-G3
3900 CALB 91302 559-G6
CORAL ST
2300 LA 90031 635-C1
3300 LBCH 90810 795-A1
CORAL WY
900 LCF 91011 535-B3
4900 LVRN 91750 570-E6
4900 POM 91767 600-G4
22700 SCTA 91390 4460-J3
S CORAL WY
- UPL 91786 601-J4
CORALBELL LN
22200 WdHl 91367 529-J7
CORAL BELL WY
8000 BPK 90620 767-J2
CORALEE AV
6500 LACo 91007 596-J1
CORALES PL
29100 SCTA 91387 4462-F7
CORALGLEN DR
2800 LACo 90265 628-C6
CORALINE CIR
20300 Chat 91311 500-D3
CORALINE PL
10600 Chat 91311 500-D3
E CORALITE ST
5100 LBCH 90808 796-B1
CORAL PINK CIR
6100 WdHl 91367 529-J7
CORAL REEF CIR
16800 CRTS 90703 736-F6
CORAL REEF LN
11800 VeCo 90265 625-F5
CORAL RIDGE CIR
5100 BPK 90621 738-A5
CORALRIDGE PL
500 LACo 91746 637-J6
CORAL RIDGE RD
2600 RPV 90275 823-G3
CORAL SEA TER
20900 Top 90290 590-C4
S CORAL TREE DR
700 WCOV 91791 639-B2
CORALTREE LN
- RHE 90274 822-H2
CORAL TREE PL
12800 LA 90066 672-D7
E CORAL VIEW ST
100 MONP 91755 636-B5
CORANADA WY
11200 MTCL 91763 641-E3
CORANTO ST
12900 LA 91342 482-D4
CORAVIEW LN
2400 RowH 91748 679-E7
CORAY WY
800 LACo 91302 589-A7
CORAZON CIR
- Tarz 91356 560-J3
CORBETT ST
5600 LA 90016 673-A1
CORBIN AV
3700 Tarz 91356 560-F3
3800 Tarz 91356 560-E6
3800 Tarz 91356 560-F6
4900 Tarz 91356 560-F3
4900 Tarz 91356 560-F4
4900 WdHl 91364 560-F3
4900 WdHl 91364 560-F4
5600 WdHl 91367 560-F1
6000 Tarz 91356 530-F5
6000 WdHl 91367 530-F5
6300 Res 91335 530-F2
6500 Win 91306 530-F2
8200 Nor 91324 530-F2
8800 Nor 91324 500-F6
10300 Chat 91311 500-E3
11200 Nor 91326 500-D1
CORBIN WY
- NLB 90805 735-C6

CORBY AV
9100 SFSP 90670 706-H2
10900 NRWK 90650 706-G6
12300 NRWK 90650 736-G1
17200 ART 90701 736-G7
18400 ART 90701 766-H2
19500 CRTS 90703 766-H3
19900 LKWD 90715 766-H3
CORCORAN PL
12900 LA 91340 482-D6
CORCORAN ST
12800 LA 91340 482-D6
13500 LA 91340 502-C1
CORD AV
- THO 91362 557-B4
5000 PRV 90660 676-H4
7400 PRV 90660 706-F1
9000 DWNY 90240 706-E3
10200 DWNY 90241 706-D5
CORD CIR
700 BHLS 90210 592-G6
CORDA DR
3000 Brwd 90049 561-E7
3000 Brwd 90049 591-E1
CORDA LN
2900 Brwd 90049 591-E1
CORDARY AV
1300 TOR 90503 763-E6
12800 HAW 90250 733-E3
15100 LACo 90260 733-E5
16900 TOR 90504 733-E7
17700 TOR 90504 763-E1
CORDELIA AV
1100 GLDR 91740 569-J7
CORDELIA RD
2400 Brwd 90049 591-C7
CORDELL DR
9100 LA 90069 592-G5
CORDELL MEWS
1200 LA 90069 592-G5
CORDELL PL
1300 LA 90069 592-G5
CORDELLA CT
- BPK 90621 737-F6
CORDER RD
32600 LACo 91390 4373-D7
CORDERA CT
24600 SCTA 91355 4550-E6
CORDERO AV
9400 Tuj 91042 504-B6
CORDERO RD
8100 WHIT 90605 707-J1
CORDILLERA DR
24500 CALB 91302 559-C5
CORDIVA CT
5500 LAN 93536 4104-G4
CORDO DR
21600 SCTA 91350 4551-B3
CORDOBA CIR
5000 LPMA 90623 767-C4
CORDOBA CT
- CRSN 90745 794-B1
- MANB 90266 732-J4
6200 LBCH 90803 826-D1
20100 WHIT 90601 677-D4
CORDOBA PL
3100 Cstc 91384 4459-E2
3100 PMDL 93551 4195-C4
N CORDON DR
1300 City 90063 635-E3
CORDOVA AV
700 GLDL 91206 564-F3
800 ELA 90022 635-F4
1000 GLDL 91207 564-F2
CORDOVA CIR
1800 LVRN 91750 600-H4
CORDOVA CT
400 Ven 90291 671-H6
3000 WCOV 91791 639-C2
CORDOVA DR
3400 CALB 91302 559-D7
3400 CALB 91302 589-D1
CORDOVA RD
15100 LMRD 90638 737-G1
CORDOVA ST
100 PAS 91105 565-J5
200 PAS 91101 565-J5
500 PAS 91101 566-A5
800 PAS 91106 566-A5
1300 POM 91767 601-D6
1600 LA 90007 634-A6
1800 LA 90007 633-J6
1900 LA 90018 633-J6
N CORDOVA ST
- ALH 91801 596-B3
200 BURB 91505 563-C2
S CORDOVA ST
- ALH 91801 596-C4
100 BURB 91522 563-D4
100 BURB 91505 563-D4
1800 ALH 91801 636-C1
N CORDOVA WK
100 LBCH 90803 826-D2
CORDOVAN LN
- SCTA 91351 4551-H2
CORDOZA AV
2200 RowH 91748 678-J6
CORE LN
- LA 91343 501-H6
CORE WY
- LA 91343 501-H6
CORELLA AV
9800 WHIT 90603 708-B3

CORELLIAN CT
12500 CRTS 90703 767-A3
CORETTA AV
5800 LA 91607 562-H1
COREY ST
7500 DWNY 90242 705-H6
E COREY ST
7400 DWNY 90242 705-H6
COREYELL PL
8400 LA 90046 592-H1
CORFU LN
10400 BelA 90077 592-A4
CORIA PL
2700 PMDL 93550 4286-F4
CORIANDER CT
25000 StvR 91381 4640-E2
CORIANDER DR
700 LACo 90502 794-B2
CORIE LN
6700 LACo 91307 529-D6
CORINA CT
15900 HacH 91745 678-C5
CORINGA DR
4900 HiPk 90042 565-B7
5200 HiPk 90042 595-B1
CORINNA DR
3100 RPV 90275 823-F5
CORINNE AV
1800 LBCH 90806 795-F5
CORINTH AV
1500 WLA 90025 632-A5
2200 LA 90064 632-A5
3100 LA 90066 672-C1
4200 CULC 90066 672-E4
4200 LA 90066 672-E4
4300 LA 90230 672-E4
CORINTHIAN DR
17500 Enc 91316 561-B3
CORINTHIAN PL
5800 LAN 93536 4104-F5
6100 LACo 93536 4104-E5
N CORINTHIAN WK
- LBCH 90803 826-C2
CORINTHIAN WY
1000 POM 91768 600-G7
CORIOLANUS DR
900 MONP 91755 636-D4
CORISCO ST
20300 Chat 91311 500-D7
CORK CIR
1300 LVRN 91750 570-F6
CORK PL
14700 LA 91342 481-J7
CORK ST
800 LA 91342 481-J7
800 SFER 91342 481-J7
CORK OAK LN
24300 SCTA 91321 4641-B2
CORK OAK ST
- PMDL 93551 4195-E6
CORKWOOD AV
45200 LAN 93534 4015-H4
N CORLETT AV
1800 COMP 90059 734-E2
12800 Wbrk 90059 734-E2
S CORLETT AV
14300 LACo 90220 734-F3
CORLEY DR
10300 LACo 90604 707-F5
12200 LACo 90604 737-E1
12700 LMRD 90638 737-E1
CORLINGTON RD
2500 GLDL 91206 565-A4
CORLISS ST
4400 Eagl 90041 564-J7
4500 Eagl 90041 565-A7
CORNELIA PL
- SCTA 91354 4460-F7
CORNELIA ST
1100 POM 91768 640-D1
1300 POM 91768 600-D7
CORNELIUS ST
13200 Pcma 91331 482-D7
13300 Pcma 91331 502-C1
CORNELL AV
100 CLAR 91711 601-C3
100 FUL 92831 738-J6
N CORNELL AV
100 FUL 92831 738-J7
CORNELL CT
43300 LAN 93536 4105-C2
CORNELL DR
200 BURB 91504 533-G5
500 ARCD 91007 567-C4
1000 GLDL 91205 564-F7
CORNELL RD
600 PAS 91106 566-A6
2700 Ago 91301 588-B2
3900 Ago 91301 558-A7
4400 AGRH 91301 558-A6
CORNELL WY
4600 AGRH 91301 558-A6
9200 BPK 90620 767-F6
CORNELL SCHOOL RD
30300 Ago 91301 587-G3
CORNERSTONE WY
- BqtC 91354 4460-E6
CORNET AV
15300 SFSP 90670 737-B5
CORNETT DR
8100 LA 90046 592-J1

CORNFLOWER CIR
8000 BPK 90620 767-J3
CORNFLOWER WY
- PMDL 93551 4285-E3
S CORNING AV
5100 LadH 90056 673-A5
S CORNING ST
1000 LA 90035 632-J4
1900 LA 90034 632-J5
CORNISH AV
10700 LYN 90262 705-D6
12000 LYN 90262 735-C1
CORNISHCREST RD
13000 LACo 90605 707-B3
14000 LACo 90604 707-D5
CORNISHON AV
4300 LCF 91011 535-B4
CORNUTA AV
12100 DWNY 90242 706-C7
12600 DWNY 90242 736-C2
13400 BLF 90706 736-C3
CORNWALL CIR
5000 LPMA 90623 767-F1
CORNWALL CT
- RowH 91748 708-J2
CORNWALL DR
3000 GLDL 91206 565-B1
5000 LPMA 90623 767-C5
CORNWALL PL
3200 GLDL 91206 565-C1
22500 SCTA 91350 4550-J5
CORNWELL DR
- FUL 92833 738-C6
CORNWELL ST
300 Boyl 90033 635-B3
CORO TER
1800 GLDL 91208 534-H7
CORONA AV
- LBCH 90803 826-B1
4700 VER 90058 675-C4
5100 MYWD 90270 675-C4
5900 HNTP 90255 675-C6
6200 BELL 90201 675-C7
7000 BELL 90201 705-C1
CORONA CT
400 LAN 93535 4106-A1
5200 LBCH 90803 826-B1
CORONA DR
200 PAS 91104 565-H1
300 LCF 91011 535-D6
1200 GLDL 91205 564-G7
4100 LA 90032 595-F4
CORONA ST
1200 HMB 90254 762-H2
CORONA DEL MAR
14800 LA 90402 631-A7
14800 PacP 90272 631-A7
CORONADO
15300 MsnH 91345 501-H2
CORONADO AV
- LBCH 90803 825-J1
300 LBCH 90814 795-J7
300 LBCH 90814 825-J1
700 LBCH 90804 795-J5
1800 SIGH 90755 795-J5
6200 NLB 90805 765-H1
6300 NLB 90805 735-H7
S CORONADO AV
1100 WCOV 91790 638-H2
CORONADO CT
- MANB 90266 732-H4
26000 SCTA 91355 4550-F4
CORONADO DR
700 ARCD 91007 567-A6
800 GLDL 91206 564-F3
800 ARCD 91007 566-J6
2300 FUL 92835 738-G1
7500 BPK 90621 737-H5
CORONADO LN
4600 LVRN 91750 570-G7
CORONADO ST
400 SDMS 91773 600-C2
N CORONADO ST
100 Echo 90026 634-C1
600 Echo 90026 594-D6
S CORONADO ST
100 LA 90057 634-B2
W CORONADO ST
1100 UPL 91786 571-H7
CORONADO TER
400 Echo 90026 634-C1
600 Echo 90026 594-D7
CORONEL CT
900 WAL 91789 639-D6
CORONEL PZ
- PVE 90274 792-H6
CORONEL ST
600 SFER 91340 502-A1
700 LA 90012 634-G1
1000 SFER 91340 482-A7
1500 SFER 91340 481-J7
CORONET AV
1000 PAS 91107 566-H2
CORONET CIR
6400 BPK 90621 767-G1
CORONET CT
2300 LACo 91724 639-E2
42400 LAN 93536 4104-G5
CORONET DR
4300 Enc 91316 561-B5
CORONET ST
1000 GLDR 91741 569-G3

CORPORATE CT
38500 PMDL 93551 4195-J7
CORPORATE PL
2400 MONP 91754 635-G4
CORPORATE CENTER DR
500 MONP 91754 635-G4
700 POM 91768 640-C1
1000 UPL 91786 601-F1
CORPORATE POINTE
- CULC 90230 672-H6
CORPORATE POINTE WK
5600 CULC 90230 672-H6
CORRADI TER
4400 Actn 93510 4374-J2
CORRAL CT
21200 WAL 91789 639-H6
CORRAL MTWY
2200 LHH 90631 708-G1
CORRAL PL
- SFSP 90670 707-A6
CORRAL CANYON RD
300 LACo 90265 628-B1
3000 MAL 90265 628-D4
CORRALITAS DR
2400 LA 90039 594-E4
CORRAL RIDGE RD
- LACo 93591 4200-B2
CORRAL SUNSHINE MTWY
- GmH 91344 480-G2
- StvR 91381 480-G2
CORREA WY
1700 Brwd 90049 631-E2
CORREGIDOR ST
500 COMP 90220 734-H5
CORRENTI ST
12400 Pcma 91331 502-E4
CORRIDA DR
600 COV 91724 599-E6
CORRIGAN AV
11700 DWNY 90241 706-B6
13000 DWNY 90242 736-B2
CORRIGAN CT
1500 LVRN 91750 600-F4
CORRINGTON AV
16600 CRTS 90703 737-A6
CORRINNE LN
19800 RowH 91748 679-E6
CORRY PL
27200 SCTA 91350 4460-J6
CORRYNE PL
5600 CULC 90230 672-G6
CORSA AV
5700 WLKV 91362 557-F4
CORSAIR ST
6300 CMRC 90040 675-J4
6300 CMRC 90040 676-A4
CORSAIR WY
100 SLB 90740 826-E3
CORSHAM RD
1600 Top 90290 589-J1
1600 Top 90290 590-A2
CORSICA CIR
6100 LBCH 90803 826-C1
CORSICA DR
900 PacP 90272 631-C5
4700 CYP 90630 767-C7
CORSICA PL
- Cstc 91384 4459-E2
CORSINI PL
6400 RPV 90275 823-G4
CORSO CIR
4800 CYP 90630 767-C7
CORSO DI NAPOLI
5700 LBCH 90803 826-C3
CORSO DI ORO
- LBCH 90803 826-D3
CORSON ST
100 PAS 91103 565-H4
300 PAS 91106 566-C4
500 PAS 91107 566-C4
E CORSON ST
- PAS 91103 565-J4
200 PAS 91101 565-J4
500 PAS 91101 566-E4
800 PAS 91106 566-E4
1800 PAS 91107 566-E4
CORTA CALLE
3700 LACo 91107 566-H4
CORTA CRESTA DR
100 WAL 91789 679-F1
CORTADA ST
8900 RSMD 91770 636-H2
9400 ELMN 91733 636-J2
9400 SELM 91733 636-J2
9500 ELMN 91733 637-A2
9500 LACo 91733 637-A2
N CORTE BLANCO
400 UPL 91786 601-H3
W CORTE CABALLO
1500 UPL 91786 601-H3
CORTEEN PL
5200 LA 91607 562-F2
CORTE FINA LN
- BLF 90706 736-D7
W CORTE HACIENDA
1500 UPL 91786 601-H3
N CORTE ROJO
300 UPL 91786 601-H3
CORTE SANTANA
1500 UPL 91786 601-H3
CORTESE DR
3200 OrCo 90720 796-J4

STREET Block City ZIP Pg-Grid

N CORTE VERDE
400 UPL 91786 601-H3
CORTEZ DR
- LACo 91733 636-J4
1000 GLDL 91207 564-G3
CORTEZ RD
300 ARCD 91007 566-J6
9300 SBdC 92371 (4472-F7 See Page 4471)
11700 SBdC 92372 (4472-F1 See Page 4471)
CORTEZ ST
1300 Echo 90026 634-D2
E CORTEZ ST
1700 WCOV 91791 638-J1
1900 WCOV 91791 639-A1
CORTEZ WY
11200 MTCL 91763 641-E3
CORTINA DR
14500 LMRD 90638 737-F3
25700 SCTA 91355 4550-G5
CORTINA WY
38700 PMDL 93550 4196-H7
CORTLAND AV
5100 LYN 90262 735-D1
7200 PRM 90723 735-F2
7400 SGAT 90280 735-F2
CORTLAND ST
3800 LYN 90262 705-C7
3800 LYN 90262 735-D1
7100 PRM 90723 735-F1
CORTNER AV
3500 LBCH 90808 766-J7
3500 HGDN 90716 766-J7
12300 LKWD 90715 766-J4
17100 CRTS 90703 736-J7
18300 CRTS 90703 766-J2
CORTNEY CT
18000 INDS 91748 678-J3
CORTO AV
17600 CRTS 90703 737-A7
CORTO DR
6000 VeCo 93063 499-B3
E CORTO PL
3000 LBCH 90803 825-H1
CORTO RD
- ARCD 91007 566-J5
CORTO ST
300 ALH 91801 596-C5
CORTO WY
800 LHB 90631 708-C5
CORTOLANE DR
5300 LaCr 91214 504-F6
CORTON ST
9700 SBdC 92371 (4472-H1 See Page 4471)
CORTONA DR
8900 WHIT 90603 707-J2
CORTONA WY
- Nor 91326 500-D1
CORVAL ST
5000 SGAT 90280 705-E4
CORVALLIS PL
- LACo 93536 4105-A5
CORVETTE ST
5900 CMRC 90040 675-J3
6100 CMRC 90040 676-A3
CORVO CT
900 LBCH 90813 795-C6
CORVO WY
21700 Top 90290 590-A1
CORWIN AV
600 GLDL 91206 564-H3
CORWIN ST
1800 TOR 90504 763-H1
CORY AV
1000 WHWD 90069 592-G6
1100 LA 90069 592-H6
3700 Actn 93510 4465-A2
CORY CIR
7600 LPMA 90623 767-C3
W CORY DR
700 ING 90302 703-A1
CORY ST
6200 SIMI 93063 499-B2
CORYDON DR
- LA 90017 634-D4
E CORYDON ST
2100 COMP 90220 734-F4
COSBEY AV
3100 BALD 91706 637-H1
3100 BALD 91706 597-H7
COSBEY ST
13800 BALD 91706 597-J6
13800 BALD 91706 598-A6
COSGROVE ST
9300 PRV 90660 676-G5
COSLIN AV
19000 CRSN 90746 764-F3
COSMIC WY
1300 GLDL 91201 564-A2
1600 GLDL 91201 563-J2
COSMO ST
1600 Hlwd 90028 593-F4
COSMOPOLITAN ST
3600 LA 90004 634-A1
COSMOS CT
3500 PMDL 93550 4286-H3
COSSACKS PL
1200 GLDR 91741 569-G6
COSTA CT
- PMDL 93551 4195-A4
COSTA DR
12600 LACo 90250 733-B1
COSTA BELLA DR
100 WAL 91789 679-F1
COSTA BRAVA
20900 SCTA 91321 4641-B2
COSTA DEL REY
6100 LBCH 90803 826-D1
COSTA DEL SOL
- LBCH 90803 826-D1
COSTA DEL SOL WY
300 LACo 90265 629-C2
COSTA DE SOL
- LVRN 91750 570-H3
COSTA GLEN AV
10100 WHIT 90603 707-J4
COSTA MESA DR
14300 LMRD 90638 737-H3
COSTANSO ST
20900 WdHl 91364 560-A2
22100 WdHl 91364 559-J2
COSTELLO AV
4200 Shrm 91423 562-B3
5400 VanN 91401 562-B2
5900 VanN 91401 532-B7
6600 VanN 91405 532-B4
8300 PanC 91402 532-B1
8700 PanC 91402 502-A7
COSTILLA DR
21000 DBAR 91765 679-H7
COTA AV
600 TOR 90501 763-G6
1300 LBCH 90813 795-A6
1800 LBCH 90810 795-A4
COTA ST
- LACo 91390 4461-G2
5100 CULC 90230 672-G4
COTEAU DR
13900 LACo 90604 707-D7
COTHARIN RD
11700 VeCo 90265 625-E1
COTNER AV
1500 WLA 90025 632-A4
2200 LA 90064 632-C7
COTSWOLD DR
- SCTA 91387 4552-D5
COTTAGE CIDR
- SCTA 91354 4460-F7
COTTAGE CIR
14300 CHLS 91709 680-J4
W COTTAGE DR
100 COV 91723 599-B5
COTTAGE LN
- BLF 90706 736-C6
- HAW 90250 733-F4
100 BREA 92821 709-D4
14300 CHLS 91709 680-G4
43200 LAN 93536 4105-B3
COTTAGE PL
200 PAS 91101 565-J3
900 LA 90015 634-D5
2000 LVRN 91750 600-G2
COTTAGE ST
6100 HNTP 90255 674-H7
7200 LACo 90255 674-H7
7200 LACo 90255 704-H1
COTTAGE GROVE AV
1200 GLDL 91205 564-F6
COTTAGE GROVE DR
30000 Cstc 91384 4459-C6
COTTAGE HOME ST
400 LA 90012 634-G1
COTTEGE LN
- LA 91342 481-J1
COTTER AV
800 DUAR 91010 568-A5
COTTER PL
16900 Enc 91436 561-C6
COTTER RIM LN
3500 DBAR 91765 709-G1
COTTON ST
- Cstc 91384 4459-C6
COTTON BLOSSOM LN
- StvR 91381 4640-B2
COTTONTAIL DR
- POM 91766 640-F5
COTTONTAIL LN
31800 MAL 90265 626-G7
COTTONTAIL PL
18000 RowH 91748 678-H7
COTTONTAIL ST
39400 PMDL 93551 4195-E5
COTTONTAIL TR
10300 LACo 91390 4373-F4
COTTONWOOD AV
800 BREA 92821 709-A4
12100 CHNO 91710 641-H5
38800 LACo 93591 4199-B5
COTTONWOOD CIR
- RHE 90274 793-A7
- RHE 90274 823-A1
3600 WCOV 91792 679-C1
COTTONWOOD CT
- CRSN 90746 764-D3
- SCTA 91354 4460-F4
- StvR 91381 4550-C4
COTTONWOOD DR
600 BREA 92821 709-B7
16100 CRTS 90703 736-J5
19700 SCTA 91351 4551-E2
COTTONWOOD LN
- SLB 90740 826-E3
600 SDMS 91773 600-C3
COTTONWOOD LN
5000 LPMA 90623 767-C3
21200 DBAR 91789 679-H2
21200 INDS 91789 679-H2
COTTONWOOD PL
2500 POM 91766 641-A6
COTTONWOOD ST
37700 PMDL 93552 4286-J2
37700 PMDL 93552 4287-A2
COTTONWOOD TR
2300 CHLS 91709 640-J7
2600 CHLS 91709 641-A7
COTTONWOOD WY
800 WAL 91789 639-J5
COTTONWOOD COVE DR
100 DBAR 91765 640-A7
COTTONWOOD GROVE TR
3800 CALB 91301 588-G1
3800 CALB 91301 558-G7
COUGAR PASS
38400 PMDL 93551 4195-G7
38400 PMDL 93551 4285-G1
COUGAS CREEK RD
23900 DBAR 91765 640-D4
COULSON ST
20300 WdHl 91367 560-D2
COULTER AV
- LACo 93551 4285-H4
COUNCIL ST
1500 Echo 90026 634-B1
3400 LA 90004 634-A1
4000 LA 90004 633-H1
COUNTESS DR
3200 HNTB 92649 826-J6
COUNTESS PL
17000 Enc 91436 561-C5
COUNTRY CT
29800 Cstc 91384 4459-D4
40600 PMDL 93551 4194-H2
COUNTRY LN
- RHE 90274 822-J1
- RHE 90274 823-A2
400 BREA 92821 709-B6
800 LHB 90631 708-F4
1700 LACo 91107 536-F7
2600 WLKV 91361 557-A7
2600 WLKV 91361 587-A1
6000 LACo 93536 4104-F4
COUNTRY PL
1000 MONP 91755 636-D3
COUNTRY RD
- SCTA 91354 4550-H1
800 MONP 91755 636-D3
COUNTRY TER
- LHB 90631 738-D1
W COUNTRY VW
800 LHB 90631 738-D1
COUNTRY WY
2900 Actn 93510 4465-C4
S COUNTRY WY
1300 LHB 90631 738-D1
COUNTRY BREEZE LN
34700 LACo 91390 4373-H3
COUNTRY CANYON RD
1900 HacH 91745 678-E5
COUNTRY CLUB CIR
3700 Bxby 90807 765-C7
COUNTRY CLUB CT
100 GLDR 91741 569-J5
COUNTRY CLUB DR
- AVA 90704 5923-G4
100 BREA 92821 709-E7
100 SGBL 91775 596-E3
100 SGBL 91776 596-E3
1100 BURB 91501 533-J5
1400 BURB 91501 534-A4
1900 GLDR 91741 569-J6
2000 GLDR 91741 570-A6
2200 Alta 91001 536-B6
2900 GLDR 91208 534-G4
3100 LA 90019 633-F4
3300 LKWD 90712 765-J5
3600 Bxby 90807 765-C6
3900 LKWD 90712 766-A5
4800 LVRN 91750 570-G4
7300 DWNY 90241 705-J3
8100 BPK 90621 737-J5
8300 BPK 90621 738-A5
39600 PMDL 93551 4195-H4
COUNTRY CLUB LN
4300 Bxby 90807 765-D5
COUNTRY CLUB PL
- Tarz 91356 560-H6
100 BURB 91501 533-J5
N COUNTRY CLUB RD
100 GLDR 91741 569-J4
S COUNTRY CLUB RD
100 GLDR 91741 569-J5
COUNTRY CLUB WY
- LACo 90601 637-G4
COUNTRY CLUB VISTA
200 GLDR 91741 570-A5
COUNTRY COMFORT RD
- Actn 93510 4464-J2
COUNTRY CREEK CT
15300 CHLS 91709 680-G6
COUNTRY CREEK LN
- CALB 91302 558-H7
COUNTRY ESTATES WY
- Ago 91301 588-A1
COUNTRY GLEN RD
27200 AGRH 91301 558-E7
COUNTRY HILL LN
1900 Brwd 90049 591-F4
E COUNTRY HILLS DR
100 FUL 92835 738-E2
100 LHB 90631 738-E2
W COUNTRY HILLS DR
300 LHB 90631 738-D2
COUNTRY HILLS RD
2200 BREA 92821 709-E7
COUNTRY HOLLOW DR
1200 WAL 91789 639-D4
COUNTRY KNOLL PL
1800 HacH 91745 677-J2
COUNTRYMAN LN
2100 LCF 91011 534-H1
COUNTRY MEADOW CIR
- HacH 91745 637-H6
COUNTRY MEADOW RD
- RHE 90274 822-J2
- RHE 90274 823-A2
COUNTRY MILE RD
- POM 91766 640-H6
COUNTRY OAK RD
500 SDMS 91740 570-A7
COUNTRY OAKS CIR
100 ARCD 91006 567-D4
COUNTRY OAKS DR
100 ARCD 91006 567-D4
COUNTRY OAKS LN
700 ARCD 91006 567-D4
COUNTRYPARK LN
17000 HacH 91745 678-F4
COUNTRY PARK RD
- DBAR 91765 680-B6
COUNTRY RANCH RD
1300 LACo 91361 586-H2
1300 THO 91361 586-H2
COUNTRY RIDGE RD
- POM 91766 640-G5
COUNTRYSIDE
12400 ELMN 91732 637-G7
COUNTRYSIDE DR
1000 WAL 91789 639-D5
28800 Ago 91301 588-B1
43600 LAN 93536 4105-H3
44000 LAN 93536 4015-A7
COUNTRYSIDE LN
- Cstc 91384 4369-G7
- Cstc 91384 4459-G1
2500 LaCr 91214 534-D1
3600 LBCH 90806 765-C7
COUNTRYSIDE RD
300 VeCo 91377 558-A1
COUNTRY VALLEY RD
100 THO 91362 557-E1
COUNTRY VIEW DR
23600 DBAR 91765 680-C3
COUNTRY WALK LN
14000 CHLS 91709 680-H3
COUNTRYWIDE WY
43000 LAN 93535 4105-J3
COUNTRYWOOD AV
1300 HacH 91745 678-E3
COUNTRY WOOD DR
- POM 91766 640-F5
COUNTRYWOOD LN
- WCOV 91791 639-B3
S COUNTRYWOOD LN
1300 LHB 90631 738-D1
COUNTY RD
- SCTA 91350 4551-A3
100 POM 91766 640-J6
100 POM 91766 641-A6
3400 CHNO 91710 641-C6
COUNTY LINE RD
23200 Chat 91311 499-F6
COUNTY OAK RD
5900 WdHl 91367 559-C1
6000 WdHl 91367 529-C7
6200 CanP 91307 529-C7
COURBET LN
13100 GrnH 91344 481-C4
COURBET ST
17100 GrnH 91344 481-C4
COURSER AV
11800 LMRD 90638 707-G7
S COURSON DR
600 ANA 92804 767-H7
COURSON RANCH RD
- PMDL 93550 4286-B6
COURT AV
1700 SPAS 91030 596-A3
5800 WHIT 90601 677-B5
COURT PL
5400 PMDL 93551 4104-G7
COURT ST
500 MNRO 91016 567-F3
900 LA 90012 634-F3
1200 Echo 90026 634-D1
COURT TER
1300 PAS 91105 565-E6
COURT WY
5100 HAW 90250 733-B4
COURT ADAIR
10700 ELMN 91731 597-C7
COURT DE LA GAIR
- BALD 91706 598-D5
COURTLAND AV
1400 LA 90006 634-B5
2000 SMRO 91108 596-B2
COURTLAND ST
600 Ven 90291 671-J4
COURTLAND WY
28200 SCTA 91350 4461-A4
COURTLEIGH DR
11700 LA 90066 672-E5
COURTNAY CIR
2700 WCOV 91792 638-J7
COURTNEY AV
1500 LA 90046 593-B4
COURTNEY PL
200 FUL 92833 738-C7
COURTNEY ST
10100 Wats 90002 704-F4
COURTNEY TER
- Actn 93510 4375-F5
1800 LA 90046 593-B4
COURTNEY WY
3600 TOR 90505 793-D4
S COURTRIGHT ST
1200 ANA 92804 767-H7
COURTVIEW DR
27300 SCTA 91354 4460-G6
COURT YARD PL
- CRTS 90703 737-A7
COURTYARD PL
700 LA 90036 633-C3
COUTIN LN
400 GLDL 91206 565-B4
COUTS AV
2200 CMRC 90040 675-F3
COVALA CT
25700 SCTA 91355 4550-G4
COVE AV
2000 LA 90039 594-E5
COVE CT
- PMDL 93551 4195-A3
COVE PL
28900 Ago 91301 588-B4
COVE WY
1000 BHLS 90210 592-D6
2200 LA 90039 594-E5
COVECREST CT
- SBdC 91766 641-D3
COVECREST DR
28200 RPV 90275 792-J7
28600 RPV 90275 822-J1
COVECREST WY
3100 POM 91767 600-J2
W COVELLE AV
700 ING 90301 703-A3
COVELLO ST
9900 LA 91504 533-C3
11200 SunV 91352 532-J3
11900 NHol 91605 532-E3
14100 VanN 91405 532-A4
14600 VanN 91405 531-J4
15300 VanN 91406 531-B4
18600 Res 91335 530-F4
19700 Win 91306 530-C4
21000 CanP 91303 530-A4
22000 CanP 91303 529-J4
22400 CanP 91307 529-G4
23200 LA 91304 529-F4
COVENANT WY
- LA 90068 563-G4
COVENTRY CIR
2300 FUL 92833 738-B3
7000 LPMA 90623 767-C2
7200 BPK 90621 767-D1
16000 WHIT 90605 708-A1
COVENTRY CT
1400 SDMS 91773 599-J4
COVENTRY PL
100 GLDL 91206 565-B1
1100 GLDR 91741 569-B4
1200 PMDL 93551 4195-E5
10600 LA 90064 632-D7
COVENTRY ST
45600 LAN 93534 4015-F4
COVENTRY WY
5200 MTCL 91763 641-G2
COVER ST
2000 LBCH 90808 766-A6
2000 LKWD 90712 765-H6
2000 Bxby 90807 765-G6
2000 LKWD 90712 765-G6
2300 LBCH 90808 765-G6
COVERED WAGON DR
300 DBAR 91765 640-D7
COVERED WAGON LN
- RHE 90274 822-J2
COVERIDGE DR
28300 RPV 90275 792-J7
COVERLY ST
300 SPed 90731 824-C5
COVERT AV
9900 Tuj 91042 504-C4
COVESIDE CT
- BPK 90621 738-A6
COVEVIEW DR
- RPV 90275 823-C2
COVEY CT
2700 BREA 92821 709-F7
COVINA AV
- LBCH 90803 826-B2
COVINA BLVD
100 LACo 91746 637-G4
E COVINA BLVD
100 COV 91722 599-B3
900 COV 91724 599-E3
1300 LACo 91724 599-E3
19200 LACo 91722 599-B3
21100 LACo 91773 599-F3
21100 SDMS 91773 599-F3
W COVINA BLVD
300 SDMS 91773 600-A3
700 SDMS 91773 599-H3
700 COV 91722 598-J3
700 LACo 91722 598-J3
700 LACo 91722 599-A3
18200 COV 91722 599-A3
COVINA LN
100 LACo 91746 637-G3
COVINA ST
2900 LA 90032 595-G7
COVINA HILLS RD
1000 COV 91724 599-E6
19500 LACo 91724 599-E6
20700 SDMS 91773 599-H7
21400 SDMS 91724 599-H7
21400 SDMS 91724 639-J1
21400 SDMS 91773 639-J1
COVINGTON PL
500 PAS 91105 565-G7
COVINGTON ST
13200 WHIT 90602 707-C2
COW TR
20900 Top 90290 590-C3
COWAN AV
6500 Wch 90045 702-F1
COWBELL CT
18100 RowH 91748 678-J7
COWBOY CT
- BqtC 91354 4460-F2
1500 SIMI 93063 499-D3
COWBOY ST
6700 SIMI 93063 499-D3
COW CREEK CT
700 LACo 91746 637-H6
COW FIRE RD
- HacH 91745 677-H5
COWGILL AL
300 PAS 91104 565-J2
COWGIRL CT
6700 SIMI 93063 499-D3
COWLES CT
2000 LBCH 90813 795-B5
W COWLES ST
400 LBCH 90813 795-C5
COWLEY AV
12600 DWNY 90242 736-A1
13500 BLF 90706 736-A2
COWLIN AV
2100 CMRC 90040 675-G3
COWPER AV
7800 LA 91304 529-E3
COY DR
3200 Shrm 91423 562-A7
COYA TR
21100 Chat 91311 500-B1
COYLE AV
300 ARCD 91006 597-E1
COYLE PL
4600 WdHl 91364 559-J4
COYNE ST
12000 Brwd 90049 631-G3
COYOTE
- LA 91342 481-H1
COYOTE DR
800 WAL 91789 639-J5
COYOTE LN
- CRSN 90745 794-G2
12800 NRWK 90650 737-A1
COYOTE RD
2500 SBdC 92371 (4472-H4 See Page 4471)
2500 SBdC 92372 (4472-G4 See Page 4471)
3000 PMDL 93550 4286-G5
COYOTE TR
34200 LACo 91390 4373-F4
COYOTE BRUSH ST
- LAN 93536 4014-F7
S COYOTE CANYON DR
3500 LA 90068 563-D6
N COYOTE CANYON RD
3700 LA 90068 563-D5
COYOTE CANYON WY
500 BREA 92821 709-C6
COYOTE CREEK CT
7500 BPK 90621 737-H6
COYOTE HILLS DR
1700 FUL 92833 738-B3
COYOTE SPRINGS DR
23400 DBAR 91765 680-C4
COZYCROFT AV
6700 Win 91306 530-C1
9500 Chat 91311 500-C3
COZYWOOD CT
6600 WHIT 90601 677-D6
COZZENS AV
12900 SBdC 91710 641-D7
CRABAPPLE CT
24500 CanP 91307 529-D5
CRABAPPLE DR
- POM 91767 600-J3
CRABAPPLE WY
- CRSN 90746 764-F1
CRACKING ST
- CRSN 90746 764-G4
CRAFT CT
22200 CALB 91302 559-J5
CRAFTON AV
6400 BELL 90201 675-F7
6600 BELL 90201 705-F1
7900 CDHY 90201 705-E2
CRAFTON WY
8200 CDHY 90201 705-F2
CRAFTSMAN RD
23900 LACo 91302 559-E4
CRAFTSMEN CT
- SCTA 91350 4550-J2
CRAGGY VIEW ST
22200 Chat 91311 499-J4
CRAGGYVIEW ST
21800 Chat 91311 500-A4
22000 Chat 91311 499-J4
CRAGMONT ST
14000 BALD 91706 598-B3
CRAGS DR
- LACo 91302 588-D5
28900 Ago 91301 588-A4
CRAGUN TR
14700 CHLS 91709 680-J5
CRAIG AV
700 LCF 91011 535-B3
7600 BPK 90621 737-H6
N CRAIG AV
- PAS 91107 566-D3
600 PAS 91104 566-D2
1200 LACo 91104 566-D1
1600 Alta 91001 536-D7
S CRAIG AV
- PAS 91107 566-D5
200 LACo 91107 566-D5
CRAIG CT
21500 CRSN 90745 764-D6
CRAIG DR
3200 LA 90068 563-D6
S CRAIG DR
700 WCOV 91790 638-F2
CRAIG PL
1500 LA 90732 823-H5
CRAIG WY
1900 LVRN 91750 600-G2
CRAIG ALLEN DR
1300 AZU 91702 568-H4
CRAIGHURST TER
600 MONP 91755 636-B3
CRAIGJON AV
19300 CRSN 90746 764-H3
CRAIGLEE CIR
3500 WCOV 91791 599-E7
CRAIGLEE ST
9600 TEML 91780 596-J2
9700 TEML 91780 597-A1
CRAIGMITCHELL LN
9800 SunI 91040 503-C3
CRAIGTON AV
1700 HacH 91745 678-C4
S CRAIGVIEW AV
3400 LA 90066 672-D1
CRAIL WY
3300 GLDL 91206 535-B7
CRAIN DR
8200 LACo 91770 636-F4
CRAMER ST
7800 LBCH 90808 796-H1
CRANBERRY CT
- PMDL 93551 4285-E3
CRANBERRY LN
2500 HacH 91745 678-E5
CRANBROOK AV
800 TOR 90503 763-F5
12500 HAW 90250 733-E1
15100 LACo 90260 733-E5
16700 TOR 90504 733-E7
17600 TOR 90504 763-E1
CRANBROOK PL
1200 FUL 92833 738-B5
CRANDALL ST
200 LA 90057 634-C2
CRANE
200 POM 91767 601-A2
CRANE AV
1000 COMP 90221 735-B5
N CRANE AV
100 COMP 90221 735-B4
CRANE BLVD
300 LA 90065 595-A3
CRANE CT
- PMDL 93551 4194-F3
600 CLAR 91711 571-E5
S CRANE ST
500 COMP 90221 735-B5
CRANER AV
4800 NHol 91601 563-A1
5900 NHol 91601 533-A7
6000 NHol 91606 533-A7
7200 SunV 91352 533-A4
CRANFORD AV
8400 SunV 91352 532-F1
8700 SunV 91352 502-E7
9000 Pcma 91331 502-C5
CRANKS RD
10600 CULC 90230 672-H5
CRANLEIGH ST
- CRTS 90703 767-B2
CRANLEY AV
5100 LACo 91722 598-G3
CRANMER DR
1400 WAL 91789 639-G3
CRANSHAW LN
- PMDL 93551 4285-E3
CRANSTON AV
11500 LA 91342 482-B2
CRANSTON CT
400 LBCH 90803 796-F7
CRAPE MYRTLE CT
6000 WdHl 91367 559-H7
6100 WdHl 91367 529-J7
CRAPE MYRTLE DR
- AZU 91702 569-A4
CRAPE MYRTLE LN
16500 WHIT 90603 708-A6
CRARY ST
1700 LACo 91104 566-C1
CRATER LN
1500 BelA 90077 592-B4
CRATER WY
- PMDL 93552 4286-H2
CRATER CAMP DR
500 LACo 91302 628-H1
500 LACo 91302 588-H7
CRATER OAK DR
700 LACo 91302 588-J7
CRAVATH CT
2300 WCOV 91792 679-B1
CRAVELL AV
7200 PRV 90660 676-E7
8100 PRV 90660 706-E2
CRAVEN ST
900 Wilm 90744 794-D7
CRAVENS AV
800 TOR 90501 763-G5
CRAVO AV
43000 LACo 93535 4109-D2
CRAW AV
11700 CHNO 91710 641-G4
CRAWFORD AL
1400 PAS 91104 566-B3
1900 PAS 91107 566-B3
CRAWFORD AV
2100 Alta 91001 536-A6
CRAWFORD PL
- Cstc 91384 4459-G4
CRAWFORD ST
3600 LA 90011 674-D2
CREBS AV
5100 Tarz 91356 560-H1
6200 Res 91335 530-H2
8200 Nor 91324 530-H1
9100 Nor 91324 500-H4
10700 Nor 91326 500-H2
CREE TR
11400 Chat 91311 500-A1
CREED AV
4000 LA 90008 673-F3
CREEDMORE DR
13500 LACo 90601 637-G5
CREEK LN
9500 OrCo 90631 708-C4
9500 WHIT 90603 708-C4
CREEK TR
11700 LACo 91342 482-J7
N CREEK TR
500 Top 90290 590-A5
CREEKBED RD
- Cstc 91384 4459-G5
CREEKSIDE CT
1200 UPL 91784 571-G4
1500 LACo 91107 566-E1
1500 LACo 91107 536-E7
CREEKSIDE DR
500 WAL 91789 639-C6
900 FUL 92833 738-C6
24100 SCTA 91321 4640-H3
CREEKSIDE LN
- SCTA 91354 4460-F7
- SCTA 91354 4550-F1
CREEKSIDE PL
- LMRD 90638 738-B3
CREEKSIDE RD
- LACo 90265 628-D5
7700 SBdC 92372 (4562-E4 See Page 4471)
23700 SCTA 91355 4550-F2
CREEKSIDE RUN
2300 CHLS 91709 680-J3
CREEK VIEW DR
- SCTA 91354 4460-G4
CREEKVIEW RD
- GrnH 91344 480-J6
CREEKWOOD AV
12200 CRTS 90703 766-J3
CREEKWOOD CT
200 BREA 92821 709-D7
CREEKWOOD DR
1500 LVRN 91750 570-F5
CREEKWOOD LN
2000 UPL 91784 571-G4
2200 CHLS 91709 680-J4
CREEKWOOD ST
2100 THO 91361 557-A6
CREELAND ST
8600 PRV 90660 676-G3
CREEMORE DR
9200 LA 91214 504-C5
9600 Tuj 91042 504-C5
CREEMORE LN
6400 Tuj 91042 504-C5
CREEMORE PL
9500 Tuj 91042 504-C6
CREIGHTON AV
8100 Wch 90045 702-E2
CREIGHTON CIR
200 CLAR 91711 601-D4
CREMONA WY
600 VeCo 91377 557-H2
CRENSHAW BLVD
300 TOR 90503 763-F3
600 LA 90005 633-F4
600 LA 90010 633-F4
600 TOR 90501 763-F3
900 LA 90019 633-F4
1900 LA 90018 633-E7
1900 LA 90016 633-E7
2400 TOR 90501 793-F4
3100 GAR 90249 733-F3
3100 HAW 90250 733-F3
3100 LACo 90250 733-F3
3400 LA 90018 673-E2
3400 LA 90016 673-E2
3600 LA 90008 673-E2
4400 LA 90043 673-F7
7100 LA 90043 703-F2
7900 ING 90305 703-F6
10000 ING 90303 703-F6
11400 HAW 90303 703-F6
11500 ING 90250 703-F6
11800 HAW 90250 703-F6
11900 HAW 90303 733-F3
14300 LACo 90249 733-F5
15800 LACo 90506 733-F5
16100 GAR 90247 733-F5
16200 TOR 90247 733-F5
16200 TOR 90504 733-F4
17100 TOR 90504 763-F3
22500 TOR 90505 793-F4
23900 LMTA 90717 793-F4
25900 LACo 90274 793-C7
25900 TOR 90274 793-F4
25900 RHE 90274 793-F4
26500 LACo 90274 823-B1
26500 RHE 90274 823-B1
28000 RPV 90275 823-B2
CRENSHAW DR
8100 ING 90305 703-F2
CRENSHAW PL
18700 TOR 90504 763-G2
CREOLE RD
22700 WdHl 91364 559-H4
CREOSOTE CANYON DR
35200 LACo 93552 4377-B1
CREPE MYRTLE AV
12300 CHNO 91710 641-J5
CRESCENDA ST
11700 Brwd 90049 631-G2
CRESCENT AV
300 AVA 90704 5923-H3
2100 Mont 91020 534-H2
4200 CYP 90630 767-B5
4200 LKWD 90715 767-B5
4200 LACo 90630 767-B5
4700 LPMA 90623 767-E4
4900 LPMA 90630 767-E4
5600 CYP 90620 767-E4
5600 BPK 90620 767-E4
S CRESCENT AV
1500 SPed 90731 824-C7
CRESCENT CT
- LACo 91390 4373-A4
- SCTA 91355 4550-E1
37200 PMDL 93550 4286-E4
CRESCENT DR
300 AZU 91702 568-H5
700 MNRO 91016 567-E3
1200 GLDL 91205 564-F7
1900 SIGH 90755 795-H4
2000 Alta 91001 536-D5
8400 LA 90046 592-H3
9100 BHLS 90210 592-G3
N CRESCENT DR
100 BHLS 90210 632-F1
600 BHLS 90210 592-E6
S CRESCENT DR
100 BHLS 90212 632-G3
CRESCENT PK E
- LA 90094 702-D1
CRESCENT PK W
- LA 90094 702-C1
CRESCENT PL
600 Ven 90291 671-F6
CRESCENT ST
6300 HiPk 90042 595-E2
CRESCENT WY
- RCUC (542-D7 See Page 511)
2200 PMDL 93550 4286-E3
2800 THO 91362 557-A2
CRESCENT GLEN DR
100 GLDR 91741 570-A5
N CRESCENT HEIGHTS BLVD
100 LA 90048 633-A1
300 LA 90048 593-A6
700 LA 90046 593-A6
1000 WHWD 90046 593-A4
1500 LA 90069 593-A4
S CRESCENT HEIGHTS BLVD
100 LA 90048 633-B2
1000 LA 90035 633-A5
1900 LA 90034 632-J5
1900 LA 90034 633-A5
CRESCENT HEIGHTS ST
1600 SIGH 90755 795-G3
CRESCENT VIEW DR
18300 WCOV 91791 639-B3
CRESPI LN
2100 THO 91361 557-A5
CRESPI ST
22000 WdHl 91364 560-A3
22600 WdHl 91364 559-G3
CRESSEY ST
300 COMP 90222 734-G3
CRESSON ST
10800 NRWK 90650 706-E6
CREST AV
- LA 91342 481-H6
CREST CIR
3600 LBCH 90808 766-H7
8000 LPMA 90623 767-D4
CREST CT
12000 LA 90210 592-F1
CREST DR
800 SLB 90740 826-F3
1300 Alta 91001 536-C5
2300 Bxby 90807 795-D1
3300 HMB 90254 732-E3
3400 MANB 90266 732-E3
3800 ELSG 90245 732-E3
5500 PMDL 93551 4194-G1
28900 Ago 91301 588-B4
N CREST DR
100 MANB 90266 732-E4
S CREST DR
1100 LA 90035 632-H3
1900 LA 90034 632-H4
CREST LN
4400 CHNO 91710 641-E5
15800 GAR 90249 733-G6
20800 DBAR 91789 679-G6
CREST PL
11900 LA 90210 592-G1
CREST RD
2900 RPV 90275 823-A2
2900 RPV 90275 823-F5
3900 RHLS 90275 823-F5
3900 RHLS 90274 823-F5
5700 RHE 90274 823-A2
5900 RPV 90275 822-G2
5900 RHE 90274 822-J3
25700 TOR 90505 793-F5
CREST RD E
- RHLS 90274 823-D3
CREST RD W
- RHLS 90274 823-C2
- RPV 90275 823-C2
CREST WY
1400 POM 91767 600-F6
2200 LA 90068 593-F3
E CREST WY
1000 MONP 91754 635-J4
W CREST WY
1200 MONP 91754 635-J4
N CRESTA AV
100 SGBL 91775 596-E3
100 SGBL 91776 596-E3
CRESTA DR
9000 LA 90035 632-G5
10000 LA 90064 632-F5
CRESTA PL
2700 LA 90064 632-F5
CRESTA TR
2000 Actn 93510 4375-F4
CRESTALOMA LN
15300 LMRD 90638 707-H7
15300 LMRD 90638 737-H1
CRESTA VERDE DR
11800 LACo 90601 677-C3
CRESTA VERDES DR
- RHE 90274 822-H2
CRESTBROOK CT
1100 DBAR 91765 680-E3
CRESTBROOK ST
9800 BLF 90706 736-C3
11000 NRWK 90650 736-F3
CRESTFIELD DR
800 DUAR 91010 568-D5
CRESTFORD DR
2900 Alta 91001 535-F4
3200 PAS 91001 535-F4
CRESTGLEN RD
200 GLDR 91741 569-E3
CRESTHAVEN CT
- SCTA 91351 4551-F4
29400 AGRH 91301 557-J3
CRESTHAVEN DR
800 HiPk 90042 595-E1
1000 HiPk 90042 565-E7
1100 PAS 91105 565-E7
3600 THO 91362 557-C1
CRESTHAVEN LN
- POM 91766 640-F7
CRESTHAVEN WY
- POM 91766 640-J4
1100 MONP 91754 635-J4
CREST HEIGHTS DR
- SCTA 91387 4552-A1
CRESTHILL DR
400 VeCo 91377 558-A1
CRESTHILL RD
8400 LA 90069 592-J5
8400 LA 90069 593-A5
CRESTKNOLL DR
15000 LA 91342 481-H7
CRESTLAKE AV
2000 SPAS 91030 595-H4
CREST LAKE DR
400 BREA 92821 708-H6
CRESTLAND DR
42000 LAN 93536 4104-E6
CRESTLANE CIR
1200 UPL 91786 601-J1

STREET Block City ZIP Pg-Grid

CRESTLAWN ST
24300 WdHl 91367 559-D2
CRESTLINE DR
500 Brwd 90049 631-G2
16000 LMRD 90638 737-J2
16100 LMRD 90638 738-A1
20300 LACo 91789 679-F7
20500 LACo 91765 679-F7
CRESTLINE TER
2500 ALH 91803 635-J2
CRESTLINE TR
- LACo 91390 4461-A3
CRESTMONT AV
3500 Echo 90026 594-C5
CRESTMONT CT
1800 GLDL 91208 564-H1
CRESTMONT DR
1300 DBAR 91765 680-D3
CRESTMONT LN
- RPV 90275 822-H4
CRESTMOORE PL
600 Ven 90291 671-J6
800 Ven 90291 672-A5
2400 LA 90065 594-H2
CRESTOAK DR
14800 LMRD 90638 737-G3
CRESTON AV
1600 SIGH 90755 795-G3
CRESTON CT
28000 SCTA 91387 4552-A2
CRESTON DR
2400 LA 90068 593-F2
CRESTON WY
2300 LA 90068 593-F2
CREST RANCH LN
- LA 91342 481-G6
CREST RIDGE DR
2900 BURB 91504 533-E3
CRESTRIDGE DR
400 VeCo 91377 558-A1
CRESTRIDGE RD
5500 RPV 90275 823-B1
5800 RHE 90274 823-A1
CRESTRIDGE WY
- PMDL 93551 4195-B3
CRESTSHIRE DR
1900 GLDL 91208 564-J1
CRESTVALE DR
400 SMAD 91024 566-J1
CRESTVIEW AV
900 GLDL 91202 534-B7
1000 SLB 90740 826-F3
1400 UPL 91784 571-H3
2500 PMDL 93551 4195-D7
CRESTVIEW CIR
2200 BREA 92821 709-E6
3900 THO 91362 557-C1
5700 LPMA 90623 767-D3
CREST VIEW CT
- POM 91768 600-F6
CRESTVIEW CT
- DUAR 91010 568-D3
1400 Wwd 90024 632-D2
1600 LAN 93535 4016-C6
CREST VIEW DR
2400 LA 90046 592-H2
CRESTVIEW DR
- DBAR 91765 680-C2
- LVRN 91750 570-G6
500 GLDR 91741 569-G4
900 PAS 91107 566-G2
1000 FUL 92833 738-E5
19700 SCTA 91351 4551-E1
24300 SCTA 91321 4640-H3
CRESTVIEW LN
15500 GrnH 91344 481-G7
CRESTVIEW PL
400 MNRO 91016 567-H2
5200 RCUC (542-D7
See Page 511)
CRESTVIEW RD
3800 CULC 90232 672-J2
CREST VIEW TR
- LACo 93551 4375-H5
CREST VISTA DR
600 MONP 91754 635-J5
600 MONP 91754 636-A3
CRESTWAY DR
3700 LACo 90043 673-D4
CRESTWAY PL
3700 LACo 90043 673-D4
CRESTWICK DR
1800 LACo 90210 592-E3
CRESTWIND DR
- RPV 90275 823-B2
CRESTWOLD AV
3400 LACo 90043 673-E4
CRESTWOOD CT
43200 LAN 93536 4105-B3
W CRESTWOOD DR
1200 UPL 91786 601-J1
CRESTWOOD LN
- BREA 92821 709-A4
400 WAL 91789 639-C7
400 WAL 91789 679-C1
CRESTWOOD ST
1000 SPed 90731 824-A3
1000 LA 90732 824-A3
1800 RPV 90275 823-H3
1800 RPV 90732 823-H3
W CRESTWOOD ST
600 SPed 90731 824-B3
CRESTWOOD TER
800 HiPk 90042 565-C7
CRESTWOOD WY
6000 HiPk 90042 565-D7
CRESWICK DR
15700 LMRD 90638 707-H7
15800 LACo 90604 707-H7
CRETE DR
13200 LMRD 90638 737-E2
CREWE ST
10400 NRWK 90650 706-D7
12200 NHol 91605 532-D5
13400 VanN 91405 532-C5
13700 LACo 90605 707-C7
CRICKET LN
40200 PMDL 93551 4195-A3
CRICKETT LN
4100 BALD 91706 598-C5
CRICKLEWOOD PTH
- LACo 91107 536-F7
CRICKLEWOOD ST
3100 TOR 90505 793-D3
CRIDER AV
7200 PRV 90660 676-D6
8200 PRV 90660 706-C1
8600 DWNY 90240 706-C1
CRIMSON CT
19700 SCTA 91321 4551-F5
36500 PMDL 93550 4286-F5
CRIMSON CREST DR
17800 RowH 91748 678-H6
CRINKLAW LN
5600 SIMI 93063 499-A3
5600 VeCo 93063 499-A3
CRISLER WY
1700 LA 90069 593-A4
CRISP CANYON RD
4000 Shrm 91403 561-J5
CRISPI LN
40600 PMDL 93551 4194-F1
41600 LACo 93536 4104-F7
CRISTALINO AV
- PMDL 93551 4104-D6
CRISTALINO ST
15300 HacH 91745 677-J5
15300 HacH 91745 678-A5
CRISTALLO CT
- PMDL 93550 4286-H5
CRISTI LN
11800 LHB 90631 708-G4
CRISTINE PL
1800 FUL 92835 738-G4
CRISTO LN
- RowH 91748 679-E6
CRISTOBAL AV
800 Wilm 90744 794-G6
CRISWELL ST
22200 CanP 91303 529-J6
22400 CanP 91307 529-H6
CROCKER AV
17200 CRSN 90746 734-D7
18200 CRSN 90746 764-D2
CROCKER ST
300 LA 90013 634-F6
600 LA 90021 634-F6
4300 LA 90011 674-D4
5800 LA 90003 674-D6
7800 LA 90003 704-D1
13200 LACo 90061 734-D2
CROCKETT BLVD
7200 Flor 90001 674-H7
7400 Flor 90001 704-H2
CROCKETT LN
25500 StvR 91381 4550-C7
25500 StvR 91381 4640-C1
CROCKETT PL
10300 SunV 91352 533-B2
CROCKETT ST
10400 SunV 91352 533-A2
CROCO PL
28000 SCTA 91387 4552-A2
CROCUS CIR
5800 LPMA 90623 767-E4
7600 BPK 90620 767-J3
E CROCUS DR
16300 LACo 91744 638-G4
CROCUS PL
- PMDL 93551 4285-C3
CROESUS AV
7900 Flor 90001 704-H2
9200 Wats 90002 704-H2
9200 Wats 90002 704-H4
10700 LA 90059 704-H5
11600 Wbrk 90059 704-H7
N CROFT AV
100 LA 90048 633-A1
300 LA 90048 593-A7
500 WHWD 90048 593-A7
700 LA 90069 593-A5
1000 WHWD 90069 593-A6
S CROFT AV
100 LA 90048 633-A1
5800 LA 90056 673-A6
5800 LadH 90056 673-A6
CROFTER DR
1100 DBAR 91789 679-G3
W CROFTON CT
1300 UPL 91786 601-J2
CROFTON WY
1600 PAS 91103 535-E7
CROLL CT
22200 DBAR 91765 680-A4
CROMARTY DR
24100 DBAR 91765 640-D7
CROMER PL
5400 WdHl 91367 560-C2
CROMLEY CT
42900 LAN 93534 4105-E3
CROMWELL AV
4000 LFlz 90027 594-A2
4800 LFlz 90027 593-J3
29500 SCTA 91384 4459-D6
CROMWELL LN
- ING 90305 703-D4
CROMWELL ST
1100 POM 91768 600-D7
1100 POM 91768 640-D1
CROMWELL WY
- RowH 91748 709-A2
CRONE ST
1900 SGBL 91776 596-E7
CRONIN DR
1400 RowH 91748 679-D4
CRONIUS CT
- SCTA 91351 4551-G7
CRONUS ST
3000 LA 90032 595-F6
CROOKED TR
1800 Top 90290 590-C2
CROOKED ARROW DR
500 DBAR 91765 640-C7
CROOKED CREEK DR
- LACo 91765 709-G1
2500 DBAR 91765 679-J6
3400 DBAR 91765 709-G1
CROOK SHANK DR
27700 SCTA 91350 4460-J4
CROSBY LN
1000 Echo 90026 594-E7
1000 Echo 90026 634-E1
CROSBY PL
1500 Echo 90026 634-E1
CROSBY ST
200 Alta 91001 535-F6
CROSNOE AV
7900 PanC 91402 532-C2
CROSS AV
500 LA 90065 595-A3
700 HiPk 90042 595-A3
CROSS MTWY
- Nwhl 91321 4640-H4
- SCTA 91321 4640-H3
CROSS ST
2100 LCF 91011 534-H1
2400 LaCr 91214 534-G1
24000 SCTA 91321 4640-H2
CROSSBOW RD
- Actn 93510 4375-C4
CROSS CREEK CIR
700 WAL 91789 639-C6
CROSS CREEK LN
3500 MAL 90265 629-A6
CROSS CREEK RD
3200 LACo 90265 629-A7
3200 MAL 90265 629-A7
CROSSDALE AV
10800 DWNY 90241 706-F6
11200 NRWK 90650 706-F6
12600 NRWK 90650 736-F2
17700 CRTS 90703 736-F7
19100 CRTS 90703 766-F2
CROSSFIELD DR
27500 RHE 90274 793-A7
CROSS GATE CT
- LACo 91387 4551-J4
- LACo 91387 4552-A4
CROSSGLADE AV
27000 SCTA 91351 4551-G2
CROSSHAVEN DR
18000 RowH 91748 678-J5
CROSSHILL AV
22600 TOR 90505 793-B1
CROSSON DR
23700 WdHl 91367 559-E1
CROSSPATH AV
27700 SCTA 91351 4551-F2
CROSSPOINTE DR
- PMDL 93550 4286-E5
CROSSROADS CT
- DUAR 91010 568-D5
CROSSROADS PKWY N
- LACo 90601 637-F6
13200 INDS 91745 637-F6
CROSSROADS PKWY S
12900 HacH 91745 637-E6
12900 INDS 90601 637-E6
12900 INDS 91745 637-E6
CROSSVALE AV
1300 ELMN 91732 597-E5
CROSSWAY DR
6300 PRV 90660 676-E5
7900 PRV 90660 706-D1
CROSSWINDS ST
23200 SCTA 91321 4640-H3
CROSSWOOD RD
14700 LMRD 90638 737-F3
CROTHERS CT
8000 LA 91304 529-E3
CROTON AV
3700 LACo 90601 677-A2
CROW FOOT LN
2500 DBAR 91765 680-C5
CROWLEY CIR
8100 BPK 90621 737-J6
CROWLEY ST
12800 Pcma 91331 502-D7
13100 Pcma 91331 532-D1
13400 PanC 91402 532-C1
CROWN AV
4500 LCF 91011 535-D4
CROWN CIR
2000 LVRN 91750 570-G7
CROWN CT
- CRTS 90703 766-J3
28600 SCTA 91390 4461-D4
CROWN DR
300 Brwd 90049 631-F2
CROWN ST
500 GLDR 91740 599-F1
CROWN WY
2500 FUL 92833 738-B4
CROWN COURT CIR
- SCTA 91354 4460-F5
CROWNDALE AV
7900 LACo 90606 677-B7
7900 LACo 90606 707-B1
CROWNE DR
1000 PAS 91107 566-F2
3000 PMDL 93551 4195-C5
CROWNFIELD CT
4200 WLKV 91361 557-D6
CROWN HEIGHTS CT
- SCTA 91387 4552-B1
CROWN HILL AV
1500 Echo 90026 634-D2
CROWN HILL DR
800 VeCo 93063 499-B4
CROWN LAKE CIR
600 BREA 92821 708-H6
CROWN POINT CT
- SCTA 91350 4550-H5
CROWN POINT DR
600 DBAR 91765 680-B1
CROWNRIDGE DR
3500 Shrm 91403 561-G6
CROWNRIDGE PL
15600 Shrm 91403 561-G6
CROWN VALLEY RD
- Actn 93510 4464-J5
3600 Actn 93510 4465-B2
32500 Actn 93510 4375-B1
CROWNVIEW DR
2800 RPV 90275 823-F3
CROWN VISTA DR
300 LACo 90248 734-C4
CROYDON AV
7800 Wch 90045 702-H2
CROYDON LN
20200 Top 90290 630-A1
E CRUCES ST
900 Wilm 90744 794-G4
W CRUCES ST
1000 Wilm 90744 794-C5
CRUCITA CT
- Actn 93510 4465-C1
W CRUMLEY ST
800 WCOV 91790 638-E1
CRUMMER RANCH RD
5000 LACo 91302 559-B2
23600 VeCo 91302 559-B2
CRUSADER AV
17700 CRTS 90703 736-E7
17700 CRTS 90703 766-E1
CRUSADO LN
1300 Boyl 90033 635-C3
CRUTHERS CREEK RD
28000 Pear 93553 4469-A7
28000 Pear 93553 (4559-A2
See Page 4470)
28400 Valy 93563 4469-A7
CRYSTAL AV
11700 CHNO 91710 641-F4
CRYSTAL CIR
4200 CYP 90630 767-A4
CRYSTAL CT
- ARCD 91006 567-D7
- CHNO 91710 641-F5
3500 PMDL 93550 4286-H3
N CRYSTAL CT
200 LBCH 90802 795-C7
200 LBCH 90802 825-C1
700 LBCH 90813 795-C7
CRYSTAL LN
- LA 90068 563-F5
- LACo 91107 536-F6
200 PAS 91104 565-J1
CRYSTAL PL
400 SLB 90740 826-F4
2100 POM 91767 601-C5
CRYSTAL RD
- PMDL 93550 4376-E7
CRYSTAL ST
1100 LA 90031 594-H5
2100 LA 90039 594-E3
CRYSTALAIRE DR
31500 Llan 93544 4469-F1
31800 Llan 93544 4379-G7
CRYSTALAIRE PL
16900 GrnH 91344 481-C6
CRYSTAL AIRE RD
- SBdC 92372 (4562-A1
See Page 4471)
9400 SBdC 92372 (4472-A4
See Page 4471)
CRYSTALAIRE WASH RD
- Llan 93544 4469-D1
- Pear 93553 4469-D1
CRYSTAL CANYON DR
300 AZU 91702 568-H3
E CRYSTAL COVE DR
6200 LBCH 90803 826-E1
6200 LBCH 90803 796-E7
CRYSTAL COVE WY
1200 SLB 90740 826-F4
CRYSTAL CREEK LN
16100 CRTS 90703 736-J5
CRYSTAL GLEN WY
12000 Nor 91326 480-F6
CRYSTAL HEIGHTS CT
- SCTA 91387 4552-A1
CRYSTAL HILLS DR
19600 Nor 91326 480-E6
CRYSTAL HILLS LN
20000 Nor 91326 480-E6
CRYSTAL HILLS WY
12200 Nor 91326 480-F6
CRYSTAL LAKE RD
- LACo - 4649-G7
- LACo - (4729-G1
See Page 4649)
CRYSTAL LANTERN DR
14400 HacH 91745 677-H1
CRYSTAL PEAK CIR
1700 WAL 91789 639-E3
CRYSTAL RIDGE CT
- SCTA 91351 4551-F4
CRYSTAL RIDGE LN
19300 Nor 91326 480-E6
CRYSTAL RIDGE RD
- DBAR 91765 679-J7
CRYSTAL RIDGE WY
12100 Nor 91326 480-F6
CRYSTAL SPRING CT
19600 SCTA 91321 4551-F6
CRYSTAL SPRINGS CIR
19500 Nor 91326 480-E6
CRYSTAL SPRINGS CT
100 BREA 92821 709-E7
CRYSTAL SPRINGS DR
3400 LFlz 90027 594-C1
4100 LFlz 90027 564-B5
CRYSTAL SPRINGS RD
1100 SDMS 91773 570-B7
27100 LACo 91387 4552-E4
27100 SCTA 91387 4552-E4
CRYSTAL VIEW DR
9300 Tuj 91042 504-B5
CRYSTAL WATER LN
800 WAL 91789 639-H4
CTL III RD
23600 VeCo 93063 529-A1
CUATRO DR
2300 RowH 91748 678-J6
CUATRO MILPAS ST
26800 SCTA 91354 4460-J7
26800 SCTA 91354 4550-H1
CUBA CIR
5500 BPK 90620 767-D3
CUBA DR
- LACo 91724 599-G7
CUCAMONGA AV
200 CLAR 91711 601-E4
CUDAHY AV
4400 MYWD 90270 675-D5
5100 VER 90058 675-D5
CUDAHY DR
5100 CDHY 90201 705-F2
CUDAHY ST
900 LA 90032 595-D5
2400 LACo 90255 704-J1
2600 SGAT 90255 704-J1
2700 LACo 90255 705-A2
3200 HNTP 90255 705-C2
CUERNAVACA PL
600 CLAR 91711 601-E2
CUERNO CT
40600 PMDL 93551 4194-G2
CUERVO DR
22900 SCTA 91354 4460-H7
CUESTA DR
12200 CRTS 90703 736-J6
12500 CRTS 90703 737-A6
CUESTA LN
12900 CRTS 90703 737-B6
CUESTA ST
12600 CRTS 90703 737-A6
CUESTA WY
400 BelA 90077 592-B6
1300 MTBL 90640 636-D7
CUESTA CALA RD
19400 Top 90290 590-A6
CUESTA LINDA DR
1400 PacP 90272 630-G1
CUESTPORT DR
- SCTA 91354 4460-H6
CULFORD PL
42900 LACo 93532 4102-F4
N CULLEN AV
100 GLDR 91741 569-E4
S CULLEN AV
100 GLDR 91741 569-E5
600 GLDR 91740 569-E6
CULLEN ST
2600 LA 90034 632-J7
12600 WHIT 90602 707-C1
13600 WHIT 90605 707-D2
14400 WHIT 90603 707-F3
CULLEN WY
- ING 90301 703-E3
- ING 90305 703-E3
CULLIVAN ST
2000 LACo 90047 703-G6
2200 ING 90303 703-G6
CULLMAN AV
9800 WHIT 90603 708-A3
11500 LACo 90604 708-A6
12400 LACo 90604 738-A1
12600 LMRD 90638 738-A1
CULLY AV
7000 LACo 90606 676-H6
CULMORE ST
3100 CLAR 91711 601-B2
CULP CT
- BPK 90621 737-F5
CULP DR
8300 PRV 90660 676-F2
CULP ST
14500 LPUE 91744 638-B4
CULPER CT
200 HMB 90254 762-H3
CULTURA ST
11000 SFSP 90670 706-G2
CULVER AL
3100 PAS 91107 566-G4
CULVER AV
100 COMP 90220 734-J4
1100 COMP 90222 734-J3
1700 Wbrk 90222 734-J3
CULVER BLVD
- PdlR 90293 702-A3
400 LA 90094 702-B2
3800 LA 90232 632-H7
9000 CULC 90232 632-H7
9000 CULC 90232 672-G2
9000 LA 90232 672-G2
10700 CULC 90230 672-G2
11300 CULC 90066 672-E5
11300 LA 90066 672-E5
11300 LA 90230 672-E5
12900 LA 90094 672-C7
13000 MdlR 90292 702-B2
CULVER CTR
3800 CULC 90232 672-F2
CULVER DR
11200 LA 90230 672-F5
CULVER PL
6700 PdlR 90293 702-A3
CULVER PARK DR
11200 CULC 90230 672-G5
CULVER PARK PL
5500 CULC 90230 672-G5
CULVIEW ST
5900 CULC 90230 672-H5
CUMBERLAND AV
3900 LFlz 90027 594-B4
E CUMBERLAND CT
3300 THO 91362 557-C2
W CUMBERLAND CT
3000 THO 91362 557-B2
CUMBERLAND DR
1900 WCOV 91792 638-H5
5000 CYP 90630 767-C7
CUMBERLAND LN
11300 SBdC 91766 641-C3
25400 LACo 91302 559-A3
CUMBERLAND PL
700 CLAR 91711 601-D5
CUMBERLAND RD
- FUL 92833 738-A3
100 GLDL 91202 564-B1
1900 GLDR 91741 569-J5
2100 GLDR 91741 570-A5
2300 SMRO 91108 566-D7
CUMBERLAND TER
1600 GLDL 91202 564-E1
CUMBRE DR
1700 LA 90732 823-H6
1900 RPV 90275 823-H6
CUMBRE ST
400 MONP 91754 635-G3
CUMBRE ALTA CT
1100 PacP 90272 630-G2
CUMBRE VERDE CT
16600 PacP 90272 630-G2
CUMIN CT
27500 SCTA 91350 4461-A6
CUM LAUDE AV
9100 Wch 90045 702-C4
9100 PdlR 90293 702-C4
CUMMINGS DR
1900 LFlz 90027 593-J3
CUMMINGS LN
2000 LFlz 90027 593-J3
E CUMMINGS LN
200 NLB 90805 735-C7
CUMMINGS RD
800 COV 91724 599-E4
N CUMMINGS ST
100 Boyl 90033 635-B3
S CUMMINGS ST
100 Boyl 90033 635-A5
W CUMMINGS ST
200 NLB 90805 735-B7
CUMNOCK PL
18600 Nor 91326 480-H6
CUMORAH CREST DR
23000 WdHl 91364 559-G4
CUMPSTON ST
10400 NHol 91601 563-A2
11000 NHol 91601 562-H2
12400 LA 91607 562-E2
12900 VanN 91401 562-E2
14700 VanN 91411 561-J2
17300 Enc 91316 561-C2
CUNARD ST
2600 LA 90065 564-H7
CUNNINGHAM DR
- SCTA 91354 4460-G6
S CUNNINGHAM DR
700 LACo 90601 637-F5
CUPANIA
1300 RowH 91748 679-B4
CUPANIA CIR
- MONP 91755 636-C5
CURACO TR
11400 Chat 91311 480-A7
11400 Chat 91311 500-A1
CURASSOW CT
20000 SCTA 91351 4551-E4
CURLEW CT
4500 LA 90065 564-H7
CURRAN PL
500 POM 91766 640-F2
CURRAN ST
1400 LCF 91011 535-A3
1500 Echo 90026 594-F5
CURRANT WY
- PMDL 93551 4285-E2
CURRIER RD
20600 INDS 91789 679-F2
20800 LACo 91789 679-F2
N CURRIER ST
500 POM 91768 640-G1
S CURRIER ST
600 POM 91766 640-G2
CURRITUCK DR
11900 Brwd 90049 631-G4
CURRY AV
11400 GrnH 91344 501-C1
11600 GrnH 91344 481-C7
CURRY LN
11400 ART 90701 736-G7
E CURRY ST
1600 NLB 90805 765-G1
CURSON AV
1300 LA 90019 633-B4
E CURSON AV
300 LA 90036 633-C2
N CURSON AV
300 LA 90036 633-C1
300 LA 90036 633-C1
700 LA 90046 593-C3
900 WHWD 90046 593-C5
S CURSON AV
300 LA 90036 633-C2
1000 LA 90019 633-B5
1900 LA 90016 633-B6
W CURSON AV
300 LA 90036 633-C2
CURSON PL
1900 LA 90046 593-C3
CURSON TER
7600 LA 90046 593-B4
CURT PL
17900 GAR 90248 763-J1
CURT WY
700 WAL 91789 639-F6
CURTIS AV
- NLB 90805 735-H7
500 COV 91723 599-C4
1300 MANB 90266 732-H7
1900 RBCH 90278 732-J7
1900 RBCH 90278 733-A7
N CURTIS AV
- ALH 91801 596-A4
6700 NLB 90805 735-H6
S CURTIS AV
- ALH 91801 596-A5
300 ALH 91803 596-A7
1800 ALH 91803 636-A1
CURTIS CT
800 POM 91766 641-B6
2300 GLDR 91741 570-A6
S CURTIS LN
800 ALH 91803 596-A7
CURTIS ST
500 LA 90012 634-G1
CURTIS ALAN PL
- Saug 91350 4461-E5
CURTIS AND KING RD
12100 NRWK 90650 706-E7
12300 NRWK 90650 736-E1
CURTISS CT
- LVRN 91750 600-F4
CURTISS WY
25000 TOR 90505 793-E4
CURTS AV
3100 LA 90034 632-H7
CURVE CIR
500 LAN 93535 4016-A7
CURWOOD PL
9800 LA 90210 592-C3
CUSHDON AV
10500 LA 90064 632-D6
CUSHING AV
800 Wilm 90744 794-J6
CUSHMAN CT
2000 SIMI 93063 499-A2
CUSTER AV
- LA 90012 634-F2
CUSTOZA AV
1300 RowH 91748 679-C4
CUSWALE WK
- Cstc 91384 4459-D6
CUTHBERT RD
29600 MAL 90265 627-C7
CUTLER AV
4000 BALD 91706 598-B3
CUTLER PL
13100 LA 91342 482-D3
CUTOFF CT
2500 LACo 91789 679-F6
CUTTER ST
4500 LA 90039 564-B4
N CUTTER WY
500 COV 91722 598-H5
CUTWOOD RD
42600 LACo 93532 4102-H5
S CUZCO AV
16300 RDom 90221 735-B6
16700 COMP 90221 735-B6
CYCLAMEN WY
7800 BPK 90620 767-J3
CYCLOPS ST
11700 NRWK 90650 706-G7
CYCOD PL
500 BREA 92821 709-C6
CYGNET RD
2600 SBdC 92371 (4562-G3
See Page 4471)
CYNTHIA AV
800 LA 90065 595-A2
900 PAS 91107 566-H2
CYNTHIA CT
1100 LVRN 91750 570-E7
3400 WCOV 91792 679-C1
26700 SCTA 91351 4551-F4
CYNTHIA ST
400 ALH 91801 596-B3
400 POM 91766 641-A5
6200 SIMI 93063 499-B2
8800 WHWD 90069 592-H6
CYPREAN DR
2000 LA 90046 592-H3
CYPRESS
18800 RowH 91748 679-B5
CYPRESS AV
- KeCo 93560 3835-F2
300 ALH 91801 595-H5
300 LA 90065 594-H4
400 PAS 91103 565-G3
500 GLDR 91741 569-G4
500 HMB 90254 762-H2
3600 ELMN 91731 597-D6
5200 KeCo 93560 3834-B2
5500 PMDL 93551 4194-G1
8100 SGAT 90280 705-A3
8500 CYP 90630 767-D5
E CYPRESS AV
100 BURB 91502 533-H6
100 MNRO 91016 567-H5
400 BURB 91501 533-H6
W CYPRESS AV
100 BURB 91502 533-G7
100 MNRO 91016 567-G5
700 SDMS 91773 600-A4
700 SDMS 91773 599-H4
CYPRESS CIDR
2300 LMTA 90717 793-G4
CYPRESS CIR
- CRSN 90746 764-F1
400 COMP 90220 734-H5
1700 LVRN 91750 570-F7
CYPRESS CT
- SCTA 91354 4460-F4
300 AZU 91702 568-H3
CYPRESS DR
- CRSN 90745 794-C1
- CYP 90630 767-B5
- LACo 91724 639-H1
4500 LCF 91011 535-A3
22000 WdHl 91364 559-J6
22000 WdHl 91364 560-A6
CYPRESS GRV
- PMDL 93551 4194-G2
CYPRESS LN
- LA 90065 594-F1
- LACo 91768 640-B1
CYPRESS PL
- LACo 91390 4460-J2
- LACo 91390 4461-A2
22300 SCTA 91390 4460-J2
CYPRESS ST
400 COMP 90220 734-H5
900 ELSG 90245 702-F7
1200 LHH 90631 708-E3
2100 LAN 93535 4016-D6
4700 LCF 91011 534-H1
5200 CYP 90630 767-C5
6000 VeCo 93063 499-B4
22800 TOR 90501 793-G5
E CYPRESS ST
- LACo 91773 599-E4
100 BREA 92821 709-B7
100 COMP 90220 734-J5
100 COMP 90220 735-B5
100 COV 91723 599-C4
100 GLDL 91205 564-F7
100 COV 91722 599-C4
500 COMP 90221 735-B5
700 LACo 91723 599-C4
900 COV 91722 598-G4
1000 COV 91724 599-E4
1000 LACo 91724 599-E4
1600 COV 91773 599-E4
1600 SDMS 91773 599-E4
16500 LACo 91722 598-G4
17700 LACo 91722 599-C4
N CYPRESS ST
100 LHB 90631 708-F4
100 POM 91768 640-H1
1300 OrCo 90631 708-F4
1600 LHH 90631 708-F4
S CYPRESS ST
100 LHB 90631 708-F7
200 POM 91768 640-H2
1100 LHB 90631 738-E1
W CYPRESS ST
100 BREA 92821 709-B7
100 COMP 90220 734-E5
100 GLDL 91204 564-E7
15500 IRW 91706 598-E4
15700 LACo 91722 598-E4
18000 COV 91723 599-A4
18000 LACo 91722 599-A4
18000 COV 91722 599-A4
CYPRESS WY
- Cstc 91384 4369-H5
- SDMS 91773 599-H4
- RHE 90274 793-A7
- RHE 90274 823-A1
400 PAS 91103 565-G3
E CYPRESS WY
100 LBCH 90813 795-E6
W CYPRESS WY
100 LBCH 90813 795-D6
CYPRESS GROVE LN
1600 DBAR 91765 680-A4
CYPRESS KNOLL LN
12600 HAW 90250 733-H1
CYPRESS POINT AV
8500 BPK 90621 738-A6
15500 Llan 93544 4469-E1
CYPRESS POINT DR
- LACo 90606 676-H6
- PRV 90660 676-H6
2400 FUL 92833 738-B6
19400 Nor 91326 480-F7
CYPRESS RIDGE CIR
27600 SCTA 91354 4460-H5
CYRENE DR
1500 CRSN 90746 764-G4
CYRENE PL
14300 LA 91342 482-A3
CYRENE ST
800 CRSN 90746 764-E4
CYRIL AV
1900 LA 90032 635-E1
CYRUS LN
1000 ARCD 91006 567-C4
39800 PMDL 93551 4195-C4

D

D
- PRM 90723 735-F6
18600 LACo 91744 679-B2
D CT
1000 Wilm 90744 794-D7
D ST
- LACo 90220 764-J3
- LACo 91724 599-E2
- LKWD 90712 766-A3
- PdlR 90293 702-C7
- SPed 90731 794-C7
- SPed 90731 824-B1
700 Wilm 90744 794-C7
1800 LVRN 91750 600-G2
E D ST
100 Wilm 90744 794-F7
W D ST
100 Wilm 90744 794-C7
900 ONT 91762 601-J7
D WK
1000 Wilm 90744 794-D7
DAB CT
1500 DBAR 91789 679-G4
DABLON AV
21900 CRSN 90745 764-G6
DABNEY LN
400 BHLS 90210 592-G4
DABNEY ST
3200 Alta 91001 535-G4
DABNY LN
8000 LPMA 90623 767-B4
DACE ST
12200 NRWK 90650 736-J1
DACIAN DR
2000 LACo 91789 679-E5
DACONA AV
3900 ELMN 91732 597-F7
DACOSTA ST
7700 DWNY 90240 706-B2
S DACOTAH ST
100 LA 90063 635-B6
200 Boyl 90033 635-B6
900 LA 90023 635-A7
1200 LA 90023 675-A1
DACRE PL
300 MTBL 90640 636-E7
N DADE AV
700 LACo 91744 638-D5
DADION AV
49000 LACo 93536 3923-J2
DAEMAS PL
17200 GrnH 91344 481-C5
DAFFODIL AV
- LHB 90631 708-C7
14800 SCTA 91387 4462-F6
DAGANA AV
- LACo 93591 4200-F4
E DAGGETT ST
5200 LBCH 90815 796-B4
DAGMAR AV
13900 LACo 90061 734-D3
DAGMAR WY
- LACo 91387 4552-A3
DAGUE DR
200 WAL 91789 639-G7
DAGUERRE AV
3800 CALB 91302 559-H6
DAGWOOD AV
5800 LKWD 90712 766-B2
DAHA PL
8000 NHol 91605 532-E2
DAHL DR
3200 HacH 91745 678-C6
DAHLGREN AV
3000 LA 90066 672-B1
DAHLIA AV
1300 ONT 91762 641-J3
3400 Echo 90026 594-C5
12300 ELMN 91732 637-F2
12400 DWNY 90242 705-H6
N DAHLIA AV
400 ONT 91762 601-J7
DAHLIA CIR
1300 LVRN 91750 570-F7
7900 BPK 90620 767-J3
DAHLIA CT
- Boyl 90033 634-J4
1800 PMDL 93550 4286-D4
N DAHLIA CT
1500 ONT 91762 601-J5
DAHLIA DR
5100 Eagl 90041 565-B5
DAHLIA ST
- LHB 90631 708-C6
44000 LAN 93535 4016-F7
DAHLIA WY
1100 LACo 90502 794-A1
DAHLIA RIDGE DR
14600 SCTA 91387 4462-G5
DAILY CIR
1300 GLDL 91208 534-F5
DAILY DR
16300 VanN 91406 531-E2
DAINES DR
8700 LACo 91776 596-G4
9400 TEML 91780 596-J4
9500 TEML 91780 597-B3
10200 TEML 91007 597-B3
11600 ARCD 91006 597-F3
DAIREN ST
19300 RowH 91748 679-C6
DAIRY AV
5400 NLB 90805 765-D3
DAIRY RD
- Cstc 91384 4459-J4
- Cstc 91384 4460-A4
DAISETTA DR
23500 SCTA 91321 4640-G3
DAISETTA ST
18900 RowH 91748 679-B4
DAISY AV
100 LBCH 90831 825-C1
700 LBCH 90813 795-C3
1800 LBCH 90806 795-C3
4700 NLB 90805 765-C4
N DAISY AV
- PAS 91107 566-F3
200 LBCH 90802 795-C7
200 LBCH 90802 825-C1
1300 LBCH 90813 795-C5
2200 LBCH 90806 795-C5
S DAISY AV
- PAS 91107 566-F5
DAISY CIR
100 BREA 92821 709-D7
5700 LPMA 90623 767-D4
DAISY CT
30400 Cstc 91384 4459-H3
DAISY DR
- PanC 91402 502-A6
DAISY LN
500 SBdC 92372 (4472-B4
See Page 4471)
2200 LCF 91011 534-H1
3600 SBdC 92371 (4472-J4
See Page 4471)
DAISY PL
18600 Nor 91326 500-H1
DAISY ST
- PMDL 93552 4287-A1
- SIMI 93063 499-A2
2200 UPL 91784 571-H4
37000 PMDL 93550 4286-D4
DAISY TR
23500 CALB 91302 589-F1
DAISY MEADOW ST
14600 SCTA 91387 4462-F5
DAKIN ST
19300 RowH 91748 679-C5
DAKOTA
- Ago 91301 587-F4
DAKOTA AV
11500 SGAT 90280 705-G7
11500 SGAT 90280 735-G1
DAKOTA CT
300 SDMS 91773 600-C2
DAKOTA DR
- BgtC 91354 4460-F3

STREET Block City ZIP Pg-Grid

DAKOTAH CT
- LACo 91387 4462-C6
DALADIER DR
2000 RPV 90275 823-G5
DALAMAN AV
21000 LKWD 90715 766-G5
DALARK ST
16200 LACo 91744 638-G4
DALATA RD
4800 WdHl 91364 559-H4
DALBERG ST
9000 BLF 90706 736-A2
DALBEY DR
23000 SCTA 91321 4550-H7
23000 SCTA 91355 4550-H7
DALBO ST
2500 DUAR 91010 568-D4
DALE AV
700 GLDL 91202 564-C3
9500 Sunl 91040 503-B5
DALE CT
200 BREA 92821 709-B4
22700 Chat 91311 499-H5
DALE DR
1500 MNRO 91016 567-F6
W DALE DR
- LAN 93536 4013-J5
DALE PL
6000 FUL 92833 738-A7
DALE RD
1700 GLDR 91740 599-D2
10400 LACo 91390 4373-F3
23300 CALB 90290 559-F7
DALE ST
900 PAS 91106 566-A6
5700 BPK 90621 738-A6
6000 FUL 92833 738-A6
DALEBURY DR
8400 PRV 90660 676-E5
DALECREST AV
6100 WdHl 91367 529-F7
6100 WdHl 91367 559-F1
DALEGROVE DR
9500 LA 90210 592-F2
DALEHURST AV
300 Wwd 90024 632-B1
DALEMEAD ST
2500 TOR 90505 793-E4
DALEN ST
7800 DWNY 90242 705-H7
8400 DWNY 90242 735-J1
8700 DWNY 90242 736-A1
DALEPARK DR
2700 SDMS 91773 570-B6
DALERIDGE RD
4500 LCF 91011 535-D5
DALEROSE AV
10000 ING 90304 703-B5
10000 Lenx 90304 703-B5
11100 HAW 90304 703-B5
DALESFORD DR
300 LPUE 91744 678-E1
DALESIDE AV
11600 HAW 90250 703-H7
12900 GAR 90249 733-H2
DALEVIEW AV
3800 ELMN 91731 597-D4
5000 TEML 91780 597-D4
DALEWOOD AV
8300 PRV 90660 706-F3
9000 DWNY 90240 706-E4
DALEWOOD CT
- LMRD 90638 738-B2
DALEWOOD DR
2100 FUL 92833 738-D3
DALEWOOD PL
100 BREA 92821 709-B6
DALEWOOD ST
12700 BALD 91706 637-H1
13300 BALD 91706 638-A1
14400 WCOV 91706 638-C1
E DALEWOOD ST
1000 WCOV 91790 598-H7
DALFSEN AV
19700 CRSN 90746 764-H3
DALGO DR
24100 SCTA 91355 4550-F6
DALHART AV
2700 COMP 90222 734-G1
DALI DR
12500 GrnH 91344 480-J5
12500 GrnH 91344 481-A5
DALKEITH AV
300 Brwd 90049 631-J2
DALLAS DR
7300 LPMA 90623 767-D2
DALLAS RD
500 SDMS 91773 600-B1
DALLAS ST
- BPK 90621 737-J5
2300 LA 90031 594-G5
DALLIN ST
2200 LAN 93536 4105-D1
DALMAN ST
14500 WHIT 90603 707-F3
DALMATIA DR
1300 LA 90732 823-J1
DALMATIAN AV
10400 LACo 90604 707-G5
13500 LMRD 90638 737-G2
DALTON AV
2600 LA 90018 633-J7
3600 LA 90018 673-J1

DALTON AV
3900 LA 90062 673-J3
7000 LA 90047 673-J4
7000 LA 90047 703-J1
15800 GAR 90247 733-J6
18000 GAR 90248 763-J1
18200 LA 90248 763-J2
21200 LA 90501 763-J2
E DALTON AV
400 GLDR 91741 569-F5
N DALTON AV
100 AZU 91702 568-J4
S DALTON AV
20800 LA 90501 763-J5
DALTON CT
1100 POM 91767 601-C7
DALTON PL
18000 GAR 90248 763-J1
DALTON RD
600 SDMS 91773 570-D7
1600 PVE 90274 792-E6
DALTON ST
19100 SCTA 91321 4551-G5
W DALTON ST
700 GLDR 91741 569-C5
DALTON CANYON RD
- GLDR (540-B7 See Page 509)
- GLDR 570-B1
- LACo (540-C6 See Page 509)
DALTON SPRINGS LN
900 GLDR 91741 569-H3
DALWOOD AV
10900 DWNY 90241 706-F6
11200 NRWK 90650 706-F6
12700 NRWK 90650 736-F1
DALY AV
1600 LVRN 91750 600-F1
DALY ST
1700 Boyl 90033 635-A1
1700 LA 90031 635-A1
2400 LA 90031 595-A7
DALZELL ST
37100 PMDL 93550 4286-F2
DAMAR CT
28000 SCTA 91351 4551-G1
DAMAR ST
8000 LBCH 90808 796-J1
DAMASCO ST
18800 LACo 91744 679-B2
18800 LACo 91792 679-B2
DAMASK AV
5900 LadH 90056 673-B6
6100 LA 90056 673-B6
DAMATO DR
900 COV 91724 599-E4
DAMERAL DR
20000 LACo 91724 639-E2
W DAMERON ST
- NLB 90805 765-C1
DAMIAN ST
13700 CRTS 90703 737-C6
DAMIEN AV
400 LACo 91750 600-E2
400 LVRN 91750 600-E2
3400 LVRN 91750 570-E7
DAMIETTA DR
20200 DBAR 91789 679-F3
DAMON ST
2200 LA 90021 634-H7
5700 SIMI 93063 499-A3
9000 RSMD 91770 596-H5
DAMON WY
3100 BURB 91505 533-B4
DAMREL DR
16700 LACo 91744 638-G6
DAN CT
20700 SCTA 91350 4461-C4
DANA AV
6200 SIMI 93063 499-C3
23100 TOR 90501 793-H1
DANA CT
- LACo 91387 4462-C6
2300 CLAR 91711 571-D6
23000 TOR 90501 793-H1
DANA DR
4600 LPMA 90623 767-B3
7100 PMDL 93551 4104-C6
43700 LAN 93535 4106-D1
DANA PL
- LBCH 90803 826-C3
DANA ST
1400 LA 90007 634-A7
1800 GLDL 91201 563-J2
DANAHA ST
2800 TOR 90505 793-E4
DANALDA DR
2900 LA 90064 632-F6
DANBRIDGE ST
9000 PRV 90660 676-E6
W DANBROOK AV
3400 ANA 92804 767-G6
DANBROOK DR
12600 WHIT 90602 707-C2
13400 WHIT 90605 707-D3
14500 LACo 90604 707-F4
S DANBROOK DR
800 ANA 92804 767-G7
W DANBROOK DR
300 ANA 92804 767-G6
DANBURY LN
3700 ING 90305 703-E3

DANBURY LN
13300 SLB 90740 796-G7
DANBURY PL
5500 WdHl 91367 560-D2
DANBURY RD
1600 CLAR 91711 601-B1
1700 CLAR 91711 571-B7
DANBURY ST
9300 CYP 90630 767-B6
10500 TEML 91780 597-C3
DANBY AV
5700 LACo 90606 676-J4
8500 LACo 90606 706-G1
9000 SFSP 90670 706-G3
DANCER ST
13800 LACo 91746 638-A2
14500 LACo 91744 638-C3
S DANCOVE DR
300 WCOV 91791 639-B1
DANCY ST
18400 RowH 91748 679-A7
18400 RowH 91748 709-A1
DANDELION DR
27800 SCTA 91350 4461-C6
DANDELION LN
- SCTA 91354 4460-F6
DANE AL
1100 PAS 91104 566-B1
DANECROFT AV
100 SDMS 91773 599-J2
700 GLDR 91740 569-J7
DANEHURST AV
500 COV 91724 599-E2
700 GLDR 91740 569-E7
1600 GLDR 91740 599-E2
3600 LACo 91724 599-E6
N DANEHURST AV
400 COV 91724 599-E4
DANELAND ST
- LKWD 90712 766-A3
2400 LKWD 90712 765-G3
5800 LKWD 90713 766-C3
E DANES DR
1400 WCOV 91791 598-H6
DANESWOOD DR
10700 TEML 91780 597-C3
DANETTE ST
6400 SIMI 93063 499-C2
DANFORTH DR
700 LA 90065 595-A3
N DANGLER AV
100 ELA 90022 635-G5
S DANGLER AV
100 ELA 90022 635-G6
DANIA ST
700 PMDL 93551 4195-H4
DANIEL AV
2500 CMRC 90040 675-G4
DANIEL CT
1700 BREA 92821 709-A4
DANIEL DR
- LACo 91387 4551-J3
42300 LAN 93536 4104-E5
DANIEL LN
15900 Enc 91436 561-F3
DANIELLA CT
3400 CALB 91302 589-C1
DANIELLE AV
18700 CRTS 90703 767-A2
DANIELS AV
1100 BHLS 90212 632-F3
1200 LA 90035 632-F3
E DANIELS AV
2000 WCOV 91791 639-A1
DANIELSON CT
6700 CMRC 90040 676-A7
DANIELSON DR
10900 SELM 91733 637-B5
DANIELSON ST
17700 LACo 91387 4551-J3
17700 LACo 91387 4552-A3
DANIMERE AV
300 ARCD 91006 597-E1
DANLEE ST
500 AZU 91702 568-H5
DANMAR CT
2300 LMTA 90274 793-G5
DANNA CT
8100 RSMD 91770 636-F1
DANNY AV
5500 CYP 90630 767-D5
DANNY DR
3500 GLDL 91214 504-E6
DANNY ST
3700 GLDL 91214 504-D6
DANNY WY
- SCTA 91350 4461-A4
DANNYBOYAR AV
6300 CanP 91307 529-G6
DANNYHILL DR
3000 LA 90064 632-F6
DANS PL
- BREA 92821 708-J5
DANTE ST
12500 NRWK 90650 736-J2
12500 NRWK 90650 737-A2
DANTE WY
500 VeCo 91377 557-G1
DANTES VIEW DR
5000 CALB 91301 558-F6
DANTON CT
- SCTA 91354 4460-F6

E DANTON DR
18600 GLDR 91741 569-B5
18700 LACo 91741 569-B5
DANTON ST
1100 LVRN 91750 570-E7
DANUBE AV
9700 LA 91343 501-G5
10300 GrnH 91344 501-G2
DANVERS PL
28000 Cstc 91384 4459-G5
DANVERS ST
7700 DWNY 90240 706-B1
DANVILLE DR
800 CLAR 91711 571-F7
DANVILLE ST
9500 PRV 90660 676-J1
DANYA LN
- LAN 93536 4105-B1
44200 LAN 93536 4015-B7
DANZA ST
4600 WdHl 91364 560-C4
DANZIG PL
3300 ALH 91803 635-G1
DAPHNE AV
11800 HAW 90250 703-G7
12500 HAW 90250 733-G1
12900 GAR 90249 733-G2
16100 TOR 90504 733-G6
17500 TOR 90504 763-G1
DAPHNE PL
1400 FUL 92833 738-C5
DAPPLEGRAY CIR
100 BREA 92821 709-D7
DAPPLEGRAY LN
- RHE 90274 793-F7
N DAPPLEGRAY RD
- VeCo 91307 529-B4
DAPPLE GREY CIR
600 WAL 91789 639-D7
DARBUN DR
23900 SCTA 91321 4640-F3
DARBY AV
1400 POM 91767 601-D6
6300 Res 91335 530-J2
8300 Nor 91325 530-J1
8800 Nor 91325 500-J6
9100 Nor 91330 500-J6
10100 ING 90303 703-F5
10200 Nor 91326 500-J1
11800 Nor 91326 480-H6
DARBY CT
100 LHB 90631 708-E6
DARBY PL
6300 Res 91335 530-J2
DARBY RD
900 SMRO 91108 596-B3
DARBY ST
43200 LAN 93535 4106-G2
DARCIA PL
16200 Enc 91436 561-E5
DARCY DR
1700 MTBL 90640 636-C7
DARCY LN
23400 SCTA 91321 4640-H4
DARCY ST
11200 SFSP 90670 706-F5
DARDENNE ST
22100 CALB 91302 560-A7
22200 CALB 91302 559-H6
DARE CT
900 DBAR 91765 680-C2
DARE ST
12500 NRWK 90650 736-J2
12500 NRWK 90650 737-A2
DARECK CT
1500 KeCo 93560 3835-E2
DARFIELD AV
100 COV 91724 599-F3
4800 LACo 91724 599-F3
DARGAN ST
28900 AGRH 91301 558-A3
DARIEN PL
4800 TOR 90503 763-C3
DARIEN ST
4500 TOR 90503 763-C3
22900 WdHl 91364 559-G5
DARIN DR
- PMDL 93550 4466-B1
DARIO AV
30200 CynC 91351 4462-B4
DARIUS AV
800 DBAR 91789 679-G3
DARIUS CT
1300 INDS 91745 678-E3
DARK TKTR
- LACo 505-C4
- LACo 91011 505-C4
- PAS 91011 505-C4
DARK CANYON DR
3000 LA 90068 563-D6
DARK CANYON RD
- LACo 90601 677-D3
- WHIT 90601 677-D3
DARK CANYON TKTR
- LACo 505-C3
DARK CREEK RD
25700 LACo 91302 588-J7
25700 LACo 91302 589-A7
DARKWOOD LN
3100 LAN 93536 4105-B3
DARLA AV
12600 GrnH 91344 481-C5

DARLA CT
- Saug 91350 4461-E6
DARLAN ST
400 LACo 90248 734-D5
800 LACo 90220 734-E5
DARLENE CIR
7400 LPMA 90623 767-D2
DARLENE DR
1300 LHH 90631 708-E3
DARLENE LN
8400 LA 91304 529-G2
DARLEY AV
1600 HacH 91745 677-J2
DARLING RD
10700 LACo 91390 4373-C6
DARLINGTON AV
5600 BPK 90621 737-J7
6300 BPK 90621 767-J1
11600 Brwd 90049 631-G5
12200 SMCA 90403 631-G5
12400 LA 90403 631-G5
DARLINGTON ST
500 LACo 91770 636-H5
DARLOW AV
4500 RSMD 91770 596-H5
DARNELL AV
1200 UPL 91784 571-J5
DARNELL ST
9400 BLF 90706 736-B4
DARNEY AV
500 LACo 91792 679-C2
DARNOCH WY
6900 CanP 91307 529-E4
DAROCA AV
200 SGBL 91775 596-E2
300 LBCH 90803 796-E7
2500 RSMD 91770 636-E2
DAROCA WY
4800 BPK 90621 737-J4
DARRELL DR
100 GLDL 91202 564-E1
DARRIN DR
24300 DBAR 91765 640-D7
DARRO RD
5200 WdHl 91364 560-A3
DARROW AV
28600 SCTA 91390 4461-D4
28700 LACo 91390 4461-D4
DART CT
5500 AGRH 91301 557-G5
DART ST
13100 BALD 91706 637-J1
DARTER DR
18800 SCTA 91351 4551-G1
DARTFORD PL
8700 ING 90305 703-E3
DARTFORD WY
15800 Shrm 91403 561-F7
DARTMOOR AV
14300 NRWK 90650 736-J3
14400 NRWK 90650 737-A4
21100 LKWD 90715 767-A5
DARTMOUTH AV
200 CLAR 91711 601-D4
4900 LA 90032 635-E1
5100 LA 90032 595-E7
N DARTMOUTH AV
700 CLAR 91711 601-D2
DARTMOUTH CIR
100 SLB 90740 796-F5
DARTMOUTH DR
1300 GLDL 91205 564-G7
2700 LAN 93536 4105-C2
11500 NRWK 90650 736-G5
DARTMOUTH LN
- RowH 91748 708-J2
2200 PMDL 93550 4286-E3
11300 SBdC 91766 641-D3
DARTMOUTH PL
500 LCF 91011 535-D6
DARTMOUTH RD
400 BURB 91504 533-F5
DARTMOUTH WY
- BPK 90620 767-F6
DARVALLE ST
13400 CRTS 90703 767-C1
DARWELL AV
6300 BGDN 90201 675-H7
6300 CMRC 90040 675-H7
6500 BGDN 90201 705-H1
DARWIN AV
1700 LA 90031 634-J1
2000 LA 90031 635-A1
DARWIN RD
9100 SBdC 92371 (4562-H1 See Page 4471)
9100 SBdC 92371 (4472-H7 See Page 4471)
N DARWOOD AV
500 SDMS 91773 599-H1
S DARWOOD AV
400 SDMS 91773 599-H3
DARYL AV
12400 GrnH 91344 481-B5
DARYN DR
6600 LACo 91307 529-D6
DASHI PL
- CanP 91307 530-B4
- LA 91304 530-B4
DASHWOOD ST
2000 LKWD 90712 765-G3
5800 LKWD 90713 766-C3

DASHWOOD WY
- PMDL 93552 4287-D1
DATE AV
300 ALH 91803 595-H6
1200 TOR 90503 763-F6
1700 ALH 91803 635-J1
22700 TOR 90505 793-F1
44000 LAN 93534 4015-G4
44000 LAN 93534 4105-H1
DATE CIR
2500 TOR 90505 793-F1
DATE ST
300 MTBL 90640 676-C5
1400 TOR 90503 763-F6
11900 NRWK 90650 706-J7
12300 NRWK 90650 736-J1
N DATE ST
500 POM 91768 640-G1
DATE PALM DR
- CRSN 90746 764-F1
1000 PMDL 93551 4195-E7
DATETREE DR
14300 LACo 93532 4102-G5
DAUBERT ST
14000 LA 91340 502-A2
14500 MsnH 91345 502-A2
DAUM DR
13200 INDS 91746 637-J2
DAUNTLESS DR
3900 RPV 90275 823-D5
DAUPHIN AV
5800 CULC 90232 633-A6
5800 LA 90034 633-A6
6000 LA 90034 632-J6
DAVAN ST
21200 DBAR 91789 679-H3
DAVANA RD
3800 Shrm 91423 562-C5
DAVANA TER
13800 Shrm 91423 562-B5
DAVE DR
300 LA 90732 823-H5
DAVENPORT CIR
700 CLAR 91711 601-F1
DAVENPORT DR
3100 LA 90065 594-H4
DAVENPORT RD
11200 OrCo 90720 796-J3
11300 LACo 91390 4373-D7
11800 LACo 91390 4463-A1
13000 LACo 91390 4462-H1
DAVENRICH ST
10900 SFSP 90670 706-F4
DAVENTRY ST
12700 Pcma 91331 482-E7
13000 Pcma 91331 502-D1
DAVER AV
5100 LaCr 91214 504-F6
DAVERIC DR
1000 PAS 91107 566-G2
DAVEY AV
23100 SCTA 91321 4640-J3
DAVEY JONES DR
30700 AGRH 91301 557-G5
DAVID AV
2500 LHB 90631 708-B5
5800 CULC 90232 633-A6
5800 LA 90034 633-A6
6000 LA 90034 632-H5
DAVID ST
- WCOV 91790 598-E5
43600 LAN 93535 4106-D1
DAVID WY
18000 CRTS 90703 767-C1
28600 LACo 91390 4461-D4
28600 Saug 91350 4461-D4
DAVIDS RD
3800 Ago 91301 588-F1
DAVIDSON CT
1100 BREA 92821 709-C6
DAVIDSON DR
- Cstc 91384 4459-D6
- Wch 90045 702-G4
2400 MONP 91754 635-G4
5300 WHIT 90601 677-A3
DAVIDSON LN
500 POM 91768 640-G1
1600 SIMI 93063 499-B2
DAVIE AV
2000 CMRC 90040 676-A3
DAVIES DR
1300 BelA 90077 592-B5
1300 LA 90210 592-B5
DAVIES WY
1900 LA 90046 592-J3
DA VINCI AV
4400 WdHl 91364 560-A5
DAVIS AV
300 GLDL 91201 564-A2
600 MTBL 90640 676-C3
DAVIS DR
100 ING 90301 703-C3
DAVIS LN
- FUL 92833 738-C5
DAVIS ST
4600 CHNO 91710 641-F6
8300 DWNY 90241 706-A5
23300 Chat 91311 499-F7
DAVISTA DR
8100 WHIT 90602 707-F1
8400 WHIT 90605 707-F2

DAVIT CIR
1300 LHB 90631 708-G4
DAVLINA LN
- PMDL 93551 4195-E7
DAVON WY
39300 PMDL 93551 4195-B5
DAWES AV
4400 LA 90230 672-E4
5100 CULC 90230 672-F5
DAWKINS AV
29000 Cstc 91384 4459-B6
DAWLEY AV
1400 LACo 91744 638-H4
S DAWLEY AV
500 WCOV 91790 638-H1
DAWN AV
4100 LVRN 91750 570-J7
4200 LACo 91750 570-J7
DAWN CIR
8000 LPMA 90623 767-C4
DAWN CT
- LAN 93536 4014-J7
- PMDL 93551 4195-A3
DAWN DR
12900 CRTS 90703 737-A6
DAWN LN
12400 CRTS 90703 736-J6
DAWN ST
2000 LMTA 90717 793-H3
DAWN CREEK
- LA 90094 702-D1
DAWN HAVEN RD
16600 HacH 91745 678-E5
DAWN RIDGE CT
1700 PMDL 93551 4195-E7
DAWNRIDGE DR
1300 LA 90210 592-D5
DAWNRIDGE PL
2600 WCOV 91792 638-J6
DAWN RIDGE WY
1100 COV 91724 599-E7
DAWNVIEW AV
3000 POM 91767 600-J2
DAWNVIEW PL
5100 LACo 90043 673-C5
DAWSON AV
100 GLDR 91740 599-D1
400 LBCH 90814 795-G7
700 LBCH 90804 795-G4
1800 SIGH 90755 795-G3
DAWSON CT
200 GLDR 91740 599-D1
DAWSON DR
37000 PMDL 93550 4286-H4
DAWSON ST
200 Echo 90026 634-D2
DAWSON WY
200 CLAR 91711 571-D6
DAWSON CREEK PL
19400 WAL 91789 639-C5
DAY ST
6100 GLDL 91214 504-B4
6100 Tuj 91042 504-A4
7500 Tuj 91042 503-J4
7900 Sunl 91040 503-G4
DAYBREAK
3600 ELMN 91732 637-G1
DAYBREAK S
3500 ELMN 91732 637-G7
DAYBREAK DR
- LVRN 91750 570-H5
200 WAL 91789 639-H7
1800 AZU 91702 568-H2
DAYBREAK ST
1300 UPL 91784 571-H3
37300 PMDL 93550 4286-H3
DAYDREAM WY
- SCTA 91354 4460-G5
DAYKIN ST
15500 HacH 91745 678-B3
DAYLIGHT DR
6300 AGRH 91301 558-A3
DAY LILY DR
24300 SCTA 91321 4641-C1
DAY LILY LN
- PanC 91402 502-A6
DAYLILY PL
39400 PMDL 93551 4195-D5
DAYLILY ST
1400 UPL 91784 571-H3
E DAYMAN ST
300 LBCH 90806 795-E5
6200 LBCH 90815 796-D4
DAYTON AV
900 POM 91766 640-H5
DAYTON CT
5000 PMDL 93552 4287-B4
E DAYTON ST
- PAS 91105 565-H5
W DAYTON ST
- PAS 91105 565-H5
DAYTON WY
8800 BHLS 90211 632-G1
9100 BHLS 90210 632-G1
9500 BHLS 90212 632-G2
DAYTONA AV
2500 HacH 91745 677-J4
DE ADALENA ST
8500 RSMD 91770 596-G7
9400 RSMD 91770 597-A7
DEAD HORSE CANYON
26500 StvR 91381 4640-A1

DEAKIN AV
2200 UPL 91784 571-H3
DEAL DR
4500 Bxby 90807 765-D5
DE ALCALA DR
13100 LMRD 90638 737-E2
DEAN CIR
2000 Brwd 90049 591-F4
DEANA LN
17800 LACo 91387 4551-J4
DEANA ST
11800 ELMN 91732 597-F7
12000 ELMN 91732 637-G1
DEANE AV
5100 LACo 90043 673-E6
5700 LA 90043 673-E6
DEANE ST
2300 LA 90039 594-E4
DEANNA AV
1600 SIMI 93063 499-A3
DEANNA CT
14100 GAR 90247 734-A3
DEANNA DR
900 BREA 92821 708-J5
DEANNA ST
100 LHB 90631 708-C6
DEANNE DR
2600 HacH 91745 678-B5
DEANWOOD DR
4300 WdHl 91364 560-D5
DE ANZA DR
4300 PMDL 93551 4194-J3
4300 PMDL 93551 4195-A3
DE ANZA PL
1100 ARCD 91007 566-J5
S DE ANZA ST
100 SGBL 91776 596-D4
DE ANZA HEIGHTS DR
300 SDMS 91773 600-C3
400 LVRN 91750 600-D3
DEARBORN AV
2800 PMDL 93551 4195-B5
8100 SGAT 90280 705-B3
DEARBORN CT
11500 Pcma 91331 502-H4
DEARBORN DR
- SCTA 91354 4460-F7
2500 LA 90068 593-F2
DEARBORN ST
100 PAS 91103 535-H7
100 Nor 91325 501-A7
300 PAS 91104 535-H7
14200 PanC 91402 502-A7
14800 PanC 91402 501-J6
15300 LA 91343 501-E7
17900 Nor 91330 501-A7
18400 Nor 91324 500-G7
18400 Nor 91325 500-H7
19700 Chat 91311 500-C7
DEAUVILLA CT
3600 CALB 91302 559-D7
DEBANN PL
1800 RowH 91748 679-E5
DEBBY ST
11100 NHol 91606 532-F7
11100 NHol 91606 533-A7
13000 VanN 91401 532-C7
DE BELL DR
- BURB 91501 533-H4
DEBELL ST
12500 Pcma 91331 502-E5
DE BELL RANCH RD
- LACo 90265 628-F5
- MAL 90265 628-F5
DE BERRY DR
26000 CALB 91301 558-F6
DE BIE AV
18400 CRTS 90703 767-B1
DE BIE DR
6900 PRM 90723 735-F2
DEBLYNN AV
15500 LACo 90248 734-D5
DEBLYNN CT
37700 PMDL 93550 4285-J2
DEBORAH AV
1200 AZU 91702 568-H4
DEBORAH DR
300 POM 91767 601-A5
DEBORAH ST
900 UPL 91784 571-J4
9500 CYP 90630 767-E7
E DEBORAH ST
5500 LBCH 90815 796-C2
DEBORAH KAY LN
2100 HacH 91745 678-A4
DEBRA AV
8700 LA 91343 501-E5
8700 LA 91343 531-E1
10300 GrnH 91344 501-E1
DEBRA DR
1600 LVRN 91750 570-F4
DEBRA LN
16400 CRTS 90703 736-E6
DEBRA ANN PL
37900 PMDL 93550 4286-G2
DEBS AV
6100 WdHl 91367 529-E7
6500 CanP 91307 529-E7
DEBS PARK RD
3800 LA 90032 595-C5
DEBSTONE AV
3700 Shrm 91423 562-C6

DE BUTTS TER
5700 LACo 90265 627-G7
5700 MAL 90265 627-G7
6100 MAL 90265 667-H1
DEBWOOD PL
1200 LHB 90631 738-E1
DECAMP DR
1700 LA 90210 592-B4
DECATUR CIR
900 CLAR 91711 571-F6
DECATUR DR
5000 LPMA 90623 767-C2
DECATUR ST
700 LA 90021 634-H6
E DECCA ST
8300 LBCH 90808 767-A7
DE CELIS PL
4500 Enc 91436 561-E4
6500 VanN 91406 531-D5
8300 LA 91343 531-D1
11400 GrnH 91344 501-D1
11500 GrnH 91344 481-D7
DECENTE CT
11400 LA 91604 562-J6
DECENTE DR
11400 LA 91604 562-J6
DECI ST
15200 LA 91342 481-G2
DECIMA DR
3000 HacH 91745 678-A5
DECKER LN
300 POM 91766 641-A4
DECKER CANYON RD Rt#-23
1400 LACo 90265 586-F7
1400 LACo 90265 626-D2
3100 MAL 90265 626-D5
DECKER EDISON RD
- MAL 90265 626-D5
DECKER SCHOOL LN
1300 LACo 90265 626-E1
DECKER SCHOOL RD
33000 LACo 90265 626-B2
DECLARATION AV
3800 CALB 91302 559-H6
DECLIFF DR
13600 WHIT 90601 677-E5
DECORAH RD
23600 DBAR 91765 640-C6
DECORO DR
- BqtC 91354 4460-E6
- SCTA 91355 4460-E6
22500 SCTA 91350 4460-H6
22800 SCTA 91354 4460-G6
DECOSTA AV
8300 LACo 90606 706-H1
8700 SFSP 90670 706-H2
DEDHAM CT
38600 PMDL 93551 4196-J7
DEDHAM PL
- HacH 91745 678-F6
DEDRE LN
- Saug 91350 4461-E6
DEE AV
2800 ELMN 91732 637-D2
DEE LN
2900 WCOV 91792 639-A7
DEE ST
14900 LACo 90248 734-D4
DEEBLE ST
9200 SGAT 90280 705-A4
DEEBOYAR AV
4100 LKWD 90712 765-G4
DEED AV
30100 Cstc 91384 4459-C3
DEE DEE CT
4000 LAN 93536 4015-A7
DEEGAN PL
1400 MANB 90266 732-F5
DEELANE PL
4800 TOR 90503 763-C3
DEELANE ST
4500 TOR 90503 763-A3
DEENA PL
- LACo 91390 4461-A4
DEEPBROOK DR
26500 RPV 90275 793-B6
DEEP CANYON DR
2600 LA 90210 592-C1
3000 LA 90210 562-C7
DEEP CANYON PL
9800 LA 90210 592-C1
DEEP CANYON RD
2000 LHH 90631 708-E1
DEEP CREEK CT
14600 CHLS 91709 680-H5
DEEP CREEK DR
28000 SCTA 91387 4552-B2
DEEP CREEK RD
21600 WAL 91789 639-H5
DEEPDALE AV
8400 BPK 90621 738-A5
DEEP DELL PL
6300 LA 90068 593-F2
DEEPGROVE AV
2200 RowH 91748 678-J6
DEEP HILL RD
400 DBAR 91765 640-A6
DEEPLAKE AV
16200 LACo 93591 4199-F3
DEEPLAWN DR
1200 DBAR 91765 680-A3

DEEPMEAD AV
400 LACo 91744 679-A2
DEEP RIVER DR
13500 LACo 91746 637-G5
DEEPRIVER DR
13700 LACo 91746 637-H5
DEEP SHADOW DR
29200 AGRH 91301 558-A5
DEEP SPRINGS DR
800 CLAR 91711 571-E4
DEEPSPRINGS DR
24400 DBAR 91765 640-E7
DEEPTREE AV
27500 SCTA 91351 4551-F2
DEEP VALLEY DR
600 RHE 90274 823-B1
DEEP VIEW LN
1000 COV 91724 599-D6
1000 LACo 91724 599-D6
DEEPVIEW LN
19800 LACo 91724 599-E6
DEEPWATER AV
1400 Wilm 90744 794-F3
DEEPWELL LN
3300 LAN 93536 4105-B2
DEEPWELL RD
24500 HIDH 91302 559-D3
DEEPWOOD DR
800 THO 91362 557-C1
DEER AV
3900 Shrm 91423 562-C6
DEER CT
- SCTA 91351 4461-G7
DEERBANK DR
14600 LACo 93532 4102-G5
DEERBROOK LN
12300 Brwd 90049 631-F1
14100 CHLS 91709 680-H3
DEER BROOK ST
2900 POM 91767 600-H3
DEER CREEK AV
11200 MTCL 91763 641-G3
DEER CREEK DR
1100 WAL 91789 639-E5
DEER CREEK LN
3300 GLDL 91208 534-F5
26400 SCTA 91387 4552-D7
DEER CREEK RD
- POM 91766 640-H5
1300 SDMS 91773 570-C7
14700 VeCo 90265 625-B2
DEER CROSSING DR
1500 DBAR 91765 680-C3
DEERFIELD AV
17400 BLF 90706 736-A7
N DEERFIELD AV
6200 LACo 91775 596-G2
DEERFIELD CIR
1200 UPL 91784 571-J6
DEERFIELD DR
200 WAL 91789 639-G7
DEERFIELD LN
- SCTA 91354 4460-G6
10200 Nor 91324 500-G4
DEERFIELD PL
1200 DBAR 91765 680-E3
DEERFLATS DR
800 SDMS 91773 570-D6
DEERFOOT DR
1400 DBAR 91765 679-J4
1400 DBAR 91765 680-A4
DEERFORD ST
2400 LKWD 90712 765-G4
5900 LKWD 90713 766-D4
DEERGLEN LN
33000 LACo 91390 4373-G7
DEER HAVEN DR
1900 CHLS 91709 680-H4
8100 SBdC 92371 (4562-H2 See Page 4471)
9000 SBdC 92371 (4472-H7 See Page 4471)
DEERHAVEN DR
1500 HacH 91745 678-A2
DEERHEAD RD
5800 MAL 90265 627-B7
5800 MAL 90265 667-B1
DEERHILL DR
- RHE 90274 823-F1
DEERHILL RD
800 VeCo 91377 558-A1
DEERHILL TR
1700 Top 90290 590-C2
DEERHORN DR
4000 Shrm 91403 561-H6
DEERHORN RD
15400 Shrm 91403 561-G6
DEERING AV
6900 CanP 91303 530-B5
7500 LA 91304 530-B2
9100 Chat 91311 500-B3
DEERING CIR
20900 CanP 91303 530-C6
DEERING CT
21200 LA 91304 530-B3
DEERLANE DR
2900 DUAR 91010 568-F3
DEER LICK DR
23900 LA 91304 529-E2
DEERMONT RD
1800 GLDL 91207 564-E1
DEERPARK CT
4300 WLKV 91361 557-D6

STREET Block City ZIP Pg-Grid

DEERPASS RD
3600 GLDL 91208 534-F2
DEERPATH LN
- Llan 93544 4470-D7
16300 LPUE 91744 638-E7
21400 MAL 90265 629-F6
DEERPATH PL
- POM 91766 640-G7
DEER PATH RD
- Actn 93510 4375-G6
DEERPEAK DR
1900 HacH 91745 678-C4
DEER RUN LN
1900 Brwd 90049 591-F4
DEER RUN RD
38800 LACo 93551 4195-F7
DEER SKIN LN
700 WAL 91789 639-F6
DEER SPRING LN
23500 DBAR 91765 680-C2
DEER SPRINGS DR
- LACo 91390 4461-B4
DEER SPRINGS LN
2100 BREA 92821 709-E7
DEER TRAIL CT
26900 CALB 91301 558-G7
DEER TRAIL DR
16800 HacH 91745 678-E5
DEERVALE DR
3700 Shrm 91403 562-A6
3700 Shrm 91423 562-A6
DEERVALE PL
14500 Shrm 91403 561-J6
14500 Shrm 91403 562-A6
DEER VIEW CT
18100 Enc 91316 561-A6
DEERVIEW CT
29400 AGRH 91301 557-J4
DEERVIEW ST
1700 GLDR 91740 569-J6
DEERWALK DR
42600 LACo 93532 4102-G4
DEERWEED TR
20900 CALB 91301 558-G7
DEERWOOD DR
1700 FUL 92833 738-D3
W DEERWOOD DR
3200 ANA 92804 767-G7
DEERWOOD TR
6100 Tuj 91042 504-C4
DEESWOOD DR
18100 LACo 93532 4101-H2
DEFENDER DR
4000 AGRH 91301 558-E7
DEFIANCE AV
9500 Wats 90002 704-G4
12200 Wbrk 90059 734-G1
DE FOE AV
10800 Pcma 91331 502-D1
12500 LA 91342 482-A5
13200 LA 91342 481-G2
DE FOE ST
900 SFER 91340 482-B6
DEFOE WY
- StvR 91381 4550-A7
DE FOREST AV
800 LBCH 90813 795-C6
1800 LBCH 90806 795-C2
5100 NLB 90805 765-D2
DEFOREST ST
20500 WdHl 91364 560-C3
DEGAMA ST
600 WCOV 91791 638-J1
DE GARMO AV
3800 ELMN 91731 597-B7
7800 SunV 91352 533-B1
9000 SunV 91352 502-J7
11000 Pcma 91331 502-E1
11500 Pcma 91331 482-C7
11600 LA 91340 482-C7
11700 SFER 91340 482-C7
12700 LA 91342 482-A4
12800 LA 91342 481-G2
DE GARMO DR
1000 City 90063 635-D4
DE GARMO ST
700 SFER 91340 482-B6
DEGAS AV
5200 TEML 91780 597-B4
DEGAS LN
- SCTA 91355 4550-D3
DEGAS PL
11800 CRTS 90703 766-H2
DEGNAN BLVD
3600 LA 90018 673-F2
3700 LA 90008 673-F2
DEGOVIA AV
4600 WdHl 91364 559-G4
DEGRASSE DR
22300 CALB 91302 559-J5
DE GROOT PL
17000 CRTS 90703 737-A7
DE HAVEN AV
10500 Pcma 91331 502-D1
12700 LA 91342 482-A4
12900 LA 91342 481-J4
DE HAVEN ST
700 SFER 91340 482-C6
DE HAVILAND AV
8800 Wch 90045 702-H3
S DEHN AV
11400 ING 90303 703-F7

DEHOUGNE ST
11500 NHol 91605 532-F5
DEITZ DR
- LACo 91390 4373-F6
DEJAY ST
43600 LAN 93536 4105-E2
DE JUR ST
800 BREA 92821 708-H5
DEKALB AV
4700 VER 90058 675-C4
DE KALB DR
22300 CALB 91302 559-G5
DEL BLVD
12400 LA 90066 672-D6
DELA ST
2300 LACo 90601 637-E6
N DE LACEY AV
- PAS 91103 565-C3
S DE LACEY AV
- PAS 91105 565-H5
DELACOUR DR
38100 PMDL 93550 4285-J1
38100 PMDL 93550 4286-A1
DELACROIX RD
4900 RPV 90275 793-B7
DE LA CUMBRE PL
3500 Shrm 91423 562-A7
DELAFIELD AV
13200 HAW 90250 733-A2
DELAFIELD DR
4500 OrCo 90638 737-J4
DE LA FUENTE ST
300 MONP 91754 636-A3
800 MONP 91754 635-J4
DE LA GUERRA ST
20600 WdHl 91364 560-A3
DE LA GUERRA WY
- SCTA 91355 4460-D6
DE LA LUZ AV
21800 WdHl 91364 560-A4
DELAMARE DR
1600 LACo 90601 637-F5
DELAMERE DR
1400 RowH 91748 679-D4
DEL AMO BLVD
1700 TOR 90501 763-G4
2100 TOR 90503 763-A4
2400 LKWD 90712 765-H4
4000 LKWD 90712 766-A4
4300 LBCH 90808 766-A4
5500 LKWD 90713 766-A4
5600 RBCH 90277 763-A4
6500 CRTS 90703 766-F4
6500 LKWD 90715 766-G4
12400 LKWD 90715 767-A4
12400 CRTS 90703 767-A4
E DEL AMO BLVD
- NLB 90805 765-A4
100 CRSN 90745 764-C4
500 CRSN 90746 764-E4
600 Bxby 90807 765-E4
1900 CRSN 90810 764-E4
1900 LACo 90220 764-E4
2000 LKWD 90712 765-E4
2400 CRSN 90810 765-A4
2400 LACo 90220 765-A4
2500 RDom 90221 765-A4
W DEL AMO BLVD
- LA 90501 764-A4
- LACo 90745 764-C4
- NLB 90805 765-C4
100 CRSN 90745 764-C4
200 LBCH 90810 765-C4
500 LACo 90502 764-A4
600 LA 90502 764-A4
1500 LA 90501 763-J4
DEL AMO CIR E
21600 TOR 90503 763-D7
21800 TOR 90505 763-D7
DEL AMO CIR N
3500 TOR 90503 763-C6
DEL AMO CIR W
21400 TOR 90503 763-C6
21800 TOR 90505 763-C6
DEL AMO ST
1000 RBCH 90277 762-J4
1200 RBCH 90277 763-A4
DELAMO WOODS DR
23500 Hrbr 90710 794-A2
DELANCEY AV
400 SDMS 91773 600-C1
DELAND AV
4100 PRV 90660 676-H2
DELANEY DR
- BREA 92821 708-J5
DELANO ST
10600 NHol 91606 533-A7
11200 NHol 91606 532-H7
13000 VanN 91401 532-A7
14500 VanN 91411 532-A7
14600 VanN 91411 531-H7
17500 Enc 91316 531-A7
18100 Res 91335 531-A7
18200 Res 91335 530-G7
19800 WdHl 91367 530-E7
S DELANO ST
100 ANA 92804 767-J6
DELANTE WY
- GmH 91344 480-J6
- GmH 91344 481-A6
DELANY CT
500 LACo 91746 637-J3

DELANY LN
- LA 91304 530-A3
DELANY ST
1400 POM 91767 601-C7
DE LA OSA ST
21200 WdHl 91364 560-B3
22000 WdHl 91364 559-J4
DELAPLANE RD
6200 MAL 90265 667-G1
DEL ARROYO DR
9100 SunV 91352 503-C7
DELASONDE DR
1800 RPV 90275 823-H2
DE LA TORRE WY
1300 LA 90023 675-B1
DELAVAN AV
5000 WdHl 91364 560-D3
DELAVAN DR
13500 NRWK 90650 736-J2
DE LA VINA WY
- SCTA 91355 4460-D6
DELAWARE AV
1500 SMCA 90404 671-G2
1800 SMCA 90404 631-J7
DELAWARE DR
- PMDL 93550 4286-C4
600 CLAR 91711 601-C1
DELAWARE RD
200 BURB 91504 533-G6
DE LAY AV
1200 GLDR 91740 599-D3
4800 LACo 91722 599-D3
DELAY AV
1000 GLDR 91740 569-D7
1000 GLDR 91740 599-D1
N DE LAY AV
100 COV 91723 599-D5
3300 LACo 91723 599-D4
S DE LAY AV
100 COV 91723 599-D5
DELAY DR
2900 LA 90065 594-F2
DELAY ST
1000 BREA 92821 708-H5
DELBANA AV
31800 Pear 93553 4468-G1
32500 Pear 93553 4378-G7
DEL BAY ST
2000 LKWD 90712 765-G3
DEL BONITA ST
18400 RowH 91748 679-A7
DEL CAMPO PL
20300 WdHl 91364 560-D2
DEL CERRO AV
800 WCOV 91791 639-A2
DEL CERRO CIR
23600 LA 91304 529-E4
DEL CERRO PL
300 FUL 92835 738-G1
DELCO AV
1800 SELM 91733 637-C2
2600 ELMN 91733 637-C2
5700 WdHl 91367 560-D1
6600 Win 91306 530-D1
9500 Chat 91311 500-D3
DELCO PL
7400 Win 91306 530-D4
DELCOMBRE AV
15500 PRM 90723 735-E5
DEL COURT PL
400 GLDL 91206 565-A4
DELDEN RD
20000 Nwhl 91321 4641-E1
E DE LEON ST
6400 LBCH 90815 796-E5
DEL ESTE CIR
5100 LPMA 90623 767-C4
DELEVAN DR
2400 LA 90065 564-H7
2800 LA 90065 594-H1
DELFERN DR
100 BelA 90077 592-C6
DELFINO ST
6200 Tuj 91042 504-C4
DELFORD AV
1500 DUAR 91010 568-A6
22700 CRSN 90745 794-C1
DELFS LN
2300 RowH 91748 679-E6
DELGADO CT
43800 LAN 93535 4016-F7
43800 LAN 93535 4106-F1
DEL GADO DR
15000 Shrm 91403 561-G5
DEL GADO PL
15500 Shrm 91403 561-G5
DELGANY AV
8100 PdlR 90293 702-B3
W DELHAVEN AV
1000 WCOV 91790 638-D3
W DELHAVEN ST
1400 WCOV 91790 638-D2
DELHI CT
15600 LMRD 90638 737-H4
DEL HOLLOW ST
2000 LKWD 90712 765-G4
DELIA AV
7500 SunV 91352 533-C3
16600 TOR 90504 733-F7
17300 TOR 90504 763-F1
DELIA CT
22300 CALB 91302 559-J6
DELIA PL
2900 WCOV 91792 639-A7

DELIBAN AV
10700 Tuj 91042 504-A2
DELICIA
2400 LA 90732 823-F7
DELICIOUS LN
- PMDL 93551 4285-E3
DELIGHT ST
18500 SCTA 91351 4551-D2
DELINDA LN
900 LCF 91011 535-B2
DELISLE CT
2300 GLDL 91208 534-J6
DELITA DR
20100 WdHl 91364 560-D3
DELITA PL
5000 WdHl 91364 560-D3
DELL AL
3600 MdlR 90292 671-J7
3600 LA 90292 671-J7
3700 MdlR 90292 701-J1
3700 LA 90292 701-J1
DELL AV
800 SBdC (512-A5 See Page 511)
1800 Ven 90291 671-H6
14700 BLF 90706 736-A3
DELL CT
31300 Cstc 91384 4369-F7
DELL DR
1200 MONP 91754 635-J4
DELL ST
2600 LAN 93535 4016-E5
DELLA DR
1000 BHLS 90210 592-D6
DELLMONT DR
11400 Tuj 91042 503-J1
DELL OAK DR
5500 LA 90068 593-H2
N DEL LOMA AV
5400 SGBL 91776 596-G4
5500 LACo 91776 596-G4
5900 LACo 91775 596-F2
DELLROSE AV
7800 LACo 91770 636-E3
DELLVALE PL
3600 Enc 91436 561-E6
DELLWOOD LN
2100 BelA 90077 592-A3
DEL MAR
- RSMD 91770 636-E1
- SGBL 91776 636-E1
- TOR 90505 793-F5
DEL MAR AV
700 SGBL 91776 596-E2
1400 SMRO 91108 566-E7
1400 SMRO 91108 596-E2
1600 LACo 91770 636-E3
2000 SGBL 91775 596-E2
2400 RSMD 91770 636-E3
3000 Bxby 90807 795-D1
3700 Bxby 90807 765-C6
3900 LA 90029 594-B5
9000 MTCL 91763 601-H4
11400 SBdC 91710 641-D3
N DEL MAR AV
100 SGBL 91775 596-E3
100 SGBL 91776 596-E3
2800 LBCH 90806 795-D2
S DEL MAR AV
100 SGBL 91776 596-E6
2000 RSMD 91776 636-E1
2000 SGBL 91776 636-E1
3400 RSMD 91770 636-E3
E DEL MAR BLVD
- PAS 91105 565-H5
200 PAS 91101 565-H5
500 PAS 91101 566-A5
800 PAS 91106 566-A5
1000 PAS 91125 566-A5
1800 PAS 91107 566-E5
3100 LACo 91107 566-E5
W DEL MAR BLVD
- PAS 91105 565-G5
DEL MAR CIR
4600 LVRN 91750 570-H7
DEL MAR CT
800 COMP 90221 735-A4
DEL MAR DR
9200 PRV 90660 676-H1
DEL MAR LN
7300 LPMA 90623 767-C3
DEL MAR RD
2200 Mont 91020 534-H3
DEL MAR ST
37200 PMDL 93552 4287-C2
DEL MAR TR
6800 VeCo 93063 499-D4
DEL MARINO
2200 LVRN 91750 570-H4
DEL MARINO PL
100 SGBL 91776 596-E4
DELMAS TER
3700 LA 90034 672-G1
3800 CULC 90232 672-G1
3800 LA 90232 672-G1
DELMESA AV
2100 HacH 91745 678-C4
DELMONICO AV
8600 LA 91304 529-J1
DELMONT PL
15100 LMRD 90638 707-G6
DEL MONTE DR
1400 GLDL 91207 564-G2

DEL MONTE DR
3000 Echo 90026 594-C6
13000 SLB 90740 796-H7
23500 SCTA 91355 4550-F4
W DEL MONTE DR
- SCTA 91355 4550-F4
3000 ANA 92804 767-G6
DEL MONTE RD
4800 LCF 91011 535-D4
DEL MONTE ST
200 PAS 91103 565-F1
DEL MONTE WEST
400 FUL 92832 738-G6
DEL MORENO DR
4500 WdHl 91364 560-D4
DEL MORENO PL
4700 WdHl 91364 560-D3
DELNICE AV
2200 ELMN 91732 637-E4
DEL NORDE AV
1000 POM 91767 601-B5
DEL NORTE CIR
5100 LPMA 90623 767-C4
DEL NORTE ST
400 LA 90065 595-A5
W DEL NORTE ST
1400 WCOV 91790 598-F7
DELOISE AV
18300 CRTS 90703 766-E1
DE LONE ST
16300 SCTA 91387 4552-C2
DELONG ST
5200 CYP 90630 767-C5
8600 LPMA 90623 767-C5
8600 LPMA 90630 767-C5
DE LONGPRE AV
3800 LFlz 90027 594-B4
5100 LFlz 90027 593-H5
5500 Hlwd 90028 593-D5
7100 LA 90046 593-B5
8200 WHWD 90046 593-A5
8300 WHWD 90069 593-A5
DELOR DR
2900 LA 90032 595-F7
DELOR RD
2700 LA 90065 564-H7
DELORAINE DR
20600 WAL 91789 639-F7
DELORAS DR
700 Wilm 90744 794-E3
700 CRSN 90745 794-E3
DELORES ST
2000 WCOV 91792 639-A7
DEL ORO DR
1600 LCF 91011 505-A7
DEL ORO LN
2800 FUL 92835 738-H2
8100 LPMA 90623 767-C4
DELOS DR
26100 TOR 90505 793-F6
DELOZ AV
1700 LFlz 90027 594-C4
DEL PASO AV
1800 LA 90032 635-E2
DEL PASO CT
4700 LA 90032 635-D2
DELPENA CT
- PMDL 93550 4286-H4
DELPHEY AV
12200 CHNO 91710 641-F6
DELPHI ST
6000 HiPk 90042 595-D1
DELPHIA AV
100 BREA 92821 709-A7
DELPHIN PL
4900 SBdC 91737 (542-G7 See Page 511)
DELPHINE DR
20900 WAL 91789 639-G7
DELPHINE LN
- LA 91302 589-B5
DELPHINE PL
400 FUL 92833 738-D6
DELPHINIUM AV
29600 SCTA 91387 4462-F6
DELPHINIUM CIR
7900 BPK 90620 767-J3
DEL PINO DR
8400 LACo 91770 636-G4
DEL PRADO
- LVRN 91750 570-H4
1700 POM 91768 600-F6
DEL PRADO DR
15100 HacH 91745 677-J5
15700 HacH 91745 678-A5
DELRESTO DR
1200 LA 90210 592-C6
DEL REY
1700 POM 91768 600-F6
DEL REY AL
2500 PAS 91107 566-E1
DEL REY AV
200 PAS 91107 566-E2
4000 CULC 90292 672-B6
4000 LA 90292 672-B6
N DEL REY CT
200 LBCH 90802 795-D7
200 LBCH 90802 825-D1
700 LBCH 90813 795-D7
DEL REY DR
900 GLDL 91207 564-F2
DEL RIO AV
800 SGBL 91776 596-F4

DEL RIO AV
1000 LA 90065 594-J5
DEL RIO CT
- NRWK 90650 706-D7
- NRWK 90650 736-D1
DEL RIO PL
16900 GmH 91344 481-C6
18700 CRTS 90703 766-E2
DEL RIO WY
600 FUL 92835 738-G3
9700 CYP 90630 767-E7
DEL ROBLES DR
6300 VeCo 93063 499-C4
DEL ROBLES PL
1000 VeCo 93063 499-C4
DEL ROSA DR
400 PAS 91105 565-G5
DELROSA DR
2000 Eagl 90041 565-A6
DEL ROSA PL
600 POM 91768 640-F1
DEL ROSA RD
100 Llan 93544 4471-J2
100 SBdC 92372 4471-J2
200 SBdC 92372 (4472-A2 See Page 4471)
2800 SBdC 92371 (4472-F2 See Page 4471)
6500 BPK 90621 767-G1
DEL SERRA CIR
5100 LPMA 90623 767-C4
DEL SOL CIR
5100 LPMA 90623 767-C4
DEL SOL CT
- Boyl 90033 634-J4
N DEL SOL LN
200 DBAR 91765 640-D5
S DEL SOL LN
200 DBAR 91765 640-D6
DEL SOL FIRE RD
- PVE 90274 792-H4
DEL SUR AV
800 LHB 90631 708-D7
DEL SUR CIR
5100 LPMA 90623 767-C4
DEL SUR ST
12900 LA 91340 482-D6
13400 LA 91340 502-C1
13700 Pcma 91331 502-B1
DEL SUR RIDGE RD
- LACo 91390 4281-J5
- LACo 91390 (4282-E1 See Page 4281)
- LACo 91390 (4371-H1 See Page 4281)
- LACo 91390 4461-B1
DELTA AV
400 BREA 92821 708-J6
2000 LBCH 90810 795-B2
2400 RSMD 91770 636-G1
3500 LBCH 90810 765-B7
3600 RSMD 91770 596-G6
6600 NLB 90805 735-B7
DELTA CT
8300 LACo 91770 636-G4
DELTA DR
24200 DBAR 91765 680-D3
DELTA LN
- PMDL 93551 4195-J3
100 ARCD 91007 597-C2
DELTA PL
800 CLAR 91711 601-B2
3000 RSMD 91770 636-G1
DELTA ST
1200 LACo 91770 636-G4
1600 Echo 90026 594-E6
7800 RSMD 91770 636-G4
N DELTA ST
5400 LACo 91776 596-F4
5400 SGBL 91776 596-F4
S DELTA ST
1400 SGBL 91776 596-G6
DELTA WY
- PMDL 93551 4195-D7
DELUNA DR
3000 RPV 90275 823-F5
DELVALE ST
15100 LACo 91744 638-D3
W DELVALE ST
1200 WCOV 91790 638-C3
DEL VALLE AV
400 INDS 91744 638-E5
400 LPUE 91744 638-E5
1200 LACo 91744 638-E5
1600 GLDL 91208 534-H6
DEL VALLE DR
6100 LA 90048 633-B3
DEL VALLE RD
29000 Cstc 91384 4459-D6
DEL VALLE ST
5300 WdHl 91364 559-J2
22000 WdHl 91364 560-A3
DEL VINA ST
2700 PAS 91107 566-F3
DEL VISTA DR
2600 HacH 91745 678-B5
12100 LMRD 90638 707-G7
DELWOOD ST
30000 Cstc 91384 4459-A6
DEL ZURO DR
7400 LA 90046 593-C1
DEMANDA RD
14600 LMRD 90638 737-E3

DEMARET CT
- LHB 90631 738-C2
DEMARET PL
16600 GmH 91344 481-D6
DEMBLON ST
13300 BALD 91706 598-A4
DEMETER AV
19100 CRTS 90703 766-H3
DE MILLE DR
1900 LFlz 90027 593-J3
DE MINA ST
20900 WdHl 91364 560-C3
DEMING AV
8700 DWNY 90241 706-B6
13100 DWNY 90242 735-J2
13200 DWNY 90242 736-A2
DEMPSEY AV
4400 Enc 91436 561-G3
6400 VanN 91406 531-G4
8300 LA 91343 531-F1
8800 LA 91343 501-F4
10300 GmH 91344 501-F2
DEMPSTER AV
13400 DWNY 90242 735-J2
DENA ST
- PMDL 93551 4196-E7
11400 ART 90701 766-G1
DENAIR ST
3600 PAS 91107 566-H1
11300 Brwd 90049 631-H2
DENARA ST
- PMDL 93550 4286-H4
DENBIGH DR
9800 LA 90210 592-C1
DENBO ST
8000 PRM 90723 735-H2
DENBY AV
2700 LA 90039 594-F4
DENBY CT
6500 SIMI 93063 499-C2
DE NEVE DR
200 LA 90095 631-J1
200 LA 90095 632-A1
DE NEVE LN
1300 Boyl 90033 635-C3
DENFIELD ST
43400 LACo 93536 4104-J2
DENHAM DR
3300 PMDL 93551 4195-B3
DENHOLM DR
12000 ELMN 91732 637-E2
DENISE CIR
7700 LPMA 90623 767-B3
DENISE CT
1300 BREA 92821 708-J4
DENISE LN
- LACo 91390 4461-A4
8300 LA 91304 529-G2
DENISE PL
24400 SCTA 91321 4640-E2
DENISE ST
700 LACo 93551 4285-G3
3300 LAN 93536 4015-B7
S DENISON AV
2400 SPed 90731 824-B7
2600 SPed 90731 854-B1
DENISON ST
1700 POM 91766 640-E3
S DENISON ST
2400 SPed 90731 824-B7
DENIVELLE CT
7600 Tuj 91042 503-J1
DENIVELLE PL
11200 Tuj 91042 503-H1
DENIVELLE RD
7700 Tuj 91042 503-H1
7800 Sunl 91040 503-H1
DENKER AV
1300 LA 90018 633-J7
3400 LA 90018 673-J1
3700 LA 90062 673-J3
20300 LA 90501 763-J5
22500 LA 90501 793-J1
S DENKER AV
5800 LA 90062 673-J7
5800 LA 90047 673-J7
7200 LA 90047 703-J2
10000 LACo 90047 703-J6
12000 LACo 90047 733-J1
14300 GAR 90247 733-J4
17800 GAR 90248 763-J1
18200 LA 90248 763-J2
21300 LA 90501 763-J2
DENLEY ST
14400 HacH 91745 677-J1
15000 HacH 91745 678-A1
DENMAN AV
1500 CMRC 90022 676-B3
DENMEAD ST
2000 LKWD 90712 765-G3
5800 LKWD 90713 766-C3
DENMORE AV
43000 LAN 93535 4106-B2
44200 LAN 93535 4016-B5
DENNI ST
7800 CRTS 90703 767-B4
7800 LPMA 90623 767-B4
8200 CYP 90630 767-B4
E DENNI ST
100 Wilm 90744 794-E5
W DENNI ST
100 Wilm 90744 794-C6

DENNING AV
1500 DUAR 91010 568-B6
DENNIS AV
2400 CMRC 90040 675-F3
DENNIS DR
8700 RSMD 91770 636-G1
DENNIS LN
7200 CanP 91307 529-F5
W DENNIS PL
1500 WCOV 91790 598-E7
DENNIS RD
22800 TOR 90505 793-B1
DENNIS WY
9300 Chat 91311 499-F6
DENNISON ST
3800 LACo 90023 675-D1
E DENNISON ST
6000 ELA 90022 675-J2
6000 ELA 90022 676-A2
DENNIS RANCH RD
34800 Actn 93510 4375-D3
DENNY AV
4000 LA 91604 563-A5
4200 LA 91602 563-A5
4800 NHol 91601 563-A1
6000 NHol 91606 533-A7
6600 NHol 91605 533-A4
7300 SunV 91352 533-A4
DENNY RD
25200 TOR 90505 793-E4
DE NOVA ST
600 LCF 91011 535-C3
DENOYA DR
27300 SCTA 91350 4460-J5
DENROCK AV
7400 Wch 90045 702-F1
DENSLOW AV
100 Brwd 90049 631-J1
400 Wwd 90024 631-J2
DENSMORE AV
4300 Enc 91436 561-G3
6400 VanN 91406 531-F3
8300 LA 91343 531-F2
8800 LA 91343 501-F4
10300 GmH 91344 501-F2
DENSMORE ST
900 POM 91767 601-C7
DENTON AV
1900 SGBL 91776 596-E7
2300 RSMD 91770 636-F3
12800 LA 91342 482-A4
DENVER AV
1600 CLAR 91711 601-E1
1700 CLAR 91711 571-E7
3400 LBCH 90810 765-B7
3400 LBCH 90810 795-B1
5800 LA 90044 674-B6
8600 LA 90044 704-B3
12300 LA 90044 734-B1
15400 LA 90248 734-B6
S DENVER AV
14300 LA 90248 734-B4
17400 LA 90248 764-C1
DENVER CT
37500 PMDL 93552 4286-J3
DENVER ST
4200 MTCL 91763 601-E6
7800 PRM 90723 735-G2
DENVER SPRINGS DR
32900 WLKV 91361 586-J1
DENVIEW DR
42900 LACo 93532 4102-F4
DENWALL DR
800 CRSN 90746 764-E4
DEODAR
- LA 91342 481-G1
DEODAR AV
2100 WCOV 91791 599-A7
DEODAR CIR
300 SMAD 91024 566-J1
2500 PAS 91107 566-E3
DEODAR LN
- MNRO 91016 567-J4
- BRAD 91010 567-J4
- BRAD 91010 568-A3
800 LACo 91010 568-B4
4800 WdHl 91364 560-E4
DEODAR PL
28800 SCTA 91390 4460-J2
DEODAR RD
- SMRO 91108 566-C7
2300 POM 91767 601-A4
DEODAR ST
5400 MTCL 91763 601-H5
W DEODAR ST
1300 ONT 91762 601-H5
DEODARA DR
300 Alta 91001 535-J5
600 Alta 91001 536-A6
DEODARA ST
- Boyl 90033 634-J4
DEODAR WEST
- BRAD 91010 567-J3
DEODORA AV
100 COMP 90220 734-F4
14900 LACo 90220 734-F4
DEOLINDA DR
2900 HacH 91745 678-B6
DEON PL
12700 GmH 91344 481-B5
E DE ORA WY
3900 LBCH 90815 795-J4
3900 LBCH 90815 796-A4

DE ORO CIR
17800 CRTS 90703 737-D7
DE ORO CT
17400 CRTS 90703 737-D7
DE ORO PL
17600 CRTS 90703 737-D7
DE PALMA ST
6000 DWNY 90241 705-J5
6000 SGAT 90280 705-G4
8000 DWNY 90241 706-A6
DE PALMA WY
700 MTBL 90640 676-E1
DE PAUL RD
300 CLAR 91711 601-C4
DE PAUW ST
15200 PacP 90272 631-A6
DEPOT CT
- FUL 92832 738-H7
DEPUTY JAKE DR
- SCTA 91321 4641-B1
DEPUTY YAMAMOTO PL
11600 LYN 90262 704-J7
DE QUINCY CT
24100 LA 91304 529-D3
DE QUINCY PL
- StvR 91381 4550-A7
S DEQUINE AV
2700 RSMD 91770 636-D2
DERBY CIR
4000 LAN 93536 4105-A7
4100 LAN 93536 4104-J7
4500 LVRN 91750 570-F7
DERBY CT
1600 PMDL 93551 4195-F5
DERBY LN
15500 LMRD 90638 737-H1
DERBY PL
22700 SCTA 91350 4550-J5
DERBY RD
500 SDMS 91773 599-J3
DERBYSHIRE LN
- CRTS 90703 767-A3
DEREK CT
1200 WCOV 91792 638-H5
DEREK DR
800 ARCD 91006 567-F7
DEREK LN
11700 SunV 91352 502-G7
DERIAN DR
24400 SCTA 91321 4640-H2
N DERN AV
1900 COMP 90059 734-E2
DE ROJA AV
5300 WdHl 91364 560-A2
DERONDA DR
3100 LA 90068 563-G7
3100 LA 90068 593-F1
DERRICK DR
38400 LACo 93591 4198-F7
DERRINGER LN
1500 DBAR 91765 680-D5
DERRY AV
5300 AGRH 91301 558-B6
DERRY ST
800 LHB 90631 708-D7
DERWENT AV
12200 Nor 91326 480-G6
DERWENT PL
19100 Nor 91326 480-G6
DERWIN DR
15000 LMRD 90638 737-G2
DERWOOD DR
2000 LCF 91011 504-J6
N DE SALES ST
500 SGBL 91775 596-D2
DE SANTIS AV
12700 LA 91342 481-G5
DESCANSO AV
200 AVA 90704 5923-H4
6200 BPK 90620 737-E7
6300 BPK 90620 767-E1
DESCANSO BAY
300 LBCH 90803 826-C1
DESCANSO CIR
6200 BPK 90620 737-E7
DESCANSO DR
900 LCF 91011 535-A4
1900 LHH 90631 708-G3
3200 Echo 90026 594-C6
DESCANSO MTWY
3600 GLDL 91208 534-J4
3600 GLDL 91208 535-A5
3600 LCF 91011 534-J4
3600 LCF 91011 535-A5
DESCANSO PL
2300 GLDL 91208 534-G7
DESCANSO RD
11400 SBdC 92372 (4472-A2 See Page 4471)
DESCANSO ST
7400 DWNY 90242 705-G7
DESCANSO WY
2200 TOR 90504 763-G1
DESCENDING DR
2900 HacH 91745 677-H3
DESERET DR
4400 WdHl 91364 559-G4
DESERT AV
24500 SCTA 91321 4641-B1
DESERT PL
27700 Cstc 91384 4459-G4
DESERT RD
33800 Actn 93510 4375-E5

DESERTA DR
1800 GLDR 91740 569-J7
DESERT AIRE AV
4000 PMDL 93552 4286-J1
DESERT CALICO DR
700 LAN 93534 4015-G3
DESERT CANYON RD
500 BREA 92821 709-C6
DESERT CREEK AV
2100 SIMI 93063 499-B2
DESERT FLOWER DR
38400 PMDL 93551 4285-G1
38400 PMDL 93551 4195-G7
DESERT FRONT RD
1700 SBdC 92372 (4562-C3 See Page 4471)
2100 SBdC (4562-D4 See Page 4471)
DESERT GARDEN DR
- SMRO 91108 566-D7
DESERT HAWK DR
- PMDL 93552 4287-D1
DESERT HAZE RD
- LACo 93591 4200-B2
DESERT HILLS DR
42100 LAN 93536 4104-E5
DESERT HOLY LN
- PMDL 93551 4195-D6
DESERT LILLY CT
- PMDL 93551 4195-D5
DESERT OAK DR
2300 PMDL 93550 4286-E5
DESERT POPPY RD
18800 LACo 93591 4200-B2
DESERT ROSE DR
- LAN 93536 4105-A5
29900 Cstc 91384 4459-H3
DESERT ROSE ST
- PMDL 93551 4195-D5
DESERT SAGE AV
- LAN 93536 4105-D6
DESERT SHADOW RD
30700 Cstc 91384 4459-B1
31000 Cstc 91384 4369-B7
DESERT SPRINGS DR
45800 LAN 93534 4015-G3
DESERT SPRINGS RD
- LACo 93551 4285-J7
DESERT STAR RD
29200 Llan 93544 4471-C5
DESERT VIEW CT
5300 SBdC 92397 (4652-E3 See Page 4651)
DESERT VIEW DR
5200 SBdC 92397 (4652-E3 See Page 4651)
DESERT VIEW LN
- SBdC 92397 (4652-E4 See Page 4651)
DESERT VIEW RD
8300 SBdC 92372 (4562-C1 See Page 4471)
9300 SBdC 92372 (4472-C1 See Page 4471)
DESERT VISTA
- LACo 93534 3925-D4
- LACo 93536 3925-D4
DESERT VISTA DR
- LACo 93591 4200-B2
DESERT WILLOW DR
- AZU 91702 569-A4
36800 PMDL 93550 4286-E4
DESERT WILLOW LN
1300 DBAR 91765 680-B3
36800 PMDL 93550 4286-E3
DESFORD DR
2000 LA 90210 592-D3
E DESFORD ST
300 CRSN 90745 764-D6
W DESFORD ST
100 CRSN 90745 764-C6
1100 LACo 90502 764-A6
DESHIRE PL
10700 CULC 90230 672-H4
DESIDIA ST
18200 RowH 91748 678-J4
18200 RowH 91748 679-A4
DESIRE AV
1700 RowH 91748 679-B5
DESMAN RD
14800 LMRD 90638 737-F6
DES MOINES AV
10400 Nor 91326 500-F3
DESMOND ST
12800 Pcma 91331 482-E6
13200 Pcma 91331 502-C1
DESMOND ESTATES RD
2600 LA 90046 593-C2
DE SOTO AV
5300 WdHl 91367 560-B1
6000 WdHl 91367 530-C7
6300 CanP 91303 530-C4
7500 LA 91304 530-C4
8900 LA 91304 500-C7
8900 Chat 91311 500-C7
E DE SOTO ST
2700 LBCH 90814 795-H7
DE SOTO WY
11200 MTCL 91763 641-E3
DESPERADO DR
2200 CHLS 91709 680-G5

STREET
Block City ZIP Pg-Grid

DES PLAIN PL
10600 Chat 91311 500-D3
DESSIE PL
800 POM 91768 600-G7
D ESTE DR
13500 PacP 90272 631-D3
DESTINO CIR
10600 CRTS 90703 736-E7
DESTINO LN
13000 CRTS 90703 737-B7
DESTINO PL
13100 CRTS 90703 737-B7
DESTINO ST
10200 BLF 90706 736-D7
12400 CRTS 90703 736-J7
12500 CRTS 90703 737-A7
DESTOYA AV
1400 RowH 91748 678-J4
DETER ST
40500 LACo 93535 4200-C1
DETOUR DR
2400 LA 90068 593-G2
DETROIT CT
13000 CHNO 91710 641-E7
N DETROIT ST
100 LA 90036 633-D1
300 LA 90036 593-D7
700 LA 90046 593-D4
1100 WHWD 90046 593-D5
S DETROIT ST
100 LA 90036 633-D1
DEUKMEJIAN DR
4600 LBCH 90804 796-A6
DEVANAH ST
100 COV 91722 599-A3
15400 BALD 91706 598-E3
16500 LACo 91722 598-G3
DEVELL RD
26000 SCTA 91387 4552-E7
DEVENIR AV
8000 DWNY 90242 735-H1
DEVENIR ST
7800 DWNY 90242 705-H7
7900 DWNY 90242 735-J1
DEVENTER DR
1500 LVRN 91750 570-F6
DEVERE CT
18200 LACo 93532 4101-H2
E DEVERE CT
18000 LACo 93532 4101-J2
DEVERON CT
1100 SDMS 91773 599-J4
DEVERON DR
10200 WHIT 90601 677-A3
DEVERON PL
1200 POM 91767 601-C7
DEVERON RIDGE RD
6900 CanP 91307 529-E5
W DEVERS ST
1200 WCOV 91790 638-D1
DEVILLE ST
37400 PMDL 93552 4287-C3
DEVILLE WY
23900 MAL 90265 628-J7
DEVILLO DR
10300 LACo 90604 707-D5
DEVILS CANYON MTWY
- Chat 91311 480-A7
- Chat 91311 499-J1
21400 Chat 91311 500-A1
DEVILS CANYON DAM
TKTR
- LACo - 507-G7
- LACo - (508-C5
See Page 507)
- LACo - 509-A5
DEVILS GATE RES SHR
- PAS 91011 535-E5
- PAS 91103 535-E5
DEVILS PUNCHBOWL RD
27900 Pear 93553 (4559-D1
See Page 4470)
28400 Pear 93553 4469-B6
28700 Valy 93563 4469-B6
DEVILS PUNCHBOWL
RD Rt#-N6
29300 Pear 93553 4469-A6
29300 Valy 93563 4469-A6
DEVIRIAN PL
400 Alta 91001 535-G4
DEVISTA DR
7500 LA 90046 593-B2
DEVISTA PL
2600 LA 90046 593-B2
DEVLIN AV
14300 NRWK 90650 736-H4
17900 ART 90701 766-H1
20300 LKWD 90715 766-H4
21700 HGDN 90716 766-H6
DEVLIN DR
1300 LA 90069 592-H5
DEVLIN PL
8900 LA 90069 592-H5
DEVOL ST
44200 LAN 93535 4016-C7
DEVON AV
700 Wwd 90024 632-C2
DEVON CIR
3200 HNTB 92649 826-J7
4100 CYP 90630 767-A7
8600 LPMA 90623 767-C5
DEVON CT
- GLDR 91741 569-C5
DEVON LN
28000 SCTA 91350 4461-B5
DEVON PL
500 Bxby 90807 765-C6
1200 DBAR 91765 680-D3
DEVON RD
1600 PAS 91103 535-E7
DEVONPORT LN
- Tarz 91356 560-G6
2400 BelA 90077 591-G3
DEVONPORT RD
2500 SMRO 91108 566-E6
DEVONSHIRE CT
22600 SCTA 91350 4550-J5
DEVONSHIRE DR
6000 PMDL 93551 4104-F6
DEVONSHIRE LN
400 GLDL 91206 565-B4
1200 LHB 90631 738-F1
2400 Alta 91001 536-A6
DEVONSHIRE ST
10300 Chat 91311 499-J4
14600 Pcma 91331 502-A4
14700 MsnH 91345 501-H4
14700 MsnH 91345 502-A4
15600 GrnH 91344 501-D4
17000 Nor 91325 501-A4
17900 Nor 91330 501-A4
17900 Nor 91326 501-A4
17900 Nor 91325 500-H4
18100 Nor 91326 500-H4
18300 Nor 91324 500-H4
19600 Chat 91311 500-B4
DEVONSHIRE WY
- RowH 91748 708-J2
DEVONWOOD RD
400 Alta 91001 536-A3
DEVORE CT
5500 AGRH 91301 558-C5
DE VOSS AV
18700 CRTS 90703 767-A2
W DE VOY DR
2800 ANA 92804 767-J7
DE VRIES LN
8000 LPMA 90623 767-D4
DEVYN LN
43600 LAN 93535 4106-G1
DEWAP RD
100 LA 90012 634-F3
DEWAR ST
3200 MTBL 90640 636-A6
3400 MTBL 90640 635-J6
5200 ELA 90022 635-J6
DEWBERRY CT
2000 THO 91361 557-A5
DEWBERRY TER
- PMDL 93551 4285-D4
DEWCREST CT
- SBdC 91710 641-C4
DEWDROP AV
27300 SCTA 91351 4551-G3
DEWDROP CT
- PMDL 93552 4287-A5
DEWEY AV
- LACo 90073 631-J4
100 SGBL 91776 596-E7
900 LA 90006 634-A4
21700 TOR 90503 763-B6
DEWEY CIR
100 MTBL 90640 676-E1
DEWEY PL
1700 SMCA 90405 671-H3
DEWEY ST
500 Ven 90291 671-J3
500 SMCA 90405 671-G4
12000 LA 90066 672-B2
13100 LA 90066 671-J3
DEWEY WY
- UPL 91786 601-F2
DE WITT DR
3200 LA 90068 563-D7
DE WOLFE RD
25000 SCTA 91321 4640-F1
N DEXFORD DR
100 LHB 90631 708-B5
S DEXFORD DR
100 LHB 90631 708-B6
DEXTER AL
1300 PAS 91103 565-E1
DEXTER AV
1100 ARCD 91006 566-J3
DEXTER DR
27800 SCTA 91350 4460-J4
DEXTER MTWY
- LACo 91342 482-J6
DEXTER ST
900 HiPk 90042 595-A2
14900 BALD 91706 598-D5
E DEXTER ST
100 COV 91723 599-C5
1300 COV 91724 599-E5
19500 LACo 91724 599-D5
N DEXTER ST
300 LHB 90631 708-G5
S DEXTER ST
100 LHB 90631 708-G6
W DEXTER ST
100 COV 91723 599-B5
DEXTER PARK RD
12500 LACo 91342 482-J6
DIABLO CT
37800 PMDL 93550 4286-A2
DIABLO DR
600 CLAR 91711 571-C6
DIABLO PL
29100 Cstc 91384 4459-H6
DIAL AV
300 LPUE 91744 678-E1
DIAMANTE DR
16600 Enc 91436 561-E6
DIAMANTE PL
3800 Enc 91436 561-D6
DIAMANTE RD
100 PMDL 93550 4195-J3
DIAMOND
- BREA 92823 710-C6
700 AZU 91702 598-H1
DIAMOND AV
900 SPAS 91030 595-H3
DIAMOND CIR
7200 LPMA 90623 767-D2
DIAMOND CT
- CRTS 90703 767-A3
1500 DBAR 91789 679-G4
DIAMOND DR
2400 CHLS 91709 680-J1
DIAMOND LN
21800 Cstc 91384 4369-H6
DIAMOND PL
- SCTA 91350 4551-B4
500 WAL 91789 639-C7
DIAMOND ST
- ARCD 91006 567-D6
- RBCH 90277 763-A4
300 RBCH 90277 762-J4
500 MNRO 91016 567-F6
900 LA 90012 634-E3
4000 PMDL 93552 4286-J3
4700 PMDL 93552 4287-A3
DIAMONDALE DR
700 CRSN 90746 764-E4
DIAMONDBACK RD
6100 Actn 93510 4374-E5
DIAMOND BAR BLVD
1200 DBAR 91765 680-B4
2200 DBAR 91765 679-H7
N DIAMOND BAR BLVD
200 DBAR 91765 640-C5
300 POM 91765 640-C5
S DIAMOND BAR BLVD
200 DBAR 91765 640-B7
400 DBAR 91765 680-C1
DIAMOND CANYON RD
- DBAR 91765 679-G7
- LACo 91765 679-G7
- LACo 91765 709-G1
DIAMOND CREST LN
20900 DBAR 91789 679-G4
21000 DBAR 91765 679-G4
DIAMOND HEAD
- SCTA 91321 4641-C2
DIAMONDHEAD LN
26800 RPV 90275 793-B7
DIAMOND KNOLL LN
1800 DBAR 91765 680-C4
DIAMOND POINT RD
5200 LCF 91011 535-E3
DIAMOND RANCH RD
- DBAR 91765 640-F7
- POM 91766 640-F7
DIAMOND RIDGE RD
2900 DBAR 91765 679-H7
DIAMOND VALLEY LN
1600 CHLS 91709 680-G3
DIAMOND VIEW LN
31800 LACo 91390 4462-H1
DIAMONTE LN
- RPV 90275 823-G5
DIANA AV
800 POM 91766 641-B6
DIANA CT
30100 AGRH 91301 557-H5
W DIANA CT
1200 UPL 91786 601-J1
DIANA PL
300 FUL 92833 738-D7
DIANA ST
2700 PAS 91107 566-F5
3100 LA 90020 634-A1
DIANE AV
16500 BLF 90706 736-A6
DIANE DR
5900 LVRN 91750 570-F5
E DIANE DR
1600 COMP 90221 735-B2
DIANE PL
1000 WCOV 91792 638-G5
DIANE WY
100 MONP 91755 636-B3
2000 LA 90046 592-J3
DIANE MARIE CIR
27400 SCTA 91350 4461-B7
DIANORA DR
3100 RPV 90275 823-F5
DIANRON RD
38800 PMDL 93551 4195-F6
39000 LACo 93551 4195-F6
N DIANTHUS ST
100 MANB 90266 732-G6
S DIANTHUS ST
100 MANB 90266 732-G7
DIAZ DR
26600 SCTA 91350 4550-J1
DIAZ ST
5400 IRW 91706 598-F2
DICE RD
8500 SFSP 90670 706-J3
DICHA
2300 LA 90732 823-G7
DICKASON DR
- BqtC 91354 4460-E5
- SCTA 91355 4460-E7
DICKENS CT
25800 StvR 91381 4550-D7
DICKENS LN
700 LVRN 91750 600-D2
DICKENS ST
12900 LA 91604 562-D5
14000 Shrm 91423 562-A5
14400 Shrm 91403 562-A5
14500 Shrm 91403 561-G4
15400 Enc 91436 561-E4
19600 Tarz 91356 560-F2
DICKERMAN PL
2200 POM 91766 641-A5
DICKERSON AV
100 City 90063 635-E6
DICKS ST
8900 WHWD 90069 592-H6
DICKSON AV
1200 City 90063 635-D3
DICKSON CT
19900 WAL 91789 679-E2
W DICKSON CT
- LA 90095 632-B1
DICKSON LN
8000 LA 90046 593-A3
DICKSON ST
800 LA 90292 672-A6
DICKY ST
9400 PRV 90660 676-G5
10900 LACo 90606 676-J6
11400 LACo 90606 677-A7
13300 LACo 90605 707-C3
14800 LACo 90604 707-E5
DICTURN ST
2700 LA 90065 564-H7
DIEHL ST
20100 WAL 91789 679-E1
20200 WAL 91789 639-E7
DIGBY AV
900 POM 91767 601-B4
DIJON LN
39400 PMDL 93551 4195-C5
DIKE ST
19000 GLDR 91740 599-C1
DILL PL
6100 WdHl 91367 559-E1
DILLARD AV
3600 CLAR 91711 571-D5
DILLER AV
11300 CULC 90230 672-G5
DILLERDALE ST
14000 LACo 91746 638-B1
DILLING ST
11200 LA 91602 562-H5
11200 LA 91604 562-H5
DILLMAN ST
6500 LKWD 90713 766-E2
DILLON CT
700 Ven 90291 671-H4
DILLON ST
400 Echo 90026 594-C5
N DILLON ST
100 Echo 90026 634-B1
300 Echo 90026 594-B7
S DILLON ST
100 LA 90057 634-B1
DILLOW DR
2300 HacH 91745 678-F5
DILO ST
10600 ELMN 91731 597-C6
DILWORTH ST
12700 NRWK 90650 737-A2
13800 LMRD 90638 737-D2
DIMAS CT
1600 AZU 91702 568-J3
DIMMICK AV
200 Ven 90291 671-G4
DIMMICK DR
500 LA 90065 595-A3
DIMONDALE DR
1100 CRSN 90746 764-F4
1600 CRSN 90746 764-G4
1600 CRSN 90746 764-H4
DINA PL
18300 CRTS 90703 767-A1
19800 Chat 91311 500-E4
DINARD AV
13800 SFSP 90670 737-B3
14300 NRWK 90650 737-B4
DINCARA RD
1000 BURB 91506 563-G3
DINO CT
24300 CALB 91302 559-D5
DINSDALE ST
7300 DWNY 90240 706-A2
DINWIDDIE ST
7000 DWNY 90241 705-H3
DIONE WY
2700 RowH 91748 679-B7
DIRECTORS DR
- SMRO 91108 566-C6
DIRK CIR
5400 LPMA 90623 767-D3
DISCOVERY DR
37600 PMDL 93550 4286-G2
DISCOVERY PL
- RowH 91748 679-C4
DISCOVERY WY
1900 SIGH 90755 795-H4
DISCOVERY CREEK
- LA 90094 702-D1
DISCOVERY RIDGE DR
- LACo 91390 4461-A1
DISNEY AV
8200 LACo 90606 706-J1
14300 NRWK 90650 736-J3
DISTRIBUTION WY
15900 CRTS 90703 737-C5
DISTRICT BLVD
4100 VER 90058 675-B4
5100 VER 90040 675-E5
5100 MYWD 90270 675-F6
6000 MYWD 90201 675-F6
DISTRICT CT
- FUL 92832 738-H7
N DITMAN AV
100 City 90063 635-D3
1800 LA 90032 635-D1
2400 LA 90032 595-D7
S DITMAN AV
100 City 90063 635-D6
600 LACo 90023 635-D7
900 LACo 90023 675-D1
DITSON ST
10300 Sunl 91040 503-B6
DITTMAR DR
13200 WHIT 90602 707-C2
13400 WHIT 90605 707-D2
14300 WHIT 90603 707-G5
DITWOOD PL
1300 LHB 90631 738-E1
DIVAN PL
12600 NHol 91605 532-E3
DIVER ST
16500 LACo 91387 4552-B5
DIVERSEY DR
5400 RPV 90275 793-A5
DIVIDE TER
8300 LA 91304 529-E2
DIVIDE TR
1300 LACo 90704 5923-E5
DIVINA ST
4300 WdHl 91364 560-B5
S DIVINA VISTA ST
700 MONP 91754 636-A4
DIVINE DR
2100 MONP 91754 635-J5
DIVINO
2400 LA 90732 823-F7
DIVINO DR
20100 LACo 91789 679-E4
DIVISION PL
4100 LA 90065 594-J2
DIVISION ST
- KeCo 93523 3835-H1
200 PMDL 93550 4285-J2
200 PMDL 93550 4286-A3
2800 LA 90065 594-J2
6200 SBdC 92397 (4652-B1
See Page 4651)
37900 PMDL 93551 4285-J1
38400 PMDL 93550 4195-J2
38400 PMDL 93551 4195-J2
41900 PMDL 93551 4105-J6
41900 PMDL 93550 4105-J6
42100 LAN 93534 4105-J1
42100 LAN 93535 4105-J1
44000 LAN 93534 4015-J2
44000 LAN 93535 4015-J2
45800 LACo 93535 4015-J2
46800 LACo 93535 3925-J5
46800 LACo 93534 4015-J2
46800 LACo 93535 3925-J5
E DIVISION ST
4300 LBCH 90803 826-A2
DIVONNE DR
20500 WAL 91789 679-F1
20500 WAL 91789 639-G7
DIVOT DR
5600 LVRN 91750 570-G4
DIX RD
900 SPed 90731 854-A1
DIX ST
1600 LA 90068 593-F3
DIXFORD LN
400 LACo 91744 638-G7
DIXIE DR
37600 PMDL 93550 4285-J2
37600 PMDL 93550 4286-A3
N DIXIE DR
1100 SDMS 91773 570-C7
DIXIE CANYON AV
3300 LA 90210 562-C7
3300 Shrm 91423 562-D5
DIXIE CANYON PL
3400 Shrm 91423 562-D6
DIXON AV
10100 ING 90303 703-F5
DIXON ST
100 AZU 91702 598-J1
300 COMP 90222 734-J1
400 COMP 90222 705-A7
400 COMP 90222 735-A1
1400 GLDL 91205 564-H5
1600 RBCH 90278 762-J1
DIXON TRAIL RD
5500 HIDH 91302 559-B3
DOAN DR
700 BURB 91506 533-F7
DOANE AV
500 CLAR 91711 601-C5
DOANE CANYON RD
- LACo 91342 (4723-G6
See Page 4643)
- Sunl 91040 (4723-G7
See Page 4643)
DOBBIN LN
- RHE 90274 793-D6
DOBBINS DR
500 SGBL 91775 596-D2
DOBBINS PL
13200 Brwd 90049 631-D4
DOBBS ST
2300 LA 90032 635-F1
DOBINSON ST
2600 Boyl 90033 635-C4
3100 LA 90063 635-C4
3100 City 90063 635-E4
DOBKIN AV
4900 Tarz 91356 560-J3
DOBLAS ST
45900 LACo 93536 4013-A3
DOBLE AV
22600 LACo 90502 794-B1
24300 Hrbr 90710 794-B3
25000 Hrbr 90710 794-B4
S DOBLE AV
20800 LACo 90502 764-B5
DOBSON WY
5100 CULC 90230 672-G4
DOCHAN CIR
100 MTBL 90640 676-E1
DOCK ST
3500 LBCH 90802 824-H2
DOCKWEILER DR
- SCTA 91321 4641-C2
DOCKWEILER PL
5300 LA 90019 633-C4
DOCKWEILER ST
4500 LA 90019 633-D4
DODDS AV
1200 City 90063 635-D4
5400 BPK 90621 737-H6
DODDS CIR
1200 City 90063 635-D3
DODGE AV
25300 Hrbr 90710 794-B5
DODGE CT
800 POM 91766 641-B6
E DODGE WY
2100 LBCH 90803 825-H1
DODRILL DR
15600 HacH 91745 678-B4
S DODSON AV
600 LA 90732 823-J5
DODSON ST
11000 ELMN 91733 637-D2
11400 ELMN 91732 637-D2
DODSWORTH AV
800 GLDR 91740 569-D7
4900 LACo 91724 599-D3
5500 GLDR 91740 599-D1
N DODSWORTH AV
200 COV 91724 599-D4
DOEBAY DR
- LACo 91390 4373-B3
DOESKIN PL
24200 DBAR 91765 640-D5
DOGWOOD
3500 WCOV 91792 679-J2
DOGWOOD AV
6500 KeCo 93560 3834-B2
DOGWOOD CT
500 BREA 92821 708-H6
25000 StvR 91381 4640-E2
DOGWOOD DR
700 LVRN 91750 570-D6
DOGWOOD LN
500 BREA 92821 709-A5
DOGWOOD PL
1500 HiPk 90042 565-C7
DOGWOOD RD
5500 SBdC 92397 (4652-E3
See Page 4651)
42500 LACo 93532 4102-G5
DOGWOOD ST
1200 UPL 91784 571-J3
DOHENY CT
4600 CHNO 91710 641-F7
DOHENY DR
4700 CHNO 91710 641-F7
N DOHENY DR
100 BHLS 90211 632-H1
100 LA 90048 632-H1
100 WHWD 90048 592-H7
100 WHWD 90048 632-H1
100 BHLS 90210 592-H7
100 BHLS 90210 632-H1
500 WHWD 90069 592-H7
1000 BHLS 90210 592-H4
S DOHENY DR
100 BHLS 90211 632-H1
100 LA 90048 632-H1
100 BHLS 90212 632-H3
1100 LA 90035 632-H4
DOHENY LN
36800 PMDL 93552 4287-B4
DOHENY PL
1300 LA 90069 592-H5
DOHENY RD
400 BHLS 90210 592-F6
9200 WHWD 90069 592-G6
DOIDGE CT
1200 LBCH 90813 795-F6
DOLAN AV
9700 DWNY 90240 706-C3
10300 DWNY 90241 706-B4
12000 DWNY 90242 706-A6
12400 DWNY 90242 705-J7
12400 DWNY 90242 735-J1
DOLAN ST
10300 DWNY 90241 706-B4
DOLAN WY
18300 SCTA 91387 4551-J2
DOLCE CT
- StvR 91381 4640-D1
DOLCEDO WY
10500 BelA 90077 592-A5
DOLE CT
500 DBAR 91765 640-E7
DOLE DR
- WLKV 91362 557-E5
DOLE PL
1100 LACo 93551 4195-G6
DOLLAR ST
2400 LKWD 90712 765-G3
DOLLISON DR
10700 DWNY 90241 706-F5
11500 NRWK 90650 706-G6
DOLLY AV
5500 BPK 90621 737-G6
16500 LMRD 90638 737-G6
DOLO WY
700 BelA 90077 592-A7
DOLOMITE AV
3000 PMDL 93550 4286-F5
DOLOMITE DR
2200 CHLS 91709 680-J7
DOLONITA AV
3100 HacH 91745 677-J5
3400 HacH 91745 678-A6
DOLORES
2400 LACo 90220 764-J1
2500 LACo 90220 765-A1
DOLORES AV
10500 SGAT 90280 704-J5
DOLORES DR
900 Alta 91001 536-A5
1000 FUL 92833 738-E5
DOLORES PL
- Actn 93510 4465-F1
DOLORES PZ
1100 PVE 90274 792-F6
DOLORES RD
1100 SPed 90731 824-A5
DOLORES ST
1000 LHB 90631 708-C4
2100 PAS 91107 566-D3
3000 GLDL 91204 594-E1
3000 LA 90065 594-E1
21000 CRSN 90745 764-D6
22300 CRSN 90745 794-D2
E DOLORES ST
400 Wilm 90744 794-F4
W DOLORES ST
1000 Wilm 90744 794-C4
DOLORITA AV
1000 GLDL 91208 534-F3
DOLOROSA ST
20700 WdHl 91367 560-C2
22200 WdHl 91367 559-F2
DOLPHIN
1900 LBCH 90810 765-A7
1900 LBCH 90810 795-A1
DOLPHIN AV
- SLB 90740 826-F5
2600 SPed 90731 853-J1
N DOLPHIN DR
200 LBCH 90803 826-E1
300 LBCH 90803 796-E7
DOLPHIN ST
1100 LA 90732 823-J6
S DOLPHIN ST
3700 SPed 90731 853-J1
DOLTON DR
27400 SCTA 91351 4551-F2
DOMAINE ST
8800 RSMD 91770 596-H5
DOMAL LN
3800 GLDL 91206 535-B6
3800 LCF 91011 535-B6
DOMAN AV
4900 Tarz 91356 561-A3
5100 Tarz 91356 560-J3
DOMART AV
12600 NRWK 90650 736-E1
DOME TR
21500 Top 90290 590-B5
DOMINGO
18000 LACo 90220 764-J1
W DOMINGO DR
700 SGBL 91775 596-C2
DOMINGO PL
500 FUL 92835 738-G2
DOMINGO RD
1300 FUL 92833 738-E5
1900 FUL 92835 738-F2
22400 WdHl 91364 559-J4
DOMINGUEZ AV
600 Wilm 90744 794-F6
DOMINGUEZ PL
200 AZU 91702 569-A7
DOMINGUEZ ST
100 CRSN 90745 764-C5
1800 TOR 90501 763-F5
2000 TOR 90501 763-F5
2400 TOR 90503 763-F5
E DOMINGUEZ ST
700 CRSN 90746 764-E5
1900 CRSN 90810 764-J5
2500 CRSN 90810 765-A5
2800 LBCH 90810 765-A5
DOMINGUEZ WY
2200 TOR 90501 763-G5
DOMINGUEZ HILLS DR
2500 COMP 90220 764-J2
18400 LACo 90220 764-J2
DOMINICA AV
10000 LA 91342 503-C1
DOMINION AV
1200 PAS 91104 566-C2
1300 LACo 91104 566-C2
DOMINION CIR
7200 CMRC 90040 676-A7
DOMINION WY
8000 LA 90046 593-A2
DOMINO ST
15100 VanN 91411 531-H7
18200 Res 91335 530-J7
DOMINO HILL DR
33500 LACo 91390 4373-D5
N DOMMER AV
100 WAL 91789 679-E1
100 WAL 91789 639-E7
S DOMMER AV
100 WAL 91789 679-E1
DOMO ST
9900 LACo 90601 677-A2
E DON ST
100 Wilm 90744 794-E4
W DON ST
1000 Wilm 90744 794-C4
DONA ALICIA PL
11600 LA 91604 562-H7
DONA CECILIA DR
11400 LA 91604 562-H7
DONA CHRISTINA PL
3100 LA 91604 562-H7
3100 LA 91604 592-H1
DONA CLARA PL
3100 LA 91604 563-A7
3100 LA 91604 593-A1
DONA CONCHITA PL
3100 LA 91604 562-J7
3100 LA 91604 592-H1
DONA DOLORES PL
11400 LA 91604 562-H7
DONA DOROTEA DR
11300 LA 91604 592-H1
DONA ELENA PL
3100 LA 91604 592-H1
DONA EMILIA DR
2900 LA 91604 592-J1
3100 LA 91604 562-J7
DONA EVITA DR
11400 LA 91604 562-H7
11400 LA 91604 592-J1
DONAHUE PL
4700 ELMN 91732 597-G5
DONAIRE WY
1100 PacP 90272 630-H4
DONA ISABEL DR
11200 LA 91604 592-J1
DON ALANIS PL
4200 LA 90008 673-D3
DON ALBERTO PL
4700 LA 90008 673-C4
DONALD PL
- POM 91766 641-A6
DONALDALE ST
14000 LACo 91746 638-B1
DONALD DOUGLAS DR
4100 LBCH 90808 796-A1
DONALD DOUGLAS LP N
- LA 90064 672-A2
- LA 90066 672-A2
2700 SMCA 90405 671-J3
2700 SMCA 90405 672-A2
DONALD DOUGLAS LP S
- SMCA 90405 671-J3
3100 LA 90066 672-A2
3100 SMCA 90405 672-A2
DONALDO CT
1100 SPAS 91030 595-H2
DONALDSON ST
1500 Echo 90026 594-F5
DON ALEGRE PL
4200 LA 90008 673-C3
DONA LISA DR
11200 LA 91604 562-J7
DONA LOLA DR
11200 LA 91604 562-J7
DONA LOLA PL
3300 LA 91604 562-J7
DON ALVARADO DR
1000 ARCD 91006 567-A4
DONA MARIA DR
3100 LA 91604 592-H1
3100 LA 91604 562-H7
DONA MARTA DR
3000 LA 91604 592-J1
3100 LA 91604 562-J7
DONA MEMA PL
3100 LA 91604 562-J7
3100 LA 91604 592-J1
DONA NENITA PL
3000 LA 91604 592-J1
DONA PEGITA DR
11100 LA 91604 593-A1
11100 LA 91604 562-J7
11100 LA 91604 563-A7
DONA PEPITA PL
11500 LA 91604 592-H1
DONA RAQUEL PL
3200 LA 91604 562-H7
DON ARELLANES DR
4200 LA 90008 673-D3
DONA ROSA DR
3300 LA 91604 562-J7
DON ARTURO PL
4500 LA 90008 673-C3
DONA SARITA PL
3100 LA 91604 562-J7
DONA SOFIA DR
3100 LA 91604 562-J7
3100 LA 91604 592-J1
3100 LA 91604 563-A7
DONA SUSANA DR
2900 LA 91604 592-J1
3000 LA 91604 562-J7
DONATELLO ST
1200 LAN 93535 4016-C6
DONA TERESA DR
11300 LA 91604 562-H7
DON BAPTISTA AV
300 LACo 91744 679-A1
DON BENITO CT
3700 PAS 91107 566-H1
DON CARLOS AV
1600 GLDL 91208 534-H6
DON CARLOS DR
4200 LA 90008 673-C3
DON COTA PL
4400 LA 90008 673-C3
DONCREST ST
200 MONP 91754 636-A5
DON DIABLO DR
1000 ARCD 91006 567-A4
3900 LA 90008 673-D3
DON DIEGO
8900 BPK 90620 767-G5
DON DIEGO DR
4500 LA 90008 673-C3
DONELLA CIR
2300 BelA 90077 591-H2
DONER DR
900 MTBL 90640 636-F7
DON FELIPE DR
3700 LA 90008 673-C3
DON GEE CT
21700 SCTA 91350 4461-B4
DONHILL DR
1400 LA 90210 592-E5
DONI RD
14200 LA 90402 631-C6
DON IBARRA PL
4500 LA 90008 673-C3
DONINGTON PL
9700 LA 90210 562-C7
DONINGTON ST
600 GLDR 91741 569-C4
W DONINGTON ST
900 GLDR 91741 569-C4
1000 LACo 91741 569-C4
DON JAY PL
7100 LACo 91775 566-H7
DON JOSE DR
1100 GLDL 91207 564-G2
4100 LA 90008 673-C3
DON JUAN PL
4800 WdHl 91364 560-E4
DON JULIAN RD
13100 LACo 91746 637-H4
14200 INDS 91746 637-H4
14400 INDS 91746 638-A6
15000 INDS 91745 638-A6
15200 INDS 91745 678-C1
E DON JULIO ST
6400 LBCH 90815 796-E3
DONLEY ST
800 LACo 91750 600-D1
DON LORENZO DR
4600 LA 90008 673-C4
DON LUIS DR
4000 LA 90008 673-D3
DON MARIANO DR
4100 LA 90008 673-D3
DONMAR RANCH RD
24700 LACo 90265 629-B3
DONMETZ ST
15500 MsnH 91345 501-G1
16300 GrnH 91344 501-A2
18100 Nor 91326 500-J2
DON MIGUEL DR
4400 LA 90008 673-C4
DON MILAGRO DR
4400 LA 90008 673-C3
DONNA
10900 MsnH 91345 501-H2
DONNA AV
5000 Tarz 91356 560-G1
6400 Res 91335 530-G5
8300 Nor 91324 530-G2
9300 Nor 91324 500-G4
10300 Nor 91326 500-G4
19500 CRTS 90703 766-F3
DONNA CT
19000 Res 91335 530-G4
DONNA DR
4700 LPMA 90623 767-B4
DONNA LN
- LACo 91390 4373-D6
DONNA ST
6600 NLB 90805 735-C7
DONNA WY
800 MTBL 90640 636-B7
DONNA ANTONIA AV
300 LACo 91744 679-A1
DONNA BETH AV
600 WCOV 91791 638-J2
600 AZU 91702 598-J2
5200 LACo 91702 598-J2
S DONNA BETH AV
1300 WCOV 91791 638-J3
DONNAGLEN AV
2000 SFER 91340 482-B5
DONNAGLEN LN
400 LHB 90631 708-D6
DONNA MARIA LN
5200 LCF 91011 535-A1
DONNA YNEZ LN
16900 PacP 90272 630-G5
DONNELLY AV
7200 LACo 91775 566-H7
DONNER AV
5400 BPK 90621 737-J6
DONNER CT
4500 MTCL 91763 641-E1
DONNER DR
600 WAL 91789 639-C7
DONNER PL
800 MONP 91754 635-J3
42600 LACo 93532 4102-F4
DONNIE ANN RD
3100 OrCo 90720 796-H3
DONNIS RD
11000 OrCo 90720 796-H3
DONNYBROOK AV
800 LHB 90631 708-F4
DONNYBROOK CIR
8400 LACo 90606 706-G1
DONNYBROOK RD
100 BREA 92821 709-D7
DONORA AV
19300 TOR 90503 763-B3
DON ORTEGA PL
4200 LA 90008 673-C3
DONOSA DR
2300 RowH 91748 678-H6
DONOVAN RD
11300 OrCo 90720 796-H4
DONOVAN ST
8200 DWNY 90242 705-J7
8400 DWNY 90242 706-A7
8700 DWNY 90242 736-A1
DON PABLO DR
1000 ARCD 91006 566-J4
DON PABLO PL
4500 LA 90008 673-C3
DON PIO CT
- WdHl 91364 560-A4
DON PIO DR
4500 WdHl 91364 560-A3
DON PORFIRIO PL
4700 LA 90008 673-C4
DON QUIXOTE DR
4500 LA 90008 673-C4
DON RICARDO DR
1000 ARCD 91006 566-J4
4400 LA 90008 673-C2
DON ROBLES DR
1000 ARCD 91006 567-A4
DON RODOLFO PL
4500 LA 90008 673-C3
DON TAPIA PL
4200 LA 90008 673-D3
DON TIMOTEO DR
4500 LA 90008 673-C4
DON TOMASO DR
3800 LA 90008 673-C3
DON TONITO DR
4500 LA 90008 673-C3
DON VALDES DR
4500 LA 90008 673-C3
DONWAY DR
20100 LACo 91789 679-F5
DON ZAREMBO DR
4400 LA 90008 673-C4
DOOLITTLE AV
2400 ARCD 91006 597-F1
DOOLITTLE DR
3600 RBCH 90278 733-A5
DORA CT
2200 SIMI 93063 499-B1
DORA ST
10500 SunV 91352 503-A7
10800 SunV 91352 533-A1
11100 SunV 91352 532-J1
DORADO CT
500 VeCo 91377 558-A1
DORADO DR
2000 RPV 90275 823-H3
16400 Enc 91436 561-E6
25600 SCTA 91355 4550-F6
DORADO PL
- RHE 90274 793-H6
DORA GUZMAN AV
500 LPUE 91744 678-G2
DORAL
12500 ELMN 91732 637-G1

STREET
Block City ZIP Pg-Grid

DORAL AV
11400 Nor 91326 500-G1
11600 Nor 91326 480-F7
DORAL LN
- PMDL 93551 4195-A3
DORAL PL
19100 Nor 91326 480-G7
DORAL ST
3400 LVRN 91750 600-F1
DORAL WY
- Tarz 91356 560-J6
DORAMA AV
- Actn 93510 4465-A1
32700 Actn 93510 4375-A7
DORAN PL
12300 NHol 91605 532-F4
DORAN ST
1000 SPAS 91030 595-F2
E DORAN ST
100 GLDL 91206 564-G4
W DORAN ST
100 GLDL 91203 564-D4
100 LA 90039 564-B4
4500 GLDL 91202 564-D4
DORA VERDUGO DR
3200 GLDL 91208 534-G5
DORAY CIR
2600 MNRO 91016 597-G1
DORCAS PL
6100 LA 90068 563-G7
DORCHESTER AV
1800 SMCA 90404 631-J7
2100 SMCA 90404 671-J1
2900 LA 90032 595-G6
DORCHESTER DR
19100 Nor 91324 500-E7
DORCHESTER LN
800 LHB 90631 738-F1
DORE DR
1800 HacH 91745 678-E4
DORE ST
1000 WCOV 91792 638-G5
DOREEN AV
1700 SELM 91733 637-B2
2600 ELMN 91733 637-B2
4600 ELMN 91731 597-C5
4800 TEML 91780 597-C4
DOREEN DR
9600 CYP 90630 767-F7
DOREEN PL
1000 Ven 90291 671-J4
DOREMUS RD
1200 PAS 91105 565-E7
DORER ST
37200 PMDL 93552 4287-E3
DORESTA RD
2700 PAS 91108 596-A1
2700 SMRO 91108 596-A1
DORIA AV
25000 LMTA 90717 793-H4
DORIA CT
25000 LMTA 90717 793-H4
DORIAN ST
15200 LA 91342 481-G2
DORIC ST
17400 GrnH 91344 481-B5
DORIE DR
7400 LA 91304 529-E4
DORILEE LN
16200 Enc 91436 561-E7
DORINA CT
4800 CHNO 91710 641-F7
DORINA PL
12600 GrnH 91344 481-C5
DORION ST
8700 DWNY 90242 735-J3
DORIS AV
8200 LACo 91775 596-G1
DORIS WY
5200 TOR 90505 793-A1
DORISGLEN LN
400 LHB 90631 708-D6
DORK ST
9300 PRV 90660 676-H2
DORLAND PL
6200 WHIT 90606 677-A5
6300 LACo 90606 677-A5
DORLAND ST
10400 LACo 90606 676-J5
10400 WHIT 90606 676-J5
10800 WHIT 90606 677-A5
11500 WHIT 90601 677-B5
DORLON DR
19000 Tarz 91356 560-G6
DORMAN AV
18200 TOR 90504 763-H2
DORMER RD
35600 LACo 91390 4373-H1
DORMIE PL
16900 Enc 91436 561-D4
DORMONT AV
24500 TOR 90505 793-G3
DORNER DR
1200 MONP 91754 635-H5
DORNES ST
11600 ART 90701 736-G6
DORNIE ST
19300 GLDR 91741 569-D6
DORO PL
3300 CALB 90290 589-G1
DOROTHEA RD
500 LHH 90631 708-E2

DOROTHY AV
1400 SIMI 93063 499-C3
8900 SGAT 90280 705-D5
10600 LYN 90262 705-D5
DOROTHY DR
400 FUL 92831 738-H6
1200 GLDL 91202 564-D2
26400 LACo 91302 588-G7
28000 AGRH 91301 558-C6
N DOROTHY DR
1500 BREA 92821 708-J4
W DOROTHY DR
1000 BREA 92821 708-J4
DOROTHY LN
500 FUL 92831 738-J5
DOROTHY RD
3300 CALB 90290 589-G1
DOROTHY ST
- CynC 91351 4461-D7
2000 WCOV 91792 639-A7
2300 LaCr 91214 504-H6
7800 RSMD 91770 636-E1
11700 Brwd 90049 631-G5
20000 SCTA 91351 4461-D7
DORRINGTON AV
8400 PanC 91402 532-C1
8600 Pcma 91331 532-C1
8700 WHWD 90048 592-H7
8800 Pcma 91331 502-A5
DORRINGTON PL
9200 Pcma 91331 502-A6
DORRIS PL
2200 LA 90031 594-G5
DORSET AV
1000 POM 91766 641-B4
11200 SBdC 91766 641-E3
11200 MTCL 91763 641-E3
DORSET CT
18000 RowH 91748 708-H2
DORSET DR
2500 TOR 90503 763-E4
4100 CYP 90630 767-A6
DORSET PL
4100 LCF 91011 535-D6
23300 Hrbr 90710 793-J2
DORSEY ST
4100 LA 90011 674-F3
DORSO RD
35100 Actn 93510 4374-H2
DORWOOD AV
1400 LHB 90631 738-E1
DORY CIR
16600 CRTS 90703 736-F6
DORY WY
500 SLB 90740 826-E3
DOSHIER AV
100 ARCD 91006 567-D2
DOSKE RD
- Tuj 91042 (4724-F5
See Page 4643)
DOS PALOS DR
3200 LA 90068 563-C7
3200 LA 90068 593-C1
DOS RIOS DR
7100 Tuj 91042 504-A2
DOS RIOS RD
6400 DWNY 90240 706-A1
DOS ROBLES PL
600 ALH 91801 595-J4
DOSS CT
13100 GrnH 91344 481-C4
DOSS TER
19200 Tarz 91356 560-G5
DOT AV
1800 LHB 90631 708-G5
DOT ST
20700 SCTA 91350 4461-C5
DOTTA LN
- WAL 91789 639-G6
DOTY AV
11400 HAW 90250 703-E7
11900 HAW 90250 733-E3
15100 LACo 90260 733-E5
17700 TOR 90504 763-E1
S DOTY AV
3800 HAW 90250 703-E6
10000 ING 90303 703-E5
DOUBLE ST
300 CRSN 90745 764-D6
1800 TOR 90501 763-H6
DOUBLE EAGLE DR
11500 LACo 90604 707-F7
DOUBLE EE RANCH RD
- WdHl 91364 560-C6
DOUBLEGROVE ST
900 WCOV 91790 638-E3
1600 LACo 91744 638-E3
13200 BALD 91706 597-J7
13700 BALD 91706 598-A7
17000 WCOV 91791 638-H3
E DOUBLEGROVE ST
1500 WCOV 91791 638-J4
W DOUBLEGROVE ST
14300 WCOV 91790 638-C2
DOUBLETREE LN
2300 RowH 91748 679-A6
N DOUBLE TREE LN
700 LBCH 90815 796-E6
DOUBLETREE RD
800 VeCo 91377 558-A1
DOUBLETREE WY
- Cstc 91384 4369-G7

DOUG RD
15100 SCTA 91387 4462-F5
DOUGLAS AL
- PAS 91103 565-C3
DOUGLAS AV
100 COMP 90222 734-J3
DOUGLAS CIR
7300 LPMA 90623 767-D2
DOUGLAS DR
1000 POM 91768 600-F7
DOUGLAS PL
800 Ven 90291 671-G5
DOUGLAS ST
100 Echo 90026 634-E2
200 PAS 91104 565-J2
500 PAS 91104 566-A2
1300 Echo 90026 594-F7
10600 ELMN 91731 597-C5
N DOUGLAS ST
100 ELSG 90245 732-J1
500 ELSG 90245 702-J7
S DOUGLAS ST
100 ELSG 90245 732-J2
DOUGLAS WK
- Cstc 91384 4459-D6
DOUGLAS FIR CT
5500 PMDL 93552 4287-C4
DOUGLAS FIR RD
5100 LACo 91302 559-E4
DOVE
200 POM 91767 601-A1
DOVE CIR
4800 LPMA 90623 767-C4
DOVE CT
1600 LACo 91107 566-F1
26500 SCTA 91351 4551-E4
DOVE LN
- StvR 91381 4640-C1
1400 FUL 92833 738-E5
DOVE PL
21300 Chat 91311 500-B2
DOVE RD
500 LA 90065 595-A3
DOVECOTE LN
- CRSN 90745 794-G2
DOVE CREEK LN
2600 LACo 91107 566-E1
DOVE HOUSE ST
17800 LACo 91387 4551-J4
DOVER AV
2000 LVRN 91750 600-G1
DOVER CIR
4100 CYP 90630 767-A6
DOVER CT
2200 RowH 91748 708-H2
DOVER DR
400 LHB 90631 708-E7
5100 LPMA 90623 767-C5
19100 Nor 91324 500-G7
39600 PMDL 93551 4195-F5
DOVER LN
- ING 90305 703-E3
DOVER PL
- MANB 90266 732-J5
1800 POM 91766 641-B4
3700 LA 90039 594-D1
DOVER RD
500 COV 91722 598-J5
4000 LCF 91011 535-D6
DOVER ST
500 GLDR 91740 599-F1
3400 LA 90039 594-D1
5400 CHNO 91710 641-G3
S DOVER ST
600 GLDR 91740 599-F1
DOVER WY
1100 MONP 91754 635-J4
DOVERDALE AV
400 LACo 91744 678-J2
DOVERFIELD AV
900 HacH 91745 637-J7
1000 HacH 91745 677-J2
DOVERGLEN WY
1800 HacH 91745 678-F6
DOVERRIDGE DR
28700 RPV 90275 792-H7
28700 RPV 90275 822-H1
DOVERWOOD CT
31900 WLKV 91361 557-C6
43200 LAN 93536 4105-C3
DOVERWOOD DR
900 GLDL 91207 564-G1
5800 CULC 90230 672-H7
DOVE SPRINGS DR
37700 PMDL 93550 4286-E5
DOVETAIL DR
5800 AGRH 91301 557-G4
DOVETAIL LN
- BRAD 91010 567-J3
DOVEWEED WY
26400 SCTA 91350 4551-B2
DOVE WILLOW ST
- LACo 91387 4552-A5
DOVEY AV
800 LACo 90601 637-G5
DOVEY DR
22100 LBCH 90808 766-G6
DOVLEN PL
900 CRSN 90746 764-E4
DOW AV
3000 RBCH 90278 733-B6
DOWEL AV
4500 PMDL 93552 4287-A2

DOWEL DR
6400 SIMI 93063 499-C2
DOWELL DR
28100 SCTA 91351 4461-E7
DOWLING AV
5500 PRV 90660 676-G4
DOWLING ST
- FUL 92833 738-D6
DOWNES RD
400 Brwd 90049 631-G1
DOWNEY AV
4500 LKWD 90712 765-J3
5800 NLB 90805 765-J2
6200 BLF 90706 765-J2
6300 NLB 90805 735-J7
8200 PRM 90723 735-J3
9200 DWNY 90242 706-C2
10100 DWNY 90241 706-B4
11900 DWNY 90242 706-A6
12200 DWNY 90242 705-J7
12600 DWNY 90242 735-J1
13400 PRM 90242 735-J1
16800 BLF 90706 735-J7
DOWNEY RD
2700 VER 90023 675-B2
3800 LACo 90023 675-B2
3800 LACo 90058 675-B2
3800 VER 90058 675-B2
5700 LACo 90270 675-B2
S DOWNEY RD
300 City 90063 635-E7
600 LACo 90063 635-E7
900 LACo 90023 675-E2
1800 VER 90023 675-B4
4300 LACo 90058 675-B4
4300 VER 90058 675-B4
5200 LACo 90270 675-B4
5200 MYWD 90270 675-B4
DOWNEY WY
1000 LA 90089 674-A1
DOWNEY & NORWALK RD
9800 DWNY 90241 706-D7
9800 NRWK 90650 706-D7
DOWNEY & SANFORD BRIDGE RD
9700 DWNY 90240 706-D4
DOWNEY NORWALK RD
10400 NRWK 90650 706-D7
DOWNIE CIR
900 SDMS 91773 570-C6
DOWNING AV
3200 GLDL 91208 534-H4
3700 BALD 91706 598-C3
DOWNING CT
2800 RowH 91748 679-C7
DOWNING ST
37200 PMDL 93550 4286-C3
DOWNSVIEW RD
44300 LAN 93535 4016-C7
DOYLE CT
25400 StvR 91381 4550-B7
25400 StvR 91381 4640-B1
DOYLE DR
400 SGBL 91775 596-D3
DOYLE PL
1000 LA 90012 634-G1
DOYNE RD
3000 LACo 91107 536-F7
3000 LACo 91107 566-F1
DOYON PL
15700 LMRD 90638 737-J4
DOZIER ST
3700 City 90063 635-D5
4300 ELA 90022 635-F5
DRACAENA DR
8100 BPK 90620 767-J5
DRACENA DR
1900 LFlz 90027 594-A3
DRACO WY
23600 CanP 91307 529-F5
DRADO
2400 LA 90732 823-F7
DRAGONERA DR
18300 RowH 91748 678-J7
18300 RowH 91748 679-A7
DRAGONFLY CT
- SCTA 91350 4550-J2
DRAGONFLY ST
3000 GLDL 91206 565-C1
DRAILLE DR
22600 TOR 90505 763-B7
22600 TOR 90505 793-B1
DRAKE AV
100 FUL 92832 738-F6
N DRAKE AV
300 UPL 91786 601-G3
DRAKE LN
9700 LA 90210 592-D1
DRAKE PL
6500 Win 91306 530-C6
16800 CynC 91351 4462-A4
DRAKE RD
300 ARCD 91007 566-J6
DRAKE ST
100 POM 91767 600-J2
800 CLAR 91711 601-D5
DRAKE TER
4100 LA 90032 595-D5
DRAKEWOOD AV
10600 CULC 90230 672-H4
DRAPER AV
10500 LA 90064 632-E6

DRAPER DR
- HacH 91745 678-B7
- LHH 91745 678-B7
DRASIN DR
19800 SCTA 91351 4551-E1
DRAYER LN
8400 LACo 91770 636-G4
8400 RSMD 91770 636-G4
DRAYTON ST
3100 SCTA 91350 4550-H4
DRELL ST
14700 LA 91342 481-J2
DRESDEN AV
1100 DUAR 91010 568-C5
DRESDEN DR
7500 LA 90046 593-B3
DRESDEN PL
12000 GrnH 91344 481-C7
DRESSER RD
23600 LACo 90265 629-F1
DREW PL
1700 CLAR 91711 601-A1
DREW ST
3100 LA 90065 594-F1
DREXEL AV
5800 LA 90036 633-C2
6200 LA 90048 633-A1
6700 LA 90048 632-J1
DREXEL DR
20500 WAL 91789 639-G4
DREXEL PL
500 PAS 91105 565-H6
DREXEL ST
37400 PMDL 93550 4286-C3
DR GLENN T SEABORG WY
3500 SGAT 90280 705-B3
DRIESER PL
13600 CRTS 90703 737-C6
DRIFT DR
5900 WLKV 91362 557-F4
DRIFTON AV
300 SDMS 91773 600-B3
DRIFTSTONE DR
1900 GLDR 91740 569-J7
DRIFTWOOD AV
600 BREA 92821 709-C5
700 SLB 90740 826-F3
5500 LPMA 90623 767-D3
DRIFTWOOD CT
13500 LMRD 90638 738-A2
DRIFTWOOD DR
2000 FUL 92831 738-J4
16000 PacP 90272 630-F4
E DRIFTWOOD DR
6200 LBCH 90803 826-E1
DRIFTWOOD LN
600 SDMS 91773 600-C3
29500 RPV 90275 822-H1
DRIFTWOOD PL
- PacP 90272 630-F4
1200 BREA 92821 709-B5
5500 PMDL 93552 4287-C2
DRIFTWOOD ST
- LA 90292 671-H7
44500 LAN 93535 4016-D6
DRIGGS AV
3100 ELMN 91770 636-J1
3100 RSMD 91770 636-J1
DRIGGS CT
10600 LACo 91390 4373-F4
DRILL RD
33000 LACo 91390 4373-D5
DRINKWATER CANYON RD
- LACo 91390 4281-A6
- LACo 91390 (4370-J1
See Page 4279)
- LACo 91390 (4371-A2
See Page 4281)
DRISCOLL AV
7900 VanN 91406 531-C3
E DRISCOLL ST
1500 LBCH 90815 796-E5
DRIVER AV
5200 Ago 91301 558-G6
5200 CALB 91301 558-G6
28100 AGRH 91301 558-B5
29600 Cstc 91384 4459-C6
DRIVER LN
2000 LVRN 91750 570-G4
DRIVERS WY
43200 LAN 93534 4105-G3
DRONFIELD AV
9700 SunV 91352 502-J4
10900 Sunl 91040 502-G2
11600 Pcma 91331 482-D7
11900 LA 91340 482-D7
12100 SFER 91340 482-D7
12900 LA 91342 482-A3
13400 LA 91342 481-J2
DRONFIELD PL
13800 LA 91342 481-H2
DRONFIELD ST
14700 LA 91342 481-J2
DRONFIELD TER
- Pcma 91331 502-F1
DROVER CT
1000 SDMS 91773 570-A7
DROXFORD CIR
12300 CRTS 90703 766-J2

DROXFORD PL
12300 CRTS 90703 766-J2
DROXFORD ST
6000 LKWD 90713 766-D2
10600 CRTS 90703 766-E2
11900 ART 90701 766-H2
12700 CRTS 90703 767-B1
DRUCKER ST
4200 LACo 90032 635-E2
4200 LA 90032 635-E2
DRUID LN
2900 OrCo 90720 796-H6
DRUID ST
4600 LA 90032 635-D1
DRUMHILL DR
1500 HacH 91745 678-A2
DRUMM AV
1200 Wilm 90744 794-G5
DRUMMOND ST
14600 PacP 90272 631-B5
DRUMS CT
22100 CALB 91302 559-J5
DRURY CT
2000 CLAR 91711 571-E7
DRURY DR
16700 WHIT 90603 708-B3
DRURY LN
400 BHLS 90210 592-G5
2200 LA 90039 594-C4
2400 GLDL 91206 564-J3
2400 GLDL 91206 565-A3
10700 LYN 90262 705-A6
DRUSILLA WY
1900 LACo 91789 679-E5
DRYAD RD
500 LA 90402 631-C7
DRYANDER DR
800 DBAR 91789 679-H3
DRYBANK DR
5300 RHE 90274 793-B7
5300 RHE 90274 823-A1
DRYBROOK DR
15300 HacH 91745 678-A3
DRY CANYON RD
28700 LACo 91390 4460-J2
28800 LACo 91390 (4370-J7
See Page 4279)
DRY CANYON COLD CREEK RD
23200 CALB 90290 559-F7
23200 CALB 91302 559-F7
24100 CALB 91302 589-C2
24300 LACo 91302 589-C4
DRYCLIFF ST
19000 SCTA 91351 4551-F2
DRY CREEK CT
- SCTA 91350 4550-H6
DRYCREEK LN
16200 CRTS 90703 736-J5
DRY CREEK RD
8700 SBdC 92372 (4562-C2
See Page 4471)
22600 DBAR 91765 640-B6
DRYDEN LN
1900 WCOV 91792 638-J5
DRYDEN PL
300 Echo 90026 634-C1
15500 HacH 91745 678-B3
E DRYDEN ST
100 GLDL 91207 564-F3
W DRYDEN ST
100 GLDL 91202 564-C3
DRYFIELD DR
23800 CALB 91302 559-E7
DRY GULCH RD
- LACo 91390 (4280-H5
See Page 4279)
- LACo 91390 4281-A5
DRYSDALE AV
3800 LA 90032 595-E5
DRYSDALE DR
- LAN 93535 4016-G4
DRYSDALE LN
11300 OrCo 90720 796-H3
DRY WELL CIR
28000 Cstc 91384 4369-G7
N DUANE AV
200 SGBL 91775 596-D3
DUANE ST
1500 Echo 90026 594-F6
2100 LA 90039 594-D5
DUANE WY
3200 SGAT 90280 705-B4
DUARTE RD
700 ARCD 91007 566-J7
700 ARCD 91007 567-H6
900 DUAR 91010 567-H6
1100 DUAR 91010 568-A6
1600 DUAR 91706 568-A6
1600 IRW 91706 568-A6
2800 SMRO 91108 596-E1
E DUARTE RD
- ARCD 91006 567-D6
100 MNRO 91016 567-D6
700 MNRO 91010 567-D6
8200 LACo 91775 596-G1
8900 LACo 91775 566-H7
W DUARTE RD
- ARCD 91007 567-A7
100 MNRO 91016 567-F6
DUARTE ST
5200 LA 90058 674-G5

DUBARRY DR
17500 BLF 90706 736-E7
DUBARRY ST
10500 BLF 90706 736-D7
DUBESOR ST
15600 LACo 91744 638-E4
17000 LACo 91744 638-H4
17000 WCOV 91791 638-H4
17000 WCOV 91792 638-H4
DUBLIN AV
3700 LA 90008 673-G2
3700 LA 90018 673-G2
14400 GAR 90249 733-G4
DUBLIN DR
2800 GLDL 91206 535-A7
DUBLIN LN
2000 DBAR 91765 680-A5
2200 DBAR 91765 679-J5
DUBLIN WY
- RowH 91748 708-H1
DUBNOFF WY
10500 LA 91505 533-B6
10500 NHol 91606 533-B6
DUBOIS AV
5300 WdHl 91367 559-F2
DUBOIS ST
28900 Cstc 91384 4459-D6
DUBONNET AV
2500 RSMD 91770 636-H3
3600 RSMD 91770 596-G5
N DUBONNET AV
5400 LACo 91776 596-G4
DUBUQUE AV
1300 WAL 91789 639-F4
DUCAL ST
40300 LACo 93551 4193-G3
DUCASSE AL
700 LA 90021 634-F6
DUCAT ST
14300 LA 91340 502-A2
14500 MsnH 91345 501-J2
14500 MsnH 91345 502-A2
DUCHESNE CT
300 CLAR 91711 571-D7
DUCHESS DR
6400 LACo 90606 677-A6
6800 LACo 90606 676-J7
7700 SFSP 90606 676-J7
8400 LACo 90606 706-H1
DUCHESS LN
- LBCH 90815 795-J4
DUCHESS PL
- SCTA 91350 4551-D5
DUCHY WY
2500 VeCo 91361 586-D2
DUCOMMUN ST
400 LA 90012 634-G4
DUCOR AV
7600 LA 91304 529-G2
DUDLEXT AV
8900 SGAT 90280 705-E4
DUDLEY AL
1400 PAS 91104 566-B2
DUDLEY AV
- Ven 90291 671-G5
S DUDLEY AV
500 POM 91766 640-G2
DUDLEY CIR
- LBCH 90755 795-H4
- SIGH 90755 795-H4
DUDLEY CT
- Ven 90291 671-G5
DUDLEY DR
4400 LA 90032 595-D7
DUDLEY LN
- SCTA 91321 4641-C1
DUDLEY ST
1200 POM 91768 600-F7
2000 PAS 91104 566-D2
14000 CHLS 91709 680-H4
N DUDLEY ST
500 POM 91768 640-F1
1000 POM 91768 600-F7
S DUDLEY ST
900 POM 91766 640-G3
DUDLEY WY
4500 LA 90032 595-D6
DUELL ST
1700 GLDR 91740 569-J7
2100 GLDR 91740 570-A7
19000 LACo 91740 569-C7
E DUELL ST
100 GLDR 91740 569-E7
500 AZU 91702 569-A7
18500 LACo 91702 569-B7
W DUELL ST
200 GLDR 91740 569-E7
300 AZU 91702 568-H7
DUENAS DR
2000 RowH 91748 679-A5
DUENDE LN
1300 PacP 90272 630-H3
DUESENBERG DR
2500 THO 91362 557-B3
DUESLER LN
8000 DWNY 90242 705-J6
DUESLER ST
8100 DWNY 90242 705-J6
8100 DWNY 90242 706-A6
DUFF AV
400 LPUE 91744 638-E3
600 LACo 91744 638-C5
800 WCOV 91790 638-F2

DUFFEL ST
37600 PMDL 93552 4287-A2
DUFFIELD AV
12400 LACo 90605 737-D1
12800 LMRD 90638 737-D2
DUFFY ST
9100 TEML 91780 596-H3
9900 TEML 91780 597-A3
DUFOUR AV
1900 RBCH 90278 733-A6
DUFRESNE CT
3700 LA 90034 672-E2
DUGGAN AV
500 AZU 91702 598-G2
DUKAS ST
18100 Nor 91326 500-H1
DUKE AV
3300 CLAR 91711 601-B2
DUKE DR
- BPK 90620 767-F6
- BqtC 91354 4460-F2
5200 LPMA 90623 767-C3
DUKE LN
1200 WAL 91789 639-F4
DUKE ST
3700 LA 90031 635-C1
DULCE LN
22200 SCTA 91350 4460-J7
DULCE RANCH RD
34900 LACo 91390 4373-G2
DULCET AV
11100 Nor 91326 500-H1
DULCE YNEZ LN
16900 PacP 90272 630-G5
DULCINEA CT
4500 WdHl 91364 560-A5
DULEY RD
100 ELSG 90245 732-J1
DULIN AV
5100 PRV 90660 676-F4
DULUTH LN
1500 BelA 90077 592-A5
DULZURA DR
3200 HacH 91745 678-C6
E DUMA ST
3700 RDom 90221 735-C6
DUMAINE AV
800 SDMS 91773 599-J4
DUMAINE DR
5000 LPMA 90623 767-C2
DUMALSKI ST
- LKWD 90712 765-H3
DUMB DIRT RD
100 Llan 93544 4471-J3
100 SBdC 92372 4471-J3
100 SBdC 92372 (4472-A3
See Page 4471)
DUME DR
6500 MAL 90265 667-E2
DUME CANYON MTWY
- LACo 90265 627-F4
DUME CANYON RD
- LACo 90265 587-D7
DUMETZ RD
20900 WdHl 91364 560-A4
22000 WdHl 91364 559-J4
DUMFRIES RD
2700 LA 90064 632-E6
DUMONT AV
11000 DWNY 90241 706-E6
11200 NRWK 90650 706-E6
13900 NRWK 90650 736-E3
17400 CRTS 90703 736-E7
17400 CRTS 90703 766-E1
DUMONT PL
5000 WdHl 91364 560-D3
DUMONT ST
20500 WdHl 91364 560-C3
DUMP RD
- AVA 90704 5923-J5
- Cstc 91384 4459-J5
- LACo 90704 5923-J5
- SBdC - (4562-G7
See Page 4471)
- SBdC - (4652-F1
See Page 4651)
DUNA DR
4400 LACo 91722 598-G4
DUNAS LN
4600 Tarz 91356 561-A4
DUNBAR PL
14400 Shrm 91403 562-A5
14400 Shrm 91423 562-A5
DUNBAR ST
8700 BLF 90706 735-J5
8800 BLF 90706 736-A5
39100 PMDL 93551 4195-F5
DUNBARTON AV
7300 Wch 90045 702-F1
DUNBARTON PL
300 CLAR 91711 571-D6
DUNBLANE AV
12000 Nor 91326 480-G6
DUNBROOKE AV
19000 CRSN 90746 764-E3
DUNCAMP PL
8700 LA 90046 592-H3
DUNCAN AV
800 MANB 90266 732-G7
900 ELA 90022 675-F1
10900 LYN 90262 705-E7
11300 LYN 90262 735-D2

S DUNCAN AV
600 ELA 90022 635-F7
900 ELA 90022 675-F2
1300 CMRC 90040 675-F2
DUNCAN DR
1100 MANB 90266 732-H7
DUNCAN PL
800 MANB 90266 732-G7
DUNCAN RD
100 Llan 93544 4471-J1
100 SBdC 92372 4471-J1
200 SBdC 92372 (4472-A1
See Page 4471)
DUNCAN ST
17700 Enc 91316 531-A7
18800 Res 91335 530-H7
DUNCAN WY
5100 SGAT 90280 705-E4
DUNCANNON AV
800 DUAR 91010 568-A5
DUNDAS DR
11200 NHol 91601 562-J2
DUNDAS ST
1000 LA 90063 635-C4
3200 City 90063 635-D4
DUNDEE CT
600 BREA 92821 709-C5
16500 LMRD 90638 738-A1
DUNDEE DR
4100 LFlz 90027 594-A2
DUNDEE PL
2600 LFlz 90027 594-B2
DUNDRY AV
1700 BALD 91706 638-B1
3800 BALD 91706 598-D6
DUNE LN
3400 LVRN 91750 600-G1
28900 SCTA 91387 4552-D1
29000 SCTA 91387 4462-D7
DUNE ST
800 ELSG 90245 702-D7
11000 NRWK 90650 706-F7
DUNEGAL CT
5900 AGRH 91301 557-G3
DUNES CT
40500 PMDL 93551 4194-J3
40500 PMDL 93551 4195-A3
DUNFIELD AV
7100 Wch 90045 672-G7
7200 Wch 90045 702-G1
DUNFORD AV
36400 Litl 93543 4287-J4
DUNFORD LN
3800 ING 90305 703-E3
DUNHAM AL
1500 PAS 91104 566-C3
DUNHAM ST
4300 LACo 90023 675-E2
4400 LACo 90040 675-E2
4500 CMRC 90040 675-E2
DUNIA ST
13400 BALD 91706 598-A4
DUNKIRK AV
10300 WLA 90025 632-D3
DUNLAP AV
11800 CHNO 91710 641-G4
DUNLAP PL
12000 CHNO 91710 641-F5
DUNLAP CROSSING RD
8600 PRV 90660 676-F4
10300 LACo 90606 676-H6
DUNLEER DR
10200 LA 90064 632-E6
DUNLEER PL
2700 LA 90064 632-E6
DUNLIN CT
800 THO 91361 557-A5
DUNLIN ST
- LACo 93591 4200-D5
DUNLO PL
6400 CanP 91307 529-D7
DUNMAN AV
4600 WdHl 91364 559-G3
DUNMORE AV
38600 PMDL 93550 4196-G7
DUNMORE DR
22300 CALB 91302 559-J6
DUNN AV
1400 City 90063 635-D3
N DUNN AV
700 LA 90732 824-A3
DUNN DR
3500 LA 90034 632-F7
3600 LA 90034 672-G1
3800 LA 90232 672-G1
DUNN ST
100 SPed 90731 824-A4
DUNNE CT
27000 CALB 91301 588-G1
DUNNET AV
14400 LMRD 90638 737-J3
DUNNICLIFFE CT
11900 Nor 91326 480-H6
DUNNING ST
11000 SFSP 90670 706-F4
DUNNING WY
1200 SDMS 91773 599-J2
DUNOON LN
12100 Brwd 90049 631-G4
DUNRAVEN CT
31700 WLKV 91361 557-D6
DUNROBIN AV
4500 LKWD 90713 766-C2

DUNROBIN AV
9600 DWNY 90242 736-C1
12100 DWNY 90242 706-C7
13400 BLF 90706 736-C3
DUNSHILL CT
16500 WHIT 90603 708-A5
DUNSMERE RD
3200 GLDL 91206 565-C1
DUNSMORE AV
3900 GLDL 91214 534-E1
4000 GLDL 91214 504-E5
DUNSMORE LN
23600 SCTA 91354 4460-G7
DUNSMUIR AV
1200 LA 90019 633-C4
S DUNSMUIR AV
600 LA 90036 633-C3
1000 LA 90019 633-C5
1900 LA 90016 633-C6
3400 LA 90016 673-B1
3800 LA 90008 673-B2
DUNSMUIR LN
700 WAL 91789 639-B7
DUNSTAN WY
11600 Brwd 90049 631-H3
DUNSVIEW AV
400 LACo 91744 638-G7
DUNSWELL AV
1100 HacH 91745 678-B2
S DUNSWELL AV
1900 HacH 91745 678-B3
DUNTON DR
9000 WHIT 90602 707-B2
13400 WHIT 90605 707-C3
13900 LACo 90605 707-D3
14600 LACo 90604 707-F5
DUNURE PL
19100 Nor 91326 480-G6
DUNWICH AV
1200 LACo 90502 764-A7
DUNWOOD RD
26300 RHE 90274 793-B5
DUOMO ST
- PMDL 93550 4286-F6
DUOMO VIA
15400 BelA 90077 591-G1
DU PAGE AV
9700 LACo 90605 707-B4
DU PONT PL
500 POM 91768 640-C1
DU PONT ST
200 POM 91768 640-C2
DUPONT ST
21600 Chat 91311 500-A5
DUPRE DR
6600 RPV 90275 822-H3
DUQUE DR
11500 LA 91604 562-H7
11500 LA 91604 592-H1
DUQUESNE AV
3900 CULC 90232 672-G1
DURAND DR
2800 LA 90068 593-F1
2800 LA 90068 563-F7
S DURANGO AV
1400 LA 90035 632-H4
1900 LA 90034 632-H5
3700 LA 90034 632-G7
DURANGO CT
900 SDMS 91773 570-C7
900 SDMS 91773 600-C1
2000 LVRN 91750 570-G4
43200 LAN 93536 4104-H3
DURANGO DR
2000 MONP 91754 635-G2
4500 BPK 90621 737-J4
DURANGO LN
11300 LACo 91390 4373-D5
DURANGO PL
13300 CRTS 90703 737-C7
37800 PMDL 93550 4286-G2
DURANGO ST
900 MTBL 90640 636-E7
DURANT DR
9800 BHLS 90212 632-E2
DURANT PL
- StvR 91381 4550-A7
DURANT ST
300 AZU 91702 568-H3
DURAY PL
2700 LA 90016 633-B7
3800 LA 90008 673-B2
DURAZNO DR
1900 HacH 91745 678-C4
DURBIN ST
3700 IRW 91706 597-H6
DURFEE AV
100 LACo 90660 636-J6
100 LACo 91733 636-J6
100 LACo 90660 637-C5
100 WHIT 90660 637-A6
100 LACo 91733 637-A6
700 SELM 91733 637-D4
2100 ELMN 91733 637-D4
2200 ELMN 91732 637-F1
3100 INDS 91732 637-F1
3600 PRV 90660 676-H2
3800 ELMN 91732 597-H4
5400 ARCD 91006 597-H4
DURHAM CT
- BURB 91504 533-E2
DURHAM PL
3800 LCF 91011 535-C6

STREET
Block City ZIP Pg-Grid

DURHAM PL
28000 SCTA 91350 4461-A5
DURHAM RD
13800 LA 90210 562-B6
13800 Shrm 91423 562-B6
DURHAM ST
700 LHB 90631 708-E7
DURKEE AV
10100 Tuj 91042 504-C4
DURKLYN CT
1700 SMRO 91108 596-D1
DURNESS ST
800 WCOV 91790 638-D1
13800 BALD 91706 598-B7
DURRELL AV
400 AZU 91702 569-A6
DURWARD WY
2100 LVRN 91750 600-G1
DURWOOD DR
600 LCF 91011 535-C3
DURYEA AV
1300 LACo 90601 637-G5
DUSK ST
18200 RowH 91748 678-J7
DUSKY WILLOW ST
\- LAN 93536 4014-F7
DUSON ST
\- Actn 93510 4465-A1
DUSSEN LN
13100 CRTS 90703 767-B2
DUSTIN DR
400 LA 90065 595-B4
DUSTIN ALLAN LN
7200 VanN 91405 531-J4
DUSTY DR
35400 LACo 91390 4374-D2
DUSTY RD
44100 LAN 93536 4015-B7
DUSTY WILLOW CT
\- LACo 91387 4552-A4
DUTCH ST
14700 BALD 91706 598-D7
DUTHIE ST
12800 BALD 91706 637-H1
DUVAL CT
\- PMDL 93552 4287-E1
DUVAL ST
800 LVRN 91750 570-D7
DUVALL ST
2100 LA 90031 594-H6
DUXBURY CIR
2200 LA 90034 632-G5
DUXBURY LN
9500 LA 90034 632-G5
DUXBURY PL
\- SCTA 91354 4460-G6
2400 LA 90034 632-G6
DUXBURY RD
9300 LA 90034 632-G5
DUXFORD AV
4600 LACo 91722 598-J4
5400 AZU 91702 598-J2
5400 LACo 91702 598-J2
DWIGGINS ST
3600 City 90063 635-D3
N DWIGHT AV
100 COMP 90220 734-G4
S DWIGHT AV
100 COMP 90220 734-G4
DWIGHT DR
1400 GLDL 91207 564-E2
DWIGHT LEE ST
3000 Actn 93510 4375-B2
DWP RD
\- LA 90068 563-E7
DYER AV
4800 LaCr 91214 504-F7
DYER LN
100 GLDR 91741 569-D5
DYER ST
4400 LaCr 91214 534-F1
4600 LaCr 91214 504-F7
13200 LA 91342 482-C2
14500 LA 91342 481-J5
DYLAN PL
11400 Nor 91326 500-H1
DYLAN ST
18500 Nor 91326 500-H1
DYMOND ST
2100 BURB 91505 533-B6
DYOTT WY
39900 PMDL 93551 4195-J4
DYSON AV
4800 ELMN 91732 597-F5

E

E
\- PRM 90723 735-F6
18600 LACo 91744 679-B2
E CT
1000 Wilm 90744 794-D7
E ST
\- LA 90245 732-D1
\- LACo 90220 764-J3
\- LACo 91724 599-E3
\- PdlR 90293 702-C7
\- PdlR 90293 732-D1
\- SPed 90731 794-B7
\- Wilm 90744 794-B7
1900 LVRN 91750 600-G3
10600 LACo 90230 672-H3
E E ST
100 Wilm 90744 794-E7
W E ST
100 Wilm 90744 794-C7
1000 ONT 91762 601-H7
E WK
1000 Wilm 90744 794-D7
EA WY
\- LA 90094 702-C1
EADALL AV
13900 LACo 90061 734-D3
EADBROOK DR
14400 HacH 91745 677-H2
EADBURY AV
1900 RowH 91748 679-C6
EADHILL PL
4100 LACo 90601 677-C2
EADINGTON DR
800 BREA 92821 738-J1
EADMER AV
39700 PMDL 93551 4195-H4
EADS ST
2300 LA 90031 594-G5
EAGAN DR
10300 LACo 90604 707-F5
EAGAN ST
6800 Tuj 91042 504-B6
EAGER RD
34600 Actn 93510 4374-J3
EAGLE CT
6200 LAN 93536 4104-E4
EAGLE DR
2100 LVRN 91750 570-H4
7000 BPK 90620 767-E2
EAGLE LN
\- StvR 91381 4550-C4
W EAGLE LN
39900 PMDL 93551 4195-J4
EAGLE RD
900 SBdC 92397 (4652-C2 See Page 4651)
EAGLE ST
1500 Boyl 90033 634-J5
2700 Boyl 90033 635-B5
3000 LA 90063 635-C6
3600 City 90063 635-D6
4300 ELA 90022 635-F6
E EAGLE ST
100 LBCH 90806 795-D3
5100 LBCH 90815 796-B3
W EAGLE ST
100 LBCH 90806 795-D3
EAGLE WY
\- LAN 93536 4015-B6
EAGLEBROOK DR
30300 AGRH 91301 557-G5
EAGLE BUTTE RD
1400 LACo 93551 4375-F2
EAGLECLIFF DR
1600 SDMS 91773 570-D6
EAGLECREST AV
28000 SCTA 91351 4551-H1
EAGLECREST PL
2700 DBAR 91789 679-G6
EAGLEDALE AV
5200 Eagl 90041 564-H5
EAGLEFEN DR
1300 DBAR 91765 680-A3
EAGLE GROVE AV
200 CLAR 91711 571-D6
EAGLEHAVEN CIR
31300 RPV 90275 823-F6
EAGLEHELM DR
27300 SCTA 91387 4552-D5
EAGLEMONT AV
1000 LACo 90601 637-G5
S EAGLEMONT DR
900 LACo 90601 637-G5
EAGLE MOUNTAIN RD
24000 LA 91304 529-D2
EAGLE MOUNTAIN ST
24000 LA 91304 529-D1
EAGLE NEST DR
200 DBAR 91765 640-A7
EAGLE PARK RD
1400 HacH 91745 678-E4
EAGLE PASS DR
20600 MAL 90265 629-G6
EAGLE PEAK AV
28000 SCTA 91387 4552-B2
EAGLE POINT CIR
4800 THO 91362 557-F1
EAGLE POINT DR
3400 GLDL 91208 534-J4
EAGLE POINTE DR
\- FUL 92833 738-B3
EAGLE RIDGE CT
13600 LMRD 90638 738-A2
EAGLERIDGE CT
\- PMDL 93551 4195-B2
EAGLE RIDGE DR
1500 GLDR 91740 569-H7
EAGLE RIDGE LN
19400 Nor 91326 480-E6
EAGLE RIDGE WY
11900 Nor 91326 480-E6
EAGLE ROCK BLVD
2900 LA 90065 594-H1
4200 Eagl 90041 594-H1
4400 Eagl 90041 564-J7
4700 Eagl 90041 565-A6
EAGLE ROCK VIEW DR
800 Eagl 90041 565-D5
EAGLES CREST CT
\- SCTA 91351 4461-G7
\- SCTA 91351 4551-G1
EAGLESET AV
\- LACo 91390 (4372-J7 See Page 4281)
EAGLES LANDING DR
7600 PMDL 93550 4286-G3
EAGLE SPRINGS FIRE RD
\- PacP 90272 590-E4
EAGLESPUR RD
22700 DBAR 91765 640-A6
EAGLETON ST
28600 AGRH 91301 558-B3
EAGLE VIEW CIR
5000 Eagl 90041 564-J6
EAGLE VISTA DR
1000 Eagl 90041 565-C5
EAGLEWOOD DR
2300 CHLS 91709 680-J3
EAGLEWOOD PL
1500 LHB 90631 738-D1
EAMES AV
8900 Nor 91324 500-H7
EARHART AV
8800 Wch 90045 702-H3
EARHART CT
1500 LVRN 91750 600-F4
EARL AV
13200 BALD 91706 597-J6
13300 BALD 91706 598-A6
N EARL AV
2100 LBCH 90806 795-D3
EARL CT
2200 LA 90039 594-E5
EARL DR
5100 LCF 91011 535-A1
EARL ST
2200 LA 90039 594-E5
20300 TOR 90503 763-C5
EARL CANYON MTWY
\- LACo - 504-J7
\- LACo - 505-A6
\- LCF 91011 504-J7
\- LCF 91011 505-A6
\- LCF 91011 534-J1
EARLDOM AV
7000 PdlR 90293 702-B3
EARLE AV
2400 RSMD 91770 636-G1
3600 RSMD 91770 596-G5
N EARLE AV
5500 LACo 91776 596-G3
5600 SGBL 91776 596-G3
EARLE CT
2200 RBCH 90278 763-A2
EARLE LN
500 RBCH 90278 763-A2
EARLE ST
400 SPed 90731 824-E4
5700 SGBL 91775 596-F3
5700 SGBL 91776 596-F3
5800 LACo 91775 596-F3
EARLGATE ST
20500 DBAR 91789 679-F3
EARLHAM DR
700 CLAR 91711 601-E1
13400 WHIT 90602 677-E6
13400 WHIT 90608 677-E6
EARLHAM ST
600 PAS 91101 566-A3
15200 PacP 90272 631-A6
EARLIE AV
19600 CRSN 90746 764-H4
EARLINGTON AV
1800 DUAR 91010 568-A6
EARLMAR DR
3000 LA 90064 632-F6
EARLMONT AV
1500 LCF 91011 535-A1
1700 LCF 91011 534-J1
EARLS CT
\- PMDL 93552 4287-C4
2200 BelA 90077 591-G3
24800 CALB 91302 559-C7
EARLS RANCH RD
7300 SBdC 92371 (4562-J5 See Page 4471)
EARLSWOOD DR
3300 RSMD 91770 636-H1
EARL WARREN DR
1300 LBCH 90840 796-C5
EARLY AV
23200 TOR 90505 793-E2
EARNFORD DR
3600 CALB 91302 559-E7
EARNSHAW AV
13400 DWNY 90242 735-J3
EARNSLOW DR
2100 LCF 91011 504-H6
EARNWAY ST
29500 CynC 91351 4462-B6
EASLEY CANYON RD
700 GLDR 91741 569-E3
EAST AV
200 AZU 91702 568-G7
1000 BURB 91504 533-F6
16000 LA 91342 481-F3
EAST BLVD
3800 LA 90066 672-D3
4200 CULC 90066 672-D3
EAST DR
\- Hrbr 90710 794-B4
\- NRWK 90650 736-G5
EAST LN
16900 CHLS 91709 710-F3
N EAST PKWY
700 ING 90302 673-E7
EAST RD
100 LHH 90631 708-D2
1300 LA 90810 794-J4
26400 SCTA 91355 4550-D4
EAST ST
\- AZU 91702 598-J2
24000 CRSN 90745 794-E3
EAST TR
\- LFlz 90027 563-J6
\- LFlz 90027 564-A6
11700 LACo 91342 482-J7
EAST WY
\- LA 91342 481-J2
10000 Wch 90045 702-G5
EASTBORNE AV
10200 Wwd 90024 632-D3
EAST BOUND DR
\- SMRO 91108 566-D7
EASTBROOK AV
4500 LKWD 90713 766-C2
12100 DWNY 90242 706-C7
12600 DWNY 90242 736-C2
13800 BLF 90706 736-C3
EASTBURY AV
600 COV 91723 599-A7
N EASTBURY AV
1100 COV 91722 599-A3
4400 LACo 91722 599-A3
EAST CANYON CT
5300 SBdC 92397 (4652-F4 See Page 4651)
EASTEDGE DR
2100 GLDL 91206 564-J3
EAST END AV
11300 SBdC 91710 641-C5
11300 SBdC 91766 641-C5
12100 CHNO 91710 641-C5
N EAST END AV
100 POM 91767 641-C1
600 POM 91767 601-C7
S EAST END AV
\- POM 91767 641-C2
100 POM 91766 641-C2
1100 SBdC 91766 641-C2
EASTER CIR
3300 HNTB 92649 826-J7
EASTER DR
5400 SBdC 92397 (4652-F3 See Page 4651)
EASTERLY RD
5500 AGRH 91301 558-C5
EASTERLY TER
1400 Echo 90026 594-D5
EASTERN AV
6100 BGDN 90201 675-G7
6500 BGDN 90201 705-G1
33300 LACo 91390 4373-A4
N EASTERN AV
100 ELA 90022 635-E4
100 City 90063 635-E4
1600 LACo 90032 635-E1
2000 LA 90032 635-E1
2400 LA 90032 595-E7
S EASTERN AV
\- PAS 91107 566-F5
100 ELA 90022 635-F7
100 City 90063 635-F7
300 LACo 90023 635-F7
900 ELA 90022 675-F1
900 LACo 90023 675-F1
1200 CMRC 90022 675-F1
1300 CMRC 90040 675-F1
2800 BELL 90040 675-G4
2800 BELL 90201 675-G4
EASTERN CT
2200 Ven 90291 671-H6
EASTERN CANAL WK
2300 Ven 90291 671-H6
EASTERN PINES CT
\- LACo 91387 4552-A4
EASTFIELD DR
\- RHLS 90274 823-F3
EASTFORD AV
800 DUAR 91010 568-B5
EAST FORK RD
\- LACo - 509-H5
23500 LACo - (510-D6 See Page 509)
EASTGATE DR
24400 DBAR 91765 680-E2
EASTGATE PL
2300 GLDL 91208 534-J7
S EASTGATES ST
1200 ANA 92804 767-H7
EASTGLEN DR
900 LVRN 91750 570-E6
EASTHAM DR
3500 CULC 90232 632-J7
3500 CULC 90232 672-J1
EASTHAVEN LN
\- CanP 91307 529-E5
EAST HILLS DR
900 WCOV 91791 639-D2
EASTLAKE AV
1400 Boyl 90033 635-B2
1500 LA 90031 635-B1
EASTLAKE AV
2500 LA 90031 595-B7
EASTLAND CENTER DR
2600 WCOV 91791 599-B7
EASTLEIGH AV
1400 HacH 91745 678-D3
EASTLYN PL
1200 LACo 91104 566-D1
N EASTMAN AV
100 City 90063 635-D5
S EASTMAN AV
100 City 90063 635-D6
600 LACo 90023 635-D7
900 LACo 90023 675-D1
1300 CMRC 90023 675-D1
EASTMAN PL
800 SPed 90731 824-A2
EASTMAN ST
12000 CRTS 90703 766-J3
S EASTMONT AV
400 ELA 90022 635-H7
600 ELA 90022 675-H1
EASTNOR AV
4000 WCOV 91792 679-B2
EASTON DR
9700 LA 90210 592-C3
EASTON LN
28300 SCTA 91350 4461-B4
EASTON PL
\- RowH 91748 679-B7
EASTON ST
2100 MTBL 90640 676-B2
38600 PMDL 93552 4196-J7
E EASTON ST
5900 ELA 90022 675-J2
6000 ELA 90022 676-A2
6700 MTBL 90640 676-A2
EASTONDALE AV
6800 NLB 90805 735-E6
EASTPARK DR
1300 LHB 90631 708-G5
12100 NHol 91606 532-F7
EASTRIDGE CT
16100 CHLS 91709 710-G1
EASTRIDGE DR
7300 WHIT 90602 677-E7
14200 WHIT 90602 707-F1
EAST RIDGE LN
\- CRSN 90745 794-G2
EASTRIDGE WY
900 BREA 92821 709-C7
EASTRIDGE KNOLL
1000 FUL 92835 738-F5
EASTSIDE BLVD
3000 LA 90063 635-C5
EASTVALE CT
29900 AGRH 91301 557-H4
EASTVALE RD
26600 LACo 90274 793-C7
27600 LACo 90274 823-C1
EASTVIEW DR
400 HiPk 90042 595-D1
500 HiPk 90042 565-D7
EASTWARD ST
23600 Chat 91311 499-F6
EASTWIND CIR
1300 THO 91361 557-B6
EASTWIND DR
900 BPK 90621 738-B6
EASTWIND ST
\- LA 90292 671-J7
\- LA 90292 701-H1
EASTWIND WY
\- SIGH 90755 795-H3
EASTWOOD AV
14500 LNDL 90260 733-D5
16900 TOR 90504 733-D7
20300 TOR 90503 763-D4
22600 TOR 90505 763-D5
22600 TOR 90505 793-D1
N EASTWOOD AV
100 ING 90301 703-D2
S EASTWOOD AV
10800 Lenx 90304 703-D6
11100 HAW 90304 703-D6
EASTWOOD CT
22300 TOR 90505 763-D7
EASTWOOD PL
100 BREA 92821 709-B6
EASTWOOD RD
8500 LA 90046 592-H2
EASY AV
2000 LBCH 90810 795-B2
3500 LBCH 90810 765-B7
EASY ST
900 HiPk 90042 595-F1
4000 ELMN 91731 596-J6
4000 ELMN 91731 597-A6
5200 Actn 93510 4374-G3
6500 Res 91335 530-B7
8500 SBdC 92371 (4562-H2 See Page 4471)
12700 CHNO 91710 641-E7
43600 LAN 93535 4106-E1
EATON CIR
2600 LBCH 90815 796-C3
EATON CT
4800 SBdC 91710 641-F3
EATON DR
300 PAS 91107 566-F2
EATON PL
1700 LVRN 91750 600-G1
EATON RD
1100 SDMS 91773 599-H2
EATON ST
5000 HiPk 90042 565-B7
5500 HiPk 90042 595-C1
EATON TER
1400 HiPk 90042 565-C7
1400 HiPk 90042 595-C1
EATON CANYON DR
2600 PAS 91107 536-E7
2800 PAS 91107 566-F1
2800 LACo 91107 536-E7
2800 LACo 91107 566-F1
EATOUGH AV
8500 LA 91304 529-J1
EATOUGH PL
8500 LA 91304 529-J2
EAU CLAIRE DR
5400 RPV 90275 793-A7
EBB CT
28100 SCTA 91350 4461-D6
EBBTIDE LN
11800 VeCo 90265 625-F5
EBBTIDE PL
600 SLB 90740 826-F4
EBBTIDE WY
6200 MAL 90265 667-B2
EBELDEN AV
24500 SCTA 91321 4640-G3
EBELL ST
13000 NHol 91605 532-D2
13300 PanC 91402 532-C2
E EBELL ST
5100 LBCH 90808 766-B6
EBERLE CIR
11400 CRTS 90703 766-G3
EBERLE PL
12200 CRTS 90703 766-J3
EBERLE ST
5700 LKWD 90713 766-C3
11800 CRTS 90703 766-H3
EBEY AV
5400 HiPk 90042 595-D4
EBEY CANYON DR
11300 Sunl 91040 503-G1
EBEY CANYON RD
11000 Sunl 91040 503-F1
EBEY CANYON TKTR
\- LA 91342 (4723-F7 See Page 4643)
\- LACo 91342 (4723-F7 See Page 4643)
11500 Sunl 91040 503-F1
11500 Sunl 91040 (4723-F7 See Page 4643)
EBONY AV
\- WCOV 91790 638-E1
EBONY DR
\- PMDL 93551 4285-D3
EBONY LN
25000 LMTA 90717 793-J4
EBY DR
12000 LACo 93536 4013-B4
ECCLES ST
15800 LA 91343 531-F1
18100 Nor 91325 530-G2
18100 Nor 91325 531-F1
18500 Nor 91324 530-G2
19900 Win 91306 530-D2
21700 LA 91304 530-A2
22100 LA 91304 529-H2
ECHANDIA ST
100 Boyl 90033 634-J4
500 Boyl 90033 635-A3
ECHANDIA ST E
600 Boyl 90033 635-A3
ECHANDIA ST W
600 Boyl 90033 634-J3
600 Boyl 90033 635-A3
ECHARD AV
43200 LAN 93536 4105-C3
N ECHELON AV
800 LACo 91744 638-F5
800 INDS 91744 638-F5
ECHELON PL
8300 SunV 91352 533-C1
ECHILMAN AL
31500 Cstc 91384 4369-G7
ECHO ST
100 HiPk 90042 595-D2
ECHO CANYON PL
200 BREA 92821 709-B5
ECHO GLEN DR
1200 Alta 91001 536-B4
ECHO HILL WY
16500 HacH 91745 678-E5
ECHO LAKE WY
\- Pcma 91331 502-D6
ECHO MOUNTAIN ST
37600 PMDL 93552 4287-A2
ECHO PARK AV
600 Echo 90026 634-E1
1100 Echo 90026 594-E6
ECHO PARK TER
700 Echo 90026 634-E1
ECHO RIVER WY
12200 CRTS 90703 736-J6
E ECKERMAN AV
1000 WCOV 91790 598-G6
1400 WCOV 91791 598-H6
1900 WCOV 91791 599-A6
W ECKERMAN AV
1200 WCOV 91790 598-F6
ECKFORD ST
13500 LACo 91746 637-H4
ECKHART AV
1700 LACo 91770 636-F4
3200 RSMD 91770 636-F1
ECKLESON CIR
11400 CRTS 90703 766-G3
ECKLESON PL
12200 CRTS 90703 766-J3
ECKLESON ST
2400 LKWD 90712 765-H3
5700 LKWD 90713 766-C3
12400 CRTS 90703 766-D3
12400 CRTS 90703 767-A3
ECLIPSE CT
1000 ONT 91762 641-J3
ECLIPSE DR
3700 PMDL 93550 4286-H3
ECLIPSE WY
1000 WCOV 91792 638-G5
N ECROYD AV
2100 SIMI 93063 499-A2
ECTOR ST
13300 INDS 91746 637-J2
13300 LACo 91746 637-J3
13600 LACo 91746 638-A3
14500 LPUE 91744 638-B4
14600 LACo 91744 638-B4
EDAM ST
\- LAN 93536 4104-J1
2200 LAN 93536 4105-D1
EDANRUTH AV
1000 LACo 91746 638-B2
EDDA VILLA DR
8900 RSMD 91770 596-H7
EDDERTON AV
11100 LACo 90604 707-F6
12600 LMRD 90638 737-E1
EDDES ST
2500 WCOV 91791 639-B2
E EDDES ST
3000 WCOV 91791 639-C2
EDDIE LN
\- CynC 91351 4461-D7
EDDINGHAM AV
3500 CALB 91302 559-H7
EDDINGHAM WY
\- LA 91304 529-E4
EDDINGHILL DR
6500 RPV 90275 792-G7
EDDINGTON DR
19000 CRSN 90746 764-E3
EDDLESTON DR
11600 Nor 91326 480-H6
EDDRIDGE DR
22500 DBAR 91765 680-A3
EDDY LN
\- PMDL 93552 4287-E2
EDDY ST
18200 Nor 91325 530-J1
18500 Nor 91324 530-H1
EDDYSTONE ST
11500 LACo 90606 676-J7
12000 LACo 90606 707-A1
EDELLE PL
4600 LA 90032 635-D1
EDELWEISS CT
\- BqtC 91354 4460-E6
EDEN AV
1900 GLDL 91206 564-H4
EDEN CIR
600 CLAR 91711 571-E6
EDEN CT
\- SCTA 91350 4551-D5
EDEN DR
9400 LA 90210 592-F2
EDEN PL
2600 LA 90210 592-F2
EDEN RD
22100 Top 90290 590-A6
EDEN WY
\- BREA 92821 709-A4
EDENBERG AV
11300 Nor 91326 500-H1
EDENBORO
1600 WCOV 91791 638-J5
EDENDALE PL
2200 LA 90039 594-E5
EDENFIELD AV
100 AZU 91702 569-B7
600 COV 91723 599-B6
4700 LACo 91722 599-B3
5400 LACo 91702 599-B1
5900 LACo 91702 569-B7
N EDENFIELD AV
700 COV 91723 599-B4
1100 COV 91722 599-B3
4600 LACo 91722 599-B3
S EDENFIELD AV
500 COV 91723 599-B6
EDENHURST AV
3600 LA 90039 594-D1
4000 LA 90039 564-C5
EDENPARK DR
26000 CALB 91302 558-J3
EDENTON PL
23000 SCTA 91354 4460-H6
EDENVIEW LN
1900 WCOV 91792 638-H5
EDENWILD RD
700 LACo 91302 589-A7
EDGAR ST
16700 PacP 90272 630-H5
EDGAR ST
21800 CRSN 90745 764-F7
EDGEBROOK AV
12300 LYN 90262 735-E2
EDGEBROOK DR
\- POM 91766 640-G6
EDGEBROOK RD
13400 LMRD 90638 738-A2
EDGEBROOK WY
\- Nor 91326 500-H4
EDGECLIFF AV
11700 LA 91342 481-H5
EDGECLIFF DR
1500 FUL 92831 738-J5
EDGECLIFF LN
1400 LACo 91107 566-G1
EDGECLIFFE DR
900 Echo 90026 594-C5
E EDGECOMB ST
900 COV 91724 599-D4
EDGEFIELD ST
5900 LKWD 90713 766-D2
12300 CRTS 90703 766-J2
12700 CRTS 90703 767-A2
EDGEHILL DR
1200 POM 91767 601-C6
2600 LA 90018 633-F7
3400 LA 90018 673-F1
3700 LA 90008 673-F2
EDGEHILL PL
1300 PAS 91103 535-D7
EDGEHURST LN
\- Saug 91350 4461-F6
EDGELEY PL
2900 OrCo 90720 796-H4
10500 Wwd 90024 632-B2
EDGEMAR AV
5600 LA 90043 673-D6
5600 LACo 90043 673-D6
EDGEMERE DR
5400 TOR 90503 763-A4
EDGEMONT CIR
5100 CYP 90630 767-C6
EDGEMONT DR
38800 PMDL 93551 4195-E7
EDGEMONT LN
2600 BREA 92821 709-F7
EDGEMONT PL
100 GLDR 91741 570-A5
20200 LACo 91789 679-F7
EDGEMONT ST
1000 LHB 90631 708-C4
N EDGEMONT ST
100 LA 90004 633-J1
200 LA 90004 593-J5
700 LA 90029 593-J5
700 LA 90029 594-A6
1300 LFlz 90027 593-J2
S EDGEMONT ST
100 LA 90004 633-J1
E EDGERIDGE DR
14300 HacH 91745 677-H3
EDGERTON AV
4900 Enc 91436 561-E3
EDGEVIEW DR
600 SMAD 91024 566-H1
3700 PAS 91107 566-H1
EDGEVIEW PL
14500 SCTA 91387 4462-G6
EDGEWARE DR
5200 CALB 91301 558-G6
E EDGEWARE RD
300 Echo 90026 634-E2
N EDGEWARE RD
100 Echo 90026 634-E2
S EDGEWARE RD
100 Echo 90026 634-E3
W EDGEWARE RD
1000 Echo 90026 634-E1
EDGEWARE WY
\- PMDL 93552 4287-C4
EDGEWATER DR
\- PMDL 93551 4195-G6
13900 NRWK 90650 736-E3
19900 SCTA 91351 4551-D1
EDGEWATER LN
\- SCTA 91355 4550-F1
EDGEWATER RD
36500 PMDL 93550 4286-A5
EDGEWATER TER
2300 LA 90039 594-D4
EDGEWICK RD
2800 GLDL 91206 565-A1
EDGEWOOD CT
2700 PMDL 93551 4195-C6
EDGEWOOD DR
\- LVRN 91750 570-G6
1300 ALH 91803 595-H7
1700 ALH 91803 635-H1
1700 SIMI 93063 499-B2
1900 SPAS 91030 595-J2
N EDGEWOOD LN
1100 UPL 91786 601-J1
EDGEWOOD PL
4500 LA 90019 633-C3
N EDGEWOOD ST
400 ING 90302 703-C1
900 ING 90302 673-C7
EDGEWORTH AV
12000 LACo 90604 707-J7
EDGLEY DR
300 MONP 91755 636-C2
ED HALLEY PL
43000 LAN 93536 4105-B3
EDIE CT
2100 WCOV 91791 639-A2
EDIE DR
800 DUAR 91010 568-D5
EDIE WY
1000 LAN 93535 4106-B2
EDINBORO AV
2100 CLAR 91711 571-E7
EDINBURG CT
1200 POM 91766 640-G3
N EDINBURGH AV
100 LA 90048 633-B1
300 LA 90048 593-B7
700 LA 90046 593-B7
1000 WHWD 90046 593-B7
S EDINBURGH AV
100 LA 90048 633-B1
EDINBURGH CT
6100 AGRH 91301 557-J3
EDINBURGH LN
1400 GLDL 91206 564-G3
EDINBURGH RD
1100 SDMS 91773 599-G5
EDINGER AV
2900 HNTB 92649 826-J6
2900 SLB 90740 826-J6
EDINGER WY
20900 WAL 91789 639-G3
EDISON AV
500 LBCH 90813 795-A7
EDISON BLVD
1300 BURB 91505 563-C1
1700 BURB 91505 533-B7
EDISON LN
1000 SPAS 91030 595-H2
EDISON PL
100 LBCH 90802 825-G1
400 GLDL 91204 564-D6
EDISON RD
\- Actn 93510 4464-J6
\- Actn 93510 4465-J5
\- Actn 93510 4466-A7
\- Actn 93510 (4555-J3 See Page 4466)
\- Actn 93510 (4556-A1 See Page 4466)
\- BqtC 91354 4460-D3
\- CHLS 91709 680-H2
\- Cstc 91384 4460-D3
\- Cstc 91384 4549-D2
\- LACo - 505-D2
\- LACo - 4279-A4
\- LACo - (4555-H7 See Page 4466)
\- LACo - 4645-H1
\- LACo 90265 586-J7
\- LACo 90265 626-J2
\- LACo 90265 627-A3
\- LACo 91390 4281-J5
\- LACo 91390 (4282-A4 See Page 4281)
\- LACo 91390 (4371-E4 See Page 4281)
\- LACo 91390 4460-J3
\- LACo 91390 4461-A3
\- LACo 91390 4463-A3
\- LACo 93551 4375-G3
\- LACo 93552 4376-H6
\- MAL 90265 627-E7
\- Nwhl 91321 4640-G4
\- Nwhl 91321 4641-B6
\- PMDL 91390 (4284-B4 See Page 4283)
\- PMDL 93550 4376-G4
\- PMDL 93550 4466-A7
\- PMDL 93550 (4556-A1 See Page 4466)
\- PMDL 93551 4194-J7
\- PMDL 93551 (4284-J1 See Page 4283)
\- PMDL 93551 4285-A1
\- SCTA 91355 4460-A5
\- SCTA 91384 4460-C4
\- SCTA 91390 4460-J3
200 BURB 91506 563-E3
2600 Actn 93510 4375-C1
3500 GLDL 91208 535-A5
3500 LCF 91011 535-A5
5200 LACo 93552 4377-A4
22000 GrnH 91344 481-B1
22000 StvR 91381 481-B1
22000 StvR 91381 4641-A7
24100 SCTA 91321 4640-J2
EDISON ST
4500 LA 90032 595-D5
EDISON WK
\- LA 90032 595-F5
EDISON WY
2500 COMP 90220 764-J1
8500 RSMD 91770 636-G3
10400 NHol 91606 533-B7
EDISON LOOP RD
\- LACo - (4726-J3 See Page 4645)
\- LACo - (4727-A4 See Page 4647)
EDISON POTRERO RD
\- StvR 91381 4549-H7
\- StvR 91381 4550-A5
EDISON POWER RD
\- LACo 93551 4375-H4
EDISON RD TKTR
\- LACo - 505-C2
EDITH AV
800 ALH 91803 596-A7
N EDITH AV
500 WCOV 91790 598-F6
EDITH LN
\- LAN 93535 4106-C2
EDITH ST
3200 LA 90064 632-F7
EDITH WY
600 Bxby 90807 765-C6
EDITH ANN DR
600 AZU 91702 568-H4
EDLEEN DR
18700 Tarz 91356 560-H4
EDLOFT AV
3200 LA 90032 595-D6
EDMARU AV
800 WHIT 90605 707-E2
8100 WHIT 90602 707-E2
EDMINSTER LN
4300 LVRN 91750 570-F7
EDMOND DR
8600 RSMD 91770 596-G6
EDMONDS PL
\- Saug 91350 4461-E6
EDMONDSON AL
300 PAS 91105 565-H7
EDMONTON PL
8700 ING 90305 703-D3
EDMONTON RD
2900 GLDL 91206 565-B2
EDMORE AV
1300 RowH 91748 679-C4
EDMORE PL
9800 SunV 91352 533-C2
EDMUND AV
5800 LaCr 91214 504-H5
EDNA PL
15800 IRW 91706 598-F4
E EDNA PL
100 COV 91723 599-B4
900 COV 91724 599-E4
16100 LACo 91722 598-F4
16500 COV 91722 598-G4
W EDNA PL
100 COV 91723 599-A4
400 LACo 91723 599-A4
600 COV 91722 599-A4
600 LACo 91722 599-A4
600 COV 91722 598-H4
1100 LACo 91722 598-H4
EDNA ST
800 SBdC 92397 (4652-B1 See Page 4651)
5200 LA 90032 595-F6
8200 PRV 90660 676-F2
EDOM ST
1600 CRSN 90746 764-G4
EDRA AV
4400 BALD 91706 598-B4
EDRIDGE CT
2800 PMDL 93551 4195-C6
EDRIS DR
1200 LA 90035 632-G3
EDSEL AV
5100 LA 90066 672-E6
EDSON AV
43300 LAN 93536 4105-D2
EDUARDO ST
10000 LACo 90606 676-J3
EDUCATORS WY
\- FUL 92835 738-H5
EDWARD AV
100 FUL 92833 738-A7
2900 LA 90065 594-G3
EDWARD ST
13000 LACo 93536 4013-A3
EDWARD WY
\- LA 90065 594-F3
EDWARD EVERETT HORTON LN
5500 Enc 91316 561-C2
EDWARDS AV
2000 SELM 91733 637-B3
2700 ELMN 91733 637-B1
EDWARDS DR
10400 MTCL 91763 641-D1
EDWARDS PL
200 GLDL 91206 565-A4
EDWARDS RD
12600 LMRD 90638 737-D1
16600 CRTS 90703 737-D7
EDWIN AV
500 POM 91767 601-A3
EDWIN DR
8400 LA 90046 592-G1
EDWIN PL
2700 LA 90046 592-H1
EDWIN ALDRIN CIR
400 MTBL 90640 676-E1
EFFIE PL
3200 Echo 90026 594-C5
EFFIE ST
1700 Echo 90026 594-C6
3900 LA 90029 594-B5
EFFINGHAM PL
3700 LFlz 90027 594-C2
EGAN AV
1100 LACo 91744 638-D4
EGBERT ST
13400 LA 91342 482-C1

STREET Block City ZIP Pg-Grid

EGERER PL
3300 FUL 92835 738-H1
EGIL AV
13000 BALD 91706 597-J7
EGLEY AV
7400 RSMD 91770 636-D2
EGLISE AV
5500 PRV 90660 676-G5
7800 PRV 90660 706-F1
9000 DWNY 90240 706-E3
10200 DWNY 90241 706-D5
EGRET PL
20100 SCTA 91351 4551-E4
EHLERS DR
9300 Chat 91311 499-F6
23500 Chat 91311 499-F6
EHREN AV
11400 LA 91342 503-B1
EIDER ST
2800 LVRN 91750 570-J6
EIFFEL CIR
2100 UPL 91784 571-J4
EIGER CT
15900 CHLS 91709 710-F1
EIGHTH ST
12400 NRWK 90650 706-J7
12500 NRWK 90650 707-A7
EILAT CIR
\- SIMI 93063 499-B1
EILAT PL
5800 WdHl 91367 559-C1
EILAT ST
24400 WdHl 91367 559-C1
EILEEN AV
5400 LACo 90043 673-D6
5700 LA 90043 673-D6
S EILEEN AV
100 COV 91722 598-J5
W EILEEN CT
1100 UPL 91784 571-J6
EILEEN LN
4500 RSMD 91770 596-H6
N EILEEN ST
600 WCOV 91791 598-J6
EILINITA AV
900 GLDL 91208 534-F3
EINSTEIN AV
1800 LAN 93535 4106-D1
EISENHOWER AV
\- LACo 90073 631-J4
EISENHOWER WY
5500 PMDL 93552 4287-C5
EL ABACA PL
4500 Tarz 91356 560-H4
EL ADOBE LN
5000 LaCr 91214 504-G7
EL ADOBE PL
400 FUL 92835 738-G2
ELAINE AV
13700 NRWK 90650 736-H3
16600 ART 90701 736-H6
17100 CRTS 90703 736-H7
17800 ART 90701 766-H2
19900 CRTS 90703 766-H3
20600 LKWD 90715 766-H4
21300 HGDN 90716 766-H5
ELAINE DR
9400 LACo 91390 4373-H2
ELAINE ST
600 POM 91767 601-A6
ELANITA DR
1900 LA 90732 823-J7
EL ARBOLITA DR
1900 GLDL 91208 534-H5
EL ARCO DR
9700 WHIT 90603 707-H3
10900 WHIT 90604 707-H6
EL ATAJO ST
700 LA 90065 594-J3
700 LA 90065 595-A3
EL AZUL CIR
500 VeCo 91377 557-J1
ELBA PL
5800 WdHl 91367 559-E1
6100 WdHl 91367 529-E7
ELBA ST
8600 PRV 90660 676-G2
EL BAILE PL
2200 HacH 91745 678-C4
ELBEN AV
9200 SunV 91352 503-E6
ELBEN DR
4600 LPMA 90623 767-C4
ELBEN PL
9200 SunV 91352 503-E6
ELBERGLEN DR
2200 HacH 91745 678-F5
ELBERLAND ST
19100 LACo 91792 679-C2
W ELBERON AV
400 SPed 90731 824-B3
1000 LA 90732 824-A4
1200 LA 90732 823-J4
ELBERON ST
2000 RPV 90275 823-H4
EL BONITO AV
300 GLDL 91204 564-E7
300 GLDL 91204 594-E1
EL BOSQUE CT
1400 PacP 90272 630-G1
EL BRASO DR
9600 WHIT 90603 707-H3

S EL BRASO DR
10400 WHIT 90603 707-H5
ELBURG ST
8200 PRM 90723 735-H3
EL CABALLERO DR
4400 Tarz 91356 560-H4
EL CABALLO DR
1000 ARCD 91006 566-J4
EL CAJON ST
15400 LA 91342 481-G5
EL CAJONITA DR
2000 LHH 90631 708-B1
EL CAMINITO
2600 LaCr 91214 504-F6
3400 GLDL 91214 504-D5
EL CAMINO
1400 MTBL 90640 636-C7
1600 POM 91768 600-F6
EL CAMINO AV
14300 PRM 90723 735-E4
EL CAMINO CIR
7400 BPK 90620 767-G2
EL CAMINO DR
400 FUL 92835 738-G5
500 LHB 90631 708-D4
8500 RSMD 91770 636-G5
36200 LACo 93551 4285-J5
S EL CAMINO DR
100 BHLS 90212 632-G3
EL CAMINO WY
100 CLAR 91711 601-D4
EL CAMINO CORTO
4400 LCF 91011 535-A3
EL CAMINO ESPLANADE
3200 WAL 91789 679-D2
3200 WCOV 91792 679-D2
EL CAMINO REAL
1000 VeCo 93063 499-B4
EL CAMPO CIR
7400 BPK 90620 767-G3
EL CAMPO DR
800 LACo 91107 566-F6
EL CANEY DR
7600 BPK 90620 767-H3
EL CANO AV
\- LACo 93591 4200-F4
EL CANON AV
4800 LA 91302 559-F4
5500 WdHl 91367 559-D1
6100 WdHl 91367 529-D7
EL CANON DR
1300 LHB 90631 708-E4
EL CANTO DR
4900 Eagl 90041 564-J6
EL CAPITAN AV
2200 ARCD 91006 597-D2
EL CAPITAN CT
800 LACo 90601 637-G5
EL CAPITAN WY
7500 BPK 90620 767-H2
EL CAPRICE AV
7600 NHol 91605 532-F3
E EL CARMEN ST
6700 LBCH 90815 796-F3
EL CASCO ST
14100 LA 91342 482-A2
14500 LA 91342 481-J3
E EL CEDRAL ST
5100 LBCH 90815 796-B5
EL CEDRO CIR
7400 BPK 90620 767-G2
EL CEDRO ST
600 LA 90065 594-J3
EL CENTRO AV
700 LA 90038 593-F5
1300 Hlwd 90028 593-F5
EL CENTRO ST
300 SPAS 91030 595-F2
EL CENTRO WY
7400 BPK 90620 767-H2
EL CERCO PL
600 PacP 90272 631-A6
EL CERRITO CIR
1200 SPAS 91030 595-G2
EL CERRITO PL
1700 Hlwd 90028 593-D4
1800 LA 90068 593-D4
N EL CERRITO PL
1900 LA 90068 593-D3
EL CERRO DR
7000 BPK 90620 767-G2
EL CERRO LN
11600 LA 91604 562-H7
EL CHACO DR
7600 BPK 90620 767-H3
EL CHINO CIR
7400 BPK 90620 767-G3
EL CIELO CIR
7200 BPK 90620 767-G3
EL CIELO LN
200 BRAD 91010 568-C3
EL CINO PL
1800 GLDL 91208 534-H4
EL CIRCUITO
\- CLAR 91711 571-F3
EL CIRCULO DR
\- PAS 91105 565-F4
EL COCO WY
7800 BPK 90620 767-G3
EL CONCHO LN
\- RHLS 90274 823-D2
EL CONTENTO DR
2200 LA 90068 593-F2

EL CORONADO
400 SPAS 91030 595-F4
EL CORTEZ AV
6500 BGDN 90201 675-H7
6500 BGDN 90201 705-H1
EL CORTEZ CIR
7400 BPK 90620 767-G2
EL CORTO DR
1300 Alta 91001 536-B5
ELDA ST
2300 BRAD 91010 568-D4
2500 DUAR 91010 568-D4
ELDEN AV
900 LA 90006 634-B4
7700 WHIT 90602 677-E7
7900 WHIT 90602 707-E1
8100 WHIT 90605 707-E1
ELDEN WY
1000 BHLS 90210 592-E6
ELDENA DR
27600 RPV 90275 823-H1
ELDER AV
1500 KeCo 93560 3835-A2
3500 KeCo 93560 3834-A2
8000 KeCo 93560 3833-J2
ELDER CT
900 HiPk 90042 595-E1
E ELDER DR
100 CLAR 91711 601-E4
ELDER ST
1900 WCOV 91790 638-D1
6400 HiPk 90042 595-E1
ELDERBANK DR
3800 LA 90031 595-C5
ELDERBERRY AV
12200 CHNO 91710 641-J5
N ELDERBERRY AV
100 ONT 91762 601-J6
100 ONT 91762 641-J1
S ELDERBERRY AV
900 ONT 91762 641-J2
ELDERBERRY CIR
\- CRSN 90746 764-F1
ELDERBERRY CT
40400 PMDL 93551 4195-B3
N ELDERBERRY CT
1500 ONT 91762 601-J5
ELDERBERRY DR
600 LACo 91302 589-A7
600 LACo 91302 629-A1
ELDERBERRY ST
400 LVRN 91750 600-C3
17800 LACo 93532 4101-J2
ELDER CREEK CT
38700 PMDL 93551 4195-D6
ELDER CREEK DR
21000 SCTA 91350 4461-C6
ELDERGLEN LN
1100 Hrbr 90710 794-A2
ELDERHALL AV
5000 LKWD 90712 765-G4
ELDERIDGE DR
9700 LA 90210 592-D5
ELDERMOOR DR
2600 LACo 90265 629-E4
ELDEROAK LN
2600 VeCo 91361 586-E1
ELDEROAK RD
2700 VeCo 91361 586-E2
ELDERTREE DR
1500 DBAR 91765 679-J4
ELDER VIEW DR
27400 SCTA 91354 4460-H6
ELDERWAY DR
2000 HacH 91745 678-E4
ELDERWOOD ST
11300 Brwd 90049 631-H2
EL DIABLO CIR
7600 BPK 90620 767-H3
EL DOMINGO CIR
2100 LAN 93536 4015-E6
EL DOMINO WY
7300 BPK 90620 767-G3
N ELDON AV
300 LPUE 91744 638-D5
S ELDON AV
1100 HacH 91745 678-A1
EL DON DR
1600 LHB 90631 708-C5
ELDORA AV
10100 SunV 91040 503-G2
ELDORA PL
11000 SunV 91040 503-G2
ELDORA RD
400 PAS 91104 565-J2
400 PAS 91104 566-A2
EL DORADO AV
1500 LHB 90631 708-C5
9000 SunV 91352 502-F6
9900 Pcma 91331 502-B2
11300 LA 91340 502-B1
12100 LA 91342 481-F4
EL DORADO CT
\- LACo 91770 636-F4
\- POM 91766 640-D4
19600 SCTA 91351 4551-H3
ELDORADO CT
38000 PMDL 93551 4285-H1
EL DORADO DR
\- Actn 93510 4465-F2
800 FUL 92832 738-G6
1000 FUL 92835 738-G6
3200 LBCH 90808 796-J1

EL DORADO DR
7000 BPK 90620 767-G3
13100 SLB 90740 796-G7
13200 SLB 90740 826-G1
ELDORADO DR
4800 LVRN 91750 570-G6
N EL DORADO DR
3400 LBCH 90808 766-J7
3400 LBCH 90808 796-J1
EL DORADO LN
\- LACo 90606 676-H6
EL DORADO PZ
3600 LBCH 90808 766-H7
EL DORADO ST
400 PAS 91101 565-J5
800 MNRO 91016 567-E6
1000 WCOV 91790 598-G6
2100 TOR 90501 763-F6
2500 TOR 90503 763-F6
ELDORADO ST
\- ARCD 91006 567-D6
W EL DORADO ST
1000 WCOV 91790 598-E5
EL DORADO WY
10300 LALM 90720 796-J1
EL DORADO MEADOW RD
24700 HIDH 91302 559-C1
W ELDRED AV
1600 WCOV 91790 598-E6
ELDRED ST
4700 HiPk 90042 595-B3
ELDRED WK
4700 LA 90065 595-A3
4700 HiPk 90042 595-A3
ELDREST ST
5100 Actn 93510 4374-H2
ELDRIDGE AV
11300 LA 91342 502-H1
11500 LA 91342 482-C2
ELDRIDGE ST
\- SPed 90731 824-E4
E ELDRIDGE ST
100 Bxby 90807 795-D2
ELDROW RD
33200 LACo 91390 4373-G6
ELEANOR AV
6000 LA 90038 593-E6
ELEANOR CIR
\- LACo 91387 4552-A3
ELEANOR CT
3800 LAN 93535 4106-H1
10600 NRWK 90650 736-E2
E ELEANOR LN
200 NLB 90805 735-C7
ELEANOR PL
1900 LMTA 90717 793-H4
ELEANOR ST
1200 NLB 90805 735-F7
N ELEANOR ST
200 POM 91767 641-A1
800 POM 91767 601-A7
S ELEANOR ST
100 POM 91766 641-A2
ELEANORE DR
2000 GLDL 91206 564-J3
ELECTRA AV
1300 RowH 91748 679-C4
ELECTRA CT
\- SCTA 91351 4551-G2
1800 LA 90046 593-B4
ELECTRA DR
7800 LA 90046 593-B3
ELECTRA ST
100 POM 91766 641-C2
ELECTRIC AV
100 LHB 90631 708-E6
100 SLB 90740 826-E3
400 Ven 90291 671-H5
1400 SBdC 91784 571-H2
N ELECTRIC AV
\- ALH 91801 595-J5
S ELECTRIC AV
\- ALH 91801 595-J5
100 MONP 91754 636-A2
300 ALH 91803 595-J5
1200 ALH 91803 596-A7
1900 ALH 91803 636-A1
ELECTRIC CT
1100 LBCH 90813 795-D6
1400 Ven 90291 671-H5
ELECTRIC DR
100 PAS 91103 565-H4
S ELECTRIC LN
800 ALH 91803 595-J6
800 ALH 91803 596-A6
ELECTRIC ST
1000 LA 90248 764-A1
1000 GAR 90248 764-A1
2200 LA 90039 594-E4
8800 CYP 90630 767-D5
ELECTRONIC DR
3300 PAS 91107 566-G3
ELECTRONICS PL
4500 LA 90039 564-C5
ELEDA DR
3600 TOR 90505 793-D4
EL EMPINO DR
2200 LHH 90631 708-B1
ELENA AV
2600 WCOV 91792 639-A7
N ELENA AV
400 RBCH 90277 762-H4

S ELENA AV
1600 RBCH 90277 792-J1
1700 TOR 90277 792-J1
ELENA CT
\- LAN 93536 4104-F1
16400 WHIT 90603 708-A5
ELENA DR
\- LAN 93536 4104-F2
ELENA PL
\- LACo 93536 4104-J5
ELENA ST
\- LAN 93536 4104-F2
10800 CRTS 90703 736-E6
EL ENCANTO DR
300 PAS 91107 566-F5
1200 BREA 92821 708-H4
4200 CALB 91302 588-G1
EL ENCANTO RD
300 INDS 91745 638-C7
N EL ENCINO DR
200 DBAR 91765 640-C6
S EL ENCINO DR
200 DBAR 91765 640-C6
ELENDA ST
4000 CULC 90232 672-F3
4200 CULC 90230 672-F3
EL ESCORIAL WY
7600 BPK 90620 767-H3
EL ESCORPION RD
5900 WdHl 91367 559-D1
6000 WdHl 91367 529-E7
EL ESPEJO RD
13600 LMRD 90638 737-E3
ELEVA AV
300 SDMS 91773 600-B2
ELEVADO AV
1600 ARCD 91006 567-D2
9000 WHWD 90069 592-H6
9100 BHLS 90210 592-F7
9500 BHLS 90210 632-E1
ELEVADO LN
2700 PVE 90274 792-J4
ELEVADO ST
1400 Echo 90026 594-C6
W ELEVADO TER
400 MONP 91754 635-H3
ELEVEN CT
\- SCTA 91321 4551-F5
EL FERROL WY
7500 BPK 90620 767-H3
ELFORD DR
3600 LACo 90601 677-A2
ELFSTONE CT
1000 THO 91361 557-A5
ELFSTROM DR
\- FUL 92833 738-C6
ELFWOOD DR
300 MNRO 91016 567-J3
ELGAR AV
16700 TOR 90504 733-F7
17100 TOR 90504 763-F1
EL GATO PL
25800 SCTA 91355 4550-G4
EL GAVILAN DR
15200 HacH 91745 677-J4
E ELGENIA AV
1000 WCOV 91790 598-G5
E ELGENIA ST
16000 LACo 91722 598-F5
W ELGENIA ST
1000 WCOV 91790 598-F5
ELGERS ST
10500 BLF 90706 766-D1
10700 CRTS 90703 766-J1
13400 CRTS 90703 767-C1
ELGIN AL
500 PAS 91104 565-J2
ELGIN ST
\- ALH 91801 596-B4
6300 HiPk 90042 595-E1
ELGRACE ST
11100 SFSP 90670 706-F4
EL GRANADA AV
11400 LYN 90262 735-E1
EL GRECO CT
3200 HacH 91745 678-D6
EL HITO CIR
1200 PacP 90272 630-H3
EL HITO CT
16400 PacP 90272 630-H3
EL HITO PL
16400 PacP 90272 630-H3
ELI PL
1700 HacH 91745 678-E4
ELIAS AV
27100 SCTA 91350 4461-A7
ELIDA PL
15300 LACo 93532 4102-E4
ELINDA PL
10900 SunV 91352 503-A5
ELINDA WY
9600 SunV 91352 503-A5
ELINOR DR
500 FUL 92835 738-H2
ELIOPULOS DR
43600 LAN 93536 4105-C2
ELIOPULOS RANCH DR
\- PMDL 93551 4195-A6
ELIOT CT
25800 StvR 91381 4550-D7
ELIOT LN
300 LBCH 90814 796-B7
300 LBCH 90814 826-B1

ELIOT ST
5200 LBCH 90803 796-B7
5300 LBCH 90803 826-C1
5400 LBCH 90814 826-C1
E ELIOT ST
6300 LBCH 90803 796-E7
ELISA PL
16200 Enc 91436 561-E5
ELITE LN
43500 LAN 93535 4106-C2
ELIZA
18000 LACo 90220 764-J1
ELIZABETH AV
100 MONP 91755 636-D2
3300 LYN 90262 705-B6
8100 SGAT 90280 705-B3
ELIZABETH CIR
1200 UPL 91786 601-G2
ELIZABETH CT
30100 AGRH 91301 557-H5
ELIZABETH LN
43400 LAN 93535 4106-C2
ELIZABETH ST
200 PAS 91104 565-J1
600 PAS 91104 566-A1
1600 LACo 91104 566-C1
4100 CDHY 90255 705-D2
4200 CDHY 90201 705-D2
4800 BALD 91706 598-C3
11400 NRWK 90650 706-G6
E ELIZABETH ST
1400 COMP 90221 735-B5
2000 RDom 90221 735-B5
ELIZABETH WY
300 FUL 92833 738-E7
19700 SCTA 91351 4551-F3
ELIZABETH LAKE RD
Rt#-N2
700 PMDL 93551 4195-A6
700 LACo 93551 4195-D7
3500 PMDL 93551 4194-E4
4000 LACo 93551 4194-A3
7700 LACo 93551 4193-D1
8000 LACo 93532 4102-A2
8000 LACo 93551 4102-G4
8000 LACo 93551 4103-A7
17500 LACo 93532 4101-H2
ELIZALDE AV
8500 Nor 91324 530-H1
ELIZONDO ST
18800 LACo 91744 679-B2
18800 LACo 91792 679-B2
E EL JARDIN ST
5300 LBCH 90815 796-C5
ELK AV
29000 Cstc 91384 4459-D6
E ELK AV
100 GLDL 91205 564-F5
W ELK AV
100 GLDL 91204 564-D5
ELK CIR
4500 LVRN 91750 570-E7
ELKGROVE AV
1000 Ven 90291 671-J4
2300 CMRC 90040 675-H4
ELKGROVE CIR
1400 Ven 90291 671-J4
ELKHART PL
900 Ven 90291 671-J4
ELKHILL DR
15300 HacH 91745 678-A3
ELKHORN DR
200 DUAR 91010 568-F4
ELKHORN LN
1400 GLDR 91740 569-H6
ELKHORN RD
35100 LACo 91390 4374-E3
ELKHURST ST
11200 SFSP 90670 706-F4
ELKINS AV
100 ARCD 91006 567-D1
1100 SMAD 91024 567-D1
ELKINS PL
100 ARCD 91006 567-D1
ELKINS RD
500 Brwd 90049 631-E2
ELKLAND PL
900 Ven 90291 671-J4
ELKLANE DR
1500 HacH 91745 678-F4
ELKMONT DR
5100 RPV 90275 793-B6
E ELKO ST
4200 LBCH 90814 796-A7
ELKPORT ST
2700 LKWD 90712 765-H4
5900 LKWD 90713 766-D5
ELKRIDGE DR
4900 RPV 90275 793-C7
ELK RIDGE RD
\- Cstc 91384 4369-G5
ELKRIDGE ST
800 BREA 92821 708-J5
ELK RUN LN
41800 LACo 93536 4104-F6
ELKS HILL WY
\- FUL 92835 738-H5
ELKS RAPID LN
1000 DBAR 91765 640-D5
ELKWOOD
1600 WCOV 91791 638-J4
1600 WCOV 91791 639-A4

ELKWOOD CT
500 BREA 92821 708-H6
ELKWOOD LN
27600 Cstc 91384 4459-H3
ELKWOOD RD
20300 WAL 91789 639-F7
ELKWOOD ST
10100 SunV 91352 533-A3
11200 SunV 91352 532-H3
11400 NHol 91605 532-D3
17200 VanN 91406 531-B3
17300 Nor 91325 531-B3
17700 Res 91335 531-A3
18100 Res 91335 530-F3
20100 Win 91306 530-D3
20900 LA 91304 530-A3
22000 LA 91304 529-E3
ELLA RD
28000 RPV 90275 792-H6
EL LADO DR
3500 GLDL 91208 534-E2
3700 GLDL 91214 534-D1
3900 GLDL 91214 504-D7
ELLEN DR
4000 LACo 91722 598-G4
N ELLEN DR
100 WCOV 91790 598-F5
ELLEN PL
1100 POM 91766 641-B5
ELLEN ST
\- NLB 90805 735-G7
10600 ELMN 91731 597-C5
ELLEN WY
200 ARCD 91006 567-E6
19400 CRTS 90703 766-G3
ELLENAN ST
34600 Actn 93510 4375-C3
ELLENBOGEN ST
7800 SunI 91040 503-G1
ELLENBORO WY
4400 WdHl 91364 560-C4
ELLENDA AV
3200 LA 90034 632-D7
3200 LA 90034 672-E1
ELLENDA PL
10800 LA 90034 672-D1
ELLENDALE PL
1900 LA 90007 634-A6
ELLENITA AV
3900 Tarz 91356 560-F4
ELLENVALE AV
5300 WdHl 91367 559-D3
ELLENVIEW AV
5900 WdHl 91367 529-D7
5900 WdHl 91367 559-D1
6200 CanP 91307 529-D7
ELLENWOOD DR
4400 Eagl 90041 564-J5
4400 Eagl 90041 594-J1
ELLENWOOD PL
5100 Eagl 90041 564-J5
ELLERAY PL
900 GLDR 91741 569-C5
E ELLERFORD ST
8200 LBCH 90808 767-A7
N ELLERY DR
200 LA 90732 823-J4
S ELLERY DR
100 LA 90732 823-J4
N ELLERY PL
200 LA 90732 823-J4
ELLERY WY
\- CynC 91351 4462-A4
ELLESFORD AV
1500 RowH 91748 679-C4
S ELLESFORD AV
3900 WCOV 91792 679-C2
ELLETT PL
900 Echo 90026 594-C7
ELLICE ST
11700 VeCo 90265 625-E5
ELLINCOURT DR
1600 SPAS 91030 595-H1
ELLINGBROOK DR
100 MTBL 90640 636-F5
ELLINGTON DR
3000 LA 90068 593-C1
3100 LA 90068 563-C7
ELLINGTON LN
900 PAS 91105 565-E7
ELLINGTON VILLA DR
3300 Alta 91001 536-B3
ELLINWOOD DR
21300 TOR 90503 763-B6
22100 TOR 90505 763-B7
22600 TOR 90505 793-B1
ELLIOT GRN
8200 BPK 90621 737-J4
ELLIOTT AV
10600 SELM 91733 637-C2
10600 ELMN 91733 637-C2
11300 ELMN 91732 637-E3
15300 LPUE 91744 638-D5
S ELLIOTT AV
100 AZU 91702 568-J7
100 AZU 91702 598-J1
ELLIOTT CT
700 POM 91766 641-A3
ELLIOTT DR
500 PAS 91106 565-J7
500 PAS 91106 566-A7
1700 BURB 91504 533-F5

ELLIOTT LN
\- SCTA 91321 4640-H2
ELLIOTT PL
700 GLDL 91202 564-C1
ELLIOTT ST
900 Boyl 90033 634-H3
ELLIS AV
1800 SIGH 90755 795-H5
8900 LA 90034 632-H7
E ELLIS AV
100 ING 90302 673-C7
W ELLIS AV
100 ING 90302 673-B7
ELLIS CT
\- LHB 90631 708-D7
28000 SCTA 91350 4461-C6
ELLIS DR
3300 LA 90068 563-D7
ELLIS LN
600 FUL 92832 738-H6
3500 RSMD 91770 597-A7
4400 ELMN 91731 597-A5
4400 TEML 91780 597-A5
4500 ELMN 91780 597-A5
ELLIS PL
\- Cstc 91384 4459-B5
100 FUL 92832 738-H6
ELLIS ST
\- NLB 90805 765-D2
400 PAS 91105 565-G5
ELLISA RD
4500 Actn 93510 4374-G1
ELLIS HENRY AV
\- SCTA 91321 4551-E6
ELLISON DR
2700 LA 90210 592-D2
ELLISON ST
3400 City 90063 635-D3
ELLISON WY
27200 SCTA 91354 4460-G7
ELLITA PL
100 HiPk 90042 595-C3
EL LOBO CIR
19600 CRTS 90623 767-B3
ELLORA ST
16500 LPUE 91744 678-E1
ELLSMERE AV
1400 LA 90019 633-B5
ELLSTREE DR
18200 LACo 93532 4101-H2
E ELLSTREE DR
18100 LACo 93532 4101-H2
ELLSWORTH ST
300 AZU 91702 568-H3
3200 Echo 90026 594-B7
EL LUCERO CIR
7200 BPK 90620 767-G3
ELM
\- LA 91342 481-G2
1200 SDMS 91773 599-H2
18800 RowH 91748 679-B4
ELM AV
\- LBCH 90802 825-E1
100 LBCH 90802 795-E7
200 BURB 91502 563-H2
300 BURB 91506 563-H2
300 NLB 90805 765-D3
500 SMAD 91024 567-A1
600 SGBL 91775 596-F3
700 LBCH 90813 795-E7
800 TOR 90503 763-F6
1000 GLDL 91201 563-J1
1100 GLDL 91201 534-A7
1100 GLDL 91201 564-A1
1100 MANB 90266 732-G4
1400 ELSG 90245 732-G1
3000 Bxby 90807 795-E2
3500 Bxby 90807 765-D5
8200 LACo 91775 596-F3
8800 TEML 91780 596-G3
10700 LYN 90262 705-E6
22600 TOR 90505 793-F1
43600 LAN 93534 4105-H1
44000 LAN 93534 4015-G4
N ELM AV
1300 LBCH 90813 795-E5
2100 LBCH 90806 795-E3
3800 Bxby 90807 765-D1
5100 NLB 90805 765-D1
W ELM AV
300 ING 90301 703-B3
600 ELSG 90245 732-D1
ELM CIR
8500 BPK 90620 767-J4
ELM CT
\- CRSN 90746 764-D3
100 BURB 91502 563-J1
21300 SIMI 93063 499-B3
28800 SCTA 91390 4460-J2
ELM DR
3500 CALB 91302 559-E7
3500 CALB 91302 589-E1
N ELM DR
100 BHLS 90210 632-G1
500 BHLS 90210 592-F7
S ELM DR
100 BHLS 90212 632-G2
1100 LA 90035 632-G2
ELM LN
1000 PAS 91103 565-H2
31500 Cstc 91384 4369-G7
ELM PK
39200 PMDL 93551 4195-F5

ELM PL
\- Nor 91326 500-E1
ELM ST
\- ALH 91801 595-H5
100 MTBL 90640 676-C5
100 POM 91766 641-E3
600 LHB 90631 708-E5
1200 Ven 90291 672-A5
1300 ALH 91803 595-H7
1700 ALH 91803 635-H1
2700 LA 90065 594-H4
4400 SBdC 91710 641-E3
5600 SBdC 92397 (4652-D2
See Page 4651)
6900 CMRC 90040 676-A5
8300 Flor 90001 704-G2
8600 Wats 90002 704-G3
11000 LYN 90262 705-D7
11400 LYN 90262 735-D1
44600 LAN 93534 4015-H6
E ELM ST
100 COMP 90220 734-J3
200 COMP 90220 735-A3
200 COMP 90221 735-A3
S ELM ST
200 POM 91766 641-A2
W ELM ST
100 COMP 90220 734-H3
ELM TR
23700 CALB 91302 559-E7
ELMA RD
3700 LACo 91107 566-H5
EL MANOR AV
7200 Wch 90045 672-G7
7200 Wch 90045 702-G1
ELMBANK RD
5400 RPV 90275 793-A5
ELMBRAKE LN
100 MTBL 90640 636-F5
ELMBRIDGE DR
27400 RPV 90275 793-B7
ELMBROOK DR
13900 LMRD 90638 737-G3
ELM BROOK LN
500 POM 91767 600-H3
ELMCREST ST
1500 LVRN 91750 600-F2
10600 ELMN 91731 597-C5
11300 ELMN 91732 597-E5
ELMCROFT AV
1400 POM 91767 601-C7
10900 DWNY 90241 706-F6
11200 NRWK 90650 706-F6
12700 NRWK 90650 736-F1
16600 CRTS 90703 736-F6
16600 LACo 90703 736-F6
ELMCROFT CIR
2000 LHB 90631 708-B7
ELMDALE DR
4800 RHE 90274 793-B5
ELMDALE PL
17200 GmH 91344 481-C6
EL MEDIO AV
400 PacP 90272 630-J4
900 PacP 90272 631-A4
EL MEDIO PL
1000 PacP 90272 631-A4
ELMER AV
4000 LA 91602 562-J3
5500 NHol 91601 562-J1
6000 NHol 91606 532-J7
7000 WHIT 90602 677-B6
7400 SunV 91352 532-J3
EL MERCADO AV
400 MONP 91754 636-A3
EL MERRIE DEL DR
12200 LACo 91342 482-J6
ELMFIELD AV
1500 LBCH 90815 796-B5
E ELMGATE ST
100 MONP 91755 636-B5
W ELMGATE ST
100 MONP 91754 636-A5
ELM GLEN CIR
23000 SCTA 91354 4460-H5
ELMGROVE DR
1300 GLDR 91741 569-H4
ELMGROVE ST
2200 LA 90031 594-H6
ELM HAVEN DR
16400 HacH 91745 678-E4
ELM HILL
700 SDMS 91773 599-J4
ELM HILL DR
11500 LACo 90604 708-A6
ELM HILL LN
14500 CHLS 91709 680-H4
ELMHURST AV
1200 DUAR 91010 568-C5
ELMHURST CIR
600 CLAR 91711 571-E7
700 CLAR 91711 601-F1
ELMHURST DR
6500 Tuj 91042 504-B6
11200 NRWK 90650 736-G5
ELMHURST PL
300 FUL 92835 738-H4
ELMHURST ST
18700 RowH 91748 679-B7
ELMHURST WY
1400 UPL 91784 571-H4
EL MIO DR
5900 HiPk 90042 595-C2

ELMIRA AV
3400 CLAR 91711 571-E5
ELMIRA CT
19400 CRTS 90703 766-F3
ELMIRA ST
600 PAS 91104 566-A3
37000 PMDL 93552 4286-J4
EL MIRADERO AV
1400 GLDL 91201 534-B7
1400 GLDL 91201 564-B1
EL MIRADOR AV
1000 LBCH 90815 796-C5
EL MIRADOR DR
500 FUL 92835 738-H2
1200 PAS 91103 565-E2
5200 LA 90008 673-B2
EL MIRADOR ST
14100 LMRD 90638 737-J3
W ELMLAWN DR
2800 ANA 92804 767-J7
ELMO AV
22100 TOR 90503 763-B7
ELMO ST
6500 Tuj 91042 504-A4
EL MOLINA AV
\- SCTA 91355 4460-D6
EL MOLINO AV
\- ALH 91801 596-A2
500 SMRO 91108 596-A2
N EL MOLINO AV
\- PAS 91101 566-A3
600 PAS 91104 566-A3
1300 PAS 91104 565-J1
1600 PAS 91104 535-J7
1800 PAS 91104 536-A7
1900 Alta 91001 536-A7
S EL MOLINO AV
\- PAS 91101 566-A5
500 PAS 91106 566-A6
1200 PAS 91106 596-A1
1400 PAS 91108 596-A1
1600 SMRO 91108 596-A1
EL MOLINO PL
2100 SMRO 91108 596-A2
N EL MOLINO ST
\- ALH 91801 596-C3
S EL MOLINO ST
\- ALH 91801 596-C4
1800 ALH 91801 636-D1
ELMONT AV
8200 PRV 90660 706-D1
8700 DWNY 90240 706-C2
16300 CRTS 90703 737-D6
EL MONTE AV
1100 ARCD 91007 567-C6
1500 ARCD 91007 597-C1
3600 ELMN 91731 597-C5
4800 ELMN 91780 597-C3
4800 TEML 91780 597-C3
EL MONTE DR
7500 BPK 90620 767-G3
E EL MONTE ST
100 SGBL 91776 596-F4
W EL MORADO CT
800 ONT 91762 601-J7
EL MORADO ST
4300 MTCL 91763 601-E7
13000 LMRD 90638 737-J1
EL MORAN ST
2000 LA 90039 594-F4
ELMORE AV
9600 LACo 90604 707-F4
EL MORENO ST
2300 LaCr 91214 534-G1
3700 GLDL 91214 504-D5
EL MORO AV
12800 LMRD 90638 737-D2
EL MOROCCO WY
7900 BPK 90620 767-H3
EL MORRO WY
7300 BPK 90620 767-H3
ELM PARK DR
16500 CRTS 90703 736-J6
ELMPARK ST
1300 SPAS 91030 595-H4
ELMQUIST AV
6200 WHIT 90601 677-E5
6200 WHIT 91745 677-E5
ELMROCK AV
11700 LACo 90604 707-J6
12800 LMRD 90638 737-J1
ELMSBURY LN
7000 CanP 91307 529-D5
ELMSBURY RD
1900 THO 91361 557-A7
ELMSFORD AV
1500 LHB 90631 708-C7
ELMTREE DR
14300 LACo 93532 4102-H5
ELM TREE LN
12900 CHLS 91709 640-J7
ELMTREE RD
10600 Nor 91326 500-H3
ELM VIEW DR
4100 Enc 91316 560-J5
ELM VISTA DR
9200 DWNY 90242 706-C7
ELMWOOD AV
800 BREA 92821 709-A5
4200 LYN 90262 705-D7
4700 LA 90004 593-G7
E ELMWOOD AV
200 BURB 91502 533-J7

STREET
Block City ZIP Pg-Grid

E ELMWOOD AV
200 BURB 91502 563-J1
400 BURB 91501 533-J7
800 BURB 91501 534-A6
W ELMWOOD AV
100 BURB 91502 563-H2
300 BURB 91506 563-H2
ELMWOOD DR
300 PAS 91105 565-D6
ELM WOOD LN
14200 CHLS 91709 680-H3
ELMWOOD LN
- StvR 91381 4550-B4
W ELMWOOD ST
1300 UPL 91786 601-J2
E ELMYRA ST
100 LA 90012 634-H2
W ELMYRA ST
100 LA 90012 634-H2
EL NIDO
5800 LVRN 91750 570-H3
EL NIDO AV
100 MNRO 91016 567-F3
S EL NIDO AV
- PAS 91107 566-F5
EL NIDO DR
2800 Alta 91001 535-F5
EL NIDO LN
2700 LAN 93535 4106-F1
EL NIDO ST
700 LHB 90631 708-E7
ELNORA PL
11900 GrnH 91344 481-C6
ELNORA ST
8200 MTBL 90640 676-F2
8200 PRV 90660 676-F2
EL NORTE AV
700 MNRO 91016 567-F6
EL NORTE ST
200 LACo 91016 567-G6
200 MNRO 91016 567-G6
E EL NORTE ST
100 MNRO 91016 567-G6
W EL NORTE ST
100 MNRO 91016 567-F6
1000 ARCD 91006 567-F6
EL OESTE DR
2700 HMB 90254 732-G7
2700 HMB 90254 762-G1
ELOISE AV
- PAS 91107 566-E4
7800 SunV 91352 532-J3
ELOISE CIR
1600 SIMI 93063 499-A3
ELOISE ST
11200 CRTS 90703 766-F3
ELON AV
9600 Pcma 91331 502-B5
EL ORO LN
800 PacP 90272 630-H4
EL ORO WY
11900 GrnH 91344 481-C5
EL PARAISO DR
1200 POM 91768 600-G6
E EL PARQUE ST
5200 LBCH 90815 796-B5
EL PASEO
- LHH 90631 708-D3
2100 ALH 91803 635-H1
E EL PASEO CT
6300 LBCH 90815 796-E4
EL PASEO DR
2200 LHH 90631 707-J3
2200 WHIT 90603 707-J3
23500 SCTA 91355 4550-F4
EL PASEO RD
400 SPed 90731 824-A5
E EL PASEO ST
5600 LBCH 90815 796-C4
EL PASO CIR
7900 BPK 90620 767-H3
EL PASO CT
700 SDMS 91773 600-C1
EL PASO DR
800 HiPk 90042 595-A2
1000 Eagl 90041 595-A2
1000 Eagl 90041 594-J1
1000 LA 90065 594-J1
1000 LA 90065 595-A2
EL PASO LN
1500 FUL 92833 738-D4
EL PASO ST
2200 LAN 93535 4016-D4
EL PASO WK
2200 LA 90007 633-J6
EL PEQUENO DR
30700 MAL 90265 627-A7
EL PESCADOR LN
8200 LPMA 90623 767-C4
EL POCHE ST
9600 SELM 91733 637-C3
EL PORTAL
- PVE 90274 792-H5
EL PORTAL BLVD
700 MONP 91754 636-A3
EL PORTAL CT
- Boyl 90033 634-J4
1500 LHB 90631 708-C5
N EL PORTAL DR
100 LHB 90631 708-C5
W EL PORTAL DR
1500 LHB 90631 708-C5

EL PORTO ST
100 MANB 90266 732-E4
EL PORTOLO
- PAS 91105 565-F4
EL POSTE DR
7100 BPK 90620 767-G3
EL PRADO AV
1200 TOR 90501 763-G6
E EL PRADO AV
5200 LBCH 90815 796-B5
EL PRADO WY
7300 BPK 90620 767-G2
E EL PRESIDIO ST
2500 CRSN 90810 765-A5
EL PRIETO FIRE RD
4300 Alta 91001 535-F2
4300 PAS 91011 535-F2
4500 LACo - 535-F2
E EL PROGRESO ST
6500 LBCH 90815 796-E4
EL PROVO CIR
7000 BPK 90620 767-G3
E EL PULCRO ST
6500 LBCH 90815 796-E3
EL RANCHO DR
100 LHB 90631 708-C5
5700 WHIT 90601 677-A5
5700 WHIT 90606 677-A4
10400 WHIT 90606 676-J4
20500 WdHl 91367 530-C7
EL RANCHO VERDE DR
4600 CRTS 90623 767-B3
4700 LPMA 90623 767-B3
EL RANCHO VISTA
2000 FUL 92833 738-C4
EL REDONDO
500 RBCH 90277 762-J5
EL REDONDO CIR
7200 BPK 90620 767-G3
E EL REPETTO DR
100 MONP 91755 636-B4
W EL REPETTO DR
100 MONP 91754 636-A4
700 MONP 91754 635-J4
EL REPOSO DR
4500 LA 90065 564-H6
4600 Eagl 90041 564-H6
EL RETIRO CT
900 VeCo 91377 557-H1
EL RETIRO WY
1100 BHLS 90210 592-F5
EL REY DR
700 LHB 90631 708-C5
7100 BPK 90620 767-G3
10300 WHIT 90606 676-J4
10800 WHIT 90606 677-A5
EL REY RD
1700 LA 90732 823-H5
EL RICO PL
24300 DBAR 91765 640-D7
EL RINCON WY
5700 CULC 90230 672-H5
EL RIO AV
5100 Eagl 90041 565-A5
EL RIO ST
2200 LAN 93535 4016-E4
EL RIO VERDE CIR
19600 CRTS 90623 767-B3
EL RITA DR
8100 LA 90046 592-J2
EL RITO AV
1400 GLDL 91208 534-G7
EL ROBLE DR
2700 Eagl 90041 564-H6
EL ROBLE LN
2100 LA 90210 592-F3
E EL ROBLE ST
5100 LBCH 90815 796-B5
6400 LBCH 90815 796-E5
EL RODEO RD
6600 RPV 90275 822-H1
EL ROSA DR
2500 LA 90065 594-H2
EL ROSAL CIR
7300 BPK 90620 767-H3
ELROVIA AV
3900 ELMN 91731 597-E7
4100 ELMN 91732 597-E6
EL ROVIA CIR
7600 BPK 90620 767-G3
ELSA DR
100 FUL 92835 738-H4
ELSA ST
3900 LKWD 90712 765-J4
3900 LKWD 90712 766-A4
6100 LKWD 90713 766-D4
ELSAH AV
1100 LACo 90601 637-G5
E EL SALVADOR ST
6700 LBCH 90815 796-E3
EL SASTRE RD
32400 Actn 93510 4375-H7
32400 Actn 93510 4465-H1
ELSBERRY AV
700 LACo 91744 638-G5
ELSDALE PL
40600 PMDL 93551 4194-F1
41600 LACo 93536 4104-F7
EL SEBO AV
3100 HacH 91745 677-J5
E EL SEGUNDO BLVD
100 ELSG 90245 732-E2
100 LACo 90061 734-D1
300 COMP 90222 734-H1
400 COMP 90222 735-A1
600 Wbrk 90059 734-D1
1900 Wbrk 90222 734-H1
3100 LYN 90262 735-A1
W EL SEGUNDO BLVD
100 ELSG 90245 732-E2
100 LACo 90061 734-A1
400 LA 90061 734-A1
500 LA 90044 734-A1
600 LA 90247 734-A1
700 LACo 90250 733-B2
700 HAW 90250 733-B2
800 COMP 90222 734-F1
1000 GAR 90044 734-A1
1000 GAR 90247 734-A1
1000 LACo 90044 734-A1
1300 GAR 90247 733-F1
1300 LACo 90044 733-F1
1400 GAR 90249 733-F1
1400 LACo 90047 733-F1
1600 COMP 90059 734-F1
2400 HAW 90245 732-E2
2400 HAW 90245 733-B2
2400 ELSG 90245 733-B2
EL SELINDA AV
6200 BGDN 90201 675-G7
6500 BGDN 90201 705-G1
EL SELINDA DR
15100 HacH 91745 677-J4
EL SERENO AV
1300 PAS 91103 565-H1
1500 PAS 91103 535-H7
2000 Alta 91001 535-J3
3500 LA 90032 595-E6
4800 LaCr 91214 534-H1
4900 LaCr 91214 504-H7
EL SERENO DR
1900 ARCD 91007 597-A1
E ELSEY PL
1000 ELSG 90245 732-F2
ELSIE AV
9400 Nor 91324 500-G6
ELSIE DR
3400 CALB 91302 589-E1
ELSIE ST
7200 Flor 90001 674-F7
7200 Flor 90001 704-F1
ELSINORE AV
5500 BPK 90621 737-J6
ELSINORE RD
800 SBdC 92372 (4472-B7
See Page 4471)
2800 SBdC 92371 (4472-G7
See Page 4471)
ELSINORE ST
2100 Echo 90026 594-D7
ELSMERE DR
600 CRSN 90746 764-E3
ELSMERE CANYON MTWY
22200 Nwhl 91321 4641-D6
22300 SCTA 91321 4641-D6
ELSMORE DR
8300 LACo 91770 636-F4
N EL SOL AV
2100 Alta 91001 535-F6
EL SOL DR
2800 LAN 93535 4106-F1
ELSOL PL
200 POM 91767 600-J6
EL SONETO DR
1600 WHIT 90605 707-G3
15700 WHIT 90603 707-J3
ELSPETH AV
4600 LACo 91722 598-J4
N ELSPETH WY
100 COV 91722 598-J4
ELSTEAD ST
14600 BALD 91706 598-D5
ELSTER AV
700 LACo 91744 638-G6
ELSTON AV
8800 DWNY 90240 706-D2
EL SUENO DR
30600 MAL 90265 627-A6
EL SUR ST
1000 ARCD 91006 567-F7
E EL SUR ST
200 LACo 91016 567-G7
200 MNRO 91016 567-G7
500 LACo 91010 567-H7
W EL SUR ST
100 LACo 91016 567-G7
EL TERRAZA DR
900 LHH 90631 708-A2
EL TESORITO
700 SPAS 91030 595-G4
EL TESORO CT
2800 HacH 91745 677-J4
EL TESORO PL
3800 RPV 90275 823-G3
ELTHAM PL
1300 FUL 92833 738-B5
EL TIRO DR
15700 LMRD 90638 737-H3
EL TOMASO WY
7200 BPK 90620 767-G3
S ELTON AV
1500 ELA 90022 675-J2
ELTON CIR
19400 CRTS 90703 766-G3

ELTON ST
4200 BALD 91706 598-D3
EL TORO CIR
19600 CRTS 90623 767-B3
EL TORO WY
7800 BPK 90620 767-G3
EL TOVAR DR
3100 GLDL 91208 534-H5
EL TOVAR PL
8700 WHWD 90069 592-H7
EL TRAVESIA DR
1500 LHH 90631 708-C3
ELUSIVE DR
8000 LA 90046 592-J3
8000 LA 90046 593-A3
ELVA AV
1500 COMP 90222 734-G2
12000 Wbrk 90059 704-F7
12100 Wbrk 90059 734-F1
ELVA ST
11900 Wbrk 90059 704-F7
EL VADO RD
200 DBAR 91765 640-C7
EL VAGO ST
1000 LCF 91011 535-A1
EL VALLENCITO DR
600 WAL 91789 639-F6
EL VECINO PL
- POM 91766 640-E4
EL VELOZ WY
7000 BPK 90620 767-G3
EL VENADO DR
2500 HacH 91745 677-H3
9500 WHIT 90603 707-H3
EL VERANO AV
5000 Eagl 90041 564-H5
EL VERANO DR
7000 BPK 90620 767-G3
ELVIDO DR
2900 Brwd 90049 591-E1
3100 Brwd 90049 561-E7
EL VIENTO WY
7000 BPK 90620 767-G3
ELVILL DR
3000 Brwd 90049 591-E1
ELVINA DR
400 GLDL 91206 564-J4
EL VINO WY
7500 BPK 90620 767-G3
ELVINS ST
11400 LKWD 90715 766-G4
12400 LKWD 90715 767-A4
S ELVIRA AV
600 RBCH 90277 762-J7
ELVIRA RD
5100 WdHl 91364 560-A3
30600 Cstc 91384 4459-B6
EL VISTA CIR
1700 ARCD 91006 567-C2
EL VISTA CT
2000 GLDL 91208 534-J5
EL VOLCAN PL
2600 HacH 91745 678-C5
ELWOOD AV
1500 POM 91768 600-E7
4000 PMDL 93552 4286-H2
4500 PMDL 93552 4287-A2
N ELWOOD AV
100 GLDR 91741 569-F5
S ELWOOD AV
100 GLDR 91741 569-F6
700 GLDR 91740 569-F6
ELWOOD ST
1300 LA 90021 634-H7
1300 POM 91768 600-F7
1400 LA 90021 674-H1
ELWYN DR
13500 BALD 91706 598-A5
ELY AV
3500 LBCH 90808 766-J7
12300 LKWD 90715 766-J5
17100 CRTS 90703 736-J7
19000 CRTS 90703 766-J2
19000 ART 90701 766-J2
21400 LKWD 90716 766-J5
21400 HGDN 90715 766-J5
21400 HGDN 90716 766-J5
ELYRIA DR
800 LA 90065 594-J4
ELYSIAN AV
1400 POM 91767 601-C7
ELYSIAN PARK AV
1100 Echo 90026 634-F1
1100 LA 90012 634-F1
ELYSIAN PARK DR
- LA 90012 594-H7
- LA 90012 634-H1
1300 Echo 90026 594-G6
1300 Echo 90026 634-F1
ELZA DR
16100 HacH 91745 678-C7
ELZEVIR RD
4200 WdHl 91364 560-B5
EMANUEL DR
3500 GLDL 91208 534-F4
S EMBASSY AV
21800 CRSN 90810 765-A6
W EMBASSY AV
2900 ANA 92804 767-J6
EMBASSY CIR
4800 LPMA 90623 767-B5
EMBASSY DR
17000 Enc 91316 561-B3

EMBASSY PL
1000 POM 91767 601-C7
EMBASSY WY
4900 CYP 90630 767-C5
EMBER CT
5500 AGRH 91301 557-G5
EMBER DR
17600 RowH 91748 678-H6
EMBER LN
600 LHB 90631 708-F4
EMBER GLEN RD
16300 HacH 91745 678-E4
EMBREE DR
11500 ELMN 91732 597-F4
EMBURY ST
900 PacP 90272 631-A4
EMDEN RD
34800 LACo 93552 4377-C2
EMDEN ST
1300 Wilm 90744 794-C7
EMELITA ST
11000 NHol 91601 562-J1
11000 NHol 91601 563-A1
12000 LA 91607 562-E1
13500 VanN 91401 562-A1
17300 Enc 91316 561-A1
18200 Tarz 91356 561-A1
23600 WdHl 91367 559-F1
EMENS WY
1500 GLDL 91201 563-J2
1500 GLDL 91201 564-A3
EMERADO DR
9800 WHIT 90603 708-B3
EMERALD
- BREA 92823 710-C6
EMERALD AV
400 WCOV 91791 639-C1
3600 LVRN 91750 600-G1
3600 LVRN 91750 570-G7
EMERALD CIR
4200 CYP 90630 767-A4
EMERALD CT
- StvR 91381 4550-B4
3300 PMDL 93551 4195-B5
EMERALD DR
1300 Echo 90026 634-E3
EMERALD LN
- GAR 90247 734-A3
- POM 91767 600-J2
1500 DBAR 91789 679-G4
2500 LAN 93535 4016-E6
31900 Cstc 91384 4369-G5
EMERALD PL
400 SLB 90740 826-F4
EMERALD ST
200 Echo 90026 634-E3
400 RBCH 90277 762-J5
900 RBCH 90277 763-A5
3400 TOR 90503 763-B5
EMERALD TER
1800 GLDL 91201 534-B6
EMERALD WY
- LACo 91789 679-F6
2000 MONP 91755 636-C5
10700 CULC 90230 672-G3
E EMERALD COVE DR
6200 LBCH 90803 826-D1
EMERALD COVE WY
1500 SLB 90740 826-F4
EMERALD CREEK DR
19700 SCTA 91351 4551-E1
EMERALD DOVE DR
24600 SCTA 91355 4550-E4
EMERALD ISLE DR
2900 GLDL 91206 535-A7
EMERALD MEADOW DR
20000 LACo 91789 679-E5
EMERALD VIEW DR
- RPV 90275 823-F6
EMERSON AV
7700 Wch 90045 702-F1
E EMERSON AV
100 MONP 91755 636-C1
W EMERSON AV
100 MONP 91754 636-B1
800 ALH 91803 636-B1
EMERSON CT
4900 CHNO 91710 641-F6
5700 AGRH 91301 557-J4
EMERSON DR
6700 BPK 90620 767-F2
38900 PMDL 93551 4195-F6
EMERSON LN
25700 StvR 91381 4550-D7
EMERSON PL
900 CLAR 91711 571-B7
1100 MONP 91755 636-E1
1100 RSMD 91770 636-E1
EMERSON ST
900 PAS 91106 566-A3
W EMERSON ST
1000 UPL 91784 571-J3
EMERSON WK
- HiPk 90042 595-E4
EMERSON WY
2900 Alta 91001 535-J5
EMERY AV
2000 LHB 90631 708-H6
13100 BALD 91706 597-J7
EMERY PL
1100 Wilm 90744 794-F5
EMERY ST
3300 LA 90023 675-B2
7700 BPK 90621 737-H6
10500 ELMN 91731 597-C5
11300 ELMN 91732 597-E5
EMERY RANCH RD
2100 FUL 92833 738-A3
2300 FUL 90638 738-A3
EMERYWOOD DR
5300 BPK 90621 738-A6
EMIL AV
6200 CMRC 90040 676-A7
6400 BGDN 90201 676-A7
6500 BGDN 90201 706-A1
6600 BGDN 90201 705-J2
EMILE ZOLA ST
43600 LAN 93535 4106-C1
43900 LAN 93535 4016-C7
EMILIA LN
43400 LAN 93535 4106-C2
EMILIA PL
1900 LA 90732 823-H5
S EMILY DR
1000 WCOV 91790 638-G2
EMILY LN
7300 DWNY 90242 705-G6
S EMILY ST
900 SPed 90731 854-A1
EMIR AV
13900 LA 91342 482-B1
EMMA AV
3400 LA 90031 595-B7
EMMENS WY
12600 SFSP 90670 707-A5
EMMET RD
19800 SCTA 91351 4551-E3
EMMET TER
6600 LA 90068 593-E3
N EMMETT AV
2100 SIMI 93063 499-A2
EMMETT WILLIAMS WY
500 MTBL 90640 676-D2
EMMONS RD
1500 Eagl 90041 565-A7
EMORY DR
1600 CLAR 91711 601-B1
13800 WHIT 90605 707-E1
EMPALMO CT
25800 SCTA 91355 4550-F6
EMPANADA PL
17000 Enc 91436 561-C6
EMPEROR AV
8800 LACo 91775 596-G1
8900 TEML 91775 596-H1
9000 TEML 91780 596-J1
9600 LACo 91007 596-J1
EMPINO LN
22100 SCTA 91350 4460-J7
22100 SCTA 91350 4461-A7
EMPIRE AV
1800 BURB 91504 533-D6
3500 BURB 91505 533-D6
4700 LA 91505 533-D6
EMPIRE DR
3600 LA 90034 632-F7
3600 LA 90034 672-F1
10600 Pcma 91331 502-F3
EMPIRE LNDG
300 LBCH 90803 826-C1
EMPIRE PL
12400 Pcma 91331 502-F3
EMPIS ST
4100 WdHl 91364 560-C5
EMPORIA AV
5100 CULC 90230 672-F5
5100 LA 90230 672-F5
EMPORIA PL
5400 CULC 90230 672-F6
EMPRESS AV
2000 SPAS 91030 595-H4
4100 Enc 91436 561-D5
EMPRESS RD
500 POM 91768 640-B2
EMPRESS OAK CT
- LACo 91387 4552-B4
EMPTY SADDLE AV
1700 SIMI 93063 499-C3
EMPTY SADDLE LN
- RHE 90274 793-E6
EMPTY SADDLE RD
- RHE 90274 793-E6
19300 WAL 91789 639-C7
EMPYREAN WY
10000 CenC 90067 632-F4
ENADIA WY
13800 VanN 91405 532-A5
14700 VanN 91405 531-H5
15700 VanN 91406 531-B5
17700 Res 91335 531-A5
19100 Res 91335 530-F5
19700 Win 91306 530-C5
22500 CanP 91307 529-G5
ENCANADA DR
100 LHH 90631 708-B1
ENCANTADOR
2600 LA 90732 823-F7
ENCANTADORA LN
1100 LAN 93535 4106-B1
ENCANTO DR
- RHE 90274 793-G7
200 GLDR 91741 569-H5
900 ARCD 91007 566-J5
15000 Shrm 91403 561-H5

ENCANTO PKWY
- AZU 91010 568-E5
- DUAR 91010 568-E5
ENCANTO PL
- PMDL 93551 4195-A3
ENCANTO WY
- LAN 93536 4104-E1
42300 LACo 93536 4104-E5
44200 LAN 93536 4014-E7
ENCARO CT
33200 LACo 91390 4373-G6
ENCELIA LN
3200 LAN 93536 4015-B7
ENCHANTED PL
16900 PacP 90272 630-H4
ENCHANTED WY
600 PacP 90272 630-G4
ENCHANTED HILLS RD
1000 Actn 93510 4465-H2
ENCINA RD
21300 Top 90290 590-B6
ENCINAL AV
3000 LaCr 91214 534-E1
3300 GLDL 91214 534-E1
3400 GLDL 91214 504-D7
ENCINAL CANYON RD
100 LACo 90265 587-A7
600 LACo 90265 586-G7
1300 LACo 90265 626-F1
3600 MAL 90265 626-E6
ENCINAS DR
1400 LHH 90631 708-F3
4100 LCF 91011 535-A3
ENCINITA AV
4100 RSMD 91770 596-J6
4800 TEML 91780 596-J3
6700 LACo 91775 596-H1
6900 LACo 91775 566-H7
ENCINITAS AV
12200 LA 91342 481-F5
N ENCINITAS AV
100 MNRO 91016 567-G3
S ENCINITAS AV
100 MNRO 91016 567-G4
ENCINITAS ST
900 LHB 90631 708-E7
ENCINO AV
900 ARCD 91006 567-E7
1100 MNRO 91016 567-E5
4500 Enc 91316 561-B1
6400 VanN 91406 531-B5
7600 Nor 91325 531-B1
8700 Nor 91325 501-B5
10300 GrnH 91344 501-B1
11700 GrnH 91344 481-B7
ENCINO CT
600 ARCD 91006 567-E7
ENCINO DR
700 ARCD 91006 567-E6
1100 SMRO 91108 566-A7
1100 SMRO 91108 596-B1
1100 PAS 91106 566-A7
1100 PAS 91106 596-B1
ENCINO LN
- Enc 91316 561-B3
ENCINO PL
800 MNRO 91016 567-E6
W ENCINO PL
2200 POM 91766 641-A5
ENCINO TER
4800 Enc 91316 561-B3
ENCINO WY
800 MNRO 91016 567-E6
ENCINO HILLS DR
16700 Enc 91436 561-D7
17000 Brwd 90049 561-D7
ENCINO HILLS PL
3800 Enc 91436 561-D6
ENCINO VERDE PL
17000 Enc 91436 561-C6
END CT
2600 LAN 93536 4105-C1
END ST
6000 VeCo 93063 499-B3
ENDEAVOR CIR
- BREA 92821 708-J6
ENDEAVOR ST
27500 AGRH 91301 558-E7
ENDERBY CT
5300 LACo 91302 559-A4
ENDERLY ST
28200 SCTA 91351 4461-F7
ENDICOTT DR
800 CLAR 91711 571-F7
ENDICOTT RD
1900 SMRO 91108 596-E2
ENDICOTT ST
2400 LA 90032 595-F7
ENDRINO PL
600 BHLS 90210 592-G3
ENDSLEIGH AV
8700 ING 90305 703-D3
ENERO CT
- Boyl 90033 634-J4
ENFIELD AV
4800 Enc 91316 561-A1
6200 Enc 91316 531-A7
6400 Res 91335 531-A4
8500 Nor 91325 531-A1
8800 Nor 91325 501-A7
11000 GrnH 91344 501-A2
ENGEL DR
2600 OrCo 90720 796-G5

ENGINEERS ST
- Cstc 91384 4459-J3
ENGLAND AV
10100 ING 90303 703-F5
ENGLANDER ST
500 LACo 90248 734-D5
1000 SPed 90731 824-A1
ENGLE PL
16800 LACo 91744 638-G6
ENGLE WY
44000 LAN 93536 4015-D7
44000 LAN 93536 4105-D1
ENGLEMANN CT
- ARCD 91006 567-A4
ENGLEWILD DR
900 GLDR 91741 569-F3
ENGLEWILD LN
- GLDR 91741 569-F2
ENGLEWOOD CT
- PMDL 93551 4195-A2
ENGLISH RD
2500 CHLS 91709 680-J3
ENGLISH IVY LN
- LACo 91387 4552-B4
ENGLISH OAK CT
- LACo 91387 4552-A3
ENGLISH OAKS CT
2400 SIMI 93063 499-C1
ENGLISH OAKS DR
1000 ARCD 91006 567-A4
ENGLISH OAKS PL
1000 GLDR 91741 569-B5
ENGLISH ROSE PL
- BqtC 91354 4460-E5
ENGMAN RD
500 SBdC 92372 (4472-A6
See Page 4471)
ENGRACIA AV
1100 TOR 90501 763-G6
ENID AV
600 COV 91722 598-H4
4900 LACo 91722 598-H2
5200 LACo 91702 598-H2
5200 AZU 91702 598-H2
N ENID AV
900 AZU 91702 568-H5
S ENID AV
300 AZU 91702 598-H1
ENID ST
1300 COV 91722 598-H3
4900 LACo 91722 598-H3
ENLOE ST
9700 SELM 91733 637-A3
ENNA ST
2300 LACo 90601 637-E6
ENNIS ST
8400 Sunl 91040 503-G4
ENNISMORE AV
27600 SCTA 91351 4551-H3
ENOLA AV
22700 CRSN 90745 794-D1
ENORO DR
4200 LACo 90008 673-C4
ENRAMADA AV
8100 WHIT 90605 707-F2
ENRIQUE ST
20900 WdHl 91364 560-C5
ENRIQUEZ DR
23800 DBAR 91765 640-C7
ENROSE AV
200 LA 90732 823-H4
N ENROSE AV
300 LA 90732 823-H3
28600 RPV 90275 823-H3
ENSELVADO AV
14600 LMRD 90638 737-G3
ENSENADA DR
4200 WdHl 91364 560-B5
ENSENADA PL
4300 WdHl 91364 560-B5
ENSENADA RD
15300 LACo 91390 4192-E3
ENSIGN AV
4400 LA 91602 563-A4
5600 NHol 91601 563-A1
6000 NHol 91606 533-A6
6700 NHol 91605 533-A4
7200 SunV 91352 533-A2
ENSLEY AV
1500 Wwd 90024 632-D2
ENSLOW DR
19000 CRSN 90746 764-E3
ENTERPRISE AV
11000 SFSP 90670 706-G2
N ENTERPRISE AV
900 ING 90302 673-B7
900 ING 90302 703-B1
ENTERPRISE DR
7600 PMDL 93550 4286-G3
ENTERPRISE PKWY
100 LAN 93534 4105-H4
100 LAN 93535 4105-H4
ENTERPRISE PL
300 POM 91768 640-C3
ENTERPRISE ST
2200 LA 90021 634-H7
2800 BREA 92821 709-F7
ENTERPRISE WY
1800 MNRO 91010 567-J6
ENTERTAINMENT WY
- Wch 90045 672-H7
ENTRADA AV
11700 Nor 91326 480-J7

ENTRADA CT
18500 Nor 91326 480-J7
ENTRADA DR
100 LA 90402 631-B7
100 LA 90402 671-B1
600 SMCA 90402 631-C7
1000 LHB 90631 708-D4
1000 OrCo 90631 708-D4
ENTRADA RD
20800 PacP 90272 590-B6
20800 Top 90290 590-B6
ENTRADA ST
2200 CMRC 90040 675-H3
ENTRADA WY
700 GLDR 91741 569-F3
ENTRADERO AV
19000 TOR 90503 763-B3
ENTRADO DR
21600 Top 90290 590-A1
ENTRANCE DR
2400 LFlz 90027 594-C4
ENTRANCE RD
- CRSN 90745 764-G5
- CRSN 90746 764-G5
- LACo 90220 765-A3
ENTRAR DR
5000 PMDL 93551 4194-G2
ENTRECOLINAS PL
1600 POM 91768 600-G6
ENVILLE PL
3500 LA 90016 673-A1
ENVOY ST
14800 LA 91342 481-J6
EOLA DR
300 WAL 91789 639-E7
EOS LN
- SCTA 91351 4551-H2
EPPERSON DR
700 INDS 91748 679-A3
EPPING RD
400 PVE 90274 792-E7
EPSILON ST
22800 WdHl 91364 559-H3
EPSOM PL
9500 PRV 90660 677-A1
EQUADOR WY
5700 BPK 90620 767-D3
EQUATION RD
3600 LACo 91711 600-J2
3600 POM 91767 600-J2
EQUESTRIAN LN
13100 LACo 90601 637-F6
EQUESTRIAN WY
- Actn 93510 4374-J7
4000 LAN 93536 4105-A7
EQUITABLE RD
13900 CRTS 90703 737-D6
ERATO LN
- SCTA 91351 4551-G7
EREMLAND DR
500 COV 91723 599-C6
ERIC AV
16300 NRWK 90703 736-F6
16600 LACo 90703 736-F6
16900 CRTS 90703 736-F6
17700 CRTS 90703 766-F1
ERIC DR
2100 Brwd 90049 631-D1
ERIC PL
- THO 91362 557-A2
ERICA AV
2600 WCOV 91792 639-A7
ERICA CIR
7000 CanP 91307 529-F5
ERICA LN
2500 LAN 93536 4105-D3
ERICK CT
37000 PMDL 93550 4286-C4
ERICKSEN DR
900 POM 91768 640-F1
ERICKSON AV
12500 DWNY 90242 705-G7
13000 DWNY 90242 735-G1
ERIE
- Ago 91301 587-G4
ERIE ST
100 POM 91768 640-F1
E ERIE ST
1600 LBCH 90802 795-G7
ERIEL AV
1000 TOR 90503 763-F5
13200 LACo 90250 733-F2
15100 LACo 90249 733-F5
18400 TOR 90504 763-F2
22400 TOR 90505 793-F1
ERIK CT
18100 LACo 91387 4551-J4
ERIKA CT
1700 RowH 91748 678-H5
ERIKA LN
- PMDL 93551 4195-E7
N ERIN AV
1300 UPL 91786 601-J1
1400 UPL 91786 571-J7
1600 UPL 91784 571-J4
ERIN CIR
19400 CRTS 90703 766-F3
ERIN CT
- LACo 91789 679-F6
2600 WCOV 91792 639-A6
2900 GLDL 91206 535-B7
ERIN LN
12100 LMRD 90638 707-G7

ERIN PL
- LA 91304 529-E3
ERIN WY
2900 GLDL 91206 535-A7
10700 LACo 91390 4373-E4
ERMANITA AV
15200 LACo 90249 733-F5
16600 TOR 90504 733-F7
17500 TOR 90504 763-F1
N ERMINE PL
28000 SCTA 91351 4461-F7
ERMINE ST
18900 SCTA 91351 4461-E7
ERMITA AV
14400 LMRD 90638 737-J3
ERMONT PL
700 SMCA 90402 631-C6
E ERNA AV
300 LHB 90631 708-F5
W ERNA AV
100 LHB 90631 708-D5
ERNEST AV
1900 RBCH 90278 733-A6
5800 CULC 90232 633-A6
5800 LA 90034 633-A6
ERNESTINE AV
11200 LYN 90262 705-C7
11500 LYN 90262 735-C1
EROICA DR
900 MONP 91755 636-D4
ERSKINE DR
500 PacP 90272 630-J6
ERSKINE GRN
8200 BPK 90621 737-J4
ERVILLA PL
1900 POM 91767 600-J6
ERVILLA ST
300 POM 91767 600-J6
1100 POM 91767 601-A6
ERWIN DR
1100 PMDL 93551 4195-G5
ERWIN ST
10500 NHol 91606 533-A7
11000 NHol 91606 532-E7
13000 VanN 91401 532-C7
14500 VanN 91411 532-A7
14600 VanN 91411 531-G7
17700 Enc 91316 531-A7
18100 Res 91335 531-A7
18100 Res 91335 530-G7
21000 WdHl 91367 530-A7
22100 WdHl 91367 529-F7
23500 WdHl 91367 559-F1
ERWOOD AV
13700 NRWK 90650 736-H2
ESCALADA AV
1400 RowH 91748 678-J4
ESCALANTE
- LVRN 91750 570-H4
ESCALANTE DR
5200 LCF 91011 504-H7
ESCALON AV
4800 LACo 90043 673-D4
ESCALON DR
16700 Enc 91436 561-D7
ESCALONA RD
14700 LMRD 90638 737-G5
ESCARPA DR
1900 Eagl 90041 565-A7
ESCARPADO DR
800 LHH 90631 707-J3
ESCOBEDO DR
4700 WdHl 91364 560-B3
ESCONDIDO DR
2800 LACo 90265 627-H3
33000 LACo 91390 4373-F6
ESCONDIDO ST
21100 WdHl 91364 560-B6
ESCONDIDO TR
4300 LACo 90265 627-H5
ESCONDIDO BEACH RD
27400 MAL 90265 667-J1
27400 MAL 90265 668-A1
ESCONDIDO CANYON RD
3700 Actn 93510 4465-A1
3900 Actn 93510 4374-F5
3900 Actn 93510 4464-J1
6900 LACo 91390 4374-A6
7000 LACo 91390 4373-E7
ESCUELA ST
5000 ELA 90022 635-H7
ESCUELA WY
4500 PMDL 93551 4194-J2
ESEVERRI LN
100 LACo 90631 708-C3
ESHELMAN AV
1900 LMTA 90717 793-H4
ESHELMAN WY
1900 LMTA 90717 793-H3
ESKO AV
11200 LA 91342 503-C1
ESMERALDA AV
3700 ELMN 91731 597-D7
ESMERALDA DR
1100 GLDL 91207 564-G1
ESMERALDA ST
4300 LA 90032 595-C6
ESMOND AV
13400 NRWK 90650 736-J2
ESMOND ST
2300 POM 91767 600-J4
ESPADA PL
21300 DBAR 91765 679-H5

STREET
Block City ZIP Pg-Grid

E ESPANITA ST
6500 LBCH 90815 796-E5
ESPANOL AV
1400 MTBL 90640 676-B5
ESPARTA WY
100 SMCA 90402 631-C6
14100 LA 90402 631-C6
ESPARTO RD
4600 WdHl 91364 560-A5
ESPARZA CT
- POM 91766 640-H4
ESPELETTE PL
700 MTBL 90640 676-F1
ESPERA AV
500 PacP 90272 630-F5
ESPERANZA AV
- LBCH 90802 825-F1
- SMAD 91024 567-A2
200 LBCH 90802 795-F7
5700 LACo 90606 676-J4
5800 WHIT 90606 676-J4
5900 PRV 90606 676-J4
ESPERANZA DR
2500 LVRN 91750 570-H4
2600 LACo 91750 570-H4
ESPERANZA ST
600 LA 90023 635-C7
1000 LA 90023 675-C1
7400 DWNY 90242 705-G7
ESPERANZA TER
3300 GLDL 91208 534-F4
ESPERANZA WY
- PMDL 93551 4195-A3
- SCTA 91354 4460-G4
ESPINHEIRA DR
13000 CRTS 90703 767-B2
ESPINOSA CIR
1500 PVE 90274 792-F6
ESPINOZA DR
25800 SCTA 91355 4550-G4
ESPINOZA ST
19300 Tarz 91356 560-G5
ESPITO ST
18000 RowH 91748 678-J4
18200 RowH 91748 679-A4
ESPLANADE
400 RBCH 90277 762-H7
1300 RBCH 90277 792-H1
6200 PdlR 90293 702-A2
W ESPLANADE
100 LA 90292 701-H1
ESPRIT LN
16500 Enc 91436 561-E3
ESPUELLA DR
22300 SCTA 91350 4550-H1
ESPUMA DR
26800 SCTA 91350 4550-J1
ESQUERRA RD
- CynC 91351 4461-G3
18400 LACo 91390 4461-G3
ESQUILIME DR
15700 CHLS 91709 680-F7
16000 CHLS 91709 710-F1
ESQUILINE AV
20000 LACo 91789 679-E5
ESQUIRA PL
16900 Enc 91436 561-D4
ESQUIVEL AV
5300 LKWD 90712 765-J3
ESSEX AV
1200 POM 91767 601-C7
1700 LVRN 91750 570-G7
11000 MTCL 91763 641-E2
11200 SBdC 91766 641-E3
11300 SBdC 91710 641-E3
ESSEX CT
1300 GLDR 91740 599-F1
ESSEX DR
1300 LHB 90631 708-G5
4800 PMDL 93552 4287-B4
8900 Nor 91324 500-G7
13100 CRTS 90703 767-B1
ESSEX LN
1400 GLDL 91207 564-G1
13000 CRTS 90703 767-B1
45300 LAN 93534 4015-F4
ESSEX PL
- SCTA 91354 4460-G6
12900 CRTS 90703 767-B1
ESSEX RD
900 SDMS 91773 599-G4
ESSEX ST
200 GLDR 91740 599-E1
1400 LA 90021 634-F7
4200 MTCL 91763 641-D3
18500 CRTS 90703 766-J1
ESSEXFELLS DR
2500 ALH 91803 635-J2
N ESSEY AV
900 COMP 90221 735-B3
S ESSEY AV
100 COMP 90221 735-C5
900 RDom 90221 735-C5
ESTABAN DR
25800 SCTA 91355 4550-G4
ESTABAN WY
7300 Tuj 91042 504-A5
7300 Tuj 91042 503-J5
ESTADO ST
2800 PAS 91107 566-F3
ESTARA AV
2700 LA 90065 594-F1
ESTATE CT
800 WAL 91789 639-H5
ESTATE DR
1300 LHB 90631 708-G5
ESTATES LN
3600 LACo 90274 793-E5
41000 PMDL 93551 4194-G1
ESTEBAN RD
4200 WdHl 91364 560-B5
ESTEBAN TORRES DR
1200 SELM 91733 637-B5
ESTEL DR
- POM 91768 600-G7
ESTELLA AV
16200 CRTS 90703 736-E6
ESTELLA ST
14400 BALD 91706 598-C4
ESTELLE AV
600 GLDL 91202 564-C3
ESTEPA DR
6700 Tuj 91042 504-A5
ESTEPONA CT
- Boyl 90033 634-J4
ESTEPONA WY
4800 BPK 90621 737-J4
ESTERBROOK AV
27500 SCTA 91351 4551-F2
ESTERINA WY
10600 CULC 90230 672-J5
ESTERO RD
13400 LMRD 90638 737-E2
ESTES RD
1900 Eagl 90041 565-A5
ESTHER AV
2300 LVRN 91750 600-E2
10500 LA 90064 632-D6
ESTHER DR
600 LAN 93535 4106-A1
ESTHER ST
- PAS 91103 565-H3
9100 CYP 90630 767-C6
11400 NRWK 90650 706-G7
11600 LYN 90262 705-A7
E ESTHER ST
300 LBCH 90813 795-E5
2500 LBCH 90804 795-H5
3800 LBCH 90804 796-A5
W ESTHER ST
500 LBCH 90813 795-A5
ESTHER VIEW DR
2400 LMTA 90717 793-G5
ESTO AV
3600 ELMN 91731 597-C6
ESTON PL
600 LAN 93535 4016-A7
ESTORIL CT
- PMDL 93551 4195-B2
ESTORIL DR
22900 DBAR 91765 680-B3
ESTORIL ST
25600 SCTA 91355 4550-F6
ESTRADA CT
19300 WAL 91789 639-C6
ESTRADA LN
11900 Nor 91326 480-G7
ESTRADA ST
3200 LA 90023 675-B1
ESTRALITA PL
400 FUL 92835 738-G2
ESTRELLA AV
300 MNRO 91016 567-G6
600 ARCD 91007 597-A1
700 TEML 91780 597-A1
1900 LA 90007 634-C6
5800 LA 90044 674-B6
13100 LA 90248 734-B2
15900 LA 90247 734-B6
W ESTRELLA AV
1900 LA 90007 634-C6
ESTRELLA CT
2000 PMDL 93550 4286-D3
ESTRELLA DR
- CALB 91302 558-H6
3900 SBdC 91710 641-D7
ESTRELLA LN
- PMDL 93551 4104-E6
43800 LAN 93535 4016-F7
43800 LAN 93535 4106-F1
ESTRELLA PL
23500 SCTA 91355 4550-G5
ESTRELLITA LN
200 VeCo 91377 558-A2
ESTRELLITA WY
600 Brwd 90049 631-H1
ESTRIBO DR
2200 RHE 90274 823-G1
ESTRONDO DR
4400 Enc 91436 561-D4
ESTRONDO PL
4300 Enc 91436 561-D5
ESTUDILLO AV
400 LA 90063 635-C6
1500 LA 90023 675-B2
ESWARD DR
27000 CALB 91301 558-F6
ETERNAL VALLEY FIRE RD
- SCTA 91321 4641-A4
ETHEL AV
3800 LA 91604 562-D6
4300 Shrm 91423 562-D3
5200 VanN 91401 562-D2
5900 VanN 91401 532-D7
6500 NHol 91606 532-D6
6800 NHol 91605 532-D2
N ETHEL AV
400 ALH 91801 595-J4
S ETHEL AV
1000 ALH 91803 595-J7
1700 ALH 91803 635-J1
ETHEL ST
1000 GLDL 91207 564-G2
9100 CYP 90630 767-C6
ETHEL ANN AL
12900 NHol 91605 532-D5
ETHELDO AV
5100 CULC 90230 672-F5
5100 LA 90230 672-F5
ETHELINDA WY
800 BREA 92821 708-J4
ETIENNE DR
- PMDL 93552 4287-E1
ETIWANDA AV
5100 Tarz 91356 560-J2
6100 Res 91335 530-J2
8200 Nor 91325 530-J1
8800 Nor 91325 500-J6
9500 Nor 91330 500-J6
10300 Nor 91326 500-J1
ETON AV
6600 CanP 91303 530-B5
7500 LA 91304 530-B2
8800 LA 91304 500-B6
8900 Chat 91311 500-B2
ETON DR
400 BURB 91504 533-F5
ETON PL
2900 POM 91767 600-J3
ETONGALE AV
2200 RowH 91748 678-J6
ETTA ST
600 LA 90065 594-J5
ETTRICK ST
3100 LFlz 90027 594-C2
ETZ MELOY MTWY
- LACo 90265 586-E4
- VeCo 90265 586-E4
EUBANK AV
300 Wilm 90744 794-F4
EUCALYPTUS
3500 WCOV 91792 679-C1
15000 LA 91342 481-H1
18800 RowH 91748 679-B4
EUCALYPTUS AV
- AVA 90704 5923-H4
1400 CHLS 91709 680-H6
2000 LBCH 90806 795-D4
3500 LBCH 90806 765-C7
11400 HAW 90250 703-C7
11800 HAW 90250 733-C1
15100 BLF 90706 736-C4
N EUCALYPTUS AV
100 ING 90301 703-B2
300 ING 90302 703-C1
900 ING 90302 673-B7
2200 LBCH 90806 795-D2
S EUCALYPTUS AV
100 ING 90301 703-C3
EUCALYPTUS CIR
5000 CYP 90630 767-C6
EUCALYPTUS CT
6300 Enc 91316 531-A7
W EUCALYPTUS CT
1000 ONT 91762 641-H3
EUCALYPTUS DR
100 ELSG 90245 732-E2
700 ELSG 90245 702-E7
2000 LACo 91770 636-E3
EUCALYPTUS LN
- Ago 91301 588-B4
- LA 90065 594-F1
- LACo 91768 640-A2
- POM 91768 640-A2
- RHLS 90274 793-E7
300 LBCH 90814 795-H7
300 LBCH 90814 825-J1
1000 PAS 91103 565-G2
1900 BREA 92821 709-D7
5800 HiPk 90042 565-C7
EUCALYPTUS ST
1600 BREA 92821 709-D7
8400 DWNY 90242 705-J7
8400 DWNY 90242 706-A7
EUCALYPTUS WY
500 LHB 90631 708-C6
1900 DUAR 91010 568-B5
2000 LACo 91770 636-D3
21300 SCTA 91321 4641-B1
EUCALYPTUS PARK RD
- SDMS 91773 600-B6
N EUCLA AV
100 SDMS 91773 600-A2
S EUCLA AV
100 SDMS 91773 600-B2
EUCLID
1200 LHB 90631 708-E4
EUCLID AV
400 LA 90063 635-B6
400 Boyl 90033 635-B6
600 LA 90023 635-B6
700 LBCH 90804 795-J4
1400 SMCA 90404 671-F1
1600 SMRO 91108 595-J1
1800 SMRO 91108 596-A2
2100 LBCH 90815 795-J4
3100 LYN 90262 735-B2
7800 WHIT 90602 677-E7
7800 WHIT 90602 707-E1
8000 WHIT 90605 707-E1
29000 Cstc 91384 4459-B6
E EUCLID AV
300 COMP 90222 734-J2
300 COMP 90222 735-A2
500 LACo 91010 567-H6
N EUCLID AV
- PAS 91101 565-J3
200 LBCH 90803 825-J1
300 LBCH 90814 795-J7
300 LBCH 90814 825-J1
800 PAS 91104 565-J2
1300 LBCH 90804 795-J7
2000 LBCH 90815 796-A4
2000 LBCH 90815 795-J4
S EUCLID AV
- PAS 91101 565-J6
400 SGBL 91776 596-E4
600 PAS 91106 565-J6
1200 PAS 91106 595-J1
EUCLID CT
900 SMCA 90403 631-E7
1200 SMCA 90404 671-F1
N EUCLID PL
- LBCH 90803 825-J1
EUCLID ST
200 SMCA 90402 631-D6
800 SMCA 90403 631-D6
1000 SMCA 90403 671-G3
1200 SMCA 90404 671-G3
2000 SMCA 90405 671-G3
N EUCLID ST
100 FUL 92832 738-F4
100 LHB 90631 708-E5
100 FUL 92833 738-E2
1000 FUL 92835 738-F4
1400 LHH 90631 708-E5
3000 LHB 90631 738-E2
S EUCLID ST
100 FUL 92832 738-F7
100 LHB 90631 708-E7
100 FUL 92833 738-F7
1100 LHB 90631 738-F7
EUDORA AV
1500 Wilm 90744 794-C4
EUDORA CT
- Boyl 90033 634-J4
EUGENE DR
1000 FUL 92832 738-H5
EUGENE ST
4200 City 90063 635-F5
4300 ELA 90022 635-F5
23000 WdHl 91364 559-G4
EULA DR
100 MTBL 90640 676-E1
E EULALIA ST
100 GLDL 91205 564-E7
W EULALIA ST
100 GLDL 91204 564-E7
EULER RD
9900 LACo 91390 4373-G3
EULITA AV
400 LACo 91744 679-B2
600 LACo 91792 679-B2
EUNICE AV
3900 ELMN 91731 597-A6
5600 SIMI 93063 499-A3
6300 HiPk 90042 595-E1
EUNICE CIR
300 LHB 90631 708-C6
EUREKA AV
16600 PRM 90723 735-H6
N EUREKA AV
6900 NLB 90805 735-H6
EUREKA CT
- MTCL 91763 641-E1
EUREKA DR
3700 LA 91604 562-J6
3700 LA 91604 563-A6
W EUREKA ST
- PAS 91103 565-H4
EUREKA WY
- UPL 91784 571-H5
EUREKA RIVER PL
19300 WAL 91789 639-C5
EUSTACE ST
12700 Pcma 91331 482-D7
13200 Pcma 91331 502-C1
EUSTON PL
400 LCF 91011 535-D7
EUSTON RD
1500 SMRO 91108 596-C1
1800 SMRO 91108 566-D7
EVA CT
41300 LACo 93536 4104-H7
41300 LACo 93536 4194-H1
EVA PL
7400 VanN 91406 531-H4
EVA TER
2800 LA 90031 595-B7
EVADALE DR
3800 LA 90031 595-B5
EVA D EDWARDS
1000 COV 91722 599-B3
EVALYN AV
21200 TOR 90503 763-B6
22300 TOR 90505 763-C7
22600 TOR 90505 793-C1
N EVAN LN
- LACo 91387 4552-B5
EVAN WY
- VanN 91411 532-A6
EVANGELINA ST
2000 WCOV 91792 639-A6
EVANS AV
1500 POM 91766 641-B4
23700 SCTA 91321 4640-F2
EVANS CT
- Cstc 91384 4459-C7
2300 LMTA 90717 793-G5
EVANS RD
14200 PacP 90272 631-C4
EVANS ST
- FUL 92833 738-C5
- PMDL 93552 4287-E1
3700 LFlz 90027 594-C3
EVANSPORT DR
9000 RSMD 91770 596-H5
EVANSTON PL
100 PAS 91105 565-H5
EVANSTON ST
12700 Brwd 90049 631-E4
EVANT DR
20600 WAL 91789 639-F7
EVANVIEW DR
8800 LA 90069 592-J4
EVANWOOD AV
300 LPUE 91744 638-B5
600 LACo 91744 638-D3
5000 VeCo 91377 557-G1
S EVANWOOD AV
600 WCOV 91790 638-E1
EVARG AV
1200 COMP 90220 734-F6
EVARO DR
12500 WHIT 90606 707-B1
EVART ST
4000 MTCL 91763 601-D7
EVE AV
11000 LYN 90262 705-C6
EVELYN AV
2500 RSMD 91770 636-E2
2600 WCOV 91792 639-A7
17800 GAR 90248 763-J1
S EVELYN AV
18200 LA 90248 763-J2
EVELYN CT
45800 LAN 93534 4015-F3
EVELYN PL
- PAS 91104 566-B2
400 BHLS 90210 592-G3
400 LA 90210 592-G3
1700 PMDL 93550 4286-D3
EVELYN ST
2500 Mont 91020 534-G2
3000 LaCr 91214 534-F1
EVELYNGLEN LN
1100 LHB 90631 708-D6
EVENHAIM LN
6000 Tarz 91356 560-G1
EVENING BREEZE DR
20100 LACo 91789 679-E5
EVENING CANYON DR
5700 LCF 91011 535-C1
EVENING CANYON RD
800 BREA 92821 709-B5
EVENING PRIMROSE AV
- PMDL 93551 4195-D5
EVENINGSHADE AV
27500 SCTA 91351 4551-F2
EVENING SHADE DR
900 SPed 90731 824-A3
EVENING SIDE DR
29000 Cstc 91384 4459-B6
EVENINGSIDE DR
- PMDL 93552 4287-B5
1900 WCOV 91792 638-H5
EVENING STAR AV
17200 CRTS 90703 737-A7
EVENING STAR CT
- LACo 91390 4460-J1
- LACo 91390 4461-A1
EVENING STAR ST
- PMDL 93551 4195-D5
EVENING TERRACE DR
13700 CHLS 91709 680-J2
EVENING VIEW DR
2200 CHLS 91709 680-J3
EVENSONG DR
12300 LA 90064 672-A1
EVENSTAR AV
800 THO 91361 557-B5
EVENTIDE PL
1100 LA 90210 592-C6
EVERDING MTWY
2400 Top 90290 630-B2
EVEREST CIR
4500 CYP 90630 767-B6
EVEREST CT
900 CHLS 91709 680-F7
EVEREST DR
800 CHLS 91709 680-E7
EVEREST ST
7600 DWNY 90242 705-H6
8400 DWNY 90242 706-A7
9800 DWNY 90241 736-C1
9800 DWNY 90242 736-C1
10400 NRWK 90650 736-D1
EVERETT AV
100 MONP 91755 636-C2
4500 VER 90058 675-C4
5100 MYWD 90270 675-C5
5900 HNTP 90255 675-C5
EVERETT CT
4300 VER 90058 675-C4
EVERETT DR
25300 SCTA 91321 4640-F1
EVERETT PL
1000 LA 90012 634-F1
EVERETT ST
900 LA 90012 634-F1
900 Echo 90026 634-F1
N EVERETT ST
100 GLDL 91206 564-F4
900 GLDL 91207 564-F3
S EVERETT ST
100 GLDL 91205 564-F5
EVERGEM AV
5300 PMDL 93552 4287-B2
EVERGLADE ST
12200 LA 90066 672-B3
EVERGLADES CT
- SCTA 91387 4462-G7
EVERGREEN
12400 ELMN 91732 637-G1
EVERGREEN AV
5000 CYP 90630 767-C6
8100 SGAT 90280 705-A3
E EVERGREEN AV
100 MNRO 91016 567-G6
2200 WCOV 91791 639-B1
N EVERGREEN AV
100 LA 90063 635-C3
100 Boyl 90033 635-C3
S EVERGREEN AV
100 LA 90063 635-B5
100 Boyl 90033 635-B5
600 LA 90023 635-B6
1400 LA 90023 675-A1
W EVERGREEN AV
100 MNRO 91016 567-G6
EVERGREEN CIR
- COV 91724 599-E7
21000 WAL 91789 639-G7
EVERGREEN CT
- CRSN 90746 764-F1
200 AZU 91702 568-J3
5500 CHNO 91710 641-H3
EVERGREEN DR
- HacH 91745 678-F5
- LA 90068 563-F4
- LACo 91724 639-G1
- POM 91768 600-H6
300 BREA 92821 709-A5
500 PAS 91105 565-D6
1300 UPL 91784 571-H5
9100 CYP 90630 767-C5
EVERGREEN LN
- MANB 90266 732-H4
12300 CRTS 90703 736-J4
28200 SCTA 91390 4460-J4
EVERGREEN PL
- INDS 91745 678-F3
EVERGREEN RD
700 SBdC 92397 (4652-B1 See Page 4651)
7500 SBdC 92372 (4562-F1 See Page 4471)
9500 SBdC 92372 (4472-E2 See Page 4471)
EVERGREEN ST
100 BURB 91505 563-B1
900 DUAR 91010 567-J6
1100 DUAR 91010 568-A6
1600 BURB 91505 533-B7
1900 LVRN 91750 600-G1
6900 Wch 90045 703-A1
W EVERGREEN ST
500 ING 90302 673-A7
500 ING 90302 703-A1
EVERGREEN SPRINGS DR
1900 DBAR 91765 679-H5
EVERINGTON ST
5100 CMRC 90040 675-G2
EVERS AV
600 COMP 90220 734-G4
9600 Wats 90002 704-F4
11100 LA 90059 704-F6
13900 Wbrk 90222 734-G4
EVERSTON ST
11500 NRWK 90650 736-G4
EVERTS ST
600 PAS 91103 565-F2
EVETTE CT
- PMDL 93550 4286-C1
EVEWARD RD
5700 CULC 90230 672-H5
EVI LN
27300 LACo 91387 4551-J4
EVITA CT
5500 AGRH 91301 557-H5
EVONDA AV
21700 CRSN 90810 765-A6
S EVONDA AV
22000 CRSN 90810 765-A7
EVRON AV
27400 SCTA 91351 4551-F2
EWELL LN
1200 ARCD 91007 567-C7
EWING AV
3000 Alta 91001 535-J4
EWING CT
1800 HacH 91745 678-F6
EWING ST
1400 Echo 90026 594-F6
1900 LA 90039 594-D5
EXA CT
17700 CRSN 90746 764-E1
EXBURY PL
20500 LACo 91724 599-F7
EXCELENTE DR
4700 WdHl 91364 559-H4
EXCELLO ST
11600 ART 90701 736-G6
EXCELSIOR DR
10600 NRWK 90650 736-E4
12200 NRWK 90650 737-C4
12600 SFSP 90670 737-A4
14600 LMRD 90638 737-F4
EXCELSIOR ST
15500 LA 91342 481-F3
EXCHANGE AL
- PAS 91103 565-H4
EXCHANGE AV
4200 VER 90058 675-B3
4500 LACo 90058 675-B3
EXCHANGE LN
900 SPAS 91030 595-H2
EXCHANGE PL
100 POM 91768 640-C3
43000 LAN 93535 4106-A3
N EXCHANGE PL
100 SDMS 91773 600-B2
EXCHANGE ST
5200 LA 90039 564-C5
EXETER AV
500 LHB 90631 708-D7
9300 MTCL 91763 601-G5
EXETER CIR
400 LHB 90631 708-E7
EXETER CT
1400 WCOV 91792 638-H5
EXETER PL
17200 Nor 91325 501-C6
EXETER ST
7200 PRM 90723 735-F3
EXHIBIT CT
20700 WdHl 91367 560-C1
EXHIBIT PL
20700 WdHl 91367 560-C1
EXLINE ST
11900 ELMN 91732 637-E1
EXMOOR AV
1000 COMP 90220 734-H6
EXMOOR PL
2000 GLDR 91741 569-J5
EXMOOR RD
13000 SLB 90740 796-G7
EXPEDITION WY
- PMDL 93552 4287-C1
EXPLORER DR
50100 LACo 93536 3833-C6
EXPLORER RD
- LCF 91011 535-E4
EXPLORER ST
100 POM 91768 640-C2
300 BREA 92821 709-A6
EXPLORER WY
- PMDL 93552 4287-D1
EXPOSITION BLVD
400 LA 90007 674-A1
600 LA 90037 674-A1
600 LA 90089 674-A1
1100 LA 90007 673-J1
1100 LA 90037 673-J1
1300 LA 90018 673-F1
1300 LA 90062 673-J1
2800 SMCA 90404 631-J7
3600 LA 90016 673-B1
8800 CULC 90232 632-H7
8800 LA 90232 632-H7
8900 LA 90034 632-G7
10700 LA 90064 632-C6
12200 LA 90064 631-J7
EXPOSITION DR
9100 LA 90034 632-G7
EXPOSITION PL
2400 LA 90018 673-E1
EXPOSITION PARK DR
500 LA 90037 674-A2
N EXTON AV
400 ING 90302 703-C1
EXULTANT DR
3900 RPV 90275 823-D5
EYE ST
1000 ONT 91762 601-J6
E EYE ST
100 Wilm 90744 794-E6
3100 Wilm 90744 795-A6
W EYE ST
100 Wilm 90744 794-D6
3200 Wilm 90744 795-A6
3400 LBCH 90813 795-A6
E EZMIRLIAN ST
1400 COMP 90221 735-B3
N EZRA ST
400 LA 90063 635-C5
S EZRA ST
1500 LA 90023 675-A1

F

F
600 LACo 91744 679-B2
F ST
- LACo 90220 764-J3
- LACo 91724 599-E3
- PdlR 90293 702-C7
- SPed 90731 794-B7
- Wilm 90744 794-B7
2100 LVRN 91750 600-G3
10700 LACo 90230 672-H3
E F ST
100 Wilm 90744 794-F6
W F ST
100 Wilm 90744 794-C7
900 ONT 91762 601-J7
F WK
1000 Wilm 90744 794-D7
FABER ST
2800 RBCH 90278 733-B6
FABIAN AV
39100 LACo 93591 4200-E5
FABLE AV
8300 LA 91304 529-F2
FABRICA WY
17400 CRTS 90703 737-D7
FABRIK AV
43900 LAN 93536 4105-C1
FABRY DR
24200 Hrbr 90710 794-A3
FABUENO DR
2700 HacH 91745 678-C5
FACADE AV
7600 PRM 90723 735-G2
FACETA DR
14800 LMRD 90638 737-J4
FACILIDAD ST
15400 HacH 91745 678-A4
FACILITY RD
23600 VeCo 93063 499-B7
N FACTOR AV
6000 LACo 91702 569-B7
6200 AZU 91702 569-B7
FACTORIAL WY
9700 SELM 91733 637-A3
FACTORY DR
500 POM 91768 640-C3
FACTORY PL
1200 LA 90013 634-G5
FACULTY AV
3700 LBCH 90808 766-A4
5400 LKWD 90712 766-A2
15700 BLF 90706 736-A5
FACULTY DR
11600 NRWK 90650 736-G6
FADA DR
15600 LMRD 90638 737-H4
FADDEN ST
19300 RowH 91748 679-C6
FAGAN AV
18800 ART 90701 766-J2
19900 CRTS 90703 766-J3
FAGAN CT
19100 CRTS 90703 766-J2
FAGAN WY
19500 CRTS 90703 766-J3
FAHREN CT
27300 LACo 91387 4551-H4
FAHRINGER WY
1200 LHB 90631 708-C5
FAIN DR
24700 SCTA 91321 4640-F3
FAINRIDGE PL
2300 RowH 91748 678-H6
FAIR AV
2000 POM 91768 600-H4
4100 LA 91602 562-J5
4100 LA 91604 562-J5
5000 NHol 91601 562-J1
5900 NHol 91601 532-J7
6000 NHol 91606 532-J7
7100 NHol 91605 532-J4
7200 SunV 91352 532-J3
FAIR PL
6300 LA 90043 673-C7
N FAIR PL
1200 ING 90302 673-C7
FAIR ST
5000 CMRC 90040 675-G3
FAIRACRES DR
14600 LMRD 90638 707-F7
FAIRBANKS AV
700 LBCH 90813 795-C7
45300 LAN 93534 4015-E4
FAIRBANKS CT
- LACo 91387 4462-C7
FAIRBANKS PL
1400 Echo 90026 594-E7
FAIRBANKS WY
5000 CULC 90230 672-G4
FAIRBREEZE CIR
3900 WLKV 91361 557-C6
E FAIRBROOK ST
5200 LBCH 90815 796-B4
FAIRBURN AV
1200 Wwd 90024 632-C3
1800 WLA 90025 632-D4
FAIRBURY ST
14400 HacH 91745 637-J7
14700 HacH 91745 638-A7
FAIRCHILD AV
7800 Win 91306 530-C3
FAIRCHILD ST
3500 GLDL 91214 504-E7
FAIRCLIFF CT
- GLDL 91206 564-J3
FAIRCLIFF RD
- SCTA 91354 4460-H4
FAIRCOURT LN
700 GLDL 91203 564-C3
FAIRCOVE CT
- SBdC 91766 641-D3
FAIRCOVE DR
6800 RPV 90275 822-G1
FAIRCREST DR
8700 RSMD 91770 596-G5
W FAIRCREST DR
3200 ANA 92804 767-G7
FAIRCROSS ST
2400 TOR 90505 793-F5
FAIRDALE AV
1600 DUAR 91010 568-B6
FAIRESTA ST
3000 LaCr 91214 504-F7
3200 GLDL 91214 504-D6
N FAIRFAX AV
100 LA 90036 633-B1
100 LA 90048 633-B1
300 LA 90036 593-B7
300 LA 90048 593-B7
700 LA 90046 593-B4
900 WHWD 90046 593-B5
S FAIRFAX AV
100 LA 90036 633-B2
100 LA 90048 633-B2
1000 LA 90019 633-B2
1000 LA 90035 633-B2
1800 LA 90034 633-A5
2000 LA 90016 633-A5
2400 CULC 90232 633-A5
5000 LadH 90056 673-B5
6200 LA 90056 673-B5
6300 ING 90302 673-B5
FAIRFAX CT
600 POM 91766 641-A4
FAIRFAX LN
600 POM 91766 641-A4
11300 SBdC 91766 641-D3
FAIRFIELD AV
2600 PMDL 93550 4286-F4
7100 LA 90068 593-E3
FAIRFIELD CIR
700 PAS 91106 566-A7
FAIRFIELD DR
- LVRN 91750 570-H5
100 CLAR 91711 571-D5
FAIRFIELD LN
13200 SLB 90740 796-G7
FAIRFIELD PL
2500 SMRO 91108 566-E6
FAIRFIELD RD
18700 Nor 91326 500-H3
FAIRFIELD ST
1300 GLDL 91201 564-A3
1400 GLDL 91201 563-J3
2200 MTBL 90640 676-B2
E FAIRFIELD ST
5900 ELA 90022 675-J2
6000 ELA 90022 676-A2
FAIRFIELD WY
2300 UPL 91784 571-H3
4400 CYP 90630 767-B7
FAIRFORD AV
10700 DWNY 90241 706-F7
11200 NRWK 90650 706-F7
11200 NRWK 90650 736-F2
FAIRFORD DR
1700 FUL 92833 738-B4
FAIRGATE AV
26300 SCTA 91321 4551-G5
FAIRGLADE ST
16500 SCTA 91387 4552-C1
FAIRGLEN RD
43100 LAN 93535 4106-A2
FAIRGRANGE DR
5400 AGRH 91301 557-H5
FAIRGREEN AV
1900 LACo 91016 567-F7
FAIRGREEN DR
1700 FUL 92833 738-B4
FAIRGREEN LN
3000 PMDL 93551 4195-B2
FAIRGROUNDS ST
2100 CMRC 90040 675-H3
FAIRGROVE AV
1200 WCOV 91792 638-H5
1500 WCOV 91791 638-J4
10000 Tuj 91042 504-B4
12700 BALD 91706 597-H7
13000 BALD 91706 637-J1
13800 LACo 91746 638-A2
14900 LACo 91744 638-F4
15100 LPUE 91744 638-F4
W FAIRGROVE AV
14400 LACo 91744 638-C3
14400 WCOV 91790 638-C3
FAIRHALL ST
10600 TEML 91780 597-C5
10600 ELMN 91780 597-C5
FAIRHAVEN AV
5600 WdHl 91367 559-D1
FAIRHAVEN CT
- SCTA 91354 4460-G5
6100 AGRH 91301 558-A3
FAIRHAVEN ST
500 CRSN 90745 794-E2
FAIR HILL
700 SDMS 91773 599-J4
FAIRHILL DR
2100 RPV 90275 823-H4
FAIRHILLS FARM RD
2700 Top 90290 560-D7
2700 Top 90290 590-D1
FAIRHOPE DR
4500 OrCo 90638 737-J4
14900 LMRD 90638 737-H4
FAIRHURST DR
2100 LCF 91011 504-H7
FAIRLAIN DR
- SCTA 91355 4550-E4
FAIRLANCE DR
1300 DBAR 91789 679-F4
FAIRLAND BLVD
3600 LACo 90043 673-E4
FAIRLAND CT
17400 GmH 91344 481-B6
FAIRLANE ST
4300 Actn 93510 4374-J4
FAIRLAWN DR
4300 LCF 91011 535-A2
FAIRLAWN WY
1300 PAS 91105 565-E3
FAIRLEE AV
600 BRAD 91010 568-C4
1300 DUAR 91010 568-C5
FAIRLEE DR
- LAN 93536 4105-E3
43000 LAN 93534 4105-E3
FAIRLOCK AV
13700 PRM 90723 735-G2
FAIRMAID AV
36900 Litl 93543 4288-D4
FAIRMAN ST
2700 LKWD 90712 765-H4
3900 LKWD 90712 766-A5
5900 LKWD 90713 766-D5
FAIRMEADE RD
3500 PAS 91107 566-H3
FAIRMONT AV
700 GLDL 91203 564-C4
FAIRMONT DR
600 CLAR 91711 601-C1
FAIRMONT LN
9200 PRV 90660 676-H1
FAIRMONT NEENACH RD
12000 LACo 93536 4013-A4
FAIRMOUNT AV
500 PAS 91105 565-H6
1600 LCF 91011 535-A1
1700 LCF 91011 534-J1
2400 LaCr 91214 534-G1
2800 LaCr 91214 504-F7
3200 GLDL 91214 504-E7
FAIRMOUNT RD
400 BURB 91501 533-H5
FAIRMOUNT ST
2400 Boyl 90033 635-B4
3000 LA 90063 635-B4
3900 City 90063 635-E4
FAIR OAKS AV
200 SPAS 91030 595-H1
3400 Alta 91001 535-J3
N FAIR OAKS AV
- PAS 91103 565-H1
1500 PAS 91103 535-H6
2000 Alta 91001 535-H6
N FAIROAKS AV
- PAS 91103 565-H3
S FAIR OAKS AV
- PAS 91105 565-H6
1200 SPAS 91030 565-H6
1200 SPAS 91030 595-H1
1200 PAS 91105 595-H1
W FAIR OAKS DR
- PAS 91103 535-H7
FAIR OAK VIEW TER
2100 LA 90039 594-E5
FAIR PARK AV
1500 Eagl 90041 565-A6
2200 Eagl 90041 564-J6
FAIRPLAIN AV
1300 LACo 90601 637-F5
FAIRPLEX DR
500 POM 91768 640-E1
1000 POM 91768 600-E7
1300 LVRN 91750 600-F5
1400 POM 91773 600-E6
1400 SDMS 91773 600-E6
1400 SDMS 91768 600-E6
W FAIRPLEX DR
1900 POM 91768 600-F5
FAIRPOINT ST
3100 LACo 91107 566-G1
3300 LACo 91107 536-G7
3300 PAS 91107 566-G1
FAIRPORT AV
27400 SCTA 91351 4551-F2
FAIRRIDGE CIR
1700 WCOV 91792 638-J6
FAIRSIDE RD
26100 LACo 90265 628-C3
FAIRTON ST
8400 PRM 90723 735-H4
10400 BLF 90706 736-D4
10600 NRWK 90650 736-E4
E FAIRTON ST
10800 NRWK 90650 736-E4
FAIRVALE AV
1100 COV 91722 599-B3
5300 LACo 91722 599-B2
6000 LACo 91702 569-B7

STREET
Block City ZIP Pg-Grid

S FAIRVALE AV
200 AZU 91702 599-B1
FAIRVALLEY AV
1400 COV 91722 599-C2
5200 LACo 91722 599-C2
N FAIRVALLEY AV
1100 COV 91722 599-C3
FAIRVIEW AV
200 SPAS 91030 595-H1
300 ARCD 91007 567-A7
400 SMAD 91024 566-J1
500 Boyl 90033 634-J3
500 SGBL 91776 596-G5
700 ARCD 91007 566-J7
5200 BPK 90621 738-A5
8400 RSMD 91770 596-G5
9000 LACo 91775 566-J7
10700 TEML 91780 597-C4
11300 ELMN 91732 597-E4
26200 LMTA 90717 793-H6
E FAIRVIEW AV
100 GLDL 91207 564-E3
100 SGBL 91776 596-E5
8500 LACo 91775 566-G7
W FAIRVIEW AV
100 SGBL 91776 596-D5
200 GLDL 91202 564-E3
E FAIRVIEW BLVD
100 ING 90302 673-D7
W FAIRVIEW BLVD
100 ING 90302 673-A7
5200 LA 90056 673-A7
5200 LadH 90056 673-A7
FAIRVIEW CIR
5000 BPK 90621 738-A5
FAIRVIEW DR
- HacH 91745 637-G6
- SCTA 91354 4460-F7
1000 LCF 91011 535-B3
23500 SCTA 91354 4550-G1
FAIRVIEW LN
1500 Alta 91001 536-B5
18200 TOR 90504 763-H2
FAIRVIEW PL
1800 POM 91768 600-G5
5400 AGRH 91301 558-C4
FAIRVIEW RD
- THO 91362 557-A3
200 THO 91361 557-A3
FAIRVIEW ST
11900 ELMN 91732 597-G5
N FAIRVIEW ST
100 BURB 91505 563-D2
1300 BURB 91505 533-D7
2200 BURB 91504 533-D5
S FAIRVIEW ST
300 BURB 91505 563-E4
FAIRVIEW TER
400 SMAD 91024 566-H1
FAIRVIEW FIRE RD
400 THO 91361 557-A3
FAIRVILLA DR
14500 LMRD 90638 737-G1
FAIRWAY AV
2400 Mont 91020 534-G2
2800 GLDL 91214 534-F2
2800 LaCr 91214 534-F2
3800 LA 91604 562-E5
FAIRWAY BLVD
3600 LACo 90043 673-D4
4200 LACo 90008 673-D4
FAIRWAY CIR
1200 UPL 91784 571-J6
26400 SCTA 91321 4551-F5
FAIRWAY DR
- MANB 90266 732-H4
400 PMDL 93551 4195-H4
700 INDS 91789 679-D3
700 LACo 91789 679-D3
1800 CHLS 91709 680-H7
1800 CHLS 91709 710-H1
3800 PRV 90660 676-J1
3800 PRV 90660 677-A1
4300 LKWD 90712 765-H5
FAIRWAY LN
- StvR 91381 4550-C4
3200 WCOV 91791 599-D7
FAIRWAY ISLES DR
- FUL 92835 738-H3
S FAIRWAY KNOLLS RD
1500 WCOV 91791 639-C3
FAIR WEATHER DR
13000 SBdC 91710 641-B7
FAIRWEATHER ST
18500 SCTA 91351 4551-D2
FAIRWIND LN
21600 DBAR 91765 709-H1
FAIRWOOD ST
400 DUAR 91010 568-D4
N FAIRWOOD WY
400 UPL 91786 601-H3
1500 UPL 91786 571-H7
FAISAN CT
23200 SCTA 91355 4550-H5
FAITH CT
6400 SIMI 93063 499-C3
FAITH ST
3000 WCOV 91792 639-B7
FALCO AV
14300 NRWK 90650 736-J3
FALCON AV
- LBCH 90802 825-F1
200 LBCH 90802 795-F7
4100 Bxby 90807 765-F3
N FALCON AV
3300 Bxby 90807 795-F1
3300 SIGH 90755 795-F1
3400 Bxby 90807 765-F6
5200 NLB 90805 765-F1
6400 NLB 90805 735-F7
FALCON CIR
19700 CRTS 90703 766-J3
FALCON CT
2000 PMDL 93551 4195-E5
FALCON DR
7000 BPK 90620 767-F2
FALCON PL
17200 GmH 91344 481-B5
FALCON ST
100 Wilm 90744 824-E3
3100 POM 91767 600-J2
FALCON WY
- BREA 92823 709-G6
- CRTS 90703 736-F6
FALCONBERG DR
- LVRN 91750 570-J5
FALCONBURN WY
22400 DBAR 91765 680-A4
FALCON CREST CT
- Nor 91326 480-E6
FALCON CREST DR
- SCTA 91351 4461-G7
FALCON CREST LN
19900 Nor 91326 480-E6
FALCON CREST PL
- SCTA 91354 4460-F5
FALCON CREST WY
11800 Nor 91326 480-E6
FALCONER ST
14600 BALD 91706 598-D6
FALCONET DR
3600 CALB 91302 559-E7
FALCONGATE AV
- Actn 93510 4465-C2
FALCONHEAD DR
3700 RPV 90275 823-E5
FALCONHILL DR
11400 LACo 90604 708-A6
FALCON PARK ST
8000 LBCH 90808 796-J1
FALCON RIDGE DR
- POM 91766 640-F5
13900 CHLS 91709 680-J3
FALCON RIDGE LN
12000 Nor 91326 480-E6
FALCON RIDGE RD
3200 DBAR 91765 679-J7
3300 DBAR 91765 709-H1
FALCON RIDGE WY
12100 Nor 91326 480-E6
FALCON RIM DR
15800 SCTA 91387 4552-D5
FALCONROCK LN
400 VeCo 91377 558-A1
FALCON ROCK PL
4800 RPV 90275 793-B6
FALCONS VIEW DR
23600 DBAR 91765 680-C6
FALCONWOOD RD
33300 LACo 91390 4373-D5
FALDA AV
15500 LACo 90249 733-F5
16600 TOR 90504 733-F6
17100 TOR 90504 763-F1
FALENA AV
23100 TOR 90501 793-H2
24600 LMTA 90717 793-H3
FALKIRK LN
12200 Brwd 90049 631-G4
FALL AV
3000 Echo 90026 594-D5
FALL CT
1600 KeCo 93560 3835-E2
FALLBROOK AV
4900 WdHl 91364 559-H3
5300 WdHl 91367 559-H2
6100 WdHl 91367 529-H7
6400 CanP 91307 529-H3
7400 LA 91304 529-H3
FALLBROOK CIR
39300 PMDL 93551 4195-E5
FALLBROOK LN
- POM 91766 640-F7
- POM 91766 641-A4
FALL CANYON RD
- LACo 91390 (4282-E6 See Page 4281)
- LACo 91390 (4372-E3 See Page 4281)
FALLCREEK CIR
300 BREA 92821 709-D6
FALL CREEK CT
900 WAL 91789 639-C6
FALLCREEK CT
- SIMI 93063 499-B1
FALLCREEK LN
12400 CRTS 90703 736-J4
12500 CRTS 90703 737-A6
FALLCREEK RD
3200 DUAR 91010 568-F3
FALLEN DR
2200 RowH 91748 678-H6
FALLEN LEAF CT
- SIMI 93063 499-A1
FALLENLEAF DR
25600 TOR 90505 793-E5
FALLENLEAF PL
3400 GLDL 91206 565-C1
FALLEN LEAF RD
800 ARCD 91006 567-A3
900 ARCD 91006 566-J3
15800 LPUE 91744 638-J4
FALLEN LEAF ST
1300 LHB 90631 708-F4
FALLEN LEAF WY
- WLKV 91361 587-D1
FALLEN OAK CT
- StvR 91381 4550-B5
FALLEN OAK RD
16400 HacH 91745 678-E4
FALLHAVEN LN
5000 LCF 91011 535-B2
FALLING LEAF AL
- MNRO 91016 567-G4
FALLING LEAF AV
1900 LACo 91770 636-F3
2300 RSMD 91770 636-F1
FALLING LEAF CIR
2000 BREA 92821 709-D7
FALLINGLEAF CIR
- POM 91766 640-G6
FALLING LEAF DR
4000 Enc 91316 561-A5
14400 CHLS 91709 680-J4
FALLING SPRINGS RD
20200 WAL 91789 639-E7
FALLING STAR LN
1500 CHLS 91709 680-G2
27500 SCTA 91350 4461-B6
FALLINGSTAR PL
- PMDL 93552 4287-B6
FALLON DR
43800 LAN 93535 4106-C1
43900 LAN 93535 4016-C7
FALLON PL
- PMDL 93550 4286-H4
FALLOW FIELD DR
2400 DBAR 91765 679-G7
FALL RIVER CIR
3400 THO 91362 557-C3
FALLS CT
- PMDL 93551 4195-B3
FALLS DR
- Cstc 91384 4459-G3
600 Top 90290 590-B7
600 LA 90290 590-B7
FALLS RD
- SBdC (512-D1 See Page 511)
- SBdC (4732-D7 See Page 4651)
FALLS WY
5300 BPK 90621 737-J6
FALLS CANYON RD
- AVA 90704 5923-G4
FALLSGROVE ST
5600 LA 90016 673-A1
FALLSTON ST
5500 HiPk 90042 595-C1
FALLVIEW CT
- CHLS 91709 640-J7
FALLVIEW RD
1800 THO 91361 557-A6
1800 WLKV 91361 557-A6
FALMOUTH AV
8000 PdlR 90293 702-B2
FALSET ST
38300 PMDL 93551 4285-G1
FALSTONE AV
1100 HacH 91745 678-C2
FALTER ST
16700 LACo 91387 4552-B6
FALUN DR
10200 SunV 91352 533-C1
FAMBROUGH ST
23500 SCTA 91321 4640-G3
FAME CIR
16100 HNTB 92649 826-J6
FAMILY LN
- LKWD 90712 765-H3
FAMOSA ST
12400 LACo 90601 637-D6
FAN CT
20600 SCTA 91350 4461-D4
FANCHON AV
42800 LAN 93536 4105-D3
FANCHON LN
20200 SCTA 91351 4551-E2
FANDANGO ST
- GmH 91344 481-A6
FANDON AV
4100 ELMN 91732 597-E6
FANE ST
400 SMAD 91024 567-B2
FANITA ST
3000 Echo 90026 594-C7
FANNING ST
1700 Echo 90026 594-D5
FANO ST
2000 ARCD 91006 567-D6
2500 MNRO 91016 567-F6
FANSHAW AV
100 POM 91767 600-J2
100 POM 91767 601-A2
13400 PRM 90723 735-H2
FANTASTIC LN
25500 Cstc 91384 4369-G6
FANTASY ST
400 PMDL 93551 4195-H4
FANWOOD AV
1900 LBCH 90815 796-D2
3200 LBCH 90808 796-D1
3400 LBCH 90808 766-D7
3700 LBCH 90808 766-D7
4900 LKWD 90713 766-D2
FAR PL
2800 LA 90032 595-E7
FARADAY ST
13700 LACo 90605 707-D7
FARAGO AV
5000 TEML 91780 597-D3
FARBEN DR
600 DBAR 91765 680-C1
FARBER AV
400 COV 91724 599-E6
400 LACo 91724 599-D3
900 GLDR 91740 569-D7
5400 GLDR 91740 599-D2
FAREHOLM CT
1700 LA 90046 593-B4
FAREHOLM DR
7800 LA 90046 593-B4
FAREL AV
1000 DBAR 91789 679-H3
FARGO RD
300 SDMS 91773 600-B1
FARGO ST
1600 Echo 90026 594-F6
2100 LA 90039 594-D5
FAR HILLS RD
17600 LACo 91390 4461-J2
17600 LACo 91390 4462-A1
FARIAS AV
4500 LA 90230 672-E5
FARIMAN DR
19000 CRSN 90746 764-F3
N FARING RD
300 BelA 90077 592-C6
FARING FORD RD
2900 VeCo 91361 586-D2
FARIS DR
3600 LA 90034 632-G7
FARIS ST
- LKWD 90712 765-H3
FARJARDO ST
18300 RowH 91748 678-J6
18300 RowH 91748 679-A6
FARLAND ST
1500 COV 91724 599-F4
FARLEY CT
400 BURB 91501 533-J7
3900 LA 91604 562-J6
FARLIN ST
11300 Brwd 90049 631-H2
FARLINGTON ST
2200 WCOV 91790 638-C1
W FARLINGTON ST
1200 WCOV 91790 638-D2
FARLOW ST
12300 LKWD 90715 766-J5
12400 HGDN 90715 766-J5
12400 HGDN 90716 766-J5
12400 HGDN 90716 767-A5
FARM RD
- WAL 91789 639-H3
FARM ST
7800 DWNY 90241 706-A3
FARM CENTER RD
- Cstc 91384 4459-J4
- Cstc 91384 4460-A4
FARMDALE AV
2900 LA 90016 633-D7
3000 LA 90016 673-D1
4000 LA 91604 562-J6
4400 LA 91602 562-J4
4800 NHol 91601 562-J1
5900 NHol 91601 532-H6
6000 NHol 91606 532-H6
6800 NHol 91605 532-H3
FARMER AV
1000 LACo 90660 637-B5
1000 SELM 90660 637-B5
FARMER RIDGE FIRE RD
- PacP 90272 590-J1
FARMERS FIRE RD
2100 Brwd 90049 591-B5
2100 Brwd 90049 631-C1
2100 PacP 90272 591-A2
2100 PacP 90272 631-C1
FARMFIELD RD
26000 CALB 91302 558-H3
FARMINGTON AV
10300 SunI 91040 503-F4
FARMINGTON LN
21600 SCTA 91350 4461-B4
FARMINGTON WY
2600 RowH 91748 679-B7
FARMLAND AV
7100 PRV 90660 676-G7
7800 PRV 90660 706-F1
FARMOUTH DR
3900 LFlz 90027 594-B2
FARMSTEAD AV
1100 HacH 91745 678-B2
FARNA AV
5700 ARCD 91006 597-E3
FARNAM PL
1600 POM 91766 641-A4
FARNAM ST
900 HiPk 90042 595-A2
FARNBOROUGH AV
36800 LACo 93551 4285-F5
FARNDON AV
11400 SBdC 91710 641-D3
FARNDON PL
12400 CHNO 91710 641-D6
FARNDON ST
1500 SELM 91733 637-C4
FARNELL ST
12700 BALD 91706 637-H2
FARNESE AV
31900 Pear 93553 4468-H1
FARNHAM AV
9800 LALM 90720 767-A7
9800 LBCH 90808 767-A7
FARNHAM CT
- SCTA 91387 4462-D6
FARNHAM LN
3700 ING 90305 703-E3
FARNINGHAM AV
36900 Litl 93543 4288-E4
FARNSWORTH AV
3100 LA 90032 595-F6
N FAROLITO AV
2200 LBCH 90815 796-E4
FARQUHAR AV
3500 LALM 90720 796-J3
FARQUHAR ST
4800 LA 90032 635-E2
FARRAGUT AV
800 Wilm 90744 794-J6
FARRAGUT DR
9500 CULC 90232 672-H2
10700 CULC 90230 672-G3
FARRALONE AV
5400 WdHl 91367 559-J1
6400 CanP 91303 529-J6
7600 LA 91304 529-J1
8900 LA 91304 499-J7
9000 Chat 91311 499-J3
E FARRAR ST
5100 CMRC 90040 675-G2
FARRELL AV
1300 POM 91767 601-C7
1900 RBCH 90278 733-A6
FARRELL CT
- LHB 90631 738-C2
FARRELL RD
- Saug 91350 4461-G6
FARRINGDON AV
2200 POM 91768 600-D7
FARRINGTON DR
1100 LHB 90631 708-C4
FARRINGTON LN
- LKWD 90712 765-H3
6000 HiPk 90042 565-D7
FARROW DR
24500 SCTA 91355 4640-E1
FAR VIEW LN
2800 WCOV 91791 639-C2
FARVIEW RD
2500 FUL 92833 738-B4
FARWELL AV
2600 LA 90039 594-E3
FARYN CT
- Saug 91350 4461-F6
FASHION AV
1000 LBCH 90813 795-B6
1800 LBCH 90810 795-B2
3500 LBCH 90810 765-B7
FASHION WY
3400 TOR 90503 763-D6
FASHION SQUARE LN
- Shrm 91423 562-B4
1800 LHB 90631 708-C7
E FASLEY AV
5800 SIMI 93063 499-A1
FASTWATER CT
32400 WLKV 91361 557-B7
FATHOM AV
900 SLB 90740 826-F3
FATIMA AV
- LACo 93551 4375-G3
FAUBION PL
22500 CALB 91302 559-J7
FAULKNER AV
15100 PRM 90723 735-E4
FAULKNER DR
25800 StvR 91381 4550-A7
FAUNA LN
700 LACo 90502 794-B2
FAUNA ST
4100 MTCL 91763 601-D7
FAURE AV
- INDS 91789 639-J6
- LACo 91789 639-J6
FAUST AV
1900 LBCH 90815 796-D2
3100 LBCH 90808 796-D1
3300 LBCH 90808 766-D7
3700 LBCH 90808 766-D7
4100 LKWD 90713 766-D2
5600 WdHl 91367 559-H2
6200 BLF 90706 766-D2
6700 CanP 91307 529-H4
7600 LA 91304 529-H2
13000 DWNY 90242 736-B2
13400 BLF 90706 736-D3
FAVOLOSO CT
- StvR 91381 4640-D1
FAWCETT AV
10000 SELM 91733 637-B5
FAWN CIR
2500 LVRN 91750 600-D2
FAWN CT
8800 SBdC 92371 (4562-G2 See Page 4471)
W FAWN ST
1300 ONT 91762 601-H7
FAWNDALE PL
3600 Shrm 91403 561-J7
FAWN PATH RD
2100 CHLS 91709 680-J4
FAWNRIDGE AV
1300 BREA 92821 708-J4
FAWNRIDGE CIR
39300 PMDL 93551 4195-E6
FAWNRIDGE DR
1200 BREA 92821 708-J5
9700 LA 90210 592-D5
FAWNSKIN DR
27400 RPV 90275 793-B7
FAWN SPRINGS LN
800 GLDR 91741 569-G3
FAWN VALLEY
1400 GLDR 91740 569-H6
FAWNWOOD LN
- Nor 91326 500-H4
FAXINA AV
300 LACo 91744 679-B2
FAY AV
3200 CULC 90232 632-J7
3200 LA 90034 632-J7
FAY CIR
17900 CRTS 90703 766-F1
FAY DR
700 GLDL 91206 564-H3
FAY PL
1200 PAS 91104 565-J1
FAYE LN
400 RBCH 90277 763-A6
2900 WCOV 91792 639-B7
FAYECROFT ST
400 SFER 91340 482-B5
FAYETTE ST
5600 HiPk 90042 595-C1
S FAYLEN DR
100 ANA 92804 767-J6
FAYMONT AV
1200 MANB 90266 732-J5
FAYSMITH AV
800 TOR 90503 763-F5
15200 LACo 90249 733-F5
16600 TOR 90504 733-F7
17400 TOR 90504 763-F1
FAYWOOD ST
9100 BLF 90706 736-A4
10700 NRWK 90650 736-E4
E FEARING ST
5600 SIMI 93063 499-A2
FEATHER AV
3000 BALD 91706 598-B6
3000 BALD 91706 638-A1
N FEATHER AV
1000 LACo 91746 637-J2
1000 LACo 91746 638-A2
FEATHER HOLLOW CT
1000 CHLS 91709 710-F2
FEATHER ROCK RD
2200 DBAR 91765 680-B5
FEATHERSTAR AV
27800 SCTA 91350 4461-B5
FEATHERSTONE LN
- ING 90305 703-D4
FEATHERWOOD DR
500 DBAR 91765 640-E6
FEDALA RD
25500 SCTA 91355 4550-F6
FEDERAL AV
- WLA 90025 631-J4
1200 WLA 90025 631-J5
1600 WLA 90025 632-A6
2200 LA 90064 632-A6
2600 LA 90064 672-B1
3000 LA 90066 672-C1
3400 BELL 90201 675-C7
FEDERAL DR
- LAN 93535 4105-J3
11500 ELMN 91731 637-D1
FEDERALIST RD
22600 CALB 91302 559-H5
FEDERATION DR
600 LBCH 90814 796-B7
700 LBCH 90804 796-A6
FEDORA ST
800 LA 90005 633-J3
900 LA 90006 633-J3
FEED MILL CT
45600 LAN 93534 4015-J3
FEEDMILL RD
- Valc 91355 4550-A1
FEIJOA AV
25000 LMTA 90717 793-G4
FELA AV
3400 LBCH 90808 766-J7
FELBAR AV
800 TOR 90503 763-E6
18600 TOR 90504 763-E2
22600 TOR 90505 793-E1
S FELBERG AV
2000 LACo 91010 567-H7
FELBRIDGE ST
18800 SCTA 91351 4551-G2
FELCH AV
1300 RowH 91748 679-B4
FELDER DR
1000 LACo 91342 482-J3
FELDER ST
1000 GAR 90248 764-A1
FELDSPAR DR
15300 CHLS 91709 680-J6
FELICE PL
5300 WdHl 91364 560-E3
FELICIA AV
1400 RowH 91748 679-A6
FELICIA ST
2300 WCOV 91792 639-B7
FELICIDAD
2300 LA 90732 823-F7
FELICITAS AV
36800 LACo 93551 4285-G5
FELIPE AV
8900 MTCL 91763 601-E4
FELIPE LN
10400 MTCL 91763 641-F1
FELIPE ST
12100 ELMN 91732 637-E3
FELISE PL
19200 WAL 91789 639-C6
FELIX AV
8000 BGDN 90201 705-H3
FELIZ ST
1500 MONP 91754 635-H3
FELKER DR
5500 TOR 90503 763-A5
FELLOWS AV
10800 Pcma 91331 502-D1
11500 Pcma 91331 482-D7
11800 LA 91340 482-D7
12700 LA 91342 482-A4
13100 LA 91342 481-H2
FELLOWS PL
600 POM 91767 601-A6
FELLOWSHIP PKWY
2300 LA 90039 594-F5
FELLOWSHIP ST
15400 LACo 91744 638-E4
FELSON CIR
10700 CRTS 90703 766-E1
FELSON PL
12300 CRTS 90703 736-J7
13300 CRTS 90703 737-C7
FELSON ST
10300 BLF 90706 766-D1
11200 CRTS 90703 766-F1
12500 CRTS 90703 736-J7
12500 CRTS 90703 737-A7
FELT DR
11300 LACo 90604 707-F6
FELTON AV
900 RBCH 90278 763-B2
11500 HAW 90250 703-B7
11900 HAW 90250 733-B1
12000 LACo 90250 733-B1
S FELTON AV
9500 ING 90301 703-B4
10000 ING 90304 703-B4
10100 Lenx 90304 703-B6
FELTON LN
1300 RBCH 90278 763-B1
2000 RBCH 90278 733-B7
FENDA WY
25900 SCTA 91355 4550-F6
FENDALE AV
13600 LACo 90605 707-C6
FENDYKE AV
4500 RSMD 91770 596-H5
FENHILL LN
- MAL 90265 667-E2
FENHOLD ST
43400 LAN 93535 4016-C5
FENIMORE AV
4600 LACo 91722 599-B2
5400 LACo 91702 599-B2
N FENIMORE AV
100 AZU 91702 569-B7
700 COV 91723 599-B4
1100 COV 91722 599-B3
5400 LACo 91702 599-B3
S FENIMORE AV
500 COV 91723 599-B6
FENLEY DR
3600 LALM 90720 796-J1
FENLOCK AV
- Actn 93510 4464-G2
FENMEAD ST
2500 WCOV 91792 679-B2
FENN CT
900 CLAR 91711 571-B7
FENN ST
500 LA 90031 595-B6
FENNEL DR
- PMDL 93550 4286-F4
FENNELL PL
8600 LA 90069 592-J5
FENNELL ST
11500 ELMN 91732 637-D1
FENNER AV
42800 LAN 93536 4105-D1
44000 LAN 93536 4015-D7
FENTER AV
2200 NLB 90805 765-C1
FENTON AV
11400 LA 91342 502-G1
11500 LA 91342 482-B1
FENTON LN
14000 LA 91342 482-A1
FENTON GROVE LN
- LA 91342 482-G7
FENWALL DR
22500 SCTA 91350 4460-J5
FENWAY CT
29400 Cstc 91384 4459-H5
FENWAY ST
10900 SunV 91352 503-A5
11000 SunV 91352 502-J5
FENWICK ST
7100 Tuj 91042 504-A3
7800 SunI 91040 503-F3
FENWOOD AV
5400 WdHl 91367 559-G1
6100 WdHl 91367 529-G7
FENWORTH CT
6300 AGRH 91301 558-A3
FERAL AV
6200 AGRH 91301 558-B3
S FERDINAND AV
2200 MONP 91754 636-A5
FERGUS DR
2600 GLDL 91206 565-A3
FERGUS FALLS
- CLAR 91711 571-G2
FERGUSON DR
1700 MTBL 90640 676-A2
5400 CMRC 90022 675-H2
5800 ELA 90022 675-H2
6100 CMRC 90022 676-A2
6100 ELA 90022 676-A2
27700 Cstc 91384 4369-G7
FERGUSON GRN
8100 BPK 90621 737-J4
FERGUSON MTWY
- GLDR 91741 569-J3
- GLDR 91741 570-A3
- GLDR 91773 570-A3
- SDMS 91773 570-A4
FERINA ST
10400 BLF 90706 736-D4
11000 NRWK 90650 736-F4
FERMI DR
3200 Top 90290 560-B7
FERMO DR
1400 PacP 90272 631-D4
FERMOORE DR
1600 SFER 91340 482-C5
FERMOORE ST
100 SFER 91340 482-B5
FERN AV
1100 BREA 92821 738-J1
1200 TOR 90503 763-F6
3100 PMDL 93550 4286-G4
7400 RSMD 91770 636-D2
22600 TOR 90505 793-F1
43600 LAN 93534 4105-G1
44000 LAN 93534 4015-G7
FERN CT
200 AZU 91702 568-J3
FERN DR
- SCTA 91321 4641-C1
- PAS 91105 565-F5
500 SMAD 91024 567-B1
E FERN DR
600 FUL 92831 738-J6
W FERN DR
300 FUL 92832 738-F6
900 FUL 92833 738-D6
FERN GN
100 SMAD 91024 567-B1
FERN LN
800 WAL 91789 639-C6
1700 GLDL 91208 534-H7
FERN MTWY
- GLDL 91208 534-J6
- GLDL 91208 535-A6
FERN PL
300 DBAR 91765 640-D6
4600 LA 90032 595-D6
FERN ST
6600 NLB 90805 735-C7
9200 SELM 91733 636-J2
9600 SELM 91733 637-A2
9600 ELMN 91733 637-A2
FERN TR
23600 CALB 91302 589-F1
FERN WY
2300 LHB 90631 708-B5
FERNADEL AV
8100 PRV 90660 706-D1
FERNANDO
18000 LACo 90220 764-J1
FERNANDO CT
400 GLDL 91204 564-D7
FERNBANK AV
1800 MONP 91754 636-A5
FERNBROOK PL
1600 GLDL 91208 564-H1
FERNBROOK RD
8600 LA 91304 529-E1
FERNBURY ST
9300 CYP 90630 767-B6
FERNBUSH LN
1300 BelA 90077 592-B5
FERN CANYON TR
- LFlz 90027 564-B7
- LFlz 90027 594-B1
6200 Tuj 91042 504-C4
FERNCOLA AV
7600 SunV 91352 533-B3
FERN CREEK DR
16700 LPUE 91744 678-F1
FERNCREEK DR
4700 RHE 90274 793-B4
N FERNCROFT AV
6900 LACo 91775 566-F7
FERNCROFT RD
3400 LA 90039 594-D2
FERNDALE AV
8200 CDHY 90201 705-F3
12900 LA 90066 672-B4
FERNDALE LN
14200 HacH 91745 637-H7
FERNDALE ST
4700 LA 90016 633-C7
FERN DELL DR
2100 LFlz 90027 593-H3
2100 LA 90068 593-H3
FERN DELL PL
2100 LA 90068 593-H3
FERNDELL PL
400 GLDR 91741 569-H4
FERNDOC ST
20100 WAL 91789 639-E7
FERNFIELD DR
500 MONP 91755 636-C6
5300 ELA 90022 635-H6
E FERNFIELD DR
200 MONP 91755 636-B6
W FERNFIELD DR
100 MONP 91754 636-A6
500 MONP 91754 635-J6
FERNGLEN AV
10100 Tuj 91042 503-J4
FERN GLEN CT
21600 WAL 91789 639-H5
FERNGLEN LN
1200 SDMS 91773 570-B6
FERNGLEN WY
13800 HacH 91745 637-G6
FERN HAVEN RD
16500 HacH 91745 678-E4
FERNHILL DR
6700 MAL 90265 667-F4
FERN HOLLOW DR
1700 DBAR 91765 679-H4
FERN LAKE AV
1200 BREA 92821 708-H6
FERNLAKE DR
23900 Hrbr 90710 794-B3
FERNLEAF AV
- POM 91766 640-J3
E FERNLEAF AV
500 POM 91766 641-A3
W FERNLEAF AV
500 POM 91766 640-G3
FERNLEAF ST
2200 LA 90031 594-H6
FERNLEY DR
2500 DUAR 91010 568-D5
FERNMEAD LN
23900 Hrbr 90710 794-B3
FERNMONT ST
12900 LA 91342 482-D4
13400 LA 91340 482-C5
13500 SFER 91340 482-C5
FERNPARK DR
500 GLDR 91741 569-D4
FERN PINE CIR
13300 CRTS 90703 737-B6
FERNPINE LN
- POM 91767 600-J3
FERNREST DR
900 Hrbr 90710 794-A3
FERNRIDGE DR
1700 SDMS 91773 570-E5
FERNROCK ST
1000 CRSN 90746 764-F3
FERNSHAW DR
400 LACo 91750 600-E1
FERNSIDE DR
1200 LCF 91011 535-B3
FERNSIDE LN
- Nor 91326 500-E1
FERNTOP DR
4500 LA 90032 595-D6
FERNTOWER AV
3700 WCOV 91792 679-D2
FERNTREE PL
3900 GLDL 91214 534-D1
FERNVIEW ST
14000 LACo 90605 707-D4
14800 LACo 90604 707-F6
15400 WHIT 90604 707-H6
FERNWOOD AV
1100 BREA 92821 709-A5
2600 LYN 90262 704-J6
2800 LYN 90262 705-A6
3000 LA 90039 594-C4
3800 LFlz 90027 594-C5
3800 LYN 90262 735-C1
5400 LFlz 90027 593-H5
5500 Hlwd 90028 593-H5
FERNWOOD DR
- HacH 91745 637-J7
S FERNWOOD ST
100 WCOV 91791 598-J7
200 WCOV 91791 638-J1
FERNWOOD PACIFIC DR
400 Top 90290 590-A7
1000 Top 90290 630-A1
FERRARA CT
- POM 91766 640-D3
30800 WLKV 91362 557-G7
FERRARA LN
- Nor 91326 500-C1
FERRARA ST
6000 HiPk 90042 595-E1
FERRARI DR
1600 LA 90210 592-D4
FERRARI LN
600 WCOV 91791 639-D1
FERREE ST
1400 CHLS 91709 710-H5
1400 OrCo 92886 710-H5
FERRERO LN
400 LPUE 91744 678-F1
FERRERO PKWY
- INDS 91789 639-J7
- INDS 91789 640-A6
- INDS 91789 679-J1
FERRIER CT
- LHB 90631 738-C2
FERRIS AV
300 ELA 90022 635-G7
700 ELA 90022 675-G1
FERRIS LN
- FUL 92833 738-C5
FERRIS PL
18600 LACo 90220 764-J2
FERRIS RD
11600 ELMN 91732 597-E7
11900 ELMN 91732 637-E1
FERRIS ST
100 CLAR 91711 571-D6
FERRO CT
2000 LBCH 90815 796-A4
E FERRO ST
4900 LBCH 90815 796-A4
FERRON AV
6700 LACo 91775 596-G1
FERRY CT
- SCTA 91350 4551-B4
FERRY LN
- FUL 92833 738-D5
FERRY ST
100 SPed 90731 824-E4
FERTILE ST
5400 LYN 90262 735-E3
FES ST
10600 SunV 91352 533-A1
FESTINA DR
6700 PRM 90723 735-E5
FESTIVAL CIR
5300 LPMA 90623 767-D2
FESTIVAL CT
37200 PMDL 93552 4287-A3
FESTIVIDAD DR
22200 SCTA 91350 4550-J1
22700 SCTA 91354 4550-H1
FETLOCK LN
15800 CHLS 91709 680-H7
15800 CHLS 91709 710-J1
N FETTERLY AV
100 ELA 90022 635-G5
S FETTERLY AV
400 ELA 90022 635-G7
700 ELA 90022 675-G1
E FIAT ST
900 CRSN 90745 764-E7
W FIAT ST
100 CRSN 90745 764-C7
1000 LACo 90502 764-A7
FIBRE CT
21100 DBAR 91789 679-H2
N FICKETT ST
100 Boyl 90033 635-C3
S FICKETT ST
100 Boyl 90033 635-A6
600 LA 90023 635-A6
FICKEWIRTH AV
900 LPUE 91744 638-E5
FICUS CT
- PMDL 93551 4285-D3
FICUS DR
21200 SCTA 91321 4641-B2
FICUS ST
2700 POM 91766 641-B7
2800 CHNO 91710 641-B7
FIDALGO ST
18400 RowH 91748 679-A7
FIDDLENECK CT
36700 PMDL 93550 4286-F4
FIDDLENECK LN
29200 Llan 93544 4471-C5
FIDEL AV
11300 LACo 90605 707-B7
12100 LACo 90605 737-B1
14300 NRWK 90650 737-B3
FIDELIA AV
2400 CMRC 90040 675-H4
FIDELIDAD DR
2400 HacH 91745 678-C5
FIDLER AV
2000 LBCH 90815 796-B2
3000 LBCH 90808 796-B2
3400 LBCH 90808 766-B4
5000 LKWD 90712 766-B2
13000 DWNY 90242 736-B2
13500 BLF 90706 736-B2
FIELD AV
1100 ING 90302 673-C7
3000 LA 90016 633-D7
3000 LA 90016 673-D1

STREET Block City ZIP Pg-Grid

FIELDBROOK LN
4800 CYP 90630 767-B6
FIELDBROOK ST
18500 RowH 91748 709-B1
18500 RowH 91748 679-B7
FIELDCREST CIR
39300 PMDL 93551 4195-E6
FIELDCREST CT
13700 LMRD 90638 738-A2
FIELDCREST DR
- LA 91342 481-H7
FIELDCREST LN
40500 PMDL 93551 4194-J3
FIELDCREST ST
10500 ELMN 91731 597-C5
FIELDGATE AV
1100 HacH 91745 678-E3
FIELDGLASS CT
- PMDL 93552 4287-B6
FIELDING CIR
- LA 90094 672-E7
FIELDING DR
10800 WHIT 90604 707-H5
FIELDING ST
12700 Pcma 91331 482-E7
13800 Pcma 91331 502-B2
FIELDMONT PL
24400 CanP 91307 529-D5
FIELDSPRING ST
40100 LACo 93591 4199-G2
40400 LACo 93535 4199-G2
40800 LACo 93535 4109-G7
FIELDVIEW AV
300 DUAR 91010 568-E4
FIELDWOOD CT
- LACo 91387 4552-A4
FIERRO CIR
2700 LaCr 91214 504-G6
FIERRO ST
3000 LA 90065 594-F1
FIESEL AV
22000 CRSN 90745 764-F7
FIESTA AV
4800 TEML 91780 597-A5
FIESTA LN
- CRSN 90745 794-G2
FIESTA PL
400 FUL 92835 738-G3
FIFE AV
500 LPUE 91744 678-E1
FIFTH ST
12200 NRWK 90650 706-J7
FIG
2800 WCOV 91792 679-C1
FIG AV
100 MNRO 91016 567-G5
200 BREA 92821 709-D7
43600 LAN 93534 4105-H1
44000 LAN 93534 4015-G4
FIG CIR
4100 LVRN 91750 570-H7
FIG CT
28400 SCTA 91390 4460-J3
FIG LN
1400 MNRO 91016 567-H5
FIG ST
300 COMP 90222 734-H3
FIGTREE RD
- RPV 90275 823-A4
FIGUERAS RD
14200 LMRD 90638 737-F4
FIGUEROA DR
- Alta 91001 535-F6
1400 LA 90015 634-D6
FIGUEROA PL
500 Wilm 90744 794-C5
FIGUEROA ST
200 Wilm 90744 794-C6
200 Wilm 90744 824-C1
400 LA 90065 594-J6
400 LA 90065 595-A6
1400 CRSN 90745 794-C3
2900 GLDL 91206 565-C1
3300 GLDL 91206 535-C7
3600 LCF 91011 535-C7
7400 Eagl 90041 565-C1
30300 Cstc 91384 4459-B6
N FIGUEROA ST
100 LA 90012 634-F3
200 HiPk 90042 595-C3
1900 LA 90031 594-J6
2000 LA 90065 594-J6
3400 LA 90065 595-A5
3900 LA 90031 595-C3
6700 HiPk 90042 565-D7
7100 Eagl 90041 565-D4
7900 GLDL 91206 565-D4
7900 PAS 91105 565-D4
S FIGUEROA ST
- LA 90007 674-B3
- LA 90037 674-B3
100 LA 90012 634-D4
300 LA 90071 634-D4
400 LA 90003 674-B6
400 LA 90044 674-B6
500 LA 90003 704-B2
500 LA 90015 634-D4
500 LA 90044 704-B2
500 LA 90017 634-D4
1900 LA 90007 634-C7
3400 LA 90089 674-B3
10800 LA 90061 704-B6
12000 LA 90061 734-B3

S FIGUEROA ST
12000 LA 90044 734-B3
13000 LA 90248 734-B3
14900 LACo 90248 734-B3
16100 CRSN 90248 734-C6
17400 CRSN 90248 764-C4
17400 LA 90248 764-C4
19400 CRSN 90745 764-B7
22500 CRSN 90745 794-B1
FIGUEROA TER
700 LA 90012 634-F1
FIGUEROA WY
2300 LA 90007 634-C7
FIJI WY
13200 LA 90292 672-B7
13300 MdlR 90292 672-B7
13400 MdlR 90292 702-B1
FIKSE LN
19000 CRTS 90703 767-B2
FILAREE HEIGHTS AV
5800 MAL 90265 667-C1
FILBERT PL
800 BREA 92821 709-C7
FILBERT RD
31600 LACo 90265 587-C6
FILBERT ST
15900 LA 91342 481-E2
FILHURST AV
3900 BALD 91706 598-A5
FILION ST
3800 LA 90065 594-G1
FILLMORE CIR
8600 BPK 90620 767-H5
FILLMORE CT
2100 LVRN 91750 600-H3
FILLMORE DR
1700 MONP 91755 636-C4
7000 BPK 90620 767-G5
N FILLMORE PL
500 POM 91768 640-G1
FILLMORE ST
- PAS 91105 565-H6
200 PAS 91106 565-J6
600 PAS 91106 566-A6
5900 CHNO 91710 641-J6
FILMORE AV
- CRTS 90703 766-H3
FILMORE ST
4600 BELL 90201 675-E7
12000 LA 91342 482-E7
12500 Pcma 91331 482-E7
12600 Pcma 91331 502-D1
14500 Pcma 91331 501-J5
FINANCIAL WY
2000 GLDR 91741 569-J6
FINCH
200 POM 91767 601-A1
FINCH CT
- SCTA 91350 4551-A3
2000 SIMI 93063 499-C2
FINCH LN
- FUL 92833 738-C5
FINCH RD
900 SBdC 92397 (4652-C2 See Page 4651)
FINCH ST
- LVRN 91750 570-J5
2900 LA 90039 594-D2
FINCHGROVE AV
12600 Pear 93553 4468-H5
FINCHLEY
13200 BALD 91706 637-J1
FINCHLEY PL
1300 PAS 91103 535-D7
FINCHLEY RD
- PMDL 93552 4287-C4
FINCHLEY ST
12600 BALD 91706 597-H7
N FINDLAY AV
400 MTBL 90640 636-A7
400 MTBL 90640 676-A1
S FINDLAY AV
600 ELA 90022 676-A1
600 MTBL 90640 676-A1
2100 MONP 91754 636-A5
FINE CIR
44100 LAN 93536 4015-C7
FINE ST
44000 LAN 93536 4105-C1
44000 LAN 93536 4015-C7
FINECREST DR
5800 RPV 90275 792-J6
FINECROFT DR
1500 CLAR 91711 601-A1
FINEGROVE AV
600 HacH 91745 637-J7
900 HacH 91745 638-A7
900 HacH 91745 677-J1
FINEHILL AV
5100 GLDL 91214 504-E5
FINES RD
3400 MAL 90265 629-A6
FINEVALE DR
7200 DWNY 90240 706-A1
FINEVIEW ST
11000 ELMN 91733 637-D3
11000 SELM 91733 637-D3
12000 ELMN 91732 637-D3
FINGAL PL
6500 WHIT 90601 677-E6
FINISTERRA PL
14700 HacH 91745 677-H4

FINK PL
6400 LA 90068 593-E3
FINK ST
2200 LA 90068 593-E3
FINLEY AV
4300 LFlz 90027 594-A3
4800 LFlz 90027 593-J3
FINNEY CT
400 LACo 90248 734-D4
FINROD CT
1000 THO 91361 557-A5
FINVILLE AV
4100 PMDL 93552 4196-J7
FIONNA LN
- WCOV 91792 679-B1
FIR
200 SDMS 91773 599-J3
FIR AV
8300 Flor 90001 704-H3
8600 Wats 90002 704-H3
N FIR AV
100 ING 90301 703-C2
S FIR AV
100 ING 90301 703-C3
1900 Wats 90002 704-H3
FIR CIR
5500 LPMA 90623 767-D2
FIR CT
4400 MTCL 91763 601-E5
22800 SCTA 91390 4460-H2
FIR ST
4400 PRV 90660 676-F2
4900 LA 90016 633-C7
11400 LYN 90262 705-B7
11600 LYN 90262 735-B1
11900 NRWK 90650 707-A7
FIR WY
500 LHB 90631 708-C6
FIRCROFT AV
4600 LACo 91722 599-A4
N FIRCROFT AV
1200 COV 91722 599-A3
S FIRCROFT AV
700 COV 91723 599-A6
S FIRCROFT ST
100 WCOV 91791 599-A7
100 WCOV 91791 639-A1
FIRE RD
- HacH 91745 677-H4
- LFlz 90027 563-H5
- LFlz 90027 564-A5
3600 Shrm 91423 562-B6
FIREBIRD AV
8700 WHIT 90605 707-D2
9200 LACo 90605 707-C3
FIREBRAND DR
27600 Cstc 91384 4459-G4
FIREBRAND PL
3300 LA 90034 672-D1
FIREBRAND ST
6400 Wch 90045 702-F1
FIRECREST RD
31700 LACo 91390 4462-J1
FIRE HOLLOW DR
1600 DBAR 91765 680-C3
FIRENZA DR
4800 CYP 90630 767-C7
FIRENZE AV
7700 LA 90046 593-A1
FIRENZE DR
- PMDL 93550 4286-F6
FIRENZE LN
- Nor 91326 500-C1
FIRENZE PL
2800 LA 90046 593-B1
24400 SCTA 91355 4550-E4
FIRENZE ST
- CRSN 90745 764-B7
- CRSN 90745 794-B1
- LAN 93536 4104-J7
FIREPIT DR
600 DBAR 91765 640-B6
FIRESIDE DR
11500 LACo 90604 708-A6
W FIRESIDE SQ
1200 UPL 91786 601-G1
FIRESTONE BLVD
2100 Wats 90002 704-H3
2300 SGAT 90280 704-H3
2700 SGAT 90280 705-C3
6200 DWNY 90241 705-C3
7100 BPK 90621 737-F6
7600 DWNY 90241 706-A4
10600 NRWK 90650 706-C6
11200 NRWK 90650 736-G1
12400 NRWK 90650 737-A3
12600 SFSP 90670 737-A3
14200 LMRD 90638 737-E5
E FIRESTONE BLVD
- LACo 90280 704-F2
1100 Wats 90002 704-F2
1100 Flor 90001 704-F2
FIRESTONE DR
- PMDL 93551 4104-D6
FIRESTONE PL
5000 SGAT 90280 705-E3
7400 DWNY 90241 705-J4
FIRESTONE PZ
8800 SGAT 90280 704-J3
FIRETHORN AV
36800 PMDL 93550 4286-E5
FIRE THORN CIR
22600 DBAR 91765 680-A3

FIRETHORNE AV
2700 FUL 92835 738-J2
FIRETHORNE ST
500 BREA 92821 738-J2
FIREWOOD WY
- LAN 93536 4104-J1
FIREWORKS RD
- SCTA 91350 4551-A4
FIRMA CT
17300 GrnH 91344 481-B6
FIRMAMENT AV
4300 Enc 91436 561-G3
4700 Shrm 91403 561-G3
6400 VanN 91411 531-G6
6500 VanN 91406 531-G4
FIRMIN ST
300 Echo 90026 634-E2
FIRMONA AV
500 RBCH 90278 763-C1
14200 HAW 90250 733-C5
14200 LNDL 90250 733-C5
14300 LNDL 90260 733-C5
17300 LNDL 90260 763-C1
19000 TOR 90503 763-C3
S FIRMONA AV
10000 ING 90304 703-C5
10000 Lenx 90304 703-C5
11100 HAW 90304 703-C7
FIRST VIEW ST
43100 LAN 93535 4106-A3
FIRTH AV
600 Brwd 90049 631-G1
10300 Wats 90002 704-F5
FIRTH BLVD
9200 Wats 90002 704-F4
FIRTH DR
13400 LA 90210 562-C7
13400 LA 90210 592-C1
FIRTH GRN
8100 BPK 90621 737-G5
FIRTHRIDGE RD
29000 RPV 90275 822-J1
FIRTREE CT
- CRSN 90746 764-G2
FIRTREE DR
- LACo 93532 4102-H5
FIRVALE AV
1600 MTBL 90640 636-F5
FIRWOOD CT
10600 NRWK 90650 736-E2
FISCHER ST
300 GLDL 91205 564-G6
FISHBURN AV
1500 City 90063 635-D3
5200 MYWD 90270 675-D6
5900 HNTP 90255 675-D6
6200 BELL 90201 675-D7
6800 BELL 90201 705-D1
FISH CANYON RD
500 DUAR 91010 568-E4
3400 AZU 91010 568-F3
4000 AZU 91702 568-F3
FISHER AV
1100 MANB 90266 732-F6
FISHER CT
2200 RBCH 90278 763-A2
FISHER ST
300 HiPk 90042 595-D1
4000 City 90063 635-E5
4300 ELA 90022 635-F5
FISHERMAN PARK RD
- SDMS 91773 600-C6
FISHMAN RD
8500 PRV 90660 676-F3
FISH RIDGE TKTR
- LACo (538-G5 See Page 507)
- LACo 91702 (538-G5 See Page 507)
FISK AV
100 SGBL 91776 596-E6
FISK CT
700 RBCH 90278 763-C2
FISK LN
2400 RBCH 90278 763-B2
FISKE AV
1600 PAS 91104 536-A7
1600 PAS 91104 566-A1
FISKE ST
800 PacP 90272 631-B4
FISLER WY
- FUL 92833 738-C5
FITCH AV
29500 CynC 91351 4462-B5
FITCH DR
1900 LA 90068 593-D4
FITHIAN AV
3300 LA 90032 595-E6
FITNESS DR
1700 LA 90732 823-J1
FITZGERALD AV
2100 CMRC 90040 675-G3
25300 StvR 91381 4550-C7
FITZGERALD ST
23600 LA 91304 529-E3
FITZPATRICK CT
16400 LMRD 90638 738-A1
FITZPATRICK RD
5800 HIDH 91302 559-C2
FITZROY AV
10600 Tuj 91042 504-A3
FIUME WK
14200 Shrm 91403 561-G5

FIVE OAK CT
5600 SIMI 93063 499-A1
FIVE OAKS DR
500 SPAS 91030 595-G1
FLAG ST
5900 LA 90068 593-G3
13000 LAN 93536 4105-E2
FLAG WY
- PMDL 93551 4195-B3
FLAGLER LN
- TOR 90503 763-A3
- RBCH 90277 763-A3
300 RBCH 90278 763-A2
2300 RBCH 90278 762-J1
FLAGMOOR PL
6400 LA 90068 593-F1
FLAGSTAFF CT
1800 SLB 90740 826-G4
FLAGSTAFF ST
300 SDMS 91773 600-C1
13600 LACo 91746 637-J4
13700 LPUE 91746 637-J4
13900 LPUE 91746 638-A4
14800 LPUE 91744 638-B5
FLAGSTONE AV
2000 LACo 91010 567-H7
FLAGSTONE CT
14500 CHLS 91709 680-J4
FLAGSTONE ST
40800 PMDL 93551 4194-J2
E FLAGSTONE ST
5100 LBCH 90808 796-B1
FLAHERTY ST
9200 TEML 91780 596-J2
9800 TEML 91780 597-A2
FLAIR DR
3200 ELMN 91731 636-H1
9100 ELMN 91731 596-J7
9400 ELMN 91731 597-A7
9800 ELMN 91731 637-A1
FLALLON AV
8100 LACo 90606 676-H7
8300 LACo 90606 706-H1
9100 SFSP 90670 706-H2
11100 NRWK 90650 706-G6
13100 NRWK 90650 736-G2
17200 ART 90701 736-G7
19900 LKWD 90715 766-G3
FLAMBEAU RD
5800 RPV 90275 792-J6
FLAME FLOWER LN
2100 FUL 92833 738-A3
FLAME TREE LN
- WdHl 91367 559-H7
FLAMING ARROW CIR
19300 WAL 91789 639-C7
FLAMING ARROW DR
27600 RPV 90275 793-B7
FLAMINGO CIR
10500 LACo 90606 706-G1
FLAMINGO DR
6000 BPK 90620 767-E2
FLAMINGO ST
1000 GLDR 91741 569-G3
22500 WdHl 91364 559-H5
FLAMINGO WY
600 ARCD 91006 597-E2
900 LHB 90631 708-H4
FLAMSTEAD DR
16000 HacH 91745 678-D3
FLANAGAN ST
1500 POM 91766 641-A4
FLANCO RD
22200 WdHl 91364 559-J4
FLANDERS AV
300 POM 91768 600-H5
FLANDERS CT
2500 BREA 92821 709-E7
FLANDERS RD
900 LCF 91011 535-A3
FLANDERS ST
16300 GrnH 91344 501-B1
17400 GrnH 91344 481-B7
FLANGEL ST
2500 LKWD 90712 765-G5
FLANNER ST
13600 LACo 91746 638-A2
14400 LPUE 91746 638-B3
14600 LACo 91744 638-D5
FLAPJACK DR
20400 DBAR 91765 709-G1
FLARE RD
- SCTA 91350 4551-B5
FLASHMAN AV
8900 Pcma 91331 502-D7
FLATBUSH AV
13200 NRWK 90650 736-E2
FLATHEAD TR
1900 Ago 91301 588-B4
FLAT PEAK LN
16200 CRTS 90703 736-J6
FLAT RIVER
- CLAR 91711 571-G2
FLAVIAN AV
19300 TOR 90503 763-B3
FLAX DR
- SCTA 91321 4641-C1
FLAX PL
7600 Wch 90045 702-C3
FLAXTON ST
300 POM 91767 601-A2
10600 CULC 90230 672-H4

FLAXWOOD LN
24400 SCTA 91321 4641-C1
FLECHA CT
2800 HacH 91745 678-D6
FLEET DR
13600 SGAT 90280 735-F2
13600 PRM 90723 735-F2
13600 SGAT 90723 735-F2
FLEET ST
- LA 90292 701-H1
- LA 90292 671-J7
6400 CMRC 90040 676-A3
FLEETHAVEN RD
4100 LKWD 90712 766-A6
FLEETWELL AV
5500 LACo 91702 598-F1
N FLEETWELL AV
100 WCOV 91791 598-J7
S FLEETWELL AV
700 WCOV 91791 638-J2
S FLEETWELL ST
900 WCOV 91791 638-J2
FLEETWING AV
8900 Wch 90045 702-H3
FLEETWOOD AV
4000 CYP 90630 767-A7
FLEETWOOD DR
43200 LAN 93535 4106-G2
FLEETWOOD PL
400 GLDR 91740 599-D2
2200 POM 91767 600-J4
FLEETWOOD ST
9300 CYP 90630 767-A7
11000 SunV 91352 502-J7
11000 SunV 91352 503-A7
11100 SunV 91352 532-H1
FLEMING AV
14700 BLF 90706 736-C4
FLEMING ST
1700 POM 91766 640-E3
FLEMINGTON CT
13200 LMRD 90638 738-A1
FLEMINGTON DR
3300 WCOV 91792 679-E1
FLEMISH LN
5400 LA 90029 593-H5
FLEMMING PL
- StvR 91381 4550-A6
FLEMMING WY
13700 CRTS 90703 737-D6
FLETA DR
13200 LMRD 90638 737-E1
FLETCHER AV
1600 SPAS 91030 595-J4
3400 ELMN 91731 597-A7
3400 ELMN 91731 637-A1
FLETCHER DR
2300 LA 90039 594-F4
2900 LA 90065 594-G1
FLETCHER GRN
8100 BPK 90621 737-G5
FLETCHER PKWY
- ELMN 91731 637-B1
3400 ELMN 91733 637-B1
FLEUR DR
2700 SMRO 91108 596-A2
FLEURY LN
6100 WdHl 91367 529-J7
FLICKER PL
9200 BHLS 90210 592-G5
9200 LA 90069 592-G5
FLICKER WY
9200 LA 90069 592-G5
9200 BHLS 90210 592-G5
FLIGHT AV
6100 LA 90056 673-A6
6100 LadH 90056 673-A6
6900 Wch 90045 673-A7
7000 Wch 90045 702-H2
7000 Wch 90045 703-A1
FLIGHT PL
7800 Wch 90045 702-H2
FLINT AV
200 LBCH 90803 826-C1
300 LBCH 90814 796-C7
300 LBCH 90814 826-C1
500 Wilm 90744 794-G6
600 LBCH 90804 796-C7
9500 LA 90034 632-G7
FLINT DR
- Hrbr 90710 794-A5
FLINTGATE DR
20100 DBAR 91789 679-F3
20100 INDS 91789 679-F3
FLINT HOLLOW PL
16600 CHLS 91709 710-F2
FLINTLOCK LN
4200 WLKV 91361 557-F6
4200 AGRH 91301 557-F6
N FLINTLOCK LN
- VeCo 91307 529-A5
FLINTLOCK RD
1000 DBAR 91765 640-C5
FLINTON CT
1400 THO 91361 557-A6
FLINT POINT CIR
- POM 91766 640-H5
FLINTRIDGE AV
700 LCF 91011 535-B5
FLINTRIDGE CIR
1200 LCF 91011 535-B5
FLINTRIDGE DR
2200 GLDL 91206 535-A6

FLINTRIDGE DR
3100 FUL 92835 738-F2
41500 PMDL 93551 4104-E7
FLINTRIDGE OAKS DR
300 LCF 91011 535-D5
FLINTROCK RD
1900 DBAR 91765 680-B4
40000 LACo 93551 4193-F3
FLINT SPEAR RD
700 WAL 91789 639-E6
FLINTSTONE DR
14500 LACo 93532 4102-G4
FLINTWOOD CT
- SCTA 91351 4461-G6
FLINTWOOD DR
2400 RowH 91748 679-D6
FLO LN
26900 SCTA 91351 4551-E3
FLOMAR DR
12600 WHIT 90602 707-C1
13500 WHIT 90605 707-D2
14300 WHIT 90603 707-F4
FLOOD CONTROL RD
- BRAD 91010 568-B3
FLORA AV
3500 LA 90031 595-B7
5900 MYWD 90270 675-D6
5900 HNTP 90255 675-D6
6200 BELL 90201 675-D7
6800 BELL 90201 705-D1
7300 CDHY 90201 705-D1
FLORA DR
800 ING 90302 703-A1
FLORA ST
2300 WCOV 91792 639-B7
4200 MTCL 91763 601-D7
W FLORA ST
900 ONT 91762 601-H7
FLORABUNDA RD
29100 SCTA 91387 4462-G7
FLORAC AV
3900 CLAR 91711 600-J1
FLORAC ST
- PMDL 93552 4287-E1
FLORADALE AV
1700 SELM 91733 637-C4
2400 ELMN 91732 637-D3
FLORAL AV
8000 LA 90046 593-B4
E FLORAL AV
- ARCD 91006 567-D4
W FLORAL AV
- ARCD 91006 567-C4
FLORAL CT
600 BREA 92821 709-B7
25700 SCTA 91355 4550-G5
FLORAL DR
2100 MONP 91754 635-F5
3300 City 90063 635-D5
4300 ELA 90022 635-F5
4900 LACo 91754 635-F5
10100 LACo 90606 676-J4
10400 WHIT 90606 676-J4
10500 WHIT 90606 677-A4
11500 WHIT 90601 677-B5
E FLORAL DR
100 MONP 91755 636-B5
W FLORAL DR
100 MONP 91754 636-A5
500 MONP 91754 635-J5
2000 ELA 90022 635-J5
2000 MONP 90022 635-J5
FLORALITA AV
10200 Sunl 91040 503-F2
FLORALITA LN
10500 Sunl 91040 503-F3
FLORAL PARK TER
400 SPAS 91030 595-G1
FLORAL VISTA WY
- LAN 93536 4013-J6
FLORAMORGAN TR
7000 Tuj 91042 504-A5
FLORA VISTA
1300 POM 91766 640-G3
FLORA VISTA DR
4200 BELL 90201 675-D7
FLORA VISTA ST
9200 BLF 90706 736-A4
12200 ART 90701 766-J2
FLORAVISTA TER
- HacH 91745 637-G6
FLORCRAFT AV
20800 LKWD 90715 766-H5
FLORECITA CRES
3300 PAS 91001 535-F3
FLORECITA DR
3000 Alta 91001 535-F4
3100 PAS 91001 535-F4
FLORECITA LN
700 PAS 91001 535-G4
FLORECITA TER
700 PAS 91001 535-G4
FLORECITA WY
800 Alta 91001 535-F4
800 PAS 91001 535-F4
FLORENA CT
1900 GLDL 91208 534-J6
FLORENCE AV
2300 ARCD 91007 597-B2
3100 HNTP 90255 705-C1
3600 BELL 90201 705-C1
4500 CDHY 90201 705-C1
5500 WHIT 90601 677-A4

FLORENCE AV
5600 BGDN 90201 705-G1
5700 SGAT 90280 735-G1
7000 DWNY 90241 705-G1
7000 DWNY 90240 705-G1
7200 DWNY 90241 706-A2
7200 DWNY 90240 706-A2
10700 LACo 90605 707-B5
11300 SFSP 90670 706-H5
12500 SFSP 90670 707-B5
E FLORENCE AV
100 ING 90301 703-E1
100 LA 90003 674-E7
100 LHB 90631 708-E5
100 ING 90302 703-E1
400 WCOV 91790 638-F3
600 LA 90001 674-E7
1100 Flor 90001 674-E7
1900 HNTP 90001 674-E7
2000 LACo 90255 674-E7
2000 HNTP 90255 674-E7
2700 HNTP 90255 675-A7
2700 LACo 90255 675-A7
3100 HNTP 90255 705-A1
N FLORENCE AV
100 MONP 91755 636-D2
W FLORENCE AV
100 ING 90301 703-B2
100 ING 90302 703-B2
100 LA 90003 674-B7
100 LHB 90631 708-D5
500 LA 90044 674-B7
1300 LA 90044 673-H7
1400 LA 90047 673-H7
2200 LA 90043 673-H7
3100 LA 90043 703-B2
FLORENCE CT
- PMDL 93550 4286-F6
300 LHB 90631 708-F5
FLORENCE DR
1100 PAS 91103 565-G2
FLORENCE LN
28000 SCTA 91351 4461-E7
FLORENCE PL
200 FUL 92833 738-D7
1000 GLDL 91204 564-D6
6200 BGDN 90201 705-J1
6800 BGDN 90201 706-A1
FLORENCE ST
8200 PRM 90723 735-H2
8400 DWNY 90242 735-H2
N FLORENCE ST
100 BURB 91505 563-D1
S FLORENCE ST
200 BURB 91505 563-E3
N FLORENCE WK
- LBCH 90803 826-C3
FLORENCELL ST
34600 Actn 93510 4375-B3
FLORENCITA AV
2200 Mont 91020 534-H3
2200 GLDL 91020 534-H3
FLORENTINA AV
2300 ALH 91803 635-H2
FLORENTINE ST
14700 LA 91342 481-J5
FLORES AV
5900 LA 90056 673-B6
5900 LadH 90056 673-B6
FLORES ST
- SFSP 90670 707-B5
7300 DWNY 90242 705-G7
N FLORES ST
100 LA 90048 633-A1
300 LA 90048 593-A7
500 WHWD 90048 593-A7
1100 WHWD 90069 593-A5
S FLORES ST
100 LA 90048 633-A1
FLORES DE ORO
700 SPAS 91030 595-G3
FLORESTA AV
3400 LACo 90043 673-E4
FLORESTA PL
1400 PacP 90272 630-H3
FLORESTA WY
3700 LACo 90043 673-E4
FLORHAM AV
500 SDMS 91773 599-J1
FLORIAN PL
2200 LA 90210 592-D3
FLORIDA
3800 WCOV 91792 679-A1
E FLORIDA ST
1200 LBCH 90802 795-F7
2000 LBCH 90814 795-F7
FLORINDA ST
3100 POM 91767 600-H2
FLORINE AV
13700 PRM 90723 735-G2
FLORIS HEIGHTS RD
5900 MAL 90265 667-C1
FLORISTA ST
3200 LALM 90720 796-H2
FLORISTAN AV
4800 Eagl 90041 565-B6
FLORITA RD
14500 LMRD 90638 737-F3
FLORIZEL ST
4400 LA 90032 595-C6
FLORPARK ST
9500 PRV 90660 706-E2

FLORWOOD AV
1300 TOR 90503 763-E6
13000 HAW 90250 733-E2
15100 LACo 90260 733-E5
17800 TOR 90504 763-E1
FLORY ST
10800 LACo 90606 676-H6
FLOSSMOOR RD
8400 PRV 90660 706-D1
11200 SFSP 90670 706-F3
FLOTILLA ST
- MTBL 90640 676-A3
5500 CMRC 90040 675-H2
6400 CMRC 90040 676-A3
FLOURNOY RD
1800 MANB 90266 732-F5
FLOWER AV
100 BREA 92821 709-B7
600 Ven 90291 671-H4
1600 DUAR 91010 568-C6
1600 TOR 90503 763-E6
S FLOWER AV
200 COMP 90221 735-A4
FLOWER CT
600 Ven 90291 671-H4
FLOWER DR
3800 LA 90037 674-B2
FLOWER ST
- ARCD 91006 567-D4
100 BURB 91502 533-G7
100 BURB 91502 563-H1
200 PAS 91104 535-J7
700 GLDL 91201 564-A3
1600 GLDL 91201 563-J2
2400 LACo 90255 704-J1
2700 LACo 90255 705-A1
2900 HNTP 90255 705-A1
3000 LYN 90262 705-A7
3400 LA 90007 674-B4
3800 CDHY 90201 705-C1
4000 LA 90037 674-B4
5800 LA 90003 674-B6
8500 PRM 90723 735-J6
8600 BLF 90706 735-J6
8700 BLF 90706 736-A6
N FLOWER ST
400 ING 90301 703-D1
S FLOWER ST
100 LA 90012 634-E4
300 LA 90071 634-E4
300 LACo 90061 734-C1
400 LA 90015 634-E4
500 ING 90301 703-D3
600 LA 90017 634-E4
1900 LA 90007 634-E4
2900 LA 90007 674-B1
4600 LA 90037 674-B3
7200 LA 90003 674-B7
7200 LA 90003 704-B1
FLOWER CREEK LN
2200 HacH 91745 678-E5
FLOWERDALE CT
10300 SunV 91352 533-B1
FLOWERDALE ST
1600 SIMI 93063 499-C3
FLOWERFIELD LN
1200 LHH 90631 708-F3
FLOWER FIELDS AV
- SCTA 91321 4550-H6
- SCTA 91350 4550-H6
FLOWER GLEN DR
16500 HacH 91745 678-E4
FLOWER HILL CIR
17300 GrnH 91344 481-B7
FLOWER HILL LN
3200 HacH 91745 678-A6
FLOWER HILL ST
100 BREA 92821 709-F7
FLOWERIDGE DR
31200 RPV 90275 823-E6
FLOWERING OAK PL
- LACo 91387 4552-A4
FLOWERING PLUM CIR
16600 WHIT 90603 708-A6
FLOWERPARK DR
28800 SCTA 91387 4552-E1
28900 SCTA 91387 4462-E7
FLOWERS CT
19300 SCTA 91321 4551-F4
FLOWER VALE LN
16900 HacH 91745 678-F4
S FLOYD AL
100 ANA 92804 767-J6
W FLOYD AV
2900 ANA 92804 767-J6
FLOYD CT
- LHB 90631 738-C2
FLOYD ST
2000 BURB 91504 533-D4
2900 BURB 91504 533-D4
FLOYD TER
3300 LA 90068 563-D6
FLOYE DR
3100 LA 90046 563-B7
3100 LA 90046 593-B1
FLUFFY DUCKLING LN
- Win 91306 530-E3
FLUME CANYON DR
23300 LACo 92397 (4652-A1 See Page 4651)
FLYING HILL PL
1100 DBAR 91765 640-D5

FLYING MANE LN
- RHLS 90274 823-E4
FLYING MANE RD
- RHLS 90274 823-E4
FLYING TIGER DR
- SCTA 91387 4551-H4
FLYNN DR
18100 LACo 91387 4551-J4
FLYNN ST
13600 LACo 91746 638-A3
13800 LPUE 91746 638-A3
14300 LPUE 91744 638-B4
14600 LACo 91744 638-B4
FLYNN RANCH RD
7700 LA 90046 563-A7
FOB CIR
2100 LAN 93536 4105-D1
FOIX AV
10600 NRWK 90650 706-E7
FOIX PL
20200 Chat 91311 500-D4
FOLEY AV
21800 CRSN 90745 764-F7
FOLEY WY
500 POM 91768 640-C3
FOLGER ST
14800 HacH 91745 678-A1
FOLKESTONE TERRACE RD
1600 THO 91361 557-A6
FOLKSTONE AV
900 HacH 91745 637-J7
1100 HacH 91745 677-H1
FOLKSTONE CT
- BURB 91504 533-E2
FOLKSTONE LN
11700 BelA 90077 591-G2
FOLSOM ST
800 City 90063 635-D4
2300 Boyl 90033 635-B4
3000 LA 90063 635-C5
4300 ELA 90022 635-E4
FOND DR
3100 Enc 91436 561-F7
N FONDA ST
100 LHB 90631 708-G5
S FONDA ST
100 LHB 90631 708-G6
FONDA WY
2700 LA 90031 595-A7
FONDALE ST
1000 AZU 91702 599-B1
18000 LACo 91702 599-A1
FOND DU LAC RD
26600 RPV 90275 793-A6
FONSECA AV
12700 LMRD 90638 737-G2
FONT LN
1500 THO 91361 557-A6
FONTAINBLEAU AV
4200 CYP 90630 767-A4
4200 LACo 90630 767-A4
FONTAINBLEAU WY
8200 CYP 90630 767-B4
FONTAINE RD
20800 Top 90290 590-C5
FONTAINEBLEAU CT
42900 LAN 93536 4105-B3
FONTANA ST
7200 DWNY 90241 705-H5
8200 DWNY 90241 706-A6
FONTANET WY
700 Alta 91001 536-A5
FONTE RD
8900 CYP 90630 767-C7
FONTENELLE WY
10500 BelA 90077 592-A5
FONTENOY AV
1300 LACo 90601 637-F5
FONTES PL
900 WAL 91789 639-C6
FONTEZUELA DR
2400 HacH 91745 678-C5
FONTHILL AV
800 TOR 90503 763-E6
12500 HAW 90250 733-E1
15100 LACo 90260 733-E5
16800 TOR 90504 733-E7
17600 TOR 90504 763-E1
22600 TOR 90505 793-E1
FONTWELL CT
13400 LMRD 90638 738-A2
FOOSE RD
2600 LACo 90265 626-D3
FOOTE AV
7000 Wilm 90744 794-J6
FOOTES AL
700 LBCH 90813 795-E7
FOOTHILL AV
200 SMAD 91024 567-C1
FOOTHILL BLVD
100 LCF 91011 535-B4
100 PAS 91103 535-B4
900 LVRN 91750 570-D7
1600 LCF 91011 534-G1
2300 LACo 91011 534-G1
2400 Mont 91020 534-G1
2400 LaCr 91214 534-G1
3000 LaCr 91214 504-D6
3200 GLDL 91214 504-D6
4000 Tuj 91042 504-A5
4000 Tuj 91042 504-D6
4000 LA 91214 504-D6

STREET Block City ZIP Pg-Grid

FOOTHILL BLVD
7300 Tuj 91042 503-J4
7800 Sunl 91040 503-D2
9600 LA 91342 503-B1
10900 Sunl 91040 502-G1
10900 LA 91342 502-G1
11800 Pcma 91331 502-G1
12000 LA 91342 482-A2
12000 Pcma 91331 482-E6
12600 LA 91340 482-A2
12800 SFER 91340 482-E6
14400 LA 91342 481-C1
15700 IRW 91706 568-F6
16000 IRW 91702 568-F6
16900 LA 91342 4641-C7
FOOTHILL BLVD Rt#-66
200 POM 91767 600-G1
1000 LVRN 91750 570-E7
1200 LVRN 91750 600-G1
E FOOTHILL BLVD
- ARCD 91006 567-D3
100 AZU 91702 568-J6
100 GLDR 91741 569-F5
100 MNRO 91016 567-H3
100 SDMS 91773 570-C7
500 AZU 91702 569-A6
700 LACo 91750 570-C7
700 SDMS 91750 570-C7
700 LVRN 91750 570-C7
1900 PAS 91107 566-D4
2100 GLDR 91741 570-A5
3700 LACo 91107 566-G4
16100 IRW 91702 568-J6
E FOOTHILL BLVD Rt#-66
100 CLAR 91711 601-D2
100 POM 91767 600-J2
200 POM 91767 601-A2
W FOOTHILL BLVD
- ARCD 91006 567-A4
100 AZU 91702 568-G6
100 GLDR 91741 569-C5
100 MNRO 91016 567-F3
100 SDMS 91773 570-B6
800 ARCD 91006 566-J4
W FOOTHILL BLVD Rt#-66
100 CLAR 91711 601-B2
100 POM 91767 600-J2
100 LVRN 91750 600-J2
1000 UPL 91786 601-F2
W FOOTHILL BLVD U.S.-66 Hist
1000 UPL 91786 601-F2
FOOTHILL DR
- WCOV 91791 639-B3
1200 VeCo 93063 499-B3
1700 GLDL 91201 534-B6
1900 THO 91361 557-A3
2000 FUL 92833 738-D3
5500 AGRH 91301 558-C5
5700 LA 90068 593-G3
FOOTHILL FRWY I-210
- ARCD - 566-G4
- ARCD - 567-H6
- AZU - 568-D6
- AZU - 569-H7
- DUAR - 567-H6
- DUAR - 568-D6
- GLDL - 504-B7
- GLDL - 534-F1
- GLDR - 569-H7
- GLDR - 570-A7
- GLDR - 599-E1
- GLDR - 600-A1
- GrnH - 481-F2
- IRW - 568-D6
- LA - 481-F2
- LA - 482-D5
- LA - 502-F1
- LA - 503-C2
- LACo - 482-D5
- LACo - 566-G4
- LACo - 569-H7
- LaCr - 534-F1
- LCF - 534-F1
- LCF - 535-D6
- MNRO - 567-H6
- Mont - 534-F1
- PAS - 535-D6
- PAS - 565-G2
- PAS - 566-G4
- Sunl - 502-F1
- Sunl - 503-F5
- SunV - 503-F5
- SunV - 504-B7
- Tuj - 504-B7
FOOTHILL LN
2300 BREA 92821 709-E7
FOOTHILL PL
9700 LA 91342 503-D1
FOOTHILL RD
- Cstc 91384 4459-F3
100 BHLS 90210 632-G1
N FOOTHILL RD
500 BHLS 90210 632-G1
500 BHLS 90210 592-F6
FOOTHILL ST
1000 SPAS 91030 595-G1
FOOTHILL FRONTAGE RD
600 CLAR 91711 601-E2

FORBES AV
500 MTBL 90640 676-F1
5200 Enc 91436 561-D2
6400 VanN 91406 531-D5
8600 LA 91343 531-D1
9000 LA 91343 501-D5
10500 GrnH 91344 501-D2
N FORBES AV
2100 CLAR 91711 571-D6
FORBES DR
700 BREA 92821 709-C5
FORBES ST
42400 LAN 93534 4105-J4
FORBES WY
1500 LBCH 90810 765-B6
FORD AV
100 POM 91768 600-J5
1100 RBCH 90278 762-J1
N FORD AV
200 FUL 92832 738-G6
N FORD BLVD
100 ELA 90022 635-F5
S FORD BLVD
100 ELA 90022 635-F7
900 ELA 90022 675-F1
FORD CT
- LHB 90631 738-C2
FORD DR
1100 WCOV 91792 638-G4
FORD LN
6500 HNTP 90255 675-A7
FORD PL
400 PAS 91101 565-J4
FORD ST
800 BURB 91505 563-B3
FORDHAM PL
400 CLAR 91711 601-C4
FORDHAM RD
7800 Wch 90045 702-E2
FORDHOOK DR
1100 LCF 91011 535-B4
FORDLAND AV
400 LACo 91750 600-D1
FORDYCE AV
20400 CRSN 90810 764-J4
FORDYCE RD
300 Brwd 90049 631-G1
FORECASTLE AV
200 WAL 91789 679-D2
3500 WCOV 91792 679-D2
FOREMAN AV
2600 LBCH 90815 796-C2
FOREMAST DR
15400 LMRD 90638 737-H4
FOREST AV
600 SPAS 91030 595-F2
1100 PAS 91103 565-F1
1600 PAS 91103 535-G7
7300 WHIT 90602 677-E7
7900 WHIT 90602 707-E1
E FOREST AV
- ARCD 91006 567-D4
N FOREST AV
400 Boyl 90033 635-C4
W FOREST AV
- ARCD 91006 567-C4
FOREST DR
1800 AZU 91702 568-H2
FOREST GN
3000 LA 90046 593-B1
FOREST LN
400 SMAD 91024 567-B1
FOREST PL
100 BREA 92821 709-B6
11000 SFSP 90670 706-J6
FOREST ST
1300 UPL 91784 571-H3
10600 SFSP 90670 706-J5
N FOREST ST
1100 ING 90302 673-C7
FOREST TR
12200 LACo 91342 482-J6
FOREST CANYON DR
23200 DBAR 91765 680-B4
N FOREST CIRCLE DR
44700 LAN 93535 4015-J6
FOREST COVE LN
5300 AGRH 91301 557-H4
FORESTDALE AV
400 COV 91723 599-D6
600 WCOV 91791 639-D1
1000 GLDR 91740 569-D7
1000 GLDR 91740 599-D1
6400 GLDR 91741 569-C6
N FORESTDALE AV
100 COV 91723 599-D5
S FORESTDALE AV
100 COV 91723 599-D5
FORESTDALE ST
1100 LVRN 91750 600-E1
1100 LACo 91750 600-E1
FOREST EDGE DR
- LA 91342 481-J5
FORESTER DR
- LVRN 91750 570-J5
FOREST GATE CIR
3600 MAL 90265 628-G7
FOREST GLEN DR
1400 HacH 91745 678-E3
FORESTGLEN DR
3800 GLDL 91214 534-D1
FORESTGLEN LN
1200 SDMS 91773 570-B6

FOREST GREEN DR
700 LCF 91011 535-D2
FOREST GROVE ST
11200 ELMN 91731 597-D7
11600 ELMN 91732 597-E7
FOREST HILL DR
4000 LCF 91011 535-A5
FOREST HILLS DR
600 COV 91724 599-E7
600 COV 91791 599-E7
600 WCOV 91791 599-E7
FOREST HILLS RD
7100 CanP 91307 529-F5
FOREST KNOLL DR
1400 LA 90069 592-J5
FOREST LAKE DR
300 BREA 92821 708-H6
FOREST LAWN DR
5300 LFlz 90027 563-G4
5600 LA 90068 563-G4
FOREST MEADOW PL
28500 Cstc 91384 4369-F7
28500 Cstc 91384 4459-E1
FOREST OAKS DR
1500 GLDR 91741 569-H5
FORESTON RD
500 PMDL 93550 4376-A7
600 PMDL 93550 4375-J7
FOREST PARK DR
2500 LA 90031 595-C7
2500 LA 90032 595-C7
FOREST PARK LN
15700 WHIT 90603 707-H5
FOREST RIDGE DR
5400 AGRH 91301 557-G5
FOREST SPRING CT
15300 CHLS 91709 680-F6
FOREST VIEW AV
700 LACo 91746 637-H6
FOREST VIEW CT
- SCTA 91354 4460-F5
FORESTVIEW DR
1300 BREA 92821 708-J4
FOREST VIEW RD
- PMDL 93550 4376-A5
FORESTWOOD CT
2100 FUL 92833 738-C3
FORGE PL
15700 GrnH 91344 501-G3
E FORHAN ST
100 NLB 90805 735-C7
W FORHAN ST
- NLB 90805 735-C7
W FORK PALMER MTWY
- CLAR 91711 571-E2
- LACo 91711 571-E2
W FORK PALMER CANYON RD
- LACo 91711 571-E1
E FORK SAN DIMAS CANYON RD
- LACo - (540-G7 See Page 509)
- LACo 91750 (540-G7 See Page 509)
- LACo 91750 570-G1
W FORK SAN DIMAS CANYON RD
- LACo - (540-F6 See Page 509)
- LACo - (541-A4 See Page 511)
- LACo 91750 (540-F6 See Page 509)
- LACo 91750 570-G1
FORMAN AV
4200 LA 91602 563-C5
4800 NHol 91601 563-C5
FORMAN LN
10100 LA 91602 563-C3
FORMAN ST
2400 UPL 91784 571-J3
2400 SBdC 91784 571-J3
FORMBY DR
15700 LMRD 90638 737-J3
N FORMOSA AV
100 LA 90036 633-D1
300 LA 90036 593-D7
700 LA 90046 593-D4
1000 WHWD 90046 593-D5
S FORMOSA AV
100 LA 90036 633-D1
FORMOSA CIR
- CanP 91303 530-B5
FORNEY LN
6400 VeCo 93063 499-C4
FORNEY ST
2300 LA 90031 594-G5
FORREST AV
1600 WCOV 91790 638-D2
FORREST ST
16900 CynC 91351 4462-B6
FORRESTAL DR
32100 RPV 90275 823-D5
FORRESTAL LN
- SLB 90740 826-G3
FORRESTER DR
2300 LMTA 90717 793-G5
FORSTER ST
2700 LA 90064 632-F5
FORRY CT
- LAN 93536 4104-F1
FORRY ST
2200 LAN 93536 4105-D1

FORST CT
- Cstc 91384 4459-G3
FORSTER WY
- StvR 91381 4550-B7
FORSYTH PL
500 CLAR 91711 571-E5
FORSYTHE ST
7600 Tuj 91042 503-H2
7800 Sunl 91040 503-F2
FORSYTHE WY
- StvR 91381 4550-A7
FORT BOWIE DR
21000 WAL 91789 639-H3
FORTIN ST
4800 BALD 91706 598-D3
FORT LEWIS DR
100 POM 91767 601-A1
1200 CLAR 91711 601-A1
FORT MOORE PL
500 LA 90012 634-F3
FORTNER WY
3200 POM 91767 601-A2
FORTROSE AV
15800 WHIT 90603 707-J4
FORTSON DR
8900 LACo 91775 596-H2
9100 TEML 91780 596-H1
FORT TEJON RD
200 SBdC 92372 (4472-A3 See Page 4471)
8300 Litl 93543 4377-J3
8700 Litl 93543 4378-A3
11600 Pear 93553 4378-G7
12800 Pear 93553 4468-J1
13000 Pear 93553 4469-A2
14500 Valy 93563 4469-E1
15000 Llan 93544 4469-E1
16500 Llan 93544 4379-H7
19500 Llan 93544 4470-E1
21500 Llan 93544 4471-A1
FORT TEJON RD Rt#-138
4900 PMDL 93552 4287-B5
FORTUNA CT
35300 Litl 93543 4377-F1
FORTUNA DR
25300 SCTA 91355 4640-F1
FORTUNA ST
1500 LA 90011 674-G5
FORTUNATO CT
- PMDL 93552 4196-J7
FORTUNE PL
- RowH 91748 679-C4
6700 HiPk 90042 595-F1
FORTUNE WY
900 HiPk 90042 595-F1
1000 HiPk 90042 565-F7
FOSS AV
2600 ARCD 91006 597-F1
FOSTER AV
1800 WCOV 91790 638-D2
3700 BALD 91706 598-A6
FOSTER CIR
3700 BALD 91706 598-A6
FOSTER DR
800 LA 90048 633-A3
FOSTER RD
9200 BLF 90706 736-A2
9200 DWNY 90242 736-A2
10500 NRWK 90650 736-E2
11200 OrCo 90720 796-H4
12600 NRWK 90650 737-A2
13400 SFSP 90670 737-C2
13800 LMRD 90638 737-D2
FOSTER BRIDGE BLVD
6400 BGDN 90201 675-J7
6500 BGDN 90201 705-J1
6600 BGDN 90201 706-A1
6900 DWNY 90240 706-A1
FOSTORIA CT
39300 PMDL 93551 4195-C5
FOSTORIA ST
5100 CDHY 90201 705-F3
5600 BGDN 90201 705-G3
7400 DWNY 90241 705-J3
7600 DWNY 90241 706-A4
W FOTINI PL
600 MONP 91754 636-A3
FOUNDATION AV
100 LHB 90631 708-E7
FOUNDERS DR
22400 CALB 91302 559-J6
FOUNDERS WK
- BPK 90621 737-J7
FOUNDERS HILL RD
7000 WHIT 90608 677-D7
FOUNTAIN AV
1300 LA 90038 593-G5
1300 Hlwd 90028 593-E5
3800 Echo 90026 594-B5
3800 LFlz 90027 594-A5
3900 LA 90029 594-A5
4800 LFlz 90027 593-H5
4800 LA 90029 593-H5
7000 WHWD 90038 593-E5
7000 WHWD 90046 593-A5
7100 LA 90046 593-C5
8300 WHWD 90069 593-A5
8400 WHWD 90069 592-J5
FOUNTAIN CT
13500 BALD 91706 598-A5
FOUNTAIN PL
28500 AGRH 91301 558-C5

FOUNTAIN ST
- POM 91767 601-A4
E FOUNTAIN ST
3600 LBCH 90804 795-J6
4000 LBCH 90804 796-A5
FOUNTAIN PARK DR
- LA 90094 702-C1
FOUNTAIN PARK LN
6000 WdHl 91367 560-A1
FOUNTAIN SPRINGS LN
500 GLDR 91741 569-H3
FOUNTAIN SPRINGS RD
21300 DBAR 91765 679-H6
FOUNTAINWOOD ST
28900 AGRH 91301 558-A3
29300 AGRH 91301 557-J3
FOURL RD
24100 SCTA 91321 4640-F1
FOUR OAK CT
5600 SIMI 93063 499-A1
FOUR OAKS ST
19200 SCTA 91351 4551-F2
FOUR PALMS LN
- LA 91342 482-C4
FOURTH ST
12200 NRWK 90650 706-J7
FOUR WINDS RD
10600 Litl 93543 4468-E3
FOWLER AV
1500 POM 91766 640-J4
1500 POM 91766 641-A4
FOWLER DR
100 MNRO 91016 567-F4
FOWLER RD
6600 SIMI 93063 499-C3
FOWLER ST
2600 Boyl 90033 635-C3
2900 LA 90063 635-C3
2900 City 90063 635-D3
FOWLING ST
100 PdlR 90293 702-A3
FOX
- Ago 91301 587-G4
FOX CT
5800 LACo 93536 4104-F6
FOX DR
1300 FUL 92835 738-F4
FOX PL
- GLDL 91206 564-F3
FOX ST
100 SFER 91340 502-A2
800 LA 91340 502-A2
14400 MsnH 91345 502-A2
14500 MsnH 91345 501-J2
N FOX ST
400 SFER 91340 482-C7
FOXBERG RD
13000 SLB 90740 796-G7
FOXBORO
7600 LA 91342 481-H1
FOXBORO CT
44600 LAN 93535 4016-C6
FOXBORO DR
300 WAL 91789 639-H6
11900 Brwd 90049 631-G3
FOXBORO LN
7600 LA 91304 529-E4
FOXBOROUGH PL
2600 FUL 92833 738-B6
FOXBROOK DR
600 GLDR 91740 569-G6
FOXBURY AV
300 POM 91767 600-J2
300 POM 91767 601-A2
FOXBURY WY
9000 PRV 90660 676-E7
FOXCROFT DR
11000 LACo 90604 707-F6
FOX CROFT LN
21100 WAL 91789 639-H7
FOXCROFT PL
12300 GrnH 91344 481-C6
FOXDALE AV
2300 LHB 90631 708-B5
4000 LACo 91722 598-F5
4400 IRW 91706 598-F4
N FOXDALE AV
300 WCOV 91790 598-F6
W FOXDALE CT
1500 UPL 91786 571-H7
FOXDALE DR
2200 LHB 90631 708-B5
FOXFIELD DR
31500 WLKV 91361 557-D7
FOXFORD RD
1600 LVRN 91750 570-F4
FOXGATE LN
1800 CHLS 91709 680-H3
FOX GLEN AV
4600 LVRN 91750 570-D7
FOX GLEN DR
1600 DBAR 91765 680-A4
FOXGLOVE CT
- PMDL 93551 4285-D4
- SCTA 91321 4551-F4
800 WAL 91789 639-H5
1200 GLDR 91741 569-B4
1200 LACo 91741 569-B4
3900 THO 91362 557-C1
S FOXGLOVE DR
2400 MONP 91755 636-C6
FOXGLOVE PL
- BqtC 91354 4460-E6

FOXGLOVE RD
3500 GLDL 91206 565-C2
FOXGLOVE ST
100 BREA 92821 709-F7
FOXHAVEN PL
600 DBAR 91765 640-E7
FOX HILL LN
9400 Chat 91311 499-H6
FOX HILLS AV
5100 BPK 90621 737-J5
8300 BPK 90621 738-A5
FOX HILLS DR
100 CULC 90230 672-H6
1800 WLA 90025 632-D3
2200 LA 90064 632-D3
FOX HILLS PL
5600 BPK 90621 737-J6
FOX HOLLOW LN
11400 Pcma 91331 502-F1
FOXHOLM DR
38800 LACo 93551 4195-F6
39100 PMDL 93551 4195-G6
FOX HUNT RD
16300 CHLS 91709 710-H2
FOX INDIAN DR
2800 LACo 90265 628-B4
FOXKIRK RD
700 GLDL 91206 564-H3
900 GLDL 91208 564-H3
FOXLAKE AV
4100 WCOV 91792 679-D2
FOXLANE DR
27700 SCTA 91351 4551-G1
28100 SCTA 91351 4461-G7
FOXLEY DR
12600 WHIT 90602 707-B2
13600 WHIT 90605 707-D3
FOXMOOR CT
31900 WLKV 91361 557-C6
FOXPARK DR
400 POM 91767 601-A2
500 LACo 91711 601-A2
FOXPOINT LN
5000 RHE 90274 793-B6
FOX RIDGE DR
1900 PAS 91107 536-E6
FOX RIDGE LN
- LACo 90274 793-E5
FOX RUN CIR
28000 Cstc 91384 4369-G7
FOXTAIL CT
- AZU 91702 568-J2
25000 StvR 91381 4640-E2
FOXTAIL DR
- PMDL 93551 4195-D6
100 SMCA 90402 631-C6
FOXTAIL ST
45800 LAN 93534 4015-G3
FOXTON AV
43600 LAN 93535 4105-J1
44000 LAN 93535 4015-J4
FOX VIEW DR
5800 MAL 90265 626-J6
FOXWELL AV
21100 CRSN 90745 764-C5
FOXWOOD AV
600 BREA 92821 708-H6
FOXWOOD CT
- SCTA 91354 4460-F5
FOXWOOD DR
2300 FUL 92833 738-C3
5600 VeCo 91377 557-J1
FOXWOOD PL
2100 FUL 92833 738-C3
FOXWOOD RD
600 LCF 91011 535-C5
FOXWORTH AV
400 LPUE 91744 638-C5
600 LACo 91744 638-D4
FRACAR AV
10700 LYN 90262 705-C6
FRACKELTON PL
1300 Eagl 90041 565-C5
FRAGANCIA AV
2700 HacH 91745 678-A5
FRAGRANS WY
6000 WdHl 91367 559-H7
6100 WdHl 91367 529-J7
FRAIJO AV
4600 IRW 91706 598-E4
S FRAILEY AV
12800 COMP 90221 735-D3
12800 RDom 90221 735-D3
FRAME AV
3400 HacH 91745 677-J6
FRAMINGTON AV
36900 Litl 93543 4288-E4
FRAMPTON AV
22800 LA 90501 794-A1
24000 Hrbr 90710 794-A3
FRAMPTON CT
11800 ART 90701 736-H7
FRAN PL
600 MTBL 90640 676-E1
FRANCE AV
9900 Tuj 91042 504-B4
FRANCES AV
1200 FUL 92831 738-H5
2700 LaCr 91214 504-F6
3200 GLDL 91214 504-F6
3500 LA 90066 672-B3
FRANCES CIR
- BPK 90621 737-H5

FRANCES LN
2100 RowH 91748 679-E6
FRANCES ST
2400 LaCr 91214 504-G7
FRANCES WY
11600 CHNO 91710 641-E4
11600 SBdC 91710 641-E4
FRANCESCA DR
2200 WCOV 91792 639-B6
18700 WAL 91789 639-B6
FRANCINA DR
16300 Enc 91436 561-E6
FRANCINE CT
600 LACo 91746 637-H5
FRANCINE LN
- Chat 91311 500-B3
FRANCIS AV
1300 POM 91766 641-D4
1300 SBdC 91710 641-D4
2700 LA 90005 634-A3
2700 LA 90057 634-A3
4100 CHNO 91710 641-G4
4200 LA 90005 633-F3
E FRANCIS AV
100 LHB 90631 708-F5
W FRANCIS AV
100 LHB 90631 708-E5
FRANCIS CT
16700 TOR 90504 733-E7
FRANCIS DR
16700 CHLS 91709 710-G3
FRANCIS PL
10700 LA 90034 672-E1
11400 LA 90066 672-D2
W FRANCIS ST
1000 ONT 91762 641-J4
N FRANCISCA AV
100 RBCH 90277 762-H3
S FRANCISCA AV
100 RBCH 90277 762-J5
FRANCISCA WY
5300 AGRH 91301 557-J5
FRANCISCAN CT
10400 MTCL 91763 641-E1
FRANCISCAN PL
- POM 91766 640-E6
FRANCISCO DR
- LMRD 90638 738-A2
FRANCISCO ST
- LA 90501 763-J4
- LA 90501 764-A4
100 CRSN 90745 764-B4
200 SGBL 91775 596-F3
200 SGBL 91776 596-F3
400 HMB 90254 732-G7
400 MANB 90266 732-G7
600 LA 90017 634-D4
600 LA 90502 764-A4
900 LA 90015 634-D5
1200 LACo 90502 764-A4
FRANCISCO WY
- BqtC 91354 4460-E3
FRANCISCO RANCH RD
- LACo 90265 628-H5
FRANCISQUITO AV
900 WCOV 91744 638-B1
1000 WCOV 91790 638-B1
3600 BALD 91706 597-J6
13300 BALD 91706 598-A7
13700 BALD 91706 638-B1
13900 BALD 91706 638-B1
14000 LACo 91746 638-B1
14900 LACo 91744 638-B1
15300 LPUE 91706 638-B1
E FRANCISQUITO AV
400 WCOV 91790 638-G3
600 LACo 91744 638-G3
1600 WCOV 91791 638-G3
17000 LACo 91791 638-G3
W FRANCISQUITO AV
1200 LACo 91744 638-C2
1200 WCOV 91790 638-C2
14300 LACo 91746 638-C2
14500 WCOV 91746 638-C2
FRANCIS SCOTT KEY
- PMDL 93550 4286-C5
FRANCITA AV
800 DUAR 91010 568-D5
FRANCOIS DR
3100 HNTB 92649 826-J6
FRANDALE AV
500 LACo 91744 638-F5
S FRANDALE AV
1400 WCOV 91790 638-F3
E FRANDSEN ST
8300 LACo 91776 596-G4
FRANK AV
19600 CRTS 90703 766-F3
FRANK CT
400 LA 90013 634-F4
600 LA 90014 634-E5
FRANK ST
1900 SMCA 90404 671-H1
FRANKE ST
900 CRSN 90746 764-E1
FRANKEL AV
100 MTBL 90640 676-C4
FRANKEL ST
2500 LKWD 90712 765-G5
FRANKFORT ST
18500 Nor 91324 530-G2
FRANKFURT AV
300 LACo 91792 679-C2

FRANKIRST AV
9500 LA 91343 501-E6
FRANKLIN AV
100 ELSG 90245 732-G1
1200 LAN 93535 4106-C1
3700 LFlz 90027 594-A3
4100 BURB 91505 563-D5
4800 LFlz 90027 593-G3
5500 Hlwd 90028 593-E4
5500 LA 90068 593-G3
7100 LA 90046 593-C4
8400 LA 90069 592-J4
8400 LA 90069 593-A4
10700 CULC 90230 672-G3
E FRANKLIN AV
100 POM 91766 640-J4
100 POM 91766 641-B4
N FRANKLIN AV
100 SGBL 91775 596-D3
100 SGBL 91776 596-D3
W FRANKLIN AV
100 ELSG 90245 732-E1
100 POM 91766 640-J4
FRANKLIN CT
100 GLDL 91205 564-F5
1300 SMCA 90404 631-H6
5100 CHNO 91710 641-G6
FRANKLIN LN
25800 StvR 91381 4550-B7
25800 StvR 91381 4640-B1
FRANKLIN PKWY
27900 Valc 91355 4459-G7
28100 Valc 91355 4549-F2
FRANKLIN PL
400 LBCH 90802 795-F7
500 MNRO 91016 567-F2
6700 Hlwd 90028 593-E4
FRANKLIN ST
700 Brwd 90049 631-G5
700 SMCA 90403 631-G5
1200 SMCA 90404 631-H6
2700 LACo 91214 534-G1
2900 LaCr 91214 504-F7
3800 GLDL 91214 504-D5
9200 Chat 91311 499-F7
11100 LYN 90262 704-J6
11100 LYN 90262 705-A7
13400 WHIT 90602 677-D7
FRANKLIN WY
1600 LA 90069 592-J4
FRANKLIN CANYON DR
1700 LA 90210 592-E4
1700 LACo 90210 592-E3
2300 LA 90210 562-F7
FRANKLIN HILLS DR
2500 FUL 92833 738-B6
FRANK MODUGNO DR
200 SFER 91340 482-A6
12200 LA 91342 481-J6
12200 LA 91342 482-A6
FRANKMONT ST
10500 ELMN 91731 597-C6
11300 ELMN 91732 597-E6
FRANKS WY
- Saug 91350 4461-E6
FRANK STILES ST
1900 SELM 91733 637-D4
FRANKTON AV
14400 HacH 91745 677-H1
FRANLIE DR
10600 Sunl 91040 503-E3
FRANRIVERS AV
5500 WdHl 91367 559-D2
6400 CanP 91307 529-D7
FRANTZ AV
2000 LHB 90631 708-H5
FRANWOOD DR
20700 SCTA 91350 4461-C4
FRASCATI ST
11200 LACo 91390 4373-D7
FRASER AL
- PAS 91105 565-H5
FRASER AV
100 SMCA 90405 671-F4
300 ELA 90022 635-G7
700 ELA 90022 675-G1
12500 GrnH 91344 481-B5
FRASER PL
17400 GrnH 91344 481-B5
FRATUS DR
4800 TEML 91780 596-J4
FRAZIER ST
600 BALD 91706 637-H1
3200 BALD 91706 597-J7
3500 BALD 91706 598-A6
FRECKLES RD
2700 LKWD 90712 765-H5
6000 LKWD 90713 766-D5
FRED DR
6000 CYP 90630 767-E7
FREDA AV
100 POM 91767 600-J5
200 POM 91767 601-A5
N FREDERIC ST
100 BURB 91505 563-E1
1000 BURB 91505 533-D7
1800 BURB 91504 533-D4
S FREDERIC ST
100 BURB 91505 563-E3
FREDERICK AV
3400 GLDL 91214 504-E6

FREDERICK ST
200 Ven 90291 671-J4
2600 LA 90065 594-H4
3100 SMCA 90405 671-H4
4000 GLDL 91214 534-E1
4500 GLDL 91214 504-E7
FREDERICKS LN
1400 UPL 91786 601-H4
FREDKIN DR
1100 COV 91722 598-H4
17000 LACo 91722 598-H4
FREDONIA DR
3600 LA 90068 563-A6
FREDS LN
- SBdC 92372 (4562-C1 See Page 4471)
FREDSON ST
11300 SFSP 90670 706-H3
FREEBORN ST
2300 BRAD 91010 568-D4
2500 DUAR 91010 568-E4
FREEDEN ST
200 CRSN 90746 764-D2
FREEDOM DR
4100 CALB 91302 559-J5
FREEDOM WY
2300 LA 90065 594-G1
FREELAND ST
400 Bxby 90807 765-E5
FREEMAN AV
300 LBCH 90814 795-H7
700 LBCH 90804 795-H6
2000 SIGH 90755 795-H6
5500 LaCr 91214 504-H6
9000 SFSP 90670 707-A4
11400 HAW 90250 703-D7
11900 HAW 90250 733-D1
14500 LNDL 90260 733-D5
N FREEMAN AV
1300 LBCH 90804 795-H5
1800 SIGH 90755 795-H5
S FREEMAN AV
10000 ING 90304 703-D5
10300 Lenx 90304 703-D5
11100 HAW 90304 703-D5
FREEMAN DR
2400 CLAR 91711 571-D6
FREEMAN LN
- BPK 90621 737-H5
- BREA 92821 708-J5
FREEMONT CT
- LMRD 90638 738-B2
FREEPORT CT
1000 THO 91361 557-B5
FREEPORT RD
27000 RPV 90275 793-A6
FREEPORT TER
1600 LA 90732 823-D6
FREER ST
10200 TEML 91780 597-C4
FREER WY
44000 LAN 93536 4104-E1
44100 LAN 93536 4014-E7
FREESE LN
2200 PAS 91107 566-D4
FREESIA AV
- SIMI 93063 499-A2
FREESTONE AV
8000 SFSP 90606 707-A1
8000 SFSP 90670 707-A1
FREESTONE LN
7500 Litl 93543 4377-G1
FREETOWN LN
27400 AGRH 91301 558-E7
27400 AGRH 91301 588-E1
FRWY Rt#-22
- LBCH - 796-F7
- SLB - 796-H6
FREEWAY DR
13400 SFSP 90670 737-C4
14200 LMRD 90638 737-D5
FREEWAY CENTER CT
41300 PMDL 93551 4105-G7
FREIBURG ST
13800 WHIT 90602 677-E7
FREMANTLE LN
5300 LACo 91302 559-A3
FREMONT AV
200 SPAS 91030 595-H1
8900 MTCL 91763 601-G7
10700 MTCL 91763 641-G3
11100 MTCL 91710 641-G3
11100 SBdC 91710 641-G3
N FREMONT AV
- ALH 91801 595-H4
100 LA 90012 634-F3
S FREMONT AV
- ALH 91801 595-H6
100 MONP 91754 635-J2
300 ALH 91803 595-H6
500 LA 90071 634-E4
1700 ALH 91803 635-H1
FREMONT CT
27800 SCTA 91355 4550-C1
FREMONT DR
400 PAS 91103 565-G4
FREMONT LN
400 SPAS 91030 595-H1
FREMONT PL
- LA 90005 633-F3
- LA 90010 633-F3
- LA 90019 633-F3

W FREMONT PL
- LA 90005 633-F3
- LA 90010 633-F3
100 LA 90019 633-F3
E FREMONT SQ
100 MTBL 90640 676-E2
S FREMONT ST
1200 ANA 92804 767-F7
W FREMONT ST
900 POM 91766 640-H4
FREMONT WY
6100 BPK 90620 767-E3
FREMONTIA RD
300 SBdC 92372 (4472-A6 See Page 4471)
2100 SBdC 92371 (4472-E6 See Page 4471)
FREMONT VILLAS ST
4400 HiPk 90042 595-D4
FRENCH AV
100 LA 90065 595-A6
FRENCH CT
3900 Ago 91301 588-B1
FRENCH LN
300 POM 91767 600-H2
FRESCA DR
5900 LPMA 90623 767-D1
FRESE LN
8000 LPMA 90623 767-E4
FRESHMAN DR
4000 LACo 90230 672-H4
4900 CULC 90230 672-H4
FRESH MEADOW DR
700 LCF 91011 535-D2
FRESH MEADOW LN
13800 SLB 90740 826-G1
FRESHWATER DR
29000 AGRH 91301 558-A4
FRESHWIND CIR
3900 WLKV 91361 557-C6
N FRESNO ST
400 LA 90063 635-C5
S FRESNO ST
100 LA 90063 635-C6
600 LA 90023 635-B6
FREY AV
2300 Ven 90291 671-J6
FRIAR CIR
4300 LVRN 91750 570-G7
FRIAR DR
1700 MONP 91755 636-E5
FRIAR LN
900 POM 91766 640-H3
FRIAR PL
200 FUL 92835 738-G3
FRIAR ST
10600 NHol 91606 533-A6
11500 NHol 91606 532-H6
13300 VanN 91401 532-A7
14500 VanN 91411 532-A7
14600 VanN 91411 531-G7
18200 Res 91335 530-G7
19700 WdHl 91367 530-E7
22400 WdHl 91367 529-D7
FRIARS LN
- WLKV 91361 587-D1
FRIARSTONE CT
28600 RPV 90275 823-J2
FRIEDA CT
3000 WCOV 91792 639-B7
43700 LAN 93535 4106-B1
FRIEDA DR
4700 LA 90065 595-A2
FRIENDLY AV
38500 PMDL 93550 4196-B7
FRIENDLY LN
4100 WCOV 91792 679-C3
10800 ELMN 91731 597-D4
FRIENDLY VALLEY PKWY
19100 SCTA 91321 4551-F5
FRIENDLY WOODS LN
9400 WHIT 90605 707-H3
FRIENDS AV
5800 WHIT 90601 677-D6
7000 WHIT 90602 677-D7
7700 WHIT 90602 707-D1
FRIENDS ST
15200 PacP 90272 631-A6
FRIENDSHIP AV
8700 PRV 90660 676-G1
FRIENDSHIP PARK DR
900 LA 90732 823-H6
FRIENDSWOOD AV
3100 ELMN 91733 637-B1
FRIES AV
21300 CRSN 90745 764-E6
22400 CRSN 90745 794-E1
N FRIES AV
200 Wilm 90744 794-E5
S FRIES AV
100 Wilm 90744 794-E7
1000 Wilm 90744 824-E1
FRIGATE AV
400 Wilm 90744 794-C5
22700 CRSN 90745 794-C1
FRIJO AV
700 WCOV 91790 598-E6
3900 LACo 91722 598-E5
FRISCA DR
22900 SCTA 91354 4460-H7
FRITZ LN
13500 LA 91342 482-C1

STREET
Block City ZIP Pg-Grid

FRITZ WY
- LACo 91390 4461-A3
FRONDOSA DR
6200 MAL 90265 627-A7
FRONT ST
- ARCD 91006 567-D5
600 ALH 91801 596-A6
1100 ALH 91803 596-A6
1200 COV 91722 598-H4
1400 ALH 91803 595-G7
3200 LA 90032 595-G7
11800 NRWK 90650 736-H2
12300 NRWK 90650 737-A3
E FRONT ST
100 COV 91723 599-B4
N FRONT ST
100 BURB 91502 533-G7
600 SPed 90731 824-C3
S FRONT ST
100 BURB 91502 533-H7
100 BURB 91502 563-H1
W FRONT ST
400 COV 91723 599-A4
500 COV 91722 599-A4
700 COV 91722 598-J4
FRONTAGE RD
3400 LACo 91107 566-G4
3400 PAS 91107 566-G4
FRONTAGE RD E
9500 SGAT 90280 705-F5
FRONTAGE RD W
9500 SGAT 90280 705-F5
FRONTENAC AV
400 LA 90065 595-A4
N FRONTENAC CT
- LBCH 90802 825-E1
100 LBCH 90802 795-E7
700 LBCH 90813 795-E6
FRONTERA DR
500 PacP 90272 631-B6
FRONTIER AV
38400 PMDL 93550 4196-F7
FRONTIER PL
11300 Chat 91311 499-J2
FRONTIER RD
- POM 91766 640-G5
FRONTIER CIRCUS ST
39300 LACo 93591 4199-G5
FROST CIR
6800 BPK 90620 767-F2
FROST LN
25400 StvR 91381 4550-B7
FROSTBURG CIR
1900 CLAR 91711 571-E7
FRUIT ST
3600 LVRN 91750 600-H1
4000 LVRN 91750 570-H7
FRUITDALE ST
2700 LA 90039 594-E3
FRUITLAND AV
2400 VER 90058 674-H4
2600 HNTP 90255 674-H4
2700 VER 90058 675-A4
3400 MYWD 90270 675-C4
FRUITLAND DR
10800 LA 91604 563-A6
FRUITRIDGE CT
38800 PMDL 93551 4195-D6
FRUIT TREE RD
- RPV 90275 823-A4
FRUITVALE AV
1600 SELM 91733 637-D5
1800 LACo 91733 637-D5
FRY ST
6000 BGDN 90201 705-H1
6800 BGDN 90201 706-A1
FRYMAN PL
3300 LA 91604 562-G7
FRYMAN RD
3000 LA 91604 592-H1
3100 LA 91604 562-G7
FUCHSIA AV
900 GLDR 91740 569-D7
N FUCHSIA AV
400 ONT 91762 601-J5
S FUCHSIA AV
2200 ONT 91762 641-J5
FUCHSIA CT
22100 WdHl 91367 559-H7
FUCHSIA ST
1200 UPL 91784 571-J4
FUEGO AV
200 POM 91767 600-H2
FUEGO ST
200 NLB 90805 735-B6
FUERO DR
20200 WAL 91789 679-F1
E FUERO DR
20600 WAL 91789 679-F1
FUERTE DR
800 WAL 91789 639-F6
FUJI CT
- SCTA 91387 4462-G7
FUJITA ST
2800 TOR 90505 793-E1
FULCHER AV
5500 NHol 91601 562-J1
5900 NHol 91601 532-J7
6000 NHol 91606 532-J6
FULHAM CT
3100 PMDL 93551 4195-B3
FULLBRIGHT AV
6900 Win 91306 530-D1
8900 Chat 91311 500-D2
8900 Chat 91311 530-D1
FULLBRIGHT PL
20300 Chat 91311 500-D3
FULLBROOK CT
3300 GLDL 91206 565-C1
N FULLER AV
100 LA 90036 633-C1
300 LA 90036 593-C7
700 LA 90046 593-C4
1000 WHWD 90046 593-C5
S FULLER AV
100 LA 90036 633-C1
FULLER CIR
300 LA 90036 633-C2
FULLER DR
- CLAR 91711 571-F3
FULLERCREEK RD
2300 CHLS 91709 680-G5
FULLERFARM ST
17700 Nor 91325 501-A4
FULLERTON AV
5500 BPK 90621 737-H7
6400 BPK 90621 767-H1
FULLERTON RD
700 INDS 91748 679-A3
1300 RowH 91748 679-A5
1600 LHH 90631 708-G1
1700 RowH 91748 678-J6
2500 RowH 91748 708-H1
FULLMOON DR
3600 GLDL 91206 535-C7
FULLMOON ST
37300 PMDL 93550 4286-E3
FULMAR AV
23800 LA 90501 793-J3
23800 TOR 90501 793-J3
23900 LA 90717 793-J3
FULTON AV
- LACo 91107 566-H4
700 MONP 91755 636-B4
4100 Shrm 91423 562-D3
4200 LA 91604 562-D5
5200 VanN 91401 562-D3
5900 VanN 91401 532-D7
6700 VanN 91405 532-D5
6700 NHol 91605 532-D3
FULTON CT
13200 VanN 91401 562-D2
FULTON RD
1800 POM 91768 600-H5
2000 LVRN 91750 600-H3
2000 POM 91767 600-H3
FULTON WELLS AV
10600 SFSP 90670 706-H6
FUNCHAL RD
600 BelA 90077 591-J7
FUNSTON AV
13400 NRWK 90650 736-H3
22300 HGDN 90716 766-H7
FURLONG LN
- BRAD 91010 568-B3
FURLONG PL
4300 VER 90058 674-H4
FURMAN DR
400 CLAR 91711 571-C6
FURMAN PL
1100 GLDL 91206 564-H2
FURMAN RD
7700 LPMA 90623 767-D3
FURNESS AV
100 HiPk 90042 595-A3
100 LA 90065 595-B3
FURNIVALL AV
26800 SCTA 91351 4551-D2
FUSANO AV
13400 LA 91342 481-H2
FUSCHIA AV
12200 CHNO 91710 641-J5
FUSHIA CT
- BqtC 91354 4460-E6
FUTURE PL
3000 LA 90065 594-H4
FUTURE ST
2700 LA 90065 594-H3
FYLER PL
2700 LA 90065 564-H7

G

G
- PRM 90723 735-F6
G ST
- BELL 90201 675-F5
- LACo 90220 765-A3
- PdlR 90293 702-D7
- SPed 90731 794-B7
- Wilm 90744 794-B7
2100 LVRN 91750 600-G3
E G ST
100 Wilm 90744 794-F6
W G ST
100 Wilm 90744 794-C6
900 ONT 91762 601-J7
GABBETT DR
12600 LMRD 90638 737-F1
GABLE CIR
18900 CRTS 90703 767-B2
GABLE CT
24400 DBAR 91765 640-E6
44200 LAN 93536 4015-C7
GABLE DR
4400 Enc 91316 561-A4
GABLE LN
100 LHB 90631 738-D3
44300 LAN 93536 4015-C7
GABLE RANCH LN
- BqtC 91354 4460-D2
GABLE VIEW ST
1700 PMDL 93550 4286-D3
GABRIAL PL
- LACo 91390 4461-A3
GABRIEL DR
2300 POM 91766 640-J6
GABRIEL ST
40600 PMDL 93551 4194-H2
GABRIEL GARCIA MARQUEZ ST
100 Boyl 90033 634-J4
GABRIELINO CT
- Alta 91001 535-G3
GABRIELLA ST
3000 WCOV 91792 639-B7
GACEL CT
20900 DBAR 91789 679-H3
GADSDEN AV
43200 LAN 93534 4105-G1
44000 LAN 93534 4015-G4
GADSHILL LN
4100 AGRH 91301 558-F7
GAFF CT
21500 SCTA 91350 4461-B6
GAFFEY PL
400 SPed 90731 824-B4
N GAFFEY PL
500 SPed 90731 824-B3
N GAFFEY ST
400 SPed 90731 824-B2
2200 SPed 90731 794-A7
2800 LA 90732 794-A7
N GAFFEY ST Rt#-110
100 SPed 90731 824-B4
S GAFFEY ST
900 SPed 90731 824-B6
2600 SPed 90731 854-B2
S GAFFEY ST Rt#-110
100 SPed 90731 824-B5
S GAFFNEY AV
100 SDMS 91773 600-D2
GAFFORD ST
5000 CMRC 90040 675-G3
GAGE AV
2000 HNTP 90255 674-H6
2600 ELMN 91733 637-C2
2800 HNTP 90255 675-B6
3000 ELMN 91731 637-C2
3400 BELL 90201 675-E7
5500 BGDN 90201 675-E7
E GAGE AV
- HNTP 90255 674-F6
100 LA 90003 674-D6
100 LA 90001 674-D6
1100 Flor 90001 674-F6
1900 HNTP 90001 674-F6
5500 BGDN 90201 675-J7
6300 CMRC 90040 675-J7
6500 BGDN 90201 676-A7
6500 CMRC 90040 676-A7
7000 BGDN 90040 676-A7
N GAGE AV
100 City 90063 635-D4
S GAGE AV
100 City 90063 635-D6
100 LACo 90023 635-D7
900 LACo 90023 675-D1
W GAGE AV
100 LA 90003 674-B6
100 LA 90044 674-B6
1300 LA 90044 673-J6
1400 LA 90047 673-J6
GAGE RD
1500 MTBL 90640 676-C7
GAGELY DR
14200 LMRD 90638 737-E1
GAGER ST
11700 LA 91342 482-G7
11900 LA 91342 502-G1
12200 Pcma 91331 502-F1
GAIL CT
2400 WCOV 91792 639-B7
GAIL MTWY
- CLAR 91711 571-C4
GAIL ST
2300 LA 90031 594-G5
GAILLARD ST
100 GLDR 91740 599-D1
400 SDMS 91773 600-C1
700 LACo 91750 600-D1
900 AZU 91702 599-B1
18000 LACo 91702 599-A1
GAILXY AV
28700 SCTA 91387 4552-B1
GAIN ST
11700 LA 91342 482-G7
11800 LA 91342 502-E2
12400 Pcma 91331 502-E2
GAINES WY
- Saug 91350 4461-G6
6200 BPK 90620 767-E3
GAINFORD ST
7300 DWNY 90240 706-A2
23000 WdHl 91364 559-G3
GAINSBOROUGH AV
4400 LFlz 90027 594-A2
GAINSBOROUGH DR
800 LACo 91107 566-F7
2700 SMRO 91108 566-E7
39300 PMDL 93551 4195-G5
GAINSBOROUGH RD
1100 SDMS 91773 599-G4
GAINSWAY CT
3300 BqtC 91354 4460-F6
GAITANO RD
100 PMDL 93550 4195-J3
GALA LN
- SBdC 91762 641-G2
GALA ST
2300 LACo 90601 637-E6
GALAHAD DR
6000 MAL 90265 667-F1
GALANTE WY
25800 SCTA 91355 4550-F6
GALANTO AV
100 AZU 91702 569-C7
100 AZU 91702 599-C1
5600 LACo 91702 599-C1
5900 LACo 91702 569-C7
N GALANTO AV
6200 LACo 91702 569-C7
7000 GLDR 91741 569-C5
GALATEA ST
900 AZU 91702 569-B7
18000 LACo 91702 569-A7
18400 LACo 91702 599-B1
19000 GLDR 91740 569-C7
GALATINA ST
18000 RowH 91748 678-J6
18600 RowH 91748 679-A6
GALAVAN ST
600 CRSN 90745 794-B1
GALAX ST
10900 SELM 91733 637-C4
GALAXY CIR
8300 BPK 90620 767-J4
GALAXY PL
15700 GAR 90249 733-G6
GALAXY WY
10000 CenC 90067 632-E4
GALAXY HEIGHTS DR
700 LCF 91011 535-C2
GALBRETH CT
- Cstc 91384 4459-G3
GALBRETH RD
1800 PAS 91104 566-C1
2000 LACo 91104 566-C1
GALE AV
1900 LBCH 90810 795-B2
3400 LBCH 90810 765-B7
6400 NLB 90805 765-C1
6400 NLB 90805 735-B7
11400 HAW 90250 703-C7
11800 HAW 90250 733-C1
14400 HacH 91745 637-J7
14600 HacH 91745 677-J1
14600 HacH 91745 678-A1
15200 INDS 91745 678-D2
17200 INDS 91748 678-G3
18000 INDS 91748 679-A4
18500 RowH 91748 679-B4
GALE DR
- StvR 91381 4550-D7
N GALE DR
100 BHLS 90211 633-A2
S GALE DR
100 BHLS 90211 633-A2
GALE PL
- SMCA 90402 631-D5
E GALEANO ST
4300 LBCH 90815 796-A4
GALECREST AV
700 LACo 91744 638-H5
GALEMONT AV
800 HacH 91745 678-C1
S GALEMONT AV
1800 HacH 91745 678-B3
GALEN DR
600 LHB 90631 708-B5
GALEN ST
1000 DUAR 91010 567-J7
1000 IRW 91010 567-J7
1100 DUAR 91010 568-A7
GALENA AV
9700 MTCL 91763 601-E6
GALENA ST
3400 LA 90032 595-C6
GALENDO PL
21900 WdHl 91364 560-A5
GALENDO ST
4600 WdHl 91364 560-A5
GALER PL
500 GLDL 91206 564-G3
GALERITA DR
1900 RPV 90275 823-H2
GALESBURG ST
17000 GrnH 91344 481-C7
GALESMOORE CT
1000 THO 91361 557-A5
GALETON RD
27800 SCTA 91387 4551-J3
GALEVIEW DR
19500 RowH 91748 679-D6
GALEWOOD ST
12900 LA 91604 562-D5
13200 Shrm 91423 562-C5
GALICIA
- LVRN 91750 570-H3
GALICIA DR
14300 LMRD 90638 737-G3
GALILEE ST
22400 CALB 91302 559-J7
GALION AV
43800 LAN 93536 4105-C1
44000 LAN 93536 4015-C7
GALLANT ST
5900 BGDN 90201 705-G2
GALLARDO ST
- Boyl 90033 634-J3
GALLARNO DR
18500 LACo 91722 599-B2
GALLATIN RD
7900 DWNY 90240 706-C2
8700 PRV 90660 676-G1
8900 LACo 90660 676-G1
GALLAUDET PL
14500 PacP 90272 631-B5
GALLEANO ST
18600 LACo 91744 679-B2
18700 LACo 91792 679-B2
GALLEON ST
- LA 90292 701-H1
100 LA 90292 671-J7
GALLEON WY
400 SLB 90740 826-E3
GALLERIA LN
- Shrm 91403 561-H4
GALLERIA GATEWAY
- Shrm 91403 561-H4
GALLI ST
3200 HAW 90250 733-F3
N GALLIARD DR
300 NLB 90805 735-C6
GALLILEE WY
- SIMI 93063 499-B1
GALLINETA ST
17800 RowH 91748 678-J6
18300 RowH 91748 679-A6
GALLIO AV
2400 RowH 91748 679-A6
GALLIO DR
2700 FUL 92833 738-B4
GALLOPING CT
- Cstc 91384 4459-D5
GALLOPING WY
2000 Actn 93510 4375-F6
GALLOPING COLT CIR
600 WAL 91789 639-C7
GALLOWAY GRN
8200 BPK 90621 737-G5
GALLOWAY ST
800 PacP 90272 631-B4
GALLUP ST
5900 LKWD 90713 766-D5
GALSTER WY
- WCOV 91791 639-A4
GALT RD
8300 DWNY 90241 706-A6
GALTON RD
19000 LACo 91390 4461-G3
GALVA AV
22800 TOR 90505 793-C1
GALVESTON ST
1400 Echo 90026 594-E7
GALVEZ CT
26100 SCTA 91355 4550-G3
GALVEZ ST
21900 WdHl 91364 560-A3
GALVIN CT
2100 DBAR 91765 680-A5
GALVIN ST
10700 CULC 90230 672-H4
GALWAY AV
19000 CRSN 90746 764-E3
GALWAY PL
24000 SCTA 91355 4550-F5
GAMBIER DR
2100 POM 91766 640-J5
GAMBIER ST
4700 LA 90032 595-E7
GAMBLE AV
1400 Wilm 90744 794-G4
GAMBLE HOUSE CT
24000 SCTA 91355 4550-F4
GAMBREL GATE
- LVRN 91750 570-J5
GAMEBIRD CT
29300 AGRH 91301 558-A5
GANADO DR
30300 RPV 90275 823-E5
GANAHL ST
2500 Boyl 90033 635-C3
3000 LA 90063 635-C4
3200 City 90063 635-C4
GANDARA AV
13300 LMRD 90638 737-F2
GANDESA RD
14100 LMRD 90638 737-F3
GANELON DR
3500 CALB 91302 559-H7
GANESHA AV
2300 Alta 91001 536-B6
GANESHA PL
1500 POM 91768 600-H6
GANGEL AV
3600 PRV 90660 676-J1
GANGI LN
2000 GLDL 91202 564-D1
GANNET ST
13900 SFSP 90670 737-D4
14200 LMRD 90638 737-E4
GANTER RD
1900 LHH 90631 708-E3
GANYMEDE DR
700 LA 90065 594-J3
GAONA ST
21400 WdHl 91364 560-B4
GARA DR
15000 LMRD 90638 737-G3
GARBER ST
11300 LA 91342 482-H7
11700 LA 91342 502-G1
12300 Pcma 91331 502-F2
W GARCELON AV
100 MONP 91754 636-B2
GARCIA CT
11400 NRWK 90650 736-F4
GARCIA LN
- INDS 91789 639-J6
GARCIA RD
- LACo 90265 626-D1
GARCIA WK
3000 Echo 90026 594-C6
GARD AV
10000 SFSP 90670 706-G4
11700 NRWK 90650 706-G7
12200 NRWK 90650 736-G1
17100 ART 90701 736-G7
17900 ART 90701 766-G1
GARDA AV
400 LACo 91744 638-G7
GARDEN AV
- Cstc 91384 4459-J4
- POM 91767 601-A3
3100 LA 90039 594-D1
4100 LA 90039 564-C7
GARDEN DR
200 VeCo 91361 586-E1
S GARDEN DR
- SMRO 91108 566-C7
GARDEN LN
- HAW 90250 733-F4
500 PAS 91105 565-G7
1000 BHLS 90210 592-E6
GARDEN ST
- SIMI 93063 499-B1
1300 GLDL 91201 564-A3
1300 LFlz 90027 564-A3
1300 LFlz 90027 563-J3
1400 GLDL 91201 563-J3
GARDENA AV
1300 GLDL 91204 564-E7
1500 GLDL 91204 564-E1
2400 SIGH 90755 795-G2
E GARDENA BLVD
100 CRSN 90746 734-E6
100 CRSN 90248 734-D6
W GARDENA BLVD
100 CRSN 90248 734-C6
500 LA 90248 734-C6
500 LA 90247 734-C6
700 CRSN 90746 734-C6
900 GAR 90247 734-C6
1400 GAR 90247 733-J6
GARDENA FRWY Rt#-91
- COMP 734-E7
- COMP 735-B7
- CRSN 734-E7
- LA 734-E7
- NLB 735-B7
- RDom 735-B7
GARDENDALE LN
5400 PMDL 93551 4194-F1
GARDENDALE ST
5400 SGAT 90280 705-F7
5900 SGAT 90280 735-G1
7100 DWNY 90242 705-F7
7400 DWNY 90242 735-G1
8000 PRM 90723 735-G1
8900 DWNY 90242 736-A2
9000 BLF 90706 736-A2
GARDENERS RD
- SLB 90740 826-G4
S GARDEN GLEN ST
100 WCOV 91790 598-H7
200 WCOV 91790 638-H1
GARDEN GROVE AV
4900 Tarz 91356 561-A2
6800 Res 91335 530-J2
8000 Res 91335 531-A3
8200 Nor 91325 530-J2
8900 Nor 91325 500-J5
10300 Nor 91326 500-J1
GARDENHILL DR
14400 LMRD 90638 737-G1
GARDEN HOMES AV
4100 LA 90032 595-F5
4400 SPAS 91030 595-F5
GARDENIA AV
700 LBCH 90813 795-G7
1800 LBCH 90806 795-G2
2200 ONT 91762 641-J5
3400 Bxby 90807 765-G7
3400 Bxby 90807 765-G3
5800 NLB 90805 765-G2
6500 NLB 90805 735-G7
N GARDENIA AV
900 ONT 91762 601-J5
GARDENIA CT
- BqtC 91354 4460-E6
1600 LAN 93535 4016-C6
N GARDENIA CT
600 ONT 91762 601-J5
GARDENIA DR
- AZU 91702 569-A4
7700 BPK 90620 767-J3
GARDENIA LN
- YBLN 92886 709-J7
- YBLN 92886 710-A7
1300 LVRN 91750 570-F7
GARDENIA PL
12300 CHNO 91710 641-J5
GARDENIALANE DR
15400 SCTA 91387 4552-E1
15400 SCTA 91387 4462-E7
GARDENLAND AV
13700 BLF 90706 736-D3
GARDEN LAND RD
13100 Brwd 90049 591-C2
GARDEN OAKS CT
29000 AGRH 91301 558-A3
GARDEN OF MUMS PL
29600 SCTA 91387 4462-F6
GARDEN PARK CT
- SCTA 91354 4460-F6
GARDENSIDE LN
3400 LA 90039 594-D1
GARDENSTONE CT
2000 THO 91361 557-A5
GARDENSTONE LN
24500 CanP 91307 529-C5
GARDEN TERRACE LN
3400 HacH 91745 678-A6
GARDEN VIEW AV
8100 SGAT 90280 705-A3
GARDEN VIEW CT
14300 CHLS 91709 680-J4
GARDEN VIEW LN
1300 WCOV 91706 638-C1
1300 BALD 91706 638-C1
GARDEN VILLAGE CT
500 PAS 91101 565-J3
GARDI ST
2000 BRAD 91010 568-C4
2500 DUAR 91010 568-D4
GARDNER AV
12200 SFSP 90670 706-J5
12500 SFSP 90670 707-A5
GARDNER DR
800 MTBL 90640 636-C7
GARDNER LN
2400 GLDL 91206 565-A4
GARDNER PL
2300 GLDL 91206 565-A4
GARDNER ST
100 CRSN 90745 764-C5
800 NLB 90805 735-B7
N GARDNER ST
100 LA 90036 633-C1
300 LA 90036 593-C7
700 LA 90046 593-C5
900 WHWD 90046 593-C5
S GARDNER ST
100 LA 90036 633-C1
N GARELOCH AV
5200 LACo 91702 598-H1
GARETAL ST
11100 SFSP 90670 706-F5
GAREY AV
- POM 91766 640-J6
- POM 91766 641-A7
- SBdC 91710 641-A7
N GAREY AV
- POM 91766 640-J1
100 POM 91768 640-J1
100 POM 91767 640-J1
700 POM 91767 600-J3
700 POM 91768 600-J6
3500 POM 91711 600-J1
3600 LACo 91711 600-J1
3600 CLAR 91711 600-J1
4100 CLAR 91711 570-J7
S GAREY AV
100 POM 91766 640-J3
N GAREY ST
300 LA 90012 634-H4
S GAREY ST
100 LA 90012 634-H4
GARFIAS DR
1900 LACo 91104 566-D1
GARFIELD AV
100 POM 91767 600-J7
200 PAS 91101 565-J3
200 PAS 91104 565-J3
300 POM 91767 601-A7
400 SPAS 91030 595-J1
900 Ven 90291 672-A6
1200 SMRO 91108 595-J1
1300 SPAS 91030 596-A3
1300 SMRO 91108 596-A3
1500 CMRC 90022 676-A6
1700 ALH 91801 596-A3
1900 CMRC 90040 676-A6
3500 CMRC 90040 675-J7
6400 BGDN 90201 675-J7
6400 BGDN 90201 705-G3
8600 SGAT 90280 705-G4
10700 CULC 90230 672-G3
11200 DWNY 90242 705-F7
11500 SGAT 90280 735-G2
13700 PRM 90723 735-G2
E GARFIELD AV
100 GLDL 91205 564-F6
N GARFIELD AV
- ALH 91801 596-A3
- PAS 91101 565-J4
100 ALH 91801 636-C2
100 MONP 91755 636-C2
100 MTBL 90640 676-B1
100 MONP 91754 636-C2
400 MTBL 90640 636-B7
700 PAS 91104 565-J1
1600 PAS 91104 535-J7
2000 Alta 91001 535-J6
S GARFIELD AV
- ALH 91801 596-B7
100 MONP 91755 636-B4
100 MONP 91754 636-B4
900 MTBL 90640 676-B2
900 ELA 90022 676-B2
1800 ALH 91801 636-B4
W GARFIELD AV
100 GLDL 91204 564-D6
GARFIELD CIR
8800 BPK 90620 767-H5
GARFIELD PL
100 MNRO 91016 567-E3
1700 Hlwd 90028 593-H4
1800 MONP 91754 635-B5
10900 SGAT 90280 705-F6
GARFIELD ST
- Cstc 91384 4459-D7
5900 CHNO 91710 641-J6
E GARFORD ST
4800 LBCH 90815 796-B4
GARIBALDI AV
8700 TEML 91775 596-H2
8800 TEML 91780 596-H2
9600 TEML 91780 597-A2
9900 ARCD 91007 597-A2
E GARIBALDI AV
1100 LACo 91775 596-F2
1100 SGBL 91775 596-F2
8600 TEML 91775 596-F2
GARIBALDI LN
2100 LBCH 90815 826-C2
GARIN AV
1300 LACo 90601 637-F6
GARLAND AV
700 LA 90017 634-D4
44200 LAN 93536 4015-C7
GARLAND CT
1700 POM 91766 640-H4
23800 SCTA 91354 4550-F1
GARLAND DR
- SCTA 91355 4550-E4
10600 CULC 90232 672-F2
GARLOCK RD
34700 Actn 93510 4374-H1
GARNER ST
2000 LMTA 90717 793-H5
7800 LBCH 90808 796-H1
GARNET AV
1100 PMDL 93550 4286-C3
4200 CYP 90630 767-A4
4200 LACo 90630 767-A4
GARNET CT
- CRTS 90703 767-A3
GARNET LN
- GAR 90247 734-A3
2500 LAN 93535 4016-E7
GARNET ST
200 RBCH 90277 762-J5
800 RBCH 90277 763-A5
900 POM 91766 640-H4
2300 LA 90023 634-J6
2600 LA 90023 635-B7
3300 LA 90023 675-B1
3400 TOR 90503 763-B5
GARNET WY
19000 WAL 91789 639-C7
GARNET CANYON DR
- LACo 91390 4461-A2
GARNET HILL CT
28800 AGRH 91301 558-B4
GARNIER ST
23900 TOR 90505 793-E3
GARNISH DR
9100 DWNY 90240 706-E3
10600 DWNY 90241 706-D5
GARNSEY ST
200 RBCH 90277 762-J4
GARO ST
15400 HacH 91745 678-B2
GARONA DR
2600 HacH 91745 678-D5
GARRET DR
26900 CALB 91301 558-G6
GARRET PL
11400 Tuj 91042 503-J1
GARRETT CT
- LACo 91302 559-C4
- LACo 91744 638-F4
GARRETT ST
9000 RSMD 91770 636-H1
GARRICK AV
11400 LA 91342 502-J1
11500 LA 91342 482-C1
GARRICK ST
4700 PRV 90660 676-F3
GARRIS AV
13000 GrnH 91344 481-B4
GARRISON DR
6100 HiPk 90042 595-D2
GARSDEN AV
100 COV 91724 599-F3
5000 LACo 91724 599-F3
GARSTANG RD
34100 Actn 93510 4374-F5
GARSTON AV
21300 CRSN 90745 764-E6
GARTEL DR
20400 WAL 91789 639-F6
GARTEL DR N
500 WAL 91789 639-G6
S GARTH AV
1600 LA 90035 632-J5
1900 LA 90034 632-J5
5100 LadH 90056 673-A5
GARTHWAITE AV
4100 LA 90008 673-F3
GARTHWAITE WK
2700 LA 90008 673-G3
GARVALIA AV
7400 RSMD 91770 636-E2
GARVANZA AV
6200 HiPk 90042 595-D2
GARVEY AV
7400 RSMD 91770 636-F2
10300 ELMN 91733 637-D2
10600 ELMN 91731 637-D2
11300 ELMN 91732 637-D2
12600 BALD 91706 637-H1
13300 BALD 91706 638-A1
14400 BALD 91706 598-C7
E GARVEY AV
100 MONP 91755 636-C2
1000 MONP 91770 636-C2
1100 RSMD 91770 636-C2
9000 ELMN 91770 636-C2
9100 RSMD 91733 636-C2
9100 SELM 91733 636-C2
9100 SELM 91770 636-C2
9500 LACo 91733 637-A2
9500 SELM 91733 637-A2
9800 ELMN 91733 637-A2
S GARVEY AV
2400 ALH 91803 635-H2
W GARVEY AV
100 MONP 91754 636-A2
800 ALH 91803 636-A2
1100 MONP 91754 635-J2
1100 ALH 91803 635-J2
E GARVEY AV N
1000 WCOV 91790 598-G7
1200 COV 91724 599-D7
1800 WCOV 91791 598-J7
1800 WCOV 91791 599-A7
3500 WCOV 91724 599-D7
W GARVEY AV N
1000 WCOV 91790 598-D7
2200 BALD 91706 598-D7
E GARVEY AV S
1200 WCOV 91790 598-G7
1400 WCOV 91791 598-J7
1900 WCOV 91791 599-A7
3900 WCOV 91791 639-F1
4000 LACo 91791 639-F1
W GARVEY AV S
1100 WCOV 91790 598-D7
2300 BALD 91706 598-D7
GARVEY WY
- ING 90305 703-F4
GARVIN DR
16400 Enc 91436 561-E5
GARWICK PL
10600 SGAT 90280 705-G6
GARWOOD PL
10500 Wwd 90024 632-C2
GARY AV
800 MTBL 90640 676-C5
5600 NLB 90805 765-C2
GARY DR
29200 SCTA 91387 4462-E6
GARYDALE DR
15700 LACo 90604 707-J6
GARYFORD RD
29900 CynC 91351 4462-C5
GARZA DR
27100 SCTA 91350 4461-A7
27200 SCTA 91350 4460-J6
GARZON PL
1300 DBAR 91789 679-H3
GARZOTA DR
22400 SCTA 91350 4460-J7
22700 SCTA 91354 4460-H7
GASKELL RD
2200 KeCo 93560 3835-A1
3500 KeCo 93560 3834-A1
8200 KeCo 93560 3833-A1
GASLIGHT LN
5100 CULC 90230 672-J3
GAS LINE RD
- LACo 91390 4373-H6
- LACo 91390 4374-A4
- LACo 91390 4462-J6
- LACo 91390 4463-C2
GASPAR AV
1500 ELA 90022 675-J2
2200 CMRC 90040 675-H4
GASPE ST
16300 CynC 91351 4462-B4
GASPHER CT
- SCTA 91350 4551-D5
GASSEN PL
3200 LA 90065 594-H3
GASTINE ST
900 LACo 90502 794-B1
GASTON DR
11000 LACo 91342 482-J3
GASTON RD
1000 VeCo 93063 499-B4
N GATE RD
- Cstc 91384 4459-J2
GATE LEE CIR
5800 SGAT 90280 705-G5
GATES AV
1300 MANB 90266 732-H7
1900 RBCH 90278 732-J7
1900 RBCH 90278 733-A7
GATES PL
1300 SPAS 91030 595-G3
GATES ST
1900 LA 90031 635-B1
2400 LA 90031 595-B7
14300 BALD 91706 598-C3
GATESHEAD WY
7100 CanP 91307 529-F5
GATESIDE DR
4400 LA 90032 635-D1
GATEWAY AV
4100 LA 90029 594-B5
GATEWAY BLVD
11400 LA 90064 632-B7
11800 LA 90064 672-B1
GATEWAY CT
- FUL 92832 738-C7
- LACo 91390 4461-A2
GATEWAY DR
- MANB 90266 732-H4
- ARCD 91006 567-E5
6400 SIMI 93063 499-C3
GATEWAY LN
13300 WHIT 90602 707-D2
GATEWAY PZ
- LA 90012 634-H3
GATEWAY CENTER DR
21600 DBAR 91765 679-J3
GATEWAY TOWERS DR
- LA 90502 764-A3
GATEWOOD CT
1500 BREA 92821 708-H6
GATEWOOD LN
400 SMAD 91024 566-J1
GATEWOOD ST
2200 LA 90031 594-H6
GATEWOOD TER
600 SMAD 91024 566-H1
S GATLIN AV
1100 HacH 91745 678-B2
GATOS PL
800 PVE 90274 792-G5
GATUN ST
700 SPed 90731 824-A2
GAUCHO AV
15700 LACo 93591 4199-E5
GAUCHO CT
23400 SCTA 91355 4550-G3
GAUCHO DR
- RHE 90274 823-G1
- RPV 90275 823-G1
GAUGUIN AV
4300 WdHl 91364 560-A5
GAUGUIN LN
18000 GrnH 91344 481-A5
GAULT RD
34600 Actn 93510 4375-D3
GAULT ST
11100 NHol 91605 532-D5
13500 VanN 91405 532-A5
14400 VanN 91405 531-J5
15300 VanN 91406 531-C5
17700 Res 91335 531-A5
18100 Res 91335 530-F5
20000 Win 91306 530-C5
20900 CanP 91303 530-A5
22000 CanP 91303 529-J5
22700 CanP 91307 529-G5
GAUNTLET DR
3300 WCOV 91792 679-D1
GAVEA CIR
25500 SCTA 91355 4550-G6
GAVILAN DR
26600 SCTA 91350 4550-J1
GAVINA AV
13600 LA 91342 482-E2
GAVIOTA
- AVA 90704 5923-G2
GAVIOTA AV
- LBCH 90802 825-G1
200 LBCH 90802 795-G7
700 LBCH 90813 795-G5
2000 SIGH 90755 795-G2
3400 Bxby 90807 795-G2
3400 Bxby 90807 765-F3
4600 Enc 91436 561-F4
6400 VanN 91406 531-F3
8800 LA 91343 501-F5
10300 GrnH 91344 501-F2
N GAVIOTA AV
1300 LBCH 90813 795-G5
1800 LBCH 90806 795-G5
3800 Bxby 90807 765-F2
5800 NLB 90805 765-F2
6500 NLB 90805 735-F7
GAY ST
2800 LA 90065 594-J6
8100 CYP 90630 767-B4
N GAY ST
700 ING 90302 673-E7
S GAYBAR AV
500 WCOV 91790 638-G1
1800 LACo 91744 638-G3

STREET Block City ZIP Pg-Grid

GAYBROOK AV
10200 DWNY 90241 706-E5
GAYCREST AV
22500 TOR 90505 763-B7
22500 TOR 90505 793-B1
GAYDON AV
1900 SGBL 91776 596-F7
3400 RSMD 91770 636-F1
GAYER DR
600 LACo 91302 589-A7
600 LACo 91302 629-A1
GAYHART ST
6400 CMRC 90040 676-A3
GAYHURST AV
4800 BALD 91706 598-D3
GAYLAND AV
1100 HacH 91745 678-C2
GAYLAWN CT
600 LPUE 91744 638-D5
GAYLE DR
4200 Tarz 91356 560-G5
GAYLE PL
19100 Tarz 91356 560-G4
GAYLEMONT WY
- LACo 91387 4552-B5
GAYLEY AV
400 LA 90095 631-J2
400 Wwd 90024 631-J2
400 LA 90095 632-A1
400 Wwd 90024 632-A1
GAYLEY CT
1700 POM 91768 640-E1
GAYLIN
600 PAS 91107 566-F6
GAYLIN ST
13700 WHIT 90601 677-E5
13700 WHIT 91745 677-E5
GAYLORD CT
25500 LACo 91302 559-A3
S GAYLORD DR
500 BURB 91505 563-E4
W GAYLORD ST
1300 LBCH 90813 795-A5
GAYMONT AV
9000 DWNY 90240 706-B2
GAYMONT DR
15600 LMRD 90638 737-H4
S GAYMONT DR
800 ANA 92804 767-J7
S GAYMONT ST
600 ANA 92804 767-J7
GAYMORE CIR
5900 LVRN 91750 570-F3
GAYNOR AV
4800 Enc 91436 561-F3
6400 VanN 91406 531-F4
8300 LA 91343 531-F2
8900 LA 91343 501-F5
10300 GmH 91344 501-F2
GAY PARK LN
1700 HacH 91745 678-F4
GAYRIDGE ST
2900 POM 91767 600-J3
GAYTON PL
6200 MAL 90265 667-E1
GAYVIEW DR
11600 LMRD 90638 707-F7
GAYVILLE DR
600 CLAR 91711 571-A7
GAYWOOD DR
1500 Alta 91001 536-C5
GAZEBO CT
24300 DBAR 91765 640-E5
GAZELEY ST
16400 CynC 91351 4462-B6
GAZELLE ST
1200 LACo 93551 4285-F4
GAZETTE AV
6500 Win 91306 530-C4
9100 Chat 91311 500-C2
GEARY AV
9900 SFSP 90670 706-H4
GEDDES ST
1200 LACo 90044 704-A7
1300 LACo 90044 703-J7
GEER AV
5300 LA 90016 633-B7
GEHRIG ST
2300 WCOV 91792 679-B1
GEIGER AV
- PMDL 93551 4285-H4
36400 LACo 93551 4285-H4
GELBER PL
4000 LA 90008 673-D2
GELDING RD
31800 Cstc 91384 4369-F6
GELLER DR
23800 CALB 91302 559-E7
GEM AV
4300 CYP 90630 767-B4
GEM CIR
2600 LVRN 91750 600-H1
GEM CT
- LAN 93536 4104-F3
3800 LAN 93536 4105-A3
GEM PL
24200 DBAR 91765 640-D7
GEM ST
11600 NRWK 90650 706-G7
GEM WY
- Actn 93510 4465-E1
GEMBROOK AV
1300 HacH 91745 677-H1

GEMELOS CT
40300 PMDL 93551 4194-H3
GEMINI AV
100 BREA 92821 708-H7
GEMINI CT
- PMDL 93552 4287-D1
GEMINI ST
1700 WCOV 91792 678-J1
1900 LBCH 90810 795-A4
1900 WCOV 91792 679-A1
1900 WCOV 91792 639-A7
17400 INDS 91744 638-H7
17400 INDS 91744 678-J1
17400 LACo 91744 638-H7
17400 LACo 91744 678-J1
GEMSTONE AV
2500 PMDL 93551 4195-D5
GEMSTONE CT
13200 CHLS 91709 680-J1
GEMWOOD DR
1400 LACo 90601 637-F5
GENDEL DR
300 LACo 91744 679-B2
300 LACo 91792 679-B2
GENE CT
2000 RowH 91748 679-E6
GENE ST
9700 CYP 90630 767-E7
GENERAL AV
700 SPed 90731 824-B4
GENERAL ST
1900 RPV 90275 823-H4
W GEN THADDEUS KOSCIUSZKO WY
200 LA 90012 634-F3
GENERATION AV
- LAN 93536 4105-D1
GENESEE AV
100 LA 90036 633-B1
1300 LA 90019 633-B1
N GENESEE AV
300 LA 90036 593-B7
300 LA 90036 633-B1
700 LA 90046 593-B5
900 WHWD 90046 593-B5
S GENESEE AV
300 LA 90036 633-B1
1000 LA 90019 633-B5
1900 LA 90016 633-A6
3600 LA 90016 673-A1
3700 LA 90008 673-A1
GENESSE DR
1600 LVRN 91750 570-F7
GENESTA AV
4800 Enc 91316 561-D2
7000 VanN 91406 531-C3
9900 Nor 91325 501-C5
10400 GmH 91344 501-C2
GENEVA AV
300 CLAR 91711 601-C5
9000 MTCL 91763 601-F4
GENEVA CT
- SBdC 92397 (4652-G3 See Page 4651)
700 LAN 93535 4016-A4
GENEVA PL
2600 FUL 92833 738-B5
W GENEVA PL
100 COV 91723 599-B4
GENEVA ST
300 GLDL 91206 564-F4
700 GLDL 91207 564-F3
2300 POM 91766 640-J6
3100 LA 90020 634-B2
3100 LA 90057 634-B2
N GENEVA WK
- LBCH 90803 826-C2
GENEVIEVE AV
4800 Eagl 90041 565-C6
E GENEVIEVE ST
100 CRSN 90745 764-C5
GENOA AV
44400 LAN 93534 4015-G3
GENOA PL
3200 PMDL 93551 4195-B4
GENOA ST
- UPL 91784 571-H3
- ARCD 91006 567-D6
300 MNRO 91016 567-E6
14800 LA 91342 481-J6
S GENOA WY
- UPL 91786 601-H4
GENOLA DR
2600 HacH 91745 678-C5
GENOVA CT
30800 WLKV 91362 557-G6
GENOVA LN
- Nor 91326 500-D1
GENTIAN CT
- SCTA 91354 4460-G3
GENTILI RANCH RD
- GmH 91344 481-B1
GENTIL ROSE WY
- PMDL 93551 4104-E7
GENTLE SPRINGS LN
200 DBAR 91765 640-B7
GENTRY AV
4200 LA 91604 562-G5
4400 LA 91607 562-G2
6200 NHol 91606 532-G7
6800 NHol 91605 532-G2
GENTRY ST
100 POM 91767 600-J4

GENTRY ST
300 HMB 90254 762-J2
6300 HNTP 90255 675-A6
GEOFFREY AV
1800 SIMI 93063 499-A2
GEOFFREY CT
- POM 91766 641-A6
GEORGE AV
1900 KeCo 93560 3835-D1
5700 KeCo 93560 3834-B1
GEORGE CIR
3200 LACo 91107 566-G6
GEORGE LN
2700 DBAR 91789 679-G6
GEORGE ST
3100 LA 90031 595-A7
N GEORGE BURNS RD
100 LA 90048 632-J1
100 WHWD 90048 632-J1
S GEORGE BURNS RD
100 LA 90048 632-J1
GEORGEFF RD
- RHLS 90274 823-D3
GEORGE FREETH WY
300 RBCH 90277 762-H5
GEORGETOWN AV
1500 PMDL 93550 4286-C3
8000 Wch 90045 702-E3
GEORGETOWN DR
- BPK 90620 767-E6
21200 SCTA 91350 4461-C6
GEORGETOWN PL
300 CLAR 91711 571-D6
GEORGETTE AV
12000 LMRD 90638 707-G7
GEORGETTE PL
16900 GmH 91344 481-C6
GEORGIA AV
700 AZU 91702 568-H5
6800 BELL 90201 675-D7
6800 BELL 90201 705-D1
15100 PRM 90723 735-H5
GEORGIA CT
- LAN 93536 4015-D7
400 CLAR 91711 601-C5
GEORGIA LN
19300 Res 91335 530-G4
22300 SCTA 91350 4460-J5
22300 SCTA 91350 4461-A5
GEORGIA PL
900 AZU 91702 568-H5
GEORGIA ST
100 LA 90015 634-D5
GEORGIA WY
9200 Chat 91311 499-E7
GEORGIAN RD
300 LCF 91011 535-C5
GEORGINA AV
100 SMCA 90402 671-C1
100 SMCA 90402 631-E5
GEORGINA CIR
19500 CRTS 90703 766-H3
GEORGINA PL N
400 SMCA 90402 631-C7
GEORGIUS WY
2500 LA 90068 593-F2
GEPHART AV
7600 BGDN 90201 705-G2
GERAGHTY AV
800 City 90063 635-E4
GERALD AV
4900 Enc 91436 561-E3
6400 VanN 91406 531-E5
8800 LA 91343 501-D4
8800 LA 91343 531-E5
10300 GmH 91344 501-D1
11600 GmH 91344 481-D7
GERALDINE AV
1100 LAN 93535 4106-B2
GERALDINE ST
2600 LA 90011 674-F2
GERANIO DR
1000 ALH 91801 596-D6
1800 ALH 91801 636-D1
GERANIUM CIR
7900 BPK 90620 767-J3
GERANIUM PL
400 HiPk 90042 595-B2
GERANIUM GLEN LN
14600 SCTA 91387 4462-G5
GERARD DR
1500 DBAR 91765 680-A4
GERBER AV
11100 LACo 90604 707-F6
12100 LMRD 90638 707-F7
GERDA CT
7700 LACo 90606 676-H7
S GERHART AV
100 MTBL 90640 635-J6
100 LACo 91754 635-J6
100 ELA 90022 635-J7
600 ELA 90022 675-J1
900 CMRC 90022 675-J2
2100 MONP 91754 635-J6
GERKIN AV
14900 HAW 90250 733-E5
15100 LACo 90260 733-E5
18800 TOR 90504 763-E3
GERMAIN CIR
16400 HNTB 92649 826-J7
GERMAIN DR
1400 MTBL 90640 636-C7

GERMAIN ST
14300 MsnH 91345 502-A3
14700 MsnH 91345 501-H3
16300 GmH 91344 501-C3
18200 Nor 91326 500-F3
20200 Chat 91311 500-A3
22100 Chat 91311 499-J3
GERMAINE LN
31500 WLKV 91361 557-D7
GERMANIA CT
6300 AGRH 91301 558-A3
GERNDAL ST
21100 DBAR 91789 679-H3
GERNERT AV
3900 RSMD 91770 596-G7
GERNSIDE DR
20400 DBAR 91789 679-F4
GERONA AV
100 SGBL 91775 596-E3
100 SGBL 91776 596-E3
GERONIMO DR
28400 RPV 90275 792-G7
28800 RPV 90275 822-G1
GERONIMO LN
- CRSN 90745 794-E2
12900 NRWK 90650 737-A2
GERRAD WY
23600 CanP 91307 529-E4
GERRITT AV
16600 CRTS 90703 737-C6
GERRITT PL
17900 CRTS 90703 737-D7
17900 CRTS 90703 767-D1
GERRY ST
500 LHB 90631 708-G5
GERSHWIN CT
2700 LAN 93536 4015-C7
GERSHWIN DR
22800 WdHI 91364 559-G4
GERSHWIN PL
4600 WdHI 91364 559-H4
N GERTRUDA AV
300 RBCH 90277 762-H4
S GERTRUDA AV
400 RBCH 90277 762-J6
1200 RBCH 90277 792-J1
1300 RBCH 90277 793-A1
GERTRUDE AV
2900 LaCr 91214 504-F6
GERTRUDE CT
100 PAS 91105 565-H5
GERTRUDE DR
2600 OrCo 90720 796-G6
11300 LYN 90262 705-C7
11400 LYN 90262 735-C1
GERTRUDE ST
300 Boyl 90033 635-A5
GESELL ST
1000 GLDL 91202 564-D3
GETTY DR
- SFSP 90670 706-J6
GETTY ST
16400 LA 91343 501-E4
GETTY CENTER DR
800 Brwd 90049 591-G7
800 Brwd 90049 631-G1
GETTYSBURG AV
- Brwd 90049 631-J2
- Brwd 90049 632-A3
4300 CHNO 91710 641-E6
GETTYSBURG CIR
600 CLAR 91711 571-E7
GETTYSBURG DR
11400 NRWK 90650 736-G1
GEYER WY
4200 LACo 93536 4104-J5
GEYSER AV
5000 Tarz 91356 560-H1
6200 Res 91335 530-H2
8200 Nor 91324 530-H2
8900 Nor 91324 500-H6
GHENT ST
100 GLDR 91740 599-C1
400 SDMS 91773 600-C1
700 LACo 91750 600-D1
900 AZU 91702 599-B1
18000 LACo 91702 599-A1
W GHENT ST
500 SDMS 91773 600-A1
GHIBERTI WY
- Nor 91326 500-D1
GHOST MINE RD
32200 PMDL 93550 4466-B2
GIAMBI LN
- WCOV 91792 638-J5
GIAMILLO DR
40400 LACo 93551 4193-F3
GIAN DR
700 LACo 90502 794-A1
GIANO AV
300 LACo 91744 678-J2
300 WCOV 91792 678-J2
500 INDS 91744 678-J2
GIANO ST
3100 WCOV 91792 678-J1
GIANT OAK RD
20200 WAL 91789 639-F7
GIANT SEQUOIA ST
- PMDL 93551 4195-E6
GIARDINO WY
200 PacP 90272 630-F5
GIAVON ST
37400 PMDL 93552 4287-D2

GIBBONS ST
600 LA 90031 634-J2
GIBBS AL
- PAS 91101 565-J5
N GIBBS ST
100 POM 91767 640-J1
300 POM 91767 600-J7
800 POM 91767 600-J7
S GIBBS ST
100 POM 91766 640-J2
900 POM 91766 641-A3
GIBRALTAR AV
3800 LA 90008 673-C2
GIBRALTAR DR
3100 LA 90210 562-D7
3100 LA 90210 592-D1
GIBRALTAR LN
- Cstc 91384 4459-F5
GIBRALTAR PL
- Cstc 91384 4459-D2
S GIBSON AV
12600 COMP 90221 735-D3
12600 LYN 90262 735-D3
12800 RDom 90221 735-D4
GIBSON CT
300 BURB 91501 534-A5
45300 LAN 93534 4015-E5
GIBSON PL
2900 RBCH 90278 733-B6
27900 SCTA 91350 4460-J4
GIBSON RD
3500 ELMN 91731 597-B7
GIBSON ST
8800 LA 90034 632-H6
GIDDINGS AL
1300 PAS 91106 566-B5
GIDDINGS RANCH RD
- Alta 91001 535-G3
GIDE CT
1500 DBAR 91765 680-A3
GIDLEY ST
9400 TEML 91780 596-J5
9400 TEML 91780 597-A5
9800 ELMN 91731 597-A6
GIERSON AV
9400 Chat 91311 499-J5
GIFFORD AV
300 City 90063 635-E4
4700 VER 90058 675-D5
5100 MYWD 90270 675-D5
5900 HNTP 90255 675-D5
6200 BELL 90201 675-C7
GIFFORD ST
19600 Res 91335 530-F4
20200 Win 91306 530-D4
22200 CanP 91303 529-J4
GIGAR TER
1700 WCOV 91792 638-H4
GILA CT
7100 PMDL 93551 4104-C6
GILA DR
3500 LACo 91724 599-E6
GILBERT DR
20000 SCTA 91351 4551-E3
GILBERT PL
4500 LA 90004 593-J7
GILBERT ST
200 FUL 92833 738-C4
700 POM 91768 640-E1
N GILBERT ST
100 FUL 92833 738-D2
2600 LHB 90631 738-D2
S GILBERT ST
100 FUL 92833 738-C7
GILBERT LINDSAY DR
- LA 90015 634-D5
GILBERT LINDSAY MALL
100 LA 90012 634-G4
GILCREST DR
1500 LA 90210 592-F5
GILDAY DR
6300 LA 90068 593-F2
GILES LN
- PMDL 93551 4194-J3
GILES PL
3900 LACo 90601 676-J2
GILFORD PL
- SCTA 91354 4460-F7
GILL CIR
4500 LVRN 91750 570-F7
GILLAN AV
4500 LAN 93535 4016-B6
43700 LAN 93535 4106-B1
GILLAN CT
43900 LAN 93535 4106-B1
GILLESPIE AV
3500 Actn 93510 4465-A2
GILLESPIE ST
9000 LACo 93536 4013-H6
GILLETTE CRES
1700 SPAS 91030 595-G3
GILLETTE RD
1500 POM 91768 600-E7
GILLETTE ST
600 Boyl 90033 634-J3
GILLIG AV
3600 LA 90031 595-B6
GILLILAND AV
7800 BGDN 90201 705-H2
GILMAN LN
- Cstc 91384 4459-G3

GILMAN RD
3200 ELMN 91732 637-G1
3200 INDS 91732 637-F2
3800 ELMN 91732 597-G7
GILMAN ST
- FUL 92833 738-D5
3800 LBCH 90815 795-J3
GILMERTON AV
2900 LA 90064 632-F6
GILMORE AV
12000 LA 90066 672-D5
GILMORE LN
100 LA 90036 633-B1
GILMORE ST
6400 VanN 91406 531-B6
11500 NHol 91606 532-E6
13500 VanN 91401 532-A6
14500 VanN 91411 532-A6
14600 VanN 91411 531-H6
18500 Res 91335 530-H7
19700 WdHI 91367 530-E7
20100 Win 91306 530-D6
22000 CanP 91303 529-J7
22000 CanP 91303 530-A7
22300 CanP 91303 529-C7
GILMOUR RD
- Cstc 91384 4369-A7
30600 Cstc 91384 4459-A1
GILPIN WY
2700 ARCD 91007 597-C3
GILROY ST
2700 LA 90039 594-E3
GILSON AV
6400 NHol 91606 532-E6
GILWOOD AV
400 LPUE 91744 638-E5
GILWORTH ST
37500 PMDL 93550 4286-C2
GIMLET DR
26400 SCTA 91321 4551-G5
GINA CT
- Saug 91350 4461-E5
GINA DR
300 CRSN 90745 794-C1
GINA LN
2400 WCOV 91792 639-B7
N GINEVRA WK
100 LBCH 90803 826-D3
GINGER CT
2400 WCOV 91792 639-B7
2500 RowH 91748 679-C6
GINGER DR
300 NLB 90805 765-D1
GINGER LN
- LA 91340 502-B2
GINGER PL
19000 Tarz 91356 560-G4
GINGER WY
27600 SCTA 91350 4461-A6
GINGER ROOT LN
- BqtC 91354 4460-E5
GINGERWOOD LN
3000 LAN 93536 4105-B3
GINGERWOOD PL
24200 DBAR 91765 640-D5
GINGHAM AV
43200 LAN 93535 4106-A1
44000 LAN 93535 4016-A4
GIN LING WY
400 LA 90012 634-G2
GINNISS GRN
8100 BPK 90621 737-F5
GINSENG LN
16000 CHLS 91709 710-H1
GINZA DR
- SMRO 91108 566-C7
GIORDANO ST
13400 LACo 91746 637-J2
13400 LACo 91746 638-A3
13900 LPUE 91746 638-A3
14800 LACo 91744 638-C5
E GIORDANO ST
14800 LACo 91744 638-C5
GIOVANE ST
9500 SELM 91733 636-J2
9500 SELM 91733 637-A2
10000 ELMN 91733 637-A2
GIOVANNE WY
- WCOV 91792 679-B1
GIOVANNI CT
- LAN 93536 4104-J7
GIOVANNI LN
- Nor 91326 500-D1
GIOVANNI WY
6300 PMDL 93551 4104-E6
N GIRALDA WK
- LBCH 90803 826-D3
GIRARD AV
3800 CULC 90232 672-F2
GIRLA WY
9900 LA 90064 632-G6
GISH AV
1600 LBCH 90815 796-B5
10100 Tuj 91042 504-B4
GIST DR
14700 LACo 93532 4102-G3
GITA WY
- Saug 91350 4461-G6
GITANO RD
9300 SBdC 92371 (4472-G7 See Page 4471)
11300 SBdC 92372 (4472-G2 See Page 4471)

GIVEN PL
100 MTBL 90640 676-E3
GIVENS PL
9400 Nor 91325 501-C6
GLACIER DR
4800 Eagl 90041 565-C6
GLACIER PL
- LACo 93536 4104-J5
- LACo 93536 4105-A5
27700 Cstc 91384 4459-H2
GLACIER WY
- WCOV 91791 639-A4
GLAD WY
3000 LAN 93536 4015-B7
GLADBECK AV
8300 Nor 91324 530-H2
8900 Nor 91324 500-H4
GLADBROOK AV
4000 WCOV 91792 679-B2
GLADBROOK CT
29700 Cstc 91384 4459-D3
GLADDEN PL
4300 Eagl 90041 594-J1
GLADDING WY
- SCTA 91350 4551-A3
GLADE AV
5400 WdHI 91367 560-A1
6100 WdHI 91367 530-A7
6400 CanP 91303 529-J5
6400 CanP 91303 530-A7
7600 LA 91304 529-J4
9200 Chat 91311 499-J4
GLADE CT
300 BREA 92821 709-B5
27900 Cstc 91384 4459-G2
GLADE PL
- HacH 91745 637-G6
GLADEHOLLOW CT
5500 AGRH 91301 558-A5
GLADESIDE DR
14000 LMRD 90638 737-D2
GLADESMORE AV
6500 LACo 91007 596-J1
GLADESWORTH LN
- LACo 91387 4552-A4
GLADHILL DR
12000 LMRD 90638 707-H7
GLADHILL RD
10800 LACo 90604 707-G6
12000 LMRD 90638 707-H7
GLADIOLA CIR
7900 BPK 90620 767-J3
GLADIOLA DR
3500 CALB 91302 559-E7
3500 CALB 91302 589-E1
GLADIOLUS DR
28900 SCTA 91387 4552-E1
29000 SCTA 91387 4462-E7
GLADIOLUS PL
- BqtC 91354 4460-E5
GLADMAR ST
2300 MONP 91754 635-H6
GLADSTONE AV
11200 LA 91342 502-G1
11500 LA 91342 482-A2
GLADSTONE CT
38800 PMDL 93551 4195-C7
GLADSTONE ST
- AZU 91702 598-F1
1200 LVRN 91750 600-J3
2900 POM 91767 600-J3
15700 IRW 91706 598-F1
E GLADSTONE ST
100 GLDR 91740 599-G1
100 SDMS 91773 600-D1
700 LACo 91750 600-D1
900 AZU 91702 599-G1
900 AZU 91722 599-G1
900 LVRN 91750 600-D1
1000 LACo 91722 599-G1
1000 AZU 91702 599-G1
17500 AZU 91702 598-J1
17600 LACo 91702 598-J1
W GLADSTONE ST
100 GLDR 91740 599-C1
100 LACo 91702 598-F1
100 SDMS 91773 600-B1
100 AZU 91702 598-F1
800 SDMS 91773 599-H1
1300 AZU 91706 598-F1
GLADSTONE WY
11500 LA 91342 502-G1
GLADWICK ST
800 CRSN 90746 764-G3
1900 LACo 90220 764-H3
2200 LACo 90220 765-A3
GLADWIN ST
11300 Brwd 90049 631-H2
GLADY ST
5700 SGAT 90280 705-G6
GLADYS AV
100 MONP 91755 636-D2
300 LBCH 90814 825-H1
300 LBCH 90814 795-H7
400 LA 90013 634-G5
400 SGBL 91776 596-F7
600 LA 90021 634-G5
700 LBCH 90804 795-H6
1800 LACo 91770 636-F4
2200 RSMD 91770 636-F1
N GLADYS AV
1300 LBCH 90804 795-H5
1800 SIGH 90755 795-H5

N GLADYS AV
5700 LACo 91775 596-F3
5700 SGBL 91775 596-F3
5700 SGBL 91776 596-F3
S GLADYS AV
400 SGBL 91776 596-F5
5600 LACo 91776 596-F3
N GLADYS CT
700 PAS 91104 566-A2
GLADYS DR
1600 GLDL 91206 564-H3
GLADYS ST
500 COMP 90220 734-H5
600 MNRO 91016 567-H4
2000 PAS 91107 566-D4
E GLADYS ST
400 COMP 90221 735-A4
GLAMIS PL
12500 Pcma 91331 502-F3
GLAMIS ST
11300 LA 91342 482-H7
11600 LA 91342 502-G1
12300 Pcma 91331 502-F2
GLAMOUR TER
- LA 91304 529-D2
GLANDON ST
9500 BLF 90706 736-B3
GLASGOW AV
6900 Wch 90045 703-A1
S GLASGOW AV
100 ING 90301 703-A3
GLASGOW CT
5300 Wch 90045 703-A1
GLASGOW DR
- StvR 91381 4640-D1
GLASGOW GRN
8100 BPK 90621 737-F5
GLASGOW PL
5200 LACo 90250 733-A1
9300 Wch 90045 703-A4
13000 HAW 90250 733-A3
GLASGOW WY
5200 Wch 90045 703-A1
GLASSBORO AV
1900 CLAR 91711 571-E7
GLASSELL ST
2700 Echo 90026 634-B1
GLASSER AV
27500 SCTA 91351 4551-F1
28000 SCTA 91351 4461-F7
GLASSPORT AV
7700 LA 91304 530-B2
GLASTONBURY RD
1900 THO 91361 557-A6
GLAZEBROOK DR
15800 LMRD 90638 737-J1
GLEAM CT
5900 AGRH 91301 558-B4
GLEASON AV
2500 Boyl 90033 635-B5
3000 LA 90063 635-C6
GLEASON ST
3900 City 90063 635-E6
4500 ELA 90022 635-F6
E GLEASON ST
200 MONP 91755 636-B6
W GLEASON ST
200 MONP 91754 636-A6
300 MONP 91754 635-J6
GLEDHILL ST
14400 PanC 91402 502-A6
14600 PanC 91402 501-J6
15700 LA 91343 501-D6
17000 Nor 91325 501-B6
18500 Nor 91324 500-G6
21400 Chat 91311 500-A6
22000 Chat 91311 499-J6
GLEN AV
600 GLDL 91206 564-H3
900 POM 91768 640-F1
1000 PAS 91103 565-G2
1000 POM 91768 600-E7
1600 PAS 91103 535-G7
2600 Alta 91001 535-G5
GLEN CT
300 BREA 92821 709-C6
400 PAS 91105 565-E3
13000 CHLS 91709 641-A7
13700 WHIT 90601 677-E6
GLEN DR
1400 Top 90290 589-G4
GLEN GRN
2500 LA 90068 593-G2
GLEN PL
800 SPAS 91030 595-G3
GLEN TR
500 Top 90290 590-B5
GLEN WY
900 BHLS 90210 592-E7
1800 LVRN 91750 570-G6
3800 ELMN 91731 597-D7
4400 LACo 91711 571-B7
4400 CLAR 91711 571-B7
GLENADA AV
2100 Mont 91020 534-H3
GLEN AIRE DR
300 GLDL 91202 564-D1
GLEN AIRY
6200 LA 90068 593-F2
GLEN ALAN AV
800 WCOV 91791 639-A2
GLENALBYN DR
3400 LA 90065 594-J5

GLENALBYN DR
3400 LA 90065 595-A3
GLENALBYN PL
4000 LA 90065 595-A4
GLENALBYN WK
200 LA 90065 595-B4
GLENALBYN WY
200 LA 90065 595-B4
GLEN ALDER
6100 LA 90068 593-F2
GLEN ALDER CT
13800 LMRD 90638 738-A2
E GLENALLEN LN
1800 Alta 91001 536-C5
GLENANDALE TER
600 GLDL 91206 564-H3
GLEN ARBOR AV
900 Eagl 90041 565-D6
900 HiPk 90042 565-D6
1200 PAS 91105 565-D6
GLEN ARDEN AV
4600 LACo 91724 599-G3
E GLENARM ST
- PAS 91105 565-J7
200 PAS 91106 565-J7
500 PAS 91106 566-A7
W GLENARM ST
- PAS 91105 565-H7
GLENAVEN AV
2900 ALH 91803 635-G1
GLENAVON AV
1300 Ven 90291 671-J3
GLEN AYLSA AV
1500 Eagl 90041 565-B6
GLENBARR AV
10300 LA 90064 632-E6
GLENBRIDGE CIR
1100 THO 91361 557-B5
GLENBRIDGE RD
31400 WLKV 91361 557-D7
GLENBRIER AV
10800 LACo 90604 707-G5
GLENBROOK DR
20800 DBAR 91789 679-G3
GLENBROOK ST
9500 CYP 90630 767-D7
GLENBURN AV
16600 TOR 90504 733-F7
17100 TOR 90504 763-F1
GLENBUSH AV
37600 PMDL 93550 4286-G2
38400 PMDL 93550 4196-G7
GLENCAIRN RD
4800 LFlz 90027 593-J2
4800 LFlz 90027 594-A2
GLENCANNON DR
9400 PRV 90660 676-H4
10800 LACo 90606 676-J5
10800 WHIT 90606 676-J5
GLEN CANYON PL
- LACo 91390 4461-B3
GLEN CANYON RD
2100 Alta 91001 536-D6
GLEN CANYON WY
1000 BREA 92821 709-B5
GLENCHESTER DR
100 NLB 90805 765-D5
GLENCLAIRE DR
1000 DBAR 91789 679-G3
GLENCLIFF DR
7200 DWNY 90240 706-A1
GLENCLIFF ST
800 LHB 90631 708-C7
GLENCOE AV
1500 Ven 90291 671-J3
1500 Ven 90291 672-A3
3900 LACo 90292 672-B6
4000 CULC 90292 672-B6
4100 LA 90292 672-B6
E GLENCOE AV
1100 COMP 90221 735-B6
GLENCOE DR
1300 ARCD 91006 567-A3
1400 ARCD 91006 566-J3
W GLENCOE ST
100 COMP 90220 734-J6
GLENCOE WY
1600 GLDL 91208 534-H4
1900 LA 90068 593-D3
2200 POM 91767 600-H4
24800 TOR 90505 793-E4
GLENCOE HEIGHTS DR
900 GLDR 91741 569-F3
GLENCOVE AV
4600 GLDL 91214 504-D5
GLENCOVE DR
16000 HacH 91745 678-C6
GLEN CREEK RD
12200 CRTS 90703 736-J5
GLENCREST CIR
9900 LA 91504 533-C3
GLENCREST DR
3100 GLDL 91208 534-G5
7600 LA 91504 533-C3
8000 SunV 91352 533-B1
11700 LA 91340 482-C7
11800 SFER 91340 482-C7
GLENCREST ST
2900 POM 91767 600-J3
GLENCREST TER
1400 GLDL 91208 534-G5
GLENCROFT RD
1200 GLDR 91740 599-E2

GLENDA ST
12900 CRTS 90703 737-A7
N GLENDALE AV
100 GLDL 91206 564-F4
S GLENDALE AV
100 GLDL 91205 564-E6
1600 GLDL 91205 594-E1
1700 GLDL 91204 594-E1
1700 LA 90065 594-E1
GLENDALE BLVD
100 Echo 90026 634-D1
900 Echo 90026 594-D7
1800 GLDL 91204 594-D2
1900 LA 90039 594-D2
GLENDALE BLVD Rt#-2
- Echo 90026 594-E7
- LA 90039 594-E7
GLENDALE FRWY Rt#-2
- Eagl - 564-H6
- Echo - 594-E4
- GLDL - 534-J7
- GLDL - 564-H6
- LA - 564-H6
- LA - 594-E4
- LCF - 534-J7
GLENDALE RD
1100 SBdC 91784 571-J3
GLENDALE ST
1000 WCOV 91790 638-F1
GLENDOLA DR
8400 PRV 90660 676-E5
GLENDON AV
1000 Wwd 90024 632-B3
1800 WLA 90025 632-C5
2200 LA 90064 632-D6
3000 LA 90034 632-D7
3200 LA 90034 672-E1
GLENDON CT
1100 SPAS 91030 595-G2
GLENDON LN
800 SPAS 91030 595-G2
GLENDON PL
12900 CHLS 91709 640-J7
GLENDON WY
1000 SPAS 91030 595-G2
8800 RSMD 91770 596-H7
E GLENDON WY
- ALH 91801 596-C7
500 SGBL 91776 596-F7
W GLENDON WY
- ALH 91801 596-A7
100 SGBL 91776 596-D7
200 ALH 91803 596-A7
1400 ALH 91803 595-H7
GLENDORA AV
- LBCH 90803 826-B2
N GLENDORA AV
100 COV 91724 599-E4
100 GLDR 91741 569-E4
100 LPUE 91744 638-D7
100 INDS 91744 638-D7
5000 LACo 91724 599-E4
S GLENDORA AV
100 COV 91724 599-E5
100 GLDR 91741 569-E6
100 WCOV 91790 598-G7
200 WCOV 91790 638-G1
600 GLDR 91740 569-E7
1100 GLDR 91740 599-E2
1700 LACo 91744 638-F2
1700 LPUE 91744 638-F2
GLENDORA SQ
1000 WCOV 91790 598-G7
GLENDORA MOUNTAIN RD
- LACo - (510-E6 See Page 509)
- LACo - (539-J3 See Page 509)
- LACo - (540-C1 See Page 509)
1000 LACo - 569-G1
1000 LACo 91741 569-H1
1000 GLDR 91741 569-H4
GLENDORA RIDGE MTWY
- AZU 91702 568-J3
- AZU 91702 569-A2
- GLDR 91702 569-A2
- GLDR 91741 (539-F7 See Page 509)
- GLDR 91741 569-D1
- LACo (539-F7 See Page 509)
- LACo 91702 568-J3
- LACo 91702 569-A2
GLENDORA RIDGE RD
- LACo (510-H7 See Page 509)
- LACo 511-B7
- LACo (512-A5 See Page 511)
- LACo (540-G1 See Page 509)
GLENDOVER WY
8800 ING 90305 703-D4
GLENDOWER AV
2400 LFlz 90027 594-A2
2500 LFlz 90027 593-J2
GLENDOWER CT
- Cstc 91384 4459-F5
GLENDOWER PL
2400 LFlz 90027 594-A2

STREET	Block	City	ZIP	Pg-Grid
GLENDOWER RD				
	2700	LFlz	90027	593-J2
GLENEAGLE AV				
	600	POM	91768	640-E1
GLENEAGLE CT				
	-	SCTA	91354	4460-G5
GLENEAGLES CT				
	-	PMDL	93551	4195-C2
GLEN EAGLES DR				
	12600	HAW	90250	733-G1
GLENEAGLES DR				
	3600	Tarz	91356	560-F6
GLENEAGLES PL				
	400	LCF	91011	535-E3
	400	PAS	91011	535-E3
GLENEDEN ST				
	2600	LA	90039	594-F3
GLENELDER AV				
	1100	HacH	91745	678-D3
GLEN ELLEN PL				
	5200	HiPk	90042	595-C3
GLENFAIR ST				
	10500	ELMN	91731	597-C5
GLENFALL AV				
	16800	LACo	93591	4199-G3
	17900	LACo	93591	4200-A2
GLENFELIZ BLVD				
	3600	LA	90039	594-D1
GLENFIELD AV				
	2400	LVRN	91750	600-E2
GLENFINNAN AV				
	600	AZU	91702	569-A6
	1300	COV	91722	599-A3
	4400	LACo	91723	599-A4
	5300	LACo	91702	599-A1
	5800	LACo	91702	569-A6
GLENFLOW CT				
	-	GLDL	91206	564-J3
GLENFOLD DR				
	16800	HacH	91745	678-F5
GLENFORD AV				
	1500	DUAR	91010	568-B6
GLENFORD ST				
	5600	LA	90008	673-A2
GLENGARRY AV				
	6200	LACo	90606	677-A5
	6200	WHIT	90606	677-A5
	6500	LACo	90606	676-J6
	6600	WHIT	90606	676-J6
GLENGARRY DR				
	-	LMRD	90638	738-A1
GLENGARRY GRN				
	4700	BPK	90621	737-J4
GLENGARRY RD				
	1400	PAS	91105	565-D6
	1400	Eagl	90041	565-D6
GLENGRAY ST				
	16700	LACo	91744	638-G6
GLEN GREEN TER				
	6000	LA	90068	593-G2
GLENGROVE AV				
	100	GLDR	91741	569-J5
	600	GLDR	91740	569-J7
S GLENGROVE AV				
	100	SDMS	91773	599-J2
GLENGYLE ST				
	14000	LACo	90604	707-D5
GLEN HAVEN				
	900	POM	91766	640-G3
GLENHAVEN AV				
	800	FUL	92832	738-G6
	1000	FUL	92835	738-G5
GLENHAVEN CIR				
	4800	THO	91362	557-G1
GLENHAVEN CT				
	7200	CanP	91307	529-E5
GLENHAVEN DR				
	700	LHB	90631	708-B7
	900	PacP	90272	630-H4
	1900	LCF	91011	534-J3
GLENHILL DR				
	9800	LA	91504	533-C3
GLEN HOLLOW ST				
	2000	THO	91361	557-A5
GLEN HOLLY				
	400	PAS	91105	565-E6
	6100	LA	90068	593-F2
W GLEN HOLLY DR				
	3000	ANA	92804	767-G7
GLENHOPE DR				
	16100	LACo	91744	638-F5
GLENHURST AV				
	2900	LA	90039	594-D2
GLENHURST PL				
	2700	WCOV	91792	638-J7
	2700	WCOV	91792	639-A7
GLENHURST ST				
	3000	WCOV	91792	638-J7
	3000	WCOV	91792	639-A7
	3000	WCOV	91792	679-A1
GLEN IRIS AV				
	4900	Eagl	90041	565-A6
GLEN IVY DR				
	2100	GLDL	91206	564-J4
GLEN IVY ST				
	4700	LACo	91750	570-J6
GLEN LAKE AV				
	1200	BREA	92821	708-H5
GLENLEA ST				
	700	LACo	91750	600-D1
GLENLOCH AV				
	200	LACo	91744	638-H7
E GLENLYN DR				
	100	AZU	91702	569-B7
	18500	LACo	91702	569-B7
W GLEN LYN DR				
	200	GLDR	91740	569-C7
GLENMANOR PL				
	2900	LA	90039	594-D2
GLENMARE CT				
	1300	THO	91361	557-A6
GLENMARK DR				
	3300	HacH	91745	678-C6
W GLENMERE ST				
	900	WCOV	91790	638-D2
GLENMERE WY				
	800	Brwd	90049	631-E1
GLENMONT AV				
	700	Wwd	90024	632-B2
GLENMONT DR				
	1500	GLDL	91207	564-E1
GLENMORE BLVD				
	600	GLDL	91206	564-H3
GLENMUIR AV				
	4200	LA	90065	595-A4
GLENN AV				
	2700	LA	90023	635-A7
	2800	LA	90023	675-A1
	2900	SMCA	90405	671-H3
GLENN CT				
	1000	LAN	93535	4106-B2
	3100	SMCA	90405	671-H4
GLENN DR				
	13900	LACo	90605	707-D3
	14700	LACo	90604	707-F5
GLENN PL				
	5500	TOR	90503	763-A6
S GLENN ALAN AV				
	300	WCOV	91791	639-A1
G ANDERSN FRWY & TRNS WY I-105				
	-	DWNY	-	735-C1
	-	DWNY	-	736-D1
	-	ELSG	-	702-H6
	-	HAW	-	703-B6
	-	ING	-	703-B6
	-	LA	-	704-A7
	-	LACo	-	703-B6
	-	LACo	-	704-A7
	-	Lenx	-	703-B6
	-	LYN	-	704-A7
	-	LYN	-	705-A7
	-	LYN	-	735-C1
	-	NRWK	-	736-D1
	-	PRM	-	735-C1
	-	SGAT	-	735-C1
	-	Wbrk	-	704-A7
	-	Wch	-	702-H6
	-	Wch	-	703-B6
GLENNCROSS CT				
	1200	LA	90023	675-B1
GLENN CURTISS ST				
	1300	CRSN	90746	764-G2
	1300	CRSN	90747	764-G2
GLENNEL AV				
	3000	LAN	93536	4015-C7
GLENNFIELD CT				
	1200	LA	90023	675-B1
GLENN HILL DR				
	15200	HacH	91745	677-J4
GLENNIE LN				
	5500	LA	90016	633-A6
GLENNON DR				
	12000	WHIT	90601	677-B4
GLEN OAK				
	6100	LA	90068	593-F2
GLENOAK AV				
	1000	COV	91724	599-G3
GLEN OAKS BLVD				
	1000	PAS	91105	565-D3
	1500	GLDL	91206	565-D3
GLENOAKS BLVD				
	100	GLDL	91202	564-D3
	300	SFER	91340	482-B5
	1200	GLDL	91206	564-D3
	1900	LA	91342	482-B5
	7500	LA	91504	533-B1
	7800	LA	91505	533-B1
	7800	SunV	91352	533-B1
	8800	SunV	91352	503-A7
	9100	SunV	91352	502-G4
	10200	SunI	91040	502-E2
	10200	Pcma	91331	502-E2
	11500	Pcma	91331	482-B5
	11700	LA	91340	482-B5
	12900	LA	91342	481-G2
E GLENOAKS BLVD				
	100	GLDL	91207	564-F3
	1000	GLDL	91206	564-G3
	2200	GLDL	91206	565-B3
N GLENOAKS BLVD				
	100	BURB	91501	533-E4
	100	BURB	91502	533-E4
	1000	BURB	91504	533-E4
	3300	LA	91504	533-E4
S GLENOAKS BLVD				
	100	BURB	91501	533-H7
	100	BURB	91502	533-H7
	900	BURB	91501	563-J1
	900	BURB	91502	563-J1
	900	GLDL	91201	563-J1
W GLENOAKS BLVD				
	200	GLDL	91202	564-C3
	700	GLDL	91201	564-A1
	900	GLDL	91201	563-J1
W GLENOAKS BLVD				
	1000	BURB	91502	563-J1
	2100	GLDL	91206	564-C3
GLEN OAKS DR				
	-	LVRN	91750	570-H5
GLENOAKS ST				
	300	BREA	92821	709-A5
GLENOAKS CANYON DR				
	2800	GLDL	91206	565-B4
GLEN O PEACE PKWY				
	9400	Tuj	91042	503-J6
GLENOVER DR				
	1400	PAS	91105	565-E5
GLENPARK ST				
	1700	POM	91768	600-E7
GLEN PEAK CV				
	21600	DBAR	91765	679-J7
GLEN PINES CT				
	1400	CHLS	91709	680-G6
GLENRAVEN AV				
	38600	PMDL	93550	4196-A7
GLENRAVEN RD				
	43700	LAN	93535	4106-A1
	43900	LAN	93535	4016-A7
	44200	LAN	93535	4015-J7
GLENRIDGE AV				
	2900	ALH	91801	595-G5
GLENRIDGE CIR				
	1700	WCOV	91792	638-J6
GLENRIDGE CT				
	-	FUL	92831	738-J3
	-	LA	91342	481-H7
GLENRIDGE DR				
	3500	Shrm	91423	562-C6
	23400	SCTA	91321	4640-H3
GLEN RIDGE LN				
	-	POM	91766	640-G6
GLENROCK AV				
	500	Wwd	90024	632-A2
GLENROSE AV				
	2500	Alta	91001	535-H4
N GLENROSE AV				
	2000	Alta	91001	535-G6
	2000	PAS	91103	535-G6
N GLENROY AV				
	100	Brwd	90049	631-J1
	100	Brwd	90049	591-J7
S GLENROY AV				
	100	Brwd	90049	631-J1
GLENROY PL				
	200	Brwd	90049	631-J1
	2900	OrCo	90720	796-H4
GLENROY ST				
	2100	POM	91766	640-J5
GLENSHAW DR				
	300	LPUE	91744	638-B5
	700	LACo	91744	638-D3
	700	WCOV	91790	638-F1
GLENSHIRE RD				
	12600	DWNY	90242	736-A1
GLENSIDE PL				
	9700	LA	90210	592-C3
GLENSIDE TR				
	11800	LACo	91342	482-J7
GLEN SPRINGS RD				
	2000	LACo	91107	536-F7
GLENSTONE AV				
	1900	HacH	91745	678-B3
GLEN SUMMER RD				
	-	PAS	91105	565-E5
GLENSVIEW RD				
	400	SBdC	92372	(4472-A6 See Page 4471)
GLENTANA ST				
	700	COV	91722	598-J5
W GLENTANA ST				
	1100	COV	91722	598-H5
GLENTHORNE ST				
	17400	LACo	91744	678-H1
GLENTHORPE DR				
	1000	DBAR	91789	679-H3
GLENTIES LN				
	7900	SunI	91040	503-H4
GLENTIES WY				
	7900	SunI	91040	503-H4
GLEN TOWER				
	6100	LA	90068	593-F2
GLENTREE DR				
	2000	LMTA	90717	793-H6
GLENULLEN DR				
	200	PAS	91105	565-D6
GLENVIA ST				
	700	GLDL	91206	564-F3
GLENVIEW AV				
	2700	LA	90039	594-F3
GLEN VIEW DR				
	1100	FUL	92835	738-F4
	1700	ALH	91803	595-G7
	1700	ALH	91803	635-G1
GLENVIEW LN				
	1200	GLDR	91740	599-H2
GLENVIEW RD				
	700	GLDL	91202	564-C1
	1500	SLB	90740	796-H7
S GLENVIEW RD				
	900	WCOV	91791	638-J2
GLENVIEW TER				
	900	MONP	91754	635-J4
	1900	Alta	91001	536-D6
GLENVILLE DR				
	900	CLAR	91711	571-B6
	1100	LA	90035	632-G4
GLENVINA AV				
	4500	LACo	91723	599-D4
GLENVISTA DR				
	800	GLDL	91206	564-G3
GLENWALL ST				
	35200	LACo	91390	4374-D2
W GLENWAY DR				
	700	ING	90302	703-B1
	7000	Wch	90045	703-B1
GLENWICK AV				
	800	DBAR	91789	679-G3
GLENWOLD DR				
	20900	DBAR	91789	679-H3
GLENWOOD AV				
	3600	GLDL	91214	534-F2
	3600	GLDL	91208	534-F3
	4200	LA	90065	595-A4
	4300	LaCr	91214	534-F1
	4500	LaCr	91214	504-F7
E GLENWOOD AV				
	100	FUL	92832	738-H6
	600	FUL	92831	738-J6
N GLENWOOD AV				
	300	GLDR	91741	569-F4
	1600	UPL	91784	571-H7
S GLENWOOD AV				
	100	GLDR	91741	569-F6
W GLENWOOD AV				
	200	FUL	92832	738-G6
GLENWOOD CIR				
	800	FUL	92832	738-F6
	3000	TOR	90505	793-D5
	5100	LPMA	90623	767-C3
GLENWOOD DR				
	-	LA	91342	481-G3
	600	FUL	92832	738-F6
	38800	PMDL	93551	4195-E6
GLENWOOD PL				
	2400	SGAT	90280	704-J3
	2700	SGAT	90280	705-A3
N GLENWOOD PL				
	300	BURB	91506	563-G1
	400	BURB	91506	533-F7
S GLENWOOD PL				
	200	BURB	91506	563-G2
GLENWOOD RD				
	500	GLDL	91202	564-B2
	1300	GLDL	91201	564-A1
	1900	GLDL	91201	534-A7
	2000	GLDL	91201	533-J7
GLENWOOD TER				
	800	FUL	92832	738-F6
GLENWOOD WY				
	1900	UPL	91784	571-H5
N GLENWOOD WY				
	500	UPL	91786	601-J3
	1500	UPL	91786	571-H7
GLENWORTH ST				
	11100	SFSP	90670	706-F5
N GLESS ST				
	100	Boyl	90033	634-J4
S GLESS ST				
	100	Boyl	90033	634-J5
GLICK CT				
	2200	RBCH	90278	763-A2
GLICKMAN AV				
	4800	TEML	91780	597-B3
GLIDDEN DR				
	-	LA	90032	595-F4
GLIDE AV				
	6100	WdHl	91367	529-F7
	6100	WdHl	91367	559-F1
GLIDER AV				
	7900	Wch	90045	702-H2
GLIMMER CT				
	16400	LMRD	90638	738-A2
GLOAMING DR				
	9400	LA	90210	592-F2
GLOAMING WY				
	2200	LA	90210	592-F3
GLOBE AV				
	3600	LA	90066	672-D2
	3800	CULC	90230	672-E3
GLOBEMASTER WY				
	-	Bxby	90807	795-H1
	-	LBCH	90808	765-H7
	-	LBCH	90808	795-H1
GLORIA AV				
	4400	Enc	91436	561-F4
	6400	VanN	91406	531-F4
	8300	LA	91343	531-F2
	8800	LA	91343	501-F5
	10300	GrnH	91344	501-F2
GLORIA CT				
	11700	LKWD	90715	766-H4
GLORIA LN				
	1500	SIMI	93063	499-B3
GLORIA RD				
	500	ARCD	91006	567-A3
GLORIA ST				
	-	CHNO	91710	641-J7
	2300	WCOV	91792	639-B7
GLORIETA ST				
	-	PAS	91103	565-G2
GLORIETTA AV				
	1600	GLDL	91208	534-H6
GLORIETTA DR				
	14400	Shrm	91423	562-A7
GLORIETTA PL				
	3400	Shrm	91423	562-A7
GLORIOSA AV				
	1400	RowH	91748	678-J4
GLORIOSA LN				
	44800	LAN	93535	4016-E5
GLORISO LN				
	-	StvR	91381	4640-D1
GLORY AV				
	9300	Tuj	91042	504-B4
GLORYWHITE ST				
	6400	LKWD	90713	766-E3
GLOUCESTER DR				
	9800	LA	90210	592-C1
E GLOUCESTER ST				
	6000	ELA	90022	675-J2
	6100	ELA	90022	676-A2
GLOVER PL				
	2200	LA	90031	594-G5
GLYNDON AV				
	1400	Ven	90291	672-A4
	1500	Ven	90291	671-J3
GLYNDON CT				
	2000	Ven	90291	672-A4
GLYNN AV				
	12200	DWNY	90242	706-A7
	12300	DWNY	90242	705-J7
	12600	DWNY	90242	735-J1
GLYNN DR				
	16400	PacP	90272	630-G3
GNEISS AV				
	12100	DWNY	90242	705-J6
	12100	DWNY	90242	706-A6
	12600	DWNY	90242	735-H1
GNU CIR				
	2200	RowH	91748	678-J6
GOAT HILL RD				
	6700	SBdC	-	(512-A4 See Page 511)
GODBEY DR				
	5300	LCF	91011	535-D2
GODDARD AV				
	7600	Wch	90045	703-A2
GODDE HILL RD				
	37900	PMDL	93551	4194-F1
	38500	LACo	93551	4194-D4
GODINHO AV				
	18700	CRTS	90703	767-A2
GODOY ST				
	11000	LACo	90606	676-H7
	11000	LACo	90606	706-H1
GOETHE PL				
	12700	GrnH	91344	481-B5
GOETTING AV				
	3700	PMDL	93550	4286-H5
GOETTING LN				
	3500	PMDL	93550	4286-G5
GOLD LN				
	19000	WAL	91789	639-C7
GOLD PL				
	6600	HiPk	90042	595-F1
GOLD BLUFF DR				
	22700	DBAR	91765	640-A7
GOLD CANYON DR				
	-	LACo	91390	4460-J4
	-	LACo	91390	4461-A3
	1500	DBAR	91789	679-F4
GOLD CREEK RD				
	8800	LACo	91342	(4723-E2 See Page 4643)
GOLD CREEK TKTR				
	-	LACo	-	(4644-B7 See Page 4643)
	-	LACo	-	(4723-J2 See Page 4643)
	-	LACo	-	(4724-C1 See Page 4643)
	-	LACo	91342	(4723-G2 See Page 4643)
GOLDCREST DR				
	26300	SCTA	91355	4550-D4
E GOLDCREST ST				
	6900	LBCH	90815	796-F5
GOLD DUST CT				
	1600	SIMI	93063	499-C3
GOLD DUST LN				
	-	CRSN	90745	794-E2
GOLD DUST ST				
	1700	GLDR	91740	569-J6
GOLD DUST WY				
	13200	CHLS	91709	680-H1
GOLDEN AV				
	-	LBCH	90802	825-C1
	-	LBCH	90831	825-C1
	600	FUL	92832	738-G6
	800	LA	90017	634-D4
	1500	HMB	90254	762-H1
	8000	SGAT	90280	735-H1
	8000	PRM	90723	735-H1
	8300	PRM	90242	735-H1
	8400	DWNY	90242	735-J2
N GOLDEN AV				
	200	LBCH	90802	795-C7
	1700	LBCH	90813	795-C4
	1800	LBCH	90806	795-C2
	3400	LBCH	90806	765-C7
GOLDEN CIR				
	17400	GrnH	91344	481-B6
	37300	PMDL	93550	4286-H3
GOLDEN CT				
	-	LA	91342	481-H6
GOLDEN LN				
	2300	LAN	93536	4105-D3
	17400	GrnH	91344	481-B6
E GOLDEN ST				
	900	COMP	90221	735-A2
GOLDEN ARROW DR				
	4900	RPV	90275	793-B7
	4900	RPV	90275	823-B1
GOLDEN BOUGH DR				
	19600	LACo	91724	639-D1
GOLDEN BUSH WY				
	21200	SCTA	91351	4551-C2
GOLDEN CANYON CIR				
	11200	Chat	91311	499-H2
GOLDEN CANYON CT				
	-	DBAR	91765	679-J7
GOLDEN CARRIAGE LN				
	200	POM	91767	600-J4
GOLDEN COAST LN				
	-	RowH	91748	679-D4
GOLDEN CREST DR				
	14300	CHLS	91709	680-G4
GOLDEN CROWN CIR				
	23200	DBAR	91765	680-B1
GOLDENDALE DR				
	11600	LMRD	90638	707-F7
GOLDEN EAGLE AV				
	4900	PMDL	93552	4287-A2
GOLDEN GATE AV				
	1400	Echo	90026	594-C5
GOLDEN GLEN CT				
	26100	SCTA	91321	4551-F5
GOLDEN GROVE WY				
	700	COV	91722	598-J4
GOLDEN HILLS DR				
	-	LA	90032	595-F4
GOLDEN HILLS RD				
	1200	LVRN	91750	570-G4
	1400	SDMS	91750	570-F4
GOLDEN JUBILEE LN				
	7200	Litl	93543	4377-F1
GOLDEN KNOLL CT				
	4900	THO	91362	557-F3
GOLDEN LANTERN LN				
	15400	LMRD	90638	707-H7
	15800	LACo	90604	707-J7
	16100	LACo	90604	708-A7
GOLDENLEAF DR				
	3600	WLKV	91361	557-C7
GOLDEN MEADOW DR				
	2200	DUAR	91010	568-C3
	27900	RPV	90275	792-G7
	28700	RPV	90275	822-G1
GOLDEN MEADOW LN				
	-	SCTA	91350	4550-H5
GOLDEN OAK DR				
	36800	PMDL	93552	4287-C4
GOLDEN OAK LN				
	24500	SCTA	91321	4641-B1
	24700	SCTA	91321	4551-C7
GOLDEN OAK RD				
	-	SCTA	91350	4551-B3
GOLDEN OAKS AV				
	-	Tuj	91042	504-B4
GOLDEN PALMS LN				
	-	LA	91342	482-E5
GOLDEN POPPY CT				
	21600	WAL	91789	639-H5
GOLDEN PRADOS DR				
	400	DBAR	91765	640-B7
	400	DBAR	91765	680-B1
GOLDEN RAIN LN				
	18200	SCTA	91387	4551-J3
GOLDEN RAIN RD				
	1200	SLB	90740	826-G1
	1800	SLB	90740	796-J7
GOLDENRAIN ST				
	-	PMDL	93551	4285-D2
W GOLDEN RAIN ST				
	1000	UPL	91786	601-J2
GOLDEN RIDGE LN				
	15400	HacH	91745	678-A6
GOLDENROD CIR				
	7900	BPK	90620	767-J3
GOLDEN ROD CT				
	1900	THO	91361	557-A6
GOLDENROD CT				
	4300	CHNO	91710	641-E4
GOLDEN ROD DR				
	200	WAL	91789	639-H7
GOLDENROD PL				
	600	POM	91766	640-F3
	1000	POM	91768	640-E1
	16500	Enc	91436	561-E7
	26600	CALB	91302	558-G7
GOLDENROD ST				
	200	BREA	92821	709-F7
GOLDENROD WY				
	26300	SCTA	91350	4551-B2
GOLDEN ROSE AV				
	1500	HacH	91745	678-E4
GOLDENROSE ST				
	1000	LA	90732	824-A3
	1000	SPed	90731	824-A3
E GOLDEN SANDS DR				
	6200	LBCH	90803	826-D1
GOLDEN SHORE				
	-	LBCH	90802	825-C1
GOLDEN SPAR PL				
	-	RHE	90274	793-C6
GOLDEN SPRINGS DR				
	200	DBAR	91765	640-D5
	20300	DBAR	91789	679-F4
	21600	DBAR	91765	679-J2
	22300	DBAR	91765	680-A2
GOLDEN SPUR CIR				
	500	WAL	91789	639-C7
GOLDEN SPUR LN				
	-	RPV	90275	823-G2
GOLDEN SPUR RD				
	2900	Actn	93510	4465-D4
GOLDEN STATE FRWY I-5				
	-	Boyl	-	634-J5
	-	Boyl	-	635-A2
	-	BURB	-	533-D4
	-	BURB	-	563-H1
	-	Cstc	-	4279-C7
	-	Cstc	-	4369-D1
	-	Cstc	-	4459-H3
	-	Echo	-	594-D3
	-	GLDL	-	563-H1
	-	GLDL	-	564-B5
	-	GrnH	-	481-E4
	-	GrnH	-	4641-A7
	-	LA	-	481-E4
	-	LA	-	501-J1
	-	LA	-	502-B3
	-	LA	-	533-D4
	-	LA	-	564-B5
	-	LA	-	594-D3
	-	LA	-	634-J1
	-	LA	-	635-A2
	-	LA	-	4641-A7
	-	LACo	-	4279-A4
	-	LACo	-	4641-A7
	-	LFlz	-	564-B5
	-	MsnH	-	481-E4
	-	MsnH	-	501-J1
	-	MsnH	-	502-B3
	-	Nwhl	-	4640-F3
	-	Nwhl	-	4641-A7
	-	Pcma	-	502-B3
	-	SCTA	-	4459-H3
	-	SCTA	-	4460-A7
	-	SCTA	-	4550-C3
	-	SCTA	-	4640-F3
	-	StvR	-	4550-C3
	-	StvR	-	4640-F3
	-	StvR	-	4641-A7
	-	SunV	-	502-D6
	-	SunV	-	532-J1
	-	SunV	-	533-D4
	-	Valc	-	4459-H3
	-	Valc	-	4460-A7
	-	Valc	-	4550-C3
GOLDEN STATE RD				
	-	LA	91342	481-E3
GOLDEN TRIANGLE RD				
	20300	SCTA	91351	4551-C3
	20500	SCTA	91350	4551-B3
GOLDEN VALLEY LN				
	13300	GrnH	91344	481-C3
GOLDEN VALLEY RD				
	-	CynC	91351	4461-D7
	-	Nwhl	91321	4551-E6
	-	Saug	91350	4461-D7
	-	SCTA	91351	4551-C2
	19400	SCTA	91321	4551-E6
	25700	SCTA	91350	4551-C5
GOLDEN VIEW DR				
	1600	HacH	91745	677-J2
GOLDEN VIEW RD				
	10500	SBdC	92372	(4472-E2 See Page 4471)
GOLDENVIEW WY				
	36800	PMDL	93552	4287-A4
GOLDEN VISTA DR				
	1300	WCOV	91791	639-B3
GOLDEN WEST AV				
	1200	ARCD	91007	566-J7
	1200	LACo	91007	566-J7
	4800	TEML	91780	597-A1
	6700	LACo	91007	567-A7
	6700	ARCD	91007	567-A7
	6700	ARCD	91007	597-A1
N GOLDEN WEST AV				
	-	ARCD	91007	566-J5
	-	ARCD	91007	567-A5
S GOLDEN WEST AV				
	-	ARCD	91007	566-J5
	100	ARCD	91007	567-A6
GOLDEN WILLOW CT				
	-	YBLN	92886	709-J7
GOLDENWOOD DR				
	5200	ING	90302	673-A7
GOLDFIELD AV				
	4400	Bxby	90807	765-F5
GOLDFIELD PL				
	1600	POM	91766	640-F3
GOLDFINCH PL				
	26500	SCTA	91351	4551-E4
GOLD HILL DR				
	18900	WAL	91789	639-B6
	27900	Cstc	91384	4369-G7
GOLDING DR				
	6000	LAN	93536	4014-E7
GOLDLEAF CIR				
	4900	LadH	90056	673-A6
GOLDMINE LN				
	7800	VanN	91406	531-D3
GOLD NUGGET AV				
	23500	DBAR	91765	680-C3
GOLDPOINT PL				
	24400	DBAR	91765	640-E7
GOLDRIDGE ST				
	34400	Actn	93510	4374-J4
GOLDRING PL				
	-	RHE	90274	793-D6
GOLDRING RD				
	11600	ARCD	91006	597-F3
GOLD RUN DR				
	3500	DBAR	91765	709-G1
GOLDRUSH AV				
	2000	PMDL	93551	4195-E5
GOLD RUSH CT				
	4500	MTCL	91763	641-E1
GOLD RUSH DR				
	23300	DBAR	91765	680-B1
GOLDRUSH DR				
	1400	SDMS	91773	599-H2
GOLD SHADOW LN				
	15300	CHLS	91709	680-F6
GOLDSMITH ST				
	3000	SMCA	90405	671-G4
GOLD SPRING PL				
	800	THO	91361	557-A5
GOLD STAR DR				
	3000	LBCH	90810	795-A2
GOLDSTAR PL				
	-	POM	91766	640-G7
GOLD STONE RD				
	21700	Top	90290	590-A5
GOLDSTREAM WY				
	19500	SCTA	91321	4551-F6
GOLDWYN TER				
	3800	LA	90232	672-F1
GOLDY RD				
	1900	SDMS	91773	570-C5
GOLETA ST				
	100	COMP	90220	734-F4
	1000	LVRN	91750	600-E1
	11300	LA	91342	482-H7
	11600	LA	91342	502-H1
	12900	Pcma	91331	502-C5
	14900	LACo	90220	734-F4
GOLF PL				
	31700	Llan	93544	4469-F1
GOLF CLUB DR				
	1500	GLDL	91206	565-B1
GOLF COURSE RD				
	-	AVA	90704	5923-H5
	18800	Tarz	91356	560-G6
	24000	SCTA	91355	4550-F7
GOLFERS DR				
	39600	PMDL	93551	4195-H4
GOLFERS LN N				
	39900	PMDL	93551	4195-J4
GOLF VIEW DR				
	24500	SCTA	91355	4550-E7
GOLFWOOD CT				
	3100	LAN	93536	4105-B3
GOLL AV				
	7800	NHol	91605	532-H3
GOLLER AV				
	12900	NRWK	90650	736-J2
	13300	NRWK	90650	737-A2
GOLONDRINA PL				
	4200	WdHl	91364	560-B5
GOLONDRINA ST				
	21200	WdHl	91364	560-B5
GOLONDRINAS ST				
	7600	DWNY	90242	705-G7
GOLVA DR				
	15900	LMRD	90638	737-J4
GOMERES RD				
	5200	WdHl	91364	559-G3
GOMERO CIR				
	20300	CRSN	90746	764-F4
GOMES WY				
	300	BREA	92821	709-B7
GOMEZPALACIO DR				
	11000	SELM	91733	637-B5
GONA CT				
	1100	DBAR	91789	679-G3
GONDAR AV				
	2000	LBCH	90815	796-D2
	3000	LBCH	90808	796-D1
	3300	LBCH	90808	766-D7
	3700	LACo	90808	766-D7
	4300	LKWD	90713	766-D2
GONDOLA DR				
	4800	VeCo	91377	557-G2
GONSALVES PL				
	11000	CRTS	90703	766-F3
GONSALVES ST				
	11200	CRTS	90703	766-F3
GONZAGA AV				
	8000	Wch	90045	702-E3
GONZALES DR				
	23100	WdHl	91367	559-G3
GONZALES RD				
	1100	VeCo	93063	499-A3
GOODALL AV				
	2000	LACo	91010	567-H7
S GOODALL AV				
	2200	LACo	91010	567-H7
GOODBEE ST				
	8300	PRV	90660	676-E5
GOODE AV				
	-	GLDL	91203	564-E3
GOODHART AV				
	1300	LACo	90601	637-F5
N GOODHOPE AV				
	200	LA	90275	823-H4
	200	LA	90732	823-H4
S GOODHOPE AV				
	900	LA	90732	823-H5
GOODHOPE PL				
	900	LA	90732	823-H5
GOODHUE ST				
	14800	LACo	90604	707-F6
GOODHUE ST				
	15400	WHIT	90604	707-G6
GOODLAND AV				
	3600	LA	91604	562-E4
	5000	LA	91607	562-E1
	6000	NHol	91606	532-E6
	6800	NHol	91605	532-E2
GOODLAND CT				
	-	NHol	91605	532-E2
GOODLAND DR				
	3600	LA	91604	562-F6
GOODLAND PL				
	3900	LA	91604	562-E5
	6200	NHol	91606	532-E7
GOODMAN AV				
	200	RBCH	90278	762-J1
GOODRICH AV				
	900	Wilm	90744	794-H5
GOODRICH BLVD				
	700	CMRC	90022	675-H1
	700	ELA	90022	675-H1
GOODRICH CT				
	-	StvR	91381	4640-D1
GOODSON DR				
	700	LPUE	91744	638-D5
GOODSPRING DR				
	30300	AGRH	91301	557-G5
GOODVALE RD				
	16500	SCTA	91387	4552-B1
	18700	SCTA	91351	4551-F1
GOODVIEW TR				
	2900	LA	90068	593-C1
GOODWAY DR				
	6000	LACo	91702	569-B7
GOODWICK DR				
	3200	WCOV	91792	679-D2
GOODWIN AV				
	3900	LA	90039	564-C6
	4200	GLDL	91204	564-C6
GOODWIN ST				
	-	FUL	92833	738-D5
GOOSEBERRY DR				
	17800	RowH	91748	678-H7
GOPHER CANYON RD				
	11800	Chat	91311	480-B6
GORDON AV				
	100	GLDR	91741	569-H5
	2500	LHB	90631	708-B4
	9100	OrCo	90631	708-B4
GORDON CT				
	1600	POM	91768	600-J6
GORDON GRN				
	8100	BPK	90621	737-J5
GORDON PL				
	1400	MTBL	90640	636-D7
GORDON ST				
	1100	LA	90038	593-G5
	1300	Hlwd	90028	593-G4
	1500	POM	91768	600-J6
E GORDON ST				
	100	NLB	90805	765-C1
N GORDON ST				
	200	POM	91768	640-J1
	700	POM	91768	600-J7
S GORDON ST				
	100	POM	91766	640-J2
GORDON TER				
	300	PAS	91105	565-G6
GORDON HIGHLANDS CT				
	-	GLDR	91741	570-A4
GORDON HIGHLANDS RD				
	-	GLDR	91741	570-A4
	-	GLDR	91773	570-A4
GORDON RANCH RD				
	100	GLDR	91741	569-J4
GOREN CT				
	3100	LKWD	90712	765-H2
GOREN PL				
	11300	LA	91342	482-H7
GORGE RD				
	2800	LACo	90265	629-F4
GORGONIA ST				
	20900	WdHl	91364	560-C5
GORGONIO RD				
	3300	SBdC	92371	(4472-H1 See Page 4471)
GORHAM AV				
	-	LACo	90073	631-H4
	11600	Brwd	90049	631-H4
GORHAM LN				
	39600	PMDL	93551	4195-C3
GORHAM PL				
	11600	Brwd	90049	631-H4
GORMAN AV				
	10300	Wats	90002	704-H5
	10700	LA	90059	704-H5
	11600	Wbrk	90059	704-H7
GOSFORD AV				
	8000	NHol	91605	532-E2
GOSHEN AV				
	11600	Brwd	90049	631-H5
GOSHEN ST				
	6100	SIMI	93063	499-B2
GOSS RD				
	100	Llan	93544	4471-J3
	100	SBdC	92372	4471-J3
	200	SBdC	92372	(4472-F2 See Page 4471)
	2800	SBdC	92371	(4472-F2 See Page 4471)
GOSS ST				
	10800	SunV	91352	503-A7
	10800	SunV	91352	533-A1
GOSS ST				
	11200	SunV	91352	532-J1
E GOSSAMER ST				
	5700	LBCH	90808	766-C7
GOSS CANYON AV				
	5500	LaCr	91214	504-H6
GOTERA DR				
	3000	HacH	91745	678-D6
	3200	LHH	90631	678-D6
GOTHAM ST				
	5500	BGDN	90201	705-F2
	9000	DWNY	90241	706-C4
	14800	LA	91343	501-J5
GOTHIC AV				
	8300	LA	91343	531-E1
	8900	LA	91343	501-E5
	10200	GrnH	91344	501-E2
	11600	GrnH	91344	481-E7
GOTHIC PL				
	16400	GrnH	91344	481-E7
GOTHIC WY				
	1000	POM	91768	600-G7
GOTTES LN				
	12400	LMRD	90638	707-H7
	12400	LMRD	90638	737-H1
GOUCHER ST				
	1300	PacP	90272	631-B4
GOULD AV				
	400	HMB	90254	732-G7
	400	HMB	90254	762-G1
	700	MANB	90254	762-G1
	4400	LCF	91011	535-C2
	8000	LA	90046	593-A3
GOULD MTWY				
	-	LACo	-	535-D1
	-	PAS	91011	535-D1
	500	LCF	91011	535-D1
GOULD TER				
	600	HMB	90254	732-G7
	600	HMB	90254	762-G1
GOVERNOR AV				
	24200	Hrbr	90710	793-J3
GOVERNOR MINE RD				
	34300	Actn	93510	4375-A3
N GOWER ST				
	100	LA	90004	593-F7
	100	LA	90004	633-F1
	700	LA	90038	593-G6
	1300	Hlwd	90028	593-F3
	1900	LA	90068	593-F3
GOYA DR				
	28700	RPV	90275	823-H3
GOYA ST				
	17000	GrnH	91344	481-C4
GRABER AV				
	13700	LA	91342	482-E1
GRACE AV				
	100	LHB	90631	708-E7
	1700	ARCD	91006	597-D1
	1800	Hlwd	90028	593-E4
	1900	LA	90068	593-E3
	3600	BALD	91706	598-A4
	4700	CYP	90630	767-B5
	21000	CRSN	90745	764-D6
	22400	CRSN	90745	794-D1
E GRACE AV				
	400	ING	90301	703-D1
GRACE CT				
	-	ART	90701	766-G2
N GRACE CT				
	700	WCOV	91790	598-H6
GRACE DR				
	200	SPAS	91030	595-H1
	1200	PAS	91105	565-H7
	1200	PAS	91105	595-H1
GRACE LN				
	-	LACo	91387	4551-J3
	800	Brwd	90049	591-F7
GRACE PL				
	5300	ELA	90022	675-H1
	5400	CMRC	90022	675-H1
GRACE TER				
	-	PAS	91105	565-H7
GRACE WK				
	-	PAS	91105	565-H7
GRACEBEE AV				
	13900	NRWK	90650	737-B3
GRACELAND WY				
	2900	GLDL	91206	565-A2
GRACELDO LN				
	15900	WHIT	90603	707-J4
GRACEMONT ST				
	9000	WHIT	90602	707-C3
GRACETON DR				
	27900	SCTA	91387	4552-E3
GRACEWOOD AV				
	5500	TEML	91007	597-B3
	5500	TEML	91780	597-B3
GRACIA ST				
	2900	LA	90039	594-E3
GRACIE ALLEN DR				
	8600	LA	90048	632-J1
GRACIOSA DR				
	5800	LA	90068	593-F2
W GRACIOSA LN				
	3100	ANA	92804	767-H6
GRACIOSA ST				
	-	SCTA	91355	4460-D6
GRACITA PL				
	5300	HiPk	90042	595-C3
GRADE AV				
	13000	LA	91342	482-D4

STREET
Block City ZIP Pg-Grid

GRADWELL ST
11300 LKWD 90715 766-G5
12400 LKWD 90715 767-A5
GRADY AV
7900 LACo 90606 707-B1
GRAFF DR
12800 LMRD 90638 737-E1
GRAFTON CT
38600 PMDL 93552 4196-J7
GRAFTON ST
1600 Echo 90026 594-E7
GRAGMONT ST
200 COV 91722 599-A3
16700 LACo 91722 598-H3
GRAHAM AV
1600 COMP 90222 734-G3
1900 RBCH 90278 732-J7
1900 RBCH 90278 733-A7
7200 Flor 90001 674-G7
7200 Flor 90001 704-G1
8600 Wats 90002 704-G2
9200 Wats 90002 704-G4
11100 LA 90059 704-G6
GRAHAM CIR
9200 CYP 90630 767-D6
GRAHAM GRN
4900 BPK 90621 737-F5
GRAHAM LN
- Saug 91350 4461-G5
GRAHAM PL
100 BURB 91502 563-J1
100 GLDL 91201 563-J1
11200 LA 90064 632-C7
GRAHAM RD
3500 SBdC 92371 (4472-J2
See Page 4471)
GRAHAM ST
9300 CYP 90630 767-D7
GRAHAM ACCESS RD
- IRW 91706 597-J2
- IRW 91706 598-A2
GRAJUELO DR
26900 SCTA 91354 4550-H1
GRAMBLING PL
18800 CRSN 90746 764-E2
GRAMERCY AV
1600 TOR 90501 763-H7
2700 TOR 90501 793-G1
S GRAMERCY DR
700 LA 90005 633-H4
900 LA 90019 633-H4
GRAMERCY PK
2400 LA 90018 633-H6
E GRAMERCY PK
2400 LA 90018 633-H6
GRAMERCY PL
12900 GAR 90249 733-H2
15700 GAR 90247 733-H6
16600 TOR 90504 733-H6
17600 TOR 90504 763-H1
19000 TOR 90501 763-H3
N GRAMERCY PL
100 LA 90004 633-H1
200 LA 90004 593-H7
700 LA 90038 593-H7
1700 Hlwd 90028 593-H4
1900 LA 90068 593-G3
S GRAMERCY PL
100 LA 90004 633-H2
300 LA 90020 633-H2
600 LA 90005 633-H2
600 LA 90010 633-H2
900 LA 90019 633-H4
1900 LA 90018 633-H6
3400 LA 90018 673-H1
3700 LA 90062 673-H2
6000 LA 90047 673-H7
7200 LA 90047 703-H2
10000 LACo 90047 703-H6
GRAMERCY ST
2900 POM 91767 600-J3
6400 BPK 90621 767-G1
GRAMMAR PL
14100 PanC 91402 532-A1
GRAMMONT AV
900 COV 91724 599-G3
GRAMMONT PL
1600 GLDR 91740 599-G2
GRANADA AV
- LBCH 90803 826-B1
300 LBCH 90814 796-B7
300 LBCH 90814 826-B1
900 ALH 91801 596-B2
1200 SMRO 91108 596-B2
2300 SELM 91733 637-C3
2700 ELMN 91733 637-C2
3000 ELMN 91731 637-C1
3400 ELMN 91731 597-C7
15000 LMRD 90638 707-G7
N GRANADA AV
- ALH 91801 596-C3
600 SMRO 91108 596-C3
1300 LBCH 90804 796-B5
2200 LBCH 90815 796-B3
S GRANADA AV
- ALH 91801 596-C4
1800 ALH 91801 636-C1
GRANADA CIR
18800 Nor 91326 480-G7
GRANADA CT
200 Ven 90291 671-H6
300 LHB 90631 708-C5
4800 CHNO 91710 641-F7

W GRANADA CT
900 ONT 91762 601-H6
GRANADA DR
300 LHB 90631 708-C5
800 MONP 91754 635-G3
6500 PMDL 93551 4104-D7
7500 BPK 90621 737-H5
GRANADA LN
4800 LVRN 91750 570-G6
GRANADA PL
1600 POM 91767 601-D7
GRANADA ST
500 GLDL 91205 564-F6
1200 UPL 91784 571-J3
2600 LA 90065 594-H4
4200 MTCL 91763 601-E6
4800 HiPk 90042 595-B2
GRANARY SQ
- SCTA 91355 4550-F5
GRANBY PL
18800 RowH 91748 679-B7
GRAND AV
100 DBAR 91789 680-A2
100 INDS 91789 680-A2
100 MNRO 91016 567-H2
200 SPAS 91030 595-G1
500 DBAR 91765 680-A2
600 ELSG 90245 732-D2
600 LA 90245 732-D2
800 LBCH 90804 795-J6
1500 CHLS 91709 680-E3
2000 CLAR 91711 571-E5
2200 LBCH 90815 795-J4
2400 LACo 90255 704-J1
2700 LACo 90255 705-A1
2900 HNTP 90255 705-A1
3700 SBdC 91766 641-D3
4200 MTCL 91763 641-E3
4500 SBdC 91710 641-F3
4600 LCF 91011 535-B2
4700 MTCL 91710 641-F3
4800 SBdC 91763 641-F3
8200 BPK 90620 767-H4
8300 RSMD 91770 596-G5
8300 SGBL 91776 596-G5
8600 RSMD 91776 596-G5
10700 SBdC 91762 641-G1
10700 TEML 91780 597-C4
10800 ELMN 91780 597-C4
16200 BLF 90706 736-D6
E GRAND AV
- ALH 91801 596-C3
100 ELSG 90245 732-F1
100 POM 91766 640-J3
100 POM 91766 641-A3
100 SGBL 91776 596-F5
1600 SBdC 91766 641-A3
8300 RSMD 91770 596-F5
N GRAND AV
- INDS 91789 640-A7
- INDS 91789 680-A1
- LBCH 90803 825-J1
- PAS 91103 565-G4
100 ANA 92801 767-H5
100 COV 91724 599-D4
100 GLDR 91741 569-D3
100 LA 90012 634-G2
100 SPed 90731 824-B3
100 WCOV 91791 599-D4
100 COV 91723 599-D4
100 INDS 91789 639-J6
300 LBCH 90814 795-J7
300 LBCH 90814 825-J1
300 BPK 90620 767-H5
400 LACo 91789 639-J6
500 WAL 91789 639-H4
1300 LBCH 90804 795-J5
1300 COV 91722 599-D4
1800 LACo 91724 639-H4
1800 WCOV 91791 639-H4
2300 LBCH 90815 795-J3
4500 LACo 91724 599-D4
4500 LACo 91723 599-D4
4800 LACo 91722 599-D4
5700 GLDR 91740 599-D4
5800 GLDR 91740 569-D5
S GRAND AV
- PAS 91105 565-G6
100 ANA 92804 767-H6
100 GLDR 91741 569-D7
100 LA 90012 634-E4
100 SPed 90731 824-B6
100 WCOV 91791 599-D6
200 LA 90015 634-E4
200 WCOV 91791 639-E2
300 LA 90013 634-E4
300 LA 90071 634-E4
300 LACo 91724 639-E2
400 COV 91724 599-D6
400 COV 91723 599-D6
500 GLDR 91740 569-D7
600 LA 90014 634-E4
600 LA 90017 634-E4
1200 PAS 91105 595-G1
1300 GLDR 91740 599-D2
1900 LA 90007 634-C7
2200 LACo 91791 639-E2
2300 WCOV 91724 639-E2
2800 LA 90007 674-C2
3800 LA 90037 674-C4
5900 LA 90003 674-C7
7200 LA 90003 704-C1
10800 LA 90061 704-C6

W GRAND AV
- ALH 91801 596-A4
100 ELSG 90245 732-E1
100 POM 91766 640-G3
300 SGBL 91776 596-D5
1700 ALH 91801 595-H4
GRAND BLVD
200 Ven 90291 671-H6
GRAND CIR
9000 CYP 90630 767-F6
GRAND CANAL CT
2200 Ven 90291 671-H6
GRAND CANAL WK
2200 Ven 90291 671-H7
GRAND CANYON
800 BREA 92821 709-B5
GRAND CANYON RD
29700 SCTA 91387 4462-G6
GRAND CENTRAL AV
900 GLDL 91201 564-A2
GRAND CROSSING PKWY
- INDS 91789 679-H1
GRAND CYPRESS AV
- PMDL 93551 4195-H3
GRANDEE AV
12100 Wbrk 90059 734-G1
12400 Wbrk 90222 734-G1
19000 CRSN 90746 764-H2
N GRANDEE AV
600 COMP 90220 734-G3
1500 COMP 90222 734-G2
12300 Wbrk 90222 734-G2
S GRANDEE AV
900 COMP 90220 734-G6
9500 Wats 90002 704-G5
10400 LA 90059 704-G6
GRANDEUR AV
2700 Alta 91001 535-H4
N GRANDEUR AV
2200 Alta 91001 535-G6
GRANDEUR DR
2100 LA 90732 823-G6
GRANDEUR WY
42200 LACo 93536 4104-D5
42200 LAN 93536 4104-D5
GRANDE VISTA AV
400 LA 90063 635-B6
600 LA 90023 635-B6
1100 LA 90023 675-B1
S GRANDE VISTA AV
1200 LA 90023 675-B1
1600 VER 90023 675-B1
GRANDE VISTA DR
300 LACo 90601 677-B3
300 WHIT 90601 677-B3
GRANDE VISTA PL
11500 WHIT 90601 677-B3
GRANDEZA ST
400 MONP 91754 635-G3
GRANDIFLORAS RD
14400 SCTA 91387 4462-F5
GRANDIN AV
300 AZU 91702 598-J1
GRAND OAKS AV
1300 LACo 91104 566-D1
1500 LACo 91104 536-D7
N GRAND OAKS AV
- PAS 91107 566-D4
1600 Alta 91001 536-D7
S GRAND OAKS AV
- PAS 91107 566-D5
200 LACo 91107 566-D5
GRAND OAKS DR
- GLDR 91741 569-J5
GRANDOAKS DR
2600 WLKV 91361 557-A7
2600 WLKV 91361 587-A1
GRANDOLA AV
1500 Eagl 90041 565-B6
GRANDPARK AV
- LAN 93536 4104-E2
42300 LACo 93536 4104-E5
GRANDPOINT LN
29600 RPV 90275 823-G4
GRANDRIDGE AV
500 MONP 91754 636-A4
GRANDRIDGE PL
400 MONP 91754 636-A5
GRAND RIM CT
1200 DBAR 91765 680-C2
GRAND SUMMIT RD
2400 TOR 90505 793-E6
GRAND VIEW AV
1000 LACo 91770 636-F5
2300 Ven 90291 671-F6
2400 Ven 90291 672-A5
GRANDVIEW AV
- COV 91722 599-C3
- ARCD 91006 567-D1
600 FUL 92832 738-F6
700 GLDL 91201 564-B2
800 GLDL 91202 564-B2
1000 FUL 92835 738-F6
1200 SMAD 91024 567-D1
1500 MTBL 90640 676-C1
1600 GLDL 91202 534-B7
1600 GLDL 91201 534-B7
3300 MANB 90266 732-E4
E GRANDVIEW AV
- ARCD 91006 567-B1
200 SMAD 91024 567-B1
N GRANDVIEW AV
100 COV 91723 599-C4

N GRANDVIEW AV
900 COV 91722 599-C4
2100 MANB 90266 732-F5
S GRANDVIEW AV
100 COV 91723 599-C5
W GRANDVIEW AV
- SMAD 91024 567-A1
200 SMAD 91024 566-J1
GRAND VIEW BLVD
3000 LA 90066 672-B2
3900 CULC 90066 672-D5
GRAND VIEW DR
1500 ALH 91803 595-H7
1600 ALH 91803 635-H1
19400 Top 90290 590-B7
19400 Top 90290 630-A1
GRANDVIEW DR
- BREA 92823 709-H6
- PMDL 93551 4195-A3
- SCTA 91354 4460-G6
200 AZU 91702 598-H1
1200 CHLS 91709 710-G3
4500 PMDL 93551 4194-H3
8200 LA 90046 593-A4
8200 LA 90046 592-J4
27100 SCTA 91354 4550-F1
GRAND VIEW LN
700 LACo 91744 638-H6
1900 WCOV 91792 638-H6
GRAND VIEW ST
200 LA 90057 634-C2
900 LA 90006 634-B4
GRANDVIEW ST
1400 UPL 91784 571-H3
W GRANDVIEW ST
- PAS 91103 565-H1
300 PAS 91104 565-H1
GRANDVIEW TER
23200 Chat 91311 499-G6
GRAND VIEW TR
17800 LACo 93532 4101-J2
GRANDVIEW TR
11300 LACo 91342 482-J6
GRANDVIEW VISTA DR
18500 LACo 93591 4200-B4
GRAND VISTA PL
1200 MONP 91754 635-J4
GRAND VISTA WY
1200 MONP 91754 635-J4
GRANDWOOD DR
2300 FUL 92833 738-C3
GRANGE ST
800 GLDL 91202 564-B4
43400 LAN 93535 4106-D2
GRANGEMOUNT RD
3100 GLDL 91206 535-B7
GRANGER AV
6600 BGDN 90201 675-J7
6600 BGDN 90201 705-J1
GRANGER PL
- Cstc 91384 4459-G4
11000 Nor 91326 500-F2
GRANICY DR
1500 LAN 93535 4106-C1
GRANITE AV
400 MNRO 91016 567-H2
GRANITE CT
- SCTA 91354 4460-G4
6200 LAN 93536 4104-E5
GRANITE DR
800 PAS 91101 566-A6
800 PAS 91106 566-A6
GRANITE ST
40800 PMDL 93551 4194-H1
GRANITE RIDGE CT
- StvR 91381 4550-B4
GRANITE WELLS DR
20900 WAL 91789 639-G3
GRANITO DR
- LA 90046 593-B4
GRANO AV
27200 SCTA 91350 4461-A7
GRANT AV
- LACo 90073 631-J3
800 GLDL 91202 564-B3
1100 Ven 90291 672-A5
1700 RBCH 90278 762-J1
1900 RBCH 90278 763-A1
13300 DWNY 90242 735-J2
13300 PRM 90723 735-J2
21200 TOR 90503 763-C6
23100 TOR 90505 793-C2
GRANT CIR
8700 BPK 90620 767-H5
GRANT CT
6100 CHNO 91710 641-J6
37600 PMDL 93552 4287-C2
GRANT DR
- PMDL 93552 4287-C1
GRANT PL
1500 LVRN 91750 600-F1
GRANT PL N
1000 SMCA 90405 671-G3
GRANT ST
600 SMCA 90405 671-F3
600 Wilm 90744 794-F6
1700 MONP 91755 636-C4
11100 LYN 90262 704-J6
E GRANT ST
1600 Wilm 90744 794-H5
3200 LBCH 90755 795-J4
3200 SIGH 90755 795-J4

W GRANT ST
1100 Wilm 90744 794-C6
GRANTLAND DR
400 AZU 91702 599-B1
5300 LACo 91722 599-B2
GRANVIA ALTAMIRA
900 PVE 90274 792-J5
900 RPV 90275 792-J5
GRANVILLE AV
100 Brwd 90049 631-G3
1200 WLA 90025 631-J5
1900 WLA 90025 632-A6
2200 LA 90064 632-B7
2500 LA 90064 672-B1
3000 LA 90066 672-C2
GRANVILLE WY
1500 LAN 93535 4106-C2
GRAPE AV
200 COMP 90220 734-H4
N GRAPE AV
1600 COMP 90222 734-H2
GRAPE CIR
500 COMP 90220 734-H5
GRAPE PL
6300 LA 90068 593-F2
GRAPE ST
4600 PRV 90660 676-F3
8300 Flor 90001 704-H3
8600 Wats 90002 704-H3
9200 Wats 90002 704-H4
10700 LA 90059 704-H6
GRAPE LILY CIR
21400 SCTA 91321 4641-B2
GRAPE MYRTLE LN
- SCTA 91321 4641-C1
GRAPEVINE CT
- SIMI 93063 499-B1
GRAPEVINE DR
300 DBAR 91765 640-D7
GRAPEVINE ST
- PMDL 93551 4104-D7
GRAPEVINE FIRE RD
- Nwhl 91321 4641-C6
14500 LA 91342 481-D1
14500 LACo 91342 481-D1
14500 LACo 91342 4641-C6
GRAPHIC AV
36800 Litl 93543 4288-A4
44400 LACo 93535 4017-J6
GRASS DR
1000 PMDL 93551 4195-G7
GRASSCREEK DR
1600 SDMS 91773 570-D6
GRASSHOPPER FIRE RD
- Cstc 91384 4279-E5
- Cstc 91384 4369-F1
- LACo - 4279-C3
GRASSLAND CT
- LAN 93536 4013-J5
GRASSLANDS TR
- LACo 91302 588-F5
GRASSMERE AV
500 LACo 91792 679-B2
3900 WCOV 91792 679-B2
GRASS MOUNTAIN RD
- LACo 91390 4102-D7
GRASSWOOD AV
6900 MAL 90265 667-E3
GRASSY KNOLL LN
- SCTA 91354 4460-F6
GRATIAN ST
4300 ELA 90022 635-F6
GRATIOT ST
2200 LA 90032 635-E1
GRATLAND DR
- SCTA 91351 4551-E3
GRATTAN ST
900 LA 90015 634-C4
GRAVELIA ST
1000 Alta 91001 535-F3
GRAVES AV
5600 Enc 91316 561-C1
6400 VanN 91406 531-C7
7400 LACo 91770 636-E3
7400 RSMD 91770 636-E3
E GRAVES AV
100 MONP 91755 636-C3
900 MONP 91770 636-C3
W GRAVES AV
300 MONP 91754 636-A3
GRAVEYARD TKTR
- Tuj 91042 504-A1
- Tuj 91042 (4724-A6
See Page 4643)
GRAVINA ST
19500 RowH 91748 679-D5
GRAVINO RD
23600 SCTA 91355 4550-G5
GRAVLEY CT
500 HMB 90254 762-H2
GRAVOIS AV
1500 City 90063 635-F3
GRAY DR
- SMRO 91108 566-D7
GRAY LN
- SCTA 91351 4551-E3
GRAYBAR AV
900 LACo 91744 638-G5
GRAYBURN AV
3600 LA 90018 673-F2
3700 LA 90008 673-F2
GRAYBURN RD
3200 LACo 91107 566-G5

GRAYBURN RD
3400 PAS 91107 566-G5
GRAYBURN ST
2900 POM 91767 600-J3
GRAYCASTLE AV
1600 MTBL 90640 636-F5
S GRAYDON AV
1900 LACo 91016 567-G7
GRAYFOX ST
28700 MAL 90265 667-E3
GRAYLAND AV
14300 NRWK 90650 736-H4
17100 CRTS 90703 736-H7
17400 ART 90701 736-H7
17800 ART 90701 766-H2
19900 CRTS 90703 766-J3
GRAYLING AV
10100 WHIT 90603 708-A4
11700 LACo 90604 708-B7
12400 LACo 90604 738-B1
12700 LMRD 90638 738-B1
GRAYLOCK AV
1800 MONP 91754 636-A5
GRAYLOG ST
5500 RPV 90275 793-A5
GRAYMOUTH LN
800 LACo 90502 794-C3
GRAYNOLD AV
800 GLDL 91202 564-B2
GRAYRIDGE DR
11200 CULC 90230 672-H5
GRAYSBY AV
2500 LA 90732 823-H7
2700 LA 90732 853-H1
GRAYSLAKE RD
26200 RPV 90275 793-A5
26600 RPV 90275 792-J6
GRAYSON AV
2800 Ven 90291 671-J7
GRAYSTONE AV
11200 NRWK 90650 736-F1
11700 NRWK 90650 706-F7
16600 LACo 90703 736-F6
17400 CRTS 90703 736-F7
GRAYSTONE DR
7600 LA 91304 529-D4
GRAYSTONE ST
8000 Sunl 91040 503-G2
GRAYSTONE WY
18100 RowH 91748 708-H2
GRAYVILLE DR
2300 LHB 90631 738-B1
14200 LMRD 90638 737-E1
16100 LMRD 90638 738-A1
GRAYWOOD AV
4300 LBCH 90808 766-A5
4700 LKWD 90712 766-A2
GRAZIA LN
- StvR 91381 4640-D1
GREASEWOOD LN
1500 SBdC 92372 (4472-D2
See Page 4471)
GREAT BEND DR
400 DBAR 91765 680-B1
GREAT LAKES AV
16600 LACo 93535 4109-G6
GREAT LAKES CT
- SCTA 91350 4550-H6
GREAT MOUNTAIN DR
- WCOV 91791 639-D1
GREAT OAK CIR
5900 HiPk 90042 565-D7
E GREAT SMOKEY CT
2800 THO 91362 557-C3
W GREAT SMOKEY CT
2700 THO 91362 557-B3
GREAT WESTERN DR
3000 LAN 93536 4015-B1
3500 LAN 93536 3925-A7
GREELEY CT
800 SDMS 91773 600-C1
GREELEY ST
6400 Tuj 91042 504-A4
GREEN AV
800 LA 90017 634-C4
3500 LALM 90720 796-J3
GREEN DR
17000 INDS 91745 678-F3
GREEN LN
500 RBCH 90278 763-A2
700 LCF 91011 535-A2
2100 RBCH 90278 733-A7
GREEN RD
1600 SBdC 92372 (4472-D7
See Page 4471)
8100 SBdC 92372 (4562-C1
See Page 4471)
GREEN ST
800 GLDL 91205 564-F7
10000 TEML 91780 597-B4
E GREEN ST
- PAS 91105 565-J5
100 CLAR 91711 601-D4
200 PAS 91101 565-J5
500 PAS 91101 566-A5
800 PAS 91106 566-A5
3100 LACo 91107 566-G4
3100 PAS 91107 566-G4
W GREEN ST
- PAS 91105 565-G5
100 CLAR 91711 601-D4
GREENACRE AV
1100 WHWD 90046 593-C5

GREEN ACRE DR
500 FUL 92835 738-F4
GREEN ACRE RD
2000 FUL 92835 738-F4
GREENACRE RD
1300 POM 91768 600-E7
GREEN ACRES DR
1700 BHLS 90210 592-D6
E GREEN ACRES LN
100 LAN 93535 4015-J6
GREENBANK AV
200 DUAR 91010 568-E4
GREENBANK RD
2400 VeCo 91361 586-D1
GREENBAY DR
18500 RowH 91748 679-A4
GREENBERRY AV
4400 LACo 91722 598-G4
N GREENBERRY AV
700 WCOV 91790 598-G5
700 LACo 91722 598-G5
GREENBERRY DR
300 LPUE 91744 638-B5
700 LACo 91744 638-D3
S GREENBERRY DR
700 WCOV 91790 638-F1
GREENBLUFF DR
21400 Top 90290 590-B7
GREENBOROUGH PL
2600 WCOV 91792 638-J7
GREENBRIAR CT
5900 AGRH 91301 558-A4
GREENBRIAR DR
19400 Tarz 91356 560-F5
GREENBRIAR LN
100 LPUE 91744 638-E7
100 LPUE 91744 678-E1
GREENBRIAR PL
2600 WCOV 91792 638-J7
8900 BPK 90621 738-B6
GREENBRIAR RD
1200 GLDL 91207 564-F1
GREENBRIER AV
13500 BLF 90706 736-B3
GREENBRIER DR
- HacH 91745 637-H7
GREENBRIER LN
2200 LHB 90631 708-B7
2300 LHB 90631 738-B1
4100 Tarz 91356 560-J5
N GREENBRIER RD
1300 LBCH 90815 796-B2
3000 LBCH 90808 796-B2
3400 LBCH 90808 766-B6
GREENBRIER ST
- PMDL 93551 4285-D3
GREENBROOK CIR
16600 CRTS 90703 737-A6
GREENBROOK DR
21200 WAL 91789 639-H7
GREENBROOK LN
37600 PMDL 93550 4286-E2
GREENBURN AV
10500 Sunl 91040 503-H3
GREENBUSH AV
4100 Shrm 91423 562-C3
5400 VanN 91401 562-C2
6000 VanN 91401 532-C6
7300 NHol 91605 532-C4
7600 PanC 91402 532-D1
8800 Pcma 91331 502-B6
10400 LACo 90604 707-G5
GREEN CANYON WY
5200 PMDL 93551 4194-G3
GREENCASTLE AV
1300 RowH 91748 679-A4
GREEN COACH RD
16700 HacH 91745 678-E4
GREENCOURT DR
14500 LACo 91387 4462-G5
14500 SCTA 91387 4462-G5
GREENCRAIG RD
400 Brwd 90049 631-F2
GREENCREST DR
4600 SCTA 91321 4640-J4
GREENCREST RD
5100 LCF 91011 535-C2
GREENCREST WY
4700 PMDL 93551 4194-H1
GREENCROFT AV
100 GLDR 91741 569-J5
GREENDALE AV
3700 RSMD 91770 596-H7
8900 RSMD 91770 636-H1
GREENDALE DR
300 LACo 91746 637-H5
10300 BelA 90077 592-B6
GREENDALE LN
600 POM 91767 601-A1
GREENDALE ST
500 COV 91723 599-A6
E GREENDALE ST
1000 WCOV 91790 598-G6
W GREENDALE ST
1000 WCOV 91790 598-G6
GREENE AV
12100 LA 90066 672-D5
GREENFIELD AV
100 Brwd 90049 631-J1
1000 ARCD 91006 567-D7
1400 WLA 90025 632-B5
2200 ARCD 91006 597-D2
2200 LA 90064 632-C6

GREENFIELD AV
3000 LA 90034 632-C6
3000 LA 90034 672-D1
GREENFIELD CT
1400 GLDR 91740 599-F1
GREENFIELD PL
100 ARCD 91006 567-D7
GREEN GABLES DR
3700 Tarz 91356 560-F6
GREENGATE CT
4500 WLKV 91361 557-D6
GREENGATE DR
18700 RowH 91748 679-A4
GREENGLADE AV
3200 PRV 90660 677-A1
3200 PRV 90660 676-J1
GREEN GRASS CT
29400 AGRH 91301 557-J5
29400 AGRH 91301 558-A5
GREENGROVE DR
2200 GLDL 91206 565-A4
GREENHAVEN ST
500 COV 91722 599-D3
1300 SDMS 91773 599-H3
1700 LACo 91724 599-D3
2000 COV 91724 599-G3
19300 LACo 91722 599-D3
21300 LACo 91773 599-H3
E GREENHAVEN ST
200 COV 91722 599-C3
16600 LACo 91722 598-G3
W GREENHAVEN ST
1000 COV 91722 598-H3
GREENHEDGE LN
- POM 91766 640-F7
- POM 91766 641-A4
GREENHEDGE ST
700 LACo 90502 764-B5
W GREENHEDGE ST
1000 LACo 90502 764-A5
GREEN HILL DR
31900 Cstc 91384 4369-F5
GREENHILL DR
2500 FUL 92833 738-C5
GREENHILL RD
3500 PAS 91107 566-H3
GREEN HILLS DR
- LA 90032 595-E4
- RPV 90275 793-H7
- RPV 90275 823-J1
GREENHORN DR
600 DBAR 91765 640-B6
GREENHURST ST
10400 BLF 90706 736-D3
GREENING AV
9400 LACo 90605 707-C3
GREEN IVY DR
500 BREA 92821 709-C7
GREENJAY PL
20000 SCTA 91351 4551-E3
GREENLAKE LN
16400 CRTS 90703 736-J4
GREENLAWN AV
11100 LA 90230 672-F4
GREENLEAF AV
5400 WHIT 90601 677-C4
7000 WHIT 90602 677-C7
7700 WHIT 90602 707-C2
9200 WHIT 90605 707-C2
9200 SFSP 90670 707-B4
9300 LACo 90605 707-B4
9800 SFSP 90605 707-B4
E GREENLEAF BLVD
- NLB 90805 735-C6
100 COMP 90220 734-J6
100 COMP 90220 735-A6
300 COMP 90221 735-A6
W GREENLEAF BLVD
100 COMP 90220 734-H6
1400 CRSN 90220 734-H6
GREENLEAF CT
- StvR 91381 4550-C4
3100 WCOV 91792 639-A7
GREENLEAF DR
- SCTA 91351 4551-G7
800 COMP 90220 734-H6
1800 WCOV 91792 638-J6
1900 WCOV 91792 639-A7
GREENLEAF PL
- POM 91766 640-G7
GREENLEAF ST
3000 WCOV 91792 639-A7
12900 LA 91604 562-D5
14000 Shrm 91423 562-A5
14400 Shrm 91403 562-A5
14500 Shrm 91403 561-G4
15400 Enc 91436 561-G4
17500 Enc 91316 561-B3
GREENLEAF CANYON RD
400 Top 90290 590-A3
GREEN MEADOW CT
4100 Enc 91316 561-A5
GREEN MEADOW DR
5700 AGRH 91301 557-H4
18000 Enc 91316 561-A5
18200 Enc 91316 560-J5
GREENMEADOW DR
3300 FUL 92835 738-J2
GREENMEADOW RD
2400 LKWD 90712 765-G6
6000 LKWD 90713 766-D6
E GREENMEADOW RD
4400 LBCH 90808 766-A6

GREENMEADOWS AV
4400 TOR 90505 793-B2
GREENMEADOWS ST
5500 TOR 90505 793-A2
GREEN MILL AV
24900 SCTA 91321 4640-G2
GREENMONT DR
1300 GLDL 91208 534-G4
GREEN MOUNTAIN DR
19300 SCTA 91321 4551-F6
GREENOAK CT
- LMRD 90638 738-B3
GREEN OAK DR
5500 LA 90068 593-G2
GREEN OAK LN
900 GLDR 91741 569-F3
GREEN OAK PL
2600 LA 90068 593-H2
GREENOAKS DR
1400 ARCD 91006 566-J3
GREENOCK LN
12100 Brwd 90049 631-G2
GREEN PALMS WY
- LACo 91387 4552-A4
GREENPARK AV
600 COV 91724 599-F3
5000 LACo 91724 599-F3
GREENPORT AV
1300 RowH 91748 679-B4
GREENRIDGE DR
600 LCF 91011 535-C1
1400 LA 90210 592-D5
GREEN RIDGE TER
- WCOV 91791 639-B4
GREENRIDGE TER
- HacH 91745 637-J7
GREENRIDGE WY
23800 SCTA 91354 4460-F7
23800 SCTA 91354 4550-F1
GREEN RIVER RD
34000 LACo 91390 4373-B2
GREENRIVER RD
600 WAL 91789 639-F7
GREENROCK AV
15100 LACo 93535 4109-D7
GREENS CT
16100 CHLS 91709 710-G1
GREENS DR
1500 CHLS 91709 710-G1
GREENSBORO CT
400 CLAR 91711 601-D1
GREENSBRIER DR
- StvR 91381 4640-B2
GREENSIDE DR
20700 DBAR 91789 679-G3
GREENSLEEVES CT
21700 SCTA 91350 4461-B6
GREENSLEEVES WY
- Nor 91326 480-D7
GREEN SPRING LN
2300 HacH 91745 678-E5
GREENSTONE AV
11000 SFSP 90670 707-A7
12200 SFSP 90670 737-A1
13200 NRWK 90650 737-A3
GREENSWARD RD
3400 LA 90039 594-D2
GREEN TERRACE DR
26300 SCTA 91321 4551-E5
GREENTOP ST
2400 LKWD 90712 765-G5
5900 LKWD 90713 766-D5
GREEN TREE CT
44100 LAN 93535 4016-D7
GREENTREE CT
3000 BelA 90077 562-A7
3000 BelA 90077 592-A1
GREEN TREE LN
11000 TEML 91780 597-D3
GREENTREE LN
100 LHB 90631 708-G5
GREEN TREE PKWY E
- PMDL 93550 4106-A7
GREEN TREE PKWY W
- PMDL 93550 4106-A6
GREENTREE RD
700 PacP 90272 631-B6
GREENTREE ST
2000 LAN 93535 4016-D6
GREENVALE AV
8100 PRV 90660 706-G2
GREENVALE CIR
1200 UPL 91784 571-J6
GREEN VALLEY CIR
5900 CULC 90230 672-H6
6200 LadH 90056 672-H7
GREENVALLEY RD
2400 LA 90046 592-H2
GREEN VALLEY TER
11400 Pcma 91331 502-F1
GREEN VERDUGO DR
9500 Sunl 91040 503-D4
GREEN VERDUGO FIRE RD
8700 Sunl 91040 503-D4
GREENVIEW DR
1200 LHB 90631 708-C4
2300 GLDR 91741 570-A6
GREEN VIEW LN
1800 LVRN 91750 570-G4
GREEN VIEW PL
2400 LA 90046 592-H2

GREEN VIEW RD
400 LHH 90631 708-D1
GREENVIEW RD
5800 CALB 91302 558-J3
GREENVIEW TER
- HacH 91745 637-G6
E GREENVILLE DR
700 WCOV 91790 638-F3
1600 WCOV 91791 638-J3
1900 WCOV 91791 639-A2
GREEN VISTA CIR
7000 CanP 91307 529-F5
GREEN VISTA DR
3400 Enc 91436 561-D6
GREENWATER RD
29200 MAL 90265 667-E4
GREENWAY DR
800 BHLS 90210 632-D1
800 Wwd 90024 632-D1
GREENWAY LN
4300 CHNO 91710 641-E4
N GREENWAY ST
6000 LBCH 90803 796-D7
S GREENWAY ST
6000 LBCH 90803 796-D7
GREENWAY TER
600 LHB 90631 708-F4
GREENWELL ST
9300 BLF 90706 736-A4
GREENWICH CT
1000 DBAR 91765 680-D2
37400 PMDL 93550 4286-E3
GREENWICH DR
2300 FUL 92833 738-B3
GREENWICH RD
1700 SDMS 91773 599-H4
2700 GLDL 91206 565-B2
GREENWICH VILLAGE
2600 HMB 90254 762-F1
GREENWILLOW LN
19300 RowH 91748 679-D6
GREENWOOD AV
500 PAS 91107 566-D6
500 SMRO 91108 566-D6
1000 MTBL 90640 676-B7
1200 TOR 90503 763-F6
1900 MONP 91755 636-D5
3300 LA 90066 672-A3
3500 CMRC 90040 676-B7
6200 BGDN 90040 676-B7
6200 CMRC 90040 706-B1
6200 BGDN 90040 706-B1
9600 MTCL 91763 601-F6
22500 TOR 90505 793-F1
E GREENWOOD AV
100 LHB 90631 708-E5
8700 LACo 91775 566-H7
N GREENWOOD AV
- PAS 91107 566-D4
100 MTBL 90640 676-D1
S GREENWOOD AV
- PAS 91107 566-D5
100 MTBL 90640 676-C4
W GREENWOOD AV
100 LHB 90631 708-D5
GREENWOOD CT
300 POM 91766 641-A5
2100 FUL 92833 738-C3
GREENWOOD LN
2000 POM 91766 641-A5
GREENWOOD PL
4600 LFlz 90027 594-A3
28600 Cstc 91384 4459-F1
GREENWOOD WY
- LA 90068 563-F4
4700 SBdC 91710 641-F3
GREENWORTH DR
14500 LMRD 90638 737-E2
GREER AV
300 COV 91724 599-G4
1400 GLDR 91740 599-G2
5000 LACo 91724 599-G3
GREER RD
4200 WdHl 91364 559-G5
GREER ST
- NLB 90805 735-G7
GREG AV
7500 SunV 91352 533-C3
GREGG RD
4800 PRV 90660 676-H4
GREGORIO
18000 LACo 90220 765-A1
GREGORIO DR
16300 HacH 91745 678-D5
GREGORY AV
1600 FUL 92833 738-B7
2100 PMDL 93550 4286-E2
5500 WHIT 90601 677-B4
5800 LA 90038 593-F6
GREGORY CIR
8200 BPK 90621 737-J6
GREGORY LN
1800 LHB 90631 708-B5
26700 SCTA 91351 4551-E4
GREGORY ST
9100 CYP 90630 767-C6
GREGORY WY
800 LA 90035 632-J2
800 BHLS 90211 632-J2
6600 BHLS 90211 633-A3
6600 LA 90048 633-A3
9100 BHLS 90212 632-F3

STREET	Block	City	ZIP	Pg-Grid
GRENADA CT				
	-	MANB	90266	732-H4
GRENADIER DR				
	1700	LA	90732	823-G6
GRENOBLE AV				
	1500	WCOV	91791	638-J4
GRENOBLE CT				
	30800	WLKV	91362	557-G7
GRENOBLE LN				
	16300	HNTB	92649	826-J6
GRENOBLE ST				
	6800	Tuj	91042	504-B3
	8200	Sunl	91040	503-G3
GRENOLA ST				
	300	PacP	90272	630-H6
E GRENORA WY				
	4000	LBCH	90815	796-A4
GRENVILLE CT				
	32000	WLKV	91361	557-C6
GRESHAM PL				
	8800	LA	91304	530-A1
GRESHAM ST				
	15200	LA	91343	501-F7
	16600	LA	91343	531-D1
	16900	Nor	91325	531-A1
	18100	Nor	91325	530-J1
	18400	Nor	91324	530-E1
	20100	Win	91306	530-C1
	20900	LA	91304	530-A1
	22000	LA	91304	529-J1
GRETCHEN PL				
	400	POM	91768	640-C2
GRETCHEN ST				
	20800	Win	91306	530-C6
GRETCHEN WY				
	-	PMDL	93536	4194-H1
	-	PMDL	93551	4194-H1
GRETNA AV				
	6200	WHIT	90601	677-B6
	6500	WHIT	90606	677-B6
	6500	LACo	90606	677-A7
	7700	LACo	90606	676-J7
GRETNA GREEN WY				
	700	Brwd	90049	631-G4
S GRETNA GREEN WY				
	100	Brwd	90049	631-G3
GRETTA AV				
	900	LACo	91744	638-G5
S GRETTA AV				
	500	WCOV	91790	638-G1
	1800	LACo	91744	638-H3
	1800	WCOV	91744	638-H3
GREVE DR				
	3600	RPV	90275	823-F4
GREVELIA ST				
	800	SPAS	91030	595-G1
GREVILLEA AV				
	11400	HAW	90250	703-C7
	11800	HAW	90250	733-C2
	14300	LNDL	90260	733-C5
	17300	LNDL	90260	763-C2
	18200	TOR	90278	763-C2
	19900	TOR	90503	763-C4
N GREVILLEA AV				
	100	ING	90301	703-C2
S GREVILLEA AV				
	200	ING	90301	703-C4
	10000	ING	90304	703-C5
	10000	Lenx	90304	703-C5
	11100	HAW	90304	703-C5
E GREVILLIA ST				
	200	POM	91767	600-J4
	200	POM	91767	601-A4
W GREVILLIA ST				
	100	POM	91767	600-J4
GREY DR				
	4600	LA	90032	595-D6
GREY PL				
	-	StvR	91381	4550-A6
GREYCLIFF AV				
	600	LPUE	91744	638-F6
	1000	LACo	91744	638-F5
	11200	MTCL	91763	641-F3
GREYCLOUD LN				
	800	DBAR	91765	640-E5
GREYCREST PL				
	1200	DBAR	91765	680-D3
GREYDALE AV				
	8200	Litl	93543	4287-H5
GREYDALE DR				
	700	GLDL	91203	564-C3
GREYFIELD LN				
	3600	DBAR	91765	709-G1
GREYFORD ST				
	10900	LACo	90606	676-H7
	11800	LACo	90606	677-A7
	11800	LACo	90606	707-A1
GREY FOX RD				
	19500	WAL	91789	639-D7
GREYHALL ST				
	19200	RowH	91748	679-C5
GREY HAWK PL				
	-	GrnH	91344	481-A7
GREY ROCK RD				
	5600	AGRH	91301	558-A4
	5700	AGRH	91301	557-J3
GREY STALLION RD				
	15200	LACo	93535	4199-D1
E GREYSTONE AV				
	100	MNRO	91016	567-H3
W GREYSTONE AV				
	100	MNRO	91016	567-G3
GREYSTONE CT				
	-	SCTA	91354	4460-F5
	1500	SDMS	91773	599-G5
GREYSTONE DR				
	16500	LMRD	90638	738-B1
GRIDER AV				
	13300	HAW	90250	733-A2
GRIDLEY PL				
	16800	CRTS	90703	736-G6
GRIDLEY RD				
	10100	SFSP	90670	706-F5
	11900	NRWK	90650	706-F7
	12100	NRWK	90650	736-F2
	16600	CRTS	90703	736-G7
	16600	LACo	90703	736-G6
	17100	ART	90701	736-G7
	17800	ART	90701	766-G2
	17800	CRTS	90703	766-G2
	20700	LKWD	90715	766-G5
GRIDLEY ST				
	12500	LA	91342	482-E3
	13400	LA	91340	482-C5
	13500	SFER	91340	482-C5
GRIER ST				
	1700	POM	91766	640-E3
GRIFFIN AV				
	1700	LA	90031	635-A1
	2800	LA	90031	595-B6
	4700	HiPk	90042	595-B6
N GRIFFIN AV				
	2400	LA	90031	595-A7
	2400	LA	90031	635-A1
GRIFFITH AV				
	1400	LA	90021	634-F7
	1400	LACo	91744	638-E4
	1900	LA	90011	634-F7
	2000	LA	90011	674-E2
GRIFFITH DR				
	-	Saug	91350	4461-F5
GRIFFITH LN				
	8000	WHIT	90602	707-D1
GRIFFITH ST				
	-	AZU	91702	569-B4
	100	CRSN	90248	764-C2
	600	SFER	91340	502-A1
	1200	SFER	91340	482-A7
	1300	SFER	91340	481-J7
GRIFFITH PARK BLVD				
	1500	Echo	90026	594-C5
	1700	LA	90039	594-C5
	2700	LFlz	90027	594-C2
GRIFFITH PARK DR				
	-	LFlz	90027	563-H4
	3400	LFlz	90027	594-C1
	4100	LFlz	90027	564-A5
N GRIFFITH PARK DR				
	100	BURB	91506	563-F1
	500	BURB	91506	533-F7
S GRIFFITH PARK DR				
	200	BURB	91506	563-G2
GRIFFITH VIEW DR				
	3700	LA	90039	594-D1
GRIGGS LN				
	10200	Tuj	91042	504-B4
GRIMAUD LN				
	16400	HNTB	92649	826-J7
GRIMES PL				
	4200	Enc	91316	561-A5
GRIMKE WK				
	-	HiPk	90042	595-E4
GRIMSBY AV				
	8100	Wch	90045	702-J2
GRINDLAY ST				
	5000	CYP	90630	767-C5
GRINNELL DR				
	200	BURB	91502	533-G6
	400	BURB	91501	533-H6
W GRINNELL DR				
	400	CLAR	91711	601-C3
GRISCOM DR				
	-	Actn	93510	4374-B6
GRISHAM AV				
	4600	NLB	90805	765-D5
GRISMER AV				
	1500	BURB	91504	533-F5
GRISSOM DR				
	1500	SPed	90731	823-J7
GRISSOM PARK DR				
	1400	FUL	92833	738-E4
GRISWOLD AV				
	300	SFER	91340	482-B7
W GRISWOLD RD				
	700	COV	91722	598-J4
	17900	LACo	91722	599-A4
GRISWOLD ST				
	300	GLDL	91205	564-G5
GRIZZLY FLATS TKTR				
	-	LACo	-	505-A2
GROFF ST				
	800	POM	91768	600-G7
GROMER TER				
	3400	GLDL	91214	504-E5
GROMMON WY				
	-	SCTA	91351	4551-E3
GRONDAHL ST				
	500	COV	91722	599-A3
	800	COV	91722	598-J3
W GRONDAHL ST				
	100	COV	91722	599-A3
	700	COV	91722	598-J3
GROOM DR				
	600	DBAR	91765	640-B6
GROSS AV				
	6400	CanP	91307	529-F7
GROSSMONT DR				
	1000	LACo	90601	637-F5
GROSVENOR BLVD				
	5300	LA	90066	672-E6
	5300	LACo	90066	672-E6
W GROSVENOR ST				
	100	ING	90302	703-C1
GROTON DR				
	400	BURB	91504	533-F4
GROVE AL				
	400	SMAD	91024	566-J1
GROVE LN				
	44600	LAN	93534	4015-E6
GROVE PL				
	-	HacH	91745	637-G6
	300	FUL	92832	738-H6
	400	GLDL	91206	564-G3
GROVE ST				
	-	SMAD	91024	566-J1
	2500	LVRN	91750	600-H2
	5200	SBdC	91762	641-G1
	5200	SBdC	91763	641-G1
	7600	Tuj	91042	503-H2
	8000	Sunl	91040	503-G2
E GROVE ST				
	100	POM	91767	600-J2
	100	POM	91767	601-A2
	500	LACo	91711	601-A2
W GROVE ST				
	100	POM	91767	600-J2
GROVE TER				
	-	PRV	90660	676-F6
GROVECENTER ST				
	900	COV	91722	598-H5
E GROVECENTER ST				
	300	COV	91723	599-C5
	1000	WCOV	91790	598-G5
	1400	COV	91724	599-F5
	1800	WCOV	91791	598-G5
	15600	LACo	91722	598-E5
W GROVECENTER ST				
	1000	WCOV	91790	598-E5
	16300	LACo	91722	598-G5
GROVEDALE DR				
	9800	WHIT	90603	707-J4
	9800	WHIT	90603	708-A3
	11400	LACo	90604	707-J6
	12400	LACo	90604	737-J1
	12600	LMRD	90638	737-J1
GROVE HILL CT				
	300	BREA	92821	709-E7
GROVEHILL LN				
	15400	LMRD	90638	737-H1
GROVE HOUSE DR				
	-	SCTA	91354	4460-F4
GROVELAND AV				
	10100	WHIT	90603	707-J4
	11300	LACo	90604	707-J6
GROVELAND DR				
	2100	LA	90046	592-J3
GROVELAND LN				
	4700	LCF	91011	535-B3
GROVEOAK PL				
	6000	RPV	90275	792-J5
GROVEPARK DR				
	21500	SCTA	91350	4461-A6
	22100	SCTA	91350	4460-J6
GROVER AV				
	1000	GLDL	91201	564-A2
GROVER CIR				
	1700	SIMI	93063	499-A2
GROVERDALE ST				
	500	COV	91722	599-D3
	1300	COV	91724	599-D3
	19300	LACo	91722	599-D3
	19600	LACo	91724	599-D3
E GROVERDALE ST				
	200	COV	91722	599-B3
	16700	LACo	91722	598-H3
W GROVERDALE ST				
	500	COV	91722	599-A3
GROVERTON PL				
	100	BelA	90077	632-A1
GROVESIDE AV				
	10100	WHIT	90603	707-J4
	11300	LACo	90604	707-J6
	11900	LACo	90604	708-A7
	12400	LACo	90604	737-J1
	12600	LMRD	90638	738-A1
GROVESIDE PL				
	1300	POM	91768	600-E7
GROVESPRING DR				
	6900	RPV	90275	822-G1
GROVETON AV				
	700	SDMS	91773	600-A1
	700	GLDR	91740	600-A1
	800	GLDR	91740	570-A7
GROVETREE AV				
	12700	DWNY	90242	705-H7
GROVEVIEW LN				
	600	LCF	91011	535-C3
GRUBSTAKE DR				
	1200	DBAR	91765	680-C3
GRUEN ST				
	11600	LA	91342	482-G7
	12400	Pcma	91331	502-F2
GRUNDY LN				
	9100	Chat	91311	499-E7
GUADALAJARA CIR				
	12900	CRTS	90703	767-B1
GUADALAJARA PL				
	1400	CLAR	91711	601-E2
GUADALAJARA WY				
	4700	BPK	90621	737-J4
GUADALUPE				
	2600	LACo	90220	765-A1
N GUADALUPE AV				
	100	RBCH	90277	762-J4
S GUADALUPE AV				
	100	RBCH	90277	762-J6
GUADILAMAR DR				
	22400	SCTA	91350	4460-H6
GUANAJUATO DR				
	800	CLAR	91711	571-B6
GUARDIA AV				
	3900	LA	90032	595-F5
GUARDIAN DR				
	-	CYP	90630	767-B5
GUATEMALA AV				
	8600	DWNY	90240	706-B1
GUATEMALA WY				
	5700	BPK	90620	767-D3
GUAVA PL				
	300	BREA	92821	709-C7
GUAVA ST				
	4200	LVRN	91750	570-H7
	4200	LVRN	91750	600-H1
GUAVA WY				
	-	PMDL	93551	4285-E3
GUERIN ST				
	12000	LA	91604	562-G5
GUERNSEY AV				
	6400	MAL	90265	667-A1
GUESS ST				
	8500	RSMD	91770	596-G7
	9400	RSMD	91770	597-A7
GUEST DR				
	2200	ALH	91803	636-A1
GUIANA CIR				
	7300	BPK	90620	767-E2
GUILD DR				
	6500	PRV	90660	676-F5
GUILDFORD LN				
	18100	Nor	91326	500-J1
GUILDHALL CT				
	4400	WLKV	91361	557-E6
GUILFORD AV				
	8600	WHIT	90605	707-D2
	9400	LACo	90605	707-C3
S GUILFORD AV				
	300	CLAR	91711	601-C5
GUILFORD LN				
	28100	SCTA	91350	4461-B5
GUILFORD PL				
	1500	Hrbr	90710	793-J2
GUILFORD WY				
	7200	WHIT	90602	677-D7
GUINEA DR				
	800	LACo	90601	637-G5
GUIRADO ST				
	2600	LA	90023	635-B6
GUITA CT				
	39600	PMDL	93551	4195-C4
GULANA AV				
	8100	PdlR	90293	702-C3
	8600	Wch	90045	702-C3
GULCH RD				
	1400	SPed	90731	824-C6
GULF AV				
	200	Wilm	90744	794-D5
	4800	NLB	90805	765-C4
	22000	CRSN	90745	764-D7
	22700	CRSN	90745	794-D1
GULFCREST DR				
	3400	RPV	90275	823-E6
GULL ST				
	100	MANB	90266	732-E3
GULLO AV				
	8500	PanC	91402	532-C1
	8800	Pcma	91331	502-A5
	9900	Pcma	91331	501-J5
GUM PL				
	400	BREA	92821	709-B6
GUMBINER DR				
	16600	LACo	91744	638-G6
GUMTREE DR				
	14300	LACo	93532	4102-H5
GUMTREE PL				
	29000	SCTA	91390	4460-J2
GUN AV				
	12600	CHNO	91710	641-E6
GUN CLUB RD				
	-	AZU	91702	568-G2
GUNDERSON AV				
	13400	DWNY	90242	735-J3
GUNDRY AV				
	400	Bxby	90807	765-F3
	1300	LBCH	90813	795-F4
	2100	SIGH	90755	795-F1
	3300	Bxby	90807	795-F1
	5200	NLB	90805	765-F2
	6300	NLB	90805	735-F7
	14300	PRM	90723	735-F3
GUNDRY CT				
	1100	LBCH	90813	795-F6
GUNLOCK AV				
	1000	COMP	90220	734-G6
S GUNLOCK AV				
	19000	CRSN	90746	764-H3
GUNN AV				
	8900	WHIT	90603	707-E3
	8900	WHIT	90605	707-E3
	9400	LACo	90604	707-E3
	9400	LACo	90605	707-C5
	10400	SFSP	90605	707-C5
GUNNELL AV				
	2500	LA	90732	823-H7
GUNNER LN				
	1500	SIMI	93063	499-B3
GUNNISON TR				
	1500	Top	90290	589-G3
GUNSMOKE AV				
	-	POM	91766	640-F5
GUNSMOKE CT				
	39200	PMDL	93551	4195-E6
GUNSMOKE DR				
	100	DBAR	91765	640-B6
N GUNSTON DR				
	100	Brwd	90049	631-G1
S GUNSTON DR				
	100	Brwd	90049	631-H2
GUNTER RD				
	28600	RPV	90275	823-H2
GUNTHER ST				
	16400	GrnH	91344	481-C7
W GUNTHER WY				
	100	LBCH	90806	795-D3
GUNTON DR				
	38200	PMDL	93550	4286-A1
GUN TREE DR				
	3400	HacH	91745	678-B6
W GURDON AV				
	200	SGBL	91775	596-D3
GURLEY AV				
	11500	DWNY	90241	706-A6
	11900	DWNY	90242	706-A6
	12600	DWNY	90242	705-J7
	12600	DWNY	90242	735-J1
GURNARD AV				
	3400	LA	90732	823-G7
GURRIER AV				
	3700	Actn	93510	4465-B2
GUS CT				
	2800	LAN	93536	4105-C1
GUSTAV LN				
	8300	LA	91304	529-F2
GUSTON RD				
	10200	LACo	91390	4373-F4
GUTHRIE AV				
	5900	LA	90034	633-A6
	6000	LA	90034	632-H5
GUTHRIE CIR				
	2200	LA	90034	632-G5
GUTHRIE CT				
	2400	LA	90034	632-G6
GUTHRIE DR				
	2100	LA	90034	632-G5
GUYMAN AV				
	42900	LAN	93536	4105-A3
	44100	LAN	93536	4015-A7
GUYON AV				
	36800	LACo	93551	4285-J4
GUYSON ST				
	2000	LMTA	90717	793-H6
GWENALDA LN				
	26700	SCTA	91387	4552-E6
GWENCHRIS CT				
	15000	PRM	90723	735-G4
GWYNNE AV				
	11300	NRWK	90650	706-H7
GWYNNE LN				
	11700	BelA	90077	591-G2
GWYNWOOD AV				
	300	LHB	90631	738-E1
GYNA LN				
	-	LACo	91746	637-G4
GYPSUM CT				
	2200	CHLS	91709	680-J6
GYPSY DR				
	3100	HacH	91745	677-H5
GYPSY LN				
	20000	WdHl	91364	560-E4
GYRAL DR				
	2200	Tuj	91042	504-C4

H

STREET	Block	City	ZIP	Pg-Grid
H				
	-	PRM	90723	735-F6
H ST				
	-	BELL	90201	675-F5
	-	ELSG	90245	732-D1
	-	LA	90245	732-D1
	-	LACo	90220	765-A3
	-	PdlR	90293	702-D7
	-	PdlR	90293	732-D1
	-	SPed	90731	794-B7
	-	Wilm	90744	794-B7
W H ST				
	900	ONT	91762	601-H6
HAAS AV				
	5800	LA	90047	673-G6
	8600	LA	90047	703-G3
	10200	LACo	90047	703-G5
	11500	HAW	90250	703-G7
	12900	GAR	90249	733-H2
	16200	TOR	90504	733-H7
	18000	TOR	90504	763-H1
	23400	TOR	90501	793-H2
HABER AV				
	2200	ELMN	91733	637-D3
N HACIENDA AV				
	100	GLDR	91741	569-J5
S HACIENDA AV				
	100	GLDR	91741	569-J5
HACIENDA BLVD				
	900	LPUE	91744	638-D4
	1200	LACo	90631	708-C4
N HACIENDA BLVD				
	100	INDS	91744	638-D6
	100	LPUE	91744	638-D6
	1400	LACo	91744	638-D6
S HACIENDA BLVD				
	100	INDS	91744	638-C7
	300	INDS	91745	638-C7
	300	INDS	91745	678-C2
	700	HacH	91745	678-C2
HACIENDA DR				
	-	BqtC	91354	4460-E2
	-	ARCD	91006	567-C3
	100	LACo	93551	4285-G5
	100	PMDL	93550	4285-J5
	100	PMDL	93550	4286-A5
	400	LHB	90631	708-C5
	500	MNRO	91016	568-A4
	1400	LCF	91011	535-A1
	2700	DUAR	91010	568-E5
	12600	NRWK	90650	737-A1
	12700	LA	91604	562-E6
HACIENDA LN				
	-	CRSN	90745	794-E1
	4100	CHNO	91710	641-D7
	4100	SBdC	91710	641-D7
	24700	SCTA	91321	4550-J7
	24700	SCTA	91321	4551-A7
HACIENDA PL				
	500	MTBL	90640	636-G7
	1100	WHWD	90069	592-J5
	1400	POM	91768	600-H6
HACIENDA RD				
	900	LHB	90631	708-C4
	1200	LHH	90631	708-C3
	1400	LACo	90631	708-C3
	2400	LHH	90631	678-C7
	33800	Actn	93510	4375-D5
HACIENDA ST				
	10200	BLF	90706	736-D7
HACIENDA RANCH CT				
	-	BqtC	91354	4460-E2
HACIENDA RANCH RD				
	4500	LACo	93551	4194-F3
	4500	PMDL	93551	4194-H4
N HACKAMORE LN				
	-	VeCo	91307	529-A4
HACKAMORE RD				
	-	RHLS	90274	823-E3
HACKERS LN				
	6000	AGRH	91301	557-G3
HACKETT AV				
	1200	LBCH	90815	796-E2
	3000	LBCH	90808	796-E1
	3400	LBCH	90808	766-E7
	4100	LKWD	90713	766-E3
HACKETT PL				
	4900	HiPk	90042	595-B3
HACKLEY AV				
	3900	WCOV	91792	679-C2
HACKNEY ST				
	20400	Win	91306	530-D2
	20900	LA	91304	530-B2
	22000	LA	91304	529-J2
HADAD LN				
	-	Tarz	91356	560-J2
HADDINGTON DR				
	2800	LA	90064	632-E7
HADDOCK DR				
	23000	DBAR	91765	640-B6
HADDON AV				
	8400	SunV	91352	532-G1
	8800	SunV	91352	502-F7
	9300	Pcma	91331	502-B2
	12500	LA	91342	481-G5
HADDON ST				
	12700	LA	91342	481-G5
HADEN CT				
	23000	SCTA	91321	4640-H1
HADJIAN LN				
	22100	CanP	91303	529-J5
HADLER DR				
	11200	LACo	91342	482-J3
E HADLER ST				
	800	CRSN	90745	764-E7
HADLEY AV				
	10100	Nor	91324	500-F4
HADLEY CT				
	-	WLA	90025	631-J4
HADLEY LN				
	-	WLA	90025	631-J4
	2400	RBCH	90278	763-B2
HADLEY ST				
	11100	LACo	90606	676-J6
	11100	LACo	90606	677-A6
	11600	WHIT	90606	677-C6
	11600	WHIT	90601	677-C6
HAGAR ST				
	800	SFER	91340	482-D5
	12900	LA	91342	482-D4
	14600	LA	91340	501-J2
	14700	MsnH	91345	501-J2
N HAGAR ST				
	100	SFER	91340	482-B6
HAGEN DR				
	2300	ALH	91803	636-A2
HAGEN PL				
	12300	GrnH	91344	481-D6
HAGEN ST				
	-	LHB	90631	738-C2
HAGER AV				
	13000	LA	90066	672-C5
HAGGARD LN				
	-	AZU	91702	569-A6
HAGUE CT				
	1200	GLDL	91204	564-E7
HAGUE PL				
	5900	WdHl	91367	559-J1
HAHN AV				
	500	GLDL	91203	564-D3
HAIFA RD				
	-	SIMI	93063	499-B1
HAIG ST				
	11200	SELM	91733	637-C5
HAIGLER DR				
	19000	CRSN	90746	764-E2
HAINES AV				
	300	LBCH	90814	796-B7
HAINES CANYON AV				
	9300	Tuj	91042	504-B4
HAINES CANYON MTWY				
	-	GLDL	-	504-E2
	-	LACo	-	504-E2
	-	Tuj	91042	504-E2
HALAGA CIR				
	4600	LVRN	91750	570-G7
HALBRENT AV				
	4600	Shrm	91403	561-H4
	5400	VanN	91411	561-H1
	6200	VanN	91411	531-H7
	6900	VanN	91405	531-H5
	10000	MsnH	91345	501-H3
HALBRITE AV				
	3400	LBCH	90808	766-J7
	3400	LBCH	90808	767-A7
HALBRITE ST				
	3400	LBCH	90808	766-J7
	3400	LBCH	90808	796-J1
HALCOM AV				
	43800	LAN	93536	4105-D1
	44000	LAN	93536	4015-D7
HALCOURT AV				
	10900	DWNY	90241	706-E5
	11500	NRWK	90650	706-E7
	12600	NRWK	90650	736-E2
HALCYON WY				
	2200	POM	91767	601-A4
HALDANE ST				
	15900	WHIT	90603	707-J4
	16100	WHIT	90603	708-A4
HALDEMAN RD				
	600	LA	90402	631-C6
HALDEMAN ST				
	8600	TEML	91775	596-G2
HALDERMAN ST				
	3300	LA	90066	672-A3
HALDOR PL				
	7600	BPK	90620	767-H5
HALE AV				
	4500	LVRN	91750	570-E7
HALE ST				
	1700	GLDL	91201	563-J1
	1700	GLDL	91201	564-A2
HALEAKALA				
	-	SCTA	91321	4641-C3
HALEDON AV				
	9100	DWNY	90240	706-D3
	10200	DWNY	90241	706-C5
HALEN ST				
	4700	PMDL	93552	4287-A2
HALESCORNER RD				
	27400	RPV	90275	793-B7
E HALEY AV				
	13500	LACo	90605	707-C7
HALEY ST				
	12300	SunV	91352	502-F7
HALEY WY				
	1800	MANB	90266	732-J7
HALFMOON DR				
	37200	PMDL	93550	4286-E3
HALF MOON LN				
	20300	WAL	91789	639-F7
HALF MOON PL				
	-	LACo	91390	4461-A3
E HALFORD RD				
	8200	LACo	91775	596-F1
	8200	LACo	91775	566-F7
HALFORD ST				
	12900	LA	91342	482-D3
HALIFAX CIR				
	5000	CYP	90630	767-C7
HALIFAX DR				
	5200	CYP	90630	767-C7
HALIFAX LN				
	11300	SBdC	91766	641-D3
HALIFAX RD				
	4400	ELMN	91731	597-C6
	4800	ELMN	91780	597-C6
	4800	TEML	91780	597-C3
	5500	TEML	91007	597-C3
HALIFAX ST				
	37800	PMDL	93550	4286-E2
HALINOR AV				
	1700	BALD	91706	638-C1
	3700	BALD	91706	598-D6
S HALINOR AV				
	1300	BALD	91706	638-C1
	1300	WCOV	91706	638-C1
HALISON PL				
	19800	TOR	90503	763-B3
HALISON ST				
	4500	TOR	90503	763-A4
HALITE CT				
	2000	CHLS	91709	680-H7
HALKETT AV				
	4500	RSMD	91770	596-G5
HALKIRK ST				
	12700	LA	91604	562-E6
HALL CT				
	2200	RBCH	90278	763-A2
	4700	CHNO	91710	641-F6
S HALL DR				
	1300	LA	90015	634-C5
HALL RD				
	9000	DWNY	90241	706-C6
HALL ST				
	3900	LA	90032	595-F5
HALLACK AV				
	9900	Nor	91324	500-F5
HALL CANYON DR				
	2000	LCF	91011	534-J1
HALLDALE AV				
	1500	LACo	90047	703-J7
	1500	LA	90047	703-J2
	2600	LA	90018	633-J7
	3600	LA	90018	673-J1
	3900	LA	90062	673-J3
	5800	LA	90047	673-J7
	12000	LACo	90047	733-J2
	12800	GAR	90249	733-J2
	14300	GAR	90247	733-J4
	20800	LA	90501	763-J5
	21900	LA	90501	764-A7
	22500	LA	90501	794-A1
	23200	Hrbr	90710	794-A1
	23200	Hrbr	90710	793-J2
HALLER ST				
	1400	COV	91724	599-E4
HALLETT AV				
	2900	LA	90065	594-G3
HALLGREEN DR				
	1500	LACo	91789	679-E4
HALLIBURTON RD				
	15800	HacH	91745	678-D4
HALLIDAY AV				
	700	Brwd	90049	631-G1
S HALLIDAY ST				
	700	ANA	92804	767-J7
HALLMARK LN				
	19400	CRTS	90703	766-H3
N HALLOCK AV				
	500	SDMS	91773	600-C1
HALLOWELL AV				
	4800	TEML	91780	597-C4
	5500	TEML	91007	597-B3
HALLRICH ST				
	300	LACo	91744	679-B1
HALLWOOD AV				
	800	POM	91767	601-B5
W HALLWOOD CT				
	1300	UPL	91786	601-J2
HALLWOOD DR				
	9800	TEML	91780	597-B4
	11300	ELMN	91732	597-E4
	14400	BALD	91706	598-C4
S HALM AV				
	2300	LA	90034	632-J6
	5800	LadH	90056	673-A6
	6400	LadH	90056	672-J7
HALMA ST				
	2600	LAN	93535	4016-E5
HALO DR				
	12300	LYN	90262	735-D2
S HALO DR				
	12600	COMP	90221	735-D3
HALPER ST				
	16800	Enc	91436	561-D2
HALRAY AV				
	7100	LACo	90606	677-A7
HALSEY CT				
	3400	WCOV	91791	639-E3
HALSEY RD				
	2700	Top	90290	589-G2
HALSEY ST				
	16200	GrnH	91344	501-C1
	16200	GrnH	91344	481-E7
N HALSTEAD ST				
	-	PAS	91107	566-G4
S HALSTEAD ST				
	100	LACo	91107	566-G5
	200	PAS	91107	566-G5
E HALSTED CIR				
	-	ALH	91801	596-C3
HALSTED ST				
	16400	LA	91343	501-D6
	16900	Nor	91325	501-A6
	18100	Nor	91330	500-J6
	18100	Nor	91330	501-A6
	18100	Nor	91325	500-J6
	18300	Nor	91324	500-F6
	19700	Chat	91311	500-D6
	22100	Chat	91311	499-J6
E HALTERN AV				
	100	GLDR	91740	569-E7
W HALTERN AV				
	100	GLDR	91740	569-E7
HALTERN ST				
	19000	GLDR	91740	569-C7
	19000	LACo	91740	569-C7
E HALTERN ST				
	700	AZU	91702	569-B7
HALTON ST				
	17300	Enc	91316	561-C4
HALVERN DR				
	300	Brwd	90049	631-G1
HAMBLEDON AV				
	600	INDS	91744	678-H2
	600	LACo	91744	678-H2
N HAMBLEDON AV				
	100	LACo	91744	638-J7
	100	LACo	91744	678-H1
S HAMBLEDON AV				
	100	LACo	91744	678-H1
	500	INDS	91744	678-H1
HAMBURGER LN				
	13400	BALD	91706	638-A1
HAMDEN PL				
	11800	SFSP	90670	706-H4
HAMDEN ST				
	9600	PRV	90660	706-F3
	11500	SFSP	90670	706-G3
N HAMEL DR				
	100	BHLS	90211	632-J2
S HAMEL DR				
	100	BHLS	90211	632-J2
S HAMEL RD				
	300	LA	90048	632-J1
	400	BHLS	90211	632-J1
HAMELL RD				
	3300	FUL	92835	738-G1
HAMER CT				
	5600	LaCr	91214	504-H6
HAMILTON AV				
	300	PAS	91106	566-B3
	500	SPed	90731	824-A7
	600	PAS	91104	566-B3
	900	SPed	90731	854-A1
	1200	SPed	90731	853-J1
	16500	WHIT	90603	708-A5
	18700	LACo	90248	764-B2
	19600	LA	90502	764-B3
	19600	LACo	90502	764-B5
S HAMILTON AV				
	300	LACo	90732	824-A5
	400	LA	90732	824-A5
N HAMILTON BLVD				
	100	POM	91768	640-H1
	900	POM	91768	600-H7
	1000	POM	91766	640-H1
S HAMILTON BLVD				
	100	POM	91766	640-H2
HAMILTON CT				
	25500	LACo	91302	559-A3
HAMILTON DR				
	6300	Tuj	91042	504-C6
N HAMILTON DR				
	100	BHLS	90211	632-J2
S HAMILTON DR				
	200	BHLS	90211	632-J2
HAMILTON GRN				
	8200	BPK	90621	737-J5
HAMILTON LN				
	3900	GLDL	91214	504-D7
	4000	LA	91214	504-C6
HAMILTON PL				
	-	PMDL	93550	4286-C4
	600	SPed	90731	824-B7
HAMILTON RD				
	900	DUAR	91010	567-J6
HAMILTON WK				
	1400	SPed	90731	853-J1
HAMILTON WY				
	3100	Echo	90026	594-C6
HAMLET DR				
	600	MONP	91755	636-D3
HAMLET ST				
	100	HiPk	90042	595-D2
HAMLET WY				
	-	Cstc	91384	4459-G4
HAMLIN ST				
	10800	NHol	91606	533-A6
	11300	NHol	91606	532-E6
	13500	VanN	91401	532-A6
	14500	VanN	91411	532-A6
	14600	VanN	91411	531-H6
	15900	VanN	91406	531-B6
	19000	Res	91335	530-G6
	19700	WdHl	91367	530-F6
	20200	Win	91306	530-D6
	22200	CanP	91303	529-J6
	22600	CanP	91307	529-F6
HAMLINE PL				
	1000	BURB	91504	533-G3
HAMMACK ST				
	11700	CULC	90230	672-F6
	11800	LA	90230	672-F6
	12400	LACo	90066	672-F6
HAMMEL ST				
	3700	City	90063	635-D5
	4300	ELA	90022	635-F5
E HAMMEL ST				
	100	MONP	91755	636-B5
W HAMMEL ST				
	200	MONP	91754	636-A5
	500	MONP	91754	635-J5
HAMMER ST				
	-	PMDL	93552	4287-D2
HAMMET CIR				
	25700	StvR	91381	4550-B6
HAMMILL RD				
	5200	ELMN	91732	597-F4
N HAMMOND AV				
	6500	NLB	90805	735-H7
HAMMOND CT				
	23800	SCTA	91354	4460-F7
HAMMOND ST				
	500	POM	91767	601-A3
	800	WHWD	90069	592-H6
	1600	Boyl	90033	635-A3
	3100	BALD	91706	637-J1
E HAMMOND ST				
	-	PAS	91103	565-H2
	200	PAS	91104	565-H2
W HAMMOND ST				
	-	PAS	91103	565-G2
HAMMONS CT				
	-	Saug	91350	4461-F5
HAMNER DR				
	15400	BelA	90077	591-H1
HAMPDEN PL				
	600	PacP	90272	631-A6
N HAMPDEN TER				
	-	ALH	91801	595-G4
S HAMPDEN TER				
	-	ALH	91801	595-G5
HAMPEL AV				
	10700	Litl	93543	4378-E1
HAMPSHIRE CIR				
	8000	LPMA	90623	767-C4
HAMPSHIRE CT				
	700	POM	91768	640-H1
	1700	SDMS	91773	599-G4
HAMPSHIRE LN				
	700	LHB	90631	738-F1
	25800	RHE	90274	793-C4
HAMPSHIRE RD				
	-	THO	91362	557-A3
	100	THO	91361	557-A3
HAMPSHIRE ST				
	37300	PMDL	93550	4286-D3
HAMPSTEAD CT				
	-	VeCo	91361	586-F1
HAMPSTEAD RD				
	3600	GLDL	91206	535-B6
	3600	LCF	91011	535-B5
N HAMPSTEAD RD				
	3600	LCF	91011	535-B7
HAMPTON AV				
	7200	WHWD	90046	593-C5
W HAMPTON AV				
	100	MONP	91754	636-B1
HAMPTON CT				
	-	FUL	92831	738-J3
	-	ALH	91801	596-C4
	200	COV	91723	599-A4
	1100	SDMS	91773	599-J2
	16600	CRTS	90703	737-A6
	18300	Nor	91326	480-J7
	36900	PMDL	93552	4287-A4
HAMPTON DR				
	200	SMCA	90405	671-G5
	200	Ven	90291	671-G5
	3400	WCOV	91791	639-E3
	3700	SBdC	91766	641-C3
	12400	SCTA	91355	4550-E5
HAMPTON LN				
	100	LHB	90631	738-D3
	1900	GLDL	91201	534-B6
HAMPTON PL				
	-	MAL	90265	667-E2
	-	RowH	91748	679-B7
	25400	SCTA	91350	4550-J5
HAMPTON RD				
	500	BURB	91504	533-F4
	600	ARCD	91006	567-A3
	900	ARCD	91006	566-J3
	1400	SMRO	91108	596-C1
	3000	PMDL	93551	4195-C6
	3500	PAS	91107	566-H3
	4500	LCF	91011	535-D4
HAMPTON ST				
	-	LAN	93536	4104-F1
	800	GLDR	91740	599-G1
	4600	VER	90058	674-J4
	44200	LAN	93536	4014-F7
HAMWELL ST				
	39400	PMDL	93551	4195-F5
HANA				
	1300	WCOV	91792	638-H5
HANAN CT				
	-	Tarz	91356	560-J2
HANAN DR				
	400	LBCH	90803	826-C1
HANAN WY				
	8300	MTBL	90640	676-F3
	8300	PRV	90660	676-F3
HANAWALT RD				
	33700	LACo	91390	4373-G6
HANAWALT ST				
	2500	LVRN	91750	600-H2
E HANBURY ST				
	5100	LBCH	90808	766-B6
HANCOCK AV				
	900	WHWD	90069	592-J6
HANCOCK DR				
	-	PMDL	93550	4286-C4
HANCOCK PKWY				
	-	Cstc	91384	4459-H6
HANCOCK ST				
	1800	LA	90031	635-B1
	2400	LA	90031	595-A7
	4900	CHNO	91710	641-F5
HANCOCK WY				
	6300	BPK	90620	767-E3
HANDAH CT				
	8200	RowH	91748	679-A6
HANDEL DR				
	8300	BPK	90621	737-J7
	8300	BPK	90621	738-A7

STREET
Block City ZIP Pg-Grid

HANDLEY AV
8000 Wch 90045 702-J2
HANDORF RD
300 INDS 91744 638-F6
HANDY DR
8600 Wats 90002 704-G2
HANEMAN ST
5700 HiPk 90042 565-C7
HANEY PL
13200 Brwd 90049 631-D4
HANEY ST
8400 PRV 90660 676-E5
N HANFORD AV
100 LA 90732 824-A4
200 SPed 90731 824-A4
S HANFORD AV
100 LA 90732 824-A4
HANFORD DR
1800 LACo 91104 536-C7
HANGING ROCK AV
1600 MTBL 90640 636-F5
HANJIN RD
- LBCH 90802 825-A2
HANKINS RD
33700 LACo 91390 4373-B3
HANKS ST
700 AZU 91702 569-A7
E HANKS ST
500 AZU 91702 569-A7
HANLEY AV
500 Brwd 90049 631-E1
HANLEY PL
500 Brwd 90049 631-F2
HANLEY WY
600 Brwd 90049 631-F2
HANLIN AV
5700 LACo 91702 599-C1
6100 LACo 91702 569-C7
HANLINE WY
1300 LHB 90631 708-C5
HANNA AV
5900 WdHl 91367 560-A1
6400 CanP 91303 530-A6
7800 LA 91304 530-A1
8500 LA 91304 529-J1
8900 LA 91304 500-A7
9300 Chat 91311 499-J4
HANNAH CIR
1700 SIMI 93063 499-A3
N HANNING AV
2300 Alta 91001 535-F6
HANNON ST
6500 BGDN 90201 675-J7
6600 BGDN 90201 676-A7
6800 BGDN 90201 706-A1
7200 DWNY 90240 706-B1
HANNUM AV
5600 CULC 90230 672-G5
HANNUM DR
9800 LA 90034 632-G7
S HANOVER AV
900 ELA 90022 676-A2
HANOVER CIR
5000 CYP 90630 767-C7
HANOVER CT
11400 CRTS 90703 736-G6
HANOVER DR
1000 BelA 90077 592-C7
1000 BHLS 90210 592-C7
1000 LA 90210 592-C7
5200 CYP 90630 767-D7
HANOVER RD
1400 INDS 91748 678-H4
1800 CLAR 91711 571-C7
1800 CLAR 91711 601-C1
HANOVER ST
12700 Brwd 90049 631-E4
S HANOVER ST
13000 Brwd 90049 631-E4
HANOVER WY
5200 MTCL 91763 641-G2
HANSA CT
12600 LYN 90262 735-G4
HANSA ST
500 PMDL 93551 4195-H4
HANSARD AV
39100 LACo 93591 4200-E5
HANSCOM DR
1700 SPAS 91030 595-F3
HANSEL LN
1300 SDMS 91773 599-H3
HANSEN AV
900 POM 91766 640-G3
HANSEN ST
9300 SunV 91352 503-A6
HANSFORD AV
1200 LACo 90601 637-F5
HANSOM AV
21900 CRSN 90745 764-E7
HANSON WY
10600 SunI 91040 503-C3
HANSTEAD AV
43900 LAN 93535 4106-B1
44200 LAN 93535 4016-A5
HANSWORTH AV
13200 HAW 90250 733-A2
HANWELL AV
12700 DWNY 90242 736-A2
13600 BLF 90706 736-A2
HAPPY LN
8000 LA 90046 593-A3
HAPPY ST
7500 PRM 90723 735-G2

HAPPY TR
1700 Top 90290 590-B2
HAPPY HOLLOW RD
22700 DBAR 91765 640-B5
HAPPY VALLEY DR
23200 SCTA 91321 4640-G2
HAPPY VALLEY RD
23600 VeCo 93063 499-A7
23600 VeCo 93063 529-B1
HARBAT RD
34100 Actn 93510 4374-F4
W HARBERT ST
1600 WCOV 91790 598-E7
HARBOR AV
1300 LBCH 90813 795-B5
1800 LBCH 90810 795-B5
2100 COMP 90221 735-B7
6500 NLB 90805 735-B7
N HARBOR AV
1000 LBCH 90813 795-B6
HARBOR BLVD
1200 LHH 90631 708-G3
1300 LHB 90631 708-G3
2900 RowH 91748 708-J1
N HARBOR BLVD
100 FUL 92832 738-H7
100 LHB 90631 708-G5
100 SPed 90731 824-C4
1300 FUL 92835 738-G2
3300 LHB 90631 738-G2
S HARBOR BLVD
100 FUL 92832 738-H7
100 LHB 90631 708-G7
100 SPed 90731 824-C6
500 LHB 92835 708-G7
1100 LHB 90631 738-G1
3600 FUL 92835 708-G1
3700 FUL 92835 708-G7
HARBOR CT
4800 PMDL 93552 4287-A4
N HARBOR DR
200 RBCH 90277 762-H4
HARBOR PZ
500 LBCH 90802 825-C2
HARBOR ST
- LAN 93536 4104-F2
500 Ven 90291 671-J6
3200 LBCH 90810 795-A1
5000 CMRC 90040 675-G3
44300 LAN 93536 4014-F7
HARBOR WY
1700 SLB 90740 826-G4
HARBOR CROSSING LN
- LA 90292 672-A6
HARBOR FRWY & TRANSIT WY I-110
- CRSN - 764-B7
- CRSN - 794-B3
- Hrbr - 794-B3
- LA - 634-C6
- LA - 674-B7
- LA - 704-C5
- LA - 734-B6
- LA - 764-B7
- LACo - 704-C5
- LACo - 734-B6
- LACo - 764-B7
- LACo - 794-B3
- SPed - 824-B2
- Wilm - 794-B3
- Wilm - 824-B2
HARBOR FRWY & TRNS WY Rt#-110
- LA - 634-C7
HARBORGATE WY
- LA 90501 763-J3
HARBOR HEIGHTS DR
800 Hrbr 90710 794-A4
HARBOR LAKE AV
1200 BREA 92821 708-H6
HARBORLIGHT DR
20500 Hrbr 90710 794-B4
25100 Wilm 90744 794-B4
HARBOR RIDGE LN
22300 LACo 90502 764-B7
N HARBOR SCENIC DR
- LBCH 90802 825-C1
100 LBCH 90802 795-C7
100 LBCH 90813 795-C7
S HARBOR SCENIC DR
- LBCH 90802 825-C2
HARBOR SCENIC WY
200 LBCH 90802 825-D5
HARBOR SIGHT DR
- RHE 90274 823-G1
HARBOR VIEW AV
21000 CRSN 90810 765-A6
N HARBOR VIEW AV
100 LA 90732 823-J4
S HARBOR VIEW AV
100 LA 90732 823-J6
HARBOR VIEW LN
- PMDL 93551 4195-G6
HARBORVIEW LN
32100 WLKV 91361 557-C6
HARBOR VIEW TER
2400 SPed 90731 824-B7
HARBOR VILLAGE DR
25500 Hrbr 90710 794-A5
HARBOR VILLAGE PL
25400 Hrbr 90710 794-A5
HARBOR VISTA DR
23700 MAL 90265 628-J6

HARBOUR TOWN CT
- PMDL 93551 4195-C2
HARBY DR
24700 SCTA 91321 4640-G3
HARCLARE LN
4000 Enc 91436 561-E5
E HARCO ST
3800 LACo 90808 766-D6
5100 LBCH 90808 766-B6
HARCOURT AV
5300 LACo 90043 673-E5
6000 LA 90043 673-E6
S HARCOURT AV
1800 LA 90019 633-D6
1900 LA 90016 633-D6
2900 LA 90016 673-C1
E HARCOURT ST
100 NLB 90805 765-C1
2800 RDom 90221 765-B1
W HARCOURT ST
- NLB 90805 765-C1
HARCROSS DR
5400 LACo 90043 673-C5
HARDAWAY DR
14400 LMRD 90638 737-E2
HARDESTY AV
27900 SCTA 91351 4551-E1
28000 SCTA 91351 4461-E7
HARDIN DR
600 ING 90302 703-A1
HARDING AV
100 MTBL 90640 676-B1
100 SFER 91340 482-B6
600 ELA 90022 676-A1
700 ELA 90022 675-J1
900 Ven 90291 672-A5
1300 LACo 91104 566-E1
1500 LACo 91104 536-E7
1600 Alta 91001 536-E7
4400 LA 90066 672-D5
5700 SGAT 90280 735-G1
28600 Cstc 91384 4459-D7
S HARDING AV
100 ANA 92804 767-H6
W HARDING AV
300 MONP 91754 636-A3
HARDING CIR
7100 BPK 90620 767-G5
HARDING CT
900 Ven 90291 672-A5
1000 CLAR 91711 601-B1
11700 CHNO 91710 641-H4
HARDING ST
12400 LA 91342 482-F3
13300 LA 91340 482-C5
13400 SFER 91340 482-C5
14600 LA 91340 501-J1
E HARDING ST
300 NLB 90805 765-D1
3000 NLB 90805 765-H1
HARDISON AL
1800 SPAS 91030 595-J1
HARDISON PL
1800 SPAS 91030 595-J1
HARDISON WY
400 HiPk 90042 595-D3
HARDTREE DR
14300 LACo 93532 4102-G5
HARDWICK ST
1300 Bxby 90807 765-F3
2400 LKWD 90712 765-G3
4000 LKWD 90712 766-B3
5500 LKWD 90713 766-C3
HARDWOOD AV
43700 LAN 93534 4105-G1
44000 LAN 93534 4015-G7
HARDY DR
24300 DBAR 91765 640-E7
HARDY PL
25400 StvR 91381 4640-C1
25500 StvR 91381 4550-C7
E HARDY ST
100 ING 90301 703-D4
W HARDY ST
100 ING 90301 703-C4
2200 ING 90305 703-G4
HARE AV
1100 DBAR 91789 679-H3
HARGILL ST
9100 BLF 90706 736-A2
HARGIS ST
6000 CULC 90232 632-J7
6000 LA 90034 632-H6
HARGITT WY
14600 NRWK 90650 736-J4
HARGRAVE DR
2500 LA 90068 593-F2
HARGRAVE ST
600 ING 90302 673-D7
E HARGRAVE ST
300 ING 90302 673-C7
HARKER AV
5500 TEML 91780 596-H4
HARKER ST
500 SPed 90731 824-B4
HARKNESS AV
- PAS 91106 566-C4
HARKNESS LN
- RBCH 90277 762-J3
200 RBCH 90278 762-J2
HARKNESS ST
200 MANB 90266 732-J6

HARLAN AV
900 COMP 90220 734-G5
3900 BALD 91706 598-A4
19000 CRSN 90746 764-G3
HARLAND AV
9000 WHWD 90069 592-H7
HARLAS AV
44800 LAN 93534 4015-F5
HARLEM PL
200 LA 90012 634-F5
400 LA 90013 634-F5
600 LA 90014 634-F5
HARLENE DR
3600 Enc 91436 561-F6
HARLENE PL
5700 Tarz 91356 561-A1
HARLEQUIN CT
3300 WCOV 91791 639-E3
HARLEQUIN WY
37200 PMDL 93552 4287-A3
HARLESDEN CT
2600 LA 90046 593-A2
HARLEY AV
- LA 91342 482-B2
HARLINE CT
22500 LACo 90502 794-A1
HARLISS ST
19100 Nor 91324 500-G5
HARLOW AV
9200 LA 90034 632-G7
HARLOW CT
- LAN 93536 4015-E4
1800 LAN 93536 4015-E4
HARLOW DR
100 GLDL 91206 565-A4
HARMAN AV
11600 Wbrk 90059 704-H7
HARMAN DR
6300 Tuj 91042 504-C6
HARMON AV
18000 CRSN 90746 764-H2
HARMON PL
1800 GLDL 91208 534-H5
HARMON WY
- BPK 90621 737-H5
HARMONY AV
12700 CHNO 91710 641-E7
HARMONY DR
5200 NHol 91601 563-A2
HARMONY LN
- Litl 93543 4468-E3
700 FUL 92831 738-J5
4800 LA 90032 595-E7
5500 LAN 93536 4104-G4
HARMONY PL
500 FUL 92831 738-J5
2400 LaCr 91214 504-F5
HARMONY WY
- LACo 91390 4460-J2
400 LBCH 90806 795-E4
2600 LAN 93535 4106-E1
HARMONY HILL DR
2500 DBAR 91765 679-H6
HARMSWORTH AV
600 LPUE 91744 678-G2
HARNETT AV
4000 ELMN 91732 597-G7
HARNETT ST
18800 Nor 91326 500-G3
HARNEY PL
22500 CALB 91302 559-H7
HARNISH RD
5800 WdHl 91367 559-H1
HARO AV
11500 DWNY 90241 705-H4
HAROLD CIR
2300 BURB 91504 533-E3
HAROLD WY
5100 LFlz 90027 593-H4
5500 Hlwd 90028 593-G4
8400 LA 90069 592-J5
8400 LA 90069 593-A5
HAROLD 1ST ST
36300 PMDL 93550 4286-C5
HAROLD 2ND ST
36400 PMDL 93550 4286-B5
HAROLD 3RD ST
36400 PMDL 93550 4286-B5
HAROLD 5TH ST
36400 PMDL 93550 4286-B6
HAROLD ASH AV
1100 PMDL 93550 4286-C6
HAROLD BEECH AV
- PMDL 93550 4286-C5
HAROLD CEDAR AV
- PMDL 93550 4286-C5
HAROLD DATE AV
600 PMDL 93550 4286-B6
HARP DR
2100 HacH 91745 678-C4
HARPER AV
1100 RBCH 90278 762-H1
1200 HMB 90254 762-H1
7800 DWNY 90241 706-A3
N HARPER AV
100 LA 90048 633-A1
300 LA 90048 593-A7
700 LA 90046 593-A5
900 WHWD 90046 593-A5
S HARPER AV
100 LA 90048 633-A1
HARPER CT
1600 LVRN 91750 570-F4

HARPERS WY
1800 TOR 90501 763-H4
HARPS ST
100 SFER 91340 482-B6
13000 LA 91342 482-D4
HARPTREE DR
3600 CALB 91302 559-E7
HARQUAHALA PL
- LACo 93532 4102-E5
HARRAH RD
34300 LACo 91390 4373-G4
HARRATT ST
8800 WHWD 90069 592-H6
HARRELL ST
9000 PRV 90660 676-H2
HARRIDGE DR
1400 LA 90210 592-D5
E HARRIET ST
- Alta 91001 535-H5
W HARRIET ST
- Alta 91001 535-G5
HARRIETT ST
2400 LA 90058 674-J2
2500 VER 90058 674-J2
HARRIET TUBMAN WY
- LYN 90262 705-C7
HARRIMAN AV
3600 LA 90032 595-E4
4900 SPAS 91030 595-E4
HARRIMAN LN
1700 RBCH 90278 762-J1
1900 RBCH 90278 763-A1
HARRIMAN ST
7400 DWNY 90242 705-H7
HARRINGTON AV
3000 LA 90006 633-H4
HARRINGTON RD
800 GLDL 91207 564-F2
HARRINGTON WY
1000 WCOV 91792 638-J5
HARRIS AV
1000 City 90063 635-D4
4200 LYN 90262 735-C1
11000 LYN 90262 705-D7
S HARRIS AV
100 COMP 90221 735-C4
600 RDom 90221 735-C6
HARRIS WY
- LACo 91387 4552-A4
HARRISBURG CT
13000 CHNO 91710 641-E7
HARRISBURG RD
3500 LALM 90720 796-J3
11400 OrCo 90720 796-H4
HARRISON AV
- INDS 91789 679-E2
- LHB 90631 738-C2
100 CLAR 91711 601-B3
800 POM 91767 601-B3
1000 Ven 90291 672-A6
E HARRISON AV
100 POM 91767 600-J3
100 POM 91767 601-A3
W HARRISON AV
100 POM 91767 600-J3
HARRISON PKWY
- Valc 91355 4459-G7
HARRISON RD
500 MONP 91755 636-E5
HARRISON ST
4500 CHNO 91710 641-F5
7600 PRM 90723 735-G6
E HARRISON ST
2500 CRSN 90810 764-J5
2500 CRSN 90810 765-A5
HARRISON WY
8500 BPK 90620 767-G5
HARRLEE LN
23900 TOR 90505 793-B3
HARROW CT
37300 PMDL 93550 4286-C3
HARROW RD
20500 Top 90290 630-A3
HARROWAY AV
16600 CRTS 90703 737-C6
HARRY BRIDGES BLVD
100 Wilm 90744 794-D7
1000 Wilm 90744 824-C1
HARSHAW PL
15700 LMRD 90638 737-J4
HART AV
100 SMCA 90405 671-F4
3500 RSMD 91770 596-H7
5800 TEML 91780 596-H3
HART DR
13600 CRTS 90703 737-C7
HART PL
6900 VanN 91406 531-F5
13000 CRTS 90703 737-B7
S HART PL
- LBCH 90802 825-E1
W HART PL
600 MTBL 90640 676-D2
HART ST
- LAN 93536 4015-D4
1800 LAN 93534 4015-E4
2800 ART 90701 736-G7
11400 NHol 91605 532-D5
12000 CRTS 90703 736-H7
13400 VanN 91405 532-A5
14500 VanN 91405 531-J5
15300 VanN 91406 531-C5
17700 Res 91335 531-A5

HART ST
18100 Res 91335 530-F5
19700 Win 91306 530-D5
20800 CanP 91303 530-A5
22000 CanP 91303 529-J5
HARTCREST DR
6900 RPV 90275 792-G7
HARTDALE AV
11800 LACo 90604 707-H6
11900 LMRD 90638 707-H7
HARTE TER
4000 LA 90032 595-D5
HARTER AV
4000 CULC 90232 672-F3
4300 CULC 90230 672-F3
HARTER LN
5200 LCF 91011 535-B1
HARTFIELD CT
4200 WLKV 91361 557-D6
HARTFORD AV
400 LA 90017 634-D3
27600 Cstc 91384 4459-H5
HARTFORD LN
- PMDL 93551 4104-D6
700 LHB 90631 738-F1
11300 SBdC 91766 641-D3
11500 CRTS 90703 736-G6
HARTFORD PL
900 POM 91768 600-G7
900 POM 91768 640-G1
HARTFORD WY
900 BHLS 90210 592-D7
HARTGLEN AV
800 THO 91361 557-A4
HARTGLEN PL
5500 AGRH 91301 557-H5
HARTLAND CIR
2600 THO 91361 557-B5
HARTLAND ST
11300 NHol 91605 532-D5
13300 VanN 91405 532-A5
14500 VanN 91405 531-H5
17700 Res 91335 531-A6
18100 Res 91335 530-F6
20100 Win 91306 530-C6
22200 CanP 91303 529-H6
22400 CanP 91307 529-E6
HARTLE AV
4200 CDHY 90201 705-D1
HARTLE ST
5000 CDHY 90201 705-E1
N HARTLEY AV
4000 LACo 91722 598-G5
N HARTLEY ST
100 WCOV 91790 598-G6
700 LACo 91722 598-G6
HARTMAN CT
200 SDMS 91773 600-B1
HARTMAN WY
9300 WHil 91304 499-E7
HARTNEL PL
3700 CLAR 91711 571-F4
HARTSHORN RANCH PL
- LVRN 91750 570-H7
- LVRN 91750 600-H1
HARTSOOK ST
10800 NHol 91601 563-A2
11000 NHol 91601 562-G3
11700 LA 91607 562-F3
12900 Shrm 91423 562-B3
14300 Shrm 91423 562-A3
14600 Shrm 91403 561-H3
15700 Enc 91436 561-E3
17000 Enc 91316 561-C3
HARTSVILLE ST
13600 LACo 91746 637-J3
13600 LACo 91746 638-A3
13700 LPUE 91746 638-A3
14500 LPUE 91744 638-C6
HARTT PL
200 CLAR 91711 601-D1
HARTVIEW AV
- LACo 91744 638-G4
HARTWELL CT
- Alta 91001 535-G3
HARTWELL LN
- Hrbr 90710 794-A3
HARTWICK ST
4800 Eagl 90041 565-C5
HARTWOOD POINT DR
1200 PAS 91107 566-G1
HARTZELL ST
700 PacP 90272 631-B4
N HARVARD AV
100 CLAR 91711 601-D2
HARVARD BLVD
1200 LA 90029 593-J5
14700 GAR 90247 733-J5
17800 GAR 90248 763-J1
21700 LA 90501 763-J7
22500 LA 90501 793-J1
N HARVARD BLVD
100 LA 90004 593-J7
100 LA 90004 633-J1
700 LA 90029 593-J6
1300 LFlz 90027 593-H4
S HARVARD BLVD
100 LA 90004 633-J1
300 LA 90020 633-J1
600 LA 90005 633-J2
700 LA 90010 633-J1
900 LA 90006 633-J3

S HARVARD BLVD
1900 LA 90018 633-H7
3700 LA 90018 673-H1
3700 LA 90062 673-H3
5800 LA 90047 673-J7
7200 LA 90047 703-J2
11100 LACo 90047 703-J6
12000 LACo 90047 733-J1
18200 LA 90248 763-J2
20300 LA 90501 763-J5
HARVARD CT
1000 SMCA 90403 631-G6
1300 SMCA 90404 631-G6
HARVARD DR
300 ARCD 91007 567-B4
11200 NRWK 90650 736-F6
HARVARD LN
100 SLB 90740 796-F6
3000 PMDL 93551 4195-C5
HARVARD PL
100 CLAR 91711 601-D3
13700 GAR 90249 733-J3
W HARVARD PL
1300 ONT 91762 601-H6
HARVARD RD
300 BURB 91502 533-H5
400 BURB 91501 533-H4
HARVARD ST
800 SMCA 90403 631-G6
1200 SMCA 90404 631-G6
4300 MTCL 91763 601-E6
9100 BLF 90706 736-A5
E HARVARD ST
100 GLDL 91205 564-E5
W HARVARD ST
400 GLDL 91204 564-C5
HARVARD WK
3400 LA 90018 633-H7
3400 LA 90018 673-H1
HARVARD WY
- BPK 90620 767-F6
43300 LAN 93536 4105-C2
HARVEST AV
9900 SFSP 90670 706-F4
12000 NRWK 90650 706-F7
12100 NRWK 90650 736-F1
16600 CRTS 90703 736-F6
16600 LACo 90703 736-F6
17800 CRTS 90703 766-G1
20400 LKWD 90715 766-F4
HARVEST CT
3800 SBdC 91710 641-D6
35300 Litl 93543 4377-F1
HARVEST LN
100 PMDL 93550 4285-J2
1700 BREA 92821 709-D7
HARVEST ST
14900 MsnH 91345 501-H1
15500 GmH 91344 501-F1
HARVEST WY
19900 CRTS 90703 766-G3
HARVESTER RD
29500 MAL 90265 667-C1
30000 MAL 90265 627-B7
HARVEST MOON DR
- SFER 91340 482-G6
HARVEST MOON ST
1000 WCOV 91792 638-G4
15700 LACo 91744 638-E4
E HARVEST MOON ST
1200 WCOV 91792 638-H4
N HARVEST WALK DR
- LACo 91744 638-G4
HARVEY DR
100 GLDL 91206 564-H4
800 BREA 92821 708-J5
HARVEY ST
37600 PMDL 93550 4286-E2
HARVEY WY
- LACo 91775 596-F2
2700 LKWD 90712 765-H5
4100 LKWD 90712 766-C5
5500 LKWD 90713 766-C5
E HARVEY WY
4300 LBCH 90808 766-A5
HARWICH PL
23700 CanP 91307 529-E5
HARWICK CT
17400 CRSN 90746 734-F7
17400 CRSN 90746 764-F5
HARWICK PL
- SCTA 91354 4460-G6
HARWILL AV
16200 CRSN 90746 734-E6
HARWOOD CT
700 SDMS 91773 600-C3
HARWOOD DR
27900 SCTA 91350 4460-J4
HARWOOD PL
500 CLAR 91711 601-E3
700 UPL 91786 601-F3
HARWOOD ST
2200 LA 90031 594-H6
HASEKIAN DR
4800 Tarz 91356 560-G4
HASELTINE GRN
8200 BPK 90621 737-J5
HASKELL AV
4400 Enc 91436 561-G3
6400 VanN 91406 531-G3
8300 LA 91343 531-G2
8700 LA 91343 501-F5
10200 GmH 91344 501-F2

HASKELL RD
- LACo 92823 680-C7
- LACo 92823 710-C1
HASKELL ST
5100 LCF 91011 535-B1
HASKELL CANYON RD
- LACo 91390 4461-B3
27600 SCTA 91350 4461-B6
28100 Saug 91350 4461-B3
HASKELL VISTA LN
23200 SCTA 91321 4640-H3
HASKETT RD
31900 LACo 91390 4463-C1
HASKINS AV
1500 COMP 90220 734-E6
15400 LACo 90220 734-E5
HASKINS LN
16100 COMP 90746 734-E6
16100 CRSN 90746 734-E6
HASLAM TER
1500 LA 90069 592-J4
HASLER RD
- VeCo 90265 625-H1
HASLEY CANYON RD
26900 Cstc 91384 4459-A2
HASSON DR
- BPK 90621 737-F6
HASSTED DR
33100 LACo 90265 586-E7
33100 LACo 90265 626-E1
HASTAIN FIRE RD
- LA 90210 592-E3
- LACo 90210 592-E3
HASTING ST
5200 ELA 90022 635-H7
HASTINGS AV
8000 Wch 90045 702-D2
8100 PdlR 90293 702-D2
HASTINGS CIR
2200 CLAR 91711 571-F6
HASTINGS CT
800 POM 91768 640-G1
1100 SDMS 91773 599-J4
5000 VeCo 91377 557-H1
HASTINGS DR
11900 LACo 90605 707-C7
HASTINGS ST
19100 RowH 91748 679-C7
37900 PMDL 93550 4286-E2
HASTINGS WY
18100 Nor 91326 500-J1
HASTINGS HEIGHTS LN
1600 PAS 91107 536-G7
HASTINGS RANCH DR
300 PAS 91105 566-H2
1500 PAS 91107 536-H7
HASTON PL
21100 LKWD 90715 766-G5
HASTY AV
7000 PRV 90660 676-F7
7800 PRV 90660 706-F1
9000 DWNY 90240 706-E3
10200 DWNY 90241 706-D5
HATARI WY
- BqtC 91354 4460-F2
S HATCHER AV
900 INDS 91748 678-G3
HATCHWAY ST
1900 COMP 90222 734-H2
1900 Wbrk 90222 734-H2
HATFIELD AV
400 SDMS 91773 600-D1
HATFIELD PL
4100 LA 90032 635-C1
HATHAWAY AV
500 ALH 91803 636-A2
500 MONP 91754 636-A2
3400 LBCH 90755 795-J4
3400 LBCH 90804 795-J4
3400 LBCH 90815 795-J4
3500 LBCH 90815 796-A4
HATHAWAY DR
- SIGH 90755 795-H3
10500 SFSP 90670 706-H5
23700 SCTA 91354 4460-F6
HATHAWAY RD
500 SDMS 91773 600-B1
HATHAWAY RANCH RD
- LACo - 4643-F7
- LACo - (4723-F1
See Page 4643)
HATILLO AV
6500 WdHl 91367 530-E6
6800 Win 91306 530-E2
8800 Nor 91324 530-E1
9500 Chat 91311 500-E5
HATMOR DR
26100 CALB 91302 558-H4
HATRIDGE LN
17900 SCTA 91387 4551-J2
17900 SCTA 91387 4552-A2
HATTERAS ST
3900 BURB 91505 563-B1
10600 NHol 91601 563-A1
11000 NHol 91601 562-H1
11700 LA 91607 562-E1
13300 VanN 91401 562-A1
14500 VanN 91411 562-A1
14600 VanN 91411 561-H1
17100 Enc 91316 561-A1
18100 Tarz 91356 561-A1
18300 Tarz 91356 560-F1
19700 WdHl 91367 560-D1

HATTERAS ST
22400 WdHl 91367 559-F1
24500 HIDH 91302 559-D2
HATTON CT
10200 SunV 91352 533-B2
HATTON PL
7700 Res 91335 531-A3
HATTON ST
17800 Res 91335 531-A3
18100 Res 91335 530-F3
19700 Win 91306 530-E3
HAUCK ST
4300 City 90063 635-F3
HAUSER
- LACo 91390 (4284-C6
See Page 4283)
HAUSER BLVD
300 LA 90036 633-C2
1000 LA 90019 633-B5
1800 LA 90016 633-B7
3600 LA 90016 673-B1
3800 LA 90008 673-B1
HAVANA AV
- LBCH 90803 796-C7
300 LBCH 90814 796-C7
700 LBCH 90804 796-C7
12000 LA 91342 481-J6
HAVASU CIR
8000 BPK 90621 737-J6
HAVEL PL
8200 LACo 91775 596-F2
HAVELOCK AV
11200 LA 90230 672-F5
11200 CULC 90230 672-F5
12400 LA 90066 672-D6
HAVEMEYER LN
1400 RBCH 90278 762-J2
1900 RBCH 90278 763-A2
E HAVEN AV
100 ARCD 91006 567-D4
HAVEN CT
36800 PMDL 93552 4287-B4
HAVEN PL
43200 LAN 93536 4104-H3
HAVEN ST
1900 GLDL 91208 534-J7
2600 LA 90032 595-F7
HAVEN WY
2800 BURB 91504 533-E3
HAVENBROOK ST
14100 BALD 91706 598-B6
W HAVENBROOK ST
2300 WCOV 91790 598-C7
HAVENDALE DR
300 PAS 91105 565-G6
HAVENHURST DR
1100 WHWD 90046 593-A5
1100 BREA 92821 708-H5
1300 LA 90046 593-A5
N HAVENHURST DR
900 WHWD 90046 593-A6
HAVENHURST WY
2000 UPL 91784 571-H4
HAVENPARK AV
1500 SELM 91733 637-B4
2600 ELMN 91733 637-B2
HAVENPARK ST
- SELM 91733 637-B3
HAVEN RIDGE RD
2400 POM 91767 601-B4
HAVENWOOD DR
9000 PRV 90660 676-G4
11400 LACo 90606 677-A6
HAVENWOOD PL
10500 LACo 90606 676-J5
HAVENWOOD ST
9400 PRV 90660 676-G4
HAVERFORD AV
600 PacP 90272 631-A5
HAVERHILL DR
2400 LA 90065 594-J2
HAVERHILL PARK RD
7000 WHIT 90608 677-D6
HAVERKAMP DR
500 GLDL 91206 565-A3
HAVERLY ST
10500 ELMN 91731 597-C5
HAVERSTOCK RD
500 LCF 91011 535-D6
HAVILAND AV
5800 WHIT 90601 677-D5
HAWAII
1900 WCOV 91792 679-A1
HAWAII AV
500 TOR 90503 763-E5
HAWAII ST
600 ELSG 90245 732-J3
HAWAIIAN AV
200 Wilm 90744 794-D7
200 Wilm 90744 824-D1
20000 CRTS 90703 767-A5
20100 LKWD 90715 767-A5
21700 HGDN 90716 767-A6
HAWES ST
13700 LACo 90605 707-D3
14200 LACo 90604 707-E4
HAWES WY
25900 StvR 91381 4550-B6
HAWICK ST
2800 LA 90039 594-D4
HAWK AV
9700 KeCo 93560 3833-F3

HAWK DR
14800 LACo 93532 4102-F3
HAWK LN
300 GLDR 91741 569-F5
W HAWK LN
40000 PMDL 93551 4195-J3
HAWK RD
21200 LACo 91768 639-H2
21200 WAL 91789 639-H2
HAWKBROOK DR
1800 SDMS 91773 570-E6
HAWKBRYN AV
24900 SCTA 91321 4640-E2
HAWK CANYON LN
1000 CHLS 91709 710-F2
HAWKDEN CT
- GLDL 91206 564-J3
HAWKEYE AV
9500 KeCo 93560 3833-G3
HAWK FREE CT
2300 Actn 93510 4375-E3
HAWKHURST DR
26500 RPV 90275 793-B6
HAWKINS AV
2400 RBCH 90278 733-B6
HAWKINS CIR
1900 HNTP 90001 674-H7
HAWKINS ST
12200 SFSP 90670 706-J4
HAWKRIDGE DR
2900 LaCr 91214 504-F5
HAWKS DR
- BREA 92823 709-H6
HAWKSET ST
30100 Cstc 91384 4459-B2
HAWKS HILL RD
20000 Chat 91311 500-E3
HAWKSMOOR DR
31000 RPV 90275 823-F5
HAWKS NEST TR
2500 Top 90290 630-A2
HAWKS POINTE CT
- FUL 92833 738-A3
- LMRD 90638 738-A3
HAWKS POINTE DR
- FUL 92833 738-A3
- LMRD 90638 738-A3
HAWKS RIDGE DR
- SCTA 91351 4461-G7
HAWKSTONE AV
9800 LACo 90605 707-C4
HAWKWOOD DR
2400 CHLS 91709 680-J3
HAWKWOOD RD
3200 DBAR 91765 679-H7
3300 DBAR 91765 709-H1
HAWLEY AV
3800 LA 90032 595-D5
5300 HiPk 90042 595-D4
HAWLEY RD
32900 Actn 93510 4374-D7
HAWTHORN AV
6700 Hlwd 90028 593-D4
7100 LA 90046 593-C4
12400 DWNY 90242 705-H6
HAWTHORNE AL
12800 HAW 90250 733-C3
HAWTHORNE AV
200 BREA 92821 709-F7
1600 LVRN 91750 600-F2
4400 VER 90058 674-H4
12800 DWNY 90242 705-G7
HAWTHORNE BLVD
11900 HAW 90250 703-C7
11900 HAW 90250 733-C3
14300 HAW 90260 733-C3
14300 LNDL 90260 733-C3
17600 TOR 90504 763-D4
19200 TOR 90503 763-D4
24500 TOR 90505 793-A7
27500 RPV 90275 793-A7
27600 RPV 90275 792-J7
HAWTHORNE BLVD Rt#-N7
24100 TOR 90505 793-D5
25500 RHE 90274 793-D5
26000 RPV 90275 793-A7
27500 RPV 90275 792-J7
28800 RPV 90275 822-H2
29500 RHE 90274 822-H2
HAWTHORNE BLVD Rt#-107
1700 RBCH 90278 763-D6
2000 RBCH 90278 733-C7
16100 LNDL 90260 733-C7
17200 TOR 90504 733-C7
17200 TOR 90504 763-D6
17200 TOR 90278 733-C7
17200 TOR 90278 763-D6
19000 TOR 90503 763-D6
21900 TOR 90505 763-D6
22600 TOR 90505 793-D2
S HAWTHORNE BLVD
10000 ING 90304 703-C6
10400 Lenx 90304 703-C6
11100 HAW 90304 703-C6
11400 HAW 90250 703-C6
HAWTHORNE DR
5000 VeCo 91377 557-G1
HAWTHORNE LN
1000 SPAS 91030 595-G2
HAWTHORNE PL
- StvR 91381 4550-A7

STREET
Block City ZIP Pg-Grid

E HAWTHORNE PL
700 POM 91767 641-B1
HAWTHORNE ST
200 SPAS 91030 595-F2
400 GLDL 91204 564-D5
4500 MTCL 91763 601-E5
- PMDL 93551 4195-E5
W HAWTHORNE ST
900 ONT 91762 601-H5
HAWTHORNE WY
12000 HAW 90250 733-C1
S HAWTHORNE WY
13800 HAW 90250 733-C3
HAXBY CT
800 CRSN 90746 734-E7
HAXTON DR
27700 SCTA 91351 4551-G1
28100 SCTA 91351 4461-G7
S HAY AV
300 ELA 90022 676-A1
300 MTBL 90640 676-A1
HAY DR
16800 CHLS 91709 710-F3
N HAY ST
400 MTBL 90640 676-B1
500 MTBL 90640 636-B7
HAYCREEK AV
27800 SCTA 91351 4461-D7
HAYDEN AV
3500 CULC 90232 632-J7
3500 CULC 90232 672-J1
13300 NRWK 90650 737-B2
HAYDEN PL
8500 CULC 90232 672-H1
HAYDEN WY
- BREA 92821 709-B6
HAYES AL
- PAS 91103 565-H4
HAYES AV
1300 LBCH 90813 795-A6
2300 LBCH 90810 795-A3
5900 HiPk 90042 595-D2
HAYES CIR
7100 BPK 90620 767-G5
HAYES CT
29800 Cstc 91384 4459-C7
HAYES DR
2500 LVRN 91750 600-H2
6400 LA 90048 633-A3
HAYES ST
4400 City 90063 635-F2
N HAYFIELD DR
3200 LBCH 90808 796-D1
HAYFORD AV
11000 NRWK 90650 736-F5
HAYFORD ST
10400 BLF 90706 736-D5
10600 NRWK 90650 736-E5
12500 NRWK 90650 737-A5
15100 LMRD 90638 737-G5
HAYFORK RD
- LACo 91390 4461-F3
HAYLAND ST
14200 LACo 91746 638-B3
14900 LACo 91744 638-D4
E HAYLAND ST
14100 LACo 91746 638-B3
15400 LPUE 91744 638-D5
HAYLEY CT
- WCOV 91744 679-B1
HAYLOFT PL
1800 HacH 91745 678-F5
HAYMAN AV
4300 LCF 91011 535-B2
HAYMOND ST
11000 SELM 91733 637-B5
HAYNES AV
500 BHLS 90210 592-G4
HAYNES LN
1400 HMB 90254 762-J2
1400 RBCH 90278 762-J2
HAYNES ST
11500 NHol 91606 532-E6
13500 VanN 91401 532-A6
14500 VanN 91411 532-A6
14600 VanN 91411 531-H6
15300 VanN 91406 531-B6
18500 Res 91335 530-F6
19800 WdHl 91367 530-E6
20000 Win 91306 530-C6
22200 CanP 91303 529-J6
22400 CanP 91307 529-E6
HAYRIDE CT
2500 RowH 91748 678-J7
HAYTER AV
3800 LKWD 90712 765-J2
11200 CULC 90230 672-G5
15100 PRM 90723 735-J5
15900 BLF 90706 735-J6
HAYVENHURST AV
3600 Enc 91436 561-D5
6400 VanN 91406 531-E3
8300 LA 91343 531-E1
8700 LA 91343 501-D6
10100 GmH 91344 501-D4
11600 GmH 91344 481-E7
HAYVENHURST DR
4000 Enc 91436 561-E5
HAYVENHURST PL
7200 VanN 91406 531-E4
8300 LA 91343 531-D2
HAYWARD DR
- Cstc 91384 4459-G4

HAYWARD ST
9900 WHIT 90603 707-G4
14200 WHIT 90605 707-E3
S HAYWARD ST
700 ANA 92804 767-J7
W HAYWARD ST
600 ANA 92804 767-J7
HAYWARD WY
9900 SELM 91733 637-A4
HAYWOOD ST
- LACo 91342 482-E6
6300 Tuj 91042 504-B5
HAYWORTH AV
1200 LA 90035 633-A4
N HAYWORTH AV
100 LA 90048 633-B1
300 LA 90048 593-B7
700 LA 90046 593-B5
900 WHWD 90046 593-B5
S HAYWORTH AV
100 LA 90048 633-B1
1000 LA 90035 633-A5
N HAZARD AV
400 City 90063 635-E3
HAZBETH LN
1600 GLDL 91202 564-E1
1600 GLDL 91207 564-E1
HAZEL AV
600 LACo 91770 636-H5
HAZEL CIR
6400 SIMI 93063 499-C2
HAZEL CT
37300 PMDL 93550 4286-A3
44300 LAN 93536 4014-E7
W HAZEL CT
1500 UPL 91784 571-H6
HAZEL ST
500 GLDL 91201 564-A3
9200 Chat 91311 499-G7
22700 SCTA 91390 4460-J3
E HAZEL ST
100 ING 90302 703-C1
N HAZEL ST
100 LHB 90631 708-E5
S HAZEL ST
100 LHB 90631 708-E6
W HAZEL ST
100 ING 90302 703-C2
HAZEL WY
9200 Chat 91311 499-G7
HAZELBROOK AV
4300 LBCH 90808 766-A5
5400 LKWD 90712 766-A2
HAZELBROOK RD
3400 LA 91604 562-H7
HAZELCREST CIR
4800 THO 91362 557-F2
HAZELCREST DR
15800 LMRD 90638 737-J1
HAZELCREST LN
25100 StvR 91381 4640-E1
HAZELHURST PL
6000 NHol 91606 532-H7
HAZEL KIRK DR
4200 LFlz 90027 594-B3
HAZELL WY
100 SGBL 91776 596-E6
HAZELNUT PL
- PMDL 93551 4285-E3
HAZELRIDGE DR
27900 RPV 90275 792-H6
HAZELTINE AV
4100 Shrm 91423 562-B4
5200 VanN 91401 562-B2
5900 VanN 91401 532-B7
6500 VanN 91405 532-B5
7800 PanC 91402 532-A1
8700 PanC 91402 502-A7
HAZELWOOD AV
1400 Eagl 90041 595-A1
1500 Eagl 90041 565-A7
HAZELWOOD CT
- CRSN 90746 764-G2
HAZELWOOD PL
1300 BREA 92821 709-B5
HAZEN DR
9100 LA 90210 592-G2
HEADLAND DR
28300 RPV 90275 823-G1
HEADSTROM CANYON RD
25000 CALB 91302 589-B2
25000 LACo 91302 589-B2
HEALY TER
9300 Chat 91311 499-E6
9300 Chat 91311 499-F7
HEARD DR
- LACo 91390 (4371-G6 See Page 4281)
HEARD PL
1800 Brwd 90049 631-D2
HEARST TANK MTWY
19800 Top 90290 629-J4
19800 Top 90290 630-A4
HEARTHSIDE CT
- FUL 92831 738-J3
- SCTA 91354 4460-G5
HEARTHSTONE LN
13800 CHLS 91709 680-G3
HEARTWOOD CIR
300 BREA 92821 709-D6
HEARTWOOD CT
- SCTA 91354 4460-G5
13900 LMRD 90638 738-A2

HEATH AV
400 BHLS 90212 632-F3
2100 CenC 90067 632-F3
2100 LA 90035 632-F3
HEATH CT
44000 LAN 93535 4016-C7
E HEATH LN
200 NLB 90805 735-C7
W HEATH ST
200 NLB 90805 735-B6
E HEATH TER
1900 WCOV 91791 638-J3
1900 WCOV 91791 639-A3
HEATHCLIFF PL
200 BREA 92821 709-D7
HEATH CREEK CT
5400 SBdC 92397 (4652-E3 See Page 4651)
HEATH CREEK DR
5400 SBdC 92397 (4652-E3 See Page 4651)
HEATH CREEK LN
5400 SBdC 92397 (4652-E3 See Page 4651)
HEATHDALE AV
4400 LACo 91722 599-A4
5300 LACo 91702 599-A2
N HEATHDALE AV
100 COV 91722 599-A3
S HEATHDALE AV
100 COV 91722 599-A6
600 COV 91723 599-A7
HEATHER AV
500 LHB 90631 708-D5
3000 PMDL 93550 4286-F2
18300 CRTS 90703 767-C1
N HEATHER AV
2300 LBCH 90815 796-B3
HEATHER CIR
7600 BPK 90620 767-J3
HEATHER CT
1800 LA 90210 592-F4
29600 AGRH 91301 557-J3
HEATHER DR
1600 LVRN 91750 570-F7
6300 LA 90068 563-F7
S HEATHER DR
1800 MONP 91755 636-B5
HEATHER LN
- ART 90701 766-G1
- DUAR 91010 568-B5
- ING 90305 703-F3
8500 Nor 91324 500-G7
900 HacH 91745 637-J7
28500 Cstc 91384 4459-E1
S HEATHER LN
- ING 90305 703-E3
700 WCOV 91791 639-A2
HEATHER RD
4100 LBCH 90808 766-B5
9500 LA 90210 592-F4
N HEATHER RD
2800 LBCH 90815 796-B2
3000 LBCH 90808 796-B2
3400 LBCH 90808 766-B7
HEATHER SQ
1100 PAS 91104 566-A2
HEATHER ST
900 GLDR 91740 599-G1
HEATHER WY
300 LHB 90631 708-E5
1800 LA 90210 592-F4
2100 POM 91767 600-J5
13600 HAW 90250 733-A3
HEATHERCLIFF RD
6400 MAL 90265 667-D2
HEATHERCREST DR
38700 PMDL 93551 4195-E7
HEATHERDALE DR
5600 LACo 90043 673-C5
HEATHER FIELD DR
3300 HacH 91745 677-J5
HEATHERGLEN CT
- Nor 91325 501-A5
HEATHERGLEN LN
- SDMS 91773 570-B6
HEATHER HEIGHTS CT
200 MNRO 91016 567-F3
HEATHER HILL RD
1500 HacH 91745 678-E4
HEATHER KNOLLS PL
23500 SCTA 91321 4640-G2
HEATHERLANE CT
20800 DBAR 91765 679-J5
HEATHER LEE LN
21600 Chat 91311 500-A2
HEATHER RIDGE DR
1500 GLDL 91207 564-F1
HEATHER RIDGE LN
1400 CHLS 91709 680-J4
HEATHER RIDGE WY
- SCTA 91351 4551-G7
HEATHERSIDE RD
600 PAS 91105 565-E3
HEATHERTON AV
1300 RowH 91748 679-B4
HEATHERVALE DR
14100 CHLS 91709 680-H3
HEATHER VALE ST
- SCTA 91321 4550-H6
- SCTA 91350 4550-H6
HEATHFIELD DR
16200 WHIT 90603 708-A6

HEATHRIDGE CIR
19700 LACo 91789 679-D4
HEATHROW DR
40000 PMDL 93551 4195-B4
HEATON AV
43700 LAN 93534 4105-G1
44000 LAN 93534 4015-G7
HEATON MOOR DR
900 WAL 91789 639-D6
HEAVEN AV
4700 WdHl 91364 559-G4
HEAVENLY CT
24500 CanP 91307 529-D4
HEAVENLY WY
31200 Cstc 91384 4369-G7
31200 Cstc 91384 4459-G1
HEAVENLY VALLEY CIR
1100 WAL 91789 639-E5
HEBE AV
12000 NRWK 90650 706-H7
HEBER ST
300 GLDR 91741 569-D6
E HEBER ST
19300 GLDR 91741 569-D6
W HEBER ST
19000 GLDR 91741 569-C6
HEBRIDES CIR
7000 CanP 91307 529-F5
HEBRON LN
10400 BelA 90077 592-A4
HECLA ST
9200 TEML 91780 596-J4
HEDDA CIR
13700 CRTS 90703 767-D1
HEDDA DR
12300 CRTS 90703 766-J1
13100 CRTS 90703 767-B1
HEDDA LN
13000 CRTS 90703 767-B1
HEDDA PL
10700 CRTS 90703 766-E1
13200 CRTS 90703 767-B1
HEDDA ST
3800 LKWD 90712 765-J1
3800 NLB 90805 765-J1
4100 LKWD 90712 766-B1
5800 LKWD 90713 766-D1
12900 CRTS 90703 767-B1
E HEDDA ST
3500 NLB 90805 765-J1
HEDDING ST
6400 Wch 90045 672-F7
HEDGEPATH AV
900 HacH 91745 637-J7
900 HacH 91745 677-J2
HEDGEROW DR
3400 WCOV 91792 679-E1
HEDGEROW LN
2100 CHLS 91709 680-J4
HEDGES PL
8500 LA 90069 592-J5
HEDGES WY
8500 LA 90069 592-J5
HEDGEWALL DR
6000 WLKV 91362 557-F3
HEDGEWOOD DR
6900 RPV 90275 792-G7
HEDGEWOOD PL
1100 DBAR 91765 680-E3
HEDWIG RD
3200 OrCo 90720 796-H3
HEFFNER RD
- Actn 93510 (4554-H1 See Page 4464)
29100 Actn 93510 4464-H7
HEFFNER HILL RD
600 COV 91724 599-D6
700 LACo 91724 599-D6
HEFFRON DR
3700 BURB 91505 563-D4
HEFLIN DR
12600 LMRD 90638 737-F1
HEGEL ST
9000 BLF 90706 736-A4
HEGLIS AV
3100 RSMD 91770 636-J1
3100 ELMN 91770 636-J1
HEIDELBERG AV
1100 WAL 91789 639-F4
HEIDELBURG LN
400 CLAR 91711 571-E7
HEIDEMARIE ST
22100 Chat 91311 499-J6
HEIDI LN
3100 Top 90290 560-B7
HEIDI JO LN
27600 SCTA 91350 4461-B7
HEIDLEMAN RD
1800 LA 90032 635-E2
HEIGHTS DR
41000 PMDL 93551 4194-F1
HEINEMANN AV
- LBCH 90808 765-J7
HEINER ST
9300 BLF 90706 736-A3
HEINTZ ST
5000 BALD 91706 598-D3
HEIRLOOM PL
- SCTA 91350 4550-J2
HEISS ST
23100 WdHl 91364 559-G4
HELA AV
11300 LA 91342 502-H1

N HELBERTA AV
100 RBCH 90277 762-J4
S HELBERTA AV
100 RBCH 90277 762-J5
1200 RBCH 90277 792-J1
1200 RBCH 90277 793-A1
HELEN AV
8800 SunV 91352 503-A7
8800 SunV 91352 533-A1
9600 Sunl 91040 503-A5
N HELEN AV
1300 ONT 91762 601-H5
S HELEN AV
1300 ONT 91762 641-H3
N HELEN CT
1500 ONT 91762 601-H5
HELEN DR
100 FUL 92835 738-H4
1300 City 90063 635-F3
HELEN LN
2800 LAN 93536 4105-C2
3000 WCOV 91792 639-A7
3000 WCOV 91792 679-A1
HELEN PL
10600 Sunl 91040 503-A4
HELEN ST
1300 SBdC 92397 (4652-D2 See Page 4651)
13400 WHIT 90602 677-D7
HELENA
18000 LACo 90220 765-A1
HELENA AV
8900 MTCL 91763 601-F4
10300 MTCL 91763 641-F1
HELENA CIR
3400 LVRN 91750 570-E7
HELENA ST
12400 Brwd 90049 631-F4
HELENDALE AV
10100 Tuj 91042 503-J3
HELENSBURG ST
19300 GLDR 91740 569-D7
HELEO AV
4800 TEML 91780 596-J3
HELIOS CT
- SCTA 91351 4551-G7
HELIOS DR
2200 LA 90068 593-F3
HELIOTROPE AV
100 MNRO 91016 567-H3
4700 BELL 90201 675-E7
5500 VER 90040 675-E5
5500 MYWD 90270 675-E5
6800 BELL 90201 705-E1
S HELIOTROPE AV
100 MNRO 91016 567-H4
HELIOTROPE CIR
4700 MYWD 90270 675-E6
HELIOTROPE DR
300 LA 90004 594-A7
700 LA 90029 594-A6
HELLER CIR
- Saug 91350 4461-F6
HELLER PL
14900 LMRD 90638 707-F7
HELLMAN AV
100 MONP 91754 636-E1
100 ALH 91803 636-E1
1100 MONP 91755 636-E1
1100 RSMD 91770 636-E1
3600 LA 90032 595-D5
4900 HiPk 90042 595-E4
E HELLMAN AV
100 MONP 91755 636-C1
100 ALH 91801 636-C1
W HELLMAN AV
100 MONP 91754 636-A1
100 ALH 91801 636-A1
200 ALH 91803 636-A1
1500 ALH 91803 635-G1
E HELLMAN ST
1100 LBCH 90813 795-F6
HELLMAN WY
- LA 90089 674-B1
HELM PL
32200 RPV 90275 823-D5
HELMCREST DR
16400 LACo 90604 708-A6
HELMER DR
12900 WHIT 90602 707-C1
HELMET TR
1800 Top 90290 590-C2
HELMGATE DR
4700 ELMN 91732 597-F5
HELMICK ST
800 CRSN 90746 764-F3
HELMOND DR
26900 CALB 91301 558-F6
HELMS AV
3100 LA 90034 632-H7
3200 CULC 90232 632-J7
3500 CULC 90232 672-H1
HELMS PL
8900 LA 90034 632-H6
HELMSDALE AV
500 LACo 91744 638-G6
HELMSDALE CIR
7100 CanP 91307 529-F5
HELMSDALE RD
7000 CanP 91307 529-E5
HELTON DR
27900 SCTA 91350 4461-C6

HELVEY LN
- FUL 92833 738-D5
HELWIG AV
14300 NRWK 90650 736-J4
HEMET PL
8000 LA 90046 593-B4
HEMINGER ST
300 GLDL 91205 564-E7
HEMINGSFORD WY
- VeCo 91361 586-F1
HEMINGWAY AV
25300 StvR 91381 4550-B7
25900 StvR 91381 4640-B1
HEMLOCK AV
- LAN 93536 4104-C4
HEMLOCK DR
19700 LA 90210 592-D2
HEMLOCK LN
3600 WCOV 91792 679-J2
HEMLOCK RD
- PMDL 93551 4285-D2
10100 SBdC 92372 (4472-B4 See Page 4471)
HEMLOCK ST
900 LA 90021 634-G7
11500 ELMN 91732 597-F4
HEMLOCK WY
2400 POM 91767 601-A4
HEMMINGWAY ST
17200 VanN 91406 531-B3
17400 Nor 91325 531-B3
17700 Res 91335 531-A3
18100 Res 91335 530-F3
19700 Win 91306 530-D3
20900 LA 91304 530-B3
22100 LA 91304 529-J3
HEMP CT
6800 LACo 93536 4104-D6
HEMPHILL ST
17400 LACo 91744 638-H7
HEMPSTEAD AV
3000 ARCD 91006 597-E2
HEMPSTEAD DR
5700 AGRH 91301 557-H4
HEMSTEAD CT
3300 WCOV 91791 639-D3
HENDEE ST
1900 WCOV 91792 638-J7
1900 WCOV 91792 639-A7
N HENDERSON AV
1400 LBCH 90813 795-D5
1800 LBCH 90806 795-D5
HENDERSON GRN
8200 BPK 90621 737-J5
HENDERSON ST
5000 LA 90032 595-F4
HENDERSON WY
1200 LHB 90631 708-C5
3700 CLAR 91711 571-F4
HENDLEY DR
11300 LA 91604 562-J6
HENDON DR
38200 PMDL 93550 4285-J1
38200 PMDL 93550 4286-A1
HENDRICKS AV
24300 LMTA 90717 793-H3
S HENDRICKS AV
600 ELA 90022 676-A1
1000 ELA 90022 675-J2
2000 MONP 91754 636-A5
N HENDRICKS ST
500 MTBL 90640 636-A7
E HENDRIE ST
8300 LBCH 90808 767-A7
HENDRIX AV
500 CLAR 91711 601-C5
HENDRIX LN
- LA 91343 501-J6
HENDRON WY
1800 MONP 91755 636-B5
HENEFER AV
7400 Wch 90045 672-F7
7400 Wch 90045 702-F1
HENERY RIDGE RD
- Top 90290 589-J2
HENLEY CT
4400 WLKV 91361 557-D6
HENLEY LN
11800 BelA 90077 591-G2
HENLEY WY
- StvR 91381 4550-D7
HENNA LN
- PMDL 93551 4285-D3
HENNIGER RIDGE MTWY
- LACo - 536-E5
HENNING DR
14700 LMRD 90638 707-F7
HENNIPEN ST
500 POM 91768 640-C2
HENNY AV
13600 LA 91342 481-J2
HENRIETTA AV
2300 LaCr 91214 504-F6
3200 GLDL 91214 504-E5
HENRIETTA ST
20300 TOR 90503 763-A5
HENRILEE ST
4500 LKWD 90713 766-D4
HENRY AL
- PAS 91103 535-H7
HENRY CT
23300 TOR 90505 793-F2
HENRY FORD AV
300 Wilm 90744 794-H6
300 Wilm 90744 824-H1

HENRY MAYO DR
26800 Valc 91355 4459-J7
27000 Valc 91355 4549-H1
HENRY MAYO DR
Rt#-126
- SCTA 91355 4459-H7
- SCTA 91355 4460-A6
27100 Valc 91355 4459-H7
27100 Valc 91355 4549-F2
28500 Cstc 91384 4549-A4
HENRY RIDGE MTWY
400 Top 90290 590-A5
500 Top 90290 589-J3
HENSAL RD
9700 LA 90210 592-D2
HENSEL DR
900 LHB 90631 708-F4
900 OrCo 90631 708-F4
HENSEL ST
12700 BALD 91706 637-H2
HENSHAW AV
11300 LACo 90604 707-F6
HENSHAW CIR
7800 LPMA 90623 767-C3
8200 BPK 90621 737-J6
HENSHAW ST
19600 Tarz 91356 560-E2
19700 WdHl 91364 560-E2
HENSLOW AV
- LACo 93551 4285-J4
HENSON DR
12300 Pcma 91331 502-F4
HENTON AV
100 COV 91723 599-F4
4800 LACo 91724 599-F3
HENZIE PL
12400 GmH 91344 481-B5
HEPBURN AV
3700 LA 90008 673-F2
3700 LA 90018 673-F2
HEPBURN CIR
2200 FUL 92833 738-C3
10700 CULC 90232 672-F2
HEPNER AV
300 COV 91723 599-A6
1300 Eagl 90041 565-C7
HEPWORTH AV
2200 CMRC 90040 675-F3
HERA ST
500 SDMS 91773 600-D2
W HERALD ST
800 WCOV 91790 638-F1
HERB CT
18900 RowH 91748 679-C7
HERB ST
11300 LACo 91733 637-D4
11300 SELM 91733 637-D4
HERBERT AV
1600 GLDL 91206 564-H3
N HERBERT AV
100 City 90063 635-D3
800 SPed 90731 824-A3
S HERBERT AV
100 City 90063 635-E6
700 LACo 90023 635-E7
800 SPed 90731 824-A3
900 LACo 90023 675-E1
1300 CMRC 90023 675-E1
N HERBERT CIR
1000 City 90063 635-D4
HERBERT ST
500 PAS 91104 565-J2
11300 CULC 90066 672-D4
12000 LA 90066 672-D4
HERBERT WY
12200 CULC 90066 672-D4
HERBINE ST
900 LACo 91750 600-E1
HERBOLD ST
18100 Nor 91325 500-J6
18100 Nor 91325 501-A6
HERCULE WY
16700 CynC 91351 4462-A3
HERCULES DR
2000 LA 90046 593-A2
3000 SBdC 92371 (4562-H1 See Page 4471)
HERCULES ST
- SCTA 91355 4460-C5
11100 NRWK 90650 706-F7
HEREFORD DR
1900 MTBL 90640 676-B2
E HEREFORD DR
1400 ELA 90022 675-J2
1600 ELA 90022 676-A2
HEREFORD RD
- VeCo 91361 586-E1
HERITAGE CIR
11900 DWNY 90241 705-H5
HERITAGE CT
200 POM 91767 601-A6
600 AZU 91702 569-A6
HERITAGE DR
2700 PAS 91107 566-F2
3300 WCOV 91791 639-D2
6100 AGRH 91301 557-J3
6100 AGRH 91301 558-A3
HERITAGE LN
1700 PMDL 93551 4195-E5
24200 SCTA 91321 4640-H2
HERITAGE PL
- CULC 90230 672-G5
- RowH 91748 679-C4
500 PMDL 93550 4286-A6
1500 GLDR 91740 599-F2
12700 CRTS 90703 767-A1

HERITAGE WY
- COV 91724 599-F3
- ING 90305 703-F3
2200 FUL 92833 738-D3
HERITAGE OAK CT
800 Alta 91001 535-G3
23500 SCTA 91321 4640-G3
HERITAGE OAK DR
200 GLDR 91741 569-H5
HERITAGE OAKS DR
1000 ARCD 91006 566-J4
HERITAGE PARK DR
10400 SFSP 90670 706-H5
HERITAGE PASS PL
22300 Chat 91311 499-H2
HERITAGE VIEW LN
- StvR 91381 4550-C5
W HERKIMER ST
2800 LA 90039 594-D3
HERLINDA LN
2500 RowH 91748 679-E7
HERMAN LN
7800 LPMA 90623 767-C3
HERMANO DR
4700 Tarz 91356 560-J4
HERMANOS ST
600 PAS 91107 566-F3
HERMAR CT
3100 Alta 91001 535-H4
HERMES DR
7500 LA 90046 593-B2
HERMES LN
- SCTA 91351 4551-G7
HERMES ST
10800 NRWK 90650 706-E6
13600 LACo 90605 707-C6
HERMITAGE AV
5200 LA 91607 562-F2
HERMITAGE DR
700 MONP 91755 636-D1
2200 FUL 92833 738-C3
3500 HacH 91745 677-J7
HERMITAGE LN
300 AZU 91702 568-J4
HERMITS GN
2300 LA 90046 592-H3
HERMOSA AV
- HMB 90254 762-G1
- LBCH 90802 825-G1
200 LBCH 90802 795-G7
500 SMAD 91024 567-A1
1000 POM 91767 601-B6
2500 Mont 91020 534-F2
2600 GLDL 91020 534-F2
2800 GLDL 91214 534-F2
2900 HMB 90254 732-F7
5000 Eagl 90041 565-A5
N HERMOSA AV
- SMAD 91024 567-A2
S HERMOSA AV
- SMAD 91024 567-A3
HERMOSA CIR
6800 BPK 90620 767-E2
HERMOSA CT
6300 PMDL 93551 4104-E7
HERMOSA DR
600 SGBL 91775 596-H3
1000 LACo 91775 596-H3
8700 TEML 91775 596-H3
8800 TEML 91780 596-H3
E HERMOSA DR
100 FUL 92835 738-G2
100 SGBL 91775 596-F3
8300 LACo 91775 596-F3
8600 TEML 91775 596-F3
W HERMOSA DR
100 FUL 92835 738-F2
100 SGBL 91775 596-D3
HERMOSA PL
400 SPAS 91030 595-G1
3600 FUL 92835 738-F1
HERMOSA RD
1000 PAS 91105 565-E6
HERMOSA ST
100 Wilm 90744 824-E2
500 SPAS 91030 595-F1
HERMOSA VIEW DR
2800 HMB 90254 732-G7
HERMOSA VISTA ST
400 MONP 91754 636-A3
HERMOSILLA CT
24700 CALB 91302 559-C6
HERMOSITA DR
2300 GLDL 91208 534-G6
HERMOSURA ST
11800 NRWK 90650 736-H5
HERN DR
1200 DBAR 91789 679-G3
HERNANDEZ DR
800 LACo 93551 4285-G4
HEROIC DR
3500 RPV 90275 823-E6
HERON AV
15500 LMRD 90638 737-E5
HERON BAY
5400 LBCH 90803 796-C7
5400 LBCH 90803 826-C1
HERON CIR
- SLB 90740 826-G3
HERON LN
- LACo 91387 4551-J6
- LACo 91387 4552-A6

HERON PL
- BREA 92823 709-H6
HERONDO ST
- HMB 90254 762-H3
- RBCH 90277 762-H3
HERON POINTE
- SLB 90740 826-G3
HERR AL
300 PAS 91105 565-H6
HERRERES TKTR
- LACo 91342 (4723-C5 See Page 4643)
HERRICK AV
8600 SunV 91352 533-A1
8900 SunV 91352 502-J7
10900 Pcma 91331 502-D1
11500 LA 91340 482-C7
11500 LA 91340 502-D1
12000 LA 91342 482-A5
12700 LA 91342 481-F2
N HERRIN AV
1700 MANB 90266 732-J5
HERRIN ST
1500 RBCH 90278 762-J1
N HERRIN ST
100 MANB 90266 732-J6
S HERRIN ST
100 MANB 90266 732-J7
300 MANB 90266 762-J1
E HERRING AV
600 WCOV 91790 638-G2
1400 WCOV 91791 638-G2
HERRON ST
12600 LA 91342 482-E1
14400 LA 91342 481-J6
HERSCHER WY
- Brwd 90049 591-F1
HERSHEY AV
700 MONP 91755 636-D1
HERSHEY DR
7500 BPK 90620 767-F3
HERSHEY ST
200 POM 91767 641-C1
7800 RSMD 91770 636-E1
11000 SunV 91352 502-J5
HERSHOLT AV
4700 LBCH 90808 766-B4
4900 LKWD 90712 766-B2
HERSKIND RD
- Actn 93510 4374-D5
HERTFORD PL
3500 RowH 91748 708-J2
N HERVEY AV
300 UPL 91786 601-G3
HERVEY ST
8600 LA 90034 632-J6
HERZEL AV
1000 LAN 93535 4106-B1
HESBY ST
5000 NHol 91601 563-A3
5100 Shrm 91423 562-B3
11100 NHol 91601 562-J3
11700 LA 91607 562-E3
14500 Shrm 91403 561-H3
14500 Shrm 91403 562-A3
15500 Enc 91436 561-G3
HESPERIA AV
4800 Enc 91316 561-A1
6200 Enc 91316 531-A7
6400 Res 91335 531-A3
HESPERIAN AV
3600 LBCH 90810 764-J7
3600 LA 90810 764-J7
HESPERO ST
18200 RowH 91748 678-J6
HESSE DR
15600 LMRD 90638 737-H4
HESSEN ST
- FUL 92833 738-D5
HESTER AV
10200 WHIT 90603 707-G4
10500 LACo 90604 707-G5
HESTON ST
8400 LACo 91776 596-G4
HETEBRINK ST
- FUL 92833 738-C5
HETZLER RD
6100 CULC 90016 672-J1
6100 CULC 90232 672-J2
HEWITT AV
11200 LA 91340 502-B1
HEWITT CT
- FUL 92833 738-D5
HEWITT ST
600 SFER 91340 502-A1
1100 SFER 91340 482-A7
1400 SFER 91340 481-J7
N HEWITT ST
500 LA 90012 634-G4
S HEWITT ST
100 LA 90012 634-G4
300 LA 90013 634-G5
HEYER ST
500 LAN 93534 4105-H1
HEYWOOD DR
27700 SCTA 91350 4461-B6
E HI RD
- PMDL 93550 4376-F3
HIATT ST
1000 LHH 90631 708-E3
HIAWATHA AV
- AVA 90704 5923-G3

HIAWATHA DR
1700 GLDL 91208 564-H1
HIAWATHA ST
14600 MsnH 91345 501-H4
15600 GmH 91344 501-A4
17900 Nor 91326 501-A4
18200 Nor 91326 500-J4
19600 Chat 91311 500-E3
22000 Chat 91311 499-J4
HIBBING ST
11000 CRTS 90703 766-F2
12000 ART 90701 766-H2
HIBISCUS AV
- AZU 91702 568-J4
HIBISCUS CT
- Saug 91350 4461-B4
800 POM 91766 641-B2
HIBISCUS ST
- FUL 92835 738-H3
900 MTBL 90640 636-F7
1200 UPL 91784 571-J4
HIBISCUS HILL LN
- WdHl 91367 559-H7
HICKMAN DR
4000 TOR 90504 763-D1
HICKOCK LN
- CRSN 90745 794-G1
12900 NRWK 90650 737-A1
HICKORY AV
800 COMP 90220 734-J3
800 TOR 90503 763-F6
2300 UPL 91784 571-J3
2900 POM 91767 600-J3
22400 TOR 90505 763-F7
22400 TOR 90505 793-F1
HICKORY CIR
5100 CYP 90630 767-C6
HICKORY CT
- SCTA 91354 4460-F4
HICKORY DR
- CRSN 90746 764-F5
1300 LVRN 91750 570-F6
5800 VeCo 91377 558-A1
HICKORY LN
500 PAS 91103 565-G3
11300 SBdC 91766 641-D3
HICKORY PL
22500 SCTA 91390 4460-J3
HICKORY ST
4700 LA 90016 633-D7
5400 PMDL 93551 4104-E7
6500 PMDL 93551 4104-F7
8300 Flor 90001 704-H3
8600 Wats 90002 704-H3
9200 Wats 90002 704-H4
10700 LA 90059 704-H5
HICKORY GLEN AV
42200 LACo 93536 4104-F5
42200 LAN 93536 4104-F5
HICKORYHILL DR
15800 LMRD 90638 737-J1
HICKORY HILL LN
19000 WAL 91789 639-B6
HICKORY NUT LN
22600 DBAR 91765 680-A4
N HICKS AV
100 City 90063 635-D4
2000 LA 90032 635-D1
S HICKS AV
100 City 90063 635-D6
800 LACo 90023 635-D7
1000 LACo 90023 675-D1
1300 CMRC 90023 675-D1
HICKSON ST
10400 ELMN 91731 597-B6
HICREST RD
1200 GLDR 91741 569-B4
18000 LACo 91741 569-B4
HIDALGO AV
- ALH 91801 596-C4
2200 LA 90039 594-E4
N HIDALGO AV
- ALH 91801 596-B3
S HIDALGO AV
- ALH 91801 596-C4
1800 ALH 91801 636-C1
HIDALGO ST
7100 BPK 90621 767-G1
15800 IRW 91706 598-F2
HIDAWAY AV
27000 SCTA 91351 4551-G2
HIDDEN LN
1000 LHB 90631 708-E4
1000 LHH 90631 708-E4
1800 LBCH 90815 796-E4
3200 ELMN 91733 637-B1
3600 LACo 90274 793-E6
HIDDEN TR
12000 LACo 91342 482-J6
HIDDEN CANYON RD
1400 LHH 90631 708-C3
HIDDEN COVE LN
39200 PMDL 93551 4195-G5
HIDDEN CREEK LN
- SCTA 91354 4460-F5
HIDDEN CREEK RD
1300 SDMS 91773 570-D7
HIDDENCREEK WY
12500 CRTS 90703 737-A5
HIDDEN HIGHLAND RD
31600 Ago 91301 587-D4
31600 LACo 90265 587-D4

STREET Block City ZIP Pg-Grid

HIDDEN HILLS CIR
- POM 91766 640-G5
HIDDEN HILLS DR
- LACo 91390 4461-A4
HIDDEN OAK CT
- StvR 91381 4550-C5
HIDDEN OAK DR
10300 Sunl 91040 503-F3
HIDDEN OAK PL
29300 SCTA 91387 4462-G7
HIDDEN OAKS RD
- Enc 91316 561-B4
HIDDEN PARK DR
- Ago 91301 587-J4
HIDDEN PINE DR
7100 LACo 91775 566-G7
HIDDEN PINES DR
21200 DBAR 91765 679-H6
HIDDEN PINES PL
3800 RSMD 91770 596-G6
HIDDEN RANCH DR
- SIMI 93063 499-A3
HIDDEN RANCHO PL
3400 GLDL 91208 534-J4
HIDDEN RIDGE LN
16000 CRTS 90703 736-J4
HIDDEN SPRINGS LN
1100 GLDR 91741 569-G3
HIDDEN SPRINGS RD
19900 WAL 91789 639-E4
HIDDEN TRAIL PL
19800 WAL 91789 639-E5
HIDDEN TRAIL RD
29300 Cstc 91384 4459-H5
HIDDEN VALLEY CT
- Cstc 91384 4459-B3
HIDDEN VALLEY DR
500 AZU 91702 568-H4
S HIDDEN VALLEY DR
1200 WCOV 91791 639-A3
HIDDEN VALLEY PL
9400 LA 90210 592-G1
HIDDEN VALLEY RD
- MNRO 91016 567-F2
- POM 91766 640-F6
- RHE 90274 793-C5
9500 LA 90210 592-F1
HIDEAWAY LN
- DUAR 91010 568-D5
3100 WCOV 91792 679-D2
3200 FUL 92835 738-G1
HIDEAWAY PL
- PMDL 93551 4195-E6
HIDEOUT CT
- LACo 91390 4460-J3
HIDEOUT DR
3300 WCOV 91791 639-E3
21300 DBAR 91765 679-H6
HIERBA RD
7900 LACo 91390 4374-A2
8600 LACo 91390 4373-G2
HIERRO WY
2500 LACo 91302 589-C3
HIGA RD
5200 Actn 93510 4374-G1
HIGBEE AV
43700 LAN 93534 4105-G1
44000 LAN 93534 4015-G7
HIGGINS CT
20800 TOR 90501 763-H5
HIGGINS ST
11600 NHol 91605 532-H5
HIGH LN
700 RBCH 90278 763-B2
HIGH PL
1900 SMCA 90404 671-H1
HIGH ST
- TOR 90505 793-D4
5700 HiPk 90042 565-C7
13400 WHIT 90602 707-D1
13900 WHIT 90605 707-E2
N HIGH ST
600 ING 90302 673-E7
600 ING 90302 703-E1
HIGH TR
17800 LACo 93532 4101-J2
HIGHACRES AV
16100 LACo 93591 4199-F3
HIGHBLUFF DR
1500 DBAR 91765 680-C4
HIGHBLUFF RD
21600 DBAR 91765 709-J1
HIGH BLUFF WY
6500 LAN 93536 4104-E5
HIGHBURY AV
2200 LA 90032 635-G1
2300 LA 90032 595-G7
HIGHCASTLE ST
2500 WCOV 91792 679-B2
18800 LACo 91744 679-B2
18800 LACo 91792 679-B2
HIGH CHAPARRAL AV
16000 LACo 93591 4199-F4
HIGHCLIFF DR
2500 TOR 90505 793-F5
HIGHCLIFF ST
7600 RSMD 91770 636-E3
HIGHCLIFF TR
7000 Tuj 91042 504-A5
HIGH COUNTRY DR
1000 GLDR 91740 569-H7
20800 DBAR 91789 679-G5

HIGH COUNTRY LN
15900 SCTA 91387 4552-D1
HIGH COUNTRY RD
38000 PMDL 93551 4285-H1
HIGHCREST AV
5100 Eagl 90041 565-C5
HIGHCREST DR
23700 DBAR 91765 680-D1
HIGHCROSS DR
26000 TOR 90505 793-E6
HIGHDALE ST
9200 BLF 90706 736-A4
11300 NRWK 90650 736-F4
12600 NRWK 90650 737-A4
HIGHFALLS ST
16700 SCTA 91387 4552-B2
HIGHGATE AV
100 POM 91767 600-J3
HIGHGATE CT
2500 CHLS 91709 640-J7
2500 CHLS 91709 641-A7
HIGHGATE RD
2100 THO 91361 557-A7
2100 WLKV 91361 557-A7
HIGH GLEN WY
12200 Nor 91326 480-F5
HIGHGROVE AV
4300 TOR 90505 793-B2
HIGHGROVE ST
5300 TOR 90505 793-A2
HIGHGROVE TER
1000 HiPk 90042 565-E7
1000 HiPk 90042 595-E1
1100 PAS 91105 565-E7
HIGH KNOB RD
24000 DBAR 91765 640-D5
HIGH KNOLL LN
900 WAL 91789 639-E6
HIGH KNOLL RD
15500 Enc 91436 561-F5
HIGHLAND AV
700 GLDL 91202 564-C3
800 DUAR 91010 568-B6
1800 DUAR 91706 568-B6
2100 FUL 92835 738-F4
2300 Alta 91001 536-B6
2600 SMCA 90405 671-G4
3200 HMB 90254 732-F7
3300 MANB 90266 732-F7
6500 BPK 90621 767-G1
8800 WHIT 90605 707-F3
E HIGHLAND AV
- SMAD 91024 567-B2
N HIGHLAND AV
100 FUL 92832 738-G7
100 LA 90004 633-E1
100 MANB 90266 732-E5
100 LA 90036 633-E1
300 LA 90004 593-E7
300 LA 90036 593-E7
700 LA 90038 593-E7
1000 FUL 92835 738-G5
N HIGHLAND AV Rt#-170
1100 LA 90038 593-E5
1300 Hlwd 90028 593-E5
1400 LA 90068 593-E5
S HIGHLAND AV
100 FUL 92832 738-G7
100 LA 90004 633-E2
100 LA 90036 633-E2
300 LA 90020 633-E2
600 LA 90005 633-E2
600 LA 90010 633-E2
900 LA 90019 633-D4
2100 LA 90016 633-D6
W HIGHLAND AV
- SMAD 91024 567-A2
200 SMAD 91024 566-J2
HIGHLAND CT
- Cstc 91384 4369-E4
200 LHB 90631 708-E4
37400 PMDL 93552 4287-C2
42300 LAN 93536 4104-C5
HIGHLAND DR
- PMDL 93552 4287-C1
- SCTA 91321 4551-F6
300 LCF 91011 535-C6
300 PAS 91103 535-C6
400 GLDR 91741 569-H4
1100 MONP 91754 635-H4
1200 LVRN 91750 600-E2
S HIGHLAND DR
1900 LA 90016 633-D6
HIGHLAND GRN
4600 BPK 90621 737-G5
HIGHLAND PL
100 MNRO 91016 567-F3
700 SDMS 91773 600-A1
HIGHLAND ST
300 PAS 91104 535-J7
600 PAS 91104 536-A7
1000 SPAS 91030 595-G1
4500 MTCL 91763 601-E4
37600 PMDL 93552 4287-C2
39000 PMDL 93551 4195-D7
HIGHLAND TR
7900 LA 90046 593-B4
HIGHLAND WY
200 CRSN 90745 794-D3
HIGHLANDER AV
500 LHB 90631 708-D5

HIGHLANDER CT
- FUL 92833 738-A3
HIGHLANDER RD
- FUL 92833 738-A3
- LMRD 90638 738-A3
23700 CanP 91307 529-D5
HIGHLAND GLEN DR
23500 SCTA 91321 4640-G2
HIGHLAND GORGE DR
9600 LA 90210 592-E5
HIGHLAND OAKS DR
1100 ARCD 91006 567-D1
2100 ARCD 91006 537-E7
HIGHLAND PASS CIR
16100 CHLS 91709 710-G1
HIGHLAND PASS RD
1200 CHLS 91709 710-G1
HIGHLAND PINES RD
2400 POM 91767 601-B5
HIGHLANDS LN
27100 SCTA 91354 4460-G7
HIGHLAND TERRACE DR
- WAL 91789 639-C4
HIGHLAND VALLEY RD
23500 POM 91765 640-C5
23600 DBAR 91765 640-C5
HIGHLAND VIEW AV
4900 Eagl 90041 565-A5
HIGHLAND VIEW DR
3100 BURB 91504 533-E3
HIGHLAND VIEW PL
5300 Eagl 90041 565-A5
HIGHLAND VISTA DR
2100 ARCD 91006 537-D7
2100 ARCD 91006 567-E1
HIGHLAND VISTA LN
1900 Brwd 90049 591-F4
HIGHLAWN PL
200 Alta 91001 535-J5
HIGHLIGHT DR
1200 WCOV 91791 639-D3
HIGHLIGHT PL
5300 LA 90016 673-B1
HIGHLINE RD
900 GLDL 91205 564-H6
HIGHMEADOW DR
38700 PMDL 93551 4195-F7
HIGH MESA DR
2200 DUAR 91010 568-C3
HIGHMORE AV
29000 RPV 90275 823-J3
HIGH MOUNTAIN WY
- Nor 91326 480-E7
HIGH NOON WY
16000 SCTA 91387 4552-D1
HIGH OAK DR
2300 LA 90068 593-H2
HIGH PEAK PL
5600 AGRH 91301 557-J5
HIGH PINE ST
8800 LACo 91770 636-H5
HIGHPLAINS CT
29100 Cstc 91384 4459-G6
HIGH POINT DR
800 CLAR 91711 571-B5
1500 PMDL 93550 4286-C4
HIGHPOINT DR
2300 Ago 91301 588-B4
13300 LMRD 90638 738-A1
HIGH POINT PL
20300 SCTA 91351 4461-D7
HIGHPOINT RD
29500 RPV 90275 823-F4
HIGHPOINT ST
1400 UPL 91784 571-H3
HIGH RIDGE DR
- LACo 91390 4461-C3
HIGHRIDGE DR
2500 CHLS 91709 680-J2
9500 LA 90210 592-D3
HIGHRIDGE PL
9500 LA 90210 592-D2
HIGHRIDGE RD
2800 LaCr 91214 504-F5
5900 HIDH 91302 559-C2
27800 RPV 90275 792-J7
28300 RHE 90274 792-J7
28400 RHE 90274 822-J1
28500 RPV 90275 822-J1
28600 RHE 90274 823-A2
28600 RPV 90275 823-A2
HIGHRIM RD
2100 LCF 91011 504-J5
HIGH SIERRA TR
- LACo 91390 4461-A2
HIGHSPIRE DR
2200 WCOV 91791 639-A3
HIGHSPRING AV
24900 SCTA 91321 4640-G2
HIGH SPRINGS RD
- LACo 93551 4285-G6
HIGHTIDE DR
3400 RPV 90275 823-E5
HIGH TOP DR
9800 Tuj 91042 503-J5
HIGH TOR DR
16100 HacH 91745 678-C7
HIGH TOWER DR
2000 LA 90068 593-E3
HIGH TREE RD
1300 SIMI 93063 499-C3
HIGHTREE RD
600 LA 90402 631-B6

HIGHTREE ST
9000 PRV 90660 676-G3
HIGHVALE TR
21500 Top 90290 590-B5
HIGH VALLEY PL
16100 Enc 91436 561-F5
HIGH VALLEY RD
4100 Enc 91436 561-F5
HIGHVIEW AV
800 MANB 90266 732-F6
2600 Alta 91001 535-H5
HIGH VIEW RDG
12200 Nor 91326 480-F6
HIGH VISTA AV
1700 PMDL 93550 4286-D4
HIGH VISTA LN
16100 CHLS 91709 710-J1
HIGHWATER RD
11800 GrnH 91344 481-A6
HIGHWAY Rt#-138
200 SBdC 92372 (4472-A3 See Page 4471)
2500 SBdC 92371 (4472-F7 See Page 4471)
2600 SBdC 92371 (4562-G1 See Page 4471)
HIGHWAY ESPLANADE
900 MNRO 91016 567-F5
HIGHWOOD CT
- AZU 91702 568-J1
- AZU 91702 569-A1
HIGHWOOD RD
17000 HacH 91745 678-F5
HIGHWOOD ST
12700 Brwd 90049 631-E3
HIGMAN AV
6800 Hlwd 90028 593-D5
HIGUERA ST
3900 CULC 90232 672-H1
HILARY LN
1100 LA 90210 592-C6
HILBERT AV
500 LACo 91746 637-G4
S HILBORN AV
1000 WCOV 91791 639-A2
HILD TR
3100 LA 90068 593-D1
HILDA AV
1300 GLDL 91205 564-G6
HILDA ST
6600 NLB 90805 735-B7
HILDRETH AV
8900 SGAT 90280 705-D4
10600 LYN 90262 705-D5
HILDRETH CT
3000 LAN 93535 4106-F2
E HILE AV
2700 LBCH 90804 795-H5
HILGARD AV
100 Wwd 90024 592-B7
100 LA 90095 592-B7
200 Wwd 90024 632-B2
200 LA 90095 632-B2
HILL AV
6200 WHIT 90601 677-E5
6700 SBdC - (512-A4 See Page 511)
N HILL AV
100 PAS 91106 566-B3
500 PAS 91104 566-B3
1500 PAS 91104 536-B7
1600 LACo 91104 536-B7
1900 Alta 91001 536-B7
S HILL AV
- PAS 91106 566-B6
400 PAS 91125 566-B5
HILL CT
400 SMCA 90405 671-G4
HILL DR
- SLB 90740 826-G3
300 GLDL 91206 564-H4
1600 SPAS 91030 595-E3
1600 Eagl 90041 565-A5
2000 LA 90032 595-E3
2300 Eagl 90041 564-J5
7800 LACo 91770 636-F4
7900 MTBL 91770 636-F4
W HILL DR
1100 Eagl 90041 565-C5
HILL LN
2000 SPAS 91030 595-G2
2300 RBCH 90278 763-B2
N HILL PL
600 LA 90012 634-G2
HILL PL N
800 SMCA 90405 671-G3
HILL RD
1000 LHB 90631 708-E4
5900 CULC 90230 672-H5
6000 LACo 90230 672-H5
23300 CALB 90290 559-F7
HILL ST
100 AVA 90704 5923-H3
100 SMCA 90405 671-H3
100 HMB 90254 762-H3
200 MNRO 91016 567-H2
900 LBCH 90806 795-H3
2300 SIGH 90755 795-H3
2400 LACo 90255 704-J1
2700 LACo 90255 705-A1
2900 HNTP 90255 705-C2
4500 LCF 91011 535-B2
15700 LPUE 91744 638-D7

HILL ST
16000 INDS 91744 638-D7
30700 Cstc 91384 4459-A6
E HILL ST
100 LBCH 90806 795-E4
1100 SIGH 90755 795-G4
2800 LBCH 90755 795-H4
5000 LBCH 90815 796-B3
N HILL ST
100 LA 90012 634-G3
S HILL ST
100 LA 90012 634-E5
300 LA 90013 634-E5
600 LA 90014 634-E5
900 LA 90015 634-D6
1900 LA 90007 634-D6
2700 LA 90007 674-C2
3800 LA 90037 674-C2
W HILL ST
100 LBCH 90806 795-B4
500 ING 90302 673-B7
500 ING 90302 703-A1
1200 LBCH 90810 795-B4
6900 Wch 90045 703-A1
HILLANDALE AV
1200 LHB 90631 708-C6
HILLANDALE DR
6000 HiPk 90042 565-D7
HILLARD AV
4500 LCF 91011 534-J2
HILLARY DR
7800 LA 91304 529-F2
S HILLBORN AV
400 WCOV 91791 639-A1
HILLCASTLE LN
800 LACo 90502 794-C3
HILLCREST AV
- LA 91342 481-J1
600 LCF 91011 535-C6
1100 PAS 91106 566-A7
1300 PAS 91106 596-A1
1400 GLDL 91202 564-C1
1700 GLDL 91202 534-D7
2000 LHB 90631 708-D6
26300 LMTA 90717 793-J6
HILLCREST BLVD
300 ARCD 91006 567-E3
400 MNRO 91016 567-E3
E HILLCREST BLVD
100 ING 90301 703-C3
100 MNRO 91016 567-G2
N HILLCREST BLVD
100 ING 90301 703-D2
S HILLCREST BLVD
100 ING 90301 703-D2
W HILLCREST BLVD
100 ING 90301 703-A3
100 MNRO 91016 567-F3
HILLCREST CIR
8700 BPK 90621 738-A4
HILLCREST DR
- GLDR 91741 570-B4
- RPV 90275 793-H7
- CanP 91307 529-D5
- LA 91304 529-D5
100 FUL 92832 738-H6
100 LPUE 91744 638-E7
200 LPUE 91744 678-E1
700 POM 91768 600-F6
700 Top 90290 590-A7
900 SBdC 91784 571-J2
1600 LA 90210 592-E4
1800 HMB 90254 762-H1
1800 LACo 90210 592-E3
1900 LA 90016 633-E6
2400 THO 91362 557-A2
2700 LVRN 91750 600-F2
3400 LA 90016 673-D1
3900 LA 90008 673-D3
4900 LA 90043 673-E5
4900 LACo 90043 673-E5
12900 SBdC 91710 641-B7
36700 PMDL 93552 4287-B4
38200 PMDL 93551 4285-G1
E HILLCREST DR
2000 THO 91362 557-A1
HILLCREST DR N
- RPV 90275 793-H7
HILLCREST DR S
- RPV 90275 793-H7
HILLCREST LN
- LACo 90606 676-H6
100 FUL 92832 738-H5
HILLCREST MNR
- RHE 90274 822-J1
- RHE 90274 823-A1
HILLCREST PKWY
29100 Cstc 91384 4459-D2
HILLCREST PL
- SCTA 91354 4460-G6
800 POM 91768 600-G6
1400 PAS 91106 596-A1
HILLCREST RD
1800 LA 90068 593-D3
8500 BPK 90621 738-A4
N HILLCREST RD
500 BHLS 90210 592-G5
HILLCREST ST
- SIGH 90755 795-H3
300 ELSG 90245 732-D1
700 ELSG 90245 702-D7
800 WAL 91789 639-F6
1500 UPL 91784 571-H4
HILLCREST WY
6800 LA 90068 593-D3

HILLCREST MEADOW
- RHE 90274 822-J1
- RHE 90274 823-A1
HILLCROFT DR
8200 LA 91304 529-D1
HILLCROFT RD
900 GLDL 91207 564-G2
HILLDALE AV
800 WHWD 90069 592-H6
HILLDALE CT
12300 Pcma 91331 502-H4
HILLDALE DR
1000 WHWD 90069 592-H5
1100 LA 90069 592-H5
1900 LCF 91011 534-J3
2000 Mont 91020 534-J3
HILLDALE PL
- HacH 91745 637-H7
HILLDYKE
47600 LACo 93534 3925-E5
HILLEN DR
4300 CLAR 91711 571-A7
W HILLER PL
8000 LA 90046 593-B4
HILLFAIR DR
1700 GLDL 91208 564-J1
HILLFIELD LN
28300 SCTA 91351 4551-J1
28300 SCTA 91351 4552-A1
HILLFORD AV
19000 CRSN 90746 764-G2
N HILLFORD AV
400 COMP 90220 734-F3
S HILLFORD AV
900 COMP 90220 734-F6
13900 Wbrk 90222 734-F3
HILLGATE DR
15700 LMRD 90638 707-H7
15800 LACo 90604 707-H7
HILLGREEN DR
- LA 90035 632-F3
400 BHLS 90212 632-F3
HILLGREEN PL
200 ARCD 91006 567-D1
9700 BHLS 90212 632-F4
HILLGROVE DR
10000 LA 90210 592-C6
10100 BelA 90077 592-C6
HILLGROVE PL
1200 LA 90210 592-C5
HILLHAVEN AV
9400 Tuj 91042 503-J6
9400 Tuj 91042 504-A2
HILLHAVEN DR
3400 WCOV 91791 599-D7
HILLHAVEN PL
9500 Tuj 91042 504-A5
HILLHAVEN TER
- HacH 91745 637-G6
HILLHURST AV
1500 LFlz 90027 594-A2
HILLHURST DR
- CanP 91307 529-D5
- LA 91304 529-D5
HILLIARD AV
100 MONP 91754 636-B1
1700 SIMI 93063 499-A3
HILLIARD DR
1600 SMRO 91108 596-F1
HILLMAN LN
2400 RowH 91748 679-C7
HILLMAR DR
1200 DBAR 91765 680-A3
HILLMONT AV
5300 Eagl 90041 565-C5
HILL OAK DR
5600 LA 90068 593-G2
HILLOCK DR
3200 LA 90068 563-D6
HILLPARK DR
6700 LA 90068 593-D2
HILLRISE DR
2700 LACo 91789 679-F7
29100 AGRH 91301 558-A5
29400 AGRH 91301 557-J5
HILLROSE CIR
10600 Sunl 91040 503-F3
HILLROSE DR
2900 OrCo 90720 796-H6
HILLROSE ST
7000 Tuj 91042 504-A3
7300 Tuj 91042 503-J3
7800 Sunl 91040 503-D3
7800 Sunl 91040 503-H3
9300 Sunl 91040 503-D3
9300 Sunl 91040 503-E3
HILLSBORO
- LA 91342 481-H1
HILLSBORO AV
1800 LA 90035 632-H5
2000 LA 90034 632-H5
HILLSBORO DR
9100 LA 90034 632-H5
HILLSBORO PL
700 FUL 92833 738-D6
17700 SCTA 91387 4552-A2
HILLSBORO RD
10500 Nor 91326 500-H3
HILLSBOROUGH DR
- LMRD 90638 737-J3
16000 LMRD 90638 738-A2
HILLSBOROUGH LN
2500 CHLS 91709 640-J7

HILLSBOROUGH PKWY
- SCTA 91354 4460-G6
27000 SCTA 91354 4550-G1
HILLSBOROUGH PL
2600 WCOV 91792 638-J7
HILLSBURY RD
2200 THO 91361 557-A6
HILLSDALE AV
- LA 91342 481-H7
- LA 91342 482-G6
- SFER 91340 482-G6
HILLSDALE CT
- LA 91342 481-H6
HILLSDALE DR
1100 CLAR 91711 601-A1
4700 LA 90032 595-E6
E HILLSDALE ST
300 ING 90302 673-C7
W HILLSDALE ST
100 ING 90302 673-B7
HILLSFALL CT
26500 SCTA 91321 4551-H5
HILLSIDE AV
1800 LAN 93535 4106-C1
7000 LA 90068 593-C4
7100 LA 90046 593-B4
8200 LA 90069 593-A4
8600 LA 90069 592-J4
HILLSIDE CT
1300 LHB 90631 708-E4
2200 LHH 90631 708-D1
HILLSIDE DR
700 LBCH 90815 796-E6
1100 POM 91768 600-F6
1300 GLDL 91208 534-G7
2600 TOR 90505 793-F5
2900 WCOV 91791 639-C3
20600 Top 90290 590-B4
21300 LA 91342 481-G1
33000 PMDL 93550 4376-B6
33000 PMDL 93550 4466-B1
HILLSIDE LN
- HacH 91745 637-H6
- RHLS 90274 823-E1
400 LA 90402 631-B7
6200 WHIT 90601 677-E5
HILLSIDE PL
1100 POM 91768 600-G7
5100 PMDL 93551 4194-H2
8500 SBdC 92372 (4562-C2 See Page 4471)
HILLSIDE RD
- BREA 92823 709-J6
200 SPAS 91030 595-G1
1100 PAS 91105 565-G7
1200 PAS 91105 595-G1
2000 CHLS 91709 710-F3
HILLSIDE ST
600 LHB 90631 708-E5
1000 MONP 91754 635-H4
W HILLSIDE ST
100 LHB 90631 708-E4
HILLSIDE TER
600 PAS 91105 565-F6
HILLSIDE WY
1700 LA 90069 593-A4
HILLSLOPE ST
12100 LA 91604 562-F6
HILLSVIEW CT
7300 LA 91304 529-E4
HILLTONIA DR
3200 WCOV 91792 679-D1
HILLTOP CIR
- RPV 90275 792-J7
HILLTOP CT
20000 LACo 91390 4461-E3
HILLTOP DR
1400 AZU 91702 568-J4
1600 LACo 91702 568-J4
HILLTOP LN
200 BREA 92821 709-E7
HILLTOP PL
- LMRD 90638 737-J1
- LMRD 90638 738-A1
HILL TOP RD
5700 HIDH 91302 559-D3
HILLTOP RD
1100 VeCo 93063 499-B3
5300 Eagl 90041 564-J5
HILLTOP TER
500 PMDL 93551 4285-H2
35100 LACo 91390 4374-F3
HILLTOP WY
- THO 91362 557-A2
1800 Brwd 90049 631-D2
HILLTOP CLIMB DR
25600 LACo 91302 629-A1
HILLTREE RD
14600 LA 90402 631-B6
HILLVALE DR
900 MONP 91754 635-J5
HILLVIEW AV
8300 LA 91304 530-A2
10000 Chat 91311 500-A3
N HILLVIEW AV
2200 MONP 91754 635-J6
S HILLVIEW AV
200 ELA 90022 635-H7
600 ELA 90022 675-H1
HILLVIEW CT
11700 WHIT 90601 677-B6
HILL VIEW DR
4200 LACo 90265 627-H6

HILLVIEW DR
3100 SBdC 91710 641-B7
13600 HacH 91745 637-G6
HILLVIEW LN
- LMTA 90717 793-G3
10700 Litl 93543 4378-E6
15600 GrnH 91344 501-G1
HILLVIEW PL
3500 LA 90032 595-D6
HILLVIEW RD
1300 SBdC 92372 (4562-D2 See Page 4471)
HILLVIEW PARK AV
5700 VanN 91401 562-C1
5900 VanN 91401 532-C7
S HILLWARD AV
200 WCOV 91791 598-J7
200 WCOV 91791 599-A7
200 WCOV 91791 638-J1
200 WCOV 91791 639-A1
HILLWAY DR
3700 GLDL 91208 534-E2
HILLWOOD DR
12200 LACo 90604 707-F7
12200 LACo 90604 737-F1
HILLWORTH AV
25800 LMTA 90717 793-G5
25800 TOR 90505 793-G5
HILO CT
23800 SCTA 91355 4550-G6
HILO ST
1500 WCOV 91792 638-H4
HILSE ARC
23000 SCTA 91321 4550-H6
HILTON AV
5400 TEML 91780 596-J4
HILTON CT
18600 SCTA 91351 4551-H3
HILTON DR
1800 BURB 91504 533-F4
HILTON HEAD CT
- PMDL 93551 4195-B2
HILTON HEAD DR
22800 DBAR 91765 680-B2
HILTON HEAD WY
3600 PRV 90660 676-J1
4100 Tarz 91356 560-J5
HILTS AV
900 Wwd 90024 632-B2
HIMALAYAN CT
- SCTA 91351 4551-H2
HIMAN ST
4200 Actn 93510 4464-J1
4200 Actn 93510 4465-A1
HIMBER PL
23500 Hrbr 90710 793-J2
HINDRY AV
- ING 90301 703-A2
7700 Wch 90045 703-A2
12000 LACo 90250 733-A1
13000 HAW 90250 733-A2
14300 HAW 90260 733-A4
S HINDRY AV
100 ING 90301 703-A3
HINDRY PL
9200 Wch 90045 703-A4
HINDS AV
6500 NHol 91606 532-G5
6800 NHol 91605 532-G2
HINES AL
700 PAS 91104 565-J3
HINES AV
2500 CULC 90232 633-A7
HINES DR
2400 LA 90065 594-H2
HINNEN AV
1100 HacH 91745 678-D2
HINSDALE AV
19300 TOR 90503 763-B3
HINTON AV
5300 WdHl 91367 559-F1
HIPASS DR
21300 DBAR 91765 679-H6
HI POINT ST
1000 LA 90035 633-A4
HIPSHOT DR
31500 Cstc 91384 4369-F6
HIRONDELLE LN
9900 Tuj 91042 504-A5
HISEY RANCH RD
- Actn 93510 4374-F6
HITCHCOCK DR
2200 ALH 91803 635-J2
HITCHCOCK PL
1700 PMDL 93550 4286-D3
HITCHING POST DR
- RHE 90274 793-G7
- RHE 90274 823-F1
HITCHING POST LN
- VeCo 91307 529-A5
HITE ST
13700 BLF 90706 736-C2
HIWASSEE
- CLAR 91711 571-F3
HOADLEY AV
- Actn 93510 4375-H6
HOB AV
28500 SCTA 91350 4461-D4
HOBACK ST
9400 BLF 90706 736-B2
10900 NRWK 90650 736-F2
12700 NRWK 90650 737-A2
13800 LMRD 90638 737-D2

HOBACK GLEN RD
5400 HIDH 91302 559-C3
HOBAN AV
44000 LAN 93534 4015-G7
44000 LAN 93534 4105-G1
HOBART BLVD
14100 GAR 90249 733-J3
16100 GAR 90247 733-J6
17800 GAR 90248 763-J1
21200 LA 90501 763-J6
N HOBART BLVD
100 LA 90004 593-H7
100 LA 90004 633-H1
700 LA 90029 593-J5
1300 LFlz 90027 593-H3
S HOBART BLVD
100 LA 90004 633-H1
300 LA 90020 633-H1
600 LA 90005 633-H3
600 LA 90010 633-H1
900 LA 90006 633-J5
1700 LA 90047 703-H1
1900 LA 90018 633-H7
3700 LA 90062 673-H3
6100 LA 90047 673-H6
10800 LACo 90047 703-H6
21100 LA 90501 763-J5
HOBART DR
600 CLAR 91711 571-E7
N HOBART PL
300 LA 90004 593-H7
HOBBS DR
4400 LCF 91011 535-C4
HOBSON AV
800 Wilm 90744 794-J5
HOBSON CT
600 POM 91766 640-J4
5400 LACo 91302 559-A3
HOCKEY TR
7100 LA 90068 593-D1
HOCKNEY CT
1200 PMDL 93550 4286-C4
HODGSON CIRCLE RD
2600 Top 90290 589-G3
HODLER DR
3100 Top 90290 590-B7
HODSON AV
1400 BREA 92821 708-H5
1600 LHB 90631 708-G5
HOEFFER DR
1300 ALH 91801 596-C3
E HOEFFER DR
1200 ALH 91801 596-C3
S HOEFNER AV
400 ELA 90022 635-J7
600 ELA 90022 675-H1
2000 CMRC 90040 675-H3
HOFFMAN AV
800 LBCH 90813 795-F6
17800 CRTS 90703 736-E7
17800 CRTS 90703 766-E1
HOFFMAN ST
8600 BPK 90620 767-E5
12000 LA 91604 562-G5
HOFGAARDEN ST
500 LPUE 91745 678-E2
HOGAN CT
- LHB 90631 738-C2
HOGAN DR
25600 SCTA 91355 4550-E7
HOGAN WK
3100 LA 90008 673-F3
HOGEE DR
7100 PRM 90723 735-F1
N HOG FARM RD
- Cstc 91384 4459-J3
- Cstc 91384 4460-A2
S HOG FARM RD
- Cstc 91384 4459-J3
- Cstc 91384 4460-A3
HOIG ST
13200 LACo 91746 637-G4
HOKE AV
- CULC 90232 632-H7
- LA 90232 632-H7
HOLABIRD AV
3600 VER 90023 675-B2
3600 LA 90023 675-B2
HOLAN WY
- LMRD 90639 737-F2
HOLANDA RD
22600 WdHl 91364 559-H4
HOLBORN DR
600 CRSN 90746 764-E3
HOLBORO DR
3500 LFlz 90027 594-C2
HOLBROOK AL
1600 PAS 91104 566-C2
HOLBROOK CT
500 LBCH 90803 796-D7
HOLBROOK ST
1400 Eagl 90041 565-C6
8600 PRV 90660 676-F3
10200 LACo 90606 676-J5
HOLCOMB ST
9600 LA 90035 632-G4
HOLCOMB RIDGE RD
17600 Llan 93544 4470-B3
HOLCROFT DR
20300 LACo 91789 679-F5
HOLDEN CIR
3800 LALM 90720 796-J1

HOLDER ST
7000 BPK 90620 767-F2
9000 CYP 90630 767-F6
9200 BPK 90630 767-F6
HOLDMAN AV
- SMAD 91024 567-B2
HOLDREGE AV
3600 LA 90016 672-J1
HOLFORD ST
2300 LACo 90601 637-E6
HOLGATE SQ
2300 LA 90031 635-B1
HOLGATE ST
100 LHB 90631 708-H5
HOLGER DR
300 MTBL 90640 676-F1
HOLGUIN AV
- LAN 93535 4016-A3
HOLGUIN PL
300 LPUE 91744 638-E7
HOLGUIN ST
- LAN 93535 4016-C3
- LAN 93536 4015-D4
700 LAN 93534 4015-E4
HOLIDAY AV
1800 UPL 91784 571-H5
HOLIDAY CIR
- StvR 91381 4550-C7
HOLIDAY DR
1200 WCOV 91791 639-E2
HOLIDAY LN
9000 SBdC 92372 (4562-F1 See Page 4471)
9100 SBdC 92372 (4472-E6 See Page 4471)
9700 SBdC 92371 (4472-E5 See Page 4471)
HOLIDAY WY
12200 LA 91342 481-H6
HOLLADAY RD
600 PAS 91106 566-B6
600 SMRO 91108 566-B6
HOLLADAY WY
- MONP 91754 635-J4
HOLLAND AL
- PAS 91103 565-H3
HOLLAND AV
400 HiPk 90042 595-B2
HOLLAND DR
9900 Tuj 91042 503-J5
HOLLANDALE AV
1600 RowH 91748 679-D5
HOLLANDER ST
2900 POM 91767 601-A3
HOLLENBECK AV
4300 LACo 91723 599-A4
4300 LACo 91722 599-A4
4800 COV 91722 599-A4
N HOLLENBECK AV
100 COV 91723 599-A5
100 COV 91722 599-A5
4900 LACo 91722 599-A5
S HOLLENBECK AV
100 COV 91723 599-A6
100 COV 91722 599-A6
700 WCOV 91791 599-A6
HOLLENBECK DR
2000 LA 90023 634-J5
2000 LA 90023 635-A6
HOLLENBECK ST
6200 HNTP 90255 675-B7
S HOLLENBECK ST
100 WCOV 91791 599-A7
100 WCOV 91791 639-A3
E HOLLENCREST CIR
2200 WCOV 91791 639-A3
S HOLLENCREST DR
1200 WCOV 91791 639-A3
HOLLIFIELD CT
1700 RPV 90275 823-H2
HOLLINE CT
3000 LAN 93535 4106-F2
HOLLINGSWORTH RD
- Alta 91001 535-G3
HOLLINGWORTH ST
2700 LACo 91792 679-C2
2700 WCOV 91792 679-C2
HOLLINS AV
3600 CLAR 91711 571-F5
HOLLINS ST
900 LA 90023 634-J6
900 LA 90023 635-A6
HOLLIS AV
1300 AZU 91702 568-H4
HOLLIS CIR
400 LHB 90631 708-D7
HOLLIS LN
2200 ARCD 91006 597-E2
HOLLIS ST
15100 HacH 91745 678-A2
HOLLISTER AV
100 SMCA 90405 671-F4
2800 LA 90032 595-F7
HOLLISTER RD
900 SBdC 92372 (4562-C1 See Page 4471)
2300 SBdC 92371 (4562-G1 See Page 4471)
HOLLISTER ST
600 SFER 91340 502-A1
1000 SFER 91340 482-A7
1400 SFER 91340 481-J7

STREET
Block City ZIP Pg-Grid

HOLLISTER TER
2100 GLDL 91206 564-J4
2200 GLDL 91206 565-A4
N HOLLISTON AV
- PAS 91106 566-B4
500 PAS 91104 566-B3
1600 PAS 91104 536-B7
1600 LACo 91104 536-B7
1900 Alta 91001 536-B6
S HOLLISTON AV
- PAS 91125 566-B5
- PAS 91106 566-B5
N HOLLOW AV
300 WCOV 91790 598-F6
HOLLOWAY DR
8300 WHWD 90069 592-J6
8300 WHWD 90069 593-A6
HOLLOWAY PZ
8600 WHWD 90069 592-J6
HOLLOW BROOK AV
28900 AGRH 91301 558-B4
HOLLOW CORNER RD
4800 CULC 90230 672-H3
HOLLOWELL AV
200 HMB 90254 762-J2
W HOLLOWELL ST
900 ONT 91762 601-H7
HOLLOW GLEN CIR
10100 BelA 90077 592-B1
HOLLOWGLEN DR
3700 PMDL 93550 4286-H4
HOLLOW OAK CT
29000 AGRH 91301 558-A3
HOLLOW PINE DR
20600 DBAR 91789 679-G3
HOLLOW SPRINGS DR
11700 Nor 91326 480-F6
HOLLY AV
400 MNRO 91016 567-J4
800 ARCD 91007 567-B7
1500 ARCD 91007 597-B1
2600 LHB 90631 708-B5
3700 BALD 91706 598-C6
4800 NLB 90805 765-C4
12300 CHNO 91710 641-H6
E HOLLY AV
100 ELSG 90245 732-E1
N HOLLY AV
100 COMP 90221 735-C4
S HOLLY AV
100 COMP 90221 735-C5
W HOLLY AV
100 ELSG 90245 732-E1
HOLLY CT
28800 SCTA 91390 4460-J2
HOLLY DR
- CRSN 90746 764-F5
- Saug 91350 4461-E6
300 GLDL 91206 564-H4
1900 LA 90068 593-E2
7900 LPMA 90623 767-C4
HOLLY PL
8900 LA 90046 592-H3
S HOLLY PL
700 WCOV 91790 638-G1
HOLLY ST
- FUL 92835 738-H3
1600 BREA 92821 709-D7
E HOLLY ST
- PAS 91103 565-H4
200 PAS 91101 565-H4
S HOLLY ST
900 ING 90301 703-B4
W HOLLY ST
500 PAS 91103 565-F4
700 PAS 91105 565-F4
HOLLY TR
23500 CALB 91302 589-F1
HOLLY WY
1500 POM 91766 641-B4
HOLLY BEACH DR
- SCTA 91350 4550-H6
S HOLLYBROOK DR
2900 WCOV 91791 639-C3
HOLLYBURNE CT
3100 GLDL 91206 565-C1
HOLLYBUSH LN
1000 BelA 90077 592-B5
HOLLYCREST DR
3000 LA 90068 593-D1
3000 LA 90068 563-D7
HOLLYCREST PL
3000 LA 90068 593-D1
HOLLYDALE DR
3100 LA 90039 594-D2
N HOLLY GLEN DR
800 LBCH 90815 796-E6
HOLLYGLEN LN
100 SDMS 91773 570-B7
HOLLYGLEN PL
5100 PMDL 93551 4194-G1
12100 LA 91604 562-G6
HOLLYGROVE LN
900 Alta 91001 535-F3
HOLLY GROVE ST
3300 THO 91362 557-B3
HOLLYHILL LN
1700 GLDR 91741 569-H4
HOLLY HILL TER
2000 LA 90068 593-E3
HOLLYHOCK CT
900 THO 91362 557-C1
25000 StvR 91381 4640-E2

HOLLYHOCK ST
11200 SFSP 90670 706-G4
HOLLYHOCK FIRE RD
16500 Brwd 90049 591-D2
HOLLY KNOLL DR
4000 LFlz 90027 594-B3
HOLLY LEAF WY
1300 DBAR 91765 680-B3
HOLLYLINE AV
3800 Shrm 91423 562-B6
HOLLY MONT DR
6200 LA 90068 593-F3
HOLLY OAK CIR
13300 CRTS 90703 737-C6
HOLLYOAK CT
- StvR 91381 4550-C5
HOLLY OAK DR
1700 MONP 91755 636-D5
1800 WCOV 91791 638-J1
5600 LA 90068 593-G3
E HOLLY OAK DR
1400 WCOV 91791 638-H1
HOLLY OAK PL
800 MONP 91755 636-D5
S HOLLY OAK PL
300 WCOV 91791 638-J1
HOLLY OAK ST
1500 LVRN 91750 600-F2
HOLLYPARK DR
3100 ING 90305 703-F3
HOLLYPARK PL
3800 LA 90039 594-D1
HOLLY RIDGE DR
23300 SCTA 91354 4460-G6
HOLLYRIDGE DR
2100 LA 90068 593-G1
3000 LA 90068 563-G7
HOLLY SLOPE RD
3400 Alta 91001 535-J3
HOLLY TRAIL PTH
600 SMAD 91024 567-B1
600 SMAD 91024 537-B7
HOLLYTREE DR
5600 VeCo 91377 557-J1
5600 VeCo 91377 558-A1
HOLLY TREE RD
14700 HacH 91745 677-H4
HOLLYVALE ST
19000 LACo 91740 569-C6
19000 GLDR 91740 569-C6
E HOLLYVALE ST
500 AZU 91702 569-B6
18700 LACo 91702 569-B6
W HOLLYVALE ST
600 AZU 91702 568-G7
HOLLYVIEW CT
- LA 90068 593-D2
HOLLYVIEW DR
11600 LMRD 90638 707-F7
HOLLYVIEW TER
3800 CULC 90232 673-A2
HOLLYVISTA AV
1700 LFlz 90027 594-C4
HOLLYVISTA DR
800 PAS 91105 565-F4
HOLLYWELL PL
3000 GLDL 91206 565-B2
HOLLYWOOD BLVD
1800 Hlwd 90028 593-H4
4400 LFlz 90027 594-A4
4800 LFlz 90027 593-H4
7100 LA 90046 593-B4
8100 LA 90069 593-A4
8300 LA 90069 592-J4
HOLLYWOOD CT
- SCTA 91355 4550-G3
HOLLYWOOD FRWY
Rt#-170
- LA - 532-F6
- LA - 562-G1
- NHol - 532-E1
- NHol - 562-G1
- Pcma - 502-E7
- SunV - 502-E7
- SunV - 532-E1
HOLLYWOOD FRWY
U.S.-101
- Echo - 594-A7
- Echo - 634-D1
- Hlwd - 593-E2
- LA - 562-J4
- LA - 563-A5
- LA - 593-E2
- LA - 594-A7
- LA - 634-D1
HOLLYWOOD WY
7500 LA 91504 533-C2
7500 LA 91505 533-C3
7800 SunV 91352 533-C2
N HOLLYWOOD WY
100 BURB 91505 563-D2
1600 BURB 91505 533-C7
2300 BURB 91504 533-C7
S HOLLYWOOD WY
- BURB 91522 563-D4
HOLLYWOOD HILLS RD
8700 LA 90046 592-H2
HOLMAN AV
10300 Wwd 90024 632-C3
HOLMAR AV
1100 AZU 91702 568-J5
HOLMBURY AV
- CRTS 90703 767-B2

HOLMBY AV
600 Wwd 90024 632-C2
1800 WLA 90025 632-D4
HOLMBY CT
- Cstc 91384 4459-H3
HOLMBY PARK LN
100 BelA 90077 592-C7
HOLMES AV
1700 COMP 90222 734-G2
5000 LA 90058 674-G5
5700 Flor 90001 674-G6
7200 Flor 90001 704-G1
8600 Wats 90002 704-G2
9200 Wats 90002 704-G4
11700 Wbrk 90059 704-G7
17800 CRTS 90703 737-C7
17900 CRTS 90703 767-C1
HOLMES CIR
3400 HacH 91745 677-J6
17100 CRTS 90703 737-C7
HOLMES PL
16400 CRTS 90703 737-C6
25200 StvR 91381 4550-C6
HOLMES CREEK RD
28300 Pear 93553 (4559-B1
See Page 4470)
28500 Pear 93553 4469-B6
HOLMS CT
22500 SCTA 91350 4460-J5
N HOLSTER LN
- VeCo 91307 529-B4
HOLSTON AV
11800 LMRD 90638 707-G7
HOLT AV
300 LA 90048 632-J1
400 BHLS 90211 632-J1
1200 WCOV 91791 599-D7
15900 SCTA 91387 4552-D2
20000 COV 91724 599-D7
20000 WCOV 91724 599-D7
20100 LACo 91724 599-D7
E HOLT AV
100 POM 91767 640-J1
200 POM 91767 641-A1
1600 MTCL 91763 641-A1
3100 WCOV 91791 599-D7
S HOLT AV
800 LA 90035 632-J3
1900 LA 90034 632-J6
5100 LadH 90056 673-A5
6400 LadH 90056 672-J7
W HOLT AV
100 POM 91768 640-F1
HOLT BLVD
4000 MTCL 91763 641-E1
W HOLT BLVD
900 ONT 91762 641-H1
1300 ONT 91763 641-H1
HOLT DR
2100 LHB 90631 708-H5
HOLT ST
7700 BPK 90621 737-H6
HOLT CANYON RD
16500 LACo 91387 4552-B4
HOLTON ST
16400 LACo 91744 638-H3
17000 LACo 91791 638-H3
HOLTWOOD AV
1300 SELM 91733 637-C5
HOLY CROSS PL
8000 Wch 90045 702-E3
HOLYOKE DR
3300 LA 90065 594-H3
HOLYOKE PL
26800 SCTA 91351 4551-D2
HOMAGE AV
9300 WHIT 90603 707-F4
9900 LACo 90604 707-F4
S HOMAGE AV
10900 LACo 90604 707-D6
HOME AV
6200 BELL 90201 675-F7
E HOME ST
- NLB 90805 765-D4
W HOME ST
- NLB 90805 765-C4
HOMEBROOK ST
9000 PRV 90660 676-F6
HOMEDALE ST
11200 Brwd 90049 631-H2
HOMELAND AV
10100 WHIT 90603 707-J4
11400 LACo 90604 707-J6
HOMELAND DR
3500 LA 90008 673-E4
3500 LACo 90008 673-E4
HOMEPARK AV
2600 Alta 91001 536-A5
HOMEPARK DR
12600 WHIT 90602 707-C1
HOME PLACE DR
43600 LAN 93536 4105-C2
HOMER PL
200 MANB 90266 732-F7
HOMER RD
12700 Pear 93553 4378-H7
HOMER ST
200 HMB 90254 732-G7
200 MANB 90266 732-G7
3500 LA 90031 595-B5
HOMEREST AV
600 COV 91722 598-J4

N HOMEREST AV
100 WCOV 91791 598-J6
S HOMEREST AV
100 WCOV 91791 598-J7
200 COV 91722 598-J5
500 AZU 91702 598-J2
700 LACo 91702 598-J2
HOMERIDGE DR
7700 SBdC 92372 (4562-E4
See Page 4471)
40200 PMDL 93551 4195-A3
HOMERIDGE LN
12800 CHLS 91709 640-H7
HOMERIDGE ST
40400 PMDL 93551 4194-H2
HOMESIDE AV
5300 LA 90016 633-B7
HOMESTEAD DR
- POM 91767 601-A3
43400 LAN 93535 4106-G2
HOMESTEAD PL
- Saug 91350 4460-J4
2500 LACo 90220 765-A1
12900 CHNO 91710 641-F7
HOMESTEAD ST
- LAN 93535 4106-G3
6200 Tuj 91042 504-C7
HOMESTEAD WY
11300 SFSP 90670 706-H2
HOMESTEAD ST E
43200 LAN 93535 4106-G2
HOMET RD
1600 PAS 91106 566-C6
1600 SMRO 91108 566-D6
HOME TERRACE DR
1600 POM 91768 600-E7
HOMEWARD ST
13500 LACo 91746 638-A3
13900 LPUE 91746 638-B3
14300 LPUE 91746 638-D5
14600 LACo 91744 638-C4
HOMEWAY DR
3600 LACo 90008 673-E3
HOMEWOOD AV
2200 SIMI 93063 499-C1
5700 BPK 90621 737-H7
6300 Hlwd 90028 593-E5
6300 BPK 90621 767-H1
HOMEWOOD CT
6400 SIMI 93063 499-C1
HOMEWOOD DR
1500 Alta 91001 536-C5
HOMEWOOD LN
1200 LCF 91011 535-B4
HOMEWOOD PL
2100 FUL 92833 738-C3
HOMEWOOD RD
100 Brwd 90049 631-F2
1400 SLB 90740 826-G1
HOMEWOOD WY
12600 Brwd 90049 631-E2
HOMEWORTH DR
1800 RPV 90275 823-H3
HOMEZELL DR
23900 LA 91304 529-E1
HOMEZELL TR
24000 LA 91304 529-C1
HOMYR PL
27400 SCTA 91351 4551-H3
HONAN AV
1300 LACo 90601 637-G6
HONBY AV
26800 SCTA 91351 4551-D2
HONBY ST
29700 LACo 91390 4461-F2
HONDERO CT
- GrnH 91344 481-A6
HONDO ST
7400 DWNY 90242 705-H6
HONDO CANYON RD
22400 Top 90290 589-H6
HONDURAS ST
4300 LA 90011 674-G4
HONDURAS WY
5800 BPK 90620 767-D3
HONEY DR
8000 LA 90046 593-A3
HONEY BEE LN
15800 CHLS 91709 680-H7
HONEYBEE LN
- LAN 93536 4014-J7
11600 Litl 93543 4468-F6
43300 LAN 93536 4104-J2
HONEYBROOK LN
3300 DBAR 91765 709-H1
HONEYCOMB RD
27900 SCTA 91350 4461-C5
HONEY CREEK RD
26600 RPV 90275 793-B6
W HONEYDALE CT
1500 UPL 91786 571-H7
HONEYGLEN RD
11500 Pcma 91331 502-H4
11500 Pcma 91331 482-F7
HONEYHILL DR
1300 DBAR 91789 679-F4
HONEYMAN ST
5400 SIMI 93063 499-A2
HONEY MAPLE ST
- LACo 91387 4552-A4
HONEY RIDGE LN
13800 CHLS 91709 680-G2

HONEYSUCKLE AV
3200 PMDL 93550 4286-G1
HONEYSUCKLE LN
100 BREA 92821 709-A7
14000 LACo 90604 707-D6
HONEYSUCKLE HILL DR
30200 SCTA 91387 4462-G4
HONEYWOOD CT
1500 BREA 92821 708-H6
HONEYWOOD LN
500 LHB 90631 738-D1
HONEYWOOD RD
900 Brwd 90049 631-E1
HONIG LN
800 LA 90065 595-A2
HONITON AV
29600 CynC 91351 4462-B4
HONNINGTON ST
16200 WHIT 90603 708-A4
HONNOLD DR
22500 SCTA 91350 4460-J4
HONOLULU AV
2200 GLDL 91020 534-F2
2200 GLDL 91208 534-F2
2800 GLDL 91214 534-E1
3600 GLDL 91214 504-C7
6200 Tuj 91042 504-C7
HONOLULU PL
3200 GLDL 91214 534-E1
HONOLULU TER
12200 WHIT 90601 677-C4
HONORE ST
18700 RowH 91748 679-B5
HONORINE CT
- SCTA 91321 4551-F4
HOOD AV
4100 BURB 91505 563-D5
6200 HNTP 90255 675-B7
HOOD DR
600 CLAR 91711 601-B1
4900 WdHl 91364 560-E3
HOOD WY
- StvR 91381 4550-A7
HOOK LN
2100 LA 90210 592-B3
HOOK ST
39700 PMDL 93551 4195-H4
HOOKTREE RD
4700 LCF 91011 535-C3
HOOPER AV
900 LA 90021 634-G7
1500 LA 90021 674-F2
1900 LA 90011 674-F2
5800 Flor 90001 674-F7
7300 Flor 90001 704-F3
8600 Wats 90002 704-F3
9400 Wats 90002 704-F3
10900 LA 90059 704-F6
HOOPER DR
1200 WCOV 91791 639-D3
HOOPER PL
2300 LA 90011 674-F2
HOOVER AV
1600 POM 91767 601-D6
5500 WHIT 90601 677-B4
11700 SGAT 90280 735-G2
HOOVER BLVD
3400 LA 90089 674-B1
HOOVER CT
500 SDMS 91773 600-A1
HOOVER PL
1900 LFlz 90027 594-B3
17300 LA 90247 734-B7
N HOOVER ST
100 Echo 90026 634-B1
100 LA 90004 634-B1
300 Echo 90026 594-B7
300 LA 90004 594-B7
700 LA 90029 594-B4
1300 LFlz 90027 594-B4
S HOOVER ST
100 LA 90057 634-B1
200 LA 90004 634-B1
300 LA 90020 634-B1
300 LA 90005 634-B4
600 LA 90010 634-B1
900 LA 90006 634-B4
1900 LA 90007 634-B7
3300 LA 90007 674-B4
3900 LA 90037 674-B4
5800 LA 90044 674-B6
7200 LA 90044 704-B1
12000 LA 90044 734-B1
12800 LA 90247 734-B2
17700 LA 90248 764-B1
HOOVER WY
7000 BPK 90620 767-G5
HOPE CT
700 SPAS 91030 595-G1
HOPE DR
1800 DUAR 91010 568-B6
HOPE PL
600 LA 90071 634-E4
HOPE ST
- CLAR 91711 601-C4
- LMRD 90639 737-F3
1000 SPAS 91030 595-J1
2400 LACo 90255 704-J1
2700 LACo 90255 705-A1
2900 HNTP 90255 705-A1
6100 SIMI 93063 499-B3
N HOPE ST
100 LA 90012 634-F3

S HOPE ST
100 LA 90012 634-E5
300 LA 90071 634-E5
600 LA 90017 634-E5
900 LA 90015 634-E5
2100 LA 90007 634-C7
2900 LA 90007 674-C1
HOPE CANYON RD
- SCTA 91321 4551-C7
- SCTA 91350 4551-C7
HOPELAND AV
10200 DWNY 90241 706-A3
HOPEN PL
9000 LA 90069 592-H4
HOPETON RD
2900 LaCr 91214 504-F5
HOPEVALE DR
3700 Shrm 91403 561-H6
HOPEWELL LN
700 SPAS 91030 595-H1
HOPI
- Ago 91301 587-G4
HOPI ST
600 DBAR 91765 680-B1
HOPKINS AL
- PAS 91103 565-H4
HOPKINS AV
300 HMB 90254 762-H3
HOPKINS PL
- StvR 91381 4550-A7
- StvR 91381 4640-A1
HOPKINS WY
700 RBCH 90277 762-G4
HOPLAND ST
10400 BLF 90706 736-D4
10800 NRWK 90650 736-E4
HOPPER CT
4600 CALB 91302 559-F4
HOPPING ST
- FUL 92833 738-C5
HORACE
15400 MsnH 91345 501-G2
HORACE ST
15600 GrnH 91344 501-A2
18600 Nor 91326 500-H2
19600 Chat 91311 500-C3
HORCADA PL
700 PVE 90274 792-G4
HORIZON AV
- Ven 90291 671-G6
HORIZON CT
- Ven 90291 671-G6
18000 RowH 91748 678-H6
HORIZON DR
5200 MAL 90265 627-C7
HORIZON LN
- DBAR 91765 680-A6
- LACo 92823 680-A6
1900 LAN 93535 4016-D7
HORIZON PL
3400 WCOV 91791 639-E3
22200 Chat 91311 499-J2
HORIZON RD
100 PMDL 93550 4285-J2
HORIZON HILLS DR
- WCOV 91791 639-B4
HORLEY AV
8900 DWNY 90240 706-A2
10200 DWNY 90241 706-A3
11500 DWNY 90241 705-J5
12000 DWNY 90242 705-H6
HORMEL AV
900 LVRN 91750 570-E7
900 LVRN 91750 600-E1
HORN AV
1100 WHWD 90069 592-H5
HORNBEAM RD
- PMDL 93551 4285-D2
HORNBROOK AV
3900 BALD 91706 598-A5
HORNBY AV
8900 WHIT 90603 707-F3
HORNBY ST
400 MTBL 90640 676-B3
HORNDEAN AV
32800 Actn 93510 4375-G7
HORNELL ST
14900 LACo 90604 707-F6
15400 WHIT 90604 707-H6
15800 WHIT 90603 707-J5
HORNER ST
6000 LA 90035 633-A4
6100 LA 90035 632-G4
HORNET PL
11200 LKWD 90715 766-F4
HORNET WY
- ELSG 90245 702-J7
1000 FUL 92831 738-J6
HORSE CANYON RD
2600 SBdC (4562-H6
See Page 4471)
HORSE CREEK AV
- SunI 91040 503-B3
HORSE FLATS RD
- LACo 4647-E4
HORSE FLATS FIRE RD
- Nor 91326 480-D6
HORSE HAVEN ST
- SunV 91352 503-B7
HORSE HOLLOW RD
900 SDMS 91773 600-A4
HORSESHOE BEND
1000 WAL 91789 639-F5

HORSESHOE CIR
- LACo 91390 4460-J3
100 WCOV 91791 639-F1
HORSESHOE CT
43400 LAN 93535 4106-F2
HORSESHOE DR
19700 Top 90290 630-A1
HORSESHOE LN
- CRSN 90745 794-G1
- RHE 90274 822-J1
24800 SCTA 91321 4550-J7
E HORSESHOE RD
- VeCo 91307 529-A4
HORSESHOE CANYON RD
2400 LA 90046 592-J2
E HORSESHOE CANYON
RD
2400 LA 90046 592-J2
HORSETHIEF CANYON
PARK RD
- SDMS 91773 570-C6
HORSHOE CIR
- CALB 91302 558-H4
HORST AV
13900 NRWK 90650 736-H3
17200 CRTS 90703 736-H7
17400 ART 90701 736-H7
17800 ART 90701 766-J2
19500 CRTS 90703 766-J3
20800 LKWD 90715 766-J5
21400 HGDN 90716 766-J5
HORTENSE ST
10600 LA 91602 563-A4
11000 LA 91602 562-J4
11700 LA 91607 562-G4
12300 LA 91604 562-E4
14100 Shrm 91423 562-A4
14500 Shrm 91403 562-A4
14600 Shrm 91403 561-J4
HORTICULTURAL DR
14300 HacH 91745 677-H3
HORTON AV
200 FUL 92833 738-E7
10600 DWNY 90241 706-A3
11400 DWNY 90241 705-J5
12000 DWNY 90242 705-H5
HOSFORD AV
7700 Wch 90045 702-G1
HOSMER WK
200 HiPk 90042 595-E4
HOSPERS RD
35100 Actn 93510 4374-H2
HOSPITAL PL
1800 Boyl 90033 635-A3
HOSS ST
600 DBAR 91765 680-B2
HOSTETTER ST
2700 LA 90023 634-J7
2700 LA 90023 635-A7
HOSTETTER FIRE RD
- GLDL 91208 534-B2
- SunV 91352 504-B7
- SunV 91352 534-B2
HOT BOX CANYON RD
25200 Nwhl 91321 4641-G1
HOT SPRINGS AV
28000 SCTA 91351 4461-F7
HOT SPRINGS PL
26800 CALB 91301 558-G7
HOUGH ST
6600 HiPk 90042 595-E1
HOUGHTON AV
9200 SFSP 90670 706-G2
HOURGLASS PL
1000 DBAR 91765 640-E5
HOUSEMAN ST
400 LCF 91011 535-B4
N HOUSER DR
100 COV 91722 599-A5
S HOUSER DR
100 COV 91722 599-A6
HOUSMAN PL
- StvR 91381 4550-B7
HOUSTON AV
5000 LPMA 90623 767-C3
HOUSTON CT
- Saug 91350 4461-F7
1600 CLAR 91711 601-E1
HOUSTON RD
9500 VeCo 90265 625-D1
HOUSTON ST
2400 Boyl 90033 635-B4
6500 BPK 90620 767-F2
HOVENWEEP LN
24000 LACo 90265 629-F1
24000 LACo 91302 589-F7
24000 LACo 91302 629-F1
24000 Top 90290 589-F7
HOVEY AV
100 SGBL 91776 596-E6
HOVEY ST
8700 RSMD 91770 596-G6
HOWARD AV
500 COV 91723 599-B4
500 MTBL 90640 676-D1
700 CRSN 90746 764-E2
700 MTBL 90640 636-D7
1000 COV 91722 599-B3
21300 TOR 90503 763-A6
HOWARD CT
1800 WCOV 91792 638-J5
2700 BURB 91504 533-G3

HOWARD CT
20300 WdHl 91364 560-D5
HOWARD LN
27800 Cstc 91384 4369-G6
HOWARD ST
300 GLDL 91206 564-F4
500 ALH 91801 596-A5
700 LA 90012 634-H3
700 LA 90292 672-A6
900 GLDL 91207 564-F2
4300 MTCL 91763 641-E2
4500 SBdC 91710 641-G2
4700 MTCL 91710 641-G2
5300 SBdC 91762 641-G2
10800 WHIT 90606 677-A5
11300 WHIT 90601 677-A5
E HOWARD ST
- PAS 91103 565-J1
200 PAS 91104 565-J1
600 PAS 91104 566-A1
1600 LACo 91104 566-B1
W HOWARD ST
- PAS 91103 565-G1
1200 UPL 91786 601-J1
W HOWARD ACCESS RD
1500 UPL 91786 601-H1
HOWARD HUGHES PKWY
6000 Wch 90045 702-H1
HOWARD MARIE CT
29000 LACo 91390 4461-D3
HOWARDVIEW CT
3800 CULC 90232 672-J2
HOWE ST
7800 PRM 90723 735-G2
HOWELLHURST DR
15000 BALD 91706 598-D6
N HOWELLHURST DR
1600 WCOV 91790 598-E6
HOWERY ST
7300 SGAT 90723 735-F2
7300 SGAT 90280 735-F2
7300 PRM 90723 735-F2
HOWLAND AV
400 Ven 90291 671-H6
HOWLAND DR
600 ING 90301 703-D2
9800 TEML 91780 597-A4
HOWLAND CANAL CT
200 Ven 90291 671-H7
HOWLAND CANAL WK
200 Ven 90291 671-H6
HOWSLER PL
1800 POM 91766 640-J4
HOXIE AV
10800 NRWK 90650 736-E1
11900 NRWK 90650 706-E7
HOYA WY
16600 PRM 90723 735-F6
HOYT LN
- LA 91342 482-G7
HOYT ST
11900 LA 91342 482-G7
13100 Pcma 91331 502-D2
HOYT TKTR
- LACo - 505-B2
HOYT PARK PL
10300 ELMN 91733 637-B1
HUALPAI TR
- Ago 91301 588-B5
HUATABAMPO PL
- GAR 90247 734-A6
HUB ST
4800 HiPk 90042 595-A1
HUBARD HEIGHTS RD
- Litl 93543 4468-G4
- Pear 93553 4468-G4
N HUBBARD AV
- SFER 91340 482-A6
S HUBBARD AV
- SFER 91340 481-J6
- SFER 91340 482-A6
200 LA 91342 481-J6
HUBBARD PL
12000 LA 91342 481-J6
HUBBARD RD
4500 Actn 93510 4465-A2
4500 Actn 93510 4464-G1
6100 Actn 93510 4374-D5
HUBBARD RD S
- Actn 93510 4464-F3
HUBBARD ST
300 SFER 91340 482-A6
3700 LACo 90023 635-D7
4400 ELA 90022 635-G7
5100 ELA 90022 675-H1
6000 ELA 90022 676-A1
8800 CULC 90232 672-H1
12600 LA 91342 482-E1
14600 LA 91342 481-J7
38900 PMDL 93551 4195-C6
HUBER AV
23000 TOR 90501 793-J2
HUBERT AV
3900 LA 90008 673-F2
HUBERT WK
3000 LA 90008 673-F3
HUCKFINN LN
5100 CULC 90230 672-J3
HUCKLEBERRY CIR
21800 WAL 91789 639-J5
HUCKLEBERRY DR
25600 LACo 91302 589-A7

HUDDART AV
4300 ELMN 91731 597-E5
HUDSON AV
100 INDS 91744 638-C7
1200 LA 90019 633-E4
15600 LPUE 91744 638-D6
N HUDSON AV
- PAS 91101 566-A4
100 LA 90004 633-E1
700 LA 90038 593-E5
900 PAS 91104 566-A2
1400 Hlwd 90028 593-E4
S HUDSON AV
- PAS 91101 566-A6
100 LA 90004 633-E1
300 LA 90020 633-E1
500 PAS 91106 566-A6
600 LA 90005 633-E2
600 LA 90010 633-E2
900 LA 90019 633-E2
HUDSON CT
700 PAS 91104 566-A1
HUDSON PL
100 LA 90004 633-E1
HUDSON ST
37400 PMDL 93552 4287-B3
HUDSONIA WY
- PMDL 93552 4287-B1
HUDSPETH ST
2300 ING 90303 703-G6
HUERTA CT
4400 Enc 91436 561-D5
HUERTA DR
26100 SCTA 91355 4550-G3
HUERTA RD
16600 Enc 91436 561-D5
HUERTA VERDE RD
700 GLDR 91741 569-F3
HUFFER AL
2000 PAS 91103 535-G7
HUFFY ST
20300 SCTA 91351 4461-D7
HUGGINS DR
19000 CRSN 90746 764-F3
HUGHES AV
100 MTBL 90640 676-D3
3500 LA 90034 632-F7
3600 LA 90034 672-G1
3700 LA 90232 672-G1
3800 CULC 90232 672-G1
HUGHES DR
- FUL 92833 738-D6
W HUGHES DR
3000 ANA 92804 767-J6
HUGHES LN
- ING 90305 703-F3
HUGHES ST
1200 MTBL 90640 676-C3
HUGHES WY
900 ELSG 90245 702-H7
1300 LBCH 90810 765-B6
HUGHES WY S
1900 ELSG 90245 732-H3
HUGHES CANYON RD
5800 Actn 93510 4464-G3
HUGO AV
11600 Wbrk 90059 704-H7
HUGO REID DR
700 ARCD 91007 567-A5
900 ARCD 91007 566-J5
HUGUS AL
- PAS 91103 565-C3
HULA DR
6400 NLB 90805 735-D7
HULA LN
6400 NLB 90805 735-D7
HULA-HULA
6300 NLB 90805 765-D1
6300 NLB 90805 735-D7
HULBERT AV
7800 PdlR 90293 702-C2
HULL CT
2100 SIMI 93063 499-B2
HULL LN
1300 Alta 91001 536-B6
HULL ST
- KeCo 93560 3834-J2
HULLETT ST
100 NLB 90805 765-D2
E HULLETT ST
2700 NLB 90805 765-H2
HULLETT TURN
5800 NLB 90805 765-D2
HULME AV
10700 LYN 90262 705-D6
HULSEY CT
- Saug 91350 4461-F6
N HUMANE WY
100 POM 91768 640-D2
S HUMANE WY
100 POM 91768 640-E2
200 POM 91766 640-E2
HUMBERT AV
2700 ELMN 91733 637-A2
2700 SELM 91733 637-A2
HUMBOLDT AV
12000 SBdC 91710 641-C5
HUMBOLDT CT
4500 MTCL 91763 641-E1
HUMBOLDT DR
5300 BPK 90621 737-J5
HUMBOLDT PL
12100 CHNO 91710 641-D5

HUMBOLDT ST
1900 LA 90031 594-J7
2600 LA 90031 595-A7
HUMBOLT CT
900 SDMS 91773 570-D5
HUMBOLT WY
2700 POM 91768 640-C2
HUME AV
4600 LaCr 91214 504-F7
HUME RD
2400 LACo 90265 629-F4
HUME CANYON RD
- LACo 91390 4462-D3
HUMFORD AV
1900 HacH 91745 678-B4
HUMMINGBIRD CIR
8000 LPMA 90623 767-B4
26800 SCTA 91351 4551-E3
HUMMINGBIRD CT
5800 PMDL 93551 4194-G3
HUMMINGBIRD DR
- BREA 92823 709-G6
HUMMINGBIRD LN
- RHLS 90274 823-F2
2900 SIGH 90755 795-H4
HUMMINGBIRD PL
2200 POM 91767 600-J4
HUMMING BIRD WY
22900 CALB 91302 559-G6
HUMMINGBIRD WY
2400 LVRN 91750 570-H5
HUMPHREY WK
4200 LA 90008 673-F3
HUMPHREY WY
5000 LaCr 91214 504-G7
N HUMPHREYS AV
100 ELA 90022 635-F5
S HUMPHREYS AV
100 ELA 90022 635-F7
HUMPHREYS WY
300 GLDR 91741 569-G5
HUNGATE LN
800 ARCD 91007 567-A7
HUNGERFORD PL
10700 CRTS 90703 766-E1
HUNGERFORD ST
1200 NLB 90805 765-F2
4300 LKWD 90712 766-A1
6200 LKWD 90713 766-D1
E HUNGERFORD ST
3500 NLB 90805 765-J1
HUNGRYJACK RD
43300 LACo 93532 4102-F3
HUNNEWELL AV
11300 LA 91342 502-G1
11500 LA 91342 482-D5
HUNSAKER AV
15400 PRM 90723 735-E5
15500 COMP 90221 735-E5
HUNSTOCK AV
29500 Cstc 91384 4459-D6
HUNSTOCK DR
29900 Cstc 91384 4459-C6
HUNT AL
100 PAS 91106 566-C4
HUNT AV
800 POM 91766 641-A5
8900 SGAT 90280 705-D5
10600 LYN 90262 705-D5
HUNT LN
1800 SPAS 91030 595-G3
HUNT TER
- Hrbr 90710 794-A3
HUNTCLIFF LN
20400 LACo 91789 679-F5
HUNT CLUB LN
4000 Ago 91301 588-A1
4200 WLKV 91361 557-E6
9500 Chat 91311 499-H6
E HUNTDALE ST
5700 LBCH 90808 766-C7
HUNTER AV
10800 WHIT 90601 677-A4
HUNTER CT
44100 LAN 93536 4015-A7
HUNTER DR
700 SGBL 91775 596-E2
HUNTER GRN
4600 BPK 90621 737-F5
HUNTER LN
31500 Cstc 91384 4369-G6
HUNTER PL
3200 WCOV 91791 639-D3
HUNTER RD
1900 CHLS 91709 710-H1
HUNTER ST
300 LA 90023 675-B1
1800 LA 90021 634-G7
HUNTER POINT RD
- POM 91766 640-G4
HUNTERS TR
600 GLDR 91740 569-H6
HUNTERS GATE CIR
15000 CHLS 91709 680-G5
HUNTERS HILL DR
900 WAL 91789 639-E6
HUNTER VALLEY LN
4900 THO 91362 557-E1
HUNTINGTON AV
100 SDMS 91773 599-J3
N HUNTINGTON AV
100 MONP 91754 636-B1

STREET Block City ZIP Pg-Grid

S HUNTINGTON AV
500 MONP 91754 636-B3
N HUNTINGTON BLVD
500 POM 91768 640-H1
800 POM 91768 600-H7
HUNTINGTON CIR
700 PAS 91106 596-A1
HUNTINGTON DR
100 ALH 91801 596-B2
300 SMRO 91108 596-C1
800 LACo 91107 566-E7
800 LACo 91775 566-E7
900 DUAR 91010 567-H5
900 MNRO 91016 567-H5
1100 DUAR 91010 568-B5
1100 DUAR 91016 568-B5
1100 MNRO 91016 568-B5
2000 SPAS 91030 596-B2
2400 SMRO 91108 566-E7
2800 IRW 91706 568-B5
2800 AZU 91010 568-B5
2900 IRW 91010 568-B5
3900 ARCD 91007 566-E7
4300 LA 90032 595-F5
8200 SMRO 91775 566-E7
E HUNTINGTON DR
- ARCD 91006 567-D5
100 MNRO 91016 567-D5
N HUNTINGTON DR
600 CLAR 91711 601-E3
600 UPL 91786 601-E3
S HUNTINGTON DR
100 CLAR 91711 601-E3
4600 MTCL 91763 601-E3
W HUNTINGTON DR
- ARCD 91007 567-C5
100 MNRO 91016 567-G5
700 ARCD 91007 566-J6
1600 UPL 91786 601-G3
HUNTINGTON DR N
200 ALH 91801 595-H3
1100 SPAS 91030 595-H3
2000 SPAS 91030 596-A3
4100 LA 90032 595-E6
HUNTINGTON DR S
4300 LA 90032 595-D6
HUNTINGTON LN
1100 SPAS 91030 595-H4
1700 RBCH 90278 762-J1
1900 RBCH 90278 763-A1
25500 SCTA 91355 4460-B7
N HUNTINGTON ST
100 SFER 91340 482-B5
100 POM 91768 640-H1
S HUNTINGTON ST
100 POM 91766 640-H3
100 SFER 91340 482-A7
400 SFER 91340 481-J7
HUNTINGTON GARDEN DR
700 PAS 91108 596-A1
HUNTLEY AV
4100 CULC 90230 672-E4
HUNTLEY CIR
2200 SMRO 91108 566-D7
HUNTLEY DR
300 WHWD 90048 592-J7
600 WHWD 90069 592-J7
1100 Echo 90026 634-E3
1100 LA 90012 634-E3
3300 OrCo 90720 796-J4
HUNTLEY PL
11200 CULC 90230 672-F4
HUNTSINGER CIR
3000 LACo 90263 628-G6
3000 LACo 90265 628-G6
3400 MAL 90265 628-G6
HUNTSMAN CT
1700 RPV 90275 823-J2
HUNTSTOCK AV
29500 Cstc 91384 4459-D7
HUNTSWOOD CIR
5100 LPMA 90623 767-C3
HUNTSWOOD LN
- LACo 91387 4552-A6
HURCHEL CT
13400 LACo 90605 707-C7
HURFORD CT
5600 AGRH 91301 557-H4
HURFORD TER
4600 Enc 91436 561-F4
HURLBUT ST
100 PAS 91105 565-H7
HURLEY ST
- INDS 91748 678-H2
16800 LPUE 91744 678-F1
17300 INDS 91744 678-H2
17700 LACo 91744 678-H2
18400 LACo 91744 679-A2
HURLOCK AV
2000 DUAR 91010 567-J7
HURLOCK ST
2000 DUAR 91010 567-J7
HURON
- Ago 91301 587-G4
HURON AV
3800 CULC 90232 672-E2
4200 CULC 90230 672-F3
HURON CT
- CHNO 91710 641-H4
HURON DR
800 CLAR 91711 571-B7
HURON ST
2000 LA 90065 594-J6
43400 LAN 93535 4106-D2
HURRICANE ST
- LA 90292 701-H1
HURST PL
- BREA 92821 708-J5
E HURST ST
100 COV 91723 599-B4
600 LACo 91723 599-C4
HURSTVIEW AV
400 LACo 91010 567-H6
400 MNRO 91016 567-H6
HURSTVIEW ST
900 DUAR 91010 567-J6
HUSK AV
30300 LACo 91390 4462-E4
HUSSEY RD
100 SLB 90740 826-G3
HUSTON PL
2800 LAN 93536 4015-C7
HUSTON RD
9100 Chat 91311 499-E7
9300 Chat 91311 499-E7
HUSTON ST
2900 POM 91767 601-A3
10100 NHol 91601 563-A3
11100 NHol 91601 562-J3
11700 LA 91607 562-F3
12900 Shrm 91423 562-B3
14400 Shrm 91403 562-A3
14500 Shrm 91403 561-J3
15600 Enc 91436 561-E3
25600 StvR 91381 4550-C7
HUTAIN ST
- FUL 92833 738-C5
HUTAK LN
29900 Litl 93543 4468-C5
HUTCHCROFT ST
13400 LACo 91746 637-J3
13600 LACo 91746 638-A3
14500 LPUE 91744 638-B4
14600 LACo 91744 638-B4
HUTCHINGS CT
900 SDMS 91773 570-C7
900 SDMS 91773 600-C1
HUTCHINS DR
14900 LMRD 90638 707-F7
14900 LMRD 90638 737-F1
HUTCHISON AV
3100 LA 90034 632-H7
3200 CULC 90232 632-H7
HUTTON DR
2500 LA 90210 592-C1
3200 LA 90210 562-C7
HUTTON PL
3000 LA 90210 592-D1
HUXLEY DR
- StvR 91381 4640-D1
HUXLEY ST
3400 LFlz 90027 594-C2
HYACINTH AV
5200 LACo 91702 598-H2
N HYACINTH AV
700 WCOV 91791 598-H6
S HYACINTH AV
100 COV 91722 598-H5
1700 LACo 91791 638-H3
1700 WCOV 91791 638-H3
HYACINTH CT
36900 PMDL 93552 4287-C4
N HYACINTH CT
600 ONT 91762 601-H7
HYANNIS DR
7200 CanP 91307 529-F4
HYANNIS LN
1500 LA 90732 823-D6
HYANS ST
2700 Echo 90026 634-B1
HYATT AV
1000 Wilm 90744 794-F5
HYATT WY
4500 PMDL 93551 4194-J3
HYDE AV
800 POM 91767 601-B5
HYDE ST
5300 LA 90032 595-F6
HYDE PARK BLVD
2000 LA 90047 673-E7
2100 LA 90043 673-E7
E HYDE PARK BLVD
100 ING 90302 703-C1
500 ING 90302 673-D7
N HYDE PARK BLVD
100 ING 90301 703-A2
200 ING 90302 703-A2
W HYDE PARK BLVD
100 ING 90302 703-B1
HYDE PARK CT
11500 CRTS 90703 736-G6
HYDE PARK DR
6000 PMDL 93551 4104-F6
E HYDE PARK PL
500 ING 90302 673-C7
HYDRAFLOW WY
- FUL 92833 738-D6
HYDRANGEA WY
14600 SCTA 91387 4462-F4
HYDRO DR
8400 WHIT 90606 707-C1
HYDRO RD
20600 CRSN 90746 764-G5
HYLAND AV
1500 ARCD 91006 567-C3
HYLAND CT
- LA 91342 482-C3
HYLER AV
2500 Eagl 90041 564-J7
HYNFORD PL
23700 Hrbr 90710 793-J2
HYPERION AV
600 Echo 90026 594-C4
600 LA 90029 594-B6
1800 LA 90039 594-D2
1800 LFlz 90027 594-D2
HYPERION WY
- PdlR 90293 732-C1
HYSLO RD
- SCTA 91350 4551-B6
HYSSOP LN
27500 SCTA 91350 4461-A6
HYTE RD
26600 RPV 90275 792-J6
HYTHE CT
9800 LA 90210 592-C1

I

I ST
- BELL 90201 675-F5
- LACo 90220 765-A3
- PdlR 90293 702-D7
2200 LVRN 91750 600-H3
E I ST
100 Wilm 90744 794-E6
3100 Wilm 90744 795-A6
W I ST
100 Wilm 90744 794-C6
1000 ONT 91762 601-J6
3200 Wilm 90744 795-A6
3400 LBCH 90813 795-A6
IA LN
22700 WdHl 91364 559-H5
IANITA ST
6500 LKWD 90713 766-E3
IBANEZ AV
21300 WdHl 91364 560-B4
IBBETSON AV
5900 LKWD 90713 766-C1
6200 BLF 90706 766-C1
12600 DWNY 90242 736-C1
13600 BLF 90706 736-C3
IBERVILLE CIR
5000 LPMA 90623 767-C2
IBEX AV
14300 NRWK 90650 736-H4
17200 CRTS 90703 736-J7
17400 ART 90701 736-J7
17900 ART 90701 766-J2
19900 CRTS 90703 766-J3
20700 LKWD 90715 766-J4
21900 HGDN 90716 766-J7
IBEX CT
19500 CRTS 90703 766-J3
IBOLD RD
600 LACo 90265 586-G6
IBSEN ST
8700 PRV 90660 676-G2
ICE HOUSE CANYON RD
- SBdC - (512-B4 See Page 511)
ICHABOD WY
800 WAL 91789 639-H4
ICICLE DR
8200 SBdC 92371 (4562-G3 See Page 4471)
ICY WILLOW LN
- LACo 91387 4552-B4
IDA AV
12800 LA 90066 672-B5
IDA CT
6000 CHNO 91710 641-J7
IDA PL
23200 Chat 91311 499-F7
IDA ST
500 PacP 90272 630-H5
IDA WY
23600 WHil 91304 499-E6
S IDABEL PL
400 CRSN 90745 794-E2
IDABELL AV
23600 CRSN 90745 794-E2
IDAHO
3800 WCOV 91792 679-A1
IDAHO AV
100 SMCA 90403 671-D1
900 SMCA 90403 631-F6
11300 SGAT 90280 705-F7
11300 WLA 90025 632-A5
11500 SGAT 90280 735-F1
11600 WLA 90025 631-H6
IDAHO CT
1000 CLAR 91711 571-F6
IDAHO ST
200 PAS 91103 535-G7
3700 BALD 91706 598-B6
6600 BPK 90621 767-J1
N IDAHO ST
100 LHB 90631 708-D4
900 OrCo 90631 708-D4
S IDAHO ST
100 LHB 90631 708-D7
1000 LHB 90631 738-D1
E IDAHOME ST
400 COV 91723 599-A7
E IDAHOME ST
1000 WCOV 91790 598-H7
1400 WCOV 91791 598-J7
1900 WCOV 91791 599-A7
IDALENE ST
11100 SFSP 90670 706-F4
IDA MAY LN
400 SMAD 91024 566-J2
IDELL ST
2300 LA 90065 594-J6
IDLE DR
28900 AGRH 91301 558-B4
IDLEHOUR LN
700 SMAD 91024 537-B7
IDLEWHILE TER
- LACo 91342 482-J6
IDLEWILD WY
26100 LACo 90265 628-C3
IDLEWOOD RD
800 GLDL 91202 564-B2
1700 GLDL 91202 534-C7
IDYLLWILD AV
200 LA 90031 595-A6
IGLESIA DR
21400 WdHl 91364 560-B5
IGLESIA ST
100 SDMS 91773 600-C2
100 SDMS 91773 570-C7
IGNATIAN CIR
7400 Wch 90045 702-E1
IGUALA ST
1000 MTBL 90640 636-E7
IKEBANA RD
- SMRO 91108 566-C7
ILA JOYCE ST
300 Alta 91001 535-G5
ILANA LN
29000 LACo 91390 4461-G4
ILENE DR
100 ARCD 91006 567-D7
ILENE RD
- LACo 91390 4373-B4
ILEX AV
600 SFER 91340 502-B1
8800 SunV 91352 502-G6
8800 SunV 91352 532-H1
9900 Pcma 91331 502-C2
11300 LA 91340 502-B1
ILIFF ST
700 PacP 90272 631-B4
ILLINOIS
2000 WCOV 91792 679-A1
ILLINOIS AV
2400 SGAT 90280 704-J3
2600 SGAT 90280 705-A4
15100 PRM 90723 735-G5
31800 Actn 93510 4465-D3
ILLINOIS CT
600 ELSG 90245 732-G1
15800 TOR 90247 733-H6
15800 TOR 90504 733-H6
18200 TOR 90504 763-H2
ILLINOIS DR
1800 SPAS 91030 595-F4
ILLINOIS ST
100 ELSG 90245 732-G1
10800 WHIT 90601 677-A4
13700 BALD 91706 598-A6
N ILLINOIS ST
500 POM 91768 640-H1
ILLORA DR
15400 LMRD 90638 737-H3
ILLUSION WY
16400 LMRD 90638 738-A2
ILONA AV
10300 LA 90064 632-D5
ILOPANGO DR
2800 HacH 91745 678-C6
ILUSO AV
19900 LACo 91789 679-E4
IMBIANCO CT
- PMDL 93551 4104-E6
IMBLER CT
6300 AGRH 91301 557-J3
IMLAY AV
4700 LA 90230 672-F4
IMOGEN AV
600 Echo 90026 594-B7
IMPALA DR
12600 LYN 90262 735-G3
IMPATIENS LN
- PMDL 93551 4285-E3
IMPERIAL AV
- LAN 93534 4015-E6
E IMPERIAL AV
100 ELSG 90245 702-F7
W IMPERIAL AV
100 ELSG 90245 702-D7
IMPERIAL DR
1200 GLDL 91207 564-G2
IMPERIAL HWY
2000 LHB 90631 738-A1
8000 DWNY 90242 705-J7
8300 DWNY 90242 735-J1
8500 DWNY 90242 736-A1
10000 NRWK 90650 736-F1
12400 NRWK 90650 737-A1
12600 SFSP 90670 737-A1
13000 LACo 90605 737-A1
13800 LMRD 90638 737-G1
14000 LACo 90604 737-G1
14000 LACo 90604 738-A1
16000 LMRD 90638 738-A1
E IMPERIAL HWY
100 LA 90061 704-E6
600 LA 90059 704-E6
1100 Wbrk 90059 704-E6
2600 LYN 90262 704-H7
2600 LYN 90262 705-B6
5100 SGAT 90280 705-F6
5300 LACo 90242 705-F6
5300 LACo 90280 705-F6
5600 LA 90245 702-G7
5600 Wch 90045 702-F7
5600 ELSG 90245 702-G7
7300 DWNY 90242 705-F6
7300 SGAT 90242 705-F6
E IMPERIAL HWY Rt#-90
100 FUL 92835 708-G7
100 LHB 90631 738-E1
400 LHB 90631 708-G7
W IMPERIAL HWY
100 LA 90061 704-B6
500 LA 90044 704-B6
1000 LACo 90044 704-B6
1300 LACo 90044 703-F6
1400 LACo 90047 703-F6
2000 HAW 90250 703-F6
2200 ING 90303 703-F6
2600 ING 90250 703-E6
4000 HAW 90304 703-F6
4800 Lenx 90304 703-A7
4800 Wch 90045 703-A7
5000 Wch 90045 703-A7
5100 Wch 90045 703-A7
5300 Wch 90045 702-C7
6900 ELSG 90245 702-C7
7400 PdlR 90293 702-C7
W IMPERIAL HWY Rt#-90
100 BREA 92821 709-A7
500 BREA 92821 708-H7
500 FUL 92835 708-H7
1200 LHB 90631 738-C1
IMPERIAL ST
600 LA 90021 634-H6
1900 LA 90021 674-H1
IMPERIAL TR
1700 Top 90290 590-B2
INA DR
1600 GLDL 91206 564-H3
INA ST
14400 BALD 91706 598-C5
INADALE AV
4800 LACo 90043 673-C4
INAGLEN WY
5000 LACo 90043 673-C4
INAVALE PL
12100 Brwd 90049 631-F1
INCA TR
21600 Chat 91311 500-A1
INCA WY
16700 PRM 90723 735-F6
INCE BLVD
3900 CULC 90232 672-H1
INCLINE CT
5200 RCUC - (542-E7 See Page 511)
14000 LMRD 90638 738-A2
INCLINE DR
- RCUC - (542-D7 See Page 511)
INCLINE LN
- LACo 91390 4461-A4
INDALS PL
22400 CALB 91302 559-J7
INDEPENDENCE AV
2600 LACo 90255 704-J2
2600 SGAT 90255 704-J2
2800 SGAT 90280 705-A2
6400 WdHl 91367 530-B7
6500 CanP 91303 530-B5
7500 LA 91304 530-B1
8900 LA 91304 500-B7
8900 Chat 91311 500-B4
INDEPENDENCE CT
5100 CHNO 91710 641-G5
INDEPENDENCE DR
100 CLAR 91711 571-D5
INDEPENDENCE SQ
- PMDL 93550 4286-C4
INDEPENDENCE ST
4200 CHNO 91710 641-F5
INDEPENDENCE WY
9200 LA 91343 501-H7
INDEPENDENCIA ST
22000 WdHl 91364 560-A4
INDEX ST
14900 MsnH 91345 501-H1
15600 GmH 91344 501-A1
18100 Nor 91326 500-G2
INDIA ST
2100 LA 90039 594-E4
INDIAN BEND
1000 GLDR 91740 569-H7
INDIAN DR
5200 LCF 91011 535-A1
22000 Chat 91311 500-A2
22000 Chat 91311 499-J1
INDIAN LN
12900 NRWK 90650 737-A1
INDIANA
2000 WCOV 91792 679-A1
INDIANA AV
300 CLAR 91711 571-D6
INDIANA AV
300 Ven 90291 671-J4
900 SPAS 91030 595-F3
1800 LA 90032 635-C1
2400 SGAT 90280 704-J4
2600 SGAT 90280 705-A4
4400 LCF 91011 535-A3
6200 NLB 90805 735-H7
6200 NLB 90805 765-H1
14700 PRM 90723 735-H4
INDIANA CT
300 Ven 90291 671-J4
500 SPAS 91030 595-F2
700 ELSG 90245 702-G7
INDIANA PL
600 SPAS 91030 595-F3
INDIANA ST
- ARCD 91006 567-D5
300 ELSG 90245 732-G1
2700 Actn 93510 4465-D1
5800 BPK 90621 737-J7
6300 BPK 90621 767-J1
10800 WHIT 90601 677-A4
N INDIANA ST
100 City 90063 635-C3
100 LA 90063 635-C5
1400 Boyl 90033 635-C3
S INDIANA ST
100 City 90063 635-D7
100 LA 90063 635-D7
600 LACo 90023 635-D7
600 LA 90023 635-D7
900 LACo 90023 675-D2
900 LA 90023 675-D2
1400 CMRC 90023 675-D2
2600 VER 90023 675-C3
INDIANA TER
600 SPAS 91030 595-G3
INDIANAPOLIS ST
11700 LA 90066 672-B2
INDIAN BEND DR
11700 LACo 90601 677-C2
INDIAN CANYON MTWY
- LACo 91342 482-G5
INDIAN CANYON RD
28900 Llan 93544 4471-B6
INDIAN CANYON TKTR
- Actn 93510 (4554-A5 See Page 4464)
- LACo (4554-A5 See Page 4464)
- LACo 91390 4464-B7
- LACo 91390 (4554-A5 See Page 4464)
INDIAN CANYON LATERAL
- LACo 91342 482-H4
INDIAN CREEK RD
2100 DBAR 91765 680-D5
15900 CRTS 90703 737-A5
INDIAN DUNES LN
300 AZU 91702 568-H4
INDIAN FALLS AV
15600 LACo 93535 4109-E6
INDIAN HILL BLVD
500 POM 91767 601-D7
500 POM 91767 641-D1
N INDIAN HILL BLVD
100 CLAR 91711 601-C3
1800 CLAR 91711 571-C6
S INDIAN HILL BLVD
100 CLAR 91711 601-D5
INDIAN HILL LN
600 SDMS 91773 599-J3
24400 CanP 91307 529-D4
INDIAN HILLS RD
11400 MsnH 91345 501-H1
11500 MsnH 91345 481-H7
INDIAN MEADOWS PL
- GmH 91344 481-A6
INDIAN MESA DR
11100 LACo 91342 482-J3
INDIAN MOUND RD
29700 MAL 90265 667-D3
INDIAN OAK LN
- VeCo 91377 557-J1
- VeCo 91377 558-A1
INDIAN OAK RD
31400 Actn 93510 4465-C4
INDIANOLA WY
4500 LCF 91011 535-C3
INDIAN PEAK RD
26600 RPV 90275 793-A7
27500 RHE 90274 793-A7
28000 RHE 90274 823-A1
28000 RPV 90275 823-A1
INDIAN RIDGE CT
29000 AGRH 91301 558-A3
INDIAN ROCK DR
27900 RPV 90275 792-G7
INDIAN SAGE RD
1300 LAN 93534 4015-F4
INDIAN SCHOOL LN
- CRSN 90745 794-G1
INDIAN SPRINGS DR
1100 GLDR 91741 569-G3
INDIAN SPRINGS RD
100 SDMS 91773 570-B7
N INDIAN SUMMER AV
1000 LACo 91744 638-F4
S INDIAN SUMMER AV
800 WCOV 91790 638-G2
1400 LACo 91744 638-G3
INDIAN VALLEY RD
28800 RPV 90275 822-J1
28800 RHE 90274 822-J1
INDIAN WELL DR
1300 DBAR 91765 680-A3
INDIAN WELLS CIR
23800 SCTA 91355 4550-G6
INDIAN WELLS DR
- LACo 90606 676-H6
INDIAN WELLS LN
2000 LVRN 91750 570-G4
INDIAN WOOD RD
4900 CULC 90230 672-H3
INDIES LN
28700 SCTA 91387 4552-B1
INDIGO
400 COMP 90220 734-H5
INDIGO CT
700 POM 91767 601-A4
INDIGO LN
7500 LPMA 90623 767-C3
E INDIGO ST
100 COMP 90220 734-J5
100 COMP 90220 735-A5
W INDIGO ST
100 COMP 90220 734-J5
INDIGO WY
41000 PMDL 93551 4194-J1
INDIGO SKY AV
- PMDL 93551 4195-E5
INDUSTRIAL AV
11700 SGAT 90280 735-G2
W INDUSTRIAL AV
700 ING 90302 703-A1
INDUSTRIAL RD
- SLB 90740 826-G4
INDUSTRIAL ST
800 AZU 91702 568-G6
1000 KeCo 93560 3835-E2
1000 POM 91766 641-B3
1200 LA 90021 634-G6
INDUSTRIAL WY
1700 LA 90023 675-B2
W INDUSTRIAL PARK ST
1400 COV 91722 598-G4
INDUSTRY AV
100 LHB 90631 708-E7
3400 Bxby 90807 795-G1
3400 Bxby 90807 765-G7
3400 LKWD 90712 765-G7
3400 LKWD 90712 795-G1
5100 PRV 90660 676-F3
8200 PRV 90660 706-C1
INDUSTRY CIR
14300 LMRD 90638 737-E6
INDUSTRY DR
3200 SIGH 90755 795-J3
27800 Valc 91355 4459-F5
INDUSTRY PL
17100 LMRD 90638 737-E6
INDUSTRY WY
2400 LYN 90262 704-J7
INDUSTRY HILLS PKWY
16800 INDS 91744 638-G7
16800 INDS 91744 678-G1
INEZ AV
10600 LACo 90605 707-C5
INEZ ST
900 NLB 90805 735-E6
1700 LA 90023 634-J5
2100 LA 90023 635-A6
INFINITY CIR
- LACo 91390 4460-J4
INGLEDALE TER
2900 LA 90039 594-D2
INGLENOOK LN
12400 CRTS 90703 767-A4
INGLESIDE DR
300 HMB 90254 732-G7
3200 MANB 90266 732-H3
N INGLESIDE DR
100 MANB 90266 732-F7
INGLESIDE WY
26200 LACo 90265 628-C3
INGLETON AV
100 SDMS 91773 599-H2
INGLEWOOD AV
- ING 90301 703-B7
500 RBCH 90278 763-C2
2000 RBCH 90278 733-B4
3600 LNDL 90260 733-B7
11400 HAW 90250 733-B4
11900 HAW 90250 733-B4
12800 LACo 90250 733-B4
14300 HAW 90260 733-B4
17300 LNDL 90260 763-C2
19000 TOR 90503 763-C3
N INGLEWOOD AV
100 ING 90301 703-B2
600 ING 90302 703-B1
900 ING 90302 673-B7
S INGLEWOOD AV
100 ING 90301 703-B3
10000 ING 90304 703-B6
10000 Lenx 90304 703-B6
11200 HAW 90304 703-B6
INGLEWOOD BLVD
3000 LA 90066 672-B1
4100 CULC 90066 672-E5
4500 LA 90230 672-E5
INGLIS DR
3600 LA 90065 594-H2
INGLIS WK
2600 LA 90065 594-H2
INGOMAR ST
17800 Res 91335 531-A3
18100 Res 91335 530-F3
19700 Win 91306 530-C3
20800 LA 91304 530-A3
22100 LA 91304 529-D3
INGRAHAM ST
1000 LA 90017 634-D3
3800 LA 90005 633-G3
INGRAM CT
23200 SCTA 91354 4460-G7
INGRAM PL
4900 THO 91362 557-G1
INGRAM ST
16500 LACo 91744 638-G6
INGRES AV
13100 GmH 91344 481-C4
INGRUM WY
19900 TOR 90503 763-C4
INLAND LN
20000 MAL 90265 629-J6
S INMAN RD
600 WCOV 91791 639-B1
INNES AV
1100 Echo 90026 634-F1
1100 LA 90012 634-F1
INNES PL
1300 Ven 90291 671-G6
INNISFREE CT
- FUL 92831 738-J3
INNSBRUCK POINT CT
- LACo 91387 4552-B5
INNSDALE DR
6100 LA 90068 563-F7
INOLA AV
44800 LAN 93534 4015-E6
INOLA CT
800 LHB 90631 708-H4
INOLA ST
1700 GLDR 91740 569-J6
2400 SDMS 91773 570-A6
INSKEEP AV
5800 LA 90003 674-C6
INSKIP AV
2700 LACo 91302 589-C3
INSPIRATION DR
700 POM 91768 600-H6
INSPIRATION PT
- WCOV 91791 639-C4
INSPIRATION TR
3300 BELL 90201 675-B7
12000 LACo 91342 482-H6
INSPIRATION WY
9500 Tuj 91042 503-J5
9500 Tuj 91042 504-A5
INSTAR PL
11400 ELMN 91732 597-G6
INSTITUTE PL
5000 LA 90029 593-H6
INSTONE CT
2900 THO 91361 557-C5
INTERCEPTOR ST
5700 Wch 90045 702-J3
INTERLACHEN RD
1400 SLB 90740 796-H7
INTERLAKEN CT
- SBdC 92397 (4652-G3 See Page 4651)
INTERMODAL WY
23500 CRSN 90810 794-J2
INTERNATIONAL AV
8500 LA 91304 530-A1
INTERNATIONAL RD
10000 Wch 90045 702-J5
INTREPID DR
32100 RPV 90275 823-D5
INTREPID LN
16600 OrCo 92649 826-J7
INVALE DR
2800 GLDL 91208 534-F3
INVERGARRY ST
19000 GLDR 91741 569-C6
INVERNESS AV
800 GLDR 91740 569-J7
800 GLDR 91740 570-A7
2300 LFlz 90027 594-A2
INVERNESS CT
500 FUL 92835 738-H2
INVERNESS DR
100 LCF 91011 535-B6
1200 PAS 91103 535-E7
1200 PAS 91103 565-D1
2800 OrCo 90720 796-H4
INVERNESS GRN
8200 BPK 90621 737-J5
INVERNESS PL
200 GLDR 91741 570-A5
INWOOD CT
- PMDL 93551 4195-A2
INWOOD DR
13300 Shrm 91423 562-D6
INWOOD LN
7700 LPMA 90623 767-C3
INWOOD WK
3800 Shrm 91423 562-C6
INYO PL
3800 CHNO 91710 641-D5
INYO ST
3600 LA 90031 595-B7
16200 LPUE 91744 678-E1
IONE DR
3400 LA 90068 563-C7
IONE PL
3200 LA 90068 563-C7
IONIA WK
5900 LBCH 90803 826-D3
IOWA
3700 WCOV 91792 679-A1
IOWA AV
1300 PAS 91103 565-H1
2400 SGAT 90280 704-J3
2600 SGAT 90280 705-A3
11200 WLA 90025 632-A5
11600 WLA 90025 631-J6
IOWA CT
- CHNO 91710 641-H4
1100 CLAR 91711 571-A7
IOWA ST
8300 DWNY 90241 706-A5
33000 Actn 93510 4375-C7
IOWA TR
1800 Top 90290 590-C2
IPSWICH CT
11700 BelA 90077 591-G2
IPSWICH ST
1000 LHB 90631 708-E7
IRA AV
6400 BGDN 90201 675-H7
6500 BGDN 90201 705-H1
IRA ST
3900 LYN 90262 705-D6
IREDELL LN
3200 LA 91604 562-G7
IREDELL ST
11900 LA 91604 562-G7
N IRENA AV
100 RBCH 90277 762-J4
S IRENA AV
100 RBCH 90277 762-J5
1200 RBCH 90277 763-A7
1200 RBCH 90277 793-A1
1400 TOR 90505 793-A1
IRENE CT
500 ELSG 90245 702-F7
IRENE ST
1200 SBdC 92397 (4652-D2 See Page 4651)
1900 WCOV 91792 639-A7
10400 LA 90034 632-E7
IRIS AV
100 COV 91722 598-H5
1600 TOR 90503 763-F6
3300 TOR 90505 793-F1
22500 TOR 90505 793-F1
IRIS CIR
2500 LVRN 91750 600-H1
5800 LPMA 90623 767-E3
6600 LA 90068 593-D2
IRIS CT
- SCTA 91351 4551-G7
38600 PMDL 93551 4195-G7
N IRIS CT
600 ONT 91762 601-H5
IRIS DR
6500 LA 90068 593-D2
IRIS LN
200 BREA 92821 709-D4
10800 ELMN 91731 597-C7
IRIS PL
6600 LA 90068 593-D2
27600 Cstc 91384 4459-H3
IRIS ST
- LHB 90631 708-C6
- PMDL 93552 4287-B1
1200 VeCo 93063 499-B4
S IRIS WY
2100 MONP 91755 636-C5
IRMA AV
10200 Tuj 91042 503-J3
IROLO ST
600 LA 90005 633-J3
1600 LA 90006 633-J4
IRON CT
39800 PMDL 93551 4195-J3
IRONBARK CIR
2100 BREA 92821 709-D6
IRONBARK DR
16600 CRTS 90703 737-B6
22500 DBAR 91765 680-A3
IRONBARK LN
700 SDMS 91773 600-C3
IRONBARK ST
- FUL 92835 738-H3
IRON CANYON RD
15100 SCTA 91387 4552-D6
N IRON CANYON RD
26600 SCTA 91387 4552-F6
IRON CLUB DR
1900 LVRN 91750 570-G5
IRONDALE AV
5400 WdHl 91367 560-C2
6700 Win 91306 530-C2
9400 Chat 91311 500-C3
IRONHORSE DR
36400 PMDL 93550 4286-G6
IRON HORSE PL
- LACo 91390 4461-A2
IRON HORSE RD
700 WAL 91789 639-F6
IRONHORSE CANYON RD
23200 DBAR 91765 680-B3
IRONSHIRE ST
18500 SCTA 91351 4551-H2
IRONSHOE CT
700 WAL 91789 639-J4
IRONSIDES ST
- LA 90292 701-H1
IRONSTONE AV
1600 MTBL 90640 636-F5
IRONSTONE DR
27600 SCTA 91387 4551-J3
IRONTON DR
16800 LACo 91744 638-G6
IRONWOOD AV
1000 PMDL 93551 4285-G1
IRONWOOD CIR
200 WAL 91789 639-B4
IRONWOOD CT
1500 BREA 92821 708-H6
IRONWOOD DR
- SCTA 91355 4550-B5
5700 AGRH 91301 557-J4
IRONWOOD LN
- LACo 91390 4460-H2
- CRSN 90745 794-G1
IRONWOOD RD
100 SBdC 92372 (4472-A6 See Page 4471)
IRONWOOD ST
1200 LHB 90631 738-F1
5300 RPV 90275 793-A5
5700 RPV 90275 792-J5
IROQUOIS AV
800 LBCH 90815 796-E2
3000 LBCH 90808 796-E1
3400 LBCH 90808 766-E7
4100 LKWD 90713 766-E3
IROQUOIS DR
7400 BPK 90620 767-G2
IRVINE AV
4200 LA 91604 562-H5
4400 LA 91602 562-H4
4800 NHol 91601 562-H1
5900 NHol 91601 532-H6
6500 NHol 91606 532-H6
7200 NHol 91605 532-H3
8000 SunV 91352 532-H3
IRVING AV
100 GLDL 91201 563-J2
1000 GLDL 91201 564-A1
1200 GLDL 91201 534-B7
5800 LaCr 91214 504-H5
N IRVING BLVD
100 LA 90004 593-G7
100 LA 90004 633-G1
S IRVING BLVD
100 LA 90004 633-G2
300 LA 90020 633-G2
600 LA 90005 633-G2
600 LA 90010 633-G2
IRVING CT
4900 CHNO 91710 641-F6
IRVING DR
400 BURB 91504 533-F4
IRVING LN
25000 StvR 91381 4640-C1
IRVING PL
3900 CULC 90232 672-H1
IRVING ST
600 ALH 91801 596-A5
3700 VER 90058 674-H3
S IRVING WY
- UPL 91786 601-J4
IRVING TABOR CT
1400 Ven 90291 671-H6
IRVINGTON PL
5000 HiPk 90042 595-B2
IRVINGTON TER
5100 HiPk 90042 595-B2
IRWIN AV
10100 ING 90304 703-A5
10100 Lenx 90304 703-A5
IRWINDALE AV
100 AZU 91702 568-F7
100 AZU 91702 598-F4
4000 LACo 91722 598-F4
4000 WCOV 91790 598-F4
4300 IRW 91706 598-F4
6000 IRW 91702 568-F7
6000 IRW 91706 568-F7
IRWINGROVE DR
7200 DWNY 90241 705-J2
7300 DWNY 90241 706-A2
ISABEL AV
3000 RSMD 91770 636-E2
ISABEL DR
3000 LA 90065 594-H3
ISABEL ST
200 LA 90065 595-A5
400 LA 90065 594-H4
900 BURB 91506 533-F7
N ISABEL ST
100 GLDL 91206 564-F3
900 GLDL 91207 564-F3
S ISABEL ST
100 GLDL 91205 564-F5
ISABELLA AV
800 MONP 91754 636-B4
ISABELLA CT
5300 AGRH 91301 557-H5
ISABELLA PKWY
26700 SCTA 91351 4551-D3
ISABELLA TER
300 MONP 91754 636-B3
ISABELLE PL
22200 CRSN 90745 764-D7

STREET Block City ZIP Pg-Grid

ISADORA LN
10400 BelA 90077 592-A5
ISAMAR CT
- LA 91343 501-J6
ISELI RD
14300 SFSP 90670 737-D3
ISHIDA AV
16400 CRSN 90746 734-E6
ISIDORO
18000 LACo 90220 765-A1
ISIS AV
7700 Wch 90045 702-J2
7700 Wch 90045 703-A2
11600 Wch 90045 703-A7
11600 Lenx 90304 703-A7
11900 Lenx 90304 733-A1
12000 LACo 90250 733-A1
12700 ELSG 90245 733-A2
13200 HAW 90250 733-A2
14300 HAW 90260 733-A4
S ISIS AV
100 ING 90301 703-A3
ISLAND
1500 WCOV 91790 638-D2
ISLAND AV
100 Wilm 90744 794-E5
100 Wilm 90744 824-E1
21300 CRSN 90745 764-D6
22400 CRSN 90745 794-D1
ISLAND DR
1600 FUL 92833 738-B5
E ISLAND RD
- SCTA 91355 4550-F1
W ISLAND RD
- SCTA 91355 4550-F1
ISLANDIA AV
- CRTS 90703 736-F6
ISLAND OAK ST
- SIMI 93063 499-A3
ISLAND PALMS LN
- LA 91342 482-E5
ISLAND VIEW CT
- SCTA 91355 4550-F2
ISLAND VIEW DR
600 SLB 90740 826-G4
29600 RPV 90275 822-H2
ISLAND VILLAGE DR
6900 LBCH 90803 826-F2
ISLE OF VIEW DR
25600 LACo 91302 629-A1
ISLETA ST
11300 Brwd 90049 631-H2
ISORA RD
8700 PRV 90660 676-G1
ISORA ST
8700 PRV 90660 676-H1
ISTHMUS
300 LBCH 90803 826-C1
ISTHMUS VIEW DR
- RPV 90275 823-F7
ITALIA ST
800 COV 91723 599-D5
E ITALIA ST
100 COV 91723 599-C5
ITAPETINGA LN
13000 CRTS 90703 767-B2
ITASCA ST
16200 LA 91343 501-D5
16900 Nor 91325 501-C6
19200 Nor 91324 500-F6
19800 Chat 91311 500-B6
22100 Chat 91311 499-H6
ITATI TR
11400 Chat 91311 480-B7
11400 Chat 91311 500-B1
ITHACA AV
2200 LA 90032 635-E1
5100 LA 90032 595-F7
ITUNI ST
1000 WCOV 91790 638-C1
IVA ST
100 NLB 90805 735-B7
E IVA ST
3700 RDom 90221 735-C6
IVADEL PL
16900 Enc 91436 561-D4
IVAFERN LN
5200 LCF 91011 535-D3
IVAN CT
2700 LA 90039 594-D3
IVANELL AV
500 LPUE 91744 638-C6
IVAN HILL TER
2500 LA 90039 594-D3
IVANHOE DR
2400 LA 90039 594-D3
IVAR AV
1300 Hlwd 90028 593-F4
1900 LA 90068 593-F3
3400 RSMD 91770 636-H2
3500 RSMD 91770 596-H6
5900 TEML 91780 596-H3
IVARENE AV
6200 LA 90068 593-F3
IVERSON LN
11100 Chat 91311 499-J2
IVERSON RD
11300 Chat 91311 499-H2
11400 Chat 91311 499-H2
IVES CT
- Saug 91350 4461-F6
IVES LN
2300 RBCH 90278 763-B2
IVES ST
8400 PRM 90723 735-H4
9200 BLF 90706 736-A4
IVESBROOK ST
400 LAN 93534 4015-F5
500 LAN 93535 4016-A5
6200 LAN 93536 4014-D5
9000 LACo 93536 4013-H5
IVESCREST AV
400 COV 91724 599-E3
5000 LACo 91724 599-E3
IVESGROVE DR
42000 LACo 93536 4104-D6
IVO ST
7400 DWNY 90240 706-A2
IVORY AV
1800 PMDL 93550 4286-D5
IVORY DR
2000 DUAR 91010 567-J7
IVORY LN
- WCOV 91792 679-C1
2300 POM 91767 601-A4
IVORY WY
19100 RowH 91748 679-C7
IVREA PL
26300 SCTA 91355 4550-E4
E IVY AV
100 ING 90302 703-C1
N IVY AV
100 MNRO 91016 567-G3
S IVY AV
100 MNRO 91016 567-G5
W IVY AV
100 ING 90302 703-C2
IVY CT
300 POM 91767 600-J2
10600 NRWK 90650 736-E3
IVY DR
500 PMDL 93550 4286-A3
3500 CALB 91302 559-F7
3500 CALB 91302 589-F1
IVY LN
- SCTA 91321 4641-C2
IVY PL
2300 LHB 90631 708-B5
11200 LA 90064 632-C7
12100 LA 90064 672-B1
IVY ST
400 GLDL 91204 564-C5
700 GLDR 91740 599-G1
3100 LA 90034 632-H7
4700 PRV 90660 676-F2
8600 Wats 90002 704-H3
IVY TER
- LACo 90502 764-A5
IVY TR
3400 CALB 91302 589-F1
IVY WY
5900 CULC 90232 673-A2
5900 CULC 90232 672-J2
5900 LA 90016 672-J2
5900 LA 90016 673-A2
5900 CULC 90016 672-J2
IVY BRIDGE RD
1600 GLDL 91207 564-F1
IVYDALE CT
3600 LACo 91107 566-H6
IVY GLEN WY
3100 LA 90064 632-E7
IVY HILL RD
16800 HacH 91745 678-F4
IVYLAND AV
2000 ARCD 91007 597-C2
IVYSIDE PL
16800 Enc 91436 561-D7
IVYTON ST
- LAN 93536 4014-J5
500 LAN 93535 4016-A5
700 LAN 93534 4015-F5
IVYWOOD CT
- PMDL 93551 4285-D3
IVYWOOD DR
5200 LPMA 90623 767-C3
IZETTA AV
12100 DWNY 90242 706-C7
12600 DWNY 90242 736-C1
13600 BLF 90706 736-C2

J

J
16600 PRM 90723 735-F6
J ST
- BELL 90201 675-F5
- PdlR 90293 732-C1
W J ST
900 ONT 91762 601-H6
JABONERIA RD
6200 BGDN 90201 675-H7
6500 BGDN 90201 705-G2
JACANA CT
20000 SCTA 91351 4551-E4
JACANA DR
14700 LMRD 90638 737-G4
JACARANDA
2000 WCOV 91791 639-A4
JACARANDA AV
3300 BURB 91505 563-C3
12400 CHNO 91710 641-H6
JACARANDA DR
200 PAS 91105 565-D6
JACARANDA LN
- CYP 90630 767-E6
- SCTA 91354 4460-E7
JACARANDA PL
200 BREA 92821 709-C7
200 FUL 92832 738-G6
1200 FUL 92833 738-D6
1200 UPL 91784 571-J5
12500 CHNO 91710 641-H6
JACARANDA ST
41400 PMDL 93551 4104-G7
W JACARANDA ST
1000 ONT 91762 641-J3
JACARANDA TER
- LA 91342 481-J2
JACARANDA WY
- POM 91767 600-J3
JACARTE AV
3700 PMDL 93550 4286-H4
JACINTO AV
11200 LA 91342 503-C1
JACINTO WY
40300 PMDL 93551 4194-J3
E JACINTO WY
4100 LBCH 90815 796-A4
JACK PL
2200 SPed 90731 824-A1
JACKDAW DR
- LACo 91342 482-J3
JACK FROST DR
8100 SBdC 92371 (4562-G3
See Page 4471)
JACKIE AV
6200 WdHl 91367 529-F7
JACKLIN AV
38500 PMDL 93550 4196-D7
JACKMAN AV
500 LA 91342 481-J7
500 SFER 91342 481-J7
JACKMAN ST
- LAN 93536 4013-H5
100 LAN 93534 4015-E5
500 LAN 93535 4016-A5
3000 LAN 93536 4015-B5
4200 LAN 93536 4014-C5
7200 LACo 93535 4017-F4
7300 LACo 93536 4014-C5
9000 LACo 93536 4013-H5
JACK RABBIT LN
- CRSN 90745 794-G1
JACKRABBIT LN
4600 Actn 93510 4374-H3
JACK RABBIT RUN
7500 SBdC 92372 (4562-F4
See Page 4471)
JACK RABBIT TR
30900 Llan 93544 4471-C2
JACK RABBIT WY
- PMDL 93552 4287-E2
JACKSON AV
- AZU 91702 568-G7
300 AZU 91702 598-G1
1200 LBCH 90813 795-A6
1700 SGBL 91776 596-E7
2000 SGBL 91776 636-E2
2400 RSMD 91770 636-E2
2400 CULC 90232 672-G2
4100 CYP 90630 767-A6
9900 SGAT 90280 705-D6
10600 LYN 90262 705-D7
JACKSON CT
- LAN 93535 4016-G4
4200 CHNO 91710 641-E4
JACKSON PL
500 GLDL 91206 564-F3
7200 LACo 91775 566-H7
8300 WHIT 90602 707-E2
JACKSON ST
300 PAS 91104 565-J2
300 PAS 91104 566-A2
600 LA 90012 634-H4
1300 GLDL 91207 564-F2
1800 BURB 91504 533-E5
7000 PRM 90723 735-F5
9300 PRV 90660 676-H4
11800 CRTS 90703 766-H4
13600 WHIT 90602 707-D2
29700 Cstc 91384 4459-D7
E JACKSON ST
1100 NLB 90805 765-F3
2500 CRSN 90810 764-J5
2500 CRSN 90810 765-A5
N JACKSON ST
100 GLDL 91206 564-F4
100 GLDL 91207 564-F3
1800 NLB 90805 765-G3
S JACKSON ST
100 GLDL 91205 564-F5
JACKSON WY
7500 BPK 90620 767-H5
JACKSTADT ST
3700 SPed 90731 853-J1
JACMAR AV
9000 WHIT 90605 707-D3
JACMAR DR
300 MTBL 90640 676-D4
JACOB AV
19100 CRTS 90703 766-H2
JACOB DR
- PMDL 93551 4195-D6
JACOB ST
6000 CULC 90232 632-J7
6000 CULC 90232 633-A7
JACOB HAMBLIN RD
24800 HIDH 91302 559-C3
JACOBS LN
1000 SPAS 91030 595-G2
JACON WY
600 PacP 90272 630-H4
JACQUELINE DR
1300 POM 91768 600-F7
2900 WCOV 91792 638-J7
3000 WCOV 91792 678-J1
JACQUELINE PL
6300 HiPk 90042 565-E7
12400 GrnH 91344 481-A6
JACQUES ST
4600 TOR 90503 763-B6
JACUMBA AV
- LACo 93591 4200-F4
JADE AV
4200 CYP 90630 767-A4
4200 LACo 90630 767-A4
JADE CT
- LAN 93536 4014-G7
- WCOV 91792 679-C1
2700 PMDL 93550 4286-F5
20900 DBAR 91789 679-G4
27600 Cstc 91384 4369-G6
JADE DR
- LAN 93536 4104-J1
JADE LN
8700 RSMD 91770 636-H2
JADE ST
4500 LA 90032 635-D2
JADE WY
- POM 91767 600-J2
N JADE COVE DR
300 LBCH 90803 826-E1
JADE COVE WY
400 SLB 90740 826-F4
JADESTONE DR
14800 Shrm 91403 561-J6
JADESTONE PL
14900 Shrm 91403 561-J6
JADE TREE DR
400 MONP 91754 636-A3
JAFFREY AV
21300 LACo 90502 764-B6
JAFFREY ST
1000 LHB 90631 708-E7
JAGUAR CT
- Enc 91316 531-A7
- Res 91335 531-A7
1300 PMDL 93551 4285-F1
JAGUAR ST
14500 MsnH 91345 501-J2
14500 MsnH 91345 502-A2
JAIME CT
- PMDL 93551 4194-G1
JAKE LN
- LA 91304 529-J2
JAKES WY
- LACo 91387 4552-A3
18200 LACo 91387 4551-J4
JALAPA DR
500 COV 91724 599-F6
JALEE CT
2000 LACo 91789 679-F7
JALISCO RD
14200 LMRD 90638 737-F3
JALMIA DR
2500 LA 90046 593-B2
JALMIA PL
7600 LA 90046 593-B1
JALMIA WY
7500 LA 90046 593-B2
JALON RD
14500 LMRD 90638 737-G3
JAMACHA PL
16100 WHIT 90603 707-J1
JAMAICA CIR
7600 BPK 90620 767-D3
JAMAICA CT
6000 LAN 93536 4014-F7
JAMAICA LN
- LAN 93536 4014-F7
E JAMES AV
1500 WCOV 91791 598-H7
2100 WCOV 91791 599-A7
JAMES CT
1000 LAN 93535 4106-B3
JAMES PL
600 POM 91767 601-A6
11100 CRTS 90703 766-F3
36500 PMDL 93550 4286-H4
JAMES ST
400 LA 90065 594-J5
400 LA 90065 595-A5
4500 MTCL 91763 601-E6
9000 DWNY 90242 736-A1
11500 CRTS 90703 766-G3
JAMES WK
- Cstc 91384 4459-D6
JAMES WY
2400 FUL 92833 738-D3
5900 SIMI 93063 499-B3
JAMES ALAN CIR
22100 Chat 91311 499-J4
JAMES ALAN ST
6000 CYP 90630 767-E7
JAMES LEWIS CT
- POM 91766 641-B4
JAMES M WOOD BLVD
700 LA 90015 634-B3
800 LA 90017 634-B3
1800 LA 90006 634-A3
1800 LA 90057 634-B3
2600 LA 90005 634-A3
3000 LA 90006 633-H3
3000 LA 90005 633-H3
JAMESON CT
100 SMAD 91024 566-J2
JAMESON DR
22500 CALB 91302 559-H6
JAMESON PL
3900 CALB 91302 559-H6
JAMES STEWART AV
- Univ 91608 563-B5
JAMES TOWN
1000 MNRO 91016 567-G2
JAMESTOWN CT
2300 CLAR 91711 571-E6
JAMESTOWN RD
500 BURB 91504 533-F4
1000 PMDL 93550 4286-B4
JAMIE AV
600 LHB 90631 708-F7
10800 Pcma 91331 502-F2
13000 LA 91342 482-A4
13300 LA 91342 481-H3
JAMIE CT
44100 LAN 93536 4015-A7
JAMIESON AV
5700 Enc 91316 561-A1
6100 Enc 91316 531-A7
6400 Res 91335 531-A3
8300 Nor 91325 531-A2
JAMISON AV
20700 CRSN 90745 764-C5
JAMON LN
500 WAL 91789 639-E7
JAN CT
9300 PRV 90660 676-J1
JAN ST
20800 Win 91306 530-C6
JANALINDA AV
500 COV 91722 598-H5
JANDO DR
1600 Top 90290 589-G3
JANDY PL
5400 LA 90066 672-E7
JANE PL
900 PAS 91105 565-H7
JANEEN CIR
8000 LPMA 90623 767-D4
JANEL AV
24300 SCTA 91321 4640-H2
JANELL AV
17100 CRTS 90703 736-J7
JANET DR
- LAN 93536 4015-D7
JANET LN
1500 SIMI 93063 499-B3
23900 TOR 90505 793-C3
JANET PL
4700 Eagl 90041 564-J6
JANET WY
5900 SIMI 93063 499-B3
JANETDALE ST
13800 LACo 91746 638-B2
14900 LACo 91744 638-D3
14900 WCOV 91790 638-D3
JANET LEE DR
2300 LaCr 91214 504-G6
JANETTA WY
10000 Sunl 91040 503-A4
JANETTE AV
1000 HacH 91745 637-J7
E JANICE DR
700 NLB 90805 765-E1
JANICE LN
700 WAL 91789 639-C6
JANICE PL
9100 LA 90210 592-G2
E JANICE ST
300 NLB 90805 765-D1
JANINE DR
100 LACo 90631 708-C4
14100 WHIT 90605 707-E2
15300 WHIT 90603 707-H3
16000 WHIT 90603 708-A4
JANIS LN
1500 SIMI 93063 499-B3
JANIS ST
11100 CRSN 90746 734-F7
JANIS WY
6000 SIMI 93063 499-B3
JANISANN AV
5300 CULC 90230 672-G5
JANISON DR
9500 OrCo 90631 708-C4
17000 WHIT 90603 708-C4
JANLOR DR
30600 AGRH 91301 557-G4
30800 WLKV 91362 557-F4
JANLU AV
1400 HacH 91745 678-A2
JANNA ST
9200 BLF 90706 736-A7
JANNA WY
14000 LA 91342 482-E1
JANNETTA AV
2100 BURB 91504 533-E5
JANSEN AV
400 SDMS 91773 599-J2
JANSU PL
400 POM 91768 640-C2
JANUARY DR
25500 TOR 90505 793-E5
JANUS DR
37600 PMDL 93550 4286-H2
JANVIER WY
4600 LaCr 91214 534-G1
JANZER CT
- SCTA 91350 4551-D5
JAPANESE VILLAGE PLAZA MALL
100 LA 90012 634-G4
JAPONICA AV
4200 LACo 91750 570-H7
JARANA CT
27000 SCTA 91354 4460-H7
JARDIN CT
- Boyl 90033 634-J4
JARDINE AV
10100 Sunl 91040 503-H3
JARDINE ST
4900 CMRC 90040 675-G3
JARED CT
6100 WdHl 91367 529-D7
JARED DR
18300 Tarz 91356 560-J3
JARGONELLE CT
- PMDL 93551 4285-E4
JARMAN PL
- BALD 91706 598-A4
JARROW AV
800 HacH 91745 638-A7
800 HacH 91745 678-A1
JARVIS AV
4900 LCF 91011 535-A1
12800 LACo 90061 734-D2
JARVIS ST
1800 LA 90012 594-H7
JASMINE AV
200 MNRO 91016 567-H4
2200 UPL 91784 571-J3
3400 LA 90034 632-F7
3500 LA 90034 672-F1
3800 CULC 90232 672-G2
3800 LA 90232 672-F1
N JASMINE AV
800 ONT 91762 601-H5
JASMINE CIR
1900 WCOV 91791 638-J3
1900 WCOV 91791 639-A3
JASMINE CT
2500 LVRN 91750 570-H6
N JASMINE CT
600 ONT 91762 601-H5
JASMINE DR
300 BREA 92821 708-J7
300 BREA 92821 738-J1
11900 CHNO 91710 641-E5
JASMINE LN
- StvR 91381 4640-D1
16200 LPUE 91744 638-E7
JASMINE PL
1300 ONT 91762 641-H3
JASMINE ST
- PMDL 93551 4285-C3
JASMINE WK
- LACo 90502 764-A5
JASMINE WY
- CRTS 90703 737-D7
- CYP 90630 767-E6
- YBLN 92886 709-J7
- YBLN 92886 710-A7
JASMINE VALLEY DR
30200 SCTA 91387 4462-G4
JASON AV
7400 CanP 91307 529-F4
7700 LA 91304 529-F2
JASON CIR
3800 TOR 90505 793-D1
JASON CT
900 LAN 93534 4015-G3
JASON DR
29000 LACo 91387 4551-H5
JASON LN
23200 CanP 91307 529-F4
JASON PL
1000 DBAR 91765 680-E2
JASON RD
33800 Actn 93510 4374-G6
JASPER
- BREA 92823 710-C6
JASPER CT
- StvR 91381 4550-B4
6200 LAN 93536 4104-E1
JASPER ST
4400 LA 90032 595-D7
JASPER WY
27500 Cstc 91384 4369-H6
JATO RD
- SCTA 91350 4551-A5
JAVA DR
13300 LA 90210 562-C7
S JAVA ST
800 ING 90301 703-C3
JAVALAMBRE DR
5100 WHIT 90601 677-D4
JAVELIN ST
200 CRSN 90745 764-D5
700 LACo 90502 764-B5
E JAVELIN ST
100 CRSN 90745 764-C5
JAXINE DR
100 Alta 91001 535-H3
JAY CT
500 MTBL 90640 676-D1
JAY PL
1100 LACo 90502 764-A7
E JAY ST
100 CRSN 90745 764-D7
W JAY ST
100 CRSN 90745 764-C7
1000 LACo 90502 764-A7
JAYBROOK DR
1800 RPV 90275 823-H3
JAY CARROLL DR
20200 SCTA 91350 4461-D6
JAYDEE CIR
7800 Tuj 91042 503-H2
JAYHAWKER LN
23700 DBAR 91765 640-C5
JAYHAWKER RD
35500 LACo 91390 4373-J1
JAYLEE DR
8800 LACo 91775 596-H2
9000 TEML 91780 596-H1
JAYMA LN
2300 LaCr 91214 504-H6
JAYMILLS AV
100 NLB 90805 765-D2
JAYNES PL
- BPK 90621 738-B3
JAYSEEL ST
7500 Tuj 91042 503-H2
7800 Sunl 91040 503-F2
JAYSON CT
700 POM 91767 601-A3
JAYWOOD CT
700 BREA 92821 708-H6
JEAN LN
2800 WLKV 91361 557-A7
JEAN PL
3800 CULC 90232 672-G1
JEANETTE AV
16600 CRTS 90703 737-B7
JEANETTE LN
14300 BALD 91706 598-B7
JEANETTE PL
12000 GrnH 91344 481-C6
W JEANETTE PL
1700 LBCH 90810 795-A2
JEANETTE ST
38100 PMDL 93550 4286-D1
JEANINE PL
16900 GrnH 91344 481-C5
JEANNE LN
16000 Enc 91436 561-F7
35400 LACo 93552 4376-J1
JEANNE TER
7700 Tuj 91042 503-H2
JEANNIE DR
17900 LACo 91744 678-J2
JEANS CT
- SIGH 90755 795-H3
JEDBURGH ST
1000 GLDR 91740 599-H1
JED SMITH RD
5300 HIDH 91302 559-B3
JEFF AV
11300 LA 91342 503-A1
11500 LA 91342 (4723-A7
See Page 4643)
JEFF ST
9000 BLF 90706 736-A3
JEFFDALE AV
5100 WdHl 91364 559-H3
JEFFERS LN
21600 SCTA 91350 4461-A5
JEFFERSON AV
- PMDL 93550 4286-B4
900 POM 91767 601-B7
5300 CHNO 91710 641-G6
5700 SGAT 90280 735-G1
12800 HAW 90250 733-D3
14200 LNDL 90250 733-D3
E JEFFERSON AV
100 POM 91767 600-J7
300 POM 91767 601-A7
N JEFFERSON AV
100 FUL 92832 738-F7
W JEFFERSON AV
100 POM 91768 600-H7
JEFFERSON BLVD
800 MTBL 90640 636-D7
5600 LA 90230 672-H3
5600 CULC 90230 672-H3
5900 LA 90016 672-H3
5900 CULC 90232 672-H3
6000 CULC 90016 672-H3
E JEFFERSON BLVD
100 LA 90011 674-D2
N JEFFERSON BLVD
- CULC 90230 672-F6
11800 LA 90230 672-F6
12100 LA 90094 672-F6
W JEFFERSON BLVD
100 LA 90007 674-B1
600 LA 90089 674-B1
900 LA 90089 634-A7
900 LA 90007 634-A7
1400 LA 90007 633-F7
1500 LA 90018 633-F7
3600 LA 90016 633-A7
4300 LA 90016 673-C1
5800 LA 90016 632-J7
5800 CULC 90232 632-J7
5800 LA 90016 672-J1
5900 CULC 90232 672-J1
5900 CULC 90016 672-J1
10100 CULC 90230 672-J1
12400 LA 90094 672-E7
12400 LACo 90066 672-E7
12400 LA 90066 672-E7
12900 LA 90094 702-C1
12900 LA 90066 702-C1
JEFFERSON CT
5800 CHNO 91710 641-J6
44700 LAN 93535 4016-F6
JEFFERSON DR
- CYP 90630 767-A6
- PMDL 93551 4195-D5
1900 LACo 91104 566-D1
8800 BPK 90620 767-G5
JEFFERSON ST
- CRTS 90703 766-H3
900 UPL 91784 571-J4
2300 TOR 90501 763-F7
7200 PRM 90723 735-G4
9400 BLF 90706 736-B4
E JEFFERSON ST
2500 CRSN 90810 764-J6
2500 CRSN 90810 765-A6
JEFFERSONIA WY
2200 Brwd 90049 631-D1
JEFFREY AV
17400 CRTS 90703 737-B7
18300 CRTS 90703 767-B1
JEFFREY CIR
19600 CRTS 90703 767-B3
JEFFREY CT
3100 PAS 91107 566-F2
JEFFREY DR
5500 TOR 90503 763-A5
JEFFREY LN
- LAN 93536 4105-D1
JEFFREY PL
19700 WdHl 91364 560-E3
JEFFREY MARK CT
22400 Chat 91311 499-H4
JEFFREY MARK ST
6000 CYP 90630 767-E7
JEFFRIES AV
100 MNRO 91016 597-F1
500 ARCD 91006 597-F1
2300 BURB 91506 533-C7
2500 BURB 91505 533-C7
2600 LA 90065 594-J6
JELLICK AV
400 LACo 91744 679-A2
1600 RowH 91748 679-A5
S JELLICK AV
1100 INDS 91748 679-A4
1300 RowH 91748 679-A4
JELLICO AV
5800 Enc 91316 561-B1
6700 VanN 91406 531-B4
7600 Nor 91325 531-B1
9100 Nor 91325 501-B6
10400 GrnH 91344 501-B2
11800 GrnH 91344 481-B7
JENA DR
24600 SCTA 91321 4640-G3
JENIEL CT
22500 SCTA 91350 4550-J5
JENIFER AV
300 COV 91724 599-E5
700 GLDR 91740 569-E7
4900 LACo 91724 599-E3
5400 GLDR 91740 599-E2
JENKINS DR
15200 LACo 90604 707-G5
15400 WHIT 90604 707-G5
JENKINS ST
11400 ART 90701 736-G7
JENNA LN
36400 PMDL 93550 4286-G4
JENNER ST
- LAN 93536 4014-J5
500 LAN 93535 4016-A5
700 LAN 93534 4015-E5
JENNIE LN
1900 LHB 90631 708-G4
JENNIFER CIR
7700 LPMA 90623 767-C3
JENNIFER CT
- SCTA 91351 4551-E4
6200 SIMI 93063 499-B2
JENNIFER DR
3200 PMDL 93550 4286-G4
JENNIFER LN
- LA 91304 529-J2
43400 LAN 93535 4106-C2
JENNIFER PL
1800 WCOV 91792 638-G5
24300 SCTA 91321 4640-F2
JENNINGS DR
4000 LA 90032 595-E5
JENNY AV
9000 Wch 90045 702-H4
JENNY CT
20700 SCTA 91350 4461-C4
JENNY LN
3700 SBdC 91710 641-C7
41800 LAN 93536 4104-D6
JENNY WY
8800 RSMD 91770 636-H1
JENSEN DR
23900 LA 91304 529-E2
JENSEN WY
100 FUL 92833 738-B7
JEREMIE ST
14500 BALD 91706 598-C5
JEREMY PL
12500 GrnH 91344 481-A6
JERENE LN
800 LACo 90502 794-C3
JEREZ ST
- AZU 91702 598-G1
JERI LN
38000 PMDL 93550 4286-E1
JEROME CT
13200 CHLS 91709 680-J1
JEROME ST
12100 SunV 91352 502-F7
JERRY AV
3900 BALD 91706 598-B3
JERRY PL
- Saug 91350 4461-E5
11000 CRTS 90703 766-F3
JERRY ST
11500 CRTS 90703 766-G3
JERSEY
15400 MsnH 91345 501-G2
JERSEY AV
9400 SFSP 90670 706-G4
11100 NRWK 90650 706-G6
12300 NRWK 90650 736-G1
16600 ART 90701 736-G6
17800 ART 90701 766-G1
19500 CRTS 90703 766-G3
19900 LKWD 90715 766-G4
JERSEY CIR
19400 CRTS 90703 766-G3
JERSEY ST
16000 GrnH 91344 501-C2
JERSEYDALE AV
1600 MTBL 90640 636-F5
JESLEW CT
2100 RowH 91748 678-F5
JESS ST
1500 POM 91766 640-F3
8900 SGAT 90280 705-E3
JESSE AV
100 GLDL 91201 563-J3
JESSE ST
1500 LA 90021 634-H6
2200 LA 90023 634-J6
JESSEN DR
5100 LCF 91011 534-J1
JESSICA CIR
16200 CRTS 90703 736-E6
JESSICA CT
1800 WCOV 91792 638-J7
JESSICA DR
4500 LA 90065 594-J2
4500 LA 90065 595-A2
JESSICA PL
12400 GrnH 91344 481-A5
JESSIE ST
- SFER 91340 502-B1
- SFER 91340 482-B7
JESSIE NELSON CIR
2100 SIGH 90755 795-G4
JESTER CT
- LA 91343 501-H6
JESUS CANYON RD
28400 Llan 93544 4471-E6
JETMORE AV
13400 PRM 90723 735-H2
JETTY LN
- SCTA 91355 4550-H3
JEWEL AV
2700 VER 90058 674-J2
JEWEL CT
21000 DBAR 91789 679-H4
JEWEL DR
- CRTS 90703 767-C2
- LPMA 90623 767-C2
JEWEL ST
3000 Echo 90026 594-C7
JEWETT DR
- FUL 92833 738-C6
1800 LA 90046 592-J3
JIB ST
- LA 90292 701-J1
JILL CT
2000 SIMI 93063 499-C2
JILL LN
34700 Actn 93510 4375-E3
JILL PL
4000 Enc 91436 561-D5
JILL WY
1000 UPL 91784 571-J4
JILLIENE LN
- PRV 90660 676-F3
JILLSON ST
4900 CMRC 90040 675-E3
JIM BOWIE RD
3900 Ago 91301 558-F7
3900 AGRH 91301 558-F7
3900 AGRH 91301 588-F1
3900 Ago 91301 588-F1
JIM BRIDGER RD
24800 HIDH 91302 559-B4
JIMENEZ PL
10300 LA 91342 503-B1
JIMENEZ ST
10000 LA 91342 503-A1
JIMENO AV
12600 GrnH 91344 481-C4
JIMILYN ST
6400 SIMI 93063 499-C2
JIMPSON WY
21200 SCTA 91351 4551-B2
J LEE CIR
1300 GLDL 91208 534-G5
JOAN CIR
8000 LPMA 90623 767-C4
JOAN CT
1800 WCOV 91792 638-J7
JOAN DR
1400 HacH 91745 678-B2
JOAN LN
8300 LA 91304 529-F2
JOAN ST
500 LHB 90631 708-G5
JOANBRIDGE ST
5000 BALD 91706 598-B3
JOANN WY
1400 POM 91767 601-B6
JOANNA AV
16200 CRTS 90703 736-E6
JOAQUIN CT
5400 CMRC 90040 675-H3
JOAQUIN DR
2600 BURB 91504 533-F3
13500 CRTS 90703 737-C6
JOAQUIN LN
13700 CRTS 90703 737-C6
JOAQUIN RD
300 ARCD 91007 567-A6
700 ARCD 91007 566-J6
32200 Actn 93510 4465-F2
JOCELYN DR
500 LHB 90631 708-F5
JODEE DR
3300 WCOV 91791 639-D1
JODI PL
22000 SCTA 91350 4461-A5
JODI ST
19000 RowH 91748 679-C4
JODON CT
1900 RowH 91748 678-F5
JODY AV
9600 LACo 90605 707-B3
JODY LN
- PMDL 93551 4195-H3
22600 CRSN 90745 794-C1
JOEL CIR
9800 CYP 90630 767-E7
JOEL DR
2200 RowH 91748 679-E6
2400 LACo 91789 679-E6
JOEL ST
20600 SCTA 91350 4461-D5
E JOEL ST
800 CRSN 90745 764-E7
JOELLA ST
800 DUAR 91010 567-J7
E JOELLA ST
300 LACo 91016 567-H7
700 LACo 91010 567-H7
JOELTON DR
4000 AGRH 91301 558-E7
JOE VARGAS WY
9800 SELM 91733 637-A4
JOEY RD
42700 LACo 93532 4102-D4
JOFFRE ST
11300 Brwd 90049 631-H2
JOHANNA AV
4300 LKWD 90713 766-F5
10100 Sunl 91040 503-C3
JOHANNA PL
9700 Sunl 91040 503-D4
JOHN AV
8600 Wats 90002 704-F3
N JOHN AV
5800 NLB 90805 765-F2
JOHN PL
200 MANB 90266 732-G6
JOHN ST
200 MANB 90266 732-G5
3400 Echo 90026 594-B7
9400 SFSP 90670 707-A3
JOHN WY
300 LA 90732 823-H5
6000 SIMI 93063 499-B3
JOHN COLTER RD
24500 HIDH 91302 559-C4
JOHNELL RD
9200 Chat 91311 499-F7
JOHNETTA ST
24300 WdHl 91367 559-D1
JOHN FREMONT RD
24900 HIDH 91302 559-B3
JOHN IRWIN DR
21100 WAL 91789 639-H7
JOHN K DR
500 LBCH 90803 796-D7
JOHN MONTGOMERY DR
27400 LA 90732 823-J1
JOHN MUIR RD
- HIDH 91302 559-C1
JOHNNIE RD
35400 LACo 91390 4374-A2
JOHNNY GRANT WY
- Hlwd 90028 593-D4
JOHN REED CT
1100 INDS 91745 678-F3
JOHN RUSSEL DR
23400 SCTA 91355 4550-G5

STREET
Block City ZIP Pg-Grid

JOHNS CT
- LAN 93536 4105-E1
JOHNS CANYON RD
- RHLS 90274 823-C2
JOHN S GIBSON BLVD
1100 SPed 90731 824-B2
1400 Wilm 90744 824-B2
JOHN SLOAT PL
27600 LA 90732 823-J1
JOHNS MANVILLE ST
22300 CRSN 90745 764-J7
22300 CRSN 90745 794-H1
22300 CRSN 90810 764-J7
JOHNSON AL
700 PAS 91104 566-A2
JOHNSON AV
- Cstc 91384 4459-D6
2500 LHB 90631 708-B5
3500 ELMN 91731 597-D7
3500 ELMN 91731 637-D1
6200 NLB 90805 735-J7
6200 NLB 90805 765-J1
JOHNSON CIR
8700 BPK 90620 767-H5
JOHNSON CT
2000 TOR 90504 733-H7
JOHNSON DR
1200 INDS 91745 678-E3
JOHNSON LN
- BREA 92821 708-J5
JOHNSON PL
1500 FUL 92833 738-E6
9300 Chat 91311 499-F6
JOHNSON RD
11000 LACo 93536 4103-B4
11000 LAN 93536 4103-B4
11400 LACo 93532 4102-H4
11400 LACo 93532 4103-B4
16400 CynC 91351 4462-C5
27800 Cstc 91384 4369-G6
34900 LACo 91390 4373-F2
JOHNSON ST
200 MANB 90266 732-H6
E JOHNSON ST
100 COMP 90220 734-J6
100 COMP 90220 735-A6
100 COMP 90221 735-A6
W JOHNSON ST
100 COMP 90220 734-J6
JOHNSON PASTURE MTWY
- CLAR 91711 571-C2
JOHNSTON AV
2900 RBCH 90278 733-B5
JOHNSTON ST
1800 LA 90031 635-A1
2400 LA 90031 595-A7
JOHNSTONE PEAK TKTR
- GLDR - (540-D7 See Page 509)
- GLDR - 570-C2
- GLDR 91773 570-C2
- LACo - (540-F4 See Page 509)
- SDMS 91773 570-C2
JOHNSTON KNOLL
1500 FUL 92835 738-G4
JOHNSWOOD DR
4000 WdHl 91364 560-A6
JOHN TYLER DR
3500 LACo 90263 628-G6
3500 MAL 90265 628-G6
JOJOBA TER
2700 PMDL 93550 4286-F4
JOLEE LN
- RPV 90275 822-J1
JOLENE CT
7500 NHol 91605 532-F4
JOLETTE AV
12200 GrnH 91344 481-B4
JOLIE WY
- PMDL 93552 4287-E1
JOLIET AV
21900 HGDN 90716 766-J7
JOLINE AV
39600 PMDL 93551 4195-H5
JOLLEY DR
2000 BURB 91504 533-F4
JOLLY DR
- Top 90290 590-B2
JON CT
500 DBAR 91765 640-D7
W JON ST
1200 LACo 90502 764-A4
JONAH CT
- Tarz 91356 560-J2
JONALLAN DR
7000 NHol 91605 532-F5
JONATHAN CT
3900 LAN 93536 4105-A1
JONATHAN DR
- BREA 92821 709-A4
JONATHAN ST
23100 LA 91304 529-F3
JONATHON ST
- LAN 93536 4105-A1
6200 LAN 93536 4104-E1
JON DODSON DR
5300 AGRH 91301 557-H5
JONES AL
2100 PAS 91107 566-D4
JONES AV
1800 LA 90032 635-D2
JONES CT
1500 WCOV 91792 638-H4
JONES DR
- BREA 92821 708-J5
JONES PL
2900 SIGH 90755 795-G2
JONES RD
- HacH 91745 678-A6
- WHIT 91745 678-A6
19900 MAL 90265 629-J6
19900 MAL 90265 630-A6
JONESBORO AV
2200 SIMI 93063 499-C1
JONESBORO CIR
5400 BPK 90621 738-B5
JONESBORO DR
1300 Brwd 90049 631-D4
JONESBORO PL
13200 Brwd 90049 631-D4
JONESBORO WY
5400 BPK 90621 738-B6
JONES CANYON RD
4400 Actn 93510 4374-H7
JONFIN
15400 MsnH 91345 501-G2
JONFIN ST
16300 GrnH 91344 501-E2
JONQUIL CT
- PMDL 93551 4285-D3
JONQUIL TR
23800 CALB 91302 589-E1
JONQUIL FIELD RD
3300 WLKV 91361 557-B7
3300 WLKV 91361 587-C1
JOPLIN AV
19600 CRSN 90746 764-H3
JORDAN AV
6800 CanP 91303 530-A5
7500 LA 91304 530-A4
9100 Chat 91311 500-A4
JORDAN CIR
9700 SFSP 90670 706-J4
JORDAN LN
8900 SunV 91352 503-B7
JORDAN RD
10600 WHIT 90603 708-A5
JORDAN ST
29800 Llan 93544 4471-F5
JORDAN WY
5100 CULC 90232 672-G3
JOSARD AV
8300 LACo 91775 566-F7
JOSE WY
500 FUL 92835 738-F3
JOSEL DR
26300 SCTA 91387 4552-E7
JOSEPH CT
1300 LHB 90631 708-C4
15800 LA 91342 481-F2
JOSEPH LN
100 PMDL 93551 4195-J4
JOSEPH HOOPER DR
27000 SCTA 91387 4552-E5
E JOSEPHINE CT
3600 COMP 90221 735-B5
3600 RDom 90221 735-B5
JOSEPHINE RD
- LACo - 505-H1
- LACo - (4725-H6 See Page 4645)
JOSEPHINE ST
3100 LYN 90262 705-A7
3200 LYN 90262 735-B1
JOSEPHO WY
- PacP 90272 591-B7
JOSHUA
2800 WCOV 91792 679-J2
JOSHUA AV
32900 Actn 93510 4375-G7
JOSHUA CIR
8100 BPK 90620 767-J5
JOSHUA CT
- LACo 91775 596-F2
JOSHUA DR
- BqtC 91354 4460-E3
JOSHUA LN
1200 POM 91767 601-B7
12800 NRWK 90650 737-A1
JOSHUA RD
10700 Litl 93543 4468-E5
JOSHUA ST
5500 PMDL 93551 4104-G7
6400 VeCo 91377 558-B2
JOSHUA GROVE AV
17100 LACo 93591 4199-J3
17100 LACo 93591 4200-A3
JOSHUA HILLS DR
2500 PMDL 93550 4286-F5
JOSHUA RANCH RD
- PMDL 93551 4195-A5
JOSHUA TREE CT
23600 SIMI 93063 499-C3
JOSHUA TREE DR
14300 LACo 93532 4102-H5
JOSHUA TREE WY
- WCOV 91791 639-A3
JOSIE AV
1300 LBCH 90815 796-E2
3000 LBCH 90808 796-E1
3300 LBCH 90808 766-E7
4700 LKWD 90713 766-E3
JOSLIN ST
11100 SFSP 90670 706-F4
JOTHAM CT
- SIGH 90755 795-H4
JOTHAM PL
3800 Bxby 90807 765-F6
JOUETT ST
11700 LA 91342 482-G7
12300 Pcma 91331 502-F1
JOURNEYS END DR
1200 LCF 91011 535-A2
JOVAN ST
18200 Res 91335 530-G7
JOVENITA CANYON RD
8000 LA 90046 593-A2
JOVITA AV
9700 Chat 91311 500-D4
JOVITA PL
9800 Chat 91311 500-D5
JOY ST
200 HiPk 90042 595-B3
1000 HMB 90254 762-H2
3000 WCOV 91791 599-C7
JOYCE AV
200 ARCD 91006 567-E4
8100 KeCo 93560 3834-A1
8300 KeCo 93560 3833-J1
JOYCE DR
900 BREA 92821 708-J5
JOYCE PL
25300 StvR 91381 4640-B1
JOYCE ST
500 MTBL 90640 676-B3
JOYCEDALE ST
13800 LACo 91746 638-B2
15000 LACo 91744 638-D4
W JOYCEDALE ST
1400 WCOV 91790 638-C3
JOYGLEN DR
13600 LACo 90605 707-C5
JUAN AV
4600 TOR 90505 793-B1
21000 HGDN 90716 766-J5
JUAN BAUTISTA DR
500 SDMS 91773 600-D3
JUANITA AV
1900 PAS 91104 535-J7
E JUANITA AV
100 GLDR 91740 599-F2
300 SDMS 91773 600-C2
700 LVRN 91750 600-C2
700 LACo 91750 600-C2
N JUANITA AV
100 RBCH 90277 763-A5
200 LA 90004 594-A7
200 LA 90004 634-A1
200 RBCH 90277 762-J3
S JUANITA AV
100 RBCH 90277 763-A5
200 LA 90004 634-A1
700 RBCH 90277 762-J7
W JUANITA AV
100 GLDR 91740 599-D2
1100 SDMS 91773 599-H2
JUANITA PL
2900 FUL 92835 738-F2
JUANITA ST
300 LHB 90631 708-G5
9500 CYP 90630 767-E7
JUAREZ AV
5700 LACo 90606 676-J4
JUAREZ ST
700 MTBL 90640 636-D7
15800 IRW 91706 598-F3
JUBILEE LN
23500 DBAR 91765 640-C7
JUBILEE RD
100 Llan 93544 4471-J7
100 Llan 93544 (4472-A6 See Page 4471)
100 SBdC 92372 (4472-A6 See Page 4471)
27500 Llan 93544 (4561-H1 See Page 4471)
27900 Pear 93553 (4559-D2 See Page 4470)
JUBILEE TRAIL AV
16100 LACo 93591 4199-F5
JUBILO DR
4200 Tarz 91356 560-H5
JUBUEDLY DR
500 AZU 91702 569-A5
JUDAH AV
11500 Wch 90045 703-A7
11600 Lenx 90304 703-A7
11900 Lenx 90304 733-A1
12100 LACo 90250 733-A1
13300 HAW 90250 732-J2
13400 HAW 90250 733-A3
JUDAH LN
20900 SCTA 91321 4641-B2
JUDAY FLATS MTWY
- LACo 93532 4101-G1
JUDD ST
12200 LA 91342 482-F7
12500 Pcma 91331 482-E7
12500 Pcma 91331 502-E1
JUDGE JOHN AISO ST
100 LA 90012 634-G4
JUDILEE DR
3300 Enc 91436 561-E7
JUDITH CT
2100 ARCD 91007 597-B2
JUDITH PL
22000 CRSN 90745 764-E7
JUDITH ST
13000 BALD 91706 637-J1
13400 LACo 91746 638-A2
JUDSON AV
1400 LBCH 90813 795-A5
JUDSON CT
1900 CLAR 91711 571-D7
JUDSON ST
600 Boyl 90033 635-A3
JUDY DR
500 RBCH 90277 762-J6
JUDY WY
16600 CRTS 90703 736-J6
JUILLIARD DR
300 CLAR 91711 571-E6
JULEP PL
3400 ALH 91803 635-G2
JULIA AV
700 RBCH 90277 763-A6
JULIA LN
- CynC 91351 4461-D7
JULIAN AV
3000 LBCH 90808 796-H1
3400 LBCH 90808 766-H7
JULIAN CT
500 DBAR 91765 640-E6
JULIAN LN
- PMDL 93552 4287-B4
5900 Tarz 91356 560-G1
JULIANNA LN
21400 WdHl 91367 560-A2
JULIANNA PL
- WdHl 91367 560-A2
JULIANNE CT
15100 SCTA 91387 4462-F6
JULIE AV
1900 FUL 92833 738-D7
JULIE CT
3100 WCOV 91792 678-J1
JULIE DR
1800 RowH 91748 679-D5
JULIE LN
6600 LACo 91307 529-D6
7100 LACo 91775 566-G7
JULIE BETH ST
4700 CYP 90630 767-B7
JULIET CT
1700 BREA 92821 709-A4
JULIET ST
2200 LA 90007 634-A6
JULIUS AV
9600 DWNY 90240 706-A2
10200 DWNY 90241 706-A3
11400 DWNY 90241 705-J4
12000 DWNY 90242 705-H6
JULLIARD DR
20300 WAL 91789 639-F7
JULLIEN ST
100 LA 90063 635-B5
JUMILLA AV
5100 WdHl 91364 560-F3
5600 WdHl 91367 560-F1
6000 WdHl 91367 530-F7
6600 Win 91306 530-F2
8700 Nor 91324 530-F1
9500 Chat 91311 500-E5
9500 Nor 91324 500-E5
JUMPING CACTUS TR
- PMDL 93550 4286-E7
- PMDL 93550 4376-E1
JUNALUSKA WY
15900 PacP 90272 630-J5
JUNCTION ST
5900 Flor 90001 674-G6
JUNE CT
1800 WCOV 91792 638-J7
1800 WCOV 91792 678-J1
JUNE LN
1700 GLDL 91208 534-H7
JUNE ST
100 NLB 90805 735-B7
N JUNE ST
100 LA 90004 633-E1
300 LA 90004 593-E7
700 LA 90038 593-E5
1300 Hlwd 90028 593-E5
S JUNE ST
100 LA 90004 633-E1
300 LA 90020 633-E2
600 LA 90005 633-E2
600 LA 90010 633-E2
JUNEAU PL
20400 WdHl 91364 560-D4
JUNEBERRY LN
- LA 91343 501-H6
JUNEDA DR
28100 SCTA 91350 4461-C5
JUNE MOUNTAIN DR
5100 MTCL 91763 601-G6
JUNE ROSE CT
- Cstc 91384 4459-F3
S JUNEWAY RD
2400 MONP 91755 636-B6
JUNEWOOD PL
600 DBAR 91765 680-C1
JUNGFRAU AV
- LACo 93551 4285-J7
- PMDL 93550 4285-J7
- PMDL 93550 4286-A7
JUNG JING RD
400 LA 90012 634-G2
JUNIETTE ST
11800 LA 90230 672-F6
12400 LACo 90066 672-F6
JUNIPER AV
1600 TOR 90503 763-E6
22600 TOR 90505 793-E1
JUNIPER BEND
- WAL 91789 639-C5
JUNIPER CIR
5000 LPMA 90623 767-C3
JUNIPER CT
- LAN 93536 4104-H1
- Saug 91350 4461-B4
- SIMI 93063 499-B3
5000 SBdC 91710 641-F4
JUNIPER DR
400 PAS 91105 565-E6
2600 PMDL 93550 4286-F4
5400 SBdC 92397 (4652-F3 See Page 4651)
JUNIPER RD
100 Llan 93544 4471-J5
100 SBdC 92372 4471-J5
100 SBdC 92372 (4472-A5 See Page 4471)
2100 SBdC 92371 (4472-E5 See Page 4471)
JUNIPER RDG
1600 POM 91766 640-F3
JUNIPER ST
300 BREA 92821 738-J2
500 LVRN 91750 600-D3
5600 CHNO 91710 641-H4
8600 Wats 90002 704-H3
10100 Wats 90002 704-H5
10700 LA 90059 704-H5
12900 DWNY 90242 705-G7
S JUNIPER ST
100 WCOV 91791 598-J7
200 WCOV 91791 638-J1
W JUNIPER ST
100 ING 90302 703-C1
1400 ONT 91762 641-J4
JUNIPER WY
500 LHB 90631 708-C6
JUNIPER CREST RD
6000 LACo 91390 4374-E3
JUNIPER HILLS RD
10600 Litl 93543 4468-E5
12200 Pear 93553 4468-G7
JUNIPER MESA RD
10600 Litl 93543 4468-E5
JUNIPERO AV
- LBCH 90803 825-G1
300 LBCH 90814 825-G1
300 LBCH 90814 795-G7
700 LBCH 90804 795-G4
1800 SIGH 90755 795-G2
2800 LBCH 90808 795-G2
JUNIPERO DR
1300 DUAR 91010 568-A5
JUNIPERO PL
300 SGBL 91776 596-D4
JUNIPERO ST
- LBCH 90803 825-G1
3500 VeCo 93063 499-B4
JUNIPERO SERRA DR
100 SGBL 91776 596-D4
E JUNIPER RIDGE LN
- PMDL 93550 4466-C1
W JUNIPER RIDGE LN
- PMDL 93550 4466-A1
JUNIPER TREE RD
38400 PMDL 93551 4195-F7
38400 PMDL 93551 4285-F1
38600 LACo 93551 4195-F7
JUNIPER VALLEY RD
34500 Actn 93510 4374-F4
34500 LACo 91390 4374-F3
JUNO AV
12000 NRWK 90650 706-H7
JUPITER AV
3500 PMDL 93550 4286-G2
JUPITER DR
2300 LA 90046 593-B3
JUPITER PL
15700 GAR 90249 733-G6
JUPITER ST
14800 WHIT 90603 707-G3
JURA RD
22700 DBAR 91765 640-A6
JURADO AV
2300 HacH 91745 678-A4
JURICH PL
3300 ALH 91803 635-G1
JUSTAMERE AV
29000 Cstc 91384 4459-B5
JUSTICE ST
23200 LA 91304 529-F3
JUSTIN AV
200 GLDL 91201 563-J3
600 GLDL 91201 564-A2
JUSTIN CT
1000 LAN 93535 4106-B3
7700 LA 91304 529-G4
36800 PMDL 93550 4286-G4
JUSTINE CT
1800 WCOV 91792 638-J7
JUTEWOOD
1700 WCOV 91791 638-J5
JUTEWOOD CT
14100 LMRD 90638 738-A2
JUTLAND AV
9800 Nor 91325 501-B5
JUTLAND ST
7800 Nor 91325 531-B3

K

K ST
- BELL 90201 675-F5
- CMRC 90040 675-F5
- LA 90245 732-C1
- PdlR 90293 732-C1
KAASTAD CT
45600 LAN 93534 4015-E3
KACHINA CT
- LAN 93535 4106-F1
KADLETZ RD
- GLDL 91214 534-E2
KADOTA AV
10700 MTCL 91763 641-D3
10900 SBdC 91766 641-D3
11500 SBdC 91710 641-D4
12100 CHNO 91710 641-D5
KADOTA ST
15000 LA 91342 481-H2
KAGAWA ST
800 PacP 90272 631-B4
KAGEL CANYON RD
11700 LACo 91342 482-J5
KAGEL CANYON ST
11200 LACo 91342 482-J7
11200 LA 91342 482-J7
11400 LA 91342 502-G1
11900 Pcma 91331 502-C5
KAGEL CANYON TKTR
- LACo - 4643-A7
- LACo - (4723-A2 See Page 4643)
- LACo 91342 482-H2
- LACo 91342 (4723-A2 See Page 4643)
KAHLENBERG LN
12700 LA 91607 562-E3
KAHNS DR
9100 RSMD 91770 636-H1
KAHOOLAWE
- SCTA 91321 4641-C3
KAIA LN
2000 SMAD 91024 567-C1
KAIBAB CT
- LACo 93532 4102-E4
KAILUA LN
10400 Tuj 91042 503-J3
KAISER CIR
20300 CRSN 90746 764-F4
KAISER WY
- LA 90034 633-A6
KAKKIS DR
400 LBCH 90803 796-D7
KALB CT
26400 SCTA 91321 4551-G5
KALE ST
9800 ELMN 91733 637-A3
9800 SELM 91733 637-A3
KALEIN DR
5300 CULC 90230 672-G5
KALISHER ST
100 SFER 91340 482-A7
600 SFER 91340 481-J7
700 SFER 91340 501-J1
800 LA 91340 501-J1
15000 MsnH 91345 501-H1
15600 GrnH 91344 501-B1
KALLIN AV
800 LBCH 90815 796-F4
3000 LBCH 90808 796-F1
3200 LBCH 90808 766-F7
KALLIN WY
6800 LBCH 90815 796-F6
KALLIOPE AV
- LAN 93534 4105-E3
- LAN 93536 4105-E3
KALMAN ST
2600 Actn 93510 4375-A5
KALMAR AV
24600 SCTA 91321 4640-G3
KALMIA ST
9200 Wats 90002 704-H4
10200 Wats 90002 704-H4
10700 LA 90059 704-H6
KALNOR AV
11000 NRWK 90650 706-H6
12600 NRWK 90650 736-H1
KALSMAN AV
600 COMP 90220 734-F4
2000 COMP 90222 734-F2
13900 Wbrk 90222 734-F2
KALSMAN DR
3600 LA 90016 673-A1
KALUA DR
10200 Sunl 91040 503-C5
KAM CT
1700 WCOV 91792 638-J7
KAMAN CT
11800 GrnH 91344 481-A7
KAMAS AV
1100 HacH 91745 678-A1
KAMLOOPS PL
11400 LA 91342 502-H1
KAMLOOPS ST
11100 LA 91342 482-J7
11300 LA 91342 502-H1
12800 Pcma 91331 502-C5
KAMLYN LN
19200 WAL 91789 639-C6
KAMM ST
1800 CRSN 90746 764-H3
KAMSTRA AV
18300 CRTS 90703 767-B2
KANAINA CT
- Chat 91311 499-J1
KANAN RD
- VeCo 91377 558-A1
600 VeCo 91377 557-H1
5200 AGRH 91301 558-A5
KANAN RD Rt#-N9
400 LACo 90265 587-E4
600 Ago 91301 587-H2
3200 Ago 91301 588-B1
4100 Ago 91301 558-A7
4100 AGRH 91301 558-A7
KANAN DUME RD Rt#-N9
100 LACo 90265 587-D7
1000 LACo 90265 627-D1
3700 MAL 90265 627-F5
5800 MAL 90265 667-F1
KANDI CT
25600 SCTA 91321 4551-H5
KANE AV
10700 LACo 90604 707-F5
KANOLA RD
1700 LHH 90631 708-G2
KANOW AV
36800 Litl 93543 4287-J4
KANSAS
3600 WCOV 91792 679-A1
KANSAS AV
2300 SMCA 90404 671-H1
2400 SGAT 90280 704-J4
2600 SGAT 90280 705-A4
4000 LA 90037 674-A3
5800 LA 90044 674-A6
7500 LA 90044 704-A1
13300 GAR 90247 734-A2
13600 PRM 90723 735-F2
KANSAS ST
100 ELSG 90245 732-G1
24500 SCTA 91321 4640-H1
KAPLAN AV
16000 INDS 91744 638-F5
KARA PL
18400 RowH 91748 679-A7
KARAK RD
1200 LACo 93551 4375-G4
KARDASHIAN AV
5400 ARCD 91006 597-G3
KAREEM CT
- ING 90305 703-E3
KARELIA ST
4000 LA 90065 594-J3
KAREN AV
3000 LBCH 90808 796-F1
3300 LBCH 90808 766-F6
5500 CYP 90630 767-D6
KAREN CIR
4700 LPMA 90623 767-B3
5100 CULC 90230 672-G4
KAREN CT
- Cstc 91384 4459-E2
W KAREN CT
1200 UPL 91786 601-J1
KAREN DR
17600 Enc 91316 561-B4
18100 Tarz 91356 561-A4
18100 Tarz 91356 560-J4
41600 PMDL 93551 4104-E7
KAREN ST
1800 BURB 91504 533-F4
N KAREN WY
800 LBCH 90815 796-F6
KARENA AV
31300 Cstc 91384 4369-G7
KAREN LYNN DR
3800 GLDL 91206 535-C7
KAREN SUE LN
3600 LCF 91011 535-D7
KARESH AV
600 POM 91767 601-C7
600 POM 91767 641-C1
KARI WY
100 ARCD 91006 567-D7
KARIE LN
25100 SCTA 91350 4551-B6
N KARIN PL
6600 LACo 91775 596-G1
KARINE ST
- KeCo 93560 3833-H1
KARL BARNUM WY
900 MONP 91754 635-J3
KARLING PL
4000 PMDL 93552 4286-H3
4700 PMDL 93552 4287-A3
KARMONT AV
9200 SGAT 90280 705-G4
KARNS AV
400 LACo 91746 637-G4
KARNS CT
27000 LACo 91387 4551-J4
KARROO WY
16700 PRM 90723 735-F6
KASHIWA CT
23100 TOR 90505 793-E1
KASHIWA ST
2800 TOR 90505 793-E1
KASHLAN RD
1200 LHH 90631 708-F3
KASHMERE CANYON RD
2600 Actn 93510 4465-D1
KASHMIR CT
18600 SCTA 91351 4551-H2
KASS DR
- BPK 90621 767-J2
KATE CT
1700 WCOV 91792 638-J7
KATEE LN
600 PMDL 93550 4376-C3
KATELLA AV
2800 LALM 90720 796-J3
KATELLA RD
5200 SGAT 90280 705-E6
KATHERINE AV
4400 Shrm 91423 562-A3
5400 VanN 91401 562-A2
6700 VanN 91405 532-A4
8000 PanC 91402 532-A1
8700 PanC 91402 502-A7
KATHERINE CT
200 PMDL 93550 4286-A2
19700 CRTS 90703 766-G3
KATHERINE DR
400 MTBL 90640 676-F1
KATHERINE LN
700 ARCD 91006 567-A4
1500 SIMI 93063 499-B3
KATHERINE RD
600 VeCo 93063 499-B4
6500 SIMI 93063 499-B3
KATHERINE ST
5500 SIMI 93063 499-A3
KATHERINE WY
5900 SIMI 93063 499-B3
KATHERINEL AV
34600 Actn 93510 4375-C3
KATHLEEN AV
12300 LACo 90601 637-D6
28500 SCTA 91350 4461-D4
28600 SCTA 91390 4461-D4
28600 LACo 91390 4461-D4
KATHLEEN CT
1700 WCOV 91792 678-J1
KATHLEEN DR
9600 CYP 90630 767-F7
KATHRYN AV
2000 POM 91766 641-B6
22000 TOR 90503 763-C7
22300 TOR 90505 763-C7
22500 TOR 90505 793-C1
KATHY
15300 MsnH 91345 501-H2
KATHY DR
4500 LPMA 90623 767-B3
KATHY WY
2000 TOR 90501 793-H1
KATHYANN ST
11800 LA 91342 482-G7
KATIE LN
8700 RSMD 91770 636-H1
KATRINA LN
- LFlz 90027 594-A3
KATRINA PL
4700 PMDL 93552 4287-C2
KATRINA ST
- Actn 93510 4375-F4
- LACo 93551 4375-F4
KATRINA WY
2000 UPL 91784 571-H4
KATRINE CIR
19700 LACo 91789 679-D4
W KATY CT
1100 UPL 91784 571-J5
KATY LN
1100 VeCo 93063 499-B4
KATY ST
12500 NRWK 90650 736-J1
KATYGLEN LN
600 LHB 90631 708-D7
KATYS LN
25100 SCTA 91355 4550-H7
KAUAI
1400 WCOV 91792 638-H4
KAUFFMAN AV
4800 TEML 91780 597-A2
6500 LACo 91007 596-J1
6500 LACo 91780 596-J1
8900 SGAT 90280 705-D4
10600 LYN 90262 705-D5
KAUFFMAN ST
11000 ELMN 91731 597-D7
KAVENAGH LN
25900 StvR 91381 4550-A6
KAWEAH DR
1500 PAS 91105 565-D6
KAY AV
1600 SIMI 93063 499-C3
19000 CRTS 90703 767-B2
KAY CT
17800 CRTS 90703 737-B7
17800 CRTS 90703 767-B1
KAY DR
20500 SCTA 91321 4641-D1
KAY ST
100 NLB 90805 735-B7
1500 COMP 90221 735-B3
E KAY ST
800 COMP 90221 735-B3
KAYAK ST
3200 LAN 93535 4106-G1
KAYANN PL
1400 SELM 91733 637-D5
KAYDEL DR
2200 LACo 90601 637-D6
N KAYE LN
44600 LAN 93535 4015-J6
KAY FIORENTINO
1700 LA 90732 853-G1
KAYFORD AV
1300 SELM 91733 637-B4
KAYLOR AV
9900 LALM 90720 767-A7
9900 LBCH 90808 767-A7
KAYLYN ST
3000 LAN 93535 4106-C2
KAYREID DR
12300 LACo 90605 707-D7
12300 LACo 90605 737-D1
KAYS AV
800 MONP 91755 636-D3
2100 LACo 91770 636-D3
KAYS LN
21700 Ago 91301 588-F1
KAYS PL
2200 LACo 91770 636-D3
KAYWOOD DR
23000 LACo 90502 794-B1
KEANSBURG AV
4000 WCOV 91792 679-B2
KEARN CREEK CT
- INDS 91745 678-F2
KEARNEY DR
29000 Cstc 91384 4459-D6
KEARNEY ST
1600 Boyl 90033 634-J4
KEARNY LN
2600 LHB 90631 738-B1
KEARNY ST
1100 Boyl 90033 634-H4
22400 CALB 91302 559-J6
KEARSARGE ST
11700 Brwd 90049 631-G3
KEATING DR
14500 LMRD 90638 738-A3
KEATON CT
19800 SCTA 91351 4461-E7
KEATON WY
- LAN 93536 4015-E4
1700 LAN 93534 4015-E4
KEATS LN
25200 StvR 91381 4640-C1
KEATS ST
200 ALH 91801 595-G5
200 LA 90032 595-G5
KEEGAN AV
16900 CRSN 90746 734-F7
KEEL CT
- LBCH 90803 826-G2
3300 LAN 93535 4106-G2
KEEL ST
700 SPed 90731 824-D3
KEELER DR
16200 GrnH 91344 481-E7
KEELER ST
1600 BURB 91504 533-F5
S KEENAN AV
500 ELA 90022 635-J7
500 ELA 90022 675-J1
KEENAN ST
600 MTBL 90640 635-J7
KEENE AV
12800 Wbrk 90059 734-E2
17400 CRSN 90746 734-F7
17400 CRSN 90746 764-F1
N KEENE AV
1900 COMP 90059 734-E2
S KEENE AV
400 COMP 90220 734-F5
14300 LACo 90220 734-F4
KEENE DR
600 LHB 90631 708-D7
KEEPSAKE WY
- SCTA 91354 4460-G5
KEESE DR
14200 LACo 90604 707-E7
14200 LACo 90604 737-E1
E KEESE DR
14700 LACo 90604 737-F1
KEESHEN DR
2200 LA 90066 672-B2
KEEVER AV
4100 Bxby 90807 765-F5
KEEVER PL
1500 Bxby 90807 765-F5
KEGA CT
3300 LAN 93535 4106-G2
KEIM ST
8200 RSMD 91770 636-F3
KEITH AV
8900 WHWD 90069 592-H7
KEITH CIR
7500 LPMA 90623 767-C3
KEITH CT
37000 PMDL 93550 4286-G4
KEITH DR
7000 LACo 90606 677-A5
KEITH GRN
8100 BPK 90621 737-F5
KEITH ST
2000 LA 90031 635-B1
KEITHLEY DR
12800 OrCo 90720 796-H6
KELBURN AV
2100 LACo 91770 636-F3
2300 RSMD 91770 636-E1
KELBY ST
17900 LACo 91722 599-A4
E KELBY ST
100 COV 91723 599-B4
KELFIELD DR
20600 DBAR 91789 679-G4
KELFORD ST
14100 LACo 90604 707-D7
KELI CT
5100 LA 90066 672-E6
KELLA AV
2200 LACo 90601 637-D6
2300 INDS 90601 637-D6
KELLAM AV
1300 Echo 90026 634-E1
KELLAM LN
8400 PRV 90660 706-D2
KELLEN DR
1600 BREA 92821 709-A4
KELLER CIR
18200 CRTS 90703 767-D1
KELLER RD
20900 Top 90290 590-C3
KELLER ST
100 MONP 91755 636-B4
500 LA 90012 634-H3
KELLERTON DR
1800 HacH 91745 678-C3
KELLETT AV
3600 CLAR 91711 571-F5
KELLEY AV
25400 LMTA 90717 793-G5
KELLNER AV
1700 LACo 91770 636-G4
KELLOGG AV
100 FUL 92833 738-B7
600 GLDL 91202 564-B3
12300 CHNO 91710 641-F6
KELLOGG CT
- DUAR 91010 568-D5
2300 Alta 91001 535-H6
KELLOGG DR
- LACo 91768 640-B2
- SDMS 91773 640-B2
3800 POM 91768 640-A2
KELLOGG PARK DR
2100 POM 91768 640-C1
KELLOGG VALLEY RD
- LACo 93532 4102-J5
- LACo 93551 4102-J5
- LACo 93551 4103-A5
- LACo 93551 4193-F1
KELLS PL
9400 PRV 90660 676-J1
KELLWIL WY
1000 DUAR 91010 567-J6
1100 DUAR 91010 568-A7
KELLWOOD CT
- LMRD 90638 738-B3
900 VeCo 91377 557-H1
N KELLY AV
1000 UPL 91784 571-J3
1400 UPL 91786 571-J7
KELLY CIR
7700 LPMA 90623 767-B3
KELLY CT
37000 PMDL 93550 4286-G4
KELLY DR
2100 SIGH 90755 795-G4
N KELLY DR
44700 LAN 93535 4015-J6
KELLY LN
2800 POM 91767 601-A3
W KELLY LN
- LACo 91387 4552-B5
KELLY RD
700 SBdC 92372 (4472-B6 See Page 4471)
KELLY ST
5000 LA 90066 672-D7
KELLY WY
2000 WCOV 91792 638-G5
KELLY JOHNSON PKWY
- SCTA 91355 4460-C5
KELLYS WY
500 PMDL 93550 4196-A3
KELMORE ST
10700 CULC 90230 672-H4
KELMSCOTT CT
2200 THO 91361 557-A6
KELOWNA ST
11300 LA 91342 482-J7
11400 LA 91342 502-H1
12800 Pcma 91331 502-D5
KELP ST
100 MANB 90266 732-E4
KELSEY CT
- PMDL 93551 4195-D7
KELSEY RD
300 SDMS 91773 570-C6
KELSEY ST
11500 LA 91604 562-H6
KELSFORD CT
1100 THO 91361 557-A5
KELSLOAN ST
16600 VanN 91406 531-D4
KELSO RD
200 WAL 91789 639-E6
E KELSO ST
100 ING 90301 703-D3

STREET Block City ZIP Pg-Grid

01 703-B3
d 90024 631-J2
Wwd 90024 632-A2
LA 90034 672-E1
WLA 90025 632-B4
1200 LA 90064 632-D7
3000 LA 90034 632-D7
KELTONVIEW DR
6400 PRV 90660 676-E5
KELVIN AV
4500 WdHl 91364 560-C3
5600 WdHl 91367 560-C1
6500 Win 91306 530-C2
9200 Chat 91311 500-C7
KELVIN PL
20800 WdHl 91367 560-C1
KELWOOD ST
16500 LACo 91744 638-G5
KEM WY
1400 WAL 91789 639-G3
KEM BAR LN
7200 Litl 93543 4377-F2
KEMBLE AV
3400 LBCH 90808 766-J7
KEMERTON PL
16900 HacH 91745 678-F6
KEMMETT CT
- Boyl 90033 634-J4
KEMP AV
19000 CRSN 90746 764-H2
N KEMP AV
100 COMP 90220 734-G4
1100 COMP 90222 734-G3
S KEMP AV
100 COMP 90220 734-G4
KEMP CT
- COMP 90220 734-G4
KEMP PL
700 COV 91722 599-D3
KEMP ST
800 BURB 91505 563-C3
S KEMP ST
1000 COMP 90220 734-H6
KEMPER AV
2100 CLAR 91711 571-F7
2400 LaCr 91214 504-G7
KEMPER CIR
1900 LA 90065 594-H4
KEMPER CT
3000 LA 90065 594-H4
KEMPER ST
1500 LA 90065 594-H4
KEMPTON AV
600 MONP 91755 636-C3
KEMPTON DR
2600 OrCo 90720 796-G5
3500 LALM 90720 796-J5
KEMPTON PL
200 MONP 91755 636-B4
KEMPTON RD
200 GLDL 91202 564-D1
KEN AV
4900 LKWD 90713 766-E4
KENBRIDGE DR
500 CRSN 90746 734-D7
KENDALL AL
- PAS 91103 565-H4
KENDALL AV
400 HiPk 90042 595-D4
700 SPAS 91030 595-G4
1000 LA 90032 595-E4
8900 SGAT 90280 705-E3
KENDALL DR
1000 SGBL 91775 596-C2
KENDALL LN
- StvR 91381 4550-A7
KENDALL ST
2500 LVRN 91750 600-H2
KENDALL WY
200 COV 91723 599-C5
KENDRA CT
6700 LA 90068 593-E3
KENDRICK CIR
37000 PMDL 93550 4286-D4
KENDRICK DR
1700 LVRN 91750 600-F1
KENESAW AV
2700 COMP 90222 734-G1
KENFEL DR
27400 SCTA 91350 4461-B7
KENFIELD AV
900 Brwd 90049 591-F7
900 Brwd 90049 631-F1
KENGARD AV
7100 LACo 90606 677-A7
KENGARY LN
2200 Alta 91001 536-D6
KENILWORTH AV
1200 SMRO 91108 566-D7
1400 SMRO 91108 596-E1
1500 PAS 91103 565-F1
1600 PAS 91103 535-F7
2000 LA 90039 594-D4
N KENILWORTH AV
100 GLDL 91203 564-D4
800 GLDL 91202 564-C2
S KENILWORTH AV
200 GLDL 91204 564-D6
KENILWORTH DR
3200 OrCo 90720 796-H4

KENINGSTON RD
28900 Cstc 91384 4459-B6
KENISTON AV
700 LA 90005 633-E4
700 LA 90010 633-E4
900 LA 90019 633-E4
1400 ING 90302 673-D6
4600 LACo 90043 673-D4
5800 LA 90043 673-D6
KENITRA PT
2700 PMDL 93550 4286-F5
KENMERE AV
2100 BURB 91504 533-E5
KENMORE AV
3800 BALD 91706 598-A4
N KENMORE AV
100 LA 90004 593-J7
100 LA 90004 633-J1
700 LA 90029 593-J5
1300 LFlz 90027 593-J3
S KENMORE AV
100 LA 90004 633-J2
300 LA 90020 633-J2
600 LA 90005 633-J2
600 LA 90010 633-J2
800 LA 90005 634-A3
900 LA 90006 634-A3
900 LA 90006 633-J4
KENMORE CIR
14200 BALD 91706 598-B7
KENMORE DR
600 SGBL 91776 596-F6
KENMORE RD
1400 PAS 91106 596-A1
KENNARD ST
15500 HacH 91745 678-B3
KENNEBEC AV
- LBCH 90803 825-G1
KENNEDY CT
4000 CHNO 91710 641-D6
KENNEDY DR
- LA 91342 482-A1
- PMDL 93551 4195-D5
KENNEDY RD
200 SDMS 91773 599-H2
KENNEDY ST
4400 CHNO 91710 641-E6
KENNERLY ST
9200 TEML 91780 596-J4
9500 TEML 91780 597-A4
KENNETH DR
3100 LA 90032 595-D6
KENNETH PL
15700 SCTA 91387 4462-D7
E KENNETH RD
100 GLDL 91207 564-E2
N KENNETH RD
100 BURB 91501 533-G5
1000 BURB 91504 533-E4
S KENNETH RD
100 BURB 91501 533-J6
800 BURB 91501 534-A7
900 BURB 91201 534-A7
900 GLDL 91201 534-A7
W KENNETH RD
100 GLDL 91202 564-D1
1400 GLDL 91201 564-B1
1700 GLDL 91201 534-A7
KENNETH WY
1500 PAS 91103 535-F7
1500 PAS 91103 565-F1
KENNEY ST
10800 NRWK 90650 706-E6
KENNEYDALE AV
1200 LACo 91770 636-F4
KENNINGTON DR
2600 GLDL 91206 565-A2
KENNSINGTON PL
43800 LAN 93536 4105-C1
KENNY DR
12200 GmH 91344 481-D5
KENNY LN
- CynC 91351 4461-D7
KENOAK DR
15200 BALD 91706 598-D5
E KENOAK DR
600 COV 91723 599-C5
W KENOAK DR
400 POM 91768 600-H7
400 COV 91723 599-A5
700 COV 91722 598-J5
1800 WCOV 91790 598-E5
1900 BALD 91706 598-E5
1900 BALD 91790 598-E5
W KENOAK PL
400 POM 91768 600-H7
KENOAK WY
1300 POM 91768 600-H7
KENOBI CT
12500 CRTS 90703 767-A3
KENOMA ST
1900 GLDR 91740 569-J7
2100 GLDR 91740 570-A6
2400 SDMS 91773 570-A7
KENRICH CT
2200 LHB 90631 708-B5
KENROSE CIR
26100 CALB 91302 558-H4
KENROY AV
28600 SCTA 91387 4552-C1
KENS WY
- LA 91304 529-G4

KENSINGTON AV
17600 CRTS 90703 737-D7
17900 CRTS 90703 767-D1
KENSINGTON CIR
17500 CRTS 90703 737-D7
41700 PMDL 93551 4104-F6
KENSINGTON CT
7400 CanP 91307 529-E4
KENSINGTON DR
7100 BPK 90621 737-G6
9000 Nor 91324 500-G7
KENSINGTON LN
- ING 90305 703-E3
100 LHB 90631 738-D3
KENSINGTON PL
400 PAS 91103 565-G4
KENSINGTON RD
600 SMCA 90405 671-F3
1400 SMRO 91108 596-C1
4300 CULC 90066 672-E5
4300 LA 90066 672-E5
11100 OrCo 90720 796-H4
E KENSINGTON RD
500 Echo 90026 634-F1
1200 LA 90012 634-F1
W KENSINGTON RD
800 Echo 90026 634-E1
KENSINGTON WY
200 MTBL 90640 676-B2
5600 CULC 90230 672-J6
38900 PMDL 93551 4195-F6
KENSLEY DR
3600 ING 90305 703-E3
KENSLEY PL
- RowH 91748 679-B7
KENT
15400 LA 91342 481-G2
KENT AV
21200 TOR 90503 763-C6
22300 TOR 90505 763-C7
22600 TOR 90505 793-C1
KENT CIR
4700 LPMA 90623 767-B4
KENT DR
500 BURB 91504 533-F4
800 CLAR 91711 601-B1
1600 LVRN 91750 570-F4
KENT LN
20000 SCTA 91351 4461-E7
KENT PL
1300 GLDL 91205 564-G6
KENT ST
900 LACo 91011 535-F5
1000 SDMS 91773 599-J3
1700 Echo 90026 634-D1
2200 Echo 90026 594-C7
KENT WY
19100 Nor 91324 500-E7
N KENTER AV
100 Brwd 90049 631-E1
1100 Brwd 90049 591-E7
S KENTER AV
100 Brwd 90049 631-G3
KENTER WY
900 Brwd 90049 631-E1
KENTFIELD CT
31700 WLKV 91361 557-D6
KENTFIELD PL
2900 LACo 92821 679-B7
2900 LACo 92821 709-B1
2900 RowH 91748 679-B7
2900 RowH 91748 709-B1
KENTLAND AV
5800 WdHl 91367 559-H1
6100 WdHl 91367 529-H7
6500 CanP 91307 529-H5
7600 LA 91304 529-H2
9600 Chat 91311 499-H6
KENTON DR
1100 MONP 91755 636-E4
KENTON LN
28000 SCTA 91350 4461-A5
KENTUCKY
2100 WCOV 91792 679-H2
KENTUCKY AV
10100 WHIT 90603 707-J4
11300 LACo 90604 707-J6
KENTUCKY DR
3900 LA 90068 563-B6
6100 BPK 90620 767-E5
KENTUCKY PL
3200 GLDL 91214 504-E7
KENTUCKY SPRINGS RD
1100 Actn 93510 4375-H7
1100 Actn 93510 4376-A7
KENTWOOD AV
6900 Wch 90045 672-G7
7400 Wch 90045 702-G1
KENTWOOD CT
6400 Wch 90045 672-G7
KENTWOOD BLUFFS DR
6500 Wch 90045 672-G7
KENTWORTHY AV
23400 Hrbr 90710 794-A2
KENWATER AV
5900 WdHl 91367 559-E1
6100 WdHl 91367 529-E7
6400 CanP 91307 529-E7
KENWATER PL
6400 CanP 91307 529-E7
KENWAY AV
3900 LACo 90008 673-D4

KENWOOD AV
2600 LA 90007 633-J7
4200 LA 90037 673-J3
5100 BPK 90621 738-A6
22100 LACo 90502 764-A7
29000 Cstc 91384 4459-C5
S KENWOOD AV
20400 LACo 90502 764-A4
KENWOOD CT
- LAN 93536 4105-C3
KENWOOD DR
1400 POM 91768 600-F6
KENWOOD PL
400 GLDL 91206 564-E3
KENWOOD RD
1200 SLB 90740 796-G7
KENWOOD ST
1200 LHB 90631 738-E1
2500 LAN 93536 4105-C3
3100 BURB 91505 533-C4
N KENWOOD ST
100 GLDL 91206 564-E4
1800 BURB 91505 533-C7
S KENWOOD ST
100 GLDL 91205 564-E5
900 ING 90301 703-B4
KENWORTHY DR
100 PAS 91105 565-E5
KENWYN CT
21100 Top 90290 560-C7
KENYA PL
11000 Nor 91326 500-G2
KENYA ST
18600 Nor 91326 500-G2
KENYON AV
4100 CULC 90066 672-C5
4100 LA 90066 672-C5
7800 Wch 90045 702-F2
KENYON PL
1600 CLAR 91711 601-E1
KEOKUK AV
5500 WdHl 91367 560-D1
6500 Win 91306 530-D1
9500 Chat 91311 500-D4
KEPLER RD
35400 LACo 93552 4377-D1
KERCKHOFF AV
2600 SPed 90731 824-B7
2600 SPed 90731 854-B1
KERMAN AV
4200 ELMN 91731 597-D6
N KERN AV
100 ELA 90022 635-G5
S KERN AV
100 ELA 90022 635-G7
700 ELA 90022 675-F1
1400 MONP 91754 635-G4
KERN RD
3700 CHNO 91710 641-C6
KERN ST
500 LHB 90631 708-B6
KERNER WY
1000 LHB 90631 708-F5
KERNS AV
1900 SGBL 91775 596-E2
1900 SMRO 91108 596-E2
KERNVILLE AV
1600 MTBL 90640 636-F5
KERR GRN
8000 BPK 90621 737-J5
KERR ST
- LA 90039 594-F3
KERRICK ST
1300 LAN 93534 4015-F5
KERRMOOR DR
6000 WLKV 91362 557-F3
KERRWOOD ST
1500 BREA 92821 708-H6
11400 ELMN 91732 597-E6
KERRY CT
1700 WCOV 91792 638-J7
1700 WCOV 91792 678-J1
KERRY LN
1700 Top 90290 630-A2
KERRYHILL CT
6300 AGRH 91301 558-A3
KERRY ROBIN DR
25000 SCTA 91321 4640-F2
KERSTING CT
- SMAD 91024 567-A2
KERTH DR
3000 OrCo 90720 796-H3
KERVIN AV
15600 PRM 90723 735-J5
KERWIN PL
2500 Eagl 90041 564-J6
KERWOOD AV
2000 WLA 90025 632-D4
2200 LA 90064 632-D4
KESLEY ST
20400 SCTA 91351 4461-D7
KESSLER AV
6400 WdHl 91367 530-E7
9500 Chat 91311 500-E4
KESSLER CT
- Cstc 91384 4459-G3
E KESSLER RD
2500 LKWD 90712 765-H6
KESSOCK AV
11900 LACo 90604 707-E7
KESTER AV
4100 Shrm 91403 561-J4
5200 VanN 91411 561-J2

KESTER AV
6000 VanN 91411 531-J7
6600 VanN 91405 531-J5
7900 PanC 91402 531-J1
8700 PanC 91402 501-J6
9600 LA 91343 501-J5
9900 MsnH 91345 501-H2
KESTRAL DR
23800 SCTA 91355 4550-G6
KESWICK AV
10300 LA 90064 632-D4
KESWICK PL
900 GLDR 91741 569-C5
KESWICK RD
3800 LCF 91011 535-B6
KESWICK ST
9900 LA 91504 533-C3
10000 LA 91505 533-C3
10000 SunV 91352 533-A3
11000 SunV 91352 532-H3
11400 NHol 91605 532-D3
13400 PanC 91402 532-C3
14500 VanN 91405 532-A3
14500 VanN 91405 531-H3
15300 VanN 91406 531-D3
17300 Nor 91325 531-B4
17900 Res 91335 531-A3
18100 Res 91335 530-F3
20100 Win 91306 530-C3
21000 LA 91304 530-A4
22200 LA 91304 529-F4
KETCH CT
100 LA 90292 701-J1
KETCH MALL
- LA 90292 701-J1
KETCH ST
- LA 90292 701-J1
KETTERING ST
100 LAN 93534 4015-F5
300 LAN 93535 4015-H5
300 LAN 93535 4016-A5
4200 LACo 93535 4016-J5
4700 LACo 93535 4017-A5
6200 LAN 93536 4014-D6
12000 LACo 93535 4018-F4
KETTLER AV
5300 LKWD 90713 766-E3
KEVIN CT
18300 Nor 91325 500-J4
KEVIN LN
7500 LPMA 90623 767-D3
KEVIN PL
27600 SCTA 91350 4461-A6
E KEVIN ST
8200 LBCH 90808 766-J7
8200 LBCH 90808 767-A7
KEVIN WY
- LACo 91387 4462-C6
KEW DR
2000 LA 90046 592-J3
KEW ST
600 ING 90302 703-A1
7100 Wch 90045 703-A1
KEWANEE ST
4300 LA 90032 595-D7
KEWEN AV
8400 SunV 91352 532-G1
8800 SunV 91352 502-F6
9600 Pcma 91331 502-B2
11200 LA 91340 502-B1
KEWEN DR
800 PAS 91106 566-A7
800 SMRO 91108 566-A7
KEWEN PL
- SMRO 91108 566-B7
KEWEN ST
600 SFER 91340 502-A1
1100 SFER 91340 482-A7
1300 SFER 91340 481-J7
KEY CT
2500 LAN 93536 4015-D7
20400 SCTA 91390 4461-D3
KEY ST
8800 LA 90035 632-H4
KEY LARGO CT
4800 VeCo 91377 557-G2
E KEYNOTE ST
5100 LBCH 90808 766-B7
KEYPOINTE PL
14200 LMRD 90638 737-J2
14200 LMRD 90638 738-A2
W KEYS LN
3300 ANA 92804 767-G7
KEYSTONE AV
1600 POM 91767 601-D7
3300 LA 90034 632-E7
3400 LA 90034 672-F1
3800 LA 90232 672-F1
4100 CULC 90232 672-G2
KEYSTONE CT
1400 UPL 91784 571-H5
KEYSTONE ST
1700 PAS 91106 566-C5
1800 PAS 91107 566-C5
2200 SIMI 93063 499-C1
17800 INDS 91748 678-H4
N KEYSTONE ST
100 BURB 91506 563-E1
900 BURB 91506 533-E7
1800 BURB 91504 533-E4
S KEYSTONE ST
100 BURB 91506 563-F3
400 BURB 91521 563-F3

KEY VISTA DR
500 SMAD 91024 566-J1
KEY WEST AV
10300 Nor 91326 500-F2
KEY WEST ST
4900 LACo 91776 596-H5
9200 TEML 91780 596-J5
9800 TEML 91780 597-C4
KIAN CT
- VanN 91406 531-F5
KIBBEE AV
10400 WHIT 90603 707-H4
10800 WHIT 90604 707-H6
11500 LACo 90604 707-H6
11900 LMRD 90638 707-H7
KICKAPOO TR
21200 Chat 91311 500-A1
KICKING HORSE DR
22300 DBAR 91765 680-A6
KIDD DR
23400 DBAR 91765 680-C1
KIDD WY
- PMDL 93552 4287-E1
KIDDER AV
600 COV 91724 599-F4
5000 LACo 91724 599-F3
KIDDIE LN N
- CRSN 90745 794-E1
KIDDIE LN S
600 CRSN 90745 794-E2
KIEL ST
11300 Brwd 90049 631-H2
KIKI PL
- PacP 90272 630-F4
KILAMANJARO CT
- SCTA 91387 4462-H7
KILBOURN ST
1600 LA 90065 594-H4
KILBURN HIGH RD
- PMDL 93552 4287-C4
KILDARE CT
- BURB 91504 533-E2
KILDARE ST
- LAN 93536 4015-B5
100 LAN 93534 4015-F5
300 LAN 93535 4015-J5
300 LAN 93535 4016-A5
KILDONAN DR
1000 GLDL 91207 564-F1
1100 GLDL 91207 534-G7
KILFINAN PL
19000 Nor 91326 480-G5
KILFINAN ST
18800 Nor 91326 480-F5
KILGARRY AV
5300 PRV 90660 676-G4
7500 PRV 90660 706-F1
KILHAM AV
42800 LAN 93534 4105-E3
N KILKEA DR
100 LA 90048 633-A1
300 LA 90048 593-A7
700 LA 90046 593-A7
S KILKEA DR
100 LA 90048 633-A1
KILKENNY CT
13300 LMRD 90638 738-A1
KILLARNEY AV
1300 LA 90065 594-H4
E KILLDEE ST
5100 LBCH 90808 796-B1
KILLDEER ST
- KeCo 93560 3833-H1
E KILLEN CT
2300 COMP 90221 735-B2
E KILLEN PL
1600 COMP 90221 735-C2
KILLIAN AV
19000 RowH 91748 679-C5
KILLIAN ST
11600 ELMN 91732 597-F6
KILLIMORE AV
11500 Nor 91326 500-G1
11500 Nor 91326 480-G7
KILLIMORE CT
18900 Nor 91326 480-H7
KILLION ST
11300 NHol 91601 562-H1
12200 LA 91607 562-E2
12900 VanN 91401 562-A2
14500 VanN 91411 562-A2
14600 VanN 91411 561-H2
16800 Enc 91436 561-D2
17100 Enc 91316 561-A2
18100 Tarz 91356 560-J2
18100 Tarz 91356 561-A2
23700 WdHl 91367 559-E2
KILLOCH PL
19100 Nor 91326 480-G6
KILLOCH WY
18800 Nor 91326 480-G6
KILMARY LN
900 GLDL 91207 534-F7
KILNALECK LN
700 GLDR 91741 569-F3
KILPACK DR
23700 CALB 91302 559-E7
KILRENNEY AV
10200 LA 90064 632-F6
KILROY AIRPORT WY
3500 LBCH 90815 795-J2
3500 LBCH 90815 796-A2

KILROY CENTER RD
- ELSG 90245 702-J7
KILT CT
- LAN 93535 4106-F2
KILTY AV
7100 CanP 91307 529-F5
KILTY PL
23400 CanP 91307 529-F5
KIM CT
3600 LAN 93536 4015-A7
19100 RowH 91748 679-C6
KIM LN
3800 Enc 91436 561-D6
KIM TR
21400 Top 90290 590-B5
KIMA CT
8700 BLF 90706 766-A1
8700 LKWD 90712 765-J1
8700 LKWD 90712 766-A1
8700 BLF 90706 765-J1
KIMBALL AV
2300 POM 91767 601-A3
KIMBALL ST
4900 LA 90032 595-E7
KIMBARK AV
10300 LACo 90601 677-B2
KIMBERLY AV
400 SDMS 91773 599-H3
4000 LVRN 91750 600-H1
9700 MTCL 91763 601-E6
10300 MTCL 91763 641-E2
10300 Wats 90002 704-G5
11300 SBdC 91766 641-E3
KIMBERLY CIR
12300 ELMN 91732 597-G5
KIMBERLY CT
19700 CRTS 90703 766-G3
KIMBERLY DR
2800 WCOV 91792 638-J7
2900 LACo 91744 638-J7
2900 WCOV 91792 678-J1
2900 LACo 91744 678-J1
29600 AGRH 91301 557-H3
KIMBERLY LN
1800 Brwd 90049 631-E2
37400 PMDL 93550 4286-A3
KIMBROUGH ST
18500 SCTA 91351 4551-G2
KIMDALE LN
7500 LA 90046 593-B1
KIMDALE RD
6600 LACo 91775 596-F1
KIMLIN DR
600 GLDL 91206 564-H3
KIMMORE TER
23100 SCTA 91355 4550-H7
KIMRIDGE RD
2300 LA 90210 592-F2
KINARD AV
21200 CRSN 90745 764-C6
22500 CRSN 90745 794-C1
KINBRACE ST
18800 Nor 91326 480-G6
KINBRAE AV
800 HacH 91745 638-A7
800 HacH 91745 678-A1
KINBROOK ST
13600 LA 91342 482-B1
W KINCAID AV
800 ING 90302 703-B1
KINCARDINE AV
9100 LA 90034 632-G6
10200 LA 90064 632-F6
KINCHELOE DR
5300 Eagl 90041 565-B5
KINCLAIR DR
1900 LACo 91107 536-F6
KINDA DR
41500 PMDL 93551 4104-F7
KINDLING CT
4700 LAN 93536 4104-F2
KING AV
200 Wilm 90744 794-D6
200 Wilm 90744 824-D1
4500 BELL 90201 675-E7
5200 MYWD 90270 675-E6
6800 BELL 90201 705-E1
KING CT
10700 ELMN 91731 597-C7
KING PL
300 FUL 92833 738-E7
KING ST
700 SGBL 91776 596-E5
2900 LVRN 91750 600-H2
W KING ST
500 MNRO 91016 567-F5
KING WY
2500 CLAR 91711 571-D6
KING ARTHUR CT
28700 RPV 90275 822-J1
KINGBEE ST
7800 DWNY 90242 705-H6
KINGBIRD AV
9000 KeCo 93560 3833-B2
KINGBIRD WY
- Actn 93510 4374-B6
KINGCUP TER
- PMDL 93551 4285-E4
KING DAVID DR
- LA 90068 563-G4
KINGFISHER CT
- LBCH 90803 826-C1
- KeCo 93560 3833-G3

KING FISHER RD
4100 CALB 91302 559-G6
KINGHAM CT
5900 AGRH 91301 558-A4
KINGHAM WY
1500 FUL 92833 738-C4
KINGHORN ST
11400 SFSP 90670 706-G5
KINGHURST RD
2900 SMRO 91108 596-F1
2900 SMRO 91108 566-F7
E KINGHURST RD
8200 LACo 91775 566-F7
KINGLAKE DR
1200 DBAR 91789 679-F4
KINGLET DR
9200 LA 90069 592-H4
KINGLET PL
26500 SCTA 91351 4551-F4
KINGMAN AV
600 LA 90402 631-C7
5500 BPK 90621 737-H7
6400 BPK 90621 767-H1
KINGMAN DR
5400 PMDL 93552 4287-C5
KINGRIDGE WY
3100 GLDL 91206 535-B7
KINGS CT
3100 BelA 90077 561-J7
KINGS PL
- WLKV 91361 587-D1
2400 LA 90032 595-E7
KINGS RD
1200 PMDL 93551 4195-F5
1500 LA 90069 592-J4
1500 LA 90069 593-A4
N KINGS RD
100 LA 90048 633-A1
300 LA 90048 593-A7
500 WHWD 90048 593-A7
700 LA 90069 593-A5
800 WHWD 90069 593-A5
1500 LA 90069 592-J4
S KINGS RD
100 LA 90048 633-A1
5800 LadH 90056 673-A6
6000 LA 90056 673-A6
KINGS RW
4800 ELMN 91731 597-E5
KINGS WY
1800 LA 90069 592-J4
KINGSBORO WY
20600 WdHl 91364 560-C4
KINGSBRIDGE CT
2200 SDMS 91724 599-F5
KINGSBURY CT
- SLB 90740 796-J6
KINGSBURY RD
- PMDL 93552 4287-C4
KINGSBURY ST
14300 MsnH 91345 502-A3
14600 MsnH 91345 501-G3
15700 GrnH 91344 501-A3
18200 Nor 91326 500-G3
19600 Chat 91311 500-A3
KINGS CANYON LN
- SCTA 91387 4462-H6
KINGS CANYON RD
800 BREA 92821 709-C5
KINGS CREST DR
2100 WCOV 91791 639-A3
KINGSCREST DR
20800 SCTA 91350 4461-C5
S KINGS CROSS LN
- ING 90305 703-D4
KINGSDALE AV
1200 RBCH 90278 763-C2
14300 LNDL 90260 733-C4
18200 TOR 90278 763-C2
KINGSDOWN CT
1700 RPV 90275 823-H2
KINGSFORD ST
- MONP 91754 635-J4
300 MONP 91754 636-A3
KINGSGLEN CIR
19700 LACo 91789 679-D4
KINGS HARBOR DR
6700 RPV 90275 822-G1
KINGSHILL PL
700 CRSN 90746 734-E7
KINGSIDE DR
1100 COV 91722 598-H4
15800 LACo 91722 598-F4
KINGSLAND ST
10800 LA 90034 632-E7
10800 LA 90034 672-E1
11300 LA 90066 672-C1
E KINGSLEY AV
100 POM 91767 600-J7
300 POM 91767 601-C7
W KINGSLEY AV
100 POM 91768 600-J7
KINGSLEY DR
800 ARCD 91007 567-A6
900 ARCD 91007 566-J5
14100 GAR 90249 733-J3
14700 GAR 90247 733-J4
N KINGSLEY DR
100 LA 90004 593-J7
100 LA 90004 633-J1
700 LA 90029 593-J5
1300 LFlz 90027 593-J4

S KINGSLEY DR
100 LA 90004 633-J2
300 LA 90020 633-J2
600 LA 90005 633-J2
600 LA 90010 633-J2
900 LA 90006 633-J4
KINGSLEY ST
4000 MTCL 91763 601-E7
5600 MTCL 91762 601-E7
KINGSLY CT
37800 PMDL 93552 4287-A2
KINGSMILL AV
1200 RowH 91748 679-D4
KINGSPARK CT
31900 WLKV 91361 557-C6
KINGSPINE RD
4800 RHE 90274 793-B5
KINGSPOINT DR
1600 WAL 91789 639-F3
KINGSPORT DR
18000 LACo 90265 630-D6
KINGSRIDGE DR
30100 RPV 90275 823-H5
KINGS ROW AV
18600 CRTS 90703 766-E2
KINGS RUN PL
17700 RowH 91748 678-H6
KINGSTON AV
1000 Boyl 90033 635-A3
KINGSTON CT
3800 SBdC 91766 641-D3
25500 LACo 91302 559-A3
KINGSTON DR
1000 LHB 90631 708-E4
KINGSTON PL
- SCTA 91354 4460-G6
KINGSVIEW AV
17000 CRSN 90746 734-E7
KINGS VIEW DR
2100 HacH 91745 678-E5
KINGSWAY DR
800 BURB 91504 533-F3
KINGSWELL AV
4300 LFlz 90027 594-A4
KINGSWOOD LN
- CRSN 90745 794-G1
15300 Shrm 91403 561-H6
KINGSWOOD RD
3800 Shrm 91403 561-H6
KINGTON WY
8400 LPMA 90630 767-D4
KINGTREE AV
44100 LAN 93534 4015-G3
KINLEY ST
300 LHB 90631 708-B5
E KINMOUNT ST
3800 LALM 90720 767-A7
3800 LBCH 90808 767-A7
KINNARD AV
10400 Wwd 90024 632-C3
N KINNELOA AV
- PAS 91107 566-F4
S KINNELOA AV
- PAS 91107 566-F5
KINNELOA CANYON RD
1700 LACo 91107 536-F7
1700 PAS 91107 536-F7
KINNELOA MESA RD
1300 LACo 91107 536-F7
1300 LACo 91107 566-F1
KINNELOA RANCH RD
- LACo 91107 536-G7
KINNEY CIR
3600 LA 90065 594-H2
KINNEY PL
3600 LA 90065 594-H2
KINNEY ST
100 SMCA 90405 671-G4
3500 LA 90065 594-H2
KINNOW PL
3000 RowH 91748 679-A7
KINROSS AV
10800 Wwd 90024 632-A3
KINROSS CT
2200 THO 91361 557-A6
KINSELLA AV
100 COV 91724 599-F4
5000 LACo 91724 599-F3
KINSEY DR
- LA 90037 674-B2
KINSIE ST
4900 CMRC 90040 675-F3
KINSLER CT
1500 BREA 92821 708-H6
KINSTON AV
5200 CULC 90230 672-G4
KINZIE ST
14600 PanC 91402 501-J5
14800 LA 91343 501-E5
16900 Nor 91325 501-A5
18100 Nor 91325 500-J5
18400 Nor 91324 500-F5
19800 Chat 91311 500-D5
22000 Chat 91311 499-J5
KIOWA
- Ago 91301 587-G4
KIOWA AV
11600 Brwd 90049 631-H5
KIOWA WY
1000 SDMS 91773 570-D7
KIOWA CREST DR
1500 DBAR 91765 679-J4
1600 DBAR 91765 680-A4

KIP DR
9900 LA 90210 592-C4
KIPLING AV
1000 Eagl 90041 565-C5
KIPLING PL
- StvR 91381 4550-A6
KIPPEN ST
23700 Hrbr 90710 793-J2
KIPPER CT
3300 LAN 93535 4106-G2
KIPTON PL
18600 Tarz 91356 560-J4
KIPTREE DR
14300 LACo 93532 4102-G5
KIPWAY DR
12700 DWNY 90242 736-A1
KIRBY CT
- BqtC 91354 4460-E6
W KIRBY CT
1100 UPL 91786 571-J7
KIRBY DR
800 LHB 90631 708-D4
KIRBY ST
300 HiPk 90042 595-D1
KIRKBY RD
1700 GLDL 91208 564-H1
KIRKCALDY CIR
24000 CanP 91307 529-E5
KIRKCOLM CT
12000 Nor 91326 480-H6
KIRKCOLM LN
18600 Nor 91326 480-G6
KIRKFORD WY
1200 THO 91361 557-C5
KIRKHAM DR
3000 GLDL 91206 535-B7
KIRKLAND AV
43500 LAN 93535 4106-A1
44000 LAN 93535 4015-J7
44200 LAN 93535 4016-A7
KIRKLAND DR
2800 LA 90210 592-D1
KIRKSIDE RD
9300 LA 90035 632-G4
KIRKTON PL
900 GLDL 91207 564-G1
KIRK VIEW DR
16900 HacH 91745 678-F5
KIRKWALL RD
700 GLDR 91740 599-F1
1000 AZU 91702 598-G2
1100 SDMS 91773 599-H1
16700 LACo 91702 598-G2
17900 LACo 91702 599-A2
E KIRKWALL RD
100 AZU 91702 598-J2
18200 LACo 91702 599-A2
W KIRKWALL RD
200 AZU 91702 598-J2
KIRKWOOD AV
100 CLAR 91711 601-D4
500 POM 91767 601-A4
900 PAS 91103 565-H2
KIRKWOOD DR
8100 LA 90046 593-A3
8300 LA 90046 592-J4
KIRKWOOD LN
400 MNRO 91016 567-H2
500 LHB 90631 738-D1
KIRSCH CT
- SCTA 91321 4641-B1
KIRST ST
200 LCF 91011 535-D4
KIRSTENGARY WY
24000 SCTA 91355 4550-F5
KIRSTEN LEE DR
1800 WLKV 91361 586-J1
1800 WLKV 91361 587-A1
KIRTLAND AV
5300 LKWD 90713 766-E3
KIRUNA PL
23600 WdHl 91367 559-E3
KISKA AV
2400 HacH 91745 678-C5
KISMET AV
11300 LA 91342 502-H1
11600 LA 91342 482-B2
KITAOKA LN
- BREA 92821 708-J5
KIT CARSON RD
24900 HIDH 91302 559-B3
KITFOX PL
25700 SCTA 91355 4550-F7
KITSY LN
1500 SIMI 93063 499-B3
KITTERING RD
800 SDMS 91773 599-J4
KITTRICK DR
3000 OrCo 90720 796-H3
KITTRIDGE ST
100 SFER 91340 482-B7
2300 BURB 91506 533-D7
10700 NHol 91606 533-A6
11000 NHol 91606 532-D6
13200 VanN 91401 532-A6
13800 VanN 91405 532-A6
14500 VanN 91411 532-A6
14600 VanN 91411 531-H6
14600 VanN 91405 531-H6
15900 VanN 91406 531-C6
17700 Res 91335 531-A6
18100 Res 91335 531-A6
18100 Res 91335 530-G6

STREET Block City ZIP Pg-Grid

KITTRIDGE ST
18200 Res 91335 530-J6
18900 Res 91335 530-H6
19700 Win 91306 530-C6
20800 CanP 91303 530-A6
22000 CanP 91303 529-H6
22300 CanP 91307 529-D6
24500 LACo 91307 529-C6
KITTS HWY
- SLB 90740 826-H3
KITTY RD
- LACo 90660 637-A6
KITTYHAWK AV
6900 Wch 90045 673-A7
6900 Wch 90045 703-A1
7600 Wch 90045 702-H2
KITTYHAWK LN
37800 PMDL 93550 4286-A2
KITTYS LN
6300 Tuj 91042 504-C6
KIVA CT
29100 AGRH 91301 558-A5
KIVIK ST
23500 WdHl 91367 559-F3
KIWI PL
- PMDL 93551 4285-E2
KIYOT WY
- LA 90094 702-D1
KLAMATH CT
- LACo 91390 4461-A3
800 SDMS 91773 570-D5
KLAMATH LN
42300 LACo 93536 4104-J5
KLAMATH PL
4700 LA 90032 595-E7
KLAMATH ST
4600 LA 90032 595-D7
15400 LPUE 91744 638-D5
16200 LACo 91744 638-F5
KLEE ST
16700 LA 91343 501-D7
17400 Nor 91325 501-B7
KLEIN PL
2200 POM 91766 641-A5
KLEVINS CT
28300 SCTA 91387 4552-A1
KLINEDALE AV
8600 PRV 90660 706-F3
9200 DWNY 90240 706-E3
KLING ST
4100 BURB 91505 563-C3
10200 LA 91602 563-A4
11000 LA 91602 562-J4
11700 LA 91607 562-F4
12400 LA 91604 562-F4
12800 Shrm 91423 562-C4
14400 Shrm 91403 562-A4
KLINGERMAN ST
8200 RSMD 91770 636-F3
9200 SELM 91733 636-J3
9600 SELM 91733 637-A3
10900 ELMN 91733 637-B3
11400 ELMN 91732 637-D3
KLONDIKE AV
5100 LKWD 90712 765-J3
8400 DWNY 90242 735-H2
KLUM PL
18500 RowH 91748 679-B7
KLUMP AV
4100 LA 91602 562-J5
4800 NHol 91601 562-J2
6000 NHol 91606 532-J6
7700 SunV 91352 532-J3
KNAPP RD
700 SBdC 92372 (4472-B6 See Page 4471)
7600 Chat 91311 499-F6
KNAPP ST
15200 LA 91343 501-D6
16900 Nor 91325 501-B6
18600 Nor 91324 500-G7
20900 Chat 91311 500-B7
KNAPP WY
9300 Chat 91311 499-F7
KNAPP RANCH RD
- WHil 91304 499-C7
- WHil 91304 529-C1
KNEWOOD CT
3000 LAN 93536 4105-C3
KNIGHT AV
6200 NLB 90805 765-H1
KNIGHT DR
28200 AGRH 91301 558-C7
KNIGHT ST
- Cstc 91384 4459-G4
KNIGHT WY
200 LCF 91011 535-C3
5000 PMDL 93552 4287-A2
KNIGHTSBRIDGE CT
- PMDL 93552 4287-C4
KNIGHTSBRIDGE ST
45600 LAN 93534 4015-E3
KNIGHTSGATE RD
4500 WLKV 91361 557-D6
KNOB DR
3000 LA 90065 594-H4
KNOB HILL AV
100 RBCH 90277 762-J7
700 RBCH 90277 763-A7
KNOBHILL DR
3500 Shrm 91423 561-J6
3500 Shrm 91423 562-A6
4000 Shrm 91403 562-A6

KNOB HILL RD
12800 Pear 93553 4378-J7
KNOCHAVEN DR
15500 SCTA 91387 4552-E6
KNODE ST
2800 TOR 90501 793-H1
KNOLL CT
- Cstc 91384 4459-F2
- StvR 91381 4550-B5
300 BREA 92821 709-B4
24300 DBAR 91765 680-D4
KNOLL DR
200 SPed 90731 824-C3
1100 MONP 91754 635-J2
1100 MONP 91754 636-A2
41000 PMDL 93551 4194-G2
N KNOLL DR
3200 LA 90068 563-D7
3200 LA 90068 593-D1
KNOLL CREST AV
3400 LACo 90043 673-E4
KNOLLCREST DR
1000 COV 91724 599-D6
1000 LACo 91724 599-D6
KNOLL CREST PL
2200 THO 91361 557-A4
KNOLL HILL
- GmH 91344 480-J7
KNOLL LAKE AV
700 BREA 92821 708-J6
KNOLL RIDGE DR
- POM 91766 640-F6
KNOLL STONE CIR
16400 CRTS 90703 736-J6
KNOLLVIEW CT
500 PMDL 93551 4285-H1
KNOLL VIEW DR
29600 RPV 90275 823-G4
KNOLLVIEW DR
- POM 91766 640-G5
KNOLLWOOD AV
2900 LVRN 91750 600-H2
KNOLLWOOD CT
- CanP 91307 529-E5
- PMDL 93551 4195-A2
8400 BPK 90621 738-A4
KNOLLWOOD DR
1600 PAS 91103 565-D1
16300 GmH 91344 481-D5
KNOLLWOOD LN
- SCTA 91355 4550-B5
700 SDMS 91773 600-C3
KNOLLWOOD RD
1200 SLB 90740 826-G1
KNOLLWOOD TER
1500 PAS 91103 565-D1
KNOLLWOOD WY
- WdHl 91364 559-H3
KNOPF ST
2000 COMP 90222 734-H2
2000 Wbrk 90222 734-H2
KNOTT AV
5500 BPK 90621 737-G6
6000 BPK 90620 737-G7
6200 BPK 90621 767-G2
6200 BPK 90620 767-G2
16600 LMRD 90638 737-G6
S KNOTT AV
100 ANA 92804 767-G6
600 BPK 90620 767-G6
KNOTT CT
3400 LAN 93535 4106-G2
KNOTTINGTON
1300 LHB 90631 738-D3
KNOWLES AV
1400 City 90063 635-E2
KNOWLTON PL
6900 Wch 90045 703-A1
KNOWLTON ST
5300 Wch 90045 673-A7
5900 Wch 90045 703-A1
KNOX AV
2600 LA 90039 594-F4
KNOX PL
800 CLAR 91711 571-B7
KNOX ST
- LA 90501 763-J3
- LA 90501 764-A3
100 CRSN 90248 764-C3
600 LA 90502 764-A3
600 LACo 90248 764-C3
1100 LACo 90502 764-A3
1100 SFER 91340 482-B5
1900 LA 91340 482-B5
1900 LA 91342 482-B5
KNOXVILLE AV
1200 LBCH 90815 796-E2
3000 LBCH 90808 796-E1
3400 LBCH 90808 766-E6
4100 LKWD 90713 766-E3
KNUDSEN PKWY
- Valc 91355 4550-A1
KNUDSON ST
200 LHB 90631 708-D6
KOBE RD
33700 LACo 91390 4373-E5
KOBE FIRE RD
- Nor 91326 480-G3
KODAK DR
800 Echo 90026 594-B6
KOEHLER CRSG
- BPK 90621 737-J7
- BPK 90621 738-A7

KOHLENBERGER DR
- FUL 92833 738-C6
KOHLER ST
600 LA 90021 634-G6
KOJI CT
- SCTA 91351 4551-F4
KOLEETA DR
900 Hrbr 90710 794-A3
KOLLE AV
1200 SPAS 91030 595-E3
KOLSTER ST
300 Boyl 90033 634-J5
KOMAR DR
19700 Tarz 91356 560-F4
KOMORI CIR
17000 GAR 90247 734-A7
KONA CT
4000 PMDL 93552 4286-J3
KONA DR
1600 COMP 90220 764-G1
KONA LN
- CRTS 90703 737-B7
300 NLB 90805 735-D7
KONTIKI WY
16000 PacP 90272 630-F4
KONYA DR
4000 TOR 90503 763-A4
KOOLISH ST
2200 POM 91766 641-A5
KOONTZ AV
10800 SFSP 90670 706-H6
KOONTZ RD
34800 LACo 91390 4373-E2
KOONTZ WY
21800 Top 90290 590-A1
KOOPMAN AV
11400 DWNY 90241 706-A5
KOOPMANS WY
1300 OrCo 90631 708-B4
1300 LHB 90631 708-B4
KOOTENIA DR
- LACo 93532 4102-E4
KOPANY AV
13900 LA 91342 482-B1
KORAT DR
- PMDL 93551 4285-F1
KORNBLUM AV
800 TOR 90503 763-E6
11500 HAW 90250 703-E7
11500 ING 90303 703-E7
11900 HAW 90303 703-E7
11900 HAW 90303 733-E3
11900 HAW 90250 733-E3
15100 LACo 90260 733-E5
16700 TOR 90504 733-E7
17400 TOR 90504 763-E1
KOSTER AV
3600 Shrm 91423 562-C6
KOSTURAS PL
6600 Win 91306 530-D6
KOTLER CT
- BqtC 91354 4460-E6
KOUDEKERK ST
12100 ART 90701 736-H7
KOUFAX DR
3600 LAN 93535 4016-A4
S KOURI LN
800 ANA 92804 767-G7
KOURY DR
15100 HacH 91745 677-J6
N KRAEMER BLVD
200 BREA 92821 709-F7
S KRAEMER BLVD
100 BREA 92821 709-F7
KRAFT AV
4000 LA 91604 562-J5
4400 LA 91602 562-J4
6200 NHol 91606 532-J6
7200 NHol 91605 532-J3
KRAKE AL
600 PAS 91101 565-J3
600 PAS 91104 565-J3
KRAMER DR
1100 CRSN 90746 764-F3
KRAMERWOOD PL
8900 LA 90034 632-G6
KRATT LN
3900 PRV 90601 637-B7
KREGMONT DR
900 GLDR 91741 569-G3
KRENZ AV
3000 Alta 91001 535-G4
KRESS AV
6500 BGDN 90201 675-J7
6500 BGDN 90201 705-H2
KRESS ST
2100 LA 90046 592-J3
KRIM DR
2700 LA 90064 632-G6
KRINKE WY
- SMAD 91024 567-A1
KRISTIN AV
16500 TOR 90504 733-G7
17500 TOR 90504 763-G1
KRISTIN DR
9200 DWNY 90240 706-C2
KRISTIN LN
27600 SCTA 91350 4461-A6
KRISTINA CT
7000 LAN 93536 4104-D5
KRISTINE CT
- SCTA 91387 4462-D6

KRISTOPHER PL
12100 Nor 91326 480-H6
KROEGER AV
1000 FUL 92831 738-J5
KRUEGER ST
8900 CULC 90232 672-H1
KRUSE AV
200 MNRO 91016 567-G7
KRUSE RD
9300 PRV 90660 676-J1
9600 PRV 90660 677-A1
KRYSTAL AV
- LAN 93536 4105-E3
KUDOS CT
3400 LAN 93535 4106-G2
KUEHNER DR
1300 SIMI 93063 499-C1
KUEN PL
13100 VanN 91401 562-D2
KUHL DR
7100 CMRC 90040 676-B7
KUHN DR
100 MANB 90266 732-H7
KUMQUAT LN
- RPV 90275 823-B4
KURL WY
6700 Res 91335 530-H6
KURT AV
2500 CMRC 90040 675-H4
KURT ST
10200 LA 91342 503-A1
10700 LA 91342 (4723-A7 See Page 4643)
KURTALLEN CT
- LAN 93535 4016-E6
KURTZ AV
1400 City 90063 635-D3
KWIS AV
1100 HacH 91745 678-B3
S KWIS AV
2300 HacH 91745 678-A4
KYLE CT
7400 CanP 91307 529-G4
KYLE DR
13700 CRTS 90703 737-C6
KYLE PL
- PMDL 93551 4195-E7
13500 CRTS 90703 737-C6
KYLE ST
7300 Tuj 91042 504-A1
7300 Tuj 91042 504-A2
7800 Sunl 91040 503-F2
9900 LALM 90720 767-A7
KYRA CT
- LACo 91390 4461-B3

L

L ST
1100 Wilm 90744 794-B6
E L ST
100 Wilm 90744 794-F5
W L ST
100 Wilm 90744 794-C5
S LA ALAMEDA AV
100 SPed 90731 824-A4
1100 SPed 90731 824-A4
W LA ALAMEDA AV
900 SPed 90731 824-A5
LA ALBA DR
9000 WHIT 90603 707-H3
LA ALTURA RD
1100 BHLS 90210 592-F6
LA AMISTAD PL
18800 Tarz 91356 560-H5
LA AMISTAD WY
4300 Tarz 91356 560-H5
LABAIG AV
1500 Hlwd 90028 593-G4
LA BAJADA AV
8200 WHIT 90605 707-G2
LA BALLEN DR
300 WAL 91789 639-E7
LA BARCA DR
4300 Tarz 91356 560-G4
15100 LMRD 90638 737-G4
LA BARCA PL
4500 Tarz 91356 560-G4
LA BARCA RD
14000 LMRD 90638 737-F3
LA BARRA PL
15800 HacH 91745 678-B4
LA BARRANCA RD
1700 LCF 91011 534-J3
1700 LCF 91011 535-A3
LA BAYA DR
5600 WLKV 91362 557-E4
LABEL AV
27500 SCTA 91351 4461-D7
27500 SCTA 91351 4551-D1
E LA BELLE ST
15200 HacH 91745 677-J5
15300 HacH 91745 678-A5
LA BELLORITA
800 SPAS 91030 595-G3
LABIN CT
18900 RowH 91748 679-B4
LA BOICE
1100 GLDL 91205 564-F6
LA BONITA CIR
17800 CRTS 90703 737-D7
LA BONITA DR
2800 HacH 91745 677-J4

LA BONITA PL
17600 CRTS 90703 737-D7
LA BONITA RD
200 DBAR 91765 640-C7
LA BONITA WY
17400 CRTS 90703 737-D7
LABRADOR ST
14600 PanC 91402 501-J5
14700 LA 91343 501-D5
16900 Nor 91325 501-A5
18100 Nor 91325 500-J5
18500 Nor 91324 500-F5
19700 Chat 91311 500-D5
N LA BREA AV
100 ING 90301 703-C1
100 LA 90036 633-D1
200 ING 90302 703-C1
300 LA 90036 593-D7
700 LA 90038 593-D7
700 LA 90046 593-D4
900 ING 90302 673-C7
1000 WHWD 90038 593-D4
1000 WHWD 90046 593-D4
1300 Hlwd 90028 593-D4
1500 LA 90043 673-C7
S LA BREA AV
100 ING 90301 703-C2
100 LA 90036 633-D3
1000 LA 90019 633-D3
1900 LA 90016 633-D6
3000 LA 90016 673-C1
3800 LA 90008 673-C1
4200 LACo 90008 673-C1
5000 LACo 90043 673-B5
5000 LadH 90056 673-B5
6200 LA 90043 673-B5
6200 LA 90056 673-B5
E LA BREA DR
700 ING 90301 703-D3
LA BREA TER
2000 LA 90046 593-D3
LA BREDA AV
400 WCOV 91791 598-J6
1000 COV 91722 598-J4
LA BRIDA DR
12700 SBdC 91710 641-C7
LA BRISA DR
30700 MAL 90265 627-A7
LA CADENA AV
800 ARCD 91007 567-B7
LA CADENA WY
500 LHB 90631 708-C5
LA CALANDRIA DR
4900 LA 90032 595-E7
4900 LA 90032 635-E1
LA CALANDRIA WY
4900 LA 90032 595-E7
4900 LA 90032 635-E1
LA CALLA PL
2000 SMRO 91108 596-A2
LA CALMA DR
15100 WHIT 90605 707-G3
15900 WHIT 90603 707-J3
LA CANA DR
1900 HacH 91745 678-D4
LA CANADA
- GLDR 91740 599-C2
LA CANADA BLVD
4500 LCF 91011 535-B2
LA CANADA CIR
6000 BPK 90620 767-E3
LA CANADA DR
1300 BREA 92821 708-H4
1400 LHB 92821 708-H4
LA CANADA PL
10500 Sunl 91040 503-D3
LA CANADA WY
9500 Sunl 91040 503-C3
LA CANADA CREST DR
2100 LCF 91011 534-H2
LA CANADA PLAZA RD
4400 LCF 91011 534-H2
LA CANADA VERDUGO RD
800 Alta 91001 535-E6
800 LACo 91103 535-E6
800 PAS 91103 535-E6
LA CAPELLE RD
14700 LMRD 90638 737-F4
E LA CARA ST
4000 LBCH 90815 796-A4
LA CARLITA PL
2900 HMB 90254 732-G7
LA CARTA CIR
7700 BPK 90620 767-E3
LA CASA AV
800 LHB 90631 708-D7
LA CASA LN
12100 Brwd 90049 631-F1
LA CASA WY
7700 BPK 90620 767-E3
LA CASITA LN
500 MNRO 91016 568-A4
LA CASTANA DR
2700 LA 90046 593-B1
LA CASTANA WY
7700 BPK 90620 767-E3
LA CAUSEY CT
4600 CHNO 91710 641-F4
LA CESTA PL
4600 Tarz 91356 560-H4
LACEWOOD DR
1500 LACo 90601 637-F5

LACHMAN LN
600 PacP 90272 630-G3
LA CIENAGA DR
6100 BPK 90620 767-F3
LA CIENEGA AV
2600 LA 90034 632-J7
3100 CULC 90232 632-J7
LA CIENEGA BLVD
12900 LACo 90250 733-B3
13000 HAW 90250 733-B3
N LA CIENEGA BLVD
100 BHLS 90211 632-J2
300 LA 90048 632-J2
300 LA 90048 592-J7
500 WHWD 90048 592-J7
600 WHWD 90069 592-J7
600 LA 90069 592-J7
S LA CIENEGA BLVD
- LA 90232 673-A1
100 LA 90048 632-J1
200 BHLS 90211 632-J1
800 LA 90035 632-J1
1900 LA 90034 632-J6
2700 LA 90034 633-A7
2800 CULC 90232 633-A7
3000 LA 90016 633-A7
3400 LA 90016 673-A1
3700 LA 90008 673-A1
3700 CULC 90232 673-A1
3800 LACo 90008 673-A4
4000 LACo 90230 673-A1
4900 LadH 90056 673-A4
5800 LA 90056 673-A4
6000 ING 90302 673-A4
6200 Wch 90045 673-A4
6500 Wch 90045 703-A1
6500 ING 90302 703-A1
10000 Lenx 90304 703-A6
11800 LACo 90250 733-A1
11800 Lenx 90304 733-A1
S LA CIENEGA PL
3300 LA 90016 633-A7
LA CIENEGA WEST WY
6600 LA 90056 673-A7
LA CIMA DR
9600 WHIT 90603 707-H3
10800 LACo 90604 707-H6
11900 LMRD 90638 707-H7
LA CITY W&P RD
- Cstc 91384 4279-E4
- LACo 4279-E4
LA CLEDE AV
3000 LA 90039 594-E1
LACLEDE AV
4300 LA 90039 564-D7
E LA COLINA DR
300 ING 90302 703-D1
LACOLLE PL
6500 LAN 93536 4104-D5
LA COLLINA DR
1100 LA 90069 592-G5
1100 WHWD 90069 592-G5
LA COLMENA WY
3500 LALM 90720 796-J4
LACOMB DR
28000 SCTA 91351 4461-F7
LACON AV
800 LACo 91744 638-G6
LA CONDESA DR
2400 Brwd 90049 591-C7
2400 Brwd 90049 631-C1
14600 LMRD 90638 737-H3
LACONIA BLVD
400 LACo 90061 734-B1
400 LA 90061 734-B1
600 LA 90044 734-B1
LACONIA PL
700 LA 90044 734-B1
LA CONTEMPO AV
37000 PMDL 93550 4286-D4
LA CORONA AV
3000 Alta 91001 535-H4
LA CORONA CT
600 VeCo 91377 557-J2
LA CORONA WY
7700 BPK 90620 767-F3
LA CORTITA ST
18200 RowH 91748 678-J6
18400 RowH 91748 679-A6
LA COSTA CIR
7700 BPK 90620 767-F3
LA COSTA CT
4000 LHB 90631 738-D2
LA COSTA PL
- POM 91766 640-E5
2600 PVE 90274 822-F1
LA COTA DR
40100 PMDL 93550 4195-J3
LA COTA PL
14600 Shrm 91403 561-J5
LA CRESCENTA AV
2400 ALH 91803 635-H2
3200 GLDL 91208 534-G4
3700 GLDL 91214 534-G3
3700 GLDL 91020 534-G1
4100 LaCr 91214 534-G1
4100 Mont 91020 534-G1
4600 LaCr 91214 504-G7
LA CRESTA CT
5300 LA 90038 593-H6
LA CRESTA DR
1300 LHH 90631 708-G3
1600 PAS 91103 535-F7

LA CRESTA PL
900 PVE 90274 792-G5
1100 FUL 92835 738-F5
LA CRESTA WY
- LA 91342 482-E4
LA CROIX DR
6300 RPV 90275 822-H3
LA CROSSE CIR
2200 CLAR 91711 571-E6
LA CROSSE ST
600 GLDR 91741 569-C4
19000 LACo 91741 569-C4
LA CRUZ DR
15200 PacP 90272 631-A5
LA CUARTA ST
1400 WHIT 90605 707-G2
8000 WHIT 90602 707-C1
LA CUESTA DR
2600 LA 90046 593-B1
LA CUESTA LN
17400 Enc 91316 561-B4
LA CUEVA DR
2000 RowH 91748 679-A5
LA CUMBRE DR
900 PAS 91105 565-F4
14800 PacP 90272 631-B7
S LA CUTA CIR
500 WCOV 91791 638-J1
LACY ST
2400 LA 90031 594-J6
2600 LA 90031 595-A6
LADANA CT
13000 SFSP 90670 707-B6
LADBROOK WY
2500 VeCo 91361 586-D1
LADD AV
4900 LA 90032 595-E7
LADDIE LN
2200 LaCr 91214 504-H6
LADEENE AV
20600 TOR 90503 763-C5
22300 TOR 90505 763-C7
22500 TOR 90505 793-C1
LADELLE AV
38500 PMDL 93550 4196-E7
W LA DENEY DR
900 ONT 91762 601-H5
LA DENEY ST
4400 MTCL 91763 601-E5
LA DERA DR
1000 Bxby 90807 765-F5
LADERA DR
100 BHLS 90210 592-D7
100 BelA 90077 592-D7
LADERA LN
- WdHl 91364 560-A4
LADERA ST
100 MONP 91754 635-G3
E LADERA ST
400 PAS 91104 565-J1
600 PAS 91104 566-A1
LADERA TER
1400 LHB 90631 738-G1
LADERA WY
- LACo 93536 4104-J5
LADERA CREST DR
5200 LadH 90056 673-A5
LADERA PARK AV
5800 LadH 90056 673-B6
LADERMAN LN
37600 PMDL 93550 4286-E2
LADLEY CT
28300 SCTA 91387 4552-A1
LADNER ST
16400 WHIT 90603 708-A5
LA DOCENA LN
8300 PRV 90660 706-D1
11300 SFSP 90670 706-H3
LADO DE LOMA DR
15800 HacH 91745 678-B5
LADOGA AV
2400 LBCH 90815 796-E2
3000 LBCH 90808 796-E1
3400 LBCH 90808 766-E6
4100 LKWD 90713 766-E5
LA DONNA WY
15000 HacH 91745 677-J4
LADRILLO ST
23200 WdHl 91367 559-F2
LA DUE WY
5400 HiPk 90042 595-D4
LADYBIRD DR
2600 LACo 91302 589-C3
LADYFACE CT
29800 AGRH 91301 557-H6
LADYFERN LN
- PMDL 93551 4285-C3
LADY LINDA LN
- LACo 91390 4460-G1
LADYSMITH ST
15500 HacH 91745 678-B3
LADYWOOD PL
800 MTBL 90640 636-C7
LA ENCINA WY
3200 LACo 91107 566-F7
LA ENTRADA AV
8500 WHIT 90605 707-G3
E LA ENTRADA PL
100 FUL 92835 738-G2
W LA ENTRADA PL
100 FUL 92835 738-G2
LA FALDA PL
3400 LA 90068 563-D7

LA FARINA DR
36700 LACo 93551 4285-F5
LAFAYETTE CT
- MANB 90266 732-H4
LAFAYETTE PL
4000 CULC 90232 672-H1
LA FAYETTE RD
1600 LA 90019 633-E5
LAFAYETTE RD
1300 CLAR 91711 601-C1
LAFAYETTE ST
300 GLDL 91205 564-H5
1100 SGBL 91776 596-F6
3400 RSMD 91770 636-F1
S LAFAYETTE ST
400 SGBL 91776 596-F5
N LAFAYETTE PARK PL
300 Echo 90026 634-C1
600 Echo 90026 594-C7
S LAFAYETTE PARK PL
100 LA 90057 634-B2
LA FETRA DR
19000 GLDR 91741 569-C4
19000 LACo 91741 569-C4
LA FIESTA AV
2500 Alta 91001 535-H5
LA FIESTA DR
7700 BPK 90620 767-F3
LAFLER DR
1400 City 90063 635-F3
LAFLER RD
2200 LA 90032 635-F1
LA FLORA LN
1100 GLDR 91741 569-G4
LA FLORESTA DR
1700 LCF 91011 534-J2
15800 HacH 91745 678-C4
LA FOLLETTE DR
200 HiPk 90042 595-D2
LA FONDA DR
14300 LMRD 90638 737-H3
LA FONTAINE CT
1700 LA 90210 592-F4
LA FOREST DR
5200 LCF 91011 534-J1
5400 LCF 91011 504-J7
LA FORGE ST
13500 WHIT 90605 707-D2
14300 WHIT 90603 707-F4
LA FORTUNA DR
15400 LMRD 90638 737-H4
LA FRANCE AV
200 ALH 91801 595-H4
1900 SPAS 91030 595-H4
LA FREMONTIA
1900 SPAS 91030 595-G4
LA GABRIELLA DR
42300 LACo 93536 4104-J5
LA GARITA DR
6500 RPV 90275 792-H7
LA GLORIA DR
6100 MAL 90265 627-A7
LA GLORIA ST
14000 LMRD 90638 737-J3
LA GLORITA CIR
24200 SCTA 91321 4640-E2
LAGO LINDA RD
100 PMDL 93550 4285-J5
100 PMDL 93550 4286-A5
LA GOLONDRINA AV
1600 ALH 91803 595-H7
1700 ALH 91803 635-H1
LAGOON
1400 WCOV 91790 638-D2
LAGOON AV
200 Wilm 90744 794-D5
LAGOON CIR
- CRTS 90703 736-F6
LAGOON DR
- Wilm 90744 794-C6
LAGOS RD
10000 LACo 91390 4373-F4
LA GOSTA PL
25500 SCTA 91355 4550-F7
LAGO VISTA DR
1200 BHLS 90210 592-F5
1200 LA 90210 592-F5
LAGO VISTA PL
1200 BHLS 90210 592-F5
LA GRANADA CIR
8200 LPMA 90623 767-C4
LA GRANADA DR
2200 LA 90068 593-E3
LA GRANADA WY
1900 LCF 91011 534-J3
4500 LCF 91011 535-A3
LA GRANGE AV
10300 WLA 90025 632-D3
11800 WLA 90025 631-J7
LA GRANJA DR
23000 SCTA 91354 4550-H1
LAGROSS WY
9400 Chat 91311 499-F6
LA GUARDIA ST
18200 RowH 91748 678-J6
18400 RowH 91748 679-A6
LAGUNA
- Ago 91301 587-F4
LAGUNA AV
800 Echo 90026 634-E1
1000 Echo 90026 594-E7
LAGUNA CT
- DUAR 91010 568-A4

LAGUNA CT
- MANB 90266 732-H4
6100 LBCH 90803 826-D1
26000 SCTA 91355 4550-G4
LAGUNA DR
200 FUL 92835 738-G4
1700 LHB 90631 708-B4
LAGUNA PL
- LBCH 90803 826-C3
500 SLB 90740 826-F4
LAGUNA RD
100 FUL 92835 738-F3
300 PAS 91105 565-E6
LAGUNA ST
- LMRD 90638 738-B2
LAGUNA TER
1000 FUL 92833 738-E4
LAGUNA WY
5700 CYP 90630 767-D7
LAGUNA CANYON WY
500 BREA 92821 709-C6
LAGUNA CIRCLE DR
2300 Ago 91301 588-B3
LAGUNITA DR
39600 PMDL 93551 4195-J4
LAGUNITA RD
1000 PAS 91105 565-E6
LA HABRA
2500 GLDR 91740 599-C2
E LA HABRA BLVD
100 LHB 90631 708-F5
1600 BREA 92821 708-F5
W LA HABRA BLVD
100 LHB 90631 708-B6
LA HABRA CIR
7700 BPK 90620 767-F3
LA HABRA RD
2100 LHH 90631 708-G1
2400 LHH 90631 678-G7
LA HABRA HILLS DR
- LHB 90631 738-C1
LAHAINA
- SCTA 91321 4641-C3
LAHAINA ST
1500 WCOV 91792 638-H4
LA HERMOSA DR
16500 WHIT 90603 708-A5
LA HERRAN RD
31300 MAL 90265 626-H7
LAHEY ST
15600 GmH 91344 501-A2
18100 Nor 91326 500-G2
LA HOMA ST
8500 CYP 90630 767-D5
LAIDLAW LN
40600 PMDL 93551 4194-F1
41600 LACo 93536 4104-F7
LAINIE ST
1800 WCOV 91792 638-J6
1800 WCOV 91792 639-A6
LAIRD DR
2400 GLDL 91206 565-A3
LAIRPORT ST
600 ELSG 90245 702-H7
600 ELSG 90245 732-H1
LA JARA CIR
12900 CRTS 90703 767-A1
LA JARA CT
5000 LKWD 90712 766-B1
LA JARA LN
12300 CRTS 90703 766-J1
LA JARA ST
5800 LKWD 90713 766-C1
10700 CRTS 90703 766-D1
13000 CRTS 90703 767-B1
E LA JARA ST
3200 NLB 90805 765-H1
LA JARRA CIR
13700 CRTS 90703 767-D1
LA JOLLA AV
200 LBCH 90803 826-C1
N LA JOLLA AV
100 LA 90048 633-A1
300 LA 90048 593-A7
700 LA 90046 593-A7
900 WHWD 90046 593-A7
S LA JOLLA AV
100 LA 90048 633-A2
1000 LA 90035 633-A3
LA JOLLA CIR
13500 LMRD 90638 737-J2
LA JOLLA DR
4100 PMDL 93552 4286-H4
LA JOLLA WY
5700 CYP 90630 767-D7
LA JUNTA DR
4000 CLAR 91711 600-J1
4000 CLAR 91711 601-A1
4000 CLAR 91711 571-A7
LAKE AV
800 LVRN 91750 570-D7
2400 Alta 91001 535-A5
16600 PRM 90723 735-G6
N LAKE AV
- PAS 91101 566-A2
600 PAS 91104 566-A2
1600 PAS 91104 536-A7
1700 LACo 91104 536-A7
1800 Alta 91001 536-A7
6900 NLB 90805 735-G6
S LAKE AV
- PAS 91101 566-A6
500 PAS 91106 566-A6

LAKE DR
1800 LACo 90210 592-E3
1900 Ago 91301 588-A4
2100 LA 90210 592-E3
LAKE ST
900 Ven 90291 671-J4
1300 Ven 90291 672-A3
1400 GLDL 91201 564-A3
1500 GLDL 91201 563-J2
1900 BURB 91502 563-J2
3800 CHNO 91710 641-D5
13100 LA 90066 672-A3
N LAKE ST
100 BURB 91502 563-G1
100 Echo 90026 634-D1
300 BURB 91502 533-G7
S LAKE ST
100 BURB 91502 563-H1
100 LA 90057 634-C2
900 LA 90006 634-B4
LAKE TER
600 FUL 92835 738-F2
LAKE WY
1700 LAN 93534 4015-E4
LAKE CANYON DR
20100 LACo 91789 679-F4
20800 DBAR 91789 679-G5
LAKE CENTER DR
- LA 90094 672-F7
LAKE CENTER PARK LN
10700 SFSP 90670 706-G5
LAKECREST AV
28600 SCTA 91387 4552-C1
LAKE CREST CT
3300 WLKV 91361 557-C7
LAKE CREST DR
5300 AGRH 91301 557-F6
14000 LMRD 90638 737-D1
LAKE CREST LN
2200 LHB 90631 708-H6
LAKEDALE DR
23700 CALB 91302 559-E7
LAKE ENCINO DR
18000 Enc 91316 561-A5
18100 Enc 91316 560-J5
LAKE ERIE DR
20300 WAL 91789 639-F4
LAKEFIELD DR
15900 LMRD 90638 737-J1
LAKEFIELD RD
100 THO 91361 557-B4
LAKE FOREST CIR
2200 LHB 90631 708-H6
LAKE FOREST DR
1000 CLAR 91711 571-B7
LAKE FOREST WY
12600 LMRD 90638 737-D1
LAKE FRANKLIN DR
1200 LA 90210 592-E4
1200 LACo 90210 592-E4
LAKE FRONT DR
10600 NRWK 90650 736-D3
LAKEFRONT DR
30600 AGRH 91301 557-G5
LAKE GLEN DR
2200 LHB 90631 708-H6
3000 LA 90210 562-E7
14000 LMRD 90638 737-D1
LAKEGROVE AV
1600 MTBL 90640 636-G5
LAKE GROVE WY
500 LHB 90631 708-H6
LAKE HARBOR LN
3800 WLKV 91361 557-C6
LAKEHILLS RD
31200 Cstc 91384 4459-G1
31200 Cstc 91384 4369-G7
LAKE HOLLYWOOD DR
2600 LA 90068 563-D7
2600 LA 90068 593-E1
LAKE HUGHES RD
- LACo 91390 (4280-E4 See Page 4279)
27500 Cstc 91384 4369-G6
33100 BqtC 91354 (4370-B3 See Page 4279)
33100 Cstc 91384 (4370-B3 See Page 4279)
33100 LACo 91390 (4370-B3 See Page 4279)
41600 LACo 91390 4101-A6
41700 LACo 93532 4101-G4
LAKE HUGHES FIRE RD
- LACo 91390 4102-A4
- LACo 93532 4101-J2
- LACo 93532 4102-A4
LAKEHURST AV
27200 SCTA 91351 4551-E1
27700 SCTA 91351 4461-E7
LAKE KNOLL DR
3200 FUL 92835 738-F2
7900 LACo 91770 636-F3
LAKEKNOLL DR
- BPK 90621 737-J6
- BPK 90621 738-A6
LAKELAND RD
10800 NRWK 90650 706-E6
11500 SFSP 90670 706-H6
12500 SFSP 90670 707-A6
13000 LACo 90605 707-C6
13000 SFSP 90605 707-C6
LAKELAND TER
24000 LA 91304 529-C1

STREET Block City ZIP Pg-Grid

LAKE LINDERO DR
5300 AGRH 91301 557-G3
LAKE LOS ANGELES AV
17200 LACo 93591 4199-H3
17800 LACo 93591 4200-A3
LAKE MANOR DR
23200 Chat 91311 499-F7
23400 Chat 91311 499-F7
LAKEMEADOW DR
31600 Actn 93510 4465-D3
LAKEMEADOW LN
32100 WLKV 91361 557-C6
LAKEMONT DR
14700 LACo 93532 4102-F4
LAKEMOOR PL
2600 WCOV 91792 638-J6
LAKEMORE DR
20000 SCTA 91351 4551-D2
LAKE NADINE PL
6000 AGRH 91301 557-G3
LAKE PALMDALE DR
200 PMDL 93550 4286-A5
LAKE PARK WY
400 LHB 90631 708-H6
1200 BREA 92821 708-J6
12700 LMRD 90638 737-D1
LAKE PLACID ST
4500 CRTS 90703 767-B3
LAKE PLEASANT DR
32300 WLKV 91361 557-B7
LAKEPOINTE LN
36300 PMDL 93550 4286-B5
LAKEPORT DR
3300 WLKV 91361 557-C7
LAKER CT
21400 Chat 91311 500-A2
LAKERIDGE DR
2900 LA 90068 593-E1
LAKERIDGE LN
1300 THO 91361 557-B5
LAKERIDGE PL
6600 LA 90068 593-D1
LAKERIDGE RD
6500 LA 90068 593-D1
LAKE RIDGE WY
400 LHB 90631 708-H6
LAKES DR
1000 WCOV 91790 598-G7
1000 WCOV 91790 638-G1
LAKE SHORE AV
1300 Echo 90026 594-E6
1900 LA 90039 594-E5
LAKE SHORE DR
2000 CHLS 91709 680-H3
LAKESHORE DR
5900 CYP 90630 767-E6
E LAKESHORE DR
2000 Ago 91301 588-B4
17600 LACo 93532 4101-J2
S LAKESHORE DR
28800 Ago 91301 588-A4
W LAKESHORE DR
18000 LACo 93532 4101-H2
LAKE SHORE TER
200 Echo 90026 634-E2
LAKESIDE
\- LACo 93536 3925-D4
LAKE SIDE DR
2000 LHB 90631 708-H6
14000 LMRD 90638 737-D1
LAKESIDE DR
\- BPK 90621 738-A6
400 FUL 92835 738-F2
4400 BURB 91505 563-D5
LAKESIDE RD
\- SCTA 91355 4550-F2
LAKESIDE ST
13800 LA 91342 482-A2
14600 LA 91342 481-J4
LAKESIDE LATERAL
\- LACo 90265 587-J5
\- LACo 90265 588-A5
LAKESIDE PLAZA DR
6900 LA 90068 563-D5
6900 Univ 91608 563-D5
7000 Univ 91608 563-D5
LAKESPRING AV
17100 LACo 93591 4199-H3
17800 LACo 93591 4200-A3
LAKE TERRACE DR
2300 CHLS 91709 680-J3
LAKE TERRACE LN
2200 LHB 90631 708-H6
LAKETRAIL CV
\- BPK 90621 738-A6
LAKEVIEW E
\- LACo 93534 3925-D4
LAKEVIEW S
\- LACo 93534 3925-D4
\- LACo 93536 3925-D4
LAKEVIEW W
\- LACo 93536 3925-D4
LAKE VIEW AV
2200 LA 90039 594-E4
LAKEVIEW AV
300 LBCH 90803 826-B1
1200 LHB 90631 708-F7
1200 LHB 90631 738-F1
3700 FUL 92835 738-F1
LAKEVIEW CIR
3000 FUL 92835 738-F2
LAKEVIEW CT
3000 FUL 92835 738-F2

LAKE VIEW CV
\- SCTA 91355 4550-F1
LAKE VIEW DR
\- RPV 90275 793-H7
\- RPV 90275 823-H1
2000 LHB 90631 708-H6
14000 LMRD 90638 737-D1
LAKEVIEW DR
\- LVRN 91750 570-J5
200 LACo 93551 4285-G6
200 PMDL 93550 4285-J6
200 PMDL 93550 4286-A6
2800 LBCH 90806 795-E2
2900 FUL 92835 738-F2
LAKEVIEW LN
2200 CHLS 91709 680-J3
LAKE VIEW RD
43700 LACo 93532 4101-J1
LAKEVIEW RD
400 PAS 91105 565-E6
2200 Ago 91301 588-B4
LAKEVIEW TER
500 AZU 91702 569-A5
3000 FUL 92835 738-F2
9200 Chat 91311 499-F7
LAKEVIEW TER E
2500 LA 90039 594-D3
LAKEVIEW TER W
2600 LA 90039 594-D3
LAKEVIEW WY
2900 FUL 92835 738-F2
31200 Cstc 91384 4369-G7
31200 Cstc 91384 4459-G1
LAKEVIEW CANYON RD
\- THO 91362 557-G1
100 THO 91361 557-C5
300 WLKV 91361 557-C5
5200 VeCo 91362 557-G1
LAKE VISTA CT
3900 Enc 91316 561-A6
LAKE VISTA DR
17900 Enc 91316 561-A6
28800 Ago 91301 588-A4
29400 Ago 91301 587-J4
LAKEWAY DR
22700 DBAR 91765 680-B2
LAKEWOOD AV
1800 UPL 91784 571-H6
2400 LA 90039 594-D3
N LAKEWOOD AV
1300 UPL 91786 601-J1
1600 UPL 91784 571-J6
LAKEWOOD BLVD
9100 DWNY 90240 706-C4
10200 DWNY 90241 706-C4
12200 DWNY 90242 706-B7
12300 DWNY 90242 736-A2
13400 BLF 90706 736-A2
LAKEWOOD BLVD Rt#-19
11400 DWNY 90241 706-C6
11800 DWNY 90242 706-B7
12300 DWNY 90242 736-A1
13300 BLF 90706 736-A7
14300 PRM 90723 736-A1
17800 BLF 90706 766-A1
17900 LKWD 90712 766-A1
N LAKEWOOD BLVD
1900 LBCH 90815 796-A4
4400 LKWD 90712 766-A5
4700 LBCH 90808 766-A4
N LAKEWOOD BLVD Rt#-19
1800 LBCH 90815 796-A3
3100 LBCH 90808 796-A1
3400 LBCH 90808 766-A6
4100 LKWD 90712 766-A4
LAKEWOOD CT
1300 THO 91361 557-C5
5300 PMDL 93552 4287-B2
LAKEWOOD DR
4100 LKWD 90712 765-J6
4100 LKWD 90712 766-A5
LAKEWOOD PL
600 PAS 91106 566-A6
2700 THO 91361 557-B5
N LAKEWOOD WY
500 UPL 91786 601-J3
1500 UPL 91786 571-H7
LAKME AV
200 Wilm 90744 794-E3
LA LINDA DR
\- Bxby 90807 765-D6
LA LINDURA DR
15700 WHIT 90603 707-J2
LA LOMA AV
38200 PMDL 93551 4285-J1
LA LOMA PL
3200 FUL 92835 738-G2
LA LOMA RD
400 GLDL 91206 564-G4
400 PAS 91105 565-F6
800 Eagl 90041 565-D6
LA LUNA DR
5000 LPMA 90623 767-C4
LA LUNA WY
2000 POM 91767 600-J5
LA LUZ TER
\- PMDL 93551 4194-G2
LAMA AV
3100 LBCH 90808 796-H1
3400 LBCH 90808 766-H7

LA MADERA AV
3000 ELMN 91732 637-E2
3600 ELMN 91732 597-G5
LA MADRID DR
\- Saug 91350 4461-F5
LA MADRINA AV
9900 SELM 91733 637-A4
LA MADRINA DR
8500 LACo 91770 636-G4
8500 RSMD 91770 636-G4
LA MAIDA ST
10500 NHol 91601 563-A3
11000 NHol 91601 562-J3
11700 LA 91607 562-F3
12800 Shrm 91423 562-B3
14500 Shrm 91403 561-G3
14500 Shrm 91403 562-A3
15500 Enc 91436 561-D3
LA MANCHA
1500 POM 91768 600-F6
LA MANCHA CT
\- Actn 93510 4465-C1
38700 PMDL 93550 4196-H7
LA MANCHA ST
13000 LMRD 90638 737-J1
13000 LMRD 90638 738-A1
LAMANDA ST
12000 LA 90066 672-D4
LA MANGA CT
\- PMDL 93551 4195-J4
LA MANZANITA
1800 SPAS 91030 595-F3
LAMAR CT
3100 LKWD 90712 765-H2
LAMAR DR
200 CLAR 91711 571-C6
LAMAR ST
600 LA 90031 634-J2
LAMAR WY
45400 LAN 93534 4015-E4
E LA MARIMBA ST
6700 LBCH 90815 796-E3
LAMARR AV
3900 CULC 90232 672-F2
LA MASINA CT
24300 CALB 91302 559-D5
LA MASITA CT
4600 CHNO 91710 641-F4
LAMAT RD
500 LHH 90631 708-D3
LAMBERT AV
11600 ELMN 91732 597-E6
E LAMBERT AV
10900 ELMN 91731 597-D6
11300 ELMN 91732 597-D6
LAMBERT DR
500 PAS 91107 566-E3
2000 PAS 91104 566-D3
2800 LA 90068 593-G2
LAMBERT RD
500 LHB 90631 708-C7
1200 LHB 92835 708-C7
2600 LACo 90604 708-A6
11500 FUL 92835 708-C7
11800 LACo 90606 677-A7
12400 WHIT 90606 707-B1
12600 WHIT 90602 707-B1
13400 WHIT 90605 707-E3
14300 WHIT 90603 707-E3
14400 LACo 90604 707-E3
15200 WHIT 90604 707-H5
E LAMBERT RD
100 BREA 92821 709-C6
100 LHB 90631 708-F6
3000 OrCo 92821 709-G6
W LAMBERT RD
100 BREA 92821 709-A6
100 LHB 90631 708-J6
600 BREA 92821 708-J6
LAMBERTON AV
20900 CRSN 90810 764-J5
LAMBERTON PL
27000 SCTA 91354 4550-G1
LAMBETH LN
\- ING 90305 703-F3
LAMBETH ST
3400 LFlz 90027 594-C2
LAMEGO DR
1600 GLDL 91207 564-G1
LAMER ST
2600 BURB 91504 533-E3
N LAMER ST
100 BURB 91506 563-F1
800 BURB 91506 533-E7
2000 BURB 91504 533-E2
S LAMER ST
100 BURB 91506 563-F3
LA MERCED RD
7800 LACo 91770 636-E3
8100 RSMD 91770 636-E3
LA MESA CT
2700 LAN 93535 4106-F1
LA MESA DR
1000 FUL 92833 738-E5
1600 LVRN 91750 570-F5
1800 SMCA 90402 631-D5
14300 LMRD 90638 737-H3
LA MESA PL
1000 FUL 92833 738-E5
1000 PAS 91103 565-G2
LA MESA ST
14900 LA 91342 481-H2

S LA MESA ST
200 POM 91766 641-B2
LA MESA WY
2500 SMCA 90402 631-E5
7700 BPK 90620 767-F3
LA MESA OAKS DR
1700 SDMS 91773 570-E6
LA MESETA WY
16000 WHIT 90603 707-J2
LA MESITA DR
1500 HacH 91745 678-A2
S LA MESITA DR
1700 HacH 91745 678-A2
1700 HacH 91745 677-J3
LA MIRADA AV
300 SMRO 91108 596-A2
4500 LA 90029 594-A5
5300 LA 90029 593-H5
5500 LA 90038 593-E5
LA MIRADA BLVD Rt#-N8
7500 BPK 90621 737-G4
10400 LACo 90604 707-G7
11500 LMRD 90638 707-G7
12200 LMRD 90638 737-G2
12900 LMRD 90639 737-G2
LA MIRADA CIR
7700 BPK 90620 767-F3
LA MIRADA RD
200 PAS 91105 565-E4
LA MIRADA ST
1000 LHB 90631 708-B4
LAMKINS ST
10800 SunV 91352 503-A7
LA MOINE ST
15500 HacH 91745 678-A5
E LA MOINE ST
15600 HacH 91745 678-B5
LA MONA CIR
7700 BPK 90620 767-F3
LA MONDE ST
15500 HacH 91745 678-B4
E LA MONDE ST
15800 HacH 91745 678-B4
LAMONETTE ST
1000 CLAR 91711 571-F5
LA MONT DR
500 MONP 91755 636-B3
LAMONT DR
200 HiPk 90042 595-D2
LA MONTANA CIR
4800 Tarz 91356 560-H4
LA MONTANA PL
18900 Tarz 91356 560-H4
LA MORADA PL
\- POM 91766 640-F5
LAMOS ST
500 ING 90302 703-C1
900 ING 90302 673-C7
N LAMOS ST
700 ING 90302 703-C1
LA MOUR CT
23800 TOR 90501 793-H2
LAMOUR CT
44800 LAN 93535 4016-D5
LAMOUR DR
100 LCF 91011 535-D5
LAMPARA DR
23500 SCTA 91355 4550-G5
LAMPASAS RD
5200 Actn 93510 4374-G1
LAMPLIGHT PL
\- SCTA 91350 4550-J2
\- SCTA 91350 4551-A2
LAMPLIGHTER LN
4300 CHNO 91710 641-E5
21800 LACo 90265 629-E5
LAMP POST LN
1900 LCF 91011 534-J1
LAMPSON AV
3500 SLB 90740 796-J6
LAMPSON ST
9900 LACo 90601 676-J2
9900 LACo 90601 677-A2
LANA CT
2200 SIMI 93063 499-C1
LANACA ST
18100 LACo 91744 678-J2
18100 LACo 91744 679-A1
LANAI DR
16500 Enc 91436 561-E5
LANAI RD
4100 Enc 91436 561-E5
LANAI ST
1800 WCOV 91792 638-H4
5100 LBCH 90808 796-B1
E LANAI ST
7100 LBCH 90808 796-F1
LANARK ST
1000 Eagl 90041 565-D6
9800 SunV 91352 533-A2
13700 PanC 91402 532-A2
14500 PanC 91402 531-H2
15300 VanN 91406 531-C2
17500 Nor 91325 531-C2
17700 Res 91335 531-A2
18500 Res 91335 530-F2
19700 Win 91306 530-C2
20800 LA 91304 530-A3
22100 LA 91304 529-G3
LANCASHIRE CIR
8000 LPMA 90623 767-B4

LANCASHIRE PL
1400 PAS 91103 565-D1
LANCASTER AV
2400 Boyl 90033 635-C3
LANCASTER BLVD
100 LAN 93534 4015-H5
100 LAN 93535 4015-J6
300 LAN 93535 4016-C5
2000 LAN 93536 4015-A6
4000 LAN 93536 4014-D6
4000 LACo 93535 4016-F5
4600 LAN 93535 4017-A5
4600 LACo 93535 4017-A5
8700 LACo 93536 4013-D6
9000 LACo 93535 4018-B5
10000 LAN 93536 4013-D6
LANCASTER CT
800 CLAR 91711 571-F7
LANCASTER DR
800 CLAR 91711 571-F7
LANCASTER RD
12100 LACo 93536 4013-B4
LANCASTER WY
1000 LAN 93534 4015-G6
LANCE CT
\- VanN 91405 532-B5
N LANCE CT
\- LPUE 91744 638-E7
LANCE PL
24000 CanP 91307 529-E5
LANCEBROOK DR
27200 SCTA 91351 4551-E2
LANCELOT AV
13400 NRWK 90650 737-A2
LANCELOT LN
11700 BelA 90077 591-G3
LANCER AV
2800 POM 91768 640-B2
LANCER CT
10000 LA 90210 592-B3
LANCEWOOD AV
1200 HacH 91745 678-C2
LANCEWOOD PL
\- PMDL 93551 4285-D3
LANDA ST
1400 Echo 90026 594-F5
1500 LA 90039 594-C5
3000 LA 90039 594-D5
LANDALE ST
10600 LA 91602 563-A4
11000 LA 91602 562-H4
11700 LA 91607 562-G4
12200 LA 91604 562-E4
13100 Shrm 91423 562-D4
LANDALUCE LN
20100 WAL 91789 639-E5
LANDAU AV
44800 LAN 93535 4016-D5
LANDAU PL
1700 HacH 91745 678-E4
6100 LACo 93536 4104-E4
LANDER CIR
500 CLAR 91711 571-E7
LANDER DR
20300 WdHl 91364 560-D4
LANDEROS AV
4100 LVRN 91750 570-H7
LANDFAIR AV
400 Wwd 90024 632-A2
LANDFAIR RD
3400 PAS 91107 566-G3
LANDING AV
1100 SLB 90740 826-F4
LANDING PL
\- LAN 93536 4014-J5
LANDINO DR
6100 WLKV 91362 557-F3
LANDIS AV
4300 BALD 91706 598-C3
LANDIS ST
1700 BURB 91504 533-E5
LANDIS VIEW LN
8600 RSMD 91770 636-G5
LANDMARK CT
39300 PMDL 93551 4195-C5
LANDMARK DR
15800 LACo 90604 707-J7
16100 LACo 90604 708-A7
LANDMARK LN
\- BREA 92823 709-H6
LANDMARK ST
3900 CULC 90232 632-H7
39300 PMDL 93551 4195-C6
LANDMARK WY
\- SCTA 91354 4460-G4
LANDON AV
36600 PMDL 93550 4286-H2
38500 PMDL 93550 4196-H7
LANDON PL
\- SCTA 91354 4460-G6
LANDOR LN
500 PAS 91106 566-C6
LANDRA RD
\- LACo 91390 (4371-G7 See Page 4281)
LANDSBURN CIR
1100 THO 91361 557-C5
LANDSEER ST
10100 TEML 91780 597-B4
LANDSFORD ST
300 LAN 93535 4015-J5
300 LAN 93535 4016-A5

LANE CT
1200 CLAR 91711 571-A7
23400 SCTA 91354 4550-G1
LANE RANCH DR
42400 LAN 93536 4104-G5
LANESBORO DR
3100 WCOV 91792 679-D3
LANESBORO PL
23800 SCTA 91354 4550-F1
LANETT AV
9400 LACo 90605 707-D3
10300 SFSP 90605 707-C4
LANETT ST
8700 CYP 90630 767-C5
LANEWOOD AV
100 ALH 91801 595-G5
7000 Hlwd 90028 593-D4
LANFAIR AV
15100 LACo 93535 4109-D6
LANFRANCA DR
\- Saug 91350 4461-F5
LANFRANCO ST
1600 Boyl 90033 634-J5
2700 Boyl 90033 635-B6
2900 LA 90063 635-B6
3600 City 90063 635-D7
LANG AV
300 LPUE 91744 638-B4
1000 LACo 91744 638-B4
3900 LACo 91722 598-E5
N LANG AV
100 WCOV 91790 598-E6
S LANG AV
1600 WCOV 91790 638-C2
LANGDALE AV
2300 Eagl 90041 564-J7
LANGDON AV
2200 MsnH 91345 501-G2
6200 VanN 91411 531-G7
6400 VanN 91406 531-G2
8300 LA 91343 531-G2
8700 LA 91343 501-G6
LANGFIELD AV
16300 CRTS 90703 737-C6
LANGFORD AL
600 PAS 91106 565-J7
LANGFORD PL
3000 RSMD 91770 636-G2
LANGFORD ST
3800 City 90063 635-E7
LANGHALL CT
6300 AGRH 91301 557-J3
LANGHAM AV
700 COV 91724 599-E3
900 GLDR 91740 569-E7
S LANGHAM AV
5000 LACo 91724 599-E3
LANGHILL DR
14400 HacH 91745 677-H2
LANGHORN ST
300 LAN 93535 4015-J5
300 LAN 93535 4016-A5
LANGLEY PL
\- Cstc 91384 4459-G4
LANGLEY ST
300 GLDL 91205 564-H5
LANGLEY WY
1000 MONP 91755 636-B4
LANGMUIR AV
10100 Sunl 91040 503-H1
LANGPORT AV
5500 NLB 90805 765-H2
LANGSIDE AV
27000 SCTA 91351 4551-E2
28000 SCTA 91351 4461-E7
LANGSPUR CT
31800 WLKV 91361 557-D6
LANGSPUR DR
2100 HacH 91745 678-F5
LANG STATION RD
14300 LACo 91387 4552-H1
LANGSTON PL
\- RowH 91748 679-B7
LANGSTON ST
25400 SCTA 91355 4550-F6
LANHAM DR
700 LACo 91744 638-H6
LANIA LN
9500 LA 90210 592-F4
LANIGAN AV
9100 SunV 91352 503-B7
LANKERSHIM BLVD
2700 LA 91604 563-A6
3600 LA 90068 563-A6
3800 Univ 91608 563-A6
4000 LA 91602 563-A3
4800 NHol 91601 563-A3
5000 NHol 91601 562-H1
5800 NHol 91601 532-H6
6000 NHol 91606 532-H6
6800 NHol 91605 532-H4
8400 SunV 91352 532-H4
8700 SunV 91352 502-H7
LANKIN ST
8200 DWNY 90242 705-J7
LANNING DR
9900 LACo 90604 707-E4
13400 LACo 90605 707-C3
LANNY AV
600 LPUE 91744 638-E6
LANSBURY AV
3000 CLAR 91711 601-B3

LANSDALE ST
11700 ELMN 91732 637-E1
LANSDOWNE AV
1800 LACo 90032 635-E2
1800 LA 90032 635-F1
LANSDOWNE PL
\- LACo 92821 709-B1
LANSFORD ST
8800 RSMD 91770 596-H5
LANSING AV
800 Wilm 90744 794-G6
LANTANA AV
700 BREA 92821 738-J2
2700 FUL 92835 738-J2
LANTANA CT
3100 PMDL 93551 4195-C3
LANTANA DR
1000 HiPk 90042 565-E7
LANTANA LN
2600 CULC 90230 672-G5
LANTANA PL
\- RHE 90274 793-H6
LANTANA ST
600 LVRN 91750 600-D3
2600 COMP 90220 734-E6
LANTANA WY
\- CYP 90630 767-E6
1600 POM 91766 641-B4
LANTE ST
4800 BALD 91706 598-E3
LANTERMAN LN
1200 LCF 91011 535-A4
LANTERMAN TER
2400 LA 90039 594-C3
LANTERN LN
13000 LMRD 90638 737-J1
LANTO ST
5500 BGDN 90201 675-G7
6700 CMRC 90040 676-A7
LANVIEW LN
\- Saug 91350 4461-F6
E LANZIT AV
100 LA 90061 704-D6
600 LA 90059 704-E6
LA PALMA AV
1600 PMDL 93550 4286-D4
4400 CRTS 90703 767-B4
4400 LPMA 90623 767-B4
6000 BPK 90620 767-H3
W LA PALMA AV
8300 BPK 90620 767-J3
LA PALMA CT
26000 SCTA 91355 4550-F4
LA PALMA LN
7000 LACo 91775 566-H7
LA PALOMA
\- AVA 90704 5923-G2
LA PALOMA AV
\- ALH 91801 595-H5
300 ALH 91803 595-H5
600 Wilm 90744 824-E2
1900 ALH 91803 635-H1
LA PALOMA CANYON RD
\- LACo - (4724-H6 See Page 4643)
\- Tuj 91042 (4724-H6 See Page 4643)
E LA PASADA ST
5300 LBCH 90815 796-C6
LA PASAITA CT
17700 RowH 91748 678-H5
LA PAZ DR
500 LACo 91107 566-E6
500 SMRO 91108 566-E6
2200 CLAR 91711 571-D7
3000 LA 90039 594-C3
LA PAZ LN
2900 DBAR 91765 679-J7
3600 MAL 90265 629-A6
7100 LPMA 90623 767-C2
43600 LAN 93535 4106-F1
LA PAZ RD
1700 Alta 91001 536-C6
11000 WHIT 90603 708-A5
LA PAZ ST
5500 LBCH 90803 826-C1
40300 PMDL 93551 4195-C3
N LA PEER DR
100 BHLS 90211 632-H2
100 LA 90048 632-H1
100 WHWD 90048 592-H7
100 WHWD 90048 632-H1
600 WHWD 90069 592-H7
S LA PEER DR
100 BHLS 90211 632-H3
100 LA 90048 632-H1
1100 LA 90035 632-H3
LA PENA AV
15800 LMRD 90638 737-J2
LA PERLA AV
1400 LBCH 90815 796-C5
LAPINE AV
28600 SCTA 91390 4461-D3
LA PINTORESCA DR
1200 PAS 91103 565-H2
LAPLANTE WY
28000 SCTA 91350 4461-D6
LA PLATA AV
2800 HacH 91745 678-A6
LA PLAZA CT
400 LHB 90631 708-C5
LA PLAZA DR
200 LHB 90631 708-C5

LA PLUMA DR
14400 LMRD 90638 737-H3
LA POMELO RD
12200 LMRD 90638 707-H7
12200 LMRD 90638 737-H1
LA PORTADA
600 SPAS 91030 595-G3
LA PORTE DR
700 LCF 91011 535-C4
LA PORTE ST
\- ARCD 91006 567-D4
LA PRADA ST
6000 HiPk 90042 565-D7
6000 HiPk 90042 595-D1
LA PRADA TER
5900 HiPk 90042 595-D1
5900 HiPk 90042 565-D7
LA PRESA AV
1000 RSMD 91770 636-G3
4700 RSMD 91770 596-G5
5300 LACo 91776 596-G4
6700 LACo 91775 596-G1
6700 LACo 91775 566-G7
LA PRESA DR
200 LHB 90631 708-D4
300 PAS 91107 566-F5
800 LACo 91107 566-F6
6900 LA 90068 593-D3
LAPS CT
\- LACo 91390 4373-D6
LA PUEBLA AV
8700 WHIT 90605 707-G3
LA PUENTE DR
20900 WAL 91789 639-G3
LA PUENTE RD
3000 WCOV 91792 679-D1
19400 WAL 91789 679-D1
19800 WAL 91789 639-J5
E LA PUENTE RD
2700 WCOV 91792 679-C2
17900 LACo 91744 678-J1
18100 LACo 91744 679-A1
19000 LACo 91792 679-C2
LA PUERTA ST
1100 LA 90023 675-C1
LA PUNTA DR
6300 LA 90068 593-F2
LAPWORTH DR
5800 AGRH 91301 558-C4
LA QUILLA DR
22400 Chat 91311 499-H1
LA QUINTA CT
\- PMDL 93551 4195-B3
2000 LHB 90631 738-E2
LA QUINTA DR
200 GLDR 91741 570-A6
LA QUINTA LN
\- PMDL 93551 4195-H3
LA QUINTA ST
13200 LMRD 90638 737-J1
LA QUINTA WY
16500 WHIT 90603 708-A5
LARA ST
1000 Boyl 90033 635-C4
LARAINE CIR
1600 LA 90732 823-H4
LA RAMADA AV
1600 ARCD 91006 567-C2
LA RAMADA PL
\- POM 91766 640-D4
LA RAMBLA
900 BURB 91501 534-B6
LARAMIE AV
5600 WdHl 91367 560-D1
6500 Win 91306 530-D1
9500 Chat 91311 500-D4
LARAMIE DR
900 SDMS 91773 570-D7
900 SDMS 91773 600-D1
LARAMIE PL
10500 Chat 91311 500-D4
LARAMIE ST
37300 PMDL 93552 4286-J3
LARAMIE WY
11700 LACo 91390 4373-C5
S LARAWAY AV
9500 ING 90301 703-B4
LARBERT ST
19800 SCTA 91351 4461-E7
LARBOARD LN
5800 AGRH 91301 557-G4
LARBROOK DR
16900 HacH 91745 678-F5
LARCH AV
10800 Lenx 90304 703-D6
11100 HAW 90304 703-D6
14300 LNDL 90260 733-D5
LARCH CIR
8100 BPK 90620 767-J4
LARCH LN
\- LA 90065 594-F1
LARCH PL
3700 LVRN 91750 570-F7
LARCH ST
1400 ALH 91801 595-H4
1400 ALH 91801 596-A4
10300 Lenx 90304 703-D5
S LARCH ST
700 ING 90301 703-D3
10200 ING 90304 703-D4
LARCHBLUFF DR
27400 RPV 90275 793-B7

LARCHFORK RD
35300 Actn 93510 4375-B2
N LARCHMONT BLVD
100 LA 90004 593-F7
100 LA 90004 633-F1
S LARCHMONT BLVD
100 LA 90004 633-F1
LARCHMONT ST
2100 POM 91767 601-B5
LARCHWOOD AV
800 HacH 91745 678-C1
LARCHWOOD CIR
6900 CanP 91307 529-F6
LARCHWOOD DR
700 BREA 92821 738-J2
37300 PMDL 93550 4286-B3
LARCO WY
1600 GLDL 91202 564-E1
1600 GLDL 91207 564-E1
LA REATA DR
3500 SBdC 91710 641-D6
LAREDO AV
700 POM 91768 600-H4
700 LVRN 91750 600-H4
14000 PRM 90723 735-G3
LAREDO DR
900 SDMS 91773 570-D7
900 SDMS 91773 600-D1
LAREDO VISTA AV
17100 LACo 93591 4199-H4
LA REINA AV
9200 DWNY 90240 706-C2
10200 DWNY 90241 706-B4
12600 DWNY 90242 705-J7
12600 DWNY 90242 735-J1
LA REINA DR
6300 Tuj 91042 504-C6
LA REINA PL
9400 Tuj 91042 504-C6
E LA REINA WY
100 LBCH 90813 795-E7
W LA REINA WY
100 LBCH 90813 795-D7
LARGA AV
3000 LA 90039 594-E2
S LARGO AV
13100 Wbrk 90222 734-J2
N LARGO ST
1600 COMP 90222 734-J2
LARGO VISTA RD
39500 LACo 93591 4200-G3
40400 LACo 93535 4110-G3
40400 LACo 93535 4200-G3
LARGO VISTA RD Rt#-N4
27400 Llan 93544 4470-F5
27400 Llan 93544 (4560-F2 See Page 4470)
27400 Valy 93563 (4560-F2 See Page 4470)
LARIAT CIR
700 LBCH 90815 796-E6
LARIAT CT
21100 WAL 91789 639-H5
LARIAT LN
3400 RHE 90274 793-E6
3500 LACo 90274 793-E6
12900 NRWK 90650 737-A1
LARIAT PL
3800 FUL 92835 738-G1
LARIAT WY
\- Actn 93510 4375-B5
LA RIATA DR
1400 LHH 90631 708-A3
LA RIBA WY
6200 HiPk 90042 595-D2
LA RICA AV
3900 BALD 91706 598-B3
LARIME RD
18500 LACo 93591 4200-B3
LARIMORE AV
600 LPUE 91744 638-E5
1200 LACo 91744 638-E4
1200 WCOV 91790 638-E3
LARISA DR
17300 CRTS 90703 736-J7
LARISSA DR
3200 Echo 90026 594-C6
LARK CT
700 LA 90065 595-A3
LARK DR
\- LACo 92397 (4652-A2 See Page 4651)
400 SBdC 92397 (4652-A2 See Page 4651)
LARK LN
\- BREA 92823 709-H6
\- PMDL 93550 4376-E7
\- PMDL 93550 4466-E1
8000 LA 90046 593-A3
LARK RD
500 SBdC 92397 (4652-B1 See Page 4651)
LARK WY
\- LACo 91387 4551-J5
LARK BAY LN
2000 LKWD 90712 765-G3
LARKDALE RD
8400 LACo 91775 596-F1
LARKE ELLEN CIR
9000 LA 90035 632-H5
LARK ELLEN AV
4400 LACo 91722 598-H2

LARK ELLEN AV
4700 COV 91722 598-H3
N LARK ELLEN AV
100 COV 91722 598-H5
100 WCOV 91791 598-H5
100 WCOV 91790 598-H7
600 LACo 91722 598-H5
S LARK ELLEN AV
100 COV 91722 598-H7
100 WCOV 91791 598-H7
100 WCOV 91790 598-H7
100 WCOV 91791 638-H2
100 WCOV 91790 638-H2
500 AZU 91702 598-H2
1400 LACo 91744 638-H2
1400 WCOV 91792 638-H4
1700 LACo 91791 638-H2
5200 LACo 91702 598-H2
LARKELLEN CT
6000 VeCo 91377 558-A2
LARK ELLEN LN
4400 LACo 91722 598-H4
LARKER AV
900 HiPk 90042 595-F1
1000 HiPk 90042 565-F7
LARKFIELD AV
2800 MNRO 91006 597-F2
LARKHALL AV
300 DUAR 91010 568-E4
LARKHAVEN PL
26200 SCTA 91321 4551-G5
E LARK HILL DR
2600 WCOV 91791 639-B2
LARKIN AV
37300 PMDL 93550 4286-A3
38400 PMDL 93550 4196-A7
LARKIN DR
100 COV 91722 599-A3
4400 LACo 91722 599-A4
5500 LACo 91702 599-A1
LARKIN PL
100 SMCA 90402 631-C6
LARKIN WY
1600 POM 91768 600-H6
LARKMAIN DR
27800 SCTA 91350 4461-C6
LARKPORT DR
13900 LACo 91746 637-H6
LARK SPRING TER
22500 DBAR 91765 680-A4
LARKSPUR AV
1200 POM 91767 601-D7
2700 BREA 92821 709-F7
LARKSPUR CT
\- BqtC 91354 4460-E6
LARKSPUR DR
7500 BPK 90620 767-J3
39700 PMDL 93551 4195-F4
LARKSPUR LN
400 GLDR 91740 569-D7
4600 LVRN 91750 570-F7
29200 MAL 90265 667-E2
45800 LAN 93534 4015-G3
LARKSPUR ST
1200 VeCo 93063 499-B4
14800 LA 91342 481-H2
LARKSPUR WY
\- SCTA 91354 4460-G3
LARKSPUR FIELD ST
14700 SCTA 91387 4462-G6
LARKSTONE DR
20600 DBAR 91789 679-G4
LARKSTONE LN
900 GLDL 91206 565-A3
LARK TREE WY
1500 HacH 91745 678-F4
LARKVALE DR
6900 RPV 90275 792-G7
LARKVANE RD
1500 RowH 91748 678-J5
LARKWOOD AV
4500 WdHl 91364 559-G4
LARKWOOD DR
2500 FUL 92833 738-B5
E LARKWOOD ST
1000 WCOV 91790 638-G1
1400 WCOV 91791 638-H1
1900 WCOV 91791 639-A1
LARMAR RD
2600 LA 90068 593-C2
LARMONA DR
2900 LACo 91107 566-F1
LARMOR AV
1300 RowH 91748 679-D4
LARNE ST
18700 RowH 91748 679-B4
LARNED LN
10500 BelA 90077 592-A4
LARO DR
28900 AGRH 91301 558-A3
29300 AGRH 91301 557-J4
LA ROCHA DR
6300 LA 90068 593-F2
LA ROCHELLE DR
22400 SCTA 91350 4460-H5
LA RODA AV
4700 Eagl 90041 565-B5
LA RONDA CIR
15900 HacH 91745 678-C4
LA ROSA DR
4800 VeCo 91377 557-G1
8900 LACo 91776 596-H5
9100 TEML 91780 596-J5

STREET
Block City ZIP Pg-Grid

LA ROSA DR
9500 TEML 91780 597-A4
LA ROSA RD
1100 ARCD 91007 566-J5
LA ROSA ST
10700 TEML 91780 597-C4
LA ROTONDA DR
3000 RPV 90275 823-E6
LARRABEE ST
1100 WHWD 90069 592-H5
1300 LA 90069 592-H5
LARRES CANYON RD
\- StvR 91381 4549-G5
LARRY AV
4600 BALD 91706 598-C3
LARRYAN DR
5700 WdHl 91367 559-E1
LARRYLYN DR
9900 WHIT 90603 708-A4
11800 LACo 90604 708-A7
12400 LACo 90604 738-A1
LARRYLYNN DR
12700 LMRD 90638 738-A1
LARSON WY
9300 Chat 91311 499-F6
9300 Chat 91311 499-F6
LARSSON ST
200 MANB 90266 732-G7
LA RUE AV
900 LVRN 91750 570-E6
LA RUE ST
13800 LA 91340 502-A2
LARWIN AV
10000 Chat 91311 499-H4
LARWIN CIR
13600 SFSP 90670 737-C2
LARWIN RD
12700 NRWK 90650 737-A2
13800 LMRD 90638 737-D2
LARWOOD ST
3000 LAN 93536 4105-B3
LA SABANA AV
12000 LMRD 90638 707-G7
12000 LMRD 90638 737-G1
LASAINE AV
5600 Enc 91316 561-C1
6500 VanN 91406 531-C4
7600 Nor 91325 531-B1
9300 Nor 91325 501-B5
11100 GrnH 91344 501-B2
LA SALINA ST
13200 LMRD 90638 737-J1
LA SALLE AV
1600 LA 90047 703-J1
1900 LA 90018 633-J6
3700 LA 90018 673-J1
3700 LA 90062 673-J3
4000 CULC 90232 672-G2
7200 LA 90047 673-J3
11100 LACo 90047 703-J6
14700 GAR 90247 733-J4
17800 GAR 90248 763-J1
20900 LA 90501 763-J5
LA SALLE ST
8600 CYP 90630 767-C5
LA SALLE CANYON DR
23700 SCTA 91321 4640-F3
LA SALOS DR
15200 WHIT 90603 707-H4
LAS ALTURAS ST
2800 LA 90068 593-C1
LA SARRA DR
6500 LAN 93536 4104-C4
LAS BRISAS
5700 LVRN 91750 570-H4
41900 LAN 93536 4105-A6
LAS BRISAS CIR
100 POM 91768 640-G1
LAS BRISAS DR
2300 DUAR 91010 568-C5
LAS BRISAS RD
\- BqtC 91354 4460-E3
LAS BRISAS TER
5700 PMDL 93551 4194-F2
LAS BRISAS WY
900 SIGH 90755 795-E3
1100 LACo 91107 566-F7
LAS CANOAS RD
1300 PacP 90272 630-J4
LAS CASAS AV
300 PacP 90272 630-H6
4000 CLAR 91711 600-J1
4100 CLAR 91711 570-J7
LAS CASAS PL
16500 PacP 90272 630-H4
LAS COLIMAS
1100 LVRN 91750 570-H4
LAS COLINAS AV
2000 Eagl 90041 565-A7
2200 Eagl 90041 564-J7
LAS COLINAS LN
4700 LCF 91011 535-B3
LAS CRUCES DR
4200 Shrm 91403 561-H5
LAS CUMBRES DR
16100 WHIT 90603 707-J2
16200 WHIT 90603 708-A2
S LA SEDA RD
300 LACo 91744 679-A2
LA SELVA PL
2400 PVE 90274 793-B3
LA SENA AV
700 WCOV 91790 598-E6

LA SENA AV
3900 BALD 91706 598-E3
N LA SENA AV
200 WCOV 91790 598-E6
LA SENA CT
700 POM 91768 600-H4
LA SENDA DR
1000 FUL 92835 738-E2
LA SENDA PL
1700 SPAS 91030 596-A3
LA SERENA DR
500 COV 91723 599-C6
800 GLDR 91740 569-C7
1200 GLDR 91740 599-C1
1300 BREA 92821 708-H4
6100 LACo 91740 569-C7
10100 WHIT 90603 707-H4
S LA SERENA DR
300 WCOV 91791 639-C1
LA SERNA AV
300 LHB 90631 708-D4
LA SERNA DR
9400 WHIT 90603 707-H5
9400 WHIT 90605 707-H3
10800 LACo 90604 707-H6
11900 LMRD 90638 707-H7
LAS ESTRELLAS DR
30600 MAL 90265 627-A7
LASEY WK
400 LA 90065 595-B3
LAS FALDAS DR
3100 FUL 92835 738-G2
LAS FLORES AV
900 MTBL 90640 636-F7
1600 SMRO 91108 595-J1
1600 SMRO 91030 595-J1
15100 LMRD 90638 737-G1
15100 LMRD 90638 707-G7
E LAS FLORES AV
\- ARCD 91006 597-D1
W LAS FLORES AV
\- ARCD 91007 597-B1
LAS FLORES CT
3700 LA 90034 672-F2
LAS FLORES DR
1200 Eagl 90041 565-A5
1600 GLDL 91207 564-G1
1900 SPAS 91030 595-J1
2300 Eagl 90041 564-J5
3500 ELMN 91731 597-C7
E LAS FLORES DR
\- Alta 91001 535-J4
300 Alta 91001 536-A5
W LAS FLORES DR
100 Alta 91001 535-H4
LAS FLORES MTWY
\- GLDL 91202 534-E7
\- GLDL 91207 534-E7
\- GLDL 91208 534-E7
LAS FLORES ST
2500 ALH 91803 635-H2
LAS FLORES CANYON RD
1900 LACo 90265 629-E3
3500 MAL 90265 629-F3
LAS FLORES HEIGHTS RD
\- Top 90290 629-G3
20200 LACo 90265 629-F3
LAS FLORES MESA DR
20600 LACo 90265 629-G6
20600 MAL 90265 629-G6
LASH LN
6600 LA 90068 593-D2
LASHBROOK AV
2600 SELM 91733 636-J2
3000 ELMN 91733 636-J2
3500 RSMD 91770 596-J7
LASHBURN ST
600 LA 91342 481-J7
600 SFER 91342 481-J7
14900 LACo 90604 707-G5
15400 WHIT 90604 707-H5
15700 WHIT 90603 707-J5
16200 WHIT 90603 708-A5
LASHEART DR
4500 LCF 91011 535-A2
LA SHELL DR
9200 Tuj 91042 504-B6
LASHER RD
5200 HIDH 91302 559-D3
E LAS HERMANAS ST
2800 RDom 90221 765-B1
LA SIERRA AV
8200 WHIT 90605 707-G2
LA SIERRA DR
\- POM 91766 640-E5
5200 LCF 91011 534-J1
13400 CHLS 91709 680-H1
E LA SIERRA DR
100 ARCD 91006 567-D7
W LA SIERRA DR
\- ARCD 91007 567-C7
LA SIERRA WY
2100 CLAR 91711 571-B7
LASITA PL
1900 RPV 90275 823-H1
LASKER AV
37300 PMDL 93550 4286-C2
S LASKY DR
100 BHLS 90212 632-E2
LAS LANAS CIR
1500 FUL 92833 738-D4

LAS LANAS CT
26100 SCTA 91355 4550-G4
LAS LANAS LN
1700 FUL 92833 738-C4
LAS LOMAS AV
\- AVA 90704 5923-G3
600 PacP 90272 630-J4
LAS LOMAS DR
100 LHB 90631 708-D7
1300 BREA 92821 708-H4
LAS LOMAS PL
1200 PacP 90272 630-J4
LAS LOMAS RD
200 DUAR 91010 568-D4
1200 IRW 91706 568-D5
E LAS LOMAS ST
5200 LBCH 90815 796-B5
S LAS LOMITAS DR
1900 HacH 91745 678-A3
2400 HacH 91745 677-J4
LAS LOMITAS WY
2500 LACo 91724 639-E2
LAS LUNAS ST
1400 PAS 91106 566-C3
1800 PAS 91107 566-D3
LAS LUNITAS AV
10300 Tuj 91042 504-A2
LAS MANANITAS DR
22900 SCTA 91354 4550-H1
26800 SCTA 91354 4460-H7
S LAS MARIAS AV
2700 HacH 91745 678-A5
LA SOLANA DR
1300 Alta 91001 536-B6
LA SOMBRA DR
3400 LA 90068 563-D7
LA SOMBRA WY
3100 FUL 92835 738-F2
LA SONORA DR
30600 MAL 90265 627-A6
LAS PALMAS AV
3300 GLDL 91208 534-G4
3700 PMDL 93550 4196-H7
N LAS PALMAS AV
100 LA 90004 633-E1
300 LA 90004 593-E7
700 LA 90038 593-E5
1300 Hlwd 90028 593-E4
1900 LA 90068 593-E3
S LAS PALMAS AV
100 LA 90004 633-E2
300 LA 90020 633-E2
LAS PALMAS CT
\- BqtC 91354 4460-E3
E LAS PALMAS DR
100 FUL 92835 738-H1
100 LHB 90631 738-H1
W LAS PALMAS DR
100 FUL 92835 738-F1
LAS PALMAS RD
800 PAS 91105 565-F4
LAS PALMAS ST
\- SCTA 91355 4460-D6
LAS PALMERAS AV
15800 LMRD 90638 737-J2
LAS PALMITAS
1700 SPAS 91030 595-F3
LAS PALOMAS DR
1500 LHH 90631 708-B1
15800 WHIT 90605 677-J7
15800 WHIT 90605 678-A7
15800 WHIT 90605 708-A1
LAS PASADAS DR
8200 WHIT 90605 707-G2
LAS PIEDRAS TER
\- PMDL 93551 4194-G2
LAS PILAS RD
21300 WdHl 91364 560-B5
LASPINO LN
200 DBAR 91765 640-D6
LAS PLUMAS LN
7200 Tuj 91042 504-A5
LAS POSADAS DR
\- DUAR 91010 568-A5
LAS POSAS ST
8800 PRV 90660 676-G2
LAS POSITAS RD
2400 GLDL 91208 534-J6
LAS POSITAS WY
\- SCTA 91355 4460-D6
LAS PUERTAS ST
14000 LMRD 90638 737-J3
LAS PULGAS PL
1100 PacP 90272 630-J4
LAS PULGAS RD
900 PacP 90272 630-J4
LAS RIENDAS CT
\- FUL 92835 738-J1
LAS RIENDAS DR
200 FUL 92835 738-G1
1200 LHB 90631 738-G1
LAS RIENDAS WY
1100 LACo 91107 566-G7
LAS ROCAS DR
300 SMAD 91024 567-B1
LAS ROSAS DR
1000 WCOV 91791 639-C3
LASSALETTE ST
13400 LACo 91746 637-J3
13600 LACo 91746 638-A3
13600 LPUE 91746 638-A3
14300 LPUE 91744 638-B4
14600 LACo 91744 638-B4

LASSEN AV
1800 CLAR 91711 571-E7
LASSEN CIR
6600 BPK 90620 767-F7
LASSEN CT
\- ANA 92804 767-J7
1100 SDMS 91773 570-E5
17300 Nor 91325 501-B5
LASSEN DR
6500 BPK 90620 767-F7
LASSEN ST
14700 LA 91343 501-E5
14700 PanC 91402 501-H5
14700 MsnH 91345 501-H5
16900 Nor 91325 501-A5
17900 Nor 91330 501-A5
18100 Nor 91325 500-H5
18300 Nor 91324 500-G5
19700 Chat 91311 500-B5
22000 Chat 91311 499-H5
27800 Cstc 91384 4459-G3
LASSERON DR
\- PMDL 93552 4287-E1
LASSITER DR
1400 WAL 91789 639-F3
LASSO DR
19000 LACo 93591 4200-C3
21300 DBAR 91765 679-H6
LASSO LN
21700 WAL 91789 639-J5
LAS TERRENO LN
\- BqtC 91354 4460-E3
LAS TUNAS DR
\- ARCD 91007 597-B3
8800 TEML 91780 596-H3
9600 TEML 91780 597-B3
14700 HacH 91745 677-H2
E LAS TUNAS DR
100 SGBL 91776 596-F3
W LAS TUNAS DR
100 SGBL 91776 596-D3
900 ALH 91801 596-D3
LAS TUNAS TR
\- LACo 91390 4460-G1
LA SUBIDA DR
15100 HacH 91745 677-J4
15200 HacH 91745 678-A4
LA SUBIDA PL
4600 Tarz 91356 560-J4
LA SUVIDA DR
3100 LA 90068 563-D7
LAS VECINAS DR
13600 LACo 91746 637-J3
13700 LPUE 91746 637-J3
13700 LPUE 91746 638-B5
14800 LPUE 91744 638-B5
E LAS VECINAS DR
13900 LPUE 91746 638-A4
LAS VEGAS AV
2100 POM 91767 600-J5
LAS VEGAS ST
1500 Boyl 90033 634-J4
LAS VIRGENES RD
5100 CALB 91302 558-H3
5100 LACo 91302 558-H3
5700 VeCo 91302 558-H3
LAS VIRGENES RD Rt#-N1
1000 LACo 91302 588-G3
2200 CALB 91302 588-G3
2700 CALB 91301 588-G3
2700 Ago 91301 588-G3
3700 CALB 91302 558-H7
4800 LACo 91302 558-H7
LAS VIRGENES CANYON RD
1600 LACo 91302 588-G5
E LAS VIRGENES CANYON RD
23600 VeCo 91302 529-A7
23600 VeCo 91302 558-H2
LASZLO ST
44800 LAN 93534 4015-E6
LATANA CT
23600 SCTA 91355 4550-G5
LA TAZA DR
1700 LCF 91011 534-J2
1700 LCF 91011 535-A2
LATCHFORD AV
900 HacH 91745 638-A7
1000 HacH 91745 677-J1
1000 HacH 91745 678-A1
LATCHWOOD LN
300 LHB 90631 738-E1
LATENTE DR
100 PMDL 93550 4195-J3
LATERINA WY
\- PMDL 93552 4287-D3
LA TERRAZA
400 SPAS 91030 595-F4
LATHAM ST
5100 LA 90011 674-F4
LATHROP ST
5000 LA 90032 595-F4
LA TIENDA RD
31600 THO 91362 557-D5
31600 WLKV 91362 557-D5
LA TIERRA CT
11700 Nor 91326 480-H7
LA TIERRA ST
2600 PAS 91107 566-E4
LA TIERRA WY
\- LA 91342 482-E3

LATIGO LN
\- RHE 90274 793-C5
LATIGO BAY VIEW DR
27400 MAL 90265 627-J6
LATIGO CANYON RD
200 LACo 90265 587-D6
1400 LACo 90265 627-F1
4200 MAL 90265 627-J6
4700 MAL 90265 628-A7
6300 MAL 90265 668-B1
LATIGO SHORE DR
26500 MAL 90265 628-C7
26500 MAL 90265 668-B1
LATIGO SHORE PL
26700 MAL 90265 668-B1
LA TIJERA BLVD
1100 ING 90302 673-A7
1100 LA 90056 673-A7
5000 LadH 90056 673-A7
6800 Wch 90045 673-A7
6900 Wch 90045 703-A1
7200 Wch 90045 702-H3
10100 PdlR 90293 702-D4
LATIJERA PKWY
8800 Wch 90045 702-G3
LATIMER LN
10300 BelA 90077 592-A3
LATIMER RD
500 LA 90402 631-B6
6300 SIMI 93063 499-C3
LATIN WY
1000 LA 90065 594-J2
LATIUM WY
20000 LACo 91789 679-E5
LATONA AV
4200 LA 90031 595-B5
LATONA RD
4300 LA 90031 595-B5
LA TORRE DR
\- POM 91766 640-F5
LA TORTOLA DR
200 WAL 91789 679-E1
300 WAL 91789 639-E7
LA TOUR WY
4200 LCF 91011 534-J3
4200 GLDL 91011 534-J3
LA TRAVESIA DR
2900 FUL 92835 738-E2
LA TREMOLINA LN
8500 WHIT 90605 707-G3
LA TREVESIA DR
3100 FUL 92835 738-E2
LATROBE ST
3600 LA 90031 595-C5
LA TUNA CANYON RD
6300 SunV 91352 504-A6
6300 Tuj 91042 504-A6
6700 SunV 91352 503-B7
LAUDER ST
1100 CRSN 90745 764-F6
LAUDERDALE AV
4000 GLDL 91214 504-D7
4000 GLDL 91214 534-D1
LAUGHLIN CT
600 LA 90013 634-G5
LAUGHLIN ST
2200 LCF 91011 504-H7
2400 LaCr 91214 504-G7
LAUGHLIN PARK DR
1900 LFlz 90027 593-H3
LAUGHTON WY
11800 Nor 91326 480-J6
LAUN ST
200 Alta 91001 535-G7
LAUNER DR
1200 LHB 90631 708-D4
LAUNER RD
\- BREA 92821 708-J5
LAURA AV
400 LPUE 91744 678-G1
1900 HNTP 90255 674-H5
LAURA LN
7300 Res 91335 530-G5
LAURA ST
500 LHB 90631 708-G5
1300 SBdC 92397 (4652-D2
See Page 4651)
7400 DWNY 90242 705-H5
LAURA ANN LN
\- VanN 91405 531-J4
LAURA LA PLANTE DR
28100 AGRH 91301 558-C6
LAURA LEE LN
1900 LMTA 90717 793-H4
LAUREL AV
100 BREA 92821 709-B7
100 ARCD 91006 567-D4
1100 MANB 90266 732-G4
1400 GLDR 91741 569-H4
1400 POM 91768 640-D1
5400 PMDL 93552 4287-C4
8300 WHIT 90605 707-D2
9100 LACo 90605 707-C3
10500 SFSP 90670 707-B6
10700 SFSP 90605 707-B6
12100 LACo 90605 737-B1
12400 DWNY 90242 705-H6
E LAUREL AV
\- SMAD 91024 567-B2
400 GLDR 91741 569-F4
N LAUREL AV
100 LA 90048 633-B1
300 LA 90048 593-B7

N LAUREL AV
700 LA 90046 593-B5
1000 WHWD 90046 593-B5
S LAUREL AV
100 LA 90048 633-B1
W LAUREL AV
\- SMAD 91024 567-A2
200 SMAD 91024 566-J2
300 GLDR 91741 569-D4
500 POM 91768 640-F1
LAUREL CIR
700 MONP 91755 636-D4
LAUREL CT
14600 SCTA 91387 4462-G4
21600 WAL 91789 639-H5
37500 PMDL 93552 4287-A3
LAUREL DR
\- Alta 91001 535-H4
\- RPV 90275 822-F2
1700 MONP 91755 636-D4
LAUREL LN
600 MNRO 91016 567-H2
1200 BHLS 90210 592-E6
12000 LA 91604 562-G6
LAUREL PL
700 MONP 91755 636-D4
2700 SGAT 90280 704-J3
2800 SGAT 90280 705-A3
9700 Wats 90002 704-H4
22400 SCTA 91390 4460-J3
24000 CALB 91302 589-E1
LAUREL ST
1100 PAS 91103 565-E1
1300 LACo 90044 703-J7
1400 SPAS 91030 595-H3
8700 BLF 90706 735-J6
8700 BLF 90706 736-A6
9200 Wats 90002 704-H4
12800 DWNY 90242 705-G7
E LAUREL ST
100 GLDL 91205 564-E7
300 COMP 90221 735-A4
W LAUREL ST
100 GLDL 91204 564-E7
300 COMP 90220 734-G5
LAUREL WY
500 LHB 90631 708-C6
1000 BHLS 90210 592-E6
1300 LA 90210 592-E5
LAUREL BAY DR
1800 PAS 91105 565-D6
LAUREL BLUFF PL
5600 AGRH 91301 557-J5
LAURELBROOK CIR
18300 CRTS 90703 767-D1
LAURELBROOK CT
17400 CRTS 90703 737-C7
LAURELBROOK PL
17900 CRTS 90703 737-C7
17900 CRTS 90703 767-C1
LAURELBROOK WY
16600 CRTS 90703 737-C6
LAUREL CANYON BLVD
1500 LA 90046 593-A3
1700 LA 90069 593-A3
2500 LA 90046 592-J2
3100 LA 91604 592-J1
3300 LA 91604 562-G5
4800 LA 91607 562-G5
5900 LA 91607 532-G7
6000 NHol 91606 532-G7
6800 NHol 91605 532-G4
8100 SunV 91352 532-F1
8800 SunV 91352 502-D5
9100 Pcma 91331 502-D5
10700 LA 91340 502-A2
11300 LA 91340 501-J1
11700 LA 91342 501-J1
11700 LA 91342 481-H6
N LAUREL CANYON PL
2800 LA 90046 592-J1
2800 LA 90046 593-A1
LAUREL CANYON RD
1800 LA 90046 593-A3
LAUREL CREEK CIR
27700 SCTA 91354 4460-H5
LAURELCREST DR
3500 LA 91604 562-H6
LAUREL CREST LN
\- SCTA 91351 4461-G7
LAURELCREST LN
24700 StvR 91381 4640-D2
LAURELCREST RD
11400 LA 91604 562-H6
LAURELDALE AV
12900 DWNY 90242 735-J1
LAUREL GLEN CIR
27400 SCTA 91354 4460-H6
LAURELGROVE AV
3800 LA 91604 562-F4
4700 LA 91607 562-F3
6000 NHol 91606 532-F7
6700 NHol 91605 532-F2
LAUREL HILLS RD
11800 LA 91604 562-G6
LAURELHURST DR
10600 ELMN 91731 637-C1
LAURELMONT DR
8000 LA 90046 593-A2
LAURELMONT PL
2300 LA 90046 593-A3
LAUREL OAK CT
\- StvR 91381 4550-C5

E LAUREL OAK DR
800 AZU 91702 569-B5
LAUREL PARK RD
18400 LACo 90220 765-A3
LAUREL PASS AV
2400 LA 90046 592-H2
LAUREL RIDGE DR
24700 MAL 90265 628-G6
LAURELRIM DR
21600 DBAR 91765 679-J5
LAUREL TERRACE DR
12000 LA 91604 562-F6
LAURELVALE DR
3200 LA 91604 562-H7
LAUREL VALLEY DR
400 AZU 91702 568-H4
LAUREL VIEW DR
8000 LA 90069 593-A4
LAURELWOOD AV
\- SIMI 93063 499-A2
6400 ING 90302 673-A7
LAURELWOOD DR
11600 LA 91604 562-G6
LAUREL WOOD LN
14200 CHLS 91709 680-H3
LAURELWOOD LN
\- SCTA 91354 4460-F5
7600 LPMA 90623 767-C3
43200 LAN 93536 4105-C3
S LAURELWOOD LN
9900 DWNY 90242 736-D2
LAURELWOOD WY
700 WAL 91789 639-J5
LAUREN CT
\- LACo 91789 679-F6
LAUREN LN
\- LA 91304 529-G4
\- Saug 91350 4461-F6
LAURENS AV
4100 BALD 91706 598-C4
LAURENT ST
20800 Chat 91311 500-C2
LAURETTE ST
4500 TOR 90503 763-A7
LAURICE AV
3200 Alta 91001 535-J4
LAURIE CT
1600 LAN 93535 4016-C5
LAURIE DR
11200 LA 91604 562-J6
LAURIE LN
\- PMDL 93551 4195-E7
2700 LVRN 91750 600-H3
LAURIE PL
3400 LA 91604 562-J6
W LAURIN ST
1500 ONT 91762 641-H5
LAURINDA AV
300 LBCH 90803 796-E7
LAURISTON AV
10300 WLA 90025 632-E4
10400 LA 90064 632-D5
LAURITA AV
3700 LACo 91107 566-H6
LAURRIE LN
13700 LACo 90601 637-H6
LAUSANNE CT
14000 LACo 90604 707-D6
LAUSANNE DR
2200 SBdC 92397 (4652-F3
See Page 4651)
LAUSANNE RD
700 BelA 90077 592-A6
LAUSINDA AV
600 LBCH 90803 796-F7
LAUTERBACH ST
1600 LAN 93535 4106-C1
LAUTREC DR
600 FUL 92831 738-J4
LAUTREC PL
6600 RPV 90275 822-H3
LAVA PL
8700 LA 91304 529-E1
LAVAGNA WY
10600 BelA 90077 591-J4
LA VALLE ST
14200 LA 91342 482-A2
14800 LA 91342 481-J3
E LAVANTE ST
4400 LBCH 90815 796-A4
LAVE AV
1800 LBCH 90815 796-C4
LA VEDA AV
16700 SCTA 91387 4552-B1
LA VELA AV
8400 WHIT 90605 707-F2
LAVELL DR
3500 LA 90065 594-H2
LA VELLA DR
4800 VeCo 91377 557-G1
LAVENDER DR
\- DBAR 91765 680-A2
\- YBLN 92886 709-J7
LAVENDER LN
200 BREA 92821 709-D4
1000 LCF 91011 535-B2
LAVENDER PL
\- BqtC 91354 4460-E6
600 LVRN 91750 600-D3
LAVENDER WY
\- AZU 91702 569-A4
LAVENDER BELL LN
22300 WdHl 91367 529-J7

LA VENEZIA CT
\- Alta 91001 535-H6
LA VENTA DR
1200 THO 91361 557-B6
LA VEQUE ST
1200 City 90063 635-D3
N LA VERE DR
2600 LBCH 90810 795-A2
LA VEREDA DR
600 LHB 90631 708-D4
LA VEREDA RD
100 PAS 91105 565-F4
LA VEREDA ESCARPADA
\- LACo 91711 571-E3
LAVERNA AV
2100 Eagl 90041 565-A6
2200 Eagl 90041 564-J6
LA VERNE AV
\- LBCH 90803 826-B2
E LA VERNE AV
100 POM 91767 600-J5
200 POM 91767 601-A6
S LA VERNE AV
300 ELA 90022 635-G7
700 ELA 90022 675-G1
W LA VERNE AV
100 POM 91768 600-J5
100 POM 91767 600-J5
LAVERY CANYON RD
34200 LACo 91390 4373-C2
LAVETA TER
300 Echo 90026 634-E1
1100 Echo 90026 594-E7
LAVI CT
\- Tarz 91356 560-G1
LA VIDA DR
2700 LAN 93535 4016-F7
LA VIDA LN
700 ARCD 91007 597-A2
LAVIDA RD
\- BREA 92823 710-D4
\- OrCo 92823 710-B4
LA VILLA ST
8300 DWNY 90241 706-B4
LA VILLA MARINA
4700 LA 90292 672-C7
LA VINA LN
\- Alta 91001 535-G3
\- LACo 90604 707-D5
LA VINA WY
3200 LACo 91107 566-G7
LAVINIA AV
4100 LYN 90262 735-C2
LA VISTA AV
3400 BALD 91706 598-D7
LA VISTA CT
5100 LA 90004 593-G7
LA VISTA PL
1600 PAS 91103 535-E7
1600 PAS 91103 565-E1
LA VISTA TER
1400 GLDL 91208 534-G7
LA VISTA VERDE
30300 RPV 90275 823-G5
LAVITA AV
1500 POM 91768 600-F7
LA VITA CT
26100 SCTA 91355 4550-G4
LA VITA PL
1300 LHB 90631 708-D4
LAW BEHM TER
3300 FUL 92835 738-G1
LAWFORD ST
1200 GLDR 91741 569-H6
LAWLEN WY
9600 LA 90210 592-E5
LAWLER ST
10700 LA 90034 672-E1
11900 LA 90066 672-B2
LAWNDALE DR
2800 LA 90065 564-H6
LAWNHILL DR
15800 LMRD 90638 737-J1
LAWNSIDE DR
23700 SCTA 91321 4640-G2
LAWNWOOD DR
2100 FUL 92833 738-C3
LAWNWOOD ST
15500 LPUE 91744 638-E5
16300 LACo 91744 638-G5
LAWRENCE AV
500 FUL 92832 738-J7
900 Wilm 90744 794-J6
1000 LACo 91770 636-F5
1000 MTBL 90640 636-F5
1000 RSMD 91770 636-F5
2500 LAN 93536 4015-C7
8800 RSMD 91770 596-H6
N LAWRENCE AV
100 FUL 92832 738-J7
S LAWRENCE AV
100 FUL 92832 738-J7
LAWRENCE CIR
900 CLAR 91711 571-F7
LAWRENCE DR
9100 CYP 90630 767-E7
LAWRENCE LN
10000 LA 90210 592-C6
LAWRENCE PL
1600 POM 91766 641-B4
LAWRENCE ST
\- ING 90303 703-F5
700 LA 90021 634-G7

LAWRENCE ST
6000 CYP 90630 767-E7
LAWSON CT
\- Actn 93510 4465-E3
LAWSON PL
300 GLDL 91202 564-D1
S LAWSON ST
900 INDS 91748 678-J3
LAWTON ST
\- FUL 92833 738-C5
9900 SELM 91733 637-B4
LAXFORD RD
18000 LACo 91702 599-A2
E LAXFORD RD
16500 AZU 91702 598-G2
16500 LACo 91702 598-G2
17600 LACo 91702 599-A2
18500 LACo 91722 599-C2
E LAXFORD ST
100 GLDR 91740 599-E2
W LAXFORD ST
100 GLDR 91740 599-D2
S LAXORE ST
100 ANA 92804 767-J5
LAYLA AV
2500 PMDL 93551 4195-D5
LAYMAN AV
3900 PRV 90660 676-G2
N LAYTON DR
100 Brwd 90049 631-G2
S LAYTON DR
100 Brwd 90049 631-H2
LAYTON ST
1800 LACo 91104 566-C1
LAYTON WY
300 Brwd 90049 631-G1
2400 WCOV 91791 639-B2
LA ZANJA DR
1100 GLDL 91207 564-G2
LAZARD ST
12600 LA 91342 482-E2
13500 LA 91340 482-C4
13600 SFER 91340 482-C4
N LAZARD ST
200 SFER 91340 482-A6
S LAZARD ST
\- SFER 91340 482-A7
300 SFER 91340 481-J7
LAZARE LN
16400 HNTB 92649 826-J7
LAZIO WY
4900 VeCo 91377 557-G2
LAZULITE LN
1300 POM 91767 601-C6
LAZY BROOK LN
2400 HacH 91745 678-D5
LAZY CREEK CIR
500 FUL 92831 738-H5
LAZY CREEK LN
\- RHE 90274 793-C5
LAZY MEADOW DR
2900 TOR 90505 793-E5
22500 DBAR 91765 680-A5
LAZY MEADOW RD
\- POM 91766 640-G7
LAZY OAK PL
29600 AGRH 91301 557-J5
LAZY TRAIL LN
\- POM 91766 640-G5
LAZY TRAIL RD
22800 DBAR 91765 680-B5
LEA CT
\- SCTA 91354 4460-G4
8200 LACo 91770 636-F4
LEA WK
\- Cstc 91384 4459-D6
LEACH ST
12700 LA 91342 482-E2
13600 LA 91340 482-B4
13700 SFER 91340 482-B4
LEACREST DR
28500 RPV 90275 792-H7
LEADHILL DR
42800 LACo 93532 4102-J4
LEADORA AV
1200 GLDR 91741 569-G4
19000 LACo 91741 569-G4
E LEADORA AV
100 GLDR 91741 569-F4
W LEADORA AV
100 GLDR 91741 569-D4
18600 LACo 91741 569-B4
LEADWELL ST
11000 SunV 91352 533-A4
11000 SunV 91352 532-H4
11500 NHol 91605 532-D4
13500 VanN 91405 532-A4
14500 VanN 91405 531-J4
15300 VanN 91406 531-B4
18700 Res 91335 530-F4
19800 Win 91306 530-C4
22000 CanP 91303 529-J4
22000 CanP 91303 530-A4
22500 CanP 91307 529-H4
LEAF AV
100 COV 91722 598-H4
5200 LACo 91702 598-H2
N LEAF AV
500 WCOV 91791 598-H6
S LEAF AV
100 WCOV 91791 598-H7
200 WCOV 91791 638-H2

LEAF CIR
1400 UPL 91786 571-H7
LEAF ST
1700 LVRN 91750 600-F1
LEAFDALE AV
1400 SELM 91733 637-C4
2400 ELMN 91732 637-E2
LEAFLOCK AV
2400 THO 91361 557-B5
LEAFWOOD CT
700 BREA 92821 708-H6
LEAFWOOD DR
1600 MNRO 91016 567-E6
LEAFWOOD LN
2000 ARCD 91007 597-B1
LEAGUE AV
600 LPUE 91744 638-B4
900 LACo 91744 638-B4
N LEAGUE AV
300 LPUE 91744 638-A5
LEAGUE ST
12700 NHol 91605 532-E2
LEAH CIR
28800 RPV 90275 792-H7
28800 RPV 90275 822-H1
LEAHY AV
13000 DWNY 90242 736-C2
14000 BLF 90706 736-C3
LEAHY ST
4600 CULC 90232 672-H2
LEAL AV
17000 CRTS 90703 737-B7
LEAL CIR
19400 CRTS 90703 767-B2
LEALMA AV
3900 CLAR 91711 601-A1
LEANDER DR
\- LACo 91342 482-J3
15900 HacH 91745 678-B6
LEANDER PL
9100 LA 90210 592-G2
LEANDRA LN
1000 ARCD 91006 567-B4
LEANDRO RD
1900 Actn 93510 4465-F2
LEANDRY RD
\- LMRD 90638 738-A1
LEANING OAK CT
1700 GLDR 91741 569-J5
LEANING PINE DR
1700 DBAR 91765 679-J4
LEANNA DR
2400 WCOV 91792 639-A6
LEANNE TER
1500 LACo 91789 679-F4
LEAP CT
20400 LACo 91789 679-F6
LEAPWOOD AV
19000 CRSN 90746 764-E2
LEAR CT
16100 LACo 91744 638-F5
LEARY MERRIAM DR
\- SPed 90731 854-B1
LEATA LN
4500 LCF 91011 534-J2
LEATART AV
13900 PRM 90723 735-F2
LEATHERWOOD AV
44400 LAN 93534 4015-F4
LEAVENWORTH DR
800 SPed 90731 854-A1
LEAVEY RD
\- Wch 90045 702-D2
LEAYN CT
12200 NHol 91605 532-F4
LEBANON ST
500 LA 90015 634-E4
600 LA 90017 634-E4
LEBEC PL
6500 RPV 90275 822-H3
LEBEC RD
8200 SBdC 92371 (4562-J2
See Page 4471)
9200 SBdC 92371 (4472-J1
See Page 4471)
LE BERTHON ST
7600 Tuj 91042 503-H2
7900 Sunl 91040 503-F2
LE BLANC PL
6400 RPV 90275 822-H2
LEBO ST
16400 WHIT 90603 708-A6
LE BORGNE AV
300 LACo 91746 637-J3
700 LACo 91746 638-A1
1400 BALD 91746 638-A1
LE BOURGET AV
4100 CULC 90232 672-G2
LECCO LN
17800 PacP 90272 630-F6
LECHNER PL
6000 LA 90068 593-G1
LECHUSA RD
1700 LACo 90265 626-E1
LE CLAIRE PL
1000 LA 90019 633-F3
LE CONTE AV
10400 Wwd 90024 632-C2
10800 LA 90095 632-A2
LE CONTE PL
\- LA 90095 632-A2
LECOUVREUR AV
200 Wilm 90744 794-F6

STREET Block City ZIP Pg-Grid

LEDA LN
300 ARCD 91006 567-E7
LEDAN ST
18900 Nor 91324 500-H7
LEDEEN DR
10600 LA 91342 503-A1
LEDERER AV
6100 WdHl 91367 559-F1
6100 WdHl 91367 529-F7
6400 CanP 91307 529-F7
LEDFORD ST
12700 BALD 91706 637-H1
LEDGE AV
800 BURB 91505 563-B5
4200 LA 91602 563-B5
4800 NHol 91601 563-B5
7800 SunV 91352 533-B3
9000 SunV 91352 503-B7
LEDGESTONE LN
- POM 91767 601-C6
LEDGEWOOD DR
2900 LA 90068 593-F1
3200 LA 90068 563-F7
LEDGEWOOD RD
5200 SGAT 90280 705-E5
LEDO WY
600 Brwd 90049 591-J7
LE DOUX RD
400 LA 90048 632-J1
400 BHLS 90211 632-J1
N LE DOUX RD
100 BHLS 90211 632-J2
S LE DOUX RD
100 BHLS 90211 632-J3
800 LA 90035 632-J3
5800 LadH 90056 673-A6
LE DROIT DR
2000 SPAS 91030 595-J2
LEE AV
200 FUL 92833 738-E7
300 CLAR 91711 601-E1
1600 ARCD 91006 597-D1
2000 SELM 91733 636-J3
N LEE AV
1300 LBCH 90804 796-A5
LEE CIR
4400 RSMD 91770 596-H6
LEE CT
- StvR 91381 4550-D7
LEE DR
400 AZU 91702 569-A6
1400 GLDL 91201 534-A7
6000 CYP 90630 767-E7
7500 BPK 90620 767-E3
LEE LN
10100 SGAT 90280 705-G5
11400 ELMN 91731 597-D7
LEE PL
600 AZU 91702 569-A6
2000 POM 91766 641-B5
LEE ST
3400 LA 90023 635-C7
3600 RSMD 91770 596-H7
3700 LA 90023 675-C1
4600 TOR 90503 763-B6
9700 CYP 90630 767-E7
LEEBE AV
2400 POM 91768 640-D2
LEE CREEK DR
500 DBAR 91765 640-D7
LEEDS AL
400 PAS 91107 566-E3
LEEDS AV
1200 Wilm 90744 794-H5
LEEDS CT
1000 SDMS 91773 599-J3
LEEDS ST
5500 SGAT 90280 705-F6
6000 SGAT 90242 705-G6
7700 DWNY 90242 705-H7
10400 NRWK 90650 736-D1
LEEDY AV
13900 LA 91342 482-B1
LEERIDGE TER
500 GLDL 91206 564-H4
LEES AV
800 LBCH 90815 796-F4
3000 LBCH 90808 796-F1
3200 LBCH 90808 766-F7
E LEES WY
6800 LBCH 90815 796-F6
LEESBURY WY
- RowH 91748 679-B7
LEESCOTT AV
7200 VanN 91406 531-C4
LEESDALE AV
26400 Hrbr 90710 793-J6
LEESIDE ST
300 GLDR 91741 569-D6
LEEVIEW CT
3800 CULC 90232 673-A2
LEEWARD
- WCOV 91790 638-D2
LEEWARD AV
2800 LA 90005 634-A3
2800 LA 90057 634-A3
4000 LA 90005 633-G3
16700 CRTS 90703 736-F6
LEEWARD CIR
2300 THO 91361 557-B6
W LEEWOOD ST
1000 WCOV 91790 638-D1

LEFFCO RD
16100 WHIT 90603 707-J5
16100 WHIT 90603 708-A5
LEFFINGWELL AV
- SFSP 90670 737-B1
LEFFINGWELL RD
10600 NRWK 90650 736-F2
12600 NRWK 90650 737-B1
13200 LACo 90605 737-B1
13400 WHIT 90603 708-A6
14100 LACo 90604 707-E7
LE FLORE DR
1200 LHH 90631 708-A1
LEFLOSS AV
11000 DWNY 90241 706-E6
11200 NRWK 90650 706-E6
12600 NRWK 90650 736-E2
LEGACY CT
5100 WdHl 91364 559-H3
LEGACY LN
- ING 90305 703-F3
- LAN 93536 4015-B5
- PMDL 93551 4195-H3
LEGACY PL
- RowH 91748 679-C4
LEGARY PL
700 LA 90732 823-H5
LEGATO CT
- POM 91766 640-D4
LEGEND AV
21300 CRSN 90745 764-G6
LEGEND LN
2500 RowH 91748 678-J7
LEGENDS WY
2700 LAN 93536 4015-C7
LEGGE AL
- PAS 91103 565-H4
LEGGETT LN
2000 FUL 92833 738-C4
LEGHORN AV
5200 Shrm 91423 562-E2
5200 VanN 91401 562-E2
N LEGION DR
2200 SIGH 90755 795-G3
LEGION LN
3700 LA 90039 594-D1
LE GRANDE TER
1400 LA 90732 823-J6
LE GRAY AV
900 HiPk 90042 595-C1
LEHIGH AV
8300 SunV 91352 533-A1
8700 SunV 91352 532-J1
9700 MTCL 91763 601-E6
10300 MTCL 91763 641-E1
10800 Pcma 91331 502-D2
11400 LA 91340 502-C1
LEHIGH DR
600 CLAR 91711 601-C5
LEHIGH ST
900 LACo 91011 535-F5
900 PAS 91103 535-F5
LEHMAN RD
4000 GLDL 91214 504-D7
S LEHMEN DR
100 ANA 92804 767-J6
LEI DR
300 NLB 90805 735-D7
LEIBACHER AV
11000 DWNY 90241 706-E6
11400 NRWK 90650 706-E7
12600 NRWK 90650 736-E1
LEICESTER CT
3600 CLAR 91711 571-F5
LEICESTER DR
2500 LA 90046 593-A2
LEIGH CT
1200 LBCH 90806 795-F4
LEIGHTON AL
900 PAS 91104 565-J2
900 PAS 91104 566-A2
LEIGHTON AV
900 LA 90037 674-A2
1100 LA 90037 673-J2
1500 LA 90062 673-H2
LEIGHTON POINT RD
3800 CALB 91301 558-G7
LEILANI WY
3500 Alta 91001 535-H3
LEIMERT BLVD
2600 LA 90008 673-F3
4400 LA 90043 673-F3
LEI MIN WY
400 LA 90012 634-G2
LEIR DR
4600 LCF 91011 534-H2
LEISURE DR
14200 LMRD 90638 737-E1
LEISURE LN
- LACo 93536 3925-D4
LEISURE LAKE PKWY
- LACo 93534 3925-D4
- LACo 93536 3925-D4
LEITH RD
2300 GLDL 91206 564-J3
2300 GLDL 91206 565-A3
LELA DR
23000 DBAR 91765 640-B6
LELAND AV
10700 LACo 90605 707-C7
12400 LACo 90605 737-C1
N LELAND AV
200 WCOV 91790 598-D6

S LELAND AV
1200 WCOV 91790 638-C1
LELAND DR
600 FUL 92832 738-F6
LELAND PL
4500 LCF 91011 535-A3
N LELAND ST
400 LA 90732 824-A4
S LELAND ST
700 SPed 90731 824-A6
2600 SPed 90731 854-A1
3700 SPed 90731 853-J2
LELAND WY
200 ARCD 91006 567-E7
1100 BURB 91504 533-F6
6800 Hlwd 90028 593-E5
LELIA LN
10200 BelA 90077 592-B4
LEMA DR
24200 SCTA 91355 4550-F7
LEMAC ST
15300 VanN 91406 531-G3
17300 Nor 91325 531-B3
LEMAN ST
1900 SPAS 91030 595-J3
LE MANS DR
- CALB 91302 560-A7
LEMAR PARK DR
600 GLDR 91740 569-F6
LEMARSH ST
15200 MsnH 91345 501-G4
15600 LA 91343 501-F4
17400 Nor 91325 501-A4
18100 Nor 91325 500-J4
18400 Nor 91324 500-F4
19700 Chat 91311 500-B4
22000 Chat 91311 499-J4
LEMAY PL
17400 VanN 91406 531-B6
LEMAY ST
10900 NHol 91606 533-A6
11000 NHol 91606 532-D6
13600 VanN 91401 532-C6
14100 VanN 91405 532-B6
14700 VanN 91405 531-H6
15300 VanN 91406 531-B6
18100 Res 91335 531-A6
18500 Res 91335 530-F6
20600 Win 91306 530-C6
24000 CanP 91307 529-D6
LEMBO LN
- PMDL 93550 4286-F7
- PMDL 93550 4376-F1
LEMMER DR
19300 Tarz 91356 560-G6
LEMMER ST
20600 Chat 91311 500-C5
LEMMING ST
11300 LKWD 90715 766-F4
12500 LKWD 90715 767-A4
LEMOLI AV
13100 LACo 90250 733-F4
13500 HAW 90250 733-F4
14700 LACo 90249 733-F5
S LEMOLI AV
10700 ING 90303 703-F6
LEMOLI WY
14000 HAW 90250 733-F3
LEMON AV
100 WAL 91789 639-C4
100 WAL 91789 679-F2
200 GLDR 91741 569-E6
400 INDS 91789 679-F2
700 ARCD 91007 597-A1
700 DBAR 91789 679-G4
1300 LBCH 90813 795-F5
1800 LBCH 90806 795-F4
2200 SIGH 90755 795-F1
3300 Bxby 90807 795-F1
3400 Bxby 90807 765-F4
4900 CYP 90630 767-C6
5200 NLB 90805 765-E2
6300 LACo 91775 596-G1
6300 NLB 90805 735-E7
6300 TEML 91775 596-G1
9200 TEML 91780 596-J1
9600 LACo 91007 596-J1
9700 TEML 91780 597-A1
E LEMON AV
- ARCD 91006 597-D1
100 MNRO 91016 567-J4
1100 MNRO 91016 568-A4
1200 BRAD 91010 568-A4
N LEMON AV
500 AZU 91702 568-H6
S LEMON AV
100 AZU 91702 568-H7
100 AZU 91702 598-H1
100 WAL 91789 679-F1
W LEMON AV
- ARCD 91007 597-B1
100 MNRO 91016 567-F4
LEMON CIR
4500 CYP 90630 767-B6
8100 BPK 90620 767-J4
LEMON CT
- CRSN 90746 764-D4
LEMON DR
15300 LMRD 90638 707-H7
15300 LACo 90604 707-H7
LEMON ST
100 LHB 90631 708-F5
500 FUL 92832 738-H7

LEMON ST
1200 LA 90021 634-H7
1700 ALH 91803 595-J6
1700 LA 90021 674-H1
22400 SCTA 91390 4460-J3
N LEMON ST
100 FUL 92832 738-H6
1100 FUL 92831 738-H6
S LEMON ST
100 FUL 92832 738-H7
W LEMON ST
800 BREA 92821 738-J1
LEMONA AV
4500 Shrm 91403 561-J4
5200 VanN 91411 561-J2
6100 VanN 91411 531-J7
6600 VanN 91405 531-H3
7900 PanC 91402 531-H3
8700 LA 91343 501-H6
8700 LA 91343 531-H1
9900 MsnH 91345 501-H3
LEMON CREEK DR
300 WAL 91789 679-E1
LEMONCREST AV
11300 LA 91342 503-B1
LEMONGRASS PL
- LACo 91744 638-G4
LEMON GROVE AV
4800 LA 90029 593-H6
5300 LA 90038 593-G6
N LEMON GROVE DR
1400 UPL 91786 571-G7
LEMON HEIGHTS DR
- UPL 91784 571-H6
LEMON HILL TER
500 FUL 92832 738-F6
LEMON SWIRL DR
- AZU 91702 569-A4
LEMON TREE CIR
1300 UPL 91786 571-J7
LEMON TREE CT
1400 LHB 90631 738-C1
LEMON TREE DR
1200 LHB 90631 738-C1
LEMONWOOD CIR
7800 LPMA 90623 767-D3
LEMONWOOD DR
- PMDL 93551 4285-E3
600 LHB 90631 738-F1
3000 LAN 93536 4105-B3
E LEMONWOOD DR
1300 UPL 91786 601-H1
1300 UPL 91786 571-J7
W LEMONWOOD DR
1300 UPL 91786 571-G7
1400 UPL 91786 601-H1
LEMONWOOD LN
500 BREA 92821 709-A5
LEMONWOOD ST
1600 LVRN 91750 570-F6
LEMORAN AV
5300 PRV 90660 676-G4
7500 PRV 90660 706-E1
9000 DWNY 90240 706-D3
10500 DWNY 90241 706-D5
LEMOYNE ST
1100 Echo 90026 594-E6
1900 LA 90039 594-E6
LEMP AV
4200 LA 91604 562-H5
4400 LA 91602 562-H5
5200 NHol 91601 562-H1
5900 NHol 91601 532-H6
6600 NHol 91606 532-H6
6900 NHol 91605 532-H4
LEMSFORD AV
37600 PMDL 93550 4286-G1
38600 PMDL 93550 4196-G7
LENA AV
6200 WdHl 91367 529-G7
6800 CanP 91307 529-G4
7600 LA 91304 529-G3
LENA CT
43700 LAN 93535 4106-B1
LENA DR
5100 LPMA 90623 767-C4
LENAHAN ST
- FUL 92833 738-D6
LENAWEE AV
3600 LA 90016 673-A1
3700 CULC 90232 673-A2
LENCHO PL
19600 WAL 91789 679-D2
LE NICHE LN
1700 LAN 93535 4106-D1
LENNON CT
- SCTA 91350 4550-H6
LENNON ST
100 LACo 90248 734-C4
E LENNON ST
800 LACo 90220 734-E4
LENNOX AV
4400 Shrm 91423 562-A3
5200 VanN 91401 562-A2
6600 VanN 91405 532-A4
8000 PanC 91402 532-A1
LENNOX BLVD
4000 ING 90304 703-B6
4000 Lenx 90304 703-B6
LENNOX CIR
400 FUL 92835 738-H4
LENNOX CT
600 BREA 92821 709-C5

LENNOX CT
3100 PMDL 93551 4195-B3
LENNOX ST
2400 POM 91767 601-B4
LENNY ST
18400 LACo 91390 4461-G1
LENORE AV
5700 ARCD 91006 597-E3
LENORE DR
2100 GLDL 91206 535-B7
LENORE LN
700 POM 91767 601-B5
LENORE ST
4000 TOR 90503 763-B6
LENTA LN
2200 ARCD 91006 597-E2
LENVALE AV
5400 WHIT 90601 677-A3
W LENWOOD SQ
1200 UPL 91786 601-G2
LENZGROVE LN
4200 LCF 91011 535-A3
LEO AV
2000 CMRC 90040 675-J3
LEO CIR
- PMDL 93552 4286-J2
LEOLA ST
1800 LMTA 90717 793-H4
LEOLANG AV
10300 Sunl 91040 503-H2
LEON
- LVRN 91750 570-H3
LEON CIR
19400 CRTS 90703 766-G3
LEONA AV
8700 LACo 93551 4193-F3
8700 LACo 93551 4194-A3
10000 Tuj 91042 504-B4
LEONA DR
1200 BHLS 90210 592-D6
LEONA DIVIDE RD
- LACo 91390 4102-D6
- LACo 93551 4102-D6
LEONA DIVIDE FIRE RD
- LACo 91390 4192-G1
- LACo 91390 4193-A3
- LACo 93551 4102-G7
- LACo 93551 4192-G1
LEONA JOAN AV
6100 PRV 90660 676-G6
LEONARD AV
1000 PAS 91107 566-H2
S LEONARD AV
500 ELA 90022 635-J7
500 ELA 90022 675-J1
S LEONARD PL
900 ELA 90022 675-J1
LEONARD RD
800 Brwd 90049 631-E1
N LEONARD ST
600 MTBL 90640 636-A7
LEONARD J PIERONI ST
- PAS 91103 565-H4
LEONARD TREE LN
24400 SCTA 91321 4641-B1
LEONA VIEW WY
- LACo 93551 4193-J2
LEONG CT
- Saug 91350 4461-E5
LEONIS BLVD
2600 VER 90058 674-J4
2800 VER 90058 675-A4
LEONIS ST
4500 CMRC 90040 675-F3
LEONORA DR
22700 WdHl 91367 559-F3
LEOPARD CT
1300 PMDL 93551 4285-F1
1300 PMDL 93551 4195-F7
LEOPOLD AV
2700 HacH 91745 678-C6
LEORA AV
100 LHB 90631 708-D5
LEORITA ST
900 BALD 91706 637-J1
LEOSE LN
700 GLDR 91741 569-D4
LEOTA LN
7100 WHil 91304 499-E7
22700 WHil 91304 499-E7
LEOTA ST
2100 LACo 90255 704-H1
LEOTI TER
8100 LA 90069 593-A4
LE PAGE RANCH RD
12400 Pear 93553 4468-H5
12500 Valy 93563 4468-H5
LE PARC BLVD
13000 CHLS 91709 641-A7
LERDO AV
11500 GrnH 91344 481-A7
11500 GrnH 91344 501-A1
LERIDA PL
2000 LACo 91770 636-E3
10500 Chat 91311 500-D3
LERMA RD
1200 SELM 91733 637-A5
9800 LACo 91733 637-A5
LERONA AV
1800 RowH 91748 679-C5

E LE ROY AV
- ARCD 91006 567-D7
W LE ROY AV
- ARCD 91007 567-B7
LE ROY ST
9000 LACo 91775 596-H1
9100 LACo 91775 566-J7
LEROY ST
- LA 90012 634-H2
8300 LACo 91775 596-F1
9600 LACo 91007 566-J7
LE SAGE AV
5600 WdHl 91367 559-F1
6100 WdHl 91367 529-F7
LE SAGE ST
3700 LYN 90262 705-C6
LESINA DR
42700 LACo 93532 4102-E4
LESLIE AV
5600 NLB 90805 765-C2
16800 CRTS 90703 737-C7
LESLIE CT
1700 POM 91767 601-B6
44700 LAN 93535 4016-E5
LESLIE DR
800 LACo 91775 596-F3
800 SGBL 91775 596-F3
8700 TEML 91775 596-G3
W LESLIE DR
200 SGBL 91775 596-D3
LESLIE LN
500 BHLS 90210 592-G4
LESLIE ST
- LAN 93535 4016-F6
900 LHB 90631 708-F7
19000 RowH 91748 679-C5
LESLIE WY
300 HiPk 90042 595-C3
LESMAR DR
500 LACo 91750 600-E1
LESNER AV
8000 VanN 91406 531-C2
LESNY ST
10700 LA 91342 503-A1
LESSER ST
11800 NRWK 90650 736-H2
LESSERMAN ST
2500 TOR 90503 763-F5
LESTER AV
11700 CHNO 91710 641-G5
LESTER CT
12100 CHNO 91710 641-G5
LESTER LN
8300 LA 91304 529-F2
LESTER PL
11800 CHNO 91710 641-G4
LESTER ST
5700 NLB 90805 765-D2
LESTERFORD AV
9800 DWNY 90240 706-E4
10200 DWNY 90241 706-E6
LESTERWEST WY
500 GLDR 91741 569-E5
LETA ST
2600 LA 90011 674-F2
LETICIA CT
30100 AGRH 91301 557-H5
LETICIA DR
2600 HacH 91745 678-B5
25600 SCTA 91355 4550-G5
LETICIA PL
- VanN 91406 531-G4
LETON AV
700 AZU 91702 598-J2
LEUCADIA RD
100 LHH 90631 678-C7
LEV AV
8900 Pcma 91331 502-A4
10500 MsnH 91345 502-A3
11200 MsnH 91345 501-H1
LEVANDA AV
2200 LA 90032 635-F1
LEVEL ST
700 COV 91723 599-D6
1300 COV 91724 599-E6
19300 LACo 91723 599-D6
LEVELGLEN DR
2900 WCOV 91792 679-D1
LEVELSIDE AV
4100 LKWD 90712 765-H3
LEVELWOOD ST
13100 LACo 91746 637-G4
LEVEN LN
12100 Brwd 90049 631-G2
LEVERETT AV
400 LPUE 91744 678-G1
LEVERING AV
400 Wwd 90024 631-J2
400 Brwd 90049 631-J2
500 Wwd 90024 632-A2
LEVICO WY
10600 BelA 90077 591-J5
10700 BelA 90077 592-A5
LEVINSON ST
1100 LACo 90502 764-A6
LEVITT LN
4200 Shrm 91403 561-J5
LEW AV
200 LACo 91744 638-H7
E LEW DAVIS ST
4700 LBCH 90808 766-A6
LEWENDO CT
20300 SCTA 91351 4461-D7

LEWIS AV
1000 LBCH 90813 795-F6
2000 Alta 91001 536-A7
12300 CHNO 91710 641-F6
N LEWIS AV
1700 LBCH 90813 795-F1
1900 LBCH 90806 795-F1
2300 SIGH 90755 795-F1
3300 Bxby 90807 795-F1
3400 Bxby 90807 765-F7
5200 NLB 90805 765-E2
6300 NLB 90805 735-E7
LEWIS CT
400 CLAR 91711 601-D4
LEWIS DR
2700 LVRN 91750 600-F2
LEWIS LN
5500 AGRH 91301 558-C5
LEWIS PL
28400 AGRH 91301 558-C6
LEWIS RD
4900 AGRH 91301 558-C5
10700 LYN 90262 705-C6
LEWIS ST
400 HiPk 90042 595-E1
900 POM 91768 600-G7
11500 LYN 90262 705-B7
N LEWIS ST
500 POM 91768 640-G1
LEWIS TER
2100 LA 90046 592-J3
LEWIS WY
- StvR 91381 4550-A7
LEWIS & CLARK RD
24900 HIDH 91302 559-B3
LEWIS HILL RD
11100 LACo 91390 4373-D5
LEWISTON ST
800 DUAR 91010 567-J6
LEXHAM AV
900 SELM 91733 637-C4
LEXICON AV
11500 LA 91342 502-H1
11500 LA 91342 482-C1
LEXICON PL
13500 LA 91342 482-C2
LEXINGTON AV
- CHNO 91710 641-D4
700 MTBL 90640 636-D7
700 MTBL 90640 676-D1
1100 LACo 91104 536-B7
2600 ELMN 91733 637-C2
3000 ELMN 91731 637-C2
3400 ELMN 91731 597-C7
4200 LA 90029 594-A5
4200 SBdC 91710 641-D4
4800 LA 90029 593-H5
5500 LA 90038 593-D5
7000 WHWD 90038 593-D5
7100 WHWD 90046 593-C5
E LEXINGTON AV
100 POM 91766 640-J5
100 POM 91766 641-A4
W LEXINGTON AV
100 POM 91766 640-H5
LEXINGTON CIR
11700 CRTS 90703 766-G3
LEXINGTON CT
500 LBCH 90803 796-F7
4000 PMDL 93552 4286-J3
4900 CHNO 91710 641-F4
LEXINGTON DR
1800 FUL 92835 738-H4
30000 Cstc 91384 4459-C6
E LEXINGTON DR
100 GLDL 91206 564-F4
W LEXINGTON DR
100 GLDL 91203 564-D4
LEXINGTON RD
1000 BHLS 90210 592-E6
4700 PRV 90660 676-G3
8300 DWNY 90241 706-B3
LEXINGTON ST
3900 SBdC 91710 641-C4
6800 LA 90038 593-D5
9200 CYP 90630 767-A6
LEXINGTON WY
30900 AGRH 91301 557-F6
30900 WLKV 91361 557-F6
LEXINGTON-GALLATIN RD
700 LACo 90660 637-B5
700 LACo 91733 637-B5
700 SELM 91733 637-B5
8300 PRV 90660 706-D2
LEY DR
3300 LFlz 90027 594-B2
LEYBURN DR
3200 RSMD 91770 636-H2
LEYCROSS DR
1600 LCF 91011 535-A4
LEYDEN LN
600 CLAR 91711 601-C3
LEYDON AV
4400 WdHl 91364 559-G5
LEYLAND DR
700 DBAR 91765 680-D1
LEYTE DR
22200 TOR 90505 763-C7
22500 TOR 90505 793-C2
LEYVA ST
12800 NRWK 90650 737-A4

LIAHONA PL
23200 WdHl 91364 559-G4
LIANA LN
- PMDL 93551 4285-D4
23200 SCTA 91354 4460-G4
LIBBIT AV
4400 Enc 91436 561-E3
LIBBY WY
5900 LA 90068 593-G2
LIBERATOR AV
8600 Wch 90045 702-F3
LIBERTY
- PMDL 93550 4286-C4
LIBERTY AV
700 MTBL 90640 636-D6
3900 GLDL 91214 534-F2
LIBERTY BLVD
2600 SGAT 90280 704-J2
2800 SGAT 90280 705-A2
N LIBERTY CT
200 LBCH 90802 795-E7
700 LBCH 90813 795-E6
LIBERTY DR
- VanN 91405 531-J5
LIBERTY LN
2400 Top 90290 590-A1
LIBERTY ST
500 LHB 90631 708-E6
1300 Echo 90026 594-D7
4800 CHNO 91710 641-F5
LIBERTY WY
- Actn 93510 4465-A1
LIBERTY BELL RD
22300 CALB 91302 559-H6
LIBERTY CANYON RD
3000 Ago 91301 588-E2
3000 AGRH 91301 588-E1
3900 AGRH 91301 558-E7
4000 Ago 91301 558-E7
LIBLEN AV
14600 BLF 90706 736-A4
LIBRA DR
14600 LMRD 90638 737-H3
31300 Llan 93544 4470-G2
LIBRARY LN
1100 SPAS 91030 595-H2
LIBRARY ST
500 SFER 91340 482-A6
LICK ST
1400 Eagl 90041 565-C6
LIDA LN
1300 PAS 91103 565-D1
LIDA ST
1100 PAS 91103 565-D1
1700 GLDL 91206 565-D1
LIDCOMBE AV
1400 SELM 91733 637-C4
LIDDINGTON ST
- CRTS 90703 767-A3
LIDFORD AV
500 LACo 91744 638-F5
LIDLE DR
- WCOV 91792 638-J5
LIDO CT
3500 CALB 91302 559-J7
LIDO DR
38000 PMDL 93552 4287-B1
LIDO LN
5900 LBCH 90803 826-D2
E LIDO LN
5700 LBCH 90803 826-D3
LIDO PL
200 FUL 92835 738-G3
LIDO WY
9700 CYP 90630 767-E7
S LIDO WY
- UPL 91786 601-H4
LIEBE DR
9900 LA 90210 592-B2
LIFFORD ST
100 CRSN 90746 764-D2
LIFUR AV
3400 LA 90032 595-F6
LIGGETT ST
9800 BLF 90706 736-C3
10600 NRWK 90650 736-E3
12900 NRWK 90650 737-B3
14300 PanC 91402 502-A6
15700 LA 91343 501-D6
16900 Nor 91325 501-D6
18600 Nor 91324 500-G6
22000 Chat 91311 499-J6
22000 Chat 91311 500-A6
LIGHT ST
13800 LACo 90605 707-D4
14100 LACo 90604 707-D4
LIGHTCAP ST
300 LAN 93535 4015-J5
300 LAN 93535 4016-A5
LIGHTFOOT PL
26600 RPV 90275 792-J5
W LIGHTHALL ST
1300 WCOV 91790 638-D1
LIGHTHILL DR
21100 Top 90290 560-B7
LIGHTHOUSE CT
100 LA 90292 701-J1
LIGHTHOUSE DR
25000 Hrbr 90710 794-B4
LIGHTHOUSE LN
- SLB 90740 796-J6
5500 PMDL 93552 4287-C3
44200 LAN 93536 4015-B7

LIGHTHOUSE MALL
- LA 90292 701-J1
LIGHTHOUSE ST
- LA 90292 701-J1
LIGHTHOUSE LATERAL
- LACo 90265 627-H5
LIGHTVIEW ST
1200 MONP 91754 635-H4
LIGHTWOOD AV
44100 LAN 93534 4015-F7
LIGURE
100 BREA 92823 710-D6
LILA LN
1700 LCF 91011 534-J2
1700 LCF 91011 535-A2
LILAC CIR
6000 LAN 93536 4104-F5
LILAC CT
- CRSN 90746 764-H2
22600 SCTA 91390 4460-J3
LILAC DR
- PMDL 93552 4287-A1
LILAC LN
100 BREA 92823 710-C5
700 GLDR 91741 569-H3
2000 GLDL 91206 564-J4
10200 VeCo 93063 499-F3
10200 SIMI 93063 499-F3
LILAC PL
900 POM 91768 640-E1
1100 Echo 90026 634-F1
1100 LA 90012 634-F1
LILAC RD
3000 SBdC 92371 (4562-H1 See Page 4471)
LILAC TER
600 LA 90012 634-G1
1300 Echo 90026 634-F1
LILAC TR
3400 CALB 91302 589-F1
LILAC CANYON LN
- Alta 91001 535-G2
LILACVIEW AV
36600 PMDL 93550 4286-G2
38600 PMDL 93550 4196-G7
LIL DIRT RD
10200 SBdC 92372 (4472-B5 See Page 4471)
LILIANA CT
17700 RowH 91748 678-H5
LILIANO DR
1900 SMAD 91024 567-C1
LILIANO PL
1900 SMAD 91024 567-C1
LILIENTHAL AV
8300 Wch 90045 702-H3
LILIENTHAL LN
700 RBCH 90278 763-B2
LILITA ST
3700 LYN 90262 705-C6
LILLA PL
7500 LA 91304 529-E4
LILLIAN CT
1000 LAN 93535 4106-B2
4500 LCF 91011 535-C4
LILLIAN LN
10900 SGAT 90280 705-G7
LILLIAN PL
15300 HacH 91745 677-J5
LILLIAN ST
5100 TOR 90503 763-B6
5900 Flor 90001 674-G6
LILLIAN WY
500 LA 90004 593-F7
700 LA 90038 593-F7
LILLIANNE ST
34600 Actn 93510 4375-C3
LILLY AV
3100 LALM 90808 796-J1
3100 LBCH 90808 796-J1
3400 LBCH 90808 766-J7
LILLY CT
9600 Nor 91325 500-J6
LILLYGLEN DR
28900 SCTA 91387 4462-E7
28900 SCTA 91387 4552-F1
LILLYVALE AV
2200 LA 90032 635-G1
2300 LA 90032 595-G7
LILY AV
2200 UPL 91784 571-H4
LILY DR
3500 CALB 91302 559-F7
LILY WY
- PMDL 93552 4287-A1
E LILY WY
100 LBCH 90813 795-D6
W LILY WY
100 LBCH 90813 795-D6
LILY CREST AV
4600 LA 90029 593-J6
4600 LA 90029 594-A6
LILYFIELD LN
- SCTA 91354 4460-F6
LIMA AV
4400 PMDL 93552 4286-J4
LIMA ST
4300 LA 90011 674-F3
N LIMA ST
- SMAD 91024 566-J2
100 BURB 91505 563-D1
1400 BURB 91505 533-C6
2800 BURB 91504 533-C4

S LIMA ST
- SMAD 91024 566-J3
LIME
1200 SDMS 91773 599-J2
LIME AV
- LBCH 90802 825-E1
100 SGBL 91776 596-E6
100 LBCH 90802 795-E7
700 LBCH 90813 795-E7
3300 Bxby 90807 795-E1
3300 SIGH 90755 795-E1
3400 Bxby 90807 765-E6
5300 NLB 90805 765-E3
5500 CYP 90630 767-D6
E LIME AV
100 MNRO 91016 567-J4
N LIME AV
1300 LBCH 90813 795-E6
1800 LBCH 90806 795-E3
2600 SIGH 90755 795-E3
6600 NLB 90805 735-E6
S LIME AV
12800 COMP 90221 735-D3
12800 RDom 90221 735-D3
W LIME AV
100 MNRO 91016 567-F4
LIME CIR
8000 BPK 90620 767-J4
9200 CYP 90630 767-E6
LIME RD
6600 LAN 93536 4104-D4
LIME ST
200 LHB 90631 708-B5
500 AZU 91702 568-H6
600 AZU 91702 569-A6
2100 SBdC 92372 (4562-E2 See Page 4471)
W LIME ST
100 ING 90301 703-B3
700 BREA 92821 738-J1
LIMECREST DR
19900 LACo 91724 639-E2
LIMEDALE ST
14600 PanC 91402 501-J6
LIMEKILN CANYON RD
- Nor 91326 480-F3
- Nor 91326 480-G5
10400 Nor 91326 500-F4
LIMEKILN CANYON TR
- LA 91342 482-G2
- LACo 91342 482-G2
LIMELIGHT WY
- PMDL 93551 4285-E3
LIME ORCHARD RD
9500 LA 90210 592-F1
LIMERICK AV
6700 Win 91306 530-C2
10000 Chat 91311 500-C2
LIMERIDGE DR
42800 LACo 93532 4102-J4
LIMEROCK TR
8600 LA 91304 529-E1
LIMESTONE CT
15300 CHLS 91709 680-J6
LIMESTONE PL
3700 Shrm 91403 561-J6
LIMESTONE RD
2700 CLAR 91711 571-D5
LIMETREE LN
- RPV 90275 823-B4
LIMEWOOD LN
2100 LAN 93536 4105-C3
LIMOGES CT
- LACo 91302 558-G3
LINARD ST
11200 SELM 91733 637-C5
LINARES AV
300 LBCH 90803 796-E7
LINARO DR
4700 CYP 90630 767-C7
LINCOLN AV
100 FUL 92831 738-J7
300 GLDL 91205 564-H6
400 PAS 91103 565-G2
700 DBAR 91789 679-H2
800 POM 91767 601-B7
1200 LAN 93535 4106-B1
1600 PAS 91103 535-G4
1700 TOR 90501 793-H1
1800 TOR 90501 763-G7
2400 LACo 91010 567-H7
2600 Alta 91001 535-G4
3800 ELMN 91731 597-D7
4000 CULC 90232 672-G2
4000 CYP 90630 767-B6
4400 Eagl 90041 594-J1
4500 Eagl 90041 595-A1
4700 HiPk 90042 595-A1
4800 CHNO 91710 641-F7
5600 BPK 90620 767-E5
5700 SGAT 90280 735-G1
28500 Cstc 91384 4459-C6
E LINCOLN AV
100 MTBL 90640 676-F1
100 POM 91767 600-J7
300 POM 91767 601-A7
700 MTBL 90640 636-H7
N LINCOLN AV
100 MONP 91755 636-C2
500 FUL 92831 738-J6
2000 Alta 91001 535-G6
S LINCOLN AV
100 MONP 91755 636-C3

STREET Block City ZIP Pg-Grid

W LINCOLN AV
100 MTBL 90640 676-E1
1200 MTBL 90640 636-B7
2800 ANA 92804 767-H5
2800 ANA 92801 767-H5
7000 BPK 90620 767-H5
LINCOLN BLVD
300 SMCA 90402 631-C7
600 SMCA 90402 671-D1
800 SMCA 90403 671-D1
1200 SMCA 90401 671-E1
1600 SMCA 90404 671-E1
LINCOLN BLVD Rt#-1
100 Ven 90291 671-G3
1100 Ven 90291 672-A6
1700 SMCA 90404 671-G3
1900 SMCA 90405 671-G3
4000 LA 90292 672-A6
4400 MdlR 90292 672-A6
4800 LA 90094 672-A6
4800 LA 90094 702-D2
4800 MdlR 90292 702-D2
8100 Wch 90045 702-D2
LINCOLN CT
- SMCA 90401 671-E1
- BPK 90620 767-F5
800 SMCA 90403 631-D7
800 SMCA 90403 671-D1
1400 Ven 90291 671-J5
2100 SMCA 90405 671-F3
LINCOLN LN
- PMDL 93551 4195-D6
N LINCOLN PL
100 MNRO 91016 567-E3
S LINCOLN PL
300 MNRO 91016 567-E4
LINCOLN ST
- KeCo 93560 3835-E2
300 CRSN 90745 794-D2
N LINCOLN ST
100 BURB 91506 563-E1
900 BURB 91506 533-E7
2000 BURB 91504 533-E4
S LINCOLN ST
100 BURB 91506 563-F3
W LINCOLN ST
1500 LBCH 90810 765-A7
2300 LBCH 90810 764-J7
LINCOLN TER
8200 LA 90069 593-A5
LINCOLN WY
28800 Cstc 91384 4459-D6
LINCOLN CENTER DR
9000 CYP 90630 767-A6
LINCOLN HIGH CT
3800 LA 90031 595-C7
LINCOLN HIGH DR
2400 LA 90031 595-C7
2400 LA 90031 635-C1
LINCOLN HIGH PL
3800 LA 90031 595-C7
LINCOLN PARK AV
2000 LA 90031 635-B1
2400 LA 90031 595-B7
LINCOLN PLAZA WY
4300 CYP 90630 767-B6
LINCOLNSHIRE AV
4700 BPK 90621 738-A4
LINCROFT ST
18500 RowH 91748 679-A7
LINDA AV
600 LHB 90631 708-D4
1700 LAN 93534 4015-E5
18600 CRTS 90703 767-C1
LINDA CIR
18500 CRTS 90703 767-C1
LINDA CT
200 PMDL 93550 4286-A2
800 WAL 91789 639-D6
LINDA DR
5300 TOR 90505 793-A1
19400 TOR 90503 763-A3
21800 TOR 90505 763-B7
LINDA LN
- CynC 91351 4461-D7
3000 SMCA 90405 671-H3
5600 LVRN 91750 570-F4
5600 SDMS 91750 570-F4
7700 LPMA 90623 767-B3
9500 CYP 90630 767-F7
LINDA TER
200 COV 91723 599-D5
4500 LACo 91723 599-D4
16600 PacP 90272 630-H5
LINDA WY
1300 ARCD 91006 567-F7
6000 CULC 90230 672-J4
17400 CRTS 90703 737-C7
S LINDA WY
- UPL 91786 601-J4
W LINDACITA LN
3100 ANA 92804 767-H6
LINDACREST DR
1300 BHLS 90210 592-F5
1300 LA 90210 592-F5
LINDA FLORA DR
700 Brwd 90049 591-H6
2100 BelA 90077 591-H3
LINDA GLEN DR
1000 PAS 91105 565-E3
LINDA JOYCE DR
27500 SCTA 91350 4461-B6

LINDALE PL
- SCTA 91350 4551-D6
LINDALE ST
9900 BLF 90706 736-C3
10600 NRWK 90650 736-E3
14400 NRWK 90650 737-A3
LINDA LEE AV
3500 RSMD 91770 596-J7
LINDALOA LN
2700 LACo 91107 536-F7
LINDA LOU AV
5000 LACo 91724 599-D3
LINDAMERE DR
10600 BelA 90077 591-J4
LINDAMERE PL
1600 BelA 90077 591-J4
LINDA MESA RD
11000 Litl 93543 4468-F6
LINDANTE DR
8200 WHIT 90603 707-J2
8200 WHIT 90603 708-A1
LINDA RAE WY
- ARCD 91006 567-D7
LINDARAXA PK N
500 ALH 91801 596-B4
LINDARAXA PK S
600 ALH 91801 596-C4
LINDA RIDGE RD
1200 PAS 91103 565-E3
1200 PAS 91105 565-E3
LINDA ROSA AV
200 PAS 91107 566-D3
1200 Eagl 90041 565-B6
LINDA ROSA CT
1900 PAS 91107 566-D3
LINDAUER DR
1500 LHB 90631 708-B4
LINDA VIEW PL
11500 Tuj 91042 504-A1
LINDA VISTA AV
- PAS 91105 565-F5
700 PAS 91103 565-E3
1500 LAN 93535 4016-C5
1500 PAS 91103 535-E7
1800 LCF 91011 535-E7
E LINDA VISTA AV
- ALH 91801 596-C6
W LINDA VISTA AV
- ALH 91801 596-B6
LINDA VISTA DR
5200 LCF 91011 535-A1
14200 WHIT 90602 677-F7
14200 WHIT 90602 707-F1
LINDA VISTA MTWY
- GLDL 91206 565-D2
LINDA VISTA RD
3100 GLDL 91206 565-B1
LINDA VISTA ST
- SCTA 91387 4462-A7
1800 WCOV 91791 638-J2
1900 WCOV 91791 639-A2
28300 SCTA 91387 4552-A1
LINDA VISTA TER
3300 LA 90032 595-F6
LINDA VISTA WY
1000 PAS 91103 565-E2
LINDBERGH AV
11500 LYN 90262 705-A7
11700 LYN 90262 735-A1
LINDBERGH CT
1500 LVRN 91750 600-F4
LINDBERGH LN
5300 BELL 90201 675-F4
LINDBERGH ST
16100 VanN 91406 531-E3
LINDBLADE DR
4200 CULC 90066 672-D5
4200 LA 90066 672-D5
4600 LA 90230 672-E5
LINDBLADE PL
4500 LA 90230 672-E5
LINDBLADE ST
5100 LA 90230 672-E5
8900 CULC 90232 632-H7
8900 CULC 90232 672-H1
10800 CULC 90230 672-F4
LINDBROOK DR
10300 Wwd 90024 632-C2
LINDCOVE LN
8700 RSMD 91770 636-G1
LINDELL AV
4100 PRV 90660 676-H2
8100 PRV 90660 706-E1
8800 DWNY 90240 706-D2
LINDEN AV
700 LBCH 90813 795-E5
1000 GLDL 91201 563-J1
1100 GLDL 91201 564-A1
1200 GLDL 91201 534-A7
1400 Ven 90291 671-J5
2000 LBCH 90806 795-E3
3000 Bxby 90807 795-E2
3400 Bxby 90807 765-E5
5000 NLB 90805 765-E1
11400 LYN 90262 735-D1
E LINDEN AV
100 BURB 91502 563-J1
100 GLDL 91201 563-J1
N LINDEN AV
- LBCH 90802 825-E1
100 LBCH 90802 795-E7
S LINDEN AV
- LBCH 90802 825-E1

W LINDEN AV
100 BURB 91502 563-J2
300 BURB 91506 563-H2
LINDEN CIR
8100 BPK 90620 767-J4
LINDEN CT
100 BURB 91502 563-J2
1500 Ven 90291 671-J5
5200 PMDL 93552 4287-B4
N LINDEN DR
400 BHLS 90210 632-E1
400 BHLS 90212 632-E1
S LINDEN DR
100 BHLS 90212 632-F2
LINDEN LN
600 LHB 90631 708-F4
27300 SCTA 91354 4460-G7
LINDEN ST
800 LA 90021 634-G6
9400 BLF 90706 736-B5
11000 LYN 90262 705-D7
11300 LYN 90262 735-D1
N LINDEN ST
200 POM 91767 641-A1
S LINDEN ST
100 POM 91766 641-A2
LINDEN TER
23900 CALB 91302 589-E1
LINDEN WY
500 BREA 92821 738-J1
LINDENCLIFF ST
900 LACo 90502 794-B2
LINDENGROVE AV
1200 RowH 91748 679-D4
LINDENGROVE ST
2000 THO 91361 557-A4
LINDENHURST AV
5700 LA 90036 633-B2
6100 LA 90048 633-A2
LINDENVALE RD
10400 LACo 90606 676-G7
10400 LACo 90606 706-G1
LINDENWOOD DR
700 CLAR 91711 571-E7
LINDENWOOD LN
1000 Brwd 90049 591-F7
1000 Brwd 90049 631-F1
LINDER AL
1800 PAS 91103 535-H7
LINDERO AV
- LBCH 90803 825-H1
9000 MTCL 91763 601-F4
LINDERO ST
300 SBdC 92372 (4472-A6 See Page 4471)
2500 SBdC 92371 (4472-F6 See Page 4471)
LINDERO CANYON RD
100 THO 91362 557-G3
100 WLKV 91362 557-G3
5400 WLKV 91361 557-E5
5900 VeCo 91362 557-G3
6000 VeCo 91377 557-G3
W LINDERO CANYON RD
5300 WLKV 91362 557-C7
5400 WLKV 91361 557-C7
32100 WLKV 91361 587-C1
LINDESMITH AV
10100 WHIT 90603 708-A4
12600 LMRD 90638 738-A1
LINDHALL WY
14800 LACo 90604 707-F5
LINDIE LN
13300 LA 91342 482-C4
LINDLEY AV
4500 Enc 91316 561-A2
4500 Tarz 91356 561-A2
6000 Enc 91316 531-A6
6000 Res 91335 531-A4
6000 Res 91335 561-A2
6700 WHIT 90601 677-C6
8200 Nor 91325 531-A4
8800 Nor 91325 501-A7
9600 Nor 91330 501-A5
10300 Nor 91326 501-A3
10400 GrnH 91344 501-A3
LINDLEY PL
500 LA 90013 634-F4
LINDO ST
3100 LA 90068 563-D7
LINDSAY CIR
19200 WAL 91789 639-C6
LINDSAY LN
2400 LA 90039 594-D4
LINDSAY WY
2200 GLDR 91740 570-A7
LINDSAY CANYON DR
30600 LACo 91390 4462-C3
LINDSAY CANYON RD
30400 LACo 91390 4462-C4
LINDSEY AV
4000 PRV 90660 676-H2
9300 DWNY 90240 706-E3
LINDSEY CT
2300 WCOV 91792 679-B1
LINDSEY LN
9700 CYP 90630 767-D7
LINDSKOG DR
15700 WHIT 90603 707-J4
LINDY AV
2700 RSMD 91770 636-D2
LINDY ST
700 RSMD 91770 636-D1

LINE DR
2400 LAN 93536 4015-D5
LINFIELD AV
13500 LA 91342 482-D2
LINFIELD ST
700 AZU 91702 569-A7
1700 GLDR 91740 569-J7
2100 GLDR 91740 570-A7
E LINFIELD ST
100 GLDR 91740 569-E7
18500 AZU 91702 569-B7
18500 LACo 91702 569-B7
19000 LACo 91740 569-C7
W LINFIELD ST
200 GLDR 91740 569-E7
LINFORTH DR
6000 LA 90068 563-G7
6000 LA 90068 593-G1
LINGARD ST
400 LAN 93535 4015-J6
400 LAN 93535 4016-E5
2000 LAN 93534 4015-E6
2000 LAN 93536 4015-B6
LINK RD
- DWNY 90242 705-G7
LINK ST
11400 LA 90061 704-D6
LINKS RD
8600 BPK 90621 738-A6
LINLEY LN
7500 LA 91304 529-E4
LINLEY ST
900 LACo 90502 764-B5
LINN AV
2400 SELM 91733 637-A3
LINN WY
1700 LAN 93535 4016-A4
LINNET CT
- SBdC 92397 (4652-D3 See Page 4651)
26700 SCTA 91351 4551-E3
LINNET RD
1200 SBdC 92397 (4652-E2 See Page 4651)
LINNET ST
18300 Tarz 91356 560-F2
19800 WdHl 91364 560-E2
LINNIE AV
400 Ven 90291 671-H6
LINNIE CANAL CT
200 Ven 90291 671-H6
LINNIE CANAL WK
200 Ven 90291 671-H6
LINNINGTON AV
2000 WLA 90025 632-D4
2200 LA 90064 632-D4
LINS AV
8200 LACo 90606 706-J1
LINSCOTT PL
4800 LA 90016 673-C1
LINSLEY CT
1800 LBCH 90806 795-F5
E LINSLEY ST
4100 COMP 90221 735-C5
4200 RDom 90221 735-C5
LINTON DR
3500 LACo 91724 599-E6
LINVILLE AL
1100 PAS 91104 565-J2
LINWALT ST
8100 LACo 91770 636-F4
LINWOOD AV
200 MNRO 91016 567-F4
1300 LA 90017 634-D4
LINWOOD DR
5100 LFlz 90027 593-J3
LINWOOD PL
100 FUL 92831 738-J7
LION WY
- PMDL 93551 4195-F7
LIONEL PL
6700 Win 91306 530-C7
LIONEL ST
7300 PRM 90723 735-F2
LIONS MTWY
- CHLS 91709 710-E3
- LACo 92823 710-D2
LIONS CANYON RD
- BREA 92823 710-E2
- CHLS 91709 710-E2
- LACo 92823 710-D2
LIPARI CIR
9600 CYP 90630 767-B7
LIPTON AV
3000 SMCA 90403 631-G6
LIQUID AMBER DR
1900 DUAR 91010 568-B5
LIRIO LN
3800 GLDL 91214 504-D7
LISA AV
16500 BLF 90706 736-A6
LISA CT
500 DBAR 91765 640-E7
1100 LAN 93535 4106-B2
LISA LN
19900 Nor 91326 480-E6
LISA PL
3400 Shrm 91403 561-H7
LISA ST
700 LACo 93551 4285-H4
2400 WCOV 91792 638-J6
27700 Cstc 91384 4369-G7

LISA ELLEN ST
600 GLDR 91740 599-F1
LISA GAIL DR
20300 SCTA 91350 4461-D6
LISA KELTON PL
24400 SCTA 91321 4640-F2
LISBON CT
5700 PMDL 93552 4287-C2
10600 WHIT 90601 677-A3
LISBON LN
1500 BelA 90077 592-A4
LISBON ST
- UPL 91784 571-H6
LISBURN PL
11600 LMRD 90638 707-G6
13200 LMRD 90638 737-G2
18700 Nor 91326 480-H6
LISCO DR
2200 SBdC 92372 (4562-F4 See Page 4471)
LISCO PL
2600 LA 90046 593-C2
LISCO ST
16100 WHIT 90603 707-J5
16100 WHIT 90603 708-A5
LISCOMB ST
11800 ELMN 91732 597-F7
N LISE LN
- LACo 91387 4552-B5
LISETTE ST
17000 GrnH 91344 481-C5
LISMAN AV
38100 PMDL 93550 4285-J1
38100 PMDL 93550 4286-A1
LISMORE LN
- BURB 91504 533-E2
LISSO ST
3700 HAW 90250 733-E3
LISTIE AV
32800 Actn 93510 4375-F6
LITA PL
23000 WdHl 91364 559-G5
N LITCHFIELD AV
1800 LBCH 90815 796-B4
LITCHFIELD LN
3500 Tarz 91356 560-G7
LITCHFIELD ST
37400 PMDL 93550 4286-C3
LITCHI LN
1100 SBdC 92372 (4472-C7 See Page 4471)
LITHUANIA DR
12300 GrnH 91344 481-C5
LITHUANIA PL
17200 GrnH 91344 481-C5
LITTCHEN ST
10900 NRWK 90650 736-E2
LITTLE ST
600 LA 90017 634-C3
LITTLEBOW RD
5300 RPV 90275 793-A6
LITTLEBOY DR
14700 LACo 93532 4102-F3
LITTLE CEDAR WY
- Actn 93510 4465-B3
- SCTA 91350 4550-H6
LITTLE FALLS CT
- SCTA 91350 4550-H6
LITTLEFIELD DR
27000 SCTA 91354 4550-G1
E LITTLEFIELD ST
8300 LBCH 90808 767-A7
LITTLE HOLLOW RD
5600 HIDH 91302 559-D3
LITTLEHORN DR
13300 LACo 93532 4102-J4
LITTLE JOHN CT
- WLKV 91361 587-D1
LITTLE JOHN LN
- WLKV 91361 587-D1
LITTLE JOHN ST
4400 BALD 91706 597-J4
4400 IRW 91706 597-J4
LITTLE LAKE RD
10700 DWNY 90241 706-E6
LITTLE LAS FLORES RD
2100 Top 90290 629-G2
LITTLE LEAF DR
36600 PMDL 93550 4286-F4
LITTLE OAK LN
6000 WdHl 91367 529-C7
6000 WdHl 91367 559-C1
24600 SCTA 91321 4640-G3
LITTLE PARK LN
100 Brwd 90049 631-G3
LITTLE QUAIL AV
1400 DBAR 91765 680-C3
LITTLER CT
5600 LHB 90631 738-B2
LITTLER PL
12400 GrnH 91344 481-D5
LITTLERIVER LN
12300 CRTS 90703 736-J4
LITTLE ROCK
900 CLAR 91711 571-F4
LITTLE ROCK LN
- PMDL 93552 4287-E2
LITTLE ROCK RD
- LACo - 4467-D4
- Litl 93543 4467-D4
- Litl 93543 (4557-H1 See Page 4467)

LITTLE ROCK RD
- Litl 93543 (4558-A1 See Page 4467)
LITTLE ROCK TKTR
- LACo - (4557-H7 See Page 4467)
- LACo - (4558-A3 See Page 4467)
- LACo - 4647-F2
- Litl 93543 (4558-A2 See Page 4467)
LITTLE ROCK WY
20300 MAL 90265 629-H6
LITTLEROCK RANCHOS RD
36800 Litl 93543 4288-A4
LITTLE ROCK WASH RD
5600 LACo 93552 4377-C3
6800 Litl 93543 4377-E3
LITTLE SANTA MONICA BLVD
10000 CenC 90067 632-C4
10100 WLA 90025 632-C4
E LITTLESTONE DR
8800 LACo 91776 596-H5
LITTLE SYCAMORE ST
36600 PMDL 93552 4287-A3
LITTLE SYCAMORE CANYON RD
100 VeCo 90265 586-D4
200 LACo 90265 586-D4
LITTLETON PL
4500 LCF 91011 534-J2
LITTLETON WY
23500 SCTA 91354 4460-G7
LITTLE TUJUNGA RD
11700 LA 91342 482-J7
11700 LA 91342 (4723-A6 See Page 4643)
11700 LACo 91342 (4723-A6 See Page 4643)
11700 LACo 91342 482-J7
13400 LACo - 4643-B6
13400 LACo - (4723-A6 See Page 4643)
15000 LACo - 4642-G4
LITTLE VALLEY RD
24200 HIDH 91302 559-D2
LITTLEWOOD DR
27500 RPV 90275 793-B7
LIVELY AV
43600 LAN 93536 4105-D1
44200 LAN 93536 4015-D7
LIVELY CT
43900 LAN 93536 4105-D1
LIVE OAK AV
- ARCD 91006 597-G2
100 IRW 91016 597-G2
100 MNRO 91016 597-G2
100 IRW 91706 597-G2
100 MNRO 91706 597-G2
200 BREA 92821 709-B6
800 IRW 91706 598-A2
8300 LACo 91776 596-J3
8700 SGBL 91776 596-J3
9200 TEML 91780 596-J3
9500 TEML 91780 597-A3
9900 ARCD 91007 597-A3
13700 BALD 91706 598-A2
E LIVE OAK AV
- ARCD 91006 597-E2
4400 MNRO 91006 597-E2
4400 MNRO 91016 597-E2
N LIVE OAK AV
100 GLDR 91741 569-F4
W LIVE OAK AV
- ARCD 91007 597-B3
- TEML 91780 597-B3
100 SGBL 91776 596-E4
10200 TEML 91007 597-B3
LIVE OAK CIR
- SCTA 91387 4552-D3
LIVE OAK CT
26800 CALB 91301 558-G7
LIVE OAK DR
- DUAR 91010 568-C5
400 LACo 91750 571-A7
3700 POM 91767 600-J1
E LIVE OAK DR
2000 LA 90068 593-H2
W LIVE OAK DR
2100 LA 90068 593-H3
LIVE OAK LN
3000 IRW 91706 598-A2
7300 CDHY 90201 705-F1
LIVE OAK RD
27600 Cstc 91384 4459-H5
LIVE OAK ST
2400 LACo 90255 704-H1
2500 THO 91362 557-A2
2700 LACo 90255 705-A1
2900 HNTP 90255 705-A1
3700 CDHY 90201 705-C1
4200 BELL 90201 705-C1
5700 BGDN 90201 705-G1
E LIVE OAK ST
100 SGBL 91776 596-E4
8200 LACo 91776 596-F3
W LIVE OAK ST
500 SGBL 91776 596-D4
LIVE OAK TER
22600 Chat 91311 499-H5

LIVE OAK TR
6700 VeCo 93063 499-D4
LIVE OAK CANYON RD
- CLAR 91711 571-A6
4100 LACo 91750 571-A6
4100 LACo 91750 570-J6
4800 LVRN 91750 570-J6
LIVE OAK CIRCLE DR
500 LACo 91302 628-H1
LIVE OAK CUTOFF
- LACo 91711 571-A4
- LACo 91750 570-J4
- LACo 91750 571-A4
LIVE OAK MEADOW RD
2300 LACo 90265 629-F3
LIVE OAKS AV
500 PAS 91103 565-G4
LIVE OAK SPRINGS CANYON RD
15300 LACo 91387 4552-E4
15300 SCTA 91387 4552-D4
LIVE OAK VIEW AV
5200 Eagl 90041 564-J5
LIVERMONT LN
800 DUAR 91010 568-D5
LIVERMORE PL
4200 CYP 90630 767-B6
LIVERMORE TER
200 HiPk 90042 595-D2
LIVERPOOL CT
- Cstc 91384 4459-F5
1200 SDMS 91724 599-G5
1200 SDMS 91773 599-G5
LIVERPOOL DR
1300 PAS 91103 565-D1
LIVERPOOL WY
- PMDL 93552 4287-C4
LIVERY WY
15900 SCTA 91387 4462-D7
LIVEWOOD LN
23600 Hrbr 90710 794-A2
LIVIA AV
4500 RSMD 91770 596-H5
6300 TEML 91780 596-H1
LIVINGSTON AV
28100 Valc 91355 4459-E6
LIVINGSTON CT
- CLAR 91711 571-E6
E LIVINGSTON DR
3700 LBCH 90803 825-J2
3900 LBCH 90803 826-A1
LIVINGSTON WY
8200 LA 90046 593-A4
LIVIUS WY
2000 LACo 91789 679-E5
LIVONIA AV
1400 LA 90035 632-H4
1900 LA 90034 632-H5
LIVORNO CT
30800 WLKV 91362 557-G6
LIVORNO DR
16700 PacP 90272 630-G6
LIVORNO WY
- Nor 91326 500-D1
LIZ CT
7400 LA 91304 529-E4
LLANO CTO
17500 Llan 93544 4379-J6
LLANO DR
4800 WdHl 91364 559-J3
LLEWELLYN DR
- SIGH 90755 795-H3
LLEWELLYN ST
100 LA 90012 634-H2
LLOYD AV
100 FUL 92833 738-C7
7900 NHol 91605 532-D3
LLOYD PL
8900 WHWD 90069 592-H6
LLOYDCREST DR
9300 LA 90210 592-F4
LLOYD HOUGHTON PL
23500 SCTA 91321 4640-G2
LLOYDS CT
40000 PMDL 93551 4195-B3
LMU DR
12300 Wch 90045 702-D2
LOADSTONE DR
3400 Shrm 91403 561-H7
LOBBY CIR
1400 Hrbr 90710 793-J3
1400 Hrbr 90710 794-A3
LOBDELL PL
1500 Echo 90026 594-E6
LOBELIA AV
1300 UPL 91784 571-J3
LOBELIA LN
- SCTA 91354 4460-G3
LOBER PL
6500 LACo 91775 596-G1
LOBIVIA WY
16500 PRM 90723 735-G6
LOBO CT
1600 LAN 93535 4016-C5
LOBO CANYON RD
30900 Ago 91301 587-E2
LOBOS RD
4100 WdHl 91364 560-B5
LOBO VISTA RD
31100 Ago 91301 587-E2
LOBROOK DR
28000 RPV 90275 792-G7

LOCARNO DR
- SBdC 92397 (4652-F3 See Page 4651)
LOCH ALENE AV
6300 PRV 90660 676-F6
LOCHALENE AV
7500 PRV 90660 676-E7
LOCH AVON AV
- LACo 90606 676-H5
LOCH AVON DR
9200 PRV 90660 676-G4
10300 LACo 90606 676-J5
10900 WHIT 90606 676-J5
11000 LACo 90606 677-A6
LOCHGLEN CT
1800 HacH 91745 678-F6
LOCHGREEN DR
19100 Tarz 91356 560-F6
LOCHINVAR DR
9200 PRV 90660 676-F6
LOCHINVAR ST
9400 PRV 90660 676-F6
10600 LACo 90606 676-G7
11600 LACo 90606 706-J1
LOCHLEVEN ST
19200 GLDR 91741 569-C6
LOCH LOMOND DR
8300 PRV 90660 676-F3
10100 LACo 90606 676-H5
10800 WHIT 90606 676-J5
11400 LACo 90606 677-A6
LOCH LOMOND RD
11100 OrCo 90720 796-H3
LOCHMERE AV
300 LACo 91744 679-B2
LOCHMOOR RD
25600 SCTA 91355 4550-F6
LOCHNEVIS AV
14000 NRWK 90650 737-A3
LOCHRIN LN
13400 LA 91342 482-C1
LOCHVALE DR
6200 RPV 90275 792-J7
LOCKE AV
3500 LA 90032 595-E5
LOCKEARN ST
700 Brwd 90049 631-F1
LOCKERBIE CT
3800 GLDL 91208 534-E2
LOCKERBIE LN
3700 GLDL 91208 534-E2
LOCKFORD ST
9600 LA 90035 632-G4
LOCKHART AV
36000 PMDL 93552 4287-C6
LOCKHAVEN AV
4800 Eagl 90041 564-J5
LOCKHAVEN DR
1000 BREA 92821 708-J5
5300 BPK 90621 737-J6
LOCKHAVEN ST
400 PAS 91105 565-G6
LOCK HAVEN WY
1800 CLAR 91711 571-A7
LOCKHEED AV
5700 LACo 90606 676-J4
5700 WHIT 90606 676-J4
LOCKHEED DR
7500 LA 91505 533-C3
LOCKHEED WY
1000 PMDL 93550 4196-B4
LOCKHEED VIEW DR
1200 BURB 91504 533-H4
LOCKHURST DR
5300 WdHl 91367 559-E1
6000 WdHl 91367 529-E7
6300 CanP 91307 529-E7
LOCKLAND DR
3700 LA 90008 673-E3
LOCKLAND PL
4100 LA 90008 673-D3
LOCKLAYER ST
1000 SDMS 91773 599-J4
LOCKLENNA LN
6500 RPV 90275 822-H1
LOCKLIN WY
2600 FUL 92833 738-B4
LOCKNESS AV
22800 LA 90501 793-J1
23200 Hrbr 90710 793-J2
LOCKNESS PL
1500 LA 90501 793-J1
LOCKPORT PL
11000 SFSP 90670 707-A6
LOCKRIDGE RD
11900 LA 91604 562-G7
11900 LA 91604 592-G1
LOCKRIDGE ESTATE RD
- LA 91604 562-G7
- LA 91604 592-G1
LOCKSLEY DR
3500 LACo 91107 566-G6
LOCKSLEY PL
2600 LA 90039 594-D3
5800 LA 90068 593-G2
LOCKWOOD AV
4200 LA 90029 594-A6
LOCKWOOD LN
- POM 91766 640-F7
LOCKWOOD RD
1800 GLDL 91208 534-H6
26200 LACo 90265 628-C3

LOCUST AV
- VeCo 91377 558-A2
600 LBCH 90802 795-D6
700 LBCH 90813 795-D5
1800 LBCH 90806 795-D4
3100 Bxby 90807 795-D1
3400 Bxby 90807 765-D6
4900 NLB 90805 765-D3
N LOCUST AV
100 COMP 90221 735-C2
S LOCUST AV
100 COMP 90221 735-C4
LOCUST CIR
500 COMP 90221 735-C5
LOCUST DR
3500 CALB 91302 559-E7
8200 BPK 90620 767-J5
N LOCUST DR
400 FUL 92833 738-D6
LOCUST RD
300 SBdC 92372 (4472-A4 See Page 4471)
LOCUST ST
- ONT 91762 641-H3
- SIMI 93063 499-B2
500 LA 90065 594-J5
600 PAS 91101 566-A4
800 PAS 91106 566-C4
1700 PAS 91107 566-C4
3800 SBdC 91710 641-G3
5400 CHNO 91710 641-G3
N LOCUST ST
100 ING 90301 703-D2
200 POM 91767 640-J1
S LOCUST ST
100 ING 90301 703-D2
100 POM 91766 640-J2
W LOCUST ST
1100 ONT 91762 641-J3
LOCUST TR
3500 CALB 91302 559-F7
LOCUST RIDGE CIR
23100 SCTA 91354 4460-H5
LODESTAR DR
28100 SCTA 91350 4461-B5
LODESTONE LN
15700 HacH 91745 678-B5
LODGE AV
5300 HiPk 90042 595-D4
LODGEPOLE CT
14600 CHLS 91709 680-J4
LODGE POLE RD
24000 DBAR 91765 680-D4
LODGEPOLE RD
5500 SBdC 92397 (4652-E3 See Page 4651)
LODI PL
1100 LA 90038 593-F5
LODI CREEK RD
1300 SDMS 91773 570-D7
LODI LATERAL MTWY
- SDMS 91773 570-D2
LODOSA DR
8100 WHIT 90605 707-G1
LOFIELD CT
3500 LACo 91107 566-G4
LOFTHILL DR
14900 LMRD 90638 737-H4
LOFTUS DR
100 SGBL 91776 596-E7
8700 RSMD 91770 596-G7
9700 RSMD 91770 597-A7
9800 ELMN 91731 597-A7
LOFTYGROVE DR
6900 RPV 90275 792-G6
LOFTY HEIGHTS DR
- LACo 90265 587-D7
LOFTYHILL DR
400 LACo 90265 587-C7
LOFTYVIEW DR
2400 TOR 90505 793-E6
LOGAN CT
- BURB 91504 533-E2
LOGAN ST
1100 Echo 90026 594-E7
2200 POM 91767 601-B5
3300 LVRN 91750 600-F1
LOGANBERRY CIR
- PMDL 93551 4285-E2
LOGANBERRY DR
12700 LMRD 90638 738-A1
LOGANBERRY RD
- CRSN 90746 764-F1
LOGANDALE DR
6300 LA 90068 593-F2
LOGANRITA AV
1000 ARCD 91006 567-F7
1600 ARCD 91006 597-F1
LOGANSIDE DR
1900 LACo 90047 703-H7
1900 LACo 90250 703-H7
LOG CABIN TR
43700 LACo 93532 4101-J1
LOGDELL AV
24200 SCTA 91321 4640-J2
LOGGERS LN
- WCOV 91792 679-J2
S LOGGERS LN
2200 ONT 91762 641-J5
LOGUE AV
44800 LAN 93535 4016-A5
LOGUE CT
45000 LAN 93535 4016-A5

LOGWOOD DR
26600 LACo 92397 (4652-A1 See Page 4651)
LOGWOOD RD
5800 WLKV 91362 557-G4
LOHART AV
300 MTBL 90640 676-D3
LOHENGRIN ST
1800 LACo 90047 703-H6
LOHMAN LN
700 SPAS 91030 595-F2
LOIRE CT
30800 WLKV 91362 557-F5
LOIS AV
900 SPed 90731 824-A3
LOIS CIR
1100 LVRN 91750 600-E2
LOIS CT
- GrnH 91344 481-A7
LOIS LN
300 LA 90732 823-J5
800 FUL 92832 738-F6
800 LAN 93535 4106-B3
LOIS ST
100 LHB 90631 708-E5
2400 WCOV 91792 639-A6
LOLA AV
200 PAS 91107 566-D3
LOLA LN
- SCTA 91321 4640-H1
LOLETA AV
4600 Eagl 90041 565-C6
LOLETA PL
4600 Eagl 90041 565-C7
LOLINA LN
5000 CYP 90630 767-C5
7500 LA 90046 593-B1
S LOLITA ST
800 WCOV 91791 639-A2
LOMA AV
- LBCH 90815 795-J4
700 LBCH 90804 795-J4
1000 LACo 91733 636-J4
1400 MNRO 91016 567-F6
1500 LVRN 91750 600-F1
2000 SELM 91733 636-J4
4000 RSMD 91770 596-J6
4900 TEML 91780 596-H1
N LOMA AV
- LBCH 90803 825-J1
300 LBCH 90814 795-J5
300 LBCH 90814 825-J1
1300 LBCH 90804 795-J5
6700 LACo 91775 596-H1
LOMA DR
100 Echo 90026 634-D2
100 HMB 90254 762-G1
300 LA 90017 634-D3
11900 LACo 90604 707-D7
12200 LACo 90604 737-D1
LOMA LN
1000 VeCo 93063 499-B4
3500 BALD 91706 597-J7
3500 BALD 91706 598-A7
LOMA PL
- UPL 91786 601-G3
200 Echo 90026 634-D2
N LOMA PL
- UPL 91786 601-G3
LOMA RD
1400 MTBL 90640 636-C7
LOMA ST
1200 RBCH 90277 763-A5
LOMA ALTA DR
2100 FUL 92833 738-C4
E LOMA ALTA DR
- Alta 91001 535-J4
300 Alta 91001 536-A3
W LOMA ALTA DR
- Alta 91001 535-G4
LOMACITAS LN
16100 WHIT 90603 707-J1
16100 WHIT 90603 708-A1
LOMA CONTENTA
- LACo 91390 4373-E7
LOMA CREST
1600 GLDL 91205 564-G7
LOMA CREST DR
3400 Alta 91001 535-J3
LOMA LADA DR
3400 LA 90065 594-H3
LOMA LINDA
- LACo 91390 4373-E7
LOMA LINDA AV
5300 LFlz 90027 593-H4
LOMA LINDA DR
1100 BHLS 90210 592-E5
S LOMA LINDA DR
200 ANA 92804 767-H6
LOMA LISA LN
1000 ARCD 91006 567-B4
LOMA METISSE RD
100 LACo 90265 629-C1
LOMA NORTE PL
1000 LHB 90631 708-H4
LOMAS VERDES
2300 LA 90732 823-F7
LOMA VERDE AV
400 LHB 90631 708-E6
6900 CanP 91303 530-C5
7600 LA 91304 530-C3
LOMA VERDE DR
1000 ARCD 91006 566-J4

STREET Block City ZIP Pg-Grid

LOMA VERDE DR
2100 FUL 92833 738-C4
LOMA VERDE MTWY
30300 Cstc 91384 4459-A7
LOMA VERDE ST
700 MONP 91754 636-A4
LOMA VIEW DR
3400 Alta 91001 535-H4
LOMA VISTA
41900 LAN 93536 4105-B6
LOMA VISTA AV
4500 VER 90058 675-C4
5100 MYWD 90270 675-C4
5900 HNTP 90255 675-C5
6200 BELL 90201 675-C6
LOMA VISTA CT
1000 SPAS 91030 595-G2
LOMA VISTA DR
- GLDL 91208 534-J7
700 LBCH 90813 795-C6
800 BHLS 90210 592-G4
1600 GLDL 91208 564-J1
2000 LA 90210 592-G3
2500 ALH 91803 635-H2
4500 LCF 91011 535-A3
45100 LAN 93535 4016-C5
LOMA VISTA PL
1000 FUL 92833 738-B6
2100 LA 90039 594-E5
6400 BELL 90201 675-C7
LOMA VISTA ST
100 ELSG 90245 732-D1
700 ELSG 90245 702-D7
1300 PAS 91104 566-B2
E LOMA VISTA ST
100 COV 91723 599-B6
1300 WCOV 91790 598-H6
W LOMA VISTA ST
600 POM 91768 600-G6
LOMAX LN
1400 RBCH 90278 762-J3
LOMAY PL
1300 PAS 91103 565-E1
LOMBARD AV
300 PacP 90272 631-A6
LOMBARD ST
200 POM 91768 640-D2
LOMBARDY BLVD
2400 LA 90032 595-E7
2400 LA 90032 635-F1
LOMBARDY CT
4300 CHNO 91710 641-E5
LOMBARDY DR
1900 LCF 91011 534-J2
LOMBARDY PL
600 SMRO 91108 566-E6
LOMBARDY RD
1200 PAS 91106 566-B6
1600 SMRO 91108 566-C6
2900 LACo 91107 566-E6
3000 PAS 91107 566-G6
LOMBARDY ST
3900 SBdC 91710 641-D5
4000 CHNO 91710 641-E5
LOMELA CT
15700 LMRD 90638 737-H4
LOMELI LN
2300 LVRN 91750 600-H2
LOMINA AV
4100 LKWD 90713 766-C4
N LOMINA AV
2000 LBCH 90815 796-C2
3000 LBCH 90808 796-C1
3600 LBCH 90808 766-D7
LOMIRA ST
1800 COV 91724 599-F5
E LOMITA AV
100 GLDL 91205 564-E5
W LOMITA AV
100 GLDL 91204 564-D6
LOMITA BLVD
1700 LMTA 90717 793-H3
2500 TOR 90505 793-D2
5200 TOR 90505 763-B7
E LOMITA BLVD
100 CRSN 90745 794-D4
100 Wilm 90744 794-F3
W LOMITA BLVD
- LACo 90745 794-B4
100 Wilm 90744 794-B4
100 CRSN 90745 794-B4
800 Hrbr 90710 794-B4
800 Hrbr 90710 794-B4
1400 Hrbr 90710 793-J4
1700 LA 90717 793-J4
1700 LMTA 90717 793-J4
LOMITA CT
1400 PAS 91106 595-J1
LOMITA DR
1300 PAS 91106 595-J1
1300 PAS 91106 596-A1
24100 LMTA 90717 793-G3
29000 Cstc 91384 4459-D6
LOMITA ST
100 ELSG 90245 732-F2
600 ELSG 90245 702-F7
4500 LA 90019 633-E5
N LOMITA ST
100 BURB 91506 563-G1
400 BURB 91506 533-F7
S LOMITA ST
200 BURB 91506 563-G2

LOMITA PARK PL
2000 LMTA 90717 793-H3
LOMITAS AV
9400 BHLS 90210 592-F7
9600 BHLS 90210 632-E1
13500 LACo 90601 637-G5
13600 LACo 91746 637-H6
14200 INDS 91746 637-H6
LOMITAS DR
3700 LA 90032 595-D5
5800 HiPk 90042 595-E4
LOMO DR
27900 RPV 90275 792-H7
LOMOND AV
400 Wwd 90024 632-C1
LOMORA AV
600 PAS 91107 566-F2
LOMPOC ST
2700 Eagl 90041 564-H7
2700 LA 90065 564-H7
LONDELIUS ST
15800 LA 91343 531-D1
17100 Nor 91324 530-F1
17200 Nor 91325 531-B1
18600 Win 91306 530-C1
21900 LA 91304 529-J1
21900 LA 91304 530-A1
LONDON PL
25800 StvR 91381 4550-C7
LONDON ST
2500 Echo 90026 634-C1
2700 Echo 90026 594-B7
LONDONDERRY PL
1300 LA 90069 592-J5
1300 WHWD 90069 592-J5
LONDONDERRY VW
1300 LA 90069 592-J5
LONDRINA LN
700 LACo 90502 794-C3
LONECREST DR
15800 HacH 91745 678-B6
LONE EAGLE RD
600 WAL 91789 639-F7
LONE GROVE WY
5800 LCF 91011 535-C1
N LONE HILL AV
100 GLDR 91741 569-J4
100 SDMS 91773 599-J2
S LONE HILL AV
100 GLDR 91741 569-J6
100 SDMS 91773 599-J3
600 GLDR 91740 569-J6
1200 GLDR 91740 599-J1
LONEOAK AV
43800 LAN 93534 4105-F1
44400 LAN 93534 4015-F6
LONEOAK CT
29800 Cstc 91384 4459-D4
LONE OAK DR
400 THO 91362 557-A1
17900 GrnH 91344 481-A5
LONE OAK RD
12600 Pear 93553 4378-G2
12700 Pear 93553 4288-J7
LONE PINE LN
4500 LCF 91011 534-J2
LONE PINE TR
16500 LACo 93532 4101-J2
16500 LACo 93532 4102-A2
LONE PINE CANYON RD
4800 SBdC (4652-F3 See Page 4651)
5100 SBdC 92397 (4652-E2 See Page 4651)
LONE RIDGE PL
15700 LMRD 90638 707-H7
15800 LACo 90604 707-H7
LONE RIDGE RD
- POM 91766 640-H6
LONE ROCK CT
- StvR 91381 4550-B4
LONE ROCK ST
19000 SCTA 91351 4551-F2
LONESOME VALLEY RD
- LACo 91390 4193-D5
- LACo 93551 4193-D5
S LONESS AV
14400 LACo 90220 734-F4
LONESTAR PL
27600 Cstc 91384 4459-H4
E LONE STAR ST
14000 LACo 91746 637-H6
E LONE STAR WY
- LACo 91390 4461-B4
LONESTAR WY
2000 THO 91362 557-A1
LONE TREE DR
13200 LACo 93532 4102-J4
LONE VALLEY DR
4700 RPV 90275 793-B7
LONG LN
100 INDS 91746 638-A5
3600 SBdC 92371 (4562-J2 See Page 4471)
LONG PT
300 LBCH 90803 826-C1
LONG ST
6000 LA 90043 673-E6
N LONG ST
600 ING 90302 673-E7
LONGACRE AV
11500 GrnH 91344 480-J5
11500 GrnH 91344 481-A7

LONGACRES AV
9200 PRV 90660 676-H1
LONG BEACH AV
900 LA 90021 634-G7
LONG BEACH AV E
- Flor 90001 674-G4
1500 LA 90021 634-G7
1500 LA 90021 674-G1
1900 LA 90058 674-G2
LONG BEACH AV W
1900 LA 90058 674-G3
1900 LA 90011 674-G3
5700 Flor 90001 674-G5
LONG BEACH BLVD
- NLB 90805 735-B1
700 LBCH 90813 795-E6
900 COMP 90221 735-B1
8000 SGAT 90255 704-J2
8000 SGAT 90280 704-J2
8000 LACo 90255 704-J2
8800 SGAT 90280 705-A4
9900 LYN 90262 705-A4
11800 LYN 90262 735-B1
N LONG BEACH BLVD
- LBCH 90802 825-E1
100 COMP 90221 735-B2
100 NLB 90805 735-B2
200 Bxby 90807 765-D7
200 LBCH 90802 795-E7
1300 LBCH 90813 795-D4
1800 LBCH 90806 795-D4
2200 LYN 90262 735-B2
3000 Bxby 90807 795-D4
4600 NLB 90805 765-C1
S LONG BEACH BLVD
100 COMP 90221 735-B5
LONG BEACH FRWY
I-710
- KeCo 93560 3833-G3
- ALH 595-G7
- ALH 635-F4
- BELL 675-F5
- BELL 705-F5
- BGDN 675-F5
- BGDN 705-F5
- CDHY 705-F5
- CMRC 675-F5
- COMP 735-D6
- CRSN 765-B5
- ELA 635-F4
- ELA 675-F5
- LACo 705-F5
- LACo 735-D6
- LBCH 765-B5
- LBCH 795-B4
- LBCH 825-C1
- LYN 705-F5
- LYN 735-D6
- MONP 635-F4
- NLB 735-D6
- NLB 765-B5
- PRM 735-D6
- RDom 735-D6
- RDom 765-B5
- SGAT 705-F5
- VER 675-F5
LONG BEACH FRWY Rt#-710
- PAS 565-G5
LONGBOW CT
3400 Shrm 91403 561-H7
LONGBOW DR
15300 Shrm 91403 561-G7
LONGBRANCH CIR
200 BREA 92821 709-D7
LONG CANYON RD
- BRAD 91010 568-B3
LONGDALE LN
3000 LA 90068 593-D1
LONGDEN AV
100 IRW 91016 597-G2
100 IRW 91706 597-G2
100 MNRO 91016 597-G2
300 ARCD 91006 597-G2
700 ARCD 91007 597-G2
8200 LACo 91775 596-F2
8600 TEML 91775 596-G2
8800 TEML 91780 596-H2
9600 TEML 91780 597-G2
E LONGDEN AV
- ARCD 91006 597-D2
1200 MNRO 91016 597-D2
1300 MNRO 91016 597-D2
W LONGDEN AV
- ARCD 91007 597-B2
E LONGDEN DR
100 SGBL 91775 596-E2
W LONGDEN DR
100 SGBL 91775 596-E2
LONGDON
1600 WCOV 91791 638-J5
LONGFELLOW AV
- HMB 90254 732-F7
500 MANB 90266 732-G7
LONGFELLOW DR
1100 MANB 90266 732-H7
6500 BPK 90620 767-F1
LONGFELLOW PL
25400 StvR 91381 4550-C7
25400 StvR 91381 4640-C1
LONGFELLOW ST
3100 SMCA 90405 671-H4
5100 HiPk 90042 595-C3

LONGFORD PL
- MNRO 91016 567-H2
LONGFORD ST
10600 LA 91342 503-A1
10900 LA 91342 502-J1
LONGHILL DR
1400 MONP 91754 635-H4
27400 RPV 90275 793-B7
LONGHILL WY
1100 MONP 91754 635-H4
LONGHORN CT
39300 PMDL 93551 4195-E5
LONGHORN RD
1300 SDMS 91773 570-C7
LONGLEAF DR
12600 LMRD 90638 737-E1
LONGLEY WY
100 ARCD 91007 597-C2
LONGMEADOW AV
17000 LACo 93591 4199-H4
17100 LACo 93591 4200-A4
N LONGMONT AV
6300 LACo 91775 596-F1
6700 LACo 91775 566-F7
LONG OAK DR
26300 SCTA 91321 4551-E5
LONGRIDGE AV
3200 Shrm 91423 562-D3
3400 LA 91604 562-D6
5200 VanN 91401 562-D2
6000 VanN 91401 532-D6
6800 NHol 91605 532-D3
LONGRIDGE DR
1200 LHB 90631 738-D2
LONGRIDGE TER
3200 Shrm 91423 562-D7
LONGSPUR ST
- KeCo 93560 3833-G3
LONGVALE AV
11900 LYN 90262 735-A1
LONG VALLEY RD
23400 WdHI 91364 559-C2
23400 WdHI 91367 559-C2
23400 HIDH 91302 559-C2
23400 LA 91302 559-C2
23600 VeCo 91302 559-C2
LONGVIEW AV
6300 LA 90068 593-F3
LONG VIEW DR
- RPV 90275 793-H7
LONGVIEW DR
900 DBAR 91765 680-E2
1100 FUL 92831 738-J4
LONGVIEW RD
28500 Pear 93553 4468-J7
34300 Pear 93553 4378-J3
38000 LACo 93591 4199-A7
40400 LACo 93535 4198-J1
40700 LACo 93535 4199-A1
40900 LACo 93535 4109-A1
LONGVIEW RD Rt#-N6
29600 Valy 93563 4468-J2
31300 Pear 93553 4468-J2
31800 Pear 93553 4378-J5
LONGVIEW VALLEY RD
3600 Shrm 91423 562-A6
LONGWOOD AV
1600 CLAR 91711 601-E1
S LONGWOOD AV
700 LA 90005 633-D4
700 LA 90010 633-D4
700 LA 90019 633-D4
1900 LA 90016 633-D6
LONGWOOD LN
500 PAS 91103 565-G3
LONGWOOD PL
1100 LA 90019 633-E4
LONGWORTH AV
- LACo 90703 736-F6
10000 SFSP 90670 706-F5
10800 DWNY 90241 706-F6
11200 NRWK 90650 706-F6
12100 NRWK 90650 736-F1
20400 LKWD 90715 766-F4
LONGWORTH DR
1300 Brwd 90049 631-D4
E LONNA LINDA DR
5500 LBCH 90815 796-C6
LONSDALE CT
- PMDL 93551 4195-A3
LONZO ST
7100 Tuj 91042 504-A2
LOOKABOUT RD
43200 LACo 93532 4102-F3
LOOKING GLASS DR
500 DBAR 91765 640-E5
LOOKING GLASS WY
1900 UPL 91784 571-H5
LOOK OUT CIR
- LVRN 91750 570-H5
LOOKOUT CT
1300 UPL 91784 571-H3
LOOKOUT DR
- Actn 93510 4374-D4
- Brwd 90049 631-J2
- LACo 91390 4374-C4
600 LA 90012 634-G1
1700 Ago 91301 588-B4
LOOKOUT RD
- SCTA 91350 4551-B5
1700 LACo 90265 628-C3
LOOKOUT TR
400 Top 90290 590-A7

LOOKOUT MOUNTAIN AV
8100 LA 90046 592-J2
LOOKOUT ROCK TR
1000 VeCo 93063 499-C4
LOOM PL
15400 Shrm 91403 561-G7
LOOMIS CT
37000 PMDL 93550 4286-F4
LOOMIS ST
2500 LKWD 90712 765-G4
5900 LKWD 90713 766-D4
LOOMIS RANCH RD
- LACo 4647-B5
LOOP AV
26500 LACo 91387 4552-B6
LOOP BRANCH
- CLAR 91711 571-F3
LOOSCHEN RD
31300 MAL 90265 626-H7
LOOSMORE ST
2600 LA 90065 594-H5
LOPE LN
1100 GLDR 91740 569-J6
LOPEZ AV
800 ELA 90022 635-F4
LOPEZ LN
- PMDL 93552 4287-E2
N LOPEZ RD
- LA 91342 482-F6
- LACo 91342 482-F6
LOPEZ ST
21100 WdHI 91364 560-A3
LOPEZ CANYON RD
10300 LACo 91342 482-H3
12600 LA 91342 482-F5
LOQUAT LN
5700 PMDL 93551 4104-F7
LORA ST
10600 TEML 91780 597-C4
LORADO WY
3700 LACo 90043 673-D5
LORAE PL
5800 LA 90068 593-G2
LORAIN RD
1000 SMRO 91108 596-E1
E LORAIN RD
8200 LACo 91775 566-F7
LORAINE AV
12300 CHNO 91710 641-E6
N LORAINE AV
100 GLDR 91741 569-G3
S LORAINE AV
100 GLDR 91741 569-G6
LORAINE ST
1900 WCOV 91792 639-A6
E LORAINE ST
400 GLDL 91207 564-F2
W LORAINE ST
200 GLDL 91202 564-D2
LORALYN DR
100 ARCD 91006 567-C2
LORANNE AV
700 POM 91767 641-B1
800 POM 91767 601-B7
N LORANNE AV
100 POM 91767 641-B1
LORAWOOD ST
1200 LHB 90631 738-F1
LORCA RD
12700 LMRD 90638 737-G1
LORD ST
1000 Boyl 90033 635-A3
LORDS RD
11400 LACo 91390 4373-D7
LORDSBURG CT
- LVRN 91750 600-H4
LOREE WY
25600 LACo 91302 589-A7
LORELEI AV
4700 LBCH 90808 766-B4
4900 LKWD 90712 766-B2
LORELLA AV
1200 LHB 90631 708-C6
15500 LACo 90248 734-D5
N LOREN AV
700 AZU 91702 568-G6
LOREN LN
1900 LACo 91770 636-F3
LOREN ST
4400 City 90063 635-F3
LORENA AV
600 ARCD 91006 567-D4
LORENA DR
24900 CALB 91302 559-C6
N LORENA ST
100 LA 90063 635-C5
S LORENA ST
100 LA 90063 635-C6
600 LA 90023 635-C6
1100 LA 90023 675-B1
LORENCITA DR
19700 LACo 91724 639-E1
19900 WCOV 91791 639-E1
LORENE ST
10400 WHIT 90601 676-J4
10400 WHIT 90601 677-A4
LORENZA CT
5400 LACo 91776 596-H4
LORENZANA DR
20200 WdHI 91364 560-D3
LORENZO CT
24900 CALB 91302 559-C7

LORENZO DR
500 VeCo 91377 557-G1
2300 LA 90068 593-E2
10300 LA 90064 632-F5
LORENZO LN
- SCTA 91355 4460-D6
LORENZO PL
10400 LA 90064 632-E6
N LORETA WK
100 LBCH 90803 826-C2
LORETO DR
1300 GLDL 91207 564-G2
LORETO ST
300 LA 90065 595-A6
400 LA 90065 594-J6
LORETTA DR
14900 LMRD 90638 707-F7
LORETTA LN
28800 SCTA 91387 4552-D1
LORETTO CT
100 CLAR 91711 571-D7
LORI LN
1300 LACo 91770 636-G4
LORI ANN AV
600 AZU 91702 568-H4
LORI ANN LN
17400 CRTS 90703 737-B7
LORICA ST
9600 RSMD 91770 597-A6
LORIKEET LN
24500 SCTA 91355 4550-E5
LORILLARD ST
16600 GrnH 91344 481-C7
LORIMER AV
44200 LAN 93534 4015-E4
LORIN AV
2400 SELM 91733 637-C3
LORIN LN
200 LACo 90265 629-C1
LORINDA DR
900 GLDL 91206 564-H3
LORING AV
100 Wwd 90024 592-B7
200 Wwd 90024 632-C1
LORING DR
3100 OrCo 90720 796-H4
LORITA LN
- Saug 91350 4461-F6
LORJEN RD
27800 LACo 91387 4552-C3
LORNA CT
11700 Brwd 90049 631-H3
LORNA LN
500 Brwd 90049 631-H3
LORNA ST
5200 TOR 90503 763-A5
LORNE ST
10300 SunV 91352 533-A2
11000 SunV 91352 532-J2
11900 NHol 91605 532-D2
14200 PanC 91402 532-A2
14800 PanC 91402 531-H2
16900 VanN 91406 531-C2
17400 Nor 91325 531-B2
17800 Res 91335 531-A2
18200 Res 91335 530-F3
19900 Win 91306 530-D2
LORRAIN ST
10700 LYN 90262 704-J6
LORRAINE BLVD
200 LA 90004 633-G3
300 LA 90020 633-G3
600 LA 90005 633-G3
600 LA 90010 633-G3
LORRAINE DR
1200 UPL 91784 571-J4
LORRAINE RD
4000 RPV 90275 823-H3
LORRAINE ST
43000 LAN 93534 4105-E3
LORRAINE WK
6000 LA 90003 674-C6
LORRI WY
800 WAL 91789 639-C6
LOS ADORNOS WY
5100 LFlz 90027 593-H3
LOS ALAMITOS BLVD
10300 LALM 90720 796-J3
10300 LALM 90808 796-J3
11000 OrCo 90720 796-J3
LOS ALAMITOS CIR
Rt#-1
- LBCH 90804 796-A5
100 LBCH 90815 796-A5
LOS ALAMOS DR
3200 WCOV 91791 639-D2
LOS ALAMOS ST
5600 BPK 90620 767-D4
LOS ALIMOS ST
15000 MsnH 91345 501-H2
15800 GrnH 91344 501-A3
18200 Nor 91326 500-F2
19600 Chat 91311 500-A3
LOS ALISOS
300 SPAS 91030 595-F4
LOS ALISOS CIR
11800 NRWK 90650 706-H6
LOS ALISOS ST
13100 LMRD 90638 737-J1
LOS ALTOS AV
300 LBCH 90814 796-C7
400 ARCD 91007 597-B2
700 LBCH 90804 796-C6

LOS ALTOS AV
1100 LBCH 90815 796-C6
LOS ALTOS DR
- SCTA 91355 4550-D3
- PAS 91105 565-F4
1400 BREA 92821 708-H4
8100 BPK 90620 767-D4
15200 HacH 91745 677-J4
15300 HacH 91745 678-A5
N LOS ALTOS DR
15000 HacH 91745 677-J4
LOS ALTOS PL
6800 LA 90068 593-D3
E LOS ALTOS PZ
5200 LBCH 90815 796-B6
E LOS AMIGOS AV
200 MTBL 90640 636-F7
W LOS AMIGOS AV
100 MTBL 90640 636-E7
LOS AMIGOS ST
2000 LCF 91011 534-H1
2300 LaCr 91214 534-G1
3600 GLDL 91214 504-D5
5600 BPK 90620 767-D4
LOS AMORES CT
- PMDL 93551 4194-G2
LOS AMORES ST
8300 BPK 90620 767-D4
LOS ANGELES AV
100 MNRO 91016 567-G5
100 MTBL 90640 676-C2
E LOS ANGELES AV
5400 SIMI 93063 499-A2
LOS ANGELES ST
700 GLDL 91204 564-D6
9000 BLF 90706 736-A5
13000 IRW 91706 597-J5
13300 BALD 91706 597-J5
13300 BALD 91706 598-A4
14800 IRW 91706 598-A4
N LOS ANGELES ST
100 LA 90012 634-G4
S LOS ANGELES ST
100 LA 90012 634-F4
200 LA 90015 634-F4
300 LA 90013 634-F4
600 LA 90014 634-F4
1900 LA 90011 634-D7
5800 LA 90003 674-D6
12200 LACo 90061 734-D1
LOS ANGELES WY
5700 BPK 90620 767-D4
LOS ANGELES CITY
WTR & PWR RD
17500 Llan 93544 4379-J1
- LACo 4279-C1
LOS ANGELES DWP
EASEMENT
- KeCo 93560 3833-C2
LOS ARBOLES LN
500 SMRO 91108 566-E6
LOS ARCOS DR
5300 VeCo 91377 557-H1
LOS ARCOS ST
5600 LBCH 90815 796-C3
E LOS ARCOS ST
6300 LBCH 90815 796-E3
LOS ARCOS WY
5700 BPK 90620 767-D4
LOS ARQUEROS DR
- StvR 91381 4550-C3
LOS BENTOS DR
2300 HacH 91745 678-B4
LOS BERROS DR
18500 RowH 91748 679-A5
LOS BONITOS WY
5100 LFlz 90027 593-H3
LOS CABALLEROS WY
5100 LFlz 90027 593-H3
LOS CERILLOS DR
2900 WCOV 91791 639-C2
LOS CERRITOS CTR
- CRTS 90703 766-F1
LOS CERRITOS RD
600 GLDR 91740 569-G7
LOS CERRITOS PARK
PL
500 Bxby 90807 765-C7
LOS CERROS DR
1800 DBAR 91765 679-H5
LOS CIENTOS CIR
5800 BPK 90620 767-E5
LOS CODONA AV
23000 TOR 90505 793-D1
LOS COYOTES AV
11800 LMRD 90638 707-G7
12100 LMRD 90638 737-G1
LOS COYOTES BLVD
20000 LKWD 90715 766-G4
E LOS COYOTES DIAG
4400 LBCH 90815 796-A4
N LOS COYOTES DIAG
2600 LBCH 90815 796-D2
3000 LBCH 90808 796-D2
3300 LBCH 90808 766-E7
4100 LKWD 90713 766-F5
LOS COYOTES DR
- POM 91766 640-D4
8300 BPK 90621 737-J4
8400 BPK 90621 738-A4
8700 FUL 92833 738-A5
LOS DIEGOS WY
5100 LFlz 90027 593-H3

LOS ENCANTOS CIR
5100 LPMA 90623 767-C4
LOS ENCANTOS WY
5100 LFlz 90027 593-H3
LOS ENCINOS AV
1800 GLDL 91208 534-H6
LOS ENCINOS DR
- SCTA 91355 4550-E3
LOS ENCINOS ST
5700 BPK 90620 767-E5
LOS ENCINOS WY
23300 WdHI 91367 559-F3
LOSETO LN
- SunV 91352 502-G7
LOS FELIS DR
- POM 91766 640-E4
LOS FELIZ
1700 GLDR 91740 599-C2
LOS FELIZ BLVD
2800 LA 90039 564-D7
2900 LA 90039 594-C1
3500 LFlz 90027 594-A3
4800 LFlz 90027 593-H3
5400 LA 90068 593-H3
LOS FELIZ DR
2000 THO 91362 557-A2
5700 BPK 90620 767-E5
LOS FELIZ PK
3700 LFlz 90027 594-C2
LOS FELIZ PL
3400 LA 90039 564-D7
E LOS FELIZ RD
100 GLDL 91205 564-E7
W LOS FELIZ RD
100 GLDL 91204 564-E7
LOS FLORES AV
8700 BPK 90620 767-E5
LOS FLORES BLVD
2800 LYN 90262 704-J6
2800 LYN 90262 705-A6
LOS FLORES ST
2100 POM 91767 601-B5
E LOS FLORES ST
5100 LBCH 90815 796-B5
LOS FRANCISCOS WY
5100 LFlz 90027 593-H3
LOS FUENTES RD
14500 LMRD 90638 737-E4
LOS GATOS DR
300 WAL 91789 679-D1
400 WAL 91789 639-D7
LOS GRANDES WY
5100 LFlz 90027 593-H2
LOS HERMOSOS WY
5100 LFlz 90027 593-H2
E LOS HIGOS ST
- ALH 91801 596-C6
LOS INDIOS CIR
5700 BPK 90620 767-E5
LOS JORDANS RD
10700 LACo 91390 4373-E4
LOS LAGOS
900 POM 91766 640-G3
LOS LAURELES
200 SPAS 91030 595-F3
LOS LIONES DR
300 PacP 90272 630-F5
LOS LOTES AV
14900 WHIT 90605 707-G2
LOS MACHOS DR
18500 RowH 91748 679-A5
LOS MOLINOS DR
5700 BPK 90620 767-D4
LOS MOLINOS ST
15400 HacH 91745 678-A5
LOS NIETOS DR
4100 LFlz 90027 594-B3
LOS NIETOS RD
11100 SFSP 90670 706-H2
12000 SFSP 90670 707-A3
13200 LACo 90605 707-B4
LOS NIETOS ST
5700 BPK 90620 767-E5
LOS OLAS WY
6700 MAL 90265 667-D3
LOS OLIVOS
15400 MsnH 91345 501-G2
LOS OLIVOS DR
500 SGBL 91775 596-F2
8500 LACo 91775 596-G2
LOS OLIVOS LN
2400 LaCr 91214 534-G1
2700 LaCr 91214 504-E7
3200 GLDL 91214 504-D5
LOS OLIVOS RD
- LA 91342 481-G3
LOS OLIVOS ST
15000 MsnH 91345 501-H2
LOS PACOS ST
8700 BPK 90620 767-E5
LOS PADRES DR
1700 RowH 91748 679-A5
LOS PADRES PL
- POM 91766 640-D4
LOS PADRINOS DR
12200 DWNY 90242 705-G6
LOS PALACIOS DR
18000 INDS 91748 678-J4
18000 RowH 91748 678-J4
18200 RowH 91748 679-A4
LOS PALOS CIR
5500 BPK 90620 767-D4

LOS PALOS ST
100 LA 90023 675-C1
LOS PINETOS RD
- Nwhl 91321 4641-C5
- SCTA 91321 4641-C5
LOS PINETOS WATER
TANK RD
- Nwhl 91321 4641-J4
- Nwhl 91321 4642-A4
LOS PINOS DR
19700 WAL 91789 639-D7
LOS RAMOS CIR
5900 BPK 90620 767-E5
LOS RANCHITOS RD
2100 CHLS 91709 680-J4
LOS RANCHOS DR
5700 BPK 90620 767-E5
LOS RAPIDOS CIR
5800 BPK 90620 767-E5
LOS REYES AV
12000 LMRD 90638 707-G7
LOS ROBLES
4100 LVRN 91750 570-F6
LOS ROBLES AV
400 ALH 91801 596-A2
1200 MNRO 91016 567-E5
1500 SMRO 91108 595-J1
1600 SMRO 91108 596-A2
6200 BPK 90621 737-J7
6300 BPK 90621 767-J1
14400 HacH 91745 677-H1
14900 HacH 91745 678-A2
E LOS ROBLES AV
15200 HacH 91745 678-A2
N LOS ROBLES AV
- PAS 91101 565-J2
600 PAS 91104 565-J2
1600 PAS 91104 535-J7
S LOS ROBLES AV
- PAS 91101 565-J7
600 PAS 91106 565-J7
1200 PAS 91106 595-J1
LOS ROBLES PL
1200 POM 91768 600-G6
LOS ROBLES RD
2700 THO 91362 557-A2
LOS ROBLES ST
4900 Eagl 90041 565-C6
LOS ROGUES DR
22400 SCTA 91350 4460-H6
LOS ROSAS ST
23900 LA 91304 529-E2
E LOS SANTOS DR
5600 LBCH 90815 796-C4
LOS SANTOS WY
5700 BPK 90620 767-E5
LOS SERRANOS DR
10500 LACo 90601 677-B2
LOST CANYON RD
- LACo 91387 4551-H5
14600 LACo 91387 4462-G7
14600 LACo 91387 4552-G1
15500 LACo 91387 4552-C2
LOST CREEK RD
18200 LACo 91390 4461-H2
LOST HILLS RD
3900 CALB 91301 588-G1
3900 CALB 91302 588-G1
4100 CALB 91301 558-G7
4100 CALB 91301 588-G1
4800 Ago 91301 558-F5
5000 LACo 91302 558-G7
LOS TIGRES DR
22300 SCTA 91350 4550-J1
LOS TILOS RD
6900 LA 90068 593-D3
LOSTINE AV
21300 CRSN 90745 764-G6
LOST OAK CT
26900 CALB 91301 558-G7
LOS TOROS AV
4500 PRV 90660 676-G2
LOS TRANCOS CIR
7500 LPMA 90623 767-B3
LOST RIVER DR
21500 DBAR 91765 679-J5
LOST SPRINGS DR
3800 CALB 91301 558-G7
4000 CALB 91301 588-G1
LOST SPRINGS RD
27700 SCTA 91387 4552-A2
LOST TRAIL AV
- Sunl 91040 503-A3
LOST TRAIL DR
1600 WAL 91789 639-G3
LOST VALLEY RANCH
RD
9100 LACo 93551 4193-F5
9100 LACo 93551 4194-A5
LOSTWOOD AV
44400 LAN 93534 4015-F4
LOS VERDES DR
6700 RPV 90275 822-G3
LOTA LN
- AGRH 91301 558-C5
LOTONE ST
400 MNRO 91016 567-F2
LOTT AV
1300 City 90063 635-D3
LOTTA AV
8900 SGAT 90280 705-E3
LOTTA DR
1300 City 90063 635-F3

LOTUS AL
1800 LACo 91104 536-C7
N LOTUS AV
- LACo 91107 566-G4
6600 LACo 91775 596-H1
6900 LACo 91775 566-H7
S LOTUS AV
- LACo 91107 566-H5
3600 LACo 91775 566-H5
LOTUS CIR
900 SDMS 91773 570-C6
LOTUS CT
44100 LAN 93536 4015-B7
LOTUS DR
3200 HacH 91745 678-B6
LOTUS LN
- LAN 93536 4015-B6
500 SMAD 91024 567-C1
LOTUS PL
300 BREA 92821 709-B5
1800 BREA 92821 708-G6
LOTUS ST
500 LA 90065 595-A5
LOTUSGARDEN DR
15100 SCTA 91387 4462-E7
28900 SCTA 91387 4552-E1
LOTUS PETAL CT
14600 SCTA 91387 4462-G6
LOU LN
- PMDL 93550 4286-H4
LOU DILLON AV
7600 Flor 90001 704-H2
10300 Wats 90002 704-H5
10700 LA 90059 704-H5
11600 Wbrk 90059 704-H7
LOUDON CT
- Cstc 91384 4459-H3
LOUDON LN
13100 INDS 91746 637-H2
LOUELLA AV
1500 Ven 90291 671-J3
1500 Ven 90291 672-A4
LOUER DR
- LAN 93536 4105-B7
LOUIS AV
29500 CynC 91351 4462-B4
S LOUIS AV
11600 LACo 90605 707-B7
12100 LACo 90605 737-B1
LOUIS PL
5100 ELA 90022 675-G1
E LOUISA AV
1000 WCOV 91790 598-G5
1400 WCOV 91791 598-J5
W LOUISA AV
1000 WCOV 91790 598-E5
LOUISE AV
1000 ARCD 91006 567-D7
1500 ARCD 91006 597-D1
1700 LAN 93534 4015-E5
4200 Enc 91316 561-C1
4800 TOR 90505 793-B2
6400 VanN 91406 531-C5
7800 Nor 91325 531-C1
8800 Nor 91325 501-B5
10300 GrnH 91344 501-B3
11000 LYN 90262 705-E7
11300 LYN 90262 735-E1
11600 GrnH 91344 481-A5
11900 CULC 90066 672-C5
11900 LA 90066 672-D5
N LOUISE AV
500 AZU 91702 568-H6
S LOUISE AV
100 AZU 91702 568-H7
100 AZU 91702 598-H1
1700 ARCD 91006 597-D1
LOUISE DR
5000 LCF 91011 535-A2
LOUISE LN
- PMDL 93551 4195-E7
7800 LPMA 90623 767-C3
LOUISE PL
1600 FUL 92833 738-D7
LOUISE ST
3100 LYN 90262 705-A7
3500 LYN 90262 705-B7
9000 BLF 90706 736-A3
E LOUISE ST
- NLB 90805 765-D3
N LOUISE ST
100 GLDL 91206 564-E4
800 GLDL 91207 564-E3
S LOUISE ST
100 GLDL 91205 564-E6
W LOUISE ST
- NLB 90805 765-C3
LOUISE TER
200 GLDL 91207 564-E2
LOUISIANA
3600 WCOV 91792 679-H2
LOUISIANA AV
2100 WLA 90025 632-D4
10500 LA 90064 632-D4
LOUKELTON ST
15400 LPUE 91744 638-E5
16000 INDS 91744 638-E5
16000 LACo 91744 638-G5
LOUMONT ST
13200 LACo 90601 637-G6
LOUVRE ST
12600 Pcma 91331 482-E7
12600 Pcma 91331 502-E1

STREET
Block City ZIP Pg-Grid

LOVAGE CT
27500 SCTA 91350 4461-A6
LOVE CIR
1700 SIMI 93063 499-B2
LOVE LN
100 PMDL 93551 4195-J4
LOVEJOY AV
38800 LACo 93591 4199-B3
LOVEJOY ST
2200 POM 91767 601-B5
LOVELACE AV
1900 LA 90007 634-C6
LOVELAND DR
2200 LA 90065 594-J2
LOVELAND ST
5500 BGDN 90201 675-G7
6300 BGDN 90201 705-J1
LOVELANE PL
10100 LA 90064 632-F6
LOVELL AV
1200 ARCD 91007 567-A7
1300 ARCD 91007 597-A1
LOVELL PL
400 FUL 92835 738-H1
LOVETT PL
16200 Enc 91436 561-E4
LOVETT ST
4300 LACo 90023 675-E2
4400 CMRC 90040 675-E2
LOVILA LN
2000 Alta 91001 535-J7
LOW LN
1600 CHLS 91709 710-G1
LOWDER ST
10000 LA 90210 592-B4
LOWE DR
15000 LMRD 90638 737-G4
LOWE ST
1800 LA 90039 594-F4
7800 LBCH 90808 796-H1
LOWELL AV
- SMAD 91024 567-A2
1500 CLAR 91711 601-D1
2900 LA 90032 595-G5
3900 GLDL 91214 504-D7
4500 LA 91214 504-D5
4600 Tuj 91042 504-D5
N LOWELL AV
7000 GLDR 91741 569-C5
LOWELL ST
400 COV 91723 599-C6
LOWEMONT ST
10400 BLF 90706 736-D5
11400 NRWK 90650 736-G5
W LOWEN ST
1000 Wilm 90744 794-C4
N LOWENA DR
200 LBCH 90803 825-G1
LOWER RD
- LFlz 90027 594-A4
100 AVA 90704 5923-H4
LOWER AZUSA RD
9000 RSMD 91770 596-H5
9200 TEML 91780 596-H5
9400 TEML 91780 597-A5
9600 ELMN 91780 597-A5
9700 ELMN 91731 597-A5
11300 ELMN 91732 597-D5
12300 ARCD 91706 597-J5
12500 IRW 91706 597-J5
LOWER BLACKWATER CANYON RD
- RHLS 90274 793-D7
- RHLS 90274 823-D1
LOWER BREWSTER RD
- LACo 90265 587-E5
LOWER BROWN MOUNTAIN FIRE RD
- LACo - 505-F7
- LACo - 535-G1
- PAS 91011 535-F3
LOWER CLAMSHELL MTWY
- MNRO 91016 537-G7
- MNRO 91016 567-G1
LOWER CLAMSHELL TKTR
- ARCD 91006 537-E7
- MNRO 91016 537-E7
- MNRO 91016 567-E1
LOWER EAST MANDEVILLE FIRE RD
2400 Brwd 90049 591-D5
LOWER EAST TERRACE RD
- AVA 90704 5923-H4
LOWER FRYMAN FIRE RD
11800 LA 91604 592-G1
12000 LA 90210 592-G1
LOWER LIVE OAK CANYON RD
- LACo 91711 571-A6
- LACo 91750 570-J6
- LACo 91750 571-A6
LOWER PASEO LA CRESTA
1400 PVE 90274 792-G6
LOWER PASTURE RD
- LACo 91750 570-J4
LOWES DR
- PMDL 93551 4195-G5

LOWHILL DR
42800 LACo 93532 4102-F4
LOWMAN AV
8000 DWNY 90240 706-C1
8200 PRV 90660 706-C1
LOWNES PL
1200 POM 91766 640-G4
LOWRIDGE PL
23100 LACo 91390 4460-G2
LOWRY RD
3200 LFlz 90027 594-B2
LOWTREE AV
44200 LAN 93534 4015-F6
LOXLEY PL
1100 DBAR 91789 679-G3
LOY CT
45300 LAN 93534 4015-E4
LOY LN
2300 Eagl 90041 564-J5
LOYAL TR
7000 LA 90068 593-D1
LOYALTON DR
20400 WAL 91789 639-F4
LOYNES DR
5700 LBCH 90803 826-D1
6000 LBCH 90803 796-D7
LOYOLA AV
600 CRSN 90746 764-E2
LOYOLA BLVD
7700 Wch 90045 702-E2
LOYOLA CT
- SBdC 91710 641-C5
1900 CLAR 91711 571-E7
LOYOLA PZ
100 SLB 90740 796-F6
LOYOLA WY
- SBdC 91710 641-D5
9200 BPK 90620 767-F6
LOYTAN ST
25200 TOR 90505 793-E4
LOZANO DR
- BALD 91706 598-D5
L RON HUBBARD WY
1300 LFlz 90027 594-A5
LUANA LN
2200 Mont 91020 534-H2
LUANDA ST
11500 LA 91342 482-H7
LUANN DR
39600 PMDL 93551 4195-H4
LUANNE AV
1200 FUL 92831 738-H5
LUBAO AV
5100 WdHl 91364 560-E2
5600 WdHl 91367 560-E1
6000 WdHl 91367 530-E7
6800 Win 91306 530-E1
8800 Nor 91324 530-E1
9500 Chat 91311 500-E4
LUBAO PL
19900 Chat 91311 500-E4
LUBEC ST
5500 BGDN 90201 705-G1
7400 DWNY 90240 706-A2
LUBEN LN
100 ARCD 91006 597-D1
LUBICAN ST
13300 BALD 91706 598-A6
LUBLIN ST
200 POM 91767 601-A3
LUCANIA DR
30500 RPV 90275 823-F5
LUCAS AV
100 Echo 90026 634-D3
300 LA 90017 634-D3
LUCAS LN
12900 CRTS 90703 737-A6
LUCAS PL
13400 CRTS 90703 737-C6
LUCAS ST
800 SFER 91340 482-B5
2000 LA 91342 482-B5
11200 CRTS 90703 736-F6
12600 CRTS 90703 737-A6
LUCASZ CT
1500 LAN 93535 4106-C1
LUCAYAN DR
4400 LACo 90601 677-B2
LUCCA DR
13500 PacP 90272 631-D4
LUCCA WY
- PMDL 93550 4286-F6
LUCE PL
9300 PRV 90660 676-J1
LUCERA CIR
4400 PVE 90274 793-C4
LUCERA CT
- POM 91766 640-D4
LUCERNE AV
9000 CULC 90232 672-H1
11100 LA 90230 672-G4
S LUCERNE AV
2300 LA 90016 633-D6
W LUCERNE AV
4600 LA 90016 633-D6
N LUCERNE BLVD
100 LA 90004 593-F7
100 LA 90004 633-F1
S LUCERNE BLVD
100 LA 90004 633-F2
300 LA 90020 633-F2
600 LA 90005 633-F3
600 LA 90010 633-F2

S LUCERNE BLVD
900 LA 90019 633-F4
LUCERNE CT
26000 SCTA 91355 4550-F5
LUCERNE PL
6200 SBdC 92397 (4652-B1
See Page 4651)
LUCERNE ST
22100 CRSN 90745 764-F7
22500 CRSN 90745 794-F1
LUCERO AV
500 PacP 90272 630-G5
3400 LVRN 91750 600-F1
LUCERO PL
500 PacP 90272 630-G5
LUCIA AV
8700 WHIT 90605 707-E2
N LUCIA AV
100 RBCH 90277 763-A5
200 RBCH 90277 762-J3
S LUCIA AV
100 RBCH 90277 763-A5
LUCIA PL
8700 SunV 91352 533-A1
E LUCIA WK
5700 LBCH 90803 826-C3
E LUCIEN ST
2000 COMP 90222 734-H2
2000 Wbrk 90222 734-H2
LUCIENNE ST
1100 POM 91766 641-B4
LUCILE AV
600 Echo 90026 594-C5
1800 LA 90039 594-C5
LUCILE ST
11800 LA 90230 672-F6
LUCILLE AV
300 LBCH 90814 796-A7
800 WCOV 91790 638-E3
900 Ven 90291 671-J5
900 Ven 90291 672-A5
6400 BELL 90201 675-B7
12900 LA 90066 672-A5
23700 TOR 90501 793-G2
24300 LMTA 90717 793-G3
E LUCILLE AV
400 WCOV 91790 638-F3
LUCILLE CT
15600 SCTA 91387 4462-E7
LUCILLE ST
- ARCD 91006 567-D6
12400 LACo 90066 672-E7
LUCILLE TR
- RPV 90275 822-F2
8000 LA 90046 593-A3
LUCINDA DR
14700 LACo 90604 737-F1
LUCKY PL
15700 LA 91342 481-G4
LUCRETIA AV
1500 Echo 90026 594-E6
LUCY CT
22000 SCTA 91350 4461-A5
W LUCY DR
3000 ANA 92804 767-J6
LUDDINGTON ST
10900 SunV 91352 503-A7
11300 SunV 91352 532-H1
LUDELL ST
5800 BGDN 90201 705-G1
LUDER AV
1800 SELM 91733 637-B2
2600 ELMN 91733 637-B2
LUDGATE DR
5000 CALB 91301 558-F6
LUDLOW ST
11000 GrnH 91344 501-A2
15400 MsnH 91345 501-G2
18100 Nor 91326 500-G2
LUELLA DR
1300 City 90063 635-E3
LUEON LN
- Llan 93544 4471-J3
- SBdC 92372 4471-J3
LUFKIN ST
1900 WCOV 91790 638-C2
LUGANO PL
3300 LA 90068 563-F7
LUGANO WY
- Nor 91326 500-C1
400 VeCo 91377 557-G3
LUGAR DE ORO DR
22700 SCTA 91354 4460-H7
26700 SCTA 91354 4550-H1
LUGGER WY
2000 LBCH 90813 795-A6
LUGO AV
3600 LYN 90262 705-C7
3900 LYN 90262 735-D1
7300 PRM 90723 735-F1
LUGO ST
2800 LA 90023 674-J1
2800 LA 90023 675-A1
7100 PRM 90723 735-F1
LUGO WY
10700 CULC 90230 672-H4
LUGO PARK AV
11600 LYN 90262 735-E1
LUIS DR
5400 AGRH 91301 557-H5
LUJON ST
14600 HacH 91745 677-J2
15500 HacH 91745 678-B3

LUKAY ST
13400 LACo 90605 707-C6
LUKENS CT
- FUL 92833 738-D5
LUKENS PL
100 GLDL 91206 564-H5
LULL ST
7600 LA 91304 529-F4
9900 LA 91504 533-C3
10700 SunV 91352 533-A3
11000 SunV 91352 532-H3
11600 NHol 91605 532-D3
13500 PanC 91402 532-C3
14600 VanN 91405 531-J3
15300 VanN 91406 531-G3
17400 Nor 91325 531-B3
17700 Res 91335 531-A4
18100 Res 91335 530-G4
19700 Win 91306 530-C4
20900 LA 91304 530-B4
LULLABY LN
8000 PanC 91402 532-A1
LULU CARR RD
1700 LACo 90265 626-F2
LULU GLEN DR
7800 LA 90046 593-A1
LUMBER RD
3200 SBdC 92371 (4562-H3
See Page 4471)
LUMBER ST
400 LAN 93534 4015-H5
2000 LAN 93536 4015-B6
6200 LAN 93536 4014-E6
LUMBER ST E
4600 LACo 93535 4016-J5
LUNA CT
- CALB 91302 558-H6
- KeCo 93560 3835-E2
400 Alta 91001 535-G3
6300 PMDL 93551 4104-E7
LUNA PL
400 LBCH 90802 795-D7
12300 GrnH 91344 481-C5
LUNADA CIR
29600 RPV 90275 793-J7
LUNADA LN
5700 LBCH 90814 796-D7
LUNADA BAY PZ
2500 PVE 90274 822-E1
LUNADA RIDGE DR
28300 RPV 90275 792-J7
LUNADA VISTA
- RPV 90275 822-F2
LUNAR AV
600 BREA 92821 709-A6
LUNAR DR
1500 MONP 91754 635-J4
LUNA VISTA DR
1300 PacP 90272 630-G3
LUND ST
23600 WdHl 91367 559-E3
LUNDAHL DR
9500 PRV 90660 676-F7
LUNDENE DR
10200 LACo 90601 677-A3
LUNDY AV
1800 PAS 91104 535-J7
LUNES
- LVRN 91750 570-H3
LUNITA RD
6400 MAL 90265 626-J7
LUNSFORD DR
5100 Eagl 90041 565-D5
LUPIN LN
400 GLDR 91741 569-J6
S LUPIN LN
700 WCOV 91791 639-A2
LUPIN TER
300 LA 90031 595-B6
LUPIN WY
- LAN 93536 4105-C5
LUPINE AV
1500 MONP 91755 636-B4
7700 LACo 91390 4374-B3
LUPINE DR
22600 TOR 90505 763-B7
22600 TOR 90505 793-B1
LUPINE LN
3800 CALB 91302 588-G1
LUPINE PL
200 MONP 91755 636-B4
2000 LVRN 91750 600-D3
LUPINE ST
- Cstc 91384 4459-F3
37600 PMDL 93552 4287-B2
LUPIN HILL RD
2300 LHH 90631 708-B1
24000 HIDH 91302 559-D3
LUPITA DR
23700 SCTA 91355 4550-G5
LURA ST
- PAS 91125 566-B5
E LURAY ST
600 Bxby 90807 765-E4
LURIE CT
- StvR 91381 4640-C1
LURIE PL
10700 Nor 91326 500-H3
LURING DR
700 GLDL 91206 564-H3
LURLINE AV
6700 Win 91306 530-C2
8900 Chat 91311 500-C4

LUSE TANK RD
1200 Top 90290 590-A3
LUSK AV
19400 CRTS 90703 766-G3
LUSS DR
30100 CynC 91351 4462-B5
LUTGE AV
300 BURB 91506 563-H2
LUTHER DR
27000 SCTA 91351 4551-G3
LUTHER LN
- ING 90305 703-E3
LUTHER ST
3500 LA 90031 595-C6
LUTON DR
500 GLDL 91206 564-G3
LUVERNE PL
17200 Enc 91316 561-C5
LUXOR ST
6000 DWNY 90241 705-H4
6000 SGAT 90280 705-H4
8300 DWNY 90241 706-A6
LUY RD
3600 LA 90034 672-E2
LUY ST
1700 MONP 91755 636-C4
LUZON DR
- LACo 91390 (4371-G7
See Page 4281)
28900 LACo 91390 4461-G1
LYALL AV
4400 LACo 91722 598-G4
N LYALL AV
300 WCOV 91790 598-G6
LYANS DR
1900 LCF 91011 534-J2
LYCEUM AV
3800 LA 90066 672-B5
3900 CULC 90066 672-B5
LYCOMING ST
20600 DBAR 91789 679-F2
LYDIA DR
3100 LA 90023 675-A1
LYDIA ST
100 LHB 90631 708-D5
2400 WCOV 91792 639-A6
LYDLE CREEK PL
19200 WAL 91789 639-C5
LYFORD DR
400 LACo 91750 600-D1
900 SDMS 91750 570-D7
900 SDMS 91750 600-D1
1000 LACo 91750 570-D7
2500 LVRN 91750 600-D2
LYLE ST
10200 WHIT 90601 676-J3
13800 LA 91342 482-B2
14400 LA 91342 481-J4
LYLEDALE ST
9000 TEML 91780 596-H3
LYMAN AV
600 COV 91724 599-G3
1200 GLDR 91740 599-G1
4000 SDMS 91724 599-G5
4000 SDMS 91773 599-G5
4100 LACo 91724 599-G3
LYMAN PL
1100 LA 90029 594-A5
1300 LFlz 90027 594-A4
LYMAN ST
1400 GLDR 91740 599-G1
LYNALAN AV
6800 LACo 90606 677-A7
LYNBROOK AV
2000 HacH 91745 678-B4
LYND AV
4300 MNRO 91006 597-F3
LYNDA LN
1900 WCOV 91792 638-G5
7900 BGDN 90201 705-F2
LYNDALE AV
2400 POM 91768 640-C2
LYNDBROOK CT
31900 WLKV 91361 557-C6
LYNDHURST AV
1400 HacH 91745 678-D3
LYNDON DR
2400 LACo 91302 589-D3
LYNDON ST
- HMB 90254 762-G3
800 SPAS 91030 595-G2
LYNDON WY
1100 ARCD 91007 567-B7
LYNDORA ST
3800 LYN 90262 705-C6
7800 DWNY 90242 705-H7
8300 DWNY 90242 735-J1
8500 DWNY 90242 736-A1
10500 NRWK 90650 736-D1
LYNETTE LN
21900 SCTA 91350 4461-A4
LYNGLEN DR
1500 GLDL 91206 564-H4
LYNHAM PL
23400 SCTA 91354 4460-G6
LYNMARK ST
14000 LMRD 90638 737-D2
LYNN CIR
3500 LVRN 91750 600-G1
5000 LPMA 90623 767-C3
LYNN CT
2300 WCOV 91792 639-A6

LYNN DR
20200 WAL 91789 639-G3
LYNN LN
- Ago 91301 588-C2
8800 RSMD 91770 636-H1
LYNN ST
4800 HiPk 90042 595-B3
LYNN WY
- LAN 93536 4013-J5
LYNNE CT
- LACo 91387 4552-A3
LYNNFIELD CIR
2700 LA 90032 595-E7
LYNNFIELD ST
4400 LA 90032 595-D7
LYNNGROVE DR
1100 MANB 90266 732-J6
LYNNHAVEN LN
700 LCF 91011 535-B2
LYNOAK DR
600 CLAR 91711 571-A7
1700 CLAR 91711 601-A1
3200 LACo 91711 601-A2
3300 POM 91767 601-A2
LYNRIDGE DR
18900 WAL 91789 639-B6
W LYNROSE DR
2800 ANA 92804 767-J7
LYNROSE ST
10000 TEML 91780 597-B3
10600 ARCD 91007 597-C3
11300 ARCD 91006 597-D3
LYNTON AV
1400 Wilm 90744 794-C4
21200 CRSN 90745 764-B5
LYNVUE PL
500 POM 91768 640-D1
LYNWOOD DR
1000 BREA 92821 709-A5
LYNWOOD RD
2700 LYN 90262 704-J7
2700 LYN 90262 705-A7
3600 LYN 90262 735-B1
LYNWOOD ST
1200 LHB 90631 738-F1
LYNX WY
- PMDL 93551 4195-F7
LYNX GULCH RD
- LACo - (4646-E6
See Page 4645)
- LACo - (4726-F2
See Page 4645)
LYON AV
2200 PMDL 93550 4286-E4
LYON CT
- LACo 91302 558-G3
LYON PL
6100 VeCo 93063 499-B4
14200 LMRD 90638 738-A2
LYON ST
900 LA 90012 634-H3
LYONS AV
22500 SCTA 91321 4640-E1
23100 SCTA 91355 4640-E1
LYONS RANCH RD
24700 StvR 91381 4640-D3
LYONWOOD AV
700 DBAR 91789 679-H2
LYRIC AV
2000 LA 90039 594-C4
2100 LFlz 90027 594-C3
5600 LAN 93536 4104-C4
LYSANDER DR
17400 CRSN 90746 734-E7
17400 CRSN 90746 764-E1
LYSTER AV
11400 Nor 91326 480-H7
11400 Nor 91326 500-H1
LYTELLE PL
2700 Eagl 90041 564-J7
2700 Eagl 90041 594-H1
2700 LA 90065 594-H1
LYTLE CT
- LACo 91390 4461-A4
LYTLE CREEK RD
3000 SBdC - (4732-J1
See Page 4651)
3400 SBdC - (4652-H7
See Page 4651)

M

E M ST
100 Wilm 90744 794-F5
W M ST
100 Wilm 90744 794-C5
MAAG PL
- FUL 92833 738-C6
MABANA DR
34200 LACo 91390 4373-G4
MABBIT RD
- Actn 93510 4465-J1
MABEL AV
1100 MONP 91754 635-J2
1100 MONP 91754 636-J2
2700 SELM 91733 636-J2
E MABEL AV
700 MONP 91755 636-D2
W MABEL AV
800 MONP 91754 636-A2
MABEN AV
20600 SCTA 91351 4551-D2

MABERY RD
100 LA 90402 631-B7
100 LA 90402 671-B1
MACADAM CT
6000 AGRH 91301 558-A3
MACAFEE RD
4600 TOR 90505 793-B2
MACAL PL
6300 LA 90068 593-F2
MACALESTER DR
200 WAL 91789 639-E7
MACALESTER PL
500 CLAR 91711 571-E6
MACAPA DR
7000 LA 90068 593-D2
MAC ARTHUR AV
500 SPed 90731 824-B3
1100 LA 90732 824-A3
MACARTHUR AV
- LACo 90073 631-H3
3400 FUL 92833 738-B7
MACARTHUR BLVD
2400 SPed 90731 824-C7
2500 SPed 90731 854-C1
MACARTHUR DR
36700 PMDL 93552 4287-C5
MAC ARTHUR ST
1800 RPV 90275 823-H3
MACARTHUR WY
6000 BPK 90620 767-E3
MACAW ST
14300 LMRD 90638 737-E4
MACBETH ST
1400 Echo 90026 594-F7
MACCULLOCH DR
600 Brwd 90049 631-G1
MACDEVITT ST
2200 WCOV 91790 598-C6
14100 BALD 91706 598-C6
MACDONALD ST
200 PAS 91103 565-G1
MACE PL
7200 Flor 90001 674-F7
7200 Flor 90001 704-F1
MACENTA LN
500 DBAR 91765 640-D7
MACEO ST
2600 LA 90065 594-H5
MACFARLANE DR
2500 LAN 93536 4015-C7
22200 WdHl 91364 559-H3
MACFARLANE LN
5000 WdHl 91364 559-H3
MACGOVERN AV
11500 DWNY 90241 706-A5
MACHADO AV
1300 City 90063 635-F3
MACHADO DR
700 Ven 90291 671-H4
MACHADO RD
5400 CULC 90230 672-G4
MACHLIN CT
- INDS 91789 640-A6
MACHREA ST
7600 Tuj 91042 503-H3
MACIEL AV
20900 CRSN 90810 764-J5
MACKAY LN
1000 RBCH 90278 763-B2
2000 RBCH 90278 733-B7
MACKEL TER
19600 WAL 91789 679-D2
MACKENNAS GOLD AV
16400 LACo 93591 4199-G4
MACKENZIE CT
13500 LACo 91746 637-H4
MACKENZIE WY
- StvR 91381 4550-B7
MACKESON CT
17800 CRSN 90746 764-F1
MACKLIN AV
28600 SCTA 91387 4552-C1
MACLAREN ST
16800 LPUE 91744 678-F1
17700 LACo 91744 678-H2
18400 LACo 91744 679-A2
N MACLAY AV
- SFER 91340 482-B7
S MACLAY AV
- SFER 91340 482-A7
500 SFER 91340 502-A1
800 LA 91340 502-A1
MACLAY ST
12900 LA 91342 482-E4
13200 LA 91340 482-D5
13300 SFER 91340 482-D5
14500 LA 91340 501-J2
14500 LA 91340 502-A1
14600 MsnH 91345 501-J2
MACMILLAN RANCH RD
26300 SCTA 91387 4552-D6
MACNEIL DR
- AZU 91702 569-B4
- GLDR 91702 569-B4
- GLDR 91741 569-B4
MACNEIL ST
100 SFER 91340 482-C6
12800 LA 91342 482-D5
14500 LA 91340 501-J2
14600 MsnH 91345 501-J2
MACOMB RD
35400 Actn 93510 4374-G2

MACOMBER AL
900 PAS 91103 565-H2
MACON ST
2700 LA 90065 594-H4
MACY ST
1000 OrCo 90631 708-B4
1000 WHIT 90603 708-B4
1100 LHB 90631 708-B4
MADDEN AV
5800 LA 90043 673-F6
MADDOX ST
1200 LBCH 90810 765-B7
MADEIRA CT
19200 CRTS 90703 767-B2
MADEIRA LN
- BqtC 91354 4460-E2
MADELEINE WY
800 POM 91767 601-B7
MADELENA DR
100 LACo 90631 708-C3
MADELIA AV
3900 Shrm 91403 561-J6
MADELINE DR
100 MNRO 91016 567-J3
200 PAS 91105 565-G7
MADELINE COVE DR
6500 RPV 90275 822-H1
MADERA AV
3100 LA 90039 594-D2
MADERA DR
4600 LVRN 91750 570-G7
6000 WdHl 91367 559-H7
MADERA PL
800 FUL 92833 738-F3
MADERA RD
500 SBdC 92372 (4472-A1
See Page 4471)
2800 SBdC 92371 (4472-F1
See Page 4471)
MADERA ST
400 SGBL 91776 596-E4
E MADERA ST
6400 LBCH 90815 796-E4
MADERA BAY LN
11600 Nor 91326 500-E1
11600 Nor 91326 480-E7
MADERO CT
3100 WCOV 91791 639-C3
MADERO ST
1000 MTBL 90640 636-E7
MADGE AV
10700 SGAT 90280 705-G6
MADIA CIR
8000 LPMA 90623 767-B4
MADIA ST
1100 PAS 91103 565-E1
MADIGAN DR
26700 SCTA 91351 4551-F4
MADILL AV
3600 LACo 91724 599-E6
MADISON AV
- CRTS 90703 766-H4
300 POM 91767 601-A6
2100 LVRN 91750 600-H3
2500 Alta 91001 536-A6
3900 CULC 90232 672-G1
8100 SGAT 90280 705-A3
8300 WHIT 90602 707-D2
8600 BPK 90620 767-H5
9000 CYP 90630 767-A6
E MADISON AV
100 MTBL 90640 676-E2
N MADISON AV
- PAS 91101 565-J3
100 MNRO 91016 567-E3
200 LA 90004 634-A1
200 LA 90004 594-A7
400 PAS 91104 565-J2
700 LA 90029 594-A7
1600 PAS 91104 535-J7
1900 Alta 91001 535-J7
S MADISON AV
- PAS 91101 565-J6
100 LA 90004 634-A1
100 MNRO 91016 567-E4
600 PAS 91106 565-J6
W MADISON AV
100 MTBL 90640 676-C1
MADISON CIR
7400 BPK 90620 767-H5
MADISON CT
- LAN 93536 4104-F1
3500 TOR 90505 793-D3
MADISON RD
3700 LCF 91011 535-C6
MADISON ST
4900 CHNO 91710 641-F6
7100 PRM 90723 735-F5
20300 TOR 90503 763-D5
22300 TOR 90505 763-D7
22500 TOR 90505 793-D1
29700 Cstc 91384 4459-C7
37400 PMDL 93552 4286-J3
E MADISON ST
2500 CRSN 90810 764-J6
2500 CRSN 90810 765-A6
MADISON WY
- LHB 90631 708-D7
300 GLDL 91205 564-F7
29800 Cstc 91384 4459-C6
MADLER ST
2800 Actn 93510 4375-C7

MADLOY ST
30000 Cstc 91384 4459-C2
MADONA ST
18200 RowH 91748 678-J4
18200 RowH 91748 679-A4
MADONNA DR
2700 FUL 92835 738-H1
MADONNA LN
2000 LHB 90631 708-H4
MADORA AV
7200 Win 91306 530-E5
MADRE LN
400 SMAD 91024 567-B1
MADRE ST
- LACo 91107 566-G5
- PAS 91107 566-G5
MADRE VISTA RD
1000 Alta 91001 536-A5
MADRID AV
400 TOR 90501 763-G4
MADRID CIR
9900 CYP 90630 767-D7
MADRID CT
5700 PMDL 93552 4287-C2
10600 WHIT 90601 677-D4
MADRID LN
5700 LBCH 90814 796-D7
5700 LBCH 90814 826-D1
MADRID PL
- Cstc 91384 4459-D3
500 SBdC 92372 (4472-A1
See Page 4471)
1200 SGAT 90280 704-J2
MADRID PZ
4600 BPK 90621 737-J4
MADRID WY
42200 LAN 93536 4104-E5
MADRILLO CT
2700 PAS 91107 566-F6
2700 SMRO 91108 566-F6
MADRIS AV
14100 NRWK 90650 736-J4
MADRONA AV
20300 TOR 90503 763-D7
21800 TOR 90505 763-E7
22600 TOR 90505 793-E1
N MADRONA AV
100 BREA 92821 709-A7
S MADRONA AV
100 BREA 92821 709-A7
MADRONO LN
300 BelA 90077 592-B7
MADRUGADA DR
2300 CHLS 91709 680-J2
MAEMURRAY DR
5400 Eagl 90041 565-B4
MAESTRO AV
7600 LA 91304 529-F3
MAESTRO LN
40200 PMDL 93551 4194-H3
MAESTRO PL
23400 LA 91304 529-F4
MAGALA LN
13300 CHLS 91709 680-J2
MAGDA CT
5600 LACo 93552 4287-C7
MAGDA LN
700 LHB 90631 708-F4
700 OrCo 90631 708-F4
MAGDALENA DR
2400 WCOV 91792 639-B6
26000 SCTA 91355 4550-G4
MAGDALENA ST
1300 LA 90012 634-H2
MAGDELENA
18000 LACo 90220 765-A1
MAGED CT
- LACo 91390 4461-A3
MAGEE AV
11400 Pcma 91331 502-D1
MAGEE PL
11400 Pcma 91331 502-D1
MAGELLAN DR
19500 LA 90502 764-A4
MAGELLAN RD
200 ARCD 91007 566-J6
MAGELLAN ST
1700 WCOV 91791 638-J1
MAGIC MOUNTAIN LN
27900 SCTA 91387 4552-A2
27900 SCTA 91387 4551-J2
MAGIC MOUNTAIN PKWY
23200 SCTA 91355 4550-C2
25400 Valc 91355 4550-B3
25400 StvR 91381 4550-C2
MAGIC VIEW PL
29800 Cstc 91384 4459-D4
MAGINN DR
1800 GLDL 91202 564-D1
1900 GLDL 91202 534-D7
MAGINN PL
1700 GLDL 91202 534-D7
MAGNA CARTA RD
4000 CALB 91302 559-H6
E MAGNA VISTA AV
- ARCD 91006 567-D7
W MAGNA VISTA AV
- ARCD 91007 567-C7
MAGNA VISTA CT
400 PMDL 93551 4285-H1
MAGNA VISTA ST
2900 PAS 91107 566-F2

MAGNETIC TER
1600 LA 90069 592-G4
MAGNIS ST
900 ARCD 91006 597-F1
MAGNOL LN
- WdHl 91367 559-H7
MAGNOLIA
18800 RowH 91748 679-B4
MAGNOLIA AV
100 GLDL 91204 564-D7
100 LBCH 90831 825-D1
100 LBCH 90802 825-D1
200 LBCH 90802 795-D5
600 PAS 91106 565-J7
700 LA 90005 634-B3
700 LBCH 90813 795-D5
900 LA 90006 634-B4
900 GAR 90247 734-A5
1000 WCOV 91791 639-B2
1100 MANB 90266 732-H6
1800 LBCH 90806 795-D5
1900 LA 90007 634-B6
2300 LVRN 91750 600-F2
3200 LYN 90262 735-B1
5400 WHIT 90601 677-B6
12300 CHNO 91710 641-J7
N MAGNOLIA AV
100 FUL 92833 738-B7
100 MNRO 91016 567-G3
200 LBCH 90802 795-C3
2200 LBCH 90806 795-C3
3500 LBCH 90806 765-C7
S MAGNOLIA AV
100 FUL 92833 738-B7
100 MNRO 91016 567-G5
400 ONT 91762 641-J4
600 WCOV 91791 639-B1
2200 CHNO 91710 641-J4
2200 CHNO 91762 641-J4
W MAGNOLIA AV
300 ING 90301 703-B3
MAGNOLIA BLVD
4500 NHol 91601 563-A2
4700 BURB 91505 563-A2
11100 NHol 91601 562-E2
11700 LA 91607 562-E2
12800 Shrm 91423 562-A2
14400 Shrm 91403 562-A2
14500 Shrm 91403 561-H3
15700 Enc 91436 561-F3
16900 Enc 91316 561-A3
E MAGNOLIA BLVD
- BURB 91502 533-G7
400 BURB 91501 533-H6
W MAGNOLIA BLVD
- BURB 91502 533-G7
200 BURB 91502 563-D2
900 BURB 91506 563-D2
2500 BURB 91505 563-D2
MAGNOLIA CIR
100 WAL 91789 639-B4
MAGNOLIA CT
100 COMP 90220 734-H4
2100 LA 90007 634-B6
MAGNOLIA DR
- CRSN 90746 764-F1
- LA 90068 563-G5
- Saug 91350 4461-B4
600 SGBL 91775 596-C2
1900 MONP 91755 636-D5
8500 LA 90069 592-J4
43900 LAN 93535 4106-C1
MAGNOLIA LN
- LACo 91768 640-A1
- PMDL 93551 4285-D2
- StvR 91381 4640-C2
600 SPAS 91030 595-G2
800 ARCD 91006 567-F7
MAGNOLIA PL
- AZU 91702 569-B6
- Hrbr 90710 794-C3
- SCTA 91354 4550-F1
MAGNOLIA ST
- WAL 91789 639-H6
400 SPAS 91030 595-G1
11300 ELMN 91732 637-D2
E MAGNOLIA ST
100 POM 91767 600-J4
100 POM 91767 601-A4
W MAGNOLIA ST
100 POM 91767 600-J4
300 COMP 90220 734-G4
MAGNOLIA TER
5300 WHIT 90601 677-B4
MAGNOLIA TR
3400 CALB 91302 589-E1
MAGNOLIA VIA
- FUL 92832 738-J7
- FUL 92801 738-J7
MAGNOLIA WY
500 LHB 90631 708-C6
22700 SCTA 91390 4460-H2
MAGNOLIA GLEN DR
22900 SCTA 91354 4460-H5
MAGUIRE DR
4000 LACo 90265 627-J5
S MAHALO PL
2300 COMP 90220 764-G1
W MAHALO PL
1400 COMP 90220 764-G1
MAHANNA AV
1000 LBCH 90813 795-F6

STREET Block City ZIP Pg-Grid

MAHAR AV
800 Wilm 90744 794-G5
MAHOGANY
2800 WCOV 91792 679-C1
MAHOGANY CIR
8100 BPK 90620 767-J5
MAHOGANY CT
1300 DBAR 91789 679-G3
MAHOGANY RW
- SCTA 91351 4551-G2
MAHOGANY ST
43500 LAN 93535 4106-G2
MAHOGANY TR
10100 Tuj 91042 504-C4
MAHONEY DR
10500 Sunl 91040 503-B3
MAHONIA AV E
37200 PMDL 93552 4287-B3
MAHONY PL
17600 GmH 91344 481-A6
MAI ST
4900 RCUC 91737 (542-J7 See Page 511)
MAIDEN LN
100 AVA 90704 5923-H3
200 MTBL 90640 676-F2
1900 Alta 91001 536-A5
16800 GmH 91344 481-D7
MAIDENHAIR LN
- PMDL 93551 4285-D3
MAIDSTONE AV
10800 SFSP 90670 706-G6
11100 NRWK 90650 706-G6
12200 NRWK 90650 736-G1
17500 ART 90701 736-G7
MAIDSTONE CIR
1500 Hrbr 90710 793-J2
MAIDSTONE PL
23700 Hrbr 90710 793-J2
MAIE AV
7200 Flor 90001 674-G7
7200 Flor 90001 704-G1
8600 Wats 90002 704-G3
9100 Wats 90002 704-G4
11100 LA 90059 704-G6
N MAIE AV
100 COMP 90220 734-G4
S MAIE AV
100 COMP 90220 734-G4
MAIMONE AV
100 SDMS 91773 599-J2
100 SDMS 91773 600-A2
MAIN CT
1900 SMCA 90405 671-F3
MAIN ST
- Univ 91608 563-B6
- SLB 90740 826-E4
100 ELSG 90245 732-E2
200 Ven 90291 671-G5
600 ELSG 90245 702-E7
900 SPed 90731 854-A1
1600 SMCA 90401 671-E3
1900 SMCA 90405 671-E3
3800 CULC 90232 672-G1
3800 LA 90232 672-G1
5500 SGAT 90280 735-F1
15800 LPUE 91744 638-D7
16300 LPUE 91744 678-F1
E MAIN ST
- ALH 91801 596-B4
100 SGBL 91776 596-E4
N MAIN ST
- POM 91766 640-J1
100 LA 90012 634-H2
100 POM 91768 640-J1
200 LHB 90631 708-E5
1600 LA 90031 634-H2
2000 LA 90031 635-A2
S MAIN ST
100 LA 90012 634-E6
100 POM 91766 640-J2
100 LA 90061 704-C6
200 LHB 90631 708-E6
300 LA 90013 634-E6
400 BURB 91506 563-G2
600 LA 90014 634-E6
900 LA 90015 634-E6
1900 LA 90011 634-E6
1900 LA 90007 634-E6
2600 LA 90011 674-D1
2600 LA 90007 674-D1
3800 LA 90037 674-C3
5800 LA 90003 674-C6
7300 LA 90003 704-C2
12000 LACo 90061 704-C6
12000 LACo 90061 734-C2
14800 LACo 90248 734-C5
16100 CRSN 90248 734-C5
16500 CRSN 90746 734-C5
17400 CRSN 90746 764-C1
17400 CRSN 90248 764-C1
19200 CRSN 90745 764-C4
22500 CRSN 90745 794-D2
W MAIN ST
- ALH 91801 596-A5
100 SGBL 91776 596-D4
1400 ALH 91801 595-H4
MAINE
2100 WCOV 91792 679-H2
MAINE AV
100 LBCH 90831 825-C1
200 LBCH 90802 795-C7
200 LBCH 90802 825-C1

MAINE AV
700 LBCH 90813 795-C7
1300 BALD 91706 638-A1
1800 LBCH 90806 795-C2
3100 BALD 91706 598-C5
3500 LBCH 90806 765-C7
N MAINE AV
2200 LBCH 90806 795-C3
MAINE RD
4500 RPV 90275 823-G4
MAINMAST DR
30500 AGRH 91301 557-G5
MAINMAST PL
5600 AGRH 91301 557-G5
MAINSAIL CIR
3800 WLKV 91361 557-B6
MAINTENANCE WY
- Wch 90045 702-D5
MAIN WAY DR
2600 OrCo 90720 796-G5
MAIREMONT DR
1900 LACo 91789 679-F5
MAISON AV
5100 Eagl 90041 565-C5
MAITLAND AV
7900 ING 90305 703-G2
MAITLAND LN
- Saug 91350 4461-F7
MAITLAND ST
5300 SBdC 91762 641-G2
MAJELLA AV
800 LVRN 91750 600-D2
MAJESTIC CT
- LACo 91390 4460-J3
MAJESTIC ST
- WCOV 91791 639-B3
MAJESTIC WY
1500 GLDL 91207 564-G1
MAJOR ST
11800 LA 90230 672-G6
MAJORCA CIR
6200 LBCH 90803 826-D1
MAJORCA DR
11700 LACo 93536 3833-C7
MAJORCA PL
800 Brwd 90049 631-F1
MAJOR SEAWAY
20100 MAL 90265 629-J6
20100 MAL 90265 630-A6
MAKEE AV
5800 Flor 90001 674-F7
MAKENZIE CT
- THO 91362 557-A1
MAKIN AV
300 PMDL 93551 4195-H4
MALABAR ST
2400 Boyl 90033 635-B4
3000 LA 90063 635-B4
3300 City 90063 635-D5
5100 VER 90058 674-J5
5200 HNTP 90255 674-J5
5200 HNTP 90058 674-J5
MALACHITE CT
15300 CHLS 91709 680-J6
MALAD CT
21100 DBAR 91765 679-G7
MALAFIA DR
3600 GLDL 91208 534-G4
MALAGA CIR
2800 DBAR 91765 679-H7
MALAGA CT
3400 CALB 91302 559-C7
5500 PMDL 93552 4287-C3
6200 LBCH 90803 826-D1
MALAGA DR
4900 LPMA 90623 767-C4
MALAGA LN
- PVE 90274 792-H4
MALAGA PL
5700 LBCH 90814 796-D7
MALAGA PL E
- MANB 90266 732-H4
MALAGA PL W
- MANB 90266 732-H5
MALAGA RD
2200 LA 90068 593-D3
MALAGA ST
1200 UPL 91784 571-J3
MALAGA WY
- MANB 90266 732-H5
MALAGA COVE PZ
- PVE 90274 792-H4
MALAKOFF RD
- Cstc 91384 4459-E3
MALAMAR DR
900 SDMS 91773 570-C6
MALAT WY
11200 CULC 90230 672-H5
MALATI CIR
2100 UPL 91784 571-J4
MALBURG WY
5900 VER 90058 675-B6
MALBY AV
38500 PMDL 93550 4196-E7
MALCOLM AV
700 Wwd 90024 632-B2
1800 WLA 90025 632-C5
2200 LA 90064 632-D6
3000 LA 90034 632-E7
MALCOLM DR
- PAS 91105 565-E5
N MALDEN AV
100 FUL 92832 738-G6
S MALDEN AV
100 FUL 92832 738-H7

MALDEN CIR
16400 HNTB 92649 826-J7
MALDEN DR
1700 MTBL 90640 676-C2
MALDEN LN
- ING 90305 703-F3
MALDEN ST
14900 PanC 91402 531-H1
15800 LA 91343 531-E1
17000 Nor 91325 531-A1
18300 Nor 91325 530-H1
18500 Nor 91324 530-G1
19700 Win 91306 530-C1
21700 LA 91304 530-A1
22300 LA 91304 529-H1
MALDONADO LN
- MONP 91755 636-C3
MALDONADO PL
- Saug 91350 4461-F5
MALEZA PL
4600 Tarz 91356 560-H4
N MALGREN AV
200 LA 90275 823-H4
200 LA 90732 823-H4
S MALGREN AV
700 LA 90732 823-H6
MALIA CT
- Actn 93510 4375-E4
MALIBU DR
29000 Ago 91301 588-A5
MALIBU RD
23600 MAL 90265 628-F7
23600 MAL 90265 629-A7
23900 MAL 90265 668-G1
MALIBU CANYON RD
900 BREA 92821 709-C5
W MALIBU CANYON RD
Rt#-N1
100 LACo 91302 628-H1
500 LACo 91302 588-H7
S MALIBU CANYON RD
Rt#-N1
100 LACo 90265 628-J3
100 LACo 91302 628-G2
2600 MAL 90265 628-J3
3700 LACo 90263 628-H7
MALIBU CANYON WY
1000 BREA 92821 709-C5
MALIBU COLONY DR
23300 MAL 90265 629-A7
23600 MAL 90265 628-J7
MALIBU COLONY RD
3900 MAL 90265 629-A7
MALIBU COUNTRY DR
3500 MAL 90265 628-G6
MALIBU COVE COLONY DR
26800 MAL 90265 668-A1
MALIBU CREST DR
23800 MAL 90265 628-J6
23800 MAL 90265 629-A6
MALIBU HILLS RD
26700 CALB 91301 558-G7
26700 CALB 91302 558-G7
MALIBU KNOLLS RD
23800 MAL 90265 628-J6
MALIBU MEADOWS DR
800 LACo 91302 588-H7
800 LACo 91302 628-J1
MALIBU PARK LN
6300 MAL 90265 667-B1
MALIBU RANCHO RD
28800 Ago 91301 588-B4
MALIBU VIEW CT
- Ago 91301 587-J1
- Ago 91301 588-A1
MALIBU VISTA DR
3600 LACo 90265 630-D6
MALINTA AV
32900 Actn 93510 4375-G7
MALI VISTA DR
2200 LACo 91302 589-D3
MALLARD ST
2500 LA 90032 595-C7
MALLISON AV
9200 SGAT 90280 705-C5
10600 LYN 90262 705-C6
MALL LOOP RD
2300 LAN 93536 4015-D5
MALLORCA LN
13300 CHLS 91709 680-J2
MALLORCA PL
- Cstc 91384 4459-E3
MALLORCA ST
1200 UPL 91784 571-J3
MALLORY DR
- StvR 91381 4550-A6
MALLORY ST
2500 LA 90032 595-E7
MALLOT PL
11900 GmH 91344 481-D7
MALLOW CT
- SCTA 91321 4551-F5
4700 PMDL 93551 4194-H1
44000 LAN 93535 4016-C7
MALLOY AV
16200 CRSN 90746 734-E6
MALL RING RD
- PMDL 93551 4195-F4
MALMO RD
29000 LACo 91390 4461-G3
MALONE DR
800 MTBL 90640 636-C7

MALONE ST
12200 LA 90066 672-B1
MALPASO RD
8300 SBdC 92371 (4562-J3 See Page 4471)
MALT AV
2400 CMRC 90040 676-A5
3400 CMRC 90040 675-J6
MALTA CT
- LAN 93536 4013-J6
MALTA ST
4800 HiPk 90042 595-B3
E MALTA ST
4700 LBCH 90815 796-B5
E MALTA WY
600 LBCH 90802 825-E1
MALTBY PL
23200 Hrbr 90710 793-J2
MALTMAN AV
600 Echo 90026 594-C5
1800 LA 90039 594-C5
E MALTON AV
5800 SIMI 93063 499-A1
N MALTON AV
2100 SIMI 93063 499-B2
MALTON PL
15600 HacH 91745 678-B3
MALVA ROSA DR
- PMDL 93551 4195-E6
MALVERN AV
700 FUL 92832 738-C6
1000 FUL 92833 738-C6
1400 LA 90006 634-B5
2500 BPK 90621 738-A6
5300 BPK 90621 737-J5
W MALVERN AV
100 FUL 92832 738-G6
MALVINA AV
1800 LA 90012 594-G7
MAMERS RD
6000 Actn 93510 4374-F4
MAMIE AV
4900 LKWD 90713 766-E4
MAMMOTH AV
4100 Shrm 91423 562-C3
5500 VanN 91401 562-C2
5900 VanN 91401 532-C6
6400 VanN 91405 532-C4
7800 PanC 91402 532-B1
7900 CRTS 90703 767-B3
MAMMOTH CIR
9700 MTCL 91763 601-G6
MAMMOTH DR
- UPL 91784 571-H6
MAMMOTH LN
- SCTA 91387 4462-G7
MAMMOTH PL
- Shrm 91423 562-C4
MAMOTA WY
9500 CYP 90630 767-F7
MANADA CT
21800 DBAR 91765 679-J5
MANADA RD
7500 SBdC 92372 (4562-E5 See Page 4471)
MANAGUA PL
2800 HacH 91745 678-B5
MANANTONGA TER
700 HiPk 90042 565-C7
MANATEE ST
8200 DWNY 90241 706-A5
MANATO ST
39600 LACo 93591 4199-F4
MANCERO AV
300 LACo 91744 678-J1
MANCHA PL
300 MONP 91755 636-C4
S MANCHA WY
1700 MONP 91755 636-C5
E MANCHESTER AV
100 LA 90003 704-D2
100 LA 90044 704-A3
600 Wats 90002 704-D2
600 LA 90001 704-D2
1200 LA 90044 703-H2
1400 LA 90047 703-H2
2100 Wats 90002 704-H2
2100 Flor 90001 704-H2
W MANCHESTER AV
200 PdlR 90293 702-B3
5500 Wch 90045 702-E3
E MANCHESTER BLVD
100 ING 90301 703-C2
W MANCHESTER BLVD
100 ING 90301 703-B2
1200 ING 90301 702-J3
2200 ING 90305 703-E3
MANCHESTER CT
700 CLAR 91711 571-F7
MANCHESTER DR
600 ING 90301 703-D2
MANCHESTER PL
4200 CYP 90630 767-B6
MANCHESTER RD
1300 SDMS 91724 599-F5
MANCHESTER ST
37400 PMDL 93552 4286-J3
MANCHESTER TER
500 ING 90301 703-D2
MANCHESTER WY
25400 SCTA 91350 4550-J5

MANCO DR
16000 HacH 91745 678-C5
MANDALAY DR
4100 City 90063 635-E3
16200 Enc 91436 561-E6
MANDALAY RD
- SCTA 91387 4552-D5
MANDALE ST
9200 BLF 90706 736-A3
MANDAN ST
18600 SCTA 91351 4551-H3
MANDARIN CT
17100 GmH 91344 481-C6
S MANDARIN DR
200 BREA 92821 709-C7
MANDARIN LN
- DUAR 91010 568-A6
22300 LACo 91390 4460-J3
22300 SCTA 91390 4460-J3
MANDEL CT
- Saug 91350 4461-F6
MANDELL ST
20400 Win 91306 530-C2
22300 LA 91304 529-J2
MANDERA CT
- SCTA 91355 4460-D6
MANDERLY ST
3900 WCOV 91792 679-C2
MANDEVILLE DR
400 WAL 91789 679-C1
MANDEVILLE LN
1700 Brwd 90049 631-E2
MANDEVILLE CANYON RD
1600 Brwd 90049 631-D1
2300 Brwd 90049 591-C1
W MANDEVILLE FIRE RD
2400 Brwd 90049 591-C1
MANDY CT
24800 WdHl 91367 559-C1
MANDY ST
18700 RowH 91748 679-B4
MANE DR
23400 DBAR 91765 680-C1
MANE ST
4400 MTCL 91763 641-E2
MANECITA DR
14300 LMRD 90638 737-H3
MANET LN
2400 SIMI 93063 499-B1
MANETTE PL
12500 LYN 90262 735-D2
S MANETTE PL
12600 COMP 90221 735-D3
12800 RDom 90221 735-D3
MANFORD WY
300 PAS 91105 565-E4
MANGAF ST
- Actn 93510 4465-A1
MANGATE AV
400 LACo 91744 638-H7
MANGO CT
800 POM 91766 641-A4
MANGO LN
6100 SIMI 93063 499-B3
MANGO PL
- PMDL 93551 4285-E2
MANGO ST
800 BREA 92821 709-C6
8900 SBdC 92371 (4562-J1 See Page 4471)
9700 SBdC 92371 (4472-J6 See Page 4471)
MANGO WY
1600 POM 91766 641-B4
1800 Brwd 90049 631-E2
8300 BPK 90620 767-J4
MANGROVE AV
100 COV 91724 599-E5
4800 LACo 91724 599-E5
MANGROVE DR
- PMDL 93551 4285-D3
MANGRUM CT
- LHB 90631 738-B2
MANGUM ST
3100 BALD 91706 637-H1
3300 BALD 91706 597-J7
MANHATTAN AV
100 HMB 90254 762-G1
2500 Mont 91020 534-G2
2600 GLDL 91020 534-G2
2800 GLDL 91214 534-F2
2800 HMB 90254 732-F7
3300 MANB 90266 732-F7
N MANHATTAN AV
100 MANB 90266 732-E4
MANHATTAN PL
12900 GAR 90249 733-H2
15800 GAR 90247 733-H7
17800 TOR 90504 763-H1
20500 TOR 90501 763-H5
N MANHATTAN PL
100 LA 90004 633-H1
200 LA 90004 593-H7
700 LA 90038 593-H7
S MANHATTAN PL
100 LA 90004 633-H2
300 LA 90020 633-H2
600 LA 90005 633-H2
600 LA 90010 633-H2
900 LA 90019 633-H3
2000 LA 90018 633-H6

S MANHATTAN PL
5100 LA 90062 673-H5
6000 LA 90047 673-H6
8900 LA 90047 703-H4
10800 LACo 90047 703-H6
MANHATTAN WY
2300 GAR 90249 733-G6
MANHATTAN BEACH BLVD
1100 MANB 90266 732-G6
1900 RBCH 90278 732-G6
1900 RBCH 90278 733-A6
2200 GAR 90249 733-E6
3100 LACo 90506 733-E6
3100 LACo 90249 733-E6
3600 LACo 90260 733-E6
4000 LNDL 90260 733-A6
MANILA AV
- LBCH 90814 826-C1
300 LBCH 90814 796-C7
600 LBCH 90804 796-C7
S MANINGTON PL
400 WCOV 91791 639-D1
MANISTEE DR
2000 LCF 91011 504-J6
MANITOBA ST
400 PdlR 90293 702-B4
MANITOU AV
2100 LA 90031 634-J1
2100 LA 90031 635-A1
MANITOU PL
2300 LA 90031 635-C1
MANITOWAC DR
5300 RPV 90275 793-A6
MANKATO
15400 MsnH 91345 501-G2
MANKATO CT
1500 CLAR 91711 601-F1
MANKATO ST
14900 MsnH 91345 501-H2
MANLEY CT
25900 LACo 91302 558-J3
MANLEY DR
500 SGBL 91776 596-E5
MANNING AV
700 Wwd 90024 632-B2
1800 WLA 90025 632-C4
2200 LA 90064 632-E6
N MANNING AV
1900 BURB 91505 533-B7
MANNING CT
3300 LA 90064 632-F7
MANNING DR
- LA 90095 632-B2
MANNING RD
- PRV 90660 676-H3
MANNING ST
500 AZU 91702 569-A7
MANNING WY
15900 CRTS 90703 737-B5
MANNIX DR
8100 LA 90046 593-A4
MANNS RD
2300 SBdC - (4562-F5 See Page 4471)
MANOA CT
1400 Hlwd 90028 593-E5
MANOLA WY
5900 LA 90068 593-G3
MANOR CIR
1600 POM 91766 640-H4
23700 SCTA 91354 4550-G1
MANOR CT
4100 LA 90065 594-H1
MANOR DR
3700 LKWD 90712 765-J5
11800 HAW 90250 703-C7
11800 HAW 90250 733-C1
N MANOR DR
2100 MANB 90266 732-F5
S MANOR DR
13800 HAW 90250 733-C3
MANOR LN
- LACo 91390 4463-C2
1500 GLDR 91741 569-H6
12900 LA 90066 672-B4
E MANOR ST
- Alta 91001 535-H5
W MANOR ST
- Alta 91001 535-H5
MANOR WY
1700 SGBL 91776 596-D7
MANOR GATE RD
1500 HacH 91745 678-F4
MANORS PL
- LMRD 90638 738-A1
MANSA DR
12800 NRWK 90650 737-A2
13800 LMRD 90638 737-D2
MANSARD DR
13700 LACo 91342 482-J2
MANSEL AV
4500 TOR 90278 763-C2
14300 LNDL 90260 733-C5
19900 TOR 90503 763-C4
S MANSEL AV
10000 Lenx 90304 703-C6
11100 HAW 90304 703-C6
N MANSFIELD AV
100 LA 90036 633-D1
300 LA 90036 593-D7
700 LA 90038 593-D5
1300 Hlwd 90028 593-D5

S MANSFIELD AV
100 LA 90036 633-D2
1000 LA 90019 633-D4
2100 LA 90016 633-C6
3000 LA 90016 673-C6
5800 LACo 90043 673-C6
MANSFIELD CT
- SCTA 91354 4460-G6
1500 UPL 91784 571-H4
MANSFIELD DR
800 CLAR 91711 571-F7
2700 BURB 91504 533-F3
MANSFIELD PL
1200 ALH 91801 596-A3
MANSFIELD WY
- BELL 90201 675-G5
- CMRC 90040 675-G5
MANSIE LN
22500 LACo 90265 629-E3
MANSION CT
4300 LVRN 91750 570-F6
MANSION LN
- LACo 91724 640-A1
- LACo 91768 640-A1
MANSON AV
4200 WdHl 91364 559-H5
MANTECA ST
17400 VanN 91406 531-B4
MANTIS AV
1700 LA 90732 823-H7
MANTON AV
5300 WdHl 91367 559-F2
6100 WdHl 91367 529-F7
MANTOVA DR
4000 LA 90008 673-B3
E MANTOVA ST
1300 LBCH 90815 796-E5
MANTUA RD
200 PacP 90272 630-H6
MANU LN
2400 WCOV 91792 639-B6
MANUEL AV
1200 TOR 90501 763-G6
MANVILLE ST
2400 POM 91767 601-B5
E MANVILLE ST
100 COMP 90220 765-A1
W MANVILLE ST
100 COMP 90220 764-H1
100 COMP 90220 765-A1
MANZANA AV
15300 PRM 90723 735-J4
MANZANAR AV
5000 PRV 90660 676-G4
8200 PRV 90660 706-D2
8800 DWNY 90240 706-C2
10400 DWNY 90241 706-B4
MANZANARES RD
15000 LMRD 90638 737-G3
MANZANILLO DR
2400 RowH 91748 678-J6
MANZANITA AV
200 SMAD 91024 566-J3
200 SMAD 91024 567-A3
700 PAS 91103 565-G2
MANZANITA CIR
4800 LVRN 91750 570-H6
MANZANITA DR
1200 FUL 92833 738-E3
1700 SBdC 92372 (4562-E5 See Page 4471)
2400 SBdC - (4562-F5 See Page 4471)
2700 SBdC 92371 (4562-G1 See Page 4471)
41400 PMDL 93551 4104-E7
E MANZANITA DR
15300 HacH 91745 678-A3
S MANZANITA DR
100 WCOV 91791 599-B7
700 WCOV 91791 639-B1
MANZANITA LN
- BqtC 91354 4460-E3
- THO 91362 557-A3
200 THO 91361 557-A3
1100 MANB 90266 732-J5
18300 LACo 91387 4551-H4
MANZANITA ST
800 LA 90029 594-B6
1300 LFlz 90027 594-B5
2200 LaCr 91214 504-H5
4700 MTCL 91763 641-F1
MANZANITA TR
17700 LACo 93532 4101-J1
MANZANITA MESA RD
10800 Litl 93543 4468-E5
MANZANITA PARK AV
1700 LACo 90265 629-E2
MANZANO CT
26000 SCTA 91355 4550-G4
MANZANO DR
30700 MAL 90265 627-A7
MAPACHE DR
21200 DBAR 91765 679-H7
MAPES AV
- LACo 90703 736-F6
17100 CRTS 90703 736-F7
19600 CRTS 90703 766-G3
MAPLE
1100 SDMS 91773 599-H3
18800 RowH 91748 679-B4
MAPLE AV
- ELSG 90245 702-H7

MAPLE AV
200 TOR 90503 763-E7
300 LA 90015 634-F5
500 LA 90013 634-F5
600 LA 90014 634-F5
1900 LA 90011 634-D7
2200 POM 91767 601-A4
2200 TOR 90505 763-E7
2400 LA 90011 674-D1
2500 MANB 90266 732-G4
3900 ELMN 91731 597-E7
10900 TOR 90505 793-E1
14000 LACo 90061 734-D3
14500 LACo 90248 734-D4
16100 CRSN 90248 734-D6
E MAPLE AV
100 ELSG 90245 702-E7
100 MNRO 91016 567-H5
N MAPLE AV
100 MTBL 90640 676-C1
600 MTBL 90640 636-D7
S MAPLE AV
100 MTBL 90640 676-B4
900 ING 90301 703-C4
W MAPLE AV
100 ELSG 90245 702-D7
100 MNRO 91016 567-F5
MAPLE CT
1500 ALH 91803 595-J6
23600 SIMI 93063 499-B3
W MAPLE CT
1400 ONT 91762 641-H3
MAPLE DR
- CRSN 90746 764-F5
8000 BPK 90620 767-J4
8200 LA 90046 593-A4
N MAPLE DR
100 BHLS 90210 632-G2
400 BHLS 90210 592-G7
S MAPLE DR
100 BHLS 90212 632-G2
MAPLE LN
- Hrbr 90710 794-C3
MAPLE PL
200 MTBL 90640 676-C2
MAPLE ST
500 PAS 91103 565-H4
500 LHB 90631 708-F5
800 SMCA 90405 671-G3
1100 SPAS 91030 595-G4
4000 SBdC 91710 641-D4
5700 SBdC 92397 (4652-D3 See Page 4651)
8700 BLF 90706 735-J6
8700 BLF 90706 736-A6
9900 LALM 90720 767-A7
9900 LBCH 90808 767-A7
11000 WHIT 90601 677-A4
12200 LACo 90061 734-D1
23200 SCTA 91321 4640-G3
40600 PMDL 93551 4194-F1
E MAPLE ST
- PAS 91103 565-J4
100 COMP 90220 734-J3
100 GLDL 91205 564-E6
200 COMP 90220 735-A3
200 PAS 91101 565-J4
500 PAS 91101 566-A4
800 PAS 91106 566-C3
1800 PAS 91107 566-F3
N MAPLE ST
100 BURB 91505 563-C1
1600 BURB 91505 533-C7
W MAPLE ST
100 GLDL 91204 564-E6
300 COMP 90220 734-G3
MAPLE WY
300 PAS 91101 566-A4
1200 SPAS 91030 595-H4
E MAPLE WY
100 LBCH 90802 795-E7
W MAPLE WY
300 LBCH 90802 795-D7
MAPLEBAY CT
19200 SCTA 91321 4551-G6
MAPLEDALE AV
10700 NRWK 90650 736-E4
MAPLEDALE ST
10200 BLF 90706 736-D4
10800 NRWK 90650 736-E3
12500 NRWK 90650 737-B3
MAPLEFIELD ST
11000 SELM 91733 637-B5
MAPLEGATE ST
1800 MONP 91755 636-B5
MAPLEGROVE ST
6400 VeCo 91377 558-B2
15300 LPUE 91744 638-E4
15400 LACo 91744 638-E4
E MAPLEGROVE ST
1100 WCOV 91792 638-H4
16000 LACo 91744 638-F4
MAPLE HILL RD
1300 DBAR 91765 680-A3
MAPLEHURST PL
- LACo 91387 4551-J5
- LACo 91387 4552-A5
MAPLELEAF ST
2500 LACo 90265 628-C5
MAPLELEAF TER
- PMDL 93551 4285-D3
MAPLEPARK DR
29000 RPV 90275 822-G1

MAPLE RIDGE CIR
27600 SCTA 91354 4460-H5
MAPLESIDE ST
9000 BLF 90706 736-A2
MAPLE SPRING DR
23600 DBAR 91765 640-C7
N MAPLETON DR
100 BelA 90077 592-C7
S MAPLETON DR
100 Wwd 90024 592-C7
300 Wwd 90024 632-C1
MAPLE TREE CT
1200 LHB 90631 738-C1
MAPLETREE CT
- StvR 91381 4550-C4
MAPLE VIEW DR
1100 POM 91766 640-F4
MAPLEWOOD AV
3200 LA 90066 672-A3
4400 LA 90004 593-G7
5500 LPMA 90623 767-D3
N MAPLEWOOD AV
100 WCOV 91790 598-G7
MAPLEWOOD LN
500 BREA 92821 709-A5
10800 Nor 91326 500-H4
MAPLEWOOD ST
1500 LVRN 91750 600-F2
9500 BLF 90706 736-B3
43700 LAN 93535 4106-E1
MAQUOKETAH TR
29000 Ago 91301 588-B5
MARABOU PL
- LACo 91387 4551-J5
MARACAIBO PL
15900 HacH 91745 678-B6
MARAND ST
1300 DUAR 91010 568-A6
MARANVILLE CT
3400 WCOV 91792 679-B1
MARATHON RD
- Alta 91001 535-J4
MARATHON ST
2100 Echo 90026 594-B6
3900 LA 90029 594-A6
4500 LA 90029 593-H6
5100 LA 90038 593-G6
MARAVILLA CT
25600 SCTA 91355 4550-G5
MARAVILLA DR
2200 LA 90068 593-D2
40300 PMDL 93550 4195-J3
MARBEL AV
10500 DWNY 90241 706-C4
11900 DWNY 90242 706-A7
MARBELLA AV
21000 CRSN 90745 764-D5
22400 CRSN 90745 794-D1
MARBELLA CT
24900 CALB 91302 559-C6
MARBELLA LN
3100 PMDL 93550 4286-G2
4100 Tarz 91356 560-J6
MARBELLA ST
- LAN 93536 4014-J5
- LAN 93536 4104-J1
42200 LACo 93536 4104-J5
MARBER AV
1800 LBCH 90815 796-C3
3100 LBCH 90808 796-C1
3400 LBCH 90808 766-C7
4100 LKWD 90713 766-C5
MARBLE CT
40800 PMDL 93551 4194-H1
MARBLE DR
15000 Shrm 91403 561-H6
MARBLE LN
1200 LHB 90631 738-D2
MARBLE RD
- LHH 90631 678-F7
MARBLE COVE WY
400 SLB 90740 826-F4
MARBLECREST DR
2100 HacH 91745 678-F5
MARBLEHEAD WY
18300 Tarz 91356 560-J6
MARBORA CT
400 LBCH 90803 796-D7
MARBRING CT
5700 LACo 90606 676-J4
MARBRISA AV
6100 HNTP 90255 674-H7
7200 LACo 90255 674-H7
7200 LACo 90255 704-H2
MARBRISSA AV
- PMDL 93551 4195-J4
MARBRO DR
16400 Enc 91436 561-E5
MARBURN AV
5000 LACo 90043 673-C5
MARBURY ST
500 COV 91723 599-A6
E MARBURY ST
1000 WCOV 91790 598-G6
1400 WCOV 91790 598-H6
W MARBURY ST
1000 WCOV 91790 598-G6
MARBY DR
2500 LACo 90265 628-C5
MARC CT
1000 DBAR 91765 680-E2
MARCASEL AV
3800 LA 90066 672-D4

MARCASEL AV
4100 CULC 90066 672-D4
MARCASEL CT
11800 LA 90066 672-D4
MARCASITE LN
31800 Cstc 91384 4369-H6
MARCELINA AV
1400 TOR 90501 763-H6
MARCELLA AV
2400 WCOV 91792 639-B6
MARCELLA ST
2500 LAN 93536 4015-D7
MARCELLE ST
1100 COMP 90221 735-B5
6600 PRM 90723 735-E5
E MARCELLE ST
1400 COMP 90221 735-C5
1400 RDom 90221 735-C5
MARCELLO PL
17700 Enc 91316 561-B4
MARCELLUS ST
1000 Bxby 90807 765-E5
MARCH AV
7500 LA 91304 529-F3
MARCHANT AV
13600 LA 91342 482-E2
MARCHEETA PL
1800 LA 90069 592-H4
MARCHENA DR
4000 LA 90065 594-J3
MARCHENA ST
21400 WdHl 91364 560-B4
MARCHETA ST
800 Alta 91001 536-A6
MARCHLAND AV
27200 SCTA 91351 4551-G3
MARCHMONT AV
1100 HacH 91745 678-C3
MARCI WY
25100 SCTA 91355 4550-H6
MARCIA DR
1300 LHB 90631 708-B4
3600 Echo 90026 594-B6
17900 LACo 91387 4551-J3
MARCIA RD
2900 GLDL 91208 534-H6
N MARCILE AV
300 GLDR 91741 569-C5
S MARCILE AV
6800 GLDR 91741 569-C5
MARCINE ST
1000 LHB 90631 708-G4
MARCO CT
700 Ven 90291 671-J5
2800 LVRN 91750 600-H2
MARCO PL
700 Ven 90291 671-J5
1000 Ven 90291 672-A4
11500 LA 90066 672-D2
MARCOLA DR
18600 RowH 91748 679-A5
MARCON DR
20600 WAL 91789 639-F6
MARCONI ST
800 MTBL 90640 636-C7
6300 HNTP 90255 675-A7
MARCOS AV
200 SDMS 91773 600-D2
MARCOS RD
4100 WdHl 91364 560-C6
MARCUS AV
1700 PMDL 93550 4286-D4
9700 Tuj 91042 504-B4
MARCUS DR
- GmH 91344 481-A5
MARCUS LN
9700 Tuj 91042 504-B5
MAR DE CORTEZ
- AVA 90704 5923-G2
MARDEL AV
2200 LACo 90601 637-D6
MARDINA ST
100 WCOV 91790 598-G7
E MARDINA ST
1200 WCOV 91790 598-H7
1400 WCOV 91791 598-H7
2000 WCOV 91791 599-A7
N MARDINA ST
100 WCOV 91790 598-H7
MARDINA WY
600 LHB 90631 708-B5
MAREK DR
200 MTBL 90640 636-E7
MAREK MTWY
- LACo 91342 482-J5
- LACo 91342 (4723-A4 See Page 4643)
MARELEN DR
1400 FUL 92835 738-G5
MARELLEN PL
4600 LaCr 91214 534-G1
MARELLEN WY
1900 POM 91767 601-C6
MARENDALE LN
1500 ARCD 91006 567-D3
MARENGO AL
1100 SPAS 91030 595-J2
MARENGO AV
1000 SPAS 91030 595-J4
1000 ALH 91803 595-J4
N MARENGO AV
- ALH 91801 595-J5
- PAS 91103 565-H2

STREET Block	City	ZIP	Pg-Grid
N MARENGO AV			
-	PAS	91101	565-J4
600	PAS	91104	565-H2
1600	PAS	91103	535-H7
1600	PAS	91104	535-H7
2000	Alta	91001	535-J6
3200	Alta	91001	536-A4
S MARENGO AV			
-	ALH	91801	595-J6
-	PAS	91105	565-J6
-	PAS	91101	565-J6
300	ALH	91803	595-J6
500	PAS	91106	565-J6
1200	PAS	91106	595-J1
1300	SMRO	91106	595-J1
1300	SMRO	91108	595-J1
1700	ALH	91803	635-J1
MARENGO DR			
1000	GLDL	91206	565-C2
1900	RowH	91748	678-G5
MARENGO PL			
2000	Boyl	90033	635-B3
MARENGO ST			
1600	Boyl	90033	635-A3
2900	City	90063	635-C3
2900	LA	90063	635-C3
MARETO WY			
700	VeCo	91377	557-H1
MARFIELD AV			
-	Tarz	91356	560-G7
MARGARET AV			
5300	LA	90230	672-F6
S MARGARET AV			
200	ELA	90022	635-H7
600	ELA	90022	675-H1
MARGARET CT			
2200	RBCH	90278	763-A2
W MARGARET CT			
1100	UPL	91786	601-J1
MARGARET DR			
2900	PAS	91107	566-F5
MARGARET LN			
800	WAL	91789	639-C6
3000	SMCA	90405	671-H3
MARGARET ST			
9000	DWNY	90241	706-C6
9500	CYP	90630	767-E7
20800	CRSN	90745	764-C5
MARGARITA DR			
1100	WCOV	91790	638-F1
1200	FUL	92833	738-F5
22600	WdHl	91364	559-H5
MARGARITA WY			
-	PMDL	93551	4104-D6
MARGARITA HILLS DR			
33100	Actn	93510	4374-D7
MARGATE PL			
3000	PMDL	93551	4195-C3
MARGATE RD			
1600	PVE	90274	792-E6
MARGATE SQ			
-	PVE	90274	792-F6
MARGATE ST			
10300	NHol	91601	563-B2
11600	NHol	91601	562-H2
13100	VanN	91401	562-A2
14500	VanN	91411	562-A2
14600	VanN	91411	561-J2
16800	Enc	91436	561-D2
17100	Enc	91316	561-A2
18200	Tarz	91356	560-J2
18200	Tarz	91356	561-A2
MARGAY AV			
17000	CRSN	90746	734-E7
MARGO AV			
300	LBCH	90803	796-E7
MARGO ST			
1300	LA	90015	634-D6
MARGUERITA AV			
100	MONP	91754	636-A2
100	SMCA	90402	671-C1
400	SMCA	90402	631-E6
N MARGUERITA AV			
-	ALH	91801	596-A4
S MARGUERITA AV			
-	ALH	91801	596-A7
300	ALH	91803	596-A7
1700	ALH	91803	636-A1
MARGUERITA DR			
1400	COMP	90221	735-B3
MARGUERITA LN			
200	PAS	91106	565-J7
200	PAS	91106	595-J1
MARGUERITE DR			
-	RPV	90275	822-E2
MARGUERITE ST			
3200	LA	90065	594-G2
MARIA AV			
-	RBCH	90277	763-A6
800	LVRN	91750	600-D2
16700	CRTS	90703	737-A7
18700	CRTS	90703	767-A1
N MARIA AV			
400	RBCH	90277	762-J3
S MARIA AV			
300	RBCH	90277	763-A5
MARIA CIR			
43900	LAN	93535	4016-F7
43900	LAN	93535	4106-F1
MARIA CT			
2700	WCOV	91792	639-B6
MARIA PL			
18300	CRTS	90703	767-A1
MARIA RD			
100	SBdC	92372	(4472-A7 See Page 4471)
MARIA ST			
1600	BURB	91504	533-E6
E MARIA ST			
2900	RDom	90221	765-B2
MARIACHI PLAZA DE LOS ANGELES			
1700	Boyl	90033	634-J2
MARIALINDA ST			
5500	TOR	90503	763-A4
MARIAM PL			
27500	SCTA	91350	4461-A6
MARIAN CT			
2200	Ven	90291	671-F6
MARIAN PL			
2200	Ven	90291	671-J5
2200	Ven	90291	672-A5
N MARIAN ST			
100	LHB	90631	708-D5
S MARIAN ST			
100	LHB	90631	708-D6
S MARIAN WY			
800	ANA	92804	767-G7
MARIANA ST			
1200	WCOV	91790	638-E1
MARIANITA DR			
1300	LACo	90631	708-C3
N MARIANNA AV			
100	City	90063	635-E5
1800	LA	90032	635-E2
S MARIANNA AV			
100	City	90063	635-E6
1100	LACo	90023	675-E2
1200	CMRC	90023	675-E2
1400	CMRC	90040	675-E2
1400	LACo	90040	675-E2
MARIANNA RD			
1300	PAS	91105	565-E7
MARIANO ST			
22600	WdHl	91367	559-G2
MARIBEL AV			
23200	CRSN	90745	794-D2
MARICIO DR			
23600	SCTA	91355	4550-G5
MARICOPA DR			
2100	LA	90065	594-J2
MARICOPA PL			
2300	TOR	90501	763-G5
MARICOPA ST			
2200	TOR	90501	763-E5
2500	TOR	90503	763-A5
MARICOTTE DR			
3000	PMDL	93550	4286-F2
MARIE AV			
200	FUL	92833	738-F7
300	HiPk	90042	595-E1
500	HiPk	90042	565-E7
MARIE DR			
-	PMDL	93552	4287-B4
MARIE ST			
200	LHB	90631	708-B6
MARIE ELLEN ST			
1300	WHIT	90603	708-C3
MARIEL WY			
-	Saug	91350	4461-F6
MARIETTA AV			
2200	CLAR	91711	571-C6
10800	CULC	90232	672-F3
MARIETTA CT			
700	LBCH	90813	795-E1
3300	Bxby	90807	795-E1
3300	SIGH	90755	795-E1
N MARIETTA CT			
-	LBCH	90802	825-E1
200	LBCH	90802	795-E7
MARIETTA LN			
10600	CULC	90230	672-H4
MARIETTA ST			
900	LA	90023	635-A7
MARIGOLD AV			
-	LHB	90631	708-C6
1000	PMDL	93551	4195-G7
14700	GAR	90249	733-G4
21200	LACo	90502	764-A6
23000	LACo	90502	794-A2
24300	Hrbr	90710	794-A3
25000	Hrbr	90710	794-A4
42200	LAN	93536	4104-E5
MARIGOLD CIR			
30400	Cstc	91384	4459-H3
MARIGOLD CT			
26600	CALB	91302	558-G7
MARIGOLD LN			
2000	WCOV	91791	638-J3
2000	WCOV	91791	639-A3
MARIGOLD ST			
1400	UPL	91784	571-H3
1900	POM	91767	601-B6
E MARIGOLD ST			
300	Alta	91001	535-J5
400	Alta	91001	536-A5
W MARIGOLD ST			
300	Alta	91001	535-G4
MARILLA AV			
100	AVA	90704	5923-G3
14300	NRWK	90650	737-C3
MARILLA ST			
15400	LA	91343	501-D5
17100	Nor	91325	501-A5
18100	Nor	91325	500-J5
18500	Nor	91324	500-F5
19800	Chat	91311	500-A5
22200	Chat	91311	499-H5
MARILYN DR			
1000	BHLS	90210	592-E6
6000	CYP	90630	767-E7
16200	GrnH	91344	481-E7
28800	SCTA	91387	4552-E1
29000	SCTA	91387	4462-E7
MARILYN LN			
15500	Enc	91436	561-G4
MARILYN PL			
200	ARCD	91006	537-E7
MARILYN WY			
700	COV	91722	599-D4
MARILYNN ST			
3200	LAN	93536	4015-A7
MARIMBA ST			
18400	RowH	91748	679-A7
MARIN CT			
-	MANB	90266	732-J4
S MARIN CT			
1200	ANA	92804	767-J7
MARIN ST			
200	LHB	90631	708-C6
MARINA CT			
15600	SCTA	91387	4552-E1
MARINA DR			
-	LBCH	90803	826-D4
-	SLB	90740	826-D4
1800	LA	90732	823-H7
26000	RHE	90274	793-B5
E MARINA DR			
1600	LBCH	90803	826-D2
N MARINA DR			
-	LBCH	90803	826-E3
MARINA EXWY Rt#-90			
12800	LA	90066	672-C6
12800	LA	90094	672-C6
12800	LA	90292	672-C6
MARINA FRWY Rt#-90			
-	CULC	-	672-D7
-	LA	-	672-D7
MARINA PL			
2000	LA	90732	823-H7
MARINA WY			
-	RBCH	90277	762-H4
100	SPed	90731	824-E6
MARINA CITY DR			
4200	MdlR	90292	671-J6
4200	MdlR	90292	672-A6
MARINA PACIFICA			
-	LBCH	90803	826-D2
MARINA PARK LN			
400	LBCH	90803	826-B1
MARINA POINT LN			
-	SCTA	91355	4550-H3
MARINA POINTE DR			
13600	LA	90292	672-B6
E MARINA VIEW DR			
6200	LBCH	90803	796-E7
6200	LBCH	90803	826-E1
MARINA VISTA DR			
30700	MAL	90265	627-A7
MARINE AV			
100	MANB	90266	732-F5
100	Wilm	90744	794-E5
100	Wilm	90744	824-E1
1500	SLB	90740	826-F5
1900	RBCH	90278	732-G5
1900	RBCH	90278	733-A5
3400	LACo	90249	733-C5
3400	LACo	90250	733-C5
3500	LACo	90260	733-C5
3600	HAW	90250	733-C5
3900	HAW	90260	733-A5
4000	LNDL	90260	733-C5
5300	HAW	90261	733-A5
5400	HAW	90261	732-G5
22300	CRSN	90745	764-E7
22500	CRSN	90745	794-E1
W MARINE AV			
1000	GAR	90247	734-A4
1300	GAR	90247	733-G4
1800	GAR	90249	733-G4
3100	LACo	90249	733-G4
MARINE CT			
-	SMCA	90405	671-F5
-	Ven	90291	671-F5
MARINE PL			
100	MANB	90266	732-E5
N MARINE PL			
12300	LA	90066	672-B2
MARINE PL N			
600	SMCA	90405	671-G4
MARINE ST			
100	SMCA	90405	671-J3
100	Ven	90291	671-G4
12000	LA	90066	672-B2
MARINE TER			
-	SMCA	90401	671-E3
MARINER AV			
19600	TOR	90503	763-D4
MARINER CIR			
4000	WLKV	91361	557-C6
MARINER CT			
-	PMDL	93552	4287-D1
MARINER CV			
-	BPK	90621	738-B6
MARINER DR			
2500	SPed	90731	823-J7
2500	SPed	90731	853-J1
15900	HNTB	92649	826-H6
15900	SLB	90740	826-H6
MARINER ST			
700	BREA	92821	708-J7
MARINER WY			
-	SCTA	91355	4550-F1
7000	LBCH	90803	826-G2
MARINERS VIEW LN			
300	LCF	91011	535-E3
MARINETTE RD			
1200	PacP	90272	631-B4
MARINETTE ST			
1700	TOR	90501	793-H1
MARINO CT			
5000	PMDL	93551	4194-H2
MARINO ST			
40600	PMDL	93551	4194-H2
MARINO TER			
1900	SMRO	91108	595-J2
1900	SMRO	91108	596-A2
1900	SPAS	91030	595-J2
1900	SPAS	91030	596-A2
MARION AV			
-	MTCL	91763	641-G3
-	PAS	91106	566-C4
1100	LA	90012	634-F1
1100	Echo	90026	634-F1
1200	LAN	93535	4106-C2
4800	BALD	91706	598-C3
4900	TOR	90505	793-B2
9500	MTCL	91763	601-G6
MARION BLVD			
100	FUL	92835	738-H4
MARION CIR			
4900	BALD	91706	598-C3
MARION CT			
1300	INDS	91745	678-E3
MARION DR			
-	RPV	90275	823-F3
600	CLAR	91711	601-D5
1000	GLDL	91205	564-G6
1600	LA	90065	564-G7
MARION PL			
600	GLDR	91740	569-F6
MARION WY			
-	BqtC	91354	4460-F2
4000	Bxby	90807	765-C6
MARIONDALE AV			
2200	LA	90032	635-F1
2300	LA	90032	595-F7
MARIONWOOD DR			
4700	LA	90230	672-E5
MARIOTA AV			
4300	LA	91602	563-C4
MARIPOSA AV			
-	SMAD	91024	567-A2
3000	PMDL	93551	4195-B3
13500	GAR	90247	734-A3
18400	LA	90248	764-A2
20600	LACo	90502	764-A4
22800	LACo	90502	794-A2
24200	Hrbr	90710	794-A3
E MARIPOSA AV			
100	ELSG	90245	732-F1
N MARIPOSA AV			
100	LA	90004	633-J1
200	LA	90004	593-J7
700	LA	90029	593-J5
1300	LFlz	90027	593-J4
S MARIPOSA AV			
100	LA	90004	633-J2
300	LA	90020	633-J2
600	LA	90005	633-J3
600	LA	90010	633-J2
900	LA	90006	633-J4
1900	LA	90007	633-J6
7900	LA	90044	703-J2
11100	LACo	90044	704-A6
W MARIPOSA AV			
100	ELSG	90245	732-D1
100	SMAD	91024	566-J2
100	SMAD	91024	567-A2
MARIPOSA CIR			
-	LACo	90265	628-F6
MARIPOSA CT			
-	LA	91304	529-E2
MARIPOSA DR			
1000	BREA	92821	709-B5
44100	LAN	93536	4015-B6
MARIPOSA LN			
-	Cstc	91384	4369-G5
1000	MTBL	90640	676-C4
1600	FUL	92833	738-D4
10300	SGAT	90280	705-B5
10300	LYN	90262	705-B5
16300	LPUE	91744	638-G7
MARIPOSA PL			
-	SCTA	91354	4460-F7
MARIPOSA ST			
-	SCTA	91355	4460-E6
500	LHB	90631	708-B7
800	GLDL	91205	564-F6
2200	POM	91767	600-J4
E MARIPOSA ST			
-	Alta	91001	535-H5
500	Alta	91001	536-A5
N MARIPOSA ST			
300	BURB	91506	563-F1
500	BURB	91506	533-F6
S MARIPOSA ST			
200	BURB	91506	563-G2
W MARIPOSA ST			
-	Alta	91001	535-G5
MARIPOSA WY			
100	BREA	92823	710-C6
MARIPOSA BAY LN			
11400	Nor	91326	500-E1
11600	Nor	91326	480-E7
MARIPOSA CREEK WY			
19700	Nor	91326	500-E1
MARIPOSA DE ORO			
23100	MAL	90265	629-A6
MARIPOSA PINES WY			
-	Nor	91326	480-E7
E MARIQUITA ST			
2700	LBCH	90803	825-H1
6300	LBCH	90803	796-E7
MARIS AV			
4000	PRV	90660	676-G1
MARISA DR			
-	LACo	91387	4551-J4
MARISCAL LN			
2300	LA	90046	592-H2
MARISCAL RD			
-	BqtC	91354	4460-F3
E MARITA ST			
5800	LBCH	90815	796-D4
MARITIME RD			
4100	RPV	90275	823-D6
MARJAN AV			
5400	LadH	90056	672-J5
MARJORAM CT			
21900	SCTA	91350	4461-A6
MARJORIE AV			
1400	CLAR	91711	601-E1
21200	TOR	90503	763-C6
22300	TOR	90505	763-C7
22600	TOR	90505	793-C1
MARJORIE ST			
9400	PRV	90660	676-G6
MARK AV			
2200	PMDL	93550	4286-E2
MARK CIR			
7500	LPMA	90623	767-C3
MARK CT			
5300	AGRH	91301	557-H5
MARK LN			
1500	SIMI	93063	499-B3
MARK PL			
10000	LA	90210	592-B3
MARK ST			
1000	Boyl	90033	635-A3
MARKDALE AV			
11800	NRWK	90650	706-J7
13100	NRWK	90650	736-J2
13700	NRWK	90650	737-A2
MARKEL DR			
25100	SCTA	91321	4640-F2
MARKER LN			
300	NLB	90805	735-C7
E MARKER ST			
100	NLB	90805	735-C7
MARKET AL			
700	PAS	91101	566-A4
800	PAS	91106	566-A4
MARKET CT			
-	FUL	92832	738-C7
700	LA	90021	634-G6
MARKET LN			
1400	ALH	91801	596-D7
MARKET PL			
-	MANB	90266	732-J4
25900	LMTA	90717	793-J5
43100	LAN	93535	4105-J3
MARKET ST			
-	Ven	90291	671-G6
3500	GLDL	91208	534-H4
22300	SCTA	91321	4641-A1
22400	SCTA	91321	4640-J1
42400	LAN	93534	4105-J4
E MARKET ST			
-	NLB	90805	765-D3
2000	LKWD	90712	765-F3
N MARKET ST			
200	ING	90301	703-C1
300	ING	90302	703-C1
900	ING	90302	673-C7
S MARKET ST			
100	ING	90301	703-C3
W MARKET ST			
-	NLB	90805	765-C3
MARKET TR			
12100	LACo	91342	482-J6
MARKETPLACE			
-	POM	91766	641-A7
MARKETPLACE DR			
-	LACo	93551	4195-G5
700	PMDL	93551	4195-G5
MARKHAM LN			
-	ING	90305	703-F3
MARKHAM PL			
200	PAS	91105	565-G6
MARK KEPPEL ST			
-	COMP	90221	735-E4
6500	PRM	90723	735-E4
E MARKLAND DR			
100	MONP	91755	636-B6
W MARKLAND DR			
200	MONP	91754	636-A6
500	MONP	91754	635-J6
MARKLEIN AV			
8500	LA	91343	531-G1
9700	LA	91343	501-G5
9900	MsnH	91345	501-G2
MARKRIDGE RD			
2800	LaCr	91214	504-F5
3100	GLDL	91214	504-D4
3800	Tuj	91042	504-D4
MARKS RD			
3800	Ago	91301	588-F1
3800	Ago	91301	558-F7
MARKSTAY ST			
19500	RowH	91748	679-D4
MARKTON ST			
400	LACo	90061	734-D3
MARKWAY LN			
300	POM	91767	600-J2
MARKWOOD ST			
2500	DUAR	91010	568-D4
MARLA AV			
8300	LA	91304	529-E2
MARLAND ST			
13900	LPUE	91746	638-B3
MARLAY DR			
1500	LA	90069	593-A4
MARLBORO CT			
700	CLAR	91711	571-F6
N MARLBORO LN			
-	VeCo	91307	529-A3
MARLBORO ST			
1000	LHB	90631	708-E7
12700	Brwd	90049	631-E4
MARLBOROUCH LN			
3000	LA	90065	594-G1
N MARLBOROUGH AV			
500	ING	90302	703-D1
600	ING	90302	673-D7
MARLBOROUGH CT			
7600	LA	91304	529-F4
MARLEI RD			
900	LHB	90631	708-D4
MARLENA ST			
2500	WCOV	91792	639-B6
MARLETTE DR			
13000	LMRD	90638	737-E2
MARLEWOOD POINT CT			
-	LACo	91387	4552-B5
MARLEY WY			
-	LA	91343	501-J6
MARLIA CT			
3600	Tarz	91356	560-G6
E MARLIES AV			
5800	SIMI	93063	499-A1
N MARLIES AV			
2100	SIMI	93063	499-A2
MARLIES ST			
28900	AGRH	91301	558-A3
MARLIN AV			
1200	SLB	90740	826-F4
MARLIN CIR			
6700	LPMA	90623	767-D2
MARLIN PL			
1500	VanN	91405	531-H5
15700	VanN	91406	531-B5
22200	CanP	91303	529-J5
22400	CanP	91307	529-H5
MARLINDA AV			
3100	BALD	91706	637-H1
MARLINTON DR			
15700	LACo	90604	707-H7
16100	LACo	90604	708-A6
MARLITA PL			
700	HMB	90254	732-G7
MARLOMA DR			
4500	RHE	90274	793-C5
MARLOW AV			
6500	BGDN	90201	675-G7
6500	BGDN	90201	705-G1
MARLOWE CT			
-	StvR	91381	4550-A6
MARLTON AV			
3900	LA	90008	673-D3
MAR LU DR			
2600	LA	90046	592-J2
MARMADUKE PL			
16800	Enc	91436	561-D5
MARMAY PL			
8200	SunV	91352	532-J2
MARMION WY			
100	HiPk	90042	595-C2
100	SPAS	91030	595-E2
3400	LA	90065	595-A5
MARMOL DR			
4900	WdHl	91364	560-B3
MARMON AV			
-	THO	91362	557-B3
MARMONT AV			
1500	LA	90069	593-A4
MARMONT LN			
8200	LA	90069	593-A5
8200	WHWD	90069	593-A5
MARMORA AL			
-	PAS	91105	565-H5
MARMORA DR			
20900	WdHl	91364	560-C5
MARMORA ST			
20900	WdHl	91364	560-C5
MARNA AV			
3000	LALM	90808	796-H1
3000	LBCH	90808	796-H1
3400	LBCH	90808	766-J7
MARNE AV			
-	Brwd	90049	632-A3
MARNE DR			
30800	RPV	90275	822-H3
MARNEY AV			
1800	LACo	90032	635-E2
1800	LA	90032	635-E2
MARNICE AV			
9800	Tuj	91042	504-C4
MAROGE CIR			
20300	Saug	91350	4461-D5
20300	SCTA	91350	4461-D5
W MARONDE WY			
100	MONP	91754	636-B4
MARONEY LN			
1000	PacP	90272	630-J4
MAROON DR			
4500	CRTS	90703	767-B3
4500	LPMA	90623	767-B3
MAROON ST			
10100	ELMN	91733	637-B2
MAROON BELL RD			
2400	CHLS	91709	680-J1
MARQUAND AV			
7700	LA	91304	529-E3
MARQUARDT AV			
6600	LPMA	90623	767-D1
11400	LACo	90605	707-C7
11800	CRTS	90703	767-D1
12600	LMRD	90638	737-D3
12600	SFSP	90670	737-D3
16000	CRTS	90703	737-D6
MARQUESAS WY			
300	LA	90292	671-J7
300	LA	90292	701-J1
13900	MdlR	90292	671-J7
13900	MdlR	90292	672-A7
13900	MdlR	90292	701-J1
MARQUETTE AV			
2100	POM	91766	641-B6
MARQUETTE DR			
1200	WAL	91789	639-F4
2600	Top	90290	589-G2
6600	BPK	90620	767-F6
MARQUETTE LN			
11300	SBdC	91766	641-D3
MARQUETTE ST			
500	PacP	90272	630-H5
MARQUEZ AV			
16600	PacP	90272	630-H5
MARQUEZ PL			
100	PacP	90272	630-H6
MARQUEZ TER			
16600	PacP	90272	630-H5
MARQUIS CT			
-	SCTA	91350	4551-D5
MARQUITA LN			
-	LACo	90604	707-C5
MARR ST			
500	Ven	90291	671-J6
600	Ven	90291	672-A6
800	LA	90292	672-A6
MARRIOTT WY			
-	StvR	91381	4640-E1
MARRON AV			
3800	Bxby	90807	765-F6
N MARRON AV			
1100	Bxby	90807	765-F6
MARRON PL			
1100	Bxby	90807	765-F6
MARS CT			
400	LBCH	90802	795-E7
700	LBCH	90813	795-E6
3300	Bxby	90807	795-E1
3300	SIGH	90755	795-E1
MARS LN			
10500	BelA	90077	592-A5
MARSALA DR			
23600	SCTA	91355	4550-E4
37800	PMDL	93552	4287-C1
MARSDEN CT			
25900	LACo	91302	558-J3
MARSDEN ST			
1500	Echo	90026	594-F6
MARSEILLE PL			
-	Cstc	91384	4459-E2
MARSEILLE WY			
30800	WLKV	91362	557-F5
MARSEILLES CT			
5000	PMDL	93552	4287-B1
MARSEILLES DR			
-	PMDL	93552	4287-C1
MARSEN ST			
10400	ELMN	91731	597-C5
MARSH AV			
7400	LACo	91770	636-E3
MARSH ST			
2700	LA	90039	594-F3
MARSHA AV			
6200	SIMI	93063	499-B3
MARSHA LN			
14000	WHIT	90602	677-E7
MARSHALL AV			
5700	BPK	90621	737-J7
6300	BPK	90621	767-J1
12300	CHNO	91710	641-G6
MARSHALL CT			
100	SDMS	91773	570-B7
600	CLAR	91711	601-E1
N MARSHALL CT			
100	SPed	90731	824-B4
MARSHALL DR			
4700	LA	90230	672-E5
MARSHALL PL			
200	Bxby	90807	765-D6
MARSHALL ST			
800	SGBL	91776	596-F7
800	RSMD	91776	596-F7
800	RSMD	91770	596-H7
9500	RSMD	91770	597-A7
9800	ELMN	91731	597-A7
11800	LA	90230	672-E6
12400	LA	90066	672-E6
E MARSHALL ST			
-	RSMD	91770	596-F7
100	SGBL	91776	596-F7
800	RSMD	91776	596-F7
W MARSHALL ST			
100	SGBL	91776	596-E7
MARSHALL WY			
1800	SGBL	91776	596-D7
3900	Bxby	90807	765-F6
20700	SCTA	91350	4461-C6
MARSHALL CREEK DR			
4800	LVRN	91750	570-G6
MARSHALLFIELD LN			
1300	RBCH	90278	762-J2
1800	RBCH	90278	763-A2
MARSHALL VILLAS ST			
4000	LA	90032	595-D5
MARSHFIELD WY			
7000	Hlwd	90028	593-D4
7100	LA	90046	593-D4
MARSH HAWK PL			
-	LVRN	91750	570-J4
MARSON ST			
14900	PanC	91402	531-H3
MARSTON AV			
400	LPUE	91744	678-G1
MARSTON CT			
22300	SCTA	91350	4460-J4
MARSUERITE WY			
42400	LAN	93536	4104-E5
MART DR			
16000	LMRD	90638	737-J3
16000	LMRD	90638	738-A3
MARTA LN			
-	LACo	91387	4552-A4
N MARTEL AV			
100	LA	90036	633-C1
300	LA	90036	593-C7
700	LA	90046	593-C4
900	WHWD	90046	593-C5
S MARTEL AV			
100	LA	90036	633-C1
MARTELLO ST			
1700	POM	91767	601-C6
MARTELLUS DR			
-	Saug	91350	4461-F5
MARTELO AV			
200	PAS	91107	566-D3
600	PAS	91104	566-D2
1200	LACo	91104	566-D2
MARTES			
-	LVRN	91750	570-H3
MARTHA AV			
2600	TOR	90501	793-J1
17400	CRTS	90703	737-B7
19000	CRTS	90703	767-C2
MARTHA CIR			
3300	LACo	91107	566-G6
MARTHA CT			
600	LAN	93535	4106-A1
MARTHA PL			
200	FUL	92833	738-D7
17800	CRTS	90703	737-B7
17900	CRTS	90703	767-B1
MARTHA ST			
11300	NHol	91601	562-J1
11900	LA	91607	562-E1
13300	VanN	91401	562-A1
14500	VanN	91411	562-A1
14600	VanN	91411	561-H1
17100	Enc	91316	561-A1
18700	Tarz	91356	560-F1
19700	WdHl	91367	560-C2
24200	WdHl	91367	559-D2
24400	WdHl	91367	559-D2
24400	WdHl	91367	559-D2
MARTHA ANN DR			
11100	OrCo	90720	796-G4
MARTIN AL			
-	PAS	91105	565-H5
MARTIN CT			
100	BREA	92821	709-B7
MARTIN LN			
400	BHLS	90210	592-G4
16300	HNTB	92649	826-J6
MARTIN RD			
5700	IRW	91706	568-E7
5700	IRW	91706	598-E1
MARTIN ST			
5100	LA	90032	595-F7
21000	CRSN	90745	764-G5
MARTIN WY			
500	CLAR	91711	571-E6
36500	PMDL	93550	4286-A5
MARTINA AV			
1700	TOR	90501	763-H7
MARTINA ST			
13100	CHNO	91710	641-F7
MARTINDALE AV			
9000	SunV	91352	503-C7
MARTINDALE RIDGE RD			
-	LACo	91390	(4282-J1 See Page 4281)
-	LACo	91390	4283-A1
MARTINEZ DR			
500	LHB	90631	708-B7
MARTINEZ RD			
-	Actn	93510	4465-A1
MARTINEZ ST			
16000	IRW	91706	598-F3
20600	WdHl	91364	560-A3
22000	WdHl	91364	559-J3
MARTINGALE CT			
1400	SDMS	91773	599-H4
MARTINGALE DR			
-	Actn	93510	4375-B5
-	RPV	90275	823-F2
2400	LACo	91724	639-F1
MARTINIQUE WY			
8400	CYP	90630	767-B5
MARTIN LUTHER KING JR AV			
600	LBCH	90802	795-F6
700	LBCH	90813	795-F6
1800	LBCH	90806	795-F6
MARTIN LUTHER KING JR BLVD			
2600	LYN	90262	704-J5
2700	SGAT	90280	704-J5
2900	LYN	90262	705-A5
2900	SGAT	90280	705-A5
4300	LYN	90262	735-D1
E MARTIN LUTHER KING JR BLVD			
100	LA	90011	674-D2
1700	LA	90058	674-F2
W MARTIN LUTHER KING JR BLVD			
100	LA	90037	674-A2
1100	LA	90011	674-A2
1200	LA	90037	673-F2
1400	LA	90062	673-F2
2100	LA	90008	673-F2
4500	LA	90016	673-D1
MARTINO CT			
-	Saug	91350	4461-G6
MARTINQUE DR			
13600	CHLS	91709	680-J2
MARTIN RANCH RD			
6100	Actn	93510	4374-E5
MARTINSHIRE ST			
400	CRSN	90745	794-B1
MARTONA DR			
4900	VeCo	91377	557-G1
MARTOS DR			
500	SPAS	91030	595-G2
MARTSON DR			
4500	Enc	91316	561-A4
MARVA AV			
12400	GrnH	91344	481-A5
MARVALE DR			
5100	LACo	90043	673-C5
MARVENE DR			
16300	HacH	91745	678-E5
MARVIEW AV			
900	LA	90012	634-F1
MARVIEW DR			
5100	LPMA	90623	767-C3
MARVIN AV			
30000	Cstc	91384	4459-C6
S MARVIN AV			
1700	LA	90019	633-B6
1800	LA	90016	633-B6
MARVIN RD			
-	LACo	91390	4373-C5
MARVIN ST			
4500	LCF	91011	535-B3
MAR VISTA AV			
200	Wilm	90744	794-C7
200	Wilm	90744	824-C1
1500	PAS	91104	566-B1
1600	LACo	91104	536-B6
1600	PAS	91104	536-B6
2400	Alta	91001	536-B6
MARVISTA AV			
700	SLB	90740	826-E3
N MAR VISTA AV			
-	PAS	91106	566-B3
400	PAS	91104	566-B3
1500	PAS	91104	536-B7
1900	Alta	91001	536-B7
MAR VISTA DR			
4100	LACo	90265	627-J5
MAR VISTA MTWY			
-	LACo	90265	627-J3
-	LACo	90265	628-A3
MAR VISTA ST			
8100	WHIT	90605	707-H1
12400	WHIT	90602	677-C7
14000	WHIT	90602	707-F1
15700	WHIT	90605	708-A1
MAR VISTA RIDGE RD			
1300	LACo	90265	627-J2
MARWICK AV			
4100	LKWD	90713	766-C6
N MARWICK AV			
2200	LBCH	90815	796-C4
3000	LBCH	90808	796-C1
3700	LBCH	90808	766-C7
MARWOOD AV			
300	FUL	92832	738-F7
MARWOOD DR			
4600	Eagl	90041	564-J7
4600	LA	90065	564-J7
MARWOOD ST			
14400	HacH	91745	637-J7
14800	HacH	91745	638-A7
15000	HacH	91745	678-A1
MARY AV			
8600	Wats	90002	704-F3
10300	Wats	90002	704-F5
MARY CIR			
1100	LVRN	91750	600-E2
MARY CT			
2600	WCOV	91792	639-B6
MARY LN			
10600	Sunl	91040	503-G3
MARY PL			
900	CLAR	91711	571-F6
MARY RD			
-	Actn	93510	4375-F4
-	LACo	93551	4375-F4
MARY ST			
2400	Mont	91020	534-G1
2600	LaCr	91214	534-F1
3300	GLDL	91214	504-E7
8400	PRV	90660	676-E5
MARY ANN CT			
200	AZU	91702	598-F1
MARYANN DR			
500	RBCH	90278	763-B3
MARY ANN LN			
19800	LACo	91789	679-E7
19800	RowH	91748	679-E7
MARYANN LN			
300	POM	91767	601-A5
MARY ANN MNR			
-	LVRN	91750	570-H5
MARYANN ST			
3200	GLDL	91214	504-E7
MARYANNA LN			
600	MNRO	91016	567-F6
MARY BELL AV			
10300	Sunl	91040	503-C3
MARYBETH AV			
2600	SELM	91733	636-J2
2600	SELM	91733	637-A2
3100	ELMN	91733	637-A1
3500	RSMD	91770	596-J7
MARY ELLEN AV			
3900	LA	91604	562-D6
4400	Shrm	91423	562-D3
5200	VanN	91401	562-D2
6000	VanN	91401	532-D6
7000	NHol	91605	532-D2
7000	NHol	91605	532-D5
MARYE MARGO CIR			
2800	PMDL	93550	4286-F4
MARYFIELD AV			
46000	LACo	93535	4018-D2
MARYGLEN LN			
800	LHB	90631	708-D6
MARYGROVE RD			
300	CLAR	91711	601-C4
MARY HILL LN			
-	AZU	91702	569-B6
MARYHILL RD N			
4700	Actn	93510	4464-J7
MARYHILL RD W			
5100	Actn	93510	4464-H7
MARYHURST DR			
800	CLAR	91711	601-B1
MARYKNOLL AV			
8800	WHIT	90605	707-D3
9200	LACo	90605	707-D3
MARY KNOLL CIR			
700	MNRO	91016	567-H3
MARYLAND AV			
4200	GLDL	91214	534-E1
4300	GLDL	91214	504-E6
N MARYLAND AV			
100	GLDL	91206	564-E3
1100	GLDL	91207	564-E3
S MARYLAND AV			
100	GLDL	91205	564-E5
MARYLAND DR			
5800	LA	90036	633-C2
6100	LA	90048	633-A2
MARYLAND PL			
200	GLDL	91206	564-E3
MARYLAND ST			
100	ELSG	90245	732-F2
600	ELSG	90245	702-F7
1200	LA	90017	634-D3
1800	LA	90057	634-D3
W MARYLAND ST			
1900	LA	90057	634-C2
MARYLEE ST			
21700	WdHl	91367	560-A1
22100	WdHl	91367	559-F1
MARYLIE LN			
700	WAL	91789	639-C6
MARYLIND AV			
-	CLAR	91711	601-F2
-	UPL	91786	601-F2
E MARYLIND AV			
600	CLAR	91711	601-E1
MARYMOUNT LN			
800	CLAR	91711	571-B6
MARYMOUNT PL			
100	BelA	90077	632-A1
MARYPORT AV			
600	SDMS	91773	600-C1
MARYTON AV			
13800	SFSP	90670	737-B3
14400	NRWK	90650	737-B4
MARYVILLE DR			
200	WAL	91789	639-F7
200	WAL	91789	679-F1
MARYVINE ST			
11200	ELMN	91733	637-D3
12100	ELMN	91732	637-D3
MARYWOOD AV			
200	CLAR	91711	601-B4

STREET
Block City ZIP Pg-Grid

MARZELLA AV
700 Brwd 90049 631-G1
MASCAGNI ST
4400 LA 90066 672-D6
MASCARELL AV
10900 MsnH 91345 501-J2
MASCOT ST
4600 LA 90019 633-D5
MASEFIELD CT
8000 LA 91304 529-E3
MASLINE CT
- BALD 91706 598-E3
MASLINE ST
1000 COV 91722 598-H3
13800 BALD 91706 598-B3
16500 LACo 91722 598-G3
MASON AV
- Nor 91326 480-C6
- Nor 91326 500-C1
5500 WdHl 91367 560-D2
6500 Win 91306 530-D2
8900 Chat 91311 500-D3
8900 Chat 91311 530-D2
MASON CT
200 BREA 92821 709-C7
20300 TOR 90503 763-A4
22600 SCTA 91350 4460-J4
MASON RD
- LACo 90265 586-D7
MASON ST
100 AZU 91702 598-J1
400 AZU 91702 599-A1
4300 SGAT 90280 705-D3
6200 WdHl 91367 530-D7
N MASON WY
200 INDS 91746 637-J4
MASONCREST DR
8000 PRV 90660 706-G2
MASONGATE DR
- RHE 90274 793-C5
MASONHILL DR
13300 LACo 93532 4102-J4
MASSA CT
- PMDL 93552 4287-D3
MASSACHUSETTS AV
10700 Wwd 90024 632-B4
10900 WLA 90025 632-B4
E MASSACHUSETTS ST
3900 LBCH 90814 796-A7
MASSELIN AV
600 LA 90036 633-C3
1000 LA 90019 633-C3
S MASSELIN AV
1000 LA 90019 633-C4
MASSENA AV
1600 RBCH 90277 793-A1
MASSER PL
1300 MTBL 90640 676-D1
MASSEY AV
300 HMB 90254 762-J2
MASSINGER ST
11500 LKWD 90715 766-G5
MAST CT
100 LA 90292 701-J1
MAST MALL
- LA 90292 701-J1
MAST ST
- LA 90292 701-J1
S MASTERS LN
1200 ANA 92804 767-G7
MASTERS PL
32000 Llan 93544 4469-F1
W MASTERS CUP WY
24600 SCTA 91355 4550-E7
MASTERSON CT
21600 SCTA 91350 4461-B6
MASTHEAD CT
600 SLB 90740 826-G4
MATADOR DR
2400 RowH 91748 678-H6
MATADOR PL
- LACo 91390 4460-J4
MATALON LN
5500 LPMA 90630 767-D4
MATANA DR
22600 SCTA 91350 4460-H5
MATARO ST
2600 PAS 91107 566-F4
MATCHLEAF AV
1400 HacH 91745 678-C3
MATCHWOOD PL
600 AZU 91702 569-A6
E MATCHWOOD ST
700 AZU 91702 569-A6
MATEL RD
24400 SCTA 91355 4550-E6
MATEO AV
300 SDMS 91773 600-D2
1700 LHB 90631 708-G5
MATEO PL
2000 LA 90021 674-H1
MATEO ST
400 LA 90013 634-H5
600 LA 90021 634-H6
1600 LA 90021 674-H1
MATER DEI CIR
300 CLAR 91711 571-E7
MATERN PL
9900 SFSP 90670 706-H4
MATFIELD DR
25800 TOR 90505 793-F5
MATHER AV
10100 Sunl 91040 503-G3

MATHEWS AV
1500 MANB 90266 732-J7
1500 MANB 90266 762-J1
1900 RBCH 90278 732-J7
1900 RBCH 90278 733-A7
N MATHEWS ST
100 Boyl 90033 635-B5
S MATHEWS ST
100 Boyl 90033 635-A5
600 LA 90023 635-A6
MATHILDE LN
- Saug 91350 4461-F5
MATILIJA AV
4200 Shrm 91423 562-C3
5200 VanN 91401 562-C2
5900 VanN 91401 532-C7
6600 VanN 91405 532-B5
7800 PanC 91402 532-B1
8800 PanC 91402 502-B7
MATILIJA RD
800 GLDL 91202 534-B7
MATISSE AV
4100 WdHl 91364 560-A5
MATISSE CIR
15100 LMRD 90638 737-G4
MATISSE DR
30000 RPV 90275 822-H3
MATISSE LN
- SCTA 91355 4550-D3
MATLEY RD
4800 LCF 91011 534-H1
MATLOCK AV
12700 BALD 91706 637-H1
MATNEY AV
4700 Bxby 90807 765-F3
MATRANGA PL
9100 SunV 91352 503-C7
MATTEO ST
4800 VeCo 91377 557-G2
MATTESON AV
10800 CULC 90232 672-D3
11200 CULC 90230 672-D3
11300 CULC 90066 672-D3
11300 LA 90066 672-D3
MATTHEW PL
- SCTA 91321 4641-A1
MATTHEW ST
- PMDL 93551 4104-G7
MATTHEWS LN
- BREA 92821 708-J5
MATTHEWS PL
1800 POM 91766 640-H4
N MATTHISEN AV
100 COMP 90220 734-H4
1100 COMP 90222 734-H4
S MATTHISEN AV
100 COMP 90220 734-H4
MATTHISEN CIR
500 COMP 90220 734-H5
MATTOCK AV
9500 DWNY 90240 706-E5
9500 DWNY 90241 706-D5
MATULA DR
4900 Tarz 91356 560-H3
MAUBERT AV
4600 LFlz 90027 594-A4
MAUCH ST
28900 LACo 91390 4461-D3
MAUDE AV
9900 Sunl 91040 503-B5
MAUI
1800 WCOV 91792 638-H4
MAUI CT
17300 CRTS 90703 737-B7
MAULSBY DR
13400 WHIT 90602 707-D1
MAUNA LOA AV
19000 LACo 91740 569-C7
19000 GLDR 91740 569-C7
E MAUNA LOA AV
100 GLDR 91740 569-E7
18500 AZU 91702 569-C7
18500 LACo 91702 569-C7
W MAUNA LOA AV
100 GLDR 91740 569-E7
MAUNA LOA DR
100 MNRO 91016 567-F3
MAUPIN AV
4300 BALD 91706 598-C5
MAUREEN ST
2600 WCOV 91792 639-B6
37600 PMDL 93550 4286-D1
E MAURETANIA ST
1000 Wilm 90744 794-G5
W MAURETANIA ST
1000 Wilm 90744 794-C5
MAURICE AV
2200 LaCr 91214 504-H5
16900 CRTS 90703 737-B7
MAURICE CIR
16600 CRTS 90703 737-B6
MAURICE CT
16800 CRTS 90703 737-B6
MAURICE ST
1000 MNRO 91016 567-J4
MAURINE AV
700 GLDL 91201 564-A2
MAURITA PL
700 GLDL 91206 564-F3
MAURY AV
4200 Bxby 90807 765-F5
5800 WdHl 91367 559-C1
5900 WdHl 91367 529-C7

MAUSOLEUM DR
- SMRO 91108 566-C6
MAVERICK CIR
- POM 91766 640-F4
2000 LVRN 91750 570-G6
MAVERICK DR
100 SDMS 91773 570-C6
MAVERICK LN
- RHLS 90274 823-E3
MAVIS AV
5400 WHIT 90601 677-A4
MAVIS DR
300 LA 90065 595-A4
MAXELLA AV
12500 LA 90066 672-C5
12600 CULC 90066 672-C5
13000 LA 90292 672-B6
MAXFIELD ST
1100 LACo 90502 764-A7
MAX GODDE LN
- PMDL 93551 4194-G1
MAXIMUM RD
- Cstc 91384 4460-A3
MAXINE LN
28300 SCTA 91350 4461-B4
MAXINE ST
8000 PRV 90660 706-C1
11200 SFSP 90670 706-H2
MAXINE WY
4200 Actn 93510 4465-A1
MAXON LN
3700 CHNO 91710 641-C5
3800 SBdC 91710 641-D6
MAXON PL
12300 SBdC 91710 641-D6
MAXON ST
3600 CHNO 91710 641-C5
MAX SHAPIRO WY
9800 SELM 91733 637-A4
MAXSON CT
- SIGH 90755 795-H3
MAXSON DR
5700 CYP 90630 767-E7
MAXSON PL
3300 ELMN 91732 637-F2
MAXSON RD
1600 SELM 91733 637-C5
2100 ELMN 91733 637-D4
2200 ELMN 91732 637-F1
3800 ELMN 91732 597-G6
MAXWELL RD
- LACo 93532 4101-B1
MAXWELL ST
- FUL 92833 738-C5
1100 MTBL 90640 676-C5
2900 LFlz 90027 594-C2
W MAXWELL ST
1300 UPL 91786 601-J4
MAXWELL FIRE RD
- LA 90210 562-F7
- LA 91604 562-F7
MAXWELLTON RD
12000 LA 91604 562-G6
MAY AL
- PAS 91105 565-H5
MAY AV
100 MNRO 91016 567-H3
1800 LBCH 90806 795-F5
2800 RBCH 90278 733-B6
MAY CT
2100 SIMI 93063 499-C2
2600 RowH 91748 679-D7
8900 SGAT 90280 705-E3
MAY ST
3500 LA 90066 672-B3
MAY WY
- SCTA 91351 4551-E4
MAYA PL
8700 LA 91343 531-F1
MAYALL ST
14800 MsnH 91345 501-G4
15600 LA 91343 501-D4
16900 Nor 91325 501-B4
18500 Nor 91324 500-G4
19700 Chat 91311 500-E4
21900 Chat 91311 499-J4
MAYAN DR
11000 Chat 91311 500-A2
21300 Chat 91311 500-A1
MAYAPAN RD
1300 LHH 90631 708-E3
MAYBANK AV
4100 LKWD 90712 765-H4
MAYBERRY ST
2300 Echo 90026 594-D6
MAYBROOK AV
10300 WHIT 90603 708-A4
11500 LACo 90604 708-A6
12400 LACo 90604 738-A1
MAYBROOK DR
1000 BelA 90077 592-C6
1000 LA 90210 592-C6
MAYBURY CIR
4500 CYP 90630 767-B6
MAY CANYON TKTR
- LA 91342 482-D1
- LACo 91342 482-D1
- LACo 91342 4642-C6
- Nwhl 91321 4642-B5
MAYCOTTE RD
22400 WdHl 91364 559-J3
MAYCREST AV
2000 SPAS 91030 595-G4

MAYCREST AV
4200 LA 90032 595-G5
MAYCROFT DR
6900 RPV 90275 792-G6
MAYDEE ST
300 LACo 91016 567-G7
500 LACo 91010 567-H7
MAYDOCK PL
7000 Tuj 91042 504-A3
MAYENNE CT
30800 WLKV 91362 557-F5
MAYER AL
2000 Alta 91001 536-A7
MAYERLING CT
- GrnH 91344 481-A6
MAYERLING ST
- GrnH 91344 480-J6
17200 GrnH 91344 481-A6
MAYES DR
10800 WHIT 90604 707-H5
11700 LACo 90604 707-H6
11900 LMRD 90638 707-H7
MAYESDALE AV
6400 LACo 91775 596-H1
7200 LACo 91775 566-G7
MAYFAIR AV
500 POM 91766 640-J4
3100 ELMN 91733 637-B1
MAYFAIR DR
- SCTA 91354 4460-G3
3600 PAS 91107 566-H3
3700 LA 90065 594-J4
MAYFAIR LN
- ING 90305 703-D4
MAYFAIR PL
8900 Nor 91324 500-E7
MAYFARE ST
28900 Cstc 91384 4459-C6
MAYFIELD AV
2300 Mont 91020 534-G2
2600 GLDL 91020 534-G2
2800 LaCr 91214 534-F2
3700 GLDL 91214 504-D7
4000 LA 91214 504-C6
11600 Brwd 90049 631-H5
MAYFIELD CT
37400 PMDL 93550 4286-E3
MAYFIELD RD
1200 SLB 90740 796-G7
E MAYFIELD ST
3700 LBCH 90804 795-J6
3800 LBCH 90804 796-A6
MAYFLOWER AV
5200 MYWD 90270 675-E6
6200 BELL 90201 675-E7
6800 BELL 90201 705-E1
N MAYFLOWER AV
100 MNRO 91016 567-F3
S MAYFLOWER AV
100 MNRO 91016 567-F7
900 ARCD 91006 567-F7
1600 ARCD 91006 597-F1
MAYFLOWER CIR
600 CLAR 91711 601-C3
16800 GAR 90247 734-A7
MAYFLOWER DR
17400 GrnH 91344 481-B7
17400 GrnH 91344 501-B1
MAYFLOWER PL
6800 BELL 90201 675-E7
MAYFLOWER RD
500 CLAR 91711 601-C3
MAYGREEN CT
- GLDL 91206 564-J3
MAYHILL DR
12600 LMRD 90638 737-J1
MAYLAKE DR
1600 SLB 90740 796-H7
MAYLAND AV
300 LPUE 91746 637-J4
300 LPUE 91746 638-A4
900 LACo 91746 638-B2
1600 WCOV 91790 638-B1
3400 BALD 91706 598-D6
MAYLIN ST
400 PAS 91105 565-G5
MAYME RD
35300 LACo 91390 4374-A3
MAYMONT DR
4900 LACo 90043 673-C4
MAYNARD AV
5600 WdHl 91367 559-H2
6800 CanP 91307 529-H4
7600 LA 91304 529-H2
MAYNARD DR
900 DUAR 91010 567-J5
1000 DUAR 91010 568-A5
25600 LACo 91302 589-A7
MAYNARD ST
100 GLDL 91205 564-H5
MAYNARD WY
100 MTBL 90640 676-C6
MAYNE ST
8600 BLF 90706 735-J5
8700 BLF 90706 736-A5
MAYO AV
- INDS 91789 639-H7
- INDS 91789 679-H1
N MAYO AV
100 COMP 90221 735-B4
S MAYO AV
100 COMP 90221 735-B5

MAYO CT
1700 LAN 93535 4016-C4
MAYO ST
900 HiPk 90042 595-A2
MAYOR DR
4600 TOR 90505 793-C1
MAY PATH RD
29800 Litl 93543 4468-C5
MAYPOP AV
300 LPUE 91744 638-C7
MAYPORT AV
13800 NRWK 90650 737-A3
MAYS AL
800 SGBL 91776 596-D4
MAYS CT
- LAN 93535 4016-G4
MAYS ST
46000 LAN 93535 4016-G4
MAYSTONE PL
2200 RowH 91748 678-H6
MAYTERN AV
42300 LACo 93536 4104-E5
MAYTIME LN
4600 CULC 90230 672-H4
MAYTOR PL
1100 BHLS 90210 592-G4
MAYVIEW DR
1900 LFlz 90027 594-C4
MAYVIEW LN
100 PAS 91103 565-G3
MAYWIND WY
2200 HacH 91745 678-E5
MAYWOOD
4200 VER 90058 675-B3
MAYWOOD AV
1700 UPL 91784 571-J6
4500 VER 90058 675-B4
4800 Eagl 90041 565-A6
5100 MYWD 90270 675-B4
5900 HNTP 90255 675-B6
6200 BELL 90201 675-B6
N MAYWOOD AV
1300 UPL 91786 601-J1
1500 UPL 91786 571-J6
1600 UPL 91784 571-J6
4900 Eagl 90041 565-A5
MAYWOOD CT
300 THO 91362 557-G2
N MAYWOOD WY
500 UPL 91786 601-J3
MAZA ST
10900 NRWK 90650 736-E2
MAZATZAL CT
- LACo 93532 4102-E5
MAZUR DR
26500 RPV 90275 793-A6
MCALPINE DR
2800 LACo 90265 628-C6
MCANANY WY
3600 MAL 90265 629-H5
3600 LACo 90265 629-H5
N MCARTHUR WY
200 UPL 91786 601-H3
MCATEE DR
10400 WHIT 90603 707-H4
MCAULEY ST
5700 LKWD 90713 766-C2
MCBAIN AV
3300 RBCH 90278 733-B5
MCBAIN ST
2800 RBCH 90278 733-B6
MCBEAN DR
11600 ELMN 91732 597-F3
MCBEAN PKWY
- BqtC 91354 4460-G4
- LACo 91390 4460-G4
- SCTA 91354 4460-G4
- SCTA 91354 4550-E2
22800 SCTA 91355 4550-E2
24900 StvR 91381 4550-E6
MCBRIDE AV
- ELA 90022 635-F4
- MONP 90063 635-F4
S MCBRIDE AV
300 ELA 90022 635-F6
900 ELA 90022 675-F1
1300 CMRC 90040 675-F2
MCBROOM ST
9800 Sunl 91040 503-A3
10800 Sunl 91040 502-J4
MCCABE
1400 WCOV 91791 638-J5
N MC CADDEN PL
100 LA 90004 633-E1
300 LA 90004 593-E7
700 LA 90038 593-E5
1300 Hlwd 90028 593-E4
S MC CADDEN PL
100 LA 90004 633-E2
300 LA 90020 633-E2
600 LA 90005 633-E2
600 LA 90010 633-E2
MCCAHILL ST
8700 DWNY 90241 706-B5
MCCALLUM AV
5100 SGAT 90280 705-E4
MCCALLUM ST
8700 DWNY 90242 706-B7
MCCAMENT AL
800 SPAS 91030 595-G2
MCCANN DR
12200 SFSP 90670 706-J4
12500 SFSP 90670 707-A4

MCCANN PL
15200 LMRD 90638 707-G7
MCCART AV
1400 BREA 92821 708-H5
2300 LHB 90631 708-H5
MCCART CIR
900 BREA 92821 708-H5
MCCARTHY CT
800 ELSG 90245 702-F7
MC CARTHY DR
3200 LA 90065 564-G7
MC CARTHY VISTA
700 LA 90048 633-A3
S MCCARTY DR
100 BHLS 90212 632-F2
MCCLEAN DR
6800 ARCD 91007 566-J7
6800 LACo 91007 566-J7
MCCLEAN WY
9100 Wch 90045 702-E4
MCCLELLAN DR
1100 Brwd 90049 631-G5
1200 WLA 90025 631-G5
MCCLELLAN WY
6300 BPK 90620 767-E3
MCCLEMONT AV
10100 Tuj 91042 503-J3
MC CLINTOCK AV
3000 LA 90007 634-B7
3200 LA 90089 634-B7
3200 LA 90089 674-A1
MCCLINTOCK AV
4900 TEML 91780 597-D4
MCCLOUD DR
- LACo 93532 4102-J4
MC CLUNG DR
3900 LA 90008 673-E3
MCCLURE AV
13700 PRM 90723 735-G3
MC CLURE ST
2600 LA 90065 594-J6
MCCOLLUM PL
1400 Echo 90026 594-D6
MCCOLLUM ST
1300 Echo 90026 594-D6
MC COMAS ST
1500 POM 91766 640-G3
MC COMB WY
1000 MONP 91755 636-B4
MCCOMBER PL
- BPK 90621 737-H5
MCCOMBER RD
5000 BPK 90621 737-H5
MCCONNELL AV
- LA 90094 672-E7
- LA 90094 702-E1
4300 LA 90066 672-D6
7400 Wch 90045 702-E2
MC CONNELL BLVD
4100 CULC 90066 672-C5
4300 LA 90066 672-C5
MCCONNELL DR
2700 LA 90064 632-F5
MCCONNELL PL
2800 LA 90064 632-F6
MCCOOL AV
7200 Wch 90045 672-G7
7200 Wch 90045 702-G1
MCCORMICK AL
- PAS 91105 565-C3
MCCORMICK ST
10300 NHol 91601 563-A2
11100 NHol 91601 562-H2
12700 LA 91607 562-E2
13200 VanN 91401 562-C2
13900 Shrm 91423 562-B2
14600 VanN 91411 561-J2
14600 VanN 91411 562-A2
16600 Enc 91436 561-D3
17000 Enc 91316 561-B2
18200 Tarz 91356 560-J2
18200 Tarz 91356 561-B2
MCCOVEY CT
- LAN 93535 4016-G4
MCCOY AV
25000 Hrbr 90710 794-B4
MCCRAY LN
1900 LACo 90265 629-F3
MC CREADY AV
2400 LA 90039 594-E4
MCCROSKY RD
12900 SBdC 91710 641-B7
MCCUE CT
8300 Win 91306 530-C2
MCCULLOCH AV
5300 TEML 91780 597-C3
5600 ARCD 91007 597-C3
MC CUNE AV
10700 LA 90034 672-F2
11900 LA 90066 672-C3
MCCUNE AV
11300 LA 90066 672-D3
MCDANIEL RD
- LACo 91107 566-F1
MCDERMOTT AV
8000 Res 91335 531-A3
N MCDIVITT AV
1100 COMP 90221 735-A3
MCDONALD AV
200 Wilm 90744 794-D4
MCDONALD ST
11100 CULC 90230 672-F5
11700 LA 90230 672-F6

MCDONIE AV
5700 WdHl 91367 560-D1
MCDONIE PL
20100 WdHl 91367 560-E1
N MCDONNELL AV
100 ELA 90022 635-F5
S MCDONNELL AV
100 ELA 90022 635-F6
800 ELA 90022 675-F1
1400 CMRC 90040 675-F2
MCDONOUGH AV
800 Wilm 90744 794-J6
MC DOWELL AL
900 PAS 91104 566-A2
MCDUFF ST
1300 Echo 90026 594-E7
MCENNERY CANYON RD
- Actn 93510 4375-E4
MCFADDEN DR
- FUL 92833 738-C5
MCFADDEN ST
400 LHB 90631 708-D6
MCFALL LN
100 LPUE 91744 638-E7
MCFARLAND AV
100 Wilm 90744 794-F6
MC FARLANE AV
4100 BURB 91505 563-D4
MC FARLANE ST
1800 SMRO 91108 595-J2
MCGARRY ST
800 LA 90021 634-G7
1600 LA 90021 674-G1
1900 LA 90058 674-G1
MCGARVEY ST
- FUL 92833 738-D5
MCGEE DR
12500 WHIT 90606 707-B2
12600 WHIT 90602 707-B2
13500 LACo 90605 707-C3
14500 LACo 90604 707-E4
S MCGHEE DR
100 ANA 92804 767-J6
MCGILL DR
20200 WAL 91789 639-F7
MCGILL RD
16200 LMRD 90638 738-A1
MC GILL ST
1100 COV 91722 598-H5
MCGILL ST
15900 LACo 91722 598-F5
MCGILVREY AV
1500 City 90063 635-F3
MCGIRK AV
11000 ELMN 91731 597-D5
11300 ELMN 91732 597-F6
MC GREW AL
600 PAS 91101 565-J3
600 PAS 91104 565-J3
MCGROARTY ST
400 SGBL 91776 596-D4
7500 Tuj 91042 503-H4
7800 Sunl 91040 503-G4
MCGROARTY TER
7500 Tuj 91042 503-J4
S MCHELEN AV
21800 CRSN 90810 765-A6
22100 LBCH 90810 765-A6
MC HENRY RD
300 GLDL 91206 564-G4
MCINTYRE ST
15100 LA 91342 481-H6
MCKAIN ST
1900 LACo 91302 589-D5
MCKAY DR
20100 WAL 91789 639-E7
N MC KEEVER AV
700 AZU 91702 568-H5
MCKEEVER ST
15500 MsnH 91345 501-G1
15600 GrnH 91344 501-C1
MCKENDREE AV
14700 PacP 90272 631-A4
MCKENNA CT
- LMTA 90717 793-G4
MCKENNA ST
- CLAR 91711 601-C3
MCKENZIE AV
3500 LA 90032 595-D6
E MC KENZIE ST
1600 NLB 90805 735-F7
MCKEON CT
10600 LACo 91390 4373-F4
MCKEON WY
- SCTA 91350 4551-C3
MCKIM CT
8100 LA 90046 593-A3
MCKINLEY AV
100 POM 91767 600-E4
200 POM 91767 601-A7
1000 POM 91768 600-E4
1000 POM 91773 600-E4
1000 SDMS 91750 600-E4
1000 SDMS 91773 600-E4
1000 LVRN 91750 600-E4
1000 LVRN 91773 600-E4
1100 COMP 90059 734-E3
2300 Ven 90291 671-J6
3400 LA 90011 674-E3
5500 SGAT 90280 735-F1
6400 LA 90001 674-E7
7300 LA 90001 704-E2
8000 PRM 90723 735-G1

MCKINLEY AV
8600 Wats 90002 704-E4
10800 LA 90059 704-E4
12000 Wbrk 90059 704-E4
12100 Wbrk 90059 734-E1
12700 SBdC 91710 641-C7
16200 CRSN 90746 734-E5
E MCKINLEY AV
1600 POM 91767 601-D6
S MCKINLEY AV
1200 COMP 90220 734-E6
15000 LACo 90220 734-E4
16100 CRSN 90746 734-E6
16100 COMP 90746 734-E6
W MCKINLEY AV
100 POM 91768 600-G6
MCKINLEY CIR
7400 BPK 90620 767-H5
MCKINLEY CT
- Cstc 91384 4459-C7
MCKINLEY PL
100 MNRO 91016 567-E3
8600 Wats 90002 704-E3
MCKINLEY ST
300 AZU 91702 568-J7
400 AZU 91702 569-A7
1500 AZU 91702 598-F1
MCKINNEY WY
1800 SLB 90740 796-H7
MCKNIGHT DR
6000 LKWD 90713 766-D3
MCKOOL CIR
1200 CRSN 90746 764-F4
MCLAREN AV
6200 WdHl 91367 529-H7
6800 CanP 91307 529-H5
7500 LA 91304 529-H3
MC LAREN ST
10600 NRWK 90650 736-E3
MCLAREN ST
11400 NRWK 90650 736-G3
12900 NRWK 90650 737-A3
MCLAUGHLIN AV
3300 LA 90066 672-C2
4000 CULC 90066 672-D3
E MCLEAN ST
- ALH 91801 596-B3
MCLENNAN AV
5500 Enc 91436 561-D2
6400 VanN 91406 531-D4
8700 LA 91343 531-D1
8800 LA 91343 501-D5
10400 GrnH 91344 501-D2
11500 GrnH 91344 481-C5
MC LEOD DR
1700 LA 90046 592-J4
MC LEOD PL
1500 POM 91768 600-G6
MC MANUS AV
3200 CULC 90232 632-J7
3200 LA 90034 632-J7
MCMANUS ST
7000 LKWD 90713 766-F5
E MCMILLAN ST
1600 COMP 90221 735-B2
2200 LYN 90262 735-C3
4900 RDom 90221 735-C3
5000 LACo 90262 735-C3
5000 LYN 90221 735-C3
MCNAB AV
2200 LBCH 90815 796-D3
3000 LBCH 90808 796-D1
3400 LBCH 90808 766-D7
3700 LACo 90808 766-D7
4300 LKWD 90713 766-D4
13600 BLF 90706 736-D3
17800 BLF 90706 766-D4
MCNALLY AV
2600 Alta 91001 535-J4
MCNALLY RD
13000 LMRD 90638 738-A1
MCNEES AV
5800 WHIT 90606 676-J5
6000 LACo 90606 676-J5
MCNEIL LN
7000 BPK 90620 767-G2
MCNEIL WY
7400 BPK 90620 767-G2
MCNERNEY AV
8900 SGAT 90280 705-C4
10600 LYN 90262 705-C6
MCNULTY AV
7600 Win 91306 530-C2
MCNULTY PL
20700 Win 91306 530-C3
N MC PHERRIN AV
100 MONP 91754 636-B2
S MCPHERRIN AV
100 MONP 91754 636-B3
1900 MONP 91754 635-J5
MC PHERSON AV
2000 LA 90032 635-E1
MC PHERSON PL
2000 LA 90032 635-E1
2400 LA 90032 595-E7
N MCPHERSON ST
100 LHB 90631 708-F5
S MCPHERSON ST
100 LHB 90631 708-F6
MCQUEEN ST
15800 LA 91342 481-F2
MC RAE AV
16300 NRWK 90650 736-G6

MCRAE AV
12900 NRWK 90650 736-G2
MCRAE DR
2100 LA 90732 823-G7
MCREYNOLDS FIRE RD
2100 LACo 90265 627-H1
MCSPADEN CT
- LHB 90631 738-C2
MCVINE AV
10100 Sunl 91040 503-G3
MCVINE TR
10000 Sunl 91040 503-G4
MCWILTON PL
500 Alta 91001 536-A4
E MC WOOD ST
1200 WCOV 91790 638-H3
1400 WCOV 91791 638-H3
16500 LACo 91744 638-G3
MEACHAM ST
300 GLDR 91740 569-D7
MEAD AL
900 PAS 91107 566-H2
MEAD AV
4500 RSMD 91770 596-H5
MEAD DR
5200 BPK 90621 737-J5
MEADBROOK ST
800 CRSN 90746 764-E1
MEADBURY DR
28100 SCTA 91350 4461-B5
MEADCLIFF PL
23600 DBAR 91765 640-C7
MEADE DR
3100 SPed 90731 854-A1
MEADE PL
2200 Ven 90291 671-J5
W MEADOW CIR
1200 LAN 93534 4105-F1
MEADOW CT
- MAL 90265 667-J1
300 BREA 92821 709-B6
1200 UPL 91784 571-J4
MEADOW DR
1200 LA 90210 592-F5
1200 BHLS 90210 592-F5
12200 ART 90701 766-J2
15600 SCTA 91387 4552-E1
MEADOW LN
- DUAR 91010 568-B5
- StvR 91381 4640-B2
500 POM 91767 601-A4
900 MNRO 91016 567-J3
2200 DBAR 91789 679-G5
38200 PMDL 93551 4285-H1
MEADOW PL
4600 LACo 93536 4104-J5
MEADOW RD
5500 SGAT 90280 705-F6
8500 DWNY 90242 736-A1
10400 NRWK 90650 736-D1
N MEADOW RD
100 WCOV 91791 599-A7
S MEADOW RD
100 WCOV 91791 599-A7
100 WCOV 91791 639-A1
MEADOW ST
4200 LVRN 91750 570-J7
4200 LVRN 91750 600-J1
MEADOWBROOK AV
1000 LA 90019 633-D4
MEADOWBROOK LN
- SCTA 91354 4460-F7
- SCTA 91354 4550-F1
300 ING 90302 703-B2
2000 GLDR 91741 569-J5
2000 GLDR 91741 570-A5
16300 CRTS 90703 736-J6
16400 CRTS 90703 737-A6
20200 WAL 91789 679-E1
MEADOWBROOK RD
1100 Alta 91001 536-B6
MEADOWBROOK WY
8800 BPK 90621 738-B6
MEADOW CREEK CIR
20000 WAL 91789 639-E5
MEADOW CREEK LN
- CALB 91302 588-G1
MEADOWCREEK RD
100 BREA 92821 709-D7
27800 SCTA 91351 4461-E7
27800 SCTA 91351 4551-E1
MEADOWCREST RD
15900 Shrm 91403 561-F6
MEADOWCREST WY
- PMDL 93551 4195-A4
MEADOWDALE LN
5400 RPV 90275 823-B1
MEADOW FALLS DR
23700 DBAR 91765 640-D6
MEADOWGATE RD
15500 Enc 91436 561-G5
MEADOW GATE ST
3900 THO 91362 557-C3
MEADOW GLEN DR
- LVRN 91750 570-H5
MEADOWGLEN LN
1200 SDMS 91773 570-B6
1200 SDMS 91740 570-B6
MEADOWGLEN RD
1400 DBAR 91765 680-B4
MEADOWGLEN ST
1500 UPL 91784 571-H3

MEADOW GLEN WY
1500 HacH 91745 678-E4
MEADOWGRASS DR
28500 Cstc 91384 4369-F7
28600 Cstc 91384 4459-E1
MEADOW GREEN RD
12600 LMRD 90638 737-J1
MEADOW GROVE LN
200 THO 91362 557-E3
MEADOW GROVE PL
500 LCF 91011 535-D5
MEADOW GROVE ST
300 LCF 91011 535-D5
MEADOW HAVEN DR
6300 AGRH 91301 558-A3
MEADOW HEIGHTS CT
- SCTA 91387 4552-B1
MEADOWLAND CT
2300 THO 91361 557-B5
MEADOWLAND DR
1200 LHH 90631 708-G3
MEADOWLARK
3600 ELMN 91732 637-G1
MEADOWLARK S
3500 ELMN 91732 637-G7
MEADOWLARK AV
12600 GrnH 91344 481-C4
MEADOWLARK CT
- SCTA 91354 4460-G3
MEADOW LARK DR
3900 CALB 91302 559-G6
6100 LVRN 91750 570-H5
MEADOWLARK LN
- RHLS 90274 793-E7
100 VeCo 91377 557-J3
8300 LPMA 90623 767-C4
37900 PMDL 93551 4285-H2
MEADOW LARK ST
900 LHB 90631 708-F4
MEADOWLARK WY
21600 WAL 91789 639-H4
MEADOWMIST DR
28300 RPV 90275 792-J7
28600 RPV 90275 822-J1
MEADOWMIST WY
29500 AGRH 91301 557-J4
MEADOWMONT ST
25500 SCTA 91355 4550-F6
MEADOW OAK DR
3200 WLKV 91361 557-C7
MEADOW OAKS LN
100 GLDR 91741 569-B5
MEADOW PARK LN
3800 TOR 90505 793-C1
MEADOWPASS HTS
500 WAL 91789 639-E7
MEADOW PASS RD
700 WAL 91789 639-E6
MEADOW RIDGE CIR
- POM 91766 640-G5
MEADOW RIDGE DR
2300 CHLS 91709 680-J4
23600 SCTA 91321 4641-B3
MEADOW RIDGE PL
4100 Enc 91436 561-E5
MEADOW RIDGE RD
16200 Enc 91436 561-E5
MEADOW RIDGE ST
- Sunl 91040 503-A3
MEADOW RIDGE WY
16200 Enc 91436 561-E5
N MEADOWS AV
100 MANB 90266 732-H6
S MEADOWS AV
100 MANB 90266 732-H7
700 MANB 90266 762-H1
MEADOWS CIR
19700 CRTS 90703 767-A3
MEADOWS CT
19900 CRTS 90703 767-A3
MEADOWS DR
400 GLDL 91202 564-D1
MEADOWS END DR
1000 LACo 91302 588-J7
MEADOWSIDE ST
1000 WCOV 91792 638-G4
15800 LACo 91744 638-F4
E MEADOWSIDE ST
16000 LACo 91744 638-F4
MEADOWSWEET DR
- PMDL 93551 4194-G2
MEADOWVALE AV
2200 LA 90031 594-G5
MEADOW VALLEY TER
2000 LA 90039 594-C4
MEADOW VIEW CT
36800 PMDL 93552 4287-B5
MEADOW VIEW DR
- POM 91766 640-G5
400 LCF 91011 535-D3
16100 Enc 91436 561-F5
MEADOW VIEW LN
2400 CHLS 91709 680-J2
MEADOWVIEW LN
11400 Pcma 91331 502-F1
W MEADOW VIEW LN
1200 LAN 93534 4105-F1
MEADOW VIEW PL
4300 Enc 91436 561-F5
MEADOWVIEW ST
40400 PMDL 93551 4194-H2
MEADOWVIEW TER
- HacH 91745 637-G6

STREET
Block City ZIP Pg-Grid

MEADOW VISTA WY
5400 AGRH 91301 557-J5
MEADOW WOOD AV
5000 LKWD 90712 765-G3
MEADOW WOOD DR
1100 COV 91724 599-E7
MEADOW WOOD LN
13300 GrnH 91344 481-C3
MEADOW WOOD ST
38000 PMDL 93552 4286-J1
38600 PMDL 93552 4196-J7
MEADSTONE RD
16300 CynC 91351 4462-C4
MEADVIEW AV
24500 SCTA 91321 4641-A1
24600 SCTA 91321 4551-A7
MEADVILLE DR
3600 Shrm 91403 561-H6
MEAFORD AV
- Nwhl 91321 4640-J5
MEALY ST
100 COMP 90222 734-J3
MEANDER RD
33600 LACo 91390 4373-E5
MEANDERING CREEK DR
23500 DBAR 91765 680-C2
MEARS PL
3900 LACo 90601 677-A2
MECATE DR
22000 SCTA 91350 4461-A7
MECCA AV
4900 Tarz 91356 560-J2
MECHAM WY
6000 LA 90043 673-D6
E MEDA AV
100 GLDR 91741 569-E5
W MEDA AV
100 GLDR 91741 569-D5
MEDEA CT
37700 PMDL 93550 4286-H1
MEDEA LN
- AGRH 91301 558-A5
MEDEABROOK PL
5600 AGRH 91301 557-J5
MEDEA CREEK LN
- VeCo 91377 558-A1
MEDEA CREEK RD
3700 Ago 91301 588-B1
MEDEA MESA RD
28800 Ago 91301 588-B1
MEDEA VALLEY DR
5500 AGRH 91301 558-A5
MEDFIELD ST
28500 AGRH 91301 558-B5
MEDFORD CT
400 LBCH 90803 796-D7
MEDFORD PL
- Cstc 91384 4459-G4
MEDFORD RD
900 PAS 91107 566-H2
MEDFORD ST
1600 Boyl 90033 635-C2
1800 MTBL 90640 676-B2
3200 City 90063 635-D2
MEDIA DR
5500 HiPk 90042 595-C3
MEDIA CENTER DR
- LA 90039 594-F3
- LA 90065 594-F3
MEDIAN RD
- SMRO 91108 566-C7
MEDICAL CENTER DR
- PMDL 93551 4195-G7
7100 CanP 91307 529-G5
23200 TOR 90505 793-E2
MEDICI CT
- SCTA 91350 4551-D5
MEDICI LN
- ING 90301 703-E3
- ING 90305 703-E3
N MEDICINE BOW CT
200 THO 91362 557-B3
S MEDICINE BOW CT
100 THO 91362 557-B3
MEDILL PL
2800 LA 90064 632-G6
MEDINA CT
11300 ELMN 91731 597-E7
MEDINA DR
4900 WdHl 91364 560-A4
MEDINA RD
4900 WdHl 91364 560-A3
MEDINA ST
600 POM 91768 640-B2
MEDINAC LN
13500 SLB 90740 826-G1
MEDINA ESTATE RD
21600 WdHl 91364 560-A4
S MEDIO DR
100 Brwd 90049 631-F3
E MEDIO ST
600 LBCH 90802 825-E1
MEDLAR DR
- SCTA 91354 4460-G4
MEDLEY DR
17900 Enc 91316 561-A5
MEDLEY LN
20400 Top 90290 630-A2
MEDLEY PL
4400 Enc 91316 561-A5
MEDLEY RIDGE DR
- LACo 91387 4552-A4

MEDLOW AV
2400 Eagl 90041 564-J7
2500 LA 90065 564-J7
2700 Eagl 90041 594-H1
2700 LA 90065 594-H1
N MEDNIK AV
100 ELA 90022 635-G5
S MEDNIK AV
100 ELA 90022 635-G6
MEDWAY AV
41200 LACo 93536 4194-H1
MEEKER AV
500 LPUE 91746 638-A4
1000 LACo 91746 638-A4
2600 ELMN 91732 637-D1
3100 ELMN 91731 637-D1
S MEEKER AV
900 WCOV 91790 598-D7
900 WCOV 91790 638-D1
MEEKER RD
3200 ELMN 91731 637-D1
3500 ELMN 91731 597-D7
MEERHELM DR
50400 LACo 93536 3833-G6
MEGAN AV
8800 LA 91304 530-A1
8900 LA 91304 500-A7
9400 Chat 91311 500-A6
MEGAN DR
- SCTA 91387 4462-E6
MEGAN PL
8900 LA 91304 500-A7
MEGANWOOD PL
15900 LMRD 90638 738-A2
MEGHAN CT
- LACo 91789 679-F6
MEGUIAR DR
2500 LACo 91107 566-E1
MEHDEN AV
22800 CRSN 90745 794-C1
MEIER ST
3300 LA 90066 672-B3
3900 CULC 90066 672-C5
MEI LING WY
900 LA 90012 634-G2
MEISNER ST
3500 City 90063 635-D4
MELA LN
- RPV 90275 823-B2
MELANIE LN
1400 ARCD 91007 567-A7
1400 ARCD 91007 597-A1
4600 GLDL 91214 504-E7
MELANIE ST
1600 ARCD 91007 597-A1
MELBA AV
6200 WdHl 91367 529-G7
6600 CanP 91307 529-F4
7500 LA 91304 529-F2
MELBOURNE AV
2600 POM 91767 601-A3
3900 LFlz 90027 594-A4
MELBOURNE CT
25600 LACo 91302 559-A3
MELBOURNE DR
5000 CYP 90630 767-C7
MEL CANYON RD
100 DUAR 91010 568-E3
MELDAR AV
8800 DWNY 90240 706-C2
MELETO LN
- Nor 91326 500-D1
MELGAR DR
9800 WHIT 90603 707-J4
MELGRE AV
5300 WdHl 91367 559-F3
MELHAM AV
300 LPUE 91744 638-C6
700 LACo 91744 638-D4
MELHILL WY
1800 Brwd 90049 631-D2
MELHORN DR
2300 ALH 91803 636-A1
MELIA ST
6200 SIMI 93063 499-B3
MELIA WY
29200 SCTA 91387 4462-E7
MELINDA DR
9800 LA 90210 592-C1
MELINDA LN
5700 LVRN 91750 570-G4
MELINDA WY
10100 Nor 91325 501-A5
MELISA CT
25700 SCTA 91355 4550-G5
MELISSA LN
5800 WdHl 91367 559-H1
MELISSA ST
900 LACo 90502 764-B5
2700 WCOV 91792 639-B6
MELITA AV
7600 NHol 91605 532-D3
MELITA ST
9300 PRV 90660 676-H2
MELLISSA ST
10900 CRTS 90703 736-E5
MELLO CT
1000 WCOV 91792 638-J5
MELLON AV
1900 LA 90039 594-F3
MELLOW LN
200 LCF 91011 535-D3

MELLUS DR
26800 LACo 90265 627-H4
MELODI LN
22300 SCTA 91350 4460-J6
MELODY LN
900 FUL 92831 738-J5
7400 SBdC 92372 (4562-E5 See Page 4471)
9700 SBdC 92372 (4472-E6 See Page 4471)
43400 LAN 93535 4106-C2
MELROSE AL
- PAS 91105 565-E5
MELROSE AV
100 MNRO 91016 567-F3
600 LA 90048 593-A7
600 LA 90069 593-A7
1000 GLDL 91202 564-D3
1300 PAS 91105 565-E5
3800 Echo 90026 594-A6
3900 LA 90004 594-A6
3900 LA 90029 594-A6
4300 LA 90004 593-D6
4400 LA 90029 593-H6
5000 LA 90038 593-H6
6600 LA 90036 593-D6
7100 LA 90046 593-D6
7400 RSMD 91770 636-D3
8400 WHWD 90048 593-A7
8400 WHWD 90069 593-A7
8400 WHWD 90048 592-J7
8400 WHWD 90069 592-J7
13000 SBdC 91710 641-D7
MELROSE PL
8400 LA 90069 593-A6
8400 LA 90069 592-J7
MELROSE ST
7000 BPK 90621 767-G1
E MELROSE WY
400 LBCH 90802 795-E7
W MELROSE WY
200 LBCH 90802 795-C7
MELROSE HILL
800 LA 90029 593-H6
MELTON AV
37600 PMDL 93550 4286-C2
MELT POUR
- SCTA 91350 4551-B5
MELVA ST
7800 DWNY 90242 705-J6
8600 DWNY 90242 706-A7
MELVIL ST
6100 CULC 90232 632-J7
6100 LA 90034 632-J7
MELVILLE AV
12400 GrnH 91344 481-B6
MELVILLE CT
- StvR 91381 4550-A7
MELVILLE DR
100 FUL 92835 738-H4
2100 SMRO 91108 596-D1
MELVILLE PL
17500 GrnH 91344 481-B5
MELVIN AV
5100 Tarz 91356 560-F1
6000 Tarz 91356 530-F7
6200 Res 91335 530-F3
8300 Nor 91324 530-F2
9500 Nor 91324 500-F5
10300 Nor 91326 500-F4
MELVIN LN
17700 Nor 91325 531-A1
MELWOOD DR
1400 GLDL 91207 564-F1
MEMO CT
18800 Nor 91326 480-H7
MEMORIAL DR
- LA 90068 563-F5
- LACo 91724 599-H7
- LACo 91724 639-H1
MEMORIAL RD
- AVA 90704 5923-F6
- LACo 90704 5923-E5
MEMORIAL TERRACE DR
- RPV 90275 793-H7
MEMORY CIR
- LACo 91724 639-G1
MEMORY DR
7600 Tuj 91042 503-J2
MEMORY LN
- CYP 90630 767-B5
- GLDL 90065 594-F1
- GLDL 91205 594-F1
- LA 90065 594-F1
- LA 90068 563-G5
- LA 91205 594-F1
- SCTA 91354 4460-G5
2200 WLKV 91361 587-A1
MEMORY WY
- LACo 91724 639-H1
MEMORY PARK AV
8700 LA 91343 531-H1
8800 LA 91343 501-H6
9900 MsnH 91345 501-H1
MEMPHIS AV
9900 WHIT 90603 707-G4
10400 LACo 90604 707-G5
12100 LA 91342 481-J6
MEMPHIS CT
1300 POM 91768 600-E7
MENARD PL
19100 Tarz 91356 560-G5

MENCKEN AV
7900 LA 91304 529-E3
MENDEL DR
12500 GrnH 91344 481-B5
MENDENHALL CT
21000 Top 90290 560-C7
MENDENHALL RIDGE RD
- LACo - 4643-C5
- LACo - (4644-B4 See Page 4643)
MENDEZ DR
- FUL 92833 738-C5
E MENDEZ ST
4100 LBCH 90815 796-A4
MENDIPS RIDGE RD
11300 LA 91604 592-H1
MENDOCINO CT
4400 LA 90065 564-H6
MENDOCINO LN
1900 Alta 91001 536-D6
MENDOCINO PL
12100 CHNO 91710 641-D5
MENDOCINO ST
900 Alta 91001 536-A6
E MENDOCINO ST
100 Alta 91001 535-J6
600 Alta 91001 536-A6
W MENDOCINO ST
- Alta 91001 535-G5
MENDON DR
2000 RPV 90275 823-H3
MENDON PL
20400 Chat 91311 500-D3
MENDOTA AV
4700 HiPk 90042 595-A2
MENDOZA DR
25800 SCTA 91355 4550-G4
MENDY ST
7400 PRM 90723 735-F2
MENEELY AL
900 PAS 91106 566-A6
MENLO AV
900 LA 90006 634-A5
900 LA 90089 674-A3
2000 LA 90007 634-A6
3700 LA 90037 674-A3
5800 LA 90044 674-B6
8600 LA 90044 704-A3
11400 HAW 90250 703-D7
11900 HAW 90250 733-D1
12100 LA 90044 734-B1
12800 LA 90247 734-B2
20900 LACo 90502 764-B5
22600 LACo 90502 794-B1
MENLO DR
300 CLAR 91711 571-E7
1100 Alta 91001 536-B5
3000 GLDL 91208 534-H5
MENLO ST
6300 SIMI 93063 499-C2
MENOMINEE PL
26600 RPV 90275 792-J6
26600 RPV 90275 793-A5
MENSHA CT
1700 DBAR 91765 680-A4
MENTON WY
- LMRD 90638 737-H4
MENTONE AV
1100 PAS 91103 565-G2
1600 PAS 91103 535-G7
3300 LA 90034 632-E7
3400 LA 90034 672-F1
3800 LA 90232 672-F1
4100 CULC 90232 672-G2
N MENTOR AV
- PAS 91106 566-A3
500 PAS 91104 566-A3
S MENTOR AV
- PAS 91106 566-A5
MENTOR CT
37700 PMDL 93550 4286-H1
MENTOR ST
- PMDL 93550 4286-H1
MENTRY DR
24100 SCTA 91321 4640-G3
MENTZ AV
15600 LPUE 91744 638-D6
MENTZ ST
16000 LPUE 91744 638-E6
MERALDA AV
2400 SIMI 93063 499-A1
MERAMEC AV
1000 SPed 90731 824-A4
MERAWEATHER PL
- SCTA 91354 4460-G5
MERCADO AV
4500 OrCo 90638 737-J4
14400 LMRD 90638 737-J3
MERCANTILE PL
- PAS 91105 565-H5
MERCED AV
1200 SELM 91733 637-B3
1600 LHB 90631 708-B6
2600 ELMN 91733 637-B2
3700 BALD 91706 598-A5
E MERCED AV
300 WCOV 91790 638-F3
1400 WCOV 91791 638-J3
1800 WCOV 91791 639-A3
W MERCED AV
800 WCOV 91790 638-D1
2300 BALD 91706 598-C7
2300 BALD 91706 638-D1

MERCED CT
15000 LA 91343 501-H7
MERCED PL
300 WCOV 91790 638-F3
MERCED ST
2600 LA 90065 594-J5
MERCEDES AV
300 PAS 91107 566-F3
8900 Pcma 91331 502-B5
MERCER CT
2100 CLAR 91711 571-C7
MERCER ST
12000 LA 91342 482-F7
12500 Pcma 91331 502-E1
MERCHANT ST
700 LA 90021 634-G6
MERCURY AV
3500 LA 90032 595-C6
3700 LA 90031 595-C6
MERCURY CIR
100 POM 91768 640-C2
MERCURY CT
600 LA 90014 634-E5
N MERCURY DR
8300 BPK 90620 767-J4
MERCURY LN
- PRV 90660 676-E6
400 BREA 92821 709-A7
400 PAS 91107 566-G3
MEREDITH AV
5300 PMDL 93552 4287-B2
MEREDITH CT
23900 LA 91304 529-E3
MEREDITH PL
9000 LA 90210 592-G3
MEREDITH ST
100 CLAR 91711 601-D5
MERIAM WY
1300 LBCH 90840 796-D5
MERIDEN PL
23500 SCTA 91354 4550-G1
MERIDIAN AV
300 SPAS 91030 595-G1
2000 ALH 91803 635-H1
S MERIDIAN AV
- ALH 91801 595-H5
300 ALH 91803 595-H5
1700 ALH 91803 635-H1
MERIDIAN DR
7200 PRM 90723 735-F6
MERIDIAN LN
1500 SPAS 91030 595-G3
MERIDIAN ST
- IRW 91010 568-A7
- LACo 91010 567-H7
700 IRW 91010 567-J7
700 DUAR 91010 567-H7
800 IRW 91010 597-J1
800 DUAR 91010 597-J1
4900 HiPk 90042 595-B1
MERIDIAN TER
500 HiPk 90042 595-D1
MERIDIAN WY
42600 LAN 93536 4104-D4
N MERIDITH AV
- PAS 91106 566-C4
S MERIDITH AV
- PAS 91106 566-C5
MERIMAC CT
17400 CRSN 90746 734-F7
17400 CRSN 90746 764-F1
MERION DR
19000 Nor 91326 500-G1
MERION LN
100 WAL 91789 639-B4
MERION WY
1300 SLB 90740 826-G1
1700 LACo 91789 679-F5
MERIT AV
16800 LA 90247 734-B7
MERIT LN
11700 WHIT 90601 677-B5
MERIT PL
3800 TOR 90505 793-C1
MERITA PL
200 LCF 91011 535-D3
MERITAGE CT
- SunV 91352 533-C2
MERIT PARK DR
1500 GAR 90247 733-J5
MERIVALE LN
16600 PacP 90272 630-H4
MERKEL AV
8100 PRM 90723 735-H2
MERLE DR
1900 MTBL 90640 636-C7
MERLE ST
4400 MTCL 91763 641-E2
MERLIN PL
4700 Enc 91436 561-D4
MERLINDA ST
1000 WCOV 91790 638-G2
MERLON AV
- LACo 91107 566-H4
MERLOT DR
- PMDL 93551 4104-D7
MERMAID DR
1700 LA 90732 823-G7
MERO LN
200 LCF 91011 535-D3
MERRETT DR
700 PAS 91104 566-A2

MERRICK ST
300 LA 90013 634-H5
MERRIDY ST
17700 Nor 91325 501-A5
18500 Nor 91324 500-F5
19700 Chat 91311 500-A5
MERRIFIELD AV
3200 POM 91767 601-A2
MERRIFIELD DR
- BREA 92823 709-J6
MERRILL AV
100 SMAD 91024 567-B2
300 GLDL 91206 564-H4
MERRILL DR
3000 TOR 90503 763-E6
MERRILL ST
4000 TOR 90503 763-C6
MERRIMAC AV
2000 LBCH 90810 795-A4
MERRIMAC RD
3400 Brwd 90049 591-D4
MERRIMAN DR
1400 GLDL 91202 564-D1
MERRIT RD
- Actn 93510 4374-F7
- Actn 93510 4464-G1
MERRIT HILL DR
11400 LACo 91390 4373-D5
MERRITT DR
6000 MAL 90265 667-C2
MERRYGROVE ST
3000 WCOV 91792 679-D2
MERRYHILL ST
19700 SCTA 91351 4461-E7
MERRYL LN
1200 WCOV 91792 638-G5
MERRY OAK LN
100 WLKV 91361 587-D1
1000 ARCD 91006 567-B4
MERRYVALE LN
- PMDL 93551 4104-D7
MERRYWOOD CT
700 BREA 92821 708-H6
MERRYWOOD DR
2200 LA 90046 592-J2
2200 LA 90046 593-A2
MERRYWOOD ST
2400 POM 91767 601-B5
MERRYWOOD TER
2200 LA 90046 592-J3
MERSIN PL
10900 SFSP 90670 706-G2
MERTEN AV
4700 CYP 90630 767-C5
MERTON AV
2000 Eagl 90041 565-A6
2200 Eagl 90041 564-J6
MERV GRIFFIN WY
- BHLS 90212 632-E2
MERVILLE DR
200 LACo 91746 637-J5
MERWIN ST
800 Echo 90026 594-D7
MERWYN C GILL WY
4000 ELMN 91731 596-J6
4000 ELMN 91731 597-A6
MESA AV
900 SBdC - (512-A5 See Page 511)
5900 HiPk 90042 595-C2
MESA CIR
400 MNRO 91016 567-G2
MESA CT
23600 SCTA 91355 4550-G5
MESA DR
- PMDL 93552 4287-D1
1700 LAN 93535 4016-D7
3600 LVRN 91750 600-H1
7800 VeCo 93063 499-F4
E MESA DR
2700 WCOV 91791 639-C1
MESA LN
39500 PMDL 93551 4195-D5
MESA MTWY
- LACo 91711 571-G2
MESA RD
100 LA 90402 631-B7
100 WHil 91304 499-D6
1200 SMRO 91108 566-B7
1200 SMRO 91108 596-B1
MESA ST
3800 TOR 90505 793-C3
N MESA ST
100 SPed 90731 824-C4
S MESA ST
100 SPed 90731 824-C5
W MESA TER
2400 SBdC 91784 571-J2
MESA WY
500 Bxby 90807 765-C6
S MESA WY
200 MONP 91754 635-G2
MESABA DR
27100 RPV 90275 792-J7
27100 RPV 90275 793-A7
MESA BLUFF CT
13200 CHLS 91709 680-J1
MESA DEL SOL
1200 FUL 92833 738-E5
MESA GRANDE
30500 LACo 91390 4463-H4
MESAGROVE AV
5400 WHIT 90601 677-A3

MESAGROVE AV
5500 WHIT 90601 676-J4
MESA LILA LN
3600 GLDL 91208 534-E3
MESA LILA RD
200 GLDL 91208 534-E3
MESALOA LN
3100 LACo 91107 536-F7
MESA OAK LN
100 POM 91767 600-G4
MESA OF THE OAKS
19500 SCTA 91321 4551-F5
MESA PEAK MTWY
- LACo 90265 628-C1
- LACo 91302 628-F2
MESA PEAK TRACTOR WY
- LACo 91302 628-G1
MESARICA RD
20700 LACo 91724 599-G5
20700 SDMS 91724 599-G5
MESA RIDGE DR
- POM 91766 640-G6
MESA ROBLES DR
9300 WHIT 90603 707-J3
16000 HacH 91745 678-C4
MESA VERDE
1400 FUL 92833 738-E3
8900 BPK 90620 767-F5
MESA VERDE AV
300 PMDL 93551 4285-H1
MESA VERDE DR
- BqtC 91354 4460-E3
3000 BURB 91504 533-E3
9300 MTCL 91763 601-F5
MESA VERDE RD
900 PAS 91105 565-F7
MESA VERDE WY
- LA 91342 482-E4
MESA VISTA DR
4200 LCF 91011 535-B4
MESCAL ST
18000 RowH 91748 678-J6
18300 RowH 91748 679-A6
MESCAL CANYON MTWY
25500 Valy 93563 (4561-B4 See Page 4471)
27500 Llan 93544 4471-B1
27500 Llan 93544 (4561-B4 See Page 4471)
MESCALERO RD
3200 SBdC 92371 (4562-J2 See Page 4471)
9700 SBdC 92371 (4472-H3 See Page 4471)
MESCALERO ST
18200 RowH 91748 678-J6
18600 RowH 91748 679-A6
MESCAL HIGHLANDS DR
29100 Llan 93544 4471-B5
MESERVE ST
1500 POM 91766 640-F3
MESETA DR
10900 Sunl 91040 503-A4
E MESITA AV
2000 WCOV 91791 639-A1
MESITA PL
800 FUL 92835 738-H2
S MESITA PL
400 WCOV 91791 639-A1
MESITA RD
1000 PAS 91107 566-G2
MESITA WY
14000 LA 90402 631-C6
MESMER AV
5100 LA 90230 672-F5
5300 CULC 90230 672-F5
MESNAGER ST
200 LA 90012 634-H1
MESQUIT ST
600 LA 90021 634-H6
MESQUITE CT
- StvR 91381 4550-C4
MESQUITE DR
3500 CALB 91302 559-F7
3500 CALB 91302 589-F1
MESQUITE LN
- CRSN 90745 794-G1
12700 NRWK 90650 737-A1
20200 LACo 91724 639-F1
MESQUITE PL
- POM 91766 640-G7
MESQUITE RD
300 SBdC 92372 (4472-A6 See Page 4471)
3600 SBdC 92371 (4562-J3 See Page 4471)
38600 PMDL 93551 4195-F7
38800 LACo 93551 4195-F6
MESQUITE ST
2300 SBdC 92371 (4562-F3 See Page 4471)
2300 SBdC 92372 (4562-F3 See Page 4471)
MESQUITE RIDGE RD
- LACo 91342 482-J2
MESSINA
1400 MTBL 90640 636-C6
MESSINA CIR
9900 CYP 90630 767-B7
MESSINA DR
10200 WHIT 90603 707-H4

MESSINA PL
600 VeCo 91377 557-G1
1200 POM 91766 640-E3
META DR
14900 LACo 90604 707-F6
METATE LN
6800 MAL 90265 667-D3
METCALF AL
300 PAS 91101 565-J5
METEORA WY
- RowH 91748 679-E6
METRO CT
- FUL 92832 738-H7
METRO DR
700 MONP 91755 636-D3
METRO ST
9500 DWNY 90240 706-E3
METRO CENTER DR
- NRWK 90650 736-J1
METROPOL DR
15200 HacH 91745 677-J6
15200 HacH 91745 678-A6
METROPOLE AV
100 AVA 90704 5923-G4
METROPOLITAN PL
2800 POM 91767 600-J3
METROPOLITAN PZ
5900 LA 90036 633-B2
METTLER AV
13200 LACo 90061 734-D2
18000 CRSN 90746 764-D2
METTLER DR
- RBCH 90278 733-A5
17100 CRSN 90746 734-D7
METTLER ST
3600 LA 90011 674-D2
5800 LA 90003 674-D6
8600 LA 90003 704-D3
METZ PL
8600 LA 90069 592-J5
E METZ ST
6200 LBCH 90808 796-E1
METZLER DR
2400 LA 90031 595-C7
2400 LA 90031 635-C1
MEUSE AV
- Brwd 90049 632-A3
MEVEL PL
3400 GLDL 91214 504-E5
MEXICO PL
700 PVE 90274 792-G4
MEXICO WY
7500 BPK 90620 767-D3
MEYDA RD
400 SBdC 92372 (4472-A6 See Page 4471)
MEYER CT
- HMB 90254 762-H3
MEYER DR
44300 LAN 93536 4015-A7
MEYER LN
500 RBCH 90278 763-B3
MEYER RD
13000 LACo 90605 707-B6
13000 SFSP 90605 707-B6
13700 LACo 90604 707-B6
13700 LACo 90605 737-D1
13700 LACo 90604 737-D1
N MEYER ST
200 SFER 91340 482-B5
S MEYER ST
100 SFER 91340 481-J6
100 SFER 91340 482-A6
200 LA 91342 481-J6
MEYERLOA LN
2900 LACo 91107 536-F7
MEYERS CREEK RD
- Actn 93510 4375-E5
MEYLER AV
21300 LACo 90502 764-A6
22900 LACo 90502 794-A1
24300 Hrbr 90710 794-A3
MEYLER RD
400 SPed 90731 824-B7
MEYLER ST
21400 LACo 90502 764-A6
22500 LACo 90502 794-A1
N MEYLER ST
100 SPed 90731 824-A3
S MEYLER ST
100 SPed 90731 824-A6
100 SPed 90731 824-A6
2600 SPed 90731 854-A2
E MEZZANINE WY
3200 LBCH 90808 796-B1
MGM DR
10100 CenC 90067 632-E3
10100 WLA 90025 632-E3
MIAMI CT
800 CLAR 91711 571-B7
MIAMI WY
15800 PacP 90272 630-J5
MICA ST
13800 SFSP 90670 737-D4
MICAELA DR
5400 AGRH 91301 557-H5
MICHAEL AV
200 FUL 92833 738-E7
4000 CULC 90066 672-B5
4000 LA 90066 672-B5
17190 CRTS 90703 737-A7
MICHAEL DR
1700 LAN 93535 4106-D1

MICHAEL LN
- SCTA 91387 4462-D6
1500 PacP 90272 590-F7
1500 PacP 90272 630-F1
MICHAEL PL
2400 POM 91768 640-D1
MICHAEL ST
7100 LACo 91390 4374-C2
W MICHAEL ST
3900 CULC 90066 672-B5
3900 LA 90066 672-B5
MICHAEL COLLINS CIR
600 MTBL 90640 636-E7
MICHAEL CREST DR
15000 LACo 91387 4552-E5
MICHAEL HUNT DR
10800 SELM 91733 637-C4
MICHAELS ST
- PanC 91402 532-A3
MICHALE ST
20500 Win 91306 530-C1
21700 LA 91304 530-A1
22100 LA 91304 529-H1
MICHELANGELO AV
4200 WdHl 91364 560-A5
MICHELE CT
1000 MTBL 90640 676-D1
MICHELLE AV
1500 LAN 93535 4106-C1
MICHELLE CIR
13100 LACo 90605 707-B7
MICHELLE DR
3500 TOR 90503 763-A4
28800 AGRH 91301 558-B4
MICHELLE ST
11300 CRTS 90703 766-F1
E MICHELLE ST
300 WCOV 91790 638-F3
1600 WCOV 91791 638-J3
1900 WCOV 91791 639-A3
W MICHELLE ST
800 WCOV 91790 638-E3
MICHELSON ST
1200 NLB 90805 765-F2
3100 LKWD 90712 765-H2
4000 LKWD 90712 766-A2
5500 LKWD 90713 766-D2
MICHELTORENA ST
300 Echo 90026 594-C6
1900 LA 90039 594-C3
MICHENER AL
600 PAS 91103 565-H3
MICHIGAN AV
700 SMCA 90401 671-F2
700 SMCA 90404 671-H1
1500 Boyl 90033 634-J4
1900 Boyl 90033 635-A4
2400 SMCA 90404 631-H7
3200 LYN 90262 705-C5
3200 SGAT 90280 705-C5
3400 City 90063 635-D5
4300 ELA 90022 635-E5
7900 WHIT 90602 707-E1
8200 WHIT 90605 707-E1
N MICHIGAN AV
- PAS 91106 566-B3
400 PAS 91104 566-B3
1600 PAS 91104 536-B7
1600 LACo 91104 536-B7
S MICHIGAN AV
- PAS 91106 566-B5
400 PAS 91125 566-B5
MICHIGAN BLVD
400 LACo 91107 566-H6
MICHIGAN DR
800 CLAR 91711 571-E6
MICHIGAN ST
2800 Actn 93510 4465-C1
32700 Actn 93510 4375-C7
N MICHILLINDA AV
- LACo 91107 566-H3
- SMAD 91024 566-H3
200 PAS 91107 566-H3
600 ARCD 91006 566-H3
600 ARCD 91007 566-H3
S MICHILLINDA AV
- LACo 91107 566-J6
- ARCD 91007 566-J6
MICHILLINDA DR
3800 LACo 91107 566-H6
N MICHILLINDA WY
500 SMAD 91024 566-H1
MICHU LN
4600 HAW 90250 733-C1
MICON CIR
15700 LACo 90248 734-D5
MIDAS LN
- SCTA 91351 4551-H2
MIDBURY ST
1900 BREA 92821 708-H3
MIDCREST DR
14800 LACo 90604 707-F6
15400 WHIT 90604 707-G6
MIDDLE RD
1300 LA 90810 794-J4
1500 LA 90810 795-A3
3700 City 90063 635-D3
MIDDLEBANK DR
23100 SCTA 91321 4640-J2
MIDDLEBROOK RD
1800 TOR 90501 793-H1
MIDDLEBURY CIR
4500 CYP 90630 767-B6

MIDDLEBURY CT
- CLAR 91711 571-E7
MIDDLEBURY ST
3700 LA 90004 594-A7
37400 PMDL 93550 4286-D3
MIDDLECOFF CT
- LHB 90631 738-B2
MIDDLECOFF PL
12500 GrnH 91344 481-D5
MIDDLE CREST DR
5600 AGRH 91301 557-H4
MIDDLECREST RD
5200 RPV 90275 823-B1
MIDDLE EAST TERRACE RD
- AVA 90704 5923-H4
MIDDLE FORK CIR
4700 THO 91362 557-D1
MIDDLEGATE RD
3900 WLKV 91361 557-D6
MIDDLE RANCH RD
- LACo 90704 5923-A1
MIDDLERIDGE LN
- RHLS 90274 793-D7
MIDDLERIDGE LN N
- RHLS 90274 793-D7
MIDDLERIDGE LN S
- RHLS 90274 793-D7
- RHLS 90274 823-D1
MIDDLESBURY RIDGE CIR
7000 CanP 91307 529-E5
MIDDLESEX LN
- ING 90305 703-F3
MIDDLETON AV
900 LHB 90631 708-C7
16500 WHIT 90603 708-A5
MIDDLETON PL
1600 LA 90062 673-G2
MIDDLETON RD
1500 SDMS 91773 599-H4
MIDDLETON ST
5900 HNTP 90255 674-H7
39400 PMDL 93551 4195-B5
MIDFIELD AV
7400 Wch 90045 702-J1
7400 Wch 90045 703-A1
7600 ING 90302 703-A1
MIDFIELD LN
16500 CRTS 90703 736-J4
MIDFORK CIR
1400 WAL 91789 639-E4
MIDHURST DR
700 COV 91724 599-D6
MIDLAND ST
3800 LA 90031 595-A5
MIDLOTHIAN DR
1700 LACo 91104 536-D7
1700 Alta 91001 536-D6
MID PINES LN
- Nor 91326 480-E7
MIDSITE AV
600 COV 91723 599-A6
1300 COV 91722 599-A3
4600 LACo 91722 599-A4
MIDTOWN AV
19200 CRSN 90746 764-G3
MIDVALE AV
400 Wwd 90024 632-A2
1800 WLA 90025 632-B4
2200 LA 90064 632-D6
3000 LA 90034 632-D6
3200 LA 90034 672-E1
MIDVALE DR
1800 POM 91768 600-G6
13900 WHIT 90602 677-E7
MIDVALE PL
1000 ALH 91803 595-G7
1000 LA 90032 595-G7
MIDWAY AV
3800 CULC 90232 672-F2
10600 CRTS 90703 736-E5
MIDWAY PL
900 LA 90015 634-E5
12900 CRTS 90703 737-A5
MIDWAY ST
10200 BLF 90706 736-D6
13600 CRTS 90703 737-C5
E MIDWAY ST
3900 LBCH 90803 825-J2
3900 LBCH 90803 826-A2
MIDWICK DR
1600 Alta 91001 536-C6
2800 ALH 91803 635-G1
MIDWICK LN
19500 Tarz 91356 560-F6
MIDWICKHILL DR
1200 ALH 91803 636-A1
1500 ALH 91803 635-J2
MIDWOOD DR
15600 GrnH 91344 501-G1
17000 GrnH 91344 481-C7
17300 GrnH 91344 481-B7
MIGNONETTE ST
1000 LA 90012 634-E2
MIGUEL AV
3900 PRV 90660 676-J2
19600 CRTS 90703 766-J3
MIGUEL CT
25700 SCTA 91355 4550-G4
MIGUEL PL
200 FUL 92835 738-F3

STREET / Block City ZIP Pg-Grid

...CH 90803 826-D1
...RD
SCTA 91321 4551-D7
...HAIL ST
- LACo 91390 4461-A4
MIKI WY
- LAN 93535 4106-C2
MIKINDA AV
1500 LHB 90631 708-C4
9300 OrCo 90631 708-B4
MIKINDA CT
15900 WHIT 90603 707-J4
MIKOSASKY AV
43700 LAN 93535 4106-C1
MIKUNI AV
8900 Nor 91324 500-F7
MILA DR
7200 PRM 90723 735-F6
MILACA PL
4000 Shrm 91423 562-A6
MILAGRO WY
3000 FUL 92835 738-F2
MILAM PL
1200 MONP 91755 636-B4
MILAN AV
600 SPAS 91030 595-J2
MILAN DR
39600 PMDL 93551 4195-C3
MILAN LN
1900 LMTA 90717 793-H4
MILAN PL
1900 LA 90732 823-H5
MILANO
1700 MTBL 90640 636-C6
MILANO AV
10900 NRWK 90650 706-G6
MILANO LN
25800 SCTA 91355 4550-F5
MILANO PL
1200 POM 91766 640-E3
MILANO TER
- CHLS 91709 710-J3
MILANO WY
9900 SunV 91352 533-C2
MILBANK ST
12300 LA 91604 562-E4
13700 Shrm 91423 562-A4
14400 Shrm 91403 562-A4
15400 Shrm 91403 561-G4
15500 Enc 91436 561-G4
MILBROOK PL
- Cstc 91384 4459-F5
MILBURN DR
4200 City 90063 635-F3
9800 LA 91504 533-C2
9800 SunV 91352 533-C2
MILDAS DR
200 LACo 91302 589-E7
200 LACo 91302 629-E1
MILDINE DR
1400 GLDL 91208 534-G4
MILDRED AV
100 Ven 90291 671-H6
4100 CULC 90066 672-C5
19400 TOR 90503 763-A3
MILDRED DR
1700 GLDL 91206 564-H3
MILDRED ST
1000 LVRN 91750 570-E6
1100 ELMN 91733 637-B1
10600 ELMN 91731 637-D1
MILDURA AV
1200 UPL 91784 571-J3
MILDWOOD CT
2500 LAN 93536 4105-B3
2500 LAN 93536 4105-B3
3100 LAN 93536 4105-B3
3100 LAN 93536 4105-C3
MILES AV
5900 HNTP 90255 675-A7
MILES ST
400 PAS 91106 565-J6
12400 CRTS 90703 766-J3
12400 CRTS 90703 767-A3
MILESTONE ST
- LACo 91390 4461-A4
MILFORD AV
900 POM 91766 640-H4
MILFORD CT
37200 PMDL 93550 4286-D3
MILFORD ST
6100 HiPk 90042 595-E3
6300 SPAS 91030 595-E3
E MILFORD ST
100 GLDL 91206 564-E4
W MILFORD ST
100 GLDL 91203 564-C4
MILITARY AV
2400 LA 90064 632-C6
3000 LA 90034 632-C6
3000 LA 90034 672-D1
MILKYWAY CT
3600 PMDL 93550 4286-H3
MILKYWAY PL
800 DBAR 91765 640-D5
MILL LN
1100 SMRO 91108 596-B1
1100 FUL 92831 738-J3
20700 DBAR 91789 679-G6
MILL RD
1900 SPAS 91030 595-J1

MILL RD
6000 SBdC 92397 (4652-C2 See Page 4651)
MILL RD E
6000 SBdC 92397 (4652-C2 See Page 4651)
MILL RD W
6000 SBdC 92397 (4652-B2 See Page 4651)
MILL RUN
100 MNRO 91016 567-G2
MILL ST
600 LA 90021 634-H6
900 SBdC 92397 (4652-C2 See Page 4651)
MILLAR DR
1400 GLDL 91206 564-G4
MILLARD PL
17200 Nor 91325 501-C6
MILLARD CANYON RD
700 Alta 91001 535-G3
MILLBORO PL
9700 LA 90210 592-C3
MILLBRAE ST
2500 DUAR 91010 568-D5
MILLBROOK DR
14300 Shrm 91423 562-A5
MILLBROOK LN
37600 PMDL 93550 4286-D2
MILLBURGH AV
800 GLDR 91740 599-C2
17600 LACo 91702 598-J2
MILLBURGH RD
16700 LACo 91702 598-H2
MILLBURY AV
300 LACo 91746 637-J4
600 LACo 91746 638-A2
3200 BALD 91706 598-D6
MILL CANYON RD
- SMRO 91108 596-B1
MILLCREEK
1400 WCOV 91791 638-J3
MILL CREEK LN
300 SGBL 91775 596-C3
MILLCREEK WY
2000 PMDL 93551 4195-E5
MILLDALE CT
12200 NHol 91605 532-F3
MILLDALE DR
15400 BelA 90077 591-G1
MILLEN LN
- BREA 92821 708-J5
MILLENNIUM
- LA 90094 672-F7
- LA 90094 702-E1
MILLENNIUM PKWY
- LAN 93536 4105-D1
MILLER AL
- PAS 91103 565-C3
MILLER AV
700 AZU 91702 568-G5
900 City 90063 635-E2
13000 NRWK 90650 737-B2
14700 GAR 90249 733-G4
MILLER CT
1200 UPL 91784 571-J4
MILLER DR
1300 LA 90069 592-J5
1300 WHWD 90069 592-J5
9300 TEML 91780 596-J5
MILLER PL
1300 LA 90069 592-J5
MILLER RD
11200 LACo 90604 707-F6
MILLER ST
500 POM 91766 641-A5
4300 LVRN 91750 570-G7
7300 BPK 90620 767-E2
MILLER WK
- Cstc 91384 4459-D6
MILLER WY
1400 LA 90069 592-J5
9800 SGAT 90280 705-F5
MILLERGROVE DR
8000 LACo 90606 676-H7
8200 LACo 90606 706-H1
8700 SFSP 90670 706-G2
MILLER LATERAL
- CLAR 91711 571-B2
- LACo 91711 571-B2
MILLER RANCH RD
- CLAR 91711 571-A4
- LACo 91711 571-A4
MILLET AV
1400 SELM 91733 637-B4
2600 ELMN 91733 637-B2
MILLETTE AV
19800 WAL 91789 679-E2
MILLFORD CT
23800 SCTA 91354 4460-F7
MILLHOUSE DR
- SCTA 91350 4550-J2
MILLICENT WY
2700 PAS 91107 566-F5
MILLIKEN AV
8000 WHIT 90602 707-E1
8300 WHIT 90605 707-E2
MILLIKEN DR
27900 SCTA 91350 4460-J4
MILLING ST
400 LAN 93534 4015-E6
1800 LAN 93535 4016-D6
2000 LAN 93536 4015-C6

MILLIS ST
1900 MTBL 90640 676-C2
MILLMARK AV
6600 NLB 90805 735-E7
MILLMARK GROVE ST
800 SPed 90731 824-A2
MILLMEADOW RD
15700 SCTA 91387 4552-D6
MILLMONT ST
1100 CRSN 90746 764-F3
MILLOU LN
14600 WHIT 90602 707-F1
MILLPOINT AV
21000 CRSN 90745 764-G5
MILLRACE AV
12300 LYN 90262 735-D2
MILLRACE PL
8400 SunV 91352 532-D1
MILLRACE ST
13100 SunV 91352 532-D1
MILLRIDGE DR
3200 WCOV 91792 679-D1
21100 SCTA 91350 4461-C6
MILLS AV
3100 GLDL 91214 534-E1
3800 CLAR 91711 571-E4
3800 LACo 91711 571-E4
8900 WHIT 90605 707-G3
9000 WHIT 90603 707-F4
9100 MTCL 91763 601-D7
9100 CLAR 91711 601-E5
9500 LACo 90604 707-F4
9600 POM 91711 601-E5
9600 POM 91767 601-E5
10000 LACo 90605 707-C5
10400 MTCL 91763 641-D1
12300 CHNO 91710 641-C6
12300 POM 91766 641-C6
35200 LACo 91390 4374-D2
N MILLS AV
100 CLAR 91711 601-E1
1700 CLAR 91711 571-E6
S MILLS AV
200 CLAR 91711 601-E4
300 MTCL 91763 601-E4
MILLS PL
- PAS 91105 565-H5
MILLS ST
200 SMCA 90405 671-F4
MILLSTON CT
23500 SCTA 91354 4550-G1
MILLSTONE CT
3800 SBdC 91766 641-C3
MILLSTONE DR
16900 LACo 91744 638-H6
MILL STREAM DR
1500 CHLS 91709 680-G3
MILLSTREAM DR
900 FUL 92833 738-C6
26100 SCTA 91387 4552-E7
MILLSTREAM LN
16300 CRTS 90703 736-J6
MILLSWEET DR
- UPL 91784 571-H6
MILLUX AV
5000 PRV 90660 676-H4
MILL VALLEY RD
23600 SCTA 91355 4550-F7
MILL VALLEY WY
24700 CRSN 90745 794-D3
MILLWARD LN
- CRSN 90745 794-G1
MILLYGLEN LN
1100 LHB 90631 708-D6
MILMAC DR
1000 LHH 90631 708-F2
MILMADA DR
800 LCF 91011 535-B3
MILMORE AV
18200 CRSN 90746 764-C2
MILNA AV
5700 LACo 90606 676-J4
8600 LACo 90606 706-H1
MILNE DR
4600 TOR 90505 793-B1
4700 TOR 90505 763-B7
MILNER RD
6700 LA 90068 593-E3
MILO TER
600 HiPk 90042 595-B2
MILOANN ST
9800 TEML 91780 597-A4
MILROY PL
13700 SFSP 90670 737-C3
MILTA AV
11900 DWNY 90242 705-G5
MILTON AV
1300 ALH 91803 595-G7
4100 CULC 90232 672-F3
5700 WHIT 90601 677-C6
7000 WHIT 90602 677-C7
7700 WHIT 90602 707-C1
MILTON CIR
9800 CYP 90630 767-E7
MILTON CT
400 CLAR 91711 601-C5
500 LA 90065 595-A3
500 LBCH 90803 796-F7
MILTON DR
200 SGBL 91775 596-D2
W MILTON DR
800 GLDR 91741 569-B4

W MILTON DR
18600 LACo 91741 569-B4
MILTON PL
5600 WHIT 90601 677-C5
MILTON ST
900 LACo 90502 764-A4
3100 LACo 91107 566-G5
3100 PAS 91107 566-G5
12400 LA 90066 672-D6
MILTONWOOD AV
800 DUAR 91010 568-B5
MILVERN DR
15900 LACo 90604 707-J6
MILWAUKEE AV
400 HiPk 90042 595-C2
MILWOOD AV
500 Ven 90291 671-H5
6800 CanP 91303 530-B5
7500 LA 91304 530-B5
10000 Chat 91311 500-B3
MILWOOD CT
600 Ven 90291 671-H5
MIMOSA CT
5600 VeCo 91377 557-J2
W MIMOSA CT
1500 UPL 91784 571-H7
MIMOSA DR
3500 LA 90065 594-H2
MIMOSA LN
4100 LVRN 91750 570-H7
MIMOSA ST
2700 ALH 91803 595-H6
MIMOSA WY
- PMDL 93551 4285-D3
MINA AV
9500 LACo 90605 707-C4
MINA ST
10600 LACo 90605 707-C5
MINARD RD
2400 Top 90290 629-J2
MINARET CT
- Cstc 91384 4459-G2
MINA RICA DR
9500 Tuj 91042 504-C6
MINDANAO WY
13000 LA 90292 672-C6
13300 MdlR 90292 672-B7
MINDEN PL
4800 Eagl 90041 565-D6
MINDO DR
1100 POM 91767 601-C7
MINDORA AV
13500 LA 91342 482-D2
MINDORA CT
17000 GmH 91344 481-C6
MINDORA DR
4500 TOR 90505 793-C1
4600 TOR 90505 763-B7
MINEOLA ST
12500 Pcma 91331 502-E5
MINER ST
1600 SPed 90731 824-C6
2400 SPed 90731 854-D1
8800 Wats 90002 704-H3
MINERAL WELLS TR
- LFlz 90027 563-J5
- LFlz 90027 564-A5
MINERO RD
9300 SBdC 92371 (4472-G6 See Page 4471)
10500 SBdC 92372 (4472-G1 See Page 4471)
MINERS RD
37100 PMDL 93552 4287-B3
MINERS TR
13200 CHLS 91709 680-J1
MINERVA AV
3800 LA 90066 672-D3
4000 CULC 90066 672-D3
MINERVA CT
1000 LBCH 90813 795-E6
3300 Bxby 90807 795-E1
3300 SIGH 90755 795-E1
MINERVA PK
1000 LBCH 90813 795-G6
MINERVA ST
2300 LA 90058 674-H2
2500 VER 90058 674-H2
MINES AV
100 MTBL 90640 676-C3
3200 LA 90023 675-B1
8600 PRV 90660 676-G5
14000 LACo 90605 707-D4
MINES BLVD
10800 LACo 90606 676-J6
11400 LACo 90606 677-A7
S MINES ST
4400 ELA 90022 675-F1
MINFORD CT
2700 LAN 93536 4015-C6
MINFORD ST
2000 LAN 93536 4015-E6
2000 LAN 93536 4015-C6
MING LN
10600 SBdC 92372 (4472-B4 See Page 4471)
MINGUS DR
30800 WLKV 91362 557-F3
MINK DR
23000 DBAR 91765 640-B6
MINNEAPOLIS ST
3200 LA 90039 594-E2

MINNEHAHA ST
14200 MsnH 91345 502-A3
14600 MsnH 91345 501-H3
15700 GmH 91344 501-A3
18200 Nor 91326 500-F4
20300 Chat 91311 500-A4
MINNEQUA DR
23800 DBAR 91765 640-C5
MINNESOTA AV
3200 LYN 90262 705-A4
3200 SGAT 90280 705-A4
15100 PRM 90723 735-G6
N MINNESOTA AV
100 GLDR 91741 569-E5
6600 NLB 90805 735-G7
S MINNESOTA AV
100 GLDR 91741 569-E6
300 GLDR 91740 569-E7
MINNESOTA ST
3000 LA 90031 595-A7
MINNEWA LN
4300 BELL 90201 675-D6
MINNIE AV
- Actn 93510 4375-F7
MINOA AV
400 LACo 91107 566-H5
MINORCA DR
1200 PacP 90272 631-C5
MINORCA WY
4600 BPK 90621 737-J4
MINORU DR
1900 Alta 91001 536-C7
MINSON WY
1200 MTBL 90640 676-B5
MINSTREL AV
6900 CanP 91307 529-G4
7600 LA 91304 529-G3
MINSTREL DR
4700 PMDL 93552 4287-A3
42700 LAN 93536 4104-G4
W MINT CANYON RD
- LACo 91390 4373-C3
MINTER CT
16600 SCTA 91387 4552-B2
MINTER WY
- LAN 93534 4015-E4
1700 LAN 93534 4015-E4
MINTO CT
2800 LA 90032 595-E6
MINTURN AV
4900 LKWD 90712 765-J3
MINUET PL
8300 PanC 91402 532-B1
MINUTEMAN WY
30900 AGRH 91301 557-F6
30900 WLKV 91361 557-F6
MIOLAND DR
4600 LACo 90043 673-C5
MIRA ST
1500 HMB 90254 762-H1
MIRABEAU AV
100 LA 90732 823-J4
MIRABILE CT
- StvR 91381 4640-D1
MIRACLE PL
1500 CMRC 90022 676-A3
MIRACOSTA ST
1600 LA 90732 823-H4
MIRADA CIRCULO
- BqtC 91354 4460-F3
MIRADERO RD
1100 BHLS 90210 592-F5
MIRADOR CIR
3100 FUL 92835 738-G2
MIRADOR DR
1800 AZU 91702 568-H2
MIRADOR PL
4600 Tarz 91356 560-G4
W MIRAFLORES AV
700 SPed 90731 824-A3
1000 LA 90732 824-A3
MIRAGE LN
23500 DBAR 91765 680-C5
MIRAGE RD
3300 SBdC 92371 (4562-J1 See Page 4471)
MIRAGE WY
3800 PMDL 93551 4195-A3
MIRALESTE DR
100 LA 90732 823-H4
100 RPV 90732 823-H4
2000 RPV 90275 823-H4
MIRALESTE PZ
29500 RPV 90275 823-G4
MIRALINDA DR
1600 LACo 91770 636-E4
MIRA LOMA AV
200 GLDL 91204 594-E1
S MIRA LOMA DR
400 AZU 91702 598-G1
MIRALOMA WY
19500 WAL 91789 639-D6
MIRA MAR AV
- LBCH 90803 825-J1
300 LBCH 90814 795-J6
300 LBCH 90814 825-J1
1300 LBCH 90804 795-J6
2100 LBCH 90815 795-J4
MIRAMAR AV
700 CLAR 91711 571-E6
E MIRA MAR AV
600 LBCH 90814 795-J6
700 LBCH 90804 795-J6

MIRA MAR DR
- LA 91342 482-E4
MIRAMAR DR
400 RBCH 90277 762-J6
700 FUL 92831 738-J5
3600 HacH 91745 677-J7
MIRAMAR LN
- PMDL 93551 4104-D6
MIRAMAR PL
1000 FUL 92831 738-J5
MIRAMAR ST
1100 LA 90012 634-D3
1200 Echo 90026 634-D3
1700 POM 91767 601-B6
1800 LA 90057 634-C2
MIRA MESA AV
- SBdC 91710 641-D7
MIRAMONTE AV
38000 PMDL 93551 4285-H1
E MIRA MONTE AV
- SMAD 91024 567-A1
W MIRA MONTE AV
- SMAD 91024 567-A1
MIRAMONTE BLVD
5800 Flor 90001 674-G7
7200 Flor 90001 704-G1
MIRAMONTE CT
2000 CHLS 91709 680-H1
MIRAMONTE DR
- POM 91768 600-G5
100 FUL 92835 738-F4
1800 LVRN 91750 600-H4
MIRA MONTE PL
600 PAS 91101 566-A5
MIRA MONTES
7800 VeCo 93063 499-F3
MIRANDA CT
2700 PMDL 93551 4195-D6
MIRANDA PL
20500 WdHl 91367 560-D2
MIRANDA ST
2700 WCOV 91792 639-B6
11200 NHol 91601 562-H1
11900 LA 91607 562-E1
14300 VanN 91401 562-A1
17400 Enc 91316 561-B1
18100 Tarz 91356 561-A1
18700 Tarz 91356 560-G1
20400 WdHl 91367 560-C1
22200 WdHl 91367 559-F1
MIRASOL DR
1400 SMRO 91108 566-E7
1400 SMRO 91108 596-E1
MIRASOL ST
- SCTA 91355 4550-D3
1100 LA 90023 675-C1
MIRA VALLE ST
800 MONP 91754 636-A4
MIRA VERDE DR
200 LHH 90631 708-D2
MIRA VISTA AV
2200 Mont 91020 534-H3
MIRA VISTA DR
2700 GLDL 91208 534-H6
MIRA VISTA ST
- SCTA 91355 4460-E6
MIRA VISTA TER
300 PAS 91105 565-F4
MIRIAM DR
3400 WCOV 91791 599-D7
MIRIAM ST
5100 HiPk 90042 595-B2
MIRKWOOD CT
6000 PMDL 93551 4104-F6
MIRROR WY
27800 SCTA 91351 4551-J2
MIRROR LAKE DR
6300 LA 90068 593-F1
MISHA LN
41600 PMDL 93551 4104-E7
MISS GRACE DR
16200 SCTA 91387 4552-B2
MISSION AL
1800 SPAS 91030 595-J2
MISSION BLVD
3800 MTCL 91763 641-F2
3800 POM 91766 641-F2
3800 MTCL 91766 641-F2
3800 SBdC 91766 641-F2
5200 SBdC 91763 641-F2
5300 SBdC 91762 641-F2
E MISSION BLVD
100 POM 91766 640-J2
300 POM 91766 641-A2
W MISSION BLVD
100 POM 91766 640-F2
1000 ONT 91762 641-J2
MISSION CIR
11300 Chat 91311 499-H1
MISSION DR
- CRSN 90745 794-E1
100 SGBL 91776 596-H6
9000 RSMD 91770 596-H6
41000 PMDL 93551 4194-F1
41300 PMDL 93551 4104-F7
E MISSION DR
4700 RSMD 91770 596-G5
N MISSION DR
100 SGBL 91775 596-D2
100 SGBL 91776 596-D2
S MISSION DR
100 SGBL 91776 596-D4

MISSION PL
1200 DUAR 91010 568-C5
7000 HNTP 90255 675-A7
MISSION RD
- ALH 91801 596-D4
100 SGBL 91776 596-D4
300 GLDL 91205 564-E7
900 RSMD 91770 596-E5
E MISSION RD
- ALH 91801 596-C5
N MISSION RD
100 Boyl 90033 634-J3
800 Boyl 90033 635-A2
1100 LA 90031 635-A2
4000 LA 90031 595-C7
4000 LA 90032 595-C7
S MISSION RD
100 Boyl 90033 634-H4
600 LA 90023 634-J6
W MISSION RD
- ALH 91801 596-A6
1100 ALH 91803 596-A6
1400 ALH 91803 595-G7
3000 LA 90032 595-G7
MISSION ST
100 LHB 90631 708-B6
300 SPAS 91030 595-G2
2100 SMRO 91108 596-A1
2500 SMRO 91108 596-A2
7300 BPK 90621 737-H7
MISSION TR
- Actn 93510 4465-B1
MISSION WY
5400 CMRC 90040 675-H3
MISSIONARY RIDGE RD
20500 LACo 91789 679-F5
20700 DBAR 91789 679-F5
MISSION DUMP RD
3000 Brwd 90049 591-E1
3100 Brwd 90049 561-E7
MISSION GLEN LN
14800 LA 91342 481-J7
MISSION HILLS RD
15000 MsnH 91345 481-H7
15100 MsnH 91345 501-G1
MISSION MILL RD
10100 LACo 90601 677-B1
E MISSION MILL RD
10000 INDS 90601 677-B1
10000 PRV 90601 677-B1
MISSION PUEBLA
- BqtC 91354 4460-F3
MISSION RIDGE WY
12100 GmH 91344 481-B6
MISSION TIERRA
13200 GmH 91344 481-C3
MISSION TRAIL LN
- BqtC 91354 4460-F2
MISSISSIPPI AV
10200 WLA 90025 632-D4
11000 WLA 90025 632-B5
MISSOURI
3600 WCOV 91792 679-H2
MISSOURI AV
2400 SGAT 90280 704-J4
2600 SGAT 90280 705-A4
10200 WLA 90025 632-D3
11800 WLA 90025 631-J6
MIST CT
28300 SCTA 91350 4461-C4
MISTLETOE CT
26500 SCTA 91355 4550-E4
MISTLETOE RD
9600 Tuj 91042 504-B5
MISTON DR
22200 WdHl 91364 559-J3
MISTRIDGE DR
5500 RPV 90275 823-A1
MISTY CT
1300 DBAR 91765 680-D3
5900 AGRH 91301 558-B4
MISTY PL
12600 CRTS 90703 767-A2
MISTY ACRES RD
- RHE 90274 822-J2
- RHE 90274 823-A2
MISTY CANYON AV
600 THO 91362 557-G1
MISTY ISLE DR
800 GLDL 91207 564-F1
MISTY MORNING RD
2800 TOR 90505 793-E5
MISTY RIDGE PL
- LACo 91387 4551-J6
MITCHELL AV
12000 LA 90066 672-C4
12200 CULC 90066 672-C4
MITCHELL PL
- StvR 91381 4550-A6
1300 Boyl 90033 634-J3
1400 Boyl 90033 635-A3
MITLA AV
11600 DWNY 90241 705-H4
MITONY AV
11200 LACo 90605 707-C6
MITZI CT
2000 UPL 91784 571-H5
MIXER RD
- SCTA 91350 4551-C5
MOAB DR
1000 CLAR 91711 571-F6
MOANA WK
- Shrm 91423 562-A6

E MOBECK ST
900 WCOV 91790 638-G1
1600 WCOV 91791 638-J1
3200 WCOV 91791 639-D1
MOBERLY PL
20400 Win 91306 530-D6
S MOBILE AV
700 ELA 90022 676-A1
MOBILE ST
19500 Res 91335 530-F6
20200 Win 91306 530-D6
22300 CanP 91303 529-J7
22600 CanP 91307 529-E7
MOCCASIN LN
- RHE 90274 793-C5
MOCCASIN PL
- LAN 93536 4014-J5
- LAN 93536 4104-J1
43600 LACo 93536 4104-J2
MOCCASIN ST
300 LPUE 91744 638-B4
13400 LACo 91746 637-J3
13700 LPUE 91746 637-J3
13700 LPUE 91746 638-A4
MOCHA DR
26700 SCTA 91350 4550-J1
MOCKINGBIRD CT
- VeCo 91377 557-J2
24400 SCTA 91355 4550-E4
MOCKINGBIRD LN
- BREA 92823 709-G6
- SCTA 91350 4461-A5
100 WCOV 91791 599-B7
100 SPAS 91030 565-H7
100 SPAS 91030 595-H1
400 WAL 91789 639-H6
N MOCKINGBIRD LN
100 WCOV 91791 599-B7
MOCKINGBIRD PL
1300 LA 90069 592-H5
MOCKING BIRD RD
900 SBdC 92397 (4652-C2 See Page 4651)
MOCKINGBIRD HILL DR
15300 HacH 91745 678-A3
MOCKINGBIRD KNOLL
3100 LVRN 91750 570-J4
MOCO LN
5300 LA 90068 593-H2
5300 LFlz 90027 593-H2
MODENA LN
- Nor 91326 500-C1
MODENA PL
5500 AGRH 91301 557-G5
MODERNO PL
200 FUL 92835 738-F1
MODESTO AV
2700 TOR 90501 793-H1
MODJESKA PL
11900 LA 90066 672-C3
MODJESKA ST
1900 LA 90039 594-F4
MODOC DR
19000 WAL 91789 639-B7
MODOC PL
12100 CHNO 91710 641-C5
MODOC ST
2400 LA 90021 674-H1
MODOC TR
- Ago 91301 588-B5
MOFFATT ST
600 SPAS 91030 595-G4
MOHALL LN
10500 LACo 90604 707-F5
MOHAVE ROSE DR
42000 LAN 93536 4104-D6
42000 LACo 93536 4104-D5
MOHAWK
- Ago 91301 587-G4
- CLAR 91711 571-F3
3200 Top 90290 560-B6
MOHAWK AV
- THO 91362 557-A2
11200 Chat 91311 500-A1
MOHAWK CIR
7400 BPK 90620 767-G2
MOHAWK ST
1000 Echo 90026 594-D7
2300 PAS 91107 566-E5
3700 LACo 91107 566-H4
MOHEGAN
- Ago 91301 587-G4
MOHICAN DR
6500 BPK 90620 767-F2
42800 LACo 93532 4102-E4
MOJAVE TR
21700 Chat 91311 500-A1
MOJAVE SCENIC DR
1900 SBdC 92397 (4652-F4 See Page 4651)
MOLETTE ST
10400 BLF 90706 736-D4
10800 NRWK 90650 736-E4
12600 NRWK 90650 737-A4
13000 SFSP 90670 737-B4
MOLINA LN
1600 LA 90248 763-J2
MOLINAR AV
600 LPUE 91744 638-E5
MOLINE DR
12200 LACo 90604 707-F7
12200 LACo 90604 737-F1

MOLINO AV
- LBCH 90803 825-H1
300 LBCH 90814 795-H7
300 LBCH 90814 825-H1
700 LBCH 90804 795-H7
2200 SIGH 90755 795-H4
N MOLINO AV
1300 LBCH 90804 795-H5
1800 SIGH 90755 795-H5
MOLINO ST
400 LA 90013 634-H5
W MOLLY CT
1100 UPL 91786 601-J1
MOLLYKNOLL AV
9900 WHIT 90603 707-J4
11300 LACo 90604 707-J6
MOLOKAI
- SCTA 91321 4641-C3
MOLONY RD
1800 WCOV 91792 638-H4
10700 CULC 90230 672-H5
MOMAX ST
- AZU 91702 598-G1
N MONA BLVD
1300 COMP 90222 734-J3
S MONA BLVD
3000 COMP 90222 704-J7
3000 COMP 90222 734-J1
3000 LYN 90262 704-J7
10700 LYN 90059 704-H6
10700 LA 90059 704-H6
10700 Wats 90002 704-H6
10700 Wats 90059 704-H6
10700 Wbrk 90059 704-H6
12000 Wbrk 90222 704-J7
12000 Wbrk 90222 734-J1
MONA CT
43700 LAN 93535 4106-B1
MONACAN PL
43000 LACo 93532 4102-E4
MONACO CT
10600 WHIT 90603 677-D4
30800 WLKV 91362 557-G6
MONACO DR
- PMDL 93552 4287-C1
1200 Brwd 90049 631-D3
1200 PacP 90272 631-D3
9500 CYP 90630 767-C7
17200 CRTS 90703 736-J7
MONACO LN
5000 PMDL 93552 4287-A1
MONACO WY
- LMRD 90638 737-G4
MONAKEA
- SCTA 91321 4641-C3
MONARCA DR
4600 Tarz 91356 560-F4
MONARCH CT
900 WAL 91789 639-E6
MONARCH DR
800 LCF 91011 535-C7
MONARCH ST
37400 PMDL 93552 4287-B3
MONARCH RIDGE DR
- SCTA 91351 4551-F4
MONCADO DR
1100 GLDL 91207 564-G2
MONDAVI WY
- Nor 91326 500-E1
MONDELL PINE AV
- PMDL 93551 4195-E6
MONDINO DR
17500 RowH 91748 678-G5
MONDO DR
500 LACo 90631 708-D3
MONDON AV
11200 SFSP 90670 706-G6
11300 NRWK 90650 706-G6
11300 SFSP 90650 706-G6
MONDORF RD
700 SBdC 92372 (4472-B6 See Page 4471)
MONERO DR
6100 RPV 90275 792-H6
MONET AV
4100 WdHl 91364 560-A6
MONET LN
- SCTA 91355 4550-D3
MONET PL
11800 CRTS 90703 766-H3
MONETA AV
19600 CRSN 90745 764-C3
22500 CRSN 90745 794-C1
MONETTE PL
3200 LA 90006 633-H4
MONICA AV
3500 LBCH 90808 766-J7
MONICA CIR
16200 CRTS 90703 736-E6
MONICA CT
1700 RowH 91748 678-H5
MONICA WY
900 WAL 91789 639-F5
MONIQUE WY
8200 CYP 90630 767-B4
E MONITA ST
6200 LBCH 90803 796-E7
MONITEAU PL
2100 DBAR 91765 679-J5
MONITOR AV
2000 LBCH 90810 795-A4
11100 LA 90059 704-G6

E MONLACO RD
3500 LBCH 90808 766-B7
MONMOUTH AV
2600 LA 90007 634-B7
MONMOUTH WY
- PRV 90660 676-H1
MONNOW RD
33000 Actn 93510 4374-A7
MONO CIR
2500 LVRN 91750 600-H1
MONO RD
800 SBdC 92372 (4472-B3 See Page 4471)
3500 SBdC 92371 (4472-J3 See Page 4471)
MONO ST
1300 Boyl 90033 634-J4
MONOGRAM AV
2400 LBCH 90815 796-E3
3000 LBCH 90808 796-E1
3300 LBCH 90808 766-E6
4100 LKWD 90713 766-E5
8700 LA 91343 501-E4
8700 LA 91343 531-E1
10300 GmH 91344 501-E1
11600 GmH 91344 481-E7
MONON ST
1900 LFlz 90027 594-B3
MONOVALE DR
100 BelA 90077 592-D7
MONROE AV
100 POM 91767 600-J7
5400 SGAT 90280 705-F7
7000 BPK 90620 767-G5
W MONROE AV
2800 ANA 92801 767-H5
MONROE CIR
7000 BPK 90620 767-G5
MONROE CT
200 AZU 91702 568-J3
MONROE LN
44300 LAN 93536 4015-C7
MONROE PL
- PMDL 93550 4286-C4
200 MNRO 91016 567-G3
MONROE ST
- CRTS 90703 766-H3
4000 LA 90029 594-A6
4500 LA 90029 593-J6
5300 LA 90038 593-H6
5700 CHNO 91710 641-H6
7500 PRM 90723 735-G5
29700 Cstc 91384 4459-C7
E MONROE ST
2500 CRSN 90810 764-J5
2500 CRSN 90810 765-A5
MONROE WY
- PMDL 93551 4195-D5
MONROVIA AV
200 LBCH 90803 826-B1
400 LBCH 90814 796-B7
11600 LYN 90262 705-A7
MONROVIA PL
- AZU 91702 569-B5
- GLDR 91702 569-B5
- GLDR 91741 569-B5
MONROVIA CANYON TKTR
- DUAR 91010 (538-C2 See Page 507)
- LACo - (538-C2 See Page 507)
- MNRO 91016 (538-B6 See Page 507)
700 MNRO 91016 537-H7
700 MNRO 91016 567-H1
MONROVISTA AV
400 MNRO 91016 567-H6
MONSON LN
300 SGBL 91776 596-D4
MONTAGUE CT
17900 GmH 91344 481-A5
MONTAGUE LN
10000 Pcma 91331 502-F4
MONTAGUE ST
12100 Pcma 91331 502-E5
13800 Pcma 91331 532-B1
MONTAIGNE WY
4000 LACo 90274 793-C6
MONTAIR AV
1800 LBCH 90815 796-C2
3000 LBCH 90808 796-C2
3400 LBCH 90808 766-C4
4900 LKWD 90712 766-C3
MONTAIRE PL
6500 LPMA 90623 767-D1
MONTALCINO WY
- Nor 91326 500-C1
MONTALLEGRO ST
- LAN 93536 4104-J6
MONTALVO ST
3600 LA 90065 594-J5
3600 LA 90065 595-A5
MONTANA
2200 WCOV 91792 679-H2
MONTANA AV
100 MNRO 91016 567-G5
100 SMCA 90403 671-C1
100 SMCA 90402 671-C1
800 SMCA 90403 631-F6
800 SMCA 90402 631-F6
11100 Wwd 90024 631-F6
11100 Brwd 90049 631-J2

STREET
Block City ZIP Pg-Grid

MONTANA AV
11600 Brwd 90049 631-H2
E MONTANA AV
15700 LPUE 91744 638-D6
MONTANA DR
- PMDL 93551 4104-D6
MONTANA LN
1000 CLAR 91711 571-F6
MONTANA PL N
100 SMCA 90402 671-C1
MONTANA PL S
2900 SMCA 90403 631-F5
MONTANA ST
400 MNRO 91016 567-F5
1300 Echo 90026 594-D7
1300 Echo 90026 634-F1
E MONTANA ST
- PAS 91103 535-H7
200 PAS 91104 535-J7
W MONTANA ST
- PAS 91103 535-G7
MONTANA WY
- SCTA 91354 4550-F1
MONTANA CALVA CIR
9500 PRV 90660 676-H4
MONTANERO AV
17000 CRSN 90746 734-F7
MONTANZA WY
9500 BPK 90620 767-G7
MONTARA AV
9900 SGAT 90280 705-A5
MONTARA RD
8100 SBdC 92371 (4562-J3
See Page 4471)
10300 SBdC 92371 (4472-J2
See Page 4471)
MONTAU DR
19800 Top 90290 630-B1
MONTBROOK ST
16100 LACo 91744 638-F5
MONT CALABASAS DR
- Ago 91301 558-G3
- LACo 91302 558-G3
MONTCALM AV
2800 LA 90046 593-C1
MONTCLAIR CIR
5300 LPMA 90623 767-D2
MONTCLAIR CT
- PMDL 93552 4287-E2
MONTCLAIR ST
3100 LA 90018 633-F7
MONTE PL
200 ARCD 91006 537-D7
MONTE ST
15100 LA 91342 481-G2
MONT EAGLE PL
4300 Eagl 90041 594-J1
4500 Eagl 90041 595-A1
MONTE ALTO PL
16600 PacP 90272 630-G1
N MONTEBELLO BLVD
100 MTBL 90640 676-D2
500 MTBL 90640 636-F6
500 RSMD 90640 636-F6
500 RSMD 91770 636-F6
S MONTEBELLO BLVD
100 MTBL 90640 676-C4
E MONTEBELLO PKWY
5800 ELA 90022 675-J1
MONTEBELLO WY
400 MTBL 90640 676-D3
MONTE BONITO DR
5000 Eagl 90041 565-C5
MONTE CARLO CT
3300 LAN 93536 4105-B3
MONTECHICO DR
300 MONP 91754 636-A2
MONTE CIELO CT
1600 BHLS 90210 592-F4
1600 LA 90210 592-F4
MONTE CIELO DR
1200 BHLS 90210 592-F4
1200 LA 90210 592-F4
MONTECILLO DR
- RHE 90274 793-G7
MONTECITO AV
- SMAD 91024 567-A2
E MONTECITO AV
200 SMAD 91024 567-B2
W MONTECITO AV
- SMAD 91024 567-A2
200 SMAD 91024 566-J2
MONTECITO CIR
- LPMA 90623 767-B3
1300 LA 90031 595-C5
MONTECITO CT
- DUAR 91010 568-A4
- SMAD 91024 567-A2
MONTECITO DR
400 LA 90031 595-B5
500 SGBL 91776 596-D5
1900 GLDL 91208 534-H5
2100 SMRO 91108 566-D7
10800 ELMN 91731 597-C6
MONTECITO PL
- SCTA 91354 4460-G4
MONTECITO RD
11500 OrCo 90720 796-J5
12200 SLB 90740 796-J5
MONTECITO ST
2700 LA 90031 595-B6
21300 WAL 91789 639-B4

MONTECITO WY
400 AZU 91702 568-H4
5700 CYP 90630 767-E7
MONTECLARO DR
2300 CHLS 91709 680-J2
MONTE COLLINS WY
- LALM 90720 796-J2
MONTE CRISTO AV
16600 CRTS 90703 737-A6
MONTE CRISTO DR
16400 HacH 91745 678-D6
MONTE DIABLO LN
- POM 91766 640-D4
MONTEEL RD
8100 LA 90046 593-A5
8100 LA 90069 593-A5
MONTEFINO AV
1200 DBAR 91765 680-B3
MONTEFINO DR
4600 CYP 90630 767-B7
MONTEGO DR
1000 Brwd 90049 591-G7
MONTE GRANDE PL
1400 PacP 90272 630-G1
MONTE GRIGIO DR
200 PacP 90272 630-F5
MONTE HERMOSO
16600 PacP 90272 630-G2
MONTEITH DR
3700 LACo 90043 673-C4
MONTE LADO DR
30700 MAL 90265 627-A7
MONTE LEON DR
800 BHLS 90210 592-G6
MONTE LEON LN
9300 BHLS 90210 592-G6
MONTE LEON WY
11700 Nor 91326 480-G7
MONTELEONE AV
800 VeCo 91377 557-H1
MONTELL CT
19000 RowH 91748 679-C4
MONTELLANO AV
2700 HacH 91745 677-J4
2700 HacH 91745 678-A4
3000 PMDL 93551 4195-B4
MONTELLO DR
42600 LACo 93532 4102-F4
E MONTELLO DR
300 AZU 91702 568-J4
MONTEMALAGA DR
5300 RPV 90275 793-A5
5800 RPV 90275 792-J5
MONTEMALAGA PZ
2300 PVE 90274 792-H5
MONTE MAR DR
9000 LA 90035 632-G4
10100 LA 90064 632-F5
MONTE MAR PL
2600 LA 90064 632-G5
MONTE MAR TER
2700 LA 90064 632-F5
MONTE MAR VISTA DR
700 FUL 92832 738-F6
MONTE NIDO DR
500 LACo 91302 589-A7
25600 LACo 91302 629-A1
MONTE ORO DR
16600 WHIT 90603 708-A3
MONTE PLACENTIA WY
1300 LA 90210 592-E5
MONTE PUESTO DR
9300 WHIT 90603 707-J2
MONTERA AV
3000 PMDL 93551 4195-C4
MONTERA DR
2000 HacH 91745 678-C4
MONTEREINA DR
2100 RPV 90275 823-H1
MONTEREY AV
- SCTA 91355 4550-E4
600 MNRO 91016 567-F5
1500 BURB 91506 533-D6
2500 BURB 91505 533-B6
3600 ELMN 91731 597-C7
3700 BALD 91706 598-A4
9400 BLF 90706 736-B7
E MONTEREY AV
100 POM 91767 640-J1
200 POM 91767 641-B1
W MONTEREY AV
100 POM 91768 640-H1
MONTEREY BLVD
- HMB 90254 762-G1
MONTEREY CIR
25300 LMTA 90717 793-J4
MONTEREY CT
- MNRO 91016 567-E4
- MANB 90266 732-H4
1400 DUAR 91010 568-B5
30400 Cstc 91384 4459-F2
MONTEREY DR
200 CRSN 90745 794-D4
MONTEREY LN
- LMRD 90638 738-A2
- SMAD 91024 567-C2
7100 LPMA 90623 767-C2
MONTEREY PL
600 SMAD 91024 567-C2
1300 SMRO 91108 596-B2
2300 BURB 91506 533-D6
2500 FUL 92833 738-B6
5700 PMDL 93552 4287-C2

MONTEREY RD
100 GLDL 91206 564-E3
100 SPAS 91030 595-E2
1300 SLB 90740 826-G2
2100 SPAS 91030 596-B1
2100 SMRO 91108 595-G2
2100 SMRO 91108 596-B1
3400 LA 90032 595-D4
4300 HiPk 90042 595-E2
MONTEREY ST
1000 LHB 90631 708-C4
2500 TOR 90501 763-F7
2500 TOR 90503 763-F7
4100 LA 90065 595-A4
5700 LVRN 91750 570-G4
10200 BLF 90706 736-D7
N MONTEREY ST
200 ALH 91801 596-A3
S MONTEREY ST
- ALH 91801 596-B4
1800 ALH 91801 636-C1
MONTEREY PARK DR
1700 LACo 91770 636-E3
MONTEREY PASS RD
100 MONP 91754 635-G4
MONTEREY PINE CT
- HacH 91745 678-F6
MONTEREY PINES DR
- ARCD 91006 567-D2
MONTEREY PINES LN
- LACo 91387 4552-B4
MONTERO AV
12300 LA 91342 482-A2
MONTEROSA AV
3300 Alta 91001 536-A4
MONTEROSA DR
3500 Alta 91001 536-A3
MONTE ROYALE DR
2300 CHLS 91709 680-J2
MONTERRA WY
600 BPK 90620 767-F7
MONTERREY DR
100 CLAR 91711 571-D7
MONTESANO ST
15200 HacH 91745 677-J5
MONTESINO DR
9300 WHIT 90603 707-J2
MONTE VERDE AV
4200 SBdC 91766 641-E3
MONTE VERDE DR
- SIGH 90755 795-G4
800 ARCD 91007 566-J4
800 ARCD 91007 567-A5
1200 LACo 91107 566-J4
2800 LACo 91724 639-E1
2800 WCOV 91791 599-E7
2800 WCOV 91791 639-E1
2800 LACo 91724 599-E7
MONTEVERDE DR
13400 CHLS 91709 680-H2
MONTE VERDE ST
- MTCL 91762 641-G3
4500 MTCL 91763 641-E3
MONTEVIDEO DR
14600 WHIT 90605 707-F2
MONTE VIENTO DR
1500 LACo 90265 629-E2
MONTE VISTA
4900 ELMN 91731 597-D4
4900 ELMN 91780 597-D4
MONTE VISTA AV
100 COV 91723 599-D6
200 MTCL 91763 601-F7
200 UPL 91763 601-F2
200 UPL 91786 601-F2
500 GLDL 91202 564-D2
1100 CLAR 91711 601-F2
1400 CLAR 91711 571-F7
10300 MTCL 91763 641-F4
11000 SBdC 91710 641-F4
11100 SBdC 91763 641-F4
11700 CHNO 91710 641-F6
26200 LMTA 90717 793-H6
37000 PMDL 93550 4286-F4
N MONTE VISTA AV
100 SDMS 91773 600-B1
900 SDMS 91773 570-B7
S MONTE VISTA AV
- SDMS 91773 600-B2
MONTEVISTA CIR
- BqtC 91354 4460-E6
MONTE VISTA DR
10800 WHIT 90601 677-A4
22100 Top 90290 590-A6
22200 Top 90290 589-J6
MONTE VISTA LN
- SMAD 91024 567-B3
MONTE VISTA RD
300 ARCD 91007 566-J5
MONTE VISTA ST
1400 PAS 91106 566-C3
1800 PAS 91107 566-D3
4800 HiPk 90042 595-B3
N MONTE VISTA ST
100 LHB 90631 708-D5
S MONTE VISTA ST
100 LHB 90631 708-D6
MONTE VISTA WK
6100 HiPk 90042 595-E4
MONTE VISTA WY
9600 LA 90210 592-E5
MONTEZUMA AV
2100 ALH 91803 635-J1

MONTEZUMA AV
3000 MONP 91754 635-G2
MONTEZUMA PL
1700 Echo 90026 634-D1
MONTEZUMA ST
5000 HiPk 90042 595-B2
S MONTEZUMA WY
300 WCOV 91791 639-B1
MONTFORD ST
12600 Pcma 91331 482-E7
12900 Pcma 91331 502-D1
MONTGOMERY AV
1400 GLDL 91202 564-C2
6400 VanN 91406 531-F6
9900 LA 91343 501-F5
10200 GrnH 91344 501-F2
MONTGOMERY CIR
1300 CLAR 91711 601-E1
MONTGOMERY CT
- PMDL 93550 4286-H4
MONTGOMERY DR
900 HMB 90254 762-H2
MONTGOMERY RD
9200 Chat 91311 499-F7
MONTGOMERY ST
12200 DWNY 90242 705-J7
MONTICELLO AV
5500 BPK 90621 738-A6
MONTICELLO DR
11700 LMRD 90638 707-G7
MONTICELLO RD
2600 CLAR 91711 571-D5
MONTICELLO ST
5700 CHNO 91710 641-H5
W MONTICELLO ST
1200 ONT 91762 641-J5
MONTIFLORA AV
1800 Eagl 90041 565-A6
MONTLAKE DR
2700 LA 90068 563-F7
2700 LA 90068 593-F2
MONTLINE LN
800 BelA 90077 592-B6
MONTMARTE CT
43000 LAN 93536 4105-B3
MONTOLLA LN
26100 SCTA 91355 4550-F4
MONTREAL ST
100 PdlR 90293 702-A3
MONTROBLES PL
1800 SMRO 91108 596-A2
MONTROSE
12400 ELMN 91732 637-G1
MONTROSE AV
600 SPAS 91030 595-J2
2000 GLDL 91020 534-F2
2000 Mont 91020 534-H3
2800 GLDL 91214 534-E1
2800 LaCr 91214 534-F2
3600 GLDL 91214 504-D7
S MONTROSE AV
- UPL 91786 601-H4
MONTROSE LN
1000 SPAS 91030 595-J2
2200 GLDL 91020 534-H3
MONTROSE ST
1800 Echo 90026 594-D7
MONTSERRAT CT
13400 CHLS 91709 680-H1
MONTURA DR
23200 DBAR 91765 680-B1
MONTUSO PL
3700 Enc 91436 561-C6
MONTVIEW CT
- BqtC 91354 4460-E4
2700 WLKV 91361 557-A7
E MONTWOOD AV
100 LHB 90631 738-E1
W MONTWOOD AV
100 LHB 90631 738-E1
MONUMENT ST
900 PacP 90272 631-A4
MONUMENT CANYON DR
23500 DBAR 91765 680-C2
MOODY PL
- CLAR 91711 571-F3
MOODY ST
7500 LPMA 90623 767-C7
8500 LPMA 90630 767-C7
8600 CYP 90630 767-C7
14600 PanC 91402 501-J5
MOODY CANYON TKTR
- Actn 93510 4465-A7
- Actn 93510 (4555-B3
See Page 4466)
- LACo - (4555-A6
See Page 4466)
- LACo - 4645-A1
MOOMAT AHIKO WY
1500 SMCA 90401 671-E3
MOON AV
700 LA 90065 595-A3
24600 LMTA 90717 793-G3
MOONBEAM AV
8700 PanC 91402 502-A6
8700 PanC 91402 532-A1
MOONBEAM CIR
1900 UPL 91784 571-J5
MOONBEAM DR
900 MONP 91754 635-J5
MOONBEAM PL
1500 FUL 92833 738-C5

MOONCREST CIR
800 BREA 92821 708-J4
MOONCREST DR
16800 Enc 91436 561-C5
MOON CREST LN
14600 CHLS 91709 680-J5
MOONCREST PL
4200 Enc 91436 561-C5
MOONDANCE DR
37900 PMDL 93552 4287-A2
MOON DUST CT
- LACo 91390 4461-A2
MOON DUST DR
2400 CHLS 91709 680-J5
MOONEY DR
200 MONP 91755 636-C3
900 LACo 91770 636-E3
MOONFLOWER CT
2000 PMDL 93550 4286-D3
MOONGATE DR
6000 RPV 90275 792-J7
MOONGLOW CIR
17300 CRTS 90703 736-J7
MOONHILL RD
11400 LACo 91342 482-H5
MOONLAKE ST
20700 DBAR 91789 679-G3
MOONLIGHT CT
2000 PMDL 93550 4286-D3
MOONLIGHT PL
30000 Cstc 91384 4459-H4
MOONLIGHT SUMMIT DR
1100 DBAR 91765 640-D5
MOONMIST DR
- RPV 90275 823-C3
MOONRAKER RD
4500 PMDL 93552 4287-A2
MOONRIDGE CT
- AZU 91702 568-J1
- AZU 91702 569-A1
1500 UPL 91784 571-H3
MOONRIDGE DR
11500 LACo 90601 677-C3
15400 Shrm 91403 561-G6
MOONRIDGE LN
- PMDL 93550 4286-E3
27700 Cstc 91384 4459-G1
MOONRIDGE TER
9500 LA 90210 592-F1
S MOONRISE DR
100 LACo 90265 629-E1
100 LACo 91302 629-E1
W MOONRISE DR
- LACo 90265 629-E1
MOON RISE LN
14600 CHLS 91709 680-G5
MOON SHADOW CIR
19800 WAL 91789 639-E4
MOON SHADOWS DR
23400 LACo 90265 629-E2
MOONSHADOWS RANCH RD
- PMDL 93550 4376-E4
MOONSTONE
300 LBCH 90803 826-C1
MOONSTONE CT
2800 LA 90032 595-C7
MOONSTONE DR
2800 SIGH 90755 795-H4
4200 LA 90032 595-C7
MOONSTONE ST
100 MANB 90266 732-E3
1600 BREA 92821 708-H7
MOONSTONE WY
- GAR 90247 734-A3
MOON VIEW DR
2100 HacH 91745 678-F5
MOONVIEW ST
40400 PMDL 93551 4194-G2
MOONWORT TER
- PMDL 93551 4285-D4
MOORBROOK AV
16600 CRTS 90703 737-C6
MOORCROFT AV
5900 WdHl 91367 559-J1
6500 CanP 91303 529-J4
7600 LA 91304 529-J1
8800 LA 91304 499-J7
MOORCROFT PL
8700 LA 91304 529-J1
MOORE AV
2300 FUL 92833 738-B6
N MOORE AV
100 MONP 91754 636-B2
S MOORE AV
100 MONP 91754 636-B3
MOORE DR
6400 LA 90048 633-A3
MOORE LN
- StvR 91381 4550-B7
MOORE PL
300 SDMS 91773 600-C2
MOORE ST
2200 LA 90039 594-E5
3300 LA 90066 672-A3
3900 CULC 90066 672-C5
4500 GLDL 91214 504-D6
12800 CRTS 90703 737-A6
MOORE CANYON RD
- CanP 91307 529-C7
23600 VeCo 91302 529-C7
23600 VeCo 91307 529-C7

MOOREHAVEN DR
400 CRSN 90746 734-D7
MOORELAND DR
13200 WHIT 90602 707-D1
MOORESQUE DR
300 PAS 91105 565-E4
MOORGATE DR
4400 LPMA 90623 767-B4
MOORGATE RD
9600 LA 90210 592-C1
MOORHEN CT
24500 SCTA 91355 4550-E4
MOORLAND PL
2600 WCOV 91792 638-J7
2600 WCOV 91792 639-A7
MOORPARK ST
10000 LA 91602 563-A4
11100 LA 91602 562-G4
11400 LA 91604 562-E4
11700 LA 91607 562-G4
13100 Shrm 91423 562-B4
14400 Shrm 91403 562-A4
14600 Shrm 91403 561-H4
15500 Enc 91436 561-D3
MOORPARK WY
4400 LA 91602 563-B4
MOORSHIRE DR
- CRTS 90703 767-A3
MOORSHIRE PL
- CRTS 90703 767-B2
MOORSIDE DR
900 GLDL 91207 564-F1
MOPENA WY
- Nor 91326 500-C1
MORA CT
- LAN 93536 4013-J5
2600 LAN 93535 4016-E5
MORA DR
11900 SFSP 90670 706-H5
MORADA AV
4000 LACo 91722 598-G5
N MORADA AV
100 WCOV 91790 598-G6
700 LACo 91722 598-G6
MORADA PL
700 Alta 91001 536-A7
MORADA ST
5200 IRW 91706 598-G2
MORAGA DR
800 Brwd 90049 591-G6
800 Brwd 90049 631-H1
2700 BelA 90077 591-H1
MORAGA LN
11700 Brwd 90049 591-H6
MORAINE AV
3600 CLAR 91711 571-F5
MORAY AV
1900 LA 90732 823-H7
MORE CT
18500 SCTA 91351 4551-G7
MOREA WY
22300 WdHl 91367 559-H7
MOREHART AV
8500 SunV 91352 532-F1
8800 SunV 91352 502-E7
9100 Pcma 91331 502-C4
MOREHOUSE DR
18800 CRSN 90746 764-E2
MOREHOUSE ST
12200 ELMN 91732 637-E3
12600 ELMN 91732 637-F4
MORELAND DR
1900 LACo 90210 592-E3
MORELIA AV
2000 FUL 92835 738-G4
E MORELIA DR
600 CLAR 91711 601-E2
MORELIA PL
2300 FUL 92835 738-G3
MORELLA AV
4400 LA 91607 562-H1
6000 NHol 91606 532-G7
6800 NHol 91605 532-G3
MORENO AV
500 Brwd 90049 631-F5
700 LVRN 91750 600-E1
3400 LVRN 91750 570-E7
MORENO DR
1500 GLDL 91207 564-G2
2100 LA 90039 594-D3
25900 SCTA 91355 4550-G4
S MORENO DR
100 BHLS 90212 632-E2
100 CenC 90067 632-E2
MORENO ST
4400 MTCL 91763 601-E4
5600 MTCL 91786 601-E4
MORESBY DR
4600 TOR 90505 763-B7
MORETON ST
2400 TOR 90505 793-F3
MORGAN AV
1800 BURB 91504 533-F5
1800 CLAR 91711 571-C7
3200 LA 90011 674-F3
MORGAN CIR
- MTCL 91763 641-E1
MORGAN CT
21100 WAL 91789 639-H6
MORGAN LN
- Actn 93510 4375-E7
- FUL 92833 738-D5
- RHLS 90274 823-B1

MORGAN LN
1100 HMB 90254 762-J2
1100 RBCH 90278 762-J2
1800 RBCH 90278 763-A2
MORGAN RD
11300 LACo 91390 4373-D7
MORGAN ST
- PMDL 93551 4195-A6
4100 BALD 91706 598-A5
5400 SBdC 91762 641-H3
MORGAN WY
2000 LVRN 91750 570-G6
6300 BPK 90620 767-E3
MORGANFIELD AV
3600 WAL 91789 679-D2
3600 WCOV 91792 679-D2
MORGAN HILL CIR
2000 LA 90068 593-G3
MORGAN HILL DR
2000 LA 90068 593-G3
MORGAN RANCH DR
2200 GLDR 91741 570-A5
MORGAN RANCH RD
100 GLDR 91741 570-A4
100 GLDR 91741 569-J5
MORIAH LN
- Saug 91350 4461-F5
MORIAH RD
- LA 90068 563-G4
MORISAN AV
1700 PMDL 93550 4286-D4
MORISAN CT
1600 PMDL 93550 4286-D4
MORITZ DR
3100 HNTB 92649 826-J6
MORLAN PL
- ARCD 91007 567-C5
MORLEY AV
6200 LA 90056 673-B6
6200 LadH 90056 673-B6
MORLEY ST
5700 Wch 90045 702-J4
MORMON CANYON MTWY
- Nor 91326 480-C5
MORNING AV
10300 DWNY 90241 706-A3
11600 DWNY 90241 705-J5
12000 DWNY 90242 705-J6
12800 DWNY 90242 735-H1
MORNING CIR
37300 PMDL 93550 4286-H3
MORNING CANYON RD
1700 DBAR 91765 679-J4
MORNING DEW DR
2400 BREA 92821 709-E6
MORNING DEW LN
1500 CHLS 91709 680-F4
MORNING DEW ST
- PMDL 93551 4195-D5
MORNING DOVE PL
- BREA 92823 709-H6
MORNINGFLOWER CIR
100 BREA 92821 709-D7
MORNING GLORY PL
- Cstc 91384 4459-H3
MORNING GLORY ST
100 BREA 92821 709-F7
MORNING GLOW WY
8900 SunV 91352 503-C7
MORNING GROVE LN
- WAL 91789 639-C5
MORNING MIST DR
- StvR 91381 4640-B2
MORNINGRAIN AV
12400 CRTS 90703 736-J7
MORNINGSIDE
12400 ELMN 91732 637-G1
MORNINGSIDE AV
1400 UPL 91784 571-H4
2000 LAN 93535 4106-D1
MORNINGSIDE CIR
- LVRN 91750 570-G5
400 FUL 92835 738-H4
MORNINGSIDE CT
900 SFER 91340 482-B7
1400 Hlwd 90028 593-F5
1800 AZU 91702 568-H2
MORNINGSIDE DR
100 WAL 91789 639-H7
800 FUL 92835 738-J3
1100 CLAR 91711 601-A1
1300 BURB 91506 563-G3
2500 HMB 90254 762-G1
2700 HMB 90254 732-G7
3300 MANB 90266 732-G7
11100 WHIT 90603 708-A6
28900 Cstc 91384 4459-C6
N MORNINGSIDE DR
100 MANB 90266 732-F6
S MORNINGSIDE DR
- MANB 90266 732-G7
MORNINGSIDE ST
- NLB 90805 765-D3
E MORNINGSIDE ST
2500 PAS 91107 566-E5
MORNINGSIDE TER
300 PMDL 93551 4285-H1
MORNINGSIDE WY
1200 Ven 90291 671-J4
1300 Ven 90291 672-A3
13000 LA 90066 672-A3

MORNING STAR CT
- SBdC 92397 (4652-E3
See Page 4651)
MORNING STAR WY
- LACo 91390 4461-A1
MORNING SUN AV
1600 DBAR 91789 679-F4
1600 LACo 91789 679-F4
MORNING SUN DR
1100 POM 91767 641-C1
MORNING TERRACE DR
1500 CHLS 91709 680-G3
MORNINGTON DR
24300 SCTA 91355 4550-E6
MORNING VIEW DR
14100 CHLS 91709 680-J3
30000 MAL 90265 667-B1
MORO BAY DR
28900 RPV 90275 823-A1
MOROCCO LN
9300 WHil 91304 499-E7
MORPATH LN
1100 GLDR 91740 599-H1
MORRILL AV
5800 WHIT 90606 676-J5
5800 WHIT 90606 677-A4
6000 LACo 90606 676-J5
8300 LACo 90606 706-H1
9000 SFSP 90670 706-G2
MORRIS AV
2100 LHB 90631 708-B5
N MORRIS AV
200 WCOV 91790 598-E5
MORRIS PL
300 MTBL 90640 676-B1
500 MTBL 90640 636-B7
MORRISON AV
12800 LA 91607 562-E3
MORRISON ST
1700 POM 91766 640-H4
10800 NHol 91601 563-A3
11100 NHol 91601 562-H3
12100 LA 91607 562-E3
13100 Shrm 91423 562-B3
14500 Shrm 91403 562-A3
14500 Shrm 91403 561-G3
15400 Enc 91436 561-D3
MORRISON RANCH RD
- Ago 91301 558-F4
26400 CALB 91302 558-F4
26400 LACo 91302 558-F4
MORRISSEY WY
- SCTA 91350 4550-H5
MORRO DR
200 CRSN 90745 794-C1
4100 WdHl 91364 560-B4
17600 RowH 91748 678-H5
MORRO PL
1100 LBCH 90813 795-D6
MORRO BAY DR
- SCTA 91354 4550-H1
MORROW PL
1300 ELA 90022 675-G2
MORSE AV
4400 LA 91604 562-E4
4600 Shrm 91423 562-E3
6100 NHol 91606 532-D6
6700 NHol 91605 532-D2
MORSE DR
1600 LA 90732 823-H6
MORSLAY RD
2300 Alta 91001 536-C5
MORTIMER AV
2100 HNTP 90255 674-H7
MORTON AV
900 PAS 91103 565-H2
1500 Echo 90026 594-F6
7900 Flor 90001 704-G2
MORTON CIR
1300 CLAR 91711 601-E1
MORTON PL
1400 Echo 90026 594-F6
MORTON TER
1500 Echo 90026 594-E6
MORTON WK
1700 Echo 90026 594-F7
MORVALE DR
2900 VeCo 91361 586-D2
MORVEN ST
1000 LAN 93535 4016-B6
MORY ST
8600 DWNY 90242 706-A7
MOSBY ST
23000 WdHl 91364 559-G4
MOSCADA AV
1000 LACo 91789 679-E3
MOSHER AV
4300 LA 90031 595-B5
MOSLEY AV
6200 LA 90056 673-B6
6200 LadH 90056 673-B6
MOSS AV
- SMCA 90401 671-E3
1200 UPL 91784 571-J3
2100 LA 90065 594-G2
MOSS CIR
2400 LVRN 91750 600-H3
MOSS ST
1100 BURB 91502 563-J2
N MOSS ST
400 BURB 91502 533-G7
MOSSBANK DR
5900 RPV 90275 792-J6

MOSSBANK DR
26300 RPV 90275 793-A6
W MOSSBERG AV
1300 WCOV 91790 638-D1
2200 WCOV 91790 598-D7
MOSSBERG ST
14200 BALD 91706 598-B6
MOSSDALE AV
15600 LACo 93535 4109-E7
MOSSDALE CT
- AZU 91702 568-J2
MOSSY ROCK CIR
10200 BelA 90077 592-A1
MOTOR AV
2400 LA 90064 632-F4
3200 LA 90034 632-F6
3400 LA 90034 672-F1
3700 LA 90232 672-F1
4100 CULC 90232 672-G2
S MOTOR AV
100 AZU 91702 568-F7
100 AZU 91702 598-F1
MOTOR LN
1000 LAN 93534 4105-G2
MOTOR PL
10100 LA 90064 632-F5
MOTOR ST
- Cstc 91384 4459-J3
- Cstc 91384 4460-A3
MOTT ST
600 SFER 91340 502-A1
1200 SFER 91340 481-J7
1200 SFER 91340 482-A7
N MOTT ST
100 Boyl 90033 635-B4
S MOTT ST
100 Boyl 90033 635-B6
600 LA 90023 635-A7
MOTTLEY DR
15000 LMRD 90638 737-H4
MOTZ ST
6500 PRM 90723 735-E5
MOULTON AV
600 LA 90031 634-J2
MOUND AV
500 SPAS 91030 595-H1
MOUND ST
2000 LA 90068 593-F3
MOUND VIEW AV
3500 LA 91604 562-G6
MOUND VIEW PL
12000 LA 91604 562-G6
MOUNT ST
600 DBAR 91765 680-B1
MOUNTAIN AV
600 POM 91767 601-C6
600 POM 91767 641-C1
1200 DUAR 91010 567-J7
1200 MNRO 91016 567-J7
1700 MNRO 91010 567-J7
1900 CLAR 91711 601-C6
1900 LACo 91010 567-J7
2300 LaCr 91214 534-G1
2400 IRW 91010 567-J7
2400 IRW 91010 597-H1
2500 IRW 91706 597-H1
2500 SBdC 91784 571-J1
2700 LACo - (541-H7
See Page 511)
2700 SBdC 91784 (541-H7
See Page 511)
2800 SBdC - (541-H7
See Page 511)
2900 CLAR 91711 571-J1
N MOUNTAIN AV
- UPL 91786 601-J2
100 CLAR 91711 601-B3
100 MNRO 91016 567-J2
100 ONT 91762 601-J6
100 ONT 91762 641-J1
1400 UPL 91786 571-J4
1700 CLAR 91711 571-B5
1900 UPL 91784 571-J4
2300 SBdC 91784 571-J2
2300 LACo 91711 571-B7
N MOUNTAIN AV Rt#-30
1600 UPL 91784 571-J7
S MOUNTAIN AV
- UPL 91786 601-J4
100 MNRO 91016 567-J5
100 ONT 91762 641-J4
300 POM 91767 601-C5
400 ONT 91762 601-J4
400 ONT 91786 601-J4
2100 CLAR 91711 601-C5
MOUNTAIN CT
100 BREA 92821 709-B5
MOUNTAIN DR
500 BHLS 90210 592-F6
MOUNTAIN LN
- LACo 91387 4462-C7
800 GLDR 91741 569-H3
N MOUNTAIN LN
2400 SBdC 91784 571-J2
2400 UPL 91784 571-J2
MOUNTAIN PL
800 PAS 91104 565-J3
34200 Actn 93510 4375-E4
MOUNTAIN RD
9300 SBdC 92372 (4472-B2
See Page 4471)

MOUNTAIN RD
9300 SBdC 92372 (4562-B1
See Page 4471)
E MOUNTAIN ST
- PAS 91103 565-H2
100 GLDL 91207 564-E2
200 PAS 91104 565-H2
600 PAS 91104 566-B2
1500 GLDL 91206 564-H2
1500 GLDL 91208 564-H2
W MOUNTAIN ST
- PAS 91103 565-G2
100 GLDL 91202 564-C1
800 GLDL 91202 534-B7
1400 GLDL 91201 534-B7
MOUNTAIN VW
- LACo 93534 3925-D4
- LACo 93536 3925-D4
MOUNTAIN BROOK DR
2300 HacH 91745 678-E5
MOUNTAIN CREEK RD
12400 CRTS 90703 736-J6
MOUNTAIN CREST CIR
- THO 91362 557-A1
MOUNTAIN CREST LN
12500 Brwd 90049 591-E4
MOUNTAIN CREST RD
200 DUAR 91010 568-E4
MOUNTAIN DALE CT
18800 SCTA 91321 4551-G5
MOUNTAINEER RD
20700 WAL 91789 639-G3
MOUNTAINEERING LN
800 LACo 90502 794-C3
MOUNTAINGATE DR
11900 Brwd 90049 591-E4
MOUNTAIN GATE RD
1100 UPL 91786 601-J1
MOUNTAIN GREEN DR
500 LACo 91302 588-H7
500 LACo 91302 628-H1
MOUNTAIN LAUREL WY
- AZU 91702 568-J1
22300 DBAR 91765 680-A4
MOUNTAIN MEADOW LN
5300 LCF 91011 535-B1
MOUNTAIN OAK DR
2200 LA 90068 593-H3
MOUNTAIN PARK DR
3000 CALB 91302 589-D2
MOUNTAIN PARK RD
26300 LACo 91387 4552-B6
MOUNTAIN PASS RD
25500 SCTA 91321 4551-F6
MOUNTAIN PINE DR
2600 LaCr 91214 504-F6
MOUNTAIN RANCH RD
- GrnH 91344 481-A7
MOUNTAIN RIDGE RD
- WCOV 91791 639-B4
MOUNTAIN SHADOW DR
- UPL 91784 571-G6
MOUNTAIN SHADOW RD
- UPL 91784 571-H7
31900 Actn 93510 4464-J2
MOUNTAIN SHADOWS CT
- PMDL 93551 4195-B2
MOUNTAIN SHADOWS DR
4200 LACo 90601 677-C2
MOUNTAIN SHADOWS PL
- POM 91766 640-G7
MOUNTAIN SHADOWS RD
3600 CALB 91301 588-G1
MOUNTAINSIDE DR
37700 PMDL 93550 4285-J2
MOUNTAIN SPRING ST
14600 HacH 91745 677-J1
15000 HacH 91745 678-A2
MOUNTAIN SPRINGS RD
- PMDL 93550 4376-A4
1400 LACo 93551 4375-G4
2100 Actn 93510 4375-E3
4400 Actn 93510 4374-J2
7300 SBdC 92371 (4562-J5
See Page 4471)
MOUNTAIN SPRINGS RANCH RD
5700 LVRN 91750 570-G3
MOUNTAIN TERRACE LN
200 MTBL 90640 636-E5
N MOUNTAIN TRAIL AV
- SMAD 91024 567-B2
S MOUNTAIN TRAIL AV
- SMAD 91024 567-B3
MOUNTAIN VIEW AV
100 LHB 90631 708-E6
100 MTBL 90640 676-D2
200 POM 91767 641-B1
500 SBdC 92397 (4652-B1
See Page 4651)
700 MNRO 91016 567-H3
1300 SPAS 91030 595-F3
3000 LA 90066 672-B2
3500 LACo 91107 566-G5
6900 HNTP 90255 675-A7
7200 HNTP 90255 705-A2
7200 LACo 90255 675-A7
7200 LACo 90255 705-A2
8000 SGAT 90280 705-A2
E MOUNTAIN VIEW AV
200 GLDR 91741 569-F5
N MOUNTAIN VIEW AV
100 Echo 90026 634-D2

STREET
Block City ZIP Pg-Grid

N MOUNTAIN VIEW AV
1000 POM 91767 601-B7
S MOUNTAIN VIEW AV
100 LA 90057 634-C2
1300 POM 91766 641-B3
W MOUNTAIN VIEW AV
200 GLDR 91741 569-D5
MOUNTAIN VIEW CIR
- AZU 91702 568-G4
MOUNTAIN VIEW CT
- LA 91342 482-D1
MOUNTAIN VIEW DR
- LACo 91302 558-J3
- PMDL 93552 4287-A5
2600 LVRN 91750 600-F2
5300 LACo 91302 559-A3
MOUNTAIN VIEW LN
1600 CHLS 91709 710-G2
MOUNTAIN VIEW PL
- LA 91342 482-E2
MOUNTAIN VIEW RD
2000 ELMN 91733 637-D3
2000 SELM 91733 637-D3
2400 ELMN 91732 637-D3
43700 LACo 93532 4102-A2
MOUNTAIN VIEW ST
- Alta 91001 535-G5
1100 SFER 91340 482-C5
E MOUNTAIN VIEW ST
- NLB 90805 765-D3
W MOUNTAIN VIEW ST
- NLB 90805 765-C3
MOUNTAINVIEW TER
900 ALH 91801 596-C4
MOUNTAIN VIEW TR
12000 LACo 91342 482-J6
19700 Top 90290 590-A7
19700 Top 90290 630-A1
MOUNTAIN VISTA DR
1400 LACo 91770 636-F4
MOUNTAIN VISTA PZ
1200 DUAR 91010 567-J5
MOUNTAIN WILLOW LN
- LACo 91387 4552-B4
MOUNTAIR AV
10000 Tuj 91042 503-J2
MOUNT ANGELUS DR
6100 HiPk 90042 595-D2
MOUNT ANGELUS PL
6100 HiPk 90042 595-D2
MOUNT ANGELUS WK
- HiPk 90042 595-D2
MOUNT BALDY CIR
6600 BPK 90620 767-F7
MOUNT BALDY RD
- LACo - 511-J7
- LACo - (541-H3
See Page 511)
- LACo 91711 (541-H7
See Page 511)
800 SBdC - (512-D1
See Page 511)
900 LACo - (512-B4
See Page 511)
900 SBdC - (4732-E7
See Page 4651)
3800 CLAR 91711 571-G2
3900 LACo 91711 571-G2
MOUNT BARNARD DR
9600 BPK 90620 767-G7
MOUNTBATTEN DR
1100 GLDL 91207 534-G7
1100 GLDL 91207 564-G1
MOUNT BEACON TER
2500 LA 90068 593-G2
MOUNT CARMEL DR
300 GLDL 91206 564-J4
400 CLAR 91711 571-C6
MOUNTCASTLE DR
11100 LA 91604 562-J7
11100 LA 91604 563-A7
MOUNT CRAIG CIR
- LMRD 90638 738-B2
MOUNTCREST AV
1600 LA 90069 592-J4
MOUNT CURVE AV
400 Alta 91001 536-A4
MOUNT DANA CIR
9600 BPK 90620 767-G7
MOUNT DISAPPOINTMENT RD
- LACo - (506-C4
See Page 505)
MOUNT DUME LN
- MAL 90265 667-E2
MOUNT EMMA RD
- PMDL 93550 4466-E4
4300 LACo 93552 4376-J4
4300 LACo 93552 4377-B4
4600 PMDL 93550 4376-H7
5700 Litl 93543 4377-G3
8700 Litl 93543 4378-A3
MOUNT GLEASON AV
10100 Tuj 91042 503-H1
10100 Sunl 91040 503-H2
MOUNT GLEASON RD
- LACo - (4554-C5
See Page 4464)
- LACo - (4555-C7
See Page 4466)
- LACo - (4556-F4
See Page 4466)

MOUNT GLEASON RD
- LACo - (4644-F1
See Page 4643)
- LACo - 4645-A1
MOUNT HELENA AV
5000 Eagl 90041 565-C5
MOUNT HOLLY DR
12500 WHIT 90601 677-C4
MOUNT HOLLYWOOD DR
3100 LFlz 90027 593-H1
3300 LFlz 90027 563-H5
MOUNT HOLYOKE AV
300 PacP 90272 630-J6
300 PacP 90272 631-A6
MOUNT HOOD CT
28600 RPV 90275 823-J2
MOUNT LANGLEY CT
28700 RPV 90275 823-J2
MOUNT LASSEN LN
28600 RPV 90275 823-J2
MOUNT LEE DR
- LA 90068 563-G6
MOUNT LOWE DR
1000 Alta 91001 536-B4
6500 BPK 90620 767-F7
MOUNT LOWE MTWY
- Alta 91001 535-J2
- Alta 91001 536-B1
- LACo - (506-D6
See Page 505)
- LACo - 535-J2
- LACo - 536-B1
MOUNT LUKENS TKTR
- LA - 504-F1
- LACo - 504-H3
- LACo - 505-A4
- PAS 91011 505-B6
- Tuj 91042 504-F1
MOUNT MAHOGANY RD
2000 SBdC 92397 (4652-F4
See Page 4651)
MOUNT MARTY DR
1700 WAL 91789 639-F3
MOUNT OLIVE DR
100 DUAR 91010 568-C5
100 BRAD 91010 568-C3
MOUNT OLIVE LN
2400 BRAD 91010 568-D4
MOUNT OLYMPUS DR
1700 LA 90046 593-A3
MOUNT PALOMAR DR
6500 BPK 90620 767-F7
MOUNT PALOMAR PL
28600 RPV 90275 823-J2
MOUNT PLEASANT ST
1400 HiPk 90042 595-A1
MOUNT PROSPECT DR
1900 Top 90290 589-H3
MOUNT RAINIER RD
1200 RPV 90275 823-J2
1200 RPV 90275 824-A2
MOUNT RIPLEY DR
6200 CYP 90630 767-F7
6500 BPK 90620 767-F7
MOUNT ROSE RD
28600 RPV 90275 824-A2
MOUNT ROYAL DR
4800 Eagl 90041 565-B5
MOUNT RUSHMORE RD
28600 RPV 90275 823-J2
MOUNT SAC WY
1000 WAL 91789 639-G4
MOUNT SAINT MARYS FIRE RD
1600 Brwd 90049 591-E5
MOUNT SAWTOOTH DR
28600 RPV 90275 823-J2
28700 LA 90732 823-J2
MOUNT SHASTA CIR
6600 BPK 90620 767-F7
MOUNT SHASTA DR
1900 LA 90732 823-J1
28500 LA 90275 823-J2
28500 RPV 90275 823-J2
MOUNT SINAI DR
- LA 90068 563-G4
23600 SIMI 93063 499-C1
MOUNT STEPHEN AV
17200 SCTA 91387 4552-B2
MOUNT TRICIA AV
- WCOV 91791 639-B4
MOUNT VANCOUVER CT
28600 RPV 90275 824-A2
MOUNT VERNON AV
1500 POM 91768 640-E2
4700 CHNO 91710 641-F6
MOUNT VERNON DR
300 SGBL 91775 596-C3
3500 LACo 90043 673-C4
3500 LACo 90008 673-C4
W MOUNT VERNON DR
3400 LACo 90043 673-D4
3400 LACo 90008 673-D4
MOUNT VERNON PL
1200 PAS 91103 565-E1
MOUNT VERNON ST
4300 CHNO 91710 641-E6
MOUNT WASHINGTON DR
200 LA 90065 595-A4
500 LA 90065 594-J4
MOUNT WATERMAN DR
6800 BPK 90620 767-G7

MOUNT WHITNEY DR
6500 BPK 90620 767-F7
MOUNT WHITNEY WY
28600 RPV 90275 823-J2
MOUNT WILSON RD
- Alta 91001 536-E5
- LACo - (506-J7
See Page 505)
- LACo - 507-A7
- LACo - 536-H4
- PAS - 536-E5
MOUNT WILSON TR
400 SMAD 91024 537-B6
400 SMAD 91024 567-B1
MOUNT WILSON- RED BOX RD
- LACo - (506-F6
See Page 505)
MOURNING DOVE WY
4100 CALB 91302 559-G6
MOY LN
10000 Sunl 91040 503-H4
MOZART ST
1600 LA 90031 634-J1
2000 LA 90031 635-A1
MOZART WY
13000 CRTS 90703 737-B6
MUERDAGO RD
100 Top 90290 590-B6
MUIR AV
500 POM 91766 640-H3
MUIR CT
12300 CHNO 91710 641-E6
12300 WHIT 90601 677-C6
MUIR DR
5500 BPK 90621 737-J5
43600 LACo 93532 4101-H2
MUIR ST
5800 SIMI 93063 499-A2
MUIR TR
- SCTA 91354 4550-G1
MUIR WY
2100 LHB 90631 708-H5
MUIRFIELD
3700 ELMN 91732 637-G1
MUIRFIELD AV
1900 UPL 91784 571-H4
MUIRFIELD DR
- SCTA 91355 4550-B5
32000 Llan 93544 4469-F1
32000 Llan 93544 4379-F7
MUIRFIELD LN
300 WAL 91789 639-H7
39400 Cstc 91384 4459-H6
MUIRFIELD RD
1200 LA 90019 633-E4
S MUIRFIELD RD
100 LA 90004 633-F2
300 LA 90020 633-F2
600 LA 90005 633-F2
600 LA 90010 633-F2
900 LA 90019 633-F3
3500 LA 90016 673-D1
3700 LA 90008 673-D2
MUIR GROVE PL
- Cstc 91384 4369-G5
MUIRKIRK DR
18800 Nor 91326 480-G6
MUIR TRAIL DR
- FUL 92833 738-A3
MUIR WOODS CT
- WCOV 91791 639-B4
MULBERRY AV
2200 LAN 93535 4106-E1
8200 BPK 90620 767-J4
12200 CHNO 91710 641-J5
MULBERRY DR
- CRSN 90746 764-F5
- WAL 91789 639-C4
300 POM 91767 601-A3
8700 Sunl 91040 503-E3
12600 WHIT 90605 707-B2
12600 WHIT 90602 707-B2
13100 LACo 90605 707-C3
14000 LACo 90604 707-E4
15200 WHIT 90604 707-G5
MULBERRY LN
- ING 90305 703-E3
- PMDL 93551 4285-D3
MULBERRY PL
23600 SIMI 93063 499-B3
MULBERRY ST
1100 COMP 90222 734-J3
8100 CYP 90630 767-B4
MULBERRY GLEN DR
22900 SCTA 91354 4460-H6
MULEDEER LN
29800 Cstc 91384 4459-G4
MULFORD AV
3300 LYN 90262 705-B7
MULHALL ST
10400 ELMN 91731 597-C5
11300 ELMN 91732 597-E5
MULHOLLAND DR
2900 LA 90068 593-C2
4900 WdHl 91364 559-F4
7200 LA 90046 593-C2
7500 LA 90046 563-A7
7500 LA 90068 563-A7
7700 LA 91604 563-A7
7800 LA 91604 593-C2
7900 LA 90046 592-J1
7900 LA 91604 592-G2

MULHOLLAND DR
8500 LA 90210 592-D1
12400 LA 90210 562-B7
14000 Shrm 91423 562-A7
14200 BelA 90077 562-A7
14700 BelA 90077 561-H7
14900 Shrm 91403 561-H7
15600 BelA 90077 591-F1
15700 Brwd 90049 591-C1
15800 Brwd 90049 561-C7
16500 Enc 91436 561-D7
17400 PacP 90272 591-A1
18100 PacP 90272 590-H1
18200 PacP 90272 560-J7
18300 Tarz 91356 590-F1
19400 WdHl 91364 560-A5
19400 Tarz 91356 560-E7
MULHOLLAND HWY
5500 LFlz 90027 563-H6
5700 LA 90068 563-H6
6200 LA 90068 593-F1
22200 CALB 91302 559-F7
22200 WdHl 91364 559-F7
22500 LACo 91302 559-F7
23000 CALB 90290 559-F7
23800 CALB 91302 589-D2
24400 LACo 91302 589-A5
25100 LACo 91302 588-G4
26800 CALB 91302 588-G4
28100 Ago 91301 588-B4
29400 Ago 91301 587-F4
30600 LACo 90265 587-A5
32400 LACo 90265 586-J5
34300 LACo 90265 626-A1
35500 LACo 90265 625-J3
MULHOLLAND HWY Rt#-23
33000 LACo 90265 586-G6
MULHOLLAND PL
15700 Brwd 90049 561-F7
MULHOLLAND TER
8100 LA 90046 592-J1
MULHOLLAND WY
22000 WdHl 91364 560-A4
MULLAGHBOY RD
900 GLDR 91741 569-F3
MULLDAE AV
3400 LA 90732 823-H7
MULLEN AV
1200 LA 90019 633-E4
3700 LACo 90043 673-E4
S MULLEN AV
700 LA 90005 633-E3
700 LA 90010 633-E3
900 LA 90019 633-E3
4400 LACo 90043 673-E4
MULLEN PL
3700 LACo 90043 673-E4
MULLENDER AV
1500 LACo 91744 638-F4
S MULLENDER AV
1200 WCOV 91790 638-F3
1300 LACo 91744 638-F3
MULLER ST
5600 BGDN 90201 705-G2
7400 DWNY 90241 705-J3
7400 DWNY 90241 706-A3
11400 SFSP 90670 706-G6
MULLIN AV
1300 TOR 90501 763-H6
MULTIVIEW DR
3500 LA 90068 563-B7
MULTNOMAH ST
4100 LA 90032 635-D1
MULVANE ST
15500 LPUE 91744 638-E5
16500 LACo 91744 638-G6
MULVILLE ST
- FUL 92833 738-D5
MUMFORD ST
14600 PanC 91402 501-J5
MUMS DR
29600 SCTA 91387 4462-F6
MUMS MEADOW CT
14600 SCTA 91387 4462-G5
MUNDARE AV
17900 ART 90701 766-G1
W MUNGALL DR
3500 ANA 92804 767-G7
MUNGER DR
2700 LACo 90265 628-C5
MUNHALL AV
1900 POM 91766 641-B5
MUNNINGS WY
2700 VeCo 91361 586-C1
MUNSON AV
1500 HiPk 90042 595-A1
MUNSTER ST
2200 POM 91768 600-H4
MUNZ RANCH RD
43400 LACo 93532 4102-F2
43400 LACo 93536 4102-F2
45300 LACo 93536 4013-A4
MURAD AV
22400 LMTA 90717 793-H6
MURAL DR
1400 CLAR 91711 601-A2
3100 POM 91767 601-A2
MURCHISON AV
800 POM 91768 600-D7
MURCHISON ST
1600 Boyl 90033 635-C3

MURDOCK AV
900 Wilm 90744 794-H6
MUREAU RD
24700 CALB 91302 559-B5
24700 LACo 91302 559-A5
24700 HIDH 91302 559-B5
25400 LACo 91302 558-J5
25400 CALB 91302 558-J5
MURFIELD CT
400 FUL 92835 738-H3
MURIEL AV
6300 NLB 90805 765-C1
6400 NLB 90805 735-C7
14300 COMP 90221 735-C3
S MURIEL AV
900 COMP 90221 735-C6
12600 RDom 90221 735-C6
MURIEL DR
11300 LYN 90262 705-C7
11500 LYN 90262 735-C1
MURIETTA AV
3900 Shrm 91423 562-B3
5400 VanN 91401 562-B2
6100 VanN 91401 532-B6
6600 VanN 91405 532-B4
8100 PanC 91402 532-A1
8700 PanC 91402 502-A7
MURIETTA DR
800 ARCD 91007 567-A4
800 ARCD 91007 566-J4
MURMURING PINES RD
- LACo 91724 639-G1
MUROC PL
200 FUL 92833 738-C7
MUROC ST
9200 BLF 90706 736-A2
10900 NRWK 90650 736-E2
12700 NRWK 90650 737-A2
13800 LMRD 90638 737-D2
MUROS PL
2000 PVE 90274 792-G7
MURPHY MTWY
4000 LACo 90265 627-G5
MURPHY RD
16300 LMRD 90638 738-A1
MURPHY HILL DR
13400 WHIT 90601 677-D6
MURPHYS LN
12100 Pear 93553 4468-G6
MURRAY AV
100 AZU 91702 569-A7
100 AZU 91702 599-A1
900 POM 91767 601-D7
MURRAY CIR
1500 Echo 90026 594-C6
MURRAY DR
1400 Echo 90026 594-C6
MUSCADINE LN
14400 CHLS 91709 680-H4
MUSCAT RD
- PMDL 93551 4104-D6
MUSCATEL AV
700 LACo 91770 636-H5
1000 RSMD 91770 636-H1
3700 RSMD 91770 596-H7
5800 TEML 91780 596-H7
5800 SGBL 91775 596-H7
5800 TEML 91775 596-H7
N MUSCATEL AV
1200 LACo 91775 566-G7
4900 LACo 91776 596-H4
5500 SGBL 91775 596-H3
5600 TEML 91780 596-H3
5700 SGBL 91775 596-H3
6300 LACo 91775 596-G1
MUSCATEL CIR
3500 RSMD 91770 596-H7
MUSCATINE ST
12700 Pcma 91331 502-E6
13400 Pcma 91331 532-C1
MUSE DR
3500 LACo 91724 599-E6
MUSEUM DR
- LA 90037 674-B2
200 LA 90065 595-A4
MUSGROVE AV
2700 ELMN 91732 637-D2
MUSKINGUM AV
500 PacP 90272 630-J5
MUSKINGUM PL
500 PacP 90272 630-J5
MUSTANG
15500 LA 91342 481-G1
MUSTANG CIR
- MTCL 91763 641-E1
- WAL 91789 639-D7
2000 LVRN 91750 570-G7
MUSTANG CT
400 SDMS 91773 600-A1
W MUSTANG CT
1200 UPL 91786 571-J7
MUSTANG DR
32300 Cstc 91384 4369-F5
MUSTANG LN
- LA 91343 531-H1
36500 PMDL 93550 4286-G5
MUSTANG RD
4100 SBdC 91710 641-D4
28500 RPV 90275 823-F1
40000 LACo 93551 4193-G3
MUSTANG WY
9600 Sunl 91040 503-D3

MYDA AV
5800 TEML 91780 596-H3
MYERS PL
- Saug 91350 4461-G6
S MYERS PL
300 ING 90301 703-B3
MYERS ST
600 LA 90023 634-J5
N MYERS ST
100 Boyl 90033 634-H4
1000 BURB 91506 563-E2
1000 BURB 91506 533-E7
2400 BURB 91504 533-E4
S MYERS ST
100 Boyl 90033 634-H4
100 BURB 91506 563-F3
600 LA 90023 634-J6
MYOSOTIS ST
6000 HiPk 90042 595-D1
MYRA AV
900 LA 90029 594-B5
1500 LFlz 90027 594-B3
MYRA CT
2600 WCOV 91792 639-B6
W MYRA CT
1100 UPL 91786 601-J1
MYRA LN
16400 CRTS 90703 736-E6
MYRA TER
- LA 90046 593-A3
MYRIN CT
27600 SCTA 91350 4460-J5
MYRNA ST
10400 NHol 91601 563-B2
MYRON ST
9000 PRV 90660 706-E1
MYRRH LN
500 COMP 90220 734-H5
MYRRH ST
- COMP 90221 735-F4
6600 PRM 90723 735-F4
E MYRRH ST
100 COMP 90220 734-J5
100 COMP 90220 735-A5
300 COMP 90221 735-A5
4100 RDom 90221 735-C5
W MYRRH ST
100 COMP 90220 734-G5
MYRTLE AV
1000 LBCH 90813 795-E6
2400 HMB 90254 762-G1
2600 IRW 91706 597-G1
2800 IRW 91016 597-G1
2800 MNRO 91016 597-G1
3300 Bxby 90807 795-E1
3300 SIGH 90755 795-E1
E MYRTLE AV
400 GLDR 91741 569-F6
N MYRTLE AV
100 MNRO 91016 567-G2
100 POM 91768 640-G1
1300 LBCH 90813 795-E5
1800 LBCH 90806 795-E4
2600 SIGH 90755 795-E3
3400 Bxby 90807 765-E5
3400 Bxby 90807 795-E3
5400 NLB 90805 765-E2
6300 NLB 90805 735-E6
S MYRTLE AV
100 MNRO 91016 567-G4
100 POM 91766 640-G2
600 ING 90301 703-D3
2100 LACo 91016 567-G7
2500 MNRO 91016 597-G1
2600 IRW 91016 597-G1
2600 IRW 91706 597-G1
MYRTLE CT
- SIMI 93063 499-B2
5100 VeCo 91377 557-H1
MYRTLE ST
- CRSN 90746 764-F5
300 GLDL 91203 564-D4
1300 LA 90015 634-E6
4600 PRV 90660 676-F3
10500 DWNY 90241 706-B4
41000 PMDL 93551 4194-F1
41300 PMDL 93551 4104-F7
MYRTLE WY
20100 SCTA 91350 4461-D5
N MYRTLEWOOD AV
700 WCOV 91791 598-J6
S MYRTLEWOOD ST
100 WCOV 91791 598-J7
200 WCOV 91791 638-J1
MYRTUS AV
5700 ARCD 91006 597-D3
MYSTERY CT
16400 LMRD 90638 738-A2
MYSTERY MESA DR
30300 CynC 91351 4462-A4
MYSTIC LN
7300 CanP 91307 529-E5
MYSTIC ST
13300 LACo 90605 707-C3
14000 LACo 90604 707-E4
MYSTIC VIEW PL
2900 BURB 91504 533-F3

N

N ST
100 Wilm 90744 794-E5

NABAL RD
1500 LHH 90631 708-F2
NACE PL
1600 HacH 91745 678-E4
NACHAZEL WY
1700 LAN 93534 4015-E3
NACHI WY
900 MONP 91754 635-J3
NACO PL
1600 HacH 91745 678-E4
NACORA ST
19500 RowH 91748 679-D5
NADA ST
200 LHB 90631 708-C5
7000 DWNY 90242 705-G5
8200 DWNY 90242 706-A6
NADAL ST
18700 SCTA 91351 4551-F1
NADEAU DR
1400 LA 90019 633-E5
NADEAU ST
1100 Flor 90001 704-F1
2100 LACo 90255 704-F1
NADER PL
15000 GAR 90249 733-G4
NADEU MTWY
- SCTA 91387 4551-J6
- SCTA 91387 4552-A6
NADINA ST
10300 LA 91342 503-B1
NADINE CIR
22500 TOR 90505 793-E1
NADINE ST
2400 WCOV 91792 638-J6
8700 LACo 91776 596-G4
9500 TEML 91780 596-J4
9500 TEML 91780 597-A4
NADIR ST
23600 LA 91304 529-E2
NADULA DR
1900 RowH 91748 678-F5
NAFFA AV
23500 CRSN 90745 794-C2
NAGLE AV
4100 Shrm 91423 562-D3
5200 VanN 91401 562-D1
5800 VanN 91401 532-D6
6600 VanN 91405 532-D5
6900 NHol 91605 532-D2
8300 SunV 91352 532-D1
8600 PanC 91402 532-D1
8800 Pcma 91331 502-A5
8800 Pcma 91331 532-C1
NAGOYA WY
1000 SPed 90731 824-C6
S NAIRN AV
1500 ELA 90022 675-J2
NALIN DR
2300 BelA 90077 591-H2
NALIN PL
15500 BelA 90077 591-H2
NAN CT
24300 DBAR 91765 680-E2
NAN ST
9000 PRV 90660 676-F6
11600 LACo 90606 706-J1
NANBERRY RD
16600 Enc 91436 561-D4
NANCE AV
11200 DWNY 90241 706-D6
NANCE ST
8100 DWNY 90241 706-A5
10800 NRWK 90650 706-E7
17100 Enc 91316 561-C5
17100 Enc 91436 561-C5
NANCY CIR
7700 LPMA 90623 767-C3
19500 CRTS 90703 766-H3
W NANCY CT
1200 UPL 91786 601-J1
NANCY LN
700 FUL 92831 738-J5
NANCY PL
22000 SCTA 91350 4461-A5
NANCY RD
6500 RPV 90275 823-G3
NANCY ST
2400 WCOV 91792 638-J6
6300 Wch 90045 672-G7
9200 CYP 90630 767-E6
NANCY WY
300 LCF 91011 535-D4
NANCYLEE LN
23900 TOR 90505 793-B2
NANDINA DR
2600 PMDL 93550 4286-F4
NANDINA LN
21300 SCTA 91321 4641-B1
NANETTE AV
1600 WCOV 91792 638-J6
1800 WCOV 91792 639-A6
NANETTE ST
16800 GmH 91344 481-C5
NANNESTAD ST
7800 LACo 91770 636-F4
NANRY ST
14700 LACo 90604 707-F5
NANSEN DR
- LACo 91342 482-J2
NANTASKET DR
32600 RPV 90275 822-H5
N NANTES AV
300 LPUE 91744 638-D5

S NANTES AV
1100 HacH 91745 678-B1
NANTUCKET DR
37700 PMDL 93550 4286-D2
NANTUCKET LN
1600 LA 90732 823-J6
NANTUCKET PL
- SLB 90740 796-J5
- MANB 90266 732-H4
NANTUCKET ST
800 LHB 90631 708-G4
28000 Cstc 91384 4459-G5
NANWOOD ST
1200 LHB 90631 738-E1
NAOMA LN
13400 CRTS 90703 737-C6
NAOMI AV
- ARCD 91007 567-A7
700 ARCD 91007 566-J7
3200 LA 90011 674-E2
6100 Flor 90001 674-F6
6500 BPK 90620 767-F3
7900 Flor 90001 704-F2
8900 LACo 91775 596-J1
9400 LACo 91007 596-J1
9500 LACo 91007 566-J7
E NAOMI AV
8700 LACo 91775 596-G1
S NAOMI AV
800 LA 90021 634-G7
1700 LA 90021 674-F1
1900 LA 90011 674-F1
NAOMI ST
800 BURB 91505 563-E2
1000 BURB 91505 533-D3
1600 WCOV 91792 638-J6
3000 BURB 91504 533-D3
N NAOMI ST
100 BURB 91505 563-E1
1300 BURB 91505 533-D7
2200 BURB 91504 533-D4
S NAOMI ST
200 BURB 91505 563-E3
NAPA CIR
17300 CRTS 90703 736-H7
NAPA CT
700 CLAR 91711 571-B5
3700 SCTA 91355 4550-E4
NAPA DR
- SCTA 91354 4550-H1
3700 CHNO 91710 641-C6
NAPA PL
200 FUL 92833 738-C7
NAPA ST
14900 PanC 91402 531-H1
15500 LA 91343 531-D1
16900 Nor 91325 531-A1
18100 Nor 91325 530-G1
18400 Nor 91324 530-G1
19700 Win 91306 530-C1
21700 LA 91304 530-A1
22100 LA 91304 529-H1
NAPA WY
3700 PMDL 93550 4286-H5
NAPLES AV
2300 UPL 91784 571-J3
2500 Ven 90291 672-A5
NAPLES DR
9500 CYP 90630 767-C7
E NAPLES LN
5600 LBCH 90803 826-C2
N NAPLES LN
- LBCH 90803 826-C2
E NAPLES PZ
5800 LBCH 90803 826-D2
NAPLES ST
800 MNRO 91016 567-E6
NAPOLEON ST
100 PdlR 90293 702-B4
NAPOLI
6200 LBCH 90803 826-D1
NAPOLI DR
100 BREA 92821 709-A7
700 PacP 90272 631-D4
12100 CRTS 90703 736-J7
NAPOLI PL
1200 POM 91766 640-D3
9500 CYP 90630 767-C7
NARAMORE WY
2200 RBCH 90278 763-B2
NARANJA AV
15300 PRM 90723 735-J4
NARANJA DR
400 GLDL 91206 564-G3
NARANJA RD
20900 WdHl 91364 560-C5
NARATO PL
21800 DBAR 91765 679-J5
NARBONNE AV
24000 LMTA 90717 793-G5
NARCISSA DR
- RPV 90275 823-A4
W NARCISSA DR
- RPV 90275 823-A4
NARCISSUS CT
2100 Ven 90291 671-J6
NARCISSUS CREST AV
14800 SCTA 91387 4462-F6
NARDIAN WY
7800 Wch 90045 702-E2
E NARDO CT
100 LBCH 90813 795-E6

W NARDO WY
100 LBCH 90813 795-D6
NARES DR
28000 Cstc 91384 4369-G7
NARINO DR
30800 RPV 90275 823-F5
NARROT ST
4500 TOR 90503 763-B3
NARROW BRIDGE LN
16000 CRTS 90703 736-J4
NARROWS DR
9300 PRV 90660 676-J1
NARVA ST
1700 LA 90031 635-A2
NASH AV
11200 DWNY 90241 706-B6
NASH DR
8500 LA 90046 592-J3
N NASH ST
100 ELSG 90245 732-H1
600 ELSG 90245 702-H7
S NASH ST
800 ELSG 90245 732-H4
NASHOTAH
- CLAR 91711 571-F3
NASHPORT ST
900 LVRN 91750 570-E7
NASHUA ST
800 LHB 90631 708-E7
NASHUA WY
25700 SCTA 91355 4550-F6
NASHVILLE AV
4200 PMDL 93552 4286-J3
10400 LACo 90604 707-G4
11900 LMRD 90638 707-G7
NASHVILLE CT
1100 POM 91768 600-F7
NASHVILLE ST
18900 Nor 91326 500-F2
19600 Chat 91311 500-B2
NASSAU AV
400 City 90063 635-D6
10200 Sunl 91040 503-G2
NASSAU CT
400 City 90063 635-D6
NASSAU DR
13000 SLB 90740 796-F7
NASSAU PL
100 CLAR 91711 571-D5
NASTURTIUM DR
15400 SCTA 91387 4552-E1
NATALIE AV
1600 WCOV 91792 638-J6
NATALIE DR
14600 LACo 90604 707-E6
NATALIE LN
- LACo 91390 4461-A3
8300 LA 91304 529-F2
NATALIE WY
27500 SCTA 91350 4461-B7
NATASHA CT
5300 AGRH 91301 557-H5
NATASHA LN
- MTBL 90640 676-E3
N NATCHEZ PL
1300 SPed 90731 824-A3
NATCHEZ ST
900 SPed 90731 824-A2
NATHAN HILL RD
18600 SCTA 91351 4551-G2
NATHENE DR
500 LPUE 91744 678-F1
NATICK AV
4500 Shrm 91403 561-J4
5300 VanN 91411 561-J2
7000 VanN 91405 531-J5
8000 PanC 91402 531-J2
9200 LA 91343 501-J5
9900 MsnH 91345 501-J5
NATIONAL AV
4100 BURB 91505 563-C4
8700 SGAT 90280 705-G4
NATIONAL BLVD
8400 CULC 90232 632-J7
8400 LA 90016 632-J7
8400 LA 90016 633-A7
8800 LA 90232 632-G7
8900 LA 90034 632-F7
9900 LA 90064 632-C7
11200 LA 90064 672-B1
11200 LA 90064 632-C7
11200 LA 90066 672-B1
NATIONAL PL
5800 CHNO 91710 641-H5
10400 LA 90034 632-D7
NATIVE AV
2600 RowH 91748 678-J7
NATOMA AV
4100 WdHl 91364 560-D4
NATOMA ESTATE DR
- WdHl 91364 560-C5
NAU AV
18600 Nor 91326 500-H1
NAUD ST
1400 LA 90012 634-H2
NAUSET CT
17400 CRSN 90746 734-F7
17400 CRSN 90746 764-F1
NAUSIKA AV
1600 RowH 91748 679-D5
NAUTICAL LN
- SCTA 91355 4550-H3

NAUTILUS DR
32400 RPV 90275 823-D6
NAVA ST
10400 BLF 90706 736-D5
11400 NRWK 90650 736-G5
NAVAHO
- Ago 91301 587-F4
NAVAHO TRAIL LN
- POM 91766 640-H5
NAVAJO
21600 Top 90290 560-B6
21700 WdHl 91364 560-B6
NAVAJO AV
2700 THO 91362 557-A2
NAVAJO CT
27600 Cstc 91384 4459-H4
NAVAJO DR
6500 BPK 90620 767-F2
NAVAJO LN
- CRSN 90745 794-G2
12800 NRWK 90650 737-A1
NAVAJO PL
3600 PVE 90274 793-B3
NAVAJO ST
4200 LA 91602 563-C5
NAVAJO TR
28800 Ago 91301 588-B5
NAVAJO SPRINGS RD
23600 DBAR 91765 640-B6
NAVARETH WY
- Boyl 90033 634-J4
NAVARO LN
800 LACo 91791 639-D2
2300 WCOV 91791 639-D2
NAVARRE CT
1200 Ven 90291 671-H6
NAVARRO AV
1300 PAS 91103 565-H1
1500 PAS 91103 535-H7
2000 Alta 91001 535-H7
N NAVARRO AV
2100 Alta 91001 535-H6
NAVARRO DR
2200 CLAR 91711 571-D6
NAVARRO ST
4800 LA 90032 595-E6
NAVIGATION PL
- PMDL 93552 4287-A5
NAVILLA PL
1300 COV 91724 599-E6
15100 BALD 91706 598-D6
E NAVILLA PL
100 COV 91723 599-B6
900 COV 91724 599-D6
900 LACo 91724 599-D6
19300 LACo 91723 599-D6
NAVOJOA PL
10900 SFSP 90670 706-G2
NAVY CT
- Ven 90291 671-G5
NAVY ST
- Ven 90291 671-F5
600 SMCA 90405 671-J3
11700 LA 90066 672-B2
NAVY WY
100 SPed 90731 824-F3
NAVY MOLE RD
- LBCH 90802 824-G3
- LBCH 90802 825-A4
NAWA LN
14600 NRWK 90650 736-G4
NAYLOR AV
7400 Wch 90045 702-G1
NCO RD
- SPed 90731 854-B1
NEAL DR
5300 Eagl 90041 565-A5
NEAPOLITAN LN E
9900 LBCH 90803 826-C3
NEAPOLITAN LN W
- LBCH 90803 826-C3
NEARBANK DR
17700 RowH 91748 678-H6
NEARBROOK ST
17900 SCTA 91387 4551-J3
18900 SCTA 91351 4551-G3
NEARCLIFF ST
2300 TOR 90505 793-F5
NEARDALE ST
8600 PRM 90723 735-J3
NEARFIELD LN
7600 LPMA 90623 767-C3
NEARFIELD ST
900 AZU 91702 599-B1
18000 LACo 91702 599-A1
NEARGATE DR
23500 SCTA 91321 4640-G2
NEARGLEN AV
300 COV 91724 599-E6
3600 LACo 91724 599-E3
5400 GLDR 91740 599-E2
N NEARGLEN AV
100 COV 91724 599-E5
NEARGROVE RD
14200 LMRD 90638 737-F3
NEARPOINT DR
3800 WCOV 91792 679-D2
NEARSIDE DR
14800 LACo 93532 4102-F4
NEARSIDE ST
16500 WHIT 90603 708-A4
NEARTREE RD
14700 LMRD 90638 737-F4

STREET Block City ZIP Pg-Grid

NEARVIEW DR
16500 SCTA 91387 4552-C1
18800 SCTA 91351 4551-G1
NEARWOOD RD
11600 Litl 93543 4468-H6
12300 Pear 93553 4468-H6
NEBLINA CT
25600 SCTA 91355 4550-G5
NEBO DR
25600 LACo 91302 629-A1
NEBRASKA
2100 WCOV 91792 679-H2
NEBRASKA AV
400 LBCH 90802 795-F7
2500 SGAT 90280 704-J4
2600 SGAT 90280 705-A4
2900 SMCA 90404 631-H7
11100 WLA 90025 632-A6
11700 WLA 90025 631-J6
13600 PRM 90723 735-F2
NECTAR AV
20600 LKWD 90715 766-G5
NECTAR LN
- VanN 91401 562-D2
NECTARINE AV
12200 CHNO 91710 641-J5
NECTARINE DR
37600 PMDL 93550 4286-D2
W NECTARINE ST
300 ING 90301 703-B3
NEDDY AV
5900 WdHl 91367 559-D1
6100 WdHl 91367 529-D7
6400 CanP 91307 529-D7
NEDRA AV
10600 DWNY 90241 706-B4
NEDRA DR
12400 GrnH 91344 481-D5
NEDRA ST
4300 LYN 90262 705-E6
NEECE AV
24000 TOR 90505 793-D3
E NEECE ST
100 NLB 90805 735-C7
NEEDLES ST
14800 LA 91343 501-J5
19500 Nor 91324 500-F5
19800 Chat 91311 500-D5
22100 Chat 91311 499-J5
NEELY ST
31400 Cstc 91384 4369-H7
NEENACH ST
11700 SunV 91352 502-G7
11800 SunV 91352 532-G1
NEENAH ST
7500 CMRC 90040 676-B7
S NEFF AV
1000 WCOV 91790 638-G3
1800 LACo 91744 638-G3
NEFF CT
- SCTA 91351 4551-D3
NEFF RD
13100 LMRD 90638 738-A1
N NEIL AV
700 WCOV 91791 598-J6
N NEIL ST
400 WCOV 91791 598-J6
NEIL ARMSTRONG ST
1600 MTBL 90640 636-F5
W NEILSON ST
300 CRSN 90745 794-C1
NEILSON WY
1900 SMCA 90405 671-F4
NEINDORFF DR
5500 LA 90068 593-G3
NEKO DR
25000 LMTA 90717 793-G4
NEKOMA ST
2600 Eagl 90041 564-J6
E NELDA ST
5900 SIMI 93063 499-B2
NELDOME ST
600 Alta 91001 535-F6
NELL AV
19900 CRTS 90703 766-H3
NELLAS ST
8800 WHWD 90069 592-H6
NELLA VISTA AV
2200 LFlz 90027 594-B2
NELLIEMAY LN
29900 CynC 91351 4462-B5
NELROSE AV
1100 Ven 90291 672-A5
NELSON AL
1400 PAS 91104 566-C3
NELSON AV
200 LPUE 91744 638-C6
1500 MANB 90266 732-J7
1900 RBCH 90278 732-J7
1900 RBCH 90278 733-A7
13400 INDS 91746 637-J3
13400 LACo 91746 637-J3
13700 LPUE 91746 637-J3
13800 INDS 91746 638-A4
13800 LPUE 91746 638-A4
14300 INDS 91744 638-A4
E NELSON AV
13200 INDS 91746 637-H3
NELSON CT
- LHB 90631 738-B2
NELSON DR
4800 BELL 90201 675-E7

NELSON LN
5300 LPMA 90623 767-D3
NELSON PL
200 MTBL 90640 676-D2
3600 FUL 92835 738-F1
NELSON RD
- PanC 91402 532-A3
NELSON ST
500 SPed 90731 824-C5
1400 WCOV 91792 638-H4
2200 POM 91766 641-A5
5300 CYP 90630 767-D6
NELSONBARK AV
4200 LKWD 90712 765-H5
NEMAHA ST
100 POM 91767 600-J6
NEMO ST
9000 WHWD 90069 592-H7
NEO ST
7300 DWNY 90241 705-H4
NEOLA PL
4800 Eagl 90041 565-C6
NEOLA ST
900 Eagl 90041 565-C6
NEOLA WY
- LAN 93536 4015-A7
NEON WY
12500 GrnH 91344 481-B5
NEOSHO AV
4100 CULC 90066 672-C5
4100 LA 90066 672-C5
NEPTUNE AV
- SLB 90740 826-F5
100 HMB 90254 732-F7
500 BREA 92821 708-J6
1000 Wilm 90744 794-D5
21000 CRSN 90745 764-D5
22400 CRSN 90745 794-D1
N NEPTUNE AV
200 Wilm 90744 794-D6
NEPTUNE ST
2400 POM 91767 600-H4
NESBITT RD
2600 Top 90290 589-G3
NESMUTH RD
400 GLDL 91202 534-D7
NESS DR
17800 LACo 91387 4551-J3
NESSA DR
1800 LAN 93535 4106-D1
N NESTER AV
- COMP 90222 734-F2
NESTLE AV
4800 Tarz 91356 560-J3
5100 Tarz 91356 561-A3
6100 Res 91335 530-J2
8200 Nor 91325 530-J1
8800 Nor 91325 500-J5
10800 Nor 91326 500-J1
NESTOR AV
19000 CRSN 90746 764-G2
N NESTOR AV
100 COMP 90220 734-F3
2000 COMP 90222 734-F2
S NESTOR AV
100 COMP 90220 734-F5
13900 Wbrk 90222 734-F5
NESTOR CT
- SCTA 91351 4551-G7
NETHERLY AV
3200 LBCH 90810 795-A1
NETTIE RD
- Actn 93510 4465-C3
NETTLEBROOK ST
1900 THO 91361 557-A4
NETTLETON ST
10500 SunV 91352 533-A1
NETTO RIDGE CT
- LMRD 90638 738-B3
NEURASCHEL ST
28900 Cstc 91384 4459-C6
NEUTRA PL
2200 LA 90039 594-D5
NEVA LN
1100 POM 91766 641-B4
NEVA PL
300 HiPk 90042 595-D1
NEVADA
3600 WCOV 91792 679-H2
NEVADA AV
100 City 90063 635-E6
2600 ELMN 91733 637-C2
3000 ELMN 91731 637-C1
3400 ELMN 91731 597-C7
5700 SGAT 90280 735-G2
5800 WdHl 91367 559-J1
6100 WdHl 91367 529-J7
6500 CanP 91303 529-J6
7700 LA 91304 529-J1
8700 RSMD 91770 596-G7
8900 LA 91304 499-J7
8900 LA 91304 500-A7
9600 Chat 91311 499-J3
11800 LYN 90262 735-A1
E NEVADA AV
1000 SIGH 90755 795-F3
NEVADA ST
100 ELSG 90245 732-G1
3500 BELL 90201 675-B7
E NEVADA ST
200 LBCH 90806 795-D3
900 SIGH 90755 795-E3

S NEVEEN LN
1200 ANA 92804 767-H7
NEVELSON LN
5900 SIMI 93063 499-B1
NEVERS ST
13900 LPUE 91746 638-A3
NEVETTE CT
17100 SCTA 91387 4552-B1
NEVILL AV
8600 SGAT 90280 705-E3
NEVIN AV
2400 LA 90011 674-F2
NEW AV
- MONP 91755 636-D1
200 MONP 91770 636-D1
900 ALH 91801 596-D6
1300 SGBL 91776 596-D6
1400 SGBL 91776 636-D1
1400 ALH 91801 636-D1
2400 RSMD 91770 636-D1
N NEW AV
100 MONP 91755 636-D2
700 RSMD 91770 636-D2
S NEW AV
100 RSMD 91770 636-D2
100 MONP 91770 636-D2
NEW ST
10600 DWNY 90241 706-B4
NEWACRE RD
- SCTA 91355 4550-G3
NEWARK AV
5200 LA 90032 595-F7
NEWARK CT
3800 CLAR 91711 571-F4
NEW BEDFORD AV
3700 CLAR 91711 600-J1
NEW BEEKLEY RD
- SBdC 92371 (4562-H2
See Page 4471)
NEWBIRD DR
27900 SCTA 91350 4461-C5
NEWBOLT CIR
3200 HacH 91745 678-A6
NEWBRIDGE CIR
19800 LACo 91789 679-E4
NEWBROOK AV
17800 CRTS 90703 737-C7
17800 CRTS 90703 767-C1
NEWBROOK CIR
16600 CRTS 90703 737-C6
18500 CRTS 90703 767-C1
NEWBURGH ST
100 AZU 91702 598-J2
200 GLDR 91740 599-D2
16800 LACo 91702 598-J2
17600 LACo 91702 599-A2
17900 AZU 91702 599-A2
18600 LACo 91722 599-B2
E NEWBURGH ST
100 AZU 91702 598-G2
16500 LACo 91702 598-G2
NEWBURRY CT
16700 CRTS 90703 736-G6
NEWBURY PL
37200 PMDL 93552 4287-C2
NEWBURY RD
11600 OrCo 90720 796-H4
NEWBURY WY
700 DBAR 91765 680-D1
NEWBY AV
8900 RSMD 91770 596-H6
E NEWBY AV
100 SGBL 91776 596-F6
W NEWBY AV
200 SGBL 91776 596-D6
NEWBY ST
1000 GLDL 91201 564-B2
NEWCASTLE AV
4800 Enc 91316 561-A1
6200 Enc 91316 531-A7
6300 Res 91335 531-A3
8500 Nor 91325 531-A1
8800 Nor 91325 501-A7
11100 Nor 91326 501-A2
11400 GrnH 91344 481-A7
11400 GrnH 91344 501-A1
NEWCASTLE CT
25500 SCTA 91350 4550-J5
NEWCASTLE DR
8000 WHIT 90605 708-A1
NEW CASTLE LN
4800 LACo 91724 599-F3
NEWCASTLE LN
- SDMS 91724 599-G4
- SDMS 91773 599-G4
1100 FUL 92833 738-B5
5200 LACo 91302 559-A3
8900 CYP 90630 767-C7
NEW CENTURY DR
15600 LACo 90248 734-C5
NEWCOMB AV
9800 WHIT 90603 708-A3
12600 LMRD 90638 738-A1
NEWCOMB DR
13200 Shrm 91423 562-D6
NEWCOMB PL
1500 CLAR 91711 601-B1
E NEWCREST DR
1400 WCOV 91791 638-H4
1400 WCOV 91792 638-H4
NEWDALE DR
4200 LFlz 90027 594-B3

NEW DEAL AV
2800 ELMN 91733 637-D2
NEW DEPOT ST
600 LA 90012 634-F2
NEW DOCK ST
200 LBCH 90802 824-G2
1100 SPed 90731 824-G2
NEWELL AV
500 FUL 92832 738-J7
NEWELL PL
300 FUL 92832 738-J7
NEWELL RD
1500 LACo 90265 628-D4
NEWELL ST
1900 LA 90039 594-F4
6000 HNTP 90255 675-B7
6900 HNTP 90255 705-B1
NEW ENGLAND LN
- CRTS 90703 736-G6
NEW ENGLAND ST
1700 LA 90006 634-B6
1900 LA 90007 634-B6
NEWFIELD CT
28000 SCTA 91350 4461-B5
NEWFIELD ST
200 LACo 90248 734-D5
NEWGARD AV
12100 LA 91342 481-H6
NEWGARDEN ST
19500 RowH 91748 679-D4
NEWGATE AV
10700 LACo 90605 707-C6
S NEWGATE AV
12300 LACo 90605 707-C7
NEWGATE RD
6900 CanP 91307 529-E5
NEWGROVE ST
100 LAN 93534 4015-E6
500 LAN 93535 4016-A6
2000 LAN 93535 4015-C6
7000 LACo 93536 4014-B6
7000 LAN 93536 4014-B6
9500 LACo 93535 4018-A5
NEWHALL AV
23100 SCTA 91355 4550-H7
24100 SCTA 91321 4640-H1
24700 SCTA 91321 4550-H7
NEWHALL RANCH RD
- SCTA 91350 4550-H2
- SCTA 91350 4551-A2
- SCTA 91355 4550-F1
23000 SCTA 91355 4550-F1
23000 SCTA 91354 4550-F1
24200 SCTA 91355 4460-A6
NEW HAMPSHIRE AV
- CLAR 91711 571-E4
13300 GAR 90247 734-A2
18400 LA 90248 764-B2
N NEW HAMPSHIRE AV
100 LA 90004 634-A1
200 LA 90004 594-A6
700 LA 90029 594-A5
1300 LFlz 90027 594-A4
S NEW HAMPSHIRE AV
100 LA 90004 634-A2
300 LA 90020 634-A2
600 LA 90005 634-A2
600 LA 90010 634-A2
900 LA 90006 634-A5
900 LA 90044 704-A2
7900 LA 90044 704-A2
11100 LACo 90044 704-A6
20300 LACo 90502 764-B5
NEWHAMPTON ST
15600 HacH 91745 678-B4
NEW HAVEN AV
2000 CLAR 91711 571-E7
NEWHAVEN CT
1400 GLDR 91740 599-F1
NEW HAVEN DR
- PMDL 93551 4195-G5
1300 POM 91766 640-G3
NEWHAVEN DR
1800 BREA 92821 709-D7
NEWHAVEN LN
300 GLDR 91740 599-F2
NEWHAVEN RD
3500 PAS 91107 566-H3
NEW HAVEN ST
10700 SunV 91352 533-A1
NEWHAVEN ST
4900 VeCo 91377 557-G1
NEW HIGH CT
200 RBCH 90277 762-J5
NEW HIGH ST
100 LA 90012 634-G2
E NEWHILL ST
18600 GLDR 91741 569-B5
NEWHOME AV
8600 SunI 91040 503-F3
NEWHOUSE ST
19000 SCTA 91351 4551-F2
NEWINGTON ST
600 LACo 91010 567-H6
800 DUAR 91010 567-J6
NEW JERSEY
3600 WCOV 91792 679-H2
NEW JERSEY ST
1600 Boyl 90033 634-J4
1600 Boyl 90033 635-A4
NEWKIRK AV
500 FUL 92832 738-J7
21900 CRSN 90745 764-E7
NEWLAND ST
200 HiPk 90042 595-D1

NEWLEE ST
1100 MONP 91754 635-J2
1100 MONP 91754 636-A2
NEWLIN AV
5600 WHIT 90601 677-C6
7000 WHIT 90602 677-C7
7700 WHIT 90602 707-C1
NEWMAN AV
4500 CYP 90630 767-B6
E NEWMAN AV
- ARCD 91006 567-D4
W NEWMAN AV
- ARCD 91007 567-D4
NEWMAN ST
100 POM 91768 640-G1
5500 CYP 90630 767-D6
9700 LA 90035 632-F3
W NEWMAN ST
1300 SBdC 91784 571-H2
NEWMANOR AV
1300 POM 91768 600-E7
NEWMARK AV
7400 RSMD 91770 636-D2
E NEWMARK AV
100 MONP 91755 636-C2
900 MONP 91770 636-C2
W NEWMARK AV
100 MONP 91754 636-A2
1100 MONP 91754 635-J2
NEWMARK MALL
600 MTBL 90640 676-D2
NEWMARKET ST
13100 LACo 90601 637-F6
NEW MEXICO LN
4700 CYP 90630 767-B5
NEWMIRE AV
12000 NRWK 90650 706-D7
12700 NRWK 90650 736-D1
NEWMONT AV
15100 LACo 93535 4199-D1
NEW ORLEANS CT
800 CLAR 91711 571-E5
NEW PINE DR
16800 HacH 91745 678-F5
NEWPORT AV
1600 PAS 91103 535-G7
1600 PAS 91103 565-G1
N NEWPORT AV
200 LBCH 90803 825-J1
300 LBCH 90814 795-J7
300 LBCH 90814 825-J1
700 LBCH 90804 795-J5
NEWPORT CIR
7000 CanP 91307 529-E5
NEWPORT PL
29600 Cstc 91384 4459-G5
NEWPORT RD
38900 PMDL 93551 4195-F6
NEWPORT TER
- LA 90732 823-J6
NEWPORT WY
9800 CYP 90630 767-E7
NEWQUIST PL
300 INDS 91745 638-C7
NEWRIDGE DR
3400 RPV 90275 823-F4
NEW ROCHELLE ST
20300 WAL 91789 639-F4
NEWSTAR DR
28900 RPV 90275 823-A1
NEWTON AL
400 PAS 91106 566-B3
NEWTON AV
6900 NLB 90805 735-G6
NEWTON CT
21600 SCTA 91350 4461-B4
NEWTON MTWY
- LACo 90265 587-H7
1700 LACo 90265 627-G1
NEWTON PL
1100 SFER 91340 482-D6
NEWTON ST
300 SFER 91340 482-C6
400 COV 91723 599-C6
1300 LA 90021 634-F7
2900 TOR 90505 793-B2
12600 LA 91342 482-D5
E NEWTON ST
2100 HacH 91745 678-A3
NEWTON CANYON RD
28400 LACo 90265 587-F7
28800 LACo 90265 627-D1
NEWTONIA DR
5200 LA 90032 595-F4
NEWTREE AV
45300 LAN 93534 4015-F4
NEWVALE DR
17900 LACo 93532 4101-H2
NEWVIEW DR
18000 LACo 93532 4101-H2
NEWVILLE AV
9600 DWNY 90241 706-D5
9800 DWNY 90240 706-E4
NEW VISTA PL
14900 HacH 91745 677-J2
NEW YORK
3700 WCOV 91792 679-H2
NEW YORK AV
3800 GLDL 91214 534-E1
4200 GLDL 91214 504-E6
4700 CYP 90630 767-B5
NEW YORK DR
- Alta 91001 536-A7

NEW YORK DR
500 POM 91768 640-F1
900 LACo 91104 536-A7
2600 LACo 91107 536-D7
2600 PAS 91107 536-D7
2600 PAS 91107 566-F1
2900 LACo 91107 566-F1
NEW YORK ST
4300 ELA 90022 635-F5
E NEW YORK ST
500 LBCH 90813 795-E5
NIAGARA AV
1400 CLAR 91711 601-B1
17300 CRTS 90703 736-J7
N NIAGARA ST
100 BURB 91505 563-D1
1300 BURB 91505 533-D7
2200 BURB 91504 533-D5
S NIAGARA ST
100 BURB 91505 563-E4
NIAGARA WY
2500 Eagl 90041 564-J5
NIBUS ST
400 BREA 92821 709-A6
NICADA DR
2700 BelA 90077 592-A1
3000 BelA 90077 562-A7
NICARAGUA CIR
7300 BPK 90620 767-E2
NICE CT
2600 LAN 93536 4015-C7
NICHOLAS AV
19500 CRTS 90703 766-H3
NICHOLAS CIR
28300 Saug 91350 4461-D5
NICHOLAS LN
700 ARCD 91006 567-E7
W NICHOLAS ST
1000 UPL 91784 571-J4
NICHOLAS BEACH RD
33800 MAL 90265 626-A6
NICHOLAS FLATS RD
- LACo 90265 626-A3
NICHOLAS RIDGE MTWY
- LACo 90265 626-B3
- MAL 90265 626-C5
NICHOLET ST
2700 POM 91768 640-C2
NICHOLS LN
- Cstc 91384 4369-G7
- Cstc 91384 4459-G1
NICHOLS ST
2000 POM 91768 600-J5
9000 BLF 90706 736-A4
NICHOLS CANYON PL
2800 LA 90046 593-B1
NICHOLS CANYON RD
1700 LA 90046 593-B2
3200 LA 90046 563-B7
N NICHOLS CANYON RD
2700 LA 90046 593-B1
3000 LA 90046 563-B7
NICHOLSON AV
800 Wilm 90744 795-A5
N NICHOLSON AV
100 MONP 91755 636-C2
S NICHOLSON AV
100 MONP 91755 636-C2
NICHOLSON ST
8000 PdlR 90293 702-B2
NICKELS AV
3700 Actn 93510 4465-A2
NICKIE LN
20500 SCTA 91350 4461-D5
NICKLAUS AV
- LHB 90631 738-B2
NICKLAUS DR
- LA 91342 481-D2
W NICKLAUS DR
24400 SCTA 91355 4550-E7
NICKLE ST
36400 PMDL 93550 4286-G5
NICOBAR ST
100 LAN 93534 4015-J6
NICOLA AV
1500 CMRC 90022 676-A3
NICOLAS DR
2300 FUL 92833 738-E3
NICOLAS ST
- FUL 92833 738-D5
NICOLAS WY
- FUL 92833 738-D5
NICOLE CT
1100 GLDR 91740 570-A7
1100 GLDR 91740 600-A1
NICOLE DR
- PMDL 93551 4195-D6
NICOLE ST
43600 LAN 93535 4106-D1
NICOLET AV
3700 LA 90016 673-C2
3800 LA 90008 673-C2
NICOLLE AV
21200 CRSN 90745 764-C6
22600 CRSN 90745 794-C1
NICOYA DR
16500 HacH 91745 678-D6
NIDO CT
23200 SCTA 91354 4550-G1
40200 PMDL 93551 4194-H2
NIELD CT
- Saug 91350 4461-F6

NIELSON RD
400 SBdC 92372 (4562-A1
See Page 4471)
1700 SBdC 92372 (4472-E7
See Page 4471)
2700 SBdC 92371 (4472-G7
See Page 4471)
NIETO AV
- LBCH 90803 826-B1
300 LBCH 90803 796-B7
300 LBCH 90814 796-B7
300 LBCH 90814 826-B1
NIETO LN
1300 Boyl 90033 635-C3
NIETO PL
- BPK 90621 738-A6
3900 FUL 92835 738-G1
NIGHTINGALE CT
7200 LACo 91387 4551-H5
NIGHTINGALE DR
9200 LA 90069 592-H4
NIGHTINGALE LN
42100 LAN 93536 4104-C6
NIGHTSKY PL
- PMDL 93552 4287-B5
NIGUEL DR
5200 LPMA 90623 767-C2
NIGUEL CANYON WY
1100 BREA 92821 709-B5
NIHAV
- SCTA 91321 4641-C3
NIKE LN
- SCTA 91351 4551-G2
NIKKI CT
2400 WCOV 91792 638-J6
NILAND ST
4200 LYN 90262 735-D2
NILES PL
1800 Echo 90026 594-F5
NILGON ST
5600 LACo 93552 4287-C7
NIMES CT
13600 CHLS 91709 680-J2
NIMES PL
800 BelA 90077 592-B6
NIMES RD
600 BelA 90077 592-B6
NIMITZ AV
- LACo 90073 631-H3
NIMITZ RD
- LBCH 90802 824-H4
2700 LBCH 90802 825-A4
NIMROD PL
13100 Brwd 90049 631-E4
NIMROD ST
17800 LACo 93532 4101-J2
NINA LN
- ING 90305 703-E3
NINA PL
11300 LA 90230 672-F5
NINA RD
- PMDL 93550 4376-A7
- PMDL 93550 4466-A2
NINA ST
2400 WCOV 91792 638-J6
2500 PAS 91107 566-E4
NINDE PL
200 PAS 91101 565-J4
NINFA CT
22200 WdHl 91364 559-J4
NINITA PKWY
300 PAS 91106 566-C5
NINTH CT
- SMCA 90401 671-F2
NINTH ST
12400 NRWK 90650 706-J7
12500 NRWK 90650 707-A7
NIODRARA DR
1800 GLDL 91208 564-H1
1800 GLDL 91208 534-H7
NIPOMO AV
1900 LBCH 90815 796-F3
3100 LBCH 90808 796-E1
3400 LBCH 90808 766-E7
4100 LKWD 90713 766-F4
NIRVANA LN
- SCTA 91350 4551-E6
NITA AV
5900 WdHl 91367 559-J1
6200 WdHl 91367 529-J7
6800 CanP 91303 529-J4
7600 LA 91304 529-J3
9600 Chat 91311 499-J5
NITA CT
- LACo 90605 707-B7
NITHSDALE RD
900 PAS 91105 565-E6
NIXON ST
6400 LKWD 90713 766-E3
NOAH CT
400 SDMS 91773 600-A1
NOAKES ST
1500 CMRC 90040 675-F2
3600 LA 90023 675-C2
3900 CMRC 90023 675-C2
4300 LACo 90023 675-E2
NOBEL ST
4700 CMRC 90040 675-F3
NOBEL WY
- ING 90305 703-F3
NOB HILL DR
4600 LA 90065 594-J2
4600 LA 90065 595-A2

NOBHILL DR
1400 AZU 91702 568-J4
NOBLE AV
100 AZU 91702 568-J7
100 AZU 91702 598-J1
4200 Shrm 91403 561-H4
5200 VanN 91411 561-H2
6100 VanN 91411 531-H7
6600 VanN 91405 531-H3
7900 PanC 91402 531-H2
8300 LA 91343 531-H1
8700 LA 91343 501-H6
9900 MsnH 91345 501-H2
NOBLE CT
37800 PMDL 93552 4287-A2
NOBLE PL
100 AZU 91702 568-J7
100 AZU 91702 598-J1
NOBLE ST
10800 MsnH 91345 501-H3
NOBLE CANYON WY
2300 LACo 91789 679-E6
NOBLE FIR CT
- SCTA 91354 4460-F4
NOBLE LAKE DR
9600 LACo 93536 3833-G6
NOBLES AV
10000 LACo 90606 676-J4
NOBLETREE CT
700 VeCo 91377 557-H1
NOBLETT DR
43800 LACo 93532 4101-J1
NOBLE VIEW DR
2000 RPV 90275 823-H3
NOEL DR
5300 TEML 91780 596-H4
NOEL PL
1800 LA 90210 592-F4
NOELINE AV
4200 Enc 91436 561-E3
NOELINE WY
4500 Enc 91436 561-E4
NOELL CIR
19500 CRTS 90703 766-J3
NOELLE CT
25300 LMTA 90717 793-G4
NOFRAL RD
4900 WdHl 91364 560-B4
NOGA DR
- Tarz 91356 560-H6
NOGA WY
15700 LA 91343 501-G6
NOGAL AV
8600 WHIT 90606 707-B2
NOGAL CIR
2500 LVRN 91750 570-H7
NOGALES DR
4000 Tarz 91356 560-G5
NOGALES ST
1700 RowH 91748 679-B5
S NOGALES ST
100 WAL 91789 679-C3
100 WCOV 91792 679-C3
200 WAL 91789 639-B7
400 LACo 91792 679-C3
600 INDS 91748 679-C3
800 RowH 91748 679-C3
2200 WCOV 91792 639-B7
3600 LACo 91744 679-C3
NOHLES DR
10600 SunI 91040 503-E3
NOKOMIS RD
26600 RPV 90275 793-B6
NOLA PL
12600 GrnH 91344 481-A5
NOLAN AV
300 GLDL 91202 534-D7
400 GLDL 91202 564-D1
NOLAN ST
10900 ELMN 91731 597-D6
NOLANDALE ST
13800 LACo 91746 638-B2
W NOLANDALE ST
1700 WCOV 91790 638-C3
NOLDEN ST
500 HiPk 90042 595-C2
1400 HiPk 90042 565-C7
1900 Eagl 90041 565-C7
NOLINA AV
700 BALD 91706 637-H1
NOLINA CIR
3700 LAN 93536 4015-A7
NOLINA ST
3300 BALD 91706 597-J7
NOLINA WY
16700 PRM 90723 735-F6
NOLL DR
3700 PMDL 93550 4286-H4
NOLLAN PL
- PanC 91402 532-A3
NOLTE CT
28300 SCTA 91387 4552-B1
NOMAD DR
4600 WdHl 91364 560-E4
NOMAR ST
23900 WdHl 91367 559-E1
NONA LN
14000 WHIT 90602 677-F7
NONPAREIL DR
41400 PMDL 93551 4104-F7
NORA AV
1500 LACo 91722 598-E5
4600 IRW 91706 598-F4

N NORA AV
300 WCOV 91790 598-E6
NORA PL
14900 LA 91342 481-J6
NORAH AV
19300 CRTS 90703 767-B2
NORA LYNN DR
5900 WdHl 91367 559-C1
NORAN AV
18300 CRTS 90703 767-B1
NORAN CIR
17800 CRTS 90703 737-B7
NORANDA LN
3600 MAL 90265 626-F5
NORANN CIR
7700 LPMA 90623 767-C3
NORBECK DR
13700 LMRD 90638 737-D2
NORBERRY ST
100 LAN 93534 4015-E6
500 LAN 93535 4016-A6
2000 LAN 93536 4015-A6
NORBY LN
1100 FUL 92833 738-E6
NORCO AV
4600 BALD 91706 598-A4
NORCREST DR
15900 LACo 90604 707-J6
NORCROFT AV
300 Wwd 90024 632-B1
NORCROSS DR
33800 Actn 93510 4374-B5
E NORD ST
2000 COMP 90222 734-H2
2000 Wbrk 90222 734-H2
W NORD ST
700 COMP 90222 734-H2
NORDBY ST
900 CRSN 90746 734-E6
NORDESTA DR
12100 NRWK 90650 706-D7
12300 NRWK 90650 736-D1
NORDHOFF PL
19400 Nor 91324 500-E7
19700 Chat 91311 500-E7
NORDHOFF ST
13900 Pcma 91331 502-A7
14100 PanC 91402 502-A7
14500 PanC 91402 501-H7
14800 LA 91343 501-D7
16800 Nor 91325 501-A7
17900 Nor 91330 501-A7
18100 Nor 91325 500-G7
18100 Nor 91330 500-G7
18400 Nor 91324 500-F7
20100 Win 91306 500-D7
20100 Chat 91311 500-D7
20100 Chat 91311 530-D1
20100 Win 91306 530-D1
22000 Chat 91311 499-J7
NORDHOFF WY
19500 Nor 91324 500-F7
NORDIC AV
1800 CHLS 91709 680-H5
NORDICA DR
900 LA 90065 594-J2
NORDLAND AV
2800 LVRN 91750 600-H2
NORDMAN ST
1900 LMTA 90717 793-H3
NORDYKE ST
5400 HiPk 90042 565-C7
W NOREEN CT
1100 UPL 91784 571-J5
NORELLE ST
4600 LA 90032 635-D1
NOREMA ST
2100 ELMN 91733 637-D3
NOREN ST
200 LCF 91011 535-D3
7400 DWNY 90240 706-A2
NORFIELD CT
2100 BelA 90077 591-G3
NORFOLK AV
1000 Ven 90291 671-H5
NORFOLK ST
1500 Boyl 90033 635-B2
NORFORK PL
25500 SCTA 91350 4550-J5
NORGATE ST
1100 SDMS 91773 599-J1
E NORGATE ST
300 GLDR 91740 599-E1
W NORGATE ST
100 GLDR 91740 599-E1
NORGROVE LN
11600 OrCo 90720 796-H4
NORGROVE PL
1200 PAS 91103 535-D7
NORHAM PL
900 LCF 91011 535-C7
3600 GLDL 91206 535-C7
NORINO DR
11500 WHIT 90601 677-B4
NORITSU AV
6800 BPK 90620 767-G2
NORLAIN AV
9700 DWNY 90240 706-A2
10700 DWNY 90241 705-J3
12200 DWNY 90242 705-H6
NORLAND RD
15200 LACo 91387 4552-D1

NORLINA PL
12700 GrnH 91344 481-B5
E NORMA AV
200 WCOV 91791 598-H7
1900 WCOV 91791 599-A7
2200 WCOV 91791 639-A1
NORMA CT
200 WCOV 91791 599-A7
200 WCOV 91791 639-A1
NORMA PL
8900 WHWD 90069 592-H6
NORMA ST
200 LHB 90631 708-C6
NORMA WY
6000 SIMI 93063 499-B3
NORMAL AV
4100 LA 90029 594-A6
NORMALLIN ST
2700 TOR 90505 793-F5
NORMAN AV
600 WAL 91789 639-F6
E NORMAN AV
100 ARCD 91006 597-D1
W NORMAN AV
- ARCD 91007 597-B1
N NORMAN CT
1000 LBCH 90813 795-F6
NORMAN PL
200 SMCA 90405 671-F4
800 Brwd 90049 631-F1
900 Brwd 90049 591-F7
1500 City 90063 635-E3
NORMANDALE AV
19500 CRTS 90703 766-H3
N NORMANDIE AV
100 LA 90004 633-J1
200 LA 90004 593-J7
700 LA 90029 593-J5
1300 LFlz 90027 593-J3
S NORMANDIE AV
100 LA 90004 633-J2
300 LA 90020 633-J2
600 LA 90005 633-J2
600 LA 90010 633-J2
900 LA 90006 633-J3
1400 LACo 90044 703-J2
1400 LACo 90047 703-J6
1900 LA 90007 633-J6
1900 LA 90018 633-J6
3200 LA 90007 673-J3
3200 LA 90018 673-J3
3700 LA 90062 673-J3
3700 LA 90037 673-J3
5800 LA 90044 673-J5
5800 LA 90047 673-J5
7200 LA 90044 703-J2
7200 LA 90047 703-J2
12000 LACo 90044 733-J4
12000 LACo 90047 733-J4
12800 GAR 90247 733-J4
12800 GAR 90249 733-J4
15400 GAR 90247 734-A6
17500 GAR 90248 734-A6
17500 GAR 90248 764-A2
17700 LA 90248 764-A2
19000 LACo 90502 764-A3
19000 LA 90501 764-A6
20200 LA 90502 764-A3
22500 LACo 90501 764-A6
22500 LACo 90502 794-A2
22500 LACo 90501 794-A2
23400 Hrbr 90710 794-A2
25000 Hrbr 90710 794-A5
26000 Wilm 90744 794-A5
NORMANDIE PL
300 LA 90004 593-J7
NORMANDIE WY
15400 GAR 90247 734-A5
NORMANDY CT
- LCF 91011 535-E6
38800 PMDL 93551 4195-E6
NORMANDY DR
- LACo 91302 558-G3
1400 PAS 91103 535-E7
1400 LCF 91011 535-E7
NORMANDY LN
- LAN 93536 4015-B6
100 LCF 91011 535-E6
15200 LMRD 90638 737-G4
42800 LAN 93536 4105-B1
NORMANDY WY
- RowH 91748 708-J2
9500 CYP 90630 767-B7
NORMANS WY
24900 CALB 91302 589-C1
NORMANTON DR
2100 LCF 91011 504-H6
NOROCO DR
6000 PRV 90660 676-F5
NORRIS AV
8400 SunV 91352 533-A1
8700 SunV 91352 532-J1
8800 SunV 91352 502-J7
10200 Pcma 91331 502-D2
11500 LA 91340 502-C1
11500 LA 91340 482-C7
12500 LA 91342 482-A5
12500 LA 91342 481-F2
NORSALL CT
- GLDL 91206 564-J3
N NORSE WY
4100 LBCH 90808 766-A6

STREET Block City ZIP Pg-Grid

NORSEWOOD DR
2600 RowH 91748 679-B7
3000 RowH 91748 709-B1
NORSTADT WY
6100 BPK 90620 767-E2
W NORTE DAME ST
1300 UPL 91786 601-H1
NORTE VISTA DR
2400 CHLS 91709 680-J1
NORTH AL
1900 SPAS 91030 595-J2
5600 VanN 91401 562-B1
NORTH DR
- Hrbr 90710 794-A3
- SMRO 91108 566-C6
5700 CULC 90230 672-H5
NORTH PL
2100 LA 90031 635-A1
NORTH SPUR
- BREA 92823 710-F4
- BREA 92886 710-F4
- OrCo 92823 709-J5
- OrCo 92823 710-A4
- OrCo 92886 710-F4
NORTH ST
100 AZU 91702 598-J2
1200 AZU 91702 568-G6
1300 CRSN 90746 764-F4
NORTH TR
4200 LFlz 90027 563-J4
4200 LFlz 90027 564-A4
11000 LACo 91342 482-J6
NORTHAM DR
- FUL 92833 738-C5
NORTHAM ST
14600 LMRD 90638 737-F5
16600 LPUE 91744 678-F1
17400 LACo 91744 678-H1
18100 LACo 91744 679-A2
18800 LACo 91792 679-B2
NORTH AMERICAN CUT OFF
23600 VeCo 93063 499-C5
NORTHAMPTON AV
3700 CLAR 91711 600-J1
NORTHAMPTON ST
20700 DBAR 91789 679-G3
NORTHAMPTON WY
800 FUL 92833 738-B5
NORTHAVEN LN
2800 Alta 91001 536-C5
NORTHBAY RD
28900 RPV 90275 823-A1
NORTH BOUND DR
- SMRO 91108 566-D6
NORTHBROOK AV
27800 SCTA 91351 4461-E7
NORTHBROOKE LN
- SCTA 91355 4550-H3
NORTHCAPE AV
600 SDMS 91773 600-C1
NORTHCLIFF DR
19700 SCTA 91351 4551-E1
NORTHCLIFF RD
300 LACo 91107 566-E5
NORTHFIELD CT
23500 SCTA 91354 4460-G7
NORTHFIELD ST
15900 PacP 90272 630-J5
NORTHFLEET WY
19200 Tarz 91356 560-G6
NORTHFORD DR
6800 Tuj 91042 504-B6
NORTHGATE AV
7900 LA 91304 530-A2
NORTHGATE ST
10700 CULC 90230 672-H4
NORTHGATE WY
200 LHB 90631 708-G5
NORTH HILL RD
800 POM 91768 600-G6
NORTH HILLS DR
1200 UPL 91784 571-J6
1300 LHB 90631 708-G4
NORTHLAKE CIR
2400 THO 91361 557-B5
NORTHLAND DR
3600 LACo 90008 673-E4
NORTH PARK AV
1800 LA 90066 672-D3
NORTHPARK DR
- SCTA 91354 4460-G4
NORTH RANCH RD
- POM 91766 640-G4
NORTH RIDGE AV
1400 GLDR 91741 569-H4
NORTHRIDGE AV
1100 GLDR 91741 569-G4
E NORTHRIDGE AV
500 GLDR 91741 569-F4
W NORTHRIDGE AV
300 GLDR 91741 569-D4
NORTHRIDGE DR
4200 LACo 90043 673-C5
4600 PMDL 93551 4194-F1
NORTH RIDGE PL
1100 MONP 91754 635-H4
NORTHRIDGE RD
19800 Chat 91311 500-D3
NORTH RIDGE TR
- BREA 92823 710-B7
NORTHRIDGE HILL DR
10500 Chat 91311 500-F3

NORTHROCK DR
- LACo 93532 4102-J4
NORTHSHORE LN
1100 THO 91361 557-B5
NORTH SIDE DR
9000 LACo 93551 4193-G1
NORTHSIDE DR
1900 MTBL 90640 676-B2
E NORTHSIDE DR
5900 ELA 90022 675-J1
5900 ELA 90022 676-A2
6600 MTBL 90640 676-A2
NORTHSIDE PKWY
- Wch 90045 702-E4
NORTH SLOPE LN
- POM 91766 640-H5
NORTHSTAR CT
100 LA 90292 701-J1
NORTHSTAR DR
4500 PMDL 93552 4287-A1
NORTHSTAR LN
1300 UPL 91784 571-H4
NORTHSTAR MALL
- LA 90292 701-J1
NORTHSTAR ST
- LA 90292 701-J1
NORTHUP AV
- LACo 91107 566-G5
- PAS 91107 566-G5
NORTHVALE RD
10300 LA 90064 632-E6
NORTH VALLEY DR
500 THO 91362 557-C2
NORTH VIEW AV
800 ARCD 91006 567-E4
NORTHVIEW CIR
- LVRN 91750 570-H5
NORTHVIEW CT
300 AZU 91702 568-H2
37000 PMDL 93550 4286-H4
NORTHVIEW DR
20900 WAL 91789 639-G6
NORTHVIEW PL
24300 DBAR 91765 640-D7
NORTHVIEW TER
- HacH 91745 677-J4
NORTHWEST PASG
13800 MdlR 90292 702-A1
NORTHWESTERN DR
500 CLAR 91711 601-B3
NORTHWIND LN
- LA 91343 501-H6
NORTHWOOD AV
600 BREA 92821 709-A4
600 OrCo 92821 709-A4
700 BREA 92821 708-J4
19000 CRSN 90746 764-G3
N NORTHWOOD AV
600 COMP 90220 734-G3
S NORTHWOOD AV
400 COMP 90220 734-G5
13900 Wbrk 90222 734-G3
NORTHWOOD PL
700 POM 91767 601-B1
NORTHWOOD RD
1100 SLB 90740 796-G7
NORTHWOODS LN
- GLDL 91214 534-F1
NORTHWOODS VIEW RD
23800 CanP 91307 529-E5
NORTON AV
800 GLDL 91202 564-C2
1100 LA 90019 633-G4
2600 LYN 90262 704-J6
2800 LYN 90262 705-B6
7500 WHWD 90046 593-A5
9800 MTCL 91763 601-E6
11300 SBdC 91766 641-E3
11400 SBdC 91710 641-E3
11700 CHNO 91710 641-E6
N NORTON AV
100 LA 90004 593-G7
100 LA 90004 633-G1
S NORTON AV
100 LA 90004 633-G2
300 LA 90020 633-G2
600 LA 90005 633-G2
600 LA 90010 633-G2
900 LA 90019 633-F5
2800 LA 90018 633-E7
3400 LA 90018 673-E2
3700 LA 90008 673-E2
NORTON DR
22700 SCTA 91350 4460-H4
NORTON ST
100 NLB 90805 765-D2
5300 TOR 90503 763-A4
NORUMBEGA CT
3900 LA 90037 673-J2
NORUMBEGA DR
100 MNRO 91016 567-J2
900 MNRO 91016 568-A2
900 BRAD 91010 567-J2
NORUMBEGA RD
- MNRO 91016 567-H2
NORVAL AV
4200 LACo 93536 4104-J5
NORVAL ST
1600 POM 91766 641-B4
NORWALK AV
1900 Eagl 90041 565-A6
2200 Eagl 90041 564-J6

NORWALK BLVD
5400 WHIT 90601 677-A4
5700 WHIT 90606 677-A4
5900 WHIT 90606 676-H6
6000 LACo 90606 676-H6
7700 SFSP 90606 676-H6
8100 LACo 90606 706-H4
8100 SFSP 90606 706-H4
9000 SFSP 90670 706-H4
11000 NRWK 90650 706-J6
12200 NRWK 90650 736-J1
16000 CRTS 90703 736-J6
17400 ART 90701 736-J6
17800 ART 90701 766-J2
19100 CRTS 90703 766-J2
20300 LKWD 90715 766-J2
21000 HGDN 90716 766-J6
N NORWALK BLVD
3200 LALM 90808 796-J1
3200 LBCH 90808 796-J1
3400 LBCH 90808 766-J7
3500 HGDN 90716 766-J7
NORWAY LN
700 Brwd 90049 631-G1
NORWIC PL
2200 Alta 91001 536-A6
NORWICH AV
3000 ALH 91803 595-G6
4600 Shrm 91403 561-H4
5200 VanN 91411 561-H1
5400 LA 90032 595-G6
6200 VanN 91411 531-H6
6600 VanN 91405 531-H4
7900 PanC 91402 531-H2
8500 LA 91343 531-H1
8700 LA 91343 501-H4
9900 MsnH 91345 501-H4
NORWICH DR
400 CLAR 91711 571-C7
400 WHWD 90048 592-J7
37400 PMDL 93550 4286-E3
NORWICH LN
1400 LHB 90631 738-F1
NORWICH PL
- RowH 91748 708-J2
NORWOOD CT
600 SDMS 91773 600-D1
1600 BREA 92821 708-H6
W NORWOOD CT
1400 UPL 91786 601-H2
NORWOOD DR
600 SDMS 91773 600-D1
600 PAS 91105 565-F6
NORWOOD PL
8400 RSMD 91770 596-G7
27200 SCTA 91354 4460-G7
E NORWOOD PL
- ALH 91801 596-C7
100 SGBL 91776 596-E7
W NORWOOD PL
- ALH 91801 596-A7
100 SGBL 91776 596-D7
200 ALH 91803 596-A7
1900 ALH 91803 595-G7
NORWOOD ST
1900 LA 90007 634-C6
W NOSTRAND DR
700 SGBL 91775 596-C2
NOTRE DAME AV
2100 POM 91766 641-B6
9200 Chat 91311 499-F7
9200 Chat 91311 499-F7
9200 Chat 91311 499-F6
NOTRE DAME DR
- BPK 90620 767-F6
NOTRE DAME RD
300 CLAR 91711 601-C5
NOTTEARGENTA RD
200 PacP 90272 630-F6
NOTTINGHAM AV
2200 LFlz 90027 593-J2
NOTTINGHAM CT
24200 SCTA 91355 4550-E4
NOTTINGHAM LN
- ING 90305 703-E3
- RowH 91748 708-J2
- RowH 91748 709-A2
1800 SDMS 91773 599-G4
NOTTINGHAM PL
400 FUL 92835 738-H4
2600 LFlz 90027 593-J2
8700 Nor 91325 531-C1
NOTTINGHAM RD
- WLKV 91361 587-C1
NOTTINGHAM ST
- CRTS 90703 767-A2
NOTTINGWOOD CIR
1200 THO 91361 557-B5
NOUGUIER CT
400 SGBL 91776 596-D4
NOUTARY DR
- FUL 92833 738-C5
NOVA AV
- PMDL 93552 4286-J2
NOVA CT
2400 RowH 91748 679-D7
NOVA DR
6200 LAN 93536 4014-E7
NOVA ST
9700 PRV 90660 706-F2
11200 SFSP 90670 706-G3
NOVAK ST
14400 HacH 91745 637-J7

NOVAK ST
14800 HacH 91745 638-A7
14900 HacH 91745 678-A1
N NOVARA DR
200 LBCH 90803 826-C2
NOVARA LN
9800 CYP 90630 767-B7
NOVARA WY
500 VeCo 91377 557-G1
S NOVARRO ST
900 WCOV 91791 639-A2
NOVATO PL
2500 PVE 90274 792-J5
NOVEL CT
3500 HacH 91745 677-J6
NOVEL ST
1400 POM 91768 600-G7
NOVELA WY
25500 SCTA 91355 4550-F6
NOVELDA RD
600 ALH 91801 596-A3
NOVGOROD ST
4900 LA 90032 595-E5
NOVIA WY
40600 PMDL 93551 4194-G2
NOVICE LN
200 MNRO 91016 597-G1
NOVICE PL
14800 LA 91343 501-J6
NOVICE ST
14600 PanC 91402 501-J6
14800 LA 91343 501-J6
NOWELL AV
1800 RowH 91748 679-B5
NOWITA CT
600 Ven 90291 671-J5
NOWITA PL
700 Ven 90291 671-J5
NOYA PL
2000 PVE 90274 792-G6
NOYES ST
9900 LACo 90601 677-A2
NOYON ST
1300 DUAR 91010 568-A6
NUANU DR
15500 GAR 90247 733-J5
NUBIA ST
500 COV 91722 599-C3
13800 BALD 91706 598-A3
E NUBIA ST
200 COV 91722 599-C3
16500 LACo 91722 598-G3
20300 LACo 91724 599-F3
W NUBIA ST
100 SDMS 91773 600-B2
300 COV 91722 599-A3
NUEVA VISTA DR
1800 LHH 90631 708-D2
NUEZ WY
2400 Top 90290 590-B1
NUGENT DR
11700 GrnH 91344 481-B6
NUGENT PL
17200 GrnH 91344 481-C5
NUGENT ST
100 LAN 93534 4015-H6
200 LAN 93535 4015-H6
300 LAN 93535 4016-A6
6500 LACo 93535 4017-D6
9500 LACo 93535 4018-E5
NUGGET CT
200 SDMS 91773 599-H2
NUGGET DR
27500 SCTA 91387 4551-J3
NUGGET RD
10100 SBdC 92371 (4472-J3
See Page 4471)
NUNEZ DR
18800 RowH 91748 679-B5
NURENBURG RD
- Cstc 91384 4459-J1
NURMI ST
12000 LA 91342 482-B2
14600 LA 91342 481-J4
NUTCRACKER CT
20000 SCTA 91351 4551-E3
NUTMEG AV
11300 LA 90066 672-E4
NUTMEG LN
21600 SCTA 91350 4461-B5
NUTRIR WY
21800 Top 90290 590-A1
NUTWOOD AV
800 FUL 92831 738-J6
NUTWOOD CIR
5700 SIMI 93063 499-A2
NUTWOOD DR
- CRSN 90746 764-F1
NUTWOOD PL
300 FUL 92832 738-H6
NUTWOOD ST
300 BREA 92821 709-A5
E NUTWOOD ST
100 ING 90301 703-D3
NUVOLA CT
- RPV 90275 822-H4
NYE AV
6200 CMRC 90040 676-A7
N NYLIC CT
200 LBCH 90802 795-C7
200 LBCH 90802 825-C1
700 LBCH 90813 795-C6

O

E O ST
200 Wilm 90744 794-F4
OAHU
1300 WCOV 91792 638-H4
OAK
300 SDMS 91773 599-J3
OAK AV
100 POM 91766 640-G2
800 DUAR 91010 568-B5
1100 MANB 90266 732-G4
5700 TEML 91780 596-J1
6500 TEML 91775 596-J1
26700 SCTA 91351 4551-C2
E OAK AV
100 ELSG 90245 702-E7
N OAK AV
- PAS 91107 566-D3
600 PAS 91104 566-D3
6700 LACo 91007 596-J1
6700 LACo 91780 596-J1
6700 LACo 91775 596-J1
6800 LACo 91007 566-D4
6800 LACo 91775 566-D4
6800 ARCD 91007 566-D4
S OAK AV
- PAS 91107 566-D5
300 LACo 91107 566-D5
W OAK AV
100 ELSG 90245 702-E7
OAK CIR
- SCTA 91321 4641-C2
OAK CT
8500 LA 90046 592-J4
9200 MTCL 91763 601-E5
OAK DR
- Saug 91350 4461-B4
400 GLDR 91741 569-C4
400 LACo 91741 569-C4
1600 Top 90290 589-G3
4300 LCF 91011 534-J3
5500 LPMA 90623 767-D3
OAK GRV
100 MNRO 91016 567-G1
OAK LN
- LA 90068 563-G5
- LACo 91768 640-A2
- SCTA 91350 4550-H6
400 SGBL 91775 596-D2
1000 SMRO 91108 566-B7
4400 LACo 91711 571-B7
OAK PK
900 MNRO 91016 567-H1
OAK PL
200 BREA 92821 709-C7
1900 LCF 91011 534-J3
OAK RD
1400 SIMI 93063 499-B3
OAK ST
300 SMRO 91108 596-A3
400 GLDL 91204 564-D5
500 HMB 90254 762-H2
900 BURB 91506 563-F2
1100 SMCA 90405 671-G3
1100 SPAS 91030 595-G3
1200 UPL 91784 571-J3
1400 LA 90015 634-C5
1700 TOR 90501 763-G7
1900 LA 90007 634-B6
2000 SPAS 91030 596-A3
2400 CMRC 90023 675-D3
2500 BURB 91505 563-D3
4400 PRV 90660 676-F2
5500 SBdC 92397 (4652-D3
See Page 4651)
6000 HNTP 90255 675-A6
8500 LA 90046 592-J4
8700 BLF 90706 735-J5
8700 BLF 90706 736-A5
10600 LALM 90720 796-J2
11000 ELMN 91731 637-D1
12300 LYN 90262 735-B2
12700 WHIT 90602 707-C1
13300 LACo 91390 (4372-J4
See Page 4281)
13600 WHIT 90605 707-E2
22900 SCTA 91321 4640-H1
24700 LMTA 90717 793-H5
N OAK ST
100 ING 90301 703-B2
300 ING 90302 703-B2
S OAK ST
100 ING 90301 703-B3
OAK TR
17500 LACo 93532 4101-J1
OAK WY
500 LHB 90631 708-C6
OAKADO PL
4700 LCF 91011 534-H2
OAK BANK
- VeCo 91377 557-J1
OAKBANK AV
400 COV 91723 599-C5
OAKBANK DR
5200 LACo 91722 599-C2
6000 LACo 91702 569-C7
N OAKBANK DR
7000 GLDR 91741 569-C5
7200 LACo 91741 569-C5
OAKBAR CT
25600 SCTA 91321 4551-F6

OAK BARREL CT
- PMDL 93551 4104-D7
OAKBAY RD
26000 TOR 90505 793-F6
OAK BEND DR
5000 LVRN 91750 570-F6
9600 Tuj 91042 504-A5
OAK BLUFF RD
16200 LACo 91387 4552-C4
16200 SCTA 91387 4552-C4
OAK BRANCH CIR
26700 SCTA 91321 4551-F4
OAK BRANCH DR
700 VeCo 91377 558-B1
OAKBRIDGE LN
23100 SCTA 91321 4640-J3
OAKBRIDGE WY
- PMDL 93551 4194-H2
E OAKBROOK ST
5700 LBCH 90815 796-C2
N OAKBROOK ST
2700 LBCH 90815 796-D3
OAKBROOKE CT
- StvR 91381 4550-B5
OAKBURN DR
1200 LACo 91789 679-E4
OAKBURY DR
14900 LMRD 90638 737-H3
OAK CANYON AV
13600 Shrm 91423 562-C6
E OAK CANYON DR
14300 HacH 91745 677-H3
OAK CANYON LN
- LVRN 91750 570-H5
1000 GLDR 91741 569-F3
2000 CHLS 91709 710-H1
OAK CANYON RD
- Cstc 91384 4459-A2
- LACo 91387 4551-H4
600 COV 91724 599-E7
600 WCOV 91791 599-D7
OAK CANYON WY
1000 BREA 92821 709-C5
OAK CIRCLE DR
1200 GLDL 91208 534-G3
OAKCLIFF AV
39500 PMDL 93551 4195-E5
OAK CLIFF DR
- POM 91766 640-F6
OAKCLIFF RD
300 MNRO 91016 567-J2
OAKCREEK AV
24600 SCTA 91321 4551-B7
24600 SCTA 91321 4641-B1
OAK CREEK CT
17400 Enc 91316 561-B2
OAK CREEK LN
- AGRH 91301 558-A5
OAKCREEK LN
12500 CRTS 90703 736-J6
12500 CRTS 90703 737-A6
E OAKCREEK LN
16300 CRTS 90703 736-J4
OAK CREEK RD
1300 SDMS 91773 570-D7
OAKCREST
- LA 91342 481-G1
OAK CREST AV
1400 SPAS 91030 595-F3
OAKCREST AV
700 BREA 92821 709-A4
700 BREA 92821 708-H4
2300 PMDL 93550 4286-E2
OAK CREST DR
500 SMAD 91024 566-J1
600 SMAD 91024 536-J7
13700 CRTS 90703 737-D6
20600 LACo 91765 679-G7
31200 WLKV 91361 557-E6
OAKCREST DR
3100 LA 90068 593-D1
S OAKCREST PL
900 ANA 92804 767-J7
OAK CREST ST
12800 CRTS 90703 737-A6
OAK CREST WY
6100 HiPk 90042 565-D7
OAK CROSSING RD
19300 SCTA 91321 4551-F4
OAKDALE AV
700 MNRO 91016 567-H4
3700 LACo 91107 566-H5
4900 WdHl 91364 560-E3
5600 WdHl 91367 560-E1
6000 WdHl 91367 530-E7
6600 Win 91306 530-E2
8700 Nor 91324 530-E2
8800 Nor 91324 500-E7
9100 Chat 91311 500-E3
W OAKDALE CT
1500 UPL 91786 571-H7
OAKDALE DR
300 CLAR 91711 601-E4
500 SMAD 91024 567-B1
4300 CHNO 91710 641-E5
OAKDALE LN
1000 ARCD 91006 567-C4
OAKDALE ST
1000 WCOV 91790 638-F1
1400 PAS 91106 566-B5
1900 LACo 91107 566-D5
4500 CLAR 91711 601-E4
4500 MTCL 91763 601-E4

OAKDALE CANYON LN
- LACo 91387 4551-H6
OAKDELL LN
3100 LA 91604 592-H1
3200 LA 91604 562-H7
OAKDELL RD
3200 LA 91604 562-H7
OAKDEN DR
1800 LA 90046 593-A3
OAK DYKE AV
1200 LACo 90631 708-G3
OAKENDALE PL
2900 GLDL 91214 534-F3
OAKENGATE DR
1600 GLDL 91207 564-F1
OAKENGATE RD
1100 SDMS 91773 599-J4
OAKFAIR LN
1100 Hrbr 90710 794-A2
OAKFEN CT
5500 AGRH 91301 557-G5
OAK FENCE LN
- LAN 93536 4104-E3
3200 LAN 93536 4105-B3
OAK FERN CT
- SIMI 93063 499-A3
OAKFERN LN
1100 Hrbr 90710 794-A3
OAKFIELD DR
3400 Shrm 91423 562-A6
OAKFIELD RD
23600 HIDH 91302 559-E4
23600 LACo 91302 559-E4
OAKFLAT CT
26100 SCTA 91321 4551-G6
OAK FLAT DR
- LACo 91342 482-J2
OAKFORD DR
400 ELA 90022 635-H7
600 ELA 90022 675-H1
S OAKFORD DR
200 ELA 90022 635-H6
OAK FOREST CIR
- GLDR 91741 569-H5
OAK FOREST DR
6500 VeCo 91377 558-A1
OAKFOREST LN
- SCTA 91321 4641-B2
1000 LACo 91107 566-G6
OAKFORT AV
21200 CRSN 90745 764-H5
OAKGALE AV
27200 SCTA 91351 4551-E2
27900 SCTA 91351 4461-E7
OAK GARDEN CT
26700 SCTA 91321 4551-F4
OAKGATE AV
1900 WCOV 91792 639-A7
OAKGATE ST
1700 MONP 91755 636-B5
E OAKGATE ST
10300 BLF 90706 736-D7
OAKGLADE DR
700 MNRO 91016 567-H1
OAK GLEN AV
10500 MTCL 91763 641-D1
OAKGLEN AV
1200 ARCD 91006 567-D3
10100 MTCL 91763 601-D7
OAKGLEN CT
400 SDMS 91773 599-H3
OAK GLEN DR
3300 LA 90068 563-C7
OAK GLEN PL
2000 LA 90039 594-E5
OAK GLEN RD
2900 GLDL 91208 534-H5
OAK GLEN ST
4300 CALB 91302 558-H7
S OAKGREEN AV
1700 WCOV 91792 638-H4
OAK GROVE AV
800 PAS 91106 566-A7
800 SMRO 91108 566-B7
1100 LACo - (512-A5
See Page 511)
OAK GROVE CIR
4600 Eagl 90041 565-B7
OAK GROVE CT
3900 GLDL 91214 504-D7
OAKGROVE CT
- PMDL 93551 4194-H2
OAK GROVE DR
- LCF 91103 535-E5
600 GLDR 91741 569-F3
1000 Eagl 90041 565-B7
1000 LCF 91011 535-E5
1000 PAS 91103 535-E5
2100 Alta 91001 535-E5
OAKGROVE DR
4800 MTCL 91763 601-F5
OAK GROVE PL
1000 SMRO 91108 566-B7
1500 Eagl 90041 565-B7
OAK GROVE RD
3100 OrCo 90720 796-H5
OAK GROVE ST
44400 LAN 93535 4016-C6
OAKGROVE ST
44000 LAN 93536 4104-E1
44100 LAN 93536 4014-E7
OAKHART DR
100 GLDR 91741 570-A5

OAK HAVEN CT
400 VeCo 91377 558-B1
OAKHAVEN DR
1600 ARCD 91006 567-C2
2100 DUAR 91010 568-C4
S OAKHAVEN DR
800 ANA 92804 767-H7
OAKHAVEN LN
1200 ARCD 91006 567-D3
OAKHAVEN RD
1200 ARCD 91006 567-D3
OAKHEATH DR
1100 Hrbr 90710 794-A2
1300 Hrbr 90710 794-A2
OAKHEATH PL
23700 Hrbr 90710 794-A2
OAK HIGHLAND DR
26300 SCTA 91321 4551-F5
OAK HILL AV
1200 SPAS 91030 595-E3
3600 LA 90032 595-D6
4900 HiPk 90042 595-E3
N OAKHILL CIR
- CRSN 90746 764-F1
S OAKHILL CIR
- CRSN 90746 764-F1
OAK HILL CT
- Cstc 91384 4369-E4
OAKHILL DR
- GLDR 91741 570-A4
OAK HILL LN
100 SPAS 91030 595-E3
OAK HILL PL
1200 SPAS 91030 595-E3
6000 LA 90032 595-E3
6000 HiPk 90042 595-E3
OAK HILL ST
36600 PMDL 93552 4287-A3
OAK HILL TER
100 SPAS 91030 595-E3
OAK HILL WY
11500 Nor 91326 500-E1
OAK HILLS CT
1000 LHB 90631 738-D2
OAK HILLS DR
300 VeCo 91377 558-A2
500 VeCo 91377 557-J1
13000 SLB 90740 796-G7
OAK HOLLOW CIR
900 THO 91362 557-C1
OAK HOLLOW RD
4100 CALB 91302 559-G6
4100 CLAR 91711 571-A7
4100 CLAR 91711 601-A1
OAKHORN AV
31500 Cstc 91384 4369-F6
OAKHORNE DR
900 Hrbr 90710 794-A3
1300 Hrbr 90710 794-A2
1400 Hrbr 90710 793-J1
OAKHURST
3700 ELMN 91732 637-G1
OAKHURST AV
2700 LA 90034 632-G6
OAKHURST CT
2100 UPL 91784 571-H4
OAKHURST DR
- SCTA 91321 4641-B2
800 POM 91767 601-B4
N OAKHURST DR
100 BHLS 90210 632-H1
400 BHLS 90210 592-H7
S OAKHURST DR
100 BHLS 90212 632-H3
1100 LA 90035 632-H4
OAKHURST LN
200 ARCD 91007 567-B4
OAKHURST WY
- Nor 91326 480-E7
OAK KNOLL AV
1600 PAS 91108 596-B2
1600 SMRO 91108 596-B2
N OAK KNOLL AV
- PAS 91101 566-A4
S OAK KNOLL AV
- PAS 91101 566-A6
600 PAS 91106 566-A7
1200 PAS 91106 596-A1
1500 PAS 91108 596-A1
OAK KNOLL CIR
- LVRN 91750 570-G6
600 PAS 91106 566-A7
OAK KNOLL DR
- CRSN 90745 794-C1
200 GLDR 91741 569-H4
200 WCOV 91791 599-C7
1000 POM 91768 600-G6
2600 DBAR 91765 679-J6
2600 OrCo 90720 796-G5
2800 DBAR 91765 680-A7
OAK KNOLL LN
- BRAD 91010 568-B3
OAK KNOLL RD
1800 GLDL 91208 564-H1
OAK KNOLL ST
700 BREA 92821 708-J4
700 BREA 92821 709-A4
OAK KNOLL TER
- PAS 91106 596-A1
1000 LVRN 91750 570-E6
OAK KNOLL GARDENS DR
- PAS 91106 566-A6

OAK KNOLLS RD
5800 VeCo 93063 499-A3
N OAKLAND AV
- PAS 91101 565-J3
500 PAS 91104 565-J2
S OAKLAND AV
- PAS 91101 565-J7
500 PAS 91106 565-J7
1100 PAS 91106 595-J1
OAKLAND CT
23900 SCTA 91355 4550-F4
OAKLAND DR
300 LHB 90631 708-B6
OAKLAND RD
200 GLDR 91741 569-J5
OAKLAND ST
5100 LA 90032 595-F5
OAKLAND WY
12900 CHLS 91709 640-J7
OAK LANE DR
4900 Enc 91316 561-C4
OAKLAR DR
28000 SCTA 91350 4461-C5
OAKLAWN AV
200 SPAS 91030 595-H1
OAKLAWN LN
3600 PRV 90660 676-H1
OAKLAWN PL
400 SPAS 91030 595-H1
1400 ARCD 91006 567-A3
OAKLAWN RD
1200 ARCD 91006 567-B3
10500 LA 90064 632-E6
OAKLEAF
- LA 91342 481-H1
OAKLEAF AV
- VeCo 91377 558-B2
1000 MNRO 91016 567-J4
OAK LEAF CT
- StvR 91381 4550-C5
OAK LEAF DR
9400 Chat 91311 499-J6
12000 OrCo 90720 796-H5
OAK LEAF LN
- LVRN 91750 570-H7
- LVRN 91750 600-H1
OAKLEAF CANYON DR
- SCTA 91321 4641-C2
OAKLEAF CANYON RD
2300 LACo 91789 679-E6
W OAKLEY CT
1300 UPL 91786 571-J7
OAKLEY DR
3100 LA 90068 563-B7
OAKLEY RD
400 PVE 90274 792-E7
400 PVE 90274 822-E1
OAKLON DR
5000 RPV 90275 793-B7
OAKMALL LN
26400 SCTA 91321 4551-F5
OAKMAN DR
800 LACo 90601 637-G5
OAKMEAD LN
1600 LVRN 91750 570-F4
OAK MEADOW DR
- StvR 91381 4550-C5
OAK MEADOW LN
- LACo 91765 679-G7
- LACo 91765 709-F1
1500 SPAS 91030 595-J3
OAK MEADOW PL
- SMAD 91024 567-B2
5900 VeCo 91377 558-A2
OAK MEADOW RD
100 SMAD 91024 567-B3
1300 ARCD 91006 567-B3
OAKMERE DR
900 Hrbr 90710 794-B3
OAK MESA DR
1200 LVRN 91750 570-F6
OAKMILL AV
900 MTBL 90640 636-G5
900 RSMD 91770 636-G5
OAK MIRAGE PL
1000 THO 91362 557-D1
OAKMONT CT
- PMDL 93551 4195-B2
OAKMONT DR
- LACo 91387 4551-H4
- Brwd 90049 631-E1
300 Brwd 90049 631-E2
900 Brwd 90049 631-E1
1800 GLDL 91208 534-J7
E OAKMONT DR
300 MTBL 90640 636-F7
W OAKMONT DR
100 MTBL 90640 636-E7
200 MTBL 90640 676-E1
OAKMONT LN
12700 HAW 90250 733-H2
12800 Brwd 90049 631-E2
OAKMONT PL
2100 FUL 92831 738-J4
8200 BPK 90621 737-J6
8300 BPK 90621 738-J4
23900 LA 91304 529-E1
OAKMONT RD
1100 SLB 90740 796-G7
1100 SLB 90740 826-G1
OAKMONT TER
1800 GLDL 91208 534-J7

OAKMONT WY
16100 CHLS 91709 710-H1
OAKMONT VIEW DR
3100 GLDL 91208 534-G4
OAKMOOR ST
18500 SCTA 91351 4551-G1
OAKMORE RD
9300 LA 90035 632-G5
OAKMOUNT ST
9600 CYP 90630 767-D7
OAK MOUNTAIN PL
- Sunl 91040 503-A3
OAK MOUNTAIN RD
- BRAD 91010 568-A2
OAK ORCHARD RD
21100 SCTA 91321 4551-A7
22200 SCTA 91321 4550-J7
OAK PARK AV
4800 Enc 91316 561-C2
6800 VanN 91406 531-C4
8500 Nor 91325 531-C1
8700 Nor 91325 501-C4
11000 GrnH 91344 501-C2
OAK PARK CT
- Enc 91316 561-C3
E OAK PARK DR
100 CLAR 91711 601-D5
W OAK PARK DR
100 CLAR 91711 601-D4
OAK PARK LN
4900 VeCo 91377 557-G1
5200 Shrm 91423 562-D2
OAK PARK PL
800 WCOV 91790 638-F1
OAK PARK RD
800 COV 91724 599-E7
2200 GLDR 91741 570-A5
OAK PASS RD
9500 LA 90210 592-C2
OAK PATH CT
700 VeCo 91377 558-B1
OAKPATH DR
28800 AGRH 91301 558-A4
OAK PLAIN DR
26300 SCTA 91321 4551-F5
OAK PLAZA CT
19300 SCTA 91321 4551-F4
OAK PLUMA CT
19400 SCTA 91321 4551-F4
OAK POINT DR
600 VeCo 91377 558-A1
2800 LA 90068 593-C1
OAK RANCH CT
31800 WLKV 91361 557-D7
OAKRANCH RD
2300 LHH 90631 708-G1
OAKREST LN
23500 Hrbr 90710 794-A2
OAKRIDGE
15400 LA 91342 481-G1
OAKRIDGE CIR
1700 WCOV 91792 638-J6
OAKRIDGE CT
19900 WAL 91789 679-E1
OAK RIDGE DR
- SCTA 91321 4550-H5
1100 LVRN 91750 570-E6
22800 SCTA 91350 4550-H5
OAKRIDGE DR
1200 GLDL 91205 564-F7
OAKRIDGE PL
9500 Chat 91311 499-H6
OAKRIDGE RD
- LA 91304 529-C1
- StvR 91381 4640-C2
OAKRIDGE TER
3100 CALB 91302 589-D1
OAKRIM DR
30800 WLKV 91362 557-F4
OAKRIVER LN
- SCTA 91321 4641-C2
OAKROCK CT
17800 GrnH 91344 481-A5
OAKROW DR
16300 HacH 91745 678-E4
OAKROY RD
23100 Top 90290 589-F7
23100 Top 90290 629-G1
OAKRUN LN
23300 SCTA 91321 4640-H2
OAK RUN TR
- VeCo 91377 557-J1
OAKS AV
100 MNRO 91016 567-G3
12200 CHNO 91710 641-J7
12200 CHNO 91762 641-J7
12200 ONT 91762 641-J7
N OAKS AV
200 ONT 91762 601-H6
S OAKS AV
100 ONT 91762 641-J1
N OAKS CT
1500 ONT 91762 601-H5
OAKS PL
1900 ARCD 91006 567-D1
E OAKS ST
300 COMP 90221 734-J2
300 COMP 90221 735-A2
OAK SAVANNAH CT
- StvR 91381 4550-C5
OAKSBORO CIR
20600 WdHl 91364 560-C4

STREET
Block City ZIP Pg-Grid

OAK SHADE RD
2200 BRAD 91010 568-C4
OAKSHIRE DR
3100 LA 90068 563-C7
OAKSHORE DR
2400 THO 91361 557-B6
2600 WLKV 91361 557-B6
OAKSIDE CT
20000 LACo 91390 4461-D3
OAKSIDE LN
1200 GLDL 91208 534-G3
OAK SPRING CANYON RD
27800 LACo 91390 4552-D3
28000 LACo 91387 4552-D2
28100 SCTA 91387 4552-D2
29000 SCTA 91387 4462-D7
OAK SPRINGS DR
6500 VeCo 91377 558-B1
OAK SPRINGS LN
12100 Nor 91326 480-F6
OAK SPRINGS VALLEY RD
1700 SBdC 92372 (4562-E5 See Page 4471)
OAKSPUR DR
26300 SCTA 91321 4551-F5
OAKSTAFF CT
2000 THO 91361 557-A6
OAKSTONE WY
2000 LA 90046 592-H3
OAK SUMMIT RD
27300 AGRH 91301 588-F1
OAK TERRACE DR
4900 HiPk 90042 595-B4
OAK TERRACE PL
- StvR 91381 4550-B5
OAKTHORN LN
12600 LMRD 90638 737-H1
OAKTON WY
2500 POM 91768 640-C2
OAK TREE CIR
100 GLDR 91741 569-H5
1300 CHLS 91709 710-G1
OAK TREE CRSG
1100 CHLS 91709 710-F1
OAK TREE CT
- COV 91723 599-B6
1500 LHB 90631 738-C1
1600 GLDR 91741 569-H5
OAK TREE DR
100 GLDR 91741 569-H4
600 COV 91723 599-D6
1800 Eagl 90041 565-A6
OAK TREE LN
1600 GLDR 91741 569-H5
OAKTREE LN
- RHE 90274 793-A7
OAK TREE PL
- SCTA 91354 4460-F7
1600 GLDR 91741 569-H5
OAK TREE ST
- FUL 92835 738-H3
OAK TREE TER
1600 GLDR 91741 569-H5
OAK TREE WY
10600 Sunl 91040 503-G3
OAK TWIG LN
3900 LACo 91724 599-G5
OAK VALE DR
24000 SCTA 91355 4550-F7
OAKVALE RD
1200 SDMS 91750 570-F4
OAK VALLEY PL
- LACo 91765 679-G7
- LACo 91765 709-G1
OAK VALLEY RD
- Cstc 91384 4369-E5
2000 GLDL 91208 534-H4
OAK VIEW AV
1300 SMRO 91108 566-C7
OAK VIEW CT
- Cstc 91384 4369-E4
16500 Enc 91436 561-D4
OAK VIEW DR
- THO 91362 557-A2
16600 Enc 91436 561-D4
17000 Enc 91316 561-C4
OAKVIEW DR
200 AZU 91702 568-H6
OAK VIEW LN
- SCTA 91321 4641-C2
1200 LVRN 91750 570-F6
OAKVIEW LN
1800 ARCD 91006 567-C1
19100 RowH 91748 679-C6
40900 PMDL 93551 4194-G2
OAKVIEW ESTATES DR
- StvR 91381 4550-C6
OAKVILLE CT
- Nor 91326 500-E1
OAKVISTA CT
29900 AGRH 91301 557-H4
OAKWATER ST
1000 LACo 90502 794-A2
N OAKWAY AV
700 SDMS 91773 600-A1
OAK WAY DR
12300 OrCo 90720 796-H5
OAK WAY LN
16700 CHLS 91709 710-F3
OAKWELL DR
100 WAL 91789 639-F7

OAKWELL DR
100 WAL 91789 679-F1
OAKWELL RD
16200 LACo 91387 4642-C1
16200 Nwhl 91321 4642-C1
16200 SCTA 91321 4642-C1
16200 SCTA 91387 4642-C1
OAKWILDE LN
8800 LA 90046 592-H2
OAKWOOD
- LA 91342 481-G1
OAKWOOD AV
800 GLDR 91741 569-F4
900 FUL 92835 738-J3
1000 Ven 90291 671-H5
1600 ARCD 91006 567-D2
1800 GLDL 91208 534-H6
1900 SMAD 91024 567-D2
2500 Ven 90291 672-A6
2900 LYN 90262 705-A6
3600 LA 90004 594-A7
4100 LA 90004 593-H7
4200 LCF 91011 535-C3
6600 LA 90036 593-B7
7900 LA 90048 593-A7
8400 LA 90048 592-J7
30200 Cstc 91384 4459-C5
OAKWOOD CT
2000 Ven 90291 671-J5
OAKWOOD DR
1100 ARCD 91006 567-D3
1100 SMRO 91108 566-D7
1200 Top 90290 590-B4
OAKWOOD LN
500 BREA 92821 709-A5
700 LCF 91011 535-C3
2000 DUAR 91010 568-C5
2900 TOR 90505 793-E5
12800 LMRD 90638 737-G1
OAKWOOD PL
800 PAS 91106 566-A6
1100 SMAD 91024 567-C1
OAKWOOD ST
300 MTBL 90640 676-C5
1600 LACo 91104 536-C7
2100 LACo 91104 566-D1
OAKWOOD WY
- POM 91767 601-D6
21800 WAL 91789 639-J5
OASIS DR
900 LACo 90502 794-B2
OASIS RD
- Actn 93510 4374-J6
8900 SBdC 92372 (4562-B1 See Page 4471)
9300 SBdC 92372 (4472-B3 See Page 4471)
OATES DR
1200 DBAR 91765 680-C3
OAT MOUNTAIN MTWY
- Nor 91326 480-A2
- StvR 91381 480-A1
OBAN DR
900 LA 90065 594-J2
OBAR DR
500 LACo 91746 637-G4
OBECK AV
9300 Pcma 91331 502-A4
OBEE LN
11700 ELMN 91732 597-F6
OBER AV
26200 LMTA 90717 793-H6
E OBERG ST
100 SDMS 91773 570-C7
OBERLE CT
4600 LVRN 91750 570-G7
N OBERLIN AV
100 CLAR 91711 601-C3
OBERLIN DR
1000 GLDL 91205 564-G7
OBERLIN ST
12900 LA 91342 482-D4
OBERON ST
10500 LACo 90606 676-G7
OBERT AV
11500 LACo 90604 707-E7
OBISPO AV
300 LBCH 90814 795-J7
700 LBCH 90804 795-J7
3200 LKWD 90712 765-H2
5800 NLB 90805 765-H2
13400 PRM 90723 735-H2
N OBISPO AV
200 LBCH 90803 825-J1
300 LBCH 90814 825-J1
1000 LBCH 90814 795-H4
1300 LBCH 90804 795-H4
1800 SIGH 90755 795-H3
2000 LBCH 90755 795-H4
2800 LBCH 90808 795-H3
OBISPO AVEX
6300 NLB 90805 735-H7
6300 NLB 90805 765-H1
OBISPO DR
- LMRD 90638 738-A2
OBOE CIR
2800 HacH 91745 677-J5
OBREGON ST
10000 LACo 90606 676-J3
OBSERVATION DR
19700 Top 90290 630-A1
OBSERVATION LN
16200 CHLS 91709 710-H2

OBSERVATION WY
- PMDL 93552 4287-A5
OBSERVATORY AV
2200 LFlz 90027 594-B2
E OBSERVATORY RD
2800 LFlz 90027 593-J1
OBSIDIAN CT
2200 CHLS 91709 680-J7
39400 PMDL 93551 4195-D5
OCALA AV
600 LPUE 91744 638-E6
OCAMPO DR
400 PacP 90272 631-B5
OCANA AV
4100 LKWD 90713 766-C2
13600 BLF 90706 736-C2
N OCANA AV
2000 LBCH 90815 796-C3
3000 LBCH 90808 796-C1
3200 LBCH 90808 766-C7
OCASEY PL
- StvR 91381 4550-A6
OCASO AV
5000 BPK 90621 737-H5
12300 LMRD 90638 707-G7
12300 LMRD 90638 737-H1
N OCCIDENTAL BLVD
100 Echo 90026 634-C1
400 Echo 90026 594-C6
S OCCIDENTAL BLVD
100 LA 90057 634-B2
300 LA 90020 634-B2
OCCIDENTAL DR
100 SLB 90740 796-F6
W OCCIDENTAL DR
500 CLAR 91711 571-B7
OCEAN
100 WCOV 91790 598-E7
OCEAN AV
100 LA 90402 631-C7
100 LA 90402 671-C1
100 SLB 90740 826-E4
100 SMCA 90402 671-C1
800 SMCA 90403 671-C1
1100 SMCA 90401 671-C1
2100 Ven 90291 671-H6
3800 TOR 90503 763-C6
15800 LACo 90604 707-J7
22100 TOR 90505 763-C7
22600 TOR 90505 793-C2
N OCEAN AV
1900 SMCA 90405 671-E4
OCEAN BLVD
2100 LBCH 90802 824-G3
E OCEAN BLVD
100 LBCH 90802 825-F1
2000 LBCH 90803 825-F1
3900 LBCH 90803 826-A2
W OCEAN BLVD
- LBCH 90802 825-B1
500 LBCH 90831 825-B1
2200 LBCH 90802 824-H2
OCEAN CT
2200 SMCA 90405 671-F4
2300 Ven 90291 671-H6
OCEAN DR
200 MANB 90266 732-F6
800 HMB 90254 762-H2
10600 CULC 90232 672-G4
10700 CULC 90230 672-G4
N OCEAN DR
1100 MANB 90266 732-E5
OCEAN VW
16000 PacP 90272 630-F4
OCEAN WY
1900 SMCA 90405 671-E3
14700 LA 90402 631-B7
14700 LA 90402 671-B1
OCEANA CT
18500 SCTA 91351 4551-H2
OCEANAIRE DR
- RPV 90275 823-B2
OCEANAIRE LN
11900 VeCo 90265 625-F5
N OCEANBLUFF AV
600 SDMS 91773 600-C1
OCEAN BLUFF DR
- Wch 90045 702-C2
OCEAN CREST CT
- RPV 90275 822-H2
OCEAN CREST DR
6500 RPV 90275 822-H2
OCEAN FRONT WK
100 Ven 90291 671-G5
1200 SMCA 90401 671-D2
1200 SMCA 90403 671-D2
1900 SMCA 90405 671-E4
3100 LA 90292 671-G6
3400 LA 90292 701-J1
6100 PdlR 90293 702-A2
OCEANGATE
- LBCH 90802 825-C1
OCEAN GATE AV
12800 LACo 90250 733-B3
14200 HAW 90250 733-B3
S OCEAN GATE AV
5000 Lenx 90304 703-B5
9500 ING 90301 703-B4
10100 ING 90304 703-B5
14300 HAW 90250 733-B4
OCEANGROVE DR
32100 RPV 90275 823-E5

OCEANHILL WY
3600 LACo 90265 630-E5
S OCEAN MANOR PL
- LBCH 90803 825-J2
OCEANO DR
200 Brwd 90049 631-G4
OCEANO PL
11900 Brwd 90049 631-G3
OCEAN PARK BLVD
100 SMCA 90405 671-G3
2900 SMCA 90405 672-A1
11800 LA 90064 672-A1
OCEAN PARK PL N
1700 SMCA 90405 671-H2
OCEAN PARK PL S
400 SMCA 90405 671-H3
OCEANPORT RD
29500 RPV 90275 823-A2
OCEANRIDGE DR
29100 RPV 90275 823-A1
OCEANSIDE DR
4600 CHNO 91710 641-F7
OCEANSIDE ST
800 Wilm 90744 794-E3
OCEAN TERRACE DR
5800 RPV 90275 823-A2
5900 RPV 90275 822-J3
OCEAN TRAILS DR
- RPV 90275 823-D6
OCEANUS DR
7800 LA 90046 593-A3
OCEAN VIEW AV
300 HMB 90254 762-H3
700 MNRO 91016 567-H3
2200 LA 90057 634-B2
3500 LA 90066 672-B3
7900 WHIT 90602 677-G7
7900 WHIT 90602 707-F2
8300 WHIT 90605 707-F2
26200 LMTA 90717 793-H6
OCEAN VIEW BLVD
3400 GLDL 91208 534-H4
3800 GLDL 91020 534-H2
3800 Mont 91020 534-H2
4400 LCF 91011 534-H2
5100 LCF 91011 504-H7
OCEAN VIEW DR
- SIGH 90755 795-G3
700 FUL 92832 738-F6
2400 SBdC 91784 571-J2
S OCEAN VIEW DR
4200 LACo 90265 627-J6
4300 MAL 90265 627-J6
W OCEAN VIEW DR
26500 LACo 90265 627-J5
OCEAN VIEW TER
- SPed 90731 824-B7
OCHO RIOS WY
300 VeCo 91377 557-G2
OCIO LN
5300 PMDL 93551 4194-G2
OCONTO AV
5100 RPV 90275 793-B7
OCOTILLO DR
38800 LACo 93551 4195-F7
OCOTILLO LN
- CRSN 90745 794-G2
OCOTILLO ST
2100 SBdC 92371 (4472-E5 See Page 4471)
OCOTILLO SCHOOL DR
- LACo 93551 4195-F7
OCTAGON ST
12200 Brwd 90049 631-F1
OCTAVIA PL
16700 Enc 91436 561-D5
OCTILLO RD
2100 SBdC 92371 (4472-E5 See Page 4471)
ODD RD
39600 LACo 93551 4193-J5
39600 LACo 93551 4194-A5
ODELL AV
10200 Sunl 91040 503-G2
ODELL PL
1900 FUL 92833 738-D7
ODESSA AV
4900 Enc 91436 561-E3
6400 VanN 91406 531-E6
8600 LA 91343 531-E1
8700 LA 91343 501-E4
10200 GmH 91344 501-E1
11600 GmH 91344 481-E7
S ODGEN DR
200 LA 90036 633-B2
ODIN ST
2200 LA 90068 593-E3
ODONNELL LN
9900 Tuj 91042 504-C5
ODYSSEY DR
15500 GmH 91344 481-G7
OESTE AV
3900 LA 91604 562-E7
W OFARRELL ST
100 SPed 90731 824-B4
1200 LA 90732 824-A4
1200 LA 90732 823-H4
1600 RPV 90275 823-H4
OFFICE LN
- BLF 90706 736-B5
OFFICERS RD
2500 SPed 90731 824-B7
2500 SPed 90731 854-C1

OFFLEY AV
10800 DWNY 90241 706-F6
11600 NRWK 90650 706-F7
N OGDEN DR
300 LA 90036 593-B7
300 LA 90036 633-B1
700 LA 90046 593-B4
900 WHWD 90046 593-B5
S OGDEN DR
300 LA 90036 633-B1
1000 LA 90019 633-B4
OGDEN LN
2100 LAN 93535 4106-D2
OGELSBY AV
7000 Wch 90045 672-G7
7200 Wch 90045 702-G1
OGRAM AV
15500 LACo 90249 733-F5
16600 TOR 90504 733-F7
OHAN CT
2800 DBAR 91765 679-G6
W OHARA CT
1100 UPL 91786 571-J7
OHARA LN
2600 StvR 91381 4550-B6
O'HARE CT
- SCTA 91387 4462-D7
OHIO AV
400 LBCH 90814 795-H7
700 LBCH 90804 795-H7
2200 SIGH 90755 795-H4
2400 SGAT 90280 704-J4
2600 SGAT 90280 705-A4
3100 CLAR 91711 571-E6
10500 Wwd 90024 632-C3
10900 WLA 90025 632-C3
11200 LACo 90073 632-A5
11500 WLA 90025 631-J5
N OHIO AV
1300 LBCH 90804 795-H4
2100 SIGH 90755 795-H4
OHIO ST
200 PAS 91106 565-J7
2800 Actn 93510 4465-D2
13700 BALD 91706 598-A4
OHM AV
10600 NRWK 90650 706-E7
OIL FIELD RD
13000 BREA 92821 709-A4
13000 OrCo 92821 709-A4
OIL WELL RD
- CHLS 91709 710-H5
- OrCo 92886 710-H5
OIL WELL CANYON RD
- HacH 91745 677-G2
S OJAI CIR
700 MONP 91754 636-A3
OJAI DR
7200 PMDL 93551 4104-C6
OJIBWA PL
15100 LACo 93532 4102-E4
OKEAN PL
2900 LA 90046 593-A1
OKEAN TER
8000 LA 90046 593-A1
OKELL DR
2900 LA 90032 595-D7
OKI ST
4000 Actn 93510 4465-A1
OKLAHOMA AV
10200 Chat 91311 500-C2
11300 SGAT 90280 705-F7
11500 SGAT 90280 735-F1
OKOBOJI DR
9000 ARCD 91007 566-J7
9000 LACo 91775 566-J7
OLA AV
9000 WHIT 90603 707-F3
OLAF PL
12600 GmH 91344 481-B5
OLAF HILL DR
3300 HacH 91745 677-J6
OLANCHA DR
900 LA 90065 595-A2
1000 LA 90065 594-J2
OLAND AV
8700 SunV 91352 533-B1
OLAND ST
12600 NRWK 90650 737-A5
OLANDA ST
4100 LYN 90262 735-C2
4200 COMP 90221 735-C2
8200 PRM 90723 735-H2
OLAS DR
2100 LA 90732 823-G7
OLCOTT ST
6300 Tuj 91042 504-B4
OLD RD
27700 MAL 90265 667-H1
OLD ADOBE CT
- PMDL 93552 4287-E2
OLD ADOBE LN
- BqtC 91354 4460-E3
OLD BADILLO ST
1400 COV 91724 599-F5
OLD BREA CANYON RD
22300 DBAR 91789 679-J2
22300 DBAR 91789 680-A2
22300 INDS 91789 679-J2
22300 INDS 91789 680-A2
OLD BUCKBOARD LN
9000 SunV 91352 503-C7

OLD CANYON DR
1100 HacH 91745 677-H1
OLD CARBON CANYON RD
2000 CHLS 91709 680-J7
2100 CHLS 91709 710-J1
OLD CARRIAGE CT
29000 AGRH 91301 558-A3
OLD CASTLE RD
- WLKV 91361 587-C1
OLD CHESEBORO RD
34800 LACo 93552 4377-B1
35600 LACo 93552 4287-B7
OLD CHIMNEY RD
26800 LACo 90265 627-G5
OLD CHURCH RD
100 Top 90290 590-A6
OLD COACH CT
- LACo 91390 4461-C3
OLD COLONY WY
30900 AGRH 91301 557-F6
30900 WLKV 91361 557-F6
OLD COPPER LN
2200 HacH 91745 678-E5
OLD COURSE WY
25500 SCTA 91355 4550-F6
OLD DEPOT PLAZA RD
9900 Chat 91311 500-A5
OLDEN ST
15400 LA 91342 481-F3
OLDENBERG WY
6000 SIMI 93063 499-B1
OLDENBURG LN
- GmH 91344 480-J6
OLD FARM RD
5200 HIDH 91302 559-E3
OLDFIELD ST
100 LAN 93534 4015-J6
500 LAN 93535 4016-A6
2000 LAN 93536 4015-A6
OLDFIELD RANCH RD
21500 Top 90290 590-A4
22100 Top 90290 589-J4
OLD FOREST RD
16400 HacH 91745 678-E4
OLD FORT RD
400 SPed 90731 824-B7
OLD FORT TEJON RD
5700 LACo 93552 4287-C7
5700 LACo 93552 4377-D1
6900 Litl 93543 4377-D1
OLD FRIEND RD
28100 SCTA 91351 4461-F7
OLD GROVE PL
- WAL 91789 639-D4
OLD GROVE RD
- LA 91342 481-G3
1700 LACo 91107 536-G7
OLDGROVE WY
40900 PMDL 93551 4194-H1
OLDHAM LN
6500 LACo 91775 596-F1
OLDHAM PL
16600 Enc 91436 561-D6
OLDHAM ST
16400 Enc 91436 561-D6
OLD HARBOR CT
- SLB 90740 796-J6
OLD HARBOR LN
13900 MdlR 90292 702-A2
OLD HAROLD RD
2300 PMDL 93550 4286-D5
OLD HOMESTEAD RD
12600 Pear 93553 4468-H3
12600 Valy 93563 4468-H3
OLD HOUSE RD
1400 PAS 91107 566-G1
OLD LANDMARK LN
800 LCF 91011 535-B3
OLD MALIBU RD
3700 LACo 90265 630-D6
OLD MILL RD
500 SMRO 91108 595-J1
500 SMRO 91108 596-B2
600 PAS 91108 596-A1
1000 AZU 91702 569-A5
1400 BREA 92821 708-J4
11900 OrCo 90720 796-J5
OLD MILL CREEK LN
29100 Ago 91301 588-A1
OLD MINE RD
34100 Actn 93510 4374-E5
OLD MINER RD
32900 Actn 93510 4375-E7
OLD MINT CANYON RD
10700 LACo 91390 4373-D6
OLD MOTOR AV
3100 LA 90064 632-E7
OLD NADEAU RD
2000 PMDL 93550 4376-D1
2200 PMDL 93550 4286-E7
OLD OAK LN
200 SMAD 91024 567-A3
1600 ARCD 91006 567-C2
13200 Brwd 90049 631-D3
OLD OAK RD
1500 Brwd 90049 631-E3
3700 Ago 91301 588-B1
OLD OAK SPRING RANCH RD
100 SBdC 92372 (4562-A2 See Page 4471)

OLD OAK SPRING RANCH RD
1000 SBdC (4562-C4 See Page 4471)
OLD ORCHARD RD
1800 Brwd 90049 631-E2
OLD PHILLIPS RD
900 GLDL 91207 564-F1
1000 GLDL 91207 534-F7
OLD POMONA RD
- POM 91766 640-G5
OLD POST RD
500 WAL 91789 639-F7
OLD RANCH CIR
11300 Chat 91311 499-J1
OLD RANCH PKWY
3000 SLB 90740 796-H6
OLD RANCH RD
- INDS 91789 639-H7
200 INDS 91789 679-J1
200 SMAD 91024 567-B1
300 BRAD 91010 568-A3
1700 Brwd 90049 631-D2
1800 PacP 90272 631-D2
4900 LVRN 91750 570-E6
N OLD RANCH RD
200 ARCD 91007 567-A5
1000 ARCD 91006 567-A4
S OLD RANCH RD
- ARCD 91007 567-A6
OLD RANCH RAVINE RD
18800 RowH 91748 679-B6
OLDRIDGE DR
2200 HacH 91745 678-E5
OLD RIVER SCHOOL RD
10200 DWNY 90241 706-A2
10300 DWNY 90241 705-H6
11900 DWNY 90242 705-H6
12700 SGAT 90280 705-G7
OLD ROCK RD
- StvR 91381 4550-B5
OLD SALT LN
5500 AGRH 91301 557-G5
OLD SAN GABRIEL CANYON RD
- LACo 569-B1
- AZU 91702 569-B1
- LACo 91702 569-B1
OLD SCANDIA LN
23900 LACo 91302 559-D4
OLD SETTLERS LN
1400 POM 91768 600-H6
OLD SIERRA HWY
- Actn 93510 4375-H6
- LACo 93551 4375-H6
- LACo 93550 4376-A5
- PMDL 93550 4376-A5
OLD SPANISH TR
- LACo 91390 4461-B4
OLD STAGE RD
9200 LACo 91390 4373-H6
OLDSTONE CT
1700 RPV 90275 823-H2
OLD STONE RD
9200 SBdC 92372 (4472-F7 See Page 4471)
9200 SBdC 92372 (4562-F1 See Page 4471)
OLD STONE WY
24900 StvR 91381 4640-B2
OLD TOLL RD
- Alta 91001 535-G3
OLD TOPANGA CANYON RD
100 Top 90290 590-A6
400 Top 90290 589-G2
2700 CALB 90290 589-F1
3500 CALB 90290 559-F7
3600 CALB 91302 559-G7
OLD TRAIL DR
600 DBAR 91765 640-B6
OLD VALLEY BLVD
15800 INDS 91744 638-D7
15800 INDS 91744 678-E1
15800 LPUE 91744 678-E1
15800 LPUE 91744 638-D7
16300 INDS 91745 678-E1
16300 LPUE 91745 678-E1
OLD WHEELER RD
1400 LVRN 91750 570-F5
OLD WILEY CANYON RD
24900 SCTA 91321 4640-F2
OLDWOOD CT
1700 BREA 92821 708-H6
OLD WOOD RD
- POM 91766 640-F5
OLD ZAFERIA WY
2500 LBCH 90804 795-H5
OLEANDER AV
1200 UPL 91784 571-J4
12300 CHNO 91710 641-J6
N OLEANDER AV
100 COMP 90220 734-J3
1100 COMP 90222 734-J3
1700 Wbrk 90222 734-J3
S OLEANDER AV
100 COMP 90220 734-J6
13000 Wbrk 90222 734-H2
OLEANDER CIR
7800 BPK 90620 767-J3
OLEANDER CT
3900 CALB 91302 588-G1
15200 SCTA 91387 4462-E6

OLEANDER DR
- DUAR 91010 568-C5
500 HiPk 90042 565-D7
500 HiPk 90042 595-D1
OLEANDER RD
1400 LHH 90631 708-G3
OLEANDER ST
600 BREA 92821 738-J1
900 BREA 92821 708-J7
43600 LAN 93535 4106-E1
OLEANDER TER
- LA 91342 481-J1
OLEANDER TR
3400 CALB 91302 589-E1
OLEMA ST
9100 TEML 91780 596-J1
E OLETA ST
5400 LBCH 90815 796-C6
OLETA TURN
5400 LBCH 90815 796-C6
OLETHA LN
10300 BelA 90077 592-A3
OLIN DR
9200 Chat 91311 499-F7
E OLIN PL
2000 WCOV 91791 639-A1
OLIN ST
8600 LA 90034 632-H6
OLINDA AV
200 LHB 90631 708-E4
OLINDA DR
100 BREA 92823 710-D5
200 OrCo 92823 710-D5
W OLINDA LN
3100 ANA 92804 767-G6
OLINDA PL
100 BREA 92823 710-C6
OLINDA RD
- BREA 92823 710-B5
- OrCo 92823 710-B4
S OLINDA RD
- BREA 92823 710-B6
- OrCo 92823 710-B6
OLINDA ST
10700 SunV 91352 533-A1
11000 SunV 91352 532-J2
OLIVA AV
3900 LKWD 90712 766-A2
4100 LKWD 90712 765-J3
15100 PRM 90723 735-J5
OLIVA CT
21800 SCTA 91350 4461-A4
OLIVAS PARK RD
25700 SCTA 91355 4550-F6
OLIVE
- LA 91342 481-G1
200 SDMS 91773 599-H3
OLIVE AV
- SMAD 91024 567-A1
500 BREA 92821 709-D6
500 Ven 90291 671-J6
700 LBCH 90813 795-E1
1800 SPAS 91030 596-A3
2400 LaCr 91214 504-G6
2600 Alta 91001 535-G5
2900 SIGH 90755 795-E1
3300 Bxby 90807 795-E1
3400 Bxby 90807 765-E5
5300 NLB 90805 765-E3
31900 Cstc 91384 4369-F6
E OLIVE AV
- BURB 91502 533-H6
100 LHB 90631 708-E6
100 MNRO 91016 567-G4
400 BURB 91501 533-H6
N OLIVE AV
- ALH 91801 596-A4
200 LBCH 90802 795-E7
1300 LBCH 90813 795-E6
1800 LBCH 90806 795-E3
2200 Alta 91001 535-G6
2700 SIGH 90755 795-E2
6600 NLB 90805 735-E6
S OLIVE AV
- ALH 91801 596-A5
800 ALH 91803 596-A6
1800 ALH 91803 636-A1
W OLIVE AV
- BURB 91502 533-H7
- BURB 91502 563-E3
100 MNRO 91016 567-E4
500 BURB 91506 563-E3
900 BURB 91505 563-E3
3200 BURB 91523 563-E3
3600 BURB 91522 563-E3
OLIVE CT
- CRSN 90746 764-D4
- LCF 91011 535-A2
900 MNRO 91016 567-E4
5400 TEML 91780 597-A4
N OLIVE CT
700 AZU 91702 569-B5
OLIVE DR
- WdHI 91364 560-A5
1100 WHWD 90069 593-A5
2500 PMDL 93550 4286-F4
13400 WHIT 90608 677-D6
13400 WHIT 90601 677-D6
OLIVE LN
- LA 90065 594-F1
1000 LCF 91011 535-A2
2500 LACo 91768 640-A1

OLIVE PL
200 BREA 92821 709-C7
700 MONP 91755 636-D5
1400 ALH 91803 596-A7
12100 CHNO 91710 641-D6
OLIVE ST
100 CLAR 91711 601-D4
100 GLDL 91206 564-G5
100 AVA 90704 5923-H3
600 Ven 90291 671-J6
600 Ven 90291 672-A6
2400 LACo 90255 704-J1
2500 LVRN 91750 600-H1
2700 LACo 90255 705-A1
2800 TOR 90501 793-H1
2900 HNTP 90255 705-A1
3900 SBdC 91710 641-D5
4000 CDHY 90201 705-A1
4000 CDHY 90255 705-A1
4500 MTCL 91763 601-E4
8700 BLF 90706 735-J5
9000 BLF 90706 736-A5
9000 TEML 91780 596-H4
9500 TEML 91780 597-A4
11100 LA 90061 704-J1
11600 LYN 90262 705-B7
11600 LYN 90262 735-B1
11900 NRWK 90650 736-H1
13600 BALD 91706 598-A3
14800 IRW 91706 598-C3
E OLIVE ST
100 POM 91766 640-J6
100 POM 91766 641-B5
S OLIVE ST
100 LA 90012 634-F4
200 LA 90015 634-E5
300 LA 90013 634-F4
600 LA 90014 634-F4
1900 LA 90007 634-D7
2800 LA 90007 674-C1
4500 LA 90037 674-D5
5800 LA 90003 674-C6
8400 LA 90003 704-C2
10800 LA 90061 704-C5
W OLIVE ST
100 POM 91766 640-J6
200 ING 90301 703-B2
OLIVE WY
1900 LACo 91104 566-D1
OLIVE BRANCH DR
15400 LMRD 90638 737-H1
OLIVEGROVE AV
10600 Sunl 91040 503-E3
OLIVE GROVE LN
13900 LA 91342 482-B1
N OLIVE GROVE LN
- LACo 91744 638-G4
OLIVEGROVE PL
9000 Sunl 91040 503-E3
OLIVE HILL DR
600 SDMS 91773 599-J4
4000 LACo 91711 571-E4
OLIVE KNOLL PL
4000 LACo 91711 571-E4
OLIVE MILL CT
- SCTA 91354 4460-F7
OLIVEMILL RD
16100 LMRD 90638 738-A1
OLIVE POINT PL
4000 LACo 91711 571-E4
OLIVER DR
900 FUL 92832 738-F6
W OLIVER DR
3000 ANA 92804 767-J6
OLIVER LN
36200 LACo 93551 4285-H5
OLIVER ST
900 SPAS 91030 595-G1
W OLIVER ST
200 SPed 90731 824-A4
1000 LA 90732 824-A4
OLIVER WY
- StvR 91381 4550-D7
OLIVERA DR
1800 Ago 91301 588-A4
OLIVERA LN
200 SMAD 91024 567-C3
OLIVERA PL
42300 LACo 93536 4104-J5
OLIVERAS AV
2300 Alta 91001 535-J6
OLIVER VICKERY CIRCLE WY
- SPed 90731 854-C2
OLIVETA PL
300 LCF 91011 535-D3
OLIVE TREE DR
1100 LHB 90631 738-C1
OLIVE TREE LN
300 SMAD 91024 567-A1
OLIVE VIEW DR
13800 LA 91342 481-J2
14400 LA 91342 481-J2
OLIVE VIEW LN
14500 LA 91342 482-A2
OLIVEWOOD CT
1800 LVRN 91750 570-G6
OLIVIA TER
10000 SunV 91352 533-C2
OLIVINE DR
15600 CHLS 91709 680-J7
OLIVOS DR
19300 Tarz 91356 560-G4

OLMSTED AV
3700 LA 90018 673-F2
3700 LA 90008 673-F2
OLMSTED DR
500 GLDL 91202 564-B1
OLNEY PL
2900 BURB 91504 533-F3
OLNEY ST
800 SGBL 91776 596-F7
800 RSMD 91770 596-F7
9500 RSMD 91770 597-A7
10100 ELMN 91731 597-B7
OLNEY WY
13100 Brwd 90049 631-E1
OLSON DR
- FUL 92833 738-C5
OLSON LN
23900 LMTA 90717 793-H3
OLSON ST
4700 Eagl 90041 565-A6
OLVERA ST
600 LA 90012 634-G3
OLYMPIA PL
10600 Nor 91326 500-G3
OLYMPIA ST
18900 Nor 91326 500-G3
OLYMPIA WY
- LACo 93536 4104-J5
OLYMPIAD DR
3400 LACo 90043 673-D4
OLYMPIAD LN
16000 VanN 91406 531-F6
OLYMPIAN CT
18500 SCTA 91351 4551-H2
OLYMPIC BLVD
300 SMCA 90401 671-F2
600 SMCA 90404 671-F2
2300 SMCA 90404 631-H7
8400 PRV 90660 676-F3
8800 BHLS 90211 632-F3
9100 BHLS 90212 632-F3
10300 LA 90064 632-F3
10300 WLA 90025 632-F3
E OLYMPIC BLVD
100 LA 90015 634-E6
1000 ELA 90022 675-E1
1000 LA 90021 634-G6
2400 LA 90023 634-G6
2700 LA 90023 635-A7
2700 LA 90023 675-B1
3900 LACo 90023 675-E1
5400 CMRC 90022 675-H1
6100 ELA 90022 676-B2
W OLYMPIC BLVD
- SMCA 90404 631-J7
100 LA 90015 634-C4
400 MTBL 90640 676-C2
1000 LA 90006 634-C4
2100 ELA 90022 676-C2
2800 LA 90006 633-G4
3300 LA 90019 633-G4
5100 LA 90036 633-C3
12100 LA 90064 631-J7
12100 WLA 90025 631-J7
OLYMPIC CT
- CLAR 91711 571-F5
OLYMPIC DR
- WdHI 91367 530-D7
2600 GLDL 91206 565-A2
OLYMPIC LN
200 MTBL 90640 676-E3
W OLYMPIC PL
6500 LA 90035 633-A3
E OLYMPIC PZ
4000 LBCH 90803 826-A2
OLYMPIC ST
30300 Cstc 91384 4459-H3
OLYMPIC WY
9100 PRV 90660 676-G3
OLYMPIC CREST DR
- SCTA 91351 4551-G1
OLYMPIC VIEW DR
2400 CHLS 91709 680-J1
OLYMPUS
1400 WCOV 91790 638-D2
OLYMPUS AV
800 HacH 91745 678-C2
OLYMPUS DR
44200 LAN 93536 4015-B7
OMAHA CT
300 CLAR 91711 601-E4
OMAHA ST
5700 HiPk 90042 595-C3
O MALLEY AV
100 AZU 91702 569-A7
100 AZU 91702 599-A1
1100 COV 91722 599-A2
5300 LACo 91702 599-A2
N OMALLEY AV
1000 UPL 91784 571-J3
1400 UPL 91786 571-J7
OMALLEY LN
1400 LHB 90631 738-B1
N OMALLEY WY
1700 UPL 91784 571-J5
OMALLY CT
16400 LMRD 90638 738-A2
OMAR ST
300 LA 90013 634-G5
500 POM 91768 640-C2
700 GLDL 91202 564-C3
OMBU LN
- SMRO 91108 566-C7

STREET
Block City ZIP Pg-Grid

OMELIA RD
12500 WHIT 90601 677-C4
OMELVENY AV
600 SFER 91340 502-A1
1100 SFER 91340 501-J1
1300 SFER 91340 481-J7
8400 SunV 91352 532-G1
8800 SunV 91352 502-F7
9500 Pcma 91331 502-C3
11000 LA 91340 502-A2
OMER LN
1000 BURB 91502 563-H2
ONACREST DR
5100 LACo 90043 673-C5
ONAKNOLL AV
5100 LACo 90043 673-D4
ONARGA AV
700 HiPk 90042 565-D7
ONAWA PL
21800 DBAR 91765 679-J5
ONEAL CT
9600 Nor 91325 500-J6
ONEIDA AV
8800 SunV 91352 502-F7
10200 Pcma 91331 502-B2
11000 LA 91340 502-A1
ONEIDA CT
- CHNO 91710 641-G4
ONEIDA DR
300 PAS 91107 566-G5
ONEIDA ST
2300 LACo 91107 566-E5
2300 PAS 91107 566-F5
ONEIL ST
4300 LA 90032 595-D7
W ONEIL ST
1100 UPL 91784 571-J6
O NEILL AV
2400 CMRC 90040 675-G3
ONEILL CIR
- StvR 91381 4640-B1
ONE OAK LN
2400 SIMI 93063 499-A1
ONEONTA AL
1500 ALH 91801 595-J3
1600 SPAS 91030 595-H3
ONEONTA DR
800 LA 90065 594-J2
800 LA 90065 595-A2
1800 SPAS 91030 595-G3
ONEONTA KNOLL
1400 SPAS 91030 595-H3
ONIZUKA ST
100 LA 90012 634-G4
ONLEE AV
27300 SCTA 91350 4460-J6
27300 SCTA 91350 4461-A6
ONRADO ST
2700 TOR 90503 763-E6
ONTARE RD
- ARCD 91006 567-D3
ONTARIO AV
1300 PAS 91103 565-E1
ONTARIO ST
1100 BURB 91505 563-D1
1100 BURB 91505 533-D4
7500 LA 91504 533-D4
N ONTARIO ST
100 BURB 91505 563-E3
1400 BURB 91505 533-D7
1900 BURB 91504 533-D5
ONTEORA WY
4900 Eagl 90041 564-J6
ONTIVEROS PL
10500 SFSP 90670 706-H5
ONYX
- BREA 92823 710-C6
ONYX CT
- CRTS 90703 767-A3
ONYX DR
1300 PMDL 93550 4286-C3
1900 WAL 91789 639-H2
2500 LA 90032 595-C7
ONYX LN
27500 Cstc 91384 4369-G6
ONYX ST
3400 TOR 90503 763-B5
ONYX WY
- WCOV 91792 679-C1
OPAL AV
4200 CYP 90630 767-A4
4200 LACo 90630 767-A4
4700 PMDL 93552 4287-C1
OPAL CT
- CRTS 90703 767-A3
5600 WHIT 90601 677-C4
OPAL LN
- POM 91767 600-J2
2300 WCOV 91792 679-B1
OPAL PL
400 LBCH 90813 795-D6
OPAL ST
700 RBCH 90277 762-J6
700 RBCH 90277 763-A6
2300 LA 90023 634-J7
2900 TOR 90503 763-E6
3300 LA 90023 675-B1
OPAL WY
- GAR 90247 734-A3
OPAL CANYON RD
200 DUAR 91010 568-E4
OPAL COVE WY
400 SLB 90740 826-F4

OPALINE CT
37500 PMDL 93550 4286-C3
OPECHEE WY
1300 GLDL 91208 534-G7
OPEN BRAND RD
- RHLS 90274 823-E3
OPEN CREST DR
27500 SCTA 91350 4461-A6
OPEN SKY DR
2200 FUL 92833 738-C3
OPHIR CIR
500 SDMS 91773 570-C6
OPHIR DR
10900 Wwd 90024 632-A2
11000 Wwd 90024 631-J2
OPORTO DR
6900 LA 90068 593-D3
E OPP ST
100 Wilm 90744 794-J5
W OPP ST
100 Wilm 90744 794-D6
OPTICAL DR
1300 AZU 91702 568-F6
1300 IRW 91702 568-F6
ORACLE PL
14700 PacP 90272 631-B4
ORACLE ST
12100 NRWK 90650 706-H6
ORACLE HILL RD
33400 PMDL 93550 4376-E7
ORAH AV
500 MTBL 90640 676-B1
500 MTBL 90640 636-B7
ORAL ST
18700 RowH 91748 679-B7
ORAN CIR
6800 BPK 90621 767-G2
ORANGE
200 SDMS 91773 599-J2
ORANGE AV
- LBCH 90802 825-F1
200 LBCH 90802 795-F7
500 MNRO 91016 567-J4
700 LBCH 90813 795-F6
900 AZU 91702 568-A4
1100 MNRO 91016 568-A4
1300 DUAR 91010 568-A4
1800 LBCH 90806 795-F3
2200 SIGH 90755 795-F3
2400 LaCr 91214 504-F6
2600 Bxby 90807 795-F3
2700 TOR 90501 763-G7
2700 TOR 90501 793-G1
3200 GLDL 91214 504-E6
3400 Bxby 90807 765-F6
4000 CYP 90630 767-C7
5100 NLB 90805 765-F3
6300 NLB 90805 735-F6
6500 ANA 90620 767-C7
6500 BPK 90620 767-C7
6900 PRM 90723 735-F1
8100 PRV 90660 706-F2
9900 SGAT 90280 705-D6
10600 LYN 90262 705-D6
N ORANGE AV
100 AZU 91702 568-H5
100 BREA 92821 709-B7
100 FUL 92833 738-F7
100 INDS 91744 638-B4
100 MONP 91755 636-D2
100 WCOV 91790 598-E6
100 INDS 91746 638-B4
300 LPUE 91744 638-B4
300 LPUE 91746 638-B4
700 LACo 91722 598-E6
900 LACo 91744 638-B4
900 LACo 91746 638-B4
1500 WCOV 91790 638-B4
S ORANGE AV
100 AZU 91702 568-H7
100 BREA 92821 709-B7
100 FUL 92833 738-F7
100 MONP 91755 636-D3
100 AZU 91702 598-H1
700 WCOV 91790 598-E7
800 WCOV 91790 638-C2
1700 LACo 91746 638-C2
W ORANGE AV
2900 ANA 92804 767-H6
3500 BPK 90620 767-H6
3800 ANA 90620 767-H6
ORANGE CIR
700 COV 91723 599-B6
ORANGE DR
600 SMAD 91024 567-B1
600 SMAD 91024 537-B7
1300 LBCH 90806 795-F3
10200 LACo 90606 676-J4
10200 WHIT 90606 676-J4
10600 WHIT 90606 677-A5
11300 WHIT 90601 677-A5
N ORANGE DR
100 LA 90036 633-D1
300 LA 90036 593-D7
1300 LA 90038 593-D5
1200 Hlwd 90028 593-D4
S ORANGE DR
100 LA 90036 633-D2
1000 LA 90019 633-D4
3800 LA 90008 673-C2
ORANGE FRWY Rt#-57
- BREA - 709-D7
- DBAR - 640-C3

ORANGE FRWY Rt#-57
- DBAR - 679-H6
- DBAR - 709-E3
- GLDR - 569-J7
- GLDR - 570-A7
- GLDR - 599-J1
- GLDR - 600-A5
- INDS - 679-H6
- LACo - 709-E3
- OrCo - 709-E3
- POM - 640-C3
- SDMS - 570-A7
- SDMS - 599-J1
- SDMS - 600-A5
- SDMS - 640-C3
ORANGE PL
- WHIT 90606 677-A5
- PAS 91105 565-H5
600 MONP 91755 636-D4
5100 LA 90008 673-B2
N ORANGE PL
300 AZU 91702 568-H7
ORANGE ST
- GLDL 91204 564-E5
100 COV 91723 599-B5
100 LHB 90631 708-E4
1400 LHH 90631 708-E4
1500 ALH 91803 595-H6
2500 LVRN 91750 600-H1
4600 PRV 90660 676-F3
6100 LA 90048 633-A2
8000 DWNY 90242 705-J6
8100 LACo 91770 636-F4
8200 RSMD 91770 636-F4
8400 DWNY 90242 706-A7
8600 LACo 90606 706-H2
11800 NRWK 90650 736-H3
N ORANGE ST
100 GLDL 91203 564-E4
S ORANGE ST
100 GLDL 91210 564-E7
1200 GLDL 91204 564-E7
W ORANGE ST
100 SGBL 91776 596-E4
ORANGE TER
- PRV 90660 706-F2
ORANGE BLOSSOM AV
100 LACo 91746 637-J2
800 LACo 91746 638-A2
ORANGE BLOSSOM LN
4700 SBdC 91710 641-F3
5600 CHNO 91710 641-H3
ORANGE BLOSSOM RD
4800 SBdC 91710 641-F3
ORANGE COVE AV
2300 LaCr 91214 504-H7
ORANGECREST AV
5500 LACo 91702 599-A1
5900 LACo 91702 569-A7
N ORANGECREST AV
300 AZU 91702 569-A7
ORANGECREST RD
600 GLDR 91741 569-F3
ORANGEDALE AV
3800 GLDL 91020 534-H3
3800 Mont 91020 534-H3
ORANGEGLEN AV
5500 LACo 91702 599-A1
ORANGE GROVE AV
- SFER 91340 482-A6
400 SPAS 91030 595-G2
600 GLDL 91205 564-F5
1800 ALH 91803 635-H2
10200 WHIT 90601 676-J3
10400 WHIT 90601 677-A4
14400 HacH 91745 677-H2
E ORANGE GROVE AV
- ARCD 91006 567-D3
- BURB 91502 533-H6
- SMAD 91024 567-D3
400 BURB 91501 533-H6
N ORANGE GROVE AV
200 POM 91767 600-J6
300 LA 90036 593-B7
300 LA 90036 633-B1
700 LA 90046 593-B5
900 WHWD 90046 593-B5
2000 POM 91767 601-A5
S ORANGE GROVE AV
300 ALH 91803 595-H6
300 LA 90036 633-B2
1000 LA 90019 633-A5
W ORANGE GROVE AV
- ARCD 91006 567-A3
- SMAD 91024 567-A3
100 POM 91768 600-H7
200 BURB 91502 563-G1
200 SMAD 91024 566-J3
500 BURB 91506 563-G1
800 ARCD 91006 566-J3
1000 POM 91768 640-D1
E ORANGE GROVE BLVD
200 PAS 91103 565-H3
200 PAS 91104 565-H3
200 PAS 91104 566-A3
300 PAS 91107 566-A3
N ORANGE GROVE BLVD
- PAS 91103 565-G4
S ORANGE GROVE BLVD
100 PAS 91105 565-G6
200 SPAS 91030 595-G2
1200 PAS 91105 595-G2

ORANGE GROVE CIR
400 PAS 91105 565-G7
ORANGE GROVE DR
13300 LMRD 90638 738-A1
ORANGE GROVE LN
- BREA 92823 709-J6
ORANGE GROVE PL
400 PAS 91105 565-G3
800 SPAS 91030 595-G2
ORANGE GROVE RD
- DUAR 91010 568-B5
- HacH 91745 677-H2
ORANGE GROVE TER
700 SPAS 91030 595-G1
1100 BURB 91501 533-J5
E ORANGE HILL CT
- LACo 91744 638-J5
ORANGE KNOLL AV
4500 LCF 91011 535-C3
ORANGEPATH ST
500 GLDR 91741 569-C6
700 LACo 91741 569-C6
ORANGETHORPE AV
5300 LPMA 90623 767-C2
5300 CRTS 90703 767-C2
5600 BPK 90620 767-E2
7000 BPK 90621 767-E2
ORANGETREE DR
- CRSN 90746 764-F1
ORANGE TREE LN
1600 LCF 91011 535-A3
ORANGEWOOD AV
1700 UPL 91784 571-H6
3200 OrCo 90720 796-H4
3700 LALM 90720 796-H4
N ORANGEWOOD AV
1600 UPL 91784 571-H7
ORANGEWOOD CT
500 PMDL 93550 4286-B3
ORANGEWOOD DR
500 COV 91723 599-C6
900 BREA 92821 709-B5
ORANGEWOOD LN
700 SDMS 91773 600-C3
1700 ARCD 91006 567-C2
ORANGEWOOD PL
2200 POM 91767 600-J4
ORANGEWOOD ST
1200 LHB 90631 738-F1
1600 LVRN 91750 570-F6
1700 PAS 91107 566-C5
ORANGEWOOD WY
1700 UPL 91784 571-H6
ORANUT LN
200 LACo 91746 637-J5
ORBIT CT
2500 RowH 91748 679-C6
ORBIT LN
- LA 90732 823-J7
ORBITAL WY
- Pcma 91331 502-E3
ORC RD
- SPed 90731 854-B1
ORCAS AV
9700 SunI 91040 503-A2
11300 LA 91342 503-A1
11400 LA 91342 (4723-A7
See Page 4643)
ORCHARD AV
1300 LA 90006 634-A6
1700 GLDL 91206 564-H4
1900 LA 90007 634-B6
3200 LYN 90262 735-B2
3300 COMP 90221 735-B2
4400 LA 90037 674-B4
5800 LACo 90606 676-J4
6100 HNTP 90255 675-C6
6200 BELL 90201 675-C6
8600 LA 90044 704-B3
10500 WHIT 90606 676-J4
10700 WHIT 90606 677-A5
14300 LA 90247 734-B4
15900 BLF 90706 736-B6
20800 LACo 90502 764-B5
22600 CRSN 90745 794-B1
N ORCHARD AV
100 FUL 92833 738-E7
S ORCHARD AV
100 FUL 92833 738-E7
ORCHARD CIR
1300 UPL 91786 601-J1
ORCHARD CT
400 BREA 92821 709-B6
2600 LVRN 91750 600-H3
ORCHARD DR
2500 BURB 91504 533-E4
5200 SBdC 92397 (4652-F3
See Page 4651)
11900 CHNO 91710 641-E5
N ORCHARD DR
200 BURB 91506 563-F1
600 BURB 91506 533-E7
2200 BURB 91504 533-E7
S ORCHARD DR
100 BURB 91506 563-F3
800 ING 90301 703-C4
ORCHARD LN
1900 LCF 91011 534-J2
44600 LAN 93534 4015-F6
ORCHARD LP
700 AZU 91702 569-B5
ORCHARD PL
600 LHB 90631 708-D5

ORCHARD PL
2700 SGAT 90280 704-J3
2800 SGAT 90280 705-A3
ORCHARD RD
1200 DUAR 91010 568-B5
ORCHARD ST
- Cstc 91384 4459-J3
4100 MTCL 91763 601-E7
5600 MTCL 91762 601-E7
11100 ELMN 91731 597-D7
E ORCHARD ST
1500 COMP 90221 735-B2
ORCHARD TR
11800 LACo 91342 482-J7
ORCHARD WY
2300 UPL 91784 571-H3
ORCHARD FLAT LN
16500 CRTS 90703 736-J6
ORCHARD HILL LN
1500 HacH 91745 678-F4
ORCHARDVIEW CT
4200 WLKV 91361 557-D6
ORCHARD VILLAGE RD
24800 SCTA 91355 4640-H1
24900 SCTA 91355 4550-G7
ORCHID AV
2200 LHB 90631 708-H4
N ORCHID AV
1700 Hlwd 90028 593-D4
1800 LA 90068 593-D4
ORCHID DR
4500 LACo 90043 673-C6
7700 BPK 90620 767-H2
ORCHID LN
300 POM 91766 641-A6
300 NLB 90805 735-E7
1600 LAN 93535 4016-C6
1800 BURB 91504 533-E4
3800 CALB 91302 588-G1
6300 NLB 90805 765-E1
9000 PRV 90660 676-F6
12300 CHNO 91710 641-J5
ORCHID TR
3400 CALB 91302 589-E1
ORCHID WY
2100 WCOV 91791 639-A3
ORCHID COVE DR
29900 SCTA 91387 4462-G5
ORCHID TREE DR
2500 PMDL 93550 4286-F5
ORCUTT AV
6400 NLB 90805 765-C1
6400 NLB 90805 735-C7
ORCUTT DR
400 MTBL 90640 676-F1
700 MTBL 90640 636-F7
ORCUTT LEASE TRAIL RD
- GrnH 91344 480-H3
- LA 91381 480-H3
- StvR 91381 480-H3
N ORD CT
300 LBCH 90802 795-C7
ORD ST
100 LA 90012 634-G2
ORDCO ST
- SCTA 91350 4551-A4
ORDEN DR
- SFSP 90670 737-B1
ORDIN RANCH RD
- VanN 91401 532-B7
OREGANO CIR
27900 SCTA 91350 4461-A5
OREGON AV
1100 LBCH 90813 795-C5
1800 LBCH 90806 795-C2
4700 NLB 90805 765-C5
10700 CULC 90232 672-F2
16200 BLF 90706 736-D5
OREGON CT
2800 TOR 90503 763-E4
OREGON ST
100 ELSG 90245 732-G2
2700 LA 90023 635-B6
6700 BPK 90621 767-J2
OREO PL
800 PacP 90272 630-J4
OREY PL
20400 Win 91306 530-D6
ORGAN LN
4100 Mont 91020 534-J3
ORGREN AV
12600 CHNO 91710 641-E5
ORGREN CT
- CHNO 91710 641-E6
ORGREN ST
11900 CHNO 91710 641-E5
E ORIENTA DR
1200 ALH 91801 596-C3
ORILLA AV
3200 LA 90065 564-G6
12700 DWNY 90242 705-H7
ORIN AV
4500 LaCr 91214 504-F7
ORINDA AV
4800 LACo 90043 673-D4
ORINOCO PL
2900 HacH 91745 678-B6
ORIOL RD
9100 SBdC 92372 (4562-D1
See Page 4471)
9200 SBdC 92372 (4472-D7
See Page 4471)

ORIOLE AV
- LVRN 91750 570-J4
ORIOLE CT
- LACo 91387 4551-J5
500 SBdC 92397 (4652-B2
See Page 4651)
2400 PMDL 93550 4286-E3
ORIOLE DR
1400 LA 90069 592-H4
7000 BPK 90620 767-E2
ORIOLE LN
1500 LA 90069 592-H4
ORIOLE PL
1500 UPL 91784 571-H4
ORIOLE RD
300 LCF 91011 535-D5
500 SBdC 92397 (4652-B1
See Page 4651)
ORIOLE WY
9000 LA 90069 592-H5
ORION AV
4600 Shrm 91403 561-G4
6200 VanN 91411 531-G7
6400 VanN 91406 531-G2
8300 LA 91343 531-G2
8700 LA 91343 501-G6
9900 MsnH 91345 501-G2
ORION CT
19700 RowH 91748 679-D7
ORION LN
- LACo 91390 4461-A1
- SCTA 91351 4551-H2
E ORIS ST
100 COMP 90222 734-J2
1900 Wbrk 90222 734-J2
ORIZABA AV
- LBCH 90803 825-H1
300 LBCH 90814 825-H1
300 LBCH 90814 795-H7
700 LBCH 90804 795-H7
2000 SIGH 90755 795-H7
2100 LBCH 90755 795-H7
9100 DWNY 90240 706-C2
11900 DWNY 90242 706-A6
12000 DWNY 90242 705-J6
12600 DWNY 90242 735-H2
13300 PRM 90723 735-H2
N ORIZABA AV
1300 LBCH 90804 795-H5
1800 SIGH 90755 795-H5
5500 NLB 90805 765-H1
6300 NLB 90805 735-H6
ORKNEY ST
400 AZU 91702 598-J1
16900 LACo 91702 598-H1
17900 LACo 91702 599-A1
N ORLANDO AV
100 LA 90048 633-A1
300 LA 90048 593-A7
500 WHWD 90048 593-A7
700 LA 90069 593-A7
1000 WHWD 90069 593-A7
S ORLANDO AV
100 LA 90048 633-A1
1000 LA 90035 633-A3
5800 LadH 90056 673-A6
ORLANDO DR
1400 ARCD 91006 567-B3
ORLANDO PL
900 SMRO 91108 566-B7
ORLANDO RD
1100 SMRO 91108 566-B7
1500 PAS 91106 566-C6
3100 OrCo 90720 796-H5
3100 LACo 91107 566-G6
3100 PAS 91107 566-G6
ORLANDO WY
200 COV 91723 599-B6
ORLANES LN
- FUL 92833 738-D5
ORLEANS CT
30800 WLKV 91362 557-F4
ORLEANS LN
7400 LPMA 90623 767-C3
ORLEANS WY
200 NLB 90805 735-C6
ORLENA AV
300 LBCH 90814 796-B7
ORLON AV
1100 PacP 90272 630-J4
ORLON DR
17600 RowH 91748 678-G6
ORME AV
600 LA 90023 635-A6
1300 LA 90023 675-A1
ORMOND LN
1300 RBCH 90278 762-H1
ORMOND ST
10300 SunI 91040 503-B6
ORMSKIRK AV
12300 Nor 91326 480-H5
ORNA DR
17400 GrnH 91344 481-A5
ORNELAS ST
15800 IRW 91706 598-F2
ORO CT
6000 PMDL 93552 4287-D2
ORO TER
700 SPed 90731 824-A5
ORO FINO MTWY
- SCTA 91350 4551-B7
21500 SCTA 91321 4551-B7

ORO GRANDE ST
13400 LA 91342 482-C2
14400 LA 91342 481-J5
OROS ST
2100 LA 90031 594-H6
OROSCO DR
1500 GLDL 91207 564-G2
ORO VISTA AV
10100 SunI 91040 503-G1
11400 SunI 91040 (4723-G7
See Page 4643)
OROZCO ST
17000 GrnH 91344 481-C4
ORR AND DAY RD
9500 SFSP 90670 706-F4
11200 NRWK 90650 706-G7
12200 NRWK 90650 736-G1
ORRICK AV
21300 CRSN 90745 764-D6
ORRIN RD
33400 LACo 91390 4373-E6
ORRINGTON AV
800 LPUE 91744 638-D5
ORRVILLE AV
5000 WdHl 91367 559-E3
ORSA DR
15700 LMRD 90638 737-H3
16000 LMRD 90638 738-A3
ORSINI AV
27400 SCTA 91351 4551-H3
ORTANO LN
9600 CYP 90630 767-B7
ORTEGA PL
1700 LA 90732 823-H6
ORTEGA ST
12900 NHol 91605 532-E4
ORTLEY PL
13100 VanN 91401 532-D6
ORTON AV
10200 LA 90064 632-E4
ORTUNO DR
- AZU 91702 569-A4
ORUM RD
11500 Brwd 90049 591-H6
ORVILLE ST
11100 CULC 90230 672-G5
OSAGE
- Ago 91301 587-G4
OSAGE AV
7300 Wch 90045 702-J2
14500 LNDL 90260 733-D5
16900 TOR 90504 733-D7
17800 TOR 90504 763-D1
20400 TOR 90503 763-D5
N OSAGE AV
400 ING 90301 703-D1
S OSAGE AV
300 ING 90301 703-D3
10600 Lenx 90304 703-D5
10800 ING 90304 703-D6
OSAGE CT
1700 LAN 93534 4105-E1
22300 TOR 90505 763-D7
OSAGE RIDGE RD
23100 SCTA 91354 4460-G6
N OSBORN AV
300 WCOV 91790 598-G6
OSBORNE CT
- FUL 92833 738-E5
OSBORNE PL
11300 LA 91342 502-H1
12200 Pcma 91331 502-F3
OSBORNE ST
11000 LA 91342 482-J7
11000 LA 91342 502-J1
12000 SunI 91040 502-J1
12000 Pcma 91331 502-E4
14000 PanC 91402 502-A7
14500 PanC 91402 501-F7
15800 LA 91343 501-D7
17000 Nor 91325 501-A7
18100 Nor 91325 500-J7
20900 LA 91304 500-A7
OSCAR ST
13300 LA 91342 482-C2
OSCEOLA ST
900 GLDL 91205 564-H6
14800 LA 91342 481-H6
OSGOOD AV
10700 LYN 90262 705-A6
OSGOOD ST
100 NLB 90805 765-D2
OSGOOD FARLEY RD
- SPed 90731 854-A1
N OSLER AV
3900 LBCH 90808 766-B6
OSLO CIR
6800 BPK 90621 767-G2
OSMOND AV
17000 LMRD 90638 737-G6
OSMUNDA CT
- PMDL 93551 4285-D4
OSO AV
5500 WdHl 91367 560-D1
6500 Win 91306 530-D2
8900 Chat 91311 500-D2
8900 Chat 91311 530-D2
OSO WY
5700 PMDL 93551 4194-F2
OST ST
37700 PMDL 93552 4287-A2
OSTEGO LN
- CHNO 91710 641-G4

OSTEND DR
14300 LMRD 90638 737-E2
OSTIA WY
20000 LACo 91789 679-E5
OSTIN AV
5500 WdHl 91367 559-D2
OSTROM AV
1800 LBCH 90815 796-F3
3000 LBCH 90808 796-F1
3600 LBCH 90808 766-F7
4100 LKWD 90713 766-F4
5300 Enc 91316 561-C2
7200 VanN 91406 531-C3
11400 GrnH 91344 481-C7
11400 GrnH 91344 501-C1
OSTRONIC DR
22800 WdHl 91367 559-F3
OSTRONIC PL
23300 WdHl 91367 559-G3
OSULLIVAN DR
4800 LA 90032 635-E1
OSWALD ST
14900 LA 91342 481-H5
OSWEGO ST
2300 PAS 91107 566-E5
7800 SunI 91040 503-E3
OTAY DR
4500 LA 90065 594-J2
OTERO DR
- LA 90032 595-D7
OTIS AV
2100 LHB 90631 708-B5
5000 Tarz 91356 560-J3
5900 HNTP 90255 675-D6
5900 MYWD 90270 675-D6
6200 BELL 90201 675-D6
7000 BELL 90201 705-C1
7300 CDHY 90201 705-C1
7800 CDHY 90255 705-C1
7900 HNTP 90255 705-C1
OTIS CT
300 POM 91766 640-J6
OTIS ST
8100 SGAT 90280 705-C3
10600 LYN 90262 705-C5
OTISH WY
- PMDL 93551 4195-A3
OTSEGO CT
5100 Enc 91436 561-D3
OTSEGO ST
10400 NHol 91601 563-A3
11000 NHol 91601 562-J3
11700 LA 91607 562-E3
12900 Shrm 91423 562-C3
14500 Shrm 91403 562-C3
14600 Shrm 91403 561-H3
15500 Enc 91436 561-E3
16900 Enc 91316 561-C3
OTT PL
4400 BALD 91706 598-C4
OTTAWA DR
800 CLAR 91711 601-B1
OTTAWA PL
- CHNO 91710 641-H4
OTTER CT
- PMDL 93551 4194-J1
OTTERBEIN AV
1100 RowH 91748 679-C6
S OTTERBEIN AV
900 RowH 91748 679-C5
900 INDS 91748 679-C4
OTTIE RD
- Tuj 91042 (4724-E4
See Page 4643)
OTTO LN
- Hrbr 90710 794-A3
OTTO ST
6700 BGDN 90201 705-J2
7300 DWNY 90240 706-A2
11400 SFSP 90670 706-G5
OTTOMAN ST
12700 Pcma 91331 502-E6
13500 Pcma 91331 532-C1
OTTONE WY
10500 BelA 90077 592-A5
OUTER DR
3700 POM 91767 601-A2
3700 LACo 91711 601-A2
OUTER HWY
1900 SBdC 92397 (4652-E2
See Page 4651)
OUTER ST
2200 SPed 90731 824-C7
OUTER HWY S
3700 SBdC 92371 (4472-J7
See Page 4471)
OUTER TRAFFIC CIR
1700 LBCH 90815 796-A4
3400 LBCH 90804 796-A4
OUTLAND VIEW DR
8300 SunV 91352 533-B1
OUTLET TR
2200 Ago 91301 587-J3
OUTLOOK AV
6100 HiPk 90042 595-D2
OUTLOOK LN
- WCOV 91791 639-B3
1100 GLDL 91206 564-J2
4400 CHNO 91710 641-E5
OUTPOST CIR
1900 LA 90068 593-D3
OUTPOST DR
1800 LA 90068 593-D2

OUTPOST LN
1600 LACo 91107 536-F7
1600 PAS 91107 536-F7
OUTPOST COVE DR
7200 LA 90068 593-C2
OUTRIDER RD
- RHLS 90274 823-F3
OUTRIGGER
1400 WCOV 91790 638-D2
OUTRIGGER CIR
16800 CRTS 90703 736-F6
OUTRIGGER CT
- LBCH 90803 826-F2
100 LA 90292 701-J1
OUTRIGGER MALL
- LA 90292 701-J1
OUTRIGGER ST
- LA 90292 701-J1
OVADA PL
11300 Brwd 90049 631-H1
OVAL DR
12700 WHIT 90602 707-B2
13900 LACo 90605 707-D3
14100 LACo 90604 707-E4
OVERCREST DR
4000 LACo 90601 677-C2
OVERDALE DR
5200 LACo 90043 673-C5
OVERDEN ST
1200 POM 91766 640-E3
OVEREST AV
9000 LACo 90605 707-C4
OVERFALL DR
30800 WLKV 91362 557-F4
OVERHILL DR
1300 ING 90302 673-C6
5000 LACo 90043 673-C6
6200 LA 90043 673-C6
OVERHILL RD
1900 Ago 91301 588-B4
OVERHOLTZER DR
5900 LVRN 91750 570-F5
OVERING DR
5300 WdHl 91367 559-E3
OVERLAND AV
1800 WLA 90025 632-C4
1800 WLA 90025 632-D5
2200 LA 90064 632-D5
3000 LA 90034 632-D5
3300 LA 90034 672-E1
3800 LA 90232 672-E1
3800 CULC 90232 672-F2
4100 CULC 90232 672-F2
4100 CULC 90230 672-F2
4100 CULC 90230 672-H5
11200 CULC 90230 672-H5
44400 LAN 93536 4015-C6
OVERLAND CT
900 SDMS 91773 599-J2
1200 UPL 91786 571-J7
OVERLAND DR
24500 LA 91304 529-C4
OVERLAND TR
33500 LACo 91390 4373-D5
OVERLOOK RD
1900 FUL 92831 738-J4
OVERLOOK TR
11300 LACo 91342 482-J6
OVERLOOK RIDGE RD
1000 DBAR 91765 640-C5
OVERMAN AV
10600 Chat 91311 500-D3
OVERTON ST
1000 LA 90015 634-D4
OVID AV
2000 LMTA 90717 793-H6
OVINGTON ST
100 LAN 93534 4015-F6
700 LAN 93535 4016-A6
OWEN AV
17700 CRTS 90703 737-C7
18100 CRTS 90703 767-C1
OWEN CT
- Alta 91001 535-G3
- Saug 91350 4461-G5
1500 LACo 91770 636-E4
OWEN WY
10600 ELMN 91733 637-C2
19000 CRTS 90703 767-C2
OWENS DR
- FUL 92833 738-D6
OWENS LN
100 POM 91766 640-J6
OWENS PL
10700 Tuj 91042 504-A3
OWENS ST
7000 Tuj 91042 504-A3
7500 Tuj 91042 503-J3
7800 SunI 91040 503-F3
8100 BPK 90621 737-J6
OWENSMOUTH AV
5400 WdHl 91367 560-A2
6100 WdHl 91367 530-A6
6400 CanP 91303 530-A6
7500 LA 91304 530-A4
8700 LA 91304 500-A7
9000 Chat 91311 500-A2
OWL AV
9500 KeCo 93560 3833-F2
OWL CT
- LACo 91387 4551-H6
OWL PL
- BREA 92823 709-G6

OWL CREEK WY
- Nor 91326 480-E7
OWOSSO AV
900 HMB 90254 762-H2
OXBOW CT
21900 DBAR 91765 679-J4
OXFORD AV
600 Ven 90291 671-J6
600 Ven 90291 672-A6
700 LA 90292 672-A6
800 CLAR 91711 601-C2
1200 PAS 91104 566-C1
1300 LACo 91104 566-C1
1600 LACo 91104 536-C7
1600 PAS 91104 536-C7
2100 CLAR 91711 571-C7
5400 LA 90029 593-H5
7300 BPK 90621 737-H6
11400 HAW 90250 703-D7
11900 HAW 90250 733-D1
N OXFORD AV
100 LA 90004 593-H7
100 LA 90004 633-H1
700 LA 90029 593-H6
1300 CLAR 91711 601-C1
1700 CLAR 91711 571-C7
1900 LFlz 90027 593-H3
S OXFORD AV
100 LA 90004 633-H1
300 LA 90020 633-H1
600 LA 90005 633-H3
600 LA 90010 633-H3
900 LA 90006 633-H5
1900 LA 90018 633-H5
OXFORD CIR
3500 LVRN 91750 600-F1
OXFORD CT
- RowH 91748 709-A2
800 SDMS 91773 599-H4
1500 WCOV 91791 638-J4
OXFORD DR
300 ARCD 91007 567-B4
5000 CYP 90630 767-C7
12200 LMRD 90638 707-H7
12200 LMRD 90638 737-H1
37400 PMDL 93550 4286-E3
OXFORD LN
- Nor 91326 500-E1
100 LHB 90631 738-D2
22200 SCTA 91350 4550-J5
22200 SCTA 91350 4551-A5
OXFORD PL
1100 POM 91768 640-D1
OXFORD RD
800 SMRO 91108 566-D6
1300 SMRO 91108 596-D1
15600 LMRD 90638 737-H1
OXFORD WY
- Nor 91324 500-E7
900 BHLS 90210 592-F7
1000 LCF 91011 535-C6
7200 CMRC 90040 676-A7
E OXHOLM ST
5700 LBCH 90808 766-C7
OXLEY AL
1700 SPAS 91030 595-H2
OXLEY ST
1100 SPAS 91030 595-H2
OXNARD ST
4300 BURB 91505 533-A7
10400 NHol 91601 533-A7
10400 NHol 91606 533-A7
11000 NHol 91606 532-E7
11000 NHol 91601 532-H7
11700 LA 91607 532-E7
12900 VanN 91401 532-A7
14300 VanN 91401 562-A1
14500 VanN 91411 562-A1
14600 VanN 91411 561-H1
17100 Enc 91316 561-C7
17200 Enc 91316 561-A1
18100 Tarz 91356 560-F1
18100 Tarz 91356 561-A1
19700 WdHl 91367 560-B1
22000 WdHl 91367 559-D1
OXSEE AV
6200 WHIT 90606 677-A5
OZARK WK
20900 Top 90290 590-C3
OZETA TER
1200 LA 90069 592-H5
1200 WHWD 90069 592-H5
OZMUN CT
1400 SPAS 91030 595-H1
OZONE AV
- Ven 90291 671-G5
900 SMCA 90405 671-H4
26200 Hrbr 90710 793-J6
OZONE CT
- Ven 90291 671-G5
2400 HMB 90254 762-G1
OZONE PK
1200 SMCA 90405 671-H4
OZONE ST
600 SMCA 90405 671-G4

P

PABLO PL
1700 PVE 90274 792-G4
PABLO ST
- CHNO 91710 641-J7

STREET
Block City ZIP Pg-Grid

PACATO RD
18600 LACo 91744 679-A2
PACE AV
9200 Wats 90002 704-F4
10400 Wats 90002 704-F5
PACER CT
600 WAL 91789 639-J6
PACHECO DR
- BALD 91706 598-C5
3900 Shrm 91403 561-H6
PACIFIC AL
1600 SPAS 91030 595-G2
PACIFIC AV
- WCOV 91790 598-E7
- LBCH 90802 825-D1
100 SLB 90743 826-H6
100 Ven 90291 671-H6
500 MANB 90266 732-G5
700 LBCH 90813 795-D5
1800 BURB 91506 533-C6
1800 LBCH 90806 795-D1
2500 BURB 91505 533-C6
2500 SLB 90740 826-H6
3100 LA 90292 671-H6
3200 Bxby 90807 795-D1
3400 Bxby 90807 765-C4
3700 LA 90292 701-J1
4700 NLB 90805 765-C4
6000 LA 90292 702-A3
6000 PdlR 90293 702-A3
7400 BPK 90621 737-H6
9400 BLF 90706 736-B5
10700 LHB 90631 708-E7
11800 LA 90066 672-B4
14400 BALD 91706 598-C5
N PACIFIC AV
100 GLDL 91203 564-D4
100 SPed 90731 824-B4
200 LBCH 90802 795-D7
200 LBCH 90802 825-D1
200 RBCH 90277 762-H5
900 GLDL 91202 564-D1
2200 LBCH 90806 795-D3
3800 Bxby 90807 765-D6
4600 NLB 90805 765-C3
16000 SunB 90742 826-J7
16000 Surf 90743 826-J7
S PACIFIC AV
100 GLDL 91204 564-D6
100 SPed 90731 824-B6
2500 SPed 90731 854-B2
16000 SLB 90743 826-J7
16000 SunB 90742 826-J7
16000 Surf 90743 826-J7
W PACIFIC AV
1600 WCOV 91790 598-D7
PACIFIC BLVD
600 COMP 90220 734-G3
4400 VER 90058 674-H3
5100 HNTP 90255 674-J7
7200 LACo 90255 674-J7
7300 LACo 90255 704-J1
7900 SGAT 90255 704-J1
PACIFIC CIR
4100 LVRN 91750 600-H1
16200 HNTB 92649 826-H3
PACIFIC CT
1200 DUAR 91010 568-D5
3300 LA 90292 671-H7
3700 LA 90292 701-H1
PACIFIC DR
200 FUL 92833 738-D7
3200 LBCH 90810 795-A1
3500 LBCH 90810 765-A7
6200 CMRC 90040 676-A7
20400 WAL 91789 639-F6
PACIFIC LN
700 TOR 90501 763-G5
W PACIFIC LN
1800 WCOV 91790 598-E7
PACIFIC PL
- PAS 91103 565-H4
500 MANB 90266 732-G6
3200 LBCH 90806 795-D1
5300 ELA 90022 675-H2
16000 PacP 90272 630-F4
E PACIFIC PL
7600 WHIT 90602 677-C7
N PACIFIC PL
3500 LBCH 90806 765-C7
3500 LBCH 90806 795-D1
PACIFIC PL N
900 SMCA 90405 671-G3
PACIFIC ST
100 POM 91768 640-C2
100 SMCA 90405 671-G2
400 CRSN 90745 794-E3
11900 SFSP 90670 706-J3
PACIFIC TER
- SMCA 90401 671-E3
PACIFIC WY
4000 CMRC 90023 675-D2
4400 CMRC 90040 675-E3
PACIFICA AV
4700 PMDL 93552 4287-B2
PACIFICA CT
- LACo 91390 4461-A2
32700 WLKV 91361 587-A1
PACIFICA DR
32000 RPV 90275 822-J3
32000 RPV 90275 823-A3
PACIFICA PL
2200 LACo 90220 764-J4

PACIFICA PL
2200 LACo 90220 765-A4
PACIFICA DEL MAR
- RPV 90275 822-H4
PACIFIC COAST HWY
2600 TOR 90505 793-B2
PACIFIC COAST HWY
Rt#-1
- HMB 90254 762-H1
100 SLB 90740 826-G4
400 MANB 90266 732-H7
600 HMB 90266 762-H1
600 MANB 90266 762-H1
1700 LA 90717 793-F5
1700 LMTA 90717 793-F5
2400 TOR 90505 793-F5
2600 MANB 90254 732-H7
2600 MANB 90254 762-H1
2700 HMB 90254 732-H7
9000 VeCo 90265 625-A3
12300 LACo 90265 625-F5
14700 LA 90402 671-B1
14800 LA 90402 631-A7
14900 PacP 90272 630-H6
14900 PacP 90272 631-A7
15900 SLB 90743 826-G4
16100 HNTB 92649 826-G4
16300 SunB 90742 826-G4
16300 Surf 90743 826-G4
16500 HNTB 90742 826-G4
16600 OrCo 92649 826-G4
17600 LA 90265 630-H6
17900 LACo 90265 630-A6
18700 MAL 90265 630-A6
19800 MAL 90265 629-G6
23500 MAL 90265 628-C7
24200 LACo 90263 628-G7
26300 MAL 90265 668-A1
27200 MAL 90265 667-A1
30800 MAL 90265 626-A6
30800 MAL 90265 627-A7
34100 MAL 90265 625-F5
E PACIFIC COAST
HWY Rt#-1
- SLB 90740 826-D1
100 LBCH 90813 795-E5
100 Wilm 90744 794-F5
100 LBCH 90806 795-E5
200 LBCH 90804 796-A5
600 LBCH 90814 796-A5
2000 LBCH 90804 795-E5
2100 SIGH 90755 795-E5
2300 LA 90813 794-F5
2300 LA 90810 794-F5
2400 LBCH 90813 794-F5
2400 LBCH 90810 794-F5
4200 LBCH 90815 796-A5
5900 LBCH 90803 796-A5
6200 LBCH 90803 826-D1
N PACIFIC COAST
HWY Rt#-1
- HMB 90254 762-H4
- RBCH 90277 762-H4
- RBCH 90278 762-H4
6000 LBCH 90803 796-D7
6000 LBCH 90803 826-D1
S PACIFIC COAST
HWY Rt#-1
100 RBCH 90277 762-J6
1300 RBCH 90277 792-J1
1500 TOR 90277 792-J1
1700 RBCH 90277 793-C2
1700 TOR 90277 793-C2
5700 TOR 90505 793-C2
W PACIFIC COAST
HWY Rt#-1
100 LBCH 90813 795-C5
100 Wilm 90744 794-B5
100 LBCH 90806 795-C5
800 Hrbr 90710 794-B5
1100 LBCH 90810 795-C5
1400 Hrbr 90710 793-J5
2300 LBCH 90813 794-B5
2300 LBCH 90810 794-B5
PACIFIC COMMERCE DR
2900 RDom 90221 765-B3
PACIFIC CONCOURSE
DR
5200 Wch 90045 703-A7
PACIFIC GATEWAY DR
19000 LA 90502 764-A3
PACIFIC HIGHLAND ST
- PMDL 93551 4195-D6
PACIFICO WY
9700 CYP 90630 767-E7
PACIFIC OAK DR
22400 Chat 91311 499-H5
PACIFIC OAKS PL
- RowH 91748 679-D4
PACIFICO MOUNTAIN
RD
- LACo - (4556-F6
See Page 4466)
- LACo - (4557-A7
See Page 4467)
- LACo - 4647-C1
PACIFIC PARK DR
2500 LACo 90601 637-C7
PACIFIC PARK WY
- WCOV 91791 639-A4
PACIFIC PROMENADE
- LA 90094 702-D1

PACIFIC RIDGE RD
6300 VeCo 93063 499-C4
PACIFIC STAR DR
- PMDL 93552 4286-H2
PACIFIC TELEPHONE
ACCESS RD
- PMDL 93550 4376-E6
PACIFIC VIEW DR
6800 LA 90068 593-C1
PACIFIC VIEW RD
10700 VeCo 90265 625-A1
PACIFIC VIEW TR
2700 LA 90068 593-C1
PACINO ST
12500 CRTS 90703 767-A2
PACKARD CIR
100 THO 91362 557-C4
PACKARD DR
900 POM 91766 641-B3
PACKARD ST
5000 LA 90019 633-B4
5900 LA 90035 633-A4
6100 LA 90035 632-J3
PACKERS AV
3300 VER 90058 675-B3
PACKET RD
- RPV 90275 822-J4
PACKSADDLE LN
700 WAL 91789 639-D6
PACKSADDLE RD E
- RHLS 90274 823-D4
PACKSADDLE RD W
- RHLS 90274 823-D4
PACKWOOD TR
7200 LA 90068 593-C1
PACOIMA CT
12000 LA 91604 562-G6
PACOIMA MTWY
- LACo 91342 482-G3
PACOIMA CANYON RD
13500 LA 91342 482-F3
13600 LACo 91342 482-F1
15300 LACo 91342 4642-F7
PACOIMA CANYON TKTR
- LACo - 4643-H3
- LACo - (4644-D2
See Page 4643)
PACOIMA CANYON TR
- LACo 91342 482-F1
PACY ST
25300 Nwhl 91321 4642-C1
PAD CT
18600 SCTA 91321 4551-H5
PADDINGTON DR
- PMDL 93552 4287-C4
PADDINGTON PL
4200 GLDL 91206 565-A1
PADDINGTON RD
1000 GLDR 91740 569-F7
3000 GLDL 91206 565-A1
PADDISON AV
11000 NRWK 90650 706-H6
12500 NRWK 90650 736-H1
PADDOCK
- Actn 93510 4375-E7
PADDOCK CT
1000 WAL 91789 639-J4
PADDOCK ST
13700 LA 91342 482-B2
14500 LA 91342 481-J5
PADDOCK WY
4000 LAN 93536 4105-A7
4100 LAN 93536 4104-J7
PADDY LN
3100 BALD 91706 598-B6
3100 BALD 91706 638-A1
PADILLA PL
5200 LA 90008 673-B3
PADILLA ST
500 SGBL 91776 596-D4
PADONIA AV
1200 WHIT 90603 708-C4
PADOVA CT
30800 WLKV 91362 557-F5
PADOVA DR
15900 HacH 91745 678-B6
PADRE DR
400 WCOV 91790 598-E6
W PADRE DR
1600 WCOV 91790 598-E6
PADRE LN
8000 LA 90046 593-A3
PADRE TER
6600 LA 90068 593-E3
PADRE PATRICIO
18000 LACo 90220 765-A1
PADRES TR
1200 LCF 91011 535-A4
PADRINO AV
20100 LACo 91789 679-E4
PADRON PL
24600 LMTA 90717 793-H3
PADUA AV
2100 CLAR 91711 571-F6
N PADUA AV
700 CLAR 91711 571-F5
PADUA AV N
4400 CLAR 91711 571-F3
PADUA DR
700 COV 91723 599-C6
PADUA PL
2300 Ven 90291 671-J5

PAGE DR
2400 Alta 91001 536-B6
PAGE ST
7900 BPK 90621 767-J2
PAGEANT PL
16700 Enc 91436 561-D6
PAGEANT ST
8100 DWNY 90240 706-C2
E PAGEANTRY CT
5800 LBCH 90808 796-D1
E PAGEANTRY ST
5100 LBCH 90808 796-B1
PAGET AV
43600 LAN 93536 4103-H2
PAGODA CT
1100 LA 90031 595-B6
PAGODA PL
1000 LA 90031 595-B6
PAGOSA CT
300 PMDL 93551 4285-H2
PAIGE DR
1400 POM 91768 600-H6
PAIGE PL
- Saug 91350 4461-E6
PAIGE ST
3900 LA 90031 595-C5
PAINE AL
1000 PAS 91104 566-C2
PAINE CIR
25500 StvR 91381 4550-C7
PAINE CT
1600 CLAR 91711 601-B1
PAINTBRUSH DR
- PMDL 93551 4285-D3
PAINT BRUSH LN
21800 DBAR 91765 679-J5
21900 DBAR 91765 680-A5
PAINTED DESERT CT
- LAN 93536 4015-B6
PAINTER AV
5800 WHIT 90601 677-D5
6700 WHIT 90608 677-D5
7000 WHIT 90602 677-D7
7800 WHIT 90602 707-D1
8400 WHIT 90605 707-C3
9100 LACo 90605 707-B7
9800 SFSP 90605 707-C3
10000 SFSP 90670 707-B4
12200 LACo 90605 737-B1
14400 NRWK 90650 737-B3
PAINTER CT
900 POM 91766 641-A3
PAINTER ST
- PAS 91103 565-H3
200 LHB 90631 708-B6
PAISLEY CT
18700 Nor 91326 480-H7
PAISLEY LN
12200 Brwd 90049 631-G4
PAIUTE AV
11200 Chat 91311 499-J2
PAIUTE DR
29100 Ago 91301 588-A4
PAIZ PL
12400 NRWK 90650 736-J4
PAJARITO CT
25700 SCTA 91355 4550-G5
PALA AV
6100 MYWD 90270 675-F6
6200 BELL 90201 675-F7
8400 SunV 91352 532-J1
10700 Pcma 91331 502-D2
13400 LA 91342 481-F3
PALACETE DR
26800 SCTA 91354 4550-H1
26800 SCTA 91354 4460-H7
PALACIOS DR
17000 LA 90732 823-H6
PALADORA AV
900 PAS 91104 566-D2
PALAIS PL
5300 PMDL 93551 4104-G7
22100 CALB 91302 559-J7
PALA MESA DR
- POM 91766 640-F5
4500 LACo 90601 677-C2
11300 Nor 91326 500-G1
11600 Nor 91326 480-G7
PALA MESA PL
19100 Nor 91326 500-G1
PALAMOS AV
300 LACo 91744 679-A1
PALAMOS PL
13200 CHLS 91709 680-J1
PALATINE DR
- ALH 91801 595-G5
PALAWAN WY
13900 MdlR 90292 671-J7
13900 MdlR 90292 672-A7
PALEN RD
9000 LACo 91390 4373-J6
PALENCIA AV
- WdHl 91364 560-B4
PALERMO AV
2300 UPL 91784 571-H3
PALERMO CT
- LAN 93536 4104-J7
PALERMO DR
- CHLS 91709 710-J3
100 PMDL 93550 4195-J2
24500 CALB 91302 559-C6
PALERMO LN
600 SPAS 91030 595-H1

N PALERMO WK
- LBCH 90803 826-C3
PALERMO WY
- SCTA 91355 4550-E6
400 LHB 90631 708-H5
9500 CYP 90630 767-C7
PALES RD
13800 LACo 91390 4462-J1
PALGRAVE RD
34800 Actn 93510 4374-G3
PALI AV
9200 Tuj 91042 504-C5
PALI DR
300 NLB 90805 735-D7
300 NLB 90805 765-D1
PALI WK
300 NLB 90805 765-D1
PALIO ST
- PMDL 93550 4286-F5
PALI POINT LN
5300 LCF 91011 535-E3
PALISADE ST
200 PAS 91103 565-F1
PALISADE WY
400 WAL 91789 679-C1
PALISADES AV
100 SMCA 90402 671-C1
PALISADES CIR
16900 PacP 90272 630-F1
PALISADES CT
1800 PacP 90272 630-F1
PALISADES DR
400 PacP 90272 630-F1
1800 FUL 92831 738-J4
PALISADES BEACH RD
1500 SMCA 90401 671-E3
PALISADES BEACH RD
Rt#-1
200 LA 90402 671-C1
300 SMCA 90402 671-C1
800 SMCA 90403 671-C1
1200 SMCA 90401 671-C1
PALISAIR PL
1000 PacP 90272 630-J4
1000 PacP 90272 631-A4
PALJAY AV
2400 RSMD 91770 636-G3
PALLAS CT
- PMDL 93551 4195-F7
- PMDL 93551 4285-F1
PALLETT CREEK RD
12800 Valy 93563 4468-J3
13100 Valy 93563 4469-A3
PALLETT MESA RD
12600 Pear 93553 4468-H7
PALM
1900 LBCH 90810 795-A1
PALM AV
800 WHWD 90069 592-J6
900 SGBL 91776 596-E5
900 SPAS 91030 595-G2
1400 RowH 91748 679-B4
1800 MANB 90266 732-G4
1900 MONP 91755 636-D5
2200 ALH 91803 635-J1
3200 LYN 90262 735-B2
3600 COMP 90221 735-B2
5100 WHIT 90601 677-B3
6100 MYWD 90270 675-E6
6200 BELL 90201 675-E6
13300 BALD 91706 597-J5
13300 BALD 91706 598-A5
14400 HacH 91745 677-J1
14800 HacH 91745 678-A1
E PALM AV
- BURB 91502 533-H6
100 MNRO 91016 567-J4
400 BURB 91501 533-H6
500 ELSG 90245 702-F7
N PALM AV
- ALH 91801 595-J5
S PALM AV
- ALH 91801 595-J6
300 ALH 91803 595-J6
1700 ALH 91803 635-J1
W PALM AV
100 ELSG 90245 702-E7
100 MNRO 91016 567-F4
200 BURB 91502 563-G1
200 ELSG 90245 732-D1
600 BURB 91506 563-G1
PALM CIR
600 COMP 90220 734-H4
2200 ARCD 91007 597-D2
PALM CT
- COMP 90220 734-J4
- CRSN 90746 764-D4
- LA 91342 481-J5
300 CRSN 90745 764-D7
400 SPAS 91030 595-F2
12400 CHNO 91710 641-J6
22600 SCTA 91390 4460-J3
PALM DR
- AZU 91702 569-A5
- CALB 91302 559-G6
- PAS 91106 566-C6
- SFSP 90670 706-J4
- SMRO 91108 566-C6
- HMB 90254 762-G1
200 SDMS 91773 599-J3
400 GLDL 91202 564-C3
800 MTBL 90640 676-D2
1100 COV 91724 599-E5

PALM DR
2300 LA 90007 634-C7
2900 HMB 90254 732-F7
3500 ELMN 91731 597-C7
4500 LCF 91011 534-J1
5200 LCF 91011 505-A7
5200 LCF 91011 535-A1
E PALM DR
- ARCD 91006 597-D2
100 GLDL 91205 564-F7
500 GLDR 91741 569-F3
1300 COV 91724 599-F5
N PALM DR
100 BHLS 90210 632-G1
400 BHLS 90210 592-G7
600 AZU 91702 569-B5
2400 SIGH 90755 795-H3
S PALM DR
100 BHLS 90212 632-H3
W PALM DR
- ARCD 91007 597-B2
400 COV 91723 599-A5
400 GLDR 91741 569-D3
700 COV 91722 599-B5
1000 WCOV 91790 598-E5
PALM LN
- LAN 93535 4106-D2
1300 RBCH 90278 762-J1
44000 LAN 93535 4016-D3
PALM PL
200 POM 91767 641-A1
800 MTBL 90640 676-D2
2400 LACo 90255 704-J2
2400 SGAT 90280 704-J2
13000 CRTS 90703 737-B6
PALM ST
200 COMP 90220 734-H4
3900 FUL 92835 708-H7
3900 FUL 92835 738-H1
8600 BLF 90706 735-J7
9000 BLF 90706 736-A7
11300 CRTS 90703 736-F7
12600 CRTS 90703 737-A6
E PALM ST
- COMP 90221 735-B4
- Alta 91001 535-J5
500 Alta 91001 536-A5
N PALM ST
100 LHB 90631 708-H4
900 OrCo 90631 708-H4
1400 LACo 90631 708-H4
S PALM ST
400 LHB 92821 708-H7
400 LHB 90631 708-H7
500 BREA 92821 708-H7
2500 BREA 90631 708-H7
4000 FUL 92835 708-H7
W PALM ST
- Alta 91001 535-G4
300 COMP 90220 734-J4
PALM TER
900 PAS 91104 566-A1
PALM WY
20500 TOR 90503 763-C5
PALMA DR
2100 RowH 91748 678-G5
PALMA ALTA DR
25500 SCTA 91355 4550-H5
PAL MAL AV
4600 ELMN 91731 597-C5
4800 TEML 91780 597-C3
PALMAS CT
40300 PMDL 93551 4194-J3
PALMAS DR
1800 SMRO 91108 596-C2
PALMA VISTA ST
8500 LACo 91775 566-G7
PALM BREEZE LN
- Hrbr 90710 794-B4
- Wilm 90744 794-B4
PALM CANYON DR
- TOR 90505 793-F5
PALM CANYON LN
23100 MAL 90265 629-A5
23400 LACo 90265 629-A5
PALM COURT WY
10700 CULC 90232 672-F2
PALM CREEK DR
8700 LACo 91770 636-H5
8700 RSMD 91770 636-H5
PALMDALE BLVD
4200 PMDL 93552 4197-B7
6000 LACo 93552 4197-F7
8000 Litl 93543 4198-B7
9000 Litl 93543 4198-B7
9000 LACo 93591 4197-F7
9000 LACo 93591 4198-B7
12900 LACo 93591 4199-B7
16500 Llan 93544 4199-F7
17500 Llan 93544 4200-A7
17500 LACo 93591 4200-A7
PALMDALE BLVD
Rt#-N2
200 PMDL 93551 4195-H7
PALMDALE BLVD
Rt#-138
200 PMDL 93551 4195-J7
200 PMDL 93551 4285-J1
400 PMDL 93550 4285-J1
400 PMDL 93550 4286-A1
2700 PMDL 93550 4196-H7
3700 PMDL 93552 4196-H7
4200 PMDL 93552 4197-A7

PALMDALE HILLS DR
4200 LACo 93552 4376-J1
4400 LACo 93552 4377-A1
PALMDALE-LLANO RD
7100 Litl 93543 4287-F6
PALMER AV
10900 SGAT 90280 705-F6
E PALMER AV
100 GLDL 91205 564-F7
W PALMER AV
100 GLDL 91204 564-D7
700 COMP 90220 734-G4
PALMER CT
- LHB 90631 738-C2
700 LBCH 90813 795-E7
1800 LBCH 90806 795-E7
N PALMER CT
1300 LBCH 90813 795-D5
PALMER DR
2800 LA 90065 594-G6
PALMER ST
- COMP 90220 734-J4
E PALMER ST
300 COMP 90221 735-A4
4100 RDom 90221 735-C4
W PALMER ST
300 COMP 90220 734-H4
1500 POM 91766 640-G3
PALMERA AV
500 PacP 90272 630-J5
PALMER CANYON RD
4500 CLAR 91711 571-E2
4600 LACo 91711 571-E2
PALMER-EVEY MTWY
- CLAR 91711 571-G1
- LACo - (541-F7
See Page 511)
- LACo 91711 (541-F7
See Page 511)
- LACo 91711 571-G1
PALMERO BLVD
4200 LA 90008 673-E3
PALMERO DR
4100 LA 90065 594-J2
4500 LA 90065 595-A2
PALMERSTON PL
1900 LFlz 90027 593-J3
PALMERSTONE DR
700 LCF 91011 535-C7
E PALMERSTONE ST
4200 RDom 90221 735-C3
PALMETTO AV
700 COV 91723 599-B7
N PALMETTO AV
400 ONT 91762 601-J5
PALMETTO DR
- ALH 91801 596-B6
- PAS 91105 565-G6
40000 PMDL 93551 4195-B3
PALMETTO PL
800 BREA 92821 709-C6
13600 CHLS 91709 680-J2
PALMETTO ST
1100 LA 90013 634-H5
PALMETTO RIDGE DR
27800 SCTA 91354 4460-G4
PALM GROVE AV
1900 LA 90016 633-D6
3000 LA 90016 673-D1
PALMGROVE AV
1700 POM 91767 601-B6
PALM HILL LN
- LACo 91010 567-J3
PALMILLA DR
24900 CALB 91302 559-C6
PALM ROSE ST
14400 BALD 91706 598-C5
PALMS BLVD
500 Ven 90291 671-J4
1200 Ven 90291 672-A4
10000 LA 90034 632-F7
10300 LA 90034 672-D2
11200 LA 90066 672-D2
PALMS PL
38000 PMDL 93552 4286-H1
38600 PMDL 93552 4196-H7
PALM TERRACE CT
- LCF 91011 534-J2
PALM TREE WY
38800 LACo 93551 4195-F6
38800 PMDL 93551 4195-F6
PALM VIEW DR
800 HiPk 90042 595-E1
PALM VIEW PL
600 PAS 91101 565-J5
600 PAS 91101 566-A5
PALM VISTA AV
37700 PMDL 93550 4286-C2
43800 LAN 93535 4106-B1
44000 LAN 93535 4016-B6
PALMWOOD CT
- PMDL 93551 4194-J2
PALMWOOD DR
4000 LA 90008 673-D2
PALMYRA RD
4000 LA 90008 673-D2
PALO DR
4800 Tarz 91356 560-F3
PALO ALTO DR
800 ARCD 91007 566-J6
800 ARCD 91007 567-A6
PALO ALTO ST
1000 MTBL 90640 636-G7

PALO ALTO ST
1600 Echo 90026 634-D1
N PALO CEDRO DR
100 DBAR 91765 640-A7
S PALO CEDRO DR
100 DBAR 91765 640-A7
200 DBAR 91765 680-A1
PALO COMADO DR
5900 AGRH 91301 558-D4
PALO COMADO CANYON
RD
5000 AGRH 91301 558-D6
PALOMA AV
- LBCH 90803 825-H1
- Ven 90291 671-G5
1600 GLDL 91208 534-H4
3200 LVRN 91750 600-E1
5600 LA 90011 674-E5
9900 Wats 90002 704-E5
PALOMA CT
- BREA 92823 709-H6
- CYP 90630 767-E6
- Ven 90291 671-G5
30800 WLKV 91362 557-F5
43200 LAN 93536 4104-H3
PALOMA DR
200 POM 91767 641-A1
500 SPAS 91030 595-F1
900 ARCD 91007 566-J5
PALOMA PL
900 FUL 92835 738-F3
PALOMA ST
- LAN 93536 4104-H2
700 PAS 91107 566-F2
1200 LA 90021 634-F7
1400 PAS 91104 566-C3
2600 LA 90011 674-E1
PALOMA BLANCA DR
23200 LACo 90265 629-E3
PALOMA BLANCA RD
- Actn 93510 (4554-J1
See Page 4464)
PALOMAR DR
1900 GLDR 91741 569-J5
4900 Tarz 91356 560-G4
PALOMAR PL
19300 Tarz 91356 560-G3
PALOMAR RD
800 SMRO 91108 566-F6
PALOMARES AV
700 LVRN 91750 600-E3
700 SDMS 91773 600-E3
N PALOMARES ST
100 POM 91767 641-A1
800 POM 91767 601-A6
S PALOMARES ST
100 POM 91766 641-A3
PALOMINO
- Actn 93510 4375-E7
1800 WCOV 91791 638-J4
PALOMINO AV
1700 UPL 91784 571-J6
N PALOMINO AV
1300 UPL 91786 601-J1
1400 UPL 91786 571-J7
PALOMINO CIR
- MTCL 91763 641-E1
19900 WAL 91789 639-E6
PALOMINO CT
11300 LA 91342 503-B2
36500 PMDL 93550 4286-H5
PALOMINO DR
2500 Actn 93510 4465-D1
2500 LACo 91724 639-F1
2700 LACo 91791 639-F1
18600 Tarz 91356 560-J4
23400 DBAR 91765 640-C6
PALOMINO LN
- SBdC 91710 641-B7
- CRSN 90745 794-G2
3400 RHE 90274 793-E7
PALOMINO PL
29000 SCTA 91387 4462-C7
29000 SCTA 91387 4552-C1
PALOMINO WY
22200 SCTA 91321 4550-J7
PALOMITA DR
25900 SCTA 91355 4550-G4
PALOPINTO AV
1500 GLDR 91741 569-H6
PALORA ST
17300 Enc 91316 561-A3
18200 Tarz 91356 560-J3
PALOS WY
43400 LAN 93535 4106-D2
PALO SOLO MTWY
- StvR 91381 480-A1
- StvR 91381 4640-A7
PALOS VERDES BLVD
100 TOR 90277 792-H3
200 RBCH 90277 792-J1
1000 RBCH 90277 793-A1
1000 TOR 90505 793-A1
5400 TOR 90505 763-B7
21200 TOR 90503 763-B7
PALOS VERDES DR E
4200 RPV 90275 823-G1
26200 RHE 90274 793-G7
27300 RHE 90274 823-G1
28900 RHLS 90274 823-G1
PALOS VERDES DR N
200 PVE 90274 792-J3
1300 LA 90732 794-A6

PALOS VERDES DR N
1300 Hrbr 90710 794-A6
1400 LA 90732 793-F7
1400 Hrbr 90710 793-F7
1700 LMTA 90732 793-F7
1800 LMTA 90717 793-F7
2000 RHE 90274 793-C6
2700 RHLS 90274 793-C6
3000 PVE 90274 793-A3
3800 LACo 90274 793-C6
PALOS VERDES DR S
2200 LA 90732 823-D6
2200 RPV 90275 823-B5
5700 RPV 90275 822-G5
PALOS VERDES DR W
100 TOR 90277 792-G4
100 PVE 90274 792-G4
2500 PVE 90274 822-F2
3000 RPV 90275 822-F2
PALOS VERDES LN
4100 LNDL 90260 733-D4
4100 RHE 90274 793-C5
N PALOS VERDES ST
100 SPed 90731 824-C4
S PALOS VERDES ST
100 SPed 90731 824-C5
PALO VERDE AV
300 LBCH 90803 826-E1
400 PAS 91107 566-D3
600 PAS 91104 566-D3
800 LBCH 90815 796-E6
1200 LBCH 90840 796-E5
3000 LBCH 90808 796-E2
3300 LBCH 90808 766-E6
3700 LACo 90808 766-E6
4100 LKWD 90713 766-E2
5600 CRTS 90703 766-E2
17200 BLF 90706 736-E7
17600 CRTS 90703 736-E7
17800 BLF 90706 766-E2
PALO VERDE DR
- BqtC 91354 4460-E2
PALO VERDE PL
27300 LACo 91387 4551-J4
PALO VERDE ST
4300 MTCL 91763 601-E5
5600 MTCL 91763 601-G5
44200 LAN 93536 4015-A7
PALO VISTA DR
3000 RPV 90275 823-E6
7400 LA 90046 593-B1
45000 LAN 93535 4016-C5
PAM CT
20600 SCTA 91350 4461-D4
PAM PL
2700 WCOV 91792 638-J7
PAMELA AV
5000 ELMN 91732 597-F4
PAMELA CIR
700 ARCD 91006 567-E7
PAMELA CT
17500 RowH 91748 678-G6
PAMELA DR
1000 BHLS 90210 592-D6
3800 SBdC 91710 641-C7
26700 SCTA 91351 4551-E3
PAMELA LN
500 POM 91766 641-A5
1400 LHB 90631 708-G4
2400 RowH 91748 679-E7
PAMELA PL
- ARCD 91006 567-F7
E PAMELA RD
- ARCD 91006 567-D7
100 LACo 91016 567-E7
400 LACo 91010 567-H7
W PAMELA RD
- ARCD 91007 567-C7
PAMELA ST
2500 RSMD 91770 636-E2
PAMELA KAY LN
300 LACo 91746 637-H5
700 LACo 90601 637-G5
PAMPAS CIR
4100 LVRN 91750 570-H7
PAMPAS RD
4300 WdHl 91364 560-A5
PAMPAS ST
- PMDL 93551 4195-B4
PAMPAS RICAS BLVD
14800 PacP 90272 631-B6
PAMPLICO DR
22000 SCTA 91350 4461-A6
22300 SCTA 91350 4460-J5
22800 SCTA 91354 4460-H6
PANAMA AV
300 LBCH 90814 796-B7
23100 CRSN 90745 794-D2
PANAMA DR
5500 BPK 90620 767-D3
PANAMA ST
12800 LA 90066 672-C6
PANAMINT CT
100 PMDL 93550 4286-A2
E PANAMINT CT
2800 THO 91362 557-C3
W PANAMINT CT
2700 THO 91362 557-B3
PANAMINT DR
2000 LA 90065 594-H3
PANAMINT ST
4200 LA 90065 594-H1

PANAY WY
13900 MdlR 90292 671-J7
13900 MdlR 90292 672-A7
PANCHOY PL
2400 LHH 90631 678-C7
2400 LHH 90631 708-D1
PANDO DR
2000 HacH 91745 678-D4
PANDORA AV
1400 Wwd 90024 632-D3
1800 WLA 90025 632-D3
PANDORA WY
2000 POM 91766 641-A5
PANDY CT
19800 SCTA 91351 4551-E3
PANGBORN AV
9800 DWNY 90240 706-E4
10200 DWNY 90241 706-D6
12100 DWNY 90242 706-D7
PANHANDLE DR
700 DBAR 91765 680-B1
N PANNES AV
900 COMP 90221 735-C2
S PANNES AV
100 COMP 90221 735-C4
900 RDom 90221 735-C6
PANORAMA CT
- BqtC 91354 4460-D4
- WCOV 91791 639-B4
100 BREA 92821 709-B6
PANORAMA DR
900 ARCD 91007 566-J5
2200 SIGH 90755 795-G3
2300 LaCr 91214 504-H7
5600 WHIT 90601 677-C4
PANORAMA MTWY
- Llan 93544 (4562-A2
See Page 4471)
20500 Llan 93544 4470-F5
23300 Llan 93544 4471-C7
25400 Llan 93544 (4561-H1
See Page 4471)
PANORAMA PL
700 PAS 91105 565-E3
PANORAMA RD
500 FUL 92831 738-J4
2000 FUL 92835 738-J4
17500 Llan 93544 4469-J4
17500 Llan 93544 4470-B4
21300 Llan 93544 4471-A6
PANORAMA ST
1300 UPL 91784 571-H3
PANORAMA TER
2100 LA 90039 594-C4
PANSY AV
1300 UPL 91784 571-J4
PANSY CT
- Cstc 91384 4459-F2
PANSY DR
3400 CALB 91302 589-E1
3500 CALB 91302 559-E7
PANSY ST
- SIMI 93063 499-A2
PANTANO RD
40300 PMDL 93550 4195-J3
PANTERA DR
600 DBAR 91765 640-D7
600 DBAR 91765 680-D1
PANTERRA WY
37800 PMDL 93550 4286-G2
PANTHEON ST
11200 NRWK 90650 706-F7
PANTHER DR
- PMDL 93551 4195-F7
PAOLA AV
2900 LA 90032 595-E6
PAOLI WY
5000 LBCH 90803 796-B7
5000 LBCH 90803 826-C1
PAOLINO PL
26100 SCTA 91355 4550-E5
PAPADAKIS WY
2000 SIGH 90755 795-H4
PAPAGAYO WY
1900 PMDL 93550 4286-D1
PAPAGO TER
8400 LA 91304 529-D1
PAPAYA DR
2000 LHH 90631 708-E1
PAPAYA PL
900 BREA 92821 709-C6
PAPAYA WY
- PMDL 93551 4285-E3
PAPAZIAN CT
- SCTA 91321 4551-F5
W PAPEETE ST
1000 Wilm 90744 794-C5
PAPYRUS DR
500 LACo 90631 708-D4
PAQUET PL
28000 MAL 90265 627-G7
PAQUITA DR
17800 RowH 91748 678-H6
PAR PL
- PRV 90660 676-J1
- PRV 90660 677-A1
31600 Llan 93544 4469-E2
PARA WY
- LA 90094 702-D1
- Wch 90045 702-D1
PARADA DR
25700 SCTA 91355 4550-F6

STREET
Block City ZIP Pg-Grid

W PARADE ST
1300 LBCH 90810 795-B5
PARADISE DR
2600 LA 90032 595-C7
4900 ELMN 91731 597-D4
4900 ELMN 91780 597-D4
18000 LACo - (4560-A4
See Page 4470)
PARADISE LN
6300 NLB 90805 735-D7
6300 NLB 90805 765-D1
20200 Top 90290 590-D2
PARADISE RD
28900 Cstc 91384 4459-A6
PARADISE CANYON LN
5100 LCF 91011 535-D3
PARADISE COVE RD
- MAL 90265 667-G2
PARADISE VALLEY N
- CRSN 90745 794-G2
PARADISE VALLEY S
- CRSN 90745 794-G2
PARADISE VALLEY RD
5300 HIDH 91302 559-E3
PARAGON DR
- LACo 91390 4460-J4
22400 Saug 91350 4460-J4
22400 SCTA 91350 4460-H4
PARAGUAY DR
5500 BPK 90620 767-D3
22000 SCTA 91350 4550-J1
PARAISO ST
1100 SPed 90731 824-A3
PARAISO WY
2700 LaCr 91214 504-F6
3300 GLDL 91214 504-D5
PARALTA AV
5200 WdHl 91364 560-B3
5300 WdHl 91367 560-B3
PARAMONT BLVD
4800 PRV 90660 676-G3
PARAMOUNT BLVD
1000 LACo 91770 636-F5
1500 MTBL 90640 636-F5
3800 LKWD 90712 765-H5
4000 PRV 90660 676-D6
5300 NLB 90805 765-H5
8000 PRV 90660 706-B3
8500 DWNY 90240 706-B3
10200 DWNY 90241 706-A5
11700 DWNY 90241 705-H7
11900 DWNY 90242 705-H7
12800 DWNY 90242 735-H2
13000 SGAT 90280 735-H2
13700 PRM 90723 735-H2
N PARAMOUNT BLVD
5400 NLB 90805 765-H2
6300 NLB 90805 735-H7
PARAMOUNT DR
2000 LA 90068 593-D3
PARAMOUNT LN
- PRV 90660 676-F4
PARAMOUNT PL
- PRM 90723 735-J3
- PRM 90723 736-A3
7600 PRV 90660 676-D7
W PARAMOUNT ST
100 AZU 91702 598-F1
PARANA DR
11400 Chat 91311 480-A7
11400 Chat 91311 500-A1
E PARAPET ST
3400 LBCH 90808 766-C7
PARASOL PL
- StvR 91381 4640-B2
N PARCELS ST
200 POM 91768 640-J1
S PARCELS ST
100 POM 91766 640-J2
PARCHED DR
22200 CALB 91302 559-J6
PARCHER PL
2100 GLDL 91206 564-J2
PARCHER TR
9600 Tuj 91042 504-A5
PARCHMAN AV
24800 SCTA 91321 4640-G2
PARDEE ST
5200 Wch 90045 703-A4
PARHAM AV
5100 LaCr 91214 504-F6
PARIMA ST
6200 LBCH 90803 796-E7
PARION CT
5300 WdHl 91367 559-E3
PARIS CIR
2100 UPL 91784 571-J4
PARIS CT
30800 WLKV 91362 557-F5
PARIS LN
- Nwhl 91321 4640-J5
- Nwhl 91321 4641-A5
- SCTA 91321 4640-J5
PARISE DR
9100 WHIT 90603 707-F4
10200 LACo 90604 707-E5
12900 LMRD 90638 737-D2
S PARISE DR
11900 LACo 90604 707-D7
12100 LACo 90604 737-D1
N PARISH PL
100 BURB 91506 563-F1
800 BURB 91506 533-E7
1900 BURB 91504 533-E4
S PARISH PL
100 BURB 91506 563-F3
PARK AV
- LBCH 90803 826-B1
- SFER 91340 482-B7
- SFER 91340 502-B1
- SMAD 91024 566-J3
- Ven 90291 671-G5
300 LBCH 90814 796-B7
300 LBCH 90814 826-B1
400 MONP 91754 636-B3
500 COV 91723 599-B4
600 SPAS 91030 595-H1
700 LBCH 90804 796-B5
900 ARCD 91007 567-C6
1000 LHB 90631 708-D7
1100 GLDL 91205 564-G6
1600 Echo 90026 594-D7
1600 Echo 90026 634-E1
2000 LVRN 91750 600-F3
2200 HMB 90254 762-G1
2300 Mont 91020 534-J2
2300 LCF 91011 534-H2
4400 IRW 91706 598-D4
4400 BALD 91706 598-D3
4800 CYP 90630 767-C6
6500 Res 91335 530-B7
7900 CDHY 90201 705-F2
9000 SGAT 90280 705-E4
10400 CULC 90232 672-G2
12200 SFSP 90670 706-J5
12500 SFSP 90670 707-A5
15900 PacP 90272 630-J6
43600 LAN 93534 4105-H2
N PARK AV
- POM 91766 640-J1
100 MTBL 90640 676-C2
100 POM 91768 640-J1
600 ING 90302 673-D7
600 ING 90302 703-D1
700 COV 91723 599-B4
800 POM 91768 600-J6
900 COV 91722 599-B4
1500 LBCH 90815 796-A3
S PARK AV
100 MTBL 90640 676-C2
100 POM 91766 640-J3
W PARK BLVD
2300 SBdC 91784 571-J3
PARK CIR
700 LBCH 90813 795-C6
8200 ING 90305 703-G2
PARK CT
- Ven 90291 671-G5
N PARK CT
300 LBCH 90802 795-D7
700 LBCH 90813 795-D7
PARK DR
- WdHl 91364 559-J5
- WdHl 91364 560-A5
1400 SMCA 90404 631-G7
1800 Echo 90026 594-F6
3600 PRV 90660 676-J1
5200 LKWD 90712 765-G3
6000 SBdC 92397 (4652-D1
See Page 4651)
6800 BELL 90201 675-C7
13400 CRTS 90703 737-C6
W PARK DR
200 PMDL 93551 4195-H7
PARK LN
- HAW 90250 733-F4
- SCTA 91354 4550-F1
- WdHl 91364 559-J6
600 BREA 92821 709-B6
3100 Bxby 90807 795-D1
7900 BGDN 90201 705-H2
8300 Flor 90001 704-G2
PARK PL
- MANB 90266 732-H4
- RPV 90275 823-B3
100 Ven 90291 671-G5
500 LHB 90631 708-E5
1400 SMRO 91108 596-B1
2000 ELSG 90245 732-H4
2600 HNTP 90255 674-J6
3300 GLDL 91020 534-J4
3300 GLDL 91208 534-J4
3800 Mont 91020 534-J4
4200 BALD 91706 598-D5
5300 CHNO 91710 641-H7
9200 SGAT 90280 705-E4
14100 CRTS 90703 737-D6
E PARK PL
2100 ELSG 90245 732-J3
PARK PZ S
- CRTS 90703 767-A1
PARK PZ W
- CRTS 90703 767-A1
PARK RD
- LA 90012 594-G6
- SDMS 91773 600-D5
1700 LBCH 90810 795-A1
16000 INDS 91744 638-E6
PARK RW
1500 Ven 90291 671-H6
PARK ST
- ART 90701 766-H2
- ALH 91801 596-B5
4300 CHNO 91710 641-E7
8200 RSMD 91770 636-F2
8500 BLF 90706 735-J6
8900 BLF 90706 736-A6
11100 CRTS 90703 736-F6
12600 CRTS 90703 737-A6
12900 SFSP 90670 707-A5
13200 WHIT 90601 677-D6
22200 SCTA 91321 4641-A2
24200 TOR 90505 793-D4
PARK TER
6700 Wch 90045 672-H7
6700 Wch 90045 702-H1
PARK TR
12200 LACo 91342 482-J6
PARK WY
- LACo 91724 639-H1
900 LHB 90631 708-D7
1200 BHLS 90210 632-F1
3500 MANB 90266 732-H4
PARK ADELFA
23200 CALB 91302 559-F5
PARK ALISAL
23000 CALB 91302 559-G5
PARK ALLEGRA
4500 CALB 91302 559-F5
PARK ANDORRA
23600 CALB 91302 559-F5
PARK ANTIGUA
23700 CALB 91302 559-E5
PARK ANTONIO
3900 CALB 91302 559-F6
PARK ARROYO
4200 CALB 91302 559-G5
PARK ATHENA
24200 CALB 91302 559-D5
PARK AURORA
4400 CALB 91302 559-F5
PARK BASILICO
23200 CALB 91302 559-F6
PARK BELMONTE
23500 CALB 91302 559-E6
PARK BLANCO
23100 CALB 91302 559-G5
PARK BLU
4300 CALB 91302 559-G5
PARKBROOK LN
700 GLDR 91741 569-D4
PARKBYRN PL
7200 LACo 91775 566-H7
PARK CAPRI
23600 CALB 91302 559-E5
PARK CASINO
24000 CALB 91302 559-D6
PARK CENTER DR
2900 LA 90068 593-D1
PARK CENTRE
- CALB 91302 559-E4
PARK CENTRE ST
13400 BALD 91706 598-A4
PARK CIRCLE DR
- SLB 90740 826-J6
1000 LACo 90502 794-A1
1700 LAN 93535 4016-C7
PARKCLIFF ST
8700 DWNY 90242 735-J3
PARK COLOMBO
23300 CALB 91302 559-F6
PARK COLONY CT
3700 AGRH 91301 588-F1
PARK CONTESSA
23100 CALB 91302 559-F5
PARK CORDERO
4500 CALB 91302 559-F5
PARK CORNICHE
23200 CALB 91302 559-F6
PARK CORONA
4300 CALB 91302 559-F5
PARK CREST
700 BREA 92821 708-J5
PARKCREST DR
- LVRN 91750 570-H5
PARKCREST ST
1400 UPL 91784 571-H3
E PARKCREST ST
5100 LBCH 90808 766-B6
6000 LACo 90808 766-D6
PARKDALE PL
1900 LCF 91011 534-J3
PARK DEL AMO
2200 TOR 90503 763-F7
PARK DULCE
23000 CALB 91302 559-G5
PARKE ST
200 PAS 91101 565-J3
PARK ENCINO LN
4800 Enc 91436 561-D4
PARK ENSENADA
23200 CALB 91302 559-F5
PARK ENTRADA
4200 CALB 91302 559-D6
PARK ENTRANCE RD
- LACo 91302 588-F5
PARKER AL
300 PAS 91106 565-J6
PARKER AV
500 MNRO 91016 567-F5
PARKER DR
6000 PMDL 93551 4104-E7
S PARKER DR
500 GLDR 91741 569-D6
PARKER PL
12100 PRM 90723 735-F1
21800 LA 91304 530-A3
PARKER RD
27000 Cstc 91384 4369-G7
W PARKER RD
28300 Cstc 91384 4369-F7
PARKER ST
3600 SPed 90731 854-A2
28900 Cstc 91384 4459-C6
N PARKER ST
100 SPed 90731 824-A4
S PARKER ST
1300 SPed 90731 824-A6
PARKER CANYON RD
1300 WAL 91789 639-E4
PARKER MOUNTAIN MTWY
- Actn 93510 4464-H2
PARKERTON DR
36800 LACo 93551 4285-F5
PARK ESPERANZA
23200 CALB 91302 559-F5
PARK ESTE
4600 CALB 91302 559-G5
PARKFIELD LN
5700 LVRN 91750 570-F4
PARK FOREST CT
37400 PMDL 93552 4287-C2
PARK FORTUNA
4300 CALB 91302 559-F5
PARK FRONT WK
400 LA 90011 674-D4
PARKGLEN AV
4800 LACo 90043 673-C4
PARKGLEN PL
29600 SCTA 91387 4462-G6
PARK GLENN DR
- LA 90068 593-D2
PARK GRANADA
4500 CALB 91302 559-D5
PARK GROVE AV
1900 LA 90007 634-C6
PARK HACIENDA
23300 CALB 91302 559-F6
PARK HAVEN CIR
5000 LaCr 91214 504-G7
PARK HAVEN LN
- LMTA 90717 793-H3
PARKHEATH DR
28900 AGRH 91301 558-B5
PARK HEIGHTS TER
3400 LA 90031 635-B1
PARK HELENA
4000 CALB 91302 559-F6
PARK HERMOSA
23400 CALB 91302 559-F6
PARK HILL DR
8000 Wch 90045 702-D3
PARKHOUSE LN
21400 Top 90290 629-H2
PARKHURST DR
3200 RPV 90275 823-F5
PARK INDUSTRIAL DR
400 LHB 90631 708-F6
PARKINSON AV
9900 LACo 90605 707-C4
PARK JACARANDA
4700 CALB 91302 559-F4
PARK JAZMIN
4400 CALB 91302 559-G5
PARKLAND CIR
13200 LA 91342 482-D1
PARKLAND DR
15800 HacH 91745 678-B6
PARK LANE CIR
16500 Brwd 90049 561-E7
16500 Brwd 90049 591-E1
PARK LANE DR
16500 Brwd 90049 561-E7
16500 Brwd 90049 591-E1
PARK LANE PL
16600 Brwd 90049 561-D7
16600 Brwd 90049 591-D1
PARKLANE WY
23900 SCTA 91354 4460-F7
23900 SCTA 91354 4550-F1
PARK LAWN RD
1500 HacH 91745 678-F4
PARK LIDO
4200 CALB 91302 559-G6
PARK LIVORNO
4500 CALB 91302 559-G5
PARKLYNN DR
6400 RPV 90275 822-H1
PARK MADRID
23700 CALB 91302 559-E5
PARK MALLORCA
4400 CALB 91302 559-F5
PARKMAN AV
300 Echo 90026 594-C7
300 Echo 90026 634-C1
PARKMAN DR
800 LCF 91011 535-C3
PARKMAN ST
200 Alta 91001 535-J4
200 Alta 91001 536-A4
PARK MANOR AV
7000 NHol 91605 532-C5
PARK MARBELLA
4500 CALB 91302 559-E5
PARK MARCO POLO
23100 CALB 91302 559-G6
PARK MARIPOSA
23300 CALB 91302 559-F5
PARK MCCOMBER CIR
7700 BPK 90621 737-H5
PARKMEAD ST
11200 SFSP 90670 706-F5
PARKMEADOW CT
- PMDL 93551 4195-B4
PARK MEADOW DR
27900 SCTA 91387 4552-A2
PARK MELINDA
4000 CALB 91302 559-F6
PARK MILANO
4300 CALB 91302 559-F6
PARK MIRAMAR
24600 CALB 91302 559-D6
PARK MIRASOL
4600 CALB 91302 559-F4
PARK MONACO
4500 CALB 91302 559-F5
PARKMONT DR
42000 LACo 93536 4104-C6
42000 LAN 93536 4104-C6
PARK MONTE NORD
4300 CALB 91302 559-G5
PARKMOR RD
5300 CALB 91302 558-H3
PARKMOUNT DR
2000 GLDL 91206 564-J2
2000 GLDL 91208 564-J2
PARK OAK CT
2500 LA 90068 593-H2
PARK OAK DR
2400 LA 90068 593-G2
PARK OAK PL
5600 LA 90068 593-H2
PARK OESTE
3800 CALB 91302 559-F6
PARK OLIVO
4700 CALB 91302 559-F4
PARK ORA
22900 CALB 91302 559-G5
PARK PALOMA
4200 CALB 91302 559-G5
PARK PASEO
- Boyl 90033 634-J4
PARKPATH TR
6300 Tuj 91042 504-C4
PARK PINTA
23100 CALB 91302 559-F6
PARK PLAZA DR
1300 LBCH 90804 796-B6
17700 CRTS 90703 737-A7
17700 CRTS 90703 767-A1
PARK PRIVADO
23000 CALB 91302 559-G5
PARKRIDGE DR
1600 GLDL 91202 564-D1
21000 WAL 91789 639-G7
PARKRIDGE LN
- PMDL 93551 4195-B4
28000 SCTA 91387 4552-A2
PARKRIDGE PL
- LAN 93536 4104-C6
- LAN 93551 4104-C6
PARK RIVIERA
24100 CALB 91302 559-D5
PARK ROCK DR
16700 LPUE 91744 678-F1
PARK ROSE AV
1300 DUAR 91010 567-J5
PARKROSE AV
200 MNRO 91016 567-J4
1300 DUAR 91010 567-J4
2400 IRW 91010 567-J4
2400 IRW 91010 597-J1
PARK ROSSO
24100 CALB 91302 559-D5
PARK ROW DR
100 LA 90012 634-H1
100 LA 90012 594-H7
PARKS RD
1300 FUL 92833 738-D4
PARK SERENA
4500 CALB 91302 559-F5
PARK SEVILLA
23600 CALB 91302 559-F5
PARK SHADOW CT
14200 BALD 91706 598-C5
PARKSHIRE CT
16400 PRM 90723 735-H6
PARKSIDE AV
1300 BURB 91506 563-F3
2100 LA 90031 635-C1
2700 BURB 91505 563-E4
16600 CRTS 90703 736-J6
PARKSIDE CT
14200 CHLS 91709 680-J4
PARKSIDE DR
- BqtC 91354 4460-E4
200 SFER 91340 482-C7
200 SFER 91340 502-B1
1300 WCOV 91792 638-H5
PARKSIDE LN
7100 LAN 93536 4104-C5
PARKSIDE ST
- AZU 91702 568-G7
PARKSIDE TER
- Hrbr 90710 794-A3
PARKSIDE CROSSING LN
- FUL 92833 738-A3
PARK SIENNA
23000 CALB 91302 559-F5
PARK SOLDI
23300 CALB 91302 559-F6
PARK SOMERSET DR
1500 LAN 93534 4105-H2
PARK SORRENTO
23000 CALB 91302 559-F4
PARKSOUTH ST
23500 CALB 91302 559-E7
PARK SPRING LN
900 DBAR 91765 680-C2
PARK SPRINGS CT
400 VeCo 91377 558-B1
PARKSQUARE WY
- POM 91767 601-A3
PARK TERRA
23100 CALB 91302 559-G6
PARK TERRACE DR
4300 WLKV 91361 557-E6
4900 LBCH 90804 796-B6
PARKVALE DR
27800 SCTA 91350 4461-C5
PARKVALLE AV
16900 CRTS 90703 737-D6
18300 CRTS 90703 767-D1
PARKVALLE CIR
18100 CRTS 90703 767-D1
PARKVALLE PL
17500 CRTS 90703 737-D7
PARKVALLEY AV
16900 LACo 93591 4199-H2
PARK VENETO
23000 CALB 91302 559-G5
PARK VERDI
4200 CALB 91302 559-F6
PARK VERONA
4500 CALB 91302 559-F5
PARK VICENTE
4300 CALB 91302 559-F6
PARK VIEW AV
1200 MANB 90266 732-H4
PARKVIEW AV
1200 PAS 91103 565-E1
PARKVIEW CIR
1200 UPL 91784 571-J6
W PARKVIEW CIR
3100 ANA 92804 767-H7
PARK VIEW CT
- DUAR 91010 568-D5
PARKVIEW CT
- Ago 91301 588-E1
21600 WAL 91789 639-H5
PARK VIEW DR
- RPV 90275 793-H7
100 FUL 92835 738-H4
100 VeCo 91377 558-A2
1000 COV 91724 599-E7
1900 ALH 91803 635-G1
3500 BALD 91706 597-H7
3600 LKWD 90712 765-J5
23000 SCTA 91321 4640-J2
38000 PMDL 93551 4285-A1
PARKVIEW DR N
- ELSG 90245 702-J7
PARKVIEW DR S
- ELSG 90245 702-J7
- ELSG 90245 732-J1
PARKVIEW LN
2200 CHLS 91709 680-J3
44000 LAN 93535 4016-D3
PARK VIEW RD
26200 SCTA 91355 4550-E4
N PARK VIEW ST
100 Echo 90026 634-C1
S PARK VIEW ST
100 LA 90057 634-C2
900 LA 90006 634-B3
S PARKVIEW ST
600 ANA 92804 767-H7
PARKVILLE RD
5000 CALB 91301 558-G6
5100 Ago 91301 558-G6
PARK VISTA CIR
3900 PAS 91107 566-J1
PARK VISTA DR
3200 GLDL 91214 534-E1
3900 PAS 91107 566-H1
4000 PAS 91107 536-J7
27900 Cstc 91384 4459-F3
PARK VISTA LN
2200 CHLS 91709 680-J3
PARK VISTA PL
3200 GLDL 91214 534-E2
PARK VISTA RD
27300 AGRH 91301 588-F1
PARK VISTA TER
- LA 90032 595-D5
PARKWAY AV
1900 LAN 93535 4016-D7
PARKWAY DR
1800 LACo 91733 637-D5
2000 ELMN 91733 637-E4
2200 ELMN 91732 637-F3
PARKWAY TR
- Top 90290 630-A1
PARKWAY CALABASAS
- CALB 91302 589-B1
5000 LACo 91302 559-D4
24100 CALB 91302 559-D6
PARKWEST CIR
5600 LPMA 90623 767-D4
PARK WESTERN DR
1100 SPed 90731 824-A3
1100 LA 90732 824-A3
1200 LA 90732 823-J3
PARK WESTERN PL
1200 LA 90732 823-J3
E PARKWOOD AV
300 LHB 90631 738-F1
N PARKWOOD AV
- PAS 91107 566-C4
S PARKWOOD AV
- PAS 91107 566-C5
W PARKWOOD AV
100 LHB 90631 738-E1
PARKWOOD DR
- PMDL 93551 4285-D2
300 GLDL 91202 564-D2
N PARKWOOD DR
300 BelA 90077 592-C6
PARKWOOD LN
- SCTA 91350 4550-H5
- SCTA 91355 4550-G1
300 GLDL 91202 564-E2
600 POM 91767 601-A1
PARKWOOD PL
13100 BALD 91706 637-J1
PARK WOODLAND PL
28700 LACo 91390 4461-D4
PARKYNS ST
12700 Brwd 90049 631-E3
PARLIN ST
11200 SELM 91733 637-C5
PARMA CT
25800 SCTA 91355 4550-F5
PARMA DR
4800 VeCo 91377 557-G1
PARMELEE AV
1300 Wbrk 90059 704-F7
6300 Flor 90001 674-F7
7300 Flor 90001 704-F1
9200 Wats 90002 704-F4
10400 Wats 90002 704-F5
11200 LA 90059 704-F6
12000 Wbrk 90059 734-F1
N PARMELEE AV
1400 COMP 90222 734-F3
1400 Wbrk 90222 734-F3
S PARMELEE AV
13900 Wbrk 90222 734-F3
PARMER AV
1500 Echo 90026 594-E7
PARMERTON AV
5300 TEML 91780 597-C3
PARNA WY
16600 PRM 90723 735-F6
PARNELL AV
1800 WLA 90025 632-C4
2200 LA 90064 632-C4
PARNELL WY
2000 PAS 91101 535-F7
2000 Alta 91001 535-F7
2300 LACo 91103 535-F7
PARR AV
10100 Sunl 91040 503-G2
PARRA CIR
- FUL 92833 738-A3
PARRAL PL
4200 Shrm 91403 561-H5
PARRIOTT PL
400 INDS 91745 678-C1
E PARRIOTT PL
500 INDS 91745 678-C1
PARRISH AV
3500 LA 90065 594-H3
PARRON AV
14700 GAR 90249 733-H5
PARROT AV
8500 DWNY 90240 706-B2
10600 DWNY 90241 706-A4
12000 DWNY 90242 705-J6
12700 DWNY 90242 735-H1
PARSONS LNDG
300 LBCH 90803 826-C1
PARSONS ST
300 LHB 90631 708-B5
PARSONS TR
6800 Tuj 91042 504-A3
PARTEN DR
4100 LACo 90265 627-H5
PARTHENIA PL
8600 LA 91343 531-H1
8700 LA 91343 501-H7
18400 Nor 91325 530-J1
PARTHENIA ST
13900 PanC 91402 532-A1
14500 PanC 91402 531-H1
14900 LA 91343 531-H1
16800 Nor 91325 531-A1
18100 Nor 91325 530-F1
18400 Nor 91324 530-F1
19700 Win 91306 530-B1
20800 LA 91306 530-A1
22000 LA 91304 529-J1
PARTON CIR
- LAN 93536 4105-C2
PARTON CT
- LAN 93536 4104-H2
PARTRIDGE AV
2700 LA 90039 594-F3
PARTRIDGE CIR
8400 LPMA 90623 767-C4
PARTRIDGE DR
- BREA 92823 709-G5
- LACo 91387 4551-J6
PARTRIDGE LN
1400 GLDR 91740 569-H7
PARTRIDGE PL
2600 LVRN 91750 570-H4
PARTRIDGE RD
900 SBdC 92397 (4652-B2
See Page 4651)
PARVA AV
4000 LFlz 90027 594-B2
PARVIN
21500 SCTA 91350 4551-A6
PARWAY DR
1500 GLDL 91206 565-B1
PASADA DR
16200 WHIT 90603 708-A4
PASADENA AV
- SPAS 91030 595-E2
100 GLDR 91741 569-E5
1700 LA 90031 634-J1
2000 LA 90031 594-J7
2200 LA 90031 595-A7
3000 Bxby 90807 795-E2
3400 LA 90065 595-A7
4500 Bxby 90807 765-E5
4600 NLB 90805 765-E5
N PASADENA AV
- PAS 91103 565-G3
100 AZU 91702 569-A7
400 AZU 91702 568-J5
400 GLDR 91741 569-E4
1800 LBCH 90806 795-E3
S PASADENA AV
- PAS 91105 565-H6
300 GLDR 91741 569-E6
600 GLDR 91740 569-E6
1100 PAS 91105 595-H1
PASADENA FRWY
Rt#-110
- HiPk - 595-B5
- LA - 594-H7
- LA - 595-B5
- LA - 634-F2
- PAS - 565-H7
- PAS - 595-B5
- SPAS - 595-B5
PASADENA ST
12300 WHIT 90601 677-C5
E PASADENA ST
100 POM 91767 640-J1
200 POM 91767 641-A1
PASADENA AVENUE TER
100 HiPk 90042 595-B3
PASADENA GLEN RD
1600 LACo 91107 536-G7
PASADERO DR
18600 Tarz 91356 560-H5
PASADERO PL
4200 Tarz 91356 560-H5
PASADO DR
3400 DBAR 91765 709-H1
PASA GLEN DR
1800 GLDL 91208 534-H6
PASALA CT
24000 SCTA 91355 4550-F4
PASATIEMPO LN
23700 Hrbr 90710 794-A3
PASCAL CT
1400 LAN 93535 4106-C1
PASCAL PL
4100 LACo 90274 793-C6
PASCO CT
21100 DBAR 91765 679-G7
PASEO AV
1500 LVRN 91750 600-F1
PASEO DR
3500 LA 90065 594-H2
12300 CRTS 90703 766-J3
PASEO PL
600 FUL 92835 738-H1
PASEO ST
8700 PRM 90723 735-J4
8800 PRM 90723 736-A4
E PASEO ST
100 COV 91723 599-B6
PASEO AGUA AZUL
1200 PacP 90272 630-F2
PASEO ALAMOS
1300 SDMS 91773 599-J6
PASEO ALDEANO
800 SDMS 91773 600-A5
PASEO ALICIA
1200 SDMS 91773 599-J7
PASEO ALLEGRE
1200 PacP 90272 630-D3
PASEO ALONDRA
1200 SDMS 91773 599-J7
PASEO AMBAR
2000 SDMS 91773 600-B7
PASEO ANACAPA
1200 PacP 90272 630-D3
PASEO ANITGUO
1300 SDMS 91773 599-H5
PASEO AZUL
1800 RowH 91748 678-J5
2000 SDMS 91773 600-B7
PASEO BONITA
11600 LALM 90720 796-J5
PASEO BRAVO
4500 PMDL 93551 4194-J2
PASEO BRILLANTE
1300 PacP 90272 630-D3
PASEO BUENA VISTA
17700 LACo 91744 638-J7
PASEO CANCUN
2300 WCOV 91792 639-A6
PASEO CANYON DR
5700 MAL 90265 627-A7
6400 MAL 90265 667-A1
PASEO CARMEL
1600 SDMS 91773 599-H6
PASEO CASTANOS
1400 SDMS 91773 599-H5
PASEO CIELO
1300 SDMS 91773 599-H5
PASEO CORRIDO
1300 SDMS 91773 599-J5
PASEO CORTO
1300 SDMS 91773 599-J5
PASEO CUMBRE
800 SDMS 91773 600-A5
PASEO DE ARENA
100 TOR 90277 793-A3
100 TOR 90505 793-A3
PASEO DE CASTANA
29700 RPV 90275 823-F4
PASEO DE CIMA
3100 GLDL 91206 535-A6
PASEO DE GRACIA
100 TOR 90277 792-J2
200 TOR 90277 793-A2
PASEO DE GRANADA
100 TOR 90277 793-A3
PASEO DE LA CONCHA
100 TOR 90277 792-H2
PASEO DE LA ESTRELLA
1300 PacP 90272 630-D3
PASEO DE LA FORTUNA
1300 PacP 90272 630-D3
PASEO DE LA LORA
1300 PacP 90272 630-F2
PASEO DE LA LUZ
- RPV 90275 822-F3
PASEO DE LA PALIZADA
500 WAL 91789 679-D2
PASEO DE LA PAZ
1300 PacP 90272 630-F1
1500 SDMS 91773 599-H5
PASEO DE LA PLAYA
100 RBCH 90277 792-H2
200 TOR 90277 792-H2
PASEO DE LA PLAZA
100 LA 90012 634-G3
PASEO DE LA RISA
1300 PacP 90272 630-D3
PASEO DE LAS CASADAS
1600 PacP 90272 630-D3
PASEO DE LAS DELICIAS
100 TOR 90277 792-J2
1800 RBCH 90277 792-J2
1800 RBCH 90277 793-A1
PASEO DE LAS ESTRELLAS
400 TOR 90277 792-J2
PASEO DE LAS FLORES
1300 PacP 90272 630-D3
PASEO DE LAS LOMAS ALTAS
1300 PacP 90272 630-D3
PASEO DE LAS TORTUGAS
3800 TOR 90505 793-C3
PASEO DE LA SUERTE
1400 PacP 90272 630-D3
PASEO DE LA VIDA
1400 PacP 90272 630-F1
PASEO DEL CABALLO
100 WAL 91789 679-C1
PASEO DEL CAMPO
3000 PVE 90274 792-J3
3000 PVE 90274 793-B4
PASEO DEL CASTILLO
1300 PacP 90272 630-D3
PASEO DEL MAR
- RPV 90275 823-E7
300 PVE 90274 792-G3
2200 PVE 90274 822-E1
S PASEO DEL MAR
700 SPed 90731 854-B2
1000 SPed 90731 853-H1
2000 LA 90732 853-G1
2200 LA 90732 823-G7
PASEO DEL MONTE
300 LACo 91744 638-J7
PASEO DELORES
1500 SDMS 91773 599-H6
PASEO DE LOS ARBOLES
1200 PacP 90272 630-D3
PASEO DE LOS REYES
500 TOR 90277 792-J3
PASEO DEL PAJARO
1300 PacP 90272 630-D3
PASEO DEL PALACIO
2200 CHLS 91709 680-J6
PASEO DEL PAVON
5000 TOR 90505 793-B3
PASEO DEL PRADO
20200 WAL 91789 679-F1
PASEO DEL PUERTO
1600 PacP 90272 630-F1
PASEO DEL RANCHO
24800 CALB 91302 589-C1
PASEO DEL REY
7700 PdlR 90293 702-C3
PASEO DEL RIO
- BGDN 90040 676-B7
- BGDN 90040 706-B1
PASEO DEL SERRA
2900 LA 90068 593-D3
PASEO DEL SOL
- CALB 91302 589-C1
1800 PVE 90274 792-H4
PASEO DEL VILLA
200 LACo 91744 638-H7
PASEO DE MONCLOVA
1700 PacP 90272 630-D3
PASEO DE ORO
4100 CYP 90630 767-A7
16700 PacP 90272 630-G1
PASEO DE PABLO
5000 TOR 90505 793-B3
PASEO DE PINO
29600 RPV 90275 823-F4
PASEO DE PLATA
4100 CYP 90630 767-A7
PASEO DE ROCHA
16300 HacH 91745 678-D5
PASEO DESCANSO
1300 SDMS 91773 599-J5
PASEO DE SEVILLA
19600 WAL 91789 679-D2
PASEO DE SUENOS
100 TOR 90277 792-H2
PASEO DE TERRADO
23000 DBAR 91765 680-B3
PASEO DE TONER
- BREA 92821 709-B7
PASEO DORADO
400 LBCH 90803 796-F7
900 FUL 92835 738-E4
1000 FUL 92833 738-E4
1200 SDMS 91773 599-J7
PASEO ENCANTO
1300 SDMS 91773 599-J5
PASEO ENCINAS
1300 SDMS 91773 599-J6
PASEO FELIZ
1700 SDMS 91773 600-A6
PASEO FORTUNA
4700 PMDL 93551 4194-H2
PASEO FORTUNO
1300 SDMS 91773 599-J5
PASEO GABRIELA
1900 SDMS 91773 599-J7
PASEO GRACIA
1200 SDMS 91773 600-A5
PASEO GRANADA
1700 SDMS 91773 599-J6
20100 CRTS 90703 766-J4
PASEO GRANDE
1300 FUL 92833 738-E3
2000 CHLS 91709 680-J6
PASEO GRANDE CIR
900 DUAR 91010 568-E5
PASEO HERMOSO
4500 PMDL 93551 4194-J2
PASEO HIDALGO
3800 MAL 90265 629-F6
PASEO ISABELLA
1300 SDMS 91773 599-J5
PASEO JACINTA
2200 SDMS 91773 600-A7
PASEO JARDIN
1700 SDMS 91773 600-A6
PASEO LA CRESTA
900 PVE 90274 792-G5
PASEO LAGUNA
1700 SDMS 91773 600-A6
PASEO LA PAZ
1900 POM 91768 600-G6
2600 WCOV 91792 639-A6
PASEO LAS LOMAS
1600 PacP 90272 630-D3
PASEO LAURO CT
25600 SCTA 91355 4550-G5
PASEO LA VALLE
1700 PacP 90272 630-D3
PASEO LA VISTA
6100 WdHl 91367 529-C7
6100 WdHl 91367 559-C1
PASEO LOS GAVILANES
1200 SDMS 91773 599-J5
1200 SDMS 91773 600-A5
PASEO LOS LAGOS
1500 PacP 90272 630-F1
PASEO LOS MONTEROS
1500 PacP 90272 630-F1
PASEO LOS POCITOS
1600 PacP 90272 630-D3
PASEO LUCER
19800 WAL 91789 679-E1
PASEO LUCINDA
2000 SDMS 91773 599-G6
PASEO LUNADO
500 PVE 90274 822-F1
PASEO MADRONAS
1400 SDMS 91773 599-H6
PASEO MALAGUENA
1300 PacP 90272 630-D3
PASEO MANZANA
1400 SDMS 91773 600-A5
PASEO MARAVILLA
1400 SDMS 91773 600-A5
PASEO MARIPOSA
1300 PacP 90272 630-D3

STREET
Block City ZIP Pg-Grid

PASEO MARLENA
1400 SDMS 91773 599-H6
PASEO MERIDA
2600 WCOV 91792 639-A6
PASEO MIRAMAR
- TOR 90277 792-J2
300 PacP 90272 630-G5
PASEO MONTE COVINA
200 LACo 91744 638-H7
PASEO MONTE VERDE
17500 LACo 91744 638-H7
PASEO MORELOS
1300 SDMS 91773 599-J5
PASEO MUNDO
1700 SDMS 91773 600-A6
PASEO NOGALES
1300 SDMS 91773 599-J6
PASEO NUEVO DR
18600 Tarz 91356 560-H5
PASEO OLIVAS
2600 WCOV 91792 639-A6
PASEO OLIVOS
1400 SDMS 91773 599-H6
PASEO OTONO
1700 SDMS 91773 600-A6
PASEO PALOMA
1300 PacP 90272 630-F2
PASEO PAS
1300 PacP 90272 630-D3
PASEO PERDIDO
100 WAL 91789 679-E1
PASEO PLACITA
1300 SDMS 91773 599-H5
PASEO PORTOLA
21400 MAL 90265 629-F6
PASEO PRIMARIO
3600 CALB 91302 559-C7
PASEO RANCHO CASTILLA
1600 LACo 90032 635-F1
1800 LA 90032 635-F1
5400 ALH 90032 635-F1
PASEO REDONDO
1200 BURB 91501 534-B6
PASEO REGINA
1100 SDMS 91773 599-J7
PASEO ROBLES
1400 SDMS 91773 599-H6
20500 WAL 91789 679-F1
PASEO SANDI
1100 SDMS 91773 599-J6
PASEO SERENO
1300 SDMS 91773 599-H5
PASEO SERRA
21500 MAL 90265 629-F6
PASEO SOMBRA
1200 SDMS 91773 599-J5
PASEO SONRISA
300 WAL 91789 679-F1
PASEO SUENO
1500 SDMS 91773 599-H5
PASEO SUSANA
2000 SDMS 91773 599-H6
PASEO TEPIC
2200 WCOV 91792 639-A6
PASEO TERESA
1200 SDMS 91773 599-J7
PASEO TERRAZA
22500 SCTA 91350 4460-J7
PASEO TESORO
300 WAL 91789 679-F1
PASEO TORTUGA
2500 CHLS 91709 680-J5
PASEO VALLE VISTA
1300 SDMS 91724 599-F5
PASEO VERANO
1700 SDMS 91773 599-J6
1700 SDMS 91773 600-A6
PASEO VERDE
13000 LACo 90601 637-E6
PASEO VICTORIA
1400 SDMS 91773 599-H7
PASEO VIENTO
900 SDMS 91773 599-J5
900 SDMS 91773 600-A5
PASEO VILLA CAPRI
10600 LACo 90604 707-F5
PASEO VISTA HERMOSA
1300 PacP 90272 630-F1
PASEO YNEZ
2000 SDMS 91773 599-H7
PASEO ZACATE
1300 SDMS 91773 600-A5
PASHA PL
13300 LA 91342 482-D3
PASHA ST
13100 LA 91342 482-D3
PASHLEY ST
15900 SCTA 91387 4552-D3
PASKENTA RD
1200 PacP 90272 631-B4
PASO ALTO
1000 PAS 91105 565-F4
PASO REAL AV
1400 RowH 91748 679-B5
PASO ROBLES AV
4800 Enc 91316 561-D3
7200 VanN 91406 531-D3
8300 Nor 91325 531-C1
8700 Nor 91325 501-C5
10800 GrnH 91344 501-C1
11600 GrnH 91344 481-C7

W PASO ROBLES DR
3100 ANA 92804 767-H6
PASO VERDE DR
1900 HacH 91745 678-D5
PASQUAL AV
300 SGBL 91775 596-C2
PASQUAL LN
100 SGBL 91775 596-C3
PASQUAL PL
100 SGBL 91775 596-C3
PASQUALITO DR
500 SMRO 91108 596-A2
PASS AV
100 BURB 91505 563-C1
1600 BURB 91505 533-C7
N PASS AV
- BURB 91505 563-C2
- BURB 91522 563-D4
PASSAGE AV
14400 PRM 90723 735-J3
16800 BLF 90706 735-J6
PASSAGEWAY PL
30300 AGRH 91301 557-G5
PASSAIC ST
6200 HNTP 90255 675-A6
PASS AND COVINA RD
1400 LACo 91744 638-G4
1700 WCOV 91792 638-G4
PASSIFLORA DR
500 LACo 90631 708-D3
PASSMORE DR
2900 LA 90068 593-C1
3000 LA 90068 563-C7
PASSONS BLVD
4800 PRV 90660 676-H3
7500 PRV 90660 706-E2
8800 DWNY 90240 706-E3
PASTEL PL
3700 LA 91604 562-H6
PASTEL WK
16100 LACo 91390 4192-C3
PASTEUR DR
1200 LAN 93535 4106-C1
PASTRANA DR
15300 LMRD 90638 737-H3
PAT AV
5900 WdHl 91367 559-D1
5900 WdHl 91367 529-D7
6200 CanP 91307 529-D7
PAT PL
24500 WdHl 91367 559-D1
PATAGONIA DR
2100 LCF 91011 534-H2
PATATA ST
4700 CDHY 90201 705-E3
5000 SGAT 90280 705-E3
PATE PL
12600 CHNO 91710 641-D6
E PATERO WY
4000 LBCH 90815 796-A4
PATHFINDER RD
1300 DBAR 91765 679-G5
18000 RowH 91748 708-J1
18000 RowH 91748 678-J7
18000 RowH 91748 679-D6
19700 LACo 91789 679-G5
20100 DBAR 91789 679-G5
PATHWAY TR
10200 Tuj 91042 504-C4
PATIO PL
3600 LA 90032 595-F6
PATIRENE PL
19300 Res 91335 530-G6
PAT MIRANDA LN
5100 IRW 91706 598-F3
PAT MOORE WY
6800 LA 90068 593-E2
PATOM DR
11200 CULC 90230 672-G5
PATRAE ST
4800 LA 90066 672-D6
PATRICE PL
500 LA 90248 764-B1
PATRICIA AV
2100 WLA 90025 632-D4
2100 LA 90064 632-D4
PATRICIA CIR
4500 LPMA 90623 767-B3
PATRICIA DR
12400 CRTS 90703 766-J2
12400 CRTS 90703 767-A2
PATRICIA LN
37500 PMDL 93552 4287-A3
PATRICIA PL
- Saug 91350 4461-E5
PATRICIA ST
3400 WCOV 91792 639-B7
3400 WCOV 91792 679-B1
PATRICIA WY
400 ARCD 91006 567-E7
PATRICIAGLEN LN
100 LHB 90631 708-D6
PATRICIA HILL DR
28300 SCTA 91387 4552-B1
PATRICIAN WY
- Eagl 90041 565-D5
- PAS 91105 565-E4
400 MNRO 91016 567-F2
PATRICIAN VIEW DR
2300 RowH 91748 679-B6
PATRICK AV
800 POM 91767 601-B7
8900 Pcma 91331 502-B3

PATRICK ST
1600 UPL 91784 571-J6
5100 TOR 90503 763-B4
PATRICK HENRY PL
- PMDL 93550 4286-B4
3600 AGRH 91301 588-E1
3800 AGRH 91301 558-E7
PATRITTI AV
3100 BALD 91706 637-H1
3200 BALD 91706 597-H7
PATRONELLA AV
800 TOR 90503 763-F5
15300 LACo 90249 733-F5
16600 TOR 90504 733-F7
17500 TOR 90504 763-F1
PATTERSON AV
500 GLDL 91203 564-C3
700 GLDL 91202 564-C3
1000 KeCo 93560 3835-D1
1000 POM 91766 641-B4
PATTERSON DR
300 MNRO 91016 567-G2
PATTERSON PL
10700 SFSP 90670 707-A5
15200 PacP 90272 631-A6
PATTERSON RD
- KeCo 93560 3835-D1
PATTERSON ST
5100 LBCH 90815 796-B2
E PATTERSON ST
300 LBCH 90806 795-E2
600 SIGH 90755 795-E2
W PATTERSON ST
500 LBCH 90806 795-C2
PATTERSON WY
- PMDL 93552 4287-E2
400 FUL 92832 738-J7
500 FUL 92831 738-J7
PATTI LN
- LAN 93535 4106-F2
PATTIE ST
1400 COMP 90221 735-B4
PATTIGLEN AV
2000 LVRN 91750 600-D2
PATTILAR AV
5500 WdHl 91367 559-E2
PATTIZ AV
1600 LBCH 90815 796-F4
3000 LBCH 90808 796-G2
PATTON AV
- LACo 90073 631-H3
N PATTON AV
100 LA 90732 823-J4
S PATTON AV
100 LA 90732 823-J5
300 LACo 90732 823-J5
700 SPed 90731 823-J6
2500 SPed 90731 853-J1
PATTON CT
1200 SMRO 91108 596-C1
PATTON RD
11200 DWNY 90241 706-A7
11900 DWNY 90242 706-A7
PATTON ST
200 Echo 90026 634-E2
PATTON WY
1200 SMRO 91108 566-C7
1200 SMRO 91108 596-C1
6000 BPK 90620 767-E3
PATTY CT
2400 WCOV 91792 679-B1
37600 PMDL 93550 4285-J3
PATTY LN
1000 LAN 93535 4106-B3
PATWOOD DR
1200 LHB 90631 738-D1
E PATWOOD DR
400 LHB 90631 738-F1
PAUL AV
21600 TOR 90503 763-B6
PAUL DR
7700 WHIT 90606 677-B7
PAUL TER
1500 Echo 90026 594-E6
PAULA AV
300 GLDL 91201 564-A3
PAULA DR
3000 SMCA 90405 671-H3
PAULA LN
3700 LAN 93535 4106-H1
PAULA ST
3400 WCOV 91792 639-B7
3400 WCOV 91792 679-B1
4400 LKWD 90713 766-F5
4600 LA 90032 595-D6
PAUL BUNYON MTWY
- LACo 92823 709-G3
- OrCo 92823 709-G3
PAULCREST DR
3000 LA 90046 593-A1
PAULETTE PL
400 LCF 91011 535-D3
16900 GrnH 91344 481-C5
PAULHAN AV
4500 Eagl 90041 564-J7
4500 Eagl 90041 565-A7
PAULHAN ST
2000 LACo 90220 764-H2
N PAULINA AV
400 RBCH 90277 762-J3
400 RBCH 90277 763-A4
PAULINE AV
2000 LA 90046 592-H3

PAULINE CT
- LACo 91387 4552-A3
PAULINE DR
9600 CYP 90630 767-F7
PAULINE ST
2400 WCOV 91792 639-B7
E PAULINE ST
2300 COMP 90221 735-C6
3600 RDom 90221 735-C6
PAUL JONES AV
900 Wilm 90744 794-J5
900 Wilm 90744 795-A5
PAUL REVERE DR
22400 CALB 91302 559-H5
PAUL REVERE PL
- PMDL 93550 4286-C5
PAULSEN AV
200 COMP 90220 734-H4
N PAULSEN AV
100 COMP 90220 734-H4
1100 COMP 90222 734-H2
PAULSEN CIR
500 COMP 90220 734-H5
PAULSON AV
2500 SELM 91733 637-C2
2500 ELMN 91733 637-C2
PAUMA VALLEY DR
19100 Nor 91326 500-F1
PAVAROTTI DR
500 VeCo 91377 557-G2
PAVAS CT
1800 RowH 91748 678-J5
PAVIA PL
1300 PacP 90272 631-D4
PAVILION DR
900 POM 91768 600-G7
PAVILLION DR
1700 POM 91768 640-E1
E PAVO ST
5300 LBCH 90808 796-D1
PAVO REAL AV
1600 MONP 91754 636-A4
PAWNEE
100 Top 90290 560-B6
PAWNEE ST
10600 SunV 91352 533-A1
PAXSON LN
2500 ARCD 91007 597-D2
PAXTON AV
2500 PMDL 93551 4195-C5
PAXTON ST
- LA 91342 482-D7
- LACo 91342 482-D7
12600 Pcma 91331 482-D7
13000 Pcma 91331 502-C2
PAYERAS ST
20300 Chat 91311 500-C6
PAYETTE DR
10400 WHIT 90603 707-H5
PAYNE AV
21300 LACo 90502 764-B6
PAYSON ST
200 SDMS 91773 600-C1
700 LACo 91750 600-D1
18200 LACo 91702 599-A1
18800 LACo 91722 599-C1
E PAYSON ST
100 AZU 91702 598-J1
100 GLDR 91740 599-E1
800 LACo 91702 598-H2
17900 LACo 91702 599-A2
W PAYSON ST
100 GLDR 91740 599-E1
200 AZU 91702 598-J2
1200 SDMS 91773 599-H1
PAZ CT
6000 PMDL 93552 4287-D2
PEABODY ST
6100 LBCH 90808 766-D7
E PEABODY ST
5100 LBCH 90808 766-B7
E PEACE ST
300 NLB 90805 765-D4
PEACEFUL WY
2600 LAN 93535 4106-E1
PEACEFUL HILLS RD
1800 DBAR 91789 679-G5
PEACEFUL VALLEY RD
34200 LACo 93551 4375-G1
34200 PMDL 93550 4375-H3
34200 PMDL 93550 4376-A4
36200 LACo 93551 4285-F7
PEACH
200 SDMS 91773 599-H2
10900 MsnH 91345 501-G2
PEACH AV
4800 Shrm 91403 561-H4
5800 VanN 91411 561-H1
6200 VanN 91411 531-H7
6400 VanN 91406 531-G3
9800 LA 91343 501-G5
10300 MsnH 91345 501-G4
PEACH CT
22700 SCTA 91390 4460-J3
PEACH DR
37600 PMDL 93550 4286-D2
PEACH MTWY
23200 SCTA 91321 4640-H3
PEACH PL
- PAS 91105 565-H5
PEACH RD
24700 SCTA 91321 4640-G2

PEACH ST
300 MONP 91755 636-C3
300 COMP 90222 734-H3
9200 CYP 90630 767-D6
11000 LYN 90262 705-A7
11800 LYN 90262 735-A1
12600 COMP 90221 735-A1
PEACH BLOSSOM RD
20400 WAL 91789 639-F5
PEACH GROVE ST
10800 NHol 91601 563-A3
11200 NHol 91601 562-J3
13900 Shrm 91423 562-B3
PEACHLAND AV
24500 SCTA 91321 4640-G1
PEACHTREE AV
7700 PanC 91402 532-B2
E PEACHTREE CT
- LACo 91744 638-J5
PEACH TREE LN
32600 Pear 93553 4378-J6
PEACHTREE LN
- CRSN 90746 764-F1
500 ARCD 91006 567-E7
700 COV 91723 599-C7
7100 Litl 93543 4377-F1
PEACHTREE ST
5700 CMRC 90040 675-G6
PEACHTREE WY
800 POM 91767 601-B4
PEACHWOOD DR
3000 LAN 93536 4105-B4
3700 SBdC 91766 641-D3
PEACHWOOD PL
- PMDL 93551 4285-E3
32700 WLKV 91361 586-J1
32700 WLKV 91361 587-A1
PEACOCK CT
23000 CALB 91302 559-G5
PEACOCK LN
- RHE 90274 793-F7
200 MTBL 90640 636-E7
1600 FUL 92833 738-E5
PEACOCK PL
- StvR 91381 4550-A6
2600 LVRN 91750 570-H5
PEACOCK RIDGE DR
28100 RPV 90275 792-J7
PEACOCK RIDGE RD
3700 CALB 91301 588-G1
3700 CALB 91301 558-F7
5900 RPV 90275 792-J7
PEAJAY WY
26700 SCTA 91351 4551-F4
PEAK CT
24200 DBAR 91765 680-D2
PEAK TR
- Top 90290 590-A7
PEAKLAND RD
- LACo 93551 4375-H5
- LACo 93551 4376-A5
PEALE DR
22500 CALB 91302 559-H5
PEAR CT
22700 SCTA 91390 4460-J4
PEAR ST
300 COMP 90222 734-H3
900 BREA 92821 738-J1
11400 LYN 90262 705-A7
PEAR BLOSSOM CT
16500 WHIT 90603 708-A6
PEARBLOSSOM HWY
4000 PMDL 93552 4286-G6
4300 LACo 93552 4286-G6
4500 PMDL 93552 4287-B6
4500 LACo 93552 4287-B6
15700 PMDL 93550 4286-G6
35300 PMDL 93550 4376-D1
36200 PMDL 93550 4286-E7
PEARBLOSSOM HWY Rt#-138
5600 PMDL 93552 4287-C6
5700 LACo 93552 4287-C6
5800 PMDL 93552 4377-F1
5800 LACo 93552 4377-F1
6100 Litl 93543 4377-F1
9100 Litl 93543 4378-B1
11600 Pear 93553 4378-G3
13300 Pear 93553 4379-A3
14100 Llan 93544 4379-G3
PEARBLOSSOM ST
- FUL 92835 738-J3
PEARBLOSSOM VISTA
32700 Pear 93553 4378-H6
PEARCE AV
4900 LKWD 90712 766-B2
N PEARCE AV
4700 LBCH 90808 766-B4
PEARL AV
400 MNRO 91016 567-H3
N PEARL AV
100 COMP 90221 735-A3
S PEARL AV
100 COMP 90221 735-A5
PEARL CIR
4200 CYP 90630 767-A5
4200 LACo 90630 767-A5
PEARL CT
- CRTS 90703 767-A3
2400 WCOV 91792 679-B1
4300 CYP 90630 767-B5
5100 LACo 93536 4104-H5

PEARL PL
300 PAS 91101 565-J4
500 LBCH 90802 795-D7
2400 SMCA 90405 671-J2
11500 LA 90064 632-A7
36600 PMDL 93550 4286-G5
PEARL PL N
900 SMCA 90405 671-G3
PEARL ST
100 RBCH 90277 762-J6
700 RBCH 90277 763-A6
800 SMCA 90405 671-H2
3200 SMCA 90405 672-A1
5600 TOR 90503 763-A6
11200 LA 90064 632-B7
12000 LA 90064 672-A1
E PEARL ST
100 POM 91767 640-J1
100 SGBL 91776 596-F5
200 POM 91767 641-A1
W PEARL ST
100 POM 91768 640-J1
PEARLANNA DR
500 SDMS 91773 600-A1
PEARLE ST
7800 PRM 90723 735-G2
PEARLWOOD DR
3000 LAN 93536 4105-C3
PEARMAIN DR
- PMDL 93551 4285-E3
PEAR ORCHARD LN
3600 PAS 91107 566-G1
PEARSON AV
2200 LACo 90601 637-D6
PEARSON CT
22500 SCTA 91350 4460-J5
PEARSON PL
10400 Sunl 91040 503-D3
PEARSON ST
4600 CULC 90232 672-H2
PEART AV
- LACo 93551 4375-J5
PEARTREE CT
100 WAL 91789 679-E1
PEARTREE LN
- RHE 90274 822-J2
9500 CYP 90630 767-E7
PEARTREE PL
23300 CALB 91302 559-F6
PEAR TREE WY
2200 HacH 91745 678-E5
PEARWOOD AV
1600 LA 91342 481-J7
1600 SFER 91342 481-J7
PEARY DR
24400 SCTA 91355 4550-E6
PEAVINE DR
9700 LA 90210 592-D4
PEBBLE CT
2000 MONP 91754 635-G4
PEBBLE DR
- Hrbr 90710 794-A5
PEBBLE LN
2200 DBAR 91789 679-G5
PEBBLE ST
- Actn 93510 4375-A7
- Actn 93510 4465-A1
PEBBLE WY
40400 PMDL 93551 4195-B3
PEBBLE BEACH AV
300 LHB 90631 738-D2
PEBBLE BEACH CT
- PRV 90660 676-J1
- PRV 90660 677-A1
8400 BPK 90621 738-A4
PEBBLE BEACH DR
- LCF 91011 535-C2
- PMDL 93551 4195-B2
- StvR 91381 4550-C4
300 LACo 90606 676-H6
8400 BPK 90621 737-J4
8400 BPK 90621 738-A4
PEBBLE BEACH LN
300 AZU 91702 568-H4
PEBBLE BEACH PL
400 FUL 92835 738-H3
19200 Nor 91326 480-G7
PEBBLE CREEK LN
900 WAL 91789 639-C6
PEBBLEDON ST
1100 MONP 91754 635-G4
PEBBLE HURST ST
1300 MONP 91754 635-H4
PEBBLE RIDGE PL
- StvR 91381 4550-B4
PEBBLESHIRE RD
900 GLDL 91207 564-G1
PEBBLE SPRGS LN
1300 GLDR 91741 569-H4
PEBBLE VALE ST
1300 MONP 91754 635-H4
PEBBLEWOOD DR
1100 DBAR 91765 680-E3
PEBBLY BEACH RD
100 AVA 90704 5923-H4
PECAN CT
- CRSN 90746 764-G2
PECAN PL
200 BREA 92821 709-B7
22500 SCTA 91390 4460-J4
PECAN ST
900 BREA 92821 738-J1
9200 CYP 90630 767-C6

PECAN ST
40400 PMDL 93551 4194-G2
S PECAN ST
100 Boyl 90033 634-J5
600 LA 90023 634-J5
PECAN WY
500 LHB 90631 708-C6
PECAN GROVE DR
1300 DBAR 91765 680-A3
PECK AV
2500 SPed 90731 824-B7
2600 SPed 90731 854-B1
N PECK AV
100 MANB 90266 732-H5
S PECK AV
100 MANB 90266 732-H7
600 MANB 90266 762-J1
PECK CIR
4500 LVRN 91750 570-G7
PECK CT
37000 PMDL 93550 4286-F4
S PECK DR
100 BHLS 90212 632-F3
400 LA 90035 632-F3
PECK RD
1000 LACo 90601 637-C6
1000 LACo 90660 637-C6
1000 SELM 91733 637-D4
1700 MNRO 91016 567-G6
1800 LACo 91016 567-G6
2000 ELMN 91733 637-D2
2200 ELMN 91732 637-D2
2300 INDS 90601 637-C6
2600 MNRO 91016 597-F3
3000 ELMN 91731 637-D2
3200 IRW 91706 597-F3
3200 ARCD 91706 597-F3
3200 MNRO 91706 597-F3
3200 ARCD 91006 597-F3
3500 ELMN 91732 597-E6
3500 ELMN 91731 597-E6
S PECK RD
1900 MNRO 91016 567-G7
1900 LACo 91016 567-G7
2400 MNRO 91016 597-G1
E PECK ST
400 COMP 90221 735-A3
PECKAM DR
500 LACo 91746 637-G4
600 LACo 90601 637-G4
S PECKHAM RD
100 AZU 91702 568-F7
100 AZU 91702 598-F1
PECOS AV
12600 NRWK 90650 736-E1
PECOS CT
27600 Cstc 91384 4459-H4
43600 LAN 93535 4106-E2
PEDLEY DR
1300 ALH 91803 636-A1
1500 ALH 91803 635-J1
PEDRO PL
1800 PVE 90274 792-G4
PEEKABOO RD
43100 LACo 93532 4102-G3
PEERLESS PL
1400 LA 90035 632-F4
PEERLESS BLUFF CT
- SCTA 91351 4551-G1
PEG PL
1400 LA 90035 632-F4
PEGASE DR
- PMDL 93551 4104-D6
PEGASUS DR
11300 LACo 91342 482-J2
PEGASUS WY
- PMDL 93552 4286-J2
PEGFAIR LN
1300 PAS 91103 565-D1
PEGFAIR ESTATES DR
1400 PAS 91103 565-D1
PEGGY AV
600 LPUE 91744 638-F6
PEGGY CT
3400 WCOV 91792 639-B7
3400 WCOV 91792 679-B1
PEGGY JOYCE LN
21400 SCTA 91350 4461-B6
PELANCONI AV
800 GLDL 91202 564-B3
PELE CT
2700 WCOV 91792 679-B1
PELHAM AV
1800 WLA 90025 632-C4
2200 LA 90064 632-C4
PELHAM PL
2700 LA 90068 593-G2
23200 SCTA 91354 4550-G1
PELHAM RD
1300 SLB 90740 826-G1
1400 SLB 90740 796-G7
PELICAN AV
1700 LA 90732 823-H6
PELICAN DR
7000 BPK 90620 767-E2
PELION CT
37700 PMDL 93550 4286-H1
PELLET ST
7000 DWNY 90241 705-H3
9300 DWNY 90241 706-D6
PELLEUR ST
4600 LYN 90262 735-D2

PELLISSIER PL
2100 INDS 90601 637-C7
2100 LACo 90601 637-C7
PELLISSIER RD
12200 LACo 90601 637-D6
PELON WY
1000 MONP 91754 636-B4
PELONA RD
10700 LACo 91390 4373-E3
PELONA CANYON RD
- Actn 93510 4374-J3
- Actn 93510 4375-A3
PELONA VALLEY RD
34600 LACo 91390 4373-F2
PELONA VISTA DR
3900 LAN 93536 4105-A2
PELORUS AV
1800 SLB 90740 826-G4
PELTON AV
13900 PRM 90723 735-F2
PELUSO AV
10700 Sunl 91040 503-E3
PEMBERTON DR
14900 LMRD 90638 737-F4
PEMBERTON RD
11200 OrCo 90720 796-J3
PEMBINA RD
27100 RPV 90275 793-A7
PEMBRIDGE CT
2000 BelA 90077 591-G3
PEMBROKE CT
1900 CLAR 91711 571-E7
PEMBROKE LN
- LA 90017 634-E5
1100 LA 90015 634-E5
S PEMBROKE LN
1300 LA 90015 634-D6
PEMBROKE RD
900 SDMS 91773 599-G4
PEMBROOK AV
300 POM 91766 641-A5
PEMBROOK DR
400 PAS 91107 566-H3
PEMBROOK PL
25500 SCTA 91350 4550-J5
PEMBURY DR
5200 LPMA 90623 767-C3
PEMBURY PL
4100 LCF 91011 535-B5
PEN ST
18800 RowH 91748 709-B1
PENA RD
- MAL 90265 630-B6
PENARA ST
37400 PMDL 93552 4286-H3
PENARTH AV
700 DBAR 91789 679-G2
PENBYRN RD
33200 LACo 91390 4373-E6
PENCA AV
4200 PMDL 93552 4286-J5
PENCIN DR
600 LACo 90601 637-G5
600 LACo 91746 637-G5
PENDER AV
11000 GrnH 91344 501-C2
PENDLETON AV
4100 LYN 90262 705-D6
5100 SGAT 90280 705-D6
PENDLETON CT
5000 LadH 90056 673-A4
PENDLETON LN
2600 LHB 90631 738-B1
PENDLETON ST
10900 SunV 91352 503-A6
10900 SunV 91352 502-H7
11600 SunV 91352 532-G1
PENFIELD AV
5100 WdHl 91364 560-E2
5600 WdHl 91367 560-E1
6100 WdHl 91367 530-E7
6800 Win 91306 530-E1
8700 Nor 91324 530-E1
9300 Chat 91311 500-E3
15500 LACo 93535 4109-E5
PENFIELD ST
100 POM 91768 600-H5
PENFOLD ST
600 NLB 90805 735-E7
PENFORD DR
11800 LACo 90604 707-H6
12000 LMRD 90638 707-H7
PENGRA ST
1300 DUAR 91010 568-A6
PENGUIN DR
7000 BPK 90620 767-E2
PENGUIN LN
6200 SBdC 92397 (4652-B1
See Page 4651)
PENHAVEN LN
8700 LACo 93551 4193-J2
8700 LACo 93551 4194-A2
PENHILL CT
- GLDL 91206 564-J3
PENINA WY
39900 PMDL 93551 4195-J4
PENINSULA AV
800 CLAR 91711 571-E4
PENINSULA CTR
- RHE 90274 793-A7
PENINSULA RD
300 Wilm 90744 824-G1

PENINSULA VERDE DR
1800 RPV 90275 793-H7
1800 RPV 90732 793-H7
N PENLAN AV
2100 SIMI 93063 499-B2
PENLAND PL
24000 HIDH 91302 559-D3
PENLAND RD
5500 HIDH 91302 559-D3
PENLEY DR
- PMDL 93551 4104-D6
PENLON RD
19600 SCTA 91351 4551-E3
PENMAN RD
35300 LACo 91390 4374-C3
PENMAR AV
200 LHB 90631 708-E7
1400 Ven 90291 671-J4
1900 Ven 90291 672-A4
PENMAR CT
2300 Ven 90291 672-A5
PENMAR LN
600 POM 91766 641-A3
PENN ST
- PAS 91103 565-J1
100 ELSG 90245 732-F1
200 PAS 91104 565-J1
600 ELSG 90245 702-F7
11100 LYN 90262 704-J6
12300 WHIT 90602 677-C7
13800 WHIT 90608 677-D7
E PENN ST
100 SDMS 91773 570-C7
PENNANT PL
12500 WHIT 90606 707-B1
PENNEKAMP CT
1200 MANB 90266 732-H7
PENNELL DR
1200 SDMS 91740 570-B7
PENNERTON DR
2300 GLDL 91206 565-A4
PENNEY AV
10900 ING 90303 703-G6
PENN MAR AV
1200 SELM 91733 637-C4
2200 ELMN 91732 637-E2
3600 ELMN 91732 597-F7
PENNSWOOD AV
5400 LKWD 90712 766-A2
16600 BLF 90706 736-A6
PENNSYLVANIA AV
1200 GLDR 91740 599-D1
1300 Boyl 90033 634-J4
1700 Boyl 90033 635-A4
2100 SMCA 90404 671-G1
2700 SMCA 90404 631-H7
3800 GLDL 91214 534-F2
4100 LaCr 91214 534-F2
4300 LaCr 91214 504-F7
4300 GLDL 91214 504-F6
11300 SGAT 90280 705-F7
11500 SGAT 90280 735-F1
22500 TOR 90501 793-G2
23900 LMTA 90717 793-G3
26000 LMTA 90274 793-G6
N PENNSYLVANIA AV
100 GLDR 91741 569-D5
S PENNSYLVANIA AV
100 GLDR 91741 569-D5
600 GLDR 91740 569-D7
PENNSYLVANIA DR
2200 RHE 90274 793-G6
PENNSYLVANIA LN
700 GLDR 91741 569-D4
PENNSYLVANIA PL
3600 CLAR 91711 571-E5
PENNSYLVANIA ST
300 LBCH 90802 824-G3
PENNY LN
19700 CRTS 90703 766-F3
PENNY RD
1300 Top 90290 590-D3
PENNY ST
2500 WCOV 91792 679-B1
PENNYROYAL ST
45800 LAN 93534 4015-G3
PENNYWOOD CT
1700 BREA 92821 708-H6
PENNYWOOD PL
2000 POM 91767 601-B6
PENOBSCOT DR
- LA 91304 529-D4
PENRIDGE PL
8700 ING 90305 703-E3
PENRITH DR
600 LA 90023 635-A6
PENROD DR
800 CRSN 90746 764-E1
30400 AGRH 91301 557-G5
PENROSE AV
13000 Wbrk 90222 734-J2
PENROSE CT
24400 DBAR 91765 680-E3
PENROSE LN
- Cstc 91384 4459-H4
PENROSE ST
10200 SunV 91352 503-A7
10900 SunV 91352 532-J1
10900 SunV 91352 533-A1
PENSACOLA DR
15300 LACo 93532 4102-E4
PENSHORE TER
900 GLDL 91207 564-F1

E PENTAGON ST
200 Alta 91001 535-J5
W PENTAGON ST
400 Alta 91001 535-G4
PENTLAND ST
9000 TEML 91780 596-J4
9500 TEML 91780 597-A4
PENTLAND WY
23900 CanP 91307 529-E5
PENWOOD WY
23600 SCTA 91354 4460-G6
PEONIA RD
4800 WdHl 91364 559-J4
PEONY WY
- PMDL 93551 4195-D6
PEONZA LN
40300 PMDL 93551 4194-J2
PEORIA ST
10900 SunV 91352 503-A5
10900 SunV 91352 502-J6
11900 SunV 91352 532-F1
E PEORIA ST
- PAS 91103 565-H3
W PEORIA ST
- PAS 91103 565-H3
PEPPER AV
2600 LA 90065 594-J5
S PEPPER AV
300 GLDR 91741 569-F6
PEPPER CIR
8100 BPK 90620 767-J5
PEPPER CT
500 ING 90302 703-B1
PEPPER DR
100 Bxby 90807 795-D1
1300 LACo 91104 566-D1
1600 LACo 91104 536-D7
1600 Alta 91001 536-D7
PEPPER PL
28800 SCTA 91390 4460-J2
PEPPER ST
- PAS 91103 565-G1
700 MONP 91755 636-D4
800 ELSG 90245 702-E7
1400 BURB 91505 563-C1
1600 BURB 91505 533-C7
1700 ALH 91801 595-J5
2300 LVRN 91750 600-H2
PEPPER WY
800 GLDL 91205 564-F6
PEPPER BROOK WY
16800 HacH 91745 678-F4
PEPPERCORN DR
21800 SCTA 91350 4461-A6
PEPPER CREEK LN
12500 CRTS 90703 736-J5
12500 CRTS 90703 737-A5
PEPPERDALE DR
1700 RowH 91748 679-D6
3000 LACo 92821 679-E7
3000 LACo 92821 709-E1
PEPPERDINE CT
4200 LVRN 91750 600-J1
PEPPERDINE DR
- BPK 90620 767-E6
18800 CRSN 90746 764-E2
PEPPERDINE LN
800 CLAR 91711 601-B1
PEPPERGLEN DR
700 ARCD 91007 597-A2
PEPPERHILL RD
900 PAS 91107 566-H2
PEPPERIDGE DR
24500 SCTA 91321 4641-B1
24600 SCTA 91321 4551-B7
PEPPERMILL LN
- POM 91766 640-F6
PEPPERMILL WY
12600 LMRD 90638 738-A1
PEPPERMINT LN
24300 SCTA 91321 4641-B1
PEPPERTREE CIR
1300 WCOV 91792 638-H5
PEPPERTREE CT
100 WAL 91789 679-E1
PEPPER TREE DR
400 BREA 92821 709-B6
PEPPERTREE DR
- StvR 91381 4550-C4
- RPV 90275 823-B5
1200 LHH 90631 708-F3
E PEPPER TREE DR
800 AZU 91702 569-B6
PEPPER TREE LN
- RHE 90274 822-H2
1200 DUAR 91010 568-B5
16000 IRW 91706 598-F3
16000 LMRD 90638 737-J2
16000 LMRD 90638 738-A2
PEPPERTREE LN
- CYP 90630 767-B4
- MNRO 91016 567-E4
1000 UPL 91784 571-J4
1700 FUL 92835 738-G4
6000 VeCo 93063 499-B3
35400 LACo 91390 4373-H2
E PEPPER TREE LN
700 LBCH 90815 796-E7
PEPPER TREE PL
22000 TOR 90501 793-G1
PEPPER TREE WY
- PanC 91402 532-C2

LOS ANGELES CO.

STREET	Block	City	ZIP	Pg-Grid
PEPPERTREE WY				
	-	CYP	90630	767-B4
	-	POM	91767	601-A3
PEPPERWOOD AV				
	5400	LKWD	90712	766-A2
	13300	BLF	90706	736-A2
N PEPPERWOOD AV				
	2200	LBCH	90815	796-A3
	4200	LBCH	90808	766-A5
PEPPERWOOD CIR				
	-	POM	91766	640-G6
PEPPERWOOD CT				
	-	CRSN	90746	764-D3
PEPPERWOOD DR				
	600	BREA	92821	709-B7
PEPPERWOOD LN				
	500	BREA	92821	709-A5
	2000	DUAR	91010	568-C5
PEQUENA LN				
	1200	LCF	91011	535-A2
PEQUENO PL				
	16600	PacP	90272	630-H4
PERA RD				
	22700	WdHl	91364	559-H4
PERALTA AV				
	300	LBCH	90803	796-E7
PERALTA DR				
	21400	CRSN	90745	764-F6
PERCH ST				
	1700	LA	90732	823-H7
PERCHERON DR				
	900	WAL	91789	639-J4
PERCHERON LN				
	-	SBdC	92371	(4562-J1 See Page 4471)
PERCIVAL PL				
	2200	LA	90046	593-A3
PERCY ST				
	3400	LA	90023	635-C7
	3800	LACo	90023	635-D7
	5400	ELA	90022	675-H1
PERDIDO LN				
	10400	BelA	90077	592-A2
PEREGRINE CIR				
	-	VeCo	91377	558-B3
PEREZ LN				
	1300	LA	90063	635-C3
PEREZ PL				
	-	BALD	91746	637-G3
	12900	INDS	91746	637-G3
	12900	LACo	91746	637-G3
PERFECT PL				
	2800	LAN	93536	4105-C1
PERGOLA TER				
	-	PMDL	93551	4285-D4
PERHAM DR				
	3800	CULC	90016	672-J2
	3800	CULC	90232	672-J2
PERICO DR				
	9100	WHIT	90603	707-J2
PERIDOT LN				
	36400	PMDL	93550	4286-G5
PERIDOT WY				
	27600	Cstc	91384	4369-G6
PERIGEE CIR				
	-	LA	90732	823-J7
PERIGORD CT				
	-	Tuj	91042	503-J1
PERILLA AV				
	14400	PRM	90723	735-J3
PERIMETER RD				
	-	CRSN	90746	764-F2
	-	CRSN	90747	764-F2
PERIWINKLE DR				
	8100	BPK	90620	767-J3
PERIWINKLE LN				
	-	BqtC	91354	4460-E6
PERIWINKLE ST				
	-	FUL	92835	738-H3
PERIWINKLE WY				
	-	WdHl	91367	529-J7
PERKINS AL				
	900	PAS	91104	566-A1
PERKINS AV				
	11500	SFSP	90606	706-H2
	11500	LACo	90606	706-H2
	20300	TOR	90503	763-D4
PERKINS CIR				
	2600	GLDL	91206	565-A4
PERKINS DR				
	-	ARCD	91006	567-C2
PERKINS LN				
	1400	RBCH	90278	763-B1
	2000	RBCH	90278	733-B6
PERKINS ST				
	-	FUL	92833	738-D5
	9100	PRV	90660	676-E7
PERLITA AV				
	1700	LA	90039	594-E2
	4000	LA	90039	564-D7
PERLITA ST				
	3400	LVRN	91750	570-E7
	3400	LVRN	91750	600-E1
PERLMAN PL				
	25600	StvR	91381	4550-C7
PERNELL AV				
	10900	DWNY	90241	705-H3
	11900	DWNY	90242	705-G5
PERRIN ST				
	1500	POM	91766	640-J3
PERRINO PL				
	1500	LA	90023	674-J1
PERRIS ST				
	1600	Boyl	90033	635-C2
PERRY AV				
	800	MTBL	90640	636-C7
	1000	Wilm	90744	794-J5
	1900	RBCH	90278	733-A6
PERRY CT				
	2300	CLAR	91711	571-C6
PERRY DR				
	5800	CULC	90232	633-A7
PERRY RD				
	6400	BGDN	90201	675-J7
	6600	BGDN	90201	705-H2
PERRY ST				
	3900	City	90063	635-E3
	21300	CRSN	90745	764-F6
PERSELL ST				
	32900	Pear	93553	4378-H6
PERSHING AV				
	-	LACo	90073	631-J3
PERSHING CT				
	200	COV	91723	599-B4
PERSHING DR				
	200	PdlR	90293	702-B3
	9200	Wch	90045	702-B3
PERSHING WY				
	6100	BPK	90620	767-E2
N PERSHORE AV				
	600	SDMS	91773	600-C1
PERSIAN WY				
	-	PMDL	93551	4195-F7
	-	PMDL	93551	4285-F1
PERSIMMON AV				
	4800	ELMN	91780	597-C3
	4800	TEML	91780	597-C3
	5600	ARCD	91007	597-C3
PERSIMMON DR				
	-	CRSN	90746	764-F1
PERSIMMON LN				
	-	PMDL	93551	4285-E3
	28700	SCTA	91390	4460-J2
PERSING DR				
	12500	WHIT	90606	707-C1
PERSONNEL RD				
	1900	DUAR	91010	568-A7
PERTH AV				
	300	LPUE	91744	638-C6
PERTHSHIRE CIR				
	6900	CanP	91307	529-E6
PERU CIR				
	7500	BPK	90620	767-D3
PERU ST				
	2300	LA	90039	594-F4
PERUGIA WK				
	200	LBCH	90803	826-D3
N PERUGIA WY				
	500	BelA	90077	592-A7
PESARO ST				
	400	VeCo	91377	557-G1
PESARO WY				
	-	Nor	91326	500-C2
PESCADERO AV				
	10100	SGAT	90280	705-A5
PESCADORES AV				
	1700	LA	90732	823-H6
PESCADOS DR				
	15500	LMRD	90638	737-H3
PESEBRE DR				
	40600	PMDL	93551	4194-G2
PESQUERA DR				
	2400	Brwd	90049	591-C7
PESTO WY				
	5300	VeCo	91377	557-H2
PETAL AV				
	5200	PMDL	93552	4287-B2
PETALUMA AV				
	1600	LBCH	90815	796-F3
	3000	LBCH	90808	796-F1
	3300	LBCH	90808	766-F7
	4200	LKWD	90713	766-F4
PETALUMA DR				
	8300	SunV	91352	533-C1
PETALUMA LN				
	24800	CRSN	90745	794-D3
PETALUMA PL				
	10100	SunV	91352	533-C1
PETERKIN PL				
	-	BREA	92821	708-J5
PETERS CIR				
	3100	GLDL	91208	534-F5
PETERS RD				
	-	LACo	91342	482-J5
PETERSEN RD				
	34700	LACo	91390	4373-F2
PETERSON AV				
	1700	SPAS	91030	595-E4
	6100	WdHl	91367	529-E7
	6100	WdHl	91367	559-E1
	6500	CanP	91307	529-E6
N PETERSON AV				
	1300	LBCH	90813	795-F6
PETERSON DR				
	8000	WHIT	90603	708-A1
	8000	WHIT	90605	708-A1
PETES WY				
	-	Actn	93510	4465-F1
PETIT AV				
	4300	Enc	91436	561-D3
	6400	VanN	91406	531-D5
	8600	LA	91343	531-D1
	8900	LA	91343	501-D4
	10100	GrnH	91344	501-D1
PETIT DR				
	4400	Enc	91436	561-D4
PETITE CT				
	3000	LA	90039	594-E3
	4300	PMDL	93552	4286-J3
PETITE LN				
	4500	CYP	90630	767-B4
PETRA CT				
	2500	WCOV	91792	679-B1
PETRA DR				
	2700	PMDL	93550	4286-F4
PETREL CT				
	-	LACo	91387	4551-J5
PETRO PL				
	2800	LAN	93536	4105-C1
E PETROL ST				
	7200	PRM	90723	735-F4
PETROLEUM AV				
	22800	LACo	90502	794-B1
	25000	Hrbr	90710	794-A4
PETROLIA AV				
	900	COMP	90221	735-A5
E PETTERSON LN				
	7200	PRM	90723	735-F2
PETTICOAT LN				
	11700	NRWK	90650	736-G3
PETTINGER CANYON RD				
	-	LACo	91390	(4371-A4 See Page 4281)
	-	LACo	91390	4461-B1
PETULA PL				
	10800	CRTS	90703	736-E6
PETUNIA ST				
	-	LHB	90631	708-D6
	200	GLDR	91740	569-E7
	2000	GLDR	91740	570-A7
	2600	WCOV	91792	679-B1
	18500	LACo	91702	569-B7
PETUNIA WY				
	8300	BPK	90620	767-J2
PETWORTH AV				
	11500	LA	91342	482-F7
PEVERO CT				
	40100	PMDL	93551	4195-J3
PEWTER AV				
	3200	PMDL	93550	4286-F5
PEWTER CT				
	1800	HacH	91745	678-F5
PEWTER RD				
	33100	LACo	91390	4373-C5
PEYTON AV				
	1600	BURB	91504	533-E5
PEYTON DR				
	12800	CHLS	91709	641-A7
	12800	SBdC	91710	641-A7
PEYTON RD				
	1900	LVRN	91750	600-G2
PFEIFFER LN				
	200	CLAR	91711	571-D6
PFLUEGER AV				
	100	GLDR	91741	569-G5
PHAETON AV				
	6500	PRV	90660	676-E5
PHAETON DR				
	20100	WdHl	91364	560-E5
PHAETON LN				
	6100	LACo	93536	4104-E5
PHANTOM DR				
	32200	RPV	90275	823-E6
PHANTOM TR				
	-	LACo	91390	4461-B2
PHEASANT CIR				
	6400	BPK	90620	767-F2
PHEASANT CT				
	1400	FUL	92833	738-E5
	26400	SCTA	91355	4550-E4
PHEASANT DR				
	600	LA	90065	595-A3
	6200	BPK	90620	767-F2
PHEASANT LN				
	-	BREA	92823	709-H6
	-	RHLS	90274	823-D1
PHEASANT RD				
	-	POM	91766	640-G6
	900	SBdC	92397	(4652-B2 See Page 4651)
	2100	SBdC	92372	(4562-E5 See Page 4471)
PHEASANT ST				
	3400	GLDL	91206	565-C1
PHEASANT HILL RD				
	10200	SBdC	92372	(4472-A5 See Page 4471)
PHEASANT RUN DR				
	2400	CHLS	91709	680-J3
PHELAN AV				
	4400	BALD	91706	598-D4
PHELAN LN				
	-	PMDL	93552	4287-E2
	500	RBCH	90278	763-B1
	2000	RBCH	90278	733-B7
PHELAN RD				
	1900	SBdC	92372	(4472-E6 See Page 4471)
	2000	SBdC	92371	(4472-E6 See Page 4471)
PHELPS AV				
	2700	LA	90032	595-E7
PHELPS WY				
	-	AZU	91702	569-B4
PHILADELPHIA ST				
	3500	POM	91766	641-D5
	3500	SBdC	91710	641-D5
	3500	CHNO	91710	641-D5
	5600	ONT	91710	641-D5
	12000	WHIT	90602	677-B6
	12000	WHIT	90601	677-B6
	13400	WHIT	90608	677-D6
E PHILADELPHIA ST				
	100	POM	91766	640-J5
	100	POM	91766	641-A5
W PHILADELPHIA ST				
	1000	ONT	91762	641-J5
	1400	CHNO	91710	641-J5
PHILADELPHIA WY				
	11600	LYN	90262	704-J7
PHILBERT DR				
	1600	LA	90210	592-B4
PHILBROOK AV				
	23700	SCTA	91354	4460-F7
PHILBROOK ST				
	18600	RowH	91748	679-A7
PHILIP AV				
	5800	MAL	90265	627-B7
	5900	MAL	90265	667-B1
PHILIPRIMM ST				
	22200	WdHl	91367	559-D2
PHILLIPPI AV				
	11100	Pcma	91331	502-F1
	11600	Pcma	91331	482-E7
	11900	LA	91340	482-D7
	12800	LA	91342	482-A3
	13300	LA	91342	481-H2
PHILLIPPI ST				
	1100	SFER	91340	482-B5
	1900	LA	91342	482-B5
PHILLIPS AV				
	12000	LYN	90262	735-E2
N PHILLIPS AV				
	200	WCOV	91791	598-J5
PHILLIPS BLVD				
	3700	SBdC	91710	641-D3
	3900	SBdC	91766	641-D3
	4500	MTCL	91710	641-D3
	4600	MTCL	91763	641-D3
	4600	SBdC	91763	641-D3
	5200	CHNO	91710	641-D3
	5300	SBdC	91762	641-D3
	5300	CHNO	91762	641-D3
	5600	ONT	91762	641-D3
E PHILLIPS BLVD				
	100	POM	91766	640-J3
	100	POM	91766	641-A3
	1400	SBdC	91710	641-A3
W PHILLIPS BLVD				
	100	POM	91766	640-G3
PHILLIPS CT				
	3700	SBdC	91766	641-C3
PHILLIPS DR				
	-	FUL	92833	738-C5
W PHILLIPS DR				
	1600	POM	91766	640-E3
PHILLIPS ST				
	100	SLB	90743	826-H6
E PHILLIPS ST				
	1200	NLB	90805	765-F2
W PHILLIPS ST				
	1000	ONT	91762	641-J3
PHILLIPS WY				
	1700	HiPk	90042	595-B1
	1800	HiPk	90042	565-B7
PHILLIPS RANCH RD				
	-	POM	91766	640-G7
PHILO ST				
	3200	LA	90064	632-F7
	5400	CYP	90630	767-D5
PHILODENDRON WY				
	8300	BPK	90620	767-J3
PHILPRIMM ST				
	18700	Tarz	91356	560-H2
PHILRICH CIR				
	2600	CALB	91302	558-J4
PHLOX ST				
	7500	DWNY	90241	705-J4
	7800	DWNY	90241	706-A5
PHOEBE AV				
	15500	LMRD	90638	737-F5
PHOEBE CT				
	3400	WCOV	91792	679-B1
PHOENIX DR				
	12000	CRTS	90703	766-J2
	16000	INDS	91745	678-D2
PHOENIX ST				
	600	LA	90012	594-G7
PHOSPHOROUS RD				
	-	SCTA	91350	4551-B5
PHOTOFLASH RD				
	-	SCTA	91350	4551-A4
PHYLLIS AV				
	9000	WHWD	90069	592-H6
PHYLLIS CT				
	3500	WCOV	91792	679-B1
PHYLLIS ST				
	2200	LaCr	91214	504-H6
	9100	BHLS	90210	592-H6
	9100	WHWD	90069	592-H6
PHYLLISGLEN LN				
	400	LHB	90631	708-C6
PIAZZA CT				
	-	LAN	93536	4104-J6
	9700	CYP	90630	767-B7
PIAZZA PL				
	-	PMDL	93552	4287-D3
PIAZZA DI SARRO				
	-	SCTA	91321	4551-E5
PICAACHO DR				
	500	LHH	90631	708-B2
PICADILLY LN				
	16700	CRTS	90703	736-G6
PICADILLY PL				
	-	Cstc	91384	4459-G5
PICADILLY ST				
	45800	LAN	93534	4015-F3
PICARDIE RD				
	2600	RPV	90275	823-G3
PICASO LN				
	2400	SIMI	93063	499-B1
PICASO ST				
	43600	LAN	93535	4106-C1
PICASSO AV				
	4100	WdHl	91364	560-A6
PICASSO PL				
	21400	WdHl	91364	560-A6
PICCADILLY PTH				
	1900	LACo	91107	536-F7
PICCOLO ST				
	3100	LACo	91107	566-F7
PICFORD PL				
	-	Cstc	91384	4459-G5
PICHER AL				
	500	PAS	91105	565-H6
PICKADILLY PL				
	13900	LA	91342	482-E1
PICKENS ST				
	2600	GLDL	91020	534-G2
PICKENS TKTR				
	-	LACo	-	504-G3
PICKENS CANYON RD				
	2300	LaCr	91214	504-H6
PICKERING AV				
	5600	WHIT	90601	677-C7
	7000	WHIT	90602	677-C7
	7900	WHIT	90602	707-C1
PICKERING WY				
	300	MTBL	90640	676-B2
	11600	ELMN	91732	597-F5
PICKFAIR WY				
	1100	BHLS	90210	592-D5
PICKFORD AV				
	45200	LAN	93534	4015-E5
PICKFORD LN				
	-	CRTS	90703	736-F6
PICKFORD PL				
	6000	LA	90035	633-A4
	6100	LA	90035	632-J4
PICKFORD ST				
	4500	LA	90019	633-D5
	5800	LA	90035	633-A4
	6100	LA	90035	632-H4
	11200	LA	90064	632-C7
PICKFORD WY				
	5000	CULC	90230	672-G4
PICKNEY DR				
	4000	CALB	91302	559-H6
PICKWICK PL				
	1700	FUL	92833	738-D3
PICKWICK ST				
	6500	HiPk	90042	595-E1
PICO AL				
	500	SPAS	91030	595-F2
PICO AV				
	100	LBCH	90802	825-B1
	200	LBCH	90802	795-B7
	400	LBCH	90813	795-B7
PICO BLVD				
	-	SMCA	90401	671-F3
	-	SMCA	90405	671-F3
	700	SMCA	90404	671-F3
	3300	SMCA	90405	631-J7
	3300	SMCA	90404	631-J7
	3400	SMCA	90405	632-A7
	3400	SMCA	90404	632-A7
E PICO BLVD				
	100	LA	90015	634-F6
	700	LA	90021	634-F6
	2800	LA	90023	674-J1
	2800	LA	90023	675-A1
W PICO BLVD				
	100	LA	90015	634-C5
	1300	LA	90006	633-H4
	1800	LA	90006	634-C5
	3100	LA	90019	633-B4
	5800	LA	90035	633-B4
	9800	LA	90035	632-F4
PICO CIR				
	3400	LVRN	91750	570-E7
PICO CT				
	9200	PRV	90660	676-H3
PICO PL				
	600	SMCA	90405	671-F3
PICO PL S				
	200	SMCA	90405	671-F3
PICO ST				
	-	PAS	91105	565-H6
	100	POM	91766	641-B2
	600	SFER	91340	502-B1
	1000	SFER	91340	482-A7
	1300	FUL	92833	738-E6
	1500	SFER	91340	481-J6
PICO WY				
	41800	PMDL	93551	4104-C6
PICO CANYON RD				
	-	SCTA	91321	4640-C1
	-	SCTA	91355	4640-C1
	24600	StvR	91381	4640-A1
PICO VISTA RD				
	7000	PRV	90660	676-G7
	7400	PRV	90660	706-F1
	9100	DWNY	90240	706-F3
	10200	DWNY	90241	706-E6
PICOVISTA RD				
	5100	PRV	90660	676-H5
PICTON ST				
	15900	LPUE	91744	638-E6
PICTORIAL ST				
	100	PMDL	93550	4195-J5
	100	PMDL	93550	4196-A5
PICTURESQUE DR				
	11600	LA	91604	562-H6
PIDGEON RD				
	-	CHLS	91709	680-H2
PIEDMONT AV				
	100	CLAR	91711	601-B4
	400	GLDL	91206	564-G4
	2500	Mont	91020	534-G2
	2600	GLDL	91020	534-G2
	2600	OrCo	90720	796-G4
	2800	GLDL	91214	534-F2
	5800	HiPk	90042	595-C2
PIEDMONT CIR				
	-	HNTB	92649	826-H6
PIEDMONT DR				
	1200	SBdC	91784	571-J2
	4800	VeCo	91377	557-G2
PIEDMONT MESA DR				
	4200	CLAR	91711	571-A7
PIEDRA WY				
	1400	MONP	91754	636-A4
PIEDRA CHICA RD				
	20000	MAL	90265	629-J6
PIEDRA MORADA DR				
	1100	PacP	90272	630-G2
PIEDROS DR				
	26700	SCTA	91350	4550-J1
PIENZA LN				
	-	Nor	91326	500-D1
PIER AV				
	100	HMB	90254	762-G2
	100	SMCA	90405	671-J3
PIER PL				
	-	LBCH	90802	825-D1
PIER PZ				
	-	HMB	90254	762-G2
PIER A PL				
	100	Wilm	90744	824-D2
PIER A PZ				
	-	Wilm	90744	794-H7
PIER A ST				
	400	Wilm	90744	824-D2
PIER A WY				
	-	LBCH	90813	794-J7
	500	Wilm	90744	794-H7
PIER B ST				
	-	LBCH	90813	794-J6
	1200	LBCH	90813	795-A6
	2000	Wilm	90744	795-A6
	2500	Wilm	90744	794-J6
PIER C ST				
	1300	LBCH	90813	795-B7
PIERCE AV				
	6200	WHIT	90601	677-C6
	7000	WHIT	90602	677-C6
PIERCE CIR				
	7200	BPK	90620	767-H5
PIERCE DR				
	8200	BPK	90620	767-G5
PIERCE PL				
	1800	MONP	91755	636-C4
PIERCE ST				
	6100	CHNO	91710	641-J6
	11700	LA	91342	482-G7
	12000	LA	91342	502-G1
	12200	Pcma	91331	502-E2
PIERCE ARROW AV				
	-	THO	91362	557-B4
PIERCY AV				
	5400	LKWD	90712	765-H2
PIER D AV				
	100	LBCH	90802	825-A1
PIER D ST				
	1100	LBCH	90802	795-B7
	1100	LBCH	90802	825-A1
PIER E ST				
	1000	LBCH	90802	825-B1
PIER F AV				
	500	LBCH	90802	825-C2
PIER G AV				
	800	LBCH	90802	825-C3
PIER G AV N				
	1100	LBCH	90802	825-C3
PIER G AV S				
	1100	LBCH	90802	825-C4
PIER G WY				
	1500	LBCH	90802	825-D4
PIER J AV E				
	1200	LBCH	90802	825-E4
PIERMONT DR				
	1700	HacH	91745	678-D4
PIERPONT CT				
	-	SCTA	91355	4550-F2
PIERRE RD				
	100	WAL	91789	679-G1
	100	WAL	91789	639-F6
PIER S AV				
	-	LBCH	90802	824-H2
	-	SPed	90731	824-H2
PIER S LN				
	-	LBCH	90802	824-J2
PIER T AV				
	400	LBCH	90802	825-A2
	2200	LBCH	90802	824-J2
PIER T LN				
	-	LBCH	90802	824-J1
	-	LBCH	90802	825-A1
PIER T WY				
	-	LBCH	90802	825-A2
PIETRO DR				
	-	BqtC	91354	4460-F4
	2800	HacH	91745	678-A5
PIGGOTT DR				
	11100	CULC	90232	672-E3
PIKE PL				
	23300	SCTA	91355	4550-G1
PIKE RD				
	10300	LACo	91390	4373-F6
PIKE ST				
	11600	SFSP	90670	706-H3
PIKES CT				
	24400	DBAR	91765	640-E6
PILAR RD				
	20900	WdHl	91364	560-C5
PILARIO ST				
	18500	RowH	91748	679-B5
PILCHARD ST				
	500	SPed	90731	824-E4
PILGRAM CT				
	-	BqtC	91354	4460-F2
PILGRIM CT				
	4600	CHNO	91710	641-F5
PILGRIM PL				
	400	SMRO	91108	596-A3
PILGRIM WY				
	1400	MNRO	91016	567-F6
	11700	WHIT	90601	677-B5
PILGRIMAGE BRDG				
	2600	LA	90068	593-E2
PILGRIMAGE TER				
	2400	LA	90068	593-E2
PILGRIMS WY				
	3700	SBdC	91710	641-D7
PILLSBURY ST				
	100	LAN	93534	4015-F6
	700	LAN	93535	4016-A6
	2800	LAN	93536	4015-A6
	8600	LACo	93535	4017-J6
	9000	LACo	93535	4018-A6
S PIMA AV				
	200	WCOV	91790	598-H7
	200	WCOV	91790	638-H1
PIMENTA AV				
	4600	LKWD	90712	766-A1
	15200	PRM	90723	736-A4
	16400	BLF	90706	736-A6
PIN CT				
	20300	SCTA	91350	4461-D4
PINAFORE PL				
	2000	POM	91766	641-A5
PINAFORE ST				
	4400	LA	90008	673-C2
PINALE LN				
	2500	PVE	90274	792-J4
PINATA PL				
	400	FUL	92835	738-G4
PINCAY DR				
	3100	ING	90305	703-D3
	3600	ING	90301	703-D3
PINCHOT CT				
	7700	BPK	90621	767-H1
PINCKARD AV				
	2800	RBCH	90278	733-B6
PINE				
	1300	SDMS	91773	599-H2
	18800	RowH	91748	679-B4
PINE AV				
	200	LBCH	90802	795-D7
	200	LBCH	90802	825-D1
	700	LBCH	90813	795-D5
	1100	MANB	90266	732-G4
	1800	LBCH	90806	795-D3
	3100	Bxby	90807	795-D1
	3500	Bxby	90807	765-D6
	3700	ELMN	91731	597-D7
	4100	ELMN	91732	597-E6
	4300	BELL	90201	675-D6
	5100	NLB	90805	765-D3
	5200	MYWD	90270	675-D6
	5500	PMDL	93551	4104-G7
	6800	BELL	90201	705-D1
	10900	LYN	90262	705-D6
E PINE AV				
	100	ELSG	90245	732-G1
	6100	MYWD	90270	675-D6
N PINE AV				
	-	LBCH	90802	825-D1
S PINE AV				
	-	LBCH	90802	825-D1
W PINE AV				
	100	ELSG	90245	732-E1
PINE CIR				
	5000	LPMA	90623	767-C3
PINE CT				
	-	CRSN	90746	764-D4
	600	ING	90302	703-B1
	1600	LAN	93535	4016-C6
	5600	CYP	90630	767-D7
PINE DR				
	200	FUL	92833	738-C7
	600	TOR	90501	763-F5
	1100	BHLS	90210	592-E6
	1500	LHB	90631	708-C6
PINE LN				
	39100	LACo	93551	4195-G5
	39100	PMDL	93551	4195-G5
PINE PL				
	2600	SGAT	90280	704-J2
PINE ST				
	500	HMB	90254	762-H2
	700	SMCA	90405	671-G3
	800	WCOV	91790	638-E2
	1100	SPAS	91030	595-G3
	1200	VeCo	93063	499-C4
	2100	LACo	91770	636-F3
	2300	RSMD	91770	636-F3
	4400	PRV	90660	676-F3
	5700	SBdC	92397	(4652-C2 See Page 4651)
	10700	LALM	90720	796-J2
	11000	LYN	90262	705-D7
	12000	NRWK	90650	736-H2
	23300	SCTA	91321	4641-A1
	24200	SCTA	91321	4640-J1
	24600	SCTA	91321	4550-J7
E PINE ST				
	-	ALH	91801	596-B3
	-	Alta	91001	535-H5
	300	COMP	90222	734-J2
	300	COMP	90222	735-A2
	600	Alta	91001	536-A5
	700	COMP	90221	735-A2
N PINE ST				
	100	SGBL	91775	596-F3
	100	SGBL	91776	596-F3
	2300	POM	91767	600-J4
S PINE ST				
	100	SGBL	91776	596-F4
	2400	CMRC	90023	675-D3
W PINE ST				
	-	ALH	91801	596-A3
	-	Alta	91001	535-H5
	1000	UPL	91786	601-J1
	1100	SPAS	91030	596-A3
	1400	ALH	91801	595-J3
	2000	SPAS	91030	595-J3
S PINE AVENUE CIR				
	200	LBCH	90802	825-D1
PINEBANK DR				
	27900	SCTA	91350	4461-C5
PINE BLUFF DR				
	1000	PAS	91107	566-G2
	6600	WHIT	90601	677-D6
PINEBLUFF PL				
	32500	WLKV	91361	557-B7
PINE CANYON RD Rt#-N2				
	18200	LACo	93532	4101-F1
PINECASTLE DR				
	28900	RPV	90275	823-A1
PINECLIFF DR				
	42600	LACo	93532	4102-E5
PINE CLIFF PL				
	-	StvR	91381	4550-B4
PINE CONE CT				
	1700	LAN	93535	4016-D7
PINECONE PL				
	27600	Cstc	91384	4459-H4
PINECONE RD				
	5300	LaCr	91214	504-F5
PINE COVE CIR				
	27700	SCTA	91354	4460-H5
PINE CREEK LN				
	1400	Wilm	90744	794-C4
PINE CREEK RD				
	12300	NRWK	90650	736-J5
	12400	CRTS	90703	736-J5
	12400	CRTS	90650	736-J5
	12500	CRTS	90703	737-A5
PINE CREEK TER				
	1500	Wilm	90744	794-B5
	24700	Hrbr	90710	794-B5
PINE CREST DR				
	6000	HiPk	90042	595-D3
	6300	SPAS	91030	595-D3
PINECREST DR				
	1800	Alta	91001	536-D5
PINE CREST LN				
	600	WAL	91789	639-B7
PINE CREST PL				
	-	Cstc	91384	4369-G5
PINECREST RD				
	2200	Ago	91301	588-B4
PINECREST MESA RD				
	10600	Litl	93543	4468-E6
PINEDALE PL				
	31000	Cstc	91384	4459-A5
PINE EDGE DR				
	1400	LACo	90631	708-G3
PINE FALLS AV				
	800	DBAR	91789	679-G3
PINEFALLS AV				
	700	DBAR	91789	679-G2
PINEFALLS DR				
	2900	WCOV	91792	679-D1
PINEFOREST LN				
	23500	Hrbr	90710	794-A2
PINEGLEN RD				
	5400	LaCr	91214	504-G6
PINEGROVE				
	1400	WCOV	91791	638-J3
PINE GROVE AV				
	900	HiPk	90042	565-D6
PINEGROVE LN				
	12400	CRTS	90703	736-J6
	12500	CRTS	90703	737-A6
PINEGROVE ST E				
	16500	CRTS	90703	737-A6
PINEGROVE ST W				
	16500	CRTS	90703	736-J4
PINEHAVEN WY				
	18800	Nor	91326	500-H4
PINE HILL DR				
	-	Sunl	91040	503-A4
PINEHILL LN				
	21300	DBAR	91765	679-H4
PINE HILLS AV				
	27100	SCTA	91351	4551-E1
	27700	SCTA	91351	4461-E7
PINE HOLLOW CT				
	-	StvR	91381	4550-C4
PINE HOLLOW RD				
	4100	CALB	91302	559-G6
PINEHURST AV				
	9500	SGAT	90280	705-E5
	10600	LYN	90262	705-E5
E PINEHURST AV				
	100	LHB	90631	708-E5
W PINEHURST AV				
	100	LHB	90631	708-D5
PINEHURST CT				
	400	FUL	92835	738-H3
PINEHURST DR				
	-	SCTA	91355	4550-D4
	600	PAS	91106	566-A7
PINE HURST LN				
	1100	HAW	90250	733-H1
PINEHURST PL				
	2000	POM	91766	641-A5
PINEHURST RD				
	1900	LA	90068	593-D3
PINEHURST ST				
	1900	GLDR	91741	569-J5
	2000	GLDR	91741	570-A5
	12500	ELMN	91732	637-G1
PINEHURST WY				
	21000	WAL	91789	639-G7
PINEKNOLL AV				
	26400	Hrbr	90710	793-J6
PINELAKE DR				
	8400	LA	91304	529-F2
PINELAND AV				
	2800	LVRN	91750	600-H2
PINELAWN DR				
	2600	LaCr	91214	504-F5
PINE MOUNTAIN TKTR				
	-	LACo	-	(508-J7 See Page 507)
PINE NEEDLE CT				
	1200	AZU	91702	568-J4
PINE NUT DR				
	4000	Enc	91316	560-J6
PINE OAK LN				
	1000	PAS	91103	565-F3
	1000	PAS	91105	565-F3
PINE OAK PL				
	-	StvR	91381	4550-B5
PINE PARK CIR				
	23700	Hrbr	90710	794-A2
PINERIDGE DR				
	5300	LaCr	91214	504-G6
	5500	LPMA	90623	767-D4
	16500	GrnH	91344	481-D6
PINERIDGE PL				
	2700	LaCr	91214	504-G6
PINERIDGE ST				
	300	BREA	92821	709-A5
PINE RIDGE KNOLL				
	800	FUL	92835	738-F5
PINE ROCK RD				
	27900	Pear	93553	(4559-D2 See Page 4470)
PINE SHADOWS RD				
	10300	Litl	93543	4468-D6
PINE TREE CT				
	1500	LHB	90631	738-C1
PINETREE CT				
	100	WAL	91789	679-E1
PINE TREE LN				
	-	RHLS	90274	823-D1
	300	MNRO	91016	567-H2
PINETREE LN				
	1300	LACo	91770	636-G4
	12900	LMRD	90638	737-G1
PINE TREE PL				
	8600	LA	90069	592-J5
PINE TREE RD				
	7500	SBdC	-	(4562-D4 See Page 4471)
	7500	SBdC	92372	(4562-D2 See Page 4471)
	9900	SBdC	92372	(4472-D1 See Page 4471)
PINE VALLEY AV				
	19000	Nor	91326	480-F7
	19500	Nor	91326	500-F1
PINE VALLEY CT				
	36600	PMDL	93552	4287-C4
PINE VALLEY DR				
	-	StvR	91381	4550-C4
	1100	HAW	90250	733-G1
	2400	ALH	91803	636-A2
PINE VALLEY PL				
	11700	Nor	91326	480-F7
PINE VALLEY WY				
	19600	Nor	91326	480-E7
PINEVIEW RD				
	9800	SBdC	92372	(4472-A6 See Page 4471)
	16200	SCTA	91387	4552-C7
PINEVILLE ST				
	12100	ELMN	91732	637-D3
PINE VISTA LN				
	4700	LNDL	90260	733-C4
PINEWOOD AV				
	-	BREA	92821	709-A5
	-	AGRH	91301	558-B2
	-	VeCo	91377	558-B2
	9600	Tuj	91042	504-A3
	37500	PMDL	93550	4286-H3
PINEWOOD CIR				
	18800	CRTS	90703	767-B2
PINEWOOD CT				
	-	LACo	91390	4461-B4
	400	POM	91767	600-J3
	22400	CALB	91302	559-H7
PINEWOOD LN				
	600	SDMS	91773	600-C3
	3000	GLDL	91214	534-F2
W PINEWOOD LN				
	1200	ONT	91762	641-J5
PINEWOOD PL				
	100	GLDR	91741	569-G5
	1500	LHB	90631	738-D1
PINHIERO PL				
	-	BALD	91706	637-H1
PININA CT				
	-	PMDL	93551	4195-B2
PINION RD				
	-	PMDL	93550	4466-F1
PINION ST				
	6300	VeCo	91377	558-B2
PINKERTON RD				
	1500	GLDR	91740	599-F2
PINK PANSY CT				
	30200	SCTA	91387	4462-G5
PINKSAND RD				
	-	SCTA	91321	4550-J7
PINNACLE CT				
	14300	SCTA	91387	4462-G7
PINNACLE PL				
	11900	LA	90210	592-G1
PINNACLE RD				
	-	CHLS	91709	680-J7
	16000	CHLS	91709	710-J1
PINNACLE WY				
	20600	MAL	90265	629-H6
	40300	PMDL	93551	4194-J3
PINNEY ST				
	12200	LA	91342	482-F7
	12400	Pcma	91331	482-F7
	12400	Pcma	91331	502-D2
PINO AV				
	700	LAN	93535	4106-B3
PINON				
	2800	WCOV	91792	679-J2
PINON CT				
	38000	PMDL	93552	4286-J1
PINON RD				
	100	SBdC	92372	(4472-A6 See Page 4471)
	28900	Llan	93544	4471-A5
PINON HILLS RD				
	9300	SBdC	92372	(4472-A2 See Page 4471)
	9300	SBdC	92372	(4562-B1 See Page 4471)
PINON PINE LN				
	30300	Litl	93543	4468-C4
PINON PINES LN				
	3300	SBdC	92371	(4562-J4 See Page 4471)
PINON PINES RD				
	3300	SBdC	92371	(4562-J3 See Page 4471)
PINON RIDGE TKTR				
	18500	Valy	93563	(4560-B2 See Page 4470)
	21700	Valy	93563	(4561-A4 See Page 4471)
PINON SPRINGS DR				
	44600	LAN	93535	4016-C6
PINON VIEJO RD				
	-	SBdC	92372	(4562-C2 See Page 4471)
PINOSITAS RD				
	8200	WHIT	90605	707-H2
PINOT CIR				
	2100	UPL	91784	571-J4
PINTADO DR				
	100	DBAR	91765	640-B7
S PINTADO DR				
	100	DBAR	91765	640-B7
PINTAIL ST				
	5300	LVRN	91750	570-J6
PINTO				
	15300	LA	91342	481-G1
PINTO CIR				
	700	WAL	91789	639-D6
PINTO CT				
	-	PMDL	93551	4195-A6
PINTO DR				
	1100	LHH	90631	708-F1
PINTO LN				
	-	RHE	90274	793-E7
PINTO PL				
	8800	LA	90069	592-H4
	28000	Cstc	91384	4369-F5
PINTO RD				
	-	RHLS	90274	823-D4

STREET Block City ZIP Pg-Grid

PINTO ST
2100 LVRN 91750 570-G7
PINTO WY
21800 WAL 91789 639-J5
PINTO MESA DR
500 DBAR 91765 640-D7
PINTORESCA DR
200 PacP 90272 630-H5
PINTURA DR
15000 HacH 91745 677-J4
15300 HacH 91745 678-A4
PINYON AV
10300 Tuj 91042 504-A3
PINYON PL
2000 LVRN 91750 600-D3
PINYON ST
8500 BPK 90620 767-J5
PIOCHE DR
14300 LMRD 90638 737-E2
PIONEER AV
600 Wilm 90744 794-G5
1500 FUL 92833 738-B5
19800 TOR 90503 763-D4
PIONEER BLVD
4800 LACo 90601 677-A3
5300 WHIT 90601 677-A3
5300 WHIT 90601 676-J4
5700 LACo 90606 676-H7
5700 WHIT 90606 676-J4
6300 PRV 90606 676-H5
8100 LACo 90606 706-G3
8700 SFSP 90670 706-G3
11100 NRWK 90650 706-G6
12300 NRWK 90650 736-G3
16600 ART 90701 736-H7
17800 ART 90701 766-H2
18700 CRTS 90703 766-H2
19700 LKWD 90715 766-H5
21500 HGDN 90716 766-H6
21700 LBCH 90808 766-H6
N PIONEER BLVD
3600 LBCH 90808 766-G7
PIONEER CT
43600 LAN 93534 4105-J1
PIONEER DR
\- PMDL 93552 4197-D7
\- PMDL 93552 4287-D1
300 GLDL 91203 564-D4
E PIONEER DR
1400 WCOV 91791 598-H6
PIONEER MTWY
\- DBAR 91765 680-B6
\- LACo 92823 680-B6
PIONEER PL
100 POM 91768 640-D2
PIONEER RD
\- DBAR 91765 680-B5
PIONEER ST
1200 BREA 92821 708-H7
5100 CHNO 91710 641-G7
PIONEER TR
\- Actn 93510 4374-H6
PIONEER WY
1400 WAL 91789 639-E4
PIONEER HILL CT
\- SCTA 91351 4551-G1
PIONERO RD
8900 SBdC 92371 (4562-G1 See Page 4471)
9700 SBdC 92371 (4472-G1 See Page 4471)
PIPELINE AV
10900 SBdC 91766 641-D5
11100 MTCL 91763 641-D5
11400 SBdC 91710 641-D5
12100 CHNO 91710 641-D5
PIPELINE RD
\- LACo - 4279-C5
2800 SBdC 92371 (4562-J5 See Page 4471)
PIPER AV
7400 Wch 90045 702-J1
PIPER PL
7500 Wch 90045 702-J1
PIPIT CT
26500 SCTA 91351 4551-E4
PIPPIN DR
43800 LACo 93532 4101-J2
PIPPIN PL
37300 PMDL 93551 4285-E3
PIRATE DR
3800 RPV 90275 823-E5
PIRES AV
17000 CRTS 90703 737-B7
17800 CRTS 90703 767-B1
PIRTLE ST
2600 LA 90039 594-F4
PIRU ST
300 LACo 90061 734-D3
E PIRU ST
2000 COMP 90222 734-H2
2000 Wbrk 90222 734-H2
W PIRU ST
1200 COMP 90222 734-F2
PISA PL
1900 LA 90732 823-H5
PISANI PL
2000 Ven 90291 671-J5
PISCES CIR
\- PMDL 93552 4286-J2
PISCES ST
28700 AGRH 91301 558-B3

PISMO DR
22800 CRSN 90745 794-C1
PISTACHE LN
\- RSMD 91770 596-G6
PISTACHIO PL
6700 PMDL 93551 4104-D7
PISTACIA LN
\- POM 91767 600-J3
PISTACIO LN
200 BREA 92821 709-D4
PISTOL CREEK CT
500 SDMS 91773 600-C3
PITAYA WY
16700 PRM 90723 735-F6
PITCAIRN WY
24800 TOR 90505 793-E4
PITCHER RD
2700 LA 90068 593-F2
PITCHESS PL
13300 INDS 91746 637-H3
PITKIN ST
9200 RSMD 91770 596-J5
PITMAN AV
1000 GLDL 91202 564-D3
PITSCH CANYON RD
31600 LACo 90265 587-C6
E PITTMAN ST
5600 SIMI 93063 499-A1
PITTS AV
15600 PRM 90723 735-J5
15900 BLF 90706 735-J5
PITTSFIELD CT
500 LBCH 90803 796-F7
PIUMA AV
12000 NRWK 90650 706-E7
12300 NRWK 90650 736-E1
15900 CRTS 90703 736-E5
15900 NRWK 90703 736-E5
PIUMA RD
24200 LACo 90265 629-C2
24800 LACo 91302 629-A1
24800 LACo 91302 628-J1
26100 LACo 91302 588-H7
PIUMA MEADOWS RD
\- LACo 90265 629-A2
\- LACo 91302 629-A2
PIUTE
\- Ago 91301 587-G4
PIUTE AV
2700 THO 91362 557-A2
PIUTE CT
23100 LACo 91390 4460-G2
PIUTE DR
13800 LACo 91342 482-J2
PIUTE RD
10300 Litl 93543 4468-D5
PIUTE MESA RD
29800 Litl 93543 4468-D5
PIVOT ST
7500 DWNY 90241 705-J4
8100 DWNY 90241 706-A5
PIXIE AV
3800 LKWD 90712 765-G5
E PIXLEY ST
1700 COMP 90221 735-C3
4500 RDom 90221 735-D3
PIZARRO ST
300 Echo 90026 634-D2
PIZZO RANCH RD
5200 LCF 91011 535-C1
PLACENTIA CT
3500 CHNO 91710 641-C6
PLACENTIA DR
1900 HacH 91745 678-D4
PLACENTIA RD
3700 SBdC 91710 641-C6
PLACER DR
600 SDMS 91773 600-A1
PLACER PL
4400 LA 90032 595-F4
PLACERITA MTWY
\- LACo 91387 4551-H7
\- LACo 91387 4552-A7
\- Nwhl 91321 4551-H7
\- SCTA 91321 4551-H7
\- SCTA 91387 4551-H7
\- SCTA 91387 4552-A7
\- SCTA 91387 4642-A1
PLACERITA CANYON RD
5300 Nwhl 91321 4641-D1
16000 LACo 91387 4642-A1
16000 SCTA 91387 4642-A1
16200 Nwhl 91321 4642-A1
16700 SCTA 91321 4642-A1
20500 SCTA 91321 4641-A1
22200 SCTA 91321 4550-J7
22200 SCTA 91321 4551-A7
PLACERITA MOTORWAY LATERAL
\- SCTA 91321 4642-A1
\- SCTA 91387 4552-A7
\- SCTA 91387 4642-A1
PLACERITOS BLVD
21000 SCTA 91321 4641-C1
21600 SCTA 91321 4551-A7
22100 SCTA 91321 4550-J7
PLACERVIEW TR
\- LACo 91390 4461-B3
PLACID DR
13400 LACo 90605 737-C1
13900 LACo 90604 707-D7
13900 LACo 90604 737-E1
15300 LMRD 90638 737-H1

PLACID DR
16100 LACo 90604 738-A1
PLACIDIA AV
4400 LA 91602 563-B4
4800 NHol 91601 563-B4
PLACITA PL
10900 SFSP 90670 706-G2
PLAID WY
16700 PRM 90723 735-F6
PLAIN TR
500 Top 90290 590-B5
PLAINFIELD DR
28300 RPV 90275 792-H7
PLAINS DR
42400 LAN 93536 4104-E5
PLAINVIEW AV
10000 Tuj 91042 503-H2
PLANADA AV
6300 HiPk 90042 595-E1
PLANEO DR
5300 PMDL 93551 4194-G2
PLANET CIR
44000 LAN 93536 4015-C7
44000 LAN 93536 4105-C1
PLANETARY DR
8300 BPK 90620 767-J4
PLANE TREE DR
21400 SCTA 91321 4641-B2
PLANETT AV
10600 DWNY 90241 706-B4
12200 DWNY 90242 706-A7
PLANEWOOD DR
21700 WdHl 91364 560-A6
PLANO DR
2700 RowH 91748 679-A7
PLANT AV
1900 RBCH 90278 733-A6
PLANTAIN LN
\- PMDL 93551 4285-E3
PLANTANA DR
14200 LMRD 90638 737-E1
PLANTATION LN
700 WAL 91789 639-G5
PLANTATION LATERAL
\- GLDL 91208 534-A1
\- SunV 91352 534-A1
PLANTER ST
9500 PRV 90660 706-F1
PLASCENCIA CT
\- BALD 91706 598-A4
PLASKA AV
6200 HNTP 90255 675-B7
7100 HNTP 90255 705-B1
PLATA LN
26300 CALB 91302 558-H4
PLATA ST
2500 Echo 90026 634-C1
3400 Echo 90026 594-B7
PLATEAU AV
800 MONP 91755 636-D3
PLATEAU DR
200 WCOV 91791 599-C7
200 WCOV 91791 639-C1
10700 Sunl 91040 503-E3
PLATEAU RD
\- PMDL 93552 4287-B4
PLATINA DR
23500 SCTA 91355 4550-G5
N PLATINA DR
200 DBAR 91765 640-C6
S PLATINA DR
200 DBAR 91765 640-C6
PLATINUM CT
\- BqtC 91354 4460-D3
PLATT AV
3400 LYN 90262 705-B7
5500 WdHl 91367 559-F1
6100 WdHl 91367 529-F7
6400 CanP 91307 529-F5
7300 LA 91304 529-F3
PLATT BLVD
200 CLAR 91711 601-E2
PLATT CT
\- SCTA 91387 4462-G7
PLATT ST
\- NLB 90805 765-D3
PLATT RIVER DR
19300 WAL 91789 639-C5
PLATZ RD
3500 Actn 93510 4465-B3
PLAYA CT
11200 CULC 90230 672-H5
PLAYA ST
11200 CULC 90230 672-G5
PLAYA WY
5700 CYP 90630 767-E7
PLAYA AZUL
\- AVA 90704 5923-G2
PLAYA SERENA DR
\- StvR 91381 4550-C3
PLAYA VISTA DR
\- LA 90066 702-D1
\- LA 90094 672-C7
\- LA 90094 702-D1
PLAYER AV
\- LHB 90631 738-C2
N PLAYER DR
25600 SCTA 91355 4550-E7
PLAYGROUND ST
1400 Boyl 90033 635-C2
PLAZA CT
5500 PMDL 93552 4287-C3

PLAZA DR
\- MTBL 90640 636-G6
900 WCOV 91790 598-F7
1600 COMP 90220 735-A6
PLAZA LN
\- LCF 91011 535-C3
5200 MTCL 91763 601-G4
S PLAZA LN
4900 MTCL 91763 601-F5
PLAZA PKWY
\- LA 91604 563-A6
PLAZA ST
2100 CMRC 90040 675-H3
PLAZA WK
5100 LCF 91011 535-C2
PLAZA ANDRES
1300 PVE 90274 792-G7
PLAZA CHIVA
25500 SCTA 91355 4550-F7
PLAZA DE CORDOBA
20100 CRTS 90703 766-H3
PLAZA DEL AMO
1300 LA 90501 794-A1
1400 LA 90501 793-J1
1500 LA 90501 763-J7
1700 TOR 90501 763-H7
2500 TOR 90503 763-F7
PLAZA DEL SOL
\- Boyl 90033 634-J4
PLAZA DE MADRID
20100 CRTS 90703 766-J4
PLAZA DE ORO
\- BqtC 91354 4460-E4
PLAZA DE TIERRA
800 FUL 92833 738-C6
PLAZA DE VISTA
2400 FUL 92833 738-C6
PLAZA ESCONDIDO
900 FUL 92833 738-B6
PLAZA ESCOVAR
25400 SCTA 91355 4640-F1
PLAZA FRANCISCO
1400 PVE 90274 822-G1
PLAZA GAVILAN
23900 SCTA 91355 4550-F7
PLAZA LARIOS
25000 SCTA 91355 4640-H1
PLAZA LIBRE
2500 MTBL 90640 676-B1
PLAZA LIBRE N
2500 MTBL 90640 636-B7
2500 MTBL 90640 676-B1
PLAZA LIBRE S
2500 MTBL 90640 676-B1
PLAZA LUNETA
24000 SCTA 91355 4550-F7
PLEASANT AV
1200 Boyl 90033 634-J4
PLEASANT ST
200 PAS 91101 565-J6
3200 LYN 90262 705-A7
3200 LYN 90262 735-A1
4300 LVRN 91750 570-G7
E PLEASANT ST
100 NLB 90805 765-D4
W PLEASANT ST
\- NLB 90805 765-D4
PLEASANT WY
1500 PAS 91105 565-D7
2400 THO 91362 557-A2
10500 LACo 90606 676-J5
10500 WHIT 90606 676-J5
PLEASANT CREST LN
1500 LHH 90631 708-E2
PLEASANT DALE PL
400 THO 91362 557-G1
PLEASANTDALE ST
19000 SCTA 91351 4551-F2
PLEASANT HILL DR
\- RHE 90274 793-C5
1500 CHLS 91709 680-G3
PLEASANT HILL LN
300 SMAD 91024 567-B1
PLEASANTHOME DR
100 LPUE 91744 638-F7
200 LPUE 91744 678-F1
PLEASANT LAKE PL
1500 BREA 92821 708-H6
1500 LHB 90631 708-H6
PLEASANT MEADOW RD
23400 DBAR 91765 680-B5
PLEASANT RIDGE DR
1200 Alta 91001 536-B4
PLEASANT VIEW AV
900 Ven 90291 671-H5
1100 LA 90065 594-J5
PLEASANT VIEW DR
42000 LAN 93536 4104-C5
PLEASANT VIEW TER
700 GLDL 91202 564-C1
PLEASURE WY
3800 GLDL 91020 534-G3
PLENTY ST
200 NLB 90805 765-D4
PLEVKA AV
8600 Wats 90002 704-F3
PLOVER WY
24600 MAL 90265 628-G7
PLUM AV
200 BREA 92821 709-D7
2600 TOR 90501 763-G7
2700 TOR 90501 793-G1

PLUM CT
\- LA 91340 502-B1
PLUM ST
\- FUL 92835 738-H3
400 COMP 90222 734-H3
11400 LYN 90262 705-A7
PLUM WY
40300 PMDL 93551 4194-H3
PLUMA ST
3100 LYN 90262 705-A6
PLUMA WY
600 MONP 91754 636-A5
PLUMAS CIR
18900 WAL 91789 639-B7
PLUMAS ST
1400 LA 90065 564-G6
1400 GLDL 91205 564-G6
PLUM CANYON RD
19600 Saug 91350 4461-D5
20200 SCTA 91350 4461-D5
PLUM CANYON FIRE RD
\- CynC 91351 4461-H6
\- CynC 91351 4462-A5
PLUME DR
13900 LMRD 90638 737-D3
PLUMERIA AV
1200 UPL 91784 571-J4
PLUMERIA CT
600 BREA 92821 709-B7
PLUMERIA LN
\- CYP 90630 767-D7
\- PMDL 93551 4195-D6
PLUM HOLLOW LN
14000 CHLS 91709 680-H3
PLUMMER PL
1200 WHWD 90046 593-C5
PLUMMER ST
14300 PanC 91402 502-A6
14500 PanC 91402 501-H6
14700 LA 91343 501-E6
16800 Nor 91325 501-A6
18300 Nor 91330 500-D6
18300 Nor 91325 500-D6
18400 Nor 91324 500-D6
19700 Chat 91311 500-A6
22000 Chat 91311 499-H6
PLUMOSA DR
300 PAS 91107 566-F5
PLUM TREE CT
24400 CanP 91307 529-D5
PLUM TREE DR
200 AZU 91702 568-J5
PLUMTREE LN
10500 Nor 91326 500-H3
PLUMTREE RD
\- RPV 90275 823-A4
PLUMWOOD AV
27200 SCTA 91351 4551-G2
E PLUNKETT ST
10100 BLF 90706 736-C7
E PLURIBUS ST
7100 LBCH 90808 766-F7
PLUTON ST
10800 NRWK 90650 706-E6
N PLYMOUTH BLVD
100 LA 90004 593-G7
100 LA 90004 633-G1
S PLYMOUTH BLVD
100 LA 90004 633-F2
300 LA 90020 633-F2
600 LA 90005 633-F3
600 LA 90010 633-F2
900 LA 90019 633-F4
PLYMOUTH CT
37300 PMDL 93550 4286-D3
PLYMOUTH DR
\- SLB 90740 796-J5
200 PAS 91104 565-H1
PLYMOUTH LN
1500 LA 90732 823-J6
PLYMOUTH RD
400 SMRO 91108 596-A2
29300 Cstc 91384 4459-H5
W PLYMOUTH RD
600 CLAR 91711 601-C3
PLYMOUTH ST
300 GLDR 91740 599-F2
5700 CHNO 91710 641-H5
E PLYMOUTH ST
\- NLB 90805 765-D3
100 ING 90302 703-C1
W PLYMOUTH ST
\- NLB 90805 765-C3
100 ING 90302 703-B1
PLYMOUTH WY
9200 LA 91343 501-H6
POCAHANTAS DR
30100 Cstc 91384 4459-C5
POCASSET DR
11800 LACo 90601 677-C3
POCATELLO AV
2400 RowH 91748 678-J7
POCHO TR
11600 Chat 91311 480-A7
W POCO WY
300 MONP 91754 636-A4
POCONO CT
9000 PRV 90660 676-H1
POCONO ST
15700 LPUE 91744 638-E5
16100 LACo 91744 638-G5
PODD CT
26900 SCTA 91351 4551-E3

POE AV
4400 WdHl 91364 560-D4
POE PKWY
\- StvR 91381 4549-J6
\- StvR 91381 4550-A7
25600 StvR 91381 4640-B1
POEMA PL
14100 Chat 91311 499-J1
22000 Chat 91311 500-A1
POETS LN
\- ING 90305 703-F3
POINCIANA ST
9500 PRV 90660 706-F1
10500 LACo 90606 706-G1
POINDEXTER ST
1200 LACo 90044 704-A7
POINSETTA TR
3400 CALB 91302 589-E1
POINSETTIA AV
100 MNRO 91016 567-H3
300 BREA 92821 708-J4
300 BREA 92821 738-J1
900 THO 91362 557-F1
12300 ELMN 91732 637-E3
N POINSETTIA AV
100 COMP 90221 735-B4
100 MANB 90266 732-G4
S POINSETTIA AV
100 COMP 90221 735-B5
100 MANB 90266 732-G7
POINSETTIA CT
9000 CULC 90232 672-H1
POINSETTIA DR
7700 BPK 90620 767-J2
N POINSETTIA DR
1100 WHWD 90046 593-C5
POINSETTIA LN
7400 BPK 90620 767-J2
N POINSETTIA PL
100 LA 90036 633-C1
300 LA 90036 593-C7
700 LA 90046 593-C5
1000 WHWD 90046 593-D5
S POINSETTIA PL
100 LA 90036 633-C1
E POINSETTIA ST
1200 NLB 90805 765-F1
POINT ARENA CT
19100 SCTA 91321 4551-G5
POINT ARENA PL
13000 CRTS 90703 767-B1
POINT ARGUELLO PL
17900 CRTS 90703 767-B1
POINT CEDAR DR
3100 WCOV 91792 679-D2
POINT CONCEPTION PL
18000 CRTS 90703 767-B1
POINTE DR
400 BREA 92821 709-D6
N POINTE PL
6000 WdHl 91367 560-D1
POINTED OAK PL
5500 AGRH 91301 558-A5
POINTER DR
2200 LACo 91789 679-F6
POINTER LN
2200 BelA 90077 592-A3
POINT LECHUZA DR
6500 MAL 90265 626-H7
POINT O WOODS
500 AZU 91702 568-H4
POINT REYES PL
13000 CRTS 90703 767-B1
S POINT VIEW ST
1000 LA 90035 633-A4
1900 LA 90034 633-A6
POINT VISTA LN
2400 CHLS 91709 680-J2
POKER PLANT CT
2500 PMDL 93550 4286-F5
POLARIS DR
1900 GLDL 91208 534-G7
POLARIS WY
2500 LVRN 91750 600-H1
POLICE ACADEMY RD
\- HacH 91745 637-D7
\- HacH 91745 677-E1
\- LACo 90601 637-D7
POLIS DR
5200 LPMA 90623 767-C3
POLK AV
\- CYP 90630 767-A6
W POLK AV
2800 ANA 92801 767-H5
POLK CT
4000 CHNO 91710 641-D6
POLK ST
4400 CHNO 91710 641-E6
13400 LA 91342 482-B2
14400 LA 91342 481-H5
POLK WY
1700 MONP 91755 636-C4
POLLARD LN
500 COV 91723 599-B5
POLLARD ST
6400 HiPk 90042 595-E1
POLLOCK ST
1100 LACo 91770 636-F4
POLLY AV
15100 LACo 90260 733-E5
POLO CT
\- PMDL 93551 4195-B3
1700 LAN 93535 4016-C4

POLSON LN
\- Cstc 91384 4459-G3
POLYNESIAN DR
6300 NLB 90805 765-D1
6300 NLB 90805 735-D7
POLY VISTA
3400 POM 91768 640-B3
POMANDER PL
600 LCF 91011 535-C5
POMEGRANATE LN
\- WdHl 91367 559-H7
POMEGRANATE PL
5900 PMDL 93551 4104-F7
E POMEGRANATE RD
\- RPV 90275 823-B5
W POMEGRANATE RD
\- RPV 90275 823-B4
E POMELLO DR
100 CLAR 91711 571-D5
POMELO AV
300 BREA 92821 709-C7
S POMELO AV
300 MONP 91755 636-D3
POMELO DR
6900 CanP 91307 529-E5
7400 LA 91304 529-E4
POMERING RD
9600 DWNY 90240 706-A2
10300 DWNY 90241 706-A3
10500 DWNY 90241 705-J4
11900 DWNY 90242 705-H5
POMEROY AV
1600 Boyl 90033 635-A3
POMEROY ST
3300 City 90063 635-D4
POMITA PL
23400 SCTA 91355 4550-G4
POMMEL CT
22100 WAL 91789 639-J4
POMONA AV
\- LBCH 90803 826-B2
E POMONA AV
100 MNRO 91016 567-H6
N POMONA AV
100 FUL 92832 738-H7
S POMONA AV
100 FUL 92832 738-H7
W POMONA AV
100 MNRO 91016 567-G6
POMONA BLVD
\- MONP 90022 635-H6
5100 ELA 90022 635-H6
E POMONA BLVD
\- MTBL 90640 636-B6
100 MONP 91755 636-B6
W POMONA BLVD
100 MONP 91754 636-A6
500 MTBL 90640 635-J6
500 MTBL 90640 636-A6
500 MONP 91754 635-J6
700 LACo 91754 635-J6
2200 POM 91768 640-D2
3500 POM 91789 640-B3
POMONA CT
900 CLAR 91711 601-B2
POMONA DR
1300 WAL 91789 639-G3
POMONA FRWY Rt#-57
\- DBAR - 680-B1
POMONA FRWY Rt#-60
\- CHLS - 640-D6
\- CHNO - 641-D6
\- City - 635-C7
\- DBAR - 640-D6
\- DBAR - 679-D4
\- DBAR - 680-A1
\- DBAR - 680-B1
\- ELA - 635-C7
\- HacH - 637-G6
\- HacH - 677-J1
\- HacH - 678-A2
\- INDS - 637-G6
\- INDS - 678-A2
\- INDS - 679-D4
\- LA - 634-J7
\- LA - 635-C7
\- LACo - 635-C7
\- LACo - 636-H5
\- LACo - 637-A5
\- LACo - 679-D4
\- MONP - 635-C7
\- MONP - 636-D6
\- MTBL - 635-C7
\- MTBL - 636-H5
\- ONT - 641-D6
\- POM - 640-D6
\- POM - 641-B6
\- RowH - 679-D4
\- RSMD - 636-H5
\- SBdC - 641-D6
\- SELM - 637-A5
POMONA ST
3400 LA 90031 595-B7
POMPANO ST
23300 LACo 90265 629-E3
POMPEII WY
\- LAN 93536 4104-J6
8000 LA 91504 533-E2
8000 BURB 91504 533-E2
PONCA AV
4300 LA 91602 563-C4
PONCE AV
5200 WdHl 91364 559-H2

PONCE AV
5300 WdHl 91367 559-H2
6300 WdHl 91367 529-H7
6400 CanP 91307 529-H4
7600 LA 91304 529-H2
POND AV
36800 PMDL 93550 4286-G4
38500 PMDL 93550 4196-G7
POND CIR
3400 LVRN 91750 570-E7
3400 LVRN 91750 600-E1
PONDERA CIR
7200 CanP 91307 529-E5
PONDERA ST
100 LAN 93534 4015-H6
400 LAN 93535 4015-H6
400 LAN 93535 4016-A6
2600 LAN 93536 4015-A7
PONDEROSA
1400 ELMN 91732 637-G1
PONDEROSA AV
1100 BREA 92821 709-B4
PONDEROSA CT
5000 LKWD 90712 766-B1
PONDEROSA DR
13200 Brwd 90049 631-D1
E PONDEROSA DR
800 AZU 91702 569-B6
PONDEROSA LN
\- RHE 90274 793-B4
1100 SDMS 91773 599-J4
PONDEROSA RD
8800 SBdC 92372 (4562-C1 See Page 4471)
9300 SBdC 92372 (4472-C3 See Page 4471)
PONDEROSA ST
\- Cstc 91384 4459-F2
\- LAN 93535 4016-D6
100 LPUE 91744 638-E7
10300 BLF 90706 766-D1
43600 LAN 93535 4106-E1
PONDEROSA WY
\- CRSN 90746 764-F1
\- UPL 91784 571-H6
3500 PMDL 93550 4286-H6
N PONDOSA AV
5300 LACo 91776 596-F4
5300 SGBL 91776 596-F4
PONER ST
14500 LMRD 90638 737-E2
PONET DR
2100 LA 90068 593-H3
PONTE CORVO RD
\- LACo 91390 (4372-H7 See Page 4281)
13800 LACo 91390 4462-G1
PONTENOVA AV
800 HacH 91745 678-C2
PONTEVEDRA DR
27800 RPV 90275 823-H2
PONTIAC ST
2600 LaCr 91214 534-G1
3100 LaCr 91214 504-E7
3200 GLDL 91214 504-D6
PONTINE AV
21000 CRSN 90745 764-G5
PONTIUS AV
1500 WLA 90025 632-A4
2200 LA 90064 632-A4
PONTLAVOY AV
14200 SFSP 90670 737-B3
14300 NRWK 90650 737-B3
PONTOON PL
13100 Brwd 90049 631-E4
PONTY ST
1600 LACo 90047 703-J6
PONY LN
\- LA 91342 481-E2
\- RHE 90274 793-E7
PONY CROSS RD
400 LACo 91302 588-J7
400 LACo 91302 628-J1
PONY EXPRESS CT
100 SDMS 91773 600-C2
PONY EXPRESS RD
100 SDMS 91773 600-C2
POOLE AV
8300 SunV 91352 533-A1
9000 Sunl 91040 503-B5
POOR RD
\- LACo 93551 4193-J1
\- LACo 93551 4194-A1
\- PMDL 93551 4194-C2
POPE AV
10900 LYN 90262 705-E7
11300 LYN 90262 735-D1
POPE PL
\- StvR 91381 4550-A7
POPENOE RD
1200 LHH 90631 708-F3
POPLAR AV
100 MTBL 90640 676-E2
700 MTBL 90640 636-F7
E POPLAR AV
15000 HacH 91745 678-A1
N POPLAR AV
100 BREA 92821 709-B7
S POPLAR AV
100 BREA 92821 709-B7
POPLAR BLVD
\- ALH 91801 595-G5
2600 ALH 91803 595-G5

POPLAR BLVD
5300 LA 90032 595-G5
POPLAR CIR
41400 PMDL 93551 4104-G7
POPLAR CT
\- CRSN 90746 764-D3
\- LAN 93535 4016-E6
43600 LAN 93535 4106-E2
POPLAR DR
\- Ago 91301 588-B4
2900 LYN 90262 705-A6
POPLAR LN
100 PAS 91103 565-H2
POPLAR PL
2400 LACo 90255 704-J2
2500 SGAT 90280 704-J2
POPLAR ST
\- FUL 92835 738-H3
\- LHB 90631 708-C6
2600 LA 90065 594-J6
22400 SCTA 91390 4460-J3
E POPLAR ST
200 COMP 90220 734-J4
200 COMP 90220 735-A4
300 COMP 90221 735-A4
W POPLAR ST
200 COMP 90220 734-G4
POPLAR WY
100 MTBL 90640 676-E2
POPLAR GLEN CIR
23100 SCTA 91354 4460-H6
POPLAR POINT LN
\- LACo 91387 4552-A4
POPLAR VIEW DR
700 AZU 91702 568-H5
POPPY AV
100 MNRO 91016 567-H3
1400 UPL 91784 571-H3
E POPPY AV
900 COMP 90221 735-A2
POPPY DR
\- CRSN 90746 764-F1
3500 CALB 91302 559-F7
3500 CALB 91302 589-F1
POPPY LN
300 GLDR 91741 569-J6
300 POM 91766 640-J5
POPPY RD
32900 Actn 93510 4375-B7
POPPY ST
\- Actn 93510 4465-D1
\- FUL 92835 738-H3
900 HiPk 90042 565-D7
E POPPY ST
300 NLB 90805 765-D1
POPPY TR
\- RHLS 90274 823-E2
POPPY WY
8300 BPK 90620 767-J3
E POPPYFIELDS DR
200 Alta 91001 535-J4
300 Alta 91001 536-A5
W POPPYFIELDS DR
\- Alta 91001 535-H4
POPPYGLEN CT
\- AZU 91702 568-J2
POPPYGLEN LN
16500 CRTS 90703 736-J6
POPPY HILLS CT
1000 LHB 90631 738-D2
POPPY MEADOW ST
15100 SCTA 91387 4462-E6
28900 SCTA 91387 4552-F1
POPPY PEAK DR
1400 PAS 91105 565-E7
6100 HiPk 90042 565-D7
POPPYSEED LN
15400 SCTA 91387 4552-E1
POPPYSEED PL
3900 CALB 91302 588-H1
3900 CALB 91302 558-H7
POPPYVIEW DR
6600 VeCo 91377 558-A1
POPS RD
1200 DUAR 91010 568-B5
POPULAR PL
\- NRWK 90650 736-E1
POPULUS AV
37100 PMDL 93552 4287-B3
POQUITO LN
300 Top 90290 590-A6
PORT AV
\- PMDL 93551 4104-E7
PORT RD
11200 CULC 90230 672-G5
11800 LA 90230 672-F6
PORTADA DR
9300 WHIT 90603 707-H3
11000 WHIT 90604 707-H6
PORTAFINO CT
\- POM 91766 640-D3
PORTAFINO PL
8400 WHIT 90603 707-J1
8400 WHIT 90603 708-A1
PORTAGE CIRCLE DR
22800 Top 90290 589-H2
S PORTAL RD
\- LACo 91390 4102-B7
\- LACo 91390 4192-A1
\- LACo 93532 4102-C4
PORTAL PASS RD
40400 LACo 93551 4193-F3

PORTAL RIDGE RD
\- LACo 93532 4101-J1
\- LACo 93532 4102-B2
PORTER AV
2300 Alta 91001 536-C6
PORTER LN
600 HMB 90254 762-G1
PORTER MTWY
\- LACo 91342 482-J2
PORTER RD
16000 VanN 91406 531-F6
PORTER ST
300 GLDL 91205 564-G6
2300 LA 90021 634-H7
PORTERDALE DR
6200 MAL 90265 627-H7
6200 MAL 90265 667-H1
PORTER RANCH DR
\- Chat 91311 500-D1
11700 Nor 91326 480-E7
11700 Nor 91326 500-D1
PORTER VALLEY DR
11200 Nor 91326 500-G1
11600 Nor 91326 480-F7
PORTIA ST
1300 Echo 90026 594-E7
PORTICO PL
4400 Enc 91316 561-C4
PORTLAND AV
4100 PMDL 93552 4286-J3
4500 PMDL 93552 4287-A3
PORTLAND LN
42300 LACo 93536 4105-A5
PORTLAND ST
2100 LA 90007 634-B6
PORTLAND TER
800 ALH 91801 596-A6
PORTNER ST
3300 LA 90065 594-G2
E PORTNER ST
700 WCOV 91790 638-G2
1400 WCOV 91791 638-J2
PORTOBELLO DR
2600 TOR 90505 793-E5
PORTOFINO CIR
3100 HNTB 92649 826-J6
4600 CYP 90630 767-B7
PORTOFINO LN
15000 LA 91343 501-H7
PORTOFINO PL
10800 BelA 90077 591-J5
PORTOFINO WY
\- RBCH 90277 762-H5
37600 PMDL 93552 4287-E2
PORTO GRANDE DR
1200 DBAR 91765 680-B3
PORTOLA
15300 MsnH 91345 501-H2
PORTOLA AV
400 LHB 90631 708-E6
600 TOR 90501 763-G6
700 GLDL 91206 564-F3
3200 LA 90032 595-F5
4400 SPAS 91030 595-F5
PORTOLA CIR
18800 WAL 91789 639-B7
PORTOLA CT
\- POM 91766 640-D5
5700 WLKV 91362 557-G6
PORTOLA DR
900 ARCD 91007 566-J6
1000 DUAR 91010 568-A5
4300 PMDL 93551 4194-J3
4300 PMDL 93551 4195-A3
9800 LA 90210 592-C3
PORTOLA LN
2100 THO 91361 557-A5
PORTOLA PL
\- LA 90095 632-B1
PORTOLA PZ
\- LA 90095 632-B1
PORTOLA ST
400 SDMS 91773 600-C2
PORTOLA TER
600 HiPk 90042 595-E4
PORTOLA WY
\- CRSN 90745 794-E1
\- LA 91342 482-E4
11200 MTCL 91763 641-E3
PORTO MARINA WY
17600 PacP 90272 630-F6
PORTO RICO DR
13900 LACo 91746 637-H6
PORTSHEAD RD
6500 MAL 90265 667-E2
PORTSIDE DR
20100 LACo 91789 679-E7
PORTSIDE LN
900 Hrbr 90710 794-B5
PORTSIDE PL
30500 AGRH 91301 557-G5
PORTSMOUTH CT
700 VeCo 91377 557-H1
12200 CHNO 91710 641-J5
PORTSMOUTH DR
37700 PMDL 93550 4286-E2
PORTSMOUTH LN
1700 LA 90732 823-D6
PORTSMOUTH ST
5700 CHNO 91710 641-H5
PORTSMOUTH WY
\- MANB 90266 732-H5
\- RowH 91748 709-A2

STREET Block City ZIP Pg-Grid

PORTUGAL CT
12000 NRWK 90650 736-H5
PORTUGUESE BEND RD
- RHLS 90274 793-D7
- RHLS 90274 823-D3
PORTULACA PL
3900 THO 91362 557-C1
PORTULACA WY
8300 BPK 90620 767-J2
POSADA DR
22900 SCTA 91354 4460-H7
22900 SCTA 91354 4550-H1
POSEIDON
1400 WCOV 91790 638-D2
POSEIDON AV
19100 CRTS 90703 766-H2
POSEIDON DR
37600 PMDL 93552 4286-J2
POSEIDON LN
- SCTA 91351 4551-G7
POSETANO RD
17400 PacP 90272 630-F6
POSEY LN
23600 LA 91304 529-E4
POSEY WY
29200 RPV 90275 822-H1
POSSUM RIDGE RD
- RHLS 90274 823-D3
POST AV
500 POM 91766 640-J5
1600 TOR 90501 763-G6
POST RD
1100 FUL 92833 738-B5
POST ST
3100 SGAT 90280 705-A2
POST WY
- Wch 90045 702-G5
POSTAL RD
10000 Wch 90045 702-J5
POSTMASTER AV
24200 Hrbr 90710 793-J3
POSTON CT
700 LAN 93534 4105-G1
POTOMAC
1500 WCOV 91791 638-J6
POTOMAC AV
2800 LA 90016 633-D7
3000 LA 90016 673-D1
3800 LA 90008 673-D2
POTOMAC WY
400 CLAR 91711 601-C1
POTOSI AV
3600 LA 91604 562-E6
POTRERO AV
1300 LACo 91733 637-A4
1300 SELM 91733 637-A4
2400 ELMN 91733 637-A2
POTRERO DR
3600 FUL 92835 738-G1
POTRERO RD
- LACo 90265 626-E4
- MAL 90265 626-E4
- StvR 91381 4550-A4
- Valc 91355 4550-A3
POTRERO CANYON RD
- Cstc 91384 4549-B5
- Nwhl 91382 4549-B5
- StvR 91381 4549-F6
- StvR 91381 4640-A1
POTRERO GRANDE DR
400 MONP 91755 636-D5
900 MTBL 90640 636-E4
1300 LACo 91770 636-E4
2000 RSMD 91770 636-E4
POTRILLO RD
- RHE 90274 823-G1
POTTER AV
8100 NHol 91605 532-E2
POTTER DR
- LACo 90265 628-J5
- MAL 90265 628-J5
37000 PMDL 93550 4286-F4
POTTER PL
- StvR 91381 4550-A6
POTTER ST
9800 BLF 90706 736-C3
10600 NRWK 90650 736-E3
POTTER FIRE RD
- GrnH 91344 480-G4
- Nor 91326 480-G4
POULSEN AV
- MTCL 91762 641-G3
- MTCL 91763 641-G2
9500 MTCL 91763 601-G7
POULSEN CT
10300 MTCL 91763 601-G7
POULTER DR
14600 LACo 90604 707-E6
POUNDS AV
9800 WHIT 90603 708-A3
11700 LACo 90604 708-A6
12400 LACo 90604 738-A1
POWAY ST
11500 LA 90061 704-C7
POWDER CANYON MTWY
2300 RowH 91748 678-G7
2500 LHH 90631 678-G7
POWDER HORN RANCH RD
100 Top 90290 589-J7
POWELL AV
100 AZU 91702 569-B6
POWELL CT
- ART 90701 736-G7
- ART 90701 766-G1
POWELL DR
23700 SCTA 91321 4640-F2
POWER ST
100 LA 90012 634-J2
2000 HMB 90254 762-G1
POWERHOUSE LATERAL
- LACo 91390 (4370-H1 See Page 4279)
POWER LINE RD
- Cstc 91384 4459-J4
- Cstc 91384 4460-A5
- LACo 93536 4103-D6
- LACo 93551 4103-D6
POWERLINE RD
30400 Llan 93544 4471-H3
POWER LINE FIRE RD
- BelA 90077 561-J7
- BelA 90077 591-J1
POWERS AV
9100 PRV 90660 676-G3
POWERS PL
1800 LA 90006 634-B5
POWERS ST
2100 POM 91766 640-J5
POXON PL
100 WCOV 91790 598-G7
POYNETTE ST
3500 GLDL 91214 534-E1
3500 GLDL 91214 504-E7
POZO DR
3100 HacH 91745 678-D6
PRA DR
4600 PRV 90660 676-G2
PRADERA AV
9300 MTCL 91763 601-E5
10300 MTCL 91763 641-D1
PRADERA WY
- CYP 90630 767-E6
PRADO CT
100 SBdC 92372 4471-J1
PRADO RD
11200 SBdC 92372 4471-J2
PRADO ST
1000 LA 90023 675-C1
PRADO DE AMARILLO
- CALB 91302 559-A7
PRADO DE AMBAR
- CALB 91302 559-B7
- CALB 91302 589-B1
PRADO DE AMOR
- CALB 91302 559-A6
PRADO DE AZUL
- CALB 91302 559-A7
PRADO DE FUCSIA
- CALB 91302 559-A7
PRADO DE LA FELICIDAD
- CALB 91302 589-A1
PRADO DE LA LUNA
- CALB 91302 559-B7
PRADO DE LA MAGIA
- CALB 91302 589-B1
PRADO DE LA MARIPOSA
- CALB 91302 559-B7
PRADO DE LA PUMA
- CALB 91302 559-B6
PRADO DE LAS BELLOTAS
- CALB 91302 559-A7
PRADO DE LAS CABRAS
- CALB 91302 559-B6
PRADO DE LAS CALABAZAS
- CALB 91302 559-A6
PRADO DE LAS ESTRELLAS
- CALB 91302 559-B7
PRADO DE LAS FLORES
- CALB 91302 559-A7
PRADO DE LAS FRESAS
- CALB 91302 559-A7
PRADO DE LAS FRUTAS
- CALB 91302 559-A7
PRADO DE LAS PANTERAS
- CALB 91302 559-B6
PRADO DE LAS PERAS
- CALB 91302 559-B6
PRADO DE LAS UVAS
- CALB 91302 559-B7
PRADO DEL GRANDIOSO
- CALB 91302 559-C7
- CALB 91302 589-B1
PRADO DEL MAIZ
- CALB 91302 559-A7
PRADO DEL MISTERIO
- CALB 91302 589-B1
PRADO DE LOS ARBOLES
- CALB 91302 559-B7
PRADO DE LOS CABALLOS
- CALB 91302 559-B6
PRADO DE LOS CIERVOS
- CALB 91302 559-B6
PRADO DE LOS GANSOS
- CALB 91302 559-B6
PRADO DE LOS PAJAROS
- CALB 91302 559-B6
PRADO DE LOS SUENOS
- CALB 91302 589-B1
PRADO DE LOS ZORROS
- CALB 91302 559-B6
PRADO DEL TRIGO
- CALB 91302 559-B7
PRADO DE NARANJA
- CALB 91302 559-B7
PRADO DE ORO
- CALB 91302 559-A7
PRADO DE ROSADO
- CALB 91302 589-B1
PRADO DE VERDE
- CALB 91302 559-A7
PRAGER AV
11400 LA 91342 502-G1
11600 LA 91342 482-F7
PRAIRIE AV
11400 HAW 90250 703-D7
11900 HAW 90250 733-D3
14200 LNDL 90250 733-D3
14300 LNDL 90260 733-D6
15000 HAW 90260 733-D3
15200 LACo 90260 733-D6
16900 TOR 90504 733-D6
17300 TOR 90504 763-E3
19000 TOR 90503 763-E3
N PRAIRIE AV
100 ING 90301 703-D2
S PRAIRIE AV
100 ING 90301 703-D4
400 ING 90305 703-D4
10000 ING 90303 703-D4
10000 ING 90304 703-D4
PRAIRIE CT
300 BREA 92821 709-B6
6400 LAN 93536 4104-E4
PRAIRIE DR
100 SDMS 91773 570-C6
PRAIRIE LN
3800 PMDL 93550 4286-H1
28800 SCTA 91387 4552-D1
PRAIRIE PL
100 GLDR 91741 569-J5
PRAIRIE ST
17000 Nor 91325 501-C6
17900 Nor 91330 501-A6
18300 Nor 91330 500-H6
18400 Nor 91324 500-H6
18400 Nor 91325 500-H6
19700 Chat 91311 500-C6
22000 Chat 91311 499-J7
PRAIRIE FALCON DR
5800 LVRN 91750 570-H5
PRAIRIE VIEW RD
39600 LACo 93591 4200-B2
PRAIRIEVISTA PL
41400 LACo 93536 4104-H7
PRASA RD
4100 WdHl 91364 560-C5
PRATHER AV
11600 LACo 90606 677-B6
11600 WHIT 90606 677-B6
PRATTY RD
- LACo 91390 4373-H4
- LACo 91390 4374-A4
PRAY ST
- FUL 92833 738-D5
PREBLE AV
800 Wilm 90744 794-H6
PRECIADO AV
13000 CHNO 91710 641-E7
13000 SBdC 91710 641-E7
PRECIADO ST
300 POM 91768 600-H7
PRECISE ST
44000 LAN 93536 4105-C1
44000 LAN 93536 4015-C7
PREMIERE AV
4700 LBCH 90808 766-B4
5300 LKWD 90712 766-B2
13000 DWNY 90242 736-B2
13500 BLF 90706 736-B3
PREMIERE HILLS CIR
5200 WdHl 91364 560-C3
PREMIERE HILLS DR
5200 WdHl 91364 560-C2
E PREMIUM ST
600 LBCH 90808 796-E1
PRENTISS AV
37600 PMDL 93550 4286-D2
PRESADO DR
2300 DBAR 91765 679-J5
PRESCOTT AV
900 SDMS 91773 599-H4
W PRESCOTT CT
3000 LA 90018 633-G7
PRESCOTT ST
400 PAS 91104 565-J1
400 PAS 91104 566-A1
9200 PRV 90660 676-H1
PRESIDENT AV
23400 Hrbr 90710 793-J2
PRESIDENT DR
24400 LACo 90263 628-G6
PRESIDIO DR
4400 LACo 90008 673-D4
4700 LACo 90043 673-D4
PRESLEY CIR
18900 CRTS 90703 767-B2
PRESNELL ST
12500 LA 90066 672-D6
PRESSON PL
8200 LA 90069 593-A4
PRESTBURY LN
- VeCo 91361 586-E2
PRESTINA WY
20400 WAL 91789 639-F6
PRESTON AV
1800 Echo 90026 594-E6
PRESTON CT
1400 POM 91766 641-A3
W PRESTON CT
1200 UPL 91786 571-J7
PRESTON LN
- BPK 90621 737-J7
- BPK 90621 738-A7
PRESTON RD
- PMDL 93551 4195-A3
PRESTON WK
- Cstc 91384 4459-D6
PRESTON WY
1200 Ven 90291 671-J4
1200 Ven 90291 672-A4
12400 LA 90066 672-B3
23200 SCTA 91354 4460-G7
PRESTON TRAILS AV
11700 Nor 91326 480-F7
PRESTWICK
12500 ELMN 91732 637-G1
PRESTWICK DR
3700 LFlz 90027 594-B2
PRESTWICK LN
- PMDL 93551 4195-A2
PRESTWICK RD
1300 SLB 90740 796-G7
PRESTWICK WY
21000 WAL 91789 639-B4
PRETTY-O-RANCH RD
19900 Llan 93544 4470-E3
S PREUSS RD
1600 LA 90035 632-H5
1900 LA 90034 632-H5
PREWETT ST
2700 LA 90031 595-B7
PRIAM DR
6500 BGDN 90201 676-A7
6500 BGDN 90201 706-A1
7600 BGDN 90201 705-J2
PRICE DR
600 BURB 91504 533-F4
2500 LVRN 91750 600-H2
PRICE LN
45000 LAN 93535 4016-D5
PRICE ST
900 POM 91767 641-B1
N PRICE ST
4300 LFlz 90027 594-B3
S PRICEDALE AV
1000 WCOV 91790 638-G2
PRICETOWN AV
19100 CRSN 90746 764-G4
PRICHARD ST
8400 DWNY 90242 735-J2
9300 BLF 90706 736-A3
13600 LACo 91746 637-J3
13700 LPUE 91746 637-J3
13700 LPUE 91746 638-A4
14500 LPUE 91744 638-B5
PRIER RD
20300 Top 90290 590-C4
PRIEST DR
5900 LPMA 90623 767-E4
PRIMAVERA AV
3600 LA 90065 594-J3
N PRIMAVERA DR
700 GLDR 91741 569-F3
PRIMAVERA LN
- CYP 90630 767-E6
PRIMAVERA RD
9000 SBdC 92372 (4562-C1 See Page 4471)
9300 SBdC 92372 (4472-B1 See Page 4471)
PRIMAVERA ST
3100 PAS 91107 566-G2
PRIMAVERA WK
- LA 90065 594-J3
PRIME CT
100 PAS 91104 566-A1
S PRIMEAUX AV
1200 WCOV 91790 638-H3
PRIMERA AV
3200 LA 90068 563-D7
PRIMERA PL
3200 LA 90068 563-D7
PRIMM WY
3300 TOR 90505 793-E4
PRIMROSE AV
1900 SPAS 91030 595-H4
2900 BREA 92821 709-F7
5700 TEML 91780 596-J2
6100 LA 90068 593-F3
N PRIMROSE AV
- ALH 91801 595-H4
100 MNRO 91016 567-G3
S PRIMROSE AV
- ALH 91801 595-H5
100 MNRO 91016 567-G5
1300 ALH 91803 595-H7
1700 ALH 91803 635-H1
2200 LACo 91016 567-G7
PRIMROSE CT
- PMDL 93552 4287-A1
39400 PMDL 93551 4195-E5
PRIMROSE DR
- PRV 90660 676-F6
45800 LAN 93534 4015-G3
PRIMROSE LN
- Cstc 91384 4459-H3
- YBLN 92886 710-A7
2900 FUL 92833 738-A3
8100 DWNY 90240 706-C3
PRIMROSE PL
400 GLDR 91740 569-D7
PRIMROSE ST
- LHB 90631 708-C6
6500 Res 91335 530-B7
W PRIMROSE ST
1300 UPL 91786 601-H4
PRIMROSE WY
2000 POM 91766 641-A5
PRINCE AV
8600 Wats 90002 704-F3
PRINCE CT
- LA 90069 592-J4
PRINCE RD
6000 VeCo 93063 499-B3
PRINCE ST
2300 LA 90031 635-C1
PRINCE ISLAND
5500 LBCH 90803 826-D1
PRINCELY CT
37800 PMDL 93552 4287-A2
PRINCES DR
1500 GLDL 91207 564-G2
PRINCESS DR
6700 HiPk 90042 595-E2
PRINCESSA DR
- PMDL 93551 4104-D6
PRINCESS ANNE RD
5000 LCF 91011 535-B2
PRINCESS PALM
900 WCOV 91790 638-H6
PRINCETON AV
100 CLAR 91711 601-C4
2100 Echo 90026 594-F5
N PRINCETON AV
100 FUL 92831 738-J6
S PRINCETON AV
100 FUL 92831 738-J7
PRINCETON CIR
100 SLB 90740 796-F6
PRINCETON CIR E
500 FUL 92831 738-J6
PRINCETON CIR W
500 FUL 92831 738-J6
PRINCETON CT
1000 SMCA 90403 631-G6
1400 SMCA 90404 631-H7
PRINCETON DR
900 LA 90292 672-A6
1100 GLDL 91205 564-G7
1200 WAL 91789 639-F4
PRINCETON RD
500 ARCD 91007 567-B4
PRINCETON ST
- CYP 90630 767-F7
800 SMCA 90403 631-F6
1200 SMCA 90404 631-F6
1800 GLDL 91204 594-E1
3700 LACo 90023 635-D7
4300 MTCL 91763 601-F5
W PRINCETON ST
800 ONT 91762 601-H5
PRINCETON WY
- BPK 90620 767-F6
2800 LAN 93536 4105-C2
PRINCEVILLE CT
- PMDL 93551 4195-C2
PRINCIPIA DR
1000 GLDL 91206 564-H3
PRINCIPIO DR
30700 MAL 90265 627-A7
PRIOR AV
500 LACo 91744 638-G5
PRIORY ST
5500 BGDN 90201 705-G2
PRISCILLA AV
8000 DWNY 90242 735-H1
PRISCILLA DR
3400 WCOV 91792 639-B7
3400 WCOV 91792 679-B1
PRISCILLA LN
500 CLAR 91711 601-C3
600 BURB 91505 563-C3
PRISCILLA ST
8400 DWNY 90242 735-J1
8900 DWNY 90242 736-A2
10500 NRWK 90650 736-D2
12800 NRWK 90650 737-A2
14100 LMRD 90638 737-D2
PRISMO DR
2600 LA 90065 564-H7
PRITCHARD AV
200 FUL 92833 738-B7
N PRITCHARD AV
100 FUL 92833 738-B7
S PRITCHARD AV
100 FUL 92833 738-B7
PRITCHARD WY
1800 HacH 91745 678-F6
PRIVATEER CT
100 LA 90292 701-J1
PRIVATEER MALL
- LA 90292 701-J1
PRIVATEER ST
- LA 90292 701-J1
PRIVET AV
5000 ELMN 91732 597-F4
PROCK ST
900 POM 91768 640-E1
PROCTOR AV
13600 LACo 91746 637-H4
13700 INDS 91746 637-H4
14200 LACo 91746 638-A5
14400 INDS 91746 638-A5
15200 INDS 91745 638-A6
15200 INDS 91744 638-A6
PROCTOR ST
400 Wilm 90744 794-F4
E PROCTOR ST
13000 LACo 91746 637-G3
PRODUCE CT
800 LA 90021 634-F6
PRODUCE RW
2100 LA 90021 634-F6
PRODUCE ST
1200 LA 90021 634-G6
PRODUCER WY
3100 POM 91768 640-C3
PROGRESS LN
1200 PAS 91103 565-H2
16100 IRW 91706 598-F3
PROGRESS PL
400 Boyl 90033 634-J3
PROGRESS ST
3300 WHIT 90601 677-E5
PROJECT ST
2000 Wats 90002 704-H4
PROMENADE DR
11500 SFSP 90670 706-G4
14400 CHLS 91709 680-H4
PROMENADE PZ
- Wch 90045 672-H7
PROMENADE WY
14000 MdlR 90292 671-J7
14000 MdlR 90292 672-A6
PROMENADE MALL DRIVEWAY
- WdHl 91367 560-A1
PROMINENTE DR
1100 LAN 93535 4106-B1
PROMISA WY
- CYP 90630 767-E6
PROMONTORY DR
2300 SIGH 90755 795-H3
PROMONTORY LN
- BqtC 91354 4460-E5
PROMONTORY PL
1600 WCOV 91791 639-C3
15900 LMRD 90638 737-J2
16000 LMRD 90638 738-A1
29400 AGRH 91301 557-J5
PROMONTORY RD
12400 Brwd 90049 591-E4
15900 CHLS 91709 710-J1
PRONDALL CT
17400 CRSN 90746 734-F7
17400 CRSN 90746 764-F1
PROSA CT
20000 LACo 91789 679-E4
PROSPECT AV
- LBCH 90803 826-A1
100 RBCH 90278 762-H2
100 HMB 90254 762-H1
200 MNRO 91016 567-H2
300 LBCH 90814 796-A7
300 LBCH 90814 826-A1
400 MANB 90266 732-H7
500 SPAS 91030 595-G2
600 MANB 90266 762-H1
1000 LBCH 90804 796-A6
1000 SGBL 91776 596-D6
2200 Ven 90291 672-A5
2400 Mont 91020 534-G1
2600 LaCr 91214 534-F1
2700 RSMD 91770 636-D1
3000 SMCA 90405 671-H3
3200 GLDL 91214 504-E7
3200 GLDL 91214 534-F1
3800 CULC 90232 672-E2
3900 LFlz 90027 594-A4
6000 MYWD 90270 675-E6
6200 BELL 90201 675-E7
6800 BELL 90201 705-E1
21000 CRSN 90810 765-A5
E PROSPECT AV
100 BURB 91502 563-J1
N PROSPECT AV
100 RBCH 90277 763-A4
500 RBCH 90277 762-J3
900 RBCH 90278 762-J3
900 HMB 90254 762-J3
S PROSPECT AV
100 RBCH 90277 793-A6
1200 RBCH 90277 793-A1
PROSPECT BLVD
400 PAS 91103 565-G3
PROSPECT CIR
400 SPAS 91030 595-G1
PROSPECT CRES
600 PAS 91103 565-G3
PROSPECT CT
3000 SMCA 90405 671-H3
PROSPECT DR
700 GLDL 91205 564-F7
800 SPAS 91030 595-G1
1100 POM 91766 640-G3
1700 LA 90046 593-A4
PROSPECT LN
600 SPAS 91030 595-G1
PROSPECT PL
- WAL 91789 639-D4
PROSPECT SQ
400 PAS 91103 565-G4
PROSPECT ST
- KeCo 93560 3833-H1
PROSPECT TER
400 PAS 91103 565-G3
PROSPECT TR
2000 LA 90046 593-A3
PROSPECTOR LN
13200 CHLS 91709 680-J1
PROSPECTOR PL
2000 PMDL 93551 4195-E5
N PROSPECTORS RD
100 DBAR 91765 640-B7
S PROSPECTORS RD
100 DBAR 91765 640-B7
PROSPECT VALLEY DR
20500 DBAR 91765 640-C6
PROSPERO DR
400 COV 91723 599-C6
1200 GLDR 91740 599-C1
5800 GLDR 91740 569-C7
N PROSPERO DR
300 COV 91723 599-C5
1000 COV 91722 599-C3
S PROSPERO DR
500 WCOV 91791 639-C1
PROSSER AV
1800 WLA 90025 632-C4
2100 LA 90064 632-C4
PROVENCE DR
- Ago 91301 558-G3
- LACo 91302 558-G3
PROVENCE LN
- Tuj 91042 503-J1
- Tuj 91042 504-A1
PROVENCE PL
37100 PMDL 93552 4286-J4
N PROVENCE RD
6200 LACo 91775 596-F1
PROVIDENCE CT
400 LBCH 90803 796-D7
PROVIDENCE LN
1500 LA 91343 501-H7
PROVIDENCE PL
800 CLAR 91711 571-B6
PROVIDENCE WY
- POM 91767 601-A3
E PROVIDENCIA AV
- BURB 91502 563-H1
200 BURB 91502 533-J7
400 BURB 91501 533-J7
1000 BURB 91501 534-A6
W PROVIDENCIA AV
100 BURB 91502 563-H1
300 BURB 91506 563-H1
PROVIDENCIA ST
21200 WdHl 91364 560-A4
22000 WdHl 91364 559-J4
PROVIDENT RD
27300 AGRH 91301 558-E7
PROVINCETOWN ST
- SLB 90740 796-J5
PROVO AV
9900 Tuj 91042 504-B5
PROVON LN
3200 LA 90034 632-G7
PRUDENCIA DR
16300 WHIT 90603 708-A3
PRUDENT ST
900 LA 90012 634-H2
PRUESS AV
11400 DWNY 90241 706-A5
11500 DWNY 90241 705-J5
PRUITT DR
500 RBCH 90278 763-B2
19300 TOR 90503 763-B3
PRYOR PL
23200 Hrbr 90710 793-J1
PSOMAS WY
13000 LA 90066 672-A3
PT&T RD
- LACo 91390 4373-C7
- LACo 91390 4463-C1
PUDDINGSTONE DR
100 SDMS 91773 600-C4
800 LVRN 91750 600-E4
PUEBLA DR
1500 GLDL 91207 564-G1
PUEBLO
3300 Top 90290 560-B6
PUEBLO AV
3100 LA 90032 595-E4
PUEBLO CT
1400 CLAR 91711 601-C1
5400 CMRC 90040 675-H3
PUEBLO DR
8500 RSMD 91770 636-G5
25900 SCTA 91355 4550-G4
W PUEBLO DR
600 MONP 91754 635-H3
PUEBLO PL
600 FUL 92835 738-H1
PUEBLO ST
22100 Chat 91311 499-J2
PUEBLO CREST LN
1700 LHH 90631 708-D3
PUENTE AV
1400 BALD 91706 638-B1
1400 LACo 91746 638-B1
1900 WCOV 91746 638-B1
2000 BALD 91706 598-D5
3100 WCOV 91790 598-C7
E PUENTE AV
1000 WCOV 91790 598-J6
1400 WCOV 91791 598-J6
1900 WCOV 91791 599-A6
N PUENTE AV
100 INDS 91746 637-J4
300 LPUE 91746 637-J4
300 LACo 91746 637-J4
400 LPUE 91746 638-A3
400 LACo 91746 638-A3
W PUENTE AV
1000 WCOV 91790 598-F6
PUENTE LN
1300 BREA 92821 708-J4
PUENTE RD
20900 WdHl 91364 560-C5
PUENTE ST
800 SDMS 91773 600-A7
1000 SDMS 91773 599-H6
1600 COV 91724 599-H6
2700 FUL 92835 738-J2
E PUENTE ST
100 COV 91723 599-C6
700 LACo 91723 599-E6
1100 COV 91724 599-E6
1100 LACo 91724 599-E6
1800 SDMS 91724 599-E6
20800 SDMS 91773 599-E6
N PUENTE ST
100 BREA 92821 708-J5
S PUENTE ST
100 BREA 92821 708-J7
300 FUL 92835 708-J7
300 FUL 92835 738-J1
300 BREA 92821 738-J1
W PUENTE ST
100 COV 91723 599-A6
500 COV 91722 599-A6
1900 WCOV 91791 599-A6
PUERCO MTWY
- LACo 90265 628-E4
- MAL 90265 628-E5
PUERCO CANYON RD
3100 LACo 90265 628-F6
3100 MAL 90265 628-F6
PUERTA AV
38600 PMDL 93550 4196-E7
PUERTA DEL SOL
3300 LA 90732 823-G7
PUERTO DEL MAR
300 PacP 90272 630-J6
PUERTO RICO DR
7400 BPK 90620 767-D3
7400 LPMA 90623 767-D3
PUESTA DEL SOL
1600 POM 91768 600-F6
4900 MAL 90265 626-E6
PUESTA DEL SOL DR
16000 WHIT 90603 707-J3
PUFFIN PL
- LACo 91387 4551-J5
PUGET WY
42300 LACo 93536 4105-A5
PULIDO CT
4000 CALB 91302 559-H6
PULLMAN AV
2000 SIMI 93063 499-A2
PULLMAN LN
1700 RBCH 90278 762-J2
1800 RBCH 90278 763-A2
PULLMAN ST
400 HiPk 90042 595-D4
900 LA 90032 595-E4
PUMA DR
7600 SBdC 92372 (4562-E2 See Page 4471)
PUMA LN
38600 PMDL 93551 4285-F1
PUMA CANYON LN
700 GLDR 91740 569-G7
PUMICE ST
13400 NRWK 90650 737-C3
13600 SFSP 90670 737-C3
PUNAHOU ST
300 Alta 91001 535-J4
300 Alta 91001 536-A4
PUNCH BOWL RD
31100 Pear 93553 4468-H1
31100 Valy 93563 4468-H1
PUNTA PL
1700 PVE 90274 792-G5
S PUNTA WY
1100 MONP 91754 636-A4
PUNTA ALTA DR
4000 LA 90008 673-B3
PUNTA DEL ESTE DR
2000 HacH 91745 678-D4
PUNTA DEL ESTES DR
3200 HacH 91745 678-D6
PUNTO DE VISTA DR
25700 LACo 91302 588-J7
PURCELL DR
4100 City 90063 635-E4
PURCHE AV
2400 GAR 90249 733-G3
11800 HAW 90250 703-G7
16500 TOR 90504 733-G7
17500 TOR 90504 763-G1
PURDIN AV
13900 PRM 90723 735-F2
PURDUE AV
1500 WLA 90025 632-A5
2200 LA 90064 632-A5
3100 LA 90066 672-C1
4300 CULC 90066 672-E4
4400 LA 90230 672-E4
5100 CULC 90230 672-F5
PURDUE CIR
400 SLB 90740 796-G6
PURDUE DR
600 CLAR 91711 601-C2
W PURDUE ST
1300 UPL 91786 601-H1
PURDY AV
6500 BGDN 90201 675-G7
6500 BGDN 90201 705-G1
PURITAN AV
8000 DWNY 90242 735-H1
PURITAN ST
7800 DWNY 90242 735-H1
PURITAN MINE RD
- Actn 93510 4374-E4
PURPLEBRUSH AV
42000 LACo 93536 4104-E6
42100 LAN 93536 4104-E6
PURPLE MARTIN CT
20100 SCTA 91351 4551-E3
PURPLE RIDGE AV
- LACo 91342 482-J3
PURPLE RIDGE DR
6900 RPV 90275 792-G7
6900 RPV 90275 822-G1
PURPLE SAGE LN
100 Alta 91001 535-J3
2800 PMDL 93550 4286-G6
PURPLE SAGE RD
7200 SBdC (4562-F6 See Page 4471)
7500 SBdC 92372 (4562-F5 See Page 4471)
PURTELL DR
4300 LCF 91011 534-J3
PURVIS DR
2500 BURB 91504 533-E4
PUTNAM ST
2800 LA 90039 594-D3
12400 WHIT 90602 677-B7
12400 WHIT 90602 707-C1
12500 WHIT 90606 707-C1
13600 WHIT 90605 707-D2
PUTNEY RD
- ING 90305 703-F3
1700 PAS 91103 535-E7
10500 LA 90064 632-D6
PUTNEY WY
- PMDL 93552 4287-C4
PUTT PL
31700 Llan 93544 4469-F1
PUZZLE CANYON RD
28200 Llan 93544 4471-G3
PYRAMID DR
7300 LA 90068 593-C1
7300 LA 90046 593-C1
PYRAMID PL
7200 LA 90046 593-C1
PYRAMID PEAK DR
- SCTA 91350 4550-H6
PYRENEES DR
1600 ALH 91803 595-G7
PYRITE CT
15600 CHLS 91709 680-J7
PYRITES ST
2800 LA 90032 595-C7

Q

Q ST
1500 Wilm 90744 794-G4
E Q ST
100 Wilm 90744 794-E4
W Q ST
100 Wilm 90744 794-C4
QUADRO VECCHIO DR
200 PacP 90272 630-F5
QUAIL CIR
800 BREA 92821 708-J4
QUAIL CT
6600 LVRN 91750 570-H4
QUAIL DR
400 LA 90065 595-A3
4900 LPMA 90623 767-C4
W QUAIL DR
- PMDL 93551 4195-J4
QUAIL LN
- LACo 91390 4373-E7
1300 BREA 92821 708-J4
12700 NRWK 90650 737-A1
15200 LMRD 90638 737-G1
QUAIL RD
900 SBdC 92397 (4652-C2 See Page 4651)
3300 SBdC 92371 (4562-J2 See Page 4471)
6200 LACo 91390 4374-E3
QUAIL ST
36400 PMDL 93552 4286-J5
QUAIL TR
- LACo 91390 (4370-G5 See Page 4279)
QUAIL WY
6100 LAN 93536 4104-F6
QUAILBROOK CIR
2000 PMDL 93550 4286-D1
QUAIL CANYON RD
- AVA 90704 5923-F5
5300 GLDL 91214 504-F5
5300 LaCr 91214 504-F5
35600 LACo 91390 4374-E1
QUAIL COVE WY
18000 RowH 91748 678-H7
QUAIL CREEK CT
- SCTA 91350 4550-H6
QUAILCREEK DR
42000 LAN 93536 4104-F5
QUAIL CREEK LN
- POM 91766 640-G6
QUAIL CREEK PL
19500 Nor 91326 500-F1
QUAIL CREEK RD
11300 Nor 91326 500-F1
QUAIL GLEN DR
2300 CHLS 91709 680-J3
QUAIL HAVEN
1800 SBdC 92372 (4562-E5 See Page 4471)
QUAIL HAVEN RD
2100 SBdC 92372 (4562-E4 See Page 4471)
QUAIL HAVEN TR
- LACo 91390 4460-G1
QUAILHILL DR
28400 RPV 90275 792-J7
28500 RPV 90275 822-J1
QUAIL HOLLOW CT
1300 AZU 91702 568-H4
QUAIL KNOLL DR
4800 MTCL 91763 601-F5
QUAIL OAKS DR
29500 Cstc 91384 4459-D4
QUAIL RIDGE CIR
19700 WAL 91789 639-D5
QUAIL RIDGE LN
6100 LAN 93536 4104-F5
QUAIL RIDGE RD N
- RHLS 90274 823-D2
QUAIL RIDGE RD S
- RHLS 90274 823-D3
QUAIL ROW LN
- CRSN 90745 794-G2
QUAIL RUN DR
20800 DBAR 91789 679-G5
29100 AGRH 91301 558-A5
29400 AGRH 91301 557-H5
QUAIL RUN RD
3000 OrCo 90720 796-H3
QUAIL RUN WY
42100 LAN 93536 4104-E6
QUAIL SPRINGS PTH
800 GLDR 91741 569-G3
QUAIL SUMMIT CIR
- POM 91766 640-G5
QUAIL SUMMIT DR
23200 DBAR 91765 680-B3
QUAIL VALLEY LN
700 WCOV 91791 639-D2
QUAIL VALLEY RD
4500 LACo 91750 570-J6
31200 Cstc 91384 4459-F1
31200 Cstc 91384 4369-F7
QUAIL VIEW CT
700 VeCo 91377 558-B1
QUAILWOOD DR
29300 RHE 90274 823-A2
29300 RPV 90275 823-A2
QUAINT ST
28600 AGRH 91301 558-B3
QUAKERTOWN AV
5100 WdHl 91364 530-E7
6400 WdHl 91367 530-E7
6600 Win 91306 530-E3
8700 Nor 91324 530-E1
9500 Chat 91311 500-E6
QUAKERTOWN CT
8200 Win 91306 530-E2
QUARRY DR
- LACo 91342 482-J2
QUARRY LN
2600 DBAR 91789 679-G6
QUARRY RD
3000 PMDL 93550 4286-G5
QUARRY ST
4900 MTCL 91763 601-F4
QUARRY RIDGE RD
42000 LAN 93536 4103-J6
42000 LAN 93551 4103-J6
QUARTER ST
- LAN 93536 4014-H7
- LAN 93536 4104-H1
QUARTERDECK CT
100 LA 90292 701-J1
QUARTERDECK MALL
- LA 90292 701-J1
QUARTERDECK ST
- LA 90292 701-J1
QUARTER HORSE
- Actn 93510 4375-E7
QUARTER HORSE DR
- PMDL 93551 4195-A6

STREET
Block City ZIP Pg-Grid

QUARTER HORSE LN
900 VeCo 91377 558-A1
QUARTERHORSE LN
- RHE 90274 822-J2
QUARTERMASTER CT
200 SPed 90731 824-C7
QUARTERMASTER RD
2200 SPed 90731 824-C7
QUARTZ AV
6300 WdHl 91367 530-F6
6600 Win 91306 530-E2
8400 SGAT 90280 705-D3
8700 Nor 91324 530-E1
8900 Nor 91324 500-E7
9500 Chat 91311 500-E6
QUARTZ LN
31900 Cstc 91384 4369-G6
W QUARTZ HILL
37000 PMDL 93551 4194-C7
QUARTZ HILL RD
4300 LACo 93536 4104-H6
4400 LAN 93536 4104-H6
QUARTZITE CT
1800 PMDL 93550 4286-D5
QUARTZITE ST
- PMDL 93550 4286-D5
QUARTZ MESA LN
- StvR 91381 4550-B4
QUAY AV
200 Wilm 90744 794-F7
QUEBEC DR
6200 LA 90068 593-F2
QUEDO DR
20400 WdHl 91364 560-C4
QUEDO PL
4800 WdHl 91364 560-C4
QUEEN ST
2600 LA 90039 594-F4
E QUEEN ST
200 ING 90301 703-C2
W QUEEN ST
100 ING 90301 703-B2
QUEEN ANNE CT
1200 GLDR 91740 599-G1
QUEEN ANNE PL
- PMDL 93551 4285-E4
1000 LA 90019 633-E4
QUEEN ANNES WK
1900 POM 91767 600-J5
QUEEN FLORENCE LN
4800 WdHl 91364 560-E3
QUEEN OAK DR
4000 Enc 91436 561-G5
QUEENRIDGE DR
6100 RPV 90275 792-J7
QUEENS CT
1500 CLAR 91711 601-C1
1700 LA 90069 592-J4
18800 CRTS 90703 767-B2
QUEENS HWY
- LBCH 90802 825-D3
QUEENS RD
1400 LA 90069 592-J4
1400 WHWD 90069 592-J4
QUEENS WY
- LBCH 90802 825-D2
1400 LA 90069 592-J5
29300 AGRH 91301 557-J4
29300 AGRH 91301 558-A4
QUEENSBERRY RD
1000 PAS 91104 566-C2
QUEENSBORO CT
37800 PMDL 93552 4287-A2
QUEENSBOROUGH LN
1900 BelA 90077 591-G3
QUEENSBOROUGH ST
- CRTS 90703 767-A2
QUEENSBURY AV
800 LVRN 91750 600-D2
QUEENSBURY DR
2900 LA 90064 632-F6
QUEENSCLIFF CT
25600 LACo 91302 559-A4
E QUEENSDALE ST
1500 COMP 90221 735-B3
4200 RDom 90221 735-C3
QUEENSFERRY RD
2100 Brwd 90049 631-C1
2100 PacP 90272 631-C1
QUEENS GARDEN CT
23600 VeCo 91361 586-F1
QUEENS GARDEN DR
23600 VeCo 91361 586-E1
QUEENSGLEN AV
17000 LACo 93591 4199-H4
17300 LACo 93591 4200-A4
QUEENSIDE DR
15800 LACo 91722 598-F4
E QUEENSIDE DR
17000 LACo 91722 598-H4
W QUEENSIDE DR
1100 COV 91722 598-H4
1100 LACo 91722 598-H4
QUEENSLAND ST
10700 LA 90034 632-D7
10900 LA 90034 672-D1
S QUEEN SUMMIT DR
1400 WCOV 91791 639-A3
QUEENSVIEW LN
2500 LaCr 91214 534-G1
QUEENSWAY DR
500 LBCH 90802 825-C2

QUEEN VICTORIA RD
4700 WdHl 91364 560-E4
QUEMADA RD
16200 Enc 91436 561-E5
QUESAN PL
17200 Enc 91316 561-C5
QUESTA CT
400 PMDL 93551 4285-H1
QUEZADA WY
14800 SCTA 91387 4462-F7
QUICK ST
- PMDL 93551 4195-E6
QUICKSILVER LN
3200 PMDL 93550 4286-G5
19500 RowH 91748 679-D6
31200 Actn 93510 4465-B4
QUIET WY
2500 LAN 93535 4106-E1
QUIET BROOK CIR
500 FUL 92831 738-H5
QUIET CANYON CIR
- POM 91766 640-G5
QUIET CREEK LN
1000 DBAR 91765 680-C2
2200 CHLS 91709 680-J3
QUIET HILLS CIR
- POM 91766 640-H6
QUIET HILLS CT
8200 LA 91304 529-E3
QUIET HILLS RD
- POM 91766 640-G6
QUIET HOLLOW RD
- POM 91766 640-H5
QUIGLEY AV
4100 LKWD 90713 766-F5
N QUIGLEY AV
- LACo 91107 566-H4
S QUIGLEY AV
- LACo 91107 566-H5
QUIGLEY RD
21200 SCTA 91321 4551-C7
21200 SCTA 91350 4551-C7
QUIGLEY ST
4900 CMRC 90040 675-G3
QUIGLEY CANYON RD
24600 SCTA 91321 4551-A7
24600 SCTA 91321 4641-A1
QUILL AV
10200 Sunl 91040 503-G2
QUILL DR
7200 DWNY 90242 705-G6
QUILLA RD
25700 SCTA 91355 4550-F6
QUIMBY AV
7400 CanP 91307 529-G4
7600 LA 91304 529-G4
QUIMBY ST
7300 PRM 90723 735-F3
N QUIMBY ST
8200 PRM 90723 735-H3
QUINCE CIR
16300 HacH 91745 678-E4
QUINCE CT
- ONT 91762 641-J3
W QUINCE CT
1000 ONT 91762 641-J3
W QUINCE ST
1100 ONT 91762 641-J3
QUINCY AV
- LBCH 90803 826-A1
300 LBCH 90814 796-A7
300 LBCH 90814 826-A1
1300 LBCH 90804 796-A5
2400 LBCH 90815 796-A3
QUINCY ST
27600 Cstc 91384 4459-H5
QUINCY WY
- Nor 91326 480-E5
QUINLIN DR
4100 LACo 90274 793-C6
QUINN DR
- LACo 91387 4462-B6
QUINN PL
21500 SCTA 91350 4461-B6
QUINN ST
5500 BGDN 90201 705-F2
7400 DWNY 90241 705-J3
7500 DWNY 90241 706-A3
11400 SFSP 90670 706-G6
QUINNELL DR
2900 WCOV 91792 679-D2
QUINTA RD
4600 WdHl 91364 559-J4
QUINTA VISTA DR
- THO 91362 557-A2
QUINTERO ST
1300 Echo 90026 594-F7
1300 Echo 90026 634-F1
QUINTON LN
6500 Tuj 91042 504-B5
N QUIRK RD
1000 Actn 93510 4465-J2
QUIROZ CT
19800 INDS 91789 679-E4
19800 LACo 91789 679-E4
QUITO LN
10400 BelA 90077 592-A4
QUITO WY
- PMDL 93550 4286-F5
QUIXLEY ST
20100 CRSN 90746 764-E4
QUOIT ST
8000 DWNY 90242 705-J7

R

E R ST
100 Wilm 90744 794-E4
W R ST
100 Wilm 90744 794-C4
RABBIT RD
3300 SBdC 92371 (4472-H3
See Page 4471)
14000 LA 91342 482-C1
RABER ST
5200 HiPk 90042 565-B7
E RABORN ST
500 SDMS 91773 600-D1
RACE ST
23900 SCTA 91321 4641-A1
RACELAND RD
13400 LMRD 90638 737-E2
RACHEL AV
3400 WCOV 91792 639-B7
3400 WCOV 91792 679-B1
4900 LKWD 90713 766-E3
45000 LAN 93535 4016-C5
RACHMANINOV ST
9200 LACo 93536 3833-G6
RACIMO DR
12900 LACo 90605 707-B3
RACINE AV
7500 PRM 90723 735-G2
RACQUET LN
3100 PMDL 93551 4195-A3
RACQUET CLUB CT
28200 SCTA 91351 4551-H2
RACQUET CLUB DR
100 COMP 90220 734-J4
100 COMP 90220 735-A4
RACQUET CLUB RD
700 DBAR 91765 680-A1
RADA RD
1700 HacH 91745 678-E4
RADAR AV
44700 LAN 93534 4015-J6
RADBARD ST
800 CRSN 90746 764-E1
RADBROOK CT
28500 RPV 90275 823-J2
RADBROOK PL
25500 SCTA 91355 4550-F7
RADBURN AV
14600 SFSP 90670 737-D4
RADBURY PL
600 DBAR 91765 640-D7
600 DBAR 91765 680-D1
RADBY ST
18900 RowH 91748 679-B5
RADCLAY DR
1900 LACo 91789 679-F5
RADCLAY ST
16500 LACo 91387 4552-B6
RADCLIFF DR
400 WAL 91789 639-F7
RADCLIFF PL
1000 LHB 90631 708-B7
RADCLIFFE AV
500 PacP 90272 631-A6
RADCLIFFE CT
44100 LAN 93536 4015-A7
E RADCLIFFE DR
100 CLAR 91711 571-D7
W RADCLIFFE DR
100 CLAR 91711 571-D7
RADCOURT DR
2200 HacH 91745 678-F5
RADECKI CT
- INDS 91748 678-H3
RADFALL CT
27800 SCTA 91350 4461-C6
RADFORD AV
1800 CLAR 91711 571-B7
4000 LA 91604 562-G5
4400 LA 91607 562-G1
5900 LA 91607 532-G7
6000 NHol 91606 532-G7
6800 NHol 91605 532-G3
RADFORD PL
1600 MNRO 91016 567-F6
RADIAN LN
44100 LAN 93536 4015-C7
RADIAN WY
2900 LAN 93536 4015-C7
RADIANT CT
16600 LACo 91722 598-G3
RADIO DR
3300 LA 90031 595-B6
11700 LA 90064 672-B1
RADIO RD
- LHH 90631 678-E7
3300 LA 90031 595-B6
RADIO ST
3800 LFlz 90027 594-C4
RADIO LATERAL
- GLDL 91206 565-C2
RADIUM DR
4300 LA 90032 595-C7
RADIUS PL
15100 SFSP 90670 737-C4
RADLETT AV
19100 CRSN 90746 764-G3
RADLEY ST
11500 ART 90701 766-G1
RADLOCK AV
6600 LadH 90056 673-A7

RADLOCK AV
6600 LadH 90056 672-J7
RADNOR AV
4100 LKWD 90713 766-D4
N RADNOR AV
2000 LBCH 90815 796-C3
3600 LBCH 90808 766-D7
RADON DR
- LACo 91342 482-J2
RADSTOCK AV
600 LPUE 91744 678-G2
RADWAY AV
400 LPUE 91744 638-B5
600 LACo 91744 638-B5
S RADWAY AV
1800 WCOV 91790 638-C3
RADWIN AV
10600 Sunl 91040 503-D3
RAE CT
- WCOV 91792 679-B1
1100 UPL 91784 571-J4
E RAE ST
1000 PMDL 93550 4286-C6
RAEBERT ST
9000 DWNY 90241 706-B6
RAELYN PL
2100 WCOV 91792 638-G5
RAFAEL DR
1000 ARCD 91006 566-J4
RAFAEL TER
2000 GLDL 91208 534-J5
N RAFAEL WK
200 LBCH 90803 826-D3
RAGAN DR
14600 LMRD 90638 737-F1
RAGING WATERS DR
- SDMS 91773 600-B4
RAGLEY ST
15700 HacH 91745 678-B3
RAGOSA CT
- SCTA 91321 4551-F5
RAGUS ST
1000 LACo 91746 638-A2
14400 LACo 91744 638-C4
RAHN AV
6100 NLB 90805 765-B1
12100 GrnH 91344 481-E6
RAIL WY
- FUL 92832 738-C6
RAILROAD AV
100 MNRO 91016 567-G6
3800 BALD 91706 598-C5
13000 INDS 91746 637-G3
24100 SCTA 91321 4641-A1
24200 SCTA 91321 4640-J1
RAILROAD DR
10100 ELMN 91731 597-B6
RAILROAD MTWY
- Nwhl 91321 4641-A5
- SCTA 91321 4641-A5
RAILROAD PL
900 MANB 90266 732-F6
W RAILROAD PL
400 ING 90302 703-B2
RAILROAD ST
- PAS 91030 565-H7
- PAS 91105 565-H7
- SPAS 91030 565-H7
400 GLDL 91204 564-D7
1400 GLDL 91204 594-D1
10800 ELMN 91731 597-C7
17100 INDS 91748 678-G3
18200 INDS 91748 679-A3
RAILTON ST
8600 PRV 90660 676-G3
RAILWAY AV
- BREA 92823 709-H6
W RAILWAY ST
200 SDMS 91773 600-B2
RAINBOW AV
400 LA 90065 595-A4
RAINBOW CT
19500 CRTS 90703 766-J3
RAINBOW DR
300 AZU 91702 568-J4
700 GLDR 91741 569-D4
29000 Cstc 91384 4459-C6
RAINBOW LN
2300 BREA 92821 709-E7
RAINBOW PL
600 DBAR 91765 640-E7
RAINBOW TER
300 PMDL 93551 4285-H1
RAINBOW WK
16000 LACo 91390 4192-C3
RAINBOW WY
19900 CRTS 90703 766-J3
RAINBOW ACRES RD
10600 Litl 93543 4468-E4
RAINBOW BEND DR
33600 Actn 93510 4374-D6
N RAINBOW CREST DR
5500 AGRH 91301 557-G5
W RAINBOW CREST DR
29800 AGRH 91301 557-H5
RAINBOW GLEN DR
26000 SCTA 91321 4551-E4
26300 SCTA 91351 4551-E3
RAINBOW HILL RD
5700 AGRH 91301 557-G3
RAINBOW KNOLL
14400 CHLS 91709 680-G4

RAINBOW RIDGE CIR
17300 GrnH 91344 481-B7
RAINBOW RIDGE RD
- POM 91766 640-H5
16200 CHLS 91709 710-H2
27300 LACo 90274 793-C7
RAINBOWS END
5000 CULC 90230 672-J3
RAINBOW TERRACE LN
1800 MTBL 90640 636-F5
RAINBOW VIEW DR
30300 AGRH 91301 557-G4
RAINDANCE PL
27400 SCTA 91350 4461-B7
RAINER AV
2300 RowH 91748 679-A6
RAINER RD
27700 Cstc 91384 4459-G2
RAINEY RD
1200 VeCo 93063 499-A3
RAINFOREST
1400 WCOV 91790 638-D2
RAINIER AV
13000 LACo 90605 707-B6
RAINIER DR
4500 CYP 90630 767-B6
RAINIER ST
10300 SunV 91352 533-A2
RAINIER WY
2600 LHB 90631 708-B5
RAINS ST
12400 ELMN 91732 597-G7
RAINSBURY AV
17500 CRSN 90746 734-E7
17500 CRSN 90746 764-E1
RAINSFORD PL
29500 MAL 90265 667-D2
RAINSGATE LN
13900 CHLS 91709 680-H3
RAINSTAR LN
2400 CHLS 91709 680-G5
RAINTREE AV
3200 TOR 90505 793-D4
RAINTREE CIR
1000 CULC 90230 672-H3
RAINTREE CT
800 THO 91361 557-A4
RAIN TREE DR
1100 LHB 90631 738-C1
RAINTREE DR
2300 BREA 92821 709-E7
8600 WHIT 90605 707-G3
RAINTREE LN
10500 Nor 91326 500-H3
28700 SCTA 91390 4460-J2
28800 LACo 91390 4460-H2
38000 PMDL 93552 4286-J1
RAINTREE RD
1700 FUL 92835 738-G4
RAINWATER LN
800 WAL 91789 639-H5
RAINWOOD DR
21100 DBAR 91789 679-H2
RAITT LN
- FUL 92833 738-C5
RAJAH ST
12400 LA 91342 482-E2
RALE DR
- PMDL 93550 4376-E1
RALEIGH CT
- Nor 91326 480-D6
RALEIGH DR
2500 SMRO 91108 566-E7
RALEIGH LN
- StvR 91381 4549-J7
RALEIGH ST
400 GLDL 91205 564-F6
5100 LA 90004 593-G7
RALEO AV
1300 RowH 91748 679-C4
RALL AV
300 LACo 91746 637-G4
3400 BALD 91706 598-A7
RALPH CT
500 POM 91766 641-A6
RALPH ST
8500 RSMD 91770 596-G7
9400 RSMD 91770 597-B7
10200 ELMN 91731 597-B7
19900 WAL 91789 639-E7
E RALPH ST
200 SGBL 91776 596-E7
W RALPH ST
200 SGBL 91776 596-D7
RALPH LIEBERMAN AV
2400 CMRC 90040 675-F3
RALSTON AV
9200 SunV 91352 502-H6
10000 Pcma 91331 502-D2
12200 LA 91342 482-A6
12200 SFER 91340 482-A6
12300 LA 91342 481-G3
RALSTON LN
2300 RBCH 90278 763-B2
W RALSTON ST
1000 ONT 91762 641-J2
RAMA DR
500 LPUE 91746 638-A4
1400 LACo 91746 638-A4
S RAMA DR
1400 WCOV 91790 638-D1
RAMADA AV
100 LACo 91746 637-G3

RAMADA DR
25600 SCTA 91355 4550-G5
RAMADA PZ
2400 FUL 92833 738-C6
RAMAGE ST
700 WHWD 90069 592-H7
RAMARA AV
5600 WdHl 91367 559-E2
RAMBLA DEL ORTO DR
5800 MAL 90265 626-J6
RAMBLA ORIENTA
3800 MAL 90265 629-F6
RAMBLA PACIFICO
1500 LACo 90265 629-E3
2900 MAL 90265 629-E6
RAMBLA VISTA
21300 MAL 90265 629-E6
RAMBLER AV
38800 PMDL 93550 4196-B7
S RAMBLEWOOD DR
800 ANA 92804 767-H7
RAMBLING RD
19800 LACo 91724 599-E6
RAMBOZ DR
3500 City 90063 635-D3
RAMBOZ PL
1300 City 90063 635-E3
RAMCO WY
17600 Enc 91316 561-B3
RAMER ST
12600 ELMN 91732 637-E4
RAMERA MTWY E
3900 LACo 90265 627-G4
RAMESA RIDGE WY
3800 LACo 90265 627-G4
RAMEY RD
7300 LACo 90606 677-B7
RAMHURST DR
13900 LMRD 90638 737-D1
RAMILLO AV
1100 LBCH 90815 796-B5
RAMILLO WY
24100 SCTA 91355 4550-F6
RAMINDA AV
400 LACo 91744 638-G7
RAMIREZ ST
500 LA 90012 634-H3
RAMIREZ CANYON RD
5600 LACo 90265 627-G7
5600 MAL 90265 627-G7
5900 MAL 90265 667-G1
RAMIREZ MESA DR
6200 MAL 90265 667-G1
RAMIREZ RIDGE TR
2900 LACo 90265 627-G5
RAMIRO RD
1600 PAS 91108 596-A1
1600 SMRO 91108 596-A1
RAMISH AV
7600 BGDN 90201 705-J2
RAMLI DR
14700 SCTA 91387 4462-G7
RAMO DR
14200 LMRD 90638 737-E2
RAMON CT
5800 CMRC 90040 676-B7
RAMON ST
- PMDL 93551 4195-A3
RAMONA AV
100 SMAD 91024 566-J2
100 SMAD 91024 567-A2
300 LVRN 91750 600-D1
400 LACo 91750 600-D1
900 LVRN 91750 570-D7
1500 SPAS 91030 595-H3
1600 GLDL 91208 534-H6
2000 LHB 90631 708-H5
8900 MTCL 91763 601-E4
10300 MTCL 91763 641-E2
11300 SBdC 91763 641-E2
11300 SBdC 91766 641-E2
11400 HAW 90250 703-C7
11400 SBdC 91710 641-E2
11800 HAW 90250 733-C1
11800 CHNO 91710 641-E7
S RAMONA AV
100 MONP 91754 636-B3
RAMONA BLVD
2100 WCOV 91790 598-D5
2100 WCOV 91706 598-D5
2300 BALD 91706 598-D5
8600 RSMD 91770 636-H1
9200 RSMD 91770 596-J7
10600 ELMN 91731 597-E7
11600 ELMN 91732 597-E7
12400 BALD 91732 597-H6
12400 IRW 91732 597-H6
12400 BALD 91706 597-H6
12400 IRW 91706 597-H6
W RAMONA BLVD
100 SGBL 91776 636-D1
3100 MONP 91754 635-F2
3400 City 90063 635-F2
3400 MONP 90063 635-F2
RAMONA CT
6300 LA 90048 633-A3
RAMONA DR
100 FUL 92833 738-F6
13400 WHIT 90602 707-D1
13800 WHIT 90605 707-E1
RAMONA PKWY
13300 BALD 91706 598-A6

RAMONA PL
100 PAS 91107 566-F5
4600 SBdC 91710 641-F3
RAMONA RD
1200 ARCD 91006 567-C3
10800 MsnH 91345 501-H2
36300 PMDL 93550 4286-F6
E RAMONA RD
100 ALH 91801 636-C1
W RAMONA RD
100 ALH 91801 636-A1
200 ALH 91803 636-A1
1400 ALH 91803 635-H1
3000 MONP 91754 635-G2
RAMONA ST
200 PAS 91101 565-J4
8500 BLF 90706 735-J7
8700 BLF 90706 736-A7
S RAMONA ST
400 SGBL 91776 596-D5
W RAMONA ST
300 COV 91723 599-C6
W RAMONA TER
1900 ALH 91803 635-H1
RAMOS PL
14900 PacP 90272 631-B7
N RAMPART BLVD
100 Echo 90026 634-C1
600 Echo 90026 594-C7
S RAMPART BLVD
100 LA 90057 634-B2
RAMPART LN
7000 LPMA 90623 767-C2
RAMSAY DR
2300 GLDL 91206 564-J3
RAMSDELL AV
3700 GLDL 91214 534-F3
4100 LaCr 91214 534-F1
4500 LaCr 91214 504-F7
RAMSEY DR
11600 LACo 90605 707-D7
12300 LACo 90605 737-D1
12800 LMRD 90638 737-D1
RAMSEY WY
2000 POM 91767 601-A5
RAMSGATE AV
7000 Wch 90045 703-A1
7900 Wch 90045 702-J2
RAMSGATE PL
7000 Wch 90045 703-A1
RAMS HORN CT
1900 GLDL 91207 564-E1
N RAMUDA LN
- VeCo 91307 529-A5
RAN DR
37000 PMDL 93550 4286-E4
RANA DR
25700 SCTA 91355 4550-F6
S RANBURN AV
100 AZU 91702 569-B7
200 AZU 91702 599-B1
RANCE DR
20400 LACo 91789 679-F6
RANCH LN
500 GLDR 91741 569-G4
700 PacP 90272 631-B5
16000 LMRD 90638 737-J2
16000 LMRD 90638 738-A2
RANCH RD
- Actn 93510 4465-H6
1400 AZU 91702 568-J2
4700 CHNO 91710 641-F7
10600 CULC 90230 672-H4
RANCH CENTER DR
38300 PMDL 93551 4195-A6
38300 PMDL 93551 4285-A1
RANCH CLUB RD
- LACo 93551 4102-F6
42500 LACo 93532 4102-F4
RANCH CREEK CT
- POM 91766 640-F5
RANCH CREEK LN
14500 CHLS 91709 680-J4
RANCH CREEK RD
900 COV 91724 599-D6
RANCHERIA RD
400 DBAR 91765 640-C7
RANCHERO RD
- RHLS 90274 823-D3
W RANCHERO ST
1800 WCOV 91790 598-E5
RANCHEROS PL
1100 PAS 91103 565-E3
RANCHEROS RD
1100 PAS 91103 565-E3
RANCHGROVE DR
2400 WLKV 91361 586-J1
RANCH HILL DR
1800 LHH 90631 708-G2
RANCH HOUSE RD
900 THO 91361 557-A5
2100 CHLS 91709 710-J1
RANCHILL DR
13600 CRTS 90703 737-C5
RANCHITO AV
4800 Shrm 91423 562-B3
5200 VanN 91401 562-B2
5900 VanN 91401 532-B7
6600 VanN 91405 532-B5
7800 PanC 91402 532-B1
8700 PanC 91402 502-B7
RANCHITO LN
- Actn 93510 4465-B1

RANCHITO RD
500 MNRO 91016 568-A4
RANCHITO ST
10500 ELMN 91731 597-C5
11300 ELMN 91732 597-F5
RANCHITOS DR
6600 Actn 93510 4374-D6
RANCHO AV
1500 GLDL 91201 563-J3
1500 LFlz 90027 563-J3
RANCHO CIR
700 FUL 92835 738-F3
RANCHO CT
- BqtC 91354 4460-E4
RANCHO DR
300 MTBL 90640 676-F1
700 LBCH 90815 796-E6
12700 NRWK 90650 737-A1
RANCHO LN
- LACo 90604 707-C5
RANCHO RD
- SMAD 91024 567-C3
100 Llan 93544 4471-J4
100 SBdC 92372 4471-J4
200 SBdC 92372 (4472-D3
See Page 4471)
1000 ARCD 91006 567-C3
1000 DUAR 91010 568-E5
2900 SBdC 92371 (4472-G3
See Page 4471)
7400 SBdC 92371 (4562-J5
See Page 4471)
RANCHO ST
17000 Enc 91316 561-A4
18100 Tarz 91356 560-J4
18100 Tarz 91356 561-A4
RANCHO WY
- Actn 93510 4375-B7
- Actn 93510 4465-B1
19600 LACo 90220 765-A3
20200 LACo 90220 764-J4
RANCHO ADOBE RD
25600 SCTA 91355 4550-G5
RANCHO ALEGRE DR
400 COV 91724 599-G6
RANCHO AMERICANA PL
- Actn 93510 4375-B7
- Actn 93510 4465-B1
RANCHO ARROYO ST
8000 PRM 90723 735-H2
RANCHO BERNARDO
6700 BPK 90620 767-G5
RANCHO CABALLO DR
9800 Sunl 91040 503-C4
RANCHO CAMINO
12100 PRM 90723 735-F1
12100 SGAT 90280 735-F1
RANCHO CAMINO DR
- POM 91766 640-H6
RANCHO CANADA RD
2000 LCF 91011 534-J2
RANCHO CAPISTRANO RD
15100 PRM 90723 735-J4
RANCHO CENTINA RD
15100 PRM 90723 735-J4
RANCHO CERONA DR
8600 PRM 90723 735-J4
RANCHO CLEMENTE DR
15100 PRM 90723 735-J4
RANCHO CONTENTO DR
2600 SBdC 92371 (4562-G5
See Page 4471)
RANCHO CORTO DR
400 COV 91724 599-G6
RANCHO CULEBRA DR
1900 COV 91724 599-G6
RANCHO DEL AMO PL
- CRSN 90810 765-A4
20200 LACo 90220 764-J4
20200 LACo 90220 765-A4
RANCHO DEL MONICO RD
3200 LACo 91724 599-F6
RANCHO DEL ORO ST
8000 PRM 90723 735-H2
RANCHO DEL SOL DR
400 COV 91724 599-G6
RANCHO DEL VALLE
- GrnH 91344 501-A1
RANCHO DORADO RD
8200 PRM 90723 735-H2
RANCHO EL ENCINO DR
3200 LACo 91724 599-F7
RANCHO EL FUERTE DR
1100 COV 91724 599-E7
RANCHO GRANDE DR
1800 COV 91724 599-F6
RANCHO HILLS DR
1400 CHLS 91709 680-G5
RANCHO JURUPA PL
- POM 91766 640-E4
RANCHO LA CARLOTA RD
3200 LACo 91724 599-F7
RANCHO LA CUESTA RD
15100 PRM 90723 735-J4
RANCHO LA FLORESTA RD
20400 LACo 91724 599-F6
RANCHO LAGUNA DR
- POM 91766 640-D4

RANCHO LA MERCED DR
2000 COV 91724 599-G6
RANCHO LA PUENTE DR
600 LACo 91744 678-J2
RANCHO LINDO DR
400 COV 91724 599-G6
RANCHO LOS CERRITOS RD
20400 LACo 91724 599-F6
20400 COV 91724 599-F6
RANCHO LOS NOGALES RD
400 COV 91724 599-G6
RANCHO MANGANA RD
8500 LACo 91775 566-G7
RANCHO NOVATO DR
- POM 91766 640-D4
RANCHO OBISPO RD
15100 PRM 90723 735-J4
RANCHO POLERMO RD
15100 PRM 90723 735-J4
RANCHO PONDEROSA RD
8000 PRM 90723 735-H2
RANCHO REAL RD
9000 TEML 91780 596-H4
RANCHO RIO RD
- PRM 90723 735-E5
RANCHO RIO BONITA RD
3300 LACo 91724 599-F6
RANCHO SAN JOSE DR
20400 LACo 91724 599-F6
RANCHO SANTORO DR
3300 LACo 91724 599-F6
RANCHO SERANO DR
15200 PRM 90723 735-J4
RANCHO SIMI DR
500 COV 91724 599-G6
RANCHO SINALOA DR
700 COV 91724 599-E6
RANCHO TESORO DR
- BqtC 91354 4460-E3
RANCHO TUJUNGA DR
1800 COV 91724 599-G6
RANCHO VALERO RD
8000 PRM 90723 735-H2
RANCHO VERDE DR
11700 LACo 90601 677-C2
15200 PRM 90723 735-J4
RANCHO VISTA BLVD
300 PMDL 93550 4195-J5
300 PMDL 93550 4196-B5
500 PMDL 93551 4195-A3
4300 PMDL 93551 4194-H2
RANCHO VISTA DR
500 COV 91724 599-G6
12400 CRTS 90703 736-J6
RANCHO VISTA PL
- POM 91766 640-E5
RANCHO VISTA ST
8500 PRM 90723 735-J4
RANCH TOP RD
3400 PAS 91107 536-G7
RANCH VIEW PL
600 THO 91362 557-A1
RANCHVIEW RD
- RHE 90274 793-C6
RANCHVIEW TER
- LACo 91390 4461-C3
14600 CHLS 91709 680-G5
RANCHWOOD AV
44400 LAN 93536 4015-C6
RANCHWOOD PL
1100 DBAR 91765 680-D3
RAND CT
4000 Shrm 91423 562-C6
RAND DR
13400 Shrm 91423 562-C6
RAND ST
5900 BPK 90621 737-J7
RANDA LN
- ING 90305 703-E3
RANDALL AV
1000 OrCo 90631 708-B4
9000 LHB 90631 708-B4
RANDALL CT
1400 LA 90065 594-H4
RANDALL ST
- OrCo 90631 708-B4
1300 GLDL 91201 564-A3
1400 GLDL 91201 563-J3
5100 LA 90230 672-E6
10900 SunV 91352 503-A6
11000 SunV 91352 502-J7
11800 SunV 91352 532-G1
W RANDALL WY
1200 WCOV 91790 638-D2
RANDEE WY
3600 FUL 92833 738-B7
RANDI AV
6200 WdHl 91367 529-J7
6400 CanP 91303 529-J7
6500 CanP 91303 530-A6
RANDIWOOD LN
6600 LACo 91307 529-C6
RANDOLPH AV
500 PAS 91107 566-F6
3600 LA 90032 595-E5
N RANDOLPH AV
100 BREA 92821 709-C7
S RANDOLPH AV
100 BREA 92821 709-C7

RANDOLPH PL
200 Bxby 90807 765-D6
3500 BELL 90201 675-C6
3500 HNTP 90255 675-C6
RANDOLPH ST
600 POM 91768 600-H7
1100 LA 90032 595-E5
1700 Flor 90001 674-H6
1900 HNTP 90001 674-H6
1900 HNTP 90255 674-H6
2800 HNTP 90255 675-A6
3800 BELL 90201 675-E6
4300 MYWD 90270 675-D6
5200 MYWD 90201 675-E6
5500 CMRC 90040 675-G6
11600 ARCD 91006 597-F3
E RANDOLPH ST
100 GLDL 91207 564-E2
W RANDOLPH ST
100 GLDL 91202 564-E2
300 POM 91768 600-H7
RANDOM LN
800 DUAR 91010 568-C5
RANDSBURG ST
13400 CRTS 90703 737-C6
RANDWICK DR
10000 TEML 91780 597-B4
RANDY ST
200 POM 91768 640-D1
W RANDY ST
1300 UPL 91786 601-J3
RANETTO PL
11200 LA 91342 503-C1
RANGE CT
1600 DBAR 91765 680-D4
RANGE DR
- PMDL 93551 4195-J3
RANGE RD
2600 Eagl 90041 564-J7
2600 LA 90065 564-J7
RANGE HORSE LN
5000 RHE 90274 793-B5
RANGE LATERAL
- GLDL 91208 534-J5
- GLDL 91208 535-A5
RANGELY AV
8700 WHWD 90048 592-H7
RANGELY ST
8400 WHWD 90048 593-A7
8400 WHWD 90048 592-J7
RANGER AV
100 BREA 92821 709-F7
4200 ELMN 91731 597-C6
RANGER DR
- PMDL 93552 4287-D1
300 AZU 91702 599-B1
1300 COV 91722 599-B3
5300 LACo 91722 599-B2
N RANGER DR
1400 COV 91722 599-B2
6000 LACo 91702 569-B7
7000 GLDR 91741 569-B5
RANGER RD
- LCF 91011 535-E4
- PAS 91103 535-E4
RANGETON DR
1300 DBAR 91789 679-G3
RANGE VIEW AV
5100 HiPk 90042 595-C1
RANGEVIEW AV
4800 Eagl 90041 595-B1
4900 HiPk 90042 595-B1
RANGEVIEW DR
1900 GLDL 91201 534-A6
RANGEWOOD RD
29100 Cstc 91384 4459-H6
RANGOON ST
12700 Pcma 91331 502-E6
13300 Pcma 91331 532-C1
RANIER DR
38000 PMDL 93552 4287-B1
RANIER PL
- LACo 93536 4104-J5
- LACo 93536 4105-A5
RANIER ST
19200 SCTA 91351 4551-F1
RANLETT AV
500 LACo 91744 638-F5
RANMORE DR
16300 HacH 91745 678-E5
RANNEY HOUSE CT
23900 SCTA 91355 4550-F4
RANONS AV
3900 LA 90065 594-G1
4100 LA 90065 564-G7
RANSOM RD
1800 GLDL 91201 534-B6
RANSOM ST
2200 CMRC 90040 675-F3
E RANSOM ST
3200 LBCH 90804 795-J5
4000 LBCH 90804 796-A5
RANSOM WY
200 MONP 91755 636-C3
RANTHOM AV
5500 WdHl 91367 559-D2
S RAPALLO AV
600 LA 90732 823-H5
RAPALLO PL
1900 LA 90732 823-H5
RAPHAEL LN
39200 PMDL 93551 4195-D6

STREET
Block City ZIP Pg-Grid

RAPHAEL ST
5000 HiPk 90042 595-B2
43800 LAN 93535 4106-C1
RAPID BROOK RD
1200 DBAR 91765 680-C2
RAPID GROVE DR
26600 LACo 92397 (4652-A1
See Page 4651)
RAPIDVIEW DR
1200 DBAR 91789 679-G3
RAPTOR CT
- WAL 91789 639-C5
RAQUEL LN
14800 SCTA 91387 4462-F7
RARITAN DR
14700 LACo 90604 707-F7
RASHDALL AV
21800 CRSN 90745 764-C6
22700 CRSN 90745 794-C1
RASIC RIDGE RD
900 GLDL 91207 564-F1
RASKIN DR
19400 RowH 91748 679-D4
RATH ST
1000 LACo 91746 638-A2
14400 LACo 91744 638-C3
RATHBURN AV
8300 Nor 91325 530-J2
8900 Nor 91325 500-J4
10600 Nor 91326 500-J2
RATHER ST
10900 SunV 91352 533-A2
RATLIFFE ST
10900 NRWK 90650 736-E1
13800 LMRD 90638 737-D1
RATNER ST
11900 NHol 91605 532-D2
13400 PanC 91402 532-C2
RATON CIR
5000 Bxby 90807 765-G3
RATTLESNAKE RD
- LACo 90265 586-G7
- LACo 90265 626-F1
1200 SBdC 92372 (4562-C3
See Page 4471)
RATTLESNAKE GULCH
1700 SBdC 92372 (4562-D4
See Page 4471)
RATTLESNAKE GULCH RD
2200 SBdC 92372 (4562-E4
See Page 4471)
RAUSCH RD
15600 INDS 91744 638-D7
RAVARI DR
9600 CYP 90630 767-C7
RAVEN CT
3800 CALB 91301 588-G1
9700 KeCo 93560 3833-G3
RAVEN DR
37400 PMDL 93550 4286-E3
W RAVEN DR
- PMDL 93551 4195-J3
RAVEN LN
- LAN 93536 4014-H7
- LAN 93536 4104-H1
RAVEN RD
26700 LACo 92397 (4652-A2
See Page 4651)
RAVEN ST
13200 LA 91342 482-C2
RAVENCREST CIR
- POM 91766 640-F5
RAVENCREST LN
44400 LAN 93536 4015-C6
E RAVENDALE RD
8200 LACo 91775 596-F1
RAVENFALL AV
2200 RowH 91748 678-H6
RAVENGLEN RD
16000 LACo 91387 4552-C7
16000 SCTA 91387 4552-C7
RAVENHILL DR
- POM 91766 640-F6
RAVENHILL RD
26100 SCTA 91387 4552-D7
26100 SCTA 91387 4642-D1
RAVENNA AV
1000 Wilm 90744 794-D5
21300 CRSN 90745 764-D6
22400 CRSN 90745 794-D1
RAVENNA DR
- Actn 93510 4464-H6
N RAVENNA DR
100 LBCH 90803 826-C2
RAVENNA LN
- Nor 91326 500-C2
RAVENNA WY
9800 CYP 90630 767-C7
RAVENSFIELD LN
1900 BelA 90077 591-G3
RAVENSPUR DR
5600 RHE 90274 793-A7
5600 RPV 90275 792-J7
5600 RPV 90275 793-A7
RAVENSWOOD AV
10500 Lenx 90304 703-D5
RAVENSWOOD WY
2100 POM 91767 600-J5
RAVENWOOD CT
2700 DBAR 91789 679-G6
10400 BelA 90077 592-A2
RAVENWOOD DR
13900 CHLS 91709 680-J3
RAVIA ST
5500 LKWD 90713 766-C5
RAVILLER DR
7800 DWNY 90240 706-B2
RAVINE LN
1600 CHLS 91709 710-H2
RAVINE RD
2200 LA 90039 594-F5
RAVISTA LN
1900 LCF 91011 534-J1
RAVOLI DR
1000 PacP 90272 631-C4
RAWDON AV
44300 LAN 93535 4016-C7
RAWHIDE
- WCOV 91791 638-J4
- WCOV 91791 639-A4
RAWHIDE AV
15500 LACo 93591 4199-E4
RAWHIDE CIR
500 WAL 91789 639-D7
RAWHIDE LN
- RHE 90274 793-D6
- CRSN 90745 794-G2
12700 NRWK 90650 737-A1
RAWHIDE ST
- MTCL 91763 641-E2
- POM 91766 640-F5
RAWLINGS AV
5500 SGAT 90280 705-F6
5600 WdHl 91367 560-E1
RAWLINGS CIR
- StvR 91381 4640-D1
RAWLINSDALE LN
500 SDMS 91773 600-D3
500 LVRN 91750 600-D3
RAWLINSON CT
400 BURB 91505 563-E4
RAWSON RD
- LACo 91390 4373-C3
500 SBdC 92372 (4472-A5
See Page 4471)
RAY CIR
19500 CRTS 90703 766-H3
RAY CT
4800 Eagl 90041 565-C6
28500 SCTA 91350 4461-D4
RAYBET RD
10400 BelA 90077 592-A1
RAYBORN ST
4600 LYN 90262 735-D2
RAYBURN RD
100 PMDL 93550 4285-J2
100 PMDL 93551 4285-J2
RAYEN ST
13500 Pcma 91331 502-B7
14200 PanC 91402 502-A7
14600 PanC 91402 501-H7
14900 LA 91343 501-D7
16900 Nor 91325 501-A7
18100 Nor 91325 500-J7
18400 Nor 91324 500-H7
22000 LA 91304 529-J1
22000 LA 91304 530-A1
23900 WHil 91304 529-E1
RAYFIELD DR
14500 LMRD 90638 737-J3
RAYFORD DR
8000 Wch 90045 702-D2
RAYLAND DR
900 LACo 90502 794-A1
RAYLANDS DR
11300 LACo 91342 482-J2
RAYLENE CT
6200 SIMI 93063 499-C2
RAYLENE PL
1300 POM 91767 601-A6
RAYMER AV
1900 FUL 92833 738-B7
RAYMER ST
12500 NHol 91605 532-D4
14500 VanN 91405 531-H3
14500 VanN 91405 532-A3
15300 VanN 91406 531-E2
17100 Nor 91325 531-A1
RAYMOND AV
200 GLDL 91201 563-J2
400 SMCA 90405 671-G4
700 LBCH 90804 795-G7
1000 GLDL 91201 564-A1
1300 GLDL 91201 534-B7
1600 HMB 90254 762-H1
1600 MNRO 91016 567-G6
1900 LA 90007 633-J6
3400 LA 90007 673-J4
4000 GLDL 91020 534-G2
4000 LA 90037 673-J4
4300 LaCr 91214 534-G1
4700 LaCr 91214 504-G7
5800 LA 90044 674-A6
7200 LA 90044 704-A1
11100 LACo 90044 704-A6
11800 LACo 90044 703-J7
12000 LACo 90044 734-A1
13500 GAR 90247 734-A3
18400 LA 90248 764-A2
N RAYMOND AV
- ALH 91801 595-J5
- PAS 91103 565-H2
1300 LBCH 90804 795-G4
1600 PAS 91103 535-H7
1800 FUL 92831 738-J4
1800 SIGH 90755 795-G3
2000 Alta 91001 535-J4
6200 NLB 90805 765-G1
6300 NLB 90805 735-G7
S RAYMOND AV
- PAS 91105 565-H7
800 ALH 91803 595-J6
1600 ALH 91801 595-J6
1700 ALH 91803 635-J1
20400 LACo 90502 764-A5
RAYMOND CT
400 SMCA 90405 671-G4
RAYMOND DR
400 LACo 91107 566-H5
4600 LVRN 91750 570-G7
RAYMOND LN
800 SPAS 91030 595-H2
2200 Alta 91001 535-H6
RAYMOND PL
16800 GAR 90247 734-A7
RAYMOND ST
200 LHB 90631 708-B6
23200 Chat 91311 499-F7
E RAYMOND ST
100 COMP 90220 734-J5
100 COMP 90220 735-A5
W RAYMOND ST
100 COMP 90220 734-F5
RAYMONDALE DR
300 SPAS 91030 595-H1
RAYMOND HILL RD
1600 SPAS 91030 595-H1
1600 SPAS 91030 565-H7
RAY MURRISET LN
- CHNO 91710 641-E5
RAYNETA DR
15000 Shrm 91403 561-H5
RAYNOL ST
4100 LA 90032 595-C6
RAYO AV
8600 SGAT 90280 705-F3
RAYO DE SOL DR
30600 MAL 90265 627-A7
RAYSACK AV
43800 LAN 93535 4106-A1
44000 LAN 93535 4016-A4
RAYSEL RD
2400 LA 90065 594-H3
RAYWOOD AV
400 MTBL 90640 676-F1
700 MTBL 90640 636-F7
RAYWOOD DR
- LAN 93536 4104-D4
13700 Brwd 90049 591-C7
RAYWOOD LN
16500 WHIT 90603 708-A6
RAYWOOD PL
900 MTBL 90640 636-F7
RAZZAK CIR
2500 DBAR 91765 679-J5
REA DR
500 MTBL 90640 676-F1
READCREST DR
9300 LA 90210 592-F5
READE PL
- StvR 91381 4640-B1
READING AV
7900 Wch 90045 702-J2
REAGAN RD
- LA 91342 482-A1
REAGAN ST
10600 LALM 90720 796-J3
REAL CT
23600 SCTA 91355 4550-G5
REALITOS DR
600 LACo 91750 570-H7
600 LVRN 91750 570-H7
REALTY ST
400 CRSN 90745 794-E3
S REALTY ST
300 CRSN 90745 794-D3
REATA LN
- RHLS 90274 823-E2
REATA PL
2500 DBAR 91765 679-J6
REATA RD
40200 PMDL 93550 4195-J3
REAZA PL
20300 WdHl 91364 560-D2
REBECCA AV
4600 GLDL 91214 504-E6
REBECCA CT
- POM 91766 640-J3
REBECCA DR
100 SDMS 91773 600-C4
1200 LHB 90631 708-C4
REBECCA ST
2200 WCOV 91792 679-A1
N REBECCA ST
100 POM 91768 640-H1
S REBECCA ST
100 POM 91766 640-H2
REBEL RD
- LACo 93551 4375-G1
RECADO RD
1400 LHH 90631 708-C3
RECINTO AV
2400 RowH 91748 679-A7
N RECORD AV
100 City 90063 635-E5
S RECORD AV
400 City 90063 635-E6
600 LACo 90023 635-E7
1000 LACo 90023 675-E1
N RECORD DR
700 City 90063 635-E5
RECREATION RD
21700 CRSN 90745 764-F6
RECREATION LODGE DR
- Echo 90026 594-F7
RECTOR PL
900 LA 90029 594-B6
RECYCLE WY
1800 SMCA 90404 671-H1
RED APPLE LN
1400 CHLS 91709 710-G2
REDBANK ST
11800 SunV 91352 532-G1
REDBAY AV
200 BREA 92821 709-D7
REDBEAM AV
19400 TOR 90503 763-A4
22100 TOR 90505 763-A7
REDBERRY ST
11200 ELMN 91733 637-D3
12100 ELMN 91732 637-D3
REDBIRD DR
6000 PRV 90660 676-E5
REDBIRD RD
- CHLS 91709 680-H2
RED BLUFF CT
- SCTA 91321 4550-H6
1400 SDMS 91773 570-C6
RED BLUFF DR
26000 CALB 91302 558-J4
RED BLUFF LN
1400 DBAR 91789 679-G4
RED BLUFF TR
21500 Top 90290 590-B5
REDBRIDGE LN
- Tarz 91356 560-G7
REDBUD LN
3000 PMDL 93551 4195-B2
RED BUD PL
27300 LACo 91387 4551-J4
REDBUD PL
1700 POM 91766 640-F3
17800 LACo 91744 638-J7
REDBUD ST
900 BREA 92821 709-C6
REDBUD RIDGE CIR
23200 SCTA 91354 4460-H5
REDBURN AV
600 LACo 91746 637-J6
REDBUSH LN
8100 PanC 91402 532-B2
RED CEDAR DR
20200 WAL 91789 639-E7
RED CEDAR PL
28500 SCTA 91390 4460-H3
RED CEDAR WY
- LACo 91387 4552-A4
REDCLIFF ST
1600 Echo 90026 594-C5
1700 LA 90039 594-C5
RED CLOUD DR
100 DBAR 91765 640-B7
RED COACH LN
2300 LHB 90631 708-B7
16000 LACo 90604 707-J7
16100 LACo 90604 708-A7
REDCOAT LN
4200 WLKV 91361 557-F6
REDDING AV
1700 LACo 91770 636-E4
REDELL AV
2100 LACo 91016 567-G7
REDESDALE AV
1600 Echo 90026 594-C5
1900 LA 90039 594-C5
S REDFERN AV
9500 ING 90301 703-B4
10100 Lenx 90304 703-B5
REDFIELD AV
400 HiPk 90042 595-D3
REDFIELD ST
- FUL 92833 738-D5
RED FIR LN
22600 DBAR 91765 680-A4
REDFORD LN
8000 LPMA 90623 767-B4
RED FOX ST
1500 LAN 93535 4016-C6
REDGATE CIR
21900 DBAR 91765 679-J4
RED GATE RANCH RD
33300 LACo 91390 4373-A2
REDGROVE WY
1500 UPL 91784 571-H4
RED GULCH RD
- LACo - (4560-A4
See Page 4470)
RED GUM RD
- LACo 91768 640-A1
RED HAT LN
3000 INDS 90601 637-C7
REDHAWK PL
- SCTA 91350 4551-D5
RED HAWK RD
400 WAL 91789 639-C7
REDINGTON ST
2600 PMDL 93551 4195-D6
REDLANDS AV
400 CLAR 91711 571-C6
REDLANDS ST
200 PdlR 90293 702-C3
7700 Wch 90045 702-C3
REDLEN AV
700 LACo 90601 637-G6
REDLINE DR
4100 LKWD 90713 766-F5
REDMAN AV
5700 WHIT 90606 676-J5
5700 LACo 90606 676-J5
RED MAPLE CT
- LACo 91387 4552-B4
REDMESA DR
10900 Chat 91311 499-J2
REDMONT AV
9800 Tuj 91042 503-J2
10000 Tuj 91042 504-A4
RED OAK CIR
- POM 91766 640-F5
RED OAK CT
- Cstc 91384 4369-E4
- SCTA 91321 4641-C2
RED OAK DR
5300 LA 90068 593-H2
REDONDA LN
700 LACo 90502 794-C3
REDONDELA DR
1800 RPV 90275 823-H1
REDONDO AV
700 LBCH 90804 795-J5
N REDONDO AV
- LBCH 90803 825-J1
100 MANB 90266 732-J4
300 LBCH 90814 795-J7
300 LBCH 90814 825-J1
1300 LBCH 90804 795-J4
1800 SIGH 90755 795-J4
1900 LBCH 90755 795-J4
2100 LBCH 90815 795-J4
2700 LBCH 90808 795-J4
S REDONDO AV
100 MANB 90266 732-J7
700 MANB 90266 762-J1
REDONDO BLVD
800 ING 90302 703-E1
900 ING 90302 673-E7
S REDONDO BLVD
1000 LA 90019 633-C5
1900 LA 90016 633-B7
2900 LA 90016 673-B1
3800 LA 90008 673-B2
REDONDO PL
2000 FUL 92835 738-F4
REDONDO WY
2300 GAR 90249 733-G6
REDONDO BEACH AV
3600 RBCH 90278 733-A5
REDONDO BEACH BLVD
2800 TOR 90247 733-D7
3000 RBCH 90278 733-D7
3000 RBCH 90278 763-C1
3100 TOR 90504 733-D7
3100 LACo 90506 733-D7
3300 LACo 90260 733-D7
4000 LNDL 90260 733-D7
4400 LNDL 90260 763-C1
17100 TOR 90260 733-D7
E REDONDO BEACH BLVD
100 LACo 90248 734-D5
600 LACo 90220 734-D5
1000 COMP 90220 734-D5
W REDONDO BEACH BLVD
100 LACo 90248 734-B5
500 LA 90248 734-B5
600 LA 90247 734-B5
1000 GAR 90247 734-B5
1300 GAR 90247 733-H6
1800 GAR 90249 733-H6
2000 TOR 90247 733-H6
RED PINE RD
- YBLN 92886 709-J7
RED PINE WY
- LACo 91390 4460-H2
RED PLUM CIR
- MONP 91755 636-C5
RED PLUM ST
13300 CRTS 90703 737-B6
REDPOST CT
1400 DBAR 91765 679-J3
RED RIVER CIR
500 WAL 91789 639-C7
RED ROCK CT
- Cstc 91384 4459-F2
REDROCK CT
2000 PMDL 93551 4195-C5
2100 LA 90039 594-C4
RED ROCK DR
1900 WAL 91789 639-H2
REDROCK LN
- POM 91766 640-G5
RED ROCK RD
23100 Top 90290 589-F4
23500 LACo 91302 589-E5
RED ROSE DR
3300 Enc 91436 561-E7
RED ROVER TR
- Actn 93510 4374-J3
RED ROVER MINE RD
33800 Actn 93510 4374-J3
RED SAIL CIR
1300 THO 91361 557-B6
REDSTART CT
20000 SCTA 91351 4551-E3
RED START DR
26700 SBdC 92397 (4652-A1
See Page 4651)
26700 LACo 92397 (4652-A1
See Page 4651)
REDSTONE CT
13200 CHLS 91709 680-J1
REDSTONE ST
12000 ELMN 91732 637-D3
REDTAIL CT
- WAL 91789 639-C5
RED TAIL DR
4200 PMDL 93551 4194-J7
4200 PMDL 93551 4195-A7
REDTAIL DR
- BREA 92823 709-H6
REDWILLOW LN
5000 LCF 91011 535-D3
RED WILLOW RD
1700 FUL 92833 738-B5
REDWING ST
18700 Tarz 91356 560-G2
19700 WdHl 91364 560-E2
REDWOOD AV
100 BREA 92821 709-B7
700 ELSG 90245 702-D7
3000 LYN 90262 705-A7
3300 LA 90066 672-A3
3900 CULC 90066 672-B5
4000 CULC 90292 672-B5
4000 LA 90292 672-B5
5600 PMDL 93551 4194-F1
17900 BLF 90706 766-D1
44100 LAN 93534 4015-J5
N REDWOOD AV
600 UPL 91786 601-H2
REDWOOD CIR
7300 LPMA 90623 767-D2
REDWOOD CT
- CRSN 90746 764-F1
- LACo 91390 4460-H2
W REDWOOD CT
- COV 91723 599-B6
REDWOOD DR
100 GLDR 91741 569-J5
200 PAS 91105 565-D6
1000 VeCo 93063 499-C4
2100 GLDR 91741 570-A5
16400 CRTS 90703 736-J6
REDWOOD LN
200 LHB 90631 738-E1
600 SDMS 91773 600-C3
3600 WCOV 91792 679-J2
REDWOOD RD
11000 SBdC 92372 (4472-D1
See Page 4471)
REDWOOD ST
500 BURB 91505 563-E4
9300 CYP 90630 767-C6
REDWOOD WY
- Cstc 91384 4369-H5
N REDWOOD WY
1500 UPL 91786 571-H7
1600 UPL 91784 571-H6
REDWOOD BLUFF LN
- StvR 91381 4550-C4
REDWOOD CANYON PL
- LACo 91390 4461-A4
REDWOOD GLEN RD
27900 SCTA 91354 4460-H4
REDWOOD VIEW DR
1200 POM 91766 640-F4
REED DR
800 CLAR 91711 601-B2
25600 LMTA 90717 793-G5
REED ST
100 COV 91723 599-B4
1700 RBCH 90278 762-J1
25800 LMTA 90717 793-H5
REEDER AV
900 COV 91724 599-F3
5000 LACo 91724 599-F3
N REEDER AV
100 COV 91724 599-F4
S REEDER AV
- COV 91724 599-F5
100 SDMS 91724 599-F5
REEDLEY ST
13100 Pcma 91331 532-D1
13200 PanC 91402 532-C2
REEDVALE LN
1700 Brwd 90049 631-E2
REEDVIEW DR
19700 RowH 91748 679-E5
REEF
1400 WCOV 91790 638-D2
REEF CT
100 LA 90292 701-J1
REEF MALL
100 LA 90292 701-J1
REEF ST
- LA 90292 701-J2
REEF WY
11800 VeCo 90265 625-F5
REEFTON CT
5800 LACo 91302 559-A3
REES ST
100 PdlR 90293 702-A3
REES WK
8300 PdlR 90293 702-B3
REESE CT
- PMDL 93552 4287-B3
100 Ven 90291 671-G5
REESE DR
6400 LBCH 90815 796-E6
N REESE PL
100 BURB 91506 563-F1
600 BURB 91506 533-E7
2200 BURB 91504 533-E4
S REESE PL
100 BURB 91506 563-F2
REESE RD
4600 TOR 90505 793-A1
REEVE DR
16100 LMRD 90638 738-A1
REEVE RD
7700 PRV 90660 706-E1
E REEVE ST
100 COMP 90220 734-J5
100 COMP 90220 735-A5
W REEVE ST
100 COMP 90220 734-G5
REEVER WY
- Alta 91001 535-H4
REEVES AV
- LBCH 90802 824-G3
700 SPed 90731 824-G3
16600 BLF 90706 736-A6
20400 CRSN 90810 764-J4
S REEVES DR
100 BHLS 90212 632-G3
REEVES PL
700 POM 91767 641-B1
800 GLDL 91205 564-F7
REEVES ST
1400 LA 90035 632-G4
REEVESBURY DR
9900 LA 90210 592-B3
REFINERY RD
- Cstc 91384 4459-J2
22200 Nwhl 91321 4641-C6
REFLECTION WY
- PMDL 93552 4287-B5
REFLECTIONS RD
- LACo 91724 639-H1
REFORMA RD
4600 WdHl 91364 559-H3
REFUGIO RD
16400 Enc 91436 561-E6
REGAL CT
1000 LVRN 91750 570-E7
2600 LAN 93535 4016-E5
REGAL LN
- PMDL 93551 4195-C6
REGAL PL
3600 LA 90068 563-B7
E REGAL WY
100 LBCH 90813 795-D6
W REGAL WY
100 LBCH 90813 795-D6
REGALADO ST
15300 HacH 91745 678-A4
REGAL CANYON DR
800 WAL 91789 639-G4
REGALO RD
4700 WdHl 91364 559-H4
REGAL OAK DR
4100 Enc 91436 561-G5
REGAL VISTA DR
3700 Shrm 91403 561-G6
REGAL WOODS PL
15700 Shrm 91403 561-G7
REGAN CT
16900 HacH 91745 678-F6
REGAN ST
100 SPed 90731 824-C3
REGATTA AV
9600 LACo 90604 707-F4
REGATTA WY
300 SLB 90740 826-E3
REGENCY CIR
2500 FUL 92833 738-B4
17600 BLF 90706 736-D7
REGENCY CT
3500 RowH 91748 708-J2
4900 ELMN 91731 597-E4
20800 WAL 91789 639-G4
REGENCY PL
36800 PMDL 93552 4287-B4
REGENCY ST
8100 LPMA 90623 767-B4
REGENCY WY
3000 PMDL 93551 4195-C5
17500 GrnH 91344 481-B6
REGENE ST
1500 POM 91766 641-A4
S REGENE ST
500 POM 91766 641-A2
REGENT AV
26000 LMTA 90717 793-H6
REGENT CIR
200 ING 90301 703-D2
REGENT ST
5900 HNTP 90255 674-H6
8700 LA 90034 632-G7
9700 LA 90034 672-F1
11200 LA 90066 672-D2
E REGENT ST
- ING 90301 703-D2
W REGENT ST
- ING 90301 703-B2
REGENT HILL TER
5500 PMDL 93551 4194-F2
REGENT PARK DR
900 LCF 91011 535-C7
REGENTS CT
4400 WLKV 91361 557-D6
REGENTS ST
1100 LAN 93534 4015-E3
REGENTS PARK CIR
24000 SCTA 91355 4550-F5
REGENTVIEW AV
11200 DWNY 90241 706-D7
13400 BLF 90706 736-D3
17800 BLF 90706 766-D1
REGGIO PL
1200 POM 91766 640-E3
REGIE LN
100 PMDL 93551 4195-J4
REGINA AV
17500 TOR 90504 763-D1
20300 TOR 90503 763-D4
S REGINA CT
8700 LA 90044 704-B3
REGINA ST
2300 WCOV 91792 639-B7
2300 WCOV 91792 679-A1
REGIO AV
6200 BPK 90620 737-F7
6300 BPK 90620 767-F1
REGIS AV
1000 CLAR 91711 601-B2
REGIS WY
8000 Wch 90045 702-E2
REGISTRY WY
- PMDL 93551 4195-B4
N REGWAY AV
2600 LBCH 90810 795-A2
REHNBORG DR
- BPK 90621 737-J6
- BPK 90621 738-A6
REICHLING LN
7400 LACo 90606 677-A6
8600 PRV 90660 676-F4
10400 LACo 90606 676-H5
REID AV
3000 CULC 90232 632-J7
REID ST
6200 Tuj 91042 504-C5
REIFER ST
8300 LACo 91770 636-F4
REIGATE RD
20200 Top 90290 630-A2
REIMS ST
400 POM 91767 601-A1
1200 CLAR 91711 601-A1
REINA CT
3600 CALB 91302 559-D7
REINHART AV
19000 CRSN 90746 764-E3
REINWAY CT
500 PAS 91101 565-J3
REIS ST
12900 LACo 90605 707-B3
14000 LACo 90604 707-D5
REISLING AV
- PMDL 93551 4104-D7
REISNER WY
5300 SGAT 90280 705-F3
REITER DR
1800 PAS 91107 566-C5
REITHE AV
600 LACo 91302 589-A7
600 LACo 91302 629-A1
REJECT RD
- SCTA 91350 4551-A5
REKLAW DR
3700 LA 91604 562-H6
RELA WY
5000 LACo 93536 4104-H7
RELIANCE ST
13000 Pcma 91331 502-D7
13300 Pcma 91331 532-C1
REMAH VISTA DR
1500 GLDL 91207 564-F1
REMBERT LN
9400 LA 90210 592-F3
REMBRANDT ST
43600 LAN 93535 4106-B1
REMER CT
- SCTA 91350 4551-D5
REMER ST
9600 SELM 91733 637-A4
REMEY AV
3400 BALD 91706 597-J7
3400 BALD 91706 598-A7
REMICK AV
8500 SunV 91352 532-F1
8800 SunV 91352 502-E7
9000 Pcma 91331 502-B3
10900 LA 91340 502-A2
REMINGTON RD
30300 Cstc 91384 4459-B2
REMINGTON ST
11500 LA 91342 482-G7
12200 Pcma 91331 502-F2
REMMET AV
6800 CanP 91303 530-A5
7500 LA 91304 530-A1
10100 Chat 91311 500-A3
REMO AV
18600 RowH 91748 679-A4
REMORA DR
2300 RowH 91748 678-G6
REMORA DR
3100 OrCo 92649 826-J7
REMSEN ST
- SCTA 91321 4641-B4
REMSTOY DR
5100 LA 90032 595-F4
REMUDA DR
1300 GLDR 91740 569-H6
REMY AV
8300 Win 91306 530-D2
REMY PL
2900 BURB 91504 533-F3
RENAISSANCE DR
- Tuj 91042 503-J2
RENAISSANCE PL
- WLKV 91362 557-G6
RENAISSANCE WY
- ING 90305 703-F3
RENAULT ST
17400 INDS 91744 678-H1
17400 LACo 91744 678-H1
18100 LACo 91744 679-A1
RENDALIA ST
9000 BLF 90706 736-A5
RENDALL PL
1500 Echo 90026 594-C6
E RENDINA ST
6400 LBCH 90815 796-E5
RENDOVA ST
12000 ART 90701 736-H7
RENEE CT
1800 WCOV 91792 638-J5
RENEE DR
28100 AGRH 91301 558-C7
RENEE ST
1600 LAN 93535 4016-C5
RENE VELUZAT BRYCE CT
- SCTA 91321 4551-F6
RENFREW RD
12200 Brwd 90049 631-F2
RENNELL AV
400 SDMS 91773 599-J3
N RENNELL AV
100 SDMS 91773 599-J2
RENNIE AV
200 Ven 90291 671-G4
RENO AV
5800 TEML 91780 596-H3
6300 LACo 91775 596-H1
N RENO ST
100 Echo 90026 634-B1
300 Echo 90026 594-C7
S RENO ST
100 LA 90057 634-B1
RENOA AV
10300 SGAT 90280 705-G5
RENOAK WY
200 ARCD 91007 567-B4
RENOIR LN
- SCTA 91355 4550-E3
RENO RIDGE DR
1100 DBAR 91765 640-C4
RENO RIDGE LN
900 DBAR 91765 640-C5
RENOVO ST
4900 LA 90032 595-E5
RENOWN TER
1500 WCOV 91792 638-H5
RENSHAW ST
1800 SDMS 91724 599-F5
1800 COV 91724 599-F5
20500 LACo 91724 599-F5
RENSSELAER DR
2100 ALH 91803 635-J2
E RENTON ST
900 CRSN 90745 764-F7
RENTON MINE RD
- AVA 90704 5923-J5
- LACo 90704 5923-J5
RENVILLE ST
11400 LKWD 90715 766-G4
12400 LKWD 90715 767-A4
RENWICK CT
26600 SCTA 91350 4460-J5
RENWICK RD
16700 LACo 91702 598-H2
17100 AZU 91702 598-H2
E RENWICK RD
100 GLDR 91740 599-E2
17600 LACo 91702 598-J2
17700 AZU 91702 598-J2
17700 AZU 91702 599-A2
17700 LACo 91702 599-A2
W RENWICK RD
100 AZU 91702 598-J2
1400 SDMS 91773 599-H2
19500 GLDR 91740 599-D2
RENZ CIR
2600 FUL 92833 738-B5
REPETTO AV
2300 MTBL 90640 676-B1
6500 LACo 90640 676-B1
REPETTO ST
5100 ELA 90022 635-H6
5800 MTBL 90640 635-H6
REPOSA LN
2800 Alta 91001 536-B5
REPOSADO DR
100 LHH 90631 708-D1
800 LHH 90631 678-E7
REPPERT CT
2600 LA 90046 593-A2
REPTON ST
6300 HiPk 90042 595-E1
REPUBLIC ST
100 LA 90012 634-G3
REQUA AV
3900 CLAR 91711 601-A1
RESEDA BLVD
3000 Tarz 91356 560-J2
6000 Res 91335 530-J3
6000 Res 91335 560-J2
8200 Nor 91324 530-J3
8800 Nor 91324 500-J7
10300 Nor 91326 500-J3
11600 Nor 91326 480-H7
RESERVOIR AV
13100 LACo 91390 (4372-J4
See Page 4281)
13100 LACo 91390 4373-A4
RESERVOIR DR E
3400 LBCH 90804 795-J4
RESERVOIR DR W
1800 LBCH 90804 795-J4
1800 SIGH 90755 795-J4
RESERVOIR RD
- Cstc 91384 4460-A3
29400 Valy 93563 4469-F5
RESERVOIR ST
1900 Echo 90026 594-D7
N RESERVOIR ST
200 POM 91767 641-B1
500 POM 91767 601-B7
S RESERVOIR ST
100 POM 91766 641-B2
100 POM 91767 641-B2
12800 CHNO 91710 641-C6
RESIN PL
15600 SFSP 90670 737-C5
RESOLANO DR
600 PacP 90272 630-G5
RESORT LN
1300 POM 91768 600-F7
RESORT ST
1400 UPL 91784 571-H5
RESORT WY
- PMDL 93551 4195-A3
RESSER DR
4600 LA 90032 595-D5
RESTAURANT DR
- POM 91768 600-E6
RESTHAVEN DR
2400 Eagl 90041 564-J6
RETA ST
3300 GLDL 91214 504-E6
RETFORD ST
1300 COV 91724 599-E4
RETFORD KNOLL
400 COV 91724 599-F4
RETREAT CT
3200 LACo 90265 629-A5
3200 MAL 90265 629-A5
RETSINA ST
- PMDL 93551 4104-D7
REUNION CT
- SCTA 91354 4460-G4
REVA CIR
13400 CRTS 90703 767-C1
REVA CT
5000 LKWD 90712 766-B1
REVA PL
10700 CRTS 90703 766-E1
13500 CRTS 90703 767-C1
REVA ST
10500 BLF 90706 766-D1
12300 CRTS 90703 766-J1
13300 CRTS 90703 767-C1
E REVA ST
5900 LKWD 90713 766-D1
REVAL CT
300 BURB 91505 563-E4
REVELLO DR
17400 PacP 90272 630-F6
REVERE AL
1700 PAS 91106 566-C4
REVERE AV
800 MTBL 90640 636-E6
3600 LA 90039 594-D1
3900 LA 90039 564-D7
REVERE CT
- CHNO 91710 641-F5
REVERE PL
4200 CULC 90232 672-G2
REVERE ST
4800 CHNO 91710 641-F5
19400 CRTS 90703 766-G2
REVERE WY
- AGRH 91301 588-E1
27400 Ago 91301 588-E1
REVERIE RD
9300 Tuj 91042 503-J6
9400 Tuj 91042 504-A5
REVLON DR
4800 LCF 91011 535-D4
REVUELTA WY
10400 BelA 90077 592-B7
REX CT
- SCTA 91387 4462-D6
700 POM 91767 601-A3
5600 WHIT 90601 677-C4
REX RD
8300 PRV 90660 676-D6
REX ST
13900 LA 91342 482-B2
14600 LA 91342 481-J4

STREET Block City ZIP Pg-Grid

REXALL AV
8200 LACo 90606 706-H1
REXBON RD
10800 GrnH 91344 481-A7
REXFORD AV
1000 PAS 91107 566-H2
REXFORD CT
800 DBAR 91765 680-E1
REXFORD DR
1100 LA 90035 632-G4
9300 BHLS 90210 632-G4
N REXFORD DR
100 BHLS 90210 632-F1
600 BHLS 90210 592-E6
S REXFORD DR
100 BHLS 90212 632-G3
REXFORD PL
27100 SCTA 91354 4460-G7
REXTON ST
12600 NRWK 90650 737-A2
REXWOOD AV
13500 BALD 91706 598-A7
REXWOOD ST
1600 WCOV 91790 638-C1
14000 BALD 91706 598-B7
REY ALBERTO CT
25000 CALB 91302 559-C6
REYBURN LN
- SCTA 91354 4460-F6
REY DE COPAS LN
28200 MAL 90265 667-G2
REYDON ST
8900 DWNY 90242 735-J2
REYES
2500 LACo 90220 765-A1
REYES AV
18600 RDom 90221 765-B2
REYES DR
600 INDS 91789 679-G2
4200 Tarz 91356 560-H5
REYES ADOBE RD
4900 AGRH 91301 557-G3
REYES ADOBE WY
- BqtC 91354 4460-E2
REYNARD AV
5000 GLDL 91214 504-D5
REYNIER AV
2600 LA 90034 632-H6
5100 LadH 90056 673-A5
REYNOLDS AV
1800 LACo 91770 636-F4
1800 RSMD 91770 636-F4
3300 LA 90032 595-C6
3500 LA 90031 595-C6
REYNOLDS DR
1200 GLDL 91205 564-F6
2800 BURB 91504 533-F3
20400 TOR 90503 763-B5
22200 TOR 90505 763-B7
REYNOLDS LN
400 RBCH 90278 762-J2
400 HMB 90254 762-J2
REYNOLDS RD
5000 TOR 90505 793-B1
18600 TOR 90505 763-B7
REYNOLDS WY
1300 GLDR 91740 599-E1
REYNOSA DR
1800 TOR 90501 793-H1
REYNOSO PKWY
- BREA 92821 708-J5
RHAPSODY DR
4800 VeCo 91377 557-G2
RHAPSODY RD
20100 LACo 91789 679-E5
RHEA AV
5300 Tarz 91356 560-H1
6300 Res 91335 530-H2
8200 Nor 91324 530-H2
8900 Nor 91324 500-H5
E RHEA ST
300 LBCH 90806 795-E4
RHEA VISTA DR
7900 WHIT 90602 677-D7
7900 WHIT 90602 707-D1
RHEEM AV
8600 SGAT 90280 705-D3
RHINE PL
18600 CRTS 90703 766-E2
RHINESTONE DR
14900 Shrm 91403 561-J6
RHODA CIR
20100 CRTS 90703 766-J4
RHODA ST
5700 Enc 91316 561-B1
20500 WdHl 91367 560-D1
RHODA WY
5000 CULC 90230 672-G4
RHODE ISLAND AV
12000 WLA 90025 631-H5
RHODELIA AV
500 CLAR 91711 601-B3
4400 LACo 91711 571-B7
RHODES AL
1000 PAS 91106 566-A4
RHODES AV
3800 LA 91604 562-F5
4800 LA 91607 562-F2
5900 LA 91607 532-F7
6000 NHol 91606 532-F6
6700 NHol 91605 532-F2
RHODES LN
3600 BALD 91706 597-J7
RHODES PL
12900 CHNO 91710 641-F7
RHODES ST
1800 HMB 90254 762-H1
RHODESIA AV
10500 Sunl 91040 503-H1
RHODODENDRON DR
15300 SCTA 91387 4462-E7
RHONA CT
5300 AGRH 91301 557-H5
RHONA PL
- Saug 91350 4461-E5
RHONE DR
30100 RPV 90275 822-H3
RHUBARB LN
- PMDL 93551 4285-E3
RHYOLITE CT
2200 CHLS 91709 680-J7
RIAL LN
1800 BelA 90077 592-A4
RIALTO AV
400 Ven 90291 671-H6
RIALTO CT
600 Ven 90291 671-J5
RIALTO DR
43700 LAN 93535 4106-D1
RIALTO ST
11700 SunV 91352 532-G1
RIALTO WY
900 POM 91767 601-B7
RIBBON ST
- PMDL 93552 4287-D3
RICARDO CT
2600 LVRN 91750 600-H3
RICARDO ST
1100 Boyl 90033 635-C3
RICCI AV
100 WAL 91789 679-E1
RICE ST
5700 HiPk 90042 565-C7
RICH LN
2000 RPV 90275 823-G5
RICH ST
2600 LA 90039 594-F4
RICHARD CIR
4400 LA 90032 595-G4
RICHARD DR
4400 LA 90032 595-F4
RICHARD PL
1200 GLDL 91206 564-G4
RICHARD ST
1700 POM 91767 601-C6
1800 BURB 91504 533-F4
RICHARD M NIXON DR
13300 WHIT 90602 677-D7
RICHARDSON DR
3600 LA 90065 594-H3
RICHARDSON LN
500 GLDR 91741 569-D4
RICHBROOK DR
600 LACo 91711 601-A2
600 POM 91767 601-A2
RICHBURN AV
300 LACo 91744 679-B2
RICHDALE AV
1900 HacH 91745 678-B3
RICHELIEU AV
2200 LA 90032 635-E1
2400 LA 90032 595-D7
RICHELIEU PL
4600 LA 90032 635-D1
RICHELIEU TER
4600 LA 90032 595-D7
RICHEON AV
9600 DWNY 90240 706-A2
10600 DWNY 90241 706-A4
11500 DWNY 90241 705-J5
12000 DWNY 90242 705-H6
RICHEVILLE ST
- PMDL 93552 4287-D1
RICHEY DR
2200 LCF 91011 534-H1
RICHFIELD ST
7200 PRM 90723 735-F3
RICHFORD AV
200 LACo 91744 678-J1
RICHGROVE CT
31900 WLKV 91361 557-C6
RICHLAND AV
200 GLDL 91206 564-H4
2200 LFlz 90027 594-B2
10700 LA 90064 632-D6
RICHLAND PL
1000 PAS 91103 565-F2
RICHLEE AV
10200 SGAT 90280 705-G5
RICHMAN AV
500 FUL 92832 738-G7
N RICHMAN AV
100 FUL 92832 738-G6
1000 FUL 92835 738-G5
S RICHMAN AV
100 FUL 92832 738-G7
RICHMAN KNOLL
1000 FUL 92835 738-F4
RICHMOND CT
9900 TEML 91780 597-A5
25900 LACo 91302 558-J3
RICHMOND DR
900 CLAR 91711 601-B2
5100 PRV 90660 676-G4
RICHMOND RD
300 LCF 91011 535-D4
RICHMOND ST
100 ELSG 90245 732-E1
600 ELSG 90245 702-E7
900 Boyl 90033 634-J3
900 Boyl 90033 635-A2
900 LA 90031 635-A2
4300 CHNO 91710 641-E7
37400 PMDL 93552 4286-J3
RICHMOND WY
9800 TEML 91780 597-A5
N RICHMONT DR
100 ANA 92801 767-J5
RICHTER LN
1900 PMDL 93550 4376-F4
RICHTON ST
4900 MTCL 91763 601-F3
RICHVALE DR
14600 LMRD 90638 707-F7
15500 LACo 90604 707-H6
16100 LACo 90604 708-A6
RICHVIEW DR
3100 HacH 91745 678-B6
RICHVILLE DR
25900 TOR 90505 793-F5
RICHWOOD AV
3000 ELMN 91732 637-D2
3800 ELMN 91732 597-F5
RICHWOOD DR
12200 Brwd 90049 631-F2
RICKENBACKER RD
5600 BELL 90201 675-G5
5700 CMRC 90040 675-G5
RICKI CT
- Saug 91350 4461-E5
RICKIE LN
6300 PMDL 93551 4104-E7
RICO PL
1600 PVE 90274 792-F6
RIDA ST
3100 PAS 91107 566-G3
RIDDLE AV
1900 COMP 90059 734-E2
RIDEAU ST
9900 LACo 90601 677-A2
RIDEOUT PL
12100 WHIT 90601 677-B4
RIDE OUT WY
800 FUL 92835 738-F2
RIDEOUT WY
5200 WHIT 90601 677-B4
RIDER CT
500 CLAR 91711 571-C7
RIDERWOOD AV
1100 HacH 91745 678-A1
1200 HacH 91745 677-J2
RIDERWOOD DR
8800 Sunl 91040 503-E3
RIDERWOOD VW E
9100 Sunl 91040 503-E3
RIDERWOOD VW W
9100 Sunl 91040 503-E2
RIDGE AV
13000 LACo 91390 4373-A4
RIDGE CIR
12300 Brwd 90049 591-F3
RIDGE CT
5700 LCF 91011 535-D1
RIDGE DR
- BRAD 91010 568-A3
600 GLDL 91206 564-J2
2000 Brwd 90049 591-F4
RIDGE MTWY
1500 GLDL 91208 534-J7
1500 GLDL 91208 564-J1
1500 GLDL 91208 565-A1
2500 GLDL 91206 535-A6
2500 GLDL 91208 535-A7
RIDGE RD
- SCTA 91350 4551-B4
12400 Brwd 90049 591-F4
13700 WHIT 90601 677-E6
RIDGE WY
1300 PAS 91106 596-A1
1400 Echo 90026 634-E1
RIDGEBLUFF CT
27900 RPV 90275 792-J7
RIDGEBROOK CT
27900 RPV 90275 792-J7
RIDGEBROOK DR
5700 AGRH 91301 557-H4
RIDGEBYRNE CT
6400 RPV 90275 792-H7
RIDGECLIFF LN
1000 LCF 91011 535-B1
RIDGECOVE CT
27900 RPV 90275 792-J7
RIDGE CREST CIR
- POM 91766 640-G4
RIDGECREST CIR
19000 WAL 91789 639-B7
RIDGECREST CT
- BqtC 91354 4460-E3
- DBAR 91765 680-C1
1200 MONP 91754 635-G4
RIDGE CREST LN
13300 CRTS 90703 767-C2
RIDGECREST RD
1300 BHLS 90210 592-F5
1300 LA 90210 592-F5
RIDGECREST ST
700 MONP 91754 635-H4
RIDGECREST WY
1500 MONP 91754 635-H4
RIDGECROFT CT
28400 RPV 90275 792-H7
RIDGEDALE DR
1000 BHLS 90210 592-D7
1000 BelA 90077 592-D7
RIDGE ESTATES CT
19900 WAL 91789 639-E7
RIDGEFALLS CT
28300 RPV 90275 792-H7
RIDGEFERN CT
28100 RPV 90275 792-H7
RIDGEFIELD CT
21600 SCTA 91350 4461-B5
RIDGEFIELD DR
500 CLAR 91711 571-A7
RIDGE FIRE RD
- WHIT 90601 677-C3
RIDGEFORD DR
3200 WLKV 91361 557-D7
RIDGEFOREST CT
28000 RPV 90275 792-J7
RIDGEGATE DR
6000 RPV 90275 792-H7
11300 LACo 90601 677-C2
RIDGEGATE LN
40800 PMDL 93551 4194-G2
RIDGEGLADE CT
6300 RPV 90275 792-H7
RIDGEGROVE DR
27800 SCTA 91350 4461-B6
RIDGEHAVEN CT
28100 RPV 90275 792-H7
RIDGEHAVEN DR
700 LHB 90631 708-B7
1100 LHB 90631 738-B1
RIDGELAND RD
2400 TOR 90505 793-F6
RIDGE LATERAL
- GLDL 91206 535-A7
- GLDL 91208 535-A7
S RIDGELEY DR
600 LA 90036 633-C3
1000 LA 90019 633-C4
2000 LA 90016 633-B6
3500 LA 90016 673-B1
3800 LA 90008 673-B2
RIDGE LINE RD
22400 DBAR 91765 680-A5
RIDGELINE ST
40400 PMDL 93551 4194-G2
RIDGEMAR CT
6300 RPV 90275 792-H7
RIDGEMIST ST
40000 LACo 93591 4199-J2
RIDGEMONT CIR
- LVRN 91750 570-H5
RIDGEMONT CT
2000 UPL 91784 571-H5
RIDGEMONT DR
2100 LA 90046 592-H3
2100 BHLS 90210 592-H3
3800 MAL 90265 629-B6
RIDGEMONT LN
200 WAL 91789 639-H7
RIDGEMONT WY
2300 UPL 91784 571-H3
RIDGEMOOR DR
3800 LA 91604 562-J6
RIDGE OAK DR
5500 LA 90068 593-H2
RIDGE PARK DR
16900 HacH 91745 678-F4
RIDGEPATH CT
6300 RPV 90275 792-H7
RIDGEPINE DR
2600 LaCr 91214 504-G5
RIDGEPOINT CT
28100 RPV 90275 792-H7
RIDGE POINT DR
3100 LACo 91765 679-G7
12500 Brwd 90049 591-E4
RIDGE ROUTE RD
31300 Cstc 91384 4369-G4
33000 Cstc 91384 4279-B3
33000 LACo - 4279-B3
RIDGESIDE CIR
1000 MONP 91754 635-J4
RIDGESIDE DR
700 MNRO 91016 567-H1
800 MONP 91754 635-J4
RIDGE TERRACE LN
200 MTBL 90640 636-F5
RIDGETHORN CT
28100 RPV 90275 792-H7
RIDGE TOP LN
- Cstc 91384 4369-E4
RIDGETOP RANCH RD
9900 LACo 93551 4193-G4
RIDGETREE AV
19800 WAL 91789 679-E2
RIDGE VALE DR
26200 SCTA 91321 4551-G5
RIDGEVIEW AV
2000 Eagl 90041 565-A7
2300 Eagl 90041 564-J7
2500 RowH 91748 679-C7
RIDGEVIEW CIR E
37800 PMDL 93550 4286-A2
RIDGEVIEW CIR S
100 PMDL 93550 4285-J2
100 PMDL 93550 4286-A2
RIDGEVIEW CIR W
37800 PMDL 93550 4285-J2
RIDGEVIEW CT
- DBAR 91765 680-D1
15000 CHLS 91709 680-G5
RIDGE VIEW DR
- AZU 91702 568-J3
7300 LAN 93536 4104-C5
28200 SCTA 91387 4552-A1
RIDGEVIEW DR
- LVRN 91750 570-H5
1500 GLDL 91207 564-E1
14500 CHLS 91709 680-J5
W RIDGEVIEW DR
800 Alta 91001 535-F4
RIDGEVIEW LN
- LACo 90606 677-A7
15900 LMRD 90638 737-J2
15900 LMRD 90638 738-A2
RIDGE VIEW RD
3400 SBdC 92371 (4562-J5
See Page 4471)
RIDGEVIEW ST
4900 LVRN 91750 570-G6
RIDGEVIEW TER
- SIGH 90755 795-H4
1300 FUL 92831 738-J5
RIDGEWAY CT
- Cstc 91384 4459-B3
4800 THO 91362 557-F1
RIDGEWAY DR
1500 GLDL 91202 564-D1
7400 BPK 90620 767-E3
29500 AGRH 91301 557-J3
RIDGEWAY RD
1500 SMRO 91108 596-D1
2200 SMRO 91108 566-D7
17600 GrnH 91344 501-B1
17600 GrnH 91344 481-A7
RIDGEWAY ST
100 POM 91768 640-D1
1300 POM 91768 600-C7
N RIDGEWAY ST
100 ANA 92801 767-J5
S RIDGEWAY WY
100 ANA 92804 767-J6
RIDGEWOOD CT
- POM 91766 640-F5
4500 PMDL 93552 4286-J2
4500 PMDL 93552 4287-A2
RIDGEWOOD DR
2400 WCOV 91792 638-J6
RIDGEWOOD LN
500 PAS 91103 565-G3
N RIDGEWOOD PL
100 LA 90004 593-G7
100 LA 90004 633-G1
700 LA 90038 593-G6
1300 Hlwd 90028 593-G5
S RIDGEWOOD PL
100 LA 90004 633-G1
RIDGEWOOD RD
4500 LACo 91390 4373-B3
RIDGEWOOD ST
900 Bxby 90807 765-E4
RIDGLEA AV
4800 BPK 90621 737-J5
8300 BPK 90621 738-A4
RIDGWAY LN
500 LHB 90631 708-C5
RIDING LN
100 Top 90290 590-A6
RIDLEY AV
800 HacH 91745 638-A7
900 HacH 91745 678-A1
1200 HacH 91745 677-J1
RIDPATH DR
8200 LA 90046 593-A3
8300 LA 90046 592-J4
RIEGEL DR
2300 ALH 91803 636-A1
RIEGO DR
21100 DBAR 91765 679-G7
RIENDO LN
1500 LCF 91011 535-A2
RIESHEL ST
9600 PRV 90660 676-G6
RIESS RD
900 VeCo 93063 499-B4
RIFLE RANGE RD
- AVA 90704 5923-G5
RIGALI AV
3900 LA 90039 564-C7
RIGEL DR
27900 SCTA 91351 4551-E1
RIGGER RD
30500 AGRH 91301 557-G5
E RIGGIN ST
100 MONP 91755 636-B5
W RIGGIN ST
100 MONP 91754 636-A6
500 MONP 91754 635-J6
RIGGS PL
6300 Wch 90045 672-G7
RIGOLETTO ST
4900 WdHl 91364 559-H3
RIGSBY ST
100 LHB 90631 708-B6
RILEY CT
- PMDL 93552 4287-B4
RILEY ST
- LACo 91390 4461-G2
RIM LN
20700 DBAR 91789 679-G5
RIM RD
500 PAS 91107 566-G2
2200 DUAR 91010 568-C3
RIMBANK AV
5700 PRV 90660 676-H5
RIM CANYON RD
7800 Sunl 91040 503-H1
RIM CREST CIR
2300 THO 91361 557-B4
RIM CREST DR
2200 THO 91361 557-B4
RIMCREST DR
1900 GLDL 91202 564-E1
1900 GLDL 91207 564-E1
2000 GLDL 91207 534-E7
2100 GLDL 91202 534-E7
RIMCREST RD
2500 BREA 92821 709-E6
RIMFIELD AV
41500 LACo 93536 4104-J7
RIMFIELD DR
41000 PMDL 93551 4194-H1
RIM FIRE LN
22100 DBAR 91765 679-J6
22100 DBAR 91765 680-A6
RIMFORD DR
15100 LACo 93532 4102-E4
RIMFORD PL
24300 DBAR 91765 680-D4
RIMGATE CIR
- POM 91766 640-G5
RIMGATE DR
10300 LACo 90604 707-E5
RIMGROVE DR
400 LACo 91744 638-H6
RIMHILL RD
3200 GLDL 91214 504-E5
RIMHURST AV
100 COV 91724 599-E4
1300 GLDR 91740 599-E2
4800 LACo 91724 599-E3
RIMMELE DR
9800 LA 90210 592-C3
RIMMER AV
1200 PacP 90272 631-A4
RIMPATH DR
21100 LACo 91724 599-H5
RIMPAU BLVD
5100 LACo 90043 673-E6
5800 LA 90043 673-E6
S RIMPAU BLVD
200 LA 90004 633-F2
300 LA 90020 633-F2
600 LA 90005 633-F2
600 LA 90010 633-F2
900 LA 90019 633-E4
1900 LA 90016 633-D6
3000 LA 90016 673-C1
RIM RIDGE RD
20200 WAL 91789 639-E7
RIMROCK AV
12800 CHLS 91709 640-H7
RIMROCK CIR
- FUL 92833 738-A3
800 WAL 91789 639-C6
RIM ROCK CT
- LACo 91390 4460-J1
RIMROCK DR
11700 LMRD 90638 707-F7
RIM ROCK LN
27800 SCTA 91351 4551-E1
RIMSDALE AV
900 COV 91722 598-J4
5500 LACo 91702 598-F1
N RIMSDALE AV
300 COV 91722 598-J3
S RIMSDALE DR
1000 WCOV 91791 638-J2
RIMSIDE AV
- PMDL 93550 4376-A7
RIMVALE AV
43700 LAN 93534 4105-F1
RIMVIEW DR
4100 LACo 90601 677-C2
RIMVIEW LN
300 BREA 92821 709-E6
RIMVIEW PL
20300 LACo 91789 679-F7
RIMWOOD DR
16900 WHIT 90603 708-B3
RINALDI PL
18100 Nor 91326 500-J1
RINALDI ST
14600 LA 91340 481-J7
14600 LA 91340 501-G1
14800 MsnH 91345 501-G1
15500 GrnH 91344 501-A1
17900 Nor 91326 500-D2
17900 Nor 91326 501-A1
20700 Chat 91311 500-B2
N RINARD AV
4500 LACo 91722 599-A4
RINCON AV
4100 Mont 91020 534-H3
8400 SunV 91352 532-G1
8700 SunV 91352 502-F7
9300 Pcma 91331 502-C3
11100 LA 91340 502-A1
11300 LA 91340 501-J1
11600 LA 91340 481-J7
11600 LA 91342 481-J7
RINCON DR
1400 LHH 90631 708-G3
10800 WHIT 90606 676-J5
10900 WHIT 90606 677-A5
11100 LACo 90606 677-A5
RINCON LN
800 PVE 90274 792-H4
RINCONIA DR
2400 LA 90068 593-F2
RINCONIA PL
2700 LA 90068 593-F2
RINCON RED BOX TKTR
- LACo - (506-E3
See Page 505)
- LACo - 507-B5
- LACo - (508-F7
See Page 507)
- LACo - 509-D6
- LACo - 537-H1
- LACo - (538-A1
See Page 507)
- LACo - (539-A1
See Page 509)
RINDGE AV
6900 PdlR 90293 702-B3
RINDGE LN
500 RBCH 90278 763-A2
2000 RBCH 90278 733-A7
RINDGE MESA RD
- LACo 90265 629-C5
- MAL 90265 629-C5
RINETTI LN
4500 LCF 91011 535-C4
E RING ST
7600 LBCH 90808 766-H7
RINGBIT RD E
- RHLS 90274 823-E4
RINGBIT RD W
- RHLS 90274 823-D4
RINGE CT
1100 POM 91767 601-C7
RINGER PL
15300 HacH 91745 678-B2
RINGGOLD DR
- LA 90032 595-F4
RINGLING ST
18600 Tarz 91356 560-H3
RINGSTEM AV
42000 LACo 93536 4104-D5
RINGWOOD AV
10800 SFSP 90670 706-G6
11500 NRWK 90650 706-F7
RINZLER ST
16900 LA 91343 501-D5
16900 Nor 91325 501-D5
RIO
- CMRC 90040 706-B1
RIO AV
4600 NLB 90805 765-D4
RIO CT
17600 RowH 91748 678-G5
RIO ST
600 LA 90023 634-J6
4500 LVRN 91750 570-H7
RIO WY
5700 BPK 90620 767-D2
RIO BLANCO AV
1200 MTBL 90640 636-E6
RIO BLANCO RD
14500 LMRD 90638 737-F3
RIO BONITO DR
1800 RowH 91748 678-H5
RIO BOSQUE DR
27000 SCTA 91354 4460-H7
RIO BRANCA DR
2400 HacH 91745 678-C5
RIO BUENO CT
22700 SCTA 91354 4460-H7
RIO CHICO DR
22700 SCTA 91354 4460-H7
RIO CLARA DR
22800 SCTA 91354 4460-H6
RIO CLARO DR
2800 HacH 91745 678-A5
RIO DELL ST
8600 RSMD 91770 596-G6
RIO DEL SOL AV
600 MTBL 90640 676-G1
N RIO DEL SOL ST
800 MTBL 90640 636-G7
800 MTBL 90640 676-G1
E RIO DE ORO DR
17500 WCOV 91791 638-J3
RIODOSA TR
5500 VeCo 91377 557-J1
RIO FLORA PL
7100 DWNY 90241 705-J3
RIO FLORIDA DR
15800 WHIT 90603 707-J2
RIO GARZA DR
27100 SCTA 91354 4460-H6
RIO GRANDE ST
400 PAS 91104 565-J1
600 PAS 91104 566-A1
RIO GUSTO CT
22700 SCTA 91354 4550-H1
RIO HONDO AV
3300 ELMN 91731 596-J7
3300 ELMN 91731 636-J1
3500 RSMD 91770 596-J6
4800 TEML 91780 596-J3
RIO HONDO CIR
- LMRD 90638 737-J2
RIO HONDO DR
10900 DWNY 90241 705-H3
RIO HONDO PKWY
9700 ELMN 91733 637-A1
11600 ELMN 91732 597-F4
RIO HONDO PL
7300 DWNY 90241 705-J3
RIO LEMPA DR
2700 HacH 91745 678-D6
RIO LINDA DR
6300 RPV 90275 792-H6
RIO LOBO WY
- BqtC 91354 4460-F2
RIO LOBOS RD
22800 DBAR 91765 680-B2
RIO NORTE DR
- BqtC 91354 4460-E4
RIO PECOS DR
26900 SCTA 91354 4460-H7
RIO POCO
- LACo 91390 4373-E7
RIO PRADO DR
27000 SCTA 91354 4460-H7
RIO RANCH WY
- BqtC 91354 4460-F3
RIO RANCHO RD
100 POM 91766 640-J5
RIO RANDO LN
- Actn 93510 4375-E7
RIO REYES CT
22700 SCTA 91354 4550-J1
RIOS ST
20900 WdHl 91364 560-B5
RIO SECO DR
18100 RowH 91748 678-J5
18500 RowH 91748 679-A5
RIO TAJO CT
22700 SCTA 91354 4460-H7
RIO VERDE DR
2000 LHB 90631 708-B5
E RIO VERDE DR
1400 WCOV 91791 638-H1
1900 WCOV 91791 639-A1
RIO VISTA AV
1200 LA 90023 634-J7
1400 LA 90023 674-J1
RIPLEY AV
1700 RBCH 90278 762-J3
1800 RBCH 90278 763-A2
RIPLEY LN
1600 RBCH 90278 762-J3
RIPON AV
15700 BLF 90706 736-D5
RIPPLE PL
2800 LA 90039 594-F3
RIPPLE ST
1800 LA 90039 594-E3
RIPTON RD
14800 LACo 93532 4102-F4
RISA DR
2200 GLDL 91208 534-H6
RISA PL
1800 GLDL 91208 534-H6
RISE CT
- PMDL 93551 4194-H2
RISING DR
4000 LA 90032 595-C7
RISING GLEN PL
8800 LA 90069 592-H5
RISING GLEN RD
1400 LA 90069 592-H4
RISING HILL RD
- POM 91766 640-G4
RISINGHILL RD
4300 Alta 91001 535-G2
4900 LACo - 535-G2
RISING STAR DR
2600 DBAR 91765 679-J6
RISLEY ST
15600 WHIT 90603 707-H5
16100 WHIT 90603 708-A5
RISNER WY
600 LHB 90631 738-D2
RISTA DR
5700 AGRH 91301 557-J4
RITA AV
5900 HNTP 90255 674-J7
RITA LN
3400 WCOV 91792 639-A7
RITA ST
700 RBCH 90277 763-A6
38100 PMDL 93550 4286-D1
E RITCHIE ST
7800 LBCH 90808 766-H7
RITNER ST
1200 LACo 90502 764-A6
W RITNER ST
200 CRSN 90745 764-C6
RITTER MTWY
- LACo 91390 (4284-D6
See Page 4283)
- PMDL 91390 (4284-D6
See Page 4283)
RITTER ST
500 DBAR 91765 680-B1
RIVA LN
5400 CYP 90630 767-D5
RIVAS CANYON RD
900 PacP 90272 631-B5
RIVER AV
2000 LBCH 90810 795-A4
2600 RSMD 91770 636-H2
3600 LBCH 90810 765-A7
3700 CRSN 90810 765-A7
RIVER CIR
17900 SCTA 91387 4551-J3
17900 SCTA 91387 4552-A3
RIVER DR
6200 BELL 90201 675-F7
6400 BELL 90201 705-F1
RIVER RD
7700 CDHY 90201 705-F2
N RIVER ST
500 LA 90065 594-J6
RIVER WY
7700 BPK 90621 737-H6
RIVERA CT
- Boyl 90033 634-J4
RIVERA DR
1000 SBdC 92397 (4652-C1
See Page 4651)
RIVERA PL
800 PVE 90274 822-F2
RIVERA RD
9000 PRV 90660 676-E7
9200 PRV 90660 706-F1
10400 LACo 90606 706-G1
11600 SFSP 90606 706-H1
11900 SFSP 90670 707-A1
12000 WHIT 90670 707-A1
12100 WHIT 90606 707-A1
RIVERA ST
100 LA 90063 635-B5
RIVER ACCESS RD
- LACo 90601 637-D5
RIVERBEND ST
39300 PMDL 93551 4195-E5
RIVER BIRCH CT
- LACo 91387 4552-B4
RIVERDALE
1400 WCOV 91791 638-J5
RIVERDALE AV
2200 LA 90031 594-G5
RIVERDALE DR
300 GLDL 91204 564-D6
RIVERDALE PL
- Cstc 91384 4459-F1
RIVER FARM DR
3700 WLKV 91361 557-C7
RIVERGRADE RD
3000 IRW 91706 598-B2
4400 IRW 91706 597-J4
4700 BALD 91706 597-J4
4900 BALD 91706 598-A3
RIVERGROVE DR
6400 DWNY 90240 706-A1
RIVEROCK LN
40800 PMDL 93551 4194-H2
RIVER RIDGE CT
14600 CHLS 91709 680-J5
RIVERROCK CIR
400 THO 91362 557-G1
RIVERROCK CT
- AZU 91702 569-A2
RIVERROCK DR
- Hrbr 90710 794-A5
RIVERS RD
13000 Brwd 90049 631-D1
RIVERSBRIDGE WY
23400 SCTA 91354 4550-G1
RIVERSEA RD
- SLB 90740 826-E3
RIVERSIDE AV
5900 HNTP 90255 675-C6
6200 BELL 90201 675-C7
RIVERSIDE DR
- SCTA 91354 4460-F7
400 BURB 91506 563-F4
1000 LA 90031 594-G5
1200 LFlz 90027 563-H3
1200 LFlz 90027 564-A4
1500 GLDL 91201 563-H3
1700 Echo 90026 594-G5
1700 LA 90039 594-D3
2100 BURB 91521 563-F4
2400 BURB 91505 563-D4
2800 SBdC 91710 641-C7
2900 POM 91766 641-C7
3000 LFlz 90027 594-C2
3100 CHNO 91710 641-G7
3200 BURB 91522 563-F4
10000 LA 91602 563-A4
11000 LA 91602 562-J3
11300 NHol 91601 562-G3
11700 LA 91607 562-G3
12400 LA 91604 562-D3
12600 Shrm 91423 562-A3
14400 Shrm 91403 562-A3
18900 Res 91335 530-B7
RIVERSIDE PL
2400 LA 90039 594-E4
RIVERSIDE TER
2500 LA 90039 594-E4
RIVERSIDE TR
2900 SBdC 91710 641-B7
RIVERSIDE WY
13000 SBdC 91710 641-B7
RIVERTON AV
3800 LA 91604 563-A6
4000 LA 91602 563-A4
4800 NHol 91601 563-A1
5900 NHol 91601 533-A6
6000 NHol 91606 533-A6
6600 NHol 91605 533-A4
7200 SunV 91352 533-A4
RIVER TRAIL LN
- SCTA 91354 4460-F4
RIVERVIEW AV
3800 ELMN 91731 597-D5
RIVERVIEW LN
- SCTA 91354 4550-F1
RIVERVIEW RD
100 MTBL 90640 676-E3
23000 LACo 91390 (4370-H7
See Page 4279)
RIVERWALK LN
- StvR 91381 4640-B2
RIVER WOOD CT
23600 SIMI 93063 499-B3
RIVERWOOD DR
11400 Sunl 91040 503-F1
11400 Sunl 91040 (4723-F7
See Page 4643)
RIVERWOOD TER
11200 Sunl 91040 503-F1
RIVES AV
8400 DWNY 90240 706-B1
10200 DWNY 90241 706-A4
11200 DWNY 90241 705-H6
11900 DWNY 90242 705-H6
RIVIERA AV
1300 Ven 90291 671-H6
RIVIERA CIR
1200 PAS 91107 566-G1
6300 LBCH 90815 796-E6
RIVIERA CT
200 LHB 90631 738-E2
500 FUL 92835 738-H3
38000 PMDL 93552 4287-B1
RIVIERA DR
- SLB 90740 826-F4
900 PAS 91107 566-G2
17200 CRTS 90703 736-J7
19200 WAL 91789 639-C7
19200 WAL 91789 679-C1
RIVIERA LN
- LACo 90606 676-H6
15200 LMRD 90638 737-G4
E RIVIERA WK
5500 LBCH 90803 826-C2
RIVIERA WY
5400 TOR 90505 793-A2
RIVIERA RANCH RD
13100 Brwd 90049 631-D3
RIVKIND LN
10000 Sunl 91040 503-C3
RIVO ALTO CANAL
- LBCH 90803 826-C2
RIVOL RD
7000 CanP 91307 529-D5
RIXFORD AV
15700 LNDL 90260 733-D5
ROA DR
16900 CRSN 90746 734-D7
ROAD WY
- LMRD 90639 737-F2
ROAD 3
- SPed 90731 794-C7
- SPed 90731 824-C1
- Wilm 90744 794-C7
ROAD 8
- SPed 90731 794-B7
- SPed 90731 824-C1
ROAD 10
- SPed 90731 794-B7
- SPed 90731 824-B1
ROAD 12
- SPed 90731 794-B7
- SPed 90731 824-B1
ROAD C
- SLB 90740 826-H2
ROAD RUNNER DR
- BREA 92823 709-H6
ROADRUNNER DR
- LVRN 91750 570-H5
W ROADRUNNER DR
- PMDL 93551 4195-J4
ROAD RUNNER LN
14600 CHLS 91709 680-G5
ROADRUNNER LN
11600 Litl 93543 4468-G6
ROAD RUNNER RD
16400 LACo 91387 4552-C3
16400 SCTA 91387 4552-C3
ROADRUNNER RD
- RHLS 90274 823-F1
ROADRUNNER ST
39600 PMDL 93551 4195-J4
ROADRUNNER WY
42600 LAN 93536 4105-C4
ROADS END
300 GLDL 91205 564-E7
ROADSIDE DR
28300 AGRH 91301 558-A6
29300 AGRH 91301 557-J6
ROAN RD
28600 RPV 90275 823-F2
ROANNE DR
1300 LHB 90631 708-F4
1400 LHH 90631 708-F4
ROANOAK
1400 WCOV 91791 638-J5
ROANOKE PL
1100 LCF 91011 535-B6
ROANOKE RD
800 SMRO 91108 596-D1
1800 CLAR 91711 571-C7
1800 CLAR 91711 601-C1

STREET
Block City ZIP Pg-Grid

ROANOKE RD
8500 LACo 91775 566-G7
ROANOKE ST
1200 LHB 90631 708-B4
ROANWOOD DR
- RHE 90274 793-C6
ROARK DR
2200 ALH 91803 635-J1
2300 ALH 91803 636-A1
ROB CIR
900 WAL 91789 639-F5
ROBALO AV
2400 LA 90732 823-H7
ROBBIE CT
14400 BALD 91706 638-C1
ROBBINS DR
400 ARCD 91006 567-E6
9900 BHLS 90212 632-E2
ROBERT AV
8400 SunV 91352 533-A1
8600 SunV 91352 532-J1
14600 BLF 90706 736-A3
ROBERT CT
1300 BREA 92821 709-A4
W ROBERT DR
3000 ANA 92804 767-J6
ROBERT LN
400 BHLS 90210 592-G5
ROBERT PL
20400 WdHl 91364 560-D4
ROBERT RD
2300 RowH 91748 679-E6
23100 TOR 90505 793-A1
ROBERT WY
7000 Tuj 91042 504-A3
ROBERTA ST
3700 LA 90031 595-C6
3800 LA 90032 595-C6
10900 CRTS 90703 736-E6
ROBERT C. LEE PKWY
- SCTA 91350 4551-D5
ROBERT F KENNEDY DR
500 LA 91340 502-B1
500 SFER 91340 502-B1
ROBERT GUY RD
24700 HIDH 91302 559-C3
N ROBERTO AV
100 WCOV 91790 598-E7
ROBERTO CT
45100 LAN 93535 4016-A5
ROBERTO LN
1100 BelA 90077 591-J5
ROBERTS AV
3100 CULC 90232 632-J7
ROBERTS RD
- LACo 90265 628-B6
- MAL 90265 628-B6
3900 Actn 93510 4465-A1
ROBERTS ST
100 POM 91767 600-J5
ROBERTS WK
- Cstc 91384 4459-D6
N ROBERTSON BLVD
100 BHLS 90211 632-H2
100 LA 90048 632-H2
100 WHWD 90048 592-H7
100 WHWD 90048 632-H2
600 WHWD 90069 592-H6
S ROBERTSON BLVD
100 BHLS 90211 632-H6
100 LA 90048 632-H6
800 LA 90035 632-H6
1900 LA 90034 632-H6
3700 CULC 90232 632-H6
3700 LA 90232 632-H6
3700 CULC 90232 672-H1
ROBERTSON PL
2900 LA 90034 632-H6
ROBERTSON RD
23600 VeCo 93063 499-D4
ROBERT STOCKTON PL
27700 LA 90732 823-J1
ROBERTS VIEW PL
3600 LA 91604 562-H6
ROBERT W PRESCOTT WY
- Wch 90045 702-H6
E ROBIDOUX ST
900 Wilm 90744 794-G5
W ROBIDOUX ST
1000 Wilm 90744 794-C5
ROBIN AV
28000 SCTA 91350 4461-C5
ROBIN DR
4200 LPMA 90623 767-B4
9200 LA 90069 592-H4
ROBIN LN
2300 LMTA 90717 793-G4
37400 PMDL 93550 4286-E3
ROBIN MTWY
- BREA 92823 710-D3
- LACo 92823 710-D3
ROBIN RD
1000 SBdC 92397 (4652-C2 See Page 4651)
1600 LVRN 91750 570-F5
1800 SGBL 91775 596-E2
1800 SMRO 91108 596-E2
S ROBIN RD
100 WCOV 91791 598-H7
200 WCOV 91791 638-H3
ROBIN ST
11600 Wbrk 90059 704-F7

ROBIN WY
300 POM 91767 600-J2
1200 LHB 90631 708-C5
1500 FUL 92835 738-G4
6100 BPK 90620 767-E2
16000 INDS 91745 678-D2
ROBINA AV
37800 PMDL 93550 4286-B2
ROBINBROOK PL
23400 DBAR 91765 680-C3
ROBIN CIRCLE LN
1000 SBdC 92397 (4652-C2 See Page 4651)
ROBIN CREST CT
28200 SCTA 91387 4552-B2
ROBIN CREST LN
14000 CHLS 91709 680-J3
ROBINCROFT DR
200 PAS 91104 565-J1
ROBINDALE PL
- SCTA 91354 4460-F5
ROBINDALE ST
800 WCOV 91790 638-F2
W ROBINDALE ST
1000 WCOV 91790 638-E1
ROBINETTE AV
3100 BALD 91706 637-J1
3400 BALD 91706 597-J7
3400 BALD 91706 598-A7
ROBIN GLEN DR
500 GLDL 91202 534-C7
500 GLDL 91202 564-C1
ROBIN HILL RD
3900 LCF 91011 535-B5
ROBINHOOD AV
4800 TEML 91780 597-B3
ROBIN HOOD LN
- WLKV 91361 587-C1
ROBINHOOD LN
2500 LA 90046 592-H2
ROBINLINDA LN
1700 MONP 91755 636-E4
1800 LACo 91770 636-E4
ROBIN OAKS TER
22400 DBAR 91765 680-A4
ROBINS PL
- BREA 92823 709-H6
ROBINSON CT
1100 LAN 93535 4106-B2
ROBINSON DR
3600 LAN 93535 4016-G4
ROBINSON RD
200 PAS 91104 565-H1
700 Top 90290 590-B5
ROBINSON ST
100 Echo 90026 634-B1
200 Echo 90026 594-B7
1900 RBCH 90278 733-A7
ROBINSON WY
25100 TOR 90505 793-E4
ROBINSON RANCH RD
- SCTA 91387 4552-D3
ROBINVIEW LN
28500 RPV 90275 823-B1
ROBINWOOD DR
400 Brwd 90049 631-F2
ROBINWOOD LN
19200 WAL 91789 639-C7
ROBLAR PL
14200 Shrm 91423 562-A5
ROBLAR RD
14000 Shrm 91423 562-B5
ROBLE AV
6400 HiPk 90042 595-E2
ROBLE LN
5500 LVRN 91750 570-H4
E ROBLE WY
300 LBCH 90802 795-E7
W ROBLE WY
200 LBCH 90802 795-C7
ROBLES AV
2100 SMRO 91108 566-D7
ROBLES LN
5300 AGRH 91301 557-H5
ROBLE VISTA DR
3800 LFlz 90027 594-C2
ROBLIN ST
100 CRSN 90746 764-D2
ROBMAR DR
1400 LA 90210 592-E5
ROBOJO DR
9900 LACo 93551 4193-F2
ROB ROI CT
- SCTA 91387 4462-E6
ROBRUCE DR
2200 HacH 91745 678-B4
ROBRUCE LN
2500 HacH 91745 678-B4
ROBSON AV
1700 SMCA 90405 671-H3
ROCA DR
1600 GLDL 91207 564-H2
ROCA TR
3400 Actn 93510 4375-B1
ROCA WY
100 MONP 91754 636-A4
ROCA CHICA DR
20100 MAL 90265 629-J6
ROCCA CT
10500 BelA 90077 592-A6
ROCCA DR
- Cstc 91384 4369-G7

ROCCA PL
10500 BelA 90077 592-A6
ROCCA WY
10500 BelA 90077 592-A5
ROCCUS LN
23500 Chat 91311 499-F7
ROCHDALE AV
8600 TEML 91775 596-G2
ROCHDALE CT
900 SDMS 91773 599-J4
ROCHEDALE LN
12300 Brwd 90049 631-F1
ROCHEDALE WY
700 Brwd 90049 631-F1
ROCHELLE AV
2200 LACo 91016 567-G7
2600 MNRO 91016 597-G1
18700 CRTS 90703 767-A2
E ROCHELLE LN
6300 LBCH 90815 796-E6
ROCHELLE PL
4400 Enc 91316 561-C5
ROCHEMONT DR
20200 PacP 90272 590-D3
20200 Top 90290 590-D3
ROCHESTER AV
10200 Wwd 90024 632-B2
11400 WLA 90025 631-J5
ROCHESTER CIR
1900 LA 90018 673-G1
ROCHESTER ST
3100 RPV 90275 823-G2
ROCHESTER WY
11500 CRTS 90703 736-F6
ROCHLEN ST
15200 HacH 91745 678-A1
ROCK LN
1800 LVRN 91750 600-G1
ROCK ST
2100 LA 90039 594-C4
ROCK TR
500 Top 90290 590-B5
ROCKBLUFF DR
4600 RHE 90274 793-B6
ROCK BLUFF RD
- POM 91766 640-G4
ROCKBRIDGE RD
400 DBAR 91765 640-A6
ROCKBURY DR
24400 DBAR 91765 640-E7
ROCK CANYON DR
- LACo 91390 4461-A2
ROCK CASTLE DR
5400 LCF 91011 504-H7
ROCKCLIFF CT
39300 PMDL 93551 4195-E5
ROCKCLIFF DR
6100 LA 90068 563-G7
ROCKCLIFF PL
- POM 91766 640-G7
ROCK CREEK DR
- SCTA 91354 4550-H1
ROCK CREEK RD
5600 AGRH 91301 558-A4
ROCK CREST LN
- POM 91766 640-J7
12800 CHLS 91709 640-J7
ROCKCROFT DR
20600 MAL 90265 629-H5
ROCKDALE AV
900 Eagl 90041 565-D6
N ROCKDALE AV
2000 SIMI 93063 499-B1
ROCKDALE ST
1200 UPL 91784 571-H5
ROCKDELL ST
2300 LaCr 91214 504-G6
ROCKEDGE DR
300 VeCo 91377 558-A1
ROCKEFELLER LN
1700 RBCH 90278 762-J1
1900 RBCH 90278 763-A1
ROCKENBACH ST
13300 BALD 91706 598-A4
ROCKET RD
- SCTA 91350 4551-B5
ROCKET ST
5500 LKWD 90713 766-C2
ROCKETDYNE RD
23700 LA 91304 499-D7
23900 WHil 91304 499-D7
24900 VeCo 93063 499-B7
ROCKETDYNE DRIVEWAY
- CanP 91303 530-B6
ROCKFIELD ST
4800 THO 91362 557-G1
4900 VeCo 91362 557-G1
5000 VeCo 91377 557-H1
ROCKFOLD DR
15000 HacH 91745 677-J2
15000 HacH 91745 678-A3
ROCKFORD DR
300 CLAR 91711 601-E1
ROCKFORD LN
11300 SBdC 91766 641-D3
ROCKFORD RD
1900 LA 90039 594-D5
ROCK GLEN AV
1400 GLDL 91205 564-H5
2600 Eagl 90041 564-H5
ROCKGROVE AV
27200 SCTA 91351 4551-G3
ROCK HAMPTON DR
4100 Tarz 91356 560-J5
ROCK HAVEN ST
1300 MONP 91754 635-H4

ROCK HILL DR
600 SDMS 91773 599-J3
ROCKHILL DR
14700 HacH 91745 677-H3
ROCKHOLD AV
3000 RSMD 91770 636-G1
3600 RSMD 91770 596-G6
6700 LACo 91775 566-F7
6700 LACo 91775 596-F1
ROCKHURST LN
26500 RPV 90275 793-B6
ROCKIE LN
37200 PMDL 93552 4287-D2
N ROCKINGHAM AV
100 Brwd 90049 631-E3
S ROCKINGHAM AV
100 Brwd 90049 631-E4
ROCKINGHAM DR
1300 SIMI 93063 499-C4
ROCKINGHORSE LN
1100 LHB 90631 708-G4
ROCKING HORSE RD
- LACo 91390 4373-D3
600 WAL 91789 639-D6
ROCKINGHORSE RD
- RPV 90275 823-F2
ROCKING HORSE SPUR
3100 RPV 90275 823-G2
ROCK ISLAND DR
44800 LAN 93535 4016-C3
ROCKLAND AV
5100 Eagl 90041 565-A5
ROCKLAND PL
4400 LCF 91011 534-H2
4400 Mont 91020 534-H2
ROCK LANDING WY
- SLB 90740 796-J5
ROCKLEDGE DR
5300 BPK 90621 738-A6
ROCKLEDGE LN
- WAL 91789 639-C5
ROCKLEDGE RD
2100 LA 90068 593-E3
ROCKMEAD CT
15400 HacH 91745 678-A6
ROCKMERE WY
4400 LCF 91011 534-J2
ROCKMONT AV
700 LACo 91711 571-C7
ROCKNE AV
5400 WHIT 90601 677-A4
5800 WHIT 90606 676-J5
6000 LACo 90606 676-J5
ROCK PARK DR
29200 RPV 90275 822-G1
ROCK PINE LN
2700 LaCr 91214 504-G5
ROCKPOINT RD
20600 MAL 90265 629-H6
ROCKPORT DR
- PMDL 93551 4195-G5
ROCKPORT WY
20100 MAL 90265 629-J6
20100 MAL 90265 630-A6
ROCKRIDGE CT
24000 SCTA 91355 4550-F4
ROCKRIDGE LN
2400 BREA 92821 709-E6
2500 DBAR 91789 679-G6
ROCK RIDGE RD
100 SBdC 92372 (4472-A5 See Page 4471)
ROCKRIDGE TER
2100 LCF 91011 534-H2
7100 CanP 91307 529-E5
ROCK RIDGE WY
16600 CHLS 91709 710-F2
ROCK RIVER DR
100 DBAR 91765 640-B6
ROCK RIVER RD
200 DBAR 91765 640-B7
400 DBAR 91765 680-A1
ROCK ROSE LN
27300 LACo 91387 4551-J4
ROCKROSE LN
100 VeCo 91377 557-J2
ROCK ROSE ST
100 LACo 91016 567-G6
ROCKROSE ST
- PMDL 93551 4195-D6
ROCK SPRINGS DR
2300 CHLS 91709 640-J7
2300 CHLS 91709 680-J1
2500 CHLS 91709 641-A7
ROCK SPRINGS WY
- AZU 91702 568-J1
- AZU 91702 569-A2
ROCK TREE DR
5500 AGRH 91301 558-A5
N ROCKVALE AV
100 AZU 91702 569-A6
5300 LACo 91702 599-A1
5800 LACo 91702 569-A7
ROCKVALLEY RD
4900 RPV 90275 793-B6
ROCK VIEW CT
1800 MONP 91754 635-H4
ROCKVIEW DR
5100 TOR 90505 793-A1
ROCK VIEW ST
1100 Eagl 90041 565-C5

ROCK VIEW ST
1200 MONP 91754 635-H4
ROCKVIEW TER
2000 Top 90290 629-H2
5300 Eagl 90041 565-C5
ROCKVIEW WY
- POM 91766 641-A4
ROCK VISTA DR
29000 AGRH 91301 558-A5
ROCK VISTA LN
16200 CHLS 91709 710-F2
ROCKWALL ST
11700 LKWD 90715 766-H5
ROCKWAY DR
2200 WCOV 91790 638-C1
13400 BALD 91706 598-A5
ROCKWELL AV
3500 ELMN 91731 597-B7
ROCKWELL CANYON RD
26000 SCTA 91355 4550-E4
ROCKWOOD RD
600 PAS 91105 565-F6
ROCKWOOD ST
1500 Echo 90026 634-D2
3900 City 90063 635-E4
ROCKY CT
18400 RowH 91748 679-A6
ROCKY RD
- UPL 91784 571-H6
1200 VeCo 93063 499-D4
ROCKYFORD RD
- PMDL 93550 4375-J6
- PMDL 93550 4376-A6
ROCKY HILL AV
900 MTBL 90640 636-D7
900 MTBL 90640 676-D1
ROCKY KNOLL RD
16700 HacH 91745 678-E5
ROCKY LEDGE RD
1600 Top 90290 630-A1
ROCKY MESA PL
9200 WHil 91304 499-D7
ROCKY MOUNTAIN
- CLAR 91711 571-F3
ROCKY MOUNTAIN CT
- SCTA 91387 4462-H7
ROCKY MOUNTAIN VIEW RD
- Tuj 91042 503-J1
ROCKY PEAK FIRE RD
15900 SIMI 93063 499-F1
23600 VeCo 93063 499-F1
ROCKY POINT LN
20800 DBAR 91789 679-G6
ROCKY POINT PL
2200 PVE 90274 792-D7
ROCKY POINT RD
100 PVE 90274 792-D7
25100 Hrbr 90710 794-B4
25200 Wilm 90710 794-B4
ROCKYRIVER LN
16100 CRTS 90703 736-J5
ROCKY TRAIL RD
2600 DBAR 91765 680-A6
ROCKY VIEW RD
2000 DBAR 91765 680-B5
ROCOSO PL
18600 Tarz 91356 560-J5
ROCTON DR
1000 PAS 91107 566-F2
ROD AV
5900 WdHl 91367 559-C1
6000 WdHl 91367 529-C7
ROD PL
24600 WdHl 91367 559-C1
RODARTE WY
18000 Enc 91316 561-A5
RODAX ST
20400 Win 91306 530-C2
21000 LA 91304 530-A2
22700 LA 91304 529-H2
RODDY DR
1000 LHB 90631 708-F4
RODDY WY
1000 LHB 90631 708-F4
RODECKER DR
100 AZU 91702 569-A7
RODEFFER PL
22000 SCTA 91350 4461-A4
E RODELL PL
- ARCD 91006 597-D2
W RODELL PL
- ARCD 91007 597-D2
RODEO CT
200 SDMS 91773 570-C7
W RODEO CT
1200 UPL 91786 571-J7
RODEO DR
5800 LA 90016 672-J1
5800 LA 90016 673-A1
N RODEO DR
200 BHLS 90210 632-F1
200 BHLS 90212 632-F1
700 BHLS 90210 592-F7
S RODEO DR
100 BHLS 90212 632-F3
1100 LA 90035 632-F3
RODEO LN
4500 LA 90016 673-D1
4600 LVRN 91750 570-H7
RODEO PL
3500 LA 90018 673-E1
3500 LA 90016 673-B1

RODEO RD
200 GLDR 91741 569-J6
600 FUL 92835 738-F5
900 ARCD 91006 567-C2
1800 LA 90062 673-E1
1800 LA 90018 673-E1
2000 LA 90008 673-E1
3600 LA 90016 673-B1
3600 CULC 90232 672-J1
3600 LA 90016 672-J1
W RODEO RD
- LA 90016 673-D1
RODEO ST
4200 MTCL 91763 641-E2
4200 SBdC 91763 641-D2
36400 PMDL 93552 4286-J5
RODEO WY
600 WAL 91789 639-H6
RODEO GROUNDS
3700 LACo 90265 630-D5
RODEO HEIGHTS CIR
400 WAL 91789 639-E7
RODERICK AV
500 POM 91767 601-A4
RODERICK PL
3000 LA 90065 594-G1
RODERICK RD
3600 LA 90065 594-G1
RODGERS DR
20500 SCTA 91350 4461-D6
28200 Saug 91350 4461-D5
RODGERTON DR
6000 LA 90068 593-F1
RODILEE AV
400 WCOV 91791 639-A1
S RODILLE AV
1000 WCOV 91791 639-A2
RODIN AV
43700 LAN 93535 4106-A1
44000 LAN 93535 4016-A3
RODIN LN
- SCTA 91355 4550-E3
RODIN PL
2900 LA 90065 564-H6
N RODLOY RD
2700 LBCH 90810 795-A1
RODMAN AV
1000 POM 91767 601-B6
RODMAN CIR
500 MONP 91754 635-J3
RODNEY DR
1500 LFlz 90027 594-A3
RODNEY RD
1500 WCOV 91792 638-H5
RODS WY
800 LA 91340 482-D6
800 SFER 91340 482-D6
ROEBLING AV
10900 Wwd 90024 632-A2
ROEBUCK ST
10500 BLF 90706 736-D7
ROESSLER CT
4100 LACo 90274 793-C6
ROGAN CT
19500 RowH 91748 679-D6
ROGEN DR
4000 Enc 91436 561-D5
E ROGENE ST
5800 LBCH 90815 796-D2
ROGER CT
100 BREA 92821 709-B7
500 POM 91766 641-A6
8600 PRV 90660 676-F4
ROGER RD
- Actn 93510 4465-A1
32900 Actn 93510 4375-A7
ROGERS AV
2200 LA 90023 635-A6
W ROGERS CT
2900 ANA 92804 767-J6
ROGERS PL
1700 BURB 91504 533-F5
ROGERS ST
1600 NLB 90805 765-F2
3900 City 90063 635-F2
ROGERS FIRE RD
- PacP 90272 590-G4
- PacP 90272 591-A7
- PacP 90272 631-A1
ROGIER ST
43700 LAN 93535 4106-C1
ROGUE WY
- Cstc 91384 4369-F7
ROHNER AV
2000 SIMI 93063 499-C2
ROHNER CT
2200 SIMI 93063 499-C1
ROHR ST
1700 GLDL 91202 564-D1
1800 GLDL 91202 534-D7
ROJAS ST
15400 HacH 91745 678-A5
ROKEBY ST
2600 LA 90039 594-D3
ROLAINE ST
10500 BLF 90706 736-D6
ROLAND AV
- KeCo 93560 3835-D1
7500 KeCo 93560 3834-C1
ROLAND ST
6300 BPK 90621 738-A7
E ROLAND ST
100 AZU 91702 598-J1

ROLAND WY
- SCTA 91354 4460-G6
E ROLANDA ST
5500 LBCH 90815 796-C3
ROLANDEE ST
2600 Actn 93510 4375-B3
ROLKEL PL
11100 Nor 91326 500-H2
ROLLA RD
18400 LACo 91390 4461-G3
ROLLAND CURTIS PL
1000 LA 90037 673-J2
1000 LA 90037 674-A2
1200 LA 90062 673-J2
ROLLANDO DR
4600 RHE 90274 793-C5
ROLLE ST
3600 LA 90031 595-B6
3700 LA 90032 595-B6
ROLLIN ST
800 SPAS 91030 595-G3
ROLLING DR
10700 ELMN 91780 597-D4
ROLLING RD
5700 WdHl 91367 559-J1
5700 WdHl 91367 560-A1
ROLLING GREENS WY
- SCTA 91321 4550-H6
1600 LACo 90601 637-E5
ROLLING HILL DR
1400 MONP 91754 635-H4
ROLLING HILLS AV
26700 LACo 91387 4552-C4
ROLLING HILLS DR
- POM 91766 640-G5
700 FUL 92835 738-J2
ROLLING HILLS LN
27700 Cstc 91384 4369-G7
ROLLING HILLS RD
- WCOV 91791 639-B3
3300 TOR 90505 793-D4
26000 LACo 90274 793-D4
26000 RHE 90274 793-E7
ROLLING HILLS WY
25400 TOR 90505 793-F5
ROLLING KNOLL RD
1300 DBAR 91765 680-C3
ROLLING MEADOWS RD
4900 RHE 90274 793-B5
ROLLING PINES RD
- PMDL 93550 4286-F7
ROLLINGRIDGE AV
3200 PMDL 93550 4286-G1
ROLLING RIDGE DR
- POM 91766 640-F6
2900 BURB 91504 533-F3
22000 SCTA 91350 4550-J6
22000 SCTA 91350 4551-A6
29900 AGRH 91301 557-H4
ROLLING RIDGE RD
5200 RPV 90275 793-A5
5200 PVE 90274 793-A5
ROLLING VIEW RD
24200 HIDH 91302 559-D3
ROLLING VISTA DR
26400 LMTA 90717 793-H6
ROLLINGWOOD DR
- RHE 90274 793-B5
ROLLINS DR
1300 MONP 90063 635-F3
1300 City 90063 635-F3
ROLLINS RD
9300 Chat 91311 499-F6
ROLLINS WY
2100 POM 91767 601-A5
ROLOMAR DR
4100 Enc 91436 561-D5
ROLYN PL
200 ARCD 91007 567-D5
ROMA CT
- PMDL 93550 4196-H7
4100 LA 90292 701-J1
ROMA DR
14200 LMRD 90638 737-F3
14200 LMRD 90639 737-F3
ROMA PL
1200 POM 91766 640-D3
ROMA ST
9700 PRV 90660 706-F2
11200 SFSP 90670 706-G3
ROMAINE ST
4900 LA 90029 593-J6
5400 LA 90038 593-F6
7000 WHWD 90038 593-C6
7100 LA 90046 593-A6
7100 WHWD 90046 593-A6
8300 LA 90069 593-A6
8300 WHWD 90069 593-A6
8400 LA 90069 592-J6
ROMAN CT
- Saug 91350 4461-F7
ROMANDEL AV
9900 SFSP 90670 707-A4
ROMANO PL
23100 TOR 90505 793-B1
ROMANY DR
13500 PacP 90272 631-C4
ROMAR LN
20500 SCTA 91350 4461-D5
ROMAR PL
19300 Nor 91324 500-F4
ROMAR ST
15000 MsnH 91345 501-G4

ROMAR ST
15600 LA 91343 501-D4
17000 Nor 91325 501-A4
18700 Nor 91324 500-F4
19700 Chat 91311 500-B4
22000 Chat 91311 499-J4
ROMBERG PL
4600 WdHl 91364 559-H4
ROME AV
5200 CYP 90630 767-D7
W ROME AV
2800 ANA 92804 767-G7
ROME CT
3900 LA 90065 595-A4
ROME DR
700 LA 90065 595-A4
800 LA 90065 594-H3
S ROME PL
800 ANA 92804 767-G7
ROME ST
9700 CYP 90630 767-D7
ROMEO CANYON RD
- Cstc 91384 4459-H1
ROMERO CT
800 WAL 91789 639-D6
ROMERO DR
4300 Tarz 91356 560-F5
14700 WHIT 90605 707-G1
ROMERO PL
15100 LA 91343 501-H6
ROMERO CANYON RD
30000 Cstc 91384 4459-C2
30600 Cstc 91384 4369-B5
ROMERO-SLOAN CTO
29700 Cstc 91384 4369-D7
29700 Cstc 91384 4459-D1
ROMNEY DR
1000 DBAR 91789 679-G3
1100 PAS 91105 565-F7
ROMNEY WY
1200 PAS 91105 565-E7
ROMOLA AV
4600 LVRN 91750 570-D7
4800 SDMS 91773 570-D7
ROMONT ST
12900 LA 91342 482-D4
ROMULO ST
600 LA 90065 594-J5
ROMULUS DR
1200 GLDL 91205 564-G6
1400 LA 90065 564-G6
RONALD AV
19200 TOR 90503 763-A3
RONALD CIR
6000 CYP 90630 767-E7
RONALD CT
- AZU 91702 569-B6
RONALD DR
6100 CYP 90630 767-E7
11700 LMRD 90638 707-F7
RONALD REAGAN FRWY
Rt#-118
- Chat - 499-E2
- Chat - 500-D2
- GrnH - 501-A1
- LA - 482-D7
- LA - 502-B2
- LACo - 482-D7
- MsnH - 501-A1
- MsnH - 502-B2
- Nor - 500-D2
- Nor - 501-A1
- Pcma - 482-D7
- Pcma - 502-B2
- SIMI - 499-E2
RONAN AV
800 Wilm 90744 794-D5
21300 CRSN 90745 764-D6
22600 CRSN 90745 794-D1
RONAR ST
40100 LACo 93591 4199-F2
RONDA CIR
1000 LVRN 91750 570-E7
RONDA DR
1100 MANB 90266 732-H7
1800 LA 90032 635-D2
RONDA VISTA DR
2200 LFlz 90027 594-C3
RONDA VISTA PL
3800 LFlz 90027 594-C4
RONDELL ST
4100 AGRH 91301 558-E7
RONDERO RIDGE WY
28300 LACo 90265 627-G5
RONDOUT ST
100 LA 90012 634-H2
RONMAR PL
4700 WdHl 91364 560-D4
RONNIE ST
1200 WCOV 91792 638-H5
RON RIDGE DR
27600 SCTA 91350 4461-A5
RONSARD DR
2100 RPV 90275 823-H2
RONWOOD AV
400 LHB 90631 738-E1
RONWOOD ST
19800 GLDR 91740 569-E7
RON YARY WY
10300 BLF 90706 736-D5
ROOD ST
7300 PRM 90723 735-F2

ROOKS RD
2400 INDS 90601 637-C6
12200 LACo 90601 637-C6
12200 PRV 90601 637-C6
ROOSEVELT AV
100 FUL 92832 738-F7
100 MTBL 90640 676-D3
200 POM 91767 600-J6
200 POM 91767 601-A6
1600 LA 90006 633-J5
5700 SGAT 90280 735-G1
8400 DWNY 90242 735-J2
28500 Cstc 91384 4459-D7
N ROOSEVELT AV
- PAS 91107 566-D4
1300 LACo 91104 566-D1
1500 LACo 91104 536-D7
1600 Alta 91001 536-D7
S ROOSEVELT AV
- PAS 91107 566-D5
200 LACo 91107 566-D5
ROOSEVELT CIR
8600 BPK 90620 767-H5
ROOSEVELT CT
4300 CHNO 91710 641-E6
ROOSEVELT DR
36600 PMDL 93552 4287-C5
E ROOSEVELT RD
100 Bxby 90807 765-E6
W ROOSEVELT RD
200 Bxby 90807 765-D6
ROOSEVELT ST
2900 LVRN 91750 600-H3
4300 CHNO 91710 641-E6
W ROOSEVELT ST
1500 AZU 91702 598-F1
ROOT ST
- FUL 92833 738-C5
1800 WCOV 91790 598-E6
1900 BALD 91706 598-E6
ROPER AV
13200 NRWK 90650 737-A2
ROPER ST
7800 LBCH 90808 796-H1
RORIMER ST
16600 LPUE 91744 678-F1
18400 LACo 91744 679-A2
RORY LN
1600 SIMI 93063 499-B2
RORY WY
- PMDL 93551 4195-D5
5900 SIMI 93063 499-B3
ROSA AV
200 LVRN 91750 600-D2
ROSA CT
6000 CHNO 91710 641-J7
ROSA LN
- LACo 91387 4552-A3
ROSA RD
4800 WdHl 91364 559-H4
ROSABELL ST
800 LA 90012 634-H3
4000 CULC 90066 672-C5
ROSADA ST
4300 LBCH 90815 796-A4
ROSADO RD
11400 SBdC 92372 (4472-E2 See Page 4471)
ROSALES AL
15500 PRM 90723 735-G5
ROSALES ST
14600 LA 91342 481-J3
ROSALIA RD
1500 LFlz 90027 594-B3
ROSALIND AV
1100 LA 90023 635-A7
ROSALIND PL
2900 LA 90023 635-A7
2900 LA 90023 675-A1
ROSALIND RD
800 PAS 91106 566-B7
800 SMRO 91108 566-B7
S ROSALINDA AV
300 AZU 91702 599-A1
ROSALITA DR
15000 LMRD 90638 737-G3
ROSALYNN DR
100 GLDR 91740 599-E1
ROSAMOND DR
27800 SCTA 91351 4551-F1
ROSANNA CT
23200 LACo 90502 794-B2
ROSANNA ST
2800 LA 90039 594-F3
ROSA PARKS FRWY
I-10
- LA - 632-B7
- LA - 633-F6
- LA - 634-A6
ROSARIO AV
- LMRD 90638 737-J2
44600 LAN 93535 4016-E6
ROSARIO DR
1100 Top 90290 590-C4
ROSARIO RD
4100 WdHl 91364 560-C5
ROSARIO ST
5900 CHNO 91710 641-J7
ROSARITA DR
400 FUL 92835 738-H2
500 BREA 92821 738-J2
ROSATI WY
- PMDL 93552 4196-J7

ROSCOE BLVD
9900 SunV 91352 533-B1
11100 SunV 91352 532-E2
11700 NHol 91605 532-E2
13200 PanC 91402 532-A2
14600 PanC 91402 531-G2
15400 VanN 91406 531-A2
15400 LA 91343 531-G2
19700 Win 91306 530-F2
22000 LA 91304 529-D2
24000 WHil 91304 529-D2
ROSCOE PL
16500 LA 91343 531-D2
ROSCOE ST
100 LHB 90631 708-H5
100 BREA 92821 708-H6
ROSCOMARE RD
900 BelA 90077 591-H4
2900 BelA 90077 561-H7
S ROSCOMMON AV
100 ELA 90022 635-H5
2300 MONP 91754 635-H5
ROSE AL
2700 PAS 91107 566-E5
ROSE AV
- Actn 93510 4375-F6
- Ven 90291 671-G5
400 LBCH 90802 795-G7
700 LBCH 90813 795-G6
700 SGBL 91775 596-E1
1500 SMRO 91108 596-E1
2200 SIGH 90755 795-G2
3300 HNTP 90255 675-B7
3300 BELL 90201 675-B7
4100 Bxby 90807 765-G3
5100 NLB 90805 765-G3
8900 MTCL 91763 601-G4
9900 ELMN 91731 597-A6
10500 LA 90034 632-E7
10500 MTCL 91763 641-G1
10700 LA 90034 672-D1
10700 SBdC 91762 641-G2
11200 LA 90066 672-B2
12400 DWNY 90242 736-A1
13000 LA 90066 671-G5
E ROSE AV
100 LHB 90631 708-E5
N ROSE AV
100 COMP 90221 735-A3
900 PAS 91107 566-E2
1300 LBCH 90813 795-G5
1800 LBCH 90806 795-G5
3400 Bxby 90807 795-G5
3400 Bxby 90807 765-G7
5100 NLB 90805 765-F1
6300 NLB 90805 735-F7
S ROSE AV
100 COMP 90221 735-A4
W ROSE AV
100 LHB 90631 708-E5
ROSE CIR
10600 CRTS 90703 766-E1
ROSE CT
- Ven 90291 671-H4
2000 WCOV 91791 638-J3
ROSE DR
800 GLDR 91741 569-F3
3400 BREA 92823 709-H7
3400 OrCo 92823 709-H7
10500 WHIT 90606 676-J4
10500 WHIT 90606 677-A4
12100 WHIT 90601 677-C5
N ROSE DR
100 FUL 92833 738-E6
ROSE LN
- MNRO 91016 567-J3
100 MTBL 90640 676-C2
10700 ELMN 91731 597-D4
10700 SBdC 91762 641-G2
16200 LPUE 91744 638-G7
23200 Top 90290 589-G4
ROSE PL
400 LBCH 90802 795-G7
ROSE ST
100 LA 90012 634-G4
1200 VeCo 93063 499-B4
1300 SBdC 92397 (4652-D2 See Page 4651)
7800 LPMA 90623 767-E3
7800 PRM 90723 735-G3
8500 BLF 90706 765-J1
8700 BLF 90706 766-A1
9200 RSMD 91770 596-J6
10100 BLF 90706 736-C7
11100 CRTS 90703 736-F7
12200 ART 90701 736-J7
12500 CRTS 90703 737-A7
36600 PMDL 93552 4287-A3
E ROSE ST
4300 RDom 90221 735-D4
4800 COMP 90221 735-D4
N ROSE ST
100 BURB 91505 563-B1
1600 BURB 91505 533-B7
S ROSE ST
100 BURB 91505 563-D5
ROSE WK
- Cstc 91384 4459-D6
ROSEAPPLE RD
- RPV 90275 823-B4
ROSEBANK AV
2000 LCF 91011 534-J1

STREET Block City ZIP Pg-Grid

ROSEBANK DR
4400 LCF 91011 534-J2
ROSEBAY ST
2000 THO 91361 557-A5
E ROSEBAY ST
5300 LBCH 90808 796-C1
ROSEBERRY AV
7200 LACo 90255 674-H7
7200 LACo 90255 704-H1
ROSE BOWL DR
900 PAS 91103 565-F2
ROSEBROOK LN
1800 RSMD 91770 636-F4
ROSEBUD AV
1900 LA 90039 594-F4
ROSE BUD DR
- PMDL 93551 4195-E5
ROSEBUD TR
3500 CALB 91302 559-E7
3500 CALB 91302 589-E1
ROSE CANYON LN
- LACo 91390 4461-A4
ROSE COURT DR
14600 SCTA 91387 4462-G5
ROSECRANS AV
100 MANB 90266 732-E4
400 ELSG 90245 732-H4
1000 FUL 92833 738-A4
2500 GAR 90249 733-D4
3000 BPK 90621 738-A4
4000 LNDL 90260 733-D4
4000 LNDL 90250 733-D4
4300 HAW 90260 733-D4
4300 HAW 90250 733-D4
6400 PRM 90221 735-E3
6500 PRM 90723 735-E3
8300 BPK 92833 738-A4
8300 LMRD 90638 737-E3
8300 LMRD 90638 738-A4
8700 DWNY 90242 735-J3
8700 DWNY 90242 736-A3
8700 BLF 90706 736-A3
10400 NRWK 90650 736-G3
12500 NRWK 90650 737-B3
12600 SFSP 90670 737-B3
E ROSECRANS AV
100 COMP 90220 734-E3
100 LACo 90248 734-D3
100 COMP 90222 734-E3
100 LACo 90061 734-D3
200 COMP 90220 735-B3
200 COMP 90222 735-B3
200 COMP 90221 735-B3
600 LACo 90220 734-E3
600 COMP 90059 734-E3
600 Wbrk 90059 734-D3
4200 RDom 90221 735-B3
4900 PRM 90221 735-B3
W ROSECRANS AV
100 COMP 90220 734-E3
100 LACo 90248 734-C3
100 COMP 90222 734-E3
100 LACo 90061 734-C3
400 LA 90248 734-C3
400 LA 90061 734-C3
600 LA 90247 734-C3
1000 GAR 90247 734-C3
1000 Wbrk 90222 734-E3
1100 LACo 90220 734-E3
1200 GAR 90247 733-F3
1400 GAR 90249 733-F3
2000 COMP 90059 734-E3
3100 HAW 90250 733-B4
4500 LNDL 90260 733-B4
4500 LNDL 90250 733-B4
4600 HAW 90260 733-B4
5400 HAW 90260 732-J4
5400 HAW 90250 732-J4
ROSECRANS PL
100 MANB 90266 732-E4
E ROSECREST AV
100 LHB 90631 708-E7
W ROSECREST AV
100 LHB 90631 708-E7
ROSECREST DR
2300 GLDL 91208 534-J4
28900 Ago 91301 588-B4
ROSEDALE AV
- AZU 91702 569-A5
1000 GLDL 91201 564-B2
ROSEDALE CT
- LACo 91770 636-E3
W ROSEDALE CUR
2300 SBdC 91784 571-J3
ROSEDELL DR
21100 SCTA 91350 4461-B6
ROSEGATE PL
24400 DBAR 91765 640-E6
ROSE GLEN AV
900 RSMD 91770 636-G5
ROSEGLEN AV
1600 SPed 90731 824-A1
ROSEGLEN PL
1600 PMDL 93550 4286-D3
ROSEGLEN ST
9200 TEML 91780 596-J5
10600 TEML 91780 597-C4
11600 ELMN 91732 597-F5
ROSEHAVEN LN
15600 SCTA 91387 4552-D1
ROSE HEDGE DR
10400 LACo 90606 676-H5
11400 LACo 90606 677-A6
ROSE HEDGE DR
12000 WHIT 90606 677-A7
ROSEHEDGE DR
3300 FUL 92835 738-H1
8600 PRV 90660 676-F4
E ROSE HEDGE LN
- ING 90305 703-D4
200 VeCo 91377 557-J2
ROSEHEDGE ST
8900 PRV 90660 676-G5
E ROSE HILL DR
4500 LA 90032 595-C6
W ROSE HILL DR
4300 LA 90032 595-C6
ROSE HILLS RD
- PRV 90660 677-B1
9900 PRV 90601 677-B1
9900 INDS 90601 677-B1
10100 LACo 90601 677-B1
ROSE HILLS NO 1 FIRE RD
- HacH 91745 677-F3
ROSE HILLS NO 2 FIRE RD
- HacH 91745 677-F4
ROSE HILLS NO 3 FIRE RD
- HacH 91745 677-E5
- LACo 90601 677-E5
- WHIT 90601 677-E5
ROSELAKE AV
100 Echo 90026 634-C1
ROSELAND ST
4900 LA 90016 633-B7
ROSELAWN AV
3400 GLDL 91208 534-G3
3700 GLDL 91020 534-G3
ROSELAWN PL
100 HiPk 90042 595-C3
ROSELAWN ST
100 POM 91768 640-D2
ROSE LEE CT
21600 SCTA 91350 4461-B7
ROSELIN PL
2100 LA 90039 594-E4
ROSELLA ST
14000 LACo 91746 637-H6
ROSELLE AV
12800 HAW 90250 733-E2
15200 LACo 90260 733-E5
18800 TOR 90504 763-E3
ROSELLI ST
600 BURB 91501 533-J7
600 BURB 91501 534-A7
W ROSELYN PL
100 MONP 91754 636-B2
ROSELYN WY
200 MONP 91754 636-B2
ROSE MALLOW LN
- LACo 91387 4552-B4
ROSEMARIE CT
- CYP 90630 767-C7
ROSEMARIE DR
400 ARCD 91007 597-B2
ROSE MARIE LN
12000 Brwd 90049 631-G3
ROSEMARIE ST
37800 PMDL 93550 4286-D1
ROSEMARY AV
3400 GLDL 91208 534-H4
ROSEMARY DR
4800 Eagl 90041 565-A6
5100 CYP 90630 767-E7
E ROSEMARY DR
2800 WCOV 91791 639-C1
ROSEMARY LN
100 BREA 92821 709-D4
500 BURB 91505 563-D2
1000 LVRN 91750 570-E6
16700 CHLS 91709 710-F3
ROSEMEAD AV
3700 LA 90032 595-E5
ROSEMEAD BLVD
4700 PRV 90660 676-F6
8700 DWNY 90240 706-D2
ROSEMEAD BLVD Rt#-19
- ELMN 91731 596-H7
300 LACo 91733 636-J7
3000 SELM 91733 636-H1
3000 SELM 91770 636-H1
3100 ELMN 91770 636-H1
3200 ELMN 91731 636-H1
3200 RSMD 91770 636-H1
3500 RSMD 91770 596-H7
3800 LACo 90660 636-J7
3800 LACo 90660 676-G2
3900 PRV 90660 676-G2
4800 TEML 91780 596-H4
4800 TEML 91776 596-H4
5100 LACo 91775 596-H4
7700 PRV 90660 706-D2
N ROSEMEAD BLVD
100 LACo 91107 566-H5
100 PAS 91107 566-G3
N ROSEMEAD BLVD Rt#-19
1000 LACo 91733 636-J4
1500 SELM 91733 636-J4
S ROSEMEAD BLVD
200 LACo 91107 566-H7
3700 LACo 91775 566-H7
6300 TEML 91775 596-H2
S ROSEMEAD BLVD
6300 TEML 91780 596-H2
6300 LACo 91775 596-H2
ROSEMEAD PL
3000 RSMD 91770 636-H2
ROSEMERE LN
- POM 91767 601-A3
ROSEMIST LN
1600 CHLS 91709 680-G4
ROSEMONT AV
100 Echo 90026 634-C1
300 PAS 91103 565-F1
800 Echo 90026 594-D7
1600 PAS 91103 535-F7
2900 LaCr 91214 534-G2
2900 Mont 91020 534-G2
3800 GLDL 91020 534-G3
4800 LaCr 91214 504-G7
ROSEMONT BLVD
100 SGBL 91775 596-D3
100 SGBL 91776 596-D3
ROSEMONT LN
27200 SCTA 91354 4460-G7
ROSEMOUNT AV
1800 CLAR 91711 571-C7
ROSEMOUNT RD
900 GLDL 91207 564-G2
ROSEMOUNT WY
- PMDL 93551 4104-D6
ROSENDA ST
400 SGBL 91776 596-E4
ROSENELL TER
400 Echo 90026 634-C1
ROSEPARK CT
24800 SCTA 91321 4640-G2
E ROSES RD
100 SGBL 91775 596-E2
W ROSES RD
100 SGBL 91775 596-D2
ROSETON AV
10100 SFSP 90670 706-G4
11800 NRWK 90650 706-G7
12200 NRWK 90650 736-G1
17000 ART 90701 736-G7
17800 ART 90701 766-G1
19200 CRTS 90703 766-G2
20300 LKWD 90715 766-G4
ROSE TREE LN
32700 Pear 93553 4378-J6
ROSETTA DR
1100 Top 90290 590-C4
ROSETTA WY
16700 PRM 90723 735-G6
ROSETTE LN
- BqtC 91354 4460-E3
ROSEVALE DR
5100 TEML 91780 597-B4
ROSEVIEW AV
1000 LA 90065 594-J4
ROSE VILLA ST
1400 PAS 91106 566-B5
1800 PAS 91107 566-B5
1900 LACo 91107 566-B5
ROSEWALK WY
- PAS 91103 565-G2
W ROSEWAY ST
1200 WCOV 91790 638-E1
ROSEWOOD AV
2300 LAN 93535 4106-E1
3200 LA 90066 672-A3
4000 LA 90004 594-A7
4200 LA 90004 593-F7
6600 LA 90036 593-B7
7900 LA 90048 593-A7
8200 WHWD 90048 593-A7
8400 LA 90048 592-J7
8400 WHWD 90048 592-H7
9900 SGAT 90280 705-E6
10600 LYN 90262 705-E6
37500 PMDL 93550 4286-H3
S ROSEWOOD AV
900 ING 90301 703-B4
ROSEWOOD CT
- StvR 91381 4550-B3
W ROSEWOOD CT
1200 ONT 91762 601-H6
ROSEWOOD DR
1600 MNRO 91016 567-E6
ROSEWOOD LN
500 BREA 92821 709-A5
500 PAS 91103 565-G3
600 LHB 90631 738-F1
600 SDMS 91773 600-C3
ROSEWOOD ST
1500 UPL 91784 571-H6
1800 LVRN 91750 570-G7
4300 MTCL 91763 601-E6
N ROSEWOOD WY
1700 UPL 91784 571-H6
W ROSEWOOD WY
1300 UPL 91784 571-H6
ROSILLA PL
2000 LA 90046 592-H3
ROSILYN DR
4200 City 90063 635-F3
ROSIN AV
10100 WHIT 90603 708-A4
ROSINA ST
7800 LBCH 90808 796-H1
ROSITA AV
1800 BURB 91504 533-E5
ROSITA DR
1800 GLDL 91208 534-H7
ROSITA DR
21400 CRSN 90745 764-F6
ROSITA LN
300 PAS 91105 565-E6
ROSITA PL
2200 PVE 90274 792-H3
4700 Tarz 91356 560-G4
ROSITA ST
17900 Enc 91316 561-A4
18100 Tarz 91356 561-A4
18200 Tarz 91356 560-F4
ROSLIN AV
17500 TOR 90504 763-D1
20300 TOR 90503 763-D4
ROSLYNDALE AV
8600 Pcma 91331 532-D1
8700 Pcma 91331 502-A5
ROSLYNDALE CT
14100 Pcma 91331 502-A5
ROSNICK PL
17000 GmH 91344 481-C6
ROSS AV
600 ALH 91801 636-D1
W ROSS AV
1800 ALH 91803 635-G1
ROSS CT
200 CLAR 91711 601-D1
ROSS PL
- SMAD 91024 566-J2
300 Wilm 90744 794-E6
ROSS RD
10600 Litl 93543 4468-E3
10600 Pear 93553 4468-E3
ROSS ST
400 GLDL 91207 564-E2
1200 POM 91767 601-C7
1400 SBdC 92397 (4652-E2 See Page 4651)
2000 VER 90058 674-G2
13200 NRWK 90650 737-B2
ROSSBURN AV
13700 HAW 90250 733-A3
ROSSBURY PL
10000 LA 90064 632-E6
ROSSELLEN PL
300 COV 91723 599-C6
ROSSER ST
9100 BLF 90706 736-A3
ROSSFORD AV
19900 LKWD 90715 766-H3
ROSSINI PL
3100 Top 90290 560-B7
ROSSITER AV
11900 LA 91342 481-J7
ROSS LOOS PL
1800 Echo 90026 634-D1
ROSSLYN ST
3000 GLDL 91204 594-F1
3000 LA 90065 594-F1
ROSSMOOR WY
3200 OrCo 90720 796-J4
3400 LALM 90720 796-J4
ROSSMOOR CENTER WY
3300 SLB 90740 796-J5
N ROSSMORE AV
300 LA 90004 593-F7
300 LA 90004 633-F2
S ROSSMORE AV
100 LA 90004 633-F1
300 LA 90020 633-F1
600 LA 90005 633-F1
600 LA 90010 633-F1
ROSSMOYNE AV
1000 GLDL 91207 564-G3
ROSSWOOD TER
6300 HiPk 90042 565-E7
ROSTRATA AV
5600 BPK 90621 737-G7
6400 BPK 90621 767-H1
ROSWELL AV
- LBCH 90803 826-A2
700 LBCH 90804 796-A6
10900 SBdC 91766 641-D3
11400 SBdC 91710 641-D5
12100 CHNO 91710 641-D6
N ROSWELL AV
100 LBCH 90803 826-A1
300 LBCH 90814 796-A7
300 LBCH 90814 826-A1
2200 LBCH 90815 796-A4
ROSWELL CT
3900 SBdC 91710 641-D4
27000 SCTA 91354 4550-G1
ROSWELL RD
11300 SBdC 92371 (4472-J2 See Page 4471)
ROSWELL ST
3000 LA 90065 594-F2
ROSY CIR
12500 LA 90066 672-E6
ROTARY DR
1600 Echo 90026 594-C5
1900 LVRN 91750 570-J5
ROTELLA ST
37800 PMDL 93550 4286-G2
ROTH ST E
43600 LAN 93535 4106-D1
ROTHDELL TR
8000 LA 90046 593-A3
ROTHKO LN
6000 SIMI 93063 499-B1
ROTHROCK DR
28300 RPV 90275 792-H7
ROTTA AV
9600 Sunl 91040 503-B5
ROTUNDA RD
23700 SCTA 91355 4550-F7
24000 SCTA 91355 4640-F1
ROTUNDE MESA RD
24700 LACo 90265 629-C2
ROUGE ST
12400 SunV 91352 502-F7
ROUGH RD
- PMDL 93550 4376-D3
ROUGHRIDER RD
200 LACo 91750 570-H6
ROULETTE LN
43100 LAN 93536 4105-B3
ROUND DR
2600 LA 90032 595-F7
ROUNDABOUT DR
100 LPUE 91744 638-E7
100 LPUE 91744 678-E1
ROUND HILL DR
7300 LAN 93536 4104-C6
ROUNDHILL DR
6200 WHIT 90601 677-E5
ROUND HILL LN
19800 WAL 91789 639-E6
ROUND MEADOW RD
5000 HIDH 91302 559-C4
ROUND ROCK DR
2600 DBAR 91765 679-J6
ROUNDTABLE CT
900 WAL 91789 639-E5
ROUND TOP DR
4400 LA 90065 564-H6
4800 Eagl 90041 564-H6
ROUNDTOP RD
- LACo (4556-H7 See Page 4466)
- LACo (4646-H3 See Page 4645)
ROUNDTREE CIR
1700 DBAR 91765 679-H4
ROUNDTREE CT
200 BREA 92821 709-E7
19900 WAL 91789 679-E2
ROUNDTREE LN
4300 CHNO 91710 641-E5
ROUNDTREE PL
4800 THO 91362 557-F1
ROUNDUP DR
9300 MTCL 91763 601-F5
22000 WAL 91789 639-J5
ROUNDUP RD
- RHLS 90274 823-F2
100 GLDR 91741 569-H5
N ROUNDUP RD
- VeCo 91307 529-A5
ROUND VALLEY DR
14500 Shrm 91403 562-A5
14500 Shrm 91403 561-J5
ROUNTREE RD
10500 LA 90064 632-E6
ROUSSEAU LN
4000 LACo 90274 793-C6
15200 LMRD 90638 737-H4
E ROUTE 66
100 GLDR 91741 569-G6
300 GLDR 91740 569-H6
2000 GLDR 91740 570-A6
2000 GLDR 91741 570-A6
W ROUTE 66
100 GLDR 91740 569-D6
100 GLDR 91741 569-D6
ROUTH DR
2500 RowH 91748 679-C7
ROUX LN
- PMDL 93551 4195-C5
ROVER RIDGE RD
4400 Actn 93510 4374-J2
ROW AL
1900 PAS 91103 535-G7
ROW CT
28500 SCTA 91350 4461-D4
N ROWAN AV
100 City 90063 635-D4
1800 LA 90032 635-D2
S ROWAN AV
100 City 90063 635-D6
600 LACo 90023 635-D7
900 LACo 90023 675-D1
1300 CMRC 90023 675-D1
ROWAN CT
39400 PMDL 93551 4195-E5
ROWE LN
5300 LPMA 90623 767-D3
ROWEL CT
31600 Actn 93510 4465-E3
ROWELL AV
9200 Chat 91311 499-F6
9200 Chat 91311 499-F7
N ROWELL AV
100 MANB 90266 732-H5
S ROWELL AV
100 MANB 90266 732-H7
ROWENA AV
2700 LA 90039 594-C3
3100 LFlz 90027 594-B3
ROWENA DR
3000 OrCo 90720 796-H6
ROWHER TKTR
- LACo 91390 (4282-J6 See Page 4281)
- LACo 91390 4283-A6
ROWHER CANYON RD
- LACo 91390 (4372-H5 See Page 4281)
ROWLAND AV
3900 ELMN 91731 597-A5
5700 TEML 91780 597-A2
5800 ARCD 91007 597-A1
E ROWLAND AV
100 COV 91723 599-C6
1000 WCOV 91790 598-H6
1400 WCOV 91790 598-H6
1900 WCOV 91791 599-C6
19200 LACo 91723 599-C6
W ROWLAND AV
100 COV 91723 599-A6
1000 WCOV 91790 598-F6
W ROWLAND CIR
2900 ANA 92804 767-J6
ROWLAND ST
17500 INDS 91748 678-H3
18100 INDS 91748 679-A3
E ROWLAND ST
15800 LPUE 91744 638-D7
ROWLES CT
- LA 90066 672-D4
ROWLEY CT
37600 PMDL 93552 4287-A2
ROWLEY PL
7200 Tuj 91042 504-A2
ROWLEY ST
8700 Litl 93543 4377-J1
ROXABEL ST
8400 SFSP 90670 706-H2
ROXANNE AV
800 LBCH 90815 796-F4
3000 LBCH 90808 796-F1
3200 LBCH 90808 766-F7
3900 LA 90008 673-D2
E ROXANNE WY
6800 LBCH 90815 796-F6
ROXBURGH AV
4400 LACo 91722 598-H3
N ROXBURGH AV
5200 LACo 91702 598-H1
ROXBURGH PL
18700 Nor 91326 480-H6
ROXBURY CT
1500 UPL 91784 571-H4
ROXBURY DR
800 FUL 92833 738-B6
800 PAS 91104 566-D2
1100 LA 90035 632-F3
1100 LA 90212 632-F3
N ROXBURY DR
400 BHLS 90210 632-E1
800 BHLS 90210 592-D7
S ROXBURY DR
100 BHLS 90212 632-F3
400 LA 90035 632-F3
ROXBURY RD
900 SMRO 91108 596-B3
8200 LA 90069 593-A5
8200 WHWD 90069 593-A5
ROXBURY ST
3600 SPed 90731 854-A2
W ROXBURY ST
1300 WCOV 91790 638-D3
ROXBURY TER
1100 LHB 90631 708-B7
1100 LHB 90631 738-B1
ROXCOVE DR
5300 RHE 90274 823-B1
ROXDALE AV
400 LACo 91744 638-H7
ROXFORD PL
15000 LA 91342 481-H2
ROXFORD ST
14900 LA 91342 481-G3
16000 GmH 91344 481-F4
ROXHAM AV
600 LPUE 91744 678-F1
ROXIE ST
10200 ELMN 91731 597-B7
ROXLEY DR
600 LACo 91744 638-H6
ROXTON AV
3700 LA 90008 673-G2
14400 GAR 90249 733-G4
ROY DR
20500 SCTA 91321 4641-D1
ROY ST
6000 HiPk 90042 595-D1
ROYAL BLVD
1300 GLDL 91207 564-F1
20900 LACo 91502 764-A5
ROYAL CT
700 Ven 90291 671-G5
37400 PMDL 93552 4287-B3
ROYAL RD
28000 Cstc 91384 4369-F6
ROYAL ST
3000 LA 90007 634-B7
3200 LA 90007 674-B1
ROYAL COACH AV
200 POM 91767 600-J5
200 POM 91767 601-A5
ROYALCREST CT
13200 LMRD 90638 738-A1
ROYAL CREST PL
4100 Enc 91436 561-G5
ROYALE CIR
4000 LAN 93536 4195-A1
4100 LAN 93536 4194-J1
ROYALE PL
2500 FUL 92833 738-B4
ROYAL ESTATES DR
15800 LACo 91722 598-F4
ROYAL GLEN RD
3900 WLKV 91361 557-C6
ROYAL HAVEN PL
15800 Shrm 91403 561-F7
ROYAL HILLS DR
16300 Enc 91436 561-E7
ROYAL LYTHAM CT
- PMDL 93551 4195-C2
ROYAL MEADOW PL
15800 Shrm 91403 561-G6
ROYAL MEADOW RD
3600 Shrm 91403 561-G6
ROYAL MOUNT DR
16000 Enc 91436 561-F5
ROYAL OAK PL
3900 Enc 91436 561-F6
ROYAL OAK RD
15600 Enc 91436 561-F6
ROYAL OAKS DR
400 MNRO 91016 567-H4
1100 MNRO 91016 568-A5
1100 DUAR 91010 568-D4
3000 THO 91362 557-A3
ROYAL OAKS DR N
1400 DUAR 91010 568-A4
1400 BRAD 91010 568-A4
1600 LACo 91010 568-A4
ROYAL OAKS RD
- StvR 91381 4640-B2
ROYAL PALM
- WCOV 91790 638-H6
ROYAL PALM CIR
12900 CHNO 91710 641-F7
ROYAL PALMS DR
1600 LA 90732 853-H1
1600 SPed 90731 853-H1
ROYAL RIDGE RD
15500 Shrm 91403 561-G6
ROYAL STONE DR
20400 MAL 90265 629-J6
ROYALTON DR
9600 LA 90210 592-F3
ROYALTON PL
2000 LA 90210 592-F3
ROYALTY DR
1900 POM 91767 601-A6
ROYAL VIEW RD
16800 HacH 91745 678-F5
ROYALVIEW ST
400 DUAR 91010 568-D4
ROYAL VISTA CT
- SCTA 91351 4551-F4
5000 THO 91362 557-E1
ROYAL WOODS DR
3500 Shrm 91403 561-G6
ROYAL WOODS PL
15600 Shrm 91403 561-G6
ROYCE CT
9700 LA 90210 592-C1
36800 PMDL 93552 4287-B4
ROYCE DR
- LA 90095 632-B1
ROYCE DR W
17600 Enc 91316 561-B3
ROYCE ST
400 Alta 91001 535-F5
ROYCETON CT
32000 WLKV 91361 557-C6
ROYCOVE DR
3000 LACo 91724 599-G7
ROYCROFT AV
- LBCH 90803 826-A1
300 LBCH 90814 796-A7
300 LBCH 90814 826-A1
1300 LBCH 90804 796-A5
2300 LBCH 90815 796-A3
ROYCROFT LN
7600 LPMA 90623 767-D3
ROYCROFT ST
10800 SunV 91352 503-A6
ROYER AV
5200 WdHl 91367 559-G2
6200 WdHl 91367 529-G7
6400 CanP 91307 529-G5
7500 LA 91304 529-G2
ROYMOR DR
26100 CALB 91302 558-H4
ROYSTON PL
- RowH 91748 679-B7
2800 LA 90210 592-C1
ROYSTON ST
12700 BALD 91706 597-H7
ROYWOOD DR
1600 LAN 93535 4016-C7
ROZALEE DR
36400 PMDL 93550 4286-B5
ROZICH RD
33800 LACo 91390 4373-C3
ROZIE AV
5400 WdHl 91367 559-E2
RUBENS AV
12400 LA 90066 672-D6
RUBERTA AV
300 GLDL 91201 563-J3
RUBERTA AV
500 GLDL 91201 564-A2
RUBICON RD
20900 Top 90290 590-B2
RUBIDOUX ST
300 MTBL 90640 676-C1
RUBIO AV
4500 Enc 91436 561-E4
6500 VanN 91406 531-D5
8500 LA 91343 531-D1
8800 LA 91343 501-D4
10300 GmH 91344 501-D1
RUBIO DR
1400 SMRO 91108 566-E7
1400 SMRO 91108 596-E1
RUBIO ST
1000 Alta 91001 536-B5
RUBIO CANYON RD
3000 Alta 91001 536-B4
RUBIO CREST DR
3300 Alta 91001 536-B4
RUBIO VISTA RD
1200 Alta 91001 536-B4
RUBY CT
- CRTS 90703 767-A3
- GAR 90248 764-A1
1300 UPL 91784 571-H5
1500 DBAR 91789 679-H4
2300 WCOV 91792 679-A1
5100 LACo 93536 4104-H5
RUBY LN
- PMDL 93552 4287-D2
27500 Cstc 91384 4369-G6
RUBY PL
400 LBCH 90813 795-D7
5600 TOR 90503 763-A6
6000 HiPk 90042 595-D1
RUBY ST
100 RBCH 90277 762-J6
1000 RBCH 90277 763-B6
5100 TOR 90503 763-B6
6200 HiPk 90042 595-E2
RUBY WY
- POM 91767 600-J2
RUBY GLEN CT
13000 CHLS 91709 680-G3
RUBYRED LN
- PMDL 93551 4285-E3
RUCHEL ST
12100 NRWK 90650 706-H7
RUCHTI RD
10600 SGAT 90280 705-F6
RUCKER CT
- LAN 93535 4106-F1
RUCKER ST
- LAN 93535 4016-F7
- LAN 93535 4106-F1
RUDALL AV
37800 PMDL 93550 4286-F1
E RUDDOCK ST
600 COV 91723 599-D5
900 COV 91724 599-D5
RUDELL RD
1700 BURB 91501 534-A5
RUDISILL ST
4100 MTCL 91763 601-D7
RUDMAN DR
11200 CULC 90230 672-H5
RUDNICK AV
5600 WdHl 91367 559-J1
6600 CanP 91303 529-J6
7600 LA 91304 529-J1
9500 Chat 91311 499-J5
RUDY ST
2500 RowH 91748 679-E7
RUDYARD ST
900 WCOV 91790 638-D3
RUE BEAUPRE
7400 RPV 90275 822-F3
RUEBENS ST
43800 LAN 93535 4106-C1
RUE CREVIER
20300 SCTA 91351 4551-D3
RUE DANIEL
28900 SCTA 91387 4552-E1
RUE DE LA PIERRE
30500 RPV 90275 822-G3
RUE DE VALLE
500 AZU 91702 598-F1
7400 LA 90046 593-B1
RUE ENTREE
28800 SCTA 91387 4552-D1
RUE GODBOUT
7200 RPV 90275 822-F2
RUE LA FLEUR
7200 RPV 90275 822-G3
RUE LANGLOIS
30500 RPV 90275 822-F3
RUELAS ST
2400 IRW 91010 567-J7
2400 IRW 91010 597-J1
RUE LE CHARLENE
1900 LA 90732 823-G5
1900 RPV 90275 823-G5
1900 RPV 90732 823-G5
1900 LA 90275 823-G5
RUE ROYALE
500 COV 91723 599-C5
RUETHER AV
- SCTA 91350 4551-D3
26800 SCTA 91351 4551-D2
RUE VALOIS
30600 RPV 90275 822-F3
RUEZ LN
1500 Boyl 90033 635-C3
RUFF DR
16800 HacH 91745 678-E5
RUFFNER AV
6500 VanN 91406 531-D3
8700 LA 91343 531-D1
8800 LA 91343 501-D5
10200 GmH 91344 501-D2
11500 GmH 91344 481-D7
RUFUS AV
8900 WHIT 90603 707-F3
9500 LACo 90604 707-E4
9800 LACo 90605 707-D4
RUGBY AV
5900 HNTP 90255 674-J7
RUGBY DR
8500 WHWD 90069 592-J6
RUGBY PL
8000 LA 90046 592-J3
8000 LA 90046 593-A3
RUGGIERO AV
11300 LA 91342 503-A1
RUGGLES ST
1100 LVRN 91750 570-E6
RUHLAND AV
1500 MANB 90266 732-J6
1900 RBCH 90278 732-J7
1900 RBCH 90278 733-A7
RUIZ PL
2200 HacH 91745 678-D5
RUIZ ST
1500 POM 91768 600-G6
RULEN ST
41000 LACo 93551 4193-H2
RUMBOLD ST
1000 GAR 90248 764-A1
RUMFORD AV
3000 ELMN 91732 637-F2
RUMPOLE CT
- CynC 91351 4462-A4
RUMSON ST
15700 HacH 91745 678-B3
RUNAN WK
- LACo 91390 4192-D3
E RUNDELL ST
7400 DWNY 90242 705-H6
RUNNING DR
- AZU 91702 568-J4
RUNNING BRANCH RD
20900 DBAR 91765 709-G1
RUNNING BRAND CIR
19600 WAL 91789 639-D7
RUNNING BRAND RD
- RHLS 90274 823-C4
RUNNING BROOK LN
700 WAL 91789 639-H5
RUNNING BROOK WY
15200 CHLS 91709 680-G6
RUNNING CREEK LN
1200 UPL 91784 571-J4
RUNNINGCREEK LN
12400 CRTS 90703 736-J5
RUNNING DEER RD
600 WAL 91789 639-C7
RUNNING HORSE RD
25200 Nwhl 91321 4641-G1
25200 Nwhl 91321 4551-G7
RUNNING RIVER CT
21400 DBAR 91765 679-H4
RUNNING SPRINGS RD
14500 HacH 91745 637-H7
14500 HacH 91745 677-J1
RUNNYMEDE ST
11000 SunV 91352 532-J4
11700 NHol 91605 532-F4
13600 VanN 91405 532-A4
14500 VanN 91405 531-J4
15300 VanN 91406 531-B4
18600 Res 91335 530-F4
20100 Win 91306 530-C4
20800 CanP 91303 530-A4
22000 CanP 91303 529-J4
22700 CanP 91307 529-G4
RUNWAY LN
- LA 90094 702-E1
RUNWAY RD
- LA 90094 702-D1
RUNYAN ST
- LHB 90631 738-C1
RUNYON CANYON RD
1900 LA 90046 593-C2
RUOFF AV
9400 WHIT 90603 707-F4
10100 LACo 90604 707-D5
RUPERT AV
4900 Enc 91316 561-A4
RUPERT LN
4900 LCF 91011 535-D4
29800 Cstc 91384 4459-D2
RUPP RD
8700 DWNY 90242 736-A1
N RURAL DR
100 MONP 91755 636-C2
S RURAL DR
100 MONP 91755 636-C2
RUSH ST
8200 RSMD 91770 636-F3
8600 LACo 91770 636-G3
9200 LACo 91733 636-J3
9200 SELM 91733 636-J3
9400 SELM 91733 637-A3
12300 LACo 91733 637-D4
RUSH ST
17000 BLF 90706 736-C6
RUSH CANYON RD
- LACo 91390 (4372-F3 See Page 4281)
35300 PMDL 93550 4376-E2
RUSHFORD ST
15700 WHIT 90603 707-H5
16200 WHIT 90603 708-A5
RUSHING DR
17400 GmH 91344 481-B6
RUSHING CREEK TR
- PMDL 93550 4376-F1
RUSHLIGHT AV
7700 Litl 93543 4377-G2
RUSHMORE CT
- SCTA 91387 4462-G7
4300 CHNO 91710 641-E7
RUSHMORE ST
9600 PRV 90660 676-G6
RUSKIN ST
3000 SMCA 90405 671-G4
RUSS PL
5300 PMDL 93552 4287-B2
S RUSSELEE DR
900 WCOV 91790 638-F3
RUSSELL AV
200 FUL 92833 738-E7
4100 LFlz 90027 594-A3
5300 LFlz 90027 593-H4
12300 CHNO 91710 641-F7
S RUSSELL AV
100 MONP 91755 636-C3
N RUSSELL DR
1400 LBCH 90804 796-B6
N RUSSELL LN
- LACo 91387 4552-B5
RUSSELL PL
600 POM 91767 601-A6
RUSSELL ST
100 INDS 91744 638-D7
100 INDS 91744 678-C1
900 LHB 90631 708-C4
2500 OrCo 90631 708-A4
13400 WHIT 90602 707-D1
13800 WHIT 90605 707-E1
15800 WHIT 90603 707-J4
16100 WHIT 90603 708-A4
E RUSSELL ST
100 AZU 91702 598-J1
100 AZU 91702 599-A1
RUSSELL RANCH RD
31300 WLKV 91362 557-E5
RUSSET LN
1700 SMRO 91108 596-F1
RUSSETT AV
10200 Sunl 91040 503-F2
RUSS JAY ST
20600 SCTA 91350 4461-D5
RUSSO ST
5100 LA 90230 672-E6
RUST CT
1400 CLAR 91711 601-C1
RUSTIC CT
100 BREA 92821 709-B6
1500 DBAR 91765 680-D3
RUSTIC DR
400 LA 90065 595-A3
RUSTIC LN
- PacP 90272 631-C5
2700 GLDL 91208 534-H6
E RUSTIC RD
300 LA 90402 631-B7
W RUSTIC RD
400 LA 90402 631-B6
RUSTICA CT
- BqtC 91354 4460-F3
RUSTIC CANYON RD
- PacP 90272 591-A6
- PacP 90272 631-C2
RUSTIC CREEK LN
- PacP 90272 631-C5
RUSTIC GATE WY
2500 HacH 91745 678-E5
RUSTIC GLEN DR
- POM 91766 640-F6
RUSTIC HILL DR
10900 LACo 90601 677-C2
RUSTIC OAK DR
31500 WLKV 91361 557-D6
RUSTLER LN
- RHE 90274 793-B5
RUSTLING OAKS DR
5900 AGRH 91301 558-A3
RUSTON RD
19900 WdHl 91364 560-D4
RUSTY FIG CIR
13300 CRTS 90703 737-B6
RUSTY PUMP RD
23500 DBAR 91765 680-C5
RUSTY SPUR RD
2000 DBAR 91765 680-B4
RUTAN WY
700 PAS 91104 566-A1
RUTGERS AV
13000 DWNY 90242 736-B2
N RUTGERS AV
2000 LBCH 90815 796-B2
3300 LBCH 90808 796-B1
3500 LBCH 90808 766-B5
RUTGERS CT
1200 WAL 91789 639-F4
1600 CLAR 91711 601-B1

STREET Block	City	ZIP	Pg-Grid
RUTGERS PL			
1500	Hrbr	90710	793-J2
RUTH AV			
200	Ven	90291	671-G4
4800	Eagl	90041	565-C6
10900	LYN	90262	705-C6
N RUTH AV			
4600	NLB	90805	765-D5
RUTH CT			
-	LAN	93535	4016-G4
2300	RowH	91748	679-E6
2300	WCOV	91792	679-A1
RUTH LN			
-	LAN	93536	4105-C3
44200	LAN	93536	4015-C7
RUTH WY			
1200	UPL	91784	571-J5
RUTHBAR DR			
3700	HAW	90250	733-E4
N RUTHCREST AV			
500	LACo	91744	638-F5
RUTH ELAINE DR			
3000	OrCo	90720	796-H3
RUTHELEN AV			
11000	LACo	90047	703-H6
12900	GAR	90249	733-H2
15600	GAR	90247	733-H5
RUTHELEN ST			
3600	LA	90018	673-H1
5100	LA	90062	673-H5
8600	LA	90047	703-H3
RUTHER AV			
13400	PRM	90723	735-H2
13400	SGAT	90280	735-H2
RUTHERFORD CT			
3700	ING	90305	703-E3
RUTHERFORD DR			
1500	PAS	91103	565-D2
2600	LA	90068	593-G2
RUTHERFORD PL			
-	SCTA	91354	4460-F7
RUTHERFORD HILL DR			
-	LA	91304	529-D4
RUTHERGLEN ST			
16200	WHIT	90603	708-A6
N RUTHLEE AV			
6400	LACo	91775	596-F1
6800	LACo	91775	566-F7
RUTHRON AV			
44000	LAN	93536	4015-B6
44000	LAN	93536	4105-B1
RUTHSPRING DR			
15700	SCTA	91387	4552-D7
RUTH SWIGGETT DR			
2600	LA	90032	595-E7
RUTHUPHAM ST			
3700	LA	90031	595-C5
3700	LA	90032	595-C5
RUTHVEN LN			
10300	BelA	90077	592-A3
RUTHWOOD DR			
5400	CALB	91302	558-H3
RUTLAND AV			
900	HiPk	90042	595-F1
1000	HiPk	90042	565-F7
9400	LACo	90605	707-C3
RUTLEDGE PL			
1300	BREA	92821	708-H5
10000	SunV	91352	533-C2
RUXTON AV			
1800	RBCH	90278	763-C1
RYAN AV			
500	LHB	90631	708-D4
5300	LKWD	90712	765-H3
RYAN CT			
-	LA	91343	501-G6
RYAN LN			
-	LACo	91387	4462-C6
12400	CRTS	90703	766-J2
RYAN ST			
14000	LA	91342	482-A2
14500	LA	91342	481-J3
RYAN WY			
2200	UPL	91784	571-J3
RYANDALE DR			
11200	CULC	90230	672-G5
RYAN RIDGE WY			
-	WdHl	91367	559-J2
RYANS PL			
-	LAN	93536	4104-E2
2500	LAN	93536	4105-B2
RYCKEBOSCH LN			
43600	LAN	93535	4106-G1
43900	LAN	93535	4016-G7
RYE AV			
500	LHB	90631	708-D7
RYE CIR			
400	LHB	90631	708-E7
RYE CT			
-	THO	91362	557-A1
RYE ST			
11200	LA	91602	562-J4
12300	LA	91604	562-E4
13500	Shrm	91423	562-C4
RYE CANYON RD			
-	Valc	91355	4550-B1
25000	SCTA	91355	4460-C7
25300	SCTA	91355	4550-B1
RYERSON AV			
10700	SGAT	90280	705-G6
10800	SGAT	90242	705-G6
10900	DWNY	90241	705-H3
12400	DWNY	90242	705-G6
RYGATE AV			
1100	LPUE	91744	638-E5
RYLAND AV			
4800	TEML	91780	597-B3
RYNGLER RD			
12000	LA	91604	562-G6
RYON AV			
14700	BLF	90706	736-B4
S			
SABADO CT			
26100	SCTA	91355	4550-G4
SABAL AV			
37000	PMDL	93552	4287-B2
SABAL ST			
37400	PMDL	93552	4287-B3
SABANA DR			
23200	DBAR	91765	640-B7
23200	DBAR	91765	680-B1
SABANA LN			
16000	Enc	91436	561-F7
SABANA RD			
11300	SBdC	92372	4471-J2
SABBIADORO WY			
17700	PacP	90272	630-F5
SABINA CIR			
1500	SIMI	93063	499-A3
SABINA DR			
2400	Top	90290	630-A2
SABINA ST			
3300	LA	90023	635-C7
SABINE DR			
14500	LMRD	90638	737-F1
SABLE AV			
10600	Sunl	91040	503-F3
SABLE LN			
19200	WAL	91789	679-C1
SABRA AV			
-	VeCo	91377	558-A2
SABRA LN			
-	PMDL	93552	4287-E2
SABRE LN			
-	IRW	91706	598-F3
SABRINA AV			
18700	CRTS	90703	767-B2
SABRINA CT			
19600	CRTS	90703	767-B3
SACHE ST			
2500	Actn	93510	4374-J4
2500	Actn	93510	4375-D4
SACHS DR			
42800	LAN	93536	4105-B3
SACHS PL			
1600	COV	91724	599-F4
SACK CT			
-	SCTA	91351	4551-E3
SACO ST			
2900	VER	90058	674-H2
SACRAMENTO AV			
2700	Actn	93510	4465-A1
4500	Actn	93510	4464-H2
SACRAMENTO ST			
600	Alta	91001	535-F6
1700	LA	90021	634-H7
E SACRAMENTO ST			
-	Alta	91001	535-J6
600	Alta	91001	536-A7
SADDLE AV			
15700	LACo	93591	4199-E4
SADDLE DR			
-	PMDL	93551	4195-A6
E SADDLE DR			
6400	LBCH	90815	796-E6
SADDLE RD			
27600	RHE	90274	823-H1
28400	RPV	90275	823-H2
SADDLE BACK DR			
18500	LACo	93591	4200-B3
SADDLEBACK DR			
-	PMDL	93550	4286-H1
SADDLEBACK PL			
12900	CHNO	91710	641-F7
SADDLEBACK RD			
-	RHLS	90274	793-E7
-	RHLS	90274	823-E1
4000	PMDL	93552	4286-J1
15100	LACo	91387	4552-E5
15300	SCTA	91387	4552-E5
SADDLEBACK ST			
4500	MTCL	91763	641-E3
SADDLEBACK RIDGE RD			
18900	SCTA	91351	4551-G1
SADDLEBOW LN			
-	RHE	90274	793-C5
SADDLEBROOK CT			
-	PMDL	93551	4195-B2
SADDLEBROOK DR			
29000	AGRH	91301	558-A4
SADDLE CREEK RD			
5200	HIDH	91302	559-E4
SADDLECREST DR			
19600	WAL	91789	639-D6
SADDLE CREST LN			
4200	WLKV	91361	557-E6
SADDLE HORN LN			
-	LACo	91750	570-H6
-	RHE	90274	793-E6
SADDLEHORN WY			
-	WAL	91789	639-C5
SADDLE HORSE RD			
19200	LACo	93591	4200-C2
SADDLE MOUNTAIN DR			
32300	WLKV	91361	557-C7
SADDLE PEAK CT			
32500	Actn	93510	4465-D1
SADDLE PEAK RD			
21000	Top	90290	629-G1
23100	Top	90290	589-F7
W SADDLE PEAK RD			
24500	LACo	90265	629-C2
SADDLE PEAK TR			
23600	SCTA	91354	4550-G1
SADDLE RIDGE DR			
2500	LACo	91724	639-F1
SADDLE RIDGE LN			
19800	WAL	91789	639-E6
SADDLERIDGE LN			
-	CALB	91302	558-H4
SADDLE RIDGE RD			
13900	LA	91342	481-F1
SADDLERIDGE WY			
27700	Cstc	91384	4459-H6
SADDLETREE CT			
-	LA	91342	481-E2
SADDLE TREE DR			
31500	WLKV	91361	557-D7
SADDLE VIEW RD			
25900	LMTA	90717	793-G6
SADDLEWOOD PL			
-	POM	91766	640-G7
SADIE RD			
400	Top	90290	589-G7
500	Top	90290	629-G1
SADLER AL			
2300	MANB	90266	732-F5
N SADLER AV			
2300	MONP	91754	635-J6
S SADLER AV			
200	ELA	90022	635-J7
600	ELA	90022	675-J1
SADRING AV			
5200	WdHl	91367	559-F1
7800	LA	91304	529-F3
SAED ST			
700	POM	91768	640-E1
SAFARI CT			
1300	LACo	93551	4195-F7
1300	PMDL	93551	4195-F7
SAFARI DR			
13300	LACo	90605	707-C3
SAFE CIR			
2700	LAN	93536	4105-C1
SAFED RD			
-	SIMI	93063	499-B1
SAFFRON AV			
4300	PMDL	93552	4286-J4
SAFFRON LN			
27500	SCTA	91350	4461-A6
SAGA ST			
1000	GLDR	91741	569-G3
SAGAMORE WY			
2900	LA	90065	564-G7
SAGE			
1800	WCOV	91791	639-A4
SAGE CT			
300	BREA	92821	709-B4
4000	PMDL	93552	4286-J4
26800	CALB	91301	588-G1
SAGE LN			
-	Tarz	91356	560-J3
300	LA	90402	631-C7
E SAGE LN			
-	VeCo	91307	529-A4
SAGE PL			
400	GLDR	91741	569-J6
SAGE RD			
100	SBdC	92372	(4472-A7 See Page 4471)
SAGE ST			
2000	LVRN	91750	600-D3
W SAGE ST			
600	CLAR	91711	571-B6
600	LACo	91711	571-B6
SAGE TR			
17700	LACo	93532	4101-J2
SAGEBANK ST			
900	CRSN	90746	764-E1
SAGEBROOK RD			
-	Chat	91311	499-J3
-	Chat	91311	500-A3
SAGEBRUSH AV			
-	Chat	91311	499-H6
SAGEBRUSH CIR			
-	POM	91766	640-F4
SAGEBRUSH DR			
6800	LACo	93536	4104-D6
SAGE BRUSH LN			
900	WAL	91789	639-D6
SAGEBRUSH LN			
-	RHLS	90274	823-D1
SAGEBRUSH WY			
-	AZU	91702	568-J2
-	CRSN	90746	764-F1
23400	SCTA	91321	4640-H3
SAGE CANYON RD			
-	POM	91766	640-G3
SAGECREST CIR			
24500	StvR	91381	4640-D2
SAGECREST WY			
-	Cstc	91384	4459-B4
SAGE HILL RD			
-	LACo	91342	482-J2
SAGEHURST DR			
3400	DUAR	91010	568-F3
SAGE MESA LN			
-	LACo	91390	4461-G1
SAGEMONT PL			
1200	Alta	91001	536-B5
SAGE TREE ST			
38500	LACo	93551	4195-G7
38600	PMDL	93551	4195-G7
SAGE VIEW CT			
-	FUL	92833	738-A3
SAGEVIEW CT			
-	SCTA	91354	4460-G5
SAGEWIND DR			
-	FUL	92833	738-A3
SAG HARBOR CT			
24000	SCTA	91355	4550-F4
SAGINAW ST			
1200	Eagl	90041	565-C6
SAGO ST			
3800	LAN	93536	4015-A7
SAGO PALM			
800	WCOV	91790	638-F2
SAGORA WY			
2400	CHLS	91709	680-J1
SAGUARO ST			
-	PMDL	93550	4286-D5
29700	Cstc	91384	4459-H4
SAHUAYO ST			
43400	LAN	93535	4105-J2
SAIGON AV			
45200	LAN	93534	4015-E4
SAILBOAT CIR			
5300	AGRH	91301	557-G6
SAILFISH AV			
16600	LACo	93535	4109-G6
SAIL VIEW AV			
-	RPV	90275	822-J3
-	RPV	90275	823-A2
SAILVIEW LN			
32100	WLKV	91361	557-C6
SAINT ALBANS AV			
1200	SPAS	91030	595-E3
SAINT ALBANS DR			
2600	OrCo	90720	796-H4
SAINT ALBANS RD			
500	SGBL	91775	596-C2
1000	SMRO	91108	596-B1
SAINT ALBANS ST			
6100	HiPk	90042	565-D7
6100	HiPk	90042	595-D1
SAINT ANDRES AV			
4800	LVRN	91750	570-E6
SAINT ANDREWS AV			
300	LHB	90631	738-D2
4600	BPK	90621	737-J4
4800	BPK	90621	738-A5
SAINT ANDREWS CIR			
4900	BPK	90621	737-J4
4900	BPK	90621	738-A4
SAINT ANDREWS CT			
-	PMDL	93551	4195-B2
-	PRV	90660	676-J1
SAINT ANDREWS DR			
2500	GLDL	91206	565-A3
13100	SLB	90740	796-G7
13400	SLB	90740	826-H1
SAINT ANDREWS LN			
300	AZU	91702	568-H4
24100	CALB	91302	559-D7
24100	CALB	91302	589-D1
SAINT ANDREWS PL			
2100	CLAR	91711	571-F7
12900	GAR	90249	733-H3
15800	GAR	90247	733-H5
17800	TOR	90504	763-H2
N SAINT ANDREWS PL			
100	LA	90004	633-H1
200	LA	90004	593-H7
700	LA	90038	593-H5
1300	Hlwd	90028	593-H4
1900	LA	90068	593-H4
S SAINT ANDREWS PL			
100	LA	90004	633-H2
300	LA	90020	633-H2
600	LA	90005	633-H2
600	LA	90010	633-H2
900	LA	90019	633-H3
2400	LA	90018	633-H7
3400	LA	90018	673-H1
3900	LA	90062	673-H3
5900	LA	90047	673-H7
7200	LA	90047	703-H2
10800	LACo	90047	703-H6
SAINT ANDREWS ST			
45600	LAN	93534	4015-E4
SAINT ANDREWS WY			
-	PMDL	93551	4195-H3
1100	HAW	90250	733-H1
SAINT ANN AV			
5500	CYP	90630	767-D5
5600	BPK	90620	767-D5
SAINT ANNE DR			
31800	Llan	93544	4469-F1
SAINT ANNE PL			
31700	Llan	93544	4469-F1
SAINT ANNES CT			
-	PMDL	93551	4195-C2
SAINT ANNES RD			
-	SCTA	91355	4550-B5
SAINT AUGUSTA LN			
1100	HAW	90250	733-H1
SAINT AUGUSTINE AV			
400	CLAR	91711	601-D4
SAINT BERNARD ST			
7600	Wch	90045	702-C3
7600	PdlR	90293	702-C3
SAINT BONAVENTURE AV			
300	CLAR	91711	601-D5
SAINT CATHERINE WY			
-	AVA	90704	5923-G3
900	CLAR	91711	571-B6
SAINT CHALON RD			
11700	Brwd	90049	591-G7
SAINT CHARLES PL			
4200	LA	90019	633-D5
SAINT CHARLES ST			
4400	VER	90058	674-H4
SAINT CHARLES TER			
1100	ALH	91801	596-A4
SAINT CLAIR AV			
2100	SIMI	93063	499-B2
4100	LA	91604	562-F5
4600	LA	91607	562-F1
5900	LA	91607	532-F7
6000	NHol	91606	532-F6
7000	NHol	91605	532-F3
8300	SunV	91352	532-F3
E SAINT CLAIR CT			
2200	SIMI	93063	499-B2
SAINT CLOUD			
-	CLAR	91711	571-F3
SAINT CLOUD DR			
3300	OrCo	90720	796-J6
3300	SLB	90740	796-J6
SAINT CLOUD RD			
300	BelA	90077	592-B6
SAINT CRISPEN AV			
200	BREA	92821	709-A7
SAINT CROIX CT			
4800	VeCo	91377	557-G2
SAINT DENIS CT			
24600	SCTA	91355	4550-E5
SAINT EDENS CIR			
24200	CanP	91307	529-D5
SAINT ELIZABETH RD			
3600	GLDL	91206	535-C7
SAINT ELMO DR			
4500	LA	90019	633-D5
SAINT ESTABAN ST			
6600	Tuj	91042	504-A5
SAINT FRANCIS PL			
4400	LCF	91011	535-A3
E SAINT FRANCIS PL			
3200	NLB	90805	765-H1
SAINT FRANCIS ST			
100	SGBL	91776	596-E4
SAINT FRANCIS TER			
6600	Hlwd	90028	593-E4
SAINT GEORGE CIR			
9700	CYP	90630	767-D7
SAINT GEORGE DR			
1100	SDMS	91773	599-H2
SAINT GEORGE ST			
2300	LFlz	90027	594-C3
SAINT GREGORY RD			
2900	GLDL	91206	565-B2
SAINT GREGORY ST			
300	CLAR	91711	571-D5
E SAINT IRMO WK			
5500	LBCH	90803	826-C2
SAINT IVES CT			
24400	DBAR	91765	680-E3
SAINT IVES DR			
8700	LA	90069	592-H5
SAINT IVES PL			
1200	LA	90069	592-G5
SAINT JAMES AV			
10400	SGAT	90280	705-E6
SAINT JAMES CIR			
-	BALD	91706	597-J6
13400	BALD	91706	598-A6
SAINT JAMES CT			
1000	SDMS	91773	599-H4
1800	LAN	93534	4015-E3
SAINT JAMES DR			
6000	CULC	90230	672-J4
6000	LACo	90230	672-J4
6100	TEML	91780	596-J2
SAINT JAMES PK			
700	LA	90007	634-C7
SAINT JAMES PK W			
2300	LA	90007	634-B7
SAINT JAMES PL			
2300	LA	90007	634-B7
2600	Alta	91001	535-J6
2700	Alta	91001	536-A5
12700	BALD	91706	597-H7
SAINT JEAN CT			
30800	WLKV	91362	557-F5
SAINT JOHN AV			
-	PAS	91103	565-G5
-	PAS	91105	565-G5
SAINT JOHN CIR			
9700	CYP	90630	767-D7
SAINT JOHN PL			
500	ING	90301	703-D2
800	CLAR	91711	571-B7
SAINT JOHN RD			
1700	SLB	90740	796-H7
SAINT JOHN ST			
1500	LA	90012	634-H2
SAINT JOHNSWOOD DR			
3700	WdHl	91364	560-A6
SAINT JOSEPH AV			
-	LBCH	90803	826-B1
300	LBCH	90814	796-B7
300	LBCH	90814	826-B1
2300	LBCH	90815	796-B3
E SAINT JOSEPH ST			
-	ARCD	91006	567-D5
W SAINT JOSEPH ST			
-	ARCD	91007	567-D4
SAINT JOSEPHS PL			
1300	LA	90015	634-E6
SAINT JULIEN WY			
-	PMDL	93551	4285-D3
SAINT KATHERINE DR			
200	LCF	91011	535-C7
200	PAS	91103	535-D7
SAINT LAURENT DR			
-	PMDL	93552	4287-C1
5800	AGRH	91301	557-G3
SAINT LAURENT PL			
5000	PMDL	93552	4287-B1
SAINT LAWRENCE ST			
28900	Cstc	91384	4459-C6
SAINT LOUIS AV			
400	LBCH	90814	795-G7
700	LBCH	90804	795-G4
1800	SIGH	90755	795-G2
3200	Bxby	90807	795-G1
6300	NLB	90805	765-G1
6300	NLB	90805	735-G7
SAINT LOUIS CT			
4900	CULC	90230	672-H3
SAINT LOUIS DR			
10700	ELMN	91731	597-C6
SAINT LOUIS PL			
6200	NLB	90805	765-G1
N SAINT LOUIS ST			
100	Boyl	90033	635-A4
S SAINT LOUIS ST			
100	Boyl	90033	635-A5
600	LA	90023	635-A5
700	LA	90023	634-J6
SAINT MALO AV			
500	LACo	91744	638-D4
500	LPUE	91744	638-C6
4500	LACo	91722	598-G3
SAINT MALO ST			
400	WCOV	91790	638-E2
SAINT MARK AV			
4300	LACo	91750	570-H7
SAINT MARTIN LN			
1000	GLDL	91206	565-A3
SAINT MARYS CT			
1100	LBCH	90813	795-E6
SAINT MICHEL AV			
-	Brwd	90049	632-A3
SAINT MORITZ DR			
18300	Tarz	91356	560-J5
24000	SCTA	91355	4550-F5
SAINT NICHOLAS AV			
4600	CULC	90230	672-G4
4600	LA	90230	672-G4
SAINT PANCRATIUS PL			
3500	LKWD	90712	765-J2
SAINT PAUL AV			
600	LA	90017	634-E4
SAINT PAUL PL			
600	LA	90017	634-E3
SAINT PAUL ST			
500	POM	91767	601-C7
500	POM	91767	641-D1
N SAINT PIERRE AV			
2400	Alta	91001	535-F6
SAINT PIERRE RD			
200	BelA	90077	592-B6
SAINT REGIS DR			
-	CenC	90067	632-E3
SAINTS CT			
600	SDMS	91773	599-J3
SAINT SUSAN PL			
3400	LA	90066	672-C2
SAINT THIRA CT			
900	WCOV	91790	638-F2
SAINT THOMAS DR			
4800	VeCo	91377	557-G2
SAINT TROPEZ DR			
12100	CRTS	90703	736-J7
SAINT TROPEZ PL			
-	Cstc	91384	4459-E2
SAINT TROPEZ ST			
2300	UPL	91784	571-H3
SAINT VINCENT CT			
600	LA	90014	634-F4
SAINT VINCENT DR			
300	VeCo	91377	557-G2
SAINT VLADIMIR ST			
1200	GLDR	91741	569-G6
SAL AV			
8500	LACo	90606	706-G1
SALA PL			
10300	SunV	91352	533-B1
SALADA RD			
13700	LMRD	90638	737-F3
SALAIS ST			
10700	LPUE	91744	678-F1
17400	INDS	91744	678-F1
17400	LACo	91744	678-H1
SALAMANCA			
-	LVRN	91750	570-H3
SALAMANCA AV			
21400	WdHl	91364	560-B4
SALAMEA AV			
5900	WdHl	91367	559-D1
SALANO RD			
100	Llan	93544	4471-J3
100	SBdC	92372	4471-J3
SALAZAR DR			
16200	HacH	91745	678-C4
SALCEDA RD			
25600	SCTA	91355	4550-G5
SALDEE DR			
17100	CRSN	90746	734-D7
SALE AV			
5200	WdHl	91364	559-H3
5400	WdHl	91367	559-H1
6100	WdHl	91367	529-H7
6400	CanP	91307	529-H4
7600	LA	91304	529-H2
SALE PL			
2400	LACo	90255	704-J2
2400	SGAT	90280	704-J2
SALEM CT			
1800	CLAR	91711	571-C7
27600	Cstc	91384	4459-H5
37300	PMDL	93550	4286-C3
SALEM DR			
11900	GrnH	91344	481-C6
SALEM LN			
1000	POM	91766	641-B3
SALEM ST			
300	GLDL	91203	564-C4
6100	CHNO	91710	641-J7
SALEM VILLAGE CT			
4800	CULC	90230	672-J3
SALEM VILLAGE DR			
4800	CULC	90230	672-J3
SALEM VILLAGE PL			
4000	CULC	90230	672-J3
SALERNO			
1000	MTBL	90640	636-D6
SALERNO DR			
400	PacP	90272	630-H5
5500	WLKV	91362	557-F5
SALERNO WY			
-	Nor	91326	500-C2
SALEROSO DR			
1700	RowH	91748	678-G6
SALFORD AV			
11600	DWNY	90241	705-H4
SALIDA AV			
700	LBCH	90815	796-F6
10900	LACo	90604	707-F6
SALIENT DR			
5000	HiPk	90042	595-B2
SALINAS AV			
13000	Wbrk	90059	734-E2
N SALINAS AV			
1900	COMP	90059	734-E2
2200	Wbrk	90059	734-E2
SALINAS CT			
5400	SIMI	93063	499-A1
SALINGER LN			
26000	StvR	91381	4550-B6
SALISBURY CIR			
8500	CYP	90630	767-C5
8500	LPMA	90623	767-C5
SALISBURY CT			
1000	LCF	91011	535-B3
SALISBURY LN			
400	CLAR	91711	571-E7
8500	LPMA	90623	767-C7
9500	CYP	90630	767-C7
SALISBURY RD			
800	LCF	91011	535-A3
7000	CanP	91307	529-D5
SALISBURY ST			
12700	BALD	91706	597-H7
SALLY AV			
19700	CRTS	90703	766-G3
SALLY CT			
2200	WCOV	91792	679-A1
SALLY RD			
20500	SCTA	91321	4641-D1
SALLY LEE AV			
500	AZU	91702	598-J2
SALLY TANNER DR			
11000	ELMN	91731	637-C1
SALMON AV			
21800	CRSN	90810	764-J6
SALMON DR			
2600	OrCo	90720	796-G6
SALMON RIVER CIR			
3400	THO	91362	557-C2
SALOMA AV			
4500	Shrm	91403	561-J4
5200	VanN	91411	561-J2
6200	VanN	91411	531-J7
6600	VanN	91405	531-J6
7900	PanC	91402	531-J2
9500	LA	91343	501-J6
9900	MsnH	91345	501-J4
SALONICA ST			
6700	HiPk	90042	595-E2
N SALTAIR AV			
100	Brwd	90049	631-G2
S SALTAIR AV			
100	Brwd	90049	631-G3
1200	WLA	90025	631-H5
SALTAIR PL			
12000	Brwd	90049	631-G3
SALTAIR TER			
11900	Brwd	90049	631-G4
SALTA VERDE PT			
300	LBCH	90803	826-C1
SALT BUSH CT			
2500	PMDL	93550	4286-F5
SALT CANYON RD			
-	Nwhl	91382	4549-A7
SALTEE AV			
19900	TOR	90503	763-B4
SALTER AV			
6300	TEML	91780	597-A1
SALTILLO ST			
4100	WdHl	91364	560-B4
SALTINO WY			
4800	VeCo	91377	557-G2
SALT LAKE AV			
6400	HNTP	90255	675-B7
6400	BELL	90201	675-B7
6900	HNTP	90255	705-C1
7300	CDHY	90201	705-C1
7800	CDHY	90255	705-C1
9500	SGAT	90280	705-F4
11000	Nor	91326	500-H2
14600	INDS	91745	637-J7
14600	INDS	91745	638-A7
14900	HacH	91745	638-A7
14900	HacH	91745	678-C1
15200	INDS	91745	678-C1
SALT LAKE PL			
18800	Nor	91326	500-G2
E SALT LAKE ST			
1000	LBCH	90806	795-F4
SALTO DR			
1900	HacH	91745	678-D4
SALTY DOG RD			
33300	Actn	93510	4374-G6
SALUDA AV			
9600	Tuj	91042	504-C5
9600	LA	91214	504-C5
SALVATIERRA ST			
15700	IRW	91706	598-E2
SALVESON RD			
-	BREA	92821	708-J5
-	BREA	92821	709-A5
SALVIA CANYON RD			
1000	PAS	91103	565-E2
SAM PL			
28800	SCTA	91387	4552-D1
29000	SCTA	91387	4462-D7
SAMANTHA AV			
3200	WCOV	91792	679-A1
5400	LKWD	90712	765-J3
SAMANTHA CT			
-	Saug	91350	4461-E6
SAMAR AV			
1100	HacH	91745	678-A1
SAMARA DR			
1800	RowH	91748	678-H5
SAMARKAND PL			
1800	GLDL	91208	534-H7
1800	GLDL	91208	564-J1
SAM GERRY DR			
600	LACo	91744	638-G6
SAM LITTLETON ST			
2000	COMP	90059	734-E2
SAMMY DR			
43900	LAN	93535	4016-D7
43900	LAN	93535	4106-D1
SAMOA AV			
9700	Tuj	91042	504-A3
SAMOA PL			
7100	Tuj	91042	504-A2
SAMOA WY			
15900	PacP	90272	630-J6
SAMOLINE AV			
7800	DWNY	90242	705-H7
8200	PRV	90660	706-C1
8600	DWNY	90240	706-C1
10300	DWNY	90241	706-B3
11700	DWNY	90241	705-J5
12800	DWNY	90242	735-H1
SAMOLINE LN			
12000	DWNY	90242	705-J6
SAMPAN CIR			
16600	CRTS	90703	736-F6
SAMPSON AV			
800	Wilm	90744	794-H6
10700	LYN	90262	705-D6
SAMPSON PL			
1500	City	90063	635-E3
SAMPSON WY			
400	SPed	90731	824-C5
SAMRA AV			
1200	LAN	93535	4106-C2
SAMRA DR			
8300	LA	91304	529-G2
SAMUAL DR			
20400	SCTA	91350	4461-D5
20400	Saug	91350	4461-D5
SAMUEL ST			
22700	TOR	90505	793-D1
SAMUEL DUPONT AV			
27400	LA	90732	793-J7
27400	LA	90732	823-J1
SAMUELSON ST			
1100	INDS	91748	678-J3
SAN CIR			
9700	LA	90210	592-D4
SAN ADRIANO WY			
8500	BPK	90620	767-G5
SAN ALANO CIR			
6500	BPK	90620	767-F5
SAN ALANO LN			
8800	BPK	90620	767-F5
SAN ALFREDO CIR			
6900	BPK	90620	767-G5
SAN ALTO WY			
6700	BPK	90620	767-F5
SAN ANDREAS AV			
4400	LA	90065	594-J3
4500	LA	90065	595-A3
SAN ANDRES WY			
2500	CLAR	91711	571-B6
SAN ANGELO AV			
100	LACo	91746	637-G4
700	MTBL	90640	636-G7
700	MTBL	90640	676-G1
SAN ANGELO DR			
2600	CLAR	91711	571-C5
SAN ANSELINE AV			
1800	LBCH	90815	796-C4
3800	LBCH	90808	766-C7
4100	LKWD	90713	766-C6
4800	LBCH	90808	796-C2
SAN ANSELMO AV			
9900	SGAT	90280	705-A5
SAN ANTONIO			
-	GLDR	91740	599-C2
SAN ANTONIO AV			
1000	FUL	92835	738-J2
8100	SGAT	90280	705-B3
8500	BPK	90620	767-F5
10400	LYN	90262	705-B5
14700	PRM	90723	735-E4
15900	LMRD	90638	737-J2
N SAN ANTONIO AV			
100	POM	91767	641-B1
700	POM	91767	601-B7
S SAN ANTONIO AV			
100	POM	91766	641-B3
SAN ANTONIO DR			
700	COV	91723	599-C7
700	MTBL	90640	636-C7
3500	PMDL	93550	4286-H4
12900	NRWK	90650	736-H3
E SAN ANTONIO DR			
100	Bxby	90807	765-F4
W SAN ANTONIO DR			
100	Bxby	90807	765-C6
SAN ANTONIO PL			
600	Bxby	90807	765-E5
SAN ANTONIO RD			
200	ARCD	91007	567-C5
500	SDMS	91773	600-B3
SAN ANTONIO WY			
5300	MTCL	91763	641-G3
SAN ANTONIO CREEK RD			
7600	SBdC	-	(512-A5 See Page 511)
SAN ARDO CIR			
15500	LMRD	90638	737-F4
SAN ARDO DR			
7500	BPK	90621	737-G5
7500	LMRD	90638	737-E3
SAN ARDO ST			
1800	TOR	90501	763-H7
1800	TOR	90501	793-H1
SAN ARTURO CIR			
6700	BPK	90620	767-F5
SAN AUGUSTINE DR			
3700	GLDL	91206	535-C7
SAN BENITO CT			
2300	CLAR	91711	571-C6
SAN BENITO ST			
200	Boyl	90033	635-A4
SAN BENITO WY			
6700	BPK	90620	767-F5
SAN BERNARDINO AV			
300	POM	91767	601-B6
SAN BERNARDINO CT			
4200	MTCL	91763	601-E6
SAN BERNARDINO FRWY I-10			
-	ALH	-	635-C3
-	ALH	-	636-A1
-	BALD	-	598-H7
-	BALD	-	637-E1
-	BALD	-	638-C1
-	Boyl	-	634-J3
-	Boyl	-	635-C3
-	City	-	635-C3
-	CLAR	-	601-A6
-	COV	-	599-A7
-	COV	-	639-J1
-	ELMN	-	596-G7
-	ELMN	-	597-A7
-	ELMN	-	637-E1
-	INDS	-	637-E1
-	LA	-	634-J3
-	LA	-	635-C3
-	LACo	-	599-A7
-	LACo	-	635-C3
-	LACo	-	639-J1
-	LACo	-	640-A1
-	MONP	-	635-C3
-	MONP	-	636-A1
-	MTCL	-	601-A6
-	POM	-	600-D7
-	POM	-	601-A6
-	POM	-	640-A1
-	RSMD	-	596-G7
-	RSMD	-	597-A7
-	RSMD	-	636-A1
-	SDMS	-	639-J1
-	SDMS	-	640-A1
-	SGBL	-	636-A1
-	UPL	-	601-A6
-	WCOV	-	598-H7
-	WCOV	-	599-A7
-	WCOV	-	639-J1
E SAN BERNARDINO RD			
100	COV	91723	599-C4
W SAN BERNARDINO RD			
100	COV	91723	599-A5
500	COV	91722	599-A5
600	COV	91722	598-G5
1500	WCOV	91790	598-E5
1500	LACo	91722	598-E5
1900	BALD	91706	598-E5
SAN BERNARDINO ST			
4200	MTCL	91763	601-E6
5500	MTCL	91762	601-E6
SAN BERNARDO CIR			
6800	BPK	90620	767-G5
SAN BLAS AV			
4400	WdHl	91364	560-B5
SANBORN AV			
-	SBdC	-	(512-A5 See Page 511)
800	LA	90029	594-B5
1300	LFlz	90027	594-B5
2700	LaCr	91214	534-G1
2800	Ven	90291	671-H7
3300	LYN	90262	705-B7
SANBORN WY			
1900	POM	91766	641-B5
SAN BRUNO DR			
6700	BPK	90620	767-F5
14300	LMRD	90638	737-E3
SAN CALVINO CIR			
8500	BPK	90620	767-F4
SAN CAPISTRANO WY			
8300	BPK	90620	767-F4
SAN CARLOS AV			
8100	SGAT	90280	705-B3
10400	LYN	90262	705-B5
SAN CARLOS CT			
800	SDMS	91773	600-B3
SAN CARLOS DR			
2200	POM	91767	601-B5
SAN CARLOS RD			
1000	ARCD	91006	567-B3
SAN CARLOS ST			
4000	City	90063	635-E5
4900	COMP	90221	735-D3
4900	RDom	90221	735-D3
6500	PRM	90723	735-E3
SAN CARLOS WY			
8200	BPK	90620	767-E4
37800	PMDL	93550	4286-F2
SAN CATALDO AV			
1800	LBCH	90815	796-F4
SANCHEZ DR			
-	GLDL	91203	564-E3
5100	LA	90008	673-B2
SANCHEZ ST			
700	MTBL	90640	676-F1
700	MTBL	90640	636-F7
SAN CLEMENTE AV			
300	Wilm	90744	824-E2
2200	ALH	91803	635-H2
SAN CLEMENTE CT			
3400	PMDL	93550	4286-G3
SAN CLEMENTE DR			
25900	SCTA	91321	4551-F6
29700	RPV	90275	823-B2
SAN CLEMENTE LN			
13000	CHNO	91710	641-F7
SAN CLEMENTE PL			
5500	RPV	90275	823-B2
SAN CLEMENTE WY			
5100	MTCL	91763	641-G2
8300	BPK	90620	767-E4
SANCOLA AV			
4400	LA	91602	563-C4
4800	NHol	91601	563-C4
4900	BURB	91505	563-C4
7600	SunV	91352	533-C3
SAN CRISTOBAL DR			
14200	LMRD	90638	737-E3
SANCROFT AV			
44100	LAN	93535	4016-A3
SANDAL LN			
10400	BelA	90077	592-A4
SANDALIA DR			
25900	SCTA	91355	4550-G4
SANDALWOOD AV			
800	FUL	92835	738-J3
N SANDALWOOD AV			
100	LACo	91744	638-H7
100	LACo	91744	678-H1
S SANDALWOOD AV			
100	LACo	91744	678-H1
SANDALWOOD DR			
1500	BREA	92821	708-H4
6400	SIMI	93063	499-C3
SANDALWOOD PL			
100	GLDR	91741	569-G5
41400	LACo	93536	4104-G7
SANDALWOOD ST			
23300	CanP	91307	529-E4
SANDBAR DR			
2300	FUL	92833	738-C5
SAND BROOK DR			
37400	PMDL	93550	4286-F3
SANDBROOK DR			
6000	RPV	90275	792-J5
SANDBURG CIR			
6800	BPK	90620	767-F1
SANDBURG DR			
6800	BPK	90620	767-F2
SANDBURG PL			
26000	StvR	91381	4550-C6

STREET	Block	City	ZIP	Pg-Grid
SANDBURN PL				
	-	StvR	91381	4550-A7
SAND CANYON RD				
	7500	SBdC	92372	(4562-E5 See Page 4471)
	17000	LACo	-	4642-F1
	19100	LACo	91387	4642-F1
	19100	Nwhl	91321	4642-D2
	20000	SCTA	91387	4642-D1
	22900	SCTA	91387	4552-C2
	28800	SCTA	91387	4462-C6
	29100	LACo	91387	4462-C6
SAND CANYON WY				
	400	BREA	92821	709-B5
SANDCASTLE CT				
	7100	LBCH	90803	826-G2
SAND CREEK CT				
	-	LMRD	90638	738-B3
SAND CREEK DR				
	2400	Actn	93510	4375-C4
	5200	Actn	93510	4374-G4
SAND CREEK RD				
	1300	SDMS	91773	570-D7
SANDEE LN				
	12500	CRTS	90703	737-A6
SANDEFUR ST				
	1500	DUAR	91010	568-B6
SANDEL AV				
	15500	LACo	90248	734-D5
SANDELWOOD LN				
	500	BREA	92821	709-A5
SANDERS CT				
	-	LHB	90631	738-C2
SANDGATE DR				
	3700	TOR	90504	763-E1
SANDHILL AV				
	-	LACo	91390	4462-E4
	800	CRSN	90746	734-E7
SANDHURST LN				
	1700	LVRN	91750	570-G4
	23700	Hrbr	90710	794-B2
	44400	LAN	93536	4015-C6
SANDI CIR				
	20200	WAL	91789	639-F6
SANDIA AV				
	300	LPUE	91746	638-A4
	900	LACo	91746	638-B3
S SANDIA AV				
	1400	WCOV	91790	638-C2
SAN DIEGO				
	1800	WCOV	91790	598-E7
SAN DIEGO CIR				
	8100	BPK	90620	767-F4
SAN DIEGO CT				
	2400	CLAR	91711	571-C6
SAN DIEGO DR				
	6400	BPK	90620	767-F4
SAN DIEGO FRWY I-405				
	-	BelA	-	561-G7
	-	BelA	-	591-F3
	-	Brwd	-	561-G7
	-	Brwd	-	591-F3
	-	Brwd	-	631-J3
	-	Bxby	-	765-A7
	-	Bxby	-	795-G2
	-	CRSN	-	764-C4
	-	CRSN	-	765-A7
	-	CULC	-	672-D1
	-	Enc	-	531-G3
	-	Enc	-	561-G3
	-	GrnH	-	481-G7
	-	GrnH	-	501-G7
	-	HAW	-	703-A6
	-	HAW	-	733-B4
	-	ING	-	703-A1
	-	ING	-	703-A6
	-	LA	-	481-G7
	-	LA	-	501-G7
	-	LA	-	531-G3
	-	LA	-	631-J3
	-	LA	-	632-A4
	-	LA	-	672-D1
	-	LA	-	763-G2
	-	LA	-	764-C4
	-	LACo	-	631-J3
	-	LACo	-	632-A4
	-	LACo	-	703-A6
	-	LACo	-	733-B4
	-	LACo	-	764-C4
	-	LBCH	-	765-A7
	-	LBCH	-	795-G2
	-	LBCH	-	796-A3
	-	Lenx	-	703-A6
	-	LNDL	-	733-B4
	-	MsnH	-	481-G7
	-	MsnH	-	501-G7
	-	RBCH	-	733-B4
	-	Shrm	-	561-G3
	-	SIGH	-	795-G2
	-	SLB	-	796-J6
	-	TOR	-	733-B4
	-	TOR	-	763-G2
	-	VanN	-	531-G3
	-	VanN	-	561-G3
	-	Wch	-	672-D1
	-	Wch	-	702-J1
	-	Wch	-	703-A1
	-	WLA	-	632-A4
SAN DIEGO WY				
	700	LA	90048	633-B3
SAN DIEGUITO DR				
	14400	LMRD	90638	737-E3
SANDIMAN ST				
	5500	SIMI	93063	499-A2
SAN DIMAS AV				
	100	SDMS	91773	600-A7
	100	SDMS	91773	640-A1
N SAN DIMAS AV				
	100	SDMS	91773	600-B1
	900	SDMS	91773	570-C7
S SAN DIMAS AV				
	100	SDMS	91773	600-C3
	1200	LACo	91773	600-A4
SAN DIMAS CIR				
	8000	BPK	90620	767-F4
SAN DIMAS CANYON RD				
	1100	LACo	91750	570-F2
	1100	SDMS	91773	570-D7
	1300	LVRN	91750	570-F5
	1300	SDMS	91750	570-F5
	1800	LVRN	91750	600-D2
	2800	LVRN	91773	570-F2
	2800	LACo	91773	570-F2
N SAN DIMAS CANYON RD				
	100	LVRN	91750	600-D2
	100	SDMS	91773	600-D2
	400	LACo	91750	600-D2
	800	SDMS	91750	600-D2
	900	SDMS	91750	570-D7
	900	SDMS	91773	570-D7
	1000	LACo	91750	570-D7
S SAN DIMAS CANYON RD				
	100	SDMS	91773	600-D3
	400	LVRN	91750	600-D3
E SANDISON ST				
	300	Wilm	90744	794-E4
W SANDISON ST				
	100	Wilm	90744	794-D4
SANDLAKE AV				
	17400	CRSN	90746	734-E7
	17500	CRSN	90746	764-E1
SANDLEWOOD AV				
	1000	LHB	90631	738-D1
SANDLEWOOD LN				
	-	Nor	91326	500-H4
SANDLOCK ST				
	8800	PRV	90660	676-F5
SANDOVAL AV				
	3200	PRV	90660	677-A1
	3300	PRV	90660	676-J1
SANDOVAL ST				
	12900	SFSP	90670	707-A5
SANDOWN CT				
	13300	LMRD	90638	738-A2
SANDOWN RD				
	9200	PRV	90660	676-H1
SANDOWN ST				
	1000	LHB	90631	708-D7
SAND PALM WY				
	42200	LAN	93536	4104-E5
SANDPEBBLE LN				
	2400	BREA	92821	709-E6
SANDPIPER				
	900	WCOV	91790	638-F2
SANDPIPER CIR				
	800	THO	91361	557-A5
SANDPIPER CT				
	3600	WLKV	91361	557-B7
	9900	KeCo	93560	3833-F2
SANDPIPER DR				
	1300	SLB	90740	826-F4
	4400	LPMA	90623	767-C4
	7200	LAN	93536	4104-C6
N SAND PIPER DR				
	300	LBCH	90803	826-D1
SANDPIPER PL				
	5500	PMDL	93552	4287-C3
	19800	SCTA	91321	4551-E5
SAND PIPER ST				
	21000	WAL	91789	639-G7
SANDPIPER ST				
	100	PdlR	90293	702-B4
SANDPIPER WY				
	-	BREA	92823	709-G6
SANDPOINT CT				
	800	CRSN	90746	764-E1
SANDRA AV				
	-	ARCD	91007	597-C2
E SANDRA AV				
	100	ARCD	91006	597-D2
SANDRA CIR				
	-	VanN	91406	531-E4
SANDRA CT				
	900	BREA	92821	708-J5
W SANDRA CT				
	1200	UPL	91786	601-J1
SANDRA LN				
	15500	LA	91342	481-G4
	37600	PMDL	93550	4285-J2
	37600	PMDL	93550	4286-A2
SANDRA ST				
	14900	MsnH	91345	501-H2
SANDRA GLEN DR				
	2300	RowH	91748	679-A6
SANDRAGLEN LN				
	400	LHB	90631	708-D6
SAND RIDGE RD				
	23400	DBAR	91765	680-C3
SANDRINGHAM CT				
	18100	Nor	91326	500-J1
SANDRINGHAM DR				
	1300	GLDL	91207	564-G1
SAND RIVER RD				
	19100	LACo	93591	4200-C2
SANDROCK DR				
	14500	LACo	93532	4102-E4
SANDS LN				
	2000	LACo	93534	3925-D4
	2000	LACo	93536	3925-D4
SAND SPOLING AV				
	700	LACo	90601	637-G5
SAND SPRING DR				
	19700	RowH	91748	679-D5
SANDSPRINGS DR				
	500	LPUE	91746	638-B4
	1000	LACo	91746	638-B3
S SANDSPRNGS DR				
	1400	WCOV	91790	638-C2
SANDSTARR CT				
	-	LAN	93535	4106-D1
SANDSTONE CT				
	-	SCTA	91354	4460-G5
	2000	PMDL	93551	4195-B5
	2400	CHLS	91709	680-J7
	6400	LAN	93536	4104-E5
SANDSTONE DR				
	900	GLDR	91740	569-J7
SANDSTONE LN				
	-	Hrbr	90710	794-A5
SANDSTONE ST				
	13900	BALD	91706	598-B3
SANDSTONE WY				
	-	AZU	91702	568-J2
SANDTRAP DR				
	30400	AGRH	91301	557-G4
SANDUSKY AV				
	9000	Pcma	91331	502-B5
SAND WEDGE LN				
	24600	SCTA	91355	4550-E7
SANDWOOD PL				
	800	SPed	90731	824-A1
SANDWOOD ST				
	2700	LKWD	90712	765-H4
	5900	LKWD	90713	766-D4
E SANDWOOD ST				
	5200	LBCH	90808	766-B4
SANDWOOD WY				
	-	PMDL	93552	4287-D1
SANDY CIR				
	4800	LPMA	90623	767-C3
SANDY DR				
	18200	LACo	91387	4551-H3
SANDY LN				
	8200	PRM	90723	735-H4
	12900	DWNY	90242	735-J1
	16100	Enc	91436	561-F7
SANDY CAPE DR				
	18000	LACo	90265	630-E5
	18000	PacP	90272	630-E5
SANDYCREEK DR				
	2500	WLKV	91361	587-A1
SANDYCREEK LN				
	12500	CRTS	90703	736-J5
	12500	CRTS	90703	737-A5
E SANDY HILL DR				
	1200	WCOV	91791	639-B3
SANDY HOOK AV				
	500	LPUE	91744	638-C6
	600	LACo	91744	638-D4
	1100	MTBL	90640	636-D7
SANDY HOOK ST				
	400	WCOV	91790	638-G1
SANDYOAK LN				
	15700	SCTA	91387	4552-D6
SANDY POINT CT				
	6500	RPV	90275	822-H4
SANDY RIDGE RD				
	14700	LACo	93532	4102-F4
SANDY ROCK ST				
	12200	CRTS	90703	736-J6
SAN ESTEBAN DR				
	14300	LMRD	90638	737-E3
SAN FABIO CIR				
	8700	BPK	90620	767-F5
SAN FELICIANO DR				
	4500	WdHl	91364	559-J3
	5000	WdHl	91364	560-A3
	14200	LMRD	90638	737-E3
SAN FELICIANO PL				
	22200	WdHl	91364	559-J4
SAN FELIPE AV				
	11300	SBdC	91766	641-E3
	11300	SBdC	91710	641-E3
SAN FELIPE CIR				
	8700	BPK	90620	767-F5
SAN FELIPE CT				
	3400	PMDL	93550	4286-G3
SAN FELIPE ST				
	100	POM	91767	600-J5
	200	POM	91767	601-A5
	13100	LMRD	90638	737-J1
N SAN FERNANDO BLVD				
	900	BURB	91504	533-G7
S SAN FERNANDO BLVD				
	100	BURB	91502	533-H7
	500	BURB	91502	563-J1
SAN FERNANDO CT				
	2400	CLAR	91711	571-C6
SAN FERNANDO RD				
	-	LA	91342	4641-A2
	600	SFER	91340	502-B1
	700	SFER	91340	482-A7
	1600	SFER	91340	481-G4
	1700	LA	91342	481-G4
	3600	GLDL	91204	594-E1
	3800	GLDL	91204	564-C5
	5100	LA	90031	594-E1
	5100	LA	90065	594-E1
	5200	GLDL	91203	564-C5
	5700	GLDL	91202	564-A2
	6100	GLDL	91201	564-A2
	6700	GLDL	91201	563-J1
	7400	BURB	91505	533-A2
	7400	SunV	91352	533-A2
	7400	LA	91505	533-A2
	8200	SunV	91352	532-J1
	8700	SunV	91352	502-G6
	9700	Pcma	91331	502-E4
	11200	LA	91340	502-B1
	13800	GrnH	91344	481-D2
	20500	SCTA	91321	4641-A2
	24100	SCTA	91321	4640-J1
	24600	SCTA	91321	4550-H4
	25200	SCTA	91355	4550-H4
	25400	SCTA	91350	4550-H4
N SAN FERNANDO RD				
	100	LA	90031	594-J7
	100	LA	90031	634-J1
	500	LA	90065	594-F1
SAN FERNANDO RD W				
	4700	LA	90039	564-C4
SAN FERNANDO MISSION BLVD				
	100	SFER	91340	482-A7
	600	SFER	91340	502-A1
	700	SFER	91340	501-F2
	800	LA	91340	501-F2
	14700	MsnH	91345	501-F2
	15500	GrnH	91344	501-B2
	18000	Nor	91326	501-B2
	18100	Nor	91326	500-H2
	18900	Chat	91311	500-C2
S SAN FIDEL AV				
	100	LACo	91746	637-G3
SANFORD AV				
	500	Wilm	90744	794-F5
SANFORD DR				
	4600	LA	90230	672-E5
SANFORD ST				
	12000	LA	90230	672-E6
	12400	LA	90066	672-E7
SANFORD WY				
	27100	SCTA	91354	4460-G7
	27100	SCTA	91354	4550-G1
SAN FRANCISCO AV				
	200	POM	91767	640-J1
	300	LBCH	90802	795-C7
	300	POM	91767	641-A1
	900	LBCH	90806	795-C2
	1300	LBCH	90813	795-C5
	43600	LAN	93535	4106-F1
	43800	LAN	93535	4016-F7
SAN FRANCISCO DR				
	6200	BPK	90620	767-F5
SAN FRANCISQUITO MTWY				
	-	BqtC	91354	(4370-F7 See Page 4279)
	-	BqtC	91354	4460-D2
	-	Cstc	91384	4460-D2
	-	LACo	91390	(4280-H7 See Page 4279)
	-	LACo	91390	(4370-F7 See Page 4279)
SAN FRANCISQUITO CANYON RD				
	28500	LACo	91390	4460-G3
	28500	SCTA	91354	4460-G3
	28500	SCTA	91390	4460-G3
	29100	LACo	91390	(4370-G7 See Page 4279)
	35600	LACo	91390	(4280-J7 See Page 4279)
	35600	LACo	91390	4281-A6
	38200	LACo	91390	4192-B4
	40500	LACo	93551	4102-G7
	40500	LACo	93551	4192-B4
	42000	LACo	93532	4102-G7
SAN GABRIEL				
	-	GLDR	91740	599-C2
SAN GABRIEL AV				
	-	LACo	93551	4375-H6
	200	AZU	91702	568-J7
	200	AZU	91702	598-J1
	1600	GLDL	91208	534-G5
	1900	LBCH	90810	795-A4
	3400	PMDL	93550	4286-G2
	8100	SGAT	90280	705-C3
	10400	LYN	90262	705-B5
	17200	CRTS	90703	766-E1
	17700	CRTS	90703	736-E7
	33700	Actn	93510	4375-H6
N SAN GABRIEL AV				
	100	AZU	91702	568-J7
SAN GABRIEL BLVD				
	-	MTBL	90640	636-G4
	-	LACo	91770	636-F4
	200	RSMD	90640	636-G4
	500	RSMD	91770	636-F2
	1900	SGBL	91776	596-F7
	3500	RSMD	91770	596-F7
	3500	SGBL	91776	636-F2
	9000	LACo	90640	636-G4
	9100	LACo	90660	636-G4
	9100	LACo	91733	636-G4
N SAN GABRIEL BLVD				
	-	PAS	91107	566-E4
	100	SGBL	91775	596-F3
	100	SGBL	91776	596-F3
	700	LACo	91775	596-F3
	700	SMRO	91108	596-F3
S SAN GABRIEL BLVD				
	-	PAS	91107	566-F6
	100	SGBL	91776	596-F6
	500	SMRO	91108	566-F6
	600	LACo	91107	566-F6
	1300	SMRO	91108	596-F1
	1700	LACo	91775	596-F1
	6900	LACo	91775	566-F6
	7000	SMRO	91775	566-F6
SAN GABRIEL CIR				
	6500	BPK	90620	767-F4
SAN GABRIEL CT				
	100	SMAD	91024	567-B2
SAN GABRIEL PL				
	300	AZU	91702	568-H7
	4800	PRV	90660	676-G3
SAN GABRIEL RD				
	-	UPL	91784	571-H7
SAN GABRIEL WY				
	700	LA	90048	633-A3
SAN GABRIEL CANYON RD				
	1600	AZU	91702	568-H2
	2300	AZU	91702	569-A2
SAN GABRIEL CANYON RD Rt#-39				
	-	LACo	-	509-D4
	-	LACo	-	4649-E7
	-	LACo	-	(4729-E2 See Page 4649)
	9300	LACo	-	(539-E2 See Page 509)
	9300	LACo	-	569-B1
	9300	LACo	91702	569-B1
SAN GABRIEL RIVER FRWY I-605				
	-	BALD	-	597-H6
	-	BALD	-	637-E5
	-	CRTS	-	736-E4
	-	CRTS	-	766-F1
	-	DUAR	-	568-B7
	-	DWNY	-	706-F3
	-	HGDN	-	766-G5
	-	INDS	-	637-E5
	-	INDS	-	677-A2
	-	IRW	-	568-B7
	-	IRW	-	597-H6
	-	IRW	-	598-A2
	-	LACo	-	637-E5
	-	LACo	-	676-J3
	-	LACo	-	677-A2
	-	LACo	-	706-F3
	-	LALM	-	796-H2
	-	LBCH	-	766-G5
	-	LBCH	-	796-H2
	-	LKWD	-	766-G5
	-	NRWK	-	706-F3
	-	NRWK	-	736-E4
	-	PRV	-	637-E5
	-	PRV	-	676-J3
	-	PRV	-	677-A2
	-	SFSP	-	706-F3
	-	SLB	-	796-H2
	-	WHIT	-	676-J3
	-	WHIT	-	677-A2
SAN GABRIEL RIVER PKWY				
	3400	BALD	91706	597-H7
	3500	INDS	90660	677-A2
	3500	PRV	90660	677-A2
	3800	PRV	90660	676-J2
SAN GABRIEL VALLEY DR				
	20100	WAL	91789	639-F3
SANGAMON AV				
	7900	SunV	91352	533-C2
SANGER AV				
	8300	LACo	90606	706-H1
SAN GORGONIO RD				
	1700	SBdC	92372	(4562-D2 See Page 4471)
	2200	LCF	91011	504-H7
SAN HACIENDA CIR				
	8000	BPK	90620	767-F4
SAN HARCO CIR				
	6200	BPK	90620	767-E5
SAN HAROLDO WY				
	6500	BPK	90620	767-F5
SAN HELICE CIR				
	8000	BPK	90620	767-F4
SAN HERNANDO WY				
	6500	BPK	90620	767-F4
SAN HERON CIR				
	8000	BPK	90620	767-F4
SAN HILARIO CIR				
	8000	BPK	90620	767-G4
SAN HOMERO WY				
	6500	BPK	90620	767-F5
SAN HUERTA CIR				
	8000	BPK	90620	767-F4
SAN HUGO WY				
	6500	BPK	90620	767-F5
SAN IGNACIO DR				
	3000	ELMN	91732	637-D1
SAN JACINTO				
	13000	LMRD	90638	737-J1
SAN JACINTO CT				
	2400	CLAR	91711	571-C6
SAN JACINTO ST				
	1800	Echo	90026	594-C5
SAN JOAQUIN				
	-	GLDR	91740	599-C2
SAN JOAQUIN AV				
	3600	LALM	90720	796-J1
SAN JOAQUIN CIR				
	6900	BPK	90620	767-G4
SAN JOAQUIN CT				
	2300	CLAR	91711	571-C6
SAN JOAQUIN RD				
	700	COV	91724	599-E6
	3300	LACo	91724	599-E6
SAN JOAQUIN ST				
	14100	LMRD	90638	737-J3
SAN JOSE				
	-	GLDR	91740	599-C2
SAN JOSE AV				
	-	COMP	90221	735-E4
	300	BURB	91502	533-H6
	400	BURB	91501	533-H6
	1800	LHB	90631	708-B6
	10100	LYN	90262	705-A6
	10100	SGAT	90280	705-A5
	14500	PRM	90723	735-E4
	15800	LPUE	91744	638-D7
	16100	INDS	91744	638-D7
	18300	INDS	91748	679-A3
	19000	RowH	91748	679-C3
	19200	LACo	91789	679-C3
	19500	INDS	91789	679-C3
E SAN JOSE AV				
	100	CLAR	91711	601-D5
N SAN JOSE AV				
	100	COV	91723	599-C5
S SAN JOSE AV				
	100	COV	91723	599-C6
W SAN JOSE AV				
	100	CLAR	91711	601-C5
SAN JOSE CIR				
	8000	BPK	90620	767-G4
N SAN JOSE DR				
	100	GLDR	91741	569-G5
S SAN JOSE DR				
	100	GLDR	91741	569-G6
SAN JOSE PL				
	1600	POM	91768	600-G6
SAN JOSE ST				
	-	Actn	93510	4465-C1
	4400	MTCL	91763	601-F5
	5600	MTCL	91762	601-H5
	14000	LA	91340	502-B2
	14200	MsnH	91345	502-A3
	14500	MsnH	91345	501-G3
	15600	GrnH	91344	501-A3
	18200	Nor	91326	500-H3
	20500	Chat	91311	500-B3
	22000	Chat	91311	499-J4
SAN JOSE HILLS RD				
	20400	WAL	91789	639-F4
SAN JUAN AV				
	200	Ven	90291	671-H5
	8100	SGAT	90280	705-C3
	10400	LYN	90262	705-B5
SAN JUAN CIR				
	800	DUAR	91010	568-E4
	6900	BPK	90620	767-G4
SAN JUAN CT				
	500	Ven	90291	671-H5
SAN JUAN DR				
	-	ARCD	91007	567-C5
	1300	BREA	92821	708-H4
	2900	FUL	92835	738-G2
	4900	LPMA	90623	767-C3
SAN JUAN PL				
	300	PAS	91107	566-F5
	2900	FUL	92835	738-G2
SAN JUAN ST				
	200	POM	91767	600-J6
	6500	PRM	90723	735-E3
E SAN JUAN ST				
	4900	RDom	90221	735-D3
SAN JUAN WY				
	300	LCF	91011	535-D4
	11000	MTCL	91763	641-G2
SAN JUAN HILL AV				
	-	Brwd	90049	631-J2
SAN JULIAN				
	-	GLDR	91740	599-C2
SAN JULIAN CIR				
	6900	BPK	90620	767-G4
SAN JULIAN PL				
	500	LA	90014	634-F5
SAN JULIAN ST				
	500	LA	90013	634-E6
	600	LA	90014	634-E6
	900	LA	90015	634-E6
SAN LAZARO CIR				
	8000	BPK	90620	767-E4
SAN LEANDRO CIR				
	8000	BPK	90620	767-E4
SAN LEANDRO DR				
	300	DBAR	91765	640-C7
	19300	SCTA	91321	4551-F6
SAN LEON CIR				
	8000	BPK	90620	767-E4
SAN LEON DR				
	3100	ELMN	91732	637-D1
SANLO PL				
	5000	WdHl	91364	560-D3
SAN LORENZO DR				
	6000	BPK	90620	767-E4
SAN LORENZO ST				
	100	POM	91766	641-C2
	600	LA	90402	631-C6
SAN LUCAS CIR				
	8000	BPK	90620	767-E4
SAN LUCAS CT				
	500	SDMS	91773	600-B3
SAN LUCAS DR				
	8000	WHIT	90605	707-G1
SAN LUIS AV				
	6800	BELL	90201	675-C7
	6800	BELL	90201	705-C3
	8100	SGAT	90280	705-C3
	10600	LYN	90262	705-B6
SAN LUIS CIR				
	8000	BPK	90620	767-E4
SAN LUIS DR				
	2800	LAN	93535	4106-F1
SAN LUIS PL				
	200	CLAR	91711	571-C6
SAN LUIS ST				
	200	POM	91767	600-J5
	6400	PRM	90723	735-E4
E SAN LUIS ST				
	1600	COMP	90221	735-C4
	4100	RDom	90221	735-C4
SAN LUIS POTOSI PL				
	-	PRV	90660	676-F2
SAN LUIS REY DR				
	200	SDMS	91773	600-B3
	1100	GLDL	91208	534-F7
SAN LUIS REY RD				
	200	ARCD	91007	567-C4
SAN MARCELLO CIR				
	8000	BPK	90620	767-F4
SAN MARCO CIR				
	6400	LA	90068	593-E2
SAN MARCO DR				
	200	LBCH	90803	826-D2
	2200	LA	90068	593-E2
SAN MARCO WY				
	5800	LBCH	90803	826-C2
SAN MARCOS DR				
	2500	PAS	91107	566-E5
SAN MARCOS PL				
	2100	CLAR	91711	571-D7
	3900	FUL	92835	738-J1
	4800	HiPk	90042	595-A3
	12900	CHNO	91710	641-E7
SAN MARCOS RD				
	500	SDMS	91773	600-B3
SAN MARCOS ST				
	200	SGBL	91776	596-D4
SAN MARCOS WY				
	6300	BPK	90620	767-E4
SAN MARCUS LN				
	800	DUAR	91010	568-E5
SAN MARCUS ST				
	6400	PRM	90723	735-E4
E SAN MARCUS ST				
	1600	COMP	90221	735-C4
	4100	RDom	90221	735-D4
SAN MARINO AV				
	500	SMRO	91108	566-D7
	800	MTBL	90640	676-D3
	2000	SGBL	91775	596-D1
	2000	SMRO	91108	596-D1
	14700	PRM	90723	735-F4
E SAN MARINO AV				
	-	ALH	91801	596-C6
N SAN MARINO AV				
	-	PAS	91107	566-D4
	100	SGBL	91775	596-D3
	100	SGBL	91776	596-D3
S SAN MARINO AV				
	-	PAS	91107	566-D5
	100	SGBL	91776	596-E3
	200	LACo	91107	566-D5
	500	SMRO	91108	566-D5
	1000	ALH	91801	596-E4
	1300	SMRO	91108	596-E3
W SAN MARINO AV				
	-	ALH	91801	596-A6
SAN MARINO CIR				
	6300	BPK	90620	767-F4
SAN MARINO CT				
	19400	SCTA	91321	4551-F6
SAN MARINO DR				
	7800	BPK	90620	767-E4
SAN MARINO ST				
	2500	LA	90006	634-A3
	3000	LA	90006	633-H3
	3500	LA	90019	633-H3
SAN MARINO OAKS				
	300	SGBL	91775	596-D2
SAN MARTIN WY				
	6300	BPK	90620	767-F4
SAN MARTINEZ RD				
	29800	Cstc	91384	4459-A6
SAN MARTINEZ GRANDE CYN RD				
	27300	Cstc	91384	4549-A1
SAN MATEO AV				
	38000	PMDL	93551	4285-J1
SAN MATEO CIR				
	8000	BPK	90620	767-F4
SAN MATEO CT				
	2400	CLAR	91711	571-C6
SAN MATEO LN				
	6300	BPK	90620	767-F4
SAN MATEO ST				
	6400	PRM	90723	735-E4
E SAN MATEO ST				
	4900	RDom	90221	735-D4
SAN MICHELE CT				
	-	PMDL	93550	4196-H7
SAN MIGUEL				
	-	RHE	90274	822-J2
SAN MIGUEL AV				
	700	Ven	90291	671-H5
	8100	SGAT	90280	705-C3
	10600	LYN	90262	705-C6
SAN MIGUEL CIR				
	8000	BPK	90620	767-F4
SAN MIGUEL CT				
	-	MANB	90266	732-H4
SAN MIGUEL DR				
	100	ARCD	91007	567-C5
	2800	LAN	93535	4106-F1
	3800	FUL	92835	738-H1
SAN MIGUEL RD				
	-	PAS	91105	565-E5
	800	WAL	91789	639-D6
SAN MIGUEL ST				
	6500	PRM	90723	735-E3
	21000	WdHl	91364	560-B3
	22000	WdHl	91364	559-J4
E SAN MIGUEL ST				
	4900	RDom	90221	735-D3
SAN MIGUEL WY				
	11000	MTCL	91763	641-G2
SAN MINA CT				
	-	CHNO	91710	641-E6
SAN NICOLAS DR				
	800	WAL	91789	639-D6
	27900	RPV	90275	792-H6
SANO CT				
	1100	ARCD	91007	566-J6
SANO ST				
	4100	LA	90065	594-J3
SAN OAKS DR				
	400	SDMS	91773	599-J3
SANOME MTWY				
	-	LACo	92823	710-C1
SAN ONOFRE DR				
	1600	PacP	90272	631-D3
SAN PABLO CT				
	-	POM	91766	640-D4
	500	SDMS	91773	600-B3
E SAN PABLO CT				
	800	LBCH	90813	795-F6
SAN PABLO DR				
	1400	GLDL	91207	564-G2
	3800	FUL	92835	738-H1
	8100	BPK	90620	767-F4
SAN PABLO ST				
	1300	Boyl	90033	635-B3
SAN PABLO WY				
	800	DUAR	91010	568-D4
SAN PACIFICO CIR				
	8100	BPK	90620	767-G4
SAN PACO CIR				
	6800	BPK	90620	767-G4
SAN PACO LN				
	8300	BPK	90620	767-G4
SAN PADRE CIR				
	6900	BPK	90620	767-G4
SAN PALO CIR				
	8100	BPK	90620	767-G4
SAN PALO PL				
	300	PAS	91107	566-F5
SAN PASCUAL AV				
	100	HiPk	90042	595-E2
	1200	PAS	91105	565-F7
	1200	PAS	91105	595-E2
	1200	SPAS	91030	595-E2
	10900	MTCL	91763	641-E2
SAN PASQUAL				
	700	GLDR	91740	599-C2
SAN PASQUAL AV				
	11000	MTCL	91763	641-E2
	11300	SBdC	91766	641-E3
SAN PASQUAL CIR				
	6700	BPK	90620	767-F4
SAN PASQUAL DR				
	300	ALH	91801	596-C5
SAN PASQUAL LN				
	8400	BPK	90620	767-G4
SAN PASQUAL ST				
	800	PAS	91101	566-A6
	800	PAS	91106	566-A6
	1000	PAS	91125	566-A6
	1800	PAS	91107	566-F6
	1900	LACo	91107	566-C6
SAN PATRICIO DR				
	900	MONP	91755	636-D4
SAN PEDRO CIR				
	6800	BPK	90620	767-G4
SAN PEDRO PL				
	4100	LA	90011	674-C3
	5800	LA	90003	674-D4
SAN PEDRO ST				
	16600	CRSN	90746	734-E6
S SAN PEDRO ST				
	100	LA	90012	634-F6
	200	LA	90061	704-D6
	300	LA	90013	634-F6
	500	LA	90011	674-D1
	600	LA	90021	634-E6
	600	LA	90014	634-F6
	900	LA	90015	634-E6
	1900	LA	90011	634-E6
	5800	LA	90003	674-D7
	7300	LA	90003	704-D4
	12000	LACo	90061	704-D7
	12000	LACo	90061	734-D2
	14300	LACo	90248	734-D4
SAN PIERRE DR				
	3100	ELMN	91732	637-D1
SAN RAFAEL				
	200	GLDR	91740	599-C2
SAN RAFAEL AV				
	1000	GLDL	91202	564-D3
	3700	LA	90065	594-J4
	3800	LA	90065	595-A3
	4200	HiPk	90042	595-B2
N SAN RAFAEL AV				
	-	PAS	91105	565-E4
S SAN RAFAEL AV				
	-	PAS	91105	565-F5
SAN RAFAEL DR				
	6000	BPK	90620	767-E3
	13100	CHLS	91709	680-H1
	25800	SCTA	91321	4551-F6
SAN RAFAEL LN				
	1000	PAS	91105	565-F5
SAN RAFAEL RD				
	-	ARCD	91007	567-C5
SAN RAFAEL ST				
	200	POM	91767	600-J5
	6800	PRM	90723	735-E3
E SAN RAFAEL ST				
	4900	RDom	90221	735-D3
	4900	COMP	90221	735-D3
SAN RAFAEL TER				
	700	PAS	91105	565-F7
SAN RAFAEL WY				
	11000	MTCL	91763	641-G2
SAN RAMON AV				
	300	AZU	91702	568-G7
SAN RAMON DR				
	1000	FUL	92835	738-H1
	2700	RPV	90275	823-F5
	2800	LAN	93535	4106-F1
	6700	HiPk	90042	595-F1
	6700	SPAS	91030	595-F1
SAN RAMON WY				
	6100	BPK	90620	767-E4
SAN RAPHAEL PL				
	-	POM	91766	640-E4
SAN REMO DR				
	1300	PacP	90272	631-D3
	1300	SIMI	93063	499-C3
N SAN REMO DR				
	200	LBCH	90803	826-C2
SAN REMO PL				
	-	Cstc	91384	4459-E3
SAN REMO RD				
	700	PAS	91105	565-F7
SAN REMO WY				
	4100	Tarz	91356	560-J5
	6000	BPK	90620	767-E5
SAN RENALDO CIR				
	6200	BPK	90620	767-F5
SAN RICARDO WY				
	6100	BPK	90620	767-E4
SAN RIO DR				
	8500	BPK	90620	767-E5
SAN RIO ST				
	12000	ELMN	91732	597-G4
SAN ROBERTO CIR				
	6200	BPK	90620	767-F5
SAN RODOLFO WY				
	6000	BPK	90620	767-E5
SAN ROLANDO CIR				
	6200	BPK	90620	767-E5
SAN ROLANDO WY				
	6000	BPK	90620	767-E5
SAN ROMOLO WY				
	8500	BPK	90620	767-E5
SAN ROQUE DR				
	300	WAL	91789	679-D1
	400	WAL	91789	639-D7
SAN RUBEN CIR				
	6200	BPK	90620	767-F5
SAN RUFO CIR				
	6200	BPK	90620	767-F5
SAN SALVADOR CIR				
	8800	BPK	90620	767-F5
SAN SALVADOR PL				
	13000	CRTS	90703	767-B2
SAN SALVATORE PL				
	1900	SGBL	91775	596-E2
	1900	SMRO	91108	596-E2
SAN SEBASTIAN DR				
	4700	WdHl	91364	559-H4
SAN SIMEON CIR				
	8300	BPK	90620	767-F4
SAN SIMEON DR				
	5600	LPMA	90623	767-D3
SAN SIMEON LN				
	13000	CHNO	91710	641-F7
SAN SIMEON RD				
	300	SDMS	91773	600-B3
	800	ARCD	91007	567-A4
SAN SIMEON ST				
	1700	POM	91767	601-C6
	13000	CRTS	90703	767-B1
SAN SIMON LN				
	15200	LMRD	90638	737-H4
SANSINENA LN				
	1400	LHB	90631	708-C4
SANTA ANA AV				
	-	LBCH	90803	826-B2
	2800	SGAT	90280	705-A2
	15100	BLF	90706	736-A5
SANTA ANA BLVD N				
	1700	Wats	90002	704-H5
	1800	LA	90059	704-H5
	2400	Wbrk	90059	704-H5
SANTA ANA BLVD S				
	1900	LA	90059	704-H6
	2300	Wbrk	90059	704-H6
SANTA ANA CIR				
	7000	BPK	90620	767-G4
SANTA ANA CT				
	12300	CHNO	91710	641-E6
SANTA ANA FRWY I-5				
	-	BPK	-	737-B4
	-	BPK	-	767-H1
	-	CMRC	-	675-F2
	-	CMRC	-	676-A6
	-	DWNY	-	676-A6
	-	DWNY	-	706-D3
	-	LA	-	634-J6
	-	LA	-	635-B7
	-	LA	-	675-F2
	-	LACo	-	675-F2
	-	LMRD	-	737-B4
	-	NRWK	-	706-D3
	-	NRWK	-	736-J2
	-	NRWK	-	737-B4
	-	SFSP	-	706-D3
	-	SFSP	-	737-B4
SANTA ANA FRWY U.S.-101				
	-	Boyl	-	634-G3
	-	LA	-	634-G3
SANTA ANA PL				
	12400	CHNO	91710	641-E6
SANTA ANA ST				
	2400	LACo	90255	704-H2
	2400	SGAT	90280	704-J2
	2600	SGAT	90255	704-J2
	2700	SGAT	90280	705-D2
	3200	HNTP	90255	705-D2
	4300	CDHY	90201	705-D2
	4300	CDHY	90255	705-D2
SANTA ANA PINES				
	8100	CDHY	90201	705-E2
SANTA ANITA				
	800	GLDR	91740	599-C2
SANTA ANITA AV				
	200	PAS	91107	566-E5
	200	LACo	91107	566-E5
	500	LACo	90660	637-A5
	500	SMRO	91108	566-E5
	500	LACo	91733	637-A5
	700	SELM	91733	637-C4
	1800	ARCD	91006	597-C7
	1800	ARCD	91007	597-C7
	2600	ELMN	91733	637-C4
	2900	Alta	91001	535-J5
	2900	Alta	91001	536-A5
	3000	ELMN	91731	637-C4
	3400	ELMN	91731	597-C7
	4900	ELMN	91780	597-C7
	5100	TEML	91780	597-C7
	9800	MTCL	91763	601-H6
	11400	CHNO	91710	641-H3
E SANTA ANITA AV				
	-	BURB	91502	563-H1
	100	BURB	91502	533-J7
	400	BURB	91501	533-J7
	1000	BURB	91501	534-A6
N SANTA ANITA AV				
	-	ARCD	91007	567-D3
	-	ARCD	91006	567-D3
	1900	SMAD	91024	567-D3
	2100	Alta	91001	535-J6
S SANTA ANITA AV				
	-	ARCD	91007	567-D6
	-	ARCD	91006	567-D6
	600	SMRO	91108	566-E7
	1500	ARCD	91007	597-D2
	1500	ARCD	91006	597-D2
W SANTA ANITA AV				
	200	BURB	91502	563-G1
SANTA ANITA CIR				
	7000	BPK	90620	767-G4
SANTA ANITA CT				
	100	SMAD	91024	567-B2
N SANTA ANITA ST				
	100	SGBL	91775	596-D3
	100	SGBL	91776	596-D3
S SANTA ANITA ST				
	100	SGBL	91776	596-D4
W SANTA ANITA ST				
	600	SGBL	91776	596-D4
E SANTA ANITA TER				
	-	ARCD	91006	567-D7
W SANTA ANITA TER				
	-	ARCD	91007	567-C7
SANTA ANITA CANYON RD				
	-	MNRO	91016	537-D7
	2200	LACo	91024	537-D7
	2400	ARCD	91006	567-C1
	2400	ARCD	91024	537-D7
	2400	SMAD	91006	567-C1
	2400	SMAD	91024	537-D7
	2400	SMAD	91024	567-C1
	2500	ARCD	91024	567-C1
SANTA BARBARA AV				
	500	FUL	92835	738-F3
	1600	GLDL	91208	534-H6
SANTA BARBARA CIR				
	800	DUAR	91010	568-E5

STREET
Block City ZIP Pg-Grid

SANTA BARBARA CT
3400 PMDL 93550 4286-G3
3900 LA 90037 674-A2
SANTA BARBARA DR
- RPV 90275 823-A2
700 CLAR 91711 601-C2
SANTA BARBARA ST
- LMRD 90638 738-A2
600 PAS 91101 566-A3
SANTA BELLA RD
- RHE 90274 793-C6
SANTA BERTA WY
8300 BPK 90620 767-G4
SANTA BIANCA DR
16200 HacH 91745 678-C5
SANTA CARLOTTA ST
2900 LaCr 91214 504-F6
3300 GLDL 91214 504-D5
SANTA CATALINA CIR
7100 BPK 90620 767-G4
SANTA CATALINA DR
5500 RPV 90275 823-A3
SANTA CATALINA VW
12400 Brwd 90049 631-F4
SANTA CATALINA FERRY
- AVA 90704 5923-H3
- LACo - 854-E1
- LACo 90704 5923-H2
- SPed 90731 824-D6
- SPed 90731 854-E1
SANTA CATARINA RD
- Saug 91350 4461-E5
SANTA CLARA AV
400 Ven 90291 671-H5
W SANTA CLARA AV
700 CLAR 91711 601-B2
SANTA CLARA CT
500 Ven 90291 671-H5
SANTA CLARA DR
- POM 91766 640-E5
SANTA CLARA ST
- ARCD 91007 567-C5
1900 LA 90021 674-H1
7100 BPK 90620 767-G4
20500 SCTA 91351 4551-C2
E SANTA CLARA ST
- ARCD 91006 567-D5
SANTA CLARA TKTR
- LACo - (4553-F7 See Page 4464)
- LACo - (4554-A5 See Page 4464)
- LACo - 4642-G3
- LACo - 4643-B3
- Nwhl 91321 4641-G4
- Nwhl 91321 4642-A4
- SCTA 91321 4641-D3
SANTA CLARITA RD
26900 SCTA 91350 4460-H5
SANTA CRUZ
- RHE 90274 822-J2
SANTA CRUZ CIR
7100 BPK 90620 767-G4
SANTA CRUZ CT
- MANB 90266 732-H4
600 SDMS 91773 600-B3
2100 TOR 90501 793-G1
2300 TOR 90501 763-F7
SANTA CRUZ RD
100 ARCD 91007 567-C5
W SANTA CRUZ ST
100 SPed 90731 824-A4
1000 LA 90732 824-A4
1200 LA 90732 823-H4
SANTA DOMINGO WY
7400 BPK 90620 767-H4
SAN TAELA CT
4500 WdHl 91364 560-B5
SANTA ELENA DR
7300 BPK 90620 767-H4
SANTA ELISE CIR
7300 BPK 90620 767-H4
SANTA ELVIRA WY
8200 BPK 90620 767-H4
SANTA FE AV
100 AZU 91702 568-J5
600 GLDR 91740 569-E6
700 FUL 92831 738-J7
1300 LBCH 90813 795-A5
1600 GLDR 91740 599-E2
1700 TOR 90501 793-H1
1900 LBCH 90810 795-A5
2100 TOR 90501 763-F7
2300 COMP 90222 735-A1
2700 RBCH 90278 733-B5
3100 LYN 90262 735-A1
3400 LBCH 90810 765-A7
E SANTA FE AV
100 FUL 92832 738-H7
800 SGBL 91776 596-F4
N SANTA FE AV
100 COMP 90221 735-A4
100 LA 90012 634-H4
900 LBCH 90813 795-A2
1800 LBCH 90810 795-A2
1900 COMP 90222 735-A4
2100 LYN 90262 735-A4
S SANTA FE AV
100 COMP 90221 735-A5
100 LA 90012 634-H5
300 LA 90013 634-H5
600 LA 90021 634-H6
S SANTA FE AV
1600 LA 90021 674-H2
2400 LA 90058 674-H2
2500 VER 90058 674-H2
5700 HNTP 90058 674-H6
5900 HNTP 90255 674-H6
7200 LACo 90255 674-H6
7300 LACo 90255 704-H1
8600 SGAT 90280 704-J2
10500 LYN 90262 704-J5
17500 RDom 90221 735-A6
17600 RDom 90221 765-A2
20400 CRSN 90810 765-B5
21300 LBCH 90810 765-A6
W SANTA FE AV
100 FUL 92832 738-G7
SANTA FE CT
700 SDMS 91773 600-C1
SANTA FE DR
8200 BPK 90620 767-G4
SANTA FE LN
700 SPAS 91030 595-G2
SANTA FE PL
1800 MNRO 91016 567-G6
SANTA FE RD
300 BREA 92821 709-F6
3400 BREA 92823 709-H6
SANTA FE ST
100 CLAR 91711 601-C4
100 POM 91767 600-J4
15800 WHIT 90603 707-J5
16100 WHIT 90603 708-A5
SANTA FE WY
39900 PMDL 93551 4195-J4
SANTA FE SPRINGS RD
8000 WHIT 90602 707-A4
8100 WHIT 90606 707-A4
9000 WHIT 90605 707-A4
9000 SFSP 90670 707-A4
SANTA GERTRUDES AV
9800 WHIT 90603 707-J4
11000 WHIT 90604 707-J4
11400 LACo 90604 707-J6
11800 LMRD 90638 707-J6
12200 LMRD 90638 737-H4
SANTA GERTRUDES RD
8200 DWNY 90240 706-C2
SANTA INEZ CIR
7100 BPK 90620 767-G4
SANTA INEZ DR
8000 BPK 90620 767-G3
SANTA INEZ PL
8200 BPK 90620 767-G4
SANTA INEZ WY
200 LCF 91011 535-D3
7100 BPK 90620 767-G4
SANTA IRENE CIR
7000 BPK 90620 767-G4
SANTA ISABEL CIR
7000 BPK 90620 767-G4
SANTA ISABEL DR
7100 BPK 90620 767-G4
SANTA LUCIA CIR
7100 BPK 90620 767-G4
SANTA LUCIA DR
4500 WdHl 91364 560-A4
SANTA LUNA DR
30500 RPV 90275 823-G5
SANTA MARGARITA DR
1300 ARCD 91006 567-A3
SANTA MARGARITA LN
8100 LPMA 90623 767-C4
8600 CYP 90630 767-C4
SANTA MARIA AV
1600 GLDL 91208 534-H6
3200 FUL 92835 738-G2
SANTA MARIA CIR
800 DUAR 91010 568-E5
SANTA MARIA DR
19300 SCTA 91321 4551-F6
SANTA MARIA RD
200 ARCD 91007 567-C4
2000 Top 90290 590-C1
2000 Top 90290 560-D7
2000 WdHl 91364 560-D7
SANTA MARIA ST
- ANA 92801 767-J5
6200 VeCo 93063 499-B4
SANTA MARIANA AV
100 LACo 91746 637-G4
SANTA MARTA CIR
7000 BPK 90620 767-G4
SANTA MONICA AV
3200 FUL 92835 738-G2
SANTA MONICA BLVD
100 SMCA 90401 671-E1
1200 SMCA 90404 671-E1
1800 SMCA 90404 631-G7
4000 LA 90029 594-A5
4800 LA 90029 593-E5
9900 CenC 90067 632-B5
9900 Wwd 90024 632-B5
10200 WLA 90025 632-B5
SANTA MONICA BLVD Rt#-2
5300 LA 90029 593-A6
5500 LA 90038 593-A6
7000 WHWD 90038 593-A6
7100 WHWD 90046 593-A6
8300 WHWD 90069 593-A6
8400 WHWD 90069 592-G7
9200 BHLS 90210 592-G7
9200 BHLS 90210 632-E2
SANTA MONICA BLVD Rt#-2
9800 BHLS 90212 632-E2
11200 WLA 90025 632-E2
11500 WLA 90025 631-H6
S SANTA MONICA BLVD
9300 BHLS 90210 632-F2
9700 BHLS 90212 632-E2
SANTA MONICA FRWY I-10
- LA - 632-F7
- LA - 633-B6
- LA - 634-A6
- LA - 674-G1
- SMCA - 631-J7
- SMCA - 632-F7
- SMCA - 671-J1
SANTA MONICA FRWY Rt#-1
- SMCA - 671-F3
SANTA MONICA PL N
2600 SMCA 90404 631-G7
SANTA MONICA PL S
2600 SMCA 90404 631-H6
SANTANA AV
3000 PMDL 93551 4195-C3
18300 CRTS 90703 766-E1
SANTA PAULA AV
200 PAS 91107 566-G3
SANTA PAULA CIR
7000 BPK 90620 767-G4
SANTA PAULA CT
600 SDMS 91773 600-B3
SANTA PAULA PL
1700 GLDL 91208 534-H6
SANTAQUIN DR
1400 DBAR 91765 679-J4
SANTAR ST
18400 RowH 91748 679-A4
SANTA RENA DR
1800 RPV 90275 823-H2
SANTA RITA CIR
7000 BPK 90620 767-G4
SANTA RITA ST
700 LACo 90220 734-E4
17800 Enc 91316 561-A3
19000 Tarz 91356 560-F2
19800 WdHl 91364 560-D2
SANTA ROSA
- RHE 90274 822-J2
SANTA ROSA AV
1600 GLDL 91208 534-H6
1800 PAS 91104 535-J6
2000 Alta 91001 535-J6
2500 Alta 91001 536-A5
SANTA ROSA CIR
43600 LAN 93535 4106-F1
SANTA ROSA CT
700 SDMS 91773 600-B3
1800 CLAR 91711 571-C7
1800 CLAR 91711 601-C1
3400 PMDL 93550 4286-G3
SANTA ROSA DR
- Nor 91326 500-E1
SANTA ROSA PL
3100 FUL 92835 738-G2
SANTA ROSA RD
200 ARCD 91007 567-C5
SANTA ROSALIA DR
3700 LA 90008 673-D2
SANTA SUSANA DR
25900 SCTA 91321 4551-F6
SANTA SUSANA PL
- Chat 91311 500-A6
8600 LA 91304 530-A1
SANTA SUSANA TR
8600 VeCo 93063 499-C4
SANTA SUSANA FIRE RD
23600 VeCo 93063 499-E4
SANTA SUSANA PASS RD
6600 SIMI 93063 499-G2
6700 VeCo 93063 499-D4
7600 Chat 91311 499-G2
10800 Chat 91311 500-A2
SANTA SUSANNA PL
- Chat 91311 500-A7
SANTA TERESA
1400 SPAS 91030 595-F3
SANTA TERESA CIR
7100 BPK 90620 767-G4
SANTA VALERA ST
7300 BPK 90620 767-H4
SANTA YNEZ DR
100 ARCD 91007 567-C4
SANTA YNEZ LN
600 SGBL 91775 596-F3
SANTA YNEZ RD
- PacP 90272 630-F1
SANTA YNEZ ST
1800 Echo 90026 634-D1
1900 Echo 90026 594-D7
E SANTA YNEZ ST
8200 LACo 91775 596-F3
8200 SGBL 91775 596-F3
SANTA YNEZ WY
- SCTA 91355 4550-E4
800 LA 90048 633-A3
SANTA YSABELA DR
1700 RowH 91748 679-A5
SANTEE ST
700 LA 90014 634-E6
900 LA 90015 634-E6
1900 LA 90011 634-D7
SANTEZ DR
2800 POM 91768 640-B2
SANTIAGO
- LVRN 91750 570-H3
SANTIAGO AV
300 LBCH 90814 796-C7
700 LBCH 90804 796-C7
SANTIAGO DR
4700 CRTS 90623 767-B3
4700 LPMA 90623 767-B3
SANTIAGO RD
32600 Actn 93510 4465-E1
32800 Actn 93510 4375-F6
SANTIAGO ST
2100 LACo 91724 639-F2
2900 THO 91362 557-C3
SANTIAGO TKTR
- LACo - 4466-E6
- LACo - 4467-A5
- PMDL 93550 4466-E6
SANTIAGO CANYON WY
500 BREA 92821 709-C5
SANTINA ST
23600 Chat 91311 499-F7
SANTINI LN
- Nor 91326 500-C1
SANTO DR
4900 VeCo 91377 557-G1
SANTO DOMINGO AV
1200 DUAR 91010 568-B5
SANTOL DR
11300 LACo 91342 482-H6
SANTOLINA DR
36600 PMDL 93550 4286-F4
SANTONA DR
28000 RPV 90275 792-H6
SANTO ORO AV
1200 LPUE 91744 638-D6
SANTORINI DR
4600 CYP 90630 767-B7
SANTORO WY
37800 PMDL 93550 4286-G2
SANTOS DIAZ ST
6100 IRW 91702 568-F7
SANTO TOMAS DR
3900 LA 90008 673-C2
SAN TROPEZ CT
13500 CHLS 91709 680-H2
N SAN VICENTE AV
1900 LBCH 90815 796-D2
SAN VICENTE BLVD
100 SMCA 90402 671-C1
100 SMCA 90402 631-D6
4500 LA 90019 633-A2
5900 LA 90036 633-A2
6300 LA 90048 633-A2
6500 BHLS 90211 633-A2
11400 Brwd 90049 631-F4
11500 LACo 90073 631-F4
N SAN VICENTE BLVD
100 LA 90048 632-J1
100 WHWD 90048 632-J1
300 WHWD 90048 592-H6
600 WHWD 90069 592-H6
S SAN VICENTE BLVD
100 LA 90048 632-J1
100 LA 90048 633-A2
400 BHLS 90211 632-J1
400 BHLS 90211 633-A2
SAN VICENTE CIR
20100 WAL 91789 639-E7
SAN VICENTE DR
600 WAL 91789 639-E7
SAN VICENTE PL N
100 SMCA 90402 631-C7
100 SMCA 90402 671-C1
SAN VICENTE RD
800 ARCD 91007 567-A4
SAN VINCENTE AV
8100 SGAT 90280 705-C2
10600 LYN 90262 705-C6
SAN VINCENTE ST
6400 PRM 90723 735-E4
E SAN VINCENTE ST
1600 COMP 90221 735-C4
4100 RDom 90221 735-C4
SAN YSIDRO AV
- SCTA 91355 4550-E4
SAN YSIDRO CIR
6000 BPK 90620 767-E4
SAN YSIDRO DR
1100 BHLS 90210 592-D6
1100 LA 90210 592-D3
SAN YSIDRO LN
32900 Actn 93510 4375-B7
SAN YSIDRO WY
37600 PMDL 93550 4286-G2
SAN YUBA WY
6000 BPK 90620 767-E4
SAO PAULO PL
1400 POM 91768 600-F7
SAPOTA DR
2100 LHH 90631 708-F1
SAPPHIRE
- BREA 92823 710-D6
SAPPHIRE CT
- CRTS 90703 767-A3
800 POM 91766 640-H4
SAPPHIRE DR
3600 Enc 91436 561-F5
SAPPHIRE LN
- GAR 90248 764-A1
800 DBAR 91789 679-G4
31800 Cstc 91384 4369-G6
SAPPHIRE ST
100 RBCH 90277 762-J6
SAPPHIRE CANYON RD
23800 DBAR 91765 640-C5
SAPPHIRE HILL LN
14000 CHLS 91709 680-G3
SARA DR
3500 TOR 90503 763-A4
SARA ST
27300 LACo 91387 4551-J4
SARABANDE LN
27900 SCTA 91387 4551-J2
SARABETH ST
7500 DWNY 90242 705-H5
SARAGOSA ST
10700 LACo 90606 676-H7
SARAGOSSA
1800 POM 91768 600-F6
SARAH CT
- SIGH 90755 795-H3
2000 WCOV 91792 679-A1
SARAH LN
44600 LAN 93535 4016-F6
SARAH PL
3200 FUL 92835 738-H2
SARAH ST
4800 BURB 91505 563-C4
8400 LACo 91770 636-G4
10100 LA 91602 563-A4
11000 LA 91602 562-G4
11700 LA 91607 562-G4
12300 LA 91604 562-E4
12900 Shrm 91423 562-C4
SARAHGLEN LN
600 LHB 90631 708-D7
SARALYNN DR
9100 Chat 91311 499-F7
SARALYNN LN
100 Chat 91311 499-E6
SARA MAR LN
5400 TEML 91780 597-A3
SARAN DR
8100 PdlR 90293 702-C3
8600 Wch 90045 702-C3
SARANAC AV
- LA 91342 482-A1
SARANAC DR
13700 LACo 90605 737-C1
13800 LACo 90604 707-D7
E SARANAC DR
11800 LACo 90604 707-D7
SARANDI GRANDE DR
2300 HacH 91745 678-C5
SARANNE ST
2200 LCF 91011 534-H2
SARAPE CT
25700 SCTA 91355 4550-G5
SARATOGA AV
9800 MTCL 91763 601-G6
SARATOGA CT
2500 PMDL 93551 4195-D6
SARATOGA DR
4300 LYN 90262 735-G3
SARATOGA LN
- CHLS 91709 640-J7
- CULC 90230 672-H3
2200 GLDR 91741 569-J6
2200 GLDR 91741 570-A6
SARATOGA PL
2600 CHLS 91709 640-J7
SARATOGA ST
3600 PRV 90660 676-H1
N SARATOGA ST
100 Boyl 90033 635-B5
S SARATOGA ST
200 Boyl 90033 635-B5
SARATOGA WY
18000 SCTA 91387 4551-J2
SARAZEN CT
- LHB 90631 738-C2
SARAZEN DR
1200 ALH 91803 636-A2
1600 ALH 91803 635-J2
SARAZEN PL
12200 GmH 91344 481-D6
SARBONNE LN
- BelA 90077 591-H4
SARBONNE RD
600 BelA 90077 591-J7
600 BelA 90077 592-A7
SARCO DR
11700 LMRD 90638 707-G7
SARDA RD
23700 SCTA 91355 4550-F7
SARDINE ST
300 SPed 90731 824-E5
SARDINIA CT
25800 SCTA 91355 4550-F5
SARDINIA WY
- Nor 91326 500-C1
SARDIS AV
11000 LA 90064 632-C7
11600 LA 90064 672-B1
SARDIUS
- BREA 92823 710-D6
SARDONYX ST
4300 LA 90032 595-C6
SARELDA RD
23800 WHil 91304 499-E7
SARENTINA CT
- BLF 90706 736-D7
SARGASSO CT
25000 StvR 91381 4640-E2
SARGENT AV
7900 WHIT 90602 677-F7
7900 WHIT 90602 707-E1
8000 WHIT 90605 707-E1
SARGENT CT
1600 Echo 90026 594-F7
SARGENT PL
1500 Echo 90026 594-E7
SARGENT ST
3400 LVRN 91750 600-G1
SARI AV
7400 Nor 91325 501-D7
7400 Nor 91325 531-D1
SARI PL
9700 LA 91343 501-D5
9700 Nor 91325 501-D5
SARILEE AV
4100 RSMD 91770 596-G6
SARITA AV
17300 SCTA 91387 4552-A2
SARITA PL
19100 Tarz 91356 560-G5
SARK PL
- Saug 91350 4461-G6
SARKIS CT
22600 SCTA 91350 4460-J5
SARNIA AV
6600 NLB 90805 735-G7
SARTELL DR
20400 LACo 91789 679-F5
SARTORI AV
600 TOR 90501 763-G5
SARVISTREE CT
- LACo 91387 4552-A4
SASPARILLA ST
6600 SIMI 93063 499-D2
SASSAFRAS CT
- LA 91343 501-H6
- LACo 91387 4551-J5
SASSARI LN
- Nor 91326 500-C1
SASSOON PL
- Saug 91350 4461-E5
SASTRE AV
2000 SELM 91733 637-A3
2500 ELMN 91733 637-A1
SATHER CT
- BREA 92821 709-B6
SATICOY ST
2100 POM 91767 601-A5
9900 LA 91504 533-C3
10600 SunV 91352 533-A3
11000 SunV 91352 532-J3
11400 NHol 91605 532-F3
13400 PanC 91402 532-B3
14400 VanN 91405 532-A3
14500 VanN 91405 531-F4
15300 VanN 91406 531-F4
17300 Nor 91325 531-B4
17700 Res 91335 531-B4
18100 Res 91335 530-G4
19700 Win 91306 530-A4
20700 LA 91304 530-A4
22000 CanP 91303 529-G4
22000 CanP 91303 530-A4
22200 CanP 91307 529-G4
22800 LA 91304 529-F4
SATICOY ST S
12500 NHol 91605 532-E4
SATIN CT
3400 PMDL 93551 4195-B3
SATINWOOD AV
100 VeCo 91377 558-B2
SATINWOOD DR
6500 WHIT 90601 677-E6
20700 SCTA 91350 4461-C6
SATINWOOD LN
- PMDL 93551 4285-D2
SATSUMA AV
4200 LA 91602 563-A5
4800 NHol 91601 563-A1
5900 NHol 91601 533-A7
6100 NHol 91606 533-A7
6600 NHol 91605 533-A4
7200 SunV 91352 533-A4
SATTES DR
6200 RPV 90275 822-H2
SATURN AV
2000 HNTP 90255 674-J7
2700 HNTP 90255 675-A7
3500 PMDL 93550 4286-H2
SATURN ST
1800 MONP 91755 636-C5
4500 LA 90019 633-B4
5800 LA 90035 633-A4
9700 LA 90035 632-G4
SATURN WY
- SLB 90740 826-G2
SAUDER ST
13600 LACo 91746 638-A2
14500 LACo 91744 638-C4
SAUGUS AV
4000 Shrm 91403 561-H5
SAUGUS RD
11600 Chat 91311 480-B7
11700 Chat 91311 500-B1
SAUGUS TO THE SEA RD
- StvR 91381 480-G1
- StvR 91381 4640-H6
- StvR 91381 4641-A7
SAUL CT
15600 SCTA 91387 4462-E7
SAUNDERS ST
2200 POM 91767 601-B5
E SAUNDERS ST
1600 COMP 90221 735-B3
4100 RDom 90221 735-C3
SAUSALITO AV
6000 WdHl 91367 559-J1
6500 CanP 91307 529-J5
7600 LA 91304 529-J2
SAUSALITO CIR
- MANB 90266 732-J4
5000 LPMA 90623 767-C4
SAUSALITO DR
16700 WHIT 90603 708-B3
SAUSALITO ST
3200 LALM 90720 796-J2
SAVAGE AV
9700 DWNY 90240 706-D4
SAVANNA CIR
- LA 91342 482-G6
W SAVANNA ST
3500 ANA 92804 767-G7
SAVANNAH PL
1700 LVRN 91750 600-D3
SAVANNAH ST
800 MTBL 90640 636-E6
4400 CHNO 91710 641-E7
N SAVANNAH ST
100 Boyl 90033 635-B5
S SAVANNAH ST
100 Boyl 90033 635-B6
SAVANNA PLAIN DR
- LAN 93536 4013-J6
SAVANO RD
- SBdC 92372 (4562-E3 See Page 4471)
SAVARONA WY
100 CRSN 90746 764-C1
SAVILLE AV
5200 Enc 91436 561-D2
SAVONA CT
- SBdC 91710 641-C4
SAVONA DR
2200 SBdC 92372 (4562-F4 See Page 4471)
SAVONA PL
1200 POM 91766 640-E3
SAVONA RD
10800 BelA 90077 591-H5
N SAVONA WK
100 LBCH 90803 826-D3
SAVONA WY
500 VeCo 91377 557-G1
SAVORY PL
- SCTA 91354 4460-G5
SAVOY CIR
6400 BPK 90621 767-G1
SAVOY CT
400 VeCo 91377 557-H2
SAVOY ST
400 LA 90012 634-H1
SAWGRASS CT
19200 LHB 90631 738-D2
SAWGRASS DR
- PMDL 93551 4194-J2
- PMDL 93551 4195-A2
SAWGRASS LN
43200 LAN 93536 4104-H3
SAWMILL LN
- SCTA 91350 4550-J2
SAWPIT LN
- BRAD 91010 567-J3
SAWTELLE BLVD
1500 WLA 90025 632-A5
2200 LA 90064 632-B5
2800 LA 90064 672-C1
3000 LA 90066 672-C1
3800 CULC 90230 672-E3
3800 CULC 90066 672-E3
4400 LA 90230 672-F4
S SAWTOOTH CT
100 THO 91362 557-B2
SAWYER AV
1600 WCOV 91790 638-E1
SAWYER ST
2800 NLB 90805 765-H1
5800 LA 90019 633-A5
5900 LA 90034 633-A5
5900 LA 90035 633-A5
6000 LA 90034 632-G5
6000 LA 90035 632-G5
9700 LA 90064 632-G5
E SAXON AV
100 SGBL 91776 596-E7
W SAXON AV
100 SGBL 91776 596-D7
SAXON DR
2600 LA 90065 564-H7
SAYBROOK AV
600 ELA 90022 676-A1
1900 CMRC 90040 676-A3
SAYLER AV
15700 LNDL 90260 733-D5
SAYLIN LN
6200 HiPk 90042 595-D1
SAYRE DR
14600 LA 91342 481-J5
SAYRE LN
800 Echo 90026 594-C6
SAYRE ST
13000 LA 91342 482-B4
13000 LACo 91342 482-B4
14500 LA 91342 481-J6
SCADLOCK LN
3300 Shrm 91403 561-G6
SCALEA CT
6000 PMDL 93552 4287-C3
SCALES WY
7200 BPK 90621 767-G1
SCALLION DR
21800 SCTA 91350 4461-A6
SCANDIA WY
3800 LA 90065 594-H2
SCANNEL AV
21500 TOR 90503 763-A6
SCANNO DR
400 VeCo 91377 557-G2
SCARBORO ST
3300 LA 90065 594-H4
SCARBOROUGH AV
- CHNO 91710 641-J7
SCARBOROUGH CT
- CHNO 91710 641-J7
SCARBOROUGH LN
- CRTS 90703 767-B2
1900 SDMS 91773 599-G5
SCARBOROUGH PEAK DR
6900 CanP 91307 529-D5
SCARECROW PL
2600 RowH 91748 678-H7
SCARFF ST
2300 LA 90007 634-B7
SCARLET CT
4700 PMDL 93551 4194-J1
SCARLET MEADOW DR
19700 SCTA 91321 4551-F5
SCARLET OAK CIR
100 POM 91767 600-J1
SCELINA AV
6500 BELL 90201 675-C7
SCENARIO LN
2000 BelA 90077 592-A3
SCENIC AV
6000 LA 90068 593-F3
SCENIC DR
1200 GLDL 91205 564-G7
1400 PAS 91103 565-D1
2900 WCOV 91792 679-C3
7700 SBdC 92372 (4562-C4 See Page 4471)
8300 LACo 91770 636-F4
11500 WHIT 90601 677-B3
E SCENIC DR
100 MNRO 91016 567-G2
W SCENIC DR
100 MNRO 91016 567-F2
SCENIC PL
16900 PacP 90272 630-H4
SCENIC WY
200 BREA 92821 709-B4
SCENIC RIDGE DR
- CHLS 91709 640-H7
- POM 91766 640-J7
2600 CHLS 91709 641-A7
SCEPTER LN
21700 SCTA 91350 4461-A5
SCHABARUM AV
12700 IRW 91706 597-H6
SCHADER DR
2200 SMCA 90404 631-G7
SCHAEFER RD
- LACo 91390 4463-E2
SCHAEFER ST
3500 CULC 90232 632-J7
3500 CULC 90232 672-J1
SCHAMISE ST
45700 LAN 93534 4015-H3
SCHARN LN
9200 BLF 90706 736-A3
SCHAUFELE AV
- LBCH 90808 765-J7
SCHERER AV
100 WAL 91789 679-E1
100 WAL 91789 639-E7
SCHERZINGER LN
17500 SCTA 91387 4552-A2
17700 SCTA 91387 4551-J2
SCHICK AV
1200 City 90063 635-D3
SCHICK LN
12100 LKWD 90715 766-J4
SCHILLING AV
6600 NLB 90805 735-G7
SCHILLING CT
1700 TOR 90501 793-H2
E SCHINNER ST
1300 COMP 90221 735-B6
SCHLAEPFER DR
- FUL 92833 738-C5
SCHLEY AV
800 Wilm 90744 794-J6
SCHLITZ ST
13700 VanN 91405 532-B4
SCHMIDT RD
2400 ELMN 91732 637-D3
10300 SELM 91733 637-B3
10900 ELMN 91733 637-C2
SCHMIDT ST
- SELM 91733 637-B3
SCHOENBORN ST
13000 SunV 91352 532-D1
15000 LA 91343 531-D2
17900 Nor 91325 531-A2
18100 Nor 91325 530-J2
18700 Nor 91324 530-F2
20300 Win 91306 530-C2
21400 LA 91304 530-A2
22200 LA 91304 529-E2
SCHOLL DR
300 GLDL 91206 564-J4
SCHOLL CANYON RD
7600 Eagl 90041 565-D5
7600 PAS 91105 565-D5
SCHOLLVIEW AV
17100 LACo 93591 4199-H2
S SCHOOL AV
500 ELA 90022 675-J1
SCHOOL ST
100 COMP 90220 734-G4
100 COV 91723 599-B5
1300 GLDL 91202 564-C2
11600 LYN 90262 705-B7
11600 LYN 90262 735-B1
14300 BALD 91706 598-C3
SCHOOLCRAFT ST
16900 VanN 91406 531-C5
18300 Res 91335 530-G5
19700 Win 91306 530-C5
20900 CanP 91303 530-A5
22000 CanP 91303 529-J5
22300 CanP 91307 529-F6
SCHOOL HOUSE CT
5500 CMRC 90040 675-H3
SCHOOLING RD
9500 PRV 90660 676-F7
SCHOOLSIDE AV
2300 MONP 91754 635-H5
SCHOOLWOOD DR
600 LHB 90631 738-D1
SCHOONER
1900 LBCH 90810 795-A1
SCHOONER AV
3400 LA 90292 671-H7
SCHOONER DR
32200 RPV 90275 823-D5
SCHOONER WY
300 SLB 90740 826-E3
SCHRADER BLVD
1500 Hlwd 90028 593-E4
SCHREY PL
- SCTA 91351 4551-E3
SCHROLL ST
7000 LKWD 90713 766-F6
SCHUBERT CIR
- StvR 91381 4550-C7
6300 BPK 90621 738-A7
SCHUEREN RD
100 LACo 90265 629-E1
100 LACo 91302 589-E7
100 LACo 91302 629-E1
100 Top 90290 589-E7
SCHULTZE DR
- HGDN 90716 766-J5
SCHUMACHER DR
700 LA 90048 633-A3
900 LA 90048 632-J3
SCHUMACHER RD
4900 LACo 91302 559-D4
SCHUMANN RD
23100 Chat 91311 499-G7
SCHUYLER RD
1000 BHLS 90210 592-F6
1200 LA 90210 592-F5
SCHUYLKILL DR
4000 CALB 91302 559-H6
SCHWEITZER DR
3100 Top 90290 560-B7
SCHWIND RD
5600 LACo 90265 626-H4
SCIOTO RD
1200 SLB 90740 796-G7
SCOBEE LN
1700 LCF 91011 534-J1
SCOBEY AV
19000 CRSN 90746 764-F3
SCOFIELD DR
1100 GLDL 91205 564-G7
SCOMAR ST
37600 PMDL 93550 4286-E2
SCORIA CT
2400 CHLS 91709 680-J6
SCORPIUS WY
- PMDL 93552 4286-J2
SCOTCH PINE PL
- LACo 91387 4552-A4
SCOTGROVE DR
6500 RPV 90275 792-H7
SCOTLAND ST
3000 LA 90039 594-C4
SCOTMIST DR
6000 RPV 90275 792-J7
SCOTMONT DR
9200 Tuj 91042 504-B6
SCOTSVIEW DR
28900 RPV 90275 822-H1
SCOTT AV
300 AZU 91702 599-A1
900 MTBL 90640 636-G7
1100 Echo 90026 594-D6
1100 LA 90012 594-F7
SCOTT AV
1200 POM 91767 601-B7
2100 PMDL 93550 4286-E2
9900 WHIT 90603 707-H6
10600 WHIT 90604 707-H6
10800 LACo 90604 707-H6
11000 SGAT 90280 705-F7
SCOTT CIR
5000 LPMA 90623 767-C3
SCOTT LN
4100 RSMD 91770 596-G6
W SCOTT LN
- LACo 91387 4552-A4
SCOTT PL
300 PAS 91103 565-G4
400 ARCD 91006 567-E6
600 GLDR 91740 569-F6
2700 Echo 90026 594-C4
14300 BALD 91706 598-C4
SCOTT RD
1000 BURB 91504 533-E3
2000 WCOV 91792 638-G5
9600 LA 91504 533-D3
SCOTT ST
800 SGBL 91776 596-F6
4000 TOR 90503 763-B6
8600 RSMD 91770 596-G6
9000 BLF 90706 736-A3
E SCOTT ST
100 NLB 90805 765-C1
W SCOTT ST
- NLB 90805 765-C1
SCOTT WY
- Actn 93510 4375-F4
3100 LA 91504 533-D3
6000 BPK 90620 767-E2
6000 CMRC 90040 675-H7
SCOTTDALE AV
1300 GLDR 91740 569-J7
SCOTT ROBERTSON RD
5200 HIDH 91302 559-C4
SCOTTSBLUFF DR
500 CLAR 91711 571-E7
SCOTTSDALE DR
- CRSN 90745 794-G1
SCOTTSDALE DR N
- CRSN 90745 794-E2
SCOTTSDALE DR S
- CRSN 90745 794-E2
SCOTWOOD DR
5500 RPV 90275 823-A2
5800 RHE 90274 823-A2
SCOUT AV
6500 BGDN 90201 706-A1
7200 BGDN 90201 705-J2
SCOUT WY
2200 Echo 90026 634-C1
SCOVILLE AV
1100 POM 91767 601-C6
10100 Sunl 91040 503-G2
SCRANTON CT
37300 PMDL 93552 4286-J3
N SCREENLAND DR
100 BURB 91505 563-C2
1800 BURB 91505 533-C7
SCRIBNER AV
9900 LACo 90605 707-B4
SCRIBNER LN
- ING 90305 703-E3
SCRIPPS DR
400 CLAR 91711 601-C1
500 CLAR 91711 571-B7
SCRIPPS LN
2600 Alta 91001 535-J5
SCRIPPS PL
2700 Alta 91001 535-J5
E SCRIVENER ST
5300 LBCH 90808 796-C1
SCROLL ST
19400 Res 91335 530-F5
SCRUB OAK DR
- SBdC 92371 (4472-G7 See Page 4471)
2600 SBdC - (4562-G5 See Page 4471)
7400 SBdC 92371 (4562-G1 See Page 4471)
SCUDDER CT
17400 CRSN 90746 734-F7
17400 CRSN 90746 764-F1
SCUDDER WY
- MONP 91754 635-J4
SEA LNDR
28000 MAL 90265 667-H1
SEA WY
100 SLB 90743 826-H6
SEAACA ST
9700 DWNY 90241 706-D7
SEABEC CIR
15800 PacP 90272 630-J6
SEA BISCUIT CT
900 WAL 91789 639-F5
SEABLUFF DR
- LA 90094 702-D1
- Wch 90045 702-D1
SEABOARD LN
2800 NLB 90805 765-H1
SEABOARD RD
20400 MAL 90265 629-H6
SEABOARD WY
20700 MAL 90265 629-H6
SEABORN ST
5300 LBCH 90808 766-C5

STREET Block City ZIP Pg-Grid

SEABORN ST
6100 LKWD 90713 766-D5
11300 LKWD 90715 766-G5
SEA BREEZE AV
- RPV 90275 822-J3
SEA BREEZE DR
600 SLB 90740 826-F4
2700 LACo 90265 628-D6
17900 PacP 90272 630-E5
E SEA BREEZE DR
6200 LBCH 90803 826-E1
6200 LBCH 90803 796-D7
SEA BREEZE LN
44200 LAN 93536 4015-B7
SEABRIGHT AV
1300 LBCH 90813 795-A5
2200 LBCH 90810 795-A3
3600 LBCH 90810 765-A7
N SEABRIGHT AV
2800 LBCH 90810 795-A2
SEABRIGHT DR
1300 LA 90210 592-D5
SEABRYN DR
6400 RPV 90275 822-H1
SEABURY LN
10200 BelA 90077 592-A3
SEACLAIRE DR
21400 RPV 90275 823-F6
SEACLIFF CIR
3400 NLB 90805 735-H6
SEACLIFF DR
3200 RPV 90275 823-E6
SEA COLONY DR
2900 SMCA 90405 671-F5
SEACOVE DR
- RPV 90275 822-H5
SEA COVE LN
- SCTA 91355 4550-H4
SEACREST CT
- LBCH 90803 826-G2
SEA CREST DR
- RPV 90275 823-B3
SEACREST DR
- BPK 90621 738-A6
SEA DAISY DR
29500 MAL 90265 667-D3
SEADLER DR
18400 RowH 91748 679-A4
SEA DRIFT CV
6200 MAL 90265 667-B1
SEAFARER CIR
1500 SPed 90731 823-H7
SEAFIELD DR
31800 MAL 90265 626-G7
SEAFORTH AV
14300 NRWK 90650 736-J4
SEA GATE DR
32600 RPV 90275 822-J4
SEAGLEN DR
3400 RPV 90275 823-E5
SEAGREEN DR
24200 DBAR 91765 640-D5
SEA GRIT AV
- SCTA 91387 4552-C5
SEAGROVE AV
1400 Wilm 90744 794-E3
24200 CRSN 90745 794-F3
SEAGULL DR
- MAL 90265 668-B1
SEAGULL WY
26600 MAL 90265 668-B1
SEAHILL DR
32500 RPV 90275 822-H4
SEAHORN DR
3600 LACo 90265 630-E5
SEA HORSE LN
4100 RPV 90275 823-D6
SEAHURST RD
- RHE 90274 793-B6
N SEA ISLE DR
- LBCH 90803 826-C3
SEAL WK
- Cstc 91384 4459-D6
SEAL WY
1000 SLB 90740 826-E5
SEAL BEACH BLVD
200 SLB 90740 826-H1
12000 LALM 90720 796-J7
12000 SLB 90740 796-J7
12300 OrCo 90720 796-J7
SEA LEVEL DR
31500 MAL 90265 626-G7
SEA LION PL
29200 MAL 90265 667-E4
SEALPOINT CT
6400 RPV 90275 822-H4
SEAMAN AV
1300 SELM 91733 637-A3
2600 ELMN 91733 637-A1
SEAMOOR DR
3800 MAL 90265 629-J6
SEAMOUNT DR
28200 RPV 90275 792-H7
SEAPINE LN
2600 LaCr 91214 504-G5
SEA RANCH WY
28700 MAL 90265 667-F3
SEA RAVEN DR
32200 RPV 90275 823-E6
SEARCHLIGHT RANCH RD
500 Actn 93510 4465-J1

SEA REEF DR
18000 PacP 90272 630-E5
SEA RIDGE CIR
32000 RPV 90275 822-J3
SEA RIDGE DR
- SIGH 90755 795-G3
SEARIDGE DR
2700 LACo 90265 628-D5
SEARLS DR
19500 RowH 91748 679-D4
SEARS ST
2700 VER 90058 674-J5
2700 VER 90058 675-A5
SEARS WY
3600 PAS 91107 566-H3
SEASCAPE RD
200 RPV 90275 823-C5
W SEASHELL CT
1000 ONT 91762 641-J2
SEASHELL WY
28000 RPV 90275 823-B1
N SEASIDE AV
200 SPed 90731 824-F3
1000 LBCH 90802 824-F3
S SEASIDE AV
600 SPed 90731 824-D5
SEASIDE TER
- SMCA 90401 671-E3
SEASIDE WK
5500 LBCH 90803 826-C3
E SEASIDE WY
100 LBCH 90802 825-E1
W SEASIDE WY
100 LBCH 90802 825-C1
SEASIDE HEIGHTS DR
5500 RPV 90275 823-A1
SEASON AV
1600 WCOV 91791 638-H3
1600 LACo 91744 638-H3
SEASONAL
3500 Actn 93510 4465-B3
SEASPRAY DR
29400 RPV 90275 822-H1
SEA SPRING DR
2000 HacH 91745 678-D4
SEASTAR DR
6400 MAL 90265 627-B7
6400 MAL 90265 667-A1
SEA TERRACE AV
- RPV 90275 822-J2
SEATON ST
400 LA 90013 634-G5
SEATTLE
1800 WCOV 91790 598-E7
SEATTLE DR
2800 LA 90046 593-B1
SEATTLE PL
7600 LA 90046 593-B1
SEA URCHIN LN
- RPV 90275 823-C5
SEAVER CT
22500 SCTA 91350 4460-J5
SEAVER DR
24200 LACo 90263 628-G6
24200 LACo 90265 628-G6
SEA VIEW AV
4400 LA 90065 594-J3
4500 LA 90065 595-A3
SEA VIEW DR
4400 LA 90065 594-J3
4400 LA 90065 595-A3
5600 MAL 90265 627-B7
SEAVIEW DR
2000 FUL 92833 738-C3
16000 PacP 90272 630-J6
SEAVIEW DR N
- RHE 90274 823-A2
SEAVIEW DR S
29500 RHE 90274 823-A2
SEA VIEW LN
1300 SLB 90740 796-G7
4400 LA 90065 594-J3
4500 LA 90065 595-A3
SEAVIEW ST
100 MANB 90266 732-E3
SEAVIEW TER
- SMCA 90401 671-E3
SEAVIEW TR
1700 LA 90046 593-B4
SEA VISTA DR
26800 MAL 90265 668-A1
SEAWALK DR
- LA 90094 702-D1
SEA WALL RD
- RPV 90275 823-C5
SEAWATCH LN
6700 MAL 90265 667-D3
SEAWIND DR
7000 LBCH 90803 826-F2
SEA WIND PL
3900 CALB 91302 559-J6
SEAWOLF DR
32500 RPV 90275 822-H4
SEBALD AV
2400 RBCH 90278 733-B6
SEBASTAPOL ST
600 CLAR 91711 571-E6
SEBEC PL
15700 LMRD 90638 737-H4
SEBREN AV
4100 LKWD 90713 766-C5
N SEBREN AV
3700 LBCH 90808 766-C7

SEBRING ST
1400 POM 91767 601-B6
SECKER DR
23600 WHil 91304 499-D6
SECLUSION LN
600 GLDL 91207 564-F2
SECLUSION PL
3300 Actn 93510 4465-B3
SECO CT
17500 RowH 91748 678-G6
SECO ST
500 PAS 91105 565-F3
500 PAS 91103 565-F3
SECO CANYON RD
26800 SCTA 91350 4460-H5
26800 SCTA 91350 4550-J1
26800 SCTA 91354 4460-H4
26800 SCTA 91354 4550-J1
27800 SCTA 91390 4460-J2
28600 LACo 91390 4460-J2
SECOND ST
12200 NRWK 90650 706-J6
SECREST DR
5500 LACo 90043 673-C5
SECTION CENTER ST
18400 COV 91722 599-B3
18400 LACo 91722 599-B3
SECURA WY
8100 SFSP 90670 707-A1
SECURE PL
43600 LAN 93536 4105-C1
SECURITY AV
7500 LA 91504 533-C3
SEDALIA AV
400 LVRN 91750 600-E2
400 LACo 91750 600-E2
SEDAN AV
5500 WdHl 91367 559-G2
6600 CanP 91307 529-G4
7600 LA 91304 529-G2
SEDGEWICK CT
7500 LA 91304 529-D4
SEDGWICK CT
- StvR 91381 4640-D1
SEDONA CT
900 SDMS 91773 570-C7
900 SDMS 91773 600-C1
41900 PMDL 93551 4104-C6
SEDONA DR
- SCTA 91354 4550-H1
SEDONA WY
27500 Cstc 91384 4459-H4
44200 LAN 93536 4015-A7
SEE DR
9500 PRV 90660 676-H4
10900 WHIT 90606 676-H4
10900 WHIT 90606 677-A5
11100 LACo 90606 677-A5
SEELERT LN
1300 LACo 91770 636-F4
SEELEY PL
21100 LKWD 90715 766-H5
SEEP WILLOW WY
21200 SCTA 91351 4551-B2
SEFTON AV
100 MONP 91755 636-C3
SEGAL ST
18200 CRTS 90703 767-A2
SEGO RD
13600 LACo 91390 4462-J2
SEGOVIA
- LVRN 91750 570-H3
N SEGOVIA AV
100 SGBL 91775 596-E3
100 SGBL 91776 596-E3
SEGOVIA WY
37200 PMDL 93552 4287-C2
SEGRELL WY
11200 CULC 90230 672-G5
SEGURO DR
10900 Chat 91311 500-F2
10900 Nor 91326 500-F2
SEIGNEUR AV
1800 LA 90032 635-E2
1800 LACo 90032 635-E2
SEINE AV
17900 ART 90701 766-H1
20300 LKWD 90715 766-H4
21200 HGDN 90716 766-H5
SEINE CT
5400 WLKV 91362 557-F5
SEINNE CT
13500 CHLS 91709 680-J2
SEKIO AV
1500 RowH 91748 679-D4
SELANDIA LN
100 CRSN 90746 764-D1
SELBY AV
1000 Wwd 90024 632-B3
1800 WLA 90025 632-C4
2200 LA 90064 632-D6
3200 LA 90034 632-E7
3700 LA 90034 672-F1
SELBY ST
900 ELSG 90245 702-H7
SELDNER ST
4800 LA 90032 635-E2
SELDON PL
2000 POM 91768 600-J5
SELENE CT
- Nor 91326 500-E1
- SCTA 91351 4551-G2

SELFLAND AV
6500 BGDN 90201 675-G7
SELFRIDGE DR
28800 MAL 90265 667-F2
SELIG PL
3800 LA 90031 635-C1
SELKIRK AV
1100 POM 91767 601-C6
SELKIRK CT
4000 CYP 90630 767-A6
SELKIRK LN
10500 BelA 90077 592-A3
SELKIRK ST
700 PAS 91103 535-F7
SELLERS ST
300 GLDR 91741 569-H6
SELMA AV
6000 Hlwd 90028 593-E4
7700 LA 90046 593-B4
SELMA DR
1500 LA 90046 593-A4
SELMARAINE DR
5100 CULC 90230 672-F5
SELVAS PL
1300 GLDL 91208 534-G7
SELWYN AV
21300 CRSN 90745 764-E6
SEMANA
- LVRN 91750 570-H3
SEMINOLE AV
2500 LYN 90262 704-J5
2500 SGAT 90280 704-J5
2900 SGAT 90280 705-A5
3200 LYN 90262 705-A5
SEMINOLE CIR
11500 Nor 91326 480-F7
11500 Nor 91326 500-F1
SEMINOLE DR
- Ago 91301 587-F4
1800 Ago 91301 588-A5
SEMINOLE PL
19500 Nor 91326 480-F7
19500 Nor 91326 500-F1
SEMORA DR
13000 CRTS 90703 737-B7
SEMORA PL
12300 CRTS 90703 736-J7
13100 CRTS 90703 737-B7
SEMORA ST
10200 BLF 90706 736-D7
10600 CRTS 90703 736-E7
12500 CRTS 90703 737-A7
SEMRAD RD
6900 CanP 91307 529-E5
SENA CT
27100 SCTA 91354 4460-G7
SENADALE ST
15600 HacH 91745 678-B3
SENALDA RD
7000 LA 90068 593-D2
SENASAC AV
1900 LBCH 90815 796-D2
3100 LBCH 90808 796-D1
3400 LBCH 90808 766-D7
3700 LACo 90808 766-D7
5100 LKWD 90713 766-D3
SENATOR AV
24200 Hrbr 90710 794-A3
24700 Hrbr 90710 793-J5
SENDA CALMA
3700 CALB 91302 559-D7
SENDA PAJARO
24700 CALB 91302 559-D7
SENDA SALVIA
24600 CALB 91302 559-D7
SENDERO PL
4500 Tarz 91356 560-H4
SENECA
1600 WCOV 91791 639-A4
SENECA AV
3600 LA 90039 594-D1
3800 LA 90039 564-D7
11200 Chat 91311 500-A1
SENECA CT
2600 BREA 92821 709-F7
SENECA DR
100 WAL 91789 639-G7
SENECA PL
1100 DBAR 91765 680-E3
1500 CLAR 91711 601-B1
SENECA ST
2300 LACo 91107 566-E5
SENECA WY
- CHNO 91710 641-H4
SENEFELD DR
3500 TOR 90505 793-D4
SENFORD AV
5200 LadH 90056 672-J5
5500 LadH 90056 673-A5
SENITA WY
16700 PRM 90723 735-G6
SENNA LN
- PMDL 93551 4285-D2
SENTA AV
2300 CMRC 90040 675-H4
SENTAR RD
22200 WdHl 91364 559-J4
SENTENO ST
18200 RowH 91748 678-J7
SENTINEL AV
1000 LA 90063 635-C4
SENTINEL DR
900 LVRN 91750 570-E7

SENTINEL LN
- ING 90305 703-F3
SENTNEY AV
2900 CULC 90232 632-J7
SENTOUS ST
3400 WCOV 91792 679-C1
S SENTOUS ST
300 LACo 91792 679-C2
600 WCOV 91792 679-C3
800 INDS 91748 679-C3
SENTRY DR
24300 DBAR 91765 640-D7
24300 DBAR 91765 680-D1
SENTRY LN
43700 LAN 93536 4105-C1
SENWOOD ST
9600 BLF 90706 736-B2
11500 NRWK 90650 736-G2
E SEPTIMO ST
6800 LBCH 90815 796-F6
SEPTO ST
14700 MsnH 91345 501-G5
15600 LA 91343 501-D5
17000 Nor 91325 501-B5
18200 Nor 91325 500-J5
19700 Chat 91311 500-A5
19700 Nor 91324 500-E5
22000 Chat 91311 499-J5
SEPULVEDA BLVD
1700 TOR 90501 793-G1
2500 TOR 90505 793-G1
2600 TOR 90505 763-B7
7400 VanN 91405 531-H4
12900 GrnH 91344 481-E3
15300 PanC 91402 531-H2
E SEPULVEDA BLVD
100 CRSN 90745 794-F2
1800 CRSN 90810 794-F2
2300 LA 90810 794-F2
2300 LA 90810 795-A3
2500 LBCH 90810 795-A3
N SEPULVEDA BLVD
100 Brwd 90049 631-H1
800 Brwd 90049 591-F2
2900 Brwd 90049 561-G6
3100 Enc 91436 561-G6
3100 Shrm 91403 561-H3
5200 VanN 91411 561-H3
6000 VanN 91411 531-H6
6400 VanN 91406 531-H3
6800 VanN 91405 531-H3
8000 PanC 91402 531-H3
8300 LA 91343 531-H3
8800 LA 91343 501-G6
9900 MsnH 91345 501-G1
N SEPULVEDA BLVD Rt#-1
100 ELSG 90245 732-G1
100 MANB 90266 732-H6
600 ELSG 90245 702-G7
S SEPULVEDA BLVD
100 Brwd 90049 631-H1
500 Brwd 90049 631-J2
500 LACo 90073 631-J2
700 Brwd 90049 632-A4
700 LACo 90073 632-A4
900 WLA 90025 632-A4
2200 LA 90064 632-A4
3000 LA 90034 632-A4
3000 LA 90034 672-D1
3700 LA 90066 672-D1
3800 CULC 90232 672-D1
3800 CULC 90230 672-F4
4400 LA 90230 672-F4
6200 Wch 90045 672-G7
6700 Wch 90045 702-G1
S SEPULVEDA BLVD Rt#-1
100 MANB 90266 732-H7
100 ELSG 90245 732-G3
9400 Wch 90045 702-G5
W SEPULVEDA BLVD
- LACo 90745 794-C2
100 CRSN 90745 794-C2
600 Hrbr 90710 794-C2
600 LACo 90502 794-C2
1300 Hrbr 90710 794-C2
1300 LA 90501 794-C2
1300 LACo 90501 794-C2
1400 Hrbr 90710 793-J1
1400 LA 90501 793-J1
SEPULVEDA LN
3500 Shrm 91403 561-F6
SEPULVEDA PL
- Brwd 90049 561-F7
2900 Brwd 90049 591-F1
8100 PanC 91402 531-H2
W SEPULVEDA ST
200 SPed 90731 824-A4
1000 LA 90732 824-A4
1200 LA 90732 823-J4
SEPULVEDA WY
2200 TOR 90501 793-G1
SEPULVEDA EASTWAY
8700 Wch 90045 702-G4
E SEPULVEDA FIRE RD
1200 Brwd 90049 591-G5
1600 BelA 90077 591-G5
SEPULVEDA WESTWAY
7600 Wch 90045 702-G3
SEQUIT DR
2800 LACo 90265 628-C6
2900 MAL 90265 628-C6

SEQUOIA AV
300 BREA 92821 708-J7
300 BREA 92821 738-J1
5000 CYP 90630 767-C6
13000 CHNO 91710 641-J7
19400 CRTS 90703 766-J2
19600 CRTS 90703 767-C6
41200 PMDL 93551 4194-G1
41200 PMDL 93551 4104-G7
SEQUOIA CIR
- MNRO 91016 567-J5
2800 WCOV 91792 679-C1
SEQUOIA CT
- Cstc 91384 4459-G2
100 CLAR 91711 571-D6
900 SDMS 91773 570-E6
SEQUOIA DR
- LYN 90280 704-J5
- PAS 91105 565-E6
100 CLAR 91711 571-D6
2400 COMP 90220 764-G1
2400 COMP 90746 764-G1
2500 SGAT 90280 704-J5
2900 SGAT 90280 705-A5
3100 LYN 90262 705-A5
6500 BPK 90620 767-F7
7300 SBdC - (4562-F5 See Page 4471)
7300 SBdC 92372 (4562-F5 See Page 4471)
21100 Chat 91311 500-B1
SEQUOIA GN
1100 POM 91766 640-F4
SEQUOIA LN
16200 LPUE 91744 638-G7
N SEQUOIA LN
600 AZU 91702 569-B5
SEQUOIA RD
- SCTA 91387 4462-G7
3700 SBdC 92371 (4472-J1 See Page 4471)
SEQUOIA ST
2500 SBdC 92372 (4472-F1 See Page 4471)
2700 SBdC 92371 (4472-F1 See Page 4471)
3900 LA 90039 564-C6
SEQUOIA GLEN DR
27600 SCTA 91354 4460-H5
SERANATA DR
8200 WHIT 90603 708-A1
8600 LHH 90631 708-A1
8600 WHIT 90603 707-J2
SERAPIS AV
7400 PRV 90660 676-E7
7600 PRV 90660 706-E2
8700 DWNY 90240 706-D2
SERATT PL
4600 LA 91607 562-G4
SERENA CIR
- Tarz 91356 560-J3
SERENA CT
3100 PMDL 93551 4195-C3
SERENA DR
23500 SCTA 91355 4550-G5
S SERENA DR
1900 WCOV 91791 639-B3
SERENA ST
5800 SIMI 93063 499-B1
S SERENADE AV
700 WCOV 91790 638-G2
SERENDIPITY WY
36800 PMDL 93552 4286-J5
SERENE AV
4200 LACo 93536 4104-J5
5700 CHNO 91710 641-H6
SERENITY CT
43600 LAN 93535 4106-E1
SERENITY LN
23200 LACo 90502 794-B2
SERENO DR
4900 TEML 91780 596-H4
SERPENTINE DR
3500 LALM 90720 796-J2
SERPENTINE LN
4500 PMDL 93551 4194-J2
SERPENTINE ST
700 RBCH 90277 762-J6
900 RBCH 90277 763-A7
SERRA AV
11700 CHNO 91710 641-F4
SERRA DR
- CRSN 90745 794-E1
- POM 91766 640-E4
SERRA LN
- SCTA 91355 4460-D6
SERRA RD
3200 MAL 90265 629-A6
SERRA WY
- PMDL 93552 4287-D1
15300 MsnH 91345 501-H2
SERRANIA AV
4700 WdHl 91364 560-C3
5700 WdHl 91367 560-C1
N SERRANO AV
100 LA 90004 593-H7
100 LA 90004 633-H1
900 LA 90029 593-H6
1300 LFlz 90027 593-H3
S SERRANO AV
100 LA 90004 633-H1
200 LA 90020 633-H2
600 LA 90005 633-H3

S SERRANO AV
600 LA 90010 633-H2
900 LA 90006 633-H4
SERRANO PL
- SCTA 91351 4551-D3
100 POM 91767 600-J2
800 LA 90029 593-H6
2100 FUL 92833 738-D4
SERRANO RD
3200 SBdC 92371 (4562-J4 See Page 4471)
SERRANO WY
- LA 91342 482-E3
SERVAL WY
- PMDL 93551 4195-F7
S SERVER AV
900 ELA 90022 676-A2
SERVIA DR
26700 SCTA 91350 4550-J1
E SERVICE AV
900 WCOV 91790 638-H1
W SERVICE AV
600 WCOV 91790 638-F1
SERVICE DR
600 PAS 91103 565-F2
SERVICE RD
- Wch 90045 702-H5
1000 WAL 91789 639-H4
15400 BelA 90077 561-H7
SERVICE ST
3800 City 90063 635-E3
SERVICE AREA RD
23600 VeCo 93063 499-A7
SERVICE RD K
- Wch 90045 702-D6
SERVILLA PL
- Cstc 91384 4459-E2
SESAME ST
23200 LACo 90502 794-B2
SESMAS ST
- DUAR 91010 568-C5
1100 MNRO 91016 567-J5
1100 MNRO 91016 568-C5
SESNON BLVD
16900 GrnH 91344 481-C4
18100 GrnH 91344 480-H5
18700 Nor 91326 480-C6
SESPE AV
4100 Shrm 91403 561-J5
SESSLER ST
10600 SGAT 90280 705-F6
SETH ST
8400 LACo 91776 596-G4
SETON CT
2200 CLAR 91711 571-C6
SETON HILL DR
20400 WAL 91789 639-F3
SETTLER CT
22100 WAL 91789 639-J5
SEURAT LN
- SCTA 91355 4550-E3
SEVENHILLS DR
10700 Tuj 91042 504-A2
SEVENHILLS PL
7300 Tuj 91042 504-A2
SEVENOAKS CT
4400 WLKV 91361 557-D6
SEVENTH ST
12400 NRWK 90650 706-J7
12500 NRWK 90650 707-A7
SEVERANCE ST
2600 LA 90007 634-B7
SEVERING DR
100 LPUE 91744 678-F1
SEVERN DR
6800 PRM 90723 735-E4
SEVERO PL
16800 Enc 91436 561-D7
SEVERY ST
8100 DWNY 90240 706-C2
SEVILLA CT
10600 WHIT 90601 677-A3
SEVILLA ST
- MONP 91754 635-J4
- MONP 91754 636-A4
SEVILLE AV
3000 PMDL 93551 4195-C4
3700 VER 90058 674-J4
5500 HNTP 90255 674-J5
7200 LACo 90255 674-J7
7300 LACo 90255 704-J1
8000 SGAT 90280 704-J1
SEVILLE CIR
5200 LPMA 90623 767-C2
42300 LAN 93536 4104-D5
SEVILLE CT
400 Ven 90291 671-H6
6200 LBCH 90803 826-D1
SEVILLE LN
- Enc 91436 561-F4
SEVILLE PL
500 SBdC 92372 (4472-B1 See Page 4471)
1100 FUL 92833 738-B5
2700 SBdC 92371 (4472-G1 See Page 4471)
SEVILLE RD
100 Llan 93544 4471-J1
100 SBdC 92372 4471-J1
100 SBdC 92372 (4472-A1 See Page 4471)
SEVILLE WY
300 LBCH 90814 796-D7

SEVILLE WY
9500 CYP 90630 767-B7
SEVY LN
3300 LA 90210 562-C7
3300 Shrm 91423 562-C7
SEWANEE CT
8600 SunV 91352 533-B1
SEWANEE LN
2200 ARCD 91007 597-C2
SEWARD ST
600 LA 90004 593-E6
700 LA 90038 593-E5
1300 Hlwd 90028 593-E5
SEWELL AL
- PAS 91107 566-F5
SEWER RD
11900 Wch 90045 672-F7
12500 LA 90094 702-F1
12500 Wch 90045 702-F1
12500 LA 90094 672-F7
SEXTON LN
- BREA 92821 708-J5
SEYMOUR PL
100 MNRO 91016 567-G2
SEYMOUR ST
3300 LA 90065 594-J5
SHABLOW AV
13500 LA 91342 482-D2
SHAD PL
3800 LA 90732 823-G7
SHAD ST
44000 LAN 93536 4105-C1
44000 LAN 93536 4015-C6
SHADE LN
300 LPUE 91744 638-J4
8500 PRV 90660 706-D1
11100 SFSP 90670 706-H2
SHADED WOOD RD
1800 DBAR 91789 679-G5
SHADEHILL PL
21900 DBAR 91765 679-J4
SHADELAND DR
24300 SCTA 91321 4640-J2
SHADETREE CIR
2200 BREA 92821 709-E6
SHADE TREE LN
500 FUL 92831 738-H5
7000 CanP 91307 529-D5
SHADE TREE PL
- WAL 91789 639-C4
SHADEWAY RD
4300 LKWD 90713 766-F4
SHADOW CIR
1200 UPL 91784 571-J6
SHADOW CT
16400 LMRD 90638 738-A2
SHADOW LN
- SCTA 91350 4550-J5
- RHE 90274 793-E6
300 MNRO 91016 567-H2
1000 SFER 91340 482-C5
1300 FUL 92831 738-H5
SHADOW PL
- Cstc 91384 4459-G4
SHADOW WY
9800 Sunl 91040 503-D5
SHADOW BROOK LN
2900 THO 91361 557-C5
SHADOWBROOK TER
- Hrbr 90710 794-A3
SHADOW CANYON DR
2600 DBAR 91765 679-J6
SHADOW CANYON PL
4800 THO 91362 557-F1
SHADOW CANYON RD
- Actn 93510 4465-F2
1000 BREA 92821 709-C5
13100 Brwd 90049 591-D7
SHADOW CLIFF CT
- SCTA 91350 4550-H6
SHADOW CREEK DR
- Ago 91301 587-J4
SHADOW CREEK LN
- PRV 90660 677-A1
3300 PRV 90660 676-J1
SHADOWCREST DR
44400 LAN 93536 4015-C6
SHADOWCREST PL
23500 DBAR 91765 680-B3
SHADOW GLEN CIR
19500 Nor 91326 480-E6
SHADOW GLEN LN
12000 Nor 91326 480-F6
SHADOW GROVE RD
3500 PAS 91107 566-G3
SHADOWGROVE ST
700 BREA 92821 708-J5
700 BREA 92821 709-A5
SHADOW HILL WY
1000 BHLS 90210 592-E5
SHADOW HILLS AV
- Sunl 91040 503-A3
SHADOW HILLS CT
20000 LACo 91390 4461-E3
SHADOW HILLS DR
6100 LAN 93536 4104-E6
9900 Sunl 91040 503-C3
SHADOW HILLS RD
- CALB 91301 558-G7
SHADOW HILLS ST
- PMDL 93550 4286-G4
SHADOW ISLAND DR
9700 Sunl 91040 503-C5

SHADOW ISLAND DR
19700 SCTA 91351 4551-E1
SHADOW LAKE DR
300 BREA 92821 708-H6
SHADOW LAKE LN
- Cstc 91384 4369-G5
SHADOWLAWN AV
2800 LA 90039 594-D3
SHADOW MOUNTAIN DR
7300 LAN 93536 4104-C6
16200 PacP 90272 630-H3
SHADOW MOUNTAIN RD
8800 SBdC 92372 (4562-E2 See Page 4471)
20100 WAL 91789 639-F3
SHADOW OAK DR
2600 WCOV 91792 639-A7
10400 Chat 91311 499-J4
18900 WAL 91789 639-A7
SHADOW OAK LN
23400 SCTA 91321 4640-G2
SHADOWOOD DR
9300 MTCL 91763 601-F5
SHADOW PINES BLVD
29000 SCTA 91387 4462-G7
SHADOW RIDGE CT
7100 CanP 91307 529-D5
SHADOW RIDGE DR
13700 CHLS 91709 680-J2
SHADOW RIDGE LN
15400 HacH 91745 678-A6
SHADOW RIDGE WY
12000 Nor 91326 480-F6
SHADOW ROCK LN
- StvR 91381 4550-A4
SHADOW SPRING PL
2200 THO 91361 557-B4
SHADOW SPRINGS WY
19500 Nor 91326 480-F6
SHADOWTREE LN
- StvR 91381 4550-C4
SHADOW VALLEY CIR
22200 Chat 91311 499-J1
SHADOW VALLEY LN
28700 LACo 91390 4461-E3
SHADOW VIEW DR
- POM 91766 640-F5
SHADOW WOOD DR
26600 RPV 90275 793-A6
SHADWELL CT
23400 SCTA 91354 4460-G7
W SHADWELL ST
200 CRSN 90745 764-C7
SHADY CT
300 BREA 92821 709-B6
SHADY DR
12400 Brwd 90049 631-F4
SHADY LN
- KeCo 93560 3835-F2
900 GLDR 91740 599-G1
3800 LACo 90265 630-D6
20900 Top 90290 590-C4
SHADY PL
600 DBAR 91765 640-D7
600 DBAR 91765 680-D1
SHADYBEND DR
14400 HacH 91745 637-H7
14400 HacH 91745 677-J1
14800 HacH 91745 678-A1
SHADY BROOK DR
1600 FUL 92831 738-H5
SHADYBROOK DR
1200 LA 90210 592-C5
SHADY BROOK WY
1900 UPL 91784 571-H5
SHADY COVE AV
7700 LA 91504 533-D3
SHADY COVE CT
- AZU 91702 568-J2
SHADYCREEK DR
6000 AGRH 91301 558-A3
SHADY CREST LN
1600 MONP 91754 635-J5
SHADYCREST LN
11800 OrCo 90631 708-G4
SHADYCROFT AV
22200 TOR 90505 763-A7
22200 TOR 90505 793-A2
SHADYDALE AV
400 LPUE 91744 638-B5
600 LACo 91744 638-B5
900 WCOV 91790 638-B5
4000 LACo 91722 598-F4
N SHADYDALE AV
200 WCOV 91790 598-F7
700 LACo 91722 598-F7
S SHADYDALE AV
1100 WCOV 91790 638-C3
SHADYDALE LN
12500 CRTS 90703 737-A6
SHADY ELM TER
22400 DBAR 91765 680-A4
SHADY GLADE AV
6000 NHol 91606 532-F7
7600 NHol 91605 532-F7
SHADYGLADE AV
4000 LA 91604 562-F5
7400 NHol 91605 532-F2
SHADY GLEN CT
- StvR 91381 4640-C2
SHADYGLEN DR
700 COV 91724 599-D6
3600 LACo 91724 599-D6

SHADYGLEN DR
5700 GLDR 91740 599-D1
N SHADYGLEN DR
200 COV 91724 599-D5
SHADYGLEN LN
2500 SDMS 91740 570-B7
2500 SDMS 91773 570-B7
SHADYGLEN RD
1400 GLDL 91208 534-G5
SHADY GROVE LN
13900 CHLS 91709 680-G3
SHADY GROVE PL
25800 LACo 91302 559-A3
25800 LACo 91302 558-J3
SHADYGROVE ST
6600 Tuj 91042 504-A5
SHADY HILLS DR
22000 DBAR 91765 679-J5
SHADY HOLLOW CT
12100 Nor 91326 480-F6
SHADY HOLLOW LN
12200 Nor 91326 480-F6
14300 CHLS 91709 680-J4
43300 LAN 93536 4104-H2
SHADYLANE PL
- SCTA 91354 4460-F5
SHADY LANE RD
8000 LACo 91390 4374-B3
SHADYLAWN DR
3200 DUAR 91010 568-E3
SHADYLAWN PL
13500 BALD 91706 598-A5
SHADY MEADOW DR
16900 HacH 91745 678-F3
SHADY MOSS CT
800 WAL 91789 639-J5
SHADY OAK CT
1700 AZU 91702 568-H3
SHADYOAK CT
400 POM 91767 600-J3
SHADY OAK DR
1200 LVRN 91750 570-E6
SHADYOAK DR
7200 DWNY 90240 706-A1
SHADY OAK LN
- StvR 91381 4550-C5
5500 SIMI 93063 499-A1
38200 PMDL 93551 4285-H1
SHADY OAK RD
3600 LA 91604 562-F6
SHADY OAKS DR
500 MNRO 91016 567-H2
SHADY OAKS RD
2200 GLDR 91741 570-A6
SHADY PALMS LN
- LA 91342 482-C4
N SHADYPARK DR
3000 LBCH 90808 796-D1
SHADY POINT DR
10100 WHIT 90603 708-A4
SHADY RIDGE LN
2600 DBAR 91765 680-C6
SHADYSIDE AV
8100 LACo 90606 676-G7
8200 LACo 90606 706-G1
SHADYSPRING DR
7700 LA 91504 533-C3
SHADYSPRING PL
7700 LA 91504 533-C3
SHADY SPRINGS CT
12100 Nor 91326 480-F6
SHADY STREAM LN
12300 CRTS 90703 736-J4
SHADY TREE LN
16200 CHLS 91709 710-H1
SHADYVALE LN
300 BREA 92821 709-E6
SHADY VALLEY LN
2500 LHB 90631 708-A4
10300 WHIT 90603 708-A4
SHADYVIEW DR
28700 SCTA 91387 4552-B1
28800 SCTA 91387 4462-C7
SHADY VISTA RD
- RHE 90274 793-B6
SHADYWOOD CT
15800 LMRD 90638 737-J1
SHAFER PL
12400 LACo 91342 482-J5
SHAFFER CT
1500 BREA 92821 708-H6
SHAFTER WY
6100 HiPk 90042 595-E3
SHAFTSBURY AV
400 SDMS 91773 600-D1
900 SDMS 91773 570-D7
SHAIN LN
41700 LACo 93536 4104-F6
SHAKESPEARE DR
2400 WCOV 91792 679-B1
2700 OrCo 90720 796-H3
2700 SMRO 91108 566-E7
3000 LACo 91107 566-E7
3400 WCOV 91792 639-C7
19000 WAL 91789 679-B1
19000 WAL 91789 639-C7
SHAKESPEARE LN
- StvR 91381 4550-A7
- StvR 91381 4640-A1
SHALE AV
1800 LACo 91744 638-H3
SHALE RD
3000 PMDL 93550 4286-G5

STREET Block City ZIP Pg-Grid

SHALE HOLLOW LN
1400 DBAR 91765 680-C3
SHALENE ST
1200 WCOV 91792 638-H5
SHALLOT CT
21700 SCTA 91350 4461-A6
SHALLOWBROOK RD
- LACo 90601 677-C1
SHALLOW CREEK RD
33600 LACo 91390 4373-H6
SHALLOWFORD CIR
19300 CRTS 90703 766-H2
SHALLOW SPRINGS RD
40400 LACo 93551 4194-A2
SHAMHART DR
16300 GrnH 91344 481-D7
SHAMROCK AV
1800 MNRO 91010 567-H6
1800 PMDL 93550 4286-D5
1800 MNRO 91016 567-H6
1900 LACo 91010 567-H6
2800 BREA 92821 709-F7
N SHAMROCK AV
100 MNRO 91016 567-H3
S SHAMROCK AV
100 MNRO 91016 567-H4
SHAMROCK DR
6200 SBdC 92397 (4652-B1
See Page 4651)
SHAMROCK PL
20400 Chat 91311 500-D3
E SHAMWOOD ST
400 COV 91723 599-A7
1000 WCOV 91790 598-H7
1400 WCOV 91791 598-J7
1900 WCOV 91791 599-A7
SHANA PL
- Saug 91350 4461-E5
SHANE CT
1000 UPL 91784 571-J3
SHANER RD
200 LACo 93551 4285-H6
SHANGRI-LA DR
18500 SCTA 91351 4551-H2
SHANGRI LA DR
18600 LA 90210 592-C4
SHANLEY AV
200 HiPk 90042 595-B3
SHANNON CT
- DBAR 91765 680-A5
- LACo 91387 4462-C6
SHANNON LN
2000 DBAR 91765 680-A5
SHANNON RD
3600 LFlz 90027 594-B1
W SHANNON ST
1000 UPL 91784 571-H6
SHANNON WY
3600 GLDL 91206 535-B7
SHANNONDALE RD
34800 Actn 93510 4374-F2
SHANNON RIDGE PL
- LACo 91387 4551-H6
SHANNON VALLEY RD
2700 Actn 93510 4375-C1
4500 Actn 93510 4374-E2
5800 LACo 91390 4374-E2
SHANNON VIEW RD
4500 Actn 93510 4374-H1
SHAPIRO ST
- FUL 92833 738-C5
SHARON AV
4400 LaCr 91214 534-G1
10700 SunI 91040 503-D3
SHARON DR
100 POM 91767 600-J5
4500 LPMA 90623 767-B3
SHARON LN
37500 PMDL 93551 4287-A3
SHARON PL
1700 SMRO 91108 596-E1
SHARON RD
200 ARCD 91007 597-A1
SHARON ST
11200 CRTS 90703 766-F1
SHARON WY
9000 LHB 90631 708-B4
9000 OrCo 90631 708-B4
SHARONHILL DR
15500 LACo 90604 707-H6
16100 LACo 90604 708-A6
S SHARONLEE DR
800 WCOV 91790 638-F2
SHARONS WY
4100 BALD 91706 598-E5
SHARP AV
8400 SunV 91352 532-F1
8900 Pcma 91331 502-A3
10600 MsnH 91345 502-A2
11000 MsnH 91345 501-J1
SHARP PL
800 POM 91768 600-G7
SHARP RD
30100 Cstc 91384 4459-C3
SHARPLESS CT
2200 LHH 90631 708-F1
SHARPLESS DR
1800 LHH 90631 708-F1
SHARPLESS ST
1100 OrCo 90631 708-B4
1300 LHB 90631 708-B4
SHARYNNE LN
4500 TOR 90505 793-A1

SHASTA CIR
4500 CYP 90630 767-B6
5700 LPMA 90623 767-D3
11900 CRTS 90703 736-H7
SHASTA CIR N
3000 LA 90065 564-G7
SHASTA CIR S
3000 LA 90065 564-H7
SHASTA CT
900 SDMS 91773 570-D5
3700 CHNO 91710 641-C6
27800 Cstc 91384 4459-G2
SHASTA DR
- SCTA 91354 4550-H1
SHASTA LN
- BqtC 91354 4460-E3
SHASTA PL
300 PMDL 93550 4286-A6
4400 ELMN 91731 597-C6
SHASTA ST
3000 POM 91767 600-J2
3600 CHNO 91710 641-C6
S SHASTA ST
600 WCOV 91791 639-A1
SHASTA DAISY PL
29600 SCTA 91387 4462-F6
SHATTO PL
400 LA 90020 634-A3
600 LA 90005 634-A3
600 LA 90010 634-A3
SHATTO ST
1300 LA 90017 634-C3
SHATTUCK ST
- BREA 92821 709-B5
SHAUER ST
2000 COMP 90222 734-H2
2000 Wbrk 90222 734-H2
SHAUNA WY
- LACo 91387 4552-A3
SHAVER ST
13100 BALD 91706 637-J1
13700 LACo 91746 638-A2
14300 LACo 91744 638-C4
SHAW AV
6700 LACo - (512-A4
See Page 511)
6700 SBdC - (512-A4
See Page 511)
SHAW CT
13200 LMRD 90638 738-A1
SHAW PL
1600 CLAR 91711 601-E1
2200 LA 90032 635-F1
25400 StvR 91381 4550-B7
E SHAW ST
4100 LBCH 90803 826-A1
SHAWNA PL
22600 SCTA 91350 4550-H5
SHAWNAN LN
200 LHH 90631 708-C2
SHAWNEE CT
23100 LACo 91390 4460-H1
SHAWNEE DR
- Chat 91311 499-J1
SHAWNEE LN
13100 SLB 90740 796-H7
SHAW RANCH RD
3500 LACo 91107 536-G7
SHAY AV
200 LPUE 91744 678-E1
SHAYNA CT
- PMDL 93552 4287-D1
SHEA LN
400 LBCH 90803 796-F7
SHEA PL
8500 RSMD 91770 596-G7
SHEARER AV
20600 CRSN 90745 764-C5
SHEARIN AV
5000 Eagl 90041 565-A5
SHEARWATER LN
6700 MAL 90265 667-D3
SHEBA CT
2000 WCOV 91792 639-A7
2000 WCOV 91792 679-A1
SHEDD TER
3900 CULC 90232 672-J2
SHEDDON ST
- FUL 92833 738-D5
SHEELIN LN
700 GLDR 91741 569-F3
SHEEP CREEK DR
5500 SBdC 92397 (4652-E3
See Page 4651)
SHEFFIELD AV
1400 WCOV 91790 638-E3
3100 LA 90032 595-G6
SHEFFIELD CT
800 SDMS 91773 599-H4
SHEFFIELD DR
1500 LHB 90631 708-B7
37200 PMDL 93550 4286-C3
SHEFFIELD LN
18200 Nor 91326 480-J7
25400 SCTA 91350 4550-J5
SHEFFIELD PL
1000 GLDR 91741 569-B5
SHEFFIELD RD
2800 SMRO 91108 596-F1
8200 LACo 91775 596-F1
SHEFFIELD ST
- LAN 93535 4016-D3
1400 LAN 93534 4015-F3

SHEFFIELD WY
11600 Nor 91326 480-J7
SHEFFORD ST
15300 HacH 91745 678-A3
SHEILA CT
600 WAL 91789 639-F6
1000 MTBL 90640 676-D1
19600 RowH 91748 679-E6
W SHEILA CT
1100 UPL 91784 571-J5
SHEILA DR
- VanN 91406 531-E5
SHEILA ST
4000 CMRC 90023 675-D2
4400 CMRC 90040 675-G4
SHELBOURNE WY
2100 TOR 90503 763-F7
SHELBURN CT
4000 LA 90065 595-A5
SHELBURNE DR
- SCTA 91354 4460-G7
SHELBURNE ST
800 LHB 90631 708-G4
SHELBY DR
3000 LA 90034 632-G7
3000 LA 90064 632-G7
SHELBY PL
4800 Eagl 90041 565-D6
SHELDON AV
- SCTA 91351 4551-D3
SHELDON ST
100 ELSG 90245 732-F2
600 ELSG 90245 702-F7
11000 SunI 91040 502-J4
11100 SunV 91352 502-J4
12500 SunV 91352 532-E1
SHELFORD DR
- CRTS 90703 767-A3
SHELL AV
1400 Ven 90291 671-J5
SHELL CT
1600 Ven 90291 671-J5
SHELL DR
- CRSN 90745 794-C1
SHELL ST
100 MANB 90266 732-E3
SHELLBARK CT
- PMDL 93551 4285-E3
SHELLCREEK PL
2800 WLKV 91361 557-A7
SHELLER DR
- FUL 92833 738-C5
SHELLEY PL
- StvR 91381 4550-A7
- StvR 91381 4640-A1
SHELLEY ST
1100 MANB 90266 732-H7
5300 LA 90032 595-G5
N SHELLMAN AV
400 SDMS 91773 599-H1
S SHELLMAN AV
400 SDMS 91773 599-H3
SHELLY CT
1700 BREA 92821 708-J4
SHELLY ST
900 LACo 91011 535-F6
SHELLYFIELD RD
9200 DWNY 90242 706-D3
10500 DWNY 90241 706-C5
SHELLY VISTA DR
11500 Tuj 91042 503-J1
SHELTER COVE DR
28100 SCTA 91350 4461-C5
SHELTER GROVE DR
3800 CLAR 91711 600-J1
3800 CLAR 91711 601-A1
N SHELTON ST
400 BURB 91506 563-F1
400 BURB 91506 533-F7
S SHELTON ST
500 BURB 91506 563-G2
SHELTONDALE AV
6200 WdHl 91367 529-D6
6300 CanP 91307 529-D6
SHELYN DR
19500 RowH 91748 679-D6
SHEMIRAN ST
6900 LVRN 91750 570-H5
SHENANDOAH AV
5000 LadH 90056 673-A5
5100 LadH 90056 672-J5
8800 PRV 90660 676-G4
16600 CRTS 90703 737-A6
SHENANDOAH DR
800 CLAR 91711 571-F7
1500 CLAR 91711 601-F1
SHENANDOAH LN
- SCTA 91387 4462-H6
- SCTA 91390 4462-H6
2200 GLDR 91741 570-A5
SHENANDOAH RD
1100 SMRO 91108 566-B7
1200 SMRO 91108 596-B1
S SHENANDOAH ST
800 LA 90035 632-J3
1900 LA 90034 632-H5
SHENANGO DR
19400 Tarz 91356 560-F6
SHENLEY ST
12700 LA 91342 482-E1
SHEOD TER
- CULC 90232 672-J2

SHEPARD ST
500 SPed 90731 854-B2
SHEPHARD CANYON
- SCTA 91321 4641-C2
SHEPHERD DR
1500 DUAR 91010 568-A6
SHEPHERD ST
3400 INDS 90601 677-A2
SHEPHERD WY
400 CLAR 91711 571-A7
SHEPHERD HILLS RD
20500 LACo 91789 679-F5
SHEPHERDS LN
4200 LCF 91011 535-B4
SHEPLEY PL
18200 Nor 91326 500-J3
SHEPPARD CT
1100 FUL 92831 738-J5
SHEPPARD RD
3700 SBdC 92371 (4472-J5
See Page 4471)
SHERATON DR
1100 LCF 91011 535-B4
SHERATON ST
- PMDL 93551 4195-B4
SHERBOURNE DR
1100 WHWD 90069 592-J5
3200 LA 90034 632-J7
3200 CULC 90232 632-J7
N SHERBOURNE DR
300 WHWD 90048 592-J7
300 WHWD 90048 632-J1
S SHERBOURNE DR
300 LA 90048 632-J1
400 BHLS 90211 632-J1
800 LA 90035 632-J3
1900 LA 90034 632-J5
5100 LadH 90056 673-A5
5800 LadH 90056 672-J7
SHERBOURNE PL
18700 RowH 91748 679-B7
SHERBROOK AV
2400 MONP 91754 635-H6
SHERER LN
1600 GLDL 91208 564-H1
N SHERER PL
100 COMP 90220 734-H4
S SHERER PL
200 COMP 90220 734-H4
E SHERI LN
6300 LBCH 90815 796-E6
SHERIDAN AV
800 POM 91767 601-C7
SHERIDAN CIR
1100 POM 91767 601-C7
SHERIDAN CIR E
43700 LAN 93534 4105-E1
SHERIDAN CIR W
43700 LAN 93534 4105-E1
SHERIDAN RD
1500 GLDL 91206 565-A1
2700 FUL 92833 738-B5
29000 Cstc 91384 4459-C6
SHERIDAN ST
1900 Boyl 90033 635-A3
12200 NRWK 90650 736-J3
SHERIDAN WY
6000 BPK 90620 767-E2
SHERIDELL AV
8400 PRV 90660 706-E2
9100 DWNY 90240 706-D3
SHERIDGE DR
3600 Shrm 91403 561-H6
SHERIFF RD
1000 City 90063 635-F4
1000 MONP 90063 635-F3
1500 MONP 91754 635-F3
SHERINGHAM LN
1900 BelA 90077 591-G3
SHERINGTON CT
4500 CYP 90630 767-B7
SHERLOCK DR
900 BURB 91501 534-A6
1100 GLDL 91201 534-A6
SHERMAN AV
200 CRSN 90248 734-C7
400 Ven 90291 671-J6
500 LA 90248 734-B7
1200 MNRO 91016 567-H5
SHERMAN CIR
14500 VanN 91405 531-J4
14500 VanN 91405 532-A5
SHERMAN DR
300 CRSN 90746 734-D7
SHERMAN LN
900 GLDL 91207 564-E3
SHERMAN PL
- LACo 91387 4462-C7
1700 LBCH 90804 795-G5
10600 SunV 91352 533-A4
23100 CanP 91307 529-G5
SHERMAN RD
11900 NHol 91605 532-G4
SHERMAN WY
6200 BPK 90620 767-F3
6400 BELL 90201 675-F7
6700 BELL 90201 705-F1
10600 BURB 91505 533-A4
10600 SunV 91352 533-A4
11000 NHol 91605 532-E4
11000 NHol 91605 533-A4
11000 SunV 91352 532-G4
13500 VanN 91405 532-B4

SHERMAN WY
14500 VanN 91405 531-F5
15300 VanN 91406 531-F5
17700 Res 91335 531-A5
18100 Res 91335 530-G5
19700 Win 91306 530-D5
20800 CanP 91303 530-B5
22000 CanP 91303 529-G5
22300 CanP 91307 529-F5
SHERMAN CANAL CT
200 Ven 90291 671-H7
SHERMAN CANAL WK
200 Ven 90291 671-H7
SHERMAN GROVE AV
10200 SunI 91040 503-F3
SHERMAN OAKS AV
4200 Shrm 91403 561-G5
4200 Enc 91436 561-G5
SHERMAN OAKS CIR
4400 Shrm 91403 561-G4
SHERNOLL PL
3400 Shrm 91403 561-H7
SHERRI DR
- PMDL 93551 4195-D6
SHERRILL ST
10200 WHIT 90601 676-J3
10200 WHIT 90601 677-A3
SHERRY AV
10300 DWNY 90241 705-J2
SHERRY LN
13100 Brwd 90049 591-C1
SHERRY WY
- PMDL 93551 4104-E7
SHERRYGLEN LN
800 LHB 90631 708-D6
SHERVIEW DR
3800 Shrm 91403 561-H6
SHERVIEW PL
15000 Shrm 91403 561-H6
SHERWAY ST
2200 WCOV 91790 598-D7
W SHERWAY ST
1700 WCOV 91790 638-E1
SHERWIN WY
2700 LVRN 91750 600-H3
SHERWOOD AV
3000 ALH 91801 595-G5
3200 LA 90032 595-G5
SHERWOOD CIR
600 MONP 91754 635-J5
SHERWOOD CT
1000 SDMS 91773 599-G4
SHERWOOD DR
- WLKV 91361 587-C1
5000 LVRN 91750 570-G5
8500 LA 90069 592-J6
8500 WHWD 90069 592-J6
SHERWOOD PL
200 POM 91768 600-H5
2200 GLDL 91206 535-B7
2200 LCF 91011 535-B7
3800 Shrm 91423 562-B6
23200 SCTA 91354 4550-G1
SHERWOOD RD
900 SMRO 91108 596-D1
SHERWOOD FOREST LN
9500 LA 90210 592-F2
SHERWOOD HILLS DR
- Ago 91301 587-E1
SHERYL AV
19200 CRTS 90703 766-G2
SHERYL CIR
600 CRSN 90745 794-B2
19400 CRTS 90703 766-G3
SHERYL PL
2000 WCOV 91792 638-G5
SHETLAND AV
11000 MTCL 91763 641-E2
SHETLAND LN
12100 Brwd 90049 631-G4
SHETLAND PL
- GrnH 91344 480-H6
SHETLAND WY
21800 WAL 91789 639-J6
SHIELDS DR
3600 SPed 90731 824-B3
SHIELDS ST
2200 LaCr 91214 504-H6
SHILENO PL
16800 Enc 91436 561-D5
SHILOH AV
9900 WHIT 90603 708-B3
SHILOH DR
- Brwd 90049 631-J2
SHILOH LN
43700 LAN 93535 4016-G7
43700 LAN 93535 4106-G1
SHILOH RANCH RD
- Ago 91301 587-E1
SHINE DR
20800 SCTA 91350 4461-C5
SHINEDALE DR
16600 SCTA 91387 4552-B2
SHINING AV
- LACo 91775 566-H7
SHINNECOCK CT
- PMDL 93551 4194-J2
SHIPLEY GLEN CT
5000 HiPk 90042 595-B2
SHIPLEY GLEN DR
5000 HiPk 90042 595-B3
N SHIPMAN AV
100 LACo 91744 678-J1

N SHIPMAN AV
100 LACo 91744 638-J7
S SHIPMAN AV
100 LACo 91744 678-J1
SHIPWAY AV
1800 LBCH 90815 796-F4
3000 LBCH 90808 796-F2
3400 LBCH 90808 766-F7
SHIRA DR
5200 LA 91607 562-E2
SHIRE CT
100 SDMS 91773 599-H2
SHIRE LN
- AZU 91702 569-C6
SHIRE PL
10700 WHIT 90601 677-A4
SHIRE WY
- AZU 91702 569-B6
E SHIRE WY
6400 LBCH 90815 796-E6
SHIRE OAKS DR
28600 RPV 90275 792-H7
28600 RPV 90275 822-J1
SHIRL ST
5700 CYP 90630 767-D6
SHIRLEE ST
2100 WCOV 91792 679-A1
SHIRLEY AV
3800 LYN 90262 705-C7
3900 ELMN 91731 597-B6
5000 Tarz 91356 560-F1
6000 Tarz 91356 530-F7
6200 Res 91335 530-F6
8200 Nor 91324 530-F2
9100 Nor 91324 500-F5
10300 Nor 91326 500-F4
SHIRLEY CT
3100 PAS 91107 566-F2
19400 Tarz 91356 560-F3
SHIRLEY DR
5000 LPMA 90623 767-C3
SHIRLEY LN
- Saug 91350 4461-E6
100 PMDL 93551 4195-J4
5500 MTCL 91763 601-H7
9500 LA 90210 592-F2
SHIRLEY PL
- LACo 91387 4552-A3
1500 POM 91767 601-A6
S SHIRLEY PL
400 BHLS 90212 632-E3
SHIRLEY J LN
1600 SBdC 92397 (4652-E3
See Page 4651)
SHIRLEY JEAN ST
100 GLDL 91208 534-F3
SHIRLMAR AV
300 SDMS 91773 600-B3
1300 SDMS 91773 570-B6
SHIVA LN
1500 POM 91766 641-B4
SHMILY CT
- LAN 93536 4105-C5
SHOEMAKER AV
8600 WHIT 90602 707-C2
10000 SFSP 90670 707-B7
11000 SFSP 90605 707-B7
11100 LACo 90605 707-B7
12200 LACo 90605 737-B1
12200 SFSP 90670 737-B1
12900 NRWK 90650 737-B2
12900 CRTS 90703 737-B6
13900 CRTS 90703 767-B2
15900 NRWK 90703 737-B5
SHOEMAKER CANYON RD
- LACo - (510-C5
See Page 509)
SHOENBORN ST
21000 LA 91304 530-B2
SHOLANDER AV
12500 CHNO 91710 641-D6
SHOOTING STAR CT
6800 MAL 90265 667-D3
SHOOTING STAR WY
36700 PMDL 93552 4287-A5
SHOPKEEPER RD
- LBCH 90803 826-E2
SHOPPERS LN
- PAS 91106 566-A5
E SHOPPERS LN
600 COV 91723 599-B6
E SHORB ST
- ALH 91801 596-C6
W SHORB ST
- ALH 91801 596-B6
1100 ALH 91803 596-A7
1500 ALH 91803 595-H7
SHORE DR
- PacP 90272 630-J6
SHORE RD
200 Wilm 90744 824-G1
SHOREBREAK LN
- SCTA 91355 4550-H3
SHORE CLIFF DR
- Wch 90045 702-C2
SHOREDALE AV
2200 LA 90031 594-H6
SHOREHAM DR
8700 WHWD 90069 592-J5
8900 LA 90069 592-H6
SHOREHEIGHTS DR
3400 LACo 90265 630-E5

SHORELAND DR
1600 LA 90012 594-F7
SHORELINE DR
10600 NRWK 90650 736-E3
E SHORELINE DR
100 LBCH 90802 825-E1
W SHORELINE DR
- LBCH 90802 825-D1
SHOREVIEW CIR
2800 THO 91361 557-C6
SHOREVIEW DR
3300 WLKV 91361 557-C7
5500 RPV 90275 793-A6
SHOREWOOD RD
26600 RPV 90275 793-A6
SHOREY PL
1500 City 90063 635-F3
SHORT AV
1700 COMP 90221 735-B2
12400 LA 90066 672-C6
12800 CULC 90066 672-C6
SHORT CIR
1100 WAL 91789 639-E5
SHORT ST
- KeCo 93560 3834-G1
- PMDL 93550 4286-F3
100 FUL 92832 738-G7
300 POM 91768 640-E1
500 ING 90302 673-A7
1200 ARCD 91006 567-E7
2200 LACo 90255 704-H2
2600 LA 90023 634-J7
6800 Wch 90045 673-A7
11400 LACo 90606 706-H2
14800 LA 90402 631-B7
SHORT TR
400 Top 90290 590-B7
12200 LACo 91342 482-J6
SHORT WY
6500 HiPk 90042 595-E3
6500 SPAS 91030 595-E3
SHORTLINE WY
9000 LACo 91390 4373-G3
SHOSHONE AV
5100 Enc 91316 561-B1
6100 Enc 91316 531-B7
6800 VanN 91406 531-B4
7800 Nor 91325 531-B1
8700 Nor 91325 501-B4
10500 GrnH 91344 501-B1
11300 Chat 91311 499-J1
11500 GrnH 91344 481-B6
SHOSHONE CT
1000 SDMS 91773 570-C7
SHOSHONEAN RD
3000 SPed 90731 854-C1
SHOSHONEE WY
6700 BPK 90620 767-F2
SHOTGUN LN
1500 DBAR 91765 680-D3
SHOUP AV
5300 WdHl 91364 559-J2
5400 WdHl 91367 559-J2
6100 WdHl 91367 529-J7
6400 CanP 91307 529-J4
7600 LA 91304 529-J4
9300 Chat 91311 499-J6
S SHOUP AV
12800 LACo 90250 733-B3
14200 HAW 90250 733-B3
SHOUSE AV
400 COV 91724 599-E6
500 LACo 91724 599-E6
SHOW CT
1600 SELM 91733 637-D5
SHOWBOAT LN
5100 CULC 90230 672-J3
SHOWBOAT PL
5000 CULC 90230 672-J3
SHREVE AV
2200 SIMI 93063 499-C1
SHREVE RD
12600 WHIT 90602 707-B2
SHREWSBURY CIR
24300 CanP 91307 529-D5
SHRINE PL
3000 LA 90007 634-B7
3000 LA 90007 674-B1
SHRODE AV
100 LACo 91016 567-G7
400 LACo 91010 567-H7
700 IRW 91010 597-H1
E SHRODE ST
400 ARCD 91006 567-F7
SHROPSHIRE CT
4100 WLKV 91361 557-D6
SHUBIN LN
- LACo 90606 677-A7
SHULL ST
5600 BGDN 90201 705-G3
SHULMAN AV
8400 WHIT 90602 707-C1
SHULTS ST
300 HiPk 90042 595-D3
SHUNK RD
1700 SIMI 93063 499-B2
SHURTLEFF CT
3500 LA 90065 595-A5
SHUTTLE LN
1800 Top 90290 630-B2

SHY ST
12100 NRWK 90650 706-H6
12100 SFSP 90670 706-H6
SIALIC PL
1600 LHH 90631 708-C3
SIAMESE LN
- PMDL 93551 4195-F7
- PMDL 93551 4285-F1
SIBERIAN CT
1500 PMDL 93551 4195-F7
SIBERT ST
11100 SFSP 90670 706-H2
SIBLEY ST
11200 NRWK 90650 736-F4
E SIBLEY ST
6400 SIMI 93063 499-C2
SICHEL ST
1700 LA 90031 635-A1
2400 LA 90031 595-A7
N SICILIAN WK
- LBCH 90803 826-C3
SICOMORO DR
30600 MAL 90265 627-A7
SIDANI LN
- Saug 91350 4461-F6
SIDE FIRE RD
- LACo 90601 677-D5
- WHIT 90601 677-D5
SIDEVIEW DR
7400 PRV 90660 676-F7
7800 PRV 90660 706-F1
9100 DWNY 90240 706-E3
SIDLEE PL
23200 Hrbr 90710 794-A2
23400 Hrbr 90710 793-J2
SIDNEY AV
- NLB 90805 765-C2
600 PAS 91107 566-F6
SIDON AV
2000 LHB 90631 708-B6
SIDWELL ST
17600 GrnH 91344 481-A5
SIEBERT LN
- FUL 92833 738-D5
SIEMERIO WY
- LACo 91390 4192-C3
SIENA CT
2300 CLAR 91711 571-D6
N SIENA DR
100 LBCH 90803 826-C2
SIENA WY
600 BelA 90077 592-A7
26500 SCTA 91355 4550-E4
SIENNA CT
- PMDL 93550 4196-H7
SIENNA WY
5500 WLKV 91362 557-F5
SIENNA CREST
- WCOV 91790 598-D7
SIENNA RIDGE RD
- SCTA 91351 4551-H2
SIERKS WY
3900 MAL 90265 629-G6
SIERRA CIR
- WCOV 91792 679-C1
7600 LPMA 90623 767-C3
SIERRA CT
- SCTA 91354 4550-H1
100 PMDL 93550 4105-J6
1200 DUAR 91010 568-D5
SIERRA DR
17900 COMP 90220 764-G1
17900 COMP 90746 764-G1
E SIERRA DR
3300 THO 91362 557-C3
N SIERRA DR
500 BHLS 90210 592-G6
W SIERRA DR
2700 THO 91362 557-B2
SIERRA HWY
100 PMDL 93550 4376-D1
200 PMDL 93550 4375-G7
200 LACo 93551 4375-G7
200 LACo 93551 4376-A5
1000 KeCo 93560 3835-E1
1100 Actn 93510 4375-A6
4200 Actn 93510 4374-G4
6000 LACo 91390 4374-B3
8500 LACo 91390 4373-G2
13100 LACo 91390 (4372-G6
See Page 4281)
14600 LACo 91390 4462-E3
15300 LA 91342 4641-B6
16300 LACo 91390 4462-B7
16300 CynC 91351 4462-B7
16700 SCTA 91351 4462-B7
16700 SCTA 91387 4462-B7
17300 SCTA 91387 4552-A1
17300 SCTA 91351 4552-A1
17700 SCTA 91387 4551-H3
17700 SCTA 91351 4551-H3
18500 LACo 91351 4551-H3
18600 CynC 91351 4551-H3
21500 Nwhl 91321 4641-B6
22000 SCTA 91321 4641-C2
24700 SCTA 91321 4551-G5
25800 SCTA 91350 4551-D7
36600 PMDL 93550 4286-C6
36900 PMDL 93550 4286-B2
38400 PMDL 93550 4196-A2
38800 PMDL 93550 4196-A6
41100 PMDL 93550 4105-J5
41100 PMDL 93550 4195-J1

SIERRA HWY
42000 LAN 93535 4105-J5
42600 LAN 93534 4105-H1
44000 LAN 93534 4015-G1
46800 LACo 93534 3925-F2
46800 LACo 93534 4015-G1
49200 LACo 93534 3835-F5
SIERRA LN
11900 Nor 91326 480-G7
SIERRA PL
- SMAD 91024 567-B2
500 ELSG 90245 732-F1
1000 TOR 90501 763-G5
2000 GLDL 91208 534-G7
N SIERRA PL
100 UPL 91786 601-H3
800 BHLS 90210 592-G6
S SIERRA PL
- UPL 91786 601-H3
SIERRA RD
900 SBdC 92372 (4472-C1
See Page 4471)
2700 SBdC 92371 (4472-J1
See Page 4471)
SIERRA ST
100 ELSG 90245 732-F2
600 ELSG 90245 702-F7
2100 TOR 90501 763-F5
2500 TOR 90503 763-F5
2500 LVRN 91750 600-H1
2800 LA 90031 595-B7
SIERRA TER
1000 MNRO 91016 568-A5
SIERRA TR
17800 LACo 93532 4101-J2
SIERRA WY
2500 LVRN 91750 600-H4
11200 MTCL 91763 641-E3
14500 BALD 91706 598-C6
SIERRA ALTA WY
1100 WHWD 90069 592-G5
1100 LA 90069 592-G5
1800 MONP 91754 635-H2
SIERRA ANCHA DR
800 LACo 93551 4285-F4
SIERRA BLANCA DR
900 MNRO 91016 567-E5
SIERRA BONITA AV
8100 LACo 91770 636-F4
N SIERRA BONITA AV
- PAS 91106 566-C3
300 LA 90036 593-C7
300 LA 90036 633-C1
600 PAS 91104 566-C3
700 LA 90046 593-C4
900 WHWD 90046 593-C5
1600 PAS 91104 536-C7
1700 LACo 91104 536-C7
S SIERRA BONITA AV
200 PAS 91106 566-C6
500 LA 90036 633-C2
1000 LA 90019 633-B5
SIERRA BONITA LN
1600 PAS 91106 566-C5
SIERRA CANYON WY
- Chat 91311 500-B2
2800 HacH 91745 678-D6
SIERRA CREEK RD
2300 Ago 91301 587-G3
SIERRA CREST WY
2200 HacH 91745 678-C6
SIERRA CROSS AV
28200 SCTA 91387 4552-A1
28200 SCTA 91351 4552-A1
SIERRA ESTATES DR
18800 SCTA 91321 4551-F5
SIERRA GLEN RD
3400 GLDL 91208 534-J4
SIERRA GRANDE AV
38000 PMDL 93551 4285-H2
SIERRA GRANDE ST
2700 PAS 91107 566-F4
SIERRA HILL ST
16500 SCTA 91387 4552-C1
17600 SCTA 91351 4552-A1
SIERRA HILLS LN
1000 PMDL 93550 4286-B6
SIERRA KEYS DR
400 SMAD 91024 566-J1
SIERRA LEONE AV
1700 RowH 91748 679-A5
SIERRA MADRE AV
- AZU 91702 568-J4
- AZU 91702 569-A4
- GLDR 91702 569-A4
- GLDR 91741 569-A4
E SIERRA MADRE AV
100 AZU 91702 568-J4
100 GLDR 91741 569-F4
3300 LACo 91741 569-F4
18400 GLDR 91702 569-F4
18600 LACo 91741 569-F4
W SIERRA MADRE AV
100 AZU 91702 568-G4
100 GLDR 91741 569-D4
SIERRA MADRE BLVD
500 SMRO 91108 566-E7
1200 SMRO 91108 596-D1
E SIERRA MADRE BLVD
- ARCD 91006 567-D2
- SMAD 91024 567-A2
2700 PAS 91107 566-E2
3300 LACo 91107 566-F2

N SIERRA MADRE BLVD
- PAS 91107 566-E4
S SIERRA MADRE BLVD
- PAS 91107 566-E5
200 LACo 91107 566-E5
1300 SMRO 91108 566-E6
W SIERRA MADRE BLVD
- ARCD 91006 567-C2
- SMAD 91024 567-A2
200 SMAD 91024 566-J2
SIERRA MADRE VILLA AV
- PAS 91107 566-G1
900 LACo 91107 566-G1
N SIERRA MADRE VILLA AV
1600 LACo 91107 536-G7
1600 LACo 91107 566-G1
SIERRA MAR DR
9200 LA 90069 592-G5
9200 BHLS 90210 592-G5
SIERRA MAR PL
9400 LA 90069 592-G5
SIERRA MEADOW DR
500 SMAD 91024 567-A1
600 SMAD 91024 537-A7
SIERRA MEADOWS LN
- Nor 91326 480-E7
SIERRA MESA RD
10600 Litl 93543 4468-E5
SIERRA MORENA AV
10600 WHIT 90601 677-A3
SIERRA MORENA CT
11700 Nor 91326 480-H7
SIERRA OAK TR
- Cstc 91384 4369-E4
SIERRA OAKS DR
200 ARCD 91006 567-B4
SIERRA PASS PL
11200 Chat 91311 499-J2
SIERRA PASS WY
16000 HacH 91745 678-C6
SIERRA PEAK WY
2900 HacH 91745 678-C6
SIERRA PELONA MTWY E
- LACo 93551 4285-A3
- PMDL 93551 (4284-J3
See Page 4283)
- PMDL 93551 4285-A3
SIERRA PELONA RD
- LACo 91390 (4282-G5
See Page 4281)
- LACo 91390 4283-A4
- LACo 91390 (4372-A1
See Page 4281)
34300 LACo 91390 4373-F3
SIERRA PELONA TKTR
- LACo 91390 4283-G3
- PMDL 91390 4283-G3
- PMDL 91390 (4284-B3
See Page 4283)
SIERRA PELONA E MTWY
- PMDL 91390 (4284-E5
See Page 4283)
- PMDL 93551 (4284-H6
See Page 4283)
SIERRA PELONA W MTWY
- PMDL 91390 (4284-D3
See Page 4283)
SIERRA PINE AV
2600 VER 90023 675-A2
SIERRA RANCH VIEW RD
- Tuj 91042 503-J1
SIERRA RIDGE WY
16200 HacH 91745 678-D6
SIERRA SKY DR
1000 GLDR 91740 569-H7
11500 LACo 90601 677-C2
SIERRA SUNRISE LN
- SCTA 91387 4552-A1
SIERRA TRIAL CT
16300 HacH 91745 678-D5
SIERRA VALLEJO RD
33600 LACo 91390 4373-B3
SIERRA VIEW AV
1700 LAN 93535 4016-C6
SIERRA VIEW DR
1200 SDMS 91740 570-A7
1200 SDMS 91773 570-A7
SIERRA VIEW RD
100 PAS 91105 565-F5
35000 LACo 91390 4374-E3
SIERRA VILLA DR
4900 Eagl 90041 564-J6
SIERRA VISTA
4900 ELMN 91731 597-D4
SIERRA VISTA AV
400 MNRO 91016 567-H3
500 LACo 91107 566-D6
500 SMRO 91108 566-D6
3400 GLDL 91208 534-G4
5300 LA 90029 593-H6
5400 LA 90038 593-H6
S SIERRA VISTA AV
600 ALH 91801 596-C7
1800 ALH 91803 636-C1
SIERRA VISTA CIR
- PRV 90660 706-E1

STREET Block City ZIP Pg-Grid

SIERRA VISTA CT
700 LPUE 91744 638-D6
SIERRA VISTA DR
400 RBCH 90277 762-J5
900 FUL 92832 738-F6
900 LHB 90631 708-D4
1400 LHH 90631 708-D4
1400 LACo 90631 708-D4
35300 LACo 91390 4373-J2
43400 LAN 93536 4105-A1
44000 LAN 93536 4015-A7
N SIERRA VISTA ST
100 MONP 91755 636-C2
S SIERRA VISTA ST
100 MONP 91755 636-C2
SIERRA VISTA WY
- LAN 93536 4105-A7
16800 CRTS 90703 737-A6
16800 CRTS 90703 736-J6
SIERRA WOODS DR
200 SMAD 91024 566-J1
SIESTA AV
300 LPUE 91746 637-H6
300 LPUE 91746 638-A3
700 LACo 91746 637-H6
1800 BALD 91706 638-A3
N SIESTA AV
100 LACo 91746 638-B2
1500 BALD 91706 638-B2
1600 WCOV 91790 638-C1
S SIESTA AV
200 LACo 91746 637-J5
1300 BALD 91706 638-C1
1300 WCOV 91706 638-C1
1300 WCOV 91790 638-C1
SIESTA DR
10300 Sunl 91040 503-B5
SIGMAN ST
15700 HacH 91745 678-C3
SIGNAL DR
1000 POM 91767 601-C7
N SIGNAL DR
600 POM 91767 641-C1
600 POM 91767 601-C7
S SIGNAL DR
1300 POM 91766 641-C3
SIGNAL PKWY
2600 SIGH 90755 795-H2
SIGNAL PL
1800 SPed 90731 824-D6
SIGNAL PT
2800 SIGH 90755 795-H4
SIGNAL RD
- SLB 90740 826-H5
SIGNAL ST
2200 SPed 90731 824-D7
SIGNATURE CT
42800 LAN 93535 4106-A3
SIGNATURE DR
17000 GrnH 91344 481-B7
SIGSBEE AV
800 Wilm 90744 794-H6
SILENT RANCH DR
- GLDR 91741 569-C3
SILHOUCTTE
- BqtC 91354 4460-E6
SILICA DR
38800 LACo 93551 4195-F6
38900 PMDL 93551 4195-F6
SILICON AV
10500 MTCL 91763 641-D1
10800 MTCL 91766 641-D2
11800 SBdC 91710 641-D5
SILK TREE LN
37400 PMDL 93550 4286-D2
SILK TREE WY
- LACo 91387 4552-B4
SILKWOOD CT
- LACo 91390 4460-H2
SILLIKER AV
1200 LHB 90631 708-C4
SILMAN ST
1500 HacH 91745 678-B3
SILTON AV
300 SDMS 91773 600-B2
SILTSTONE CT
40800 PMDL 93551 4194-J2
SILVA DR
- FUL 92833 738-C5
SILVA PL
12100 CRTS 90703 766-J3
SILVA ST
- LKWD 90712 766-A4
300 NLB 90805 765-D4
700 Bxby 90807 765-E4
2400 LKWD 90713 765-G4
5700 LKWD 90713 766-C3
SILVAN PL
1000 CRSN 90745 764-F6
SILVER LN
1500 DBAR 91789 679-G4
17200 Enc 91316 561-C2
SILVER ST
1500 HMB 90254 762-H1
2800 LA 90065 594-H4
7500 BPK 90620 767-F3
29600 Cstc 91384 4459-D6
SILVERA AV
300 LBCH 90803 796-E7
SILVERADO
23700 SCTA 91321 4641-B2
SILVERADO DR
2100 LA 90039 594-C4
36500 PMDL 93550 4286-H5
SILVERADO LN
- Actn 93510 4465-F2
7500 LPMA 90623 767-C3
SILVER ARROW DR
4900 RPV 90275 793-A7
SILVERBANK PL
2300 RowH 91748 678-H6
SILVERBAY AV
2200 ELMN 91732 637-E4
SILVERBELL LN
- LACo 91387 4551-J4
SILVER BERRY CIR
13300 CRTS 90703 737-C6
SILVERBERRY LN
- PMDL 93551 4195-D6
S SILVER BIRCH PL
1000 WCOV 91790 638-F2
SILVER BIT CT
1400 SDMS 91773 599-H4
SILVERBIT LN
- RHE 90274 793-G7
SILVERBOW AV
12900 NRWK 90650 736-J2
SILVER BOW RD
43800 LAN 93535 4106-C1
SILVER BRIDLE RD
600 WAL 91789 639-C6
SILVER BULLET DR
20800 DBAR 91765 709-G1
SILVER CANYON AV
13300 LACo 91390 (4372-J4 See Page 4281)
SILVER CANYON WY
500 BREA 92821 709-C6
SILVER CLOUD DR
21000 DBAR 91765 679-G6
SILVER CREEK RD
28900 Ago 91301 558-B7
28900 Ago 91301 588-B1
SILVER CREST CT
- SCTA 91350 4550-H6
SILVERCREST WY
1700 WAL 91789 639-F3
SILVERDALE DR
600 LACo 91711 601-A2
3200 POM 91767 601-A2
SILVER EAGLE RD
- RHE 90274 793-B5
SILVERETTE DR
6300 PRV 90660 676-E5
SILVER FIR RD
800 DBAR 91789 679-G2
SILVERFISH TKTR
- DUAR 91010 (538-D4 See Page 507)
- LACo (538-G3 See Page 507)
- LACo (539-A5 See Page 509)
SILVER FOREST CT
- AZU 91702 569-A2
SILVER FOX AV
4900 PMDL 93552 4287-A2
SILVER FOX CT
500 WAL 91789 639-C7
SILVER FOX RD
11600 OrCo 90720 796-H4
SILVERGROVE DR
15800 LACo 90604 707-J7
16100 LACo 90604 708-A7
SILVER HAWK DR
1700 DBAR 91765 679-J4
1900 DBAR 91765 680-A5
SILVER HAWK LN
- Tarz 91356 560-J6
SILVERHAWK PL
- SCTA 91354 4460-G6
SILVERKING TR
- LACo 91390 4461-B4
SILVER LAKE AV
2100 LA 90039 594-E4
SILVER LAKE BLVD
100 LA 90004 594-A7
300 Echo 90026 594-B7
1900 LA 90039 594-E3
SILVER LAKE CT
2200 LA 90039 594-E3
W SILVER LAKE DR
1700 Echo 90026 594-D4
1900 LA 90039 594-D4
SILVER LAKE PL
1500 BREA 92821 708-H6
SILVER LAKE TER
2500 LA 90039 594-D4
SILVER LANTERN DR
1800 HacH 91745 678-A3
SILVER LEA TER
2300 LA 90039 594-C4
SILVERLEAF DR
- RHE 90274 793-D5
SILVER MAPLE DR
- YBLN 92886 709-J7
1300 HacH 91745 677-J1
1500 LHB 90631 708-C6
E SILVER MAPLE DR
800 AZU 91702 569-B5
SILVER MOON LN
27000 RPV 90275 793-B7
SILVER OAK CT
- LACo 91390 4460-J1
SILVER OAK LN
- LACo 91387 4551-H4
SILVER OAK TER
1600 Eagl 90041 565-B7
SILVER OAKS DR
- LA 91342 481-E2
SILVER PALMS LN
- LA 91342 482-E5
SILVER PINE ST
- FUL 92835 738-H3
SILVER PUFFS DR
42000 LACo 93536 4104-D6
SILVER RAIN DR
1500 DBAR 91765 680-B4
SILVER RIDGE AV
2200 LA 90039 594-E3
SILVER RIDGE DR
2500 SBdC 92371 (4562-G2 See Page 4471)
8500 RSMD 91770 636-G5
SILVER RIDGE RD
13200 CHLS 91709 680-H1
SILVER RIDGE WY
2300 LA 90039 594-E4
SILVER ROCK RD
7400 SBdC 92372 (4562-E2 See Page 4471)
9200 SBdC 92372 (4472-E2 See Page 4471)
9700 SBdC 92371 (4472-E4 See Page 4471)
SILVER SADDLE LN
- RHE 90274 793-C6
5100 Actn 93510 4374-H3
SILVER SADDLES CIR
28800 SCTA 91387 4552-C1
28900 SCTA 91387 4462-C7
SILVERSET RD
31200 Actn 93510 4465-D4
SILVER SHOALS AV
500 SLB 90740 826-F4
N SILVER SHOALS DR
300 LBCH 90803 826-E1
SILVERSMITH DR
- BqtC 91354 4460-E3
SILVER SPRAY DR
23700 DBAR 91765 640-D6
SILVER SPRING DR
- RHE 90274 793-B6
2100 THO 91361 557-A4
SILVER SPRING LN
23500 DBAR 91765 680-C2
SILVER SPRUCE LN
- Alta 91001 535-H4
SILVER SPUR CT
14700 CHLS 91709 680-H5
SILVER SPUR LN
- Actn 93510 4375-B5
- LCF 91011 529-A5
SILVERSPUR LN
2400 LHB 90631 708-B7
36500 PMDL 93550 4286-G5
SILVER SPUR RD
600 RHE 90274 793-A5
600 RHE 90274 823-B1
600 RPV 90275 793-A5
800 RPV 90275 823-B1
SILVERSPUR WY
700 LHB 90631 708-B7
SILVER STAR LN
15800 SCTA 91387 4552-D7
SILVERSTONE LN
- BqtC 91354 4460-E5
SILVERSTRAND AV
2400 HMB 90254 762-G1
SILVERSTREAM CT
- SIMI 93063 499-A1
SILVERSTREAM DR
17700 SCTA 91387 4552-A2
SILVER TIP DR
4500 LACo 90601 677-B2
SILVERTIP DR
900 DBAR 91765 680-E2
SILVERTON AV
10000 Tuj 91042 504-A3
SILVERTON CT
- SCTA 91354 4460-G5
SILVER TREE RD
200 GLDR 91741 570-A5
2100 CLAR 91711 571-B7
SILVER TREE ST
600 CLAR 91711 571-B6
600 LACo 91711 571-B6
SILVER VALLEY AV
5600 AGRH 91301 557-J5
SILVER VALLEY TR
600 WAL 91789 639-G5
SILVERWIND WY
10700 LACo 93536 4103-E2
N SILVERWOOD AV
400 UPL 91786 601-J3
SILVERWOOD DR
1400 HiPK 90042 565-B7
1500 Eagl 90041 565-B7
2600 OrCo 90720 796-H4
SILVER WOOD LN
1100 SDMS 91773 599-J4
SILVERWOOD LN
- POM 91766 640-F5
1900 HiPK 90042 565-C7
SILVERWOOD TER
1500 Echo 90026 594-D5
SILVIA AV
1500 LAN 93535 4016-C5
SILVIUS AV
1200 SPed 90731 853-J1
SILVRETTA DR
9900 CYP 90630 767-B7
SIM LN
- FUL 92833 738-D5
SIMAY LN
21200 SCTA 91321 4551-B7
21200 SCTA 91321 4641-B1
SIMES LN
30400 Ago 91301 587-G4
SIMI ST
- PMDL 93552 4287-D2
SIMILAX CT
- PMDL 93551 4285-C3
SIMION LN
- LA 91304 530-A4
SIMLA ST
- LACo 93551 4375-H4
SIMMONS AV
600 MTBL 90640 635-J7
600 ELA 90022 635-J7
S SIMMONS AV
500 ELA 90022 635-J7
600 ELA 90022 675-J1
900 CMRC 90022 675-J1
SIMMONS CT
1700 CLAR 91711 571-C7
1700 CLAR 91711 601-C1
SIMMONS ST
- Cstc 91384 4459-D6
SIMMS AV
12800 HAW 90250 733-F2
S SIMMS AV
11400 ING 90303 703-F7
SIMON CT
20500 WAL 91789 639-F6
SIMON ST
- FUL 92833 738-C5
SIMONDS ST
14900 MsnH 91345 501-H1
15600 GrnH 91344 501-A1
SIMONE WY
4600 CYP 90630 767-B4
SIMON RAMO DR
- RBCH 90278 733-A5
SIMPSON AV
4300 LA 91604 562-H4
4400 LA 91607 562-H1
5900 LA 91607 532-H7
6000 NHol 91606 532-H6
6800 NHol 91605 532-H4
SIMPSON PL
25700 LACo 91302 559-A3
SIMS CT
21900 SCTA 91350 4461-A5
SIMS PL
1200 DBAR 91765 680-C3
SIMSALIDO AV
28300 SCTA 91387 4552-B2
SIMSBURY ST
1700 PMDL 93550 4286-D3
SIMSHAW AV
13400 LA 91342 482-D1
SINALOA AV
400 PAS 91106 566-C3
600 PAS 91104 566-C2
1300 LACo 91104 566-C2
1600 LACo 91104 536-C7
1800 Alta 91001 536-C6
SINALOA DR
1300 GLDL 91207 564-G2
SINALOA RD
8100 PdlR 90293 702-B2
SINALOA ST
36400 PMDL 93552 4286-J5
SINATRA ST
12500 CRTS 90703 767-A2
SINCLAIR AV
100 GLDL 91206 564-H4
11300 Nor 91326 500-H1
S SINCLAIR AV
- UPL 91786 601-J4
SINCLAIR CT
- LA 90094 672-E7
SINCLAIR PL
- StvR 91381 4550-B7
11300 Nor 91326 500-H1
SINCLAIR ST
2100 POM 91767 601-A5
SINGER PL
26000 StvR 91381 4550-B6
SINGING HILLS DR
19200 Nor 91326 500-F1
25800 SCTA 91355 4550-E6
SINGING WIND RD
23100 DBAR 91765 680-B4
SINGINGWOOD AV
1300 POM 91767 601-B7
SINGING WOOD DR
700 ARCD 91006 567-A3
800 ARCD 91006 566-J3
SINGINGWOOD DR
- LACo 91390 4460-J2
- RowH 91748 679-C4
3100 TOR 90505 793-D4
SINGINGWOOD LN
200 BREA 92821 709-D6
SINGING WOOD RD
15800 LPUE 91744 638-J4
SINGLETON DR
11600 LMRD 90638 707-F7
SINGLETREE LN
3400 RHE 90274 793-E6
SINNOTT ST
43200 LACo 93536 4104-J3
SINO AV
800 DUAR 91010 568-D5
SINOVA ST
4000 LA 90031 595-C5
4400 LA 90032 595-C5
SIOUX
- Ago 91301 587-G4
SIOUX DR
22000 Chat 91311 500-A2
22000 Chat 91311 499-J1
SIPES PL
35000 LACo 91390 4374-E3
SIPHON RD
9400 LACo 90660 636-J7
9400 LACo 90660 637-A7
9400 WHIT 90660 637-A7
SIRANI CT
- SCTA 91355 4460-D6
SIREL LN
2000 WCOV 91792 679-A1
SIR HENRY
14500 LA 91342 481-G2
SIRIUS DR
19700 RowH 91748 679-E6
SIR KAY WY
- Actn 93510 4374-B6
SISAL PL
2900 HacH 91745 678-C6
SISCHO DR
20000 Top 90290 630-A1
SISKIYOU ST
3300 LA 90023 635-C7
3700 LA 90023 675-C1
SISSON AL
1300 PAS 91104 566-A1
SISTER ELSIE DR
6000 Tuj 91042 504-C4
SITE DR
800 BREA 92821 709-A5
SITKA CT
1400 CLAR 91711 601-C1
SITKA ST
1200 ELMN 91732 637-F1
11600 ELMN 91732 597-F7
SIVAL CT
26200 SCTA 91355 4550-F4
SIWANOY DR
1200 ALH 91803 636-A1
1500 ALH 91803 635-J2
SIWASH TR
28900 Ago 91301 588-B4
SIX OAK CT
2400 SIMI 93063 499-A1
SIXTH ST
12400 NRWK 90650 706-J7
12500 NRWK 90650 707-A7
SIXTH STWY
- LMRD 90639 737-F2
SKABO AV
8600 LACo 90606 706-J2
8700 SFSP 90606 706-J2
SKAGWAY ST
16200 WHIT 90603 708-A4
SKELTON CIR
4000 CULC 90232 672-F3
SKELTON CANYON CIR
3800 THO 91362 557-C1
SKILLEN AL
- PAS 91101 565-J4
SKINNER PL
3800 FUL 92835 738-G1
SKIPPING STONE DR
- SCTA 91350 4550-J2
- SCTA 91350 4551-A2
SKIRBALL CENTER DR
2600 Brwd 90049 591-G1
2600 BelA 90077 591-G1
SKOKIE RD
1300 SLB 90740 826-G1
SKOURAS DR
20500 Win 91306 530-C6
SKY CT
600 DBAR 91765 640-E7
SKY LN
12200 Brwd 90049 591-F7
SKY WY
- Wch 90045 702-G5
100 MNRO 91016 567-G2
SKYBURST CT
5300 PMDL 93551 4194-G1
SKYCREST CIR
- SCTA 91354 4460-F5
SKYCREST DR
1900 FUL 92831 738-J4
3800 PAS 91107 536-H7
SKYCREST RD
300 LHH 90631 708-D3
SKYEWAY RD
300 Brwd 90049 631-F2
SKYHAVEN
4300 CHNO 91710 641-E5
SKYHAWK LN
20200 Top 90290 630-A2
SKYHILL DR
7700 LA 90068 563-A7
SKY LAKE AV
1200 BREA 92821 708-H6
SKYLAKE PL
- LACo 91390 4460-J3
SKYLAND DR
600 SMAD 91024 537-B7
600 SMAD 91024 567-B1
SKYLAND RD
11400 Sunl 91040 503-G1
SKYLANE DR
3600 Alta 91001 535-J3
SKYLARK DR
2500 TOR 90505 793-E5
SKYLARK LN
1400 LA 90069 592-H4
SKYLARK WY
- BREA 92823 709-G6
SKYLER WY
- BREA 92821 708-J5
- BREA 92821 709-B4
SKYLINE CIR
- LVRN 91750 570-G5
SKYLINE CT
32000 Cstc 91384 4369-G5
SKY LINE DR
8100 SBdC 92371 (4562-G3 See Page 4471)
SKYLINE DR
- DBAR 91765 680-C1
- RCUC - (542-E7 See Page 511)
- TOR 90505 793-F5
- BURB 91501 533-J5
700 Top 90290 590-A7
1300 FUL 92831 738-H5
1500 LHH 90631 678-A7
1600 LHH 90631 708-F1
2000 SIGH 90755 795-G3
2300 BREA 92821 709-E6
8100 LA 90046 592-H2
14100 HacH 91745 677-G3
15600 HacH 91745 678-A7
E SKYLINE DR
100 LHH 90631 678-C7
19800 WAL 91789 639-E4
N SKYLINE DR
100 THO 91362 557-A2
S SKYLINE DR
- THO 91362 557-A3
100 THO 91361 557-A3
W SKYLINE DR
100 LHH 90631 678-B7
SKYLINE LN
- POM 91766 640-H5
SKYLINE RD
5200 RCUC - (542-D7 See Page 511)
SKYLINE TR
- LFlz 90027 563-H4
600 Top 90290 590-A7
SKYLINE WY
1800 FUL 92831 738-J5
2300 UPL 91784 571-H3
SKYLINE EASEMENT RD
1100 Top 90290 589-H3
SKYLINE FIRE RD
- HacH 91745 677-F2
- WHIT 91745 677-H6
500 HacH 91745 678-A7
500 LHH 90631 678-A7
500 WHIT 90631 678-A7
500 WHIT 91745 678-A7
500 LHH 91745 678-A7
SKYLINE NO 2 FIRE RD
- HacH 91745 677-G4
SKYLINE VIEW DR
24600 MAL 90265 628-G6
SKYLINE VISTA DR
1900 LHH 90631 708-G1
SKY MEADOW PL
900 WAL 91789 639-G5
SKYPARK DR
2500 TOR 90505 793-D2
SKYPARK WY
- PMDL 93552 4287-A5
SKY RANCH RD
16100 SCTA 91387 4552-D4
SKY RIDGE DR
5100 GLDL 91214 504-D4
SKYRIDGE DR
24300 SCTA 91321 4640-G3
SKY RIDGE LN
3100 HacH 91745 678-A5
SKYTOP RD
15900 Enc 91436 561-F6
SKY VALLEY RD
13000 Brwd 90049 591-C1
SKY VIEW CIR
- POM 91766 640-G5
SKY VIEW CT
- SCTA 91351 4551-F4
SKY VIEW DR
- SCTA 91351 4551-F4
SKYVIEW DR
- LMRD 90638 738-A1
1700 Alta 91001 536-C5
SKY VIEW LN
24600 GLDL 91214 504-D4
SKYVIEW LN
- WCOV 91791 639-B3
SKYVIEW TER
9300 Tuj 91042 504-B6
SKYVIEW WY
5700 AGRH 91301 558-A4
SKY VISTA TER
- LACo 93551 4285-H7
- LACo 93551 4375-H1
SKYWAY CT
3500 PMDL 93550 4286-H4
SKYWAY LN
1400 POM 91768 600-E7
SKYWIN WY
2600 LA 90046 592-G1
SKYWOOD CIR
1300 Alta 91001 536-B6
W SKYWOOD CIR
2900 ANA 92804 767-J6
SKYWOOD ST
300 BREA 92821 709-B6
1800 BREA 92821 708-G6
SLATE AV
- Hrbr 90710 794-A5
SLATE CT
- StvR 91381 4550-B4
40800 PMDL 93551 4194-H2
SLATE CREEK DR
19200 WAL 91789 639-C6
SLATER AV
1700 COMP 90222 734-F2
2700 Wbrk 90222 734-F1
11000 LA 90059 704-F6
11000 Wbrk 90059 704-F6
11600 Wbrk 90059 734-F1
SLATER ST
11700 Wbrk 90059 704-F7
SLATER TER
9200 Chat 91311 499-F7
SLAUSON AV
2800 HNTP 90255 674-J5
2800 HNTP 90255 675-C5
3300 VER 90058 675-C5
3300 LACo 90270 675-C5
3400 MYWD 90270 675-C5
4400 LA 90230 672-E4
5000 MYWD 90040 675-C5
5000 VER 90040 675-C5
8000 MTBL 90640 676-C7
8000 PRV 90660 676-C7
8900 PRV 90660 706-F1
9400 SFSP 90670 706-F1
10400 LACo 90606 706-H1
11500 SFSP 90606 706-H1
11800 SFSP 90670 707-A1
12200 WHIT 90670 707-A1
12400 WHIT 90606 707-A1
E SLAUSON AV
100 LA 90003 674-F5
100 LA 90011 674-F5
600 LA 90011 674-F5
1100 Flor 90001 674-F5
1700 LA 90058 674-F5
1900 HNTP 90001 674-F5
1900 HNTP 90058 674-F5
2300 HNTP 90058 674-F5
2300 VER 90058 674-F5
2300 VER 90255 674-F5
3100 VER 90058 675-G6
5000 MYWD 90270 675-G6
5000 MYWD 90040 675-G6
5000 VER 90040 675-G6
5100 BELL 90201 675-G6
5100 BELL 90270 675-G6
5100 BELL 90040 675-G6
5300 CMRC 90040 675-G6
6800 CMRC 90040 676-A6
8000 MTBL 90640 676-A6
S SLAUSON AV
5000 CULC 90230 672-F5
W SLAUSON AV
100 LA 90003 674-B5
100 LA 90037 674-B5
500 LA 90044 674-B5
1300 LA 90044 673-G5
1300 LA 90037 673-G5
1400 LA 90047 673-G5
1400 LA 90062 673-G5
2100 LA 90043 673-G5
3700 LACo 90043 673-D6
4700 LadH 90056 673-D6
5400 LadH 90056 672-J6
5600 CULC 90230 672-H6
5700 LACo 90230 672-H6
SLAUSON LN
900 RBCH 90278 763-A2
SLAYTON ST
- PMDL 93551 4195-E7
3500 HAW 90250 733-F3
SLEEPY CREEK LN
29600 Cstc 91384 4459-D2
SLEEPY HOLLOW CT
21600 WAL 91789 639-H4
SLEEPY HOLLOW DR
2400 GLDL 91206 565-A4
SLEEPY HOLLOW LN
200 BREA 92821 709-E7
19800 Tarz 91356 560-E5
SLEEPYHOLLOW LN
12500 CRTS 90703 737-A6
SLEEPY HOLLOW PL
2600 GLDL 91206 565-B4
SLEEPY HOLLOW TER
200 GLDL 91206 565-A4
SLEEPY HOLLOW ACCESS
1200 CHLS 91709 710-F3
SLEEPY SPRING WY
2500 HacH 91745 678-E6
SLICERS CIR
5600 AGRH 91301 557-G5
SLIPPERY ELM RD
2000 SBdC 92397 (4652-E4 See Page 4651)
N SLOAN AV
100 COMP 90221 735-B4
S SLOAN AV
100 COMP 90221 735-B4
SLOAN DR
2200 LVRN 91750 570-H4
16300 Brwd 90049 561-E7
SLOAN PL
5600 LACo 91302 559-A3
SLOAN CANYON RD
27800 Cstc 91384 4369-E7
29700 Cstc 91384 4459-D2
SLOAT ST
400 LA 90063 635-C5
SLOOP
3600 LBCH 90810 765-A7
SLOPE DR
500 WAL 91789 679-E2
SLUSHER AV
10100 Tuj 91042 504-C4
SLUSHER DR
10300 SFSP 90670 706-H5
SMALL RD
35400 PMDL 93550 4376-E1
SMALLWOOD AV
8500 DWNY 90240 706-C1
10400 DWNY 90241 706-A4
12000 DWNY 90242 705-J6
12900 DWNY 90242 735-H1
SMEAD WY
500 SDMS 91773 600-C1
SMILAX ST
3500 LA 90004 594-B7
SMILEY CT
22400 SCTA 91350 4460-J4
SMILEY DR
5300 LA 90016 633-A7
5800 CULC 90232 633-A7
5900 CULC 90232 632-J7
SMITH AL
- PAS 91103 565-C3
SMITH AV
3600 Actn 93510 4465-A2
11600 SFSP 90670 706-H3
SMITH CT
- LHB 90631 738-C2
E SMITH DR
100 CLAR 91711 600-J1
W SMITH DR
100 CLAR 91711 600-J1
SMITH PL
1200 LBCH 90806 795-F4
SMITH RD
6500 SIMI 93063 499-C3
23100 Chat 91311 499-F7
SMITH ST
3300 LA 90031 595-A6
3500 BELL 90201 675-C7
E SMITH ST
100 NLB 90805 765-D1
W SMITH ST
1500 POM 91766 640-G3
SMITHWAY ST
5600 CMRC 90040 675-H3
SMITHWOOD DR
400 BHLS 90212 632-G3
400 LA 90035 632-G3
SMOKETREE AV
- VeCo 91377 558-A2
SMOKE TREE CIR
6500 LAN 93536 4104-E5
SMOKE TREE CT
1300 LHB 90631 738-C1
SMOKE TREE DR
1300 LHB 90631 738-C1
SMOKETREE DR
400 LACo 91750 570-H7
600 LVRN 91750 570-H7
SMOKE TREE LN
- LACo 91387 4552-A4
SMOKETREE LN
- StvR 91381 4550-B4
24200 DBAR 91765 680-D3
S SMOKETREE LN
2200 ONT 91762 641-J5
SMOKETREE PL
- WAL 91789 639-D4
SMOKE TREE RD
100 Llan 93544 4471-H5
100 SBdC 92372 4471-H5
100 SBdC 92372 (4472-F4 See Page 4471)
2100 SBdC 92371 (4472-F4 See Page 4471)
SMOKE TREE ST
37700 PMDL 93552 4287-B2
SMOKEWOOD AV
1800 FUL 92831 738-J4
SMOKEWOOD DR
700 SDMS 91773 600-C3
SMOKEWOOD WY
- StvR 91381 4640-D1
SMOKIE LN
12000 CRTS 90703 766-H2
SMUGGLERS CV
300 LBCH 90803 826-D1
SMYTH DR
- SCTA 91355 4460-D6
SNAKE LN
- PMDL 93551 4194-G3
SNAPDRAGON CT
36900 PMDL 93552 4287-B4
SNAPDRAGON PL
29200 SCTA 91387 4462-E7
SNARK ST
11400 LALM 90720 796-J3
SNEAD DR
2300 ALH 91803 635-J2
SNEAD ST
- LHB 90631 738-B2
SNELLING ST
11700 SunV 91352 502-G7
SNOW DR
3900 City 90063 635-E3
SNOWAPPLE LN
14700 CHLS 91709 680-G5
SNOWBERRY LN
2400 CHLS 91709 680-J5
SNOWBERRY WY
39400 PMDL 93551 4195-D5
SNOWBIRD CIR
4400 CRTS 90703 767-B3
SNOWBIRD PL
26500 SCTA 91351 4551-E4
SNOW BIRD RD
800 SBdC 92397 (4652-C1 See Page 4651)
SNOW CAP AV
8100 SBdC 92371 (4562-G3 See Page 4471)
SNOW CAP CT
2600 SBdC 92371 (4562-G3 See Page 4471)
SNOW CREEK DR
21100 WAL 91789 639-H5
SNOWDALE ST
14000 LACo 91746 638-B1
SNOWDEN AV
1800 LBCH 90815 796-D2
3000 LBCH 90808 796-D2
3700 LBCH 90808 766-D7
4300 LKWD 90713 766-D2
8400 PanC 91402 532-C1
8400 Pcma 91331 532-C1
8700 Pcma 91331 502-B7
SNOW DROP CT
14500 SCTA 91387 4462-G4
SNOWFIELD ST
2600 BREA 92821 709-F7
SNOW LINE DR
1700 SBdC 92372 (4562-E3 See Page 4471)
2000 SBdC 92371 (4562-G2 See Page 4471)
SNOWMASS DR
9700 MTCL 91763 601-G6
SNOWPEAK DR
32400 WLKV 91361 557-B7
SNOWSHOE THOMPSON RD
6000 LACo 91390 4374-F3
SNOW VALLEY RD
8300 SBdC 92371 (4562-H3 See Page 4471)
SNOWY OWL CT
24400 SCTA 91355 4550-E5
SNYDER AV
11700 CHNO 91710 641-G4
SNYDER LN
- MONP 91754 635-J4
SNYDER PL
300 WCOV 91791 639-D1
SOBEY WY
- PMDL 93552 4287-D2
SOBRECOLINAS PL
800 POM 91768 600-G6
SOCO DR
- FUL 92832 738-H7
SODERBERG AV
1200 GLDR 91740 599-C1
SOFT AV
44100 LAN 93536 4015-D7
SOFTWIND DR
24200 DBAR 91765 680-D3
SOFTWIND WY
3000 TOR 90505 793-E5
5400 AGRH 91301 557-J5
5400 AGRH 91301 558-A5
SOFTWOOD CT
3100 LAN 93536 4105-B3
SOHN DR
500 LACo 91302 629-A1
SOISSONS AV
- Brwd 90049 631-J2
SOLADERA WY
- SCTA 91351 4551-D3
SOLAMINT RD
- SCTA 91387 4551-J3
SOLANA CIR
1300 MTBL 90640 636-D7
SOLANA CT
- Boyl 90033 634-J4
N SOLANA CT
300 LBCH 90802 795-D7
700 LBCH 90813 795-D5
SOLANA LN
16500 CynC 91351 4462-B4
SOLANO AV
400 LA 90012 634-H1
500 LA 90012 594-H7
SOLANO CT
100 LBCH 90802 825-D1
SOLANO DR
3900 ANA 90620 767-F7
3900 BPK 90620 767-F7
SOLANO PL
19700 LACo 91724 599-E6
SOLANO RD
100 Llan 93544 4471-J3
100 SBdC 92372 4471-J3
100 SBdC 92372 (4472-A3 See Page 4471)
3100 SBdC 92372 (4472-H3 See Page 4471)
SOLANO CANYON DR
- LA 90012 594-G6
SOLAR DR
1400 MONP 91754 635-H4
2400 LA 90046 593-C2
N SOLDANO AV
100 AZU 91702 568-J5
SOLDANO DR
1100 AZU 91702 568-J4
SOLDEA DR
10700 Chat 91311 500-E3
SOLDON CT
19600 SCTA 91351 4461-F7
SOLEDAD AV
6500 KeCo 93560 3834-B1
9000 KeCo 93560 3833-G1
SOLEDAD RD
- SBdC 92372 (4562-A1 See Page 4471)
11100 SBdC 92372 (4472-A1 See Page 4471)
SOLEDAD ST
20500 SCTA 91351 4551-C2
SOLEDAD CANYON RD
1200 Actn 93510 4375-F7
1200 LACo 93551 4375-F7
1200 PMDL 93550 4375-F7
1400 Actn 93510 4465-D2
4300 Actn 93510 4464-C7
7300 LACo 91390 4464-C7
8000 LACo 91390 4463-G6
10800 LACo 91390 (4553-C1 See Page 4464)
13800 LACo 91387 4462-G7
13800 LACo 91390 4462-G7
14000 LACo 91387 4552-C1
14600 SCTA 91387 4462-G7
15000 SCTA 91387 4552-C1
18000 SCTA 91387 4551-F3
18500 SCTA 91351 4551-F3
21300 SCTA 91350 4551-A3
22600 SCTA 91350 4550-H2
SOLEDAD PASS RD
1200 PMDL 93550 4376-B6
SOLEJAR DR
1200 WHIT 90603 708-C4
1300 LHH 90631 708-B3
SOLEM ST
- AZU 91702 598-G1
SOLERA LN
- DBAR 91765 680-A3
SOLITA RD
1100 PAS 91103 565-F2
SOLLIDEN LN
5100 LCF 91011 534-J1
SOLMIRA PL
3100 PMDL 93551 4195-C3
SOLMONTE RD
9600 LA 90210 592-D4
SOLO ST
10400 NRWK 90650 706-D7
SOLON AV
28300 SCTA 91387 4552-C1
SOLSTICE CANYON RD
3300 MAL 90265 628-B6
SOLTAIRE ST
23900 DBAR 91765 640-D4
SOLVANG ST
12600 NHol 91605 532-E3
SOLVAY ST
36700 PMDL 93552 4286-J5
SOL VISTA LN
27900 RPV 90275 823-G2
SOL VISTA WY
900 WAL 91789 639-D6
SOLWAY ST
500 GLDL 91206 564-H3
SOMBRA AV
15600 LNDL 90260 733-D5
SOMBRA DR
1700 GLDR 91208 534-H6
SOMBRA TER
9700 Sunl 91040 503-D4
SOMBRAS CT
26000 SCTA 91355 4550-G4
SOMBRA VALLEY DR
9600 Sunl 91040 503-D4
SOMBRERO
14500 LA 91342 481-G1
W SOMBRERO DR
1300 MONP 91754 635-H2
SOMBRERO RD
500 MNRO 91016 568-A4
SOMERA RD
900 BelA 90077 591-J5
SOMERDALE LN
8100 LPMA 90623 767-B4
SOMERS AV
4000 LA 90065 594-H1

STREET
Block City ZIP Pg-Grid

SOMERS AV
4100 LA 90065 564-H7
SOMERSET
12400 ELMN 91732 637-G1
SOMERSET AV
800 POM 91767 601-B6
SOMERSET BLVD
- PRM 90221 735-F4
6400 PRM 90723 735-F4
6400 COMP 90221 735-F4
8800 PRM 90723 736-B4
9000 BLF 90706 736-B4
SOMERSET CIR
5100 BPK 90621 737-J5
5100 BPK 90621 738-A5
SOMERSET CT
- Cstc 91384 4459-G5
300 AZU 91702 568-H2
SOMERSET DR
1300 SDMS 91773 599-H4
2600 LA 90016 633-E7
2900 WCOV 91792 679-C3
3400 LA 90016 673-E1
3700 LA 90008 673-D3
16400 LMRD 90638 738-A3
21200 WAL 91789 639-H7
21300 LACo 91789 639-H7
SOMERSET LN
1800 FUL 92833 738-C3
2100 CRSN 90810 764-J4
9300 CYP 90630 767-A7
SOMERSET PL
400 LCF 91011 535-D5
1300 Bxby 90807 765-F6
2700 RowH 91748 679-B7
2800 SMRO 91108 596-E2
6300 LACo 91775 596-F1
SOMERSET ST
4900 BPK 90621 737-J5
5100 BPK 90621 738-A5
5300 LA 90032 595-F6
13200 WHIT 90602 707-C3
SOMERSET WY
2100 UPL 91784 571-H4
SOMERSET RANCH RD N
8300 DWNY 90242 735-H2
8300 PRM 90723 735-H2
13500 SGAT 90280 735-H2
SOMERSET RANCH RD S
8100 PRM 90723 735-H2
8100 SGAT 90280 735-H2
8400 DWNY 90242 735-H2
SOMMA WY
10600 BelA 90077 592-A6
SOMMERSET CIR
7000 LPMA 90623 767-C2
SOMMERSET DR
2200 BREA 92821 709-E6
SONATA LN
4800 HiPk 90042 595-A3
SONDI DR
- LAN 93536 4104-F1
SONGBIRD LN
2500 RowH 91748 679-C6
SONGFEST DR
7400 PRV 90660 676-F7
7400 PRV 90660 706-F1
9100 DWNY 90240 706-E3
SONNET PL
15000 HacH 91745 678-A3
SONOITA DR
20900 WAL 91789 639-G3
SONOMA CT
3700 CHNO 91710 641-C5
SONOMA DR
1100 Alta 91001 536-B7
SONOMA PL
22000 Chat 91311 499-J6
SONOMA RD
- PMDL 93551 4104-D6
SONOMA ST
2200 TOR 90501 763-E6
2500 TOR 90503 763-E6
SONOMA WY
11900 Nor 91326 480-F6
SONORA
6700 BPK 90620 767-F5
SONORA AV
100 LFlz 90027 563-J3
100 GLDL 91201 563-J3
400 GLDL 91201 564-A2
800 LHB 90631 708-D7
17400 CRTS 90703 737-C7
SONORA CT
700 SDMS 91773 600-C1
900 SDMS 91773 570-C7
SONORA PL
200 CLAR 91711 571-C6
300 LHB 90631 708-H5
SONORA ST
700 BREA 92821 708-H6
900 MTBL 90640 636-E7
2100 POM 91767 601-A5
SONORA WY
3700 PMDL 93550 4196-H7
6300 CYP 90630 767-F7
SONORAN ST
- LAN 93536 4015-B6
SONRISA ST
9100 BLF 90706 736-A3
SONTERA AV
45200 LAN 93535 4016-E4

SONWELL PL
9500 CYP 90630 767-E7
SONYA CT
2000 WCOV 91792 679-A1
SONYA WY
2100 UPL 91784 571-H4
SOPER DR
2800 LA 90046 593-B1
SOPHIA AV
4700 Enc 91436 561-E3
7000 VanN 91406 531-E5
8300 LA 91343 531-E1
8700 LA 91343 501-E5
10300 GmH 91344 501-E1
11600 GmH 91344 481-E7
SOPHIA LN
18500 Tarz 91356 560-J2
N SOPHIA LN
- LACo 91387 4552-B5
SOPHOMORE DR
4000 LACo 90230 672-H3
SOQUEL CANYON RD
1400 OrCo 92886 710-F5
18600 BREA 92823 710-F5
SORBONNE ST
15500 LA 91342 481-G2
SORBONNE WY
- BPK 90620 767-F6
SORDELLO ST
18200 RowH 91748 678-J5
18200 RowH 91748 679-A6
SORENSEN AV
6700 WHIT 90606 677-A7
6900 LACo 90606 677-A7
7900 LACo 90606 707-A1
8000 SFSP 90606 707-A1
8000 SFSP 90670 707-A1
SORIANO DR
1500 HacH 91745 678-C5
SOROCK DR
900 LACo 90502 794-B1
SORORITY LN
23800 WHil 91304 499-E7
SORREL CT
- SCTA 91354 4460-G5
21900 WAL 91789 639-J4
SORREL LN
- RHE 90274 793-F7
44000 LAN 93535 4016-C7
SORREL ST
2700 BREA 92821 709-F7
SORRELL AV
4000 PMDL 93552 4286-H4
SORRELWOOD CT
800 THO 91361 557-A4
SORRENTO CIR
800 DUAR 91010 568-E5
5200 LPMA 90623 767-C2
SORRENTO CT
24300 SCTA 91355 4550-E4
SORRENTO DR
1500 PacP 90272 631-D3
4500 CYP 90630 767-B7
E SORRENTO DR
5400 LBCH 90803 826-C2
SORRENTO LN
- Nor 91326 500-C1
SORRENTO PL
- Cstc 91384 4459-D2
SORRENTO RD
- POM 91766 640-D3
SOTELLO ST
100 LA 90012 634-H1
SOTO ST
5200 VER 90058 675-A5
5600 HNTP 90255 675-A5
N SOTO ST
100 Boyl 90033 635-B3
1800 LA 90032 635-C1
1800 LA 90031 635-C1
2200 LA 90032 595-C7
2500 LA 90031 595-C7
S SOTO ST
100 Boyl 90033 635-B4
600 LA 90023 635-A6
1100 LA 90023 634-J7
1400 LA 90023 674-J2
1800 VER 90023 674-J2
3200 VER 90058 674-J3
5000 VER 90058 675-A4
SOTO GRANDE DR
100 PMDL 93551 4195-J3
SOTRO ST
15800 INDS 91744 638-D7
SOUDAN AV
- PMDL 93552 4287-E1
SOURDOUGH RD
3800 Actn 93510 4375-A5
SOURWOOD WY
- LACo 91387 4552-A4
SOUTH AL
1900 SPAS 91030 595-J2
SOUTH AV
5900 Flor 90001 674-G7
SOUTH DR
- Hrbr 90710 794-A4
5700 CULC 90230 672-H5
SOUTH LN
100 SPAS 91030 595-E3
SOUTH RD
500 SBdC 92372 (4472-B7
See Page 4471)

SOUTH SPUR
- BREA 92823 709-J6
- BREA 92823 710-A6
- OrCo 92823 710-A6
SOUTH ST
100 AZU 91702 598-J2
100 NLB 90805 765-D2
500 GLDL 91202 564-C2
2900 LKWD 90712 765-H2
4100 LKWD 90712 766-C2
5500 LKWD 90713 766-C2
6600 CRTS 90703 766-G2
11400 ART 90701 766-G2
12300 CRTS 90703 767-B2
13400 LPMA 90623 767-B2
SOUTHALL CT
4900 BELL 90201 675-E7
4900 BELL 90201 705-E1
SOUTHALL LN
4900 BELL 90201 675-E7
5000 BELL 90201 705-E1
SOUTHAMPTON CT
11700 BelA 90077 591-G3
SOUTHAMPTON DR
26300 SCTA 91355 4550-F4
SOUTH BOUND DR
800 SMRO 91108 566-C6
SOUTHBY DR
7500 LA 91304 529-D4
SOUTHCLIFF ST
1000 SDMS 91773 599-J4
SOUTHCLIFF WY
39400 PMDL 93551 4195-F5
SOUTHCOAST DR
500 WAL 91789 639-F6
SOUTHERLAND AV
800 Wilm 90744 794-H6
SOUTHERN AV
- LACo 90280 704-J3
2400 SGAT 90280 704-J3
2700 SGAT 90280 705-B3
SOUTHERN LN
4800 SGAT 90280 705-E4
SOUTHERN PL
4800 SGAT 90280 705-E4
SOUTHERN OAK AV
- SIMI 93063 499-A3
SOUTHERN OAKS DR
- StvR 91381 4640-B1
SOUTHERN PACIFIC DR
2400 Wilm 90744 794-J5
SOUTHERN WILLOW CT
- LACo 91387 4552-B4
SOUTHFIELD DR
- RHLS 90274 823-E4
SOUTH FORK RD
4700 CHNO 91710 641-F7
SOUTH GATE AV
7900 LACo 90255 705-A2
8100 SGAT 90280 705-A3
SOUTH HILLS DR
- LACo 90606 676-H6
S SOUTH HILLS DR
1200 WCOV 91791 639-A3
SOUTH HILLS MTWY
- GLDR 91740 569-E7
- GLDR 91740 599-E1
SOUTH PARK AV
11800 LA 90066 672-D4
SOUTH PARK DR
500 LA 90037 674-B2
SOUTH PARK LN
17000 GAR 90247 734-A7
SOUTHPORT DR
1100 THO 91361 557-A5
SOUTHPORT LN
13100 SLB 90740 796-G7
SOUTHRIDGE AV
4800 LACo 90043 673-C4
SOUTHRIDGE DR
300 VeCo 91377 558-A1
1200 BREA 92821 708-H5
SOUTH SHORE DR
17200 LACo 93532 4101-J2
17500 LACo 93532 4102-A2
SOUTHSHORE DR
600 SLB 90740 826-F4
SOUTHSHORE PL
32500 WLKV 91361 557-B7
SOUTHSIDE DR
1900 MTBL 90640 676-B2
E SOUTHSIDE DR
5800 ELA 90022 675-J2
6100 ELA 90022 676-A2
SOUTHVIEW CT
3500 PMDL 93550 4286-H4
SOUTHVIEW PL
900 POM 91766 640-E3
SOUTHVIEW RD
700 ARCD 91007 567-A6
9000 LACo 91775 566-H7
SOUTHWEST BLVD
11200 LA 90044 704-A6
SOUTHWEST DR
2200 LA 90043 673-F7
SOUTHWIND CIR
1300 THO 91361 557-B6
SOUTHWIND CT
- StvR 91381 4640-D2
8500 SGBL 91776 596-G3
8500 LACo 91776 596-G3
SOUTHWIND DR
6100 WHIT 90601 677-E6

SOUTHWIND VILLAGE LN
1500 LA 90732 823-J6
W SOUTHWOOD LN
1200 UPL 91786 601-J1
SOVEREIGN LN
- ING 90305 703-F3
SOWMA WY
5100 CYP 90630 767-C6
SPACE CT
2600 LAN 93536 4105-C1
SPACE PARK DR
- RBCH 90278 732-J5
- RBCH 90278 733-A5
SPAD PL
3800 CULC 90232 672-F2
SPADE LETTEAU TKTR
35600 LACo 91390 4283-G5
35600 LACo 91390 4373-E1
SPADE SPRING CANYON RD
10000 LACo 91390 4373-B2
SPADRA RD
- LACo 91768 640-A2
SPAHN AV
5400 LKWD 90713 766-D2
SPAHN LN
- LAN 93535 4016-G4
S SPALDING DR
100 BHLS 90212 632-F2
SPANDAU DR
27500 SCTA 91350 4460-J5
SPANGLER PL
14800 LMRD 90638 707-F7
SPANISH LN
500 LACo 91789 679-G2
500 INDS 91789 679-G2
SPANISH BIT DR
- Actn 93510 4375-B4
SPANISH BROOM DR
1900 PMDL 93550 4286-D4
SPANISH CANYON MTWY
- BRAD 91010 568-A1
- MNRO 91016 567-J1
- MNRO 91016 568-A1
SPANISH OAK DR
19700 SCTA 91321 4551-F5
SPANISH OAK LN
5400 VeCo 91377 557-J1
SPANISH TRAILS
3900 PRV 90660 676-J2
SPANNER ST
100 MNRO 91016 567-G6
SPARKLER DR
3200 HNTB 92649 826-J6
SPARKLETT ST
9200 TEML 91780 596-J5
9500 TEML 91780 597-C4
N SPARKS ST
100 BURB 91506 563-F1
500 BURB 91506 533-F7
2300 BURB 91504 533-E4
S SPARKS ST
100 BURB 91506 563-F2
SPARLAND ST
3400 BALD 91706 598-A7
SPARR BLVD
3000 GLDL 91208 534-H4
SPARROW DR
14900 LMRD 90638 707-F7
37400 PMDL 93551 4286-E3
SPARROW LN
800 WCOV 91790 638-F2
8300 LPMA 90623 767-C4
SPARROW RD
1600 SBdC 92397 (4652-D3
See Page 4651)
SPARROW ST
- LAN 93536 4014-H7
- LVRN 91750 570-J4
SPARROW DELL DR
22700 CALB 91302 559-G6
SPARROWHAWK LN
100 VeCo 91377 557-J3
SPARROW HILL LN
2100 LKWD 90712 765-G4
SPARTA DR
2200 RPV 90275 823-G3
SPARTON AV
8300 PanC 91402 532-C1
8500 Pcma 91331 532-C1
8700 Pcma 91331 502-B7
SPARWOOD LN
12600 LMRD 90638 737-H1
N SPAULDING AV
300 LA 90036 593-B7
300 LA 90036 633-B1
700 LA 90046 593-C5
900 WHWD 90046 593-C5
S SPAULDING AV
500 LA 90036 633-B2
1000 LA 90019 633-B3
1900 LA 90016 633-A6
E SPAULDING CT
2100 LBCH 90804 795-G5
N SPAULDING PL
2100 Alta 91001 535-G6
E SPAULDING ST
2100 LBCH 90804 795-H5
E SPAULDING WY
2000 LBCH 90804 795-G5
SPAZIER AV
1100 GLDL 91201 563-J1

SPAZIER AV
1100 GLDL 91201 533-J7
1100 GLDL 91201 534-A7
E SPAZIER AV
1000 GLDL 91201 563-J1
1000 BURB 91502 563-J1
W SPAZIER AV
100 BURB 91502 563-J1
300 BURB 91506 563-H2
SPEARING AV
3500 LA 90732 823-G7
SPEARMAN AV
44700 LAN 93534 4015-J4
SPECHT AV
6200 BGDN 90201 675-G7
6500 BGDN 90201 705-G1
SPECHT ST
8200 BGDN 90201 705-F3
SPECTRUM LN
37600 PMDL 93552 4287-C2
SPEEDWAY
100 Ven 90291 671-G5
500 SMCA 90405 671-G5
3100 LA 90292 671-H7
3600 LA 90292 701-J1
6200 PdlR 90293 702-A3
SPEEDWAY DR
- IRW 91706 597-J2
SPEEDWAY ST
8700 PRV 90660 676-G3
SPEER CT
500 POM 91766 641-A6
SPENCE ST
600 LA 90023 635-C7
1100 LA 90023 675-B1
SPENCER AV
2100 POM 91767 601-A5
S SPENCER AV
- UPL 91786 601-J4
SPENCER CT
- LACo 91387 4552-A3
300 POM 91767 601-A5
25900 LACo 91302 558-J3
SPENCER DR
- SCTA 91387 4462-D7
SPENCER PL
900 DBAR 91765 680-E2
SPENCER ST
200 GLDL 91202 564-D2
800 RBCH 90277 762-J5
900 RBCH 90277 763-A4
3400 TOR 90503 763-B4
SPERRY ST
4500 LA 90039 564-B4
SPEYER LN
1400 RBCH 90278 762-J2
1800 RBCH 90278 763-A2
SPEZIA PL
1200 PacP 90272 631-C5
SPHYNX DR
- PMDL 93551 4195-F7
- PMDL 93551 4285-F1
SPICE CT
21600 SCTA 91350 4461-B5
SPICE ST
- LAN 93536 4104-E2
2100 LAN 93536 4105-A2
SPICEPECAN WY
- PMDL 93551 4285-D3
E SPICER ST
100 CRSN 90745 764-F7
SPICEWOOD LN
24100 Hrbr 90710 794-B3
SPIELBERG DR
- LA 91302 559-F4
- WdHl 91364 559-F4
SPIGNO PL
7200 LACo 91390 4374-C2
SPINDLEWOOD DR
12700 LMRD 90638 738-A1
SPINDRIFT DR
4400 RPV 90275 823-C5
SPINDRIFT LN
- RPV 90275 823-C5
SPINKS CANYON RD
100 DUAR 91010 568-C3
SPINNAKER CT
- SCTA 91355 4550-F2
100 LA 90292 701-J1
SPINNAKER MALL
- LA 90292 701-J1
SPINNAKER ST
- LA 90292 701-J2
11000 CRTS 90703 736-E6
SPINNAKER WY
300 SLB 90740 826-E3
6900 LBCH 90803 826-F2
S SPINNAKER WY
- UPL 91786 601-H4
SPINNAKER BAY DR
5100 LBCH 90803 826-C1
SPINNING AV
11500 HAW 90250 703-G7
12900 GAR 90249 733-G3
16100 TOR 90504 733-G6
18500 TOR 90504 763-G2
S SPINNING AV
10800 ING 90303 703-G6
SPINNING WHEEL LN
2300 RHE 90274 823-G1
SPINNING WHEEL RD
19500 WAL 91789 639-D7

SPIRAL LN
44100 LAN 93536 4015-C7
SPIRAL WY
2800 LAN 93536 4015-C7
SPIRES ST
23200 LA 91304 529-F3
SPIRIT CT
- SCTA 91350 4551-B4
16400 LMRD 90638 738-A2
SPIROS DR
11700 Brwd 90049 591-H7
SPIROS PL
900 Brwd 90049 591-H7
SPIRSA WK
1700 GLDL 91206 565-A1
SPLENDIDO CT
- StvR 91381 4640-D1
SPLENDORA DR
13100 LACo 90605 737-B1
SPLIT ROCK RD
3200 LA 90210 562-E7
SPOKANE ST
5500 LA 90016 633-A7
SPOLETO DR
500 PacP 90272 631-C6
SPORT CHALET DR
- LCF 91011 535-B3
SPORTSMAN DR
1400 COMP 90221 735-D6
1400 NLB 90805 735-D6
SPOTTED PONY RD
500 WAL 91789 639-D7
SPRAGUE AV
5500 CYP 90630 767-D5
SPRAGUE ST
1300 COMP 90222 734-F2
19000 Tarz 91356 560-G3
SPRAY LN
3900 LACo 90265 630-E5
SPREADING OAK DR
5600 LA 90068 593-G2
SPRECKELS CT
2900 RBCH 90278 763-B2
SPRECKELS LN
1400 RBCH 90278 762-J2
1800 RBCH 90278 763-A2
SPRING AV
- Actn 93510 4465-B3
14600 SFSP 90670 737-C4
N SPRING AV
100 COMP 90221 735-A3
SPRING CT
100 BREA 92821 709-B6
7200 CanP 91307 529-F5
SPRING ST
- LAN 93536 4104-J1
100 CLAR 91711 601-D4
3100 SPed 90731 854-A1
13300 BALD 91706 597-J4
21300 WAL 91789 639-H6
33000 LACo 91390 (4372-J4
See Page 4281)
E SPRING ST
100 LBCH 90806 795-H2
100 Bxby 90807 795-H2
600 SIGH 90755 795-H2
2200 LBCH 90808 795-H2
3400 LBCH 90815 795-H2
4000 LBCH 90815 796-F2
4000 LBCH 90808 796-A1
7900 LALM 90815 796-F2
N SPRING ST
100 LA 90012 634-G2
1700 LA 90031 634-H2
S SPRING ST
100 LA 90012 634-F5
300 LA 90013 634-F5
600 LA 90014 634-E5
9400 LA 90003 704-C4
10800 LA 90061 704-C6
12100 LACo 90061 734-C1
14700 LACo 90248 734-C4
W SPRING ST
100 LBCH 90806 795-C2
1200 LBCH 90810 795-B2
SPRING TR
12100 LACo 91342 482-J6
SPRINGBROOK AV
25600 SCTA 91350 4550-H3
SPRING CANYON LN
4500 PMDL 93552 4286-J2
4500 PMDL 93552 4287-F2
SPRING CANYON RD
- LACo 91387 4462-J7
- LACo 91390 4283-E6
- LACo 91390 4373-C2
- LACo 91390 4463-C2
SPRINGCREEK CIR
2000 UPL 91784 571-G4
SPRING CREEK RD
6000 RPV 90275 792-J6
SPRING CREEK WY
1300 CHLS 91709 710-F1
SPRING CREST DR
14200 CHLS 91709 680-J4
SPRINGDALE AV
10400 SFSP 90670 706-J5
SPRINGDALE DR
3000 LBCH 90810 795-A2
4400 LACo 90043 673-C5
SPRINGER ST
7800 DWNY 90242 705-H6
8600 DWNY 90242 706-A7

SPRINGFIELD AV
1800 HMB 90254 762-H1
10700 Nor 91326 500-G3
SPRINGFIELD CT
- SCTA 91355 4550-D4
SPRINGFIELD PL
2800 LAN 93536 4105-C1
SPRINGFIELD ST
300 CLAR 91711 601-D5
37000 PMDL 93552 4286-J3
W SPRINGFIELD ST
1000 UPL 91786 601-H1
SPRINGFORD DR
8300 SunV 91352 533-C1
12800 LMRD 90638 737-F1
13300 LMRD 90639 737-F1
SPRING FOREST LN
4000 THO 91362 557-D1
SPRINGHAVEN ST
800 LCF 91011 535-B2
SPRING HILL CT
4800 THO 91362 557-F1
SPRINGHILL PL
5600 LACo 90043 673-C6
SPRINGLAND DR
9900 LACo 90601 677-A2
9900 PRV 90601 677-A2
9900 PRV 90660 677-A2
SPRINGLAND LN
2000 UPL 91784 571-G4
SPRING LEAF CT
- BqtC 91354 4460-E4
SPRINGLET TR
3100 LA 90068 593-C1
SPRINGLINE DR
1200 PMDL 93550 4286-C3
SPRING MEADOW CT
- LACo 91765 679-G7
SPRING MEADOW DR
900 WCOV 91791 639-C2
2300 CHLS 91709 680-J4
S SPRING MEADOW DR
1000 WCOV 91791 639-C3
SPRING MEADOW LN
1200 LHB 90631 738-B1
SPRING OAK DR
5700 LA 90068 593-G2
SPRING OAK TER
5700 LA 90068 593-G2
SPRING OAK WY
1100 CHLS 91709 710-F2
S SPRINGPARK AV
6400 LadH 90056 672-J7
6400 LadH 90056 673-A7
SPRING PARK LN
16200 CRTS 90703 736-J6
SPRINGPARK LN
- PMDL 93551 4195-B3
SPRING POINT DR
600 BRAD 91010 568-C4
SPRINGPORT DR
19100 RowH 91748 679-C5
SPRINGRIDGE WY
- PMDL 93551 4195-B3
SPRINGSNOW CIR
12600 CRTS 90703 737-A7
SPRINGSONG WY
- PMDL 93552 4287-A5
SPRING TREE CT
1100 LHB 90631 738-D1
SPRING TREE LN
1400 POM 91768 600-E7
SPRINGTREE PL
- SCTA 91354 4460-G5
SPRINGVALE DR
5800 HiPk 90042 595-C1
SPRINGVALE LN
- Cstc 91384 4459-G5
SPRINGVALE ST
1300 POM 91766 641-B3
SPRING VALLEY RD
5900 HIDH 91302 559-C2
6200 WdHl 91367 559-C2
7500 LACo 93536 3834-A4
SPRINGVIEW DR
11900 LMRD 90638 707-F7
12100 LACo 90604 707-F7
12300 LACo 90604 737-E1
SPRINGVIEW WY
- PMDL 93551 4195-B3
SPRING VISTA LN
14200 CHLS 91709 680-J4
SPRINGWATER DR
- BPK 90621 738-A6
SPRINGWATER ST
14500 HacH 91745 677-J1
SPRINGWOOD DR
24200 DBAR 91765 680-D3
SPRINGWOOD ST
11200 SELM 91733 637-C4
SPRONG LN
500 LPUE 91744 678-F1
SPROUL AV
10800 LA 90064 632-D7
SPROUL ST
11800 NRWK 90650 736-H2
SPROULE AV
11100 Pcma 91331 502-E1
11700 Pcma 91331 482-E7
11900 LA 91340 482-D6
12800 LA 91342 482-A3
13500 LA 91342 481-H2

SPRUCE AV
500 PMDL 93550 4286-A3
E SPRUCE AV
100 ING 90301 703-C3
W SPRUCE AV
200 ING 90301 703-A3
SPRUCE CIR
7300 LPMA 90623 767-D2
SPRUCE CT
200 AZU 91702 568-J3
500 PMDL 93550 4286-B3
9600 CYP 90630 767-D7
W SPRUCE CT
1400 ONT 91762 641-J5
SPRUCE DR
- LACo 91302 559-J6
- LACo 91724 639-J1
- WdHl 91364 559-J6
- WdHl 91364 560-A6
SPRUCE LN
900 PAS 91103 565-H2
SPRUCE RD
8800 SBdC 92372 (4562-D1
See Page 4471)
9200 SBdC 92372 (4472-D7
See Page 4471)
SPRUCE ST
- CRSN 90746 764-F5
600 LA 90012 594-G7
800 WCOV 91790 638-E2
1100 ALH 91801 596-A3
1200 SPAS 91030 595-H3
5700 SBdC 92397 (4652-C2
See Page 4651)
8500 PRV 90660 676-F3
10300 BLF 90706 766-D1
11400 LYN 90262 705-B7
24500 SCTA 91321 4640-J1
24600 SCTA 91321 4550-J7
E SPRUCE ST
100 COMP 90220 734-J3
200 COMP 90220 735-A3
N SPRUCE ST
100 MTBL 90640 676-D2
600 UPL 91786 601-J2
S SPRUCE ST
100 MTBL 90640 676-D3
W SPRUCE ST
300 COMP 90220 734-F3
SPRUCE TR
43700 LACo 93532 4101-J1
SPRUCE WY
500 LHB 90631 708-C6
28500 RHE 90274 822-J1
28500 RHE 90274 823-A1
SPRUCE CREEK CIR
27800 SCTA 91354 4460-H4
SPRUCEGROVE DR
28900 RPV 90275 822-G1
SPRUCE LAKE DR
800 Hrbr 90710 794-B2
SPRUCE MEADOW CT
- SCTA 91354 4460-F4
SPRUCE MEADOW PL
400 THO 91362 557-D2
SPRUCE TREE DR
1300 DBAR 91765 680-B4
SPRUCE TREE LN
24000 Hrbr 90710 794-A3
SPRUCEVIEW
1700 POM 91766 640-F3
SPRUCEWOOD AV
300 VeCo 91377 558-A1
SPRUCEWOOD LN
1800 BelA 90077 592-A4
SPRY ST
9600 DWNY 90242 706-C7
10400 NRWK 90650 706-E7
SPUNKY CANYON RD
- LACo 91390 4193-A7
- LACo 91390 4283-A1
13800 LACo 91390 4192-E3
SPUNKY EDISON FIRE RD
- LACo 91390 4192-G5
- LACo 91390 4193-A4
SPUR AV
- LAN 93536 4104-H1
SPUR LN
- RHLS 90274 823-D3
12800 OrCo 90720 796-H6
SPURGEON AV
2400 RBCH 90278 733-B6
SPUR RANCH RD
9000 KeCo 93560 3833-H2
SPUR RIDGE RD
16000 LA 91342 481-F2
SPUR TRAIL AV
600 WAL 91789 639-H6
SPY GLASS DR
11600 Nor 91326 480-F7
11600 Nor 91326 500-F1
SPYGLASS DR
- PMDL 93552 4287-B5
SPYGLASS LN
200 WAL 91789 639-H7
27800 SCTA 91351 4551-E1
SPYGLASS HILL CT
1800 LHB 90631 738-D2
SPY GLASS HILL RD
10300 LACo 90601 677-B2
SQUAW PEAK LN
- CRSN 90745 794-E1

SQUAW VALLEY WY
7800 CRTS 90703 767-B4
SQUIB ST
- SCTA 91350 4550-J4
- SCTA 91350 4551-A3
SQUIRE DR
19800 LACo 91724 599-E6
STAATS PL
1600 PAS 91108 596-A1
STABLE WY
- RHE 90274 822-J2
STACEY AV
6900 KeCo 93560 3834-C1
STACEY CT
2000 WCOV 91792 679-A1
STACY ST
4900 HAW 90250 733-B1
4900 LACo 90250 733-B1
STADIA HILL LN
29200 RPV 90275 822-H1
STADIUM CT
46000 LAN 93535 4016-G4
STADIUM LN
- LAN 93535 4016-G4
STADIUM WY
- GLDR 91741 569-B6
700 LA 90012 634-F1
1100 Echo 90026 594-F5
1100 Echo 90026 634-F1
1700 LA 90039 594-F5
20200 WdHl 91367 530-D7
STAFF CT
15000 LACo 90248 734-C4
STAFF TR
21500 Top 90290 590-B5
STAFFORD AV
5900 HNTP 90255 674-J7
STAFFORD LN
10300 Chat 91311 500-D4
W STAFFORD RD
2200 VeCo 91361 586-D1
STAFFORD ST
15200 INDS 91744 638-C6
STAFFORD CANYON RD
25600 StvR 91381 4640-C1
25600 StvR 91381 4550-B7
STAFFORDSHIRE DR
1600 LAN 93534 4105-E3
STAGE RD
- AVA 90704 5923-G3
- LACo 90704 5923-C1
7600 BPK 90621 737-G5
13800 SFSP 90670 737-D3
14200 LMRD 90638 737-G5
STAGECOACH AV
10900 MTCL 91763 641-F2
16100 LACo 93591 4199-F5
STAGECOACH CIR
100 WCOV 91791 599-E7
100 WCOV 91791 639-E1
STAGECOACH DR
- POM 91766 640-F5
4800 MTCL 91763 601-F5
STAGECOACH LN
- CRSN 90745 794-E1
12700 NRWK 90650 737-A1
STAGECOACH RD
- VeCo 90265 625-G1
- RHE 90274 793-B4
E STAGECOACH RD
- VeCo 91307 529-A4
STAGECOACH TR
2500 CHLS 91709 640-J7
2500 CHLS 91709 641-A7
STAGECOACH WY
- BqtC 91354 4460-F2
STAGELINE RD
27800 Cstc 91384 4459-G6
STAGG ST
10100 SunV 91352 533-A3
11000 SunV 91352 532-J3
11400 NHol 91605 532-D3
13400 PanC 91402 532-B3
15100 VanN 91405 531-H3
15300 VanN 91406 531-C3
17300 Nor 91325 531-B3
17700 Res 91335 531-A3
18600 Res 91335 530-F3
19700 Win 91306 530-C3
21000 LA 91304 530-B3
22100 LA 91304 529-D3
STAG HOLLOW CT
- SCTA 91350 4551-D6
STAGIO DR
1900 LACo 91016 567-G6
STALLION AV
11000 MTCL 91763 641-F2
13100 CHNO 91710 641-E7
STALLION CIR
19600 WAL 91789 639-D7
STALLION DR
- PMDL 93551 4195-A5
STALLION PL
27800 Cstc 91384 4369-G6
STALLION RD
28500 RPV 90275 823-F2
STALLION MEADOW
- Actn 93510 4375-E6
- GrnH 91344 480-J6
STALLO AV
3300 RSMD 91770 636-G1
STALWART DR
3900 RPV 90275 823-D5

STAMPS AV
9100 DWNY 90240 706-C2
STAMPS RD
8700 DWNY 90240 706-D2
10200 DWNY 90241 706-B4
STAMY RD
10300 WHIT 90603 707-G5
10400 LACo 90604 707-G5
11500 LMRD 90638 707-G6
STAN PL
9800 LA 90210 592-D3
STANBRIDGE AV
2100 LBCH 90815 796-B2
3400 LBCH 90808 766-B5
3400 LBCH 90808 796-B2
12800 DWNY 90242 736-B2
13400 BLF 90706 736-B2
STANBROOK DR
15600 LMRD 90638 737-H4
STANCLIFF AV
43600 LAN 93535 4106-D1
STANCREST DR
3400 GLDL 91208 534-J4
STANCREST FRONTAGE RD
3300 GLDL 91208 534-J5
STANCROFT ST
4800 BALD 91706 598-D3
STANDARD AV
1700 GLDL 91201 563-J1
1700 GLDL 91201 564-A2
10700 LYN 90262 705-D6
STANDARD ST
100 ELSG 90245 732-E1
STANDARD OIL FIRE RD
- GrnH 91344 480-F3
- LA 91381 480-F3
- Nor 91326 480-F3
- StvR 91381 480-F3
STANDELL AV
4500 ELMN 91732 597-G5
STANDISH DR
3400 Enc 91436 561-C7
STANDISH PL
- PMDL 93551 4285-E3
1300 ARCD 91006 567-F7
STANDISH ST
100 LACo 91016 567-F7
300 ARCD 91006 567-F7
STANDRIDGE AV
- LAN 93535 4015-J4
STANFIELD DR
2700 Top 90290 589-G2
STANFORD AV
400 LA 90013 634-F6
600 LA 90021 634-F6
1100 COMP 90059 734-E3
1100 RBCH 90278 762-H1
1900 LA 90011 634-E7
2100 POM 91766 641-B6
2100 LA 90011 674-D2
2900 LA 90292 672-A6
6400 LA 90001 674-E7
7300 LA 90001 704-E2
8800 Wats 90002 704-E4
9200 SGAT 90280 705-A4
10100 SGAT 90280 704-J5
10700 LYN 90262 704-J5
10800 LA 90059 704-E6
12800 Wbrk 90059 734-E2
14300 LACo 90220 734-E4
S STANFORD AV
15300 LACo 90220 734-E5
STANFORD CT
- CYP 90630 767-F7
1300 SMCA 90404 631-H6
20100 WAL 91789 639-F5
STANFORD DR
- BPK 90620 767-E6
300 CLAR 91711 601-C3
400 ARCD 91007 567-B4
1400 GLDL 91205 564-G7
STANFORD LN
100 SLB 90740 796-G6
STANFORD PL
6700 WHIT 90601 677-D6
STANFORD RD
400 BURB 91504 533-F5
STANFORD ST
200 LHB 90631 708-B6
800 SMCA 90403 631-G5
1200 SMCA 90404 631-H6
STANFORD TER
- HiPk 90042 595-D4
STANFORD WY
6200 WHIT 90601 677-D5
6700 WHIT 90608 677-D6
STANGATE ST
11600 LKWD 90715 766-G4
STANHILL DR
12700 LMRD 90638 737-E1
STANHURST AV
1900 LMTA 90717 793-H3
23800 TOR 90501 793-H3
STANISLAUS CIR
600 CLAR 91711 601-E1
STANLEAF DR
15000 LMRD 90638 737-F4
STANLEY AV
600 LBCH 90814 795-H6
700 LBCH 90804 795-H6
1100 GLDL 91206 564-G4

STREET Block	City	ZIP	Pg-Grid
STANLEY AV			
2100	SIGH	90755	795-H3
6900	NLB	90805	735-G6
N STANLEY AV			
300	LA	90036	593-C7
300	LA	90036	633-C1
700	LA	90046	593-C4
900	WHWD	90046	593-C7
1800	SIGH	90755	795-H5
S STANLEY AV			
700	LA	90036	633-B3
1000	LA	90019	633-B3
STANLEY CT			
28200	SCTA	91351	4461-E7
N STANLEY DR			
100	BHLS	90211	632-J2
S STANLEY DR			
100	BHLS	90211	632-J2
STANLEY PL			
2500	SIGH	90755	795-H4
E STANLEY ST			
-	COMP	90220	735-A7
-	COMP	90220	765-A1
STANLEY HILLS DR			
2000	LA	90046	592-J3
STANLEY HILLS PL			
2000	LA	90046	592-J3
STANMONT ST			
15900	WHIT	90603	707-J5
STANMOOR DR			
8200	Wch	90045	702-D3
STANRIDGE AV			
38400	PMDL	93550	4196-A7
43600	LAN	93535	4105-J1
43900	LAN	93535	4015-J6
STANSBURY AV			
3900	Shrm	91423	562-B3
5500	VanN	91401	562-B2
7000	VanN	91405	532-B4
7800	PanC	91402	532-A1
8700	PanC	91402	502-A7
STANSBURY LN			
100	LHB	90631	738-D2
STANSBURY WAY WK			
3200	LA	90011	674-F2
STANSFIELD LN			
-	Saug	91350	4461-F6
STANSTEAD AV			
13400	NRWK	90650	737-A2
STANTON AV			
1700	GLDL	91201	563-H3
2500	LHB	90631	708-B6
5600	BPK	90621	737-J6
6300	BPK	90621	767-J4
7200	BPK	90620	767-J4
8600	ANA	92801	767-J4
14400	LMRD	90638	737-J4
S STANTON AV			
4500	OrCo	90638	737-J4
14900	LMRD	90638	737-J4
STANTON DR			
4500	LA	90065	564-H6
STANTON PL			
1500	LBCH	90804	795-G5
STANTON ST			
200	PAS	91103	565-G1
600	PAS	91103	535-F7
2900	POM	91767	601-A3
STANWELL ST			
21100	Chat	91311	500-A3
STANWICK DR			
1300	SDMS	91773	599-H2
STANWIN AV			
8900	Pcma	91331	502-A4
10500	MsnH	91345	501-J2
10500	MsnH	91345	502-A3
STANWOOD AV			
600	POM	91767	601-A3
STANWOOD DR			
11300	LA	90066	672-C1
STANWOOD PL			
12400	LA	90066	672-B2
STAPLETON CT			
11400	CRTS	90703	736-G6
STAR CIR			
4500	CULC	90230	672-F4
19500	CRTS	90703	767-A3
STAR CT			
24400	DBAR	91765	640-E7
STAR LN			
5700	WdHl	91367	559-D2
STAR ST			
12200	ELMN	91732	597-G6
STAR WY			
19500	CRTS	90703	767-A3
STARBIRD DR			
200	MONP	91755	636-B4
STARBUCK ST			
-	FUL	92833	738-C5
10100	WHIT	90603	707-G4
13500	WHIT	90605	707-D2
STARBURST DR			
1500	WCOV	91790	638-C3
STARBURY AV			
16000	LACo	93591	4199-E5
STARCA AV			
10300	LACo	90601	677-B2
STAR CANYON PL			
-	Cstc	91384	4459-F3
STARCREST DR			
900	COV	91722	599-C3
2500	DUAR	91010	568-D3
6000	GLDR	91740	569-C7
STAR CREST LN			
27800	SCTA	91351	4551-E1
STARCREST ST			
800	BREA	92821	708-J4
37300	PMDL	93550	4286-H3
STARDALE DR			
27700	SCTA	91350	4461-B6
STARDELL ST			
12800	WHIT	90601	677-C5
STARDUST DR			
1300	DBAR	91765	680-D3
1500	WCOV	91790	638-C3
STARDUST PL			
16900	GrnH	91344	481-C6
37900	PMDL	93552	4287-A2
STARDUST RD			
4900	LCF	91011	535-E3
STARE ST			
100	POM	91767	600-J4
14700	MsnH	91345	501-G4
15600	LA	91343	501-E4
17000	Nor	91325	501-B4
18500	Nor	91324	500-F5
20100	Chat	91311	500-D5
STARFALL CIR			
-	LVRN	91750	570-H5
STARFALL DR			
1800	WCOV	91790	638-C3
2700	LaCr	91214	504-G5
STARFALL LN			
2000	CHLS	91709	710-H1
STARFALL WY			
-	LACo	91390	4461-A2
STARFALL RIDGE RD			
-	Actn	93510	4375-G5
STARFIRE WY			
16700	PRM	90723	735-F6
STARFISH LN			
11800	VeCo	90265	625-F4
N STARFLOWER ST			
100	BREA	92821	709-F7
S STARFLOWER ST			
100	BREA	92821	709-F7
STARGAZE DR			
1800	WCOV	91790	638-C3
STARGAZER AV			
3700	LA	90732	823-G7
STARGAZER CT			
-	BqtC	91354	4460-E6
STARGAZER PL			
-	PMDL	93552	4287-A5
STARGLEN DR			
100	COV	91724	599-F5
STARHAVEN AV			
2000	DUAR	91010	567-J7
2000	DUAR	91010	568-A7
STARHAVEN ST			
1300	DUAR	91010	568-A7
STARHILL LN			
13700	LACo	91746	637-H5
STARK AV			
4500	WdHl	91364	559-H4
17100	CRTS	90703	736-J7
18700	CRTS	90703	766-J2
STARKLAND AV			
8300	LA	91304	529-E2
STARKUS WY			
24500	SCTA	91355	4550-E5
STARLAND DR			
3900	LCF	91011	535-B6
STARLAND ST			
1300	LHB	90631	708-E4
STARLANE DR			
200	LCF	91011	535-E4
STARLIGHT AV			
2300	UPL	91784	571-H3
11400	LACo	90604	707-D7
STARLIGHT CIR			
1900	BURB	91504	533-G4
STARLIGHT DR			
1500	WCOV	91790	638-C3
19300	Tarz	91356	560-G3
STARLIGHT LN			
-	SIGH	90755	795-G3
4300	CHNO	91710	641-E4
24500	CanP	91307	529-D4
27700	Cstc	91384	4459-G1
STARLIGHT CREST DR			
100	LCF	91011	535-D2
200	PAS	91011	535-E3
STARLIGHT HEIGHTS DR			
700	LCF	91011	535-C2
STARLIGHT MESA LN			
5200	LCF	91011	535-E4
STARLINE DR			
3200	RPV	90275	823-F5
STARLINE ST			
6800	LVRN	91750	570-H4
STARLING CIR			
4900	LPMA	90623	767-C4
STARLING CT			
-	LACo	91387	4551-J5
STARLING WY			
-	BREA	92823	709-G6
4500	LA	90065	595-A4
STARLIT LN			
1100	MNRO	91016	567-J2
1100	MNRO	91016	568-A2
STARLITE DR			
-	BRAD	91010	568-A3
STAR OF INDIA LN			
100	CRSN	90746	764-D1
STARPATH DR			
14600	LMRD	90638	707-F7
STAR PINE CT			
200	AZU	91702	568-J3
STARPINE DR			
-	DUAR	91010	568-D3
STAR RIDGE DR			
1400	MONP	91754	635-H4
STARSET DR			
34700	Actn	93510	4375-E3
STARSHINE RD			
1700	LACo	91789	679-F5
20800	DBAR	91789	679-G5
STARSTONE CT			
40800	PMDL	93551	4194-H2
STARSTONE DR			
6900	RPV	90275	792-G7
STARTOUCH DR			
3600	PAS	91107	536-H7
3600	PAS	91107	566-H1
STARTREE LN			
28700	SCTA	91390	4460-H2
28800	LACo	91390	4460-H2
STAR TREK DR			
700	LCF	91011	535-C2
STARVALE RD			
1700	GLDL	91207	564-E1
STARVIEW DR			
-	LAN	93536	4104-E1
STAR VIEW LN			
-	Actn	93510	4375-H6
STARWOOD DR			
16300	LACo	90604	708-A6
STARWOOD PL			
-	LACo	91390	4460-H1
STARWOOD WY			
20100	LACo	91390	4461-D4
STASSEN ST			
14800	LA	91343	501-J5
STASSI LN			
500	LA	90402	631-C7
STATE DR			
500	LA	90037	674-A2
STATE RD			
-	CHLS	91709	710-C1
-	LACo	92823	710-C1
-	OrCo	92823	709-J4
-	OrCo	92823	710-A3
20000	CRTS	90703	766-F4
STATE ST			
500	GLDL	91203	564-C4
1700	PAS	91105	595-J1
1700	PAS	91106	595-J1
1700	SPAS	91030	595-J1
3000	POM	91769	640-C4
3500	POM	91768	640-B3
4000	MTCL	91763	641-E1
5200	MTCL	91762	641-H1
5200	SBdC	91762	641-H1
5200	SBdC	91763	641-H1
6000	HNTP	90255	675-A6
7100	HNTP	90255	705-B1
8100	SGAT	90280	705-B2
9900	LYN	90262	705-A6
11900	LYN	90262	735-A1
E STATE ST			
-	PAS	91105	565-H7
-	SPAS	91030	565-H7
1600	SPAS	91030	595-H1
N STATE ST			
100	Boyl	90033	635-A2
S STATE ST			
100	Boyl	90033	635-A5
400	Boyl	90033	634-J5
W STATE ST			
-	PAS	91105	565-G7
1000	ONT	91762	641-J1
N STATE COLLEGE BLVD			
100	BREA	92821	709-B6
S STATE COLLEGE BLVD			
200	BREA	92821	709-C7
STATEN PL			
27200	SCTA	91354	4460-G7
STATE ROUTE 210 FRWY Rt#-210			
-	CLAR	-	570-A7
-	CLAR	-	571-C7
-	GLDR	-	569-J7
-	GLDR	-	570-A7
-	GLDR	-	600-A1
-	LACo	-	570-A7
-	LVRN	-	570-A7
-	SDMS	-	570-A7
-	UPL	-	571-C7
STATE UNIVERSITY DR			
-	MONP	90032	635-F2
-	MONP	91754	635-F2
4300	LACo	90032	635-F2
4300	LA	90032	635-F2
E STATE UNIVERSITY DR			
6200	LBCH	90815	796-E6
6200	LBCH	90840	796-E6
STATLER ST			
800	SPed	90731	824-A1
STAUNTON AV			
1600	LA	90021	674-G1
1900	LA	90058	674-G1
STEALTH PKWY			
-	PRV	90660	676-E6
STEAMBOAT DR			
9700	MTCL	91763	601-G6
STEARNLEE AV			
1800	LBCH	90815	796-B3
3600	LBCH	90808	766-C7
STEARNS AV			
600	LHB	90631	708-F5
STEARNS DR			
900	LA	90048	633-A3
1000	LA	90035	633-A4
1900	LA	90034	633-A5
STEARNS ST			
-	BREA	92821	709-F6
4000	LBCH	90815	796-A4
E STEARNS ST			
3400	LBCH	90815	795-J4
3900	LBCH	90815	796-B4
STEBBINS TER			
1400	LA	90069	592-J5
STEDDOM DR			
7600	LACo	91770	636-E4
STEDLEY PL			
3800	LVRN	91750	600-F1
STEDMAN PL			
100	MNRO	91016	567-G3
STEED CT			
2400	LMTA	90717	793-G5
STEELE AV			
33300	LACo	91390	4373-A4
N STEELE AV			
1400	City	90063	635-F3
STEELE DR			
800	BREA	92821	708-J5
STEELE RD			
33300	LACo	91390	4373-A3
STEELE ST			
4700	TOR	90503	763-C3
8700	RSMD	91770	596-G6
9400	RSMD	91770	597-A6
STEEN PL			
11800	LMRD	90638	707-F7
STEEP CANYON RD			
1200	DBAR	91765	680-C2
STEEPLECHASE LN			
2500	DBAR	91765	679-J6
22100	DBAR	91765	680-A6
STEERS WY			
-	LA	90290	560-E7
-	Top	90290	560-E7
-	Top	90290	590-E1
-	WdHl	91364	560-E7
STEFANI AV			
18700	CRTS	90703	766-J2
18700	CRTS	90703	767-A2
STEFFEN LN			
800	VeCo	93063	499-B4
STEFFEN ST			
1100	GLDR	91741	569-G6
STEIF ST			
43600	LAN	93535	4106-C1
STEIN LN			
700	AZU	91702	569-A6
STEIN WY			
25900	StvR	91381	4550-B6
STEINBECK AV			
25000	StvR	91381	4550-D7
STEINER AV			
3000	SMCA	90405	671-H3
STEINHART AV			
1100	RBCH	90278	762-J1
STEIN STRAUSS ST			
-	FUL	92833	738-C5
STEINWAY ST			
19400	SCTA	91351	4461-E7
STELLA AV			
3200	WCOV	91792	679-A1
STELLBAR PL			
9800	LA	90064	632-G6
STELLER DR			
8400	CULC	90232	672-J1
STEPHANIE AV			
2700	PMDL	93551	4195-C6
STEPHANIE CT			
1000	LAN	93535	4106-B2
4100	KeCo	93560	3834-J2
STEPHANIE DR			
500	COV	91722	599-C3
3100	WCOV	91792	639-A7
3100	WCOV	91792	679-A1
19700	LACo	91724	599-E2
20700	Win	91306	530-C6
E STEPHANIE DR			
200	COV	91722	599-B3
STEPHANIE PL			
6700	Win	91306	530-C6
STEPHANIE WY			
6000	SIMI	93063	499-B3
STEPHEN AV			
1100	CLAR	91711	601-C2
STEPHEN LN			
8300	LA	91304	529-F2
STEPHEN RD			
600	BURB	91504	533-F4
STEPHEN HORN WY			
-	DWNY	90242	706-C7
STEPHEN M WHITE DR			
3600	SPed	90731	854-C2
STEPHENS AV			
700	FUL	92833	738-E6
STEPHENS CIR			
3300	GLDL	91208	534-F5
STEPHENS ST			
9300	PRV	90660	676-H3
16100	INDS	91745	678-D1
STEPHENS PASTURE RD			
-	LACo	91750	570-J4
-	LACo	91750	571-A3
STEPHENS RANCH RD			
-	LACo	91711	571-A3
-	LACo	91750	571-A3
5800	LACo	91750	570-H3
5800	LVRN	91750	570-H3
STEPHEN S WISE DR			
15400	BelA	90077	561-H7
15400	BelA	90077	591-G1
STEPHON TER			
10700	CULC	90230	672-H5
STEPHORA AV			
100	COV	91724	599-F3
1200	GLDR	91740	599-F1
5000	LACo	91724	599-F2
E STEPNEY PL			
700	ING	90302	673-D7
700	ING	90302	703-D1
E STEPNEY ST			
200	ING	90302	703-C1
STEPROCK DR			
14800	LMRD	90638	707-F7
STERLING DR			
3500	PMDL	93550	4286-H3
STERLING LN			
-	BqtC	91354	4460-D3
-	Cstc	91384	4460-D3
-	SCTA	91350	4551-D6
STERLING PL			
500	SPAS	91030	595-F1
2800	Alta	91001	535-F5
STERLING ST			
2900	POM	91767	601-A3
STERLING WK			
6100	HiPk	90042	595-E4
STERLING WY			
4000	BALD	91706	598-C6
STERLING CENTER DR			
5300	WLKV	91361	557-E6
STERLING GROVE LN			
-	LACo	91387	4552-A4
STERN AV			
4200	Shrm	91423	562-B3
13100	LMRD	90638	737-H2
STERN GOODMAN ST			
-	FUL	92833	738-C6
STETSON			
-	LA	91342	481-G1
STETSON AV			
7600	Wch	90045	702-G1
STETSON WY			
13200	CHLS	91709	680-J1
STEUBEN ST			
1000	PAS	91106	566-B5
STEVEANN ST			
5000	TOR	90503	763-B6
STEVE JON ST			
20600	SCTA	91350	4461-D5
STEVELY AV			
800	LBCH	90815	796-G4
3400	LBCH	90808	766-F6
3800	LA	90008	673-C2
4100	LKWD	90713	766-E2
N STEVELY AV			
3000	LBCH	90808	796-G1
3300	LBCH	90808	766-G7
STEVEN DR			
3100	Enc	91436	561-F7
STEVEN PL			
10300	Chat	91311	500-E4
STEVEN WY			
1100	BHLS	90210	592-E5
STEVE N AMBERS WY			
34900	PMDL	93550	4376-E3
STEVENS AV			
200	LHB	90631	708-E4
1300	SGBL	91776	596-D6
2400	RSMD	91770	636-D1
11200	CULC	90230	672-H5
15100	BLF	90706	736-B5
STEVENS CIR			
5100	CULC	90230	672-G4
STEVENS PL			
600	LA	90012	634-F2
5300	CMRC	90040	675-G3
STEVENS ST			
2700	LaCr	91214	504-F7
3300	GLDL	91214	504-E6
17000	GAR	90247	734-A7
STEVENS WY			
9000	LA	91304	499-E7
9000	WHil	91304	499-E7
STEVENS CREEK LN			
900	WAL	91789	639-C5
STEVENSON AV			
13900	LACo	91342	482-J2
STEVENSON LN			
18700	RowH	91748	679-B5
STEVENSON RANCH PKWY			
25000	StvR	91381	4550-C7
25200	StvR	91381	4640-C1
STEVER CT			
5700	CULC	90230	672-H5
STEVER ST			
10800	CULC	90230	672-H5
STEVEY ST			
3100	LAN	93536	4015-B7
STEVIE CT			
-	SCTA	91351	4551-E4
STEWART AL			
-	PAS	91107	566-E5
STEWART AV			
3100	LA	90066	672-A2
3100	IRW	91706	598-B5
3800	BALD	91706	598-B5
7400	Wch	90045	702-F1
STEWART CT			
-	RowH	91748	679-C7
STEWART DR			
-	LMRD	90638	737-F3
-	LMRD	90639	737-F3
500	COV	91723	599-C6
STEWART RD			
-	Cstc	91384	4459-J1
STEWART ST			
1600	SMCA	90404	631-H7
1900	SMCA	90404	671-J1
11300	ELMN	91731	597-D7
11500	ELMN	91732	597-D7
11500	ELMN	91732	637-E1
STEWART WY			
200	Bxby	90807	765-C6
STEWART AND GRAY RD			
7000	DWNY	90242	705-G4
7000	DWNY	90241	705-G4
8000	DWNY	90242	706-A6
8000	DWNY	90241	706-A6
STEWARTON DR			
11800	Nor	91326	480-H6
STEWARTON WY			
900	GLDL	91207	534-F7
STICHMAN AV			
3100	BALD	91706	598-D5
N STICHMAN AV			
700	LACo	91746	637-J3
700	LACo	91746	638-A2
N STICHMAN ST			
300	LACo	91746	637-J3
STILL KNOLL LN			
16200	CRTS	90703	736-J6
S STILLMAN AV			
300	UPL	91786	601-J4
STILLMAN ST			
11200	LKWD	90715	766-F4
12500	LKWD	90715	767-A4
S STILLMAN WY			
1300	UPL	91786	601-J4
STILL MEADOW LN			
-	LAN	93536	4104-J2
STILLMEADOW LN			
-	LAN	93536	4104-E2
2500	LAN	93536	4105-B2
STILLMORE ST			
17800	SCTA	91387	4552-A3
17900	SCTA	91387	4551-G3
18900	SCTA	91351	4551-F3
STILLWATER DR			
5300	LA	90008	673-B2
44400	LAN	93536	4015-C6
STILLWATER LN			
12200	CRTS	90703	736-J4
STILLWATER PL			
23500	SCTA	91321	4640-G3
STILLWELL AV			
4100	LA	90032	595-G5
N STIMSON AV			
100	LPUE	91744	638-D5
1200	LACo	91744	638-E4
S STIMSON AV			
100	LPUE	91744	638-D7
100	LPUE	91744	678-D1
300	INDS	91744	678-D1
500	INDS	91745	678-D1
1100	HacH	91745	678-C3
STINGLE AV			
2600	RSMD	91770	636-H2
STIPA WY			
1800	Brwd	90049	631-D2
STIPE CT			
-	Saug	91350	4461-G6
STIRLING ST			
45600	LAN	93534	4015-F3
STIRRUP CT			
-	PMDL	93551	4195-A5
STIRRUP DR			
23300	DBAR	91765	680-B1
STIRRUP LN			
-	RPV	90275	823-G2
N STIRRUP LN			
-	VeCo	91307	529-B3
STIRRUP RD			
-	RPV	90275	823-G2
STITES DR			
20000	Top	90290	630-B1
STITESWOOD AV			
600	GLDR	91740	569-D6
STOAKES AV			
8800	DWNY	90240	706-D2
STOCKBRIDGE AV			
100	ALH	91801	595-H5
2900	LA	90032	595-G5
STOCKDALE ST			
14700	BALD	91706	598-D6
STOCKER PL			
3000	LA	90008	673-F3
STOCKER PZ			
2800	LA	90008	673-F3
STOCKER ST			
2100	POM	91767	601-A5
3000	LA	90008	673-F3
3600	LACo	90008	673-C3
4300	LACo	90043	673-C4
4900	LadH	90056	673-A4
10600	LACo	90230	672-H4
E STOCKER ST			
100	GLDL	91207	564-E2
W STOCKER ST			
100	GLDL	91202	564-C2
STOCKHAM PL			
11900	ELMN	91732	637-E1
STOCKTON DR			
-	BPK	90621	737-J7
E STOCKTON ST			
900	COMP	90221	735-A2
STOCKTON PASS RD			
21400	WAL	91789	639-H2
STOCKWELL DR			
11000	LYN	90262	705-C6
E STOCKWELL ST			
2000	COMP	90222	734-H2
2000	Wbrk	90222	734-H2
W STOCKWELL ST			
700	COMP	90222	734-F2
STODDARD PL			
2000	POM	91768	600-J5
STODDARD WELLS RD			
1600	WAL	91789	639-G3
E STOKE CT			
6100	SIMI	93063	499-B1
STOKES CANYON RD			
2100	CALB	91302	589-A3
2100	LACo	91302	589-A3
2500	LACo	91302	588-H4
STOKOWSKI DR			
28600	RPV	90275	823-H2
STOLL DR			
5600	HiPk	90042	595-C2
STONE CIR			
4200	LVRN	91750	600-J1
4200	LVRN	91750	570-J7
STONE CT			
2200	MONP	91754	635-G4
STONE LN			
1500	GLDL	91202	564-B1
STONE ST			
900	LA	90063	635-C3
N STONEACRE AV			
1600	COMP	90221	735-C2
12400	LYN	90262	735-C2
S STONEACRE AV			
900	COMP	90221	735-D6
12800	RDom	90221	735-C3
STONEBANK ST			
10300	BLF	90706	736-D7
STONEBRIDGE DR			
600	BREA	92821	709-A4
STONEBRIDGE LN			
-	ING	90305	703-F3
44500	LAN	93536	4015-D6
STONEBROOK LN			
2000	UPL	91784	571-J4
STONEBROOK ST			
1400	AZU	91702	568-H4
STONEBRYN DR			
900	Hrbr	90710	794-A3
STONE CANYON AV			
3500	Shrm	91403	561-J6
STONE CANYON LN			
-	SCTA	91351	4461-G7
STONE CANYON RD			
1400	BelA	90077	591-J1
1400	BelA	90077	592-A5
2400	BelA	90077	561-J7
N STONE CANYON RD			
300	BelA	90077	592-A5
S STONE CANYON RD			
100	BelA	90077	592-B7
100	BelA	90077	632-B1
STONE CANYON WY			
500	BREA	92821	709-C5
STONECHAT CT			
24400	SCTA	91355	4550-E4
STONECLIFF LN			
23700	Hrbr	90710	794-A2
STONE COURT CIR			
23800	Hrbr	90710	794-A2
STONECREEK DR			
-	SCTA	91354	4460-F7
STONE CREEK RD			
1300	SDMS	91773	570-C7
30700	Cstc	91384	4459-C2
STONECREST CIR			
1300	BREA	92821	708-J4
STONECREST DR			
5700	AGRH	91301	557-H4
STONECREST PL			
1400	DBAR	91765	680-D3
STONECREST RD			
29200	RHE	90274	823-A2
29300	RPV	90275	823-A2
STONE CREST WY			
6500	WHIT	90601	677-D6
STONECROFT CT			
2000	THO	91361	557-A5
STONEFORD CT			
21300	Top	90290	560-B6
STONEGATE CIR			
-	POM	91766	640-F6
STONEGATE DR			
-	StvR	91381	4550-B4
24500	LA	91304	529-D4
STONEGATE LN			
-	RowH	91748	708-J2
-	RowH	91748	709-A2
37400	PMDL	93552	4287-B3
STONEGATE RD			
12000	Pcma	91331	482-F7
12000	Pcma	91331	502-F1
STONE GATE ST			
1300	MONP	91754	635-G4
STONEGATE ST			
39300	PMDL	93551	4195-E5
STONE GATE WY			
11800	Nor	91326	480-E6
STONEGLEN DR			
4800	LCF	91011	535-C2
STONE GROVE LN			
16200	CRTS	90703	736-J6
STONEHAM CT			
500	LBCH	90803	796-F7
STONEHAM WY			
1500	LHB	90631	708-C7
STONE HARBOR CIR			
500	LHB	90631	708-D7
STONEHAVEN CT			
16500	LMRD	90638	738-A2
18700	Nor	91326	480-H7
STONEHAVEN DR			
-	Hrbr	90710	794-A5
STONEHAVEN LN			
300	VeCo	91377	557-J2
STONEHAVEN PL			
2600	WCOV	91792	639-A7
STONEHAVEN WY			
100	Brwd	90049	631-G3
STONEHEDGE DR			
1000	GLDR	91740	569-G6
STONEHEDGE LN			
1300	LHB	90631	738-D2
STONEHENGE CT			
19800	WdHl	91367	530-E7
STONEHENGE DR			
1200	SDMS	91773	599-H4
STONEHENGE LN			
4800	CYP	90630	767-B6
11700	BelA	90077	591-G3
STONEHILL CT			
2500	CLAR	91711	571-D6
STONEHILL DR			
2800	Alta	91001	536-B5
STONEHILL LN			
900	Brwd	90049	631-F1
STONE HILL PL			
3500	Shrm	91423	562-C7
STONEHILL WY			
27800	SCTA	91351	4551-J2
STONE HOUSE RD			
1800	ARCD	91006	567-C1
1900	SMAD	91024	567-C1
STONEHURST AV			
9500	Sunl	91040	503-A5
9500	SunV	91352	503-A5
9900	SunV	91352	502-J4
10100	Sunl	91040	502-G2
STONEHURST DR			
400	Alta	91001	535-F6
STONEHURST PL			
9900	Sunl	91040	502-J4
9900	Sunl	91040	503-A4
9900	SunV	91352	502-J4
9900	SunV	91352	503-A4
STONELEY DR			
3000	LACo	91107	566-F7
STONEMAN AV			
1100	ALH	91801	596-A3
2300	SMRO	91108	596-A3
N STONEMAN AV			
-	ALH	91801	596-B4
S STONEMAN AV			
400	ALH	91801	596-B5
1800	ALH	91801	636-C1
STONE OAK DR			
3100	Brwd	90049	561-D7
3100	Brwd	90049	591-D1
STONE OAK PK			
2900	Brwd	90049	561-D7
2900	Brwd	90049	591-D1
STONE PINE CT			
-	HacH	91745	678-F7
STONEPINE DR			
21800	DBAR	91765	679-J5
STONER AV			
1200	WLA	90025	631-J5
1700	WLA	90025	632-A6
2200	LA	90064	632-B7
2600	LA	90064	672-B1
3000	LA	90066	672-C2
4500	LA	90230	672-E5
STONER CREEK RD			
1200	INDS	91748	678-J4
STONE RIDGE CT			
14500	SCTA	91387	4462-G6
STONERIDGE CT			
3400	CALB	90290	559-J7
3400	CALB	91302	559-J7
W STONERIDGE CT			
1100	ONT	91762	601-J7
1100	ONT	91762	641-H1
STONERIDGE DR			
900	PAS	91105	565-G7
8000	WHIT	90605	708-A1
STONERIDGE LN			
3300	Shrm	91403	561-J7
STONERIDGE PL			
13200	Shrm	91423	562-D6
STONERIVER CT			
3400	THO	91362	557-C2
STONESBORO PL			
14900	Shrm	91403	561-J6
STONESGATE ST			
1800	THO	91361	557-A5
STONE VIEW CT			
-	LA	90068	593-D2
STONEVIEW DR			
5900	CULC	90232	672-J2
5900	CULC	90232	673-A2
13600	Shrm	91423	562-C6
STONEWALL CIR			
1200	THO	91361	557-B5
STONEWALL TER			
21000	Top	90290	590-B4
STONEWELL ST			
1300	MONP	91754	635-G4
STONEWOOD CT			
1100	LA	90732	823-J2
1100	LA	90732	824-A2
STONEWOOD DR			
500	BHLS	90210	592-F6
1200	DUAR	91010	568-C5
3500	Shrm	91403	561-H7
STONEWOOD ST			
800	LHB	90631	708-F4
9000	DWNY	90241	706-C5
STONEWOOD TER			
15300	Shrm	91403	561-H7
STONEY DR			
400	SPAS	91030	595-F1
400	HiPk	90042	595-F1
STONEY LN			
12500	Brwd	90049	591-E4
STONEYBROOK DR			
4000	Shrm	91403	561-J5
STONEYBROOK LN			
1100	THO	91361	557-C5
STONEY CREEK RD			
-	BqtC	91354	4460-F2
STONEY HILL RD			
2100	Brwd	90049	591-E3
STONEYVIEW LN			
6400	SIMI	93063	499-C3
STONINGTON LN			
28100	SCTA	91350	4461-B5
STONY LN			
2300	BREA	92821	709-E6
S STONY PL			
600	ANA	92804	767-H7
STONYBROOK			
13500	ELMN	91732	637-G7
STONY BROOK AV			
10500	SGAT	90280	705-G6
STONYBROOK DR			
21000	WAL	91789	639-G5
W STONYBROOK DR			
2800	ANA	92804	767-H7
STONYCREEK RD			
5000	CULC	90230	672-H3
STONY POINT PL			
-	POM	91766	640-G7
STONYVALE RD			
-	LACo	-	504-J1
-	LACo	-	(4724-E4 See Page 4643)
2200	Tuj	91042	(4724-E4 See Page 4643)
STORAGE RD			
-	Cstc	91384	4459-J4
-	Cstc	91384	4460-A3
STORE ST			
500	MTBL	90640	676-B3
STORES ST			
1400	CRSN	90746	764-G5
1700	CRSN	90745	764-G5
STORK PL			
11200	LKWD	90715	766-F4
STORM PKWY			
1200	LA	90501	794-A1
1200	LACo	90501	794-A1
STORMCROFT CT			
2300	THO	91361	557-B5
STORM HILL LN			
-	RHLS	90274	823-C2
STORRS PL			
900	POM	91766	640-F3
STORY AV			
2000	LHB	90631	708-B6
STORY PL			
300	ALH	91801	596-A3
2500	GLDL	91206	565-A4
STORY ST			
3200	City	90063	635-D3
STOUGH CANYON AV			
-	BURB	91501	533-H3
-	BURB	91504	533-H3
STOUGH CANYON MTWY			
-	BURB	91501	533-H2
-	BURB	91504	533-H2
STOVALL AV			
1100	HacH	91745	678-B2
STOVER FLATS CT			
-	LACo	91390	4461-B4
STOW ST			
1500	SIMI	93063	499-A1
STOWE CT			
1900	CLAR	91711	571-D7
STOWE LN			
27700	Cstc	91384	4459-H5
STOWE TER			
300	HiPk	90042	595-D2
STOWELL LN			
9900	LA	90210	592-B3
STOWERS AV			
16400	CRTS	90703	737-C6
17900	CRTS	90703	767-C1
STRADA CORTA RD			
100	BelA	90077	592-B7
STRADA VECCHIA RD			
800	BelA	90077	592-A6
STRADELLA CT			
10700	BelA	90077	591-J5
STRADELLA RD			
700	BelA	90077	591-H3
700	BelA	90077	592-A6
STRAMBINO CT			
26500	SCTA	91355	4550-E4
STRANAHAN DR			
2200	ALH	91803	635-J2
STRAND CT			
1000	WCOV	91792	638-J5
STRAND PL N			
100	SMCA	90405	671-F4
STRAND ST			
100	SMCA	90405	671-F3
STRANG AV			
3500	RSMD	91770	597-A7
STRANG ST			
3900	City	90063	635-E6
4600	ELA	90022	635-G6
STRANGE CREEK DR			
23800	DBAR	91765	640-C5
STRANWOOD AV			
11000	MsnH	91345	501-H2
11300	GrnH	91344	501-G1
STRASBOURG CT			
-	CLAR	91711	571-E4
STRATFORD			
-	MANB	90266	732-H4
1700	WCOV	91791	638-J3
STRATFORD AV			
600	SPAS	91030	595-J1
STRATFORD CIR			
1900	BelA	90077	591-G3
5000	LPMA	90623	767-F1
5500	BPK	90621	737-H6
41700	PMDL	93551	4104-F6
STRATFORD DR			
1000	LCF	91011	535-B6
2300	LMTA	90717	793-G5
5000	LACo	93536	4104-H7
25400	SCTA	91350	4550-J5
36900	PMDL	93552	4287-A4
STRATFORD LN			
-	ING	90305	703-E3
600	SPAS	91030	595-J1
1100	SDMS	91773	599-J3
STRATFORD PL			
1800	POM	91768	600-G5
STRATFORD RD			
2000	SMRO	91108	566-D7
4800	HiPk	90042	595-A1
4800	Eagl	90041	595-A1
STRATFORD ST			
1700	LAN	93534	4015-E3
STRATFORD WY			
2100	LVRN	91750	600-D2
STRATHERN ST			
10200	SunV	91352	533-A2
11000	SunV	91352	532-H2
11400	NHol	91605	532-D2
13400	PanC	91402	532-B2
14700	PanC	91402	531-H2
15600	VanN	91406	531-C3
17300	Nor	91325	531-B3
17700	Res	91335	531-B3
18100	Res	91335	530-H3
19700	Win	91306	530-D3
20800	LA	91304	530-A3
22000	LA	91304	529-E3
STRATHMORE AV			
1800	SGBL	91776	596-E7
2200	LACo	91770	636-E3
2400	RSMD	91770	636-E3
STRATHMORE DR			
500	Wwd	90024	632-B1
10900	Wwd	90024	632-A2
STRATHMORE PL			
-	LA	90095	632-A2
1800	WCOV	91792	638-J7
STRATTFORD ST			
1300	BREA	92821	709-A4
STRATTON AV			
13800	LA	91342	482-C1
STRATTON LN			
600	SPAS	91030	595-H1
STRATTON PL			
-	PAS	91101	565-J4
STRATTON WY			
3100	PMDL	93551	4195-B6
STRAWBERRY CT			
3500	PMDL	93550	4286-H4
STRAWBERRY DR			
16900	Enc	91436	561-C5
STRAWBERRY LN			
-	RHE	90274	793-F7
100	BREA	92821	709-D7
1000	GLDR	91740	599-G2
STRAWBERRY PL			
4000	Enc	91436	561-C6
5800	CHNO	91710	641-J6

STREET Block City ZIP Pg-Grid

STRAWBERRY HILL DR
29600 AGRH 91301 557-J5
STRAWBERRY PINE CT
- LACo 91387 4552-B3
STRAWFLOWER LN
1500 DBAR 91765 680-B4
STREAMVIEW LN
- LA 91604 562-J7
STREAMVIEW ST
800 WAL 91789 639-E6
STRELNA PL
20300 WdHl 91364 560-D4
STRETTO WY
17400 PacP 90272 630-G6
STRICKLAND AV
6100 HiPk 90042 565-D7
STRICKLER DR
- FUL 92833 738-C5
STRINGER AV
1100 City 90063 635-D4
STROHM AV
4200 LA 91602 563-B5
4800 NHol 91601 563-B3
STRONG AV
2200 CMRC 90040 675-G3
10200 LACo 90601 677-A3
10400 WHIT 90601 677-A3
STRONGBOW DR
600 DBAR 91765 640-B6
STRONGS DR
1800 Ven 90291 671-H6
3100 LA 90292 671-J7
STROUD ST
13900 PanC 91402 532-B3
STROZIER AV
1300 SELM 91733 637-B3
2600 ELMN 91733 637-B3
STRUB AV
8000 WHIT 90602 707-F1
8000 WHIT 90605 707-E2
STRUIKMAN RD
13800 CRTS 90703 737-D7
E STUART AV
1200 WCOV 91790 638-H1
1400 WCOV 91791 638-H1
STUART LN
9500 LA 90210 592-F2
STUART WK
2500 GLDL 91206 565-A2
STUART RANCH RD
23700 MAL 90265 628-J6
STUBBS LN
10700 CULC 90230 672-H4
STUBBY WY
28100 Cstc 91384 4369-G6
STUDEBAKER RD
10600 DWNY 90241 706-E7
11200 NRWK 90650 706-E7
12300 NRWK 90650 736-E3
15900 CRTS 90703 736-F5
15900 NRWK 90703 736-F5
17600 CRTS 90703 766-F3
20300 LKWD 90715 766-F4
N STUDEBAKER RD
100 LBCH 90803 826-F1
300 LBCH 90803 796-E7
2500 LBCH 90815 796-F2
3400 LBCH 90808 766-F7
STUDENT CENTER DR
- GLDR 91741 569-B5
STUDIO DR
5200 CULC 90230 672-G4
STUDIO RD
7100 VeCo 93063 499-E5
W STUHR DR
800 SGBL 91775 596-C3
STULMAN AV
15600 LACo 90248 734-D5
STULMAN ST
14800 LACo 90248 734-D4
STUNT RD
100 LACo 91302 589-D5
100 Top 90290 589-D7
STUNT RANCH RD
- LACo 91302 589-D6
STURBRIDGE DR
700 LHB 90631 708-B7
28000 Cstc 91384 4459-G5
STURGESS DR
19200 TOR 90503 763-B3
STURTEVANT DR
200 SMAD 91024 567-B1
STYLES ST
22500 WdHl 91367 529-F7
SUANA DR
2000 RPV 90275 823-H5
SUBIDO ST
18300 RowH 91748 679-A6
SUBTROPIC DR
1500 LHH 90631 708-B1
SUCCESS AV
1400 Wbrk 90059 704-F7
9200 Wats 90002 704-F5
9200 Wats 90002 704-F4
11200 LA 90059 704-F5
SUDAN ST
7200 BGDN 90201 705-J2
SUDBURY CT
17400 CRSN 90746 734-E7
17500 CRSN 90746 764-E1
SUE AV
11000 LYN 90262 705-C7

SUE DR
20600 SCTA 91350 4461-D4
N SUEDE AV
2000 SIMI 93063 499-B2
SUENO RD
22400 WdHl 91364 559-J4
SUFFIELD ST
8100 LPMA 90623 767-C4
SUFFOLK AV
- SMAD 91024 567-A2
800 MTBL 90640 636-E7
1300 GLDR 91740 599-F1
SUFFOLK CT
1600 PMDL 93551 4195-E4
3700 PRV 90660 676-H1
SUFFOLK DR
9700 LA 90210 562-C7
45800 LAN 93534 4015-F3
SUFFOLK LN
- ING 90305 703-D4
SUFFOLK PL
1600 GLDR 91740 599-F2
SUGAR ST
43000 LAN 93536 4105-D2
SUGAR BLISS PL
- LACo 91390 4461-B3
SUGARGROVE DR
11700 LACo 90604 708-A7
SUGAR GUM RD
14700 HacH 91745 677-H4
SUGARHILL DR
4500 RHE 90274 793-C4
SUGARLOAF AV
1800 UPL 91784 571-H5
SUGAR LOAF CT
3500 SCTA 91387 4462-H7
SUGARLOAF CT
3500 PMDL 93550 4286-H4
SUGAR LOAF DR
300 LACo 93551 4285-H6
1300 LCF 91011 535-A6
1500 GLDL 91206 535-A6
3200 GLDL 91208 535-A6
SUGARLOAF DR
2300 Ago 91301 588-A4
SUGARMAN ST
18200 Tarz 91356 560-J3
18200 Tarz 91356 561-A3
SUGARPINE LN
16000 CRTS 90703 736-J5
SUGARPINE PL
2800 DBAR 91765 679-J6
SUGAR PINE WY
28500 SCTA 91390 4460-H3
SUGARWOOD ST
6000 LKWD 90713 766-D4
SULLIVAN AV
3000 RSMD 91770 636-H2
SULLIVAN PL
7500 BPK 90621 767-H1
W SULLIVAN ST
1100 UPL 91784 571-H6
SULLIVAN FIRE RD
2200 PacP 90272 631-C1
3000 PacP 90272 591-A2
SULLY DR
10000 SunV 91352 533-C2
SULPHUR SPRING FIRE RD
- GrnH 91344 480-J4
- GrnH 91344 481-A4
SULPHUR SPRINGS RD
36600 PMDL 93552 4287-A3
SULTAN CIR
1200 CRSN 90746 764-F3
SULTANA AV
4500 RSMD 91770 596-H5
4900 TEML 91780 596-H3
6300 TEML 91775 596-H1
N SULTANA AV
6600 LACo 91775 596-H1
7100 LACo 91775 566-H7
SULTUS ST
- LACo 91387 4552-C5
16100 SCTA 91387 4552-C5
SUMAC AV
37400 PMDL 93550 4286-A2
38400 PMDL 93550 4196-A7
SUMAC CT
27300 LACo 91387 4551-H4
SUMAC DR
3900 Shrm 91403 562-A6
3900 Shrm 91423 562-A6
SUMAC LN
300 LA 90402 631-C7
SUMAC ST
1700 LVRN 91750 600-D3
SUMAC TR
700 SMAD 91024 537-B7
SUMACH LN
16800 CHLS 91709 710-F3
SUMACRIDGE DR
3100 MAL 90265 629-F5
SUMATRA DR
3300 LA 90210 562-D7
SUMIYA DR
17400 Enc 91316 561-B5
SUMMER AV
10100 SFSP 90670 706-G4
11700 NRWK 90650 706-G7
12200 NRWK 90650 736-G1
17500 ART 90701 736-G7
17800 ART 90701 766-G1

SUMMER CT
- Chat 91311 499-J3
SUMMER LN
3600 BALD 91706 597-H6
42000 LAN 93536 4104-G6
SUMMER PL
1000 WCOV 91792 638-J5
SUMMERBREEZE CT
- PMDL 93552 4287-A5
SUMMER CANYON RD
1000 CHLS 91709 710-F2
SUMMERDALE DR
1300 POM 91766 640-G3
SUMMERFIELD AV
8100 LACo 90606 676-G7
8300 LACo 90606 706-G1
SUMMERFIELD CIR
1700 BREA 92821 709-D7
SUMMERFIELD DR
3500 Shrm 91423 562-A7
SUMMERGLEN PL
- SCTA 91354 4460-G5
SUMMER GROVE PL
- SCTA 91354 4460-F6
SUMMERHILL DR
5500 LACo 90043 673-C5
SUMMERHILL LN
- SCTA 91354 4460-F6
- StvR 91381 4640-D2
SUMMER HILL RANCH RD
20400 Top 90290 590-C2
SUMMER HOLLY CIR
10200 BelA 90077 592-A1
SUMMERHOLLY CIR
36500 PMDL 93550 4286-H5
SUMMER LAKE CIR
1500 BREA 92821 708-H6
SUMMERLAND AV
400 SPed 90731 824-B3
W SUMMERLAND AV
700 SPed 90731 824-A4
1000 LA 90732 824-A4
1200 LA 90732 823-J4
1400 LA 90275 823-J4
SUMMERLAND PL
700 SPed 90731 824-B4
SUMMERLAND ST
1500 RPV 90275 823-H4
1900 LA 90275 823-H4
1900 LA 90732 823-H4
SUMMER LAWN WY
1500 HacH 91745 678-F4
SUMMER LILAC DR
2600 PMDL 93550 4286-F5
SUMMER MAPLE WY
- LACo 91387 4552-B4
SUMMER OAK CT
- LACo 91390 4460-H1
SUMMERPLACE DR
1800 WCOV 91792 638-G4
SUMMERSET DR
14300 CHLS 91709 680-H4
SUMMERSET PL
3600 ING 90305 703-E3
SUMMERSHADE DR
2600 LHB 90631 738-A1
16000 LMRD 90638 737-J1
16100 LMRD 90638 738-A1
SUMMERSHORE LN
3600 WLKV 91361 557-C7
SUMMERSWORTH PL
1200 FUL 92833 738-B5
SUMMERTIME LN
4800 CULC 90230 672-H3
SUMMERTOWN ST
20500 LACo 91789 679-F5
SUMMERWIND DR
1600 PMDL 93551 4195-F5
SUMMERWIND ST
12400 CRTS 90703 736-J7
12500 CRTS 90703 737-A7
SUMMERWOOD AV
700 DBAR 91789 679-H2
SUMMERWOOD DR
1700 FUL 92833 738-D3
SUMMIT AV
300 PAS 91103 565-H1
1500 Boyl 90033 634-J4
1600 PAS 91103 535-H7
2000 Alta 91001 535-J4
SUMMIT CIR
- SCTA 91350 4551-B4
1500 FUL 92833 738-C4
12000 LA 90210 592-F1
SUMMIT CT
- UPL 91784 571-H6
12100 LA 90210 592-F1
SUMMIT DR
600 Top 90290 590-A7
800 SPAS 91030 595-G3
1000 BHLS 90210 592-D5
1100 LA 90210 592-D5
5400 SBdC 92397 (4652-F3 See Page 4651)
13900 WHIT 90602 677-E7
23500 CALB 91302 589-E1
23500 WHil 91304 499-E6
N SUMMIT DR
23500 WHil 91304 499-E6
SUMMIT PL
900 MONP 91754 635-J4
12100 LA 90210 592-F1

SUMMIT PL
26000 SCTA 91355 4550-E6
41000 PMDL 93551 4194-G1
SUMMIT RD
100 LACo 91750 570-J6
200 LVRN 91750 570-J6
21100 Top 90290 590-B4
W SUMMIT ST
1200 LBCH 90810 795-B4
SUMMIT TR
12200 LACo 91342 482-J6
21500 Top 90290 590-B5
43700 LACo 93532 4101-J2
SUMMIT CREST DR
5700 LCF 91011 535-C1
SUMMIT HILLS DR
- SCTA 91387 4552-A1
SUMMIT KNOLL CT
400 VeCo 91377 558-B1
SUMMIT KNOLL RD
13000 LACo 91390 4462-H1
13000 LACo 91390 4463-A1
SUMMIT POINT DR
21500 Brwd 90049 591-E4
SUMMIT POINTE DR
3200 Top 90290 560-C7
N SUMMIT RIDGE CIR
22300 Chat 91311 499-H6
S SUMMIT RIDGE CIR
22300 Chat 91311 499-H6
SUMMIT RIDGE CT
3900 THO 91362 557-C1
SUMMIT RIDGE DR
19000 WAL 91789 639-C6
SUMMITRIDGE DR
900 DBAR 91765 680-D3
1300 LA 90210 592-D2
SUMMITRIDGE PL
1300 BHLS 90210 592-D5
1300 LA 90210 592-D5
SUMMITROSE ST
7000 Tuj 91042 504-A3
7300 Tuj 91042 503-J3
7800 Sunl 91040 503-J3
SUMMIT TO SUMMIT MTWY
22100 CALB 90290 559-J7
22100 CALB 90290 589-G1
22100 CALB 91302 559-J7
22100 CALB 91302 560-A7
22100 LACo 91302 560-A7
22100 Top 90290 560-A7
22100 Top 90290 589-H1
22100 WdHl 91364 560-A7
SUMMIT TRAIL RD
15300 CHLS 91709 680-G6
SUMMIT VIEW CT
900 WAL 91789 639-F6
19800 SCTA 91351 4551-E1
SUMMIT VIEW DR
4900 THO 91362 557-E1
19900 SCTA 91351 4551-D1
SUMMITVIEW DR
2200 FUL 92833 738-C3
SUMMITVIEW LN
41000 PMDL 93551 4194-G1
SUMMIT VUE DR
- WdHl 91367 529-J7
- WdHl 91367 559-J1
SUMMIT VUE DR E
- WdHl 91367 529-J7
SUMMIT VUE DR N
- WdHl 91367 529-J7
SUMMIT VUE DR W
- WdHl 91367 559-H7
SUMMIT VUE LN
- WdHl 91367 559-J1
SUMNER AV
100 AVA 90704 5923-H4
1400 CLAR 91711 601-A2
1800 CLAR 91711 571-A7
2800 POM 91767 601-A2
5200 Eagl 90041 564-J5
27700 SCTA 91350 4460-J5
SUMNER PL
8500 CYP 90630 767-B5
SUMNER WY
5600 CULC 90230 672-J6
SUMTER DR
2000 HiPk 90042 595-D2
SUN CT
1400 LAN 93535 4106-C1
SUN LN
5500 BGDN 90201 675-G7
7800 LACo 91770 636-E3
SUNBEAM DR
3800 LA 90065 594-H2
SUNBIRD AV
1300 LACo 90631 708-C4
SUNBIRD CT
26500 SCTA 91355 4550-E4
SUNBLUFF DR
1500 DBAR 91765 679-J4
SUNBLUFF WY
5400 PMDL 93551 4194-G1
SUNBRIGHT DR
2400 DBAR 91765 679-H6
SUNBROOK DR
10100 BelA 90077 592-C5
10100 LA 90210 592-C5
SUNBURST CIR
400 LAN 93535 4106-A1

SUNBURST DR
4900 PMDL 93552 4287-A4
SUNBURST ST
11100 LA 91342 482-J7
11100 LA 91342 502-H1
12700 Pcma 91331 502-D5
14200 PanC 91402 502-A7
15000 LA 91343 501-D7
17000 Nor 91325 501-A7
18100 Nor 91325 500-J7
18500 Nor 91324 500-H7
20100 Chat 91311 500-D7
40400 PMDL 93551 4194-H2
SUNBURST TR
- CHLS 91709 640-J7
SUNBURY ST
900 LA 90015 634-D4
SUNCOURT TER
500 GLDL 91206 565-A4
SUNCREST CIR
300 BREA 92821 709-D7
SUNCREST CT
1600 LHH 90631 678-F7
1600 LHH 90631 708-F1
SUNCUP LN
45900 LAN 93534 4015-G3
SUNDALE AV
11500 HAW 90250 703-B7
12100 HAW 90250 733-B1
SUNDALE DR
7200 Tuj 91042 504-A5
SUNDANCE
12400 ELMN 91732 637-G1
SUNDANCE AV
13300 LACo 90605 707-B5
SUNDANCE CT
200 AZU 91702 568-H2
2000 PMDL 93551 4195-E5
44100 LAN 93535 4016-C7
SUNDANCE DR
- POM 91766 640-F5
5100 MTCL 91763 601-G6
SUNDANCE LN
- BqtC 91354 4460-E3
8000 LPMA 90623 767-D4
SUNDANCE PL
14700 SCTA 91387 4462-F5
SUNDANCE ST
21200 WAL 91789 639-H7
SUNDANCE CREEK DR
- SCTA 91354 4550-H6
SUNDAY TR
2800 LA 90068 593-C1
SUNDELL AV
44200 LAN 93536 4015-D7
SUNDELL CT
43900 LAN 93536 4105-D1
SUNDERLAND CT
23600 SCTA 91354 4460-G7
SUNDERLAND DR
17100 GrnH 91344 481-B6
SUNDEW WY
44100 LAN 93535 4016-C7
SUNDIAL CT
35100 Litl 93543 4377-G2
SUNDIAL DR
2400 CHLS 91709 680-G5
SUNDIAL LN
10000 LA 90210 592-C6
SUNDOWN DR
2400 LA 90065 594-H2
27600 RHE 90274 823-G1
SUNDOWN LN
12800 CHLS 91709 640-H7
SUNDOWNER LN
1800 WAL 91789 639-G2
SUNDOWNER WY
18000 SCTA 91387 4551-J2
SUNFIELD AV
4300 LBCH 90808 766-B5
5000 LKWD 90712 766-B2
SUNFIELD CT
300 THO 91362 557-F2
SUNFLOWER AV
- LHB 90631 708-C6
- POM 91767 601-A4
100 SDMS 91724 599-G4
100 SDMS 91773 599-G4
200 LACo 91724 599-G4
700 COV 91724 599-G4
1900 LA 90039 594-F4
N SUNFLOWER AV
1100 COV 91724 599-G3
1100 LACo 91724 599-G3
S SUNFLOWER AV
1000 GLDR 91740 599-G1
SUNFLOWER CIR
6800 MAL 90265 667-D3
SUNFLOWER CT
- SCTA 91354 4460-G5
26600 CALB 91302 588-G1
SUNFLOWER LN
7800 LPMA 90623 767-E3
SUNFLOWER PL
100 CLAR 91711 571-D6
SUNFLOWER ST
- FUL 92835 738-H3
- SIMI 93063 499-A1
100 BREA 92821 709-F7
SUNFLOWER WY
44100 LAN 93535 4016-C7
SUNGATE DR
- PMDL 93551 4195-A3

SUNGATE DR
4300 PMDL 93551 4194-H3
SUNGLOW ST
9200 PRV 90660 706-E2
11600 SFSP 90670 706-H3
SUNGLOW WY
9800 SunV 91352 503-C7
SUNGROVE PL
800 BREA 92821 709-C6
SUNKEN TR
19500 Top 90290 590-A7
SUNKIST AV
300 LPUE 91746 638-A4
900 LACo 91746 638-C2
N SUNKIST AV
100 WCOV 91790 598-D7
S SUNKIST AV
800 WCOV 91790 598-D7
800 WCOV 91790 638-D1
SUNKIST DR
13700 LPUE 91746 638-A3
W SUNKIST PL
2000 WCOV 91790 598-D7
SUNKIST ST
- PMDL 93551 4195-A4
SUNLAND BLVD
8100 SunV 91352 533-A2
8800 SunV 91352 503-A6
9300 Sunl 91040 503-C5
SUNLAND PL
9500 Sunl 91040 503-B5
SUNLAND WY
9900 Sunl 91040 503-D4
SUNLAND PARK DR
9300 SunV 91352 503-A6
SUNLIGHT PL
5100 LA 90016 673-A1
SUNLIGHT WK
- LA 90016 673-C1
SUNMIST CT
44100 LAN 93535 4016-C7
SUNMIST DR
5600 RPV 90275 823-A2
SUNMORE LN
800 Alta 91001 535-F2
SUN MUN WY
900 LA 90012 634-G2
SUNNINGDALE RD
1600 SLB 90740 796-H7
SUNNY CIR
9800 CYP 90630 767-E7
SUNNY CT
10600 WHIT 90603 707-J5
SUNNY CV
6800 LA 90068 593-D1
SUNNY DR
- LA 91342 481-J5
SUNNY LN
- AVA 90704 5923-H4
18500 Tarz 91356 560-J2
36500 PMDL 93551 4286-F5
42800 LAN 93536 4105-D3
SUNNYBANK DR
2000 LCF 91011 534-H1
SUNNY BRAE AV
6600 Win 91306 530-D3
SUNNYBRAE AV
8300 Win 91306 530-D2
10000 Chat 91311 500-C2
SUNNYBROOK AV
4700 BPK 90621 738-A4
8300 BPK 90621 737-J5
SUNNYBROOK CIR
8300 BPK 90621 737-G5
8300 BPK 90621 738-A5
SUNNY BROOK CT
400 VeCo 91377 558-B1
SUNNYBROOK DR
700 LHB 90631 708-B5
SUNNY BROOK LN
10800 LACo 91390 4373-E5
SUNNYBROOK LN
10300 LACo 90604 707-E5
13000 LMRD 90638 737-D2
S SUNNYBROOK LN
12200 LACo 90604 737-D1
SUNNYBROOK TR
21200 WAL 91789 639-H6
SUNNYCANYON LN
12300 CRTS 90703 736-J4
SUNNYCREEK CT
2000 UPL 91784 571-H5
SUNNY CREEK DR
- SCTA 91354 4460-F6
SUNNYCREEK LN
12400 CRTS 90703 736-J5
SUNNYCREST CT
24300 DBAR 91765 680-E2
SUNNY CREST DR
1300 FUL 92835 738-G5
SUNNYCREST DR
1500 FUL 92835 738-G4
4400 LA 90065 564-G6
6000 VeCo 91377 558-A1
SUNNYCREST TR
7000 Tuj 91042 504-A4
SUNNYDALE DR
2600 DUAR 91010 568-D3
14700 LACo 93532 4102-F3
SUNNYDELL TR
6900 LA 90068 593-D1
SUNNYDIP TR
7200 LA 90068 593-C1

SUNNYFIELD DR
- RHE 90274 793-E7
SUNNY GLEN RD
2800 TOR 90505 793-E5
19900 WAL 91789 639-E6
SUNNY GLENN WY
7100 LACo 91775 566-G7
SUNNY GROVE LN
- GLDR 91741 569-F3
SUNNY HEIGHTS DR
1600 LA 90065 594-J3
SUNNYHILL DR
600 LA 90065 595-A3
1400 MONP 91754 635-H4
SUNNY HILL PL
7500 LA 90046 593-B1
SUNNYHILL TER
13600 HacH 91745 637-G6
SUNNYHILLS AV
1100 BREA 92821 708-J5
SUNNY HILLS RD
400 FUL 92835 738-F1
SUNNY HILLS TER
2300 FUL 92833 738-C5
SUNNY KNOLL
1700 FUL 92835 738-G4
SUNNY LEAF LN
2000 LMTA 90717 793-H4
SUNNYMEAD DR
14600 LMRD 90638 707-F7
SUNNYNOOK DR
2900 LA 90039 594-D1
SUNNY OAK RD
3900 Shrm 91403 561-J6
SUNNY OAKS CIR
1200 Alta 91001 536-B4
SUNNY PALMS LN
- LA 91342 482-C4
SUNNY POINT PL
5200 RPV 90275 793-A7
SUNNYRIDGE CIR
- POM 91766 640-F5
SUNNY RIDGE CT
16800 CRTS 90703 736-F6
SUNNY RIDGE DR
800 FUL 92833 738-B4
SUNNYRIDGE DR
30000 AGRH 91301 557-H4
SUNNY RIDGE PL
2000 FUL 92833 738-B4
SUNNYRIDGE RD
27000 LACo 90274 793-C7
27000 LACo 90274 823-C1
SUNNYSEA DR
8200 PdlR 90293 702-B2
SUNNYSIDE AV
4100 LA 90066 672-B5
N SUNNYSIDE AV
- SMAD 91024 566-J1
400 SMAD 91024 536-J7
S SUNNYSIDE AV
- SMAD 91024 566-J3
300 SMAD 91024 537-B7
E SUNNYSIDE PL
12900 SFSP 90670 707-A6
S SUNNYSIDE PL
11100 SFSP 90670 707-A6
SUNNYSIDE TER
1400 LA 90732 823-J6
SUNNYSIDE RIDGE RD
2400 RPV 90275 823-G2
SUNNYSLOPE AV
4000 Shrm 91423 562-C3
5200 VanN 91401 562-C2
6000 VanN 91401 532-C6
6800 VanN 91405 532-C6
N SUNNYSLOPE AV
- PAS 91107 566-F3
S SUNNYSLOPE AV
- PAS 91107 566-F5
SUNNYSLOPE BLVD
3100 LACo 91107 566-F6
3100 PAS 91107 566-F6
SUNNYSLOPE DR
1300 MONP 91754 635-H4
7300 LAN 93536 4104-C5
8400 LACo 91775 566-G7
SUNNYSLOPE LN
8800 SBdC 92371 (4562-J1 See Page 4471)
SUNNYSLOPE PL
1300 MONP 91754 635-H4
SUNNYSLOPE RD
- POM 91766 640-H5
900 SBdC 92372 (4562-D1 See Page 4471)
2200 SBdC 92371 (4562-G1 See Page 4471)
SUNNYSLOPE ST
12300 WHIT 90602 677-B7
SUNNYSLOPE WY
- HacH 91745 637-J7
SUNNYVALE CT
- SCTA 91354 4460-G5
SUNNYVALE LN
- PMDL 93552 4287-E2
SUNNYVALE PL
- HacH 91745 637-H7
SUNNYVALE RD
- LAN 93536 4105-C4
SUNNYVALE ST
38700 PMDL 93551 4195-D7

SUNNYVALE WY
1000 BHLS 90210 592-E6
SUNNYVIEW LN
13400 VanN 91401 562-C1
SUNNYVIEW ST
5300 TOR 90505 763-B7
5300 TOR 90505 793-A1
SUNNYVIEW TER
16100 HacH 91745 678-C4
SUNNYVISTA AV
- VeCo 91377 558-A3
SUNNYWOOD DR
2800 FUL 92835 738-G2
SUNNYWOOD LN
7500 LA 90046 593-B1
N SUNOL DR
100 City 90063 635-E5
S SUNOL DR
100 City 90063 635-E6
900 LACo 90023 635-E6
900 LACo 90023 675-E1
2700 VER 90023 675-E4
SUN RANCH CT
22100 Chat 91311 499-J2
SUNRIDGE CT
3200 PMDL 93550 4286-G2
SUN RIDGE DR
2100 CHLS 91709 680-J4
SUNRIDGE PL
30000 SCTA 91387 4462-F5
SUNRIDGE ST
100 PdlR 90293 702-A3
SUNRIDGE WK
8300 PdlR 90293 702-B3
SUNRISE
500 SDMS 91773 600-A3
E SUNRISE BLVD
600 LBCH 90806 795-E3
800 SIGH 90755 795-E3
SUNRISE CIR
- LVRN 91750 570-H5
SUNRISE CIR E
1300 UPL 91784 571-G4
SUNRISE CIR N
1300 UPL 91784 571-J4
SUNRISE CIR S
1300 UPL 91784 571-H4
SUNRISE CIR W
1400 UPL 91784 571-H4
SUNRISE CT
800 LAN 93535 4016-A5
SUNRISE DR
- CYP 90630 767-B5
1300 MONP 91754 635-J5
10600 Litl 93543 4378-D7
13600 WHIT 90602 707-D1
17700 RowH 91748 678-H7
SUNRISE LN
1500 FUL 92833 738-D4
27800 SCTA 91351 4551-E1
SUNRISE PL
1400 MONP 91754 635-J4
SUNRISE RD
200 BREA 92821 709-E7
3200 WCOV 91791 639-D3
SUNRISE ST
2300 LA 90023 634-J6
2900 LA 90023 635-B7
SUNRISE TER
300 PMDL 93551 4285-H1
SUNRISE HILL DR
- Brwd 90049 591-F4
SUNRISE HILL LN
700 SMAD 91024 567-C1
SUNRISE HILLS RD
- LACo 91390 4462-D3
SUNRISE RIDGE LN
3100 HacH 91745 678-A6
SUNRISE RIDGE RD
- LA 91342 481-H5
SUNRISE SUMMIT DR
- SCTA 91351 4551-F4
SUNRISE VIEW LN
- Actn 93510 4375-H6
SUNRISE VIEW PL
- LACo 91390 4461-A3
SUNRISE VIEW ST
- Actn 93510 4375-H6
SUNRIVER DR
800 DBAR 91765 680-E1
W SUN RIVER ST
1400 UPL 91784 571-H6
SUNROSE CT
- BREA 92823 709-J6
SUNROSE PL
30200 SCTA 91387 4462-G4
SUN ROSE ST
400 LVRN 91750 600-C3
SUNSET
500 SDMS 91773 600-A3
1900 LBCH 90810 795-A1
SUNSET AV
- Ven 90291 671-H4
700 PAS 91103 565-G2
1200 SMCA 90405 671-H3
3800 GLDL 91020 534-G3
3800 Mont 91020 534-G2
4700 LaCr 91214 534-G1
4800 LaCr 91214 504-G7
E SUNSET AV
100 SGBL 91776 596-F4
N SUNSET AV
100 INDS 91744 638-B5

N SUNSET AV
100 WCOV 91790 598-F7
300 LPUE 91744 638-B5
600 LACo 91744 638-B5
900 AZU 91702 568-H4
3900 LACo 91722 598-F7
S SUNSET AV
100 AZU 91702 568-H6
100 AZU 91702 598-H1
500 WCOV 91790 598-F7
600 WCOV 91790 638-D3
SUNSET BLVD
9200 BHLS 90210 592-E7
9700 BHLS 90210 632-D1
9900 Wwd 90024 592-E7
S SUNSET BLVD
500 ARCD 91007 566-J6
1100 LACo 91007 566-J6
W SUNSET BLVD
500 LA 90012 634-G2
1100 Echo 90026 634-F1
1400 Echo 90026 594-D7
1500 Hlwd 90028 593-E4
1500 LFlz 90027 594-A4
3900 LA 90029 594-B5
4800 LFlz 90027 593-H4
7100 LA 90046 593-B5
8100 LA 90069 593-B5
8200 WHWD 90046 593-B5
8200 WHWD 90069 593-B5
8400 WHWD 90069 592-H6
10000 BelA 90077 592-B7
10100 Wwd 90024 592-B7
10500 LA 90095 592-B7
10500 LA 90095 632-A1
10500 BelA 90077 632-A1
10700 LA 90095 631-J1
10700 BelA 90077 631-J1
11000 Brwd 90049 631-J1
13300 PacP 90272 631-A5
15600 PacP 90272 630-J5
SUNSET CT
- Ven 90291 671-G5
1100 SBdC 91784 571-J3
S SUNSET CT
500 RBCH 90277 762-H6
SUNSET CUR
2300 SBdC 91784 571-J3
SUNSET DR
- CYP 90630 767-A5
- THO 91362 557-A3
100 THO 91361 557-A3
500 Alta 91001 536-A4
600 HMB 90254 762-G2
700 POM 91768 600-H6
1400 AZU 91702 568-H4
2200 PMDL 93550 4286-E3
3800 LFlz 90027 594-B4
13400 WHIT 90602 677-D7
14000 WHIT 90602 707-E1
18900 Res 91335 530-H6
SUNSET LN
1500 FUL 92833 738-C4
SUNSET PL
- DBAR 91765 680-A2
2800 LA 90005 634-B3
2800 LA 90057 634-B3
N SUNSET PL
100 MNRO 91016 567-E3
S SUNSET PL
100 MNRO 91016 567-E4
SUNSET RD
500 GLDL 91202 564-C1
1500 SBdC 92372 (4472-D2 See Page 4471)
3200 SBdC 92371 (4472-H2 See Page 4471)
SUNSET ST
- NLB 90805 765-D3
N SUNSET ST
100 LHB 90631 708-F5
S SUNSET ST
300 LHB 90631 708-F6
SUNSET TER
500 PMDL 93551 4285-H2
SUNSET TR
17500 LACo 93532 4102-A2
19700 Top 90290 630-A1
SUNSET VW
2800 SIGH 90755 795-H4
SUNSET WY
- Actn 93510 4374-D4
16700 CHLS 91709 710-F3
SUNSET WY E
- SLB 90740 826-H6
SUNSET BLUFF RD
1000 WAL 91789 639-F5
SUNSET CANYON CT
6200 LAN 93536 4104-E6
N SUNSET CANYON DR
100 BURB 91501 533-H5
1000 BURB 91504 533-H4
S SUNSET CANYON DR
100 BURB 91501 533-J6
300 BURB 91501 534-A6
SUNSET CREEK
30100 Cstc 91384 4459-D4
SUNSET CREST DR
2100 LA 90046 592-H3
SUNSET CREST PL
8800 LA 90046 592-H3
SUNSET CROSSING RD
22600 DBAR 91765 640-A6

SUNSET CROSSING RD
22600 INDS 91789 640-A6
SUNSET HEIGHTS DR
2200 LA 90046 592-H3
E SUNSET HILL DR
400 WCOV 91791 639-B1
1400 WCOV 91791 638-H1
SUNSET HILLS DR
- SCTA 91354 4460-F5
SUNSET HILLS RD
1100 WHWD 90069 592-G6
1100 LA 90069 592-G6
SUNSET MEADOW CIR
1400 WAL 91789 639-D4
SUNSET PARK WY
12200 LA 90064 672-A1
SUNSET PEAK MTWY
- LACo - 511-C7
- LACo (541-E1 See Page 511)
- LACo 91711 (541-B7 See Page 511)
- LACo 91711 571-A1
- LACo 91750 570-H1
- LACo 91750 571-A1
- LVRN 91750 570-H1
SUNSET PLAZA DR
1200 LA 90069 592-H4
1200 WHWD 90069 592-H5
1900 LA 90046 592-H3
SUNSET PLAZA PL
8700 LA 90069 592-J4
SUNSET PLAZA TER
8700 LA 90069 592-J4
SUNSET RIDGE CIR
17400 GrnH 91344 481-B7
SUNSET RIDGE CT
6800 CanP 91307 529-D6
SUNSET RIDGE DR
- POM 91766 640-G4
SUNSET RIDGE LN
15400 HacH 91745 678-A5
SUNSET RIDGE RD
- Alta 91001 535-G4
SUNSET SPRINGS RD
- LA 91342 (4723-F6 See Page 4643)
- LACo 91342 (4723-F6 See Page 4643)
- Sunl 91040 (4723-F6 See Page 4643)
SUNSET VALE AV
1100 LA 90069 592-G6
1100 WHWD 90069 592-G6
SUNSET VIEW DR
8300 LA 90069 593-A4
SUNSET VISTA RD
19700 WAL 91789 639-E4
SUNSHINE AV
6200 LAN 93536 4104-E5
12800 SFSP 90670 707-B7
13000 LACo 90605 707-B7
SUNSHINE CT
- SGBL 91776 596-F6
1800 GLDL 91208 564-H1
3800 LA 91604 562-H6
18300 LACo 91744 679-A2
E SUNSHINE CT
1500 LBCH 90813 795-F6
SUNSHINE DR
1100 GLDL 91207 534-G7
1100 GLDL 91208 534-G7
1200 GLDL 91207 564-G1
1300 GLDL 91208 564-G1
SUNSHINE PKWY
- PMDL 93551 4195-E6
SUNSHINE TER
11100 LA 91604 562-G6
11100 LA 91604 563-A6
SUNSHINE CANYON MTWY
- GrnH 91344 481-B1
- StvR 91381 481-B1
- StvR 91381 4641-A7
SUNSHINE CANYON RD
- GrnH 91344 481-C2
SUNSHINE VALLEY CT
- SIMI 93063 499-B1
SUNSIDE DR
7600 LACo 91770 636-E4
SUNSIDE ST
1200 LA 90732 824-A5
W SUNSONG CT
1000 ONT 91762 641-J2
SUNSTAR ST
- PMDL 93551 4195-B4
SUNSTONE PL
15000 Shrm 91403 561-H6
SUNSTONE ST
4800 THO 91362 557-G1
SUNSTREAM AV
3700 PMDL 93550 4286-H3
SUNSWEPT CIR
2100 LAN 93536 4105-D1
SUNSWEPT DR
3600 LA 91604 562-E5
SUN VALLEY CT
5400 AGRH 91301 557-J5
SUN VALLEY DR
9700 MTCL 91763 601-G6
SUNVIEW CT
44000 LAN 93535 4016-C7

STREET Block City ZIP Pg-Grid

SUNVIEW DR
1500 GLDL 91208 534-G4
4400 CHNO 91710 641-E5
SUNVUE PL
1100 LA 90012 634-F2
E SUNWOOD DR
21100 DBAR 91789 679-H2
SUPERBA AV
600 Ven 90291 671-J5
SUPERBA CT
700 Ven 90291 671-J5
SUPERIOR AV
1200 LHB 90631 708-G6
2200 Ven 90291 672-A5
SUPERIOR CT
- LACo 91390 4461-A4
4100 LA 90032 595-C7
SUPERIOR ST
15000 LA 91343 501-D5
16900 Nor 91325 501-A5
18100 Nor 91325 500-J5
18300 Nor 91324 500-F5
19700 Chat 91311 500-D5
SUPI
1100 Top 90290 560-B7
SUPPLY AV
2700 CMRC 90040 676-B5
SUPPLY ST
2300 POM 91767 600-J4
SUPREME CT
4100 LA 90032 595-C7
SUREE ELLEN LN
2200 Alta 91001 536-D6
SURF CT
800 Hrbr 90710 794-B4
SURF PL
100 SLB 90740 826-E3
SURF ST
- PdlR 90293 702-A3
SURFSIDE AV
100 SLB 90740 826-H6
100 SLB 90743 826-H6
SURFSIDE WY
6400 MAL 90265 667-A1
SURFVIEW DR
100 LA 90265 630-E5
100 LACo 90265 630-E6
100 PacP 90272 630-E5
SURFVIEW LN
17900 PacP 90272 630-F5
SURFWOOD RD
3500 LACo 90265 630-E5
SURREY AV
9000 MTCL 91763 601-F4
11100 SBdC 91710 641-F3
SURREY CT
42400 LACo 93536 4104-F5
SURREY DR
2500 LACo 91724 639-G1
4200 CYP 90630 767-B6
E SURREY DR
6400 LBCH 90815 796-E6
SURREY LN
- ING 90305 703-F3
- RPV 90275 823-F2
1700 POM 91768 600-E7
5600 WHIT 90601 677-C5
15400 LMRD 90638 707-H7
SURREY PL
16400 HacH 91745 678-E4
SURRY CT
300 BREA 92821 709-B5
SURRY ST
3000 LFlz 90027 594-C3
SURVEYOR AV
200 BREA 92821 709-G7
SURVEYOR ST
3000 POM 91768 640-C2
SUSAN AV
- DWNY 90240 706-A2
10300 DWNY 90241 705-J2
11900 DWNY 90242 705-H5
14600 BLF 90706 736-A3
SUSAN CIR
7400 LPMA 90623 767-D2
SUSAN CT
1000 LVRN 91750 570-E7
39600 PMDL 93551 4195-H4
SUSAN DR
1200 CRSN 90745 764-F6
11800 GrnH 91344 481-D7
SUSAN LN
1400 LHB 90631 708-G4
SUSAN PL
18300 CRTS 90703 767-A1
SUSAN WY
100 MONP 91755 636-B3
SUSANA
2600 LACo 90220 765-A1
SUSANA AV
400 RBCH 90277 763-A6
22200 TOR 90505 763-A7
22400 TOR 90505 793-A1
SUSANA RD
20400 CRSN 90810 765-B4
S SUSANA RD
17400 COMP 90221 735-B7
17400 RDom 90221 735-B7
17600 COMP 90221 765-B1
17600 RDom 90221 765-B1
18400 NLB 90805 765-B1
SUSAN BETH WY
27600 SCTA 91350 4461-B6

SUSAN BROOK PL
- DUAR 91010 568-D3
SUSAN CAROLE DR
20900 SCTA 91350 4461-C6
SUSANGLEN CIR
- LHB 90631 708-D6
S SUSANNA AV
700 WCOV 91790 638-G2
SUSANNAH CT
- AZU 91702 568-H3
SUSAN RUTH ST
20600 SCTA 91350 4461-D5
SUSQUEHANNA AV
13900 BALD 91706 598-B6
SUSQUEHANNA CIR
- BALD 91706 598-B6
SUSSEX CIR
4100 CYP 90630 767-A6
SUSSEX CT
1600 PMDL 93550 4286-D3
1900 GLDL 91206 565-B1
SUSSEX LN
- ING 90305 703-F3
2900 LA 90023 675-A1
SUSSEX RD
800 SMRO 91108 596-B2
SUTHERLAND CT
- BPK 90621 737-F6
SUTHERLAND ST
1300 Echo 90026 594-E7
1500 LAN 93534 4015-E3
SUTHERLAND WY
13600 LMRD 90639 737-F2
SUTOW AL
400 SPAS 91030 595-F2
SUTRO AV
3700 LA 90008 673-G2
3700 LA 90018 673-G2
14700 GAR 90249 733-G4
SUTRO WK
3000 LA 90008 673-F3
SUTTER AV
9200 SunV 91352 502-H6
10600 Pcma 91331 502-C2
SUTTER CT
100 SDMS 91773 599-H2
SUTTER ST
4900 CHNO 91710 641-F6
SUTTER WY
2300 FUL 92833 738-A3
SUTTER CREEK
100 MNRO 91016 567-G2
SUTTER CREEK DR
18800 WAL 91789 639-B7
SUTTERS MILL CT
- LACo 91390 4461-B4
SUTTERS MILL DR
2400 DBAR 91765 679-G6
SUTTERS POINTE DR
27600 SCTA 91350 4461-B6
SUTTON CT
300 POM 91767 601-A5
SUTTON PL
4300 Shrm 91403 561-J5
SUTTON ST
13000 CRTS 90703 737-B7
13100 CRTS 90703 767-B1
14600 Shrm 91403 561-G5
15400 Enc 91436 561-F4
SUTTON WY
- SBdC 91710 641-B7
100 BHLS 90210 592-E5
100 LA 90210 592-E5
SUVA ST
6500 BGDN 90201 705-J1
6700 BGDN 90201 706-A1
6900 DWNY 90240 706-B2
N SUZANNE LN
- LACo 91387 4552-B5
SUZANNE RD
100 WAL 91789 639-G6
SUZANNE MARIE CT
200 AZU 91702 598-J1
SWAIN ST
1200 GLDR 91740 599-H1
15700 LA 91342 481-F2
N SWALL DR
100 BHLS 90211 632-H2
100 LA 90048 632-H1
100 WHWD 90048 592-H7
100 WHWD 90048 632-H1
S SWALL DR
100 BHLS 90211 632-H3
100 LA 90048 632-H1
1100 LA 90035 632-H3
SWALLOW CT
19900 SCTA 91351 4551-E3
SWALLOW DR
9200 LA 90069 592-H3
SWALLOW GN
900 WCOV 91790 638-H6
SWALLOW LN
- BREA 92823 709-H6
2400 PMDL 93550 4286-E3
SWALLOW HILL DR
- SBdC 92397 (4652-A1
See Page 4651)
26600 LACo 92397 (4652-A1
See Page 4651)
SWAN CIR
8000 LPMA 90623 767-B4
SWAN DR
1100 PMDL 93550 4286-C4

SWAN LN
- LACo 91387 4551-J5
SWAN PL
2900 Echo 90026 594-C5
SWANEE LN
400 COV 91723 599-A6
15100 BALD 91706 598-D6
19300 LACo 91723 599-C6
E SWANEE LN
1000 WCOV 91790 598-G6
W SWANEE LN
1000 WCOV 91790 598-E6
SWANSEA CIR
1800 LHB 90631 708-G4
SWAN SEA PL
1000 LA 90029 593-H6
SWARTHMORE AV
300 PacP 90272 631-A6
N SWARTHMORE AV
1000 PacP 90272 631-A5
SWARTHMORE CT
- CLAR 91711 571-E4
SWARTHMORE DR
1200 GLDL 91206 564-H2
SWARTHOUT LN
- SBdC 92397 (4652-E3
See Page 4651)
SWEET AV
200 FUL 92833 738-E7
SWEET PL
15700 HacH 91745 678-B3
SWEETAIRE AV
15200 LACo 93535 4199-E2
SWEETBAY RD
- RPV 90275 823-B4
SWEETBRIAR DR
100 CLAR 91711 571-D5
1100 GLDL 91206 564-G3
SWEETBRIAR LN
12300 Pcma 91331 502-H4
SWEETBRIER ST
1500 PMDL 93550 4196-C7
SWEETBRUSH ST
37700 PMDL 93552 4287-B2
SWEETCAP LN
9700 LACo 91390 4373-G3
SWEET ELM DR
18000 Enc 91316 561-A6
18100 Enc 91316 560-J5
SWEET GRASS LN
14000 CHLS 91709 680-H3
SWEETGRASS LN
- RHE 90274 823-F1
SWEET GUM LN
16500 WHIT 90603 708-A6
SWEETGUM LN
- LACo 91387 4551-J4
- LACo 91387 4552-A4
SWEET JASMINE LN
- WdHl 91367 559-H7
SWEETLAND ST
800 CLAR 91711 601-B3
SWEET SHADE LN
24300 SCTA 91321 4641-B2
SWEET WATER CT
2400 CHLS 91709 680-J4
SWEETWATER DR
2300 BREA 92821 709-E6
34500 LACo 91390 4373-G3
SWEETWATER LN
- SCTA 91354 4460-G5
SWEETWATER CANYON RD
3600 MAL 90265 629-B6
SWEETWATER MESA RD
3300 MAL 90265 629-B6
N SWEETZER AV
100 LA 90048 633-A1
300 LA 90048 593-A7
500 WHWD 90048 593-A7
700 LA 90046 593-A5
700 LA 90069 593-A5
800 WHWD 90069 593-A5
900 WHWD 90046 593-A5
S SWEETZER AV
100 LA 90048 633-A2
SWENSON DR
22100 Top 90290 629-G2
SWIFT CT
- LVRN 91750 570-H6
SWIFT DR
14300 LMRD 90638 737-E2
SWIFTWATER WY
2200 GLDR 91741 570-A6
N SWINDON AV
2000 SIMI 93063 499-C2
SWINFORD ST
100 SPed 90731 824-D3
SWING PATH DR
- PMDL 93550 4106-A6
SWINTON AV
4800 Enc 91436 561-F3
8700 LA 91343 501-E5
8700 LA 91343 531-E1
10400 GrnH 91344 501-E1
11500 GrnH 91344 481-E7
SWISS TRAIL RD
900 DUAR 91010 568-D5
SWITZER AL
1300 PAS 91107 566-E1
1300 LACo 91107 566-E1

E SWOPE ST
300 CRSN 90745 764-D7
SYBLE AV
14500 BLF 90706 736-A3
SYBRANDY AV
17400 CRTS 90703 736-J7
17600 CRTS 90703 766-J1
SYCAMORE
1400 RowH 91748 679-B4
2800 WCOV 91792 679-C1
15400 LA 91342 481-G1
SYCAMORE AV
- LA 91342 481-J1
- LA 91342 482-A1
- ARCD 91006 567-C3
400 GLDR 91741 569-F5
700 LHB 90631 708-F4
1000 SPAS 91030 595-E2
1400 GLDL 91201 534-A7
2600 GLDL 91208 534-F2
2600 GLDL 91020 534-F2
2800 GLDL 91214 534-F2
3700 LACo 91107 566-H5
12300 CHNO 91710 641-J6
E SYCAMORE AV
- ARCD 91006 567-D3
200 ELSG 90245 702-F7
N SYCAMORE AV
- LACo 91107 566-G4
100 LA 90036 633-D1
300 LA 90036 593-D7
700 LA 90038 593-D5
1300 Hlwd 90028 593-D4
1800 LA 90068 593-D3
S SYCAMORE AV
100 LA 90036 633-D2
300 CLAR 91711 601-E4
1000 LA 90019 633-D4
2100 LA 90016 633-C6
3000 LA 90016 673-C1
3800 LA 90008 673-C2
W SYCAMORE AV
100 ELSG 90245 702-D7
SYCAMORE CT
- Saug 91350 4461-B4
SYCAMORE DR
- Saug 91350 4461-B4
800 AZU 91702 569-B5
1600 Top 90290 589-G3
1800 SMRO 91108 596-E2
2500 LVRN 91750 600-H2
4900 LA 90230 672-F4
12800 NRWK 90650 736-J1
13500 WHIT 90601 677-D5
N SYCAMORE DR
100 SGBL 91775 596-D3
100 SGBL 91776 596-D3
W SYCAMORE DR
600 SGBL 91775 596-C3
SYCAMORE GN
200 PAS 91105 565-D6
1800 CHLS 91709 680-H3
SYCAMORE LN
- BPK 90621 737-J6
- BRAD 91010 568-A3
- CYP 90630 767-D7
- LACo 91768 640-A1
- RHE 90274 823-A1
2300 PMDL 93551 4195-D5
6500 PMDL 93551 4104-D7
SYCAMORE PK
- DBAR 91765 680-B1
SYCAMORE PL
- WdHl 91364 559-J5
100 SMAD 91024 567-B1
1600 POM 91768 600-G6
S SYCAMORE PL
500 ING 90301 703-B3
SYCAMORE RD
300 LA 90402 631-B7
700 SBdC 92372 (4472-B5
See Page 4471)
SYCAMORE ST
- CRSN 90746 764-D4
100 MTBL 90640 676-B5
1200 CMRC 90040 676-B5
5300 SBdC 92372 (4652-E3
See Page 4651)
11900 NRWK 90650 736-H3
SYCAMORE TER
4800 HiPk 90042 595-B3
SYCAMORE TR
7100 LA 90068 593-C1
SYCAMORE WY
- Hrbr 90710 794-C3
SYCAMORE CANYON DR
1600 THO 91361 586-H1
1600 WLKV 91361 586-H1
SYCAMORE CANYON RD
- LACo 90601 677-A3
- WHIT 90601 677-A3
1700 SDMS 91773 570-C5
SYCAMORE CONNECTOR RD
- MTBL 90640 676-B5
SYCAMORE CREEK DR
22900 SCTA 91354 4460-H6
27900 SCTA 91390 4460-H6
SYCAMORE FLATS MTWY
2500 SDMS 91773 570-C2
SYCAMORE MEADOW DR
- StvR 91381 4550-C4
6200 MAL 90265 668-A1

SYCAMORE PARK DR
100 LA 90031 595-B4
SYCAMORE VILLAGE DR
12800 NRWK 90650 736-J1
N SYDNEY AV
700 ELA 90022 635-F5
S SYDNEY DR
400 ELA 90022 635-F7
1400 CMRC 90040 675-F2
SYLMAR AV
4400 Shrm 91423 562-A3
5200 VanN 91401 562-A2
6100 VanN 91401 532-A6
6600 VanN 91405 532-A4
8100 PanC 91402 532-A1
8700 PanC 91402 502-A6
SYLVAN DR
6100 VeCo 93063 499-B3
43600 LACo 93532 4101-H2
SYLVAN LN
2300 GLDL 91208 534-H7
SYLVAN ST
10700 NHol 91606 533-A7
11100 NHol 91606 532-F7
13100 VanN 91401 532-A7
14500 VanN 91411 532-A7
14600 VanN 91411 531-G7
18200 Res 91335 530-F7
22200 WdHl 91367 529-E7
37000 PMDL 93552 4286-J4
SYLVAN GLEN RD
24000 LACo 91302 589-D5
24100 DBAR 91765 640-D6
SYLVANIA LN
1700 Top 90290 590-D3
SYLVANOAK DR
700 GLDL 91206 564-G3
SYLVANWOOD AV
13900 NRWK 90650 736-G3
20400 LKWD 90715 766-G4
SYLVESTER ST
12000 LA 90066 672-D4
SYLVIA AV
5300 Tarz 91356 560-G1
6100 Res 91335 530-G4
8300 Nor 91324 530-G2
9500 Nor 91324 500-G5
10300 Nor 91326 500-G3
W SYLVIA CT
1400 UPL 91786 601-H1
SYLVIA DR
29000 SCTA 91387 4552-E1
29000 SCTA 91387 4462-E7
SYLVIA ST
2100 WCOV 91792 679-A1
SYLVIAN LN
2400 LVRN 91750 600-E2
SYMPHONY CT
5500 LAN 93536 4104-G4
SYMPHONY LN
4800 VeCo 91377 557-G2
16600 CRTS 90703 737-B6
SYRACUSE AV
600 BALD 91706 637-H1
3200 BALD 91706 597-H7
3300 Actn 93510 4465-A2
SYRACUSE DR
800 CLAR 91711 601-B1
SYRACUSE ST
14100 LACo 90604 707-E6
N SYRACUSE WK
100 LBCH 90803 826-D2
SYRINGA ST
11200 SFSP 90670 706-F4

T

TABARD RD
600 LACo 90265 629-F1
TABLE MOUNTAIN RD
- Valy 93563 (4561-F6
See Page 4471)
4500 PMDL 93552 4287-F2
TABLER AV
4500 LAN 93535 4016-A6
TABOR LN
1300 LVRN 91750 600-F1
TABOR PL
9800 SFSP 90670 706-J4
TABOR ST
9600 LA 90034 632-F7
10100 LA 90034 672-E1
11200 LA 90066 672-D2
TACANA ST
4700 LA 90008 673-C2
TACKABERRY CT
29000 AGRH 91301 558-A3
TACKSTEM ST
37700 PMDL 93552 4287-B2
TACOMA AV
3500 LA 90065 594-J4
TACOMA CT
37500 PMDL 93552 4286-J3
TACOMA ST
37600 PMDL 93552 4286-J2
TACUBA DR
14500 LMRD 90638 737-E1
TACUBA ST
800 LA 90065 594-J3
TADDY ST
11200 NRWK 90650 736-F3
TADMORE ST
17400 LACo 91744 678-H1

TAFT AV
1600 Hlwd 90028 593-G4
1900 LA 90068 593-G3
3700 SBdC 91710 641-C4
5700 SGAT 90280 705-G7
5700 SGAT 90280 735-G1
TAFT CT
600 MONP 91755 636-D4
28600 Cstc 91384 4459-C7
TAFT LN
- PMDL 93551 4195-D5
TAFT ST
4900 CHNO 91710 641-F4
TAFT WY
700 SMCA 90401 671-F2
TAGUS ST
9900 LACo 90601 676-J2
9900 PRV 90660 676-J2
TAHITI AV
100 PacP 90272 630-J6
TAHITI WY
13700 LA 90292 701-J1
13900 MdlR 90292 701-J1
13900 MdlR 90292 702-A1
TAHOE AV
11700 HAW 90250 703-B7
12000 LACo 90250 733-B1
TAHOE CIR
5600 BPK 90621 737-J6
TAHOE CT
- LACo 91390 4460-J4
TAHOE DR
- SCTA 91354 4550-H1
6300 LA 90068 563-F7
6400 LA 90068 593-E1
TAHOE LN
- WCOV 91791 639-A4
TAHOE PL
3200 LA 90068 563-E7
TAHOE WY
44000 LAN 93536 4104-E1
44100 LAN 93536 4014-E7
TAHQUITZ PL
200 PMDL 93550 4286-A3
500 PacP 90272 630-J5
TAINTOR RD
100 PMDL 93550 4285-J1
TAJAUTA AV
19000 CRSN 90746 764-G3
N TAJAUTA AV
100 COMP 90220 734-G4
1400 COMP 90222 734-G4
1400 Wbrk 90222 734-G4
S TAJAUTA AV
100 COMP 90220 734-G5
13800 Wbrk 90222 734-G3
TALAVERA LN
- BqtC 91354 4460-F3
TALAVERA ST
- LBCH 90814 796-C7
TALBERT ST
400 PdlR 90293 702-B3
W TALBERT ST
7800 PdlR 90293 702-C3
7800 Wch 90045 702-C3
TALBOT DR
- LMRD 90639 737-F2
12400 LMRD 90638 737-H4
TALC ST
13600 SFSP 90670 737-C4
TALENTO WY
4500 PMDL 93551 4194-J2
TALI ST
43400 LAN 93535 4106-C2
TALISMAN ST
19400 TOR 90503 763-C4
TALLAC DR
800 ARCD 91007 566-J5
800 ARCD 91007 567-A5
TALL PINE CT
- SunV 91352 533-A2
TALL PINE DR
2200 DUAR 91010 568-C3
TALLYHAND RD
- RHLS 90274 823-D1
TALLYRAND DR
24400 DBAR 91765 680-E2
TALMADGE ST
1300 LFlz 90027 594-B3
TALMAGE V BURKE WY
- ALH 91801 596-B4
TALOFA AV
4300 LA 91602 563-C4
TALOGA ST
15500 HacH 91745 678-A5
TALUS PL
12000 LA 90210 592-G1
TAM CT
2000 SIMI 93063 499-B2
TAMAR DR
400 LPUE 91746 638-A4
1600 WCOV 91790 638-C2
14300 LACo 91746 638-C2
W TAMARA DR
3000 ANA 92804 767-J6
TAMARA LN
- LACo 90606 676-H6
TAMARA PL
- Saug 91350 4461-D5
37800 PMDL 93550 4286-G2
TAMARAC DR
200 PAS 91105 565-D6

TAMARACK
12500 ELMN 91732 637-G1
TAMARACK AV
400 BREA 92821 709-B5
8600 SunV 91352 532-H1
9200 SunV 91352 502-G6
9800 Pcma 91331 502-C2
11300 LA 91340 502-B1
E TAMARACK AV
100 ING 90301 703-C3
TAMARACK CT
- LA 91343 501-H6
N TAMARACK DR
800 FUL 92832 738-G6
TAMARACK LN
5500 PMDL 93552 4287-C4
22600 SCTA 91390 4460-H2
TAMARACK RD
400 SBdC 92372 (4472-B7
See Page 4471)
TAMARACK ST
1900 THO 91361 557-A4
TAMARIND AV
1100 LA 90038 593-G5
1300 Hlwd 90028 593-G4
1900 LA 90068 593-G3
N TAMARIND AV
100 COMP 90220 734-J3
1100 COMP 90222 734-J3
1600 Wbrk 90222 734-J3
S TAMARIND AV
100 COMP 90220 734-J4
500 COMP 90220 735-A6
TAMARIND CT
- PMDL 93551 4285-D3
TAMARIND ST
6000 VeCo 91377 558-A3
TAMARIND WY
- SCTA 91354 4460-G5
TAMARISK CIR
1200 UPL 91784 571-J6
TAMARISK DR
- PMDL 93551 4195-B3
5000 LVRN 91750 570-G4
TAMARISK PL
25700 SCTA 91355 4550-F7
TAMARIX DR
14700 HacH 91745 677-H3
TAMBERLY LN
- Tuj 91042 503-J2
TAMBO PL
21300 DBAR 91765 679-H5
TAMBOR CT
1900 RowH 91748 678-J5
TAMBOR DR
1700 GLDL 91208 564-J1
TAMBORA DR
27700 SCTA 91351 4551-G1
28100 SCTA 91351 4461-G7
TAMCLIFF AV
17800 CRSN 90746 764-E1
TAMERLANE DR
1800 GLDL 91208 534-H7
TAMORA AV
2400 ELMN 91733 637-A3
2400 SELM 91733 637-A3
TAM O SHANTER DR
20400 LACo 91789 679-F4
TAM OSHANTER DR
1200 AZU 91702 568-H4
TAMOSHANTER LN
4300 Tarz 91356 560-F5
TAM OSHANTER RD
32000 Llan 93544 4469-F1
TAMOSHANTER RD
1600 SLB 90740 826-H1
TAMPA AV
5100 Tarz 91356 560-G1
6000 Tarz 91356 530-G7
6100 Res 91335 530-G3
8200 Nor 91324 530-G3
8800 Nor 91324 500-G6
10300 Nor 91326 500-F1
11600 Nor 91326 480-F7
TAMPA CT
37300 PMDL 93552 4286-J3
TAMPA LN
- SBdC 92397 (4652-E4
See Page 4651)
TAMPA ST
2400 POM 91766 641-A6
TAMPICO AV
3800 LA 90032 595-E5
TAMPICO DR
26000 SCTA 91355 4550-G4
TAMPICO WY
800 MTBL 90640 636-E7
TAMWORTH AV
7100 LACo 91775 566-G7
TANA AV
11500 LACo 90604 707-F6
TANAGER AV
2700 CMRC 90040 676-B5
TANAGER CT
20000 SCTA 91351 4551-E4
TANAGER WY
1400 LA 90069 592-H5
TANAMACHI LN
15600 LA 90247 734-B5
TANBARK CT
1500 THO 91361 557-A6
TANBARK PL
3900 GLDL 91214 534-D1

TANBARK FLATS RD
- LACo - (540-F3
See Page 509)
TANCYN RD
500 DUAR 91010 568-E4
TANDEM WY
25200 TOR 90505 793-E4
TANFIELD DR
12000 LMRD 90638 707-F7
12200 LACo 90604 707-F7
12200 LACo 90604 737-F1
12600 LMRD 90638 737-F1
N TANFORAN LN
200 DBAR 91765 640-D6
TANGELO LN
1100 LHH 90631 708-F3
TANGELO PL
6000 SIMI 93063 499-B3
TANGENT LN
11300 LKWD 90715 766-F4
TANGERINE DR
- BREA 92823 709-J6
TANGERINE RD
- RPV 90275 823-B4
TANGERINE ST
- PMDL 93551 4285-E3
TANGIER AV
13500 BLF 90706 736-B2
TANGIER PL
600 POM 91768 640-B2
TANGLEWOOD
- WCOV 91791 639-A4
TANGLEWOOD DR
- POM 91766 640-G5
100 SDMS 91773 600-C3
TANGLEWOOD LN
- HacH 91745 637-H7
3400 RHE 90274 793-E6
14600 CHLS 91709 680-H4
TANGLEWOOD ST
1200 LPUE 91744 638-G7
1600 BREA 92821 708-H6
5300 LBCH 90808 766-B4
5700 LKWD 90713 766-C4
TANGLEWOOD WY
5100 PMDL 93551 4194-H1
TANGO DR
- BqtC 91354 4460-E3
N TANK RD
- BREA 92823 710-D3
S TANK RD
- BREA 92823 710-D4
- OrCo 92823 710-D4
TANK FARM RD
20400 CRSN 90746 764-G5
20900 CRSN 90745 764-G5
TANK FIRE RD
- HacH 91745 677-D3
- LACo 90601 677-D3
- WHIT 90601 677-D3
TANNAHILL AV
26800 SCTA 91387 4552-D6
TANNENCREST DR
3400 DUAR 91010 568-F3
TANNERBERG CT
800 CRSN 90746 764-E1
TANNER BRIDGE RD
1500 BelA 90077 591-J4
TANNER RIDGE AV
400 THO 91362 557-G1
TANNERS RD
13100 Brwd 90049 631-D1
TANOAK LN
900 VeCo 91377 557-G1
TANOBLE DR
2300 Alta 91001 536-C6
TAN PAN TR
3300 CALB 90290 589-F1
TANTALUS DR
6200 MAL 90265 668-A1
TANYA AV
22100 CRSN 90810 765-A7
TAOS CIR
4400 CRTS 90703 767-B3
TAOS CT
1400 UPL 91784 571-H5
TAOS DR
5100 MTCL 91763 601-G6
TAOS PL
200 PMDL 93550 4286-A3
TAOS RD
- Alta 91001 535-J3
TAPER AV
400 COMP 90220 734-F5
1600 SPed 90731 824-A1
2200 LA 90732 823-J1
2200 SPed 90731 823-J1
TAPER DR
600 SLB 90740 826-F4
TAPER ST
1200 LBCH 90810 795-B1
TAPIA DR
6100 MAL 90265 627-A7
TAPIA ST
15800 IRW 91706 598-F3
TAPIA CANYON RD
26900 BqtC 91354 (4370-D7
See Page 4279)
26900 Cstc 91384 (4370-D7
See Page 4279)
26900 Cstc 91384 4459-H1
26900 Cstc 91384 4460-A1

TAPLEY CT
1900 SIMI 93063 499-C2
TAPLEY ST
6500 SIMI 93063 499-C2
TARA CT
- LAN 93536 4013-J5
1600 LAN 93535 4016-C5
TARA DR
4500 Enc 91436 561-D4
TARA TER
4900 CULC 90230 672-H3
TARANTO AV
24300 SCTA 91355 4550-F6
TARANTO WY
4800 VeCo 91377 557-G2
10600 BelA 90077 592-A5
TARAPACA RD
30500 RPV 90275 823-G6
TARCUTO WY
800 BelA 90077 591-J7
TARECO DR
3200 LA 90068 593-D1
3200 LA 90068 563-D7
TARLETON ST
1600 LA 90021 674-F1
1900 LA 90011 674-F1
E TARMA ST
7800 LBCH 90808 796-H1
8000 LBCH 90808 766-J7
TARO WY
800 BelA 90077 592-A6
TARPAN PL
- WAL 91789 639-C5
TARQUIN ST
12900 LA 91342 482-D3
TARR PL
1800 POM 91766 640-J4
TARRAGON DR
44400 LAN 93536 4015-D6
TARRAGON RD
6300 RPV 90275 822-J4
TARRANT AV
15200 LACo 90220 734-E4
16300 CRSN 90746 734-E6
S TARRANT AV
15400 LACo 90220 734-E5
TARRASA DR
27600 RPV 90275 823-J1
TARRON AV
11500 HAW 90250 703-H7
TARRYBRAE TER
3900 Tarz 91356 560-F6
TARRYGLEN LN
1200 SDMS 91773 570-B7
TARRYTON AV
8700 WHIT 90605 707-D2
9200 LACo 90605 707-D3
TARRYTOWN DR
2500 FUL 92833 738-B5
TARRYTOWN LN
3900 AGRH 91301 558-E7
TARTA CT
1000 LACo 91789 679-E4
S TARTAR LN
1600 COMP 90221 735-A6
TARYN DR
27600 SCTA 91350 4460-J5
TARZANA DR
18200 Tarz 91356 560-J3
TARZANA ST
17200 Enc 91316 561-A3
18100 Tarz 91356 561-A3
18200 Tarz 91356 560-J3
TARZANA ESTATES DR
4200 Tarz 91356 560-F5
TARZANA FIRE RD
2900 Tarz 91356 560-G7
2900 Tarz 91356 590-G1
TARZANA WOODS DR
4900 Tarz 91356 560-F3
TARZON ST
4400 City 90063 635-F2
TASMAN AV
300 POM 91767 601-A5
TATAVIAM RD
33600 LACo 91390 4373-H6
TATE AV
300 GLDR 91741 569-F6
TATE ST
200 POM 91767 600-J6
TATINA LN
- LACo 91390 4463-C2
TATUM ST
3000 LA 90065 594-H4
TAU PL
20300 Chat 91311 500-D3
TAVENER AV
11200 LA 90230 672-F4
TAVERN TR
2100 LA 90046 593-A3
TAVISTOCK AV
200 Brwd 90049 631-J1
TAWNY CT
1500 DBAR 91765 679-J4
TAYLOR AV
- CYP 90630 767-A6
700 MTBL 90640 636-D7
N TAYLOR AV
100 MTBL 90640 676-D1
600 MTBL 90640 636-D7
S TAYLOR AV
100 MTBL 90640 676-C2

TAYLOR CT
- LACo 91390 4461-A4
100 BREA 92821 709-B7
16200 TOR 90504 733-H6
18200 TOR 90504 763-H2
N TAYLOR CT
500 WCOV 91790 598-F6
TAYLOR DR
300 CLAR 91711 601-B3
500 MONP 91755 636-C5
TAYLOR ST
100 MNRO 91016 567-G7
200 NLB 90805 735-B6
8000 BPK 90621 737-J6
29700 Cstc 91384 4459-C7
TAYLOR CANYON MTWY
- LACo 91390 (4280-D6
See Page 4279)
TEA LN
100 BREA 92821 709-A7
TEAGARDEN LN
2000 ALH 91801 595-J5
TEAGUE DR
200 SDMS 91773 600-C3
TEAK CT
- SCTA 91354 4460-F4
TEAK ST
900 BREA 92821 738-J1
TEAKWOOD AV
300 LHB 90631 738-D1
TEAKWOOD LN
500 BREA 92821 709-A5
700 SDMS 91773 600-C3
TEAKWOOD RD
700 Brwd 90049 631-E1
TEAL CT
- BURB 91505 563-E4
- LACo 91387 4551-J6
TEAL ST
2800 LVRN 91750 570-J6
37600 PMDL 93552 4287-D2
TEAL TER
28800 MAL 90265 667-F1
TEALE ST
11800 LA 90230 672-G6
TEAL RIDGE CT
- LMRD 90638 738-B3
TEASDALE DR
1200 CLAR 91711 601-A1
TEASDALE ST
6500 LAN 93536 4104-D5
TEASEDALE PL
- Cstc 91384 4459-G5
TEASLEY ST
2300 LaCr 91214 504-G7
TEAZLE CANYON RD
9700 Sunl 91040 503-D4
TEBO AV
12300 CHNO 91710 641-G6
TECHNOLOGY DR
300 PMDL 93550 4195-J6
300 PMDL 93550 4196-A6
400 PMDL 93551 4195-G6
26200 SCTA 91355 4460-A7
TECHNOLOGY PL
2000 LBCH 90810 795-A4
TECUM RD
9700 DWNY 90240 706-A2
TECUMSEH AV
3100 SGAT 90280 705-A5
3200 LYN 90262 705-A5
TEDEMORY DR
13400 WHIT 90602 707-D1
13800 WHIT 90605 707-E1
E TEDFORD DR
14000 LACo 90604 737-D1
14200 LACo 90604 707-E7
TEDFORD WY
400 MONP 91754 635-J3
TEDREGAL CT
4400 CALB 91302 559-D6
TEDROW DR
100 GLDR 91740 569-E7
TEE PL
31700 Llan 93544 4469-E1
TEED ST
600 LA 90012 634-G3
TEESDALE AV
4200 LA 91604 562-E4
5100 LA 91607 562-E3
6000 NHol 91606 532-E6
6700 NHol 91605 532-E2
TEGNER DR
700 MONP 91755 636-D4
700 LACo 91770 636-D4
TEHACHAPI DR
700 Bxby 90807 765-F5
TEHAMA ST
5500 HiPk 90042 565-C7
TEJON PL
300 PVE 90274 792-H4
TELAMON LN
800 POM 91766 641-B4
TELECHRON AV
- LACo 90605 707-C7
S TELECHRON AV
12300 LACo 90605 707-C7
TELEGA PL
200 PMDL 93550 4286-A3
TELEGRAPH RD
4300 LACo 90023 675-F1
4400 CMRC 90023 675-F1
4400 CMRC 90022 675-F1

STREET Block City ZIP Pg-Grid

TELEGRAPH RD
4400 ELA 90022 675-F1
5400 CMRC 90040 675-J3
6300 CMRC 90040 676-B6
7100 MTBL 90640 676-B6
7700 PRV 90660 676-B6
7800 DWNY 90240 676-B6
7800 DWNY 90240 706-D1
7800 PRV 90660 706-D1
9700 SFSP 90670 706-G4
12400 SFSP 90670 707-A4
13300 LACo 90605 707-A4
13300 SFSP 90605 707-A4
13600 LACo 90604 707-D5
14500 LMRD 90638 707-D5
14700 LACo 90604 737-F1
14700 LMRD 90638 737-F1
TELEGRAPH CANYON TR
- BREA 92823 710-A7
17600 OrCo 92886 710-A7
TELEGRAPH HILL CT
24000 SCTA 91355 4550-F4
TELEPHONE AV
11300 SBdC 91710 641-G4
11700 CHNO 91710 641-G5
TELEPHONE RD
- LACo 91390 4373-G5
- LACo 93551 4285-A7
- PMDL 93551 (4284-J6 See Page 4283)
36000 Actn 93510 (4284-J7 See Page 4283)
36000 Actn 93510 4374-J1
36000 LACo 93551 (4284-J7 See Page 4283)
TELEPHONE CO RD
- LACo 91390 4373-B2
TELEPHONE LINE RD
- CHLS 91709 710-H4
TELFAIR AV
8300 SunV 91352 532-H1
8800 SunV 91352 502-F6
9700 Pcma 91331 502-C3
11300 LA 91340 502-B1
12300 LA 91342 481-F4
TELFORD ST
2400 MONP 91754 635-H6
5000 ELA 90022 635-H6
TELLEFSON RD
5700 CULC 90230 672-H5
TELLEM DR
1000 PacP 90272 630-H4
TELLER AV
32600 LACo 91390 (4372-J7 See Page 4281)
TELLEZ ST
17900 Res 91335 531-A6
TELLGATE DR
23600 DBAR 91765 640-C5
TELLURIDE DR
13200 CHLS 91709 680-J1
14300 BALD 91706 598-C7
TELLURIDE ST
4100 LA 90031 595-C7
4100 LA 90032 595-C7
TELO AV
23500 TOR 90505 793-E2
TELSTAR AV
9000 ELMN 91731 636-J1
9400 ELMN 91731 637-A1
9600 ELMN 91731 597-A7
TELSTAR WY
- BREA 92821 709-B7
TEMECULA CT
1000 SDMS 91773 570-C7
TEMECULA ST
15900 PacP 90272 630-J5
TEMESCAL CANYON RD
100 PacP 90272 630-J3
100 PacP 90272 631-A5
TEMESCAL FIRE RD
- PacP 90272 590-G3
1300 PacP 90272 631-A3
1400 PacP 90272 630-H1
TEMMA CT
4200 CALB 91302 559-G5
TEMMERA LN
200 GLDR 91740 599-E1
TEMPE DR
3200 HNTB 92649 826-J6
5400 PMDL 93552 4287-C5
TEMPE WY
32300 WLKV 91361 557-C7
TEMPLAR DR
14900 LMRD 90638 737-G3
TEMPLE AL
1300 PAS 91104 566-B2
TEMPLE AV
- LBCH 90803 825-H1
100 INDS 91746 637-H2
100 LACo 91746 637-H3
300 LBCH 90814 825-H1
300 LBCH 90814 795-H7
500 LBCH 90814 795-H7
500 LPUE 91746 638-B4
700 LBCH 90804 795-H7
2200 SIGH 90755 795-H2
2400 LBCH 90808 795-H2
2400 WCOV 91792 638-H7
2500 LACo 91744 638-H7
3000 POM 91765 640-C3
3200 POM 91766 640-C3
3200 POM 91769 640-C3
3200 POM 91768 640-C3

TEMPLE AV
13600 LACo 91746 638-B4
14300 LPUE 91744 638-B4
16000 INDS 91744 638-F6
20100 WAL 91789 639-H3
21700 LACo 91768 639-H3
21900 LACo 91768 640-A3
23900 DBAR 91765 640-C3
N TEMPLE AV
1800 SIGH 90755 795-H4
2100 LBCH 90755 795-H4
2800 LBCH 90808 795-H4
S TEMPLE AV
1000 COMP 90221 735-B6
E TEMPLE ST
100 LA 90012 634-G4
W TEMPLE ST
100 LA 90012 634-F2
300 Echo 90026 634-C1
3200 Echo 90026 594-B7
3400 LA 90004 594-B7
TEMPLE TER
4600 HiPk 90042 595-E4
E TEMPLE WY
1500 Wwd 90024 632-C4
3300 WCOV 91791 599-D7
N TEMPLE WY
10700 Wwd 90024 632-C4
TEMPLE CITY BLVD
3500 RSMD 91770 597-A7
4100 ELMN 91731 597-A4
4300 TEML 91780 597-A4
5700 TEML 91780 596-J1
6500 LACo 91007 596-J1
6700 LACo 91007 566-J7
TEMPLE HILL DR
6100 LA 90068 593-F3
TEMPLETON ST
4700 LA 90032 595-E6
5900 HNTP 90255 674-J6
6600 HNTP 90255 675-A7
TEMPLIN HWY
- LACo - 4279-A3
TEMPO DR
42600 LAN 93536 4104-G4
TEMRE LN
19300 RowH 91748 679-D5
TENANGO DR
4000 CLAR 91711 600-J1
4000 CLAR 91711 570-J7
4500 WdHl 91364 560-D5
TENAYA AV
3100 SGAT 90280 705-B5
3200 LYN 90262 705-A5
TENDA DR
27900 SCTA 91351 4551-E1
28100 SCTA 91351 4461-F7
TENDE ST
- PMDL 93552 4287-E1
TENDERFOOT WY
21800 DBAR 91765 679-J6
TENDERFOOT TRAIL RD
18800 Nwhl 91321 4641-H1
18900 Nwhl 91321 4551-G7
TENDILLA AV
5000 WdHl 91364 560-A3
TENHAEFF AL
300 PAS 91105 565-H6
TENINO AV
11300 LA 90066 672-E4
TENNEB DR
300 Brwd 90049 631-G4
TENNESSEE AV
10200 LA 90064 632-E4
TENNESSEE PL
11600 LA 90064 632-A7
TENNESSEE TR
19900 WAL 91789 639-E6
TENNESSEE WALKER
- Actn 93510 4375-E7
TENNEYSON DR
5700 AGRH 91301 557-J4
TENNIS CT
17500 Enc 91316 561-B2
TENNYSON LN
- StvR 91381 4550-A6
TENNYSON PL
2800 HMB 90254 732-G7
17000 GrnH 91344 481-B4
TENNYSON ST
1100 MANB 90266 732-H7
TENSHAW PL
1700 Eagl 90041 565-B6
TEPIC DR
8400 PRM 90723 735-H5
TEPIC RD
4100 WdHl 91364 560-B5
TEPOCA RD
4400 WdHl 91364 560-C5
TERAMO WY
- Nor 91326 500-C1
W TERANIMAR DR
3000 ANA 92804 767-H7
TERECITA PL
10800 Tuj 91042 504-A2
TERECITA RD
10700 Tuj 91042 504-A2
TERESA AV
800 LACo 91770 636-D3
800 MONP 91755 636-D3
TERESA CT
19700 CRTS 90703 767-A3

TERESA PL
2500 POM 91766 641-A6
W TERESA ST
1000 WCOV 91790 598-G7
TERESA WY
19000 CRTS 90703 767-A2
TERESINA DR
2500 HacH 91745 678-B5
TERESITA CIR
1100 MNRO 91016 567-J5
1100 MNRO 91016 568-A5
TERHUNE AV
8300 SunV 91352 533-A1
9000 SunV 91352 503-A7
9900 Sunl 91040 503-A5
TERHUNE DR
2700 LACo 90265 628-C5
TERI AV
800 TOR 90503 763-E6
TERI CT
- LA 91304 529-J2
TERMINAL ST
700 LA 90021 634-G6
6100 NLB 90805 765-G1
TERMINAL WY
- LBCH 90802 824-F4
100 SPed 90731 824-F4
TERMINAL ISLAND FRWY Rt#-47
- LBCH - 824-H1
- Wilm - 794-H7
- Wilm - 824-H1
TERMINAL ISLAND FRWY Rt#-103
- LBCH - 794-H7
- LBCH - 795-A3
- Wilm - 794-H7
TERMINO AV
500 SPed 90731 824-B4
N TERMINO AV
- LBCH 90803 826-A1
300 LBCH 90814 795-J7
300 LBCH 90814 796-A7
300 LBCH 90814 825-J1
700 LBCH 90804 796-A3
1800 LBCH 90815 796-A3
TERMINO PL
3900 FUL 92835 738-H1
S TERMINO ST
- LBCH 90803 826-A2
TERN BAY LN
2100 LKWD 90712 765-G3
TERRA LN
1900 ARCD 91007 597-B1
TERRA BELLA ST
11400 LA 91342 482-H7
11600 LA 91342 502-G1
12000 Pcma 91331 502-F2
14200 PanC 91402 502-A6
TERRACE AV
2900 ALH 91803 595-G7
TERRACE CIR
16400 PacP 90272 630-H6
TERRACE CT
20000 LACo 91390 4461-E3
TERRACE DR
- RHE 90274 822-J1
- RHE 90274 823-A1
- PAS 91105 565-G5
500 SDMS 91773 600-A3
700 Bxby 90807 765-F6
900 SBdC 91784 571-J3
2000 SIGH 90755 795-H4
2900 WCOV 91792 679-C2
5500 LaCr 91214 504-H6
5900 HiPk 90042 595-C2
15900 PacP 90272 630-J6
TERRACE LN
300 HiPk 90042 595-B2
1700 POM 91768 600-E7
2300 Ago 91301 588-A4
TERRACE LN E
- DBAR 91765 680-A2
TERRACE LN W
- DBAR 91765 680-A3
TERRACE PL
13500 WHIT 90601 677-D6
16000 PacP 90272 630-F4
E TERRACE ST
- Alta 91001 535-H5
W TERRACE ST
- Alta 91001 535-G4
TERRACE 49
700 HiPk 90042 595-A2
TERRACE 52
200 HiPk 90042 595-C3
TERRACEDALE DR
15200 LMRD 90638 707-G7
TERRACE HEIGHTS AV
- BqtC 91354 4460-E2
TERRACE HILL CIR
2200 LA 90023 635-A6
TERRACE HILL DR
4900 THO 91362 557-G1
TERRACE HILL LN
2300 CHLS 91709 680-J4
TERRACE LAKE AV
700 BREA 92821 708-H6
TERRACE VIEW CT
23900 SCTA 91321 4640-G2
TERRACE VIEW DR
200 MNRO 91016 567-E3
3500 Enc 91436 561-D7
TERRACINA PL
- Cstc 91384 4459-E3

TERRACITA LN
4900 LCF 91011 535-A2
TERRA COTTA WY
16600 PRM 90723 735-F6
TERRADELL ST
8300 PRV 90660 706-D1
10900 SFSP 90670 706-G3
TERRADO DR
500 MNRO 91016 568-A4
TERRADO PZ
700 COV 91723 599-B7
TERRAFINA ST
- GrnH 91344 481-A6
TERRAINE AV
300 LBCH 90814 796-C7
700 LBCH 90804 796-C7
N TERRAINE AV
2400 LBCH 90815 796-C3
TERRA MIA WY
- PMDL 93552 4196-J7
TERRAPIN WY
7000 Tuj 91042 504-A3
TERRA VERDE DR
- PMDL 93552 4196-H7
TERRAVISTA CT
- SCTA 91351 4551-D3
TERRA VISTA WY
11000 LA 91342 482-G7
11000 LACo 91342 482-G7
TERRAZA CT
- Cstc 91384 4459-D2
TERRAZA DR
4100 LA 90008 673-B2
TERRAZA PL
100 MANB 90266 732-H7
2000 FUL 92835 738-F2
TERRAZA TER
19600 WAL 91789 679-D2
TERRAZAS WY
- PRV 90660 676-E6
TERRAZA SAN ANGELO
100 LHB 90631 738-E1
TERRAZA SAN BENITO
100 LHB 90631 738-E1
TERRAZA SAN CARLOS
100 LHB 90631 738-E1
TERRAZA SANTA ELENA
100 LHB 90631 738-E2
TERRAZZO DR
41400 PMDL 93551 4104-D7
TERREBONNE AV
1900 SDMS 91773 570-D5
TERRELL PL
400 POM 91767 600-J3
TERRI DR
19700 SCTA 91351 4551-E3
S TERRI ANN DR
600 WCOV 91791 638-J2
TERRILL AV
400 HiPk 90042 595-D4
TERRITORY RD
34200 LACo 91390 4373-E3
TERRY AV
4600 CHNO 91710 641-F6
TERRY PL
3000 LA 90031 595-A7
TERRY ST
4300 CHNO 91710 641-E6
TERRY WY
300 LHB 90631 708-E4
21100 LACo 91724 599-H7
N TERRY WY
400 UPL 91786 601-J3
TERRYHILL PL
11600 Brwd 90049 631-H3
TERRYKNOLL DR
14300 LACo 90604 707-E4
TERRY LYN LN
17400 CRTS 90703 737-B7
TERRYLYNN CIR
4000 Bxby 90807 765-C6
TERRY LYNN LN
15000 HacH 91745 677-J4
TERRYLYNN PL
600 Bxby 90807 765-C6
TERRYVIEW AV
800 POM 91767 601-B5
TERRY VIEW DR
10900 LA 91604 563-A6
TERZILLA PL
3200 LA 90065 564-G7
TESLA AV
2700 LA 90039 594-D4
TESLA TER
2400 LA 90039 594-D3
TESORO LN
39600 PMDL 93551 4195-C3
TESORO DEL VALLE DR
- BqtC 91354 4460-E2
TETLEY ST
15400 HacH 91745 678-B4
TETLOW AV
1700 SIMI 93063 499-C2
TETON DR
3300 FUL 92835 738-H1
14500 HacH 91745 677-H4
TETON ST
1100 GAR 90247 734-A3
TETON TR
- SCTA 91354 4550-J4
TEVIOT ST
2300 LA 90039 594-E4

TEVIS AV
1800 LBCH 90815 796-D3
3000 LBCH 90808 796-D1
3400 LBCH 90808 766-E7
TEXACO AV
14300 PRM 90723 735-F4
S TEXACO AV
16300 PRM 90723 735-F5
TEXANIA TER
- LA 91304 529-D2
TEXAS AV
11600 WLA 90025 631-H6
TEXAS RD
- Cstc 91384 4460-A4
TEXAS ST
8300 DWNY 90241 706-A5
W TEXAS ST
400 POM 91768 640-H1
TEXAS CANYON RD
- LACo 91390 (4282-J7 See Page 4281)
- LACo 91390 4283-A7
- LACo 91390 (4371-J7 See Page 4281)
- LACo 91390 (4372-F3 See Page 4281)
- LACo 91390 4373-A3
TEXAS OIL COMPANY RD
- Cstc 91384 4460-A4
TEXCOCO ST
700 MTBL 90640 636-D7
TEXHOMA AV
4800 Enc 91316 561-B1
6800 VanN 91406 531-B5
7600 Nor 91325 531-B3
9300 Nor 91325 501-B5
THACKERY LN
- StvR 91381 4550-A7
E THACKERY ST
1000 WCOV 91791 638-G2
1400 WCOV 91791 638-J2
2000 WCOV 91791 639-A2
THALIA LN
- SCTA 91351 4551-H2
THAMES CT
900 SDMS 91773 599-H4
39200 PMDL 93551 4195-F5
THAMES PL
2500 LA 90046 593-A2
19100 Nor 91324 500-E7
THAMES ST
2500 LA 90046 593-A2
THATCHER AV
2900 LA 90292 672-A6
THATCHER ST
- FUL 92833 738-D5
THAXTON AV
3200 HacH 91745 678-B6
THAYER AV
600 Wwd 90024 632-B2
1800 WLA 90025 632-D4
THE MALL
- LACo 91724 639-G1
2700 LA 90023 635-A7
2900 LA 90023 675-A1
21100 LACo 91724 599-H7
N THE COLONNADE CANAL
- LBCH 90803 826-C3
THE GRAND CANAL
200 Ven 90291 671-H6
THE GROVE DR
100 LA 90036 633-C1
THE GROVES
- PMDL 93551 4285-D2
THEIS AV
10700 LACo 90604 707-E6
E THELBORN ST
500 COV 91723 599-C6
1000 WCOV 91790 598-G6
1400 WCOV 91791 598-H6
19200 LACo 91723 599-C6
W THELBORN ST
500 COV 91723 599-A6
1000 WCOV 91790 598-E6
THELEN RD
11900 LACo 91390 4373-C3
THELMA AV
2100 LA 90032 635-E1
3300 LA 90032 595-E6
5500 LPMA 90623 767-D3
5500 BPK 90623 767-F3
11100 SunV 91352 502-J4
THELMA LN
2300 RowH 91748 679-E6
THELMA ST
3300 GLDL 91214 504-E7
12200 SunV 91352 502-F7
THE MIDWAY
1500 GLDL 91208 564-H1
THEO AV
4800 TOR 90505 793-B2
THEODORA DR
2800 LACo 91724 639-E1
THEODORE CT
6300 PMDL 93551 4104-E6
21900 SCTA 91350 4461-A5
THE OLD RD
21600 LA 91342 4641-A6
21700 Nwhl 91321 4641-A6
22700 Nwhl 91321 4640-H5
23700 StvR 91381 4640-D1

THE OLD RD
24000 SCTA 91321 4640-F4
24000 SCTA 91381 4640-F4
25500 StvR 91381 4550-C2
27900 Valc 91355 4550-B1
28100 Valc 91355 4459-H5
28100 Valc 91355 4460-A7
28800 Cstc 91384 4459-H3
31000 Cstc 91384 4369-E4
THE OLD DIRT RD
30500 LACo 91390 4462-E3
THE PALMS DR
- CRTS 90703 736-J7
THE PASEO
- LBCH 90802 825-D1
3300 LA 90065 594-H2
THE PLAZA ST
13900 NRWK 90650 736-G3
THE PROMENADE
- AZU 91702 569-A5
- GLDR 91702 569-A5
- GLDR 91741 569-A5
THE PROMENADE N
- LBCH 90802 825-D1
200 LBCH 90802 795-D7
THE PROMENADE S
- LBCH 90802 825-D1
THERESA LN
300 SMAD 91024 567-B1
THERESA ST
200 LA 90065 595-A5
E THERESA ST
2800 LBCH 90814 795-H7
4000 LBCH 90814 796-A7
THERMAL DR
11700 LMRD 90638 707-F7
THERMO ST
12000 LA 90066 672-B2
THE STRAND
- HMB 90254 762-F1
2600 HMB 90254 732-D3
3900 MANB 90266 732-D3
4400 ELSG 90245 732-D3
4400 LA 90245 732-D3
4400 PdlR 90293 702-A3
4400 PdlR 90293 732-D3
N THE STRAND
3400 HMB 90254 732-F7
3500 MANB 90266 732-E5
THE TERRACE
2200 Brwd 90049 591-E3
THE TOLEDO
200 LBCH 90803 826-B1
THE VILLAGE
100 RBCH 90277 762-H5
THE VILLAGE GRN
5100 LA 90016 673-B1
THE VISTA
12500 Brwd 90049 591-E4
THE WYE ST
11800 ELMN 91732 597-G4
THICKET DR
- CRSN 90746 764-F1
16300 LACo 91744 638-G4
THIENES AV
10400 SELM 91733 637-B4
11300 LACo 91733 637-D4
THIRD ST
12200 NRWK 90650 706-J7
THISBE CT
37700 PMDL 93550 4286-H2
THISTLE AV
1800 PMDL 93550 4286-D4
13100 NRWK 90650 736-J2
13500 NRWK 90650 737-A2
THISTLE CT
24400 SCTA 91321 4640-G3
N THISTLE RD
100 BREA 92821 709-F7
S THISTLE RD
100 BREA 92821 709-F7
THISTLE ST
45800 LAN 93534 4015-G3
THISTLEGATE RD
900 VeCo 91377 558-A1
THISTLEWOOD WY
28500 RPV 90275 823-J2
THOMAS AV
2200 PMDL 93550 4286-E4
2400 RBCH 90278 733-B6
THOMAS CT
11500 NRWK 90650 706-G7
THOMAS DR
1500 LAN 93535 4106-C2
21300 CRSN 90745 764-F6
THOMAS PL
2700 WCOV 91792 639-A7
12500 CHNO 91710 641-F6
THOMAS RD
7400 LACo 91390 4374-C2
THOMAS ST
1900 LA 90031 635-B1
2400 LA 90031 595-B7
N THOMAS ST
2200 POM 91768 640-J1
S THOMAS ST
200 POM 91766 640-J2
THOMAS WY
1800 FUL 92833 738-D6
THOMAS PAYNE LN
- PMDL 93550 4286-C4
THOMICIA PL
5700 WdHl 91367 559-E1

THOMPSON AL
2700 PAS 91107 566-F4
THOMPSON AV
100 FUL 92833 738-B7
200 GLDL 91201 563-J2
900 GLDL 91201 564-A1
1200 GLDL 91201 534-B7
9400 Chat 91311 499-F6
THOMPSON CT
2000 GLDL 91020 534-H3
2000 Mont 91020 534-H3
THOMPSON DR
500 PAS 91104 565-J2
THOMPSON LN
200 Chat 91311 499-F6
500 VeCo 93063 499-F6
9200 Chat 91311 499-F7
THOMPSON RD
300 Chat 91311 499-F6
9200 Chat 91311 499-F6
9200 Chat 91311 499-F6
E THOMPSON ST
2300 NLB 90805 735-G6
THOMPSON WK
- Cstc 91384 4459-D6
THOMPSON CREEK RD
2100 POM 91767 600-J3
THOMPSON RANCH DR
- SCTA 91387 4462-D7
THOR AV
3500 LALM 90720 796-J3
THOR PL
300 BREA 92821 709-B7
THOREAU ST
1800 LACo 90047 703-G6
2300 ING 90303 703-G6
THOREAU WY
- StvR 91381 4550-B7
- StvR 91381 4640-A1
THORLEY CT
28100 SCTA 91351 4461-F7
THORLEY PL
2200 PVE 90274 792-E7
THORLEY RD
2100 PVE 90274 792-E7
THORNBURGH AV
16800 TOR 90504 733-E7
THORNBURGH PL
3900 TOR 90504 733-E7
THORNBURN ST
5200 Wch 90045 703-A1
5600 Wch 90045 702-J1
THORNBUSH AV
42000 LACo 93536 4104-D6
THORN CREST CT
- SCTA 91351 4461-G7
THORNCREST DR
1700 GLDL 91207 564-F1
THORNCROFT CIR
- PMDL 93551 4285-E3
THORNCROFT WY
3800 ING 90305 703-E3
THORNDALE RD
3200 PAS 91107 566-G5
3500 LACo 91107 566-G5
THORNDIKE RD
2700 PAS 91107 566-F6
THORNE AV
2300 LHB 90631 708-B5
THORNE CT
- Cstc 91384 4459-G3
THORNE RD
1500 Eagl 90041 565-A7
THORNE ST
200 HiPk 90042 595-E2
THORNEWOOD DR
23400 SCTA 91321 4640-G3
THORNHILL RD
600 LACo 91302 589-A7
600 LACo 91302 629-A1
THORNHURST AV
400 GLDR 91741 569-H4
THORNLAKE AV
3500 LBCH 90808 766-J4
6800 LACo 90606 677-A6
7700 LACo 90606 676-J7
8300 LACo 90606 706-J1
14800 NRWK 90650 736-J5
17500 ART 90701 736-J7
17800 ART 90701 766-J1
19500 CRTS 90703 766-J3
20300 LKWD 90715 766-J4
N THORNLAKE AV
3400 LBCH 90808 766-J7
S THORNLAKE AV
14600 NRWK 90650 736-J4
THORNTON AV
- Ven 90291 671-G5
2300 BURB 91504 533-C5
THORNTON CT
- Ven 90291 671-G5
THORNTON PL
100 Ven 90291 671-G5
THORNTON ST
1000 LA 90063 635-C4
1000 City 90063 635-C4
THORNWOOD AV
45200 LAN 93534 4015-F5
THORNWOOD ST
1000 GLDL 91206 565-C2
THORNY LN
5000 LVRN 91750 570-H4

E THOROUGHBRED WY
13000 LACo 90601 637-E7
THORPE AV
2600 LA 90065 594-H5
THORSON AV
11200 LYN 90262 705-D7
11600 LYN 90262 735-D1
N THORSON AV
700 COMP 90221 735-C3
1100 RDom 90221 735-C3
S THORSON AV
100 COMP 90221 735-C5
15900 RDom 90221 735-C6
THOUSAND OAKS BLVD
25800 LACo 91302 558-H4
26000 CALB 91302 558-H4
28700 AGRH 91301 558-A4
29400 AGRH 91301 557-G4
30700 WLKV 91361 557-G4
E THOUSAND OAKS BLVD
2400 THO 91362 557-A3
30700 WLKV 91362 557-E4
THOUSAND OAKS DR
7500 Tuj 91042 503-H4
THOUSAND PEAKS RD
24900 LACo 91302 589-C4
THRACE DR
11200 LACo 90604 707-F6
THRASHER AV
8800 LA 90069 592-H4
THREE OAK CT
2400 SIMI 93063 499-A1
THREE OAKS LN
- WAL 91789 639-D5
THREE PALMS ST
15400 HacH 91745 678-B2
THREE RANCH RD
1100 DUAR 91010 567-J6
1100 DUAR 91010 568-A6
THREE SPRINGS DR
2200 WLKV 91361 587-A1
2600 WLKV 91361 557-A7
THREEWOODS LN
- FUL 92831 738-J3
THRIFT RD
400 LACo 90265 587-E6
THROOP AL
800 SPAS 91030 595-G2
THRUSH CT
1200 LACo 91104 566-D1
THRUSH RD
1600 SBdC 92397 (4652-D3 See Page 4651)
THRUSH WY
9200 LA 90069 592-H4
THRUST DR
20400 LACo 91789 679-F6
THUNDER TR
24300 DBAR 91765 680-E2
THUNDERBIRD AV
11700 Nor 91326 480-F7
THUNDERBIRD CT
400 FUL 92835 738-H2
THUNDERBIRD DR
- LA 91343 531-H1
2300 THO 91362 557-A2
13700 SLB 90740 826-H1
THURBER PL
1600 GLDL 91201 534-B6
1600 BURB 91501 534-B6
THURBER WY
- StvR 91381 4550-A7
THURGOOD MARSHALL ST
200 PAS 91101 565-D4
THURIN AV
3000 Alta 91001 535-G4
THURLENE RD
1400 GLDL 91206 565-A1
THURLOW ST
500 MTBL 90640 676-C3
THURMAN AL
1400 PAS 91106 566-C4
THURMAN AV
1800 LA 90019 633-B6
1800 LA 90016 633-B6
N THURSTON AV
100 Brwd 90049 631-H1
S THURSTON AV
100 Brwd 90049 631-H1
THURSTON CIR
11300 Brwd 90049 631-H1
THURSTON PL
11300 Brwd 90049 631-H1
THURZAL PL
7200 VanN 91406 531-E4
THYME PL
- RPV 90275 823-B4
THYNNE ST
42000 LAN 93536 4104-G6
TIANA ROSE ST
- LAN 93534 4015-E4
TIANNA RD
8100 LA 90046 592-J2
TIARA CT
16700 SCTA 91387 4462-B7
16700 SCTA 91387 4552-C1
TIARA LN
7100 LPMA 90623 767-D2
TIARA ST
10400 NHol 91601 533-A7
10900 NHol 91601 532-J7

TIARA ST
11800 LA 91607 562-E1
13400 VanN 91401 562-A1
14500 VanN 91411 562-A1
14600 VanN 91411 561-J1
17100 Enc 91316 561-A1
20400 WdHl 91367 560-A1
22100 WdHl 91367 559-E1
TIBANA ST
7800 LBCH 90808 766-H7
TIBBETTS ST
12400 LA 91342 482-E2
TIBETAN CT
18600 SCTA 91351 4551-G7
TIBURON CT
- MANB 90266 732-H4
1900 RowH 91748 678-J5
TIBURON DR
- SCTA 91355 4550-D3
TIBURON PL
16500 HNTB 92649 826-J7
TICA DR
3300 LFlz 90027 594-B2
TICATICA DR
2600 HacH 91745 678-C5
E TICHENOR ST
100 COMP 90220 734-J6
100 COMP 90220 735-A6
1100 COMP 90221 735-B5
W TICHENOR ST
100 COMP 90220 734-F6
TICK CANYON RD
30000 LACo 91387 4462-H4
30000 LACo 91390 4462-H4
TICONDEROGA RD
22600 CALB 91302 559-H5
TIDE DR
24400 SCTA 91355 4550-E6
TIDEWATER CV
9300 BPK 90621 738-B6
TIDWELL AV
11500 LACo 90604 707-J6
TIERNAN AV
11500 LA 91342 482-F7
11500 LA 91342 502-F1
TIERRA DR
26000 SCTA 91355 4550-G4
TIERRA ALTA DR
1000 PAS 91104 566-D2
1200 LACo 91104 566-D1
TIERRA ANTIGUA DR
5000 WHIT 90601 677-B3
TIERRA BLANCA DR
9400 WHIT 90603 707-J3
TIERRA BONITA DR
5200 WHIT 90601 677-B3
TIERRA CIMA
1400 LACo 91789 679-E4
TIERRA DULCE RD
35600 LACo 91390 4374-B1
TIERRA ENCANTA DR
5200 WHIT 90601 677-D4
TIERRA GRANADA DR
5100 WHIT 90601 677-D4
TIERRA LOMA DR
2000 DBAR 91765 679-J5
TIERRA LUNA
1000 LACo 91789 679-E4
TIERRA MAJORCA DR
5100 WHIT 90601 677-D4
TIERRA MONTE DR
5200 WHIT 90601 677-D4
TIERRA NAVARRA DR
10600 WHIT 90601 677-D4
TIERRA SIESTA
1300 LACo 91789 679-F4
TIERRA SUBIDA AV
35500 LACo 93551 4285-H5
35500 LACo 93551 4375-H1
37200 PMDL 93551 4285-H1
38400 PMDL 93551 4195-G7
TIFAL AV
2400 IRW 91010 567-J7
2400 IRW 91010 597-J1
TIFFANY CIR
1200 UPL 91786 601-G2
2900 BelA 90077 562-A7
2900 BelA 90077 592-A1
37800 PMDL 93550 4286-F2
TIFFANY CT
3800 Ago 91301 588-E1
22800 TOR 90505 793-D1
TIFFANY LN
3100 WCOV 91792 679-D3
3800 TOR 90505 793-C1
28000 SCTA 91387 4551-J2
TIFFANY PL
2500 FUL 92833 738-B4
TIFFANY ST
42000 LAN 93536 4104-G6
TIFFANY TER
700 ARCD 91006 567-E7
TIFFIN WY
1400 CLAR 91711 601-C1
TIGER TR
1700 Top 90290 590-C2
TIGER WY
- PMDL 93551 4194-F3
TIGER EYE DR
- Hrbr 90710 794-A5
E TIGER MOUNTAIN RD
- PMDL 93550 4466-C2

TIGERTAIL CT
1500 PMDL 93551 4195-F7
TIGERTAIL DR
2800 OrCo 90720 796-H6
TIGERTAIL RD
500 Brwd 90049 631-F1
1000 Brwd 90049 591-F7
N TIGERTAIL RD
100 Brwd 90049 631-G3
TIGRINA AV
10100 WHIT 90603 708-A4
11600 LACo 90604 708-A6
12400 LACo 90604 738-A1
12600 LMRD 90638 738-A1
TIKI WK
300 NLB 90805 735-D7
TIKITA PL
10000 LA 91602 563-C5
TILBURY DR
40000 PMDL 93551 4195-B4
TILBURY ST
5500 LKWD 90713 766-C6
12100 HGDN 90716 766-J6
12300 LKWD 90715 766-J6
TILDEN AV
200 Brwd 90049 631-J1
2500 LA 90064 632-C6
3000 LA 90034 632-C6
3200 LA 90034 672-D1
3800 CULC 90232 672-F3
4600 Shrm 91403 562-A3
5000 Shrm 91423 562-A2
5200 VanN 91401 562-A1
8000 PanC 91402 532-A1
8700 PanC 91402 502-A7
TILE AV
300 LBCH 90802 795-F7
TILE ST
9100 PRV 90660 676-G3
TILFORD CT
17400 GrnH 91344 481-B6
TILLIE CT
1900 WCOV 91792 679-A1
TILLIE ST
3000 LA 90065 594-H4
TILLMAN AV
19000 CRSN 90746 764-F2
TILMONT AV
8700 PRV 90660 676-G2
TILMONT ST
9300 PRV 90660 676-H2
TILTON DR
41800 PMDL 93551 4104-C6
42000 LACo 93536 4104-C6
TIM AV
1700 LACo 90032 635-E2
TIMBER PL
31900 Cstc 91384 4369-G6
TIMBER BRANCH PL
- LACo 91387 4551-J6
TIMBERCREEK CIR
2200 BREA 92821 709-E7
TIMBERCREEK LN
12400 CRTS 90703 736-J5
TIMBERHILL LN
16000 CRTS 90703 736-J5
TIMBERLAKE DR
2600 LaCr 91214 504-G6
TIMBER LAKE TER
5000 CULC 90230 672-J3
TIMBERLAND LN
700 WAL 91789 639-J5
TIMBERLANE AV
2100 SIMI 93063 499-A2
TIMBERLANE CT
- SCTA 91354 4460-G5
TIMBERLANE ST
6200 AGRH 91301 558-A3
TIMBERLINE CT
100 BREA 92821 709-B6
TIMBERLINE DR
- SBdC 92397 (4652-A2 See Page 4651)
400 AZU 91702 568-H4
23200 LACo 92397 (4652-A2 See Page 4651)
TIMBERLINE LN
20600 DBAR 91789 679-G6
TIMBERLINE ST
- SCTA 91351 4551-F4
TIMBERLINE TER
- StvR 91381 4550-B4
TIMBERLYN TRAIL RD
- FUL 92833 738-A3
- LMRD 90638 738-A3
TIMBERRIDGE CT
32400 WLKV 91361 557-B7
TIMBER RIDGE DR
16900 GrnH 91344 481-C3
TIMBER RIDGE LN
1600 WAL 91789 639-G3
TIMBERTOP LN
22700 DBAR 91765 680-A6
TIMBERVIEW CT
- SCTA 91351 4551-G7
TIMELESS WY
- PMDL 93551 4195-E6
TIMES MTWY
- LACo 92823 709-J3
- LACo 92823 710-A3
- OrCo 92823 710-A3
TIMMONS TR
6400 LA 90068 593-F2

STREET Block City ZIP Pg-Grid

TIMMS WY
1300 SPed 90731 824-C6
TIMON LN
24400 SCTA 91321 4640-H2
TIMOR ST
7800 LBCH 90808 766-H7
TIMOTHY AV
2800 RBCH 90278 733-B6
TIMOTHY CT
44400 LAN 93535 4016-C3
TIMOTHY DR
28200 SCTA 91350 4461-D5
TIMPANGOS DR
25600 LACo 91302 589-A7
TIN DR
23400 DBAR 91765 680-C1
TINA CT
600 LAN 93535 4106-A1
TINA LN
1200 WCOV 91792 638-H4
TINA PL
19000 Tarz 91356 560-G4
TINA ST
11400 NRWK 90650 706-G7
TINAJA RD
2200 Ago 91301 587-F2
TINA LOUISE LN
5100 Actn 93510 4374-H3
TINDALL AV
- Actn 93510 4465-F1
32800 Actn 93510 4375-F7
TINDALO RD
800 ARCD 91006 567-D4
TINER CT
24400 LACo 90263 628-H6
TINKER AV
10200 Tuj 91042 503-H2
TINKER ST
3400 WCOV 91792 679-B1
TINKERMAN ST
5500 SIMI 93063 499-A2
TINTAH DR
1800 DBAR 91765 679-J4
1800 DBAR 91765 680-A4
TIOGA CT
12300 CHNO 91710 641-E6
36500 PMDL 93550 4286-H5
TIOGA DR
23200 DBAR 91765 680-B1
TIOGA PL
22200 LA 91304 529-J1
TIONE RD
900 BelA 90077 592-A6
TIPICO ST
20000 Chat 91311 500-E4
TIPTON TER
700 HiPk 90042 565-C7
TIPTON WY
5800 HiPk 90042 565-C7
TISTOU TR
- LACo 90265 628-B3
TITAN CT
1500 LACo 91770 636-E4
37200 PMDL 93550 4286-H3
TITAN DR
- SPed 90731 823-H7
TITAN WY
1200 BREA 92821 708-H7
TITIAN AV
12800 GmH 91344 481-C4
TITLEY AV
100 PAS 91107 566-F4
TITUS AV
1900 POM 91766 641-B5
TITUS ST
14400 PanC 91402 532-A2
14500 PanC 91402 531-J2
TIVERTON AV
900 Wwd 90024 632-B3
TIVERTON CT
800 SDMS 91773 599-H4
TIVERTON DR
- LA 90095 632-B2
TIVOLI AV
3900 CULC 90066 672-B5
3900 LA 90066 672-B5
TIVOLI CIR
9500 CYP 90630 767-C7
TIVOLI DR
100 LBCH 90803 826-C2
TOBAGA WY
300 VeCo 91377 557-G2
TOBERMAN ST
1300 LA 90015 634-C5
1800 LA 90007 634-B6
TOBIAH PL
31300 Cstc 91384 4369-G7
TOBIAS AV
4400 Shrm 91403 561-J3
4400 PRV 90660 676-H3
5900 VanN 91411 561-J1
6600 VanN 91405 531-J3
8300 PanC 91402 531-J2
8700 PanC 91402 501-J7
TOBIN WY
15800 Shrm 91403 561-F7
TOBIRA DR
36800 PMDL 93550 4286-E4
TOBRUK CT
6200 LBCH 90803 826-D1
TOBY LN
30000 Llan 93544 4471-F4

N TOBY PL
200 POM 91767 641-A1
TOCALOMA LN
4800 LCF 91011 535-A2
TOCATTA LN
- POM 91766 640-D4
TOCCOA FALLS
- CLAR 91711 571-F3
TOCINO DR
300 DUAR 91010 568-E4
TODD AV
600 AZU 91702 568-G5
3600 CMRC 90040 676-B7
TODD CT
12200 NHol 91605 532-F3
TODD LN
400 MNRO 91016 567-H2
TODD PL
1400 MTBL 90640 636-D7
1700 LVRN 91750 600-G1
3700 LVRN 91750 570-G7
TODD VIEW CT
8600 LA 91304 529-C1
TOERGE DR
11500 LMRD 90638 707-G6
TOKAY RD
6400 Tuj 91042 504-B4
TOKEN ST
9500 LBCH 90808 766-J7
TOLA AV
2700 Alta 91001 535-G5
TOLA ST
800 MTBL 90640 676-C5
TOLAND AV
3800 LALM 90720 796-J1
7700 Wch 90045 702-J2
7700 Wch 90045 703-A2
N TOLAND AV
100 WCOV 91790 598-G7
TOLAND PL
4300 Eagl 90041 594-J1
TOLAND WY
3700 LA 90065 594-H2
4300 Eagl 90041 594-J1
4500 Eagl 90041 595-A1
4600 HiPk 90042 595-A1
TOLANI CT
21900 DBAR 91765 679-J4
TOLBERT AV
4500 Bxby 90807 765-D5
TOLEDO CT
200 Ven 90291 671-H6
TOLEDO DR
1400 GLDL 91207 564-G2
TOLEDO PL
2200 LHB 90631 708-B6
TOLEDO ST
400 HiPk 90042 595-C1
TOLEDO WK
700 LBCH 90813 795-F7
TOLEDO WY
4500 BPK 90621 737-J4
TOLENAS DR
12500 LA 91604 562-F6
TOLER AV
6300 BGDN 90201 705-H1
6500 BGDN 90201 675-J7
TOLIMA DR
27700 SCTA 91351 4551-G2
TOLL DR
7200 LACo 91770 636-D4
TOLLBOOTH RD
- Univ 91608 563-B6
TOLLY ST
9600 BLF 90706 736-B2
10600 NRWK 90650 736-E2
TOLMAN DR
15100 LACo 90604 707-G5
TOLMIE AV
1500 CMRC 90022 676-A3
TOLTEC DR
- Chat 91311 500-B1
TOLTEC WY
6100 HiPk 90042 595-D3
TOLUCA AV
600 POM 91767 601-A5
700 WCOV 91790 598-E7
700 WCOV 91790 638-E1
20500 TOR 90503 763-B5
TOLUCA RD
- LA 91602 563-B5
N TOLUCA ST
100 Echo 90026 634-E2
S TOLUCA ST
200 Echo 90026 634-E3
TOLUCA ESTATES DR
4000 LA 91602 563-B5
TOLUCA LAKE AV
4100 BURB 91505 563-D5
9900 LA 91602 563-C5
TOLUCA LAKE LN
4200 BURB 91505 563-D5
TOLUCA PARK DR
500 BURB 91505 563-C3
TOLUENE RD
20400 CRSN 90746 764-G5
TOMAHAWK LN
- CRSN 90745 794-G1
12700 NRWK 90650 737-A1
TOMAHAWK PL
43600 LACo 93536 4104-J2
TOMAHAWK TER
8400 LA 91304 529-D1

TOMAS CT
1800 RowH 91748 678-J5
TOMBUR DR
2000 RowH 91748 678-F5
TOMICH RD
1900 RowH 91748 678-F5
TOMIK CIR
4300 RSMD 91770 596-H6
TOMLEE AV
19300 TOR 90503 763-A3
TOMPKINS WY
6300 CULC 90232 672-H1
TOM WHITE WY
13000 NRWK 90650 737-B2
TONALE WY
400 VeCo 91377 557-G1
TONALEA DR
- LACo 93532 4102-E5
TONAWANDA AV
1500 Eagl 90041 564-J7
1500 Eagl 90041 594-J1
TONDOLEA LN
1900 LCF 91011 534-H2
TONGA ST
11500 VeCo 90265 625-F5
TONGAREVA ST
11400 VeCo 90265 625-F5
E TONI DR
3300 WCOV 91791 639-D1
TONIA AV
3200 Alta 91001 535-J4
TONIBAR ST
10700 NRWK 90650 736-E2
TONNER DR
700 POM 91768 600-H6
TONNER CANYON RD
- CHLS 91709 680-F3
- LACo 92823 680-B7
- LACo 92823 710-A1
500 DBAR 91765 640-G7
500 DBAR 91765 680-F3
500 POM 91766 640-G7
15500 OrCo 92821 709-H4
16000 BREA 92821 709-D5
17900 LACo 92823 709-H4
17900 OrCo 92823 709-H4
TONNER FIRE RD
- LACo 92823 710-A1
TONONI AV
900 GLDL 91202 564-C2
TONOPAH AV
300 LPUE 91744 638-B5
900 LACo 91744 638-C4
S TONOPAH AV
1500 WCOV 91790 638-D2
TONOPAH CT
700 SDMS 91773 600-C4
TONOPAH ST
12600 Pcma 91331 502-D7
13000 Pcma 91331 532-D1
13200 PanC 91402 532-D1
TONY AV
6100 WdHl 91367 529-E7
6100 WdHl 91367 559-E1
6400 CanP 91307 529-E6
TOOLEN PL
400 PAS 91103 535-F7
TOOMEY PL
1300 Hrbr 90710 794-A2
TOP CIR
2100 LAN 93536 4105-D1
TOP CT
24400 DBAR 91765 640-E7
W TOPACIO DR
700 MONP 91754 635-G3
S TOPANGA DR
100 ANA 92804 767-H6
TOPANGA BEACH RD
18600 LACo 90265 630-D6
18600 MAL 90265 630-D6
TOPANGA CANYON BLVD Rt#-27
- Chat 91311 500-A3
3000 LACo 90265 630-D4
3500 WdHl 91364 560-A5
3600 Top 90290 560-B7
4200 WdHl 91364 560-A5
5400 WdHl 91367 560-A2
6100 WdHl 91367 530-A7
6400 CanP 91303 530-A4
7500 LA 91304 530-A4
8900 Chat 91311 500-A3
8900 LA 91304 530-A4
9500 Chat 91311 499-J6
N TOPANGA CANYON BLVD Rt#-27
100 Top 90290 590-B1
2800 Top 90290 560-B7
3300 WdHl 91364 560-B7
S TOPANGA CANYON BLVD Rt#-27
100 Top 90290 590-B6
500 LA 90290 590-B6
1500 LA 90290 630-C1
1500 Top 90290 630-C1
2700 LACo 90265 630-C1
TOPANGA CANYON LN
3800 LACo 90265 630-D6
TOPANGA CANYON PL
5800 WdHl 91367 560-A1
9500 Chat 91311 499-J6
9500 Chat 91311 500-A6

TOPANGA FIRE RD
- PacP 90272 630-E3
- Top 90290 630-E3
E TOPANGA FIRE RD
- PacP 90272 590-E3
- PacP 90272 630-D2
- Top 90290 630-D2
TOPANGA RIDGE MTWY
200 Top 90290 589-F7
400 LACo 91302 589-F7
TOPANGA SCHOOL RD
22000 Top 90290 590-A6
TOPANGA SKYLINE DR
1400 Top 90290 589-G2
TOPAZ
- BREA 92823 710-D6
TOPAZ AV
2000 LHB 90631 708-H5
TOPAZ CT
- CRTS 90703 767-A3
31900 Cstc 91384 4369-H6
37600 PMDL 93552 4287-C2
TOPAZ LN
- GAR 90247 734-A3
- WCOV 91792 679-C1
TOPAZ PL
300 ARCD 91006 537-E7
TOPAZ ST
100 RBCH 90277 762-J6
2400 CHLS 91709 680-J7
3500 LA 90032 595-C6
TOPAZ WY
900 POM 91766 641-B4
TOPE AV
8800 SGAT 90280 704-J3
TOPEKA DR
4800 Tarz 91356 560-H1
6100 Res 91335 530-H3
8300 Nor 91324 530-H2
9700 Nor 91324 500-G5
10300 Nor 91326 500-G3
TOPEKA ST
900 PAS 91104 566-A1
1000 PAS 91104 536-A7
TOPHAM ST
17900 Enc 91316 531-A7
18100 Res 91335 530-J7
18100 Res 91335 531-A7
19200 Tarz 91356 560-G1
19600 WdHl 91367 530-F7
TOPIA ST
7800 LBCH 90808 766-H7
TOPLEY LN
7500 Tuj 91042 503-J4
7900 Sunl 91040 503-F4
TOPOCHICO DR
21000 WdHl 91364 560-B5
TOPOCK ST
1800 GLDL 91204 594-E1
3500 LA 90039 594-E1
TOPPER CT
25900 StvR 91381 4550-C6
TOPPINGTON DR
3100 LA 90210 592-C1
TOPRAIL LN
- RPV 90275 823-G2
TOPSAIL CIR
2300 THO 91361 557-B6
TOPSAIL CT
100 LA 90292 701-J1
TOPSAIL MALL
- LA 90292 701-J2
TOPSAIL ST
- LA 90292 701-J2
TOPSFIELD ST
300 LACo 91107 566-E5
2600 PAS 91107 566-E5
TOP SIDE CT
- LBCH 90803 826-G2
TOPSIDE PL
500 DBAR 91765 640-E7
TOQUET DR
17300 Enc 91316 561-C4
TORBAY CT
1500 LAN 93534 4015-E4
TORCH ST
12600 BALD 91706 637-H1
24200 WdHl 91367 559-D1
TORCHWOOD PL
32600 WLKV 91361 587-A1
TORCIDA DR
1600 LCF 91011 535-A2
TORIN ST
7800 LBCH 90808 766-H7
TORINO
1000 MTBL 90640 636-C6
TORINO PL
1200 POM 91766 640-F3
TORINO WY
- Nor 91326 500-C1
TORITO LN
300 DBAR 91765 640-C7
TORNADO CT
4200 PMDL 93552 4286-J5
TORO DR
2500 RowH 91748 678-H6
TORRANCE BLVD
100 RBCH 90277 762-H5
700 RBCH 90277 763-B5

TORRANCE BLVD
1000 TOR 90503 763-B5
1200 TOR 90501 763-H5
1300 LA 90501 764-A5
1300 LA 90501 763-J5
E TORRANCE BLVD
100 CRSN 90745 764-C5
W TORRANCE BLVD
- LACo 90745 764-A5
100 CRSN 90745 764-A5
600 LACo 90502 764-A5
TORREON DR
4200 WdHl 91364 560-B5
TORREON PL
4200 WdHl 91364 560-B5
TORREON ST
- AZU 91702 568-H7
- AZU 91702 598-H1
TORREPINES PL
30000 AGRH 91301 557-H5
TORRES DR
1300 GLDL 91207 564-G2
TORRES LN
16200 LPUE 91744 638-G7
TORREY CIR
3700 BALD 91706 597-J7
TORREY ST
3700 BALD 91706 598-A6
TORREY PINE CT
- HacH 91745 678-F6
TORREY PINES CT
3000 LHB 90631 738-D2
TORREY PINES DR
- ARCD 91006 567-E2
- LACo 90606 676-H6
26300 SCTA 91321 4551-G5
TORREY PINES LN
18500 Tarz 91356 560-J5
TORREY PINES WY
- PRV 90660 676-J1
- PRV 90660 677-A1
TORREYSON DR
7700 LA 90046 563-A7
TORREYSON PL
3100 LA 90046 563-A7
3100 LA 90046 593-A1
TORRINGTON ST
37400 PMDL 93550 4286-D3
TORTOSA AV
2400 RowH 91748 679-A6
TORTUGA ST
1800 Actn 93510 4375-F7
TORTUOSO WY
700 BelA 90077 592-A6
TORY ST
2700 WCOV 91792 638-J7
TOSCA RD
4200 WdHl 91364 560-B5
TOSCANA CT
- SCTA 91387 4552-D5
TOSCANA DR
- BqtC 91354 4460-F4
TOSCANINI DR
1400 RPV 90275 823-H2
TOSCANY CT
3600 PMDL 93550 4286-H4
TOSCO LN
- SPed 90731 794-B6
TOSSANO DR
24100 SCTA 91355 4550-F6
TOTANA DR
4400 Tarz 91356 560-F5
TOTH PL
5700 AGRH 91301 558-C5
TOTHILL DR
28000 SCTA 91350 4461-C5
TOTTENHAM CT
9700 LA 90210 592-C1
TOUCAN PL
- LACo 91387 4551-J5
TOUCAN ST
4500 TOR 90503 763-C3
TOUCHSTONE PL
- LACo 91390 4460-J3
TOUCHWOOD AV
14900 BLF 90706 736-A4
TOUL AV
- Brwd 90049 631-J3
- Brwd 90049 632-A3
TOULON DR
800 PacP 90272 631-C5
TOULOUSE DR
5000 LPMA 90623 767-C2
TOURELLE PL
26000 SCTA 91355 4550-E6
TOURMALINE LN
3000 PMDL 93550 4286-G5
TOURMALINE ST
3300 LA 90032 595-C6
TOURNAMENT DR
- LACo 93551 4195-A2
- PMDL 93551 4195-A2
TOURNAMENT RD
25400 SCTA 91355 4640-F1
25500 SCTA 91355 4550-F7
N TOURNAMENT RD
25700 SCTA 91355 4550-E6
TOURNEY RD
26800 SCTA 91355 4550-C2
TOUSSAU DR
700 FUL 92831 738-J5
TOVEY AV
36200 LACo 93551 4285-G5

TOWER DR
200 BHLS 90211 633-A2
TOWER LN
9900 LA 90210 592-D6
TOWER RD
- BREA 92823 710-A6
- OrCo 92823 710-A4
1000 BHLS 90210 592-D5
1100 LA 90210 592-D5
TOWER GROVE DR
1100 BHLS 90210 592-D5
1100 LA 90210 592-D4
TOWER GROVE PL
10000 LA 90210 592-D6
TOWERS ST
4700 TOR 90503 763-A3
TOWHEE CT
19900 SCTA 91351 4551-E3
TOWHEE DR
3900 CALB 91302 559-H6
TOWN AV
600 MONP 91755 636-D3
TOWN CT
- FUL 92832 738-H7
TOWN CTR
- Nor 91326 500-E2
TOWN & COUNTRY RD
- POM 91766 640-H6
TOWN CENTER DR
- MTBL 90640 636-G5
- RSMD 90640 636-G5
- RSMD 91770 636-G5
3000 PMDL 93551 4195-A3
24500 SCTA 91355 4550-E3
TOWNCENTER VILLAS
- DUAR 91010 568-A4
TOWN CRIER RD
22600 CALB 91302 559-H6
TOWNE AV
300 LA 90013 634-F6
600 LA 90021 634-F6
4400 LA 90011 674-D4
4400 LACo 91711 571-B7
4400 CLAR 91711 571-B7
5800 LA 90003 674-D6
7300 LA 90003 704-D1
11100 LA 90061 704-D6
12800 LACo 90061 734-D2
18200 CRSN 90746 764-D2
N TOWNE AV
100 POM 91767 641-A1
700 POM 91767 601-B3
1500 CLAR 91711 601-B3
1700 CLAR 91711 571-B7
3200 LACo 91711 601-B3
S TOWNE AV
100 POM 91766 641-A3
2600 SBdC 91710 641-A5
13000 LACo 90061 734-D3
TOWNE CT
17300 CRSN 90746 734-D7
TOWNE ST
1700 GLDL 91208 564-H1
TOWNE CENTER CT
- LAN 93534 4015-H4
TOWNE CENTER DR
800 POM 91767 601-B4
3400 LVRN 91750 600-H2
12600 CRTS 90703 737-A7
12800 CRTS 90703 767-A1
TOWNE PARK CIR
100 POM 91767 601-A2
TOWNE WAY DR
9700 ELMN 91733 637-A1
TOWNLEY CIR
1700 SIMI 93063 499-A3
TOWNLEY DR
8600 PRV 90660 676-F4
10300 LACo 90606 676-H5
11800 LACo 90606 677-A7
TOWNSEND AV
4600 Eagl 90041 565-B5
4600 HiPk 90042 565-B7
N TOWNSEND AV
100 City 90063 635-D4
S TOWNSEND AV
100 City 90063 635-D6
800 LACo 90023 635-D7
900 LACo 90023 675-D1
TOWNSEND PL
200 PAS 91103 565-H4
TOWNSGATE RD
2100 THO 91361 557-B4
TOWNSITE DR
3200 WCOV 91792 679-D1
TOWNSLEY CT
- Saug 91350 4461-F6
TOWSLEY CANYON RD
24100 SCTA 91381 4640-D5
24100 StvR 91381 4640-D5
TOYON
3500 WCOV 91792 679-C1
TOYON BAY
5200 LBCH 90803 826-C1
TOYON CIR
4300 LVRN 91750 570-G7
TOYON DR
- LACo 91390 (4371-G7 See Page 4281)
- LACo 91390 4461-G1
TOYON LN
- LACo 91768 640-B1

TOYON RD
200 SMAD 91024 567-A1
TOYOPA DR
200 PacP 90272 631-B5
TRABUCO LN
7500 CRTS 90703 767-C3
7500 LPMA 90623 767-C3
TRABUCO PL
- POM 91766 640-E5
TRABUCO ST
10200 BLF 90706 736-D5
TRABUCO CANYON WY
300 BREA 92821 709-B5
TRACIE DR
900 BREA 92821 708-H5
TRACTION AV
500 LA 90012 634-H5
700 LA 90013 634-H5
TRACY CT
19900 SCTA 91351 4551-E3
TRACY LN
7600 LPMA 90623 767-C3
TRACY ST
3600 LA 90039 594-C4
3700 LFlz 90027 594-B3
13200 BALD 91706 597-J7
13200 BALD 91706 598-A7
13300 BALD 91706 638-A1
TRACY TER
2200 LFlz 90027 594-C4
TRADE CENTER DR
38800 PMDL 93551 4195-G5
TRADEPOST RD
33600 Actn 93510 4375-F5
TRADEWINDS
1400 WCOV 91790 638-D2
TRAFALGAR AV
500 LACo 91744 679-A2
TRAFALGAR CT
45800 LAN 93534 4015-E3
TRAFALGAR DR
4500 LPMA 90623 767-B4
45600 LAN 93534 4015-E3
TRAFALGER DR
1000 GLDL 91207 564-G1
W TRAFFORD ST
- NLB 90805 765-C1
TRAIL RD
31900 LACo 91390 4463-C1
W TRAIL RD
12300 LACo 91390 4463-B2
TRAIL 1
12400 LACo 91342 482-J5
TRAIL 10
12400 LACo 91342 482-H5
TRAIL 12
11200 LACo 91342 482-J5
TRAIL 2
12400 LACo 91342 482-J5
TRAIL 3
12400 LACo 91342 482-J5
TRAIL 4
12300 LACo 91342 482-J5
TRAIL 5
12300 LACo 91342 482-J5
TRAIL 6
- LACo 91342 482-H6
TRAIL 7
12400 LACo 91342 482-H6
TRAIL 8
- LACo 91342 482-H6
TRAIL A
43700 LACo 93532 4101-J2
TRAIL B
43700 LACo 93532 4101-J2
N TRAIL CANYON RD
- LACo (4724-E4 See Page 4643)
TRAIL CREEK DR
29900 AGRH 91301 557-H5
TRAIL E
43600 LACo 93532 4101-J2
TRAILER CANYON FIRE RD
- PacP 90272 590-F7
- PacP 90272 630-F1
TRAIL F
43600 LACo 93532 4101-J2
TRAIL G
43600 LACo 93532 4101-J2
TRAIL H
43600 LACo 93532 4101-J2
TRAIL I
43600 LACo 93532 4101-J2
TRAIL K
43600 LACo 93532 4101-J2
43600 LACo 93532 4102-A2
TRAIL L
43600 LACo 93532 4102-A2
TRAIL M
43600 LACo 93532 4102-A2
TRAIL N
17500 LACo 93532 4102-A2
TRAIL RANCH RD
33300 LACo 91390 4373-D5
TRAILRIDERS DR
28200 RPV 90275 792-G7
28800 RPV 90275 822-H1
TRAIL RIDGE CIR
- POM 91766 640-G4
TRAIL RIDGE RD
27500 SCTA 91387 4552-D4

TRAILRIDGE ST
40400 PMDL 93551 4194-H2
TRAILS END
10700 ELMN 91731 597-D4
TRAILS LN
- DUAR 91010 568-D5
TRAILS END DR
23600 Chat 91311 499-F6
TRAILS END RD
20300 WAL 91789 639-F6
W TRAILS END RD
2400 Actn 93510 4465-D2
TRAILSIDE DR
14100 LACo 91746 637-H6
TRAILVIEW CIR
200 BREA 92821 709-D7
TRAIL VIEW CT
- LA 91342 481-H6
TRAIL VIEW LN
- CHLS 91709 640-H7
TRAILWAY LN
29200 AGRH 91301 558-A5
29400 AGRH 91301 557-J5
TRAINING CENTER RD
- LACo 92823 709-H3
TRAMAT LN
- Tarz 91356 560-F3
TRAMMELL LN
- Chat 91311 500-E2
TRAMMELL RD
2700 GLDL 91206 565-A2
TRAMONTO DR
- RPV 90275 822-H4
17300 PacP 90272 630-F5
TRANA CIR
26000 CALB 91302 558-J3
TRANBARGER ST
19000 RowH 91748 679-C4
TRANCAS PL
4400 Tarz 91356 560-H5
TRANCAS CANYON RD
5700 LACo 90265 626-J6
5700 MAL 90265 626-J6
5800 MAL 90265 627-A7
6400 MAL 90265 667-A1
TRANCAS LAKES DR
- LACo 90265 586-H6
TRANE RD
8100 LACo 91390 4374-B4
TRANQUIL DR
7200 Tuj 91042 503-J6
7200 Tuj 91042 504-A6
TRANQUIL LN
300 VeCo 91377 558-A1
TRANQUIL PL
7200 Tuj 91042 504-A6
TRANQUILITY CT
43600 LAN 93535 4106-E1
TRANQUILLO RD
200 PacP 90272 630-F5
TRANSIT AV
1200 POM 91766 641-B3
TRANSPORTATION CENTER DR
- PMDL 93550 4196-A6
TRAPANI LN
- Nor 91326 480-C7
- Nor 91326 500-C1
TRASK AV
7000 PdlR 90293 702-B3
TRAUB AV
13300 Wbrk 90059 734-E2
TRAVELER CIR
20100 WAL 91789 639-F5
TRAVERS AV
2200 CMRC 90040 675-J3
TRAVERS CT
- Saug 91350 4461-F6
TRAVIS AV
3500 CMRC 90040 676-B7
TRAVIS LN
27100 LACo 90274 793-D7
TRAVIS RD
- BPK 90621 738-B3
TRAVIS ST
12100 Brwd 90049 631-F1
TRAVIS PAUL DR
5800 LAN 93536 4104-F5
TRAVISTUCK PL
8500 BPK 90621 738-A6
TRAYER AV
300 GLDR 91741 569-C4
TRAYMORE AV
400 COV 91723 599-C5
5400 LACo 91722 599-C2
5600 LACo 91702 599-C1
6000 LACo 91702 569-C7
N TRAYMORE AV
1000 COV 91722 599-C3
TREADWELL ST
3000 LA 90065 594-F1
TREANOR AV
400 GLDR 91741 569-G4
1400 GLDR 91740 599-G2
N TREANOR AV
700 SDMS 91773 599-H4
4900 LACo 91724 599-H3
S TREANOR AV
100 GLDR 91741 599-G5
TREASURE TR
6800 LA 90068 593-D1
TREASURE ISLAND DR
5500 LBCH 90803 826-B2

TREASURE ISLAND LN
5500 LBCH 90803 826-B2
TREASURES WY
- FUL 90638 738-A3
TREASURE VALLEY
- CLAR 91711 571-F2
TREASURE VISTA DR
24400 SCTA 91321 4640-H2
TREBERT PL
9400 Tuj 91042 504-C6
TREE LN
1400 POM 91768 600-E7
TREEFERN DR
2900 DUAR 91010 568-E4
TREEHAVEN CT
6000 LAN 93536 4014-E7
TREE HOLLOW GN
29300 AGRH 91301 558-A5
TREELANE AV
2200 LACo 91016 567-G7
TREERIDGE CIR
2100 BREA 92821 709-D6
TREE ROSE TER
5800 TEML 91775 596-G3
TREETOP CIR
20200 DBAR 91765 679-H4
TREFOIL AV
6400 VeCo 91377 558-B1
TREGO PL
13400 LA 91342 482-C1
TREGO ST
13300 LA 91342 482-C1
TRELAWNEY AV
6300 TEML 91780 596-J1
TRELLIS RD
30200 Cstc 91384 4459-B6
TRELLIS WY
- PMDL 93551 4104-D7
S TREMAINE AV
700 LA 90005 633-E4
700 LA 90010 633-E4
900 LA 90019 633-E4
TREMAINE DR
- BREA 92821 709-A5
TREMEZZO DR
4800 CYP 90630 767-C7
TREMONT AV
300 LBCH 90814 796-A7
N TREMONT AV
2000 SIMI 93063 499-C2
E TREMONT CIR
6600 SIMI 93063 499-C2
TREMONT LN
- BLF 90706 736-D5
TREMONT ST
100 AVA 90704 5923-G4
1000 Boyl 90033 635-C3
E TREMONT ST
- PAS 91103 535-H7
W TREMONT ST
- PAS 91103 535-H7
TREND CT
20500 DBAR 91789 679-F4
TREND TER
4900 GLDL 91214 504-D5
TRENMAR DR
34400 Actn 93510 4374-G2
TRENT CT
2700 LA 90065 564-H7
TRENT WY
- StvR 91381 4550-A7
4100 LA 90065 564-H7
TRENTHAM AV
- CRTS 90703 767-B3
TRENTINO DR
9500 CYP 90630 767-C7
TRENTINO LN
- Nor 91326 480-C7
- Nor 91326 500-C1
TRENTLY LN
2100 LA 90210 592-F3
TRENTON AV
1500 GLDL 91206 564-H3
4200 PMDL 93552 4286-J3
TRENTON CT
300 GLDR 91740 599-F1
TRENTON DR
600 BHLS 90210 632-E2
TRENTON PL
27200 SCTA 91354 4460-H7
TRENTON WY
1000 WCOV 91790 638-D3
TRESSY AV
1200 GLDR 91740 569-J7
TREVAN RD
3300 PAS 91107 566-G1
TREVECCA PL
- CLAR 91711 571-F4
TREVES DR
7100 PRM 90723 735-F1
TREVI PL
400 VeCo 91377 557-G2
TREVI ST
9800 CYP 90630 767-C7
W TREVINO DR
24200 SCTA 91355 4550-E7
TREVINO ST
- LHB 90631 738-C2
TREVINO WY
4500 BPK 90621 737-J4
TREVOR AV
44400 LAN 93534 4015-H4

TREVYELON ST
30000 Cstc 91384 4459-C6
TRIAD DR
13900 LMRD 90638 737-D2
TRIANA PL
700 MONP 91754 636-A3
TRIANA ST
700 MONP 91754 636-A3
TRIANGLE DR
5800 CMRC 90040 676-A7
TRIANGLE PL
3300 GLDL 91208 534-H4
TRI BAY CIR
5100 LKWD 90712 765-G3
N TRIBUNE CT
100 LBCH 90802 825-D1
100 LBCH 90802 795-D7
700 LBCH 90813 795-D7
TRIBUNE PL
17900 GmH 91344 501-A2
TRIBUNE ST
16300 GmH 91344 501-D2
18000 Nor 91326 500-F3
18000 Nor 91326 501-A3
20600 Chat 91311 500-A3
TRICIA LN
15000 LMRD 90638 737-G4
TRICKLING CREEK DR
4900 LVRN 91750 570-H4
TRIDENT WY
7000 LBCH 90803 826-F2
TRIER AV
500 LACo 91744 678-H2
TRIESTE LN
- Nor 91326 500-C1
TRIESTE WY
2500 FUL 92833 738-B5
TRIGGER LN
20900 DBAR 91765 679-G6
TRIGGER PL
9700 Chat 91311 499-H5
TRIGGER ST
22700 Chat 91311 499-G6
TRIGGS ST
4300 LACo 90023 675-E2
4400 CMRC 90023 675-E2
4400 CMRC 90040 675-G2
5100 CMRC 90022 675-G2
TRILLIUM LN
- BqtC 91354 4460-E6
TRILLIUM DRIVEWAY
- WdHl 91367 530-B7
TRILPORT AV
- PMDL 93552 4287-E1
N TRIMBLE CT
300 LBCH 90814 796-B7
TRIMINGHAM ST
- CRTS 90703 767-A2
TRI NET CT
- WAL 91789 639-G6
TRINIDAD CIR
1900 CLAR 91711 571-E7
TRINIDAD CT
- SCTA 91354 4460-G7
TRINIDAD RD
4000 WdHl 91364 560-C6
TRINIDAD WY
5800 BPK 90620 767-D2
TRINITY CT
3700 CHNO 91710 641-C5
TRINITY LN
- AZU 91702 569-B6
700 CLAR 91711 571-F7
7800 LPMA 90623 767-B3
TRINITY PL
- LACo 91390 4460-J3
- LACo 91390 4461-A3
TRINITY RD
900 SBdC 92372 (4562-B1 See Page 4471)
3700 SBdC 92371 (4562-J1 See Page 4471)
TRINITY ST
1600 LA 90015 634-E7
1900 LA 90011 634-E7
2300 LA 90011 674-D1
12200 LACo 90061 734-D1
TRINO WY
200 PacP 90272 630-H6
TRIPOLI AV
11500 LA 91342 502-H1
13000 LA 91342 482-D3
TRIPPET LATERAL
- PacP 90272 590-C6
TRIPPETT LATERAL
20800 PacP 90272 590-C6
20800 Top 90290 590-C6
TRISH WY
- WCOV 91792 679-C1
TRISTAN CT
16400 WHIT 90603 708-A5
TRISTAN DR
9800 DWNY 90240 706-C4
10300 DWNY 90241 706-C4
11900 DWNY 90242 706-B7
TRISTANIA WY
- POM 91767 600-J3
TRISTE PL
4500 Tarz 91356 560-H4
TRISTIN DR
23300 SCTA 91355 4550-G7
TRITON CT
4100 PMDL 93552 4286-J2

STREET
Block City ZIP Pg-Grid

TRITON DR
3900 PMDL 93550 4286-H2
4000 PMDL 93552 4286-H2
6400 PRV 90660 676-E5
TRIUMPH AV
26700 LACo 91387 4552-C4
26700 SCTA 91387 4552-C6
TRIUMPH ST
5900 CMRC 90040 675-J3
TRIUNFO DR
29100 Ago 91301 588-A4
29600 Ago 91301 587-J3
TRIUNFO PL
2200 Ago 91301 588-A4
TRIUNFO CANYON RD
100 THO 91361 557-B4
1100 WLKV 91361 557-A5
2700 Ago 91301 587-E1
3400 WLKV 91361 587-C1
TRIUNFO RIDGE FIRE TR
- LACo 90265 586-D4
- VeCo 90265 586-D4
TRIXIS AV
500 LAN 93534 4015-G3
TROJAN AV
11900 LACo 90047 703-J7
TROJAN CT
- LAN 93536 4014-H7
TROJAN ST
8400 PRV 90660 676-D7
TROJAN WY
1700 POM 91766 641-A4
15900 LMRD 90638 737-F6
S TROJAN WY
1200 WCOV 91790 638-D2
TROLLEY CT
- BREA 92823 709-H6
TROLLEY PL
6800 PdlR 90293 702-A3
TROLLEYWAY
6800 PdlR 90293 702-A3
S TRONA AV
400 WCOV 91791 639-D1
TRONKEEL AV
5700 CHNO 91710 641-H7
TROON AV
10400 LA 90064 632-E6
TROOST AV
4000 LA 91604 562-H5
4400 LA 91602 562-H5
5400 NHol 91601 562-H1
5900 NHol 91601 532-H7
6200 NHol 91606 532-H6
6800 NHol 91605 532-H3
TROPEZ DR
- LAN 93536 4104-G6
TROPEZ LN
16400 HNTB 92649 826-J7
TROPHY TR
600 Top 90290 590-B5
TROPICAL AV
1100 PAS 91107 566-H1
1700 BHLS 90210 592-D6
TROPICAL DR
3900 LA 91604 562-J6
TROPICANA CT
1400 ONT 91762 641-H3
W TROPICANA CT
1000 ONT 91762 641-J3
TROPICANA ST
1200 ONT 91762 641-H3
TROPICANA WY
800 LHB 90631 708-H4
TROPICO AV
10200 WHIT 90603 707-G4
10800 LACo 90604 707-G6
TROPICO WY
4000 LA 90065 594-J3
TROSA ST
17200 GmH 91344 481-B5
TROT AV
18600 RowH 91748 679-A4
TROTTER CT
700 WAL 91789 639-H5
TROTTER TER
1900 CHLS 91709 710-H2
TROTTERS LN
- Cstc 91384 4459-D5
N TROTWOOD AV
200 LA 90732 823-H4
29200 RPV 90275 823-H3
S TROTWOOD AV
1000 LA 90732 823-H6
TROUSDALE DR
- LAN 93536 4015-B5
TROUSDALE PKWY
3400 LA 90089 674-B1
TROUSDALE PL
300 BHLS 90210 592-G4
TROUTDALE DR
2300 Ago 91301 587-H3
TROWBRIDGE CT
3900 WLKV 91361 557-D6
TROY AV
2000 SELM 91733 636-J3
TROY CT
400 CLAR 91711 601-C4
4300 PMDL 93552 4286-J4
TROY DR
3300 LA 90068 563-D6
TROYTON LN
21300 CRSN 90745 764-F6

TRUBA AV
9200 SGAT 90280 704-J4
TRUCK WY
800 MTBL 90640 676-D3
TRUCKE WY
18900 WAL 91789 639-B7
TRUDEAU LN
- PMDL 93551 4195-C6
TRUDGEON AV
1800 LAN 93535 4106-D1
TRUDI LN
3000 BURB 91504 533-E3
TRUDIE AV
11000 WHIT 90604 707-J6
TRUDIE DR
1800 RPV 90275 823-H3
TRUDY DR
2900 LA 90210 592-C1
TRUDY PL
2500 POM 91766 641-B6
TRUE AV
8000 PRV 90660 706-F2
9400 DWNY 90240 706-E4
TRUE GRIT CT
- BqtC 91354 4460-F2
TRUEGRIT PL
22900 DBAR 91765 680-B2
TRUE KNOLL DR
9300 Tuj 91042 504-C6
TRUESDALE ST
11500 SunV 91352 502-F6
13200 SunV 91352 532-C2
13300 PanC 91402 532-C2
TRUITT ST
1300 GLDL 91201 564-A3
TRUJILLO DR
4500 LACo 91722 598-G4
N TRUJILLO DR
4600 LACo 91722 598-G4
TRULL BROOK DR
19600 Tarz 91356 560-F7
TRUMAN AV
400 FUL 92832 738-F6
TRUMAN CT
28200 SCTA 91350 4461-A4
E TRUMAN PL
400 WCOV 91790 638-F2
TRUMAN ST
600 LA 91340 502-B1
600 SFER 91340 502-B1
700 SFER 91340 482-A6
1700 SFER 91340 481-J6
1700 LA 91342 481-J6
43800 LAN 93535 4106-C1
TRUMBALL ST
10800 LACo 90604 707-D5
13200 LACo 90605 707-C4
13200 SFSP 90605 707-B4
TRUMBOWER AV
200 MONP 91755 636-B4
TRUMPET DR
21200 SCTA 91321 4641-B2
TRURO AV
11400 HAW 90250 703-C7
11800 HAW 90250 733-C1
S TRURO AV
900 ING 90301 703-C4
10400 Lenx 90304 703-C6
11100 HAW 90304 703-C6
E TRUSLOW AV
100 FUL 92832 738-J7
W TRUSLOW AV
100 FUL 92832 738-G7
TRUSS CT
1500 DBAR 91789 679-G4
TRUXTON AV
7600 Wch 90045 702-H2
TRYON PL
400 GLDL 91206 565-A4
TRYON RD
5600 LA 90068 593-H3
TUALLITAN RD
400 Brwd 90049 631-F2
TUBA ST
14800 MsnH 91345 501-G4
15600 LA 91343 501-D4
17000 Nor 91325 501-B4
18300 Nor 91325 500-J4
18700 Nor 91324 500-F4
19700 Chat 91311 500-A4
22100 Chat 91311 499-J4
S TUBEWAY AV
1900 CMRC 90040 675-J4
1900 CMRC 90040 676-A3
TUCKAWAY LN
1200 DUAR 91010 568-A7
TUCKER AV
13800 LA 91342 482-E1
TUCKER LN
900 INDS 91789 679-F3
2600 OrCo 90720 796-G5
E TUCKER ST
400 COMP 90221 735-A3
TUCKERWAY RANCH RD
35000 LACo 93551 4375-H2
TUCSON CT
700 SDMS 91773 600-C1
41800 PMDL 93551 4104-C6
TUCSON ST
2200 LAN 93535 4016-E4
TUDOR AV
9500 MTCL 91763 601-F6
10400 MTCL 91763 641-F1

TUDOR AV
11100 SBdC 91710 641-F3
TUDOR DR
16300 Enc 91436 561-E6
TUDOR ST
500 COV 91722 599-C3
1300 COV 91724 599-E3
19300 LACo 91722 599-D3
19600 LACo 91724 599-D3
21200 LACo 91773 599-H3
E TUDOR ST
200 COV 91722 599-C3
16500 LACo 91722 598-G3
W TUDOR ST
100 COV 91722 599-A3
200 LACo 91722 599-A3
1100 SDMS 91773 599-H3
TUESDAY DR
2100 WCOV 91792 679-A1
TUFTS AV
400 BURB 91504 533-G5
TUFTS CIR
20400 WAL 91789 639-F7
TUJUNGA AV
4000 LA 91604 562-J6
4000 LA 91602 562-J3
4800 NHol 91601 562-J3
5900 NHol 91601 532-J7
6000 NHol 91606 532-J7
6800 NHol 91605 532-J4
7200 SunV 91352 532-J2
9000 SunV 91352 502-H7
E TUJUNGA AV
100 BURB 91502 533-J7
400 BURB 91501 533-J7
1100 BURB 91501 534-A5
W TUJUNGA AV
200 BURB 91502 563-G1
TUJUNGA CANYON BLVD
9000 Tuj 91042 504-A1
10300 Tuj 91042 503-J2
TUJUNGA CANYON PL
9600 Tuj 91042 504-C5
TUJUNGA VALLEY ST
8500 Sunl 91040 503-F2
TULA DR
22400 SCTA 91350 4460-J6
TULA ST
7800 LBCH 90808 766-H7
E TULA ST
8200 LBCH 90808 766-J7
TULANE AV
1800 LBCH 90815 796-C2
3400 LBCH 90808 766-C5
3600 LBCH 90808 796-C2
N TULANE AV
4500 LBCH 90808 766-B5
TULANE RD
1300 CLAR 91711 601-C1
TULARE AV
1600 BURB 91504 533-C4
TULARE LN
28400 AGRH 91301 558-C6
TULARE ST
7500 BPK 90621 737-H6
TULAROSA DR
600 Echo 90026 594-B7
TULE DIVIDE FIRE RD
- LACo 91390 4101-J7
- LACo 91390 4102-A6
- LACo 93551 4102-F6
TULETTE LN
- PMDL 93552 4287-E1
TULIP AV
- SIMI 93063 499-A2
2200 UPL 91784 571-H3
TULIP CIR
6000 LAN 93536 4104-F5
TULIP CT
22500 SCTA 91390 4460-J3
TULIP LN
- BREA 92821 709-D4
1700 ARCD 91006 597-F1
TULIP ST
- LHB 90631 708-C7
TULIP GROVE ST
- StvR 91381 4640-B2
TULIPLAND AV
14800 SCTA 91387 4462-F5
TULIP TREE LN
1900 LCF 91011 534-J1
12700 RowH 91748 678-J7
TULIP WOOD CT
500 OrCo 90631 708-F4
TULLER AV
3500 LA 90034 672-D2
3700 LA 90066 672-E2
3800 CULC 90230 672-E3
TULLER RD
2200 LA 90032 635-F1
TULLIS DR
9500 LA 90210 592-F4
TULSA
15400 MsnH 91345 501-G2
TULSA AV
2200 CLAR 91711 571-C6
TULSA LN
10900 Chat 91311 500-D2
TULSA PL
17900 GmH 91344 501-A2
TULSA ST
15500 MsnH 91345 501-F2
15600 GmH 91344 501-A2

TULSA ST
18600 Nor 91326 500-F2
19600 Chat 91311 500-D2
22000 Chat 91311 499-J3
TUMBLEWEED DR
2700 PMDL 93550 4286-F5
TUMBLEWEED RD
11000 Litl 93543 4468-F5
11800 Pear 93553 4468-H5
12900 Valy 93563 4468-H5
13500 Valy 93563 4469-A5
TUMBLEWEED RD Rt#-N6
13100 Pear 93553 4468-J5
13100 Pear 93553 4469-A5
13100 Valy 93563 4468-J5
13100 Valy 93563 4469-A5
TUMBLEWEED WY
21400 SCTA 91350 4551-B3
TUMBLEWOOD WY
42800 LAN 93536 4105-C4
TUMIN RD
1800 LHH 90631 708-F2
S TUNA ST
600 SPed 90731 824-D5
TUNA CANYON RD
1700 Top 90290 630-A1
2300 Top 90290 629-J3
3200 LACo 90265 630-A3
3600 MAL 90265 630-A3
TUNALES DR
3600 FUL 92835 738-H1
TUNBRIDGE CT
11700 BelA 90077 591-G3
TUNDRA DR
- LA 91342 481-J6
TUNDRA WY
18500 LACo 93591 4200-B3
TUNE PL
2500 LAN 93536 4105-D1
TUNNEY AV
6200 Res 91335 530-F2
8300 Nor 91324 530-F2
9500 Nor 91324 500-F4
10300 Nor 91326 500-F4
TUOLUMNE DR
600 WAL 91789 639-B7
TUPELO LN
10300 BelA 90077 592-A3
TUPELO RIDGE DR
22800 SCTA 91354 4460-H4
28000 SCTA 91390 4460-H4
TUPPER ST
14300 PanC 91402 502-A6
14500 PanC 91402 501-H6
14900 LA 91343 501-D6
16900 Nor 91325 501-D6
TURA LN
2600 SMRO 91108 566-E6
E TURBO ST
7800 LBCH 90808 766-H7
TURIN ST
400 VeCo 91377 557-G1
TURK DR
16800 LPUE 91744 678-F1
TURLOCK RD
14800 LMRD 90638 737-F3
TURMERIC CT
21600 SCTA 91350 4461-A5
TURMONT ST
600 CRSN 90746 764-E3
TURNBERRY CT
- PMDL 93551 4195-B2
TURNBERRY DR
19900 Tarz 91356 560-E6
19900 WdHl 91364 560-E6
TURNBERRY LN
- Cstc 91384 4459-H5
TURNBOW DR
10600 Sunl 91040 503-F3
TURNBULL CANYON RD
100 INDS 91744 638-B7
100 INDS 91746 638-B7
100 LACo 91746 638-B7
300 INDS 91745 638-B7
500 HacH 91745 638-B7
600 INDS 91745 678-A2
1700 HacH 91745 677-H4
3800 LACo 90601 677-E5
3800 WHIT 90601 677-E5
TURNDELL RD
500 OrCo 90631 708-F4
TURNER AV
- FUL 92833 738-A7
S TURNER AV
100 WCOV 91791 598-H7
200 WCOV 91791 638-H1
TURNER CT
5300 LKWD 90712 765-J3
TURNER DR
36400 PMDL 93550 4286-F4
TURNER LN
1000 LHB 90631 708-E4
TURNER ST
400 LA 90012 634-G4
TURNERGROVE DR
5900 LKWD 90713 766-D3
TURNING BEND DR
100 CLAR 91711 600-J1
1100 CLAR 91711 601-A1
TURNING LEAF WY
- AZU 91702 568-J1

TURNPOST LN
- POM 91766 640-H5
1600 HacH 91745 678-F4
TURNSTONE CT
26500 SCTA 91355 4550-E4
TURPIN ST
8500 RSMD 91770 596-G5
TURQUESA DR
25700 SCTA 91355 4550-G4
TURQUESA LN
1200 PacP 90272 630-H4
TURQUOISE CIR
2100 CHLS 91709 680-H6
TURQUOISE CIR N
2000 CHLS 91709 680-J6
TURQUOISE LN
3600 LVRN 91750 600-G1
3900 LVRN 91750 570-G7
TURQUOISE ST
4100 LA 90032 595-C6
TURRELL ST
1900 LMTA 90717 793-H3
TURTLE CREEK RD
3000 CALB 91302 589-D2
TURTLE POND CT
15000 CHLS 91709 680-G5
TURTLE RIDGE LN
19400 Nor 91326 480-F6
TURTLE RIDGE PL
12200 Nor 91326 480-F6
TURTLE RIDGE WY
12600 Nor 91326 480-F6
TURTLE SPRINGS CT
12000 Nor 91326 480-F6
TURTLE SPRINGS LN
11800 Nor 91326 480-F7
TURTLE SPRINGS WY
19500 Nor 91326 480-E6
TUSCAN CT
- PMDL 93551 4287-D1
17700 GmH 91344 481-A5
TUSCAN DR
17400 GmH 91344 481-A5
TUSCANI DR
4500 CYP 90630 767-B7
TUSCANY AV
8100 PdlR 90293 702-B3
TUSCANY CT
- PMDL 93550 4286-F5
TUSCANY DR
- VeCo 91377 557-G2
TUSTIN RD
- PAS 91105 565-D5
TUSTIN ST
14600 Shrm 91403 561-J5
TUTHILL LN
34600 LACo 91390 4374-A4
TUTTLE ST
4300 LACo 90023 675-E2
4400 CMRC 90023 675-E2
4400 CMRC 90040 675-E2
TUTTLE CREEK PL
19200 WAL 91789 639-C6
TUXEDO TER
5500 LA 90068 593-G2
TUXFORD PL
10800 SunV 91352 503-A7
TUXFORD ST
10400 SunV 91352 503-A6
11000 SunV 91352 502-J7
11300 SunV 91352 532-H1
11600 NHol 91605 532-H1
TWAIN PL
25900 StvR 91381 4550-B6
TWAIN ST
4900 CHNO 91710 641-F4
TWEED LN
7800 SBdC 92372 (4562-F4
See Page 4471)
12200 Brwd 90049 631-G4
TWEEDY BLVD
2500 LACo 90280 704-J4
2500 SGAT 90280 704-J4
2600 SGAT 90280 705-B4
3100 LYN 90262 705-B4
TWEEDY LN
8400 DWNY 90240 706-C1
TWEEDY PL
5300 SGAT 90280 705-F5
S TWICKENHAM AV
200 ELA 90022 635-J7
TWIG CIR
1400 UPL 91786 601-H1
TWILIGHT AV
- LA 91342 481-J5
TWILIGHT CT
2200 PMDL 93550 4286-E3
TWILIGHT DR
3000 FUL 92835 738-H1
TWILIGHT LN
17800 Enc 91316 561-B5
TWILIGHT CANYON TR
- VeCo 93063 499-E3
TWILIGHT VISTA DR
100 Alta 91001 535-J3
TWIN AV
1900 SGBL 91776 596-F7
3400 RSMD 91770 636-F1
TWINBERRY LN
600 LAN 93534 4015-G3
TWIN BUTTE RD
- LACo 93551 4375-G2

TWIN CANYON LN
1000 DBAR 91765 640-D5
TWIN CIRCLE LN
6400 SIMI 93063 499-C3
TWINCREEK AV
2200 PMDL 93551 4195-B5
TWINCREEK CT
3300 PMDL 93551 4195-B5
TWINFOOT CT
1000 THO 91361 557-B5
TWIN HARBORS VIEW DR
- RPV 90275 823-F7
TWIN HILL DR
16800 HacH 91745 678-E5
TWIN HILLS AV
11400 Nor 91326 500-F1
TWIN HILLS DR
13200 SLB 90740 796-H7
TWIN HILLS PL
19400 Nor 91326 500-F1
TWINING ST
4500 LA 90032 595-D6
TWINING WY
- LA 91304 530-A4
TWINKLE CIR
16100 HNTB 92649 826-J6
TWIN LAKE RDG
3400 WLKV 91361 557-B7
TWIN LAKES DR
1000 SBdC 92397 (4652-D2
See Page 4651)
5300 CYP 90630 767-D5
TWIN OAK ST
2500 LA 90039 594-F5
TWIN OAKS CT
400 THO 91362 557-A1
TWIN OAKS PL
- StvR 91381 4550-C5
TWIN OAKS RD
5200 HIDH 91302 559-F3
TWIN PALMS DR
1800 SMRO 91108 596-C2
N TWIN PALMS DR
500 SGBL 91775 596-C2
TWIN PALMS LN
- LA 91342 482-E6
TWIN PINES LN
23800 DBAR 91765 640-C6
TWINSLOPE TR
1700 Top 90290 590-C2
TWIN SPRING LN
23500 DBAR 91765 680-C2
TWIN SPRINGS AV
6300 VeCo 91377 558-A1
TWIN TIDES DR
- SCTA 91355 4550-E1
TWINTREE AV
5500 LACo 91702 599-B1
N TWINTREE AV
200 AZU 91702 569-A7
TWISTED OAK DR
- CanP 91307 529-C7
TWO OAK CT
2400 SIMI 93063 499-A1
TWO TREE AV
3300 LA 90031 595-B7
TYBURN RD
600 PVE 90274 822-E1
TYBURN ST
1800 GLDL 91204 594-E1
2900 LA 90039 594-D2
3500 LA 91204 594-E1
3500 LA 90065 594-E1
TYE CIR
4500 LVRN 91750 570-E7
TYE PL
37000 LACo 93551 4285-H3
TYLEEN PL
1000 POM 91768 600-F7
TYLER AL
1200 PAS 91106 566-B3
TYLER AV
1400 SELM 91733 637-C3
2400 ELMN 91733 637-C2
3000 ELMN 91731 637-C2
3400 ELMN 91731 597-D5
5000 ELMN 91006 597-D4
5000 ELMN 91780 597-D4
5700 ARCD 91006 597-D4
W TYLER AV
2800 ANA 92801 767-H5
TYLER DR
1700 MONP 91755 636-D4
TYLER LN
27900 SCTA 91387 4551-J2
TYLER ST
1000 GLDL 91205 564-G7
2800 CRSN 90810 765-B5
4900 CHNO 91710 641-F6
13900 LA 91342 482-A3
14400 LA 91342 481-J4
E TYLER ST
2500 CRSN 90810 764-J5
2500 CRSN 90810 765-A5
N TYLER WY
400 UPL 91786 601-J3
TYNDALL RD
33100 LACo 91390 4373-F6
TYNE CT
- LACo 91390 4373-H5
TYNEBOURNE CT
31800 WLKV 91361 557-D6

TYPHOON LN
16100 HNTB 92649 826-J6
TYROLEAN DR
- LA 90068 563-F7
TYRONE AV
4300 Shrm 91423 562-A3
5200 VanN 91401 562-A2
5900 VanN 91401 532-A7
6600 VanN 91405 532-A4
8000 PanC 91402 532-A1
8700 PanC 91402 502-A7
TYRRELL PL
3300 GLDL 91206 565-C1
TYSON PL
12700 GmH 91344 481-B5

U

UCLAN DR
600 BURB 91504 533-G5
UDELL CT
3800 LFlz 90027 594-C4
UDELL MTWY
- Ago 91301 588-D2
UDINE WY
100 BelA 90077 632-B1
UHEA RD
22500 WdHl 91364 559-H5
UINTAH ST
1100 LCF 91011 535-B3
E ULEN ST
5500 LBCH 90815 796-C3
ULMUS DR
21600 WdHl 91364 560-A6
ULTIMO AV
300 LBCH 90814 796-C7
300 LBCH 90814 826-C1
600 LBCH 90804 796-C7
ULVERSTON ST
4900 VeCo 91377 557-H1
ULYSSES ST
300 LA 90065 595-A5
UMATILLA AV
1100 LBCH 90804 795-J6
UMBRELLA TER
- PMDL 93551 4285-D3
UMBRIA ST
600 HiPk 90042 595-B2
UMEO RD
1500 PacP 90272 631-D3
UNDERHILL DR
100 GLDR 91741 569-H5
UNDERHILL TER
1400 GLDR 91741 569-H5
UNDERWOOD ST
8800 PRV 90660 676-G3
UNDINE RD
24200 SCTA 91355 4550-F7
UNION AV
- CRTS 90703 766-H3
2500 LHB 90631 708-B6
7200 WHIT 90602 677-C7
17900 BLF 90706 766-A1
E UNION AV
100 FUL 92832 738-H6
1000 FUL 92831 738-J6
N UNION AV
100 Echo 90026 634-D2
100 POM 91768 640-E1
S UNION AV
100 Echo 90026 634-D3
300 LA 90017 634-D3
900 LA 90015 634-C5
1900 LA 90007 634-C5
W UNION AV
100 FUL 92832 738-F6
UNION CT
5400 CHNO 91710 641-H4
UNION DR
400 LA 90017 634-D3
UNION PL
100 Echo 90026 634-D2
300 LA 90017 634-D2
UNION ST
300 MTBL 90640 676-B6
4400 LCF 91011 535-A3
5100 CHNO 91710 641-G4
9000 PRV 90660 676-G3
11800 NRWK 90650 736-H1
E UNION ST
- PAS 91103 565-J4
200 PAS 91101 565-J4
500 PAS 91101 566-A4
800 PAS 91106 566-A4
W UNION ST
- PAS 91103 565-H4
UNION HILLS LN
- CRSN 90745 794-G1
UNION JACK MALL
- LA 90292 701-J2
100 LA 90292 702-A4
UNION JACK ST
- LA 90292 701-J2
UNION PACIFIC AV
3200 LA 90023 675-A1
3900 CMRC 90023 675-D1
3900 LACo 90023 675-D1
4400 CMRC 90040 675-F1
4700 ELA 90022 675-F1
5400 CMRC 90022 675-H2
UNIT ST
11200 LA 90059 704-E6

UNITED RD
3800 AGRH 91301 588-F1
3900 AGRH 91301 558-F7
UNIVERSAL PL
10600 LA 91604 563-B6
UNIVERSAL CENTER DR
3500 Univ 91608 563-C6
UNIVERSAL CITYWALK DR
- Univ 91608 563-C6
UNIVERSAL HOLLYWOOD DR
- Univ 91608 563-B6
400 Univ 91608 563-B6
UNIVERSAL STUDIOS BLVD
3400 LA 90068 563-C7
UNIVERSITY AV
100 BURB 91504 533-G5
2700 LA 90007 634-B7
3200 LA 90007 674-B1
UNIVERSITY CIR
- FUL 92835 738-H5
400 CLAR 91711 601-C2
UNIVERSITY DR
- LACo 91768 639-J2
- LACo 91768 640-B1
- POM 91768 640-A2
600 CRSN 90746 764-F2
700 CRSN 90747 764-F2
1600 LACo 91104 536-C7
1600 PAS 91104 536-C7
1600 PAS 91104 566-C1
1900 LACo 90220 764-H2
13300 LMRD 90639 737-F2
E UNIVERSITY DR
9100 Nor 91330 501-A7
N UNIVERSITY DR
18100 Nor 91330 500-J6
18100 Nor 91330 501-A6
W UNIVERSITY DR
- LACo 91768 640-A3
- POM 91768 640-A3
9100 Nor 91330 500-J7
UNIVERSITY PKWY
400 POM 91768 640-B3
UNIVERSITY WY
- AZU 91702 569-B6
- BPK 90620 767-F6
UNIVERSITY CENTER DR
- SCTA 91355 4550-E5
N UNRUH AV
100 INDS 91744 638-C6
300 LPUE 91744 638-D5
600 LACo 91744 638-D5
UNSER ST
8600 PRV 90660 676-E5
UPLAND AV
500 SPed 90731 824-A3
1000 LA 90732 824-A3
UPLAND CT
36500 PMDL 93550 4286-A5
UPLAND ST
1900 RPV 90275 823-H3
UPLANDER WY
5700 CULC 90230 672-H6
UPPER CT
1700 PMDL 93550 4286-D4
UPPER RD
- LFlz 90027 594-A4
UPPER TER
700 SDMS 91773 600-A3
2500 LaCr 91214 504-G6
UPPER BARREL W
1000 PVE 90274 792-G5
UPPER BEACON TR
- LFlz 90027 564-B7
- LFlz 90027 594-B1
UPPER BIG TUJUNGA CANYON RD
- LACo - 507-B1
- LACo - (4646-B7
See Page 4645)
- LACo - (4726-B2
See Page 4645)
- LACo - (4727-A5
See Page 4647)
UPPER BLACKWATER CANYON RD
- RHLS 90274 823-D1
UPPER BREWSTER MTWY
- LACo 90265 587-E6
UPPER EAST TERRACE RD
- AVA 90704 5923-H4
UPPER KRESS ST
2100 LA 90046 592-J3
UPPER LAKE RD
- VeCo 91361 586-F1
UPPER MAREK MTWY
- LACo 91342 482-J3
- LACo 91342 (4723-A4
See Page 4643)
UPPER MESA RD
400 LA 90402 631-B7
UPPER MONROE TKTR
- LACo - 509-H6
- LACo - (510-A5
See Page 509)
- LACo - (540-A1
See Page 509)

UPPER RAMIREZ MTWY
29000 LACo 90265 627-D1
UPPERTON AV
1700 HiPk 90042 565-C7
UPPERTON PL
1900 HiPk 90042 565-C7
UPTON CT
5200 Eagl 90041 565-C5
UPTON DR
- PMDL 93552 4287-C4
UPTON PL
1200 Eagl 90041 565-C5
URBAN AV
2900 SMCA 90404 671-J1
3000 SMCA 90404 631-J7
URBANA AV
8800 Pcma 91331 502-B6
8800 Pcma 91331 532-D1
URBANA LN
43400 LAN 93535 4106-D2
URBANDALE AV
27700 SCTA 91350 4461-B5
28100 Saug 91350 4461-B5
URELL DR
1100 LHB 90631 708-E4
URMSTON PL
2000 SMRO 91108 596-A2
URQUIDEZ AV
3600 GLDL 91208 534-G4
URSINUS CIR
2200 CLAR 91711 571-D6
URSULA AV
3900 LA 90008 673-C2
USC MCCARTHY WY
600 LA 90089 674-B1
USC PARDEE WY
- LA 90089 674-B1
USHER PL
500 BHLS 90210 592-G4
USREY DR
- AZU 91702 569-A4
USS ANTIETAM ST
15200 LA 90732 793-J6
USS DUNCAN CT
15100 LA 90732 794-A7
USS MISSOURI ST
15200 LA 90732 794-A7
USS NEW JERSEY ST
15100 LA 90732 794-A7
15300 LA 90732 793-J7
USS OGDEN CT
15100 LA 90732 794-A6
USS PRAIRIE CT
15100 LA 90732 794-A6
15100 LA 90732 793-J6
USS PRINCETON CT
15200 SPed 90731 794-A7
15300 LA 90732 793-J7
15300 LA 90732 794-A7
UTAH AV
2300 ELSG 90245 732-J3
3200 ELMN 91731 637-D1
8100 BPK 90621 767-J1
11300 SGAT 90280 705-F7
11500 SGAT 90280 735-F1
UTAH CT
300 CLAR 91711 601-E4
N UTAH ST
100 Boyl 90033 634-J4
S UTAH ST
100 Boyl 90033 634-J5
UTICA DR
8200 LA 90046 593-A3
8400 LA 90046 592-J3
UTICA ST
13500 LACo 90605 707-C7
UTILITY WY
22700 CRSN 90745 794-F1
UTLEY RD
2300 LaCr 91214 504-H6
UTOPIA AV
1200 LA 90230 672-F5
UTOPIA CT
- SCTA 91351 4551-H2

V

VACA AV
31300 Cstc 91384 4369-F7
VACCARO AV
20500 TOR 90503 763-B5
VACCO ST
10300 SELM 91733 637-B4
VACHON DR
3900 RSMD 91770 596-G6
VADO DR
2400 LA 90046 592-J2
VADO PL
8600 LA 90046 592-H2
VAGA AV
11500 LACo 90604 707-F6
VAGABOND RD
1200 MONP 91754 635-H3
VAGNONE WY
15900 CRTS 90703 736-J5
15900 CRTS 90650 736-J5
VAHAN CT
- LAN 93536 4104-F1
2700 LAN 93536 4105-A1
VAHN LN
- LAN 93536 4105-B1
VAIL AV
1200 CMRC 90040 676-B5

VAIL AV
1200 MTBL 90640 676-B5
1500 UPL 91784 571-H5
2000 RBCH 90278 733-B7
2000 RBCH 90278 763-B1
N VAIL AV
100 MTBL 90640 676-C1
600 MTBL 90640 636-C6
S VAIL AV
100 MTBL 90640 676-B3
VAIL DR
9800 MTCL 91763 601-G6
10500 Sunl 91040 503-B3
VAIL LN
- LA 91342 482-C3
VAIL ST
4400 CRTS 90703 767-B4
VAIL WY
- ING 90305 703-F3
1800 UPL 91784 571-H6
VAL ST
700 ARCD 91007 597-A1
700 TEML 91780 597-A1
9600 TEML 91780 596-J1
VALAHO DR
7200 Tuj 91042 504-A4
7300 Tuj 91042 503-J4
VALAHO LN
7300 Tuj 91042 503-J4
7300 Tuj 91042 504-A4
VALANE DR
1400 GLDL 91208 534-G5
VALARESSA LN
13000 LACo 90601 637-E5
VALBERG ST
- PMDL 93552 4287-E1
VALCARLOS AV
1400 RowH 91748 678-J4
VALCOUR DR
28000 SCTA 91387 4552-A2
VALCOURT LN
2300 GLDR 91741 570-A5
VALDEMAR DR
15100 HacH 91745 677-J5
VALDERAS DR
2000 GLDL 91208 534-H4
VALDERRAMA DR
- StvR 91381 4550-C3
VALDEZ DR
19500 Tarz 91356 560-F4
VALDEZ PL
4500 Tarz 91356 560-F4
VALDEZ RD
23100 CALB 90290 589-F1
23100 Top 90290 589-F1
VALDINA DR
8100 DWNY 90240 706-B3
VALDINA PL
4500 LACo 90043 673-C5
VALE CT
- SCTA 91354 4460-G3
VALE DR
7600 WHIT 90602 677-E7
8000 WHIT 90602 707-E1
VALE WY
- HacH 91745 637-H7
VALEBROOK PL
1200 SDMS 91740 570-A7
VALECREST DR
8300 SunV 91352 533-B1
VALEDA DR
14300 LMRD 90638 737-E1
VALEMONT AV
1900 RowH 91748 679-C5
VALENCIA AV
800 HacH 91745 678-A1
1300 LACo 91104 566-E1
1500 LACo 91104 536-E7
1900 OrCo 92823 709-H5
1900 OrCo 92821 709-H5
1900 BREA 92823 709-H5
1900 BREA 92821 709-G6
E VALENCIA AV
200 BURB 91502 533-J7
200 BURB 91502 563-J1
400 BURB 91501 533-J7
1000 BURB 91501 534-A6
S VALENCIA AV Rt#-142
2500 OrCo 92823 709-G7
2500 BREA 92821 709-G7
2500 OrCo 92821 709-G7
3000 BREA 92823 709-G7
W VALENCIA AV
100 BURB 91502 563-H2
300 BURB 91506 563-H2
VALENCIA BLVD
- StvR 91381 4550-B5
23000 SCTA 91355 4550-F3
VALENCIA CT
1100 Ven 90291 671-H6
VALENCIA DR
4600 LVRN 91750 570-G7
E VALENCIA DR
200 FUL 92832 738-J7
W VALENCIA DR
400 FUL 92832 738-F7
VALENCIA LN
1900 DUAR 91010 568-A6
VALENCIA PL
100 COV 91723 599-A4
1500 POM 91768 600-G6

STREET Block City ZIP Pg-Grid

VALENCIA ST
100 GLDR 91741 569-C4
600 LA 90017 634-C5
900 LA 90015 634-C5
1800 RowH 91748 679-C6
2500 LVRN 91750 600-H1
11800 NRWK 90650 736-H3
12500 CRTS 90703 767-A3
N VALENCIA ST
- ALH 91801 596-C3
100 LHB 90631 708-F5
S VALENCIA ST
- ALH 91801 596-C4
100 LHB 90631 708-F5
1800 ALH 91801 636-D1
VALENCIA WY
1100 ARCD 91006 567-E3
E VALENCIA MESA DR
100 FUL 92835 738-G4
W VALENCIA MESA DR
100 FUL 92835 738-E5
1000 FUL 92833 738-E5
VALENS ST
12700 BALD 91706 637-H1
VALENTINE DR
400 GLDL 91202 534-D7
400 GLDL 91202 564-D1
VALENTINE PL
2100 SMRO 91108 596-A2
VALENTINE ST
2000 Echo 90026 594-F5
VALENZA AV
1400 RowH 91748 678-J4
VALEPORT AV
15600 LACo 93535 4199-E1
E VALEPORT ST
8300 LBCH 90808 767-A7
VALERA AV
300 POM 91767 601-A2
VALERA DR
400 MTBL 90640 676-F1
VALERA WY
3000 FUL 92835 738-E2
VALERIE AV
5500 WdHl 91367 559-D1
VALERIE CT
1900 WCOV 91792 679-A1
VALERIE LN
4200 CHNO 91710 641-D5
VALERIO CT
- SCTA 91354 4460-G4
VALERIO ST
4500 BURB 91505 533-B4
10600 SunV 91352 533-A4
11000 SunV 91352 532-H4
11400 NHol 91605 532-G4
13500 VanN 91405 532-A4
14500 VanN 91405 531-H4
15300 VanN 91406 531-B4
17700 Res 91335 531-A4
18100 Res 91335 530-F4
19700 Win 91306 530-D4
20800 CanP 91303 530-A4
22000 CanP 91303 529-H4
22300 CanP 91307 529-F4
23200 LA 91304 529-F4
VALERO CIR
4900 VeCo 91377 557-G2
VALEVIEW AV
1300 SDMS 91773 570-A7
VALEVIEW DR
1400 DBAR 91765 680-D3
VALEVISTA TR
3000 LA 90068 593-C1
VALEWOOD ST
2400 SDMS 91773 570-A7
VALHALLA DR
3100 BURB 91505 533-C6
VALHALLA ST
2400 POM 91767 601-B5
VALIANT ST
- LAN 93536 4015-E3
1000 LAN 93534 4015-F3
2000 GLDR 91741 569-J5
2100 GLDR 91741 570-A5
VALIDO RD
500 ARCD 91007 566-J4
VALIENTE DR
40300 PMDL 93551 4194-H3
VALIHI WY
3600 GLDL 91208 534-J4
VALINDA AV
400 LACo 91744 638-G6
1500 WCOV 91790 638-G6
S VALINDA AV
600 WCOV 91790 638-G2
1000 LACo 91744 638-G2
1700 WCOV 91792 638-G2
VALITA ST
700 Ven 90291 671-J4
VALJEAN AV
4800 Enc 91436 561-F3
6400 VanN 91406 531-E4
8300 LA 91343 531-E1
8700 LA 91343 501-E5
10500 GrnH 91344 501-E1
VALLE CT
- LACo 90502 764-A5
VALLE DR
2100 LHH 90631 708-F1
VALLECITO
1500 POM 91768 600-F6
VALLECITO DR
1600 HacH 91745 678-A3
1700 LA 90732 823-G6
2600 HacH 91745 677-J5
VALLE CONTENTO DR
15800 HacH 91745 678-B5
VALLE DEL ORO
23700 SCTA 91321 4641-B1
VALLEJO DR
200 GLDL 91206 564-H4
W VALLEJO DR
3100 ANA 92804 767-H6
VALLEJO ST
200 LHB 90631 708-G6
700 BREA 92821 708-G6
2100 LA 90031 635-A1
VALLEJO WY
11200 MTCL 91763 641-E3
VALLEJO VILLAS ST
600 HiPk 90042 595-D5
600 LA 90032 595-D5
VALLEJO VISTA DR
34700 LACo 91390 4374-B3
VALLE LINDO LN
100 LACo 90265 629-A3
VALLETA DR
1800 RPV 90275 823-H1
VALLE VERDE CT
4600 LVRN 91750 570-H7
VALLE VIEW LN
40000 LACo 93551 4194-C4
VALLE VISTA AV
200 MNRO 91016 567-H3
13400 BALD 91706 598-A6
VALLE VISTA DR
600 SMAD 91024 567-C1
1200 FUL 92831 738-J5
2600 Eagl 90041 565-A4
2600 GLDL 91206 565-A4
2900 LA 90065 594-H1
VALLE VISTA MTWY
3100 GLDL 91206 565-C4
VALLEY BLVD
900 SGBL 91776 596-G6
1400 ALH 91803 595-F7
2100 POM 91768 640-D1
3100 Boyl 90033 635-B2
3100 LA 90031 635-B2
3500 POM 91789 640-A4
3900 LA 90032 635-E2
4000 LA 90063 635-E2
5200 LA 90032 595-F7
5500 ALH 90032 595-F7
8300 RSMD 91770 596-G6
9400 ELMN 91731 596-G6
9500 ELMN 91731 597-A6
9500 RSMD 91770 597-A6
11200 ELMN 91731 637-E1
11500 ELMN 91732 637-E1
12400 INDS 91746 637-E1
12400 LACo 91746 637-E1
12400 INDS 91732 637-E1
14000 INDS 91746 638-A5
14200 LACo 91746 638-A5
14300 INDS 91744 638-A5
15500 INDS 91745 638-A5
15600 INDS 91745 678-D1
15600 INDS 91744 678-D1
16100 LPUE 91745 678-D1
16100 LPUE 91744 678-D1
17300 INDS 91748 678-H2
17700 LACo 91744 678-H2
18200 INDS 91748 679-A2
18200 LACo 91744 679-A2
18300 INDS 91744 679-A2
18600 LACo 91792 679-A2
18600 WCOV 91792 679-A2
E VALLEY BLVD
- ALH 91801 596-C7
100 SGBL 91776 596-F6
1700 INDS 91748 679-C3
2500 WCOV 91792 679-C3
3200 INDS 91789 679-F1
3200 WAL 91789 679-F1
4100 WAL 91789 639-J6
4100 LACo 91789 640-A5
4100 POM 91789 640-A5
4100 WAL 91789 639-J6
4100 WAL 91789 640-A5
13100 LACo 91746 637-H4
13100 INDS 91746 637-H4
16100 LPUE 91745 678-F2
16100 LPUE 91744 678-F2
16300 INDS 91745 678-F2
17300 INDS 91744 678-F2
20700 LACo 91789 679-F1
W VALLEY BLVD
- ALH 91801 596-A7
100 SGBL 91776 596-D7
200 ALH 91803 596-A7
1500 ALH 91803 595-H7
3100 LA 90032 595-H7
VALLEY CIR
300 MNRO 91016 597-H1
8300 LA 91304 529-E2
VALLEY CT
8100 SBdC 92371 (4562-G3
See Page 4471)
VALLEY DR
- LA 90068 563-F4
- LACo 91724 639-H1
- MANB 90266 732-G7
- HMB 90254 762-G1
1500 Top 90290 589-G3
2500 HMB 90254 732-G7
N VALLEY DR
100 MANB 90266 732-G5
S VALLEY DR
100 MANB 90266 732-G7
VALLEY LN
1600 FUL 92833 738-C4
VALLEY MALL
10500 ELMN 91731 597-C7
VALLEY ST
300 ELSG 90245 732-D1
1500 BURB 91505 563-B1
1600 BURB 91505 533-B7
2000 LA 90057 634-C2
24100 SCTA 91321 4640-H1
N VALLEY ST
100 BURB 91505 563-B2
1600 BURB 91505 533-B6
S VALLEY ST
100 BURB 91505 563-D5
W VALLEY ST
- PAS 91105 565-H5
VALLEY TR
17800 LACo 93532 4101-J2
VALLEY VW
200 PMDL 93550 4286-A3
700 SDMS 91773 600-A3
VALLEY WY
- LA 90065 594-F1
VALLEYBRINK RD
3600 LA 90039 594-D1
VALLEY CANYON RD
13800 LACo 91390 4462-H7
13900 LACo 91387 4462-H7
N VALLEY CENTER AV
100 GLDR 91741 569-H5
S VALLEY CENTER AV
100 GLDR 91741 569-H6
100 SDMS 91773 599-H4
1200 GLDR 91740 599-H2
4600 LACo 91773 599-H2
4900 LACo 91724 599-H2
VALLEY CENTER DR
- SCTA 91351 4551-C2
VALLEY CENTRAL WY
44400 LAN 93536 4015-D5
VALLEY CIRCLE BLVD
4900 WdHl 91364 559-E2
4900 WdHl 91367 559-E2
6000 WdHl 91367 529-D6
6300 CanP 91307 529-D5
6900 LACo 91307 529-D5
7100 LA 91304 529-E2
8600 LA 91304 499-G7
9000 Chat 91311 499-H5
9200 Chat 91311 499-G7
VALLEY CIRCLE TER
6300 CanP 91307 529-D7
VALLEYCREST RD
11600 LA 91604 592-H1
VALLEY CREST ST
800 LCF 91011 535-B2
VALLEY CROSSING RD
- BREA 92823 709-H6
VALLEYDALE AV
4900 LACo 90043 673-C4
VALLEY FALLS RD
3500 Shrm 91403 561-F7
VALLEY FLORES DR
7800 LA 91304 529-E1
VALLEY FORGE RD
900 PMDL 93550 4286-B4
VALLEY GLEN ST
- Cstc 91384 4459-B4
VALLEY GLEN WY
5600 LACo 90043 673-D5
VALLEY GLOW DR
10300 SunI 91040 503-B4
VALLEY HEART DR
2900 BURB 91505 563-E5
10600 LA 91604 563-A6
10800 LA 91602 563-A5
VALLEYHEART DR
1300 BURB 91506 563-G3
12000 LA 91604 562-D5
13100 Shrm 91423 562-B4
N VALLEY HEART DR
14700 Shrm 91403 561-H3
VALLEY HEIGHTS DR
28900 AGRH 91301 558-A5
VALLEY HIGH DR
14600 CHLS 91709 680-H5
VALLEY HOME AV
100 WHIT 90603 708-B6
200 LHB 90631 708-B6
VALLEY HOME RD
3500 Shrm 91403 561-F7
VALLEYLIGHTS DR
3600 PAS 91107 566-H1
VALLEY LINE RD
42000 LAN 93535 4105-J4
42700 LAN 93534 4105-J4
VALLEY MEADOW PL
15900 Enc 91436 561-F6
VALLEY MEADOW RD
3400 Shrm 91403 561-F6
3700 Enc 91436 561-F5
VALLEY OAK CT
23800 SCTA 91321 4640-F3
VALLEY OAK DR
5500 LA 90068 593-G3
VALLEY OAK LN
- StvR 91381 4550-B5
100 POM 91767 600-G4
VALLEY OAK PL
- LACo 91390 4460-H1
VALLEY PARK AV
1700 HMB 90254 762-G1
VALLEY POINT LN
26200 SCTA 91321 4551-G5
VALLEY RANCH RD
- LACo 93551 4193-J5
- LACo 93551 4194-A6
16200 SCTA 91387 4552-C4
16500 LACo 91387 4552-C4
VALLEY RIDGE AV
4400 LACo 90008 673-D4
4600 LACo 90043 673-D4
5700 LA 90043 673-D5
VALLEY SAGE RD
5900 Actn 93510 4374-D4
7500 LACo 91390 4374-A6
VALLEY SPRING LN
10000 LA 91602 563-A5
11100 LA 91602 562-J5
11400 LA 91604 562-E5
VALLEY SPRING PL
11100 LA 91602 562-J5
11100 LA 91602 563-A5
VALLEY SPRING RD
2000 CHLS 91709 710-H1
VALLEY SPRINGS DR
600 WAL 91789 639-B7
VALLEY SPRINGS RD
36000 PMDL 93550 4286-G7
36000 PMDL 93550 4286-G7
VALLEY SUN LN
1000 LCF 91011 535-B3
VALLEY VIEW AV
700 MNRO 91016 567-H3
900 PAS 91107 566-H2
2700 WCOV 91792 679-C2
2700 LACo 91792 679-C2
7300 WHIT 90602 677-D7
8900 WHIT 90603 707-G3
9100 WHIT 90603 707-F4
10200 LACo 90604 707-F5
11900 LACo 90604 737-E3
12600 LMRD 90638 737-E3
14100 SFSP 90670 737-E3
16500 CRTS 90703 737-E7
17300 BPK 90620 737-E7
17900 BPK 90620 767-E1
17900 CRTS 90703 767-E1
VALLEYVIEW CT
15800 LA 91342 481-F4
VALLEY VIEW DR
2300 Echo 90026 594-F5
2400 CHLS 91709 680-J3
19600 Top 90290 590-A7
21100 WAL 91789 639-H7
E VALLEY VIEW DR
100 FUL 92832 738-H5
W VALLEY VIEW DR
100 FUL 92832 738-G5
100 FUL 92835 738-G5
1000 FUL 92833 738-E6
VALLEY VIEW LN
13900 CHLS 91709 680-G3
VALLEY VIEW PL
900 FUL 92833 738-F6
VALLEY VIEW RD
- RPV 90275 823-B2
700 SPAS 91030 595-G4
1200 GLDL 91202 564-D1
1300 SBdC 92372 (4562-D1
See Page 4471)
5900 SBdC 92397 (4652-E2
See Page 4651)
23500 CALB 91302 589-E1
VALLEY VIEW ST
5900 BPK 90620 767-E3
6500 LPMA 90623 767-E3
7700 BPK 90623 767-E3
9000 CYP 90630 767-E7
VALLEY VIEW WY
30800 Cstc 91384 4459-J1
VALLEY VIEW CREST
1800 BURB 91504 533-G4
VALLEY VISTA BLVD
4200 LA 91604 562-B5
13200 Shrm 91423 562-B5
14400 Shrm 91403 562-A5
14500 Shrm 91403 561-H5
15400 Enc 91436 561-F4
17700 Enc 91316 561-A3
18100 Tarz 91356 561-A3
18200 Tarz 91356 560-J4
VALLEY VISTA CT
- SCTA 91351 4461-G7
3900 Shrm 91403 561-J5
VALLEY VISTA DR
1200 DBAR 91765 679-H4
1400 MONP 91754 635-H5
42000 LAN 93536 4104-C5
VALLEY VISTA LN
1600 CHLS 91709 710-G2
VALLEY VISTA WY
- LA 91342 482-E4
VALLEY WELLS CT
26000 SCTA 91321 4551-F6
VALLEY WOOD RD
15900 Shrm 91403 561-F7
VALLOMBROSA DR
500 LACo 91107 566-H6
VALLON DR
6600 RPV 90275 822-G4
VALMAR RD
4200 CALB 91302 559-G5
4200 LA 91302 559-G5
4200 WdHl 91364 559-G5
4200 WdHl 91364 559-G5
VALMERE DR
2900 LACo 90265 628-D6
VALMEYER AV
17500 GAR 90248 764-A1
VALMONT DR
500 MNRO 91016 567-H2
VALMONT PL
500 MNRO 91016 567-H2
VALMONT ST
6300 Tuj 91042 504-B4
7300 Tuj 91042 503-J4
VALMONTE PZ
3900 PVE 90274 793-B4
VALNA DR
13400 WHIT 90602 707-D1
13900 WHIT 90605 707-E1
VALONA DR
1800 BALD 91706 638-C1
VALOR PL
32200 RPV 90275 823-D5
VALPARAISO DR
600 CLAR 91711 571-B6
VALPARAISO ST
10500 LA 90034 632-E7
VALPICO PL
22300 DBAR 91765 680-A5
VALPREDA ST
1800 BURB 91504 533-E6
VAL VERDE AV
3100 LBCH 90808 796-H1
3400 LBCH 90808 766-H7
6500 BPK 90621 767-G1
VALVERDE AV
200 BREA 92821 709-D7
VALVERDE CT
3600 GLDL 91208 534-G4
E VAL VERDE CT
2900 RDom 90221 765-B3
VAL VERDE DR
8400 LA 91304 529-D1
8500 WHil 91304 529-D1
VALVERDE PL
1400 GLDL 91208 534-G4
VAL VERDE RD
29000 Cstc 91384 4459-C6
VAL VISTA ST
600 POM 91768 600-F6
VALWOOD AV
2300 ELMN 91732 637-E4
VALWOOD DR
1800 FUL 92831 738-J4
VALWOOD ST
1200 LHB 90631 738-E1
VALYERMO RD
14600 Pear 93553 4379-B5
15500 Pear 93553 4469-D2
29200 Valy 93563 4469-D2
VAMANA ST
2900 POM 91767 601-A3
VANADA RD
15100 LMRD 90638 737-F4
VAN AKEN ST
9400 PRV 90660 676-H1
VANALDEN AV
3600 Tarz 91356 560-G1
6100 Res 91335 530-G2
8200 Nor 91324 530-G2
8900 Nor 91324 500-G7
10300 Nor 91326 500-G4
VAN ALLEN PL
3300 Top 90290 560-B7
VANANBEV WY
39000 LACo 93551 4195-F6
VAN BUREN AV
- CYP 90630 767-B6
1000 Ven 90291 672-A6
11100 LACo 90044 704-A6
13600 GAR 90247 734-A3
VAN BUREN CT
14100 GAR 90247 734-A3
VAN BUREN DR
400 MONP 91755 636-C4
VAN BUREN PL
1200 LA 90007 634-A7
3900 CULC 90232 672-H1
4200 LA 90037 674-A3
VAN BUREN ST
2800 CRSN 90810 765-B5
4100 CHNO 91710 641-D6
29700 Cstc 91384 4459-D7
E VAN BUREN ST
2500 CRSN 90810 764-J5
2500 CRSN 90810 765-A5
VAN BUREN WY
7000 BPK 90620 767-G5
VANCE ST
200 LA 90402 631-B7
200 PacP 90272 631-B7
VANCEBORO CT
4400 WdHl 91364 560-C4
VANCOUVER AV
800 ELA 90022 675-G1
S VANCOUVER AV
100 ELA 90022 635-H6
700 ELA 90022 675-G2
2000 MONP 91754 635-H5
2000 MONP 90022 635-H5
VANCOUVER LN
- LACo 93536 4105-A5
VANDA WY
10100 SunI 91040 502-J4
VANDAL WY
- PMDL 93551 4195-H7
- PMDL 93551 4285-G1
VANDALIA AV
2200 LA 90032 635-G1
2300 LA 90032 595-G7
VAN DEENE AV
20800 LACo 90502 764-B5
22500 LACo 90502 794-B1
VANDEMERE ST
12500 LKWD 90715 767-A4
VANDERBILT AV
900 CLAR 91711 601-B2
VANDERBILT LN
1800 RBCH 90278 762-J1
1900 RBCH 90278 763-B1
VANDERBILT PL
1500 GLDL 91205 564-G7
VANDERBILT WY
- SCTA 91355 4460-A6
VANDERGRIFT AV
- LACo 90073 631-H3
VANDERGRIFT LN
500 POM 91766 640-J4
VANDERHILL RD
4600 TOR 90505 793-B1
E VANDERHOOF DR
2600 WCOV 91791 639-B1
2800 WCOV 91791 599-C7
VANDERLIP RD
- RPV 90275 823-B3
VANDERWELL AV
700 LACo 91744 638-G4
1700 WCOV 91792 638-G4
S VANDERWELL AV
600 WCOV 91790 638-G1
VANDORF PL
15600 Enc 91436 561-G5
VANDORF ST
7700 RSMD 91770 636-E3
VAN DUSEN RD
1600 LVRN 91750 600-E3
VAN DYKE CIR
5200 LPMA 90623 767-C3
VANDYKE RD
1300 SMRO 91108 566-F7
1300 SMRO 91108 596-F1
VANE AV
3100 ELMN 91733 636-J1
N VANE AV
3500 RSMD 91770 596-J7
VANEGAS LN
1300 Boyl 90033 635-C3
VANESSA CIR
8500 LACo 90606 706-G1
VANESSA CT
5700 WdHl 91367 559-H2
VANETTA DR
4100 LA 91604 562-F6
VANETTA PL
12500 LA 91604 562-F6
VAN GOGH LN
- SCTA 91355 4550-E3
VAN GOGH ST
17100 GrnH 91344 481-C4
VANGOLD AV
4300 LKWD 90712 765-G5
VAN GORDER WY
21700 Cstc 91384 4369-H6
VANGUARD AV
100 LACo 91744 638-H7
100 LACo 91744 678-H1
VANGUARD LN
- PMDL 93551 4195-D5
VANGUARD WY
500 BREA 92821 709-A7
VAN HORN AV
800 WCOV 91790 598-D7
800 WCOV 91790 638-D1
VAN HORNE AV
4000 LA 90032 595-F5
4300 SPAS 91030 595-F5
VAN HORNE LN
1200 RBCH 90278 762-J3
1200 HMB 90254 762-J3
VAN KARAJAN DR
2000 RPV 90275 823-H2
VANLAND TR
6900 LA 90068 593-D1
VAN METER ST
500 IRW 91706 597-H1
VANNA DR
7100 PRM 90723 735-F1
VAN NESS AV
300 TOR 90501 763-G5
12800 GAR 90249 733-G3
15700 GAR 90247 733-H7
15900 TOR 90247 733-H7
15900 TOR 90504 733-H7
17400 TOR 90504 763-H2
N VAN NESS AV
100 LA 90004 593-G7
100 LA 90004 633-G1
700 COMP 90221 735-A3
700 LA 90038 593-G6
1300 Hlwd 90028 593-G4
1900 LA 90068 593-G4
S VAN NESS AV
100 LA 90004 633-G1
300 LA 90020 633-G2
600 LA 90005 633-G2
600 LA 90010 633-G2
1200 LA 90019 633-G5
3500 LA 90018 673-G1
3700 LA 90062 673-G5
3700 LA 90008 673-G3
4400 LA 90043 673-G4
5800 LA 90047 673-G5
7200 LA 90047 703-G2
7200 LA 90043 703-G2
7600 ING 90305 703-G2
10000 LACo 90047 703-G4
10000 ING 90303 703-G6
11400 HAW 90250 703-G6
12000 HAW 90250 733-G1
12100 LACo 90047 733-G1
S VAN NESS PL
5300 LA 90043 673-G5
VAN NESS WY
300 TOR 90501 763-G4
VAN NOORD AV
3900 LA 91604 562-E4
4600 Shrm 91423 562-E3
5400 VanN 91401 562-E2
6000 VanN 91401 532-D7
6500 NHol 91606 532-E6
6800 NHol 91605 532-D2
VAN NORMAN RD
100 PRV 90660 676-F3
100 MTBL 90640 676-F3
VAN NOSTRAN DR
3100 LKWD 90712 765-H3
VAN NUYS BLVD
4200 Shrm 91403 562-A4
5200 VanN 91401 562-A1
5200 VanN 91411 562-A1
6000 VanN 91401 532-A6
6000 VanN 91411 532-A6
6600 VanN 91405 532-A3
7700 PanC 91402 532-A3
8700 PanC 91402 531-J1
8700 PanC 91402 501-J7
12000 LA 91342 482-F7
12300 Pcma 91331 482-F7
12300 Pcma 91331 502-E2
14500 PanC 91402 502-A5
VAN NUYS PL
14600 PanC 91402 501-J5
VANORA DR
10600 SunI 91040 503-E3
VANOWEN PL
4100 BURB 91505 533-B6
VANOWEN ST
2500 BURB 91505 533-C6
4500 LA 91505 533-A5
10700 NHol 91605 533-A5
11100 NHol 91606 532-E5
11100 NHol 91606 533-A5
11100 NHol 91605 532-E5
11300 NHol 91606 532-J5
13200 VanN 91405 532-A5
13400 VanN 91401 532-E5
14500 VanN 91405 531-F6
15200 VanN 91411 531-F6
15300 VanN 91406 531-F6
17700 Res 91335 531-A6
18100 Res 91335 530-F6
19700 Win 91306 530-A6
20800 CanP 91303 530-A6
21900 CanP 91303 529-G6
22200 CanP 91307 529-D6
24400 LACo 91307 529-D6
VAN PELT AV
900 City 90063 635-E4
VAN PELT PL
2900 Echo 90026 594-D5
VANPORT AV
6700 LACo 90606 676-J7
6700 LACo 90606 677-A6
8300 LACo 90606 706-J1
11400 LA 91342 482-F7
11400 LA 91342 502-G1
VAN RUITEN ST
9200 BLF 90706 736-A3
10800 NRWK 90650 736-E3
VANS ST
8700 PRM 90723 735-J4
8800 PRM 90723 736-A4
VANSCOY AV
6800 NHol 91605 532-F2
VANTAGE AV
3700 LA 91604 562-G5
4300 LA 91607 562-G1
6000 NHol 91606 532-G6
6600 NHol 91605 532-G3
VANTAGE DR
- DBAR 91765 680-A2
VANTAGE POINT TER
24500 MAL 90265 628-G7
VANTAGE POINTE DR
3400 RowH 91748 708-H2
18700 RowH 91748 709-A2
VAN TASSEL MTWY
- AZU 91010 568-E2
- DUAR 91010 (538-C7
See Page 507)
- DUAR 91010 568-E2
- LACo - (538-C7
See Page 507)
- MNRO 91010 568-C1
- MNRO 91016 (538-C7
See Page 507)
- MNRO 91016 568-C1
VAN TASSEL WY
3300 DUAR 91010 568-F4
VAN TRESS AV
1500 Wilm 90744 794-C4
VAN VELSIR DR
500 LACo 91302 629-A1
VAN WICK ST
1900 LACo 90047 703-G6
2300 ING 90303 703-G6
VAN WICKLIN AV
12300 LA 91342 481-H6
VAN WIG AV
600 LACo 91746 637-J3
600 LACo 91746 638-A3
1500 BALD 91706 638-A3
3300 BALD 91706 598-C7
VAQUERO
2000 WCOV 91791 639-A4
VAQUERO AV
2000 LHB 90631 708-H5
2800 LA 90032 595-F7
VAQUERO CT
25800 SCTA 91355 4550-G4
VAQUERO LN
- GLDL 91208 564-H2
- CRSN 90745 794-G1
VAQUERO RD
200 ARCD 91007 567-A4
300 ARCD 91007 566-J4
600 MNRO 91016 568-A4
VARA PL
11900 GmH 91344 480-J6
11900 GmH 91344 481-A6
VARDEN ST
15400 Shrm 91403 561-G4
VARESE CT
24600 SCTA 91355 4550-E6
VARGAS WY
2500 RBCH 90278 733-B6
VARIEL AV
5900 WdHl 91367 560-B1
6000 WdHl 91367 530-B7
6500 CanP 91303 530-B5
7500 LA 91304 530-B1
9500 Chat 91311 500-B3
VARILLA DR
1700 WCOV 91792 638-H4
1700 WCOV 91791 638-H4
VARNA AV
4500 Shrm 91423 562-D3
5500 VanN 91401 562-C1
5900 VanN 91401 532-D7
6600 VanN 91405 532-C5
7000 NHol 91605 532-C3
7900 PanC 91402 532-D2
8800 Pcma 91331 502-A5
8800 Pcma 91331 532-C1
VARNELL AV
5100 LACo 91722 598-G3
N VARNEY ST
400 BURB 91502 533-G7
S VARNEY ST
400 BURB 91502 563-H1
VARSITY DR
20400 WAL 91789 639-F4
VARUS ST
5500 ARCD 91006 597-G3
VASANTA WY
2200 LA 90068 593-F2
VASCONES DR
1900 HacH 91745 678-D4
VASQUEZ WY
16000 LACo 91390 4462-D3
VASQUEZ CANYON RD
- LACo 91390 (4372-C7
See Page 4281)
16100 CynC 91351 4462-A2
16100 LACo 91390 4462-A2
16800 CynC 91351 4461-G2
16800 LACo 91390 4461-G2
VASQUEZ CANYON TKTR
- LACo 91390 (4372-C7
See Page 4281)
- LACo 91390 4461-J1
- LACo 91390 4462-A1
VASQUEZ ROCK CT
- SCTA 91350 4550-H6
VASSAR AV
1800 GLDL 91204 594-E1
5900 WdHl 91367 560-A1
7000 CanP 91303 530-A4
7500 LA 91304 530-A2
9500 Chat 91311 500-A4
VASSAR DR
- BPK 90620 767-F6
VASSAR LN
1200 WAL 91789 639-F4
VASSAR ST
700 CLAR 91711 601-B5
800 POM 91767 601-B5
VAUGHN ST
12700 LA 91342 482-D7
12800 Pcma 91331 482-D7
12800 LA 91340 482-D7
13300 Pcma 91331 502-B2
13300 LA 91340 502-C1
23600 Chat 91311 499-G6
VAUGHT CT
1000 WCOV 91792 638-J5
VAYA CON DIOS
- POM 91766 640-D4
VECINO AV
6500 GLDR 91741 569-C6
6500 LACo 91741 569-C6
N VECINO AV
100 GLDR 91741 569-C4
VECINO DR
400 COV 91723 599-C6
1200 GLDR 91740 599-D2
4800 LACo 91722 599-D3
6000 GLDR 91740 569-C7
N VECINO DR
100 COV 91723 599-C5
S VECINO DR
100 COV 91723 599-C5
VECINO LN
1200 LHB 90631 708-D4
1200 OrCo 90631 708-D4
VECINO ST
800 LHB 90631 708-H4
VEDADO AV
3500 LA 91604 562-E7
VEDANTA PL
1900 LA 90068 593-F3
VEDANTA TER
6300 LA 90068 593-F3
VEDDER MTWY
- VeCo 90265 586-C3
- VeCo 91361 586-C3
VEGA CIR
1200 LVRN 91750 600-E2
VEGA DR
2800 LAN 93535 4106-F1
VEGA ST
100 ALH 91801 596-C4
N VEGA ST
- ALH 91801 596-C3
S VEGA ST
100 ALH 91801 596-D6
1800 ALH 91801 636-D1
VEGA WK
28900 Cstc 91384 4459-C6
VEGA WY
19600 RowH 91748 679-D6
VEJAR DR
4900 AGRH 91301 558-B6
VEJAR RD
20100 WAL 91789 679-E1
20200 WAL 91789 639-F7
W VEJAR ST
1400 POM 91766 640-F2
VELA PL
6500 PRV 90660 676-E5
VELAN DR
25600 SCTA 91355 4550-F7
VELASCO ST
100 LA 90063 635-C6
1200 LA 90023 675-B1
VELEZ DR
1800 RPV 90275 823-H2
VELICATA ST
21200 WdHl 91364 560-A3
VELLANO CLUB DR
- CHLS 91709 710-J2
VELMA AV
3800 ELMN 91731 597-B7
VELMA DR
3200 LA 90068 563-D6
VELMA LN
10000 LA 90210 592-B3
VELOZ AV
5000 Tarz 91356 560-H3
VELUTINA WY
37000 PMDL 93550 4286-D4
VELVET LN
5100 CULC 90230 672-H3
VELVET OAK CT
- SIMI 93063 499-A4
VENA AV
9000 Pcma 91331 502-A3
10800 MsnH 91345 502-A2
10900 MsnH 91345 501-J1
VENADA DR
9500 BPK 90620 767-G6
VENADO DR
1600 LHH 90631 708-C2
VENADO WY
900 WAL 91789 639-C6
VENADO VISTA DR
600 LCF 91011 535-C2
VENANGO AV
900 LA 90029 594-B6
VENANGO CIR
900 LA 90029 594-B6
VENDALE DR
20500 LKWD 90715 766-F4
VENDELL RD
27400 AGRH 91301 558-E7
N VENDOME ST
100 Echo 90026 634-B1
300 Echo 90026 594-C7
S VENDOME ST
100 LA 90057 634-B1
W VENETIA DR
100 LBCH 90803 826-C2
VENEZA WY
- Nor 91326 500-C1
VENEZIA AV
500 Ven 90291 671-J5
VENEZIA CT
600 Ven 90291 671-J5
VENEZIA PL
1200 POM 91766 640-E3
VENICE AV
1500 MNRO 91016 567-E6
VENICE BLVD
100 LA 90015 634-C5
1100 LA 90006 634-A5
1800 LA 90006 633-G5
2300 LA 90019 633-G5
5900 LA 90034 633-G5
VENICE BLVD Rt#-187
1000 Ven 90291 672-D3
6000 LA 90034 633-A6
6000 LA 90034 632-H7
8800 LA 90232 632-H7
9100 LA 90232 672-D3
9200 LA 90034 672-D3
10700 CULC 90232 672-D3
11200 CULC 90230 672-D3
11200 LA 90066 672-D3
11300 CULC 90066 672-D3
N VENICE BLVD
- Ven 90291 671-H6
800 Ven 90291 672-A5
S VENICE BLVD
- Ven 90291 671-H6
900 Ven 90291 672-A5
VENICE ST
- CRSN 90745 764-C7
- CRSN 90745 794-C1
VENICE WY
100 Ven 90291 671-H6
W VENICE WY
300 ING 90302 703-B1
VENIDO RD
22400 WdHl 91364 559-J3
VENITA ST
10400 ELMN 91731 597-B6
VENTANA AV
300 LACo 91744 679-A1
VENTANA DR
41400 PMDL 93536 4104-G7
41400 PMDL 93551 4104-G7
VENTANA LN
9100 LA 91343 501-H6
VENTON ST
1100 SDMS 91773 599-J3
20100 LACo 91724 599-H3
E VENTON ST
1700 COV 91724 599-F3
1700 LACo 91724 599-F3
VENTURA BLVD
10600 LA 91604 562-A6
11100 LA 91604 562-D5
13200 Shrm 91423 562-B5
14400 Shrm 91403 562-B5
14600 Shrm 91403 561-F4
15400 Enc 91436 561-F4
16900 Enc 91316 561-B3
18100 Tarz 91356 561-B3
18200 Tarz 91356 560-E2
19700 WdHl 91364 560-E2
19700 WdHl 91367 560-A2
22100 WdHl 91364 559-G3
22100 WdHl 91367 559-G3
23800 LACo 91302 559-E4
VENTURA CT
12300 LA 91604 562-F5
VENTURA FRWY Rt#-134
- BURB - 563-B4
- Eagl - 564-F3
- Eagl - 565-A5
- GLDL - 564-F3
- LA - 562-J4
- LA - 563-B4
- LA - 564-F3
- LFlz - 563-G4
- LFlz - 564-F3
- PAS - 565-A5
VENTURA FRWY U.S.-101
- Ago - 558-D6
- AGRH - 557-G6
- AGRH - 558-D6
- CALB - 558-D6
- CALB - 559-B5
- Enc - 561-C2
- HIDH - 559-B5
- LA - 559-B5
- LA - 562-A4
- LACo - 558-D6
- LACo - 559-B5
- Shrm - 561-C2
- Shrm - 562-A4
- Tarz - 560-H1
- Tarz - 561-C2
- THO - 557-B4
- WdHl - 559-B5
- WdHl - 560-B2
- WLKV - 557-B4
VENTURA PL
200 FUL 92833 738-C7
12000 LA 91604 562-G5
VENTURA ST
- Alta 91001 535-G5
800 PAS 91011 535-G5
VENTURA WY
100 Chat 91311 499-F7

STREET	Block	City	ZIP	Pg-Grid
VENTURA WY				
	400	CLAR	91711	601-C1
	9200	Chat	91311	499-F7
VENTURA CANYON AV				
	3600	Shrm	91423	562-C3
	5200	VanN	91401	562-C2
	6000	VanN	91401	532-C7
	7100	VanN	91405	532-C5
	7500	PanC	91402	532-C3
	8400	Pcma	91331	532-C3
VENTURE DR				
	3200	HNTB	92649	826-J6
VENTURE PL				
	4000	PMDL	93552	4196-H7
VENTURE ST				
	43000	LAN	93535	4106-A3
W VENTURI DR				
	24300	SCTA	91355	4550-F7
VENUS DR				
	2300	LA	90046	593-A2
VENUS PL				
	15700	GAR	90249	733-G6
VERA AV				
	3100	LA	90034	632-H7
E VERA CT				
	2300	LBCH	90804	795-G6
N VERA CT				
	2000	SIMI	93063	499-B2
VERA ST				
	21300	CRSN	90745	764-G6
E VERA ST				
	6000	SIMI	93063	499-B2
VERA TER				
	7100	LACo	91775	566-G7
VERA CANYON RD				
	200	LACo	90265	587-C7
E VERA CREST DR				
	6300	LBCH	90815	796-E6
VERA CRUZ				
	-	POM	91768	600-F6
VERA CRUZ ST				
	1100	MTBL	90640	636-E7
VERACRUZ ST				
	13300	CRTS	90703	737-C7
VERADA AV				
	11600	GrnH	91344	481-C7
VERADES LN				
	-	PMDL	93552	4287-E1
VERAGUA DR				
	7700	PdlR	90293	702-C2
VERANADA AV				
	1600	Alta	91001	536-E7
VERANDA CT				
	-	FUL	92831	738-J3
VERANDA DR				
	11400	LACo	91342	482-H5
VERANDAH CT				
	-	StvR	91381	4640-B2
VERANO DR				
	800	GLDR	91741	569-F3
VERANO RD				
	10900	BelA	90077	591-H5
VERANO WY				
	-	LACo	90255	704-H1
VERBECK ST				
	11600	LACo	90606	706-J2
	11600	SFSP	90606	706-J2
VERBENA AV				
	1700	UPL	91784	571-J3
VERBENA CT				
	-	PMDL	93551	4285-E3
	-	POM	91766	641-B3
VERBENA DR				
	2400	LA	90068	593-G2
VERBENA LN				
	200	BREA	92823	710-C5
VERBURG CT				
	2000	TOR	90504	733-H7
VERCELLI WY				
	-	Nor	91326	500-C1
VERCELLY CT				
	5600	WLKV	91362	557-G6
VERCOE PL				
	1200	MONP	91755	636-B4
VERDALE AV				
	29000	Cstc	91384	4459-A5
VERDANT ST				
	3900	LA	90039	564-C7
VERDE CT				
	1100	LBCH	90804	795-J6
	1100	LBCH	90804	796-A6
	1100	POM	91767	601-B5
VERDE ST				
	2000	PAS	91107	566-D5
	2400	Boyl	90033	635-C3
VERDE MESA LN				
	-	MAL	90265	667-E1
VERDEMOUR AV				
	4100	LA	90032	595-D7
VERDE OAK DR				
	2100	LA	90068	593-H3
VERDE RIDGE RD				
	6500	RPV	90275	822-G1
VERDE VISTA AV				
	1600	POM	91767	601-D6
VERDE VISTA DR				
	600	POM	91767	601-A6
W VERDE VISTA DR				
	1500	MONP	91754	635-H2
VERDI DR				
	6300	BPK	90621	737-J7
	6300	BPK	90621	767-J1
VERDI LN				
	-	Nor	91326	500-C1
VERDI ST				
	12400	LA	90066	672-E6
VERD OAKS DR				
	1400	GLDL	91205	564-H6
VERDON ST				
	-	PMDL	93552	4287-E1
VERDOSA DR				
	8400	WHIT	90605	707-H2
VERDUGO AV				
	100	GLDR	91741	569-J4
	300	POM	91767	601-A3
	1700	LHB	90631	708-G5
E VERDUGO AV				
	-	BURB	91502	563-H1
	-	BURB	91502	533-H7
	400	BURB	91501	533-J7
	1000	BURB	91501	534-A6
W VERDUGO AV				
	-	BURB	91502	563-G1
	700	BURB	91506	563-G1
	2500	BURB	91505	563-E2
VERDUGO BLVD				
	1200	LCF	91011	535-A3
	1700	LCF	91011	534-J4
	1800	GLDL	91208	534-J4
	1800	GLDL	91011	534-J4
	1900	GLDL	91020	534-J4
VERDUGO CT				
	2200	GLDL	91208	534-G7
VERDUGO DR				
	400	BURB	91502	563-G1
VERDUGO MTWY				
	-	BURB	91501	533-G2
	-	BURB	91501	534-A2
	-	BURB	91504	533-G2
	-	GLDL	91208	534-A2
	-	SunV	91352	533-G2
	-	SunV	91352	534-A2
VERDUGO PL				
	2000	FUL	92833	738-C4
	3100	LA	90065	594-G3
VERDUGO RD				
	2900	LA	90065	594-H1
	3000	GLDL	91208	534-H5
	3600	GLDL	91020	534-H5
	4100	LA	90065	564-H6
N VERDUGO RD				
	100	GLDL	91206	564-G2
	1300	GLDL	91208	564-H1
	1800	GLDL	91208	534-H6
S VERDUGO RD				
	100	GLDL	91205	564-H6
	1000	LA	90065	564-H6
VERDUGO CIRCLE DR				
	900	GLDL	91206	564-G3
VERDUGO CRESTLINE DR				
	7200	Tuj	91042	504-A5
	7300	Tuj	91042	503-J5
	7800	Sunl	91040	503-F4
VERDUGO KNOLLS DR				
	1800	GLDL	91208	564-H1
VERDUGO KNOLLS PL				
	1800	GLDL	91208	564-J1
VERDUGO LOMA DR				
	1800	GLDL	91208	564-H1
VERDUGO SPRING LN				
	1200	BURB	91501	534-A5
VERDUGO VIEW DR				
	3900	LA	90065	594-J1
VERDUGO VISTA				
	1800	GLDL	91208	564-H1
VERDUGO VISTA TER				
	3400	LA	90065	594-J1
VERDUGO WOODS HWY E				
	-	GLDL	91214	534-E2
VERDUGO WOODS HWY W				
	-	GLDL	91214	534-E1
S VERDUN AV				
	1400	ING	90302	673-D6
	4800	LACo	90043	673-D5
	5700	LA	90043	673-D6
VERDURA AV				
	3500	LKWD	90712	765-J2
	6200	NLB	90805	765-J1
	12600	DWNY	90242	736-A1
	12600	DWNY	90242	735-J1
	14900	PRM	90723	735-J4
VEREDA DR				
	40400	PMDL	93550	4195-J3
VEREDA DE LA MONTURA				
	17300	PacP	90272	630-E1
	17700	PacP	90272	590-E7
VERHALEN CT				
	3800	CULC	90232	673-A1
VERKLER				
	25000	LACo	91302	589-B3
VERMILION CREEK RD				
	500	SDMS	91773	570-D7
VERMILLION ST				
	3000	WCOV	91792	679-D2
VERMONT AV				
	100	FUL	92833	738-B7
	1600	GLDR	91740	599-E2
	15100	PRM	90723	735-G5
N VERMONT AV				
	100	GLDR	91741	569-E5
	100	LA	90004	634-A1
	200	LA	90004	594-A5
	700	LA	90029	594-A5
	1300	LFlz	90027	594-A2
S VERMONT AV				
	100	GLDR	91741	569-E6
	100	LA	90004	634-A3
	300	LA	90020	634-A3
	600	GLDR	91740	569-E6
	600	LA	90005	634-A3
	600	LA	90010	634-A3
	800	LA	90247	734-A4
	800	GAR	90247	734-A4
	800	LA	90006	634-A3
	900	LACo	90502	764-B7
	1900	LA	90007	634-A7
	3400	LA	90089	634-A7
	3400	LA	90089	674-A3
	3400	LA	90007	674-A3
	3700	LA	90037	674-A3
	5800	LA	90044	674-A7
	7200	LA	90044	704-A2
	8600	LACo	90044	704-A6
	12000	LA	90044	734-A4
	12000	LACo	90044	734-A4
	12800	GAR	90044	734-A4
	17500	LA	90248	734-B7
	17500	LA	90248	764-B3
	17500	GAR	90248	734-B7
	17500	GAR	90248	764-B3
	19000	LACo	90248	764-B3
	19000	LA	90502	764-B3
	22500	LACo	90502	794-B4
	23700	Hrbr	90710	794-B4
	25000	Hrbr	90710	794-B4
	25700	Wilm	90744	794-A5
VERMONT DR				
	24900	SCTA	91321	4640-G1
VERMONT PL				
	1600	POM	91768	600-G6
	4600	LA	90029	594-A5
VERMONT ST				
	400	Alta	91001	535-G7
	400	PAS	91103	535-G7
E VERMONT ST				
	3600	LBCH	90814	795-J7
	4000	LBCH	90814	796-A7
	6300	LBCH	90803	796-E7
VERMONT CANYON RD				
	2700	LFlz	90027	594-A2
	2700	LFlz	90027	593-J1
VERNA DR				
	17600	RowH	91748	678-G6
VERNAL WY				
	28000	SCTA	91350	4461-D6
VERNE AV				
	20700	LKWD	90715	766-J5
	21000	LKWD	90715	767-A5
	21700	HGDN	90716	766-J6
VERNE CT				
	25400	StvR	91381	4640-B1
VERNER CIR				
	500	ARCD	91006	597-E1
VERNER DR				
	5100	LPMA	90623	767-C4
VERNER ST				
	9100	PRV	90660	676-G4
VERNESS ST				
	500	COV	91723	599-A7
E VERNESS ST				
	1100	WCOV	91790	598-H7
	1400	WCOV	91791	598-H7
VERNICE DREDD ST				
	100	COMP	90220	734-J4
VERNON AV				
	300	Ven	90291	671-H4
	8900	MTCL	91763	601-G4
	10300	MTCL	91763	641-H1
	10700	SBdC	91762	641-H3
	11300	CHNO	91710	641-H4
	11300	CHNO	91762	641-H3
	29300	Cstc	91384	4459-C5
E VERNON AV				
	100	LA	90011	674-F3
	1700	LA	90058	674-F3
	1900	VER	90058	674-J3
	3000	VER	90058	675-A3
N VERNON AV				
	100	AZU	91702	568-H5
S VERNON AV				
	100	AZU	91702	568-H7
	100	AZU	91702	598-H1
W VERNON AV				
	100	LA	90037	674-B3
	1200	LA	90037	673-G3
	1400	LA	90062	673-G3
	2100	LA	90043	673-G3
	2100	LA	90008	673-G3
	3400	LACo	90043	673-G3
	3400	LACo	90008	673-G3
VERNON CT				
	500	Ven	90291	671-H4
	5500	MTCL	91763	641-H1
VERNON RD				
	1800	GLDL	91202	534-C7
VERNON ST				
	1000	LHB	90631	708-C4
	2500	LBCH	90815	796-B3
	3800	LBCH	90815	795-J3
E VERNON ST				
	200	LBCH	90806	795-D3
	900	SIGH	90755	795-D3
	3900	LBCH	90815	796-A3
VERONA AV				
	10500	WLA	90025	632-D4
VERONA CT				
	-	CHLS	91709	710-J3
	-	CRSN	90745	794-B1
	5500	WLKV	91362	557-G6
VERONA DR				
	-	BqtC	91354	4460-F4
	900	FUL	92835	738-F4
VERONA LN				
	39700	PMDL	93551	4195-B4
VERONA PL				
	1200	POM	91766	640-F3
VERONA ST				
	400	LHB	90631	708-H5
	3800	LACo	90023	675-D1
	4400	ELA	90022	675-F1
VERONDA PL				
	1900	SMRO	91108	596-A2
VERONICA				
	10900	MsnH	91345	501-H2
VERONICA AV				
	3200	WCOV	91792	679-A1
	3500	WCOV	91792	678-J1
VERONICA LN				
	25500	LMTA	90717	793-G5
VERONICA ST				
	5100	LA	90008	673-B2
VERONIQUE CT				
	43700	LAN	93535	4106-B1
VERRY ST				
	-	FUL	92833	738-D5
VERSAILLES AV				
	25900	SCTA	91355	4550-E6
VERSAILLES CT				
	3200	LAN	93536	4105-B3
VERSAILLES ST				
	-	PMDL	93552	4287-E1
VERWOOD AV				
	5000	GLDL	91214	504-D5
VESELICH AV				
	3900	LA	90039	594-D1
	4000	LA	90039	564-D7
VESEY RD				
	2200	Top	90290	589-H3
VESPER AV				
	4400	Shrm	91403	562-A3
	5200	VanN	91411	562-A2
	6000	VanN	91411	532-A7
	6600	VanN	91405	531-J6
	6600	VanN	91405	532-A7
	8500	PanC	91402	531-J1
	9600	PanC	91402	501-J5
VESPER DR				
	-	LA	90068	563-F4
VESPER RD				
	-	LACo	91724	639-G1
VESSING TER				
	-	PMDL	93552	4287-E2
VESTA AV				
	13000	Wbrk	90222	734-J2
W VESTA ST				
	700	ING	90302	703-A2
	1000	ONT	91762	601-H7
VESTAL AV				
	1900	Echo	90026	594-F6
VESTAVIA AV				
	8700	BPK	90621	738-A6
VESTAVIA CIR				
	8800	BPK	90621	738-B6
VESTONE WY				
	10500	BelA	90077	592-A4
E VESUVIAN WK				
	5500	LBCH	90803	826-C2
VETERAN AV				
	100	BelA	90077	631-J1
	100	LA	90095	631-J1
	100	Brwd	90049	631-J1
	400	Wwd	90024	631-J1
	600	Wwd	90024	632-B4
	600	Brwd	90049	631-J1
	600	Brwd	90049	632-B4
	1200	Wwd	90024	632-B4
	1300	WLA	90025	632-B4
	2200	LA	90064	632-C6
	3000	LA	90034	632-C6
	3200	LA	90034	672-D1
VETS CT				
	30600	AGRH	91301	557-G3
VEVA WY				
	26100	CALB	91302	558-H4
VIA ABBY				
	-	MTCL	91763	641-D1
VIA ACALONES				
	2000	PVE	90274	792-H5
VIA ACERO				
	28200	MAL	90265	627-F7
VIA ACORDE				
	25400	SCTA	91355	4640-E1
VIA ACOSTA				
	2400	MTBL	90640	636-B7
	2400	MTBL	90640	676-B1
VIA ADARME				
	300	PVE	90274	793-B3
VIA ADELENA				
	-	BqtC	91354	4460-F3
VIA ADORNA				
	25400	SCTA	91355	4550-F7
VIA AIDA				
	-	MTCL	91763	641-D1
VIA ALAMEDA				
	100	PVE	90274	792-J3
	100	TOR	90277	792-J3
	200	TOR	90277	793-A3
	800	SDMS	91773	600-A5
VIA ALAMITOS				
	2100	PVE	90274	792-H5
VIA ALCALDE AV				
	4100	LBCH	90810	765-B6
VIA ALCANCE				
	200	PVE	90274	793-B4
VIA ALCIRA				
	25400	SCTA	91355	4550-G7
VIA ALEGRE				
	1600	SDMS	91773	599-J6
E VIA ALEGRE				
	5900	SIMI	93063	499-B2
VIA ALISA				
	-	StvR	91381	4550-C5
VIA ALISTA				
	4800	LVRN	91750	570-F6
VIA ALMAR				
	300	PVE	90274	792-H4
E VIA ALMENDRO				
	600	NLB	90805	765-E3
VIA ALONDRA				
	4200	PVE	90274	793-C4
	5300	NLB	90805	765-H3
VIA ALTA				
	1000	BURB	91501	534-B6
VIA ALTAMIRA				
	500	MTBL	90640	676-A1
	500	MTBL	90640	636-B7
VIA ALVARADO				
	2700	PVE	90274	822-E1
VIA AMADEO				
	800	SDMS	91773	600-A7
VIA AMADO				
	23400	SCTA	91355	4640-G1
VIA AMADOR				
	2300	PVE	90274	792-F7
	2500	PVE	90274	822-F1
VIA AMARE				
	-	StvR	91381	4550-C5
VIA AMARILLA				
	100	SDMS	91773	600-B7
VIA AMISTAD				
	1400	POM	91768	600-F6
VIA AMISTOSA				
	27800	AGRH	91301	558-D6
VIA AMORE				
	-	MTCL	91763	641-D1
VIA AMORITA				
	7200	DWNY	90241	705-J2
	7400	DWNY	90241	706-A3
VIA AMOROSA				
	18000	RowH	91748	678-J5
VIA ANACAPA				
	2100	PVE	90274	822-E1
	2100	PVE	90274	792-E7
VIA ANDORRA				
	23600	SCTA	91355	4640-G1
VIA ANDRES				
	1300	PVE	90274	792-G7
VIA ANGELO				
	-	MTCL	91763	641-D1
VIA ANITA				
	100	TOR	90277	792-J3
	1300	PacP	90272	630-J3
	1400	LVRN	91750	570-F5
	2400	PVE	90274	792-H3
VIA APUESTA				
	4600	Tarz	91356	560-H4
VIA ARABELLA				
	200	SDMS	91773	600-A7
	200	SDMS	91773	640-A1
E VIA ARADO				
	1900	LACo	90220	764-H4
VIA ARANDA				
	23900	SCTA	91355	4640-F1
VIA ARBOLADA				
	4200	HiPk	90042	595-D4
	4200	LA	90032	595-D4
VIA ARCO				
	1400	PVE	90274	792-H6
VIA ARDILLA				
	100	PVE	90274	793-B3
VIA AROMITAS				
	1700	PVE	90274	792-G4
VIA ARRIBA				
	1600	PVE	90274	792-G4
VIA ARROYO				
	1400	LVRN	91750	570-G5
	1900	PVE	90274	792-G4
VIA ARROYO DR				
	6500	BPK	90620	767-F6
VIA ARTINA				
	25300	SCTA	91355	4640-F1
VIA ASTURIAS				
	1400	PVE	90274	822-G1
VIA AVANT				
	23600	SCTA	91355	4550-G6
VIA AZALEA				
	4300	PVE	90274	793-C4
VIA BALBOA				
	1100	PVE	90274	792-H5
VIA BALBOA CIR				
	9100	BPK	90620	767-F6
S VIA BANDERA				
	1800	LACo	90601	637-F6
VIA BANDINI				
	400	PVE	90274	822-E1
	500	PVE	90274	792-E7
VIA BARBARA				
	4000	LAN	93536	4015-A7
VIA BARCELONA				
	1500	PVE	90274	822-G1
	4300	LVRN	91750	570-F6
E VIA BAROLA				
	600	NLB	90805	765-E4
VIA BARON				
	6400	RPV	90275	822-H5
	19800	LACo	90220	764-J4
VIA BARRA				
	23200	SCTA	91355	4550-G6
VIA BARRI				
	2800	PVE	90274	822-E1
VIA BEELER				
	-	SCTA	91321	4551-E5
VIA BEGUINE				
	23600	SCTA	91355	4640-G1
VIA BELLAZZA				
	-	StvR	91381	4550-C5
VIA BELTERRA				
	-	BqtC	91354	4460-E4
VIA BENSA				
	4800	VeCo	91377	557-G1
VIA BERNARDO				
	9500	LA	91504	533-D3
VIA BLANCA				
	400	SDMS	91773	600-B7
VIA BOCINA				
	23900	SCTA	91355	4640-F1
VIA BODEGA				
	500	PVE	90274	793-B4
VIA BONITA				
	200	TOR	90277	792-J2
	200	TOR	90277	793-A2
	5300	NLB	90805	765-H3
VIA BORDEAUX				
	23500	SCTA	91355	4550-G6
VIA BORICA				
	3000	PVE	90274	822-F2
	30000	RPV	90275	822-F2
VIA BORONADA				
	1500	PVE	90274	792-F6
VIA BOSCANA				
	23400	SCTA	91355	4640-G1
VIA BOTTICELLI				
	-	Nor	91326	480-D5
VIA BRAMANTE				
	4000	RPV	90275	823-G4
VIA BRASA				
	25300	SCTA	91355	4640-F1
VIA BRAVA				
	25500	SCTA	91355	4550-F7
	25500	SCTA	91355	4640-F1
VIA BRENDA				
	5000	LPMA	90623	767-C5
VIA BREVE				
	3000	MTBL	90640	636-A7
E VIA BREVE				
	5900	SIMI	93063	499-B2
VIA BUENA				
	2800	PVE	90274	822-F1
	4800	LVRN	91750	570-F7
VIA BUENA VENTURA				
	100	TOR	90277	792-J2
	200	TOR	90277	793-A2
VIA CABALLOS				
	19600	LACo	91791	639-D2
VIA CABRILLO				
	6100	MAL	90265	667-B1
VIA CABRILLO MARINA				
	2200	SPed	90731	824-C7
	2500	SPed	90731	854-C1
VIA CALETA				
	2900	PVE	90274	822-E2
VIA CALIENTE				
	2100	FUL	92833	738-D4
VIA CALINDA				
	25300	SCTA	91355	4640-F1
VIA CALISERO				
	23200	SCTA	91355	4550-H7
VIA CALMA				
	18000	RowH	91748	678-J5
	23600	SCTA	91355	4550-G6
VIA CAMBRON				
	30300	RPV	90275	822-F3
VIA CAMILLE				
	1300	MTBL	90640	676-D1
	2200	MTBL	90640	636-B7
	2300	SDMS	91773	600-A7
	2300	SDMS	91773	640-A1
VIA CAMINO				
	-	Wilm	90744	794-F6
	1400	LVRN	91750	570-F7
VIA CAMPANA				
	-	BqtC	91354	4460-F3
VIA CAMPESINA				
	2400	PVE	90274	792-J4
	2900	PVE	90274	793-A4
	2900	RPV	90275	793-A4
VIA CAMPO				
	1600	LVRN	91750	570-F6
	1700	MTBL	90640	636-B6
	3400	MTBL	90640	635-J6
	5200	ELA	90022	635-J6
VIA CANADA				
	1000	SDMS	91773	599-J5
	6200	RPV	90275	823-G3
VIA CANDELA				
	24000	SCTA	91355	4550-F7
VIA CANDICE				
	25800	SCTA	91355	4550-G4
VIA CANON				
	23700	SCTA	91321	4641-B2
VIA CANTARE				
	15500	BelA	90077	591-G2
VIA CAPAY				
	100	PVE	90274	792-J3
VIA CAPRI				
	-	RPV	90275	822-G4
	7700	LA	91504	533-D3
VIA CARA				
	-	MTCL	91763	641-E1
VIA CARDELINA				
	3700	PVE	90274	793-B3
VIA CARMELITA				
	1000	BURB	91501	534-A6
E VIA CARMELITOS				
	700	NLB	90805	765-E4
VIA CARRILLO				
	2200	PVE	90274	792-F7
	2500	PVE	90274	822-F1
VIA CASSANO				
	7700	LA	91504	533-D3
VIA CASTANET				
	23400	SCTA	91355	4550-G7
	23400	SCTA	91355	4640-G1
VIA CASTILLA				
	1300	PVE	90274	792-G7
	1400	PVE	90274	822-G1
VIA CATALDO				
	6300	MAL	90265	668-B1
VIA CATALINA				
	7700	LA	91504	533-D3
	25900	SCTA	91355	4550-G4
VIA CATALUNA				
	1300	PVE	90274	792-H5
VIA CATARINA				
	100	SDMS	91773	600-B7
VIA CELLINI				
	-	Nor	91326	480-D6
VIA CERRITOS				
	2000	PVE	90274	792-H6
VIA CERRO				
	400	MTBL	90640	676-A1
VIA CHANTILLY				
	23500	SCTA	91355	4550-G6
VIA CHICO				
	300	PVE	90274	792-J4
VIA CHINO				
	1600	PVE	90274	792-G4
VIA CHISPAS				
	-	PVE	90274	792-H6
VIA CIEGA				
	6300	RPV	90275	823-G5
VIA CIELO				
	2400	HacH	91745	677-J3
VIA CLARITA				
	41800	Actn	93510	4375-E5
VIA CLASICO				
	23600	SCTA	91355	4550-G6
VIA CLASSICO				
	-	MTCL	91763	601-E7
	-	MTCL	91763	641-D1
VIA CLEMENTE				
	700	ELA	90022	676-B1
	700	LACo	90640	676-B1
	700	MTBL	90640	676-B1
VIA CODO				
	500	FUL	92835	738-F1
VIA COLINA				
	4400	HiPk	90042	595-D4
VIA COLINAS				
	-	THO	91362	557-E4
	-	WLKV	91362	557-E5
VIA COLINITA				
	2000	LA	90732	823-H4
	2000	RPV	90275	823-G4
VIA COLLADO				
	7300	RPV	90275	822-F2
VIA COLLINA				
	-	StvR	91381	4550-C4
VIA COLORIN				
	200	PVE	90274	793-C4
VIA COLUSA				
	100	TOR	90277	792-J3
	100	TOR	90277	793-A3
	100	PVE	90274	793-A3
	400	TOR	90505	793-A3
VIA CONEJO				
	800	PVE	90274	792-G4
VIA CONESO				
	5300	NLB	90805	765-H3
VIA CONSTANCE				
	4000	LAN	93536	4015-A7
VIA COPETA				
	23900	SCTA	91355	4640-F1
VIA CORDOVA				
	900	LA	90732	824-A3
	37100	PMDL	93550	4286-G4
VIA CORONA				
	1400	LVRN	91750	570-F7
	2200	MTBL	90640	676-B1
	3000	MTBL	90640	636-A7
	4500	TOR	90505	793-B3
	5100	ELA	90022	635-J7
	5800	MTBL	90640	635-J7
VIA CORONEL				
	800	PVE	90274	792-G6
VIA CORSA				
	23600	SCTA	91355	4550-G7
	23600	SCTA	91355	4640-G1
VIA CORTA				
	300	PVE	90274	792-H4
	1400	LVRN	91750	570-F6
VIA CORTA DR W				
	200	PVE	90274	792-H4
VIA CORTO				
	23300	SCTA	91355	4550-H5
VIA COSTA VERDE				
	-	RPV	90275	822-J1
VIA CREMA				
	9300	LA	91504	533-D2
VIA CRESTA				
	-	BqtC	91354	4460-E3
	1300	PacP	90272	630-J4
VIA CRUZ				
	25800	SCTA	91355	4550-G5
VIA CURVA				
	1100	PVE	90274	792-F6
VIA DABNA				
	25400	SCTA	91355	4550-G6
VIA DALIA				
	25400	SCTA	91355	4550-G7
VIA DANTE				
	-	MTCL	91763	641-D1
VIA DANZA				
	23900	SCTA	91355	4640-F1
VIA DAVALOS				
	1400	PVE	90274	792-F7
VIA DAVISO				
	2800	MTBL	90640	636-B6
VIA DE ANZAR				
	6400	RPV	90275	823-G3
VIA DE CABALLEROS				
	-	Actn	93510	4465-B1
VIA DECANO				
	23500	SCTA	91355	4550-G7
VIA DE CASA				
	-	LACo	90265	628-F5
VIA DE FLORES				
	-	LAN	93535	4016-F6
VIA DE GATO LARGO				
	-	LACo	91390	4373-E7
VIA DE LA GUERRA				
	2800	PVE	90274	822-F1
VIA DE LA PAZ				
	300	PacP	90272	631-A5
VIA DE LAS CASITAS				
	17600	LACo	91744	638-J7
VIA DE LAS OLAS				
	15200	PacP	90272	631-A7
	15500	PacP	90272	630-J6
VIA DE LA VALLE				
	-	Actn	93510	4465-C1
VIA DE LA VISTA				
	26700	RHE	90274	793-A6
VIA DEL CABALLO				
	200	VeCo	91377	558-A1
	200	VeCo	91377	557-J2
VIA DEL CIELO				
	-	RPV	90275	822-F4
VIA DEL COLLADO				
	5600	TOR	90505	793-A2
VIA DEL CORONADO				
	6500	ELA	90022	676-A1
VIA DELFINA				
	23600	SCTA	91355	4550-G6
VIA DELICIA				
	23600	SCTA	91355	4550-G6
VIA DEL LLANO				
	24700	CALB	91302	559-D7
VIA DEL MAR				
	31000	RPV	90275	822-G4
VIA DEL MIRAM				
	200	LACo	91744	638-J7
VIA DEL MONTE				
	500	PVE	90274	792-H4
VIA DEL NORTE				
	4300	MTCL	91763	641-E3
VIA DELORES				
	3300	BALD	91706	638-A1
S VIA DEL ORO				
	700	ELA	90022	676-A1
VIA DELOS				
	23600	SCTA	91355	4550-G7
VIA DEL PALMA				
	13400	WHIT	90602	677-D7
VIA DEL PARAISO				
	2200	LVRN	91750	570-H3
VIA DEL PLAZA				
	6300	RPV	90275	823-G4
VIA DEL PRADO				
	3500	CALB	91302	559-J7
VIA DEL PUENTE DR W				
	300	PVE	90274	792-H4
VIA DEL REY				
	1200	SPAS	91030	595-G2
VIA DEL RIO				
	6900	LBCH	90815	796-F5
	36800	PMDL	93550	4286-G4
VIA DEL SOL				
	-	Actn	93510	4375-C7
	-	Actn	93510	4465-C1
	1200	SDMS	91773	599-J7
	2200	LVRN	91750	570-H4
	5300	NLB	90805	765-H2
VIA DEL SOL AV				
	13000	LACo	90601	637-E6
VIA DEL SUR				
	4300	MTCL	91763	641-E3
VIA DEL VALLE				
	5100	LVRN	91750	570-G6
	5300	TOR	90505	793-A3
VIA DEL VISTA				
	17700	LACo	91744	638-J7
VIA DE MANSION				
	1400	LVRN	91750	570-F6
VIA DE PAJARO				
	900	DBAR	91765	680-E2
VIA DESCA				
	25500	SCTA	91355	4550-F7
VIA DESCANSO				
	1200	PVE	90274	792-F7
VIA DESMONDE				
	26400	LMTA	90717	793-H6
VIA DIA				
	25300	SCTA	91355	4640-F1
VIA DICHA				
	5700	LVRN	91750	570-G4
	18100	RowH	91748	678-J5
N VIA DI ROMA WK				
	-	LBCH	90803	826-C3
VIA DOLARITA				
	25500	SCTA	91355	4550-F7
	25500	SCTA	91355	4640-F1
VIA DOLCE				
	3000	MdlR	90292	671-J7
	3000	LA	90292	671-J7
	3800	LA	90292	701-J1
	4700	LA	90292	702-A4
	4700	MdlR	90292	702-A4
VIA DOMINIC				
	-	LVRN	91750	570-H3
VIA DONA CHRISTA				
	25300	SCTA	91355	4550-H6
VIA DONATELLO				
	-	Nor	91326	480-D6
VIA DONTE				
	5100	LA	90292	701-J2
	5300	LA	90292	702-A2
VIA EBANO				
	23600	SCTA	91355	4550-G7
VIA EL CAMINO				
	14600	BALD	91706	598-C4
VIA EL CHICO				
	100	TOR	90277	793-A2
	300	TOR	90505	793-A2
VIA ELDA				
	-	MTCL	91763	641-D1
VIA ELEVADO				
	2700	PVE	90274	792-J4
VIA ELISANDRA				
	23400	SCTA	91355	4550-G7
VIA ELISO				
	23500	SCTA	91355	4550-G7
VIA EL MIRO				
	2800	RPV	90275	823-F2
VIA EL PRADO				
	1700	RBCH	90277	792-J1
VIA EL SERENO				
	4800	TOR	90505	793-B3
VIA EL TORO				
	200	TOR	90277	792-H3
VIA ENCANTO				
	2000	LMTA	90717	793-H6
VIA ENCINAS				
	3900	CYP	90630	767-A7
VIA ENTRADA				
	1800	RowH	91748	678-J5
	4600	LVRN	91750	570-G5
	9500	CYP	90630	767-A7
VIA ESCONDIDA				
	8200	WHIT	90605	707-H2
VIA ESCONDIDO				
	6100	MAL	90265	628-A7
	6100	MAL	90265	668-A1
VIA ESCOVAR				
	25400	SCTA	91355	4550-G7
VIA ESPERANZA				
	1000	SDMS	91773	599-J6
VIA ESPIRITO SANTOS				
	600	CLAR	91711	571-B5
VIA ESPLANADE				
	5300	NLB	90805	765-H3
VIA ESQUINA				
	24500	CALB	91302	559-E6
VIA ESTANCIA				
	-	BqtC	91354	4460-F2
VIA ESTRADA				
	500	PVE	90274	822-E1
VIA ESTRELLA				
	1500	POM	91768	600-F6
	20900	SCTA	91321	4641-B2
VIA ESTRELLITA				
	100	TOR	90277	792-J2
	800	GLDR	91741	569-F3
VIA ESTRELUTA				
	17800	LACo	91744	638-J7
VIA ESTUDILLO				
	1600	PVE	90274	792-F6
VIA FAMERO DR				
	34800	Actn	93510	4374-H1
	35800	Actn	93510	(4284-H7 See Page 4283)
	35800	LACo	93551	(4284-H7 See Page 4283)
VIA FARALLON				
	23400	SCTA	91355	4550-G7
VIA FAROL				
	23500	SCTA	91355	4550-G7
VIA FERNANDEZ				
	1200	PVE	90274	792-G5
VIA FERRARA				
	9300	LA	91504	533-E2
VIA FLAMENCO				
	23900	SCTA	91355	4550-F7
VIA FLORED				
	23200	SCTA	91355	4550-H5
VIA FLORENCE				
	300	PacP	90272	630-G5
VIA FLORESTA				
	16500	PacP	90272	630-H3
VIA FOGGIA				
	7800	LA	91504	533-D3
VIA FORTUNA				
	1000	PVE	90274	792-F7
	5300	NLB	90805	765-H3
VIA FRANCISCA				
	1100	LA	90732	823-J3
	1100	LA	90732	824-A3
VIA FRASCATI				
	4300	RPV	90275	823-G4
VIA FRESA				
	2300	SDMS	91773	599-J7
	2300	SDMS	91773	639-J1
VIA FUENTE				
	23600	SCTA	91355	4550-G7
VIA GABRIEL				
	-	LACo	93551	4375-H5
	1200	PVE	90274	792-H5
VIA GALERA				
	23500	SCTA	91355	4550-G7
VIA GALICIA				
	1400	PVE	90274	822-G1
VIA GALILEO				
	-	Nor	91326	480-D6
VIA GANCHO CIR				
	6500	BPK	90620	767-F6
VIA GARDENIA				
	14800	SCTA	91387	4462-F7
VIA GARFIAS				
	1600	PVE	90274	792-F6
VIA GAVILAN				
	4000	PVE	90274	793-C3
VIA GAVOLA				
	23700	SCTA	91355	4550-G6
VIA GAYO				
	23400	SCTA	91355	4550-G7
VIA GENOVA				
	2600	LAN	93535	4016-E6
	7700	LA	91504	533-D3
VIA GEORGIONE				
	-	Nor	91326	480-D5
VIA GOLETA				
	1100	PVE	90274	792-F7
	5300	NLB	90805	765-H3
VIA GORRION				
	500	PVE	90274	793-C4
VIA GRACIOSO				
	25400	SCTA	91355	4550-G5
VIA GRANADA				
	-	RHE	90274	792-J7
	-	RPV	90274	792-J7
	-	RHE	90275	792-J7
	-	RPV	90275	792-J7
VIA GRANATE				
	1200	SMAD	91024	567-D1
VIA GREGORIO				
	800	SDMS	91773	600-A6
VIA GUADALANA				
	2200	PVE	90274	792-H5
VIA HALCON				
	3700	CALB	91302	559-E7
VIA HAMACA				
	23900	SCTA	91355	4550-F7
VIA HELENA				
	5000	LPMA	90623	767-C5
VIA HELINA				
	23700	SCTA	91355	4550-G6
VIA HERALDO				
	25400	SCTA	91355	4550-G6
VIA HISPANO				
	23400	SCTA	91355	4550-G7
VIA HONRADO				
	40700	PMDL	93551	4194-J2
VIA HORCADA				
	700	PVE	90274	792-G4
VIA HORQUILLA				
	600	PVE	90274	792-J4
	600	PVE	90274	793-A4
VIA IMPRESO				
	25400	SCTA	91355	4550-G6
VIA INGRESO				
	2200	FUL	92833	738-C4
VIA INGRESSO				
	4000	CYP	90630	767-A7
VIA IRANA				
	23700	SCTA	91355	4550-G6
VIA JACARA				
	23700	SCTA	91355	4550-G6
VIA JACINTO				
	2300	LVRN	91750	570-H3
VIA JARDIN				
	17800	LACo	91744	638-J7
	25400	SCTA	91355	4550-G6
VIA JOSE				
	100	PVE	90274	792-J3
VIA JOYCE DR				
	-	Saug	91350	4461-E5
VIA JUANA				
	25500	SCTA	91355	4550-G7
VIA JUANITA				
	400	WAL	91789	639-E7
VIA JUSTINO				
	1900	SDMS	91773	600-A6
VIA KALBAN				
	-	SCTA	91321	4551-E5
VIA KANNELA				
	23700	SCTA	91355	4550-G6
VIA LABRADA				
	25400	SCTA	91355	4550-G6
VIA LA BREA				
	2200	PVE	90274	792-H5
VIA LA CASA				
	-	BqtC	91354	4460-E3
VIA LA CIENEGA				
	800	MTBL	90640	676-G1

STREET Block City ZIP Pg-Grid

VIA LA CIMA
- RPV 90275 792-J7
VIA LA CIRCULA
100 TOR 90277 792-J2
200 TOR 90277 793-A2
VIA LA COSTA
1500 PacP 90272 630-H1
VIA LA CRESTA RD
30500 RPV 90275 822-H4
VIA LA CUESTA
3000 PVE 90274 792-J5
3000 PVE 90274 793-A4
3000 RPV 90275 793-A4
VIA LADERA
1700 LHH 90631 708-C2
23200 SCTA 91355 4550-H6
VIA LADO
4100 TOR 90505 793-C3
VIA LA ENTRADA
17600 LACo 91744 638-J7
VIA LA LOMA
1700 CHLS 91709 680-H6
VIA LA MESA
2200 CHLS 91709 680-J6
VIA LANDETA
1200 PVE 90274 792-G6
VIA LA PALOMA
6600 RPV 90275 823-G4
VIA LA PAZ
- StvR 91381 4550-C4
1000 LA 90732 824-A3
1700 BURB 91501 534-B6
VIA LARGAVISTA
4000 PVE 90274 793-C4
VIA LARGO
4100 CYP 90630 767-A7
VIA LA ROCCA
- RPV 90275 822-J1
VIA LA SELVA
300 CLAR 91711 601-D1
400 TOR 90277 792-J2
2400 PVE 90274 792-J3
2900 PVE 90274 793-A3
VIA LA SOLEDAD
100 TOR 90277 792-J2
VIA LAS PALMAS
16400 PacP 90272 630-H1
VIA LASTRE
3100 MTBL 90640 676-A1
VIA LAS VEGAS
100 PVE 90274 793-B3
100 TOR 90505 793-B3
1200 Boyl 90033 634-J4
VIA LA TIERRA
15000 CHLS 91709 680-J6
VIA LATINA
7900 LA 91504 533-E2
VIA LAZO
1500 PVE 90274 792-G4
VIA LEON
1500 PVE 90274 792-G7
VIA LEONARDO
22200 CALB 91302 559-J7
VIA LIDO PL
2000 POM 91767 601-A6
VIA LINDA
1500 FUL 92833 738-C4
5300 NLB 90805 765-H3
8700 WHIT 90605 707-F3
9800 CYP 90630 767-B7
26800 MAL 90265 668-B1
VIA LINDA VISTA
200 TOR 90277 792-J2
300 TOR 90277 793-A2
VIA LOPEZ
1500 PVE 90274 792-G6
VIA LORADO
7300 RPV 90275 822-F2
VIA LORENZO
6500 RPV 90275 823-G4
VIA LORETO
15100 CHLS 91709 680-J6
VIA LOS ALTOS
100 TOR 90277 793-A2
200 CLAR 91711 601-D1
1500 LHB 90631 738-E1
VIA LOS ANDES
700 CLAR 91711 571-B5
VIA LOS BONITOS
1500 LHB 90631 738-E1
VIA LOS COYOTES
1500 LHB 90631 738-F1
VIA LOS MIRADORES
100 TOR 90277 793-A2
300 TOR 90277 792-J3
VIA LOS SANTOS
700 SDMS 91773 600-D2
VIA LOS SANTOS ST
300 Boyl 90033 634-J5
VIA LUCIA
300 PacP 90272 630-G5
2400 MTBL 90640 636-B7
VIA LUNA DR
1800 LHH 90631 708-D2
VIA LUNETO
400 MTBL 90640 676-B1
VIA LUPONA
23600 SCTA 91355 4550-G6
VIA MACARENA
25400 SCTA 91355 4550-G7
VIA MACHADO
1600 PVE 90274 792-F6
VIA MADALENA
2600 LAN 93535 4016-E6
VIA MADERA
24700 CALB 91302 559-D7
VIA MADERAS
3000 Alta 91001 536-B4
VIA MADONNA
1900 LMTA 90717 793-H6
VIA MADRID
1400 LVRN 91750 570-F7
VIA MADRIGAL
- Nor 91326 480-D6
VIA MADURO
23600 SCTA 91355 4550-G6
VIA MAGDALENA
7900 LA 91504 533-E3
VIA MAJORCA
- RHE 90274 792-J7
4300 CYP 90630 767-B7
VIA MALAGA
400 TOR 90277 792-J3
VIA MALONA
- RPV 90275 822-J1
VIA MANTUA
- Nor 91326 480-D5
VIA MARCIA
4300 LVRN 91750 570-F6
27200 SCTA 91350 4460-J6
VIA MARGARITA
1300 PVE 90274 792-H5
VIA MARGATE
- PVE 90274 792-F6
VIA MARIA
300 PacP 90272 630-G5
5000 LPMA 90623 767-F1
VIA MARIE CELESTE
7300 RPV 90275 822-F2
VIA MARINA
200 LA 90292 701-J1
200 LA 90292 702-A2
200 MdlR 90292 702-A2
4000 MdlR 90292 671-J7
4200 MdlR 90292 701-J1
VIA MARINA CT
200 LA 90292 702-A4
5500 LA 90292 701-J2
VIA MARIPOSA
2400 SDMS 91773 639-J1
VIA MARISOL
3700 LA 90032 595-E4
3900 HiPk 90042 595-D3
VIA MARQUETTE
26400 LMTA 90717 793-H6
VIA MARTINEZ
1500 PVE 90274 792-G6
VIA MATEO
1400 PVE 90274 792-J6
VIA MATTONELLA
- CRSN 90745 764-B7
- CRSN 90745 794-B1
VIA MEDIA
400 PVE 90274 792-G4
9600 CYP 90630 767-B7
VIA MEDIA CIR
6700 BPK 90620 767-G6
VIA MEDICI
- Nor 91326 480-D6
VIA MERIDA
- THO 91362 557-D4
VIA MESA GRANDE
100 TOR 90277 792-J3
VIA MIA
4700 LA 90032 595-D5
VIA MIGUEL
- LHH 90631 708-D3
2700 PVE 90274 822-G2
VIA MILAGRO
- BqtC 91354 4460-E2
VIA MILANO
9500 LA 91504 533-D3
VIA MIRABEL
1000 PVE 90274 792-H5
VIA MIRADA
900 PVE 90274 792-J5
1600 FUL 92833 738-C4
VIA MIRAMONTE
300 MTBL 90640 676-B1
VIA MIRANDA
2800 NLB 90805 765-H3
VIA MIROLA
900 PVE 90274 792-F7
E VIA MONDO
3000 RDom 90221 735-B7
VIA MONIQUE
9300 LA 91504 533-D2
VIA MONTANA
100 BURB 91501 533-J5
100 BURB 91501 534-A5
23700 SCTA 91321 4641-B2
VIA MONTE D ORO
- TOR 90277 792-J2
VIA MONTEMAR
1400 PVE 90274 792-G4
VIA MONTEVIDEO
700 CLAR 91711 571-B5
VIA MORENO
300 POM 91766 640-D3
VIA MORGANA DAVIS
- MTCL 91763 601-D7
VIANA AV
25800 LMTA 90717 793-G5
VIANA DR
3000 PMDL 93550 4286-G2
VIA NAPOLI
- MTCL 91763 641-D1
1400 MTBL 90640 636-C6
7700 LA 91504 533-D3
VIA NARANJO
4400 LVRN 91750 570-F5
VIA NAUTICA
25400 SCTA 91355 4550-G6
VIA NAVAJO
200 PVE 90274 793-B4
VIA NAVARRA
1000 LA 90732 824-A3
VIA NEVE
2800 PVE 90274 822-E2
VIA NICOLAS
300 PacP 90272 630-G5
VIA NINA
2400 MTBL 90640 636-B7
VIA NIVEL
3800 PVE 90274 793-C4
VIA NOGALES
900 PVE 90274 792-H4
VIA NOLA
9700 LA 91504 533-D1
VIA NORTE
400 MTBL 90640 676-A1
400 MTBL 90640 636-A7
2800 NLB 90805 765-H2
4100 CYP 90630 767-A7
VIA NORTE AV
2300 MONP 91754 636-A6
VIA NORTE CIR
6700 BPK 90620 767-G6
VIA NOVA
2000 LMTA 90717 793-H6
2300 LVRN 91750 570-H4
VIA NOVELLA
500 VeCo 91377 557-J1
VIA NOVIA
25400 SCTA 91355 4550-F7
VIA NUEVO
40700 PMDL 93551 4194-H2
VIA OLEADAS
2700 PVE 90274 822-E1
VIA OLIVERA
1800 PVE 90274 792-F7
2500 PVE 90274 822-F1
VIA ONDA
23900 SCTA 91355 4550-F7
VIA OPATA
3900 PVE 90274 793-B4
VIA ORIOL
25300 SCTA 91355 4550-G6
VIA ORO AV
3300 BALD 91706 637-J1
VIA ORTEGA
3800 LBCH 90810 765-B6
VIA OTT
- SCTA 91321 4551-E5
VIA PACHECO
2000 PVE 90274 792-E7
2400 PVE 90274 822-F1
VIA PACIFICA
- LACo 90265 628-F5
1500 PacP 90272 630-H1
25300 SCTA 91355 4550-G6
VIA PADOVA
3900 LACo 91711 571-E3
3900 CLAR 91711 571-E3
VIA PALACIO
6500 RPV 90275 822-H5
25300 SCTA 91355 4550-G6
N VIA PALADAR
25500 SCTA 91355 4550-F7
25500 SCTA 91355 4640-E1
VIA PALERMO
1400 MTBL 90640 636-C6
VIA PALESTRA
1000 PVE 90274 792-F7
1000 PVE 90274 822-F1
VIA PALLADINO
- Nor 91326 480-D6
VIA PALMA
- MTCL 91763 601-D7
- MTCL 91763 641-D1
VIA PALOMARES
1600 SDMS 91773 599-J6
VIA PALOMINO
3300 PVE 90274 793-B4
VIA PANORAMA
900 PVE 90274 792-J5
VIA PARO
600 PVE 90274 793-C4
VIA PASEO
2700 MTBL 90640 636-B6
VIA PASQUAL
100 PVE 90274 793-A3
100 TOR 90277 792-J3
300 TOR 90277 793-A3
N VIA PASSILO
5200 NLB 90805 765-E3
VIA PATINA
- BqtC 91354 4460-D3
- Cstc 91384 4460-D3
VIA PATRICIA
9300 LA 91504 533-D2
VIA PATRICIO
- LHH 90631 708-D3
VIA PAVIA
9700 LA 91504 533-D1
VIA PAVION
3800 PVE 90274 793-B4
VIA PENA
500 PVE 90274 822-E1
VIA PERGOLA
- RPV 90275 822-J1
VIA PICAPOSTE
3800 PVE 90274 793-C4
VIA PIMA
4000 PVE 90274 793-B4
VIA PINALE
2300 PVE 90274 792-J4
VIA PINZON
4200 PVE 90274 793-C4
VIA PLATA
23500 SCTA 91355 4550-G5
W VIA PLATA ST
1400 LBCH 90810 765-B5
VIA POINTE DEL SOL
14600 LACo 90604 707-E5
VIA POLOMARES
1900 SDMS 91773 599-J6
VIA POMPEII
8000 LA 91504 533-E2
VIA PORTO GRANDE
- RPV 90275 822-J1
VIA PRADERA
24700 CALB 91302 559-D6
VIA PRIMERO
3000 PMDL 93550 4286-F4
23600 SCTA 91355 4550-G6
VIA PRINCESSA
- SCTA 91350 4551-D4
- SCTA 91355 4550-H6
18500 LACo 91387 4551-J5
18500 SCTA 91387 4551-H4
18500 Nwhl 91321 4551-H4
18500 SCTA 91321 4551-F4
18800 SCTA 91351 4551-D4
22200 SCTA 91350 4550-H6
22700 SCTA 91321 4550-H6
VIA PROVIDENCIA
500 BURB 91501 534-A6
VIA PUEBLO
- POM 91767 641-C1
VIA QUINTO
400 WAL 91789 639-D7
400 WAL 91789 679-D1
VIA RAFAEL
2400 PVE 90274 792-J6
2500 RPV 90275 792-J6
VIA RAMON
2400 PVE 90274 792-J4
25300 SCTA 91355 4550-G6
VIA RANA
23600 SCTA 91355 4550-G6
VIA RANCHO AV
3300 BALD 91706 637-J1
VIA RANCHO DR
23600 DBAR 91765 640-C7
VIA RANCHO LA VERNE
4600 LVRN 91750 570-F7
VIA RAZA
26100 SCTA 91355 4550-G4
VIA REBECCA
4000 LAN 93536 4015-A7
VIA REGATA
500 MdlR 90292 672-A6
VIA RICARDO
9500 LA 91504 533-D3
VIA RIMINI
9600 LA 91504 533-D3
VIA RINCON
900 PVE 90274 792-J4
VIA RIO NIDO
7200 DWNY 90241 705-J2
7400 DWNY 90241 706-A3
VIA RIVERA
2100 PVE 90274 792-E7
2500 PVE 90274 822-F1
30000 RPV 90275 822-F2
VIA RIVIERA
- MTCL 91763 601-E7
100 TOR 90277 792-H2
VIA RIVIERA WY
6600 BPK 90620 767-F6
VIARNA ST
12200 CRTS 90703 766-J3
VIA ROCAS
5400 WLKV 91362 557-E5
VIA RODEO DR
200 BHLS 90210 632-F2
200 BHLS 90212 632-F2
VIA ROMA
1400 MTBL 90640 636-D6
9700 LA 91504 533-D3
VIA ROMALES
2400 SDMS 91773 639-J1
2500 SDMS 91773 640-A1
VIA ROMANA
2600 LAN 93535 4016-E6
VIA ROMERO
1000 PVE 90274 822-F1
1100 PVE 90274 792-F7
VIA RONALDO
7700 LA 91504 533-D3
VIA ROSA
1600 BALD 91706 638-B1
2200 PVE 90274 792-H3
VIA ROSA LINDA
23900 SCTA 91355 4550-F4
VIA ROSA MARIA
7700 LA 91504 533-D3
VIA SAINT AMBROSE
- CLAR 91711 571-F3
VIA SALDIVAR
2200 GLDL 91208 534-F7
VIA SALERNO
9300 LA 91504 533-D3
VIA SALUDO
25300 SCTA 91355 4550-G6
VIA SAN ANSELMO
- LA 91342 482-F2
VIA SAN CARLO
2800 MTBL 90640 636-A7
VIA SANCHEZ
2500 PVE 90274 792-F7
VIA SAN CLEMENTE
400 MTBL 90640 676-A1
500 MTBL 90640 636-A7
VIA SAN DELARRO
2700 MTBL 90640 636-A7
3400 MTBL 90640 635-H6
5200 ELA 90022 635-H6
VIA SAN DIEGO
- LA 91342 482-F2
VIA SAN FELIPE
- LA 91342 482-F2
VIA SAN JOSE
17700 RowH 91748 678-H5
VIA SAN MARINO
- LA 91342 482-F2
VIA SAN MIGUEL
- LA 91342 482-E3
VIA SAN PABLO
- LA 91342 482-F3
VIA SAN RAFAEL
- LA 91342 482-F3
VIA SAN REMO
- LA 91342 482-F3
- RPV 90275 822-G4
13500 CHLS 91709 680-J2
VIA SAN RICARDO
- LA 91342 482-F3
VIA SAN SEBASTIAN
300 TOR 90277 792-J3
VIA SAN SIMON
700 CLAR 91711 571-B5
VIA SANSOVINO
- Nor 91326 480-D6
VIA SANTA BARBARA
- LA 91342 482-F2
VIA SANTA CATALINA
- LA 91342 482-F2
VIA SANTA CATARINA
700 CLAR 91711 571-B5
VIA SANTA CLARA
- LA 91342 482-F2
VIA SANTA CRUZ
8600 WHIT 90605 707-G2
VIA SANTA LUCIA
- LA 91342 482-F2
VIA SANTA MARIA
- LA 91342 482-F2
VIA SANTA MARTA
- LA 91342 482-F2
VIA SANTA ROSA
- LA 91342 482-F2
VIA SANTA VISTA
- LA 91342 482-F2
VIA SANTA YNEZ
600 PacP 90272 630-G5
VIA SANTIAGO
- LA 91342 482-F2
VIA SANTO TOMAS
700 CLAR 91711 571-B5
VIA SEBASTIAN
1100 LA 90732 823-J3
1100 LA 90732 824-A3
VIA SEGO
100 TOR 90277 793-A2
VIA SEGOVIA
2800 PVE 90274 822-E2
VIA SEGUNDA
2600 PVE 90274 792-J4
VIA SERENA DR
- LA 91342 482-E3
VIA SERENO
- BqtC 91354 4460-E2
VIA SERRANO
400 LCF 91011 535-D7
VIA SEVILLA
- RHE 90274 792-J7
100 TOR 90277 793-A3
1400 LVRN 91750 570-F7
VIA SEVILLA DR
9200 BPK 90620 767-F6
VIA SIENA
6400 RPV 90275 823-G4
9700 LA 91504 533-D1
VIA SIERRA RAMAL
8400 WHIT 90605 707-G2
VIA SINALOA
2700 CLAR 91711 571-B5
VIA SISTINE
25200 SCTA 91355 4640-G1
VIA SOBRANTE
2400 PVE 90274 792-J6
VIA SOL
40700 PMDL 93551 4194-H2
VIA SOLA
2800 PVE 90274 822-E1
VIA SOLA CIR
6700 BPK 90620 767-G6
VIA SOLANO
- BqtC 91354 4460-E2
1900 LMTA 90717 793-H6
3900 PVE 90274 793-C3
VIA SOMONTE
700 PVE 90274 792-H4
VIA SONOMA
2400 PVE 90274 792-J5
2500 RPV 90275 792-J5
9800 CYP 90630 767-A7
VIA SORELLA
1000 DBAR 91789 679-H3
VIA SORRENTO
7700 LA 91504 533-D3
VIA STEFANO
7800 LA 91504 533-D3
VIA SUBIDA
6200 RPV 90275 823-G4
VIA SUN
40700 PMDL 93551 4194-J2
VIA SUR AV
13000 LACo 90601 637-F6
VIA TAMPA
1900 LMTA 90717 793-H6
VIA TANARA
25200 SCTA 91355 4640-G1
VIA TAPIA
6000 MAL 90265 628-A7
6000 MAL 90265 668-A1
VIA TAZ
1300 LACo 90265 629-D2
VIA TECOLOTE
24600 CALB 91302 559-D7
VIA TEHAGO
23400 SCTA 91355 4550-G4
VIA TEJON
2500 PVE 90274 792-J4
VIA TELINO
25300 SCTA 91355 4550-G6
VIA TERRAZA
26800 SCTA 91350 4460-J7
VIA TESSERA
- CRSN 90745 794-B1
VIA TINA
8500 LPMA 90623 767-F1
VIA TIVOLI
9500 LA 91504 533-D1
VIA TOLEDO
4400 LVRN 91750 570-F5
VIA TOMAS
23700 SCTA 91355 4550-G4
VIA TOMAS DR
20300 WAL 91789 639-F7
VIA TORINO
9600 LA 91504 533-D3
VIA TORTONA
7800 LA 91504 533-D3
VIA TRANQILO
40800 PMDL 93551 4194-F1
VIA TRANQUILO
1900 RowH 91748 678-H5
VIA TURINA
23800 SCTA 91355 4550-F4
VIA UDINE
7800 LA 91504 533-D1
VIA URBINO
- Nor 91326 480-D5
VIA VALDES
2600 PVE 90274 822-F1
VIA VALDEZ
300 POM 91766 640-D3
VIA VALENCIA
100 RBCH 90277 792-J1
6300 TOR 90277 792-J1
VIA VALENTINA
25200 SCTA 91355 4640-G1
VIA VALER
23600 SCTA 91355 4550-G6
VIA VALLARTA
17800 Enc 91316 561-A5
VIA VALMONTE
600 PVE 90274 793-B4
4400 TOR 90505 793-D4
VIA VALOR
40700 PMDL 93551 4194-J2
VIA VAL VERDE
300 MTBL 90640 676-B1
500 MTBL 90640 636-B7
VIA VAN CLEAVE
- BALD 91706 637-H1
E VIA VAQUERO
100 SDMS 91773 600-C3
W VIA VAQUERO
100 SDMS 91773 600-B3
VIA VELADOR
25500 SCTA 91355 4550-F7
VIA VELARDO
2200 RPV 90275 823-H3
VIA VENADO ST
2100 LCF 91011 534-H1
13300 BALD 91706 637-J1
13300 BALD 91706 638-A1
VIA VENETA
- RPV 90275 822-G4
VIA VENEZIA
9300 LA 91504 533-D3
28800 MAL 90265 667-F1
VIA VENTANA
- StvR 91381 4550-C5
1000 PVE 90274 792-F7
VIA VENTI
1000 MONP 91754 635-J3
VIA VERA
1900 LMTA 90717 793-H6
N VIA VERANADA
5000 NLB 90805 765-E3
VIA VERDA
- CMRC 90040 676-B7
VIA VERDAD
40500 PMDL 93551 4194-J2
VIA VERDE
- POM 91768 600-D6
- SDMS 91768 600-D6
400 SDMS 91773 600-A6
800 SDMS 91773 599-H7
1400 LACo 91724 599-G7
4100 CYP 90630 767-A7
20300 COV 91724 599-G7
VIA VERDE AV
1500 PMDL 93550 4286-D4
7400 SBdC 92372 (4562-E4
See Page 4471)
9300 SBdC 92372 (4472-D5
See Page 4471)
VIA VERDE CT
- CALB 91302 589-D1
VIA VERDEROL
4200 PVE 90274 793-C3
4200 TOR 90505 793-C3
VIA VERITA
15300 HacH 91745 678-A4
VIA VERITA AV
2200 HacH 91745 678-A4
VIA VERONA
2600 LAN 93535 4016-E6
8000 LA 91504 533-E2
10800 BelA 90077 591-J5
VIA VICENTE
- RPV 90275 822-F4
VIA VICO
4000 RPV 90275 823-G4
VIA VICO CIR
9300 BPK 90620 767-F6
VIA VICTORIA
2800 PVE 90274 822-F1
30000 RPV 90275 822-F2
VIA VIEJO
- StvR 91381 4550-C5
VIA VIENTA
4500 MAL 90265 626-E6
VIA VIOLA
- MTCL 91763 641-D1
VIA VISALIA
1800 PVE 90274 792-H5
VIA VISTA
- BqtC 91354 4460-F3
100 MTBL 90640 676-B1
VIA VISTA CT
2000 LVRN 91750 570-G3
VIA VISTA DR
9000 BPK 90620 767-F6
VIA VIZCAYA
- BqtC 91354 4460-E2
E VIA WANDA
700 NLB 90805 765-E3
VIA YOLANDA
9400 LA 91504 533-D2
VIA ZIBELLO
9700 LA 91504 533-D3
VIA ZUMAYA
700 PVE 90274 822-F1
VIA ZURITA
1300 CLAR 91711 601-D1
1500 PVE 90274 792-G6
VIBURNUM DR
14000 LACo 90604 707-D7
VICAR ST
9800 LA 90034 632-G6
VICASA DR
4100 CALB 91302 559-G6
VICCI ST
18600 SCTA 91351 4551-G2
VICENTE AV
1000 POM 91767 601-B4
VICENTE PL
12500 CRTS 90703 737-A6
VICENTE TER
- SMCA 90401 671-E3
VICENZA LN
- SCTA 91350 4551-D5
VICENZA WY
10800 BelA 90077 591-J5
VICEROY AV
700 COV 91723 599-B4
5400 LACo 91702 599-B1
N VICEROY AV
100 AZU 91702 569-B7
1100 COV 91722 599-B3
VICINO WY
17800 PacP 90272 630-F5
VICK PL
500 BHLS 90210 592-G4
VICKER CT
13300 BALD 91706 637-J1
VICKER DR
39300 PMDL 93551 4195-C5
VICKER WY
39500 PMDL 93551 4195-B3
VICKERS DR
3000 GLDL 91208 534-H4
VICKI DR
5800 WHIT 90606 677-A5
7000 LACo 90606 676-J6
7800 SFSP 90606 676-H7
8100 LACo 90606 706-H1
9100 SFSP 90670 706-H2
VICKIE AV
17000 CRTS 90703 737-B7
18300 CRTS 90703 767-B2
VICKIVIEW DR
6600 LACo 91307 529-C6
VICKSBURG AV
7800 Wch 90045 702-G2
VICKY AV
6500 CanP 91307 529-H5
7600 LA 91304 529-H4
21500 TOR 90503 763-B6
VICLAND PL
6300 NHol 91606 533-A6
VICSTONE CT
5800 CULC 90232 673-A2
W VICTOR AV
800 ING 90302 703-B1
VICTOR CT
- WHIT 90605 707-G1
VICTOR PL
43800 LAN 93535 4106-H1
VICTOR ST
400 LA 90012 634-F2
20300 TOR 90503 763-B5
VICTORIA
100 WCOV 91790 598-E7
2400 LACo 90220 764-J1
2500 LACo 90220 765-A1
VICTORIA AV
500 Ven 90291 671-J5
1000 Ven 90291 672-A5
7400 LA 90043 703-F2
7400 ING 90305 703-F2
8100 SGAT 90280 705-B3
10000 LACo 90604 707-E4
11300 LA 90066 672-C3
15700 LPUE 91744 638-D6
45600 LAN 93534 4015-E3
E VICTORIA AV
100 MTBL 90640 676-F1
S VICTORIA AV
800 LA 90005 633-F4
900 LA 90019 633-F4
1900 LA 90016 633-E7
3400 LA 90016 673-E1
3700 LA 90008 673-E1
4100 LACo 90008 673-E3
4300 LACo 90043 673-E3
5100 LA 90043 673-F5
7100 LA 90043 703-F1
W VICTORIA AV
100 MTBL 90640 676-D1
2000 MTBL 90640 636-B7
VICTORIA CIR
6400 BPK 90621 767-G1
VICTORIA CT
- PMDL 93551 4195-F6
900 Ven 90291 671-F6
900 Ven 90291 672-A5
4500 CYP 90630 767-B7
VICTORIA DR
800 ARCD 91007 567-A6
800 PAS 91104 566-C2
900 ARCD 91007 566-J6
VICTORIA LN
- PRV 90660 676-F3
- SCTA 91355 4550-E1
- SMAD 91024 567-A2
4000 LACo 93536 4105-A5
4100 LACo 93536 4104-J5
VICTORIA PL
300 CLAR 91711 601-E4
800 BURB 91504 533-G4
1600 LVRN 91750 570-F5
2800 PVE 90274 822-F2
VICTORIA RD
28400 Cstc 91384 4369-E5
VICTORIA ST
- NLB 90805 765-C1
4400 CHNO 91710 641-E6
39300 PMDL 93551 4195-F5
E VICTORIA ST
100 CRSN 90746 764-D1
1300 CRSN 90220 764-G1
1500 COMP 90746 764-G1
2300 LACo 90220 764-J2
2300 LACo 90220 765-A2
2800 RDom 90221 765-B1
W VICTORIA ST
100 CRSN 90248 764-C2
300 COMP 90220 764-H1
1600 CRSN 90746 764-H1
1600 COMP 90746 764-H1
VICTORIA WY
- LACo 91724 639-G1
- LHB 90631 708-D7
- RowH 91748 679-E6
2100 POM 91767 600-J5
VICTORIA PARK DR
4300 LA 90019 633-E4
VICTORIA PARK PL
4300 LA 90019 633-F5
VICTORIA POINT RD
31500 MAL 90265 626-H7
VICTORINE ST
3700 LA 90031 595-C6
4200 LA 90032 595-C6
VICTORVILLE PL
42900 LAN 93534 4105-E3
VICTORVILLE ST
5600 SBdC 92397 (4652-E2
See Page 4651)
VICTORY BLVD
1000 BURB 91506 533-C7
1500 GLDL 91201 563-J2
2500 BURB 91505 533-C7
10500 NHol 91606 533-A6
10600 LA 91505 533-A6
11000 NHol 91606 532-G6
13000 VanN 91401 532-A6
VICTORY BLVD
14500 VanN 91411 532-A6
14600 VanN 91411 531-E7
15300 VanN 91406 531-B7
15600 Enc 91436 531-E7
16900 Enc 91316 531-B7
17700 Res 91335 531-B7
18100 Res 91335 530-F7
19700 WdHl 91367 530-B7
20100 Win 91306 530-B7
20500 CanP 91303 530-B7
22000 WdHl 91367 529-C7
22000 CanP 91303 529-F7
22200 CanP 91307 529-C7
23600 VeCo 91302 529-C7
N VICTORY BLVD
100 BURB 91502 563-G1
100 BURB 91506 563-G1
400 BURB 91502 533-F7
400 BURB 91506 533-F7
S VICTORY BLVD
100 BURB 91502 563-H2
100 BURB 91506 563-H2
VICTORY CT
- SCTA 91350 4551-D5
300 BURB 91506 563-G2
VICTORY PL
1000 BURB 91502 533-F6
1000 BURB 91506 533-F6
1100 BURB 91504 533-F6
VICWOOD AV
4900 LaCr 91214 504-G7
VIDA LN
5300 PMDL 93551 4194-G2
VIDALIA AV
300 LACo 91744 678-J2
VIDETTE ST
6200 HiPk 90042 595-D1
VIDOR DR
9800 LA 90035 632-F4
VIDORA DR
18400 RowH 91748 679-A5
VIEJO CT
25900 SCTA 91355 4550-G4
VIENNA WY
1200 Ven 90291 671-J4
1200 Ven 90291 672-A4
11500 LA 90066 672-D2
VIENTO CT
26000 SCTA 91355 4550-G3
VIENTOS DR
8700 LACo 93551 4193-J5
8700 LACo 93551 4194-A5
VIENTO VERANO DR
1900 DBAR 91765 679-H5
VIERIO PL
15100 LMRD 90638 737-G2
VIERRA AV
17400 CRTS 90703 737-D7
17800 CRTS 90703 767-D1
VIETA AV
11600 LYN 90262 735-E1
VIEUDELOU AV
100 AVA 90704 5923-G3
13200 NRWK 90650 737-B3
VIEW DR
- WCOV 91792 679-D2
100 LHB 90631 708-E4
600 BURB 91501 534-A6
29000 Ago 91301 588-B4
W VIEW DR
- LAN 93536 4013-J5
VIEW LN
600 DBAR 91765 680-D1
VIEW PL
29800 Cstc 91384 4459-D4
VIEWCREST AV
8000 WHIT 90602 707-E1
VIEWCREST DR
- AZU 91702 569-A3
300 MTBL 90640 636-F7
400 AZU 91702 568-J3
3300 BURB 91504 533-F3
VIEW CREST RD
300 GLDL 91202 564-D1
VIEWCREST RD
12000 LA 91604 562-F6
16300 CHLS 91709 710-F2
S VIEWFIELD AV
3300 HacH 91745 678-A6
VIEW LAKE CIR
600 BREA 92821 708-H6
VIEWLAKE LN
32000 WLKV 91361 557-C7
VIEWLAND PL
200 SPed 90731 824-C3
VIEWMONT DR
1600 LA 90069 592-J4
VIEW PARK AV
16800 BLF 90706 736-D6
VIEW PARK CT
400 VeCo 91377 558-B1
VIEWPOINT CIR
- POM 91766 640-G5
VIEWPOINT DR
9700 Tuj 91042 503-J5
VIEW POINTE DR
3200 WLKV 91361 557-C7
VIEWPOINTE LN
- SCTA 91355 4550-E1
200 WAL 91789 639-H7
VIEWRIDGE DR
2500 CHLS 91709 680-J2
VIEWRIDGE LN
15500 GmH 91344 481-G7
VIEWRIDGE RD
21000 Top 90290 560-B7
VIEWSITE DR
1500 LA 90069 592-J4
VIEWSITE TER
1500 LA 90069 592-H4
VIGILANCE DR
3500 RPV 90275 823-E5
N VIGNES ST
100 LA 90012 634-H2
S VIGNES ST
100 LA 90012 634-H4
VIKING AV
100 BREA 92821 708-J7
10100 Nor 91324 500-H4
10700 Nor 91326 500-G1
11400 Nor 91326 480-G7
VIKING WY
- PMDL 93552 4287-C1
N VIKING WY
4100 LBCH 90808 766-C6
VIKINGS WY
18700 CRTS 90703 767-C1
VILLA DR
- Boyl 90033 634-J4
8700 SBdC 92372 (4562-F2
See Page 4471)
8700 WHIT 90602 707-B2
VILLA ST
1100 MTBL 90640 636-E6
E VILLA ST
200 PAS 91103 565-J3
200 PAS 91101 565-J3
500 PAS 91101 566-A3
800 PAS 91106 566-C3
1700 PAS 91107 566-E3
W VILLA ST
- PAS 91103 565-H3
VILLA WY
2000 LAN 93535 4106-D1
2400 LVRN 91750 600-H2
5300 CYP 90630 767-D6
VILLA ALTA PL
2800 HacH 91745 678-C5
VILLA CANYON RD
27700 Cstc 91384 4459-G2
VILLA CLARA ST
18200 RowH 91748 678-J6
18300 RowH 91748 679-A6
VILLA CORTA ST
17400 LACo 91744 638-H7
17800 LACo 91744 678-J1
VILLA COSTERA
3600 MAL 90265 629-E6
VILLA DEL LAGO DR
2000 CHLS 91709 680-H3
VILLA ESCUELA
700 MANB 90266 732-G5
VILLA FLORES DR
16000 HacH 91745 678-C5
VILLAGE AV
8800 SunV 91352 503-B7
VILLAGE CIDR
- BqtC 91354 4460-E4
5200 TEML 91780 597-B4
VILLAGE CIR
- BqtC 91354 4460-F4
- MANB 90266 732-H4
VILLAGE CT
- FUL 92832 738-C6
21300 TOR 90503 763-C6
N VILLAGE CT
100 SDMS 91773 600-A2
VILLAGE DR
- LA 90094 672-E7
- WAL 91789 639-H6
800 MONP 91755 636-D3
1000 CHLS 91709 680-F7
1000 CHLS 91709 710-F1
1200 LHB 90631 708-F7
1200 LHB 90631 738-F1
3500 MANB 90266 732-H4
5100 MTCL 91763 601-G6
5400 CMRC 90040 675-G3
7000 BPK 90621 737-G7
9900 ING 90303 703-F4
9900 ING 90305 703-F4
13400 CRTS 90703 737-C5
VILLAGE GN
900 THO 91361 557-C5
VILLAGE GRN
3500 LA 90016 673-B1
VILLAGE LN
- LA 90094 672-E7
- TOR 90503 763-C6
1400 WCOV 91790 598-F5
37800 PMDL 93550 4285-J2
E VILLAGE LN
8300 RSMD 91770 636-G4
VILLAGE PL
900 MONP 91755 636-D3
VILLAGE RD
1800 DUAR 91010 568-A7
2700 LKWD 90712 765-H5
6000 LKWD 90713 766-D5
8600 PdlR 90293 702-B3
E VILLAGE RD
4400 LBCH 90808 766-A5
VILLAGE WY
1700 LA 90732 823-H5
2300 SIGH 90755 795-G5

STREET Block City ZIP Pg-Grid
VILLAGE WYDR
- LA 91342 481-H7
- LA 91342 482-G6
VILLAGE BROOK RD
31800 WLKV 91361 557-D6
VILLAGE CENTER DR
- MANB 90266 732-H4
13900 CHLS 91709 680-J4
VILLAGE CENTER RD
31600 WLKV 91361 557-D6
VILLAGE GARDEN
6800 BPK 90621 767-G1
VILLAGEGLEN LN
400 LHB 90631 708-D6
VILLAGE GREEN DR
20000 LKWD 90715 766-G4
VILLAGE LAKE MALL
700 BREA 92821 708-H6
VILLAGE LOOP RD
- POM 91766 640-F4
VILLAGE OAKS DR
800 COV 91724 599-E7
VILLAGE PARK DR
2400 SMCA 90405 671-J1
VILLAGE PARK PL
2200 CHLS 91709 680-J4
VILLAGER LN
23200 LACo 90502 794-B2
VILLAGE SCHOOL RD
31600 WLKV 91361 557-D6
VILLAGE VIEW LN
14300 CHLS 91709 680-H4
VILLAGE WAY CT
- LA 91342 481-H7
VILLA GRANDE RD
15800 HacH 91745 678-B5
VILLA GROVE DR
1000 PacP 90272 631-C5
3300 Alta 91001 536-A4
S VILLA GROVE DR
1100 PacP 90272 631-C4
VILLA HEIGHTS RD
2000 LACo 91107 536-G7
N VILLA HEIGHTS RD
2100 LACo 91107 536-G6
VILLA HIGHLANDS DR
1500 LACo 91107 566-G1
1600 PAS 91107 566-G1
VILLA KNOLLS DR
3100 LACo 91107 566-F1
E VILLA KNOLLS DR
3000 LACo 91107 566-F1
VILLA LINDA CT
- BPK 90620 767-E5
VILLA MARIA RD
2100 CLAR 91711 571-C7
VILLA MESA RD
3300 LACo 91107 536-G7
VILLA MONTES AV
600 MONP 91754 636-A3
VILLA MOURA DR
100 PMDL 93551 4195-J3
VILLANOVA AV
8700 Wch 90045 702-D3
VILLANOVA DR
100 CLAR 91711 601-D4
VILLA PACIFICA CIR
21500 CRSN 90745 764-G6
VILLA PARK DR
8500 RSMD 91770 636-G5
VILLA PARK ST
17200 LPUE 91744 678-G1
17400 LACo 91744 678-H1
18100 LACo 91744 679-A1
VILLA RICA AV
1800 LACo 91107 536-G7
VILLA RITA DR
100 LACo 90631 708-C3
17000 WHIT 90603 708-C3
VILLA ROSA DR
6300 RPV 90275 792-H6
VILLA RYAN WY
- BPK 90620 767-E5
VILLA TERRAZA
- WdHl 91364 560-D2
VILLAVERDE DR
8100 WHIT 90605 707-H1
VILLA VIEW DR
1000 PacP 90272 631-B4
VILLAWOOD CIR
5400 LACo 91302 559-A3
N VILLA WOODS DR
1200 PacP 90272 631-B4
VILLA WOODS PL
14400 PacP 90272 631-C4
VILLA ZANITA ST
500 Alta 91001 535-G4
VILLEBOSO AV
5200 WdHl 91364 560-A3
VILLENA AV
21400 WdHl 91364 560-B4
VILLEROY AV
1600 WAL 91789 639-F3
VILLETTE ST
- PMDL 93552 4287-E1
VILLOSA PL
- LA 90094 702-D1
VILNA AV
27500 SCTA 91351 4551-H3
VIMY RD
11500 GmH 91344 481-A7
11500 GmH 91344 501-A1
VINA AV
1000 LBCH 90813 795-G6
VINCA ST
- SIMI 93063 499-A2
VINCENNES CT
- CLAR 91711 571-E5
VINCENNES ST
14600 PanC 91402 501-J6
14900 LA 91343 501-D6
17000 Nor 91325 501-B6
18300 Nor 91330 500-H6
18400 Nor 91324 500-G6
18400 Nor 91325 500-H6
22000 Chat 91311 499-J6
22000 Chat 91311 500-A6
VINCENT AV
- WCOV 91790 598-G3
500 AZU 91702 598-G3
4400 LACo 91722 598-G3
4700 Eagl 90041 565-B5
4700 LACo 91706 598-G3
4700 IRW 91706 598-G3
N VINCENT AV
- WCOV 91790 598-G7
100 COV 91722 598-G7
4200 LACo 91722 598-G7
S VINCENT AV
100 WCOV 91790 598-G7
200 WCOV 91790 638-G1
VINCENT DR
- PMDL 93551 4195-F6
VINCENT PK
600 RBCH 90277 762-J4
VINCENT ST
400 RBCH 90277 762-J5
1100 RBCH 90277 763-A4
VINCENT WY
1100 GLDL 91205 564-G7
VINCENTE WY
9100 LA 91343 501-H7
VINCENT THOMAS BRDG Rt#-47
- SPed 824-F3
VINCENT VIEW RD
- PMDL 93550 4376-B5
VINE AL
200 PAS 91107 566-E4
VINE AV
200 FUL 92833 738-B7
1900 TOR 90501 763-G7
2700 TOR 90501 793-G1
3300 BELL 90201 675-B7
E VINE AV
500 WCOV 91790 638-G2
1400 WCOV 91791 638-H2
1900 WCOV 91791 639-A2
W VINE AV
900 WCOV 91790 638-E1
VINE PL
14100 CRTS 90703 737-D6
VINE ST
- POM 91767 601-A4
300 GLDL 91204 564-D5
700 LA 90038 593-F6
1300 Hlwd 90028 593-F4
1400 ALH 91801 595-J5
1400 ALH 91801 596-A5
1900 LA 90068 593-F3
VINE WY
6200 LA 90068 593-F3
VINEBURN AV
1700 LA 90063 635-D2
1800 LA 90032 635-D2
VINEDALE ST
10500 SunV 91352 533-A1
11200 SunV 91352 532-J2
N VINEDO AV
- PAS 91107 566-E2
S VINEDO AV
- PAS 91107 566-E5
200 LACo 91107 566-E5
VINEHILL DR
300 Alta 91001 535-J3
300 Alta 91001 536-A3
VINELAND AV
- PMDL 93551 4104-D7
100 LACo 91746 637-J3
100 INDS 91746 637-J3
800 LACo 91746 638-A2
1100 BALD 91746 638-A2
1100 BALD 91706 638-A2
1100 LACo 91706 638-A2
2900 BALD 91706 598-C6
3700 LA 90068 563-A6
3700 LA 91604 563-A5
4100 LA 91602 563-A2
4800 NHol 91601 563-A2
5900 NHol 91601 533-A6
6000 NHol 91606 533-A6
6700 NHol 91605 533-A2
6900 BURB 91505 533-A2
7200 SunV 91352 533-A2
VINELAND CT
- Nor 91326 500-E1
VINELAND PL
4200 LA 91602 563-A4
4800 NHol 91601 563-A4
VINEMEAD DR
700 LACo 90601 637-G5
VINETA AV
4500 LCF 91011 535-D4
VINEVALE AV
6000 MYWD 90270 675-E6
VINEVALE AV
6200 BELL 90201 675-E7
6700 BELL 90201 705-E1
VINEVALE CIR
5600 LPMA 90623 767-D4
VINEVALLEY DR
8300 SunV 91352 533-B1
VINEWOOD ST
1800 LVRN 91750 570-G7
VINEYARD AV
300 DUAR 91010 568-D4
1600 LA 90019 633-E5
1900 LA 90016 633-E6
3100 LA 90016 673-D1
VINEYARD DR
- LAN 93535 4016-F7
1000 SGBL 91775 596-C2
43200 LAN 93535 4106-F2
VINEYARD LN
- Cstc 91384 4459-F3
11500 Pcma 91331 502-F1
VINEYARD PL
400 PAS 91107 566-F3
VINEYARD TR
11700 LACo 91342 482-J7
VINEYARD WY
3900 PMDL 93550 4286-H5
VINTAGE CT
37900 PMDL 93550 4286-E2
VINTAGE DR
37600 PMDL 93550 4286-E2
VINTAGE PL
- Nor 91326 500-E1
VINTAGE ST
- LAN 93536 4014-J7
- LAN 93536 4104-J1
9900 LA 91343 501-D5
14700 MsnH 91345 501-J4
17000 Nor 91325 501-B5
18100 Nor 91325 500-J5
18500 Nor 91324 500-G5
19700 Chat 91311 500-A5
22000 Chat 91311 499-J5
VINTAGE WY
1800 FUL 92833 738-D3
VINTAGE OAK ST
- SIMI 93063 499-A3
VINTON AV
300 POM 91767 600-J6
300 POM 91767 601-A6
4000 CULC 90232 672-G2
S VINTON AV
3300 LA 90034 632-F7
3500 LA 90034 672-F1
3800 LA 90232 672-G1
VIOLA AL
2700 PAS 91107 566-F4
VIOLA AV
1200 GLDL 91202 564-E2
VIOLA CT
1900 WCOV 91792 679-A1
VIOLA PL
1500 POM 91768 600-G6
3200 LA 90292 672-A6
VIOLAN ST
34600 Actn 93510 4375-C3
VIOLET AL
2800 VER 90058 674-H2
VIOLET AV
100 MNRO 91016 567-F4
VIOLET ST
1900 LA 90021 634-H6
VIOLET TR
3400 CALB 91302 589-E1
VIOLETA AV
20300 LKWD 90715 766-H4
21700 HGDN 90716 766-H7
VIOLETA DR
600 ALH 91801 596-C7
VIOLET HILLS DR
29800 SCTA 91387 4462-G5
VIOLETLANE WY
15300 SCTA 91387 4462-E7
VIOLIN CANYON RD
27400 Cstc 91384 4369-H6
VIRAZON DR
1700 LHH 90631 708-B1
2300 LHH 90631 678-B7
VIRDEN DR
1600 GLDL 91208 564-J1
VIRDIAN AV
1700 LAN 93534 4105-E3
VIREO CT
20000 SCTA 91351 4551-E3
VIREO DR
3700 LAN 93536 4015-A7
VIRETTA LN
10300 BelA 90077 592-A4
VIRGIL AV
15300 BLF 90706 736-B4
N VIRGIL AV
100 LA 90004 634-B1
100 LA 90004 594-B6
700 LA 90029 594-B6
1200 LFlz 90027 594-B6
S VIRGIL AV
100 LA 90004 634-B2
300 LA 90020 634-B2
600 LA 90005 634-B2
600 LA 90010 634-B2
VIRGIL PL
1300 LFlz 90027 594-B5
N VIRGIL WK
- LBCH 90803 826-C3
VIRGIL WATERS WY
800 INDS 91748 678-G2
VIRGINIA AV
200 LACo 91107 566-E5
200 PAS 91107 566-E4
900 COV 91722 599-D4
1100 GLDL 91202 564-C1
1300 BALD 91706 638-A1
2000 SMCA 90404 671-H1
2100 LVRN 91750 570-G7
2900 SMCA 90404 631-J7
3900 BALD 91706 598-D5
4200 LA 90029 594-B5
4600 NLB 90805 765-C4
5200 LA 90029 593-H5
5500 LA 90038 593-G5
8100 SGAT 90280 705-B3
10400 LYN 90262 705-E7
10400 WHIT 90603 707-J5
10600 CULC 90232 672-G3
10700 CULC 90230 672-G3
11300 LYN 90262 735-D1
11400 LYN 90262 735-D1
13200 LACo 90605 707-B6
15100 BLF 90706 736-A5
15100 PRM 90723 735-H6
E VIRGINIA AV
100 GLDR 91741 569-E4
2900 WCOV 91791 599-C7
3000 WCOV 91791 639-D1
N VIRGINIA AV
100 PAS 91107 566-E4
200 AZU 91702 568-H6
S VIRGINIA AV
- PAS 91107 566-E5
100 AZU 91702 568-H7
100 BURB 91506 563-G2
100 AZU 91702 598-H1
2000 POM 91766 641-B5
W VIRGINIA AV
100 GLDR 91741 569-D4
VIRGINIA CT
- Ven 90291 671-H6
N VIRGINIA CT
200 LBCH 90802 795-D7
200 LBCH 90802 825-D1
700 LBCH 90813 795-D7
VIRGINIA LN
2800 WCOV 91791 639-C2
VIRGINIA PL
1000 GLDL 91204 564-E6
1700 SPAS 91030 595-H2
9500 BHLS 90212 632-F3
VIRGINIA RD
- ARCD 91006 567-D2
300 CLAR 91711 601-C4
300 FUL 92831 738-H5
1000 SMRO 91108 566-B7
1200 SMRO 91108 596-B1
1600 LA 90019 633-E6
1900 LA 90016 633-E6
3400 LA 90016 673-E1
3700 LA 90008 673-E1
4600 Bxby 90807 765-D5
N VIRGINIA RD
3900 Bxby 90807 765-D5
VIRGINIA ST
100 ELSG 90245 732-E2
100 LHB 90631 708-D5
700 ELSG 90245 702-E7
1600 SBdC 92397 (4652-D2 See Page 4651)
VIRGINIA TER
3000 RSMD 91770 636-E2
3100 LYN 90262 705-A7
3100 LYN 90262 735-A1
3600 GLDL 91214 504-D6
38900 PMDL 93551 4195-C6
VIRGINIA WY
400 BREA 92821 709-B7
W VIRGINIA ANN DR
500 AZU 91702 568-H4
VIRGINIA VISTA CT
4100 Bxby 90807 765-C6
VIRGO AV
- PMDL 93552 4286-H2
VIRO RD
4500 LCF 91011 535-E5
VISALIA AV
1500 COMP 90220 734-E6
14700 LACo 90220 734-E4
16200 CRSN 90746 734-E6
VISALIA LN
900 COMP 90746 734-E6
1800 PVE 90274 792-G5
VISBY PL
8500 SunV 91352 533-B1
VISCANIO RD
21900 WdHl 91364 560-A4
22000 WdHl 91364 559-J4
VISCANO DR
1100 GLDL 91207 564-G3
VISCO CT
28600 SCTA 91390 4461-D4
VISCOUNT ST
3300 ALH 91803 635-G1
VISION DR
19600 Top 90290 630-A1
VISION TR
- Top 90290 590-A7
12300 LACo 91342 482-J6
VISIONS DR
4000 FUL 90638 738-A3
E VISIONS DR
16400 LMRD 90638 738-A2
S VISIONS DR
13800 LMRD 90638 738-A3
VISIONS ST
37100 PMDL 93552 4287-B4
VISLOMA PL
2100 LMTA 90717 793-H6
VISO DR
6900 LA 90068 593-D1
VISROY AV
13700 CRTS 90703 767-D1
VISSCHER PL
2600 Alta 91001 535-J5
VISTA AV
100 PAS 91107 566-E3
1900 SMAD 91024 567-D1
2000 ARCD 91006 567-D1
11800 CHNO 91710 641-F4
VISTA CIR
800 BREA 92821 708-J5
20500 WAL 91789 639-F7
VISTA CT
- CHNO 91710 641-F5
- DBAR 91765 679-J7
800 BREA 92821 709-B4
1200 GLDL 91205 564-F6
3800 GLDL 91214 504-D6
4000 LA 91214 504-D6
4600 LVRN 91750 570-G5
17900 SCTA 91387 4551-J2
17900 SCTA 91387 4552-A2
VISTA DR
- SMRO 91108 566-C7
400 CLAR 91711 601-C5
1600 GLDL 91201 534-B7
5100 PMDL 93551 4194-G1
20500 TOR 90503 763-C5
N VISTA DR
- LA 90068 563-F4
900 FUL 92832 738-F6
900 FUL 92835 738-F6
1400 PAS 91103 565-D1
4100 WCOV 91792 679-C3
11000 ELMN 91731 597-D4
VISTA PL
- UPL 91786 601-G3
100 Ven 90291 671-G5
300 HiPk 90042 595-E1
3100 ALH 91801 595-G5
4200 LACo 90265 627-J5
4300 LCF 91011 534-J3
7400 LA 90046 593-C4
N VISTA PL
200 UPL 91786 601-G3
VISTA RD
1700 GLDL 91214 534-E2
1700 SBdC 92372 (4562-E1 See Page 4471)
2100 LHH 90631 708-G3
2200 LACo 90631 708-G3
2600 SBdC 92371 (4562-G1 See Page 4471)
5900 VeCo 93063 499-B4
VISTA RDG
1000 BURB 91504 533-G4
VISTA ST
1100 WHWD 90046 593-C5
E VISTA ST
300 LBCH 90803 826-A1
2800 LBCH 90803 825-H1
6100 LBCH 90803 796-E7
N VISTA ST
100 LA 90036 633-C1
300 LA 90036 593-C7
700 LA 90046 593-C4
1000 WHWD 90046 593-C7
5800 LACo 91775 596-G1
5800 SGBL 91775 596-G3
5800 SGBL 91776 596-G3
6800 LACo 91775 566-F7
S VISTA ST
100 LA 90036 633-C1
VISTA TER
15900 PacP 90272 630-J6
VISTA TR
17700 LACo 93532 4101-J1
VISTA WY
1900 LACo 91724 639-H1
E VISTA BELLA WY
1900 LACo 90220 764-H3
VISTA BONITA
4200 MTCL 91763 641-E2
9200 CYP 90630 767-D6
37100 PMDL 93550 4286-G4
N VISTA BONITA AV
100 GLDR 91741 569-E4
S VISTA BONITA AV
100 GLDR 91741 569-E6
VISTA BONITA ST
200 AZU 91702 568-H5
VISTA BUENA DR
24300 DBAR 91765 640-D6
VISTA CALMA
40800 PMDL 93551 4194-F2
VISTA CAMPANA
2500 PMDL 93550 4286-E4
VISTA CANADA PL
5100 LCF 91011 535-C2
VISTA CERRITOS
24600 CALB 91302 559-E6
VISTA CIRCLE CT
3900 LAN 93536 4105-A2
VISTA CIRCLE DR
- SMAD 91024 567-B1
3800 LAN 93536 4105-A2
VISTA CREST DR
3000 LA 90068 593-D1
VISTA DEL CIR
1400 AZU 91702 568-J4
VISTA DE LA LUZ
5900 WdHl 91367 559-C1
VISTA DEL ARROYO
- Ago 91301 587-J3
VISTA DEL ARROYO DR
5400 LaCr 91214 504-H6
VISTA DE LAS ONDAS
32700 MAL 90265 626-E6
VISTA DEL CANON
18700 SCTA 91321 4551-H5
VISTA DELGADO DR
22900 SCTA 91354 4460-H7
VISTA DEL GOLFO
- LBCH 90803 826-D3
VISTA DEL LAGO
15600 LACo 93532 4102-E4
36500 LACo 93551 4285-H5
VISTA DEL LLANO DR
400 LHH 90631 708-B3
400 WHIT 90603 708-B3
VISTA DEL MAR
100 RBCH 90277 792-J1
300 TOR 90277 792-J1
300 ELSG 90245 732-D2
700 LA 90245 732-D2
2800 RPV 90275 823-F6
5200 CYP 90630 767-D6
6300 PdlR 90293 702-A3
8700 PdlR 90293 732-D2
VISTA DEL MAR AV
1600 Hlwd 90028 593-F4
1900 LA 90068 593-F3
VISTA DEL MAR DR
3100 GLDL 91208 534-H5
VISTA DEL MAR LN
6900 PdlR 90293 702-A4
VISTA DEL MAR PL
2200 LA 90068 593-F3
VISTA DEL MAR RD
2600 Top 90290 630-A3
VISTA DEL MONTE AV
4400 Shrm 91403 562-A3
5600 VanN 91411 562-A1
7300 VanN 91405 532-A4
VISTA DEL MONTE DR
2400 Actn 93510 4375-E7
VISTA DEL NORTE
300 WAL 91789 639-D7
300 WAL 91789 679-C1
1600 CHLS 91709 680-H6
VISTA DEL ORO
10900 MTCL 91763 641-D2
VISTA DEL PARQUE
100 TOR 90277 793-A2
VISTA DEL PRESEAS
4400 MAL 90265 626-D5
VISTA DEL RIO
10900 MTCL 91763 641-D2
VISTA DEL RIO DR
- BqtC 91354 4460-E4
8300 DWNY 90240 706-D2
VISTA DEL ROSA
7800 DWNY 90240 706-C1
VISTA DEL ROSA ST
7900 DWNY 90240 706-C1
VISTA DEL SOL
- LACo 91390 4373-G6
- LACo 91750 570-J3
- LVRN 91750 570-J3
100 TOR 90277 792-H2
2000 CHLS 91709 680-J5
5200 CYP 90630 767-D6
10900 MTCL 91763 641-D2
40800 PMDL 93551 4194-F1
VISTA DEL SOL DR
- LA 91342 482-E3
VISTA DEL VALLE
700 SDMS 91773 600-A6
VISTA DEL VALLE DR
- LFlz 90027 563-J6
- LFlz 90027 564-A7
- LFlz 90027 594-B1
1700 ARCD 91006 567-D2
VISTA DEL VALLE RD
800 LCF 91011 535-B2
VISTA DEL VALLE WY
1400 LHH 90631 708-B3
VISTA DEL VEGAS
5000 TOR 90505 793-B3
VISTA DEL VENTADA
- MAL 90265 626-D6
VISTA DE ORA
3600 LALM 90720 796-J4
VISTA DE ORO
5700 LVRN 91750 570-H4
VISTA DE ORO AV
4500 WdHl 91364 560-D4
4800 LACo 90043 673-D4
VISTA DE ORO PL
20500 WdHl 91364 560-D4
VISTA DE RIO DR
- BqtC 91354 4460-F4
VISTA DORADO
37000 PMDL 93550 4286-E4
VISTA DORADO LN
400 VeCo 91377 557-J2
VISTA DORADO PL
1500 CHLS 91709 680-G5
VISTA EL RINCON
2500 PMDL 93550 4286-F4
VISTA ENCANTADA DR
27000 SCTA 91354 4460-H7
27000 SCTA 91354 4550-H1
VISTA ESTRADA
1300 MONP 91755 636-E4
N VISTA FAIRWAYS DR
25700 SCTA 91355 4550-E7
VISTA FLORA
4200 MTCL 91763 641-E2
VISTA FORTUNA
5300 CYP 90630 767-D6
VISTA GLEN WY
13600 HacH 91745 637-G6
VISTA GLORIOSA DR
400 LA 90065 594-J5
VISTA GORDO DR
2300 Echo 90026 594-F5
VISTA GRANDE
- LACo 91390 4373-D7
- TOR 90505 793-F5
- TOR 90717 793-F5
1000 BURB 91504 533-H4
VISTA GRANDE DR
1000 PacP 90272 630-G4
13700 CHLS 91709 680-J2
VISTA GRANDE ST
8900 WHWD 90069 592-H6
VISTA GRANDE WY
18900 Nor 91326 480-G7
VISTA HAVEN PL
15400 Shrm 91403 561-H7
VISTA HAVEN RD
3300 Shrm 91403 561-H7
VISTA HERMOSA
4300 MTCL 91763 641-E2
5200 CYP 90630 767-D6
VISTA HERMOSA DR
19500 WAL 91789 639-D7
19500 WAL 91789 679-D1
VISTA HERMOSA ST
5100 LBCH 90815 796-B5
VISTA HILLS DR
24100 SCTA 91355 4550-F7
24100 SCTA 91355 4640-E1
VISTA INDUSTRIA
2500 RDom 90221 765-A3
VISTA JUANITA
10000 MTCL 91763 641-E2
VISTA LAGUNA CIR
800 DUAR 91010 568-E4
VISTA LAGUNA TER
2300 Alta 91001 535-F5
2300 PAS 91001 535-F5
2300 PAS 91103 535-F5
2500 LACo 91011 535-F5
2500 PAS 91011 535-F5
VISTA LARGO
4200 TOR 90505 793-C3
VISTA LE JANA LN
5200 LCF 91011 535-B1
VISTA LEON
37000 PMDL 93550 4286-F4
VISTA LINDA
- PMDL 93551 4194-G1
41400 PMDL 93536 4104-G7
41400 PMDL 93551 4104-G7
VISTA LINDA DR
3800 Enc 91316 561-A6
3800 LAN 93536 4105-A2
VISTA LOMITA LN
2200 LMTA 90717 793-G6
VISTA MADERA
4200 MTCL 91763 641-E2
28500 RPV 90275 823-H2
VISTAMAR DR
2700 LACo 90265 628-C5
VISTA MESA
9200 CYP 90630 767-D6
VISTA MESA CT
900 DUAR 91010 568-E5
VISTA MESA DR
2700 RPV 90275 823-G5
VISTA MIGUEL DR
5100 LCF 91011 535-B1
VISTA MONTANA
4100 TOR 90505 793-B3
40800 PMDL 93551 4194-G2
VISTA MOORA AV
2300 CHLS 91709 680-G5
VISTA MORAGA
1300 Brwd 90049 591-H6
VISTA PACIFICA
800 PacP 90272 630-G4
6400 RPV 90275 822-H5
VISTA PACIFICA ST
3500 MAL 90265 628-H7
VISTA PANORAMA
4300 MTCL 91763 641-E2
VISTA PELONA DR
- PMDL 93551 4195-B3
VISTA PLAYA
4200 MTCL 91763 641-D2
VISTA PLAYA DR
30800 MAL 90265 627-A7
VISTA POINT LN
- LACo 91387 4462-D7
VISTA POINT PL
- Cstc 91384 4369-H5
VISTA POINT WY
- PMDL 93551 4195-A4
VISTA RAMBIA
40800 PMDL 93551 4194-G1
VISTA RAMBLA
400 WAL 91789 679-D2
VISTA RANCH AV
- LA 91342 481-H6
VISTA REAL
5200 CYP 90630 767-D6
10900 MTCL 91763 641-E2
VISTA REAL DR
- RHE 90274 793-G6
VISTA RIDGE DR
- PMDL 93551 4195-B3
24200 SCTA 91355 4640-E1
VISTA RIDGE LN
900 THO 91362 557-D1
2300 SIGH 90755 795-G3
VISTA ROSINA DR
23300 SCTA 91354 4460-G7
VISTA SANTE FE PL
1600 CHLS 91709 680-G4
VISTA SERENA
9200 CYP 90630 767-D6
VISTA SERENA CT
43500 LAN 93536 4105-A2
VISTA SERENA DR
43500 LAN 93536 4105-A2
VISTA SIERRA
5300 CYP 90630 767-D6
VISTA SIERRA CT
43600 LAN 93536 4105-A2
VISTA SIERRA DR
30600 MAL 90265 627-A7
43300 LAN 93536 4105-A2
VISTA SOL LN
- PMDL 93551 4104-D6
VISTA SUPERBA DR
4400 LA 90065 564-G7
4400 GLDL 91205 564-G7
VISTA TIERRA
28500 RPV 90275 823-H2
VISTA VALLE
40800 PMDL 93551 4194-G1
VISTA VERDE
10900 MTCL 91763 641-E2
12700 NRWK 90650 736-G1
VISTA VERDE CIR
900 DUAR 91010 568-E5
VISTA VERDE DR
800 FUL 92832 738-G6
25700 LACo 91302 588-J7
25700 LACo 91302 589-A7
VISTA VERDE WY
5100 WHIT 90601 677-A3
VISTA VERENDA
24900 WdHl 91367 559-C1
VISTA VIEW DR
27900 SCTA 91351 4551-E1
VISTA VIEW TER
- LACo 93551 4285-H7
- LACo 93551 4375-H1
VISTILLAS RD
1700 Alta 91001 536-C7
VITRINA LN
3900 PMDL 93551 4195-A3
4400 PMDL 93551 4194-H2
VIVA DR
7200 Tuj 91042 504-A5
VIVERO DR
2000 RowH 91748 679-A6
VIVIAN CT
- PMDL 93551 4194-J2
VIVIANA DR
4700 Tarz 91356 560-G4
VIVIWOOD PL
1200 LHB 90631 738-E1
VOGEL FLATS RD
- Tuj 91042 (4724-H6 See Page 4643)
VOGUE AV
4900 LACo 91722 598-H3
5200 LACo 91702 598-H2
N VOGUE AV
600 COV 91722 598-H5
4600 LACo 91722 598-H4
VOLADOR PL
12800 BALD 91706 597-H7
13200 BALD 91706 637-J1
13400 BALD 91706 638-A1
VOLANTE DR
800 ARCD 91007 566-J4
800 ARCD 91007 567-A5
VOLETTA PL
5500 LA 91607 562-E1
VOLK AV
1800 LBCH 90815 796-F4
3400 LBCH 90808 766-F6
N VOLK AV
3000 LBCH 90808 796-F2
VOLMER AV
3500 CMRC 90040 676-B7
VOLNEY DR
1300 City 90063 635-F3
1400 MONP 90063 635-F3
VOLTAIRE DR
3100 Top 90290 560-B7
VOLTAIRE PL
- StvR 91381 4550-A7
VOLTARA CT
24400 CALB 91302 559-C6
VOLUNTEER AV
11800 NRWK 90650 706-J7
12300 NRWK 90650 736-J1
VON KEITHIAN AV
300 LA 90031 595-B6
VONNIE LN
5500 CYP 90630 767-D5
VOORHEES AV
1300 MANB 90266 732-H7
1900 RBCH 90278 732-J7
1900 RBCH 90278 733-A7
VOSBURG DR
- AZU 91702 568-J4
- AZU 91702 569-A4
VOSBURG ST
3200 LACo 91107 536-G7
VOSE ST
11700 NHol 91605 532-E5
13400 VanN 91405 532-A5
14500 VanN 91405 531-J5
15300 VanN 91406 531-C5
19000 Res 91335 530-F5
20300 Win 91306 530-D5
20900 CanP 91303 530-C5
22500 CanP 91307 529-G5
VOSS ST
35400 LACo 91390 4373-H2
VOSSLER AV
8900 SGAT 90280 705-E4
VOYAGE CT
100 LA 90292 701-J2
100 LA 90292 702-A4
VOYAGE MALL
- LA 90292 702-A4
5400 LA 90292 701-J2
VOYAGE ST
- LA 90292 701-J2
VOYAGER AV
100 BREA 92821 709-G7
VOYAGER CIR
2600 SPed 90731 853-J1
VOYAGER ST
100 POM 91768 640-C2
3600 TOR 90503 763-D3
VREELAND AV
800 Wilm 90744 794-H6
VU AV
- FUL 92833 738-D6
VUELTA PL
1300 PVE 90274 792-H5
VUELTA GRANDE AV
1300 LBCH 90815 796-D2
VULCAN DR
7900 LA 90046 593-A2
VULCAN LN
20100 Top 90290 630-A2
VULCAN ST
10900 SGAT 90280 705-G7
VULTEE AV
10200 DWNY 90241 706-C4
12700 DWNY 90242 736-A1
13100 BLF 90706 736-A2

W

W & P RD
- BqtC 91354 (4370-E5 See Page 4279)
- LACo 91390 (4370-E5 See Page 4279)
WABASH AV
1200 GLDR 91740 599-E1
2400 Boyl 90033 635-B3
2900 LA 90063 635-B3
3100 City 90063 635-B3
N WABASH AV
100 GLDR 91741 569-E5
S WABASH AV
100 GLDR 91741 569-E6
600 GLDR 91740 569-E6
WABASH CT
800 CLAR 91711 571-F7
WABASH ST
1100 PAS 91103 565-E2
WABASSO WY
1400 GLDL 91208 534-G7
WABUSKA ST
24100 SCTA 91321 4640-F2
WACO ST
12800 BALD 91706 597-H7
13200 BALD 91706 637-J1
13400 BALD 91706 638-A1
WADDELL ST
10500 LACo 90606 676-G7
10600 LACo 90606 706-J1
12800 LA 91607 562-E1
WADDINGTON AV
43700 LAN 93536 4105-C1
WADE AV
22900 TOR 90505 793-F1
WADE ST
100 LHB 90631 708-H5
3200 LA 90066 672-A2
4000 CULC 90066 672-C5
WADELL ST
11300 LACo 90606 706-H1
WADENA ST
5000 LA 90032 595-F5
WADKINS AV
14300 GAR 90249 733-G4
WADLEY AV
19000 CRSN 90746 764-E3
WADSHAW AL
14700 GAR 90249 733-G4
WADSWORTH AV
100 SMCA 90405 671-F4
3200 LA 90011 674-E3
7200 LA 90001 674-E7
7300 LA 90001 704-E2
8600 Wats 90002 704-E4
10800 LA 90059 704-E7
12300 Wbrk 90059 734-E1
S WADSWORTH AV
14900 LACo 90220 734-E4
15000 COMP 90220 734-F6
WADSWORTH PL
- WLA 90025 631-J4
WAGER RD
23500 Nwhl 91321 4641-C3
23500 SCTA 91321 4641-C3
WAGNER AV
5400 LKWD 90712 765-J2
WAGNER CT
2800 Alta 91001 535-G5
WAGNER DR
100 CLAR 91711 571-D7
WAGNER PL
12100 CRTS 90703 766-H2
WAGNER ST
1600 PAS 91106 566-C3
1800 PAS 91107 566-C4
10800 CULC 90230 672-F3
11800 LA 90230 672-E5
12400 LA 90066 672-D6
WAGNER WY
25600 StvR 91381 4550-C7
WAGON LN
- RHLS 90274 823-D2
WAGON RD
28600 Ago 91301 588-A1
WAGON HORSE AV
200 LACo 91750 570-J6
WAGON MOUND RD
14000 LA 91342 481-E2
WAGON TRAIL RD
23300 DBAR 91765 680-B1
WAGON TRAIN LN
2500 DBAR 91765 680-A6
2600 DBAR 91765 679-J7
WAGON TRAIN RD
10700 SBdC 92371 (4472-H2 See Page 4471)
WAGON WHEEL CT
700 BREA 92821 709-B6
1100 SDMS 91740 570-A7
1100 SDMS 91773 570-A7
8200 LACo 91770 636-F4
WAGONWHEEL RD
100 GLDR 91741 569-J5
WAGON WHEEL WY
- LACo 91390 4462-J1
32400 LACo 91390 (4372-J7 See Page 4281)
32700 LACo 91390 4373-A6
WAHOO TR
21400 Chat 91311 500-A1
WAILEA ST
1500 WCOV 91792 638-H4
WAIN PL
16300 HacH 91745 678-E4
WAINWRIGHT AV
800 Wilm 90744 794-H6
WAINWRIGHT DR
7400 BPK 90620 767-E2
WAIST PL
7400 Wch 90045 702-D3
WAITE CT
600 LBCH 90802 795-D7
700 LBCH 90813 795-D7
WAKE CT
16000 LPUE 91744 638-E6
WAKECREST DR
18100 LACo 90265 630-D6
WAKEFIELD AV
3900 SBdC 91710 641-D5
8000 PanC 91402 532-A1
8700 PanC 91402 502-A7
WAKEFIELD CT
500 LBCH 90803 796-D7
1400 UPL 91784 571-H4
21900 SCTA 91350 4461-A4
WAKEFIELD PL
- PMDL 93551 4195-H7
38000 PMDL 93551 4285-H1
WAKEFIELD RD
27700 Cstc 91384 4459-G5
WAKE FOREST AV
1300 WAL 91789 639-F4
WAKE FOREST ST
400 BREA 92821 709-C6
WAKEMAN ST
11500 LACo 90606 706-J1
11700 SFSP 90670 707-A1
WALAVISTA RD
10300 LA 90064 632-E7
WALBROOK DR
14500 HacH 91745 637-J7
14800 HacH 91745 677-J1
14800 HacH 91745 678-A1
15100 INDS 91745 678-A1
WALBURG ST
13300 LACo 90605 707-C3

STREET
Block City ZIP Pg-Grid

WALCOTT WY
1900 LA 90039 594-F5
WALCROFT ST
11300 LKWD 90715 766-G4
12500 LKWD 90715 767-A4
WALDEN
3400 ELMN 91732 637-G1
WALDEN DR
500 BHLS 90210 632-E1
800 Wwd 90024 632-D1
WALDEN RD
- BREA 92821 709-F6
WALDEN ST
4700 CHNO 91710 641-F4
WALDIE CT
3100 LKWD 90712 765-H2
WALDO AV
100 FUL 92833 738-B7
300 PAS 91101 565-J5
WALDO CT
4500 LA 90032 595-D6
WALDO PL
5300 Eagl 90041 565-C5
WALDORF DR
700 LCF 91011 535-C7
12200 LYN 90262 735-C2
S WALDORF DR
12800 COMP 90221 735-C3
12800 RDom 90221 735-C3
WALDORF PL
- RowH 91748 709-A2
WALDRAN AV
1500 Eagl 90041 565-B6
WALDROY LN
8700 SBdC 92371 (4562-J2
See Page 4471)
WALES AV
1200 GLDR 91740 599-G1
WALES CT
- RowH 91748 708-J2
WALES ST
39400 PMDL 93551 4195-F5
WALFORD CT
30200 AGRH 91301 557-H4
WALGROVE AV
1300 LA 90066 671-J3
1300 Ven 90291 671-J3
1400 LA 90066 672-A3
1400 Ven 90291 672-A3
3900 CULC 90066 672-A3
3900 Ven 90291 672-A3
WALKATOP RD
43200 LACo 93532 4102-F3
WALKER AV
900 LHB 90631 708-D6
1800 MNRO 91016 567-G6
5900 MYWD 90270 675-F6
6100 MYWD 90201 675-F6
6200 BELL 90201 675-F7
6400 BELL 90201 705-F1
7700 CDHY 90201 705-F2
N WALKER AV
100 LA 90732 823-J4
S WALKER AV
100 LA 90732 823-J5
300 LACo 90732 823-J5
700 SPed 90731 824-A7
2600 SPed 90731 854-A1
3400 SPed 90731 853-J1
WALKER CT
5500 CYP 90630 767-D7
27700 SCTA 91350 4460-J5
WALKER DR
400 BHLS 90210 592-H3
WALKER LN
1200 OrCo 90631 708-F4
2100 FUL 92833 738-C3
WALKER PL
- StvR 91381 4550-D7
WALKER RD
400 SDMS 91773 600-A1
25100 HIDH 91302 559-B4
WALKER ST
2000 LVRN 91750 600-D3
6800 LPMA 90623 767-D2
6800 CRTS 90703 767-D2
7400 BPK 90620 767-D2
8200 BPK 90623 767-D4
8300 LPMA 90630 767-D4
8500 CYP 90630 767-D7
WALKER LEE DR
2600 OrCo 90720 796-G6
E WALKERTON ST
3800 LBCH 90808 766-B6
WALKING HORSE LN
19700 WAL 91789 639-D6
31500 WLKV 91361 557-E6
WALKINGTON LN
- FUL 92833 738-D5
WALL ST
100 LA 90003 704-D2
300 LA 90013 634-F5
500 LHB 90631 708-B6
600 LA 90014 634-F5
900 LA 90015 634-E6
2100 LA 90011 634-E7
2300 LA 90011 674-E2
5800 LA 90003 674-D6
12200 LACo 90061 734-D1
18000 CRSN 90746 764-D2
42400 LAN 93534 4105-J4
E WALL ST
2600 SIGH 90755 795-H4

S WALL ST
17200 CRSN 90746 734-D7
WALLABI AV
13800 LA 91342 482-E1
WALLACE AV
1400 Echo 90026 634-E1
9100 OrCo 90631 708-B4
WALLACE PL
- StvR 91381 4550-A7
1000 INDS 91748 678-G3
WALLACE RDG
1000 BHLS 90210 592-G5
WALLACE ST
100 LHB 90631 708-E6
WALLACE CANYON RD
35500 LACo 91390 4374-C2
WALLCREST DR
1400 CLAR 91711 601-A1
1400 POM 91767 601-A1
WALLING AV
1000 BREA 92821 708-J5
2200 LHB 90631 708-H5
WALLINGFORD DR
2500 LA 90210 592-C1
WALLINGFORD RD
2500 SMRO 91108 566-E7
3000 LACo 91107 566-F6
WALLINGSFORD RD
11000 LALM 90720 796-J3
11000 OrCo 90720 796-J3
WALLINGTON CT
31900 WLKV 91361 557-C6
WALLIS LN
5700 WdHl 91367 560-C1
WALLIS ST
100 PAS 91105 565-H7
200 PAS 91106 565-J7
WALMAR AV
4900 LCF 91011 535-C3
WALNUT
- LA 91342 481-G1
1100 SDMS 91773 599-J2
WALNUT AV
100 BREA 92821 709-A7
100 BURB 91504 533-G6
100 ARCD 91007 597-B2
300 LBCH 90802 795-G7
400 BURB 91501 533-H4
700 LBCH 90813 795-G7
1000 POM 91766 641-B6
1100 MANB 90266 732-G4
1100 LBCH 90813 795-G7
1300 LACo 91744 638-F3
1300 Ven 90291 672-A5
1300 WCOV 91790 638-F3
1500 Ven 90291 671-J3
1900 FUL 92833 738-C7
2300 UPL 91784 571-J3
2500 Ven 90291 672-A5
3000 Bxby 90807 795-G7
3200 SIGH 90755 795-G7
3400 CHNO 91710 641-C6
3600 LYN 90262 705-C7
3700 SBdC 91710 641-C6
3900 LYN 90262 735-E1
4100 Bxby 90807 765-F3
4600 PRV 90660 676-G3
7200 BPK 90620 767-G2
7300 PRM 90723 735-F1
7400 SGAT 90280 735-F1
9800 SGAT 90280 705-E5
E WALNUT AV
100 ELSG 90245 702-E7
100 FUL 92832 738-H7
100 MNRO 91016 567-H4
200 GLDR 91741 569-E6
500 FUL 92831 738-J7
N WALNUT AV
100 SDMS 91773 600-C1
900 SDMS 91773 570-C7
1300 LBCH 90813 795-G5
1800 LBCH 90806 795-G4
2000 SIGH 90755 795-F3
3300 Bxby 90807 795-F3
3400 Bxby 90807 765-F7
5200 NLB 90805 765-F1
6300 NLB 90805 735-F7
S WALNUT AV
100 SDMS 91773 600-C2
500 LVRN 91750 600-C3
1000 WCOV 91790 638-F3
W WALNUT AV
100 ELSG 90245 702-D7
100 FUL 92832 738-G7
100 MNRO 91016 567-F4
400 MTBL 90640 676-D3
1600 FUL 92833 738-D7
WALNUT CT
- MNRO 91016 567-E4
200 AZU 91702 568-J3
200 LACo 91107 566-H5
2100 Ven 90291 672-A4
17000 BLF 90706 736-B6
WALNUT DR
300 LACo 91107 566-H5
7200 Flor 90001 674-G7
7200 Flor 90001 704-G1
8400 LA 90046 592-J4
8400 LA 90046 593-A4
10600 Sunl 91040 503-A5
19300 RowH 91748 679-D4
19300 INDS 91748 679-D4
19300 INDS 91789 679-F3
19800 DBAR 91789 679-F3

WALNUT DR
19800 LACo 91789 679-F3
WALNUT DR N
19000 RowH 91748 679-C3
19000 INDS 91748 679-C3
WALNUT DR S
19300 INDS 91748 679-D4
19300 RowH 91748 679-D4
19600 LACo 91789 679-E4
19600 INDS 91789 679-D4
20100 DBAR 91789 679-E4
WALNUT LN
11900 WLA 90025 631-J6
WALNUT RD
400 SBdC 92372 (4472-A4
See Page 4471)
2700 SBdC 92371 (4472-G4
See Page 4471)
WALNUT ST
900 SGBL 91776 596-E6
1200 LHH 90631 708-E3
1300 LA 90011 674-F1
1800 LVRN 91750 600-F3
2400 LACo 90255 674-H7
2700 LACo 90255 704-J1
2700 LACo 90255 705-A1
2900 HNTP 90255 705-A1
3600 CDHY 90201 705-C1
3800 BELL 90201 705-C1
3900 BALD 91706 598-A5
4100 TOR 90505 793-H2
5600 SBdC 92397 (4652-D2
See Page 4651)
8600 BLF 90706 735-J6
8700 BLF 90706 736-A6
10600 LALM 90720 796-J2
11000 ELMN 91731 637-D1
11400 LACo 90606 706-H2
11900 NRWK 90650 736-H2
12600 WHIT 90602 677-C7
22900 TOR 90501 793-H2
23800 LMTA 90717 793-H5
24200 SCTA 91321 4640-J1
24700 SCTA 91321 4550-H7
E WALNUT ST
- PAS 91103 565-J4
200 PAS 91101 565-J4
300 CRSN 90746 734-E7
500 PAS 91101 566-B4
800 PAS 91106 566-B4
1800 PAS 91107 566-D4
3700 LACo 91107 566-H4
N WALNUT ST
100 LHB 90631 708-E4
S WALNUT ST
100 LHB 90631 708-E6
600 ING 90301 703-C3
1100 LHB 90631 738-D1
10000 ING 90304 703-C4
10000 Lenx 90304 703-C4
W WALNUT ST
- PAS 91103 565-G4
100 CRSN 90248 734-C7
300 COMP 90220 734-G7
WALNUT TER
2200 LACo 90255 704-H1
WALNUT TR
19600 Top 90290 590-A7
WALNUT WY
100 BREA 92821 709-B7
300 FUL 92832 738-H7
5900 PMDL 93551 4104-F7
E WALNUT WY
1500 LBCH 90813 795-F5
WALNUT CANYON RD
20200 WAL 91789 639-F5
WALNUT CREEK CT
- SCTA 91354 4460-F4
E WALNUT CREEK CT
1800 WCOV 91791 638-J1
WALNUT CREEK DR
1600 CHLS 91709 680-G3
WALNUT CREEK PKWY
600 WCOV 91790 638-G1
14300 BALD 91706 638-C1
E WALNUT CREEK PKWY
1000 WCOV 91790 638-H1
1500 WCOV 91791 638-H1
1900 WCOV 91791 639-A1
2300 WCOV 91791 599-B7
S WALNUT CREEK PKWY
800 WCOV 91790 638-E1
W WALNUT CREEK PKWY
2300 WCOV 91790 638-C1
S WALNUT CREEK PL
400 WCOV 91791 638-J1
WALNUT CREEK RD
1000 COV 91724 599-D7
WALNUTDALE AV
11800 NRWK 90650 736-H2
WALNUT GROVE AV
1000 RSMD 91770 636-G2
1300 LACo 91770 636-G4
3500 RSMD 91770 596-G7
4900 RSMD 91776 596-G3
5800 LACo 91775 596-G3
N WALNUT GROVE AV
100 SGBL 91776 596-G4
300 SGBL 91775 596-G4
WALNUT HALL RD
1400 INDS 91748 678-H4
WALNUTHAVEN DR
3900 LACo 91722 598-F5

N WALNUTHAVEN DR
100 WCOV 91790 598-F7
700 LACo 91722 598-F7
WALNUT LEAF DR
1500 LACo 91789 679-F4
WALNUT ORCHARD RD
30000 Cstc 91384 4549-C3
WALNUT PARK DR
1700 COMP 90220 734-G7
WALNUT PARK WY
1300 COMP 90220 734-G7
WALNUT RIDGE DR
5600 AGRH 91301 557-J5
WALNUT SPRINGS AV
27200 SCTA 91351 4551-G2
WALNUT VALLEY DR
20600 WAL 91789 639-F3
WALNUT VISTA WY
- WAL 91789 639-C4
WALPOLE DR
7000 Tuj 91042 504-A5
WALRAVEN CT
- FUL 92833 738-D5
WALRUS LN
16200 HNTB 92649 826-J6
WALRUS WY
- PMDL 93551 4194-J1
WALSH AV
12400 LA 90066 672-D6
WALSH RD
1100 VeCo 93063 499-G4
WALT DISNEY DR
15700 Brwd 90049 561-F7
WALTER AV
23700 TOR 90501 793-G2
WALTER ST
2100 LACo 90255 704-H1
WALTER WY
- BPK 90621 737-F5
WALTHALL AV
9600 LACo 90605 707-B3
WALTHALL WY
6700 PRM 90723 735-E3
WALTHAM ST
12700 BALD 91706 597-H7
WALTHAM WY
1800 LHB 90631 708-G4
WALTHER WY
600 Brwd 90049 631-F2
WALTON AV
1700 LA 90006 634-A5
2800 LA 90007 634-A7
3400 LA 90007 674-A2
3800 LA 90037 674-A2
E WALTON ST
700 SIGH 90755 795-E3
5100 LBCH 90815 796-B3
N WALTON ST
5600 LBCH 90815 796-C3
WALTONIA DR
300 GLDL 91206 564-J4
1900 Mont 91020 534-H3
WALTON OAKS LN
4100 Mont 91020 534-H3
WALWORTH AV
1600 PAS 91104 536-A7
1600 PAS 91104 566-A1
WAMEDA AV
5400 Eagl 90041 565-C5
WAMPLER ST
8300 PRV 90660 676-E5
WANAMAKER DR
900 COV 91724 599-D5
WANDA DR
4100 LFlz 90027 594-B3
N WANDA DR
200 FUL 92833 738-D7
S WANDA DR
200 FUL 92833 738-D7
WANDA ST
3500 ELMN 91732 637-F1
WANDA PARK DR
9600 LA 90210 592-C2
WANDERER DR
2200 LA 90732 823-G6
WANDERING DR
900 MONP 91754 635-J4
WANDERING LN
2200 BREA 92821 709-E7
WANDERING RIDGE DR
2400 CHLS 91709 680-J1
WANDERMERE RD
6500 MAL 90265 667-E3
WANDOO RD
- PMDL 93551 4285-D3
WANETTE AV
14900 BLF 90706 736-A4
WANSTEAD DR
5200 Actn 93510 4374-G4
WAPELLO ST
- Alta 91001 535-J4
200 Alta 91001 536-A4
WARBLER CT
26600 SCTA 91351 4551-E4
WARBLER PL
9100 LA 90069 592-H5
WARBLER WY
9100 LA 90069 592-H4
WARBURTON WY
1700 FUL 92833 738-D5
WARD AL
- PAS 91107 566-F4

N WARD AV
2000 COMP 90221 735-B2
S WARD AV
100 COMP 90221 735-B4
WARD RD
5200 Actn 93510 4374-G5
WARD ST
- FUL 92833 738-D5
500 LHB 90631 708-F5
4900 Eagl 90041 565-B6
22300 TOR 90505 763-D7
22900 TOR 90505 793-D1
WARD WY
1000 INDS 91745 678-D2
6400 BPK 90620 767-F3
WARDELL AV
1800 DUAR 91010 567-J6
WARDHAM AV
20300 LKWD 90715 767-A4
22100 HGDN 90716 767-A6
E WARDLOW RD
100 Bxby 90807 795-E1
1300 SIGH 90755 795-G1
4600 LBCH 90808 796-A1
6000 LBCH 90808 766-D7
W WARDLOW RD
100 Bxby 90807 795-C1
200 LBCH 90806 795-C1
800 LBCH 90810 765-A7
900 LBCH 90806 765-A7
2300 LBCH 90810 764-J7
2300 CRSN 90810 764-J7
2300 CRSN 90810 765-A7
WARDMAN DR
900 BREA 92821 708-J4
WARDMAN ST
12300 WHIT 90602 677-C6
WAREHOUSE ST
700 LA 90021 634-G6
WARFIELD AV
1900 RBCH 90278 732-J6
1900 RBCH 90278 733-A6
WARFIELD CIR
1700 SIMI 93063 499-A3
WARING AV
5700 LA 90038 593-D6
7100 LA 90046 593-A6
8300 LA 90069 593-A6
8400 LA 90069 592-J6
WARING DR
2300 Ago 91301 587-H3
WARING PL
28400 AGRH 91301 558-C6
WARINGWOOD RD
400 LPUE 91744 678-E1
WARMAN LN
5400 TEML 91780 597-A4
WARMOUTH ST
2100 LA 90732 853-G1
2200 LA 90732 823-F7
WARMSIDE AV
22200 TOR 90505 763-A7
WARMSPRINGS AV
5000 LVRN 91750 570-G4
WARM SPRINGS DR
15000 SCTA 91387 4552-D6
WARM SPRINGS RD
- LACo 91390 4101-A6
WARMUTH RD
- LACo 91387 4552-C5
16200 SCTA 91387 4552-C5
WARN AV
9100 SunV 91352 503-C7
WARNALL AV
1300 Wwd 90024 632-D2
WARNE ST
500 LHB 90631 708-F5
WARNER AV
500 Wwd 90024 632-B1
WARNER BLVD
2900 BURB 91523 563-E4
3300 BURB 91522 563-E4
3300 BURB 91505 563-D5
WARNER DR
6100 LA 90048 633-A2
8400 CULC 90232 672-J1
WARNER LN
400 SGBL 91775 596-D2
WARNER ST
- CLAR 91711 571-E7
WARNER CENTER LN
20900 WdHl 91367 560-B2
WARNER RANCH RD
- WdHl 91367 560-B1
WARNICK RD
29000 RPV 90275 822-H1
WARNOCK WY
3000 LBCH 90810 765-A7
WARREN AV
800 Ven 90291 671-H4
11600 LYN 90262 735-C1
12900 LA 90066 672-A3
13100 LA 90066 671-H4
N WARREN AV
1300 LBCH 90813 795-F5
WARREN CIR
7400 LPMA 90623 767-D2
WARREN CT
44700 LAN 93535 4016-F5
E WARREN LN
300 ING 90302 703-C1
WARREN PL
- AZU 91702 569-B6

WARREN PL
400 POM 91768 600-H4
WARREN ST
1100 SFER 91340 482-B5
1300 Boyl 90033 634-J4
WARREN WY
- BPK 90621 737-F6
300 ARCD 91007 597-B2
WARRINGTON AV
1800 DUAR 91010 567-J6
4000 PRV 90660 676-H2
WARRINGTON DR
17200 GmH 91344 481-B6
WARRIOR DR
27300 RPV 90275 793-B7
WARVALE ST
8400 PRV 90660 676-D7
WARWICK AV
100 SPAS 91030 595-E3
1800 SMCA 90404 631-J7
2300 LA 90032 635-F1
2800 LA 90032 595-F6
WARWICK CIR
5700 LPMA 90623 767-D3
WARWICK PL
- SPAS 91030 595-E3
WARWICK RD
1700 SMRO 91108 596-C1
2200 ALH 91803 635-G1
WARWICK ST
1700 POM 91766 640-J4
WARWOOD RD
2600 LKWD 90712 765-H5
6000 LKWD 90713 766-D5
E WARWOOD RD
4500 LBCH 90808 766-A5
WASATCH AV
3500 LA 90066 672-B3
4000 CULC 90066 672-C4
W WASATCH CT
2700 THO 91362 557-C3
WASATCH DR
4400 LCF 91011 534-J3
WASECA ST
15500 HacH 91745 678-A5
WASHBURN RD
1400 PAS 91105 565-E7
8300 DWNY 90242 706-C7
9200 DWNY 90242 706-C7
9400 DWNY 90241 706-C7
WASHINGTON AV
- CRTS 90703 766-H4
100 SMCA 90403 671-D1
800 POM 91767 601-B7
900 POM 91767 641-B1
900 SMCA 90403 631-F6
1100 SMCA 90403 631-E7
1200 GLDR 91740 599-D1
2100 TOR 90501 763-G7
2600 ELMN 91733 637-C2
3000 ELMN 91731 637-C2
3400 ELMN 91731 597-C7
5000 CHNO 91710 641-G6
5800 WHIT 90601 677-D6
7000 WHIT 90602 677-D7
7700 WHIT 90602 707-D2
9900 SGAT 90280 705-D5
10600 LYN 90262 705-D5
12800 HAW 90250 733-D3
14200 LNDL 90250 733-D3
N WASHINGTON AV
200 GLDR 91741 569-D5
S WASHINGTON AV
100 GLDR 91741 569-D5
600 GLDR 91740 569-D7
900 COMP 90221 735-D6
15100 RDom 90221 735-D5
WASHINGTON BLVD
- MTBL 90640 676-G6
- Ven 90291 671-J7
- LA 90292 671-J7
400 MdlR 90292 671-J7
600 LA 90292 672-A5
600 Ven 90291 672-A5
2400 CMRC 90040 675-E3
5700 CULC 90232 633-A7
5900 CULC 90232 632-J7
8000 PRV 90660 676-G6
8800 CULC 90232 672-E4
9700 LACo 90606 676-G6
11100 SFSP 90606 676-G6
11200 CULC 90230 672-E4
11600 CULC 90066 672-E4
11600 SFSP 90606 706-J1
11600 LACo 90606 706-J1
11600 SFSP 90606 707-A1
11600 LACo 90606 707-A1
11900 WHIT 90606 707-A1
12600 WHIT 90602 707-A1
13300 Ven 90291 672-A5
13300 CULC 90292 672-A5
E WASHINGTON BLVD
- PAS 91104 565-H1
100 LA 90011 634-E7
100 MTBL 90640 676-B4
100 LA 90015 634-E7
200 PAS 91104 566-B1
400 PAS 91104 565-H1
700 LA 90021 634-E7
700 LA 90011 674-G1
1300 LA 90011 674-G1
1600 LA 90058 674-G1
1800 LACo 91104 566-B1
2500 LACo 91107 566-F2
2500 PAS 91107 566-F2

E WASHINGTON BLVD
2600 LA 90023 674-G1
2800 LA 90023 675-A1
2800 VER 90023 675-A1
3700 CMRC 90023 675-A1
4400 CMRC 90040 675-A1
6300 CMRC 90040 676-B4
W WASHINGTON BLVD
- PAS 91103 565-E1
100 LA 90007 634-A5
100 LA 90015 634-A5
1200 LA 90006 634-A5
1700 LA 90006 633-F5
1700 LA 90007 633-F5
1900 LA 90018 633-F5
2200 LA 90019 633-F5
4200 LA 90016 633-B6
9900 CULC 90232 672-F2
9900 LA 90232 672-F2
11300 CULC 90066 672-F2
13300 CULC 90292 672-F2
WASHINGTON CIR
2300 BURB 91504 533-E5
WASHINGTON PL
700 LBCH 90813 795-E7
3200 GLDL 91214 504-E7
11000 CULC 90232 672-D4
11200 CULC 90230 672-D4
11300 CULC 90066 672-D4
11300 LA 90066 672-D4
W WASHINGTON PL
200 PAS 91103 565-G1
WASHINGTON PL S
2700 SMCA 90403 631-G6
WASHINGTON SQ
- PMDL 93550 4286-C4
WASHINGTON ST
300 ELSG 90245 732-G1
600 ALH 91801 596-A5
600 ELSG 90245 702-G7
1200 NLB 90805 765-F3
8300 BPK 90621 767-J1
10000 BLF 90706 736-C4
21000 DBAR 91789 679-G2
21200 INDS 91789 679-G2
E WASHINGTON ST
2500 CRSN 90810 764-J6
2500 CRSN 90810 765-A6
WASHINGTON WY
1700 Ven 90291 671-J6
WASOLA ST
7700 RSMD 91770 636-E2
WASSON CT
12500 CHNO 91710 641-G6
WATCHER ST
5500 BGDN 90201 675-G7
6700 CMRC 90040 676-A7
WATCHORN WK
200 SPed 90731 824-C7
WATER AV
2000 COMP 90222 734-F2
WATER ST
- SBdC 91784 571-H3
- UPL 91784 571-H3
21000 CRSN 90745 764-H5
E WATER ST
100 Wilm 90744 824-E1
W WATER ST
- LHB 90631 738-D2
100 Wilm 90744 824-E1
WATER & POWER POLE RD
3400 Brwd 90049 591-C2
WATERBURY AV
100 COV 91722 598-H5
N WATERBURY AV
600 COV 91722 598-H4
WATERBURY CT
22500 WdHl 91364 559-H5
WATERBURY WY
1500 LHB 90631 708-C7
WATERBY ST
2100 THO 91361 557-A5
WATER COURSE DR
- DBAR 91765 679-J7
WATERCRESS LN
700 WAL 91789 639-H5
WATERFALL LN
- Pcma 91331 502-D6
100 BREA 92821 709-D6
WATERFALL WY
- DUAR 91010 568-D5
- RowH 91748 679-C4
WATERFORD CT
3600 PMDL 93550 4286-H4
WATERFORD DR
27100 SCTA 91354 4550-G1
27100 SCTA 91354 4460-G7
WATERFORD ST
11300 LACo 90073 631-J3
11300 LA 90073 631-J3
WATERFORD WY
3800 CALB 91302 559-J6
42400 LACo 93536 4104-H5
WATERFRONT DR
- LA 90094 672-F7
WATERFRONT PL
- LBCH 90803 826-C1
WATERGATE CT
31900 WLKV 91361 557-C6
WATERGATE RD
2700 THO 91361 557-B5
32000 WLKV 91361 557-C6

WATER LILY CT
14600 SCTA 91387 4462-G5
WATERLOO DR
- PMDL 93552 4287-C4
WATERLOO ST
600 Echo 90026 634-D1
700 Echo 90026 594-D7
1900 LA 90039 594-E5
WATERMAN AV
36900 PMDL 93550 4286-G3
WATERMAN DR
16300 VanN 91406 531-E3
WATERMAN MTWY
30400 Cstc 91384 4459-A6
WATERMAN RD
30100 Cstc 91384 4459-C6
WATERMAN FIRE RD
- LACo - (506-B3
See Page 505)
WATEROAK LN
500 VeCo 91377 557-J1
WATERS AV
1500 POM 91766 640-H4
S WATERS AV
900 POM 91766 640-H3
WATERSIDE CT
- SCTA 91355 4550-F2
WATERSIDE CV
- BPK 90621 738-A6
WATERSIDE LN
32000 WLKV 91361 557-C7
WATERTREE CT
6200 AGRH 91301 558-A3
WATERVIEW ST
100 PdlR 90293 702-B4
WATERVILLE CT
- PMDL 93551 4195-A2
WATERWAY LN
- SCTA 91355 4550-H3
WATERWHEEL LN
200 BREA 92821 709-D7
WATFORD AV
44100 LAN 93535 4016-A5
WATFORD WY
3300 PMDL 93551 4195-B3
WATKINS DR
14400 LMRD 90638 737-J3
WATLAND AV
1300 City 90063 635-F3
WATLING DR
1600 PMDL 93551 4195-E4
WATSEKA AV
3600 LA 90034 632-G7
3700 LA 90034 672-G1
3700 LA 90232 672-G1
3800 CULC 90232 672-G1
WATSON AV
700 Wilm 90744 794-G4
1700 TOR 90501 763-G6
8800 WHIT 90605 707-E2
18800 CRTS 90703 767-C2
WATSON CIR
30300 CynC 91351 4462-A4
WATSON DR
500 CLAR 91711 601-C4
1600 ARCD 91006 597-D1
WATSON ST
- LHB 90631 738-D2
2000 GLDL 91201 534-A6
8500 CYP 90630 767-D5
WATSONCENTER RD
700 CRSN 90745 794-E1
WATSONIA CT
6700 LA 90068 593-E3
WATSONIA TER
2000 LA 90068 593-E3
WATSONIA TR
23800 CALB 91302 559-F7
WATSON PLAZA DR
4000 LKWD 90712 765-H6
WATT AV
2800 PMDL 93550 4196-F6
WATT WY
- LA 90089 674-B1
WATTLES DR
2000 LA 90046 593-B3
WATTS AV
10800 Wbrk 90059 704-J6
WAUCONDA DR
42600 LACo 93532 4102-G5
WAUKESHA PL
5900 RPV 90275 792-J6
WAUPACA RD
5300 RPV 90275 793-A7
WAVE CREST AV
- Ven 90291 671-G6
WAVERLY CIR
8300 BPK 90621 737-J4
8300 BPK 90621 738-A4
W WAVERLY CT
1300 UPL 91786 601-J2
WAVERLY DR
- ALH 91801 595-G5
- PAS 91105 565-G5
2600 LA 90039 594-D3
3000 LFlz 90027 594-C3
5000 PRV 90660 676-G4
8300 BPK 90621 738-A4
WAVERLY PL
8500 BPK 90621 738-A4
WAVERLY RD
1300 SMRO 91108 566-C7
1300 SMRO 91108 596-C1

WAVERLY TER
2200 LHB 90631 708-B7
WAVERLY GLEN WY
1600 HacH 91745 678-F4
WAVEVIEW DR
20800 Top 90290 590-B6
WAWONA PL
2700 Eagl 90041 564-J6
2700 LA 90065 564-J6
WAWONA ST
2700 LA 90065 564-H6
4600 Eagl 90041 564-H6
WAY CT
500 SDMS 91773 600-A1
WAYCOTT WY
- StvR 91381 4550-A6
WAYCROSS DR
- LACo 91302 588-F5
WAYLADN CT
- LACo 93536 4104-F6
WAYLAND CT
500 CLAR 91711 601-E4
500 MTCL 91763 601-E4
WAYLAND ST
200 HiPk 90042 595-D2
WAYMAN ST
24400 SCTA 91321 4640-H1
WAYNE AV
300 FUL 92833 738-E7
1400 SPAS 91030 595-J3
2200 LFlz 90027 594-B2
20000 TOR 90503 763-A4
WAYNE CIR
12500 CRTS 90703 767-A2
WAYNE ST
800 CLAR 91711 601-C6
1700 POM 91767 601-C6
WAYNECREST DR
1600 LA 90210 592-F4
WAYNE MILLS PL
- SCTA 91355 4550-C2
WAYNESBOROUGH LN
27400 SCTA 91354 4460-F7
WAYS ST
600 SPed 90731 824-E5
WAYSIDE DR
9300 Sunl 91040 503-D3
WAYSIDE PL
400 DBAR 91765 640-E6
E WAYSIDE ST
2000 COMP 90222 734-H2
2000 Wbrk 90222 734-H2
WAYSIDE CANYON RD
- Cstc 91384 4459-J3
- Cstc 91384 4460-A3
WAYSIDE LATERAL
- Cstc 91384 4460-B3
WAYWARD CT
2600 BREA 92821 709-F7
WEALTHA AV
9800 SunV 91352 502-J4
9800 SunV 91352 503-A5
WEATHER RD
18600 LACo 91722 599-B2
WEATHERBY RD
11200 OrCo 90720 796-J3
WEATHERFIELD DR
- SCTA 91354 4460-G6
WEATHERFORD CT
2300 CLAR 91711 571-E6
WEATHERFORD DR
5200 LA 90008 673-B2
WEATHERLY CIR
3800 WLKV 91361 557-B7
WEATHERLY PL
2100 FUL 92833 738-B3
WEATHER VANE CT
13800 CHLS 91709 680-G3
WEAVER AV
10600 SELM 91733 637-C3
WEAVER LN
- LACo 91770 636-G4
- RSMD 91770 636-G4
5800 HiPk 90042 595-D1
WEAVER ST
5800 HiPk 90042 595-C1
10300 SELM 91733 637-B3
12100 ELMN 91733 637-D3
WEBB AV
8000 NHol 91605 532-G1
8300 SunV 91352 532-G1
WEBB RD
23700 Chat 91311 499-E6
WEBB TR
19500 Top 90290 590-A7
19600 Top 90290 630-A1
WEBB WY
4100 MAL 90265 628-J7
WEBB CANYON RD
4400 CLAR 91711 571-A6
4400 LACo 91750 571-A6
4700 LACo 91711 571-A6
WEBBER WY
- BPK 90621 737-F5
WEBBER RANCH RD
7700 Litl 93543 4377-G4
8600 Litl 93543 4378-A5
WEBER AV
300 COMP 90222 734-J1
300 COMP 90222 735-A1
WEBER LN
- FUL 92833 738-D5

WEBER ST
3100 LYN 90262 735-A1
N WEBER ST
500 POM 91768 640-G1
900 POM 91768 600-F7
WEBER WY
1300 LAN 93535 4016-C7
1700 LVRN 91750 570-F7
12800 HAW 90250 733-F2
WEBSTER AL
100 PAS 91105 565-H6
WEBSTER AV
1400 CLAR 91711 601-E1
1700 Echo 90026 594-C5
2200 LBCH 90810 795-A4
3600 LBCH 90810 765-A7
N WEBSTER AV
2600 LBCH 90810 795-A2
WEBSTER CIR
1800 WCOV 91792 638-J5
WEBSTER CT
12600 CHNO 91710 641-G6
WEBSTER PL
25800 StvR 91381 4550-C7
WEBSTER WY
100 SMAD 91024 567-A2
WEDDINGTON ST
5300 VanN 91411 561-H2
10300 NHol 91601 563-A2
13000 VanN 91401 562-D2
16800 Enc 91436 561-D2
17100 Enc 91316 561-B2
18100 Tarz 91356 561-A2
18200 Tarz 91356 560-J2
WEDGE WY
- PMDL 93550 4106-A6
WEDGEPORT AV
10500 LACo 90604 707-D5
WEDGEWOOD AV
800 SGBL 91776 596-F4
1800 UPL 91784 571-J5
N WEDGEWOOD AV
600 UPL 91786 601-J1
1400 UPL 91786 571-J7
W WEDGEWOOD AV
200 SGBL 91776 596-E4
WEDGEWOOD CT
- Cstc 91384 4459-H3
400 DUAR 91010 568-D4
WEDGEWOOD LN
- BURB 91504 533-E2
200 LHB 90631 738-D1
N WEDGEWOOD LN
1100 UPL 91786 601-J1
WEDGEWOOD PL
6700 LA 90068 593-E3
WEDGEWOOD ST
1700 LVRN 91750 570-F6
8700 LACo 91775 596-G4
9200 TEML 91780 596-J4
9600 TEML 91780 597-A3
N WEDGEWOOD WY
1500 UPL 91786 571-J7
WEDGEWORTH DR
14400 HacH 91745 677-H1
15000 HacH 91745 678-A2
WEDNESDAY DR
1800 WCOV 91792 678-J1
1900 WCOV 91792 679-A1
WEEBURN CT
19500 Tarz 91356 560-F6
WEEBURN LN
19600 Tarz 91356 560-F5
WEE BURN RD
1200 SLB 90740 826-G1
WEEKS DR
14700 LMRD 90638 707-F7
15400 LACo 90604 707-H6
WEEPAH WY
1800 LA 90046 593-A3
1900 LA 90046 592-J3
WEEPING BANYAN LN
6000 WdHl 91367 559-H7
WEEPING BRANCH ST
- PMDL 93550 4286-C3
WEEPING WILLOW DR
- SCTA 91354 4460-F7
29400 AGRH 91301 557-J4
WEEPING WILLOW LN
2100 HacH 91745 678-A3
WEEPING WILLOW RD
- BREA 92823 709-H6
WEGMAN DR
16600 LPUE 91744 678-F1
WEHNER LN
1100 SDMS 91740 570-B7
WEHRLE CT
4200 LBCH 90804 796-A5
WEHRLE ST
3800 LBCH 90804 795-J5
3900 LBCH 90804 796-A5
WEID PL
2400 LA 90068 593-F2
WEIDLAKE DR
6300 LA 90068 593-F2
WEIDNER ST
12700 Pcma 91331 482-E7
12700 Pcma 91331 502-D1
WEIGAND AV
10300 Wats 90002 704-H5
10700 LA 90059 704-H5
WEIGHT AL
300 PAS 91101 565-J5

STREET Block City ZIP Pg-Grid

WEIK AV
3600 BELL 90201 675-C7
3600 BELL 90201 705-C1
N WEIMAR AV
900 Alta 91001 535-F6
WEINBERG ST
22400 Chat 91311 499-H4
WEIR AL
2500 PAS 91107 566-E4
WEIR ST
11800 LA 90230 672-F6
WEISER AV
19200 CRSN 90746 764-F3
21300 CRSN 90745 764-F6
WEISKOFF CT
- LHB 90631 738-C1
WELBY WY
2400 CanP 91307 529-D6
11100 NHol 91606 532-J5
17200 VanN 91406 531-B6
17700 Res 91335 531-A6
18100 Res 91335 530-F6
19700 Win 91306 530-E6
22100 CanP 91303 529-H6
24500 LACo 91307 529-C6
WELCH PL
4600 LFlz 90027 594-A3
WELCOME CT
2300 SIMI 93063 499-B1
WELCOME LN
- SLB 90740 826-E3
WELCOME ST
200 Echo 90026 634-D2
WELDON AV
3000 LA 90065 594-G1
WELDON CANYON MTWY
- StvR 91381 480-G1
- StvR 91381 4640-J7
- StvR 91381 4641-A7
WELDON CANYON RD
- Nwhl 91321 4641-A6
WELFLEET LN
28300 SCTA 91350 4461-B4
WELK AV
11000 Pcma 91331 502-D1
11500 Pcma 91331 482-D7
WELL ST
18600 RowH 91748 679-A4
WELLAND AV
3700 LA 90008 673-F2
3700 LA 90018 673-F2
5300 TEML 91780 597-D3
5500 ARCD 91007 597-D3
WELLBROOK DR
32700 WLKV 91361 557-A7
WELLER DR
5200 WdHl 91367 559-F3
WELLER PL
23200 WdHl 91367 559-F3
WELLER RD
- Eagl 90041 565-A7
WELLESLEY AV
800 Brwd 90049 631-G5
1200 WLA 90025 631-J6
2200 LA 90064 631-J7
2200 LA 90064 632-A7
2400 LA 90064 672-A1
WELLESLEY CT
44100 LAN 93536 4015-B7
WELLESLEY DR
600 CLAR 91711 601-C2
1400 GLDL 91205 564-G7
1600 SMCA 90405 671-H3
2500 RowH 91748 679-B7
5300 LACo 91302 559-A3
WELLESLEY RD
1900 SMRO 91108 596-F2
WELLFLEET AV
17400 CRSN 90746 734-F7
WELLFORD DR
17900 LACo 91744 678-J1
WELLHAVEN ST
17900 SCTA 91387 4551-G3
17900 SCTA 91387 4552-A3
18700 SCTA 91351 4551-G3
WELLINGTON AV
1100 PAS 91103 565-E1
WELLINGTON CT
4500 CYP 90630 767-B7
25900 LACo 91302 558-J3
27500 SCTA 91354 4460-F7
WELLINGTON DR
3000 PMDL 93551 4195-C5
WELLINGTON LN
2100 RowH 91748 708-H2
19600 Tarz 91356 560-F2
WELLINGTON RD
900 SDMS 91773 599-H4
1600 LA 90019 633-E6
1900 LA 90016 633-E6
3400 LA 90016 673-E1
3700 LA 90008 673-E1
WELLINGTON WY
19800 WdHl 91367 530-E7
WELLMAN ST
7500 CMRC 90040 676-B7
WELLS AL
1400 PAS 91104 566-B1
1500 LACo 91104 566-B1
WELLS AV
1400 CLAR 91711 601-B1
WELLS CT
25300 StvR 91381 4640-B1
WELLS DR
18400 Tarz 91356 560-F3
19600 WdHl 91364 560-D3
WELLS LN
200 WHil 91304 499-D6
WELLS PL
12500 CHNO 91710 641-D6
WELLS RD
- VeCo 90265 625-G1
WELLS ST
600 SGBL 91776 596-G6
8300 RSMD 91770 596-G6
E WELLS ST
100 SGBL 91776 596-F6
W WELLS ST
100 SGBL 91776 596-D6
WELLS FARGO AV
16000 LACo 93591 4199-F5
WELLS FARGO LN
- CRSN 90745 794-G1
WELLSFORD AV
7300 LACo 90606 677-A7
7700 LACo 90606 707-A1
WELLSFORD PL
8300 SFSP 90670 707-A1
WELLSLEY WY
- SCTA 91354 4460-G6
WELLSON DR
5700 CYP 90630 767-E7
WELLSPRING DR
1800 DBAR 91765 679-J4
WELLSTON DR
27800 SCTA 91350 4461-C5
WELLWORTH AV
10400 Wwd 90024 632-B3
WELSH WY
2800 GLDL 91206 535-A7
WELSHFIELD WY
- SCTA 91354 4460-G6
WELTON AL
2800 GAR 90249 733-F4
N WELTON WY
900 ING 90302 673-D7
900 ING 90302 703-D1
WEMAR WY
900 MTBL 90640 636-E7
WEMBLEY CT
24200 SCTA 91355 4550-F4
WEMBLEY RD
1300 SMRO 91108 596-C1
11100 OrCo 90720 796-G4
W WEMBLY ST
1300 WCOV 91790 638-C3
WENDON AV
9800 TEML 91780 597-A2
WENDON ST
8300 LACo 91775 596-F2
8700 TEML 91775 596-G2
E WENDON ST
9500 TEML 91780 596-J2
WENDOVER DR
9600 LA 90210 592-C1
WENDOVER RD
600 LCF 91011 535-C7
600 PAS 91103 535-C7
700 GLDL 91206 535-C7
WENDY DR
12200 CRTS 90703 766-J3
20700 TOR 90503 763-A5
WENDY LN
- PRV 90660 676-G1
400 LBCH 90803 826-B1
WENDY ST
12000 CRTS 90703 766-H3
WENDY WY
1200 MANB 90266 732-J5
2200 UPL 91784 571-J3
3200 OrCo 90720 796-J5
43400 LAN 93536 4105-D2
WENGER AL
2700 PAS 91107 566-F4
WENHAM RD
100 LACo 91107 566-E5
WENLOCK ST
5600 LA 90016 673-A1
WENTIFF CT
2800 LACo 91789 679-F7
WENTWORTH AV
1100 PAS 91106 566-A7
1200 PAS 91106 596-A1
WENTWORTH LN
13500 SLB 90740 796-G7
13500 SLB 90740 826-G1
WENTWORTH ST
7500 Tuj 91042 503-G2
7800 Sunl 91040 503-C2
10800 Sunl 91040 502-J4
11200 SunV 91352 502-J4
12300 Pcma 91331 502-D7
13200 Pcma 91331 532-C1
13300 PanC 91402 532-C1
E WENTWORTH ST
5900 LBCH 90815 796-D2
WENTWORTH WY
1200 UPL 91784 571-J4
WENTZEL WY
17200 GmH 91344 481-B4
WENWOOD ST
2500 LVRN 91750 600-H2
W WERBEL PL
1000 SPed 90731 824-A2
WERDIN PL
200 LA 90012 634-F4
300 LA 90013 634-F5
800 LA 90014 634-E5
E WERNER ST
1200 LBCH 90813 795-F6
WERREN PL
20200 Saug 91350 4461-D5
WESCOTT AV
10200 Sunl 91040 503-G2
WESCOTT CIR
12800 BALD 91706 597-H7
S WESCOVE PL
1100 WCOV 91790 638-F3
WESENBERG CIR
5900 LPMA 90623 767-E4
WESHAM PL
1600 BREA 92821 708-H3
WESLEY AV
- SBdC 91710 641-D4
4400 LA 90037 674-B4
10900 MTCL 91763 641-D2
11200 SBdC 91766 641-D3
N WESLEY AV
1000 PAS 91104 566-B2
WESLEY CT
37400 PMDL 93552 4287-B1
WESLEY DR
600 FUL 92833 738-E6
E WESLEY DR
1200 LBCH 90806 795-F4
WESLEY LN
1600 ARCD 91006 597-D1
WESLEY RD
- LACo 91390 4462-D3
WESLEY ST
3400 CULC 90232 632-H7
3500 CULC 90232 672-H1
WESLEY WY
500 CLAR 91711 601-E1
30700 LACo 91390 4462-D3
WESLEYAN AV
1300 WAL 91789 639-F4
WESLEYGROVE AV
2000 LACo 91010 567-H7
WESLIN AV
3500 Shrm 91423 562-C6
WEST AV
- Hrbr 90710 794-A4
15900 LA 91342 481-F3
WEST BLVD
1000 LA 90019 633-E4
1900 LA 90016 633-D7
3400 LA 90016 673-D1
3700 LA 90008 673-D3
4900 LACo 90043 673-D3
5100 LA 90043 673-E6
6400 ING 90302 673-E6
7100 LA 90043 703-E2
7100 ING 90302 703-E2
7400 ING 90305 703-E2
8500 ING 90301 703-E2
8600 PRV 90660 676-G3
WEST DR
- Hrbr 90710 794-A4
700 PAS 91103 565-E1
1600 SMRO 91108 596-D2
1900 SGBL 91775 596-D2
8300 LA 90069 593-A4
WEST PL
18700 ART 90701 766-G2
WEST RD
100 LHH 90631 708-B2
1300 LA 90810 794-J4
1700 LHH 90631 707-J3
2000 WHIT 90603 707-J3
26500 SCTA 91355 4550-D4
WEST TR
11800 LACo 91342 482-J7
21000 Top 90290 590-B2
WEST WY
- LA 91342 481-J2
- Wch 90045 702-F5
WESTAR CT
34400 Actn 93510 4375-B4
WEST BEACH LN
- MAL 90265 667-E1
WESTBEND RD
600 THO 91362 557-D1
WESTBORO AV
300 ALH 91803 595-G6
2100 ALH 91803 635-G1
WESTBORO ST
12700 Brwd 90049 631-E2
WEST BOUND DR
- SMRO 91108 566-C6
WESTBOURNE CT
9500 CYP 90630 767-B7
WESTBOURNE DR
300 WHWD 90048 592-J7
600 WHWD 90069 592-J7
WESTBOURNE PL
2700 RowH 91748 679-B7
WESTBRIDGE PL
600 PAS 91105 565-F5
WESTBROOK AV
2800 LA 90046 593-B1
WESTBROOK CT
2300 CLAR 91711 571-E6
WESTBROOK LN
- POM 91766 640-E5
16400 CRTS 90703 737-A6
WESTBURY DR
17000 GmH 91344 481-B5
WESTBURY LN
- ING 90305 703-E3
WESTCASTLE
1400 WCOV 91791 638-J3
WESTCHESTER DR
4300 WdHl 91364 560-C5
S WESTCHESTER DR
100 ANA 92804 767-H6
WESTCHESTER PKWY
5900 Wch 90045 702-G3
9700 PdlR 90293 702-C4
WESTCHESTER PL
400 FUL 92835 738-G3
800 LA 90005 633-G4
900 LA 90019 633-G4
WESTCLIFF DR
7300 LA 91304 529-D4
14900 LA 91342 481-H7
WESTCLIFF ST
- PMDL 93551 4195-A4
WESTCOATT ST
2600 Actn 93510 4375-B3
WESTCOTT AV
600 BALD 91706 637-H1
3100 BALD 91706 597-H7
S WESTCOTT AV
100 ELA 90022 635-H5
2300 MONP 91754 635-H5
WESTCOVE DR
13300 Brwd 90049 631-E3
WESTCOVE PL
800 WCOV 91790 638-F2
WEST COVINA PKWY
700 WCOV 91790 638-E1
1400 WCOV 91790 598-E7
WEST CREEK DR
- BqtC 91354 4460-E4
WESTCREEK LN
900 THO 91362 557-G1
900 VeCo 91362 557-G1
WESTDALE AV
4400 Eagl 90041 564-J7
4500 Eagl 90041 565-A7
WESTERLY TER
1100 Echo 90026 594-C6
WESTERN AV
100 GLDL 91201 563-J3
700 GLDL 91201 564-A2
1300 GLDL 91201 534-B7
1800 GAR 90248 763-J2
1800 TOR 90504 763-J2
5500 BPK 90621 737-H7
5900 WHIT 90601 677-A5
6300 BPK 90621 767-H4
6400 LACo 90606 677-A6
7000 BPK 90620 767-H4
10200 DWNY 90241 706-B4
12800 GAR 90249 733-H3
14300 GAR 90247 733-H7
17400 GAR 90248 733-H7
17400 TOR 90504 733-H7
18200 LA 90248 763-J2
WESTERN AV Rt#-213
18800 LA 90248 763-J4
18800 TOR 90504 763-J4
19000 LA 90501 763-J4
19000 TOR 90501 763-J4
N WESTERN AV
100 ANA 92801 767-H5
100 LA 90004 633-H1
200 LA 90004 593-H7
300 BPK 90620 767-H5
700 LA 90029 593-H5
700 LA 90038 593-H5
1300 LFlz 90027 593-H5
1300 Hlwd 90028 593-H5
1900 LA 90068 593-H5
N WESTERN AV Rt#-213
100 LA 90732 823-J4
200 LA 90275 823-J4
200 RPV 90275 823-J4
200 RPV 90732 823-J4
S WESTERN AV
100 ANA 92804 767-H7
100 LA 90004 633-H3
300 LA 90020 633-H3
600 LA 90005 633-H3
600 LA 90010 633-H3
900 LA 90006 633-H3
900 LA 90019 633-H3
1900 LA 90018 633-H7
3400 LA 90018 673-H2
3700 LA 90062 673-H2
5800 LA 90047 673-H5
7200 LA 90047 703-H3
10400 LACo 90047 703-H6
12000 LACo 90047 733-H1
24200 LA 90717 793-J4
24700 Hrbr 90710 793-J4
27700 RPV 90275 823-J1
S WESTERN AV Rt#-213
100 LA 90732 823-J2
2500 SPed 90731 823-H6
2500 SPed 90731 853-H1
2500 LA 90732 853-H1
21300 LA 90501 763-J7
21300 TOR 90501 763-J7
22500 LA 90501 793-J3
22500 TOR 90501 793-J3
23000 Hrbr 90710 793-J3
23800 LA 90717 793-J3
26100 Hrbr 90710 793-J3
26100 LMTA 90717 793-J3
26700 LMTA 90732 793-J7
26900 RPV 90275 793-J7
26900 RPV 90732 793-J7
26900 LA 90275 793-J7
26900 LA 90732 793-J7
26900 RPV 90275 823-J2
26900 RPV 90732 823-J2
28000 LA 90275 823-J2
WESTERN WY
- TOR 90501 763-H4
WESTERN AVENUE TR
- LFlz 90027 563-J4
WESTERN BAY DR
7400 BPK 90621 767-H1
WESTERN CANYON RD
2200 LA 90068 593-H2
2200 LFlz 90027 593-H2
WESTERN CEDAR CT
- SCTA 91354 4460-F4
WESTERN HEIGHTS WALKWAY
1900 LA 90018 633-H6
WESTERN HERITAGE WY
- LFlz 90027 564-A4
WESTFALL DR
3500 Enc 91436 561-E6
WESTFALL PL
16400 Enc 91436 561-E6
WESTFIELD CT
2200 LAN 93536 4105-D2
WESTFIELD DR
2300 LAN 93536 4105-B2
WESTFIELD PL
2700 CLAR 91711 571-D5
WESTFIELD WY
1800 LHB 90631 708-G4
WESTFORD PL
23400 SCTA 91354 4460-G7
WEST FORK
- SCTA 91350 4551-B5
WEST FORK SAN DIMAS CANYON RD
- LACo (540-G3 See Page 509)
WESTGATE AV
16600 CRTS 90703 737-A6
N WESTGATE AV
100 Brwd 90049 631-G2
S WESTGATE AV
100 Brwd 90049 631-G3
1200 WLA 90025 631-H5
1900 WLA 90025 632-A6
2200 LA 90064 632-A7
2500 LA 90064 672-B1
WESTGATE DR
36700 PMDL 93552 4287-B5
WESTGATE ST
400 PAS 91103 565-F2
S WESTHAVEN CIR
600 ANA 92804 767-H7
W WESTHAVEN CT
2900 ANA 92804 767-J7
WESTHAVEN DR
29800 Ago 91301 587-H3
W WESTHAVEN DR
3100 ANA 92804 767-H7
WESTHAVEN RD
1300 SMRO 91108 566-D7
1300 SMRO 91108 596-D1
WESTHAVEN ST
4800 LA 90016 633-C7
WEST HILL DR
8800 SBdC 92372 (4562-B2 See Page 4471)
WEST HILLS DR
- BqtC 91354 4460-E3
WESTHOFF WY
20500 WAL 91789 639-F7
WESTHOLME AV
500 LA 90095 632-B2
600 Wwd 90024 632-B2
1800 WLA 90025 632-C4
WEST HONDO PKWY
11000 ELMN 91780 597-D4
WESTIN WY
- PMDL 93551 4195-A4
WESTINGHOUSE PL
- SCTA 91355 4460-A7
WEST KNOLL DR
500 WHWD 90048 592-J6
600 WHWD 90069 592-J6
N WESTLAKE AV
100 Echo 90026 634-D2
S WESTLAKE AV
100 LA 90057 634-C3
900 LA 90006 634-B4
WESTLAKE BLVD Rt#-23
100 LACo 90265 586-H4
400 WLKV 90265 586-H4
400 WLKV 91361 586-H4
800 LACo 91361 586-H4
800 THO 91361 586-H4
N WESTLAKE BLVD
- THO 91362 557-C3
S WESTLAKE BLVD
- THO 91362 557-B5
S WESTLAKE BLVD Rt#-23
100 THO 91362 557-C4
100 THO 91361 557-C4
800 THO 91361 586-H1
WESTLAKE DR
100 LACo 91351 4285-H5
WESTLAKE VISTA LN
- THO 91362 557-A2
WESTLAND AV
7600 NHol 91605 532-F3
WESTLAND DR
3800 PMDL 93551 4285-A1
WESTLAWN AV
- LA 90094 672-E7
- LA 90094 702-F1
4300 LA 90066 672-D5
7300 Wch 90045 702-F1
WESTLEIGH PL
- RowH 91748 679-C7
WESTLYN PL
1200 LACo 91104 566-D1
WESTMAN AV
7600 LACo 90606 676-J7
8000 LACo 90606 706-J1
8000 SFSP 90606 676-J7
8000 SFSP 90606 706-J1
WESTMAN ST
8600 SFSP 90606 706-J2
WESTMINISTER AV
900 ALH 91803 595-G7
WESTMINSTER AV
- Ven 90291 671-H5
300 ALH 91803 595-H7
300 LA 90020 633-G2
2100 ALH 91803 635-H1
2100 SLB 90740 826-H2
10700 LA 90034 672-E1
11200 LA 90066 672-C2
WESTMINSTER CT
- Ven 90291 671-H5
500 SDMS 91773 599-J3
WESTMINSTER DR
600 PAS 91105 565-F5
2000 PMDL 93550 4286-E3
WESTMINSTER PL
- CLAR 91711 571-F4
11900 LA 90066 672-C2
WESTMINSTER RD
- GLDL 91205 564-F7
- GLDL 91205 594-F1
- LA 90065 594-F1
- LA 91205 594-F1
WESTMINSTER WY
42200 LAN 93536 4104-C5
WESTMONT AV
500 POM 91766 640-E3
WESTMONT CT
- PMDL 93552 4287-E2
WESTMONT DR
- LAN 93536 4013-J5
- ALH 91801 595-G6
300 ALH 91803 595-G6
700 SPed 90731 824-B1
1100 LA 90732 823-J2
1100 LA 90732 824-A2
1700 ALH 91803 635-G1
1700 LA 90275 823-J2
1700 RPV 90275 823-J2
1700 RPV 90732 823-J2
WESTMONT RD
5500 WHIT 90601 677-B4
N WESTMORELAND AV
100 LA 90004 634-A1
200 LA 90004 594-A7
1100 LA 90029 594-A5
S WESTMORELAND AV
100 LA 90004 634-A2
300 LA 90020 634-A2
600 LA 90005 634-A2
600 LA 90010 634-A2
900 LA 90006 634-A4
WESTMORELAND BLVD
1600 LA 90006 633-H5
WESTMORELAND DR
800 MTBL 90640 636-C7
WESTMORELAND PL
200 PAS 91103 565-G4
WESTMORELAND ST
1300 POM 91766 640-G3
WESTMOUNT AV
3400 LA 90043 673-E4
3400 LACo 90043 673-E4
WESTMOUNT CIR
8500 WHWD 90048 592-J7
WESTMOUNT DR
400 WHWD 90048 592-J6
600 WHWD 90069 592-J6
WESTON DR
- SCTA 91354 4460-G6
WESTON PL
2500 GLDL 91208 534-H7
3500 Bxby 90807 765-D6
19100 Tarz 91356 560-G5
WESTON RD
25200 TOR 90505 793-E4
WESTOVER PL
500 PAS 91105 565-G7
19800 WdHl 91367 530-E7
WESTOVER WY
- SCTA 91354 4460-F7
WESTPARK DR
4800 NHol 91601 562-H3
6100 NHol 91606 532-F7
WESTPARK RD
3300 LA 90210 562-B7
WEST POINT DR
300 CLAR 91711 601-E4
3800 LA 90065 595-A5
WEST POINT PL
3900 LA 90065 595-A5
WESTPORT
- MANB 90266 732-H4
WESTPORT ST
2600 WCOV 91792 638-J6
WESTRA LN
7700 LPMA 90623 767-D3
WESTRIDGE AV
1100 GLDR 91740 599-D1
3600 LACo 91724 599-D6
N WESTRIDGE AV
200 COV 91724 599-D5
300 GLDR 91741 569-D4
4700 LACo 91724 599-D4
S WESTRIDGE AV
700 GLDR 91740 569-D7
WESTRIDGE DR
- LAN 93536 4105-A1
44100 LAN 93536 4015-A7
WESTRIDGE PKWY
- StvR 91381 4550-A4
WESTRIDGE RD
- WCOV 91791 639-A3
1700 Brwd 90049 631-C1
2400 Brwd 90049 591-C7
WESTRIDGE TER
1900 Brwd 90049 631-D2
WESTRIDGE WY
800 BREA 92821 709-C7
1400 CHLS 91709 710-G1
WESTRIDGE KNOLL
1000 FUL 92835 738-F5
16100 CHLS 91709 710-G1
WESTSHIRE DR
2700 LA 90068 593-G1
WEST SHORE LN
1300 THO 91361 557-A6
WESTSHORE WY
- BPK 90621 738-A6
WESTSIDE AV
3700 LA 90018 673-F2
3700 LA 90008 673-F2
WESTSIDE DR
4700 LVRN 91750 570-E6
S WESTSIDE DR
900 ELA 90022 676-A2
WESTSLOPE LN
5000 LCF 91011 535-D3
WEST VAIL DR
23100 CanP 91307 529-F5
WESTVALE CT
2500 DUAR 91010 568-D3
S WESTVALE DR
700 ANA 92804 767-G7
WESTVALE RD
- DUAR 91010 568-D4
26600 LACo 90274 793-D7
WESTVIEW CT
4800 THO 91362 557-F1
WESTVIEW DR
37700 PMDL 93551 4286-E2
WESTVIEW LN
- PacP 90272 630-F4
27100 SCTA 91354 4550-G1
WEST VIEW ST
1900 LA 90016 633-D6
3000 LA 90016 673-C1
WESTWANDA DR
9900 LA 90210 592-B3
WESTWARD AV
22000 CRSN 90810 764-H7
WESTWARD LN
- LA 90068 563-E5
WESTWARD BEACH RD
6500 MAL 90265 667-D3
WESTWIND CIR
1300 THO 91361 557-B6
WESTWIND CT
200 LA 90292 702-A4
WESTWIND MALL
200 LA 90292 701-J2
200 LA 90292 702-A4
WESTWIND ST
- LA 90292 701-J2
WEST WIND WY
- SIGH 90755 795-G3
WESTWINDS CIR
16800 CRTS 90703 736-F6
WESTWOOD BLVD
900 Wwd 90024 632-B4
1700 WLA 90025 632-B4
2200 LA 90064 632-B4
3000 LA 90034 632-B4
3600 LA 90034 672-E1
5000 CULC 90232 672-E1
5000 CULC 90230 672-G4
WESTWOOD CT
2000 LAN 93534 4015-E6
2000 LAN 93536 4015-E6
WESTWOOD PL
1700 POM 91768 600-H5
WESTWOOD PZ
300 LA 90095 632-A1
WETHERBY LN
11700 BelA 90077 591-G3
WETHERBY RD
2500 SMRO 91108 566-E6
WETHERHEAD DR
2400 ALH 91803 636-A2
WETHERLY AV
2700 LBCH 90810 795-A2
WETHERLY CT
2200 UPL 91784 571-H4
WETHERLY DR
900 WHWD 90069 592-H6
N WETHERLY DR
100 BHLS 90211 632-H2
100 LA 90048 632-H1
100 WHWD 90048 592-H5
100 WHWD 90048 632-H1
1100 LA 90069 592-H5
1100 WHWD 90069 592-H5
S WETHERLY DR
100 BHLS 90211 632-H2
100 LA 90048 632-H1
1100 LA 90035 632-H3
WEXFORD AV
7600 LACo 90606 677-A7
7700 LACo 90606 707-A1
WEXFORD DR
9300 Tuj 91042 504-B6
WEXFORD PL
6800 Tuj 91042 504-B6
N WEXHAM WY
1200 ING 90302 673-D7
WEYAND CT
42900 LAN 93534 4105-E3
WEYBRIDGE CT
9500 CYP 90630 767-B7
WEYBRIDGE LN
2200 BelA 90077 591-G3
WEYBRIDGE PL
8700 ING 90305 703-D3
WEYBURN AV
10700 Wwd 90024 632-A3
WEYBURN PL
700 Wwd 90024 632-A3
WEYERHAEUSER WY
- SCTA 91351 4551-G4
S WEYMOUTH AV
200 LA 90732 823-J5
3700 SPed 90731 853-J1
WEYMOUTH PL
23000 SCTA 91354 4460-H6
S WEYMOUTH PL
1500 LA 90732 823-H5
WEYSE ST
1400 LA 90012 634-H2
WHALEBOAT PL
30700 AGRH 91301 557-G5
WHALERS LN
11900 VeCo 90265 625-F5
WHALERS WK
200 SPed 90731 854-C1
WHALEY AV
4500 Bxby 90807 765-E5
WHARF DR
- SLB 90740 826-F5
WHARF ST
100 SPed 90731 824-D5
WHARFF LN
15600 LNDL 90260 733-C5
WHARTON DR
- StvR 91381 4640-D1
500 CLAR 91711 601-C4
WHEATLAND AV
7500 SunV 91352 533-B1
8600 WHIT 90605 707-D2
8800 SunV 91352 503-B7
9400 Sunl 91040 503-B3
11100 LA 91342 503-B2
WHEATLAND PL
8800 SunV 91352 503-B7
8800 SunV 91352 533-B1
WHEATLEY DR
17000 WHIT 90603 708-C3
WHEATON AV
1800 CLAR 91711 571-B7
WHEATON CT
23600 SCTA 91354 4460-G6
WHEATON PL
2600 FUL 92833 738-B5
WHEATSTONE AV
14400 NRWK 90650 736-J4
WHEELER AV
- ARCD 91006 567-D5
1900 LVRN 91750 600-F2
3600 LVRN 91750 570-F5
11400 LA 91342 502-G1
11500 LA 91342 482-A2
WHEELER DR
2000 MONP 91755 636-C5
WHEELER LN
800 PAS 91103 565-H2
N WHEELER LN
600 PAS 91103 565-H3
WHEELER PL
11400 LA 91342 502-G1
WHEELER RD
25000 SCTA 91321 4640-G1
WHEELHOUSE CT
- LBCH 90803 826-G2
WHEELHOUSE LN
5800 AGRH 91301 557-G4
WHEELING WY
400 HiPk 90042 595-D3
WHEELOCK CIR
10700 LACo 90606 706-G1
WHEELOCK ST
9500 PRV 90660 706-F1
11100 LACo 90606 706-H1
WHELAN PL
4500 LACo 90043 673-C5
WHETSTONE DR
42800 LACo 93532 4102-F4
WHEY DR
21700 SCTA 91350 4461-A5
WHIETT WK
- Cstc 91384 4459-D6
WHIFFLETREE LN
3100 TOR 90505 793-E4
WHIM DR
30800 WLKV 91362 557-F4
WHIPPLE ST
10300 LA 91602 563-A5
WHIPPOORWILL DR
2700 RowH 91748 678-J7
WHIPPOORWILL PL
20000 SCTA 91351 4551-E3
WHISPERGLEN LN
1200 SDMS 91773 570-B6
WHISPERING GLEN LN
1900 BREA 92821 709-D6
WHISPERING HOLLOW CT
- WAL 91789 639-C5
WHISPERING LEAVES DR
26200 SCTA 91321 4551-G4
WHISPERING OAKS DR
100 GLDR 91741 569-H5
1000 ARCD 91006 566-J4
WHISPERING OAKS RD
- StvR 91381 4640-B2
WHISPERING PALMS
- PRV 90660 676-J1
- PRV 90660 677-A1
WHISPERING PINE LN
300 LPUE 91744 638-J4
WHISPERING PINES
4900 THO 91362 557-G1
WHISPERING PINES CT
4200 Enc 91316 560-J5
4200 Enc 91316 561-A5
WHISPERING PINES DR
200 ARCD 91006 567-D3
WHISPERING PINES PL
8500 RSMD 91770 596-G7
WHISPERING PINES RD
3600 SBdC 92371 (4562-J4 See Page 4471)
WHISPERING PINES SUMMIT
200 ARCD 91006 567-D3
WHISPERING TREES WY
25600 SCTA 91355 4550-F7
WHISPERING WILLOW CT
- AZU 91702 568-J1
WHISPERING WILLOW ST
- PMDL 93550 4286-C4
WHISTLER AV
3500 ELMN 91732 597-F6
3500 ELMN 91732 637-E1
13100 GmH 91344 481-C4
WHISTLER CT
- RowH 91748 679-E5
WHISTLER LN
13200 GmH 91344 481-C4
WHISTLER WY
- LA 91342 482-C3
WHISTLE TRAIN RD
- BREA 92823 709-H6
WHISTLING WIND CIR
600 WAL 91789 639-D7
WHITAKER AV
5200 Enc 91436 561-D2
6400 VanN 91406 531-D4
8700 LA 91343 531-D1
8800 LA 91343 501-D4
10300 GmH 91344 501-D2
WHITAKER ST
7800 BPK 90621 767-J1
WHITBURN ST
10700 CULC 90230 672-H4
E WHITCOMB AV
100 GLDR 91741 569-E4
W WHITCOMB AV
100 GLDR 91741 569-D4
WHITE AV
1800 LVRN 91750 600-H3
6000 NLB 90805 765-C1
6400 NLB 90805 735-D7
N WHITE AV
- POM 91766 640-H1
100 POM 91768 640-H1
1600 LVRN 91750 600-G5
S WHITE AV
100 POM 91766 640-H3
900 COMP 90221 735-D5
14400 RDom 90221 735-C4
WHITE CIR
2900 RBCH 90278 733-B6
WHITE CT
3500 TOR 90503 763-A4
WHITE DR
- LMRD 90639 737-F2
WHITE ST
2100 PAS 91107 566-D4
6300 SIMI 93063 499-C2
10800 SunV 91352 533-A2
WHITEASH DR
38800 LACo 93551 4195-F6
38800 PMDL 93551 4195-F6
E WHITEBIRCH DR
3200 WCOV 91791 639-D1
3300 LACo 91791 639-D1
WHITEBLUFF DR
2000 SDMS 91773 570-E5
WHITEBOOK DR
100 LHB 90631 708-C7
WHITECAP WY
20600 MAL 90265 629-J5
WHITECLIFF DR
900 DBAR 91765 680-E2
5600 RPV 90275 823-A2
WHITECLIFF ST
40600 PMDL 93551 4194-G2
WHITE CLOUD DR
3200 HacH 91745 678-B6
WHITE CLOUD TER
500 PMDL 93551 4285-H2
WHITE DEER DR
1000 LCF 91011 535-B1
WHITE DOVE LN
2300 CHLS 91709 680-J3
WHITE FEATHER RD
33700 Actn 93510 4375-F6
WHITEFIELD PL
27400 SCTA 91354 4460-G6
WHITEFIELD RD
1400 PAS 91104 566-C2
2500 PAS 91107 566-E2
WHITE FIR LN
- PMDL 93551 4195-D6
1600 DBAR 91765 680-A4
WHITEFLOWER LN
3600 ELMN 91732 637-F1
WHITEFORD AV
400 LACo 91744 679-A2
WHITEFOX DR
5300 RPV 90275 793-A6
WHITE FOX LN
9000 LACo 91390 4373-E4
WHITE FOX TR
2300 SBdC 92371 (4472-F6 See Page 4471)
WHITEGATE AV
10200 Sunl 91040 503-H2
WHITEGATE LN
10200 Sunl 91040 503-H4
WHITEHALL CT
- GLDL 91206 565-B2
WHITEHALL LN
- CanP 91307 529-D5
37300 PMDL 93550 4286-C3
WHITEHAVEN TER
900 GLDL 91207 564-F1
WHITEHEAD LN
2500 HacH 91745 678-E5
WHITEHILL DR
1300 LHB 90631 708-G3
WHITEHORN DR
26600 RPV 90275 793-B6
WHITE HORSE CIR
800 WAL 91789 639-E6
WHITEHORSE PL
26900 SCTA 91387 4552-E5
WHITE HOUSE PL
3500 LA 90004 634-A1
WHITEHURST DR
1700 MONP 91755 636-C4
WHITE KNOLL DR
800 LA 90012 634-F1
WHITELAND ST
9700 PRV 90660 706-F3
11200 SFSP 90670 706-G3
WHITEMARSH AV
1000 COMP 90220 734-H6
WHITE OAK AL
- MNRO 91016 567-G4
WHITE OAK AV
4600 Enc 91316 561-B3
6100 Enc 91316 531-B7
6400 VanN 91406 531-B4
6500 Res 91335 531-B4
7600 Nor 91325 531-A1
8800 Nor 91325 501-A7
10300 GmH 91344 501-A2
WHITE OAK CT
23600 SCTA 91321 4640-G3
WHITE OAK DR
100 ARCD 91006 567-D1
100 POM 91767 600-G4
WHITE OAK LN
100 POM 91766 640-H2
WHITE OAK PL
4400 Enc 91316 561-A4
WHITE OAK RD
21900 WAL 91789 639-J5
WHITE PALMS LN
- LA 91342 482-E6
WHITE PINE PL
22900 SCTA 91390 4460-H3
WHITEPOST LN
15800 LMRD 90638 737-J2
WHITE RABBIT TR
1900 UPL 91784 571-J5
WHITE RIVER PL
3400 WLKV 91361 557-B7
WHITE ROCK CT
- SCTA 91321 4551-F6

STREET
Block City ZIP Pg-Grid

WHITEROCK DR
13900 LMRD 90638 737-F3
WHITE ROSE WY
3400 Enc 91436 561-E7
WHITES LNDG
300 LBCH 90803 826-C1
WHITESAIL CIR
4000 WLKV 91361 557-B6
WHITESAND PL
6900 MAL 90265 667-F3
WHITES CANYON RD
- CynC 91351 4461-F7
- Saug 91350 4461-F7
19500 SCTA 91351 4551-F1
28000 SCTA 91351 4461-F7
WHITESELL ST
13800 BALD 91706 638-A1
14000 LACo 91746 638-B1
WHITESIDE PL
200 THO 91362 557-A2
WHITESIDE ST
3200 City 90063 635-D3
WHITESPEAK DR
3700 Shrm 91403 561-H6
WHITES POINT DR
2500 SPed 90731 823-J7
2600 SPed 90731 853-J1
29100 RPV 90275 822-H1
WHITESPRING DR
16000 LACo 90604 707-J7
16100 LACo 90604 708-A7
WHITE SPUR LN
- Actn 93510 4465-B4
WHITE STALLION CT
14500 CHLS 91709 680-J4
WHITE STAR DR
1900 DBAR 91765 679-H5
WHITESTAR ST
1100 SBdC 92372 (4562-C1 See Page 4471)
WHITE STONE CT
- Tarz 91356 560-G1
WHITESTONE RD
26900 RPV 90275 792-J6
WHITEWATER AV
11200 MTCL 91763 641-F2
WHITEWATER DR
- SCTA 91354 4460-F7
900 FUL 92833 738-C5
WHITEWATER LN
11800 VeCo 90265 625-F5
WHITEWATER CANYON RD
15800 SCTA 91387 4552-D2
WHITE WING LN
700 WAL 91789 639-F6
WHITE WING WY
- SCTA 91321 4550-J6
- SCTA 91350 4550-J6
WHITEWOOD AV
5400 LKWD 90712 766-A2
12700 DWNY 90242 736-A1
N WHITEWOOD AV
4300 LBCH 90808 766-B5
E WHITEWOOD ST
6500 SIMI 93063 499-C2
WHITFIELD AV
14600 PacP 90272 631-A4
WHITFIELD PL
23900 SCTA 91354 4550-F1
E WHITING AV
100 FUL 92832 738-H7
W WHITING AV
100 FUL 92832 738-G7
WHITING ST
100 ELSG 90245 732-E1
WHITINGHAM CT
29300 AGRH 91301 558-A3
WHITINGHAM DR
3400 WCOV 91792 679-D1
WHITING MANOR LN
3700 GLDL 91208 534-E2
WHITING WOODS MTWY
- GLDL 91208 534-C2
- GLDL 91214 534-C2
WHITING WOODS RD
100 GLDL 91208 534-E2
500 GLDL 91214 534-E2
WHITLATCH DR
700 LAN 93535 4106-A2
WHITLEY AV
1700 Hlwd 90028 593-E4
1900 LA 90068 593-E3
WHITLEY ST
11000 WHIT 90601 677-A4
WHITLEY TER
2000 LA 90068 593-E3
WHITLEY COLLINS DR
29200 RHE 90274 823-A1
29200 RPV 90275 823-A1
WHITLOCK AV
7500 PdlR 90293 702-B4
WHITMAN AV
1000 CLAR 91711 601-B2
6000 VanN 91406 531-G5
11100 GrnH 91344 501-F2
WHITMAN CIR
6800 BPK 90620 767-F2
WHITMAN DR
6700 BPK 90620 767-F2
WHITMAN PL
2400 LA 90068 593-G2
WHITMAN RD
24300 HIDH 91302 559-D4
WHITMAN ST
25400 StvR 91381 4640-B1
WHITMAR RANCH RD
- Actn 93510 4375-G5
WHITMORE AV
1800 LA 90039 594-F5
WHITMORE ST
1100 MONP 91755 636-D2
1100 RSMD 91770 636-G1
9100 ELMN 91770 636-J1
9200 ELMN 91731 636-J1
9500 ELMN 91733 636-J1
9500 ELMN 91733 637-A1
WHITNALL HWY
1200 BURB 91505 563-B1
5600 NHol 91601 563-B1
5800 NHol 91601 533-A7
6000 NHol 91606 533-A7
N WHITNALL HWY
100 BURB 91505 563-D3
WHITNEY AV
100 POM 91767 600-J2
WHITNEY CT
800 SDMS 91773 599-H4
WHITNEY DR
- Cstc 91384 4459-E2
2200 ALH 91803 635-J2
4400 ELMN 91731 597-C6
WHITNEY LN
3200 BURB 91504 533-F3
WHITNEY PL
500 MONP 91754 635-J3
18700 RowH 91748 679-B7
WHITNEY WY
- PMDL 93552 4287-D1
9100 CYP 90630 767-B6
WHITNEY CANYON RD
- SCTA 91321 4641-D3
WHITSETT AV
4000 LA 91604 562-F5
4800 LA 91607 562-F2
5900 LA 91607 532-F7
6000 NHol 91606 532-F7
6700 NHol 91605 532-F3
7200 Flor 90001 674-G7
7200 Flor 90001 704-G1
WHITTEMORE DR
25600 LACo 91302 629-A1
25600 LACo 91302 589-A7
WHITTIER AV
1000 BREA 92821 708-H4
1400 CLAR 91711 601-B1
1400 LHB 90631 708-H4
6300 WHIT 90601 677-C6
7000 WHIT 90602 677-C6
WHITTIER BLVD
600 Boyl 90033 634-J6
600 LA 90023 634-J6
2100 LA 90023 635-A6
3800 LACo 90023 635-C7
4400 ELA 90022 635-C7
4500 ELA 90022 675-G1
5400 CMRC 90022 675-G1
5800 WHIT 90606 676-A1
5900 LACo 90606 676-A1
6000 ELA 90022 676-A1
6500 MTBL 90640 676-A1
8200 PRV 90660 676-A1
10000 PRV 90606 676-A1
12200 WHIT 90606 677-B7
12400 WHIT 90602 677-C7
12500 WHIT 90602 707-C1
13900 WHIT 90605 707-C1
WHITTIER BLVD Rt#-72
10300 LACo 90606 676-J4
10500 WHIT 90606 676-J4
10800 WHIT 90606 677-B6
11100 LACo 90606 677-B6
11400 WHIT 90601 677-B6
12000 WHIT 90602 677-B6
12500 WHIT 90602 707-D1
13400 WHIT 90605 707-D1
14500 WHIT 90603 707-G3
16100 WHIT 90603 708-A4
E WHITTIER BLVD
100 LHB 90631 708-F4
100 MTBL 90640 676-E2
200 PRV 90660 676-F3
W WHITTIER BLVD
100 LHB 90631 708-C4
100 MTBL 90640 676-B2
2400 MTBL 90022 676-B2
W WHITTIER BLVD Rt#-72
2000 LHB 90631 708-B4
2100 OrCo 90631 708-B4
WHITTIER CT
- SBdC 91710 641-C5
WHITTIER DR
600 BHLS 90210 632-D1
700 Wwd 90024 632-D1
900 BHLS 90210 592-D7
1000 BelA 90077 592-D7
2400 LaCr 91214 504-G7
WHITTIER GLEN LN
9100 WHIT 90602 707-C2
WHITTIER WOODS CIR
1800 LACo 90601 637-E7
WHITTIER WOODS DR
1800 LACo 90601 637-E6
W WHITTLERS LN
1000 ONT 91762 641-J5
WHITTLERS PL
3600 WCOV 91792 679-J2
E WHITTLEY AV
200 AVA 90704 5923-G4
W WHITTLEY AV
100 AVA 90704 5923-G4
WHITTWOOD DR
- WHIT 90603 707-H4
WHITTWOOD LN
- WHIT 90603 707-H4
WHITWELL DR
9800 LA 90210 562-C7
9800 LA 90210 592-C1
WHITWORTH DR
5800 LA 90019 633-A3
6100 LA 90035 633-A3
6700 LA 90035 632-G3
8800 BHLS 90211 632-G3
9100 BHLS 90212 632-G3
WHOLESALE ST
1200 LA 90021 634-G6
WIATT WY
10700 LHB 90631 708-E4
WICK LN
800 GLDR 91741 569-H3
WICKER DR
12300 LMRD 90638 737-F1
12300 LACo 90604 737-F1
WICKER WY
1800 LVRN 91750 600-G1
WICKFORD AV
400 LPUE 91744 678-F2
WICKFORD DR
1300 BREA 92821 708-H5
WICKFORD WY
- PMDL 93551 4194-J3
- PMDL 93551 4195-A3
WICKHAM CT
1300 SDMS 91773 599-H4
WICKHAM LN
8100 LPMA 90623 767-B4
WICKHAM WY
3700 GLDL 91208 534-H3
3800 GLDL 91020 534-H3
3800 Mont 91020 534-H3
WICKIUP PLANTATION RD
- LACo (4726-E3 See Page 4645)
WICKLAND RD
- LACo 91302 588-H5
WICKLIFFE DR
400 PAS 91104 535-J7
500 PAS 91104 565-J1
WICKLOW RD
2900 LA 90064 632-F6
WICKS PL
11400 SunV 91352 502-H5
WICKS RD
1300 PAS 91103 565-E2
WICKS ST
10800 Sunl 91040 503-A4
10900 SunV 91352 503-A4
11000 SunV 91352 502-J5
12200 SunV 91352 532-F1
WICKSHIRE AV
1700 HacH 91745 678-B3
WICOPEE AV
4800 Eagl 90041 565-C6
WICOPY CT
- PMDL 93551 4285-D2
WIDELOOP RD
- RHLS 90274 823-E4
WIDENER AV
10700 WHIT 90603 707-H5
WIDSON CT
1800 HacH 91745 678-F6
WIEMER AV
8300 PRM 90723 735-H2
WIERFIELD DR
1300 PAS 91105 565-D3
WIERSMA AV
19000 CRTS 90703 766-F2
WIGAN PL
2000 HacH 91745 678-F6
WIGGIN ST
4800 VeCo 91377 557-G1
WIGGINS AV
3600 ELMN 91731 597-D7
WIGHT RD
28900 MAL 90265 667-F2
WIGMORE DR
200 PAS 91105 565-G7
WIGTOWN RD
2700 LA 90064 632-E6
WIGWAM AV
800 ARCD 91006 567-D4
WILADONDA DR
800 LCF 91011 535-B3
WILART PL
200 POM 91768 600-H6
WILBARN ST
8200 PRM 90723 735-H3
E WILBARN ST
4900 RDom 90221 735-D3
WILBER PL
300 MTBL 90640 676-F1
WILBUR AV
100 COV 91724 599-E5
5100 Tarz 91356 560-H1
6000 Res 91335 560-H1
6100 Res 91335 530-H4
8200 Nor 91324 530-H4
8900 Nor 91324 500-H7
10300 Nor 91326 500-G1
11500 Nor 91326 480-F7
WILBURY RD
1300 SMRO 91108 566-E7
WILCOX AV
500 LA 90004 593-F7
700 LA 90038 593-E4
1300 Hlwd 90028 593-E4
1900 LA 90068 593-E4
6100 MYWD 90270 675-F6
6200 BELL 90201 675-E7
6700 BELL 90201 705-E2
7300 CDHY 90201 705-E2
8300 SGAT 90280 705-E2
8300 CDHY 90280 705-E2
N WILCOX AV
100 MTBL 90640 676-B1
500 MTBL 90640 636-B6
S WILCOX AV
1100 MONP 91755 636-B4
WILCOX PL
1100 LA 90038 593-E5
WILCOX WY
- BPK 90621 737-F6
WILD BLOSSOM CIR
20000 WAL 91789 639-E5
WILDBRIAR DR
5700 RPV 90275 793-A5
WILD CANYON DR
14700 CHLS 91709 680-H5
WILDCAT WY
400 BREA 92821 709-D6
WILDCAT CANYON RD
19800 WAL 91789 639-E5
WILD COUNTRY WY
13400 LACo 91390 (4372-J7 See Page 4281)
WILDE AV
25500 StvR 91381 4550-B7
WILDE ST
1000 LA 90021 634-G5
WILDER AV
13200 NRWK 90650 737-A2
20300 LKWD 90715 767-A4
WILDERNESS CIR
- FUL 92833 738-A3
WILDERNESS LN
5100 CULC 90230 672-J3
WILDERNESS PL
- POM 91766 640-G7
WILDERNESS WY
- Cstc 91384 4369-G5
WILDFLOWER CIR
2100 BREA 92821 709-D7
WILDFLOWER CT
300 AZU 91702 568-H2
38200 PMDL 93551 4285-H1
WILDFLOWER DR
- HacH 91745 637-J7
2100 FUL 92833 738-C3
WILD FLOWER LN
2100 CHLS 91709 680-J4
WILDFLOWER LN
- PRV 90660 676-F6
200 WAL 91789 679-E1
WILDFLOWER PL
- POM 91766 640-G7
WILD FLOWER RD
6700 MAL 90265 667-D3
WILDFLOWER RD
10900 TEML 91780 597-D3
WILDFLOWER WY
- AZU 91702 568-J2
WILD HARE RD
34900 LACo 93551 4375-G3
WILD HORSE DR
4800 MTCL 91763 601-F5
WILDHORSE LN
- RHE 90274 793-C5
WILDHORSE CANYON RD
7100 SBdC - (4562-J6 See Page 4471)
7200 SBdC 92371 (4562-J6 See Page 4471)
WILDLIFE RD
6500 MAL 90265 667-F2
WILD OAK DR
2400 LA 90068 593-H2
WILDOMAR ST
600 PacP 90272 630-J5
WILDRIDGE LN
17800 SCTA 91387 4552-A2
WILDROSE AV
300 MNRO 91016 567-H4
1800 POM 91767 601-B6
WILD ROSE DR
25600 LACo 91302 629-A1
WILDROSE DR
800 BREA 92821 738-J2
WILD ROSE LN
600 SDMS 91773 570-A6
WILDROSE LN
14100 CHLS 91709 680-H3
WILD ROSE ST
2500 THO 91361 557-B5
WILDROSE ST
38200 PMDL 93550 4286-G1
WILDROSE WY
4600 LACo 93536 4104-J5
WILDROSE CANYON CT
- Alta 91001 535-G3
WILD TRAILS DR
- FUL 92833 738-C3
WILD TREE ST
- PMDL 93550 4286-C3
WILD WEST CIR
- POM 91766 640-F4
WILDWIND RD
28000 SCTA 91351 4461-F7
28000 SCTA 91351 4551-F1
WILDWOOD
2000 WCOV 91791 638-J4
2000 WCOV 91791 639-A4
WILDWOOD AV
500 GLDR 91741 569-C4
9000 SunV 91352 503-B6
N WILDWOOD AV
100 GLDR 91741 569-C5
S WILDWOOD AV
6800 GLDR 91741 569-C5
WILDWOOD DR
1200 Eagl 90041 565-B7
1600 HiPk 90042 565-B7
13600 HacH 91745 637-H6
25600 LACo 91302 629-A1
WILDWOOD LN
600 SDMS 91773 600-C3
WILDWOOD MTWY
- GLDR 91741 570-A5
- SDMS 91773 570-B5
WILDWOOD PL
22200 Chat 91311 499-J2
WILDWOOD RD
23100 SCTA 91321 4640-J3
WILDWOOD ST
12400 ELMN 91732 637-G1
WILDWOOD TR
12100 LACo 91342 482-J6
WILDWOOD WY
200 WAL 91789 639-B4
WILDWOOD CANYON DR
2400 GLDR 91741 570-A6
WILDWOOD CANYON RD
- BURB 91501 533-J4
- BURB 91501 534-A3
- Nwhl 91321 4640-J5
23400 SCTA 91321 4640-J3
WILDWOOD RANCH RD
2500 GLDR 91741 570-A6
WILEY CT
200 CLAR 91711 571-D7
WILEY LN
4200 GLDL 91214 504-D7
WILEY BURKE AV
9500 DWNY 90240 706-A2
10100 DWNY 90241 706-A3
10600 DWNY 90241 705-J4
WILEY CANYON RD
- StvR 91381 4640-E5
23300 SCTA 91355 4550-G7
23900 SCTA 91355 4640-F1
24100 SCTA 91321 4640-F1
24100 SCTA 91381 4640-E5
WILEY POST AV
8300 Wch 90045 702-H3
WILEY POST RD
- BELL 90201 675-G5
WILFREY AV
13500 LMRD 90638 737-E2
WILFRID CIR
14000 LA 91342 482-B1
WILGAR DR
100 LHB 90631 708-C6
WILHARDT ST
100 LA 90012 634-H1
WILHELMINA AV
5200 WdHl 91367 559-E1
WILKES CT
2100 CLAR 91711 571-C7
WILKES WY
12700 LKWD 90715 767-A4
WILKIE AV
10800 ING 90303 703-G6
11600 HAW 90250 703-G7
11600 HAW 90303 703-G7
12400 HAW 90250 733-G1
12900 GAR 90249 733-G3
16100 TOR 90247 733-G6
16100 TOR 90504 733-G6
17300 TOR 90504 763-G1
WILKIE DR
2200 POM 91767 601-A4
WILKINS AV
1100 LACo 90023 675-F1
10200 Wwd 90024 632-D2
WILKINSON AV
4000 LA 91604 562-F5
4900 LA 91607 562-F1
5900 LA 91607 532-F7
6000 NHol 91606 532-F6
7600 NHol 91605 532-F3
WILLAKE ST
9800 PRV 90660 706-F3
11500 SFSP 90670 706-G3
WILLALEE AV
4000 GLDL 91214 534-E1
4900 GLDL 91214 504-E6
N WILLAMAN DR
100 BHLS 90211 632-J2
S WILLAMAN DR
100 BHLS 90211 632-J2
300 LA 90048 632-J1
WILLAPA LN
300 DBAR 91765 640-C6
WILLARD AV
1000 GLDL 91201 564-B2
2600 RSMD 91770 636-G2
4700 RSMD 91770 596-G5
6200 LACo 91775 596-G5
N WILLARD AV
5400 SGBL 91776 596-G3
5500 LACo 91776 596-G4
5700 LACo 91775 596-G2
5700 SGBL 91775 596-G2
6800 LACo 91775 566-F7
WILLARD ST
1700 LBCH 90810 795-A4
12000 NHol 91605 532-D2
13300 PanC 91402 532-C2
14800 PanC 91402 531-J2
16900 VanN 91406 531-C2
17300 Nor 91325 531-A2
17700 Res 91335 531-A2
18500 Res 91335 530-H2
E WILLARD ST
100 LBCH 90806 795-D4
W WILLARD ST
100 LBCH 90806 795-D4
WILLAT AV
3800 CULC 90232 632-H7
WILLENS AV
4400 WdHl 91364 559-G4
WILLETA AV
42200 LACo 93536 4104-E5
42200 LAN 93536 4104-E5
WILLETTA AV
2100 LA 90068 593-F3
WILLEY LN
700 WHWD 90069 592-H7
WILL GEER RD
1100 Top 90290 590-B3
WILLIAM TR
- Actn 93510 4465-G2
WILLIAM BENT RD
6000 HIDH 91302 559-C1
WILLIAMETTE CT
1700 LAN 93534 4105-E1
WILLIAMETTE LN
400 CLAR 91711 601-C1
WILLIAM J BARNES AV
4100 LAN 93536 3924-H7
4700 LAN 93536 4014-H1
WILLIAM MORRIS PL
100 BHLS 90212 632-G2
WILLIAMS AV
3600 CLAR 91711 600-J1
3600 LVRN 91750 600-J1
3600 POM 91711 600-J1
3600 POM 91750 600-J1
3600 POM 91767 600-J1
3900 CLAR 91711 570-J7
3900 LVRN 91750 570-J7
4600 LACo 91750 570-J6
S WILLIAMS AV
12800 COMP 90221 735-D3
12800 RDom 90221 735-D3
WILLIAMS LN
600 BHLS 90210 592-G3
1600 SIMI 93063 499-B3
WILLIAMS PL
5000 LA 90032 635-E1
WILLIAMS ST
- BREA 92821 709-A5
500 POM 91768 640-G1
1100 MONP 91754 635-J3
1100 MONP 91754 636-A3
2000 LBCH 90810 795-A4
WILLIAMS WK
- Cstc 91384 4459-D6
WILLIAMS WY
5900 SIMI 93063 499-B3
13900 WHIT 90602 707-E1
WILLIAMSBURG CT
- VeCo 91361 586-G1
WILLIAMSBURG LN
- RHLS 90274 793-D7
WILLIAMSBURG PL
10600 WHIT 90603 708-A5
WILLIAMSBURG RD
2500 FUL 92833 738-B5
WILLIAMSBURG WY
- PMDL 93550 4286-C4
- VeCo 91361 586-F1
WILLIAMSON AV
500 FUL 92832 738-F7
600 FUL 92833 738-B7
S WILLIAMSON AV
400 ELA 90022 635-J7
600 ELA 90022 675-J1
WILLIMET AV
4100 LA 90039 564-D7
WILLINS ST
11500 SFSP 90670 706-G3
WILLIS AL
1100 PAS 91103 565-G2
WILLIS AV
4200 Shrm 91403 561-J4
5200 VanN 91411 561-J2
6400 VanN 91411 531-J6
6800 VanN 91405 531-J4
7700 PanC 91402 531-J2
8700 PanC 91402 501-J7
9700 LA 91343 501-J5
9900 MsnH 91345 501-J5
WILLIS ST
10400 SFSP 90670 706-J5
WILLISTON ST
1000 LACo 93551 4285-F5
WILLMONTE AV
4800 TEML 91780 597-A3
WILLMOTT LN
- MAL 90265 628-A7
WILLOUGHBY AV
5800 LA 90038 593-D6
7100 LA 90046 593-A6
7400 WHWD 90046 593-B6
8300 WHWD 90069 593-A6
8300 LA 90069 593-A6
8400 LA 90069 592-J6
WILLOW
18800 RowH 91748 679-B4
WILLOW AV
100 WCOV 91790 598-E5
300 LPUE 91746 638-B3
900 LACo 91746 638-B3
1100 GLDR 91740 599-H1
1400 WCOV 91790 638-B3
1500 WCOV 91746 638-B3
2200 UPL 91784 571-J3
3600 BALD 91706 598-E5
4900 LACo 91724 599-H3
N WILLOW AV
100 COMP 90221 735-A3
100 INDS 91746 638-A4
100 WCOV 91790 598-E6
S WILLOW AV
100 COMP 90221 735-A5
1000 WCOV 91790 598-D7
1000 WCOV 91790 638-C1
WILLOW CT
- AGRH 91301 558-A5
- Saug 91350 4461-B4
9200 MTCL 91763 601-E5
18000 RowH 91748 678-H7
WILLOW DR
- CALB 91302 559-J6
- CYP 90630 767-B4
- LACo 91302 559-J6
- WdHl 91364 559-J6
- WdHl 91364 560-A6
600 BREA 92821 709-B7
1500 Top 90290 589-G4
1700 GLDL 91208 534-H6
WILLOW LN
2200 WCOV 91790 598-D7
2400 THO 91361 557-A3
7700 LPMA 90623 767-C3
32500 LACo 91390 (4372-J7 See Page 4281)
WILLOW PL
500 LVRN 91750 600-D3
2700 SGAT 90280 704-J3
2700 SGAT 90280 705-A3
WILLOW RD
20200 WAL 91789 679-E1
WILLOW ST
100 LHB 90631 708-D5
500 Boyl 90033 634-J5
1300 LA 90013 634-H5
2600 BURB 91505 563-E3
5800 SBdC 92397 (4652-D2 See Page 4651)
E WILLOW ST
100 POM 91767 600-J6
100 LBCH 90806 795-G3
600 SIGH 90755 795-G3
1000 Bxby 90807 795-G3
2800 LBCH 90808 795-G3
3500 LBCH 90815 795-G3
3800 LBCH 90815 796-B3
7700 LALM 90720 796-F3
7700 LALM 90815 796-F3
W WILLOW ST
100 LBCH 90806 795-B3
100 POM 91768 600-H5
1000 LBCH 90810 795-A3
WILLOW TER
- Hrbr 90710 794-C3
WILLOW WY
- CRSN 90746 764-F5
- LACo 90746 764-F5
12300 Pcma 91331 502-H4
WILLOWBEND LN
- LA 91342 481-J6
- LA 91342 482-G6
- SFER 91340 482-G6
WILLOWBRAE AV
10400 Chat 91311 500-A3
WILLOWBRANCH LN
12300 CRTS 90703 736-J4
WILLOW BROOK AV
4300 LA 90029 594-A6
4700 LA 90029 593-J6
WILLOWBROOK AV
2000 PMDL 93551 4195-B5
10700 LA 90059 704-G6
10700 Wats 90002 704-G6
11600 Wbrk 90059 704-H7
12000 Wbrk 90222 704-H7
12000 Wbrk 90222 734-H1
N WILLOWBROOK AV
100 COMP 90220 734-J3
1100 COMP 90222 734-J3
1700 Wbrk 90222 734-J3
S WILLOWBROOK AV
100 COMP 90220 734-J5
2300 COMP 90220 735-A7
2300 COMP 90220 765-A1
S WILLOWBROOK AV
12800 Wbrk 90222 734-J5
WILLOWBROOK CIR
600 MNRO 91016 567-G2
WILLOWBROOK LN
- POM 91766 640-F5
1300 UPL 91784 571-G4
WILLOWBROOKE CT
- SCTA 91354 4460-F7
WILLOWBROOKE LN
- StvR 91381 4550-B4
WILLOW BUD DR
1300 DBAR 91789 679-F4
WILLOW CANYON CT
- LACo 91390 4461-A4
WILLOW CREEK LN
- SCTA 91355 4550-H3
14600 CHLS 91709 680-J5
WILLOWCREEK LN
12500 CRTS 90703 736-J5
12500 CRTS 90703 737-A5
WILLOW CREEK RD
24000 DBAR 91765 640-C6
WILLOWCREST AV
3500 LA 91604 563-B5
4500 LA 91602 563-B4
4800 NHol 91601 563-B2
5800 NHol 91601 533-B7
6000 NHol 91606 533-B7
WILLOWCREST LN
- POM 91766 640-G6
WILLOWCREST PL
10800 LA 91604 563-A6
WILLOW GLEN CT
14900 SCTA 91387 4462-F5
WILLOWGLEN DR
2500 DUAR 91010 568-D3
WILLOW GLEN LN
- WCOV 91744 679-B1
- WCOV 91792 679-B1
WILLOWGLEN LN
1200 SDMS 91740 570-B6
WILLOW GLEN RD
7500 LA 90046 593-A2
8000 LA 90046 592-J2
WILLOW GLEN ST
4300 CALB 91302 558-H7
WILLOWGREEN CT
1900 THO 91361 557-A5
WILLOWGREEN LN
- LA 91342 481-J2
WILLOWGROVE AV
400 GLDR 91741 569-G4
WILLOWHAVEN DR
2600 LaCr 91214 504-G5
WILLOW OAK CT
- LACo 91387 4552-A4
WILLOW OAKS DR
37700 PMDL 93550 4286-E5
WILLOWOOD ST
15700 LMRD 90638 737-H1
WILLOW SPRING LN
10200 Sunl 91040 503-F4
WILLOW SPRING GULCH
- LACo 91390 (4284-B7 See Page 4283)
- LACo 91390 4374-A1
WILLOW SPRINGS LN
500 GLDR 91741 569-G3
WILLOW TREE CT
- LACo 91390 4460-H2
WILLOWTREE DR
5700 AGRH 91301 557-H4
6900 RPV 90275 792-G7
WILLOWTREE LN
18700 Nor 91326 500-H3
WILLOWVALE RD
39000 LACo 93551 4195-F6
39100 PMDL 93551 4195-F6
WILLOW VIEW CIR
23000 SCTA 91354 4460-H5
WILLOW WEED WY
21200 SCTA 91351 4551-B3
WILLOW WEST CT
42800 LAN 93536 4105-D3
WILLOW WOOD LN
14200 CHLS 91709 680-H3
WILLOW WOOD RD
5000 RHE 90274 793-B6
26500 RPV 90275 793-B6
WILL ROGERS ST
5900 Wch 90045 702-H3
WILL ROGERS STATE PARK RD
1000 PacP 90272 631-C4
WILLSBROOK CT
1200 THO 91361 557-A5
WILMA AV
2100 CMRC 90040 675-G3
W WILMA PL
1800 LBCH 90810 795-A3
WILMA ST
5300 TOR 90503 763-A4
WILMAGLEN DR
15400 LACo 90604 707-H6
WILMAR PL
7500 RSMD 91770 636-D3
WILMINGTON AV
5800 Flor 90001 674-G7
5800 HNTP 90001 674-G7
9200 Wats 90002 704-G4
10700 LA 90059 704-G6
11300 Wbrk 90059 704-G6
WILMINGTON AV
12000 Wbrk 90222 704-G6
12000 Wbrk 90222 734-G1
12000 Wbrk 90059 734-G1
20400 CRSN 90810 764-H5
20400 CRSN 90746 764-H5
20800 CRSN 90745 764-H5
22300 CRSN 90745 794-F3
24400 Wilm 90744 794-F3
N WILMINGTON AV
100 COMP 90220 734-G2
1100 COMP 90222 734-G2
2700 Wbrk 90222 734-G2
S WILMINGTON AV
100 COMP 90220 734-H7
2200 COMP 90220 764-H2
2400 COMP 90746 764-H2
18000 LACo 90746 764-H2
18000 CRSN 90746 764-H2
18500 LACo 90220 764-H2
WILMINGTON BLVD
200 Wilm 90744 794-D6
WILMINGTON CT
23600 SCTA 91354 4460-G7
WILMINGTON ST
4100 TOR 90505 793-C3
WILMOT ST
- LA 90007 634-B6
WILSEY AV
10100 Tuj 91042 503-J3
WILSHIRE AV
2000 LHB 90631 708-B6
E WILSHIRE AV
100 FUL 92832 738-J7
600 FUL 92831 738-J7
W WILSHIRE AV
100 FUL 92832 738-G7
1200 FUL 92833 738-E7
WILSHIRE BLVD
100 SMCA 90401 671-D2
600 LA 90017 634-A2
700 SMCA 90403 671-D2
1200 SMCA 90404 671-D2
1500 SMCA 90404 631-H5
1500 SMCA 90403 631-F7
1800 LA 90057 634-A2
2900 LA 90010 634-A2
3400 LA 90010 633-J2
5000 LA 90036 633-D2
5000 LA 90036 633-E2
6200 LA 90048 633-B2
8400 BHLS 90211 632-G2
9100 BHLS 90212 632-G2
9100 BHLS 90210 632-G2
9900 Wwd 90024 632-B3
11000 Wwd 90024 632-B3
11000 Brwd 90049 632-B3
11000 LACo 90073 632-B3
11400 LACo 90073 631-H5
11400 WLA 90025 631-H5
11600 WLA 90025 631-H5
11600 Brwd 90049 631-H5
WILSHIRE DR
12900 WHIT 90602 707-C2
WILSHIRE PL
- SMCA 90404 631-H6
600 LA 90005 634-A3
600 LA 90010 634-A3
WILSHIRE PL N
2200 SMCA 90403 631-G6
WILSHIRE PL S
2300 SMCA 90404 631-G7
WILSON AV
500 PAS 91104 566-B3
500 PAS 91106 566-B3
1300 SMRO 91108 596-B1
1600 ARCD 91006 567-D2
1600 BURB 91504 533-E6
2300 Ven 90291 671-J6
5700 SGAT 90280 735-G1
6500 HNTP 90001 674-H7
6900 Flor 90001 674-G7
11800 LYN 90262 735-E2
E WILSON AV
100 GLDL 91206 564-F4
N WILSON AV
- PAS 91106 566-B4
300 COV 91724 599-E5
600 PAS 91104 566-A1
1000 UPL 91786 601-H1
1600 UPL 91784 571-H5
S WILSON AV
- PAS 91106 566-B5
100 COV 91724 599-E5
400 PAS 91125 566-B5
500 PAS 91126 566-B5
W WILSON AV
100 GLDL 91203 564-C4
WILSON CIR
7200 BPK 90620 767-H5
WILSON CT
700 BURB 91501 534-A6
2700 LAN 93536 4105-C1
S WILSON DR
1100 WCOV 91791 638-H3
WILSON PL
600 MONP 91755 636-D4
800 SMCA 90405 671-G4
WILSON ST
100 SMAD 91024 566-J2
300 LHB 90631 708-H5
600 POM 91768 640-G1
700 LA 90021 634-H6
WILSON ST
1400 LA 90021 674-H1
4300 CHNO 91710 641-E6
28600 Cstc 91384 4459-D7
WILSON TER
1500 GLDL 91206 564-H4
WILSON WY
- WHIT 90601 677-D6
400 INDS 91745 678-D1
2100 LA 90032 635-D1
3100 RSMD 91770 636-E1
WILSON CANYON TKTR
- LACo 91342 481-H1
- LACo 91342 4641-H7
- Nwhl 91321 4641-H7
WILSON SUMMIT ST
- HiPk 90042 595-D4
S WILTON DR
100 LA 90004 633-G1
WILTON PL
12800 GAR 90249 733-H2
16200 TOR 90504 733-H7
17800 TOR 90504 763-H1
N WILTON PL
100 LA 90004 633-G1
200 LA 90004 593-G7
700 LA 90038 593-G5
1300 Hlwd 90028 593-G3
1900 LA 90068 593-G3
S WILTON PL
100 LA 90004 633-G1
300 LA 90020 633-G1
600 LA 90005 633-G3
600 LA 90010 633-G1
900 LA 90019 633-G5
3700 LA 90018 673-H1
3900 LA 90062 673-G2
5800 LA 90047 673-H6
8600 LA 90047 703-H3
10000 LACo 90047 703-H5
11400 HAW 90250 703-H7
11500 HAW 90047 703-H7
11600 LACo 90250 703-H7
E WILTON ST
3200 LBCH 90804 795-J5
3800 LBCH 90804 796-A5
WILTON WY
1500 LHB 90631 708-C7
23500 SCTA 91354 4550-G1
WIMBERLY AV
11900 LA 91342 481-J7
WIMBERLY CT E
1300 POM 91766 640-G3
WIMBERLY CT S
1000 POM 91766 640-G3
WIMBLEDON CIR
1300 THO 91361 557-A5
WIMBLEDON CT
1500 WCOV 91791 638-J3
40600 PMDL 93551 4194-G2
WIMBLEDON LN
- ING 90305 703-E3
WIMBLEDON PL
500 LCF 91011 535-D5
WIMBLETON DR
3200 OrCo 90720 796-H4
WIMBLETON LN
2200 LHB 90631 708-B7
WIMBLEY CT
11400 CRTS 90703 736-F6
WIMER COUNTRY RD
10800 Sunl 91040 503-A4
WIMMER AV
4900 BALD 91706 598-C3
WINANS DR
6000 LA 90068 593-F2
WINCHELL ST
9600 PRV 90660 676-H6
10900 LACo 90606 676-H6
WINCHESTER AV
200 ALH 91801 595-G5
200 GLDL 91201 563-J3
300 ALH 91803 595-G5
900 LA 90032 595-G5
1000 GLDL 91201 564-A2
1300 GLDL 91201 534-B7
WINCHESTER CT
37400 PMDL 93552 4287-B3
WINCHESTER PL
200 SGBL 91776 596-F4
WINCHESTER RD
30400 Cstc 91384 4459-C3
WINCHESTER WY
- RowH 91748 708-J1
2500 CHLS 91709 680-H1
WINDBREAK CIR
300 BREA 92821 709-E6
WINDBROOK CT
1900 THO 91361 557-A7
WINDCREST
5400 PMDL 93551 4194-G1
WINDCREST PL
23400 SCTA 91321 4640-G3
WINDEMERE CT
2000 UPL 91784 571-H5
WINDEMERE DR
1700 LAN 93536 4015-E3
WINDEMERE WY
1500 UPL 91784 571-H5
WINDERMERE AV
5100 Eagl 90041 564-J5
WINDERMERE CT
1300 PMDL 93551 4195-F5

STREET Block City ZIP Pg-Grid

WINDERMERE DR
200 BREA 92821 709-E7
WINDERMERE LN
100 GLDR 91741 569-C5
WINDERMERE PL
3100 GLDL 91206 535-B6
WINDERMERE RD
800 SDMS 91773 599-J4
WINDERMERE WY
5200 LPMA 90623 767-C2
WINDFALL AV
2800 Alta 91001 536-C5
WINDFALL PL
- SCTA 91350 4551-D5
WINDHAM DR
600 CLAR 91711 601-E1
WINDHAVEN DR
4800 THO 91362 557-E2
WINDING LN
200 BREA 92821 709-E7
1900 SPAS 91030 595-J3
3000 THO 91361 557-C5
WINDING WY
1700 PAS 91107 536-H7
34000 Actn 93510 4375-D3
WINDING WY E
27300 MAL 90265 627-J7
27500 MAL 90265 667-H1
WINDING WY W
27700 MAL 90265 667-H1
WINDING BROOK LN
800 WAL 91789 639-H4
WINDING OAK LN
1000 MNRO 91016 567-J4
WINDING WAY LN
1500 GLDR 91741 569-H4
WINDJAMMER CT
- LBCH 90803 826-F2
WINDJAMMER RD
11000 CRTS 90703 736-F6
WINDMERE DR
- LA 91342 481-J6
WINDMERE LN
300 WAL 91789 639-B4
WINDMILL DR
- DBAR 91765 679-J7
- DBAR 91765 709-J1
3000 DBAR 91765 710-A1
3000 LACo 92823 710-A1
WINDMILL LN
1000 VeCo 91377 558-A1
WINDMILL RD
2800 TOR 90505 793-E4
40100 LACo 93551 4194-D4
WINDMILL CREEK RD
2400 CHLS 91709 680-J4
WINDOM ST
22800 CanP 91307 529-G4
23200 LA 91304 529-F4
WINDOVER RD
1800 LACo 91107 536-G7
WINDOVER WY
1200 MONP 91754 635-J4
WINDPORT DR
29500 RPV 90275 822-H2
WINDRIFT CIR
4500 PMDL 93552 4287-A5
WIND RIVER CIR
400 THO 91362 557-B2
WIND RIVER LN
- RowH 91748 679-E6
WINDROSE DR
19100 RowH 91748 679-C6
21000 WAL 91789 639-G7
WINDROSE PL
- LAN 93536 4014-H7
- SCTA 91354 4460-G3
43300 LAN 93536 4104-H2
WINDRUSH DR
15600 HacH 91745 678-B6
WINDRUSH RD
31900 LACo 91390 4463-D1
WINDSONG
3600 ELMN 91732 637-G1
WINDSONG AV
4600 LPMA 90623 767-B4
WINDSONG CIR
21200 WAL 91789 639-H7
WINDSONG CT
200 AZU 91702 568-H2
900 DBAR 91765 680-C2
21600 SCTA 91350 4461-B7
38200 PMDL 93551 4285-H1
WINDSONG LN
29600 AGRH 91301 557-J5
WINDSONG WY
- FUL 92833 738-C5
WINDSOR AV
3000 LA 90039 594-D5
3200 Echo 90026 594-D5
16500 WHIT 90603 708-A5
N WINDSOR AV
900 LACo 91011 535-F6
900 PAS 91011 535-F6
2100 Alta 91001 535-F6
2500 LACo 91103 535-F6
2600 PAS 91103 535-F6
N WINDSOR BLVD
100 LA 90004 593-G7
100 LA 90004 633-G1
S WINDSOR BLVD
100 LA 90004 633-G2
300 LA 90020 633-G2
S WINDSOR BLVD
600 LA 90005 633-F3
600 LA 90010 633-G2
900 LA 90019 633-F4
WINDSOR CIR
2000 DUAR 91010 568-C5
8600 LPMA 90623 767-C5
9100 CYP 90630 767-C6
WINDSOR CT
- LMRD 90638 738-B2
1500 LVRN 91750 570-F7
5500 BPK 90621 737-H6
9900 TEML 91780 597-A5
37400 PMDL 93550 4286-E3
WINDSOR DR
1300 SDMS 91773 599-H4
24500 SCTA 91355 4550-E5
WINDSOR LN
- SMAD 91024 567-A2
WINDSOR PL
- RowH 91748 679-C7
1100 SPAS 91030 595-H2
1200 PMDL 93551 4195-E5
1600 GLDR 91740 599-F2
1900 POM 91767 600-J5
3900 LCF 91011 535-B6
43800 LAN 93536 4105-C1
W WINDSOR PL
300 LBCH 90802 825-D1
WINDSOR RD
500 ARCD 91007 567-C4
1700 SMRO 91108 596-C2
28900 Cstc 91384 4459-D6
E WINDSOR RD
100 GLDL 91205 564-F6
W WINDSOR RD
100 GLDL 91204 564-D6
W WINDSOR ST
1200 WCOV 91790 638-D3
WINDSOR WY
200 LBCH 90802 825-E3
5600 CULC 90230 672-J6
9800 TEML 91780 597-A5
WINDSTAR WY
4200 PMDL 93552 4286-J5
4500 PMDL 93552 4287-A5
WINDTREE CIR
36400 PMDL 93550 4286-H4
WINDTREE DR
10400 BelA 90077 592-A1
WINDWARD
- WCOV 91790 638-D2
WINDWARD AV
- LBCH 90803 796-C7
- LBCH 90814 796-C7
- Ven 90291 671-G6
11900 LA 90066 672-C3
16600 CRTS 90703 736-F6
WINDWARD CIR
2300 THO 91361 557-B6
WINDWARD CT
- Ven 90291 671-G6
WINDWARD LN
- SCTA 91355 4550-F1
WINDWARD TER
17600 BLF 90706 736-D7
WINDWARD WY
- BPK 90621 738-A6
WINDWOOD DR
700 DBAR 91789 679-G2
2300 PMDL 93550 4286-E5
WINDWOOD LN
100 SMAD 91024 567-B3
2000 BREA 92821 709-D7
WINDY CT
9300 LACo 91390 4373-H5
WINDY WY
28100 Cstc 91384 4369-F6
WINDY CREEK ST
- PMDL 93550 4286-C4
WINEGLOW CIR
1700 LACo 91789 679-E5
WINETTA PL
200 FUL 92833 738-E7
WINFIELD AV
2900 LVRN 91750 600-H2
9900 WHIT 90603 708-B4
WINFIELD RD
20900 Top 90290 590-B5
WINFIELD ST
13200 PanC 91402 532-D1
WINFORD DR
- Tarz 91356 560-G6
WING LN
16500 LACo 91744 638-G6
WING RD
200 Chat 91311 499-F6
WING ST
300 GLDL 91205 564-G6
WINGATE CT
23700 SCTA 91354 4460-F6
WINGATE DR
1100 CRSN 90745 764-F6
WINGATE PL
1200 POM 91768 600-F7
E WINGATE ST
900 COV 91724 599-D4
WINGED FOOT CIR
19300 Nor 91326 480-F7
WINGED FOOT WY
19600 Nor 91326 480-E7
WINGFIELD RD
24500 HIDH 91302 559-C3
WINGO ST
12400 Pcma 91331 502-E4
WINGSONG CT
1400 UPL 91784 571-H5
WINIFRED AV
1100 LACo 91107 566-F7
WINIFRED ST
19500 Tarz 91356 560-F3
WINKLER AV
20300 LKWD 90715 767-A4
WINLAW AV
14000 LA 91342 482-B1
WINLOCK DR
24400 TOR 90505 793-D4
WINLOCK RD
2800 TOR 90505 793-E4
WINMAR DR
1700 LA 90065 594-H4
WINN CT
1600 POM 91768 600-E7
W WINN DR
1000 UPL 91786 601-J3
WINNEBAGO AV
10400 MsnH 91345 501-J4
WINNERS CIR
21700 WAL 91789 639-J5
WINNETKA AV
4300 WdHl 91364 560-E4
5500 WdHl 91367 560-E1
6000 WdHl 91367 530-E7
6400 Win 91306 530-E4
8700 Nor 91324 530-E4
8700 Win 91306 500-E7
8700 Nor 91324 500-E7
8900 Chat 91311 500-E4
WINNETKA CIR
4500 WdHl 91364 560-E4
WINNETKA CT
20100 WdHl 91364 560-E4
WINNETKA PL
20000 WdHl 91364 560-E3
WINNETT PL
100 SMCA 90402 631-C6
WINNIE DR
3200 LA 90068 563-D7
WINNIE WY
100 ARCD 91006 597-D1
E WINNIE WY
- ARCD 91006 597-D1
W WINNIE WY
- ARCD 91007 597-B1
N WINNIPEG PL
300 LBCH 90814 825-H1
300 LBCH 90814 795-H7
WINODEE DR
6100 PRV 90660 676-E5
WINONA AV
700 PAS 91103 565-G3
1600 BURB 91504 533-C5
E WINONA AV
100 COMP 90222 734-J2
W WINONA AV
100 COMP 90222 734-J3
WINONA BLVD
1500 LFlz 90027 593-J2
WINONA CT
6400 VeCo 91377 558-A1
WINONA DR
1600 WAL 91789 639-G3
WINONA WY
- PAS 91103 565-G3
WINROCK AV
2100 Alta 91001 536-C5
WINROW CT
2500 RowH 91748 678-H7
WINSFORD AV
7900 Wch 90045 702-J2
WINSIDE ST
4800 THO 91362 557-G2
WINSLOW AV
- LBCH 90814 826-C1
300 LBCH 90814 796-C7
600 LBCH 90804 796-C7
WINSLOW CT
- StvR 91381 4640-C1
WINSLOW DR
3400 Echo 90026 594-B6
WINSLOW PL
18300 CRTS 90703 767-A1
23500 SCTA 91354 4460-G6
WINSLOW ST
1400 UPL 91786 571-J7
WINSOME CIR
26700 SCTA 91321 4551-F4
WINSTON AV
500 BRAD 91010 568-B4
500 LACo 91107 566-E7
500 SMRO 91108 566-E7
S WINSTON AV
200 WCOV 91791 598-J7
200 WCOV 91791 638-J1
WINSTON CT
1000 THO 91361 557-B5
WINSTON DR
3700 ELMN 91731 597-D6
WINSTON PL
2600 FUL 92833 738-B3
WINSTON ST
100 LA 90013 634-F4
WINTER AV
1500 KeCo 93560 3835-E2
WINTER ST
2700 Boyl 90033 635-C4
WINTER ST
3000 LA 90063 635-C4
3200 City 90063 635-D5
WINTER CANYON RD
3500 MAL 90265 628-H6
WINTERDALE DR
28000 SCTA 91387 4552-B1
WINTERGREEN CT
25000 StvR 91381 4640-E2
WINTERGREEN RD
7700 SBdC 92372 (4562-D2 See Page 4471)
9300 SBdC 92372 (4472-D3 See Page 4471)
WINTERGREEN ST
100 BREA 92821 709-F7
WINTERHAVEN DR
3300 LVRN 91750 600-F1
WINTERHAVEN LN
2800 Alta 91001 536-C5
WINTER MESA RD
- MAL 90265 628-H7
WINTER PINE WY
- LACo 91387 4552-A4
WINTERSET DR
21100 SCTA 91350 4461-B5
WINTERWOOD DR
2000 FUL 92833 738-C4
WINTERWOOD LN
1300 DBAR 91765 680-B3
WINTHROP AV
600 CLAR 91711 571-C7
2700 ARCD 91007 597-B3
12800 GrnH 91344 481-C4
WINTHROP DR
300 ALH 91803 595-G6
2100 ALH 91803 635-G2
WINTHROP RD
400 SMRO 91108 596-A2
N WINTON AV
100 LACo 91744 638-H7
100 LACo 91744 678-H1
S WINTON AV
100 LACo 91744 678-H1
WINTON CT
5600 LACo 91302 559-A3
WINTONWOOD LN
17500 LACo 91744 638-H7
WINTRESS DR
4200 CHNO 91710 641-E5
WINWARD ST
1700 LBCH 90810 765-A7
2000 LBCH 90810 795-A1
WIOTA ST
4700 Eagl 90041 565-C6
WIRSCHING RD
- LACo 90265 627-J5
WISCASSET DR
- CanP 91307 529-C4
- LA 91304 529-D4
WISCONSIN AV
- LACo 90280 704-J4
200 LBCH 90803 825-H1
300 LBCH 90814 795-H7
300 LBCH 90814 825-H1
2500 SGAT 90280 704-J4
2900 SGAT 90280 705-A4
3100 LYN 90262 705-A4
WISCONSIN PL
400 POM 91768 600-H7
3900 LA 90037 674-A2
WISCONSIN ST
- LA 90007 674-A2
3700 LA 90037 674-A2
32300 Actn 93510 4375-C7
32300 Actn 93510 4465-C1
N WISCONSIN ST
500 POM 91768 640-H1
800 POM 91768 600-H7
WISE AV
3500 LBCH 90810 765-B7
3500 LBCH 90810 795-B1
WISEBURN ST
5200 HAW 90250 733-A2
WISH AV
5600 Enc 91316 561-C1
6800 VanN 91406 531-C3
9200 Nor 91325 501-C4
10300 GrnH 91344 501-C1
11800 GrnH 91344 481-C7
WISHBONE LN
26400 SCTA 91351 4551-B2
WISHING HILL DR
4100 LCF 91011 534-J4
4100 LCF 91011 535-A4
WISNER AV
7900 PanC 91402 531-H3
8500 LA 91343 531-H1
9900 MsnH 91345 501-H5
WISTARIA AV
700 ARCD 91007 597-A1
E WISTARIA AV
100 ARCD 91006 597-D1
W WISTARIA AV
- ARCD 91007 597-A1
WISTARIA LN
2800 FUL 92833 738-A3
WISTARIA PL
400 Alta 91001 535-J5
WISTARIA WY
200 SMAD 91024 566-J1
200 SMAD 91024 567-A1
WISTARIA VALLEY RD
29500 SCTA 91387 4462-F5
WISTERIA AV
- LHB 90631 708-C6
2200 UPL 91784 571-H3
WISTERIA DR
- PMDL 93551 4285-D3
WISTERIA LN
1700 BREA 92821 709-D7
WISTERIA TR
3400 CALB 91302 589-E1
3500 CALB 91302 559-F7
37500 PMDL 93552 4287-D2
WISTERLY CT
21600 SCTA 91350 4461-B5
WISTFULL VISTA WY
- Nor 91326 500-E1
W WIT PL
4000 LA 90029 594-B5
WITHERILL PL
1100 PMDL 93551 4195-G5
WITHERILL ST
1000 SDMS 91773 599-J4
WITHERSPOON PKWY
- Cstc 91384 4459-F6
- Valc 91355 4459-F6
WITHERSPOON RD
12600 CHNO 91710 641-D6
WITMER ST
100 Echo 90026 634-E3
300 LA 90017 634-D3
WITTICK CT
2400 LMTA 90717 793-G5
WITZEL DR
3800 Shrm 91423 562-B6
WITZMAN DR
16600 LACo 91744 638-G6
WIXOM ST
10600 SunV 91352 533-A3
11300 SunV 91352 532-H3
11600 NHol 91605 532-D3
WOBURN CT
- PMDL 93551 4195-A3
WO HE LO TR
21600 Chat 91311 500-A1
WOKING WY
4000 LFlz 90027 594-B2
WOLCOTT PL
10700 MsnH 91345 501-J2
WOLCOTT WY
- Valc 91355 4549-E2
WOLDRICH ST
10500 LA 91342 503-B2
WOLF CREEK TR
- SCTA 91354 4550-J4
WOLFE CIR
25500 StvR 91381 4550-C7
WOLFE ST
3200 LKWD 90712 765-H2
5700 LKWD 90713 766-C2
WOLFE WY
4600 WdHl 91364 560-C4
WOLFORD LN
900 SPAS 91030 595-G4
WOLFSKILL ST
- SFER 91340 502-A1
800 LA 91340 502-A1
14500 MsnH 91345 501-J2
WOLLACOTT ST
1500 RBCH 90278 762-J1
WOLLAM ST
1700 LA 90065 594-H3
WOLSEY CT
4500 WLKV 91361 557-C5
WOLVERTON LN
- CRTS 90703 767-B3
WOLVERTON RD
1000 GLDL 91207 564-F1
WONDERLAND AV
8500 LA 90046 592-H3
WONDERLAND PARK AV
8700 LA 90046 592-G2
WONDER VIEW DR
3000 LA 90068 593-D1
3000 LA 90068 563-D7
WONDERVIEW DR
100 GLDL 91202 564-D1
200 GLDL 91202 534-D7
600 LACo 91302 629-A1
600 LACo 91302 589-A7
WONDER VIEW PL
3400 LA 90068 563-D7
WONDER VIEW PZ
3300 LA 90068 563-D7
WONG CT
19900 SCTA 91351 4461-E7
WOOD AV
5100 SGAT 90280 705-E4
8700 LACo 93536 3923-J6
20500 TOR 90503 763-B5
WOOD CT
300 CLAR 91711 571-D6
40300 PMDL 93551 4195-A3
WOOD DR
- WdHl 91364 559-J5
- WdHl 91364 560-A6
WOOD TER
3300 LFlz 90027 594-B2
WOODACRE LN
300 MNRO 91016 567-J4
1000 ARCD 91006 567-B4
WOODACRE ST
2600 BREA 92821 709-F7
WOODACRES RD
- SMCA 90402 631-C6
WOODALE AV
8900 Pcma 91331 502-A4
10500 MsnH 91345 501-J3
WOODBANK WY
- PMDL 93552 4287-E2
WOODBAY DR
14900 LMRD 90638 707-F7
WOODBEND DR
1500 CLAR 91711 601-A1
1700 CLAR 91711 571-A7
3200 LACo 91711 601-A2
WOODBINE CT
- CRSN 90746 764-H2
WOODBINE RD
2200 LACo 90265 629-D4
WOODBINE ST
3200 LA 90064 632-F7
10100 LA 90034 632-E7
10600 LA 90034 672-E1
11400 LA 90066 672-C2
12400 LA 90066 672-B3
WOODBINE TER
- PMDL 93551 4285-D3
WOODBLUFF AV
400 DUAR 91010 568-E4
WOODBLUFF RD
400 LACo 91302 628-J1
WOODBRIAR PL
30100 AGRH 91301 557-H4
WOODBRIDGE AV
1600 PMDL 93550 4286-D3
WOODBRIDGE CT
2800 DBAR 91765 680-A7
WOODBRIDGE ST
10200 LA 91602 563-B5
11200 LA 91602 562-H5
11400 LA 91604 562-D5
13300 Shrm 91423 562-D5
WOODBRIER DR
2600 LACo 90604 708-A7
2600 LHB 90631 708-A7
16100 LACo 90604 707-J7
WOODBROOK DR
29500 AGRH 91301 557-J4
WOODBROOK RD
27000 RPV 90275 792-J7
27000 RPV 90275 793-A6
WOODBURN AV
2000 THO 91361 557-A7
2600 WLKV 91361 557-A7
N WOODBURN DR
100 Brwd 90049 631-G1
S WOODBURN DR
100 Brwd 90049 631-H2
W WOODBURY CT
1200 UPL 91786 601-J2
WOODBURY DR
1000 Hrbr 90710 794-A2
1300 Hrbr 90710 794-A2
1400 Hrbr 90710 793-J1
2500 TOR 90503 763-F7
WOODBURY PL
- SCTA 91354 4550-G1
WOODBURY RD
600 GLDL 91206 564-G4
900 Alta 91001 535-E6
900 PAS 91103 535-E6
E WOODBURY RD
- Alta 91001 535-J6
300 PAS 91104 535-J6
500 PAS 91104 536-A7
600 Alta 91001 536-A7
900 LACo 91104 536-A7
W WOODBURY RD
- Alta 91001 535-F6
500 LACo 91103 535-F6
500 PAS 91103 535-F6
WOODCLIFF RD
3300 Shrm 91403 561-H5
WOODCLIFFE RD
300 PAS 91105 565-D4
WOODCOCK AV
2000 LA 91342 482-A5
2000 SFER 91340 482-A5
11200 Pcma 91331 502-C1
11500 LA 91340 482-C7
11500 LA 91340 502-C1
12600 LA 91342 481-F2
WOODCREEK CIR
3200 HacH 91745 678-B6
WOODCREEK CT
29000 AGRH 91301 558-A3
WOODCREST AV
700 BREA 92821 709-A4
700 BREA 92821 708-H4
E WOODCREST AV
600 LHB 90631 708-F4
WOODCREST DR
15200 LACo 90604 707-H6
15500 Shrm 91403 561-G6
WOODCREST PL
6500 VeCo 91377 558-B2
WOODCREST WY
300 WAL 91789 639-G7
2300 UPL 91784 571-H3
WOODCROFT AV
300 GLDR 91740 599-C2
WOODCROFT ST
17000 LACo 91702 598-J2
17000 AZU 91702 598-H2
17600 LACo 91702 599-A2
WOODCROFT ST
18000 AZU 91702 599-A2
18800 LACo 91722 599-C2
WOOD DALE CT
- SCTA 91350 4550-J6
WOODED VISTA
24600 CanP 91307 529-C7
WOODFERN DR
6000 RPV 90275 792-J5
WOODFIELD CT
10500 BelA 90077 592-A1
WOODFIELD DR
2400 BREA 92821 709-E6
3800 Shrm 91403 561-G6
WOODFIELD PL
- SCTA 91354 4460-G6
15600 Shrm 91403 561-G6
WOODFIELD RD
300 LCF 91011 535-D5
WOODFORD ST
9400 PRV 90660 676-J1
WOODGATE DR
1700 WCOV 91792 638-J6
1900 WCOV 91792 639-A7
WOODGATE ST
600 LAN 93534 4015-G4
WOODGLADE LN
24500 CanP 91307 529-C5
WOODGLEN CIR
8000 LPMA 90623 767-D4
WOODGLEN CT
21100 WAL 91789 639-G5
WOODGLEN DR
200 SDMS 91773 570-B7
300 SDMS 91740 570-B7
5800 AGRH 91301 557-H4
WOODGLEN LN
1600 Alta 91001 536-C4
WOODGREEN ST
12400 LA 90066 672-B3
WOODGROVE AV
4000 LACo 91722 598-F5
WOODHALL AV
7600 LA 91304 529-F3
WOODHAVEN DR
2700 LA 90068 593-F1
WOODHILL CIR
3300 DBAR 91765 709-H1
WOODHILL LN
2000 BREA 92821 709-D6
13700 CHLS 91709 680-J2
WOODHILL CANYON PL
3700 LA 91604 562-G6
WOODHILL CANYON RD
3400 LA 91604 562-G6
WOODHOLLOW LN
12700 CHLS 91709 640-H7
WOODHOLLY CT
1900 GLDL 91207 564-E1
WOODHUE ST
9500 PRV 90660 706-F1
10400 LACo 90606 706-G1
WOODHURST DR
3600 LACo 91724 599-G5
WOODINGTON AV
15500 BLF 90706 736-B4
WOODINGTON DR
400 LAN 93535 4016-A7
WOODLAKE AV
5100 WdHl 91367 559-G2
6100 WdHl 91367 529-G7
6400 CanP 91307 529-G5
7500 LA 91304 529-G2
WOOD LAKE DR
400 BREA 92821 708-J6
WOODLAKE DR
- BPK 90621 738-B6
WOODLAND AV
300 BREA 92821 709-D6
1700 GLDL 91208 534-H6
4100 BURB 91505 563-C3
E WOODLAND AV
- ARCD 91006 567-D3
WOODLAND CT
500 DUAR 91010 568-D4
1100 MTBL 90640 676-D2
21100 WAL 91789 639-H5
WOODLAND DR
300 LA 90732 824-A5
400 SMAD 91024 567-B1
600 SMAD 91024 537-B7
1000 BHLS 90210 592-E6
WOODLAND LN
- ARCD 91006 567-C3
8000 LA 90046 593-B4
E WOODLAND LN
800 GLDR 91741 569-G5
WOODLAND RD
500 PAS 91106 595-J1
500 PAS 91106 596-A1
1700 LBCH 90810 795-A1
WOODLAND WY
500 MONP 91755 636-C6
2100 LA 90068 593-E3
WOODLAND CREST DR
21600 WdHl 91364 560-A6
WOODLAND OAKS DR
100 SDMS 91773 570-B7
WOODLANDS CT
- PMDL 93551 4195-B2
WOODLANDS DR
- SCTA 91355 4550-D3
WOODLAND VIEW DR
5900 WdHl 91367 559-C1
6000 WdHl 91367 529-C7
WOODLANE DR
1800 WCOV 91792 638-J6
WOODLARK LN
26300 SCTA 91355 4550-E5
WOODLARK ST
400 LAN 93535 4106-A1
WOODLAWN AV
500 Ven 90291 671-J6
2800 SMRO 91108 596-F1
3700 LA 90011 674-C3
3800 LYN 90262 705-C7
5700 MYWD 90270 675-E6
5800 LA 90003 674-C6
6200 BELL 90201 675-E6
WOODLAWN CT
- SCTA 91354 4460-H6
600 Ven 90291 671-J6
800 Ven 90291 672-A5
3700 LA 90011 674-C2
WOODLAWN ST
8300 LACo 91775 596-F1
W WOODLAWN ST
1700 UPL 91786 601-G2
WOODLEAF DR
23200 DBAR 91765 680-B1
WOODLEIGH LN
4100 LCF 91011 535-C5
WOODLEY AV
4400 Enc 91436 561-F1
6000 Enc 91436 531-F7
6000 VanN 91406 531-F3
8300 LA 91343 531-F3
8700 LA 91343 501-E6
10100 GrnH 91344 501-E4
11500 GrnH 91344 481-D5
WOODLEY PL
8300 LA 91343 531-E2
WOODLEY PARK LN
4500 Enc 91436 561-F4
WOODLOW CT
1300 THO 91361 557-A6
WOODLYN LN
1700 BRAD 91010 568-B4
WOODLYN RD
300 BRAD 91010 568-B4
300 LACo 91010 568-B4
1800 PAS 91104 566-C1
2500 PAS 91107 566-E1
WOODMAN AV
4100 Shrm 91423 562-C4
5200 VanN 91401 562-C2
5900 VanN 91401 532-C6
6600 VanN 91405 532-C3
7500 PanC 91402 532-C3
8300 Pcma 91331 532-B1
8800 Pcma 91331 502-A6
8800 PanC 91402 502-A6
9800 PanC 91402 501-J4
9800 Pcma 91331 501-J4
10000 MsnH 91345 501-J4
WOODMAN PL
7500 VanN 91405 532-C4
WOODMAN CANYON AV
4000 Shrm 91423 562-C6
WOODMAR DR
4400 LACo 90601 677-B2
WOODMERE CIR
700 LHB 90631 708-B7
W WOODMERE DR
1200 UPL 91786 601-J1
WOODMERE PL
400 DUAR 91010 568-F4
WOODMONT CT
800 POM 91767 601-B5
WOODMONT DR
19200 Nor 91326 480-G7
WOODMONT PL
1500 LHB 90631 738-D1
16600 HacH 91745 678-E3
WOODPARK CT
- SCTA 91354 4460-F5
WOODPECKER ST
- BREA 92823 709-G6
WOOD RANCH RD
- GrnH 91344 481-A6
WOODRICH LN
9700 ELMN 91731 597-A7
WOODRIDGE AV
12800 LMRD 90638 737-D2
S WOODRIDGE AV
12300 LACo 90605 737-D1
WOODRIDGE CIR
1700 WCOV 91792 638-J6
WOODROW AV
1800 Eagl 90041 565-A7
WOODROW WILSON DR
2700 LA 90046 593-A1
6700 LA 90068 593-B1
8000 LA 90046 592-J1
WOODRUFF AV
200 Wwd 90024 592-B7
200 Wwd 90024 632-C1
2000 LBCH 90815 796-D2
2900 LBCH 90808 796-D2
3300 LBCH 90808 766-D5
3700 LACo 90808 766-D5
4100 LKWD 90713 766-D2
9200 TEML 91780 596-J3
9600 TEML 91780 597-A2
10100 DWNY 90242 736-D3
WOODRUFF AV
10200 DWNY 90241 706-C6
12100 DWNY 90242 706-D7
12100 DWNY 90241 736-D3
13400 BLF 90706 736-D3
17900 BLF 90706 766-D2
E WOODRUFF AV
- ARCD 91006 597-D2
W WOODRUFF AV
- ARCD 91007 597-A2
WOODRUFF DR
200 WAL 91789 639-F7
WOODRUFF LN
2400 ARCD 91007 597-C2
WOODRUFF PL
100 ARCD 91007 597-C2
14700 BLF 90706 736-D4
WOODRUFF WY
2500 ARCD 91007 597-D2
WOODS AV
400 FUL 92832 738-F7
700 ELA 90022 675-G1
12600 NRWK 90650 736-G1
N WOODS AV
100 FUL 92832 738-F7
1000 FUL 92835 738-F7
S WOODS AV
- MONP 90022 635-H5
100 ELA 90022 635-H7
100 FUL 92832 738-F7
700 ELA 90022 675-G2
2000 MONP 91754 635-H5
WOODS CT
- LHB 90631 738-B2
WOODS DR
1600 LA 90069 593-A4
WOODS PL
1400 ELA 90022 675-G2
WOODSHILL TR
8200 LA 90069 593-A5
WOODSHIRE DR
2700 LA 90068 593-F1
40900 PMDL 93551 4194-G2
WOODSIA CT
- PMDL 93551 4285-D3
WOODSIDE DR
4600 LA 90065 595-B4
28700 LACo 91390 4461-D4
WOODSIDE PARK DR
3600 WCOV 91792 679-J2
WOODSON ST
8100 LBCH 90808 766-J7
8100 HGDN 90716 766-J7
8300 LBCH 90808 767-A7
8300 LBCH 90716 767-A7
12500 HGDN 90716 767-A7
WOODSPRING CV
- BPK 90621 738-A6
WOODSPRING PL
900 DBAR 91765 680-E2
WOODSTEAD AV
10300 WHIT 90603 707-H5
WOODSTOCK AV
28000 Cstc 91384 4459-G6
WOODSTOCK CT
100 CLAR 91711 571-D6
WOODSTOCK LN
2500 BURB 91504 533-F4
WOODSTOCK RD
1300 SMRO 91108 596-B1
2500 LA 90046 593-A1
2600 OrCo 90720 796-G5
WOODSTONE LN
42200 LAN 93536 4104-F5
WOODSTONE PL
7100 CanP 91307 529-C5
WOODVALE CT
7000 CanP 91307 529-F5
WOODVALE RD
15500 Enc 91436 561-F5
WOODVIEW CT
2700 DBAR 91789 679-G6
WOODVIEW DR
- LA 90068 563-F7
WOODVILLE DR
11600 ELMN 91732 597-E7
WOODWARD AV
6000 MYWD 90270 675-D6
6200 BELL 90201 675-D7
6800 BELL 90201 705-D1
9900 Sunl 91040 503-H2
24500 LMTA 90717 793-H4
E WOODWARD AV
- ALH 91801 596-B4
W WOODWARD AV
- ALH 91801 596-A4
WOODWARD BLVD
400 LACo 91107 566-H6
700 ARCD 91007 566-H6
WOODWARDIA DR
2700 BelA 90077 592-A1
WOODWORTH AL
1900 PAS 91103 535-H7
WOODWORTH AV
10100 ING 90303 703-F5
WOODWORTH CT
100 LA 90012 634-G4
WOODWORTH PL
1600 SFER 91342 481-J7
WOODWORTH ST
600 SFER 91340 502-A1
1200 SFER 91340 481-J7
1200 SFER 91340 501-J1
WOODY TR
6800 LA 90068 593-D1
WOOLFORD ST
11100 CULC 90230 672-G5
WOOLLEY ST
9000 TEML 91780 596-J1
9600 TEML 91780 597-A1
WOOLSEY LN
2100 WCOV 91792 638-H5
WOOLSEY RD
13600 LACo 91390 (4372-J7 See Page 4281)
WOOLSEY CANYON RD
23700 LA 91304 499-D7
23900 WHil 91304 499-D7
24900 VeCo 93063 499-B7
WOOLWINE DR
3600 City 90063 635-D3
WOOSTER AV
5800 LadH 90056 672-J6
S WOOSTER ST
800 LA 90035 632-J3
WORCESTER AV
700 PAS 91104 565-J3
WORDSWORTH LN
25600 StvR 91381 4550-C6
WORK ST
500 MTBL 90640 676-B3
WORKMAN AV
400 ARCD 91007 597-A3
9200 TEML 91780 596-J3
9600 TEML 91780 597-A3
E WORKMAN AV
100 COV 91723 599-B7
200 WCOV 91791 598-H7
1000 WCOV 91790 598-H7
1900 WCOV 91791 599-B7
W WORKMAN AV
200 COV 91723 599-A7
1000 WCOV 91790 598-E7
2000 WCOV 91791 599-A7
E WORKMAN LN
500 COV 91723 599-C7
WORKMAN ST
500 COV 91723 599-C7
1700 LA 90031 635-A2
2400 LA 90031 595-A7
16200 LPUE 91744 638-E7
E WORKMAN ST
15800 LPUE 91744 638-D7
N WORKMAN ST
200 SFER 91340 482-B5
S WORKMAN ST
- SFER 91340 482-A7
500 SFER 91340 481-J7
800 LA 91340 481-J7
WORKMAN MILL RD
100 INDS 91746 637-E6
100 LACo 91746 637-E6
500 LACo 90601 637-E6
2200 INDS 90601 637-E6
3400 LACo 90601 677-A2
5000 WHIT 90601 677-A2
WORLD WY
200 Wch 90045 702-F5
WORLD WY N
- Wch 90045 702-F5
WORLD WY S
400 Wch 90045 702-G5
WORLD WY W
7100 Wch 90045 702-D5
7700 PdlR 90293 702-D5
WORMWOOD DR
2200 HacH 91745 678-F5
WORNOM AV
9600 Sunl 91040 503-C5
WORSHAM AV
- LBCH 90808 765-J7
WORSHAM DR
6700 WHIT 90601 677-E6
6700 WHIT 90608 677-E6
WORTH AV
2300 LHB 90631 708-B5
WORTH ST
4300 LA 90063 635-D2
4500 City 90063 635-D2
4700 LA 90032 635-D2
WORTHEN AV
2900 LA 90039 594-F3
WORTHING LN
2200 BelA 90077 591-G3
WORTHINGTON DR
8600 TEML 91775 596-G2
WORTHINGTON ST
800 BREA 92821 708-H5
N WORTHY DR
100 GLDR 91741 569-G4
S WORTHY DR
100 GLDR 91741 569-G6
WORTSER AV
4400 LA 91604 562-D4
4600 Shrm 91423 562-D3
5300 VanN 91401 562-D2
7000 NHol 91605 532-D2
WOTKYNS DR
1100 PAS 91103 565-F2
WRANGELL LN
- SCTA 91387 4462-H6
N WRANGLER LN
- VeCo 91307 529-B3
WRANGLER RD
- RHLS 90274 823-D3

STREET Block	City	ZIP	Pg-Grid
WRANGLER WY			
400	WAL	91789	639-F7
WREDE WY			
600	WCOV	91791	639-D2
WREN AV			
1800	LACo	91744	638-H3
WREN CT			
-	LVRN	91750	570-J5
WREN DR			
-	LACo	91387	4551-J5
-	LACo	91387	4552-A5
400	LA	90065	595-A3
WREN WY			
900	WCOV	91790	638-F2
2000	FUL	92833	738-C4
WRENCH CT			
5300	LKWD	90712	765-H3
WREN CREST DR			
22900	CALB	91302	559-G6
WRIGHT AV			
700	PAS	91104	566-A3
1700	LVRN	91750	600-F4
12700	CHNO	91710	641-F7
WRIGHT CT			
2000	POM	91766	640-D3
WRIGHT PL			
4800	SGAT	90280	705-E3
18700	ART	90701	766-G2
WRIGHT RD			
5300	LYN	90262	735-E1
10000	SGAT	90280	705-E6
10900	LYN	90262	705-E7
14400	LACo	91390	4462-F1
S WRIGHT RD			
12500	LYN	90262	735-D3
12500	COMP	90221	735-D3
12600	LYN	90221	735-D3
WRIGHT ST			
1400	LA	90015	634-C5
1700	POM	91766	640-E3
WRIGHT TER			
6000	CULC	90232	672-J2
WRIGHT WY			
1100	INDS	91748	679-D4
WRIGHTCREST DR			
5800	CULC	90232	673-A2
5900	CULC	90232	672-J2
WRIGHT MOUNTAIN RD			
-	SBdC	-	(4652-F2
	See Page	4651)	
-	SBdC	92397	(4652-F2
	See Page	4651)	
WRIGHTVIEW DR			
3400	LA	91604	562-J7
WRIGHTVIEW PL			
3300	LA	91604	562-J7
WRIGHTWICK DR			
-	CRTS	90703	767-B3
WRIGHTWOOD CT			
3500	LA	91604	563-A7
WRIGHTWOOD DR			
100	LHB	90631	738-D2
3200	LA	91604	562-J7
3200	LA	91604	563-A6
WRIGHTWOOD LN			
10700	LA	90068	563-A7
10700	LA	91604	563-A7
WRIGHTWOOD PL			
11000	LA	91604	563-A6
WRIGHTWOOD WY			
3700	PMDL	93550	4286-H2
4500	PMDL	93552	4286-H2
4500	PMDL	93552	4287-A2
WRIGLEY RD			
-	AVA	90704	5923-H4
WYANDOTTE ST			
10700	SunV	91352	533-A4
11100	SunV	91352	532-H4
11500	NHol	91605	532-C4
13500	VanN	91405	532-A4
14500	VanN	91405	531-J4
15300	VanN	91406	531-B4
17700	Res	91335	531-A4
18100	Res	91335	530-F4
20200	Win	91306	530-C4
20900	CanP	91303	530-A5
22000	CanP	91303	529-J5
22700	CanP	91307	529-G5
WYANT LN			
14100	WHIT	90602	707-E1
WYATT LN			
-	StvR	91381	4549-J7
-	StvR	91381	4550-A7
WYBRO WY			
1400	City	90063	635-F3
WYCHOFF AV			
1600	SIMI	93063	499-A3
WYCKERSHAM PL			
2700	FUL	92833	738-B5
N WYCLIFF AV			
200	LA	90275	823-H4
200	LA	90732	823-H4
29600	RPV	90275	823-H4
S WYCLIFF AV			
900	LA	90732	823-H5
WYCLIFF PL			
1600	LA	90732	823-H6
WYETH DR			
11800	CRTS	90703	766-H2
W WYLAND WY			
100	MNRO	91016	597-G1
WYLIE LN			
1300	RBCH	90278	762-H1
N WYLIE LN			
1100	RBCH	90278	762-H1
WYMAN AV			
400	ELA	90022	635-G7
E WYMORE ST			
3700	RDom	90221	735-C6
WYN TER			
20200	LACo	91789	679-F4
WYNCREST WY			
4400	LCF	91011	534-J3
WYNDALE PL			
200	GLDL	91206	565-A4
WYNDHAM RD			
8200	LA	90046	592-J3
WYNFREED LN			
-	Nor	91326	480-D6
WYNGATE ST			
-	PMDL	93551	4194-J3
7000	Tuj	91042	504-A3
7600	Tuj	91042	503-J3
7900	Sunl	91040	503-F3
WYNGLEN LN			
2700	LA	90023	635-A7
WYNKOOP ST			
6400	Wch	90045	702-F1
WYNN CT			
300	THO	91362	557-A1
WYNN RD			
1200	PAS	91107	566-G1
WYNNE AV			
6200	Res	91335	530-J2
6300	Res	91335	531-A7
8200	Nor	91325	530-J2
WYNNEWOOD DR			
900	DBAR	91765	680-D2
WYNOLA ST			
400	PacP	90272	630-J6
WYNWOOD GRN			
1200	LA	90023	635-A7
WYNWOOD LN			
2700	LA	90023	635-A7
3000	LA	90023	675-B1
WYOMING AV			
2600	BURB	91505	533-D7
11500	WLA	90025	631-J5
11500	WLA	90025	632-A5
WYOMING ST			
200	PAS	91103	535-G7
WYSE RD			
33600	LACo	91390	4373-H2
WYSTERIA DR			
6100	VeCo	93063	499-B4
WYSTONE AV			
6400	Res	91335	530-G4
8300	Nor	91324	530-G2
9100	Nor	91324	500-G4
10300	Nor	91326	500-G2
WYTON DR			
-	LA	90095	632-B1
10300	Wwd	90024	632-B1
X			
XEROX CENTRE DR			
2000	ELSG	90245	732-H1
XIMENO AV			
-	LBCH	90803	826-A1
300	LBCH	90814	796-A7
300	LBCH	90814	826-A1
700	LBCH	90804	796-A5
1700	LBCH	90815	796-A4
XIMENO DR			
200	FUL	92835	738-H1
XIMENO WY			
1700	LBCH	90804	796-A5
Y			
YACHT ST			
300	Wilm	90744	824-F1
YACHT CLUB WY			
-	RBCH	90277	762-G4
YACHT HARBOR DR			
4100	RPV	90275	823-C5
YAEGER LN			
-	FUL	92833	738-D5
YAFFA ST			
43500	LAN	93535	4106-B2
YAGER WY			
3300	WLKV	91361	557-B7
YAHUALICA PL			
-	HNTP	90255	705-B1
YALE AV			
2900	LA	90292	672-A6
N YALE AV			
100	CLAR	91711	601-D2
100	FUL	92831	738-J6
S YALE AV			
100	FUL	92831	738-J7
YALE CIR			
300	SLB	90740	796-G6
YALE CT			
-	CYP	90630	767-F7
800	SMCA	90403	631-G5
1300	SMCA	90404	631-G6
43200	LAN	93536	4105-C3
YALE DR			
-	BPK	90620	767-F6
1100	GLDL	91205	564-G7
20100	WAL	91789	639-F4
YALE LN			
100	SLB	90740	796-G6
YALE ST			
-	PAS	91103	565-H3
700	LA	90012	634-G2
800	SMCA	90403	631-G5
1200	SMCA	90404	631-G5
5200	MTCL	91763	601-F5
W YALE ST			
900	ONT	91762	601-J5
YALETON AV			
4000	LACo	91722	598-F5
N YALETON AV			
100	WCOV	91790	598-F6
YANCEY LN			
41400	LACo	93536	4104-H7
YANKEE DR			
4000	AGRH	91301	558-E7
YANKEY ST			
7400	DWNY	90242	705-H5
YANKTON AV			
3300	CLAR	91711	571-E6
YARBOUGH DR			
-	FUL	92833	738-C5
YARDLEY WY			
-	SCTA	91354	4460-G6
YARMOUTH AV			
4700	Enc	91316	561-B1
6100	Enc	91316	531-B7
6300	Res	91335	531-B3
8200	Nor	91325	531-B3
10400	GrnH	91344	501-A1
YARMOUTH RD			
300	PVE	90274	792-E7
YARNELL ST			
1300	WCOV	91790	638-D2
15800	LA	91342	481-F1
W YARNELL ST			
1900	WCOV	91790	638-C1
YARROW CT			
-	PMDL	93551	4285-D3
YARROW DR			
900	LAN	93534	4015-G3
YARROW ST			
8200	LACo	91770	636-F4
YATES AV			
1500	CMRC	90022	676-B2
2000	CMRC	90040	676-A5
2000	MTBL	90640	676-B2
YATES ST			
7600	Tuj	91042	503-H4
8000	Sunl	91040	503-F4
YAVAPAI TR			
-	Ago	91301	588-A5
YAWL			
3600	LBCH	90810	765-A7
YAWL ST			
-	LA	90292	701-J2
YBARRA DR			
1500	RowH	91748	679-D5
YBARRA RD			
21700	WdHl	91364	560-A4
22000	WdHl	91364	559-J4
YEAGER AV			
1500	LVRN	91750	600-F3
YEAGER PL			
6800	LA	90068	593-D3
YEAGER WY			
-	BELL	90201	675-F4
YEARLING CIR			
11400	CRTS	90703	766-G3
YEARLING DR			
-	Actn	93510	4374-J7
YEARLING PL			
12200	CRTS	90703	766-J3
YEARLING ST			
2500	LKWD	90712	765-G3
5700	LKWD	90713	766-C3
11200	CRTS	90703	766-F3
YELLOWBLUFF PL			
18600	RowH	91748	679-B7
YELLOW BOOT LN			
-	CRSN	90745	794-G1
YELLOW BRICK RD			
3100	RPV	90275	793-A4
YELLOWBRICK RD			
20400	DBAR	91789	679-F3
YELLOWBROOK LN			
15500	LMRD	90638	737-H1
YELLOW FEATHER CIR			
20700	WAL	91789	639-G5
YELLOW HILL RD			
12000	VeCo	90265	625-G1
YELLOWSTONE DR			
1000	SBdC	92397	(4652-C1
	See Page	4651)	
YELLOWSTONE LN			
-	LACo	91387	4462-H7
-	SCTA	91387	4462-H7
YELLOWSTONE ST			
4300	LA	90032	635-D1
39200	PMDL	93551	4195-E6
YELLOWTAIL DR			
2900	OrCo	90720	796-H6
YELLOWWOOD DR			
2600	WLKV	91361	557-A7
2600	WLKV	91361	587-A1
YELLOWWOOD WY			
-	CRSN	90746	764-F1
YERBA ST			
12900	NHol	91605	532-D3
YERBA BUENA RD			
8400	VeCo	90265	586-A3
12600	VeCo	90265	625-F2
YERBA BUENA TKTR			
-	LACo	91342	(4723-E5
	See Page	4643)	
YERBA SECA AV			
6200	AGRH	91301	558-B3
YERMO PL			
1500	FUL	92833	738-D4
YERMO ST			
15600	WHIT	90603	707-H5
YEW CT			
-	Nor	91326	480-E5
YEW ST			
42800	LAN	93536	4105-B2
YNEZ AV			
900	RBCH	90277	763-A7
N YNEZ AV			
100	MONP	91754	636-B2
S YNEZ AV			
100	MONP	91754	636-B2
YNEZ CT			
3100	WCOV	91792	678-J1
YOAKUM DR			
9600	LA	90210	592-C3
YOAKUM ST			
900	LA	90032	595-E5
YOCUM ST			
1100	PAS	91103	565-E1
YODER AV			
3600	LACo	90601	677-A2
YOJOA PL			
2800	HacH	91745	678-B5
YOLANDA AV			
5100	Tarz	91356	560-H1
6100	Res	91335	530-H3
8200	Nor	91324	530-H1
8800	Nor	91324	500-H6
9300	KeCo	93560	3833-G2
10400	Nor	91326	500-G1
YOLANDA CT			
1800	WCOV	91792	678-J1
1800	WCOV	91792	679-A1
YOLIE LN			
19300	Tarz	91356	560-G1
YOLO ST			
1000	PAS	91106	566-B4
YORBA AV			
11300	SBdC	91710	641-F4
11600	CHNO	91710	641-F5
YORBA DR			
1700	POM	91768	600-H5
YORBA ST			
3500	LA	90032	595-D6
YORBITA RD			
200	LACo	91744	679-A1
YORK AV			
1200	GLDR	91740	599-G1
7700	WHIT	90602	677-E7
11400	HAW	90250	703-D7
11800	HAW	90250	733-D1
YORK BLVD			
1000	HiPk	90042	595-B1
1000	SPAS	91030	595-B1
3600	GLDL	91205	564-G7
3600	LA	90065	564-G7
3700	LA	90065	594-H1
4200	Eagl	90041	594-J1
4500	Eagl	90041	595-B1
YORK CIR			
3500	LVRN	91750	600-G1
8600	LPMA	90623	767-C5
YORK DR			
19100	Nor	91324	500-G7
YORK PL			
100	CLAR	91711	601-C4
3000	LA	90065	594-G1
45500	LAN	93534	4015-F3
YORKFIELD CT			
4400	WLKV	91361	557-D6
YORK HILL PL			
4000	Eagl	90041	564-J7
4000	Eagl	90041	594-J1
YORKSBORO LN			
20600	WdHl	91364	560-C4
YORKSHIRE AV			
1800	SMCA	90404	631-H7
1900	SMCA	90404	671-J1
YORKSHIRE CIR			
8000	LPMA	90623	767-C4
YORKSHIRE CT			
1600	SDMS	91773	599-H4
YORKSHIRE DR			
2300	LA	90065	594-H3
5000	CYP	90630	767-C7
37400	PMDL	93550	4286-E3
E YORKSHIRE DR			
-	ARCD	91006	567-C2
YORKSHIRE LN			
1400	LHB	90631	738-F1
YORKSHIRE RD			
2700	PAS	91107	566-F5
3200	LACo	91107	566-G5
YORKSHIRE WY			
2300	POM	91767	601-A4
3000	RowH	91748	708-J1
YORKTOWN AV			
800	MTBL	90640	636-D7
7800	Wch	90045	702-H2
YORKTOWN CIR			
-	LPMA	90623	767-D4
YORKTOWN CT			
4900	CHNO	91710	641-F4
YORKTOWN PL			
7800	Wch	90045	702-H1
YOSEMITE AV			
1500	SIMI	93063	499-A2
YOSEMITE CIR			
19700	Nor	91326	500-E1
YOSEMITE CT			
900	SDMS	91773	570-E5
YOSEMITE DR			
1100	Eagl	90041	565-A6
2200	Eagl	90041	564-J6
4500	MTCL	91763	641-E1
6500	BPK	90620	767-F7
30400	Cstc	91384	4459-G2
YOSEMITE PL			
-	SCTA	91354	4550-H1
YOSEMITE ST			
12500	CRTS	90703	736-J7
12500	CRTS	90703	737-A7
YOSEMITE WY			
-	WCOV	91791	639-A4
3900	LA	90065	594-H1
4200	LA	90065	564-H7
4400	Eagl	90041	564-J6
YOUNAN DR			
-	Chat	91311	499-H1
YOUNG AV			
7700	LACo	91770	636-E3
YOUNG CT			
300	POM	91766	640-J5
YOUNG DR			
4400	LCF	91011	534-H2
4400	Mont	91020	534-H2
9900	BHLS	90212	632-E3
E YOUNG ST			
600	Wilm	90744	794-F5
W YOUNG ST			
1100	Wilm	90744	794-C6
YOUNGBERRY DR			
27900	SCTA	91350	4461-B5
YOUNGBLOOD PL			
43600	LAN	93534	4105-F2
YOUNGDALE AV			
11900	LA	91342	481-H6
YOUNGDALE PL			
14900	LA	91342	481-H6
YOUNGDALE RD			
8200	LACo	91775	596-F1
E YOUNGDALE ST			
8700	LACo	91775	596-G1
YOUNGER DR			
6800	BPK	90620	767-G5
YOUNGS CANYON RD			
-	Actn	93510	4374-E7
-	Actn	93510	4464-D1
YOUNGWOOD DR			
15200	WHIT	90605	707-H3
15400	WHIT	90603	707-H3
YOUNGWORTH RD			
10600	CULC	90230	672-H4
YOUNGWORTH ST			
11300	LA	90230	672-F4
YOUTH WY			
2000	FUL	92835	738-G4
YSABEL ST			
1100	RBCH	90277	763-A6
YSIDRO PL			
16000	PacP	90272	630-J6
YUBA LN			
800	CLAR	91711	571-E5
YUBA RD			
10900	SBdC	92371	(4472-J3
	See Page	4471)	
YUCATAN AV			
21500	WdHl	91364	560-B4
YUCATAN PL			
2900	DBAR	91765	679-J7
13300	CRTS	90703	737-C7
YUCATAN RD			
11700	SBdC	92371	(4472-G1
	See Page	4471)	
YUCCA AV			
1900	FUL	92835	738-F4
44000	LAN	93534	4015-H5
YUCCA CIR			
4800	LVRN	91750	570-G6
YUCCA LN			
-	THO	91362	557-A3
2200	Alta	91001	535-F6
N YUCCA LN			
2100	Alta	91001	535-E6
2100	PAS	91103	535-E6
YUCCA PL			
1200	GLDR	91740	599-H1
27900	Cstc	91384	4459-G2
YUCCA RD			
100	SBdC	92372	(4472-A5
	See Page	4471)	
YUCCA ST			
700	ELSG	90245	702-D7
5900	Hlwd	90028	593-E4
7100	BPK	90621	767-G1
YUCCA TR			
400	SMAD	91024	537-B7
8200	LA	90046	593-A4
8200	LA	90046	592-J4
YUCCA CIRCLE DR			
23000	Llan	93544	4471-B5
YUCCA HILLS RD			
9000	LACo	91390	4373-H4
YUCCA RIDGE RD			
7400	GLDR	91741	569-B4
7400	LACo	91741	569-B4
YUCCA SPRINGS ST			
-	LACo	93591	4199-J3
YUCCA TERRACE DR			
2900	SBdC	92371	(4472-G5
	See Page	4471)	
YUCCA TREE ST			
38400	PMDL	93551	4195-G7
38400	PMDL	93551	4285-G1
38500	LACo	93551	4195-G7
YUCCA VALLEY RD			
25600	SCTA	91355	4550-F7
YUKON AV			
10000	ING	90303	703-E6
12500	HAW	90250	733-E1
13200	LACo	90250	733-E1
15200	LACo	90260	733-E5
16600	TOR	90504	733-F7
17200	TOR	90504	763-F2
YUKON TR			
8400	LA	91304	529-C2
YUMA CT			
700	SDMS	91773	600-C1
41800	PMDL	93551	4104-C6
YUMA PL			
8200	LA	90046	593-A3
YUMA WY			
2100	FUL	92835	738-F3
YVETTE AV			
16900	CRTS	90703	737-A7
YVETTE DR			
13600	LACo	90601	637-G5
YVETTE LN			
23100	SCTA	91355	4550-H7
YVETTE WY			
16600	CRTS	90703	737-A6
YVONNE AV			
5200	LACo	91776	596-G4
YVONNE ST			
1700	WCOV	91792	678-J1
1900	WCOV	91792	679-A1
Z			
ZACA PL			
4300	LA	90065	564-H7
ZACHARY CT			
1500	BREA	92821	708-H6
ZACHARY PADILLA AV			
100	AZU	91702	568-G7
ZACHARY TAYLOR WY			
-	PMDL	93550	4286-C4
ZACHAU PL			
7300	Tuj	91042	503-J2
7300	Tuj	91042	504-A2
ZADDISON CT			
-	SCTA	91350	4551-D6
ZADELL AV			
5300	TEML	91780	597-B4
ZAKON RD			
4800	TOR	90505	793-B1
ZALTANA ST			
22500	Chat	91311	499-H1
ZALVIDEA ST			
400	Echo	90026	634-D1
ZAMARA ST			
-	AZU	91702	568-G7
-	AZU	91702	598-G1
ZAMBRANO ST			
4900	CMRC	90040	675-H6
ZAMORA AV			
7900	Flor	90001	704-F2
8600	Wats	90002	704-F3
10400	Wats	90002	704-F5
11200	LA	90059	704-F6
13900	Wbrk	90222	734-F3
E ZAMORA AV			
10500	Wats	90002	704-F5
W ZAMORA AV			
10400	Wats	90002	704-F5
ZAMORA ST			
4100	LA	90011	674-F3
ZAMPERINI WY			
25300	TOR	90505	793-E4
N ZANDIA AV			
2100	LBCH	90815	796-A3
ZANE ST			
-	NLB	90805	765-C3
4500	LA	90032	595-D6
ZANE GREY TER			
2800	Alta	91001	536-B4
ZANJA ST			
400	PAS	91103	565-F1
12700	CULC	90066	672-B5
12700	LA	90066	672-B5
13300	Ven	90291	672-A5
13300	Ven	90291	672-A5
ZARA ST			
1500	GLDR	91741	569-H6
ZARING ST			
800	MONP	91754	635-J6
4100	City	90063	635-E6
ZASTROW AV			
14700	BLF	90706	736-C4
ZAYANTA DR			
7800	PdlR	90293	702-C2
ZEDLER RANCH RD			
100	Top	90290	590-A7
ZEILER AV			
8400	PanC	91402	532-C1
8800	Pcma	91331	502-B7
8800	Pcma	91331	532-C1
ZELDA WY			
9200	Chat	91311	499-G7
ZELDINS WY			
-	Brwd	90049	591-F1
ZELLA PL			
4800	LA	90032	635-E1
ZELZAH AV			
4700	Enc	91316	561-A1
6100	Enc	91316	531-A7
6400	Res	91335	531-A2
8200	Nor	91325	531-A1
8700	Nor	91325	501-A7
9100	Nor	91330	501-A6
10300	Nor	91326	501-A3
10300	GrnH	91344	501-A1
11500	GrnH	91344	481-A7
12000	GrnH	91344	480-J6
ZELZAH FIRE RD			
-	Enc	91316	561-A7
-	Enc	91316	591-A1
-	PacP	90272	591-A1
ZENITH AV			
100	LACo	91744	638-H7
100	LACo	91744	678-H1
ZENITH POINT RD			
30000	MAL	90265	627-C7
ZENO DR			
400	VeCo	91377	557-G3
ZENO PL			
2100	Ven	90291	671-J6
ZEPHYR AV			
26200	Hrbr	90710	793-J6
ZEPHYR CT			
-	PMDL	93550	4286-D5
-	Ven	90291	671-G6
ZERELDA ST			
8600	RSMD	91770	596-G5
ZERMATT DR			
5400	SBdC	92397	(4652-F3
	See Page	4651)	
ZERMATT LN			
24400	SCTA	91355	4550-E6
ZERR CT			
200	GLDL	91206	564-G4
ZEUS			
1300	WCOV	91790	638-D2
ZEUS AV			
11000	NRWK	90650	706-H6
12300	NRWK	90650	736-H1
ZEUS DR			
7900	LA	90046	593-A2
ZEUS LN			
-	SCTA	91351	4551-H2
ZEV DR			
-	LACo	91387	4551-J4
ZIEBELL ST			
-	FUL	92833	738-D4
ZIMMERMAN PL			
20100	LACo	91390	4461-D4
ZINDELL AV			
6300	CMRC	90040	676-B7
ZINFANDEL DR			
-	PMDL	93551	4104-E7
ZINNEY RD			
35400	Litl	93543	4377-F1
ZINNIA CT			
14700	SCTA	91387	4462-G4
ZINNIA LN			
500	GLDL	91205	564-H6
ZINNIA ST			
1200	UPL	91784	571-J3
36800	PMDL	93550	4286-D4
ZION CT			
27800	Cstc	91384	4459-G3
ZION LN			
-	LACo	91775	566-H7
ZION CANYON WY			
800	BREA	92821	709-C5
ZITOLA TER			
8100	PdlR	90293	702-B3
ZITOLA WK			
-	PdlR	90293	702-B3
ZITTO LN			
9900	Tuj	91042	504-C5
ZOE AV			
2000	HNTP	90255	674-H7
2800	HNTP	90255	675-A7
ZOE ANNE WY			
5000	GLDL	91214	504-D5
ZOLA AV			
4100	PRV	90660	676-G1
ZOLA ST			
17300	GrnH	91344	481-B5
ZOLTAN ST			
1600	LAN	93535	4106-C1
ZOMBAR AV			
7300	VanN	91406	531-H3
N ZONA CT			
400	LBCH	90802	795-F7
ZONAL AV			
1800	Boyl	90033	635-A2
ZOO DR			
4400	LFlz	90027	564-A4
4900	LFlz	90027	563-H4
N ZOO DR			
-	LFlz	90027	564-B4
ZOO BYPASS TR			
-	LFlz	90027	563-J4
-	LFlz	90027	564-A4
ZOOK DR			
900	GLDL	91202	564-B3
ZORADA CT			
2300	LA	90046	593-B2
ZORADA DR			
2400	LA	90046	593-B2
ZORANA PL			
100	LA	90732	823-H4
ZORILLO PL			
1900	PVE	90274	792-G7
ZORRO WY			
10700	LACo	91390	4373-E4
ZUMA BAY WY			
29500	MAL	90265	667-D3
ZUMA BEACH ACCESS RD			
29600	MAL	90265	667-A1
ZUMA MESA DR			
6300	MAL	90265	667-F2
ZUMA RIDGE MTWY			
-	LACo	90265	587-A6
-	LACo	90265	627-A1
-	MAL	90265	627-C6
ZUMA RIDGE FIRE RD			
4000	LACo	90265	587-B5
ZUMA VIEW PL			
6500	MAL	90265	667-F2
ZUMIREZ DR			
5800	MAL	90265	627-F7
5800	MAL	90265	667-F1
ZUNI LN			
-	CRSN	90745	794-G1
ZUNI ST			
21700	Top	90290	560-A6
21700	WdHl	91364	560-A6
ZUNIGA LN			
1500	Boyl	90033	635-C3
ZUNIGA RD			
23300	Top	90290	589-F3
ZURICH CT			
2300	SBdC	92397	(4652-F3
	See Page	4651)	
ZURICH DR			
5300	SBdC	92397	(4652-F3
	See Page	4651)	
#			
1ST AV			
-	SLB	90740	826-G3
3600	GLDL	91214	504-D6
10500	WHIT	90603	708-A5
11300	LACo	90604	708-A7
11600	LYN	90262	735-D1
12100	LACo	90604	738-A1
12600	LMRD	90638	738-A1
E 1ST AV			
100	LHB	90631	708-E6
N 1ST AV			
-	ARCD	91006	567-D4
100	COV	91723	599-C4
900	COV	91722	599-C4
S 1ST AV			
-	ARCD	91006	567-D6
100	COV	91723	599-C5
1400	ARCD	91006	597-D1
10200	ING	90303	703-G5
W 1ST AV			
100	LHB	90631	708-E6
1ST AV E			
-	Hrbr	90710	794-B4
1ST AV W			
-	Hrbr	90710	794-A4
1ST CT			
100	HMB	90254	762-G3
500	SMCA	90402	671-C1
800	SMCA	90403	671-D1
1ST PL			
100	MANB	90266	732-F7
600	HMB	90254	762-H3
S 1ST PL			
-	LBCH	90802	825-E1
1ST ST			
-	BELL	90201	675-F5
-	LACo	90220	765-C3
-	LBCH	90810	794-J4
-	NLB	90805	765-C3
-	HMB	90254	762-G3
-	LACo	91342	482-F6
100	HMB	90254	732-F7
100	SLB	90740	826-D4
100	MANB	90266	732-F7
900	SFER	91340	482-A6
1100	MONP	91754	635-H5
1400	DUAR	91010	568-B5
1500	LVRN	91750	600-F3
2000	Wilm	90744	794-J4
2100	LA	90810	794-J4
8000	PRM	90723	735-H4
15500	IRW	91706	568-E7
31700	Actn	93510	4465-A2
E 1ST ST			
100	AZU	91702	568-J7
100	CLAR	91711	601-D3
100	LA	90012	634-H4
100	LBCH	90802	825-E1
100	POM	91766	640-J2
100	SDMS	91773	600-C2
200	AZU	91702	569-A7
300	POM	91766	641-C1
1000	Boyl	90033	634-H4
1800	Boyl	90033	635-A5
2000	LBCH	90803	825-H1
3000	LA	90063	635-A5
3500	City	90063	635-D6
3900	LBCH	90803	826-A2
4000	MTCL	91763	641-C1
4300	ELA	90022	635-G6
4800	MONP	90022	635-G6
N 1ST ST			
-	ALH	91801	596-A3
100	BURB	91502	533-G7
100	LPUE	91744	638-D7
100	MTBL	90640	676-E1
S 1ST ST			
-	ALH	91801	596-B5
100	BURB	91502	533-H7
100	LPUE	91744	638-D7
100	LPUE	91744	678-D1
400	BURB	91502	563-H1
5700	VER	90058	674-H5
W 1ST ST			
100	AZU	91702	568-H7
100	CLAR	91711	601-C3
100	LA	90012	634-E3
100	LBCH	90802	825-D1
100	POM	91766	640-G2
100	SDMS	91773	600-B2
100	SPed	90731	824-B4
900	SPed	90731	824-B4
1100	LA	90732	824-B4
1100	LACo	90732	824-B4
1200	Echo	90026	634-E3
1200	LA	90732	823-H4
1600	IRW	91706	568-E7
1800	RPV	90732	823-H4
3300	LA	90004	634-A1
3800	LA	90004	633-F1
5400	LA	90036	633-C1
7900	LA	90048	633-A1
1ST ST W			
-	PMDL	93551	4285-J1
1ST TER			
700	SDMS	91773	600-A3
1ST ANITA DR			
12600	Brwd	90049	631-B3
1ST HELENA DR			
12300	Brwd	90049	631-G4
2ND AV			
100	LHB	90631	708-E6
1300	LA	90019	633-G6
1900	LA	90018	633-G6
3400	LA	90018	673-G1
3600	GLDL	91214	504-D6
3800	LA	90008	673-G3
4400	LA	90043	673-G5
11700	LYN	90262	735-D2
N 2ND AV			
100	ARCD	91006	567-D3
100	COV	91723	599-B5
1000	COV	91722	599-B3
S 2ND AV			
-	ARCD	91006	567-D6
100	COV	91723	599-B6
100	LACo	91746	637-H4
100	INDS	91746	637-H4
1500	ARCD	91006	597-D1
8000	ING	90305	703-G2
10000	ING	90303	703-G5
2ND AV E			
-	Hrbr	90710	794-B4
2ND AV W			
-	Hrbr	90710	794-A4
2ND CT			
800	SMCA	90403	671-D1
2ND PL			
100	MANB	90266	732-F7
200	LA	90012	634-F3
S 2ND PL			
-	LBCH	90802	825-F1
2ND ST			
-	BELL	90201	675-F5
-	LACo	90220	764-J2
-	NLB	90805	765-B3
-	PdlR	90293	702-C7
-	HMB	90254	762-G3
-	LACo	91342	482-F7
100	MANB	90266	732-F7
100	SLB	90740	826-E4
800	SMCA	90403	671-D1
1000	SFER	91340	482-A6
1100	SMCA	90401	671-D2
1500	DUAR	91010	568-B5
1500	LVRN	91750	600-F3
1700	TOR	90501	793-J2
1800	MANB	90266	733-A7
1900	RBCH	90278	732-H7
1900	RBCH	90278	733-A7
2300	LA	90810	794-J4
2300	SMCA	90405	671-F4
5300	IRW	91706	598-F2
5700	VER	90058	674-H5
5900	HNTP	90058	674-H5
5900	HNTP	90255	674-H5
7500	DWNY	90241	705-J4
7600	DWNY	90241	706-A4
8000	PRM	90723	735-H4
13000	CHNO	91710	641-F7
13800	WHIT	90605	707-E1
22200	SCTA	91321	4641-A2
31600	Actn	93510	4465-B3
E 2ND ST			
-	CLAR	91711	601-D3
100	AZU	91702	568-J7
100	LA	90012	634-G4
100	POM	91766	640-J2
100	SDMS	91773	600-C2
200	LBCH	90803	825-H1
300	POM	91766	641-A2
400	AZU	91702	569-A7
900	LBCH	90802	825-F1
1300	Boyl	90033	634-J4
1800	Boyl	90033	635-A4
1800	DUAR	91010	568-B5
2900	LA	90063	635-C6
3900	City	90063	635-E6
3900	LBCH	90803	826-B2
4300	ELA	90022	635-G6
N 2ND ST			
-	ALH	91801	596-A4
100	LPUE	91744	638-D7
100	MTBL	90640	676-E1
700	MTBL	90640	636-E7
S 2ND ST			
-	ALH	91801	596-B5
100	LPUE	91744	638-D7
100	LPUE	91744	678-D1
100	MTBL	90640	676-E2
1400	ALH	91803	596-B7
1800	ALH	91801	636-B1
1800	ALH	91803	636-B1
W 2ND ST			
100	AZU	91702	568-H7
100	CLAR	91711	601-D3
100	LA	90012	634-E3
100	POM	91766	640-F2
100	SDMS	91773	600-B2
100	SPed	90731	824-B4
900	SPed	90731	824-B4
1100	LA	90732	824-B4
1200	Echo	90026	634-D2
1200	LA	90732	823-J4
1900	LA	90057	634-B1
3200	LA	90004	634-A1
3700	LA	90004	633-E1
5400	LA	90036	633-D1
2ND ST E			
38400	PMDL	93550	4285-J1
38500	PMDL	93550	4195-J6
42400	LAN	93535	4105-J1
44000	LAN	93535	4015-J4
2ND TER			
-	LACo	91342	482-F6
700	SDMS	91773	600-A3
2ND ANITA DR			
12600	Brwd	90049	631-B3
2ND HELENA DR			
12300	Brwd	90049	631-G4
3RD AV			
300	Ven	90291	671-G5
500	LACo	91746	637-H6
700	LACo	90601	637-G6
800	LA	90005	633-G4
900	LA	90019	633-G4
1900	LA	90018	633-G6
3200	LA	90018	673-G1
3600	GLDL	91214	504-D6
3800	LA	90008	673-G3
4400	LA	90043	673-G5
7200	LA	90043	703-G1
11700	LYN	90262	735-D2
E 3RD AV			
500	LHB	90631	708-F6
N 3RD AV			
100	COV	91723	599-B5
S 3RD AV			
100	ARCD	91006	567-E7
100	COV	91723	599-B5
100	LACo	91746	637-H5
1500	ARCD	91006	597-E1
7600	ING	90305	703-G1
10200	ING	90303	703-G5
W 3RD AV			
500	LHB	90631	708-D6
3RD AV E			
-	Hrbr	90710	794-B3
3RD AV W			
-	Hrbr	90710	794-A3
3RD CT			
-	HMB	90254	762-G3
3RD PL			
100	MANB	90266	732-F7
E 3RD PL			
3500	LA	90063	635-C6
S 3RD PL			
-	LBCH	90802	825-F1
W 3RD PL			
500	LA	90013	634-F4
3RD ST			
-	AVA	90704	5923-H4
-	BELL	90201	675-F5
-	LACo	90220	764-J3
-	LACo	90220	765-A3
-	NLB	90805	765-B3
-	PdlR	90293	702-C7
-	SPed	90731	824-C1
-	TOR	90501	793-J2
-	HMB	90254	762-G3
-	LACo	91342	482-F6
100	MANB	90266	732-F7
100	SLB	90740	826-E4
200	POM	91766	641-D2
600	SFER	91340	482-B7
800	SMCA	90403	671-D1
1100	SMCA	90401	671-D1
1300	DUAR	91010	568-B5
1300	LVRN	91750	600-F3
1800	MANB	90266	733-A7
1900	SMCA	90405	671-F3
2300	LA	90810	794-J4
3100	Ven	90291	671-F3
4100	MTCL	91763	641-D2
5200	LBCH	90803	796-B7
5200	LBCH	90803	826-E4
5300	IRW	91706	598-F2

LOS ANGELES CO.

STREET Block	City	ZIP	Pg-Grid
3RD ST			
7400	DWNY	90241	705-J4
7600	DWNY	90241	706-A4
8000	PRM	90723	735-H4
12500	CHNO	91710	641-G7
22200	SCTA	91321	4641-A2
31700	Actn	93510	4465-B3
E 3RD ST			
100	AZU	91702	568-J7
100	LA	90013	634-G4
100	LBCH	90802	795-E7
100	POM	91766	640-J2
100	SDMS	91773	600-C2
100	LA	90012	634-G4
200	ELA	90022	635-G6
300	POM	91766	641-A2
400	AZU	91702	569-A7
1200	Boyl	90033	634-J5
1800	Boyl	90033	635-A5
2000	LBCH	90803	795-F7
2000	LBCH	90803	825-H1
2000	LBCH	90814	795-F7
2000	LBCH	90814	825-H1
3100	LA	90063	635-C6
3600	City	90063	635-E6
3900	LBCH	90803	826-A1
3900	LBCH	90814	826-A1
N 3RD ST			
-	ALH	91801	596-A4
100	BURB	91502	533-G6
100	LPUE	91744	638-D7
100	MTBL	90640	676-E1
100	MTBL	90640	676-E2
800	MTBL	90640	636-E7
900	BURB	91504	533-G6
S 3RD ST			
-	ALH	91801	596-B5
100	BURB	91502	533-H7
100	MTBL	90640	676-E2
1400	ALH	91803	596-B7
1800	ALH	91803	636-B1
W 3RD ST			
100	AZU	91702	568-G7
100	LA	90013	634-D3
100	LBCH	90802	795-C7
100	POM	91766	640-G2
100	SDMS	91773	600-B2
100	SPed	90731	824-B5
100	LA	90012	634-D3
600	LA	90071	634-D3
900	SPed	90731	824-B5
1000	LA	90017	634-D3
1100	LA	90732	824-B5
1100	LACo	90732	824-B5
1200	Echo	90026	634-D3
1200	LA	90732	823-J5
1300	LACo	90732	823-J5
1800	LA	90057	634-A1
3100	LA	90020	634-A1
3100	LA	90004	634-A1
3600	LA	90020	633-C1
3600	LA	90004	633-G1
5400	LA	90036	633-C1
7000	LA	90048	633-C1
8400	LA	90048	632-G1
9100	BHLS	90210	632-G1
3RD ST E			
37400	PMDL	93550	4286-A1
38400	PMDL	93550	4196-A5
41000	PMDL	93550	4195-J1
42000	LAN	93535	4106-A5
42400	LAN	93535	4105-J1
44000	LAN	93535	4015-J4
3RD ST W			
36500	LACo	93551	4285-J5
42000	LAN	93534	4105-H4
46800	LACo	93534	3925-H7
46800	LACo	93534	4015-H1
3RD TER			
-	LACo	91342	482-F6
3RD ANITA DR			
12600	Brwd	90049	631-B3
3RD HELENA DR			
12300	Brwd	90049	631-G4
3RD ST PROMENADE			
1200	SMCA	90401	671-D2
4TH AV			
100	LACo	91746	637-J5
300	Ven	90291	671-G4
900	LA	90019	633-G4
1900	LA	90018	633-G7
2400	LA	90018	673-G1
3600	GLDL	91214	504-D6
4100	LA	90008	673-G3
4400	LA	90043	673-G5
11700	LYN	90262	735-D1
E 4TH AV			
200	LHB	90631	708-F6
N 4TH AV			
100	COV	91723	599-A4
300	ARCD	91006	567-E4
S 4TH AV			
100	COV	91723	599-B5
900	ARCD	91006	567-E7
1500	ARCD	91006	597-E1
8200	ING	90305	703-G2
10200	ING	90303	703-G5
W 4TH AV			
500	LHB	90631	708-D6
4TH AV E			
-	Hrbr	90710	794-B3
4TH AV W			
-	Hrbr	90710	794-A3
4TH CT			
-	HMB	90254	762-G3
1000	SMCA	90403	671-D1
1900	SMCA	90405	671-F3
4TH PL			
100	MANB	90266	732-F7
7400	DWNY	90241	705-J3
7600	DWNY	90241	706-A4
E 4TH PL			
700	LA	90012	634-H5
700	LA	90013	634-H5
S 4TH PL			
-	LBCH	90802	825-F1
4TH ST			
-	LACo	90220	764-J3
-	PdlR	90293	702-C7
-	HMB	90254	762-G3
-	LACo	91342	482-F6
100	MANB	90266	732-F7
100	SLB	90740	826-E4
200	SMCA	90402	631-C7
400	SMCA	90402	671-D1
500	SFER	91340	482-A6
500	SFER	91340	502-C1
800	SMCA	90403	671-D1
1100	SMCA	90401	671-E2
1900	SMCA	90405	671-F3
2000	LA	91342	482-A6
3100	Ven	90291	671-F3
4900	IRW	91706	598-E2
5400	NLB	90805	765-B3
7700	BPK	90621	737-H7
7800	DWNY	90241	706-A4
8200	BPK	90621	738-A7
12900	CHNO	91710	641-G7
22200	SCTA	91321	4641-A1
E 4TH ST			
-	CLAR	91711	601-D3
100	AZU	91702	568-J6
100	LA	90013	634-G4
100	POM	91766	640-J2
100	SDMS	91773	600-C1
300	LBCH	90802	795-F7
300	POM	91766	641-A2
400	AZU	91702	569-A6
1300	Boyl	90033	634-H5
1800	Boyl	90033	635-B5
2000	LBCH	90814	795-F7
3000	LA	90063	635-B5
3600	City	90063	635-D6
3900	LBCH	90814	796-A7
4300	ELA	90022	635-F6
N 4TH ST			
-	ALH	91801	596-A4
100	MTBL	90640	676-E2
700	MTBL	90640	636-E7
S 4TH ST			
-	ALH	91801	596-B5
100	MTBL	90640	676-E3
1400	ALH	91803	596-B7
1800	ALH	91803	636-B1
W 4TH ST			
100	AZU	91702	568-G6
100	CLAR	91711	601-D3
100	LA	90013	634-F4
100	LBCH	90802	795-D7
100	POM	91766	640-H2
100	SDMS	91773	600-B2
400	SPed	90731	824-B5
600	LA	90071	634-E3
1000	ONT	91762	601-J6
1100	LA	90017	634-D3
1300	LACo	90732	823-J5
1800	LA	90057	634-C2
3000	LA	90020	634-A2
3600	LA	90020	633-E2
5400	LA	90036	633-D2
7900	LA	90048	633-A1
8400	LA	90048	632-J1
4TH ST E			
37500	PMDL	93550	4286-A3
38400	PMDL	93550	4196-A6
42000	LAN	93535	4106-A1
44000	LAN	93535	4016-A4
4TH ST W			
-	LAN	93534	4105-H6
47000	LACo	93534	3925-H7
4TH TER			
-	LACo	91342	482-F6
4TH ANITA DR			
12600	Brwd	90049	631-B3
4TH HELENA DR			
12300	Brwd	90049	631-G4
5TH AV			
100	LACo	91746	637-J5
100	LACo	91746	638-A5
100	INDS	91746	638-A5
200	Ven	90291	671-G4
700	INDS	91746	637-J6
800	LA	90005	633-G4
900	LA	90019	633-G4
1900	LA	90018	633-G6
3400	LA	90018	673-G1
3600	GLDL	91214	504-D7
4100	LA	90008	673-G3
4400	LA	90043	673-G5
7200	LA	90043	703-G1
N 5TH AV			
-	ARCD	91006	567-E4
100	MNRO	91016	567-E4
500	COV	91723	599-A4
S 5TH AV			
-	LA	90043	703-G2
-	LA	90305	703-G2
-	ARCD	91006	567-E6
100	COV	91723	599-A5
900	MNRO	91016	567-E6
1300	ARCD	91006	597-E2
7600	ING	90305	703-G2
7600	ING	90043	703-G2
10000	ING	90303	703-G5
W 5TH AV			
700	LHB	90631	708-D6
5TH AV E			
-	Hrbr	90710	794-B3
5TH AV W			
-	Hrbr	90710	794-A3
5TH AVCT			
300	MNRO	91016	567-E4
5TH CT			
-	HMB	90254	762-G3
900	SMCA	90403	671-D1
1900	SMCA	90405	671-F3
5TH PL			
100	MANB	90266	732-F7
S 5TH PL			
-	LBCH	90802	825-F1
5TH PL E			
-	PMDL	93550	4286-A1
38300	PMDL	93550	4196-A7
5TH PL W			
38200	PMDL	93551	4285-H1
5TH ST			
-	BELL	90201	675-F5
-	LACo	90220	764-J3
-	PdlR	90293	702-C7
-	HMB	90254	762-G3
-	LA	91342	482-B6
-	LACo	91342	482-F7
-	NLB	90805	765-B3
100	MANB	90266	732-G6
100	SLB	90740	826-E4
400	SFER	91340	482-B6
800	BURB	91501	533-J7
800	SMCA	90403	671-D1
1100	SMCA	90401	671-E2
1200	GLDL	91201	564-B2
1300	LVRN	91750	600-E2
2000	GLDL	91201	533-J7
2000	SMCA	90405	671-F3
7500	BPK	90621	737-H7
7800	DWNY	90241	706-A4
12900	CHNO	91710	641-G7
22200	SCTA	91321	4641-A1
22500	SCTA	91321	4640-J1
E 5TH ST			
100	AZU	91702	568-J6
100	LA	90013	634-F5
100	SDMS	91773	600-C1
100	SPed	90731	824-C5
300	LBCH	90802	795-D7
500	AZU	91702	569-A6
1600	Boyl	90033	634-J5
2300	LBCH	90814	795-H7
2700	Boyl	90033	635-B6
3000	LA	90063	635-B6
3600	City	90063	635-D7
3800	LBCH	90814	796-A7
4300	ELA	90022	635-F7
6200	LBCH	90803	796-E7
N 5TH ST			
-	ALH	91801	596-A5
100	BURB	91501	533-H6
100	LPUE	91744	638-E6
100	MTBL	90640	676-E2
1000	BURB	91504	533-F5
S 5TH ST			
-	ALH	91801	596-B5
100	BURB	91501	533-H7
100	MTBL	90640	676-E2
1400	ALH	91803	596-B7
1800	ALH	91803	636-B1
W 5TH ST			
100	AZU	91702	568-G6
100	LA	90013	634-E4
100	LBCH	90802	795-D7
100	SDMS	91773	600-B1
100	SPed	90731	824-B5
600	LA	90071	634-E4
900	SDMS	91773	599-J1
900	SPed	90731	824-B5
900	ONT	91762	601-J5
900	LA	90017	634-D3
1500	LA	90732	823-J5
1800	LA	90057	634-C2
3000	LA	90020	634-A2
3500	LA	90020	633-F2
6100	LA	90048	633-A2
5TH ST E			
4600	LAN	93535	4016-A3
37200	PMDL	93550	4286-A1
38300	PMDL	93550	4196-A4
42000	LAN	93535	4106-A1
46000	LACo	93535	4016-A1
46600	LACo	93535	3926-A5
5TH ST W			
38200	PMDL	93551	4285-H2
38600	PMDL	93551	4195-H5
42600	LAN	93534	4105-H4
47000	LACo	93534	3925-H4
5TH TER			
-	LACo	91342	482-F6
5TH ANITA DR			
12600	Brwd	90049	631-B3
5TH HELENA DR			
12300	Brwd	90049	631-B2
6TH AV			
100	INDS	91746	638-A6
100	LACo	91746	638-A6
200	Ven	90291	671-G4
300	INDS	91746	637-J6
500	LACo	91746	637-J6
800	INDS	91745	637-J7
800	HacH	91745	637-J7
900	ARCD	91006	567-E7
900	MNRO	91016	567-E7
1300	LA	90019	633-F6
1600	ARCD	91006	597-E2
1900	LA	90018	633-F6
3400	LA	90018	673-F1
3700	LA	90008	673-F2
4500	LA	90043	673-G5
S 6TH AV			
1700	ARCD	91006	597-E1
8600	ING	90305	703-G3
10200	ING	90303	703-G5
6TH AV E			
-	Hrbr	90710	794-B3
6TH CT			
-	HMB	90254	762-G3
1000	SMCA	90403	671-E1
1000	SMCA	90401	671-E1
2100	SMCA	90405	671-F3
6TH PL			
100	MANB	90266	732-F7
S 6TH PL			
-	LBCH	90802	825-F1
6TH PL W			
38200	PMDL	93551	4285-H1
6TH ST			
-	BELL	90201	675-G5
-	LACo	90220	764-J3
-	LACo	90220	765-A3
-	PdlR	90293	702-C7
-	HMB	90254	762-J2
-	LA	91342	482-F7
-	LACo	91342	482-F7
100	MANB	90266	732-G6
100	SLB	90740	826-E4
800	SMCA	90403	671-D1
1100	SMCA	90401	671-E2
1700	LVRN	91750	600-F2
1800	MANB	90266	733-A6
1900	SMCA	90405	671-F3
7800	DWNY	90241	706-A4
12900	CHNO	91710	641-G7
22200	SCTA	91321	4641-A1
22500	SCTA	91321	4640-J1
E 6TH ST			
100	AZU	91702	568-J6
100	CLAR	91711	601-E3
100	LA	90014	634-F5
100	LBCH	90802	795-E7
100	POM	91766	640-J2
100	SPed	90731	824-C5
100	LA	90013	634-F5
300	POM	91766	641-A2
500	AZU	91702	569-A6
500	LA	90021	634-F5
1500	LA	90023	634-J5
1500	Boyl	90033	634-J5
2100	LA	90023	635-A6
2100	LBCH	90814	795-G7
2100	Boyl	90033	635-A6
2900	LA	90063	635-B6
3700	LACo	90023	635-F7
3700	City	90063	635-D7
3900	LBCH	90814	796-A7
4400	ELA	90022	635-G7
5800	ELA	90022	675-J1
6000	ELA	90022	676-A1
6100	LBCH	90803	796-E7
N 6TH ST			
100	BURB	91501	533-H6
100	MTBL	90640	676-E2
700	MTBL	90640	636-E7
1000	BURB	91504	533-E4
S 6TH ST			
-	ALH	91801	596-A5
100	BURB	91501	533-J7
100	MTBL	90640	676-D3
1400	ALH	91803	596-B7
1800	ALH	91803	636-B1
2100	BURB	91201	533-J7
2100	GLDL	91201	533-J7
W 6TH ST			
100	AZU	91702	568-H6
100	CLAR	91711	601-C3
100	LA	90014	634-E4
100	LBCH	90802	795-D7
100	SDMS	91773	600-B1
100	SPed	90731	824-A5
100	LA	90013	634-E4
500	POM	91766	640-G2
600	LA	90017	634-D3
600	LA	90071	634-E4
900	SPed	90731	824-A5
900	ONT	91762	601-J5
1200	LACo	90732	823-J5
1200	LACo	90732	824-A5
1200	SPed	90731	823-J5
1500	LA	90732	823-J5
1800	LA	90057	634-A2
2800	LA	90005	634-A2
2800	LA	90020	634-A2
3400	LA	90005	633-G2
3400	LA	90020	633-G2
5200	LA	90036	633-B2
6100	LA	90048	633-B2
6TH ST E			
37200	PMDL	93550	4286-B1
38300	PMDL	93550	4196-A4
42000	LAN	93535	4106-A1
44600	LAN	93535	4016-A3
46100	LACo	93535	4016-A2
6TH ST W			
36200	LACo	93551	4285-H6
38200	PMDL	93551	4285-H1
42000	LAN	93534	4105-H5
6TH TER			
-	LACo	91342	482-F6
6TH HELENA DR			
12300	Brwd	90049	631-G4
7TH AV			
200	LACo	91746	638-A6
200	SMCA	90405	671-H4
200	Ven	90291	671-H4
200	INDS	91746	638-A6
700	INDS	91746	637-J7
700	INDS	91745	637-J7
1600	LA	90019	633-F6
1900	LA	90018	633-F6
3400	LA	90018	673-F1
4200	LA	90008	673-F3
4400	LA	90043	673-F5
7200	LA	90043	703-G1
S 7TH AV			
900	HacH	91745	637-J7
1100	HacH	91745	677-J1
1800	ARCD	91006	597-E1
7600	ING	90305	703-G3
10200	ING	90303	703-G5
7TH CT			
-	HMB	90254	762-G3
900	SMCA	90403	671-D1
1700	SMCA	90404	671-F2
2300	SMCA	90405	671-G3
7TH PL			
100	MANB	90266	732-F6
1100	BURB	91504	533-G5
1100	HMB	90254	762-J2
1800	ARCD	91006	597-E1
2100	LA	90021	634-H6
E 7TH PL			
1600	LA	90021	634-G6
S 7TH PL			
-	LBCH	90802	825-F1
7TH ST			
-	LACo	90220	764-J3
-	LACo	90220	765-A3
-	PdlR	90293	702-C7
-	HMB	90254	762-H2
-	LA	91342	482-F7
-	LACo	91342	482-F7
100	MANB	90266	732-F7
100	SLB	90740	826-E4
200	SMCA	90402	631-D7
600	SFER	91340	482-B5
600	SMCA	90402	671-D1
800	SMCA	90403	671-D1
1100	SMCA	90401	671-D1
1800	LVRN	91750	600-G2
1900	SMCA	90405	671-F3
7700	BPK	90621	737-H7
7800	DWNY	90241	706-A3
12700	CHNO	91710	641-G6
14400	WHIT	90602	707-F1
E 7TH ST			
100	CLAR	91711	601-D3
100	LA	90014	634-G6
100	LBCH	90802	795-F7
100	POM	91766	640-J2
100	LBCH	90813	795-F7
300	POM	91766	641-A2
600	LA	90021	634-G6
900	LA	90023	634-G6
1600	SBdC	91766	641-C2
2000	LBCH	90814	795-F7
2000	LBCH	90804	795-F7
2400	LA	90023	635-A7
3700	LA	90023	675-C1
3900	LBCH	90814	796-B7
3900	LBCH	90804	796-B7
E 7TH ST Rt#-22			
5600	LBCH	90804	796-D6
5600	LBCH	90815	796-D6
5700	LBCH	90803	796-D6
5700	LBCH	90822	796-D6
N 7TH ST			
100	BURB	91501	533-H6
200	MTBL	90640	676-E2
1000	BURB	91504	533-G5
S 7TH ST			
100	BURB	91501	533-J6
100	MTBL	90640	676-D2
300	ALH	91801	596-A5
1400	ALH	91803	596-A7
1800	ALH	91803	636-B1
W 7TH ST			
-	SPed	90731	824-B5
100	CLAR	91711	601-C3
100	LA	90014	634-E4
100	LBCH	90802	795-C7
100	POM	91766	640-H2
100	LBCH	90813	795-C7
600	LA	90017	634-D4
900	SPed	90731	824-B5
1200	SPed	90731	823-J5
1200	UPL	91786	601-H4
1200	SPed	90731	823-J5
1300	LACo	90732	823-J5
1300	LA	90732	823-H5
1800	LA	90057	634-A3
2700	LA	90005	634-A3
3200	LA	90005	633-H3
7TH ST E			
42000	LAN	93535	4106-A1
44000	LAN	93535	4016-A4
46100	LACo	93535	4016-A2
7TH ST W			
37200	LACo	93551	4285-H3
37200	PMDL	93551	4285-H1
42000	LAN	93534	4105-G5
46000	LAN	93534	4015-G2
7TH TER			
-	LACo	91342	482-F6
7TH HELENA DR			
12300	Brwd	90049	631-B2
8TH AV			
100	LACo	91746	638-B6
100	INDS	91746	638-B6
900	ARCD	91006	567-F7
900	MNRO	91016	567-F7
1800	LA	90019	633-F7
1900	LA	90018	633-F7
3400	LA	90018	673-F1
4000	LA	90008	673-F3
4400	LA	90043	673-F5
7200	LA	90043	703-F1
S 8TH AV			
1600	ARCD	91006	567-F7
1600	ARCD	91006	597-F1
7600	ING	90305	703-F4
7600	LA	90043	703-F4
10000	ING	90303	703-F5
8TH CT			
-	HMB	90254	762-G3
8TH PL			
100	MANB	90266	732-F6
600	HMB	90254	762-H2
S 8TH PL			
-	LBCH	90802	825-F1
10400	ING	90303	703-G5
W 8TH PL			
900	LA	90017	634-D4
8TH ST			
-	LACo	90220	764-J3
-	LACo	90220	765-A3
-	LACo	91342	482-F7
-	PdlR	90293	702-D7
-	HMB	90254	762-G2
-	SLB	90740	826-E4
100	MANB	90266	732-F6
300	SFER	91340	482-C5
500	AZU	91702	569-A5
1800	MANB	90266	733-A6
2000	LA	91340	482-C5
2000	LA	91342	482-C5
2000	LVRN	91750	600-G2
6700	BPK	90620	767-G1
7000	BPK	90621	767-H1
7800	DWNY	90241	706-A3
22500	SCTA	91321	4640-J1
E 8TH ST			
100	CLAR	91711	601-D2
100	LA	90014	634-F6
100	LBCH	90813	795-E6
200	AZU	91702	568-J5
300	POM	91766	640-J2
300	POM	91766	641-A2
500	AZU	91702	569-A5
700	LA	90021	634-F6
2000	LBCH	90804	795-H6
2500	LA	90023	634-J7
2600	LA	90023	635-A7
3100	LA	90023	675-B1
3900	LBCH	90804	796-A6
S 8TH ST			
300	ALH	91801	596-A5
1400	ALH	91803	596-A7
1800	ALH	91803	636-A1
W 8TH ST			
-	LA	90005	633-E3
100	CLAR	91711	601-C3
100	LA	90014	634-D4
100	LBCH	90813	795-D7
100	SPed	90731	824-B5
200	POM	91766	640-G2
200	UPL	91786	601-J4
600	LA	90017	634-D4
800	AZU	91702	568-G5
1200	SPed	90731	823-J5
1300	LA	90732	823-J5
1500	UPL	91763	601-J4
1800	LA	90057	634-A3
2700	LA	90005	634-A3
5100	LA	90036	633-C3
8TH ST E			
38300	PMDL	93550	4286-B1
38400	PMDL	93550	4196-B7
38800	PMDL	93550	4196-B6
42000	LAN	93535	4106-B1
44100	LAN	93535	4016-B3
8TH ST W			
42600	LAN	93534	4105-G4
46800	LACo	93534	3925-G2
46800	LACo	93534	4015-H1
8TH TER			
-	LACo	91342	482-F6
8TH HELENA DR			
12300	Brwd	90049	631-G4
9TH AV			
100	INDS	91746	638-B7
100	LACo	91746	638-B7
700	INDS	91745	638-A7
800	HacH	91745	638-A7
800	HacH	91745	678-A1
900	ARCD	91006	567-F7
1600	SBdC	91766	641-D2
1800	MNRO	91016	567-F7
2100	LA	90018	633-F7
3400	LA	90018	673-F1
4000	LA	90008	673-F3
4100	MTCL	91763	641-D2
4400	LA	90043	673-F5
7200	LA	90043	703-F1
S 9TH AV			
1300	HacH	91745	678-A2
1500	HacH	91745	677-J2
9TH CT			
-	SMCA	90403	631-D7
-	HMB	90254	762-G3
900	SMCA	90403	671-E1
1200	SMCA	90401	671-E1
1700	SMCA	90404	671-F2
9TH PL			
100	MANB	90266	732-F6
E 9TH PL			
700	LA	90021	634-F6
S 9TH PL			
-	LBCH	90802	825-F1
9TH ST			
-	AZU	91702	569-A5
-	PdlR	90293	702-C7
-	HMB	90254	762-G2
100	MANB	90266	732-F6
200	SMCA	90402	631-D7
800	SMCA	90403	631-D7
800	SMCA	90403	671-E1
1200	SMCA	90401	671-E1
1600	SMCA	90404	671-F2
1800	MANB	90266	733-A6
1900	LVRN	91750	600-G2
4000	Actn	93510	4465-A2
7000	BPK	90621	767-G1
12600	CHNO	91710	641-G7
22500	SCTA	91321	4640-J1
E 9TH ST			
100	AZU	91702	568-J5
100	LA	90015	634-F5
100	LBCH	90813	795-E6
100	POM	91766	640-J2
100	LA	90014	634-F5
300	CLAR	91711	601-E2
300	POM	91766	641-A2
500	AZU	91702	569-A5
700	LA	90021	634-F6
3800	LBCH	90804	795-J6
4100	LBCH	90804	796-A6
6700	LBCH	90815	796-F6
N 9TH ST			
100	BURB	91501	533-J6
S 9TH ST			
100	BURB	91501	533-J6
700	ALH	91801	596-A7
1400	ALH	91803	596-A7
1800	ALH	91803	636-A1
W 9TH ST			
100	AZU	91702	568-H5
100	CLAR	91711	601-C2
100	LA	90015	634-E5
100	LBCH	90813	795-A6
100	POM	91766	640-E3
100	SPed	90731	824-B5
100	LA	90014	634-E5
500	LA	90017	634-E5
1000	UPL	91786	601-H3
1200	SPed	90731	823-J5
1300	LA	90732	823-H5
1900	RPV	90275	823-H5
3600	LA	90019	633-F3
3600	LA	90005	633-F3
5000	LA	90036	633-D3
9TH ST E			
38000	PMDL	93550	4286-B1
38400	PMDL	93550	4196-B4
38800	PMDL	93550	4196-B6
9TH TER			
-	LACo	91342	482-F6
9TH HELENA DR			
12300	Brwd	90049	631-G4
10TH AV			
900	ARCD	91006	567-F7
900	MNRO	91016	567-F7
1900	LA	90018	633-F6
2500	ARCD	91006	597-F2
3400	LA	90018	673-F1
4200	LA	90008	673-F3
4400	LA	90043	673-F5
7200	LA	90043	703-F1
S 10TH AV			
1600	ARCD	91006	567-F7
1600	ARCD	91006	597-F1
7900	ING	90305	703-F2
10200	ING	90303	703-F5
10TH CT			
-	HMB	90254	762-G2
800	SMCA	90403	631-D7
1100	SMCA	90403	671-E1
1200	SMCA	90401	671-F2
1800	SMCA	90404	671-F2
2600	SMCA	90405	671-G3
10TH PL			
100	MANB	90266	732-F6
S 10TH PL			
-	LBCH	90802	825-F1
W 10TH PL			
1400	LA	90015	634-C4
10TH PL E			
38300	PMDL	93550	4196-B7
38300	PMDL	93550	4286-B1
10TH ST			
-	PdlR	90293	702-D7
-	HMB	90254	762-G2
100	MANB	90266	732-F6
100	SLB	90740	826-E4
200	SMCA	90402	631-D7
800	SMCA	90403	631-D7
900	SMCA	90403	671-E1
1200	SMCA	90401	671-F2
1600	SMCA	90404	671-F2
1800	MANB	90266	733-A6
1900	SMCA	90405	671-F3
1900	LVRN	91750	600-G2
7500	BPK	90621	767-H1
8500	DWNY	90241	706-C4
12500	CHNO	91710	641-H7
E 10TH ST			
100	AZU	91702	568-J5
100	CLAR	91711	601-D2
100	LBCH	90813	795-G6
100	POM	91766	640-J3
200	POM	91766	641-A3
500	AZU	91702	569-A5
700	LA	90021	634-F6
2000	LBCH	90804	795-G6
3800	LBCH	90804	796-A6
6800	LBCH	90815	796-F6
N 10TH ST			
100	MTBL	90640	676-D1
S 10TH ST			
100	MTBL	90640	676-D2
W 10TH ST			
100	AZU	91702	568-G5
100	CLAR	91711	601-C2
100	LBCH	90813	795-B6
100	POM	91766	640-G3
100	SPed	90731	824-A5
1200	SPed	90731	823-J5
1300	LA	90732	823-H5
2200	LA	90006	634-B4
3400	LA	90019	633-F3
4400	LA	90005	633-F3
10TH ST E			
37200	PMDL	93550	4286-B3
38300	PMDL	93550	4196-B4
38700	PMDL	93550	4196-B7
10TH ST W			
-	KeCo	93560	3835-F3
38800	LACo	93551	4195-G6
38800	PMDL	93551	4195-G2
40600	PMDL	93551	4105-G6
42000	LAN	93534	4105-G3
44000	LAN	93534	4015-G2
46800	LACo	93534	3925-G1
46800	LACo	93534	4015-G2
49200	LACo	93534	3835-F3
10TH TER			
-	LACo	91342	482-F6
10TH HELENA DR			
12300	Brwd	90049	631-G4
11TH AV			
2300	LA	90018	633-F6
3400	LA	90018	673-F1
4000	LA	90008	673-F3
4400	LA	90043	673-F5
7100	LA	90043	703-F1
S 11TH AV			
8400	ING	90305	703-F3
11TH CT			
-	HMB	90254	762-G2
800	SMCA	90403	631-E7
900	SMCA	90403	671-E1
1800	SMCA	90404	671-F2
11TH PL			
100	MANB	90266	732-F6
500	HMB	90254	762-H2
4500	LA	90019	633-F4
S 11TH PL			
-	LBCH	90802	825-F1
W 11TH PL			
1300	LA	90015	634-C4
1800	LA	90006	634-C4
11TH PL W			
48000	LACo	93534	3925-F4
11TH ST			
-	ELSG	90245	732-D1
-	LA	90245	732-D1
-	PdlR	90293	732-D1
-	HMB	90254	762-G2
100	MANB	90266	732-F6
100	SLB	90740	826-E4
1000	SMCA	90402	631-D6
1200	RBCH	90278	762-J2
1300	SMCA	90403	631-D6
1300	SMCA	90403	671-E1
1400	SMCA	90401	671-E1
1600	SMCA	90404	671-E1
1900	LVRN	91750	600-G2
2000	SMCA	90405	671-G3
2400	LA	90021	674-H1
4300	LA	90019	633-F4
7500	BPK	90621	767-H1
8500	DWNY	90241	706-C4
12900	CHNO	91710	641-H7
16800	SunB	90742	826-E4
22500	SCTA	91321	4640-J1
E 11TH ST			
100	AZU	91702	568-J5
100	CLAR	91711	601-D2
100	LA	90015	634-E6
100	POM	91766	640-J3
200	POM	91766	641-A3
300	LBCH	90813	795-E6
500	AZU	91702	569-A5
900	LA	90021	634-F6
2100	LBCH	90804	795-H6
2200	LA	90021	674-H1
2700	LA	90023	674-H1
2700	LA	90023	675-A1
3800	LBCH	90804	796-A6
6800	LBCH	90815	796-F6
W 11TH ST			
100	AZU	91702	568-H5
100	CLAR	91711	601-C2
100	LA	90015	634-D5
100	POM	91766	640-H3
100	SPed	90731	824-A6
400	LBCH	90813	795-B6
900	UPL	91786	601-G2
1200	SPed	90731	823-J6
1600	LA	90732	823-J6
1800	LA	90006	634-A4
2700	LA	90006	633-H4
3200	LA	90019	633-H4
11TH ST E			
4600	LAN	93535	4016-B4
37800	PMDL	93550	4286-C2
38300	PMDL	93550	4196-B7
43000	LAN	93535	4106-B1
11TH ST W			
38800	LACo	93551	4195-G3
38800	PMDL	93551	4195-G5
40600	PMDL	93551	4105-G6
42400	LAN	93534	4105-G5
44100	LAN	93534	4015-G4
48000	LACo	93534	3925-F4
11TH TER			
-	LACo	91342	482-F6
11TH HELENA DR			
12300	Brwd	90049	631-G4
12TH AV			
1300	LA	90019	633-F5
2300	LA	90018	633-F6
3400	LA	90018	673-F1
S 12TH AV			
8600	ING	90305	703-F3
12TH CT			
-	HMB	90254	762-G2
700	SMCA	90403	631-E7
800	MANB	90266	732-G6
900	SMCA	90403	671-E1
1400	SMCA	90404	671-E1
W 12TH DR			
1200	LA	90015	634-D5
12TH PL			
200	MANB	90266	732-F6
S 12TH PL			
-	LBCH	90802	825-G1
W 12TH PL			
1300	LA	90015	634-C5
1600	LA	90006	634-C5
3000	LA	90006	633-H4
12TH PL W			
47600	LACo	93534	3925-F5
12TH ST			
-	LA	90245	732-D1
100	MANB	90266	732-F6
100	SLB	90740	826-F4
200	SMCA	90402	631-D7
800	SMCA	90403	631-D7
1000	SMCA	90403	671-E1
1200	SMCA	90401	671-E1
1200	SMCA	90404	671-F2
1900	LVRN	91750	600-G2
2400	LA	90021	674-H1
4300	LA	90019	633-F4
12700	CHNO	91710	641-H7
16800	SunB	90742	826-J7
22300	SCTA	91321	4550-J7
22500	SCTA	91321	4640-J1
E 12TH ST			
100	CLAR	91711	601-D2
100	LA	90015	634-F6
100	LBCH	90813	795-D6
100	POM	91766	640-J3
100	POM	91766	641-A3
700	LA	90021	634-F6
2500	LA	90023	674-J1
2700	LA	90023	675-A1
N 12TH ST			
100	MTBL	90640	676-D2
W 12TH ST			
100	AZU	91702	568-H4
100	CLAR	91711	601-C2
100	LA	90015	634-C4
100	LBCH	90813	795-B6
100	POM	91766	640-H3
100	SPed	90731	824-A6
1300	LA	90732	823-J6
1300	SPed	90731	823-J6
1800	LA	90006	634-A4
2600	LA	90006	633-J4
3300	LA	90019	633-D4
12TH ST E			
37300	PMDL	93550	4286-C1
38300	PMDL	93550	4196-C7
44000	LAN	93535	4016-B4
46600	LACo	93535	4016-B1
46600	LACo	93535	3926-B7
12TH ST W			
39400	PMDL	93551	4195-G5
39900	LACo	93551	4195-G3
41300	PMDL	93551	4105-G6
42000	LAN	93534	4105-F1
44000	LAN	93534	4015-F3
12TH HELENA DR			
12300	Brwd	90049	631-G4
13TH AV			
2500	LA	90018	633-E6
13TH CT			
-	HMB	90254	762-G2
13TH PL			
100	MANB	90266	732-F6
22600	SCTA	91321	4550-J7
S 13TH PL			
-	LBCH	90802	825-G1
13TH PL W			
45600	LAN	93534	4015-F4
13TH ST			
-	PdlR	90293	732-C1
-	HMB	90254	762-G2
100	MANB	90266	732-F6
100	SLB	90740	826-F4
12700	CHNO	91710	641-H7
22400	SCTA	91321	4550-J7
22600	SCTA	91321	4640-J1
E 13TH ST			
100	AZU	91702	568-J4
W 13TH ST			
100	SPed	90731	824-A6
700	AZU	91702	568-H4
1000	UPL	91786	601-J1
1200	SPed	90731	823-J6
1200	LA	90732	823-J6
13TH ST E			
37600	PMDL	93550	4286-C1
38500	PMDL	93550	4196-C7
43600	LAN	93535	4106-C1
44300	LAN	93535	4016-C5
46800	LACo	93535	3926-B7
13TH ST W			
39900	LACo	93551	4195-F3
43400	LAN	93534	4105-F1
44000	LAN	93534	4015-F4
13TH HELENA DR			
12300	Brwd	90049	631-F4
14TH CT			
-	HMB	90254	762-G2
900	SMCA	90403	631-E7
1100	SMCA	90403	671-F1
1100	SMCA	90404	671-F1
14TH PL			
100	MANB	90266	732-F6
E 14TH PL			
700	LA	90021	634-F7
S 14TH PL			
-	LBCH	90802	825-G1
W 14TH PL			
100	LA	90015	634-E6
14TH ST			
-	PdlR	90293	732-G5
-	HMB	90254	762-G2
100	MANB	90266	732-G5
100	SLB	90740	826-F5
100	SMCA	90402	631-D6
800	SMCA	90403	631-E7
1100	SMCA	90403	671-F1
1200	MTBL	90640	676-B5
1200	SMCA	90404	671-F1
2000	SMCA	90405	671-G2
12900	CHNO	91710	641-H7
16700	SunB	90742	826-J7
22500	SCTA	91321	4550-H7
E 14TH ST			
100	LA	90015	634-E6
100	LBCH	90813	795-E5
700	LA	90021	634-F7
2000	LBCH	90804	795-H5
2100	LA	90021	674-H1
3300	LA	90023	675-B1
3800	LBCH	90804	796-A5
W 14TH ST			
100	LA	90015	634-D6
100	LBCH	90813	795-B6
100	SPed	90731	824-B6
1100	UPL	91786	601-H1
1200	SPed	90731	823-J6
1300	LA	90732	823-J6
1800	LA	90006	634-B5
2700	LA	90006	633-H5
14TH HELENA DR			
12300	Brwd	90049	631-F4
15TH CT			
-	HMB	90254	762-G2
800	SMCA	90403	631-E7
1400	SMCA	90404	671-F1
15TH DR			
600	LA	90015	634-C6
15TH PL			
100	MANB	90266	732-F6
900	HMB	90254	762-H1
S 15TH PL			
-	LBCH	90802	825-G1
15TH PL E			
-	PMDL	93550	4196-C7
15TH ST			
-	PdlR	90293	732-C1
-	HMB	90254	762-G2
100	MANB	90266	732-F5
200	SLB	90740	826-F4
200	SMCA	90402	631-D6
300	LA	90015	634-D6

STREET Block City ZIP Pg-Grid

15TH ST
800 SMCA 90403 631-D6
1100 SMCA 90403 671-F1
1200 SMCA 90404 671-F1
16700 SunB 90742 826-J7
22500 SCTA 91321 4550-H7
E 15TH ST
100 LA 90015 634-E6
100 LBCH 90813 795-F5
700 LA 90021 634-F7
1700 LA 90021 674-G1
2000 LBCH 90804 795-H5
3300 LA 90023 675-B2
3800 LBCH 90804 796-A5
W 15TH ST
100 LA 90015 634-A5
100 LBCH 90813 795-B5
100 SPed 90731 824-B6
1000 UPL 91786 571-H7
1200 SPed 90731 823-J6
1200 LA 90732 823-J6
2200 LA 90006 634-A5
2500 LA 90006 633-J5
3000 LA 90019 633-G5
15TH ST E
37600 PMDL 93550 4286-C1
39000 PMDL 93550 4196-C4
39200 PMDL 93550 4196-C4
41800 PMDL 93550 4106-C6
43300 LAN 93535 4106-C3
43800 LAN 93535 4016-C3
46000 LACo 93535 4016-C3
46800 LACo 93535 3926-C5
15TH ST W
38600 PMDL 93551 4285-F1
38600 PMDL 93551 4195-F4
38700 LACo 93551 4195-F1
42000 LAN 93534 4105-F1
42000 LAN 93551 4105-F5
44000 LAN 93534 4015-F2
46800 LACo 93534 3925-F5
46800 LACo 93534 4015-F2
50000 LACo 93534 3835-E4
15TH HELENA DR
12300 Brwd 90049 631-G4
16TH CT
- SMCA 90404 671-F1
- HMB 90254 762-G2
800 SMCA 90403 631-E7
16TH PL
100 MANB 90266 732-F6
W 16TH PL
2600 LA 90019 633-E5
16TH PL E
38700 PMDL 93550 4196-D7
16TH PL W
42800 LAN 93534 4105-F4
16TH ST
- LA 90245 732-C1
- PdlR 90293 732-C1
- HMB 90254 762-G2
100 MANB 90266 732-E6
100 SMCA 90402 631-D6
200 SLB 90740 826-F4
800 SMCA 90403 631-E7
1200 SMCA 90404 631-E7
1200 SMCA 90404 671-F1
2100 SMCA 90405 671-H3
3100 Ven 90291 671-H3
12600 CHNO 91710 641-H7
16700 OrCo 92649 826-J7
16800 SunB 90742 826-J7
22900 SCTA 91321 4550-G7
23100 SCTA 91355 4550-G7
E 16TH ST
100 LA 90015 634-E7
100 LBCH 90813 795-E5
700 LA 90021 634-F7
1600 LA 90021 674-G1
2800 LBCH 90804 795-H5
3500 LA 90023 675-B2
N 16TH ST
200 MTBL 90640 676-C1
800 MTBL 90640 636-D7
W 16TH ST
100 LBCH 90813 795-B5
100 SPed 90731 824-B6
800 UPL 91786 571-J7
800 UPL 91784 571-J7
1200 SPed 90731 823-J6
1300 LA 90732 823-J6
W 16TH ST Rt#-30
1200 UPL 91786 571-G7
1200 UPL 91784 571-G7
1600 CLAR 91711 571-G7
16TH ST E
4500 LAN 93535 4016-C5
37600 PMDL 93550 4286-C1
38600 PMDL 93550 4196-D7
43600 LAN 93535 4106-C1
46800 LACo 93535 3926-C4
16TH ST W
- Actn 93510 4465-F3
39800 LACo 93551 4195-F2
43200 LAN 93534 4105-F2
44000 LAN 93534 4015-F5
46800 LACo 93534 3925-E7
46800 LACo 93534 4015-F5
16TH HELENA DR
12300 Brwd 90049 631-F4
17TH AV
- Ven 90291 671-G6
17TH CT
- HMB 90254 762-G2
800 SMCA 90403 631-E7
1300 SMCA 90404 631-F7
1300 SMCA 90404 671-F1
17TH PL
- Ven 90291 671-G6
100 MANB 90266 732-F5
W 17TH PL
1600 LA 90006 634-A5
17TH ST
- HMB 90254 762-H1
100 MANB 90266 732-F5
100 SMCA 90402 631-D6
200 SLB 90740 826-F4
800 SMCA 90403 631-E7
1200 SMCA 90404 631-E7
1300 SMCA 90404 671-F1
1600 UPL 91784 571-G6
2300 SMCA 90405 671-H3
12500 CHNO 91710 641-J7
16700 SunB 90742 826-J7
E 17TH ST
100 LA 90015 634-E7
300 LBCH 90813 795-E5
700 LA 90021 634-E7
1400 LA 90021 674-F1
2000 LBCH 90804 795-H5
W 17TH ST
100 LA 90015 634-C6
200 LBCH 90813 795-A5
200 SPed 90731 824-A6
900 UPL 91784 571-J6
1200 SPed 90731 823-J6
1300 LA 90006 634-B5
1300 LA 90732 823-J6
2600 LA 90019 633-E5
17TH ST E
37400 PMDL 93550 4286-D2
38300 PMDL 93550 4196-D7
43600 LAN 93535 4106-C1
43900 LAN 93535 4016-C4
46800 LACo 93535 3926-C5
17TH ST W
39800 LACo 93551 4195-F1
42800 LAN 93534 4105-E2
44000 LAN 93534 4015-E3
46800 LACo 93534 3925-E5
46800 LACo 93534 4015-E3
49800 LACo 93534 3835-E4
17TH HELENA DR
12300 Brwd 90049 631-F3
18TH AV
- Ven 90291 671-G6
100 LBCH 90802 824-G2
100 SPed 90731 824-G2
18TH CT
- HMB 90254 762-G2
800 SMCA 90403 631-E6
1200 SMCA 90404 631-F7
1400 SMCA 90404 671-F1
2300 SMCA 90405 671-H2
18TH PL
- Ven 90291 671-H6
100 MANB 90266 732-E5
S 18TH PL
- LBCH 90803 825-G1
18TH ST
- HMB 90254 762-G1
100 MANB 90266 732-F5
200 SMCA 90402 631-D6
800 SMCA 90403 631-E7
1200 SMCA 90404 631-E7
1300 SMCA 90404 671-G1
2300 SMCA 90405 671-H2
12700 CHNO 91710 641-J7
16600 SunB 90742 826-J7
E 18TH ST
100 LA 90015 634-E7
700 LA 90021 634-F7
1300 LA 90021 674-F1
N 18TH ST
100 MTBL 90640 676-C1
600 MTBL 90640 636-C7
S 18TH ST
100 MTBL 90640 676-C2
W 18TH ST
100 LA 90015 634-B5
200 SPed 90731 824-A6
1000 UPL 91784 571-H6
1200 SPed 90731 823-J6
1200 LA 90732 823-J6
1300 LA 90006 634-A5
2300 LA 90019 633-D5
5800 LA 90035 633-A5
6000 LA 90035 632-J5
18TH ST E
37400 PMDL 93550 4286-D3
38600 PMDL 93550 4196-D7
43900 LAN 93535 4016-D3
43900 LAN 93535 4106-D1
46800 LACo 93535 3926-C7
18TH ST W
39800 LACo 93551 4195-E2
43100 LAN 93534 4105-E2
44600 LAN 93534 4015-E3
46800 LACo 93534 3925-E7
46800 LACo 93534 4015-E3
49800 LACo 93534 3835-E7
18TH HELENA DR
12300 Brwd 90049 631-F3
19TH AV
- Ven 90291 671-H6
19TH CT
- SMCA 90404 671-G1
- HMB 90254 762-G2
800 SMCA 90403 631-E6
19TH PL
- Ven 90291 671-G6
100 MANB 90266 732-E5
S 19TH PL
- LBCH 90803 825-G1
19TH ST
- HMB 90254 762-G1
100 MANB 90266 732-E5
700 SMCA 90402 631-D5
800 SMCA 90403 631-E6
1200 SMCA 90404 631-E6
1400 SMCA 90404 671-G1
13100 CHNO 91710 641-J7
16600 SunB 90742 826-J7
E 19TH ST
300 LBCH 90806 795-E4
2000 SIGH 90755 795-H4
N 19TH ST
100 MTBL 90640 676-C1
600 MTBL 90640 636-C7
S 19TH ST
100 MTBL 90640 676-C2
W 19TH ST
200 LBCH 90806 795-C4
300 SPed 90731 824-A7
1200 LBCH 90810 795-A4
1200 SPed 90731 823-J7
1200 UPL 91784 571-J5
1200 LA 90732 823-J7
W 19TH ST Rt#-30
1000 UPL 91784 571-J5
19TH ST E
37500 PMDL 93550 4286-D2
19TH ST W
42200 LAN 93534 4105-E3
19TH HELENA DR
12300 Brwd 90049 631-F3
20TH AV
- Ven 90291 671-G6
20TH CT
- SMCA 90404 631-F7
- HMB 90254 762-G1
800 SMCA 90403 631-F6
1600 SMCA 90404 671-G1
20TH PL
- LBCH 90803 825-H1
- Ven 90291 671-H6
100 MANB 90266 732-E5
1100 HMB 90254 762-H1
20TH ST
- HMB 90254 762-G1
100 MANB 90266 732-E5
200 SMCA 90402 631-D5
800 SMCA 90403 631-F6
1200 SMCA 90404 631-F6
1400 SMCA 90404 671-G1
2100 SMCA 90405 671-H2
16500 SunB 90742 826-J7
E 20TH ST
100 LBCH 90806 795-E4
400 LA 90011 634-E7
1100 LA 90011 674-F1
1600 SIGH 90755 795-G4
1600 LA 90058 674-G1
3200 LBCH 90755 795-J4
3400 LBCH 90804 795-J4
N 20TH ST
100 MTBL 90640 676-C1
600 MTBL 90640 636-C7
W 20TH ST
100 LBCH 90806 795-C4
300 SPed 90731 824-A7
500 LA 90007 634-A6
1000 UPL 91784 571-J5
1200 LBCH 90810 795-A4
1200 SPed 90731 823-J7
1200 LA 90732 823-J7
1800 LA 90007 633-J6
1900 LA 90018 633-H6
4900 LA 90016 633-C6
20TH ST E
37300 PMDL 93550 4286-D1
38400 PMDL 93550 4196-D4
38800 PMDL 93550 4196-D6
42200 PMDL 93550 4106-D5
42800 LAN 93535 4106-D3
43800 LAN 93535 4016-D3
46000 LACo 93535 3926-D5
46000 LACo 93535 4016-D3
20TH ST W
- KeCo 93560 3835-D3
38000 PMDL 93551 4195-E4
38000 PMDL 93551 4285-E2
39800 LACo 93551 4195-E1
41200 LACo 93551 4105-E6
41800 LACo 93534 4105-E6
42000 LAN 93534 4105-E2
44000 LAN 93534 4015-E2
46800 LACo 93534 3925-D3
46800 LACo 93534 4015-E2
49200 LACo 93534 3835-D3
20TH HELENA DR
12300 Brwd 90049 631-F3
21ST CT
- HMB 90254 762-G1
800 SMCA 90403 631-F6
21ST PL
100 MANB 90266 732-E5
100 SMCA 90402 631-E5
21ST ST
- HMB 90254 762-G1
100 MANB 90266 732-E5
200 SMCA 90402 631-E5
800 SMCA 90403 631-F6
1200 SMCA 90404 631-G7
1500 SMCA 90404 671-G1
2100 SMCA 90405 671-H2
16500 SunB 90742 826-J7
E 21ST ST
100 LA 90011 634-D7
100 LBCH 90806 795-E4
900 LA 90011 674-E1
1700 LA 90058 674-G1
1700 SIGH 90755 795-G4
N 21ST ST
100 MTBL 90640 676-C1
500 MTBL 90640 636-C7
W 21ST ST
100 LA 90007 634-A6
100 LBCH 90806 795-C4
300 SPed 90731 824-A7
1000 UPL 91784 571-J4
1200 LBCH 90810 795-B4
1200 SPed 90731 823-J7
1200 LA 90732 823-J7
1800 LA 90007 633-H6
2000 LA 90018 633-F6
4600 LA 90016 633-C6
21ST ST E
38400 PMDL 93550 4196-D7
43300 LAN 93535 4106-D2
44100 LAN 93535 4016-D6
21ST ST W
39600 PMDL 93551 4195-E5
42000 LAN 93536 4105-D1
44500 LAN 93536 4015-D4
21ST HELENA DR
12300 Brwd 90049 631-F3
22ND AV NW
- PAS 91011 535-F3
22ND CT
2100 HMB 90254 762-G1
W 22ND PL
1500 LA 90007 634-A6
4000 LA 90018 633-F6
22ND ST
- HMB 90254 762-F1
200 SMCA 90402 631-E5
800 SMCA 90403 631-F6
1100 MANB 90266 732-H5
1200 SMCA 90404 631-F6
1700 SMCA 90404 671-G1
2100 SMCA 90405 671-H2
16400 SunB 90742 826-J7
E 22ND ST
100 SPed 90731 824-C7
400 LA 90011 634-E7
700 LA 90011 674-E1
1700 LA 90058 674-G2
S 22ND ST
100 MTBL 90640 676-B2
W 22ND ST
100 LA 90007 634-A6
300 SPed 90731 824-A7
1000 UPL 91784 571-J4
1200 LA 90732 823-H7
1200 SPed 90731 823-J7
1600 LA 90007 633-J6
1800 LA 90018 633-J6
22ND ST E
- LAN 93535 4016-D2
38500 PMDL 93550 4196-E7
38500 PMDL 93550 4286-E1
42600 PMDL 93550 4106-E4
42800 LAN 93535 4106-D2
46000 LACo 93535 4016-D2
22ND ST W
2100 LAN 93536 4105-D1
39200 PMDL 93551 4195-E4
39800 LACo 93551 4195-E2
41100 LACo 93551 4105-D7
41700 LACo 93536 4105-D7
44200 LAN 93536 4015-D7
47900 LACo 93536 3925-D2
22ND HELENA DR
12300 Brwd 90049 631-F3
23RD AV
- Ven 90291 671-H7
23RD CT
1200 SMCA 90404 631-G7
23RD PL
- Ven 90291 671-H7
100 MANB 90266 732-E5
23RD ST
- HMB 90254 762-F1
100 MANB 90266 732-E5
700 SMCA 90402 631-E5
800 SMCA 90403 631-F6
1200 SMCA 90404 631-G7
2100 SMCA 90405 671-H2
16400 SunB 90742 826-J7
E 23RD ST
100 LA 90011 634-D7
100 LBCH 90806 795-E3
600 LA 90011 674-E1
1100 SIGH 90755 795-E3
1700 LA 90058 674-H1
3600 LBCH 90815 795-J3
3900 LBCH 90815 796-A3
W 23RD ST
100 LA 90007 634-A6
100 LBCH 90806 795-D3
500 SPed 90731 824-A7
1000 UPL 91784 571-J3
1000 SBdC 91784 571-J3
1200 LA 90732 823-H7
1200 LBCH 90810 795-B3
1200 SPed 90731 823-J7
1600 LA 90007 633-J6
1700 LA 90018 633-F6
4300 LA 90016 633-C6
23RD ST E
42600 PMDL 93550 4106-E4
44600 LAN 93535 4016-E4
23RD ST W
2300 LAN 93536 4015-D4
39200 PMDL 93551 4195-D5
42000 LAN 93536 4105-D3
23RD HELENA DR
12300 Brwd 90049 631-F3
24TH AV
- Ven 90291 671-H7
24TH CT
1100 SMCA 90403 631-F6
1200 SMCA 90404 631-G7
2400 SMCA 90405 671-J2
24TH PL
- Ven 90291 671-H7
100 MANB 90266 732-E5
400 HMB 90254 762-G1
24TH ST
- HMB 90254 762-G1
100 MANB 90266 732-E5
100 SMCA 90402 631-E5
900 SMCA 90403 631-F6
1200 SMCA 90404 631-G7
1800 SMCA 90404 671-H1
2200 SMCA 90405 671-H1
16400 SunB 90742 826-J7
E 24TH ST
100 LA 90011 634-D7
600 LA 90011 674-E1
1600 LA 90058 674-G2
W 24TH ST
100 LA 90007 634-A6
500 SPed 90731 824-A7
1200 LA 90732 823-J7
1200 SPed 90731 823-J7
1200 UPL 91784 571-H3
1300 SBdC 91784 571-H3
1500 LA 90007 633-J6
1700 LA 90018 633-G6
8900 LA 90034 632-H6
24TH ST W
43600 LAN 93536 4105-D2
24TH HELENA DR
12300 Brwd 90049 631-F3
25TH AV
- Ven 90291 671-H7
25TH CT
800 SMCA 90403 631-F6
25TH PL
- Ven 90291 671-H7
100 MANB 90266 732-E5
W 25TH PL
1100 LA 90007 634-B6
25TH ST
- HMB 90254 762-F1
100 MANB 90266 732-E5
200 SMCA 90402 631-E5
800 SMCA 90403 631-G6
1200 SMCA 90404 631-G6
2200 SMCA 90405 671-J1
16400 SunB 90742 826-H7
E 25TH ST
100 LA 90011 634-D7
100 LA 90011 674-E1
100 LBCH 90806 795-D3
900 SIGH 90755 795-F3
1800 VER 90058 674-H2
1800 LA 90058 674-J2
5100 LBCH 90815 796-B3
W 25TH ST
100 LA 90007 634-A6
100 LBCH 90806 795-D3
700 SPed 90731 824-A7
1000 SBdC 91784 571-H2
1200 LA 90732 823-H7
1200 LBCH 90810 795-B3
1200 SPed 90731 823-H7
1600 LA 90007 633-J6
1700 LA 90018 633-F6
5700 LA 90016 633-A6
8900 LA 90034 632-H6
25TH ST E
- PMDL 93550 4286-F7
- PMDL 93550 4376-F1
36200 PMDL 93550 4286-E3
38600 PMDL 93550 4196-E4
39000 PMDL 93550 4196-E4
41500 PMDL 93550 4106-E6
42800 LAN 93535 4106-E1
43800 LAN 93535 4016-E4
46000 LACo 93535 4016-E2
47600 LACo 93535 3926-E5
25TH ST W
1000 KeCo 93560 3835-C1
2300 LAN 93536 4105-D3
39000 PMDL 93551 4195-D7
39800 LACo 93551 4195-D1
41200 LACo 93551 4105-D7
41800 LACo 93536 4105-D7
44000 LAN 93536 4015-D6
47200 LAN 93536 3925-D5
47200 LACo 93536 3925-C2
49600 LACo 93536 3835-C7
E 25TH WY
500 LBCH 90806 795-E3
W 25TH WY
800 LBCH 90806 795-C3
25TH HELENA DR
12300 Brwd 90049 631-F3
26TH AV
- Ven 90291 671-H7
26TH CT
1100 SMCA 90403 631-G6
1200 SMCA 90404 631-G6
26TH PL
- Ven 90291 671-H7
300 MANB 90266 732-E5
W 26TH PL
1200 SPed 90731 853-J1
1200 SPed 90731 854-A1
2100 LA 90018 633-G7
26TH ST
- BELL 90201 675-F4
- VER 90040 675-F4
- VER 90201 675-F4
- HMB 90254 762-G1
100 MANB 90266 732-E5
200 SMCA 90402 631-E5
200 Brwd 90049 631-E5
800 SMCA 90403 631-G6
1200 SMCA 90404 631-G6
1700 SMCA 90404 671-H1
2200 SMCA 90405 671-J1
16300 SunB 90742 826-H7
E 26TH ST
2400 VER 90058 674-J2
2600 VER 90023 674-J2
2800 VER 90023 675-A2
4500 VER 90040 675-E3
5900 CMRC 90040 675-E3
6300 CMRC 90040 676-A5
S 26TH ST
100 SMCA 90402 631-E4
100 Brwd 90049 631-E4
W 26TH ST
500 SPed 90731 824-A7
1200 SPed 90731 823-J7
1700 LA 90732 823-H7
26TH ST E
37100 PMDL 93550 4286-F1
38500 PMDL 93550 4196-F7
44200 LAN 93535 4016-E5
47600 LACo 93535 3926-E5
26TH ST W
42400 LAN 93536 4105-D4
47300 LAN 93536 3925-C6
W 26TH WY
1400 LBCH 90810 795-B3
2600 LBCH 90806 795-C3
27TH AV
- Ven 90291 671-H7
27TH CT
200 HMB 90254 762-G1
2100 SMCA 90404 671-J1
W 27TH DR
1300 SPed 90731 853-J1
27TH PL
- Ven 90291 671-H7
100 MANB 90266 732-E5
1300 SPed 90731 853-J1
27TH PL E
37800 PMDL 93550 4286-F2
27TH ST
100 HMB 90254 762-F1
100 MANB 90266 732-F4
1200 SPed 90731 854-A1
1200 SPed 90731 853-J1
2000 SMCA 90404 671-H1
2200 SMCA 90405 671-J1
E 27TH ST
100 LA 90011 674-D1
100 LBCH 90806 795-E2
600 SIGH 90755 795-G2
1800 VER 90058 674-H2
5100 LBCH 90815 796-B2
W 27TH ST
100 LA 90007 674-D1
100 LBCH 90806 795-C2
100 LA 90007 634-A7
600 SPed 90731 854-A1
1200 LBCH 90810 795-B2
1500 LA 90007 633-G7
1600 LA 90732 823-H7
1700 LA 90018 633-F7
27TH ST E
37200 PMDL 93550 4286-F1
38500 PMDL 93550 4196-F7
43600 LAN 93535 4106-E1
43900 LAN 93535 4016-E5
47600 LACo 93535 3926-E5
27TH ST W
39600 PMDL 93551 4195-D4
39800 LACo 93551 4195-C2
41200 LACo 93551 4105-C7
41700 LACo 93536 4105-C6
42400 LAN 93536 4105-C1
44000 LAN 93536 4015-C2
47200 LAN 93536 3925-C4
49600 LACo 93536 3835-C7
49600 LACo 93536 3925-C1
28TH AV
- Ven 90291 671-H7
28TH CT
100 HMB 90254 762-F1
200 HMB 90254 732-G7
28TH PL
- Ven 90291 671-H7
100 MANB 90266 732-E5
28TH ST
100 HMB 90254 762-F1
100 MANB 90266 732-G4
200 HMB 90254 732-G7
2200 SMCA 90405 671-J1
2700 SMCA 90405 672-A2
34200 Actn 93510 4375-D4
E 28TH ST
100 LA 90011 674-D1
600 LBCH 90806 795-D2
600 SIGH 90755 795-E2
2400 VER 90058 674-H2
5100 LBCH 90815 796-B2
W 28TH ST
100 LA 90007 674-C1
100 LBCH 90806 795-C2
200 LA 90007 634-A7
400 SPed 90731 854-A1
1200 LBCH 90810 795-B2
2000 LA 90018 633-F7
4300 LA 90016 633-E7
28TH ST E
2700 PMDL 93550 4286-F2
38500 PMDL 93550 4196-F7
44900 LAN 93535 4016-F5
46100 LACo 93535 4016-F2
47600 LACo 93535 3926-E5
28TH ST W
35400 Actn 93510 4375-C2
39500 PMDL 93551 4195-C5
42100 LAN 93536 4105-C1
44000 LAN 93536 4015-C7
48000 LAN 93536 3925-C4
51000 LACo 93536 3835-C4
29TH AV
- Ven 90291 671-H7
29TH CT
100 HMB 90254 762-F1
200 HMB 90254 732-G7
29TH PL
- Ven 90291 671-H7
100 MANB 90266 732-E5
W 29TH PL
800 SPed 90731 854-A1
2000 LA 90018 633-H7
29TH PL E
37000 PMDL 93550 4286-F4
29TH ST
100 HMB 90254 762-F1
100 MANB 90266 732-F4
100 HMB 90254 732-G7
2200 SMCA 90405 671-J1
E 29TH ST
100 LA 90011 674-D1
100 LBCH 90806 795-E2
600 SIGH 90755 795-F2
2800 LBCH 90808 795-H2
5100 LBCH 90815 796-B2
W 29TH ST
100 LBCH 90806 795-C2
200 SPed 90731 854-A1
400 LA 90007 634-A7
1200 LBCH 90810 795-A2
1500 LA 90007 633-H7
1700 LA 90018 633-H7
4100 LA 90016 633-E7
29TH ST E
37000 PMDL 93550 4286-F2
38600 PMDL 93550 4196-F7
30TH AV
- Ven 90291 671-H7
30TH PL
- Ven 90291 671-H7
100 MANB 90266 732-E4
100 HMB 90254 732-G7
W 30TH PL
1300 LA 90007 634-A7
30TH ST
100 HMB 90254 732-F7
100 MANB 90266 732-F4
400 LA 90007 674-C1
2200 SMCA 90405 671-J1
2400 SMCA 90405 672-A2
E 30TH ST
100 LA 90011 674-D1
2400 VER 90058 674-H2
W 30TH ST
100 LA 90007 674-C1
400 SPed 90731 854-A1
500 LA 90007 634-A7
1500 LA 90007 633-H7
1600 LA 90018 633-F7
3800 LA 90016 633-D7
30TH ST E
36400 PMDL 93550 4286-F3
38300 PMDL 93550 4196-F6
38900 PMDL 93550 4196-F6
42000 PMDL 93550 4106-F5
42800 LAN 93535 4106-F1
43800 LAN 93535 4016-F6
46000 LACo 93535 4016-F2
46100 LACo 93535 3926-F5
30TH ST W
500 KeCo 93560 3835-B2
39200 PMDL 93551 4195-C2
39800 LACo 93551 4195-C2
41400 LAN 93551 4105-C7
41400 LAN 93551 4195-C2
41400 LACo 93551 4105-C7
41600 LACo 93536 4105-C7
41600 LAN 93536 4105-C2
44000 LAN 93536 4015-C2
46800 LAN 93536 3925-C6
48400 LACo 93536 3925-B2
49200 LACo 93536 3835-B4
W 31ST CT
300 SPed 90731 854-B1
31ST PL
100 HMB 90254 732-F7
100 MANB 90266 732-E4
31ST ST
100 HMB 90254 732-F7
100 MANB 90266 732-E4
2200 SMCA 90405 671-J1
2400 SMCA 90405 672-A1
E 31ST ST
100 Bxby 90807 795-E1
100 LA 90011 674-D1
S 31ST ST
400 SPed 90731 854-C1
W 31ST ST
100 LA 90007 674-C1
100 LBCH 90806 795-C1
600 SPed 90731 854-A1
1100 LA 90007 634-A7
1200 LBCH 90810 795-B1
2000 LA 90018 633-G7
31ST ST E
- LAN 93535 4106-F1
36700 PMDL 93550 4286-G2
38400 PMDL 93550 4196-G7
48000 LACo 93535 3926-F4
31ST ST W
34900 Actn 93510 4375-C1
44000 LAN 93536 4015-B6
44000 LAN 93536 4105-C1
32ND PL
100 MANB 90266 732-E4
100 HMB 90254 732-F7
32ND ST
100 MANB 90266 732-E4
2200 SMCA 90405 671-J1
2500 SMCA 90405 672-A1
E 32ND ST
100 LA 90011 674-D1
300 Bxby 90807 795-F1
1000 SIGH 90755 795-F1
W 32ND ST
100 LA 90007 674-C1
200 LBCH 90806 795-C1
400 SPed 90731 854-B1
700 LA 90007 634-B7
1200 LBCH 90810 795-A1
32ND ST E
- PMDL 93550 4286-G7
36000 PMDL 93550 4286-G1
38500 PMDL 93550 4196-G7
43200 LAN 93535 4106-F1
44000 LAN 93535 4016-F7
46000 LACo 93535 4016-F2
46800 LACo 93535 3926-F4
32ND ST W
40800 LACo 93551 4195-C2
42400 LAN 93536 4105-B1
44000 LAN 93536 4015-B4
47800 LAN 93536 3925-B5
48400 LACo 93536 3925-B4
50000 LACo 93536 3835-B6
32ND WY
1700 LBCH 90810 795-A1
33RD PL
100 MANB 90266 732-E4
100 HMB 90254 732-F7
33RD PL E
37900 PMDL 93550 4286-G2
33RD ST
- HAW 90260 732-J4
- HAW 90260 733-A4
100 HMB 90254 732-F7
100 MANB 90266 732-E4
2300 SMCA 90405 671-J1
2300 SMCA 90405 672-A1
E 33RD ST
100 LA 90011 674-D1
400 Bxby 90807 795-F1
600 SIGH 90755 795-F1
W 33RD ST
100 Bxby 90807 795-D1
100 LA 90007 674-C1
100 LBCH 90806 795-D1
400 SPed 90731 854-B1
1200 LBCH 90810 795-B1
33RD ST E
- PMDL 93550 4376-G1
36400 PMDL 93550 4286-G2
38600 PMDL 93550 4196-G7
43200 LAN 93535 4106-G2
46000 LAN 93535 4016-G4
47800 LACo 93535 3926-F5
33RD ST W
39900 PMDL 93551 4195-B4
43200 LAN 93536 4105-B1
44300 LAN 93536 4015-B5
49700 LACo 93536 3835-B7
W 33RD WY
200 Bxby 90807 795-C1
700 LBCH 90806 795-C1
34TH PL
100 MANB 90266 732-E4
100 HMB 90254 732-F7
34TH ST
100 HMB 90254 732-F7
100 MANB 90266 732-E4
1800 SMCA 90404 631-J7
2300 SMCA 90405 631-J7
2300 SMCA 90405 632-A7
2300 SMCA 90405 672-A1
E 34TH ST
900 LA 90011 674-E2
W 34TH ST
400 SPed 90731 854-A1
600 LA 90089 674-B1
800 LBCH 90806 795-C1
1200 LBCH 90810 795-A1
2200 LA 90732 823-G7
34TH ST W
40800 LACo 93551 4195-B1
41100 LACo 93536 4195-B1
W 35TH CT
300 SPed 90731 854-B2
400 LBCH 90806 795-C1
35TH PL
100 MANB 90266 732-E4
100 HMB 90254 732-F7
W 35TH PL
1200 LA 90007 673-H1
1200 LA 90007 674-A1
1400 LA 90018 673-H1
35TH ST
100 HMB 90254 732-F7
100 MANB 90266 732-E4
500 Bxby 90807 765-E7
E 35TH ST
100 Bxby 90807 765-D7
100 LA 90011 674-D2
W 35TH ST
100 LA 90007 674-A1
400 SPed 90731 854-B2
500 LBCH 90806 795-C1
1200 LA 90007 673-H1
1300 SPed 90731 853-J1
1400 LA 90018 673-H1
1900 LA 90732 823-G7
1900 LA 90732 853-J1
35TH ST E
- PMDL 93550 4376-G1
36600 PMDL 93550 4286-G2
38300 PMDL 93550 4196-G7
38800 PMDL 93550 4196-G4
42000 PMDL 93550 4106-G5
42800 LAN 93535 4106-G2
43600 LAN 93535 4016-G5
46000 LACo 93535 4016-G2
46000 LACo 93535 3926-G5
35TH ST W
- PMDL 93551 4195-B3
500 KeCo 93560 3835-A2
41400 LAN 93536 4105-B5
44100 LAN 93536 4015-B6
48000 LAN 93536 3925-B4
48400 LACo 93536 3925-A2
49400 LACo 93536 3835-A5
W 36TH CT
400 LBCH 90806 765-C7
36TH PL
100 MANB 90266 732-E4
E 36TH PL
100 LA 90011 674-C2
S 36TH PL
- LBCH 90803 825-J2
W 36TH PL
100 LA 90007 674-A1
1200 LA 90007 673-J1
1400 LA 90018 673-J1
36TH ST
- LBCH 90808 765-G7
100 MANB 90266 732-E4
2000 LKWD 90712 765-G7
E 36TH ST
100 Bxby 90807 765-D7
100 LA 90011 674-C2
W 36TH ST
100 Bxby 90807 765-D7
100 LA 90007 674-A1
500 LBCH 90806 765-C7
500 SPed 90731 854-A1
1100 SPed 90731 853-J1
1200 LA 90007 673-J1
1400 LA 90018 673-F1
3600 LA 90016 673-F1
36TH ST E
3500 LAN 93535 4016-G3
7600 PMDL 93550 4286-H2
38600 PMDL 93550 4196-H7
43000 LAN 93535 4106-G3
47600 LACo 93535 3926-G5
36TH ST W
40800 LACo 93551 4195-B1
41100 LACo 93536 4195-B1
42800 LAN 93536 4105-B1
44000 LAN 93536 4015-B7
47000 LAN 93536 3925-A6
W 37TH DR
1100 LA 90007 674-A1
1200 LA 90007 673-J1
1400 LA 90018 673-J1
S 37TH PL
- LBCH 90803 825-J2
W 37TH PL
- LA 90089 674-A1
100 LA 90007 674-A1
400 LA 90037 674-A1
1200 LA 90007 673-J1
1400 LA 90018 673-H1
E 37TH ST
100 LA 90011 674-C2
300 Bxby 90807 765-F7
2000 VER 90058 674-H3
W 37TH ST
100 Bxby 90807 765-D7
100 LA 90007 674-A1
400 LBCH 90806 765-C7
400 SPed 90731 854-A1
1100 SPed 90731 853-J1
1200 LA 90007 673-J1
1400 LA 90018 673-J1
2000 LA 90732 823-G7
37TH ST E
- PMDL 93550 4376-H2
36000 PMDL 93550 4286-H1
36000 PMDL 93550 4376-H2
38300 PMDL 93550 4196-H6
38800 PMDL 93550 4196-H2
42900 LAN 93535 4106-H2
45800 LAN 93535 4016-G3
46800 LACo 93535 3926-G5
37TH ST W
41900 LAN 93536 4105-A1
44000 LAN 93536 4015-A2
48000 LAN 93536 3925-A4
48400 LACo 93536 3925-A4
38TH PL
100 MANB 90266 732-E4
S 38TH PL
- LBCH 90803 825-J2
W 38TH PL
1400 LA 90062 673-H2
2700 LA 90008 673-F2
38TH ST
100 MANB 90266 732-E4
E 38TH ST
- LA 90058 674-H3
100 LA 90011 674-D2
2000 VER 90058 674-H3
W 38TH ST
100 LA 90037 674-A2
100 LA 90007 674-C2
400 SPed 90731 854-B2
500 LBCH 90806 765-C7
1100 LA 90037 673-H2
1300 LA 90062 673-H2
38TH ST E
- PMDL 93550 4286-H1
43000 LAN 93535 4106-H2
44000 LAN 93535 4016-H7
47600 LACo 93535 3926-H5
38TH ST W
40800 LACo 93551 4195-A2
41700 LAN 93536 4105-A4
45500 LAN 93536 4015-A3
39TH PL
- LBCH 90803 825-J2
W 39TH PL
1000 LA 90037 674-A2
1100 LA 90037 673-J2
1600 LA 90062 673-H2
39TH ST
100 MANB 90266 732-E4
W 39TH ST
100 LA 90037 674-A2
400 SPed 90731 854-B2
600 LBCH 90806 765-C7
1200 LA 90037 673-J2
1300 LA 90062 673-J2
2000 LA 90008 673-E2
39TH ST W
42800 LAN 93536 4105-A4
E 40TH PL
400 LA 90011 674-D2
1700 LA 90058 674-G3
W 40TH PL
100 LA 90037 674-C2
1200 LA 90037 673-J3
40TH ST
100 MANB 90266 732-E4
W 40TH ST
300 SPed 90731 854-B2
40TH ST E
4000 LACo 93535 3926-H4
4000 LACo 93523 3926-H3
35400 PMDL 93550 4286-H7
35400 PMDL 93550 4376-H1
35400 LACo 93552 4286-H7
35400 LACo 93552 4376-H1
35500 PMDL 93552 4286-H3
35500 PMDL 93550 4286-H3
38300 PMDL 93550 4196-H7
38300 PMDL 93552 4196-H3
38800 PMDL 93550 4196-H3
38800 LACo 93552 4196-H3
41100 PMDL 93550 4106-H5
41100 PMDL 93552 4106-H2
42800 LACo 93535 4106-H2
42800 LAN 93535 4106-H2
43800 LAN 93535 4016-H5
44800 LACo 93535 4016-H2
40TH ST W
- Actn 93510 4465-A3
400 KeCo 93560 3834-J3
37900 PMDL 93551 4285-A2
38200 PMDL 93551 4195-A7
40800 LACo 93551 4195-A1
41100 LACo 93536 4195-A1

LOS ANGELES CO.

STREET Block	City	ZIP	Pg-Grid
40TH ST W			
41200	LAN	93536	4195-A1
41200	LAN	93536	4105-A7
41800	LACo	93536	4105-A3
43900	LAN	93536	4015-A2
46800	LAN	93536	3925-A6
48400	LACo	93536	3924-J2
48400	LACo	93536	3925-A6
49600	LACo	93536	3834-J3
W 41ST DR			
500	LA	90037	674-A3
1700	LA	90062	673-H3
2100	LA	90008	673-H3
E 41ST PL			
100	LA	90011	674-D3
1700	LA	90058	674-F3
W 41ST PL			
100	LA	90037	674-B3
1200	LA	90037	673-J3
1400	LA	90062	673-H3
41ST ST			
100	MANB	90266	732-E4
E 41ST ST			
400	LA	90011	674-F3
1700	LA	90058	674-F3
W 41ST ST			
100	LA	90037	674-A3
1200	LA	90037	673-J3
1700	LA	90062	673-H3
3300	LA	90008	673-F3
41ST ST E			
35700	PMDL	93552	4286-J1
44600	LAN	93535	4016-H6
48400	LACo	93535	3926-H3
41ST ST W			
-	Actn	93510	4375-A7
-	LAN	93536	4105-A1
31700	Actn	93510	4465-A2
40800	LACo	93551	4195-A2
43000	LACo	93536	4105-A3
E 42ND PL			
300	LA	90011	674-E3
W 42ND PL			
100	LA	90037	674-B3
1400	LA	90062	673-H3
42ND ST			
100	MANB	90266	732-E3
E 42ND ST			
300	LA	90011	674-E3
1700	LA	90058	674-G3
W 42ND ST			
100	LA	90037	674-B3
1200	LA	90037	673-J3
1700	LA	90062	673-G3
2100	LA	90008	673-G3
42ND ST E			
35400	LACo	93552	4376-J1
35400	LACo	93552	4286-J7
35600	PMDL	93552	4286-J1
38400	PMDL	93552	4196-J7
42000	PMDL	93552	4106-J5
43000	LAN	93535	4106-J3
43000	LACo	93535	4106-J3
44800	LACo	93535	4016-H2
48800	LACo	93535	3926-H2
42ND ST W			
-	Actn	93510	4375-A7
32000	Actn	93510	4465-A3
41000	LACo	93536	4194-J1
41000	LACo	93551	4194-J1
41200	LAN	93536	4194-J1
41300	LAN	93536	4104-J1
42200	LACo	93536	4104-J3
44000	LAN	93536	4014-J3
47600	LAN	93536	3924-J6
48400	LACo	93536	3924-J1
43RD PL			
-	LBCH	90803	826-A2
E 43RD PL			
200	LA	90011	674-E3
W 43RD PL			
100	LA	90037	674-B3
1700	LA	90062	673-H3
2600	LA	90008	673-F3
43RD ST			
100	MANB	90266	732-E3
E 43RD ST			
100	LA	90011	674-E3
1700	LA	90058	674-F3
W 43RD ST			
100	LA	90037	674-A3
1200	LA	90037	673-J3
1700	LA	90062	673-G3
2100	LA	90008	673-F3
43RD ST E			
34100	LACo	93552	4376-J4
35700	PMDL	93552	4286-J1
44800	LACo	93535	4016-J5
43RD ST W			
-	LAN	93536	4014-J5
-	LAN	93536	4104-J1
40800	LACo	93551	4194-J2
43000	LACo	93536	4104-J3
44TH CIR			
400	Bxby	90807	765-E5
44TH ST			
100	MANB	90266	732-E3
E 44TH ST			
300	Bxby	90807	765-D5
2800	VER	90058	674-J3
2800	VER	90058	675-A3
44TH ST W			
-	LAN	93536	4014-J5
-	LAN	93536	4104-J1
E 44TH WY			
300	Bxby	90807	765-E5
45TH ST			
-	ELSG	90245	732-E3
-	MANB	90266	732-E3
4400	VER	90058	675-B3
E 45TH ST			
100	LA	90011	674-D3
200	Bxby	90807	765-E5
1700	LA	90058	674-G3
2000	VER	90058	674-H3
W 45TH ST			
100	LA	90037	674-C3
1200	LA	90037	673-J4
1400	LA	90062	673-J4
45TH ST E			
34100	LACo	93552	4377-A4
36400	PMDL	93552	4286-J2
38200	PMDL	93552	4196-J7
38800	LACo	93552	4196-J4
42000	PMDL	93552	4106-J5
43000	LACo	93535	4106-J3
43600	LAN	93535	4106-J1
43800	LAN	93535	4016-J7
44800	LACo	93535	4016-J1
46500	LACo	93535	3926-J2
45TH ST W			
-	KeCo	93560	3834-H1
40800	PMDL	93551	4194-J2
40800	LACo	93551	4194-J2
41100	PMDL	93536	4194-J2
41100	LACo	93536	4194-J2
41200	LAN	93536	4194-J2
41300	LAN	93536	4104-J1
41300	LACo	93536	4104-J4
44000	LAN	93536	4014-J1
47600	LAN	93536	3924-J6
48600	LACo	93536	3924-H3
49600	LACo	93536	3834-H4
E 45TH WY			
600	Bxby	90807	765-E4
E 46TH ST			
100	LA	90011	674-D4
200	Bxby	90807	765-E4
200	NLB	90805	765-D5
1700	LA	90058	674-G4
1900	VER	90058	674-H3
2800	VER	90058	675-A3
W 46TH ST			
100	LA	90037	674-B4
1200	LA	90037	673-J4
1400	LA	90062	673-J4
2800	LA	90043	673-F4
46TH ST E			
44200	LAN	93535	4016-J7
44800	LACo	93535	4016-J5
46TH ST W			
43300	LAN	93536	4104-J1
44200	LAN	93536	4014-H7
E 47TH PL			
100	LA	90011	674-C4
W 47TH PL			
100	LA	90037	674-C4
E 47TH ST			
-	NLB	90805	765-D4
100	LA	90011	674-C4
1700	LA	90058	674-F4
W 47TH ST			
100	LA	90037	674-B4
1200	LA	90037	673-J4
1400	LA	90062	673-J4
47TH ST E			
17800	PMDL	93552	4287-A7
34100	LACo	93552	4377-A3
34500	PMDL	93552	4377-A3
35200	LACo	93552	4287-A7
38300	PMDL	93552	4197-A7
44900	LACo	93535	4016-J1
46600	LACo	93535	3926-J2
47TH ST E Rt#-138			
4600	PMDL	93552	4197-A7
4600	PMDL	93552	4287-A3
47TH ST W			
41200	LACo	93536	4194-H1
41500	LACo	93536	4104-H4
43300	LAN	93536	4104-H1
44000	LAN	93536	4014-H1
47800	LAN	93536	3924-H3
48600	LACo	93536	3924-H3
50000	LACo	93536	3834-H6
E 48TH PL			
1300	LA	90011	674-F4
1700	LA	90058	674-G4
E 48TH ST			
100	LA	90011	674-D4
1900	VER	90058	674-H4
4500	VER	90058	675-C4
W 48TH ST			
-	NLB	90805	765-C4
100	LA	90037	674-A4
1200	LA	90037	673-G4
1400	LA	90062	673-G4
2100	LA	90043	673-G4
3400	LACo	90043	673-G4
48TH ST E			
35800	LACo	93552	4287-A7
37400	PMDL	93552	4287-A3
44000	LAN	93535	4017-A7
48TH ST W			
-	PMDL	93536	4194-H1
-	PMDL	93551	4194-H1
42800	LACo	93536	4104-H4
45200	LAN	93536	4014-H4
49300	LACo	93536	3924-H1
49TH AV			
-	NLB	90805	765-C4
E 49TH PL			
800	LA	90011	674-E4
W 49TH PL			
500	LA	90037	674-B4
E 49TH ST			
100	LA	90011	674-D4
100	NLB	90805	765-D4
1900	VER	90058	674-H4
4300	VER	90058	675-C4
W 49TH ST			
-	NLB	90805	765-C4
100	LA	90037	674-A4
1200	LA	90037	673-H4
1400	LA	90062	673-H4
49TH ST E			
37600	PMDL	93552	4287-A2
E 50TH PL			
1600	LA	90011	674-G4
W 50TH PL			
800	LA	90037	674-A4
E 50TH ST			
100	LA	90011	674-C4
1700	LA	90058	674-G4
2700	VER	90058	674-J4
2800	VER	90058	675-B4
W 50TH ST			
100	LA	90037	674-A4
1200	LA	90037	673-J4
1400	LA	90062	673-J4
2800	LA	90043	673-F4
50TH ST E			
29500	LACo	93535	4017-A2
35800	LACo	93552	4287-A7
36600	PMDL	93552	4287-A1
38400	PMDL	93552	4197-A7
38800	LACo	93552	4197-A3
41000	LACo	93552	4107-A6
42000	PMDL	93552	4107-A2
42800	LACo	93535	4107-A2
42800	LAN	93535	4107-A2
43800	LAN	93535	4017-A7
50TH ST W			
1000	KeCo	93560	3834-G3
40900	PMDL	93551	4194-H2
41000	PMDL	93536	4194-H1
41200	LACo	93536	4104-H3
41200	LACo	93536	4194-H1
43200	LAN	93536	4104-H1
44000	LAN	93536	4014-H3
47600	LAN	93536	3924-G4
48400	LACo	93536	3924-G4
49700	LACo	93536	3834-G5
W 51ST PL			
800	LA	90037	674-A4
1200	LA	90037	673-J4
1400	LA	90062	673-J4
E 51ST ST			
100	LA	90011	674-E4
100	NLB	90805	765-D4
1800	LA	90058	674-G4
1900	VER	90058	674-H4
W 51ST ST			
-	NLB	90805	765-C4
100	LA	90037	674-A4
1200	LA	90037	673-H4
1400	LA	90062	673-H4
51ST ST E			
37200	PMDL	93552	4287-B3
38400	PMDL	93552	4197-B7
51ST ST W			
41300	LACo	93536	4104-H3
49400	LACo	93536	3924-G1
E 52ND DR			
4500	MYWD	90270	675-E5
4500	VER	90040	675-E5
E 52ND PL			
600	LA	90011	674-E5
4400	MYWD	90270	675-E5
4800	VER	90040	675-E5
W 52ND PL			
100	LA	90037	674-B5
52ND ST			
2000	LKWD	90712	765-G3
E 52ND ST			
-	NLB	90805	765-D3
100	LA	90011	674-E4
1700	LA	90058	674-G4
1900	Bxby	90807	765-G3
1900	VER	90058	674-H4
2400	HNTP	90058	674-H4
2500	HNTP	90255	674-J4
3500	MYWD	90270	675-C4
4400	VER	90058	675-D4
W 52ND ST			
-	NLB	90805	765-C3
100	LA	90037	674-B4
1200	LA	90037	673-J5
1400	LA	90062	673-J5
2200	LA	90043	673-E5
3600	LACo	90043	673-E5
52ND ST E			
35600	LACo	93552	4287-B7
37200	PMDL	93552	4287-B1
43200	LACo	93535	4107-B2
52ND ST W			
-	KeCo	93560	3834-G3
42000	LACo	93536	4104-G5
42800	LAN	93536	4104-G3
45200	LAN	93536	4014-G3
48400	LACo	93536	3924-G4
49700	LACo	93536	3834-G5
E 53RD ST			
-	NLB	90805	765-D3
100	LA	90011	674-D5
1700	LA	90058	674-G5
2400	VER	90058	674-G5
2400	HNTP	90058	674-J4
2500	HNTP	90255	674-J4
3400	MYWD	90270	675-C4
W 53RD ST			
-	NLB	90805	765-C3
100	LA	90037	674-A5
1200	LA	90037	673-J5
1400	LA	90062	673-J5
53RD ST E			
35600	LACo	93552	4287-B6
36200	PMDL	93552	4287-B1
43100	LAN	93535	4107-B2
43200	LACo	93535	4107-B2
53RD ST W			
33900	Actn	93510	4374-G5
41100	PMDL	93551	4194-G1
41700	LACo	93536	4104-G7
46000	LAN	93536	4014-G3
48000	LAN	93536	3924-G5
49300	LACo	93536	3924-G1
54TH PL			
-	LBCH	90803	826-B2
E 54TH ST			
100	LA	90011	674-D5
1700	LA	90058	674-G5
2400	VER	90058	674-J5
2400	HNTP	90058	674-J5
2500	HNTP	90255	674-J5
2800	VER	90058	675-A5
3500	MYWD	90270	675-C5
W 54TH ST			
100	LA	90037	674-B5
1200	LA	90037	673-G5
1400	LA	90062	673-G5
2200	LA	90043	673-E5
3600	LACo	90043	673-E5
5200	LadH	90056	673-A5
55TH PL			
-	LBCH	90803	826-C3
E 55TH ST			
-	NLB	90805	765-E2
100	LA	90011	674-D5
1600	LA	90058	674-H5
1900	VER	90058	674-H5
2400	HNTP	90058	674-H5
2500	HNTP	90255	674-J5
3500	MYWD	90270	675-C5
W 55TH ST			
100	LA	90037	674-A5
1200	LA	90037	673-J5
1400	LA	90062	673-J5
5200	LadH	90056	673-A5
5400	LadH	90056	672-J5
55TH ST E			
35800	LACo	93552	4287-C7
36200	PMDL	93552	4287-B2
38200	PMDL	93552	4197-B7
42000	PMDL	93552	4107-B5
42900	LACo	93535	4107-B3
42900	LAN	93535	4107-B1
43600	LAN	93535	4017-B7
44400	LACo	93535	4017-B1
55TH ST W			
-	KeCo	93560	3834-F3
33800	Actn	93510	4374-G6
40500	PMDL	93551	4194-G2
40900	PMDL	93551	4104-G7
41100	PMDL	93536	4104-G7
41600	LACo	93536	4104-G6
42000	LAN	93536	4104-G3
45200	LAN	93536	4014-G1
47600	LAN	93536	3924-G5
48400	LACo	93536	3924-F4
49700	LACo	93536	3834-F4
E 55TH WY			
2600	NLB	90805	765-H2
56TH PL			
-	LBCH	90803	826-C3
E 56TH ST			
-	NLB	90805	765-D2
100	LA	90011	674-D5
2400	VER	90058	674-J5
2400	HNTP	90058	674-J5
2500	HNTP	90255	674-J5
2900	LKWD	90712	765-H2
3500	MYWD	90270	675-C5
W 56TH ST			
100	LA	90037	674-A5
1200	LA	90037	673-J5
1400	LA	90062	673-J5
56TH ST E			
35600	LACo	93552	4287-C6
37200	PMDL	93552	4287-C3
43200	LACo	93535	4107-B2
43200	LAN	93535	4107-B2
56TH ST W			
42400	LAN	93536	4104-G5
E 56TH WY			
2600	NLB	90805	765-H2
57TH PL			
-	LBCH	90803	826-C3
E 57TH ST			
100	LA	90011	674-D5
100	NLB	90805	765-D2
1700	LA	90058	674-G5
1900	VER	90058	674-H5
2400	HNTP	90058	674-H5
2500	HNTP	90255	674-J5
2700	HNTP	90255	675-C5
3500	MYWD	90270	675-C5
W 57TH ST			
100	LA	90037	674-A5
1200	LA	90037	673-J5
1400	LA	90062	673-J5
2200	LA	90043	673-F5
3600	LACo	90043	673-E5
4800	LadH	90056	673-B5
5400	LadH	90056	672-J5
57TH ST E			
34300	LACo	93552	4377-C3
36200	PMDL	93552	4287-C2
46000	LACo	93535	4017-B2
57TH ST W			
-	Actn	93510	4374-G7
-	Actn	93510	4464-G1
-	KeCo	93560	3834-F1
41600	LACo	93536	4104-G7
41600	LACo	93551	4104-G7
42000	LAN	93536	4104-F1
45200	LAN	93536	4014-F3
50400	LACo	93536	3834-F4
E 58TH DR			
1100	Flor	90001	674-F6
58TH PL			
-	LBCH	90803	826-C3
E 58TH PL			
1100	Flor	90001	674-F5
W 58TH PL			
100	LA	90003	674-C6
800	LA	90044	674-A6
1300	LA	90044	673-J6
1400	LA	90047	673-J6
3400	LA	90043	673-D6
4400	LACo	90043	673-D6
5000	LadH	90056	673-A6
E 58TH ST			
100	LA	90011	674-D5
2400	HNTP	90058	674-J5
2500	HNTP	90255	674-J5
2700	HNTP	90255	675-C5
3500	MYWD	90270	675-C5
W 58TH ST			
100	LA	90037	674-A5
1200	LA	90037	673-J5
1400	LA	90062	673-J5
58TH ST E			
-	PMDL	93552	4197-C7
37800	PMDL	93552	4287-C2
58TH ST W			
-	LAN	93536	4014-F7
-	PMDL	93552	4197-C7
-	PMDL	93552	4287-C1
800	KeCo	93560	3834-F1
42200	LAN	93536	4104-F1
W 59TH DR			
900	LA	90044	674-A6
59TH PL			
-	LBCH	90803	826-C3
E 59TH PL			
100	LA	90003	674-F6
1100	Flor	90001	674-F6
3500	HNTP	90255	675-C5
4500	MYWD	90270	675-E6
W 59TH PL			
100	LA	90003	674-C6
500	LA	90044	674-A6
1300	LA	90044	673-J6
1400	LA	90047	673-J6
3100	LA	90043	673-D6
4400	LACo	90043	673-D6
E 59TH ST			
100	NLB	90805	765-D2
600	LA	90001	674-E6
1100	Flor	90001	674-F6
W 59TH ST			
100	LA	90003	674-C6
500	LA	90044	674-A6
1300	LA	90044	673-J6
1400	LA	90047	673-J6
2200	LA	90043	673-D6
4400	LACo	90043	673-D6
5000	LadH	90056	673-B6
59TH ST W			
500	KeCo	93560	3834-F2
42200	LAN	93536	4104-F1
60TH PL			
-	LBCH	90803	826-C3
E 60TH PL			
2900	HNTP	90255	675-A6
4800	MYWD	90270	675-E6
W 60TH PL			
1000	LA	90044	674-A6
1300	LA	90044	673-J6
1400	LA	90047	673-J6
E 60TH ST			
100	LA	90003	674-D6
100	NLB	90805	765-D1
600	LA	90001	674-E6
1100	Flor	90001	674-F6
3500	HNTP	90255	675-C6
4300	MYWD	90270	675-E6
W 60TH ST			
100	LA	90003	674-C6
500	LA	90044	674-A6
1300	LA	90044	673-J6
1400	LA	90047	673-J6
2200	LA	90043	673-D6
4400	LACo	90043	673-D6
60TH ST E			
36100	PMDL	93552	4287-C2
38200	PMDL	93552	4197-C7
38400	LACo	93552	4197-C7
42000	PMDL	93552	4107-C3
42600	LACo	93535	4017-C2
42800	LACo	93535	4107-C3
44600	LAN	93535	4017-C7
44600	LAN	93535	4107-C1
60TH ST W			
-	KeCo	93560	3834-E3
40600	PMDL	93551	4194-F1
40700	PMDL	93551	4104-F7
41600	LACo	93536	4104-F3
41600	PMDL	93536	4104-F7
41600	LACo	93551	4104-F7
42000	LAN	93536	4104-F3
44200	LAN	93536	4014-F3
46800	LAN	93536	3924-F7
48400	LACo	93536	3924-E3
49600	LACo	93536	3834-E6
61ST PL			
-	LBCH	90803	826-C3
E 61ST PL			
3500	HNTP	90255	675-C6
E 61ST ST			
100	LA	90003	674-D6
300	NLB	90805	765-D1
600	LA	90001	674-E6
1100	Flor	90001	674-F6
2900	HNTP	90255	675-A6
4300	MYWD	90270	675-E6
5500	CMRC	90040	675-G6
W 61ST ST			
100	LA	90003	674-C6
500	LA	90044	674-A6
1300	LA	90044	673-J6
1400	LA	90047	673-J6
3600	LA	90043	673-D6
4400	LACo	90043	673-D6
5400	LadH	90056	672-J6
5400	LadH	90056	673-D6
61ST ST E			
46000	LACo	93535	4017-C2
61ST ST W			
42200	LAN	93536	4104-F1
42300	LACo	93536	4104-F5
44100	LAN	93536	4014-F7
62ND AV			
-	PdlR	90293	702-A2
62ND PL			
-	LBCH	90803	826-C3
W 62ND PL			
800	LA	90044	674-A6
4600	LA	90043	673-C6
E 62ND ST			
100	LA	90003	674-D6
600	LA	90001	674-E6
1100	Flor	90001	674-F6
W 62ND ST			
100	LA	90003	674-C6
500	LA	90044	674-A6
1300	LA	90044	673-J6
1400	LA	90047	673-H6
2300	LA	90043	673-D6
4400	LACo	90043	673-B6
4700	LadH	90056	673-A6
5400	LadH	90056	672-J6
62ND ST E			
35900	LACo	93552	4287-D6
35900	PMDL	93552	4287-D4
46000	LACo	93535	4017-C1
62ND ST W			
-	KeCo	93560	3834-E3
35600	LACo	91390	4374-F1
41500	PMDL	93551	4104-E7
42000	LAN	93536	4104-E1
42300	LACo	93536	4104-E5
44200	LAN	93536	4014-E6
48700	LACo	93536	3924-E1
50900	LACo	93536	3834-E4
63RD AV			
-	PdlR	90293	702-A3
63RD PL			
-	LBCH	90803	826-C3
W 63RD PL			
300	LA	90003	674-B6
500	LA	90044	674-B6
E 63RD ST			
300	NLB	90805	765-D1
1100	Flor	90001	674-E6
W 63RD ST			
3100	LA	90043	673-D6
4800	LA	90056	673-B7
5500	LadH	90056	672-J6
63RD ST E			
35000	LACo	93552	4377-D1
63RD ST W			
6300	PMDL	93536	4104-E6
6300	PMDL	93551	4104-E6
44000	LAN	93536	4014-E7
44000	LAN	93536	4104-E1
64TH AV			
-	PdlR	90293	702-A3
64TH PL			
-	LBCH	90803	826-C3
E 64TH PL			
100	ING	90302	673-C7
W 64TH PL			
100	ING	90302	673-B7
E 64TH ST			
100	LA	90003	674-D6
500	NLB	90805	765-E1
900	NLB	90805	735-F7
1100	Flor	90001	674-F6
1900	HNTP	90001	674-G6
W 64TH ST			
100	LA	90003	674-C6
500	ING	90302	673-B7
500	LA	90056	673-A6
800	LA	90044	674-A6
1300	LA	90044	673-J6
1400	LA	90047	673-J6
2600	LA	90043	673-F6
5200	LadH	90056	673-A6
5400	ING	90302	672-J7
5400	LadH	90056	672-J7
65TH AV			
-	PdlR	90293	702-A3
65TH PL			
-	LBCH	90803	826-C3
W 65TH PL			
1000	LA	90044	674-A7
1300	LA	90044	673-J7
1400	LA	90047	673-J7
2200	LA	90043	673-G7
E 65TH ST			
100	LA	90003	674-D7
200	NLB	90805	735-C7
700	ING	90302	673-E7
1100	Flor	90001	674-F6
1900	HNTP	90001	674-G6
W 65TH ST			
100	LA	90003	674-C7
500	LA	90044	674-A7
1300	LA	90044	673-J7
1400	LA	90047	673-J7
65TH ST E			
36200	PMDL	93552	4287-D6
38100	PMDL	93552	4197-D7
43200	LACo	93535	4107-D2
43200	LAN	93535	4107-D2
44400	LACo	93535	4017-D3
65TH ST W			
-	KeCo	93560	3834-D3
41400	PMDL	93551	4104-E7
41600	PMDL	93536	4104-E6
42000	LAN	93536	4104-E2
42000	LACo	93536	4104-E6
44100	LAN	93536	4014-E2
47300	LAN	93536	3924-E6
48400	LACo	93536	3924-D2
49700	LACo	93536	3834-D4
66TH AV			
-	PdlR	90293	702-A3
66TH PL			
-	LBCH	90803	826-C3
W 66TH PL			
3300	LA	90043	673-F7
E 66TH ST			
100	LA	90003	674-D7
1000	ING	90302	673-E7
1100	Flor	90001	674-F7
W 66TH ST			
100	LA	90003	674-C7
500	LA	90044	674-A7
1300	LA	90044	673-J7
1400	LA	90047	673-J7
3300	LA	90043	673-F7
66TH ST E			
35200	LACo	93552	4377-E1
66TH ST W			
1100	KeCo	93560	3834-D1
42400	LAN	93536	4104-E5
49000	LACo	93536	3924-D2
E 66TH WY			
1000	NLB	90805	735-E7
67TH PL			
-	LBCH	90803	826-D4
67TH ST			
500	NLB	90805	735-D7
E 67TH ST			
100	LA	90003	674-D7
100	NLB	90805	735-C7
500	ING	90302	673-E7
1100	Flor	90001	674-F7
1900	HNTP	90001	674-G7
W 67TH ST			
100	LA	90003	674-C7
1000	LA	90044	674-A7
1300	LA	90044	673-J7
1400	LA	90047	673-J7
2200	LA	90043	673-G7
67TH ST E			
37600	PMDL	93552	4287-E2
43200	LACo	93535	4107-E2
43400	LAN	93535	4107-E2
45200	LACo	93535	4017-E5
67TH ST W			
-	PMDL	93536	4104-D6
-	KeCo	93560	3834-D1
41400	PMDL	93551	4104-D6
42000	LACo	93536	4104-D6
42300	LAN	93536	4104-D5
44800	LAN	93536	4014-D1
46800	LAN	93536	3924-D5
48400	LACo	93536	3924-D2
50000	LACo	93536	3834-D5
E 67TH WY			
-	NLB	90805	735-C7
W 67TH WY			
100	NLB	90805	735-B7
68TH PL			
-	LBCH	90803	826-D4
E 68TH ST			
-	NLB	90805	735-F6
100	LA	90003	674-D7
900	ING	90302	673-E7
1100	Flor	90001	674-F7
W 68TH ST			
100	NLB	90805	735-B7
300	LA	90003	674-C7
500	LA	90044	674-A7
1300	LA	90044	673-J7
1400	LA	90047	673-J7
3100	LA	90043	673-F7
68TH ST W			
1100	KeCo	93560	3834-D1
49000	LACo	93536	3924-D2
E 68TH WY			
-	NLB	90805	735-C6
69TH PL			
-	LBCH	90803	826-D4
E 69TH ST			
-	NLB	90805	735-C6
100	LA	90003	674-D7
1100	Flor	90001	674-F7
1900	HNTP	90001	674-G7
W 69TH ST			
100	LA	90003	674-C7
500	LA	90044	674-A7
1300	LA	90044	673-J7
1400	LA	90047	673-J7
3100	LA	90043	673-F7
69TH ST W			
35300	LACo	91390	4374-D2
E 69TH WY			
-	NLB	90805	735-C6
70TH PL			
-	LBCH	90803	826-D4
E 70TH ST			
100	LA	90003	674-D7
600	NLB	90805	735-E6
1100	Flor	90001	674-F7
1200	PRM	90723	735-H6
W 70TH ST			
100	LA	90003	674-C7
100	NLB	90805	735-B6
500	LA	90044	674-A7
1300	LA	90044	673-J7
1400	LA	90047	673-J7
2200	LA	90043	673-G7
70TH ST E			
35300	PMDL	93552	4377-E1
35300	Litl	93543	4377-E1
35400	PMDL	93552	4287-E5
35400	Litl	93543	4287-E5
38200	PMDL	93552	4197-E7
38400	LACo	93552	4197-E3
40000	LACo	93552	4107-E7
42000	PMDL	93552	4107-E3
42800	LACo	93535	4107-E3
42900	LAN	93535	4107-E3
43600	LAN	93535	4017-E7
44400	LACo	93535	4017-E2
70TH ST W			
-	PMDL	93536	4104-D5
-	KeCo	93560	3834-C3
41400	PMDL	93551	4104-D7
41600	PMDL	93551	4194-D1
42000	LACo	93536	4104-D5
42000	LAN	93536	4104-D2
44000	LAN	93536	4014-D7
44400	LACo	93536	4014-D3
46800	LAN	93536	3924-D5
46800	LACo	93536	3924-C2
49700	LACo	93536	3834-C5
E 70TH WY			
900	NLB	90805	735-E6
71ST PL			
-	LBCH	90803	826-D4
E 71ST ST			
100	LA	90003	674-D7
600	NLB	90805	735-E6
1100	Flor	90001	674-F7
W 71ST ST			
100	LA	90003	674-C7
800	LA	90044	674-A7
1300	LA	90044	673-J7
1400	LA	90047	673-J7
3100	LA	90043	673-F7
71ST ST W			
1000	KeCo	93560	3834-C1
42200	LAN	93536	4104-D5
50400	LACo	93536	3834-C3
E 71ST WY			
900	NLB	90805	735-E6
72ND PL			
-	LBCH	90803	826-D4
E 72ND ST			
500	NLB	90805	735-E5
6300	PRM	90723	735-E5
72ND ST E			
4800	Litl	93543	4377-F2
36400	Litl	93543	4287-F5
36400	PMDL	93552	4287-F5
42200	PMDL	93552	4107-F5
43400	LACo	93535	4107-F2
43400	LAN	93535	4107-F2
45200	LACo	93535	4017-F2
72ND ST W			
-	KeCo	93560	3834-C3
40000	LACo	93551	4194-D4
42400	LAN	93536	4104-C5
46000	LACo	93536	4014-C3
46000	LAN	93536	4014-C3
47200	LACo	93536	3924-C3
50000	LACo	93536	3834-C4
E 73RD ST			
100	LA	90003	674-D7
600	LA	90001	674-D7
1100	Flor	90001	674-F7
W 73RD ST			
100	LA	90003	704-C1
500	LA	90044	704-B1
1300	LA	90044	703-J1
1800	LA	90047	703-G1
2200	LA	90043	703-F1
73RD ST E			
37200	PMDL	93552	4287-F3
42000	PMDL	93552	4107-F5
45700	LACo	93535	4017-F5
73RD ST W			
42300	LAN	93536	4104-C5
45000	LACo	93536	4014-C5
W 74TH PL			
3500	ING	90305	703-E1
E 74TH ST			
100	LA	90003	704-D1
600	LA	90001	704-D1
1100	Flor	90001	704-F1
1900	Flor	90001	674-G7
W 74TH ST			
100	LA	90003	704-B1
500	LA	90044	704-B1
1300	LA	90044	703-H1
1400	LA	90047	703-H1
2200	LA	90043	703-F1
3500	ING	90305	703-F1
5600	Wch	90045	702-H1
W 75TH PL			
3500	ING	90305	703-E1
6000	Wch	90045	702-H1
E 75TH ST			
100	LA	90003	704-D1
600	LA	90001	704-D1
1100	Flor	90001	704-F1
W 75TH ST			
100	LA	90003	704-B1
500	LA	90044	704-B1
1600	LA	90047	703-F1
2200	LA	90043	703-F1
5700	Wch	90045	702-H1
75TH ST E			
34800	Litl	93543	4377-G2
35400	Litl	93543	4287-F2
37200	PMDL	93552	4287-F2
38000	PMDL	93552	4197-F7
38400	LACo	93552	4197-F7
42200	PMDL	93552	4107-F5
43000	LACo	93535	4107-F2
43000	LAN	93535	4107-F2
43600	LACo	93535	4017-F1
43600	LAN	93535	4017-F6
75TH ST W			
-	KeCo	93560	3834-B3
40000	LACo	93551	4194-C4
41600	PMDL	93551	4104-C7
42300	LAN	93536	4104-C2
45200	LACo	93536	4014-C2
45200	LAN	93536	4014-C5
46800	LACo	93536	3924-B2
49700	LACo	93536	3834-B4
E 76TH PL			
100	LA	90003	704-D1
600	LA	90001	704-E1
1100	Flor	90001	704-F1
W 76TH PL			
6000	Wch	90045	702-H1
E 76TH ST			
100	LA	90003	704-D1
600	LA	90001	704-D1
1100	Flor	90001	704-F1
W 76TH ST			
100	LA	90003	704-B1
500	LA	90044	704-A1
1300	LA	90044	703-H1
1400	LA	90047	703-H1
2200	ING	90305	703-F1
2200	LA	90043	703-F1
2600	ING	90043	703-H1
5400	Wch	90045	702-H1
5400	Wch	90045	703-A1
76TH ST E			
45200	LACo	93535	4017-F5
76TH ST W			
900	KeCo	93560	3834-B1
42200	LAN	93536	4104-C5
E 77TH PL			
1100	Flor	90001	704-F1
W 77TH PL			
5800	Wch	90045	702-G1
E 77TH ST			
100	LA	90003	704-D1
600	LA	90001	704-E1
1100	Flor	90001	704-F1
W 77TH ST			
100	LA	90003	704-B1
500	LA	90044	704-A1
1300	LA	90044	703-J1
1800	LA	90047	703-F1
2200	ING	90305	703-F1
3100	LA	90043	703-F1
5400	Wch	90045	703-A1
5500	Wch	90045	702-F1
77TH ST E			
33800	Litl	93543	4377-G2
35400	Litl	93543	4287-G7
45200	LACo	93535	4017-G4
77TH ST W			
-	KeCo	93560	3834-B3
47600	LACo	93536	3924-B2
50400	LACo	93536	3834-B3
W 78TH PL			
1800	LA	90047	703-G1
2200	ING	90305	703-F1
3100	LA	90043	703-F1
5800	Wch	90045	702-G1
E 78TH ST			
-	LA	90003	704-D1
600	LA	90001	704-E1
1100	Flor	90001	704-F1
W 78TH ST			
100	LA	90003	704-B1
500	LA	90044	704-A1
1300	LA	90044	703-H1
1400	LA	90047	703-H1
2200	ING	90305	703-E1
3100	LA	90043	703-F1
5500	Wch	90045	702-G1
5500	Wch	90045	703-A2
78TH ST W			
600	KeCo	93560	3834-B2
51300	LACo	93536	3834-B4
W 79TH PL			
6300	Wch	90045	702-G1
E 79TH ST			
100	LA	90003	704-D1
600	LA	90001	704-E1
W 79TH ST			
100	LA	90003	704-B1
500	LA	90044	704-A1
1200	LA	90044	703-G1
1400	LA	90047	703-G1
2200	ING	90305	703-G1
3100	LA	90043	703-F2
5500	Wch	90045	703-A2
5500	Wch	90045	702-G1
7700	PdlR	90293	702-C2
W 80TH PL			
6300	Wch	90045	702-F2
E 80TH ST			
100	LA	90003	704-C1
600	LA	90001	704-E1
1100	Flor	90001	704-G1
W 80TH ST			
100	LA	90003	704-B1
500	LA	90044	704-B1
1200	LA	90044	703-H2
1400	LA	90047	703-H2
2300	ING	90305	703-F2
6300	Wch	90045	702-G1
7900	PdlR	90293	702-C2
80TH ST E			
34300	Litl	93543	4377-H2
34900	Litl	93543	4287-G7
36000	Litl	93543	4287-G7
37200	PMDL	93552	4287-H3
37200	LACo	93552	4287-H3
38000	PMDL	93552	4197-G7
38000	LACo	93552	4197-G7
42000	PMDL	93552	4107-G5
42800	LAN	93535	4107-G2
42800	LACo	93535	4107-G2
43700	LAN	93535	4017-G7
44400	LACo	93535	4017-G2
80TH ST W			
-	KeCo	93560	3834-A3
42000	LAN	93536	4104-B2
42000	LAN	93551	4104-B6
43600	LACo	93536	4014-B7
43600	LAN	93536	4014-B2
46800	LACo	93536	3924-B7
49700	LACo	93536	3834-A3
W 81ST PL			
1000	LA	90044	704-A2
1200	LA	90044	703-J2
E 81ST ST			
100	LA	90003	704-C2
600	LA	90001	704-E2
1100	Flor	90001	704-G2
W 81ST ST			
100	LA	90003	704-C2
500	LA	90044	704-A2
1200	LA	90044	703-H2
1400	LA	90047	703-H2
2200	ING	90305	703-F2
6300	Wch	90045	702-D2
7500	PdlR	90293	702-C2
81ST ST E			
35600	Litl	93543	4287-H7
81ST ST W			
1000	KeCo	93560	3834-A1
E 82ND PL			
100	LA	90003	704-D2
1500	Flor	90001	704-F2
W 82ND PL			
2600	ING	90305	703-F2
E 82ND ST			
100	LA	90003	704-C2
600	LA	90001	704-E2
1100	Flor	90001	704-G2
W 82ND ST			
-	LA	90003	704-C2
500	LA	90044	704-A2
1200	LA	90044	703-H2
1400	LA	90047	703-H2
2500	ING	90305	703-F2

STREET Block City ZIP Pg-Grid

W 82ND ST
5300 Wch 90045 703-A2
5500 Wch 90045 702-G2
7500 PdlR 90293 702-C2
82ND ST E
33800 Litl 93543 4377-H2
35100 Litl 93543 4287-H7
38600 LACo 93552 4197-H7
45800 LACo 93535 4017-H2
82ND ST W
1000 KeCo 93560 3834-A1
45400 LACo 93536 4014-A4
45400 LAN 93536 4014-A4
47700 LACo 93536 3924-A2
49800 LACo 93536 3834-A7
W 83RD PL
1200 LA 90044 703-J2
1200 LA 90044 704-A2
6000 Wch 90045 702-H2
E 83RD ST
100 LA 90003 704-D2
600 LA 90001 704-D2
1100 Flor 90001 704-F2
W 83RD ST
100 LA 90003 704-C2
500 LA 90044 704-A2
1200 LA 90044 703-H2
1400 LA 90047 703-H2
2200 ING 90305 703-F2
5200 ING 90302 703-A2
5200 Wch 90045 703-A2
5500 Wch 90045 702-D2
7500 PdlR 90293 702-B3
83RD ST W
1200 KeCo 93560 3834-A1
E 84TH PL
100 LA 90003 704-D2
600 LA 90001 704-D2
1100 Flor 90001 704-F2
W 84TH PL
100 LA 90003 704-C2
1000 LA 90044 704-A2
1200 LA 90044 703-H2
1400 LA 90047 703-H2
2200 ING 90305 703-E2
6200 Wch 90045 702-E2
E 84TH ST
100 LA 90003 704-D2
600 LA 90001 704-D2
1100 Flor 90001 704-F2
W 84TH ST
100 LA 90003 704-C2
500 LA 90044 704-A2
1200 LA 90044 703-H2
1400 LA 90047 703-H2
2600 ING 90305 703-F2
5900 Wch 90045 702-F2
84TH ST W
1000 KeCo 93560 3833-J1
W 85TH PL
100 LA 90003 704-C2
5700 Wch 90045 702-F3
E 85TH ST
100 LA 90003 704-D2
600 LA 90001 704-E2
1100 Flor 90001 704-F2
W 85TH ST
100 LA 90003 704-C2
500 LA 90044 704-A2
1200 LA 90044 703-H2
1400 LA 90047 703-H2
2400 ING 90305 703-E2
6300 Wch 90045 702-G2
7500 PdlR 90293 702-D3
85TH ST E
35200 Litl 93543 4377-J1
35300 Litl 93543 4287-H5
42000 PMDL 93552 4107-H3
42800 LAN 93535 4107-H1
43800 LACo 93535 4017-H2
43800 LACo 93535 4107-H1
43800 LAN 93535 4017-H4
85TH ST W
- KeCo 93560 3833-J2
42800 LAN 93536 4104-A3
43600 LACo 93536 4104-A3
44000 LAN 93536 4014-A3
44200 LACo 93536 4014-A1
46800 LACo 93536 3924-A5
48500 LACo 93536 3923-J1
49700 LACo 93536 3833-J5
W 86TH PL
100 LA 90003 704-C2
5900 Wch 90045 702-F3
86TH ST E
35300 Litl 93543 4377-J1
35600 Litl 93543 4287-J5
36700 LACo 93552 4287-J5
41800 LACo 93535 4017-H6
86TH ST W
39700 LACo 93551 4194-A5
E 87TH PL
100 LA 90003 704-D3
600 Wats 90002 704-E3
1100 Wats 90002 704-G3
W 87TH PL
100 LA 90003 704-C3
6400 Wch 90045 702-D3
E 87TH ST
100 LA 90003 704-D3
600 Wats 90002 704-E2
1100 Wats 90002 704-F2

W 87TH ST
100 LA 90003 704-C3
500 LA 90044 704-B3
1000 LACo 90044 704-A3
1200 LACo 90044 703-J3
1400 LA 90047 703-H3
6200 Wch 90045 702-D3
87TH ST E
33800 Litl 93543 4377-J1
35300 Litl 93543 4287-J4
37000 LACo 93552 4287-J4
38400 LACo 93552 4197-J7
44000 LACo 93535 4017-J5
87TH ST W
39700 LACo 93551 4194-A3
44000 LACo 93536 4013-J1
44000 LACo 93536 4103-J1
46000 LAN 93536 4013-J3
46800 LACo 93536 3923-J2
50000 LACo 93536 3833-J6
E 88TH PL
100 LA 90003 704-D3
600 Wats 90002 704-E3
1100 Wats 90002 704-E3
W 88TH PL
100 LA 90003 704-B3
500 LA 90044 704-B3
1400 LA 90047 703-H3
6500 Wch 90045 702-D3
E 88TH ST
100 LA 90003 704-D3
800 Wats 90002 704-E3
1100 Wats 90002 704-F3
W 88TH ST
100 LA 90003 704-B3
500 LA 90044 704-A3
800 Wch 90045 702-D3
900 LACo 90044 704-A3
1200 LACo 90044 703-J3
1400 LA 90047 703-H3
2200 ING 90305 703-F3
6600 Wch 90045 702-F3
7500 Wch 90045 702-D3
88TH ST E
38000 Litl 93543 4287-J1
38300 Litl 93543 4197-J7
38400 LACo 93552 4197-J7
44000 LACo 93535 4017-J6
88TH ST W
44000 LACo 93536 4013-J7
44000 LACo 93536 4103-J1
45600 LAN 93536 4013-J4
E 89TH ST
100 LA 90003 704-D3
600 Wats 90002 704-D3
1100 Wats 90002 704-F3
W 89TH ST
100 LA 90003 704-B3
500 LA 90044 704-B3
1000 LACo 90044 704-A3
1200 LACo 90044 703-J3
1400 LA 90047 703-H3
6200 Wch 90045 702-D3
89TH ST E
33800 Litl 93543 4378-A4
35200 Litl 93543 4377-J1
35300 Litl 93543 4287-J7
W 90TH PL
1200 LACo 90044 703-J3
1200 LACo 90044 704-A3
1400 LA 90047 703-J3
E 90TH ST
100 LA 90003 704-D3
600 Wats 90002 704-D3
1100 Wats 90002 704-F3
W 90TH ST
100 LA 90003 704-C3
500 LA 90044 704-B3
1000 LACo 90044 704-A3
1200 LACo 90044 703-J3
1400 LA 90047 703-J3
2200 ING 90305 703-F3
7200 Wch 90045 702-D3
90TH ST E
34000 Litl 93543 4378-A4
36700 Litl 93543 4287-J2
37000 Litl 93543 4288-A3
37200 LACo 93552 4288-A3
37500 LACo 93552 4287-J2
38200 Litl 93543 4197-J7
38400 LACo 93552 4197-J3
38400 LACo 93591 4197-J1
38900 PMDL 93552 4197-J5
38900 PMDL 93552 4198-A6
38900 PMDL 93591 4197-J5
38900 PMDL 93591 4198-A6
41200 LACo 93552 4107-J7
41200 PMDL 93552 4107-J2
41200 LACo 93591 4107-J7
41200 PMDL 93591 4107-J2
42800 LACo 93535 4107-J1
42800 LAN 93535 4107-J1
43800 LAN 93535 4017-J6
43800 LACo 93535 4017-J2
90TH ST W
- KeCo 93560 3833-H3
39600 LACo 93551 4193-J2
42100 LAN 93536 4103-J2
43600 LACo 93536 4103-J2
44000 LACo 93536 4013-J7
44000 LAN 93536 4013-J3
46800 LACo 93536 3923-H2
49700 LACo 93536 3833-H3

W 91ST PL
400 LA 90003 704-C3
1400 LA 90047 703-H3
E 91ST ST
100 LA 90003 704-D3
600 Wats 90002 704-D3
1100 Wats 90002 704-F3
W 91ST ST
100 LA 90003 704-C3
500 LA 90044 704-B3
1000 LACo 90044 704-A3
1200 LACo 90044 703-J3
1400 LA 90047 703-H3
7100 Wch 90045 702-C3
7700 PdlR 90293 702-C3
91ST ST E
38400 LACo 93591 4198-A7
42500 PMDL 93591 4107-J4
46400 LACo 93535 4017-J1
91ST ST W
44100 LAN 93536 4013-J7
44100 LAN 93536 4103-J1
44300 LACo 93536 4013-J4
47200 LACo 93536 3923-H5
E 92ND ST
100 LA 90003 704-D3
600 Wats 90002 704-G3
1100 Wats 90002 704-D3
1600 LACo 90280 704-G3
W 92ND ST
100 LA 90003 704-B3
500 LA 90044 704-B3
1000 LACo 90044 704-A3
1200 LACo 90044 703-J3
1400 LA 90047 703-H3
6300 Wch 90045 702-D4
7700 PdlR 90293 702-D4
92ND ST E
33900 Litl 93543 4378-A1
35400 Litl 93543 4288-A1
38200 Litl 93543 4198-A7
38400 LACo 93591 4198-A7
38700 PMDL 93591 4198-A6
42000 PMDL 93591 4108-A5
43600 LAN 93535 4108-A1
43800 LAN 93535 4018-A7
44400 LACo 93535 4018-A2
46400 LACo 93535 4017-J1
92ND ST W
39600 LACo 93551 4193-J4
43800 LAN 93536 4103-H1
44200 LAN 93536 4013-H7
44800 LACo 93536 4013-H4
47000 LACo 93536 3923-H3
47000 LAN 93536 3923-H7
50900 LACo 93536 3833-H5
E 93RD ST
100 LA 90003 704-D3
600 Wats 90002 704-D3
1100 Wats 90002 704-F3
W 93RD ST
100 LA 90003 704-B4
400 ING 90301 703-B4
500 LA 90044 704-A4
1000 LACo 90044 704-A4
1200 LACo 90044 703-J4
1400 LA 90047 703-H4
5200 Wch 90045 703-A4
5800 Wch 90045 702-J4
93RD ST E
37100 Litl 93543 4288-A4
38400 LACo 93591 4198-A7
38700 PMDL 93591 4198-A7
42300 PMDL 93591 4108-A4
44200 LAN 93535 4108-A6
44200 LACo 93535 4018-A1
93RD ST W
44100 LAN 93536 4013-H7
44100 LAN 93536 4103-H1
45200 LACo 93536 4013-H5
47000 LACo 93536 3923-H5
47000 LAN 93536 3923-H7
50800 LACo 93536 3833-H5
W 94TH AV
2700 ING 90305 703-G4
W 94TH PL
1400 LA 90047 703-H4
E 94TH ST
100 ING 90301 703-C4
100 LA 90003 704-D4
600 Wats 90002 704-E4
1200 Wats 90002 704-H3
W 94TH ST
- Wch 90045 702-G4
100 LA 90003 704-B4
200 ING 90301 703-B4
500 LA 90044 704-A4
900 LACo 90044 704-A4
1200 LACo 90044 703-J4
1400 LA 90047 703-H4
5200 Wch 90045 703-A4
94TH ST E
33200 Litl 93543 4378-A1
35400 Litl 93543 4288-A4
94TH ST W
50900 LACo 93536 3833-H5
95TH PL
9400 Wch 90045 703-A4
E 95TH PL
1600 Wats 90002 704-G4
W 95TH PL
5200 Wch 90045 703-A4

E 95TH ST
100 LA 90003 704-D4
600 Wats 90002 704-G4
2100 Wats 90002 704-H4
W 95TH ST
100 LA 90003 704-B4
500 LA 90044 704-B4
1000 LACo 90044 704-A4
1200 LACo 90044 703-J4
1400 LACo 90047 703-J4
1500 LA 90047 703-H4
2700 ING 90305 703-G4
4800 ING 90301 703-B4
5200 Wch 90045 703-B4
5800 Wch 90045 702-J4
95TH ST E
33900 Litl 93543 4378-B4
36800 Litl 93543 4288-A1
38200 Litl 93543 4198-A7
38400 LACo 93591 4198-A2
38700 PMDL 93591 4198-A6
40800 LACo 93591 4108-A7
41600 PMDL 93591 4108-A4
42800 LACo 93535 4108-A2
43600 LAN 93535 4108-A2
44000 LACo 93535 4018-A3
44400 LAN 93535 4018-A6
95TH ST W
- KeCo 93560 3833-G2
40000 LACo 93551 4193-H4
43600 LAN 93536 4103-H2
44100 LAN 93536 4013-H3
44400 LACo 93536 4013-H5
46800 LAN 93536 3923-H7
47000 LACo 93536 3923-G3
49600 LACo 93536 3833-G5
E 96TH PL
2300 Wats 90002 704-H4
W 96TH PL
2000 LA 90047 703-H4
5900 Wch 90045 702-H4
E 96TH ST
1200 Wats 90002 704-F4
1200 Wats 90002 704-F4
W 96TH ST
1000 LACo 90044 704-A4
1200 LACo 90044 703-J4
1400 LACo 90047 703-J4
1500 LA 90047 703-H4
4800 ING 90301 703-B4
5200 Wch 90045 703-B4
5500 Wch 90045 702-G4
96TH ST E
30600 Litl 93543 4468-B2
33300 Litl 93543 4378-B2
35200 Litl 93543 4288-B3
41600 PMDL 93591 4108-A4
42800 LACo 93535 4108-A2
96TH ST W
43600 LAN 93536 4103-H2
50500 LACo 93536 3833-G3
96TH ST BRDG
6300 Wch 90045 702-G4
W 97TH PL
5200 Wch 90045 703-A4
E 97TH ST
100 LA 90003 704-D4
300 ING 90301 703-D4
600 Wats 90002 704-H4
2100 Wats 90002 704-H4
W 97TH ST
100 LA 90003 704-C4
500 LA 90044 704-B4
1000 LACo 90044 704-A4
1200 LACo 90044 703-J4
1400 LACo 90047 703-J4
1500 LA 90047 703-H4
4800 ING 90301 703-B4
5200 Wch 90045 703-A4
97TH ST E
37200 Litl 93543 4288-B2
38200 Litl 93543 4198-B7
38400 LACo 93591 4198-B5
41600 PMDL 93591 4108-B5
42800 LACo 93535 4108-B3
44400 LACo 93535 4018-B2
97TH ST W
39600 LACo 93551 4193-H4
43600 LAN 93536 4103-G1
45200 LACo 93536 4103-G5
45200 LAN 93536 4103-G1
46800 LACo 93536 3923-G6
48000 LACo 93536 3923-G3
49600 LACo 93536 3833-G3
E 98TH ST
100 ING 90301 703-C4
100 LA 90003 704-D4
600 Wats 90002 704-D4
1200 Wats 90002 704-F4
W 98TH ST
100 ING 90301 703-A4
100 LA 90003 704-C4
500 LA 90044 704-A4
1000 LACo 90044 704-A4
1200 LACo 90044 703-J4
1400 LACo 90047 703-J4
1500 LA 90047 703-H4
5200 Wch 90045 703-A4
5500 Wch 90045 702-H4
98TH ST E
35600 Litl 93543 4288-B5
41500 PMDL 93591 4108-B5
42800 LACo 93535 4108-B2

98TH ST E
45600 LACo 93535 4018-B3
98TH ST W
40200 LACo 93551 4193-G4
43600 LAN 93536 4103-G2
44100 LAN 93536 4013-G7
50900 LACo 93536 3833-G3
E 99TH PL
2000 Wats 90002 704-H4
W 99TH PL
5300 Wch 90045 703-A5
E 99TH ST
100 LA 90003 704-D4
300 ING 90301 703-D4
600 Wats 90002 704-E4
1200 Wats 90002 704-F4
W 99TH ST
100 LA 90003 704-B4
500 LA 90044 704-A4
1000 LACo 90044 704-A4
1200 LACo 90044 703-J4
1400 LACo 90047 703-J4
1500 LA 90047 703-H4
3100 ING 90305 703-F4
4800 ING 90301 703-A4
5300 Wch 90045 703-A4
99TH ST W
44200 LAN 93536 4013-G7
50400 LACo 93536 3833-G5
E 100TH ST
1200 Wats 90002 704-F4
1200 Wats 90002 704-F4
100TH ST E
37200 Litl 93543 4288-B1
38200 Litl 93543 4198-B6
38400 LACo 93591 4198-B3
38700 PMDL 93591 4198-B6
40900 LACo 93591 4108-B7
40900 PMDL 93591 4108-B3
42800 LACo 93535 4108-B3
43100 LAN 93535 4108-B3
43700 LACo 93535 4018-B2
43700 LAN 93535 4018-B7
100TH ST W
- LACo 93551 4193-G3
- KeCo 93560 3833-F3
42600 LAN 93536 4103-G2
44000 LAN 93536 4013-G2
44400 LACo 93536 4013-G6
46800 LACo 93536 3923-F2
47000 LAN 93536 3923-F2
49600 LACo 93536 3833-F5
E 101ST ST
100 LA 90003 704-D4
700 Wats 90002 704-E4
W 101ST ST
100 LA 90003 704-B5
500 LA 90044 704-A5
1000 LACo 90044 704-A5
1200 LACo 90044 703-J5
1400 LACo 90047 703-J5
2400 ING 90303 703-G5
4000 ING 90304 703-B5
5100 Lenx 90304 703-A5
101ST ST E
33000 Litl 93543 4378-C5
36100 Litl 93543 4288-C5
40000 PMDL 93591 4198-C1
41100 PMDL 93591 4108-C7
44000 LACo 93535 4018-B3
101ST ST W
50500 LACo 93536 3833-F6
E 102ND ST
100 LA 90003 704-D5
700 Wats 90002 704-E5
W 102ND ST
100 LA 90003 704-B5
500 LA 90044 704-A5
1000 LACo 90044 704-A5
1200 LACo 90044 703-J5
1400 LACo 90047 703-H5
2200 ING 90303 703-F5
4000 ING 90304 703-D5
5200 Wch 90045 703-A5
5400 Wch 90045 702-J5
102ND ST E
37200 Litl 93543 4288-C3
40000 PMDL 93591 4198-C1
40800 PMDL 93591 4108-C3
42800 LAN 93535 4108-C3
42800 LACo 93535 4108-C3
44000 LACo 93535 4018-C3
102ND ST W
44400 LAN 93536 4013-F7
50000 LACo 93536 3833-F5
E 103RD PL
700 Wats 90002 704-E5
W 103RD PL
2000 LACo 90047 703-H5
E 103RD ST
100 LA 90003 704-D5
600 Wats 90002 704-E5
1200 Wats 90002 704-F5
2400 Wats 90002 704-H5
W 103RD ST
100 LA 90003 704-C5
500 LA 90044 704-B5
1000 LACo 90044 704-B5
1200 LACo 90044 703-J5
1400 LACo 90047 703-H5
1600 LA 90047 703-H5
4000 ING 90304 703-D5
4000 Lenx 90304 703-D5

103RD ST E
29700 Litl 93543 4468-D5
32800 Litl 93543 4378-D5
36400 Litl 93543 4288-C5
40000 PMDL 93591 4198-C3
41400 PMDL 93591 4108-C7
103RD ST W
42800 LAN 93536 4103-F3
45800 LAN 93536 4013-F3
50500 LACo 93536 3833-F4
E 104TH PL
1500 Wats 90002 704-F5
W 104TH PL
500 LA 90044 704-B5
E 104TH ST
100 LA 90003 704-E5
600 Wats 90002 704-E5
W 104TH ST
100 LA 90003 704-C5
500 LA 90044 704-A5
1000 LACo 90044 704-A5
1200 LACo 90044 703-J5
1400 LACo 90047 703-J5
1600 LA 90047 703-J5
2200 ING 90303 703-E5
4000 ING 90304 703-C5
4000 Lenx 90304 703-C5
5200 Wch 90045 703-A5
5200 Wch 90045 702-J5
104TH ST E
29600 Litl 93543 4468-D5
44400 LACo 93535 4018-C6
E 105TH ST
100 LA 90003 704-D5
600 Wats 90002 704-D5
W 105TH ST
100 LA 90003 704-C5
500 LA 90044 704-B5
1000 LACo 90044 704-A5
1200 LACo 90044 703-J5
1400 LACo 90047 703-H5
3600 ING 90303 703-E5
4000 ING 90304 703-D5
4000 Lenx 90304 703-D5
105TH ST E
- LACo 93591 4198-D7
- Litl 93543 4198-D7
37200 Litl 93543 4288-D3
38100 LACo 93591 4288-C1
40000 PMDL 93591 4198-C3
40800 PMDL 93591 4108-C4
44000 LACo 93535 4018-C2
105TH ST W
500 KeCo 93560 3833-E3
42800 LAN 93536 4103-F2
44000 LAN 93536 4013-F7
44400 LACo 93536 4013-F1
46800 LACo 93536 3923-E4
47200 LAN 93536 3923-F7
49600 LACo 93536 3833-E5
E 106TH ST
100 LA 90003 704-D5
600 Wats 90002 704-F5
W 106TH ST
100 LA 90003 704-C5
500 LA 90044 704-A5
1000 LACo 90044 704-A5
1200 LACo 90044 703-H5
1400 LACo 90047 703-H5
1800 LA 90047 703-H5
3600 ING 90303 703-E5
4000 ING 90304 703-D5
4000 Lenx 90304 703-B5
106TH ST E
- PMDL 93591 4198-D2
29000 Litl 93543 4468-E2
31900 Litl 93543 4378-D2
35300 Litl 93543 4288-D5
41600 PMDL 93591 4108-D6
106TH ST W
44400 LACo 93536 4013-F7
50000 LACo 93536 3833-E4
E 107TH ST
100 LA 90003 704-D5
600 Wats 90002 704-F5
2300 Wats 90002 704-H5
W 107TH ST
100 LA 90003 704-B5
500 LA 90044 704-B5
1000 LACo 90044 704-A5
1200 LACo 90044 703-J5
1400 LACo 90047 703-H5
3000 ING 90303 703-E5
4000 ING 90304 703-D5
4000 Lenx 90304 703-D5
107TH ST E
34000 Litl 93543 4378-D4
36400 Litl 93543 4288-D3
40800 PMDL 93591 4108-D5
40800 PMDL 93591 4198-D1
45000 LACo 93535 4018-D2
107TH ST W
39900 LACo 93551 4193-F3
50400 LACo 93536 3833-E4
E 108TH ST
100 LA 90061 704-D5
100 LA 90003 704-D5
1000 LA 90059 704-F5
1200 Wats 90002 704-F5
2400 Wbrk 90059 704-J5
2500 LYN 90059 704-J5
2600 LYN 90262 704-J5

W 108TH ST
100 LA 90061 704-B5
100 LA 90003 704-B5
500 LA 90044 704-B5
1000 LACo 90047 704-A5
1400 LACo 90047 703-G5
1800 LA 90047 703-G5
2200 ING 90303 703-G5
108TH ST E
33200 Litl 93543 4378-D4
36400 Litl 93543 4288-D5
41500 PMDL 93591 4108-D5
108TH ST W
50500 LACo 93536 3833-E6
E 109TH PL
100 LA 90061 704-D6
600 LA 90059 704-D6
W 109TH PL
100 LA 90061 704-C6
500 LA 90044 704-A6
1000 LACo 90044 704-A6
1200 LACo 90044 703-J6
1600 LACo 90047 703-H6
E 109TH ST
100 LA 90061 704-D5
600 LA 90059 704-G5
2400 Wbrk 90059 704-J6
2600 LYN 90262 704-J6
W 109TH ST
100 LA 90061 704-C6
500 LA 90044 704-B6
1000 LACo 90044 704-B6
1200 LACo 90044 703-J6
1600 LACo 90047 703-H6
2300 ING 90303 703-E6
4900 Lenx 90304 703-B6
W 110TH PL
1400 LACo 90047 703-J6
E 110TH ST
100 LA 90061 704-D6
600 LA 90059 704-D6
2400 Wbrk 90059 704-H6
2600 LYN 90262 704-J6
W 110TH ST
100 LA 90061 704-C6
500 LA 90044 704-B6
1000 LACo 90044 704-B6
1200 LACo 90044 703-J6
1400 LACo 90047 703-J6
3100 ING 90303 703-E6
4900 Lenx 90304 703-B6
110TH ST E
33400 Litl 93543 4378-E4
36400 Litl 93543 4288-E1
38000 LACo 93591 4198-E7
38000 LACo 93591 4288-E1
38700 PMDL 93591 4198-D2
41200 PMDL 93591 4108-D6
42800 LACo 93535 4108-D3
43700 LACo 93535 4018-D3
110TH ST W
- KeCo 93560 3833-D3
43200 LAN 93536 4103-E3
43200 LACo 93536 4103-E3
43700 LAN 93536 4013-E7
43700 LACo 93536 4013-E3
46800 LACo 93536 3923-D2
46800 LAN 93536 3923-D4
49800 LACo 93536 3833-D5
E 111TH DR
800 LA 90059 704-E6
E 111TH PL
100 LA 90061 704-D6
600 LA 90059 704-F6
W 111TH PL
100 LA 90061 704-C6
500 LA 90044 704-C6
1400 LACo 90047 703-J6
3100 ING 90303 703-E6
4100 Lenx 90304 703-B6
4200 HAW 90304 703-D6
E 111TH ST
100 LA 90061 704-D6
600 LA 90059 704-G6
2400 Wbrk 90059 704-J6
2600 LYN 90262 704-J6
W 111TH ST
100 LA 90061 704-B6
500 LA 90044 704-B6
1000 LACo 90044 704-A6
1400 LACo 90047 703-G6
2200 ING 90303 703-E6
4000 Lenx 90304 703-C6
4000 ING 90304 703-C6
4400 HAW 90304 703-C6
5200 Wch 90045 703-A6
5200 Wch 90045 702-J6
111TH ST E
33200 Litl 93543 4378-E4
36500 Litl 93543 4288-E3
38500 LACo 93591 4198-E7
41500 PMDL 93591 4108-E5
46000 LACo 93535 4018-D2
111TH ST W
50100 LACo 93536 3833-D6
E 112TH PL
2400 Wbrk 90059 704-H6
E 112TH ST
100 LA 90061 704-E6
600 LA 90059 704-E6
2600 LYN 90262 704-J6
W 112TH ST
100 LA 90061 704-C6

W 112TH ST
500 LA 90044 704-B6
1000 LACo 90044 704-A6
1300 LACo 90044 703-J6
1400 LACo 90047 703-H6
2300 ING 90303 703-E6
4800 Lenx 90304 703-B6
112TH ST E
29500 Litl 93543 4468-E6
33200 Litl 93543 4378-E3
36500 Litl 93543 4288-E3
38600 LACo 93591 4198-E6
38700 PMDL 93591 4198-E6
41500 PMDL 93591 4108-E5
42800 LACo 93535 4108-E3
45800 LACo 93535 4018-E2
112TH ST W
49200 LACo 93536 3923-D2
50000 LACo 93536 3833-D5
E 113TH ST
300 LA 90061 704-E6
600 LA 90059 704-E6
2400 Wbrk 90059 704-H6
W 113TH ST
100 LA 90061 704-C6
500 LA 90044 704-B6
1400 LACo 90047 703-J6
3100 ING 90303 703-E6
4000 HAW 90304 703-D6
4000 ING 90304 703-D6
113TH ST E
29500 Litl 93543 4468-F1
32200 Litl 93543 4378-F4
36500 Litl 93543 4288-E3
38500 LACo 93591 4198-E7
38700 PMDL 93591 4198-E6
113TH ST W
37600 LACo 91390 4193-D5
50100 LACo 93536 3833-D6
E 114TH ST
900 LA 90059 704-E6
2400 Wbrk 90059 704-J6
114TH ST E
42000 PMDL 93591 4108-E5
42800 LACo 93535 4108-E2
46000 LACo 93535 4018-E2
E 115TH PL
2400 Wbrk 90059 704-J6
W 115TH PL
1000 LACo 90044 704-A7
2300 HAW 90250 703-G7
E 115TH ST
300 LA 90061 704-E6
600 LA 90059 704-E6
2400 Wbrk 90059 704-J6
W 115TH ST
100 LA 90061 704-C7
500 LA 90044 704-B7
1900 LACo 90047 703-G7
2000 HAW 90250 703-B7
3300 ING 90303 703-E7
115TH ST E
33500 Litl 93543 4378-F5
36500 Litl 93543 4288-F3
38700 LACo 93591 4198-F6
38700 PMDL 93591 4198-E4
42000 PMDL 93591 4108-E5
42800 LACo 93535 4108-E2
43700 LACo 93535 4018-E3
115TH ST W
- KeCo 93560 3833-C3
37600 LACo 91390 4193-D5
43600 LACo 93536 4103-D3
43600 LACo 93536 4103-D1
47200 LACo 93536 3923-C1
49800 LACo 93536 3833-C7
E 116TH PL
100 LA 90061 704-D7
600 LA 90059 704-D7
E 116TH ST
100 LA 90061 704-E7
600 LA 90059 704-E7
W 116TH ST
100 LA 90061 704-C7
2000 HAW 90250 703-B7
2600 HAW 90303 703-G7
3000 ING 90303 703-E7
5400 Lenx 90304 703-A7
5400 Wch 90045 703-A7
5500 Lenx 90304 702-J7
5500 Wch 90045 702-J7
116TH ST E
29000 Litl 93543 4468-F1
32100 Litl 93543 4378-E3
33800 Pear 93553 4378-F3
35300 Litl 93543 4288-F2
35300 Pear 93553 4288-F5
36400 LACo 93591 4288-F2
38700 LACo 93591 4198-F6
38700 PMDL 93591 4198-F2
42900 LACo 93535 4108-E2
116TH ST W
50100 LACo 93536 3833-C6
E 117TH PL
1500 Wbrk 90059 704-G7
W 117TH PL
3300 ING 90303 703-F7
E 117TH ST
1500 Wbrk 90059 704-G7
W 117TH ST
100 LA 90061 704-B7
500 LA 90044 704-B7
1000 LACo 90044 704-A7

W 117TH ST
1800 LACo 90047 703-H7
1900 LACo 90250 703-H7
2300 HAW 90250 703-B7
3300 ING 90303 703-E7
5500 Lenx 90304 703-A7
4800 Lenx 90304 702-J7
117TH ST E
- Pear 93553 4378-F7
36400 LACo 93591 4288-F2
40300 PMDL 93591 4198-F2
42900 LACo 93535 4108-F2
43700 LACo 93535 4018-F2
117TH ST W
- KeCo 93560 3833-C1
50300 LACo 93536 3833-C5
E 118TH DR
800 LA 90059 704-E7
E 118TH PL
100 LA 90061 704-D7
600 LA 90059 704-E7
1500 Wbrk 90059 704-G7
W 118TH PL
100 LA 90061 704-C7
2500 HAW 90250 703-B7
3100 ING 90303 703-E7
5200 Lenx 90304 703-A7
5500 Lenx 90304 702-J7
E 118TH ST
100 LA 90061 704-D7
600 LA 90059 704-D7
1200 Wbrk 90059 704-G7
W 118TH ST
100 LA 90061 704-C7
500 LA 90044 704-B7
1200 LACo 90044 704-A7
2400 HAW 90250 703-B7
3300 ING 90303 703-E7
5200 Lenx 90304 703-A7
5200 Wch 90045 703-A7
5500 Lenx 90304 702-J7
5600 ELSG 90245 702-J7
118TH ST E
- Pear 93553 4378-G7
29400 Litl 93543 4468-G6
37700 LACo 93591 4288-F2
42800 LACo 93535 4108-F3
118TH ST W
50500 LACo 93536 3833-C6
W 119TH CT
- ING 90303 703-E7
W 119TH PL
1000 LACo 90044 704-A7
3700 HAW 90250 703-B7
5200 Lenx 90304 703-A7
5500 Lenx 90304 702-J7
119TH ST
2000 HAW 90250 703-D7
3000 ING 90250 703-G7
E 119TH ST
100 LA 90061 704-D7
600 LA 90059 704-F7
1200 Wbrk 90059 704-F7
W 119TH ST
100 LA 90061 704-C7
500 LA 90044 704-B7
900 LACo 90044 704-A7
3700 HAW 90250 703-B7
5200 Lenx 90304 703-A7
5500 Lenx 90304 702-J7
119TH ST W
50000 LACo 93536 3833-B6
120TH ST
- LACo 90250 733-B1
4000 HAW 90250 733-B1
11900 ELSG 90245 732-J1
E 120TH ST
100 LA 90061 704-E7
600 LA 90059 704-E7
1100 Wbrk 90059 704-F7
1900 Wbrk 90222 704-F7
W 120TH ST
100 LA 90061 704-B7
500 LA 90044 704-B7
1000 LACo 90044 704-B7
1300 LACo 90044 703-J7
1400 LACo 90047 703-H7
1800 LACo 90047 733-A1
2000 HAW 90250 703-G7
2600 HAW 90250 733-A1
3100 HAW 90303 733-A1
5000 LACo 90250 733-A1
5200 Lenx 90304 733-A1
5500 LACo 90250 732-J1
5500 Lenx 90304 732-J1
120TH ST E
37200 LACo 93591 4288-G3
38500 LACo 93591 4198-G7
38800 PMDL 93591 4198-F2
40500 LACo 93535 4198-F2
42400 LACo 93535 4108-F2
42400 PMDL 93591 4108-F2
43600 LACo 93535 4018-F3
120TH ST W
1300 KeCo 93560 3833-B3
43600 LACo 93536 4103-C2
44000 LACo 93536 4013-C3
46800 LACo 93536 3923-B2
49800 LACo 93536 3833-B5
E 121ST PL
600 Wbrk 90059 734-E1
W 121ST PL
100 LACo 90061 734-C1

121ST ST
4800 HAW 90250 733-B1
11900 LACo 90250 733-B1
E 121ST ST
100 LACo 90061 734-D1
600 Wbrk 90059 704-E7
2200 Wbrk 90222 734-H1
W 121ST ST
100 LACo 90061 734-C1
200 LA 90061 734-B1
500 LA 90044 734-B1
1000 LACo 90044 734-B1
1300 LACo 90044 733-J1
1400 LACo 90047 733-J1
5000 LACo 90250 733-A1
121ST ST E
12200 Pear 93553 4378-G3
28500 Pear 93553 4468-G7
28500 Litl 93543 4468-G7
36400 LACo 93591 4288-G1
38500 LACo 93591 4198-G7
42400 LACo 93535 4108-G4
46400 LACo 93535 4018-F1
121ST ST W
50000 LACo 93536 3833-B5
E 122ND PL
1400 Wbrk 90059 734-F1
122ND ST
4000 HAW 90250 733-D1
11900 LACo 90250 732-J1
E 122ND ST
100 LACo 90061 734-D1
600 Wbrk 90059 734-E1
1900 Wbrk 90222 734-H1
W 122ND ST
100 LACo 90061 734-C1
1000 LACo 90044 734-A1
1300 LACo 90044 733-J1
1400 LACo 90047 733-J1
5000 LACo 90250 733-A1
5400 LACo 90250 732-J1
122ND ST E
32100 Pear 93553 4378-G5
32100 Pear 93553 4468-G1
37700 LACo 93591 4288-G1
38500 LACo 93591 4198-G7
40400 LACo 93535 4198-G2
42400 LACo 93535 4108-G2
44400 LACo 93535 4018-G3
122ND ST W
44000 LACo 93536 4103-C1
44200 LACo 93536 4013-B5
49300 LACo 93536 3923-B1
49800 LACo 93536 3833-B4
123RD PL
4800 HAW 90250 733-B1
W 123RD PL
5000 LACo 90250 733-A1
5400 LACo 90250 732-J1
123RD ST
4700 HAW 90250 733-B1
E 123RD ST
1100 Wbrk 90059 734-F1
1600 Wbrk 90222 734-G1
W 123RD ST
100 LACo 90061 734-C1
700 LA 90044 734-A1
900 LACo 90044 734-A1
1300 LACo 90044 733-J1
1400 LACo 90047 733-J1
5000 LACo 90250 733-A1
5400 LACo 90250 732-J1
123RD ST E
29200 Pear 93553 4468-H1
32100 Pear 93553 4378-H5
37700 LACo 93591 4288-G1
38500 LACo 93591 4198-G7
43600 LACo 93535 4018-G1
43600 LACo 93535 4108-G1
123RD ST W
44000 LACo 93536 4103-B1
44200 LACo 93536 4013-B5
49400 LACo 93536 3923-B1
49900 LACo 93536 3833-B5
W 124TH PL
5200 LACo 90250 733-A1
124TH ST
- ELSG 90245 732-J1
12200 LACo 90250 732-J1
E 124TH ST
100 LACo 90061 734-D1
1100 Wbrk 90059 734-F1
1400 Wbrk 90222 734-H1
2500 COMP 90222 734-H1
W 124TH ST
100 LACo 90061 734-C1
500 LA 90044 734-A1
900 LACo 90044 734-A1
1300 LACo 90044 733-J1
1400 LACo 90047 733-J1
5000 LACo 90250 733-A1
5400 LACo 90250 732-J1
124TH ST E
34300 Pear 93553 4378-H3
42800 LACo 93535 4108-G3
124TH ST W
44000 LACo 93536 4103-B1
44200 LACo 93536 4013-B7
49300 LACo 93536 3923-B1
49800 LACo 93536 3833-B6
E 125TH ST
1100 Wbrk 90059 734-F1
1400 Wbrk 90222 734-J1

STREET
Block City ZIP Pg-Grid

W 125TH ST
800 LA 90044 734-B1
1700 LACo 90047 733-J1
5000 LACo 90250 733-A1
7000 LACo 90044 733-J1
7000 LACo 90044 734-A1
125TH ST E
28500 Pear 93553 4468-H7
33500 Pear 93553 4378-H3
36800 LACo 93591 4288-H1
38500 LACo 93591 4198-H6
40400 LACo 93535 4198-G2
40700 LACo 93535 4108-G2
44000 LACo 93535 4018-G1
125TH ST W
43800 LACo 93536 4103-B1
44200 LACo 93536 4013-B2
46800 LACo 93536 3923-A2
49800 LACo 93536 3833-A5
126TH ST
2200 HAW 90250 733-C1
E 126TH ST
100 LACo 90061 734-D1
900 Wbrk 90059 734-E1
1400 Wbrk 90222 734-F1
W 126TH ST
100 LACo 90061 734-C1
400 LA 90061 734-B1
700 LA 90044 734-B1
1000 LACo 90044 734-A1
1300 LACo 90044 733-J1
1400 LACo 90047 733-J1
5000 LACo 90250 733-A1
126TH ST E
28500 Pear 93553 4468-H1
32400 Pear 93553 4378-H2
35300 Pear 93553 4288-H7
36400 LACo 93591 4288-H1
38500 LACo 93591 4198-H7
45200 LACo 93535 4018-G4
126TH ST W
50800 LACo 93536 3833-A5
E 127TH PL
800 COMP 90222 734-G1
W 127TH PL
5200 LACo 90250 733-A1
E 127TH ST
100 LACo 90061 734-D1
1100 Wbrk 90059 734-F1
1400 Wbrk 90222 734-J1
W 127TH ST
100 LACo 90061 734-C1
400 LA 90061 734-C1
500 LA 90044 734-B1
900 COMP 90222 734-G1
1000 LACo 90044 734-A1
1300 LACo 90044 733-J1
1400 LACo 90047 733-J1
5200 LACo 90250 733-A1
127TH ST E
32900 Pear 93553 4378-H3
38400 LACo 93591 4198-H7
42800 LACo 93535 4108-H3
44000 LACo 93535 4018-H4
127TH ST W
45200 LACo 93536 4013-A5
49300 LACo 93536 3923-A1
49800 LACo 93536 3833-A5
128TH ST E
32900 Pear 93553 4378-J3
38500 LACo 93591 4198-H7
45200 LACo 93535 4018-H4
128TH ST W
49900 LACo 93536 3833-A6
129TH PL
2900 GAR 90249 733-G2
E 129TH PL
1000 COMP 90222 734-G2
129TH ST
1800 GAR 90249 733-G2
4000 HAW 90250 733-C2
E 129TH ST
300 LACo 90061 734-D2
2500 Wbrk 90222 734-J1
W 129TH ST
100 LACo 90061 734-B2
400 LA 90061 734-B2
700 LA 90247 734-B2
1000 COMP 90222 734-G1
1100 GAR 90247 734-A2
4800 HAW 90250 733-B2
4800 LACo 90250 733-B2
129TH ST E
34000 Pear 93553 4378-J4
129TH ST W
49300 LACo 93536 3923-A1
49800 LACo 93536 3833-A7
130TH ST
2900 GAR 90249 733-G2
3800 HAW 90250 733-C2
E 130TH ST
100 LACo 90061 734-D2
900 Wbrk 90059 734-E2
2300 Wbrk 90222 734-J2
W 130TH ST
300 LACo 90061 734-C2
400 LA 90061 734-B2
500 LA 90248 734-B2
700 LA 90247 734-A2
800 COMP 90222 734-G2
1000 GAR 90247 734-A2
1200 GAR 90247 733-J2
1400 GAR 90249 733-J2

W 130TH ST
1900 Wbrk 90222 734-G2
4800 HAW 90250 733-B2
4800 LACo 90250 733-B2
130TH ST E
29400 Pear 93553 4468-J5
29400 Valy 93563 4468-J5
34000 Pear 93553 4378-J4
37500 LACo 93591 4288-J2
38000 LACo 93591 4198-J5
40400 LACo 93535 4198-H2
42600 LACo 93535 4108-H3
43600 LACo 93535 4018-H3
130TH ST W
43600 LACo 93536 4013-A2
43600 LACo 93536 4103-A2
46800 LACo 93536 3923-A7
131ST ST
2900 GAR 90249 733-F2
3100 HAW 90250 733-F2
E 131ST ST
300 LACo 90061 734-D2
700 Wbrk 90059 734-E2
2000 COMP 90222 734-H2
2000 Wbrk 90222 734-H2
W 131ST ST
100 LACo 90061 734-C2
400 LA 90061 734-B2
700 COMP 90222 734-F2
700 LA 90247 734-B2
1000 GAR 90247 734-B2
4800 LACo 90250 733-B2
4800 HAW 90250 733-C2
131ST ST E
43400 LACo 93535 4108-J1
44000 LACo 93535 4018-J7
131TH ST E
36400 LACo 93591 4288-J4
132ND PL
2900 GAR 90249 733-G2
3600 HAW 90250 733-E2
132ND ST
1800 GAR 90249 733-G2
3700 HAW 90250 733-A2
E 132ND ST
100 LACo 90061 734-D2
2500 Wbrk 90222 734-J2
W 132ND ST
100 LACo 90061 734-C2
400 LA 90061 734-B2
500 LA 90248 734-B2
700 LA 90247 734-B2
800 COMP 90222 734-G2
1000 GAR 90247 734-A2
1200 GAR 90247 733-J2
1400 GAR 90249 733-J2
2000 COMP 90059 734-E2
3100 LACo 90250 733-B2
3300 HAW 90250 733-C2
132ND ST E
33100 Pear 93553 4378-J5
37700 LACo 93591 4288-J2
40500 LACo 93535 4198-J2
42400 LACo 93535 4108-J1
44000 LACo 93535 4018-J1
133RD ST
2900 GAR 90249 733-G2
3600 HAW 90250 733-A2
E 133RD ST
2500 Wbrk 90222 734-J2
W 133RD ST
300 LACo 90061 734-C2
700 LA 90247 734-B2
800 COMP 90222 734-G2
1000 GAR 90247 734-A2
3100 LACo 90250 733-B2
133RD ST E
29200 Pear 93553 4469-A6
33100 Pear 93553 4379-A3
33800 Pear 93553 4378-J3
37000 LACo 93591 4288-J4
40400 LACo 93535 4198-J2
42400 LACo 93535 4108-J1
44000 LACo 93535 4018-J5
134TH PL
3800 HAW 90250 733-A2
5400 HAW 90250 732-J2
W 134TH PL
800 COMP 90222 734-G2
1000 GAR 90247 734-A2
1800 GAR 90249 733-H2
3100 LACo 90250 733-B2
4800 HAW 90250 733-B2
134TH ST
2900 GAR 90249 733-G2
3800 HAW 90250 733-A2
5500 HAW 90250 732-J2
E 134TH ST
2500 Wbrk 90222 734-J2
W 134TH ST
100 LACo 90061 734-C2
700 LA 90247 734-B2
800 COMP 90222 734-F2
1200 GAR 90247 733-J2
1400 GAR 90249 733-J2
2000 COMP 90059 734-E2
3100 LACo 90250 733-B2
3500 HAW 90250 733-C2
134TH ST E
40500 LACo 93535 4198-J2
135TH PL
2900 GAR 90249 733-G3

135TH ST
2000 GAR 90249 733-E3
3700 HAW 90250 733-D2
5500 HAW 90250 732-J3
E 135TH ST
100 LACo 90061 734-D2
600 Wbrk 90059 734-D2
2500 Wbrk 90222 734-J2
W 135TH ST
100 LACo 90061 734-B2
400 LA 90061 734-B2
500 LA 90248 734-B2
600 LA 90247 734-B2
1000 GAR 90247 734-B2
1300 LACo 90247 733-G2
1400 GAR 90249 733-G2
3100 HAW 90250 733-C2
3100 LACo 90250 733-B3
135TH ST E
33100 Pear 93553 4379-A4
39900 LACo 93591 4199-A4
39900 LACo 93591 4198-J2
42400 LACo 93535 4108-J1
43600 LACo 93535 4018-J1
136TH ST
2900 GAR 90249 733-G3
4000 HAW 90250 733-A3
E 136TH ST
100 LACo 90061 734-D3
600 Wbrk 90059 734-E2
W 136TH ST
700 LA 90247 734-B3
800 COMP 90222 734-F2
4800 HAW 90250 733-C3
4800 LACo 90250 733-B3
136TH ST E
32700 Pear 93553 4379-A2
40400 LACo 93535 4199-A2
41200 LACo 93535 4109-A1
45500 LACo 93535 4018-J3
137TH PL
4400 HAW 90250 733-A3
W 137TH PL
700 LA 90247 734-B3
4800 LACo 90250 733-B3
137TH ST
4000 HAW 90250 733-A3
E 137TH ST
100 LACo 90061 734-D3
600 Wbrk 90059 734-D3
W 137TH ST
700 COMP 90222 734-F3
700 LA 90247 734-B3
1200 GAR 90247 734-A3
1300 GAR 90247 733-H3
1800 GAR 90249 733-G3
4800 LACo 90250 733-B3
137TH ST E
34000 Pear 93553 4379-A4
38200 LACo 93591 4199-A3
40400 LACo 93535 4199-A1
40900 LACo 93535 4109-A1
138TH PL
5200 HAW 90250 733-A3
138TH ST
4000 HAW 90250 733-A3
5500 HAW 90250 732-J3
E 138TH ST
100 LACo 90061 734-D3
600 Wbrk 90059 734-D3
W 138TH ST
200 LACo 90061 734-C3
700 LA 90247 734-B3
700 COMP 90222 734-F3
1100 GAR 90247 734-A3
2900 GAR 90249 733-G3
4800 LACo 90250 733-B3
138TH ST E
40800 LACo 93535 4109-A7
40800 LACo 93535 4199-A1
139TH PL
2900 GAR 90249 733-G3
139TH ST
3100 HAW 90250 733-A3
E 139TH ST
\- COMP 90222 734-F3
100 LACo 90061 734-D3
600 COMP 90059 734-F3
600 Wbrk 90059 734-D3
1200 Wbrk 90222 734-F3
W 139TH ST
700 COMP 90222 734-H3
700 LA 90247 734-B3
1200 GAR 90247 734-A3
1300 GAR 90247 733-J3
1400 GAR 90249 733-G3
4800 HAW 90250 733-B3
4800 LACo 90250 733-B3
140TH PL
1100 GAR 90247 734-A3
140TH ST
2900 GAR 90249 733-G3
4000 HAW 90250 733-A3
E 140TH ST
100 LACo 90061 734-D3
1200 Wbrk 90222 734-F3
W 140TH ST
200 LACo 90061 734-C3
500 LA 90248 734-B3
700 LA 90247 734-B3
1200 GAR 90247 734-A3
4800 HAW 90250 733-B3
4800 LACo 90250 733-B3

140TH ST E
38200 LACo 93591 4199-B5
40400 LACo 93535 4199-A2
40800 LACo 93535 4109-A7
141ST PL
1200 GAR 90247 734-A3
1300 GAR 90247 733-G3
2500 GAR 90249 733-G3
141ST ST
4000 HAW 90250 733-A3
E 141ST ST
300 LACo 90061 734-D3
1200 Wbrk 90222 734-F3
W 141ST ST
700 LA 90247 734-B3
1000 GAR 90247 734-A3
1300 GAR 90247 733-J3
1400 GAR 90249 733-G3
4800 HAW 90250 733-B3
4800 LACo 90250 733-B3
141ST ST E
33000 LACo 93591 4199-B7
34300 Pear 93553 4379-B3
43000 LACo 93535 4109-B2
142ND PL
5200 HAW 90250 733-A4
142ND ST
4000 HAW 90250 733-A3
E 142ND ST
300 LACo 90061 734-D3
1200 Wbrk 90222 734-F3
14200 COMP 90222 734-F3
W 142ND ST
700 LA 90247 734-B3
4800 HAW 90250 733-B3
4800 LACo 90250 733-B3
142ND ST E
42200 LACo 93535 4109-B2
W 143RD PL
2600 GAR 90249 733-G4
143RD ST E
43000 LACo 93535 4109-B2
144TH PL
3600 HAW 90250 733-E4
W 144TH PL
1200 GAR 90247 734-A4
144TH ST
1600 GAR 90247 733-E4
3600 HAW 90250 733-E4
8100 PRM 90723 735-H3
E 144TH ST
1100 LACo 90220 734-F3
W 144TH ST
700 LA 90247 734-B4
1200 GAR 90247 734-A4
1800 GAR 90249 733-H4
W 145TH PL
1200 GAR 90247 734-A4
1300 GAR 90247 733-J4
145TH ST
1400 GAR 90247 733-J4
1800 GAR 90249 733-H4
3600 HAW 90250 733-F4
4000 LNDL 90260 733-C4
E 145TH ST
800 LACo 90220 734-E4
W 145TH ST
700 LA 90247 734-B4
1100 GAR 90247 734-A4
1500 COMP 90220 734-F3
2000 GAR 90249 733-G4
3800 LACo 90249 733-F4
4800 HAW 90250 733-B4
145TH ST E
38800 LACo 93591 4199-C4
40800 LACo 93535 4199-B1
41300 LACo 93535 4109-B2
W 146TH PL
2000 GAR 90249 733-H4
146TH ST
600 LA 90247 734-B4
1400 GAR 90247 733-H4
1800 GAR 90249 733-H4
3600 HAW 90250 733-E4
E 146TH ST
800 LACo 90220 734-E4
W 146TH ST
200 LACo 90248 734-C4
500 LA 90248 734-B4
700 LA 90247 734-B4
1200 GAR 90247 734-A4
2000 GAR 90249 733-G4
146TH ST E
35300 Pear 93553 4379-C1
35300 LACo 93591 4379-C1
43700 LACo 93535 4109-C1
147TH PL
3800 HAW 90250 733-E4
147TH ST
1500 GAR 90247 733-H4
1800 GAR 90249 733-G4
3200 LACo 90249 733-E4
3600 HAW 90250 733-E4
4000 LNDL 90260 733-C4
W 147TH ST
500 LA 90248 734-B4
700 LA 90247 734-B4
1200 GAR 90247 734-A4
3100 LACo 90249 733-F4
3200 HAW 90249 733-F4
3500 LACo 90250 733-F4
4800 HAW 90260 733-B4

147TH ST E
40600 LACo 93535 4199-C1
43100 LACo 93535 4109-C1
W 148TH DR
700 LA 90247 734-B4
148TH PL
3600 HAW 90250 733-E4
W 148TH PL
700 LA 90247 734-B4
148TH ST
1400 GAR 90247 733-J4
1800 GAR 90249 733-H4
3800 HAW 90250 733-F4
4600 LNDL 90260 733-C4
E 148TH ST
800 LACo 90220 734-E4
W 148TH ST
500 LA 90248 734-B4
700 LA 90247 734-B4
1100 GAR 90247 734-A4
149TH ST
3900 HAW 90250 733-E4
4000 LNDL 90260 733-C4
E 149TH ST
400 LACo 90248 734-D4
1000 LACo 90220 734-E4
2000 COMP 90220 734-E4
W 149TH ST
500 LA 90248 734-B4
600 LA 90247 734-B4
1000 GAR 90247 734-A4
1300 GAR 90247 733-H4
1800 GAR 90249 733-G4
150TH ST
2500 GAR 90249 733-G4
E 150TH ST
200 COMP 90220 734-F4
1000 LACo 90220 734-F4
W 150TH ST
1100 GAR 90247 734-A4
1700 GAR 90247 733-H4
1800 GAR 90249 733-H4
150TH ST E
38000 LACo 93591 4199-D7
40400 LACo 93535 4199-D2
40800 LACo 93535 4109-C1
W 151ST ST
900 COMP 90220 734-F4
151ST ST E
38500 LACo 93591 4199-D7
40600 LACo 93535 4199-D1
41200 LACo 93535 4109-D4
W 152ND PL
3100 LACo 90249 733-F5
152ND ST
1400 GAR 90247 733-C5
4600 LNDL 90260 733-C5
W 152ND ST
500 LA 90248 734-B4
600 LA 90247 734-B4
900 COMP 90220 734-F4
1800 GAR 90249 733-G5
3100 LACo 90249 733-F5
3500 LACo 90260 733-E5
152ND ST E
38500 LACo 93591 4199-D7
40400 LACo 93535 4199-D2
41200 LACo 93535 4109-D7
153RD PL
4500 LNDL 90260 733-C5
153RD ST
4100 LNDL 90260 733-C5
E 153RD ST
700 LACo 90220 734-E5
W 153RD ST
1400 COMP 90220 734-F4
1400 GAR 90247 733-H5
1800 GAR 90249 733-H5
3100 LACo 90249 733-F5
3600 LACo 90260 733-E5
W 154TH PL
1500 GAR 90247 733-H5
1800 GAR 90249 733-H5
3100 LACo 90249 733-F5
154TH ST
4000 LNDL 90260 733-C5
E 154TH ST
500 LACo 90248 734-E5
600 LACo 90220 734-E5
900 COMP 90220 734-E5
W 154TH ST
500 LACo 90248 734-C5
600 LA 90247 734-B5
1000 COMP 90220 734-F5
1500 GAR 90247 733-H5
1800 GAR 90249 733-G5
3100 LACo 90249 733-F5
3600 LACo 90260 733-E5
154TH ST E
15100 LACo 93591 4199-E7
40500 LACo 93535 4199-D2
41200 LACo 93535 4109-D7
155TH CT
1800 GAR 90249 733-H5
155TH ST
1000 GAR 90247 734-A5
2300 GAR 90249 733-G5
W 155TH ST
500 LA 90248 734-C5
500 LA 90248 734-B5
700 LA 90247 734-B5
1400 COMP 90220 734-F5
3100 LACo 90249 733-F5

155TH ST E
33800 Llan 93544 4379-E3
38400 LACo 93591 4199-E7
40400 LACo 93535 4199-E2
40700 LACo 93535 4109-D1
156TH CT
1800 GAR 90249 733-H5
156TH PL
1200 GAR 90247 734-A5
156TH ST
4100 LNDL 90260 733-C5
W 156TH ST
500 LA 90248 734-B5
700 LA 90247 734-B5
800 COMP 90220 734-F5
1200 GAR 90247 734-A5
2000 GAR 90249 733-G5
3600 LACo 90260 733-E5
156TH ST E
38600 LACo 93591 4199-E7
40400 LACo 93535 4199-E2
40800 LACo 93535 4109-E6
E 157TH ST
100 LACo 90248 734-D5
700 LACo 90220 734-E5
W 157TH ST
100 LACo 90248 734-C5
500 LA 90248 734-C5
600 LA 90247 734-B5
1400 GAR 90247 733-J5
1800 GAR 90249 733-G5
2000 COMP 90220 734-F5
3100 LACo 90249 733-F5
3600 LACo 90260 733-F5
157TH ST E
29500 Valy 93563 4469-E5
31300 Llan 93544 4469-F2
E 158TH ST
200 LACo 90248 734-D5
W 158TH ST
500 LA 90248 734-B5
600 LA 90247 734-B5
1100 GAR 90247 734-A5
1400 GAR 90247 733-J5
2000 COMP 90220 734-F5
158TH ST E
38400 LACo 93591 4199-E2
40400 LACo 93535 4199-E1
40800 LACo 93535 4109-E6
W 159TH PL
500 LA 90248 734-B5
159TH ST
2600 RBCH 90278 733-B6
4000 LNDL 90260 733-B6
E 159TH ST
300 LACo 90248 734-D5
W 159TH ST
500 LA 90248 734-B5
700 LA 90247 734-B5
1000 GAR 90247 734-A5
1800 GAR 90247 733-H6
2000 COMP 90220 734-F5
2000 TOR 90504 733-H6
4400 LNDL 90260 733-C6
159TH ST E
38400 LACo 93591 4199-F7
40400 LACo 93535 4199-E1
40800 LACo 93535 4109-E6
160TH ST
2500 RBCH 90278 733-B6
4000 LNDL 90260 733-B6
11800 NRWK 90650 736-H5
W 160TH ST
500 LA 90248 734-B6
1000 GAR 90247 734-A6
1400 GAR 90247 733-J6
2000 TOR 90504 733-H6
4500 LNDL 90260 733-C6
160TH ST E
16000 LACo 93535 4109-E1
31000 Llan 93544 4469-F2
32800 Llan 93544 4379-F5
38400 LACo 93591 4199-E2
40400 LACo 93535 4199-F1
161ST ST
4000 LNDL 90260 733-C6
11800 NRWK 90650 736-H5
W 161ST ST
900 GAR 90247 734-A6
1900 GAR 90247 733-H6
2000 TOR 90504 733-G6
161ST ST E
31000 Llan 93544 4469-F3
38800 LACo 93591 4199-F5
40400 LACo 93535 4199-F1
40800 LACo 93535 4109-F6
162ND ST
1700 GAR 90247 733-C6
4000 LNDL 90260 733-C6
11800 NRWK 90650 736-H5
E 162ND ST
100 CRSN 90248 734-C6
W 162ND ST
900 GAR 90247 734-A6
1400 GAR 90247 733-H6
1900 TOR 90504 733-G6
162ND ST E
38800 LACo 93591 4199-F2
40400 LACo 93535 4199-F1
40800 LACo 93535 4109-F7
163RD ST
4000 LNDL 90260 733-C6
11800 NRWK 90650 736-H5

E 163RD ST
100 CRSN 90248 734-C6
900 CRSN 90746 734-E6
W 163RD ST
800 LA 90247 734-A6
1000 GAR 90247 734-A6
1400 COMP 90220 734-G6
2600 TOR 90504 733-G6
163RD ST E
32000 Llan 93544 4469-G1
32000 Llan 93544 4379-G7
38800 LACo 93591 4199-F4
40400 LACo 93535 4199-F1
40800 LACo 93535 4109-F6
164TH ST
4000 LNDL 90260 733-C6
11800 NRWK 90650 736-H6
16400 TOR 90504 733-C6
W 164TH ST
400 CRSN 90248 734-B6
600 LA 90247 734-B6
1000 GAR 90247 734-A6
1900 GAR 90247 733-G6
1900 TOR 90504 733-G6
164TH ST E
38800 LACo 93591 4199-F2
W 165TH PL
700 LA 90247 734-B6
1000 GAR 90247 734-B6
1700 GAR 90247 733-J6
165TH ST
4000 LNDL 90260 733-C6
11800 NRWK 90650 736-H6
W 165TH ST
1400 COMP 90220 734-G6
2000 TOR 90504 733-G6
165TH ST E
30800 Llan 93544 4469-G2
31900 Llan 93544 4379-G3
34800 LACo 93591 4379-G3
38000 LACo 93591 4199-F2
38000 Llan 93544 4199-G7
40400 LACo 93535 4199-G2
40800 LACo 93535 4109-G7
166TH PL
2100 TOR 90504 733-G7
166TH ST
1400 COMP 90220 734-G6
3200 TOR 90504 733-F7
4000 LNDL 90260 733-C7
10800 CRTS 90703 736-E6
11100 LACo 90703 736-G6
11100 NRWK 90650 736-G6
11200 NRWK 90650 736-G6
11500 ART 90701 736-G6
12400 CRTS 90703 737-B6
W 166TH ST
1100 GAR 90247 734-A6
1400 GAR 90247 733-H6
2000 TOR 90504 733-H6
166TH ST E
39000 LACo 93591 4199-G2
40400 LACo 93535 4199-G1
40800 LACo 93535 4109-G6
167TH ST
4000 LNDL 90260 733-C7
11300 CRTS 90703 736-F6
11300 LACo 90703 736-F6
11800 ART 90701 736-H6
W 167TH ST
700 LA 90247 734-B6
1000 GAR 90247 734-B6
2700 TOR 90504 733-G7
167TH ST E
33000 Llan 93544 4379-H5
39000 LACo 93591 4199-G2
40400 LACo 93535 4199-G1
41100 LACo 93535 4109-G7
168TH PL
600 LA 90247 734-B7
168TH ST
3600 TOR 90504 733-C7
4000 LNDL 90260 733-C7
11500 ART 90701 736-G6
W 168TH ST
100 CRSN 90248 734-B7
100 CRSN 90746 734-B7
500 LA 90248 734-B7
600 LA 90247 734-B7
1000 GAR 90247 734-B7
1300 GAR 90247 733-J7
2500 TOR 90504 733-F7
168TH ST E
33000 Llan 93544 4379-H5
39000 LACo 93591 4199-G2
40500 LACo 93535 4199-G1
40800 LACo 93535 4109-G6
169TH PL
1300 GAR 90247 734-A7
2000 TOR 90504 733-G7
W 169TH PL
800 LA 90247 734-B7
1400 GAR 90247 733-J7
169TH ST
3600 TOR 90504 733-E7
4000 LNDL 90260 733-C7
11500 ART 90701 736-G6
E 169TH ST
300 CRSN 90746 734-D7
W 169TH ST
500 LA 90248 734-B7
600 LA 90247 734-B7
1400 GAR 90247 733-H7

W 169TH ST
1400 GAR 90247 734-B7
169TH ST E
39000 LACo 93591 4199-G3
40400 LACo 93535 4199-G1
40800 LACo 93535 4109-G7
170TH ST
2200 TOR 90504 733-E7
4100 LNDL 90260 733-C7
11900 ART 90701 736-H6
14800 LMRD 90638 737-F6
W 170TH ST
500 LA 90248 734-B7
600 LA 90247 734-B7
1000 GAR 90247 734-A7
1400 GAR 90247 733-J7
170TH ST E
33100 Llan 93544 4379-H5
38000 Llan 93544 4199-H7
38400 LACo 93591 4199-H7
40400 LACo 93535 4199-H2
40700 LACo 93535 4109-G3
171ST ST
2000 TOR 90504 733-E7
4200 LNDL 90260 733-C7
W 171ST ST
600 LA 90247 734-B7
1400 GAR 90247 733-J7
1400 GAR 90247 734-B7
171ST ST E
25100 Llan 93544 4199-H7
33500 Llan 93544 4379-H5
38300 LACo 93591 4199-H3
40400 LACo 93535 4199-H2
40600 LACo 93535 4109-H2
172ND PL
1600 GAR 90247 733-J7
172ND ST
3400 TOR 90504 733-D7
4400 LNDL 90260 733-C7
W 172ND ST
500 LA 90248 734-B7
600 LA 90247 734-B7
1400 GAR 90247 733-J7
1400 GAR 90247 734-B7
172ND ST E
33000 Llan 93544 4379-J5
33400 LACo 93535 4199-H7
38400 LACo 93591 4199-H2
40200 LACo 93535 4199-H1
40900 LACo 93535 4109-H2
173RD PL
4000 TOR 90504 733-D7
W 173RD PL
700 LA 90247 734-B7
173RD ST
3700 TOR 90504 733-D7
4500 LNDL 90260 733-C7
W 173RD ST
700 LA 90247 734-B7
1400 GAR 90247 733-J7
1400 GAR 90247 734-B7
2200 TOR 90504 733-E7
173RD ST E
38100 Llan 93544 4199-H7
38400 LACo 93591 4199-H2
40800 LACo 93535 4109-H7
174TH ST E
17200 LACo 93535 4109-H7
17200 LACo 93535 4199-H1
39400 LACo 93591 4199-H2
175TH PL
4000 TOR 90504 763-D1
175TH ST
2600 TOR 90504 763-D1
11600 ART 90701 736-G7
175TH ST E
31500 Llan 93544 4469-J1
31800 Llan 93544 4379-J3
35700 Llan 93544 4199-J7
38500 LACo 93591 4199-J2
40400 LACo 93535 4199-J2
40700 LACo 93535 4109-H5
176TH CT
3800 TOR 90504 763-E1
176TH PL
17500 TOR 90504 763-H1
176TH ST
11400 ART 90701 736-G7
12200 CRTS 90703 736-J7
W 176TH ST
2100 TOR 90504 763-D1
176TH ST E
39900 LACo 93591 4199-J2
40400 LACo 93535 4199-J2
40500 LACo 93535 4199-G1
40800 LACo 93535 4109-J5
177TH ST
2000 TOR 90504 763-D1
11300 CRTS 90703 736-G7
11400 ART 90701 736-G7
W 177TH ST
1200 LA 90248 764-A1
1200 GAR 90248 764-A1
177TH ST E
40100 LACo 93591 4199-J3
40400 LACo 93535 4199-J1
40900 LACo 93535 4109-J5
178TH ST
1800 TOR 90504 763-D1
11400 ART 90701 736-G7
W 178TH ST
1400 GAR 90248 763-J1

W 178TH ST
1400 GAR 90248 764-A1
178TH ST E
39600 LACo 93591 4199-J3
40400 LACo 93535 4199-J1
40800 LACo 93535 4109-J5
W 179TH PL
1500 GAR 90248 763-J1
179TH ST
1800 TOR 90504 763-D1
12100 ART 90701 766-J1
W 179TH ST
1400 GAR 90248 763-J1
1400 GAR 90248 764-A1
179TH ST E
39600 LACo 93591 4200-A3
40100 LACo 93591 4199-J2
40400 LACo 93535 4199-J1
40800 LACo 93535 4109-J7
180TH PL
1800 TOR 90504 763-E1
180TH ST
1800 TOR 90504 763-D1
11500 ART 90701 766-G1
W 180TH ST
1400 GAR 90248 763-J1
1400 GAR 90248 764-A1
180TH ST E
31800 Llan 93544 4470-A1
35600 Llan 93544 4200-A7
38400 LACo 93591 4200-A3
40400 LACo 93535 4200-A1
40700 LACo 93535 4110-A5
42000 LACo 93535 4109-J4
181ST ST
2000 TOR 90504 763-H1
11500 ART 90701 766-G1
E 181ST ST
300 CRSN 90746 764-D1
W 181ST ST
1800 TOR 90504 763-D1
181ST ST E
40400 LACo 93535 4200-A2
40700 LACo 93535 4110-A5
182ND PL
2600 RBCH 90278 763-B2
3300 TOR 90504 763-F2
182ND ST
1800 TOR 90504 763-G1
2600 RBCH 90278 763-C2
4000 TOR 90278 763-C2
E 182ND ST
300 CRSN 90746 764-D1
W 182ND ST
500 LA 90248 764-A1
900 GAR 90248 764-A1
1400 LA 90248 763-J1
1400 GAR 90248 763-J1
182ND ST E
38800 LACo 93591 4200-A5
40400 LACo 93535 4200-A2
40700 LACo 93535 4110-A7
183RD ST
1900 TOR 90504 763-D2
2600 RBCH 90278 763-B2
5600 LPMA 90623 767-D1
10700 CRTS 90703 766-E1
11400 ART 90701 766-H1
12400 CRTS 90703 767-B1
W 183RD ST
1400 LA 90248 764-A2
1400 LA 90248 763-J2
184TH PL
3700 TOR 90504 763-D2
184TH ST
1900 TOR 90504 763-D2
2500 RBCH 90278 763-B2
11400 ART 90701 766-G1
E 184TH ST
200 CRSN 90746 764-D2
W 184TH ST
500 LA 90248 764-B1
1400 LA 90248 763-J2
184TH ST E
40700 LACo 93535 4200-A1
40700 LACo 93535 4110-A7
185TH PL
1800 TOR 90504 763-H2
12200 ART 90701 766-J1
185TH ST
1800 TOR 90504 763-G2
2500 RBCH 90278 763-B2
11500 ART 90701 766-G1
12200 CRTS 90703 766-J1
E 185TH ST
200 CRSN 90746 764-D2
W 185TH ST
1000 LA 90248 764-A2
1400 LA 90248 763-J2
3100 TOR 90504 763-D2
185TH ST E
30800 Llan 93544 4470-B3
38800 LACo 93591 4200-B5
40400 LACo 93535 4200-B2
40800 LACo 93535 4110-B6
186TH ST
1800 TOR 90504 763-E2
4400 TOR 90278 763-C2
11400 ART 90701 766-G1
E 186TH ST
200 CRSN 90746 764-D2
W 186TH ST
1000 LA 90248 764-A2

W 186TH ST
1400 LA 90248 763-J2
186TH ST E
40600 LACo 93535 4200-B1
41500 LACo 93535 4110-B6
187TH PL
1800 TOR 90504 763-F2
W 187TH PL
1000 LA 90248 764-A2
1400 LA 90248 763-J2
187TH ST
2100 TOR 90504 763-E2
11400 ART 90701 766-H1
11400 CRTS 90703 766-G2
W 187TH ST
1000 LA 90248 764-A2
1400 LA 90248 763-J2
187TH ST E
41500 LACo 93535 4110-B6
188TH ST
11600 ART 90701 766-G2
W 188TH ST
3100 TOR 90504 763-E2
188TH ST E
38800 LACo 93591 4200-B6
41500 LACo 93535 4110-B6
E 189TH ST
100 CRSN 90746 764-D2
W 189TH ST
500 LA 90248 764-C2
3200 TOR 90504 763-F2
190TH ST
1700 TOR 90501 763-G2
1700 TOR 90504 763-G2
1900 RBCH 90278 763-B3
1900 RBCH 90277 763-B3
2900 TOR 90503 763-B3
5500 TOR 90277 763-B3
W 190TH ST
500 LA 90248 764-B2
500 CRSN 90248 764-B2
500 LACo 90248 764-B2
900 LA 90502 764-B2
1200 LACo 90502 764-B2
1300 LA 90501 764-B2
1300 LA 90248 763-J2
1300 LA 90501 763-J2
190TH ST E
37700 Llan 93544 4200-C7
38400 LACo 93591 4200-C3
40400 LACo 93535 4200-C2
40700 LACo 93535 4110-C4
191ST ST
4500 TOR 90503 763-C3
191ST ST E
39700 LACo 93591 4200-C3
E 192ND ST
100 CRSN 90746 764-D3
192ND ST E
31400 Llan 93544 4470-D2
39600 LACo 93591 4200-C3
40400 LACo 93535 4200-C2
193RD ST
12600 CRTS 90703 767-A2
193RD ST E
31000 Llan 93544 4470-D3
194TH ST E
40100 LACo 93591 4200-C3
195TH ST
2000 TOR 90501 763-H3
11000 CRTS 90703 766-H3
12200 ART 90701 766-J3
12400 CRTS 90703 767-A3
195TH ST E
31000 Llan 93544 4470-D2
38400 LACo 93591 4200-D4
40400 LACo 93535 4200-D2
40700 LACo 93535 4110-D5
W 196TH ST
1200 LACo 90502 764-A3
196TH ST E
39100 LACo 93591 4200-D4
41600 LACo 93535 4110-D5
197TH ST E
38800 LACo 93591 4200-D3
40400 LACo 93535 4200-D1
40800 LACo 93535 4110-D2
198TH ST E
38800 LACo 93591 4200-E6
40400 LACo 93535 4200-D1
200TH ST E
31000 Llan 93544 4470-E3
38000 Llan 93544 4200-E7
38400 LACo 93591 4200-E7
40400 LACo 93535 4200-E7
40800 LACo 93535 4110-D2
202ND ST E
40400 LACo 93535 4200-E2
40800 LACo 93535 4110-E1
W 203RD ST
\- LA 90501 763-J4
203RD ST E
38200 Llan 93544 4200-F7
40500 LACo 93535 4200-E2
40900 LACo 93535 4110-E7
W 204TH ST
1100 LACo 90502 764-A4
1500 LA 90501 763-J4
205TH ST
1500 LA 90501 763-J4
1700 TOR 90501 763-G4
11400 LKWD 90715 766-G4

STREET Block City ZIP Pg-Grid

205TH ST E
33800 Llan 93544 4200-F7
38500 LACo 93591 4200-F3
40400 LACo 93535 4200-F2
40700 LACo 93535 4110-F3
206TH ST
11400 LKWD 90715 766-G4
12500 LKWD 90715 767-A4
W 206TH ST
1500 LA 90501 763-J4
207TH ST
11500 LKWD 90715 766-G4
12400 LKWD 90715 767-A4
W 207TH ST
1500 LA 90501 763-J5
207TH ST E
42200 LACo 93535 4110-F1
208TH ST
1700 TOR 90501 763-F5
2400 TOR 90503 763-F5
11600 LKWD 90715 766-G4
E 208TH ST
2800 CRSN 90810 765-B4
4300 LBCH 90810 765-B5
W 208TH ST
1500 LA 90501 763-J5
209TH ST
11500 LKWD 90715 766-G5
E 209TH ST
2300 CRSN 90810 764-J5
W 209TH ST
700 LACo 90502 764-A5
1300 LA 90501 764-A5
1300 LA 90501 763-J5
W 210TH ST
1000 LACo 90502 764-A5
1500 LA 90501 763-J5
210TH ST E
32700 Llan 93544 4200-G7
38400 LACo 93591 4200-G5
211TH ST
11300 LKWD 90715 766-J5
12200 HGDN 90716 766-J5
12600 LKWD 90715 767-A5
E 211TH ST
100 CRSN 90745 764-C5
W 211TH ST
1000 LACo 90502 764-A5
1300 LA 90501 764-A5
1300 LA 90501 763-J5
211TH ST E
38100 Llan 93544 4200-G7
212TH ST
1800 TOR 90501 763-H5
11300 LKWD 90715 766-G5
12200 HGDN 90716 766-J5
12400 LKWD 90715 767-A5
E 212TH ST
100 CRSN 90745 764-C5
W 212TH ST
300 CRSN 90745 764-C5
700 LACo 90502 764-A5
1300 LA 90501 764-A5
1300 LA 90501 763-J5
212TH ST E
31300 Llan 93544 4200-G7
37500 LACo 93591 4200-G3
40900 LACo 93535 4110-G4
W 213TH PL
100 CRSN 90745 764-C6
213TH ST
1200 TOR 90501 763-H6
11300 LKWD 90715 766-G5
12200 HGDN 90716 766-J5
12600 LKWD 90715 767-A5
E 213TH ST
100 CRSN 90745 764-G5
1900 CRSN 90810 764-G5
W 213TH ST
500 CRSN 90745 764-B6
700 LACo 90502 764-A6
1300 LA 90501 764-A6
1400 LA 90501 763-J6
213TH ST E
\- LACo 93591 4200-G2
29200 Llan 93544 4470-H1
214TH ST
1700 TOR 90501 763-H6
11300 LKWD 90715 766-G5
12200 HGDN 90716 766-G5
12600 LKWD 90715 767-A5
E 214TH ST
100 CRSN 90745 764-C6
12000 HGDN 90716 766-H5
W 214TH ST
100 CRSN 90745 764-B6
700 LACo 90502 764-B6
1300 LA 90501 764-A6
1400 LA 90501 763-J6
E 215TH PL
1100 CRSN 90745 764-F6
215TH ST
11300 LKWD 90715 766-G5
11800 HGDN 90716 766-H5
12400 LKWD 90715 767-A5
E 215TH ST
100 CRSN 90745 764-C6
W 215TH ST
400 CRSN 90745 764-B6
1400 LA 90501 763-J6
215TH ST E
38000 Llan 93544 4200-H7
38400 LACo 93591 4200-H2

215TH ST E
40400 LACo 93535 4200-H2
40700 LACo 93535 4110-H3
216TH ST
1700 TOR 90501 763-H6
11400 LKWD 90715 766-G6
12100 HGDN 90716 766-J5
E 216TH ST
100 CRSN 90745 764-C6
W 216TH ST
600 CRSN 90745 764-B6
1100 LACo 90502 764-A6
1300 LA 90501 763-J6
1300 LA 90501 764-A6
216TH ST E
40100 LACo 93591 4200-H2
217TH ST E
33400 Llan 93544 4200-H7
38400 LACo 93591 4200-H7
42800 LACo 93535 4110-H2
E 218TH PL
100 CRSN 90745 764-C6
2500 CRSN 90810 764-J6
2500 CRSN 90810 765-A6
218TH ST
1800 TOR 90501 763-H6
E 218TH ST
100 CRSN 90745 764-C6
2500 CRSN 90810 764-J6
2500 CRSN 90810 765-A6
W 218TH ST
300 CRSN 90745 764-B6
1300 LA 90501 763-J6
1300 LA 90501 764-A6
E 219TH PL
2500 CRSN 90810 764-J6
2500 CRSN 90810 765-A6
W 219TH PL
100 CRSN 90745 764-C6
E 219TH ST
200 CRSN 90745 764-D6
2500 CRSN 90810 764-J6
2500 CRSN 90810 765-A6
W 219TH ST
100 CRSN 90745 764-B6
700 LACo 90502 764-B6
1300 LA 90501 763-J6
1300 LA 90501 764-A6
E 220TH PL
2600 CRSN 90810 764-J7
2600 CRSN 90810 765-A7
220TH ST
1700 TOR 90501 763-H7
E 220TH ST
100 CRSN 90745 764-E7
1900 CRSN 90810 764-J6
2500 CRSN 90810 765-A6
W 220TH ST
100 CRSN 90745 764-C7
700 LACo 90502 764-A7
1300 LA 90501 764-A7
1400 LA 90501 763-J7
220TH ST E
38800 LACo 93591 4200-J3
40400 LACo 93535 4200-J2
40700 LACo 93535 4110-J3
E 221ST PL
2600 CRSN 90810 764-J7
2600 CRSN 90810 765-A7
221ST ST
11800 HGDN 90716 766-H6
12400 HGDN 90716 767-A6
E 221ST ST
100 CRSN 90745 764-D7
2600 CRSN 90810 764-J7
2600 CRSN 90810 765-A7
W 221ST ST
1200 LACo 90502 764-A7
1300 LA 90501 764-A7
1400 LA 90501 763-J7
222ND ST
1800 TOR 90501 763-H7
12200 HGDN 90716 766-J6
12400 HGDN 90716 767-A6
E 222ND ST
200 CRSN 90745 764-D7
W 222ND ST
100 CRSN 90745 764-C7
900 LACo 90502 764-A7
1300 LA 90501 764-A7
1400 LA 90501 763-J7
223RD ST
11800 HGDN 90716 766-H6
12400 HGDN 90716 767-A6
E 223RD ST
100 CRSN 90745 764-E7
1900 CRSN 90810 764-H7
2500 LA 90810 764-H7
W 223RD ST
100 CRSN 90745 764-A7
600 LACo 90745 764-A7
700 LACo 90502 764-A7
1200 LA 90501 764-A7
1400 LA 90501 763-J7
1700 TOR 90501 763-J7
223RD ST E
22300 Llan 93544 4471-A2
E 224TH PL
600 CRSN 90745 764-E7
W 224TH PL
100 CRSN 90745 764-B7
224TH ST
12200 HGDN 90716 766-J6

224TH ST
12400 HGDN 90716 767-A6
E 224TH ST
300 CRSN 90745 764-D7
W 224TH ST
300 CRSN 90745 764-B7
1400 LA 90501 763-J7
1400 LA 90501 764-B7
3400 TOR 90505 763-D7
225TH PL
2500 TOR 90505 793-F1
E 225TH ST
600 CRSN 90745 764-E7
W 225TH ST
100 CRSN 90745 764-C7
1000 LACo 90502 764-A7
1300 LA 90501 764-A7
1400 LA 90501 763-J7
2600 TOR 90505 793-F1
3400 TOR 90505 763-D7
E 226TH PL
600 CRSN 90745 794-E1
W 226TH PL
100 CRSN 90745 794-C1
226TH ST
\- LBCH 90808 766-J7
700 LACo 90502 794-A1
1400 LA 90501 793-J1
2600 TOR 90505 793-F1
3400 TOR 90505 763-C7
11900 HGDN 90716 766-H7
12400 HGDN 90716 767-A7
E 226TH ST
600 CRSN 90745 764-E7
600 CRSN 90745 794-E1
W 226TH ST
100 CRSN 90745 794-C1
2800 TOR 90505 793-E1
226TH ST E
31600 Llan 93544 4471-B1
227TH PL
700 LACo 90502 794-B1
3400 TOR 90505 793-D1
227TH ST
1000 LACo 90502 794-A1
1300 LA 90501 794-A1
1400 LA 90501 793-J1
2300 TOR 90501 793-G1
2500 TOR 90505 793-C1
E 227TH ST
100 CRSN 90745 794-D1
W 227TH ST
700 LACo 90502 794-B1
227TH ST E
31500 Llan 93544 4471-B1
228TH PL
3400 TOR 90505 793-C1
228TH ST
1400 LA 90501 793-J1
1400 LA 90501 794-A1
1700 TOR 90501 793-G1
3400 TOR 90505 793-D1
E 228TH ST
100 CRSN 90745 794-D1
W 228TH ST
100 CRSN 90745 794-C1
600 LACo 90745 794-C1
700 LACo 90502 794-A1
1200 LACo 90501 794-A1
1200 LA 90501 794-A1
228TH ST E
31300 Llan 93544 4471-B2
229TH PL
2200 TOR 90501 793-G1
3300 TOR 90505 793-D1
E 229TH PL
100 CRSN 90745 794-D1
W 229TH PL
100 CRSN 90745 794-C1
229TH ST
4100 TOR 90505 793-C1
E 229TH ST
100 CRSN 90745 794-D1
W 229TH ST
300 CRSN 90745 794-B1
800 LACo 90502 794-A1
2200 TOR 90501 793-G1
2800 TOR 90505 793-D1
230TH PL
2100 TOR 90501 793-G1
2600 TOR 90505 793-C1
230TH ST
1900 TOR 90501 793-G1
2500 TOR 90505 793-C1
E 230TH ST
100 CRSN 90745 794-D1
W 230TH ST
100 CRSN 90745 794-B1
231ST PL
3800 TOR 90505 793-C1
231ST ST
1000 LACo 90502 794-A1
4200 TOR 90505 793-C1
E 231ST ST
100 CRSN 90745 794-D1
W 231ST ST
100 CRSN 90745 794-B1
1900 TOR 90501 793-G1
2600 TOR 90505 793-C1
E 232ND PL
100 CRSN 90745 794-D1
W 232ND PL
100 CRSN 90745 794-C1

232ND ST
800 LACo 90502 794-B1
1900 TOR 90501 793-G1
2500 TOR 90505 793-C1
E 232ND ST
100 CRSN 90745 794-D1
W 232ND ST
500 CRSN 90745 794-B1
800 LACo 90502 794-B1
233RD ST
4400 TOR 90505 793-C2
E 233RD ST
100 CRSN 90745 794-F1
W 233RD ST
100 CRSN 90745 794-C2
1900 TOR 90501 793-G2
2500 TOR 90505 793-F1
233RD ST E
28500 Llan 93544 4471-C1
234TH PL
3900 TOR 90505 793-C2
E 234TH PL
100 CRSN 90745 794-D2
W 234TH PL
100 CRSN 90745 794-C2
234TH ST
2600 TOR 90505 793-C2
E 234TH ST
100 CRSN 90745 794-D2
W 234TH ST
100 CRSN 90745 794-C2
1700 TOR 90501 793-G2
2500 TOR 90505 793-E1
235TH PL
1900 TOR 90501 793-G2
W 235TH PL
100 CRSN 90745 794-C2
235TH ST
1700 TOR 90501 793-G2
2500 TOR 90505 793-E1
E 235TH ST
100 CRSN 90745 794-D2
W 235TH ST
100 CRSN 90745 794-B2
1500 Hrbr 90710 793-H2
W 236TH CT
200 CRSN 90745 794-C2
236TH PL
2000 TOR 90501 793-G2
236TH ST
1700 TOR 90501 793-G2
3700 TOR 90505 793-C2
E 236TH ST
100 CRSN 90745 794-D2
237TH PL
1900 TOR 90501 793-G2
237TH ST
1500 Hrbr 90710 793-J2
1900 TOR 90501 793-G2
2500 TOR 90505 793-E2
E 237TH ST
300 CRSN 90745 794-D2
E 238TH PL
200 CRSN 90745 794-D2
238TH ST
1400 Hrbr 90710 793-J2
1600 LA 90501 793-J2
1600 TOR 90501 793-G2
3700 TOR 90505 793-C2
E 238TH ST
300 CRSN 90745 794-D2
239TH ST
2200 TOR 90501 793-G2
4100 TOR 90505 793-C2
W 239TH ST
1700 LA 90501 793-J2
240TH ST
1900 LMTA 90717 793-H3
3600 TOR 90505 793-D3
W 240TH ST
1400 Hrbr 90710 793-J2
1400 Hrbr 90710 794-A3
1700 LA 90717 793-J3
1700 TOR 90501 793-J3
241ST ST
1900 LMTA 90717 793-G3
W 241ST ST
1700 LA 90717 793-J3
242ND PL
1800 TOR 90501 793-H3
W 242ND PL
1400 Hrbr 90710 793-J3
1400 Hrbr 90710 794-A3
1700 LA 90717 793-J3
1700 TOR 90501 793-J3
242ND ST
1700 TOR 90501 793-H3
2000 LMTA 90717 793-H3
3400 TOR 90505 793-C3
W 242ND ST
1700 LA 90717 793-J3
1700 TOR 90501 793-J3
243RD PL
1800 TOR 90501 793-H3
243RD ST
1200 Hrbr 90710 794-A3
2200 LMTA 90717 793-G3
W 243RD ST
1300 Hrbr 90710 794-A3
1400 Hrbr 90710 793-J3
1700 LA 90717 793-J3
1700 TOR 90501 793-J3

243RD ST E
30000 Llan 93544 4471-E2
244TH ST
900 Hrbr 90710 794-A3
3300 TOR 90505 793-D3
E 244TH ST
300 CRSN 90745 794-D3
W 244TH ST
1300 Hrbr 90710 794-A3
1400 Hrbr 90710 793-J3
1700 LA 90717 793-J3
1700 TOR 90501 793-J3
245TH ST
900 Hrbr 90710 794-A3
2000 LMTA 90717 793-H3
E 245TH ST
500 CRSN 90745 794-E3
W 245TH ST
1400 Hrbr 90710 793-J3
1400 Hrbr 90710 794-C3
1700 LA 90717 793-J3
1700 TOR 90501 793-J3
245TH ST E
30500 Llan 93544 4471-E3
E 246TH PL
400 CRSN 90745 794-E3
W 246TH PL
2300 LMTA 90717 793-G3
246TH ST
2300 LMTA 90717 793-G3
E 246TH ST
500 CRSN 90745 794-E3
500 Wilm 90744 794-E3
W 246TH ST
1400 Hrbr 90710 793-J3
1400 Hrbr 90710 794-C3
1700 LA 90717 793-J3
1700 LMTA 90717 793-J3
1700 TOR 90501 793-J3
W 247TH PL
1500 Hrbr 90710 793-J3
1700 LA 90717 793-J3
1700 LMTA 90717 793-J3
247TH ST
2100 LMTA 90717 793-G3
E 247TH ST
300 CRSN 90745 794-D3
600 Wilm 90744 794-E3
W 247TH ST
1400 Hrbr 90710 793-J3
1400 Hrbr 90710 794-C3
1700 LA 90717 793-J3
1700 LMTA 90717 793-J3
247TH ST E
30300 Llan 93544 4471-F4
E 248TH ST
300 CRSN 90745 794-D3
500 Wilm 90744 794-E3
W 248TH ST
1500 Hrbr 90710 793-J4
1700 LA 90717 793-J4
1700 LMTA 90717 793-G4
248TH ST E
29500 Llan 93544 4471-F1
249TH ST
2300 LMTA 90717 793-G4
E 249TH ST
300 CRSN 90745 794-E3
600 Wilm 90744 794-E3
W 249TH ST
1400 Hrbr 90710 793-J4
1700 LA 90717 793-J4
W 250TH ST
2000 LMTA 90717 793-G4
251ST ST
1100 Hrbr 90710 794-A4
2300 LMTA 90717 793-G4
W 251ST ST
1000 Hrbr 90710 794-A4
1400 Hrbr 90710 793-J4
1700 LA 90717 793-J4
1700 LMTA 90717 793-J4
252ND ST
1800 LMTA 90717 793-H4
W 252ND ST
1000 Hrbr 90710 794-A4
1400 Hrbr 90710 793-J4
1700 LA 90717 793-J4
1700 LMTA 90717 793-J4
W 253RD PL
1900 LMTA 90717 793-H4
253RD ST
1800 LMTA 90717 793-G4
W 253RD ST
800 Hrbr 90710 794-A4
1400 Hrbr 90710 793-J4
1700 LA 90717 793-J4
1700 LMTA 90717 793-H4
253RD ST E
29800 Llan 93544 4471-G4
254TH ST
1900 LMTA 90717 793-G4
W 254TH ST
1000 Hrbr 90710 794-A4
1400 Hrbr 90710 793-J4
1700 LA 90717 793-J4
1700 LMTA 90717 793-H4
255TH ST
2000 LMTA 90717 793-G5
W 255TH ST
700 Hrbr 90710 794-A4
1400 Hrbr 90710 793-J5
1700 LA 90717 793-J5

W 255TH ST
1700 LMTA 90717 793-J5
256TH ST
2100 LMTA 90717 793-G5
W 256TH ST
1100 Hrbr 90710 794-A5
1400 Hrbr 90710 793-J5
1700 LA 90717 793-J5
1700 LMTA 90717 793-J5
257TH ST
1900 LMTA 90717 793-H5
W 257TH ST
1000 Hrbr 90710 794-A5
1400 Hrbr 90710 793-J5
1700 LA 90717 793-J5
1700 LMTA 90717 793-J5
W 258TH PL
1700 LA 90717 793-J5
1700 LMTA 90717 793-J5
W 259TH PL
1600 Hrbr 90710 793-J5
1700 LA 90717 793-J5
1700 LMTA 90717 793-H5
W 259TH ST
1300 Hrbr 90710 794-A5
1400 Hrbr 90710 793-J5
1700 LA 90717 793-J5
1700 LMTA 90717 793-J5
260TH ST
1700 LMTA 90717 793-H5
W 260TH ST
1400 Hrbr 90710 794-A5
1400 Hrbr 90710 793-J5
1700 LA 90717 793-J5
1700 LMTA 90717 793-J5
261ST ST
1800 LMTA 90717 793-H5
W 261ST ST
1400 Hrbr 90710 793-H5
1400 Hrbr 90710 794-A5
1700 LA 90717 793-H5
1700 LMTA 90717 793-H5
262ND ST
1700 Hrbr 90710 793-H6
1700 LMTA 90717 793-H6
W 262ND ST
1500 Hrbr 90710 793-J6
1700 Hrbr 90710 793-J6
263RD ST
1700 Hrbr 90710 793-H6
1800 LMTA 90717 793-H6
W 263RD ST
1400 Hrbr 90710 794-A6
1500 Hrbr 90710 793-J6
1700 Hrbr 90710 793-J6
263RD ST E
11100 Llan 93544 4471-J3
264TH ST
2000 LMTA 90717 793-H6
W 264TH ST
1300 Hrbr 90710 794-A6
W 265TH ST
1600 Hrbr 90710 793-J6
W 266TH ST
1600 Hrbr 90710 793-J6
I-5 GOLDEN STATE FRWY
\- Boyl - 634-J5
\- Boyl - 635-A2
\- BURB - 533-D4
\- BURB - 563-H1
\- Cstc - 4279-C7
\- Cstc - 4369-D1
\- Cstc - 4459-H3
\- Echo - 594-D3
\- GLDL - 563-H1
\- GLDL - 564-B5
\- GrnH - 481-E4
\- GrnH - 4641-A7
\- LA - 481-E4
\- LA - 501-J1
\- LA - 502-B3
\- LA - 533-D4
\- LA - 564-B5
\- LA - 594-D3
\- LA - 634-J1
\- LA - 635-A2
\- LA - 4641-A7
\- LACo - 4279-A4
\- LACo - 4641-A7
\- LFlz - 564-B5
\- MsnH - 481-E4
\- MsnH - 501-J1
\- MsnH - 502-B3
\- Nwhl - 4640-F3
\- Nwhl - 4641-A7
\- Pcma - 502-B3
\- SCTA - 4459-H3
\- SCTA - 4460-A7
\- SCTA - 4550-C3
\- SCTA - 4640-F3
\- StvR - 4550-C3
\- StvR - 4640-F3
\- StvR - 4641-A7
\- SunV - 502-D6
\- SunV - 532-J1
\- SunV - 533-D4
\- Valc - 4459-H3
\- Valc - 4460-A7
\- Valc - 4550-C3
I-5 SANTA ANA FRWY
\- BPK - 737-B4
\- BPK - 767-H1

I-5 SANTA ANA FRWY
\- CMRC - 675-F2
\- CMRC - 676-A6
\- DWNY - 676-A6
\- DWNY - 706-D3
\- LA - 634-J6
\- LA - 635-B7
\- LA - 675-F2
\- LACo - 675-F2
\- LMRD - 737-B4
\- NRWK - 706-D3
\- NRWK - 736-J2
\- NRWK - 737-B4
\- SFSP - 706-D3
\- SFSP - 737-B4
I-10 ROSA PARKS FRWY
\- LA - 632-B7
\- LA - 633-F6
\- LA - 634-A6
I-10 SAN BERNARDINO FRWY
\- ALH - 635-C3
\- ALH - 636-A1
\- BALD - 598-H7
\- BALD - 637-E1
\- BALD - 638-C1
\- Boyl - 634-J3
\- Boyl - 635-C3
\- City - 635-C3
\- CLAR - 601-A6
\- COV - 599-A7
\- COV - 639-J1
\- ELMN - 596-G7
\- ELMN - 597-A7
\- ELMN - 637-E1
\- INDS - 637-E1
\- LA - 634-J3
\- LA - 635-C3
\- LACo - 599-A7
\- LACo - 635-C3
\- LACo - 639-J1
\- LACo - 640-A1
\- MONP - 635-C3
\- MONP - 636-A1
\- MTCL - 601-A6
\- POM - 600-D7
\- POM - 601-A6
\- POM - 640-A1
\- RSMD - 596-G7
\- RSMD - 597-A7
\- RSMD - 636-A1
\- SDMS - 639-J1
\- SDMS - 640-A1
\- SGBL - 636-A1
\- UPL - 601-A6
\- WCOV - 598-H7
\- WCOV - 599-A7
\- WCOV - 639-J1
I-10 SANTA MONICA FRWY
\- LA - 632-F7
\- LA - 633-B6
\- LA - 634-A6
\- LA - 674-G1
\- SMCA - 631-J7
\- SMCA - 632-F7
\- SMCA - 671-J1
I-105 CENTURY FRWY
\- DWNY - 735-G2
\- DWNY - 736-D2
\- ELSG - 702-H7
\- HAW - 703-E7
\- ING - 703-E7
\- LA - 704-C7
\- LACo - 703-E7
\- LACo - 704-C7
\- Lenx - 703-E7
\- LYN - 704-C7
\- LYN - 705-A6
\- LYN - 735-G2
\- NRWK - 736-D2
\- PRM - 735-G2
\- SGAT - 735-G2
\- Wbrk - 704-C7
\- Wch - 702-H7
\- Wch - 703-E7
I-105 G ANDRSN FRWY & TRNS WY
\- DWNY - 735-C1
\- DWNY - 736-D1
\- ELSG - 702-H6
\- HAW - 703-B6
\- ING - 703-B6
\- LA - 704-A7
\- LACo - 703-B6
\- LACo - 704-A7
\- Lenx - 703-B6
\- LYN - 704-A7
\- LYN - 705-A7
\- LYN - 735-C1
\- NRWK - 736-D1
\- PRM - 735-C1
\- SGAT - 735-C1
\- Wbrk - 704-A7
\- Wch - 702-H6
\- Wch - 703-B6
I-110 HARBOR FRWY & TRANS WY
\- CRSN - 764-B7
\- CRSN - 794-B3
\- Hrbr - 794-B3
\- LA - 634-C6

I-110 HARBOR FRWY & TRANS WY
\- LA - 674-B7
\- LA - 704-C5
\- LA - 734-B6
\- LA - 764-B7
\- LACo - 704-C5
\- LACo - 734-B6
\- LACo - 764-B7
\- LACo - 794-B3
\- SPed - 824-B2
\- Wilm - 794-B3
\- Wilm - 824-B2
I-210 FOOTHILL FRWY
\- ARCD - 566-G4
\- ARCD - 567-H6
\- AZU - 568-D6
\- AZU - 569-H7
\- DUAR - 567-H6
\- DUAR - 568-D6
\- GLDL - 504-B7
\- GLDL - 534-F1
\- GLDR - 569-H7
\- GLDR - 570-A7
\- GLDR - 599-E1
\- GLDR - 600-A1
\- GrnH - 481-F2
\- IRW - 568-D6
\- LA - 481-F2
\- LA - 482-D5
\- LA - 502-F1
\- LA - 503-C2
\- LACo - 482-D5
\- LACo - 566-G4
\- LACo - 569-H7
\- LaCr - 534-F1
\- LCF - 534-F1
\- LCF - 535-D6
\- MNRO - 567-H6
\- Mont - 534-F1
\- PAS - 535-D6
\- PAS - 565-G2
\- PAS - 566-G4
\- Sunl - 502-F1
\- Sunl - 503-F5
\- SunV - 503-F5
\- SunV - 504-B7
\- Tuj - 504-B7
I-405 SAN DIEGO FRWY
\- BelA - 561-G7
\- BelA - 591-F3
\- Brwd - 561-G7
\- Brwd - 591-F3
\- Brwd - 631-J3
\- Bxby - 765-A7
\- Bxby - 795-G2
\- CRSN - 764-C4
\- CRSN - 765-A7
\- CULC - 672-D1
\- Enc - 531-G3
\- Enc - 561-G3
\- GrnH - 481-G7
\- GrnH - 501-G7
\- HAW - 703-A6
\- HAW - 733-B4
\- ING - 703-A1
\- LA - 481-G7
\- LA - 501-G7
\- LA - 531-G3
\- LA - 631-J3
\- LA - 632-A4
\- LA - 672-D1
\- LA - 763-G2
\- LA - 764-C4
\- LACo - 631-J3
\- LACo - 632-A4
\- LACo - 703-A6
\- LACo - 733-B4
\- LACo - 764-C4
\- LBCH - 765-A7
\- LBCH - 795-G2
\- LBCH - 796-A3
\- Lenx - 703-A6
\- LNDL - 733-B4
\- MsnH - 481-G7
\- MsnH - 501-G7
\- RBCH - 733-B4
\- Shrm - 561-G3
\- SIGH - 795-G2
\- SLB - 796-J6
\- TOR - 733-B4
\- TOR - 763-G2
\- VanN - 531-G3
\- VanN - 561-G3
\- Wch - 672-D1
\- Wch - 702-J1
\- Wch - 703-A1
\- WLA - 632-A4
I-605 SAN GABRIEL RIVER FRWY
\- BALD - 597-H6
\- BALD - 637-E5
\- CRTS - 736-E4
\- CRTS - 766-F1
\- DUAR - 568-B7
\- DWNY - 706-F3
\- HGDN - 766-G5
\- INDS - 637-E5
\- INDS - 677-A2
\- IRW - 568-B7
\- IRW - 597-H6
\- IRW - 598-A2

I-605 SAN GABRIEL RIVER FRWY
\- LACo - 637-E5
\- LACo - 676-J3
\- LACo - 677-A2
\- LACo - 706-F3
\- LALM - 796-H2
\- LBCH - 766-G5
\- LBCH - 796-H2
\- LKWD - 766-G5
\- NRWK - 706-F3
\- NRWK - 736-E4
\- PRV - 637-E5
\- PRV - 676-J3
\- PRV - 677-A2
\- SFSP - 706-F3
\- SLB - 796-H2
\- WHIT - 676-J3
\- WHIT - 677-A2
I-710 LONG BEACH FRWY
\- ALH - 595-G7
\- ALH - 635-F4
\- BELL - 675-F5
\- BELL - 705-F5
\- BGDN - 675-F5
\- BGDN - 705-F5
\- CDHY - 705-F5
\- CMRC - 675-F5
\- COMP - 735-D6
\- CRSN - 765-B5
\- ELA - 635-F4
\- ELA - 675-F5
\- LACo - 705-F5
\- LACo - 735-D6
\- LBCH - 765-B5
\- LBCH - 795-B4
\- LBCH - 825-C1
\- LYN - 705-F5
\- LYN - 735-D6
\- MONP - 635-F4
\- NLB - 735-D6
\- NLB - 765-B5
\- PRM - 735-D6
\- RDom - 735-D6
\- RDom - 765-B5
\- SGAT - 705-F5
\- VER - 675-F5
Rt#-N1 LAS VIRGENES RD
1000 LACo 91302 588-G3
2200 CALB 91302 588-G3
2700 CALB 91301 588-G3
2700 Ago 91301 588-G3
3700 CALB 91302 558-H7
4800 LACo 91302 558-H7
Rt#-N1 N MALIBU CANYON RD
100 LACo 91302 628-H1
500 LACo 91302 588-H7
Rt#-N1 S MALIBU CANYON RD
100 LACo 90265 628-J3
100 LACo 91302 628-G2
2600 MAL 90265 628-J3
3700 LACo 90263 628-H7
Rt#-N2 ELIZABETH LAKE RD
700 PMDL 93551 4195-A6
700 LACo 93551 4195-D7
3500 PMDL 93551 4194-E4
4000 LACo 93551 4194-A3
7700 LACo 93551 4193-D1
8000 LACo 93532 4102-A2
8000 LACo 93551 4102-G4
8000 LACo 93551 4103-A7
17500 LACo 93532 4101-H2
Rt#-N2 PALMDALE BLVD
200 PMDL 93551 4195-H7
Rt#-N2 PINE CANYON RD
18200 LACo 93532 4101-F1
Rt#-N3 ANGELES FOREST HWY
\- LACo - 505-F1
\- PMDL 93550 (4556-E1 See Page 4466)
800 LACo - (4646-C7 See Page 4645)
800 LACo - (4725-G4 See Page 4645)
800 LACo - (4726-A1 See Page 4645)
1000 LACo - (4556-E7 See Page 4466)
31800 PMDL 93550 4466-B1
33100 Actn 93510 4376-B7
33100 PMDL 93550 4376-B7
Rt#-N4 BIG PINES HWY
20400 Valy 93563 (4561-A4 See Page 4471)
20500 Valy 93563 (4560-F2 See Page 4470)
Rt#-N4 LARGO VISTA RD
27400 Llan 93544 4470-F5
27400 Llan 93544 (4560-F2 See Page 4470)
27400 Valy 93563 (4560-F2 See Page 4470)

Rt#-N5 AVENUE J
700 LAN 93535 4016-H6
4500 LAN 93535 4017-B6
4800 LACo 93535 4017-B6
9000 LACo 93535 4018-C6
9300 LAN 93535 4018-C6
Rt#-N6 DEVILS PUNCHBOWL RD
29300 Pear 93553 4469-A6
29300 Valy 93563 4469-A6
Rt#-N6 LONGVIEW RD
29600 Valy 93563 4468-J2
31300 Pear 93553 4468-J2
31800 Pear 93553 4378-J5
Rt#-N6 TUMBLEWEED RD
13100 Pear 93553 4468-J5
13100 Pear 93553 4469-A5
13100 Valy 93563 4468-J5
13100 Valy 93563 4469-A5
Rt#-N7 HAWTHORNE BLVD
24100 TOR 90505 793-D5
25500 RHE 90274 793-D5
26000 RPV 90275 793-A7
27500 RPV 90275 792-J7
28800 RPV 90275 822-H2
29500 RHE 90274 822-H2
Rt#-N8 AZUSA AV
100 LACo 91744 638-H7
100 INDS 91744 638-H7
400 WCOV 91792 638-H7
800 WCOV 91791 638-H7
Rt#-N8 S AZUSA AV
100 INDS 91744 638-J4
100 INDS 91744 678-G3
100 WCOV 91791 598-J7
100 LPUE 91744 678-G3
200 WCOV 91791 638-J4
700 INDS 91748 678-G3
700 INDS 91745 678-G3
1400 HacH 91745 678-G3
1700 WCOV 91792 638-J4
Rt#-N8 COLIMA RD
3100 HacH 91745 678-C6
4000 WHIT 90605 677-J7
4000 WHIT 90605 707-H1
4000 WHIT 91745 677-J7
4000 WHIT 91745 678-C6
9800 WHIT 90603 707-G4
10200 LACo 90604 707-G4
Rt#-N8 LA MIRADA BLVD
7500 BPK 90621 737-G4
10400 LACo 90604 707-G7
11500 LMRD 90638 707-G7
12200 LMRD 90638 737-G2
12900 LMRD 90639 737-G2
Rt#-N9 KANAN RD
400 LACo 90265 587-E4
600 Ago 91301 587-H2
3200 Ago 91301 588-B1
4100 Ago 91301 558-A7
4100 AGRH 91301 558-A7
Rt#-N9 KANAN DUME RD
100 LACo 90265 587-D7
1000 LACo 90265 627-D1
3700 MAL 90265 627-F5
5800 MAL 90265 667-F1
Rt#-1 LINCOLN BLVD
100 Ven 90291 671-G3
1100 Ven 90291 672-A6
1700 SMCA 90404 671-G3
1900 SMCA 90405 671-G3
4000 LA 90292 672-A6
4400 MdlR 90292 672-A6
4800 LA 90094 672-A6
4800 LA 90094 702-D2
4800 MdlR 90292 702-D2
8100 Wch 90045 702-D2
Rt#-1 LOS ALAMITOS CIR
\- LBCH 90804 796-A5
\- LBCH 90815 796-A5
Rt#-1 PACIFIC COAST HWY
\- HMB 90254 762-H1
100 SLB 90740 826-G4
400 MANB 90266 732-H7
600 HMB 90266 762-H1
600 MANB 90266 762-H1
1700 LA 90717 793-F5
1700 LMTA 90717 793-F5
2400 TOR 90505 793-F5
2600 MANB 90254 732-H7
2600 MANB 90254 762-H1
2700 HMB 90254 732-H7
9000 VeCo 90265 625-A3
12300 LACo 90265 625-F5
14700 LA 90402 671-B1
14800 LA 90402 631-A7
14900 PacP 90272 630-H6
14900 PacP 90272 631-A7
15900 SLB 90743 826-G4
16100 HNTB 92649 826-G4
16300 SunB 90742 826-G4
16300 Surf 90743 826-G4
16500 HNTB 90742 826-G4
16600 OrCo 92649 826-G4
17600 LA 90265 630-H6
17900 LACo 90265 630-A6
18700 MAL 90265 630-A6

STREET Block City ZIP Pg-Grid

Rt#-1 PACIFIC COAST HWY
19800 MAL 90265 629-G6
23500 MAL 90265 628-C7
24200 LACo 90263 628-G7
26300 MAL 90265 668-A1
27200 MAL 90265 667-A1
30800 MAL 90265 626-A6
30800 MAL 90265 627-A7
34100 MAL 90265 625-F5

Rt#-1 E PACIFIC COAST HWY
- SLB 90740 826-D1
100 LBCH 90813 795-E5
100 Wilm 90744 794-F5
100 LBCH 90806 795-E5
600 LBCH 90804 796-A5
600 LBCH 90814 796-A5
2000 LBCH 90804 795-E5
2100 SIGH 90755 795-E5
2300 LA 90813 794-F5
2300 LA 90810 794-F5
2400 LBCH 90813 794-F5
2400 LBCH 90810 794-F5
4200 LBCH 90815 796-A5
5900 LBCH 90803 796-A5
6200 LBCH 90803 826-D1

Rt#-1 N PACIFIC COAST HWY
- HMB 90254 762-H4
- RBCH 90277 762-H4
- RBCH 90278 762-H4
6000 LBCH 90803 796-D7
6000 LBCH 90803 826-D1

Rt#-1 S PACIFIC COAST HWY
100 RBCH 90277 762-J6
1300 RBCH 90277 792-J1
1500 TOR 90277 792-J1
1700 RBCH 90277 793-C2
1700 TOR 90277 793-C2
5700 TOR 90505 793-C2

Rt#-1 W PACIFIC COAST HWY
100 LBCH 90813 795-C5
100 Wilm 90744 794-B5
100 LBCH 90806 795-C5
800 Hrbr 90710 794-B5
1100 LBCH 90810 795-C5
1400 Hrbr 90710 793-J5
2300 LBCH 90813 794-B5
2300 LBCH 90810 794-B5

Rt#-1 PALISADES BEACH RD
200 LA 90402 671-C1
300 SMCA 90402 671-C1
800 SMCA 90403 671-C1
1200 SMCA 90401 671-C1

Rt#-1 SANTA MONICA FRWY
- SMCA - 671-F3

Rt#-1 N SEPULVEDA BLVD
100 ELSG 90245 732-G1
100 MANB 90266 732-H6
600 ELSG 90245 702-G7

Rt#-1 S SEPULVEDA BLVD
100 MANB 90266 732-H7
100 ELSG 90245 732-G3
9400 Wch 90045 702-G5

Rt#-2 N ALVARADO ST
- Echo 90026 594-D7
- Echo 90026 634-D1

Rt#-2 ANGELES CREST HWY
- LACo - (506-J1 See Page 505)
- LACo - 507-A1
- LACo - 4647-H5
- LACo - (4648-D3 See Page 4647)
- LACo - 4649-C3
- LACo - (4650-A2 See Page 4649)
- LACo - 4651-J1
- LACo - (4652-F2 See Page 4651)
- LACo - (4727-F4 See Page 4647)
- LACo 91011 505-B4
- LACo 92397 (4652-F2 See Page 4651)
4100 SBdC 92371 (4562-G6 See Page 4471)
4500 LCF 91011 535-B2
5800 LACo - 505-H1
5800 PAS 91011 505-B4
5800 PAS 91011 535-B2
7200 SBdC - (4562-G6 See Page 4471)
13700 SBdC - (4652-F2 See Page 4651)
17900 SBdC 92397 (4652-F2 See Page 4651)
21600 LACo - (4560-E7 See Page 4470)
21600 Valy 93563 (4560-E7 See Page 4470)
21600 Valy 93563 (4561-A7 See Page 4471)
24900 LACo - (4561-F7 See Page 4471)

Rt#-2 GLENDALE BLVD
- Echo 90026 594-E7
- LA 90039 594-E7

Rt#-2 GLENDALE FRWY
- Eagl - 564-H6
- Echo - 594-E4
- GLDL - 534-J7
- GLDL - 564-H6
- GLDL - 564-J2
- LA - 564-H6
- LA - 594-E4
- LCF - 534-J7

Rt#-2 SANTA MONICA BLVD
5300 LA 90029 593-H6
8400 WHWD 90069 592-G7
9200 BHLS 90210 592-G7
9200 BHLS 90210 632-E2
9800 BHLS 90212 632-E2
11200 WLA 90025 632-E2
11500 WLA 90025 631-H6

Rt#-14 AEROSPACE HWY
- KeCo 93560 3835-D5
- LACo 93536 3835-D5
- LACo 93536 3925-D1

Rt#-14 ANTELOPE VALLEY FRWY
- Actn - 4374-C5
- Actn - 4375-C6
- GrnH - 481-C1
- GrnH - 4641-C4
- LA - 481-C1
- LA - 4641-C4
- LACo - 3925-D7
- LACo - 4015-D6
- LACo - 4105-F2
- LACo - 4195-F2
- LACo - 4285-J1
- LACo - 4373-J7
- LACo - 4374-C5
- LACo - 4375-C6
- LACo - 4376-B1
- LACo - 4462-G7
- LACo - 4463-B5
- LACo - 4551-F7
- LACo - 4552-D1
- LAN - 4015-D6
- LAN - 4105-F2
- Nwhl - 4551-F7
- Nwhl - 4641-C4
- PMDL - 4105-F2
- PMDL - 4195-F2
- PMDL - 4285-J1
- PMDL - 4286-A6
- PMDL - 4376-B1
- SCTA - 4462-G7
- SCTA - 4551-F7
- SCTA - 4552-D1
- SCTA - 4641-C4
- StvR - 4641-C4

Rt#-19 LAKEWOOD BLVD
11400 DWNY 90241 706-C6
11800 DWNY 90242 706-B7
12300 DWNY 90242 736-A1
13300 BLF 90706 736-A7
14300 PRM 90723 736-A1
17800 BLF 90706 766-A1
17900 LKWD 90712 766-A1

Rt#-19 N LAKEWOOD BLVD
1800 LBCH 90815 796-A3
3100 LBCH 90808 796-A1
3400 LBCH 90808 766-A6
4100 LKWD 90712 766-A4

Rt#-19 N ROSEMEAD BLVD
1000 LACo 91733 636-J4
1500 SELM 91733 636-J4

Rt#-19 ROSEMEAD BLVD
- ELMN 91731 596-H7
300 LACo 91733 636-J7
3000 SELM 91733 636-H1
3000 SELM 91770 636-H1
3100 ELMN 91770 636-H1
3200 ELMN 91731 636-H1
3200 RSMD 91770 636-H1
3500 RSMD 91770 596-H7
3800 LACo 90660 636-J7
3800 LACo 90660 676-G2
3900 PRV 90660 676-G2
4800 TEML 91780 596-H4
4800 TEML 91776 596-H4
5100 LACo 91776 596-H4
7700 PRV 90660 706-D2

Rt#-22 E 7TH ST
5600 LBCH 90804 796-D6
5600 LBCH 90815 796-D6
5700 LBCH 90803 796-D6
5700 LBCH 90822 796-D6

Rt#-22 FRWY
- LBCH - 796-F7
- SLB - 796-H6

Rt#-23 DECKER CANYON RD
1400 LACo 90265 586-F7
1400 LACo 90265 626-D2
3100 MAL 90265 626-D5

Rt#-23 MULHOLLAND HWY
33000 LACo 90265 586-G6

Rt#-23 WESTLAKE BLVD
100 LACo 90265 586-H4
400 WLKV 90265 586-H4
400 WLKV 91361 586-H4
800 LACo 91361 586-H4
800 THO 91361 586-H4

Rt#-23 S WESTLAKE BLVD
100 THO 91362 557-C4
100 THO 91361 557-C4
800 THO 91361 586-H1

Rt#-27 TOPANGA CANYON BLVD
- Chat 91311 500-A3
3000 LACo 90265 630-D4
3500 WdHl 91364 560-A5
3600 Top 90290 560-B7
4200 WdHl 91364 560-A5
5400 WdHl 91367 560-A2
6100 WdHl 91367 530-A7
6400 CanP 91303 530-A4
7500 LA 91304 530-A4
8900 Chat 91311 500-A3
8900 LA 91304 500-A6
9500 Chat 91311 499-J6

Rt#-27 N TOPANGA CANYON BLVD
100 Top 90290 590-B1
2800 Top 90290 560-B7
3300 WdHl 91364 560-B7

Rt#-27 S TOPANGA CANYON BLVD
100 Top 90290 590-B6
500 LA 90290 590-B6
1500 LA 90290 630-C1
1500 Top 90290 630-C1
2700 LACo 90265 630-C1

Rt#-30 W 16TH ST
1200 UPL 91786 571-G7
1200 UPL 91784 571-G7
1600 CLAR 91711 571-G7

Rt#-30 W 19TH ST
1000 UPL 91784 571-J5

Rt#-30 BASE LINE RD
400 LACo 91750 570-G7
600 LVRN 91750 570-E7

Rt#-30 E BASELINE RD
100 CLAR 91711 571-F7

Rt#-30 W BASELINE RD
- CLAR 91711 570-J7
- LACo 91750 570-J7
100 CLAR 91711 571-B7
600 LACo 91711 571-B7
1300 LACo 91750 571-B7

Rt#-30 N MOUNTAIN AV
1600 UPL 91784 571-J7

Rt#-39 N AZUSA AV
100 COV 91722 598-J6
100 WCOV 91791 598-J6

Rt#-39 S AZUSA AV
100 WCOV 91791 598-J5
700 COV 91722 598-J5

Rt#-39 BEACH BLVD
4600 BPK 90621 737-H7
6300 BPK 90621 767-H3
7000 BPK 90620 767-H3
8600 ANA 92801 767-H3
14900 LMRD 90638 737-H7

Rt#-39 N BEACH BLVD
100 ANA 92801 767-J5
100 LHB 90631 708-C5

Rt#-39 S BEACH BLVD
100 ANA 92804 767-J7
100 LHB 90631 708-C7
1000 LHB 90631 738-A2
1400 LMRD 90638 738-A2
13900 FUL 92833 738-A2
13900 FUL 90638 738-A2
14200 LMRD 90638 737-J3

Rt#-39 SAN GABRIEL CANYON RD
- LACo - 509-D4
- LACo - 4649-E7
- LACo - (4729-E2 See Page 4649)
9300 LACo - (539-E2 See Page 509)
9300 LACo - 569-B1
9300 LACo 91702 569-B1

Rt#-47 TERMINAL ISLAND FRWY
- LBCH - 824-H1
- Wilm - 794-H7
- Wilm - 824-H1

Rt#-47 VINCENT THOMAS BRDG
- SPed - 824-F3

Rt#-57 ORANGE FRWY
- BREA - 709-D7
- DBAR - 640-C3
- DBAR - 679-H6
- DBAR - 709-E3
- GLDR - 569-J7
- GLDR - 570-A7
- GLDR - 599-J1
- GLDR - 600-A5
- INDS - 679-H6
- LACo - 709-E3
- OrCo - 709-E3
- POM - 640-C3
- SDMS - 570-A7
- SDMS - 599-J1
- SDMS - 600-A5
- SDMS - 640-C3

Rt#-57 POMONA FRWY
- DBAR - 680-B1

Rt#-60 POMONA FRWY
- CHLS - 640-D6
- CHNO - 641-D6
- City - 635-C7
- DBAR - 640-D6
- DBAR - 679-D4
- DBAR - 680-A1
- DBAR - 680-B1
- ELA - 635-C7
- HacH - 637-G6
- HacH - 677-J1
- HacH - 678-A2
- INDS - 637-G6
- INDS - 678-A2
- INDS - 679-D4
- LA - 634-J7
- LA - 635-C7
- LACo - 635-C7
- LACo - 636-H5
- LACo - 637-A5
- LACo - 679-D4
- MONP - 635-C7
- MONP - 636-D6
- MTBL - 635-C7
- MTBL - 636-H5
- ONT - 641-D6
- POM - 640-D6
- POM - 641-B6
- RowH - 679-D4
- RSMD - 636-H5
- SBdC - 641-D6
- SELM - 637-A5

Rt#-66 FOOTHILL BLVD
200 POM 91767 600-G1
1000 LVRN 91750 570-E7
1200 LVRN 91750 600-G1

Rt#-66 E FOOTHILL BLVD
100 CLAR 91711 601-D2
100 POM 91767 600-J2
200 POM 91767 601-A2

Rt#-66 W FOOTHILL BLVD
100 CLAR 91711 601-B2
100 POM 91767 600-J2
100 LVRN 91750 600-J2
1000 UPL 91786 601-F2

Rt#-71 CHINO VALLEY FRWY
- CHLS - 641-A7
- POM - 600-C7
- POM - 640-E2
- POM - 641-A7
- SDMS - 600-B7
1100 POM - 640-E2

Rt#-72 WHITTIER BLVD
10300 LACo 90606 676-J4
10500 WHIT 90606 676-J4
10800 WHIT 90606 677-B6
11100 LACo 90606 677-B6
11400 WHIT 90601 677-B6
12000 WHIT 90602 677-B6
12500 WHIT 90602 707-D1
13400 WHIT 90605 707-D1
14500 WHIT 90603 707-G3
16100 WHIT 90603 708-A4

Rt#-72 W WHITTIER BLVD
2000 LHB 90631 708-B4
2100 OrCo 90631 708-B4

Rt#-90 E IMPERIAL HWY
100 FUL 92835 708-G7
100 LHB 90631 738-E1
400 LHB 90631 708-G7

Rt#-90 W IMPERIAL HWY
100 LHB 90631 738-C1
100 BREA 92821 709-A7
500 BREA 92821 708-H7
500 FUL 92835 708-H7
1300 LHB 90631 738-D1

Rt#-90 MARINA EXWY
12800 LA 90066 672-C6
12800 LA 90094 672-C6
12800 LA 90292 672-C6

Rt#-90 MARINA FRWY
- CULC - 672-D7
- LA - 672-D7

Rt#-91 ARTESIA FRWY
- ART - 736-A6
- BLF - 735-G7
- BLF - 736-A6
- BPK - 767-F2
- CRTS - 736-A6
- CRTS - 737-A7
- CRTS - 767-F2
- LPMA - 767-F2
- NLB - 735-G7

Rt#-91 GARDENA FRWY
- COMP - 734-E7
- COMP - 735-B7
- CRSN - 734-E7
- LA - 734-E7
- NLB - 735-B7
- RDom - 735-B7

Rt#-103 TERMINAL ISLAND FRWY
- LBCH - 794-H7
- LBCH - 795-A3
- Wilm - 794-H7

Rt#-110 N GAFFEY ST
100 SPed 90731 824-B4

Rt#-107 HAWTHORNE BLVD
1700 RBCH 90278 763-D6
2000 RBCH 90278 733-C7
16100 LNDL 90260 733-C7
17200 TOR 90504 733-C7
17200 TOR 90504 763-D6
17200 TOR 90278 733-C7
17200 TOR 90278 763-D6
19000 TOR 90503 763-D6
21900 TOR 90505 763-D6
22600 TOR 90505 793-D2

Rt#-110 HARBOR FRWY & TRNS WY
- LA - 634-C7

Rt#-110 PASADENA FRWY
- HiPk - 595-B5
- LA - 594-H7
- LA - 595-B5
- LA - 634-F2
- PAS - 565-H7
- PAS - 595-B5
- SPAS - 595-B5

Rt#-110 S ARROYO PKWY
- PAS 91105 565-J7

Rt#-110 S GAFFEY ST
100 SPed 90731 824-B5

Rt#-118 RONALD REAGAN FRWY
- Chat - 499-E2
- Chat - 500-D2
- GrnH - 501-A1
- LA - 482-D7
- LA - 502-B2
- LACo - 482-D7
- MsnH - 501-A1
- MsnH - 502-B2
- Nor - 500-D2
- Nor - 501-A1
- Pcma - 482-D7
- Pcma - 502-B2
- SIMI - 499-E2

Rt#-126 HENRY MAYO DR
- SCTA 91355 4459-H7
- SCTA 91355 4460-A6
27100 Valc 91355 4459-H7
27100 Valc 91355 4549-F2
28500 Cstc 91384 4549-A4

Rt#-134 VENTURA FRWY
- BURB - 563-B4
- BURB - 563-G4
- Eagl - 564-F3
- Eagl - 565-A5
- GLDL - 564-F3
- LA - 562-J4
- LA - 563-B4
- LA - 563-G4
- LA - 564-F3
- LFlz - 563-G4
- LFlz - 564-F3
- PAS - 565-A5

Rt#-138 47TH ST E
4600 PMDL 93552 4197-A7
4600 PMDL 93552 4287-A3

Rt#-138 ANTELOPE HWY
100 Llan 93544 4471-F1
100 SBdC 92372 4471-F1
200 SBdC 92372 (4472-A3 See Page 4471)

Rt#-138 AVENUE D
1300 LACo 93536 3925-B2
3500 LACo 93536 3924-B2
8200 LACo 93536 3923-B2

Rt#-138 FORT TEJON RD
4900 PMDL 93552 4287-B5

Rt#-138 HIGHWAY
200 SBdC 92372 (4472-A3 See Page 4471)
2500 SBdC 92371 (4472-F7 See Page 4471)
2600 SBdC 92371 (4562-G1 See Page 4471)

Rt#-138 PALMDALE BLVD
200 PMDL 93551 4195-J7
200 PMDL 93551 4285-J1
400 PMDL 93550 4285-J1
400 PMDL 93550 4286-A1
2700 PMDL 93550 4196-H7
3700 PMDL 93552 4196-H7
4200 PMDL 93552 4197-A7

Rt#-138 PEARBLOSSOM HWY
5600 PMDL 93552 4287-C6
5700 LACo 93552 4287-C6
5800 PMDL 93552 4377-F1
5800 LACo 93552 4377-F1
6100 Litl 93543 4377-F1
9100 Litl 93543 4378-B1
11600 Pear 93553 4378-G3
13300 Pear 93553 4379-A3
14100 Llan 93544 4379-G3

Rt#-142 CARBON CANYON RD
1000 BREA 92823 710-B7
1000 CHLS 91709 710-G2
1900 CHLS 91709 680-H7
3400 OrCo 92823 709-H7
3400 BREA 92823 709-H7

Rt#-142 S VALENCIA AV
2500 OrCo 92823 709-G7
2500 BREA 92821 709-G7
2500 OrCo 92821 709-G7
3000 BREA 92823 709-G7

Rt#-170 N HIGHLAND AV
1100 LA 90038 593-E5
1300 Hlwd 90028 593-E5
1800 LA 90068 593-E5

Rt#-170 HOLLYWOOD FRWY
- LA - 532-F6
- LA - 562-G1
- NHol - 532-E1
- NHol - 532-F6
- NHol - 562-G1
- Pcma - 502-E7
- SunV - 502-E7
- SunV - 532-E1

Rt#-187 VENICE BLVD
1000 Ven 90291 672-D3
6000 LA 90034 633-A6
6000 LA 90034 632-H7
8800 LA 90232 632-H7
9100 LA 90232 672-D3
9200 LA 90034 672-D3
10700 CULC 90232 672-D3
11200 CULC 90230 672-D3
11200 LA 90066 672-D3
11300 CULC 90066 672-D3

Rt#-210 STATE ROUTE 210 FRWY
- CLAR - 570-A7
- CLAR - 571-C7
- GLDR - 569-J7
- GLDR - 570-A7
- GLDR - 600-A1
- LACo - 570-A7
- LVRN - 570-A7
- SDMS - 570-A7
- UPL - 571-C7

Rt#-213 WESTERN AV
18800 LA 90248 763-J4
18800 TOR 90504 763-J4
19000 LA 90501 763-J4
19000 TOR 90501 763-J4

Rt#-213 N WESTERN AV
100 LA 90732 823-J4
200 LA 90275 823-J4
200 RPV 90275 823-J4
200 RPV 90732 823-J4

Rt#-213 S WESTERN AV
100 LA 90732 823-J2
2500 SPed 90731 823-H6
2500 SPed 90731 853-H1
2500 LA 90732 853-H1
21300 LA 90501 763-J7
21300 TOR 90501 763-J7
22500 LA 90501 793-J3
22500 TOR 90501 793-J3
23000 Hrbr 90710 793-J3
23800 LA 90717 793-J3
26100 Hrbr 90710 793-J3
26100 LMTA 90717 793-J3
26700 LMTA 90732 793-J7
26900 RPV 90275 793-J7
26900 RPV 90732 793-J7
26900 LA 90275 793-J7
26900 LA 90732 793-J7
26900 RPV 90275 823-J2
26900 RPV 90732 823-J2
28000 LA 90275 823-J2

Rt#-710 LONG BEACH FRWY
- PAS - 565-G5

U.S.-66 Hist W FOOTHILL BLVD
1000 UPL 91786 601-F2

U.S.-101 HOLLYWOOD FRWY
- Echo - 594-A7
- Echo - 634-D1
- Hlwd - 593-E2
- LA - 562-J4
- LA - 563-A5
- LA - 593-E2
- LA - 594-A7
- LA - 634-D1

U.S.-101 SANTA ANA FRWY
- Boyl - 634-G3
- LA - 634-G3

U.S.-101 VENTURA FRWY
- Ago - 558-D6
- AGRH - 557-G6
- AGRH - 558-D6
- CALB - 558-D6
- CALB - 559-B5
- Enc - 561-C2
- HIDH - 559-B5
- LA - 559-B5
- LA - 562-A4
- LACo - 558-D6
- LACo - 559-B5
- Shrm - 561-C2
- Shrm - 562-A4
- Tarz - 560-H1
- Tarz - 561-C2
- THO - 557-B4
- WdHl - 559-B5
- WdHl - 560-B2
- WLKV - 557-B4
- WLKV - 557-G6

AIRPORTS

FEATURE NAME	Address City, ZIP Code	PAGE-GRID
AGUA DULCE, LACo		4373 - G5
BARTON, Pcma		502 - E4
BRACKETT FIELD, LVRN		600 - F4
CABLE, UPL		601 - G1
COMPTON/WOODLEY, COMP		734 - G5
EL MONTE, ELMN		597 - D5
FOX, GENERAL WILLIAM J- AIRFIELD, LAN		3924 - G7
FULLERTON MUNICIPAL, FUL		738 - A7
HAWTHORNE MUNICIPAL, HAW		733 - E1
HELIPORT, Sunl		503 - E3
HELIPORT, WdHl		560 - E7
HELIPORT AT VAN NUYS, VanN		531 - D2
HOPE, BOB, BURB		533 - B5
LA/PALMDALE REGL, PMDL		4196 - G4
LONG BEACH MUNICIPAL, LBCH		765 - H7
LOS ANGELES INTL, Wch		702 - C6
QUEENSWAY BAY HELIPORT, LBCH		825 - E3
SANTA MONICA MUNICIPAL, SMCA		671 - J2
VAN NUYS, VanN		531 - D2
WHITEMAN AIRPARK, Pcma		502 - E3
ZAMPERINI FIELD, TOR		793 - F4

BEACHES, HARBORS & WATER REC

FEATURE NAME	Address City, ZIP Code	PAGE-GRID
ALAMITOS BEACH, LBCH		825 - F1
AMARILLO BEACH, MAL		628 - H7
BAY SHORE BEACH, LBCH		826 - B2
BELMONT PLAZA BEACH, LBCH		826 - A2
BELMONT SHORE BEACH, LBCH		826 - A2
BIG ROCK BEACH, MAL		629 - J6
BLOCKER, DAN CO BCH, MAL		668 - C1
CABRILLO BEACH, SPed		854 - C2
CARBON BEACH, MAL		629 - C6
CARRILLO, LEO ST BCH, VeCo		625 - G5
COUNTY LINE BEACH, VeCo		625 - E5
CRESCENT BEACH, AVA		5923 - H3
DESCANSO BEACH, AVA		5923 - H2
DOCKWEILER ST BCH, PdlR		702 - B5
EL MATADOR ST BCH, MAL		626 - F7
EL PESCADOR ST BCH, MAL		626 - D7
EL SEGUNDO BEACH, ELSG		732 - C2
EL SOL BEACH, MAL		626 - C6
ESCONDIDO BEACH, MAL		667 - H2
HAMILTON BEACH, AVA		5923 - G2
HERMOSA BEACH, HMB		762 - F1
JUNIPERO BEACH, LBCH		825 - H2
KING HARBOR, RBCH		762 - G4
LA COSTA BEACH, MAL		629 - E6
LA PIEDRA ST BCH, MAL		626 - E7
LAS FLORES BEACH, MAL		629 - G7
LAS TUNAS CO BCH, MAL		630 - B6
LECHUZA BEACH, MAL		626 - G7
MALIBU BEACH, MAL		629 - A7
MALIBU LAGOON CO BCH, MAL		629 - A7
MANHATTAN CO BCH, MANB		732 - D5
MARINA DEL REY, MdlR		672 - A7
MEYER, ROBERT H MEM ST BCH, - MAL		626 - E6
MOTHERS BEACH, MdlR		671 - J7
NICHOLAS CANYON BEACH, LACo		625 - J6
NICHOLAS CANYON CO BCH, MAL		625 - J6
PENINSULA BEACH, LBCH		826 - C3
POINT DUME CO BCH, MAL		667 - D3
POINT DUME ST BCH, MAL		667 - G3
PUERCO BEACH, MAL		628 - E7
REDONDO CO BCH, RBCH		792 - H1
ROYAL PALMS CO BCH, LA		853 - G1
SANTA MONICA ST BCH, SMCA		671 - E4
SUNSET CO BCH, SunB		826 - H7
SURFRIDER CO BCH, MAL		629 - B6
TOPANGA CO BCH, LACo		630 - D6
TORRANCE CO BCH, RBCH		792 - H2
VENICE CITY BEACH, LA		701 - H1
WHITE POINT CO BCH, SPed		853 - H1
WILL ROGERS ST BCH, PacP		630 - H6
ZUMA CO BCH, MAL		667 - C2

BUILDINGS

FEATURE NAME	Address City, ZIP Code	PAGE-GRID
FOR DOWNTOWN BUILDINGS SEE PG C		-
10 UNIVERSAL CITY PLAZA	10 UNIVERSAL CITY PZ, Univ, 91608	563 - B6
611 PLACE	611 W 6TH ST, LA, 90071	634 - E4
777 TOWER	777 S FIGUEROA ST, LA, 90017	634 - E4
ABC ENTERTAINMENT CTR	2040 AV OF THE STARS, CenC, 90067	632 - E3
AON CTR	707 WILSHIRE BLVD, LA, 90017	634 - E4
ARCO PLAZA	505 S FLOWER ST, LA, 90071	634 - E4
BANK OF AMERICA DATA CTR	1000 W TEMPLE ST, LA, 90012	634 - F2
BANK OF AMERICA TOWER	555 FLOWER ST, LA, 90071	634 - E4
BOEING CORP	LAKEWOOD BLVD, LBCH, 90808	766 - A7
BOEING NORTH AMERICAN INC	2600 WESTMINSTER AV, SLB, 90740	826 - H2
CALIFORNIA MARKET CTR	110 E 9TH ST, LA, 90015	634 - E5
CENTRE AT SYCAMORE PLAZA, THE	5000 CLARK AV, LKWD, 90712	766 - B3
CERRITOS CORPORATE YARD	166TH ST & MARQUARDT AV, CRTS, 90703	737 - D6
CITY NATL BANK	606 S OLIVE ST, LA, 90014	634 - E4
COAST SAVINGS BLDG	315 W 9TH ST, LA, 90014	634 - E5
COOPER-T SMITH STEVEDORING-COMPANY	1480 PIER F AV, LBCH, 90802	825 - B4
CROSS ROADS OF THE WORLD	6671 W SUNSET BLVD, Hlwd, 90028	593 - E4
DEL AMO FINANCIAL CTR	21515 HAWTHORNE BLVD, TOR, 90503	763 - C6
ENVIRONMENTAL MANAGEMENT CTR	780 FLOWER ST, GLDL, 91201	564 - B3
ERNST & YOUNG PLAZA	725 S FIGUEROA ST, LA, 90017	634 - D4
FAIRPLEX	1101 W MCKINLEY AV, POM, 91768	600 - G5
FASHION INSTITUTE OF DESIGN &-MERCH	919 S GRAND AV, LA, 90015	634 - E5
FIGUEROA AT WILSHIRE	601 S FIGUEROA ST, LA, 90017	634 - E4
FREMONT FOREST PRODUCTS	800 PIER T AV, LBCH, 90802	825 - A3
GAS COMPANY TOWER, THE	555 W 5TH ST, LA, 90013	634 - E4
GRAND FINANCIAL PLAZA	W 8TH ST & GRAND AV, LA, 90017	634 - E5
HARBOR STEAM PLANT	A ST & FRIES AV, Wilm, 90744	824 - E1
INTERNATIONAL TOWER	888 S FIGUEROA ST, LA, 90017	634 - E4
KPMG TOWER	355 S GRAND AV, LA, 90071	634 - F4
LEROY HAYNES CTR	233 BASE LINE RD, LACo, 91750	570 - J7
LIBRARY TOWER	633 W 5TH ST, LA, 90071	634 - E4
LOCKHEED ADVANCED DEVELOPMENT-COMPANY	1011 LOCKHEED WY, PMDL, 93550	4196 - A3
LOS ANGELES FLOWER MART	W 8TH ST & WALL ST, LA, 90014	634 - F5
LOS ANGELES MART, THE	S BROADWAY & W WASHINGTON BLVD, LA, 90007	634 - D7
NORTHROP GRUMMAN	1 SPACE PARK DR, RBCH, 90278	733 - A5
ONE CALIFORNIA PLAZA	300 S GRAND AV, LA, 90013	634 - F4
ONE WILSHIRE BLDG	624 S GRAND AV, LA, 90014	634 - E4
PACIFIC DESIGN CTR	8687 MELROSE AV, WHWD, 90069	592 - J7
PACIFIC EXCHANGE	233 S BEAUDRY ST, LA, 90012	634 - E3
PERSHING SQUARE	448 S HILL ST, LA, 90013	634 - F4
PIPER TECHNICAL CTR	555 E RAMIREZ ST, LA, 90012	634 - H3
PREMIERE TOWERS	621 S SPRING ST, LA, 90014	634 - F5
SBC PACIFIC BELL	1010 WILSHIRE BLVD, LA, 90017	634 - D4
SCIENCE EDUCATION RESOURCE CTR	700 STATE DR, LA, 90037	674 - B2
TIMES MIRROR SQUARE	145 S SPRING ST, LA, 90012	634 - F4
TOYOTA MOTOR SALES	PIER A WY & CARRACK AV, LBCH, 90813	794 - J7
TRANSAMERICA CTR	1150 S OLIVE ST, LA, 90015	634 - E5
TWO CALIFORNIA PLAZA	350 S GRAND AV, LA, 90013	634 - F4
UNION BANK PLAZA	445 S FIGUEROA ST, LA, 90071	634 - E4
UNION OIL CTR	461 S BOYLSTON ST, LA, 90017	634 - E3
US SEA LAUNCH	2700 NIMITZ RD, LBCH, 90802	825 - A4
WELLS FARGO BANK BLDG	707 WILSHIRE BLVD, LA, 90017	634 - E4
WELLS FARGO CTR	333 S GRAND AV, LA, 90071	634 - F4
WESTERN PACIFIC	1031 S BROADWAY, LA, 90015	634 - E5
WEYERHAEUSER COMPANY	280 PIER T AV, LBCH, 90802	825 - A2
WILSHIRE BIXEL BLDG	1055 WILSHIRE BLVD, LA, 90017	634 - D4
WORLD TRADE CTR	ONE WORLD TRADE CENTER, LBCH, 90831	825 - C1

BUILDINGS - GOVERNMENTAL

FEATURE NAME	Address City, ZIP Code	PAGE-GRID
AGOURA HILLS CITY HALL	30001 LADYFACE CT, AGRH, 91301	557 - H6
AIRPORT DIST LA COURTHOUSE	11701 S LA CIENEGA BLVD, Wch, 90045	703 - A7
ALHAMBRA CITY HALL	111 S 1ST ST, ALH, 91801	596 - B5
ANTELOPE VALLEY STATE PRISON	44750 60TH ST W, LAN, 93536	4014 - F6
ANTONOVICH, MICHAEL D-COURTHOUSE	42011 4TH ST W, LAN, 93534	4105 - H5
ARCADIA CITY HALL	240 W HUNTINGTON DR, ARCD, 91007	567 - C5
ARTESIA CITY HALL	18747 CLARKDALE AV, ART, 90701	766 - H2
AVALON CITY HALL	410 AVALON CANYON DR, AVA, 90704	5923 - H4
AZUSA CITY HALL	213 E FOOTHILL BLVD, AZU, 91702	568 - J6
BALDWIN PARK CITY HALL	14403 E PACIFIC AV, BALD, 91706	598 - C5
BELL CITY HALL	6330 PINE AV, BELL, 90201	675 - D7
BELLFLOWER CITY HALL	16600 CIVIC CENTER DR, BLF, 90706	736 - C6
BELL GARDENS CITY HALL	7100 GARFIELD AV, BGDN, 90201	705 - J1
BEVERLY HILLS CITY HALL	455 N REXFORD DR, BHLS, 90210	632 - G1
BEVERLY HILLS COURTHOUSE	9355 BURTON WY, BHLS, 90210	632 - G1
BRADBURY CITY HALL	600 WINSTON AV, BRAD, 91010	568 - B4
BRAND, SYBIL INSTITUTE	4500 CITY TERRACE DR, MONP, 90063	635 - F3
BREA CITY HALL	1 CIVIC CENTER CIR, BREA, 92821	709 - C7
BUENA PARK CITY HALL	6650 BEACH BLVD, BPK, 90621	767 - H1
BUENA PARK CIVIC CTR	6650 BEACH BLVD, BPK, 90621	767 - H1
BURBANK CITY HALL	275 E OLIVE AV, BURB, 91502	533 - H7
BURBANK COURTHOUSE	300 E OLIVE AV, BURB, 91502	533 - H7
CALABASAS CITY HALL	26135 MUREAU RD, CALB, 91302	558 - H5
CALIFORNIA YOUTH AUTHORITY	13200 BLOOMFIELD AV, NRWK, 90650	737 - A2
CALTRANS	100 S MAIN ST, LA, 90012	634 - G4
CAMP KARL HOLTON-(SEE PAGE 4643)	12653 LITTLE TUJUNGA CANYON RD, LACo, 91342	4723 - B5
CARSON CITY HALL	701 E CARSON ST, CRSN, 90745	764 - E6
CASTAIC LAKE WATER AGENCY	27234 BOUQUET CANYON RD, SCTA, 91350	4551 - B1
CENTRAL CIVIL WEST COURTHOUSE	600 S COMMONWEALTH AV, LA, 90005	634 - B2
CERRITOS CITY HALL	18125 BLOOMFIELD AV, CRTS, 90703	767 - A1
CHINO HILLS CITY HALL	2001 GRAND AV, CHLS, 91709	680 - H3
CITY OF COMMERCE CITY HALL	2535 COMMERCE WY, CMRC, 90040	675 - H4
CITY OF INDUSTRY CITY HALL	15651 STAFFORD ST, INDS, 91744	638 - D7
CLAREMONT CITY HALL	207 N HARVARD AV, CLAR, 91711	601 - D3
COMPTON CITY HALL	205 S WILLOWBROOK AV, COMP, 90220	734 - J4
COMPTON MUNICIPAL COURTHOUSE	200 W COMPTON BLVD, COMP, 90220	734 - J4
CORMAN, JAMES C FEDERAL BLDG	6230 VAN NUYS BLVD, VanN, 91401	532 - A7
COUNTY COURT	415 W OCEAN BLVD, LBCH, 90802	825 - D1
COUNTY HEALTH DEPARTMENT	RAMONA BLVD & TYLER AV, ELMN, 91731	597 - C7
COUNTY JUVENILE CAMP	1900 N SYCAMORE CANYON RD, SDMS, 91773	570 - D5
COUNTY MUNICIPAL COURT	14400 ERWIN ST, VanN, 91401	532 - A7
COURTHOUSE	150 W COMMONWEALTH AV, ALH, 91801	596 - B5
COVINA CITY HALL	125 E COLLEGE ST, COV, 91723	599 - B5
CUDAHY CITY HALL	5220 SANTA ANA ST, CDHY, 90201	705 - F2
CULVER CITY CITY HALL	9770 CULVER BLVD, CULC, 90232	672 - G1
CYPRESS CITY HALL	5275 ORANGE AV, CYP, 90630	767 - D7
DIAMOND BAR CITY HALL	21825 COPLEY DR, DBAR, 91765	679 - J3
DOWNEY CITY HALL	11111 BROOKSHIRE AV, DWNY, 90241	706 - B5
DUARTE CITY HALL	1600 HUNTINGTON DR, DUAR, 91010	568 - B5
EDELMAN, EDMUND D CHILDRENS-COURT	201 CENTRE PLAZA DR, MONP, 91754	635 - F3
EL MONTE CITY HALL	11333 VALLEY BLVD, ELMN, 91731	637 - D1
EL SEGUNDO CITY HALL	350 MAIN ST, ELSG, 90245	732 - E1
EMPLOYMENT DEVELOPMENT-DEPARTMENT	1525 S BROADWAY, LA, 90015	634 - D6
FEDERAL BLDG	15000 AVIATION BLVD, HAW, 90261	733 - A5
FEDERAL BLDG	300 N LOS ANGELES ST, LA, 90012	634 - G3
FEDERAL COURTHOUSE	312 N SPRING ST, LA, 90012	634 - G3
FEDERAL OFFICE BLDG	11000 WILSHIRE BLVD, Wwd, 90024	632 - A4
FULLERTON CITY HALL	303 W COMMONWEALTH AV, FUL, 92832	738 - G7
GARDENA CITY HALL	1700 W 162ND ST, GAR, 90247	733 - J6
GLENDALE CITY HALL	613 E BROADWAY, GLDL, 91206	564 - F5
GLENDALE MUNICIPAL COURT	600 E BROADWAY, GLDL, 91205	564 - F5
GLENDORA CITY HALL	116 E FOOTHILL BLVD, GLDR, 91741	569 - E5
HALL OF ADMIN	500 W TEMPLE ST, LA, 90012	634 - F3
HARBOR PATROL	13851 FIJI WY, MdlR, 90292	702 - B1
HARBOR PATROL REDONDO BEACH	280 MARINA WY, RBCH, 90277	762 - G4
HAWAIIAN GARDENS CITY HALL	21815 PIONEER BLVD, HGDN, 90716	766 - H6
HAWTHORNE CITY HALL	4455 126TH ST, HAW, 90250	733 - C1
HERMOSA BEACH CITY HALL	1315 VALLEY DR, HMB, 90254	762 - H2
HIDDEN HILLS CITY HALL	6165 SPRING VALLEY RD, HIDH, 91302	559 - C2
HUNTINGTON PARK CITY HALL	6550 MILES AV, HNTP, 90255	675 - A7
INGLEWOOD CITY HALL	1 W MANCHESTER BLVD, ING, 90301	703 - C2
INGLEWOOD JUVENILE COURT	110 E REGENT ST, ING, 90301	703 - C2
IRWINDALE CITY HALL	5050 N IRWINDALE AV, IRW, 91706	598 - F3
LA CANADA-FLINTRIDGE CITY HALL	1327 FOOTHILL BLVD, LCF, 91011	535 - A3
LA HABRA CITY HALL	201 E LA HABRA BLVD, LHB, 90631	708 - E5
LA HABRA HEIGHTS CITY HALL	1245 HACIENDA RD, LHH, 90631	708 - C4
LAKEWOOD CITY HALL	5050 CLARK AV, LKWD, 90712	766 - B3
LA MIRADA CITY HALL	13700 LA MIRADA BLVD, LMRD, 90638	737 - G2
LANCASTER CITY HALL	44933 FERN AV, LAN, 93534	4015 - G5
LA PALMA CITY HALL	7822 WALKER ST, LPMA, 90623	767 - D3
LA PUENTE CITY HALL	15900 MAIN ST, LPUE, 91744	638 - D7
LA VERNE CITY HALL	3660 D ST, LVRN, 91750	600 - G1
LAWNDALE CITY HALL	14717 BURIN AV, LNDL, 90260	733 - C4
LOMITA CITY HALL	24300 NARBONNE AV, LMTA, 90717	793 - H3
LONG BEACH ANIMAL CONTROL-SHELTER	7700 E SPRING ST, LBCH, 90815	796 - G2
LONG BEACH CITY HALL	333 W OCEAN BLVD, LBCH, 90802	825 - D1
LONG BEACH MUNICIPAL COURTHOUSE	415 W OCEAN BLVD, LBCH, 90802	825 - D1
LOS ALAMITOS CITY HALL	3191 KATELLA AV, LALM, 90720	796 - H3
LA CITY BOARD OF EDUCATION	450 N GRAND AV, LA, 90012	634 - G3
LA CITY DEPT OF WATER & POWER	111 N HOPE ST, LA, 90012	634 - F3
LA CITY HALL	200 N SPRING ST, LA, 90012	634 - G3
LA CO CHALLENGER MEM CTR	5300 W AVE I, LAN, 93536	4014 - G5
LA CO HALL OF RECORDS	12400 E IMPERIAL HWY, NRWK, 90650	736 - J1
LA CO METRO TRANS AUTHORITY	1 GATEWAY PZ, LA, 90012	634 - H3
LA CO MUNICIPAL COURT	11234 VALLEY BLVD, ELMN, 91731	637 - D1
LA CO SUPERIOR COURT	300 E WALNUT ST, PAS, 91101	565 - J4
LA CO COURTHOUSE	111 N HILL ST, LA, 90012	634 - F3
LA CO CRIMINAL COURTS	210 W TEMPLE ST, LA, 90012	634 - G3
LA CO HEALTH DEPT	313 N FIGUEROA ST, LA, 90012	634 - F3
LA CO MAIN JAIL	441 BAUCHET ST, LA, 90012	634 - H2
LA POLICE ACADEMY	1880 ACADEMY DR, Echo, 90026	594 - G7
LA PROBATION CAMP SCOTT	28700 BOUQUET CANYON RD, Saug, 91350	4461 - E4
LA PROBATION CAMP SCUDDER	28750 BOUQUET CANYON RD, LACo, 91390	4461 - E4
LOS CERRITOS MUNICIPAL COURT	10025 FLOWER ST, BLF, 90706	736 - C6
LYNWOOD CITY HALL	11330 BULLIS RD, LYN, 90262	705 - C7
MALIBU CITY HALL	23815 STUART RANCH RD, MAL, 90265	628 - J6
MALIBU CIVIC CTR	23555 CIVIC CENTER WY, MAL, 90265	629 - A7
MALIBU COURTHOUSE	23525 CIVIC CENTER WY, MAL, 90265	629 - A7
MANHATTAN BEACH CITY HALL	1400 N HIGHLAND AV, MANB, 90266	732 - F6
MARINE DEPARTMENT HEADQUARTERS	MARINA DR, LBCH, 90803	826 - D3
MAYWOOD CITY HALL	4319 E SLAUSON AV, MYWD, 90270	675 - D5
MIRA LOMA DETENTION FACILITY	45100 60TH ST W, LAN, 93536	4014 - F6
MONROVIA CITY HALL	415 S IVY AV, MNRO, 91016	567 - G4
MONTCLAIR CITY HALL	5111 BENITO ST, MTCL, 91763	601 - G6
MONTEBELLO CITY HALL	1600 W BEVERLY BLVD, MTBL, 90640	676 - C1
MONTEREY PARK CITY HALL	320 W NEWMARK AV, MONP, 91754	636 - B2
MUNICIPAL COURT	7500 E IMPERIAL HWY, DWNY, 90242	705 - H7
NEWHALL MUNICIPAL COURT	23747 VALENCIA BLVD, SCTA, 91355	4550 - F3
NORTH JUSTICE CTR	1275 N BERKELEY AV, FUL, 92832	738 - G5
NORTH VALLEY DIST COURTHOUSE	9425 PENFIELD AV, Chat, 91311	500 - E6
NORWALK CITY HALL	12700 NORWALK BLVD, NRWK, 90650	736 - J1
NORWALK COURTHOUSE	12720 NORWALK BLVD, NRWK, 90650	736 - J1
PALMDALE ADMIN BLDG	RANCHO VISTA BLVD & 25TH ST E, PMDL, 93550	4196 - E5
PALMDALE CITY HALL	38300 SIERRA HWY, PMDL, 93550	4286 - B1
PALOS VERDES ESTATES CITY HALL	340 PALOS VERDES DR W, PVE, 90274	792 - H4
PARAMOUNT CITY HALL	16400 COLORADO AV, PRM, 90723	735 - H5
PARKER CTR	150 N LOS ANGELES ST, LA, 90012	634 - G4
PASADENA CITY HALL	100 N GARFIELD AV, PAS, 91101	565 - J4
PATRIOTIC HALL	1816 S FIGUEROA ST, LA, 90015	634 - C6
PICO RIVERA CITY HALL	6615 PASSONS BLVD, PRV, 90660	676 - G6
PITCHESS, PETER J HONOR RANCHO	TEXAS OIL CO RD & POWER LINE RD, Cstc, 91384	4460 - A4
POMONA CITY HALL	505 S GAREY AV, POM, 91766	640 - J2
POMONA MUNICIPAL COURT	350 W MISSION BLVD, POM, 91766	640 - J2
PORT OF LA ADMIN OFFICES	425 S PALOS VERDES ST, SPed, 90731	824 - C5
PORT OF LONG BEACH ADMIN	925 HARBOR PZ, LBCH, 90802	825 - C2
RANCHO PALOS VERDES CITY HALL	30940 HAWTHORNE BLVD, RPV, 90275	822 - G4
REAGAN, RONALD BLDG	300 S SPRING ST, LA, 90013	634 - F4
REDONDO BEACH CITY HALL	415 DIAMOND ST, RBCH, 90277	762 - J4
ROLLING HILLS CITY HALL	2 PORTUGUESE BEND RD, RHLS, 90274	793 - E7
ROLLING HILLS ESTATES CITY HALL	4045 PALOS VERDES DR N, RHE, 90274	793 - D6
ROSEMEAD CITY HALL	8838 E VALLEY BLVD, RSMD, 91770	596 - H6
ROYBAL CTR AND FEDERAL BLDG	255 E TEMPLE ST, LA, 90012	634 - G3
SAN DIMAS CITY HALL	245 E BONITA AV, SDMS, 91773	600 - C2
SAN FERNANDO CITY HALL	117 MACNEIL ST, SFER, 91340	482 - B7
SAN FERNANDO COURTHOUSE	900 3RD ST, SFER, 91340	482 - B7
SAN GABRIEL CITY HALL	425 S MISSION DR, SGBL, 91776	596 - D4
SAN MARINO CITY HALL	2200 HUNTINGTON DR, SMRO, 91108	596 - D1
SAN PEDRO ANNEX COURTHOUSE	638 S BEACON ST, SPed, 90731	824 - C5
SAN PEDRO COURTHOUSE	505 S CENTRE ST, SPed, 90731	824 - C5
SANTA CLARITA CITY HALL	23920 VALENCIA BLVD, SCTA, 91355	4550 - F4
SANTA FE SPRINGS CITY HALL	11710 TELEGRAPH RD, SFSP, 90670	706 - G4
SANTA MONICA CITY HALL	1685 MAIN ST, SMCA, 90401	671 - E3
SANTA MONICA COURTHOUSE	1725 MAIN ST, SMCA, 90401	671 - E3
SEAL BEACH CITY HALL	211 8TH ST, SLB, 90740	826 - E4
SIERRA MADRE CITY HALL	232 W SIERRA MADRE BLVD, SMAD, 91024	567 - A2
SIGNAL HILL CITY HALL	2175 CHERRY AV, SIGH, 90755	795 - G4
SOUTH EL MONTE CITY HALL	1415 SANTA ANITA AV, SELM, 91733	637 - B4
SOUTH GATE CITY HALL	8650 CALIFORNIA AV, SGAT, 90280	705 - B3
SOUTH GATE COURTHOUSE	8640 CALIFORNIA AV, SGAT, 90280	705 - B3
SOUTH PASADENA CITY HALL	1414 MISSION ST, SPAS, 91030	595 - H2
TEMPLE CITY CITY HALL	9701 LAS TUNAS DR, TEML, 91780	597 - A3
TIDEMANSON BLDG-LA CO DEPT OF-PUB WORKS	900 S FREMONT AV, ALH, 91803	595 - H6
TORRANCE CITY HALL	3031 TORRANCE BLVD, TOR, 90503	763 - E5
TORRANCE MUNICIPAL COURTHOUSE	825 MAPLE AV, TOR, 90503	763 - E5
TRAFFIC COURT BLDG	1945 S HILL ST, LA, 90007	634 - D7
US COAST GUARD BUOY DEPT	SEASIDE AV, SPed, 90731	824 - D6
US CUSTOMS	PICO AV, LBCH, 90802	825 - B1

FEATURE NAME Address City, ZIP Code	PAGE-GRID
US CUSTOMS HOUSE 300 FERRY ST, SPed, 90731	824 - E3
US FEDERAL CORRECTIONAL-INSTITUTION 1299 S SEASIDE AV, SPed, 90731	824 - E6
US IMMIGRATION STA SEASIDE AV, SPed, 90731	824 - D6
US QUARANTINE STA SEASIDE AV, SPed, 90731	824 - E7
VERNON CITY HALL 4305 S SANTA FE AV, VER, 90058	674 - H3
VETERANS ADMIN CTR 950 S SEPULVEDA BLVD, LACo, 90073	632 - A4
WALNUT CITY HALL 21201 LA PUENTE RD, WAL, 91789	639 - H6
WEST COVINA CITY HALL 1444 W GARVEY AV, WCOV, 91790	598 - F7
WEST COVINA COURTHOUSE 1427 WEST COVINA PKWY, WCOV, 91790	598 - E7
WEST HOLLYWOOD CITY HALL 8300 SANTA MONICA BLVD, WHWD, 90069	593 - A6
WESTLAKE VILLAGE CITY HALL 31200 OAK CREST DR, WLKV, 91361	557 - F6
WEST VALLEY LOS ANGELES OFFICE 19040 VANOWEN ST, Res, 91335	530 - G6
WHITTIER CITY HALL 13230 PENN ST, WHIT, 90602	677 - D7
WHITTIER COURTHOUSE 7339 PAINTER AV, WHIT, 90602	677 - D7

CEMETERIES

FEATURE NAME Address City, ZIP Code	PAGE-GRID
ALL SOULS CEM, Bxby	765 - G5
ANGELES ABBEY MEM PK, COMP	735 - B4
ARTESIA CEM, CRTS	736 - F7
BELLEVUE MEM PK, ONT	601 - H7
BETH ISRAEL CEM, LACo	675 - E1
CALVARY CEM, LACo	635 - E7
CHAPEL OF THE PINES, LA	634 - A5
CHINESE CEM, ELA	635 - F6
DESERT LAWN MEM PK, PMDL	4286 - E4
DOWNEY CEM, DWNY	736 - A2
EDEN MEM PK, MsnH	481 - G7
EL MONTE CEM, RSMD	596 - J6
ETERNAL VALLEY MEM PK, SCTA	4641 - B3
EVERGREEN CEM, LA	635 - C5
FOREST LAWN MEM PK COVINA-HILLS, LACo	639 - G1
FOREST LAWN MEM PK CYPRESS, -CYP	767 - B5
FOREST LAWN MEM PK GLENDALE,-GLDL	564 - F7
FOREST LAWN MEM PK HOLLYWOOD-HILLS, LA	563 - F5
FOREST LAWN MEM PK LONG BEACH,-Bxby	765 - G4
GLEN HAVEN MEM PK, LACo	482 - J3
GOOD SHEPHERD CEM, LAN	4104 - D3
GRANDVIEW MEM PK, GLDL	564 - B1
GREEN HILLS MEM PK, RPV	793 - H7
HARBOR VIEW MEM CEM, SPed	824 - B7
HILLSIDE MEM PK, CULC	672 - H7
HOLLYWOOD FOREVER CEM, LA	593 - G6
HOLY CROSS CEM, POM	641 - A5
HOLY CROSS CEM, CULC	672 - J5
HOME OF PEACE MEM PK, LACo	635 - E7
INGLEWOOD PK CEM, ING	703 - E1
JOSHUA MEM PK, LAN	4016 - B6
LANCASTER CEM, LAN	4015 - J5
LA VERNE CEM, LVRN	600 - F2
LINCOLN MEM PK, CRSN	734 - F6
LITTLE LAKE CEM, SFSP	706 - H6
LIVE OAK MEM PK, MNRO	567 - H6
LOMA VISTA MEM PK, FUL	738 - H3
LONG BEACH CEM, Bxby	795 - F2
LOS ANGELES CO CEM, LA	635 - C5
LOS ANGELES NATL CEM, Brwd	631 - J2
MEMORY GARDEN MEM PK, BREA	709 - A5
MOUNTAIN VIEW CEM, Alta	535 - H6
MOUNT CARMEL CEM, CMRC	675 - J7
MOUNT OLIVE MEM PK, CMRC	676 - A6
MOUNT SINAI MEM PK, LA	563 - G4
MOUNT SINAI MEM PK, SIMI	499 - C1
OAKDALE MEM PK, GLDR	599 - C1
OAK PARK CEM, CLAR	601 - E5
OAKWOOD MEM PK, Chat	499 - H5
ODD FELLOWS CEM, LA	635 - C7
OLIVE LAWN MEM PK, LMRD	737 - G2
PACIFIC CREST CEM, RBCH	763 - C1
PALMDALE CEM, PMDL	4286 - D3
PALOMARES CEM, POM	601 - A5
PARADISE MEM PK, SFSP	706 - G5
PARK LAWN MEM PARK, CMRC	675 - J7
PIERCE BROS VALHALLA CEM, -BURB	533 - B6
POMONA CEM, POM	641 - A4
QUEEN OF HEAVEN CEM, RowH	678 - J5
RESURRECTION CEM, MTBL	636 - E4
ROOSEVELT MEM PK, LA	764 - A2
ROSEDALE CEM, LA	633 - J5
ROSE HILLS MEM PK, LACo	677 - E2
RUSSIAN MOLOKAN CHRISTIAN CEM,-CMRC	676 - A6
SAN FERNANDO MISSION CEM, -MsnH	501 - H1
SAN GABRIEL CEM, SGBL	596 - D2
SAN GABRIEL MISSION CEM, SGBL	596 - D4
SERBIAN CEM, ELA	635 - F6
SHOLOM MEM PK, LACo	482 - J4
SIERRA MADRE CEM, SMAD	567 - B2
SPADRA CEM, POM	640 - D3
SUNNYSIDE CEM, Bxby	795 - F3
VALLEY OAKS MEM PK, WLKV	557 - F5
WESTWOOD MEM PK, Wwd	632 - B3
WILMINGTON CEM, Wilm	794 - F4
WOODLAWN CEM, SMCA	671 - G2
WOODLAWN MEM PK, COMP	734 - G6
YOUNG ISRAEL CEM, NRWK	736 - D2

COLLEGES & UNIVERSITIES

FEATURE NAME Address City, ZIP Code	PAGE-GRID
ALLIANT INTERNATIONAL UNIV 1000 S FREMONT AV, ALH, 91803	595 - H6
AMERICAN COLLEGE FOR THE-APPLIED ARTS 1651 WESTWOOD BLVD, Wwd, 90024	632 - B4
AMERICAN INTERCONTINENTAL UNIV 12655 W JEFFERSON BLVD, LA, 90066	672 - E7
ANTELOPE VALLEY COLLEGE 3041 W AVE K, LAN, 93536	4105 - B1
ANTIOCH UNIV LOS ANGELES 400 CORPORATE POINTE, CULC, 90230	672 - J6
ART CTR COLLEGE OF DESIGN 1700 LIDA ST, PAS, 91103	565 - D1
ART INSTITUTE OF CALIF-LOS-ANGELES 2900 31ST ST, SMCA, 90405	672 - A2
AZUSA PACIFIC UNIV 901 E ALOSTA AV, AZU, 91702	569 - B6
BIOLA UNIV 13800 BIOLA AV, LMRD, 90639	737 - F3
BROOKS COLLEGE LONG BEACH 4825 E PACIFIC COAST HWY, LBCH, 90815	796 - B5
CALIFORNIA INSTITUTE OF-TECHNOLOGY 1200 E CALIFORNIA BLVD, PAS, 91125	566 - B6
CALIFORNIA INSTITUTE OF THE-ARTS 24700 MCBEAN PKWY, SCTA, 91355	4550 - E6
CALIFORNIA STATE POLYTECHNIC-UNIV 3801 TEMPLE AV, LACo, 91724	639 - J3
CSU DOMINGUEZ HILLS 1000 E VICTORIA ST, CRSN, 90747	764 - F2
CSU LONG BEACH 1250 N BELLFLOWER BLVD, LBCH, 90822	796 - C6
CSU LOS ANGELES 5151 STATE UNIVERSITY DR, LA, 90032	635 - F1
CSU NORTHRIDGE 18111 NORDHOFF ST, Nor, 91330	500 - J6
CERRITOS COLLEGE 11110 E ALONDRA BLVD, CRTS, 90650	736 - F5
CITRUS COLLEGE 1000 W FOOTHILL BLVD, GLDR, 91741	569 - B6
CLAREMONT COLLEGES 747 N DARTMOUTH AV, CLAR, 91711	601 - E3
CLAREMONT GRADUATE UNIV 150 E 10TH ST, CLAR, 91711	601 - D2
CLAREMONT-MCKENNA COLLEGE 500 E 9TH ST, CLAR, 91711	601 - E3
CLEVELAND CHIROPRACTIC COLLEGE 590 N VERMONT AV, LA, 90004	594 - A7
COLLEGE OF THE CANYONS 26455 ROCKWELL CANYON RD, SCTA, 91355	4550 - D5
COMPTON COMM COLLEGE 1111 E ARTESIA BLVD, COMP, 90221	735 - A7
CYPRESS COLLEGE 9200 VALLEY VIEW ST, CYP, 90630	767 - F6
DEVRY UNIV 901 CORPORATE CENTER DR, POM, 91768	640 - C1
DREW, CHARLES R UNIV OF-MEDICINE 1731 E 120TH ST, Wbrk, 90059	704 - G7
EAST LOS ANGELES COLLEGE 1301 AVD CESAR CHAVEZ, MONP, 91754	635 - H5
EL CAMINO COLLEGE 16007 CRENSHAW BLVD, LACo, 90260	733 - F6
EMBRY-RIDDLE AERONAUTICAL UNIV 5001 AIRPORT PLAZA DR, LBCH, 90815	796 - B2
FASHION INSTITUTE OF DESIGN &-MERCH 919 S GRAND AV, LA, 90015	634 - E5
FULLER THEOLOGICAL SEMINARY 135 N OAKLAND AV, PAS, 91101	565 - J4
FULLERTON COLLEGE 321 E CHAPMAN AV, FUL, 92832	738 - J6
GLENDALE COMM COLLEGE 1500 N VERDUGO RD, GLDL, 91208	564 - H2
GLENDALE UNIV COLLEGE OF LAW 220 N GLENDALE AV, GLDL, 91206	564 - F4
HARVEY MUDD COLLEGE 301 E 12TH ST, CLAR, 91711	601 - E2
HEBREW UNION COLLEGE 3077 UNIVERSITY AV, LA, 90007	634 - B7
KINGS COLLEGE & SEMINARY 14800 SHERMAN WY, VanN, 91405	531 - J5
LIFE PACIFIC COLLEGE 1100 COVINA BLVD, SDMS, 91773	599 - J3
LONG BEACH CITY COLLEGE 4901 E CARSON ST, LBCH, 90808	766 - A6
LB CITY COLLEGE PACIFIC COAST 1305 E PACIFIC COAST HWY, LBCH, 90806	795 - F4
LOS ANGELES CITY COLLEGE 855 N VERMONT AV, LA, 90029	594 - A6
LOS ANGELES HARBOR COLLEGE 1111 FIGUEROA PL, Wilm, 90744	794 - B6
LOS ANGELES MISSION COLLEGE 13356 ELDRIDGE AV, LA, 91342	482 - D3
LOS ANGELES PIERCE COLLEGE 6201 WINNETKA AV, WdHl, 91367	530 - C7
LOS ANGELES SOUTHWEST COLLEGE 1600 W IMPERIAL HWY, LACo, 90047	703 - J7
LOS ANGELES TRADE TECH COLLEGE 400 W WASHINGTON BLVD, LA, 90007	634 - D6
LOS ANGELES VALLEY COLLEGE 5800 FULTON AV, VanN, 91401	562 - D1
LOYOLA LAW 919 S ALBANY ST, LA, 90015	634 - C4
LOYOLA MARYMOUNT UNIV 7900 LOYOLA BLVD, Wch, 90045	702 - E2
MARYMOUNT COLLEGE 30800 PALOS VERDES DR, RPV, 90275	823 - F6
MASTERS COLLEGE 21726 PLACERITA CANYON RD, SCTA, 91321	4641 - A1
MOUNT SAINT MARYS COLLEGE-CHALON CAMPUS 12001 CHALON RD, Brwd, 90049	591 - F6
MOUNT SAINT MARYS COLLEGE-DOHENY CAMPUS 10 CHESTER PL, LA, 90007	634 - C7
MOUNT SAN ANTONIO COLLEGE 1100 N GRAND AV, WAL, 91789	639 - H4
OCCIDENTAL COLLEGE 1600 CAMPUS RD, Eagl, 90041	565 - A7
OTIS COLLEGE OF ART & DESIGN 9045 LINCOLN BLVD, Wch, 90045	702 - E3
PACIFIC OAKS COLLEGE 5 WESTMORELAND PL, PAS, 91103	565 - F4
PACIFIC STATES UNIV 1516 S WESTERN AV, LA, 90006	633 - H5
PASADENA CITY COLLEGE 1570 E COLORADO BLVD, PAS, 91106	566 - B5
PEPPERDINE UNIV 24255 PACIFIC COAST HWY, LACo, 90263	628 - H6
PITZER COLLEGE 1050 N MILLS AV, CLAR, 91711	601 - E2
POMONA COLLEGE 333 N COLLEGE WY, CLAR, 91711	601 - E3
REDSTONE COLLEGE 8911 AVIATION BLVD, ING, 90301	702 - J3
RIO HONDO COLLEGE 3600 WORKMAN MILL RD, LACo, 90601	637 - D7
SAINT ANDREWS ABBEY 31001 N VALYERMO RD, Valy, 93563	4469 - C3
SANTA MONICA COLLEGE 1900 PICO BLVD, SMCA, 90405	671 - H2
SCHOOL OF THEOLOGY AT CLAREMONT 1325 N COLLEGE AV, CLAR, 91711	601 - D2
SCRIPPS COLLEGE 1030 N COLUMBIA AV, CLAR, 91711	601 - E2
SO CAL INSTITUTE OF-ARCHITECTURE 960 E 3RD ST, LA, 90013	634 - H5
SO CAL UNIV OF HEALTH 16200 AMBER VALLEY DR, LACo, 90604	708 - A7
SOUTHWESTERN UNIV OF LAW 3050 WILSHIRE BLVD, LA, 90005	634 - A3
UC LOS ANGELES 405 HILGARD AV, BelA, 90077	632 - A1
UNIV OF JUDAISM 15600 MULHOLLAND DR, BelA, 90077	591 - G1
UNIV OF LA VERNE 1950 3RD ST, LVRN, 91750	600 - F3
UNIV OF LA VERNE SAN FERNANDO-VLY 4001 W ALAMEDA AV, BURB, 91505	563 - D4
UNIV OF PHOENIX 1370 VALLEY VISTA DR, DBAR, 91765	679 - H3
UNIV OF SOUTHERN CALIFORNIA 3551 UNIVERSITY AV, LA, 90089	674 - A1
UNIV OF THE WEST 1409 WALNUT GROVE AV, RSMD, 91770	636 - G4
UNIV OF WEST LOS ANGELES 1155 ARBOR VITAE ST, ING, 90301	703 - A3
USC HEALTH SCIENCES CAMPUS SAN PABLO ST & ALCAZAR ST, Boyl, 90033	635 - B2
WEBSTER UNIV (LA AFB CAMPUS) 325 CHALLENGER WY, ELSG, 90245	732 - J1
WESTERN UNIV OF HEALTH SCIENCES 309 E 2ND ST, POM, 91766	641 - A2
WEST LOS ANGELES COLLEGE 9000 OVERLAND AV, LACo, 90230	672 - J4
WHITTIER COLLEGE 13406 PHILADELPHIA ST, WHIT, 90608	677 - E6
WILLIAM CAREY INTL UNIV 1539 E HOWARD ST, PAS, 91104	566 - C1
WOODBURY UNIV 7500 GLENOAKS BLVD, LA, 91504	533 - D3

ENTERTAINMENT & SPORTS

FEATURE NAME Address City, ZIP Code	PAGE-GRID
AHMANSON THEATER 135 N GRAND AV, LA, 90012	634 - F3
ALEX THEATRE 216 N BRAND BLVD, GLDL, 91206	564 - E4
AMBASSADOR AUDITORIUM 300 W GREEN ST, PAS, 91105	565 - G5
ANTELOPE VALLEY FAIRGROUNDS 2551 AVE H, LAN, 93536	4015 - D2
AVALON HOLLYWOOD 1735 VINE ST, Hlwd, 90028	593 - F4
AZUSA SKATEPARK 320 ORANGE PL, AZU, 91702	568 - H7
BALDWIN PARK SKATE PARK 15010 BADILLO ST, BALD, 91706	598 - D5
BELL SK8 STA 4357 E GAGE AV, BELL, 90201	675 - D7
BLAIR FIELD 4700 DEUKMEJIAN DR, LBCH, 90804	796 - A6
BRENTWOOD THEATER 11302 WILSHIRE BLVD, LACo, 90073	631 - H3
BUENA PARK SKATEPARK 7725 EL DORADO DR, BPK, 90620	767 - G3
BURBANK SKATEPARK 1625 N VALLEY ST, BURB, 91505	563 - B1
CAROLINE COLEMAN STADIUM 401 S INGLEWOOD AV, ING, 90301	703 - B3
CARPENTER PERF ARTS CTR 6200 ATHERTON ST, LBCH, 90840	796 - D5
CARSON SKATEPARK 22400 MONETA AV, CRSN, 90745	764 - C7
CARUTHERS SKATEPARK FLORA VISTA ST, BLF, 90706	736 - D6
CERRITOS CTR FOR THE PERF ARTS 12700 CENTER COURT DR S, CRTS, 90703	767 - A1
CHANDLER, DOROTHY PAVILION 135 N GRAND AV, LA, 90012	634 - F3
CONVENTION CTR 1 INDUSTRY HILLS PKWY, INDS, 91744	638 - F7
DISNEY, WALT CONCERT HALL 111 S GRAND AV, LA, 90012	634 - F3
DODGER STADIUM 1000 ELYSIAN PARK AV, LA, 90012	634 - G1
DOUGLAS, KIRK THEATRE 9830 WASHINGTON BLVD, CULC, 90232	672 - G1
DOWNEY THEATER 8345 FIRESTONE BLVD, DWNY, 90241	706 - B5
DRAKE STADIUM 555 WESTWOOD PZ, LA, 90095	632 - A1
DUARTE PERF ARTS CTR 1401 S HIGHLAND AV, DUAR, 91010	568 - B5
DUARTE SKATEPARK 1401 CENTRAL AV, DUAR, 91010	568 - A5
ENCINO VELODROME 17301 OXNARD ST, Enc, 91316	531 - C7
FAIRPLEX 1101 W MCKINLEY AV, POM, 91768	600 - G5
FAIRPLEX PARK RACETRACK 1101 W MCKINLEY AV, POM, 91768	600 - G5
FALCON THEATER 4252 RIVERSIDE DR, BURB, 91505	563 - C4
FORD, JOHN ANSON THEATER 2580 CAHUENGA BLVD E, LA, 90068	593 - E2
FULLERTON SKATEPARK 801 W VALENCIA DR, FUL, 92832	738 - F7
GALEN CTR FIGUEROA ST & JEFFERSON BLVD, LA, 90007	674 - B1
GEFFEN PLAYHOUSE 10886 LE CONTE AV, Wwd, 90024	632 - B2
GIBSON AMPHITHEATRE AT UNVRSL-CITYWALK 100 UNIVERSAL CITY PZ, Univ, 91608	563 - C6
GLENDALE CIVIC AUDITORIUM 1401 N VERDUGO RD, GLDL, 91208	564 - H2
GLENDALE SKATEPARK LAS FLORES DR, GLDL, 91208	564 - H1
GRAUMANS CHINESE THEATER 6925 HOLLYWOOD BLVD, Hlwd, 90028	593 - D4
GREAT WESTERN FORUM 3900 W MANCHESTER BLVD, ING, 90305	703 - D3
GREEK THEATRE 2700 N VERMONT AV, LFlz, 90027	593 - J1
HOLLYWOOD BOWL 2301 N HIGHLAND AV, LA, 90068	593 - D2
HOLLYWOOD PALLADIUM 6215 W SUNSET BLVD, Hlwd, 90028	593 - F4
HOLLYWOOD PARK 1050 S PRAIRIE AV, ING, 90301	703 - E4
HOLLYWOOD SPORTS PK 9030 SOMERSET BLVD, BLF, 90706	736 - A4
HOME DEPOT SOCCER STADIUM 18400 AVALON BLVD, CRSN, 90747	764 - E1
HOME DEPOT TENNIS STADIUM 18400 AVALON BLVD, CRSN, 90747	764 - E2
HOUGHTON SKATEPARK 6301 MYRTLE AV, NLB, 90805	765 - E1
INDEPENDENCE SKATEPARK 12334 BELLFLOWER AV, DWNY, 90242	736 - C1
IRWINDALE SKATEPARK 5051 IRWINDALE AV, IRW, 91706	598 - F3
IRWINDALE SPEEDWAY 500 SPEEDWAY DR, IRW, 91706	597 - J2
JAPAN AMERICA THEATER &-CULTURAL CTR 244 S SAN PEDRO ST, LA, 90012	634 - G4
KNOTTS BERRY FARM 8039 BEACH BLVD, BPK, 90620	767 - H4
KNOTTS SOAK CITY USA 8039 BEACH BLVD, BPK, 90620	767 - J4
KODAK THEATER 6801 HOLLYWOOD BLVD, Hlwd, 90028	593 - D4
KRATKA SKI AREA (SEE PAGE 4647) ANGELES CREST HWY, LACo	4648 - J4
LA HABRA SKATEPARK 801 W HIGHLANDER AV, LHB, 90631	708 - D5
LA MIRADA THEATRE FOR THE PERF-ARTS 14900 LA MIRADA BLVD, LMRD, 90638	737 - G3
LANCASTER MUNICIPAL STADIUM 45116 VALLEY CENTRAL WY, LAN, 93536	4015 - D5
LANCASTER PERF ARTS CTR 750 W LANCASTER BLVD, LAN, 93534	4015 - G6
LEISURE WORLD AMPHITHEATRE 1901 GOLDEN RAIN RD, SLB, 90740	826 - H1
LONG BEACH CONV & ENT CTR 300 E OCEAN BLVD, LBCH, 90802	825 - E1
LOS ANGELES CONV CTR 1201 S FIGUEROA ST, LA, 90015	634 - D5
LOS ANGELES COUNTY RACEWAY 6850 E AVE T, Litl, 93543	4287 - F6
LOS ANGELES MEM COLISEUM 3911 S FIGUEROA ST, LA, 90037	674 - B2
LOS ANGELES SPORTS ARENA 3939 S FIGUEROA ST, LA, 90037	674 - B2
MARINE STADIUM 5255 PAOLI WY, LBCH, 90803	826 - C1
MONROVIA SKATEPARK E OLIVE AV & S MOUNTAIN AV, MNRO, 91016	567 - J4
MONTALBAN, RICARDO THEATER 1615 VINE ST, Hlwd, 90028	593 - F4
MONTEBELLO SKATEPARK 1300 WHITTER BLVD, MTBL, 90640	676 - C2
MOUNTAIN HIGH SKI AREA-(SEE PAGE 4471) ANGELES CREST HWY, Valy, 93563	4561 - E6
MOUNT BALDY SKI AREA-(SEE PAGE 4651) MT BALDY RD, SBdC	4732 - E6
MOUNT WATERMAN SKI AREA-(SEE PAGE 4647) ANGELES CREST HWY, LACo	4648 - F4
NOKIA THEATRE CHICK HEARN CT, LA, 90015	634 - D5
NORRIS THEATRE 27570 CROSSFIELD DR, RHE, 90274	793 - A7
OLYMPIC VELODROME CSU DOMINGUEZ HILLS CAMPUS, CRSN, 90747	764 - E2
PADUA HILLS THEATRE 4467 VIA PADOVA, CLAR, 91711	571 - E3
PALACE, THE 1735 VINE ST, Hlwd, 90028	593 - F4
PALMDALE PLAYHOUSE 38344 10TH ST E, PMDL, 93550	4286 - B1
PANTAGES THEATER 6233 HOLLYWOOD BLVD, Hlwd, 90028	593 - F4
PASADENA CIVIC AUDITORIUM 300 E GREEN ST, PAS, 91101	565 - J5
PASADENA PLAYHOUSE 39 S EL MOLINO AV, PAS, 91101	566 - A5
PAULEY PAVILION 555 WESTWOOD PZ, LA, 90095	632 - A2
PEDLOW SKATEPARK 17334 VICTORY BLVD, Enc, 91316	531 - B7
PICO RIVERA SPORTS ARENA 11003 ROOKS RD, PRV, 90601	637 - B7
POMONA RACEWAY 1101 W MCKINLEY AV, POM, 91768	600 - G4
POMONA SKATEPARK 499 AVD ARROW HWY, POM, 91767	601 - A4
PYRAMID, THE 1250 BELLFLOWER BLVD, LBCH, 90840	796 - D5
RAGING WATERS 111 RAGING WATERS DR, SDMS, 91773	600 - B4
REDONDO BEACH PERF ARTS CTR 1935 MANHATTAN BEACH BLVD, RBCH, 90278	733 - A5
RICKYS SKATEPARK FLORENCE PL & PERRY RD, BGDN, 90201	705 - J1
ROSE BOWL 1001 ROSE BOWL DR, PAS, 91103	565 - F2
SAN GABRIEL CIVIC AUDITORIUM 320 S MISSION DR, SGBL, 91776	596 - D4
SANTA ANITA PK 285 W HUNTINGTON DR, ARCD, 91007	567 - B6
SANTA MONICA CIVIC AUDITORIUM 1855 MAIN ST, SMCA, 90401	671 - E3
SANTA MONICA SKATEPARK 14TH ST & OLYMPIC BLVD, SMCA, 90404	671 - F1
SAUGUS SPEEDWAY 22500 SOLEDAD CANYON RD, SCTA, 91350	4550 - J3
SHRINE AUDITORIUM 649 W JEFFERSON BLVD, LA, 90007	674 - B1
SHUBERT THEATRE 2020 AV OF THE STARS, CenC, 90067	632 - E3
SIX FLAGS MAGIC MOUNTAIN 26101 MAGIC MTN PKWY, Valc, 91355	4550 - A1
SKI SUNRISE SKI AREA-(SEE PAGE 4471) BIG PINES HWY, Valy, 93563	4561 - G5
SNOWCREST SKI AREA-(SEE PAGE 4647) OFF ANGELES CREST HWY, LACo	4648 - J4
SPLASH-LA MIRADA REGL AQUATICS-CTR WEST SIDE OF LMRD REGIONAL PK, LMRD, 90638	737 - G2
STAPLES CTR 1111 S FIGUEROA ST, LA, 90015	634 - D5
STARLIGHT BOWL 1249 LOCKHEED VIEW DR, BURB, 91504	533 - H3
TAPER, MARK FORUM 135 N GRAND AV, LA, 90012	634 - F3
TERRACE THEATRE 300 E OCEAN BLVD, LBCH, 90802	825 - E1
TORRANCE SKATEPARK 2200 CRENSHAW BLVD, TOR, 90501	763 - G7
UNIVERSAL STUDIOS 100 UNIVERSAL CITY PZ, Univ, 91608	563 - C6
VETERANS MEM STADIUM 3559 CLARK AV, LBCH, 90808	766 - A6
VILLAGE SKATEPARK 7718 SOMERSET BLVD, PRM, 90723	735 - G4
WADSWORTH THEATER 11301 WILSHIRE BLVD, LACo, 90073	631 - J4
WARNER GRAND THEATRE 478 W 6TH ST, SPed, 90731	824 - B5

FEATURE NAME	Address City, ZIP Code	PAGE-GRID
WEST COVINA SKATEPARK	1615 W MERCED AV, WCOV, 91790	638 - D1
WHITTER SKATEPARK	7630 WASHINGTON AV, WHIT, 90602	677 - D7
WILSHIRE THEATER	8440 WILSHIRE BLVD, BHLS, 90211	632 - J2
WILTERN THEATRE	3790 WILSHIRE BLVD, LA, 90005	633 - H3

GOLF COURSES

FEATURE NAME	PAGE-GRID
ALHAMBRA MUNICIPAL GC, ALH	596 - C5
ALONDRA PK GC, LACo	733 - E6
ALTADENA GC, Alta	536 - B6
ANGELES NATL GC, Sunl	503 - E2
ANNANDALE GC, PAS	565 - E5
ANTELOPE VALLEY CC, PMDL	4195 - H4
ARCADIA PAR 3 GC, ARCD	597 - E3
ARROYO SECO GC, SPAS	595 - F2
AZUSA GREENS CC, AZU	568 - G4
BALBOA GC, Enc	561 - D1
BEL AIR CC, BelA	591 - J7
BIRCH HILLS GC, BREA	709 - E7
BIXBY VILLAGE GC, LBCH	796 - D7
BRAEMAR CC, Tarz	560 - H5
BREA GC, BREA	738 - J1
BRENTWOOD CC, Brwd	631 - F5
BROOKSIDE GC, PAS	535 - E7
CALABASAS GOLF & CC, CALB	559 - C6
CALIFORNIA CC, INDS	637 - F5
CANDLEWOOD CC, LACo	707 - D6
CASCADES GC, THE, LA	481 - D1
CATALINA ISLAND GC, AVA	5923 - G4
CHEVY CHASE CC, GLDL	565 - B1
CLAREMONT GC, CLAR	601 - D1
COMPTON PAR 3 GC, COMP	735 - E4
COYOTE HILLS GC, FUL	738 - J4
CRYSTALAIRE CC, Llan	4379 - F7
DE BELL MUNICIPAL GC, BURB	533 - H3
DESERT AIRE GC, PMDL	4196 - H5
DIAMOND BAR GC, DBAR	640 - B7
DOMINGUEZ HILLS GOLF & PRACTICE CTR, CRSN	764 - C4
EATON CANYON GC, LACo	566 - G2
EL CABALLERO CC, Tarz	560 - J4
EL CARISO GC, LA	482 - E3
EL DORADO PARK GC, LBCH	796 - F3
ENCINO GC, Enc	561 - E2
FORD PARK GC, BGDN	705 - H3
FRIENDLY HILLS CC, WHIT	708 - A2
FRIENDLY VALLEY GC, SCTA	4551 - F5
FULLERTON GC, FUL	738 - H2
GLENDORA CC, GLDR	569 - J6
GLENOAKS GC, GLDR	599 - E1
HACIENDA GC, LHH	678 - E7
HANSEN DAM GC, Sunl	502 - G3
HARBOR PARK MUNICIPAL GC, Wilm	794 - B5
HARDING MUNICIPAL GC, LFlz	564 - B5
HATHAWAY, MAGGIE COUNTY GC, LA	703 - H4
HEARTWELL GC, LBCH	766 - E6
HILLCREST CC, LA	632 - F4
INDUSTRY HILLS GC, INDS	638 - F7
IRON-WOOD NINE GC, CRTS	736 - E6
KNOLLWOOD COUNTY GC, GrnH	481 - D6
LA CANADA FLINTRIDGE GC, LCF	535 - D2
LAKE ELIZABETH GOLF & RANCH-CLUB, LACo	4102 - G4
LAKE LINDERO CC, AGRH	557 - G4
LAKES AT EL SEGUNDO GC, THE, ELSG	732 - H2
LAKESIDE CC, BURB	563 - C5
LAKEWOOD CC, LKWD	765 - J5
LA MIRADA GC, LMRD	737 - H2
LEISURE WORLD-SEAL BEACH GC, SLB	796 - H7
LINKS AT VICTORIA, THE, CRSN	764 - D3
LOS AMIGOS CC, DWNY	705 - G5
LOS ANGELES CC, Wwd	632 - D1
LOS ANGELES ROYAL VISTA GC, LACo	679 - E4
LOS COYOTES CC, BPK	738 - A5
LOS FELIZ MUNICIPAL GC, LA	564 - C7
LOS VERDES GC, RPV	822 - G4
MALIBU CC, LACo	586 - J6
MANHATTAN BEACH MARRIOTT GC, MANB	732 - H4
MARSHALL CANYON GC, LACo	570 - J3
MEADOWLARK GC, LAN	4104 - F1
MISSION HILLS LITTLE LEAGUE-GC, LA	501 - F5
MONTEBELLO GOLF GOURSE AND CC, MTBL	636 - A6
MONTEREY PARK GC, MONP	635 - G3
MOUNTAINGATE CC, Brwd	591 - E3
MOUNTAIN MEADOWS COUNTY GC, POM	600 - F5
NORTH RANCH CC, THO	557 - D2
NORWALK GC, NRWK	737 - A2
OAKMONT CC, GLDL	534 - G5
OLD RANCH CC, SLB	796 - J6
PALM LAKE GC, POM	640 - G4
PALOS VERDES GC, PVE	792 - J4
PALOS VERDES SHORES GC, LA	823 - G7
PENMAR GC, Ven	671 - J3
PICO RIVERA MUNICIPAL GC, PRV	677 - A1
PORTER VALLEY CC, Nor	480 - F7
RANCHO DUARTE GC, DUAR	568 - E5
RANCHO PARK GC, LA	632 - E5
RANCHO VISTA GC, PMDL	4194 - J2
RECREATION PK 9-HOLE GC, LBCH	796 - B7
RECREATION PK 18-HOLE GC, LBCH	796 - B6
RIO HONDO CC, DWNY	705 - J3
RIVIERA CC, PacP	631 - D5
ROBINSON RANCH CC, SCTA	4552 - E3
ROLLING HILLS CC, RHE	793 - F6
ROOSEVELT MUNICIPAL GC, LFlz	594 - A1
SAN DIMAS CANYON GC, SDMS	570 - E5
SAN GABRIEL CC, SGBL	596 - E2
SANTA ANITA COUNTY GC, ARCD	567 - C6
SCHOLL CANYON GC, GLDL	565 - B3
SEA-AIRE GC, TOR	793 - B1
SHERWOOD CC, VeCo	586 - E1
SIERRA LA VERNE CC, LVRN	570 - F5
SKYLINKS GC, LBCH	766 - A7
SOUTH GATE GC, SGAT	705 - E4
SOUTH HILLS CC, WCOV	639 - B2
STUDIO CITY GC, LA	562 - E5
TPC OF VALENCIA, StvR	4550 - C5
TRUMP NATL GC, RPV	823 - E6
VALENCIA CC, SCTA	4550 - D3
VAN NUYS GC, VanN	531 - E6
VERDUGO HILLS GC, Tuj	504 - C6
VIA VERDE CC, SDMS	599 - H5
VIRGINIA CC, Bxby	765 - C5
VISTA VALENCIA GC, SCTA	4550 - E7
WASHINGTON, CHESTER L GC, LACo	733 - H1
WESTCHESTER GC, Wch	702 - E3
WESTERN HILLS CC, CHLS	680 - H7
WESTLAKE VILLAGE GC, THO	557 - D5
WESTRIDGE GC, LHB	738 - B1
WHITTIER NARROWS COUNTY GC, LACo	636 - H3
WILSHIRE CC, LA	593 - E7
WILSON MUNICIPAL GC, LFlz	564 - B6
WOODLAND HILLS CC, WdHl	560 - B4
WOODLEY LAKES GC, Enc	531 - E7

HISTORIC SITES

FEATURE NAME	Address City, ZIP Code	PAGE-GRID
ALAMITOS DISCOVERY WELL	HILL ST & TEMPLE AV, SIGH, 90755	795 - H3
ANDRES PICO ADOBE	10940 SEPULVEDA BLVD, MsnH, 91345	501 - H2
ANGELS FLIGHT	351 S HILL ST, LA, 90013	634 - F4
ANTELOPE VALLEY INDIAN MUS	15701 AVE M, LACo, 93535	4109 - D3
BRADBURY BLDG	304 S BROADWAY, LA, 90013	634 - F4
CAMPO DE CAHUENGA	3919 LANKERSHIM BLVD, LA, 91604	563 - B6
CARRION ADOBE	PUDDINGSTONE DR & VAN DUSEN RD, LVRN, 91750	600 - E3
CASA ADOBE DE SAN RAPHAEL	1330 DOROTHY DR, GLDL, 91202	564 - D2
CATALINA VERDUGO ADOBE HIST-SITE	2211 BONITA DR, GLDL, 91208	534 - H7
CENTINELA ADOBE	7634 MIDFIELD AV, ING, 90302	703 - A1
EL MOLINO VIEJO	1120 OLD MILL RD, SMRO, 91108	596 - B1
EL PUEBLO DE LOS ANGELES STATE	622 N MAIN ST, LA, 90012	634 - G3
GILMORE ADOBE	6301 W 3RD ST, LA, 90036	633 - B1
HAROLD LLOYD ESTATE	1740 GREEN ACRES DR, BHLS, 90210	592 - C6
HUGO REID ADOBE	301 N BALDWIN AV, ARCD, 91007	567 - A5
INN ON MT ADA, THE	398 WRIGLEY RD, AVA, 90704	5923 - H4
JUAN MATIAS SANCHEZ ADOBE	946 ADOBE AV, MTBL, 90640	636 - G7
LEONIS ADOBE & PLUMMER HOUSE	23537 CALABASAS RD, LA, 91302	559 - F4
LITTLE TOKYO	244 S SAN PEDRO ST, LA, 90012	634 - G4
LOPEZ ADOBE	1100 PICO ST, SFER, 91340	482 - A7
LOS ANGELES STATE HIST PK	N SPRING ST & BAKER ST, LA, 90012	634 - H1
MLK JR MEM	WILLOWBROOK AV & COMPTON BLVD, COMP, 90220	734 - J4
MUCKENTHALER CULTURAL CTR	1201 W MALVERN AV, FUL, 92833	738 - E6
OLVERA STREET	622 N MAIN ST, LA, 90012	634 - G3
PATRICIO ONTIVEROS ADOBE	12100 MORA DR, SFSP, 90670	706 - H5
PIO PICO MANSION	6003 S PIONEER BLVD, WHIT, 90606	676 - J4
PIO PICO STATE HIST PK	6003 S PIONEER BLVD, WHIT, 90606	676 - H4
POINT FERMIN HIST LIGHTHOUSE	S PAS DL MAR, SPed, 90731	854 - A2
PUEBLO DE LOS ANGELES	845 N ALAMEDA ST, LA, 90012	634 - G3
QUEEN MARY	1126 QUEENS HWY, LBCH, 90802	825 - E3
RANCHO LOS ALAMITOS HIST RANCH	6400 E BIXBY HILL RD, LBCH, 90815	796 - E6
REYES ADOBE HIST SITE	5464 REYES ADOBE RD, AGRH, 91301	557 - H5
SAN FERNANDO MISSION	15151 SAN FERNANDO MISSION BL, MsnH, 91345	501 - H1
SAN GABRIEL MISSION	428 S MISSION DR, SGBL, 91776	596 - D4
SANTA SUSANA PASS STATE HIST PK	DEVONSHIRE ST, Chat, 91311	499 - G3
SCHINDLER HOUSE	835 N KINGS RD, WHWD, 90069	593 - A6
TAYLOR RANCH HOUSE	737 N MONTEBELLO BLVD, MTBL, 90640	676 - E1
TERMINAL ANNEX	900 N ALAMEDA ST, LA, 90012	634 - H3
WATTS TOWERS STATE HIST PK	1765 E 107TH ST, Wats, 90002	704 - G5
WILL ROGERS HOME	1501 WILL ROGERS STATE PARK RD, PacP, 90272	631 - C4
WILL ROGERS STATE HIST PK	1501 WILL ROGERS STATE PARK RD, PacP, 90272	631 - C3

HOSPITALS

FEATURE NAME	Address City, ZIP Code	PAGE-GRID
ALHAMBRA HOSP	100 S RAYMOND AV, ALH, 91801	595 - J5
ANAHEIM GENERAL HOSP - BUENA-PARK	5742 BEACH BLVD, BPK, 90621	737 - H6
ANTELOPE VALLEY HOSP	1600 W AVE J, LAN, 93534	4015 - E7
BARLOW RESPIRATORY HOSP	2000 STADIUM WY, Echo, 90026	594 - F7
BELLFLOWER MED CTR	9542 E ARTESIA BLVD, BLF, 90706	736 - B7
BEVERLY HOSP	309 W BEVERLY BLVD, MTBL, 90640	676 - E1
BROTMAN MED CTR	3828 DELMAS TER, CULC, 90232	672 - G1
CALIFORNIA HOSP MED CTR	1401 S GRAND AV, LA, 90015	634 - D6
CATALINA ISLAND MED CTR	100 FALLS CANYON RD, AVA, 90704	5923 - G4
CEDARS-SINAI MED CTR	8700 BEVERLY BLVD, LA, 90048	632 - J1
CENTINELA FREEMAN REGL MED CTR-MARINA	4650 LINCOLN BLVD, LA, 90292	672 - B6
CENTINELA FREEMAN REGL MED CTR-MEM	333 N PRAIRIE AV, ING, 90301	703 - D1
CENTINELA HOSP MED CTR	555 E HARDY ST, ING, 90301	703 - D4
CENTURY CITY	2070 CENTURY PARK E, CenC, 90067	632 - E3
CHILDRENS HOSP OF LOS ANGELES	4650 W SUNSET BLVD, LFlz, 90027	594 - A4
CHINO VALLEY MED CTR	5451 WALNUT AV, CHNO, 91710	641 - H6
CITRUS VLY MED CTR-INTERCOMM	210 W SAN BERNARDINO RD, COV, 91723	599 - B5
CITRUS VLY MED CTR-QUEEN OF-THE VLY	1115 S SUNSET AV, WCOV, 91790	638 - E1
CITY OF ANGELS MED CTR	1711 W TEMPLE ST, Echo, 90026	634 - D1
CITY OF HOPE NATL MED CTR	1500 E DUARTE RD, DUAR, 91010	568 - B6
COAST PLAZA DOCTORS HOSP	13100 STUDEBAKER RD, NRWK, 90650	736 - F1
COLLEGE HOSP	10802 COLLEGE PL, CRTS, 90703	736 - E5
COMM & MISSION HOSPS OF HUNTNG	2623 E SLAUSON AV, HNTP, 90255	674 - J5
COMM HOSP OF GARDENA	1246 W 155TH ST, GAR, 90247	734 - A5
COMM HOSP OF LONG BEACH	1720 TERMINO AV, LBCH, 90804	796 - A5
DOCTORS HOSP MED CTR OF-MONTCLAIR	5000 SAN BERNARDINO ST, MTCL, 91763	601 - F5
DOCTORS HOSP OF WEST COVINA	725 S ORANGE AV, WCOV, 91790	598 - E7
DOWNEY REGL MED CTR	11500 BROOKSHIRE AV, DWNY, 90241	706 - B6
EAST LOS ANGELES DOCTORS HOSP	4060 WHITTIER BLVD, LACo, 90023	635 - D7
EAST VALLEY HOSP MED CTR	150 W ROUTE 66, GLDR, 91740	569 - E6
ENCINO-TARZANA REG MED CTR-ENCINO CPS	16237 VENTURA BLVD, Enc, 91436	561 - E4
ENCINO-TARZANA REG MED CTR-TARZNA CPS	18321 CLARK ST, Tarz, 91356	560 - J2
FOOTHILL PRESBYTERIAN JOHNSTON	250 S GRAND AV, GLDR, 91741	569 - D5
GARFIELD MED CTR	525 N GARFIELD AV, MONP, 91754	636 - B1
GLENDALE ADVENTIST MED CTR	1509 WILSON TER, GLDL, 91206	564 - H4
GLENDALE MEM HOSP & HEALTH CTR	1420 S CENTRAL AV, GLDL, 91204	564 - E7
GOOD SAMARITAN HOSP	1225 WILSHIRE BLVD, LA, 90017	634 - D3
GREATER EL MONTE COMM HOSP	1701 SANTA ANITA AV, SELM, 91733	637 - B4
HOLLYWOOD COMM HOSP MED CTR	6245 DE LONGPRE AV, Hlwd, 90028	593 - F5
HOLLYWOOD COMM HOSP - VAN NUYS	14433 EMELITA ST, VanN, 91401	562 - A1
HOLLYWOOD PRES MED CTR	1300 N VERMONT AV, LFlz, 90027	594 - A5
HUNTINGTON MEM HOSP	100 W CALIFORNIA BLVD, PAS, 91105	565 - H6
KAISER PERMANENTE BALDWIN PK	1011 BALDWIN PARK BLVD, BALD, 91706	637 - J1
KAISER PERMANENTE BELLFLOWER	9400 E ROSECRANS AV, BLF, 90706	736 - B3
KAISER PERMANENTE LOS ANGELES	4867 SUNSET BLVD, LFlz, 90027	594 - A4
KAISER PERMANENTE PANORAMA CITY	13652 CANTARA ST, PanC, 91402	532 - C2
KAISER PERMANENTE SOUTH BAY	25825 S VERMONT AV, Hrbr, 90710	794 - A5
KAISER PERMANENTE WEST LOS-ANGELES	6041 CADILLAC AV, LA, 90034	632 - J6
KAISER PERMANENTE WOODLAND-HILLS	5601 DE SOTO AV, WdHl, 91367	560 - C2
KINDRED HOSP - BREA	875 N BREA BLVD, BREA, 92821	709 - B5
KINDRED HOSP - LOS ANGELES	5525 W SLAUSON AV, LadH, 90056	672 - J5
LA CO M L KING JR-HARBOR MED-CTR	12021 S WILMINGTON AV, Wbrk, 90059	704 - G7
LA CO-RANCHO LOS AMIGOS NATL-REHAB	7601 E IMPERIAL HWY, DWNY, 90242	705 - H7
LAKEWOOD REGL MED CTR	3700 SOUTH ST, LKWD, 90712	765 - J2
LANCASTER COMM HOSP	43830 10TH ST W, LAN, 93534	4105 - G1
LANTERMAN DEVELOPMENTAL CTR	3530 W POMONA BLVD, POM, 91769	640 - B5
LA PALMA INTERCOMM HOSP	7901 WALKER ST, LPMA, 90623	767 - D3
LINCOLN HOSP MED CTR	443 S SOTO ST, Boyl, 90033	635 - A5
LITTLE COMPANY OF MARY HOSP	4101 TORRANCE BLVD, TOR, 90503	763 - C5
LONG BEACH MEM MED CTR	2801 ATLANTIC AV, LBCH, 90806	795 - D2
LOS ALAMITOS MED CTR	3751 KATELLA AV, LALM, 90720	796 - J2
LA COMM HOSP	4081 E OLYMPIC BLVD, LACo, 90023	675 - D1
LA COMM HOSP OF NORWALK	13222 BLOOMFIELD AV, NRWK, 90650	737 - A2
LA CO HARBOR-UCLA MED CTR	1000 W CARSON ST, LACo, 90502	764 - A6
LA CO HIGH DESERT HOSP	44900 N 60TH ST W, LAN, 93536	4014 - F5
LA CO OLIVE VIEW-UCLA MED CTR	14445 OLIVE VIEW DR, LA, 91342	481 - H1
LA CO USC MED CTR	1200 N STATE ST, Boyl, 90033	635 - A2
LA METROPOLITAN MED CTR	2231 S WESTERN AV, LA, 90018	633 - H6
MEM HOSP OF GARDENA	1145 W REDONDO BEACH BLVD, GAR, 90247	734 - A5
METHODIST HOSP OF SOUTHERN-CALIF	300 W HUNTINGTON DR, ARCD, 91007	567 - B6
METROPOLITAN STATE HOSP	11401 BLOOMFIELD AV, NRWK, 90650	706 - J6
MISSION COMM HOSP	14850 ROSCOE BLVD, PanC, 91402	531 - J2
MISSION COMM HOSP-SAN FERNANDO-CPS	700 CHATSWORTH DR, SFER, 91340	502 - A1
MISSION HOSP	3111 E FLORENCE AV, HNTP, 90255	675 - A7
MONROVIA COMM HOSP	323 S HELIOTROPE AV, MNRO, 91016	567 - H4
MONTEREY PARK HOSP	900 S ATLANTIC BLVD, MONP, 91754	636 - A4
MOTION PICTURE & TV FUND HOSP	23388 MULHOLLAND DR, LA, 91302	559 - G4
NEWHALL, HENRY MAYO MEM HOSP	23845 MCBEAN PKWY, SCTA, 91355	4550 - F6
NORTHRIDGE HOSP MED CTR, ROSCOE	18300 ROSCOE BLVD, Res, 91335	530 - J2
OLYMPIA MED CTR	5900 W OLYMPIC BLVD, LA, 90019	633 - B3
ORTHOPAEDIC HOSP	2400 S FLOWER ST, LA, 90007	634 - C7
PACIFICA HOSP OF THE VALLEY	9449 SAN FERNANDO RD, SunV, 91352	502 - F6
PACIFIC ALLIANCE MED CTR	531 W COLLEGE ST, LA, 90012	634 - G2
PACIFIC HOSP OF LONG BEACH	2776 PACIFIC AV, LBCH, 90806	795 - D2
POMONA VALLEY HOSP MED CTR	1798 N GAREY AV, POM, 91767	600 - J6
PRESBYTERIAN INTER-COMM HOSP	12401 WASHINGTON BLVD, WHIT, 90602	707 - B1
PROVIDENCE HOLY CROSS MED CTR	15031 RINALDI ST, MsnH, 91345	481 - H7
PROVIDENCE SAINT JOSEPH MED CTR	501 S BUENA VISTA ST, BURB, 91505	563 - E4
REAGAN, RONALD UCLA MED CTR	757 WESTWOOD BLVD, LA, 90095	632 - A2
SAINT FRANCIS MED CTR	3630 E IMPERIAL HWY, LYN, 90262	705 - C6
SAINT JOHNS HOSP & HEALTH CTR	1328 22ND ST, SMCA, 90404	631 - F7
SAINT JUDE MED CTR	101 E VALENCIA MESA DR, FUL, 92835	738 - H4
SAINT MARY MED CTR	1050 LINDEN AV, LBCH, 90813	795 - E6
SAINT VINCENT MED CTR	2131 W 3RD ST, LA, 90057	634 - C2
SAN DIMAS COMM HOSP	1350 W COVINA BLVD, SDMS, 91773	599 - H3
SAN GABRIEL VALLEY MED CTR	438 W LAS TUNAS DR, SGBL, 91776	596 - D4
SAN PEDRO PENINSULA HOSP	1300 W 7TH ST, SPed, 90731	823 - J5
SANTA MONICA-UCLA MED CTR	1250 16TH ST, SMCA, 90404	671 - F1
SANTA TERESITA HOSP	819 BUENA VISTA ST, DUAR, 91010	568 - A5
SHERMAN OAKS HOSP & HEALTH CTR	4929 VAN NUYS BLVD, Shrm, 91403	562 - A3
SHRINERS HOSP FOR CHILDREN	3160 GENEVA ST, LA, 90020	634 - B2
SOUTH VALLEY MED CTR	PALMDALE BLVD & 40TH ST E, PMDL, 93552	4286 - J1
SUBURBAN MED CTR	16453 S COLORADO AV, PRM, 90723	735 - G6
TEMPLE COMM HOSP	235 N HOOVER ST, LA, 90004	594 - B7
TORRANCE MEM MED CTR	3330 W LOMITA BLVD, TOR, 90505	793 - E2
TRI-CITY REGL MED CTR	21530 PIONEER BLVD, HGDN, 90716	766 - H6
USC KENNETH NORRIS JR CANCER-HOSP	1441 EASTLAKE AV, Boyl, 90033	635 - B2
USC UNIV HOSP	1500 SAN PABLO ST, Boyl, 90033	635 - B2
VALLEY PRESBYTERIAN HOSP	15107 VANOWEN ST, VanN, 91405	531 - H5
V A SEPULVEDA AMBULATORY CARE-CTR	16111 PLUMMER ST, LA, 91343	501 - F6
VERDUGO HILLS HOSP	1812 VERDUGO BLVD, GLDL, 91208	534 - J4
VETERANS ADMIN	950 S SEPULVEDA BLVD, LACo, 90073	631 - H3
VETERANS AFFAIRS MED CTR-LONG-BEACH	5901 E 7TH ST, LBCH, 90822	796 - C6
VETERANS AFFAIRS MED CTR-WEST-LA	11301 WILSHIRE BLVD, LACo, 90073	632 - A4
WEST ANAHEIM MED CTR	3033 W ORANGE AV, ANA, 92804	767 - J6
WEST HILLS HOSP & MED CTR	7300 MEDICAL CENTER DR, CanP, 91307	529 - G4
WHITE MEM MED - ADVENTIST	1720 E CESAR E CHAVEZ AV, Boyl, 90033	635 - A4
WHITTIER HOSP MED CTR	9080 COLIMA RD, WHIT, 90605	707 - G3

HOTELS

FEATURE NAME	Address City, ZIP Code	PAGE-GRID
AITPORT PARK VIEW HOTEL	W CENTURY BLVD, ING, 90303	703 - E5
AIRTEL PLAZA HOTEL	7277 VALJEAN AV, VanN, 91406	531 - E4
AYRES HOTEL	14400 HINDRY AV, HAW, 90260	733 - A4
BELAMAR HOTEL	3501 N SEPULVEDA BLVD, MANB, 90266	732 - H4
BEST WESTERN ANTELOPE VALLEY-INN	44055 SIERRA HWY, LAN, 93534	4015 - H7
BEST WESTERN CARRIAGE INN	5525 SEPULVEDA BLVD, VanN, 91411	561 - H2
BEST WESTERN EXECUTIVE INN	18880 E GALE AV, RowH, 91748	679 - B4
BEST WESTERN GOLDEN KEY HOTEL	123 W COLORADO ST, GLDL, 91204	564 - E5
BEST WESTERN GOLDEN SAILS HOTEL	6285 E PACIFIC COAST HWY, LBCH, 90803	826 - D1
BEST WESTERN HOTEL-DIAMOND BAR	259 GENTLE SPRINGS LN, DBAR, 91765	640 - B7
BEST WESTERN JAMAICA BAY INN	4175 ADMIRALTY WY, MdlR, 90292	671 - J7
BEST WESTERN LONG BEACH	1725 LONG BEACH BLVD, LBCH, 90813	795 - D5
BEST WESTERN REDONDO BEACH INN	1850 S PACIFIC COAST HWY, RBCH, 90277	793 - A1
BEST WESTERN SANTA MONICA	1920 SANTA MONICA BLVD, SMCA, 90404	631 - F7
BEST WESTERN SOUTH BAY HOTEL	15000 HAWTHORNE BLVD, LNDL, 90260	733 - D4
BEST WESTERN SUNRISE AT RBCH	400 N HARBOR DR, RBCH, 90277	762 - H4
BEVERLY GARLAND HOLIDAY INN	4222 VINELAND AV, LA, 91602	563 - A5
BEVERLY HILLS HOTEL	9641 SUNSET BLVD, BHLS, 90210	592 - E7
BEVERLY HILTON, THE	9876 WILSHIRE BLVD, BHLS, 90212	632 - E2
BEVERLY WILSHIRE HOTEL	9500 WILSHIRE BLVD, BHLS, 90212	632 - F2
BURBANK HILTON & CONV CTR	2500 N HOLLYWOOD WY, BURB, 91504	533 - C5
CENTURY WILSHIRE HOTEL	10776 WILSHIRE BLVD, Wwd, 90024	632 - B3
CHATEAU MARMONT HOTEL	8221 W SUNSET BLVD, WHWD, 90069	593 - A5

FEATURE NAME Address City, ZIP Code	PAGE-GRID
CLARION SUITES WARNER CTR 20200 SHERMAN WY, Win, 91306	530 - D5
CONTINENTAL PLAZA HOTEL 9750 AIRPORT BLVD, Wch, 90045	702 - J4
COUNTRY INN & SUITES 23627 CALABASAS RD, CALB, 91302	559 - D5
COUNTRY INN AT CALABASAS 23627 CALABASAS RD, CALB, 91302	559 - D5
COURTYARD BY MARRIOTT 10320 W OLYMPIC BLVD, LA, 90064	632 - E4
COURTYARD BY MARRIOTT 13480 MAXELLA AV, LA, 90292	672 - B6
COURTYARD BY MARRIOTT 14635 BALDWIN PARK TOWNE CTR, BALD, 91706	598 - C7
COURTYARD BY MARRIOTT 15433 VENTURA BLVD, Shrm, 91403	561 - G4
COURTYARD BY MARRIOTT 1905 S AZUSA AV, HacH, 91745	678 - F5
COURTYARD BY MARRIOTT 2000 E MARIPOSA AV, ELSG, 90245	732 - H1
COURTYARD BY MARRIOTT 2100 EMPIRE AV, BURB, 91504	533 - E6
COURTYARD BY MARRIOTT 530 RANCHO VISTA BLVD, PMDL, 93551	4195 - H5
COURTYARD BY MARRIOTT 7621 BEACH BLVD, BPK, 90620	767 - H3
COURTYARD BY MARRIOTT AT LAX 6161 W CENTURY BLVD, Wch, 90045	702 - H4
COURTYARD BY MARRIOTT OLD-PASADENA 180 FAIR OAKS AV, PAS, 91103	565 - H4
COURTYARD BY MARRIOTT-TOR/PVE 2633 SEPULVEDA BLVD, TOR, 90503	763 - F7
COURTYARD BY MARRIOTT-TOR SOUTH 1925 W 190TH ST, TOR, 90504	763 - H2
CROWNE PLAZA BEVERLY HILLS 1150 S BEVERLY DR, LA, 90035	632 - G3
CROWNE PLAZA HOTEL 5985 W CENTURY BLVD, Wch, 90045	702 - H4
CROWNE PLAZA HOTEL 6121 TELEGRAPH RD, CMRC, 90040	675 - J4
CROWNE PLAZA LA 5985 W CENTURY BLVD, Wch, 90045	703 - A5
CROWNE PLAZA LA HARBOR HOTEL 601 S PALOS VERDES ST, SPed, 90731	824 - C5
CROWNE PLAZA REDONDO BEACH 300 N HARBOR DR, RBCH, 90277	762 - H4
CRYSTAL PARK CASINO HOTEL 123 E ARTESIA BLVD, COMP, 90220	735 - A7
DAYS INN - GLENDALE 600 N PACIFIC AV, GLDL, 91203	564 - D4
DESERT INN MOTOR HOTEL 44219 SIERRA HWY, LAN, 93534	4015 - H7
DOUBLETREE GUEST SUITES 1707 4TH ST, SMCA, 90401	671 - F3
DOUBLETREE HOTEL 2 CIVIC PLAZA DR, CRSN, 90745	764 - E6
DOUBLETREE HOTEL CLAREMONT 555 W FOOTHILL BLVD, CLAR, 91711	601 - C2
DOUBLETREE HOTEL LA/ROSEMEAD 888 MONTEBELLO BLVD, RSMD, 91770	636 - G5
DOUBLETREE HOTEL-LA/WWD/BHLS 10740 WILSHIRE BLVD, Wwd, 90024	632 - C3
DOUBLETREE HOTEL - LAX 1985 E GRAND AV, ELSG, 90245	732 - H1
DOUBLETREE HOTEL SAN PEDRO 2800 VIA CABRILLO MARINA, SPed, 90731	854 - C1
EMBASSY SUITES HOTEL 1211 E GARVEY AV, COV, 91724	599 - E7
EMBASSY SUITES HOTEL 211 E HUNTINGTON DR, ARCD, 91006	567 - D5
EMBASSY SUITES HOTEL 8425 FIRESTONE BLVD, DWNY, 90241	706 - B5
EMBASSY SUITES HOTEL 900 E BIRCH ST, BREA, 92821	709 - C7
EMBASSY SUITES - LAX NORTH 9801 AIRPORT BLVD, Wch, 90045	702 - H4
EMBASSY SUITES - LAX SOUTH 1440 E IMPERIAL AV, ELSG, 90245	702 - G7
ESSEX HOUSE 44916 N 10TH ST W, LAN, 93534	4015 - G5
FAIRFIELD INN BY MARRIOTT 25340 THE OLD RD, StvR, 91381	4640 - D1
FAIRMONT MIRAMAR HOTEL 101 WILSHIRE BLVD, SMCA, 90403	671 - D2
FOUR POINTS BY SHERATON 5990 GREEN VALLEY CIR, CULC, 90230	672 - H6
FOUR POINTS BY SHERATON 700 W HUNTINGTON DR, MNRO, 91016	567 - F5
FOUR POINTS BY SHERATON LAX 9750 AIRPORT BLVD, Wch, 90045	702 - J4
FOUR SEASONS HOTEL-BEVERY HLLS 300 S DOHENY DR, LA, 90048	632 - H1
FURAMA HOTEL 8601 LINCOLN BLVD, Wch, 90045	702 - D3
GUESTHOUSE HOTEL 5325 E PACIFIC COAST HWY, LBCH, 90815	796 - B6
HACIENDA HOTEL - LA 525 N SEPULVEDA BLVD, ELSG, 90245	732 - G1
HAMPTON INN 25259 THE OLD RD, StvR, 91381	4640 - E2
HAMPTON INN 30255 AGOURA RD, AGRH, 91301	557 - G6
HAMPTON INN 767 ALBERTONI ST, CRSN, 90746	734 - E7
HAMPTON INN & SUITES 7828 ORANGETHORPE AV, BPK, 90621	767 - H2
HAMPTON INN ARCADIA 311 E HUNTINGTON DR, ARCD, 91006	567 - E5
HAMPTON INN LAX 10300 S LA CIENEGA BLVD, Lenx, 90304	703 - A5
HILTON GARDEN INN - ARCADIA 199 N 2ND AV, ARCD, 91006	567 - D5
HILTON GARDEN INN - CALABASAS 24150 HWY SORRENTO, CALB, 91302	559 - E5
HILTON GARDEN INN - LAX 2100 E MARIPOSA AV, ELSG, 90245	732 - H1
HILTON GARDEN INN - MONTEBELLO 801 N VIA SAN CLEMENTE, MTBL, 90640	636 - A7
HILTON LONG BEACH 701 W OCEAN BLVD, LBCH, 90831	825 - C1
HILTON LOS ANGELES NORTH 100 W GLENOAKS BLVD, GLDL, 91203	564 - E3
HILTON PASADENA 168 S LOS ROBLES AV, PAS, 91101	565 - J5
HILTON TORRANCE 21333 HAWTHORNE BLVD, TOR, 90503	763 - C6
HOLIDAY INN 38630 5TH ST W, PMDL, 93551	4195 - H7
HOLIDAY INN 924 W HUNTINGTON DR, MNRO, 91016	567 - E5
HOLIDAY INN-BUENA PARK 7000 BEACH BLVD, BPK, 90621	767 - J2
HOLIDAY INN-BURBANK 150 E ANGELENO AV, BURB, 91502	533 - H7
HOLIDAY INN-CITY CTR 1020 S FIGUEROA ST, LA, 90015	634 - D5
HOLIDAY INN-DOWNTOWN 750 GARLAND AV, LA, 90017	634 - D4
HOLIDAY INN-DOWNTOWN LONG BEACH 1133 ATLANTIC AV, LBCH, 90813	795 - E6
HOLIDAY INN-HARBOR GATEWAY 19800 S VERMONT AV, LA, 90502	764 - B3
HOLIDAY INN-HLYWD WALK OF FAME 2005 N HIGHLAND AV, LA, 90068	593 - D3
HOLIDAY INN-INTL 9901 S LA CIENEGA BLVD, Wch, 90045	703 - A4
HOLIDAY INN-LONG BEACH 2640 N LAKEWOOD BLVD, LBCH, 90815	796 - A3
HOLIDAY INN-SANTA MONICA BEACH 120 COLORADO AV, SMCA, 90401	671 - E3
HOLIDAY INN SELECT-DIAMOND BAR 21725 GATEWAY CENTER DR, DBAR, 91765	679 - J3
HOLIDAY INN SELECT-GATEWAY PLZ 14299 FIRESTONE BLVD, LMRD, 90638	737 - E5
HOLLYWOOD ROOSEVELT HOTEL 7000 HOLLYWOOD BLVD, Hlwd, 90028	593 - D4
HOMESTEAD STUDIO SUITES HOTEL - LAX 1910 E MARIPOSA AV, ELSG, 90245	732 - H1
HOTEL ANGELENO 170 N CHURCH LN, Brwd, 90049	631 - H1
HOTEL BEL AIR 701 STONE CANYON RD, BelA, 90077	592 - A6
HOTEL CLAREMONT & TENNIS CLUB 840 S INDIAN HILL BLVD, CLAR, 91711	601 - D5
HOTEL QUEEN MARY 1126 QUEENS HWY, LBCH, 90802	825 - E3
HOTEL SOFITEL 8555 BEVERLY BLVD, LA, 90048	632 - J1
HUNTLEY,THE HOTEL 1111 SECOND ST, SMCA, 90403	671 - D2
HYATT REGENCY 200 S PINE AV, LBCH, 90802	825 - D1
HYATT REGENCY CENTURY PLAZA 2025 AV OF THE STARS, CenC, 90067	632 - E3
HYATT REGENCY LONG BEACH 200 S PINE AV, LBCH, 90802	825 - D1
HYATT VALENCIA 24500 TOWN CENTER DR, SCTA, 91355	4550 - E3
HYATT WEST HOLLYWOOD 8401 SUNSET BLVD, LA, 90069	593 - A5
HYATT WESTLAKE PLAZA 880 S WESTLAKE BLVD, THO, 91361	557 - C4
KNOTTS BERRY FARM RESORT HOTEL 7675 CRESCENT AV, BPK, 90620	767 - H4
LA HILTON & TOWERS 5711 W CENTURY BLVD, Wch, 90045	702 - J4
LA MARRIOTT 5855 W CENTURY BLVD, Wch, 90045	702 - J5
LA MARRIOTT DOWNTOWN 333 S FIGUEROA ST, LA, 90071	634 - E3
LE MERIDIEN AT BEVERLY HILLS 465 S LA CIENEGA BLVD, LA, 90048	632 - J2
LE MERIGOT A JW MARRIOTT HOTEL OCEAN AV, SMCA, 90401	671 - E3
LE MONTROSE SUITE HOTEL 900 HAMMOND ST, WHWD, 90069	592 - H6
LE PARC HOTEL 733 WEST KNOLL DR, WHWD, 90069	592 - J6
LOEWS SANTA MONICA BEACH HOTEL 1700 OCEAN AV, SMCA, 90401	671 - E3
LONG BEACH MARRIOTT 4700 AIRPORT PLAZA DR, LBCH, 90815	796 - A2
LOWES BEVERLY HILLS HOTEL 1224 S BEVERWIL DR, LA, 90035	632 - G3
LUXE HOTEL SUNSET BOULEVARD 11461 W SUNSET BLVD, Brwd, 90049	631 - H1
MANHATTAN BEACH MARRIOTT 1400 PARK VIEW AV, MANB, 90266	732 - H4
MARINA DEL REY HOTEL 13534 BALI WY, MdlR, 90292	672 - B7
MARINA DEL REY MARRIOTT 4100 ADMIRALTY WY, MdlR, 90292	671 - J7
MARINA INTL HOTEL 4200 ADMIRALTY WY, MdlR, 90292	671 - J6
MARRIOTT SPRINGHILL SUITES 99 N 2ND AV, ARCD, 91006	567 - D5
MID TOWN HILTON 400 N VERMONT AV, LA, 90004	594 - A7
MILLENNIUM BILTMORE HOTEL, THE 506 S GRAND AV, LA, 90013	634 - E4
MIYAKO INN 328 E 1ST ST, LA, 90012	634 - G4
MONDRIAN HOTEL 8440 SUNSET BLVD, WHWD, 90069	592 - J5
NEW OTANI HOTEL 120 S LOS ANGELES ST, LA, 90012	634 - G4
NORWALK MARRIOTT 13111 SYCAMORE DR, NRWK, 90650	736 - J2
OMNI LOS ANGELES HOTEL 251 S OLIVE ST, LA, 90012	634 - F4
OXFORD INN & SUITES 1651 W AVE K, LAN, 93534	4105 - E1
PACIFIC PALMS CONFERENCE RESORT 1 INDUSTRY HILLS PKWY, INDS, 91744	638 - G7
PARK HYATT LA AT CENTURY CITY 2151 AV OF THE STARS, CenC, 90067	632 - E4
PENINSULA BEVERLY HILLS HOTEL 9882 S SANTA MONICA BLVD, BHLS, 90212	632 - E2
PORTOFINO HOTEL & YACHT CLUB 260 PORTOFINO WY, RBCH, 90277	762 - G4
QUALITY INN 5249 W CENTURY BLVD, Wch, 90045	703 - A5
QUALITY INN-SOUTH BAY 888 DOMINGUEZ ST, CRSN, 90746	764 - E5
RADISSON HOTEL 6161 CENTINELA AV, CULC, 90230	672 - G7
RADISSON HOTEL AT LA 6225 W CENTURY BLVD, Wch, 90045	702 - G4
RADISSON HOTEL CHATSWORTH 9777 TOPANGA CANYON BLVD, Chat, 91311	500 - A5
RADISSON HOTEL MIDTOWN LA S FIGUEROA ST, LA, 90007	674 - B1
RADISSON HOTEL WHITTER 7320 GREENLEAF AV, WHIT, 90602	677 - D7
RADISSON SUITES BUENA PARK 7762 BEACH BLVD, BPK, 90620	767 - H3
RADISSON WILSHIRE PLAZA 3515 WILSHIRE BLVD, LA, 90010	633 - J2
RAFFLES LERMITAGE HOTEL 9291 BURTON WY, BHLS, 90210	632 - G1
RAMADA HOLLYWOOD 1160 N VERMONT AV, LA, 90029	594 - A5
RAMADA INN 300 W PALMDALE BLVD, PMDL, 93551	4195 - H7
RAMADA INN 7272 GAGE AV, CMRC, 90040	676 - B7
RAMADA INN 840 S INDIAN HILL BLVD, CLAR, 91711	601 - D5
RAMADA PLAZA HOTEL 5250 W EL SEGUNDO BLVD, HAW, 90250	733 - A2
RAMADA PLAZA HOTEL 8585 SANTA MONICA BLVD, WHWD, 90069	592 - J6
RAMADA PLAZA HOTEL LAX NORTH 6333 BRISTOL PKWY, CULC, 90230	672 - H7
RAMADA SUITES 1089 SANTA ANITA AV, SELM, 91733	637 - B5
RENAISSANCE AGOURA HILLS HOTEL 30100 AGOURA RD, AGRH, 91301	557 - H6
RENAISSANCE HOLLYWOOD HOTEL 1755 N HIGHLAND AV, Hlwd, 90028	593 - D4
RENAISSANCE LONG BEACH HOTEL 111 E OCEAN BLVD, LBCH, 90802	825 - D1
RENAISSANCE MONTURA HOTEL 9620 AIRPORT BLVD, Wch, 90045	702 - J4
RESIDENCE BY MARRIOTT 514 RANCHO VISTA BLVD, PMDL, 93551	4195 - H5
RESIDENCE INN BY MARRIOTT 14419 FIRESTONE BLVD, LMRD, 90638	737 - E5
RESIDENCE INN BY MARRIOTT 1700 N SEPULVEDA BLVD, MANB, 90266	732 - H5
RESIDENCE INN BY MARRIOTT 2135 E EL SEGUNDO BLVD, ELSG, 90245	732 - H1
RESIDENCE INN BY MARRIOTT 2530 THE OLD RD, StvR, 91381	4640 - E1
RESIDENCE INN BY MARRIOTT 321 E HUNTINGTON DR, ARCD, 91006	567 - E5
RESIDENCE INN BY MARRIOTT 3701 TORRANCE BLVD, TOR, 90503	763 - D5
RESIDENCE INN BY MARRIOTT 4111 E WILLOW ST, LBCH, 90815	796 - A3
RESIDENCE INN BY MARRIOTT-BHLS S BEVERLY DR, LA, 90035	632 - G3
RITZ-CARLTON HUNTINGTON HOTEL 1401 S OAK KNOLL AV, PAS, 91106	596 - A1
RITZ CARLTON MARINA DEL REY 4375 ADMIRALTY WY, MdlR, 90292	672 - A6
SANTA ANITA INN 130 W HUNTINGTON DR, ARCD, 91007	567 - C5
SHERATON CERRITOS HOTEL AT-TOWNE CTR 12725 CENTER COURT DR S, CRTS, 90703	767 - A1
SHERATON DELFINA SANTA MONICA 530 PICO BLVD, SMCA, 90405	671 - F3
SHERATON GATEWAY HOTEL 6101 W CENTURY BLVD, Wch, 90045	702 - H4
SHERATON LOS ANGELES 6101 W CENTURY BLVD, Wch, 90045	702 - H5
SHERATON LOS ANGELES DOWNTOWN 711 S HOPE ST, LA, 90017	634 - E4
SHERATON PASADENA 303 E CORDOVA ST, PAS, 91101	565 - J5
SHERATON SUITES FAIRPLEX 601 W MCKINLEY AV, POM, 91768	600 - H6
SHERATON UNIVERSAL 333 UNIVERSAL HOLLYWOOD DR, Univ, 91608	563 - B6
SHILO INN HILLTOP SUITES 3101 TEMPLE AV, POM, 91769	640 - C4
SHILO INN HOTEL 3200 TEMPLE AV, POM, 91768	640 - C3
SHUTTERS ON THE BEACH 1 PICO BLVD, SMCA, 90405	671 - E3
SPORTSMENS LODGE HOTEL 12825 VENTURA BLVD, LA, 91604	562 - E5
SPRINGHILL SUITES BY MARRIOTT 14620 AVIATION BLVD, HAW, 90260	733 - A4
SUMMERFIELD SUITES BY HYATT 1000 WESTMOUNT DR, WHWD, 90069	592 - J6
SUMMERFIELD SUITES BY HYATT 810 S DOUGLAS ST, ELSG, 90245	732 - J3
SUNSET MARQUIS HOTEL 1200 ALTA LOMA RD, WHWD, 90069	592 - J5
TORRANCE MARRIOTT 3635 FASHION WY, TOR, 90503	763 - D6
TRAVELODGE AT LAX 5547 W CENTURY BLVD, Wch, 90045	702 - J5
TRAVELODGE AT LAX SOUTH 5547 W CENTURY BLVD, Wch, 90045	702 - J5
UCLA GUEST HOUSE 330 CHARLES E YOUNG DR E, LA, 90095	632 - B1
UNIVERSAL CITY HILTON & TOWERS 555 UNIVERSAL HOLLYWOOD DR, Univ, 91608	563 - B6
VALENCIA HILTON GARDEN INN 27710 THE OLD RD, Valc, 91355	4550 - B2
VICEROY HOTEL SANTA MONICA 1819 OCEAN AV, SMCA, 90401	671 - E3
WARNER CTR MARRIOTT HOTEL 21850 OXNARD ST, WdHl, 91367	560 - A1
WEST COAST LONG BEACH HOTEL 700 QUEENSWAY DR, LBCH, 90802	825 - D2
WESTIN BONAVENTURE HOTEL 404 S FIGUEROA ST, LA, 90071	634 - E4
WESTIN HOTEL-LOS ANGELES 5400 W CENTURY BLVD, Wch, 90045	703 - A5
WESTIN LONG BEACH, THE 333 E OCEAN BLVD, LBCH, 90802	825 - E1
WESTIN - PASADENA 191 N LOS ROBLES AV, PAS, 91101	565 - J4
W HOTEL AT LOS ANGELES WESTWOOD 930 HILGARD AV, Wwd, 90024	632 - B3
WILSHIRE GRAND HOTEL & CTR 930 WILSHIRE BLVD, LA, 90017	634 - D4
WOODLAND HILLS HILTON & TOWERS 6360 CANOGA AV, WdHl, 91367	530 - B7
WYNDHAM BEL AGE HOTEL 1020 N SAN VICENTE BLVD, WHWD, 90069	592 - H6
WYNDHAM CHECKERS HOTEL 535 S GRAND AV, LA, 90071	634 - E4
WYNDHAM GARDEN HOTEL 5757 TELEGRAPH RD, CMRC, 90040	675 - H3
WYNDHAM GARDEN HOTEL 5990 GREEN VALLEY CIR, CULC, 90230	672 - H6
WYNDHAM HOTEL 6225 W CENTURY BLVD, Wch, 90045	702 - G5
WYNDHAM LOS ANGELES 6333 BRISTOL PKWY, CULC, 90230	672 - H7
ZANE GREY PUEBLO HOTEL 199 CHIMES TOWER RD, AVA, 90704	5923 - G3

LIBRARIES

FEATURE NAME Address City, ZIP Code	PAGE-GRID
AGOURA HILLS 29901 LADYFACE CT, AGRH, 91301	557 - H6
ALAMITOS 1836 E 3RD ST, LBCH, 90802	825 - G1
ALHAMBRA MAIN 410 W MAIN ST, ALH, 91801	596 - A5
ALLENDALE 1130 S MARENGO AV, PAS, 91106	565 - J7
ALONDRA 11949 E ALONDRA BLVD, NRWK, 90650	736 - H5
ALTADENA 600 E MARIPOSA ST, Alta, 91001	535 - J6
ANGELES MESA BRANCH 2700 W 52ND ST, LA, 90043	673 - G5
ARCADIA 20 W DUARTE RD, ARCD, 91007	567 - D7
ARROYO SECO REGL 6145 N FIGUEROA ST, HiPk, 90042	595 - D2
ARTESIA 18722 CLARKDALE AV, ART, 90701	766 - H2
ASCOT BRANCH 120 W FLORENCE AV, LA, 90003	674 - C7
ATLANTIC 2269 S ATLANTIC BLVD, CMRC, 90040	675 - G3
ATWATER VILLAGE BRANCH 3379 GLENDALE BLVD, LA, 90039	594 - E1
AVALON 215 SUMNER AV, AVA, 90704	5923 - H3
AZUSA 729 N DALTON AV, AZU, 91702	568 - J5
BACH 4055 N BELLFLOWER BLVD, LBCH, 90808	766 - C6
BALDWIN HILLS BRANCH 2906 S LA BREA AV, LA, 90016	633 - C7
BALDWIN PARK 4181 BALDWIN PARK BLVD, BALD, 91706	598 - B5
BAY SHORE 195 BAY SHORE AV, LBCH, 90803	826 - B2
BELL GARDENS 7110 GARFIELD AV, BGDN, 90201	705 - J1
BELL 4411 GAGE AV, BELL, 90201	675 - D7
BEVERLY HILLS 444 N REXFORD DR, BHLS, 90210	632 - G1
BILBREW, A C 150 E EL SEGUNDO BLVD, LACo, 90061	734 - D1
BRAKENSIEK, CLIFTON M 9945 FLOWER ST, BLF, 90706	736 - C6
BRAND 1601 W MOUNTAIN ST, GLDL, 91201	534 - B7
BREA 1 CIVIC CENTER CIR, BREA, 92821	709 - C7
BRENTWOOD BRANCH 11820 SAN VICENTE BLVD, Brwd, 90049	631 - H4
BREWITT 4036 E ANAHEIM ST, LBCH, 90804	796 - A6
BRISTOW PARK 1466 S MCDONNELL AV, CMRC, 90040	675 - F2
BRUGGEMEYER MEM 318 S RAMONA AV, MONP, 91754	636 - B2
BUENA PARK 7150 LA PALMA AV, BPK, 90620	767 - G3
BUENA VISTA 300 N BUENA VISTA ST, BURB, 91506	563 - E2
BURBANK 110 N GLENOAKS BLVD, BURB, 91501	533 - H7
BURNETT 560 E HILL ST, LBCH, 90806	795 - E4
CAHUENGA BRANCH 4591 SANTA MONICA BLVD, LA, 90029	594 - A5
CALABASAS 23975 PARK SORRENTO, CALB, 91302	559 - E5
CANOGA PARK BRANCH 20939 SHERMAN WY, CanP, 91303	530 - C5
CANYON COUNTRY 18601 SOLEDAD CANYON RD, SCTA, 91351	4551 - H3
CARSON 151 E CARSON ST, CRSN, 90745	764 - C6
CASA VERDUGO 1151 N BRAND BLVD, GLDL, 91202	564 - E2
CERRITOS 18025 BLOOMFIELD AV, CRTS, 90703	767 - A1
CHARTER OAK 20540 E ARROW HWY, LACo, 91724	599 - F2
CHATSWORTH BRANCH 21052 DEVONSHIRE ST, Chat, 91311	500 - B4
CHEVY CHASE 3301 E CHEVY CHASE DR, GLDL, 91206	565 - B1
CHINATOWN BRANCH 639 N HILL ST, LA, 90012	634 - G3
CHINO HILLS BRANCH 2003 GRAND AV, CHLS, 91709	680 - H4
CITY TERRACE 4025 CITY TERRACE DR, City, 90063	635 - E3
CLAREMONT 208 N HARVARD AV, CLAR, 91711	601 - D3
CLARK, WILLIAM ANDREWS MEM 2520 CIMARRON ST, LA, 90018	633 - G6
COMMERCE CENTRAL 5655 JILLSON ST, CMRC, 90040	675 - H4
COMPTON 240 W COMPTON BLVD, COMP, 90220	734 - J4
COVINA 234 N 2ND AV, COV, 91723	599 - B5
CRENSHAW-IMPERIAL 11141 CRENSHAW BLVD, ING, 90303	703 - F6
CUDAHY 5218 SANTA ANA ST, CDHY, 90201	705 - F2
CULVER CITY JULIAN DIXON 4975 OVERLAND AV, CULC, 90230	672 - G3
CYPRESS 5331 ORANGE AV, CYP, 90630	767 - D7
CYPRESS PARK BRANCH 1150 CYPRESS AV, LA, 90065	594 - H5
DANA 3680 ATLANTIC AV, Bxby, 90807	765 - E7
DIAMOND BAR 1061 GRAND AV, DBAR, 91765	680 - B3
DOWNEY CITY 11121 BROOKSHIRE AV, DWNY, 90241	706 - B5
DUARTE 1301 BUENA VISTA ST, DUAR, 91010	568 - A5
EAGLE ROCK BRANCH 5027 CASPAR AV, Eagl, 90041	565 - A6
EAST LOS ANGELES 4837 E 3RD ST, ELA, 90022	635 - G6
EAST RANCHO DOMINGUEZ 4205 E COMPTON BLVD, RDom, 90221	735 - C4
ECHO PARK BRANCH 1410 W TEMPLE ST, Echo, 90026	634 - E2
EDENDALE BRANCH 2011 W SUNSET BLVD, Echo, 90026	594 - D7
EL CAMINO REAL 4264 WHITTIER BLVD, LACo, 90023	635 - E7
EL DORADO 2900 N STUDEBAKER RD, LBCH, 90815	796 - F2
EL MONTE 3224 TYLER AV, ELMN, 91731	637 - C1
EL RETIRO 126 VIS DEL PARQUE, TOR, 90277	793 - A2
EL SEGUNDO 111 W MARIPOSA AV, ELSG, 90245	732 - E1
EL SERENO BRANCH 5226 HUNTINGTON DR S, LA, 90032	595 - F5
ENCINO-TARZANA BRANCH 18231 VENTURA BLVD, Tarz, 91356	560 - J2
EXPOSITION PARK REGL 3665 S VERMONT AV, LA, 90007	674 - A1
FAIRFAX BRANCH 161 S GARDNER ST, LA, 90036	633 - C1
FAIRVIEW 2101 OCEAN PARK BLVD, SMCA, 90405	671 - H2

FEATURE NAME / Address City, ZIP Code	PAGE-GRID
FELIPE DE NEVE BRANCH 2820 W 6TH ST, LA, 90005	634 - B2
FLORENCE 1610 E FLORENCE AV, Flor, 90001	674 - G7
FRANKLIN, BENJAMIN BRANCH 2200 E 1ST ST, Boyl, 90033	635 - A5
FREMONT, JOHN C BRANCH 6121 MELROSE AV, LA, 90038	593 - E6
FULLERTON MAIN 353 W COMMONWEALTH AV, FUL, 92832	738 - G7
GARDENA MAYME DEAR 1731 W GARDENA BLVD, GAR, 90247	733 - J6
GEISSERT, KATY 3301 TORRANCE BLVD, TOR, 90503	763 - E5
GLENDALE 222 E HARVARD ST, GLDL, 91205	564 - E5
GLENDORA CITY 140 S GLENDORA AV, GLDR, 91741	569 - E5
GRAHAM 1900 E FIRESTONE BLVD, Wats, 90002	704 - G2
GRANADA HILLS BRANCH 10640 PETIT AV, GrnH, 91344	501 - D3
GRANDVIEW 1535 5TH ST, GLDL, 91201	564 - A1
GREENWOOD 6134 GREENWOOD AV, CMRC, 90040	676 - B7
HACIENDA HEIGHTS 16010 LA MONDE ST, HacH, 91745	678 - C4
HARTE, BRET 1595 W WILLOW ST, LBCH, 90810	795 - B3
HASTINGS 3325 E ORANGE GROVE BLVD, PAS, 91107	566 - G3
HAWAIIAN GARDENS 12100 E CARSON ST, HGDN, 90716	766 - J6
HAWTHORNE 12700 GREVILLEA AV, HAW, 90250	733 - C1
HENDERSON, ISABEL 4805 EMERALD ST, TOR, 90503	763 - B5
HERMOSA BEACH 550 PIER AV, HMB, 90254	762 - H2
HILL AVENUE 55 S HILL AV, PAS, 91106	566 - B5
HOLIFIELD, CHET 1060 S GREENWOOD AV, MTBL, 90640	676 - C4
HOLLYDALE 12000 GARFIELD AV, SGAT, 90280	735 - G1
HOLLYWOOD REGL 1623 IVAR AV, Hlwd, 90028	593 - F4
HUNT BRANCH 201 S BASQUE AV, FUL, 92833	738 - D7
HUNTINGTON PARK 6518 MILES AV, HNTP, 90255	675 - A6
HYDE PARK BRANCH 6527 CRENSHAW BLVD, LA, 90043	673 - F7
HYDE PARK - MIRIAM MATTHEWS 2250 W FLORENCE AV, LA, 90043	703 - G1
IACOBONI, ANGELO M 4990 CLARK AV, LKWD, 90712	766 - B3
INGLEWOOD 101 W MANCHESTER BLVD, ING, 90301	703 - C2
IRWINDALE 5050 IRWINDALE AV, IRW, 91706	598 - F3
JEFFERSON BRANCH 2211 W JEFFERSON BLVD, LA, 90018	633 - G7
JUNIPERO SERRA BRANCH 4607 S MAIN ST, LA, 90037	674 - C4
LA CANADA-FLINTRIDGE 4545 OAKWOOD AV, LCF, 91011	535 - C4
LA CRESCENTA 4521 LA CRESCENTA AV, LaCr, 91214	534 - G1
LA HABRA 221 E LA HABRA BLVD, LHB, 90631	708 - E5
LAKE LOS ANGELES 16921 E AVE O, LACo, 93535	4199 - H2
LAKE VIEW TERRACE BRANCH 12002 OSBORNE ST, Sunl, 91040	502 - G2
LAMANDA PARK 140 S ALTADENA DR, PAS, 91107	566 - E5
LA MIRADA 13800 LA MIRADA BLVD, LMRD, 90638	737 - G2
LANCASTER 601 W LANCASTER BLVD, LAN, 93534	4015 - H5
LA PALMA 7842 WALKER ST, LPMA, 90623	767 - D3
LA PINTORESCA 1355 N RAYMOND AV, PAS, 91103	565 - H1
LA PUENTE 15920 CENTRAL AV, LPUE, 91744	638 - D7
LA VERNE 3640 D ST, LVRN, 91750	600 - G1
LAWNDALE 14615 BURIN AV, LNDL, 90260	733 - C4
LENNOX 4359 LENNOX BLVD, Lenx, 90304	703 - C5
LINCOLN HEIGHTS 2530 WORKMAN ST, LA, 90031	595 - A7
LINDA VISTA 1281 BRYANT ST, PAS, 91103	565 - E1
LITTLEROCK 35119 80TH ST E, Litl, 93543	4377 - H1
LITTLE TOKYO BRANCH 203 S LOS ANGELES ST, LA, 90012	634 - G4
LIVE OAK 4153 E LIVE OAK AV, LACo, 91006	597 - F2
LOMITA 24200 NARBONNE AV, LMTA, 90717	793 - H3
LONG BEACH 101 PACIFIC AV, LBCH, 90802	825 - D1
LOS ALAMITOS-ROSSMOOR 12700 MONTECITO RD, SLB, 90740	796 - J6
LOS ALTOS 5614 BRITTON DR, LBCH, 90815	796 - C4
LOS ANGELES COUNTY LAW 301 W 1ST ST, LA, 90012	634 - F3
LOS FELIZ BRANCH 1874 HILLHURST AV, LFlz, 90027	594 - A3
LOS NIETOS 11644 SLAUSON AV, SFSP, 90606	706 - J1
LOYOLA VILLAGE BRANCH 7114 W MANCHESTER AV, Wch, 90045	702 - E3
LUCAS, BOB MEM 2659 LINCOLN AV, Alta, 91001	535 - G5
LYNWOOD 11320 BULLIS RD, LYN, 90262	705 - C7
MALABAR BRANCH 2801 WABASH AV, Boyl, 90033	635 - C4
MALAGA COVE PLAZA 2400 VIA CAMPESINA, PVE, 90274	792 - H4
MALIBU 23519 CIVIC CENTER WY, MAL, 90265	628 - J7
MANHATTAN BEACH 1320 N HIGHLAND AV, MANB, 90266	732 - F6
MARINA DEL REY 4533 ADMIRALTY WY, MdlR, 90292	672 - B7
MAR VISTA BRANCH 12006 VENICE BLVD, LA, 90066	672 - C3
MAYWOOD CESAR CHAVEZ 4323 E SLAUSON AV, MYWD, 90270	675 - D5
MEM BRANCH 4625 W OLYMPIC BLVD, LA, 90019	633 - E3
MID-VALLEY REGL BRANCH 16244 NORDHOFF ST, LA, 91343	501 - E7
MIRALESTE 29089 PALOS VERDES DR E, RPV, 90275	823 - F3
MONROVIA 321 S MYRTLE AV, MNRO, 91016	567 - G4
MONTANA 1704 MONTANA AV, SMCA, 90403	631 - E6
MONTCLAIR BRANCH 9955 FREMONT AV, MTCL, 91763	601 - G6
MONTEBELLO 1550 W BEVERLY BLVD, MTBL, 90640	676 - C1
MONTROSE-CRESCENTA 2465 HONOLULU AV, GLDL, 91020	534 - G3
MORNINGSIDE PARK 3202 W 85TH ST, ING, 90305	703 - F2
MUIR, JOHN BRANCH 1005 W 64TH ST, LA, 90044	674 - A6
NEWHALL 22704 9TH ST, SCTA, 91321	4640 - J1
NORTH HOLLYWOOD REGL 5211 TUJUNGA AV, NHol, 91601	562 - J2
NORTH LONG BEACH 5571 ORANGE AV, NLB, 90805	765 - F2
NORTH REDONDO 2000 ARTESIA BLVD, RBCH, 90278	763 - A1
NORTHRIDGE BRANCH 9051 DARBY AV, Nor, 91325	500 - J7
NORTH TORRANCE 3604 ARTESIA BLVD, TOR, 90504	763 - E1
NORTHWEST 3323 VICTORY BLVD, BURB, 91505	533 - C7
NORWALK 12350 IMPERIAL HWY, NRWK, 90650	736 - J1
NORWOOD 4550 PECK RD, ELMN, 91732	597 - F5
NYE, GEORGE JR 6600 DEL AMO BLVD, LKWD, 90713	766 - E4
OAK PARK 899 KANAN RD, VeCo, 91377	558 - A1
OCEAN PARK 2601 MAIN ST, SMCA, 90405	671 - F4
PACIFIC PARK BRANCH 501 S PACIFIC AV, GLDL, 91204	564 - D6
PACOIMA BRANCH 13605 VAN NUYS BLVD, Pcma, 91331	502 - C3
PALISADES BRANCH 861 ALMA REAL DR, PacP, 90272	631 - A5
PALMDALE-MAIN 700 E PALMDALE BLVD, PMDL, 93550	4286 - B1
PALMDALE YOUTH 38510 SIERRA HWY, PMDL, 93550	4196 - B7
PALMS-RANCHO PARK BRANCH 2920 OVERLAND AV, LA, 90064	632 - E6
PANORAMA CITY BRANCH 14345 ROSCOE BLVD, PanC, 91402	532 - A2
PARAMOUNT 16254 COLORADO AV, PRM, 90723	735 - H5
PASADENA MAIN 285 E WALNUT ST, PAS, 91101	565 - J4
PENINSULA CTR 701 SILVER SPUR RD, RHE, 90274	823 - B1
PICO RIVERA 9001 MINES AV, PRV, 90660	676 - F5
PICO UNION BRANCH 1030 S ALVARADO ST, LA, 90006	634 - B4
PIO PICO KOREATOWN BRANCH 694 S OXFORD AV, LA, 90005	633 - H3
PLATT BRANCH 23600 VICTORY BLVD, WdHl, 91367	529 - F7
PLAYA VISTA 6400 PLAYA VISTA DR, LA, 90094	702 - D1
POMONA 625 S GAREY AV, POM, 91766	640 - J2
PORTER RANCH BRANCH 11371 TAMPA AV, Nor, 91326	500 - F1
QUARTZ HILL 42018 50TH ST W, LACo, 93536	4104 - H6
QUINN, ANTHONY 3965 CESAR E CHAVEZ AV, City, 90063	635 - E5
REDONDO BEACH MAIN 303 N PACIFIC COAST HWY, RBCH, 90277	762 - J4
RIORDAN, RICHARD J CENTRAL 630 W 5TH ST, LA, 90071	634 - E4
RIVERA 7828 SERAPIS AV, PRV, 90660	706 - E1
ROBERTSON BRANCH 1719 S ROBERTSON BLVD, LA, 90035	632 - H4
ROSEMEAD 8800 VALLEY BLVD, RSMD, 91770	596 - H6
ROWLAND HEIGHTS 1850 NOGALES ST, RowH, 91748	679 - C5
SAN DIMAS 145 N WALNUT AV, SDMS, 91773	600 - C2
SAN FERNANDO 217 N MACLAY AV, SFER, 91340	482 - B7
SAN GABRIEL 500 S DEL MAR AV, SGBL, 91776	596 - E4
SAN MARINO 1890 HUNTINGTON DR, SMRO, 91108	596 - C1
SAN PEDRO REGL 931 S GAFFEY ST, SPed, 90731	824 - B5
SAN RAFAEL 1240 NITHSDALE RD, PAS, 91105	565 - E6
SANTA CATALINA 999 E WASHINGTON BLVD, PAS, 91104	566 - A1
SANTA FE SPRINGS 11700 TELEGRAPH RD, SFSP, 90670	706 - G4
SANTA MONICA MAIN 1343 6TH ST, SMCA, 90401	671 - E2
SATOW, MASAO W 14433 CRENSHAW BLVD, LACo, 90249	733 - F4
SEAL BEACH - WILSON, MARY-BRANCH 707 ELECTRIC AV, SLB, 90740	826 - E4
SHERMAN OAKS BRANCH 14245 MOORPARK ST, Shrm, 91423	562 - A4
SIERRA MADRE 440 W SIERRA MADRE BLVD, SMAD, 91024	566 - J2
SIGNAL HILL 1770 E HILL ST, SIGH, 90755	795 - G4
SORENSEN 11405 ROSE HEDGE DR, LACo, 90606	677 - A6
SOUTHEAST TORRANCE 23115 ARLINGTON AV, TOR, 90501	793 - G1
SOUTH EL MONTE 1430 CENTRAL AV, SELM, 91733	637 - B4
SOUTH PASADENA 1100 OXLEY ST, SPAS, 91030	595 - H2
SOUTH WHITTIER 14433 LEFFINGWELL RD, LACo, 90604	707 - E7
STEVENSON, ROBERT LOUIS BRANCH 803 S SPENCE ST, LA, 90023	635 - C7
STUDIO CITY BRANCH 12511 MOORPARK ST, LA, 91604	562 - F4
SUNKIST-LA PUENTE 840 N PUENTE AV, LPUE, 91746	638 - A3
SUNLAND-TUJUNGA BRANCH 7771 FOOTHILL BLVD, Tuj, 91042	503 - J3
SUN VALLEY BRANCH 7935 VINELAND AV, SunV, 91352	533 - A2
SYLMAR BRANCH 14561 POLK ST, LA, 91342	481 - J4
TEMPLE CITY 5939 GOLDEN WEST AV, TEML, 91780	597 - A2
TWAIN, MARK 1325 E ANAHEIM ST, LBCH, 90813	795 - F6
TWAIN, MARK BRANCH 9621 S FIGUEROA ST, LA, 90044	704 - B4
VALENCIA 23743 VALENCIA BLVD, SCTA, 91355	4550 - G3
VALLEY PLAZA BRANCH 12311 VANOWEN ST, NHol, 91605	532 - F5
VAN NUYS BRANCH 6230 SYLMAR AV, VanN, 91401	532 - A7
VENICE BRANCH 501 S VENICE BLVD, Ven, 90291	671 - H6
VERMONT SQUARE BRANCH 1201 W 48TH ST, LA, 90037	674 - A4
VERNON BRANCH 4504 S CENTRAL AV, LA, 90011	674 - E3
VICTORIA PARK 17906 AVALON BLVD, CRSN, 90746	764 - E1
VIEW PARK 3854 W 54TH ST, LACo, 90043	673 - E5
VILLA PARKE COMM CTR 363 E VILLA ST, PAS, 91101	565 - J3
WALNUT 21155 LA PUENTE RD, WAL, 91789	639 - H6
WALTERIA 3815 W 242ND ST, TOR, 90505	793 - D3
WASHINGTON IRVING BRANCH 4117 W WASHINGTON BLVD, LA, 90018	633 - F6
WATTS BRANCH 10205 COMPTON AV, Wats, 90002	704 - G5
WEAVER, LELAND R 4035 TWEEDY BLVD, SGAT, 90280	705 - C4
WESTCHESTER BRANCH 8946 SEPULVEDA EAST WY, Wch, 90045	702 - H3
WEST COVINA 1601 WEST COVINA PKWY, WCOV, 91790	598 - E7
WEST HOLLYWOOD 715 N SAN VICENTE BLVD, WHWD, 90069	592 - H7
WESTLAKE VILLAGE 31220 OAK CREST DR, WLKV, 91361	557 - F6
WEST LOS ANGELES REGL 11360 SANTA MONICA BLVD, WLA, 90025	632 - A5
WEST VALLEY REGL 19036 VANOWEN ST, Res, 91335	530 - G6
WESTWOOD BRANCH 1246 GLENDON AV, Wwd, 90024	632 - B3
WHITTIER CENTRAL 7344 WASHINGTON AV, WHIT, 90602	677 - D7
WHITTWOOD 10537 SANTA GERTRUDES AV, WHIT, 90603	707 - J5
WILL & ARIEL DURANT BRANCH 7140 W SUNSET BLVD, LA, 90046	593 - D5
WILLOWBROOK 11838 WILMINGTON AV, Wbrk, 90059	704 - G7
WILMINGTON BRANCH 1300 N AVALON BLVD, Wilm, 90744	794 - E5
WILSHIRE BRANCH 149 N SAINT ANDREWS PL, LA, 90004	633 - H1
WISEBURN 5335 W 135TH ST, HAW, 90250	733 - A3
WOODCREST 1340 W 106TH ST, LACo, 90044	703 - J5
WOODLAND HILLS BRANCH 22200 VENTURA BLVD, WdHl, 91364	559 - J2
WRIGHTWOOD BRANCH- (SEE PAGE 4651) 6014 PARK DR, SBdC, 92397	4652 - C2
ZIFFERN, PAUL SPORTS RESOURCE-CTR 2141 W ADAMS BLVD, LA, 90018	633 - H6

MILITARY INSTALLATIONS

FEATURE NAME / Address City, ZIP Code	PAGE-GRID
ARMORY 220 E COLORADO ST, GLDL, 91205	564 - E5
ARMY INSTALLATION WOODLEY AV & VICTORY BLVD, Enc, 91436	531 - E7
COAST GUARD HEADQUARTERS W OCEAN BLVD & PICO AV, LBCH, 90802	825 - B1
COAST GUARD STA 13871 FIJI WY, MdlR, 90292	702 - B1
COAST GUARD STA 31501 PALOS VERDES DR W, RPV, 90275	822 - F5
EDWARDS AIR FORCE BASE ROSAMOND BLVD OFF HWY 58, LACo, 93523	3835 - H4
FORT MACARTHUR (LOWER RESV) 2800 S PACIFIC AV, SPed, 90731	824 - B7
LOS ANGELES AIR FORCE BASE 2400 E EL SEGUNDO BLVD, HAW, 90245	732 - J2
NAVAL & MARINE CORPS RESERVE-CTR BALBOA BLVD & VICTORY BLVD, Enc, 91316	531 - C7
NAVAL RESERVE S WESTERN AV, LA, 90732	793 - J7
UNITED STATES NAVAL WEAPONS STA 800 SEAL BEACH BLVD, SLB, 90740	796 - J7
US AIR FORCE PLANT 42 PALMDALE 39516 25TH ST E, PMDL, 93550	4196 - C1
US COAST GUARD SECTOR LOS-ANGELES 1001 S SEASIDE AV, SPed, 90731	824 - E7

MUSEUMS

FEATURE NAME / Address City, ZIP Code	PAGE-GRID
AEROSPACE HALL 700 STATE DR, LA, 90037	674 - B1
ANTELOPE VALLEY INDIAN MUS 15701 AVE M, LACo, 93535	4109 - E4
AVILA ADOBE 10 OLVERA ST, LA, 90012	634 - G3
BANNING MUS 401 E M ST, Wilm, 90744	794 - F5
BLACKBIRD AIRPARK AVENUE P & 25TH ST E, PMDL, 93550	4196 - E4
CALIFORNIA AFRO-AMERICAN MUS 600 EXPOSITION PARK DR, LA, 90037	674 - B2
CALIFORNIA MUS OF SCIENCE &-INDUSTRY 700 STATE DR, LA, 90037	674 - B2
CALIFORNIA SCIENCE CTR 700 EXPOSITION PARK DR, LA, 90037	674 - B2
CASA DE ADOBE 4605 N FIGUEROA ST, LA, 90065	595 - B4
CATALINA ISLAND MUS CATALINA CASINO, AVA, 90704	5923 - H3
CHILDRENS MUS AT LA HABRA 301 S EUCLID ST, LHB, 90631	708 - E6
CHILDRENS MUS OF LOS ANGELES 11800 FOOTHILL BLVD, Sunl, 91040	502 - G2
DE LA OSSA ADOBE MOORPARK ST & LA MAIDA ST, Enc, 91436	561 - D3
DIBBLE MUS 16021 GALE AV, INDS, 91745	678 - D2
DOMINGUEZ ADOBE MUS 18127 S ALAMEDA ST, LACo, 90220	765 - A1
DOWNEY ART MUS 10419 RIVES AV, DWNY, 90241	706 - A3
DRUM BARRACKS CIVIL WAR MUS 1052 BANNING BLVD, Wilm, 90744	794 - E6
EL MONTE HIST SOCIETY MUS 3150 TYLER AV, ELMN, 91731	637 - C1
FORT MACARTHUR MILITARY MUS 3601 S GAFFEY ST, SPed, 90731	854 - A2
FULLERTON MUS CTR 301 N POMONA AV, FUL, 92832	738 - H7
GEFFEN CONTEMPORARY AT MOCA,-THE 152 N CENTRAL AV, LA, 90012	634 - G4
GETTY CENTER, THE 1200 GETTY CENTER DR, Brwd, 90049	631 - G1
GETTY VILLA 17985 W PACIFIC COAST HWY, PacP, 90272	630 - F5
GILB, RUTH & CHARLES ARCADIA-HIST MUS 380 W HUNTINGTON DR, ARCD, 91007	567 - B6
HAMMER MUS 10889 WILSHIRE BLVD, Wwd, 90024	632 - B3
HART, WILLIAM S MUS 24151 SAN FERNANDO RD, SCTA, 91321	4641 - A2
HOLLYWOOD BOWL MUS 2301 N HIGHLAND AV, LA, 90068	593 - E3
HOLLYWOOD MUS, THE 1660 N HIGHLAND AV, Hlwd, 90028	593 - E4
HOLLYWOOD WAX MUS 6767 HOLLYWOOD BLVD, Hlwd, 90028	593 - E4
JAPANESE AMERICAN NATL MUS 369 E 1ST ST, LA, 90012	634 - G4
LANCASTER MUS 44801 N SIERRA HWY, LAN, 93534	4015 - H5
LOMITA RAILROAD MUS 2137 W 250TH ST, LMTA, 90717	793 - H4
LONG BEACH MUS OF ART 2300 E OCEAN BLVD, LBCH, 90803	825 - G1
LOS ANGELES COUNTY MUS OF ART 5905 WILSHIRE BLVD, LA, 90036	633 - B2
LOS ANGELES COUNTY MUS OF ART - WEST 5905 WILSHIRE BLVD, LA, 90036	633 - B2
LOS ANGELES MARITIME MUS E 6TH ST, SPed, 90731	824 - C5
MALIBU LAGOON MUS 23200 PACIFIC COAST HWY, MAL, 90265	629 - B7
MUS OF CONTEMPORARY ART 250 S GRAND AV, LA, 90012	634 - F3
MUS OF FLYING, THE 2772 DONALD DOUGLAS LP N, SMCA, 90405	672 - A2
MUS OF LATIN AMERICAN ART 628 ALAMITOS AV, LBCH, 90802	795 - F7
MUS OF TELEVISION AND RADIO 465 N BEVERLY DR, BHLS, 90210	632 - F1
MUS OF THE AMERICAN WEST 4700 WESTERN HERITAGE WY, LFlz, 90027	564 - B4
MUS OF TOLERANCE 9786 W PICO BLVD, LA, 90035	632 - F4
NATURAL HIST MUS OF LA CO 900 EXPOSITION BLVD, LA, 90037	674 - A1
NEFF HOME 14300 SAN CRISTOBAL DR, LMRD, 90638	737 - E3
NETHERCUTT MUS, THE 15200 BLEDSOE ST, LA, 91342	481 - H4
NORTON SIMON MUS OF ART 411 W COLORADO BLVD, PAS, 91103	565 - G4
OLINDA HIST MUS 4025 SANTE FE RD, BREA, 92823	709 - J6
ORTEGA-VIEARE ADOBE 428 S MISSION DR, SGBL, 91776	596 - D4
PACIFIC ASIA MUS 46 N LOS ROBLES AV, PAS, 91101	565 - J4
PAGE MUS AT LA BREA TAR PITS 5801 WILSHIRE BLVD, LA, 90036	633 - C2
PALMDALE PLANT 42 HERITAGE-AIRPARK 2041 AVE P, PMDL, 93550	4196 - D4
PALOS VERDES ART CTR 5504 CRESTRIDGE RD, RPV, 90275	823 - A1
PASADENA HIST MUS 470 W WALNUT ST, PAS, 91103	565 - G4
PETERSEN AUTOMOTIVE MUS 6060 WILSHIRE BLVD, LA, 90036	633 - B2
PETTERSON MUS OF INTERCULTURAL-ART 730 PLYMOUTH RD, CLAR, 91711	601 - C3
RANCHO LOS CERRITOS HIST SITE 4600 N VIRGINIA RD, Bxby, 90807	765 - C5
SKIRBALL CULTURAL CTR & MUS 2701 N SEPULVEDA BLVD, Brwd, 90049	591 - F1
SOUTHWEST MUS 234 MUSEUM DR, LA, 90065	595 - B4
SPROUL MUS 12203 SPROUL ST, NRWK, 90650	736 - J2
SS LANE VICTORY MEM MUS BERTH 94, SPed, 90731	824 - D4
TRAVELTOWN MUS 5200 ZOO DR, LFlz, 90027	563 - H4
WESTERN MUS OF FLIGHT 3315 AIRPORT DR, TOR, 90505	793 - E3
WORKMAN & TEMPLE HOMESTEAD MUS 15415 DON JULIAN RD, INDS, 91745	678 - C1

OPEN SPACE

FEATURE NAME / Address City, ZIP Code	PAGE-GRID
AGNES, SHEILA NATURE PRESERVE,-LA	562 - B7
ALPINE BUTTE WILDLIFE-SANCTUARY, LACo	4198 - J2
ANTONOVICH, MICHAEL D OPEN-SPACE, StvR	4640 - C5
ARBORETUM OF LOS ANGELES-COUNTY, THE, ARCD	566 - J5
BAILEY CANYON WILDERNESS PK, -SMAD	536 - J7
BELL CANYON OPEN SPACE, LA	529 - C3
BIG ROCK CREEK WILDLIFE-SANCTUARY, PMDL	4198 - F2
CANYON, GEORGE F OPEN SPACE, -RHE	793 - G7

FEATURE NAME	Address City, ZIP Code	PAGE-GRID
CHATSWORTH RESERVOIR NATURE-PRESERVE, LA		499 - E7
CLAREMONT HILLS WILDERNESS PK,-CLAR		571 - F1
COLD CREEK CANYON PRESERVE, -LACo		589 - E6
CUCAMONGA WILDERNESS, SBdC-(SEE PAGE 4651)		4732 - H7
DEFOREST WETLANDS, NLB		765 - C3
DEUKMEJIAN WILDERNESS PK, -GLDL		504 - E3
DUNSTER, JACK MARINE-BIOLOGICAL RSRVE, LBCH		826 - D1
GARDENA WILLOWS WETLAND, GAR		734 - A7
GOLDEN SHORE MARINE BIOLOGICAL-RSRVE, LBCH		825 - C1
HILTON OPEN SPACE, Brwd		591 - D6
JACKRABBIT FLATS WILDLIFE-SANCTUARY, Pear		4288 - F5
MADRONA MARSH NATURE PRESERVE,-TOR		763 - E7
POINT DUME STATE PRESERVE, -MAL		667 - E4
PRIME DESERT WOODLANDS, LAN		4105 - A3
SADDLETREE OPEN SPACE, LACo		4641 - G7
SAN GABRIEL WILDERNESS AREA, -LACo		4649 - A6
SEAL BEACH NATL WILDLIFE-REFUGE, SLB		826 - J4
SEPULVEDA BASIN WILDLIFE AREA,-Enc		561 - G1
SEPULVEDA PASS OPEN SPACE, -BelA		591 - F2
TREBEK OPEN SPACE, LA		593 - B2
WARD, ROBERT E NATURE-PRESERVE, FUL		738 - E3
WARNACK NATURE PK, PMDL		4194 - G3
WILDLIFE SANCTUARY, Pear		4379 - B5

OTHER

FEATURE NAME	Address City, ZIP Code	PAGE-GRID
20TH CENTURY FOX STUDIO	10201 W PICO BLVD, CenC, 90067	632 - F4
ABC CENTRAL SERVICES	NORWALK BLVD & CUESTA DR, CRTS, 90703	736 - J6
ABC TELEVISION CTR	4151 PROSPECT AV, LFlz, 90027	594 - B4
AMERICAN FILM INSTITUTE	2021 N WESTERN AV, LA, 90068	593 - H3
ANGELS GATE LIGHTHOUSE	ANGELS GATE, SPed, 90731	854 - F2
AQUARIUM OF THE PACIFIC	100 AQUARIUM WY, LBCH, 90802	825 - D1
ARBORETUM OF LOS ANGELES-COUNTY, THE	301 N BALDWIN AV, ARCD, 91007	567 - A5
ATLANTIC RICHFIELD CO	PIER C ST, LBCH, 90813	795 - B7
ATLANTIC RICHFIELD MARINE DEPT	PIER B ST & EDISON AV, LBCH, 90813	795 - A7
BA STUDIOS THE LOT	1041 N FORMOSA AV, LA, 90046	593 - D6
BOYS & GIRLS CLUB OF BUENA PARK	7758 KNOTT AV, BPK, 90620	767 - G3
BRAILLE INSTITUTE	741 N VERMONT AV, LA, 90029	594 - A6
BRIDGE TO NOWHERE-(SEE PAGE 4649)	ANGELES NATIONAL FOREST, LACo	4730 - J5
CABRILLO MARINE AQUARIUM	3720 STEPHEN M WHITE DR, SPed, 90731	854 - C2
CALAMIGOS RANCH (PRIVATE)	327 S LATIGO CANYON RD, LACo, 90265	587 - D6
CAL STATE UNIV BOAT HOUSE	SMUGGLERS CV, LBCH, 90803	826 - C1
CAMP BLOOMFIELD	MULHOLLAND HWY, LACo, 90265	625 - J2
CAMP KILPATRICK	427 ENCINAL CANYON RD, LACo, 90265	587 - B6
CAMP MILLER	433 ENCINAL CANYON RD, LACo, 90265	587 - B6
CAPITOL RECORDS TOWER	1750 N VINE ST, Hlwd, 90028	593 - F4
CATALINA CASINO	100 SAINT CATHERINE WY, AVA, 90704	5923 - H3
CATHEDRAL OF OUR LADY OF THE-ANGELS	555 W TEMPLE ST, LA, 90012	634 - F3
CBS RADIO & TV	6121 W SUNSET BLVD, Hlwd, 90028	593 - F4
CBS STUDIO CTR	4024 RADFORD AV, LA, 91604	562 - H5
CBS TELEVISION CITY	7800 BEVERLY BLVD, LA, 90036	633 - B1
CTR FOR MOTION PICTURE STUDY	333 S LA CIENEGA BLVD, BHLS, 90211	632 - J3
COLUMBIA MEM SPACE LEARNING CTR	LAKEWOOD BLVD, DWNY, 90242	706 - B7
COOPER BLDG, THE	860 S LOS ANGELES ST, LA, 90014	634 - F5
DISNEY STUDIOS	500 S BUENA VISTA ST, BURB, 91521	563 - F3
DRY GULCH RANCH	12420 YELLOW HILL RD, VeCo, 90265	625 - G1
EATON CANYON NATURE CTR	1750 N ALTADENA DR, PAS, 91107	536 - E7
FARMERS MARKET	6333 W 3RD ST, LA, 90036	633 - B1
FISHERMANS VILLAGE	13755 FIJI WY, MdlR, 90292	702 - B1
FLOAT CONSTRUCTION BLDG	SECO ST & ROSEMONT AV, PAS, 91103	565 - F3
FRYMAN CANYON OVERLOOK	MULHOLLAND DR & ALLENWOOD RD, LA, 91604	592 - H1
FUNLAND	525 AVE P-4, PMDL, 93551	4195 - H5
GAMBLE HOUSE	4 WESTMORELAND PL, PAS, 91103	565 - F4
GARVEY RANCH OBSERVATORY	751 S ORANGE AV, MONP, 91755	636 - D3
GOODYEAR AIRSHIP OPERATIONS CTR	19200 S MAIN ST, CRSN, 90746	764 - C3
GRAND CENTRAL MARKET	317 S BROADWAY, LA, 90013	634 - F4
GREAT WESTERN FORUM	W MANCHESTER BL & PRAIRIE AV, ING, 90301	703 - E4
GREYSTONE MANSION	501 N DOHENY RD, BHLS, 90210	592 - F5
GRIFFITH OBSERVATORY	2800 E OBSERVATORY RD, LFlz, 90027	593 - J2
GROVE OVERLOOK, THE	MULHOLLAND DR & ELVIDO DR, Brwd, 90049	561 - E7
GROVE, THE	6333 W 3RD ST, LA, 90036	633 - B1
HATHAWAY HOME (SEE PAGE 4643)	GOLD CREEK RD & DE MILLE RD, LACo, 91342	4723 - F1
HENSEL, CATHY GYMNASIUM &-YOUTH CTR	236 S TAYLOR AV, MTBL, 90640	676 - D2
HOLLYWOOD BLVD WALK OF FAME	HOLLYWOOD BLVD, Hlwd, 90028	593 - E4
HOLLYWOOD PALLADIUM	6215 W SUNSET BLVD, Hlwd, 90028	593 - F4
HOLLYWOOD SIGN	MT LEE DR, LA, 90068	563 - F7
HOME DEPOT CTR	18400 AVALON BLVD, CRSN, 90747	764 - E1
HUGHES RESEARCH LABORATORIES	3011 MALIBU CANYON RD, MAL, 90265	628 - J6
HUNTINGTON, THE	1151 OXFORD RD, SMRO, 91108	566 - C7
INDEPENDENCE HALL	8039 BEACH BLVD, BPK, 90620	767 - J4
INDUSTRY HILLS EQUESTRIAN CTR	16000 TEMPLE AV, INDS, 91744	638 - F6
JAPANESE CULTURAL INSTITUTE	1964 W 162ND ST, GAR, 90247	733 - H6
JAPANESE FISHERMANS MEM	SEASIDE AV, SPed, 90731	824 - E6
JAPANESE GARDEN	6100 WOODLEY AV, Enc, 91436	531 - F7
JET PROPULSION LAB	4800 OAK GROVE DR, LCF, 91011	535 - E4
KELLOGG ARABIAN HORSE CTR	KELLOGG DR, POM, 91768	640 - B2
KTLA TELEVISION	5800 W SUNSET BLVD, Hlwd, 90028	593 - G5
LA BREA TAR PITS	5801 WILSHIRE BLVD, LA, 90036	633 - C2
LONG BEACH ENTRANCE EAST LIGHT	QUEENS GATE, LBCH, 90802	825 - F7
LONG BEACH HARBOR LIGHT STA	QUEENS GATE, LBCH, 90802	825 - E7
LA ENTRANCE EAST LIGHT	ANGELS GATE, SPed, 90731	854 - G2
LOS ANGELES EQUESTRIAN CTR	480 RIVERSIDE DR, LFlz, 90027	563 - H3
LOS ANGELES RIVER CTR AND-GARDENS	570 W AVE 26, LA, 90065	594 - J6
LOS ANGELES ZOO	5333 ZOO DR, LFlz, 90027	564 - A4
LOWER BEL AIR BAY CLUB	16801 PACIFIC COAST HWY, PacP, 90272	630 - H6
MALIBU PIER	23000 PACIFIC COAST HWY, MAL, 90265	629 - B7
MANHATTAN BEACH CC	1330 PARK VIEW AV, MANB, 90266	732 - H4
MARINE STADIUM	5255 APPIAN WY, LBCH, 90803	826 - C1
MASONIC HOME OF CALIFORNIA	1650 OLD BADILLO ST, COV, 91724	599 - F5
MCKINLEY HOME FOR BOYS	762 W CYPRESS AV, SDMS, 91773	600 - A4
MOBIL OIL CO	EARLE ST, SPed, 90731	824 - E4
MORMON TEMPLE	10777 SANTA MONICA BLVD, Wwd, 90024	632 - C4
MOUNT WILSON OBSERVATORY-(SEE PAGE 505)	MOUNT WILSON - RED BOX RD, LACo	506 - J7
MUSCLE BEACH	OCEAN FRONT WK & 17TH AV, Ven, 90291	671 - G6
NBC STUDIOS	3000 W ALAMEDA AV, BURB, 91523	563 - E4
PARAMOUNT STUDIOS	5555 MELROSE AV, LA, 90038	593 - G6
PASADENA CTR	300 E GREEN ST, PAS, 91101	565 - J5
PASADENA CONFERENCE CTR	300 E GREEN ST, PAS, 91101	565 - J5
POINT VICENTE INTERPRETIVE CTR	31501 PALOS VERDES DR W, RPV, 90275	822 - F4
POINT VICENTE LIGHTHOUSE	31501 PALOS VERDES DR W, RPV, 90275	822 - F5
PORTS O CALL VILLAGE	590 SAMPSON WY, SPed, 90731	824 - C6
POWERINE OIL CO	PIER C ST, LBCH, 90813	795 - B7
RALEIGH STUDIOS HOLLYWOOD	5300 MELROSE AV, LA, 90004	593 - G7
RALEIGH STUDIOS MANHATTAN BEACH	1600 ROSECRANS AV, MANB, 90266	732 - J4
RAMONA CONVENT	W GLENDON WY & BENITO AV, ALH, 91803	595 - J7
RANCHO SAN ANTONIO BOYS TOWN	21000 PLUMMER ST, Chat, 91311	500 - B6
RIPLEYS BELIEVE IT OR NOT MUS	7850 BEACH BLVD, BPK, 90620	767 - H3
ROBERTS, ELEANOR GREEN AQUATIC-CTR	4526 W PICO BLVD, LA, 90019	633 - E4
SAN DIMAS CANYON NATURE CTR	1628 SYCAMORE CANYON RD, SDMS, 91773	570 - D6
SANTA CATALINA ISLAND-INTERPRETIVE CTR	1202 AVALON CANYON RD, AVA, 90704	5923 - G5
SANTA YNEZ RESERVOIR	SANTA YNEZ RD, PacP, 90272	630 - E1
SERRA RETREAT	3401 SERRA RD, MAL, 90265	629 - A5
SIMONS, GRACE E LODGE	1025 ELYSIAN PARK DR, Echo, 90026	594 - F6
SONY PICTURE STUDIOS	10202 W WASHINGTON BLVD, CULC, 90232	672 - F2
SPORTS FISHING LANDING	555 PICO AV, LBCH, 90813	795 - B7
STOUGH CANYON NATURE CTR	STOUGH CANYON AV, BURB, 91504	533 - H2
TERMINAL MARKET	E 7TH ST & TERMINAL ST, LA, 90021	634 - G6
TOPANGA COMM HOUSE	1440 N TOPANGA CANYON BLVD, Top, 90290	590 - C3
TORRANCE CULTURAL ARTS CTR	3320 CIVIC CENTER DR, TOR, 90503	763 - E5
TRIPPET RANCH	COLINA ENTRADA RD, Top, 90290	590 - C5
UCLA BOAT HOUSE	FIJI WY, MdlR, 90292	702 - B1
UCLA BOTANICAL GARDENS	405 HILGARD AV, LA, 90095	632 - B2
UNIVERSAL CITYWALK	100 UNIVERSAL CITYWALK DR, Univ, 91608	563 - C6
UNIVERSAL STUDIOS	100 UNIVERSAL CITY PZ, Univ, 91608	563 - C6
UPPER BEL AIR BAY CLUB	16801 PACIFIC COAST HWY, PacP, 90272	630 - H6
USC BOAT HOUSE	YACHT ST, Wilm, 90744	824 - F1
VENICE BEACH BOARDWALK	OCEAN FRONT WK, Ven, 90291	671 - G6
VENICE PAVILION	WINDWARD AV & OCEAN FRONT WK, Ven, 90291	671 - G6
VENICE SKILLS CTR	611 5TH AV, Ven, 90291	671 - G5
WARNER BROS RANCH	3701 OAK AV, BURB, 91505	563 - D3
WARNER BROS STUDIOS	4000 WARNER BLVD, BURB, 91522	563 - E4
WAYFARERS CHAPEL	5755 PALOS VERDES DR S, RPV, 90275	823 - A4
WESTLAKE YACHT CLUB	32123 W LINDERO CANYON RD, WLKV, 91361	557 - C7
WEST VALLEY ADULT OCC TRAINING-CTR	6200 WINNETKA AV, WdHl, 91367	530 - E7
WHITTIER NARROWS NATURE CTR	1000 DURFEE AV, LACo, 90660	637 - C6
WORLD CRUISE CTR	FRONT ST, SPed, 90731	824 - C4
WORLD OIL CO	PIER C ST, LBCH, 90813	795 - B7
WRIGLEY BOTANICAL GARDENS	MEMORIAL RD, AVA, 90704	5923 - F6
YMCA	1930 FOOTHILL BLVD, LCF, 91011	534 - J3
YMCA	2900 W SEPULVEDA BLVD, TOR, 90505	763 - E7
YMCA	6840 FOOTHILL BLVD, Tuj, 91042	504 - B5
YMCA	8015 S SEPULVEDA BLVD, Wch, 90045	702 - G2

PARK & RIDE

FEATURE NAME	Address City, ZIP Code	PAGE-GRID
ALPINE VILLAGE, LACo		764 - B4
ARTESIA, LA		764 - B1
ARTESIA STA, COMP		734 - J7
AVALON, LA		704 - D7
AVIATION, Wch		702 - J7
BADILLO/RAMONA, BALD		598 - D5
BALDWIN PARK METROLINK, BALD		598 - C5
BAPTIST, GAR		733 - J6
BREA, BREA		709 - D6
BURBANK METROLINK, BURB		533 - G7
CARSON, LACo		764 - B6
CENTURY-HARBOR JNTN, LA		704 - C7
CHATSWORTH, GrnH		501 - G3
CHATSWORTH METROLINK, Chat		500 - A4
CITADEL, CMRC		675 - H3
CITRUS COLLEGE, GLDR		569 - B5
CIVIC AUDITORIUM, SGBL		596 - D4
CLAREMONT METROLINK, CLAR		601 - D4
COMMERCE METROLINK, CMRC		676 - A5
COVINA METROLINK, COV		599 - B4
CRENSHAW, HAW		703 - F7
DEL AMO STA, RDom		765 - B4
DEL AMO TRANSIT CTR, TOR		763 - D6
DEL MAR, SGBL		596 - E7
DIAMOND BAR WEST, DBAR		640 - B6
EL SEGUNDO/NASH STA, ELSG		732 - H2
FAIRPLEX, POM		600 - E7
FIRST BAPTIST CHURCH, Wch		702 - H3
FIRST UNITED PRESBYTERIAN, -BALD		598 - B4
FULLERTON TRANS CTR, FUL		738 - H7
GAREY / RTE 10, POM		600 - J6
GLENDALE METROLINK, GLDL		594 - E1
GOLDEN VALLEY, Nwhl		4551 - G6
GRANADA HILLS MASONIC TEMPLE, -GrnH		501 - E1
GRAND AVE, GLDR		569 - D7
HARBOR PARK, Wilm		794 - C5
HAWTHORNE BLVD, HAW		703 - C6
HAYVENHURST, Enc		561 - E3
I-105 TERMINATION, NRWK		736 - E2
IMPERIAL STA, Wbrk		704 - H7
INDUSTRY METROLINK, INDS		679 - G2
KANAN RD (NW LOT), AGRH		558 - A5
KANAN RD (SE LOT), AGRH		558 - A6
KANAN RD (SW LOT), AGRH		558 - A6
LAKEWOOD BLVD, DWNY		736 - A2
LAKEWOOD WEST LOT, DWNY		706 - D2
LANCASTER, LAN		4105 - G3
LANCASTER, LAN		4105 - F2
LANCASTER, LAN		4016 - A5
LANCASTER METROLINK, LAN		4015 - H6
LANTERMAN, POM		640 - C5
LONE HILL, GLDR		569 - J7
LONG BEACH BLVD, LYN		705 - B7
LOWELL, GLDL		504 - D7
LUTHERAN, GrnH		501 - F3
MANCHESTER, LA		704 - B2
MANCHESTER, LA		704 - C2
MARINE STA, HAW		733 - A5
MLK TRANSIT CTR, COMP		734 - J4
MONROVIA, MNRO		567 - G6
MONTCLAIR TRANSCENTER, MTCL		601 - F3
NEWHALL EAST LOT, SCTA		4641 - C3
NEWHALL WEST LOT, SCTA		4641 - C3
NORTHRIDGE METROLINK, Nor		530 - H1
NORWALK/SANTA FE SPRINGS-TRANS, NRWK		737 - A1
OAK CREEK, SCTA		4641 - B2
PALMDALE - 434 AVE S, PMDL		4285 - H4
PALMDALE-AVE S, PMDL		4286 - A4
PARK & RIDE, GLDR		569 - E5
PASADENA, PAS		566 - E4
PATHFINDER RD, DBAR		679 - H5
PAXTON, LA		482 - E7
PEARBLOSSOM, PMDL		4376 - D1
PEARBLOSSOM, PMDL		4376 - C3
PENINSULA CTR, RHE		793 - A7
PLAZA AT WEST COVINA, WCOV		638 - F1
PORTER RANCH, Chat		500 - E2
PRINCESSA METROLINK, SCTA		4551 - G4
PUENTE HILLS MALL, INDS		678 - G4
RIVERTON, LA		563 - A6
ROSECRANS, LA		734 - B3
RTE 134 & 2, GLDL		564 - H5
RTE 170/OXNARD, LA		532 - G7
ST JOHNS PRSBYTRAN CHURCH, LA		632 - D7
SAINT PETER CLAVER, SIMI		499 - A1
SAN DIMAS, SDMS		600 - B6
SAN PEDRO, SPed		824 - B3
SAN PEDRO II, SPed		824 - C4
SANTA CLARITA, SCTA		4550 - J3
SEPULVEDA PASS, BelA		591 - G1
SLAUSON, LA		674 - C5
SOUTHBAY PAVILION, CRSN		764 - E5
SUNLAND K-MART, Sunl		503 - H3
SYLMAR METROLINK, LA		481 - J6
TOPANGA PLAZA, CanP		530 - A6
UNITED METHODIST CHURCH, COV		599 - A5
UNITED METHODIST CHURCH, WCOV		638 - J2
UNITED METHODIST, WAL		639 - F7
UNITED METHODIST, Tarz		561 - A2
VAN NUYS METROLINK, VanN		532 - A3
VERDUGO, LCF		534 - J3
VERMONT AV, LACo		704 - A7
VETERANS ADMIN, LACo		631 - J4
VIA VERDE, LACo		599 - H7
VINCENT GRADE METROLINK, PMDL		4376 - B5
WARDLOW STA, LBCH		795 - D1
WASHINGTON & FAIRFAX, LA		633 - A6
WEST COVINA VFW, WCOV		638 - C1
WHITTIER NARROWS, LACo		637 - B6
WILLOW STA, LBCH		795 - D3

PARKS & RECREATION

FEATURE NAME	Address City, ZIP Code	PAGE-GRID
7TH STREET PK, CHNO		641 - G7
10TH STREET PK, CHNO		641 - H7
14TH STREET PK, LBCH		795 - D6
38TH & NORMANDIE PK, LA		673 - J2
48TH STREET PK, LA		674 - B4
48TH STREET & 8TH AVENUE PK, -LA		673 - F4
109TH ST REC CTR, LA		704 - F6
ABALONE COVE SHORELINE PK, -RPV		822 - J5
ACACIA PK, ELSG		702 - D7
ACUNA PK, MTBL		636 - C7
ADAMS SQUARE MINI PK, GLDL		564 - G6
ADDAMS, JANE PK, LNDL		733 - C5
ADLENA PK, FUL		738 - D7
ADMIRAL KIDD PK, LBCH		795 - A4
ADMIRALTY PK, MdlR		672 - B6
ADVENTURE COUNTY PK, LACo		707 - D4
AIRPORT PK, SMCA		672 - A2
ALAMITOS PK, LBCH		826 - D4
ALBURTIS PK, ART		736 - G7
ALGIN SUTTON REC CTR, LA		704 - B3
ALHAMBRA PK, ALH		595 - J4
ALISO CANYON PK, GrnH		481 - A7
ALIZONDO DRIVE PK, WdHl		560 - A5
ALL AMERICAN PK, PRM		735 - H2
ALLENDALE PK, PAS		565 - J7
ALMANSOR PK, ALH		596 - C5
ALMA PK, SPed		824 - A7
ALMENDRA PK, SCTA		4550 - G5
ALONDRA COUNTY PK, LACo		733 - E6
ALPINE PK, LA		634 - G2
ALTA LOMA PK, TOR		793 - F6
ALTA VISTA PK, RBCH		762 - J6
ALVAREZ, HENRY MEM PK, Boyl		635 - C2
AMERIGE PK, FUL		738 - G7
AMIGO COUNTY PK, PRV		676 - J3
ANACONDA PK, WHIT		707 - F3
ANDERSON, GLEN PK, RBCH		733 - A6
ANDERSON PK, CRSN		764 - H3
ANDERSON PLGD, SPed		824 - C5
ANDRES PICO ADOBE PK, MsnH		501 - H2
ANDREWS PK, RBCH		762 - J1
ANGELES NATL FOREST, LACo		4279 - E2
ANGELS GATE PK, SPed		854 - B2
ANTELOPE VALLEY POPPY RESERVE-PK, LACo		3923 - A7
ANTONOVICH, MICHAEL D REGL PK-AT, Chat		480 - A5
APOLLO COUNTY PK, LAN		3924 - J6
APOLLO PK, DWNY		705 - H7
ARBOR, RAYMOND PK, SIGH		795 - G4
ARCADIA COUNTY PK, ARCD		567 - C5
ARCEO PK, ELMN		637 - C1
ARDMORE PLGD PK, LA		633 - J4
ARNOLD/ CYPRESS PK, CYP		767 - C5
AROMA PARKETTE, WCOV		639 - A3
AROVISTA PK, BREA		709 - A7
ARROYO PK, WAL		639 - D7
ARROYO PK, PAS		565 - F7
ARROYO SEQUIT, LACo		586 - D7
ARROYOSTOW PK, SIMI		499 - A3
ARTESIA PK, ART		766 - H2
ASHIYA PK, MTBL		636 - B7
ASHLAND PK, SMCA		671 - H3
ASHLEY, NORMAN PK, WAL		679 - D2
ASHWOOD PK, ING		703 - B3
ASILOMAR PK, PacP		630 - J6
ASMUS, JULIA RUSS PK, BGDN		705 - F3
ATHENS COUNTY PK, LACo		734 - C1
ATLANTIC BOULEVARD COUNTY PK, -ELA		635 - H7
ATLANTIC PLAZA PK, NLB		765 - E3
AUSTIN, AUBREY E JR PK, MdlR		702 - A2
AUTUMN HILL PK, CHLS		680 - J4
AVENUE T PK, Litl		4288 - B5
AVERILL PK, LA		823 - J6
AVIATION PK, RBCH		732 - J5
AVOCADO HEIGHTS COUNTY PK, -LACo		637 - J5
BAILEY CANYON PK, SMAD		566 - J1
BALBOA SPORTS CTR, Enc		531 - C7
BALDWIN HILLS RECREATION CTR, -LA		673 - B1
BALDWIN MINI PK, ELMN		597 - A7
BALDWIN STOCKER PK, ARCD		597 - B1
BALDY VIEW PK, UPL		601 - J2
BANDINI CANYON PK, SPed		824 - A4
BANDINI PK, CMRC		675 - F3
BANNING PK, Wilm		794 - E5
BARNARD WAY LINEAR PK, SMCA		671 - F4
BARNES MEM PK, MONP		636 - B3
BARNES PK, BALD		597 - H7
BARNSDALL PK, LFlz		593 - J4
BARRANCA PK, COV		599 - C6
BARRINGTON REC CTR, LACo		631 - H3
BASSETT COUNTY PK, LACo		637 - J3
BASSETT LITTLE LEAGUE PK, -BALD		638 - A1
BASTANCHURY PK, FUL		738 - D6
BAY SHORE PK, LBCH		826 - B3
BEACH PK, SMCA		671 - F4
BEARDSLEE PK, DUAR		568 - A7
BEAT, JOHN PK, BPK		767 - F7
BEE CANYON PK, GrnH		481 - C4
BEECHWOOD PK, FUL		738 - J2
BEGONIAS LANE PK, SCTA		4462 - F7
BEHRINGER PK, LMRD		737 - J3
BEILENSON, ANTHONY C PK, Enc		531 - D7
BEL AIRE PK, BURB		533 - G4
BELLA VISTA PK, MONP		636 - A6
BELL CANYON PK, CanP		529 - C5
BELLEVUE PK, Echo		594 - B6
BELL GARDENS VETERANS PK, -BGDN		705 - J1
BELLIS, GEORGE PK, BPK		737 - G7
BELL PK, GAR		733 - J4
BELMONT PLAZA PK, LBCH		826 - A2
BELVEDERE COUNTY PK, ELA		635 - G5
BENNETT, BERNIECE PK, WLKV		557 - D6
BETHUNE, MARY MCCLEOD COUNTY-PK, Flor		674 - F6
BETTENCOURT PK, LPMA		767 - C2

FEATURE NAME Address City, ZIP Code	PAGE-GRID
BEVERLY GARDENS PK, BHLS	592 - G7
BEVERLY GLEN PK, LA	592 - B2
BEYER PK, THO	557 - A1
BICENTENNIAL PK, HAW	733 - E2
BICENTENNIAL PK, HMB	762 - H3
BICENTENNIAL PK, ARCD	597 - E1
BICKNELL PK, MTBL	636 - B7
BIG LEAGUE DREAMS SPORTSPLEX, - WCOV	638 - J4
BIG TREE PK, GLDR	569 - E6
BIRDCAGE PK, LBCH	766 - E6
BISCAILUZ PK, LKWD	765 - H3
BIXBY KNOLLS PK, Bxby	765 - F5
BIXBY PK, LBCH	825 - G1
BLACK, DARYLE W MEM PK, LBCH	795 - E4
BLAIR HILLS PK, CULC	672 - J2
BLAISDELL PK, CLAR	601 - D4
BLANCO PK, CULC	672 - H5
BLEVINS, BILL COUNTY PK, RowH	679 - D7
BLOOMFIELD PK, LKWD	766 - H5
BLUFF PK, LBCH	825 - H1
BLUFFS PK, MAL	628 - H7
BLUFFTOP PK, SunB	826 - J7
BODGER COUNTY PK, LACo	733 - F4
BOGDANOVICH PK, LA	823 - H6
BOLIVAR, SIMON PK, LKWD	765 - J4
BONELLI, FRANK G REGL COUNT, - SDMS	600 - C5
BONITA PK, ARCD	567 - D5
BOUQUET CANYON PK, SCTA	4461 - C5
BOUTON CREEK PK, LBCH	796 - B5
BOYER, MAE PK, VeCo	558 - A2
BOYAR, MAE PK, LKWD	766 - E4
BOYAR, MAE REC CTR, CanP	529 - E6
BOYLE HEIGHTS SPORTS CTR PK, - LA	635 - A6
BRACE CANYON PK, BURB	533 - E3
BRAND PK, MsnH	501 - J2
BRAND PK, GLDL	534 - C5
BRANFORD PK, Pcma	502 - D7
BRAUDE, MARVIN GATEWAY PK, - WdHl	560 - E7
BREA DAM REC AREA, FUL	738 - H3
BRENNER, CARL PK, BPK	767 - E2
BRENNER PK, PAS	565 - G2
BRIARWOOD PK, BelA	592 - A2
BRIDGEPORT PK, SCTA	4550 - G2
BRIGGS, HOMER PK, ONT	641 - J4
BRISTOW PK, CMRC	675 - F2
BROADWAY PK, WHIT	677 - C5
BROOKHAVEN PK, CRTS	767 - B1
BROOKSHIRE CHILDRENS PK, DWNY	706 - A7
BROOKSIDE PK, PAS	565 - F3
BROWNS CREEK PK - PRIVATE, - Chat	480 - B7
BRUCES BEACH PK, MANB	732 - E5
BUENA VISTA PK, BURB	563 - E4
BURKE HERITAGE PK, ALH	595 - J4
BURNS, ROBERT PK, LA	593 - G7
BURRELL/MACDONALD PK, COMP	734 - F6
BURTON, THOMAS S COUNTY PK, - HacH	678 - D4
BUTTERFIELD PK, WAL	679 - D1
CABRILLO PK, UPL	601 - H2
CAHUILLA PK, CLAR	571 - C7
CALABASAS CREEKSIDE PK, CALB	559 - F7
CALABASAS PK LAND, CALB	558 - F7
CALAS PK, CRSN	764 - F7
CALBRISAS PK, SIGH	795 - E3
CALIFORNIA REC CTR PK, LBCH	795 - F5
CAMERON PK, WCOV	638 - H1
CAMINO GROVE PK, ARCD	567 - E7
CAMPANELLA COUNTY PK, LACo	734 - E4
CAMP LITTLE BEAR PK, BELL	675 - C7
CANDLEVERDE PK, LKWD	766 - D3
CANDY CANE PK, ELSG	732 - D2
CANYON COUNTRY PK, SCTA	4552 - A2
CANYON OAKS PK, WLKV	557 - F3
CANYON PK, AZU	568 - H4
CARAWAY PK, SCTA	4461 - B5
CARBON CANYON REGL PK, BREA	709 - J7
CAREY RANCH PK, LA	481 - H6
CARLSON, DR PAUL MEM PK, CULC	672 - G2
CARNATION PK, LYN	705 - A6
CAROUSEL PK, SMCA	671 - E3
CARRIAGE CREST PK, CRSN	794 - C2
CARRILLO, LEO STATE PK, LACo	625 - J4
CARR PK, GLDL	564 - H5
CARSON, JOHNNY PK, BURB	563 - F4
CARSON PK, CRSN	764 - C6
CARTER, WHIT PK, LAN	4015 - H3
CARTHAY CIRCLE PK, LA	633 - A2
CARUTHERS, RUTH R PK, BLF	736 - D6
CARVER, GEORGE W COUNTY PK, - Wbrk	704 - F7
CASCADES PK, MONP	636 - A3
CASTAIC COUNTY SPORTS COMPLEX,- Cstc	4459 - H1
CASTAIC LAKE STATE REC AREA, - Cstc	4369 - G3
CASTLE PEAK PK, LA	529 - D4
CEDAR MINI PK, GLDL	564 - F5
CENTENNIAL HERITAGE PK, GLDR	569 - F6
CENTENNIAL PK, POM	641 - A2
CENTER PK, ING	703 - E6
CENTRAL AVENUE JAZZ PK, LA	674 - E3
CENTRAL LIBRARY PK, LA	634 - E4
CENTRAL PK, WHIT	677 - D6
CENTRAL PK, SCTA	4461 - A7

FEATURE NAME Address City, ZIP Code	PAGE-GRID
CENTRAL PK, LPMA	767 - D3
CENTRAL REC CTR, LA	674 - F1
CERRITOS PK EAST, CRTS	737 - B6
CERRITOS REGL COUNTY PK, CRTS	767 - A3
CERRITOS PK, GLDL	594 - E1
CESAR CHAVEZ PK, COMP	735 - A2
CHACE, BURTON PK, MdlR	672 - B7
CHAFEE, ROGER PK, FUL	738 - E4
CHALLENGER PK, LVRN	600 - F3
CHANNEL VIEW PK, LBCH	796 - E7
CHAPARRAL PK, CLAR	571 - E7
CHAPARRAL PK, VeCo	557 - J2
CHARMLEE WILDERNESS PK, MAL	626 - E5
CHARTER OAK PK, LACo	599 - F3
CHASE PK, LA	529 - H2
CHATSWORTH OAKS PK, Chat	499 - G6
CHATSWORTH PK NORTH, Chat	499 - J3
CHAVEZ, CESAR E PK, LBCH	795 - C7
CHAVEZ, CESAR PK, POM	640 - C2
CHAVEZ, CESAR PK, SGAT	704 - J3
CHEESEBORO CANYON, VeCo	558 - E3
CHERRY AVENUE PK, Bxby	765 - G5
CHERRY COVE PK, LKWD	765 - G3
CHESEBROUGH COUNTY PK, SCTA	4460 - G5
CHESS PK, GLDL	564 - E4
CHESS PK, SMCA	671 - E3
CHESTERFIELD SQUARE, LA	673 - H5
CHET HOLIFIELD PK, MTBL	676 - C4
CHEVIOT HILLS PARK & REC CTR, - LA	632 - E5
CHEVY CHASE PK, LA	564 - D6
CHINO HILLS STATE PK, OrCo	710 - E7
CHITTICK FIELD PK, LBCH	795 - G4
CHUMASH PK, AGRH	558 - B5
CIRCLE J RANCH PK, SCTA	4550 - H5
CIRCLE PK, ING	703 - G2
CIRCLE X RANCH, VeCo	586 - A3
CITY TERRACE COUNTY PK, City	635 - E4
CIVIC CTR ATHLETIC FIELD, - ARCD	567 - C5
CIVIC CTR PK, COV	599 - B5
CIVIC CTR PK, SDMS	600 - C2
CIVIC CTR PK, HNTP	675 - A7
CLARA PARK-SENATOR BILL GREENE- SPORTS, CDHY	705 - E1
CLARK COMM CTR, GLDL	504 - E6
CLARKDALE PK, HGDN	766 - H6
CLARK PK, HMB	762 - H2
CLARK, RALPH B REGL PK, BPK	738 - B4
CLELAND AVENUE BICENTENNIAL- PK, HiPk	595 - A2
CLOVERCLIFF PK, PVE	792 - G7
CLOVER PK, SMCA	671 - J2
COHASSET MELBA PK, CanP	529 - F4
COLDWATER CANYON PK, LA	592 - F1
COLDWATER CANYON PK, BHLS	592 - E6
COLLEGE ESTATES PK, LBCH	796 - F6
COLLEGE PK, CLAR	601 - D4
COLONNADE, THE, LBCH	826 - C3
COLORADO LAGOON PK, LBCH	796 - B7
COLUMBIA REGL PK, TOR	763 - D2
COMM CTR PK, RSMD	596 - H7
COMM PK, HNTP	675 - B7
CONSTITUTION PK, LHB	708 - F5
CONSTITUTION PK, BLF	736 - A7
CONSTITUTION PK, ELSG	702 - G7
COOLIDGE PK, NLB	735 - D7
COOMBS PK, CULC	672 - G3
CORAL RIDGE PK, CHLS	680 - J6
CORONA PK, LHB	708 - D6
CORONEL PLAZA, PVE	792 - H6
CORRIGANVILLE PK, SIMI	499 - E3
CORTEZ PK, WCOV	639 - B1
COUNTRY CROSSING PK, POM	640 - E5
COUNTRY HILLS PK, BREA	709 - E7
COUNTRY HOLLOW PK, WAL	639 - F4
COUNTRY PK, DBAR	680 - B5
COUNTRYWOOD COUNTY PK, HacH	678 - E5
COUNTY OWNED LAND, Chat	499 - J2
COUNTY PK LAND, LACo	588 - G7
COURSON, MELVILLE J PK, PMDL	4286 - B1
COVINA PK, COV	599 - A5
COYOTE HILLS PK, FUL	738 - C3
CRAWFORD PK, DWNY	705 - H3
CREEK PK, LMRD	707 - H7
CREEKSIDE PK, WAL	639 - C6
CREEKVIEW PK, SCTA	4641 - A1
CRESCENTA VALLEY COUNTY PK, - GLDL	534 - D1
CRESCENT BAY PK, SMCA	671 - E4
CRESTWOOD HILLS PK, Brwd	591 - E7
CROSSROADS PK, CHLS	680 - J5
CUDAHY PK, CDHY	705 - F2
CULVER CITY PK, CULC	672 - H2
CULVER SLAUSON PK, LA	672 - F5
CULVER WEST PK, CULC	672 - C5
CYPRESS PK, LA	594 - J5
CZULEGER PK, RBCH	762 - H5
DAISY AVENUE GREENBELT, LBCH	795 - C4
DALTON COUNTY PK, LACo	569 - C7
DANIELS FIELD SPORTS CTR, - SPed	824 - B6
DAPPLEGRAY PK, RHE	793 - F7
DARBY PK, ING	703 - F3
DARWELL PK, BGDN	705 - H1
DAVENPORT, ED POPS PK, NLB	765 - H2
DAVIS, ZELA PK, HAW	733 - E2
DAWSON AVENUE PK, GLDR	569 - E7
DEARBORN PK, Nor	501 - C7

FEATURE NAME Address City, ZIP Code	PAGE-GRID
DEBS, ERNEST E REGL PK, LA	595 - C4
DEBS PK, BELL	675 - C7
DECKER CANYON YOUTH CAMP, MAL	626 - C5
DEERVALE PK, Shrm	561 - J6
DEFENDERS PK, PAS	565 - G5
DE FOREST PK, NLB	765 - D1
DEL AIRE COUNTY PK, LACo	733 - A1
DEL AMO PK, CRSN	764 - E4
DELANO PK, VanN	531 - H7
DEL CERRO PK, RPV	823 - B3
DEL NORTE PK, WCOV	598 - F6
DE LONGPRE PK, Hlwd	593 - E5
DEL REY LAGOON PK, PdlR	702 - A2
DELTHORNE PK, TOR	763 - E4
DEL VALLE COUNTY PK, Cstc	4369 - F7
DE NEVE SQUARE, BelA	592 - C7
DENKER REC CTR, LA	673 - J1
DENNIS THE MENACE PK, DWNY	706 - D3
DE PORTOLA PK, TOR	793 - E4
DESCANSO GARDENS, LCF	534 - J4
DESCANSO PK, LHB	708 - G5
DESCANSO PK, TOR	763 - G1
DESERT SANDS PK, PMDL	4195 - J6
DEVILS PUNCHBOWL COUNTY PK, - LACo (SEE PAGE 4470)	4559 - F2
DEVONWOOD PK, MsnH	501 - J4
DEXTER COUNTY PK, LACo	482 - J5
DILLS, RALPH C PK, PRM	735 - E3
DISCOVERY WELL PK, SIGH	795 - H3
DIXIE CANYON PK, Shrm	562 - D7
DOLPHIN PK, CRSN	764 - G5
DOMINGUEZ PK, RBCH	763 - A3
DOMINGUEZ PK, CRSN	765 - A5
DOUGLAS PK, SMCA	631 - G6
DOUGLAS PK, LBCH	766 - B7
DOWNEY PLGD, LA	634 - J1
DRAKE PK, LBCH	795 - C6
DUARTE PK, DUAR	568 - A5
DUARTE SPORTS PK, DUAR	568 - A5
DUNSMORE PK, GLDL	504 - E6
EAGLE ROCK HILLSIDE PK, Eagl	565 - B4
EAGLE ROCK REC CTR, Eagl	565 - D5
EARTHWALK PK, BURB	533 - F5
EAST GRAMERCY PK, LA	633 - H6
EAST RANCHO DOMINGUEZ CO PK, - RDom	735 - D4
EASTSIDE PK, LAN	4016 - A5
EASTVIEW PK, RPV	823 - J2
EAST VILLAGE ARTS PK, LBCH	825 - E1
EAST WILMINGTON GREENBELT, - Wilm	794 - G5
EAST WILMINGTON PK, Wilm	794 - G4
EATON BLANCHE PK, PAS	566 - G5
EATON CANYON COUNTY PK, LACo	536 - E6
ECHO PK, Echo	594 - E7
ECOLOGY PK, CRTS	736 - F7
EDDIE PK, SPAS	595 - J3
EDDLESTON PK, Nor	480 - J7
EDER PARK, A, BELL	675 - D6
EDISON PK, SLB	796 - F6
EDISON TRAILS PK, MONP	636 - B4
EDNA PK, COV	599 - B4
EISENHOWER PK, ARCD	567 - D4
EISENHOWER PK, SLB	826 - E4
EL BARRIO PK, CLAR	601 - F3
EL CARISO REGL COUNTY PK, LA	482 - D2
EL CENTRO LIONS PK, LHB	708 - E5
ELDER, GEORGE E PK, MONP	636 - B5
EL DORADO NATURE CTR PK, LBCH	796 - G2
EL DORADO PK, LAN	4016 - A6
EL DORADO PK WEST, LBCH	796 - F2
EL DORADO REGL PK, LBCH	766 - G7
EL ESCORPION PK, CanP	529 - C5
ELK MINI PK, GLDL	564 - F5
ELLERMAN PK, COMP	734 - H6
EL MARINO PK, CULC	672 - G5
EL NIDO PK, TOR	763 - C2
EL PARQUE DE LA PAZ, THO	557 - A2
EL PASEO DE CAHUENGA PK, LA	563 - C7
EL RANCHO VERDE PK, LPMA	767 - C3
EL RETIRO PK, TOR	793 - A2
EL SEGUNDO ATHLETIC FIELDS, - ELSG	732 - H1
EL SEGUNDO DOG PK, ELSG	702 - F7
EL SERENO NORTH PK, LA	595 - F4
EL SERENO REC CTR, LA	595 - E7
ELYRIA CANYON PK, LA	594 - J4
ELYSIAN PK, LA	594 - G6
ELYSIAN PK, Echo	634 - F1
ELYSIAN VALLEY PK, LA	594 - F4
ELYSIAN VALLEY REC CTR, LA	594 - F4
EMERALD ISLE PK, GLDL	535 - B7
EMERALD PK, LVRN	570 - G7
EMERY PK, ALH	595 - H6
EMERY PK, FUL	738 - B5
EMMAUS PK, SCTA	4551 - B7
ENCANTO PK, DUAR	568 - E4
ENCINO PK, Enc	561 - D3
ENGLISH CREEK PK, CHLS	680 - J4
ENGLISH SPRINGS PK, CHLS	680 - J3
ENTERPRISE COUNTY PK, Wbrk	734 - E2
ENTRADERO PK, TOR	763 - A3
ESSEX, DARRELL PK, CYP	767 - C7
ESSEX PK, MTCL	641 - E2
ESTELI PK, LHB	708 - H4
EUCALYPTUS PK, HAW	733 - B1
EVENSTAR PK, THO	557 - A5
EVERETT PK, Echo	634 - F1
EVERGREEN PK, CYP	767 - C6

FEATURE NAME Address City, ZIP Code	PAGE-GRID
EVERGREEN REC CTR, Boyl	635 - B5
EXPOSITION PK, LA	674 - A2
FAIRVIEW AVENUE PK, ARCD	567 - A7
FEHLHABERHOUK PK, Tuj	504 - C6
FERNANGELES PK, SunV	502 - F7
FERN DRIVE PK, FUL	738 - E6
FIJI GATEWAY PK, MdlR	672 - C7
FINKBINER PK, GLDR	569 - E5
FINN, HOWARD PK, Tuj	503 - J3
FIRESTONE BOY SCOUT RESV, - LACo	709 - H2
FISHER, JULIAN PK, MNRO	567 - H5
FLETCHER PK, ELMN	637 - B1
FOOTHILL PK, SIMI	499 - D2
FORD, JOHN ANSON PK, BGDN	705 - H2
FORD PK, FUL	738 - G7
FOREST AVENUE PK, ARCD	567 - C4
FOREST COVE PK, AGRH	557 - H5
FORT LOTS OF FUN PK, HMB	762 - H2
FOSSIL RIDGE PK, Shrm	562 - B6
FOUNDERS MEM PK, WHIT	677 - B5
FOUNDERS PK, RPV	823 - D6
FOUNDERS PK, BREA	708 - J5
FOXFIELD PK, WLKV	557 - C7
FOX HILLS PK, CULC	672 - H6
FOY, RALPH PK, BURB	533 - D6
FRANKLIN CANYON PK, LA	592 - E1
FRANKLIN PK, RBCH	763 - C2
FREEDOM PK, HNTP	675 - C6
FREEDOM PK, ELSG	732 - G1
FREEDOM PK, CALB	559 - J6
FREEMAN PK, GAR	733 - H5
FREMONT PK, GLDL	564 - D3
FRIENDSHIP COUNTY PK, RPV	823 - G6
FRIENDSHIP MINI PK, CRSN	764 - H6
FRIENDSHIP PK, CRTS	737 - C7
FRIENDSHIP PK, WCOV	679 - C2
FRIENDS PK, WHIT	677 - D7
FRONTIER PK, CRTS	737 - A6
FRONTIER PK, LMRD	737 - D2
FRYMAN CANYON PK, LA	592 - H1
FULLERTON SPORTS COMPLEX, FUL	738 - H3
FULLERTON TENNIS CTR, FUL	738 - G4
FULTON PK, RBCH	763 - A2
FURMAN PK, DWNY	706 - A3
GALLANT PK, BGDN	705 - H2
GALSTER WILDERNESS PK, WCOV	639 - A4
GANESHA PK, Alta	536 - B5
GANESHA PK, POM	600 - G7
GARDENHILL PK, LMRD	737 - E2
GARFIELD PK, POM	641 - B1
GARFIELD PK, PRM	735 - F4
GARFIELD PK, SPAS	595 - H1
GARVANZA PK, HiPk	595 - E1
GARVEY PK, RSMD	636 - E1
GARVEY RANCH PK, MONP	636 - C3
GATES CANYON PK, LACo	558 - J3
GENERAL FARNSWORTH COUNTY PK, - Alta	536 - A4
GENERAL SCOTT PK, CRSN	794 - D1
GENESEE AVENUE PK, LA	633 - A6
GEORGE LANE COUNTY PK, LACo	4104 - G5
GERDES PK, NRWK	736 - G4
GIBBS PK, ONT	601 - H5
GIBSON, JOHN S JR PK, SPed	824 - C5
GILBERT LINDSAY COMM CTR PK, - LA	674 - D3
GILLIAM, JIM REC CTR, LA	673 - C2
GINGRICH PK, WCOV	638 - J7
GLADSTONE PK, GLDR	599 - F1
GLADSTONE PK, AZU	599 - A1
GLASGOW STRIP PK, HAW	733 - A2
GLASSELL PK, LA	594 - H2
GLASSELL PARK & REC CTR, LA	594 - H2
GLAZIER PK, NRWK	736 - E4
GLEN ALLA PK, LA	672 - C6
GLENDALE CENTRAL PK, GLDL	564 - E5
GLENDALE SPORTS COMPLEX, GLDL	534 - J6
GLENDORA WILDERNESS PK, GLDR	570 - A1
GLENHAVEN PK, LCF	534 - J3
GLENHURST PK, LA	594 - E3
GLENOAKS PK, GLDL	565 - A4
GLENOLA PK, LCF	535 - B2
GLORIETTA PK, GLDL	534 - H6
GOLDEN HILLS WILDERNESS PK, - LVRN	570 - G4
GOLDEN PK, DWNY	735 - J2
GONSALVES, JOE A PK, CRTS	737 - C6
GONZALES, JESS SPORTS PK, - RSMD	636 - G3
GONZALES PK, COMP	734 - G3
GOOSE EGG PK, SMCA	671 - D1
GRANADA HILLS REC CTR, GrnH	501 - D3
GRANADA PK, ALH	635 - J1
GRAND AVENUE PK, CHLS	680 - G3
GRAND AVENUE PK, MNRO	567 - H2
GRANT PK, PAS	566 - B5
GRANT REA MEM PK, MTBL	676 - F1
GRAPE ARBOR PK, CALB	558 - G6
GREAVER OAK PK, LA	595 - A5
GREENBELT PK, HMB	762 - H3
GREENBELT PK, UPL	571 - H7
GREENE, TED PK, POM	600 - J5
GREEN MEADOWS REC CTR, LA	704 - D3
GREEN, WILLIAM PK, LNDL	733 - C7
GREENWOOD PK, TOR	763 - F6
GREENWOOD PK, HMB	762 - H2
GREYSTONE PK, BHLS	592 - F5
GRIDLEY PK, CRTS	766 - G3

FEATURE NAME Address City, ZIP Code	PAGE-GRID
GRIFFITH MANOR PK, GLDL	564 - A2
GRIFFITH PK, CLAR	571 - A7
GRIFFITH PK, LFlz	563 - J5
GRISSOM, VIRGIL PK, FUL	738 - E4
GROSS PK, BURB	533 - D6
GROW, PAUL C PK, DBAR	680 - B4
GUADALUPE PK, LHB	708 - D6
GUENSER PK, TOR	763 - H1
GUESS PK, RSMD	596 - G5
GUINEVERE PK, Nor	480 - D6
GUIRADO PK, WHIT	676 - J4
GUM GROVE PK, SLB	826 - F3
GWINN PK, PAS	566 - F3
HACIENDA PK, DUAR	568 - E4
HACIENDA PK, LHH	708 - C2
HAHAMONGNA WATERSHED PK, PAS	535 - E3
HAHN, KENNETH STATE REC AREA, - LACo	673 - A2
HAINES CANYON PK, Tuj	504 - A6
HAMILTON PK, PAS	566 - H2
HAMILTON PK, POM	640 - G1
HANCOCK PK, LA	633 - C2
HANNON PK, BGDN	706 - A1
HANSEN DAM PK, Sunl	502 - H2
HARBOR CITY REC CTR, Hrbr	794 - A4
HARBOR HIGHLANDS PK, SPed	824 - A2
HARTLAND MINI PK, VanN	532 - C5
HART, WILLIAM S COUNTY PK, - SCTA	4640 - J2
HART, WILLIAM S PK, WHWD	593 - A5
HARVARD MINI PK, GLDL	564 - D5
HARVARD REC CTR, LA	673 - J6
HASLEY CANYON COUNTY PK, Cstc	4459 - H5
HATHAWAY PK, LMTA	793 - G5
HAWKINS, AUGUSTUS F NATURAL- PK, LA	674 - F5
HAWTHORNE MEM PK, HAW	733 - E1
HAZARD PK, Boyl	635 - B2
HEARTWELL PK, LBCH	766 - C6
HEER, GLORIA COUNTY PK, RowH	678 - J6
HEIDELBERG PK, WAL	639 - F4
HELLMAN WILDERNESS PK, WHIT	677 - D3
HEMINGWAY, VERNON MEM PK, - CRSN	734 - E6
HENRY, HAROLD A PK, LA	633 - F3
HERITAGE PK, SFSP	706 - H5
HERITAGE PK, CRTS	767 - A1
HERITAGE PK, SFER	482 - A6
HERITAGE PK, DBAR	679 - H6
HERITAGE PK, WCOV	639 - D2
HERITAGE PK, LVRN	570 - F6
HERITAGE SQUARE, LA	595 - A6
HERMON PK IN THE ARROYO SECO, - HiPk	595 - D2
HERMOSA PK, FUL	738 - H2
HERMOSILLO PK, NRWK	736 - H5
HESSE, FRED JR COMM PK, RPV	822 - H1
HICKORY PK, TOR	793 - F1
HIDDEN HILLS PK, CHLS	680 - H4
HIGGINBOTHAM PK, CLAR	571 - C6
HIGHLAND PK, HiPk	595 - D2
HIGHLAND PK REC CTR, HiPk	595 - D2
HIGHLANDS PK, MONP	635 - H3
HIGHLANDS PK, CALB	589 - F1
HIGHRIDGE PK, RHE	822 - J1
HILLBROOK PK, SIGH	795 - H4
HILLCREST PK, FUL	738 - H5
HILLSIDE PK, PMDL	4194 - H1
HILLTOP PK, SIGH	795 - G3
HILLTOP PK, ELSG	732 - F1
HILTSCHER PK, FUL	738 - F5
HJELTE SPORTS CTR, Enc	561 - F2
HOFFMAN, ALMA PK, MTCL	601 - G6
HOGAN, FRANK PK, LNDL	733 - D7
HOLIFIELD PK, NRWK	736 - J4
HOLLENBECK PK, COV	599 - A3
HOLLENBECK PK, Boyl	635 - A5
HOLLY AVENUE PK, ARCD	567 - B7
HOLLYDALE PK, SGAT	705 - F7
HOLLY GLEN PK, HAW	733 - A3
HOLLY PK, HAW	703 - H7
HOLLY VALLEY PK, ELSG	732 - D1
HOLLYWOOD FRANKLIN PK, Hlwd	593 - D4
HOLLYWOOD REC CTR, LA	593 - F5
HOLMBY PK, Wwd	632 - C1
HOOVER-GAGE PK, LA	674 - B6
HOOVER REC CTR, LA	634 - B6
HOPE & PEACE PK, LA	634 - C4
HOPKINS WILDERNESS PK, RBCH	763 - A7
HORSETHIEF CANYON PK, SDMS	570 - C6
HOSTETTER PLGD, LA	675 - A1
HOTCHKISS, MARY PK, SMCA	671 - F3
HOUGHTON PK, NLB	765 - E1
HOUSTON, NORMAN O PK, LA	673 - C4
HOWLETT, ERNIE J PK, RHE	793 - D5
HUDSON PK, LBCH	795 - A4
HUGO REID PK, ARCD	566 - J5
HULL PK, LAN	4105 - C5
HUMPHREY, HUBERT H MEM PK, - Pcma	482 - F7
HUNTINGTON, THE, SMRO	566 - C7
IMPERIAL PARKWAY, ELSG	702 - E7
INDEPENDENCE PK, DWNY	736 - C1
INDEPENDENCE PK, ELSG	702 - G7
INDEPENDENCE PK OF FULLERTON, - FUL	738 - F7
INDIAN SPRINGS PK, VeCo	557 - H1
INDUSTRY HILLS REC CTR, INDS	638 - E7

FEATURE NAME Address City, ZIP Code	PAGE-GRID
INGOLD, RUBEN COUNTY PARKWAY, - LACo	673 - C4
IRVING SCHACHTER PK, LA	632 - G6
IRWINDALE COMM PK, IRW	598 - F3
IZAY, GEORGE PK, BURB	563 - F1
JACKSON PK, NLB	765 - F3
JACOB PK, CRTS	766 - H3
JAEGER PK, CLAR	571 - D5
JARDINE DE ROCA PK, IRW	598 - F3
JEFFERSON PK, PAS	566 - C3
JESSUP, ROGER REC CTR, Pcma	502 - E3
JOBES GLEN AT XALAPA PK, COV	599 - E7
JOHN QUIMBY PK, CanP	530 - C5
JOHNSON, EARVIN MAGIC COUNTY- REC AREA, LA	704 - E7
JOSE DEL VALLE PK, LKWD	766 - D4
JOSE SAN MARTIN PK, LKWD	766 - C3
JOSHUA HILLS PK, PMDL	4286 - G4
JOSLYN PK, SMCA	671 - F3
JUAN BAUTISTA DE ANZA PK, - CALB	588 - G1
JUNIOR HIGH PK, BREA	709 - B6
JUNTOS PK, LA	594 - F1
KAGEL CANYON PK, LA	482 - H7
KANSAS PK, ELSG	732 - G1
KELBY PK, COV	599 - C4
KELLER, HELEN COUNTY PK, LACo	734 - A1
KELLOGG PK, POM	640 - B2
KELLY PK, COMP	735 - C5
KENNEDY, JOHN F PK, POM	600 - E7
KENNEDY PK, WHIT	707 - D2
KENT, MAURICE MOSSY PK, LBCH	826 - D3
KEREDJIAN, JAKE COUNTY PK, - StvR	4640 - C1
KERR, MARIE PK, PMDL	4195 - C4
KING JR, DR MARTIN LUTHER MEM- PK, POM	640 - J5
KINGSLEY PK, MTCL	601 - H7
KINGS ROAD PK, WHWD	593 - A6
KITTRIDGE MINI PK, VanN	532 - C6
KIWANIS PK, POM	600 - G7
KLING CTR FIELDS, LMRD	737 - G1
KLINGERMAN PK, RSMD	636 - H3
KNAPP RANCH PK, CanP	529 - C7
KNOLLS PK, VeCo	499 - B3
KRONENTHAL, SYD PK, CULC	632 - J7
KUNS PK, LVRN	600 - F2
LA BELLA FONTANA DI NAPOLI, - LBCH	826 - C2
LA BONITA PK, LHB	708 - C5
LA CARRETERA PK, TOR	763 - H2
LA CIENEGA PK, BHLS	632 - J3
LACY PK, SMRO	596 - B1
LADERA CANYON PK, LadH	673 - B6
LADERA LINDA COMM CTR, RPV	823 - D5
LADERA SERRA PK, SDMS	599 - J6
LAFAYETTE PK, LA	634 - B2
LAGOS DE MORENO PK, BREA	709 - B7
LAGO SECO PK, TOR	793 - C2
LAGUNA LAKE PK, FUL	738 - F2
LAGUNA ROAD PK, FUL	738 - G3
LAKE CTR PK, SFSP	706 - G5
LAKESIDE PK, NRWK	706 - F7
LAKEVIEW PK, SFSP	706 - G4
LAKEVIEW TERRACE REC CTR, LA	502 - J1
LAKEWOOD EQUESTRIAN CTR, LKWD	766 - G5
LA LOMA PK, MONP	636 - C5
LAMBERT PK, ELMN	597 - E5
LA MIRADA REGL PK, LMRD	737 - G2
LANARK PK, LA	530 - A3
LANARK/SHELBY PK, Eagl	565 - D6
LANCASTER CITY PK, LAN	4105 - F3
LANCASTER NATL SOCCER CTR, - LAN	4106 - F3
LANGLEY SENIOR CTR & PK, MONP	636 - B1
LA PINTORESCA PK, PAS	565 - H1
LA PUENTE PK, LPUE	638 - D6
LA PUERTA SPORTS PK, CLAR	571 - D6
LARKIN PK, CLAR	601 - C3
LA ROMERIA PK, TOR	763 - C3
LAS CANCHAS RACQUET CLUB, TOR	793 - E5
LAS FLORES CREEK PK, MAL	629 - F6
LAS FLORES PK, LVRN	600 - G2
LASHBROOK PK, ELMN	636 - J2
LAS LOMAS PK, LHB	708 - E7
LASORDA, TOMMY FIELD OF- DREAMS, LA	594 - D5
LAS PALMAS PK, SFER	481 - J7
LAS VIRGENES CANYON, VeCo	558 - F1
LATHAM PK, LA	674 - F5
LA TUNA CANYON PK, SunV	503 - G7
LAUREL CANYON PK, LA	592 - J1
LAUREL PK, WHIT	707 - E2
LAYNE PK, SFER	482 - A6
LAZY J RANCH PK, LA	529 - E3
LEFFINGWELL RANCH PK, WHIT	707 - H5
LEIMERT PK, LA	673 - F3
LELAND PK, SPed	824 - A3
LEMON CREEK BICENTENNIAL PK, - WAL	679 - E1
LEMON GROVE REC CTR, LA	593 - H6
LENNOX COUNTY PK, Lenx	703 - C6
LESLIE PK, LHB	708 - F7
LEVI, SAM PK, TOR	763 - G6
LEWIS, IRENE RAILROAD PK, - LMTA	793 - H4
LEWIS, ORVILLE R PK, LALM	796 - J5
LEWIS PK, CLAR	601 - B1
LEXINGTON POCKET PK, LA	593 - H5
LIBBIT PK, Enc	561 - E3
LIBERTY PK, CHNO	641 - G4
LIBERTY PK, CRTS	766 - E2
LIBRARY PK, ELSG	702 - E7
LILIENTHAL PK, RBCH	763 - B2
LILLY PK, LBCH	796 - J1
LIMEKILN CANYON PK, Nor	480 - F7
LINCOLN HEIGHTS REC CTR, LA	635 - A1
LINCOLN MINI PK, LVRN	600 - H3
LINCOLN PK, LA	635 - B1
LINCOLN PK, BURB	563 - A2
LINCOLN PK, POM	601 - A7
LINCOLN PK, LBCH	825 - D1
LINDARAXA PK, ALH	596 - C4
LINDBERG PK, CULC	672 - G4
LINDER, CARLYLE E EQUESTRIAN- PK, GLDR	569 - H3
LIONS FIELD, FUL	738 - H5
LITTLE GREEN ACRES PK, LA	704 - A5
LITTLE LAKE PK, SFSP	706 - H6
LITTLE LANDERS PK, Tuj	504 - A4
LITTLE LEAGUE PK, DBAR	640 - A5
LIVE OAK PK, MANB	732 - F5
LIVE OAK PK, LVRN	570 - H5
LIVE OAK PK, TEML	597 - B3
LIVINGSTON DR PK, LBCH	826 - B1
LOMA ALTA COUNTY PK, Alta	535 - G4
LOMA NORTE PK, LHB	708 - H4
LOMA PK, CRTS	736 - J7
LOMA VERDE PK, LHB	708 - D6
LOMA VISTA PK, SDMS	599 - J5
LOMITA PK, LMTA	793 - H3
LONE HILL PK, SDMS	599 - H1
LONG BEACH SPORTS PK, Bxby	795 - F2
LONGDEN PK,	597 - G1
LOOKOUT POINT PK, SPed	854 - B2
LORDSBURG PK, LVRN	600 - F3
LOS ALTOS PK, LACo	707 - D7
LOS ALTOS PK, LBCH	796 - C4
LOS ALTOS PLAZA PK, LBCH	796 - B5
LOS AMIGOS PK, SMCA	671 - F3
LOS ANGELES HIGH MEM PK, LA	633 - E3
LOS ANGELES PK LAND, WdHl	560 - F7
LOS ARBOLES ROCKETSHIP PK, - TOR	793 - B2
LOS CERRITOS PK, Bxby	765 - C7
LOS COYOTES ATHLETIC FIELDS, - LMRD	737 - J3
LOS ENCINOS PK, LVRN	570 - E6
LOS ENCINOS STATE HIST PK, - Enc	561 - D3
LOS NIETOS PK, SFSP	706 - G2
LOS ROBLES COUNTY PK, HacH	677 - J2
LOUISE PK, VanN	531 - C5
LOWELL BRANDT PK, LVRN	570 - H4
LOWER ARROYO PK, PAS	565 - F5
LUEDERS PK, COMP	735 - B3
LUGO PK, CDHY	705 - D2
LUGO, VINCENT PK, SGBL	596 - D6
LUMMIS PK, LA	595 - B5
LUNADA BAY PK, PVE	792 - E7
LUNDIGAN PK, BURB	533 - D5
LYNWOOD PK, LYN	705 - B7
MACARTHUR PK, LBCH	795 - F5
MACARTHUR PK, LA	634 - C3
MACARTHUR PK, MTCL	601 - G5
MADISON PK, POM	640 - J3
MAHOOD SENIOR CTR, WLA	632 - A5
MALIBU BLUFFS STATE PK, MAL	628 - G7
MALIBU CREEK STATE PK, LACo	588 - D4
MALIBU EQUESTRIAN PK, MAL	667 - C1
MALLOWS PK, CLAR	601 - D3
MALLOY, KEN HARBOR REGL PK, - Wilm	794 - A6
MALLOY PK, CRSN	734 - E6
MALTZ PK, BHLS	632 - D1
MANHATTAN HEIGHTS PK, MANB	732 - J6
MANHATTAN VILLAGE PK, MANB	732 - H4
MANOOSHIAN, GEORGE PK, GLDR	569 - G3
MANZANITA COUNTY PK, HacH	678 - B3
MANZANITA HEIGHTS PK, PMDL	4285 - H1
MAPLE HILL PK, DBAR	680 - A3
MAPLE PK, GLDL	564 - F6
MARCHANT PK, SDMS	600 - C1
MARCH, DAVID COUNTY PK, Saug	4461 - E6
MARINA COMM PK, SLB	826 - E4
MARINA GREEN PK, LBCH	825 - E2
MARINA VISTA PK, LBCH	796 - B7
MARINE AVENUE PK, MANB	732 - J5
MARINE AVENUE SPORTS PK, MANB	732 - J5
MARINE PK, SMCA	671 - H3
MARINE PK, LBCH	826 - D2
MARINE STADIUM PK, LBCH	796 - C7
MARIPOSA PK, LAN	4015 - G3
MARLOW PK, BGDN	675 - G7
MARSH STREET PK, LA	594 - F3
MARTIN, ALLEN J COUNTY PK, - LACo	638 - C5
MARTIN, ANNA J PK, LMRD	737 - J2
MARTIN, EVERETT COUNTY PK, - Litl	4288 - A7
MARTINGALE TRAILHEAD PK, RPV	823 - E2
MLK JR PK, LBCH	795 - F4
MLK JR PK, LA	673 - H2
MAR VISTA GARDENS, LA	672 - E5
MAR VISTA REC CTR, LA	672 - C2
MARYLAND MINI PK, GLDL	564 - E6
MAS FUKAI PK, GAR	733 - J6
MASON REC CTR, Chat	500 - D3
MASSARI, DOMENIC PK, PMDL	4287 - C2
MAUNA LOA PK, GLDR	569 - F7
MAYBERRY, AMELIA COUNTY PK, - LACo	707 - B6
MAYFAIR PK, LKWD	766 - B2
MAYORS BICENTENNIAL PK, GLDL	564 - J1
MAYORS DISCOVERY PK, LCF	534 - J3
MAYWOOD PK, MYWD	675 - E5
MAYWOOD RIVERFRONT PK, MYWD	675 - F6
MCADAM, WILLIAM J PK, PMDL	4286 - F1
MCCAMBRIDGE PK, BURB	533 - F5
MCDONALD PK, PAS	566 - B2
MCGROARTY CULTURAL CTR PK, - Tuj	503 - J5
MCLEOD PK, CHNO	641 - J6
MCMASTER PK, TOR	763 - E1
MCNEES COUNTY PK, LACo	677 - A6
MEADOWS PK, PRM	735 - F5
MEDEA CREEK PK, VeCo	557 - J1
MEDIA PK, LA	632 - G7
MEM PK, SMCA	671 - F1
MEM PK, CLAR	601 - D2
MEM PK, LCF	535 - B3
MEM PK, AZU	568 - H6
MEM PK, POM	640 - H2
MEM PK, SMAD	567 - A2
MICHIGAN PK, WHIT	707 - E1
MICHILLINDA COUNTY PK, LACo	566 - H6
MILFORD MINI PK, GLDL	564 - D4
MILLER, JOAQUIN PK, BURB	533 - J7
MILLER, JOE FIELD, WHIT	677 - D7
MILLER, LOREN PK, LA	633 - J7
MILLS, DR THOMAS G MEM PK, - CRSN	764 - G4
MIRAMAR PK, TOR	792 - H2
MLK JR MINI PK, LA	674 - D2
MONA COUNTY PK, Wbrk	704 - H7
MONROVIA CANYON PK, MNRO	537 - H7
MONROVIA LIBRARY PK, MNRO	567 - G4
MONTEBELLO PK, MTBL	676 - C2
MONTEITH COUNTY PARKWAY, LACo	673 - E4
MONTE VERDE PK, LKWD	766 - F4
MONTE VISTA PK, CHNO	641 - F7
MONTROSE COMM PK, GLDL	534 - H4
MONTVUE PK, POM	601 - C6
MONTWOOD PK, LHB	738 - E1
MOONSHINE CANYON PK, Nor	480 - E7
MOORE, ALOYSIA PK, DUAR	567 - J6
MOORPARK PK, LA	562 - G4
MORENO VISTA PK, MTCL	601 - F4
MORGAN PK, BALD	598 - C5
MORRISON PK, AGRH	557 - J4
MOUNTAIN VIEW PK, ELMN	637 - E3
MOUNTAIN VIEW PK, BURB	563 - G3
MOUNT CARMEL PK, LA	674 - B7
MOUNT LOWE PK, Alta	536 - B4
MOUNT OLYMPUS PK, LA	595 - A6
MOUNT WILSON TRAIL PK, SMAD	567 - B1
MUNOZ, ANTHONY PK, ONT	601 - J5
MURPHY RANCH PK, WHIT	707 - J2
NANSEN FIELD, RHE	793 - C5
NAPLES PLAZA PK, LBCH	826 - D3
NATIONAL PK SERVICE, LACo	629 - F1
NATURE PK, CYP	767 - A7
NEFF PK, LMRD	737 - E3
NEWCASTLE PK, ARCD	567 - C4
NEWHALL MEM PK, SCTA	4550 - H7
NEW RIVER PK, NRWK	736 - E2
NEW TEMPLE PK, SELM	637 - C4
NEW YORK PK, GLDL	504 - E7
NIBLEY PK, GLDL	564 - G2
NIELSEN, CARL E YOUTH PK, Wch	702 - H3
NIXON, PATRICIA PK, CRTS	766 - J2
NOBLE PK, HMB	762 - G2
NORMANDALE REC CTR, LA	764 - A7
NORMANDIE PLGD, LA	633 - J5
NORTH ATWATER PK, LA	564 - C6
NORTHBRIDGE COUNTY PK, SCTA	4460 - F7
NORTH HILLS COMM PK, LA	501 - H7
NORTH HOLLYWOOD PK, NHol	562 - H2
NORTH OAKS PK, SCTA	4551 - F1
NORTH PK, ING	673 - D7
NORTH RANCH PLAYFIELD, THO	557 - G1
NORTHRIDGE REC CTR, Nor	500 - J5
NORTHVIEW PK, DUAR	568 - B5
NORWALK PK, NRWK	736 - J2
NORWALK SPORTS COMPLEX, NRWK	736 - J2
OAK CANYON COMM PK, VeCo	557 - J1
OAK CREEK PK, LMRD	737 - G1
OAK GROVE PK, PAS	535 - E5
OAKHURST PK, BHLS	632 - H2
OAK KNOLL PK, CYP	767 - D7
OAK MESA PK, LVRN	570 - F6
OAKMONT VIEW PK, GLDL	534 - F4
OAK SPRING PK, SCTA	4552 - D1
OAKWOOD REC CTR, Ven	671 - H5
OBREGON COUNTY PK, City	635 - E5
OBREGON PK, PRV	676 - J1
OCEAN VIEW PK, SMCA	671 - F4
OESTE PK, LHB	708 - B7
OLD AGOURA PK, AGRH	558 - D5
OLD ORCHARD PK, SCTA	4640 - G1
OLD RESERVOIR PK, LHB	708 - F4
OLE HAMMER PK, GLDR	569 - F4
OLINDA RANCH NEIGHBORHOOD PK, - BREA	709 - H6
OLIVE AVENUE PK, MNRO	567 - F4
OMELVENY PK, GrnH	480 - J3
ORANGE GROVE PK, ARCD	567 - A3
ORANGE GROVE PLGD, SPAS	595 - G2
ORANGEWOOD PK, WCOV	638 - D1
ORCAS PK, Sunl	503 - A2
ORCUTT RANCH HORTICULTURAL CTR- PK, LA	529 - F2
ORIZABA PK, LBCH	795 - H5
ORR PK, NRWK	706 - G7
OSORNIO PK, LHB	708 - C4
OTIS GORDON SPORTS PK, DUAR	568 - D5
OWENS, JESSE COUNTY PK, LA	703 - H4
OWENS, JESSE PK, VanN	531 - B5
OWENS, LEE PK, WHIT	707 - D1
OZONE PK, SMCA	671 - G4
PACIFIC DRIVE PK, FUL	738 - D7
PACIFIC PK, BURB	533 - C6
PACIFIC PK, GLDL	564 - D6
PACIFIC STREET PK, SMCA	671 - F3
PACOIMA PK, Pcma	502 - E2
PADELFORD, AJ PK, ART	736 - H6
PAGE PK, RBCH	733 - B7
PALISADES PK, PacP	630 - J6
PALISADES PK, SMCA	671 - C2
PALISADES PK, Nor	480 - G6
PALMDALE OASIS PK, PMDL	4286 - H4
PALMER PK, GLDL	564 - F7
PALM PK, BURB	533 - J5
PALM PK, WHIT	677 - A5
PALMS PK, LKWD	766 - J4
PALMS PK, LA	632 - E7
PALM VIEW PK, WCOV	598 - H6
PALO COMADO CANYON, VeCo	558 - D1
PALOMARES PK, POM	601 - A4
PALOS VERDES MEM GARDEN, PVE	792 - H3
PAMELA COUNTY PK, LACo	567 - H7
PAMPLICO PK, SCTA	4460 - J5
PAN AMERICAN PK, LBCH	766 - B4
PANORAMA REC CTR, PanC	532 - B1
PAN PACIFIC PK, LA	633 - C1
PANTERA PK, DBAR	680 - E1
PARADISE PK, TOR	763 - B6
PARAMOUNT PK, PRM	735 - H3
PARAMOUNT RANCH, Ago	588 - A2
PARK DRIVE PK, SMCA	631 - G7
PARKS, ROSA PK, LBCH	795 - F5
PARKVIEW PHOTO CTR, LA	634 - C2
PARNELL PK, WHIT	707 - H5
PARTHENIA PK, LA	530 - A1
PASADENA CENTRAL PK, PAS	565 - H5
PASADENA MEM PK, PAS	565 - H4
PASKO PK, Tuj	503 - H5
PATHFINDER COUNTY PK, RowH	708 - J1
PAXTON PK, Pcma	502 - B2
PEACE PK, LBCH	795 - E5
PEAK, WILLIAM PK, BPK	767 - G3
PEARBLOSSOM COUNTY PK, Pear	4378 - G4
PECAN PLGD, Boyl	634 - J4
PECK PARK & REC CTR, LA	823 - J3
PECK ROAD COUNTY PK, ARCD	597 - F3
PELANCONI PK, GLDL	564 - B2
PELONA VISTA PK, PMDL	4285 - H2
PELOTA PK, LVRN	600 - F1
PENMAR PLGD, Ven	671 - J3
PENN, WILLIAM PK, WHIT	677 - E7
PEPPERBROOK COUNTY PK, HacH	678 - E4
PEQUENO PK, PRM	735 - J3
PEQUENO PK, TOR	763 - D1
PERRY PK, RBCH	763 - B1
PERRY PK, CRSN	764 - F6
PERSHING SQUARE PK, LA	634 - E4
PETERSON, CARLTON PK, DBAR	640 - D6
PHILADELPHIA PK, POM	641 - A5
PHILLIPS RANCH PK, POM	640 - G5
PICO CANYON COUNTY PK, StvR	4640 - C1
PICO PK, PRV	676 - H2
PICO RIVERA BICENTENNIAL PK, - LACo	637 - B6
PICO UNION PK, LA	634 - B5
PIEDMONT PK, GLDL	564 - G4
PINE TREE PK, MONP	635 - G3
PINEWOOD PK, CYP	767 - E7
PIONEER PK, HGDN	766 - H6
PIONEER PK, SDMS	600 - B2
PIONEER PK, AZU	568 - J4
PIONEER PK, SFER	482 - B6
PIONEER PK, ELMN	597 - B7
PIO PICO PLGD, PRV	676 - G2
PIUMA RIDGE PK, LACo	629 - B3
PIXLEY PK, MYWD	675 - C5
PLACERITA CANYON NATURAL AREA,- Nwhl	4641 - G1
PLAZA ANDRES, PVE	792 - F7
PLAZA BLANCA, PVE	792 - G7
PLAZA PK, FUL	738 - H7
PLAZA ZAFERIA, LBCH	795 - J5
PLUMMER PK, WHWD	593 - C5
POINSETTIA REC CTR, LA	593 - C6
POINT FERMIN PK, SPed	853 - J2
POINT MUGU STATE PK, VeCo	625 - A1
POINT VICENTE PK, RPV	822 - G4
POLLIWOG PK, MANB	732 - J5
POMONA JAYCEE PK, POM	601 - B6
POMPEI, LOUIE SPORTS PK, GLDR	569 - H7
PORTER RANCH PK, Nor	500 - F2
PORTER RIDGE PK, Nor	480 - H5
PORTOLA PK, LHB	708 - E6
POTRERO HEIGHTS PK, MTBL	636 - F4
POTTER, BENNY H PK, LA	633 - G6
POWERS PK, POM	640 - J5
PRITCHARD FIELD, BELL	705 - F1
PROGRESS PK, PRM	735 - J5
PROSPECT PK, Boyl	634 - J3
QUEEN ANNE REC CTR, LA	633 - E4
QUEEN MARY EVENTS PK, LBCH	825 - D2
QUEEN PK, ING	703 - D2
RAINBOW HARBOR ESPLANADE, - LBCH	825 - D2
RAINBOW LAGOON PK, LBCH	825 - E1
RAINBOW PK, LPMA	767 - C1
RAMONA GARDENS PK, Boyl	635 - C3
RAMONA PK, NRWK	737 - B4
RAMONA PK, NLB	735 - H7
RAMONA PK, HAW	733 - C3
RAMON GARCIA REC CTR, LA	635 - B7
RANCHO CIENEGA SPORTS CTR PK, - LA	673 - C1
RANCHO SAN JOSE PK, CLAR	601 - C5
RANCHO SANTA ANA BOTANIC- GARDEN, CLAR	571 - D7
RANCHO SIMI REC AREA, VeCo	557 - H2
RANCHO VISTA PK, PMDL	4195 - B3
RAWLEY DUNTLEY PK, LAN	4105 - B2
RAYMOND STREET PK, COMP	734 - H5
REAGAN, RONALD PK, DBAR	679 - G5
RECREATION PK, ELSG	732 - E1
RECREATION PK, MNRO	567 - H4
RECREATION PK, SFER	482 - B7
RECREATION PK, LBCH	796 - A6
REED PK, SMCA	671 - E1
REEVES MINI PK, BHLS	632 - G2
REGGIE RODRIGUEZ PK, MTBL	676 - D3
REID, TWILA PK, ANA	767 - H7
RENA PK, LA	824 - A4
RESEDA PARK & REC CTR, Res	530 - J6
RESERVOIR HILL PK, CRTS	736 - E6
RESERVOIR PK, SIGH	795 - F1
REXFORD MINI PK, BHLS	632 - G1
REYES ADOBE PK, AGRH	557 - H5
REYNIER PK, LA	632 - H6
REYNOLDS, JANE PK, LAN	4015 - H6
RHOADS PK, SDMS	600 - B2
RICHARDSON FAMILY PK, LA	634 - A7
RIDGERIDERS MAVERICK PK, WCOV	599 - B7
RIMGROVE COUNTY PK, LACo	638 - H6
RIO HONDO PK, PRV	676 - F2
RIO SAN GABRIEL PK, DWNY	706 - D6
RIOUX, DR RICHARD H MEM PK, - StvR	4550 - B7
RIO VISTA PK, PRV	676 - F5
RIO VISTA PK, ELMN	597 - C6
RIVAS CANYON PK, PacP	631 - B3
RIVERA PK, PRV	706 - F2
RIVER PK, SCTA	4551 - E2
RIVERSIDE PK, CHNO	641 - G7
RIVIERA PK, TOR	792 - J2
ROADSIDE PK, BALD	637 - J1
ROBERTS, FRED PK, LA	674 - G4
ROBERTSON REC CTR, LA	632 - H4
ROBINSON, JACKIE COUNTY PK, - Litl	4287 - J1
ROBINSON, JACKIE PK, PAS	565 - H2
ROCKBLUFF PK, RHE	793 - C5
ROCKY OAKS, LACo	587 - C5
ROCKY PEAK PK, VeCo	499 - E1
ROCKY POINTE NATURAL PK, SIMI	499 - C3
RODAWAY PK, HMB	762 - J3
ROGERS-ANDERSON PK, LNDL	733 - D5
ROGERS PK, ING	703 - B1
ROGERS, WILL MINI PK, LBCH	796 - B7
ROOSEVELT COUNTY PK, Flor	704 - G1
ROOSEVELT PK, SGBL	596 - G4
ROSAS, CAROLYN COUNTY PK, - RowH	679 - A6
ROSCOE-VALLEY CIRCLE PK, LA	529 - D3
ROSECRANS REC CTR, LA	734 - B4
ROSE HILL PK, LA	595 - C6
ROSE HILL REC CTR, LA	595 - D6
ROSEMEAD PK, RSMD	596 - H6
ROSEN/ ACACIA PK, CYP	767 - D6
ROSE PK, LBCH	795 - H6
ROSE PK, LYN	705 - A7
ROSEWOOD PK, CRTS	736 - F7
ROSEWOOD PK, CMRC	675 - H3
ROSEWOOD PK, LA	593 - B7
ROSSMOOR PK, OrCo	796 - H3
ROSS SNYDER REC CTR, LA	674 - F3
ROTARY CENTENNIAL PK, LBCH	795 - G5
ROTARY PK, MNRO	567 - H4
ROWLAND HEIGHTS COUNTY PK, - RowH	679 - D4
ROWLEY PK, GAR	733 - H2
ROXBURY REC CTR, BHLS	632 - F3
ROYAL OAKS PK, DUAR	568 - D4
RUNNYMEDE REC CTR, Win	530 - D4
RUNYON CANYON PK, LA	593 - C3
RUSH PK, OrCo	796 - H5
RUSSELL, KAHLER PK, COV	599 - E4
RUSSELL PK, THO	557 - B2
RUSSELL RANCH PK, WLKV	557 - F5
RUSTIC CANYON PK, LVRN	570 - G3
RUSTIC CANYON PK, PacP	631 - B1
RUSTIC CANYON REC CTR, LA	631 - B6
RYAN, ROBERT E COMM PK, RPV	822 - H4
RYNERSON PK, LKWD	766 - F4
SADDLEBACK BUTTE STATE PK, - LACo	4109 - H1
SADDLEBACK PK, CRTS	737 - B7
SAGE RANCH PK, VeCo	499 - A6
SAINT ANDREWS REC CTR, LA	703 - H3

FEATURE NAME Address City, ZIP Code	PAGE-GRID
SAINT CLAIR PARKWAY, PMDL	4286 - B1
SAINT CLAIR PARKWAY, PMDL	4196 - B7
SAINT JAMES PK, LA	634 - C7
SALAZAR COUNTY PK, LACo	635 - D7
SAN ANGELO COUNTY PK, LACo	637 - G3
SAN ANTONIO PK, BPK	767 - F5
SAN ANTONIO PK, UPL	571 - J3
SAN BERNARDINO NATL FOREST, - SBdC (SEE PAGE 4471)	4562 - C7
SANDBURG PK, GLDR	569 - C4
SAND DUNE PK, MANB	732 - F4
SAN DIMAS CANYON COUNTY PK, - SDMS	570 - C5
SAN JUAN PK, FUL	738 - G2
SAN MARINO PK, BPK	767 - E5
SAN MIGUEL DE ALLENDE PK, LHB	708 - E4
SAN PEDRO PLAZA PK, SPed	824 - C5
SAN RAFAEL PK, PAS	565 - E5
SANTA CLARITA PK, SCTA	4460 - H6
SANTA CRUZ PK, LBCH	825 - C1
SANTA FE DAM REC AREA, IRW	568 - C7
SANTA FE SPRINGS PK, SFSP	706 - F4
SANTA SUSANA PK, VeCo	499 - C4
SANTA YNEZ CANYON PK, PacP	630 - G2
SAN VINCENTE MTN PK, PacP	591 - B1
SARATOGA PK, MTCL	601 - G7
SATELLITE PK, CRTS	736 - J6
SAYBROOK COUNTY PK, ELA	676 - A2
SCHABARUM REGL COUNTY PK, - RowH	678 - F6
SCHADER PK, SMCA	631 - G7
SCHERER PK, NLB	765 - E4
SCHOLL CANYON PK, GLDL	565 - B3
SCHWEITZER PK, ANA	767 - J6
SCUBIE MILLS PK, LVRN	570 - F5
SEA BRIDGE PK, HNTB	826 - J6
SEASIDE LAGOON, RBCH	762 - H5
SEAVIEW PK, HMB	762 - H1
SEBRING PK, CHNO	641 - J6
SEPULVEDA DAM REC AREA, Enc	531 - G7
SEPULVEDA GARDEN CTR, Enc	561 - D2
SEPULVEDA REC CTR, PanC	501 - J7
SEQUOIA PK, MONP	635 - J3
SERRANIA AVENUE PK, WdHl	560 - C4
SHADOW OAK PK, WCOV	639 - A7
SHADOW RANCH PK, CanP	529 - H6
SHATTO REC CTR, LA	634 - A2
SHAW, LESLIE N PK, LA	633 - G7
SHELTON PK, CLAR	601 - D3
SHIVELY PK, SELM	637 - B4
SHORELINE PK, LBCH	825 - D2
SIBRIE PK, COMP	734 - G2
SIERRA VISTA PK, MONP	636 - C1
SIERRA VISTA PK, SMAD	567 - C2
SIGNAL HILL PK, SIGH	795 - G4
SILVERADO PK, LBCH	795 - B1
SILVER LAKE REC CTR, Echo	594 - D5
SILVER SPUR PK, RHE	793 - B5
SIMINSKI PK, ING	703 - B4
SIMMS, JOHN S PK, BLF	736 - B6
SINGER PK, PAS	565 - G6
SKYTOWER PK, LAN	4106 - F2
SLAUSON PK, AZU	568 - J6
SLAUSON REC CTR, LA	674 - F5
SLAVIN PK, NHol	532 - E2
SLEEPY HOLLOW GREENBELT, NLB	765 - D4
SMITH, CARLIN PLGD PK, LA	595 - A4
SMITH-MURPHY PK, BPK	737 - J5
SMITH PK, SGBL	596 - E4
SMITH, WILLIAM A PK, PRV	676 - F5
SNOW CREEK PK, WAL	639 - H5
SOLIS, HILDA L PK, BALD	598 - D5
SOLSTICE CANYON, LACo	628 - B6
SOMERSET PK, Bxby	765 - F6
SORENSEN COUNTY PK, LACo	677 - A6
SORENSEN, STEPHEN COUNTY PK, - LACo	4199 - G4
SOROPTIMIST PK, LALM	796 - J2
SOUTH BEACH PK, SMCA	671 - F5
SOUTH COAST BOTANIC GARDEN, - LACo	793 - D6
SOUTH GARDENA PK, GAR	734 - A7
SOUTH GATE PK, SGAT	705 - D4
SOUTH HILLS PK, GLDR	569 - F7
SOUTH PK, LA	674 - D4
SOUTH PK, HMB	762 - H3
SOUTH PK, COMP	735 - A6
SOUTH SHORE HILLS PK, THO	557 - A6
SOUTH STREET PARKWAY, NLB	765 - D2
SPANE PK, PRM	735 - F3
SPORTS & SKATE PK, LVRN	600 - G2
SPORTSPLEX, SDMS	600 - A4
STANFORD AVENUE PK, SGAT	704 - J3
STARSHINE PK, DBAR	679 - G5
STATE PK LAND, AGRH	557 - H7
STATE STREET REC CTR, Boyl	635 - A3
STEARNS CHAMPIONS PK, LBCH	796 - A3
STEINMETZ COUNTY PK, HacH	678 - C3
STETSON RANCH PK, LA	481 - G1
STEVENSON PK, CRSN	734 - E7
STEWART STREET PK, SMCA	631 - H7
STONEHURST REC CTR, SunV	502 - J5
STONER PLGD, WLA	631 - J6
STONEY POINT PK, Chat	500 - A2
STORY PK, ALH	596 - B4
STOUGH PK, BURB	533 - H3
STRATHERN PK WEST, NHol	532 - E3
STRATHERN PLGD PK, NHol	532 - E2
STRAUSS, PETER RANCH, Ago	587 - H3
STREAMLAND PK, PRV	676 - H1
STUDIO CITY REC CTR, LA	562 - E4
STUNT RANCH, LACo	589 - D6
SULLIVAN CANYON PK, PacP	631 - C1
SUMAC PK, AGRH	558 - B4
SUMMITRIDGE PK, DBAR	680 - D3
SUNLAND PARK & REC CTR, Sunl	503 - F3
SUNNYGLEN PK, TOR	763 - A4
SUNNYSLOPE PK, PAS	566 - F3
SUNNYSLOPES PK, MONP	635 - H4
SUNRISE PK, MTCL	601 - H6
SUNSET AQUATIC PK, SLB	826 - J6
SUNSET FIELD, WCOV	638 - E1
SUNSET PK, CHLS	680 - G5
SUNSET PK, MTCL	601 - E7
SUNSET VIEW PK, SIGH	795 - G3
SUNSHINE COUNTY PK, LACo	679 - A2
SUNSHINE PK, CRTS	767 - B2
SUN VALLEY PARK & REC CTR, - SunV	532 - J2
SUR LA BREA PK, TOR	793 - H2
SUZANNE PK, WAL	639 - G6
SYCAMORE CANYON PK, DBAR	680 - B2
SYCAMORE CANYON PK, CLAR	571 - C5
SYCAMORE GLEN PK, CHLS	680 - H3
SYCAMORE GROVE PK, LA	595 - B4
SYCAMORE PK, ELSG	702 - G7
SYLMAR PK, LA	482 - A4
TAMARACK PK, BREA	709 - A6
TANAKA PK, LBCH	765 - B7
TANNER, SALLY PK, RSMD	596 - F5
TARZANA REC CTR, Tarz	560 - G1
TAXCO TRAILS PK, LA	529 - F3
TELLEFSON PK, CULC	672 - E3
TEMESCAL CANYON PK, PacP	631 - A4
TEMESCAL GATEWAY PK, PacP	630 - J3
TEMPLE CITY PK, TEML	597 - A2
TEMPLE PK, DWNY	705 - H5
TERRACE PK, LA	634 - B5
TERRACE PK, CHLS	680 - G4
TERRAZA PK, LHB	708 - B6
THERESA LINDSAY PK, LA	674 - B5
THIRD STREET PK, DUAR	568 - A5
THOMPSON, T MAYNE PK, BLF	736 - B3
THORNBURG PK, GAR	733 - G4
THORPE, JIM PK, HAW	733 - E3
THREE SPRINGS PK, WLKV	557 - B7
TIERRA BONITA PK, LAN	4016 - E5
TIERRA VERDE PK, ARCD	597 - E1
TOBERMAN PLGD PK, LA	634 - B5
TOBIAS PK, PanC	501 - J7
TOPANGA STATE PK, PacP	590 - E4
TORRANCE PK, TOR	763 - H7
TORRES, ROSA PK, CLAR	601 - C4
TOURNAMENT PK, PAS	566 - B6
TRAGNIEW PK, COMP	734 - F5
TRAIL REST PK, FUL	738 - J3
TRAILVIEW COUNTY PK, RowH	678 - H7
TRANCAS PK, MAL	626 - J6
TREASURE ISLAND PK, DWNY	706 - B1
TREASURE ISLAND PK, LBCH	826 - C3
TRINITY REC CTR, LA	634 - D7
TRIPOLIS PK, ARCD	566 - J7
TRIUNFO COMM PK, THO	557 - A5
TRUSLOW PK, FUL	738 - J7
TUCKER, WALTER R PK, COMP	734 - H5
TUNA CANYON, LACo	629 - H4
TWO STRIKE COUNTY PK, LaCr	504 - G7
UNION PACIFIC PK, FUL	738 - G7
UPPER ARROYO PK, PAS	535 - E7
VAIL PK, CLAR	571 - E6
VALENCIA GLEN PK, SCTA	4550 - G6
VALENCIA HERITAGE PK, SCTA	4460 - E7
VALENCIA MEADOWS PK, SCTA	4550 - F6
VALENCIA PK, FUL	738 - B7
VALENS, RICHIE PK, Pcma	502 - B3
VALENZUELA, LENA PK, DUAR	567 - J7
VALLEYDALE COUNTY PK, LACo	598 - H2
VALLEY GLEN COMM PK, VanN	532 - D7
VALLEY PK, BURB	533 - B7
VALLEY PK, HMB	732 - G7
VALLEY PLAZA PK, NHol	532 - F5
VALLEY VIEW PK, VeCo	557 - H1
VALLEY VIEW PK, DUAR	568 - E3
VAL VERDE COUNTY PK, Cstc	4459 - B6
VANALDEN PK, Nor	500 - G7
VANDERSLIP, FRANK A SENIOR PK,- RPV	822 - H5
VAN DYKE, MARY PK, SELM	637 - B4
VAN NESS REC CTR, LA	673 - G5
VAN NUYS REC CTR, VanN	532 - A5
VAN NUYS-SHERMAN OAKS PK, - Shrm	562 - A3
VASQUEZ ROCKS COUNTY PK, LACo	4373 - F7
VERDE PK, SIMI	499 - B2
VERDUGO MOUNTAIN PK, SunV	503 - E7
VERDUGO PK, GLDL	564 - H1
VERDUGO PK, BURB	563 - D2
VERMONT SQUARE, LA	673 - J4
VERNON PK, MTCL	601 - H6
VEST POCKET PK, Boyl	635 - A5
VETERANS FREEDOM PK, AZU	568 - J5
VETERANS HIST PLAZA, SCTA	4640 - J1
VETERANS MEM COUNTY PK, LACo	482 - D1
VETERANS MEM PK, LBCH	795 - D2
VETERANS MEM PK, CULC	672 - F2
VETERANS MEM PK, CMRC	676 - B7
VETERANS PK, RBCH	762 - H6
VETERANS PK, CYP	767 - B7
VETERANS PK, BELL	675 - E7
VETERANS PK, LMTA	793 - H5
VETERANS PK, POM	640 - E2
VETERANS PARK & SPORTS- COMPLEX, CRSN	764 - C7
VETERANS PARKWAY, MANB	732 - F5
VIA VERDE PK, SDMS	599 - J6
VICKROY PK, BURB	533 - D6
VICTORIA COUNTY PK, CRSN	764 - D2
VICTOR PK, TOR	763 - B5
VICTORY PK, PAS	566 - E2
VICTORY PK, LBCH	825 - E1
VICTORY VINELAND REC CTR, - NHol	532 - J6
VIKING PK, Nor	500 - H1
VILLA CABRINI PK, LA	533 - D2
VILLAGE PK, PRM	735 - G4
VILLA-PARKE CTR, PAS	565 - J3
VINA VIEJA PK, PAS	566 - F3
VINCENT, EDWARD JR PK, ING	673 - E7
VINCENT PK, RBCH	762 - J4
VINEYARD REC CTR, LA	633 - D7
VIRGINIA AVENUE PK, SMCA	671 - H1
VISTA DEL MAR PK, PdlR	702 - B5
VISTA DEL VALLE PK, LHB	738 - D2
VISTA GRANDE PK, LHB	708 - D7
VISTA VERDE PK, NRWK	736 - G1
WABASH REC CTR, Boyl	635 - C4
WALMERADO PK, WCOV	638 - F3
WALNUT CREEK COUNTY PK, SDMS	599 - H5
WALNUT CREEK NATURE PK, BALD	637 - H2
WALNUT CREEK NATURE PK, CHLS	680 - H3
WALNUT HILLS PK, WAL	679 - D1
WALNUT NATURE COUNTY PK, LACo	704 - J1
WALNUT PK, CHNO	641 - F6
WALNUT RANCH PK, WAL	639 - E4
WALNUT STREET MINI PK, CRSN	734 - D7
WALTERIA PK, TOR	793 - D3
WARDLOW PK, LBCH	766 - B7
WARE, LEE PK, HGDN	767 - A6
WAR MEM PK, SPAS	595 - H1
WARNER RANCH PK, WdHl	560 - A1
WASHINGTON, COLONEL LEON H- COUNTY PK, Wats	704 - G3
WASHINGTON IRVING POCKET PK, - LA	633 - F5
WASHINGTON PK, PAS	566 - A1
WASHINGTON PK, POM	641 - A3
WASHINGTON PK, ELSG	702 - G7
WATKINS, TED COUNTY PK, Wats	704 - F4
WATTLES GARDEN PK, LA	593 - C3
WATTS SENIOR CTR, Wats	704 - G4
WEDDINGTON PK NORTH, LA	563 - A5
WEDDINGTON PK SOUTH, LA	563 - B6
WEINER, BUD PK, HiPk	595 - D4
WELCH, RALPH PK, POM	640 - G3
WESTCHESTER REC CTR, Wch	702 - E3
WEST COYOTE HILLS TREE PK, - FUL	738 - D3
WESTERN HILLS PK, CHLS	710 - G1
WESTGATE PK, CRTS	766 - E2
WEST HILLS REC CTR, CanP	529 - D5
WEST HOLLYWOOD PK, WHWD	592 - H7
WESTMINSTER PK, Ven	671 - G6
WESTMONT PK, POM	640 - E3
WESTRIDGE CANYONBACK PK, Enc	561 - D7
WEST SAN GABRIEL RIVER- PARKWAY, LKWD	766 - F5
WESTSIDE PK, LA	633 - A7
WESTSIDE PK, HNTP	674 - H6
WEST VALLEY PK, Res	530 - H6
WESTWOOD PK, WLA	632 - A4
WHALEY PK, LBCH	796 - C5
WHEELER AVENUE PK, LVRN	600 - E3
WHEELER, STUART PK, CLAR	601 - C5
WHITAKER-JAYNES ESTATE & BACON- HOUSE, BPK	767 - H1
WHITE, CHARLES COUNTY PK, - Alta	535 - H6
WHITE, EDWARD PK, FUL	738 - E4
WHITE POINT PK, SPed	823 - H7
WHITE, ROBERT E PK, NRWK	706 - E7
WHITE, WILLIE PK, POM	601 - A3
WHITNALL HWY PK NORTH, BURB	563 - B1
WHITNALL HWY PK SOUTH, BURB	563 - D2
WHITNEY CANYON PK, SCTA	4641 - D2
WHITTIER, JG PK, WHIT	677 - C7
WHITTIER NARROWS REC AREA, - LACo	636 - J5
WILACRE PK, LA	562 - F7
WILBUR TAMPA PK, Nor	480 - F7
WILDERNESS PK, DWNY	706 - E5
WILDERNESS PK, MTCL	601 - E6
WILDERNESS PK, ARCD	537 - E7
WILD WALNUT PK, CALB	559 - G7
WILDWOOD CANYON PK, BURB	533 - J3
WILLIAMS, HENRY A NORTHSIDE- PK, AZU	568 - H4
WILLOW PK, CYP	767 - B7
WILLOW SPRINGS PK, GLDR	569 - G4
WILL ROGERS MEM PK, BHLS	592 - E7
WILMINGTON REC CTR, Wilm	794 - D7
WILMINGTON TOWN SQUARE, Wilm	794 - E6
WILSON CANYON PK, LACo	4642 - A7
WILSON, CHARLES COMM PK, TOR	763 - G7
WILSON MINI PK, GLDL	564 - G4
WILSON PK, COMP	735 - A4
WINDERMERE PK, LMRD	737 - G4
WINDSOR MINI PK, GLDL	564 - G6
WINNETKA REC CTR, Win	530 - D2
WOODBINE PK, LA	632 - F7
WOODBRIDGE PK, LA	562 - J5
WOODCREST PK, BREA	708 - J4
WOODGROVE PK, WCOV	638 - H5
WOODLAND CAMP, WHIT	637 - A7
WOODLAND HILLS REC CTR, WdHl	559 - J1
WOODLEY AVENUE PK, Enc	531 - F7
WOODS AVENUE PK, ELA	675 - G1
WRIGLEY GREENBELT, LBCH	765 - C7
YORK FIELD PK, WHIT	707 - B2
YOSEMITE REC CTR, Eagl	565 - B7
YUCCA POCKET PK, Hlwd	593 - E4
ZACATECAS PK, AZU	568 - G7
ZAMORA PK, ELMN	597 - F7
ZAPOPAN PK, RSMD	636 - F2
ZELZAH PK, GrnH	481 - A7
ZIMMERMAN PK, NRWK	737 - A1
ZINN, H BYRUM PK, BLF	736 - D2
ZOETER FIELD, SLB	826 - F4
ZUMA TRANCAS CANYONS, LACo	586 - J7

POST OFFICES

FEATURE NAME Address City, ZIP Code	PAGE-GRID
ACTON 3632 SMITH AV, Actn, 93510	4465 - B2
AGOURA HILLS 5158 CLARETON DR, AGRH, 91301	558 - B5
AIRPORT STA LOS ANGELES 9029 AIRPORT BLVD, Wch, 90045	702 - H4
ALHAMBRA 10 W BAY STATE ST, ALH, 91801	596 - B5
ALONDRA 14028 VAN NESS AV, GAR, 90249	733 - H3
ALTADENA 2271 LAKE AV, Alta, 91001	536 - A6
ARCADE 508 S SPRING ST, LA, 90013	634 - F4
ARCADIA 41 WHEELER AV, ARCD, 91006	567 - D5
ARLETA 9454 ARLETA AV, Pcma, 91331	502 - C6
ARTESIA 11721 183RD ST, ART, 90701	766 - G1
A STATION BUENA PARK 8082 COMMONWEALTH AV, BPK, 90621	737 - J7
AVALON 118 METROPOLE ST, AVA, 90704	5923 - H4
AZUSA 110 W 6TH ST, AZU, 91702	568 - J6
BAILEY 6709 WASHINGTON AV, WHIT, 90601	677 - D6
BALDWIN PARK 4230 MAINE AV, BALD, 91706	598 - C5
BARRINGTON 200 S BARRINGTON PL, LACo, 90073	631 - H2
BELL 6327 OTIS AV, BELL, 90201	675 - D7
BELLFLOWER 9835 BELLFLOWER ST, BLF, 90706	736 - C6
BELL GARDENS 7001 GARFIELD AV, BGDN, 90201	705 - J1
BELMONT SHORE 5050 E 2ND ST, LBCH, 90803	826 - B2
BEVERLY 312 S BEVERLY DR, BHLS, 90212	632 - G3
BEVERLY HILLS 325 N MAPLE DR, BHLS, 90210	632 - G1
BICENTENNIAL 7610 BEVERLY BLVD, LA, 90036	633 - C1
BIXBY 4580 ATLANTIC AV, Bxby, 90807	765 - E4
BOYLE HEIGHTS 2016 E 1ST ST, Boyl, 90033	635 - A5
BREA 700 E BIRCH ST, BREA, 92821	709 - C7
BROADWAY MANCHESTER 8525 N BROADWAY AV, LA, 90003	704 - C2
BUENA PARK 7377 LA PALMA AV, BPK, 90620	767 - H3
BURBANK 2140 HOLLYWOOD WY, BURB, 91505	533 - C6
CABRILLO 1690 W 23RD ST, LBCH, 90810	795 - B4
CALABASAS 4774 HWY GRANADA, CALB, 91302	559 - F4
CANOGA PARK 8201 CANOGA AV, LA, 91304	530 - B2
CANYON COUNTRY 18336 SOLEDAD CANYON RD, SCTA, 91387	4551 - J3
CARSON 21350 AVALON BLVD, CRSN, 90745	764 - E6
CASTAIC 31519 CASTAIC RD, Cstc, 91384	4369 - H7
CATALINA 967 E COLORADO BLVD, PAS, 91106	566 - A4
CEDAR STA LANCASTER 567 LANCASTER BLVD, LAN, 93534	4015 - H5
CENTURY CITY FINANCE 9911 W PICO BLVD, LA, 90035	632 - F4
CERRITOS 18122 CARMENITA RD, CRTS, 90703	767 - C1
CHALLENGER 21801 SHERMAN WY, CanP, 91303	530 - A5
CHANDLER 11304 CHANDLER BLVD, NHol, 91601	562 - J2
CHATSWORTH 21606 DEVONSHIRE ST, Chat, 91311	500 - A4
CHINO 5375 WALNUT AV, CHINO, 91710	641 - H6
CITY OF INDUSTRY 15421 E GALE AV, INDS, 91745	678 - B1
CITY OF INDUSTRY 15559 RAUSCH RD, INDS, 91744	638 - D7
CIVIC CTR LA HABRA 200 N EUCLID ST, LHB, 90631	708 - E5
CIVIC CTR VAN NUYS 6200 VAN NUYS BLVD, VanN, 91401	532 - A7
CLAREMONT 140 HARVARD AV, CLAR, 91711	601 - D3
COLE BRANCH 1125 N FAIRFAX AV, WHWD, 90046	593 - B5
COMMERCE 5670 E WASHINGTON BLVD, CMRC, 90040	675 - H4
COMMONWEALTH 202 E COMMONWEALTH AV, FUL, 92832	738 - H7
COMPTON 701 S SANTA FE AV, COMP, 90221	735 - A5
COVINA 545 N RIMSDALE AV, COV, 91722	598 - J5
CRENSHAW 3894 CRENSHAW BLVD, LA, 90008	673 - E2
CRENSHAW IMPERIAL 2672 W IMPERIAL HWY, ING, 90303	703 - G7
CROSSROADS PLAZA 9160 WHITTIER BLVD, PRV, 90660	676 - G3
CUDAHY 4619 ELIZBETH ST, CDHY, 90201	705 - E2
CULVER CITY 11111 JEFFERSON BLVD, CULC, 90230	672 - G5
CYPRESS 5762 LINCOLN AV, CYP, 90630	767 - D6
DEL VALLE FINANCE 819 W WASHINGTON BLVD, LA, 90015	634 - C6
DIAMOND BAR 1317 DIAMOND BAR BLVD, DBAR, 91765	680 - B3
DOCKWEILER 3585 S VERMONT AV, LA, 90007	674 - A1
DOWNEY 8111 FIRESTONE BLVD, DWNY, 90241	706 - A5
DOWNTOWN LONG BEACH 300 LONG BEACH BLVD, LBCH, 90802	795 - E7
DOWNTOWN MANHATTAN BEACH 425 15TH ST, MANB, 90266	732 - F6
DOWNTOWN 135 E OLIVE AV, BURB, 91502	533 - H7
DUARTE 1220 HIGHLAND AV, DUAR, 91010	568 - B5
EAGLE ROCK 7435 N FIGUEROA ST, Eagl, 90041	565 - D6
EAST LONG BEACH 2727 E ANAHEIM ST, LBCH, 90804	795 - H6
EAST LOS ANGELES 975 S ATLANTIC BLVD, ELA, 90022	675 - G1
EAST LYNWOOD 11634 ATLANTIC AV, LYN, 90262	735 - D1
EAST PASADENA 2609 E COLORADO BLVD, PAS, 91107	566 - E4
EASTVIEW 28648 S WESTERN AV, RPV, 90275	823 - H2
EDENDALE 1525 N ALVARADO ST, Echo, 90026	594 - E6
EL MONTE 11151 VALLEY BLVD, ELMN, 91731	597 - D7
EL SEGUNDO MAIN OFFICE 200 MAIN ST, ELSG, 90245	732 - E1
EL SERENO CARRIER ANNEX 3316 EASTERN AV, LA, 90032	595 - E6
ENCINO 5805 WHITE OAK AV, Enc, 91316	561 - B1
FEDERAL STA COVINA 170 E COLLEGE ST, COV, 91723	599 - B5
FIRESTONE 3270 FIRESTONE BLVD, SGAT, 90280	705 - B3
FOY 1808 W 7TH ST, LA, 90057	634 - C3
GARDENA 1455 W REDONDO BEACH BLVD, GAR, 90247	733 - J5
GATEWAY 9942 CULVER BLVD, CULC, 90232	672 - G1
GLASSELL 3950 EAGLE ROCK BLVD, LA, 90065	594 - H1
GLENDALE 313 E BROADWAY, GLDL, 91206	564 - E5
GLENDORA 255 S GLENDORA AV, GLDR, 91741	569 - E6
GLENOAKS 1634 N SAN FERNANDO W, BURB, 91504	533 - F6
G M F STA 2300 N REDONDO AV, LBCH, 90815	795 - J3
GRANADA HILLS 18039 CHATSWORTH ST, GrnH, 91344	501 - A3
GRAND CENTRAL 6444 SAN FERNANDO RD, GLDL, 91201	564 - A2
GREENMEAD FINANCE 12003 AVALON BLVD, LA, 90059	704 - D7
GRIFFITH 3370 GLENDALE BLVD, LA, 90039	594 - E1
HANCOCK 8200 S VERMONT AV, LA, 90044	704 - A2
HARBOR CITY 25690 FRAMPTON AV, Hrbr, 90710	794 - A5
HAWAIIAN GARDENS 21101 NORWALK BLVD, HGDN, 90716	766 - J5
HAWKINS, AUGUSTUS F. 10301 COMPTON AV, Wats, 90002	704 - G5

FEATURE NAME	Address City, ZIP Code	PAGE-GRID
HAWTHORNE	12700 INGLEWOOD AV, HAW, 90250	733 - B1
HAZARD	3729 E 1ST ST, City, 90063	635 - D6
HERMOSA BEACH	565 PIER AV, HMB, 90254	762 - H2
HIGHLAND PARK	5930 N FIGUEROA ST, HiPk, 90042	595 - D2
HILLCREST INGLEWOOD	300 E HILLCREST BLVD, ING, 90301	703 - C3
HOLLYDALE	12129 GARFIELD AV, SGAT, 90280	735 - F1
HOLLYWOOD	1615 WILCOX AV, Hlwd, 90028	593 - E4
HUB CITY	101 S WILLOWBROOK AV, COMP, 90220	734 - J4
HUNTINGTON PARK	6606 SEVILLE AV, HNTP, 90255	674 - J7
IRWINDALE	16025 CALLE DEL NORTE, IRW, 91706	598 - F3
JACKIE ROBINSON ANNEX	1100 N FAIR OAKS AV, PAS, 91103	565 - H2
LA CANADA FLINTRIDGE	607 FOOTHILL BLVD, LCF, 91011	535 - C4
LA COSTA MALIBU	21229 PACIFIC COAST HWY, MAL, 90265	629 - F6
LA CRESCENTA	3300 FOOTHILL BLVD, GLDL, 91214	504 - E7
LA HABRA	1001 W IMPERIAL HWY, LHB, 90631	708 - D7
LAKE HUGHES	16817 ELIZABETH LAKE RD, LACo, 93532	4102 - B3
LAKE LOS ANGELES	39470 170TH ST E, LACo, 93591	4199 - H4
LAKEWOOD	5200 CLARK AV, LKWD, 90712	766 - B3
LA MIRADA	14901 ADELFA DR, LMRD, 90638	737 - H4
LANCASTER	1008 W AVE J2, LAN, 93534	4015 - G7
LA PUENTE	15310 ELLIOTT AV, LPUE, 91744	638 - D5
LA TIJERA	5472 CRENSHAW BLVD, LA, 90043	673 - F5
LA VERNE	3355 N WHITE AV, LVRN, 91750	600 - H2
LAWNDALE	4320 MARINE AV, LNDL, 90260	733 - D5
LENNOX	4443 LENNOX BLVD, Lenx, 90304	703 - C6
LINCOLN RETAIL STORE	3001 N BROADWAY, LA, 90031	635 - A1
LITTLEROCK	7765 PEARBLOSSOM HWY, Litl, 93543	4377 - G1
LLANO	17234 PEARBLOSSOM HWY, Llan, 93544	4379 - J3
LOMITA	25131 NARBONNE AV, LMTA, 90717	793 - G4
LOS ALAMITOS	10650 REAGAN ST, LALM, 90720	796 - J2
LOS ANGELES	7001 S CENTRAL AV, LA, 90001	674 - E7
LOS FELIZ	1825 N VERMONT AV, LFlz, 90027	594 - A3
LOS NIETOS	8232 NORWALK BLVD, LACo, 90606	706 - J1
LUGO	3641 E 8TH ST, LA, 90023	675 - C1
LYNWOOD	11200 LONG BEACH BLVD, LYN, 90262	705 B6
MAGNOLIA PARK	3810 W MAGNOLIA BLVD, BURB, 91505	563 - C2
MALIBU	23838 PACIFIC COAST HWY, MAL, 90265	628 - J7
MANHATTAN BEACH	1007 N SEPULVEDA BLVD, MANB, 90266	732 - G6
MARCELINA	1433 MARCELINA AV, TOR, 90501	763 - H6
MARINA DEL REY	4766 ADMIRALTY WY, MdlR, 90292	672 - B7
MARINER	221 MAIN ST, SLB, 90740	826 - E4
MARKET	1122 E 7TH ST, LA, 90021	634 - G6
MAR VISTA	3826 GRAND VIEW BLVD, LA, 90066	672 - C4
MAYWOOD FINANCE	4357 E SLAUSON AV, MYWD, 90270	675 - D5
MIRACLE MILE	5350 WILSHIRE BLVD, LA, 90036	633 - D3
MISSION CITY	10919 SEPULVEDA BLVD, MsnH, 91345	501 - G2
MISSION HILLS	15305 DEVONSHIRE ST, MsnH, 91345	501 - H4
MONROVIA	225 S IVY AV, MNRO, 91016	567 - G4
MONTCLAIR	5186 BENITO ST, MTCL, 91763	601 - G6
MONTEBELLO	145 N 5TH ST, MTBL, 90640	676 - E2
MONTEREY PARK	245 W GARVEY AV, MONP, 91754	636 - B2
MORNINGSIDE PARK	3212 W 85TH ST, ING, 90305	703 - F2
MOUNT BALDY (SEE PAGE 511)	6730 MOUNT BALDY RD, SBdC	512 - A5
NEWHALL	24201 THE OLD ROAD, StvR, 91381	4640 - F4
NORTH GLENDALE	1009 N PACIFIC AV, GLDL, 91202	564 - D3
NORTH HILLS	8759 SEPULVEDA BLVD, LA, 91343	531 - G1
NORTH HOLLYWOOD	7035 LAUREL CANYON BLVD, NHol, 91605	532 - G5
NORTH INGLEWOOD	811 N LA BREA AV, ING, 90302	703 - C1
NORTH LONG BEACH	101 E MARKET ST, NLB, 90805	765 - D3
NORTH REDONDO BEACH	2215 ARTESIA BLVD, RBCH, 90278	763 - A1
NORTHRIDGE	9534 RESEDA BLVD, Nor, 91325	500 - J6
NORTH TORRANCE	18080 CRENSHAW BLVD, TOR, 90504	763 - G1
NORWALK	14011 CLARKDALE AV, NRWK, 90650	736 - H3
OAKWOOD	265 S WESTERN AV, LA, 90004	633 - H1
OCEAN PARK	2720 NEILSON WY, SMCA, 90405	671 - F4
ONTARIO PLAZA	SBDO ST & MTN AV, ONT, 91762	601 - J6
ORANGEHURST	1920 W COMMONWEALTH AV, FUL, 92833	738 - C7
ORANGEWOOD	99 CALIFORNIA BLVD, PAS, 91105	565 - H6
PACIFIC PALISADES	15209 W SUNSET BLVD, PacP, 90272	631 - A5
PACIFIC	1920 PACIFIC AV, LBCH, 90806	795 - D4
PACOIMA	13507 VAN NUYS BLVD, Pcma, 91331	502 - C3
PADDISON SQUARE	12415 NORWALK BLVD, NRWK, 90650	736 - J1
PALMS	3751 MOTOR AV, LA, 90034	672 - F1
PALOS VERDES ESTATES	2516 TEJON, PVE, 90274	792 - J4
PALOS VERDES PENINSULA	955 DEEP VALLEY DR, RHE, 90274	823 - B1
PANORAMA CITY	14416 CHASE ST, PanC, 91402	532 - A1
PARAMOUNT	7200 SOMERSET BLVD, PRM, 90723	735 - F4
PASADENA WINDOW UNIT	600 LINCOLN AV, PAS, 91103	565 - H3
PICO HEIGHTS	2390 W PICO BLVD, LA, 90006	634 - A4
PICO RIVERA	6320 PASSONS BLVD, PRV, 90660	676 - G5
PINON HILLS (SEE PAGE 4471)	10353 OASIS RD, SBdC, 92372	4472 - B5
PLAYA DEL REY	215 CULVER BLVD, PdlR, 90293	702 - A3
PLAYA VISTA	7381 LA TIJERA AV, Wch, 90045	702 - J1
PLAZA PASADENA	281 E COLORADO BLVD, PAS, 91101	565 - J4
POINT DUME	29160 HEATHERCLIFF RD, MAL, 90265	667 - E2
POMONA	580 W MONTEREY AV, POM, 91768	640 - H1
PORTER RANCH	19300 RINALDI ST, Nor, 91326	500 - F2
QUARTZ HILL	42103 50TH ST W, LACo, 93536	4104 - H5
RANCHO LOS AMIGOS STA	13003 DAHLIA ST, DWNY, 90242	735 - G1
REDONDO BEACH	1201 N CATALINA AV, RBCH, 90277	762 - H3
RESEDA	7320 RESEDA BLVD, Res, 91335	530 J4
RIMPAU	4040 W WASHINGTON BLVD, LA, 90018	633 F6
ROSEMEAD	8845 VALLEY BLVD, RSMD, 91770	596 - H6
ROWLAND HEIGHTS	1521 NOGALES ST, RowH, 91748	679 - B4
SAN DIMAS	300 E BONITA AV, SDMS, 91773	600 - C2
SAN FERNANDO MAIN	308 S MACLAY AV, SFER, 91340	482 - A7
SANFORD	3751 W 6TH ST, LA, 90020	633 - J2
SAN GABRIEL	120 S DEL MAR AV, SGBL, 91776	596 - E3
SAN MARINO	2960 HUNTINGTON DR, SMRO, 91108	566 - F7
SAN PEDRO	839 S SAN PEDRO ST, SPed, 90731	824 - C5
SANTA CLARITA	24355 CREEKSIDE RD, SCTA, 91355	4550 - E2
SANTA FE PLAZA	13445 TELEGRAPH RD, SFSP, 90605	707 - C5
SANTA FE SPRINGS	11760 TELEGRAPH RD, SFSP, 90670	706 - G4
SANTA MONICA	1248 5TH ST, SMCA, 90401	671 - E2
SANTA WESTERN	1385 N WESTERN AV, Hlwd, 90028	593 - H5
SEAL BEACH	2929 WESTMINSTER AV, SLB, 90740	826 - H2
SHERMAN OAKS	14900 MAGNOLIA BLVD, Shrm, 91403	561 - J3
SIERRA MADRE	61 S BALDWIN AV, SMAD, 91024	567 - A2
SLAUSON	9240 SLAUSON AV, PRV, 90660	706 - E1
SOUTH DOWNEY	7911 IMPERIAL HWY, DWNY, 90242	705 - J7
SOUTH EL MONTE	10452 RUSH ST, SELM, 91733	637 - C3
SOUTH GARDENA	1103 W GARDENA BLVD, GAR, 90247	734 - A6
SOUTH GATE	10120 WRIGHT RD, SGAT, 90280	705 - E5
SOUTH HILL	1418 S AZUSA AV, WCOV, 91791	638 - J3
SOUTH PASADENA	1001 FREMONT AV, SPAS, 91030	595 - H2
SOUTH SAN GABRIEL	8111 NEWMARK AV, RSMD, 91770	636 - F2
SPRING CARRIER ANNEX	3019 N BELLFLOWER BLVD, LBCH, 90808	796 - C2
STATE STREET	7800 STATE ST, HNTP, 90255	705 - B1
STUDIO CITY	3950 LAUREL CANYON BLVD, LA, 91604	562 - G6
SUNLAND	8587 FENWICK ST, Sunl, 91040	503 - F3
SUNNY HILLS	1820 SUNNYCREST DR, FUL, 92835	738 - G4
SUNSET	1425 N CHEROKEE AV, Hlwd, 90028	593 - E5
SUN VALLEY	10946 RATNER ST, SunV, 91352	533 - A2
SYLMAR	13700 FOOTHILL BLVD, LA, 91342	482 - B4
TARZANA	5609 YOLANDA AV, Tarz, 91356	560 - H2
TEMPLE CITY	5940 OAK ST, TEML, 91780	596 - J3
TERMINAL ANNEX	900 N ALAMEDA ST, LA, 90012	634 - G3
TEXTILE FINANCE	100 W OLYMPIC BLVD, LA, 90015	634 - E5
THOUSAND OAKS	3435 E THOUSAND OAKS BLVD, THO, 91362	557 - B3
TOLUCA LAKE	10063 RIVERSIDE DR, LA, 91602	563 - C4
TOPANGA	101 S TOPANGA CANYON BLVD, Top, 90290	590 - A6
TORRANCE	2510 MONTEREY ST, TOR, 90503	763 - F7
TOWN SQUARE	2220 E PALMDALE BLVD, PMDL, 93550	4286 - E1
TROPICO	120 E CHEVY CHASE DR, GLDL, 91205	564 - E6
TUJUNGA	10209 TUJUNGA CANYON BLVD, Tuj, 91042	504 - A4
VALLEY PLAZA	6242 VANTAGE AV, NHol, 91606	532 - G7
VALLEY VILLAGE	12450 MAGNOLIA BLVD, LA, 91607	562 - F2
VAN NUYS	15701 SHERMAN WY, VanN, 91406	531 - G4
VENICE	1601 MAIN ST, Ven, 90291	671 - H6
VERDUGO VIEJO	101 N VERDUGO RD, GLDL, 91206	564 - G5
VERNON	5121 HAMPTON ST, VER, 90058	674 - J4
VICTORY CTR	6535 LANKERSHIM BLVD, NHol, 91606	532 - H6
VIKING	5405 E VILLAGE RD, LBCH, 90808	766 - C5
VILLAGE STA	11000 WILSHIRE BLVD, Wwd, 90024	632 - A3
WAGNER BRANCH	2200 W CENTURY BLVD, ING, 90303	703 - G5
WALNUT	280 S LEMON AV, WAL, 91789	679 - F1
WALTERIA	4216 PACIFIC COAST HWY, TOR, 90505	793 - C3
WASHINGTON LOS ANGELES	4352 S CENTRAL AV, LA, 90011	674 - E3
WASHINGTON PASADENA	1355 N MENTOR AV, PAS, 91104	566 - A1
WEST ADAMS	4960 W WASHINGTON BLVD, LA, 90016	633 - D5
WEST ARCADIA	725 W DUARTE RD, ARCD, 91007	567 - A7
WEST BRANCH	820 SAN VICENTE BLVD, WHWD, 90069	592 - H6
WEST COVINA	396 S CALIFORNIA ST, WCOV, 91790	638 - G1
WEST HILLS	23055 SHERMAN WY, CanP, 91307	529 - G5
WEST LOS ANGELES	11270 EXPOSITION BLVD, LA, 90064	632 - C6
WEST LOS ANGELES FINANCE	11420 SANTA MONICA BLVD, WLA, 90025	632 - A5
WESTVERN	1515 W VERNON AV, LA, 90062	673 - J3
WHITTER	8520 MICHIGAN BLVD, WHIT, 90605	707 - E2
WHITTWOOD	10053 WHITTWOOD DR, WHIT, 90603	707 - H4
WILCOX	6457 SANTA MONICA BLVD, LA, 90038	593 - F5
WILLOWBROOK	2241 E EL SEGUNDO BLVD, Wbrk, 90222	734 - H1
WILL ROGERS	1217 WILSHIRE BLVD, SMCA, 90403	671 - E1
WILMINGTON	10080 N AVALON BLVD, Wilm, 90744	794 - E6
WINNETKA	7655 WINNETKA AV, Win, 91306	530 - E4
WOODLAND HILLS	22121 CLARENDON ST, WdHl, 91367	559 - J2
WRIGHTWOOD (SEE PAGE 4651)	1440 HWY 2, SBdC, 92397	4652 - D2
YORBA	2138 N GAREY AV, POM, 91767	600 - J5
YORK	5132 YORK BLVD, HiPk, 90042	595 - B1

SCHOOLS

FEATURE NAME	Address City, ZIP Code	PAGE-GRID
1ST STREET ELEM	2820 E 1ST ST, Boyl, 90033	635 - B5
2ND STREET ELEM	1942 E 2ND ST, Boyl, 90033	635 - A5
3RD STREET ELEM	201 S JUNE ST, LA, 90004	633 - E1
4TH STREET ELEM	420 AMALIA AV, ELA, 90022	635 - H7
6TH AVENUE ELEM	3109 6TH AV, LA, 90018	633 - F7
7TH STREET ELEM	1570 W 7TH ST, LA, 90732	823 - J5
9TH STREET ELEM	820 TOWNE AV, LA, 90021	634 - F6
10TH STREET ELEM	1000 GRATTAN ST, LA, 90015	634 - C4
15TH STREET ELEM	1527 S MESA ST, SPed, 90731	824 - B6
20TH STREET ELEM	1353 E 20TH ST, LA, 90011	674 - F1
24TH STREET ELEM	2055 W 24TH ST, LA, 90018	633 - H6
28TH STREET ELEM	2807 STANFORD AV, LA, 90011	674 - E1
32ND STREET USC ELEM	822 W 32ND ST, LA, 90007	634 - B7
32ND STREET USC MAGNET	822 W 32ND ST, LA, 90007	674 - B1
42ND STREET ELEM	4231 4TH AV, LA, 90008	673 - G3
49TH STREET ELEM	750 E 49TH ST, LA, 90011	674 - E4
52ND STREET ELEM	816 W 51ST ST, LA, 90037	674 - B4
54TH STREET ELEM	5501 EILEEN AV, LACo, 90043	673 - D5
59TH STREET ELEM	5939 2ND AV, LA, 90043	673 - G6
61ST STREET ELEM	6020 S FIGUEROA ST, LA, 90003	674 - B6
66TH STREET ELEM	6600 S SAN PEDRO ST, LA, 90003	674 - D7
68TH STREET ELEM	612 W 68TH ST, LA, 90044	674 - B7
74TH STREET ELEM	2112 W 74TH ST, LA, 90047	703 - G1
75TH STREET ELEM	142 W 75TH ST, LA, 90003	704 - C1
92ND STREET ELEM	9211 GRAPE ST, Wats, 90002	704 - H3
93RD STREET ELEM	330 E 93RD ST, LA, 90003	704 - D4
95TH STREET ELEM	1109 W 96TH ST, LACo, 90044	704 - A4
96TH STREET ELEM	1471 E 96TH ST, Wats, 90002	704 - F4
98TH STREET ELEM	5431 W 98TH ST, Wch, 90045	703 - A4
99TH STREET ELEM	9900 S WADSWORTH AV, Wats, 90002	704 - E4
107TH STREET ELEM	147 E 107TH ST, LA, 90003	704 - D5
109TH STREET ELEM	10915 MCKINLEY AV, LA, 90059	704 E6
112TH STREET ELEM	1265 E 112TH ST, LA, 90059	704 - F6
116TH STREET ELEM	11610 STANFORD AV, LA, 90059	704 - E7
118TH STREET ELEM	144 E 118TH ST, LA, 90061	704 - D7
122ND STREET ELEM	405 E 122ND ST, LACo, 90061	734 - D1
135TH STREET ELEM	801 W 135TH ST, LA, 90247	734 - B2
153RD STREET ELEM	1605 W 153RD ST, GAR, 90247	733 - J5
156TH STREET ELEM	2100 W 156TH ST, GAR, 90249	733 - H5
186TH STREET ELEM	1581 W 186TH ST, LA, 90248	763 - J2
232ND PLACE ELEM	23240 ARCHIBALD AV, CRSN, 90745	794 - C2
ABBOTT ELEM	5260 CLARK ST, LYN, 90262	735 - D2
ACACIA BAPTIST DAY	4712 W EL SEGUNDO BLVD, HAW, 90250	733 - B2
ACADEMIA SEMILLAS DE PUEBLO-ELEM	4736 HUNTINGTON DR S, LA, 90032	595 - E6
ACADEMY OF THE CANYONS HIGH	26455 ROCKWELL CANYON RD, SCTA, 91355	4550 - D5
ACCELERATED CHARTER	4000 S MAIN ST, LA, 90011	674 - C2
ADAMS, JOHN ELEM	2121 W 238TH ST, TOR, 90501	793 - H2
ADAMS, JOHN MID	2425 16TH ST, SMCA, 90405	671 - H2
ADAMS MID	151 W 30TH ST, LA, 90007	674 - C1
ADAMS MID	2600 RIPLEY AV, RBCH, 90278	763 - B1
ADAT ARI EL DAY ELEM	12020 BURBANK BLVD, LA, 91607	562 - G1
ADDAMS ELEM	5320 PINE AV, NLB, 90805	765 - D3
ADDAMS, JANE MID	4535 W 153RD PL, LNDL, 90260	733 - C5
ADVENTIST UNION ELEM	15548 SANTA ANA AV, BLF, 90706	736 - A4
AEOLIAN ELEM	11600 AEOLIAN ST, LACo, 90606	706 - J1
AGBU MANOOGIAN-DEMIRDJIAN	6844 OAKDALE AV, Win, 91306	530 - E6
AGOURA HIGH	28545 W DRIVER AV, AGRH, 91301	558 - B5
AGUA DULCE ELEM	11311 W FRASCATI ST, LACo, 91390	4373 - D7
ALAMEDA ELEM	8613 ALAMEDA ST, DWNY, 90242	706 - A7
ALBION STREET ELEM	322 S AVE 18, LA, 90031	634 - J1
ALCOTT ELEM	1600 S TOWNE AV, POM, 91766	641 - A4
ALDAMA ELEM	632 N AVE 50, HiPk, 90042	595 - B3
ALEXANDRIA AVENUE ELEM	4211 OAKWOOD AV, LA, 90004	593 - J7
ALEXANDRIA JR SCIENCE CHARTER	3737 S FIGUEROA ST, LA, 90037	674 - B2
AL HADI ELEM	5150 GAGE AV, BELL, 90201	675 - F7
ALHAMBRA HIGH	101 S 2ND ST, ALH, 91801	596 - B5
ALLEN AVENUE ELEM	740 E ALLEN AV, SDMS, 91750	600 - D1
ALLENDALE ELEM	1135 S EUCLID AV, PAS, 91106	565 - J7
ALLESANDRO ELEM	2210 RIVERSIDE DR, LA, 90039	594 - F4
ALLISON ELEM	1011 RUSSELL PL, POM, 91767	601 - B6
ALL SAINTS CATHOLIC ELEM	3420 PORTOLA AV, LA, 90032	595 - F6
ALL SOULS PARISH ELEM	29 S ELECTRIC AV, ALH, 91801	595 - J5
ALMONDALE MID	9330 E AVE U, Litl, 93543	4288 - A7
ALOHA ELEM	11737 214TH ST, LKWD, 90715	766 - G5
ALONDRA ELEM	16200 DOWNEY AV, PRM, 90723	735 - J5
ALPINE ELEM	8244 PEARBLOSSOM HWY, Litl, 93543	4377 - H2
ALTADENA ELEM	743 E CALAVERAS ST, Alta, 91001	536 - A6
ALTA LOMA ELEM	1745 VINEYARD AV, LA, 90019	633 - E5
ALTA VISTA ELEM	815 KNOB HILL AV, RBCH, 90277	763 - A7
ALVARADO ELEM	1900 E 21ST ST, SIGH, 90755	795 - G4
ALVARADO INTERMED	1901 DESIRE AV, RowH, 91748	679 - B5
ALVERNO HIGH	200 N MICHILLINDA AV, SMAD, 91024	566 - H2
AMARGOSA CREEK MID	44333 27TH ST, LAN, 93536	4015 - C7
AMBLER AVENUE ELEM	319 E SHERMAN DR, CRSN, 90746	734 - D7
AMERICAN MARTYRS	1701 LAUREL AV, MANB, 90266	732 - F5
AMESTOY ELEM	1048 W 149TH ST, GAR, 90247	734 - A4
ANATOLA AVENUE ELEM	7364 ANATOLA AV, VanN, 91406	531 - B4
ANAVERDE HILLS ELEM	39360 SUMMERWIND DR, PMDL, 93551	4195 - F5
ANDASOL AVENUE ELEM	10126 ENCINO AV, Nor, 91325	501 - B4
ANDERSON ELEM	2210 E 130TH ST, Wbrk, 90222	734 - H2
ANDERSON ELEM	4130 W 154TH ST, LNDL, 90260	733 - D5
ANDREWS ELEM	1010 CARAWAY DR, LACo, 90601	637 - F5
ANGELES MESA ELEM	2611 W 52ND ST, LA, 90043	673 - G5
ANIMO INGLEWOOD CHARTER HIGH	3425 W MANCHESTER BLVD, ING, 90305	703 - F2
ANIMO J ROBINSON CHARTER HIGH	3500 S HILL ST, LA, 90007	674 - C1
ANIMO LEADERSHIP HIGH	1155 W ARBOR VITAE ST, ING, 90301	703 - A4
ANIMO SOUTH LA CHARTER HS	11100 S WESTERN AV, LACo, 90047	703 - H6
ANIMO VENICE CHARTER HIGH	841 CALIFORNIA AV, Ven, 90291	671 - J5
ANITA OAKS	822 BRADBOURNE AV, DUAR, 91010	568 - C4
ANNALEE AVENUE ELEM	19410 S ANNALEE AV, CRSN, 90746	764 - F3

FEATURE NAME	Address City, ZIP Code	PAGE-GRID
ANNANDALE ELEM	6125 POPPY PEAK DR, HiPk, 90042	565 - D7
ANNENBERG, WALLIS CHARTER HIGH	4000 S MAIN ST, LA, 90011	674 - C3
ANN STREET ELEM	126 BLOOM ST, LA, 90012	634 - H2
ANNUNCIATION ELEM	1307 E LONGDEN AV,, 91006	597 - G1
ANTELOPE ELEM	37237 100TH ST E, Litl, 93543	4288 - C3
ANTELOPE VALLEY CHRISTIAN	3700 W AVE L, LAN, 93536	4105 - A4
ANTELOPE VALLEY HIGH	44900 DIVISION ST, LAN, 93535	4015 - J5
ANTHONYS ELEM	8420 CRENSHAW BLVD, ING, 90305	703 - F2
ANZA ELEM	21400 ELLINWOOD DR, TOR, 90503	763 - B6
APPERSON STREET ELEM	10233 WOODWARD AV, Sunl, 91040	503 - H4
ARAGON AVENUE ELEM	1118 ARAGON AV, LA, 90065	594 - J5
ARBOLITA	1001 BROOKDALE AV, LHB, 90631	708 - F4
ARCADIA CHRISTIAN ELEM	1900 S SANTA ANITA AV, ARCD, 91006	597 - D1
ARCADIA HIGH	180 CAMPUS DR, ARCD, 91007	567 - C6
ARCHER FOR GIRLS HIGH	11725 W SUNSET BLVD, Brwd, 90049	631 - G2
ARLETA CHRISTIAN	13821 OSBORNE ST, Pcma, 91331	502 - B7
ARLETA HIGH	14200 VAN NUYS BLVD, Pcma, 91331	502 - A5
ARLINGTON ELEM	17800 VAN NESS AV, TOR, 90504	763 - H1
ARLINGTON HEIGHTS ELEM	1717 7TH AV, LA, 90019	633 - F5
ARMENIAN MESROBIAN	8420 BEVERLY RD, PRV, 90660	676 - F2
ARMENIAN SISTERS ACADEMY	2361 FLORENCITA AV, Mont, 91020	534 - H3
ARMINTA STREET ELEM	11530 STRATHERN ST, NHol, 91605	532 - H3
ARMSTRONG ELEM	22750 BEAVERHEAD DR, DBAR, 91765	640 - B7
ARNOLD ELEM	9281 DENNI ST, CYP, 90630	767 - B6
ARNOLD, JOSEPH ELEM	4100 W 227TH ST, TOR, 90505	793 - C1
AROVISTA ELEM	900 EADINGTON DR, BREA, 92821	738 - J1
ARROW HIGH	1505 SUNFLOWER AV, GLDR, 91740	599 - G2
ARROW MONTESSORI ELEM	908 W ARROW HWY, SDMS, 91773	599 - J2
ARROYO ELEM	1605 ARROYO AV, POM, 91768	640 - F1
ARROYO HIGH	4921 CEDAR AV, ELMN, 91731	597 - E4
ARROYO SECO JR HIGH	27171 VIS DELGADO DR, SCTA, 91354	4460 - H6
ARROYO SECO MAGNET ELEM	4805 SYCAMORE TER, HiPk, 90042	595 - B4
ARROYO VISTA ELEM	335 EL CENTRO ST, SPAS, 91030	595 - F2
ARTESIA HIGH	12108 DEL AMO BLVD, LKWD, 90715	766 - J4
ASCENSION LUTHERAN ELEM	17910 PRAIRIE AV, TOR, 90504	763 - E1
ASCENSION LUTHERAN ELEM	5820 WEST BLVD, LA, 90043	673 - E6
ASCENSION	500 W 111TH PL, LA, 90044	704 - B6
ASCOT AVENUE ELEM	1447 E 45TH ST, LA, 90011	674 - F3
ASSUMPTION B V M	2660 E ORANGE GROVE BLVD, PAS, 91107	566 - E3
ASSUMPTION ELEM	3016 WINTER ST, LA, 90063	635 - C4
ATHERTON CHRISTIAN BAPTIST	2627 W 116TH ST, ING, 90303	703 - G7
ATWATER AVENUE ELEM	3271 SILVER LAKE BLVD, LA, 90039	594 - E2
AUDUBON MID	4120 11TH AV, LA, 90008	673 - F3
AURORA ELEM	1050 E 52ND PL, LA, 90011	674 - E5
AVALON ELEM	200 FALLS CANYON RD, AVA, 90704	5923 - G4
AVALON GARDENS ELEM	13940 S SAN PEDRO ST, LACo, 90061	734 - D3
AVALON JUNIOR & SENIOR HIGH	200 FALLS CANYON RD, AVA, 90704	5923 - G4
AZUSA HIGH	240 N CERRITOS AV, AZU, 91702	569 - A7
BADEN-POWELL ELEM	2911 W STONYBROOK DR, ANA, 92804	767 - J7
BADILLO ELEM	1771 E OLD BADILLO ST, COV, 91724	599 - F5
BAKER ELEM	12043 EXLINE ST, ELMN, 91732	637 - F1
BALBOA ELEM	1844 BEL AIRE DR, GLDL, 91201	534 - A7
BALBOA GIFTED MAGNET ELEM	17020 LABRADOR ST, Nor, 91325	501 - C5
BALDWIN ACADEMY	1616 GRIFFITH AV, LACo, 91744	638 - E3
BALDWIN HILLS ELEM	5421 RODEO RD, LA, 90016	673 - B1
BALDWIN, MARTHA ELEM	900 S ALMANSOR ST, ALH, 91801	596 - C6
BALDWIN PARK HIGH	3900 PUENTE AV, BALD, 91706	598 - D5
BALDWIN STOCKER ELEM	422 WEST LEMON AV, ARCD, 91007	597 - B1
BANCROFT ELEM	5301 E CENTRALIA ST, LBCH, 90808	766 - B4
BANCROFT MID	929 N LAS PALMAS AV, LA, 90038	593 - E6
BANDINI ELEM	2318 COUTS AV, CMRC, 90040	675 - F3
BANDINI STREET ELEM	425 N BANDINI ST, LA, 90732	824 - A4
BANNING ELEM	500 ISLAND AV, Wilm, 90744	794 - E7
BANNING HIGH	1527 LAKME AV, Wilm, 90744	794 - E4
BARFIELD ELEM	2181 N SAN ANTONIO AV, POM, 91767	601 - B5
BARNHART ELEM	240 W COLORADO BLVD, ARCD, 91007	567 - C4
BARRANCA ELEM	727 S BARRANCA AV, COV, 91723	599 - C6
BARREL SPRINGS ELEM	3636 PONDEROSA WY, PMDL, 93550	4286 - H5
BARRETT, CHARLES W ELEM	419 W 98TH ST, LA, 90003	704 - C4
BARTON ELEM	1100 E DEL AMO BLVD, Bxby, 90807	765 - F4
BARTON HILL ELEM	423 N PACIFIC AV, SPed, 90731	824 - B4
BASSETT HIGH	755 ARDILLA AV, LPUE, 91746	638 - A3
BASSETT STREET ELEM	15756 BASSETT ST, VanN, 91406	531 - F5
BAXTER, ALBERT ELEM	14929 CERRITOS AV, BLF, 90706	736 - A4
BAY LAUREL ELEM	24740 PAS PRIMARIO, CALB, 91302	559 - D6
BEACHY AVENUE ELEM	9757 BEACHY AV, Pcma, 91331	502 - B5
BEARDSLEE ELEM	1212 KELLWIL WY, DUAR, 91010	568 - A7
BEATITUDES OF OUR LORD	13021 S SANTA GERTRUDES AV, LMRD, 90638	737 - J1
BEATTY ELEM	8201 COUNTRY CLUB DR, BPK, 90621	737 - J5
BECKFORD AVENUE ELEM	19130 TULSA ST, Nor, 91326	500 - G3
BEECHWOOD ELEM	780 BEECHWOOD AV, FUL, 92835	738 - J3
BEETHOVEN STREET ELEM	3711 BEETHOVEN ST, LA, 90066	672 - B4
BELLARMINE-JEFFERSON HIGH	465 E OLIVE AV, BURB, 91501	533 - H6
BELLA VISTA ELEM	2410 FINDLAY AV, MONP, 91754	636 - A6
BELLEVUE PRIMARY	610 MICHELTORENA ST, Echo, 90026	594 - B7
BELLFLOWER HIGH	15301 MCNAB AV, BLF, 90706	736 - D4
BELL GARDENS CHRISTIAN	6262 GAGE AV, BGDN, 90201	675 - H7
BELL GARDENS ELEM	5620 QUINN ST, BGDN, 90201	705 - F2
BELL GARDENS HIGH	6119 AGRA ST, BGDN, 90201	675 - H7
BELL GARDENS INTERMED	5841 LIVE OAK ST, BGDN, 90201	705 - G1
BELL HIGH	4328 BELL AV, BELL, 90201	675 - D7
BELMONT HIGH	1575 W 2ND ST, Echo, 90026	634 - D2
BELMONT NEW 6 ELEM	100 N NEW HAMPSHIRE AV, LA, 90004	634 - A1
BELVEDERE ELEM	3724 E 1ST ST, City, 90063	635 - D6
BELVEDERE MID	312 N RECORD AV, City, 90063	635 - E5
BENNETT-KEW ELEM	11710 CHERRY AV, ING, 90303	703 - F7
BENTON MID	15709 OLIVE BRANCH DR, LMRD, 90638	737 - H1
BERENDO MID	1157 S BERENDO ST, LA, 90006	634 - A4
BERKELEY HALL ELEM	16000 MULHOLLAND DR, Brwd, 90049	591 - F1
BERTRAND AVENUE ELEM	7021 BERTRAND AV, Res, 91335	531 - A5
BERYL HEIGHTS ELEM	920 BERYL ST, RBCH, 90277	762 - J3
BETHANY BAPTIST ELEM	2244 CLARK AV, LBCH, 90815	796 - B3
BETHANY CHRISTIAN ELEM	93 N BALDWIN AV, SMAD, 91024	567 - A2
BETHANY LUTHERAN ELEM	5100 E ARBOR RD, LBCH, 90808	766 - B4
BETHEL CHRISTIAN ELEM	3100 AVE K, LAN, 93536	4105 - C2
BETHEL CHRISTIAN HIGH	3100 AVE K, LAN, 93536	4105 - B2
BETHEL LUTHERAN ELEM	17500 BURBANK BLVD, Enc, 91316	561 - B2
BETHUNE MID	155 W 69TH ST, LA, 90003	674 - C7
BEVERLY HILLS HIGH	241 S MORENO DR, BHLS, 90212	632 - E3
BEVERLY VISTA ELEM	200 S ELM DR, BHLS, 90212	632 - G2
BIRMINGHAM HIGH	17000 HAYNES ST, VanN, 91406	531 - C6
BIRNEY ELEM	1600 GREEN LN, RBCH, 90278	763 - A1
BIRNEY ELEM	710 W SPRING ST, LBCH, 90806	795 - C2
BIRNEY ELEM	8501 ORANGE AV, PRV, 90660	706 - F2
BISHOP ALEMANY HIGH	11111 ALEMANY DR, MsnH, 91345	501 - H1
BISHOP AMAT MEM HIGH	14301 FAIRGROVE AV, LACo, 91746	638 - C3
BISHOP CONATY OUR LADY OF-LORETTO	2900 W PICO BLVD, LA, 90006	633 - J5
BISHOP MONTGOMERY HIGH	5430 TORRANCE BLVD, TOR, 90503	763 - A6
BISHOP MORA SALESIAN HIGH	960 S SOTO ST, LA, 90023	635 - A6
BITELY, ARLENE ELEM	7501 FERN AV, RSMD, 91770	636 - D2
BIXBY ELEM	16446 WEDGEWORTH DR, HacH, 91745	678 - E4
BIXBY ELEM	5251 E STEARNS ST, LBCH, 90815	796 - B3
BLAIR HIGH	1201 S MARENGO AV, PAS, 91105	565 - J7
BLANDFORD ELEM	2601 BLANDFORD DR, RowH, 91748	679 - A7
BLESSED SACRAMENT	6641 W SUNSET BLVD, Hlwd, 90028	593 - E4
BLYTHE STREET ELEM	18730 BLYTHE ST, Res, 91335	530 - H3
BONITA HIGH	3102 D ST, LVRN, 91750	600 - G2
BONITA STREET ELEM	21929 BONITA ST, CRSN, 90745	764 - E6
BORBA, ANNA FUNDAMENTAL ELEM	12970 3RD ST, CHNO, 91710	641 - F7
BOUQUET CANYON ELEM	28110 WELLSTON DR, Saug, 91350	4461 - C5
BOWMAN, JEREANN HIGH	21508 CENTRE POINT PKWY, SCTA, 91350	4551 - B3
BRADDOCK DRIVE ELEM	4711 INGLEWOOD BLVD, LA, 90230	672 - E5
BRADLEY, TOM CHARTER MAGNET	3875 DUBLIN AV, LA, 90008	673 - G2
BRADOAKS ELEM	930 E LEMON AV, MNRO, 91016	567 - J4
BRAGG ELEM	11501 BOS ST, CRTS, 90703	766 - G2
BRAINARD AVENUE ELEM	11407 BRAINARD AV, LA, 91342	503 - A1
BRAVO, FRANCISCO MED HIGH	1200 CORNWELL ST, Boyl, 90033	635 - B3
BRAWERMAN ELEM	11661 W OLYMPIC BLVD, WLA, 90025	632 - A6
BREA CANYON HIGH	689 WILDCAT WY, BREA, 92821	709 - D6
BREA COUNTRY HILLS ELEM	150 N ASSOCIATED RD, BREA, 92821	709 - E7
BREA JR HIGH	400 N BREA BLVD, BREA, 92821	709 - B6
BREA-OLINDA FRIENDS CHRISTIAN	200 S ASSOCIATED RD, BREA, 92821	709 - D7
BREA-OLINDA HIGH	789 WILDCAT WY, BREA, 92821	709 - D5
BREED STREET ELEM	2226 E 3RD ST, Boyl, 90033	635 - A5
BRENTWOOD ELEM	100 S BARRINGTON PL, Brwd, 90049	631 - H2
BRENTWOOD MAGNET SCIENCE ELEM	740 S GRETNA GREEN WY, Brwd, 90049	631 - G4
BRENTWOOD UPPER HIGH	100 S BARRINGTON PL, Brwd, 90049	631 - H2
BRETHREN ELEM	11005 FOSTER RD, NRWK, 90650	736 - F2
BRETHREN	8101 VICKI DR, LACo, 90606	676 - H7
BRIDGEPORT ELEM	23670 NEWHALL RANCH RD, SCTA, 91355	4550 - G1
BRIDGE STREET ELEM	605 N BOYLE AV, Boyl, 90033	635 - A3
BRIGGS, LYLE S FUNDAMENTAL ELEM	11880 ROSWELL AV, SBdC, 91710	641 - D4
BRIGHT ELEM	1771 W 36TH ST, LA, 90018	673 - H1
BRIGHTWOOD ELEM	1701 BRIGHTWOOD ST, MONP, 91754	635 - H4
BROADACRES AVENUE ELEM	19424 BROADACRES AV, CRSN, 90746	764 - H3
BROAD AVENUE ELEM	24815 BROAD AV, Wilm, 90744	794 - E3
BROADOUS ELEM	12561 FILMORE ST, Pcma, 91331	482 - E7
BROADWAY ELEM	1015 LINCOLN BLVD, Ven, 90291	671 - J5
BROCKTON AVENUE ELEM	1309 ARMACOST AV, WLA, 90025	631 - H5
BROOKLYN AVENUE ELEM	4620 E CESAR E CHAVEZ AV, ELA, 90022	635 - F5
BROOKSIDE ELEM	165 SATINWOOD AV, VeCo, 91377	558 - B2
BROWN, PAT CHARTER	3801 S BROADWAY, LA, 90037	674 - C2
BRYANT ELEM	4101 E FOUNTAIN ST, LBCH, 90804	796 - A5
BRYSON AVENUE ELEM	4470 MISSOURI AV, SGAT, 90280	705 - D4
BUCHANAN STREET ELEM	5024 BUCHANAN ST, HiPk, 90042	595 - B1
BUCKLEY ELEM	3900 STANSBURY AV, Shrm, 91423	562 - B6
BUCKLEY HIGH	3900 STANSBURY AV, Shrm, 91423	562 - B6
BUDLONG AVENUE ELEM	5940 S BUDLONG AV, LA, 90044	674 - A6
BUENA PARK JR HIGH	6931 ORANGETHORPE AV, BPK, 90620	767 - G2
BUENA TERRA ELEM	8299 HOLDER ST, BPK, 90620	767 - F4
BUENA VISTA ARTS-INTERGRATED-ELEM	5685 SAN BERNARDINO ST, MTCL, 91763	601 - H6
BUENA VISTA ELEM	37005 HILLCREST DR E, PMDL, 93552	4287 - B4
BUFFUM ELEM	2350 XIMENO AV, LBCH, 90815	796 - A3
BUFORD ELEM	4919 W 109TH ST, Lenx, 90304	703 - B6
BUNCHE MID	12338 S MONA BLVD, COMP, 90222	734 - J1
BUNCHE, RALPH ELEM	16223 S HASKINS LN, CRSN, 90746	734 - E6
BURBANK BOULEVARD ELEM	12215 ALBERS ST, LA, 91607	562 - G2
BURBANK ELEM	17711 ROSETON AV, ART, 90701	736 - G7
BURBANK ELEM	2046 N ALLEN AV, Alta, 91001	536 - C6
BURBANK ELEM	501 JUNIPERO AV, LBCH, 90814	795 - G7
BURBANK HIGH	902 N 3RD ST, BURB, 91502	533 - G6
BURBANK, LUTHER MID	3700 W JEFFRIES AV, BURB, 91505	533 - C7
BURBANK MID	6460 N FIGUEROA ST, HiPk, 90042	595 - D1
BURCHAM ELEM	5610 E MONLACO RD, LBCH, 90808	766 - C7
BURKE, CAL HIGH	14630 LANARK ST, PanC, 91402	531 - J2
BURKE MID	8101 ORANGE AV, PRV, 90660	706 - F2
BURNETT ELEM	565 E HILL ST, LBCH, 90806	795 - E4
BURNETT, PETER ELEM	5403 W 138TH ST, HAW, 90250	733 - A3
BURROUGHS ELEM	1260 E 33RD ST, SIGH, 90755	795 - F1
BURROUGHS, JOHN HIGH	1920 W CLARK AV, BURB, 91506	563 - F2
BURROUGHS MID	600 S MCCADDEN PL, LA, 90005	633 - E2
BURSCH ELEM	2505 W 156TH ST, COMP, 90220	734 - F5
BURSCH ELEM	4245 MERCED AV, BALD, 91706	598 - A5
BURTON ELEM	8111 CALHOUN AV, PanC, 91402	532 - A2
BUSHNELL WAY ELEM	5507 BUSHNELL WY, HiPk, 90042	595 - D3
BUTLER ELEM	1400 E 20TH ST, LBCH, 90806	795 - F4
BYRD MID	9171 TELFAIR AV, SunV, 91352	502 - F7
CABRILLO AVENUE ELEM	732 S CABRILLO AV, SPed, 90731	824 - B5
CABRILLO ELEM	1562 W 11TH ST, UPL, 91786	601 - H2
CABRILLO HIGH	2001 SANTA FE AV, LBCH, 90810	795 - A4
CABRILLO, JUAN ELEM	30237 MORNING VIEW DR, MAL, 90265	667 - C1
CABRILLO, JUAN ELEM	5309 W 135TH ST, HAW, 90250	733 - A2
CACTUS MID	38060 20TH ST E, PMDL, 93550	4286 - D1
CAHUENGA ELEM	220 S HOBART BLVD, LA, 90004	633 - J1
CALABASAS HIGH	22855 W MULHOLLAND HWY, CALB, 91302	559 - G6
CALABASH ELEM	23055 EUGENE ST, WdHl, 91364	559 - G4
CALAHAN STREET ELEM	18722 KNAPP ST, Nor, 91324	500 - H7
CALDWELL ELEM	2300 W CALDWELL ST, COMP, 90220	734 - F6
CALIF ACADEMY OF MATH &-SCIENCE HS	1000 E VICTORIA ST, CRSN, 90747	764 - F2
CALIFORNIA ELEM	1111 CALIFORNIA AV, LACo, 91744	638 - D4
CALIFORNIA ELEM	1125 W BAINBRIDGE AV, WCOV, 91790	638 - E3
CALIFORNIA HIGH	9800 MILLS AV, LACo, 90604	707 - E4
CALIF LIBERAL STUDIES CHARTER-MID	3838 EAGLE ROCK BLVD, LA, 90065	594 - H1
CALIFORNIA TECHNICAL UNIV HIGH	1717 W CENTURY BLVD, LA, 90047	703 - J4
CALLE MAYOR MID	4800 CL MAYOR, TOR, 90505	793 - B2
CALMONT PRIVATE ELEM	1717 OLD TOPANGA CANYON RD, Top, 90290	589 - G3
CALVARY BAPTIST	2990 DAMIEN AV, LVRN, 91750	600 - E1
CALVARY CHAPEL CHRISTIAN	12808 WOODRUFF AV, DWNY, 90242	736 - C1
CALVARY CHAPELS CHRISTIAN ELEM	5202 LINCOLN AV, CYP, 90630	767 - C6
CALVARY CHRISTIAN ACADEMY	2818 MANHATTAN BEACH BLVD, GAR, 90249	733 - G6
CALVARY CHRISTIAN	2400 W 85TH ST, ING, 90305	703 - G2
CALVARY CHRISTIAN	610 N GLENDALE AV, GLDL, 91206	564 - F3
CALVARY CHRISTIAN	701 PALASADES DR, PacP, 90272	630 - G5
CALVERT STREET ELEM	19850 DELANO ST, WdHl, 91367	530 - F7
CAMELLIA AVENUE ELEM	7451 CAMELLIA AV, NHol, 91605	532 - H4
CAMERON ELEM	1225 E CAMERON AV, WCOV, 91790	638 - H2
CAMINO GROVE ELEM	700 CM GROVE AV, ARCD, 91006	567 - E7
CAMINO NUEVO CHARTER ACADEMY	635 S HARVARD BLVD, LA, 90010	633 - J2
CAMINO NUEVO CHARTER ACADEMY	697 S BURLINGTON AV, LA, 90057	634 - C3
CAMPBELL HALL EPISCOPAL HIGH	4533 LAUREL CANYON BLVD, LA, 91607	562 - F4
CAMPBELL HALL EPISCOPAL	4533 LAUREL CANYON BLVD, LA, 91607	562 - G4
CANFIELD AVENUE ELEM	9233 AIRDROME ST, LA, 90035	632 - H4
CANOGA PARK ELEM	7438 TOPANGA CANYON BLVD, CanP, 91303	530 - A4
CANOGA PARK HIGH	6850 TOPANGA CANYON BLVD, CanP, 91303	530 - A5
CANOGA PARK LUTHERAN	7357 JORDAN AV, CanP, 91303	530 - A4
CANTARA STREET ELEM	17950 CANTARA ST, Res, 91335	531 - A2
CANTERBURY AVENUE ELEM	13670 MONTAGUE ST, Pcma, 91331	502 - C7
CANTWELL - SACRED HEART OF-MARY HIGH	329 N GARFIELD AV, MTBL, 90640	676 - A1
CANYON ELEMENTARY CHARTER	421 ENTRADA DR, LA, 90402	631 - C7
CANYON HIGH	19300 NADAL ST, SCTA, 91351	4551 - F1
CANYON HILLS JR HIGH	2500 MADRUGADA DR, CHLS, 91709	680 - J2
CANYON OAKS HIGH	930 ROYAL OAKS DR, MNRO, 91016	567 - J5
CANYON SPRINGS COMM ELEM	19059 VICCI ST, SCTA, 91351	4551 - G2
CAPISTRANO AVENUE ELEM	8118 CAPISTRANO AV, LA, 91304	529 - J3
CARBON CANYON CHRISTIAN ELEM	5600 CARBON CANYON RD, BREA, 92823	710 - C6
CARBON CANYON CHRISTIAN HIGH	5600 CARBON CANYON RD, BREA, 92823	710 - C6
CARDEN CONEJO	975 EVENSTAR AV, THO, 91361	557 - B5
CARDEN ELEM	11537 GROVEDALE DR, LACo, 90604	707 - J6
CARDEN OF THE FOOTHILLS	429 WILDROSE AV, MNRO, 91016	567 - H3
CARLTHORP	438 SAN VICENTE BLVD, SMCA, 90402	631 - C7
CARMELA ELEM	13300 LAKELAND RD, SFSP, 90605	707 - B6
CARMENITA MID	13435 166TH ST, CRTS, 90703	737 - C6
CARNEGIE, ANDREW MID	21820 BONITA ST, CRSN, 90745	764 - F6
CAROLDALE AVENUE ELEM	22424 CAROLDALE AV, CRSN, 90745	764 - C7
CARPENTER AVENUE ELEM	3909 CARPENTER AV, LA, 91604	562 - G6
CARPENTER ELEM	9439 FOSTER RD, DWNY, 90242	736 - B2
CARR, EVELYN ELEM	3404 W 168TH ST, TOR, 90504	733 - F7
CARSON, BUD MID	13838 YUKON AV, HAW, 90250	733 - F3
CARSON CHRISTIAN HIGH	21828 AVALON BLVD, CRSN, 90745	764 - E6
CARSON HIGH	22328 S MAIN ST, CRSN, 90745	764 - D7
CARSON STREET ELEM	161 E CARSON ST, CRSN, 90745	764 - C6
CARTHAY CTR ELEM	6351 W OLYMPIC BLVD, LA, 90048	633 - A3
CARVER ELEM	1425 E 120TH ST, Wbrk, 90059	704 - F7
CARVER ELEM	19200 ELY AV, CRTS, 90703	766 - J2
CARVER ELEM	3100 HUNTINGTON DR, SMRO, 91775	566 - F7
CARVER ELEM	5335 E PAVO ST, LBCH, 90808	796 - C1
CARVER MID	4410 MCKINLEY AV, LA, 90011	674 - E3
CASIMIR MID	17220 CASIMIR AV, TOR, 90504	733 - G7
CASTAIC ELEM	30455 PARK VISTA DR, Cstc, 91384	4459 - F3

FEATURE NAME Address City, ZIP Code	PAGE-GRID
CASTAIC MID 28900 HILLCREST PKWY, Cstc, 91384	4459 - E3
CASTELAR STREET ELEM 840 YALE ST, LA, 90012	634 - G2
CASTLEBAY LANE ELEM 19010 CASTLEBAY LN, Nor, 91326	480 - G6
CASTLE HEIGHTS ELEM 9755 CATTARAUGUS AV, LA, 90034	632 - G6
CASTLE ROCK ELEM 2975 CASTLE ROCK RD, DBAR, 91765	679 - H7
CATHEDRAL CHAPEL ELEM 755 S COCHRAN AV, LA, 90036	633 - D3
CATHEDRAL HIGH 1253 BISHOPS RD, LA, 90012	634 - G1
CATSKILL AVENUE ELEM 23536 CATSKILL AV, CRSN, 90745	794 - D2
CEDARCREEK ELEM 27792 CAMP PLENTY RD, SCTA, 91351	4551 - F2
CEDARGROVE ELEM 1209 N GLENDORA AV, COV, 91724	599 - E3
CEDARLANE MID 16333 CEDARLANE DR, HacH, 91745	678 - D3
CENTENNIAL HIGH 2606 N CENTRAL AV, COMP, 90222	734 - F1
CENTER FOR EARLY EDUCATION 563 N ALFRED ST, WHWD, 90048	592 - J7
CENTER MID 5500 N CERRITOS AV, LACo, 91702	599 - A1
CENTER STREET ELEM 700 CENTER ST, ELSG, 90245	702 - F7
CENTINELA ELEM 1123 MARLBOROUGH AV, ING, 90302	673 - D7
CENTRAL ELEM 14741 CENTRAL AV, BALD, 91706	598 - D6
CENTRAL HIGH 716 E 14TH ST, LA, 90021	634 - F7
CENTRALIA ELEM 195 N WESTERN AV, ANA, 92801	767 - H5
CENTRAL LA NEW MID 4 3500 S HILL ST, LA, 90007	674 - C1
CENTURY COMM CHARTER MID 901 MAPLE AV, ING, 90301	703 - C4
CENTURY HIGH 20 S MARENGO AV, ALH, 91801	595 - J5
CENTURY PARK ELEM 10935 SPINNING AV, ING, 90303	703 - G6
CERES ELEM 10601 CERES AV, LACo, 90604	707 - E5
CERRITOS CHRISTIAN 12061 DEL AMO BLVD, CRTS, 90703	766 - H4
CERRITOS ELEM 120 E CERRITOS AV, GLDL, 91205	594 - E1
CERRITOS ELEM 13600 183RD ST, CRTS, 90703	767 - C1
CERRITOS HIGH 12500 183RD ST, CRTS, 90703	767 - A1
CHADWICK ELEM 26800 W ACADEMY DR, LACo, 90274	793 - C7
CHADWICK HIGH 26800 W ACADEMY DR, LACo, 90274	793 - C7
CHALLENGER MID 41725 170TH ST E, LACo, 93535	4109 - G5
CHAMINADE COLLEGE PREP HIGH 7500 CHAMINADE AV, LA, 91304	529 - F4
CHAMINADE MID 19800 DEVONSHIRE ST, Chat, 91311	500 - E4
CHANDLER ELEM 1005 ARMADA DR, PAS, 91103	565 - G3
CHANDLER ELEM 14030 WEDDINGTON ST, Shrm, 91423	562 - B2
CHAPARRAL ELEM 22601 LIBERTY BELL RD, CALB, 91302	559 - H6
CHAPARRAL ELEM 37500 50TH ST E, PMDL, 93552	4287 - A3
CHAPARRAL ELEM 451 CHAPARRAL DR, CLAR, 91711	571 - E7
CHAPARRAL HIGH 121 W ALLEN AV, SDMS, 91773	600 - B1
CHAPARRAL MID 1405 SPRUCE TREE DR, DBAR, 91765	680 - B3
CHAPMAN ELEM 1947 MARINE AV, GAR, 90249	733 - H4
CHARNOCK ROAD ELEM 11133 CHARNOCK RD, LA, 90034	672 - D2
CHARTER OAK HIGH 1430 E COVINA BLVD, COV, 91724	599 - E3
CHASE STREET ELEM 14041 CHASE ST, PanC, 91402	532 - B1
CHATSWORTH HIGH 10027 LURLINE AV, Chat, 91311	500 - C4
CHATSWORTH HILLS ACADEMY 21523 RINALDI ST, Chat, 91311	500 - A2
CHATSWORTH PARK ELEM 22005 DEVONSHIRE ST, Chat, 91311	499 - J4
CHAVEZ, CESAR ELEM 12110 WALNUT ST, NRWK, 90650	736 - H3
CHAVEZ, CESAR ELEM 5243 OAKLAND ST, LA, 90032	595 - F5
CHAVEZ, CESAR ELEM 6139 LOVELAND ST, BGDN, 90201	675 - H7
CHAVEZ, CESAR ELEM 730 W 3RD ST, LBCH, 90802	795 - C7
CHAVEZ, CESAR MID 3898 ABBOTT RD, LYN, 90262	705 - B6
CHAVEZ HIGH 12501 S WILMINGTON AV, Wbrk, 90222	734 - G1
CHEDER MENACHEM ELEM 5120 MELROSE AV, LA, 90004	593 - H7

FEATURE NAME Address City, ZIP Code	PAGE-GRID
CHEDER OF LOS ANGELES 801 N LA BREA AV, LA, 90046	593 - D6
CHEREMOYA AVENUE ELEM 6017 FRANKLIN AV, LA, 90068	593 - G3
CHERRYLEE ELEM 5025 BUFFINGTON RD, ELMN, 91732	597 - F4
CHILDRENS COMM ELEM 14702 SYLVAN ST, VanN, 91411	531 - J7
CHIME CHARTER ELEM 19722 COLLIER ST, WdHl, 91364	560 - F3
CHIME CHARTER MID 22280 DEVONSHIRE ST, Chat, 91311	499 - J4
CHIME MID 20040 PARTHENIA ST, Win, 91306	530 - E1
CHINO HIGH 5472 PARK PL, CHNO, 91710	641 - H6
CHINO HILLS CHRISTIAN 2549 MADRUGADA DR, CHLS, 91709	680 - J2
CHINO VALLEY CHRISTIAN 12410 NORTON AV, CHNO, 91710	641 - E6
CHRIST LUTHERAN ELEM 28850 S WESTERN AV, RPV, 90275	823 - J2
CHRIST LUTHERAN 311 S CITRUS ST, WCOV, 91791	639 - B1
CHRIST LUTHERAN 820 W IMPERIAL HWY, BREA, 92821	738 - J1
CHRIST THE KING ELEM 617 N ARDEN BLVD, LA, 90004	593 - F7
CIENEGA ELEM 2611 S ORANGE DR, LA, 90016	633 - C7
CIMARRON AVENUE ELEM 11559 CIMARRON AV, HAW, 90250	703 - H7
CIMARRON ELEM 36940 45TH ST E, PMDL, 93552	4286 - J4
CITY HONORS HIGH 155 W KELSO ST, ING, 90301	703 - C3
CITY OF KNOWLEDGE ELEM 3285 N GAREY AV, POM, 91767	600 - J2
CITY TERRACE ELEM 4350 CITY TERRACE DR, City, 90063	635 - F3
CLAIRBOURN ELEM 8400 HUNTINGTON DR, LACo, 91775	566 - G7
CLAREMONT HIGH 1601 N INDIAN HILL BLVD, CLAR, 91711	601 - C1
CLARK MAGNET HIGH 4747 NEW YORK AV, GLDL, 91214	504 - E6
CLAY MID 12226 S WESTERN AV, LACo, 90047	733 - J1
CLEMINSON ELEM 5213 DALEVIEW AV, TEML, 91780	597 - D4
CLEVELAND ELEM 4760 HACKETT AV, LKWD, 90713	766 - E4
CLEVELAND ELEM 524 PALISADE ST, PAS, 91103	565 - G1
CLEVELAND, GROVER HIGH 8140 VANALDEN AV, Res, 91335	530 - G2
CLIFFORD STREET ELEM 2150 DUANE ST, Echo, 90026	594 - E6
CLIFTON MID 225 S IVY AV, MNRO, 91016	567 - G4
CLINTON ELEM 6500 E COMPTON BLVD, COMP, 90221	735 - E4
CLOVER AVENUE ELEM 11020 CLOVER AV, LA, 90034	632 - D7
CLOVERLY ELEM 5476 CLOVERLY AV, TEML, 91780	596 - J4
COASTAL ACADEMY 25501 OAK ST, LMTA, 90717	793 - H5
COAST CHRISTIAN MIDDLE SCOOL 525 EARLE LN, RBCH, 90278	763 - A2
COCHRAN, JOHNNIE MID 4066 W 17TH ST, LA, 90019	633 - F5
COEUR D ALENE AVENUE ELEM 810 COEUR D ALENE AV, Ven, 90291	672 - A6
COGSWELL ELEM 11050 FINEVIEW ST, ELMN, 91733	637 - D3
COHASSET ELEM 15810 SATICOY ST, VanN, 91406	531 - F4
COLDWATER CANYON AVENUE ELEM 6850 COLDWATER CANYON AV, NHol, 91605	532 - E5
COLE, GIFFORD C MID 3126 E AVE I, LAN, 93535	4016 - F5
COLFAX AVENUE ELEM 11724 ADDISON ST, LA, 91607	562 - H3
COLISEUM STREET ELEM 4400 COLISEUM ST, LA, 90008	673 - D2
COLLEGEWOOD ELEM 20725 COLLEGEWOOD DR, WAL, 91789	639 - F3
COLLINS ELEM 6125 COKE AV, NLB, 90805	765 - J1
COLUMBIA 3400 CALIFORNIA AV, ELMN, 91731	637 - D1
COLUMBUS AVENUE 6700 COLUMBUS AV, VanN, 91405	531 - H6
COLUMBUS HIGH 12330 WOODRUFF AV, DWNY, 90242	736 - D1
COLUMBUS ELEM 425 W MILFORD ST, GLDL, 91203	564 - D4
COLUMBUS MID 22250 ELKWOOD ST, LA, 91304	529 - J3
COMMONWEALTH AVENUE ELEM 215 S COMMONWEALTH AV, LA, 90004	634 - B1
COMM CHARTER MID 1445 CELIS ST, SFER, 91340	482 - D5
COMM MAGNET 11301 BELLAGIO RD, Brwd, 90049	591 - J7
COMMUNMITY CHARTER HIGH 16930 SHERMAN WY, VanN, 91406	531 - D4

FEATURE NAME Address City, ZIP Code	PAGE-GRID
COMPTON AVENUE ELEM 1515 E 104TH ST, Wats, 90002	704 - G5
COMPTON HIGH 602 S ACACIA AV, COMP, 90220	734 - J5
CONCORDIA LUTHERAN 13633 183RD ST, CRTS, 90703	767 - C1
CONDIT ELEM 1750 N MOUNTAIN AV, CLAR, 91711	601 - C1
CONEJO ELEM 280 CONEJO SCHOOL RD, THO, 91362	557 - A1
CONSTELLATION COMM MID 620 OLIVE AV, LBCH, 90802	795 - E7
COOLIDGE ELEM 421 N MISSION DR, SGBL, 91775	596 - C3
COOMBS, NORMA HIGH 2600 PALOMA ST, PAS, 91107	566 - E3
COOPER HIGH 2210 N TAPER AV, SPed, 90731	824 - A1
COREY ELEM 7351 HOLDER ST, BPK, 90620	767 - F2
CORNERSTONE AT PEDREGAL 6069 GROVEOAK PL, RPV, 90275	792 - J5
CORNERSTONE CHRISTIAN ELEM 13000 PIPELINE AV, SBdC, 91710	641 - D7
CORNERSTONE PREP CHARTER ELEM 7651 S CENTRAL AV, LA, 90001	704 - E1
CORONA AVENUE ELEM 3825 BELL AV, BELL, 90201	675 - C7
CORONA, BERT CHARTER MID 9400 REMICK AV, Pcma, 91331	502 - E6
CORONADO HIGH 614 E VINE AV, WCOV, 91790	638 - F2
CORPUS CHRISTI ELEM 890 TOYOPA DR, PacP, 90272	631 - A5
CORTADA ELEM 3111 POTRERO AV, ELMN, 91733	637 - A1
CORTEZ, ALICE E ELEM 12750 CARISSA AV, CHNO, 91710	641 - J6
CORVALLIS MID 11032 LEFFINGWELL RD, NRWK, 90650	736 - F2
CORY, NANCY ELEM 3540 W AVE K-4, LAN, 93536	4105 - B2
COTTONWOOD ELEM 2740 W AVE P-8, PMDL, 93551	4195 - C6
COUGHLIN ELEM 11035 BORDEN AV, Pcma, 91331	502 - F2
COUNTRY ELEM 5243 LAUREL CANYON RD, LA, 91607	562 - G2
COUNTRYSIDE PREP 8756 CANBY AV, Nor, 91325	530 - J1
COUNTRY SPRINGS ELEM 14145 VILLAGE CENTER DR, CHLS, 91709	680 - J3
COVENANT LUTHERAN ELEM 310 W 95TH ST, LA, 90003	704 - C4
COVINA ELEM 160 N BARRANCA AV, COV, 91723	599 - C5
COVINA HIGH 463 S HOLLENBECK ST, COV, 91723	599 - A6
COWAN AVENUE ELEM 7615 COWAN AV, Wch, 90045	702 - F1
COX, LEONA H COMM ELEM 18643 OAKMOOR ST, SCTA, 91351	4551 - H1
CREATIVE LEARNING CTR 1729 W M LUTHER KING JR BLVD, LA, 90062	673 - H2
CRENSHAW HIGH 5010 11TH AV, LA, 90043	673 - F4
CRESCENDO CHARTER ELEM 5200 S CENTRAL AV, LA, 90011	674 - E5
CRESCENTA VALLEY HIGH 2900 COMMUNITY AV, LaCr, 91214	534 - F1
CRESCENT AVENUE CHRISTIAN 5600 CRESCENT AV, BPK, 90620	767 - D5
CRESCENT HEIGHTS BOULEVARD ELEM 1661 S CRESCENT HEIGHTS BLVD, LA, 90035	633 - A5
CRESPI CARMELITE HIGH 5031 ALONZO AV, Enc, 91316	561 - A3
CRESSON ELEM 11650 CRESSON ST, NRWK, 90650	706 - G6
CRESTVIEW PREP 140 FOOTHILL BLVD, LCF, 91011	535 - E5
CRESTWOOD STREET ELEM 1946 W CRESTWOOD ST, RPV, 90275	823 - H4
CROSSROADS HIGH 44310 HARDWOOD AV, LAN, 93534	4015 - G7
CROSSROADS ELEM 1715 OLYMPIC BLVD, SMCA, 90404	671 - G1
CROSSROADS SCH FOR ARTS &- SCIENCES 1714 21ST ST, SMCA, 90404	671 - G1
CROZIER MID 151 N GREVILLEA AV, ING, 90301	703 - C2
CUBBERLEY ELEM 3200 MONOGRAM AV, LBCH, 90808	796 - F1
CULLEN ELEM 440 N LIVE OAK AV, GLDR, 91741	569 - F4
CULTURE LANGUAGE ACADEMY ELEM 100 E NUTWOOD ST, ING, 90301	703 - C3
CULVER CHRISTIAN ELEM 11312 W WASHINGTON BLVD, CULC, 90066	672 - E4
CULVER CITY HIGH 4401 ELENDA ST, CULC, 90230	672 - F3
CULVER CITY MID 4601 ELENDA ST, CULC, 90230	672 - G3
CULVER CITY SDA ELEM 11828 W WASHINGTON BLVD, CULC, 90066	672 - E4
CULVER PARK HIGH 5303 BERRYMAN AV, CULC, 90230	672 - G5
CUMORAH ACADEMY 19545 E CIENEGA AV, LACo, 91724	599 - D3

FEATURE NAME Address City, ZIP Code	PAGE-GRID
CURTIS ELEM 15871 MULHOLLAND DR, Brwd, 90049	561 - G7
CURTISS, GLENN HAMMOND MID 1254 E HELMICK ST, CRSN, 90746	764 - F3
CYPRESS ELEM 351 W CYPRESS ST, COV, 91722	599 - A4
CYPRESS HIGH 9801 VALLEY VIEW ST, CYP, 90630	767 - E7
DAHLIA HEIGHTS ELEM 5063 FLORISTAN AV, Eagl, 90041	565 - B6
DAILY, ALLAN HIGH 220 N KENWOOD ST, GLDL, 91206	564 - F4
DAILY HIGH NORTH 3800 FOOTHILL BLVD, GLDL, 91214	504 - D6
DALTON, HENRY ELEM 500 E 10TH ST, AZU, 91702	569 - A5
DAMIEN HIGH 2280 DAMIEN AV, LVRN, 91750	600 - E2
DANA MID 1501 S CABRILLO AV, SPed, 90731	824 - B6
DANA, RICHARD HENRY MID 1401 S 1ST AV, ARCD, 91006	567 - D7
DANA, RICHARD HENRY MID 13500 AVIATION BLVD, HAW, 90250	733 - A3
DANBROOK ELEM 320 DANBROOK DR, ANA, 92804	767 - G6
DANBURY ELEM 1745 LYNOAK DR, CLAR, 91711	601 - A1
DANUBE AVENUE ELEM 11220 DANUBE AV, GrnH, 91344	501 - G2
DAPPLEGRAY ELEM 3011 PALOS VERDES DR N, RHE, 90274	793 - F7
DARBY AVENUE ELEM 10818 DARBY AV, Nor, 91326	500 - J3
DAVIS MID 621 W POPLAR ST, COMP, 90220	734 - H3
DAVIS, ZELA ELEM 13435 YUKON AV, HAW, 90250	733 - E2
DAYTON HEIGHTS ELEM 607 N WESTMORELAND AV, LA, 90004	594 - A7
DEANZA ELEM 12820 BESS AV, BALD, 91706	637 - H1
DE ANZA, JUAN ELEM 12110 HINDRY AV, LACo, 90250	733 - A1
DEARBORN STREET ELEM 9240 WISH AV, Nor, 91325	501 - C6
DECKER ELEM 20 VILLAGE LOOP RD, POM, 91766	640 - G5
DE LA HOYA ANIMO HIGH 5156 WHITTIER BLVD, ELA, 90022	675 - G1
DE LA HOYA, OSCAR HIGH 350 S FIGUEROA ST, LA, 90071	634 - E3
DEL AMO ELEM 21228 WATER ST, CRSN, 90745	764 - H5
DE LA SALLE ELEM 16535 CHATSWORTH ST, GrnH, 91344	501 - E3
DELEVAN DRIVE ELEM 4168 W AVE 42, LA, 90065	564 - H7
DEL PASO HIGH 476 S LEMON AV, INDS, 91789	679 - F2
DELPHI ACADEMY 11341 BRAINARD AV, LA, 91342	503 - A1
DEL SUR ELEM 9023 W AVE H, LAN, 93536	4013 - H3
DEL VALLE ELEM 801 DEL VALLE AV, LPUE, 91744	638 - E6
DEMILLE MID 7025 E PARKCREST ST, LBCH, 90808	766 - F6
DENA ELEM 1314 S DACOTAH ST, LA, 90023	675 - A1
DENA NEW PRIMARY 2705 HOSTETTER ST, LA, 90023	635 - A7
DENKER AVENUE ELEM 1620 W 162ND ST, GAR, 90247	733 - J6
DESERT CHRISTIAN ELEM 44662 15TH ST W, LAN, 93534	4015 - F6
DESERT CHRISTIAN MID 44662 15TH ST W, LAN, 93534	4015 - F6
DESERT CHRISTIAN 2340 AVE J-8, LAN, 93536	4105 - D1
DESERT ROSE ELEM 37730 27TH ST E, PMDL, 93550	4286 - F3
DESERT SANDS CHARTER HIGH 3030 E PALMDALE BLVD, PMDL, 93550	4286 - G1
DESERT VIEW ELEM 1555 W AVE H-10, LAN, 93534	4015 - F4
DESERT WILLOW INTERMED 36555 SUNNY LN, PMDL, 93550	4286 - F5
DESERT WINDS HIGH 45030 3RD ST E, LAN, 93535	4015 - J5
DESERT WINDS SOUTH HIGH 10801 E AVE R, Litl, 93543	4288 - D1
DESERT WINDS WEST HIGH 6300 W AVE L, LAN, 93536	4104 - E4
DEWEY AVENUE ELEM 525 DEWEY AV, SGBL, 91776	596 - F7
DEXTER MID 11532 E FLORAL DR, WHIT, 90601	677 - B5
DIAMOND BAR HIGH 21400 PATHFINDER RD, DBAR, 91765	679 - H5
DIAMOND POINT ELEM 24150 SUNSET CROSSING RD, DBAR, 91765	640 - D5
DIAMOND RANCH HIGH 100 DIAMOND RANCH RD, DBAR, 91765	640 - F7
DICKISON ELEM 905 N ARANBE AV, COMP, 90220	734 - H3
DICKRANIAN, ARSHAG ARMENIAN-ELEM 1200 N CAHUENGA BLVD, LA, 90038	593 - F5

FEATURE NAME Address City, ZIP Code	PAGE-GRID
DICKRANIAN, ARSHAG ARMENIAN-HIGH 1200 N CAHUENGA BLVD, LA, 90038	593 - F5
DICKSON ELEM 3930 PAMELA DR, SBdC, 91710	641 - D7
DISCOVERY CHARTER HIGH 12550 VAN NUYS BLVD, Pcma, 91331	502 - E1
DISNEY, WALT ELEM 1220 W ORANGE GROVE AV, BURB, 91506	563 - F1
DIVINE SAVIOUR ELEM 624 CYPRESS AV, LA, 90065	594 - J6
DIXIE CANYON AVENUE ELEM 4220 DIXIE CANYON AV, Shrm, 91423	562 - D5
DODSON MID 28014 S MONTEREINA DR, RPV, 90275	823 - H1
DOLLAND ELEM 15021 BLOOMFIELD AV, NRWK, 90650	737 - A4
DOLORES MISSION ELEM 170 S GLESS ST, Boyl, 90033	634 - J4
DOLORES STREET ELEM 22526 DOLORES ST, CRSN, 90745	764 - D7
DOMINGUEZ ELEM 21250 S SANTA FE AV, CRSN, 90810	765 - A5
DOMINGUEZ HIGH 15301 S SAN JOSE AV, COMP, 90221	735 - E4
DON BENITO ELEM 3700 DENAIR ST, PAS, 91107	566 - H1
DON BOSCO HIGH 1151 SAN GABRIEL BLVD, RSMD, 91770	636 - F5
DON JULIAN ELEM 13855 DON JULIAN RD, LACo, 91746	637 - J5
DORRIS PLACE ELEM 2225 DORRIS PL, LA, 90031	594 - G5
DORSEY, S M HIGH 3537 FARMDALE AV, LA, 90016	673 - D1
DOWNEY HIGH 11040 BROOKSHIRE AV, DWNY, 90241	706 - B5
DOWNTOWN HIGH 1081 W TEMPLE ST, LA, 90012	634 - F2
DOWNTOWN VALUE CHARTER ELEM 950 W WASHINGTON BLVD, LA, 90007	634 - C6
DREW MID 8511 COMPTON AV, Flor, 90001	704 - F2
DUARTE, ANDRES ELEM 1433 CRESTFIELD DR, DUAR, 91010	568 - D5
DUARTE HIGH 1565 CENTRAL AV, DUAR, 91010	568 - B5
DUFF ELEM 7830 DOROTHY ST, RSMD, 91770	636 - E1
DULLES ELEM 12726 MEADOW GREEN RD, LMRD, 90638	737 - J1
DUNSMORE ELEM 4717 DUNSMORE AV, GLDL, 91214	504 - D6
DURFEE ELEM 12233 STAR ST, ELMN, 91732	597 - G6
DURFEE ELEM 4220 DURFEE AV, PRV, 90660	676 - H2
DYE, JOHN THOMAS ELEM 11414 CHALON RD, Brwd, 90049	591 - H6
DYER STREET ELEM 14500 DYER ST, LA, 91342	482 - A5
DYSINGER ELEM 7770 CAMELLIA DR, BPK, 90620	767 - J3
EAGLE ROCK ELEM 2057 FAIR PARK AV, Eagl, 90041	565 - A6
EAGLE ROCK HIGH 1750 YOSEMITE DR, Eagl, 90041	565 - B7
EASISIDE CHRISTIAN HIGH 1701 W VALENCIA DR, FUL, 92833	738 - D7
EAST LOS ANGELES LIGHT & LIFE 207 S DACOTAH ST, Boyl, 90033	635 - B5
EASTMAN AVENUE ELEM 4112 E OLYMPIC BLVD, LACo, 90023	675 - D1
EAST MID 10301 WOODRUFF AV, DWNY, 90241	706 - D4
EASTMONT INTERMED 400 BRADSHAWE ST, MTBL, 90640	635 - J7
EASTSIDE CHRISTIAN MID 1701 W VALENCIA DR, FUL, 92833	738 - D7
EASTSIDE ELEM 6742 E AVE H, LACo, 93535	4017 - E2
EAST VALLEY HIGH 5525 VINELAND AV, NHol, 91601	563 - A2
EAST WHITTIER MID 14421 WHITTIER BLVD, WHIT, 90605	707 - F2
EASTWOOD ELEM 15730 PESCADOS DR, LMRD, 90638	737 - H4
ECHOS OF FAITH CHRISTIAN 11255 CENTRAL AV, SBdC, 91762	641 - G3
EDGEWOOD ACADEMY 14135 FAIRGROVE AV, LACo, 91746	638 - B2
EDGEWOOD MID 1625 W DURNESS ST, WCOV, 91790	638 - D2
EDISON ELEM 2425 KANSAS AV, SMCA, 90404	671 - H1
EDISON ELEM 3126 N GLENROSE AV, Alta, 91001	535 - H4
EDISON ELEM 3800 W 182ND ST, TOR, 90504	763 - E2
EDISON ELEM 625 MAINE AV, LBCH, 90802	795 - C7
EDISON MID 6500 HOOPER AV, Flor, 90001	674 - F7
EDISON, THOMAS ELEM 2110 CHESTNUT ST, BURB, 91506	563 - E1
EDISON, THOMAS ELEM 435 S PACIFIC AV, GLDL, 91204	564 - D6
EDMONDSON ELEM 15121 GRAYLAND AV, NRWK, 90650	736 - H4

FEATURE NAME Address City, ZIP Code	PAGE-GRID
EDWARDS MID 6812 S NORWALK BLVD, LACo, 90606	676 - J6
EGREMONT 19850 DEVONSHIRE ST, Chat, 91311	500 - E4
EKSTRAND ELEM 400 N WALNUT AV, SDMS, 91773	600 - C1
EL CAMINO ELEM 1525 W 5TH ST, ONT, 91762	601 - H5
EL CAMINO HIGH 14625 KEESE DR, LACo, 90604	707 - F7
EL CAMINO REAL HIGH 5440 VALLEY CIRCLE BLVD, WdHl, 91367	559 - E2
EL CERRITO ELEM 1051 HILLSIDE ST, LHB, 90631	708 - E4
ELDERBERRY ELEM 950 N ELDERBERRY AV, ONT, 91762	601 - J6
EL DORADO AVENUE ELEM 12749 EL DORADO AV, LA, 91342	481 - G5
EL DORADO ELEM 361 E PONDERA ST, LAN, 93535	4016 - A6
ELIOT MID 2184 N LAKE AV, Alta, 91001	536 - A6
ELIZABETH LEARNING CTR 4811 ELIZABETH ST, CDHY, 90201	705 - E2
ELLINGTON, ALICE M ELEM 5034 N CLYDEBANK AV, LACo, 91722	598 - H3
ELLIOTT ELEM 18415 CORTNER AV, ART, 90701	766 - J1
EL MARINO ELEM 11450 PORT RD, CULC, 90230	672 - G5
EL MONTE HIGH 3048 TYLER AV, ELMN, 91731	637 - D1
EL ORO WAY ELEM 12230 EL ORO WY, GrnH, 91344	481 - C6
EL PORTAL ELEM 200 NADA ST, LHB, 90631	708 - C5
EL RANCHO ELEM 5862 C ST, CHNO, 91710	641 - J7
EL RANCHO HIGH 6501 PASSONS BLVD, PRV, 90660	676 - F6
EL RINCON ELEM 11177 OVERLAND AV, CULC, 90230	672 - H5
EL ROBLE INTERMED 665 N MOUNTAIN AV, CLAR, 91711	601 - B3
EL RODEO ELEM 605 N WHITTIER DR, BHLS, 90210	632 - E2
EL SEGUNDO HIGH 640 MAIN ST, ELSG, 90245	732 - E1
EL SEGUNDO MID 332 CENTER ST, ELSG, 90245	732 - G1
EL SERENO ELEM 3838 ROSEMEAD AV, LA, 90032	595 - E5
EL SERENO MID 2839 N EASTERN AV, LA, 90032	595 - E7
ELWIN ELEM 13010 WACO ST, BALD, 91706	597 - J7
ELYSIAN HEIGHTS ELEM 1562 BAXTER ST, Echo, 90026	594 - F6
EMBLEM ELEM 22635 ESPUELLA DR, SCTA, 91350	4550 - J1
EMEK HEBREW ACADEMY 12732 CHANDLER BLVD, LA, 91607	562 - E2
EMEK HEBREW ACADEMY - MAGNOLIA-CAMPUS 15365 MAGNOLIA BLVD, VanN, 91411	561 - H2
EMELITA STREET ELEM 17931 HATTERAS ST, Enc, 91316	561 - A1
EMERSON ELEM 1011 E CALDWELL ST, COMP, 90221	735 - B6
EMERSON ELEM 7544 EMERSON PL, RSMD, 91770	636 - E1
EMERSON MID 1650 SELBY AV, Wwd, 90024	632 - C4
EMERSON MID 635 LINCOLN AV, POM, 91767	601 - A7
EMERSON PARKSIDE ACADEMY 2625 JOSIE AV, LBCH, 90815	796 - E3
EMERSON, RALPH W ELEM 720 E CYPRESS AV, BURB, 91501	533 - H6
EMERY ELEM 8600 SOMERSET ST, BPK, 90621	738 - A5
EMERY PARK ELEM 2821 W COMMONWEALTH AV, ALH, 91803	595 - H5
EMMAUS LUTHERAN ELEM 840 S ALMANSOR ST, ALH, 91801	596 - C6
EMPEROR ELEM 6415 N MUSCATEL AV, LACo, 91775	596 - G1
ENCINITA ELEM 4515 ENCINITA AV, RSMD, 91770	596 - J5
ENCINO ELEM 16941 ADDISON ST, Enc, 91316	561 - D3
ENDEAVOUR MID 831 AVE K-2, LAN, 93535	4106 - B2
ENTERPRISE MID 2600 W COMPTON BLVD, COMP, 90220	734 - E4
ENVIRONMENTAL CHARTER HIGH 4234 147TH ST, LNDL, 90260	733 - D4
EPIPHANY ELEM 10915 MICHAEL HUNT DR, SELM, 91733	637 - C4
ERWIN ELEM 943 SUNKIST AV, LACo, 91746	638 - B3
ERWIN STREET ELEM 13400 ERWIN ST, VanN, 91401	532 - D7
ESCALONA ELEM 15135 ESCALONA RD, LMRD, 90638	737 - G4
ESCUELA DE MONTESSORI 8820 SEPULVEDA EASTWAY, Wch, 90045	702 - H3
ESHELMAN AVENUE ELEM 25902 ESHELMAN AV, LMTA, 90717	793 - H5
ESPERANZA ELEM 40521 35TH ST W, PMDL, 93551	4195 - B3
ESPERANZA ELEM 680 LITTLE ST, LA, 90017	634 - C3
ETUM ACADEMY 13017 ARTESIA BLVD, CRTS, 90703	737 - B7
ETZ JACOB HEBREW ACADEMY 7951 BEVERLY BLVD, LA, 90048	633 - B1
EUCALYPTUS ELEM 12044 EUCALYPTUS AV, HAW, 90250	733 - C1
EUCLID AVENUE ELEM 806 EUCLID AV, LA, 90023	635 - B6
EVERGREEN AVENUE ELEM 2730 GANAHL ST, Boyl, 90033	635 - C4
EVERGREEN ELEM 12915 HELMER DR, WHIT, 90602	707 - C1
EVERGREEN ELEM 2450 EVERGREEN SPRINGS DR, DBAR, 91765	679 - J6
FAIR AVENUE ELEM 6501 FAIR AV, NHol, 91606	532 - J6
FAIRBURN AVENUE ELEM 1403 FAIRBURN AV, Wwd, 90024	632 - C3
FAIRFAX HIGH 7850 MELROSE AV, LA, 90036	593 - B7
FAIRFIELD ELEM 16945 SHERMAN WY, VanN, 91406	531 - D5
FAIRGROVE ACADEMY 15540 FAIRGROVE AV, LPUE, 91744	638 - E4
FAIR OAKS RANCH 26933 N SILVERBELL LN, LACo, 91387	4551 - J5
FAIRVALLEY HIGH 231 E STEPHANIE DR, COV, 91722	599 - B3
FAITH BAPTIST 7644 FARRALONE AV, LA, 91304	529 - J4
FAITH LUTHERAN 8517 S 11TH AV, ING, 90305	703 - F2
FAITH LUTHERAN 9920 MILLS AV, LACo, 90604	707 - E4
FANNING ELEM 650 N APRICOT AV, BREA, 92821	709 - C6
FARJARDO ELEM 18550 FARJARDO ST, RowH, 91748	679 - A6
FARMDALE ELEM 2660 RUTH SWIGGETT DR, LA, 90032	595 - E7
FARRAGUT ELEM 10820 FARRAGUT DR, CULC, 90230	672 - G3
FEDDE MID 21409 ELAINE AV, HGDN, 90716	766 - H5
FELTON ELEM 10417 FELTON AV, Lenx, 90304	703 - B5
FENTON AVENUE CHARTER ELEM 11828 GAIN ST, LA, 91342	502 - G1
FERNANGELES ELEM 12001 ART ST, SunV, 91352	502 - G7
FERN DRIVE ELEM 1400 W FERN DR, FUL, 92833	738 - E6
FERN ELEM 1314 FERN AV, TOR, 90503	763 - F6
FERRAHIAN HIGH 5300 WHITE OAK AV, Enc, 91316	561 - B2
FIELD ELEM 3600 SIERRA MADRE BLVD, PAS, 91107	566 - G2
FIGUEROA STREET ELEM 510 W 111TH ST, LA, 90044	704 - B6
FIREBAUGH HIGH 5246 MARTIN LUTHER KING JR BL, LYN, 90262	735 - E1
FIRST AVENUE MID 301 S 1ST AV, ARCD, 91006	567 - D6
FIRST BAPTIST CHURCH 1000 PINE AV, LBCH, 90813	795 - D6
FIRST BAPTIST LAKEWOOD ELEM 5336 E ARBOR RD, LBCH, 90808	766 - B4
FIRST CHRISTIAN ACADEMY 225 S SANTA FE AV, COMP, 90221	735 - A4
FIRST CHURCH OF GOD CHRISTIAN 2941 W 70TH ST, LA, 90043	673 - F7
FIRST LUTHERAN DAY ELEM 1300 E COLORADO ST, GLDL, 91205	564 - G5
FIRST LUTHERAN ELEM 18355 ROSCOE BLVD, Nor, 91325	530 - J2
FIRST LUTHERAN ELEM 2900 W CARSON ST, TOR, 90503	763 - E6
FIRST LUTHERAN ELEM 3119 W 6TH ST, LA, 90020	634 - A2
FIRST LUTHERAN ELEM 777 N MACLAY AV, SFER, 91340	482 - C6
FIRST LUTHERAN ELEM 9123 BROADWAY, TEML, 91780	596 - H4
FIRST LUTHERAN HIGH 13361 GLENOAKS BLVD, LA, 91342	481 - H3
FIRST LUTHERAN 1001 S GLENOAKS BLVD, BURB, 91502	563 - J1
FIRST LUTHERAN 1323 S MAGNOLIA AV, MNRO, 91016	567 - G5
FIRST LUTHERAN 815 VENICE BLVD, Ven, 90291	671 - J5
FIRST PRESBYTERIAN 10400 ZELZAH AV, GrnH, 91344	501 - A4
FISHBURN AVENUE ELEM 5701 FISHBURN AV, MYWD, 90270	675 - D5
FISLER ELEM 1350 STARBUCK ST, FUL, 92833	738 - C5
FLEMING MID 25425 WALNUT ST, LMTA, 90717	793 - H5
FLETCHER DRIVE ELEM 3350 FLETCHER DR, LA, 90065	594 - G2
FLINTRIDGE PREP 4543 CROWN AV, LCF, 91011	535 - D4
FLINTRIDGE SACRED HEART ACADEMY 440 SAINT KATHERINE DR, LCF, 91011	535 - D7
FLORENCE AVENUE ELEM 7211 BELL AV, Flor, 90001	704 - G1
FLOURNOY ELEMENTARY-MAGNET 1630 E 111TH ST, LA, 90059	704 - G6
FOOTHILL CHRISTIAN ACADEMY 13550 HERRON ST, LA, 91342	482 - C3
FOOTHILL CHRISTIAN ELEM 242 W BASE LINE RD, GLDR, 91740	569 - E7
FOOTHILL CHRISTIAN 901 S GRAND AV, GLDR, 91740	569 - D7
FOOTHILL MID 151 N FENIMORE AV, AZU, 91702	569 - A7
FOOTHILLS MID 171 E SYCAMORE AV, ARCD, 91006	567 - D3
FORD BOULEVARD ELEM 1112 S FORD BLVD, ELA, 90022	675 - F1
FOSHAY LEARNING CTR 3751 S HARVARD BLVD, LA, 90018	673 - H1
FOSTER ELEM 13900 FOSTER AV, BALD, 91706	598 - B7
FOSTER ELEM 1620 N PANNES AV, COMP, 90221	735 - C3
FOSTER ELEM 5223 BIGELOW ST, LKWD, 90712	766 - B2
FOSTER, JAMES ELEM 22500 PAMPLICO DR, SCTA, 91350	4460 - J5
FOSTER ROAD ELEM 13930 FOSTER RD, LMRD, 90638	737 - D2
FRANCIS, JOHN H POLYTECHNIC-HIGH 12431 ROSCOE BLVD, SunV, 91352	532 - F1
FRANKLIN AVENUE ELEM 1910 N COMMONWEALTH AV, LFlz, 90027	594 - B3
FRANKLIN, BENJAMIN ELEM 1610 LAKE ST, GLDL, 91201	563 - J3
FRANKLIN, BENJAMIN MID 540 CERRITOS AV, LBCH, 90802	795 - F7
FRANKLIN ELEM 2400 MONTANA AV, SMCA, 90403	631 - F6
FRANKLIN ELEM 527 W VENTURA ST, Alta, 91001	535 - G5
FRANKLIN HIGH 820 N AVE 54, HiPk, 90042	595 - C2
FREEMAN, DANIEL ELEM 2602 W 79TH ST, ING, 90305	703 - G2
FREMONT ELEM 2001 ELM ST, ALH, 91803	635 - H1
FREMONT ELEM 200 W MADISON AV, MTBL, 90640	676 - E2
FREMONT HIGH 7676 S SAN PEDRO ST, LA, 90003	704 - D1
FREMONT, JOHN C ELEM 3320 LAS PALMAS AV, GLDL, 91208	534 - H4
FREMONT, JOHN C ELEM 4000 E 4TH ST, LBCH, 90814	796 - A7
FREMONT MID 725 W FRANKLIN AV, POM, 91766	640 - J4
FRIES AVENUE ELEM 1301 N FRIES AV, Wilm, 90744	794 - E5
FRONTIER HIGH 9401 PAINTER AV, WHIT, 90605	707 - C3
FROST MID 12314 BRADFORD PL, GrnH, 91344	481 - B6
FRYER, SAMUEL A YAVNEH ACADEMY 5353 W 3RD ST, LA, 90004	633 - E1
FULLBRIGHT AVENUE ELEM 6940 FULLBRIGHT AV, Win, 91306	530 - D5
FULLERTON HIGH 201 E CHAPMAN AV, FUL, 92832	738 - H6
FULLERTON SDA ELEM 2353 W VALENCIA DR, FUL, 92833	738 - C7
FULTON, ROBERT MID 7477 KESTER AV, VanN, 91405	531 - J4
FURGESON ELEM 22215 ELAINE AV, HGDN, 90716	766 - H6
GABRIELINO HIGH 1327 S SAN GABRIEL BLVD, SGBL, 91776	596 - F6
GAGE MID 2880 E GAGE AV, HNTP, 90255	675 - A6
GAHR, RICHARD HIGH 11111 ARTESIA BLVD, CRTS, 90703	736 - F7
GAINES ELEM 7340 JACKSON ST, PRM, 90723	735 - G5
GALLATIN ELEM 9513 BROOKSHIRE AV, DWNY, 90240	706 - C3
GANESHA HIGH 1151 FAIRPLEX DR, POM, 91768	600 - D7
GANT ELEM 1854 N BRITTON DR, LBCH, 90815	796 - D5
GARDENA ELEM 647 W GARDENA BLVD, LA, 90247	734 - B6
GARDENA HIGH 1301 W 182ND ST, LA, 90248	764 - A1
GARDENA VALLEY CHRISTIAN 1473 W 182ND ST, GAR, 90248	763 - J1
GARDEN GROVE VALERIO ST, Res, 91335	531 - A4
GARDENHILL ELEM 14607 GARDENHILL DR, LMRD, 90638	737 - E2
GARDNER STREET ELEM 7450 HAWTHORN AV, LA, 90046	593 - C4
GAREY HIGH 321 W LEXINGTON AV, POM, 91766	640 - J4
GARFIELD ELEM 110 W MCLEAN ST, ALH, 91801	596 - A4
GARFIELD ELEM 2240 BALTIC AV, LBCH, 90810	795 - B4
GARFIELD ELEM 7425 GARFIELD AV, BGDN, 90201	705 - H1
GARFIELD HIGH 5101 E 6TH ST, ELA, 90022	635 - G7
GARVANZA ELEM 317 N AVE 62, HiPk, 90042	595 - D1
GARVEY, MARCUS ELEM 2916 W SLAUSON AV, LA, 90043	673 - F6
GARVEY, RICHARD INTERMED 2720 JACKSON AV, RSMD, 91770	636 - E2
GASCON, JOSEPH A ELEM 630 LEONARD AV, ELA, 90022	675 - J1
GATES STREET ELEM 3333 MANITOU AV, LA, 90031	635 - B1
GAULDIN ELEM 9724 SPRY ST, DWNY, 90242	736 - C1
GAULT STREET ELEM 17000 GAULT ST, VanN, 91406	531 - C5
GEDDES ELEM 14600 CAVETTE PL, BALD, 91706	598 - C4
GERMAIN STREET ELEM 20730 GERMAIN ST, Chat, 91311	500 - C3
GETHSEMANE BAPTIST CHRISTIAN-ELEM 6095 ORANGE AV, NLB, 90805	765 - F1
GETHSEMANE BAPTIST CHRISTIAN-HIGH 6095 ORANGE AV, NLB, 90805	765 - F1
GIANO INTERMED 3223 S GIANO AV, WCOV, 91792	678 - J1
GIBSON ELEM 9650 E PALMDALE BLVD, Litl, 93543	4198 - B7
GIDLEY ELEM 10226 LOWER AZUSA RD, ELMN, 91731	597 - B5
GILBERT ELEM 7255 8TH ST, BPK, 90621	767 - G1
GILBERT WEST HIGH 6855 LA PALMA AV, BPK, 90620	767 - G3
GIRD ELEM 4980 RIVERSIDE DR, CHNO, 91710	641 - F7
GLADSTONE ELEM 1314 W GLADSTONE ST, SDMS, 91773	599 - H1
GLADSTONE HIGH 1340 N ENID AV, COV, 91722	598 - H3
GLADSTONE STREET ELEM 1040 E GLADSTONE ST, AZU, 91722	599 - B1
GLASSELL PARK ELEM 2211 W AVE 30, LA, 90065	594 - G3
GLAZIER ELEM 10932 EXCELSIOR DR, NRWK, 90650	736 - E4
GLEDHILL STREET ELEM 16030 GLEDHILL ST, LA, 91343	501 - F6
GLEN ALTA ELEM 3410 SIERRA ST, LA, 90031	595 - C6
GLENDALE ADVENTIST ACADEMY 700 KIMLIN DR, GLDL, 91206	564 - H3
GLENDALE HIGH 1440 E BROADWAY, GLDL, 91205	564 - H5
GLENDORA HIGH 1600 E FOOTHILL BLVD, GLDR, 91741	569 - H5
GLENELDER ELEM 16234 FOLGER ST, HacH, 91745	678 - D2
GLENFELIZ BOULEVARD ELEM 3955 GLENFELIZ BLVD, LA, 90039	594 - D1
GLENN, JOHN HIGH 13520 SHOEMAKER AV, NRWK, 90650	737 - B2
GLEN OAK ELEM 1000 N SUNFLOWER AV, COV, 91724	599 - G3
GLENOAKS ELEM 2015 E GLENOAKS BLVD, GLDL, 91206	564 - J4
GLENWOOD ELEM 8001 LEDGE AV, SunV, 91352	533 - B2
GODDARD MID 859 E SIERRA MADRE AV, GLDR, 91741	569 - G3
GOLDEN DAY 4508 CRENSHAW BLVD, LA, 90043	673 - F4
GOLDEN HILL ELEM 732 BARRIS DR, FUL, 92832	738 - F6
GOLDEN POPPY ELEM 37802 ROCKIE LN, PMDL, 93552	4287 - D2
GOLDEN SPRINGS ELEM 245 BALLENA DR, DBAR, 91765	640 - C6
GOLDEN VALLEY HIGH 27051 ROBERT C LEE PKWY, SCTA, 91350	4551 - D5
GOMPERS ELEM 5206 BRIERCREST AV, LKWD, 90713	766 - C3
GOMPERS MID 234 E 112TH ST, LA, 90061	704 - D6
GONSALVES ELEM 13650 PARK ST, CRTS, 90703	737 - C6
GOODEN ELEM 192 N BALDWIN AV, SMAD, 91024	567 - A1
GOOD SHEPHERD CATHOLIC ELEM 148 S LINDEN DR, BHLS, 90212	632 - F2
GRACE CHRISTIAN 12722 WOODS AV, NRWK, 90650	736 - G1
GRACE COMM ELEM 13248 ROSCOE BLVD, NHol, 91605	532 - D2
GRACE LUTHERAN 856 W NEWGROVE ST, LAN, 93534	4015 - G6
GRAHAM ELEM 8407 S FIR AV, Flor, 90001	704 - G2
GRANADA ELEM 100 S GRANADA AV, ALH, 91801	596 - C4
GRANADA ELEM 17170 TRIBUNE ST, GrnH, 91344	501 - C3
GRANADA HILLS BAPTIST ELEM 10949 ZELZAH AV, GrnH, 91344	501 - A2
GRANADA HILLS HIGH 10535 ZELZAH AV, GrnH, 91344	501 - A3
GRANADA MID 15337 LEMON DR, LACo, 90604	707 - H7
GRAND VIEW BOULEVARD ELEM 3951 GRAND VIEW BLVD, LA, 90066	672 - C4
GRAND VIEW ELEM 455 25TH ST, MANB, 90266	732 - F5
GRANDVIEW ELEM 795 GRANDVIEW LN, LACo, 91744	638 - G6
GRANDVIEW MID 795 GRANDVIEW LN, LACo, 91744	638 - H6
GRANT ELEM 1225 E 64TH ST, NLB, 90805	735 - F7
GRANT ELEM 1530 N WILTON PL, Hlwd, 90028	593 - H4
GRANT ELEM 2368 PEARL ST, SMCA, 90405	671 - J2
GRANT, ULYSSES HIGH 13000 OXNARD ST, VanN, 91401	562 - E1
GRAPE STREET ELEM 1940 E 111TH ST, LA, 90059	704 - H6
GRATTS ELEM 309 LUCAS AV, LA, 90017	634 - D3
GRAVES MID 13243 LOS NIETOS RD, LACo, 90605	707 - B4
GRAZIDE ELEM 2850 LEOPOLD AV, HacH, 91745	678 - C5
GREEN ELEM 4520 W 168TH ST, LNDL, 90260	733 - C7
GREENWOOD ELEM 900 S GREENWOOD AV, MTBL, 90640	676 - C4
GREY HIGH 6510 ETIWANDA AV, Res, 91335	530 - J6
GRIDLEY STREET ELEM 1907 8TH ST, LA, 91340	482 - C4
GRIFFIN AVENUE ELEM 2025 GRIFFIN AV, LA, 90031	635 - A1
GRIFFITH MID 4765 E 4TH ST, ELA, 90022	635 - G6
GRIFFITHS MID 9633 TWEEDY LN, DWNY, 90240	706 - B2
GROVECENTER ELEM 775 N LARK ELLEN AV, WCOV, 91790	598 - H5
GUARDIAN ANGEL ELEM 10919 NORRIS AV, Pcma, 91331	502 - D2
GUIDANCE CHARTER ELEM, THE 1125 E PALMDALE BLVD, PMDL, 93550	4286 - C1
GULF AVENUE ELEM 828 W L ST, Wilm, 90744	794 - D5
HADDON AVENUE ELEM 10115 HADDON AV, Pcma, 91331	502 - D4
HALE MID 23830 CALIFA ST, WdHl, 91367	559 - E1
HALLDALE AVENUE ELEM 21514 HALLDALE AV, LA, 90501	764 - A6
HAMASAKI ELEM 4865 E 1ST ST, ELA, 90022	635 - G5
HAMILTON, ALEXANDER MID 1060 E 70TH ST, NLB, 90805	735 - E6
HAMILTON ELEM 2089 ROSE VILLA ST, PAS, 91107	566 - D5
HAMILTON HIGH 2955 S ROBERTSON BLVD, LA, 90034	632 - H6
HAMLIN STREET ELEM 22627 HAMLIN ST, CanP, 91307	529 - H6
HAMMEL STREET ELEM 438 N BRANNICK AV, City, 90063	635 - E5
HANCOCK PK ELEM 408 S FAIRFAX AV, LA, 90036	633 - B1
HARBOR CITY ELEM 1508 254TH ST, Hrbr, 90710	793 - J4
HARBOR MATH SCIENCE MAGNET 1214 PARK WESTERN PL, LA, 90732	823 - J3
HARBOR TEACHING PREP ACADEMY 1111 FIGUEROA PL, Wilm, 90744	794 - C6
HARDING STREET ELEM 13060 HARDING ST, LA, 91342	482 - D4
HARGITT MID 12940 FOSTER RD, NRWK, 90650	737 - A2
HARMONY ELEM 699 E 42ND PL, LA, 90011	674 - E3
HARRISON ELEM 3529 CITY TERRACE DR, City, 90063	635 - D3
HARRISON ELEM 425 E HARRISON AV, POM, 91767	601 - A3
HARTE, BRET ELEM 3200 W JEFFRIES AV, BURB, 91505	533 - C7
HARTE, BRET ELEM 1671 E PHILLIPS ST, NLB, 90805	765 - F2
HARTE PREP MID 9301 S HOOVER ST, LA, 90044	704 - B4
HART STREET ELEM 21040 HART ST, CanP, 91303	530 - B5
HART, WILLIAM S UNION HIGH 24825 NEWHALL AV, SCTA, 91321	4550 - H7
HARVARD ELEM 330 N HARVARD BLVD, LA, 90004	593 - J7
HARVARD-WESTLAKE MID 700 N FARING RD, BelA, 90077	592 - C6
HARVARD-WESTLAKE UPPER HIGH 3700 COLDWATER CANYON AV, LA, 91604	562 - E6
HASKELL ELEM 15850 TULSA ST, GrnH, 91344	501 - F2
HASKELL MID 11525 DEL AMO BLVD, CRTS, 90703	766 - G4
HAWAIIAN AVENUE ELEM 540 HAWAIIAN AV, Wilm, 90744	794 - D7

FEATURE NAME	Address City, ZIP Code	PAGE-GRID
HAWAIIAN ELEM	12350 226TH ST, HGDN, 90716	766 - J7
HAWTHORNE ACADEMY	12500 RAMONA AV, HAW, 90250	733 - C1
HAWTHORNE ELEM	624 N REXFORD DR, BHLS, 90210	592 - F7
HAWTHORNE HIGH	4859 W EL SEGUNDO BLVD, HAW, 90250	733 - B1
HAWTHORNE MATH & SCIENCE-ACADEMY	4467 W BROADWAY, HAW, 90250	733 - C1
HAWTHORNE MID	4366 W 129TH ST, HAW, 90250	733 - D2
HAYNES ELEM	6624 LOCKHURST DR, CanP, 91307	529 - E6
HAZELTINE AVENUE ELEM	7150 HAZELTINE AV, VanN, 91405	532 - B5
HEART OF THE VALLEY CHRISTIAN	18644 SHERMAN WY, Res, 91335	530 - H5
HEATH, MARGARET ELEM	14321 SCHOOL ST, BALD, 91706	598 - C3
HELIOTROPE AVENUE ELEM	5911 WOODLAWN AV, MYWD, 90270	675 - E6
HELMERS, CHARLES ELEM	27300 GRANDVIEW DR, SCTA, 91354	4460 - F7
HENRY ELEM	3720 CANEHILL AV, LBCH, 90808	766 - E7
HENRY MID	17340 SAN JOSE ST, GrnH, 91344	501 - B4
HERCHEL DAY WEST	27400 CANWOOD ST, Ago, 91301	558 - F6
HERITAGE CHARTER HIGH	603 E 115TH ST, LA, 90059	704 - E6
HERMOSA DRIVE ELEM	400 E HERMOSA DR, FUL, 92835	738 - H2
HERMOSA VALLEY	1645 VALLEY DR, HMB, 90254	762 - G2
HERMOSA VIEW	1800 PROSPECT AV, HMB, 90254	762 - H1
HERRICK AVENUE ELEM	13350 HERRICK AV, LA, 91342	481 - H3
HESBY STREET SPAN ELEM	15530 HESBY ST, Enc, 91436	561 - G3
HESCHEL DAY	17701 DEVONSHIRE ST, GrnH, 91344	501 - A4
HICKORY ELEM	2800 W 227TH ST, TOR, 90505	793 - F1
HIDDEN TRAILS ELEM	2550 RIDGEVIEW DR, CHLS, 91709	680 - J5
HIGH DESERT MID	3620 ANTELOPE WOODS RD, Actn, 93510	4375 - B6
HIGHLAND ELEM	430 VENICE WY, ING, 90302	703 - B1
HIGHLAND HALL	17100 SUPERIOR ST, Nor, 91325	501 - C5
HIGHLAND HIGH	39055 25TH ST W, PMDL, 93551	4195 - D6
HIGHLAND OAKS ELEM	10 VIRGINIA DR, ARCD, 91006	567 - D2
HIGHLANDS ELEM	27332 CATALA AV, SCTA, 91350	4461 - A7
HIGH POINT ACADEMY	1720 KINNELOA CANYON RD, LACo, 91107	536 - F7
HIGH TECH HIGH	17111 VICTORY BLVD, VanN, 91406	531 - C6
HILLCREST CHRISTIAN	17531 RINALDI ST, GrnH, 91344	501 - B1
HILLCREST HIGH	441 W HILLCREST BLVD, ING, 90301	703 - B3
HILLCREST DRIVE ELEM	4041 HILLCREST DR, LA, 90008	673 - D2
HILLCREST ELEM	795 PEPPER ST, MONP, 91755	636 - D4
HILLEL HEBREW ACADEMY	9120 W OLYMPIC BLVD, BHLS, 90212	632 - H3
HILL MID	1100 IROQUOIS AV, LBCH, 90815	796 - E6
HILLSIDE ELEM	120 E AVE 35, LA, 90031	595 - A6
HILLSIDE HIGH	1558 W 9TH ST, UPL, 91786	601 - H3
HILLVIEW MID	10931 STAMY RD, LACo, 90604	707 - G6
HILLVIEW MID	40525 PEONZA LN, PMDL, 93551	4194 - J2
HOBART BOULEVARD ELEM	980 S HOBART BLVD, LA, 90006	633 - J4
HODGE ELEM	700 W 11TH ST, AZU, 91702	568 - H4
HOLDER ELEM	9550 HOLDER ST, BPK, 90620	767 - F7
HOLLAND, JERRY D MID	4733 LANDIS AV, BALD, 91706	598 - C4
HOLLENBECK MID	2510 E 6TH ST, LA, 90023	635 - A6
HOLLENCREST MID	2101 E MERCED AV, WCOV, 91791	639 - A2
HOLLINGWORTH ELEM	3003 E HOLLINGWORTH ST, WCOV, 91792	679 - D2
HOLLY AVENUE ELEM	360 W DUARTE RD, ARCD, 91007	567 - B7
HOLLYDALE ELEM	5511 CENTURY BLVD, SGAT, 90280	735 - F1
HOLLYWOOD HIGH	1521 N HIGHLAND AV, Hlwd, 90028	593 - D4
HOLLYWOOD LITTLE RED HOUSE	1248 N HIGHLAND AV, LA, 90038	593 - E5
HOLLYWOOD PRIMARY CTR	1115 TAMARIND AV, LA, 90038	593 - G5
HOLMES AVENUE ELEM	5108 HOLMES AV, LA, 90058	674 - G4
HOLMES ELEM	5020 BARLIN AV, LKWD, 90712	765 - J3
HOLMES MID	9351 PASO ROBLES AV, Nor, 91325	501 - C6
HOLY ANGELS ELEM	360 CAMPUS DR, ARCD, 91007	567 - B6
HOLY FAMILY ELEM	400 S LOUISE ST, GLDL, 91205	564 - E5
HOLY FAMILY HIGH	400 E LOMITA AV, GLDL, 91205	564 - E6
HOLY FAMILY	1122 E ROBIDOUX ST, Wilm, 90744	794 - G5
HOLY INNOCENTS	2500 PACIFIC AV, LBCH, 90806	795 - D3
HOLY MARTYRS ARMENIAN ELEM	16617 PARTHENIA ST, LA, 91343	531 - D1
HOLY MARTYRS ARMENIAN ELEM	5300 WHITE OAK AV, Enc, 91316	561 - B2
HOLY NAME OF JESUS ELEM	1955 W JEFFERSON BLVD, LA, 90018	633 - H7
HOLY NAME OF MARY	124 S SAN DIMAS CANYON RD, SDMS, 91773	600 - D2
HOLY REDEEMER	2361 DEL MAR RD, Mont, 91020	534 - H3
HOLY SPIRIT/SAINT MARY MAGDALEN	1418 S BURNSIDE AV, LA, 90019	633 - C4
HOLY TRINITY ELEM	3716 BOYCE AV, LA, 90039	594 - D1
HOLY TRINITY	1226 W SANTA CRUZ ST, LA, 90732	824 - A4
HOOPER AVENUE ELEM	1225 E 52ND ST, LA, 90011	674 - F4
HOOVER, HERBERT HIGH	651 GLENWOOD RD, GLDL, 91202	564 - C2
HOOVER, HERBERT MID	3501 COUNTRY CLUB DR, LKWD, 90712	765 - J5
HOOVER, LOU HENRY ELEM	6302 ALTA AV, WHIT, 90601	677 - D5
HOOVER STREET ELEM	2726 FRANCIS AV, LA, 90005	634 - B3
HOPE LUTHERAN ELEM	1041 E FOOTHILL BLVD, GLDR, 91741	569 - G5
HOPE STREET NEW ELEM	7560 STATE ST, HNTP, 90255	705 - B1
HOPKINSON ELEM	12582 KENSINGTON RD, OrCo, 90720	796 - G6
HOSLER MID	11300 SPRUCE ST, LYN, 90262	705 - C7
HOWARD ELEM	4650 HOWARD ST, MTCL, 91763	641 - F2
HOWE ELEM	4100 IRVING PL, CULC, 90232	672 - G1
HUBBARD STREET ELEM	13325 HUBBARD ST, LA, 91342	482 - C3
HUDNALL, CLAUDE ELEM	331 W OLIVE ST, ING, 90301	703 - B2
HUDSON ELEM	2335 WEBSTER AV, LBCH, 90810	795 - A3
HUERTA, DELORES ELEM	11036 HAWTHORNE BLVD, Lenx, 90304	703 - C6
HUERTA ELEM	15415 PIONEER BLVD, NRWK, 90650	736 - G4
HUGHES ELEM	4242 CLARA ST, CDHY, 90201	705 - D1
HUGHES-ELIZABETH LAKES	16633 ELIZABETH LAKE RD, LACo, 93532	4102 - B3
HUGHES MID	3846 CALIFORNIA AV, Bxby, 90807	765 - F6
HULL MID	2080 W 231ST ST, TOR, 90501	793 - G2
HUMPHREYS AVENUE ELEM	500 S HUMPHREYS AV, ELA, 90022	635 - F7
HUNTINGTON DRIVE ELEM	4435 HUNTINGTON DR N, LA, 90032	595 - C6
HUNTINGTON INTERMED	1700 HUNTINGTON DR, SMRO, 91108	596 - C1
HUNTINGTON PARK 7 ELEM	6055 CORONA AV, HNTP, 90255	675 - C6
HUNTINGTON PARK BAPTIST	2665 CLARENDON AV, HNTP, 90255	674 - J6
HUNTINGTON PARK CHARTER HIGH	2701 SATURN AV, HNTP, 90255	674 - J7
HUNTINGTON PARK HIGH	6020 MILES AV, HNTP, 90255	675 - A5
HUNTINGTON PARK NEW 3 ELEM	5714 PACIFIC BLVD, HNTP, 90255	674 - J5
HURLEY ELEM	535 DORA GUZMAN AV, LPUE, 91744	678 - G1
HUTCHINSON MID	13900 ESTERO RD, LMRD, 90638	737 - E2
HYDE PARK BOULEVARD ELEM	3140 HYDE PARK BLVD, LA, 90043	673 - F7
IMMACULATE CONCEPTION	726 S SHAMROCK AV, MNRO, 91016	567 - H4
IMMACULATE CONCEPTION	830 GREEN AV, LA, 90017	634 - C4
IMMACULATE HEART HIGH	5515 FRANKLIN AV, LA, 90068	593 - H3
IMMACULATE HEART MID	5515 FRANKLIN AV, LA, 90068	593 - H3
IMMACULATE HEART OF MARY ELEM	1055 N ALEXANDRIA AV, LA, 90029	593 - J5
IMMANUEL FIRST LUTHERAN ELEM	512 S VALINDA AV, WCOV, 91790	638 - G1
IMPERIAL ELEM	8133 IMPERIAL HWY, DWNY, 90242	705 - J7
IMPERIAL MID	1450 SCHOOLWOOD DR, LHB, 90631	738 - D1
INCARNATION ELEM	123 W GLENOAKS BLVD, GLDL, 91202	564 - E3
INDEPENDENCE ELEM	8435 VICTORIA AV, SGAT, 90280	705 - B2
INDEPENDENCE HIGH	220 S 5TH ST, ALH, 91801	596 - A5
INDIAN HILLS HIGH	4345 N LAS VIRGENES RD, CALB, 91302	558 - H7
INGLEWOOD CHRISTIAN	215 E HILLCREST BLVD, ING, 90301	703 - C3
INGLEWOOD HIGH	231 S GREVILLEA AV, ING, 90301	703 - C2
INTENSIVE LEARNING CTR	4718 MICHELSON ST, LKWD, 90712	766 - A2
INTERNATIONAL ELEM	700 LOCUST AV, LBCH, 90813	795 - D7
INTERNATIONAL POLYTECHNIC HIGH	3801 TEMPLE AV, LACo, 91768	640 - A3
IRVING MID	3010 ESTARA AV, LA, 90065	594 - G2
IVANHOE ELEM	2828 HERKIMER ST, LA, 90039	594 - D3
IVY ACADEMIA CHARTER	6221 FALLBROOK AV, WdHl, 91367	529 - H7
JACKSON ELEM	593 W WOODBURY RD, Alta, 91001	535 - G6
JACKSON ELEM	8015 PAINTER AV, WHIT, 90602	707 - D1
JACKSON ELEM	7220 JACKSON ST, PRM, 90723	735 - F6
JANSON ELEM	8628 MARSHALL ST, RSMD, 91770	596 - G7
JEFFERSON ELEM	10027 ROSE ST, BLF, 90706	736 - C7
JEFFERSON ELEM	10322 CONDON AV, Lenx, 90304	703 - C5
JEFFERSON ELEM	1500 E VILLA ST, PAS, 91106	566 - C3
JEFFERSON ELEM	2508 E 133RD ST, Wbrk, 90222	734 - J2
JEFFERSON ELEM	4091 W 139TH ST, HAW, 90250	733 - D3
JEFFERSON ELEM	600 HARKNESS LN, RBCH, 90278	762 - J2
JEFFERSON LEADERSHIP ACADEMY-MID	750 EUCLID AV, LBCH, 90804	795 - J6
JEFFERSON MID	1340 E LIVE OAK ST, SGBL, 91776	596 - G3
JEFFERSON MID	21717 TALISMAN ST, TOR, 90503	763 - C6
JEFFERSON PRIMARY CTR	3601 S MAPLE AV, LA, 90011	674 - D2
JEFFERSON STREET ELEM	8600 JEFFERSON ST, PRM, 90723	735 - J4
JEFFERSON, THOMAS ELEM	1540 5TH ST, GLDL, 91201	564 - A1
JEFFERSON, THOMAS ELEM	1900 N 6TH ST, BURB, 91504	533 - F4
JEFFERSON, THOMAS HIGH	1319 E 41ST ST, LA, 90011	674 - F2
JELLICK ELEM	1400 JELLICK AV, RowH, 91748	679 - A4
JERSEY AVENUE ELEM	9400 JERSEY AV, SFSP, 90670	706 - G3
JOHNSON OPPORTUNITY HIGH	333 E 54TH ST, LA, 90011	674 - D5
JOHNSTON ELEM	13421 FAIRFORD AV, NRWK, 90650	736 - F2
JONES, CHARLES D JR HIGH	14250 MERCED AV, BALD, 91706	598 - B7
JORDAN, DAVID S HIGH	6500 ATLANTIC AV, NLB, 90805	735 - E7
JORDAN, DAVID STARR MID	420 S MARIPOSA ST, BURB, 91506	563 - G2
JORDAN ELEM	10654 JORDAN RD, WHIT, 90603	708 - A5
JORDAN FRESHMAN ACADEMY	171 W BORT ST, NLB, 90805	765 - B1
JORDAN HIGH	2265 E 103RD ST, Wats, 90002	704 - H4
JORDAN, JAMES CHARTER MID	22250 ELKWOOD ST, LA, 91304	529 - J3
JOSHUA ELEM	43926 2ND ST E, LAN, 93535	4105 - J1
JOSHUA HILLS ELEM	3030 FAIRFIELD AV, PMDL, 93550	4286 - G4
JOYNER, FLORENCE GRIFFITH ELEM	1963 E 103RD ST, Wats, 90002	704 - G5
JUAREZ ELEM	11939 ACLARE ST, CRTS, 90703	736 - H7
JUNIPER INTERMED	39066 PALM TREE WY, LACo, 93551	4195 - G6
JUNIPERO SERRA HIGH	14830 VAN NESS AV, GAR, 90249	733 - H4
JUSTICE STREET ELEM	23350 JUSTICE ST, LA, 91304	529 - F3
KATHERINE ELEM	5455 KATHERINE ST, SIMI, 93063	499 - A3
KELLER ELEM	7020 E BRITTAIN ST, LBCH, 90808	766 - F7
KELLER, HELEN ELEM	3521 PALM AV, LYN, 90262	735 - B2
KELLOGG POLYTECHNIC ELEM	610 MEDINA ST, POM, 91768	640 - C2
KELLY ELEM	2320 E ALONDRA BLVD, COMP, 90221	735 - C5
KELSO, WILLIAM H ELEM	809 E KELSO ST, ING, 90301	703 - D3
KENMORE ELEM	3823 KENMORE AV, BALD, 91706	598 - A6
KENNEDY ELEM	1305 S OLEANDER AV, COMP, 90220	734 - J6
KENNEDY ELEM	17500 BELSHIRE AV, CRTS, 90703	736 - J7
KENNEDY ELEM	4010 RAMBOZ DR, City, 90063	635 - E3
KENNEDY HIGH	11254 GOTHIC AV, GrnH, 91344	501 - E1
KENNEDY, JOHN F HIGH	8281 WALKER ST, LPMA, 90623	767 - D4
KENTER CANYON ELEM	645 N KENTER AV, Brwd, 90049	631 - E2
KENTWOOD ELEM	8401 EMERSON AV, Wch, 90045	702 - F2
KEPPEL ELEM	6630 MARK KEPPEL ST, PRM, 90723	735 - E4
KEPPEL, MARK ELEM	730 GLENWOOD RD, GLDL, 91202	564 - C2
KEPPEL, MARK HIGH	501 E HELLMAN AV, ALH, 91801	636 - C1
KESTER AVENUE ELEM	5353 KESTER AV, VanN, 91411	561 - J2
KETTERING ELEM	550 SILVERA AV, LBCH, 90803	796 - E7
KILLIAN ELEM	19100 KILLIAN AV, RowH, 91748	679 - C6
KIM ELEM	225 S OXFORD AV, LA, 90004	633 - H1
KING-DREW MED MAGNET HIGH	1656 E 118TH ST, Wbrk, 90059	704 - G7
KING-EDISON, STARR ACADEMY	145 E ARTESIA BLVD, NLB, 90805	735 - C7
KING ELEM	2270 E 122ND ST, Wbrk, 90222	734 - H1
KING ELEM	3989 S HOBART BLVD, LA, 90062	673 - H2
KING ELEM	8710 MOODY ST, CYP, 90630	767 - C5
KING MID	4201 FOUNTAIN AV, LFlz, 90027	594 - B5
KINGSLEY ELEM	1170 WASHINGTON AV, POM, 91767	601 - B7
KINGSLEY ELEM	5200 VIRGINIA AV, LA, 90029	593 - H5
KINGSLEY ELEM	5625 KINGSLEY ST, MTCL, 91763	601 - H7
KIPP LA COLLEGE PREP ELEM	1855 S MAIN ST, LA, 90031	634 - J2
KIRKWOOD EDUCATIONAL CTR	11115 PANGBORN AV, DWNY, 90241	706 - D6
KITTRIDGE STREET ELEM	13619 KITTRIDGE ST, VanN, 91401	532 - C6
KNIGHT HIGH	37423 70TH ST E, PMDL, 93552	4287 - E3
KNOLLS ELEM	6334 KATHERINE RD, SIMI, 93063	499 - C3
KNOLLWOOD ELEM	11822 GERALD AV, GrnH, 91344	481 - E7
KNOTT ELEM	7300 LA PALMA AV, BPK, 90620	767 - H4
KORNBLUM ELEM	3620 W EL SEGUNDO BLVD, HAW, 90250	733 - E2
KRANZ, CHARLES T INTERMED	12460 FINEVIEW ST, ELMN, 91732	637 - E4
KWIS ELEM	1925 KWIS AV, HacH, 91745	678 - B3
LA BALLONA ELEM	10915 WASHINGTON BLVD, CULC, 90232	672 - F2
LA CANADA HIGH	4463 OAK GROVE DR, LCF, 91011	535 - E5
LA CANADA ELEM	4540 ENCINAS DR, LCF, 91011	535 - B3
LA CANADA JR & SR HIGH	4463 OAK GROVE DR, LCF, 91011	535 - E5
LA COLIMA ELEM	11225 MILLER RD, LACo, 90604	707 - F6
LA CRESCENTA ELEM	4343 LA CRESCENTA AV, LaCr, 91214	534 - F1
LADERA PALMA ELEM	2151 BROOKDALE AV, LHB, 90631	708 - H4
LAFAYETTE ELEM	2445 CHESTNUT AV, LBCH, 90806	795 - D3
LA FETRA ELEM	547 W BENNETT AV, GLDR, 91741	569 - D5
LAGUNA NUEVA ELEM	6360 GARFIELD AV, CMRC, 90040	675 - J7
LAGUNA ROAD ELEM	300 LAGUNA RD, FUL, 92835	738 - G3
LA HABRA HIGH	801 W HIGHLANDER AV, LHB, 90631	708 - D5
LAKE CENTER MID	10503 PIONEER BLVD, SFSP, 90670	706 - G5
LAKELAND ELEM	11224 BOMBARDIER AV, NRWK, 90650	706 - H6
LAKE LOS ANGELES ELEM	16310 E AVE Q, LACo, 93591	4199 - F6
LAKE MARIE ELEM	10001 CARMENITA RD, LACo, 90605	707 - B4
LAKESIDE MID	11000 KENNEY ST, NRWK, 90650	706 - F6
LAKEVIEW ELEM	11500 JOSLIN ST, SFSP, 90670	706 - G4
LAKEWOOD ELEM	3701 MICHELSON ST, LKWD, 90712	765 - J2
LAKEWOOD HIGH	4400 BRIERCREST AV, LKWD, 90713	766 - C5
LA MERCED ELEM	724 N POPLAR AV, MTBL, 90640	676 - F1
LA MERCED INTERMED	215 E AVD D LA MERCED, MTBL, 90640	636 - F7
LA MESA JR HIGH	26623 MAY WY, SCTA, 91351	4551 - E4
LA MIRADA HIGH	13520 ADELFA DR, LMRD, 90638	737 - H2
LA MIRANDA HEIGHTS CHRISTIAN-JR HS	12900 BLUEFIELD AV, LMRD, 90638	737 - G1
LA MIRANDA HEIGHTS CHRISTIAN	12200 OXFORD DR, LMRD, 90638	707 - H7
LAMPTON ELEM	14716 ELMCROFT AV, NRWK, 90650	736 - F4
LANAI ROAD ELEM	4241 LANAI RD, Enc, 91436	561 - E5
LANCASTER BAPTIST	4024 E LANCASTER BLVD, LAN, 93535	4016 - H5
LANCASTER CHRISTIAN ELEM	44339 BEECH AV, LAN, 93534	4015 - H7
LANCASTER HIGH	44701 EAGLE WY, LAN, 93536	4015 - B6
LANDELL ELEM	9739 DENNI ST, CYP, 90630	767 - B7
LANE, ROBERT HILL ELEM	1500 AVD CESAR CHAVEZ, MONP, 91754	635 - H5
LANGDON AVENUE ELEM	8817 LANGDON AV, LA, 91343	531 - G1
LANKERSHIM ELEM	5250 BAKMAN AV, NHol, 91601	562 - J2
LANTERMAN HIGH	2328 SAINT JAMES PL, LA, 90007	634 - C7
LA PLUMA ELEM	14420 LA PLUMA DR, LMRD, 90638	737 - H3
LA PRIMARIA ELEM	4220 GILMAN RD, ELMN, 91732	597 - G7
LA PUENTE HIGH	15615 NELSON AV, LPUE, 91744	638 - D7
LARK ELLEN ELEM	4555 N LARK ELLEN AV, LACo, 91722	598 - H4
LA ROSA ELEM	9301 LA ROSA DR, TEML, 91780	596 - J5
LA SALLE AVENUE ELEM	8715 LA SALLE AV, LA, 90047	703 - J3
LA SALLE HIGH	3880 E SIERRA MADRE BLVD, PAS, 91107	566 - H2
LA SEDA ELEM	341 LA SEDA RD, LACo, 91744	679 - A1
LA SERNA HIGH	15301 YOUNGWOOD DR, WHIT, 90605	707 - H2
LAS FLORES ELEM	10039 PALM ST, BLF, 90706	736 - C6
LA SIERRA HIGH	201 W AMERIGE AV, FUL, 92832	738 - G7
LAS LOMAS ELEM	301 LAS LOMAS DR, LHB, 90631	708 - E7
LAS PALMAS MID	641 N LARK ELLEN AV, COV, 91722	598 - H4
LAS POSITAS ELEM	1400 SCHOOLWOOD DR, LHB, 90631	738 - D1
LASSALETTE ELEM	14333 LASSALETTE ST, LPUE, 91744	638 - B4
LASSEN ELEM	15017 SUPERIOR ST, LA, 91343	501 - H5
LA TIJERA ELEM	1415 S LA TIJERA BLVD, ING, 90302	673 - A7
LATONA AVENUE ELEM	4312 BERENICE AV, LA, 90031	595 - B5
LAUREL ELEM	13550 LAMBERT RD, WHIT, 90605	707 - D2
LAUREL ELEM	925 N HAYWORTH AV, LA, 90046	593 - B6
LAUREL HALL ELEM	11919 OXNARD ST, NHol, 91606	532 - G7
LAUREL STREET ELEM	1321 W LAUREL ST, COMP, 90220	734 - G5
LAURENCE	13639 VICTORY BLVD, VanN, 91401	532 - C6
LA VERNE HEIGHTS ELEM	1550 BASE LINE RD, LVRN, 91750	570 - F7
LAWNDALE HIGH	14901 INGLEWOOD AV, LNDL, 90260	733 - B4
LAWRENCE MID	10100 VARIEL AV, Chat, 91311	500 - B4
LEAL ELEM	12920 DROXFORD ST, CRTS, 90703	767 - B2
LEAPWOOD AVENUE ELEM	19302 LEAPWOOD AV, CRSN, 90746	764 - E3
LE CONTE MID	1316 N BRONSON AV, Hlwd, 90028	593 - G5
LEDESMA HIGH	12347 RAMONA BLVD, ELMN, 91732	597 - G7
LEE, CHARLES H ELEM	550 N CERRITOS AV, AZU, 91702	569 - A6
LEE ELEM	1620 TEMPLE AV, LBCH, 90804	795 - H5
LEE, RICHARD HENRY ELEM	11481 FOSTER RD, OrCo, 90720	796 - H4
LEFFINGWELL ELEM	10625 SANTA GERTRUDES AV, WHIT, 90603	707 - H5
LEGACY ACADEMY	27680 DICKASON DR, SCTA, 91355	4460 - E7
LE GORE ELEM	11121 BRYANT RD, ELMN, 91731	597 - D6
LEHIGH ELEM	10200 LEHIGH AV, MTCL, 91763	601 - E7

FEATURE NAME Address City, ZIP Code	PAGE-GRID
LELAND STREET ELEM 2120 S LELAND ST, SPed, 90731	824 - A7
LE LYCEE FRANCAIS DE LOS-ANGELES 3261 OVERLAND AV, LA, 90034	632 - E7
LEMAY STREET ELEM 17520 VANOWEN ST, VanN, 91406	531 - B6
LENNOX MATH/SCIENCE TECH-ACADEMY HIGH 10302 FIRMONA AV, Lenx, 90304	703 - C5
LENNOX MID 11033 BUFORD AV, Lenx, 90304	703 - B6
LEONA VALLEY ELEM 9063 LEONA AV, LACo, 93551	4193 - J3
LEONIS HIGH 5445 MANTON AV, WdHl, 91367	559 - F2
LEUZINGER HIGH 4118 ROSECRANS AV, LNDL, 90260	733 - D4
LEWIS ELEM 13220 BELLFLOWER BLVD, DWNY, 90242	736 - C2
LEXINGTON ELEM 550 W LEXINGTON AV, POM, 91766	640 - J5
LEXINGTON JR HIGH 4351 ORANGE AV, CYP, 90630	767 - B7
LIBERTY BOULEVARD ELEM 2728 LIBERTY BLVD, SGAT, 90280	704 - J2
LIFE CTR CHRISTIAN 305 E ARROW HWY, POM, 91767	601 - A4
LIGGETT STREET ELEM 9373 MOONBEAM AV, PanC, 91402	502 - A6
LIGHT AND LIFE CHRISTIAN ELEM 5951 DOWNEY AV, NLB, 90805	765 - J1
LILLIAN STREET ELEM 5909 LILLIAN ST, Flor, 90001	674 - G6
LIMERICK AVENUE ELEM 8530 LIMERICK AV, Win, 91306	530 - C1
LINCOLN ELEM 2223 PLANT AV, RBCH, 90278	733 - A6
LINCOLN ELEM 11031 STATE ST, LYN, 90262	705 - A6
LINCOLN ELEM 1175 E 11TH ST, LBCH, 90813	795 - F6
LINCOLN ELEM 1200 N GORDON ST, POM, 91768	600 - J7
LINCOLN ELEM 12620 BROADWAY, WHIT, 90601	677 - C5
LINCOLN ELEM 15324 CALIFORNIA AV, PRM, 90723	735 - H4
LINCOLN ELEM 1667 E 118TH ST, Wbrk, 90059	704 - G7
LINCOLN ELEM 2418 W 166TH ST, TOR, 90504	733 - G7
LINCOLN ELEM 4310 NEW YORK AV, GLDL, 91214	504 - E7
LINCOLN ELEM 44021 15TH ST E, LAN, 93535	4016 - C7
LINCOLN HIGH 3501 N BROADWAY, LA, 90031	595 - B7
LINCOLN MID 1501 CALIFORNIA AV, SMCA, 90403	631 - E7
LINDA VERDE ELEM 44924 5TH ST E, LAN, 93535	4016 - A5
LINDA VISTA ELEM 1259 LINDA VISTA AV, PAS, 91103	565 - E1
LINDBERG, CHARLES A MID 1022 E MARKET ST, NLB, 90805	765 - E3
LINDBERGH ELEM 3309 CEDAR AV, LYN, 90262	735 - A1
LINDERO CANYON MID 5844 LARBOARD LN, AGRH, 91301	557 - G4
LINDSTROM ELEM 5900 CANEHILL AV, LKWD, 90713	766 - D2
LITTLEROCK HIGH 10833 E AVE R, Litl, 93543	4288 - D1
LIVE OAK ELEM 27715 SADDLERIDGE WY, Cstc, 91384	4459 - H5
LIVING WAY CHRISTIAN ACADEMY 2495 E MOUNTAIN ST, PAS, 91104	566 - E2
LIZARRAGA ELEM 401 E 40TH PL, LA, 90011	674 - D2
LLOYDE HIGH 4951 MARINE AV, LNDL, 90260	733 - B4
LOCKE HIGH 325 E 111TH ST, LA, 90061	704 - D6
LOCKHURST DRIVE ELEM 6170 LOCKHURST DR, WdHl, 91367	529 - E7
LOCKWOOD AVENUE ELEM 4345 LOCKWOOD AV, LA, 90029	594 - A6
LOGAN STREET ELEM 1711 MONTANA ST, Echo, 90026	594 - E7
LOMA ALTA ELEM 3544 N CANON BLVD, Alta, 91001	536 - A3
LOMA ELEM 2131 LOMA AV, SELM, 91733	636 - J3
LOMA VISTA AVENUE ELEM 3629 E 58TH ST, MYWD, 90270	675 - C5
LOMA VISTA ELEM 13463 MEYER RD, LACo, 90605	707 - C7
LOMITA ELEM 2211 247TH ST, LMTA, 90717	793 - G3
LOMOND, BEN ELEM 621 E COVINA BLVD, COV, 91722	599 - C3
LONE HILL MID 700 S LONE HILL AV, SDMS, 91773	599 - J3
LONG BEACH ADVENTIST ELEM 4951 OREGON AV, NLB, 90805	765 - C4
LONG BEACH BRETHREN ELEM 3601 LINDEN AV, Bxby, 90807	765 - E7
LONG BEACH POLYTECHNIC HIGH 1600 ATLANTIC AV, LBCH, 90813	795 - E5
LONGDEN ELEM 9501 WENDON ST, TEML, 91780	596 - J2
LONGFELLOW ELEM 1065 E WASHINGTON BLVD, PAS, 91104	566 - A1
LONGFELLOW ELEM 1101 S DWIGHT AV, COMP, 90220	734 - G6
LONGFELLOW ELEM 245 W 10TH ST, AZU, 91702	568 - J5
LONGFELLOW ELEM 3800 OLIVE AV, Bxby, 90807	765 - E6
LONGFELLOW ELEM 6005 S MAGNOLIA AV, WHIT, 90601	677 - B5
LONGLEY WAY ELEM 2601 LONGLEY WY, ARCD, 91007	597 - C2
LOPEZ ELEM 701 S WHITE AV, POM, 91766	640 - H2
LORBEER MID 501 S DIAMOND BAR BLVD, DBAR, 91765	640 - C7
LORENA STREET ELEM 1015 S LORENA ST, LA, 90023	635 - B7
LORETO STREET ELEM 3408 ARROYO SECO AV, LA, 90065	595 - A6
LORNE STREET ELEM 17440 LORNE ST, Nor, 91325	531 - B3
LOS ALAMITOS HIGH 3591 CERRITOS AV, LALM, 90720	796 - J1
LOS ALISOS MID 14800 JERSEY AV, NRWK, 90650	736 - G4
LOS ALTOS BRETHREN ELEM 6505 E STEARNS ST, LBCH, 90815	796 - E4
LOS ALTOS ELEM 12001 BONA VISTA LN, LACo, 90604	707 - D7
LOS ALTOS ELEM 15565 LOS ALTOS DR, HacH, 91745	678 - A5
LOS ALTOS HIGH 15325 E LOS ROBLES AV, HacH, 91745	678 - A2
LOS AMIGOS ELEM 6640 E AVE R-8, PMDL, 93552	4287 - E2
LOS ANGELES ACADEMY MID 644 E 56TH ST, LA, 90011	674 - D5
LA ACHIEVEMENT CHARTER HIGH 20920 KNAPP ST, Chat, 91311	500 - B7
LOS ANGELES ADVENTIST 846 E EL SEGUNDO BLVD, Wbrk, 90059	734 - E1
LOS ANGELES ADVENTIST ACADEMY 846 E EL SEGUNDO BLVD, Wbrk, 90059	734 - E1
LOS ANGELES BAPTIST HIGH 9825 WOODLEY AV, LA, 91343	501 - E5
LOS ANGELES CES 5931 W 18TH ST, LA, 90035	633 - A5
LOS ANGELES CHRISTIAN 1620 W 20TH ST, LA, 90007	634 - A6
LOS ANGELES CO HIGH FOR THE-ARTS 5151 STATE UNIVERSITY DR, LA, 90032	635 - F2
LOS ANGELES ELEM 1211 S HOBART BLVD, LA, 90006	633 - H4
LOS ANGELES HEBREW HIGH 5900 SEPULVEDA BLVD, VanN, 91411	561 - H1
LOS ANGELES HIGH 4650 W OLYMPIC BLVD, LA, 90019	633 - E3
LOS ANGELES LUTHERAN HIGH 13570 ELDRIDGE AV, LA, 91342	482 - C2
LOS ANGELES PRIMARY CTR 5 987 S MARIPOSA AV, LA, 90006	633 - J4
LOS CERRITOS ELEM 14626 GUNDRY AV, PRM, 90723	735 - F3
LOS CERRITOS ELEM 515 W SAN ANTONIO DR, Bxby, 90807	765 - C6
LOS COYOTES ELEM 8122 MOODY ST, LPMA, 90623	767 - C4
LOS COYOTES MID 14640 MERCADO AV, LMRD, 90638	737 - J3
LOS FELIZ CHARTER ELEM 1265 N FAIRFAX AV, WHWD, 90046	593 - B5
LOS FELIZ ELEM 1740 N NEW HAMPSHIRE AV, LFlz, 90027	594 - A4
LOS MOLINOS ELEM 3112 LAS MARIAS AV, HacH, 91745	678 - A6
LOS NIETOS MID 11425 RIVERA RD, LACo, 90606	706 - H1
LOS ROBLES ACADEMY 1530 RIDLEY AV, HacH, 91745	677 - J2
LOUISVILLE HIGH 22300 MULHOLLAND DR, WdHl, 91364	559 - J5
LOWELL ELEM 5201 E BROADWAY, LBCH, 90803	826 - B1
LOYOLA HIGH 1901 VENICE BLVD, LA, 90006	633 - J5
LOYOLA VILLAGE ELEM 8821 VILLANOVA ST, Wch, 90045	702 - D3
LUGO ELEM 4335 PENDLETON AV, LYN, 90262	705 - E6
LUNADA BAY ELEM 520 PAS LUNADO, PVE, 90274	822 - E1
LUPIN HILL ELEM 26210 ADAMOR RD, CALB, 91302	558 - H3
LUTHERAN HIGH 3960 FRUIT ST, LVRN, 91750	600 - H1
LUTHERAN SCHOOL OF THE-FOOTHILLS 3561 FOOTHILL BLVD, GLDL, 91214	504 - E6
LUTHER, STEVE ELEM 4631 LA PALMA AV, LPMA, 90623	767 - B3
LYCEE INTL DE LOS ANGELES ELEM 4155 RUSSELL AV, LFlz, 90027	594 - B3
LYNN MID 5038 HALISON ST, TOR, 90503	763 - B4
LYNWOOD HIGH 4050 E IMPERIAL HWY, LYN, 90262	705 - D6
LYNWOOD MID 12124 BULLIS RD, LYN, 90262	735 - C1
MACARTHUR ELEM 6011 CENTRALIA ST, LKWD, 90713	766 - D5
MACARTHUR PARK PRIMARY CTR 2300 W 7TH ST, LA, 90057	634 - B3
MACK, JOHN W ELEM 3020 S CATALINA ST, LA, 90007	634 - A7
MACLAY MID 12540 PIERCE ST, Pcma, 91331	502 - E2
MACLAY PRIMARY 12513 GAIN ST, Pcma, 91331	502 - F2
MACY ELEM 2301 RUSSELL ST, LHB, 90631	708 - B4
MACY INTERMED 2101 LUPINE AV, MONP, 91755	636 - B5
MADISON ELEM 2200 MACKAY LN, RBCH, 90278	733 - B7
MADISON ELEM 2801 BOMBERRY ST, LKWD, 90712	765 - H5
MADISON ELEM 351 W PHILLIPS BLVD, POM, 91766	640 - J3
MADISON ELEM 515 ASHTABULA ST, PAS, 91104	565 - J3
MADISON MID 13000 HART ST, NHol, 91605	532 - D5
MADRID MID 3300 GILMAN RD, INDS, 91732	637 - G2
MADRONA MID 21364 MADRONA AV, TOR, 90503	763 - E6
MAGEE ELEM 8200 SERAPIS AV, PRV, 90660	706 - E1
MAGNOLIA AVENUE ELEM 1626 ORCHARD AV, LA, 90006	634 - B5
MAGNOLIA ELEM 945 E NEARFIELD ST, AZU, 91702	599 - B1
MAGNOLIA SCIENCE ACADEMY 18238 SHERMAN WY, Res, 91335	530 - J5
MAGRUDER MID 4100 W 185TH ST, TOR, 90504	763 - D2
MAIMONIDES ACADEMY 310 HUNTLEY DR, WHWD, 90048	592 - J7
MAIN STREET ELEM 129 E 53RD ST, LA, 90011	674 - C5
MALABAR STREET ELEM 3200 MALABAR ST, LA, 90063	635 - C5
MALIBU HIGH 30215 MORNING VIEW DR, MAL, 90265	667 - C1
MANCHESTER AVENUE ELEM 661 W 87TH ST, LA, 90044	704 - B2
MANHATTAN BEACH MID 1501 REDONDO AV, MANB, 90266	732 - H5
MANHATTAN PLACE ELEM 1850 W 96TH ST, LA, 90047	703 - H4
MANN ELEM 257 CORONADO AV, LBCH, 90803	825 - J1
MANN, HORACE ELEM 501 E ACACIA AV, GLDL, 91205	564 - F6
MANN, HORACE ELEM 8701 CHARLEVILLE BLVD, BHLS, 90211	632 - J2
MANN MID 7001 S SAINT ANDREWS PL, LA, 90047	673 - H7
MANUAL ARTS HIGH 4131 S VERMONT AV, LA, 90037	674 - A3
MANZANITA ELEM 38620 33RD ST E, PMDL, 93550	4196 - G7
MANZANITA ELEM 4131 N NORA AV, LACo, 91722	598 - E5
MAPLE HILL ELEM 1350 S MAPLE HILL RD, DBAR, 91765	680 - A3
MARANATHA HIGH 1610 ELIZABETH ST, PAS, 91104	566 - C1
MARENGO ELEM 1400 MARENGO AV, SPAS, 91030	595 - J2
MARGUERITA ELEM 1603 S MARGUERITA AV, ALH, 91803	596 - A7
MARIANNA AVENUE ELEM 4215 GLEASON ST, City, 90063	635 - E6
MARINA DEL REY MID 12500 BRADDOCK DR, LA, 90066	672 - D6
MARIPOSA ELEM 1111 W MARIPOSA DR, BREA, 92821	709 - B5
MARIPOSA ELEM 737 W AVE H-6, LAN, 93534	4015 - G3
MARKHAM MID 1650 E 104TH ST, Wats, 90002	704 - G5
MARLBOROUGH HIGH 250 S ROSSMORE AV, LA, 90004	633 - F1
MARQUEZ CHARTER 16821 MARQUEZ AV, PacP, 90272	630 - H5
MARSHALL ELEM 12045 TELEPHONE AV, CHNO, 91710	641 - G5
MARSHALL HIGH 990 N ALLEN AV, PAS, 91104	566 - D2
MARSHALL, JOHN ELEM 1201 E BROADWAY, GLDL, 91206	564 - G5
MARSHALL, JOHN ELEM 1817 JACKSON AV, SGBL, 91776	596 - D7
MARSHALL, JOHN HIGH 3939 TRACY ST, LFlz, 90027	594 - C3
MARSHALL, JOHN MID 1921 W ARROYO AV, POM, 91768	640 - E1
MARSHALL MID 5870 E WARDLOW RD, LBCH, 90808	796 - D1
MARSHALL, THURGOOD ELEM 3593 MARTIN LUTHER KING JR BL, LYN, 90262	705 - B6
MARVIN AVENUE ELEM 2411 S MARVIN AV, LA, 90016	633 - B6
MAR VISTA ELEM 3330 GRANVILLE AV, LA, 90066	672 - C2
MARY IMMACULATE ELEM 10390 REMICK AV, Pcma, 91331	502 - B4
MARYMOUNT HIGH 10643 W SUNSET BLVD, BelA, 90077	632 - A1
MARY STAR OF THE SEA ELEM 717 S CABRILLO AV, SPed, 90731	824 - A5
MARY STAR OF THE SEA HIGH 810 W 8TH ST, SPed, 90731	824 - A5
MAXSON ELEM 12380 FELIPE ST, ELMN, 91732	637 - E3
MAXWELL ELEM 733 EUCLID AV, LACo, 91010	567 - J6
MAYALL STREET ELEM 16701 MAYALL ST, LA, 91343	501 - D4
MAYBERRY STREET ELEM 2414 MAYBERRY ST, Echo, 90026	594 - D6
MAYFAIR HIGH 6000 WOODRUFF AV, LKWD, 90713	766 - D1
MAYFIELD HIGH 500 BELLEFONTAINE ST, PAS, 91105	565 - G7
MAYFIELD JR HIGH 405 S EUCLID AV, PAS, 91101	565 - J5
MAYFLOWER ELEM 210 N MAYFLOWER AV, MNRO, 91016	567 - F3
MAYO ELEM 915 N MAYO AV, COMP, 90221	735 - A3
MAYWOOD ACADEMY HIGH 6125 PINE AV, MYWD, 90270	675 - D6
MAYWOOD NEW ELEM 5 5200 CUDAHY AV, MYWD, 90270	675 - E5
MCALISTER HIGH 155 N OCCIDENTAL BLVD, Echo, 90026	634 - B1
MCGAUGH ELEM 1698 BOLSA AV, SLB, 90740	826 - F4
MCGRATH ELEM 21501 DEPUTY JAKE DR, SCTA, 91321	4641 - B1
MCKIBBEN ELEM 10550 MILLS AV, LACo, 90604	707 - D5
MCKINLEY AVENUE ELEM 7812 MCKINLEY AV, LA, 90001	704 - E1
MCKINLEY ELEM 325 S OAK KNOLL AV, PAS, 91101	566 - A5
MCKINLEY ELEM 1425 MANLEY DR, SGBL, 91776	596 - E6
MCKINLEY ELEM 14431 S STANFORD AV, LACo, 90220	734 - E4
MCKINLEY ELEM 2401 SANTA MONICA BLVD, SMCA, 90404	631 - G7
MCKINLEY ELEM 6822 N PARAMOUNT BLVD, NLB, 90805	735 - H6
MCKINLEY, WILLIAM ELEM 349 W VALENCIA AV, BURB, 91506	563 - H2
MCNAIR ELEM 1450 W EL SEGUNDO BLVD, COMP, 90222	734 - F2
MEADOW GREEN ELEM 12025 GROVEDALE DR, LACo, 90604	707 - J7
MEADOWLARK ELEM 3015 SACRAMENTO AV, Actn, 93510	4465 - C1
MEADOW OAKS 23456 MULHOLLAND HWY, CALB, 91302	559 - F7
MEADOWS ELEM 1200 N MEADOWS AV, MANB, 90266	732 - H5
MEADOWS ELEM 25577 FEDALA RD, SCTA, 91355	4550 - F7
MEDEA CREEK MID 1002 DOUBLETREE RD, VeCo, 91377	558 - A1
MEKHITARIST ARMENIAN 6470 FOOTHILL BLVD, Tuj, 91042	504 - C5
MELBOURNE ELEM 21314 CLARETTA AV, LKWD, 90715	766 - J5
MELLER ELEM 9115 BALFOUR ST, PRV, 90660	676 - F5
MELROSE AVENUE ELEM 731 N DETROIT ST, LA, 90046	593 - D6
MELVIN AVENUE ELEM 7700 MELVIN AV, Res, 91335	530 - F4
MENDOZA ELEM 851 S HAMILTON BLVD, POM, 91766	640 - H3
MENLO AVENUE ELEM 4156 MENLO AV, LA, 90037	674 - A3
MERCED ELEM 1545 E MERCED AV, WCOV, 91791	638 - H3
MERDINIAN ARMENIAN EVANG 13330 RIVERSIDE DR, Shrm, 91423	562 - D4
MERLINDA ELEM 1120 S VALINDA AV, WCOV, 91790	638 - G2
MERWIN ELEM 16125 CYPRESS ST, IRW, 91706	598 - F4
MESA ELEM 409 S BARRANCA ST, WCOV, 91791	639 - C1
MESA INTERMED 3243 E AVE R-8, PMDL, 93550	4286 - G2
MESA ROBLES ELEM 16060 MESA ROBLES DR, HacH, 91745	678 - C4
MESQUITE ELEM 37622 43RD ST E, PMDL, 93552	4286 - J3
METROPOLITAN HIGH 727 WILSON ST, LA, 90021	634 - H6
MEYLER STREET ELEM 1123 W 223RD ST, LACo, 90502	764 - A7
MICHELTORENA STREET ELEM 1511 MICHELTORENA ST, Echo, 90026	594 - C6
MID-CITY CHARTER MAGNET 3100 W ADAMS BLVD, LA, 90018	633 - G7
MIDDLE COLLEGE HIGH 1600 W IMPERIAL HWY, LACo, 90047	703 - J7
MIDDLETON STREET ELEM 6537 MALABAR ST, HNTP, 90255	674 - J6
MILAGRO CHARTER ELEM 1855 N MAIN ST, LA, 90031	634 - J2
MILES AVENUE 6720 MILES AV, HNTP, 90255	675 - A7
MILKEN COMM 15800 ZELDINS WY, Brwd, 90049	591 - G1
MILL ELEM 4030 S WORKMAN MILL RD, LACo, 90601	677 - C1
MILLER ELEM 7751 FURMAN RD, LPMA, 90623	767 - D3
MILLER ELEM 830 W 77TH ST, LA, 90044	704 - A1
MILLER, GRACE ELEM 1629 HOLLY OAK ST, LVRN, 91750	600 - F2
MILLER, JOAQUIN ELEM 720 E PROVIDENCIA AV, BURB, 91501	533 - J7
MILLIKAN, R A HIGH 2800 SNOWDEN AV, LBCH, 90815	796 - E2
MILLIKAN, ROBERT MID 5041 SUNNYSLOPE AV, Shrm, 91423	562 - C3
MINT CANYON COMM ELEM 16400 SIERRA HWY, LACo, 91387	4462 - C5
MIRA CATALINA ELEM 30511 LUCANIA DR, RPV, 90275	823 - F5
MIRACLE BAPTIST 8300 S CENTRAL AV, Flor, 90001	704 - E2
MIRA COSTA HIGH 701 S PECK AV, MANB, 90266	762 - H1
MIRALESTE INTERMED 29323 PALOS VERDES DR E, RPV, 90275	823 - G3
MIRAMONTE ELEM 10620 SCHMIDT RD, SELM, 91733	637 - C3
MIRAMONTE ELEM 1400 E 68TH ST, Flor, 90001	674 - F7
MIRMAN ELEM 16180 MULHOLLAND DR, Brwd, 90049	561 - F7
MISSION ELEM 5555 HOWARD ST, SBdC, 91762	641 - H2
MITCHELL COMM ELEM 16821 GOODVALE RD, SCTA, 91387	4552 - C1
MITCHELL ELEM 14429 CONDON AV, LNDL, 90260	733 - C4
MOFFETT ELEM 11050 LARCH AV, Lenx, 90304	703 - D6
MOFFITT ELEM 13323 GOLLER AV, NRWK, 90650	736 - J2
MOKLER ELEM 8571 FLOWER ST, PRM, 90723	735 - J6
MONLUX ELEM 6051 BELLAIRE AV, NHol, 91606	532 - E7
MONROE ELEM 402 W COLORADO BLVD, MNRO, 91016	567 - F4
MONROE ELEM 4400 LADOGA AV, LKWD, 90713	766 - E5
MONROE ELEM 8855 NOBLE AV, LA, 91343	501 - H7
MONROE, JAMES HIGH 9229 HASKELL AV, LA, 91343	501 - F6
MONROE MID 10711 S 10TH AV, ING, 90303	703 - F5
MONROVIA HIGH 845 W COLORADO BLVD, MNRO, 91016	567 - E4
MONTAGUE CHARTER ACADEMY 13000 MONTAGUE ST, Pcma, 91331	502 - D6
MONTARA AVENUE ELEM 10018 MONTARA AV, SGAT, 90280	705 - A4
MONTCLAIR COLLEGE PREP 8071 SEPULVEDA BLVD, VanN, 91406	531 - G2
MONTCLAIR HIGH 4725 BENITO ST, MTCL, 91763	601 - F6
MONTEBELLO BAPTIST 136 S 7TH ST, MTBL, 90640	676 - D2
MONTEBELLO GARDENS ELEM 4700 PINE ST, PRV, 90660	676 - F2
MONTEBELLO HIGH 2100 W CLEVELAND AV, MTBL, 90640	676 - C1
MONTEBELLO INTERMED 1600 W WHITTIER BLVD, MTBL, 90640	676 - C2
MONTEBELLO PARK ELEM 6300 NORTHSIDE DR, ELA, 90022	676 - A2
MONTEMALAGA ELEM 1121 VIA NOGALES, PVE, 90274	792 - H5
MONTERA ELEM 4825 BANDERA ST, MTCL, 91763	641 - F1
MONTEREY HIGH 1915 W MONTEREY AV, BURB, 91506	533 - E6
MONTEREY HIGHLANDS ELEM 400 CASUDA CANYON DR, MONP, 91754	635 - H3
MONTEREY HILLS ELEM 1624 VIA DL REY, SPAS, 91030	595 - G3
MONTEREY VISTA ELEM 901 E GRAVES AV, MONP, 91755	636 - D3
MONTE VISTA ELEM 11111 THIENES AV, SELM, 91733	637 - C4
MONTE VISTA ELEM 12000 LOMA DR, LACo, 90604	707 - D7
MONTE VISTA ELEM 1235 W KETTERING ST, LAN, 93534	4015 - F5
MONTE VISTA ELEM 1615 W ELDRED AV, WCOV, 91790	598 - E6
MONTE VISTA ELEM 2620 ORANGE AV, LaCr, 91214	504 - G7

FEATURE NAME	Address City, ZIP Code	PAGE-GRID
MONTE VISTA ELEM	4900 ORCHARD ST, MTCL, 91763	601 - F7
MONTE VISTA STREET ELEM	5423 MONTE VISTA ST, HiPk, 90042	595 - C2
MONTVUE ELEM	1440 SAN BERNARDINO AV, POM, 91767	601 - C6
MORENO ELEM	4825 MORENO ST, MTCL, 91763	601 - F4
MORNINGSIDE ELEM	576 N MACLAY AV, SFER, 91340	482 - B6
MORNINGSIDE HIGH	10500 YUKON AV, ING, 90303	703 - F5
MORRIS, C J ELEM	19875 CL BAJA, WAL, 91789	679 - E1
MORRIS ELEM	9952 GRAHAM ST, CYP, 90630	767 - D7
MORRISON ELEM	13510 MAIDSTONE AV, NRWK, 90650	736 - G2
MOTHER OF SORROWS	100 W 87TH PL, LA, 90003	704 - C3
MOUNTAIN AVENUE ELEM	2307 MOUNTAIN AV, LaCr, 91214	534 - H1
MOUNTAIN VIEW ELEM	201 N VERNON AV, AZU, 91702	568 - H7
MOUNTAIN VIEW ELEM	22201 CYPRESS PL, LACo, 91390	4461 - A2
MOUNTAIN VIEW ELEM	6410 OLCOTT ST, Tuj, 91042	504 - C5
MOUNTAIN VIEW ELEM	851 SANTA CLARA AV, CLAR, 91711	601 - B2
MOUNTAIN VIEW HIGH	2900 PARKWAY DR, ELMN, 91732	637 - F3
MOUNT BALDY JOINT ELEM- (SEE PAGE 511)	1 MOUNT BALDY RD, SBdC	512 - A4
MOUNT CALVARY LUTHERAN	23300 GOLDEN SPRINGS DR, DBAR, 91765	680 - B1
MOUNT GLEASON MID	10965 MT GLEASON AV, Sunl, 91040	503 - H2
MOUNT SAINT JOSEPH	555 E MOUNTAIN VIEW ST, Alta, 91001	535 - G5
MOUNT WASHINGTON ELEM	3981 SAN RAFAEL AV, LA, 90065	595 - A3
MUIR, J HIGH	1905 LINCOLN AV, PAS, 91103	535 - G7
MUIR, JOHN ELEM	2526 6TH ST, SMCA, 90405	671 - G4
MUIR, JOHN ELEM	3038 DELTA AV, LBCH, 90810	795 - B2
MUIR, JOHN ELEM	912 S CHEVY CHASE DR, GLDL, 91205	564 - G6
MUIR, JOHN MID	1111 N KENNETH RD, BURB, 91504	533 - G5
MUIR MID	5929 S VERMONT AV, LA, 90044	674 - A6
MULBERRY ELEM	14029 MULBERRY DR, LACo, 90604	707 - E4
MULHALL ELEM	10900 MULHALL ST, ELMN, 91731	597 - D5
MULHOLLAND MID	17120 VANOWEN ST, VanN, 91406	531 - C6
MULTNOMAH ELEM	2101 N INDIANA ST, Boyl, 90033	635 - C2
MURCHISON STREET ELEM	1501 MURCHISON ST, Boyl, 90033	635 - C2
MURPHY, DANIEL CATHOLIC HIGH	241 S DETROIT ST, LA, 90036	633 - D1
MURPHY RANCH ELEM	16021 JANINE DR, WHIT, 90603	707 - J4
MURRAY, CLIFFORD D ELEM	505 E RENWICK RD, AZU, 91702	599 - A2
MUSCATEL MID	4201 IVAR AV, RSMD, 91770	596 - H6
NAPA STREET ELEM	19010 NAPA ST, Nor, 91324	530 - G1
NAPLES ELEM	5537 THE TOLEDO, LBCH, 90803	826 - C2
NARBONNE HIGH	24300 WESTERN AV, Hrbr, 90710	793 - J3
NATIVITY ELEM	10907 SAINT LOUIS DR, ELMN, 91731	597 - C7
NATIVITY ELEM	2371 W CARSON ST, TOR, 90501	763 - G6
NATIVITY	943 W 57TH ST, LA, 90037	674 - A5
NAZARENE CHRISTIAN ELEM	15014 STUDEBAKER RD, NRWK, 90650	736 - F4
NAZARENE CHRISTIAN OF LONG-BEACH	5253 E LOS COYOTES DIAG, LBCH, 90815	796 - B3
NELSON ELEM	330 N CALIFORNIA AV, LPUE, 91744	638 - B6
NELSON ELEM	8140 VICKI DR, LACo, 90606	706 - H1
NESTLE AVENUE ELEM	5060 NESTLE AV, Tarz, 91356	561 - A3
NEVADA AVENUE ELEM	22120 CHASE ST, LA, 91304	529 - J2
NEVIN AVENUE ELEM	1569 E 32ND ST, LA, 90011	674 - F2
NEW ACADEMY CANOGA PARK	21425 COHASSET ST, CanP, 91303	530 - B4
NEW AVENUE EDUCATIONAL CTR	126 N NEW AV, MONP, 91755	636 - D2
NEWCASTLE	6520 NEWCASTLE AV, Res, 91335	531 - A6
NEW CITY CHARTER ELEM	1230 PINE AV, LBCH, 90813	795 - D6
NEWCOMB ACADEMY	3351 VAL VERDE AV, LBCH, 90808	796 - H1
NEW COMM JEWISH HIGH	7353 VALLEY CIRCLE BLVD, CanP, 91307	529 - D5
NEWHALL ELEM	24607 WALNUT ST, SCTA, 91321	4640 - J1
NEW HARVEST CHRISTIAN	11364 IMPERIAL HWY, NRWK, 90650	736 - F1
NEW HORIZON CHRISTIAN ELEM	8055 RESEDA BLVD, Res, 91335	530 - J2
NEW LEXINGTON ELEM	10410 BODGER ST, ELMN, 91733	637 - B2
NEWMAN ELEM	4150 WALNUT AV, CHNO, 91710	641 - D6
NEW RIVER ELEM	13432 HALCOURT AV, NRWK, 90650	736 - E2
NEW ROADS HIGH	3131 OLYMPIC BLVD, SMCA, 90404	631 - J7
NEW TEMPLE ELEM	11033 CENTRAL AV, SELM, 91733	637 - C5
NEWTON MID	15616 NEWTON ST, HacH, 91745	678 - B4
NEW VISTA MID	753 E AVE K-2, LAN, 93535	4106 - B2
NEW WEST CHARTER MID	11625 W PICO BLVD, LA, 90064	632 - B7
NIA EDUCATIONAL CHARTER INT	2283 FAIR OAKS AV, Alta, 91001	535 - H6
NIEMES ELEM	16715 JERSEY AV, ART, 90701	736 - G6
NIGHTINGALE MID	3311 N FIGUEROA ST, LA, 90065	594 - J6
NIMITZ MID	6021 CARMELITA AV, HNTP, 90255	675 - C6
NIXON ELEM	19600 JACOB AV, CRTS, 90703	766 - H3
NOBEL MID	9950 TAMPA AV, Nor, 91324	500 - G5
NOBLE AVENUE ELEM	8329 NOBLE AV, LA, 91343	531 - H1
NOBLE ELEM	8600 KESTER AV, PanC, 91402	531 - J1
NOGALES HIGH	401 NOGALES ST, LACo, 91792	679 - B2
NORMANDIE AVENUE ELEM	4505 S RAYMOND AV, LA, 90037	673 - J3
NORMANDIE CHRISTIAN	6306 S NORMANDIE AV, LA, 90044	673 - J6
NORMONT ELEM	1001 253RD ST, Hrbr, 90710	794 - B4
NORTHAM ELEM	17800 RENAULT ST, LACo, 91744	678 - H1
NORTH HIGH	3620 W 182ND ST, TOR, 90504	763 - E2
NORTH HOLLYWOOD HIGH	5231 COLFAX AV, LA, 91607	562 - G2
NORTH LAKE HILLS ELEM	32545 RIDGE ROUTE RD, Cstc, 91384	4369 - G4
NORTH PARK HIGH	4600 BOGART AV, BALD, 91706	598 - C4
NORTH PARK ELEM	23335 SUNSET HILLS DR, SCTA, 91354	4460 - G5
NORTH PARK MID	4450 DURFEE AV, PRV, 90660	676 - H2
NORTH RANCHITO ELEM	8837 OLYMPIC BLVD, PRV, 90660	676 - G2
NORTHRIDGE ACADEMY HIGH	9601 ZELZAH AV, Nor, 91330	501 - A5
NORTHRIDGE MID	17960 CHASE ST, Nor, 91325	531 - A2
NORTHROP, JACK ELEM	835 AVE K-4, LAN, 93535	4106 - B2
NORTHRUP, WILLIAM ELEM	409 S ATLANTIC BLVD, ALH, 91803	596 - A6
NORTHVIEW HIGH	1016 W CYPRESS ST, COV, 91722	598 - J4
NORTHVIEW INTERMED	1401 HIGHLAND AV, DUAR, 91010	568 - B5
NORWALK CHRISTIAN	11129 PIONEER BLVD, NRWK, 90650	706 - G6
NORWALK HIGH	11356 LEFFINGWELL RD, NRWK, 90650	736 - F2
NORWOOD ELEM	4520 WHISTLER AV, ELMN, 91732	597 - F6
NORWOOD STREET ELEM	2020 OAK ST, LA, 90007	634 - C6
NOTRE DAME ACADEMY	2851 OVERLAND AV, LA, 90064	632 - D6
NOTRE DAME ACADEMY	2911 OVERLAND AV, LA, 90064	632 - E7
NOTRE DAME HIGH	13645 RIVERSIDE DR, Shrm, 91423	562 - C3
NOYES ELEM	1919 PINECREST DR, Alta, 91001	536 - C5
NUEVA VISTA HIGH	755 ARDILLA AV, LPUE, 91746	638 - A3
NUEVA VISTA ELEM	4412 RANDOLPH ST, BELL, 90201	675 - D6
NUFFER ELEM	14821 JERSEY AV, NRWK, 90650	736 - G4
OAK AVENUE INTERMED	6623 OAK AV, TEML, 91775	596 - H1
OAK HILLS ELEM	1010 KANAN RD, VeCo, 91377	557 - H1
OAK HILLS ELEM	26730 OLD ROCK RD, StvR, 91381	4550 - B5
OAK KNOLL ALTERNATIVE	20350 E CIENEGA AV, LACo, 91724	599 - F3
OAK MESA ELEM	5200 WHEELER AV, LVRN, 91750	570 - F6
OAK MID	10821 OAK ST, LALM, 90720	796 - H2
OAKMONT ELEM	120 W GREEN ST, CLAR, 91711	601 - D4
OAK PARK HIGH	899 KANAN RD, VeCo, 91377	558 - A1
OAKS CHRISTIAN HIGH	31749 LA TIENDA RD, WLKV, 91362	557 - D5
OAKS CHRISTIAN MID	31749 LE TIENDA RD, WLKV, 91362	557 - E5
OAKS MID	1221 S OAKS AV, ONT, 91762	641 - J2
OAKS THE	6817 FRANKLIN AV, LA, 90068	593 - D4
OAK STREET ELEM	633 S OAK ST, ING, 90301	703 - B3
OAK TREE DAY	456 W ORANGE GROVE AV, BURB, 91502	563 - G1
OAK VIEW HIGH	5701 CONIFER ST, VeCo, 91377	558 - A2
OAKWOOD ELEM	11230 MOORPARK ST, LA, 91602	562 - J4
OAKWOOD HIGH	11600 MAGNOLIA BLVD, NHol, 91601	562 - H2
OBREGON ELEM	3300 SANDOVAL AV, PRV, 90660	676 - J1
OCEAN VIEW ELEM	14359 2ND ST, WHIT, 90605	707 - F2
OCOTILLO ELEM	38737 OCOTILLO DR, LACo, 93551	4195 - F7
ODYSSEY HIGH	8693 DEARBONE AV, SGAT, 90280	705 - B3
OHR ELIYAHU ACADEMY	5950 STONEVIEW DR, CULC, 90232	673 - A2
OLD ORCHARD ELEM	25141 AVD RONDEL, SCTA, 91355	4640 - G1
OLD RIVER ELEM	11995 OLD RIVER SCHOOL RD, DWNY, 90242	705 - H5
OLINDA ELEM	109 LILAC LN, BREA, 92823	710 - C6
OLITA ELEM	950 BRIERCLIFF DR, LHB, 90631	708 - B7
OLIVE MID	13701 OLIVE ST, BALD, 91706	598 - A3
OLIVE VISTA MID	14600 TYLER ST, LA, 91342	481 - J3
OLYMPIC HIGH	721 OCEAN PARK BLVD, SMCA, 90405	671 - G3
OLYMPIC PRIMARY CTR	950 ALBANY ST, LA, 90015	634 - D4
OMELVENY ELEM	728 WOODWORTH ST, SFER, 91340	502 - A1
ONEONTA MONTESSORI	2221 POPLAR BLVD, ALH, 91801	595 - H5
OPEN CHARTER ELEM	5540 W 77TH ST, Wch, 90045	702 - J1
OPEN CHARTER ELEM	6085 AIRDROME ST, LA, 90035	633 - A5
OPPORTUNITY UNLIMITED CHARTER-HIGH	8825 S VERMONT AV, LACo, 90044	704 - A3
OPTIMAL CHRISTIAN ACADEMY	1300 E PALMER ST, COMP, 90221	735 - B4
OPTIMIST HIGH	6957 N FIGUEROA ST, HiPk, 90042	565 - D7
OPTIONS FOR YOUTH CHARTER	310 N MOUNTAIN AV, UPL, 91786	601 - J3
ORANGE AVENUE ELEM	15733 ORANGE AV, PRM, 90723	735 - F5
ORANGE COUNTY CHRISTIAN	641 S WESTERN AV, ANA, 92804	767 - H7
ORANGE GROVE ELEM	10626 E ORANGE GROVE AV, WHIT, 90601	677 - A4
ORANGE GROVE MID	14505 ORANGE GROVE AV, HacH, 91745	677 - H2
ORANGEVIEW JR HIGH	3715 W ORANGE AV, ANA, 92804	767 - G6
ORANGEWOOD ELEM	1440 S ORANGE AV, WCOV, 91790	638 - D2
ORCHARD DALE ELEM	10625 COLE RD, LACo, 90604	707 - G5
ORR ELEM	12130 JERSEY AV, NRWK, 90650	706 - G7
ORTHOPEDIC MED MAGNET HIGH	300 W 23RD ST, LA, 90007	634 - C7
OSCEOLA STREET ELEM	14940 OSCEOLA ST, LA, 91342	481 - J6
OSWALT ELEM	19501 SHADOW OAK DR, WAL, 91789	639 - C6
OUR COMM CHARTER ELEM	16514 NORDHOFF ST, LA, 91343	501 - E7
OUR LADY HELP OF CHRISTIANS-ELEM	2024 DARWIN AV, LA, 90031	635 - A2
OUR LADY OF FATIMA ELEM	18626 CLARKDALE AV, ART, 90701	766 - H1
OUR LADY OF GRACE ELEM	17720 VENTURA BLVD, Enc, 91316	561 - B3
OUR LADY OF GUADALUPE ELEM	436 N HAZARD AV, City, 90063	635 - E5
OUR LADY OF GUADALUPE ELEM	4522 BROWNE AV, LA, 90032	595 - D6
OUR LADY OF GUADALUPE	340 MASSEY AV, HMB, 90254	762 - J3
OUR LADY OF GUADALUPE	920 W LA HABRA BLVD, LHB, 90631	708 - D6
OUR LADY OF LORETTO ELEM	258 N UNION AV, Echo, 90026	634 - D2
OUR LADY OF LOURDES ELEM	315 S EASTMAN AV, City, 90063	635 - D6
OUR LADY OF LOURDES ELEM	5303 ORCHARD ST, MTCL, 91763	601 - G7
OUR LADY OF LOURDES	18437 SUPERIOR ST, Nor, 91325	500 - J5
OUR LADY OF LOURDES	7324 APPERSON ST, Tuj, 91042	503 - J4
OUR LADY OF MALIBU	3625 WINTER CANYON RD, MAL, 90265	628 - H6
OUR LADY OF MIRACULOUS MEDAL-ELEM	840 N GARFIELD AV, MTBL, 90640	636 - B6
OUR LADY OF PEACE ELEM	9022 LANGDON AV, LA, 91343	501 - G7
OUR LADY OF PERPETUAL HELP ELEM	23225 LYONS AV, SCTA, 91355	4640 - H1
OUR LADY OF PERPETUAL HELP	10441 DOWNEY AV, DWNY, 90241	706 - B4
OUR LADY OF REFUGE	5210 E LOS COYOTES DIAG, LBCH, 90815	796 - B4
OUR LADY OF SOLEDAD ELEM	4545 DOZIER ST, ELA, 90022	635 - F5
OUR LADY OF TALPA ELEM	411 S EVERGREEN AV, Boyl, 90033	635 - B6
OUR LADY OF THE ASSUMPTION	611 W BONITA AV, CLAR, 91711	601 - C3
OUR LADY OF THE HOLY ROSARY	7802 VINELAND AV, SunV, 91352	533 - A3
OUR LADY OF THE ROSARY	14813 PARAMOUNT BLVD, PRM, 90723	735 - G4
OUR LADY OF THE VALLEY ELEM	22041 GAULT ST, CanP, 91303	530 - A5
OUR LADY OF VICTORY	601 E PALMER ST, COMP, 90221	735 - A4
OUR MOTHER OF GOOD COUNSEL ELEM	4622 AMBROSE AV, LFlz, 90027	594 - A3
OVERLAND AVENUE ELEM	10650 ASHBY AV, LA, 90064	632 - D6
OXFORD ACADEMY HIGH	5172 ORANGE AV, CYP, 90630	767 - C7
OXNARD STREET ELEM	10912 OXNARD ST, NHol, 91601	533 - A7
PACE ELEM	9625 VAN RUITEN ST, BLF, 90706	736 - B3
PACIFICA COMM CHARTER ELEM	3754 DUNN DR, LA, 90034	672 - G1
PACIFIC CHRISTIAN	625 COLEMAN AV, HiPk, 90042	595 - D3
PACIFIC DRIVE ELEM	1501 W VALENCIA DR, FUL, 92833	738 - D7
PACIFIC ELEM	1200 PACIFIC AV, MANB, 90266	732 - G6
PACIFIC HARBOR CHRISTIAN ELEM	1530 WILMINGTON BLVD, Wilm, 90744	794 - D4
PACIFIC HILLS	8628 HOLLOWAY DR, WHWD, 90069	592 - J6
PACIFIC PALISADES ELEM	800 VIA D LA PAZ, PacP, 90272	631 - A5
PACOIMA ELEM	11016 NORRIS AV, Pcma, 91331	502 - D2
PACOIMA MID	9919 LAUREL CANYON BLVD, Pcma, 91331	502 - C4
PADDISON ELEM	12100 CREWE ST, NRWK, 90650	706 - H7
PAGE OF BEVERLY HILLS	419 S ROBERTSON BLVD, BHLS, 90211	632 - H3
PAGE OF HANCOCK PARK	565 N LARCHMONT BLVD, LA, 90004	593 - F7
PALISADES HIGH	15777 BOWDOIN ST, PacP, 90272	631 - A5
PALM CREST ELEM	5025 PALM DR, LCF, 91011	534 - J1
PALMDALE HIGH	2137 E AVE R, PMDL, 93550	4286 - E1
PALM ELEM	14740 PALM AV, HacH, 91745	677 - J1
PALMS ELEM	12445 207TH ST, LKWD, 90715	766 - J4
PALMS ELEM	3520 MOTOR AV, LA, 90034	672 - F1
PALMS MID	10860 WOODBINE ST, LA, 90034	672 - E1
PALM TREE ELEM	326 E AVE R, PMDL, 93550	4286 - A2
PALOMARES MID	2211 N ORANGE GROVE AV, POM, 91767	601 - A5
PALOS VERDES HIGH	600 CLOYDEN RD, PVE, 90274	792 - E7
PALOS VERDES INTERMED	2161 VIA OLIVERA, PVE, 90274	792 - F7
PALOS VERDES PENINSULA HIGH	27118 SILVER SPUR RD, RHE, 90274	793 - A6
PANORAMA BAPTIST ELEM	8755 WOODMAN AV, PanC, 91402	532 - B1
PANORAMA HIGH	8015 VAN NUYS BLVD, PanC, 91402	532 - A2
PANTERA ELEM	801 PANTERA DR, DBAR, 91765	680 - D1
PARACLETE HIGH	42145 30TH ST W, LAN, 93536	4105 - C6
PARADISE CANYON ELEM	471 KNIGHT WY, LCF, 91011	535 - D3
PARAMOUNT ALTERNATIVE ACADEMY	3717 MICHELSON ST, LKWD, 90712	765 - J2
PARAMOUNT ELEM	409 W PARAMOUNT ST, AZU, 91702	598 - J1
PARAMOUNT HIGH	14429 S DOWNEY AV, PRM, 90723	735 - H3
PARAMOUNT PARK ELEM	14608 S PARAMOUNT BLVD, PRM, 90723	735 - H3
PARAMOUNT WEST HIGH	14708 PARAMOUNT BLVD, PRM, 90723	735 - H3
PARENT, FRANK D ELEM	5354 W 64TH ST, ING, 90302	673 - A7
PARK AVENUE ELEM	5027 LIVE OAK ST, CDHY, 90201	705 - F1
PARK ELEM	301 N MARENGO AV, ALH, 91801	595 - J4
PARKMAN MID	20800 BURBANK BLVD, WdHl, 91367	560 - C2
PARKS, ROSA ELEM	3900 AGNES ST, LYN, 90262	735 - C1
PARKS, RUSSELL JR HIGH	1710 ROSECRANS AV, FUL, 92833	738 - D4
PARKVIEW ELEM	12044 ELLIOTT AV, ELMN, 91732	637 - E3
PARK VIEW MID	808 W AVE J, LAN, 93534	4015 - G7
PARK WESTERN PLACE ELEM	1214 PARK WESTERN PL, LA, 90732	823 - J3
PARK WEST HIGH	1540 W 2ND ST, POM, 91766	640 - F2
PARMELEE AVENUE ELEM	1338 E 76TH PL, Flor, 90001	704 - F1
PARRAS, NICK G MID	200 N LUCIA AV, RBCH, 90277	763 - A4
PARRIS, R REX HIGH	38801 CLOCK TOWER PLAZA RD, PMDL, 93550	4196 - A7
PARTHENIA STREET ELEM	16825 NAPA ST, LA, 91343	531 - D1
PASADENA CHRISTIAN	1515 N LOS ROBLES AV, PAS, 91104	565 - J1
PASADENA HIGH	2925 E SIERRA MADRE BLVD, PAS, 91107	566 - F2
PASADENA TOWNE & COUNTRY	200 S SIERRA MADRE BLVD, PAS, 91107	566 - E5
PASADENA WALDORF	209 E MARIPOSA ST, Alta, 91001	535 - H5
PASEO DEL REY ELEM	7751 PAS DL REY, PdlR, 90293	702 - C3
PAYNE, BEULAH ELEM	215 W 94TH ST, ING, 90301	703 - C4
PAYNE, WILLARD F ELEM	2850 MOUNTAIN VIEW RD, ELMN, 91732	637 - E2
PEACHLAND AVENUE ELEM	24800 PEACHLAND AV, SCTA, 91321	4640 - G2
PEARBLOSSOM ELEM	12828 E AVE W, Pear, 93553	4378 - J4
PEARY MID	1415 W GARDENA BLVD, GAR, 90247	734 - A6
PENDLETON ELEM	7101 STANTON AV, BPK, 90621	767 - J2
PENINSULA HERITAGE ELEM	26944 ROLLING HILLS RD, RHE, 90274	793 - E7
PENNEKAMP ELEM	110 S ROWELL AV, MANB, 90266	732 - H7
PEPPER TREE ELEM	1045 W 18TH ST, UPL, 91784	571 - J6
PHELAN ELEM	7150 S CULLY AV, LACo, 90606	676 - J6
PHILADELPHIA ELEM	600 PHILADELPHIA ST, POM, 91766	641 - A5
PHOENIX RANCH	1845 OAK RD, SIMI, 93063	499 - A2
PICO CANYON ELEM	25255 PICO CANYON RD, StvR, 91381	4640 - C1
PILGRIM CHRISTIAN	3759 E 57TH ST, MYWD, 90270	675 - C5
PILGRIM DAY HIGH	540 S COMMONWEALTH AV, LA, 90020	634 - B2
PILGRIM DAY	540 S COMMONWEALTH AV, LA, 90020	634 - B2
PILGRIM LUTHERAN ELEM	1730 WILSHIRE BLVD, SMCA, 90404	631 - F7
PILIBOS, ALEX ARMENIAN ELEM	1615 N ALEXANDRIA AV, LFlz, 90027	593 - J4
PILIBOS, ALEX ARMENIAN HIGH	1615 N ALEXANDRIA AV, LFlz, 90027	593 - J4
PINECREST-CANYON COUNTRY	16530 LOST CANYON RD, SCTA, 91387	4552 - C2
PINECREST ELEM	2110 AVE K, LAN, 93536	4105 - E2
PINECREST PALMDALE ELEM	2320 E AVE R, PMDL, 93550	4286 - E2
PINECREST PREP-CHATSWTH	19750 MAYALL ST, Chat, 91311	500 - E5
PINECREST NORTHRIDGE	17081 DEVONSHIRE ST, GrnH, 91344	501 - C4
PINECREST VALENCIA	25443 ORCHARD VILLAGE RD, SCTA, 91355	4550 - G7
PINECREST VAN NUYS	14111 SHERMAN WY, VanN, 91405	532 - B4
PINECREST WOODLAND HILLS	5975 SHOUP AV, WdHl, 91367	559 - J1
PINETREE COMM ELEM	29156 LOTUSGARDEN DR, SCTA, 91387	4462 - E7
PINEWOOD AVENUE ELEM	10111 SILVERTON AV, Tuj, 91042	504 - A4
PINON HILLS ELEM- (SEE PAGE 4471)	878 MONO RD, SBdC, 92372	4472 - B3
PIONEER BAPTIST	11717 PIONEER BLVD, NRWK, 90650	706 - G7
PIONEER HIGH	10800 BEN AVON ST, LACo, 90606	706 - H1

FEATURE NAME	Address City, ZIP Code	PAGE-GRID
PIO PICO ELEM	1512 ARLINGTON AV, LA, 90019	633 - G5
PIO PICO ELEM	4211 COLUMBIA AV, PRV, 90660	676 - G2
PIUTE MID	425 E AVE H-11, LAN, 93535	4016 - A4
PLACERITA JR HIGH	25015 NEWHALL AV, SCTA, 91355	4550 - H7
PLAINVIEW AVENUE ELEM	10819 PLAINVIEW AV, Tuj, 91042	503 - J2
PLASENCIA, BETTY ELEM	1321 CORTEZ ST, Echo, 90026	634 - E2
PLAYA DEL REY ELEM	12221 JUNIETTE ST, LA, 90230	672 - F7
PLEASANT VIEW ELEM	14900 NUBIA ST, BALD, 91706	598 - D3
PLUM CANYON ELEM	28360 ALFREDS WY, Saug, 91350	4461 - E6
PLUMMER ELEM	9340 NOBLE AV, LA, 91343	501 - H6
PLYMOUTH ELEM	1300 BOLEY ST, MNRO, 91016	597 - G1
POINT DUME ELEM	6955 FERNHILL DR, MAL, 90265	667 - F3
POINT FERMIN ELEM	3333 S KERCKHOFF AV, SPed, 90731	854 - B1
POINT VICENTE ELEM	30540 RUE D LA PIERRE, RPV, 90275	822 - G3
POLITI ELEM	2481 W 11TH ST, LA, 90006	634 - B4
POLYTECHNIC ELEM	1030 E CALIFORNIA BLVD, PAS, 91106	566 - B6
POLYTECHNIC HIGH	1030 E CALIFORNIA BLVD, PAS, 91106	566 - A6
POMELO DRIVE ELEM	7633 MARCH AV, LA, 91304	529 - E4
POMONA ALTERNATIVE HIGH	1530 W 2ND ST, POM, 91766	640 - G2
POMONA CATHOLIC HIGH	533 W HOLT AV, POM, 91768	640 - H1
POMONA HIGH	475 BANGOR ST, POM, 91767	601 - A5
PORTER MID	15960 KINGSBURY ST, GrnH, 91344	501 - F3
PORT OF LOS ANGELES HS	250 W 5TH ST, SPed, 90731	824 - C5
PORTOLA MID	18720 LINNET ST, Tarz, 91356	560 - H2
POTRERO ELEM	2611 POTRERO AV, ELMN, 91733	637 - A2
POTRERO HEIGHTS ELEM	8026 HILL DR, MTBL, 91770	636 - F4
POWELL, COLIN L ACADEMY	150 VICTORIA ST, NLB, 90805	765 - C1
POWELL, W R ELEM	1035 E MAUNA LOA AV, AZU, 91702	569 - B7
PRAIRIE VISTA MID	13600 PRAIRIE AV, HAW, 90250	733 - E3
PRECIOUS BLOOD ELEM	307 S OCCIDENTAL BLVD, LA, 90057	634 - B2
PRESIDENT AVENUE ELEM	1465 243RD ST, Hrbr, 90710	793 - J3
PRESSMAN ACADEMY DAY	1055 S LA CIENEGA BLVD, LA, 90035	632 - J3
PRICE ELEM	9525 TWEEDY LN, DWNY, 90240	706 - B2
PRICE, FREDERICK KC III ELEM	7901 S VERMONT AV, LA, 90044	704 - A1
PRICE, FREDERICK KC III HIGH	7901 S VERMONT AV, LA, 90044	704 - B1
PRIMARY ACADEMY ELEM	9075 WILLIS AV, PanC, 91402	501 - J7
PRISK ELEM	2375 FANWOOD AV, LBCH, 90815	796 - D3
PROVIDENCE HIGH	511 S BUENA VISTA ST, BURB, 91505	563 - E4
PROVIDENCIA ELEM	1919 N ONTARIO ST, BURB, 91505	533 - D6
PUEBLO ELEM	1460 E HOLT AV, POM, 91767	641 - D1
PURCHE AVENUE ELEM	13210 PURCHE AV, GAR, 90249	733 - G2
PYLE ELEM	14500 WOODRUFF AV, BLF, 90706	736 - D3
QUAIL SUMMIT ELEM	23330 QUAIL SUMMIT DR, DBAR, 91765	680 - B3
QUAIL VALLEY ELEM	37236 58TH ST E, PMDL, 93552	4287 - C3
QUARTZ HILL ELEM	41820 50TH ST W, LACo, 93536	4104 - H6
QUARTZ HILL HIGH	6040 AVE L, LAN, 93536	4104 - E4
QUEEN ANNE PLACE ELEM	1212 QUEEN ANNE PL, LA, 90019	633 - F4
RAMONA CONVENT SECONDARY	1701 W RAMONA RD, ALH, 91803	635 - J1
RAMONA ELEM	1133 N MARIPOSA AV, LA, 90029	593 - J5
RAMONA ELEM	4225 HOWARD ST, MTCL, 91763	641 - D2
RAMONA ELEM	4617 W 136TH ST, HAW, 90250	733 - C3
RAMONA ELEM	509 W NORWOOD PL, ALH, 91803	596 - B7
RAMONA ELEM	9351 LAUREL ST, BLF, 90706	736 - B6
RAMONA JR HIGH	4575 WALNUT AV, CHNO, 91710	641 - E6
RAMONA MID	3490 RAMONA AV, LVRN, 91750	600 - E1
RAMONA OPPORTUNITY HIGH	231 S ALMA AV, LA, 90063	635 - D6
RANCH HILLS ELEM	2 TRABUCO PL, POM, 91766	640 - E5
RANCHITO AVENUE ELEM	7940 RANCHITO AV, PanC, 91402	532 - B3
RANCHO PICO JR HIGH	26250 VALENCIA BLVD, StvR, 91381	4550 - B5
RANCHO SANTA GERTRUDE ELEM	11233 CHARLESWORTH RD, SFSP, 90670	706 - H3
RANCHO STARBUCK INTERMED	16430 WOODBRIER DR, LACo, 90604	708 - A7
RANCHO VISTA ELEM	40641 PEONZA LN, PMDL, 93551	4194 - J2
RANCHO VISTA ELEM	4323 PALOS VERDES DR N, RHE, 90274	793 - C5
RAYMOND AVENUE ELEM	7511 RAYMOND AV, LA, 90044	703 - J1
REDEEMER ALTERNATIVE	900 E ROSECRANS AV, LACo, 90220	734 - E3
REDEEMER BAPTIST ELEM	10792 NATIONAL BLVD, LA, 90034	632 - D7
REDEEMER LUTHERAN ELEM	2626 LIBERTY BLVD, SGAT, 90280	704 - J2
RED OAK ELEM	4857 ROCKFIELD ST, VeCo, 91377	557 - H1
REDONDO SHORES HIGH	1000 DEL AMO ST, RBCH, 90277	762 - J4
REDONDO UNION HIGH	631 VINCENT ST, RBCH, 90277	762 - J4
REED MID	4525 IRVINE AV, LA, 91602	562 - H4
REGINA, MARIA	13510 VAN NESS AV, GAR, 90249	733 - H3
REID ALTERNATIVE HIGH	2152 W HILL ST, LBCH, 90810	795 - A4
REID HIGH	1794 CEDAR AV, LBCH, 90813	795 - D5
REID, HUGO ELEM	1000 HUGO REID DR, ARCD, 91007	566 - J5
REID, TWILA ELEM	720 S WESTERN AV, ANA, 92804	767 - H7
RENAISSANCE ACADEMY	4490 CORNISHON AV, LCF, 91011	535 - B4
RENAISSANCE ACADEMY CHARTER-HIGH	1901 S BUNDY DR, WLA, 90025	631 - J7
RENAISSANCE ARTS CHARTER-ACADEMY	1800 COLORADO BLVD, Eagl, 90041	565 - B6
RENAISSANCE HIGH	235 E 8TH ST, LBCH, 90813	795 - D6
REPETTO ELEM	650 S GRANDRIDGE AV, MONP, 91754	636 - B3
RESEDA ELEM	7265 AMIGO AV, Res, 91335	530 - H4
RESEDA HIGH	18230 KITTRIDGE ST, Res, 91335	530 - J6
RESURRECTION ELEM	3360 OPAL ST, LA, 90023	675 - B1
REVERE CHARTER MID	1450 ALLENFORD AV, Brwd, 90049	631 - E4
RIBET ACADEMY	2911 N SAN FERNANDO RD, LA, 90065	594 - G2
RICE, ELDRIDGE ELEM	2150 ANGELUS AV, RSMD, 91770	636 - G3
RICHARDSON MID	23751 NANCYLEE LN, TOR, 90505	793 - B2
RICHLAND AVENUE ELEM	11562 RICHLAND AV, LA, 90064	632 - B7
RICHMOND STREET ELEM	615 RICHMOND ST, ELSG, 90245	732 - E1
RIDGECREST INTERMED	28915 NORTHBAY RD, RPV, 90275	823 - A1
RILEY ELEM	3319 SANDWOOD ST, LKWD, 90712	765 - H4
RINCON INTERMED	2800 E HOLLINGWORTH ST, WCOV, 91792	679 - C2
RIO HONDO ELEM	11425 WILDFLOWER RD,, 91006	597 - E3
RIO HONDO ELEM	7731 MULLER ST, DWNY, 90241	706 - A3
RIO HONDO PREP	5150 FARNA AV,, 91006	597 - E3
RIO NORTE JR HIGH	28771 RIO NORTE DR, BqtC, 91354	4460 - F4
RIORDAN PRIMARY	5531 MONTE VISTA ST, HiPk, 90042	595 - C2
RIO SAN GABRIEL ELEM	9338 GOTHAM ST, DWNY, 90241	706 - D5
RIO VISTA ELEM	20417 CEDARCREEK ST, SCTA, 91351	4551 - D2
RIO VISTA ELEM	4243 SATSUMA AV, LA, 91602	563 - A5
RIO VISTA ELEM	4300 N ESTO AV, ELMN, 91731	597 - C6
RIO VISTA ELEM	8809 COFFMAN PICO RD, PRV, 90660	676 - F5
RITTER ELEM	11108 WATTS AV, Wbrk, 90059	704 - J6
RIVERA ELEM	7250 CITRONELL AV, PRV, 90660	676 - F7
RIVERA MID	7200 CITRONELL AV, PRV, 90660	676 - F7
RIVERSIDE DRIVE ELEM	13061 RIVERSIDE DR, Shrm, 91423	562 - D3
RIVIERA ELEM	365 PAS DE ARENA, TOR, 90505	793 - A3
RIVIERA HALL LUTHERAN ELEM	330 PALOS VERDES BLVD, TOR, 90277	792 - J2
ROBINSON ELEM	80 MORNINGSIDE DR, MANB, 90266	732 - G7
ROBINSON, JACKIE ACADEMY	2750 PINE AV, LBCH, 90806	795 - D2
ROCKDALE ELEM	1303 YOSEMITE DR, Eagl, 90041	565 - C6
ROGERS ELEM	11220 DUNCAN AV, LYN, 90262	705 - E7
ROGERS MID	365 MONROVIA AV, LBCH, 90803	826 - B1
ROGERS MID	4110 W 154TH ST, LNDL, 90260	733 - D5
ROGERS, WILL ELEM	2401 14TH ST, SMCA, 90405	671 - H2
ROLLING HILLS COUNTRY DAY	26444 CRENSHAW BLVD, RHE, 90274	793 - D6
ROLLING HILLS PREP	300 PAS DL MAR, PVE, 90274	792 - H3
ROOSEVELT-CARSON ELEM	3533 W MARINE AV, LACo, 90250	733 - F4
ROOSEVELT ELEM	10835 MALLISON AV, LYN, 90262	705 - C6
ROOSEVELT ELEM	13451 MERKEL AV, PRM, 90723	735 - H2
ROOSEVELT ELEM	1574 LINDEN AV, LBCH, 90813	795 - E5
ROOSEVELT ELEM	401 S WALNUT GROVE AV, SGBL, 91776	596 - G4
ROOSEVELT ELEM	700 N BRADFIELD AV, COMP, 90221	735 - C3
ROOSEVELT ELEM	701 N HUNTINGTON BLVD, POM, 91768	640 - H1
ROOSEVELT ELEM	801 MONTANA AV, SMCA, 90402	631 - D7
ROOSEVELT HIGH	456 S MATHEWS ST, Boyl, 90033	635 - A5
ROOSEVELT MID	1200 E ALONDRA BLVD, COMP, 90221	735 - B5
ROOSEVELT, THEODORE ELEM	850 N CORDOVA ST, BURB, 91505	563 - D2
ROOSEVELT, THEODORE MID	222 E ACACIA AV, GLDL, 91205	564 - E6
RORIMER ELEM	18750 RORIMER ST, LACo, 91744	679 - B2
ROSCOE ELEM	10765 STRATHERN ST, SunV, 91352	533 - A2
ROSCOMARE ROAD ELEM	2425 ROSCOMARE RD, BelA, 90077	591 - H1
ROSE CITY CONT HIGH	330 S OAK KNOLL AV, PAS, 91101	566 - A5
ROSECRANS ELEM	1301 N ACACIA AV, COMP, 90222	734 - J3
ROSEDELL ELEM	27853 URBANDALE AV, SCTA, 91350	4461 - B6
ROSEMEAD HIGH	9063 MISSION DR, RSMD, 91770	596 - H6
ROSEMONT AVENUE ELEM	421 ROSEMONT AV, Echo, 90026	634 - C1
ROSEMONT MID	4725 ROSEMONT AV, LaCr, 91214	534 - G1
ROSEWOOD AVENUE ELEM	503 N CROFT AV, LA, 90048	592 - J7
ROSEWOOD PARK ELEM	2353 COMMERCE WY, CMRC, 90040	675 - H3
ROSS, FAYE MID	17707 ELAINE AV, ART, 90701	736 - H7
ROSSMOOR ELEM	3272 SHAKESPEARE DR, OrCo, 90720	796 - H4
ROUND MEADOW ELEM	5151 ROUND MEADOW RD, HIDH, 91302	559 - C5
ROWAN AVENUE ELEM	600 S ROWAN AV, LACo, 90023	635 - D7
ROWLAND AVENUE ELEM	1355 E ROWLAND AV, WCOV, 91790	598 - H6
ROWLAND ELEM	2036 FULLERTON RD, RowH, 91748	679 - A5
ROWLAND, JOHN A HIGH	2000 OTTERBEIN AV, RowH, 91748	679 - C6
ROYAL OAK INTERMED	303 S GLENDORA AV, COV, 91724	599 - E5
ROYAL OAKS ELEM	2499 ROYAL OAKS DR, DUAR, 91010	568 - D4
ROYNON ELEM	2715 E ST, LVRN, 91750	600 - G2
RUSSELL ELEM	1263 FIRESTONE BLVD, Flor, 90001	704 - F2
SACRED HEART ELEM	45002 DATE AV, LAN, 93534	4015 - H5
SACRED HEART ELEM	2109 SICHEL ST, LA, 90031	635 - A1
SACRED HEART OF JESUS HIGH	2111 GRIFFIN AV, LA, 90031	635 - A1
SACRED HEART	360 W WORKMAN ST, COV, 91723	599 - B7
SAHAG-MESROB CHRISTIAN	2501 MAIDEN LN, Alta, 91001	536 - A5
SAINT AGNES ELEM	1428 W ADAMS BLVD, LA, 90007	634 - A6
SAINT ALBERT THE GREAT MID	823 E COMPTON BLVD, LACo, 90220	734 - E4
SAINT ALBERT THE GREAT	804 E COMPTON BLVD, LACo, 90220	734 - E4
SAINT ALOYSIUS ELEM	2023 NADEAU ST, Flor, 90001	704 - H1
SAINT ALPHONSUS ELEM	552 AMALIA AV, ELA, 90022	635 - H7
SAINT ANASTASIA ELEM	8631 STANMOOR DR, Wch, 90045	702 - D3
SAINT ANDREW ELEM	42 CHESTNUT ST, PAS, 91103	565 - H4
SAINT ANNE MISSION	2015 COLORADO AV, SMCA, 90404	671 - G1
SAINT ANSELM ELEM	7019 S VAN NESS AV, LA, 90043	673 - G7
SAINT ANTHONY ELEM	1905 S SAN GABRIEL BLVD, SGBL, 91776	596 - F7
SAINT ANTHONY HIGH	620 OLIVE AV, LBCH, 90802	795 - E7
SAINT ANTHONY OF PADUA ELEM	1003 W 163RD ST, GAR, 90247	734 - A6
SAINT ANTHONY	233 LOMITA ST, ELSG, 90245	732 - F1
SAINT ANTHONY	855 E 5TH ST, LBCH, 90802	795 - E7
SAINT ATHANASIUS	5369 LINDEN AV, NLB, 90805	765 - E3
SAINT AUGUSTINE ELEM	3819 CLARINGTON AV, LA, 90232	672 - G1
SAINT BARNABAS	3980 MARRON AV, Bxby, 90807	765 - F6
SAINT BEDE THE VENERABLE	4524 CROWN AV, LCF, 91011	535 - D4
SAINT BENEDICT ELEM	217 N 10TH ST, MTBL, 90640	676 - D2
SAINT BERNADETTE	4196 MARLTON AV, LA, 90008	673 - D3
SAINT BERNARD ELEM	3254 VERDUGO RD, LA, 90065	594 - G3
SAINT BERNARD ELEM	9626 PARK ST, BLF, 90706	736 - B6
SAINT BERNARD HIGH	9100 FALMOUTH AV, PdlR, 90293	702 - C4
SAINT BERNARDINE OF SIENA ELEM	6061 VALLEY CIRCLE BLVD, WdHl, 91367	529 - D7
SAINT BRENDAN ELEM	238 S MANHATTAN PL, LA, 90004	633 - H1
SAINT BRIDGET OF SWEDEN ELEM	7120 WHITAKER AV, VanN, 91406	531 - D5
SAINT BRUNO PARISH	15700 CITRUSTREE RD, WHIT, 90603	707 - J5
SAINT CASIMIR ELEM	2714 SAINT GEORGE ST, LFlz, 90027	594 - C3
SAINT CATHERINE LABOURE	3846 REDONDO BEACH BLVD, TOR, 90504	733 - E7
SAINT CATHERINE OF SIENA	335 N SYCAMORE AV, LA, 90036	593 - D7
SAINT CATHERINE OF SIENA ELEM	18125 SHERMAN WY, Res, 91335	531 - A4
SAINT CECILIA ELEM	4224 S NORMANDIE AV, LA, 90037	673 - J3
SAINT CHARLES BORROMEO ELEM	10850 MOORPARK ST, LA, 91602	563 - A4
SAINT CHRISTOPHER ELEM	900 W CHRISTOPHER ST, WCOV, 91790	638 - F1
SAINT COLUMBKILLE	131 W 64TH ST, LA, 90003	674 - C6
SAINT CORNELIUS	3330 N BELLFLOWER BLVD, LBCH, 90808	796 - C1
SAINT CYPRIAN ELEM	5133 E ARBOR RD, LBCH, 90808	766 - B4
SAINT CYRIL OF JERUSALEM ELEM	4548 HASKELL AV, Enc, 91436	561 - G4
SAINT DIDACUS ELEM	14325 ASTORIA ST, LA, 91342	482 - A4
SAINT DOMINIC ELEM	2005 MERTON AV, Eagl, 90041	565 - A6
SAINT DOMINIC SAVIO ELEM	9750 FOSTER RD, BLF, 90706	736 - C2
SAINT DOROTHY ELEM	215 S VALLEY CENTER AV, GLDR, 91741	569 - H5
SAINT ELISABETH ELEM	6635 TOBIAS AV, VanN, 91405	531 - J6
SAINT ELIZABETH	1840 N LAKE AV, LACo, 91104	536 - A7
SAINT EMYDIUS ELEM	10990 CALIFORNIA AV, LYN, 90262	705 - B6
SAINT EUGENE	9521 HAAS AV, LA, 90047	703 - G4
SAINT EUPHRASIA ELEM	17637 MAYERLING ST, GrnH, 91344	481 - B7
SAINT FERDINAND ELEM	1012 CORONEL ST, SFER, 91340	482 - A7
SAINT FINBAR ELEM	2120 W OLIVE AV, BURB, 91506	563 - F2
SAINT FRANCES OF ROME ELEM	734 N PASADENA AV, AZU, 91702	569 - A5
SAINT FRANCES X CABRINI	1428 W IMPERIAL HWY, LACo, 90047	703 - J7
SAINT FRANCIS DE SALES ELEM	13368 VALLEYHEART DR, Shrm, 91423	562 - D5
SAINT FRANCIS HIGH	200 FOOTHILL BLVD, LCF, 91011	535 - D5
SAINT FRANCIS OF ASSISI ELEM	1550 MALTMAN AV, Echo, 90026	594 - C6
SAINT FRANCIS XAVIER	3601 SCOTT RD, BURB, 91504	533 - E3
SAINT GENEVIEVE ELEM	14024 COMMUNITY ST, PanC, 91402	532 - B2
SAINT GENEVIEVE HIGH	13967 ROSCOE BLVD, PanC, 91402	532 - B2
SAINT GERARD MAJELLA	4471 INGLEWOOD BLVD, LA, 90066	672 - E5
SAINT GERTRUDE	6824 TOLER AV, BGDN, 90201	705 - H1
SAINT GREGORY HOVSEPIAN	2215 E COLORADO BLVD, PAS, 91107	566 - D4
SAINT GREGORY NAZIANZEN ELEM	911 S NORTON AV, LA, 90019	633 - G3
SAINT GREGORY THE GREAT	13925 TELEGRAPH RD, LACo, 90604	707 - D6
SAINT HEDWIG ELEM	3591 ORANGEWOOD AV, LALM, 90720	796 - J4
SAINT HELEN ELEM	9329 MADISON AV, SGAT, 90280	705 - A4
SAINT HILARY	5401 CITRONELL AV, PRV, 90660	676 - G4
SAINT IGNATIUS OF LOYOLA ELEM	6025 MONTE VISTA ST, HiPk, 90042	595 - D2
SAINT IRENAEUS	9201 GRINDLAY ST, CYP, 90630	767 - C6
SAINT JAMES ELEM	4625 GARNET ST, TOR, 90503	763 - B5
SAINT JAMES ELEM	625 S SAINT ANDREWS PL, LA, 90005	633 - H2
SAINT JAMES THE LESS	4635 DUNSMORE AV, GLDL, 91214	504 - D6
SAINT JANE FRANCES DE CHANTAL-ELEM	12950 HAMLIN ST, NHol, 91606	532 - D6
SAINT JEROME ELEM	5580 THORNBURN ST, Wch, 90045	702 - J1
SAINT JOAN OF ARC ELEM	11561 GATEWAY BLVD, LA, 90064	632 - B7
SAINT JOHN BOSCO HIGH	13640 BELLFLOWER BLVD, BLF, 90706	736 - C2
SAINT JOHN CHRYSOSTOM	530 E FLORENCE AV, ING, 90301	703 - D1
SAINT JOHN EUDES ELEM	9925 MASON AV, Chat, 91311	500 - D5
SAINT JOHN FISHER ELEM	5446 CREST RD, RPV, 90275	823 - B2
SAINT JOHN LUTHERAN	304 E COVINA BLVD, COV, 91722	599 - C3
SAINT JOHN OF GOD ELEM	13817 PIONEER BLVD, NRWK, 90650	736 - G2
SAINT JOHNS LUTHERAN	417 N 18TH ST, MTBL, 90640	676 - C1
SAINT JOHN THE BAPTIST ELEM	3870 STEWART AV, BALD, 91706	598 - B6
SAINT JOHN THE EVANGELIST	6028 S VICTORIA AV, LA, 90043	673 - F6
SAINT JOSEPH ELEM	11886 ACACIA AV, HAW, 90250	703 - D7
SAINT JOSEPH ELEM	1200 W HOLT AV, POM, 91768	640 - G1
SAINT JOSEPH ELEM	15650 TEMPLE AV, LPUE, 91744	638 - D6
SAINT JOSEPH ELEM	6200 E WILLOW ST, LBCH, 90815	796 - E3
SAINT JOSEPH HIGH	5825 WOODRUFF AV, LKWD, 90713	766 - C2
SAINT JOSEPH THE WORKER	19812 CANTLAY ST, Win, 91306	530 - E5
SAINT JUDE THE APOSTLE	32036 W LINDERO CANYON RD, WLKV, 91361	557 - C7
SAINT LAWRENCE BRINDISI	10044 COMPTON AV, Wats, 90002	704 - G4
SAINT LAWRENCE MARTYR ELEM	1950 S PROSPECT AV, RBCH, 90277	793 - A1
SAINT LINUS ELEM	13913 SHOEMAKER AV, NRWK, 90650	737 - B2
SAINT LOUISE DE MARILLAC	1728 E COVINA BLVD, COV, 91724	599 - F3
SAINT LOUIS OF FRANCE ELEM	13901 TEMPLE AV, LPUE, 91746	638 - A3
SAINT LUCY ELEM	2320 COTA AV, LBCH, 90810	795 - A3
SAINT LUCYS PRIORY HIGH	655 W SIERRA MADRE AV, GLDR, 91741	569 - D3
SAINT LUKE ELEM	5521 CLOVERLY AV, TEML, 91780	596 - J4
SAINT MADELEINE ELEM	935 E KINGSLEY AV, POM, 91767	601 - B7
SAINT MALACHY ELEM	1200 E 81ST ST, Flor, 90001	704 - F2
SAINT MARGARET MARY ALACOQUE-ELEM	25515 ESHELMAN AV, LMTA, 90717	793 - H5
SAINT MARGARET MARY ELEM	12664 CENTRAL AV, CHNO, 91710	641 - G6
SAINT MARIA GORETTI ELEM	3950 PALO VERDE AV, LBCH, 90808	766 - E6
SAINT MARIANNE	7911 BUHMAN AV, PRV, 90660	706 - F1
SAINT MARK ELEM	912 COEUR D ALENE AV, Ven, 90291	672 - A5
SAINT MARKS LUTHERAN	2323 LAS LOMITAS DR, HacH, 91745	678 - A4
SAINT MARKS	10354 DOWNEY AV, DWNY, 90241	706 - B3
SAINT MARKS	1050 E ALTADENA DR, Alta, 91001	536 - A5
SAINT MARTHA ELEM	440 N AZUSA AV, LACo, 91744	638 - H7
SAINT MARTHAS EPISCOPAL DAY	520 S LARK ELLEN AV, WCOV, 91791	638 - H1
SAINT MARTIN IN THE FIELDS-PARISH	7136 WINNETKA AV, Win, 91306	530 - E5
SAINT MARTIN OF TOURS ELEM	11955 W SUNSET BLVD, Brwd, 90049	631 - G3

FEATURE NAME / Address City, ZIP Code	PAGE-GRID
SAINT MARY ELEM 1600 E AVE R-4, PMDL, 93550	4286 - D2
SAINT MARY ELEM 416 S SAINT LOUIS ST, Boyl, 90033	635 - A5
SAINT MARY MAGDALEN MID 1223 CORNING ST, LA, 90035	632 - J4
SAINT MARY OF THE ASSUMPTION 7218 PICKERING AV, WHIT, 90602	677 - C7
SAINT MARYS ACADEMY 701 GRACE AV, ING, 90301	703 - D1
SAINT MARY 400 W COMMONWEALTH AV, FUL, 92832	738 - G7
SAINT MARY STAR OF THE SEA 725 WISCONSIN AV, LBCH, 90814	795 - H7
SAINT MATTHEWS PARISH 1031 BIENVENEDA AV, PacP, 90272	630 - H4
SAINT MATTHIAS ELEM 7130 CEDAR ST, HNTP, 90255	675 - A7
SAINT MATTHIAS HIGH 6003 STAFFORD AV, HNTP, 90255	674 - J5
SAINT MATTHIAS HIGH 7851 GARDENDALE ST, DWNY, 90242	735 - H1
SAINT MEL ELEM 20874 VENTURA BLVD, WdHl, 91364	560 - C3
SAINT MICHAELS ELEM 1027 W 87TH ST, LACo, 90044	704 - A3
SAINT MICHAELS HIGH 1100 W MANCHESTER AV, LACo, 90044	704 - A3
SAINT MONICA ELEM 1039 7TH ST, SMCA, 90403	671 - E1
SAINT MONICA HIGH 1030 LINCOLN BLVD, SMCA, 90403	671 - E1
SAINT NICHOLAS 9501 BALBOA BLVD, Nor, 91325	501 - C6
SAINT ODILIA ELEM 5300 S HOOPER AV, LA, 90011	674 - F5
SAINT PANCRATIUS 3601 SAINT PANCRATIUS PL, LKWD, 90712	765 - J2
SAINT PATRICK 10626 ERWIN ST, NHol, 91606	533 - B7
SAINT PAUL ELEM 1908 S BRONSON AV, LA, 90018	633 - F6
SAINT PAUL HIGH 9635 GREENLEAF AV, SFSP, 90670	707 - A3
SAINT PAUL OF THE CROSS 14030 FOSTER RD, LMRD, 90638	737 - D2
SAINT PAULS FIRST LUTHERAN 11330 MCCORMICK ST, NHol, 91601	562 - J2
SAINT PAUL THE APOSTLE ELEM 1536 SELBY AV, Wwd, 90024	632 - B4
SAINT PETERS EPISCOPAL DAY 1648 W 9TH ST, UPL, 91786	601 - H3
SAINT PHILIP BENIZI ELEM 215 PINE DR, FUL, 92833	738 - C7
SAINT PHILIP NERI 12522 STONEACRE AV, LYN, 90262	735 - D2
SAINT PHILIP THE APOSTLE 161 S HILL AV, PAS, 91106	566 - B5
SAINT PHILOMENA 21832 MAIN ST, CRSN, 90745	764 - C6
SAINT PIUS V 7681 ORANGETHORPE AV, BPK, 90621	767 - H2
SAINT PIUS X 10855 PIONEER BLVD, SFSP, 90670	706 - G5
SAINT RAPHAEL 924 W 70TH ST, LA, 90044	674 - A7
SAINT RAYMOND 12320 PARAMOUNT BLVD, DWNY, 90242	705 - J7
SAINT RITA ELEM 322 N BALDWIN AV, SMAD, 91024	567 - A1
SAINT ROBERT BELLARMINE 154 N 5TH ST, BURB, 91501	533 - H6
SAINT ROSE OF LIMA 4420 E 60TH ST, MYWD, 90270	675 - D6
SAINT SEBASTIAN ELEM 1430 FEDERAL AV, WLA, 90025	631 - J5
SAINTS FELICITAS & PERPETUA 2955 HUNTINGTON DR, SMRO, 91108	566 - F7
SAINTS PETER & PAUL ELEM 706 BAYVIEW AV, Wilm, 90744	794 - D6
SAINT STEPHEN ELEM 119 S RAMONA AV, MONP, 91754	636 - B2
SAINT TERESA OF AVILA ELEM 2215 FARGO ST, LA, 90039	594 - E5
SAINT THERESE ELEM 515 N VEGA ST, ALH, 91801	596 - C3
SAINT THOMAS AQUINAS ELEM 1501 S ATLANTIC BLVD, MONP, 91754	635 - J4
SAINT THOMAS MORE ELEM 2510 S FREMONT AV, ALH, 91803	635 - J2
SAINT THOMAS THE APOSTLE 2632 W 15TH ST, LA, 90006	633 - J5
SAINT TIMOTHY ELEM 10479 W PICO BLVD, LA, 90064	632 - E5
SAINT TURIBIUS ELEM 1524 ESSEX ST, LA, 90021	634 - F7
SAINT VINCENT ELEM 2333 S FIGUEROA ST, LA, 90007	634 - C7
SALAZAR HIGH 9426 MARJORIE ST, PRV, 90660	676 - G6
SALEM LUTHERAN 1211 N BRAND BLVD, GLDL, 91202	564 - E2
SAN ANTONIO HIGH 125 W SAN JOSE AV, CLAR, 91711	601 - D5
SAN ANTONIO DE PADUA ELEM 1500 BRIDGE ST, Boyl, 90033	634 - J4
SAN ANTONIO ELEM 6222 STATE ST, HNTP, 90255	675 - A6
SAN ANTONIO ELEM 855 E KINGSLEY AV, POM, 91767	601 - B7
SANCHEZ ELEM 11960 162ND ST, NRWK, 90650	736 - H5
SANCHEZ, GEORGE I ELEM 8470 FERN AV, RSMD, 91770	636 - G2
SANDBURG MID 819 W BENNETT AV, GLDR, 91741	569 - C5
SAN DIMAS HIGH 800 W COVINA BLVD, SDMS, 91773	600 - A3
SAN FERNANDO ELEM 1130 MOTT ST, SFER, 91340	502 - A1
SAN FERNANDO HIGH 11133 OMELVENY AV, LA, 91340	502 - A2
SAN FERNANDO MID 130 N BRAND BLVD, SFER, 91340	482 - B7
SAN FERNANDO VALLEY ACADEMY 17601 LASSEN ST, Nor, 91325	501 - B5
SAN GABRIEL AVENUE ELEM 8628 SAN GABRIEL AV, SGAT, 90280	705 - C3
SAN GABRIEL CHRISTIAN ELEM 117 N PINE ST, SGBL, 91775	596 - F3
SAN GABRIEL HIGH 801 S RAMONA ST, ALH, 91776	596 - D5
SAN GABRIEL MISSION ELEM 416 S MISSION DR, SGBL, 91776	596 - D4
SAN GABRIEL MISSION HIGH 254 S SANTA ANITA AV, SGBL, 91776	596 - D4
SAN GABRIEL SDA ACADEMY 8827 E BROADWAY, LACo, 91776	596 - G4
SAN JOSE EDISON ACADEMY 1500 E FRANCISQUITO AV, WCOV, 91791	638 - J3
SAN JOSE ELEM 2015 CADILLAC DR, POM, 91767	600 - J5
SAN JOSE STREET ELEM 14928 CLYMER ST, MsnH, 91345	501 - J3
SAN MARINO ELEM 6215 SAN ROLANDO CIR, BPK, 90620	767 - E5
SAN MARINO HIGH 2701 HUNTINGTON DR, SMRO, 91108	566 - E7
SAN MARINO MONTESSORI 444 S SIERRA MADRE BLVD, LACo, 91107	566 - E5
SAN MIGUEL AVENUE ELEM 9801 SAN MIGUEL AV, SGAT, 90280	705 - C4
SAN MIGUEL 2270 E 108TH ST, LA, 90059	704 - H6
SAN PASCUAL AVENUE ELEM 815 SAN PASCUAL AV, HiPk, 90042	595 - F1
SAN PEDRO HIGH 1001 W 15TH ST, SPed, 90731	824 - A6
SAN PEDRO STREET ELEM 1635 S SAN PEDRO ST, LA, 90015	634 - E7
SAN RAFAEL ELEM 1090 NITHSDALE RD, PAS, 91105	565 - E6
SANTA CLARITA CHRISTIAN 27249 LUTHER DR, SCTA, 91351	4551 - G3
SANTA CLARITA ELEM 27177 SECO CANYON RD, SCTA, 91354	4460 - H6
SANTA FE ELEM 4650 BALDWIN PARK BLVD, BALD, 91706	598 - C4
SANTA FE HIGH 10400 ORR AND DAY RD, SFSP, 90670	706 - G5
SANTA FE MID 148 W DUARTE RD, MNRO, 91016	567 - G6
SANTA FE SPRINGS CHRISTIAN 11457 FLORENCE AV, SFSP, 90670	706 - G5
SANTA ISABEL ELEM 2424 WHITTIER BLVD, LA, 90023	635 - A6
SANTA MONICA BLVD COMM CHARTER 1022 N VAN NESS AV, LA, 90038	593 - G6
SANTA MONICA HIGH 601 PICO BLVD, SMCA, 90401	671 - F3
SANTA MONICA MONTESSORI ELEM 1909 COLORADO AV, SMCA, 90404	671 - G1
SANTANA HIGH 1006 OTTERBEIN AV, RowH, 91748	679 - C3
SANTA ROSA DE LIMA ELEM 1309 MOTT ST, SFER, 91340	481 - J7
SANTA TERESITA ELEM 2646 ZONAL AV, Boyl, 90033	635 - C3
SATICOY ELEM 7850 ETHEL AV, NHol, 91605	532 - D3
SATURN STREET ELEM 5360 SATURN ST, LA, 90019	633 - C5
SAUGUS HIGH 21900 CENTURION WY, SCTA, 91350	4461 - A6
SAVANNAH ACADEMY HIGH W HILL ST & MONITOR AV, LBCH, 90810	795 - A4
SAVANNAH ELEM 3720 RIO HONDO AV, RSMD, 91770	596 - J7
SCHURR HIGH 820 N WILCOX AV, MTBL, 90640	636 - C7
SCOTT AVENUE ELEM 11701 SCOTT AV, LACo, 90604	707 - H6
SEASIDE ELEM 4651 SHARYNNE LN, TOR, 90505	793 - B1
SELBY GROVE ELEM 8110 PARAMOUNT BLVD, PRV, 90660	706 - D1
SELLERS ELEM 500 N LORAINE AV, GLDR, 91741	569 - G4
SELMA AVENUE ELEM 6611 SELMA AV, Hlwd, 90028	593 - E4
SENDAK, MAURICE ELEM 11414 TIARA ST, NHol, 91601	562 - J1
SEPULVEDA MID 15330 PLUMMER ST, LA, 91343	501 - H6
SEQUOAYAH 535 S PASADENA AV, PAS, 91105	565 - H6
SEQUOIA CHARTER HIGH 21515 CENTRE POINTE PKWY, SCTA, 91350	4551 - B3
SERRANIA AVENUE ELEM 5014 SERRANIA AV, WdHl, 91364	560 - C3
SERRANO MID 4725 SAN JOSE ST, MTCL, 91763	601 - F5
SHADOW HILLS INTERMED 37315 60TH ST E, PMDL, 93552	4287 - C3
SHADYBEND ELEM 15430 SHADYBEND DR, HacH, 91745	678 - B2
SHALHEVET HIGH 910 S FAIRFAX AV, LA, 90036	633 - B3
SHAMLIAM ARMENIAN 4444 LOWELL AV, GLDL, 91214	504 - D6
SHARP AVENUE ELEM 13800 PIERCE ST, Pcma, 91331	502 - B4
SHELYN ELEM 19500 NACORA ST, RowH, 91748	679 - D5
SHENANDOAH STREET ELEM 2450 S SHENANDOAH ST, LA, 90034	632 - H6
SHEPHERD OF THE VALLEY- **LUTHERAN ELEM** 23838 KITTRIDGE ST, CanP, 91307	529 - E6
SHERIDAN STREET ELEM 416 CORNWELL ST, Boyl, 90033	635 - B4
SHERMAN OAKS CES HIGH 18605 ERWIN ST, Res, 91335	530 - H7
SHERMAN OAKS HIGH 18605 ERWIN ST, Res, 91335	530 - H7
SHERMAN OAKS ELEM 14755 GREENLEAF ST, Shrm, 91403	561 - J5
SHERY HIGH 2600 VINE AV, TOR, 90501	763 - G7
SHIRLEY AVENUE ELEM 19452 HART ST, Res, 91335	530 - F5
SHIRPSER ELEM 4020 GIBSON RD, ELMN, 91731	597 - B6
SHIVELY, DEAN L MID 1431 CENTRAL AV, SELM, 91733	637 - B4
SHORT AVENUE ELEM 12814 MAXELLA AV, LA, 90066	672 - C6
SHUEY ELEM 8472 WELLS ST, RSMD, 91770	596 - G6
SHULL ELEM 825 N AMELIA AV, SDMS, 91773	600 - A1
SIERRA CANYON 11052 INDEPENDANCE AV, Chat, 91311	500 - B2
SIERRA ELEM 747 W AVE J-12, LAN, 93534	4105 - G1
SIERRA HIGH 1134 S BARRANCA AV, GLDR, 91740	599 - C1
SIERRA MADRE ELEM 141 W HIGHLAND AV, SMAD, 91024	567 - A2
SIERRA PK ELEM 3170 BUDAU AV, LA, 90032	595 - F6
SIERRA VISTA ALTERNATIVE HIGH 9401 PAINTER AV, WHIT, 90605	707 - B3
SIERRA VISTA ELEM 1800 E WHITTIER BLVD, LHB, 90631	708 - G5
SIERRA VISTA ELEM 4342 ALPHA ST, LA, 90032	595 - G4
SIERRA VISTA HIGH 3600 FRAZIER ST, BALD, 91706	598 - A7
SIERRA VISTA JR HIGH 13400 FOSTER AV, BALD, 91706	598 - A7
SIERRA VISTA JR HIGH 19425 STILLMORE ST, SCTA, 91351	4551 - F2
SIERRA VISTA MID 15801 SIERRA VISTA CT, LPUE, 91744	638 - E6
SIERRA VISTA MID 777 E PUENTE ST, COV, 91723	599 - D5
SIGNAL HILL ELEM 2285 WALNUT AV, SIGH, 90755	795 - F4
SILVER SPUR ELEM 5500 IRONWOOD ST, RPV, 90275	793 - A5
SIMI VALLEY HIGH 5400 COCHRAN ST, SIMI, 93063	499 - A1
SIMONS MID 900 E FRANKLIN AV, POM, 91766	641 - A4
SINAI AKIBA ACADEMY 10400 WILSHIRE BLVD, Wwd, 90024	632 - C2
SKYBLUE MESA ELEM 28040 HARDESTY AV, SCTA, 91351	4461 - E7
SKYWARD CHRISTIAN 7747 APPERSON ST, Tuj, 91042	503 - H4
SLAUSON MID 340 W 5TH ST, AZU, 91702	568 - J6
SOLANO AVENUE ELEM 615 SOLANO AV, LA, 90012	594 - H7
SOLEADO ELEM 27800 LONGHILL DR, RPV, 90275	793 - B7
SOLEDAD ENRICH ACT CHARTER HIGH 222 N VIRGIL AV, City, 90063	635 - D6
SOMERSET HIGH 9242 LAUREL ST, BLF, 90706	736 - A6
SONORA HIGH 401 S PALM ST, LHB, 90631	708 - G6
SONRISE CHRISTIAN ELEM 800 N BANNA AV, COV, 91724	599 - F4
SONRISE CHRISTIAN MID 1220 E RUDDOCK ST, COV, 91724	599 - E5
SORENSEN, CHRISTIAN ELEM 11493 E ROSE HEDGE DR, LACo, 90606	677 - A6
SOTO STREET ELEM 1020 S SOTO ST, LA, 90023	635 - A6
SOUTH BAY FAITH ACADEMY 101 S PACIFIC COAST HWY, RBCH, 90277	762 - J5
SOUTH BAY JUNIOR ACADEMY 4400 DEL AMO BLVD, TOR, 90503	763 - C4
SOUTH EAST HIGH 2720 TWEEDY BLVD, SGAT, 90280	704 - J4
SOUTHEAST MID 2560 TWEEDY BLVD, SGAT, 90280	704 - J4
SOUTH EL MONTE HIGH 1001 DURFEE AV, SELM, 91733	637 - C5
SOUTH GATE HIGH 3351 FIRESTONE BLVD, SGAT, 90280	705 - B3
SOUTH GATE MID 4100 FIRESTONE BLVD, SGAT, 90280	705 - C3
SOUTH GATE NEW ELEM 6 9820 MADISON AV, SGAT, 90280	705 - A4
SOUTH HIGH 4801 PACIFIC COAST HWY, TOR, 90505	793 - B2
SOUTH HILLS ACADEMY 1600 E FRANCISQUITO AV, WCOV, 91791	638 - H3
SOUTH HILLS HIGH 645 S BARRANCA ST, WCOV, 91791	639 - C1
SOUTHLAND CHRISTIAN ACADEMY 16400 WOODRUFF AV, BLF, 90706	736 - C5
SOUTHLANDS CHRISTIAN ELEM 1920 BREA CANYON CUTOFF RD, LACo, 91789	679 - E5
SOUTHLANDS CHRISTIAN HIGH 1920 BREA CANYON CUTOFF RD, LACo, 91789	679 - E5
SOUTH PARK ELEM 8510 TOWNE AV, LA, 90003	704 - D2
SOUTH PASADENA HIGH 1401 FREMONT AV, SPAS, 91030	595 - H2
SOUTH PASADENA MID 1600 OAK ST, SPAS, 91030	595 - H3
SOUTH POINTE MID 20671 LARKSTONE DR, DBAR, 91789	679 - G4
SOUTH RANCHITO ELEM 5241 PASSONS BLVD, PRV, 90660	676 - G4
SOUTH SHORES ELEM 2060 W 35TH ST, LA, 90732	823 - G7
SOUTHWESTERN ACADEMY 2800 MONTEREY RD, SMRO, 91108	596 - A2
SOUTHWESTERN LONGVIEW HIGH 4747 DAISY AV, NLB, 90805	765 - C4
SPARKS ELEM 15151 TEMPLE AV, LACo, 91744	638 - C5
SPARKS MID 15100 GIORDANO ST, LACo, 91744	638 - C5
STAGG STREET ELEM 7839 AMESTOY AV, VanN, 91406	531 - C3
STANFORD AVENUE ELEM 2833 ILLINOIS AV, SGAT, 90280	704 J3
STANFORD MID 5871 E LOS ARCOS ST, LBCH, 90815	796 - D3
STANTON ELEM 725 S VECINO DR, GLDR, 91740	569 - C7
STATE STREET ELEM 3211 SANTA ANA ST, HNTP, 90255	705 - B2
STELLA MIDDLE CHARTER ACADEMY 2636 S MANSFIELD AV, LA, 90016	633 - C7
STELLE, ALICE C MID 22450 MULHOLLAND HWY, LACo, 91302	559 - J6
STEPHENS, W L MID 1830 W COLUMBIA ST, LBCH, 90810	795 - A2
STERRY, NORA ELEM 1730 CORINTH AV, WLA, 90025	632 - A5
STEVENSON ELEM 515 LIME AV, LBCH, 90802	795 - E7
STEVENSON MID 725 S INDIANA ST, LA, 90023	635 - C7
STEVENSON RANCH ELEM 25820 CARROLL LN, StvR, 91381	4550 - B7
STEVENSON, ROBERT L ELEM 3333 W OAK ST, BURB, 91505	563 - D3
STONEHURST AVENUE ELEM 9851 STONEHURST AV, SunV, 91352	503 - A5
STONER AVENUE ELEM 11735 BRADDOCK DR, LA, 90230	672 - E5
STOWERS ELEM 13350 BEACH ST, CRTS, 90703	737 - C7
STRATHERN STREET ELEM 7939 SAINT CLAIR AV, NHol, 91605	532 - F3
STUDEBAKER ELEM 11800 HALCOURT AV, NRWK, 90650	706 - E7
SULPHUR SPRINGS COMM ELEM 16628 LOST CANYON RD, SCTA, 91387	4552 - C2
SUMAC ELEM 6050 CALMFIELD AV, AGRH, 91301	558 - B3
SUMMERWIND ELEM 39360 SUMMERWIND DR, PMDL, 93551	4195 - F5
SUMNER ELEM 1770 SUMNER AV, CLAR, 91711	571 - A7
SUNDOWN ELEM 6151 W AVE J-8, LAN, 93536	4104 - F1
SUNKIST ELEM 935 MAYLAND AV, LPUE, 91746	638 - A2
SUNLAND ELEM 8350 HILLROSE ST, Sunl, 91040	503 - G3
SUNNY BRAE AVENUE ELEM 20620 ARMINTA ST, Win, 91306	530 - C3
SUNNYDALE ELEM 1233 W AVE J-8, LAN, 93534	4105 - F1
SUNNY HILLS HIGH 1801 WARBURTON WY, FUL, 92833	738 - D5
SUNRISE ELEM 2821 E 7TH ST, LA, 90023	635 - B7
SUNSET CHRISTIAN 400 SUNSET AV, LPUE, 91744	638 - B5
SUNSET ELEM 800 TONOPAH AV, LPUE, 91744	638 - B4
SUNSET LANE ELEM 2030 SUNSET LN, FUL, 92833	738 - D4
SUN VALLEY MID 7330 BAKMAN AV, SunV, 91352	532 - J4
SUPERIOR STREET ELEM 9756 OSO AV, Chat, 91311	500 - D5
SUSSMAN MID 12500 BIRCHDALE AV, DWNY, 90242	736 - A1
SUTHERLAND ELEM 1330 AMELIA AV, SDMS, 91773	570 - A7
SUTTER ELEM 5075 DAISY AV, NLB, 90805	765 - C4
SUTTER MID 7330 WINNETKA AV, Win, 91306	530 - E4
SUVA ELEM 6740 SUVA ST, BGDN, 90201	706 - A1
SUVA INTERMED 6660 SUVA ST, BGDN, 90201	705 - J1
SUZANNE MID 525 SUZANNE RD, WAL, 91789	639 - G6
SWAIN ELEM 5851 NEWMAN ST, CYP, 90630	767 - E6
SYCAMORE ELEM 225 W 8TH ST, CLAR, 91711	601 - D2
SYCAMORE GROVE 4900 N FIGUEROA ST, HiPk, 90042	595 - B3
SYLMAR ELEM 13291 PHILLIPPI AV, LA, 91342	482 - A3
SYLMAR HIGH 13050 BORDEN AV, LA, 91342	482 - A4
SYLMAR LIGHT & LIFE CHRISTIAN- **ELEM** 14019 SAYRE ST, LA, 91342	482 - B4
SYLVAN PARK ELEM 6238 NOBLE AV, VanN, 91411	531 - H7
TAFT, WILLIAM HOWARD HIGH 5461 WINNETKA AV, WdHl, 91364	560 - E2
TAMARISK ELEM 1843 E AVE Q-5, PMDL, 93550	4196 - D7
TANNER, HOWARD ELEM 7210 ROSECRANS AV, PRM, 90723	735 - F3
TAPER AVENUE ELEM 1824 N TAPER AV, SPed, 90731	824 - A2
TARZANA ELEM 5726 TOPEKA DR, Tarz, 91356	560 - H1
TELECHRON ELEM 11200 TELECHRON AV, LACo, 90605	707 - C6
TELFAIR AVENUE ELEM 10975 TELFAIR AV, Pcma, 91331	502 - C2
TEMPLE ACADEMY 635 CALIFORNIA AV, LACo, 91744	638 - C5
TEMPLE CITY HIGH 9501 LEMON AV, TEML, 91780	596 - J1
TEMPLE ISRAEL OF HOLLYWOOD 7300 HOLLYWOOD BLVD, LA, 90046	593 - C4
TEMPLE, RAYMOND ELEM 7800 HOLDER ST, BPK, 90620	767 - F3
TEMPLE, ROGER INTERMED 8470 FERN AV, RSMD, 91770	636 - G2
TESORO DEL VALLE ELEM 29171 BERNARDO WY, BqtC, 91354	4460 - F3
TETZLAFF MID 12351 DEL AMO BLVD, CRTS, 90703	766 - J3
TIBBY ELEM 1400 W POPLAR ST, COMP, 90220	734 - G4
TIERRA BONITA ELEM 44820 27TH ST E, LAN, 93535	4016 - E5
TINCHER ELEM 1701 PETALUMA AV, LBCH, 90815	796 - F5
TOBIN WORLD ELEM 920 E BROADWAY, GLDL, 91205	564 - F5
TODAYS FRESH START CHARTER ELEM 2301 E ROSECRANS AV, RDom, 90221	735 - C3
TODAYS FRESH START CHARTER 4514 CRENSHAW BLVD, LA, 90043	673 - F4
TOLAND WAY ELEM 4545 TOLAND WY, Eagl, 90041	594 - J1
TOLL, ELEANOR J MID 700 GLENWOOD RD, GLDL, 91202	564 - C2
TOLUCA LAKE ELEM 4840 CAHUENGA BLVD, NHol, 91601	563 - B3
TOPANGA ELEM 141 N TOPANGA CANYON BLVD, Top, 90290	590 - A6
TOPEKA DRIVE ELEM 9815 TOPEKA DR, Nor, 91324	500 - G5
TORCH MID 751 VINELAND AV, INDS, 91746	637 - J2
TORRANCE ELEM 2125 LINCOLN AV, TOR, 90501	763 - G7
TORRANCE HIGH 2200 W CARSON ST, TOR, 90501	763 - G6
TOWERS ELEM 5600 TOWERS ST, TOR, 90503	763 - A3
TOWNE AVENUE ELEM 18924 TOWNE AV, CRSN, 90746	764 - D2
TRACY HIGH 12222 CUESTA DR, CRTS, 90703	736 - J6
TRACY ELEM 13350 TRACY ST, BALD, 91706	597 - J7
TRANSFIGURATION 4020 ROXTON AV, LA, 90008	673 - G2
TRAWEEK MID 1941 E ROWLAND AV, WCOV, 91791	598 - J6
TRINITY CHRISTIAN ELEM 7754 MCGROARTY ST, Tuj, 91042	503 - H4
TRINITY CHRISTIAN ELEM 10614 ORO VISTA AV, Sunl, 91040	503 - G3
TRINITY LUTHERAN 11507 STUDEBAKER RD, NRWK, 90650	706 - E7
TRINITY LUTHERAN 11716 FLORAL DR, WHIT, 90601	677 - B5

FEATURE NAME	Address City, ZIP Code	PAGE-GRID
TRINITY LUTHERAN	4783 W 130TH ST, HAW, 90250	733 - C2
TRINITY STREET ELEM	3736 TRINITY ST, LA, 90011	674 - D2
TUCKER ELEM	2221 ARGONNE AV, LBCH, 90815	796 - B4
TULITA ELEM	1520 PROSPECT AV, RBCH, 90277	793 - A1
TULSA STREET ELEM	10900 HAYVENHURST AV, GrnH, 91344	501 - E2
TUMBLEWEED ELEM	1100 E AVE R-4, PMDL, 93550	4286 - B2
TURNING POINT ELEM	1300 N SEPULVEDA BLVD, Brwd, 90049	591 - G6
TURNING POINT ELEM	8780 NATIONAL BLVD, CULC, 90232	632 - H7
TWAIN ELEM	12315 THORSON AV, LYN, 90262	735 - C2
TWAIN ELEM	5021 E CENTRALIA ST, LBCH, 90808	766 - B5
TWAIN, MARK ELEM	3728 W 154TH ST, LACo, 90260	733 - E5
TWAIN, MARK MID	2224 WALGROVE AV, LA, 90066	672 - A4
TWEEDY ELEM	PINEHURST AV, SGAT, 90280	705 - E4
TWIN LAKES ELEM	3900 GILMAN RD, ELMN, 91732	597 - G7
UNION AVENUE ELEM	150 S BURLINGTON AV, Echo, 90026	634 - D2
UNIVERSITY ELEM	330 CHARLES YOUNG DR, LA, 90095	632 - B1
UNIVERSITY HIGH	11800 TEXAS AV, WLA, 90025	631 - J5
UNSWORTH ELEM	9001 LINDSEY AV, DWNY, 90240	706 - E2
UTAH STREET ELEM	255 GABRIEL GARCIA MARQUEZ ST, Boyl, 90033	634 - J4
VAIL HIGH	1230 S VAIL AV, MTBL, 90640	676 - B4
VALENCIA ELEM	758 W GRONDAHL ST, COV, 91722	598 - J3
VALENCIA ELEM	9241 COSGROVE ST, PRV, 90660	676 - G5
VALENCIA HIGH	27801 DICKASON DR, SCTA, 91355	4460 - E6
VALENCIA PARK	3441 W VALENCIA DR, FUL, 92833	738 - B7
VALENCIA VALLEY ELEM	23601 CARRIZO DR, SCTA, 91355	4550 - G4
VALENTINE ELEM	1650 HUNTINGTON DR, SMRO, 91108	596 - C1
VALERIO STREET ELEM	15035 VALERIO ST, VanN, 91405	531 - H4
VALINDA ELEM	1030 INDIAN SUMMER AV, LACo, 91744	638 - G5
VALLEY ALTERNATIVE ELEM	6701 BALBOA BLVD, VanN, 91406	531 - D6
VALLEY ALTERNATIVE HIGH	6701 BALBOA BLVD, VanN, 91406	531 - C6
VALLEY BETH SHALOM DAY	15739 VENTURA BLVD, Enc, 91436	561 - G4
VALLEY CHRISTIAN ELEM	17408 GRAND AV, BLF, 90706	736 - D7
VALLEY CHRISTIAN HIGH	10818 ARTESIA BLVD, CRTS, 90703	736 - E7
VALLEY CHRISTIAN MID	18100 DUMONT AV, CRTS, 90703	736 - E7
VALLEY HIGH	14162 LOMITAS AV, LACo, 91746	637 - J6
VALLEYDALE ELEM	700 S LARK ELLEN AV, AZU, 91702	598 - H2
VALLEY PRESBYTERIAN ELEM	9240 HASKELL AV, LA, 91343	501 - G6
VALLEY ELEM	15700 SHERMAN WY, VanN, 91406	531 - G5
VALLEY VIEW COMM ELEM	19414 SIERRA ESTATES DR, SCTA, 91321	4551 - F5
VALLEY VIEW ELEM	237 MEL CANYON RD, DUAR, 91010	568 - E3
VALLEY VIEW ELEM	3310 W AVE L-8, LAN, 93536	4105 - B5
VALLEY VIEW ELEM	4900 MARYLAND AV, GLDL, 91214	504 - E6
VALLEY VIEW ELEM	6921 WOODROW WILSON DR, LA, 90068	593 - D1
VANALDEN AVENUE ELEM	19019 DELANO ST, Res, 91335	530 - G7
VAN DEENE AVENUE ELEM	826 JAVELIN ST, LACo, 90502	764 - B5
VAN GOGH STREET ELEM	17160 VAN GOGH ST, GrnH, 91344	481 - C4
VANGUARD MID	13305 S SAN PEDRO ST, LACo, 90061	734 - D2
VAN NESS AVENUE ELEM	501 N VAN NESS AV, LA, 90004	593 - G7
VAN NUYS ELEM	6464 SYLMAR AV, VanN, 91401	532 - A6
VAN NUYS HIGH	6535 CEDROS AV, VanN, 91411	531 - J6
VAN NUYS MID	5435 VESPER AV, VanN, 91411	561 - J2
VAN WIG ELEM	1151 VAN WIG AV, LACo, 91746	638 - A2
VASQUEZ HIGH	33630 RED ROVER MINE RD, Actn, 93510	4374 - J5
VAUGHN STREET ELEM	13330 VAUGHN ST, Pcma, 91331	502 - C1
VEJAR ELEM	20222 VEJAR RD, WAL, 91789	679 - F1
VEJAR ELEM	950 W GRAND AV, POM, 91766	640 - H3
VENA AVENUE ELEM	9377 VENA AV, Pcma, 91331	502 - D6
VENICE HIGH	13000 VENICE BLVD, LA, 90066	672 - B5
VERBUM DEI HIGH	11100 S CENTRAL AV, LA, 90059	704 - F6
VERDUGO HILLS HIGH	10625 PLAINVIEW AV, Tuj, 91042	503 - J3
VERDUGO MONTESSORI	4371 EAGLE ROCK BLVD, Eagl, 90041	594 - J1
VERDUGO WOODLANDS ELEM	1751 N VERDUGO RD, GLDL, 91208	564 - H1
VERMONT AVENUE ELEM	1435 W 27TH ST, LA, 90007	634 - A7
VERNON CITY ELEM	2360 E VERNON AV, VER, 90058	674 - H3
VERNON MID	9775 VERNON AV, MTCL, 91763	601 - H6
VICTOR ELEM	4820 SPENCER ST, TOR, 90503	763 - B5
VICTORIA AVENUE ELEM	3320 MISSOURI AV, SGAT, 90280	705 - B4
VICTORY BAPTIST DAY ELEM	892 E 48TH ST, LA, 90011	674 - E4
VICTORY BOULEVARD ELEM	6315 RADFORD AV, NHol, 91606	532 - G6
VIEW PARK PREP ELEM	3751 W 54TH ST, LACo, 90043	673 - E5
VIEW PARK PREP CHARTER HIGH	5701 CRENSHAW BLVD, LA, 90043	673 - F5
VIEW PARK PREP CHARTER MID	5749 CRENSHAW BLVD, LA, 90043	673 - F5
VIEWPOINT	23620 MULHOLLAND HWY, CALB, 91302	559 - E7
VILLACORTA ELEM	17840 VILLA CORTA ST, LACo, 91744	678 - J1
VILLAGE ACADEMY HIGH	1460 E HOLT BLVD, POM, 91767	641 - C1
VILLAGE CHRISTIAN ELEM	8930 VILLAGE AV, SunV, 91352	503 - B7
VILLAGE CHRISTIAN HIGH	8930 VILLAGE AV, SunV, 91352	503 - B7
VILLAGE ELEM	780 SWARTHMORE AV, PacP, 90272	631 - A5
VINEDALE ELEM	10150 LA TUNA CANYON RD, SunV, 91352	503 - C7
VINE ELEM	1901 E VINE AV, WCOV, 91791	638 - J2
VINELAND ELEM	3609 VINELAND AV, BALD, 91706	598 - C6
VINE STREET ELEM	955 VINE ST, LA, 90038	593 - F6
VINTAGE ELEM	15848 STARE ST, LA, 91343	501 - F5
VIRGIL MID	152 N VERMONT AV, LA, 90004	634 - A1
VIRGINIA ROAD ELEM	2925 VIRGINIA RD, LA, 90016	633 - E7
VISITATION ELEM	8740 EMERSON AV, Wch, 90045	702 - F3
VISTA HIGH	11300 WRIGHT RD, LYN, 90262	735 - E1
VISTA DEL VALLE ELEM	550 VISTA DR, CLAR, 91711	601 - C5
VISTA GRANDE ELEM	1390 W FRANCIS ST, ONT, 91762	641 - J4
VISTA GRANDE ELEM	7032 PURPLE RIDGE DR, RPV, 90275	822 - G1
VISTA HIGH	127 W ALLEN AV, SDMS, 91773	600 - B1
VISTA MID NO.2	15040 ROSCOE BLVD, PanC, 91402	531 - H2
VISTA SAN GABRIEL ELEM	18020 E AVE O, LACo, 93591	4200 - A2
VOORHIS, JERRY ELEM	3501 DURFEE AV, ELMN, 91732	637 - F1
VOYAGER CHARTER HIGH	609 W LAS TUNAS DR, SGBL, 91776	596 - D3
WADSWORTH AVENUE ELEM	981 E 41ST ST, LA, 90011	674 - E2
WAITE MID	14320 NORWALK BLVD, NRWK, 90650	736 - J3
WALGROVE AVENUE ELEM	1630 WALGROVE AV, LA, 90066	672 - A3
WALKER, JOE MID	5632 AVE L-8, LACo, 93536	4104 - G5
WALKER JR HIGH	8132 WALKER ST, LPMA, 90623	767 - D4
WALNUT AVENUE ELEM	5550 WALNUT AV, CHNO, 91710	641 - H6
WALNUT ELEM	4701 WALNUT ST, BALD, 91706	598 - A4
WALNUT ELEM	625 N WALNUT ST, LHB, 90631	708 - E5
WALNUT ELEM	841 GLENWICK AV, DBAR, 91789	679 - F3
WALNUT HIGH	400 PIERRE RD, WAL, 91789	639 - G7
WALNUT PARK ELEM	2642 OLIVE ST, LACo, 90255	704 - J1
WALTERIA ELEM	24456 MADISON ST, TOR, 90505	793 - D4
WALTON MID	900 W GREENLEAF BLVD, COMP, 90220	734 - H6
WARD ELEM	8851 ADOREE ST, DWNY, 90242	736 - A1
WARNER AVENUE ELEM	615 HOLMBY AV, Wwd, 90024	632 - C2
WARREN HIGH	8141 DE PALMA ST, DWNY, 90241	706 - A5
WARREN LANE ELEM	9330 S 8TH AV, ING, 90305	703 - G4
WASHINGTON ELEM	1100 LILIENTHAL LN, RBCH, 90278	763 - B2
WASHINGTON ELEM	1400 W MADISON AV, MTBL, 90640	676 - D1
WASHINGTON ELEM	1421 N WILMINGTON AV, COMP, 90222	734 - G3
WASHINGTON ELEM	1520 N RAYMOND AV, PAS, 91103	565 - H1
WASHINGTON ELEM	300 N SAN MARINO AV, SGBL, 91775	596 - E3
WASHINGTON ELEM	325 W GLADSTONE ST, GLDR, 91740	599 - D1
WASHINGTON ELEM	4225 SANBORN AV, LYN, 90262	705 - D7
WASHINGTON ELEM	4339 W 129TH ST, HAW, 90250	733 - D2
WASHINGTON ELEM	9725 JEFFERSON ST, BLF, 90706	736 - B4
WASHINGTON ELEM	975 E 9TH ST, POM, 91766	641 - B2
WASHINGTON, GEORGE ELEM	2322 N LINCOLN ST, BURB, 91504	533 - E5
WASHINGTON, GEORGE ELEM	7804 S THORNLAKE AV, LACo, 90606	676 - J7
WASHINGTON, GEORGE MID	1450 CEDAR AV, LBCH, 90813	795 - D5
WASHINGTON HIGH	10860 S DENKER AV, LACo, 90047	703 - J6
WASHINGTON MID	1505 N MARENGO AV, PAS, 91103	565 - H1
WASHINGTON MID	716 E LA HABRA BLVD, LHB, 90631	708 - F6
WASHINGTON PRIMARY CTR	860 W 112TH ST, LA, 90044	704 - A6
WAVERLY, THE ELEM	67 W BELLEVUE DR, PAS, 91105	565 - H6
WAVERLY, THE HIGH	396 S PASADENA AV, PAS, 91105	565 - H6
WEAVER ELEM	11872 WEMBLEY RD, OrCo, 90720	796 - G4
WEBB SCHOOLS, THE	1175 W BASELINE RD, CLAR, 91711	571 - A6
WEBSTER ELEM	1755 W 32ND WY, LBCH, 90810	795 - A1
WEBSTER ELEM	2101 E WASHINGTON BLVD, LACo, 91104	566 - D1
WEBSTER ELEM	3602 WINTER CANYON RD, MAL, 90265	628 - H6
WEBSTER MID	11330 GRAHAM PL, LA, 90064	632 - C7
WEDGEWORTH ELEM	16949 WEDGEWORTH DR, HacH, 91745	678 - F4
WEEMES ELEM	1260 W 36TH PL, LA, 90007	674 - A1
WEIGAND AVENUE ELEM	10401 WEIGAND AV, Wats, 90002	704 - H5
WELBY WAY ELEM	23456 WELBY WY, CanP, 91307	529 - F6
WESCOVE ELEM	1010 W VINE AV, WCOV, 91790	638 - E2
WESLEY, THE	4832 TUJUNGA AV, NHol, 91601	562 - J3
WEST ANGELES CHRISTIAN ACADEMY	3010 CRENSHAW BLVD, LA, 90018	633 - E7
WEST ATHENS ELEM	1110 W 119TH ST, LACo, 90044	704 - A7
WESTCHESTER HIGH	7400 W MANCHESTER AV, Wch, 90045	702 - C3
WESTCHESTER LUTHERAN	7831 S SEPULVEDA BLVD, Wch, 90045	702 - G1
WESTCHESTER NEIGHBORHOOD	5520 W ARBOR VITAE ST, Wch, 90045	703 - A4
WEST COVINA CHRISTIAN ELEM	763 N SUNSET AV, WCOV, 91790	598 - F5
WEST COVINA HIGH	1609 E CAMERON AV, WCOV, 91791	638 - H1
WEST COVINA HILLS SDA	3536 E TEMPLE WY, WCOV, 91791	599 - E7
WESTERLY	2950 E 29TH ST, LBCH, 90808	795 - H2
WESTERN AVENUE ELEM	1724 W 53RD ST, LA, 90062	673 - H5
WESTERN CHRISTIAN ELEM	3105 PADUA AV, CLAR, 91711	571 - F6
WESTERN CHRISTIAN	1115 E PUENTE ST, COV, 91724	599 - E5
WESTERN HIGH	501 S WESTERN AV, ANA, 92804	767 - H6
WEST HIGH	20401 VICTOR ST, TOR, 90503	763 - B4
WESTHOFF ELEM	1323 N COUNTRY HOLLOW DR, WAL, 91789	639 - F5
WEST HOLLYWOOD ELEM	970 HAMMOND ST, WHWD, 90069	592 - H6
WESTLAKE HIGH	100 N LAKEVIEW CANYON RD, THO, 91362	557 - D3
WESTLAKE HILLS ELEM	3333 S MEDICINE BOW CT, THO, 91362	557 - B3
WESTLAND ELEM	16200 MULHOLLAND DR, Brwd, 90049	561 - F7
WEST LOS ANGELES BAPTIST	1609 S BARRINGTON AV, WLA, 90025	631 - J6
WEST MID	11985 OLD RIVER SCHOOL RD, DWNY, 90242	705 - H5
WESTMINSTER ACADEMY	1495 COLORADO BLVD, Eagl, 90041	565 - C5
WESTMINSTER AVENUE ELEM	1010 ABBOT KINNEY BLVD, Ven, 90291	671 - H5
WESTMONT ELEM	1780 W 9TH ST, POM, 91766	640 - F3
WESTPORT HEIGHTS ELEM	6011 W 79TH ST, Wch, 90045	702 - H2
WEST RANCH HIGH	26255 VALENCIA BLVD, StvR, 91381	4550 - B5
WESTRIDGE	324 MADELINE DR, PAS, 91105	565 - G7
WESTSIDE CHRISTIAN ELEM	40027 11TH ST W, LACo, 93551	4195 - G4
WESTSIDE LEADERSHIP	104 ANCHORAGE ST, LA, 90292	671 - H7
WEST VALLEY CHRISTIAN ACADEMY	7911 WINNETKA AV, Win, 91306	530 - E3
WEST VALLEY CHRISTIAN	22450 SHERMAN WY, CanP, 91307	529 - J5
WEST VERNON AVENUE ELEM	4312 S GRAND AV, LA, 90037	674 - C3
WEST WHITTIER ELEM	6411 S NORWALK BLVD, LACo, 90606	676 - J5
WEST WIND ELEM	44044 36TH ST W, LAN, 93536	4105 - B1
WESTWOOD CHARTER ELEM	2050 SELBY AV, WLA, 90025	632 - C5
WHALEY MID	14401 S GIBSON AV, COMP, 90221	735 - D3
WHITCOMB HIGH	350 W MAUNA LOA AV, GLDR, 91740	569 - D7
WHITE, CHARLES ELEM	2401 WILSHIRE BLVD, LA, 90057	634 - B3
WHITE ELEM	744 E DORAN ST, GLDL, 91206	564 - F4
WHITE HOUSE PLACE ELEM	108 BIMINI PL, LA, 90004	634 - A1
WHITE MEM ADVENTIST ELEM	1605 NEW JERSEY ST, Boyl, 90033	634 - J4
WHITE OAK ELEM	2201 ALSCOT AV, SIMI, 93063	499 - C2
WHITE OAK ELEM	31761 W VILLAGE SCHOOL RD, WLKV, 91361	557 - D6
WHITE POINT ELEM	1410 SILVIUS AV, SPed, 90731	853 - J1
WHITE, STEPHEN M MID	22102 S FIGUEROA ST, CRSN, 90745	764 - B7
WHITMAN HIGH	7795 ROSEWOOD AV, LA, 90036	593 - B7
WHITNEY HIGH	16800 SHOEMAKER AV, CRTS, 90703	737 - B6
WHITTIER CHRISTIAN ELEM	11700 MAYBROOK AV, LACo, 90604	708 - A6
WHITTIER CHRISTIAN HIGH	2300 WORTH AV, LHB, 90631	708 - B5
WHITTIER CHRISTIAN HIGH	501 N BEACH BLVD, LHB, 90631	708 - B5
WHITTIER CHRISTIAN JR HIGH	6545 NEWLIN AV, WHIT, 90601	677 - C6
WHITTIER ELEM	1761 WALNUT AV, LBCH, 90813	795 - F5
WHITTIER HIGH	12417 PHILADELPHIA ST, WHIT, 90601	677 - C6
WILBUR AVENUE ELEM	5213 CREBS AV, Tarz, 91356	560 - H3
WILCOX ELEM	816 DONNA WY, MTBL, 90640	636 - C7
WILDERS PREP ACADEMY CHARTER-ELEM	830 N LA BREA AV, ING, 90302	703 - C1
WILDFLOWER ELEM	38136 35TH ST E, PMDL, 93550	4286 - G1
WILD ROSE ELEM	232 JASMINE AV, MNRO, 91016	567 - H4
WILDWOOD ELEM	12201 WASHINGTON BLVD, CULC, 90066	672 - C4
WILDWOOD SECONDARY	11811 W OLYMPIC BLVD, WLA, 90025	632 - A7
WILEY CANYON ELEM	24240 LA GLORITA CIR, SCTA, 91321	4640 - F2
WILKERSON ELEM	2700 DOREEN AV, ELMN, 91733	637 - B2
WILLARD ELEM	1055 FREEMAN AV, LBCH, 90804	795 - H6
WILLARD ELEM	301 S MADRE ST, PAS, 91107	566 - G5
WILLARD, FRANCES E ELEM	3152 WILLARD AV, RSMD, 91770	636 - G1
WILLARD, FRANCES ELEM	310 E EL SEGUNDO BLVD, COMP, 90222	734 - J1
WILLIAMS, DAN T ELEM	2444 DEL MAR AV, RSMD, 91770	636 - E3
WILLIAMS ELEM	13434 YUKON AV, HAW, 90250	733 - F2
WILLIAMS ELEM	301 S LORAINE AV, GLDR, 91741	569 - G6
WILLIAMS ELEM	6144 CLARK AV, LKWD, 90712	766 - B1
WILLIAMS ELEM	7530 ARNETT ST, DWNY, 90241	705 - J4
WILLOWBROOK MID	2602 N WILMINGTON AV, COMP, 90222	734 - G2
WILLOW ELEM	11733 205TH ST, LKWD, 90715	766 - H4
WILLOW ELEM	1427 WILLOW AV, GLDR, 91740	599 - H1
WILLOW ELEM	29026 LARO DR, AGRH, 91301	558 - A4
WILLOWS COMM, THE	8509 HIGUERA ST, CULC, 90232	672 - J1
WILMINGTON CHRISTIAN ELEM	24919 S AVALON BLVD, Wilm, 90744	794 - E3
WILMINGTON MID	1700 GULF AV, Wilm, 90744	794 - D4
WILMINGTON PARK ELEM	1140 MAHAR AV, Wilm, 90744	794 - G5
WILSHIRE CREST ELEM	5241 W OLYMPIC BLVD, LA, 90036	633 - D3
WILSHIRE PARK ELEM	4063 INGRAHAM ST, LA, 90005	633 - G3
WILSONA ELEM	41625 170TH ST E, LACo, 93535	4109 - G6
WILSON ELEM	11700 SCHOOL ST, LYN, 90262	735 - B1
WILSON ELEM	8317 E SHEFFIELD RD, LACo, 91775	596 - F1
WILSON HIGH	16455 WEDGEWORTH DR, HacH, 91745	678 - E3
WILSON HIGH	4500 MULTNOMAH ST, LA, 90032	635 - D1
WILSON MID	300 S MADRE ST, PAS, 91107	566 - G5
WILSON, WOODROW HIGH	4400 E 10TH ST, LBCH, 90804	796 - A6
WILSON, WOODROW MID	1221 MONTEREY RD, GLDL, 91206	564 - G3
WILTON PLACE ELEM	745 S WILTON PL, LA, 90005	633 - G3
WINDSOR HILLS MAGNET ELEM	5215 OVERDALE DR, LACo, 90043	673 - C5
WINDWARD HIGH	11350 PALMS BLVD, LA, 90066	672 - D2
WINDWARD MID	11350 PALMS BLVD, LA, 90066	672 - D2
WING LANE ELEM	16605 WING LN, LACo, 91744	638 - G6
WINNETKA AVENUE ELEM	8240 WINNETKA AV, Win, 91306	530 - E2
WINTER GARDENS ELEM	1277 CLELA AV, ELA, 90022	675 - G1
WIRTZ ELEM	8538 CONTRERAS ST, PRM, 90723	735 - J3
WISE, STEPHEN S TEMPLE DAY	15500 STEPHEN S WISE DR, BelA, 90077	591 - H1
WISE, STEPHEN S TEMPLE MID	16190 MULHOLLAND DR, BelA, 90077	591 - H1
WITTMAN ELEM	16801 YVETTE AV, CRTS, 90703	737 - A6
WONDERLAND AVENUE	8510 WONDERLAND AV, LA, 90046	592 - J2
WONDERLAND	10440 ARTESIA BLVD, BLF, 90706	736 - D7
WOODCREST ELEM	1151 W 109TH ST, LACo, 90044	704 - A5
WOODCREST NAZARENE CHRISTIAN	10936 S NORMANDIE AV, LACo, 90044	703 - J6
WOODCREST	6043 TAMPA AV, Tarz, 91356	560 - G1
WOODEN HIGH	18741 ELKWOOD ST, Res, 91335	530 - H3
WOOD, HOWARD ELEM	2250 W 235TH ST, TOR, 90501	793 - G2
WOODLAKE AVENUE ELEM	23231 HATTERAS ST, WdHl, 91367	559 - G1
WOODLAND HILLS ELEM	22201 SAN MIGUEL ST, WdHl, 91364	559 - J4
WOODLAND HILLS PRIVATE ELEM	22555 OXNARD ST, WdHl, 91367	559 - H1
WOODLAWN AVENUE ELEM	6314 WOODLAWN AV, BELL, 90201	675 - E7
WOODRUFF ELEM	15332 EUCALYPTUS AV, BLF, 90706	736 - C4
WOODWORTH, CLYDE ELEM	3200 W 104TH ST, ING, 90303	703 - F5
WORKMAN AVENUE ELEM	1941 E WORKMAN AV, WCOV, 91791	598 - J7
WORKMAN ELEM	16000 WORKMAN ST, LPUE, 91744	638 - E7
WORKMAN HIGH	16303 TEMPLE AV, INDS, 91744	638 - F6
WORTHINGTON ELEM	11101 YUKON AV, ING, 90303	703 - E6
WRIGHT, ARTHUR E MID	4029 N LAS VIRGENES RD, CALB, 91302	558 - H7
WRIGHT ELEM	11317 MCGIRK AV, ELMN, 91732	597 - E5
WRIGHT MID	6550 W 80TH ST, Wch, 90045	702 - F2
WRIGHTWOOD ELEM (SEE PAGE 4651)	1175 STATE HWY 2, SBdC, 92397	4652 - C2
YAAKOV, BAIS FOR GIRLS	7353 BEVERLY BLVD, LA, 90036	593 - C7
YBARRA ELEM	1300 BREA CANYON CTO, LACo, 91789	679 - D4
YERBA BUENA ELEM	5844 LARBOARD LN, AGRH, 91301	557 - G4
YESHIVA RAV ISACSOHN ACADEMY	540 N LA BREA AV, LA, 90036	593 - D7
YESHIVA UNIV OF LA HS-BOYS	9760 W PICO BLVD, LA, 90035	632 - G4
YNEZ ELEM	120 S YNEZ AV, MONP, 91754	636 - B2

FEATURE NAME Address City, ZIP Code	PAGE-GRID
YORBA ELEM 250 W LA VERNE AV, POM, 91768	600 - J5
YORBITA ELEM 520 VIDALIA AV, LACo, 91744	678 - J2
YORKDALE ELEM 5657 MERIDIAN ST, HiPk, 90042	595 - C1
YORK ELEM 11838 YORK AV, HAW, 90250	703 - D7
YUCCA ELEM 38440 2ND ST E, PMDL, 93550	4196 - A7
YUKON ELEM 17815 YUKON AV, TOR, 90504	763 - E1
ZION LUTHERAN 301 N ISABEL ST, GLDL, 91206	564 - F4

SHOPPING CENTERS

FEATURE NAME Address City, ZIP Code	PAGE-GRID
AMERICANA AT BRAND, THE BRAND BLVD, GLDL, 91204	564 - E5
AMERIGE HEIGHTS TOWN CTR MALVERN AV & N GILBERT ST, FUL, 92833	738 - C6
ANTELOPE VALLEY MALL RANCHO VISTA BLVD & 10TH ST W, PMDL, 93551	4195 - F4
AVENUE OF THE PENINSULA, THE INDIAN PEAK RD & CROSSFIELD DR, RHE, 90274	793 - B7
BALDWIN HILLS CRENSHAW PLAZA 3650 W MARTIN L KING JR BL, LA, 90008	673 - E3
BEVERLY CTR 8500 BEVERLY BLVD, LA, 90048	632 - J1
BREA MALL E IMPERIAL HWY & STATE COL BL, BREA, 92821	709 - C7
BUENA PARK DOWNTOWN STANTON AV & LA PALMA AV, BPK, 90620	767 - J3
BURBANK EMPIRE CTR EMPIRE AV & VICTORY PL, BURB, 91504	533 - E6
CANYON PLAZA CTR 19186 LAUREL CANYON DR, SunV, 91352	532 - F1
CERRITOS TOWNE CTR 12731 TOWNE CENTER DR, CRTS, 90703	737 - A7
CHINO TOWNE CTR PHILADELPHIA ST & CENTRAL AV, CHNO, 91710	641 - G5
CITADEL OUTLETS, THE 100 CITADEL DR, CMRC, 90040	675 - H3
CITY PLACE LONG BEACH 275 E 4TH ST, LBCH, 90802	795 - D7
CULVER CTR 3800 CULVER CTR, CULC, 90232	672 - F2
DEL AMO FASHION CTR CARSON ST & HAWTHORNE BLVD, TOR, 90503	763 - D6
FALLBROOK MALL 6633 FALLBROOK AV, CanP, 91307	529 - G6
FASHION SQUARE 14006 RIVERSIDE DR, Shrm, 91423	562 - B4
GATEWAY PLAZA CTR 13350 TELEGRAPH RD, SFSP, 90670	707 - B5
GLENDALE GALLERIA S CENTRAL AV & W BROADWAY, GLDL, 91210	564 - D5
GROVE, THE 6333 W GROVE ST, LA, 90036	633 - B1
HASTINGS RANCH PLAZA 3811 E FOOTHILL BLVD, PAS, 91107	566 - H4
HOLLYWOOD & HIGHLAND 6834 HOLLYWOOD BLVD, Hlwd, 90028	593 - D4
HUNTINGTON OAKS CTR 1321 S MAYFLOWER AV, MNRO, 91016	567 - F5
LA HABRA WESTRIDGE PLAZA S BEACH BLVD & W IMPERIAL HWY, LHB, 90631	738 - C1
LAKEWOOD CTR LAKEWOOD BLVD & DEL AMO BLVD, LKWD, 90712	766 - A3
LANCASTER COMMERCE CTR 1200 AVE K ST, LAN, 93534	4105 - G2
LAUREL PLAZA 6100 LAUREL CANYON BLVD, NHol, 91606	532 - G7
LONG BEACH TOWNE CTR E CARSON ST & I-605, LBCH, 90808	766 - G6
LOS ALTOS MARKET CTR 2100 N BELLFLOWER BLVD, LBCH, 90815	796 - C3
LOS CERRITOS CTR 239 LOS CERRITOS CTR, CRTS, 90703	766 - F1
MANHATTAN VILLAGE 3200 N SEPULVEDA BLVD, MANB, 90266	732 - H4
MARKETPLACE AT PALMDALE 10TH W, PMDL, 93551	4195 - G5
MEDIA CITY CTR E MAGNOLIA BL & N SAN FERNAN, BURB, 91502	533 - G6
MONTCLAIR PLAZA 5060 MONTCLAIR PLAZA LN, MTCL, 91763	601 - F4
MONTEBELLO TOWN CTR PARAMOUNT BLVD & POMONA FRWY, MTBL, 90640	636 - G6
NORTHRIDGE FASHION CTR 9301 TAMPA AV, Nor, 91324	500 - F6
PADDISON SQUARE 12419 NORWALK BLVD, NRWK, 90650	706 - H7
PANORAMA MALL ROSCOE BL & VAN NUYS BL, PanC, 91402	531 - J1
PASEO COLORADO E COLORADO BL & LOS ROBLES AV, PAS, 91101	565 - H5
PICO RIVERA TOWNE CTR 8770 WASHINGTON BLVD, PRV, 90660	676 - E6
PORTER RANCH TOWN CTR 19800 RINALDI ST, Nor, 91326	500 - E1
PUENTE HILLS MALL AZUSA AV & COLIMA RD, INDS, 91748	678 - G4
SANTA MONICA PLACE 395 SANTA MONICA BLVD, SMCA, 90401	671 - E2
SHOPS ON LAKE AVENUE, THE 455 S LAKE AV, PAS, 91101	566 - A5
SOUTH BAY GALLERIA ARTESIA BLVD & HAWTHORNE BLVD, RBCH, 90278	763 - C1
SOUTHBAY PAVILION AT CARSON 20700 S AVALON BLVD, CRSN, 90746	764 - E4
STONEWOOD CTR 9066 STONEWOOD ST, DWNY, 90241	706 - C5
VALENCIA MARKETPLACE 25400 THE OLD RD, StvR, 91381	4550 - D6
VALENCIA TOWN CTR 24201 VALENCIA BLVD, SCTA, 91355	4550 - F3
VALLEY CENTRAL SHOPPING CTR 44765 VALLEY CENTRAL ST, LAN, 93536	4015 - D6
VALLEY PLAZA 6329 LAUREL CANYON BLVD, NHol, 91606	532 - G6
WESTFIELD FASHION SQUARE 14006 RIVERSIDE DR, Shrm, 91423	562 - C4
WESTFIELD SHOPPINGTOWN CENTURY-CITY 10250 SANTA MONICA BLVD, CenC, 90067	632 - D3
WESTFIELD SHOPPINGTOWN EAGLE-ROCK 2700 COLORADO BLVD, Eagl, 90041	564 - H5
WESTFIELD SHOPPINGTOWN FOX-HILLS 294 FOX HILLS DR, CULC, 90230	672 - G6
WESTFIELD SHOPPINGTOWN-PROMENADE 6100 TOPANGA CANYON BLVD, WdHl, 91367	530 - A7
WESTFIELD SHOPPINGTOWN SANTA-ANITA 400 S BALDWIN AV, ARCD, 91007	567 - A5
WESTFIELD SHOPPINGTOWN TOPANGA 6600 TOPANGA CANYON BLVD, CanP, 91303	530 - A7
WESTFIELD SHOPPINGTOWN WEST-COVINA 112 PLAZA DR, WCOV, 91790	598 - F7
WESTFIELD VALENCIA TOWN CTR 24201 VALENCIA BLVD, SCTA, 91355	4550 - E3
WESTSIDE PAVILION 10800 W PICO BLVD, LA, 90064	632 - D6
WHITTWOOD TOWN CTR 15601 WHITTWOOD PKWY, WHIT, 90603	707 - H4

TRANSPORTATION

FEATURE NAME	PAGE-GRID
AMTRAK BURBANK-BOB HOPE, BURB	533 - C5
AMTRAK CHATSWORTH STA, Chat	500 - A5
AMTRAK GLENDALE STA, GLDL	594 - E1
AMTRAK POMONA STA, POM	640 - J1
AMTRAK STA - FULLERTON, FUL	738 - H7
AMTRAK UNION STA, LA	634 - G3
AMTRAK VAN NUYS STA, VanN	532 - A3
ARTESIA TRANSIT CTR, LA	764 - B1
AZUSA RAILROAD STA, AZU	568 - J5
CAL STATE LA BUS STA, LA	635 - F2
CARSON ST BUS STA, CRSN	764 - B6
CATALINA AIR & SEA TERMINAL, - SPed	824 - D3
CATALINA EXPRESS, LBCH	825 - C1
CATALINA EXPRESS - LONG BEACH, - LBCH	825 - D3
CATALINA EXPRESS - SAN PEDRO, - SPed	824 - D3
CLAREMONT TRANSCENTER, CLAR	601 - D4
EL MONTE BUS STA, ELMN	597 - B7
GATEWAY TRANSIT CTR, LA	634 - H3
GLENDALE TRANSPORTATION CTR, - GLDL	594 - E1
GREYHOUND BUS STA, NHol	562 - J2
GREYHOUND BUS STA, NRWK	736 - H2
GREYHOUND BUS STA, LA	634 - J7
GREYHOUND BUS STA, SMCA	671 - E2
GREYHOUND BUS STA, SFER	482 - A7
GREYHOUND BUS STA, LBCH	795 - E5
GREYHOUND BUS STA, Hlwd	593 - F4
GREYHOUND BUS STA, LA	634 - G6
GREYHOUND BUS STA, COMP	734 - J4
GREYHOUND BUS STA, ELMN	597 - B7
GREYHOUND BUS STA, GLDL	594 - E1
GREYHOUND BUS STA, LAN	4015 - H6
GREYHOUND BUS STA, HNTP	674 - J6
GREYHOUND BUS STA, PAS	566 - A4
GREYHOUND BUS STA, CLAR	601 - D5
HARBOR TRANSITWAY 37TH ST STA, - LA	674 - B1
HARBOR TRANSITWAY MANCHESTER-STA, LA	704 - B2
HARBOR TRANSITWAY ROSECRANS-STA, LA	734 - B3
HARBOR TRANSITWAY SLAUSON STA, - LA	674 - B5
HARBOR TRANSITWAY STA, LA	704 - B7
INGLEWOOD BUS STA, ING	703 - C3
LA CO USC MED CTR BUS STA, - Boyl	635 - A3
LAX CITY BUS CTR, Wch	702 - H4
MLK JR TRANSIT CTR, COMP	734 - J4
METRO BLUE LINE 1ST ST STA, - LBCH	825 - D1
METRO BLUE LINE 5TH ST STA, - LBCH	795 - E7
METRO BLUE LINE 7TH ST/METRO-CTR STA, LA	634 - E4
METRO BLUE LINE 103RD ST STA, - Wats	704 - G5
METRO BLUE LINE ANAHEIM STA, - LBCH	795 - E6
METRO BLUE LINE ARTESIA STA, - COMP	734 - J7
METRO BLUE LINE COMPTON STA, - COMP	734 - J4
METRO BLUE LINE DEL AMO STA, - RDom	765 - B4
METRO BLUE LINE FIRESTONE STA, - Wats	704 - G2
METRO BLUE LINE FLORENCE STA, - Flor	674 - G7
METRO BLUE LINE GRAND STA, LA	634 - D6
METRO BLUE LINE-IMPERIAL/WILMINGTON STA, Wbrk	704 - H7
METRO BLUE LINE PACIFIC STA, - LBCH	795 - D7
METRO BLUE LINE PCH STA, LBCH	795 - E5
METRO BLUE LINE PICO/CHICK-HEARN STA, LA	634 - D5
METRO BLUE LINE SAN PEDRO STA, - LA	634 - E7
METRO BLUE LINE SLAUSON STA, - Flor	674 - G6
METRO BLUE LINE TRANSIT MALL-STA, LBCH	825 - D1
METRO BLUE LINE VERNON STA, - LA	674 - G3
METRO BLUE LINE WARDLOW STA, - Bxby	795 - D1
METRO BLUE LINE WASHINGTON-STA, LA	674 - G1
METRO BLUE LINE WILLOW STA, - LBCH	795 - D2
METRO GOLD LINE ALLEN STA, - PAS	566 - C4
METRO GOLD LINE CHINATOWN STA, - LA	634 - G2
METRO GOLD LINE DEL MAR STA, - PAS	565 - H5
METRO GOLD LINE FILLMORE STA, - PAS	565 - H6
METRO GOLD LINE HERITAGE-SQUARE STA, LA	595 - A6
METRO GOLD LINE HIGHLAND PK-STA, HiPk	595 - C2
METRO GOLD LINE LAKE STA, PAS	566 - A4
METRO GOLD LINE LNCLN-HTS/CYPRESS, LA	594 - J7
METRO GOLD LINE MEM PK STA, - PAS	565 - H4
METRO GOLD LINE MISSION STA, - SPAS	595 - G2
METRO GOLD LINE SIERRA MADRE-VILLA STA, PAS	566 - G4
METRO GOLD LINE SOUTHWEST MUS-STA, LA	595 - B4
METRO GOLD LINE UNION STA, LA	634 - H3
METRO GREEN LINE AVALON STA, - LA	704 - D7
METRO GREEN LINE AVIATION/LAX-STA, Wch	703 - A7
METRO GREEN LINE CRENSHAW STA, - HAW	703 - F7
METRO GREEN LINE DOUGLAS STA, - ELSG	732 - J3
METRO GREEN LINE EL SEGUNDO-STA, ELSG	732 - J2
METRO GREEN LINE HARBOR FRWY-STA, LA	704 - C7
METRO GREEN LINE HAWTHORNE-STA, Lenx	703 - C6
METRO GREEN LINE IMP/WILM STA, - Wbrk	704 - G7
METRO GREEN LINE LAKEWOOD STA, - DWNY	736 - A2
METRO GREEN LINE LONG BEACH-STA, LYN	705 - B7
METRO GREEN LINE MARIPOSA STA, - ELSG	732 - H1
METRO GREEN LINE NORWALK STA, - NRWK	736 - E1
METRO GREEN LINE REDONDO STA, - HAW	733 - A5
METRO GREEN LINE VERMONT STA, - LA	704 - A7
METROLINK BALDWIN PARK, BALD	598 - C5
METROLINK BUENA PARK, BPK	737 - J6
METROLINK BURBANK, BURB	533 - G7
METROLINK BURBANK-BOB HOPE, - BURB	533 - C5
METROLINK CAL STATE LOS-ANGELES, LA	635 - F2
METROLINK CHATSWORTH, Chat	500 - A5
METROLINK CLAREMONT, CLAR	601 - D4
METROLINK COMMERCE, CMRC	676 - A5
METROLINK COVINA STA, COV	599 - B4
METROLINK DOWNTOWN POMONA, - POM	640 - J2
METROLINK EL MONTE, ELMN	597 - D7
METROLINK FULLERTON, FUL	738 - H7
METROLINK GLENDALE, GLDL	594 - E1
METROLINK INDUSTRY STA, INDS	679 - G2
METROLINK LANCASTER STA, LAN	4015 - H6
METROLINK MONTCLAIR STA, MTCL	601 - F4
METROLINK MONTEBELLO/COMMERCE, - MTBL	676 - C3
METROLINK NEWHALL STA, SCTA	4640 - J1
METROLINK NORTHRIDGE STA, Nor	530 - H1
METROLINK NORWALK/SANTA FE-SPRINGS STA, NRWK	737 - A1
METROLINK POMONA NORTH STA, - POM	600 - J4
METROLINK PRINCESSA STA, SCTA	4551 - G4
METROLINK SANTA CLARITA, SCTA	4551 - A3
METROLINK SUN VALLEY STA, - SunV	532 - J1
METROLINK SYLMAR/SAN FERNANDO, - LA	481 - J6
METROLINK UNION STA, LA	634 - G3
METROLINK VAN NUYS, VanN	532 - A3
METROLINK VINCENT GRADE/ACTON-STA, PMDL	4376 - B5
METRO ORANGE BUSWAY BALBOA-STA, Enc	531 - D7
METRO ORANGE BUSWAY CANOGA-STA, WdHl	530 - B7
METRO ORANGE BUSWAY DE SOTO-STA, CanP	530 - C6
METRO ORANGE BUSWAY LAUREL CYN-STA, LA	562 - G2
METRO ORANGE BUSWAY N-HOLLYWOOD STA, NHol	562 - J2
METRO ORANGE BUSWAY RESEDA-STA, Res	560 - J1
METRO ORANGE BUSWAY SEPULVEDA-STA, VanN	531 - H7
METRO ORANGE BUSWAY TAMPA STA, - Res	530 - G7
METRO ORANGE BUSWAY VALLEY-COLLEGE STA, VanN	562 - D1
METRO ORANGE BUSWAY VAN NUYS-STA, VanN	532 - A7
METRO ORANGE BUSWAY WARNER CTR-STA, WdHl	530 - A7
METRO ORANGE BUSWAY WINNETKA-STA, WdHl	530 - E7
METRO ORANGE BUSWAY WOODLEY-STA, VanN	531 - F7
METRO ORANGE BUSWAY WOODMAN-STA, VanN	532 - C7
METRO RED LINE 7TH ST/METRO-CTR STA, LA	634 - E4
METRO RED LINE CIVIC CTR STA, - LA	634 - F3
METRO RED LINE-HOLLYWOOD/HIGHLAND STA, Hlwd	593 - E4
METRO RED LINE HOLLYWOOD/VINE-STA, Hlwd	593 - F4
METRO RED LINE-HOLLYWOOD/WESTERN STA, LFlz	593 - H4
METRO RED LINE NORTH HOLLYWOOD-STA, NHol	562 - J2
METRO RED LINE PERSHING SQUARE-STA, LA	634 - F4
METRO RED LINE UNION STA, LA	634 - H3
METRO RED LINE UNIVERSAL CITY-STA, Univ	563 - B6
METRO RED LINE VERMONT/BEVERLY-STA, LA	594 - A7
METRO RED LINE VERMONT/SANTA-MONICA STA, LA	594 - A5
METRO RED LINE VERMONT/SUNSET-STA, LFlz	594 - A4
METRO RED LINE-WESTLK/MACARTHUR PK STA, LA	634 - C3
METRO RED LINE-WILSHIRE/NORMANDIE STA, LA	633 - J2
METRO RED LINE-WILSHIRE/VERMONT STA, LA	634 - A2
METRO RED LINE-WILSHIRE/WESTERN STA, LA	633 - H2
MONTCLAIR TRANSCENTER, MTCL	601 - G3
NORTH LONG BEACH BUS STA, NLB	735 - E7
PACIFIC COAST HWY BUS STA, - Wilm	794 - C5
PALMDALE TRANSPORTATION CTR, - PMDL	4196 - A6
SAN FERNANDO BUS STA, SFER	482 - A7
UNION STA, LA	634 - G3
WATERFRONT RED CAR LINE -- DOWNTOWN STA, SPed	824 - C5
WATERFRONT RED CAR LINE -- MARINA STA, SPed	824 - C7
WATERFRONT RED CAR LINE -- PORTS O CALL, SPed	824 - C6
WATERFRONT RED CAR LINE -- WORLD CRUISE, SPed	824 - C4

VISITOR INFORMATION

FEATURE NAME Address City, ZIP Code	PAGE-GRID
BEVERLY HILLS VISITORS BUREAU 239 S BEVERLY DR, BHLS, 90212	632 - G2
BUENA PARK VISITOR BUREAU BEACH BLVD & LA PALMA AV, BPK, 90620	767 - H3
CATALINA ISLAND VISITORS BUREAU CRESCENT AV & CATALINA AV, AVA, 90704	5923 - H4
GRIFFITH PK VISITORS CTR 4730 CRYSTAL SPRINGS DR, LFlz, 90027	564 - B7
LOS ANGELES CONV & VISITORS-BUREA 333 S HOPE ST, LA, 90071	634 - E3
SANTA MONICA VISITOR INFO CTR 1400 OCEAN AV, SMCA, 90401	671 - E2
WHITTIER NARROWS VISITORS CTR 750 SANTA ANITA AV, LACo, 91733	637 - A6

CUT ALONG DOTTED LINE

The Thomas Guide®

Thank you for purchasing this Rand McNally Thomas Guide! We value your comments and suggestions.

Please help us serve you better by completing this postage-paid reply card.
This information is for internal use ONLY and will not be distributed or sold to any external third party.

Missing pages? Maybe not... Please refer to the "Using Your Street Guide" page for further explanation.

Thomas Guide Title: Los Angeles County **ISBN-13# 978-0-5288-6711-8** **MKT: LAO**

Today's Date: __________ Gender: ☐M ☐F Age Group: ☐18-24 ☐25-31 ☐32-40 ☐41-50 ☐51-64 ☐65+

1. What type of industry do you work in?
   ☐Real Estate ☐Trucking ☐Delivery ☐Construction ☐Utilities ☐Government
   ☐Retail ☐Sales ☐Transportation ☐Landscape ☐Service & Repair
   ☐Courier ☐Automotive ☐Insurance ☐Medical ☐Police/Fire/First Response
   ☐Other, please specify: __________
2. What type of job do you have in this industry? __________
3. Where did you purchase this Thomas Guide? (store name & city) __________
4. Why did you purchase this Thomas Guide? __________
5. How often do you purchase an updated Thomas Guide? ☐Annually ☐2 yrs. ☐3-5 yrs. ☐Other: __________
6. Where do you use it? ☐Primarily in the car ☐Primarily in the office ☐Primarily at home ☐Other: __________
7. How do you use it? ☐Exclusively for business ☐Primarily for business but also for personal or leisure use
   ☐Both work and personal evenly ☐Primarily for personal use ☐Exclusively for personal use
8. What do you use your Thomas Guide for?
   ☐Find Addresses ☐In-route navigation ☐Planning routes ☐Other: __________
   Find points of interest: ☐Schools ☐Parks ☐Buildings ☐Shopping Centers ☐Other: __________
9. How often do you use it? ☐Daily ☐Weekly ☐Monthly ☐Other: __________
10. Do you use the internet for maps and/or directions? ☐Yes ☐No
11. How often do you use the internet for directions? ☐Daily ☐Weekly ☐Monthly ☐Other: __________
12. Do you use any of the following mapping products in addition to your Thomas Guide?
    ☐Folded paper maps ☐Folded laminated maps ☐Wall maps ☐GPS ☐PDA ☐In-car navigation ☐Phone maps
13. What features, if any, would you like to see added to your Thomas Guide? __________
14. What features or information do you find most useful in your Rand McNally Thomas Guide? (please specify)
    ____
15. Please provide any additional comments or suggestions you have. __________

We strive to provide you with the most current updated information available if you know of a map correction, please notify us here.

Where is the correction? Map Page #: __________ Grid #: __________ Index Page #: __________

Nature of the correction: ☐Street name missing ☐Street name misspelled ☐Street information incorrect
☐Incorrect location for point of interest ☐Index error ☐Other: __________

Detail: __________

I would like to receive information about updated editions and special offers from Rand McNally
☐via e-mail E-mail address: __________
☐via postal mail
Your Name: __________ Company (if used for work): __________
Address: __________ City/State/ZIP: __________

Thank you for your time and help. We are working to serve you better.
This information is for internal use ONLY and will not be distributed or sold to any external third party.

CUT ALONG DOTTED LINE

TG-noCD.06

TAPE SHUT

TAPE SHUT

get directions at

randmcnally.com

CUT ALONG DOTTED LINE

2ND FOLD LINE

NO POSTAGE
NECESSARY
IF MAILED
IN THE
UNITED STATES

BUSINESS REPLY MAIL

FIRST-CLASS MAIL PERMIT NO. 388 CHICAGO IL

POSTAGE WILL BE PAID BY ADDRESSEE

RAND MCNALLY
CONSUMER AFFAIRS
PO BOX 7600
CHICAGO IL 60680-9915

1ST FOLD LINE

CUT ALONG DOTTED LINE

SGTG_07

The Thomas Guide®

Ventura County

street guide

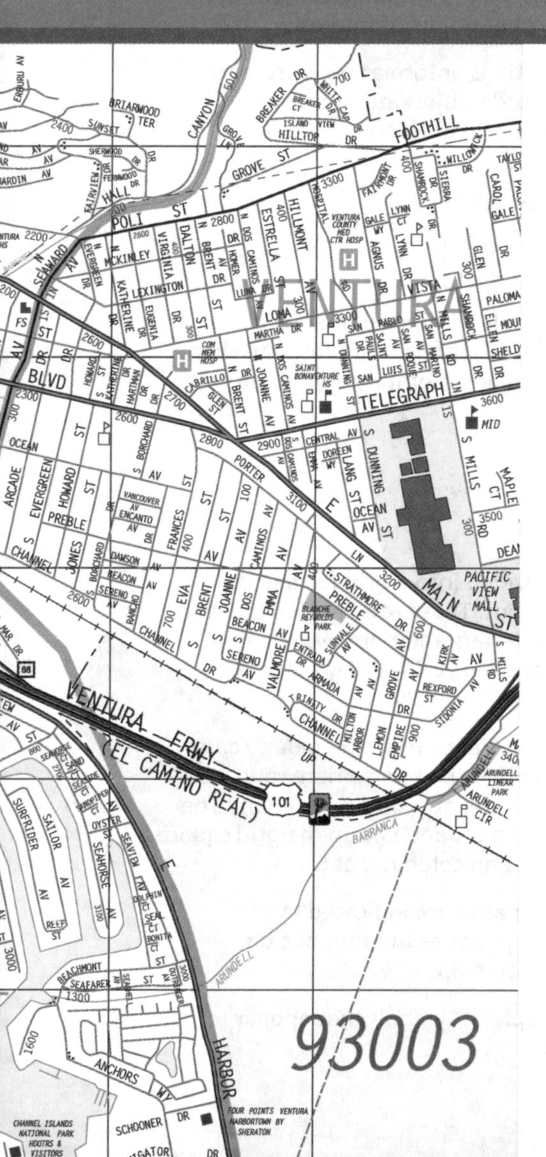

Contents

Introduction

Using Your Street Guide	B
Legend	C
PageFinder™ Map	D

Maps

Downtown Map	E
Street Guide Arterial Maps	366-387
Street Guide Detail Maps	441-625

Lists and Indexes

Cities & Communities Index	626
List of Abbreviations	627
Street Index and Points of Interest Index	628
Comment Card	Last page

RAND McNALLY

Rand McNally Consumer Affairs
P.O. Box 7600
Chicago, IL 60680-9915
randmcnally.com
For comments or suggestions, please call
(800) 777-MAPS (-6277)
or email us at:
consumeraffairs@randmcnally.com

Using Your Street Guide

PageFinder™ Map

The PageFinder™ Map

- Turn to the PageFinder™ Map. Each of the small squares outlined on this map represents a different map page in the Street Guide.
- Locate the specific part of the Street Guide coverage area that you're interested in.
- Note the appropriate map page number.
- Turn to that map page.

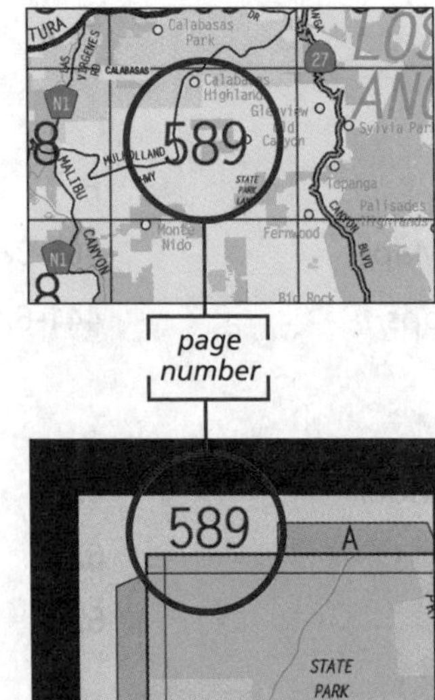

missing pages?

Please note that map pages in this book are numbered according to the PageFinder™ Map. For this reason, your book may look as though it is missing pages. For example, one page might contain map number 15 while the following page contains map number 25.

Use the PageFinder™ Map for fast and easy navigation through your Street Guide.

The Index

- The Street Guide includes separate indexes for streets, schools, parks, shopping centers, golf courses, and other points of interest.
- In the street listings, information is presented in the following order: block number, city, ZIP code, page number, and grid reference

STREET Block	City	ZIP	Pg-Grid
BROADWAY DR			
4400	SCH	60646	533-B6
6200	PLA	61644	532-D2
7800	WCH	60656	532-A3

- A grid reference is a letter-number combination (B6 for example) that tells you precisely where to find a particular street (or point of interest) on a map.

The Maps

- Each map is divided into a grid formed by rows and columns. These rows and columns correspond to letters and numbers running horizontally and vertically along the edges of each map.
- To use a grid reference from the index, search horizontally within the appropriate row and vertically within the appropriate column. The destination can be found within the grid square where the row and column meet.
- Adjacent map pages are indicated by red numbers that appear at the top, bottom, and sides of each map.
- The legend explains symbols that appear on the maps.

Legend

Freeway
Interchange/ramp
Highway
Primary road
Secondary road
Minor road
Restricted road
Alley
Unpaved road
Tunnel
Toll road
High occupancy veh. lane
Stacked multiple roadways
Proposed road
Proposed freeway
Freeway under construction
One-way road

Two-way road
Trail, walkway
Stairs
Railroad
Rapid transit
Rapid transit, underground
Ferry
City boundary
County boundary
State boundary
International boundary
Military base, Indian res.
Township, range, rancho
Section corner
River, creek, shoreline
98607 ZIP code boundary, ZIP code
A Street list marker

5 Interstate
5 Interstate (Business)
3 U.S. highway
1 4 8 9 State highways
Carpool lane
Street name continuation
Street name change
Station (train, bus)
Building (see List of Abbr. page)
Building footprint
Public elementary school
Public high school
Private elementary school
Private high school
Fire station

Library
Mission
Campground
H Hospital
Mountain
Boat Launch
Gate, locks, barricades
Lighthouse
Major shopping center
Dry lake, beach
Dam
Intermittent lake, marsh
29 Exit number

PageFinder™ Map

PageFinder™ Map
U.S. Patent No. 5,419,586
Canadian Patent No. 2,116,425
Patente Mexicana No. 188186

VENTURA CO.

366 367 386 387

441 442
450 451 452 453 454 455 456 457 458
459 460 461 462 463 464 465 466 467
469 470 471 472 473 474 475 476 477 478 479
490 491 492 493 494 495 496 497 498 499
521 522 523 524 525 526 527 528 529
551 552 553 554 555 556 557 558
583 584 585 586
625

LOS PADRES NATIONAL FOREST
ANGELES NATIONAL FOREST
SANTA BARBARA CO
VENTURA CO
LOS ANGELES CO
SESPE CONDOR PRESERVE
GIBRALTAR RESERVOIR
LAKE CASITAS
LAKE PIRU
PYRAMID LAKE
CASTAIC LAKE
SANTA BARBARA
HOPE RANCH
SUMMERLAND
SANDYLAND
CARPINTERIA
LA CONCHITA
SEACLIFF
FARIA BEACH
SOLIMAR BEACH
WHEELER SPRINGS
MEINERS OAKS
OJAI
MIRA MONTE
OAK VIEW
CASITAS SPRINGS
FOSTER PARK
VENTURA
PIERPONT BAY
MONTALVO
SATICOY
SANTA PAULA
FILLMORE
NORTH FILLMORE
BARDSDALE
PIRU
CASTAIC
VAL VERDE PARK
VALENCIA
SANTA CLARITA
NEWHALL
SAUGUS
BOUQUET CANYON
FORREST PARK
MINT CANYON
DEL VALLE
PICO
STEVENSON RANCH
MOORPARK
SOMIS
SANTA ROSA
MOORPARK HOME ACRES
SIMI VALLEY
SANTA SUSANA
CHATSWORTH
PORTER RANCH
MISSION HILLS
SAN FERNANDO
GRANADA HILLS
NORTH HILLS
ARLETA
NORTHRIDGE
PANORAMA CITY
WINNETKA
RESEDA
VAN NUYS
CANOGA PARK
WEST HILLS
BELL CANYON
HIDDEN HILLS
WARNER CTR
WOODLAND HILLS
TARZANA
ENCINO
SHERMAN OAKS
LOS ANGELES
EL RIO
CAMARILLO
LEISURE VILLAGE
NEWBURY PARK
OAK PARK
THOUSAND OAKS
OAKBROOK VILLAGE
AGOURA HILLS
AGOURA
CALABASAS
CALABASAS HIGHLANDS
WESTLAKE VILLAGE
LAKE SHERWOOD
OXNARD
COLONIA
HOLLYWOOD BEACH
HOLLYWOOD-BY-THE-SEA
SILVER STRAND
PORT HUENEME
NAVAL BASE VENTURA COUNTY
POINT MUGU
POINT MUGU STATE PARK
LEO CARRILLO STATE PARK
MALIBU CREEK STATE PARK
ZUMA TRANCAS CANYONS
EL NIDO
MALIBU
MALIBU BOWL
MALIBU LAKE
MALIBU PARK
POINT DUME
TOPANGA
TOPANGA STATE PARK
MONTE NIDO
FERNWOOD
OLD CANYON
GLENVIEW
SYLVIA PARK
PALISADES HIGHLANDS
BIG ROCK
PACIFIC PALISADES
BRENTWOOD
BEVERLY GLEN
BEL AIR ESTATES
SANTA MONICA
OCEAN PARK
VENICE
MARINA DEL REY
PLAYA DEL REY
SOUTH COAST
CHANNEL ISLANDS NATIONAL PARK
SANTA CRUZ ISLAND
ANACAPA ISLAND
PACIFIC OCEAN

RONALD REAGAN FWY
GOLDEN STATE FWY
VENTURA FWY
SANTA PAULA FWY
PACIFIC COAST HWY
TELEGRAPH RD
SOUTH MOUNTAIN RD
GUIBERSON RD
FOOTHILL RD
LA LOMA AV
POTRERO RD
OLD RIDGE ROUTE
SAN FRANCISQUITO CANYON RD
BOUQUET CANYON
HUGHES RD
GRAND AV
SULPHUR MOUNTAIN
LAS POSAS RD
LEWIS RD
KANAN RD
DECKER RD
ENCINAL CYN RD
MULHOLLAND HWY
SUNSET BL
DE SOTO AV

0 10 20 miles 1 in. = 8 mi.

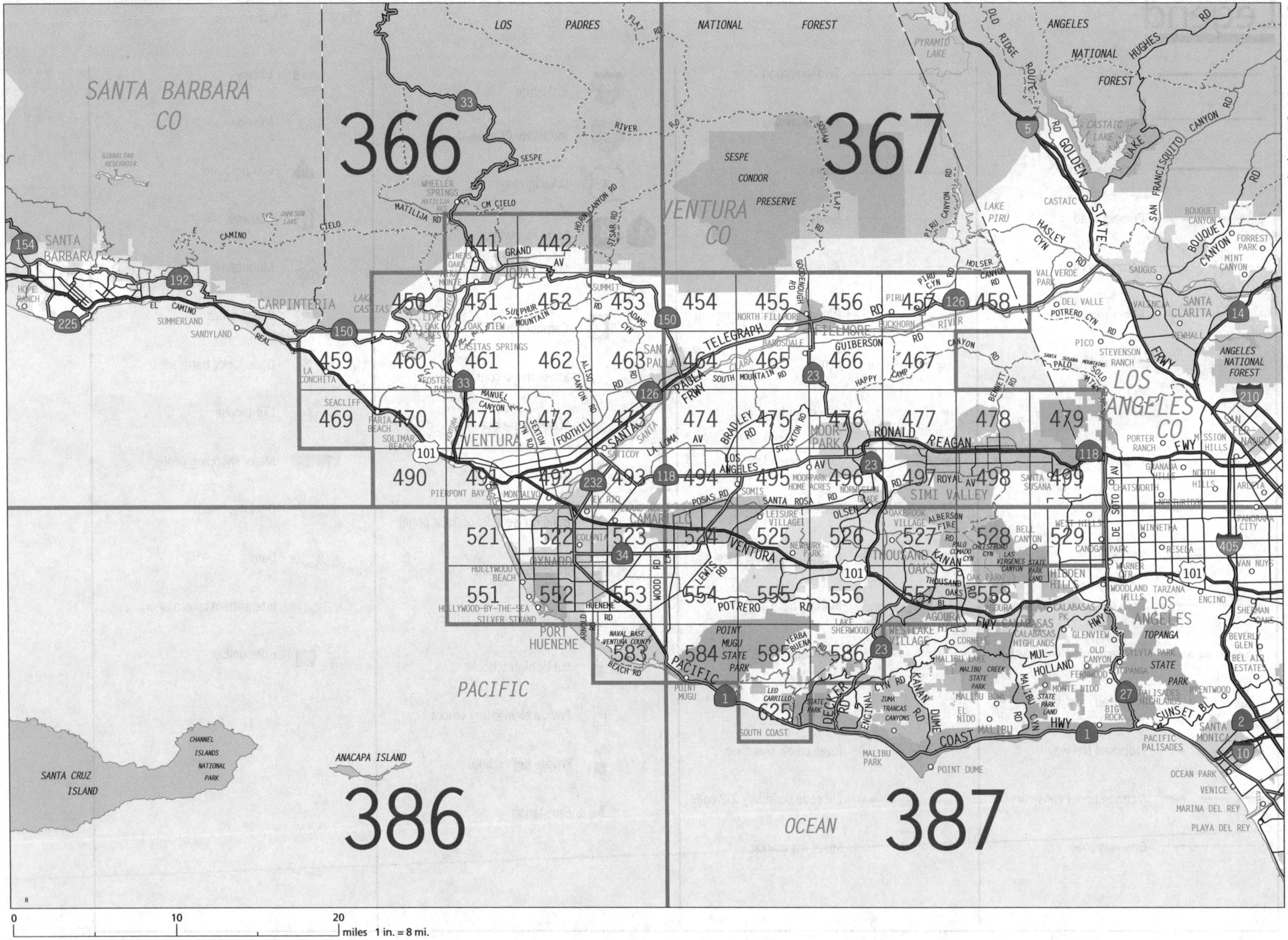

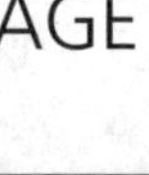

Downtown Ventura

Points of Interest

No.	Point of Interest	Grid
1	A J Comstock Fire Museum	C2
2	Albinger Archaeological Museum	C2
3	Amtrak Station	C2
4	California Street Plaza	D2
5	Channel Islands National Park HQ & Visitors Center	G7
6	Crowne Plaza Ventura Beach	C2
7	E P Foster Library	D2
8	Father Serra Cross	C1
9	Greyhound Bus Station	C2
10	Main Post Office	D2
11	Marriott Hotel	F4
12	Mission San Buenaventura	C2
13	Museum of Ventura County	C2
14	Ortega Adobe	B1
15	Ventura City Hall	D1
16	Ventura Concert Theater	D2
17	Ventura County Fairgrounds	B3
18	Ventura County Historical Courthouse	D1
19	Ventura Historical Pier	D3
20	Visitors Bureau	C2

SEE 491 MAP

SEE 490 MAP

SEE 491 MAP

VENTURA

PACIFIC OCEAN

PIERPONT BAY

CALIFORNIA COASTAL NATIONAL MONUMENT

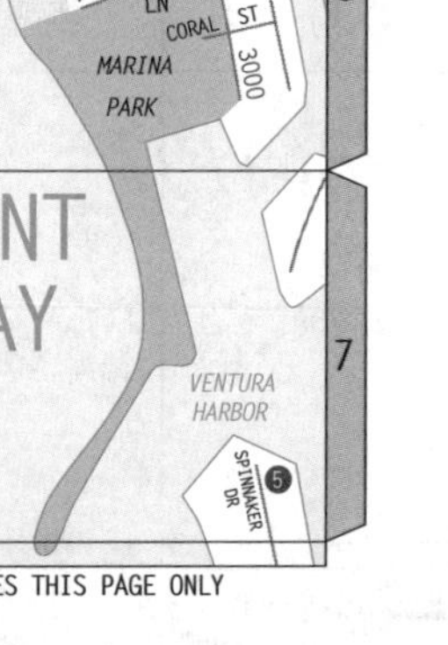

Map Scale

0 660 1320 1980 2640 Feet

0 .125 .25 .375 .5 Miles

SEE 491 MAP

GRID REFERENCES THIS PAGE ONLY

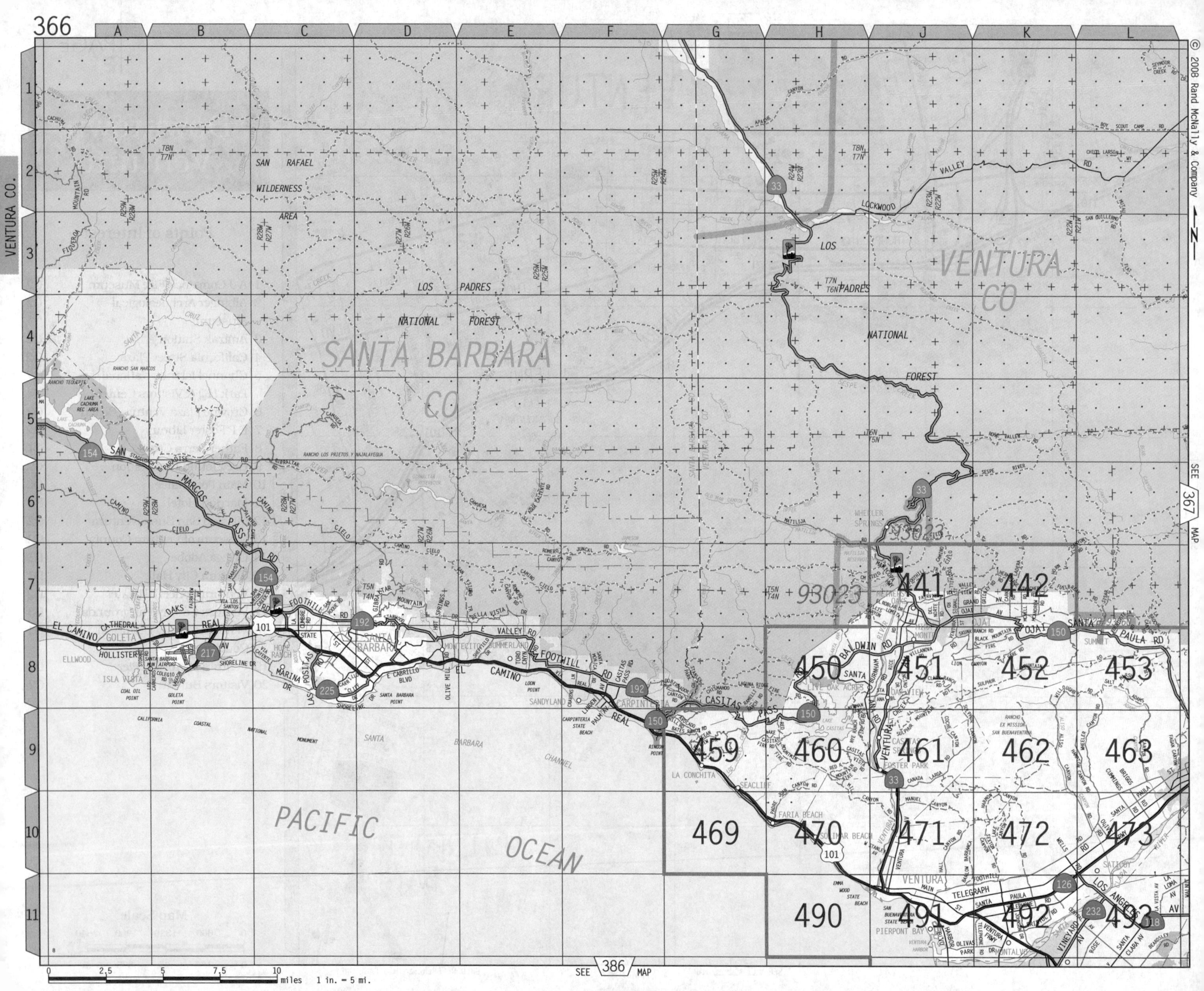
VENTURA CO.
SAN RAFAEL
WILDERNESS
AREA
LOS PADRES
NATIONAL FOREST
SANTA BARBARA
CO
VENTURA
CO
PACIFIC
OCEAN
GOLETA
HOLLISTER
ELLWOOD
ISLA VISTA
SANTA BARBARA
MONTECITO
SUMMERLAND
CARPINTERIA
LA CONCHITA
SEACLIFF
FARIA BEACH
VENTURA
PIERPONT BAY
SATICOY
FOSTER PARK
LIVE OAK ACRES
SANDYLAND
EL CAMINO REAL
SAN MARCOS PASS RD
FOOTHILL RD
CASITAS PASS RD
BALDWIN RD
LOCKWOOD VALLEY RD
93023
441
442
450
451
452
453
459
460
461
462
463
469
470
471
472
473
490
491
492
493
SEE 367 MAP
SEE 386 MAP
miles 1 in. = 5 mi.

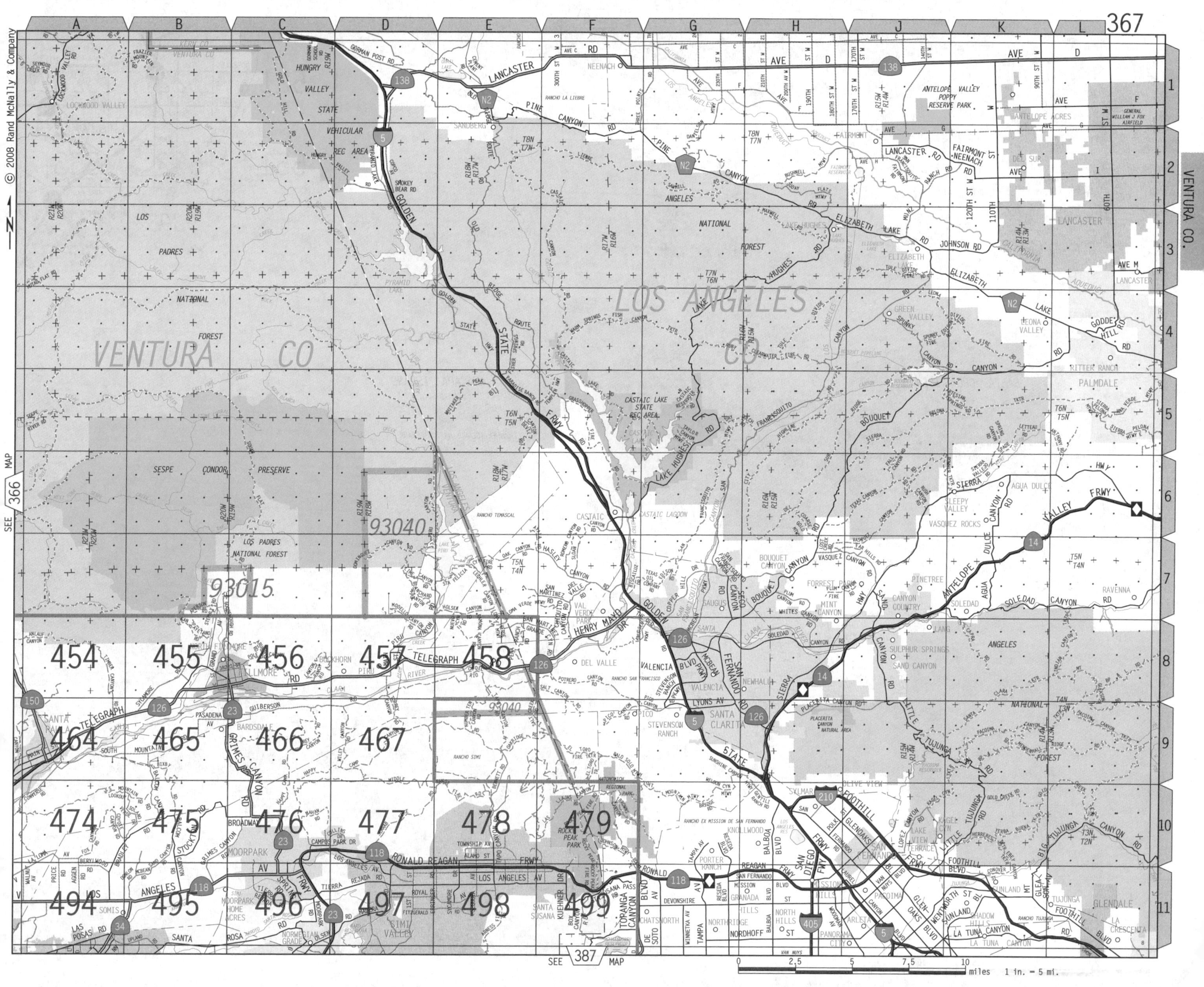
© 2008 Rand McNally & Company
VENTURA CO.
LOS ANGELES CO
VENTURA CO
LOS PADRES NATIONAL FOREST
ANGELES NATIONAL FOREST
SESPE CONDOR PRESERVE
HUNGRY VALLEY STATE VEHICULAR REC AREA
CASTAIC LAKE STATE REC AREA
ANTELOPE VALLEY POPPY RESERVE PARK
GOLDEN STATE FRWY
ANTELOPE VALLEY FRWY
RONALD REAGAN FRWY
SAN DIEGO FRWY
FOOTHILL FRWY
LANCASTER RD
PINE CANYON RD
ELIZABETH LAKE RD
LAKE HUGHES RD
BOUQUET CANYON RD
SIERRA HWY
SOLEDAD CANYON
TELEGRAPH RD
HENRY MAYO DR
LOS ANGELES AV
GRIMES CANYON RD
BIG TUJUNGA CANYON
LITTLE TUJUNGA
NEENACH
SANDBERG
FAIRMONT
ANTELOPE ACRES
DEL SUR
LANCASTER
LEONA VALLEY
PALMDALE
RITTER RANCH
AGUA DULCE
VASQUEZ ROCKS
RAVENNA
CASTAIC
VAL VERDE
SAUGUS
CANYON COUNTRY
SANTA CLARITA
VALENCIA
NEWHALL
STEVENSON RANCH
FILLMORE
PIRU
BARDSDALE
SANTA PAULA
MOORPARK
SIMI VALLEY
SANTA SUSANA
CHATSWORTH
PORTER RANCH
GRANADA HILLS
NORTHRIDGE
MISSION HILLS
SYLMAR
SAN FERNANDO
PACOIMA
ARLETA
PANORAMA CITY
SUNLAND
TUJUNGA
LA CRESCENTA
GLENDALE
93040
93015
454 455 456 457 458
464 465 466 467
474 475 476 477 478 479
494 495 496 497 498 499
SEE 366 MAP
SEE 387 MAP
miles 1 in. = 5 mi.

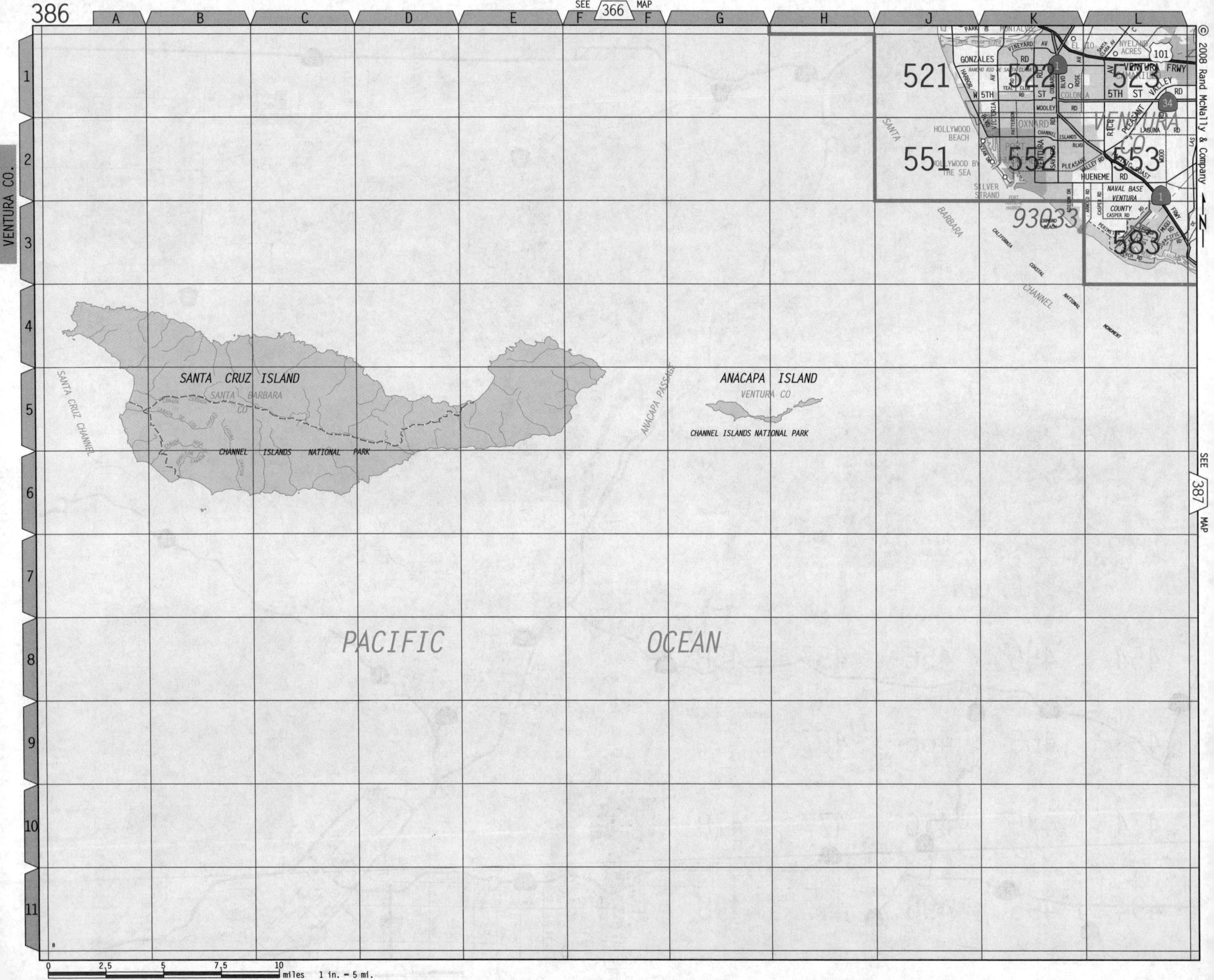
SEE 366 MAP
SEE 387 MAP
VENTURA CO.
SANTA CRUZ ISLAND
SANTA BARBARA CO
CHANNEL ISLANDS NATIONAL PARK
SANTA CRUZ CHANNEL
ANACAPA PASSAGE
ANACAPA ISLAND
VENTURA CO
CHANNEL ISLANDS NATIONAL PARK
PACIFIC OCEAN
SANTA BARBARA CHANNEL
CALIFORNIA COASTAL NATIONAL MONUMENT
521
522
523
551
552
553
583
93033
GONZALES
HOLLYWOOD BEACH
HOLLYWOOD BY THE SEA
SILVER STRAND
OXNARD
HUENEME
NAVAL BASE VENTURA COUNTY
VENTURA FRWY
NYELAND ACRES
EL RIO
COLONIA
VENTURA CO
101
1
34
0 2.5 5 7.5 10 miles 1 in. = 5 mi.

SEE 367 MAP

SEE 386 MAP

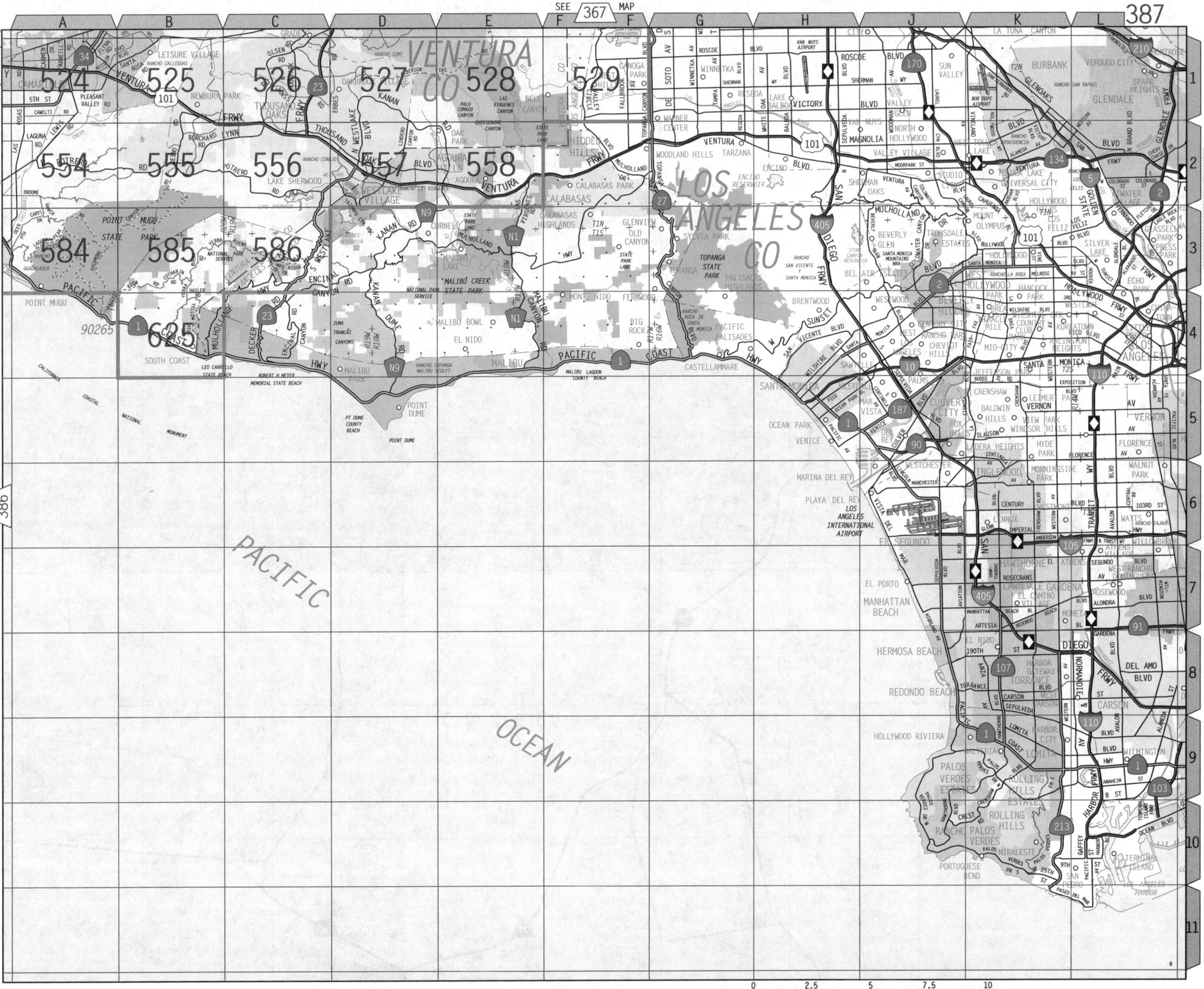

A B C D E F F G H J K L

1 2 3 4 5 6 7 8 9 10 11

VENTURA CO.

VENTURA CO

LOS ANGELES CO

524 525 526 527 528 529

554 555 556 557 558

584 585 586

625

CAMARILLO
LEISURE VILLAGE
PLEASANT VALLEY
NEWBURY PARK
THOUSAND OAKS
OAK PARK
AGOURA HILLS
AGOURA
LAKE SHERWOOD
WESTLAKE VILLAGE
CALABASAS
CALABASAS HIGHLANDS
HIDDEN HILLS
BELL CANYON
WEST HILLS
CANOGA PARK
WOODLAND HILLS
TARZANA
ENCINO
WINNETKA
RESEDA
LAKE BALBOA
WARNER CENTER
VAN NUYS
NORTH HOLLYWOOD
VALLEY VILLAGE
STUDIO CITY
SHERMAN OAKS
SUN VALLEY
BURBANK
GLENDALE
VERDUGO CITY
MONTROSE
SPARR HEIGHTS
TOLUCA LAKE
UNIVERSAL CITY
HOLLYWOOD
LOS FELIZ
SILVER LAKE
ATWATER VILLAGE
GLASSELL PARK
CYPRESS PARK
ECHO PARK
MOUNT OLYMPUS
BEVERLY GLEN
TROUSDALE ESTATES
BEL AIR ESTATES
WEST HOLLYWOOD
BEVERLY HILLS
BRENTWOOD
PACIFIC PALISADES
PALISADES HIGHLANDS
TOPANGA
TOPANGA STATE PARK
MALIBU CREEK STATE PARK
MALIBU LAKE
MALIBU BOWL
MALIBU
EL NIDO
BIG ROCK
MONTE NIDO
FERNWOOD
CASTELLAMMARE
POINT MUGU STATE PARK
POINT MUGU
POINT DUME
SOUTH COAST
LEO CARRILLO STATE BEACH
ROBERT H MEYER MEMORIAL STATE BEACH
MALIBU LAGOON COUNTY BEACH
PT DUME COUNTY BEACH
SANTA MONICA
OCEAN PARK
VENICE
MARINA DEL REY
PLAYA DEL REY
LOS ANGELES INTERNATIONAL AIRPORT
EL SEGUNDO
EL PORTO
MANHATTAN BEACH
HERMOSA BEACH
REDONDO BEACH
HOLLYWOOD RIVIERA
PALOS VERDES ESTATES
ROLLING HILLS ESTATES
ROLLING HILLS
RANCHO PALOS VERDES
MIRALESTE
PORTUGUESE BEND
SAN PEDRO
WILMINGTON
TERMINAL ISLAND
LOS ANGELES HARBOR
HARBOR CITY
LOMITA
TORRANCE
WEST CARSON
CARSON
HARBOR GATEWAY
DEL AMO
ROSEWOOD
WEST RANCHO DOMINGUEZ
WILLOWBROOK
ATHENS
EL CAMINO VILLAGE
LAWNDALE
GARDENA
HAWTHORNE
LENNOX
INGLEWOOD
MORNINGSIDE PARK
WESTMONT
WESTCHESTER
LADERA HEIGHTS
VIEW PARK
WINDSOR HILLS
BALDWIN HILLS
CRENSHAW
LEIMERT PARK
HYDE PARK
CULVER CITY
FOX HILLS
MAR VISTA
DEL REY
PALMS
SAWTELLE
WEST LOS ANGELES
CHEVIOT HILLS
RANCHO PARK
CENTURY CITY
MID-CITY
KOREATOWN
ARLINGTON HEIGHTS
HANCOCK PARK
LOS ANGELES
VERNON
FLORENCE
WALNUT PARK
WATTS
CHINATOWN
LITTLE TOKYO

PACIFIC OCEAN

CALIFORNIA COASTAL NATIONAL MONUMENT

90265

0 2.5 5 7.5 10 miles 1 in. = 5 mi.

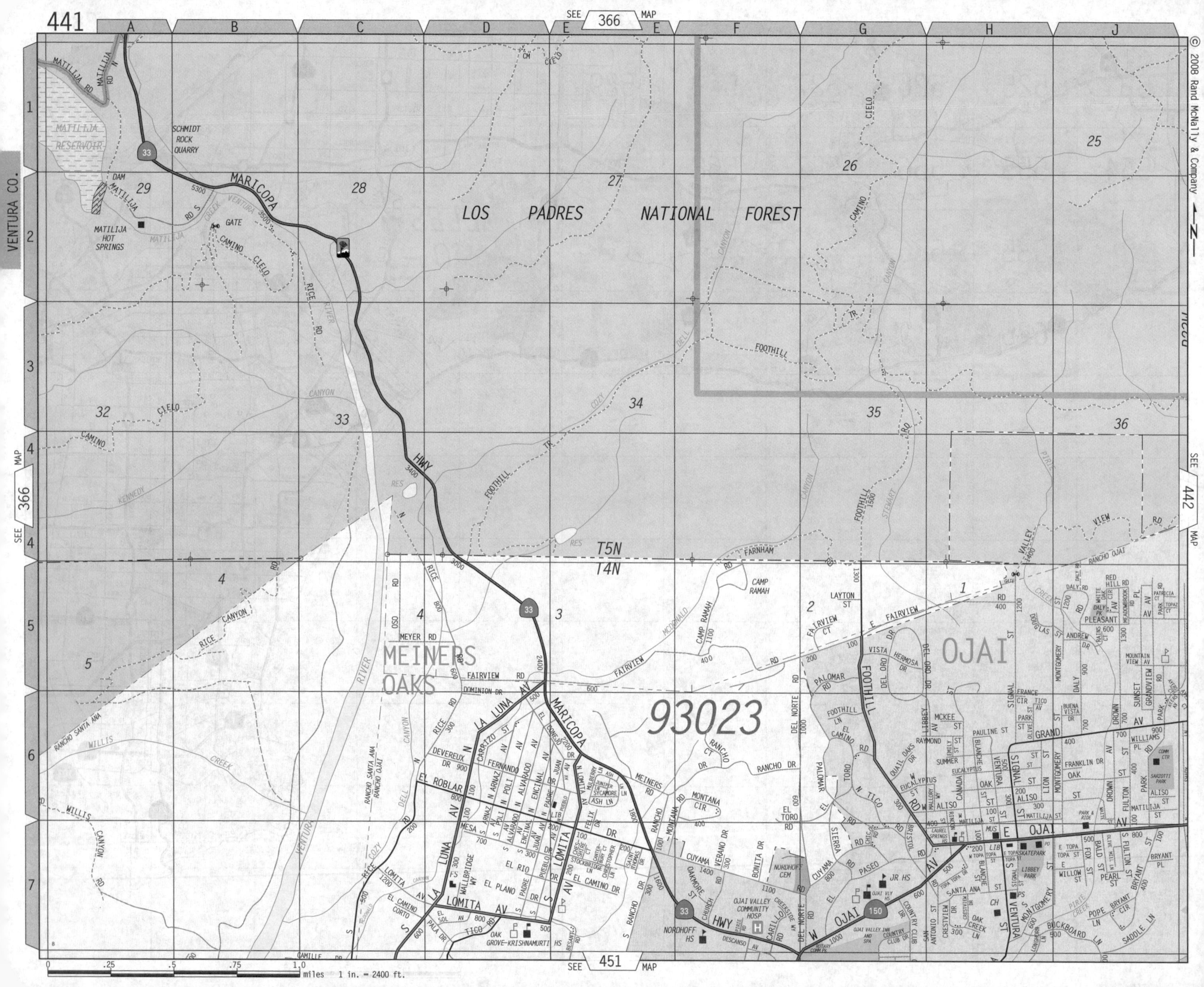

SEE 366 MAP
SEE 451 MAP
SEE 442 MAP
SEE 366 MAP
VENTURA CO.
© 2008 Rand McNally & Company
A
B
C
D
E
F
G
H
J
1
2
3
4
5
6
7
MATILIJA RESERVOIR
MATILIJA DAM
MATILIJA HOT SPRINGS
SCHMIDT ROCK QUARRY
GATE
LOS PADRES NATIONAL FOREST
MARICOPA HWY
T5N
T4N
MEINERS OAKS
OJAI
93023
CAMP RAMAH
FOOTHILL RD
FAIRVIEW RD
E OJAI AV
W OJAI AV
VENTURA ST
SIGNAL ST
GRAND AV
LA LUNA AV
EL ROBLAR DR
LOMITA AV
RICE RD
CAMINO CIELO
RANCHO SANTA ANA
WILLIS CANYON RD
OJAI VALLEY COMMUNITY HOSP
NORDHOFF HS
NORDHOFF CEM
LIBBEY PARK
SKATEPARK
SARZOTTI PARK
OAK GROVE-KRISHNAMURTI HS
OJAI VALLEY INN AND SPA
COUNTRY CLUB DR
RANCHO OJAI
VALLEY VIEW RD
25
26
27
28
29
32
33
34
35
36
1
2
3
4
5
miles 1 in. = 2400 ft.
0 .25 .5 .75 1.0

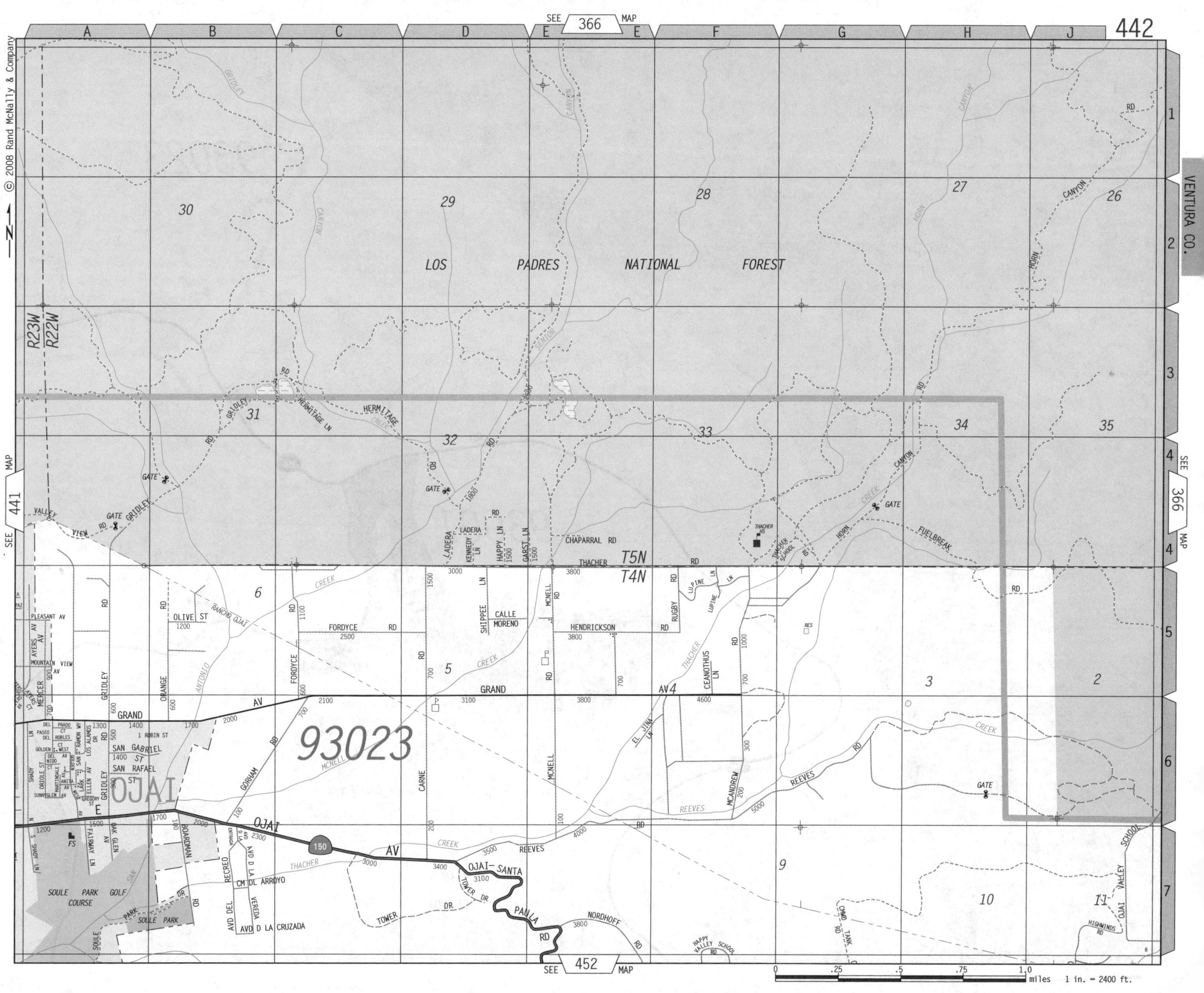
SEE 366 MAP
SEE 441 MAP
SEE 366 MAP
SEE 452 MAP
VENTURA CO.
LOS PADRES NATIONAL FOREST
93023
OJAI
T5N
T4N
R23W
R22W
GRIDLEY RD
HERMITAGE LN
HERMITAGE CREEK
THACHER RD
CHAPARRAL RD
LADERA
KENNEDY LN
HAPPY LN
GARST LN
THACHER SCHOOL
HORN CANYON
FUELBREAK
FORDYCE RD
HENDRICKSON RD
GRAND AV
OJAI AV
REEVES RD
MCNELL RD
CARNE RD
GORHAM RD
SOULE PARK GOLF COURSE
SOULE PARK
OJAI-SANTA PAULA RD
TOWER DR
NORDHOFF RD
HAPPY VALLEY SCHOOL RD
OJAI VALLEY SCHOOL
HIGHWINDS RD
CAMP TANK RD
MCANDREW RD
CEANOTHUS LN
EL JINA LN
RUGBY RD
LUPINE LN
SHIPPEE LN
CALLE MORENO
OLIVE ST
RANCHO OJAI
VALLEY VIEW RD
GATE
0 .25 .5 .75 1.0 miles 1 in. = 2400 ft.

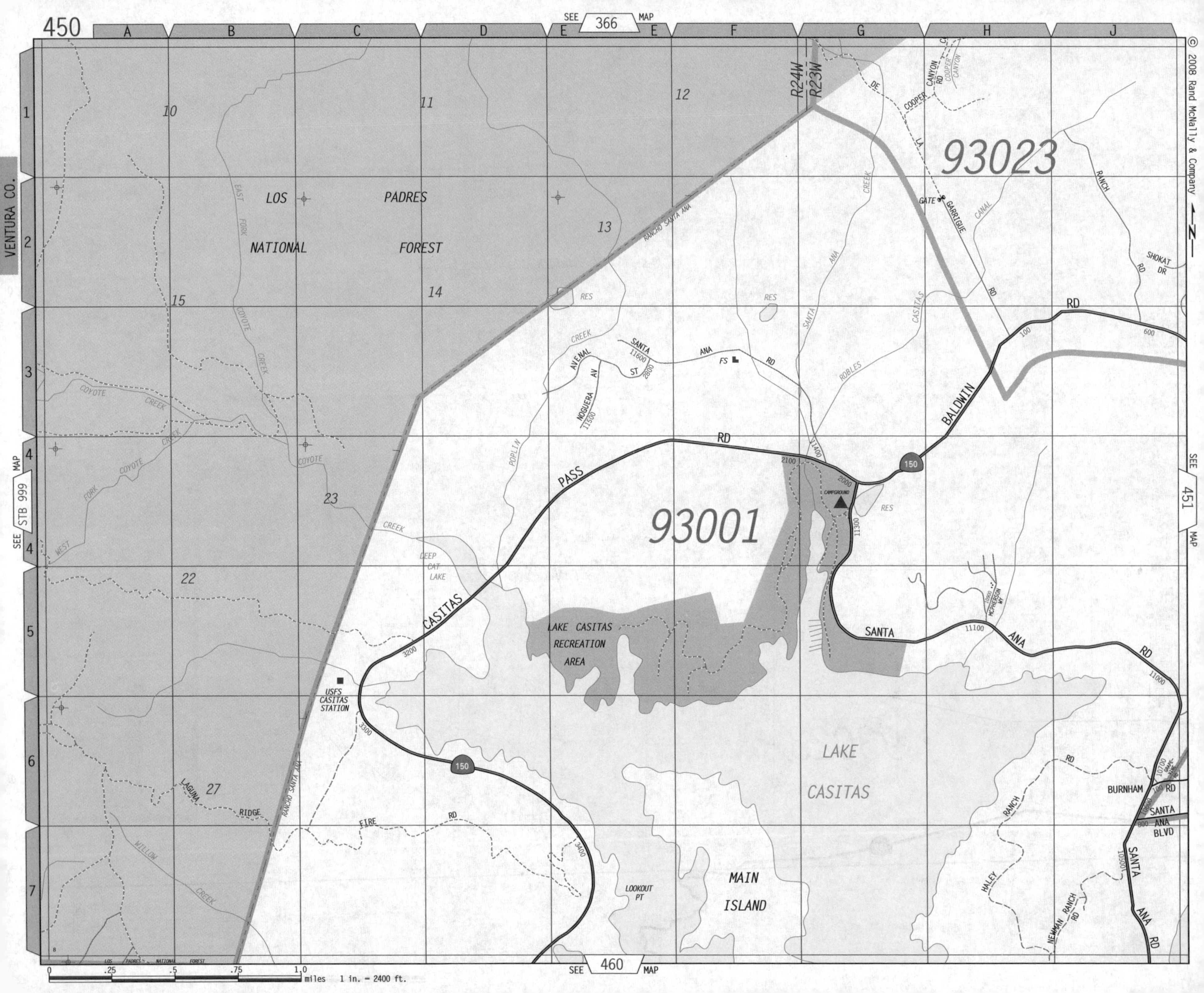
SEE 366 MAP
A B C D E E F G H J
1 2 3 4 5 6 7
VENTURA CO.
LOS PADRES NATIONAL FOREST
93023
93001
R24W R23W
RANCHO SANTA ANA
CASITAS PASS RD
BALDWIN RD
SANTA ANA RD
150
LAKE CASITAS RECREATION AREA
LAKE CASITAS
MAIN ISLAND
LOOKOUT PT
USFS CASITAS STATION
DEEP CAT LAKE
CAMPGROUND
COYOTE CREEK
LAGUNA RIDGE FIRE RD
WILLOW CREEK
HALEY RANCH RD
NEWMAN RANCH RD
BURNHAM RD
SANTA ANA BLVD
SHOKAT DR
GARRIGUE RD
COOPER CANYON RD
SEE STB 999 MAP
SEE 451 MAP
SEE 460 MAP
miles 1 in. = 2400 ft.

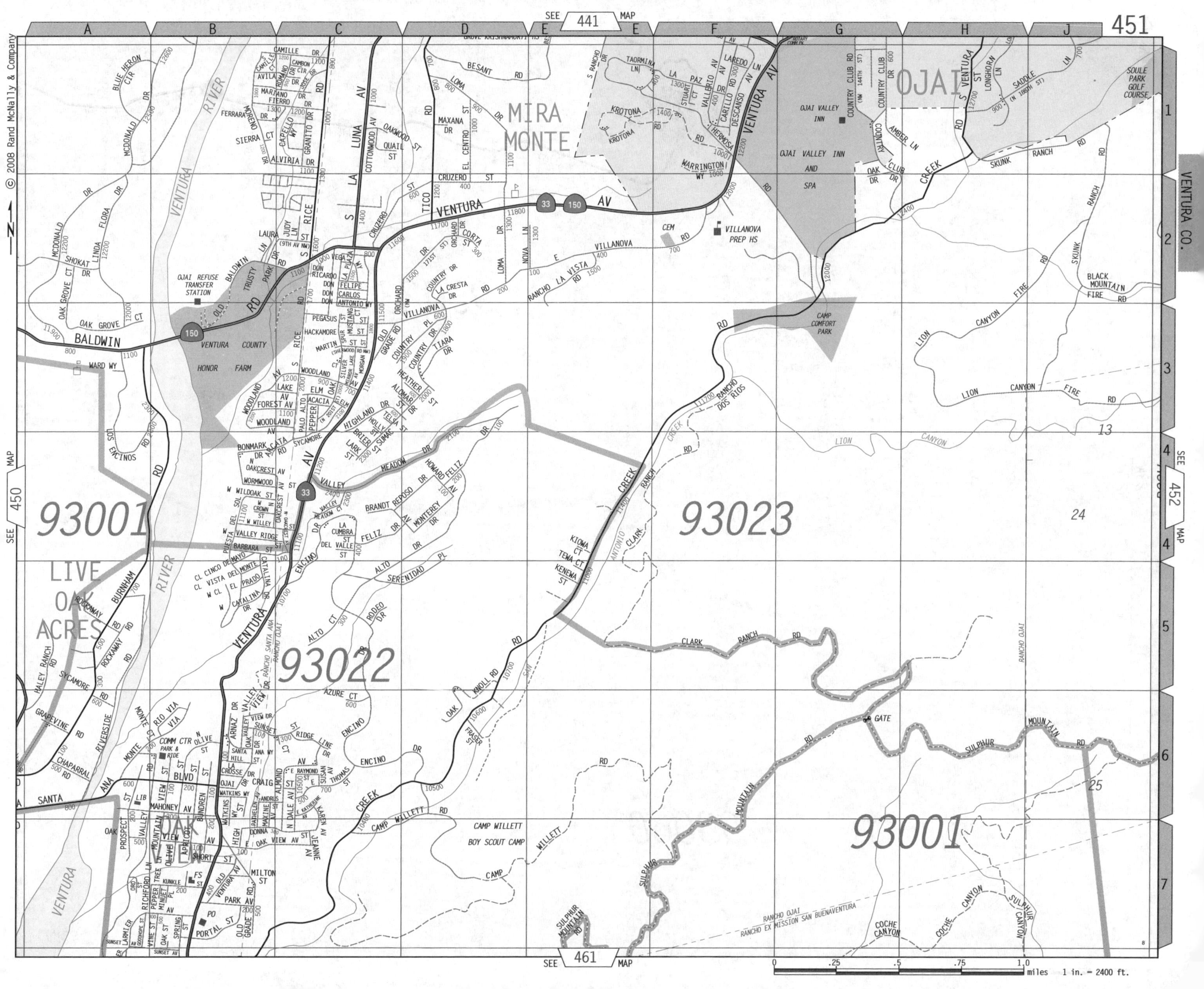

SEE 441 MAP
SEE 461 MAP
SEE 450 MAP
SEE 452 MAP
VENTURA CO.
OJAI
MIRA MONTE
LIVE OAK ACRES
OAK VIEW
93001
93023
93022
VENTURA AV
BALDWIN RD
VENTURA COUNTY HONOR FARM
OJAI REFUSE TRANSFER STATION
OJAI VALLEY INN AND SPA
OJAI VALLEY INN
SOULE PARK GOLF COURSE
VILLANOVA PREP HS
CAMP COMFORT PARK
CAMP WILLETT BOY SCOUT CAMP
CREEK RD
SULPHUR MOUNTAIN RD
CLARK RANCH RD
LION CANYON
BLACK MOUNTAIN FIRE RD
COCHE CANYON
RANCHO OJAI
RANCHO EX MISSION SAN BUENAVENTURA
GATE
VENTURA RIVER
miles 1 in. = 2400 ft.

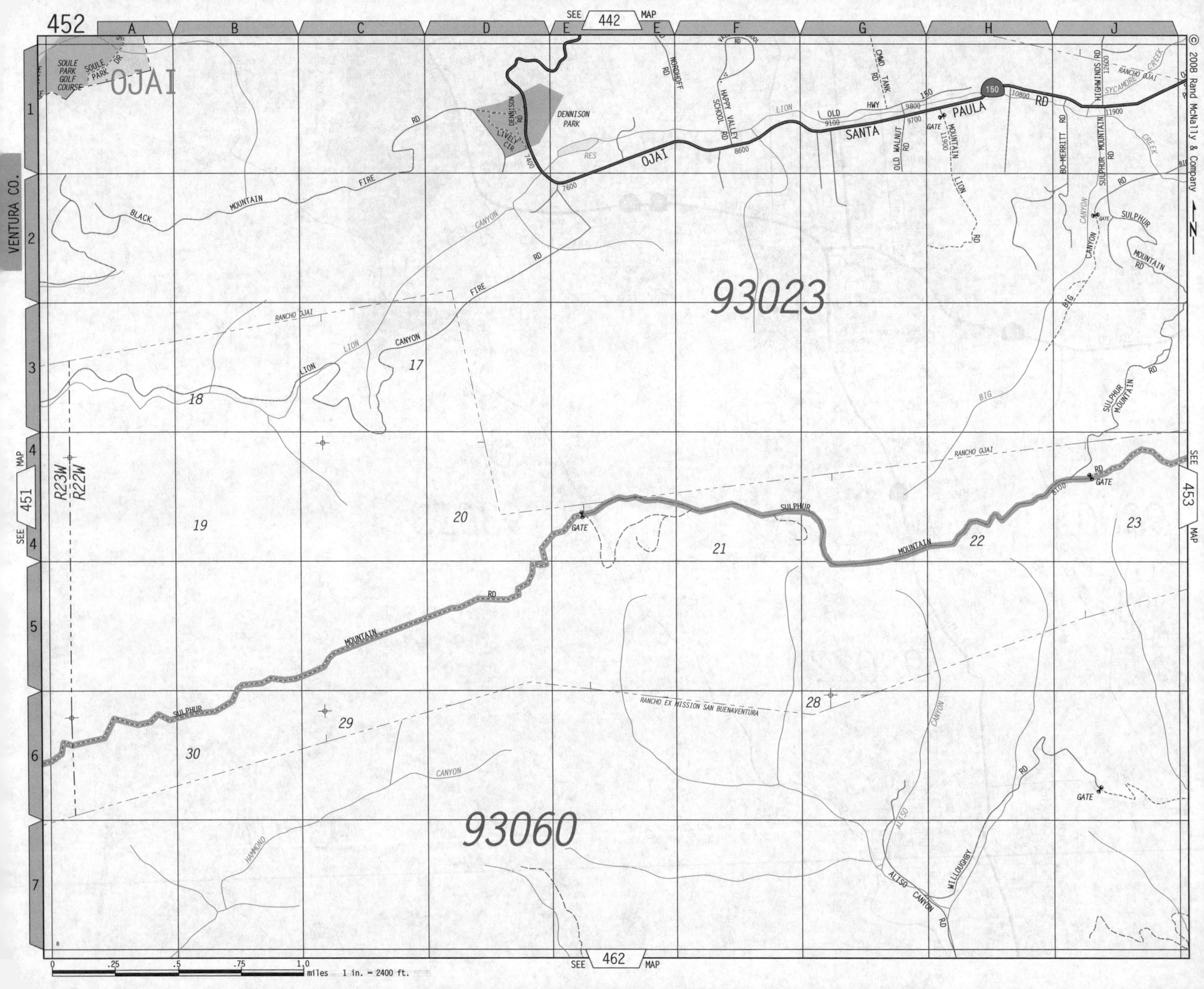

SEE 442 MAP
A
B
C
D
E
F
G
H
J
1
2
3
4
5
6
7
VENTURA CO.
OJAI
SOULE PARK GOLF COURSE
SOULE PARK DR
DENNISON PARK
DENNISON RD
LIVELY CIR
RES
OJAI
SANTA PAULA
RD
150
OLD HWY
NORDHOFF RD
HAPPY VALLEY SCHOOL RD
CMND TANK RD
OLD WALNUT RD
MOUNTAIN LION RD
GATE
BO-MERRITT RD
SULPHUR MOUNTAIN RD
HIGHWINDS RD
RANCHO OJAI
SYCAMORE CREEK
CREEK
SULPHUR MOUNTAIN RD
BIG CANYON
BLACK MOUNTAIN FIRE RD
CANYON
FIRE RD
LION CANYON
RANCHO OJAI
LION
93023
17
18
19
20
21
22
23
28
29
30
R23W
R22W
SEE 451 MAP
SEE 453 MAP
SULPHUR MOUNTAIN RD
RANCHO EX MISSION SAN BUENAVENTURA
CANYON
HAMMOND
93060
ALISO CANYON RD
ALISO
WILLOUGHBY RD
CANYON
SEE 462 MAP
0 .25 .5 .75 1.0 miles 1 in. = 2400 ft.

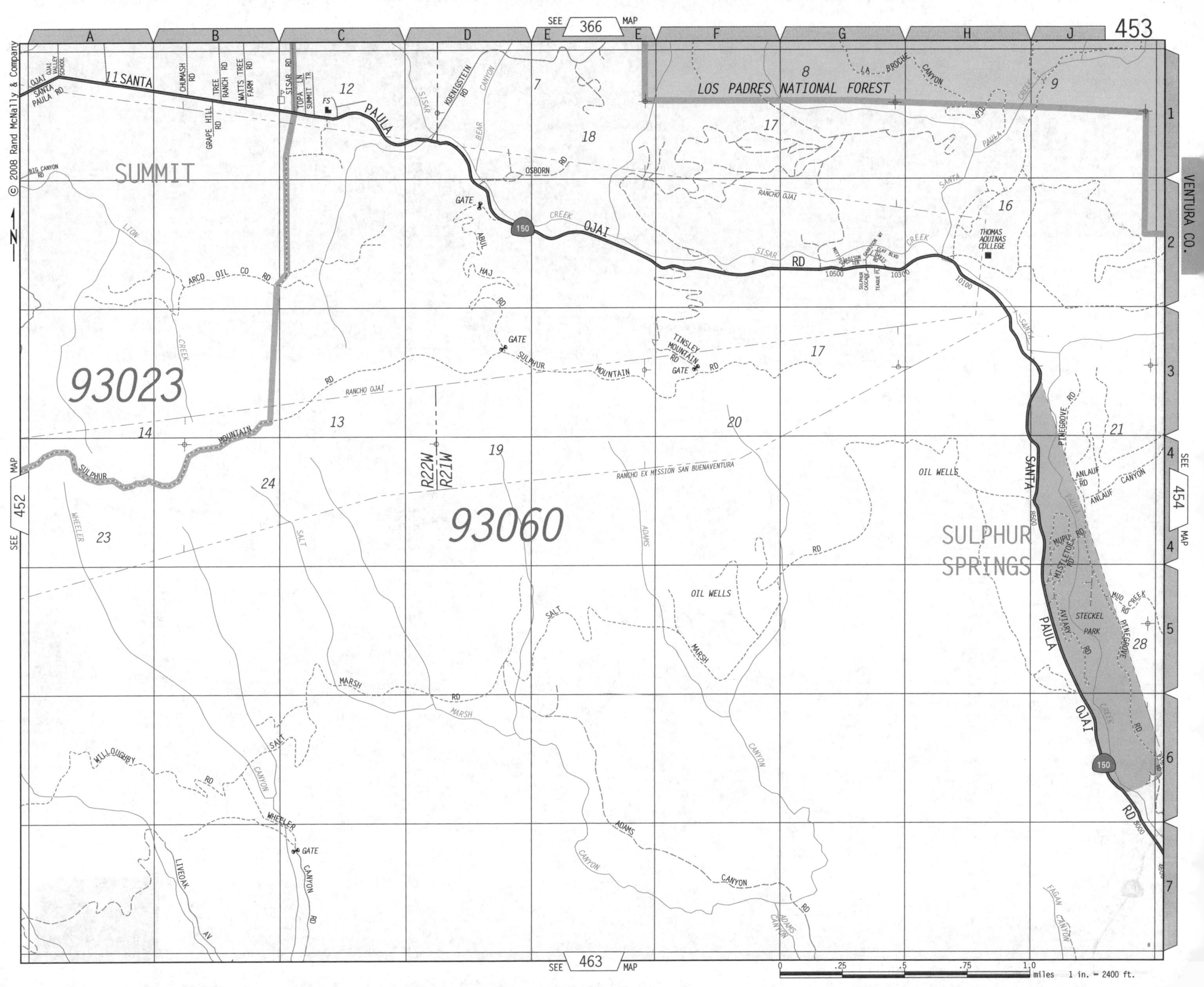
SEE 366 MAP
A
B
C
D
E
F
G
H
J
1
2
3
4
5
6
7
LOS PADRES NATIONAL FOREST
VENTURA CO.
SUMMIT
93023
93060
SULPHUR SPRINGS
SANTA PAULA OJAI RD
SANTA PAULA RD
OJAI VALLEY SCHOOL
CHUMASH RD
GRAPE HILL RD
TREE RANCH RD
WATTS TREE FARM RD
SISAR RD
TOPA LN
SUMMIT TR
FS
KOENIGSTEIN RD
BEAR CANYON
OSBORN RD
LA BROCHE CANYON RD
RANCHO OJAI
SISAR CREEK
SANTA PAULA CREEK
150
GATE
ABUL
HAJ RD
THOMAS AQUINAS COLLEGE
ARCO OIL CO RD
LION CREEK
SULPHUR MOUNTAIN RD
TINSLEY MOUNTAIN RD
RANCHO EX MISSION SAN BUENAVENTURA
R22W
R21W
OIL WELLS
PINEGROVE RD
ANLAUF RD
ANLAUF CANYON
MUPU RD
MISTLETOE RD
MUD CREEK RD
AVIARY RD
STECKEL PARK
WHEELER CANYON RD
SALT CANYON
ADAMS CANYON RD
MARSH RD
WILLOUGHBY RD
LIVEOAK AV
FAGAN CANYON
10500
10300
10100
8500
5000
SEE 452 MAP
SEE 454 MAP
SEE 463 MAP
0 .25 .5 .75 1.0 miles 1 in. = 2400 ft.

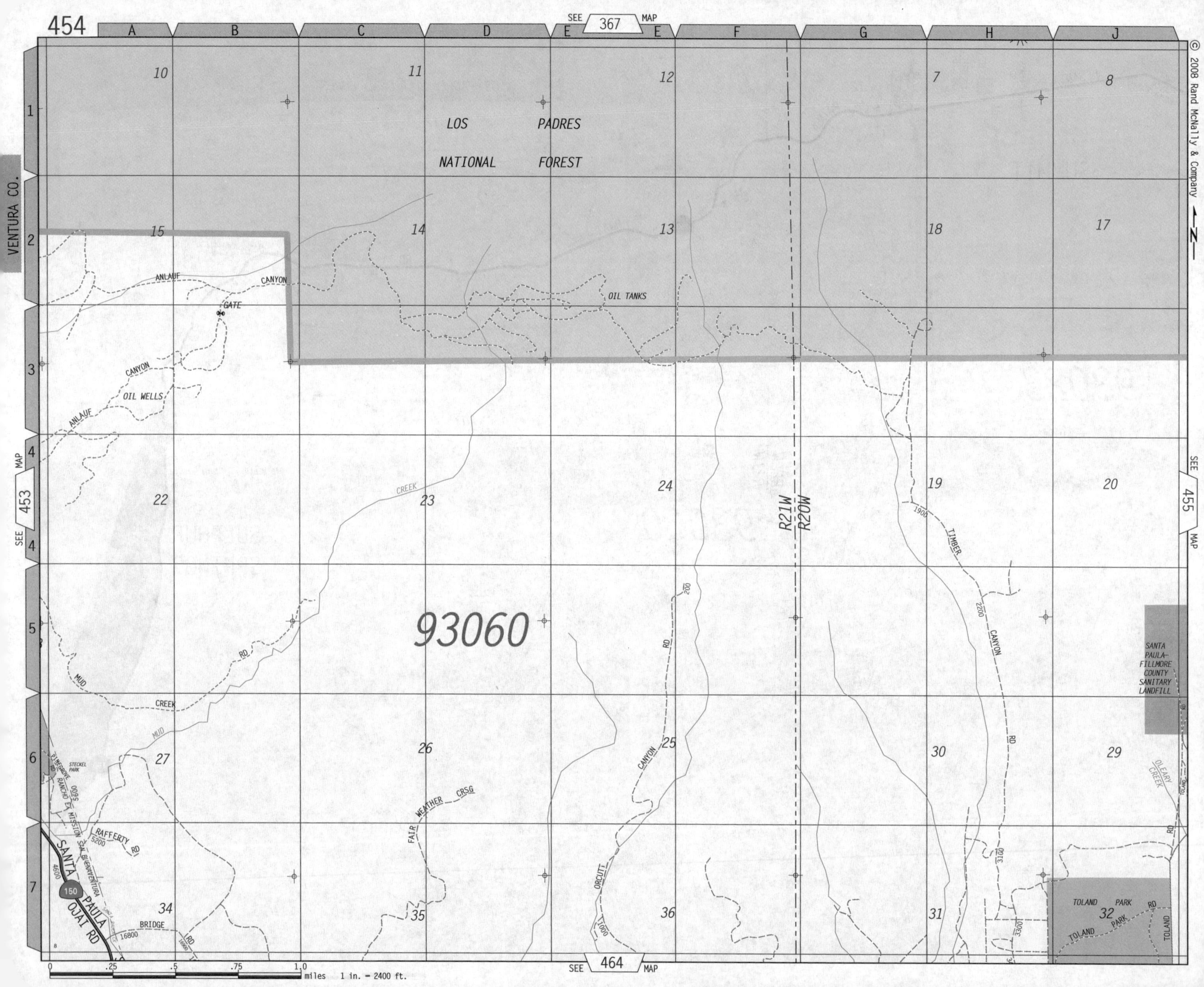
SEE 367 MAP
A
B
C
D
E
F
G
H
J
LOS PADRES
NATIONAL FOREST
VENTURA CO.
ANLAUF CANYON
GATE
OIL TANKS
CANYON
OIL WELLS
ANLAUF
CREEK
SEE MAP 453
SEE MAP 455
R21W
R20W
TIMBER
CANYON
RD
93060
MUD
RD
CREEK
MUD
SANTA PAULA-FILLMORE COUNTY SANITARY LANDFILL
CANYON
RD
FAIR WEATHER CRSG
RAFFERTY RD
MISSION
SAN BUENAVENTURA
SANTA PAULA OJAI RD
150
BRIDGE RD
ORCUTT
OLEARY CREEK
TOLAND PARK RD
TOLAND
STECKEL PARK
miles 1 in. = 2400 ft.
SEE 464 MAP

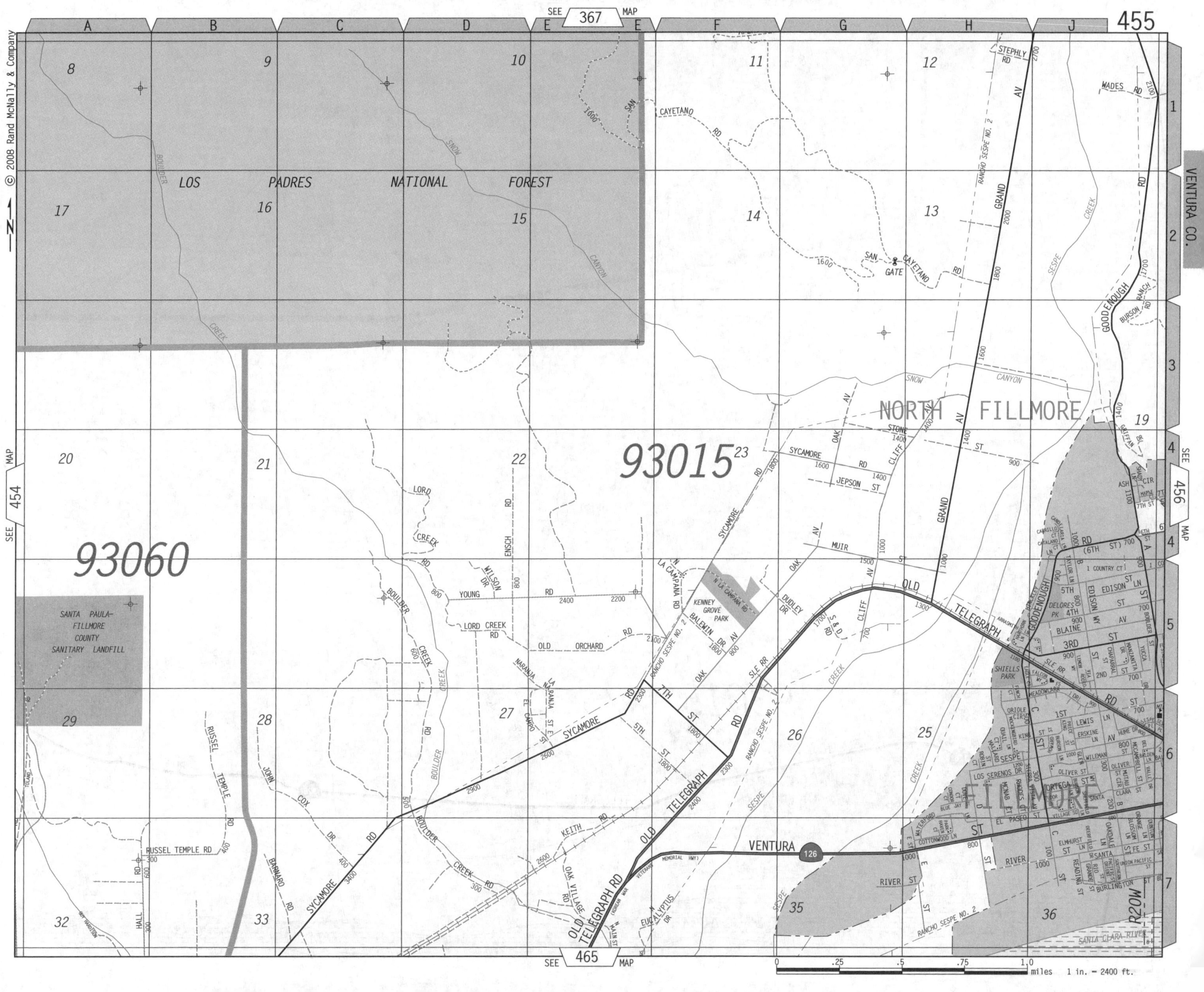

SEE 367 MAP
LOS PADRES NATIONAL FOREST
NORTH FILLMORE
FILLMORE
93015
93060
SANTA PAULA-FILLMORE COUNTY SANITARY LANDFILL
KENNEY GROVE PARK
SHIELLS PARK
DELORES PK
VENTURA CO.
SEE 454 MAP
SEE 456 MAP
SEE 465 MAP
GRAND AV
OLD TELEGRAPH RD
SYCAMORE RD
VENTURA
126
RIVER ST
SANTA CLARA RIVER
R20W
SESPE CREEK
BOULDER CREEK
SNOW CANYON
SAN CAYETANO RD
GOODENOUGH RD
0 .25 .5 .75 1.0 miles 1 in. = 2400 ft.

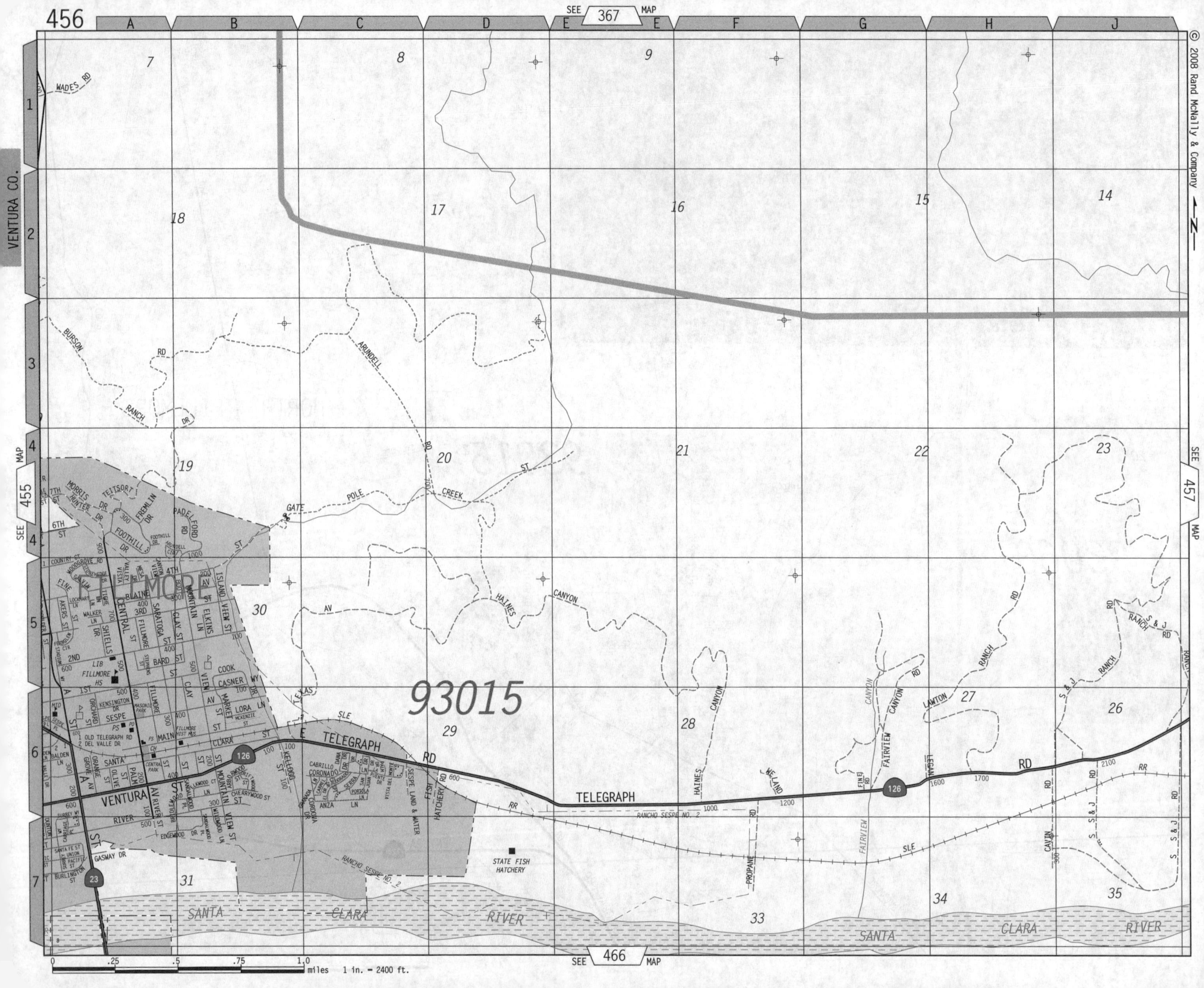

SEE 367 MAP
SEE 455 MAP
SEE 457 MAP
SEE 466 MAP
VENTURA CO.
93015
FILLMORE
TELEGRAPH RD
VENTURA ST
SANTA CLARA RIVER
HAINES CANYON AV
POLE CREEK
ARUNDELL RD
BURSON RANCH RD
WADES RD
FAIRVIEW CANYON RD
LAWTON RANCH RD
RANCHO SESPE NO. 2
STATE FISH HATCHERY
SESPE LAND & WATER
FISH HATCHERY RD
S & J RANCH RD
CAVIN RD
PROPANE RD
LEGAN
FOOTHILL DR
CENTRAL AV
MOUNTAIN VIEW ST
CLAY ST
SARATOGA ST
SANTA CLARA ST
RIVER ST
GASWAY DR
BURLINGTON ST
KELLOGG ST
CORONADO
ANZA LN
CABRILLO
1 in. = 2400 ft.
miles

SEE 367 MAP
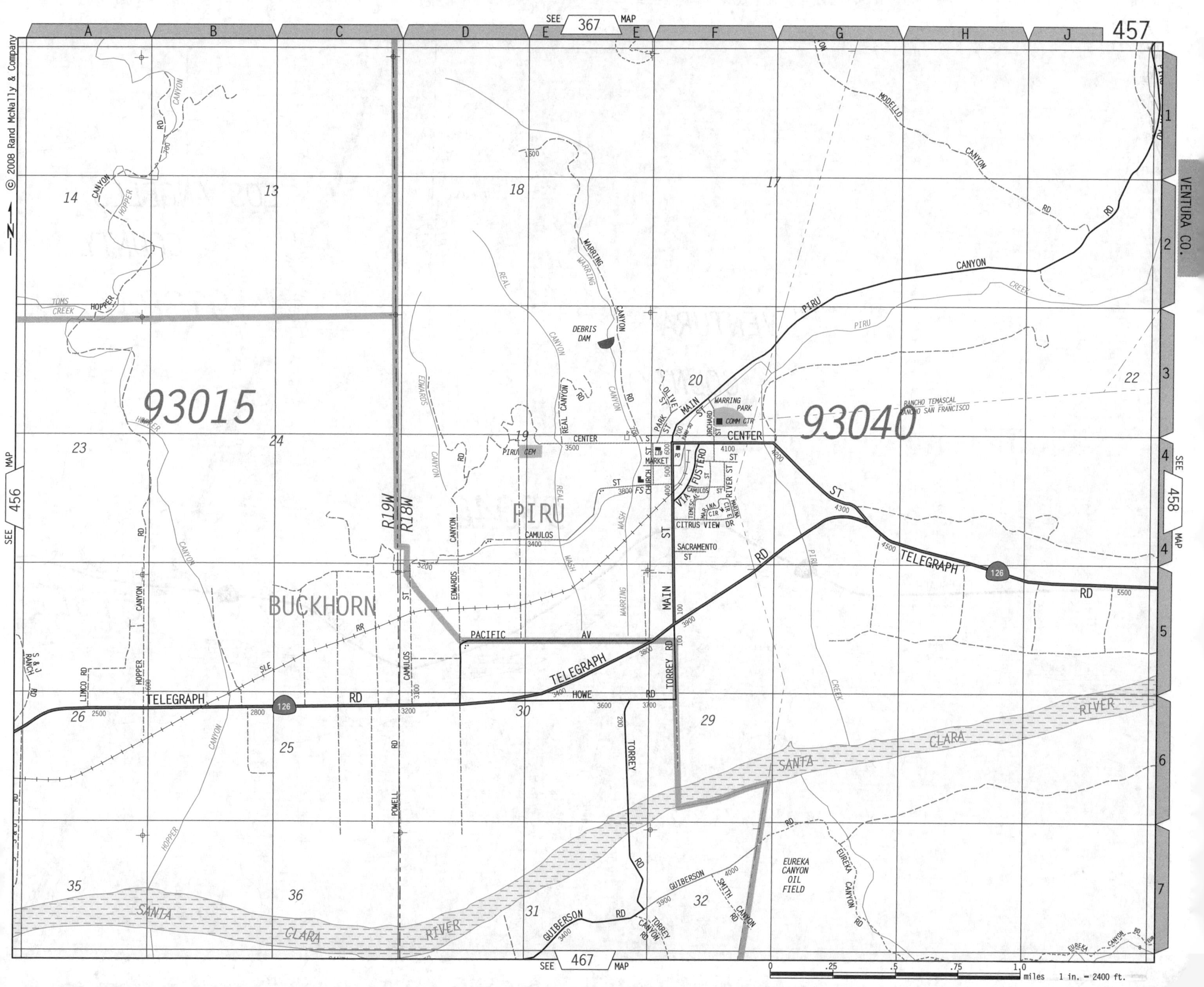

SEE 456 MAP
SEE 458 MAP
SEE 467 MAP

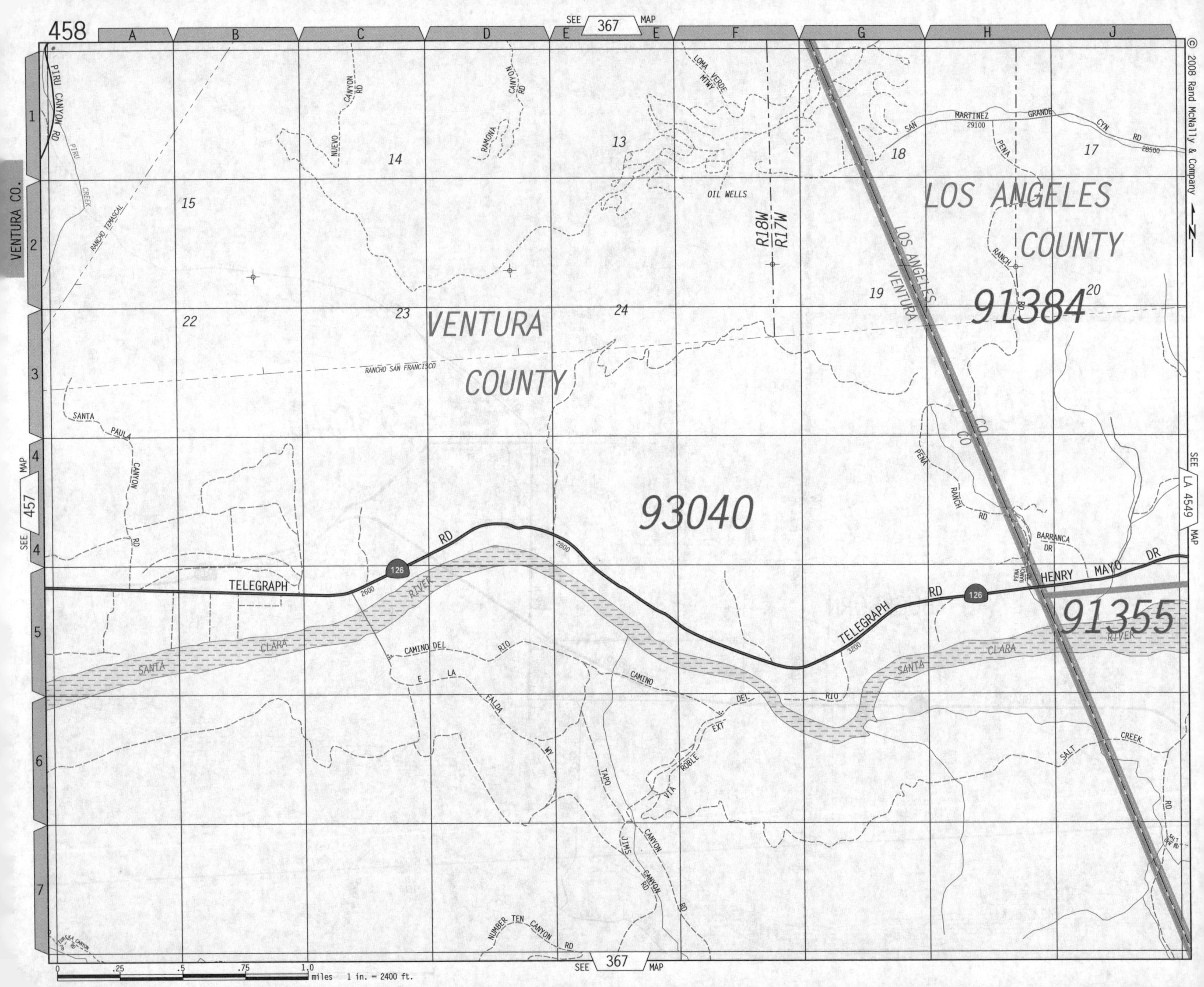
SEE 367 MAP
A
B
C
D
E
F
G
H
J
1
2
3
4
5
6
7
VENTURA CO.
SEE 457 MAP
SEE LA 4549 MAP
© 2008 Rand McNally & Company
PIRU CANYON RD
PIRU CREEK
RANCHO TEMASCAL
NUEVO CANYON RD
RAMONA CANYON RD
LOMA VERDE MTWY
SAN MARTINEZ GRANDE CYN RD
29100
28500
PENA RANCH RD
OIL WELLS
R18W
R17W
LOS ANGELES COUNTY
LOS ANGELES VENTURA CO CO
VENTURA COUNTY
RANCHO SAN FRANCISCO
91384
93040
91355
13
14
15
17
18
19
20
22
23
24
SANTA PAULA CANYON RD
TELEGRAPH RD
126
2600
2800
3200
HENRY MAYO DR
BARRANCA DR
PENA RANCH RD
SANTA CLARA RIVER
CAMINO DEL RIO
E LA FALDA WY
CAMINO DEL RIO EXT
VIA ROBLE
TAPO CANYON RD
JIMS CANYON RD
SALT CREEK
SALT CRK RD
NUMBER TEN CANYON RD
EUREKA CANYON RD
SEE 367 MAP
0 .25 .5 .75 1.0 miles 1 in. = 2400 ft.

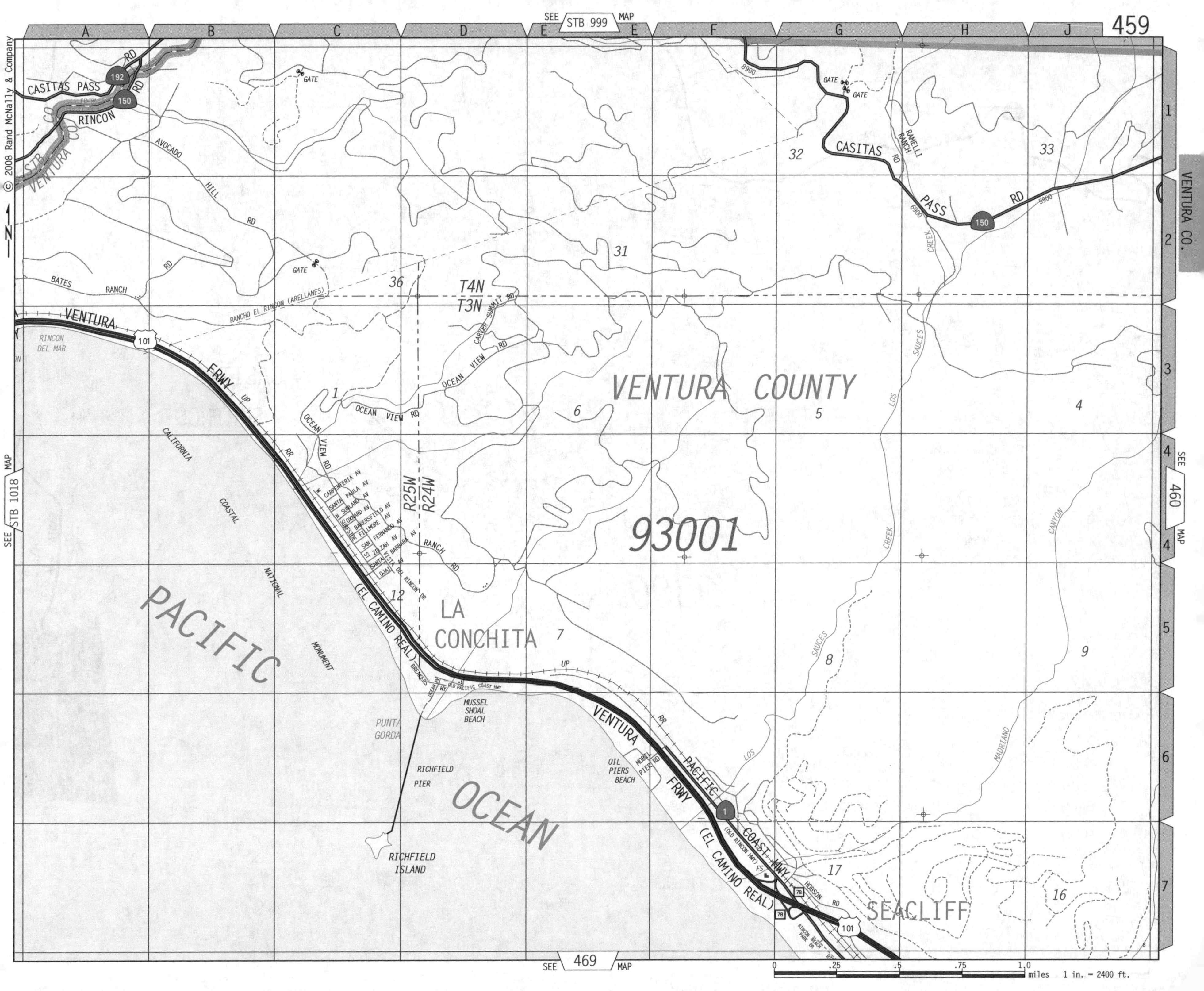

SEE STB 999 MAP
CASITAS PASS
RD
RINCON
AVOCADO
HILL
RD
BATES
RANCH
RD
GATE
RANCHO EL RINCON (ARELLANES)
VENTURA
FRWY
101
RINCON DEL MAR
T4N
T3N
R25W
R24W
CARVER SUMMIT RD
OCEAN VIEW RD
CALIFORNIA
COASTAL
NATIONAL
MONUMENT
CARPINTERIA AV
SANTA PAULA AV
N SUNLAND AV
OXNARD AV
BAKERSFIELD AV
FILLMORE AV
SAN FERNANDO AV
ZELZAH AV
SANTA BARBARA AV
OJAI AV
DEL RINCON DR
LA CONCHITA
(EL CAMINO REAL)
OLD PACIFIC COAST HWY
MUSSEL SHOAL BEACH
PUNTA GORDA
RICHFIELD PIER
RICHFIELD ISLAND
PACIFIC
OCEAN
OIL PIERS BEACH
MOBIL PIER RD
VENTURA
PACIFIC
COAST HWY
(OLD RINCON HWY)
HOBSON RD
RINCON BEACH PARK DR
SEACLIFF
VENTURA COUNTY
93001
CASITAS PASS RD
RAMELLI RANCH RD
LOS SAUCES CREEK
MADRIANO CANYON
150
192
1
78
VENTURA CO.
SEE STB 1018 MAP
SEE 460 MAP
SEE 469 MAP
miles 1 in. = 2400 ft.

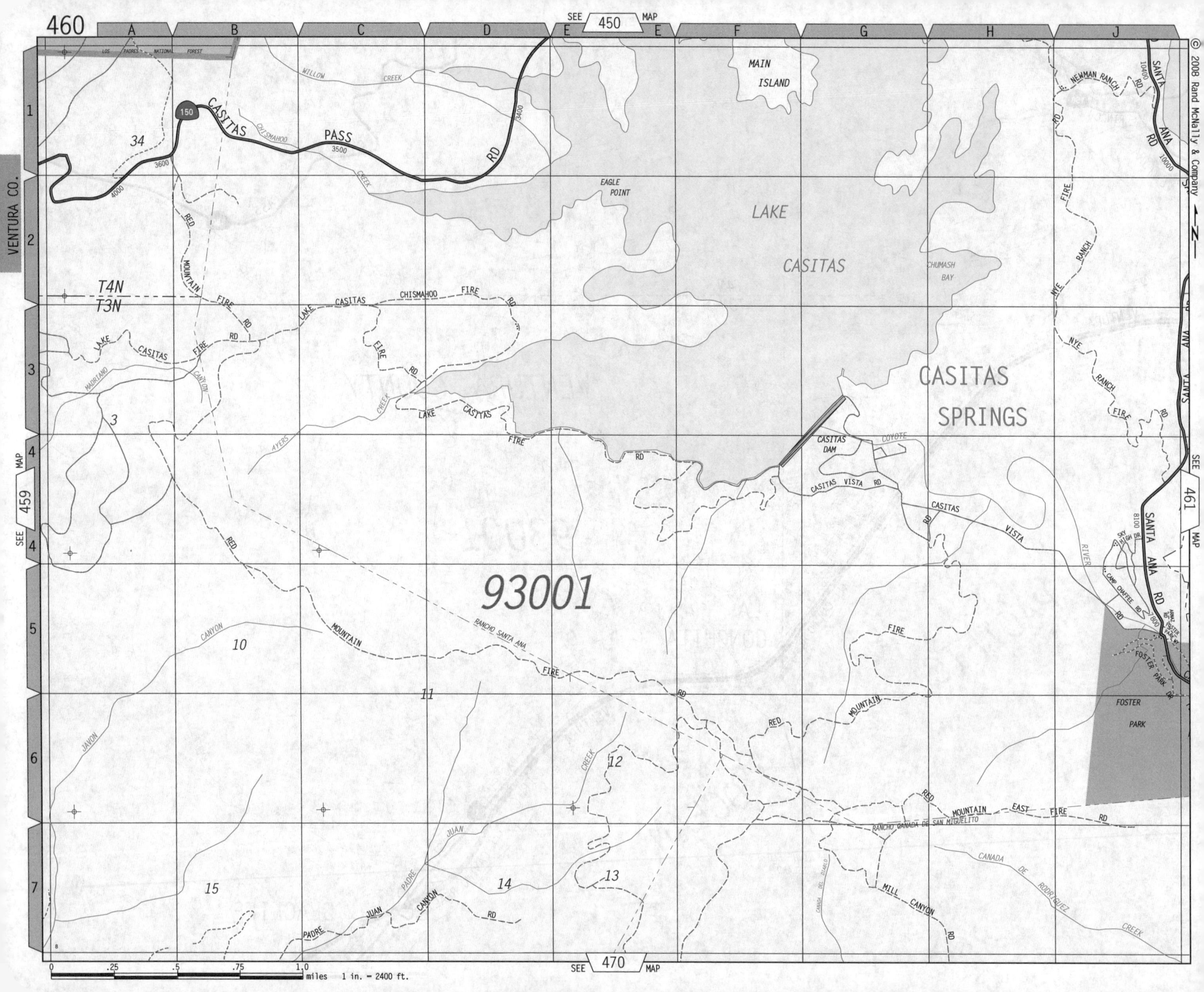
SEE 450 MAP
A
B
C
D
E
F
G
H
J
1
2
3
4
5
6
7
VENTURA CO.
SEE 459 MAP
SEE 461 MAP
SEE 470 MAP
LOS PADRES NATIONAL FOREST
150
CASITAS PASS RD
3600
4000
3500
3400
34
WILLOW CREEK
CHISMAHOO CREEK
MAIN ISLAND
EAGLE POINT
LAKE CASITAS
CHUMASH BAY
CASITAS SPRINGS
CASITAS DAM
COYOTE
CASITAS VISTA RD
NEWMAN RANCH RD
SANTA ANA RD
10400
10000
8100
7800
T4N
T3N
RED MOUNTAIN FIRE RD
LAKE CASITAS CHISMAHOO FIRE RD
LAKE CASITAS FIRE RD
MADRIANO CANYON
3
AYERS CREEK
NYE RANCH FIRE RD
SKY HIGH DR
CAMP CHAFFEE RD
RIVER
FOSTER PARK DR
FOSTER PARK
93001
RANCHO SANTA ANA
CANYON
10
11
12
13
14
15
JAVON
CREEK
RED MOUNTAIN FIRE RD
RED MOUNTAIN EAST FIRE RD
RANCHO CANADA DE SAN MIGUELITO
CANADA DE RODRIGUEZ CREEK
CANADA DEL DIABLO
MILL CANYON RD
PADRE JUAN CANYON RD
0
.25
.5
.75
1.0
miles 1 in. = 2400 ft.

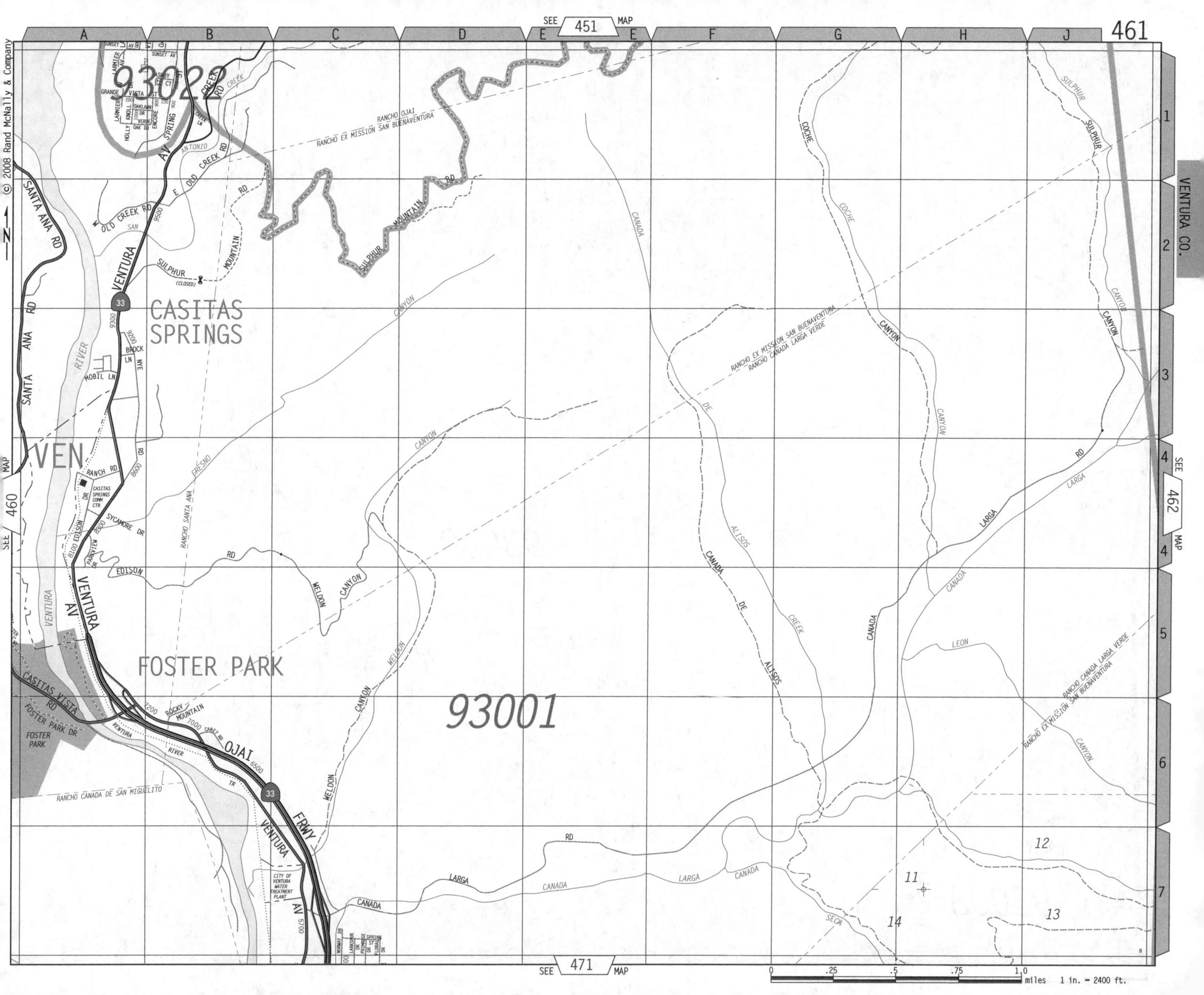

SEE 451 MAP
A
B
C
D
E
F
G
H
J
93022
93001
CASITAS SPRINGS
FOSTER PARK
VEN
VENTURA CO.
RANCHO OJAI
RANCHO EX MISSION SAN BUENAVENTURA
RANCHO EX MISSION SAN BUENAVENTURA
RANCHO CANADA LARGA VERDE
RANCHO CANADA LARGA VERDE
RANCHO CANADA DE SAN MIGUELITO
SANTA ANA RD
VENTURA AV
OJAI FRWY
CASITAS VISTA RD
FOSTER PARK DR
FOSTER PARK
SULPHUR MOUNTAIN RD
OLD CREEK RD
CREEK RD
SAN ANTONIO
VENTURA RIVER
BROCK LN
NYE
MOBIL LN
RANCH RD
CASITAS SPRINGS COMM CTR
EDISON DR
SYCAMORE DR
PARKVIEW DR
EDISON RD
WELDON CANYON
FRESNO CANYON
RANCHO SANTA ANA
ROCKY MOUNTAIN
CANADA LARGA RD
CANADA DE ALISOS
ALISOS CREEK
COCHE CANYON
SULPHUR CANYON
LEON CANYON
CANADA SECA
CITY OF VENTURA WATER TREATMENT PLANT
LARMIER
GRANDE VISTA ST
OAKLAWN
KNOLL
HOLLY
OAK DR
VERDE
ENCORE
SUNSET AV
ASHBY
33
11
12
13
14
SEE 460 MAP
SEE 462 MAP
SEE 471 MAP
0 .25 .5 .75 1.0 miles 1 in. = 2400 ft.

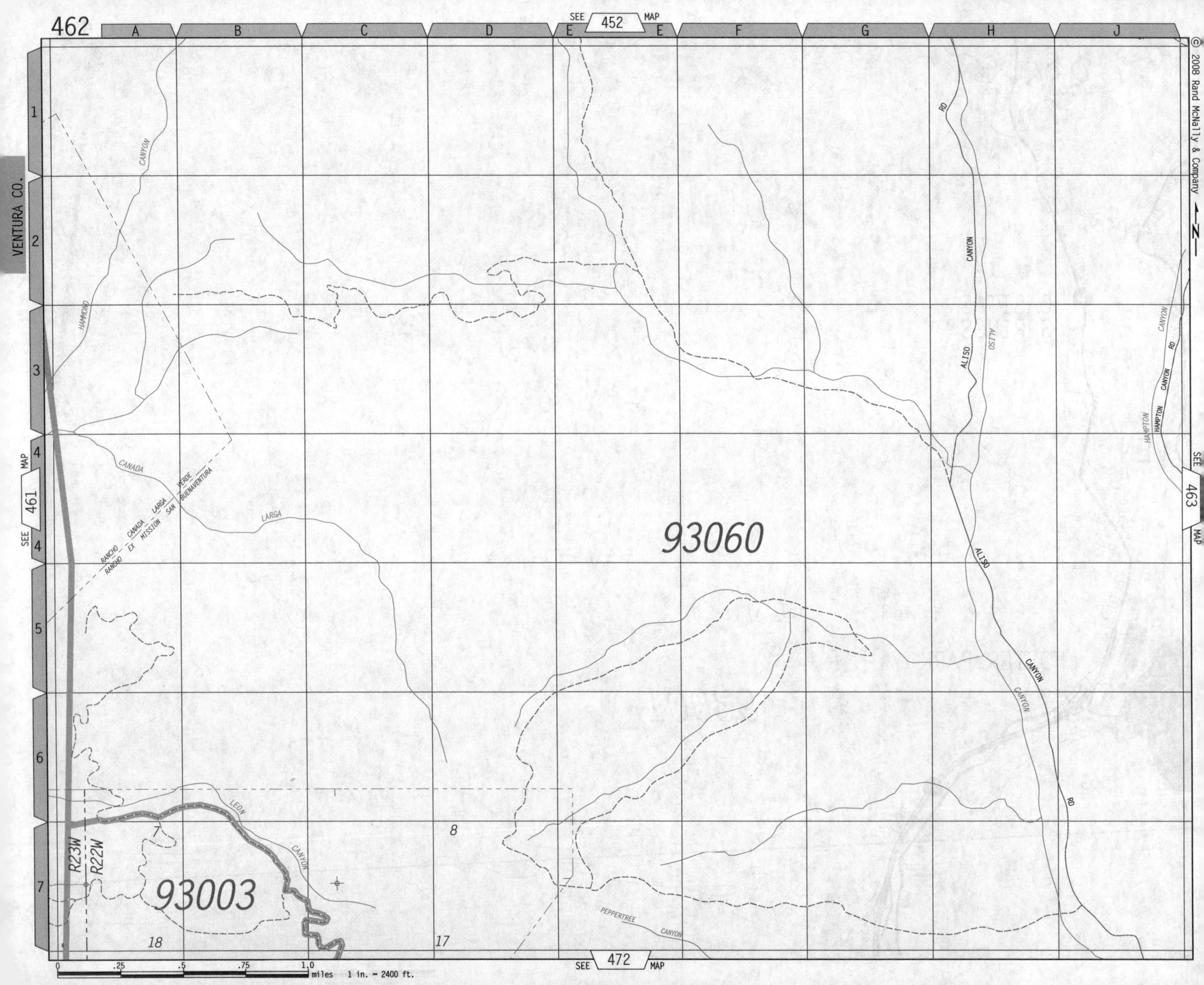
A
B
C
D
E
F
G
H
J
SEE 452 MAP
SEE 461 MAP
SEE 463 MAP
SEE 472 MAP
VENTURA CO.
1
2
3
4
5
6
7
93060
93003
HAMMOND
CANYON
CANADA
LARGA
RANCHO CANADA LARGA VERDE
RANCHO EX MISSION SAN BUENAVENTURA
ALISO
CANYON
RD
HAMPTON
CANYON
LEON
PEPPERTREE
R23W
R22W
7
8
17
18
0 .25 .5 .75 1.0 miles 1 in. = 2400 ft.

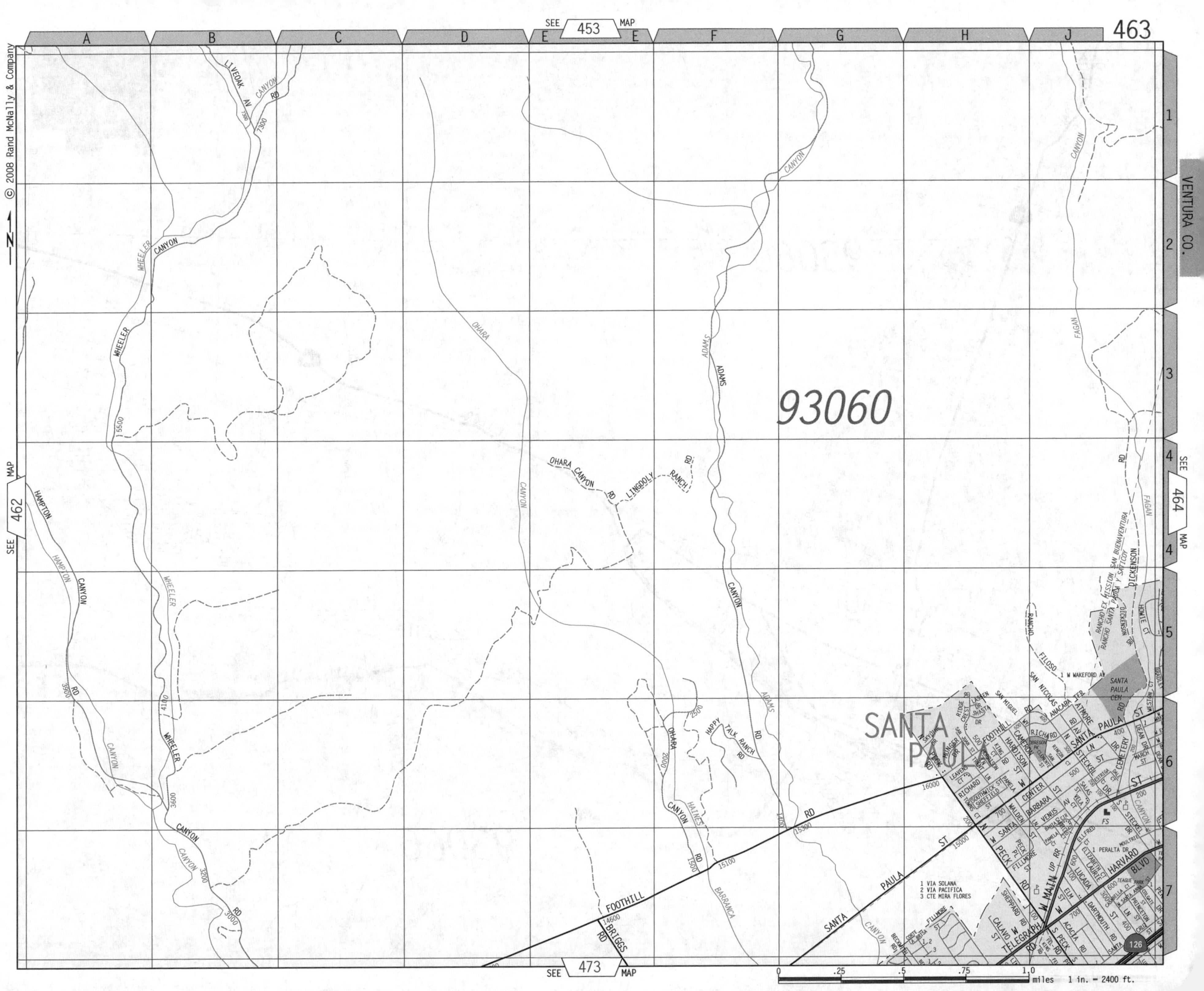

SEE 453 MAP
A
B
C
D
E
F
G
H
J
1
2
3
4
5
6
7
VENTURA CO.
SEE 462 MAP
SEE 464 MAP
SEE 473 MAP
© 2008 Rand McNally & Company
93060
SANTA PAULA
LIVEOAK AV
CANYON RD
WHEELER CANYON
WHEELER
OHARA
ADAMS
ADAMS CANYON RD
OHARA CANYON RD
LINGDOLY RANCH RD
HAMPTON CANYON RD
FAGAN CANYON
FOOTHILL RD
SANTA PAULA ST
BRIGGS RD
HAPPY TALK RANCH RD
HAINES BARRANCA
SANTA PAULA CEM
1 VIA SOLANA
2 VIA PACIFICA
3 CTE MIRA FLORES
1 W WAKEFORD AV
1 PERALTA DR
HARVARD BLVD
W MAIN ST
W TELEGRAPH RD
126
miles 1 in. = 2400 ft.
0 .25 .5 .75 1.0

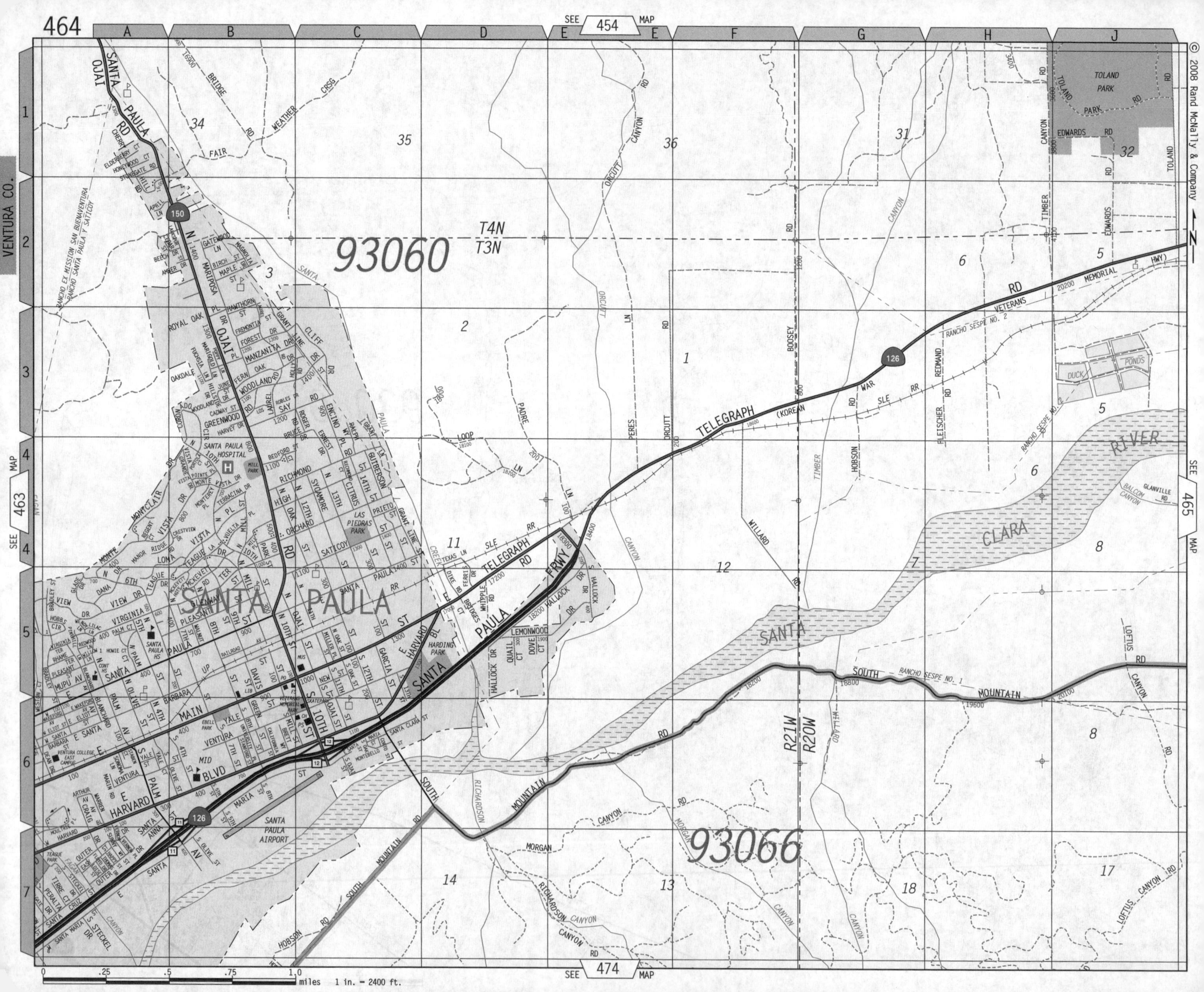

SEE 454 MAP
SEE 474 MAP
SEE 463 MAP
SEE 465 MAP
VENTURA CO.
SANTA PAULA
93060
93066
T4N
T3N
R21W
R20W
SANTA PAULA HOSPITAL
HARDING PARK
LAS PIEDRAS PARK
SANTA PAULA AIRPORT
TOLAND PARK
DUCK PONDS
SANTA CLARA RIVER
TELEGRAPH RD
SOUTH MOUNTAIN RD
SANTA PAULA FRWY
VETERANS MEMORIAL HWY
RANCHO SESPE NO. 1
RANCHO SESPE NO. 2
RANCHO EX MISSION SAN BUENAVENTURA
RANCHO SANTA PAULA Y SATICOY
miles 1 in. = 2400 ft.

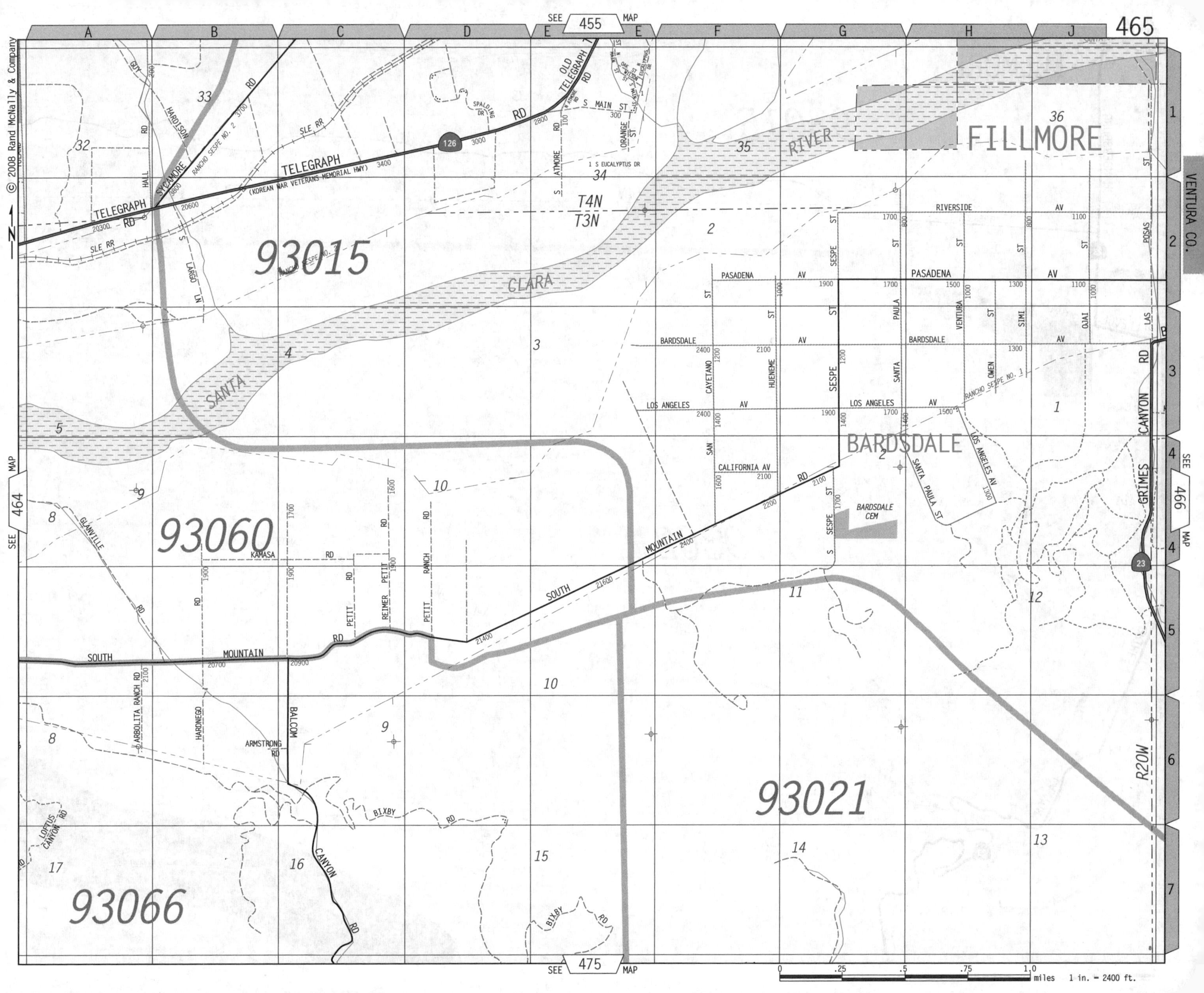
SEE 455 MAP
A
B
C
D
E
F
G
H
J
1
2
3
4
5
6
7
FILLMORE
BARDSDALE
VENTURA CO.
93015
93060
93021
93066
T4N
T3N
R20W
SANTA CLARA RIVER
TELEGRAPH RD
(KOREAN WAR VETERANS MEMORIAL HWY)
OLD TELEGRAPH RD
SYCAMORE RD
HARDISON
HALL RD
GUY
S MAIN ST
ORANGE ST
S ATMORE RD
1 S EUCALYPTUS DR
SPALDING DR
RANCHO SESPE NO. 2
RANCHO SESPE NO. 1
SLE RR
S LARGO LN
RIVERSIDE AV
PASADENA AV
BARDSDALE AV
LOS ANGELES AV
CALIFORNIA AV
SESPE ST
S SESPE ST
PAULA ST
SANTA PAULA ST
VENTURA ST
SIMI ST
OJAI ST
OWEN ST
LAS POSAS ST
CAYETANO ST
HUENEME ST
SAN
GRIMES CANYON RD
BARDSDALE CEM
SOUTH MOUNTAIN RD
GLANVILLE RD
KAMASA RD
PETIT RD
REIMER RD
PETIT RANCH RD
ARBOLITA RANCH RD
HARDNEGO
BALCOM CANYON RD
ARMSTRONG RD
BIXBY RD
LOFTUS CANYON RD
126
23
SEE 464 MAP
SEE 466 MAP
SEE 475 MAP
0 .25 .5 .75 1.0 miles 1 in. = 2400 ft.

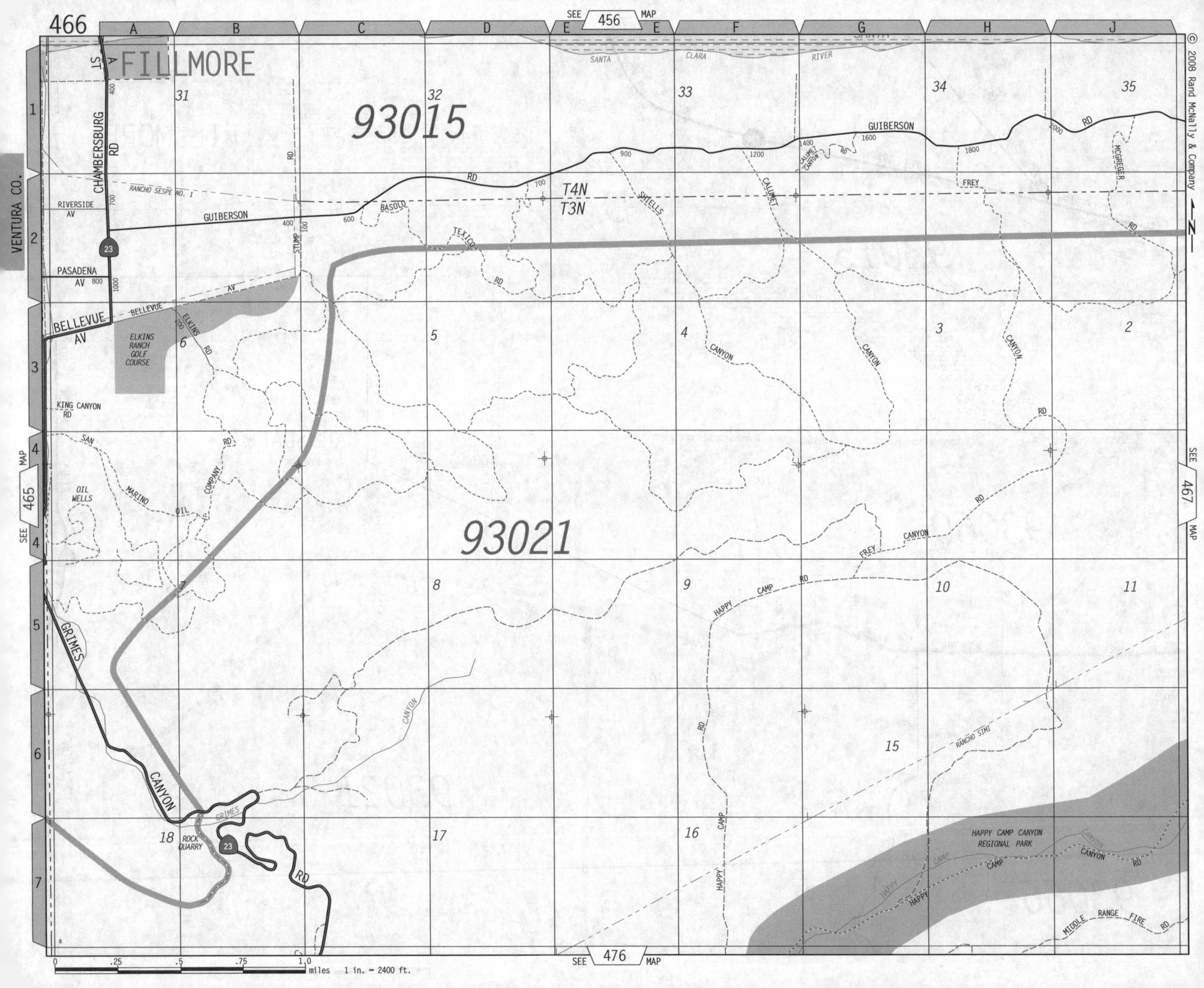

SEE 456 MAP
SEE 465 MAP
SEE 467 MAP
SEE 476 MAP

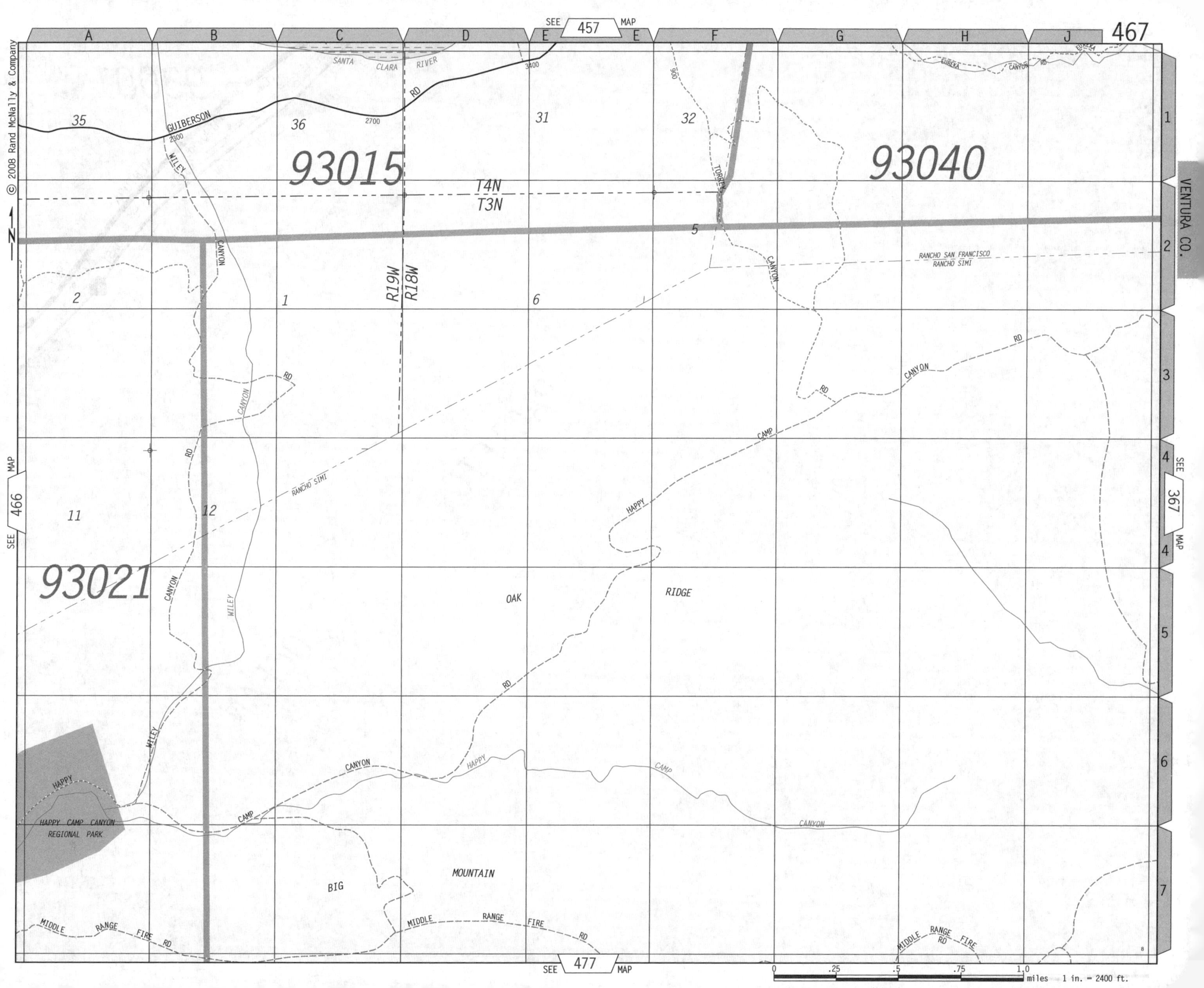

SEE 457 MAP
A
B
C
D
E
F
G
H
J
SANTA CLARA RIVER
GUIBERSON RD
WILEY CANYON
TORREY CANYON
EUREKA CANYON RD
93015
93040
93021
T4N
T3N
R19W
R18W
RANCHO SAN FRANCISCO
RANCHO SIMI
HAPPY CAMP CANYON RD
OAK RIDGE
BIG MOUNTAIN
MIDDLE RANGE FIRE RD
HAPPY CAMP CANYON REGIONAL PARK
VENTURA CO.
SEE 466 MAP
SEE 367 MAP
SEE 477 MAP
miles 1 in. = 2400 ft.

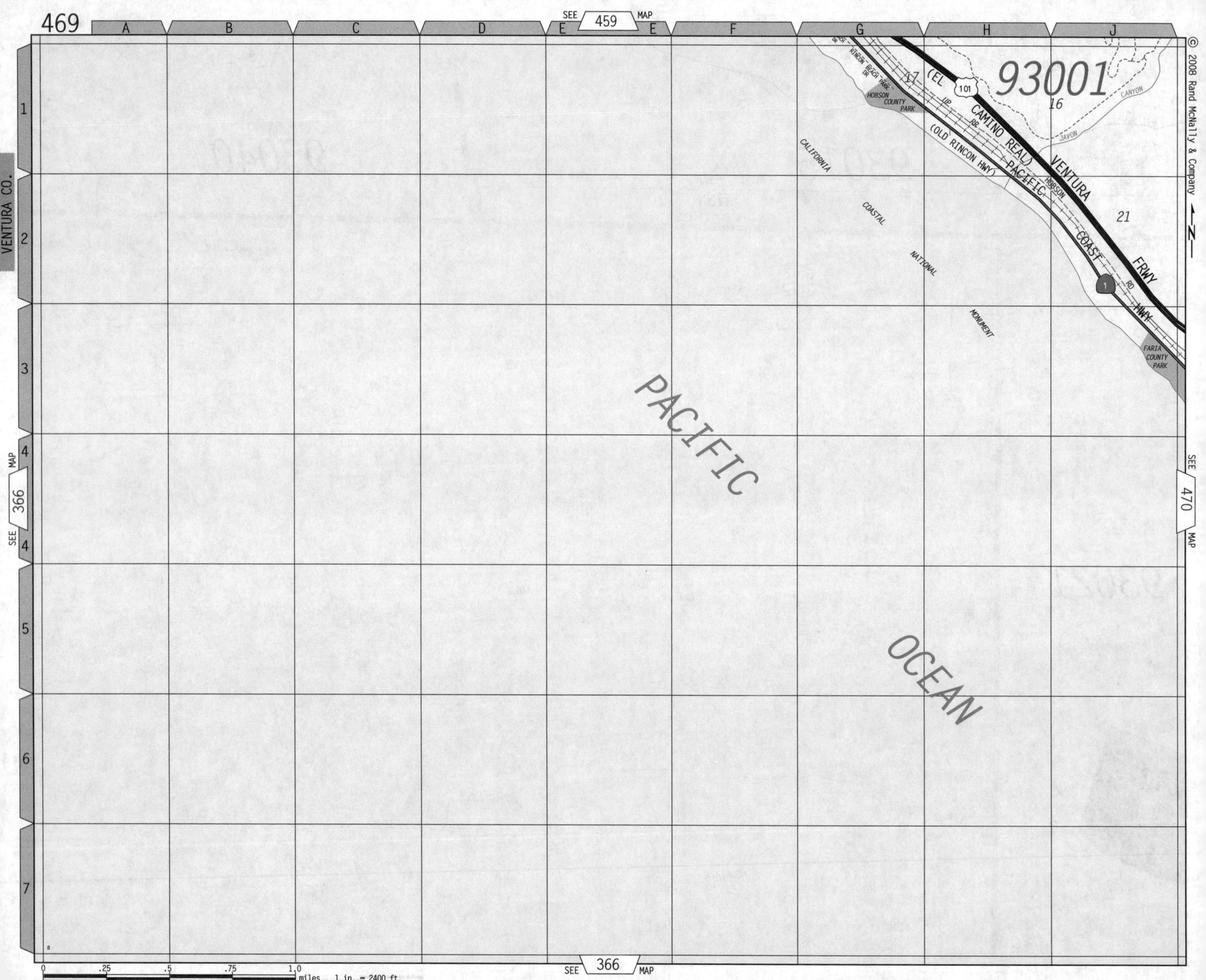

SEE 459 MAP
A
B
C
D
E
F
G
H
J
1
2
3
4
5
6
7
VENTURA CO.
SEE 366 MAP
SEE 470 MAP
SEE 366 MAP
93001
VENTURA
FRWY
101
(EL CAMINO REAL)
(OLD RINCON HWY)
PACIFIC COAST HWY
HOBSON RD
1
UP RR
HOBSON COUNTY PARK
FARIA COUNTY PARK
RINCON BEACH PARK DR
JAVON CANYON
CALIFORNIA COASTAL NATIONAL MONUMENT
PACIFIC
OCEAN
16
17
21
0 .25 .5 .75 1.0 miles 1 in. = 2400 ft.

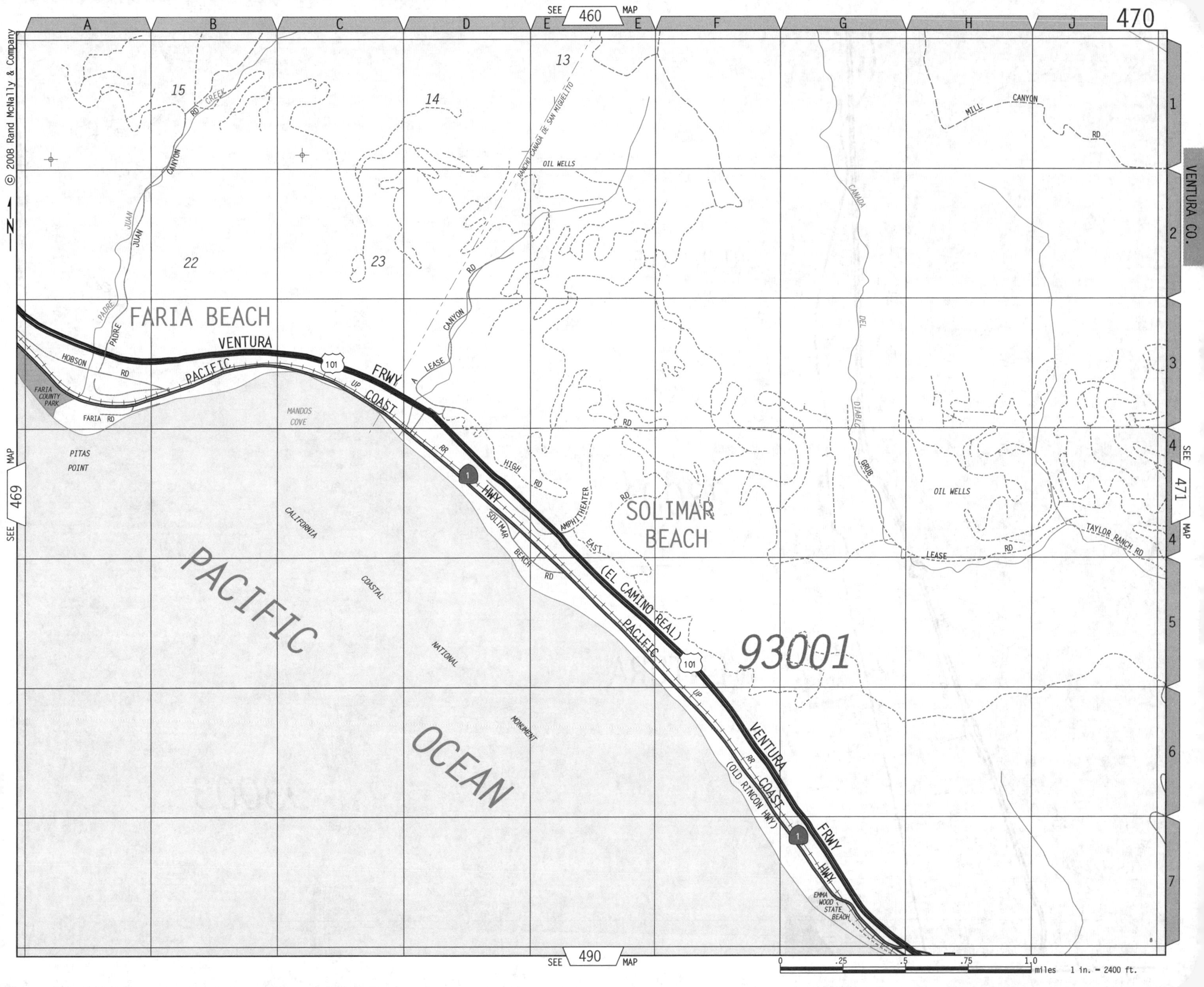

SEE 460 MAP
A
B
C
D
E
F
G
H
J
FARIA BEACH
VENTURA
FRWY
PACIFIC
COAST
HWY
HOBSON RD
FARIA COUNTY PARK
FARIA RD
MANDOS COVE
PITAS POINT
PADRE JUAN CANYON RD CREEK
OIL WELLS
RANCHO CANADA DE SAN MIGUELITO
CANYON RD
LEASE
HIGH RD
AMPHITHEATER RD
EAST (EL CAMINO REAL)
SOLIMAR BEACH RD
SOLIMAR BEACH
CANADA DEL DIABLO
GRUB
MILL CANYON RD
OIL WELLS
TAYLOR RANCH RD
LEASE RD
93001
PACIFIC OCEAN
CALIFORNIA COASTAL NATIONAL MONUMENT
UP RR
(OLD RINCON HWY)
EMMA WOOD STATE BEACH
101
1
13
14
15
22
23
VENTURA CO.
SEE 469 MAP
SEE 471 MAP
SEE 490 MAP
0 .25 .5 .75 1.0 miles 1 in. = 2400 ft.

SEE 461 MAP

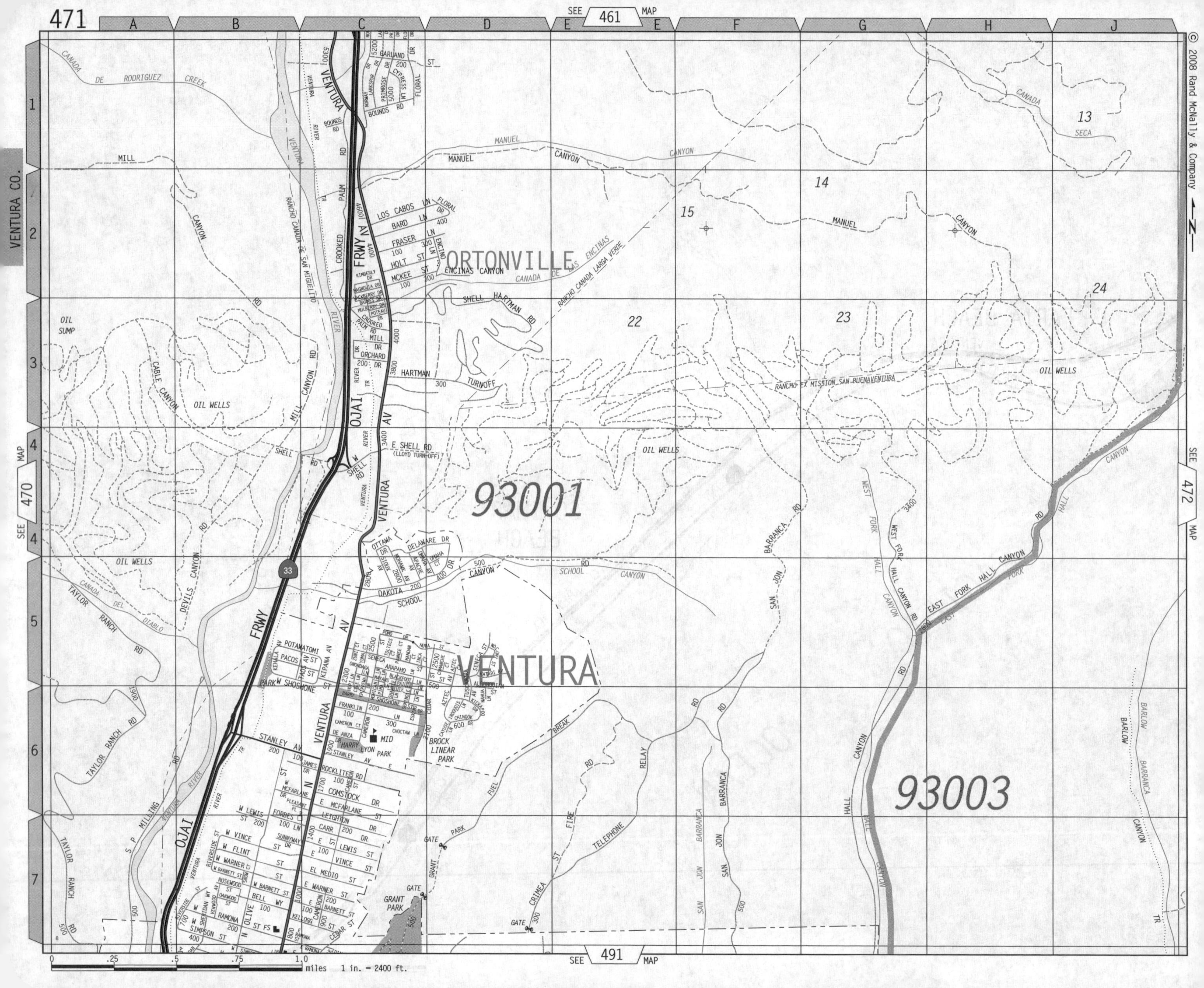

SEE 470 MAP

SEE 472 MAP

SEE 491 MAP

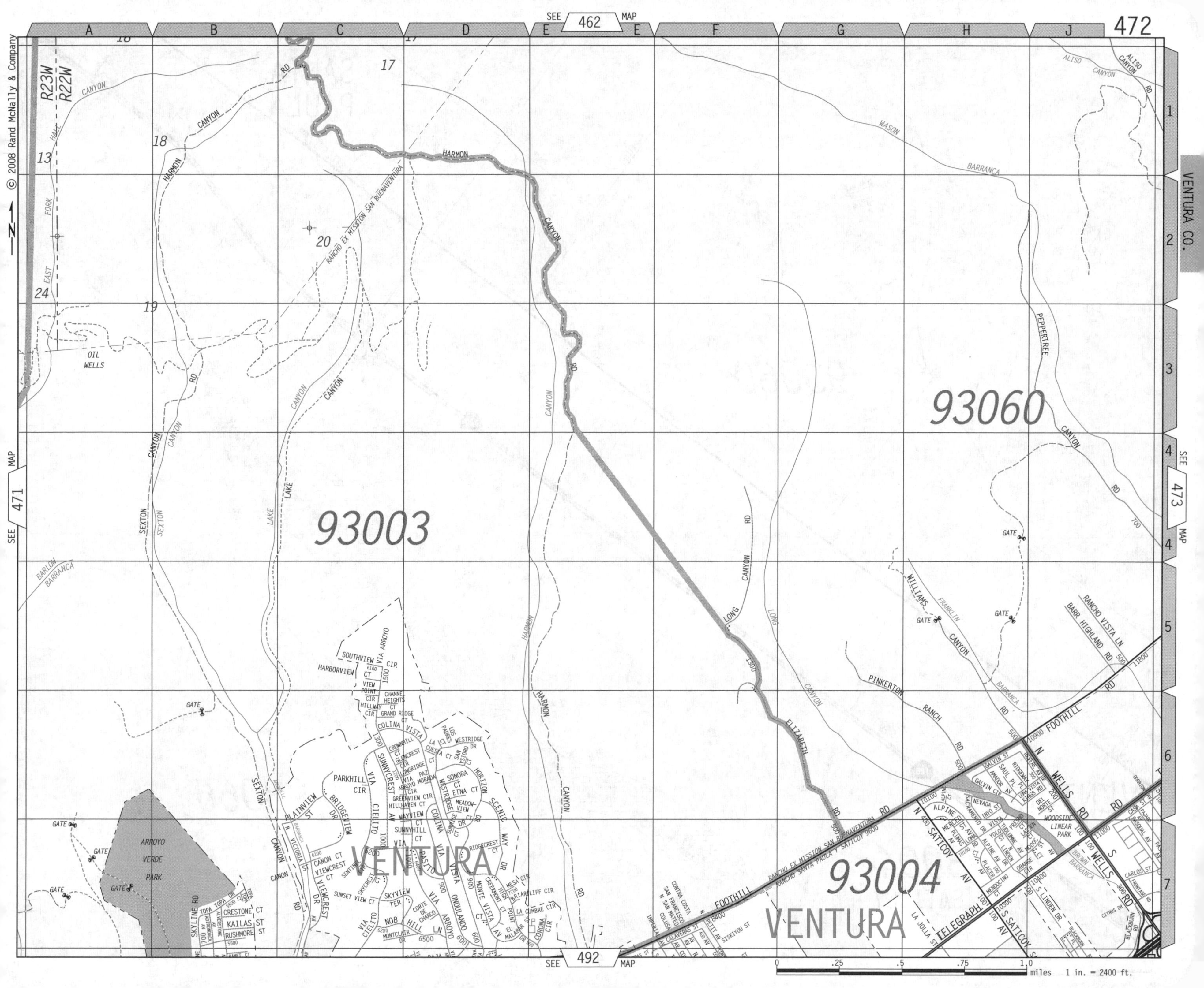
A
B
C
D
E
F
G
H
J
1
2
3
4
5
6
7
SEE 462 MAP
SEE 471 MAP
SEE 473 MAP
SEE 492 MAP
R23W
R22W
VENTURA CO.
93003
93060
93004
VENTURA
ARROYO VERDE PARK
OIL WELLS
HARMON CANYON RD
SEXTON CANYON
LAKE CANYON
LONG CANYON RD
WASON BARRANCA
ALISO CANYON RD
PEPPERTREE
WILLIAMS CANYON
PINKERTON RANCH RD
ELIZABETH RD
FOOTHILL RD
WELLS RD
TELEGRAPH RD
BARLOW BARRANCA
BROWN BARRANCA
FRANKLIN BARRANCA
RANCHO EX MISSION SAN BUENAVENTURA
WOODSIDE LINEAR PARK
GATE
0 .25 .5 .75 1.0 miles 1 in. = 2400 ft.
© 2008 Rand McNally & Company

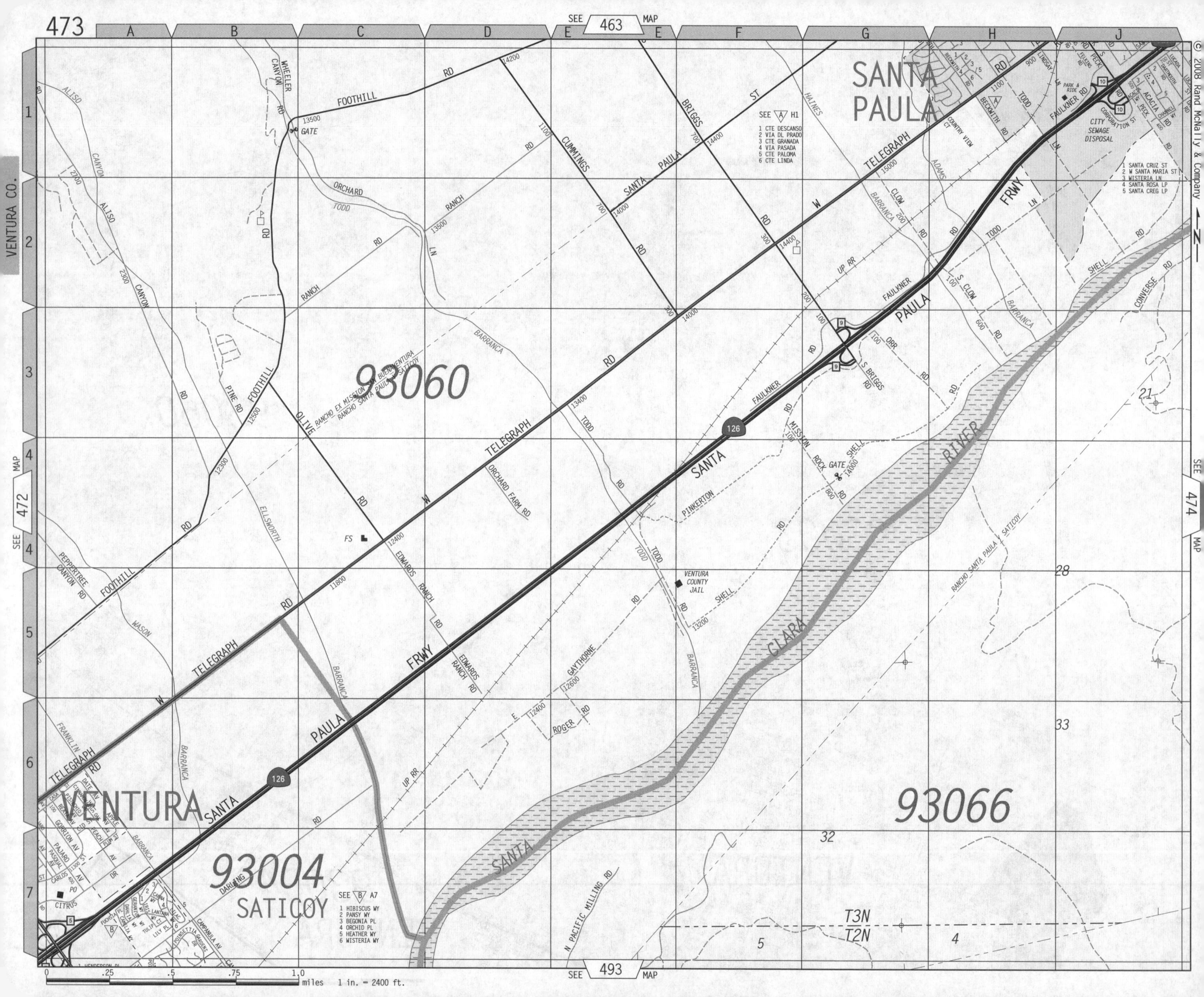

473
SEE 463 MAP
SEE 472 MAP
SEE 474 MAP
SEE 493 MAP
VENTURA CO.
© 2008 Rand McNally & Company
SANTA PAULA
VENTURA
SATICOY
93060
93066
93004
SEE A H1
1 CTE DESCANSO
2 VIA DL PRADO
3 CTE GRANADA
4 VIA PASADA
5 CTE PALOMA
6 CTE LINDA
1 SANTA CRUZ ST
2 W SANTA MARIA ST
3 WISTERIA LN
4 SANTA ROSA LP
5 SANTA CREG LP
SEE B A7
1 HIBISCUS WY
2 PANSY WY
3 BEGONIA PL
4 ORCHID PL
5 HEATHER WY
6 WISTERIA WY
CITY SEWAGE DISPOSAL
VENTURA COUNTY JAIL
PARK & RIDE
FOOTHILL RD
TELEGRAPH RD
SANTA PAULA FRWY
SANTA CLARA RIVER
BRIGGS RD
CUMMINGS RD
OLIVE RD
TODD LN
ORCHARD RD
RANCH RD
WHEELER CANYON RD
ALISO CANYON RD
PEPPERTREE CANYON RD
ELLSWORTH BARRANCA
EDWARDS RANCH RD
ORCHARD FARM RD
PINKERTON RD
SHELL RD
MISSION ROCK RD
FAULKNER RD
S BRIGGS RD
CLOW RD
ORR RD
CONVERSE RD
N PACIFIC MILLING RD
GAYTHORNE RD
ROGER RD
DARLING RD
UP RR
RANCHO EX MISION SAN BUENAVENTURA
RANCHO SANTA PAULA Y SATICOY
T3N
T2N
miles 1 in. = 2400 ft.

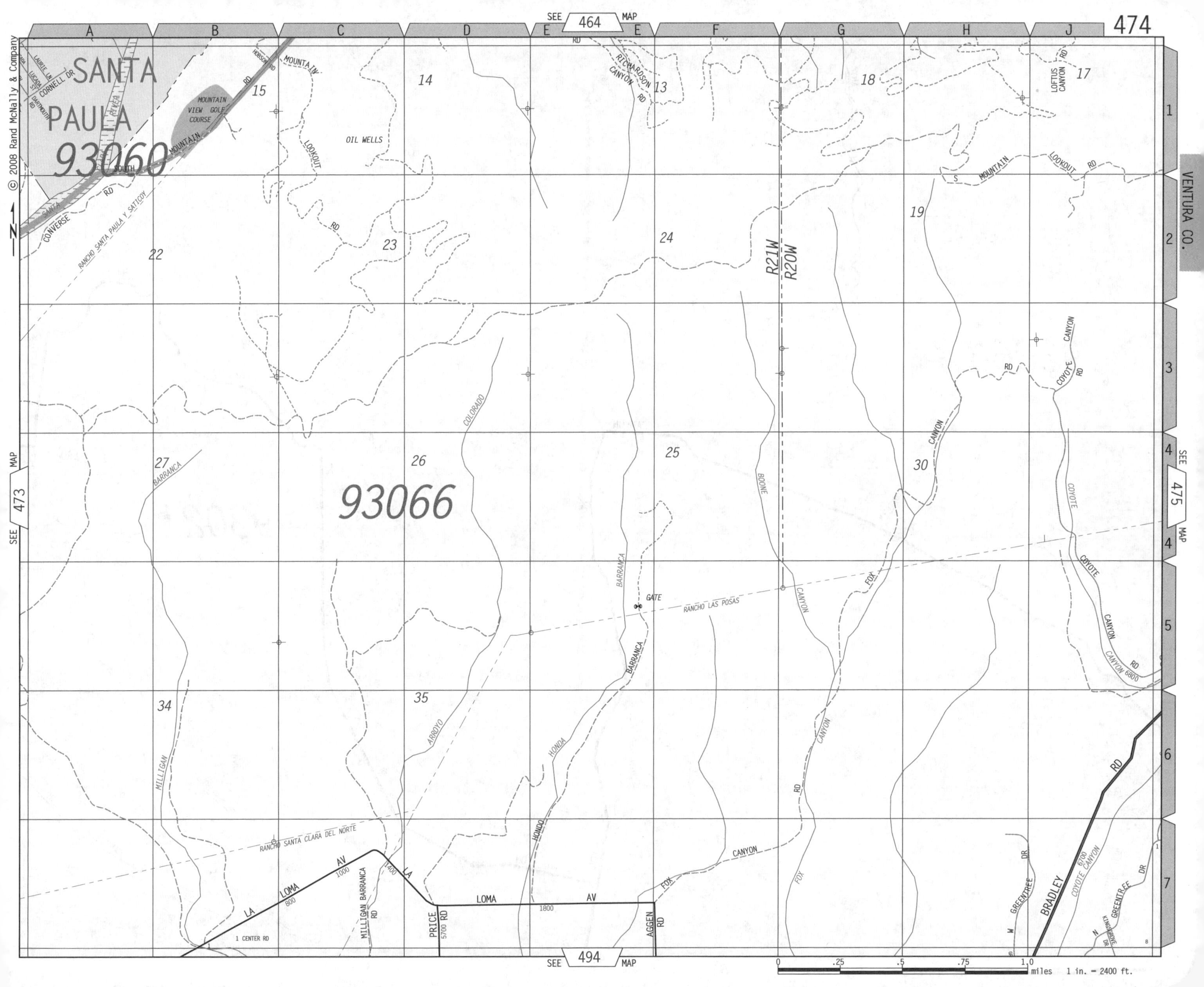
SEE 464 MAP
SANTA PAULA
93060
93066
MOUNTAIN VIEW GOLF COURSE
OIL WELLS
VENTURA CO.
R21W
R20W
GATE
RANCHO SANTA PAULA Y SATICOY
RANCHO LAS POSAS
RANCHO SANTA CLARA DEL NORTE
CONVERSE RD
LOOKOUT RD
MOUNTAIN RD
S MOUNTAIN
RICHARDSON CANYON RD
LOFTUS CANYON RD
COYOTE CANYON RD
FOX CANYON RD
BOONE
COLORADO
BARRANCA
MILLIGAN
ARROYO
HONDA
HONDO
LA LOMA AV
LOMA AV
PRICE RD
AGGEN RD
MILLIGAN BARRANCA RD
BRADLEY RD
W GREENTREE DR
N GREENTREE DR
1 CENTER RD
SEE 473 MAP
SEE 475 MAP
SEE 494 MAP
0 .25 .5 .75 1.0 miles 1 in. = 2400 ft.
© 2008 Rand McNally & Company

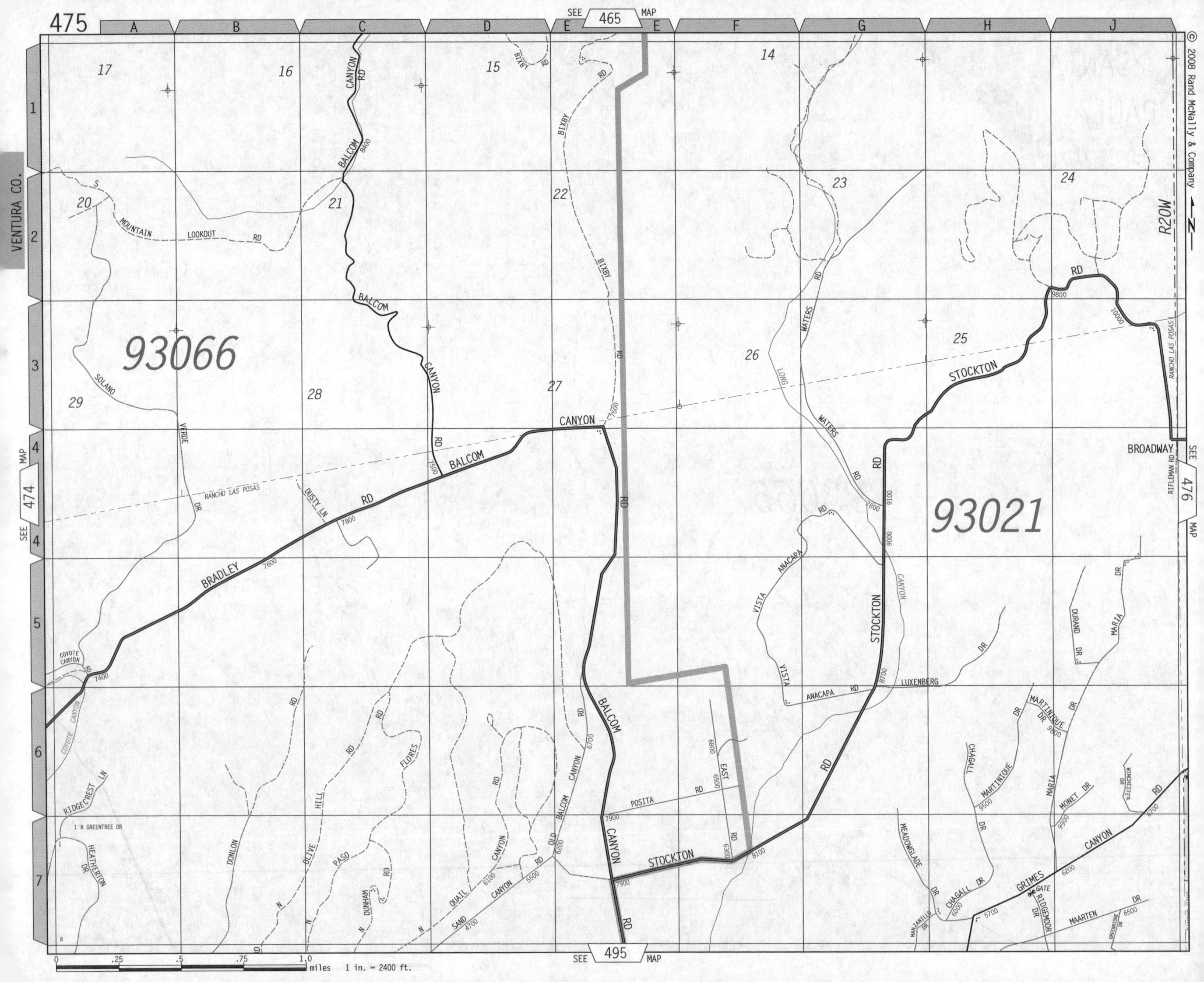

SEE 465 MAP
SEE 474 MAP
SEE 476 MAP
SEE 495 MAP
VENTURA CO.
93066
93021
R20W
BALCOM CANYON RD
MOUNTAIN LOOKOUT RD
BIXBY RD
SOLANO
VERDE DR
RANCHO LAS POSAS
DUSTY LN
BRADLEY RD
COYOTE CANYON RD
RIDGECREST LN
1 N GREENTREE DR
HEATHERTON DR
DONLON
N OLIVE
HILL RD
PASO RD
FLORES
N DUNHAM RD
N QUAIL CANYON RD
SAND CANYON RD
OLD BALCOM CANYON RD
POSITA RD
EAST RD
STOCKTON RD
LONG WATERS RD
VISTA ANACAPA RD
CANYON
LUXENBERG DR
BROADWAY
RIFLEMAN RD
RANCHO LAS POSAS RD
DURAND DR
MARIA DR
MARTINIQUE DR
CHAGALL DR
MEADOWGLADE DR
MANZANILLO DR
MONET DR
WINCHESTER DR
GRIMES CANYON RD
GATE
RIDGEMOOR DR
MAARTEN DR
GREENRIDGE DR
miles 1 in. = 2400 ft.

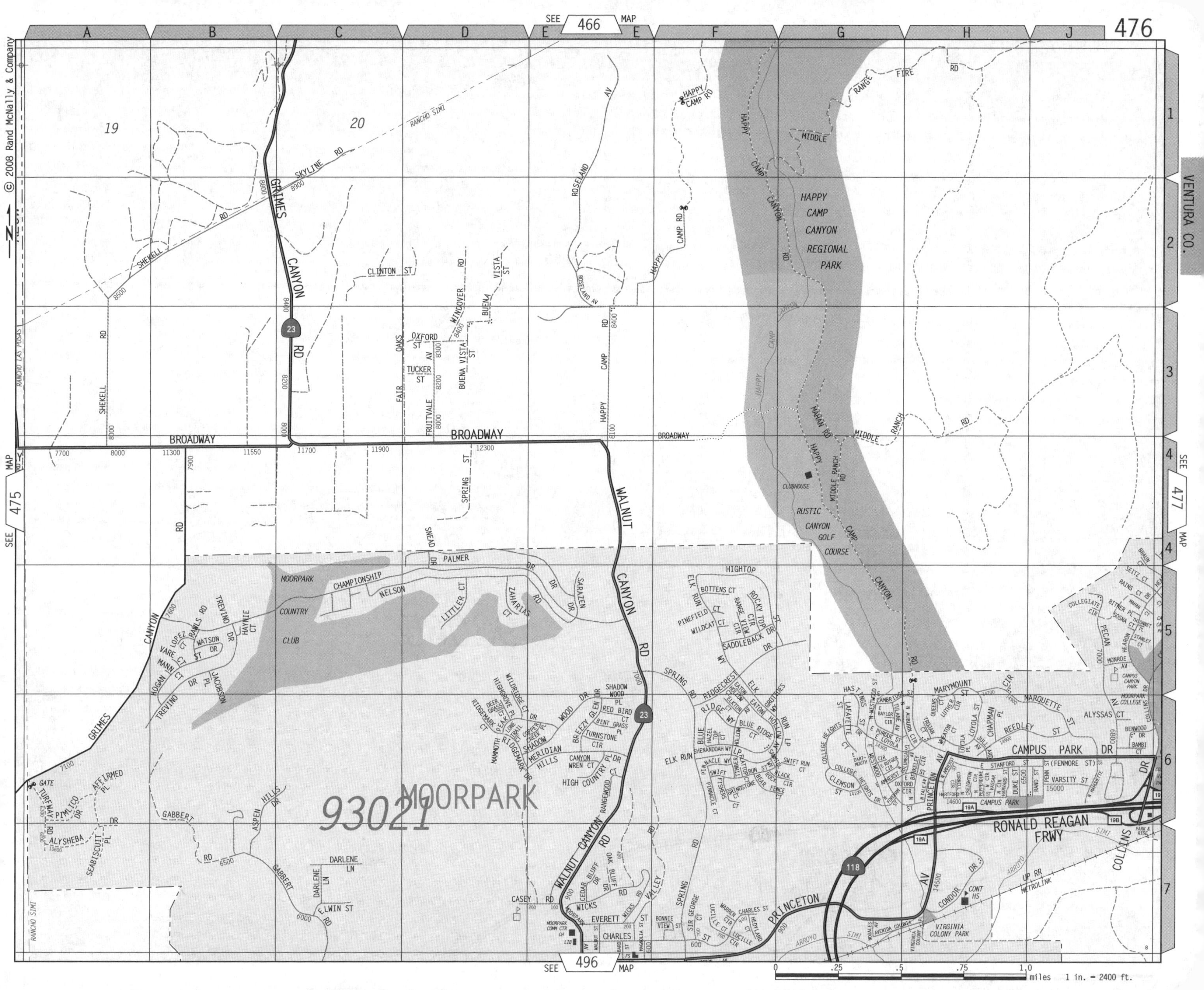

SEE 466 MAP
A
B
C
D
E
F
G
H
J
1
2
3
4
5
6
7
19
20
GRIMES CANYON RD
SKYLINE RD
RANCHO SIMI
SHEKELL RD
CLINTON ST
OXFORD ST
TUCKER ST
FAIR OAKS AV
FRUITVALE
BUENA VISTA ST
WINDOVER RD
ROSELAND AV
HAPPY CAMP RD
HAPPY CAMP CANYON RD
HAPPY CAMP CANYON REGIONAL PARK
MIDDLE RANCH RD
RANGE FIRE RD
MAHAN RD
BROADWAY
WALNUT CANYON RD
SPRING ST
CLUBHOUSE
RUSTIC CANYON GOLF COURSE
MOORPARK COUNTRY CLUB
CHAMPIONSHIP DR
NELSON
PALMER DR
SNEAD DR
LITTLER CT
ZAHARIAS CT
SARAZEN DR
TREVINO DR
HAYNIE CT
WATSON DR
HOGAN CT
JACOBSON PL
HIGHTOP
BOTTENS CT
ELK RUN
ROCKY TOP ST
PINEFIELD CT
WILDCAT CT
SADDLEBACK DR
SPRING RD
RIDGECREST
BLUE RIDGE
SHADOW WOOD PL
RED BIRD CT
TURNSTONE CIR
MERIDIAN HILLS
HIGH COUNTRY PL
RANGEWOOD CT
CANYON WREN CT
MARYMOUNT CIR
MARQUETTE ST
CAMPUS PARK DR
COLLEGE HEIGHTS
CLEMSON ST
PRINCETON AV
LOYOLA ST
CHAPMAN PL
REEDLEY ST
ALYSSAS CT
VARSITY ST
CAMPUS PARK
RONALD REAGAN FRWY
COLLINS DR
MOORPARK COLLEGE
CAMPUS CANYON PARK
COLLEGIATE CIR
PECAN AV
MONROE AV
GABBERT RD
ASPEN HILLS DR
DARLENE LN
ELWIN ST
TURFWAY RD
PIMLICO DR
AFFIRMED PL
ALYSHEBA
SEABISCUIT PL
MOORPARK
93021
CASEY RD
WICKS RD
EVERETT ST
CHARLES ST
OAK BLUFF DR
CEDAR BLUFF DR
VALLEY
SIR GEORGE CT
PRINCETON
CONDOR DR
CONT HS
VIRGINIA COLONY PARK
UP RR
METROLINK
ARROYO SIMI
SEE 475 MAP
SEE 477 MAP
VENTURA CO.
SEE 496 MAP
0 .25 .5 .75 1.0 miles 1 in. = 2400 ft.

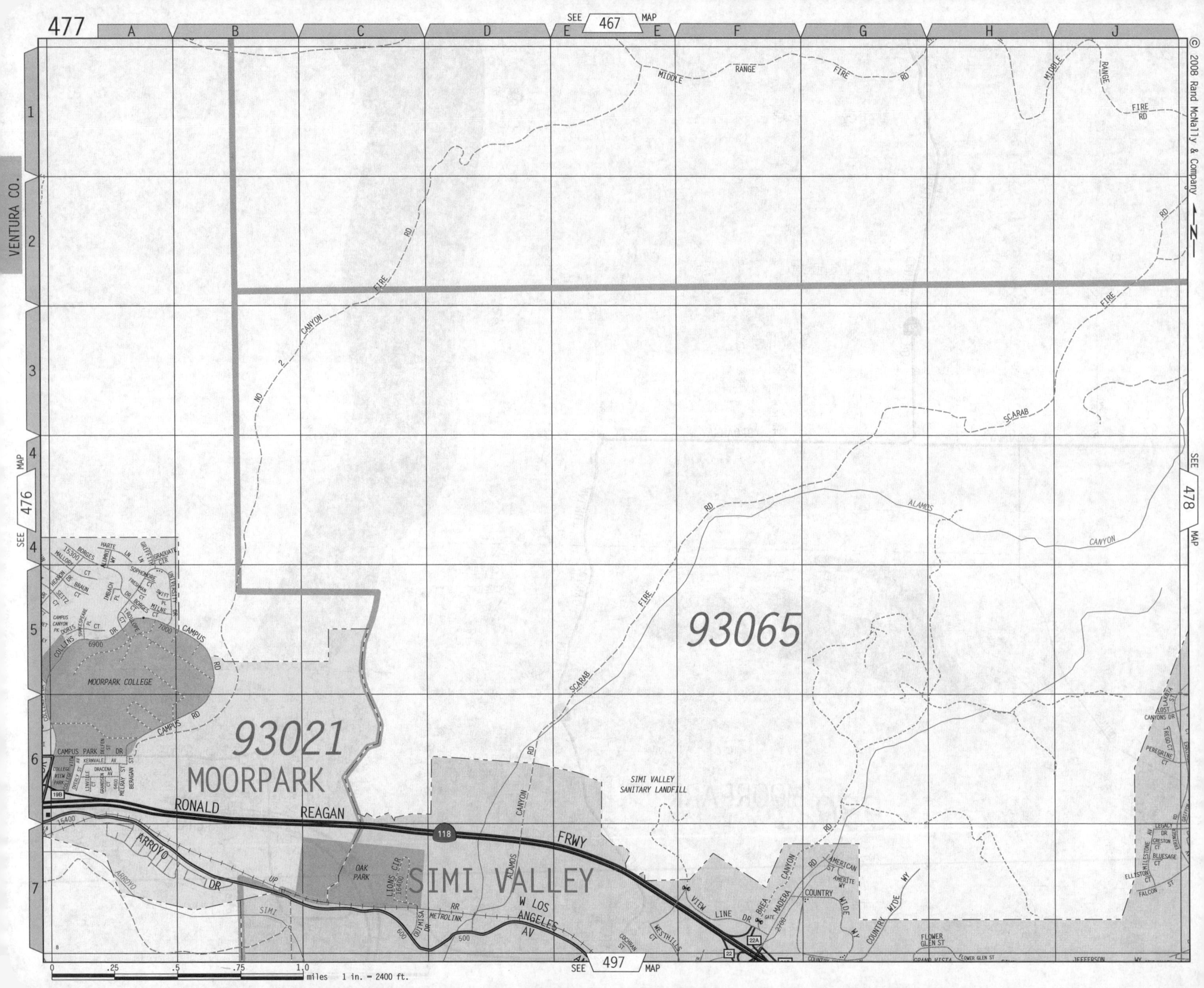
SEE 467 MAP
SEE 497 MAP
SEE 476 MAP
SEE 478 MAP
VENTURA CO.
93021
93065
MOORPARK
SIMI VALLEY
MOORPARK COLLEGE
OAK PARK
SIMI VALLEY SANITARY LANDFILL
RONALD REAGAN FRWY
118
MIDDLE RANGE FIRE RD
NO 2 CANYON FIRE RD
SCARAB FIRE RD
ALAMOS CANYON
CANYON RD
CAMPUS RD
CAMPUS PARK DR
ARROYO DR
W LOS ANGELES AV
METROLINK RR
UP
VIEW LINE DR
MADERA RD
COUNTRY WIDE WY
AMERICAN ST
FLOWER GLEN ST
JEFFERSON
LOST CANYONS DR
PEREGRINE CT
FALCON ST
BLUESAGE CT
0 .25 .5 .75 1.0 miles 1 in. = 2400 ft.
© 2008 Rand McNally & Company

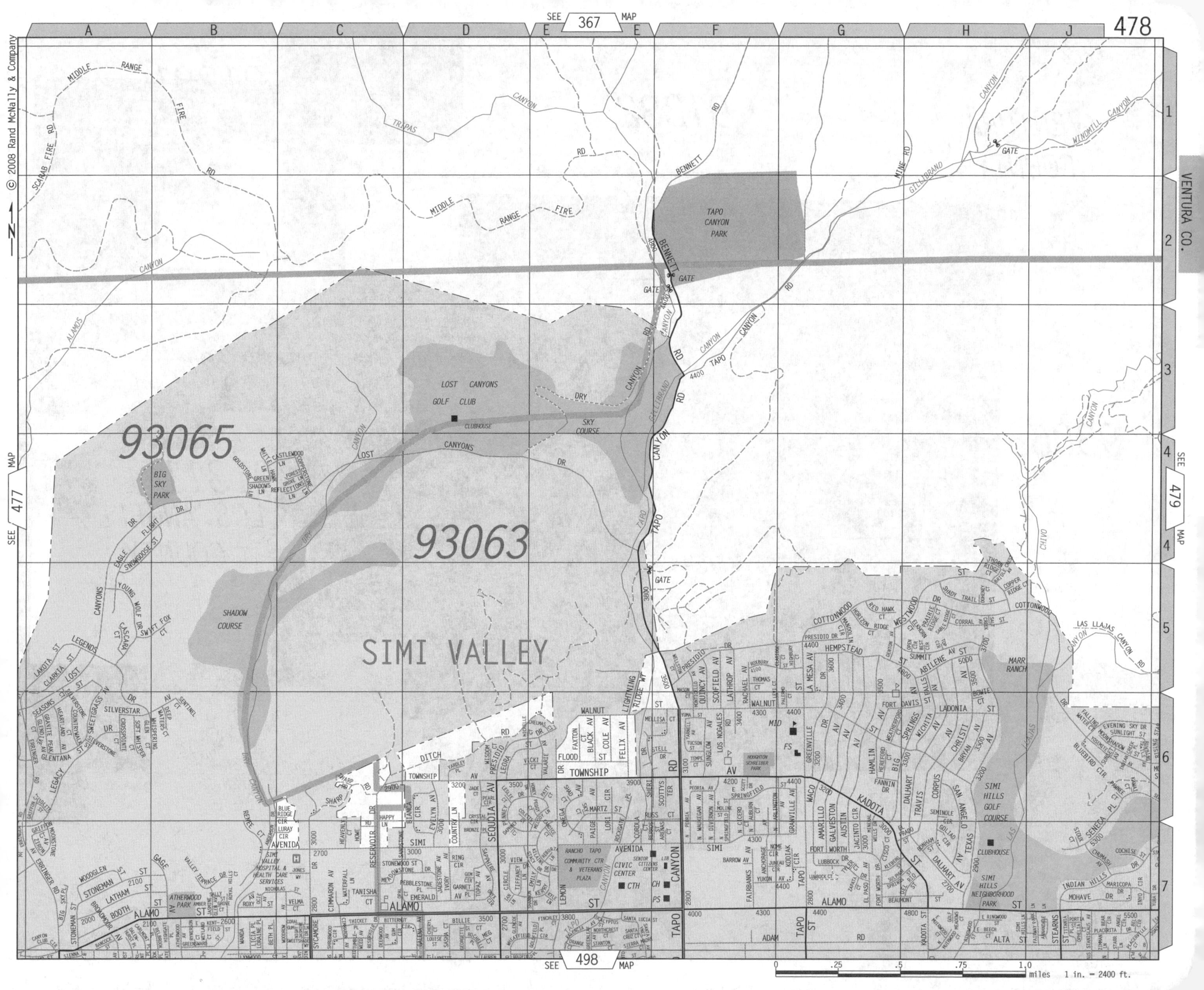
SEE 367 MAP
SEE 477 MAP
SEE 479 MAP
SEE 498 MAP
VENTURA CO.
© 2008 Rand McNally & Company
93065
93063
SIMI VALLEY
TAPO CANYON PARK
LOST CANYONS GOLF CLUB
CLUBHOUSE
SKY COURSE
SHADOW COURSE
BIG SKY PARK
MARR RANCH
SIMI HILLS GOLF COURSE
SIMI HILLS NEIGHBORHOOD PARK
ATHERWOOD PARK
HOUGHTON SCHREIBER PARK
RANCHO TAPO COMMUNITY CTR & VETERANS PLAZA
CIVIC CENTER
SENIOR CITIZENS CENTER
SIMI VALLEY HOSPITAL & HEALTH CARE SERVICES
MIDDLE RANGE FIRE RD
SCARAB FIRE RD
TRAPAS CANYON RD
BENNETT RD
TAPO CANYON RD
GILLIBRAND
WINDMILL CANYON
MINE RD
GATE
LOST CANYONS DR
DRY CANYON
ALAMOS CANYON
LAS LLAJAS CANYON RD
CHIVO
COTTONWOOD
WESTWOOD
HEMPSTEAD
PRESIDIO DR
WALNUT ST
TOWNSHIP AV
KADOTA ST
ALAMO ST
ADAM RD
SIMI
AVENIDA
SEQUOIA AV
RESERVOIR DR
TAPO ST
STEARNS
ERRINGER RD
STONEMAN ST
LEGACY
LEGENDS
EAGLE FLIGHT DR
CASCARA
SWIFT FOX CT
LIGHTNING RIDGE WY
0 .25 .5 .75 1.0 miles 1 in. = 2400 ft.

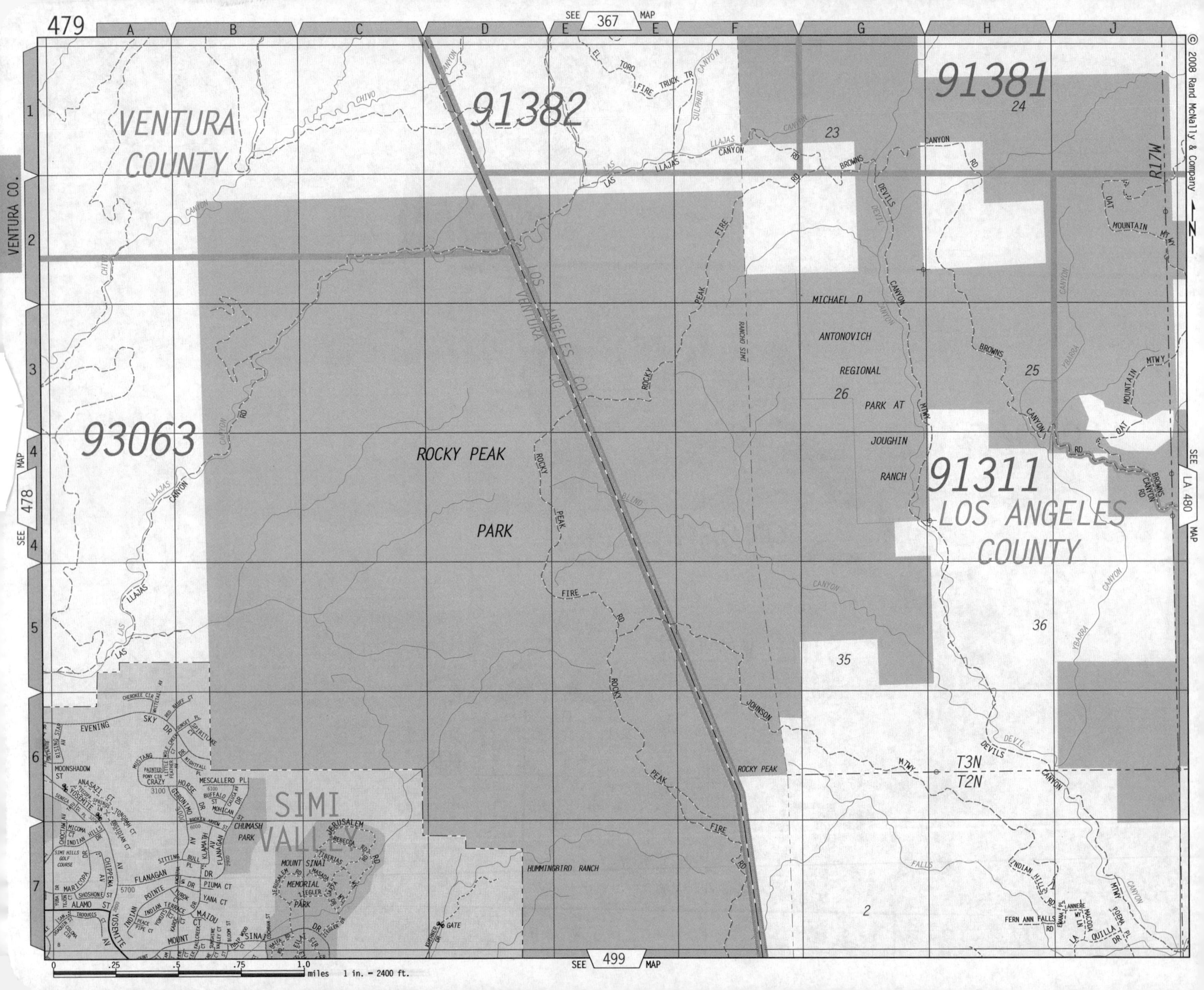

SEE 367 MAP
A B C D E E F G H J
1 2 3 4 4 5 6 7
VENTURA CO.
VENTURA COUNTY
91382
91381
93063
91311
LOS ANGELES COUNTY
SIMI VALLEY
LOS ANGELES CO
VENTURA CO
ROCKY PEAK PARK
MICHAEL D ANTONOVICH REGIONAL PARK AT JOUGHIN RANCH
EL TORO FIRE TRUCK TR
CHIVO CANYON
SULPHUR CANYON
LAS LLAJAS CANYON
BROWNS CANYON RD
DEVILS CANYON
OAT MOUNTAIN MTWY
ROCKY PEAK FIRE RD
RANCHO SIMI
JOHNSON
BLIND CANYON
YBARRA CANYON
R17W
T3N
T2N
23 24 25 26 35 36 2
HUMMINGBIRD RANCH
CHUMASH PARK
MOUNT SINAI MEMORIAL PARK
SIMI HILLS GOLF COURSE
EVENING SKY DR
MOONSHADOW ST
ANASAZI CT
YOSEMITE AV
INDIAN HILLS DR
CHIPPEWA AV
MARICOPA ST
FLANAGAN DR
INDIAN POINTE
MAIDU CT
GERONIMO AV
MESCALLERO PL
BUFFALO
MOHICAN
KLAMATH
SITTING BULL PL
CRAZY HORSE DR
JERUSALEM RD
MOUNT SINAI DR
GATE
FERN ANN FALLS RD
INDIAN HILLS RD
QUILLA DR
POEMA PL
ROCKY PEAK
SEE 478 MAP
SEE LA 480 MAP
SEE 499 MAP
0 .25 .5 .75 1.0 miles 1 in. = 2400 ft.

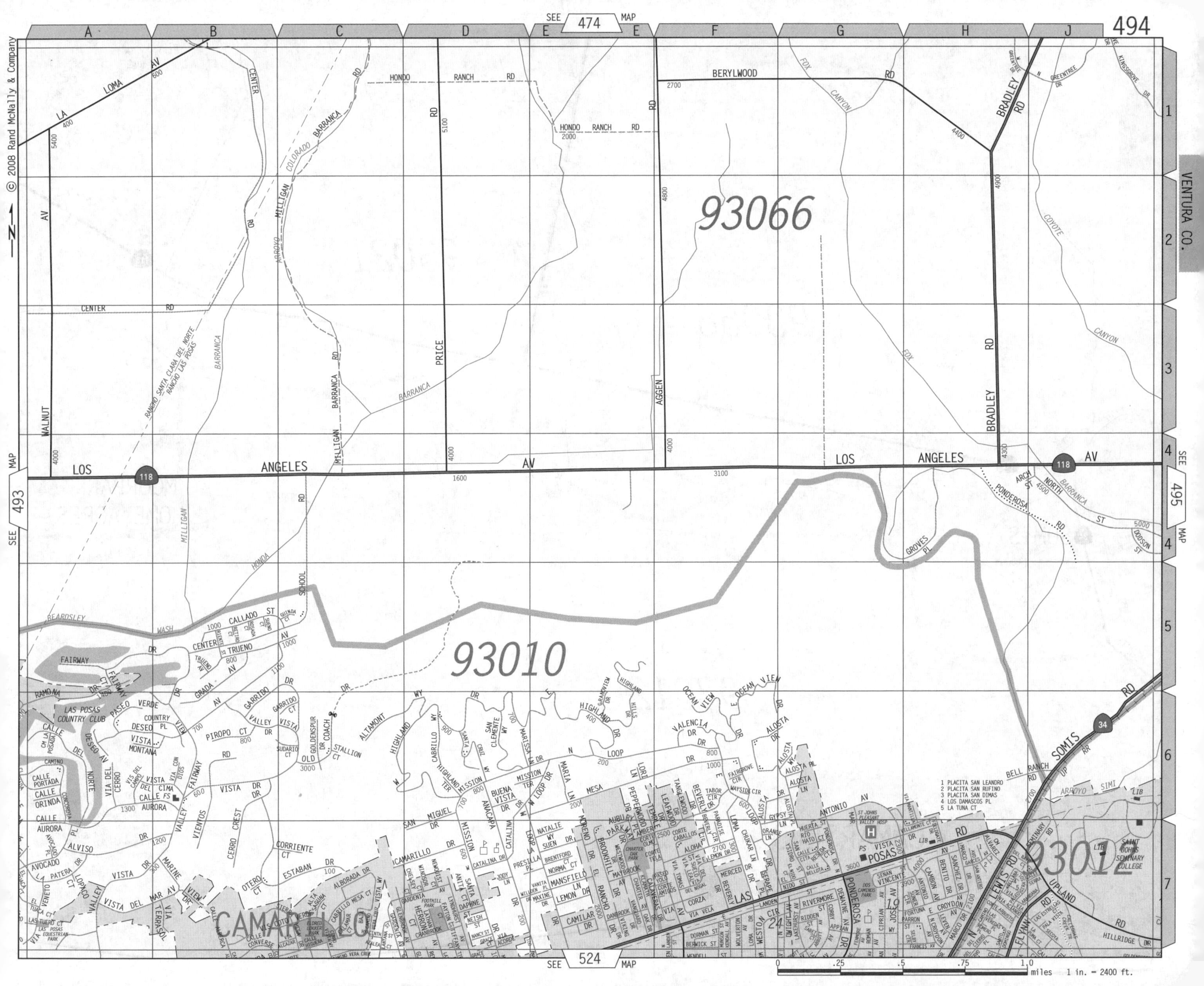

494
SEE 474 MAP
SEE 524 MAP
SEE 493 MAP
SEE 495 MAP
VENTURA CO.
© 2008 Rand McNally & Company
93066
93010
93012
LOS ANGELES AV
BERYLWOOD RD
HONDO RANCH RD
CENTER RD
WALNUT AV
LA LOMA AV
PRICE RD
AGGEN RD
BRADLEY RD
MILLIGAN BARRANCA RD
FOX CANYON
COYOTE CANYON
BEARDSLEY WASH
ARROYO SIMI
LAS POSAS COUNTRY CLUB
CAMARILLO
LAS POSAS RD
SANTA ROSA RD
SOMIS RD
UPLAND RD
LEWIS RD
PONDEROSA DR
ST JOHNS PLEASANT VALLEY HOSP
SAINT JOHNS SEMINARY COLLEGE
1 PLACITA SAN LEANDRO
2 PLACITA SAN RUFINO
3 PLACITA SAN DIMAS
4 LOS DAMASCOS PL
5 LA TUNA CT
0 .25 .5 .75 1.0 miles 1 in. = 2400 ft.

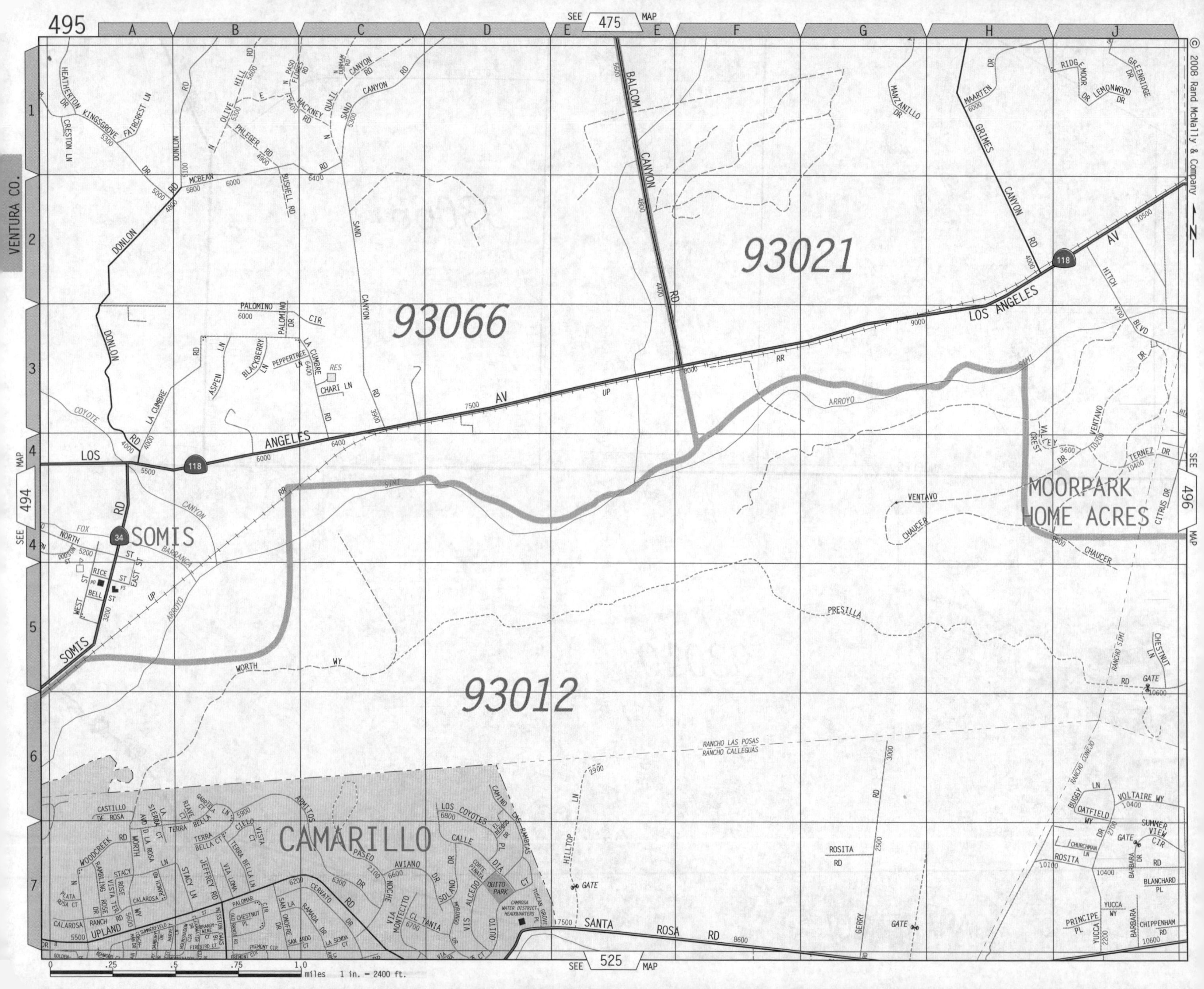

SEE 475 MAP
SEE 494 MAP
SEE 496 MAP
SEE 525 MAP
VENTURA CO.
A
B
C
D
E
F
G
H
J
1
2
3
4
5
6
7
93021
93066
93012
SOMIS
MOORPARK HOME ACRES
CAMARILLO
LOS ANGELES AV
LOS ANGELES AV
BALCOM CANYON RD
GRIMES CANYON RD
SAND CANYON RD
DONLON RD
LA CUMBRE RD
SOMIS RD
SANTA ROSA RD
UPLAND RD
HILLTOP LN
GERRY RD
ROSITA RD
SIMI ARROYO
COYOTE CANYON
BARRANCA
FOX
WORTH WY
PRESILLA
VENTAVO
CHAUCER
RANCHO LAS POSAS
RANCHO CALLEGUAS
QUITO PARK
CAMROSA WATER DISTRICT HEADQUARTERS
GATE
RES
UP
RR
118
34
MCBEAN
PHLEGER RD
BUSHELL RD
KINGSGROVE DR
FAIRCREST LN
HEATHERTON DR
CRESTON LN
OLIVE HILL RD
N PASO FLORES RD
HACKNEY RD
QUAIL
MANZANILLO DR
MAARTEN DR
RIDGEMOOR DR
LEMONWOOD DR
GREENRIDGE DR
PALOMINO CIR
BLACKBERRY LN
ASPEN LN
PEPPERTREE LN
CHARI LN
HITCH BLVD
CITRUS DR
TERNEZ DR
VALLEY CREST DR
CHESTNUT LN
RANCHO SIMI
RANCHO CONEJO
BUGGY LN
OATFIELD WY
VOLTAIRE WY
SUMMER VIEW CIR
CHURCHMAN LN
BARBARA DR
BLANCHARD PL
YUCCA WY
PRINCIPE PL
CHIPPENHAM RD
CASTILLO DE ROSA
WOODCREEK RD
CALARESA RANCH
LOS COYOTES DR
CAMINO DOS RAMBLAS
ARMITOS
PASEO AVIANO
CALLE DIA
CERVATO RD
VIA MONTECITO
CL TANIA
SOLANO DR
VIS ALCEDO
QUITO CT
TUSCAN GROVE PL
RICE ST
BELL ST
NORTH ST
EAST ST
WEST ST
0
.25
.5
.75
1.0
miles 1 in. = 2400 ft.
© 2008 Rand McNally & Company

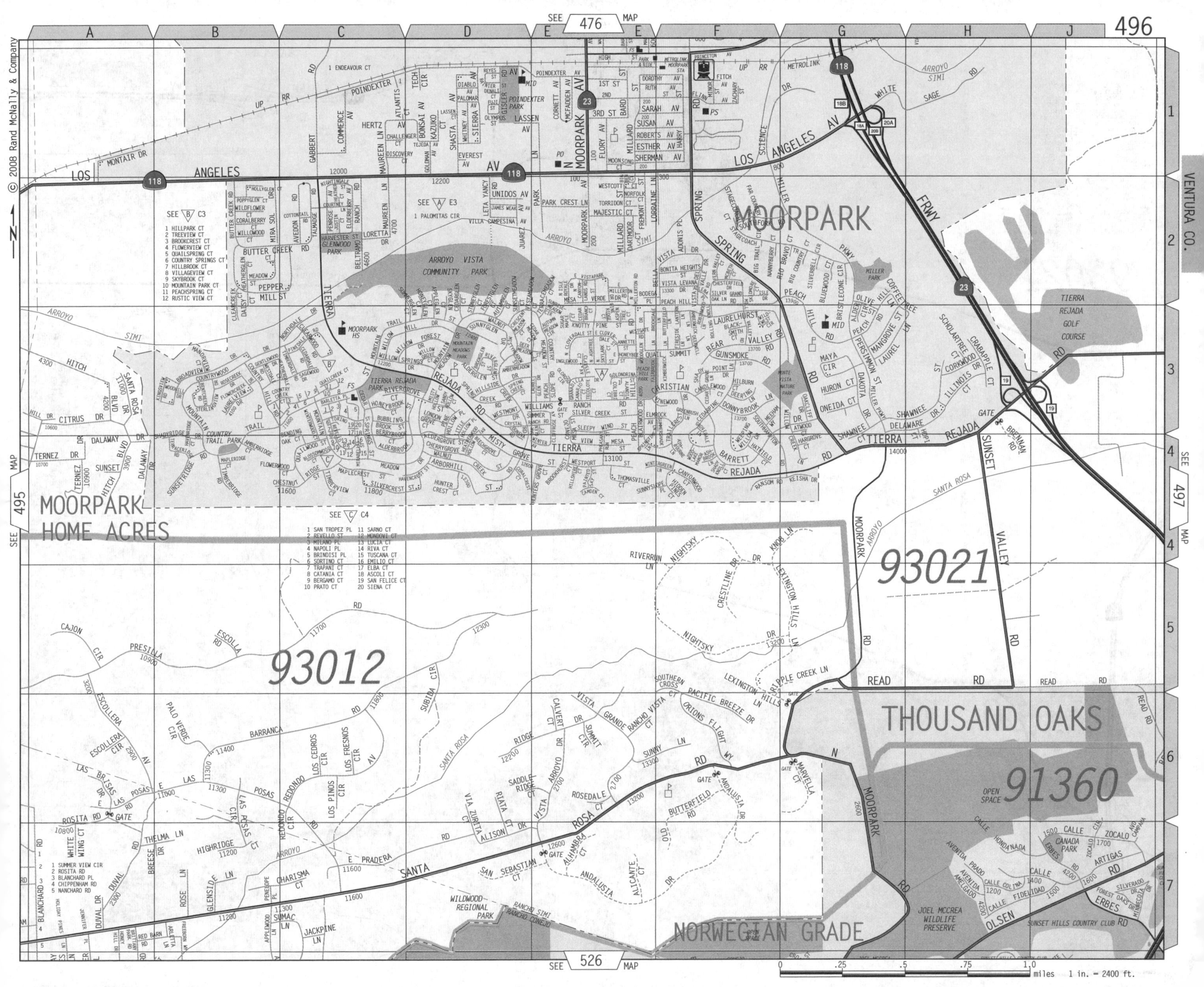
SEE 476 MAP
A
B
C
D
E
F
G
H
J
1
2
3
4
5
6
7
MOORPARK
MOORPARK HOME ACRES
THOUSAND OAKS
NORWEGIAN GRADE
VENTURA CO.
93012
93021
91360
ARROYO VISTA COMMUNITY PARK
TIERRA REJADA GOLF COURSE
TIERRA REJADA PARK
MILLER PARK
POINDEXTER PARK
GLENWOOD PARK
COUNTRY TRAIL PARK
MOUNTAIN MEADOWS PARK
MONTE VISTA NATURE PARK
PEACH HILL PARK
CANADA PARK
WILDWOOD REGIONAL PARK
JOEL MCCREA WILDLIFE PRESERVE
SUNSET HILLS COUNTRY CLUB
OPEN SPACE
MOORPARK HS
MID
PS
PO
FS
LOS ANGELES AV
118
23
FRWY
TIERRA REJADA RD
SPRING RD
MOORPARK AV
MOORPARK RD
SUNSET VALLEY RD
READ RD
SANTA ROSA RD
METROLINK
UP RR
POINDEXTER AV
HIGH ST
ARROYO SIMI
LEXINGTON HILLS LN
NIGHTSKY DR
CRESTLINE DR
RIVERRUN LN
PRESILLA CIR
CAJON CIR
ESCOLLA RD
ESCOLLERA AV
BARRANCA RD
LAS POSAS RD
RIDGE RD
VISTA GRANDE
SUNNY LN
PACIFIC BREEZE DR
ORIONS FLIGHT WY
BUTTERFIELD RD
ANDALUSIA DR
ALHAMBRA CT
SAN SEBASTIAN CT
PRADERA RD
CHARISMA CT
GLENSIDE LN
HIGHRIDGE CT
THELMA LN
ROSITA RD
GATE
SEE B C3
1 HILLPARK CT
2 TREEVIEW CT
3 BROOKCREST CT
4 FLOWERVIEW CT
5 QUAILSPRING CT
6 COUNTRY SPRINGS CT
7 HILLBROOK CT
8 VILLAGEVIEW CT
9 SKYBROOK CT
10 MOUNTAIN PARK CT
11 PEACHSPRING CT
12 RUSTIC VIEW CT
SEE C C4
1 SAN TROPEZ PL
2 REVELLO ST
3 MILANO PL
4 NAPOLI PL
5 BRINDISI PL
6 SORTINO CT
7 TRAPANI CT
8 CATANIA CT
9 BERGAMO CT
10 PRATO CT
11 SARNO CT
12 MONDOVI CT
13 LUCIA CT
14 RIVA CT
15 TUSCANA CT
16 EMILIO CT
17 ELBA CT
18 ASCOLI CT
19 SAN FELICE CT
20 SIENA CT
SEE A E3
1 PALOMITAS CIR
1 ENDEAVOUR CT
1 SUMMER VIEW CIR
2 ROSITA RD
3 BLANCHARD PL
4 CHIPPENHAM RD
5 NANCHARD RD
SEE 495 MAP
SEE 497 MAP
SEE 526 MAP
0 .25 .5 .75 1.0 miles 1 in. = 2400 ft.

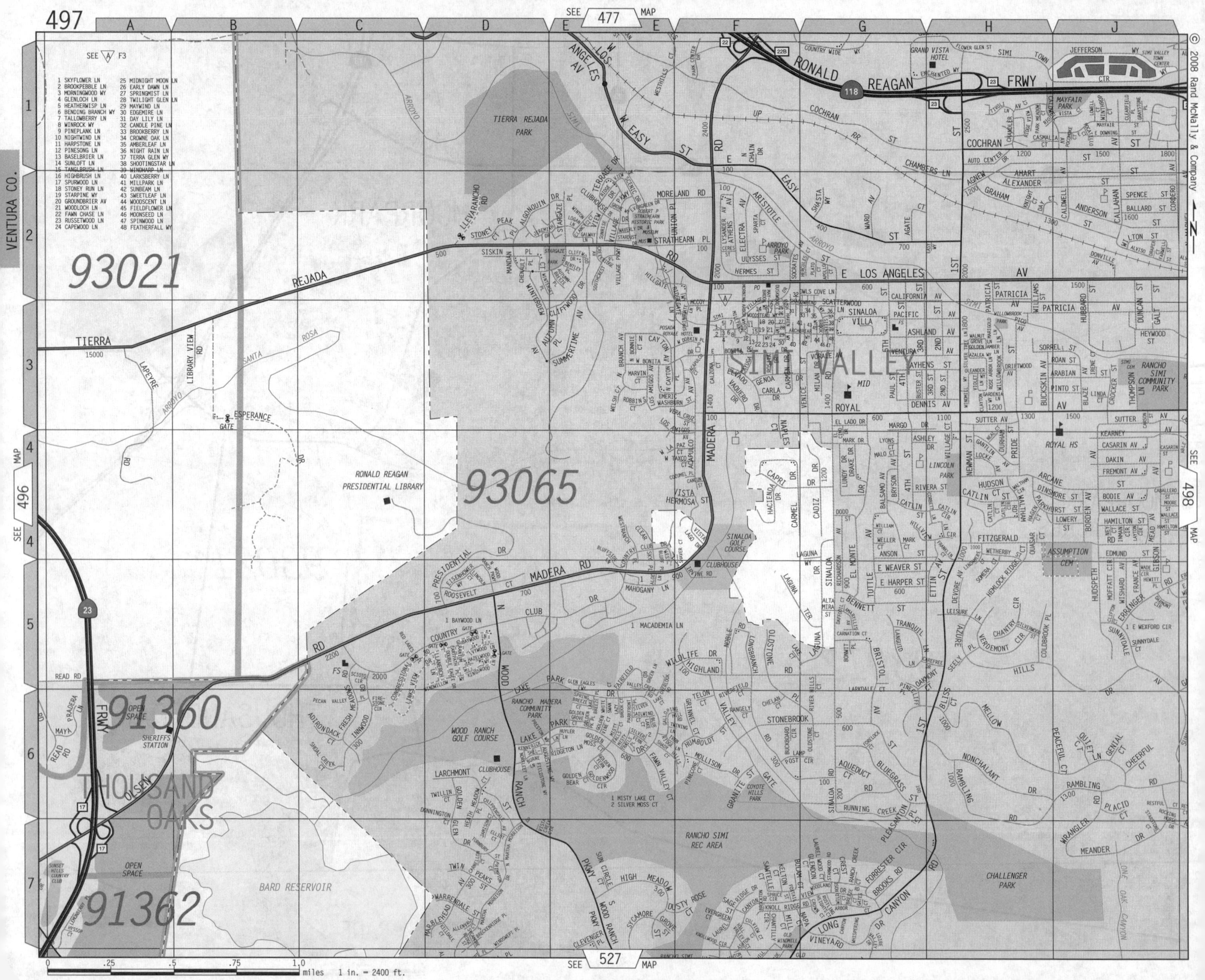
497
SEE 477 MAP
SEE 527 MAP
SEE 496 MAP
SEE 498 MAP
SEE A F3
1 SKYFLOWER LN
2 BROOKPEBBLE LN
3 MORNINGWOOD WY
4 GLENLOCH LN
5 HEATHERWISP LN
6 BENDING BRANCH WY
7 TALLOWBERRY LN
8 WINROCK WY
9 PINEPLANK LN
10 NIGHTWIND LN
11 HARPSTONE LN
12 PINESONG LN
13 BASELBRIER LN
14 SUNLOFT LN
15 TANGLEBRUSH LN
16 HIGHBRUSH LN
17 SPURWOOD LN
18 STONEY RUN LN
19 STARPINE WY
20 GROUNDBRIER AV
21 WOODLOCH LN
22 FAWN CHASE LN
23 RUSSETWOOD LN
24 CAPEWOOD LN
25 MIDNIGHT MOON LN
26 EARLY DAWN LN
27 SPRINGMIST LN
28 TWILIGHT GLEN LN
29 MAYWIND LN
30 EDGEMIRE LN
31 DAY LILY LN
32 CANDLE PINE LN
33 BROOKBERRY LN
34 CROWNE OAK LN
35 AMBERLEAF LN
36 NIGHT RAIN LN
37 TERRA GLEN WY
38 SHOOTINGSTAR LN
39 WINDHARP LN
40 LARKSBERRY LN
41 MILLPARK LN
42 SUNBEAM LN
43 SWEETLEAF LN
44 WOODSCENT LN
45 FIELDFLOWER LN
46 MOONSEED LN
47 SPINWOOD LN
48 FEATHERFALL WY
VENTURA CO.
93021
93065
91360
91362
SIMI VALLEY
THOUSAND OAKS
RONALD REAGAN FRWY
TIERRA REJADA PARK
TIERRA REJADA RD
MADERA RD
E LOS ANGELES AV
COCHRAN ST
E EASY ST
RONALD REAGAN PRESIDENTIAL LIBRARY
SINALOA GOLF COURSE
WOOD RANCH GOLF COURSE
RANCHO MADERA COMMUNITY PARK
RANCHO SIMI REC AREA
CHALLENGER PARK
RANCHO SIMI COMMUNITY PARK
ASSUMPTION CEM
ROYAL HS
LINCOLN PARK
ARROYO PARK
COYOTE HILLS PARK
BARD RESERVOIR
SHERIFFS STATION
OPEN SPACE
SUNSET HILLS COUNTRY CLUB
GRAND VISTA HOTEL
POSADA ROYALE HOTEL
ROBERT P STRATHEARN HISTORIC PARK
1 MACADEMIA LN
1 BAYWOOD LN
1 MISTY LAKE CT
2 SILVER MOSS CT
1 E WEXFORD CIR
© 2008 Rand McNally & Company
0 .25 .5 .75 1.0 miles 1 in. = 2400 ft.

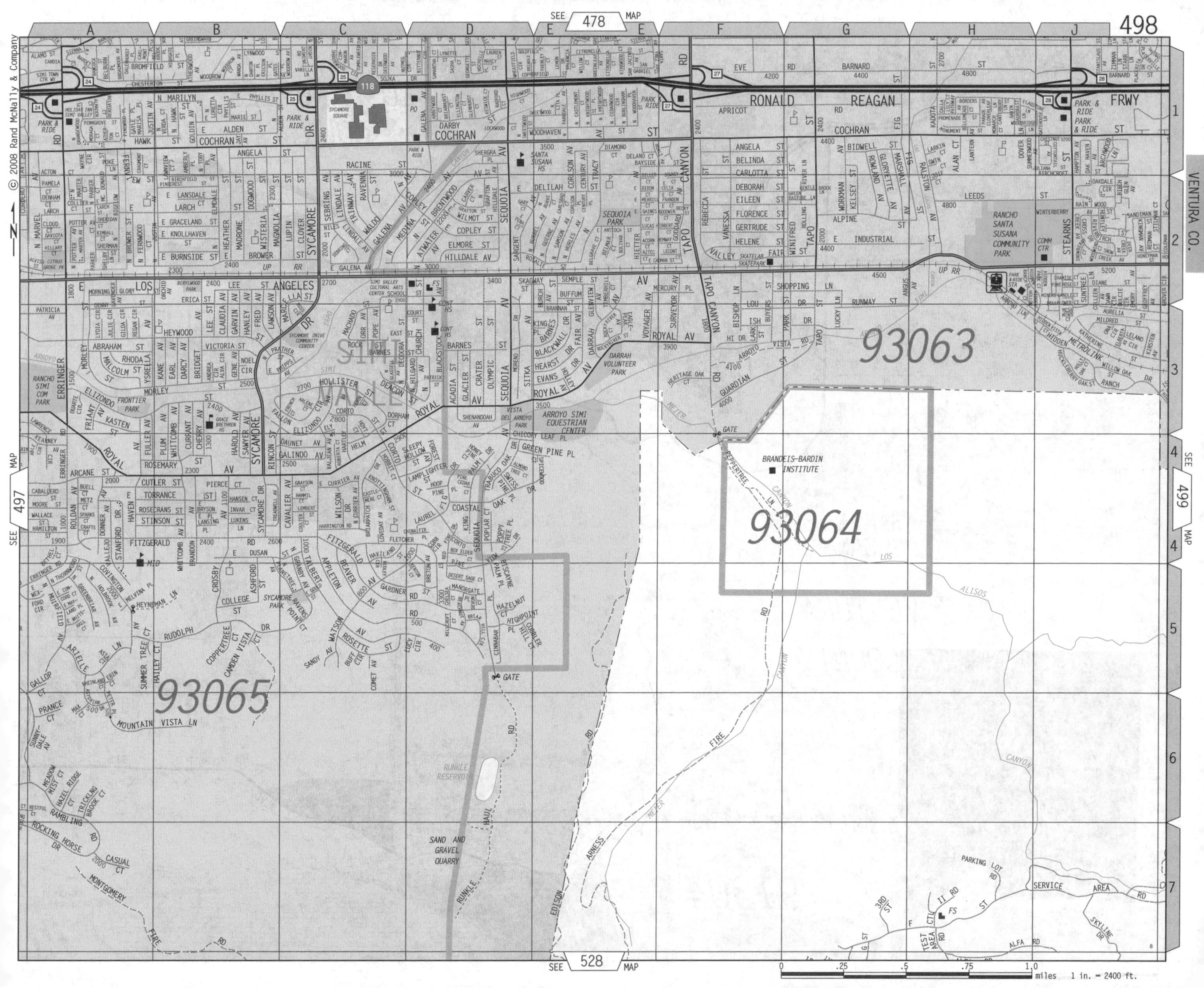
SEE 478 MAP
SEE 528 MAP
SEE 497 MAP
SEE 499 MAP
VENTURA CO.
A
B
C
D
E
F
G
H
J
1
2
3
4
5
6
7
RONALD REAGAN FRWY
118
SIMI VALLEY
SYCAMORE SQUARE
COCHRAN
LOS ANGELES AV
ROYAL AV
TAPO CANYON RD
SYCAMORE DR
SEQUOIA AV
STEARNS ST
FITZGERALD RD
ERRINGER RD
RANCHO SIMI COM PARK
SANTA SUSANA HS
SEQUOIA PARK
RANCHO SANTA SUSANA COMMUNITY PARK
SIMI VALLEY CULTURAL ARTS CENTER
SYCAMORE DRIVE COMMUNITY CENTER
DARRAH VOLUNTEER PARK
ARROYO SIMI EQUESTRIAN CENTER
FRONTIER PARK
SYCAMORE PARK
BRANDEIS-BARDIN INSTITUTE
RUNKLE RESERVOIR
SAND AND GRAVEL QUARRY
SERVICE AREA RD
PARKING LOT RD
LOS ALISOS CANYON
ARNESS
EDISON RD
METROLINK
93063
93064
93065
0
.25
.5
.75
1.0
miles
1 in. = 2400 ft.

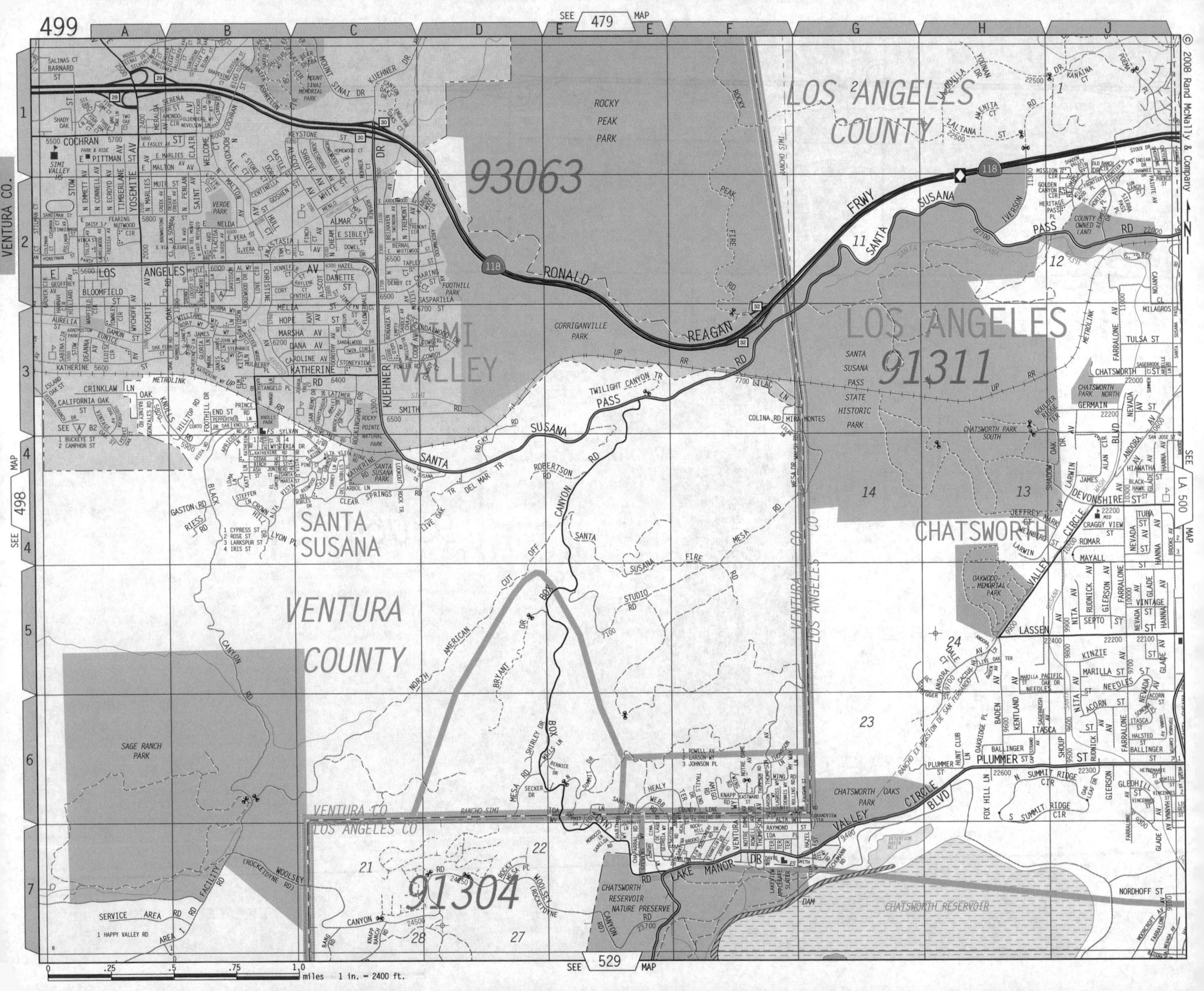
SEE 479 MAP
A
B
C
D
E
F
G
H
J
LOS ANGELES COUNTY
ROCKY PEAK PARK
93063
SIMI VALLEY
CORRIGANVILLE PARK
LOS ANGELES
91311
SANTA SUSANA PASS STATE HISTORIC PARK
CHATSWORTH
SANTA SUSANA
VENTURA COUNTY
SAGE RANCH PARK
VENTURA CO
LOS ANGELES CO
91304
CHATSWORTH RESERVOIR NATURE PRESERVE
CHATSWORTH RESERVOIR
CHATSWORTH OAKS PARK
OAKWOOD MEMORIAL PARK
COUNTY OWNED LAND
CHATSWORTH PARK NORTH
CHATSWORTH PARK SOUTH
ROCKY POINTE NATURAL PARK
SANTA SUSANA PARK
FOOTHILL PARK
VERDE PARK
MOUNT SINAI MEMORIAL PARK
KNOLLS PARK
SIMI VALLEY HS
RONALD REAGAN FRWY
SANTA SUSANA PASS RD
LOS ANGELES AV
COCHRAN ST
KATHERINE RD
KUEHNER DR
BOX CANYON RD
VALLEY CIRCLE BLVD
DEVONSHIRE ST
PLUMMER ST
LASSEN ST
LAKE MANOR DR
WOOLSEY CANYON RD
NORTH AMERICAN CUT OFF
SANTA SUSANA FIRE RD
ROCKY PEAK FIRE RD
SEE 498 MAP
SEE LA 500 MAP
VENTURA CO.
SEE 529 MAP
0 .25 .5 .75 1.0 miles 1 in. = 2400 ft.

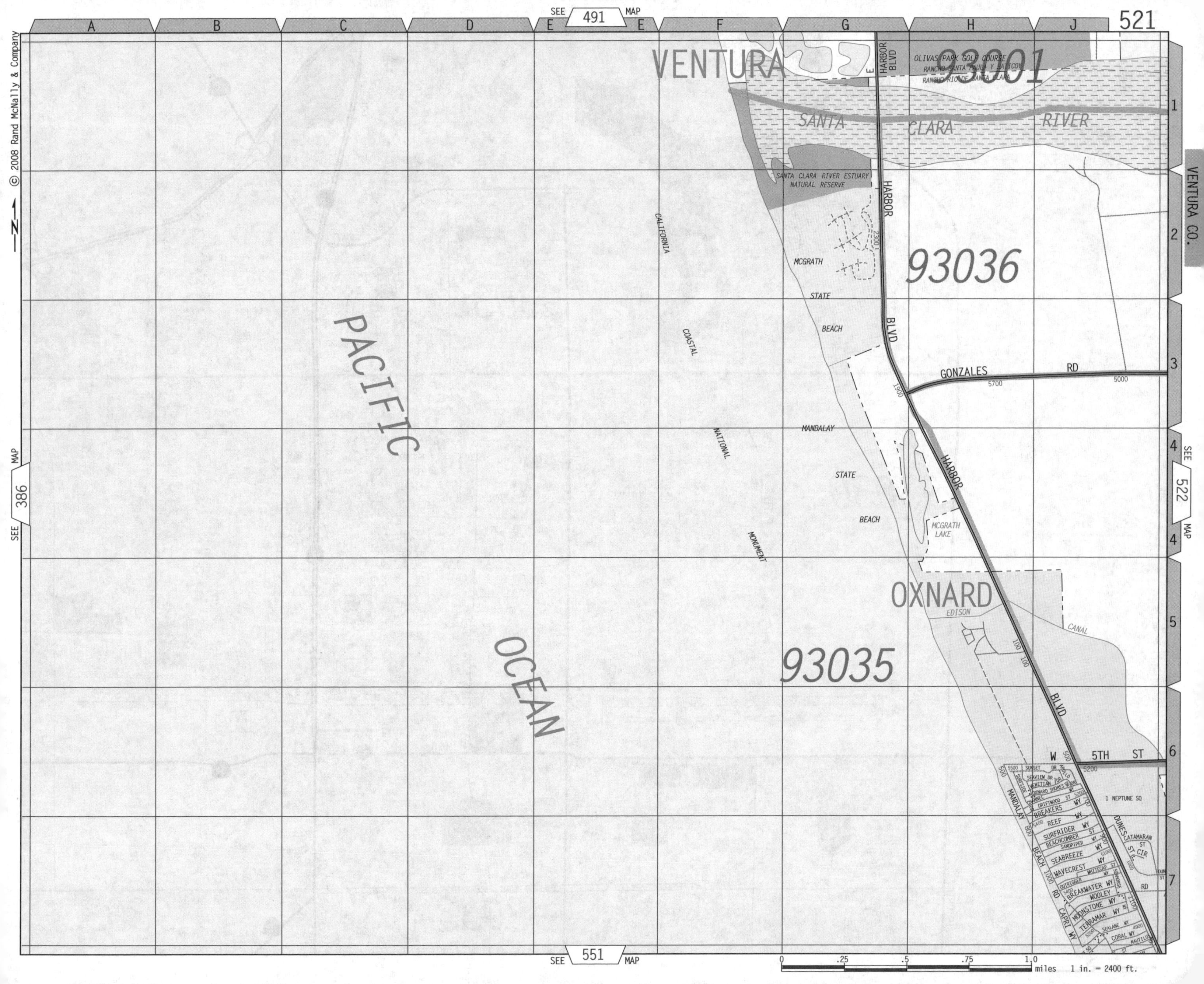
SEE 491 MAP
A
B
C
D
E
F
G
H
J
VENTURA
HARBOR BLVD
OLIVAS PARK GOLF COURSE
RANCHO SANTA PAULA Y SATICOY
RANCHO RIO DE SANTA CLARA
93001
SANTA
CLARA
RIVER
SANTA CLARA RIVER ESTUARY NATURAL RESERVE
HARBOR
CALIFORNIA
MCGRATH
93036
STATE
BEACH
PACIFIC
COASTAL
BLVD
GONZALES
RD
5700
5000
1900
MANDALAY
NATIONAL
HARBOR
STATE
BEACH
MCGRATH LAKE
MONUMENT
OXNARD
EDISON
CANAL
93035
OCEAN
BLVD
W
5TH
ST
1 NEPTUNE SQ
MANDALAY
BEACH
RD
BREAKERS
REEF
SURFRIDER
SEABREEZE
WAVECREST
BREAKWATER
WOOLEY
MOONSTONE
TERRAMAR
CAPRI WY
CORAL WY
DUNES ST
CATAMARAN
VENTURA CO.
SEE MAP 386
SEE 522 MAP
SEE 551 MAP
1 in. = 2400 ft.
miles

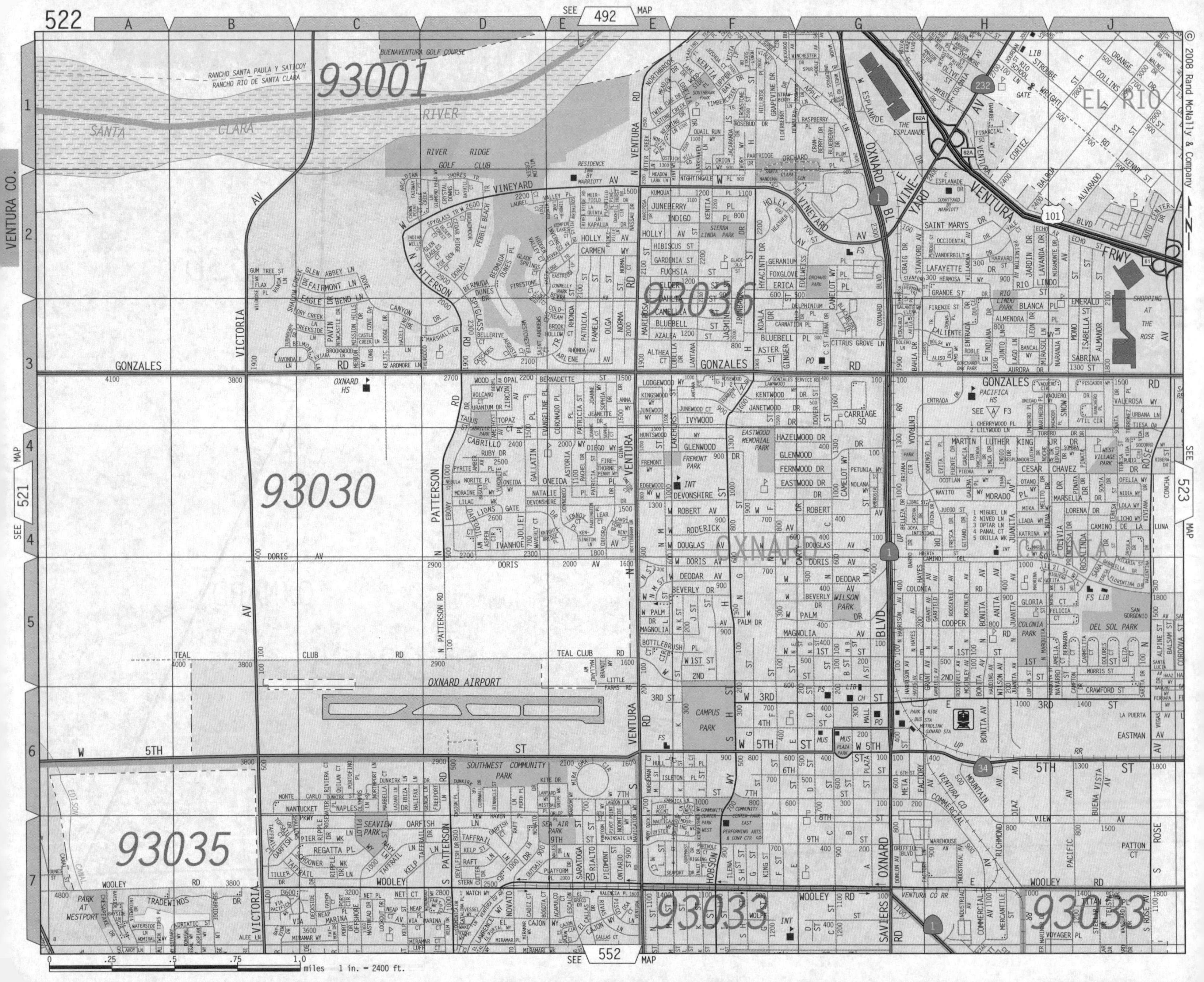

522
A B C D E F G H J
SEE 492 MAP
SEE 521 MAP
SEE 523 MAP
SEE 552 MAP
VENTURA CO.
93001
93030
93035
93036
93033
OXNARD
EL RIO
COLONIA
SANTA CLARA RIVER
RANCHO SANTA PAULA Y SATICOY
RANCHO RIO DE SANTA CLARA
BUENAVENTURA GOLF COURSE
RIVER RIDGE GOLF CLUB
OXNARD AIRPORT
OXNARD HS
PACIFICA HS
SOUTHWEST COMMUNITY PARK
SEAVIEW PARK
SEA AIR PARK
CAMPUS PARK
EASTWOOD MEMORIAL PARK
FREMONT PARK
SIERRA LINDA PARK
WILSON PARK
COLONIA PARK
DEL SOL PARK
RIO LINDO PARK
WEST VILLAGE PARK
ORCHARD PARK
SOUTHBANK PARK
PARK AT WESTPORT
COMMUNITY CENTER PARK
SHOPPING AT THE ROSE
CARRIAGE SQ
THE ESPLANADE
RESIDENCE INN BY MARRIOTT
COURTYARD BY MARRIOTT
PLAZA PARK
EAST PERFORMING ARTS & CONV CTR
METROLINK OXNARD STA
VICTORIA AV
GONZALES RD
DORIS AV
TEAL CLUB RD
W 5TH ST
WOOLEY RD
PATTERSON RD
VENTURA RD
OXNARD BL
OXNARD BLVD
SAVIERS RD
VINEYARD AV
VENTURA FRWY
ROSE AV
HOBSON WY
EDISON CANAL
1
34
101
232
0 .25 .5 .75 1.0 miles 1 in. = 2400 ft.
© 2008 Rand McNally & Company

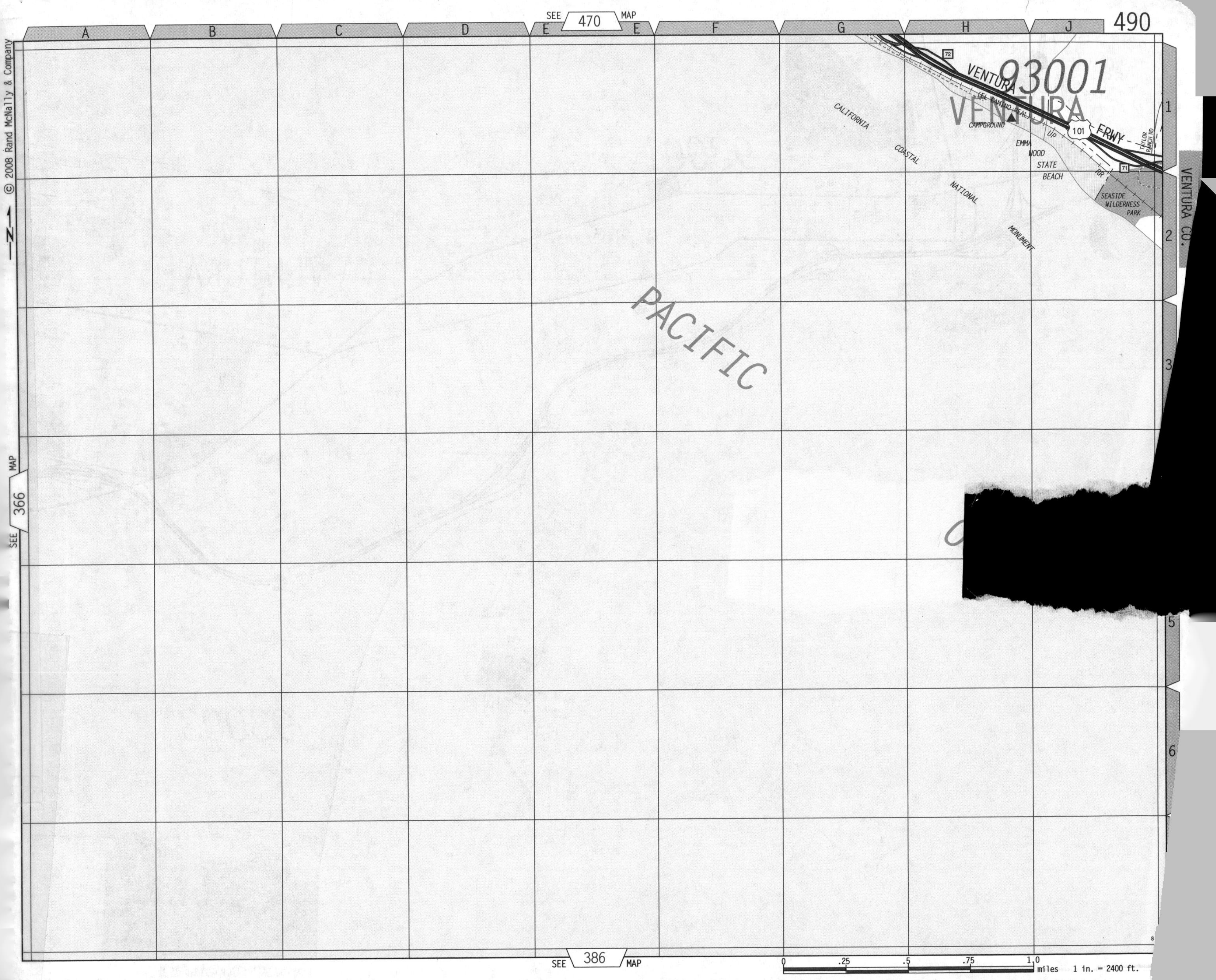
SEE 470 MAP
A
B
C
D
E
F
G
H
J
1
2
3
5
6
93001
VENTURA
VENTURA FRWY
(EL CAMINO REAL)
101
72
71
CAMPGROUND
UP
RR
TAYLOR RANCH RD
CALIFORNIA COASTAL NATIONAL MONUMENT
EMMA WOOD STATE BEACH
SEASIDE WILDERNESS PARK
VENTURA CO.
PACIFIC
SEE 366 MAP
SEE 386 MAP
0 .25 .5 .75 1.0 miles 1 in. = 2400 ft.

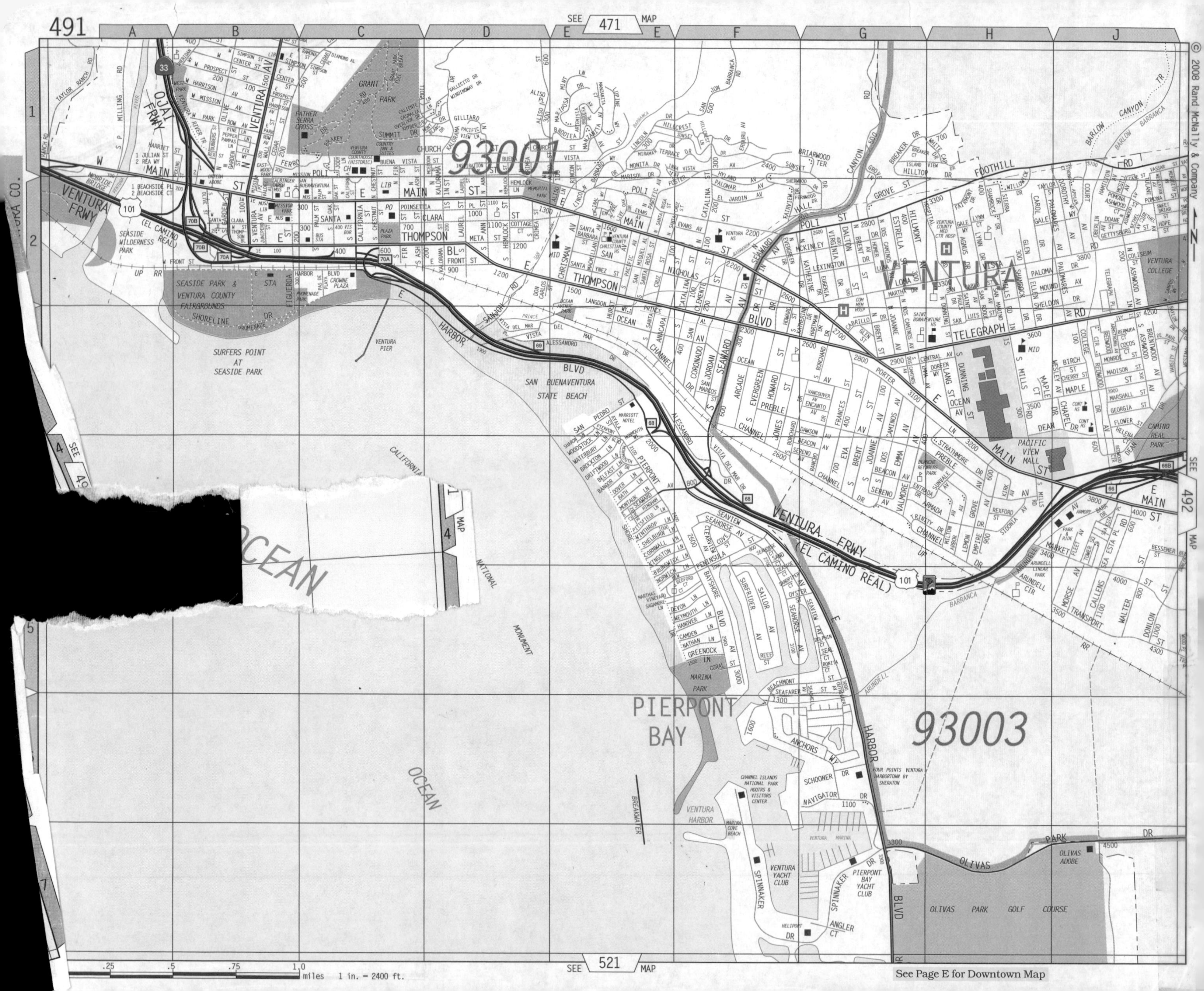
491
SEE 471 MAP
SEE 521 MAP
SEE 492 MAP
© 2008 Rand McNally & Company
93001
93003
VENTURA
PIERPONT BAY
OCEAN
VENTURA FRWY
(EL CAMINO REAL)
OJAI FRWY
SEASIDE WILDERNESS PARK
SEASIDE PARK & VENTURA COUNTY FAIRGROUNDS
SURFERS POINT AT SEASIDE PARK
VENTURA PIER
SAN BUENAVENTURA STATE BEACH
GRANT PARK
FATHER SERRA CROSS
MARINA PARK
VENTURA HARBOR
CHANNEL ISLANDS NATIONAL PARK HDQTRS & VISITORS CENTER
VENTURA YACHT CLUB
PIERPONT BAY YACHT CLUB
OLIVAS PARK GOLF COURSE
OLIVAS ADOBE
PACIFIC VIEW MALL
VENTURA COLLEGE
CAMINO REAL PARK
FOUR POINTS VENTURA HARBORTOWN BY SHERATON
MARRIOTT HOTEL
BREAKWATER
CALIFORNIA NATIONAL MONUMENT
.25 .5 .75 1.0 miles 1 in. = 2400 ft.
See Page E for Downtown Map

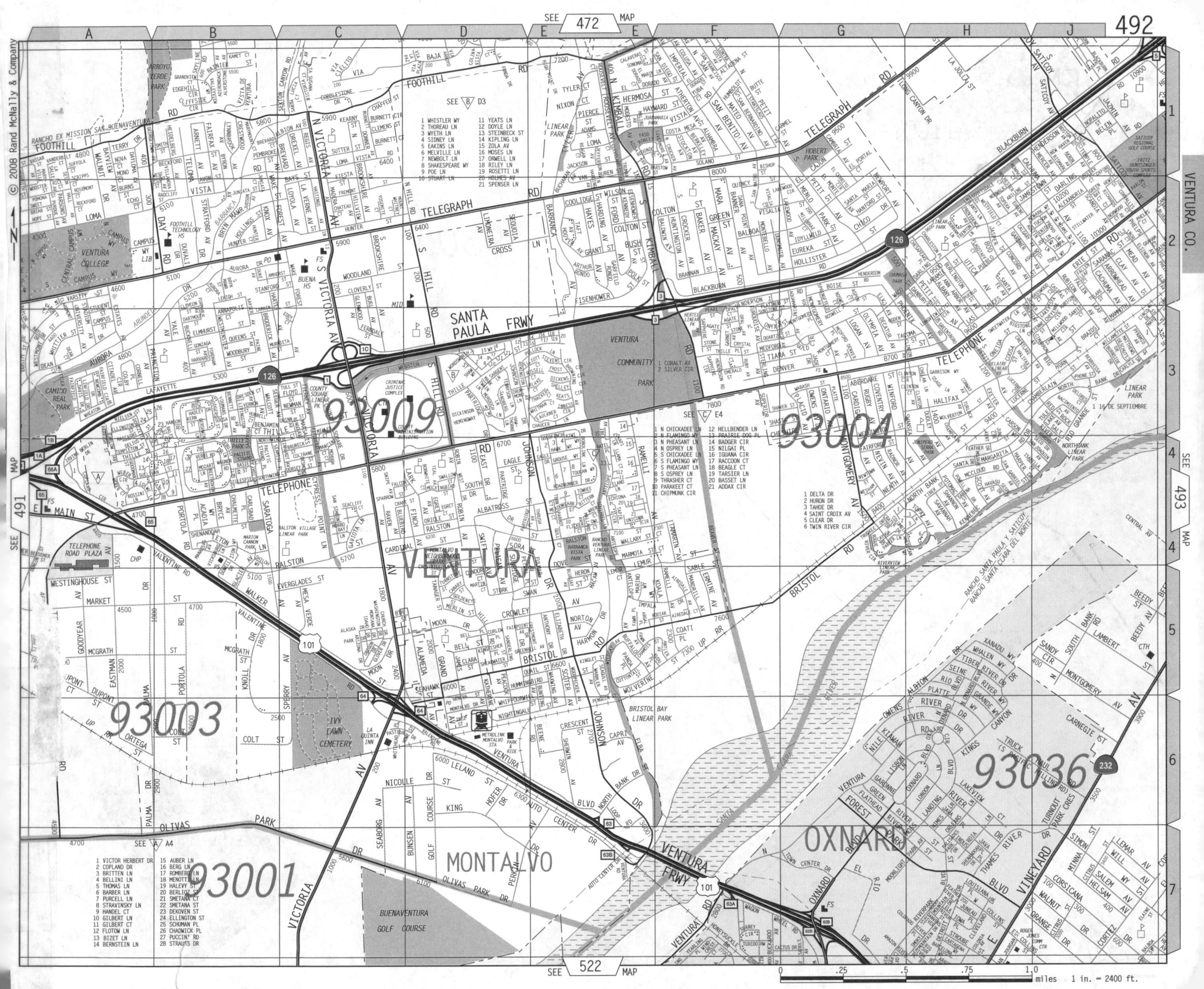
SEE 472 MAP
A
B
C
D
E
F
G
H
J
1
2
3
4
5
6
7
VENTURA CO.
SEE 493 MAP
SEE 491 MAP
SEE 522 MAP
93009
93004
93003
93036
93001
VENTURA
MONTALVO
OXNARD
SANTA PAULA FRWY
VENTURA FRWY
FOOTHILL RD
TELEGRAPH RD
TELEPHONE RD
VICTORIA AV
KIMBALL RD
JOHNSON DR
BRISTOL RD
OLIVAS PARK DR
VENTURA BLVD
VINEYARD AV
MAIN ST
VALENTINE RD
WESTINGHOUSE ST
MARKET ST
MCGRATH ST
DUPONT ST
COLT ST
LELAND ST
ARROYO VERDE PARK
VENTURA COLLEGE
FOOTHILL TECHNOLOGY HS
BUENA HS
VENTURA COMMUNITY PARK
CAMINO REAL PARK
HOBERT PARK
COUNTY SQUARE LINEAR PK
CRIMINAL JUSTICE COMPLEX
COUNTY ADMINISTRATION BUILDING
TELEPHONE ROAD PLAZA
IVY LAWN CEMETERY
LA QUINTA INN
METROLINK MONTALVO STA
PARK & RIDE
BUENAVENTURA GOLF COURSE
BRISTOL BAY LINEAR PARK
RALSTON VILLAGE LINEAR PARK
MONTALVO NEIGHBORHOOD PARK
RIVERVIEW LINEAR PARK
SATICOY REGIONAL GOLF COURSE
FRITZ HUNTSINGER YOUTH SPORTS COMPLEX
SANTA CLARA RIVER
RANCHO EX MISSION SAN BUENAVENTURA
RANCHO SANTA PAULA Y SATICOY
RANCHO SANTA CLARA DEL NORTE
SEE B D3
1 WHISTLER WY
2 THOREAU LN
3 WYETH LN
4 SIDNEY LN
5 EAKINS LN
6 MELVILLE LN
7 NEWBOLT LN
8 SHAKESPEARE WY
9 POE LN
10 STUART LN
11 YEATS LN
12 DOYLE LN
13 STEINBECK ST
14 KIPLING LN
15 ZOLA AV
16 MOSES LN
17 ORWELL LN
18 RILEY LN
19 ROSETTI LN
20 HOLMES AV
21 SPENSER LN
1 COBALT AV
2 SILVER CIR
SEE C E4
1 N CHICKADEE LN
2 N FLAMINGO WY
3 N PHEASANT LN
4 N OSPREY LN
5 S CHICKADEE LN
6 S FLAMINGO WY
7 S PHEASANT LN
8 S OSPREY LN
9 THRASHER CT
10 PARAKEET CT
11 CHIPMUNK CIR
12 HELLBENDER LN
13 PRAIRIE DOG PL
14 BADGER CIR
15 NILGAI PL
16 IGUANA CIR
17 RACCOON CT
18 BEAGLE CT
19 TARSIER LN
20 BASSET LN
21 ADDAX CIR
1 DELTA DR
2 HURON DR
3 TAHOE DR
4 SAINT CROIX AV
5 CLEAR DR
6 TWIN RIVER CIR
1 16 DE SEPTIEMBRE
SEE A A4
1 VICTOR HERBERT DR
2 COPLAND DR
3 BRITTEN LN
4 BELLINI LN
5 THOMAS LN
6 BARBER LN
7 PURCELL LN
8 STRAVINSKY LN
9 HANDEL CT
10 GILBERT LN
11 GILBERT CT
12 FLOTOW LN
13 BIZET LN
14 BERNSTEIN LN
15 AUBER LN
16 BERG LN
17 ROMBERG LN
18 MENOTTI LN
19 HALEVY ST
20 BERLIOZ ST
21 SMETANA CT
22 SMETANA ST
23 DEKOVEN ST
24 ELLINGTON ST
25 SCHUMAN PL
26 CHADWICK PL
27 PUCCINI RD
28 STRAUSS DR
0 .25 .5 .75 1.0 miles 1 in. = 2400 ft.

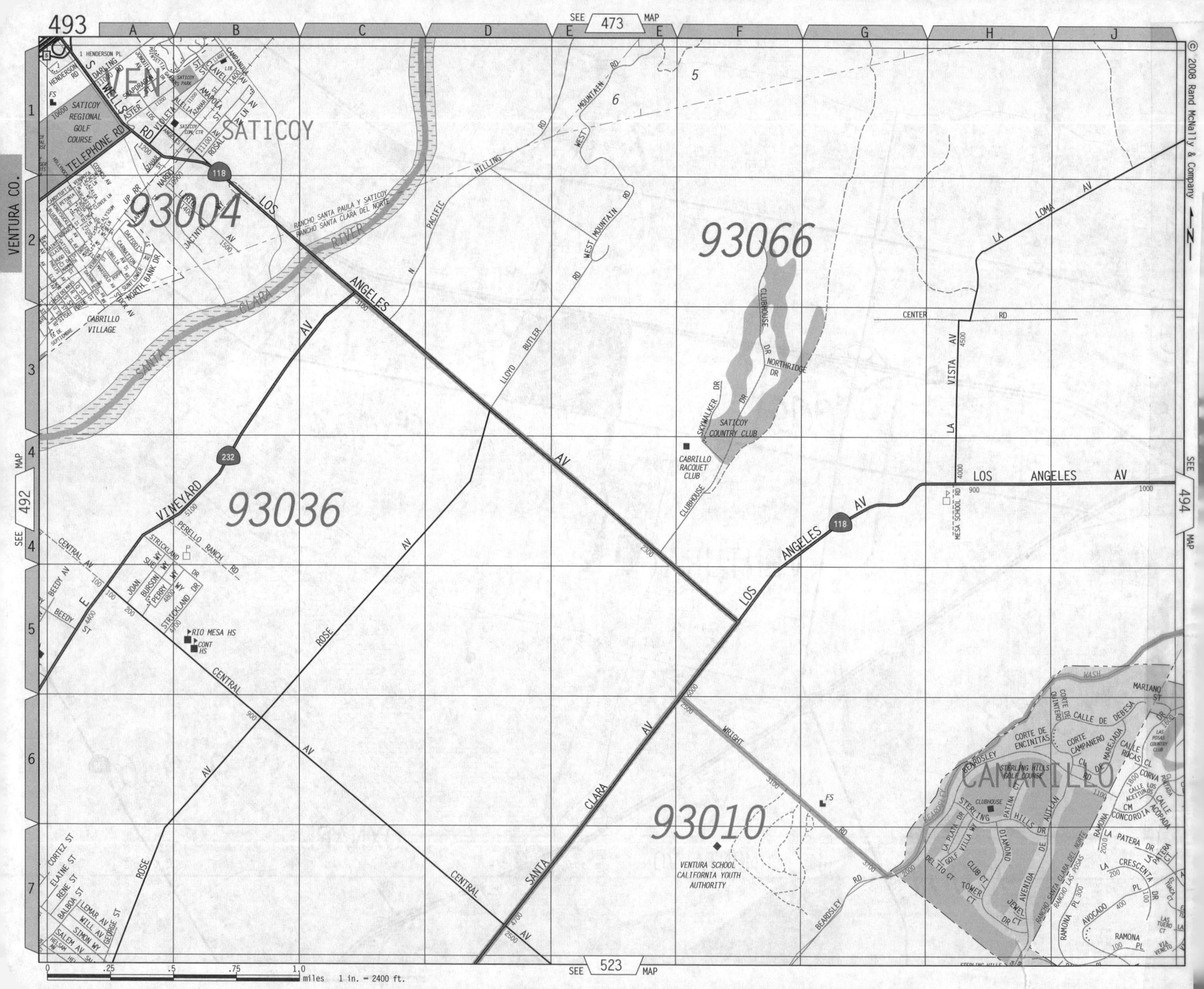

SEE 473 MAP
SEE 523 MAP
SEE 492 MAP
SEE 494 MAP
VENTURA CO.
© 2008 Rand McNally & Company
SATICOY
SATICOY REGIONAL GOLF COURSE
CABRILLO VILLAGE
93004
93066
93036
93010
SATICOY COUNTRY CLUB
CABRILLO RACQUET CLUB
RIO MESA HS
CONT HS
VENTURA SCHOOL CALIFORNIA YOUTH AUTHORITY
STERLING HILLS GOLF COURSE
LAS POSAS COUNTRY CLUB
CAMARILLO
RANCHO SANTA PAULA Y SATICOY
RANCHO SANTA CLARA DEL NORTE
SANTA CLARA RIVER
LOS ANGELES AV
VINEYARD AV
ROSE AV
CENTRAL AV
SANTA CLARA AV
WRIGHT RD
BEARDSLEY RD
LLOYD BUTLER RD
WEST MOUNTAIN RD
MILLING RD
N PACIFIC
LA LOMA AV
LA VISTA AV
CENTER RD
MESA SCHOOL RD
CLUBHOUSE DR
NORTHRIDGE DR
SKYWALKER DR
TELEPHONE RD
WELLS RD
PERELLO RANCH RD
STRICKLAND DR
BURSON WY
PERRY WY
JOAN
BEEDY AV
BEEDY ST
CORTEZ ST
ELAINE ST
RENE ST
BALBOA ST
LEMAR AV
WILL AV
GEORGE ST
SIMON WY
SALEM AV
CORTE DE ENCINITAS
CALLE DE DEBESA
CORTE CAMPANERO
MARIANO ST
CALLE ROCAS
CORVA
CM CONCORDIA
RAMONA
LA PATERA DR
LA CRESCENTA DR
AVOCADO PL
RAMONA PL
STERLING HILLS DR
DIAMOND
AVENIDA DE AUTLAN
LA PLATA DR
GOLF VILLA WY
DEL TIO CT
CLUB CT
TOWER CT
JEWEL CT
miles 1 in. = 2400 ft.

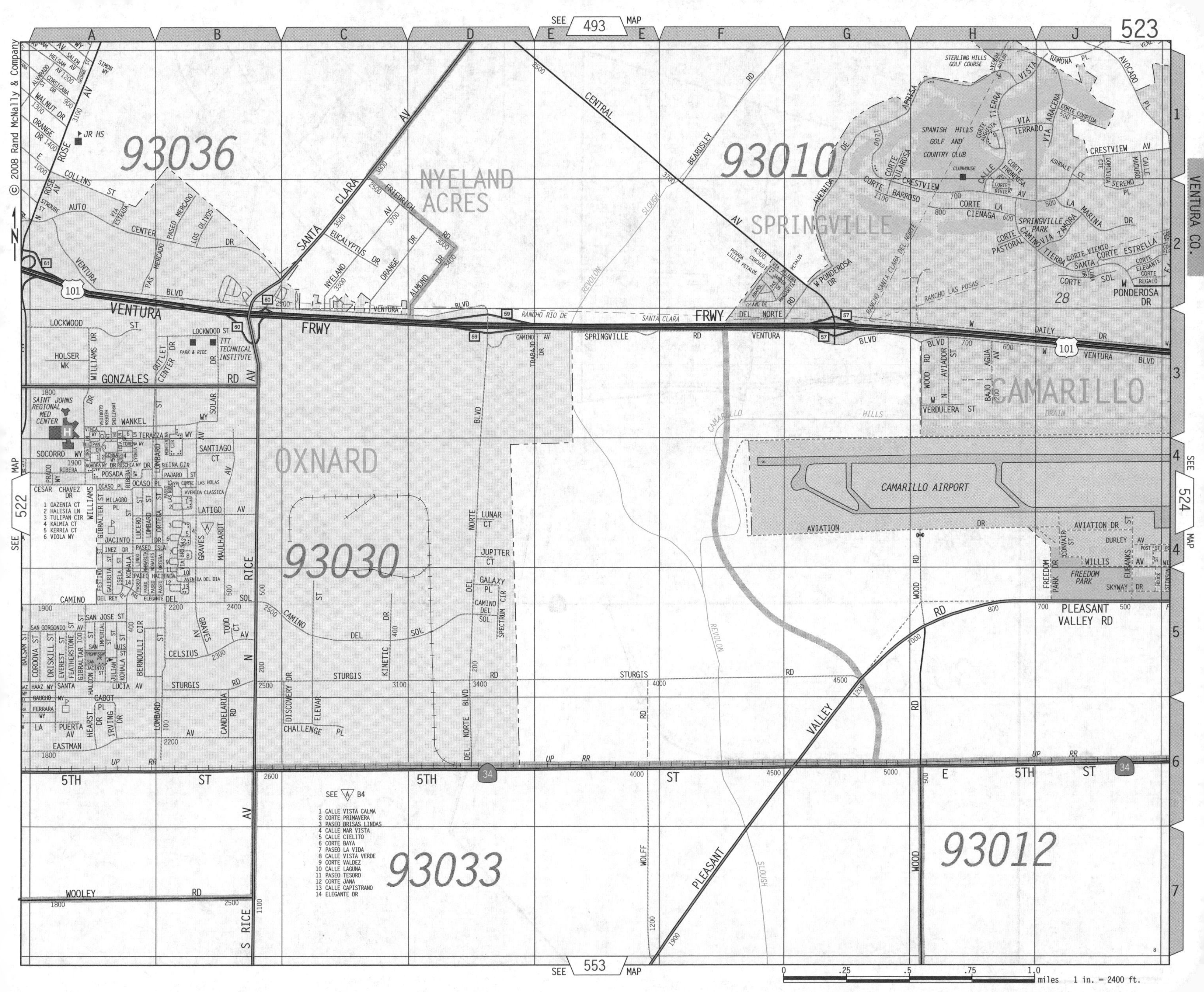
SEE 493 MAP
93036
93010
NYELAND ACRES
SPRINGVILLE
CAMARILLO
OXNARD
93030
93033
93012
CAMARILLO AIRPORT
SPANISH HILLS GOLF AND COUNTRY CLUB
STERLING HILLS GOLF COURSE
SAINT JOHNS REGIONAL MED CENTER
ITT TECHNICAL INSTITUTE
FREEDOM PARK
VENTURA FRWY
VENTURA CO.
SEE 522 MAP
SEE 524 MAP
SEE 553 MAP
1 GAZENIA CT
2 HALESIA LN
3 TULIPAN CIR
4 KALMIA CT
5 KERRIA CT
6 VIOLA WY
SEE B4
1 CALLE VISTA CALMA
2 CORTE PRIMAVERA
3 PASEO BRISAS LINDAS
4 CALLE MAR VISTA
5 CALLE CIELITO
6 CORTE BAYA
7 PASEO LA VIDA
8 CALLE VISTA VERDE
9 CORTE VALDEZ
10 CALLE LAGUNA
11 PASEO TESORO
12 CORTE JANA
13 CALLE CAPISTRANO
14 ELEGANTE DR
miles 1 in. = 2400 ft.

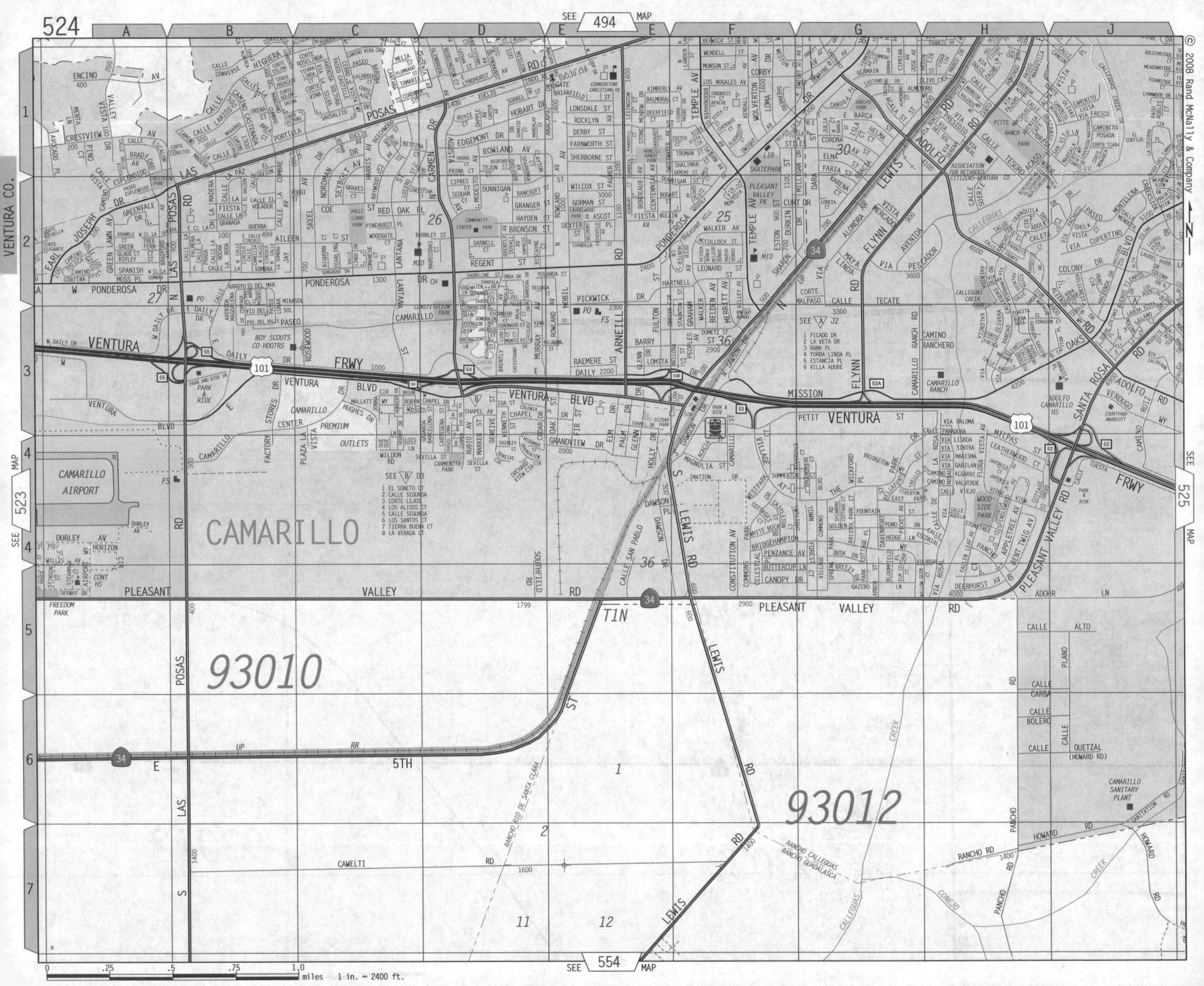

524
SEE 494 MAP
SEE 554 MAP
SEE 523 MAP
SEE 525 MAP
VENTURA CO.
© 2008 Rand McNally & Company
CAMARILLO
93010
93012
CAMARILLO AIRPORT
VENTURA FRWY
101
34
PLEASANT VALLEY RD
LEWIS RD
LAS POSAS RD
E 5TH ST
UP RR
CAWELTI RD
ARNEILL RD
ADOLFO RD
SANTA ROSA RD
FLYNN RD
MISSION OAKS
CAMARILLO CENTER
PREMIUM OUTLETS
PLEASANT VALLEY PK
CAMARILLO RANCH
CAMARILLO SANITARY PLANT
FREEDOM PARK
T1N
RANCHO CALLEGUAS
RANCHO GUADALASCA
CALLEGUAS CREEK
CONEJO CREEK
SEE A J2
1 PICADO DR
2 LA VETA DR
3 RAMA PL
4 YORBA LINDA PL
5 ESTANCIA PL
6 VILLA ADOBE
SEE B D3
1 EL SONETO CT
2 CALLE SEGUNDA
3 CORTE LEJOS
4 LOS ALISOS CT
5 CALLE SEGUNDA
6 LOS SANTOS CT
7 TIERRA BUENA CT
8 LA VERADA CT
0 .25 .5 .75 1.0 miles 1 in. = 2400 ft.

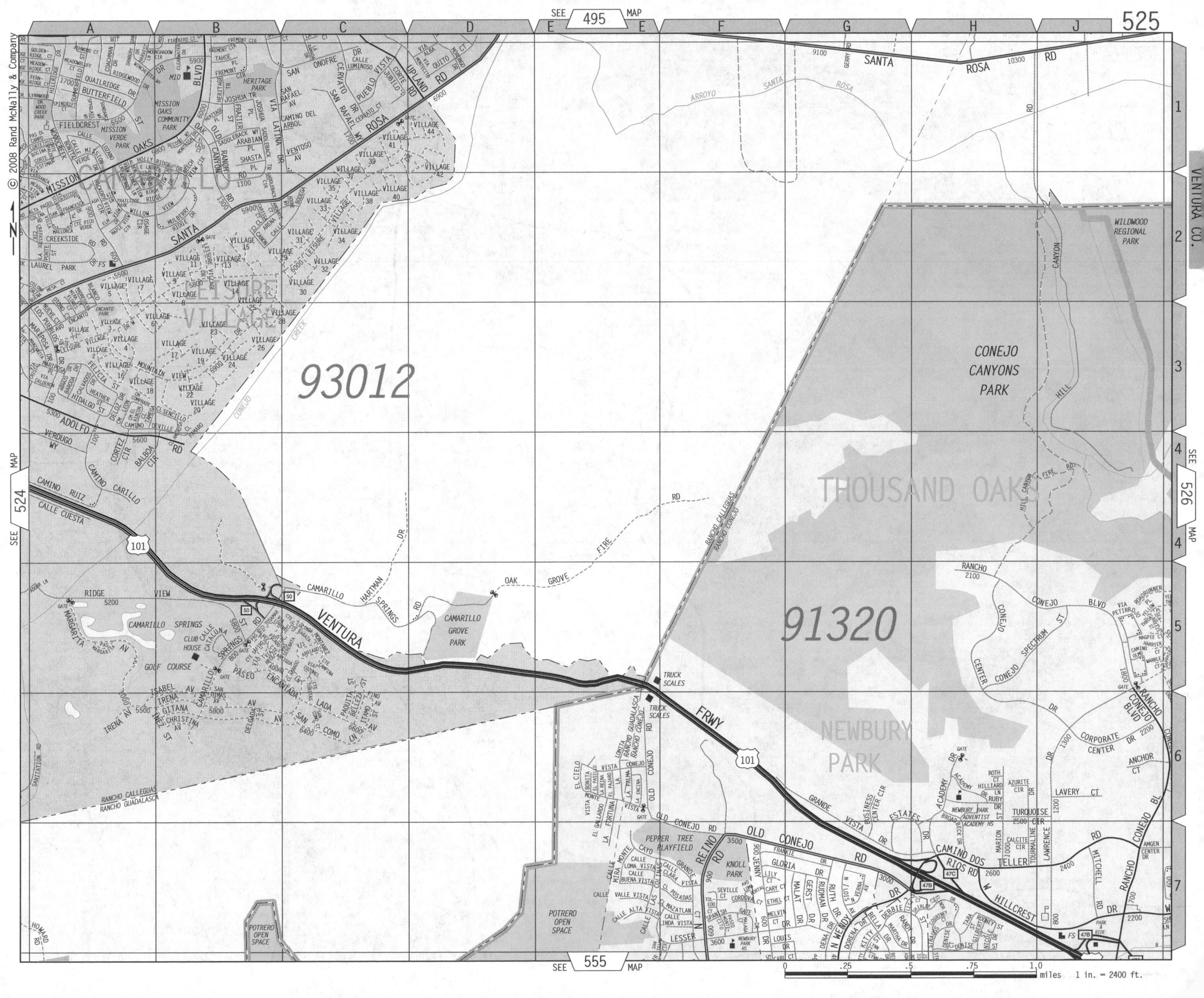

525
SEE 495 MAP
SEE 555 MAP
SEE 524 MAP
SEE 526 MAP
VENTURA CO.
© 2008 Rand McNally & Company
CAMARILLO
LEISURE VILLAGE
93012
91320
THOUSAND OAKS
NEWBURY PARK
CONEJO CANYONS PARK
WILDWOOD REGIONAL PARK
MISSION OAKS COMMUNITY PARK
MISSION VERDE PARK
HERITAGE PARK
CAMARILLO GROVE PARK
CAMARILLO SPRINGS
GOLF COURSE
CLUB HOUSE
PEPPER TREE PLAYFIELD
KNOLL PARK
POTRERO OPEN SPACE
TRUCK SCALES
SANTA ROSA RD
VENTURA FRWY
101
OLD CONEJO RD
CONEJO BLVD
CAMARILLO SPRINGS RD
OAK GROVE FIRE RD
MISSION OAKS BLVD
ADOLFO RD
UPLAND RD
HILL CANYON RD
CAMINO DOS RIOS
TELLER RD
HILLCREST DR
RANCHO CONEJO BLVD
CORPORATE CENTER DR
ARROYO SANTA ROSA
CONEJO CREEK
0 .25 .5 .75 1.0 miles 1 in. = 2400 ft.

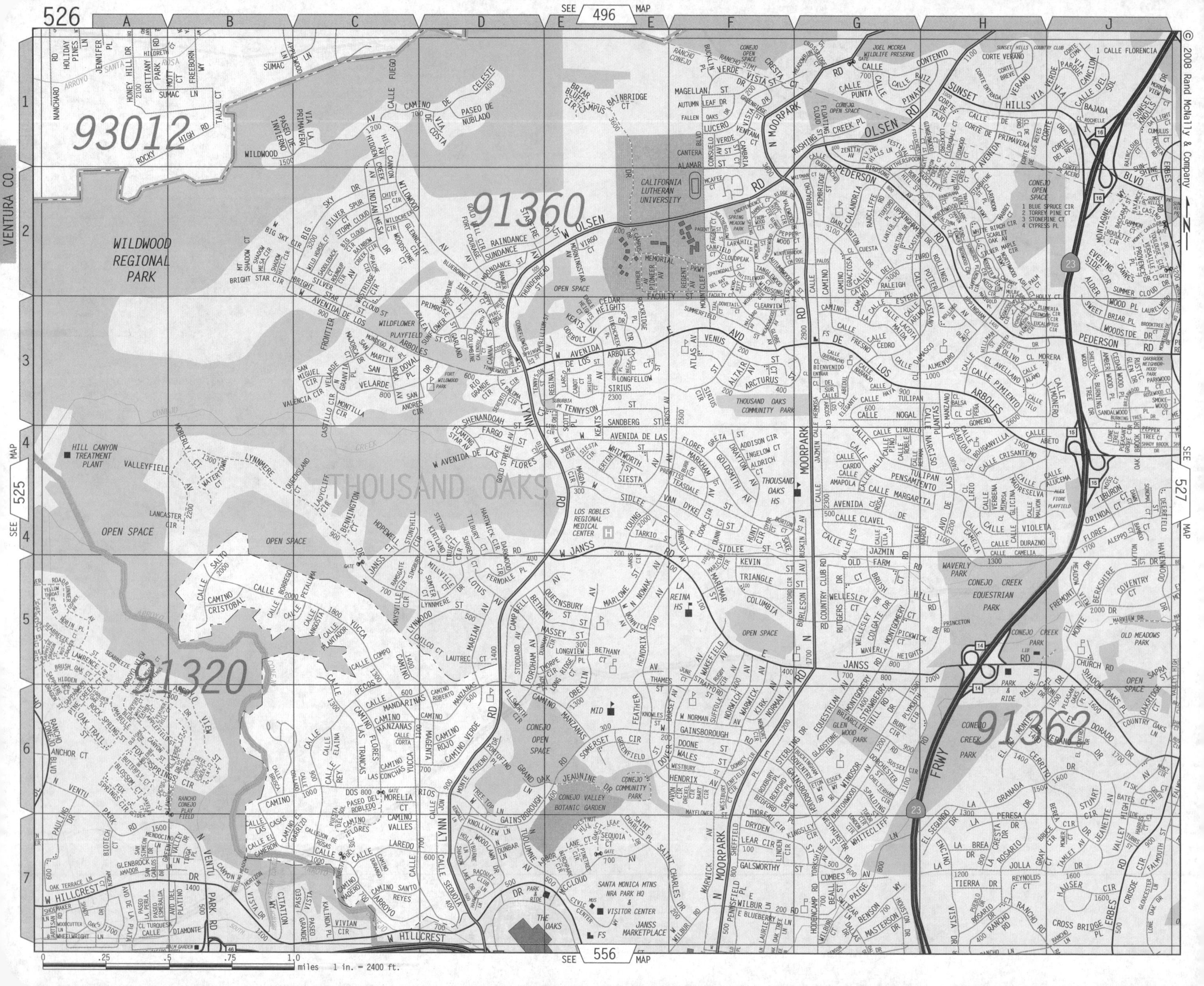
526
SEE 496 MAP
SEE 525 MAP
SEE 527 MAP
SEE 556 MAP
VENTURA CO.
© 2008 Rand McNally & Company
93012
91360
91320
91362
THOUSAND OAKS
WILDWOOD REGIONAL PARK
CALIFORNIA LUTHERAN UNIVERSITY
HILL CANYON TREATMENT PLANT
OPEN SPACE
CONEJO OPEN SPACE
LOS ROBLES REGIONAL MEDICAL CENTER
THOUSAND OAKS COMMUNITY PARK
THOUSAND OAKS HS
LA REINA HS
WAVERLY PARK
CONEJO CREEK EQUESTRIAN PARK
OLD MEADOWS PARK
CONEJO CREEK PARK
CONEJO COMMUNITY PARK
CONEJO VALLEY BOTANIC GARDEN
GLEN WOOD PARK
FORT WILDWOOD PARK
SANTA MONICA MTNS NRA PARK HQ & VISITOR CENTER
JANSS MARKETPLACE
THE OAKS
PARK & RIDE
RANCHO CONEJO PLAY FIELD
JOEL MCCREA WILDLIFE PRESERVE
W OLSEN RD
OLSEN RD
N MOORPARK RD
MOORPARK RD
LYNN RD
AVENIDA DE LOS ARBOLES
W JANSS RD
JANSS RD
W HILLCREST DR
VENTU PARK RD
PEDERSON RD
SUNSET HILLS BLVD
FRWY
1 BLUE SPRUCE CIR
2 TORREY PINE CT
3 STONEPINE CT
4 CYPRESS PL
0 .25 .5 .75 1.0 miles 1 in. = 2400 ft.

SEE 497 MAP

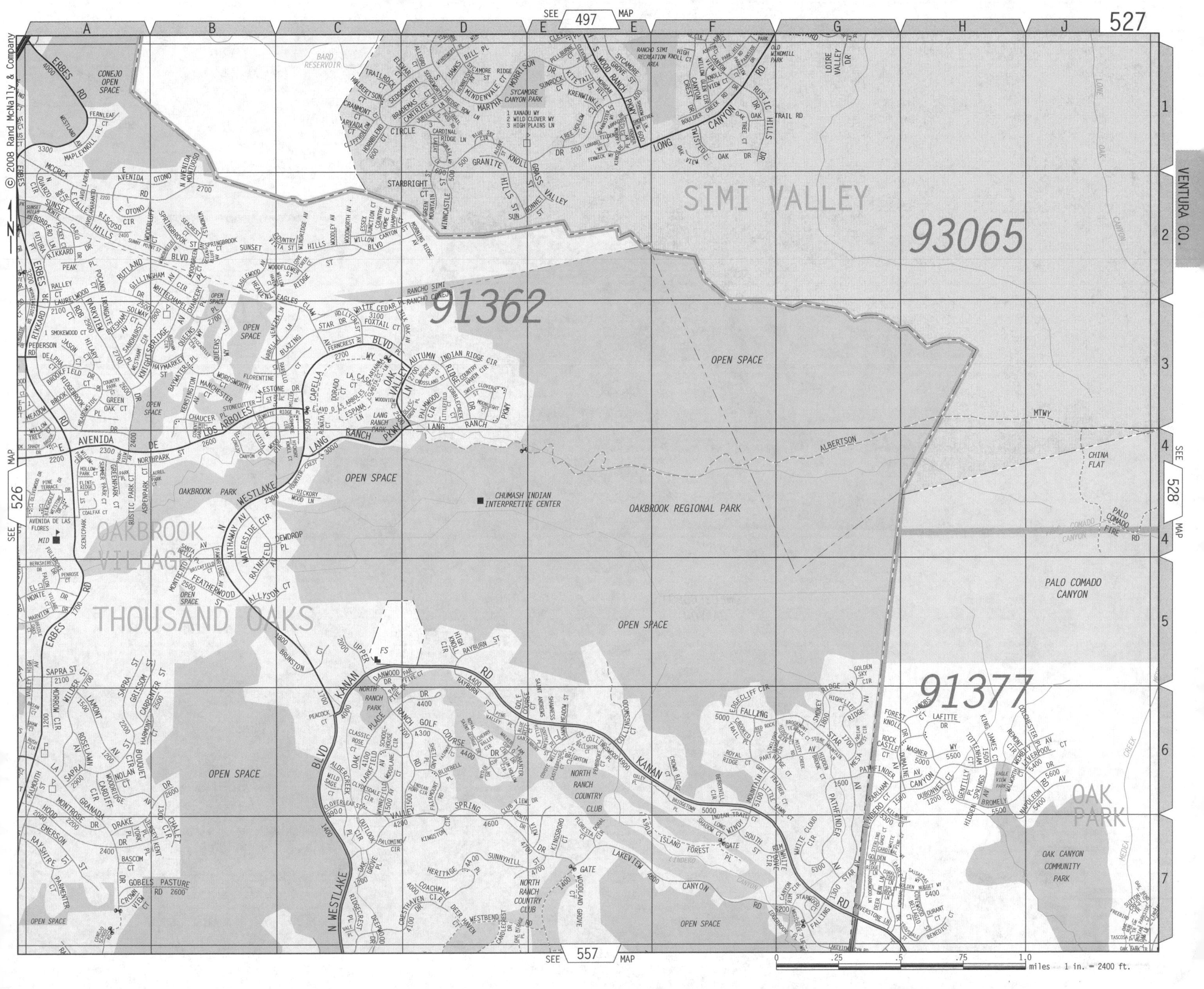

SEE 526 MAP

SEE 528 MAP

SEE 557 MAP

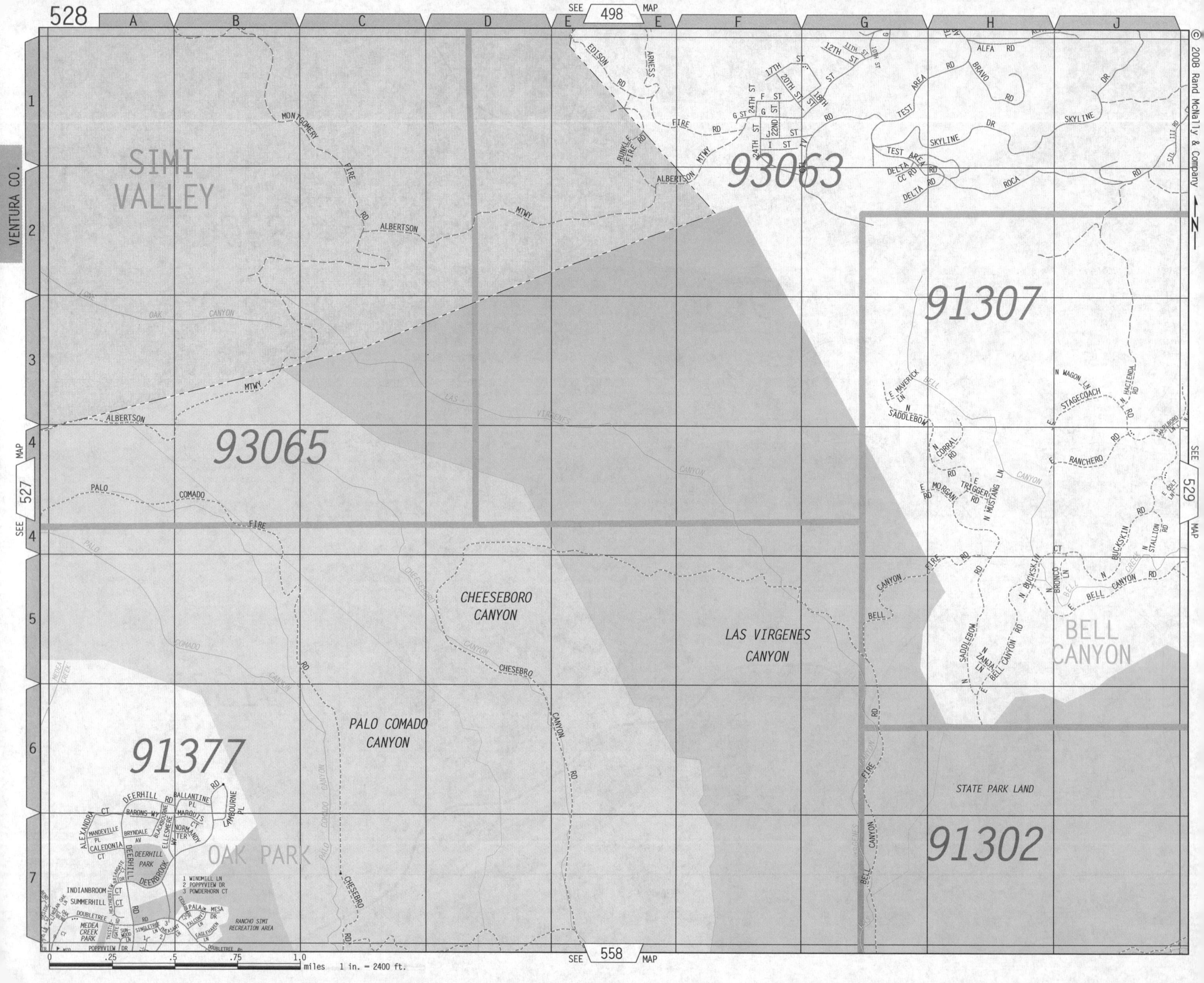

SEE 498 MAP
SEE 527 MAP
SEE 529 MAP
SEE 558 MAP
VENTURA CO.
SIMI VALLEY
93063
93065
91307
91377
91302
OAK PARK
BELL CANYON
CHEESEBORO CANYON
LAS VIRGENES CANYON
PALO COMADO CANYON
STATE PARK LAND
RANCHO SIMI RECREATION AREA
DEERHILL PARK
MEDEA CREEK PARK
1 WINDMILL LN
2 POPPYVIEW DR
3 POWDERHORN CT
0 .25 .5 .75 1.0 miles 1 in. = 2400 ft.
© 2008 Rand McNally & Company

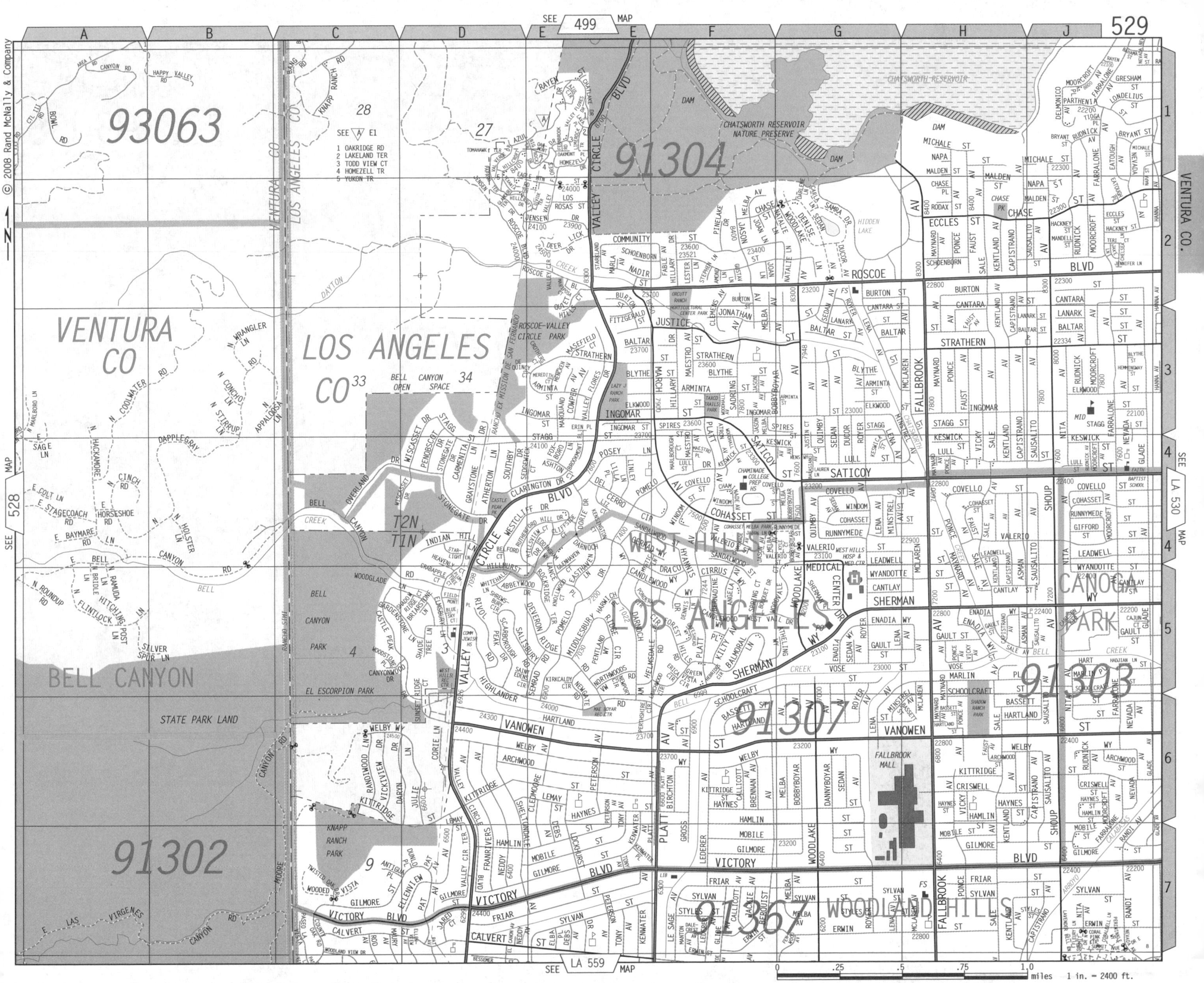

529
SEE 499 MAP
A
B
C
D
E
F
G
H
J
© 2008 Rand McNally & Company
93063
VENTURA CO
LOS ANGELES CO
91304
CHATSWORTH RESERVOIR
CHATSWORTH RESERVOIR NATURE PRESERVE
DAM
VENTURA CO.
SEE A E1
1 OAKRIDGE RD
2 LAKELAND TER
3 TODD VIEW CT
4 HOMEZELL TR
5 YUKON TR
VENTURA CO
LOS ANGELES CO
BELL CANYON OPEN SPACE
ROSCOE-VALLEY CIRCLE PARK
T2N
T1N
WEST HILLS
LOS ANGELES
CANOGA PARK
BELL CANYON
STATE PARK LAND
EL ESCORPION PARK
KNAPP RANCH PARK
91302
91307
91303
91367
WOODLAND HILLS
FALLBROOK MALL
WEST HILLS HOSP & MED CTR
CHAMINADE COLLEGE PREP HS
VALLEY CIRCLE BLVD
ROSCOE BLVD
SATICOY ST
SHERMAN WY
VANOWEN ST
VICTORY BLVD
FALLBROOK AV
PLATT AV
SEE LA 528 MAP
SEE LA 530 MAP
SEE LA 559 MAP
0 .25 .5 .75 1.0 miles 1 in. = 2400 ft.

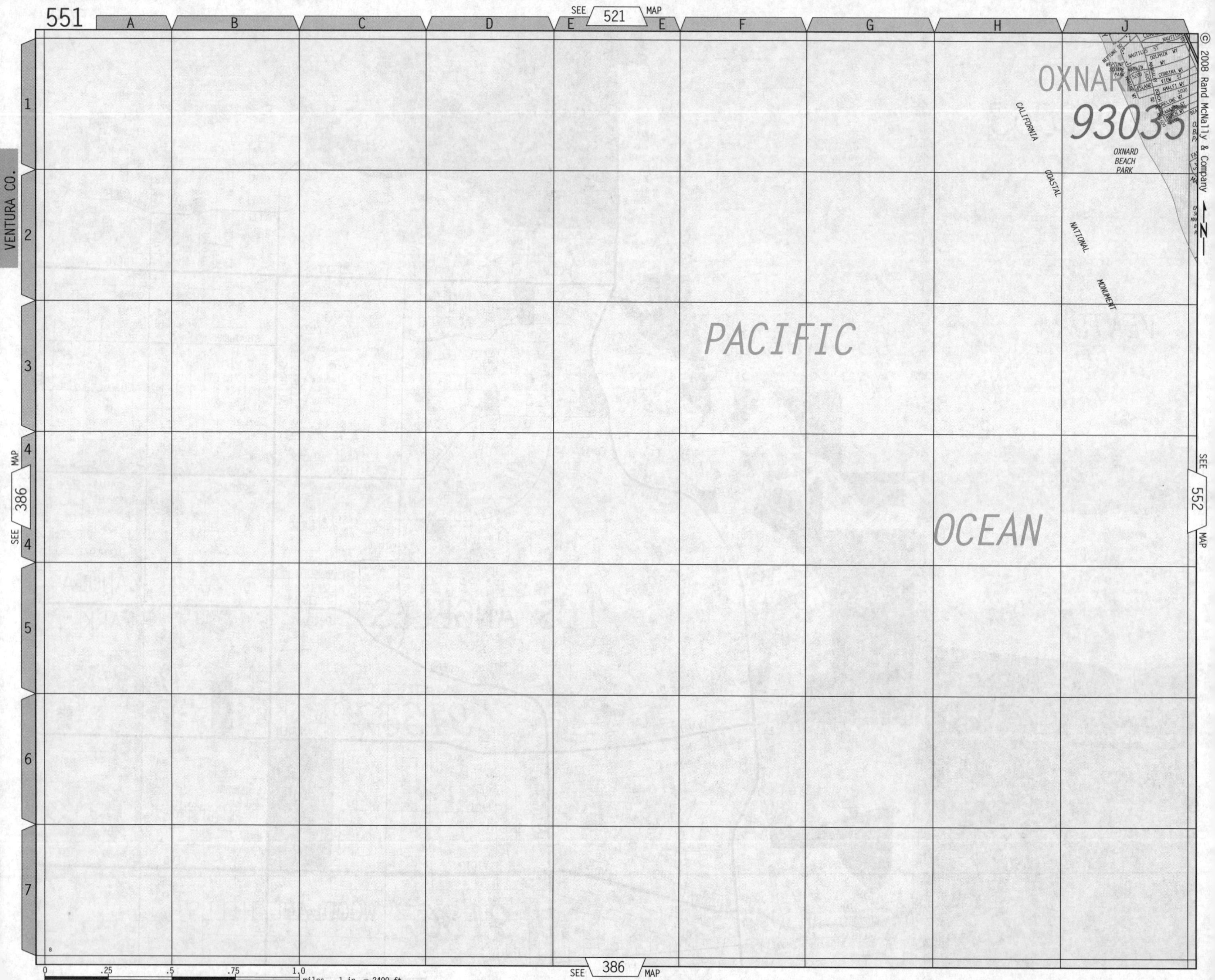
A
B
C
D
E
F
G
H
J
1
2
3
4
5
6
7
SEE 521 MAP
SEE 386 MAP
SEE 552 MAP
VENTURA CO.
OXNARD
93035
OXNARD BEACH PARK
CALIFORNIA
COASTAL
NATIONAL
MONUMENT
PACIFIC
OCEAN
NEPTUNE SQUARE PARK
NAUTILUS ST
DOLPHIN WY
CORBINA WY
VIEW ST
AMALFI WY
© 2008 Rand McNally & Company
0 .25 .5 .75 1.0 miles 1 in. = 2400 ft.

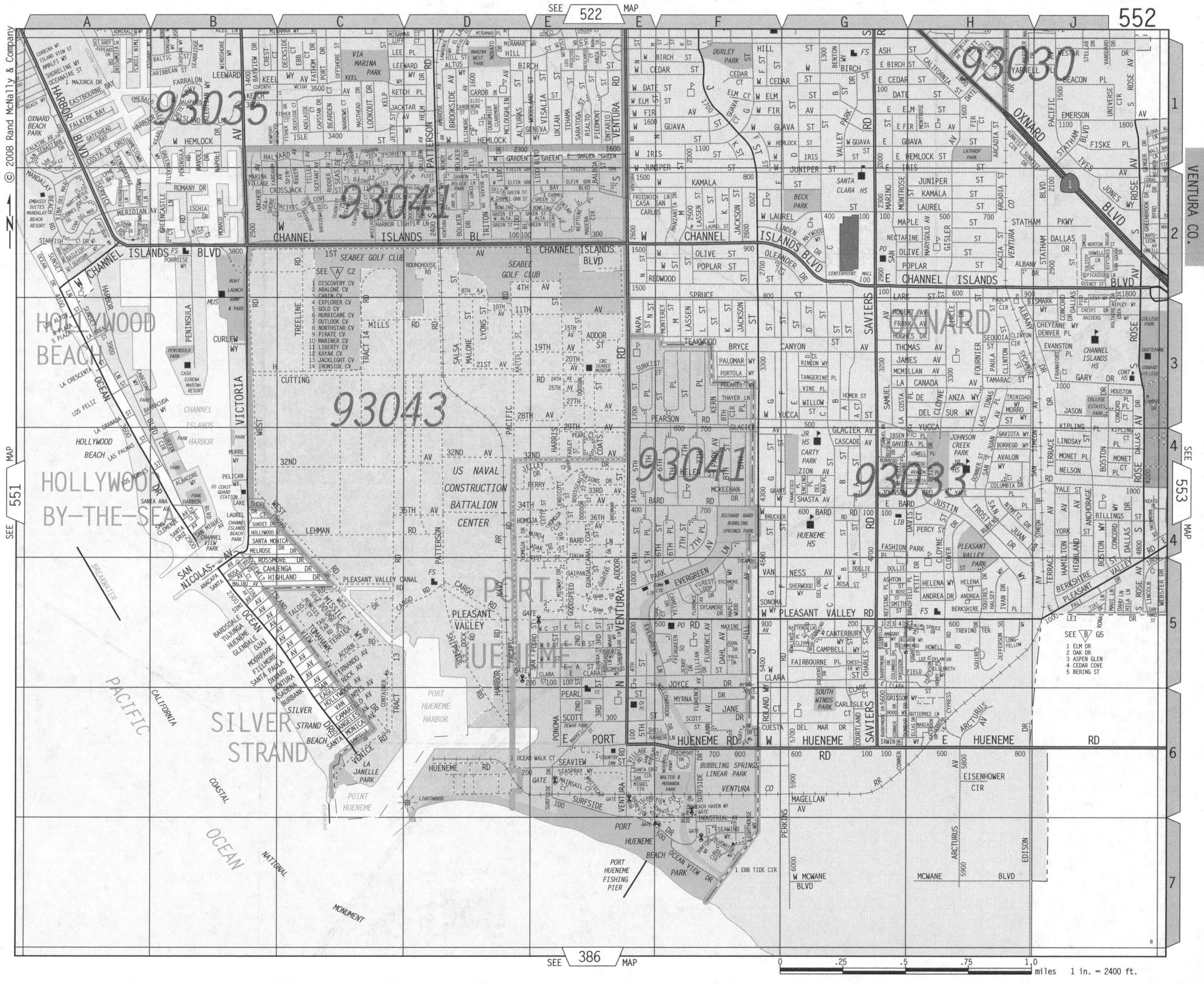

SEE 522 MAP
SEE 386 MAP
SEE 551 MAP
SEE 553 MAP
© 2008 Rand McNally & Company
A
B
C
D
E
F
G
H
J
1
2
3
4
5
6
7
VENTURA CO.
93035
93041
93043
93030
93033
OXNARD
HOLLYWOOD BEACH
HOLLYWOOD BY-THE-SEA
SILVER STRAND
PORT HUENEME
PACIFIC
OCEAN
CALIFORNIA COASTAL NATIONAL MONUMENT
US NAVAL CONSTRUCTION BATTALION CENTER
CHANNEL ISLANDS HARBOR
PORT HUENEME HARBOR
POINT HUENEME
BREAKWATER
SEABEE GOLF CLUB
VIA MARINA PARK
DURLEY PARK
BECK PARK
SANTA CLARA HS
CHANNEL ISLANDS HS
HUENEME HS
PLEASANT VALLEY PARK
JOHNSON CREEK PARK
CARTY PARK
SOUTH WINDS PARK
LA JANELLE PARK
PORT HUENEME BEACH PARK
PORT HUENEME FISHING PIER
BUBBLING SPRINGS LINEAR PARK
CHANNEL ISLANDS BLVD
HARBOR BLVD
VICTORIA AV
VENTURA RD
SAVIERS RD
OXNARD BLVD
ROSE AV
HUENEME RD
PLEASANT VALLEY RD
PATTERSON RD
MCWANE BLVD
SEE B G5
1 ELM DR
2 OAK DR
3 ASPEN GLEN
4 CEDAR COVE
5 BERING ST
SEE A C2
1 DISCOVERY CV
2 ABALONE CV
3 CABIN CV
4 EXPLORER CV
5 GOLD CV
6 HURRICANE CV
7 OUTLOOK CV
8 NORTHSTAR CV
9 PIRATE CV
10 MARINER CV
11 LIBERTY CV
12 KAYAK CV
13 JACKLIGHT CV
14 IRONSIDE CV
0 .25 .5 .75 1.0 miles 1 in. = 2400 ft.

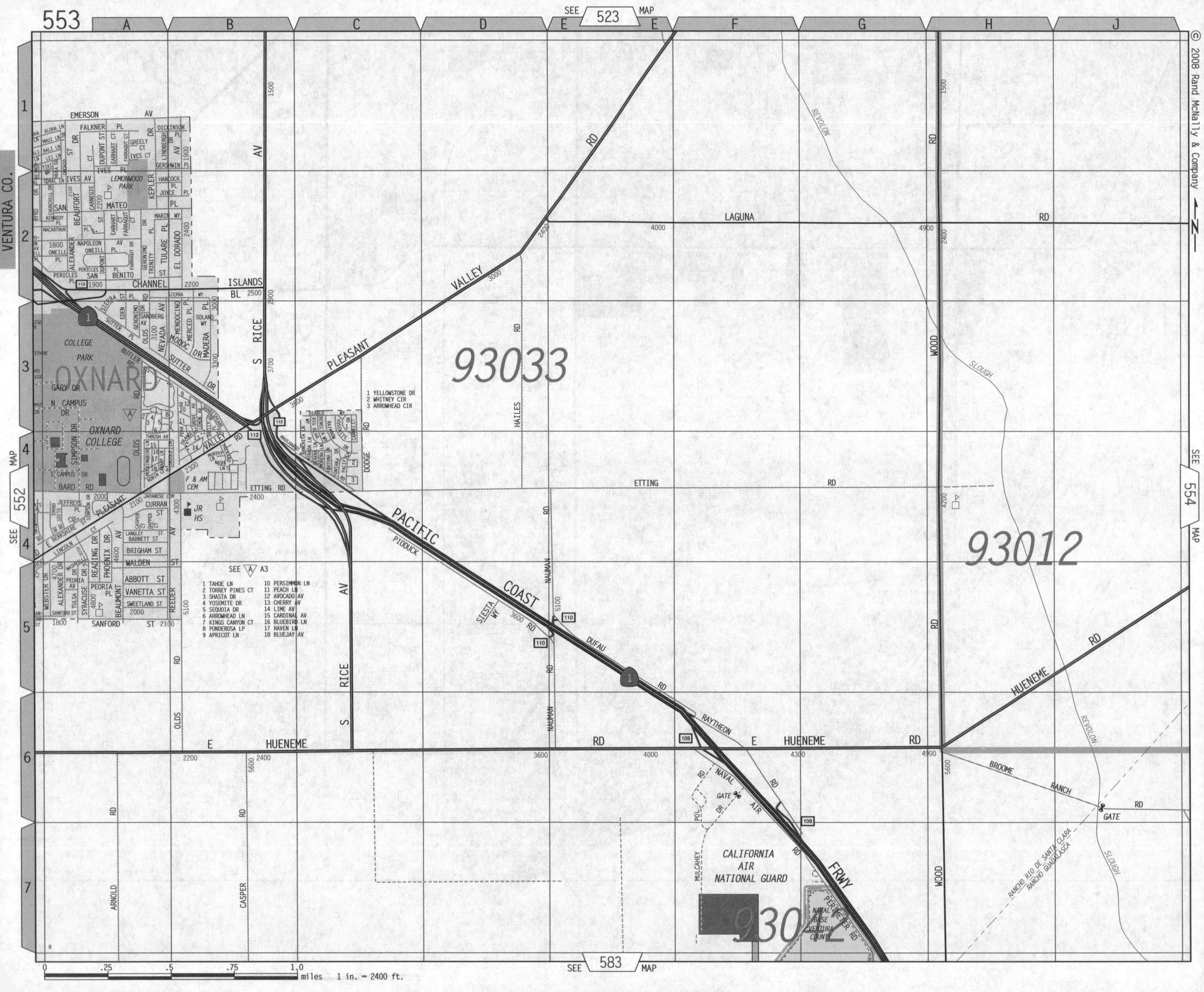

553
A B C D E F G H J
SEE 523 MAP
SEE 552 MAP
SEE 554 MAP
SEE 583 MAP
VENTURA CO.
© 2008 Rand McNally & Company
93033
93012
93042
OXNARD
OXNARD COLLEGE
COLLEGE PARK
LEMONWOOD PARK
F & AM CEM
JAPANESE CEM
JR HS
CALIFORNIA AIR NATIONAL GUARD
NAVAL BASE VENTURA COUNTY
EMERSON AV
CHANNEL ISLANDS BL
PLEASANT VALLEY RD
S RICE AV
LAGUNA RD
ETTING RD
WOOD RD
HAILES RD
NAUMAN RD
DODGE RD
PACIFIC COAST FRWY
PIDDUCK
SIESTA WY
DUFAU RD
RAYTHEON RD
E HUENEME RD
HUENEME RD
NAVAL AIR RD
BROOME RANCH RD
REVOLON SLOUGH
MULCAHEY DR
POL DR
PERIMETER RD
ARNOLD RD
CASPER RD
OLDS RD
REEDER RD
SANFORD ST
GATE
RANCHO RIO DE SANTA CLARA
RANCHO GUADALASCA
1 YELLOWSTONE DR
2 WHITNEY CIR
3 ARROWHEAD CIR
SEE A A3
1 TAHOE LN
2 TORREY PINES CT
3 SHASTA DR
4 YOSEMITE DR
5 SEQUOIA DR
6 ARROWHEAD LN
7 KINGS CANYON CT
8 PONDEROSA LP
9 APRICOT LN
10 PERSIMMON LN
11 PEACH LN
12 AVOCADO AV
13 CHERRY AV
14 LIME AV
15 CARDINAL AV
16 BLUEBIRD LN
17 RAVEN LN
18 BLUEJAY AV
0 .25 .5 .75 1.0 miles 1 in. = 2400 ft.

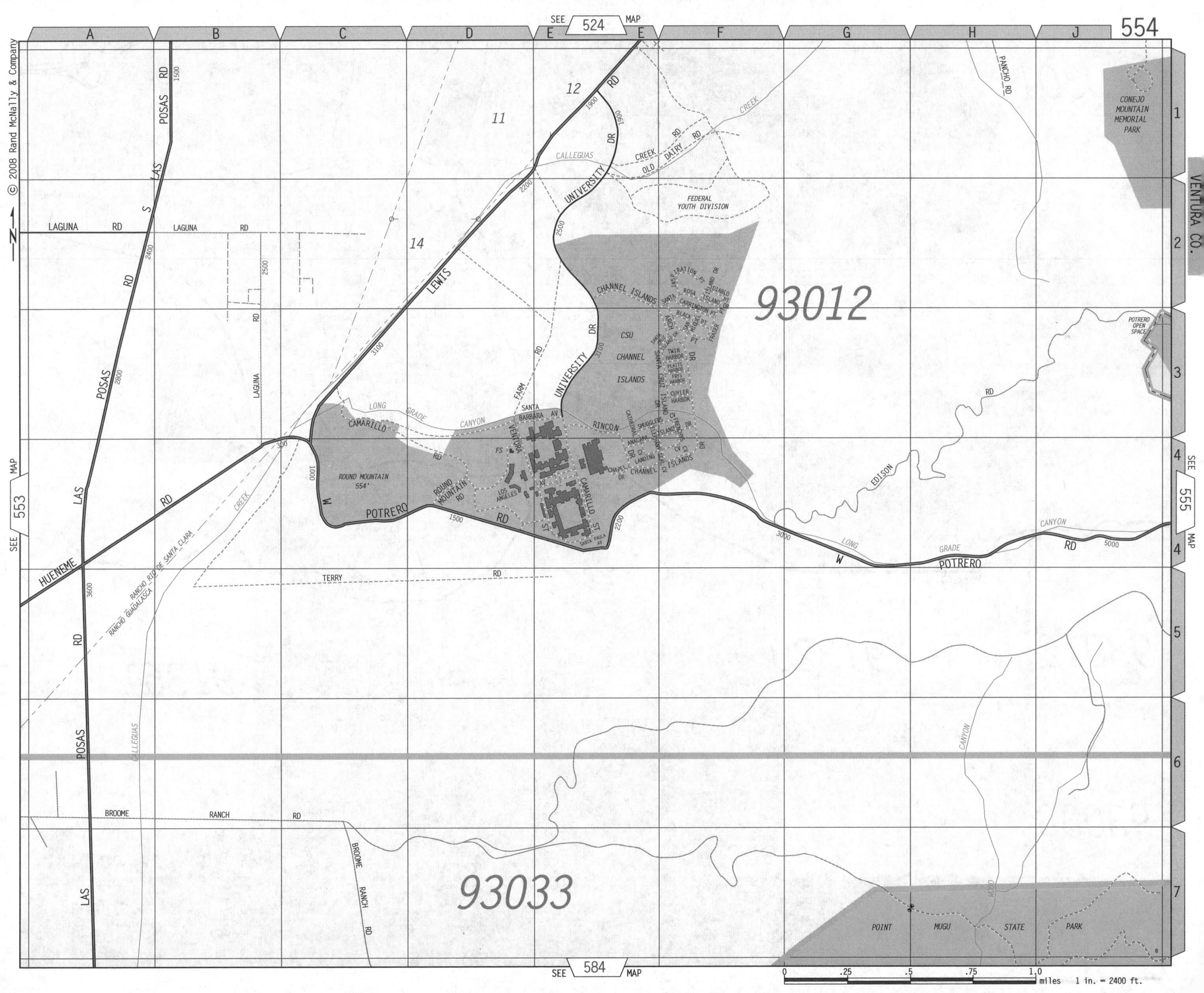
SEE 524 MAP
SEE 584 MAP
SEE 553 MAP
SEE 555 MAP
VENTURA CO.
93012
93033
CONEJO MOUNTAIN MEMORIAL PARK
POTRERO OPEN SPACE
FEDERAL YOUTH DIVISION
CSU CHANNEL ISLANDS
ROUND MOUNTAIN 554'
POINT MUGU STATE PARK
LAS POSAS RD
LAGUNA RD
LEWIS RD
UNIVERSITY DR
OLD DAIRY RD
CREEK RD
CALLEGUAS CREEK
CHANNEL ISLANDS DR
SANTA BARBARA AV
VENTURA ST
CAMARILLO ST
LOS ANGELES AV
ROUND MOUNTAIN RD
CAMARILLO RD
W POTRERO RD
FARM RD
RINCON DR
LONG GRADE CANYON
EDISON RD
PANCHO RD
HUENEME RD
TERRY RD
BROOME RANCH RD
RANCHO RIO DE SANTA CLARA
RANCHO GUADALASCA
CANYON
FS
miles 1 in. = 2400 ft.
© 2008 Rand McNally & Company

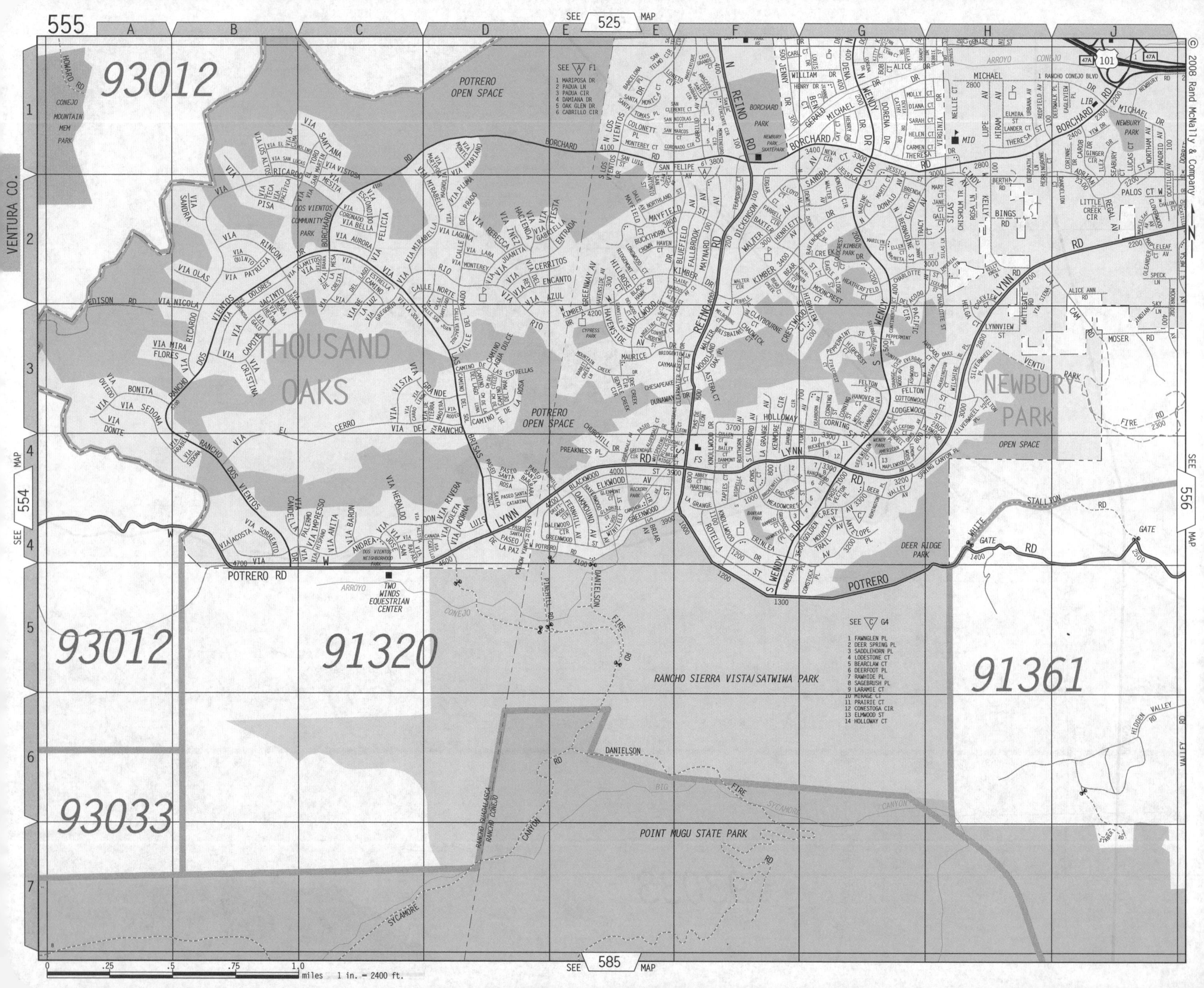

SEE 525 MAP
SEE 585 MAP
SEE 554 MAP
SEE 556 MAP
VENTURA CO.
93012
91320
93033
91361
THOUSAND OAKS
NEWBURY PARK
POTRERO OPEN SPACE
DOS VIENTOS COMMUNITY PARK
CONEJO MOUNTAIN MEM PARK
BORCHARD PARK
NEWBURY PARK SKATEPARK
CYPRESS PARK
KIMBER PARK
DOS VIENTOS NEIGHBORHOOD PARK
TWO WINDS EQUESTRIAN CENTER
DEER RIDGE PARK
OPEN SPACE
RANCHO SIERRA VISTA/SATWIWA PARK
POINT MUGU STATE PARK
BORCHARD RD
LYNN RD
REINO RD
WENDY DR
POTRERO RD
RANCHO DOS VIENTOS
VIA RIVERA
DANIELSON RD
SYCAMORE CANYON
BIG SYCAMORE CANYON
HIDDEN VALLEY RD
STALLION RD
WHITE GATE RD
SEE A F1
1 MARIPOSA DR
2 PADUA LN
3 PADUA CIR
4 DAMIANA DR
5 OAK GLEN DR
6 CABRILLO CIR
SEE C G4
1 FAWNGLEN PL
2 DEER SPRING PL
3 SADDLEHORN PL
4 LODESTONE CT
5 BEARCLAW CT
6 DEERFOOT PL
7 RAWHIDE PL
8 SAGEBRUSH PL
9 LARAMIE CT
10 MIRAGE CT
11 PRAIRIE CT
12 CONESTOGA CIR
13 ELMWOOD ST
14 HOLLOWAY CT
0 .25 .5 .75 1.0 miles 1 in. = 2400 ft.

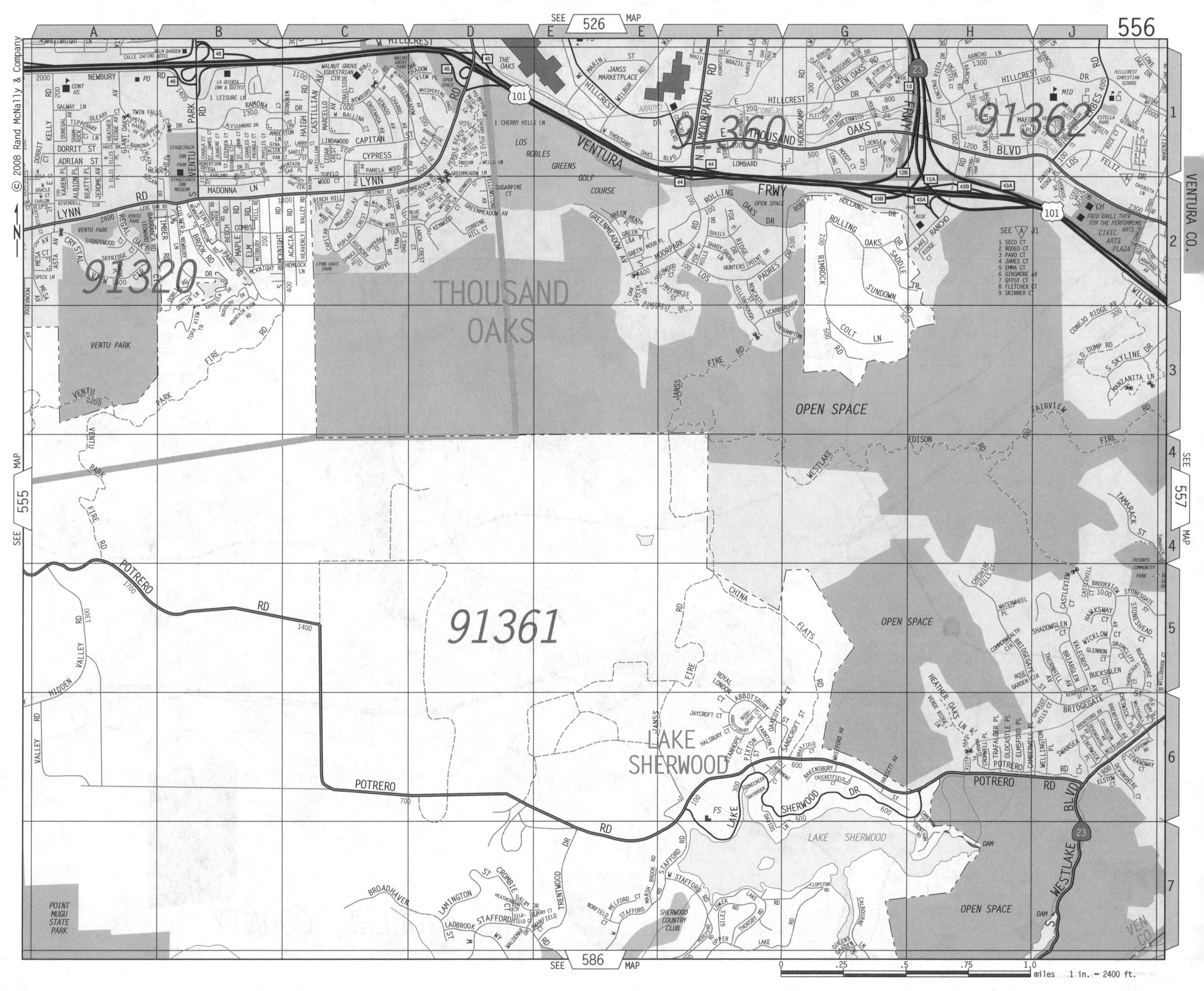
SEE 526 MAP
A
B
C
D
E
F
G
H
J
1
2
3
4
5
6
7
SEE 555 MAP
SEE 557 MAP
SEE 586 MAP
VENTURA CO.
91320
91360
91362
91361
THOUSAND OAKS
LAKE SHERWOOD
LOS ROBLES GREENS GOLF COURSE
VENTU PARK
OPEN SPACE
LAKE SHERWOOD
SHERWOOD COUNTRY CLUB
POINT MUGU STATE PARK
VENTURA FRWY
101
23
THE OAKS
JANSS MARKETPLACE
STAGECOACH INN PARK
FRED KAVLI THTR FOR THE PERFORMING ARTS
CIVIC ARTS PLAZA
HILLCREST CHRISTIAN SCHOOL
WALNUT GROVE EQUESTRIAN CTR
LYNN OAKS PARK
TRIUNFO COMMUNITY PARK
W HILLCREST DR
THOUSAND OAKS BLVD
MOORPARK RD
LYNN RD
POTRERO RD
WESTLAKE BLVD
ROLLING OAKS DR
GREENMEADOW AV
JANSS RD
EDISON RD
FAIRVIEW RD
CHINA FLATS RD
HIDDEN VALLEY RD
VENTU PARK RD
LAKE SHERWOOD DR
STAFFORD RD
TRENTWOOD DR
BRIDGEGATE ST
SEE J1
1 SECO CT
2 RODEO CT
3 PAVO CT
4 JAMES CT
5 EMMA CT
6 DINSMORE AV
7 GYPSY CT
8 FLETCHER CT
9 SKINNER CT
miles 1 in. = 2400 ft.
0 .25 .5 .75 1.0

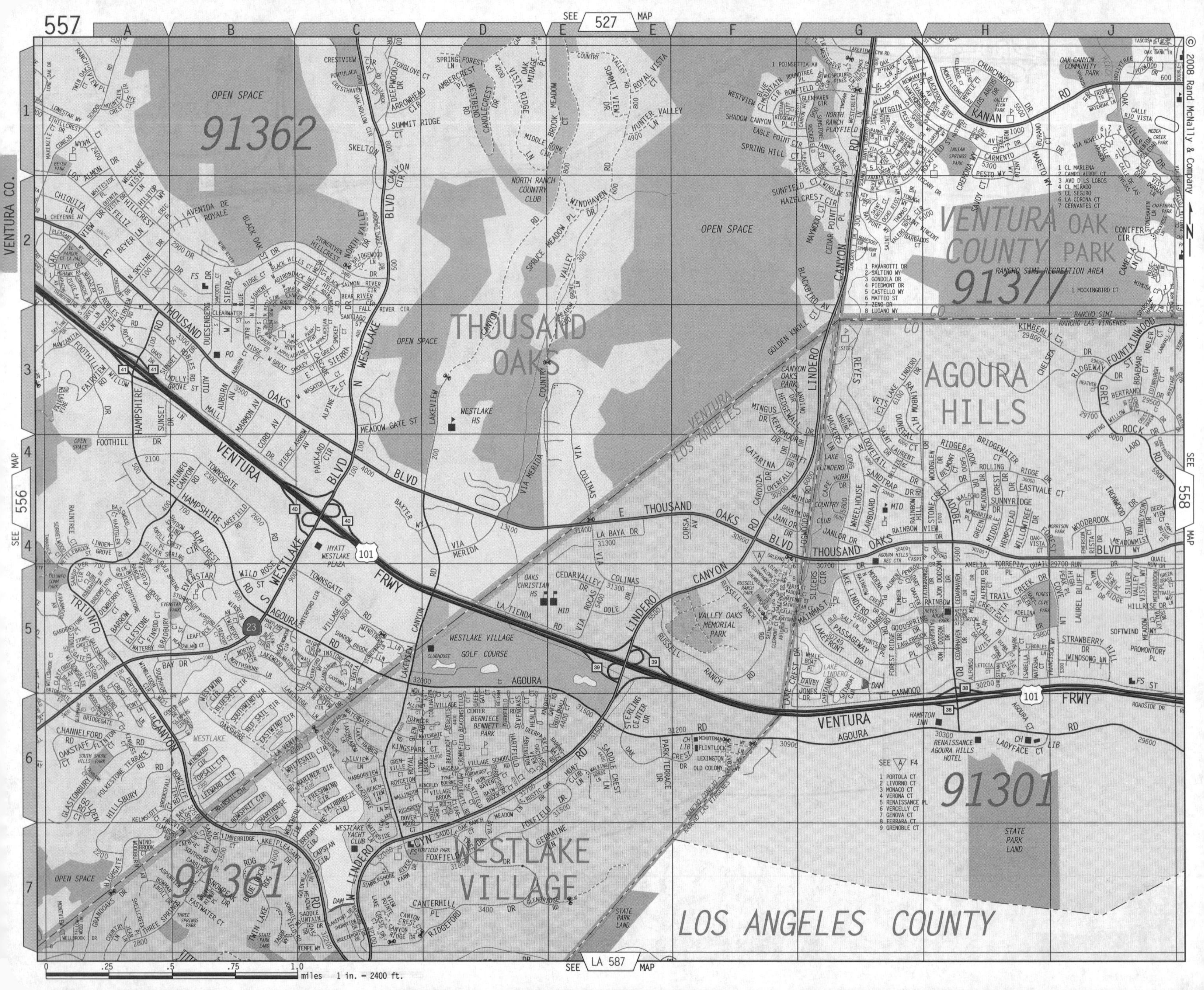

557
A
B
C
D
E
F
G
H
J
SEE 527 MAP
SEE 556 MAP
SEE 558 MAP
SEE LA 587 MAP
VENTURA CO.
OPEN SPACE
91362
91377
91301
91361
THOUSAND OAKS
AGOURA HILLS
WESTLAKE VILLAGE
VENTURA COUNTY PARK
OAK COUNTY PARK
RANCHO SIMI RECREATION AREA
NORTH RANCH COUNTRY CLUB
WESTLAKE HS
OAKS CHRISTIAN HS
WESTLAKE VILLAGE GOLF COURSE
VALLEY OAKS MEMORIAL PARK
HYATT WESTLAKE PLAZA
RENAISSANCE AGOURA HILLS HOTEL
STATE PARK LAND
LOS ANGELES COUNTY
VENTURA
LOS ANGELES
THOUSAND OAKS BLVD
E THOUSAND OAKS BLVD
VENTURA FRWY
101
23
KANAN RD
AGOURA RD
LINDERO CANYON RD
WESTLAKE BLVD
1 PAVAROTTI DR
2 SALTINO WY
3 GONDOLA DR
4 CASTELLO WY
5 CASTELLO WY
6 MATTEO ST
7 ZENO DR
8 LUGANO WY
1 CL MARLENA
2 CAMPO VERDE CT
3 AVD D LS LOBOS
4 CL MIRADO
5 CL SEGURO
6 LA CORONA CT
7 CERVANTES CT
1 PORTOLA CT
2 LIVORNO CT
3 MONACO CT
4 VERONA CT
5 RENAISSANCE PL
6 VERCELLY CT
7 GENOVA CT
8 FERRARA CT
9 GRENOBLE CT
0 .25 .5 .75 1.0 miles 1 in. = 2400 ft.
© 2008 Rand McNally & Company

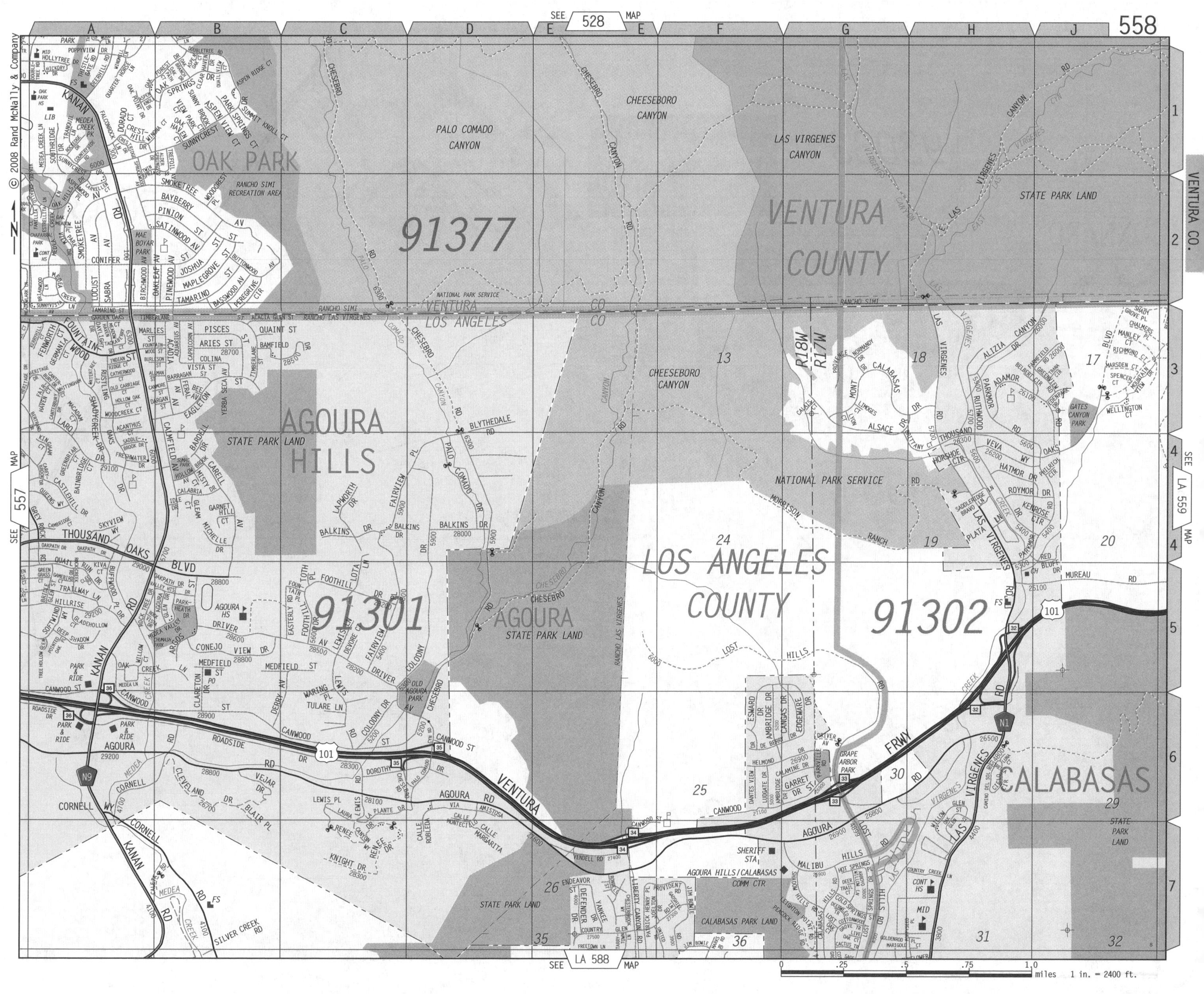
SEE 528 MAP
OAK PARK
AGOURA HILLS
VENTURA COUNTY
LOS ANGELES COUNTY
CALABASAS
91377
91301
91302
PALO COMADO CANYON
CHEESEBORO CANYON
LAS VIRGENES CANYON
STATE PARK LAND
RANCHO SIMI RECREATION AREA
NATIONAL PARK SERVICE
AGOURA STATE PARK LAND
CALABASAS PARK LAND
AGOURA HILLS/CALABASAS COMM CTR
VENTURA FRWY
THOUSAND OAKS BLVD
AGOURA RD
KANAN RD
LAS VIRGENES RD
MALIBU HILLS RD
LOST HILLS RD
MUREAU RD
CANWOOD ST
ROADSIDE DR
CORNELL RD
DRIVER AV
CONEJO VIEW DR
MEDFIELD ST
CHESEBRO RD
RANCHO LAS VIRGENES
VENTURA CO
LOS ANGELES CO
VENTURA CO.
SEE LA 559 MAP
SEE 557 MAP
SEE LA 588 MAP
miles 1 in. = 2400 ft.

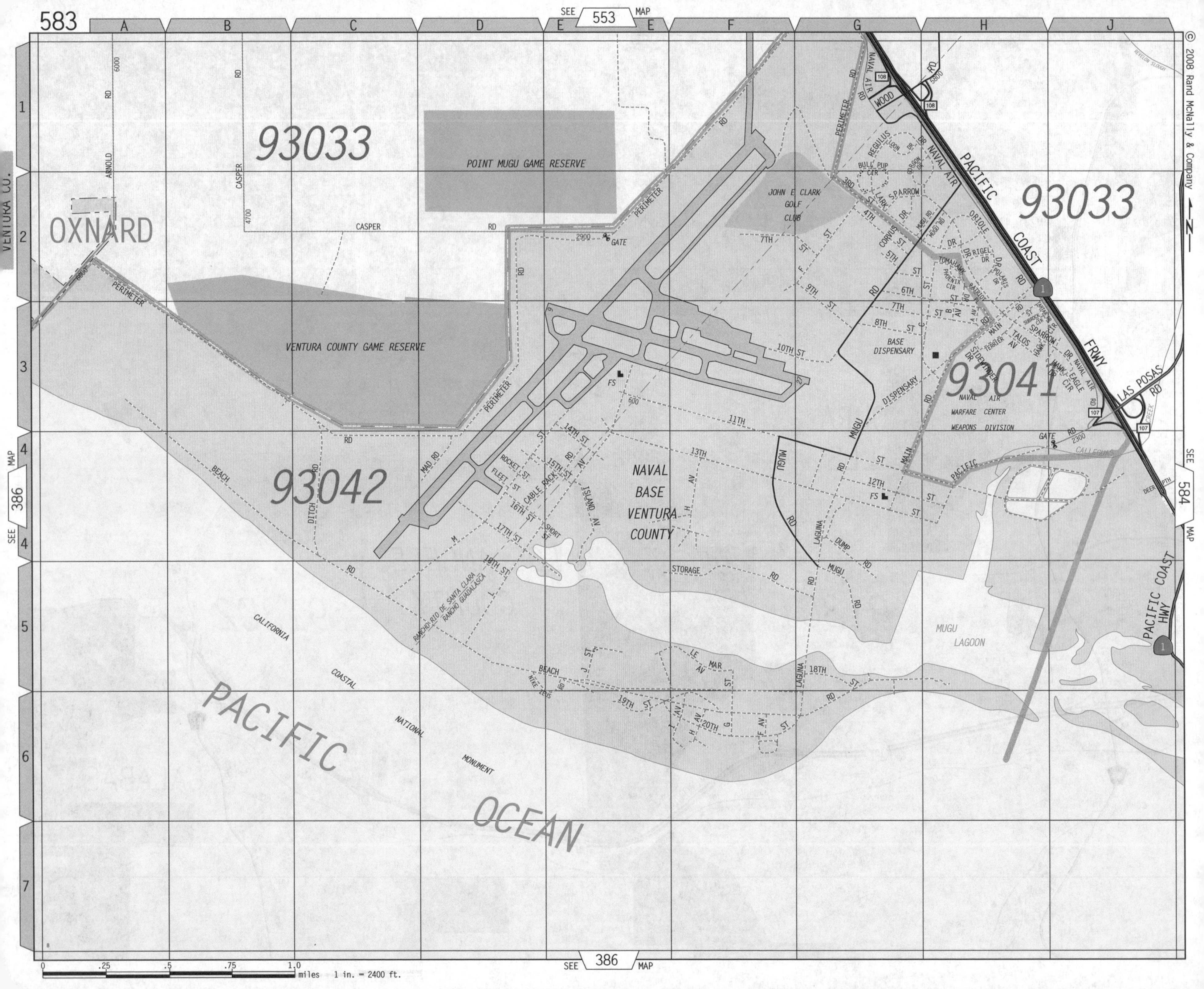
93033
POINT MUGU GAME RESERVE
OXNARD
VENTURA COUNTY GAME RESERVE
JOHN E CLARK GOLF CLUB
93033
93041
NAVAL AIR WARFARE CENTER WEAPONS DIVISION
93042
NAVAL BASE VENTURA COUNTY
BASE DISPENSARY
PACIFIC COAST FRWY
PACIFIC COAST HWY
MUGU LAGOON
CALIFORNIA COASTAL NATIONAL MONUMENT
PACIFIC OCEAN
RANCHO RIO DE SANTA CLARA
RANCHO GUADALASCA
VENTURA CO.
SEE 553 MAP
SEE 386 MAP
SEE 584 MAP
0 .25 .5 .75 1.0 miles 1 in. = 2400 ft.

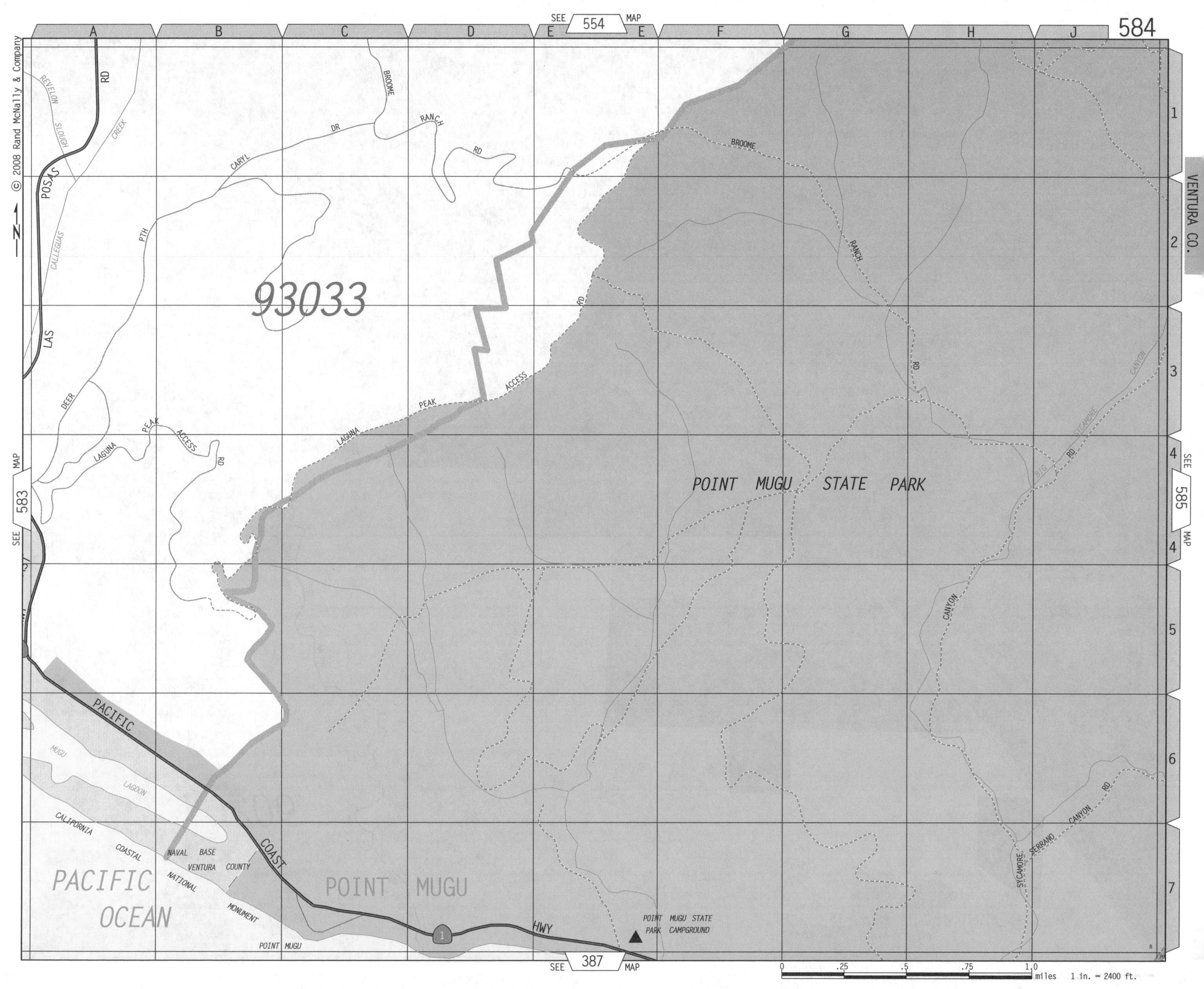
SEE 554 MAP
A
B
C
D
E
F
G
H
J
1
2
3
4
5
6
7
VENTURA CO.
SEE MAP 583
SEE MAP 585
© 2008 Rand McNally & Company
REVELON SLOUGH
CREEK
POSAS RD
LAS POSAS
CALLEGUAS
BROOME RANCH RD
CARYL DR
PTH
93033
DEER
LAGUNA PEAK ACCESS RD
BROOME RANCH RD
BIG SYCAMORE CANYON RD
POINT MUGU STATE PARK
CANYON
SYCAMORE
SERRANO CANYON RD
PACIFIC COAST HWY
MUGU LAGOON
CALIFORNIA COASTAL NATIONAL MONUMENT
NAVAL BASE VENTURA COUNTY
PACIFIC OCEAN
POINT MUGU
POINT MUGU STATE PARK CAMPGROUND
1
SEE 387 MAP
0 .25 .5 .75 1.0 miles 1 in. = 2400 ft.

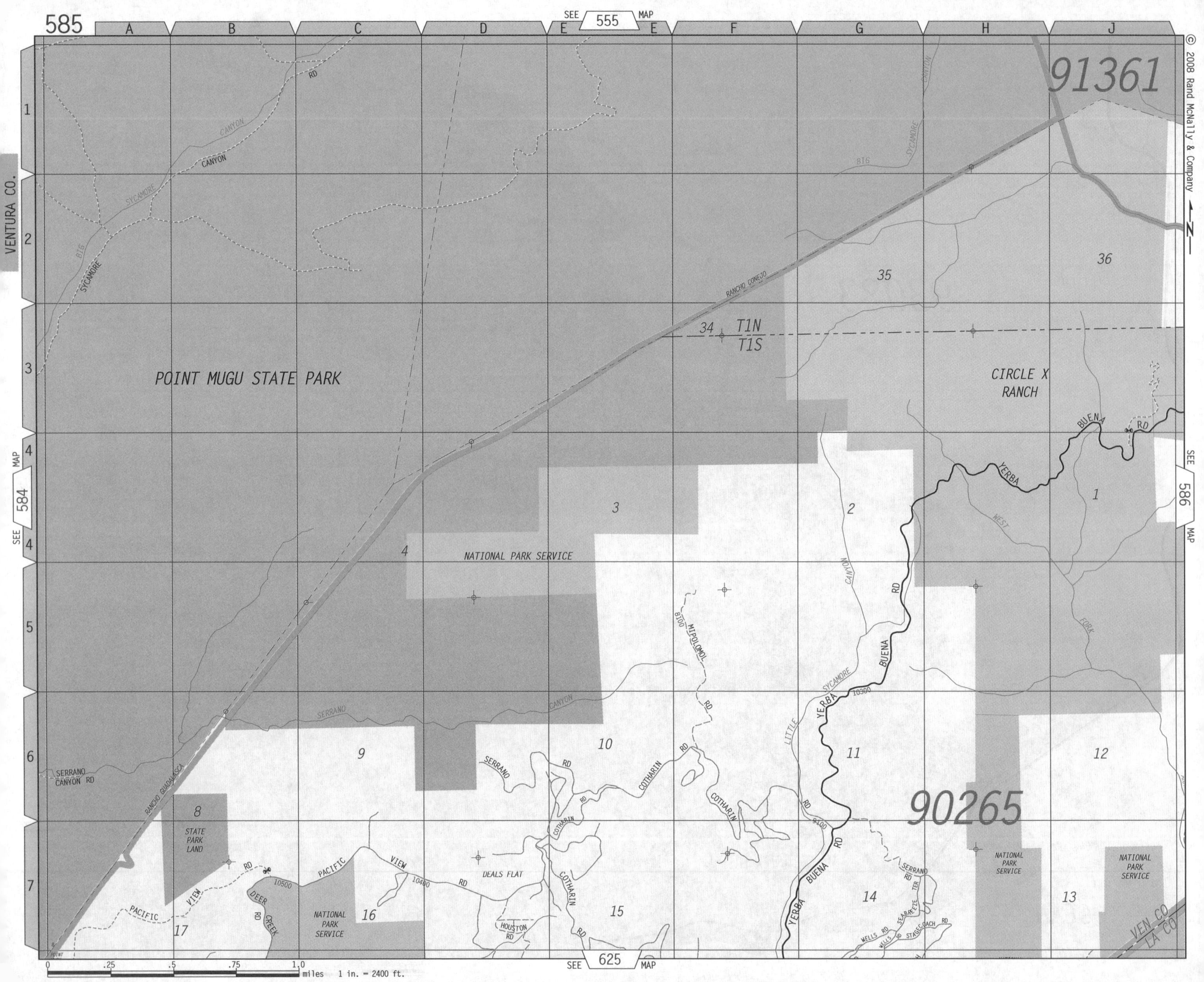
SEE 555 MAP
91361
POINT MUGU STATE PARK
RANCHO CONEJO
T1N
T1S
CIRCLE X RANCH
NATIONAL PARK SERVICE
YERBA BUENA RD
BIG SYCAMORE CANYON
MIPOLOMOL RD
COTHARIN RD
SERRANO CANYON RD
RANCHO GUADALASCA
STATE PARK LAND
PACIFIC VIEW RD
DEER CREEK RD
DEALS FLAT
HOUSTON RD
LITTLE SYCAMORE CANYON RD
WEST FORK
SERRANO RD
SEABREEZE TER
STAGECOACH RD
WELLS RD
90265
VEN CO
LA CO
VENTURA CO.
SEE 584 MAP
SEE 586 MAP
SEE 625 MAP
miles 1 in. = 2400 ft.

SEE 556 MAP

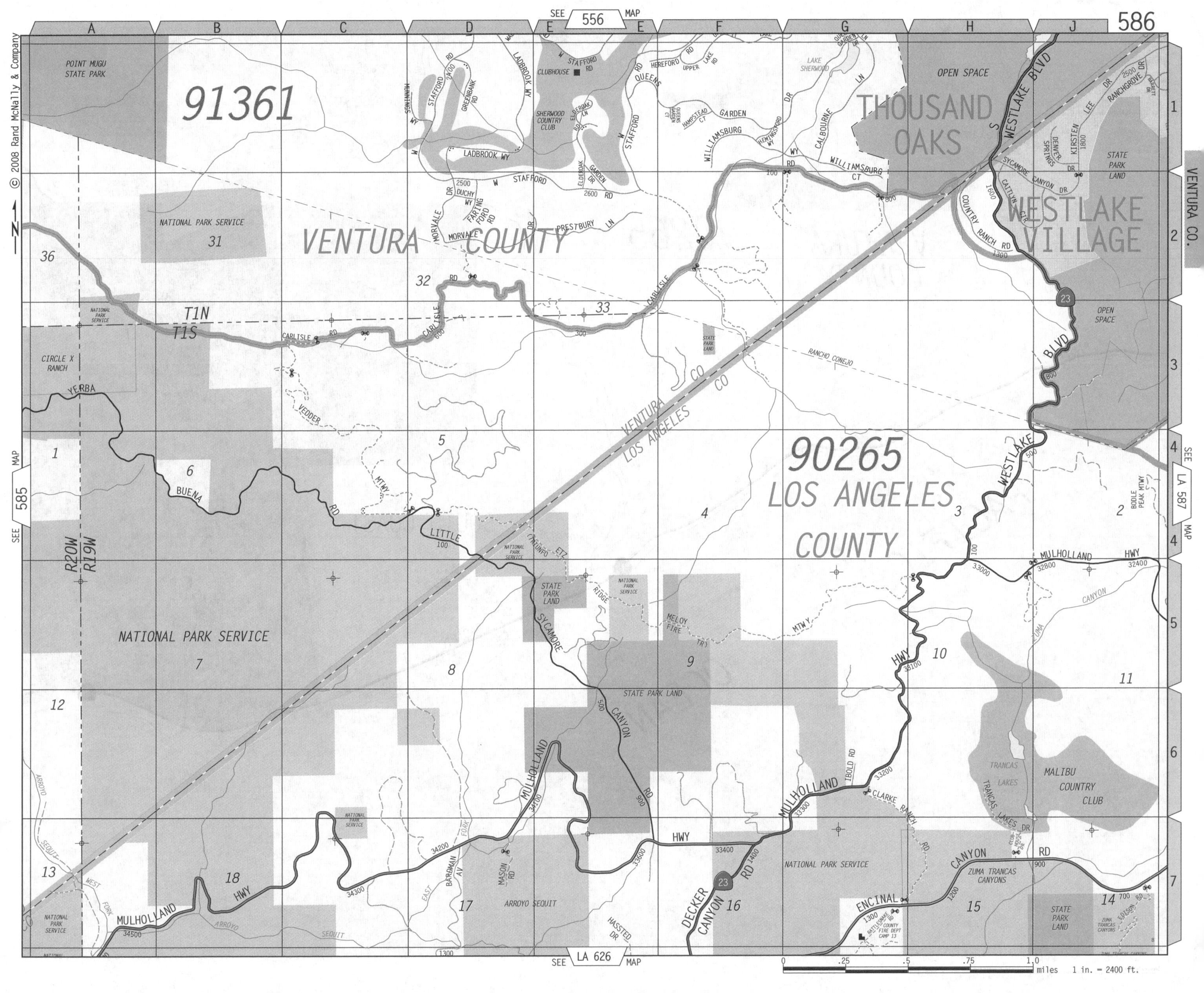

SEE 585 MAP
SEE LA 587 MAP
SEE LA 626 MAP

0 .25 .5 .75 1.0 miles 1 in. = 2400 ft.

SEE 585 MAP

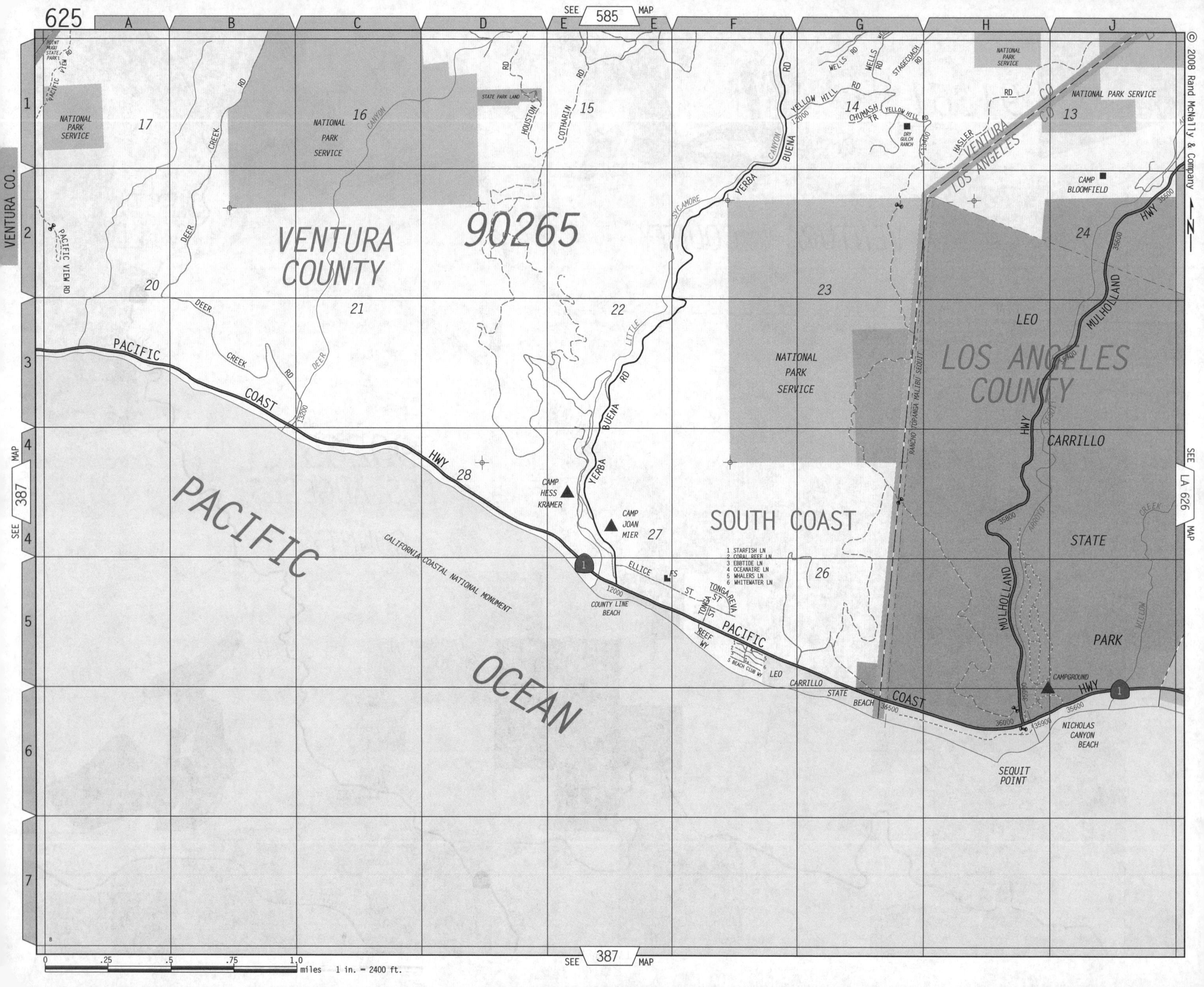

SEE 387 MAP

SEE LA 626 MAP

0 .25 .5 .75 1.0 miles 1 in. = 2400 ft.

SEE 387 MAP

Cities and Communities

Community Name	Abbr.	ZIP Code	Map Page
Bardsdale		93015	465
Bell Canyon		91307	529
Buckhorn		93015	457
* Camarillo	CMRL	93010	524
Casitas Springs		93001	460
Chrisman		93001	471
Colonia		93030	522
El Rio		93030	522
Faria Beach		93001	470
* Fillmore	FILM	93015	456
Foster Park		93001	461
Hollywood Beach		93035	552
Hollywood-By-The-Sea		93035	552
La Conchita		93001	459
Lake Sherwood		91361	556
Leisure Village		93010	525
Live Oak Acres		93022	451
Lockwood Valley			367
Meiners Oaks		93023	441
Mira Monte		93023	451
Montalvo		93003	492
* Moorpark	MRPK	93021	476
Moorpark Home Acres		93021	496
Newbury Park		91320	525
North Fillmore		93015	455
Norwegian Grade		91360	496
Nyeland Acres		93030	523
Oakbrook Village		91360	527
Oak Park		91377	558
Oak View		93022	451
* Ojai	OJAI	93023	441
Ortonville		93001	471
* Oxnard	OXN	93030	522
Pierpont Bay		93003	491
Piru		93040	457
Point Mugu		93041	387
* Port Hueneme	PHME	93041	552
* San Buenaventura (See Ventura)			
* Santa Paula	SPLA	93060	464
Santa Susana		93063	499
Saticoy		93004	473
Seacliff		93001	459
Silver Strand		93030	552
* Simi Valley	SIMI	93065	478
Solimar Beach		93001	470
Somis		93066	495
South Coast		90265	625
Springville		93010	523
Sulphur Springs		93060	453
Summit		93023	453
* Thousand Oaks	THO	91360	526
* Ventura	VEN	93001	491
-- Ventura County	VeCo		
Wheeler Springs		93023	366

*Indicates incorporated city

List of Abbreviations

PREFIXES & SUFFIXES

AL	ALLEY
ARC	ARCADE
AV,AVE	AVENUE
AVCT	AVENUE COURT
AVD	AVENIDA
AVD D LA	AVENIDA DE LA
AVD D LOS	AVENIDA DE LOS
AVD DE	AVENIDA DE
AVD DE LAS	AVENIDA DE LAS
AVD DEL	AVENIDA DEL
AVDR	AVENUE DRIVE
AVEX	AVENUE EXTENSION
AV OF	AVENUE OF
AV OF THE	AVENUE OF THE
AVPL	AVENUE PLACE
BAY	BAY
BEND	BEND
BL, BLVD	BOULEVARD
BLCT	BOULEVARD COURT
BLEX	BOULEVARD EXTENSION
BRCH	BRANCH
BRDG	BRIDGE
BYPS	BYPASS
BYWY	BYWAY
CIDR	CIRCLE DRIVE
CIR	CIRCLE
CL	CALLE
CL DE	CALLE DE
CL DL	CALLE DEL
CL D LA	CALLE DE LA
CL D LAS	CALLE DE LAS
CL D LOS	CALLE DE LOS
CL EL	CALLE EL
CLJ	CALLEJON
CL LA	CALLE LA
CL LAS	CALLE LAS
CL LOS	CALLE LOS
CLTR	CLUSTER
CM	CAMINO
CM D	CAMINO DE
CM DL	CAMINO DEL
CM D LA	CAMINO DE LA
CM D LAS	CAMINO DE LAS
CM D LOS	CAMINO DE LOS
CMTO	CAMINITO
CMTO DEL	CAMINITO DEL
CMTO D LA	CAMINITO DE LA
CMTO D LAS	CAMINITO DE LAS
CMTO D LOS	CAMINITO DE LOS
CNDR	CENTER DRIVE
COM	COMMON
COMS	COMMONS
CORR	CORRIDOR
CRES	CRESCENT
CRLO	CIRCULO
CRSG	CROSSING
CST	CIRCLE STREET
CSWY	CAUSEWAY
CT	COURT
CTAV	COURT AVENUE
CTE	CORTE
CTE D	CORTE DE
CTE DEL	CORTE DEL
CTE D LAS	CORTE DE LAS
CTO	CUT OFF
CTR	CENTER
CTST	COURT STREET
CUR	CURVE
CV	COVE
DE	DE
DIAG	DIAGONAL
DR	DRIVE
DRAV	DRIVE AVENUE
DRCT	DRIVE COURT
DRLP	DRIVE LOOP
DVDR	DIVISION DR
EXAV	EXTENSION AVENUE
EXBL	EXTENSION BOULEVARD
EXRD	EXTENSION ROAD
EXST	EXTENSION STREET
EXT	EXTENSION
EXWY	EXPRESSWAY
FOREST RT	FOREST ROUTE
FRWY	FREEWAY
FRY	FERRY
GDNS	GARDENS
GN, GLN	GLEN
GRN	GREEN
GRV	GROVE
HTS	HEIGHTS
HWY	HIGHWAY
ISL	ISLE
JCT	JUNCTION
LN	LANE
LNCR	LANE CIRCLE
LNDG	LANDING
LNDR	LAND DRIVE
LNLP	LANE LOOP
LP	LOOP
MNR	MANOR
MT	MOUNT
MTWY	MOTORWAY
MWCR	MEWS COURT
MWLN	MEWS LANE
NFD	NAT'L FOREST DEV
NK	NOOK
OH	OUTER HIGHWAY
OVL	OVAL
OVLK	OVERLOOK
OVPS	OVERPASS
PAS	PASEO
PAS DE	PASEO DE
PAS DE LA	PASEO DE LA
PAS DE LAS	PASEO DE LAS
PAS DE LOS	PASEO DE LOS
PAS DL	PASEO DEL
PASG	PASSAGE
PAS LA	PASEO LA
PAS LOS	PASEO LOS
PASS	PASS
PIKE	PIKE
PK	PARK
PKDR	PARK DRIVE
PKWY, PKY	PARKWAY
PL	PLACE
PLWY	PLACE WAY
PLZ, PZ	PLAZA
PT	POINT
PTAV	POINT AVENUE
PTH	PATH
PZ DE	PLAZA DE
PZ DEL	PLAZA DEL
PZ D LA	PLAZA DE LA
PZ D LAS	PLAZA DE LAS
PZWY	PLAZA WAY
RAMP	RAMP
RD	ROAD
RDAV	ROAD AVENUE
RDBP	ROAD BYPASS
RDCT	ROAD COURT
RDEX	ROAD EXTENSION
RDG	RIDGE
RDSP	ROAD SPUR
RDWY	ROAD WAY
RR	RAILROAD
RUE	RUE
RUE D	RUE D
RW	ROW
RY	RAILWAY
SKWY	SKYWAY
SQ	SQUARE
ST	STREET
STAV	STREET AVENUE
STCT	STREET COURT
STDR	STREET DRIVE
STEX	STREET EXTENSION
STLN	STREET LANE
STLP	STREET LOOP
ST OF	STREET OF
ST OF THE	STREET OF THE
STOV	STREET OVERPASS
STPL	STREET PLACE
STPM	STREET PROMENADE
STWY	STREET WAY
STXP	STREET EXPRESSWAY
TER	TERRACE
TFWY	TRAFFICWAY
THWY	THROUGHWAY
TKTR	TRUCK TRAIL
TPKE	TURNPIKE
TRC	TRACE
TRCT	TERRACE COURT
TR, TRL	TRAIL
TRWY	TRAIL WAY
TTSP	TRUCK TRAIL SPUR
TUN	TUNNEL
UNPS	UNDERPASS
VIA D	VIA DE
VIA DL	VIA DEL
VIA D LA	VIA DE LA
VIA D LAS	VIA DE LAS
VIA D LOS	VIA DE LOS
VIA LA	VIA LA
VW	VIEW
VWY	VIEW WAY
VIS	VISTA
VIS D	VISTA DE
VIS D L	VISTA DE LA
VIS D LAS	VISTA DE LAS
VIS DEL	VISTA DEL
WK	WALK
WY	WAY
WYCR	WAY CIRCLE
WYDR	WAY DRIVE
WYLN	WAY LANE
WYPL	WAY PLACE
VIS BUR	VISITORS BUREAU

DIRECTIONS

E	EAST
KPN	KEY PENINSULA NORTH
KPS	KEY PENINSULA SOUTH
N	NORTH
NE	NORTHEAST
NW	NORTHWEST
S	SOUTH
SE	SOUTHEAST
SW	SOUTHWEST
W	WEST

BUILDINGS

CH	CITY HALL
CHP	CALIFORNIA HIGHWAY PATROL
COMM CTR	COMMUNITY CENTER
CON CTR	CONVENTION CENTER
CONT HS	CONTINUATION HIGH SCHOOL
CTH	COURT HOUSE
FAA	FEDERAL AVIATION ADMIN
FS	FIRE STATION
HOSP	HOSPITAL
HS	HIGH SCHOOL
INT	INTERMEDIATE SCHOOL
JR HS	JUNIOR HIGH SCHOOL
LIB	LIBRARY
MID	MIDDLE SCHOOL
MUS	MUSEUM
PO	POST OFFICE
PS	POLICE STATION
SR CIT CTR	SENIOR CITIZENS CENTER
STA	STATION
THTR	THEATER

OTHER ABBREVIATIONS

BCH	BEACH
BLDG	BUILDING
CEM	CEMETERY
CK	CREEK
CO	COUNTY
COMM	COMMUNITY
CTR	CENTER
EST	ESTATE
HIST	HISTORIC
HTS	HEIGHTS
LK	LAKE
MDW	MEADOW
MED	MEDICAL
MEM	MEMORIAL
MT	MOUNT
MTN	MOUNTAIN
NATL	NATIONAL
PKG	PARKING
PLGD	PLAYGROUND
RCH	RANCH
RCHO	RANCHO
REC	RECREATION
RES	RESERVOIR
RIV	RIVER
RR	RAILROAD
SPG	SPRING
STA	SANTA
VLG	VILLAGE
VLY	VALLEY
VW	VIEW

STREET Block City ZIP Pg-Grid

A

A AV
- VeCo 93042 583-H3
A CT
3600 OXN 93033 552-G3
A ST
100 OXN 93030 522-G5
400 FILM 93015 456-A6
800 FILM 93015 455-J4
2900 OXN 93033 552-G3
A ST Rt#-23
- FILM 93015 456-A6
- FILM 93015 466-A1
E A ST
100 PHME 93041 552-E5
N A ST
100 OXN 93030 522-G5
W A ST
100 PHME 93041 552-E5
ABALONE CV
2600 PHME 93041 552-C2
ABALONE DR
2600 OXN 93035 552-A2
ABBEY CT
3600 THO 91320 555-F4
ABBEYWOOD CT
2400 SIMI 93063 498-D1
ABBEYWOOD DR
23900 CanP 91307 529-D5
ABBINGTON CT
4200 WLKV 91361 557-D6
ABBOTSBURY ST
23600 VeCo 91361 556-F6
ABBOTT AV
1700 CMRL 93010 524-G1
1700 CMRL 93010 494-G7
ABBOTT ST
2000 OXN 93033 553-A5
ABERDARE ST
8500 VEN 93004 492-G3
ABILENE ST
4700 SIMI 93063 478-H5
10100 VEN 93004 492-H2
ABLE CIR
1200 SIMI 93065 498-A4
ABRAHAM ST
2000 SIMI 93065 498-A3
ABRAZO DR
100 CMRL 93012 525-A3
ABUL HAJ RD
- VeCo 93060 453-D2
ACACIA
1000 VeCo 93023 451-C3
ACACIA LN
- VEN 93004 493-A2
ACACIA RD
100 VeCo 91320 556-C2
300 SPLA 93060 463-J7
400 SPLA 93060 473-J1
ACACIA ST
2500 OXN 93033 552-H2
2700 CMRL 93012 524-F4
ACACIA WY
23600 SPLA 93060 473-J1
ACACIA GLEN ST
28600 AGRH 91301 558-B3
ACADEMY DR
- THO 91320 525-H6
ACADIA AV
6100 AGRH 91301 558-B3
ACADIA PL
1100 VEN 93003 492-B4
ACADIA ST
1300 SIMI 93063 498-D3
ACALA ST
3500 CMRL 93010 524-G1
ACANTHUS CT
29000 AGRH 91301 558-A3
ACAPULCO AV
1200 SIMI 93065 497-F4
ACAPULCO CT
- SIMI 93065 497-F3
1100 OXN 93035 522-E7
ACORN CT
3800 SIMI 93063 498-E2
ACORN RD
- PHME 93043 552-C5
ACORN ST
22100 Chat 91311 499-J6
ACTON CT
1800 SIMI 93065 498-A1
ADAK ST
1100 PHME 93041 552-E4
ADAM RD
4000 SIMI 93063 478-F7
ADAMOR RD
26000 CALB 91302 558-H3
ADAMS ST
7300 VEN 93003 492-E1
ADAMS CANYON RD
1400 VeCo 93060 463-F3
1800 VeCo 93060 453-E7
ADDAX CIR
1600 VEN 93003 492-F4
ADDISON CIR
300 THO 91360 526-F4
ADDOR ST
- PHME 93041 552-E5
900 PHME 93043 552-E3
ADELAIDE CT
1700 OXN 93035 552-C1
ADELE PL
1400 THO 91360 526-D5
ADELINA CT
5500 AGRH 91301 557-H5
ADIRONDACK AV
600 VEN 93003 472-B7
600 VEN 93003 492-B1
ADIRONDACK CT
2100 SIMI 93065 497-C6
E ADIRONDACK CT
3300 THO 91362 557-C2
W ADIRONDACK CT
3000 THO 91362 557-B2
ADLENA PL
13500 MRPK 93021 496-F2
ADMIRAL CT
1300 VeCo 91377 527-H7
ADMIRAL WY
- OXN 93035 522-A7
ADOBE WY
800 CMRL 93012 525-C2
ADOHR LN
4500 CMRL 93012 524-H5
5100 CMRL 93012 525-A5
ADOLFO RD
3400 CMRL 93010 524-G1
3900 CMRL 93012 524-G1
5200 CMRL 93012 525-A3
ADONIS PL
4600 MRPK 93021 496-F2
ADRIAN ST
1700 THO 91320 556-A1
1900 THO 91320 555-J1
ADRIATIC ST
- OXN 93035 522-B7
AFFIRMED PL
6300 MRPK 93021 476-A6
AGATE CT
2100 SIMI 93065 497-G2
7900 VEN 93004 492-F3
AGATE ST
3500 THO 91360 526-H1
8000 VEN 93004 492-F3
AGGEN RD
4000 VeCo 93066 494-F3
5100 VeCo 93066 474-E7
AGNEW ST
1100 SIMI 93065 497-H2
AGNUS DR
200 VEN 93003 491-H2
AGOURA CT
29900 AGRH 91301 557-H6
AGOURA RD
2600 THO 91361 557-B5
2900 WLKV 91361 557-D5
26400 CALB 91302 558-G7
26600 LACo 91302 558-G7
26800 CALB 91301 558-G7
27000 Ago 91301 558-D6
27400 AGRH 91301 558-A6
29200 AGRH 91301 557-G6
AGOURA GLEN DR
5500 AGRH 91301 558-B5
AGUSTA AV
1000 CMRL 93010 524-D1
AHART ST
1200 SIMI 93065 497-H2
AHOY LN
- OXN 93035 552-A1
AILEEN ST
500 CMRL 93010 524-B2
AIREDALE AV
2000 VEN 93003 492-F5
AIREDALE CT
7300 VEN 93003 492-F5
AIRPORT WY
100 CMRL 93010 524-A5
AKERS ST
700 FILM 93015 456-A5
AKRON AV
700 VEN 93004 492-J1
AL WY
6000 SIMI 93063 499-B2
ALAMAR ST
- THO 91360 526-F2
ALAMEDA AV
2000 VeCo 93003 492-D5
2000 VEN 93003 492-D5
ALAMO ST
1700 SIMI 93065 497-J1
1700 SIMI 93065 498-A1
1900 SIMI 93065 478-H7
3300 SIMI 93063 478-C7
5400 SIMI 93063 479-A7
ALAMOS DR
1100 THO 91362 556-H1
ALAMOS CANYON RD
23600 SIMI 93065 477-D7
23600 VeCo 93065 477-D7
ALAN CT
23600 SIMI 93063 498-H1
ALANDIA CT
4200 MRPK 93021 496-E3
ALASKA DR
5700 VEN 93003 492-C5
ALBACORE WY
200 OXN 93035 552-B4
ALBANY AV
700 VEN 93004 492-H2
ALBANY DR
2800 OXN 93033 552-H2
ALBATROSS ST
6400 VEN 93003 492-D4
ALBERTSON MTWY
- VeCo 93065 527-G4
23600 SIMI 93063 528-E2
23600 SIMI 93065 527-G4
23600 SIMI 93065 528-C2
23600 THO 91362 527-G4
23600 VeCo 93063 528-E2
23600 VeCo 93065 528-A3
ALBION AV
5700 VEN 93003 492-C1
ALBION DR
- OXN 93036 492-H5
ALBION PL
- THO 91320 556-A2
ALBORADA DR
23600 CMRL 93010 494-C7
ALCOVE ST
500 SIMI 93065 527-D1
E ALDEN ST
2300 SIMI 93065 498-B1
N ALDEN ST
2400 SIMI 93065 498-C1
ALDER CIR
- MRPK 93021 496-G3
ALDERBROOK ST
11700 MRPK 93021 496-C4
ALDERCREEK PL
1300 THO 91362 527-C6
ALDERDALE CT
23600 THO 91320 555-E4
ALDERGLEN ST
12300 MRPK 93021 496-D3
ALDERGROVE ST
12100 MRPK 93021 496-D4
ALDER SPRINGS DR
300 VeCo 91377 558-B1
ALDER VIEW LN
23600 CMRL 93012 525-A1
ALDER WOOD PL
1500 THO 91362 526-J2
ALDREN CT
5500 AGRH 91301 557-G5
ALDRICH CT
300 THO 91360 526-F4
A LEASE CANYON RD
23600 VeCo 93001 470-D3
ALEE LN
- OXN 93035 522-B7
ALELIA AV
1200 VeCo 93004 493-B1
ALEPPO CT
1700 THO 91362 526-J4
ALESSANDRO DR
1200 THO 91320 556-B1
1500 VEN 93001 491-D3
ALEUTIAN WY
- OXN 93035 552-B1
ALEX CT
- THO 91320 555-E2
ALEXANDER DR
4700 OXN 93033 553-A5
ALEXANDER ST
1100 SIMI 93065 497-H2
1700 OXN 93033 553-A2
ALEXANDRA CT
23600 VeCo 91377 528-A7
ALEXANDRIA ST
10200 VEN 93004 492-J2
ALFA RD
23600 VeCo 93063 498-H7
23600 VeCo 93063 528-H1
ALFONSO DR
5300 AGRH 91301 557-H5
ALFREDO CT
5500 AGRH 91301 557-H5
ALGONQUIAN ST
700 VEN 93001 471-D5
ALGONQUIN CT
2900 CMRL 93010 524-F1
ALGONQUIN DR
2100 SIMI 93065 497-D2
ALHAMBRA AV
- VEN 93004 492-F1
4800 SIMI 93063 478-H7
ALHAMBRA CT
- VeCo 93012 496-E7
ALIANO DR
4800 VeCo 91377 557-G1
ALICANTE CT
- VeCo 93012 496-E7
ALICE DR
3000 THO 91320 555-G1
3000 VeCo 91320 555-G1
ALICE ANN RD
2400 THO 91320 555-J2
2400 VeCo 91320 555-J2
ALIENTO WY
400 CMRL 93012 524-J2
ALISO LN
100 VEN 93001 491-E2
ALISO PL
300 OXN 93036 522-H3
1300 VEN 93001 491-D1
ALISO ST
100 OJAI 93023 441-H6
200 VEN 93001 491-D1
400 VEN 93001 471-D7
N ALISO ST
100 VEN 93001 491-E1
W ALISO ST
100 OJAI 93023 441-H6
ALISO CANYON RD
2900 VeCo 93060 462-H3
6200 VeCo 93060 472-J1
6700 VeCo 93060 473-A2
23600 VeCo 93060 452-G7
ALISON DR
12400 VeCo 93012 496-D7
ALIZIA CANYON DR
26000 CALB 91302 558-H3
26000 VeCo 91302 558-H3
N ALLEGHENY CT
200 THO 91362 557-B3
S ALLEGHENY CT
100 THO 91362 557-B3
ALLEGRO CT
200 SIMI 93065 527-D1
ALLEN ST
1100 THO 91320 556-B1
ALLENBY CT
32000 WLKV 91361 557-C6
ALLENVALE CT
500 SIMI 93065 497-D7
ALLMAN ST
28900 AGRH 91301 558-A3
ALLYSON CT
23600 THO 91362 527-B5
ALMADEN CT
2500 SIMI 93065 498-A1
ALMANOR ST
1800 OXN 93030 522-J3
1800 OXN 93036 522-J3
ALMAR ST
6300 SIMI 93063 499-C2
ALMENDRA PL
800 OXN 93036 522-H3
ALMENDRO CT
1500 CMRL 93010 524-G1
ALMENDRO WY
3500 CMRL 93010 524-G1
ALMON DR
200 THO 91362 557-A2
ALMOND AV
10400 VeCo 93022 451-C6
ALMOND DR
3400 VeCo 93036 523-D2
ALMOND TREE CT
23600 SIMI 93063 498-D4
ALOE LN
23600 SIMI 93065 497-E5
ALOHA LN
1800 OXN 93033 552-J1
1800 OXN 93033 553-A1
ALOHA ST
2600 CMRL 93010 494-F7
2600 VeCo 93010 494-F7
ALOMAR ST
600 VeCo 93023 451-C3
ALOSTA DR
100 VeCo 93010 494-F6
ALOSTA LN
1300 CMRL 93010 494-G6
1300 VeCo 93010 494-G6
ALOSTA PL
300 VeCo 93010 494-G6
600 CMRL 93010 494-G6
ALOSTA WY
600 VeCo 93010 494-G6
ALPINE AV
100 VEN 93004 472-H6
ALPINE CT
400 VEN 93004 472-H6
2800 THO 91362 557-C3
ALPINE ST
100 OXN 93030 522-J5
4400 SIMI 93063 498-G2
ALSACE DR
- Ago 91301 558-G3
- LACo 91302 558-G3
ALSCOT AV
1800 SIMI 93063 499-B1
ALTA ST
4800 SIMI 93063 478-H7
ALTA WY
23200 Chat 91311 499-F6
ALTA COLINA RD
4900 CMRL 93012 524-J2
5100 CMRL 93012 525-A2
ALTADENA ST
8300 VEN 93004 492-F1
E ALTA GREEN ST
100 PHME 93041 552-E2
W ALTA GREEN ST
100 PHME 93041 552-D2
ALTAIR AV
2700 THO 91360 526-F3
ALTA MIRA ST
400 VeCo 93065 497-G5
23600 SIMI 93065 497-G5
ALTAMONT WY
- VeCo 93010 494-C6
ALTA SAGUNA CT
23600 CMRL 93010 494-C7
ALTA VISTA PL
23600 CMRL 93012 494-J7
23600 CMRL 93012 524-H1
ALTA VISTA RD
600 VeCo 93063 499-B4
ALTA VISTA RIDGE RD
6300 VeCo 93063 499-C4
ALTHEA CT
1300 OXN 93036 522-E3
ALTO CT
300 VeCo 93022 451-C5
ALTO DR
- VeCo 93022 451-C5
ALTUNA CT
3300 THO 91360 526-H2
ALTURAS ST
1300 OXN 93035 552-D1
ALTUS WY
2700 OXN 93035 552-D1
ALUMNI WY
7300 MRPK 93021 477-A4
ALVA CIR
1500 SIMI 93065 498-B3
N ALVARADO AV
100 VeCo 93023 441-D6
S ALVARADO AV
100 VeCo 93023 441-D7
ALVARADO ST
2400 OXN 93036 522-J2
2400 VeCo 93036 522-J2
3000 VeCo 93036 523-A1
ALVERSTONE AV
600 VEN 93003 492-B1
600 VEN 93003 472-B7
ALVIRIA DR
1100 VeCo 93023 451-B1
ALVISO DR
1200 VeCo 93010 494-A7
ALVISO ST
1500 SIMI 93065 497-J2
1700 SIMI 93065 498-A2
ALYSHEBA DR
10600 MRPK 93021 476-A7
ALYSSAS CT
23600 MRPK 93021 476-J6
ALYSSUM LN
- VEN 93004 493-A2
AMADOR AV
300 VEN 93004 472-H6
400 VeCo 93004 472-H6
AMADOR LN
1500 THO 91320 526-A7
AMAGRO WY
100 OXN 93033 552-G5
AMALFI DR
1300 SIMI 93063 499-C3
AMALFI WY
5000 OXN 93035 551-J1
5000 OXN 93035 552-A1
AMAPOLA AV
1200 VeCo 93004 493-B1
AMARELLE ST
1000 THO 91320 526-A6
AMARILLO AV
3000 SIMI 93063 478-G7
AMARYLLIS AV
23600 SIMI 93065 497-G5
AMAZON RIVER CT
- OXN 93036 492-G7
- OXN 93036 522-H1
AMBER AV
1100 OXN 93030 522-D4
AMBER DR
1000 SPLA 93060 464-A2
2600 CMRL 93010 494-E7
2600 VeCo 93010 494-E7
AMBER LN
800 OJAI 93023 451-G1
800 VeCo 93023 451-G1
AMBERCREST PL
4000 THO 91362 557-D1
AMBER GROVE CT
2300 SIMI 93065 478-B7
AMBERLEAF LN
23600 SIMI 93065 497-A1
AMBERLY PL
2300 SIMI 93065 498-B1
AMBERMEADOW ST
12500 MRPK 93021 496-D3
AMBERRIDGE CT
11500 MRPK 93021 496-B4
AMBERTON LN
1100 THO 91320 556-B1
AMBERWICK LN
4300 MRPK 93021 496-F3
AMBER WOOD PL
2600 THO 91362 526-J3
AMBRIDGE DR
5000 CALB 91301 558-F6
AMBROSE AV
1400 OXN 93035 552-D1
AMBROSIA ST
- OXN 93030 522-G4
AMELIA CT
100 OXN 93030 522-J5
AMELIA DR
30100 AGRH 91301 557-H5
AMERICAN ST
400 SIMI 93065 477-G7
AMERICAN WY
1800 VEN 93004 492-G4
AMERICAN OAKS AV
400 THO 91320 555-H3
AMERITE WY
2800 SIMI 93065 477-G7
AMETHYST AV
- VEN 93004 492-F3
1400 OXN 93030 522-D4
AMGEN CT
600 THO 91320 526-A7
AMGEN CENTER DR
2000 THO 91320 525-J7
2000 THO 91320 526-A7
AMHERST ST
5500 VEN 93003 492-B2
E AMHERST ST
14300 MRPK 93021 476-G6
N AMHERST ST
6400 MRPK 93021 476-H6
AMIGO RD
100 Chat 91311 499-F6
AMOND LN
8300 LA 91304 529-F2
AMONDO CIR
5900 SIMI 93063 499-A1
AMPHITHEATER RD
23600 VeCo 93001 470-E4
AMY PL
2600 PHME 93041 552-D2
ANACAPA AV
100 VeCo 93035 552-B5
ANACAPA CIR
400 THO 91320 555-F1
ANACAPA DR
100 CMRL 93010 524-E1
100 VeCo 93010 494-E7
100 VeCo 93010 524-E1
100 CMRL 93010 494-D6
ANACAPA ST
- VEN 93001 491-E3
ANACAPA TER
400 SPLA 93060 463-J6
400 VeCo 93060 463-J6
ANACAPA ISLAND DR
- VeCo 93012 554-E4
ANASAZI CT
23600 SIMI 93063 479-A6
ANASTASIA AV
6200 SIMI 93063 499-B2
ANCHOR AV
2500 PHME 93041 552-B2
2700 PHME 93035 552-B2
ANCHOR CT
2200 THO 91320 525-J6
2200 THO 91320 526-A6
ANCHORAGE AV
2900 SIMI 93063 478-F7
ANCHORAGE ST
3700 OXN 93033 552-J4
ANCHORS WY
1200 VEN 93001 491-F6
ANDALUSIA DR
- VeCo 93012 496-F6
ANDANTE CT
800 CMRL 93012 525-B2
ANDERSON DR
3100 VeCo 93065 478-B7
3100 SIMI 93065 478-B7
3300 SIMI 93063 478-B7
ANDERSON ST
1400 SIMI 93065 497-J2
ANDORA AV
9600 Chat 91311 499-J4
ANDORA PL
9800 Chat 91311 499-H5
ANDREA CIR
1500 SIMI 93065 498-B3
ANDREA CT
700 OXN 93033 552-H5
ANDREA DR
400 OXN 93033 552-H5
ANDREW DR
400 OJAI 93023 441-J5
ANDRUS ST
- VeCo 93022 451-B6
ANGEL CIR
2700 SIMI 93063 478-J7
ANGELA AV
7200 CanP 91307 529-F5
ANGELA ST
2400 SIMI 93065 498-B1
4000 SIMI 93063 498-F1
ANGELINE ST
- THO 91320 555-E3
ANGLER CT
23600 VEN 93001 491-G7
ANGUILA PL
100 CMRL 93012 524-J3
ANGUS AV
1800 SIMI 93063 498-G2
ANITA AV
200 OXN 93030 522-H5
1100 OJAI 93023 442-A6
ANLAUF RD
- VeCo 93060 453-J4
ANLAUF CANYON
- VeCo - 454-A2
- VeCo 93060 453-J4
- VeCo 93060 454-A2
ANN AV
100 PHME 93041 552-F6
N ANN ST
- VEN 93001 491-D2
S ANN ST
- VEN 93001 491-D2
ANNA WY
1400 OXN 93030 522-E3
ANNANDALE LN
2600 SIMI 93063 478-J7
ANNAPOLIS CT
5300 VEN 93003 492-B3
ANN ARBOR AV
700 VEN 93004 492-H2
ANNE CT
200 THO 91320 555-G2
ANNEPE WY
- Chat 91311 479-J7
E ANNETTE ST
13000 MRPK 93021 496-E3
ANSON ST
600 SIMI 93065 497-G4
ANTELOPE AV
1100 VEN 93003 492-E4
ANTELOPE PL
1100 THO 91320 555-G4
ANTHONY DR
2000 VEN 93003 492-E5
ANTIGUA PL
6400 CanP 91307 529-C7
ANTIGUA WY
2300 OXN 93035 552-A2
E ANTIOCH ST
3400 SIMI 93063 498-E2
ANTLER AV
2300 VEN 93003 492-F5
ANTONIO AV
2100 CMRL 93010 494-G6
2400 VeCo 93010 494-G6
ANZA CT
1300 OXN 93035 552-E1
ANZA LN
200 FILM 93015 456-C6
ANZIO WY
600 VeCo 91377 557-H1
APACHE AV
- THO 91362 557-A2
2800 VEN 93001 471-C5
APACHE CIR
3000 THO 91360 526-C2
APACHE CT
1400 CMRL 93010 524-F1
APACHE CANYON RD
- VeCo 93252 366-G1
APERSON RD
- VeCo 93015 367-B7
- VeCo 93015 455-F1
APOLLO CT
2000 SIMI 93065 497-G2
APOLLO DR
500 OXN 93035 521-J6
E APPALACHIAN CT
2800 THO 91362 557-C3
W APPALACHIAN CT
2700 THO 91362 557-B3
N APPALOOSA LN
- VeCo 91307 529-B3
APPIAN WY
300 VEN 93003 491-J2
3400 CMRL 93010 494-G7
APPLE AV
200 VEN 93004 473-A6
APPLE LN
2300 OXN 93036 522-G1
APPLEFIELD ST
1500 THO 91320 526-A6
APPLEGATE TER
9200 Chat 91311 499-F7
APPLEGLEN CT
4400 MRPK 93021 496-D2
APPLETON RD
400 SIMI 93065 498-C4
APPLETREE AV
200 CMRL 93012 524-H4
APPLETREE CT
400 CMRL 93012 524-H5
APPLEWOOD LN
2000 VeCo 93012 496-B7
2000 VeCo 93012 526-B1
APRICOT LN
1400 OXN 93033 553-B5
23600 VeCo 93063 499-B4
APRICOT RD
4000 SIMI 93063 498-F1
APRICOT ST
- VeCo 93022 451-B7
APRIL LN
1000 SPLA 93060 464-A2
AQUAMARINE AV
- VEN 93004 492-G2
AQUARIUS AV
6300 AGRH 91301 558-B3
AQUA VERDE CT
4700 CMRL 93012 524-J2
AQUEDUCT CT
600 SIMI 93065 497-G6
ARABIAN PL
6000 CMRL 93012 525-B1
ARABIAN ST
1400 SIMI 93065 497-J3
ARAGON WY
- OXN 93036 522-H1
ARANMOOR AV
900 THO 91361 557-A5
ARAPAHO AV
2300 THO 91362 556-J2
2300 THO 91362 557-A2
ARAPAHO ST
200 VEN 93001 471-C5
ARBELLA LN
- THO 91362 527-B3
ARBOL LN
6400 VeCo 93063 499-C4
ARBOLITA RANCH RD
2100 VeCo 93066 465-A6
ARBOR AV
600 VEN 93003 491-H4
ARBOR CT
- SIMI 93065 497-G7
ARBOR ST
- CMRL 93012 524-G5
ARBORHILL ST
12100 MRPK 93021 496-D4
ARBOR LANE CT
200 THO 91360 526-D7
ARBORWOOD ST
- FILM 93015 456-B6
ARCADE DR
- VEN 93003 491-F3
ARCADIA ST
1700 OXN 93033 552-H1
ARCADIAN SHORES TR
2400 OXN 93036 522-C2
ARCANE ST
1100 SIMI 93065 497-H4
1700 SIMI 93065 498-A4
ARCATA RD
1100 VeCo 93023 451-B4
ARCH PT
- VeCo 93012 554-F3
ARCH ST
4500 VeCo 93066 494-H4
ARCHBRIAR WY
300 SIMI 93065 497-F3
ARCHWOOD LN
2300 SIMI 93063 498-J1
ARCHWOOD ST
22100 CanP 91303 529-J6
22600 CanP 91307 529-D6
ARCO OIL CO RD
- VeCo 93023 453-B2
- VeCo 93060 453-B2
ARCTURUS AV
5500 OXN 93033 552-H6
ARCTURUS ST
100 THO 91360 526-F3
ARDENWOOD AV
1800 SIMI 93063 499-D2
E ARDENWOOD AV
6500 SIMI 93063 499-C2
N ARDENWOOD CIR
6600 SIMI 93063 499-D2
ARDMORE LN
- OXN 93036 522-C3
AREA I RD
23600 VeCo 93063 499-A7
23600 VeCo 93063 529-A1
ARENAS CT
3000 SIMI 93063 478-F7
ARGAL PL
2200 VEN 93003 492-E5
ARGOS ST
5300 AGRH 91301 558-B5
ARIANNA LN
2600 THO 91362 527-C3
ARIELLE LN
- Chat 91311 499-J3
23600 SIMI 93065 498-A5
ARIES ST
28700 AGRH 91301 558-B3
ARISTOTLE ST
100 SIMI 93065 497-F2
ARIZONA DR
1900 VEN 93003 492-C5
ARLENE AV
1700 OXN 93036 522-E3
ARLENE CT
2600 SIMI 93065 498-C3
ARLETTA LN
2200 VeCo 93012 496-B7
N ARLINGTON AV
3000 SIMI 93063 478-G6
ARMACOST CT
- SIMI 93065 527-E1
ARMADA DR
3100 VEN 93003 491-G4
ARMINTA ST
22900 LA 91304 529-E3
ARMITOS DR
5900 CMRL 93012 495-B6
ARMSTRONG AV
- VEN 93003 491-J3
ARMSTRONG RD
3700 VeCo 93066 465-B6
N ARNAZ AV
100 VeCo 93023 441-D6
S ARNAZ AV
100 VeCo 93023 441-D6
ARNAZ DR
- VeCo 93022 451-B6
ARNAZ RD
- VeCo 93001 460-J5
ARNEILL RD
100 CMRL 93010 524-E3
1500 CMRL 93010 494-E7
ARNESS FIRE RD
23600 VeCo 93063 498-E7
23600 VeCo 93063 528-E1
23600 VeCo 93064 498-E7
ARNETT AV
300 VEN 93003 492-B1
ARNOLD RD
6000 OXN 93033 583-A2
6000 VeCo 93033 553-A7
6000 VeCo 93033 583-A2
ARRASMITH LN
- FILM 93015 455-H5
ARROWHEAD AV
1200 VEN 93004 492-J2
ARROWHEAD CIR
100 OXN 93033 553-C3
3900 THO 91362 557-C1
ARROWHEAD LN
2200 OXN 93033 553-B5
ARROWOOD LN
5300 VeCo 91377 527-G7
ARROYO DR
900 MRPK 93021 477-A7
900 MRPK 93065 477-A7
900 SIMI 93065 477-A7
900 SIMI 93021 477-A7
15400 MRPK 93021 476-J6
ARROYO LN
- SIMI 93063 498-H2
ARROYO DEL MAR
200 CMRL 93010 524-B2
ARROYO OAKS DR
500 THO 91362 557-C2
ARROYO SECO DR
1700 VEN 93004 492-J4
ARROYO VIEW ST
1000 THO 91320 526-A6
ARROYO VISTA RD
4000 SIMI 93063 498-F3
ARROYO WILLOW LN
4100 CALB 91301 558-G7
ARTEMISIA AV
200 VEN 93001 491-E1
ARTHUR AV
100 SPLA 93060 464-A6
ARTHUR RONDO
7200 VEN 93003 492-E2
ARTISAN RD
400 THO 91320 526-A7
ARUNDELL AV
500 VEN 93003 491-H5
ARUNDELL CIR
300 FILM 93015 456-A4
3400 VEN 93003 491-H5
ARUNDELL RD
700 VeCo 93015 456-C3
ARVADA CT
800 SIMI 93065 527-C1
ASCOLI CT
11800 MRPK 93021 496-C5
ASCOT PL
2100 CMRL 93010 524-E2
ASH CIR
500 FILM 93015 455-J4
ASH CT
3000 THO 91360 526-H2
ASH LN
- VeCo 93023 441-E6
ASH ST
- VeCo 93063 499-B4
100 OXN 93033 552-G1
N ASH ST
- VEN 93001 491-C2
S ASH ST
- VEN 93001 491-C2
ASHBOURNE LN
3900 MRPK 93021 496-F4
ASHBROOK LN
13500 MRPK 93021 496-F4
ASHBURY CT
1000 CMRL 93010 524-E2
ASHBY CT
100 VeCo 93022 461-B1
ASHDALE CT
400 CMRL 93010 523-J1
ASHFORD CT
900 THO 91361 557-B5
ASHFORD ST
800 SIMI 93065 498-B5
ASHKELON CIR
- SIMI 93063 499-B1
ASHLAND AV
700 SIMI 93065 497-G3
ASHLAND ST
10000 VEN 93004 492-H2
ASHLEY DR
800 SIMI 93065 497-G4
ASHMORE CIR
2800 THO 91362 527-C3
ASHTON CT
7500 LA 91304 529-E4
23600 SIMI 93065 497-F7
23600 SIMI 93065 527-F1
ASHTON ST
200 OXN 93033 552-G5
N ASHTREE ST
4300 MRPK 93021 496-E3
ASH VIEW LN
5600 CMRL 93012 525-A2
N ASHWOOD AV
- VEN 93003 491-J2
S ASHWOOD AV
- VEN 93003 491-J3
ASHWOOD CT
500 THO 91320 555-G3
4000 VEN 93003 491-J2
5300 CMRL 93012 495-A7
5300 CMRL 93012 525-A1
ASIA CT
23600 SIMI 93065 498-A5
ASMAN AV
7100 CanP 91307 529-H5
ASPEN CIR
800 OXN 93030 522-D4
ASPEN CT
700 VEN 93004 492-G2
ASPEN GN
5100 OXN 93033 552-J5
ASPEN LN
4200 VeCo 93066 495-B3
ASPEN HILLS DR
6000 MRPK 93021 476-B7
ASPEN KNOLL DR
6100 VeCo 91377 558-A1
ASPEN OAK CT
700 VeCo 91377 558-B1
ASPENPARK CT
2100 THO 91362 527-A4
ASPEN RIDGE CT
500 VeCo 91377 558-B1
ASPEN TREE CT
4400 MRPK 93021 496-E3
ASPEN VIEW CT
500 VeCo 91377 558-B1
ASPENVIEW CT
32500 WLKV 91361 557-A7
ASPENWALL RD
1500 THO 91361 556-J6
ASPENWOOD PL
5900 VeCo 91377 558-A2
ASTA AV
200 THO 91320 556-A2
ASTA CT
2000 THO 91320 556-A2
ASTER ST
600 OXN 93036 522-F3
1200 VeCo 93063 499-B4
11000 VeCo 93004 493-A1
ASTERA CT
- THO 91320 555-F3
ASTORIA PL
1000 OXN 93030 522-E4
ASTORIAN DR
500 SIMI 93065 498-A5
ATHELING WY
7100 CanP 91307 529-G5
ATHENS AV
2000 SIMI 93065 497-F2
ATHERTON AV
200 VEN 93004 492-F1
ATHERTON CT
2400 SIMI 93065 498-A1
ATHERTON LN
7400 LA 91304 529-D4
ATHERWOOD AV
2600 SIMI 93065 498-B1
2600 SIMI 93065 478-B7
ATLANTA LN
600 VEN 93004 492-H2
ATLANTIS CT
5400 MRPK 93021 496-C1
ATLAS AV
2700 THO 91360 526-F3
ATMORE DR
200 SPLA 93060 463-J6
N ATMORE RD
100 VeCo 93015 465-E1
S ATMORE RD
100 VeCo 93015 465-E1
ATRON AV
7600 LA 91304 529-F3
N ATWATER AV
2000 SIMI 93063 498-D2
ATWOOD CT
14000 MRPK 93021 496-G3
AUBER LN
800 VEN 93003 492-B7
AUBURN AV
- THO 91362 557-B3
N AUBURN CIR
6600 MRPK 93021 476-H6

VENTURA CO.

STREET
Block City ZIP Pg-Grid

AUBURN CT
- THO 91362 557-B3
N AUBURN CT
3000 SIMI 93063 478-F6
AUBURY PL
- CMRL 93010 494-E7
AUGUSTA CT
1900 OXN 93036 522-D3
AUGUSTINE WY
300 SIMI 93065 497-D6
AURELIA ST
5300 SIMI 93063 498-J3
5400 SIMI 93063 499-A3
AURORA CT
100 VEN 93003 492-B2
AURORA DR
- OXN 93036 522-H3
4400 VEN 93003 492-B2
AURORA LN
- SIMI 93063 498-H1
AUSTIN AV
3000 SIMI 93063 478-G7
AUSTIN LN
800 VEN 93004 492-H2
AUTO CENTER DR
1100 SIMI 93065 497-H1
1500 OXN 93036 523-A2
6300 VEN 93003 492-D6
23600 OXN 93036 522-J2
AUTO MALL DR
3000 THO 91362 557-B3
AUTUMN PL
23600 SIMI 93065 497-D3
AUTUMNBREEZE PL
1800 SIMI 93065 497-E2
AUTUMNGLEN CT
4400 MRPK 93021 496-D3
AUTUMN LEAF DR
- THO 91360 526-F1
AUTUMN MEADOW CIR
4300 MRPK 93021 496-E3
AUTUMN RIDGE DR
2500 THO 91362 527-D3
AUTUMNWOOD ST
200 THO 91360 526-F2
AVALON PL
200 OXN 93033 552-H4
AVALON ST
10400 VEN 93004 492-J2
AVALON WY
700 OXN 93033 552-H4
AVEDON RD
4700 MRPK 93021 496-C2
AVENAL ST
2800 VeCo 93001 450-E3
AVENIDA ACASO
600 CMRL 93012 524-H1
AVENIDA AMARANTO
3100 THO 91362 527-A2
AVENIDA AMELGADO
4300 THO 91360 496-H7
AVENIDA CAFE
- CMRL 93012 524-H1
AVENIDA CAMPANA
4400 THO 91360 496-J7
AVENIDA CLASSICA
23600 OXN 93030 523-B4
AVENIDA COLONIA
14300 MRPK 93021 476-G7
AVENIDA DE APRISA
1900 CMRL 93010 523-G1
AVENIDA DE AUTLAN
- CMRL 93010 493-H6
- CMRL 93010 523-H1
- VeCo 93010 523-H1
AVENIDA DE LA CRUZADA
2000 VeCo 93023 442-B7
AVENIDA DE LA ENTRADA
100 VeCo 93023 442-B7
AVENIDA DE LA PLATA
400 THO 91320 526-A7
400 THO 91320 556-A1
AVENIDA DE LA ROSA
- CMRL 93012 495-A7
AVENIDA DE LAS FLORES
- THO 91360 526-F4
1600 THO 91362 526-J4
2000 THO 91362 527-A4
W AVENIDA DE LAS FLORES
- THO 91360 526-D4
AVENIDA DE LAS PLANTAS
2200 THO 91360 526-H4
AVENIDA DE LA VEREDA
100 VeCo 93023 442-B7
AVENIDA DEL DIA
23600 OXN 93030 523-B5
AVENIDA DEL MANZANO
1300 CMRL 93010 524-B1
E AVENIDA DE LOS ARBOLES
- THO 91360 526-H3
1700 THO 91362 526-H3
1800 THO 91362 527-B3
W AVENIDA DE LOS ARBOLES
- THO 91360 526-C3
AVENIDA DE LOS LOBOS
700 VeCo 91377 557-J2
AVENIDA DEL PLATINO
400 THO 91320 526-B7
400 THO 91320 556-B1
AVENIDA DEL RECREO
100 VeCo 93023 442-B7
AVENIDA DE MARGARITA
1300 CMRL 93010 523-F2
AVENIDA DE ROYALE
200 THO 91362 557-B2
AVENIDA ENCANTO
4900 CMRL 93012 525-A3
AVENIDA GAVIOTA
200 CMRL 93012 524-H3
AVENIDA LADERA
3200 THO 91362 527-A2
AVENIDA LOMA PORTAL
700 THO 91320 525-F7
AVENIDA MAGDALENA
600 CMRL 93010 524-B3
N AVENIDA MONTUOSO
3300 THO 91362 527-B2
AVENIDA NAVIDAD
- CMRL 93012 524-J1
E AVENIDA OTONO
2200 THO 91362 527-B2
AVENIDA PLACIDA
2000 SIMI 93063 499-B2
AVENIDA PRADO
4200 THO 91360 496-H7
N AVENIDA REFUGIO
2000 SIMI 93063 499-B2
AVENIDA SAN ANTERO
2200 CMRL 93010 494-H7
AVENIDA SIMI
2400 SIMI 93065 478-D7
2500 VeCo 93065 478-D7
2900 SIMI 93063 478-D7
2900 VeCo 93063 478-D7
AVENIDA SOLEDAD
700 VeCo 91377 557-J1
AVENIDA SOLTURA
1400 CMRL 93010 524-C1
1600 CMRL 93010 494-C7
AVENIDA VALENCIA
23600 CMRL 93012 524-H3
AVENIDA VERANO
3600 THO 91360 526-H1
N AVENIDA VISTA DEL MONTE
2000 SIMI 93063 499-B2
N AVIADOR ST
200 CMRL 93010 523-H3
AVIANO DR
6600 CMRL 93012 495-C7
AVIARA LN
- OXN 93036 522-C3
AVIARY RD
- VeCo 93060 453-J5
AVIATION DR
300 CMRL 93010 523-G4
600 VeCo 93010 523-G4
AVIGNON CT
5400 WLKV 91362 557-F5
AVILA DR
1100 VeCo 93023 451-B1
AVILA PL
2000 OXN 93036 522-G3
AVOCADO AV
3600 OXN 93033 553-B5
AVOCADO CT
3000 THO 91320 555-G3
AVOCADO PL
- CMRL 93010 524-A1
100 CMRL 93010 523-J1
100 VeCo 93010 493-J7
100 VeCo 93010 523-J1
100 VeCo 93010 524-A1
400 VeCo 93010 494-A7
AVOCADO HILL RD
23600 VeCo 93001 366-G9
23600 VeCo 93001 459-B1
AVON CIR
1000 THO 91360 526-F6
AVON ST
5300 VEN 93003 492-B2
AVONDALE LN
- OXN 93036 522-B3
AWENITA CT
11400 Chat 91311 499-H1
AYALA ST
2000 VEN 93001 491-E3
AYERS AV
800 OJAI 93023 441-J6
900 OJAI 93023 442-A5
AYERS CT
700 OJAI 93023 441-J5
700 OJAI 93023 442-A5
AYHENS ST
700 SIMI 93065 497-G3
AZAHAR ST
10900 VeCo 93004 493-B1
10900 VEN 93004 493-A1
AZALEA CT
300 VeCo 93010 494-C7
300 VeCo 93010 524-C1
AZALEA ST
400 THO 91360 526-C3
800 OXN 93036 522-E3
AZALEA WY
- SIMI 93065 497-H3
- VEN 93004 493-A2
AZTEC AV
2200 VEN 93001 471-D6
AZTEC CT
2500 VEN 93001 471-D5
3800 SIMI 93063 498-E2
AZUL CIR
8800 LA 91304 529-E1
AZUL DR
8700 WHil 91304 529-D1
8700 LA 91304 529-D1
AZURE CT
600 VeCo 93022 451-C6
AZURE HILLS DR
500 SIMI 93065 497-H5
AZURITE CIR
2500 THO 91320 525-H6
AZUSA AV
100 VEN 93004 492-E1

B

B AV
- VeCo 93042 583-H3
B ST
100 OXN 93030 522-G5
100 FILM 93015 455-J5
1500 OXN 93033 552-G1
E B ST
100 PHME 93041 552-E5
N B ST
100 OXN 93030 522-G5
W B ST
100 PHME 93041 552-E5
BACCARAT ST
3200 THO 91362 526-J2
BACH RD
500 VEN 93003 492-B3
BADEN AV
9500 Chat 91311 499-H5
BADGER CIR
7200 VEN 93003 492-F4
BAHAMA ST
22000 LA 91304 529-J1
BAHIA CIR
- SPLA 93060 463-J7
BAHIA DR
2000 OXN 93036 522-G3
W BAILEY CT
3600 THO 91320 555-F4
BAINBRIDGE CT
- THO 91360 526-E1
5900 AGRH 91301 558-A4
BAINBROOK CT
31700 WLKV 91361 557-D6
BAJA CT
400 CMRL 93010 524-D3
BAJA VISTA WY
1700 CMRL 93010 494-C7
BAJO AGUA AV
100 CMRL 93010 523-H3
BAKER AV
- THO 91360 556-F1
200 VEN 93004 492-F2
BAKERSFIELD AV
6900 VeCo 93001 459-C4
BALASIANO AV
- LA 91304 529-G4
BALBOA CIR
- CMRL 93012 525-A4
BALBOA ST
2400 OXN 93036 522-H2
2400 VeCo 93036 522-H2
2600 PHME 93041 552-E2
3200 VeCo 93036 492-J7
3300 VeCo 93036 493-A7
8000 VEN 93004 492-F2
BALCOM CANYON RD
1700 VeCo 93060 465-C6
4000 VeCo 93021 495-E1
4000 VeCo 93066 495-E1
5500 VeCo 93021 475-E6
5500 VeCo 93066 475-C1
8400 VeCo 93066 465-C6
BALD ST
100 OJAI 93023 441-J7
BALDEN LN
700 FILM 93015 455-J6
700 FILM 93015 456-A6
BALDWIN AV
200 VEN 93004 492-F2
BALDWIN RD Rt#-150
- VeCo 93001 450-H3
- VeCo 93023 450-H3
600 VeCo 93023 451-A3
BALEWIN DR
1800 VeCo 93015 455-F5
BALFE ST
700 VEN 93003 492-B3
BALI LN
1800 OXN 93033 552-J1
BALI LN
1800 OXN 93033 553-A1
BALKINS DR
28000 AGRH 91301 558-C4
BALLANTINE PL
7000 VeCo 91377 528-B6
BALLARD ST
1600 SIMI 93065 497-J2
W BALLINA CT
900 THO 91320 556-C1
BALLINGER ST
22000 Chat 91311 499-H6
BALMORAL CT
2400 CMRL 93010 524-E1
BALMORAL LN
23300 CanP 91307 529-F5
BALSAM ST
100 OXN 93030 522-J5
BALSAMO AV
1000 SIMI 93065 497-G4
BALTAR ST
22100 LA 91304 529-E3
BALTIC ST
- OXN 93035 552-B1
BAMBI CT
15300 MRPK 93021 476-J6
BAMBOO CT
2100 THO 91362 526-J4
BAMFIELD DR
28500 AGRH 91301 558-B3
BANCAL WY
- OXN 93036 522-H3
BANCOCK ST
2600 SIMI 93065 498-A1
2600 SIMI 93065 478-A7
BANCROFT ST
1800 CMRL 93010 524-D2
BANDERA DR
500 CMRL 93010 524-D2
BANG RD
- WHil 91304 499-C7
- WHil 91304 529-C1
BANGOR LN
1000 VEN 93001 491-E4
BANNER AV
- VEN 93004 492-F2
BANNISTER WY
- SIMI 93065 527-E1
BANTA CT
1300 OXN 93035 522-E7
1300 OXN 93035 552-E1
BARBADOS CT
4900 VeCo 91377 557-G2
BARBARA DR
1800 VeCo 93012 495-J7
BARBARA ST
- VeCo 93022 451-B4
BARBER LN
800 VEN 93003 492-A7
E BARCA ST
3400 CMRL 93010 524-G1
N BARCA ST
1400 CMRL 93010 524-G1
BARCELONA PL
3900 THO 91320 555-E1
BARCELONA ST
100 CMRL 93010 524-D4
BARCELONA WY
- OXN 93036 492-H7
- OXN 93036 522-H1
BARCLAY CT
1900 THO 91361 557-A5
BARD LN
- PHME 93041 552-E4
- VeCo 93001 471-C2
BARD RD
400 PHME 93041 552-E4
700 OXN 93033 553-A4
1800 OXN 93033 552-E4
E BARD RD
- OXN 93033 552-G4
W BARD RD
- OXN 93033 552-G4
800 PHME 93033 552-G4
800 PHME 93041 552-G4
BARD ST
300 FILM 93015 456-A5
300 MRPK 93021 496-E1
600 MRPK 93021 476-E7
BARDELL DR
28900 AGRH 91301 558-B4
BARDET PL
1900 SIMI 93065 498-A1
BARDMAN AV
1300 LACo 90265 586-D7
BARDSDALE AV
100 VeCo 93035 552-B5
800 VeCo 93015 465-F3
BARLETTA PL
11800 MRPK 93021 496-C3
BARNACLE CV
2600 PHME 93041 552-C1
BARNARD ST
4400 SIMI 93063 498-G1
5400 SIMI 93063 499-A1
BARNARD WY
1600 VEN 93001 491-E2
BARNARO RD
300 VeCo 93015 455-B7
BARNES DR
- VeCo 93001 471-C3
BARNES ST
1500 SIMI 93063 498-E3
E BARNES ST
2700 SIMI 93065 498-C3
3200 SIMI 93063 498-D3
BARNETT ST
2000 OXN 93033 553-A4
E BARNETT ST
- VEN 93001 471-C7
W BARNETT ST
- VEN 93001 471-B7
BARODA DR
- CMRL 93012 525-A3
BARONS WY
23600 VeCo 91377 528-A7
BARONSGATE RD
4200 WLKV 91361 557-E6
BARR DR
500 VEN 93003 491-J4
BARRACUDA WY
200 OXN 93035 552-A3
BARRAGAN ST
28800 AGRH 91301 558-B3
BARRANCA AV
- VEN 93003 492-E2
200 VeCo 93003 492-E2
BARRANCA DR
- Cstc 91384 458-H4
BARRANCA RD
200 THO 91320 556-A2
200 VeCo 91320 556-A2
11200 VeCo 93012 496-B6
BARRETT DR
32700 WLKV 91361 586-J1
BARR HIGHLAND RD
- VeCo 93060 472-J5
BARRINGTON CT
500 THO 91320 555-H3
BARROW AV
4200 SIMI 93063 478-F7
BARROW CT
1000 THO 91361 557-A5
BARRY DR
- VEN 93001 471-C6
BARRY ST
2300 CMRL 93010 524-E3
BARRYMORE DR
5200 OXN 93033 552-G5
BARSTOW ST
7700 VEN 93004 492-F1
BART CIR
1000 THO 91360 526-F6
BARTON AV
800 CMRL 93010 524-B2
BARVO DR
- OXN 93030 522-G5
BASALT ST
1000 OXN 93030 522-D4
BASCOM CT
2300 THO 91362 527-A7
BASELBRIER LN
23600 SIMI 93065 497-A1
BASIE ST
- VEN 93003 492-B4
BASOLO TEXICO RD
- VeCo 93015 466-C2
- VeCo 93021 466-C2
BASS CT
2600 OXN 93035 552-A2
BASSET LN
1600 VEN 93003 492-F4
BASSETT ST
22000 CanP 91303 529-H6
22400 CanP 91307 529-F6
BASSWOOD AV
- VeCo 91377 558-B3
BASSWOOD CT
1100 VEN 93004 492-J2
2100 THO 91361 557-A4
BATES CT
1700 THO 91362 526-J6
BATES RANCH RD
23600 VeCo 93001 366-G9
23600 VeCo 93001 459-A2
BATH CT
5000 VeCo 91377 557-H1
BATH LN
1000 VEN 93001 491-E4
BATTEN LN
500 OXN 93033 552-G5
BAXTER ST
3300 THO 91320 555-F2
BAXTER WY
4200 THO 91362 557-C4
E BAY BLVD
100 PHME 93041 552-E2
300 OXN 93033 552-E2
300 PHME 93033 552-E2
BAY DR
2200 THO 91361 557-A5
BAYBERRY ST
6300 VeCo 91377 558-B2
BAYBRIDGE CT
2500 PHME 93041 552-C2
BAYBROOK CT
- VeCo 91361 556-F6
BAYHAM CIR
2800 THO 91362 527-B3
BAYHILL CT
2300 OXN 93036 522-D2
E BAYLOR CIR
14400 MRPK 93021 476-G6
BAYLOR DR
- VEN 93003 491-J2
- VEN 93003 492-A3
E BAYMARE RD
- VeCo 91307 529-A4
BAYONNE CT
30800 WLKV 91362 557-F5
BAYPORT WY
300 VeCo 91377 557-G2
BAYS ST
5700 VEN 93003 492-C2
BAYSHORE AV
2400 VEN 93001 491-F5
BAYSHORE DR
32000 WLKV 91361 557-C7
BAYSIDE CIR
- OXN 93035 522-A7
BAYSIDE CT
2300 THO 91361 557-B6
BAYSIDE LN
- OXN 93035 522-A7
BAYSIDE ST
3800 SIMI 93063 498-E1
BAYVIEW AV
300 VEN 93003 492-A1
BAYVIEW DR
1300 OXN 93035 522-B7
1400 OXN 93035 552-B1
BAYWATER PL
2600 THO 91362 527-B3
BAYWOOD AV
1100 CMRL 93010 524-C2
BAYWOOD CT
1100 CMRL 93010 524-C1
BAYWOOD LN
400 SIMI 93065 497-D5
BEACH RD
- VeCo 93042 583-B4
BEACH WY
5000 OXN 93035 551-J1
5000 OXN 93035 552-A1
S BEACH CLUB WY
11800 VeCo 90265 625-F5
BEACHCOMBER ST
5000 OXN 93035 521-J7
BEACHFRONT LN
32100 WLKV 91361 557-C6
BEACH HAVEN WY
600 PHME 93041 552-F6
BEACHLAKE LN
32100 WLKV 91361 557-C6
BEACHMEADOW LN
4100 WLKV 91361 557-C6
BEACHMONT ST
1200 VeCo 93001 491-F5
1200 VEN 93001 491-F5
BEACHNUT AV
700 SIMI 93065 498-D5
BEACHPORT DR
500 PHME 93041 552-F6
BEACHSIDE CT
- VEN 93001 491-A2
BEACHSIDE PL
- VEN 93001 491-A2
BEACHVIEW LN
32100 WLKV 91361 557-C6
BEACON AV
2600 VEN 93003 491-G4
BEACON PL
1100 OXN 93033 552-J1
BEACONSFIELD CT
4400 WLKV 91361 557-D6
BEAGLE CT
7200 VEN 93003 492-F4
BEALL ST
500 THO 91360 526-G7
BEAR CIR
2600 SIMI 93063 478-J7
BEARCLAW CT
900 THO 91320 555-G5
BEAR CREEK CT
3400 THO 91320 555-F2
BEAR CREEK DR
3200 THO 91320 555-F2
BEARDEN CT
1800 OXN 93035 552-C1
BEARDSLEY RD
5600 VeCo 93010 493-G7
5600 VeCo 93010 523-F1
6100 CMRL 93010 493-H6
BEAR FENCE CT
- MRPK 93021 476-F6
BEAR RIVER CIR
3400 THO 91362 557-C2
BEAR VALLEY RD
13500 MRPK 93021 496-F3
BEATTY PL
- THO 91320 556-A2
BEAUCROFT CT
4200 WLKV 91361 557-D6
BEAUFORT DR
1800 OXN 93033 553-A2
BEAUMONT AV
4300 OXN 93033 553-A5
5000 VeCo 93033 553-A5
BEAUMONT ST
4600 SIMI 93063 478-G7
BEAVER AV
2700 SIMI 93065 498-C5
BEAVER ST
1800 VEN 93003 492-F4
BECKETT CT
2700 THO 91360 526-E3
BECKFORD ST
4900 VEN 93003 492-B1
BECKWITH RD
100 SPLA 93060 473-H1
400 SPLA 93060 463-G7
BECKY ST
3900 SIMI 93063 498-F2
BEDFORD CT
700 SPLA 93060 464-B4
1700 CMRL 93010 524-D1
BEDFORD DR
1000 CMRL 93010 524-D2
BEDFORD PL
100 THO 91360 526-F6
BEDFORD ST
1100 SPLA 93060 464-B4
BEDFORDHURST CT
31700 WLKV 91361 557-D6
BEE AV
6200 AGRH 91301 558-B3
BEE CANYON
10800 Chat 91311 499-J2
E BEECH CT
4900 SIMI 93063 478-H7
BEECH DR
1000 SPLA 93060 464-A2
BEECH RD
- THO 91320 556-B2
BEECHGROVE CT
12400 MRPK 93021 496-D4
BEECH VIEW CIR
1100 CMRL 93012 525-B2
BEECHWOOD ST
1000 CMRL 93010 524-C1
BEEDY AV
23600 VeCo 93036 492-J5
23600 VeCo 93036 493-A5
BEEDY ST
100 VeCo 93036 492-J5
100 VeCo 93036 493-A5
BEENE RD
2600 VEN 93003 492-E6
BEER SHEBA
- SIMI 93063 499-C1
BEETHOVEN AV
900 VEN 93003 492-B4
BEGONIA PL
- VEN 93004 473-C7
BEL CIR
2700 SIMI 93063 478-J7
BELAIR CT E
3100 CMRL 93010 524-F1
BELAIR CT N
1300 CMRL 93010 524-F1
BELBERT CIR
5800 CALB 91302 558-H3
BELBROOK PL
2700 SIMI 93065 478-B7
2700 SIMI 93065 498-B1
BELBURN PL
2600 SIMI 93065 498-A1
BELCARO WY
500 VeCo 91377 557-G1
BELDEN AV
400 CMRL 93010 524-F3
BELEN PL
10500 VEN 93004 492-J1
BELFAST LN
1000 VEN 93001 491-E4
BELFORD CT
24000 LA 91304 529-D4
N BELGRAVE CT
2000 SIMI 93063 498-E2
BELHAM CT
4500 WLKV 91361 557-D6
N BELHAVEN AV
1800 SIMI 93063 499-C2
BELINDA ST
4000 SIMI 93063 498-F1
BELL PL
6200 VeCo 93003 492-D5
6200 VEN 93003 492-D5
BELL ST
5300 VeCo 93066 495-A5
6200 VeCo 93003 492-D5
6200 VEN 93003 492-D5
BELL WY
- VEN 93001 471-B7
BELLA DR
400 VeCo 91320 525-G7
400 VeCo 91320 555-G1
600 THO 91320 525-G7
BELLAFONTE CT
- CMRL 93012 524-G4
BELLAGIO CT
1100 VeCo 91377 527-H7
BELLA VISTA DR
4400 MRPK 93021 496-F2
BELL CANYON RD
- CanP 91307 529-C4
- VeCo 91307 529-C4
E BELL CANYON RD
- VeCo 91307 528-H5
- VeCo 91307 529-A4
BELL CANYON FIRE RD
23600 VeCo 91302 528-G7
23600 VeCo 91307 528-G5
BELLEMEADE CT
- SIMI 93063 498-H1
BELLERIVE CT
2600 OXN 93036 522-D3
BELLEVUE AV
100 VeCo 93015 466-A3
BELLEVUE AV Rt#-23
700 VeCo 93015 465-J3
700 VeCo 93015 466-A3
BELLEZA DR
- OXN 93030 522-G4
BELLEZA ST
1000 CMRL 93012 525-C6
BELLFLOWER CT
- SIMI 93063 498-J3
BELLINI LN
900 VEN 93003 492-A7
BELL RANCH RD
4500 VeCo 93010 494-H6
4500 VeCo 93066 494-H6
BELLSHIRE CT
4800 THO 91362 527-E6
N BELMAR CT
2000 SIMI 93063 498-E2
BELMONT AV
900 CMRL 93010 524-E2
BELMONT CT
27300 AGRH 91301 557-H4
BELMONT LN
- OXN 93036 522-B3
BELSIZE PL
5800 AGRH 91301 557-G4
BELTRAMO RANCH RD
4600 MRPK 93021 496-C2
BELVEDERE CT
2500 SIMI 93065 498-A1
BEN CT
400 VeCo 91320 555-G1
BENCHLEY CT
30900 WLKV 91361 557-C6
BENDING BRANCH WY
23600 SIMI 93065 497-A1
BENDING OAK CT
11600 MRPK 93021 496-C4
BENECIA WY
100 OXN 93033 553-C3
BENEDICT CT
5300 VeCo 91377 527-H7
BENITO DR
2100 CMRL 93010 494-H7
BENJAMIN CT
- VEN 93003 492-B3
BENNETT AV
- VEN 93003 492-B3
BENNETT RD
4400 SIMI 93063 478-F2
4400 VeCo 93063 478-F2
4600 VeCo - 478-F1
23600 VeCo - 367-E9
BENNETT ST
500 SIMI 93065 497-G5
BENNINGTON CT
2000 THO 91360 526-C4
BENSON WY
600 THO 91360 526-G7
600 THO 91360 556-G1
BENTCREEK RD
4100 MRPK 93021 496-B3
BENT GRASS PL
- MRPK 93021 476-E6
BENTLEY PL
300 SIMI 93065 497-E2
BENTON WY
1300 OXN 93033 552-G1
BENT TWIG AV
300 CMRL 93012 524-H4
BENWOOD DR
15300 MRPK 93021 476-J6
15300 MRPK 93021 477-A6
BERAGAN ST
23600 MRPK 93021 477-A6
BEREA CIR
1400 THO 91362 526-J6
BERG LN
4600 VEN 93003 492-B7
BERGAMO CT
11800 MRPK 93021 496-C5
BERING ST
100 OXN 93033 552-J5
BERKELEY AV
- VEN 93004 492-F1
N BERKELEY CIR
6400 MRPK 93021 476-H6
BERKSHIRE CT
4300 OXN 93033 553-A4
BERKSHIRE DR
1600 THO 91362 526-J5
1800 THO 91362 527-A5
BERKSHIRE PL
600 OXN 93033 552-H5
BERKSHIRE ST
1000 OXN 93033 552-J5
1700 OXN 93033 553-A4
BERLIOZ ST
4900 VEN 93003 492-B7
BERMUDA CT
4000 VEN 93003 491-J3
BERMUDA DUNES DR
2300 OXN 93036 522-D2
BERMUDA DUNES PL
2000 OXN 93036 522-D2
BERNADETTE ST
1600 OXN 93030 522-D3
BERNADINE AV
7200 CanP 91307 529-F5
7400 LA 91304 529-F5
N BERNADINE ST
3000 THO 91320 555-G2
BERNAL ST
6500 SIMI 93063 499-C2
BERNARDA CT
100 OXN 93030 522-J5
BERNICE DR
23600 WHil 91304 499-E6
BERNINI CT
600 VeCo 91377 557-G1
BERNOULLI CIR
100 OXN 93030 523-A5
BERNSTEIN LN
800 VEN 93003 492-A7
BERQUIST AV
6200 WdHl 91367 529-F7
6400 CanP 91307 529-F7
BERROS ST
3000 SIMI 93063 478-F7
BERRYBROOK CT
11900 MRPK 93021 496-C3
BERRYESSA AV
- VEN 93004 492-J3
BERRYHILL CIR
1400 THO 91362 527-F6
BERTHA RD
2700 THO 91320 555-H2
BERTRAND DR
29400 AGRH 91301 557-J3
29400 AGRH 91301 558-A3
BERWICK PL
1500 THO 91361 556-J6
BERWICK ST
2700 CMRL 93010 494-F7
BERYL AV
1800 OXN 93030 522-D3
1800 OXN 93036 522-D3
BERYLWOOD RD
2700 VeCo 93066 494-F1
BESANT RD
100 VeCo 93023 441-E7
100 VeCo 93023 451-D1
BESSEMER ST
4000 VEN 93003 491-J4
4000 VEN 93003 492-A4
BEST CIR
4700 SIMI 93063 478-H5
BETH PL
2700 SIMI 93065 478-B7
2700 SIMI 93065 498-B1
BETHANY CT
200 THO 91360 526-E5
BETHANY ST
300 THO 91360 526-D5
BETHEL AV
200 VEN 93003 491-J2
BETHEL CT
900 SIMI 93065 498-A5
4200 VEN 93003 491-J2
BETTINA CT
1300 CMRL 93010 524-C1
BEVERLY CIR
300 VeCo 93010 494-F6
BEVERLY DR
- CMRL 93010 494-F7
100 VeCo 93010 494-F6
W BEVERLY DR
400 OXN 93030 522-F5
BEVRA AV
1500 OXN 93036 522-E2
BEYER LN
200 THO 91362 557-A2
BIANCA CIR
3000 SIMI 93063 478-D6
BIDWELL ST
4400 SIMI 93063 498-G1
BIENVILLE WK
5200 OXN 93033 552-G5
BIG BEAR WY
100 OXN 93033 553-C3
BIG BEN CT
- MRPK 93021 496-E2
BIG CANYON RD
23600 VeCo 93023 452-J3
23600 VeCo 93023 453-A1
BIG CLOUD CIR
3300 THO 91360 526-C2
BIG COUNTRY CT
- MRPK 93021 496-G2
N BIGELOW AV
2000 SIMI 93065 498-A2
BIGHORN CT
800 CMRL 93010 524-C2
BIG HORN ST
9800 VEN 93004 492-J3
BIG ROCK TR
8500 LA 91304 529-E1
8500 WHil 91304 529-E1
W BIG SKY CIR
900 THO 91360 526-B2
BIG SKY DR
2900 THO 91360 526-C2
BIG SKY PL
- SIMI 93065 478-A7
BIG SPRINGS AV
3000 SIMI 93063 478-G6
BIGSTONE LN
9800 VEN 93004 492-H3
BIG SUR RIVER PL
- OXN 93036 492-H7
- OXN 93036 522-H1
BIG TRAIL CIR
- MRPK 93021 496-F2
BILLIE CT
3200 SIMI 93063 478-D7
BILLINGS ST
1400 OXN 93033 552-J4
BINGS RD
2600 THO 91320 555-H2
2600 VeCo 91320 555-H2
BINNACLE ST
600 OXN 93035 522-D6
BIOTECH CT
- THO 91320 526-A7
BIRCH ST
1200 SPLA 93060 464-B2
1500 OXN 93035 552-D1
3700 VEN 93003 491-J3
6000 VeCo 93063 499-B4
E BIRCH ST
100 OXN 93033 552-G1
W BIRCH ST
100 OXN 93033 552-F1
BIRCHCREEK PL
2900 THO 91360 526-E3
BIRCHCROFT ST
5200 SIMI 93063 498-J2
BIRCHDALE CT
2000 THO 91362 527-A4
BIRCHDALE DR
1800 THO 91362 527-A4
BIRCHFIELD ST
2200 SIMI 93065 498-B2
BIRCH GLEN AV
2200 SIMI 93063 498-J2
BIRCH HILL ST
800 THO 91320 556-C2
BIRCHPARK CIR
500 THO 91360 526-E7
BIRCHSPRING WK
- CMRL 93012 524-H2
BIRCHTON AV
6600 CanP 91307 529-F6
BIRCH VIEW LN
5600 CMRL 93012 525-A2
BIRCHWOOD AV
- VeCo 91377 558-A2
BIRDSONG AV
3300 THO 91360 526-G2
BISCAYNE CT
800 CMRL 93010 524-D2
BISCAYNE PALM PL
23600 SIMI 93065 498-D5
BISHOP LN
1600 SIMI 93063 498-F3
BISHOP ST
8200 VEN 93004 492-F1
BISHOP WY
- OXN 93033 552-G5
BISMARK AV
600 VEN 93004 492-J1
BISMARK WY
800 OXN 93033 552-H3
BITNER PL
15300 MRPK 93021 476-J5
BITTERN CT
6900 VEN 93003 492-E4
BITTERNUT CIR
2600 SIMI 93065 498-D1
2700 SIMI 93065 478-C7
BIXBY RD
8400 VeCo 93066 465-C6
8400 VeCo 93066 475-D1
BIZET LN
4600 VEN 93003 492-A7
BLACK AV
3200 VeCo 93063 478-E6
BLACK PT
- VeCo 93012 554-F3
BLACKBERRY CIR
2000 OXN 93036 522-G3
BLACKBERRY LN
4200 VeCo 93066 495-B3
BLACKBIRD AV
100 THO 91362 557-G2
BLACKBOURNE
23600 VeCo 91377 528-A7
BLACKBURN PL
- VEN 93004 472-J7
- VEN 93004 492-J1
BLACKBURN RD
7700 VEN 93004 492-F2

STREET	Block	City	ZIP	Pg-Grid
BLACKBURN RD	9200	VeCo	93004	492-H1
	10600	VEN	93004	472-J7
BLACK CANYON RD	-	VeCo	93063	499-B4
BLACKFOOT LN	200	VEN	93001	471-C5
BLACKHAWK DR	300	THO	91320	555-E2
BLACKHAWK ST	-	Chat	91311	499-J4
E BLACK HILLS CT	3300	THO	91362	557-C2
W BLACK HILLS CT	3000	THO	91362	557-B2
BLACK MOUNTAIN FIRE RD	23600	VeCo	93023	451-J2
	23600	VeCo	93023	452-A2
BLACK OAK ST	2800	THO	91362	557-B2
BLACKPOOL AV	800	VeCo	91377	557-H1
BLACK ROCK CIR	-	MRPK	93021	476-F6
BLACKSMITH CT	13600	MRPK	93021	496-F3
BLACKSTOCK AV	1400	SIMI	93065	498-D3
BLACKWALL DR	1500	SIMI	93063	498-E3
BLACKWOOD ST	3700	THO	91320	555-E4
BLAINE AV	200	FILM	93015	456-A5
	700	FILM	93015	455-J5
BLAIR CT	-	THO	91320	556-A1
BLAIR PL	4800	AGRH	91301	558-B6
BLAIRWOOD DR	3900	MRPK	93021	496-E3
BLAKE CT	6800	VEN	93003	492-E3
BLAKE RIDGE CT	-	THO	91361	556-H2
BLANCA PL	800	OXN	93036	522-H3
BLANCHARD AV	200	SPLA	93060	464-A5
BLANCHARD PL	10600	VeCo	93012	495-J7
	10600	VeCo	93012	496-A7
BLANCHARD RD	2200	VeCo	93012	496-A7
BLANCHARD CANYON RD	23600	VeCo	93040	367-D7
BLANCHE ST	100	OJAI	93023	441-H6
S BLANCHE ST	100	OJAI	93023	441-H7
BLANCO CT	300	CMRL	93012	525-A2
BLAZE AV	1400	SIMI	93065	497-J3
BLAZEWOOD ST	-	SIMI	93063	499-B2
BLAZING STAR DR	3000	THO	91362	527-C3
BLISS CT	400	SIMI	93065	497-H6
BLONDELL PL	3000	THO	91320	555-G3
BLOOM ST	-	SIMI	93063	479-B7
	-	SIMI	93063	499-B1
BLOOMFIELD PL	-	CMRL	93012	524-G5
BLOOMFIELD ST	5600	SIMI	93063	499-A2
BLOSSOM CT	1600	THO	91320	526-A6
BLOSSOM ST	-	SIMI	93063	499-B1
BLOSSOMWOOD CT	11700	MRPK	93021	496-C4
BLUEBELL PL	300	OXN	93036	522-F3
	4300	THO	91362	527-D6
BLUEBELL ST	900	OXN	93036	522-E3
BLUEBERRY DR	2400	OXN	93036	522-G1
E BLUEBERRY LN	200	THO	91360	526-F7
BLUEBIRD AV	1300	VEN	93003	492-C4
BLUEBIRD CIR	3200	SIMI	93063	478-J6
BLUEBIRD LN	3900	OXN	93033	553-B5
BLUEBONNET AV	1200	VEN	93004	492-J2
	1200	VEN	93004	493-A2
BLUEBONNET CT	600	THO	91360	526-D2
BLUE CANYON ST	1500	THO	91320	526-A6
BLUE DOLPHIN DR	400	PHME	93041	552-F7
BLUEFIELD AV	-	THO	91320	555-F2
BLUEFIN CIR	200	OXN	93035	552-B4
BLUEGRASS ST	600	SIMI	93065	497-G6
BLUE HERON CIR	12500	VeCo	93023	451-A1
BLUE HILL CT	1700	THO	91362	527-D6
BLUEJAY AV	1900	VEN	93003	492-E5
	2100	OXN	93033	553-B5
BLUE JAY ST	1400	FILM	93015	455-H6
BLUE LAKE CT	400	SIMI	93065	497-E6
BLUE MEADOW LN	31600	WLKV	91361	557-D7
BLUE MESA ST	2900	THO	91362	557-C2
BLUE MOUNTAIN CIR	700	THO	91362	557-F1
BLUE OAK AV	600	THO	91320	556-D2
BLUE OAK ST	1100	CMRL	93010	524-C1
BLUE RIDGE CIR	2500	VeCo	93065	478-C6
BLUE RIDGE CT	-	MRPK	93021	476-F6
N BLUE RIDGE CT	200	THO	91362	557-B2
S BLUE RIDGE CT	100	THO	91362	557-B3
BLUE RIDGE WY	-	MRPK	93021	476-F6
BLUE ROCK RDG	32300	WLKV	91361	557-B7
BLUESAGE CT	-	SIMI	93065	477-J7
BLUESAIL CIR	1300	THO	91361	557-B6
BLUE SKY CIR	400	SIMI	93065	527-D1
BLUE SKY CT	24400	CanP	91307	529-D5
BLUESPRING DR	800	THO	91361	557-A5
BLUE SPRUCE CIR	2900	THO	91360	526-H2
BLUESTONE AV	1600	SIMI	93063	499-C3
BLUEWATER WY	600	PHME	93041	552-F7
BLUEWOOD CT	-	MRPK	93021	496-G2
BLUFFSIDE LN	23600	SIMI	93065	497-E4
BLYTHE ST	22100	LA	91304	529-E3
BLYTHEDALE RD	27800	AGRH	91301	558-D3
BOALT AV	2300	SIMI	93063	498-E1
BOARDMAN RD	100	OJAI	93023	442-B7
	100	VeCo	93023	442-B7
BOARDWALK AV	100	THO	91360	556-F1
BOB CT	400	VeCo	91320	555-G1
BOBBYBOYAR AV	6400	CanP	91307	529-G4
	7500	LA	91304	529-G3
BOBOLINK LN	1100	VEN	93003	492-E4
BOBWHITE CT	1200	VEN	93003	492-D4
BODEGA PL	13200	MRPK	93021	496-E2
BODIE AV	1500	SIMI	93065	497-J4
BODLE PEAK MTWY	600	LACo	90265	586-J4
BOE CIR	2100	THO	91362	527-A2
BOGART ST	2500	CMRL	93010	524-E2
BOGOTA CT	1100	OXN	93035	522-D7
BOISE ST	8300	VEN	93004	492-G2
BOLAM CT	23600	SIMI	93065	497-F7
BOLERO LN	200	OXN	93036	522-G3
N BOLIVAR CT	2000	SIMI	93063	498-E2
BOLKER DR	2500	PHME	93041	552-D1
	2700	PHME	93035	552-D1
BOLKER WY	2600	PHME	93041	552-D2
BOLLIN AV	1000	CMRL	93010	524-E2
BOLSA WY	300	OXN	93036	522-H3
BO-MERRITT RD	23600	VeCo	93023	452-J1
BONANZA ST	1700	SIMI	93063	499-C3
BONHAM ST	4700	SIMI	93063	478-H7
BONITA AV	100	OXN	93030	522-H6
N BONITA AV	100	OXN	93030	522-H5
BONITA CT	1100	VEN	93001	491-G5
BONITA DR	300	VeCo	93023	441-F7
E BONITA DR	100	SIMI	93065	497-F3
W BONITA DR	-	SIMI	93065	497-E3
BONITA HEIGHTS ST	13300	MRPK	93021	496-F2
BONMARK DR	1100	VeCo	93023	451-B4
N BONNIE CT	1600	SIMI	93065	497-E3
BONNIE VIEW ST	300	MRPK	93021	476-F7
BONSAI AV	200	MRPK	93021	496-D1
BONWIT PL	600	SIMI	93065	497-G5
BOOSEY RD	800	VeCo	93060	464-F3
BOOTH ST	2000	SIMI	93065	478-A7
S BORCHARD DR	-	VEN	93003	491-G3
BORCHARD RD	2200	THO	91320	555-E1
	2900	VeCo	91320	555-F1
BORDEAUX AV	1000	CMRL	93010	524-E2
BORDEN AV	1000	SIMI	93065	497-J4
BORDERO LN	3100	THO	91362	527-A2
BORDERS ST	-	SIMI	93063	498-H1
BORGES CT	15700	MRPK	93021	477-A5
BORGES DR	15300	MRPK	93021	477-A4
BORREGO AV	3900	OXN	93033	552-G4
BORREGO CT	200	OXN	93033	552-H4
BORREGO WY	700	OXN	93033	552-H4
BOSTON AV	-	VEN	93004	492-J1
BOSTON DR	3500	OXN	93033	552-J4
BOSTON WY	4400	OXN	93033	552-J5
BOTTENS CT	-	MRPK	93021	476-F5
BOTTLEBRUSH CIR	100	OXN	93030	522-E5
BOTTLEBRUSH CT	100	OXN	93030	522-E5
BOTTLEBRUSH PL	1000	OXN	93030	522-E5
BOULDER CT	10400	VEN	93004	492-J2
BOULDER ST	600	FILM	93015	455-J5
BOULDER CREEK RD	300	VeCo	93015	455-C5
	23600	SIMI	93065	527-F1
BOULDER RIDGE TER	10500	Chat	91311	499-H3
BOUNDS RD	-	VeCo	93001	471-C1
BOUNDS RD W	-	VeCo	93001	471-C1
BOUQUET CIR	1200	THO	91362	527-A6
BOUQUET DR	7200	CanP	91307	529-F5
BOWCLIFF TER	1600	THO	91361	557-B6
BOWER WY	200	THO	91360	556-G1
BOWFIELD ST	4800	THO	91362	557-F1
	4900	VeCo	91362	557-F1
	5000	VeCo	91377	557-F1
BOWIE CT	4900	SIMI	93063	478-H6
BOWL RD	23600	VeCo	93063	529-A1
BOWLINE PL	5100	OXN	93033	552-G5
E BOWLING GREEN ST	100	PHME	93041	552-E2
W BOWLING GREEN ST	100	PHME	93041	552-D2
BOWMAN KNOLL DR	32500	WLKV	91361	557-A7
BOWSPRIT CIR	3800	WLKV	91361	557-B6
BOX CANYON RD	1000	VeCo	93063	499-E5
	1000	WHil	91304	499-E5
	23600	Chat	91311	499-E6
	23700	LA	91304	499-E6
	23700	WHil	91304	499-E6
BOX ELDER CT	23600	SIMI	93065	498-D4
BOXTHORN AV	600	THO	91320	555-F4
BOXWOOD CIR	3100	THO	91360	526-H2
BOY SCOUT CAMP RD	-	VeCo	-	366-L1
BRADBURY CT	1000	THO	91361	557-A5
BRADEMAS CT	600	SIMI	93065	527-C1
BRADFIELD DR	3700	OXN	93033	552-G4
BRADFIELD PL	4700	OXN	93033	552-H5
BRADFORD AV	-	CMRL	93010	524-A1
BRADLEY RD	3900	VeCo	93066	494-H1
	5300	VeCo	93066	474-J7
	5300	VeCo	93066	475-B5
BRADLEY ST	200	SPLA	93060	464-A5
BRAEMAR CT	6100	AGRH	91301	557-J3
BRAKEY RD	100	VEN	93001	491-C1
BRAMBLE CT	-	CMRL	93010	524-A2
BRAMWELL PL	1200	THO	91361	557-C6
N BRANCH AV	1400	SIMI	93065	497-E3
BRANDON AV	900	SIMI	93065	498-B4
BRANDT AV	-	VeCo	93022	451-C4
BRANDT WY	-	OXN	93030	522-E5
BRANDYWINE CT	5700	CMRL	93012	495-B7
BRANNAN ST	3500	SIMI	93063	498-E3
	7700	VEN	93004	492-F2
BRAUN CT	15300	MRPK	93021	476-J4
	15300	MRPK	93021	477-A5
BRAVO LN	26300	CALB	91302	558-H4
BRAVO RD	23600	VeCo	93063	528-H1
BRAXFIELD CT	23600	VeCo	91361	556-G6
E BRAZIL ST	-	THO	91360	556-F1
W BRAZIL ST	-	THO	91360	556-F1
BRAZOS CT	10000	VEN	93004	492-J3
BREA CT	400	CMRL	93010	524-B1
BREA CANYON RD	2600	SIMI	93065	477-F7
	2600	VeCo	93065	477-F7
BREAKER CT	3100	VEN	93003	491-G1
BREAKER DR	300	VEN	93003	491-G1
BREAKERS WY	5100	OXN	93035	521-J7
	23600	VeCo	93001	459-D5
BREAKWATER WY	5100	OXN	93035	521-J7
BRECKENRIDGE PL	500	SIMI	93065	497-D7
	500	SIMI	93065	527-D1
BRECKFORD CT	1300	THO	91361	557-A5
BREESE DR	2500	VeCo	93012	496-A7
BREEZEPORT DR	3300	WLKV	91361	557-C7
BREEZEWATER CT	2500	PHME	93041	552-C2
BREEZY DR	-	CMRL	93012	524-G5
BREEZY GLEN DR	-	MRPK	93021	476-E6
BRENDA CT	3000	THO	91320	555-G2
BRENNAN	-	PHME	93041	552-E4
BRENNAN AV	6600	CanP	91307	529-F6
BRENNAN RD	3900	VeCo	93021	496-H3
N BRENT ST	100	VEN	93003	491-G2
S BRENT ST	100	VEN	93003	491-G4
BRENTFORD AV	1500	THO	91361	556-J6
E BRENTFORD AV	1600	THO	91361	556-J6
BRENTFORD CT	100	VeCo	93010	494-E7
BRENTLY AV	100	CMRL	93010	524-D2
BRENTWOOD AV	-	VEN	93003	491-J3
N BRENTWOOD AV	2000	SIMI	93063	498-D2
BRETON AV	800	SIMI	93065	498-D5
BRETT WY	200	SPLA	93060	464-B6
BREVARD AV	300	VEN	93003	492-C1
BREVARD CT	5600	VEN	93003	492-B1
BRIAN CIR	-	CMRL	93010	524-C3
BRIAN CT	1900	THO	91362	527-A6
BRIANA CIR	-	OXN	93030	522-G4
S BRIAR AV	800	THO	91320	555-E4
BRIAR BLUFF CIR	3800	THO	91360	526-E1
BRIARCLIFF CIR	7200	VEN	93003	472-D7
BRIARCLIFF RD	600	THO	91360	526-G6
BRIARFIELD ST	2100	CMRL	93010	524-E1
BRIARGATE CT	1200	VeCo	91377	528-A7
BRIARGLEN AV	1400	THO	91361	556-J5
BRIAR HILL CIR	700	SIMI	93065	498-D5
BRIARHURST CT	2400	SIMI	93063	498-D1
BRIARPATCH DR	2600	SIMI	93065	498-C4
BRIAR RIDGE CT	23600	THO	91320	555-E4
BRIARSTONE LN	7100	CanP	91307	529-D5
BRIARWOOD LN	-	VeCo	91377	558-A2
BRIARWOOD PL	2600	THO	91362	526-J3
BRIARWOOD TER	300	VEN	93001	491-G1
BRICKFIELD CT	23600	THO	91362	527-B5
BRIDGE RD	16800	VeCo	93060	454-A7
	16900	VeCo	93060	464-B1
BRIDGEGATE CT	2000	THO	91361	557-A6
BRIDGEGATE ST	1700	THO	91361	556-H5
	1800	THO	91361	557-A5
BRIDGEHAMPTON WY	-	CMRL	93012	524-F4
BRIDGEPORT LN	1500	CMRL	93010	524-D3
BRIDGES CT	23600	VeCo	93060	464-D5
BRIDGET AV	1500	SIMI	93065	498-B3
BRIDGETON WY	-	CMRL	93012	524-G4
BRIDGETOWN PL	4900	THO	91362	527-F6
BRIDGEVIEW DR	5800	VEN	93003	472-C6
BRIDGEVIEW LN	-	THO	91320	555-E3
BRIDGEWATER CT	5900	AGRH	91301	557-H4
BRIDGEWOOD LN	3400	THO	91362	557-C2
N BRIDLE LN	-	VeCo	91307	529-A5
BRIDLE CREST AV	-	SIMI	93063	478-H5
BRIDLE GLEN ST	5500	AGRH	91301	558-A5
BRIDLE OAKS CT	1600	THO	91362	527-A5
BRIDLEWOOD LN	100	FILM	93015	456-A7
BRIER ST	600	VeCo	93023	451-C4
BRIGANTINE CIR	3700	WLKV	91361	557-C7
BRIGGS RD	100	VeCo	93060	473-F1
	700	VeCo	93060	463-E7
S BRIGGS RD	100	VeCo	93060	473-G3
BRIGHAM ST	2000	OXN	93033	553-A4
BRIGHT GLEN CIR	2800	THO	91361	557-C5
BRIGHTON CT	4700	THO	91362	527-E6
BRIGHT STAR CIR	800	THO	91360	526-B2
BRIGHT STAR ST	700	THO	91360	526-C2
BRIGHTSTONE CT	900	THO	91361	557-A5
BRINDISI PL	4000	MRPK	93021	496-C4
BRINDLE CT	2600	SIMI	93063	498-D1
BRISBAINE AV	300	THO	91320	555-F3
BRISTLECONE CIR	-	MRPK	93021	496-G3
BRISTOL AV	400	SIMI	93065	497-G5
BRISTOL RD	-	OJAI	93023	441-G7
	6000	VeCo	93003	492-D5
	6300	VEN	93003	492-D5
	7600	VEN	93004	492-G5
	7600	VeCo	93004	492-G5
BRISTOL PARK CT	-	CMRL	93012	524-G4
BRITTANY CT	-	LACo	91302	558-G4
BRITTANY PARK RD	1800	VeCo	93012	526-A1
	2000	VeCo	93012	496-A7
BRITTEN LN	900	VEN	93003	492-A7
BROADBECK DR	-	THO	91320	525-H6
BROADHAVEN ST	-	VeCo	91361	556-C7
BROADMOOR AV	2600	SIMI	93065	498-A1
	2700	SIMI	93065	478-A7
BROADMOOR CT	2300	OXN	93036	522-D2
BROADVIEW DR	11100	MRPK	93021	496-B3
BROADWAY	13000	VeCo	93021	476-B4
	23100	VeCo	93021	475-J4
BROADWAY Rt#-23	14900	VeCo	93021	476-D4
BROCK LN	-	VeCo	93001	461-A3
BROCKTON LN	800	VEN	93001	491-E4
BROCKTON RD	23600	SIMI	93065	497-F7
BRODERICK AV	200	VEN	93003	492-B3
BRODERICK WY	400	PHME	93041	552-C2
BRODIEA AV	1300	VEN	93001	491-E1
BRODIEA PL	300	VEN	93001	491-E1
BROKEN ARROW ST	6000	SIMI	93063	479-B7
BROKENHILL ST	3400	THO	91320	555-F4
BROMELY DR	5400	VeCo	91377	527-H6
BROMFIELD ST	2100	SIMI	93065	498-A1
N BRONCO LN	-	VeCo	91307	528-J5
BRONSON ST	1700	CMRL	93010	524-D2
BRONZE PL	3300	SIMI	93063	478-D7
BRONZEWOOD CT	1700	THO	91320	556-A2
BROOK RD	200	VeCo	91320	556-B2
BROOKBERRY LN	23600	SIMI	93065	497-A1
BROOKCREST CT	4100	MRPK	93021	496-B2
BROOKDALE LN	4300	MRPK	93021	496-E3
BROOKE AV	10100	Chat	91311	499-J4
BROOKFIELD DR	2000	THO	91362	527-A3
BROOKGLEN ST	4300	MRPK	93021	496-D3
BROOKHAVEN AV	1200	CMRL	93010	524-F1
BROOKHILL DR	2600	CMRL	93010	494-E7
BROOK HOLLOW CT	2000	OXN	93036	522-E3
BROOKHURST CT	3900	MRPK	93021	496-E4
BROOK MEADOW CT	800	THO	91362	557-E1
BROOKMONT PL	7600	LA	91304	529-E4
BROOKMONT TERRACE CT	5100	THO	91362	527-G6
BROOKPEBBLE LN	23600	SIMI	93065	497-A1
BROOKS RD	23400	Chat	91311	499-F7
	23600	SIMI	93065	497-G7
BROOKSFALL CT	1700	THO	91361	557-A6
N BROOKSHIRE AV	-	VEN	93003	492-C1
S BROOKSHIRE AV	-	VEN	93003	492-C2
BROOKSHIRE CT	-	CMRL	93012	524-G4
BROOKSIDE AV	1400	OXN	93035	552-D1
BROOKSIDE PL	100	THO	91320	556-D1
BROOKTREE CT	1800	THO	91362	526-J3
BROOKTREE DR	1300	SIMI	93063	499-C3
BROOKVIEW AV	900	THO	91361	556-J5
BROOKWOOD LN	-	OXN	93036	522-C3
BROOME RANCH RD	-	VeCo	-	584-F1
	-	VeCo	93033	554-A6
	200	VeCo	93033	553-H6
	23600	VeCo	93033	584-C1
BROOMFIRTH CT	2000	THO	91361	557-A5
BROSSARD DR	500	THO	91360	556-G1
E BROWER ST	2100	SIMI	93065	498-B2
N BROWER ST	2000	SIMI	93065	498-A2
BROWNING AV	600	VEN	93003	492-E3
BROWNING DR	4200	OXN	93033	552-J4
	4400	OXN	93033	553-A4
BROWNS CANYON RD	-	StvR	91381	479-G1
	2500	Nor	91326	479-J4
	2500	Chat	91311	479-H3
BROWNSTONE CREEK AV	2100	SIMI	93063	499-A2
BRUBECK ST	-	VEN	93003	492-C4
BRUCE CIR	900	THO	91362	526-H7
BRUCE DR	1200	SPLA	93060	464-B3
BRUCKER RD	200	OXN	93033	552-F4
BRUNSTON CT	2900	THO	91362	527-C5
BRUNSWICK LN	800	VEN	93001	491-E5
BRUSH HILL RD	700	THO	91360	526-G5
BRUSH OAK CT	1800	THO	91320	526-A5
BRYAN AV	3200	SIMI	93063	478-H6
BRYANT CIR	400	OJAI	93023	441-J7
BRYANT DR	500	WHil	91304	499-D5
BRYANT PL	800	OJAI	93023	441-J7
BRYANT ST	100	OJAI	93023	441-J7
	22100	LA	91304	529-J1
BRYCE WY	1100	VEN	93003	492-B4
BRYCE CANYON AV	100	OXN	93033	552-F3
	700	PHME	93033	552-F3
	700	PHME	93041	552-F3
BRYNDALE AV	23600	VeCo	91377	528-A7
N BRYN MAWR ST	5300	VEN	93003	492-B2
S BRYN MAWR ST	-	VEN	93003	492-B2
BRYSON AV	1100	SIMI	93065	497-G4
E BRYSON PL	2300	SIMI	93065	498-B4
BUBBLING BROOK ST	11900	MRPK	93021	496-C3
BUCHANAN AV	-	VEN	93003	492-E2
BUCKAROO AV	2600	OXN	93036	492-F7
	2600	OXN	93036	522-F1
BUCKBOARD CIR	300	SIMI	93065	497-F6
BUCKBOARD LN	200	OJAI	93023	441-H7
	500	OJAI	93023	451-J1
BUCKEYE PL	3300	THO	91320	555-G4
BUCKEYE ST	-	SIMI	93063	499-A4
BUCKINGHAM DR	1000	THO	91360	526-G6
BUCKLIN PL	3900	THO	91360	526-F1
BUCKNELL AV	100	VEN	93003	492-B3
BUCKSGLEN CT	1600	THO	91361	556-J5
BUCKSKIN AV	1400	SIMI	93065	497-H3
N BUCKSKIN RD	-	VeCo	91307	528-J4
BUCKSMOORE CT	1300	THO	91361	556-J5
BUCKTHORN CT	3800	THO	91320	555-E2
BUELL CT	1900	SIMI	93065	498-A4
BUENA MESA CT	5200	CMRL	93012	525-A2
BUENA VISTA AV	500	OXN	93030	522-J6
BUENA VISTA DR	-	VeCo	93010	494-D6
	400	OJAI	93023	441-J6
BUENA VISTA ST	600	VEN	93001	491-C1
	8200	VeCo	93021	476-D3
BUENOS TIEMPOS DR	500	CMRL	93012	524-J3
BUFF CIR	2800	SIMI	93065	498-C5
BUFFALO AV	2200	VEN	93003	492-E5
BUFFALO ST	6100	SIMI	93063	479-B6
BUFFUM ST	3500	SIMI	93063	498-E2
BUFFWOOD PL	5500	AGRH	91301	558-A5
BUGGY LN	10300	VeCo	93012	495-J6
BULL PUP CIR	-	VeCo	93041	583-G1
BUMBLEBEE AV	1000	THO	91320	526-A6
BUNDREN ST	-	VeCo	93022	451-B6
BUNSEN AV	2800	VEN	93001	492-D7
	2800	VEN	93003	492-D7
BUNTING AV	2500	VEN	93003	492-E5
BURANO CT	700	VeCo	91377	557-H1
BURBANK AV	100	VeCo	93035	552-C6
BURCH AV	1800	SIMI	93063	498-E2
N BURKE CT	2200	SIMI	93063	498-E2
BURL AV	200	VEN	93003	492-C2
BURLESON AV	1800	THO	91360	526-G5
BURLESON ST	28900	AGRH	91301	558-A3
N BURLINGHAM PL	2400	SIMI	93063	498-E1
BURLINGTON AV	700	VEN	93004	492-H2
BURLINGTON ST	-	FILM	93015	455-J7
	-	FILM	93015	456-A7
BURNETT AV	200	VEN	93003	492-C1
BURNETT CIR	6300	VEN	93003	492-C1
BURNETT CT	6300	VEN	93003	492-C1
BURNHAM RD	-	VeCo	93001	450-J6
	-	VeCo	93022	450-J6
	100	VeCo	93022	451-A5
	700	VeCo	93001	451-A5
	700	VeCo	93023	451-A5
BURNING TREE DR	1700	THO	91362	526-J3
BURNLEY ST	1400	CMRL	93010	524-C2
BURNS ST	4900	VEN	93003	492-A2
BURNSIDE DR	1500	VEN	93004	492-J3
E BURNSIDE ST	2200	SIMI	93065	498-B2
BURR CIR	2300	THO	91360	526-F4
N BURREL AV	2000	SIMI	93063	498-E2
BURSON LN	200	FILM	93015	455-J6
BURSON WY	4700	VeCo	93036	493-A5
BURSON RANCH RD	-	VeCo	93015	455-J3
	-	VeCo	93015	456-A3
BURTON CT	300	THO	91360	526-F4
BURTON ST	300	THO	91360	526-G4
	22100	LA	91304	529-E2
BURTONWOOD AV	1000	THO	91360	526-G7
BURY CIR	800	THO	91360	526-G6
BUSH ST	23600	VEN	93003	492-E2
BUSHELL RD	4700	VeCo	93066	495-B2
BUSHGROVE CT	23600	VeCo	91361	556-F6
BUSINESS CENTER CIR	1000	THO	91320	525-G6
BUSTER ST	1400	SIMI	93065	497-G3
BUTLER RD	2200	OXN	93033	553-A3
BUTTE ST	8400	VEN	93004	492-F1
BUTTER CREEK RD	4900	MRPK	93021	496-B2
BUTTERCUP LN	-	CMRL	93012	524-F5
BUTTERFIELD LN	4300	MRPK	93021	496-F3
BUTTERFIELD ST	5300	CMRL	93012	525-A1
BUTTERFLY CT	1600	THO	91320	526-A6
BUTTONWOOD AV	6600	VeCo	91377	558-B2
BUYERS ST	1600	SIMI	93063	498-F3
BYRD DR	2100	OXN	93033	552-J2
BYRON AV	200	VEN	93003	492-B1
C				
C ST	-	VeCo	93042	583-H3
	-	FILM	93015	455-J6
	100	OXN	93030	522-G7
	1000	OXN	93033	522-G7
	1200	OXN	93033	552-G2
E C ST	100	PHME	93041	552-E5
N C ST	100	OXN	93030	522-G4
	1600	OXN	93036	522-G3
W C ST	-	PHME	93041	552-E5
CABALLERO ST	1700	SIMI	93065	497-J4
	1700	SIMI	93065	498-A4
CABEZONE WY	200	OXN	93035	552-A3
CABIN CV	2500	PHME	93041	552-C3
CABLE CANYON	-	VeCo	93001	471-A3
CABLE RACK RD	-	VeCo	93042	583-D4
CABOT CT	2700	THO	91360	526-E3
CABOT PL	2000	OXN	93030	523-A6
CABRILLO AV	-	THO	91320	555-F1
CABRILLO CIR	-	THO	91320	555-E1
CABRILLO CT	100	SPLA	93060	463-J6
CABRILLO DR	2700	VEN	93003	491-G3
CABRILLO LN	300	FILM	93015	456-C6
CABRILLO WY	1000	VeCo	93010	494-D6
	1600	OXN	93030	522-D4
CABRILLO MESA CT	23600	CMRL	93010	494-C7
CACHUMA AV	500	VEN	93004	492-H1
CACTUS AV	9600	Chat	91311	499-H5
CACTUS CT	800	THO	91320	526-A6
CACTUS DR	300	OXN	93036	492-F7
CACTUS TR	26800	CALB	91301	558-G7
CADIZ CT	1100	OXN	93035	522-D7
CADIZ DR	1000	VeCo	93065	497-G4
E CADMAN ST	3800	SIMI	93063	498-E2
CADWAY ST	1000	SPLA	93060	464-B3
CAHUENGA DR	200	VeCo	93035	552-B5
CAITLYN CIR	-	WLKV	91361	586-H2
CAJON CIR	10600	VeCo	93012	496-A5
CAJUN CT	-	CanP	91303	529-J5
CALABASAS HILLS RD	-	CALB	91301	558-G7
CALABRIA	28800	AGRH	91301	558-B4
CALABRIA CT	800	CMRL	93010	524-C1
CALAIS CT	-	Ago	91301	558-G3
CALAISE CT	30800	WLKV	91362	557-F5
CALAMAR CT	23600	CMRL	93010	494-C7
CALAMINE DR	26900	CALB	91301	558-F6
CALAROSA RANCH RD	-	CMRL	93012	495-A7
CALAVERAS DR	2300	CMRL	93010	494-E7
CALAVERAS ST	8000	VEN	93004	472-F7
	8000	VEN	93004	492-E1
S CALAVO ST	100	SPLA	93060	463-H7
CALBOURNE LN	-	VeCo	91361	556-G7
	-	VeCo	91361	586-G1
CALCITE CIR	2500	THO	91320	525-H7
CALDWELL AV	2100	SIMI	93065	497-H1
CALEDONIA CT	23600	VeCo	91377	528-A7
CALENDULA CT	2800	THO	91360	526-D3
CALETA CT	-	CMRL	93012	524-J2
CALETA DR	-	CMRL	93012	524-H2
CALETA RD	4300	Ago	91301	558-B7
CALGARY AV	800	VEN	93004	492-H2
CALIENTE LN	800	VEN	93001	491-C1
CALIENTE WY	600	OXN	93036	522-H3
CALIFORNIA AV	700	SIMI	93065	497-G2
	2100	VeCo	93015	465-F4
CALIFORNIA ST	200	SPLA	93060	464-B6
	1300	OXN	93033	552-H1
N CALIFORNIA ST	-	VEN	93001	491-C2
S CALIFORNIA ST	-	VEN	93001	491-C2
CALIFORNIA OAK ST	-	SIMI	93063	499-A3
CALLADO ST	700	VeCo	93010	494-B5
CALLAHAN AV	2100	SIMI	93065	497-J2
CALLA LILY CT	-	SIMI	93063	498-H1
CALLAS CT	1700	OXN	93035	522-E7
CALLAS DR	1100	OXN	93035	522-E7
	1200	OXN	93035	552-E1
CALLE ABEDUL	2500	THO	91360	526-G3
CALLE ABETO	2600	THO	91360	526-H4
CALLE ACOPADA	600	VeCo	93010	493-J6
CALLE AGRADO	600	CMRL	93012	525-C5
CALLE AGUILA	3900	CMRL	93012	524-H4
CALLE ALAMO	1500	THO	91360	526-H3
CALLE ALBERCA	1700	CMRL	93010	494-B7
	1700	CMRL	93010	524-B1
CALLE ALMENDRO	800	THO	91360	526-H3
CALLE ALTA VISTA	3700	THO	91320	525-E7
CALLE ALTO	4500	CMRL	93012	524-J5
CALLE ALUCEMA	2300	THO	91360	526-J4
CALLE AMAPOLA	500	THO	91360	526-G4
CALLE AMOROSA	-	CMRL	93012	525-B4
CALLE ANAPOL	23600	CMRL	93010	523-F2
CALLE ANGOSTA	1800	VeCo	91360	526-C5
CALLE ARAGON	600	VeCo	91377	557-J1
CALLE ARENA	5900	CMRL	93012	525-B2

VENTURA CO.

STREET	Block	City	ZIP	Pg-Grid
CALLE ARGOLLA				
	4200	CMRL	93012	524-H3
CALLE ARINO				
	2900	THO	91360	526-G3
CALLE ARROYO				
	600	VeCo	91360	526-C7
CALLE ARTIGAS				
	1300	THO	91360	496-J7
CALLE AURORA				
	1200	VeCo	93010	494-A6
CALLE AVELLANO				
	1300	THO	91360	526-H3
CALLE BALSA				
	1200	THO	91360	526-H3
CALLE BELLA VISTA				
	1400	CMRL	93010	524-A1
CALLE BELLOTA				
	3500	CMRL	93010	494-G7
CALLE BIENVENIDO				
	2600	THO	91360	526-G3
CALLE BODEGA				
	5900	CMRL	93012	525-C2
CALLE BOLERO				
	4500	CMRL	93012	524-H6
CALLE BONITA				
	1200	CMRL	93012	525-A1
CALLE BORREGO				
	1900	VeCo	91360	526-B5
CALLE BOUGANVILLA				
	2400	THO	91360	526-H4
CALLE BRISA				
	-	CMRL	93012	524-H1
CALLE BRUSCA				
	900	VeCo	91360	526-B6
CALLE BUENA VISTA				
	3800	THO	91320	525-E7
CALLE CAMELIA				
	1100	THO	91360	526-H4
CALLE CAMELLIA				
	800	CMRL	93010	524-B2
CALLE CANCUN				
	23600	CMRL	93012	494-H7
	23600	CMRL	93012	524-J1
CALLE CANON				
	600	CMRL	93012	525-B2
CALLE CAPISTRANO				
	23600	OXN	93030	523-C7
CALLE CARDO				
	500	THO	91360	526-G4
CALLE CARGA				
	4500	CMRL	93012	524-H6
CALLE CASTANO				
	2700	THO	91360	526-G2
CALLE CATALPA				
	600	THO	91360	526-G2
CALLE CATALUNA				
	-	CMRL	93012	525-B5
CALLE CEDRO				
	2800	THO	91360	526-G3
CALLE CIELITO				
	23600	OXN	93030	523-C7
CALLE CINCO DE MAYO				
	-	VeCo	93022	451-B5
E CALLE CIRCULO				
	300	CMRL	93010	524-B2
N CALLE CIRCULO				
	800	CMRL	93010	524-B2
CALLE CIRUELO				
	600	THO	91360	526-G4
CALLE CITA				
	3500	CMRL	93010	494-G7
CALLE CLARA VISTA				
	3700	THO	91320	525-F7
CALLE CLAVEL				
	600	THO	91360	526-G4
CALLE COLINA				
	1200	THO	91360	496-H7
CALLE COLLADO				
	900	VeCo	91360	526-B6
CALLE COMPO				
	1400	VeCo	91360	526-C5
CALLE CONTENTO				
	700	THO	91360	526-H1
CALLE CONVERSE				
	100	CMRL	93010	524-B1
	400	CMRL	93010	494-B7
CALLE CORTA				
	600	VeCo	91360	526-C6
CALLE CORVA				
	1700	VeCo	93010	493-J6
CALLE COVINA				
	-	CMRL	93012	524-H1
CALLE CRISANTEMO				
	1300	THO	91360	526-H4
CALLE CUESTA				
	600	THO	91360	526-G2
	4900	CMRL	93012	524-J4
	4900	CMRL	93012	525-A4
CALLE DALIA				
	2300	THO	91360	526-G4
CALLE DAMASCO				
	2700	THO	91360	526-G3
CALLE DE DEBESA				
	3000	CMRL	93010	493-J6
CALLE DE LA ROSA				
	-	CMRL	93012	524-H4
CALLE DE LAS OVEJAS				
	500	VeCo	91377	557-J2
CALLE DEL NORTE				
	800	VeCo	93010	494-A6
CALLE DEL PRADO				
	23600	THO	91320	555-D2
CALLE DEL SOL				
	3700	THO	91360	526-J1
CALLE DEL SUR				
	500	THO	91360	526-G3
CALLE DE MAREJADA				
	3000	CMRL	93010	493-J6
CALLE DE ORO				
	1200	THO	91360	526-J1
CALLE DE ORO CT				
	3300	THO	91360	526-H1
CALLE DESCANSO				
	-	CMRL	93012	524-H1
CALLE DIA				
	2000	CMRL	93012	495-D7
CALLE DIAMONTE				
	1500	THO	91320	526-B7
CALLE DURAZNO				
	1300	THO	91360	526-H4
CALLE ELAINA				
	1000	VeCo	91360	526-C6
CALLE EL AVION				
	300	CMRL	93010	524-B1
CALLE EL CAMERON				
	1200	VeCo	91360	526-B7
CALLE ELEGANTE				
	2500	THO	91360	526-G3
CALLE EL HALCON				
	1000	CMRL	93010	524-B2
W CALLE EL PRADO				
	-	VeCo	93022	451-B5
CALLE EL VOLADOR				
	300	CMRL	93010	524-B2
CALLE ENTRAR				
	500	THO	91360	526-G3
CALLE ESCALON				
	1400	CMRL	93010	524-A1
CALLE ESCORIAL				
	-	CMRL	93012	524-G4
CALLE ESTEPA				
	2900	THO	91360	526-G3
CALLE FAMILLIA				
	200	VeCo	91377	558-A2
CALLE FIDELIDAD				
	1200	THO	91360	496-H7
CALLE FLORENCIA				
	1600	THO	91360	526-J1
CALLE FRESNO				
	500	THO	91360	526-G3
CALLE FRONTE				
	-	CMRL	93012	524-H2
CALLE FUEGO				
	3500	THO	91360	526-C1
CALLE GALVEZ				
	5900	CMRL	93012	525-B5
CALLE GLADIOLO				
	2400	THO	91360	526-H4
CALLE GLICINA				
	2100	THO	91360	526-H4
CALLE GOMERO				
	1200	THO	91360	526-H3
CALLE HAYA				
	2600	THO	91360	526-G3
CALLE HERMOSA				
	2500	THO	91360	526-G3
CALLE HIGUERA				
	200	CMRL	93010	524-B1
	800	CMRL	93010	494-C7
CALLE HONDANADA				
	1400	THO	91360	496-H7
CALLE JAZMIN				
	700	THO	91360	526-G4
CALLE JON				
	800	VeCo	91360	526-D6
CALLEJON DE ROSAS				
	900	VeCo	91360	526-C7
CALLE LACOTA				
	800	THO	91360	526-G3
CALLE LA CUMBRE				
	900	CMRL	93010	524-B1
CALLE LA FIESTA				
	500	CMRL	93010	524-B2
CALLE LA GRANADA				
	-	CMRL	93010	524-B2
E CALLE LA GUERRA				
	-	CMRL	93010	524-B2
W CALLE LA GUERRA				
	-	CMRL	93010	524-A2
CALLE LAGUNA				
	23600	OXN	93030	523-C7
CALLE LA PALMERA				
	800	CMRL	93010	524-B2
CALLE LA PAZ				
	1100	CMRL	93010	524-B1
CALLE LA PRADA				
	800	CMRL	93010	524-B2
CALLE LAREDO				
	500	THO	91360	526-C7
	500	VeCo	91360	526-C7
CALLE LARIOS				
	-	CMRL	93010	524-B1
CALLE LA ROCHA				
	800	CMRL	93010	524-B2
CALLE LA RODA				
	600	CMRL	93010	524-B2
CALLE LAS CASAS				
	1300	VeCo	91360	526-B7
CALLE LAS COLINAS				
	800	THO	91320	525-E7
CALLE LA SOMBRA				
	2000	SIMI	93063	499-B2
E CALLE LA SOMBRA				
	-	CMRL	93010	524-B2
N CALLE LA SOMBRA				
	800	CMRL	93010	524-B2
W CALLE LA SOMBRA				
	-	CMRL	93010	524-A2
CALLE LAS TRANCAS				
	900	VeCo	91360	526-C6
CALLE LILA				
	2100	THO	91360	526-G4
CALLE LIMONERO				
	2600	THO	91360	526-J3
CALLE LINDA VISTA				
	3700	THO	91320	525-E7
CALLE LIRIO				
	2300	THO	91360	526-H4
CALLE LOMA VISTA				
	3800	THO	91320	525-E7
CALLE LOS ACEITUNOS				
	600	VeCo	93010	493-J6
CALLE LOS GATOS				
	800	CMRL	93010	524-A2
CALLE LOZANO				
	1100	CMRL	93012	525-A1
CALLE LUMINOSO				
	-	CMRL	93012	525-C1
CALLE LYS				
	2100	THO	91360	526-G4
CALLE MADRESELVA				
	1300	THO	91360	526-H4
CALLE MADURO				
	-	CMRL	93010	523-J1
	-	VeCo	93010	523-J1
CALLE MALVON				
	2300	THO	91360	526-H4
CALLE MANDARINAS				
	600	VeCo	91360	526-C6
CALLE MANZANO				
	2500	THO	91360	526-H3
CALLE MAPACHE				
	4600	CMRL	93012	524-H2
CALLE MARGARITA				
	500	THO	91360	526-G4
	27800	AGRH	91301	558-D7
CALLE MARLENA				
	600	VeCo	91377	557-J1
CALLE MAR VISTA				
	23600	OXN	93030	523-C7
CALLE MAZATLAN				
	3700	THO	91320	525-F7
CALLE MENDOTA				
	23600	CMRL	93012	524-J2
CALLE MIGUEL				
	23600	CMRL	93010	524-B2
CALLE MILAGROS				
	22000	Chat	91311	499-J3
CALLE MIMOSA				
	2300	THO	91360	526-H4
CALLE MIRADO				
	600	VeCo	91377	557-J2
CALLE MIRA MONTE				
	900	THO	91320	525-E7
CALLE MIRASOL				
	23600	CMRL	93010	524-B2
CALLE MONTECILLO				
	4900	AGRH	91301	558-D7
CALLE MORENO				
	3400	VeCo	93023	442-D5
CALLE MORERA				
	1500	THO	91360	526-H3
CALLE NARANJO				
	600	THO	91360	526-G3
CALLE NARCISO				
	2400	THO	91360	526-H4
CALLE NARDO				
	2100	THO	91360	526-H4
CALLE NAVARRO				
	-	CMRL	93010	524-B1
CALLE NOGAL				
	500	THO	91360	526-G3
CALLE NORTE				
	23600	THO	91320	555-D2
CALLENS RD				
	500	VEN	93003	491-J5
CALLE OLIVO				
	2600	THO	91360	526-H3
CALLE OLMO				
	2800	THO	91360	526-H3
CALLE ORINDA				
	1400	VeCo	93010	494-A6
CALLE OROVISTA				
	100	CMRL	93012	524-H3
CALLE PAMARO				
	5800	CMRL	93012	525-B4
CALLE PARADORA				
	3900	CMRL	93012	524-H3
CALLE PECOS				
	700	VeCo	91360	526-C6
CALLE PENSAMIENTO				
	500	THO	91360	526-G4
CALLE PERA				
	2500	THO	91360	526-H3
CALLE PETALUMA				
	1800	VeCo	91360	526-C5
CALLE PIMIENTO				
	1200	THO	91360	526-H3
CALLE PINATA				
	800	THO	91360	526-G1
CALLE PINO				
	2400	THO	91360	526-G4
CALLE PLANO				
	700	CMRL	93012	524-J5
CALLE PLANTADOR				
	1800	VeCo	91360	526-C5
CALLE PORTADA				
	1400	VeCo	93010	493-J6
	1400	VeCo	93010	494-A6
CALLE PORTILLA				
	100	CMRL	93010	524-B1
CALLE POSADAS				
	3700	THO	91320	525-F7
CALLE PUNTA				
	600	THO	91360	526-G1
CALLE QUEBRACHO				
	2700	THO	91360	526-G1
CALLE QUETZAL				
	4500	CMRL	93012	524-J6
CALLE RETAMA				
	2400	THO	91360	526-H4
CALLE REY				
	900	VeCo	91360	526-C6
CALLE RIO VISTA				
	5600	VeCo	91377	557-J1
E CALLE RISCOSO				
	2000	THO	91362	527-A2
CALLE ROBLE				
	2100	THO	91360	526-G4
CALLE ROBLEDA				
	4900	AGRH	91301	558-D7
CALLE ROCAS				
	1700	VeCo	93010	493-J6
CALLE ROCHELLE				
	3600	THO	91360	526-J1
CALLE ROSA				
	2200	THO	91360	526-G4
CALLE RUIZ				
	800	THO	91360	526-G1
CALLE SALTO				
	1700	VeCo	91360	526-B5
CALLE SAN JUAN				
	23600	THO	91320	555-D3
CALLE SAN PABLO				
	500	CMRL	93012	524-E5
CALLE SANTIAGO				
	23600	THO	91320	555-D3
CALLE SEGUNDA				
	23600	CMRL	93010	524-C4
CALLE SEGURO				
	600	VeCo	91377	557-J2
CALLE SENCILLO				
	5700	CMRL	93012	525-B3
CALLE SEQUOIA				
	400	THO	91360	526-D7
	400	VeCo	91360	526-D7
CALLE SERRA				
	23600	CMRL	93012	494-J7
CALLE SUERTE				
	900	CMRL	93012	524-H2
CALLE TAMEGA				
	-	CMRL	93012	525-A3
CALLE TANIA				
	6700	CMRL	93012	495-C7
CALLE TECATE				
	3600	CMRL	93012	524-G2
CALLE TESORO				
	4100	CMRL	93012	524-H1
CALLE TIERRA VISTA				
	1300	CMRL	93010	523-H1
	1700	VeCo	93010	523-H1
CALLE TILO				
	1500	THO	91360	526-H3
CALLE TULIPAN				
	1000	THO	91360	526-G3
CALLE TURQUESA				
	1500	THO	91320	526-A7
CALLE VALLE VISTA				
	3800	THO	91320	525-E7
CALLE VERACRUZ				
	23600	THO	91320	555-D3
CALLE VERBENA				
	2300	THO	91360	526-H4
CALLE VIEJO				
	3900	CMRL	93012	524-H4
CALLE VIOLETA				
	1300	THO	91360	526-H4
CALLE VISTA				
	1200	CMRL	93010	524-A2
CALLE VISTA CALMA				
	23600	OXN	93030	523-C6
CALLE VISTA DEL MONTE				
	-	VeCo	93022	451-B5
CALLE VISTA VERDE				
	23600	OXN	93030	523-C7
CALLE YUCCA				
	400	THO	91360	526-C6
	400	VeCo	91360	526-C5
CALLE ZAFIRO				
	1700	THO	91320	556-A1
CALLE ZOCALO				
	1500	THO	91360	496-J7
CALLICOTT AV				
	6200	WdHl	91367	529-F7
	6600	CanP	91307	529-F6
CALMFIELD AV				
	5800	AGRH	91301	558-B3
CALUMET CANYON				
	-	VeCo	93015	466-F2
	-	VeCo	93021	466-F2
CALUMET CANYON RD				
	23600	VeCo	93015	466-G1
CALUSA AV				
	3000	SIMI	93063	479-B6
CALVADOS DR				
	-	CMRL	93012	525-A3
CALVERT CT				
	3000	VeCo	93012	496-E6
CALVERT ST				
	23800	WdHl	91367	529-C7
CALZONA CT				
	1500	SIMI	93065	497-F3
CAMARILLO AV				
	100	VeCo	93035	552-C6
CAMARILLO DR				
	-	CMRL	93010	494-C7
	-	VeCo	93010	494-C7
CAMARILLO RD				
	-	VeCo	93012	554-C3
CAMARILLO ST				
	-	VeCo	93012	554-E4
	-	CMRL	93012	524-F4
CAMARILLO CENTER DR				
	300	CMRL	93010	524-B4
CAMARILLO RANCH RD				
	23600	CMRL	93012	524-G3
CAMARILLO SPRINGS RD				
	600	CMRL	93012	525-B6
	600	VeCo	93012	525-C5
CAMBERWELL PL				
	1500	THO	91361	556-J6
CAMBON AV				
	2100	CMRL	93010	494-H7
CAMBON CIR				
	1100	VeCo	93023	451-C1
CAMBRIA AV				
	-	VEN	93004	492-G1
CAMBRIA CT				
	1100	CMRL	93010	524-E1
	3600	THO	91360	526-F1
CAMBRIDGE CT				
	29300	AGRH	91301	558-A4
	29400	AGRH	91301	557-J4
E CAMBRIDGE ST				
	14300	MRPK	93021	476-G6
CAMDEN CT				
	12900	MRPK	93021	496-E4
CAMDEN LN				
	1300	VEN	93001	491-F5
CAMDEN VISTA CT				
	23600	SIMI	93065	498-B5
CAMELIA DR				
	800	PHME	93041	552-F5
CAMELIA LN				
	200	VeCo	91377	557-J2
CAMELIA WY				
	100	VEN	93004	473-A7
CAMELLIA ST				
	900	OXN	93036	522-E3
CAMELOT WY				
	1000	OXN	93030	522-G4
	2000	OXN	93036	522-G4
CAMEO CT				
	1100	CMRL	93010	524-F2
CAMERON CT				
	-	VEN	93001	471-C6
CAMERON ST				
	100	SPLA	93060	463-H6
	800	VEN	93001	471-C6
CAMERTON CT				
	2000	VeCo	91361	556-H6
CAMILAR DR				
	2200	CMRL	93010	494-E7
S CAMILLE CT				
	800	VeCo	93023	451-B1
CAMILLE DR				
	1100	VeCo	93023	451-C1
CAMINITO LUISA				
	-	CMRL	93012	524-J1
CAMINITO MIRADOR				
	-	CMRL	93012	524-J1
CAMINITO POSADA				
	-	CMRL	93012	524-J1
CAMINO AV				
	3400	OXN	93030	523-D3
CAMINO AGUA DULCE				
	500	THO	91320	555-D3
CAMINO ALGARVE				
	3900	CMRL	93012	524-H4
CAMINO ALVAREZ				
	2200	CMRL	93010	494-H7
CAMINO AVELLANA				
	-	CMRL	93012	494-H7
CAMINO CALANDRIA				
	2800	THO	91360	526-G2
CAMINO CARILLO				
	200	CMRL	93012	525-A4
CAMINO CASTENADA				
	1300	CMRL	93010	524-B1
CAMINO CIELO				
	-	VeCo	-	366-J6
	-	VeCo	-	441-G1
	-	VeCo	93023	366-J6
	15400	VeCo	93023	441-D1
CAMINO COMPRADE				
	5600	CMRL	93012	525-A3
CAMINO CONCORDIA				
	500	VeCo	93010	493-J6
	600	VeCo	93010	494-A6
CAMINO CORTINA				
	200	CMRL	93010	524-A2
CAMINO CRISTOBAL				
	1300	VeCo	91360	526-B5
CAMINO DE CELESTE				
	400	THO	91360	526-D1
CAMINO DE LA LUNA				
	600	THO	91320	555-D3
	23600	OXN	93030	522-J4
CAMINO DE LA LUZ				
	600	THO	91320	555-D3
CAMINO DEL ARBOL				
	6200	CMRL	93012	525-C1
CAMINO DE LA ROSA				
	4300	THO	91320	555-D3
CAMINO DEL ARROYO				
	2000	VeCo	93023	442-B7
CAMINO DE LAS ESTRELLAS				
	4300	THO	91320	555-D3
CAMINO DEL CIELO				
	500	THO	91320	555-D3
CAMINO DEL LAGO				
	500	THO	91320	555-D3
CAMINO DEL MAR				
	600	THO	91320	555-D3
CAMINO DEL RIO				
	23600	VeCo	93040	458-D5
CAMINO DEL SOL				
	-	CALB	91302	558-H6
	300	OXN	93030	522-H5
	600	THO	91320	555-D3
	1800	OXN	93030	523-B5
	1800	VeCo	93030	522-H5
	1800	VeCo	93030	523-B5
CAMINO DEL ZURO				
	2900	THO	91360	526-G2
CAMINO DEVILLE				
	5600	CMRL	93012	525-B3
CAMINO DOS PALOS				
	300	THO	91360	526-G2
CAMINO DOS RIOS				
	600	VeCo	91360	526-C6
CAMINO DOS RIOS RD				
	2800	THO	91320	525-H7
CAMINO DURANGO				
	600	VeCo	91360	526-C7
CAMINO EL CARRIZO				
	700	VeCo	91360	526-C7
CAMINO EL RINCON				
	-	CMRL	93012	525-A3
CAMINO ESPLENDIDO				
	-	CMRL	93010	524-A2
CAMINO ESTRADA				
	1300	CMRL	93010	524-B1
CAMINO FLORES				
	700	VeCo	91360	526-C6
CAMINO GRACIOSA				
	2900	THO	91360	526-G2
CAMINO LA MADERA				
	900	CMRL	93010	524-B1
CAMINO LA MAIDA				
	500	THO	91360	526-G3
CAMINO LA POSADA				
	500	VeCo	93010	494-A6
CAMINO LAS CONCHAS				
	700	VeCo	91360	526-C6
CAMINO LAS RAMBLAS				
	700	CMRL	93012	495-D6
CAMINO LEON				
	-	CMRL	93012	525-A3
CAMINO MADERO				
	800	VeCo	91360	526-C7
CAMINO MAGENTA				
	1000	VeCo	91360	526-D6
CAMINO MANZANAS				
	200	THO	91360	526-E6
	400	VeCo	91360	526-C6
CAMINO OLMO				
	23600	THO	91320	525-J5
CAMINO RANCHERO				
	23600	CMRL	93012	524-G3
CAMINO ROBERTO				
	500	VeCo	91360	526-D6
CAMINO ROJO				
	500	VeCo	91360	526-D6
CAMINO RUIZ				
	100	CMRL	93012	524-J3
	1300	CMRL	93012	525-A4
CAMINO SANTO REYES				
	600	VeCo	91360	526-C7
CAMINO TIERRA SANTA				
	300	CMRL	93010	523-J2
CAMINO TOLUCA				
	200	CMRL	93010	524-A2
CAMINO VALLES				
	600	VeCo	91360	526-C7
CAMINO VALVERDE				
	3900	CMRL	93012	524-H4
CAMINO VERA CRUZ				
	1700	CMRL	93010	494-C7
	1700	CMRL	93010	524-C1
CAMINO VERDE				
	500	VeCo	91360	526-D6
CAMPANULA AV				
	1000	VeCo	93004	473-B7
	1000	VeCo	93004	493-B1
CAMPBELL AV				
	1400	THO	91360	526-D5
CAMPBELL WY				
	200	OXN	93033	552-G5
CAMP CHAFFEE RD				
	7900	VeCo	93001	460-J5
CAMPHOR AV				
	3800	THO	91320	555-E4
CAMPHOR CIR				
	900	THO	91320	555-E4
CAMPHOR ST				
	-	SIMI	93063	499-A4
CAMPO VERDE CT				
	600	VeCo	91377	557-J2
CAMP RAMAH RD				
	1100	VeCo	93023	441-F5
CAMPTON DR				
	100	OXN	93030	522-J6
CAMPUS DR				
	3400	THO	91360	526-E1
N CAMPUS DR				
	1800	OXN	93033	552-J3
	1800	OXN	93033	553-A3
S CAMPUS DR				
	1800	OXN	93033	552-J4
	1800	OXN	93033	553-A4
	3200	THO	91360	526-E2
CAMPUS RD				
	7000	MRPK	93021	477-A6
	7000	VeCo	93021	477-B5
CAMPUS ST				
	4600	VEN	93003	492-A3
E CAMPUS WY				
	4900	VEN	93003	492-A2
N CAMPUS WY				
	4800	VEN	93003	492-A2
S CAMPUS WY				
	4300	VEN	93003	492-A2
W CAMPUS WY				
	4300	VEN	93003	491-J2
	4300	VEN	93003	492-A2
CAMPUS PARK DR				
	14300	MRPK	93021	476-H6
	15400	MRPK	93021	477-A6
CAMP WILLETT RD				
	23600	VeCo	93001	451-D7
	23600	VeCo	93022	451-C7
CAMULOS ST				
	3100	VeCo	93015	457-D5
	3100	VeCo	93040	457-E4
CANADA ST				
	100	OJAI	93023	441-H6
CANADA DE ALISOS				
	23600	VeCo	93001	461-F4
CANADA LARGA RD				
	-	VeCo	93001	461-G5
CANAL ST				
	1000	OXN	93035	522-A7
CANARIO CT				
	4200	MRPK	93021	496-E3
CANARY LN				
	4000	OXN	93033	553-A4
CANARY ST				
	-	VEN	93003	492-D5
CANCUN ST				
	-	SIMI	93065	497-F4
CANDELARIA LN				
	-	FILM	93015	455-J4
CANDELARIA RD				
	100	OXN	93030	523-B6
CANDIA CT				
	1000	SIMI	93065	498-A1
CANDICE CT				
	3000	SIMI	93063	478-E7
CANDLECREST DR				
	600	THO	91362	557-D1
	800	THO	91362	527-D7
CANDLE PINE LN				
	23600	SIMI	93065	497-A1
CANDLEWOOD CT				
	13500	MRPK	93021	496-F3
CANDLEWOOD WY				
	23400	CanP	91307	529-E5
CANDYTUFT ST				
	-	VEN	93004	493-A2
CANET RD				
	23600	VeCo	93001	461-B6
CANFIELD CT				
	-	THO	91360	526-F2
CANGAS DR				
	5200	CALB	91301	558-G6
CANMORE ST				
	28900	AGRH	91301	558-A3
CANNA ST				
	2700	THO	91360	526-D3
CANNA WY				
	200	VEN	93004	473-A7
CANNES DR				
	1700	THO	91362	526-J2
CANNES SQ				
	4600	OXN	93035	552-A2
CANOGA PL				
	3300	CMRL	93010	524-G1
CANON CT				
	5700	VEN	93003	472-C7
CANON ST				
	5600	VEN	93003	472-B7
CANOPY DR				
	-	CMRL	93012	524-F5
CANTARA ST				
	22100	LA	91304	529-J2
CANTER AV				
	1500	CMRL	93010	524-D1
CANTERA ST				
	-	THO	91360	526-F1
CANTERBURY CT				
	100	VeCo	93023	441-E7
CANTERBURY DR				
	6000	AGRH	91301	558-A3
CANTERBURY LN				
	-	SIMI	93063	498-H1
CANTERBURY ST				
	4600	THO	91362	527-D6
CANTERBURY WY				
	200	OXN	93033	552-G5
CANTERFORD CIR				
	1100	THO	91361	557-C5
CANTERHILL PL				
	32000	WLKV	91361	557-C7
CANTLAY ST				
	22000	CanP	91303	529-J5
	22400	CanP	91307	529-G5
CANTRICE ST				
	500	SIMI	93065	527-D1
CANWOOD ST				
	26800	Ago	91301	558-F6
	26800	CALB	91301	558-F6
	28000	AGRH	91301	558-A6
	29300	AGRH	91301	557-G6
CANYON RD				
	200	VeCo	91320	556-B2
	23600	VeCo	93063	529-A1
CANYON WY				
	4800	AGRH	91301	558-C7
CANYON BREEZE CT				
	-	SIMI	93065	497-G7
CANYON CLUB CIR				
	1800	SIMI	93065	497-J1
	1800	SIMI	93065	478-A7
	1800	SIMI	93065	498-A1
CANYON CREST CT				
	3500	THO	91360	526-H2
	32100	WLKV	91361	557-C7
CANYON CREST DR				
	300	SIMI	93065	497-F7
	300	SIMI	93065	527-F1
N CANYONLANDS RD				
	4500	MRPK	93021	496-E2
CANYON OAKS DR				
	6500	SIMI	93063	499-C1
CANYON RIDGE DR				
	32100	WLKV	91361	557-C7
CANYON RIM CIR				
	1300	THO	91362	527-G7
CANYON VIEW				
	800	FILM	93015	456-A5
CANYON VIEW DR				
	23600	SIMI	93065	497-F7
	23600	SIMI	93065	527-F1
CANYON VISTA DR				
	1100	THO	91320	526-B7
CANYONWOOD CT				
	13400	MRPK	93021	496-F4
CANYONWOOD DR				
	24600	CanP	91307	529-C5
CANYON WREN CT				
	-	MRPK	93021	476-E6
CAPE HORN DR				
	5800	AGRH	91301	557-G4
CAPELLA WY				
	2600	THO	91362	527-C3
CAPELLO WY				
	1100	VeCo	93023	451-C1
CAPEWOOD LN				
	23600	SIMI	93065	497-A2
CAPISTRANO AV				
	6100	WdHl	91367	529-J7
	6500	CanP	91307	529-H5
	7600	LA	91304	529-H2
	9500	Chat	91311	499-H6
CAPISTRANO CT				
	300	CMRL	93010	524-D3
CAPITAN ST				
	100	THO	91320	556-C1
CAPRI AV				
	2700	VEN	93003	492-E6
CAPRI DR				
	100	VeCo	93065	497-F4
	400	SIMI	93065	497-F4
CAPRI WY				
	1000	OXN	93035	521-J7
	1200	OXN	93035	551-J1
CAPRICORN AV				
	6300	AGRH	91301	558-B3
CAPSTAN CIR				
	3700	WLKV	91361	557-C7
CAPSTAN DR				
	1700	OXN	93035	552-C1
CAPTAINS AV				
	2500	PHME	93041	552-D2
CAPTAINS PL				
	5300	AGRH	91301	557-G6
CARAWAY CT				
	3000	THO	91360	526-H2
CARDIFF CIR				
	1100	THO	91362	527-A6
CARDIGAN AV				
	1100	VEN	93004	492-G3
CARDINAL AV				
	2100	OXN	93033	553-B5
CARDINAL ST				
	5900	VEN	93003	492-C4
CARDINAL WY				
	5300	VeCo	91377	527-G7
CARDINAL RIDGE LN				
	23600	SIMI	93065	527-D1
CARDOZA DR				
	5800	WLKV	91362	557-F4
CAREFREE DR				
	900	SIMI	93065	497-G5
CARELL AV				
	5700	AGRH	91301	558-B4
CAREYBROOK DR				
	5900	AGRH	91301	558-A4
	5900	AGRH	91301	557-J4
CARGO RD				
	-	PHME	93043	552-C5
CARIBBEAN ST				
	-	OXN	93035	552-B1
CARILLO RD				
	200	OJAI	93023	441-F7
	200	OJAI	93023	451-F1
CARINA DR				
	-	OXN	93030	522-G4
CARISSA CT				
	800	CMRL	93012	525-B2
CARISSA DR				
	-	VEN	93004	493-A2
CARL CT				
	3400	VeCo	91320	555-F1
CARLA DR				
	200	SIMI	93065	497-F3
CARLA LN				
	8400	LA	91304	529-G2
CARLISLE CT				
	100	OXN	93033	552-G6
CARLISLE RD				
	100	VeCo	90265	586-C3
	100	VeCo	91361	586-C3
	600	THO	90265	586-E3
	600	THO	91361	586-E3
CARLMONT PL				
	2700	SIMI	93065	478-A7
	2700	SIMI	93065	498-A1
CARLOS ST				
	11000	VEN	93004	472-J7
	11000	VEN	93004	473-A7
CARLOTTA ST				
	4000	SIMI	93063	498-F2
CARLSBAD CT				
	2200	SIMI	93063	498-E2
CARLSBAD PL				
	1100	VEN	93003	492-B4
CARLSON CIR				
	22200	CanP	91303	529-J5
	22200	CanP	91307	529-J5
CARLTON DR				
	3200	THO	91360	526-G2
CARLYLE ST				
	10000	VEN	93004	492-J3
CARMEL CT				
	200	OXN	93033	553-C4
CARMEL DR				
	-	FILM	93015	456-C6
	1000	VeCo	93065	497-F4
CARMEL ST				
	8400	VEN	93004	492-G1
E CARMEL GREEN ST				
	100	PHME	93041	552-E2
W CARMEL GREEN ST				
	100	PHME	93041	552-D2
CARMELITA CT				
	100	OXN	93030	522-J5
CARMEN CT				
	2900	VeCo	91320	555-G1
CARMEN DR				
	1400	SIMI	93065	497-F3
	23600	CMRL	93010	524-D4
N CARMEN DR				
	100	CMRL	93010	524-D2
CARMEN WY				
	1500	OXN	93036	522-E2
CARMENITA LN				
	7500	LA	91304	529-D4
CARMENTO DR				
	5300	VeCo	91377	557-H1
CARNATION AV				
	1500	VEN	93004	493-A2
CARNATION CT				
	23600	SIMI	93065	497-G5
CARNATION PL				
	300	OXN	93036	522-F3
CARNE RD				
	500	VeCo	93023	442-D6
CARNEGIE CT				
	1800	OXN	93033	553-A2
CARNEGIE ST				
	100	OXN	93036	492-J6
	100	VeCo	93036	492-J6
CARNELLON CT				
	200	SIMI	93065	497-D7
CAROB DR				
	-	THO	91320	555-J1
CAROB ST				
	1900	OXN	93035	552-D1
CAROL DR				
	200	VEN	93003	491-H2
CAROLINE AV				
	6200	SIMI	93063	499-B3
CARPENTER ST				
	1400	THO	91362	527-A6
CARPENTERIA AV				
	7100	VeCo	93001	459-C4
CARR DR				
	-	VEN	93001	471-C7
CARRIAGE PL				
	100	FILM	93015	456-A7
CARRIAGE SQ				
	-	OXN	93030	522-G3
CARRIE PL				
	32500	WLKV	91361	557-B7
CARRILLO CT				
	-	FILM	93015	455-J4
CARRINGTON PT				
	-	VeCo	93012	554-F2
CARRIZO ST				
	200	VeCo	93023	441-D6
CARSON ST				
	1400	SIMI	93065	497-J3
CARSON WY				
	1500	VEN	93004	492-H3
CARTAGENA WY				
	-	OXN	93036	492-H7
CARTEGENA ST				
	100	CMRL	93010	524-D4
CARTHAGE WY				
	4900	VeCo	91377	557-H1
CARTPATH PL				
	-	SIMI	93065	497-D5
CARTY DR				
	400	OXN	93030	522-G5
CARVER CT				
	2200	SIMI	93063	498-D2
CARVER SUMMIT RD				
	23600	VeCo	93001	459-D3
CARY CT				
	3400	VeCo	91320	525-F7
CARYL DR				
	23600	VeCo	93033	584-B1
CASA ST				
	11100	VEN	93004	472-J6
	11200	VEN	93004	473-A6
CASABELLA CT				
	500	SPLA	93060	463-J7
CASA GRANDE RD				
	1000	VeCo	93063	499-C4
CASARIN AV				
	1500	SIMI	93065	497-J4
CASARIN ST				
	1700	SIMI	93065	497-J4
CASA SAN CARLOS				
	1300	OXN	93033	552-E2
CASCADE AV				
	100	THO	91362	557-C3
	200	OXN	93033	552-G4
CASCADES CT				
	1900	OXN	93036	522-D3
CASCARA CT				
	-	SIMI	93065	478-A5
CASE ST				
	4200	VEN	93003	491-J1
CASEY RD				
	100	MRPK	93021	476-D7
CASINO DR				
	2900	THO	91362	526-J2
	2900	THO	91362	527-A2
CASITAS CT				
	1100	VEN	93004	492-J2
CASITAS PASS RD Rt#-150				
	2000	VeCo	93001	450-D5
	3500	VeCo	93001	460-B1
	4000	VeCo	93001	366-G8
	4000	VeCo	93001	459-G1
	7100	StBC	93013	459-G1
CASITAS PASS RD Rt#-192				
	6800	StBC	93013	459-A1
CASITAS VISTA RD				
	500	VeCo	93001	460-G4
	7200	VeCo	93001	461-A5
CASMALIA CT				
	1300	SIMI	93065	497-H1
CASMALIA LN				
	800	VEN	93001	491-C1
CASNER WY				
	100	FILM	93015	456-B5
CASPER CT				
	4300	OXN	93033	553-A4
CASPER RD				
	2900	VeCo	93033	583-B2
	2900	VeCo	93042	583-C2
	4700	VeCo	93033	553-B7
CASPIAN CT				
	-	AGRH	91301	557-G4
CASPIAN WY				
	-	OXN	93035	522-B7
	-	OXN	93035	552-B1

STREET
Block City ZIP Pg-Grid

CASTANO DR
3500 CMRL 93010 524-G1
CASTANO ST
1600 CMRL 93010 524-G1
CASTELLO WY
4800 VeCo 91377 557-G2
CASTILLIAN AV
100 THO 91320 556-C1
CASTILLIAN CT
- THO 91320 556-C1
CASTILLO CIR
2600 THO 91360 526-C4
CASTILLO DE ROSA
- CMRL 93012 495-A6
CASTLE CT
2200 SIMI 93063 499-B1
CASTLEBRIDGE CT
1600 THO 91362 527-E6
CASTLE CREEK LN
- OXN 93036 522-C3
CASTLEHILL CT
1600 THO 91361 556-J5
CASTLEHILL DR
29300 AGRH 91301 558-A4
29300 AGRH 91301 557-J4
CASTLEMERE CT
1100 SIMI 93065 498-C4
N CASTLEMONT CT
2400 SIMI 93063 498-E1
CASTLE PEAK DR
6900 CanP 91307 529-C5
CASTLETON ST
- CMRL 93012 524-F4
CASTLEVIEW CT
1500 THO 91361 556-J5
CASTLEWOOD LN
- SIMI 93065 478-B4
CASUAL CT
1900 SIMI 93065 498-A7
CATALANO CT
- FILM 93015 455-J4
CATALINA DR
- VeCo 93010 494-D7
10500 VeCo 93022 451-B4
W CATALINA DR
- VeCo 93010 494-D7
10500 VeCo 93022 451-B5
CATALINA PL
- OXN 93035 522-D7
N CATALINA ST
- VEN 93001 491-F2
S CATALINA ST
- VEN 93001 491-F2
CATAMARAN ST
900 OXN 93035 521-J7
CATANIA CT
11800 MRPK 93021 496-C5
CATARINA DR
30800 WLKV 91362 557-F4
CATHEDRAL CV
- VeCo 93012 554-E3
CATHERWOOD CT
29000 AGRH 91301 558-A3
CATHY DR
100 VeCo 91320 555-G1
CATLIN CIR
800 SIMI 93065 497-H4
CATLIN CT
1100 SIMI 93065 497-H4
CATLIN ST
700 SIMI 93065 497-G4
CAVALIER AV
1000 SIMI 93065 498-C4
CAVENWAY LN
3000 THO 91361 557-C5
CAVIN RD
300 VeCo 93015 456-H7
CAWELTI RD
- VeCo 93012 524-C7
CAY CT
200 VeCo 91320 555-G1
CAYMAN CT
- THO 91320 555-E3
CAYO GRANDE CT
500 THO 91320 525-E7
500 THO 91320 555-F1
N CAYTON AV
1600 SIMI 93065 497-E3
N CAYTON PL
1500 SIMI 93065 497-E3
CAYUGA DR
1500 SIMI 93065 497-F3
8300 VEN 93004 492-G4
CAYUSE LN
2200 VEN 93001 471-D6
CEANOTHUS LN
700 VeCo 93023 442-F5
CEANOTHUS PL
3900 CALB 91302 558-G7
CEBOLLA DR
23600 CMRL 93012 524-J3
CEDAR
5100 OXN 93033 552-J5
CEDAR CT
800 OXN 93033 552-F1
CEDAR DR
- CMRL 93010 524-D4
CEDAR PL
200 VEN 93001 491-C1
CEDAR ST
- VEN 93001 491-B1
800 VEN 93001 471-D6
1400 SPLA 93060 464-A2
6000 VeCo 93063 499-B4
E CEDAR ST
100 OXN 93033 552-G1
W CEDAR ST
200 OXN 93033 552-E1
CEDARBARK CT
6600 VeCo 91377 528-B7
CEDAR BLUFF DR
900 MRPK 93021 476-E7
CEDAR BRANCH CT
4400 MRPK 93021 496-E3
CEDARBROOK WK
- CMRL 93012 524-H1
CEDARCLIFF CT
600 THO 91362 557-F1
CEDAR CREST CT
- THO 91320 556-C1
CEDARDALE RD
4300 MRPK 93021 496-C3
CEDARGLEN CT
4400 MRPK 93021 496-D3
CEDAR GROVE LN
4200 MRPK 93021 496-F3
CEDARHAVEN DR
5300 AGRH 91301 557-H5
CEDAR HEIGHTS DR
100 THO 91360 526-E3
CEDAR MEADOW CT
4300 MRPK 93021 496-D3
CEDARPINE LN
3900 MRPK 93021 496-F3
CEDAR POINT PL
300 THO 91362 557-G2
CEDAR RIDGE CT
2200 OXN 93036 522-D2
CEDAR SPRINGS ST
3900 MRPK 93021 496-C3
CEDARVALLEY DR
31200 WLKV 91362 557-E5
N CEDARWOOD CIR
2400 SIMI 93063 498-E1
CEDAR WOOD PL
2600 THO 91362 526-J3
CELESTIAL PL
- CMRL 93012 524-F5
E CELIA CT
3900 SIMI 93063 498-F2
CELSIUS AV
2200 OXN 93030 523-B5
CEMETERY RD
100 SPLA 93060 463-J6
CENTENNIAL AV
1000 CMRL 93010 524-E2
CENTER LN
400 SPLA 93060 463-H6
CENTER RD
- VeCo 93066 493-G3
900 VeCo 93066 494-B1
1000 VeCo 93066 474-B7
CENTER ST
3400 VeCo 93040 457-E4
E CENTER ST
- VEN 93001 491-B1
W CENTER ST
- VEN 93001 491-B1
CENTER COURT DR
2300 THO 91361 557-A6
CENTER SCHOOL RD
3100 VeCo 93010 494-B5
3400 VeCo 93066 494-B5
CENTINELLA ST
6100 SIMI 93063 499-B2
CENTRAL AV
100 FILM 93015 456-A5
100 VeCo 93036 492-J4
100 VeCo 93036 493-A4
500 CMRL 93010 523-E1
2500 VeCo 93010 493-D7
2500 VeCo 93010 523-E1
3000 VEN 93003 491-G3
CENTRAL CAMPUS WY
100 VEN 93003 492-A2
CENTURY AV
2200 SIMI 93063 498-E2
CENTURY PL
2100 SIMI 93063 498-E2
CERCIS WY
1400 VEN 93004 493-A2
CERES ST
100 SIMI 93065 497-F2
CERRO CREST DR
- VeCo 93010 494-B7
CERRO VISTA WY
1300 CMRL 93010 524-C1
1700 CMRL 93010 494-C7
CERVANTES CT
600 VeCo 91377 557-J2
CERVATO CT
- CMRL 93012 525-C1
CERVATO DR
1700 CMRL 93012 525-C1
1800 CMRL 93012 495-C7
CESAR CHAVEZ DR
- OXN 93030 523-A4
- VeCo 93030 522-H4
CESAR CHAVEZ DR
- VeCo 93030 523-A4
3400 OXN 93030 522-H4
CHADWICK CT
3500 THO 91320 555-F3
CHADWICK PL
23600 VEN 93003 492-B7
CHAFFEE ST
6300 VEN 93003 492-C1
CHAGALL DR
6000 VeCo 93021 475-H6
N CHAIN DR
2400 SIMI 93065 497-F1
CHALET CIR
1000 THO 91362 527-B7
CHALLENGE PL
23600 OXN 93030 523-C6
CHALLENGER CT
11900 MRPK 93021 496-C1
CHALMERS PL
25800 LACo 91302 558-J3
CHALMETTE AV
1100 VEN 93003 492-B4
W CHALON CT
- THO 91320 556-A2
W CHALON ST
1900 THO 91320 556-A2
1900 THO 91320 555-J2
CHAMBERLAIN ST
- VEN 93004 492-J3
CHAMBERS LN
500 SIMI 93065 497-G1
CHAMBERSBURG RD
Rt#-23
300 FILM 93015 466-A2
300 VeCo 93015 466-A2
CHAMINADE AV
7400 LA 91304 529-F4
CHAMISE CT
- SIMI 93063 498-J2
CHAMOIS ST
7100 VEN 93003 492-E5
CHAMPAGNE CT
30800 WLKV 91362 557-F5
CHAMPIONSHIP DR
- MRPK 93021 476-C5
CHAMPLAIN AV
1400 VEN 93004 492-H3
CHANCERY PL
2800 THO 91362 527-B3
CHANDLER AV
2400 SIMI 93065 497-H1
CHANDLER ST
2100 CMRL 93010 524-E2
CHANNEL DR
1800 VEN 93001 491-E3
2300 VEN 93003 491-F3
CHANNEL WY
900 SPLA 93060 473-J1
5200 OXN 93035 521-H6
CHANNELFORD RD
1900 THO 91361 557-A6
CHANNEL HEIGHTS CT
6200 VEN 93003 472-C6
CHANNEL ISLANDS BLVD
1800 OXN 93033 553-A2
2200 VeCo 93033 553-A2
E CHANNEL ISLANDS BLVD
100 OXN 93033 552-H2
100 PHME 93041 552-H2
300 PHME 93043 552-H2
W CHANNEL ISLANDS BLVD
100 OXN 93033 552-F2
100 PHME 93041 552-C2
300 PHME 93043 552-E2
500 PHME 93035 552-C2
3800 OXN 93035 552-A2
4500 VeCo 93035 552-A2
CHANNEL ISLANDS DR
- VeCo 93012 554-E2
CHANTILLY CIR
23600 SIMI 93065 497-F7
CHANTRY CIR
700 SIMI 93065 497-H5
CHAPALA DR
1300 CMRL 93010 524-D2
CHAPALA ST
400 CMRL 93010 524-D2
CHAPARRAL CT
700 THO 91320 556-C2
CHAPARRAL RD
500 VeCo 93022 451-A6
3800 VeCo 93023 442-E4
9200 Chat 91311 499-E7
9200 LA 91304 499-E7
9200 WHIL 91304 499-E7
CHAPARRAL ST
600 FILM 93015 455-J5
CHAPEL AV
1600 CMRL 93010 524-D3
CHAPEL DR
- VeCo 93012 554-E4
300 VEN 93003 491-J3
1300 CMRL 93010 524-D3
CHAPMAN PL
6700 MRPK 93021 476-H6
CHAPS CT
1700 SIMI 93063 499-C3
CHARI LN
6600 VeCo 93066 495-C3
CHARING CT
1800 SIMI 93063 499-D2
CHARING ST
6500 SIMI 93063 499-C2
CHARISMA CT
11200 VeCo 93012 496-C7
CHARLA CT
- THO 91320 556-B1
CHARLES ST
100 MRPK 93021 476-E7
5100 OXN 93033 552-G5
CHARLESTON PL
- VEN 93004 492-H2
CHARLOTTE ST
3000 THO 91320 555-G2
N CHARRO AV
100 THO 91320 556-C1
CHARTER OAK DR
2000 CMRL 93010 494-E7
CHARTERWOOD CT
1300 THO 91362 556-J1
CHARTHOUSE CIR
3800 WLKV 91361 557-B6
CHASE PL
22700 LA 91304 529-H2
CHASE ST
8400 LA 91304 529-F2
CHATEAU CT
5900 VEN 93003 492-C2
CHATHAM CT
1000 THO 91360 526-H2
CHATLAKE DR
8700 LA 91304 529-E1
CHATSWORTH ST
22000 Chat 91311 499-J3
CHAUCER
9400 VeCo 93012 495-G4
9400 VeCo 93021 495-G4
CHAUCER LN
6800 VEN 93003 492-E3
CHAUCER PL
2500 THO 91362 527-B3
CHAUTAUGUA DR
1300 SIMI 93063 499-C3
N CHEAM AV
2000 SIMI 93063 499-C2
CHEERFUL CT
200 SIMI 93065 497-J6
CHELAN CT
300 SIMI 93065 497-F6
CHELAN LN
1100 VEN 93004 492-H3
CHELMAS CT
23600 SIMI 93063 478-E6
CHELSEA CT
800 SIMI 93065 498-D5
6300 AGRH 91301 557-H3
CHELSEA LN
- LA 91304 529-J2
CHELSEY CT
2200 CMRL 93010 494-D7
CHELTERHAM CIR
800 THO 91360 526-G6
CHENAULT PL
2000 SIMI 93065 497-D2
CHERBOURG CT
30800 WLKV 91362 557-F5
CHEROKEE CIR
5700 SIMI 93063 479-A6
CHEROKEE CT
1300 CMRL 93010 524-F1
CHERRY AV
1200 SIMI 93065 498-B4
1500 OXN 93033 553-B5
CHERRY ST
3700 VEN 93003 491-J3
CHERRY CREEK CIR
800 THO 91362 557-G1
CHERRYGROVE ST
12100 MRPK 93021 496-D4
CHERRY HILL RD
1600 SPLA 93060 464-A1
CHERRY HILLS CT
- THO 91320 556-D1
CHERRY HILLS LN
400 THO 91320 556-D1
CHERRY RIDGE DR
5500 CMRL 93012 525-A2
CHERRY VALLEY CIR
4500 THO 91362 527-D6
CHERRYWOOD DR
3000 THO 91360 526-F2
CHERRYWOOD PL
900 OXN 93030 522-H3
CHERRYWOOD ST
- FILM 93015 456-B6
CHERYL CT
2700 SIMI 93063 478-D7
CHESAPEAKE CT
- THO 91320 555-E3
CHESAPEAKE DR
- OXN 93035 522-A7
- OXN 93035 552-A1
CHESAPEAKE PL
- VEN 93004 492-H2
CHESEBRO RD
5000 AGRH 91301 558-D3
5300 Ago 91301 558-D3
6300 VeCo 91377 528-C7
6300 VeCo 91377 558-D3
CHESEBRO CANYON RD
- VeCo 91377 528-D5
- VeCo 91377 558-E1
5800 Ago 91301 558-E5
CHESHIRE ST
8100 VEN 93004 492-F4
CHESHIRE HILLS CT
- THO 91361 556-H5
CHESSHIRE CT
100 VeCo 93023 441-E7
CHESTER WY
200 OXN 93033 552-G5
CHESTERFIELD DR
13600 MRPK 93021 496-F2
CHESTERTON ST
2000 SIMI 93065 498-A1
CHESTNUT LN
3300 VeCo 93012 495-J5
CHESTNUT PL
5800 CMRL 93012 495-B7
CHESTNUT ST
- SIMI 93063 498-J1
700 THO 91320 556-C2
N CHESTNUT ST
- VEN 93001 491-C2
S CHESTNUT ST
- VEN 93001 491-C2
CHESTNUT HILL CT
300 THO 91360 526-E7
CHESTNUT RIDGE ST
11600 MRPK 93021 496-B4
CHESWICK PL
1500 THO 91361 556-J6
CHEVIOT HILLS CT
- THO 91361 556-J6
CHEYENNE AV
- THO 91362 557-A2
11200 Chat 91311 499-J1
CHEYENNE CIR
9900 VEN 93004 492-J3
CHEYENNE ST
9800 VEN 93004 492-H3
CHEYENNE WY
900 OXN 93033 552-J3
N CHICKADEE LN
1100 VEN 93003 492-F3
S CHICKADEE LN
1300 VEN 93003 492-F4
CHICO CT
2300 VeCo 93035 552-B5
CHICO DR
9200 VEN 93004 492-G2
CHICO RD
100 OJAI 93023 441-G7
CHICO LARSON WY
- VeCo - 366-L2
CHICORY LEAF PL
23600 SIMI 93063 498-D4
CHIEF CIR
3400 THO 91360 526-C2
CHILCO CT
1600 THO 91360 526-C5
CHINA FIR PL
23600 SIMI 93065 498-D4
CHINA FLATS RD
1000 VeCo 91361 556-F5
CHINOOK DR
600 VEN 93001 471-D6
CHIPMUNK CIR
7000 VEN 93003 492-F4
CHIPPENDALE AV
- SIMI 93065 497-D6
CHIPPENHAM RD
10600 VeCo 93012 495-J7
10600 VeCo 93012 496-A7
CHIPPEWA AV
2800 SIMI 93063 479-A7
CHIPPEWA LN
2300 VEN 93001 471-C6
CHIQUITA LN
2200 THO 91362 556-J2
2200 THO 91362 557-A2
CHISHOLM TR
- THO 91320 555-H2
CHISMAHOO RD
23600 VeCo - 366-G8
23600 VeCo 93001 366-G8
CHISMAHOO FIRE RD
23600 VeCo 93001 460-C2
CHOCTAW AV
2900 SIMI 93063 479-A7
CHOCTAW LN
400 VEN 93001 471-C6
CHRISMAN AV
- VEN 93001 491-E2
CHRISTIAN CT
5300 AGRH 91301 557-H5
CHRISTIAN BARRETT DR
13300 MRPK 93021 496-F3
CHRISTINA AV
5600 CMRL 93012 525-B6
CHRISTINA CT
1200 CMRL 93010 524-C2
CHRISTINE AV
1400 SIMI 93063 499-B2
CHRISTOPHER LN
100 VeCo 93023 441-E7
CHUKAR LN
200 VeCo 93010 494-F7
CHULA VISTA CT
4700 CMRL 93012 524-J2
CHUMASH AV
2900 SIMI 93063 478-J7
CHUMASH RD
12000 VeCo 93023 453-B1
CHUMASH TR
23600 VeCo 90265 625-G1
CHURCH DR
2000 VEN 93003 492-C5
CHURCH RD
400 OJAI 93023 441-F7
1500 THO 91362 526-J5
CHURCH ST
500 VeCo 93040 457-F4
700 VEN 93001 491-C1
N CHURCH ST
1400 SIMI 93065 498-D3
CHURCHILL DR
2100 OXN 93033 553-A2
4000 THO 91320 555-E3
CHURCHMAN LN
10200 VeCo 93012 495-J7
CHURCHWOOD DR
5100 VeCo 91377 557-H1
N CICERO CT
3000 SIMI 93063 478-F7
CID ST
11300 VEN 93004 473-A7
CIELO CIR
- CALB 91302 558-H6
CIELO VISTA CT
5800 CMRL 93012 495-B7
CIMA DE LAGO ST
9200 Chat 91311 499-E7
CIMARRON AV
1200 VEN 93004 492-J3
CIMMARON AV
2600 SIMI 93065 478-C7
2600 SIMI 93065 498-C1
N CINCH RD
- VeCo 91307 529-A4
CINCO DE MAYO
10200 VEN 93004 492-J3
10200 VEN 93004 493-A2
CINDY AV
- THO 91320 555-H1
CINDY PL
2600 PHME 93041 552-D2
CINERARIA ST
- VEN 93004 493-A2
CINNABAR PL
700 SIMI 93065 498-D5
CINNAMON OAK AV
- VEN 93004 473-A6
CIPRES CT
1400 CMRL 93010 524-D2
CIPRIAN AV
1700 CMRL 93010 494-G7
1700 CMRL 93010 524-G1
CIRCLE DR
2900 OXN 93033 552-H3
CIRCLE KNOLL DR
- SIMI 93065 527-C1
CIRCLE VIEW DR
2700 SIMI 93063 478-D7
CIRCULO JARDIN
23600 CMRL 93010 523-F2
CIRO AV
2400 THO 91360 526-E3
CIRO CIR
300 THO 91360 526-E4
CIRRUS WY
7200 CanP 91307 529-F5
CISCO CT
2900 SIMI 93063 478-G7
CITADEL AV
300 VEN 93003 492-A3
CITATION WY
400 THO 91320 526-B7
CITRONELLA CT
2600 SIMI 93063 498-E1
CITRONELLA ST
3600 SIMI 93063 498-E1
CITRUS DR
4000 VeCo 93021 496-A3
10700 VeCo 93021 495-J4
11000 VEN 93004 472-J7
11000 VEN 93004 473-A7
11100 VeCo 93004 473-A7
CITRUS ST
300 SPLA 93060 464-C4
3000 VeCo 93036 492-J7
CITRUS GROVE LN
- OXN 93036 522-G3
CITRUS VIEW DR
4000 VeCo 93040 457-F4
CIVIC ARTS PLAZA DR
1600 THO 91362 556-J2
CIVIC CENTER WY
23600 THO 91360 526-E7
CLAIRE CT
- THO 91320 555-F2
CLANCY CT
- SIMI 93065 497-E2
CLARA ST
6200 VeCo 93003 492-D5
E CLARA ST
100 OXN 93033 552-G6
100 PHME 93041 552-E5
800 PHME 93033 552-E5
W CLARA ST
100 OXN 93033 552-F5
100 PHME 93041 552-E5
CLAREMONT DR
1500 OXN 93035 552-D1
CLAREMONT WY
- VEN 93003 492-A2
CLARENDON PL
3300 THO 91360 526-H2
CLARETON DR
5100 AGRH 91301 558-B6
CLARIDGE CT
3500 SIMI 93063 478-G5
CLARINGTON DR
23900 LA 91304 529-D4
CLARITA CT
2500 THO 91362 527-C3
CLARK CT
200 OXN 93033 552-G6
CLARKE RANCH RD
- LACo 90265 586-G6
CLARKIA ST
- SIMI 93065 477-J5
- SIMI 93065 478-A5
CLARK RANCH RD
23600 VeCo 93022 451-E4
23600 VeCo 93023 451-E4
CLASSIC ROSE CT
1700 THO 91362 527-C6
CLAUDIA AV
1600 SIMI 93065 498-B3
CLAVEL AV
1200 VeCo 93004 493-B1
1200 VEN 93004 493-B1
CLAVELE AV
4300 MRPK 93021 496-E3
CLAVELE CT
4300 MRPK 93021 496-E3
CLAY AV
1100 VEN 93004 492-J2
CLAY BLVD
23600 VeCo 93060 453-G2
CLAY CT
- THO 91360 556-G1
CLAY ST
200 FILM 93015 456-A5
CLAYBOURNE CT
3500 THO 91320 555-F3
CLAYFORD AV
1100 THO 91361 557-A5
CLAYTON CT
1200 CMRL 93010 524-D1
CLAYTON WY
1400 SIMI 93065 497-H3
CLEAR DR
8600 VEN 93004 492-G4
CLEARCREEK CT
4400 MRPK 93021 496-B3
CLEARFIELD PL
2500 SIMI 93065 497-J1
CLEARFORD CT
3900 WLKV 91361 557-D6
CLEAR HAVEN DR
700 VeCo 91377 558-B1
CLEAR SKY PL
23600 SIMI 93065 497-E4
CLEAR SPRINGS RD
6400 VeCo 93063 499-C4
CLEARVIEW AV
2500 VEN 93001 491-F4
CLEARVIEW ST
100 THO 91360 526-F3
CLEARWATER DR
1700 CMRL 93012 495-B7
1700 CMRL 93012 525-B1
CLEARWATER ST
2500 THO 91362 557-B3
CLEARWATER CREEK DR
- THO 91320 555-F3
CLEARWOOD RD
4300 MRPK 93021 496-C3
CLEE CT
5500 AGRH 91301 558-A5
CLEMENS AV
8000 LA 91304 529-F3
CLEMENS ST
6300 VEN 93003 492-C1
CLEMSON ST
5200 VEN 93003 492-B2
14100 MRPK 93021 476-G6
CLEOMOORE AV
6500 CanP 91307 529-E6
CLERMONT CT
5400 WLKV 91362 557-F5
CLEVELAND CT
100 VEN 93003 492-E1
CLEVELAND DR
2800 OXN 93036 492-H7
28600 AGRH 91301 558-B6
CLEVENGER PL
100 SIMI 93065 497-E7
100 SIMI 93065 527-E1
CLIFF AV
700 VeCo 93015 455-G4
CLIFF DR
900 SPLA 93060 464-C3
CLIFFHOLLOW CT
500 SIMI 93065 527-C1
CLIFFROSE AV
4000 MRPK 93021 496-E4
CLIFFSIDE CIR
5300 VEN 93003 492-B1
CLIFFSIDE CT
- LA 91304 529-E4
CLIFFWOOD DR
200 SIMI 93065 497-E2
CLIFTON CT
700 SIMI 93065 497-J5
CLINTON AV
1000 VEN 93004 492-H3
CLINTON CIR
3100 OXN 93033 552-H3
8800 VEN 93004 492-G3
CLINTON CT
8800 VEN 93004 492-G3
CLINTON ST
3000 OXN 93033 552-H3
11800 VeCo 93021 476-C2
CLIPPER DR
500 OXN 93033 552-G5
CLIPPERS CIR
2300 THO 91361 557-B6
CLOUD CT
1800 SIMI 93065 498-A2
CLOUDCREST CT
200 THO 91320 555-G2
CLOUDPEAK ST
- THO 91360 526-F2
CLOVER DR
4300 OXN 93033 552-H5
CLOVER LN
- VEN 93004 493-A2
CLOVER ST
2000 SIMI 93065 498-C2
E CLOVERDALE ST
4300 MRPK 93021 496-E3
N CLOVERDALE ST
12800 MRPK 93021 496-E3
CLOVERLEAF LN
- SIMI 93063 498-H1
CLOVERLEAF ST
3900 THO 91362 527-C6
CLOVERLY ST
5900 VEN 93003 492-C2
CLOVERWOOD AV
100 THO 91320 555-J2
CLOW RD
200 VeCo 93060 473-G2
S CLOW RD
- VeCo 93060 473-H2
CLOYNE ST
2900 OXN 93033 552-H3
CLUB CT
- CMRL 93010 493-H7
CLUBHOUSE DR
- LACo 90265 586-H7
200 SIMI 93065 497-E2
3900 VeCo 93066 493-F2
CLUB VIEW DR
4500 THO 91362 527-D6
CLYDESDALE CIR
4100 THO 91362 527-C6
CMWD TANK RD
- VeCo 93023 442-G7
- VeCo 93023 452-G1
COACHMAN CIR
4200 THO 91362 527-D7
COACHMAN DR
1700 CMRL 93012 495-A7
1700 CMRL 93012 525-A1
COALFAX CT
2200 THO 91362 527-A4
COASTAL OAK DR
23600 SIMI 93063 498-D4
23600 SIMI 93065 498-D4
COATI PL
7300 VEN 93003 492-F5
COATS ST
- PHME 93041 552-E4
- PHME 93043 552-E4
COBALT AV
- VEN 93004 492-F3
COBB CIR
3000 SIMI 93065 498-D4
COBBLECREEK CT
2500 THO 91362 527-D3
COBBLER HILL CT
700 SIMI 93065 498-D5
COBBLESTONE DR
6000 AGRH 91301 557-J3
6000 VEN 93003 492-C1
COCHE CANYON
23600 VeCo 93001 451-G7
23600 VeCo 93001 461-G1
COCHISE ST
5400 SIMI 93063 478-J7
COCHRAN ST
- SIMI 93063 479-B7
COCHRAN ST
- SIMI 93065 497-G1
200 SIMI 93065 477-E7
1700 SIMI 93065 498-B1
3100 SIMI 93063 498-D1
5400 SIMI 93063 499-A1
COCOS CT
4000 VEN 93003 491-J3
CODY AV
1600 SIMI 93063 499-C3
COE ST
700 CMRL 93010 524-C2
COFFEETREE LN
- MRPK 93021 496-G2
COHASSET ST
22000 CanP 91303 529-J4
22600 CanP 91307 529-G4
23200 LA 91304 529-F4
COLBY CIR
300 VEN 93003 492-A3
1000 THO 91362 526-J6
COLCHESTER PL
1500 VeCo 91377 527-H6
COLDBROOK PL
600 SIMI 93065 497-H5
COLD SPRINGS ST
26800 CALB 91301 558-G7
COLD STREAM CT
2000 OXN 93036 522-E3
COLE AV
3200 VeCo 93063 478-E6
COLEMAN CT
2000 SIMI 93063 499-A2
COLETTE CT
3100 SIMI 93063 478-D6
COLGATE DR
1700 THO 91360 526-G5
COLGATE ST
300 SPLA 93060 463-J7
300 SPLA 93060 464-A7
COLIBRI CT
4200 MRPK 93021 496-E3
COLINA RD
23600 VeCo 93063 499-F3
COLINA VISTA
400 VEN 93003 472-C6
400 VEN 93003 492-D1
COLINA VISTA ST
28700 AGRH 91301 558-B3
COLISEUM ST
4100 VEN 93003 491-J2
COLLEEN AV
1700 SIMI 93063 498-J3
COLLEGE DR
- VEN 93003 491-J3
COLLEGE ST
2400 SIMI 93065 498-B5
COLLEGE HEIGHTS DR
6400 MRPK 93021 476-G6
COLLEGE VIEW AV
6400 MRPK 93021 477-A6
COLLEGIATE CIR
15200 MRPK 93021 476-J5
COLLIER CT
2200 SIMI 93065 498-A2
COLLINGSWOOD CT
1700 THO 91362 527-E6
COLLINGSWOOD PL
4800 THO 91362 527-E6
COLLINS DR
6400 MRPK 93021 476-J6
6500 MRPK 93021 477-A5
E COLLINS ST
200 VeCo 93036 492-H7
200 VeCo 93036 522-J1
700 VeCo 93036 523-A1
1000 OXN 93036 523-A1
W COLLINS ST
100 OXN 93036 492-H7
COLODNY DR
5200 AGRH 91301 558-D5
COLOMA CIR
5500 SIMI 93063 479-A7
COLONETT PL
3900 THO 91320 555-E1
COLONIA AV
2400 OXN 93036 522-H1
2700 OXN 93036 492-H7
COLONIA PL
1700 CMRL 93010 524-D3
COLONIA RD
1300 OXN 93030 522-G5
COLONY DR
4600 CMRL 93012 524-J2
5100 CMRL 93012 525-A2
COLORADO RIVER PL
- OXN 93036 492-G7
COLT LN
700 VeCo 91361 556-G3
E COLT LN
- VeCo 91307 528-J4
- VeCo 91307 529-A4
COLT ST
4800 VEN 93003 492-B6
COLTON ST
7700 VEN 93004 492-F2
23600 VEN 93003 492-E2
COLTRANE ST
- VEN 93003 492-C4
N COLUMBIA AV
6500 MRPK 93021 476-H6
COLUMBIA CT
800 OXN 93033 552-H4
COLUMBIA DR
700 OXN 93033 552-H4
1800 VEN 93004 492-G4
COLUMBIA PL
100 OXN 93033 552-H4
COLUMBIA RD
- THO 91360 526-F5
COLUMBINE CT
2800 THO 91360 526-D3
COLUMBUS PL
5100 OXN 93033 552-G5
COLUSA AV
300 VEN 93004 472-F7
300 VEN 93004 492-F1
COMANCHE AV
2700 THO 91362 557-A2
COMANCHE CT
900 CMRL 93010 524-C2
2500 VEN 93001 471-D5
COMBES AV
500 THO 91360 526-G7
COMBS RD
1100 VeCo 91320 556-B2
1200 THO 91320 556-B2
COMET AV
600 SIMI 93065 498-C5
COMMERCE AV
23600 MRPK 93021 496-C1
COMMERCIAL AV
100 OXN 93030 522-H6
1200 OXN 93030 552-H1
COMMONS PARK DR
- CMRL 93012 524-F5
COMMONWEALTH CIR
- THO 91361 556-H5
COMMUNITY ST
23200 LA 91304 529-E2
COMPASS WY
- PHME 93041 552-E5
COMSTOCK DR
- VEN 93001 471-C6
COMSTOCK PL
1200 THO 91320 555-G5
CONCERTO DR
200 VeCo 91377 557-G2
CONCHA ST
- OXN 93030 522-J4
N CONCHO LN
- VeCo 91307 529-B3
CONCORD AV
700 VEN 93004 492-H2
CONCORD CT
3700 OXN 93033 552-J3
E CONCORD CT
1900 SIMI 93065 498-A5
CONCORD DR
2900 OXN 93033 552-J3
CONCORD WY
4400 OXN 93033 552-J4
CONDOR CT
300 FILM 93015 455-H6
6300 VEN 93003 492-D5
CONDOR DR
5700 MRPK 93021 476-H7
CONEFLOWER ST
2800 THO 91360 526-D3
CONEJO BLVD
- THO 91360 556-F1
CONEJO CANYON CT
2600 THO 91362 527-B4
CONEJO CENTER DR
- THO 91320 525-H5
CONEJO MESA ST
4000 MRPK 93021 496-E4
CONEJO RIDGE AV
200 THO 91361 556-J3
CONEJO SCHOOL RD
100 THO 91361 556-J2
100 THO 91362 556-J2
200 THO 91362 557-A1
600 THO 91362 527-A7
CONEJO SPECTRUM ST
- THO 91320 525-H5
CONEJO VIEW DR
28500 AGRH 91301 558-B5
CONESTOGA CIR
800 THO 91320 555-G6
CONGRESSIONAL RD
600 SIMI 93065 497-C6
CONIFER CIR
5600 VeCo 91377 557-J2
CONIFER ST
5700 VeCo 91377 557-J2
5700 VeCo 91377 558-A2
N CONNELL AV
2100 SIMI 93063 499-A2
CONNER CT
- THO 91320 555-E3
CONNER DR
- OXN 93033 552-G6
CONSTITUTION AV
400 CMRL 93012 524-F5
CONSUELO AV
3600 THO 91360 526-F1

STREET
Block City ZIP Pg-Grid

CONTAINER WY
- PHME 93043 552-C6
CONTINENTAL CT
300 THO 91320 555-G3
CONTRA COSTA AV
200 VEN 93004 492-F1
200 VEN 93004 472-F7
CONVAIR ST
400 CMRL 93010 523-J4
CONVERSE RD
23600 VeCo 93066 473-J2
23600 VeCo 93066 474-A2
CONWAY AV
1200 VEN 93004 492-H3
COOK CIR
2100 THO 91360 526-F4
COOK DR
100 FILM 93015 456-B5
COOLHAVEN CT
4500 WLKV 91361 557-D6
COOLIDGE ST
7200 VEN 93003 492-E2
N COOLWATER RD
- VeCo 91307 529-A3
COOPER RD
100 OXN 93030 522-H5
COOPER CANYON RD
- VeCo 93023 450-G1
COOSA ST
9600 VEN 93004 492-H3
COPA DE ORO CT
1600 THO 91362 556-J1
COPLAND CIR
- VEN 93003 492-A4
- VeCo 93003 492-A4
COPLAND DR
4500 VEN 93003 492-A7
E COPLEY ST
3100 SIMI 93063 498-D2
N COPLEY ST
2100 SIMI 93063 498-D2
2100 SIMI 93065 498-D2
COPPER CREEK PL
- MRPK 93021 476-D6
COPPERFIELD ST
3500 SIMI 93063 498-D1
COPPER RIDGE CT
- SIMI 93063 478-H5
COPPERSTONE LN
- SIMI 93065 478-C4
COPPERTREE CT
23600 SIMI 93065 498-B5
CORAL LN
1800 OXN 93033 552-J2
1800 OXN 93033 553-A2
CORAL ST
1100 VEN 93001 491-F5
CORAL WY
4900 OXN 93035 521-J7
CORALBELL LN
22200 WdHl 91367 529-J7
CORALBERRY CT
11500 MRPK 93021 496-B2
CORALCREST CT
12600 MRPK 93021 496-D4
CORAL GUM LN
- SIMI 93065 478-C7
CORAL PINK CIR
6100 WdHl 91367 529-J7
CORAL REEF LN
11800 VeCo 90265 625-F5
CORAL TREE LN
5300 VeCo 91377 527-G7
CORBETT LN
1100 SIMI 93065 497-H4
CORBINA WY
5000 OXN 93035 551-J1
5000 OXN 93035 552-A1
CORBY AV
3000 CMRL 93010 524-F1
3400 CMRL 93010 494-G7
CORD AV
- THO 91362 557-B4
CORDERO AV
2100 SIMI 93065 497-J2
2100 SIMI 93065 498-A2
CORDOVA CT
3500 THO 91320 525-F7
3500 VeCo 91320 525-F7
CORDOVA DR
- FILM 93015 456-C6
CORDOVA ST
100 OXN 93030 523-A5
500 CMRL 93010 524-C1
500 VeCo 93010 524-C1
CORDUA CT
3000 SIMI 93063 478-E7
CORIE LN
6700 LACo 91307 529-D6
CORINNE DR
- THO 91320 555-J1
CORINTH WEIGH
1900 OXN 93035 552-B1
CORKWOOD DR
- MRPK 93021 496-H3
CORLSON AV
2200 SIMI 93063 498-E2
CORLSON PL
2200 SIMI 93063 498-E2

CORNELL CIR
6400 MRPK 93021 476-H6
CORNELL DR
500 SPLA 93060 473-J1
500 SPLA 93060 474-A1
CORNELL PL
300 VEN 93003 492-A3
CORNELL RD
3900 Ago 91301 558-A7
4400 AGRH 91301 558-A6
CORNELL WY
4600 AGRH 91301 558-A6
CORNETT AV
300 MRPK 93021 496-E1
CORNING ST
3300 THO 91320 555-G3
CORNWALL DR
600 OXN 93035 522-D6
CORNWALL LN
1100 VEN 93001 491-E4
CORONA CIR
500 VEN 93003 472-E7
CORONA ST
3300 CMRL 93010 524-G1
CORONADO CIR
- SPLA 93060 464-B3
3700 THO 91320 555-E1
CORONADO CT
1600 CMRL 93010 524-D3
CORONADO DR
100 FILM 93015 456-C6
CORONADO PL
500 OXN 93030 522-E4
CORONADO ST
- VEN 93001 491-F3
CORPORATE CENTER DR
2000 THO 91320 525-J6
CORPORATION ST
600 SPLA 93060 473-J1
CORPUS CHRISTI AV
2800 SIMI 93063 478-H6
N CORRAL RD
- VeCo 91307 528-H4
CORRAL ST
- SIMI 93063 478-H5
CORRIENTE CT
1100 VeCo 93010 494-C7
CORRINE HILL CT
200 THO 91320 556-D2
CORSA AV
5700 WLKV 91362 557-F4
CORSICANA DR
- VeCo 93036 492-J7
600 VeCo 93036 522-J1
700 VeCo 93036 523-A1
CORTA ST
300 VeCo 93023 451-D2
CORTE AGUACATE
600 CMRL 93010 524-B1
CORTE AMIGOS
2600 CMRL 93010 494-F7
CORTE ANTIGUA
6000 CMRL 93012 525-B5
CORTE ARBUSTO
- CMRL 93012 494-H7
CORTE AUGUSTA
800 CMRL 93010 523-H1
CORTE AZAL
800 CMRL 93010 524-C1
CORTE BARATA
6100 CMRL 93012 525-C5
CORTE BARROSO
900 CMRL 93010 523-G2
CORTE BAYA VISTA
23600 OXN 93030 523-C7
CORTE BOCINA
- CMRL 93012 524-J1
- CMRL 93012 525-A1
CORTE BREVE
1400 THO 91360 526-H1
CORTE CABALLOS
2700 CMRL 93010 494-F7
CORTE CAMPANERO
1200 CMRL 93010 493-J6
CORTE CAMPINA
6300 CMRL 93012 525-C5
CORTE CANCION
3600 THO 91360 526-J1
CORTE CASTANO
600 CMRL 93010 524-B1
CORTE CERRITOS
- CMRL 93010 524-B1
CORTE CIMA
1600 THO 91360 526-J1
CORTE COLINA
600 CMRL 93010 524-B1
CORTE CORRIDA
300 CMRL 93010 523-J1
CORTE DE ACERO
3600 THO 91360 526-J2
CORTE DE CHARCO
6500 VEN 93003 472-D7
CORTE DE ENCINITAS
1500 CMRL 93010 493-H6
CORTE DE LOS REYES
3600 THO 91360 526-H1
CORTE DEL REY
3600 THO 91360 526-J1

CORTE DE PRIMAVERA
1200 THO 91360 526-H1
CORTE DE QUINTERO
600 CMRL 93010 493-J5
CORTE DESCANSO
1000 SPLA 93060 473-F1
CORTE DE TAJO
1000 THO 91360 526-H1
CORTE ELEGANTE
- CMRL 93010 523-J2
- CMRL 93010 524-A2
CORTE ENTRADA
1300 THO 91360 526-H1
CORTE ESPALDERA
- CMRL 93012 525-A1
CORTE ESTIMA
- CMRL 93012 524-J1
- CMRL 93012 525-A1
CORTE ESTRELLA
- CMRL 93010 523-J2
- CMRL 93010 524-A2
CORTE FRESCA
23600 CMRL 93012 524-H3
CORTE FRONDOSA
600 CMRL 93010 523-H1
CORTE GOLONDRINA
600 CMRL 93010 524-B1
CORTE GRANADA
1000 SPLA 93060 473-F1
CORTE JANA
23600 OXN 93030 523-C7
CORTE JUBILO
- CMRL 93012 525-C1
CORTE LA BRISA
15500 SPLA 93060 463-H7
CORTE LA CIENAGA
600 CMRL 93010 523-H2
CORTE LAS HOLAS
23600 OXN 93030 523-B4
CORTE LEJOS
23600 CMRL 93010 524-C4
CORTE LINDA
200 SPLA 93060 473-F1
CORTE LUCINDA
6100 CMRL 93012 525-C5
CORTE MALPASO
3200 CMRL 93012 524-G2
CORTE MIRA FLORES
1000 SPLA 93060 463-H7
1000 SPLA 93060 473-H1
CORTE MONARCA
- CMRL 93012 524-J1
CORTE OLIVAS
23600 CMRL 93012 524-J1
CORTE OLMO
2600 CMRL 93010 494-E7
CORTE PALOMA
1000 SPLA 93060 473-F1
CORTE PASTORAL
600 CMRL 93010 523-H2
CORTE PICADO
6000 CMRL 93012 525-B5
CORTE PICO VERDE
5300 CMRL 93012 525-A2
CORTE PINATA
6900 CMRL 93012 495-D7
CORTE PRIMAVERA
23600 OXN 93030 523-C6
CORTE REGALO
- CMRL 93010 523-J2
- CMRL 93010 524-A2
CORTE RIVIERA
23600 CMRL 93010 523-H2
CORTE ROSELINDA
700 CMRL 93010 524-C1
CORTE SAFIRO
800 CMRL 93012 525-B5
CORTE SOL
- CMRL 93010 523-J2
CORTE TELA
2600 CMRL 93010 494-E7
CORTE TIARA
- CMRL 93012 524-J1
CORTE TULAROSA
1000 CMRL 93010 523-G1
CORTE TUNITAS
700 CMRL 93012 525-C5
CORTE VALDEZ
23600 OXN 93030 523-C7
CORTE VERANO
1400 THO 91360 526-H1
CORTE VIENTO
- CMRL 93010 523-J2
CORTE VINA
700 CMRL 93010 524-C1
CORTE VISTORA
23600 CMRL 93012 524-J2
CORTEZ CIR
- CMRL 93012 525-A4
CORTEZ ST
2400 VeCo 93036 522-H1
3000 VeCo 93036 492-J7
3500 VeCo 93036 493-A7
CORTO DR
6000 VeCo 93063 499-B3
CORTO ST
300 SPLA 93060 464-C6
2700 SIMI 93065 498-C3
14600 SIMI 93063 498-D4

CORTO TR
1900 OXN 93036 522-H3
CORVALLIS CT
1100 VEN 93004 492-J2
CORVETTE ST
400 PHME 93041 552-C1
CORVUS DR
- VeCo 93041 583-G2
CORY ST
6200 SIMI 93063 499-B2
COSMOS AV
- VEN 93004 493-A1
COSMOS CT
400 THO 91360 526-D3
COSTA DE ORO
4400 OXN 93035 552-A1
COSTA MESA ST
7800 VEN 93004 492-F1
COTA CIR
3000 OXN 93033 552-J3
COTHARIN RD
9100 VeCo 90265 585-E6
11700 VeCo 90265 625-E1
COTTAGE CT
1100 VEN 93001 491-D2
COTTAGE GROVE AV
100 CMRL 93012 524-H4
COTTAGES CT
- CMRL 93012 524-F4
COTTONTAIL AV
- SIMI 93063 498-J1
COTTONTAIL RD
23600 MRPK 93021 496-C2
COTTONTAIL ST
7000 VEN 93003 492-E5
COTTONWOOD AV
900 VeCo 93023 451-C1
COTTONWOOD CT
2800 THO 91320 555-G3
COTTONWOOD DR
- SIMI 93063 478-G5
COTTONWOOD LN
1400 FILM 93015 455-H7
COTTONWOOD GROVE TR
3800 CALB 91301 558-G7
COULTER CT
1000 SIMI 93065 498-C4
COUNTRY CT
600 FILM 93015 455-J5
600 FILM 93015 456-A5
COUNTRY DR
500 VeCo 93023 451-D2
COUNTRY LN
2600 WLKV 91361 557-A7
3000 SIMI 93063 478-D7
3000 VeCo 93063 478-D7
COUNTRY PL
1800 VeCo 93023 451-C3
COUNTRY CLUB DR
400 OJAI 93023 441-G7
400 SIMI 93065 497-D5
500 OJAI 93023 451-G1
900 VeCo 93023 451-G1
23600 VeCo 93065 497-E5
COUNTRY CLUB RD
400 OJAI 93023 451-G1
1800 THO 91360 526-G5
COUNTRY CREEK CT
11500 MRPK 93021 496-B3
COUNTRY CREEK LN
- CALB 91302 558-H7
COUNTRY GLEN RD
27200 AGRH 91301 558-E7
COUNTRY HAVEN CIR
3400 THO 91362 527-D3
COUNTRY HILL RD
4100 MRPK 93021 496-B3
COUNTRY HOME CT
- THO 91362 527-C2
COUNTRY MEADOW ST
4200 MRPK 93021 496-E3
COUNTRY OAKS LN
1700 THO 91362 526-J6
COUNTRY PARK CT
2300 THO 91362 527-A3
COUNTRY RANCH RD
1300 LACo 91361 586-H2
1300 THO 91361 586-H2
COUNTRYSIDE RD
300 VeCo 91377 558-A1
COUNTRY SPRINGS CT
11600 MRPK 93021 496-B2
COUNTRY VALLEY RD
100 THO 91362 557-E1
COUNTRY VIEW CT
100 SPLA 93060 473-H1
COUNTRY VIEW PL
500 VeCo 93010 494-A6
COUNTRY VISTA ST
- THO 91362 527-B2
COUNTRYWALK CT
- SIMI 93065 478-A6
COUNTRY WIDE WY
400 SIMI 93065 477-G7
400 SIMI 93065 497-G1
400 VeCo 93065 477-G7
COUNTRYWOOD DR
11300 MRPK 93021 496-B3

COUNTY LINE RD
23200 Chat 91311 499-F6
COUNTY OAK RD
6000 WdHl 91367 529-C7
6200 CanP 91307 529-C7
COUNTY SQUARE DR
500 VEN 93003 492-C3
COURT AV
200 VEN 93003 491-J2
COURT ST
3000 SIMI 93065 498-D3
COURTLAND ST
5100 OXN 93033 552-G6
COURTNEY CT
100 THO 91320 525-H7
COURTNEY LN
11700 MRPK 93021 496-C2
COURTYARD DR
100 PHME 93041 552-F6
100 PHME 93033 552-F6
COURTYARD WY
800 PHME 93041 552-F6
COVE DR
400 PHME 93041 552-C1
COVE ST
600 VEN 93001 491-F4
COVE CREEK CT
- THO 91362 527-C2
COVELLO ST
22000 CanP 91303 529-J4
22400 CanP 91307 529-G4
23200 LA 91304 529-F4
COVENT GARDEN CT
2400 THO 91362 527-B4
COVENTRY AV
1100 VEN 93004 492-G3
COVENTRY CT
1900 THO 91362 526-J5
COVENTRY DR
100 THO 91360 526-F6
COVEWOOD ST
1100 VeCo 91377 527-H7
COVINGTON AV
1500 THO 91361 556-J6
1900 SIMI 93065 498-A5
COWBOY CT
1500 SIMI 93063 499-D3
COWBOY ST
6700 SIMI 93063 499-D3
COWGIRL CT
6700 SIMI 93063 499-D3
COWPER AV
7800 LA 91304 529-E3
COYOTE CANYON RD
6800 VeCo 93066 474-J3
6800 VeCo 93066 475-A5
COYOTE WELLS CIR
- THO 91362 527-E6
COZUMEL PL
- SIMI 93065 497-E4
CRABAPPLE CT
- MRPK 93021 496-H3
24500 CanP 91307 529-D5
CRAFTS CT
1900 SIMI 93065 498-A4
CRAGGY VIEW ST
22200 Chat 91311 499-J4
CRAGGYVIEW ST
22000 Chat 91311 499-J4
CRAGMONT CT
2300 SIMI 93065 498-A1
CRAIG DR
100 SPLA 93060 464-A6
2000 OXN 93036 522-G2
CRAIG ST
400 VeCo 93022 451-B6
CRANBERRY DR
2400 OXN 93036 522-G1
CRANBROOK ST
1400 CMRL 93010 494-D7
CRANE ST
6000 VEN 93003 492-C4
CRANMONT CT
800 SIMI 93065 527-C1
CRAPE MYRTLE CT
6100 WdHl 91367 529-J7
CRATER DR
1800 VEN 93004 492-G4
CRATER ST
1400 SIMI 93063 498-D3
CRAWFORD ST
1300 OXN 93030 522-J6
CRAZY HORSE DR
3000 SIMI 93063 479-A6
CREE LN
2400 VEN 93001 471-C6
CREEK LN
9700 VeCo 93001 461-B1
9700 VeCo 93022 461-B1
CREEK RD
- VeCo 93012 554-E1
9800 VeCo 93001 461-B1
10200 VeCo 93022 451-E4
10200 VeCo 93022 461-B1
10800 VeCo 93023 451-E4
12000 OJAI 93023 451-H2
CREEKMONT CT
500 VEN 93003 472-D7

CREEKRIDGE AV
- SIMI 93065 497-E2
CREEKSIDE CIR
800 CMRL 93012 525-A2
CREEKSIDE LN
- OXN 93036 522-C3
CREEKSIDE RD
5000 CMRL 93012 524-J2
5000 CMRL 93012 525-A2
CREEKSIDE WY
100 OJAI 93023 441-F7
CREEKWOOD ST
2100 THO 91361 557-A6
N CREIGHTON CIR
6400 MRPK 93021 476-H6
CREMONA WY
600 VeCo 91377 557-H2
CRESCENT ST
6600 VEN 93003 492-E6
CRESCENT WY
2800 THO 91362 557-A2
CRESCENT MEADOW CT
4300 MRPK 93021 496-D3
CRESPI DR
100 FILM 93015 456-C6
1600 OXN 93033 552-J3
CRESPI LN
2100 THO 91361 557-A5
CREST CT
1400 OXN 93035 552-B1
23600 SIMI 93065 497-G7
CRESTA CT
3800 THO 91360 526-F1
CRESTHAVEN CT
29400 AGRH 91301 557-J3
CRESTHAVEN DR
3600 THO 91362 527-D7
3600 THO 91362 557-C1
CRESTHILL DR
400 VeCo 91377 558-A1
CRESTLAKE AV
1200 VEN 93004 492-H3
CRESTLINE DR
13500 VeCo 93012 496-F5
CRESTMONT DR
2100 VEN 93003 492-D5
CRESTON CT
- SIMI 93065 477-J7
CRESTON LN
5100 VeCo 93066 495-A1
CRESTONE CT
5500 VEN 93003 472-B7
CRESTRIDGE DR
400 VeCo 91377 558-A1
CRESTVIEW AV
- CMRL 93010 524-A1
- VeCo 93010 524-A1
300 CMRL 93010 523-G2
300 VeCo 93010 523-J1
CRESTVIEW CIR
3900 THO 91362 557-C1
CRESTVIEW DR
300 OJAI 93023 441-H7
700 SPLA 93060 464-B4
CRESTWOOD AV
300 VEN 93003 492-B1
CRESTWOOD CT
400 THO 91320 555-F3
CRETE LN
- OXN 93035 552-B1
CRICKETFIELD CT
400 VeCo 91361 556-G6
N CRIMEA ST
100 VEN 93001 491-D1
S CRIMEA ST
- VEN 93001 491-D2
CRIMEA ST FIRE RD
300 VeCo 93001 471-E6
CRINKLAW LN
5600 SIMI 93063 499-A3
5600 VeCo 93063 499-A3
CRISWELL ST
22200 CanP 91303 529-J6
22400 CanP 91307 529-H6
N CROCKER AV
- VEN 93004 492-F1
S CROCKER AV
- VEN 93004 492-F2
CROCKER ST
1300 SIMI 93065 497-J3
CROMBIE CT
- VeCo 91361 556-D7
CROMWELL PL
1500 THO 91361 556-H6
CROOKED PALM RD
4200 VeCo 93001 471-C2
CROOKED TRAIL PL
1700 THO 91362 527-F6
CROSBY AV
700 SIMI 93065 498-B5
CROSS AV
2600 OXN 93036 522-G1
CROSS LN
6900 VeCo 93003 492-D2
7000 VEN 93003 492-D2
CROSSBILL ST
- VEN 93003 492-D5
CROSS BRIDGE PL
1600 THO 91362 526-J7

CROSS CREEK AV
2000 SIMI 93063 498-J2
CROSSJACK ST
400 PHME 93041 552-B2
CROSSLAND ST
3200 THO 91362 527-D3
CROSSPOINTE CT
- SIMI 93065 478-A6
CROSSRIDGE CT
3800 THO 91360 526-G1
CROTHERS CT
8000 LA 91304 529-E3
CROWLEY AV
6300 VEN 93003 492-D5
CROWN CT
2300 SIMI 93065 497-G7
W CROWN ST
- VeCo 93023 451-B4
CROWNE OAK LN
23600 SIMI 93065 497-A1
CROWNFIELD CT
4200 WLKV 91361 557-D6
CROWN HAVEN CT
3700 THO 91320 555-E2
CROWNHILL CT
6200 VEN 93003 472-C6
CROWN HILL DR
800 VeCo 93063 499-B4
CROWN POINT CT
2300 OXN 93036 522-C2
CROWN RIDGE CT
1500 THO 91362 527-F6
CROWN VIEW CT
2300 THO 91362 527-A7
E CROYDON AV
4100 CMRL 93010 494-H7
N CROYDON AV
1800 CMRL 93010 494-H7
CRUSOE CIR
800 THO 91362 526-J7
CRUZERO ST
200 VeCo 93023 451-C2
CRYSTAL CIR
3300 SIMI 93063 478-D6
CRYSTAL PL
8000 VEN 93004 492-F3
CRYSTAL DOWNS CT
2300 OXN 93036 522-D2
CRYSTAL RANCH RD
12400 MRPK 93021 496-D3
CRYSTAL VIEW CIR
1600 THO 91320 556-A2
CTL II RD
23600 VeCo 93063 498-H7
CTL III RD
23600 VeCo 93063 528-J1
23600 VeCo 93063 529-A1
CTL IV RD
23600 VeCo 91307 528-G2
23600 VeCo 93063 528-G2
CUESTA DEL MAR DR
200 OXN 93033 552-F6
CULLEN CT
3600 THO 91320 555-F4
CULVER LN
100 THO 91320 556-B2
100 VeCo 91320 556-B2
CULVIEW CT
23600 SIMI 93065 497-F7
E CUMBERLAND CT
3300 THO 91362 557-C2
W CUMBERLAND CT
3000 THO 91362 557-B2
CUMMINGS RD
300 VeCo 93060 473-E1
CUMMINGS WY
- OXN 93033 552-G5
CUMULUS CT
1900 THO 91362 526-J1
CUNNINGHAM RD
- THO 91362 556-H1
CURLEW PL
6300 VEN 93003 492-D5
CURLEW WY
3800 OXN 93035 552-B3
CURRAN ST
2000 OXN 93033 553-A4
CURRANT AV
1200 SIMI 93065 498-B4
E CURRIER AV
2700 SIMI 93065 498-C4
N CURRIER AV
1000 SIMI 93065 498-C4
CURT DR
3100 CMRL 93010 524-F2
CUSHMAN CT
2000 SIMI 93063 499-A2
CUTLER ST
2000 SIMI 93065 498-A4
CUTTER DR
900 OXN 93035 522-D7
CUTTING RD
400 PHME 93041 552-C3
400 PHME 93043 552-C3
CUYAMA RD
400 OJAI 93023 441-F7
400 VeCo 93023 441-F7
CUYLER HARBOR
- VeCo 93012 554-F3

CYNTHIA ST
6200 SIMI 93063 499-B2
CYPRESS LN
5000 VeCo 93001 471-C1
CYPRESS PL
1300 THO 91360 526-H2
CYPRESS RD
5100 OXN 93033 552-H6
CYPRESS ST
600 THO 91320 556-C1
1500 OXN 93030 552-H1
6000 VeCo 93063 499-B4
CYPRESS POINT LN
1100 VEN 93003 492-C4

D

D ST
- FILM 93015 455-H6
- VeCo 93015 455-H6
100 OXN 93030 522-G6
1200 OXN 93030 522-G7
1500 OXN 93033 552-G1
N D ST
100 OXN 93030 522-G5
DAFFODIL AV
1500 VEN 93004 493-A2
DAFFODIL CT
2700 OXN 93030 522-D4
23600 SIMI 93065 497-G5
DAFFODIL WY
500 OXN 93030 522-D4
DAHL AV
400 PHME 93041 552-F5
DAHLIA ST
900 OXN 93036 522-E3
DAHLIA WY
100 VEN 93004 473-A7
E DAILY DR
- CMRL 93010 524-B3
W DAILY DR
- CMRL 93010 524-A3
200 CMRL 93010 523-J3
DAISY CT
4400 MRPK 93021 496-B3
DAISY DR
- VEN 93004 493-A2
DAISY ST
- SIMI 93063 499-A2
DAKIN AV
1400 SIMI 93065 497-J4
DAKOTA DR
- MRPK 93021 496-G3
- VEN 93001 471-C5
DALAWAY DR
3800 MRPK 93021 496-A4
3800 VeCo 93021 496-A4
DALBY DR
- VeCo 91361 556-D7
DALE AV
100 THO 91320 555-E2
N DALE AV
10400 VeCo 93022 451-C7
DALE CT
100 SPLA 93060 463-J6
22700 Chat 91311 499-H5
DALECREST AV
6100 WdHl 91367 529-F7
DALENHURST PL
2700 SIMI 93065 478-A7
2700 SIMI 93065 498-A1
DALEWOOD CIR
4200 THO 91320 555-D4
DALHART AV
2700 SIMI 93063 478-H6
DALLAS DR
500 THO 91360 526-G7
500 THO 91360 556-G1
1000 OXN 93033 552-J2
DALLAS ST
2600 OXN 93033 552-J3
DALTON ST
- VEN 93003 491-G2
DALY RD
700 OJAI 93023 441-J5
DAMIANA DR
100 THO 91320 555-E1
DAMON ST
5700 SIMI 93063 499-A3
DANA AV
6200 SIMI 93063 499-C3
DANA DR
300 SPLA 93060 464-A5
300 FILM 93015 456-C6
DANA POINT AV
- VEN 93004 492-F2
DANBROOK AV
2300 CMRL 93010 494-E7
DANBURY CT
800 VEN 93004 492-H2
DANBURY DR
1700 CMRL 93012 495-A7
1700 CMRL 93012 525-A1
DANDELION CT
- THO 91320 555-J2
DANETTE ST
6400 SIMI 93063 499-C2
DANIEL ST
3300 THO 91320 555-F2

DANIELSON FIRE RD
- VeCo - 555-E6
- VeCo 91320 555-E5
DANMONT CT
3600 THO 91320 555-F4
DANNYBOYAR AV
6300 CanP 91307 529-G6
DANTE WY
500 VeCo 91377 557-G1
DANTES VIEW DR
5000 CALB 91301 558-F6
N DANTON PL
2600 SIMI 93065 498-B1
DANUBE WY
- OXN 93036 522-H1
DANVERS CIR
700 THO 91320 555-F4
DANVERS RIVER ST
- OXN 93036 492-H7
DANVILLE AV
300 THO 91320 555-E3
DANWOOD DR
4100 THO 91362 527-C5
DAPHNE AV
1500 VEN 93004 493-A2
DAPHNE ST
1600 CMRL 93010 494-D7
DAPHNEY CT
3000 SIMI 93063 478-D7
DAPPER CT
4300 OXN 93033 553-A4
DAPPLE AV
1500 CMRL 93010 524-D1
N DAPPLEGRAY RD
- VeCo 91307 529-B4
DARA ST
800 CMRL 93010 524-G2
DARBY ST
3100 SIMI 93063 498-D1
3100 SIMI 93065 498-D1
DARCY AV
1500 SIMI 93065 498-B3
DARGAN ST
28900 AGRH 91301 558-A3
DARKWOOD CIR
1900 THO 91360 526-D4
DARLENE LN
6000 MRPK 93021 476-C7
8400 LA 91304 529-G2
DARLING RD
9400 VEN 93004 492-H2
10600 VeCo 93004 493-A1
10600 VEN 93004 493-A1
10900 VEN 93004 473-B7
10900 VeCo 93004 473-B7
DARLINGTON DR
2900 THO 91360 526-G2
DARMONT CIR
700 SIMI 93065 497-J5
DARNELL CT
1600 CMRL 93010 524-D2
DARNOCH WY
6900 CanP 91307 529-E4
DARRAH AV
1500 SIMI 93063 498-E3
DART CT
5500 AGRH 91301 557-G5
DARTMOOR CT
- MRPK 93021 496-E2
E DARTMOUTH CIR
14300 MRPK 93021 476-G6
DARTMOUTH RD
100 SPLA 93060 463-J7
400 SPLA 93060 473-J1
400 SPLA 93060 474-A1
DARTMOUTH ST
5200 VEN 93003 492-B3
DARYN DR
6600 LACo 91307 529-D6
DATE AV
- VEN 93004 473-A6
DATE ST
100 OXN 93033 552-G1
600 OXN 93030 552-H1
W DATE ST
100 OXN 93033 552-E1
DAUNET AV
2500 SIMI 93065 498-C4
DAVENPORT ST
- CMRL 93012 524-G4
DAVEY JONES DR
30700 AGRH 91301 557-G5
DAVIDS LN
200 VeCo 91361 556-F6
DAVIDSON DR
- OXN 93033 552-G5
DAVIDSON LN
1600 SIMI 93063 499-B2
DAVIS CT
4300 OXN 93033 552-H4
DAVIS DR
300 VEN 93003 492-A3
DAVIS RD
23600 VeCo 93060 453-G2
DAVIS ST
100 SPLA 93060 464-B5
DAVIS WY
23300 Chat 91311 499-F7

DAWN CIR
1700 SIMI 93063 498-J2
DAWN CT
2100 THO 91362 526-J4
DAWN MEADOW ST
1700 THO 91362 527-E6
DAWSON AV
2600 VEN 93003 491-G3
N DAWSON DR
- CMRL 93012 524-F3
S DAWSON DR
- CMRL 93012 524-E4
DAWSON PL
2500 CMRL 93012 524-E4
DAY CT
2200 SIMI 93065 497-H2
DAY RD
- VEN 93003 492-B2
DAYBREAK CIR
- THO 91320 556-A1
DAYLIGHT CT
1900 THO 91362 526-J1
DAYLIGHT DR
6300 AGRH 91301 558-A3
DAY LILY LN
23600 SIMI 93065 497-A1
DAYLOMA AV
200 VEN 93003 492-A1
DEACON ST
2900 SIMI 93065 498-C3
DEAN CT
100 VEN 93003 492-A3
DEAN DR
100 SPLA 93060 463-J6
100 SPLA 93060 464-A6
3500 VEN 93003 491-H3
4300 VEN 93003 492-A3
DEANNA AV
1600 SIMI 93063 499-A3
DE ANZA DR
- VEN 93001 471-C6
DE ANZA WY
200 OXN 93033 552-H3
DEARBORN AV
700 THO 91320 555-G3
DEBBIE ST
500 VeCo 91320 525-G7
500 VeCo 91320 555-H1
DE BERRY DR
26000 CALB 91301 558-F6
DEBORAH ST
4000 SIMI 93063 498-F2
DEBS AV
6100 WdHl 91367 529-E7
6500 CanP 91307 529-E7
DEBUSSY LN
- VEN 93003 492-B4
DECATUR AV
700 VEN 93004 492-G3
DECKER CANYON RD
Rt#-23
1400 LACo 90265 586-F7
DECKSIDE CT
1400 OXN 93035 552-C1
DECKSIDE DR
900 OXN 93035 522-C7
DEEP SHADOW DR
29200 AGRH 91301 558-A5
DEEP WATERS CT
- SIMI 93065 478-B6
DEEPWELL LN
4300 MRPK 93021 496-F3
DEEPWOOD DR
800 THO 91362 557-C1
1000 THO 91362 527-C7
DEER PTH
- VeCo 93033 583-J4
- VeCo 93033 584-A3
DEERBROOK RD
6700 VeCo 91377 528-A7
DEER CREEK AV
2000 SIMI 93063 498-J2
DEER CREEK RD
14700 VeCo 90265 585-B7
14700 VeCo 90265 625-B2
DEERFIELD CT
2400 CMRL 93010 524-E1
DEERFIELD DR
100 FILM 93015 455-J7
DEERFIELD ST
2100 THO 91362 526-J4
2100 THO 91362 527-A4
DEERFOOT PL
800 THO 91320 555-G5
DEER GRASS CT
- MRPK 93021 476-D6
DEER HAVEN CT
- THO 91362 527-D7
DEERHILL RD
800 VeCo 91377 528-A6
800 VeCo 91377 558-A1
DEER HUNTER LN
600 CMRL 93010 524-F2
DEERHURST AV
400 CMRL 93012 524-H5
DEERING LN
13600 MRPK 93021 496-F3
DEER LICK DR
23900 LA 91304 529-E2

STREET
Block City ZIP Pg-Grid

DEER MEADOW ST
12600 MRPK 93021 496-D3
DEERPARK CT
4300 WLKV 91361 557-D6
DEERPATH LN
- THO 91320 555-H2
DEER RUN LN
1200 VeCo 91377 527-G7
DEER SPRING PL
900 THO 91320 555-G5
DEER TRAIL CT
26900 CALB 91301 558-G7
DEER VALLEY AV
3100 THO 91320 555-G4
DEERVIEW CT
29400 AGRH 91301 557-J4
DEERWALK PL
300 THO 91320 555-J1
DEERWEED TR
20900 CALB 91301 558-G7
DEER WILLOW CT
700 THO 91320 555-G4
DEERWOOD AV
2600 SIMI 93065 478-C7
2600 SIMI 93065 498-C1
DEFENDER DR
4000 AGRH 91301 558-E7
DEKOVEN ST
4900 VEN 93003 492-B7
DELACODO AV
3000 THO 91320 555-G2
DE LA GARRIGUE RD
23600 VeCo 93023 450-G1
DEL AMO WY
2000 OXN 93036 522-H3
DELANO CT
3800 SIMI 93063 498-E1
DELAWARE DR
- MRPK 93021 496-G3
200 VEN 93001 471-C4
DEL CERRO CIR
23600 LA 91304 529-E4
DEL CIERVO PL
- CMRL 93012 494-H7
- CMRL 93012 524-H1
DELFEN ST
6500 MRPK 93021 477-A6
DELGADA CT
1900 CMRL 93010 524-D2
DELGADA ST
1000 CMRL 93012 525-B6
E DELILAH ST
3500 SIMI 93063 498-E2
DELIUS ST
4900 VEN 93003 492-A4
DEL MAR PL
4000 OXN 93033 552-G4
DEL MAR TR
6800 VeCo 93063 499-D4
DELMONICO AV
8600 LA 91304 529-J1
DEL NIDO CT
1100 OJAI 93023 442-A6
DEL NORTE BLVD
100 OXN 93030 523-D5
22200 OXN 93010 523-D5
DEL NORTE RD
100 OJAI 93023 441-G7
300 VeCo 93023 441-F6
1300 CMRL 93010 523-F3
DEL NORTE ST
10800 VEN 93004 472-J6
DELORES CT
- VEN 93004 492-J3
DEL ORO DR
800 OJAI 93023 441-G5
DEL ORO PL
4800 OXN 93033 552-G5
DELOZ DR
- CMRL 93012 525-A3
DELPHA CT
2100 THO 91362 527-A3
DELPHINIUM PL
200 OXN 93036 522-F3
DEL PRADO CT
1100 OJAI 93023 442-A6
DEL PRADO DR
1700 CMRL 93010 524-D2
DEL RAY CIR
- THO 91360 526-F2
DEL RAYO CT
- CMRL 93012 494-H7
DEL REY PL
- OXN 93030 523-A5
DEL RIO ST
4600 SIMI 93063 478-H7
DEL ROBLES DR
6300 VeCo 93063 499-C4
DEL ROBLES PL
1000 VeCo 93063 499-C4
DEL SUR WY
300 OXN 93033 552-H3
DELTA DR
8600 VEN 93004 492-G4
DELTA RD
23600 VeCo 93063 528-G2
DELTA CC RD
23600 VeCo 93063 528-G2

W DELTA GREEN ST
100 PHME 93041 552-D2
DEL TIO CT
- CMRL 93010 493-G7
DEL VALLE DR
200 FILM 93015 455-J6
500 FILM 93015 456-A6
DEL VALLE ST
- VeCo 93022 451-C4
DEL VERDE CT
1000 THO 91320 526-B6
DELWOOD CT
400 THO 91320 555-E2
DENA DR
100 VeCo 91320 555-G1
500 VeCo 91320 525-G7
DENALI CT
- MRPK 93021 496-D1
DENBY CT
6500 SIMI 93063 499-C2
DENHAM CT
1800 SIMI 93065 498-A2
DENISE CT
500 THO 91320 525-H7
DENISE LN
8300 LA 91304 529-G2
DENISE ST
2600 THO 91320 525-H7
DENNIS AV
700 SIMI 93065 497-G3
DENNIS LN
7200 CanP 91307 529-F5
DENNIS WY
9300 Chat 91311 499-F6
DENNISON RD
- VeCo 93023 452-D1
DENNY ST
2000 SIMI 93065 498-A3
DENTON AV
3500 SIMI 93063 478-G5
DENVER PL
900 OXN 93033 552-J3
900 VEN 93004 492-G3
DENVER ST
8000 VEN 93004 492-F3
DENVER SPRINGS DR
32900 WLKV 91361 586-J1
W DEODAR AV
100 OXN 93030 522-F5
N DEODORA ST
1400 SIMI 93065 498-C3
DE PAUL ST
4200 VEN 93003 491-J3
DE QUINCY CT
24100 LA 91304 529-D3
DERBY ST
2100 CMRL 93010 524-E1
DERRY AV
5300 AGRH 91301 558-B6
DESCANSO AV
100 OJAI 93023 441-F7
200 OJAI 93023 451-F1
DESCANSO CT
1300 OXN 93035 552-E1
DESCHUTES DR
1500 VEN 93004 492-J3
DESEO AV
400 VeCo 93010 494-A6
DESERT CREEK AV
2100 SIMI 93063 499-B2
DESERT FOREST CT
2200 OXN 93036 522-D2
DESERT SAGE CT
23600 SIMI 93065 498-D5
DESMOND AV
- VEN 93003 492-C4
DETROIT DR
2800 OXN 93036 522-H1
2800 OXN 93036 492-H7
DEVEREUX DR
900 VeCo 93023 441-D6
DEVERON RIDGE RD
6900 CanP 91307 529-E5
DEVIA DR
- VeCo 91320 555-G1
DEVILFISH DR
800 OXN 93035 522-D7
DEVILS CANYON MTWY
- Chat 91311 479-G2
- Chat 91311 499-J1
DEVILS CANYON RD
- VeCo 93001 471-B5
DEVON CT
800 SIMI 93065 498-D5
DEVON LN
1200 VEN 93001 491-F5
DEVONSHIRE AV
1500 THO 91361 556-J6
DEVONSHIRE CT
1600 THO 91361 556-J6
DEVONSHIRE DR
800 OXN 93030 522-D4
W DEVONSHIRE DR
300 OXN 93030 522-F4
DEVONSHIRE ST
10300 Chat 91311 499-J4
DEVORE AV
700 SIMI 93065 497-H5

DEVORE CT
5500 AGRH 91301 558-C5
DEWAYNE AV
1600 CMRL 93010 524-G1
1700 CMRL 93010 494-G7
DEWBERRY CT
2000 THO 91361 557-A5
DEWBERRY LN
400 OXN 93036 522-G1
DEWDROP PL
23600 THO 91362 527-C4
N DEWEY AV
- THO 91320 555-G2
S DEWEY AV
100 THO 91320 555-G2
DEXTER ST
2100 CMRL 93010 524-E2
DIABLO AV
600 MRPK 93021 496-D1
DIABLO PT
- VeCo 93012 554-F2
DIABLO WY
100 OXN 93033 553-C3
DIAMOND AL
200 VEN 93001 491-C1
DIAMOND CT
3700 SIMI 93063 498-E1
DIAMOND DR
- CMRL 93010 493-H7
DIAMOND HEAD WY
2300 OXN 93036 522-D2
DIANA CT
2900 VeCo 91320 555-G1
30100 AGRH 91301 557-H5
DIANE ST
5300 SIMI 93063 498-J2
DIAZ AV
500 OXN 93030 522-H6
DICHA DR
- OXN 93030 522-H4
DICKENS CIR
6900 VEN 93003 492-E3
DICKENS DR
5300 OXN 93033 552-G5
DICKENSON AV
- THO 91320 555-F2
DICKENSON DR
- SPLA 93060 463-J5
- VeCo 93060 463-J5
DICKENSON RD
23600 SPLA 93060 463-J5
23600 VeCo 93060 463-J5
DICKINSON LN
6600 VEN 93003 492-D3
DICKINSON PL
2100 OXN 93033 553-A1
DIEGO WY
1600 OXN 93030 522-E4
DIKE RD
- VeCo 93060 464-D5
DILLER CT
3800 SIMI 93063 498-E2
DILLON CT
2300 THO 91360 526-D4
DINSMORE AV
100 THO 91362 556-H2
DINSMORE ST
1300 SIMI 93065 497-H4
DISCOVERY CT
11900 MRPK 93021 496-C1
DISCOVERY CV
2600 PHME 93041 552-C2
DISCOVERY DR
23600 OXN 93030 523-C6
DISPENSARY RD
- VeCo 93041 583-G3
- VeCo 93042 583-G3
DITCH RD
- VeCo 93042 583-C4
2800 VeCo 93063 478-D6
2800 SIMI 93065 478-D6
2900 SIMI 93063 478-D6
N DIVERNON AV
3000 SIMI 93065 478-F7
DIVIDE TER
8300 LA 91304 529-E2
E DIXON CT
3800 SIMI 93063 498-E2
DOANE ST
4000 VEN 93003 491-J2
W DOBKIN PL
- SIMI 93065 497-F3
DOCK RD
- PHME 93043 552-D5
DOCKSIDE LN
1500 CMRL 93010 524-D3
DOCKSON PL
2500 PHME 93041 552-D2
DODD ST
500 SIMI 93065 497-G4
DODGE RD
23600 OXN 93033 553-C4
23600 VeCo 93033 553-C4
DODSON ST
- PHME 93041 552-E4
- PHME 93043 552-E3
5000 VeCo 93066 494-J4
5000 VeCo 93066 495-A4

DOE CREEK CIR
500 THO 91320 555-E3
DOGWOOD CIR
2900 THO 91360 526-H3
DOGWOOD DR
2500 OXN 93036 522-G1
DOGWOOD ST
2200 SIMI 93065 498-B2
DOHENEY CT
- SIMI 93063 478-H5
DOLE DR
- WLKV 91362 557-E5
DOLLIE ST
100 OXN 93033 552-G5
W DOLLIE ST
- OXN 93033 552-G5
DOLORES CT
100 OXN 93030 522-J5
DOLPHIN CT
1000 VEN 93001 491-G5
DOLPHIN WY
5000 OXN 93035 551-J1
DOMAR PL
2100 OXN 93036 522-H3
DOMBEY CIR
- THO 91360 526-F6
DOMINGO PL
- OXN 93030 522-H4
DOMINGUEZ CANYON RD
- VeCo - 367-D7
- VeCo 93040 367-D7
DOMINICA CTE
1400 CMRL 93010 523-J1
DOMINICA DR
- OXN 93035 522-D7
- OXN 93035 552-D1
DOMINION DR
1000 VeCo 93023 441-D6
N DONALD AV
- THO 91320 555-G2
DON ANTONIO WY
800 VeCo 93023 451-C3
DON CARLOS
800 VeCo 93023 451-C2
DON CARLOS ST
300 VEN 93001 491-D2
DONEGAL AV
100 THO 91320 556-A1
DONEGAL WY
- OXN 93035 522-B7
- OXN 93035 552-B1
DONEVA RD
4000 MRPK 93021 496-D3
DON FELIPE
800 VeCo 93023 451-C2
DONIZETTI AV
600 VEN 93003 492-A3
DONLIN LN
200 VeCo 91320 556-B3
DONLIN RD
300 VeCo 91320 556-B2
DONLON AV
800 OXN 93030 522-G7
DONLON RD
2900 VeCo 93066 495-B1
5300 VeCo 93066 475-B7
DONLON ST
100 VEN 93003 492-A5
600 VEN 93003 491-J5
DONNA ST
100 VeCo 93022 451-B7
DONNER AV
100 VEN 93003 492-C1
1100 SIMI 93065 498-A4
DONNER ST
600 OXN 93033 552-H4
W DONNICK AV
100 THO 91360 526-E5
DONNINGTON CT
700 SIMI 93065 497-C6
DONNYBROOK LN
13600 MRPK 93021 496-F3
DON RICARDO
800 VeCo 93023 451-C2
DONVILLE AV
2000 SIMI 93065 497-J2
DOONE ST
- THO 91360 526-F6
DORA CT
2200 SIMI 93063 499-B1
DORADO CT
500 VeCo 91377 558-A1
2400 THO 91362 527-C3
DORAL CIR
1400 THO 91362 527-E7
DORAL CT
2600 OXN 93036 522-D2
DORCHESTER ST
800 THO 91360 526-G6
DOREEN WY
3100 VEN 93003 491-H3
DORENA DR
100 VeCo 91320 555-G1
400 VeCo 91320 525-G7
DORHAM CT
2900 SIMI 93065 498-C3
DORIE DR
7400 LA 91304 529-E4

DORIS AV
1400 OXN 93030 522-D5
1400 VeCo 93030 522-B5
W DORIS AV
200 OXN 93030 522-F5
DORIS CT
15400 MRPK 93021 477-A5
DORMAN ST
2700 CMRL 93010 494-F7
DOROTHY AV
200 MRPK 93021 496-E1
200 VEN 93003 491-J2
400 VeCo 93003 491-J2
1400 SIMI 93063 499-C3
DOROTHY DR
28000 AGRH 91301 558-C6
DORRIT CT
- THO 91320 556-A1
DORRIT ST
1800 THO 91320 556-A1
DORSET AV
1400 THO 91360 526-F6
DORSEY ST
- VEN 93003 492-C4
DORY LN
5100 OXN 93033 552-G5
N DOS CAMINOS AV
- VEN 93003 491-G2
S DOS CAMINOS AV
- VEN 93003 491-G3
DOUBLE EAGLE DR
600 SIMI 93065 497-D5
DOUBLETREE RD
800 VeCo 91377 558-A1
900 VeCo 91377 528-A7
W DOUGLAS AV
200 OXN 93030 522-F4
DOUGLAS ST
300 OJAI 93023 441-H5
DOVE CT
300 FILM 93015 455-H6
300 SPLA 93060 464-D5
DOVE ST
6800 VEN 93003 492-E4
DOVE CANYON DR
- OXN 93036 522-C2
DOVER AV
1100 THO 91360 526-E6
DOVER LN
- SIMI 93063 498-H1
1000 VEN 93001 491-E4
DOVER ST
1500 OXN 93030 522-G3
DOVERWOOD CT
31900 WLKV 91361 557-C6
DOVETAIL CT
- THO 91360 526-F3
DOVETAIL DR
5800 AGRH 91301 557-G4
DOWEL DR
6400 SIMI 93063 499-C2
DOWELL DR
1400 VEN 93003 492-B5
DOWNEY CT
3900 SIMI 93063 498-F2
E DOWNING ST
1400 SIMI 93065 497-J1
DOWNWIND WY
500 OXN 93033 552-G5
DOYLE LN
500 VEN 93003 492-D1
DRACENA AV
15400 MRPK 93021 477-A6
DRACO WY
23600 CanP 91307 529-F5
DRAKE DR
1200 SIMI 93065 497-G4
2300 THO 91362 527-B6
4200 OXN 93033 553-A4
DRAPER CT
2000 SIMI 93065 497-J2
DRAYTON AV
2200 THO 91360 526-F4
DRESDEN CT
- VEN 93003 492-B3
DREXEL AV
200 VEN 93003 492-C1
DREXEL CIR
1000 THO 91360 526-F6
DRIFFILL BLVD
- OXN 93030 522-G7
DRIFT DR
5900 WLKV 91362 557-F4
DRIFTWOOD AV
1200 SIMI 93065 497-H3
DRIFTWOOD CIR
900 THO 91320 555-E4
DRIFTWOOD LN
1000 VEN 93001 491-E4
DRIFTWOOD ST
- FILM 93015 456-B6
5100 OXN 93035 521-J6
DRISKILL ST
100 OXN 93030 523-A5
DRIVER AV
5200 Ago 91301 558-G6
5200 CALB 91301 558-G6
28100 AGRH 91301 558-B5

DROWN AV
100 OJAI 93023 441-J6
DRUMCLIFF CT
1700 THO 91361 556-J5
DRUMMOND LN
6700 VEN 93003 492-D3
DRUMMOND PL
2700 THO 91360 526-E3
DRY CANYON RD
4500 SIMI 93063 478-E3
4500 SIMI 93065 478-E3
4500 VeCo 93063 478-E3
DRY CREEK LN
- OXN 93036 522-B3
DRYDEN ST
100 THO 91360 526-F7
DUARTE CIR
1400 SIMI 93065 498-A3
DUBBERS ST
100 VEN 93001 491-B1
DUBONNET CT
1400 VeCo 91377 527-H6
DUCHY WY
2500 VeCo 91361 586-D2
DUCOR AV
7600 LA 91304 529-G2
DUDLEY AV
1200 VEN 93004 492-H3
DUDLEY DR
1600 VeCo 93015 455-G5
DUESENBERG DR
2500 THO 91362 557-B3
DUFAU RD
3600 VeCo 93033 553-E5
DUKE AV
100 VEN 93003 492-B2
DUKE ST
6400 MRPK 93021 476-H6
DULCE DR
600 OXN 93036 522-H3
DULCIE CIR
1700 SIMI 93063 498-J2
DUMAINE AV
1400 VeCo 91377 527-G6
DUMETZ ST
2500 CMRL 93010 524-F3
DUMP RD
- VeCo 93042 583-G4
DUNAWAY DR
- THO 91320 555-E3
DUNBAR DR
- OXN 93033 552-H6
N DUNBAR LN
400 THO 91360 526-D7
DUNCAN ST
1700 SIMI 93065 497-J3
DUNEGAL CT
5900 AGRH 91301 557-G3
DUNES CIR
900 OXN 93035 521-J7
DUNES ST
800 OXN 93035 521-J7
4800 OXN 93035 522-A7
DUNHAM CIR
1600 THO 91360 526-D5
N DUNHAM RD
5600 VeCo 93066 475-C7
5600 VeCo 93066 495-C1
DUNKIRK DR
600 OXN 93035 522-C6
DUNLIN CT
800 THO 91361 557-A5
DUNLO PL
6400 CanP 91307 529-D7
DUNN CT
2100 THO 91360 526-F4
DUNNIGAN ST
1600 CMRL 93010 524-D2
N DUNNING ST
- VEN 93003 491-H2
S DUNNING ST
- VEN 93003 491-H3
DUNRAVEN CT
31700 WLKV 91361 557-D6
DUNSMUIR AV
200 VEN 93004 492-F2
DUNSMUIR CT
2500 OXN 93035 552-D1
DUNSMUIR ST
1600 OXN 93035 552-D1
DUNTON LN
100 FILM 93015 455-J7
DUPONT CT
4400 VEN 93003 492-A5
DUPONT ST
1800 OXN 93033 553-A1
4500 VEN 93003 492-A5
DURAND DR
6900 VeCo 93021 475-J5
DURANGO CT
1600 CMRL 93010 524-D2
DURANT CT
5400 VeCo 91377 527-H7
DURHAM LN
9800 VEN 93004 492-H2
DURHAM ST
1200 SIMI 93065 497-H4
DURKIN ST
700 CMRL 93010 524-F2

DURLEY AV
100 CMRL 93010 524-A4
200 CMRL 93010 523-J4
E DUSAN ST
2300 SIMI 93065 498-B4
DUSK DR
- CMRL 93012 524-G4
DUSKWOOD WY
1600 SIMI 93065 497-F2
DUSTY LN
7800 VeCo 93066 475-C4
DUSTY ROSE CT
200 SIMI 93065 497-E7
DUTCH ELM CIR
1200 THO 91360 526-H2
DUVAL DR
2200 VeCo 93012 496-A7
DUVAL RD
2300 VeCo 93012 496-A7
DUVALI DR
100 VEN 93003 492-B2
DUVALL AV
700 CMRL 93010 524-D2
N DWIGHT AV
1500 CMRL 93010 524-G1
1700 CMRL 93010 494-G7
DWIGHT AV S
3000 CMRL 93010 524-F1
DYER CT
200 THO 91360 526-F4

E

E ST
- FILM 93015 455-H7
- VeCo 93015 455-H7
100 OXN 93030 522-F7
1300 OXN 93033 552-G3
23600 OXN 93033 522-F7
N E ST
100 OXN 93030 522-F5
EAGLE CIR
- VeCo 93041 583-J3
EAGLE CT
600 FILM 93015 455-H5
EAGLE DR
6800 VEN 93003 492-E4
EAGLE ST
6500 VEN 93003 492-D4
EAGLE BEND LN
- OXN 93036 522-C3
EAGLEBROOK DR
30300 AGRH 91301 557-G5
EAGLE CREEK LN
2300 OXN 93036 522-D2
EAGLE FLIGHT DR
- SIMI 93065 478-A5
EAGLEHAVEN LN
6800 VeCo 91377 528-B7
EAGLE HEIGHTS CT
2800 THO 91360 526-E3
EAGLE MOUNTAIN RD
24000 LA 91304 529-D2
EAGLE MOUNTAIN ST
24000 LA 91304 529-D1
EAGLEPEAK AV
1600 SIMI 93063 498-E3
EAGLE POINT CIR
4800 THO 91362 557-F1
EAGLE RIDGE ST
100 THO 91320 555-G2
EAGLE ROCK AV
100 VeCo 93035 552-C6
EAGLES CLAW AV
2800 THO 91362 527-B2
EAGLESNEST PL
3400 THO 91320 555-F4
EAGLETON ST
28600 AGRH 91301 558-B3
EAGLEVIEW PL
300 THO 91320 555-J1
EAGLEWOOD AV
- THO 91362 527-B2
EAKINS LN
500 VEN 93003 492-D1
EARHART CT
1800 OXN 93033 553-A1
EARL AV
1500 SIMI 93065 498-B3
EARLHAM CT
1400 VeCo 91377 527-G6
EARL JOSEPH DR
- CMRL 93010 524-A2
EARLY DAWN LN
23600 SIMI 93065 497-A1
EAST DR
1100 VEN 93003 492-D4
EAST PK
- CMRL 93012 524-G4
EAST RD
- VeCo 93001 470-E4
6300 VeCo 93021 475-F6
6300 VeCo 93066 475-F6
EAST ST
3000 SIMI 93065 498-C3
3400 VeCo 93066 495-A5
EASTBOURNE BAY
4400 OXN 93035 552-A1

EASTERLY RD
5500 AGRH 91301 558-C5
EAST FORK HALL CANYON RD
2800 VeCo 93001 471-H5
EASTHAVEN LN
- CanP 91307 529-E5
EASTMAN AV
1500 VEN 93003 492-A5
1800 OXN 93030 522-J6
1800 OXN 93030 523-A6
EASTRIDGE CT
2200 OXN 93036 522-D3
EASTRIDGE LP
2100 OXN 93036 522-E2
EASTRIDGE TR
2000 OXN 93036 522-E2
EASTVALE CT
29900 AGRH 91301 557-H4
EASTWARD ST
23600 Chat 91311 499-F6
EASTWIND CIR
1300 THO 91361 557-B6
EASTWOOD DR
400 OXN 93030 522-F4
EASY ST
100 SPLA 93060 464-A7
E EASY ST
100 SIMI 93065 497-F1
W EASY ST
- SIMI 93065 497-E1
EASY WY
2000 SIMI 93065 497-H2
EATON HOLLOW AV
- MRPK 93021 476-F6
EATON HOLLOW CT
- MRPK 93021 476-F5
EATOUGH AV
8500 LA 91304 529-J1
EATOUGH PL
8500 LA 91304 529-J2
EBB CT
1400 OXN 93035 552-C1
EBB TIDE CIR
600 PHME 93041 552-F7
EBBTIDE LN
11800 VeCo 90265 625-F5
EBONY DR
600 OXN 93030 522-D4
ECCLES ST
22100 LA 91304 529-H2
ECHIDNA PL
7000 VEN 93003 492-E4
ECHO AV
700 OXN 93036 522-H2
ECHO CT
4900 VEN 93003 492-A2
ECHO ST
1300 OXN 93036 522-J2
N ECROYD AV
2100 SIMI 93063 499-A2
EDDINGHAM WY
- LA 91304 529-E4
EDDY CT
5500 VEN 93003 492-C3
EDELWEISS ST
2000 OXN 93036 522-G2
EDEN ST
3000 OXN 93033 553-A3
EDENPARK DR
26000 CALB 91302 558-J3
EDGAR CT
- THO 91320 555-F2
EDGAR ST
- OXN 93033 552-H5
EDGEBROOK PL
5100 THO 91362 527-F7
EDGECLIFF CIR
1800 THO 91362 527-F6
EDGEHILL CIR
5300 VEN 93003 492-B1
EDGEMIRE LN
23600 SIMI 93065 497-A1
EDGEMONT DR
1400 CMRL 93010 524-D1
EDGERTON PL
2500 PHME 93041 552-C2
EDGEVIEW CT
- THO 91320 555-H3
EDGEWARE DR
5200 CALB 91301 558-G6
EDGEWATER LN
1500 CMRL 93010 524-D2
EDGEWOOD DR
- FILM 93015 456-A7
1700 SIMI 93063 499-B2
EDGEWOOD WY
1300 OXN 93030 522-E4
EDINBURGH CT
6100 AGRH 91301 557-J3
EDISON DR
5500 OXN 93033 552-H7
6100 VeCo 93033 552-H7
8200 VeCo 93001 461-A4
EDISON LN
700 FILM 93015 455-J5
EDISON RD
- LACo 90265 586-J7
- VeCo 93001 461-A5

EDISON RD
23600 SIMI 93063 498-E7
23600 SIMI 93063 528-E1
23600 THO 91320 554-G4
23600 THO 91320 555-A3
23600 VeCo 93012 554-G4
23600 VeCo 93063 498-E7
23600 VeCo 93063 528-E1
EDISON WY
800 FILM 93015 455-J5
EDMUND ST
1500 SIMI 93065 497-J4
EDWARD RD
200 THO 91320 556-A2
200 VeCo 91320 556-A2
EDWARDS RD
23600 VeCo 93060 464-J1
EDWARDS CANYON RD
23600 VeCo 93015 457-D5
23600 VeCo 93040 457-D5
EDWARDS RANCH RD
100 VeCo 93060 473-C4
EGRET AV
1300 VEN 93003 492-D4
EGRET CT
6300 VEN 93003 492-D4
EHLERS DR
9300 Chat 91311 499-F6
23500 Chat 91311 499-F6
EILAT CIR
- SIMI 93063 479-B7
- SIMI 93063 499-B1
EILEEN ST
4000 SIMI 93063 498-F2
EISENHOWER CIR
600 OXN 93033 552-H6
EISENHOWER ST
7200 VEN 93003 492-E2
EISENHOWER WY
- SIMI 93065 497-D5
ELAINE ST
3400 VeCo 93036 492-J7
3400 VeCo 93036 493-A7
ELAND LN
7000 VEN 93003 492-E4
EL AZUL CIR
500 VeCo 91377 557-J1
ELBA CT
11800 MRPK 93021 496-C5
ELBA PL
6100 WdHl 91367 529-E7
ELBA ST
2800 VEN 93003 492-E6
ELBERTA AV
1600 SIMI 93063 498-J3
ELBURY CT
- VeCo 91361 556-E7
EL CAJON CIR
1900 OXN 93035 522-E7
EL CAJON CT
1200 OXN 93035 522-E7
1200 OXN 93035 552-E1
EL CAJON DR
1400 THO 91362 526-J5
EL CAJON ST
9200 VEN 93004 492-G2
EL CAJON WY
1600 OXN 93035 522-D7
EL CAMINO
100 OJAI 93023 441-G6
EL CAMINO DR
100 VeCo 93023 441-E7
EL CAMINO CORTO
800 VeCo 93023 441-C7
EL CAMINO REAL
1000 VeCo 93063 499-B4
EL CAMINO REAL U.S.-101
- VeCo - 366-E8
- VeCo - 459-C5
- VeCo - 469-H1
- VeCo - 470-E5
- VeCo - 490-H1
- VEN - 490-H1
- VEN - 491-G4
EL CAMPO ST
600 VeCo 93015 455-D6
EL CANON AV
6100 WdHl 91367 529-D7
EL CAPITAN PL
4200 CMRL 93012 524-J3
EL CENTRO DR
1400 THO 91362 526-J6
EL CENTRO ST
1000 VeCo 93023 451-D1
EL CERRITO CIR
1100 VEN 93004 492-G1
EL CERRITO DR
1300 THO 91362 526-H6
EL CIELO
100 THO 91320 525-E6
EL CINO DR
1100 SIMI 93065 497-G4
EL CONEJO DR
100 VeCo 93023 441-D6
EL CORAZON CT
4900 CMRL 93012 524-H3
EL CORTIJO PL
5100 CMRL 93012 524-J1

ELDER ST
900 OXN 93036 522-E2
ELDERBERRY AV
4700 MRPK 93021 496-C2
ELDERBERRY CT
1000 SPLA 93060 464-A1
ELDERBERRY DR
2400 OXN 93036 522-F1
ELDEROAK LN
2600 VeCo 91361 586-E1
ELDEROAK RD
2700 VeCo 91361 586-E2
ELDER VIEW LN
1100 CMRL 93012 525-A2
EL DORADO AV
1800 OXN 93033 553-B2
EL DORADO CT
300 VEN 93004 492-E1
EL DORADO DR
100 FILM 93015 456-C6
1400 THO 91362 526-J6
EL DORADO ST
7600 VEN 93004 492-E1
ELECTRA AV
2000 SIMI 93065 497-F2
ELEGANTE DR
- OXN 93030 523-C7
ELENA WY
200 OXN 93036 522-G3
ELEPHANT SEAL CV
- VeCo 93012 554-E3
EL ESCORPION RD
6000 WdHl 91367 529-E7
ELEVAR CT
700 SIMI 93065 527-C1
ELEVAR ST
- OXN 93030 523-C6
E ELFIN GRN
100 PHME 93041 552-E2
W ELFIN GRN
100 PHME 93041 552-D2
ELFSTONE CT
1000 THO 91361 557-A5
EL GALLARDO
200 THO 91320 525-E7
EL GRECO DR
1900 OXN 93035 522-E7
ELIAS DR
- OXN 93033 552-H6
ELINOR CT
2900 THO 91320 525-H7
ELIOT DR
4200 OXN 93033 553-A4
E ELIOT ST
100 SPLA 93060 464-A6
W ELIOT ST
100 SPLA 93060 463-J6
100 SPLA 93060 464-A6
ELIZA CT
100 OXN 93030 522-J5
ELIZABETH CT
100 SPLA 93060 463-J7
30100 AGRH 91301 557-H5
ELIZABETH DR
2000 VEN 93003 492-E5
ELIZABETH RD
500 VeCo 93003 472-G6
500 VeCo 93060 472-G6
ELIZABETH WY
- OXN 93033 552-H5
ELIZONDO AV
2500 SIMI 93065 498-C3
ELIZONDO ST
1900 SIMI 93065 498-A3
EL JARDIN AV
2100 VEN 93001 491-F2
EL JINA LN
400 VeCo 93023 442-E6
ELKHORN CT
- SIMI 93063 478-H5
ELKINS LN
600 FILM 93015 456-B5
ELKINS RD
100 VeCo 93015 466-B3
ELKO AV
700 VEN 93004 492-G2
ELK RIVER ST
- OXN 93036 492-H7
ELK RUN LP
- MRPK 93021 476-F5
ELK RUN WY
- MRPK 93021 476-F5
ELKTON CT
- MRPK 93021 476-F6
ELKWOOD AV
3700 THO 91320 555-E4
ELKWOOD CT
- FILM 93015 456-B6
ELKWOOD ST
22000 LA 91304 529-E3
EL LADO DR
500 SIMI 93065 497-G3
EL LAZO CT
1300 CMRL 93012 525-B1
ELLEN CT
3000 THO 91320 555-G2
ELLENVIEW AV
5900 WdHl 91367 529-D7
6200 CanP 91307 529-D7

STREET
Block City ZIP Pg-Grid

ELLESMERE WY
1300 VeCo 91377 528-A7
ELLFRED CT
600 SPLA 93060 463-J7
ELLICE ST
11700 VeCo 90265 625-E5
ELLINGTON CT
2400 SIMI 93063 498-D1
ELLINGTON ST
23600 VEN 93003 492-A3
ELLIOT CT
1200 SIMI 93065 497-D7
ELLIOTT CT
6800 VEN 93003 492-D3
N ELLIS PL
- THO 91320 556-A1
S ELLIS PL
- THO 91320 556-A2
ELLISTON CT
- SIMI 93065 477-J7
ELLSWORTH CIR
400 THO 91360 526-D6
ELM
700 VeCo 93023 451-C3
ELM CT
800 OXN 93033 552-F1
21300 SIMI 93063 499-B3
ELM DR
- CMRL 93010 524-E4
5100 OXN 93033 552-J5
ELM RD
100 THO 91320 556-B2
100 VeCo 91320 556-B2
ELM ST
200 SPLA 93060 463-J7
E ELM ST
100 OXN 93033 552-G1
W ELM ST
100 OXN 93033 552-E1
ELMA ST
3300 CMRL 93010 524-G1
EL MALABAR ST
7000 VEN 93003 472-D7
ELM COTTAGE CT
- CMRL 93012 524-G5
N ELMDALE AV
2000 SIMI 93065 498-B2
EL MEDIO ST
- VEN 93001 471-C7
ELMHURST LN
900 FILM 93015 455-J7
ELMHURST ST
4900 VEN 93003 492-B3
ELMIRA ST
2600 THO 91320 555-H1
EL MONTE AV
100 VEN 93004 492-G2
EL MONTE DR
900 SIMI 93065 497-G5
1100 THO 91362 526-J5
2000 THO 91362 527-A5
ELMORE ST
3200 SIMI 93063 498-D2
ELMROCK AV
13200 MRPK 93021 496-E3
ELMSBURY LN
7000 CanP 91307 529-D5
ELMSBURY RD
1900 THO 91361 557-A7
ELMSFORD PL
1500 THO 91361 556-H6
ELM VIEW DR
5400 CMRL 93012 525-A2
ELMWOOD ST
2900 THO 91320 555-G6
EL NIDO CT
2200 CMRL 93010 494-G7
EL NIDO ST
3200 CMRL 93010 494-G7
ELOISE CIR
1600 SIMI 93063 499-A3
EL PAJARO
100 THO 91320 525-E6
EL PASEO RD
300 OJAI 93023 441-G7
EL PASEO ST
1000 FILM 93015 455-H7
EL PASILLO
100 THO 91320 525-E6
EL PASO AV
2800 SIMI 93063 478-G7
EL PLANO DR
100 VeCo 93023 441-D7
EL PORTAL CT
9500 VEN 93004 492-G1
EL PORTAL WY
1200 OXN 93035 522-D7
1300 OXN 93035 552-D1
EL PRADO ST
4600 SIMI 93063 478-H7
EL RANCHO DR
1900 CMRL 93010 494-E7
EL REPOSO DR
2200 CMRL 93012 495-D7
EL RETIRO CT
900 VeCo 91377 557-H1
EL RIO DR
100 VeCo 93023 441-D7
300 OXN 93036 492-G7

EL RIO DR
300 OXN 93036 522-G1
EL ROBLAR DR
100 VeCo 93023 441-C6
EL SEGUNDO DR
800 THO 91362 526-H7
ELSINOR AV
1200 VEN 93004 492-J2
1200 VEN 93004 493-A2
ELSINOR CT
1100 VEN 93004 492-J2
ELSINORE AV
1300 OXN 93035 552-D1
ELSINORE CIR
2600 OXN 93035 552-D1
ELSINORE CT
1900 OXN 93035 552-D1
EL SOL AV
500 VeCo 93023 441-D7
EL SONETO CT
23600 CMRL 93010 524-C4
ELSTOW CT
1600 THO 91361 556-J6
EL TORO RD
700 OJAI 93023 441-G6
900 VeCo 93023 441-F6
EL TORO FIRE TRUCK TR
- Nwhl 91382 479-E1
EL TUACA CT
300 VeCo 93010 493-J7
300 VeCo 93010 494-A7
ELVADO DR
1400 SIMI 93065 497-F3
EL VERANO DR
1400 THO 91362 526-H6
ELWIN ST
11800 MRPK 93021 476-C7
ELY WY
2700 SIMI 93065 498-C3
EMBER CT
5500 AGRH 91301 557-G5
EMERALD AV
3000 SIMI 93063 478-D7
EMERALD CT
900 VEN 93004 492-F3
EMERALD ST
1300 OXN 93036 522-J3
7800 VEN 93004 492-F3
EMERALD ISLE WY
1600 OXN 93035 552-A1
EMERIC AV
1400 SIMI 93065 497-E3
EMERSON AV
1100 OXN 93033 552-J1
1600 OXN 93033 553-A1
1600 VeCo 93033 553-A1
EMERSON CT
5700 AGRH 91301 557-J4
EMERSON ST
700 THO 91362 527-A7
900 THO 91362 526-J7
EMILIO CT
11800 MRPK 93021 496-C4
EMILY LN
2800 SIMI 93063 478-E7
EMILY ST
600 OJAI 93023 441-H6
EMMA AV
- VEN 93003 491-G3
EMMA CT
2000 THO 91362 556-H2
N EMMETT AV
2100 SIMI 93063 499-A2
EMORY AV
1700 SIMI 93063 498-J2
EMPIRE AV
600 VEN 93003 491-H4
EMPRESA LN
2100 OXN 93036 522-G3
EMPRESS AV
700 CMRL 93010 524-D2
EMPTY SADDLE AV
1700 SIMI 93063 499-C3
ENADIA WY
22500 CanP 91307 529-G5
ENCANTO AV
2600 VEN 93003 491-G3
ENCHANTED WY
900 SIMI 93065 497-G1
N ENCINAL AV
100 VeCo 93023 441-D6
S ENCINAL AV
100 VeCo 93023 441-D7
ENCINAL PL
- VEN 93001 491-E2
ENCINAL WY
- VEN 93001 491-E2
ENCINAL CANYON RD
600 LACo 90265 586-G7
ENCINAS CANYON
300 VeCo 93001 471-D2
ENCINO AV
100 VeCo 93010 524-A1
300 CMRL 93010 524-A1
ENCINO DR
- VeCo 93022 451-C5
ENCINO LN
4200 VeCo 93001 471-D2

ENCINO PL
700 SPLA 93060 464-C3
4000 OXN 93033 552-G4
ENCINO VISTA CT
1200 THO 91362 556-H1
ENCINO VISTA DR
300 THO 91362 556-H1
400 THO 91362 526-H7
ENCORE ST
800 VeCo 93022 461-B1
END ST
6000 VeCo 93063 499-B3
ENDEAVOR ST
27500 AGRH 91301 558-E7
ENDEAVOUR CT
700 MRPK 93021 496-C1
ENDICOTT ST
- PHME 93041 552-E4
ENFIELD CIR
- THO 91360 526-F6
ENGLISH OAKS CT
2400 SIMI 93063 499-C1
ENID WY
10100 VEN 93004 492-J2
ENSCH RD
700 VeCo 93015 455-D4
ENSENADA AV
100 THO 91320 556-C1
ENSIGN PL
600 OXN 93035 522-D6
ENTRADA DR
- OXN 93030 522-G3
2000 OXN 93036 522-H3
3100 VEN 93003 491-G4
EQUESTRIAN AV
1100 THO 91360 526-G6
ERBES RD
100 THO 91362 556-J1
500 THO 91362 526-J7
1000 THO 91362 527-A1
3900 THO 91362 497-A7
4000 THO 91360 497-A7
4000 THO 91360 496-J7
ERBURU AV
400 VEN 93001 491-F1
ERIC PL
- THO 91362 557-A2
ERICA CIR
7000 CanP 91307 529-F5
ERICA PL
300 OXN 93036 522-F2
ERICA ST
2400 SIMI 93065 498-B2
N ERICSON PL
2600 SIMI 93065 498-B1
ERIE ST
10100 VEN 93004 492-J2
ERIN CT
23600 SIMI 93065 498-A5
ERIN PL
- LA 91304 529-E3
ERINLEA AV
3200 THO 91320 555-F4
ERMINE AV
2000 VEN 93003 492-F5
ERNEST DR
700 SPLA 93060 464-C3
ERRINGER RD
- SIMI 93065 477-J7
- SIMI 93065 478-A6
700 SIMI 93065 497-J5
800 SIMI 93065 498-A3
ERSKINE LN
900 FILM 93015 455-J6
ERTEN ST
100 THO 91360 526-E4
ERWIN ST
22100 WdHl 91367 529-F7
ESCALON DR
900 OXN 93035 522-E7
1000 OXN 93035 552-E1
ESCOLLA RD
23600 VeCo 93012 496-B5
ESCOLLERA AV
2800 VeCo 93012 496-A6
ESCOLLERA CIR
10900 VeCo 93012 496-A6
ESCONDIDO CT
1600 CMRL 93010 524-D3
ESKIMO LN
2300 VEN 93001 471-C6
ESPANA LN
3000 THO 91362 527-C3
ESPERANCE DR
- VeCo 93065 497-B3
23600 VeCo 93021 497-B3
E ESPLANADE DR
600 OXN 93036 522-H2
W ESPLANADE DR
2400 OXN 93036 522-G1
ESSEX WY
1100 THO 91360 526-G6
ESSEX JUNCTION CT
- THO 91362 527-C2
ESTABAN DR
- VeCo 93010 494-C7
ESTANCIA PL
200 CMRL 93012 524-G3

ESTATES AV
- VEN 93003 492-A2
ESTATES DR
500 THO 91320 525-G6
ESTHER AV
200 MRPK 93021 496-E1
ESTON ST
700 CMRL 93010 524-F2
ESTRELLA DR
- CALB 91302 558-H6
ESTRELLA ST
200 VEN 93003 491-G2
ESTRELLITA LN
200 VeCo 91377 558-A2
ESTRIGA CT
400 SPLA 93060 463-J6
ESTUARY WY
- OXN 93035 522-B7
- OXN 93035 552-A1
ESWARD DR
27000 CALB 91301 558-F6
ETHEL CT
3400 VeCo 91320 525-F7
ETNA CT
7000 VEN 93003 472-D6
ETON WY
1000 THO 91360 526-G6
ETTIN AV
800 SIMI 93065 497-H5
ETTING RD
1100 OXN 93033 553-B4
1100 VeCo 93033 553-E4
21200 VeCo 93012 553-E4
ETZ MELOY MTWY
- LACo 90265 586-E4
- VeCo 90265 586-E4
EUBANKS ST
400 CMRL 93010 523-J5
EUCALYPTUS CIR
1500 THO 91360 526-H3
EUCALYPTUS DR
2500 VeCo 93036 523-C2
N EUCALYPTUS DR
- VeCo 93015 465-E1
- VeCo 93015 455-E7
S EUCALYPTUS DR
100 VeCo 93015 465-E1
EUCALYPTUS ST
100 OJAI 93023 441-H6
3700 SIMI 93063 478-E7
W EUCALYPTUS ST
400 OJAI 93023 441-G6
EUCLID AV
900 CMRL 93010 524-C1
EUCLID CIR
1900 CMRL 93010 524-E1
EUGENE AV
700 VEN 93004 492-H2
EUGENIA DR
- VEN 93003 491-G2
EUNICE AV
5600 SIMI 93063 499-A3
EUREKA ST
400 PHME 93041 552-E5
8300 VEN 93004 492-G2
EUREKA CANYON RD
- VeCo 93040 457-G7
- VeCo 93040 458-A7
- VeCo 93040 467-H1
EVA ST
100 VEN 93003 491-G4
EVANGELINE PL
1500 OXN 93030 522-D4
EVANS AV
1700 VEN 93001 491-E2
EVANS DR
3500 SIMI 93063 498-E3
EVANSTON PL
900 OXN 93033 552-J3
EVANWOOD AV
5000 VeCo 91377 557-G1
EVE RD
4200 SIMI 93063 498-F1
EVELYN AV
3000 SIMI 93063 478-D7
EVENING SIDE DR
2900 THO 91362 526-J2
EVENING SKY DR
5300 SIMI 93063 478-J6
5300 SIMI 93063 479-A6
EVENSTAR AV
800 THO 91361 557-B5
EVEREST AV
700 MRPK 93021 496-D1
EVEREST ST
- OXN 93030 523-A5
EVERETT ST
- MRPK 93021 476-E7
EVERGLADES ST
5300 VEN 93003 492-C5
EVERGREEN AV
500 THO 91320 555-G3
EVERGREEN CT
23600 SIMI 93065 497-F7
EVERGREEN DR
2100 SIMI 93065 497-E2
N EVERGREEN DR
200 VEN 93001 491-F2

S EVERGREEN DR
- VEN 93003 491-F3
EVERGREEN LN
400 PHME 93041 552-E5
1100 OXN 93033 552-F5
1100 PHME 93033 552-F5
EVERGREEN SQ
400 PHME 93041 552-F5
EVESHAM AV
2800 THO 91362 527-A3
EVITA CT
5500 AGRH 91301 557-H5
EVITA PL
- OXN 93030 522-H4
EWANA PL
- Chat 91311 479-J7
EXETER AV
1300 VEN 93004 492-H3
EXETER CT
2500 CMRL 93010 524-F1
EXPLORER CV
2500 PHME 93041 552-C3

F

F AV
- VeCo 93042 583-F6
F ST
- VeCo 93041 583-G2
- VeCo 93042 583-G2
100 OXN 93030 522-F6
1300 OXN 93033 552-F1
23600 VeCo 93063 498-H7
23600 VeCo 93063 528-F1
N F ST
100 OXN 93030 522-F4
FABLE AV
8300 LA 91304 529-F2
FACILITY RD
23600 VeCo 93063 499-B7
FACTORY AV
500 OXN 93030 522-G6
FACTORY LN
300 OXN 93030 522-H7
FACTORY STORES DR
- CMRL 93010 524-B4
FACULTY CT
- THO 91360 526-F2
FACULTY ST
- THO 91360 526-E3
FAIR AV
1500 SIMI 93063 498-E3
FAIRBANKS AV
2800 SIMI 93063 478-F7
FAIRBOURNE PL
300 OXN 93033 552-G5
FAIRBREEZE CIR
3900 WLKV 91361 557-C6
FAIRBROOK LN
4300 MRPK 93021 496-E3
FAIRCHILD AV
900 CMRL 93010 524-E2
FAIRCREST LN
5100 VeCo 93066 495-A1
FAIRFAX AV
200 VEN 93003 492-B1
FAIRFIELD CIR
- VEN 93003 492-A3
FAIRFIELD RD
500 SIMI 93065 497-E5
FAIRFORD ST
8500 VEN 93004 492-G4
FAIRGRANGE DR
5400 AGRH 91301 557-H5
FAIRGROVE CIR
1000 VeCo 93012 494-F6
FAIRHAVEN CT
300 THO 91320 555-G2
6100 AGRH 91301 558-A3
FAIRMONT DR
3300 VEN 93003 491-H2
FAIRMONT LN
- OXN 93036 522-C2
FAIRMOUNT RD
1400 THO 91362 527-D6
FAIR OAKS
8000 VeCo 93021 476-D3
FAIRPOINT AV
6500 VEN 93003 492-D5
FAIRVIEW CT
1200 OJAI 93023 441-G5
1200 VeCo 93023 441-G5
FAIRVIEW DR
100 VEN 93001 491-F2
FAIRVIEW PL
5400 AGRH 91301 558-C4
FAIRVIEW RD
- THO 91362 557-A3
100 OJAI 93023 441-E5
100 VeCo 93023 441-D5
200 THO 91361 557-A3
E FAIRVIEW RD
100 OJAI 93023 441-G5
100 VeCo 93023 441-G5
FAIRVIEW CANYON RD
23600 VeCo 93015 456-G6
FAIRVIEW FIRE RD
400 THO 91361 556-J3
400 THO 91361 557-A3

FAIRWAY CT
1300 CMRL 93010 494-A5
1300 VeCo 93010 494-A5
1600 THO 91362 527-D6
2300 OXN 93036 522-C2
FAIRWAY DR
500 VeCo 93010 494-A5
FAIRWAY LN
100 OJAI 93023 442-A7
FAIRWAY PARK LN
2600 SIMI 93063 478-J7
FAIR WEATHER CRSG
23600 SPLA 93060 464-B1
23600 VeCo 93060 454-C7
23600 VeCo 93060 464-B1
FAITH CT
6400 SIMI 93063 499-C3
FALCON ST
- SIMI 93065 477-J7
- SIMI 93065 478-A7
6000 VEN 93003 492-C4
FALCON WY
1000 FILM 93015 455-J5
FALCONROCK LN
400 VeCo 91377 558-A1
FALCONVIEW LN
6800 VeCo 91377 528-B7
FALKIRK AV
1500 OXN 93035 552-A1
FALKIRK BAY
4400 OXN 93035 552-A1
FALKNER PL
1900 OXN 93033 553-A1
FALLBROOK AV
- THO 91320 555-F2
6100 WdHl 91367 529-H7
6400 CanP 91307 529-H3
7400 LA 91304 529-H3
FALLCREEK CT
- SIMI 93063 479-B7
- SIMI 93063 499-B1
FALLEN LEAF AV
300 CMRL 93012 524-H5
1100 VEN 93004 492-J2
FALLEN LEAF CT
- SIMI 93063 479-B7
- SIMI 93063 499-A1
10100 VEN 93004 492-J2
FALLEN OAKS DR
- THO 91360 526-F1
FALLING STAR AV
1200 THO 91362 527-F6
FALLING WATER CT
3300 SIMI 93063 478-J6
FALLON CIR
2500 SIMI 93065 498-B3
FALL RIVER CIR
3400 THO 91362 557-C3
FALLVIEW RD
1800 THO 91361 557-A6
1800 WLKV 91361 557-A6
FALMOUTH ST
800 THO 91362 526-J7
900 THO 91362 527-A6
FALON CT
1900 THO 91362 527-A5
FANNIN DR
4600 SIMI 93063 478-G6
FANSHELL WK
1100 OXN 93035 522-D7
FAR COUNTRY CT
- MRPK 93021 496-F2
FARGO ST
400 THO 91360 526-D4
FARIA RD
4000 VeCo 93001 470-A3
FARIA ST
3300 CMRL 93010 524-G1
FARING FORD RD
2900 VeCo 91361 586-D2
FARLAND ST
100 THO 91320 556-B2
FARLEY ST
- PHME 93043 552-E4
FARM RD
- VeCo 93012 554-D3
FARMFIELD RD
26000 CALB 91302 558-H3
FARNHAM RD
100 VeCo 93023 441-F4
FARNWORTH ST
2100 CMRL 93010 524-E1
FARRAGUT CT
1900 OXN 93033 553-A1
FARRAGUT DR
2600 OXN 93033 553-A2
FARRALON WY
- OXN 93035 552-B1
FARRALONE AV
6400 CanP 91303 529-J6
7600 LA 91304 529-J1
8900 LA 91304 499-J7
8900 Chat 91311 499-J3
FARRELL CIR
3500 THO 91320 555-F2
FARWELL ST
2000 SIMI 93065 497-J2
FASHION PARK PL
100 OXN 93033 552-G4

E FASLEY AV
5800 SIMI 93063 499-A1
FASTWATER CT
32400 WLKV 91361 557-B7
FATHOM CT
1000 OXN 93035 522-C7
FATHOM DR
1300 OXN 93035 522-C7
1300 OXN 93035 552-C1
FAULKNER CT
6800 VEN 93003 492-E3
FAULKNER RD
14900 VeCo 93060 473-G2
23600 SPLA 93060 473-H1
FAUNA DR
2000 OXN 93036 522-G3
FAUST AV
6700 CanP 91307 529-H4
7600 LA 91304 529-H2
FAWN AV
2300 VEN 93003 492-E5
FAWN PL
2100 VEN 93003 492-E5
FAWN CHASE LN
23600 SIMI 93065 497-A2
FAWNGLEN PL
900 THO 91320 555-G5
FAWNRIDGE AV
23600 THO 91362 527-B4
FAWN VALLEY CT
200 SIMI 93065 497-E6
FAXTON CT
3200 VeCo 93063 478-E6
FAYANCE PL
3300 THO 91362 526-J2
FAYTON CT
2000 CMRL 93010 494-D7
E FEARING ST
5600 SIMI 93063 499-A2
FEATHER AV
1300 THO 91360 526-E6
FEATHER ST
9000 VEN 93004 492-H4
FEATHERFALL WY
23600 SIMI 93065 497-A2
FEATHER HILL CT
1100 THO 91320 526-A6
FEATHER RIVER PL
- OXN 93036 492-H7
FEATHERSTONE ST
100 OXN 93030 523-A5
FEATHERWOOD ST
2400 THO 91362 527-B5
FELICIA CT
1200 OXN 93030 522-J5
FELICIA ST
5200 CMRL 93012 525-A3
FELIX AV
3200 VeCo 93063 478-E6
FELIX DR
100 VeCo 93023 441-E7
FELIZ DR
- VeCo 93022 451-C4
FELKINS RD
200 SPLA 93060 463-J7
200 SPLA 93060 473-J1
FELTON ST
2700 THO 91320 555-G3
FENMORE AV
1700 CMRL 93010 524-G1
1700 CMRL 93010 494-G7
FENMORE CT
1700 CMRL 93010 524-G1
FENMORE ST
14600 MRPK 93021 476-J6
FENWICK WY
- SIMI 93065 527-E1
FENWOOD AV
6100 WdHl 91367 529-G7
FENWORTH CT
6300 AGRH 91301 558-A3
FERAL AV
6200 AGRH 91301 558-B3
FERNANDO DR
100 VeCo 93023 441-D6
FERN ANN FALLS RD
- Chat 91311 479-H7
FERNBROOK RD
8600 LA 91304 529-E1
FERNCREST PL
3000 THO 91362 527-C3
FERNDALE PL
300 THO 91360 526-D5
FERNDALE ST
6000 VEN 93003 492-C3
FERNGLEN CIR
600 FILM 93015 456-A5
FERNHILL AV
800 THO 91320 555-E4
FERNHILL CT
800 THO 91320 555-D4
FERNLEAF CT
2100 THO 91362 527-A1
FERN OAK DR
1100 SPLA 93060 464-B3
FERNRIDGE CT
5200 CMRL 93012 524-J1
5200 CMRL 93012 525-A1

FERN VALLEY CT
4500 MRPK 93021 496-F2
FERNVIEW ST
2100 SIMI 93065 498-A1
N FERNWOOD CT
2000 SIMI 93065 498-A2
FERNWOOD DR
400 OXN 93030 522-F4
2400 VEN 93001 491-F2
FERRARA CT
30800 WLKV 91362 557-G7
FERRARA DR
1100 VeCo 93023 451-B1
FERRARA WY
1800 OXN 93030 522-J6
1800 OXN 93030 523-A6
FERRIS DR
4000 VeCo 93060 464-D5
FERRO DR
200 VEN 93001 491-B1
FESTIVAL CT
3600 THO 91360 526-G1
FESTIVO ST
- OXN 93030 523-A5
FICUS WY
- VEN 93004 493-A2
FIELD ST
- OXN 93033 552-H5
FIELDCREST CT
3600 THO 91360 526-G1
FIELDCREST DR
5300 CMRL 93012 525-A1
FIELDFLOWER LN
600 THO 91360 526-D4
FIELDGATE DR
5700 SIMI 93063 479-A7
FIELDMONT PL
24400 CanP 91307 529-D5
FIELDSTONE WY
300 SIMI 93065 497-D6
FIERRO DR
1100 VeCo 93023 451-B1
FIESTA AV
2300 CMRL 93010 524-E2
E FIESTA GRN
100 PHME 93041 552-E2
W FIESTA GRN
100 PHME 93041 552-D2
FIESTA ST
5900 VEN 93003 492-C2
FIG ST
2100 SIMI 93063 498-G1
FIGUEROA ST
- VEN 93001 491-B2
FILLMORE AV
100 VeCo 93035 552-B5
100 VeCo 93043 552-B5
200 VeCo 93001 459-C4
FILLMORE ST
200 FILM 93015 456-A5
700 SPLA 93060 463-H7
FINANCIAL SQ
2400 OXN 93036 522-H1
FINCH AV
1300 VEN 93003 492-D4
FINCH CT
500 FILM 93015 455-H5
2000 SIMI 93063 499-C2
FINCHLEY CT
3500 SIMI 93063 478-E7
FINE RD
700 VeCo 93015 456-G6
FINE ST
700 FILM 93015 456-A5
FINO AV
6500 CMRL 93012 525-C6
FINROD CT
1000 THO 91361 557-A5
E FIR AV
200 OXN 93033 552-G1
W FIR AV
100 OXN 93033 552-E1
FIR CT
1600 OXN 93033 552-H1
FIR ST
- CMRL 93010 524-E3
N FIR ST
- VEN 93001 491-C1
S FIR ST
- VEN 93001 491-C2
FIREBIRD CT
23600 OXN 93030 522-J5
FIREBRAND CT
5700 CMRL 93012 495-B7
FIRECREST CT
500 THO 91320 555-G3
FIRENZE ST
300 OXN 93036 522-H3
FIRESIDE LN
4300 MRPK 93021 496-F3
FIRESTONE CIR
900 SIMI 93065 497-C6
FIRESTONE CT
2100 OXN 93036 522-D2
FIRETHORNE PL
1600 OXN 93030 522-E4
FIRWOOD CT
2900 THO 91320 555-G3
FISHER CT
3600 OXN 93035 552-C1

FISHER DR
1700 OXN 93035 552-C1
FISHERS CT
- MRPK 93021 476-F6
FISH HATCHERY RD
100 FILM 93015 456-D6
FISK CT
1700 THO 91362 526-J6
FISKE PL
1200 OXN 93033 552-J1
FITCH AV
600 MRPK 93021 496-F1
FITZGERALD AV
- VEN 93003 492-C3
FITZGERALD RD
1000 SIMI 93065 497-H4
1700 SIMI 93065 498-A4
FITZGERALD ST
23600 LA 91304 529-E3
FIVE OAK CT
5600 SIMI 93063 499-A1
FIX WY
- VEN 93001 491-B1
FLAGSTAFF CT
700 VEN 93004 492-H2
FLAGSTONE LN
- SIMI 93063 498-H1
N FLAMINGO WY
1100 VEN 93003 492-F4
S FLAMINGO WY
1300 VEN 93003 492-F4
FLAMING STAR AV
600 THO 91360 526-D4
FLANAGAN DR
5700 SIMI 93063 479-A7
FLATHEAD RIVER ST
- OXN 93036 492-G6
FLATTOP CT
- MRPK 93021 476-F6
FLAX PL
- OXN 93036 522-B2
FLEET AV
700 VEN 93003 491-J4
FLEET ST
- VeCo 93042 583-D4
400 PHME 93041 552-D2
FLEISCHER REDMAND RD
23600 VeCo 93060 464-H3
FLETCHER CT
2100 THO 91362 556-H2
FLETCHER ST
2700 SIMI 93065 498-C4
FLEURY LN
6100 WdHl 91367 529-J7
FLICKER CT
6900 VEN 93003 492-E4
FLINN AV
500 MRPK 93021 496-F1
W FLINT ST
- VEN 93001 471-B7
FLINTLOCK LN
4200 WLKV 91361 557-F6
4200 AGRH 91301 557-F6
N FLINTLOCK LN
- VeCo 91307 529-A5
FLINTON CT
1400 THO 91361 557-A6
FLINTRIDGE CT
2200 THO 91362 527-A4
FLITTNER CIR
100 THO 91360 556-G1
FLOATING CLOUD ST
3600 THO 91360 526-G1
FLOOD ST
3600 VeCo 93063 478-E6
FLORA LN
- OXN 93030 523-A4
FLORADALE CT
3600 THO 91360 526-H1
FLORAL DR
4000 VeCo 93001 471-C1
4700 VeCo 93001 461-C7
FLORA VISTA AV
- CMRL 93012 524-H4
FLORENCE AV
200 PHME 93041 552-F5
FLORENCE ST
4000 SIMI 93063 498-F2
FLORENTINA DR
23600 OXN 93030 522-J5
FLORENTINE CT
- THO 91362 527-B3
FLORESTA CT
4800 THO 91362 527-E7
FLORY AV
- MRPK 93021 496-E1
FLOTOW LN
4600 VEN 93003 492-A7
FLOWER ST
3900 VEN 93003 491-J3
FLOWERCREEK DR
11500 MRPK 93021 496-B3
FLOWERDALE ST
1600 SIMI 93063 499-C3
FLOWER GLEN ST
900 SIMI 93065 477-G7
900 SIMI 93065 497-H1

FLOWERVIEW CT
4200 MRPK 93021 496-B2
FLOWERWOOD CT
11600 MRPK 93021 496-B4
FLOYD DR
300 SPLA 93060 464-A7
FLOYD ST
- VEN 93003 492-C3
FLYING HILLS LN
700 THO 91360 526-G1
FLYNN RD
- CMRL 93012 524-G2
18300 CMRL 93012 494-H7
FOGHORN CV
2600 PHME 93041 552-C1
FOLKESTONE TERRACE RD
1600 THO 91361 557-A6
FONT LN
1500 THO 91361 557-A6
FONTANA DR
100 OXN 93033 553-C4
FOOTHILL DR
400 FILM 93015 456-A4
1200 VeCo 93063 499-B3
1900 THO 91361 557-A3
5500 AGRH 91301 558-C5
FOOTHILL LN
100 OJAI 93023 441-G6
FOOTHILL RD
100 OJAI 93023 441-G5
500 SPLA 93060 463-H6
700 VeCo 93060 463-E7
1100 VeCo 93023 441-G4
2700 VEN 93003 491-H1
2800 VeCo 93003 491-H1
3800 VEN 93003 492-A1
3800 VEN 93003 492-A1
7600 VeCo 93004 472-J6
7600 VEN 93004 472-J6
7600 VEN 93004 492-D1
7600 VeCo 93004 492-D1
8300 VeCo 93003 472-F7
8300 VEN 93003 472-F7
9500 VeCo 93060 472-J6
10600 VEN 93060 472-J6
11400 VeCo 93060 473-C1
FOOTHILL TR
- VeCo 441-F3
- VeCo 93023 441-D4
FORAR CIR
1700 CMRL 93010 524-H1
FORBES LN
- VEN 93001 471-B6
FORD AV
23600 VEN 93003 492-E2
FORDHAM AV
300 VEN 93003 492-B3
1200 THO 91360 526-D5
N FORDHAM ST
14300 MRPK 93021 476-G6
FORDYCE RD
700 VeCo 93023 442-C5
FORELOCK CT
200 SIMI 93065 497-G6
FOREST AV
1100 VeCo 93023 451-B3
1200 SIMI 93065 498-D4
FOREST DR
1200 SPLA 93060 464-B3
FOREST COVE LN
5300 AGRH 91301 557-H4
FORESTGLEN CT
4400 MRPK 93021 496-D3
FOREST GROVE LN
- SIMI 93065 478-C4
FOREST HILLS RD
7100 CanP 91307 529-F5
FOREST KNOLL DR
1400 VeCo 91377 527-G6
FOREST LOOP DR
600 PHME 93041 552-F5
FOREST OAKS DR
4100 THO 91360 496-J7
FOREST PARK BLVD
- OXN 93036 492-G6
FOREST RIDGE DR
5400 AGRH 91301 557-G5
FORNEY LN
6400 VeCo 93063 499-C4
FORRESTER CIR
23600 SIMI 93065 497-G7
FORT COURAGE AV
3000 THO 91360 526-D2
FORT DAVIS ST
4600 SIMI 93063 478-G6
FORTUNA AV
3900 CMRL 93010 494-H7
FORTUNA LN
4100 OXN 93033 553-C4
FORT WORTH DR
4400 SIMI 93063 478-G7
FOSTER AV
1800 VEN 93001 491-E2
FOSTER PARK DR
- VeCo 93001 460-J5
- VeCo 93001 461-A6
FOSTER PARK WY
- VeCo 93001 460-J5

STREET
Block City ZIP Pg-Grid

FOUNTAIN PL
28500 AGRH 91301 558-C5
FOUNTAIN ST
- CMRL 93012 524-G4
FOUNTAIN CREST LN
2300 THO 91362 527-C4
FOUNTAINWOOD ST
28900 AGRH 91301 558-A3
29300 AGRH 91301 557-J3
FOURNIER ST
2900 OXN 93033 552-H3
FOUR OAK CT
5600 SIMI 93063 499-A1
FOURSITE LN
1800 THO 91362 556-J1
FOWLER AV
600 THO 91320 555-G4
FOWLER RD
6600 SIMI 93063 499-C3
FOX ST
100 OJAI 93023 441-J7
FOXBORO LN
7600 LA 91304 529-E4
FOX CANYON RD
23600 VeCo 93066 474-G5
FOXDALE CT
3700 THO 91320 555-E4
FOX DEN CT
2600 OXN 93036 522-D2
FOXFIELD DR
31500 WLKV 91361 557-D7
FOXGLOVE CT
3900 THO 91362 557-C1
FOXGLOVE PL
300 OXN 93036 522-F2
FOX HILL LN
9400 Chat 91311 499-H6
FOX HILLS DR
200 THO 91361 556-F2
FOXMOOR CT
31900 WLKV 91361 557-C6
FOX RIDGE DR
200 THO 91361 556-F2
FOX SPRINGS CIR
1500 THO 91320 526-A6
FOXTAIL CT
3100 THO 91362 527-C3
FOXTAIL ST
23600 SIMI 93065 497-F7
FOXWOOD CT
3600 THO 91360 526-H1
FOXWOOD DR
5600 VeCo 91377 557-J1
FRAGRANS WY
6100 WdHl 91367 529-J7
FRANCE AV
700 SIMI 93065 497-J5
FRANCE CIR
200 OJAI 93023 441-H6
FRANCES ST
100 VEN 93003 491-G3
FRANCIS AV
3900 CMRL 93010 494-H7
FRANCISCA WY
5300 AGRH 91301 557-J5
FRANCISCO PL
4000 OXN 93033 552-G4
E FRANDON CT
3900 SIMI 93063 498-F2
FRANK AV
100 OXN 93033 552-G3
FRANKFORT CT
3200 OXN 93033 552-J3
FRANKIE DR
3200 VeCo 91320 525-F7
FRANKLIN CT
900 SIMI 93065 497-H4
FRANKLIN DR
400 OJAI 93023 441-J6
FRANKLIN LN
- VEN 93001 471-C6
FRANKLIN ST
9200 Chat 91311 499-F7
FRANRIVERS AV
6400 CanP 91307 529-D7
FRASER LN
- VeCo 93001 471-C2
FRASER PT
- VeCo 93012 554-F3
FRASER ST
23600 VeCo 93022 451-D6
FRAZIER ST
1400 CMRL 93012 525-B1
FRAZIER MOUNTAIN RD
- VeCo - 367-B1
FRED AV
1700 SIMI 93065 498-B3
FREEBIRD LN
- VeCo 91377 527-J7
FREEBORN WY
2100 VeCo 93012 496-B7
2100 VeCo 93012 526-B1
FREEDOM PARK DR
500 VeCo 93010 523-J5
500 CMRL 93010 523-J5
FREEPORT CT
1000 THO 91361 557-B5
FREEPORT LN
2800 OXN 93035 522-D6

FREESIA AV
- SIMI 93063 499-A2
FREETOWN LN
27400 AGRH 91301 558-E7
FRWY Rt#-23
- MRPK - 496-G1
- THO - 496-J7
- THO - 497-A7
- THO - 526-J1
- THO - 556-H1
- VeCo - 496-H3
- VeCo - 497-A4
FREMLIN DR
- FILM 93015 456-A4
FREMONT AV
1500 SIMI 93065 497-J4
FREMONT CIR
5900 CMRL 93012 525-B1
5900 CMRL 93012 495-B7
FREMONT DR
1800 THO 91362 526-J5
FREMONT ST
- MRPK 93021 496-E2
5900 VEN 93003 492-C2
FREMONT WY
1300 OXN 93030 522-E4
FREMONTIA ST
1200 SPLA 93060 464-B3
FRENCH CT
2600 SIMI 93065 498-C3
FRENCHYS CV
- VeCo 93012 554-F3
FRESCA DR
- OXN 93030 522-H4
FRESHMAN CT
15700 MRPK 93021 477-A5
FRESH MEADOWS RD
300 SIMI 93065 497-C6
FRESHWATER DR
29000 AGRH 91301 558-A4
FRESHWIND CIR
3900 WLKV 91361 557-C6
FRESNO CT
10700 VEN 93004 472-H7
FREY CANYON RD
- VeCo 93015 466-H2
- VeCo 93021 466-G4
FRIANT AV
1300 SIMI 93065 498-A3
FRIAR ST
22400 WdHl 91367 529-D7
FRIEDRICH LN
1300 OXN 93033 552-E2
FRIEDRICH RD
2500 VeCo 93036 523-C2
E FRONT ST
800 VEN 93001 491-D2
W FRONT ST
200 VEN 93001 491-A2
FRONTAGE RD
300 VEN 93004 472-J7
FRONTIER AV
2900 THO 91360 526-C3
FRONTIER PL
11300 Chat 91311 499-J2
FROST AV
2500 THO 91360 526-F3
FROST CIR
6900 VEN 93003 492-E3
FROST DR
4200 OXN 93033 552-H4
FRUITVALE AV
8000 VeCo 93021 476-D3
FRYS HARBOR
- VeCo 93012 554-F3
FUCHSIA LN
1100 SPLA 93060 464-B3
FUCHSIA PL
- VEN 93004 473-A7
FUCHSIA ST
900 OXN 93036 522-E2
FUELBREAK RD
5300 VeCo - 366-L7
5300 VeCo - 442-H4
5300 VeCo 93023 366-L7
5300 VeCo 93023 442-H4
FUENTE DR
- OXN 93030 522-H4
FUJI ST
- MRPK 93021 496-D1
FULLBROKE DR
1900 THO 91362 527-A4
FULLER AV
1200 SIMI 93065 498-A4
FULMAR AV
1800 VEN 93003 492-E4
FULTON ST
100 OJAI 93023 441-J6
100 CMRL 93010 524-E3
S FULTON ST
100 OJAI 93023 441-J7
FURMAN AV
100 VEN 93003 492-B2
FUTURA PT
3100 THO 91362 527-A2

G

G ST
- VeCo 93042 583-F6
100 OXN 93030 522-F6
1200 OXN 93033 522-F7
1200 OXN 93033 552-F1
23600 VeCo 93063 498-G7
23600 VeCo 93063 528-F1
N G ST
300 OXN 93030 522-F5
GABBERT RD
5000 MRPK 93021 496-C1
5200 MRPK 93021 476-B6
GABRIELA CT
2400 CMRL 93012 495-B6
GABRIELLA DR
23600 OXN 93030 522-J5
GADSHILL LN
4100 AGRH 91301 558-F7
GAGE AV
2700 SIMI 93065 478-B7
GAIL CT
2900 THO 91320 555-H2
E GAINES CT
3800 SIMI 93063 498-E2
E GAINSBOROUGH RD
- THO 91360 526-F6
W GAINSBOROUGH RD
- THO 91360 526-F6
GALANO DR
4900 CMRL 93012 524-J3
GALANTE WY
200 OXN 93036 522-G3
GALAPAGOS WY
- OXN 93035 552-B1
GALAXY PL
3400 OXN 93030 523-D5
GALE WY
3300 VEN 93003 491-H2
GALENA AV
2100 SIMI 93065 498-D1
2100 SIMI 93065 498-D1
2700 SIMI 93063 478-D7
E GALENA AV
2700 SIMI 93065 498-C2
2800 SIMI 93063 498-C2
GALENA PL
- OXN 93030 522-H4
GALERITA ST
- OXN 93030 523-A5
GALESMOORE CT
1000 THO 91361 557-A5
GALINDO AV
2500 SIMI 93065 498-C4
GALLATIN PL
1100 OXN 93030 522-D4
1800 OXN 93036 522-D4
GALLEON AV
2600 PHME 93041 552-D1
GALLILEE WY
- SIMI 93063 499-B1
GALLOP CT
1800 SIMI 93065 497-J6
1800 SIMI 93065 498-A5
GALLOPING HILL RD
400 SIMI 93065 497-E6
GALSWORTHY ST
100 THO 91360 526-F7
GALT ST
1700 SIMI 93065 497-J3
GALVESTON AV
3000 SIMI 93063 478-G7
GALVIN CIR
400 VEN 93004 472-H6
GALVIN LN
700 FILM 93015 456-A5
GALVIN ST
10500 VEN 93004 472-H6
GALWAY LN
- SIMI 93065 497-E2
1800 THO 91320 556-A1
GAMEBIRD CT
29300 AGRH 91301 558-A5
GAMMON CT
1800 THO 91362 526-J2
GANTLIN AV
1100 SIMI 93065 497-H4
GARCES AV
4400 CMRL 93010 494-H7
GARCIA ST
100 SPLA 93060 464-C5
GARDEN DR
200 VeCo 91361 586-E1
E GARDEN GRN
100 PHME 93041 552-E1
W GARDEN GRN
100 PHME 93041 552-D1
GARDEN ST
- SIMI 93063 499-B1
N GARDEN ST
- VEN 93001 491-B1
S GARDEN ST
- VEN 93001 491-B2
GARDENIA AV
1400 CMRL 93010 494-D7
1600 VeCo 93010 494-C7
1600 VeCo 93010 524-C1

GARDENIA LN
- SIMI 93065 497-H3
GARDENIA ST
1100 OXN 93036 522-E2
GARDEN OAKS CT
29000 AGRH 91301 558-A3
GARDENSTONE CT
2000 THO 91361 557-A5
GARDENSTONE LN
24500 CanP 91307 529-C5
GARDNER AV
700 VEN 93004 492-H2
GARDNER ST
2800 SIMI 93065 498-C5
GARFIELD AV
100 OXN 93030 522-H6
N GARFIELD AV
100 OXN 93030 522-H5
GARFIELD RONDO
300 VEN 93003 492-E2
GARLAND CT
2800 THO 91360 526-D3
GARLAND ST
- VeCo 93001 471-C1
GARNET AV
700 VEN 93004 492-F3
GARNET PL
3200 SIMI 93063 478-D7
GARNET HILL CT
28800 AGRH 91301 558-B4
GARONNE ST
- OXN 93036 492-G6
GARRET DR
26900 CALB 91301 558-G6
GARRIDO CT
1000 VeCo 93010 494-B6
GARRIDO DR
900 VeCo 93010 494-B6
GARRISON WY
8900 VEN 93004 492-H3
23600 VeCo 93060 453-G2
GARST LN
1500 VeCo 93023 442-E4
GARVIN AV
1700 SIMI 93065 498-B3
GARY CT
3400 SIMI 93063 498-D2
GARY DR
1000 OXN 93033 552-J3
1800 OXN 93033 553-A3
GASTON RD
1000 VeCo 93063 499-B4
GASWAY DR
- FILM 93015 456-A7
- VeCo 93015 456-A7
GATEHOUSE LN
- SIMI 93063 498-J1
GATES PL
2600 SIMI 93065 498-B1
GATESHEAD BAY
4400 OXN 93035 552-A1
GATESHEAD WY
7100 CanP 91307 529-F5
GATEWAY DR
6400 SIMI 93063 499-C3
GATEWOOD LN
1200 SPLA 93060 464-B2
GAUCHO WY
1800 OXN 93030 522-J6
1800 OXN 93030 523-A6
GAULT ST
22000 CanP 91307 529-J5
22700 CanP 91307 529-G5
GAVIN ST
- SIMI 93063 498-H1
GAVIOTA CT
1800 SIMI 93065 498-A2
GAVIOTA LN
1300 VEN 93003 492-C4
GAVIOTA PL
100 OXN 93033 552-G4
GAVIOTA WY
700 OXN 93033 552-H4
GAY DR
- VEN 93003 492-B4
GAYLE PL
2400 SIMI 93065 498-A1
E GAYTHORNE RD
12600 VeCo 93060 473-E5
GAZANIA CT
2000 THO 91362 556-H1
GAZEBO LN
- CMRL 93012 524-G5
GAZENIA CT
- OXN 93030 523-A4
GEM CIR
3200 SIMI 93063 478-D7
GEMINI AV
1000 CMRL 93010 524-F2
GEMINI CT
2600 CMRL 93010 524-F1
GENE AV
1500 SIMI 93065 498-B3
GENEIVE CIR
200 CMRL 93010 524-D4
GENEIVE ST
- CMRL 93010 524-D4
GENEVA ST
6000 VeCo 93003 492-D6

GENEVA WY
2000 OXN 93035 552-D1
GENIAL CT
300 SIMI 93065 497-J6
GENOA DR
200 SIMI 93065 497-F3
GENOA LN
- OXN 93035 522-D6
GENOVA CT
30800 WLKV 91362 557-G6
GENTILLY PL
1400 VeCo 91377 527-H6
GENTLE BROOK LN
- SIMI 93063 498-G2
GENTLE CREEK CIR
500 THO 91320 555-E3
GENTLEWOOD DR
11500 MRPK 93021 496-B3
GEOFFREY AV
1800 SIMI 93063 498-J3
1800 SIMI 93063 499-A2
GEORGE ST
3300 VeCo 93036 523-A1
3400 VeCo 93036 493-A7
GEORGETOWN AV
400 VEN 93003 492-A1
GEORGETTE ST
2600 SIMI 93063 498-D1
2700 SIMI 93063 478-D7
GEORGIA ST
3900 VEN 93003 491-J3
GEORGIA WY
9200 Chat 91311 499-E7
GERALD DR
3100 VeCo 91320 555-G1
GERANIUM LN
600 SIMI 93065 497-D5
GERANIUM PL
200 OXN 93036 522-F2
GERANIUM WY
100 VEN 93004 473-A7
GERMAIN ST
3400 CMRL 93010 524-G1
22100 Chat 91311 499-J3
GERMAINE LN
31500 WLKV 91361 557-D7
GERMANIA CT
6300 AGRH 91301 558-A3
GERONIMO AV
2900 SIMI 93063 479-A6
GERONIMO DR
2300 OXN 93033 553-A2
GERRAD WY
23600 CanP 91307 529-E4
GERRY RD
1800 VeCo 93012 495-G7
1800 VeCo 93012 525-G1
GERSHWIN LN
600 VEN 93003 492-B3
GERSHWIN PL
2100 OXN 93033 553-A1
GERST DR
600 VeCo 91320 525-G7
GERTRUDE ST
4000 SIMI 93063 498-F2
GETMAN ST
1400 CMRL 93010 524-C1
GETTYSBURG ST
4000 VEN 93003 491-J2
GETZ AV
- VEN 93003 492-B4
GEYSER CT
1300 THO 91320 526-A6
GIANT OAK AV
- THO 91320 556-A1
GIBRALTAR ST
100 OXN 93030 523-A5
GIBRALTER ST
- OXN 93030 523-A4
- VeCo 93030 523-A4
GIBSON AV
800 SIMI 93065 497-J5
GIBSON PL
- OXN 93033 552-H5
GIERSON AV
9400 Chat 91311 499-J5
GIFFORD ST
22200 CanP 91303 529-J4
W GILA CT
1900 THO 91320 555-J2
1900 THO 91320 556-A2
GILBERT CT
4700 VEN 93003 492-A7
GILBERT LN
900 VEN 93003 492-A7
GILBERT ST
500 THO 91320 525-H7
GILDA CIR
1700 SIMI 93065 498-A3
GILES RD
100 VeCo 91361 556-F7
GILL AV
400 PHME 93041 552-F5
GILLESPIE ST
- VEN 93003 492-B4
GILLIARD LN
200 VEN 93001 491-D1
GILLINGHAM CIR
2300 THO 91362 527-A2

GILMORE ST
22000 CanP 91303 529-J7
22300 CanP 91307 529-C7
GINA DR
1200 OXN 93030 522-E4
1800 OXN 93036 522-E4
GINA ST
1200 THO 91320 556-B1
GINGER CIR
2300 THO 91320 555-J1
GINGER DR
1700 OXN 93033 552-J2
GINGER ST
1900 OXN 93036 522-F3
GINGERWOOD CT
3600 THO 91360 526-H1
GINKO CT
3200 THO 91360 526-F2
GISLER AV
1600 OXN 93033 552-H2
GISLER RD
- MRPK 93021 496-D1
GITANA AV
5600 CMRL 93012 525-B6
GITANO DR
- OXN 93030 522-H4
GLACIER AV
800 PHME 93041 552-F4
800 OXN 93033 552-F4
800 OXN 93041 552-F4
1300 VEN 93003 492-B5
W GLACIER AV
100 OXN 93033 552-G4
GLACIER ST
1400 SIMI 93063 498-D3
GLADE AV
6400 CanP 91303 529-J5
7600 LA 91304 529-J4
9200 Chat 91311 499-J4
GLADE DR
500 SPLA 93060 464-A5
GLADEHOLLOW CT
5500 AGRH 91301 558-A5
GLADE SPRINGS CT
2100 OXN 93036 522-D2
GLADHILL ST
4000 THO 91320 555-E4
GLADIOLA ST
800 OXN 93036 522-F2
GLADSTONE DR
500 THO 91360 526-G6
GLAMOUR TER
- LA 91304 529-D2
GLANVILLE RD
23600 VeCo 93060 464-J4
23600 VeCo 93060 465-A4
N GLASSELL AV
1500 SIMI 93065 498-C3
GLASTONBURY RD
1900 THO 91361 557-A6
GLEAM CT
5900 AGRH 91301 558-B4
GLEDHILL ST
22000 Chat 91311 499-J6
GLEN ST
2800 VEN 93003 491-G3
GLEN WY
200 FILM 93015 455-J6
GLEN ABBEY LN
- OXN 93036 522-C2
GLENBRIDGE CIR
1100 THO 91361 557-B5
GLENBRIDGE RD
31400 WLKV 91361 557-D7
GLENBROCK LN
1500 THO 91320 526-A7
GLENBROOK AV
- CMRL 93010 524-D1
700 CMRL 93010 494-C7
GLENCOE AV
2600 SIMI 93063 478-D7
GLENCREST CIR
6300 VEN 93003 472-C6
GLENDALE AV
100 VeCo 93035 552-B5
GLENDIVE CT
- SIMI 93065 478-A6
GLENDON CT
23600 SIMI 93065 497-G7
GLEN EAGLES CT
2600 OXN 93036 522-D2
GLEN EAGLES WY
500 SIMI 93065 497-E5
GLEN ELLEN DR
- VEN 93003 491-H2
GLENHAVEN CIR
4800 THO 91362 557-G1
GLENHAVEN CT
7200 CanP 91307 529-E5
GLEN HOLLOW ST
2000 THO 91361 557-A5
GLENHURST CT
2400 SIMI 93063 498-D1
GLENLOCH LN
23600 SIMI 93065 497-A1
GLENMARE CT
1300 THO 91361 557-A6
GLENMONT CT
4000 THO 91320 555-E4

GLENN DR
- CMRL 93010 524-E3
S GLENN DR
- CMRL 93010 524-E4
GLENNCLIFF CIR
3100 THO 91360 526-C2
GLENNON CT
1600 THO 91361 556-J5
GLEN OAKS RD
600 THO 91360 556-G1
GLENSIDE LN
2300 VeCo 93012 496-B7
GLENTANA ST
- SIMI 93065 478-A6
GLENVIEW AV
1700 SIMI 93063 498-E3
GLENWAY ST
700 SPLA 93060 464-B5
GLENWOOD AV
200 VEN 93003 492-C2
GLENWOOD DR
100 OXN 93030 522-F4
GLENWOOD PL
300 THO 91362 556-J1
GLIDE AV
6100 WdHl 91367 529-F7
GLIDER CT
1900 THO 91320 526-A6
GLOBE AV
2800 THO 91360 526-F3
GLORIA CT
1000 OXN 93030 522-H5
GLORIA DR
3200 VeCo 91320 525-F7
GLORIA LN
1500 SIMI 93063 499-B3
GLORIOSA CT
- OXN 93030 523-A3
GLORYETTE AV
2100 SIMI 93063 498-G1
GLOUCESTER LN
700 THO 91362 526-J7
GLOVER DR
2100 VEN 93003 492-C5
GOBELS PASTURE RD
2300 THO 91362 527-A7
GODDARD AV
2000 SIMI 93063 498-F2
GOLD CIR
- VEN 93004 492-G3
GOLD CV
2500 PHME 93041 552-C3
GOLD DUST CT
1600 SIMI 93063 499-C3
GOLDEN AMBER LN
- SIMI 93065 497-H3
GOLDEN BEAR CT
800 SIMI 93065 497-E6
GOLDEN CANYON CIR
11200 Chat 91311 499-H2
GOLDEN CREST AV
3200 THO 91320 555-G4
GOLDEN EAGLE DR
1200 VeCo 91377 527-G7
GOLDENEYE ST
- VEN 93003 492-D5
GOLDEN FERN CT
200 SIMI 93065 497-E6
GOLDEN GLEN DR
- SIMI 93065 497-D6
GOLDEN GROVE CT
800 SIMI 93065 497-E6
GOLDEN KNOLL CT
4900 THO 91362 557-F3
GOLDENLEAF DR
3600 WLKV 91361 557-C7
GOLDEN MOSS CT
700 SIMI 93065 497-E6
GOLDEN NUGGET WY
5300 VeCo 91377 527-H7
GOLDEN OAK ST
- THO 91320 526-A6
GOLDEN PARK PL
400 SIMI 93065 497-E6
GOLDEN POND DR
- CMRL 93012 524-G4
GOLDENRIDGE CT
5200 CMRL 93012 524-J1
5200 CMRL 93012 525-A1
GOLDEN ROD CT
1900 THO 91361 557-A6
GOLDENROD PL
26600 CALB 91302 558-G7
GOLDEN SKY CIR
1900 THO 91362 527-G5
GOLDENSPUR DR
3000 VeCo 93010 494-C6
GOLDEN VINE CT
400 SIMI 93065 497-E6
GOLDEN WEST AV
200 OJAI 93023 442-A6
200 VeCo 93023 442-A6
GOLDENWOOD CIR
500 SIMI 93065 497-E6
GOLDFIELD PL
2700 SIMI 93063 478-E7
2700 SIMI 93063 498-D1
GOLDFINCH DR
6800 VEN 93003 492-E4

GOLD HILL CIR
3100 THO 91360 526-D2
GOLD HILL RD
- VeCo - 367-C1
GOLDIN AV
2400 SIMI 93065 498-B1
GOLDMAN AV
- MRPK 93021 496-D1
GOLDSMITH AV
2200 THO 91360 526-F4
GOLD SPRING PL
800 THO 91361 557-A5
GOLDSTONE LN
- SIMI 93065 478-B4
GOLD STRIKE AV
2300 THO 91360 526-D4
GOLF COURSE CT
1800 THO 91362 527-D6
GOLF COURSE DR
2800 VEN 93003 492-D7
2900 VEN 93001 492-D7
4300 THO 91362 527-D6
GOLF MEADOWS CT
2600 SIMI 93063 478-H7
GOLF VILLA WY
- CMRL 93010 493-H7
GOLIAD CIR
4800 SIMI 93063 478-H7
GOLONDRINA ST
13100 MRPK 93021 496-E3
GONDOLA DR
4800 VeCo 91377 557-G2
GONZAGA ST
5200 VEN 93003 492-B3
GONZALES RD
- OXN 93030 522-H3
100 OXN 93036 522-F3
1100 VeCo 93063 499-A3
1800 OXN 93030 523-A3
2100 OXN 93036 523-A3
2700 VeCo 93030 522-A3
2900 VeCo 93036 522-A3
3900 VeCo 93030 521-H3
3900 VeCo 93036 521-H3
5000 VeCo 93035 521-H3
GONZALES SERVICE RD
500 OXN 93030 522-F3
GOODENOUGH RD
700 FILM 93015 455-J5
1100 VeCo 93015 455-J3
2100 VeCo 93015 367-B7
GOODHOPE ST
500 VeCo 93022 451-A7
GOODMAN ST
800 VEN 93003 492-A4
GOODSPEED ST
1000 PHME 93041 552-E5
GOODSPRING DR
30300 AGRH 91301 557-G5
E GOODWIN CT
3900 SIMI 93063 498-F2
GOODYEAR AV
1700 VEN 93003 492-A5
GORGON DR
- VeCo 93041 583-G2
GORHAM RD
100 VeCo 93023 442-B6
GORMAN ST
2100 CMRL 93010 524-E2
GORRION AV
- VEN 93004 472-J6
- VEN 93004 473-A6
GOSHEN ST
6100 SIMI 93063 499-B2
GOTITA WY
1200 OXN 93030 522-H5
E GOULD ST
2600 SIMI 93065 498-C5
GRABLE PL
700 THO 91320 555-G3
GRACE CT
- CMRL 93010 494-D7
- CMRL 93010 524-D1
E GRACELAND ST
2200 SIMI 93065 498-B2
GRACIA DR
- OXN 93030 522-H4
GRACIA ST
800 CMRL 93010 524-G2
GRADA AV
600 VeCo 93010 494-B6
GRADUATE CIR
15800 MRPK 93021 477-A4
E GRAFTON ST
3100 SIMI 93063 498-D2
N GRAFTON ST
2200 SIMI 93063 498-D2
GRAHAM AV
400 CMRL 93010 524-F3
GRAHAM CT
10100 VEN 93004 492-J2
GRAHAM ST
1100 SIMI 93065 497-H2
GRANADA LN
- FILM 93015 456-C6
GRANADA ST
- CMRL 93010 524-D4
GRANADILLA DR
4200 MRPK 93021 496-E3

N GRANBY AV
800 SIMI 93065 498-C4
GRAND AV
200 OJAI 93023 441-H6
900 VeCo 93015 455-H2
900 OJAI 93023 442-A6
1100 VeCo 93023 442-D5
1900 VEN 93003 492-D5
2000 VeCo 93003 492-D5
GRANDE ST
200 OXN 93036 522-H2
GRANDE VISTA DR
3000 THO 91320 525-G6
GRANDE VISTA ST
100 VeCo 93022 461-A1
GRAND ISLE DR
13600 MRPK 93021 496-F2
GRAND OAK LN
300 THO 91360 526-D6
GRANDOAKS DR
2600 WLKV 91361 557-A7
GRAND RIDGE CT
6200 VEN 93003 472-C6
GRANDSEN CT
6400 MRPK 93021 477-A6
GRANDVIEW AV
700 OJAI 93023 441-J6
GRANDVIEW CIR
100 CMRL 93010 524-D4
GRANDVIEW CT
5300 VEN 93003 492-B1
GRANDVIEW DR
- VeCo 93010 494-E6
2000 CMRL 93010 524-E4
GRANDVIEW TER
23200 Chat 91311 499-G6
GRANGER ST
1800 CMRL 93010 524-D2
GRANITE ST
100 SIMI 93065 497-F6
GRANITE HILLS ST
500 SIMI 93065 527-D1
GRANITE PEAK AV
- SIMI 93065 478-A6
GRANITO DR
1000 VeCo 93023 451-C1
GRANT AV
100 OXN 93030 522-H6
N GRANT AV
100 OXN 93030 522-H5
GRANT LN
500 SPLA 93060 464-C3
GRANT ST
7300 VEN 93003 492-E2
GRANT WY
600 OXN 93033 552-F4
GRANT LINE ST
300 SPLA 93060 464-B3
GRANT PARK FUEL BREAK
500 VeCo 93001 471-D7
500 VEN 93001 471-D7
500 VEN 93001 491-C1
N GRANVIA PL
2600 THO 91360 526-C3
GRANVILLE AV
3000 SIMI 93063 478-G7
GRAPE HILL RD
300 VeCo 93023 453-B1
GRAPEVINE CT
- SIMI 93063 499-B1
GRAPEVINE DR
2400 OXN 93036 522-F1
GRAPEVINE RD
- VeCo 93001 450-J6
- VeCo 93001 451-A6
- VeCo 93022 450-J6
- VeCo 93022 451-A6
GRASS VALLEY ST
500 SIMI 93065 527-E1
GRAVES AV
300 OXN 93030 523-B4
GRAVES CT
1000 CMRL 93010 524-C2
GRAY CT
800 THO 91362 526-H7
GRAYROCK ST
900 THO 91320 555-F4
GRAYSON CT
2600 SIMI 93065 498-C4
GRAYSTONE DR
7600 LA 91304 529-D4
GRAYSTONE PL
2500 SIMI 93065 497-J1
E GREAT SMOKEY CT
2800 THO 91362 557-C3
W GREAT SMOKEY CT
2700 THO 91362 557-B3
GREELY CT
2000 OXN 93033 553-A1
GREEN LN
600 SIMI 93065 497-E5
GREEN ST
100 SPLA 93060 464-B6
8000 VEN 93004 492-F2
GREENBANK RD
2400 VeCo 91361 586-D1
GREEN BAY CT
10400 VEN 93004 492-J2

N GREENBRIAR AV
700 SIMI 93065 498-A5
GREENBRIAR CT
5900 AGRH 91301 558-A4
GREENBROOK DR
2100 OXN 93033 552-J2
2600 OXN 93033 553-A2
GREENBUSH LN
4100 MRPK 93021 496-F3
GREENCASTLE CT
2500 OXN 93035 552-B2
GREENCASTLE LN
2200 OXN 93035 552-B2
GREENCASTLE WY
2000 OXN 93035 552-B1
GREENDALE AV
800 THO 91320 555-E4
GREENDALE CIR
700 THO 91320 555-E4
GREENFIELD ST
100 THO 91360 526-E6
GREENGATE CT
4500 WLKV 91361 557-D6
GREEN GLADE CT
- CMRL 93010 524-A2
GREEN GRASS CT
29400 AGRH 91301 557-J5
29400 AGRH 91301 558-A5
GREEN HEATH PL
200 THO 91361 556-E2
GREENHILL AV
6500 VEN 93003 492-D5
GREEN LAWN AV
800 CMRL 93010 524-A2
GREEN LEA PL
200 THO 91361 556-E2
GREENLEAF AV
2600 SIMI 93063 498-E1
2700 SIMI 93063 478-E7
GREENMEADOW AV
- THO 91320 556-D2
300 THO 91361 556-E2
N GREENMEADOW AV
- THO 91320 556-C1
GREEN MEADOW DR
5700 AGRH 91301 557-H4
GREENMEADOW DR
- THO 91320 556-C2
GREENMEADOW LN
600 THO 91320 556-D1
GREEN MOOR PL
200 THO 91361 556-E2
GREEN MOUNTAIN ST
500 SIMI 93065 527-D2
GREEN OAK CT
2300 THO 91362 527-A3
GREENOCK LN
1300 VEN 93001 491-F5
GREENPARK CT
2100 THO 91362 527-A4
GREEN PASTURE LN
- SIMI 93063 498-G2
GREEN PINE PL
23600 SIMI 93063 498-D4
GREENRIDGE DR
5200 VeCo 93021 475-J7
5200 VeCo 93021 495-J1
GREENRIDGE ST
100 THO 91360 526-F1
GREEN RIVER ST
- OXN 93036 492-G6
GREENSBORO RD
800 VEN 93004 492-H3
GREEN SHADOWS LN
- SIMI 93065 478-B4
GREENSWARD ST
2200 SIMI 93065 478-B7
N GREENTREE DR
5400 VeCo 93066 474-J7
5400 VeCo 93066 494-J1
5700 VeCo 93066 475-A7
W GREENTREE DR
5400 VeCo 93066 474-H7
5400 VeCo 93066 494-H1
GREENVALE DR
- CMRL 93010 524-A2
GREEN VALLEY DR
800 THO 91320 526-A7
GREENVIEW CIR
6300 VEN 93003 472-C6
GREENVIEW RD
5800 CALB 91302 558-J3
GREENVILLE DR
3200 SIMI 93063 478-G6
GREEN VISTA CIR
7000 CanP 91307 529-F5
GREENWAY AV
200 THO 91320 555-E2
GREENWICH DR
500 THO 91360 556-G1
GREENWOOD RD
900 SPLA 93060 464-B3
GREENWOOD ST
3700 THO 91320 555-D4
GREGORY ST
1200 OJAI 93023 442-A6
GRENOBLE CT
30800 WLKV 91362 557-G7

STREET Block City ZIP Pg-Grid

GRENVILLE CT
32000 WLKV 91361 557-C6
GRESHAM ST
22000 LA 91304 529-J1
GRETA ST
100 THO 91360 526-F4
GREY FEATHER CT
1500 THO 91362 527-F6
GREY ROCK RD
5600 AGRH 91301 558-A4
5700 AGRH 91301 557-J3
GRIDLEY RD
100 OJAI 93023 442-A6
400 VeCo 93023 442-B3
2300 VeCo - 442-B3
GRIFFAN DR
23600 FILM 93015 455-J3
23600 VeCo 93015 455-J3
GRIFFITH LN
7300 MRPK 93021 477-A4
GRIFFON CT
- SIMI 93065 478-A6
GRIMES CANYON RD
6700 MRPK 93021 476-A6
6700 VeCo 93021 475-H7
6700 VeCo 93021 476-A6
15100 VeCo 93021 495-H1
GRIMES CANYON RD Rt#-23
1300 VeCo 93015 465-J4
4800 VeCo 93015 466-A5
4800 VeCo 93021 466-A5
8000 VeCo 93021 476-B2
GRINDSTONE CT
- MRPK 93021 476-F6
GRINNEL CT
400 SIMI 93065 497-F6
GRISSOM ST
1400 THO 91362 527-A6
GRISSOM WY
- OXN 93033 552-G6
GROSS AV
6400 CanP 91307 529-F7
GROTTOES WY
- MRPK 93021 476-F6
GROUNDBRIER AV
23600 SIMI 93065 497-A2
GROUSE WY
6800 VEN 93003 492-E4
GROVE LN
200 VEN 93001 491-G1
200 VEN 93003 491-G1
GROVE ST
2800 VEN 93003 491-G2
GROVE WY
200 SIMI 93065 497-E2
GROVEDALE LN
13500 MRPK 93021 496-F3
GROVER CIR
1700 SIMI 93063 499-A2
GROVES PL
3700 VeCo 93066 494-H4
GRUB LEASE RD
- VeCo 93001 470-G4
GRUNDY LN
9100 Chat 91311 499-E7
GUADALCANAL ST
- PHME 93041 552-E5
N GUAM DR
1000 PHME 93041 552-E5
S GUAM DR
1000 PHME 93041 552-E5
GUARDIAN ST
4000 SIMI 93063 498-F3
GUAVA CT
1800 OXN 93033 552-F1
E GUAVA ST
100 OXN 93033 552-G1
W GUAVA ST
100 OXN 93033 552-F1
N GUERNE AV
2000 SIMI 93063 498-E2
GUIBERSON RD
- VeCo 93040 457-F7
- VeCo 93015 466-G1
2400 VeCo 93015 467-B1
3700 VeCo 93015 457-E7
GUIBERSON ST
300 SPLA 93060 464-C4
GUILDHALL CT
4400 WLKV 91361 557-E6
GUILFORD CIR
1800 THO 91360 526-F5
GUINDA CT
1100 VeCo 93010 494-C5
GULL CT
1600 VEN 93003 492-E4
GUM CIR
2600 SIMI 93065 478-C7
GUM TREE ST
- OXN 93036 522-B2
GUNNER LN
1500 SIMI 93063 499-B3
GUNSMOKE RD
13500 MRPK 93021 496-F3
GUSTAV LN
8300 LA 91304 529-F2
GUTIERREZ LN
- OXN 93033 552-H6
GUY HARDISON
100 VeCo 93015 465-A1
100 VeCo 93060 465-A1
300 VeCo 93060 455-A7
GWIN CT
4700 SIMI 93063 498-H1
GYPSY CT
2100 THO 91362 556-H2
GYPSY LN
- VeCo 93010 494-F6

H

H
- PHME 93035 552-B3
- PHME 93043 552-B3
H AV
- VeCo 93042 583-F4
H ST
100 OXN 93030 522-F5
1800 OXN 93036 522-F1
S H ST
100 OXN 93030 522-F6
1100 OXN 93033 522-F7
1200 OXN 93033 552-F1
HAAZ WY
1800 OXN 93030 522-J5
1800 OXN 93030 523-A5
HABRA CT
1300 CMRL 93010 524-D1
HACIENDA CIR
800 CMRL 93012 524-J2
HACIENDA DR
- OXN 93030 522-H4
500 CMRL 93012 524-J2
900 VeCo 93065 497-F4
N HACIENDA RD
- VeCo 91307 528-J3
N HACKAMORE LN
- VeCo 91307 529-A4
HACKAMORE ST
800 VeCo 93023 451-C3
HACKBERRY DR
- VeCo 93001 471-C3
HACKERS LN
6000 AGRH 91301 557-G3
E HACKNEY RD
6000 VeCo 93066 495-C1
HACKNEY ST
22000 LA 91304 529-J2
HADJIAN LN
22100 CanP 91303 529-J5
HADLEY DR
300 VEN 93003 492-B3
HAGEN CT
1000 SIMI 93065 497-H4
HAIFA RD
- SIMI 93063 479-B7
- SIMI 93063 499-B1
HAIGH RD
100 THO 91320 556-C1
HAILES RD
3100 VeCo 93033 553-D3
HAILEY CT
23600 SIMI 93065 498-B5
HAINES CANYON
23600 VeCo 93015 456-F6
HALCON ST
100 OXN 93030 523-A5
HALESIA LN
- OXN 93030 523-A4
HALEVY ST
600 VEN 93003 492-B7
HALEY RANCH RD
100 VeCo 93001 450-H7
100 VeCo 93001 451-A5
HALIFAX CT
1200 VEN 93004 492-H3
HALIFAX LN
- OXN 93035 522-C6
HALIFAX ST
8800 VEN 93004 492-H3
HALL RD
100 VeCo 93060 465-A2
100 VeCo 93060 455-A7
HALL CANYON RD
100 VEN 93001 491-G2
500 VeCo 93001 471-G6
500 VEN 93001 471-G6
HALLOCK DR
100 SPLA 93060 464-D5
S HALLOCK DR
200 SPLA 93060 464-E5
HALSBURY CT
23600 VeCo 91361 556-F6
HALSEY WY
4800 OXN 93033 552-H5
HALSTED ST
22100 Chat 91311 499-J6
HALYARD ST
600 PHME 93041 552-B1
HAMILTON AV
300 VEN 93003 491-J2
4200 OXN 93033 552-J5
HAMILTON ST
1500 SIMI 93065 497-J4
1700 SIMI 93065 498-A4
HAMLIN AV
3200 SIMI 93063 478-G6
HAMLIN ST
22200 CanP 91303 529-J6
22600 CanP 91307 529-F6
HAMMIL CT
2600 SIMI 93065 498-C4
HAMPSHIRE RD
1200 SIMI 93065 498-B4
- THO 91362 557-A3
100 THO 91361 557-A3
HAMPSTEAD CT
- VeCo 91361 586-F1
HAMPTON AV
2300 SIMI 93063 498-J1
HAMPTON CT
- THO 91362 527-C2
HAMPTON CANYON RD
3600 VeCo 93060 463-A4
3900 VeCo 93060 462-J3
HANCOCK PL
2100 OXN 93033 553-A2
HANDEL CT
4700 VEN 93003 492-A7
HANFORD ST
9300 VEN 93004 492-G2
HANLEY AV
1700 SIMI 93065 498-B3
HANNA AV
8500 LA 91304 529-J1
9300 Chat 91311 499-J4
HANNAH CIR
1700 SIMI 93063 499-A3
HANOVER AV
500 THO 91320 555-G3
HANOVER CT
3200 THO 91320 555-G3
HANOVER LN
1200 VEN 93001 491-F5
HANSEN CT
2400 SIMI 93065 498-B4
HANSON RD
4900 VEN 93003 492-B3
HAPPY LN
1500 VeCo 93023 442-D4
2900 VeCo 93063 478-C6
HAPPY ST
300 SPLA 93060 464-A7
HAPPY CAMP RD
7900 VeCo 93021 476-F1
9400 VeCo 93021 466-F5
HAPPY CAMP CANYON RD
- MRPK 93021 476-G4
- VeCo 93021 466-G7
- VeCo 93021 476-F1
23600 VeCo - 367-E9
23600 VeCo - 467-E4
23600 VeCo 93021 467-A6
HAPPY TALK RANCH RD
14800 VeCo 93060 463-F6
HAPPY VALLEY RD
23600 VeCo 93063 478-A7
23600 VeCo 93063 529-B1
HAPPY VALLEY SCHOOL RD
23600 VeCo 93023 442-F7
23600 VeCo 93023 452-F1
HARBOR BLVD
100 OXN 93035 521-G2
100 VeCo 93030 521-H4
100 VeCo 93035 521-H4
1200 OXN 93035 552-A1
1900 OXN 93036 521-G2
1900 VeCo 93036 521-G2
2500 VeCo 93001 521-G2
2500 VEN 93001 521-G2
3000 VeCo 93035 552-B4
E HARBOR BLVD
- VEN 93001 491-B2
2500 VEN 93001 491-D3
3300 VEN 93001 521-G1
HARBOR RD
4600 PHME 93043 552-D6
HARBOR LIGHTS LN
400 PHME 93041 552-C2
HARBORVIEW CT
6100 VEN 93003 472-C5
HARBORVIEW LN
32100 WLKV 91361 557-C6
HARBOUR ISLAND LN
4200 OXN 93035 552-A1
HARDING AV
- VEN 93003 492-E2
100 OXN 93030 522-H6
N HARDING AV
- VEN 93003 492-E1
HARDISON ST
300 SPLA 93060 463-H6
HARDISON TER
23600 VeCo 93060 453-G2
HARDNEGO RD
1800 VeCo 93060 465-B6
2100 VeCo 93066 465-B6
HARGROVE CT
14000 MRPK 93021 496-G4
HARMON DR
6800 VEN 93003 492-E5
HARMON CANYON RD
23600 VeCo 93003 472-B2
23600 VeCo 93003 492-D1
23600 VeCo 93060 472-D1
HARMON CANYON RD
23600 VEN 93003 492-E1
HARMONY CT
1400 THO 91362 527-A6
HAROLD AV
1200 SIMI 93065 498-B4
HARPER DR
1700 VEN 93004 492-H4
E HARPER ST
600 SIMI 93065 497-G5
HARPSTONE LN
23600 SIMI 93065 497-A1
HARRIER CT
- THO 91320 525-J5
- THO 91320 526-A5
HARRIET ST
300 VEN 93001 491-A1
HARRINGTON RD
2700 SIMI 93065 498-C4
HARRIS AV
1000 CMRL 93010 524-C1
HARRIS CT
900 THO 91362 526-J7
HARRIS ST
- PHME 93043 552-E4
HARRISON AV
100 OXN 93030 522-G6
E HARRISON AV
- VEN 93001 491-B1
N HARRISON AV
100 OXN 93030 522-G5
W HARRISON AV
- VEN 93001 491-B1
HARRY ST
- MRPK 93021 496-F1
HART ST
22000 CanP 91303 529-J5
HARTE AV
200 VEN 93003 492-B2
HARTE LN
15500 MRPK 93021 477-A4
HARTFIELD CT
4200 WLKV 91361 557-D6
HARTFORD ST
14600 MRPK 93021 476-H6
HARTGLEN AV
800 THO 91361 557-A4
HARTGLEN PL
5500 AGRH 91301 557-H5
HARTHORN LN
- FILM 93015 455-H5
HARTLAND CIR
2600 THO 91361 557-B5
HARTLAND ST
22200 CanP 91303 529-H6
22400 CanP 91307 529-E6
HARTLEY AV
1200 SIMI 93065 498-C4
HARTMAN DR
- VeCo 93012 525-C5
- VEN 93003 491-G3
HARTMAN WY
9300 WHil 91304 499-E7
HARTMAN TURNOFF
- VeCo 93001 471-C3
HARTNELL ST
2500 CMRL 93010 524-E2
HARTUNG CT
3600 THO 91320 555-F4
HARTWICK CIR
2000 THO 91360 526-D4
E HARVARD BLVD
100 SPLA 93060 464-C5
1300 VeCo 93060 464-C5
W HARVARD BLVD
100 SPLA 93060 464-A7
200 SPLA 93060 463-J7
HARVARD ST
300 OXN 93036 522-H2
5200 VEN 93003 492-B3
N HARVARD ST
6400 MRPK 93021 476-H6
HARVEST LN
1700 CMRL 93012 525-A1
1800 CMRL 93012 495-A7
HARVESTER ST
11800 MRPK 93021 496-C2
HARVEY DR
1000 SPLA 93060 464-B3
HARWICH PL
23700 CanP 91307 529-E5
HARWOOD LN
500 THO 91360 526-D7
HASLER RD
- VeCo 90265 625-H1
HASSETT AV
23600 VeCo 91361 556-G6
HASSTED DR
33100 LACo 90265 586-E7
HASTINGS AV
- VEN 93003 492-C2
HASTINGS CT
5000 VeCo 91377 557-H1
HASTINGS ST
6700 MRPK 93021 476-G5
HATFIELD CT
13700 MRPK 93021 496-F4
HATHAWAY AV
23600 THO 91362 527-B5
HATMOR DR
26100 CALB 91302 558-H4
HAUSER CIR
1500 THO 91362 526-J7
HAVASU ST
9000 VEN 93004 492-H4
HAVEN AV
1000 SIMI 93065 498-A4
HAVENCREST ST
12000 MRPK 93021 496-C4
HAVENRIDGE CT
4000 MRPK 93021 496-B4
HAVENSIDE AV
300 THO 91320 555-E2
HAVENWOOD DR
1800 THO 91362 526-J4
HAVILAND ST
800 SIMI 93065 498-C4
HAWK CIR
- VeCo 93041 583-H3
HAWK DR
- VeCo 93041 583-J3
HAWK ST
2100 SIMI 93065 498-A1
N HAWK ST
2400 SIMI 93065 498-B1
HAWK WY
6800 VEN 93003 492-E4
HAWKEYE PL
3600 THO 91320 555-F4
HAWKS BILL PL
500 SIMI 93065 527-D1
HAWKSWAY CT
1600 THO 91361 556-J5
HAWTHORN ST
1200 SPLA 93060 464-B3
HAWTHORNE DR
5000 VeCo 91377 557-G1
HAWTHORNE LN
900 VEN 93003 492-D3
HAYDEN ST
1700 CMRL 93010 524-D2
HAYES AV
- VEN 93003 492-E2
100 OXN 93030 522-G5
N HAYES AV
100 OXN 93030 522-G5
HAYMARKET ST
2400 THO 91362 527-B3
HAYNES ST
22200 CanP 91303 529-J6
22400 CanP 91307 529-E6
HAYNIE CT
- MRPK 93021 476-B5
HAYS DR
1700 THO 91320 556-A1
HAYWARD ST
7600 VEN 93004 492-E1
HAZEL CIR
6400 SIMI 93063 499-C2
HAZEL ST
9200 Chat 91311 499-G7
HAZEL WY
9200 Chat 91311 499-G7
HAZELCREST CIR
4800 THO 91362 557-F2
HAZELNUT CT
3400 SIMI 93065 498-D5
HAZEL RIDGE CT
200 SIMI 93065 498-A6
HAZELTINE DR
- OXN 93036 522-C3
HAZEL TOP CT
- MRPK 93021 476-F6
HAZELWOOD DR
400 OXN 93030 522-F4
HAZELWOOD WY
400 SIMI 93065 497-D5
HEALY TER
9300 Chat 91311 499-E6
9300 Chat 91311 499-F7
HEARON DR
6900 MRPK 93021 476-J5
7200 MRPK 93021 477-A5
HEARST DR
300 OXN 93030 523-A6
3500 SIMI 93063 498-E3
HEARTLAND AV
1000 SIMI 93065 478-A6
HEATHER CT
4800 MRPK 93021 496-C2
29600 AGRH 91301 557-J3
HEATHER ST
100 OXN 93036 522-F2
600 VeCo 93023 451-C3
2000 SIMI 93065 498-B2
5300 CMRL 93012 525-A3
HEATHER WY
- VEN 93004 473-C7
HEATHERBANK CT
1600 THO 91361 556-D7
HEATHERDALE CT
4200 MRPK 93021 496-B3
HEATHERFIELD CT
3200 THO 91320 555-G2
HEATHERGLEN CT
4500 MRPK 93021 496-B2
HEATHERGLOW ST
3200 THO 91360 526-F2
HEATHER OAKS LN
1400 THO 91361 556-H5
HEATHER RIDGE AV
100 THO 91320 556-A1
HEATHERTON DR
5200 VeCo 93066 475-A7
5200 VeCo 93066 495-A1
HEATHERVIEW DR
1100 VeCo 91377 528-A7
HEATHERWISP LN
23600 SIMI 93065 497-A1
HEATHERWOOD HOLLOW AV
3900 MRPK 93021 496-D4
HEATH MEADOW CT
100 SIMI 93065 497-D6
HEATH MEADOW PL
100 SIMI 93065 497-D7
HEAVENLY CT
3000 SIMI 93065 478-C7
24500 CanP 91307 529-D4
HEAVENLY RIDGE ST
- THO 91362 527-B2
HEAVENLY VALLEY RD
100 VeCo 91320 556-C2
HEBERT DR
100 CMRL 93010 524-C4
HEBRIDES CIR
7000 CanP 91307 529-F5
HEDERA LN
- OXN 93030 523-A3
HEDGE LN
- CMRL 93012 524-G4
HEDGE ROW LN
600 SIMI 93065 527-D1
HEDGEWALL DR
6000 WLKV 91362 557-F3
HEDON CIR
1700 CMRL 93010 524-H1
HEDYLAND CT
600 MRPK 93021 476-F7
HEIDELBERG AV
300 VEN 93003 492-B1
HEIDEMARIE ST
22100 Chat 91311 499-J6
HELECHO CT
- THO 91362 556-J1
HELEN CT
2900 VeCo 91320 555-G1
HELEN ST
600 PHME 93041 552-F4
HELENA CT
700 OXN 93033 552-H5
3900 VEN 93003 491-J3
HELENA WY
400 OXN 93033 552-H5
HELENE ST
4000 SIMI 93063 498-F2
HELGA CT
400 THO 91320 555-H2
HELLBENDER LN
7000 VEN 93003 492-F3
HELM DR
1200 OXN 93035 522-D7
1400 OXN 93035 552-D1
HELM ST
2800 SIMI 93065 498-C4
HELMA CT
3500 CMRL 93010 524-G1
HELMOND DR
26900 CALB 91301 558-F6
HELMSDALE CIR
7100 CanP 91307 529-F5
HELMSDALE RD
7000 CanP 91307 529-E5
HELSAM AV
200 VeCo 93036 492-J7
700 VeCo 93036 493-A7
700 VeCo 93036 523-A1
HEMINGSFORD WY
- VeCo 91361 586-F1
HEMINGWAY LN
6600 VEN 93003 492-D3
HEMLOCK LN
100 VEN 93001 491-D2
1100 VeCo 91320 556-C2
E HEMLOCK ST
200 OXN 93033 552-H1
N HEMLOCK ST
- VEN 93001 491-D2
S HEMLOCK ST
- VEN 93001 491-D2
W HEMLOCK ST
400 OXN 93033 552-F1
1500 OXN 93035 552-B1
2300 PHME 93035 552-B1
23600 PHME 93041 552-D1
HEMLOCK RIDGE CT
- SIMI 93065 497-H5
HEMMINGWAY ST
22100 LA 91304 529-J3
HEMPSTEAD DR
5700 AGRH 91301 557-H4
HEMPSTEAD ST
4400 SIMI 93063 478-G5
HEMWAY CT
3900 SIMI 93063 498-F2
HENDERSON PL
10900 VEN 93004 493-A1
HENDERSON RD
7500 VEN 93004 492-J1
10800 VEN 93004 493-A1
HENDRICKSON RD
700 VeCo 93023 442-E5
HENDRIX AV
900 THO 91360 526-F4
HENLEY CT
4400 WLKV 91361 557-D6
HENNESSY AV
300 SIMI 93065 527-D1
HENRIETTA AV
200 THO 91320 555-F2
HENRY DR
200 VeCo 91320 555-F1
HENRY PL
- OXN 93033 552-H5
HENRY MAYO DR Rt#-126
31100 Cstc 91384 458-H5
31800 VeCo 93040 458-H5
HERBERT DR
- CMRL 93010 524-C3
HERCULES CT
2000 SIMI 93065 497-G2
HEREFORD CT
3200 SIMI 93063 478-G6
HEREFORD RD
- VeCo 91361 586-E1
2400 VeCo 91361 556-F7
HERITAGE DR
6100 AGRH 91301 557-J3
6100 AGRH 91301 558-A3
HERITAGE PL
1200 THO 91362 527-D7
5900 CMRL 93012 525-B1
HERITAGE TR
1500 CMRL 93012 525-B1
HERITAGE OAK CT
3800 SIMI 93063 498-F3
HERITAGE PASS PL
22300 Chat 91311 499-H2
HERMANO TR
200 OXN 93036 522-G2
HERMES ST
100 SIMI 93065 497-F2
HERMITAGE LN
- VeCo - 442-C3
- VeCo 93023 442-C3
HERMITAGE RD
2600 VeCo - 442-C3
2600 VeCo 93023 442-C3
HERMOSA RD
23600 OJAI 93023 451-F1
23600 VeCo 93023 451-F1
HERMOSA ST
7600 VEN 93004 492-E1
HERMOSA WY
200 OXN 93036 522-H2
HERON ST
6900 VEN 93003 492-E5
HERRINGBONE CT
- THO 91320 555-H2
HERRON CT
2000 CMRL 93010 494-D7
HERTZ ST
12000 MRPK 93021 496-C1
HEWITT PL
1700 SIMI 93065 497-J5
HEWITT ST
10400 VEN 93004 492-J2
HEYNEMAN LN
2100 SIMI 93065 498-A5
HEYWOOD ST
1600 SIMI 93065 497-J3
1700 SIMI 93065 498-B3
HI DR
4000 SIMI 93063 498-F3
HIAWATHA ST
22000 Chat 91311 499-J4
HIBBERT CT
3900 SIMI 93063 498-F2
HIBISCUS ST
1100 OXN 93036 522-E2
HIBISCUS WY
- VEN 93004 473-C7
HICKORY DR
5800 VeCo 91377 558-A1
HICKORY GROVE DR
200 THO 91320 556-C2
HICKORY KNOLL CT
2800 THO 91362 527-C4
HICKORY VIEW CIR
900 CMRL 93012 525-A2
HICKORY WOOD LN
2800 THO 91362 527-C4
HIDALGO CT
300 CMRL 93010 524-D3
HIDALGO ST
5200 CMRL 93012 525-A3
HIDDEN BROOK CT
1600 THO 91362 527-G6
HIDDEN CREEK AV
3100 THO 91360 526-C1
HIDDEN GLEN CT
5100 THO 91362 527-G6
HIDDEN HOLLOW CT
- SIMI 93063 498-H2
HIDDEN MEADOW CT
- THO 91320 526-A6
HIDDEN OAK CT
1800 THO 91320 526-A5
HIDDEN PARK CT
- SIMI 93063 498-J2
HIDDEN PINES CT
3800 MRPK 93021 496-F4
HIDDEN RANCH DR
- SIMI 93063 498-H2
- SIMI 93063 499-A3
HIDDEN SPRINGS AV
1400 VeCo 91377 527-H7
HIDDEN VALLEY CT
2100 OXN 93036 522-D2
HIDDEN VALLEY RD
1100 VeCo 91361 556-A6
1400 VeCo 91361 555-J6
HIDDEN VISTA CT
- SIMI 93063 498-J3
HIETTER AV
2000 SIMI 93063 498-E2
HIGH RD
- VeCo 93001 470-D4
HIGH ST
100 MRPK 93021 496-E1
100 VeCo 93022 451-B7
1100 SPLA 93060 464-B4
HIGHBRUSH LN
23600 SIMI 93065 497-A2
HIGHBURY CT
3500 SIMI 93063 478-G5
HIGHCLIFF CT
5800 THO 91362 527-G6
HIGH COUNTRY PL
- MRPK 93021 476-E6
HIGHCREST CT
400 THO 91320 555-G3
HIGHGATE PL
2700 SIMI 93065 478-B7
2700 SIMI 93065 498-B1
HIGHGATE RD
2100 THO 91361 557-A7
2100 WLKV 91361 557-A7
HIGHGROVE PL
- MRPK 93021 476-D5
HIGH KNOLL CIR
1900 THO 91362 527-D5
HIGH KNOLL CT
23600 SIMI 93065 527-E1
HIGHLAND AV
4200 OXN 93033 552-J5
HIGHLAND DR
100 VeCo 93035 552-B5
500 VeCo 93023 451-C3
E HIGHLAND DR
- VeCo 93010 494-E6
W HIGHLAND DR
600 VeCo 93010 494-C6
HIGHLAND RD
100 SIMI 93065 497-F5
HIGHLAND TER
- VeCo 93010 494-D6
HIGHLANDER RD
23700 CanP 91307 529-D5
HIGHLAND HILLS DR
200 VeCo 93010 494-E5
HIGH MEADOW ST
100 SIMI 93065 497-E7
HIGH PEAK PL
5600 AGRH 91301 557-J5
HIGH PLAINS LN
600 SIMI 93065 527-D1
HIGH POINT DR
500 VEN 93003 472-D7
500 VEN 93003 492-E1
HIGHPOINT PL
3300 SIMI 93065 498-D5
HIGHRIDGE CT
11200 VeCo 93012 496-B7
HIGHTOP ST
- MRPK 93021 476-F5
HIGH TREE RD
1300 SIMI 93063 499-C3
HIGHVIEW ST
300 THO 91320 555-G2
HIGHWAY Rt#-33
- VeCo 93023 366-J6
- VeCo 93252 366-G1
HIGHWINDS RD
12600 VeCo 93023 442-J7
12600 VeCo 93023 452-J1
HIGHWOOD CT
3500 SIMI 93063 498-D1
HIGUERA DR
1100 OXN 93030 522-J5
HILA LN
4900 OXN 93033 552-J5
HILARIA ST
23600 OXN 93030 522-J5
HILARY CT
2700 THO 91362 527-A3
HILBURN CT
13600 MRPK 93021 496-F3
HILDRETH CT
11000 VeCo 93012 526-A1
N HILGARD AV
1400 SIMI 93065 498-D3
HILL DR
10600 VeCo 93021 495-J3
10600 VeCo 93021 496-A3
HILL RD
2000 VEN 93003 492-D5
N HILL RD
100 VEN 93003 492-D2
100 VeCo 93003 492-D2
S HILL RD
- VeCo 93003 492-D2
- VEN 93003 492-D2
500 VEN 93009 492-D3
HILL ST
- VeCo 93022 451-B6
100 OXN 93033 552-F1
1400 OXN 93035 552-D1
HILLARY CT
1800 SIMI 93065 498-A2
HILLARY DR
7800 LA 91304 529-F2
HILLBROOK CT
4200 MRPK 93021 496-B2
HILL CANYON AV
3300 THO 91360 526-C1
HILL CANYON RD
1800 VeCo 93012 525-J3
23600 THO 91320 525-J3
23600 THO 93012 525-J3
HILL CANYON FIRE RD
23600 THO 91320 525-H4
HILLCREST DR
500 CMRL 93012 524-J2
1700 VEN 93001 491-E1
2400 THO 91362 557-A2
E HILLCREST DR
- THO 91360 556-F1
1000 THO 91362 556-H1
2000 THO 91362 557-A1
W HILLCREST DR
- THO 91360 556-E1
300 THO 91360 526-C7
600 THO 91320 526-A7
600 VeCo 91360 526-C7
1000 THO 91320 556-E1
2000 THO 91320 525-H7
HILLCREST LN
400 VEN 93001 491-F1
HILLCROFT DR
8200 LA 91304 529-D1
HILLDALE AV
2000 SIMI 93063 498-D2
HILLGATE WY
1900 SIMI 93065 497-E2
HILLHAVEN CT
6300 VEN 93003 472-C6
HILLHURST DR
- CanP 91307 529-D5
- LA 91304 529-D5
HILLIARD AV
1700 SIMI 93063 499-A3
HILLIARD LN
2600 THO 91320 525-H6
HILLMAN ST
2800 THO 91360 526-H3
HILLMONT AV
200 VEN 93003 491-G2
HILLPARK CT
4100 MRPK 93021 496-B2
HILL RANCH DR
200 THO 91362 556-H1
HILLRIDGE DR
1600 CMRL 93012 525-A1
2300 CMRL 93012 494-J7
2300 CMRL 93012 495-A7
HILLRISE DR
29100 AGRH 91301 558-A5
29400 AGRH 91301 557-J5
HILLROSE CT
300 THO 91320 555-E2
HILLROSE PL
2400 OXN 93036 522-F1
HILLSBOROUGH ST
400 THO 91361 556-F2
HILLSBURY RD
2200 THO 91361 557-A6
HILLSHIRE CT
3800 MRPK 93021 496-E4
HILLSIDE DR
1000 SPLA 93060 464-B3
12400 MRPK 93021 496-D3
HILLSVIEW CT
7300 LA 91304 529-E4
HILLTOP DR
3000 VEN 93003 491-G1
HILLTOP LN
1900 VeCo 93012 495-E7
HILLTOP RD
1100 VeCo 93063 499-B3
HILLTOP WY
- THO 91362 557-A2
HILL VALLEY CT
23600 SIMI 93065 497-F7
23600 SIMI 93065 527-F1
HILLVIEW AV
- VEN 93003 492-C2
HILLVIEW CIR
800 SIMI 93065 497-G4
HILLVIEW LN
1100 SIMI 93065 497-H4
HILLWAY CIR
6100 VEN 93003 472-C6
HINCKLEY LN
- FILM 93015 455-J5
HINGHAM LN
1000 VEN 93001 491-E4
HIRAM AV
100 THO 91320 555-H1
HITCH BLVD
3800 VeCo 93021 496-A3
4000 VeCo 93021 495-J2
HITCHING POST LN
- VeCo 91307 529-A5
HOBART DR
1400 CMRL 93010 524-D1
HOBBIT CT
1200 SIMI 93065 498-C4
HOBBS CIR
- SPLA 93060 464-A5
HOBSON RD
5200 VeCo 93001 469-H2
5200 VeCo 93001 470-A3
5200 VeCo 93001 459-G7
23600 VeCo 93060 464-G4
23600 VeCo 93060 474-B1
HOBSON WY
500 OXN 93030 522-F7
HODENCAMP RD
- THO 91360 556-G1
500 THO 91360 526-G7
HOFER DR
3100 VEN 93003 492-D6
HOGAN ST
- MRPK 93021 476-B6
HOLBERTSON CT
700 SIMI 93065 527-C1
N HOLBROOK AV
700 SIMI 93065 498-A5
HOLIDAY AV
- VEN 93003 492-B4
HOLIDAY PINES LN
2100 VeCo 93012 496-A7
2100 VeCo 93012 526-A1
HOLLEY AV
1400 SIMI 93063 498-E3
HOLLINGS ST
- VEN 93003 492-B2
HOLLISTER ST
2500 SIMI 93065 498-C3
8100 VEN 93004 492-G2
HOLLOWAY CT
3100 THO 91320 555-G6
HOLLOWAY ST
3300 THO 91320 555-F3
HOLLOW BROOK AV
28900 AGRH 91301 558-B4
HOLLOW OAK CT
29000 AGRH 91301 558-A3
HOLLOWPARK CT
2200 THO 91362 527-A4
HOLLY AV
400 OXN 93036 522-E2
HOLLY CT
1500 THO 91360 526-H3
HOLLY DR
100 CMRL 93010 524-E4
HOLLY RD
900 SPLA 93060 464-B3
HOLLY ST
600 VeCo 93023 451-C3
HOLLYBURNE LN
500 THO 91360 526-D7
HOLLYCREST AV
2800 THO 91362 527-C3
HOLLYGLEN CT
4900 MRPK 93021 496-B2
HOLLY GROVE ST
3300 THO 91362 557-B3
HOLLYHOCK AV
- VEN 93004 493-A1
HOLLYHOCK CT
900 THO 91362 557-C1
HOLLY KNOLL DR
900 VeCo 93022 461-A1
HOLLY OAK CT
- SIMI 93063 498-J3
HOLLY RIDGE DR
5500 CMRL 93012 525-A1
HOLLYTREE DR
5600 VeCo 91377 557-J1
5600 VeCo 91377 558-A1
HOLLYVIEW PL
2400 THO 91362 527-B3
HOLLYWOOD AV
100 VeCo 93035 552-C6
HOLLYWOOD BLVD
200 VeCo 93035 552-B4
400 PHME 93035 552-B4
400 PHME 93043 552-B4
HOLMES AV
500 VEN 93003 492-D2
HOLSER WK
1800 OXN 93036 523-A3
HOLSER CANYON RD
23600 VeCo 93040 367-E7
N HOLSTER LN
- VeCo 91307 529-B4
HOLT ST
- VeCo 93001 471-C2

STREET Block City ZIP Pg-Grid

HOMER AV
200 VEN 93003 491-G2
HOMER ST
100 OXN 93033 552-G3
HOMESTAKE PL
1200 THO 91320 555-F5
HOMEWOOD AV
2200 SIMI 93063 499-C1
HOMEWOOD CT
6400 SIMI 93063 499-C1
HOMEZELL DR
23900 LA 91304 529-E1
HOMEZELL TR
24000 LA 91304 529-C1
HOMOJA CIR
- PHME 93041 552-E4
HOMOJA DR
1100 PHME 93041 552-D4
HONDO BARRANCA
23600 VeCo 93066 474-E7
HONDO RANCH RD
1400 VeCo 93066 494-C1
HONEY DR
3100 SIMI 93063 478-E6
E HONEYBEE ST
13100 MRPK 93021 496-E3
HONEYBROOK CT
11900 MRPK 93021 496-C3
HONEY CREEK CT
- THO 91320 526-B6
HONEYGLEN CT
4400 MRPK 93021 496-D2
HONEY HILL DR
2100 VeCo 93012 496-A7
2100 VeCo 93012 526-A1
HONEYMAN ST
5400 SIMI 93063 498-J2
5400 SIMI 93063 499-A2
HONEY PINE CT
23600 SIMI 93063 498-D4
HONEYSUCKLE AV
- VEN 93004 493-A2
HONEYSUCKLE CT
3500 THO 91360 526-H2
HONEYSUCKLE DR
2600 OXN 93036 492-F7
2600 OXN 93036 522-F1
HONEYWOOD CT
1000 SPLA 93060 464-A1
HOOD DR
2000 THO 91362 526-J6
2000 THO 91362 527-A6
HOOD WY
- OXN 93033 552-G6
HOOPER AV
- SIMI 93065 527-E1
HOOP PINE PL
23600 SIMI 93065 498-D4
HOOVER AV
- VEN 93003 492-E2
HOPE RD
100 THO 91320 556-B2
HOPE ST
4300 VEN 93003 491-J2
4300 VEN 93003 492-A2
6100 SIMI 93063 499-B3
HOPEWELL CT
2000 THO 91360 526-C4
HOPI CT
- MRPK 93021 496-H3
HOPI LN
2300 VEN 93001 471-C6
HOPPER CANYON RD
500 VeCo 93015 457-A5
1600 VeCo - 457-A3
HORIZON CIR
100 CMRL 93010 524-A4
HORIZON DR
1000 VEN 93003 472-D6
HORIZON LN
600 THO 91320 526-B7
HORIZON PL
22200 Chat 91311 499-J2
HORIZON RIDGE CT
- SIMI 93063 478-G5
HORN CT
2800 SIMI 93065 498-C3
HORNBLEND CT
400 SIMI 93065 527-C1
HORN CANYON RD
- VeCo - 442-J2
5100 VeCo 93023 442-G4
E HORSESHOE RD
- VeCo 91307 529-A4
HORSHOE CIR
- CALB 91302 558-H4
HOSPITAL RD
23600 VEN 93003 491-G2
HOT SPRINGS PL
26800 CALB 91301 558-G7
HOUCK ST
500 CMRL 93010 523-J5
HOUSTON DR
- THO 91360 556-G1
400 THO 91360 526-G7
HOUSTON PL
1500 OXN 93033 552-J3
HOUSTON RD
9500 VeCo 90265 585-D7
9500 VeCo 90265 625-D1
HOWARD AV
- VeCo 93022 451-D4
HOWARD RD
- CMRL 93012 524-J6
600 VeCo 93012 524-J7
1400 VeCo 93012 525-A7
1400 VeCo 93012 555-A1
HOWARD ST
- VEN 93003 491-F3
1000 FILM 93015 455-J6
HOWE RD
2700 VeCo 93065 478-C7
3400 VeCo 93015 457-E6
3700 VeCo 93040 457-E6
HOWE ST
23600 VEN 93003 492-D6
HOWELL RD
300 OXN 93033 552-H5
HOWIE CT
400 SPLA 93060 463-J5
400 SPLA 93060 464-A5
HOYT CT
1300 SIMI 93065 498-C3
HUBBARD ST
1800 SIMI 93065 497-J3
HUBBELL CT
- VEN 93003 492-B3
HUCKLEBERRY OAK ST
- SIMI 93063 498-J3
HUDSON CT
1100 SIMI 93065 497-H4
HUDSON LN
400 PHME 93041 552-D2
HUDSPETH AV
500 SIMI 93065 497-J5
HUENEME AV
100 PHME 93035 552-B5
100 VeCo 93035 552-B5
HUENEME RD
- PHME 93041 552-D6
- PHME 93043 552-D6
500 VeCo 93012 553-H6
500 VeCo 93012 554-A5
E HUENEME RD
100 OXN 93033 552-H6
1100 VeCo 93033 552-H6
1100 VeCo 93033 553-B6
W HUENEME RD
- OXN 93033 552-G6
HUENEME ST
1000 VeCo 93015 465-F3
HUERTA ST
- OXN 93030 522-G4
3500 CMRL 93010 494-G7
HUGHES DR
100 OXN 93033 552-G3
1000 CMRL 93010 524-C3
HUGO CT
10100 VEN 93004 493-A2
HULA DR
23600 OXN 93033 553-A2
HULL CT
2100 SIMI 93063 499-B2
HULL PL
1000 OXN 93030 522-E6
HUMBOLDT ST
100 SIMI 93065 497-F6
8300 VEN 93004 492-F1
HUME DR
400 FILM 93015 455-J6
HUMMINGBIRD ST
6300 VEN 93003 492-D5
HUNT CIR
100 THO 91360 526-F4
600 CMRL 93012 524-J2
HUNT CLUB LN
4200 WLKV 91361 557-E6
9500 Chat 91311 499-H6
HUNTER CT
- VEN 93003 492-B2
HUNTER DR
500 FILM 93015 456-A4
HUNTER ST
5400 VEN 93003 492-B2
HUNTER CREST CT
3800 MRPK 93021 496-D4
HUNTERS GROVE CT
3800 MRPK 93021 496-E4
HUNTERS POINT DR
200 THO 91361 556-F2
HUNTER VALLEY LN
4900 THO 91362 557-E1
HUNTINGTON AV
200 VEN 93004 492-F2
HUNTLEY ST
5200 SIMI 93063 498-J2
HUNTSDALE CT
23600 THO 91320 555-F3
HUNTSWOOD WY
900 OXN 93030 522-E4
HUPA ST
300 VEN 93001 471-C5
HURFORD CT
5600 AGRH 91301 557-H4
N HURLES AV
1900 SIMI 93063 498-E2
HURON CT
- MRPK 93021 496-G3
HURON DR
1800 VEN 93004 492-G4
HURRICANE CV
2600 PHME 93041 552-C3
HURST AV
- VEN 93001 491-E3
HUSTON RD
9100 Chat 91311 499-E7
9300 Chat 91311 499-E7
HUYLER LN
900 SIMI 93065 497-E6
HYACINTH CT
2900 THO 91360 526-D3
HYACINTH DR
2000 OXN 93036 522-F2
HYACINTH ST
800 CMRL 93010 494-C7
800 VeCo 93010 494-C7
HYANNIS DR
7200 CanP 91307 529-F4
HYLAND AV
2100 VEN 93001 491-F1
HYSSOP CT
2200 THO 91362 497-A7

I

I AV
- VeCo 93042 583-F6
I ST
100 OXN 93030 522-F5
1100 OXN 93033 522-F6
23600 VeCo 93063 528-F1
S I ST
1200 OXN 93033 522-F7
1200 OXN 93033 552-F1
IAN LN
2700 SIMI 93063 478-D7
IBEX SQ
1100 VEN 93003 492-E3
IBIZA LN
- OXN 93035 522-C6
IBOLD RD
600 LACo 90265 586-G6
IBSEN PL
100 OXN 93033 552-G4
ICELAND ST
2900 THO 91320 555-H2
IDA PL
23200 Chat 91311 499-F7
IDA ST
1700 CMRL 93010 524-D3
IDA WY
23600 WHil 91304 499-E6
IDAHO DR
1900 VEN 93003 492-C5
IDE CT
1700 THO 91362 526-J7
IDLE DR
28900 AGRH 91301 558-B4
IDYLLWILD ST
8300 VEN 93004 492-G2
IGUANA CIR
1300 VEN 93003 492-F4
ILENA ST
900 OXN 93030 522-F7
ILEX DR
- THO 91320 555-J1
2000 OXN 93036 522-G3
ILLINOIS CT
- MRPK 93021 496-H3
IMATION DR
2600 CMRL 93012 524-F4
IMBACH PL
7100 MRPK 93021 477-A5
IMBLER CT
6300 AGRH 91301 557-J3
IMPALA DR
7100 VEN 93003 492-E5
IMPATIENS DR
- OXN 93030 523-A3
IMPERIAL AV
- VEN 93004 492-F1
300 VEN 93004 472-E7
400 VeCo 93004 472-E7
IMPERIAL CIR
3000 THO 91320 555-H2
IMPERIAL ST
200 OXN 93030 523-A5
INCA CT
2500 VEN 93001 471-C5
INCA DR
- OXN 93030 522-H4
INDEPENDENCE CT
3200 THO 91360 526-F2
INDIAN DR
22000 Chat 91311 499-J1
INDIANA DR
2000 OXN 93036 522-H3
INDIANBROOM CT
6600 VeCo 91377 528-A7
INDIAN CREEK PL
3200 SIMI 93063 478-J6
INDIAN CREST CIR
1700 THO 91362 527-G6
INDIAN HILL LN
24400 CanP 91307 529-D4
INDIAN HILLS DR
5100 SIMI 93063 478-J7
5400 SIMI 93063 479-A7
INDIAN HILLS RD
- Chat 91311 479-H7
INDIAN MESA DR
3100 THO 91360 526-C2
INDIAN OAK LN
- VeCo 91377 527-J7
- VeCo 91377 528-A7
- VeCo 91377 557-J1
- VeCo 91377 558-A1
INDIAN POINTE DR
5700 SIMI 93063 479-A7
INDIAN PONY CIR
4200 THO 91362 527-D6
INDIAN RIDGE CIR
3200 THO 91362 527-D3
INDIAN RIDGE CT
29000 AGRH 91301 558-A3
INDIAN SKY LN
2100 THO 91320 555-J3
INDIAN TERRACE DR
5700 SIMI 93063 479-A7
INDIAN TRAIL CT
5000 THO 91362 527-F7
INDIAN WELLS CT
2700 OXN 93036 522-C2
INDIAN WELLS LN
600 THO 91320 556-D1
INDIGO PL
800 OXN 93036 522-F2
INDIO DR
- OXN 93030 522-H4
INDUS PL
- OXN 93036 492-H7
INDUSTRIAL AV
600 PHME 93041 552-F7
900 OXN 93030 522-H7
E INDUSTRIAL ST
4400 SIMI 93063 498-G2
INEZ DR
- OXN 93030 523-A4
INEZ ST
1000 CMRL 93012 525-A6
6000 VeCo 93003 492-D6
6000 VEN 93003 492-D6
INFINIDAD ST
- OXN 93030 522-G4
INGELOW CT
300 THO 91360 526-F4
INGLEWOOD ST
12800 MRPK 93021 496-E3
INGOMAR ST
22100 LA 91304 529-D3
INGRAM PL
4900 THO 91362 557-G1
INLET DR
900 OXN 93030 522-F7
INMAN CIR
1000 SIMI 93065 497-J4
INNESS CIR
6900 VEN 93003 492-E3
INNWOOD RD
100 SIMI 93065 497-C6
INSPIRATION PT
- VeCo 93012 554-F2
INSPIRATION WY
100 VEN 93001 491-D1
INSTONE CT
2900 THO 91361 557-C5
INVAR CT
2400 SIMI 93065 498-B4
INVERNESS CT
2100 OXN 93036 522-E2
INVERNESS ST
- THO 91361 556-F2
INYO CIR
2800 SIMI 93063 478-J7
INYO ST
10600 VEN 93004 472-H6
IOLITE ST
- SIMI 93065 478-A6
IOWA PL
200 OXN 93036 492-H7
IRENA AV
5400 CMRL 93012 525-A6
IRENE CT
1500 SIMI 93065 497-J3
IRIS ST
1200 VeCo 93063 499-B4
E IRIS ST
100 OXN 93033 552-G2
W IRIS ST
100 OXN 93033 552-E1
IRIS WY
200 VEN 93004 473-A7
IRONBARK CT
1700 OXN 93030 522-F3
IRONBARK DR
2000 OXN 93036 522-F3
IRONGATE PL
2600 THO 91362 527-A2
IRON RIDGE LN
300 SIMI 93065 497-E6
IRONSIDE CV
2600 PHME 93041 552-C3
IRONSTONE ST
2500 OXN 93036 522-F1
IRONWOOD CIR
200 THO 91360 526-F2
IRONWOOD DR
5700 AGRH 91301 557-J4
IROQUOIS CT
1500 CMRL 93010 524-F1
5500 SIMI 93063 479-A7
IROQUOIS LN
2300 VEN 93001 471-D6
IRVINE RD
700 SIMI 93065 497-F5
IRVING DR
300 OXN 93030 523-A6
500 THO 91360 556-G1
IRVING BERLIN DR
- VEN 93003 492-A4
IRWIN WY
- OXN 93033 552-G6
ISABEL AV
5600 CMRL 93012 525-B6
ISABELLA CT
1700 VEN 93004 492-H4
5300 AGRH 91301 557-H5
ISABELLA ST
1900 OXN 93036 522-J3
ISCHIA DR
4000 OXN 93035 552-B2
ISELA ST
- OXN 93030 523-A5
ISH DR
4100 SIMI 93063 498-F3
ISLA CT
1300 CMRL 93010 524-G1
ISLAND AV
- VeCo 93042 583-E4
ISLAND FOREST PL
4900 THO 91362 527-F7
ISLAND OAK ST
- SIMI 93063 498-J3
- SIMI 93063 499-A3
ISLAND VIEW AV
100 PHME 93043 552-B5
100 VeCo 93035 552-B5
900 VeCo 93043 552-B5
1700 PHME 93035 552-B5
ISLAND VIEW CIR
400 PHME 93041 552-E6
ISLAND VIEW DR
3000 VEN 93003 491-G1
3200 VeCo 93003 491-G1
ISLAND VIEW ST
600 FILM 93015 456-B5
1300 OXN 93035 552-A1
1600 OXN 93035 551-J1
ISLE WY
2900 OXN 93035 552-C1
N ISLE ROYALE DR
4500 MRPK 93021 496-E2
ISLETON PL
1000 OXN 93030 522-E6
ITAMO ST
1100 CMRL 93012 525-C6
ITASCA ST
22100 Chat 91311 499-H6
IVAN DR
4800 OXN 93033 552-H5
IVANHOE AV
1500 OXN 93030 522-D4
IVAR PL
- OXN 93030 522-H4
IVERSON LN
11100 Chat 91311 499-J2
IVERSON RD
11300 Chat 91311 499-H2
11400 Chat 91311 499-H2
IVES AV
1100 OXN 93033 552-J1
1800 OXN 93033 553-A2
IVES CT
2000 OXN 93033 553-A1
IVES PL
1900 OXN 93033 553-A2
IVORY AV
2800 SIMI 93063 478-D7
IVORY WY
2300 OXN 93036 522-F1
IVY ST
4000 VEN 93003 491-J3
IVYWOOD DR
400 OXN 93030 522-F3
IVYWOOD LN
400 SIMI 93065 497-D5

J

J CT
500 OXN 93030 522-F6
J ST
- VeCo 93042 583-E5
100 OXN 93030 522-F5
1100 OXN 93033 522-F7
1100 OXN 93033 552-F1
4300 PHME 93033 552-F5
23600 VeCo 93063 528-F1
JACARANDA AV
- THO 91320 556-C1
JACARANDA DR
2400 OXN 93036 522-F1
JACINTO CIR
3000 SIMI 93063 478-G7
JACINTO DR
- OXN 93030 523-A4
JACINTO WY
10000 VeCo 93004 493-B2
JACKIE AV
6200 WdHl 91367 529-F7
JACKLIGHT CV
2600 PHME 93041 552-C3
JACKPINE LN
11400 VeCo 93012 496-C7
JACKSON ST
2200 OXN 93033 552-F2
3400 PHME 93033 552-F3
3400 PHME 93041 552-F3
7300 VEN 93003 492-E1
7400 VEN 93004 492-E1
JACKTAR AV
2900 OXN 93035 552-C1
JACOBS CT
5300 VeCo 91377 527-H6
JACOBSON PL
- MRPK 93021 476-B5
JADE CT
3300 SIMI 93063 478-D6
JADE DR
900 VEN 93004 492-G3
JADESTONE AV
2800 SIMI 93063 478-D7
JAFFA RD
- SIMI 93063 479-C7
JAKE CT
- THO 91320 555-E3
JAKE LN
- LA 91304 529-J2
JALISCO CT
1600 CMRL 93010 524-D3
JAMAICA LN
1100 OXN 93030 522-E6
JAMES AV
100 OXN 93033 552-G3
2100 VeCo 93003 492-D5
JAMES CT
2000 THO 91362 556-H2
JAMES DR
- VEN 93001 471-C6
JAMES WY
5900 SIMI 93063 499-B3
JAMES ALAN CIR
22100 Chat 91311 499-J4
JAMESTOWN CT
2300 OXN 93035 552-A2
JAMESTOWN LN
2200 OXN 93035 552-A2
JAMESTOWN ST
9800 VEN 93004 492-H2
JAMESTOWN WY
2000 OXN 93035 552-A1
JAMES WEAK AV
12400 MRPK 93021 496-D2
JAMISON CT
100 SIMI 93065 497-D7
JANE CT
700 OXN 93033 552-F6
2900 THO 91320 555-H2
JANE DR
700 OXN 93033 552-F6
700 PHME 93033 552-F6
700 PHME 93041 552-F6
JANET LN
1500 SIMI 93063 499-B3
JANET WY
5900 SIMI 93063 499-B3
JANETWOOD DR
500 OXN 93030 522-F3
JANIS LN
1500 SIMI 93063 499-B3
JANIS WY
6000 SIMI 93063 499-B3
JANLOR DR
30600 AGRH 91301 557-G4
30800 WLKV 91362 557-F4
JANSS CIR
1800 THO 91360 526-E5
E JANSS RD
- THO 91360 526-G5
1000 THO 91362 526-G5
1800 THO 91362 527-A6
W JANSS RD
- THO 91360 526-E4
JANSS FIRE RD
500 THO 91361 556-F3
700 VeCo 91361 556-F6
JAPONICA AV
100 CMRL 93012 524-H4
JAPONICA CT
4300 CMRL 93012 524-H4
JAPONICA PL
4300 CMRL 93012 524-H4
JARDIN DR
2200 OXN 93036 522-H2
JARED CT
6100 WdHl 91367 529-D7
JASMINE ST
2000 OXN 93036 522-F3
JASMINE GLEN AV
2700 SIMI 93065 478-B7
JASON AV
7400 CanP 91307 529-F4
7700 LA 91304 529-F2
JASON CT
2700 THO 91362 527-A3
JASON LN
23200 CanP 91307 529-F4
JASON PL
1000 OXN 93033 552-J3
JASPER AV
500 VEN 93004 492-H2
JAVA PL
- OXN 93036 492-H6
JAVELIN CT
1600 THO 91320 526-A6
JAY AV
800 CMRL 93010 524-B2
2400 SIMI 93065 498-B1
JAYCROFT CT
23600 VeCo 91361 556-F6
JAZMIN AV
600 VEN 93004 492-J1
JEAN LN
2800 WLKV 91361 557-A7
JEANETTE AV
800 THO 91362 526-J7
JEANETTE DR
1500 OXN 93030 522-E3
JEANINE CT
- THO 91320 556-B1
JEANNE AV
10300 VeCo 93022 451-C7
JEANNE CT
400 VeCo 91320 555-G1
JEAUNINE DR
100 THO 91360 526-E6
JEFFERSON AV
100 VEN 93003 492-E1
JEFFERSON SQ
5100 OXN 93033 552-H5
JEFFERSON WY
- SIMI 93065 497-J1
JEFFREY RD
2300 CMRL 93012 495-B7
JEFFREY MARK CT
22400 Chat 91311 499-H4
JEFFREYS PL
1900 OXN 93033 553-A4
JELLEY DR
- PHME 93041 552-D4
JENNIFER CT
6200 SIMI 93063 499-B2
JENNIFER LN
- LA 91304 529-J2
JENNIFER PL
2000 VeCo 93012 496-A7
2000 VeCo 93012 526-A1
JENNY DR
300 VeCo 91320 555-F1
500 VeCo 91320 525-F7
JENSEN CT
100 THO 91360 556-G1
JENSEN DR
23900 LA 91304 529-E2
JEPSON ST
1500 VeCo 93015 455-G4
JERANIOS CT
100 THO 91362 556-J1
JEREMIAH DR
400 SIMI 93065 497-D2
JEROME AV
- THO 91320 556-A2
JERRY DR
400 PHME 93041 552-F5
JERSEY PL
1100 THO 91362 527-A7
JERUSALEM RD
- SIMI 93063 479-B7
JESSICA ST
3000 THO 91320 555-G1
JETTY ST
1800 OXN 93035 552-C1
2000 PHME 93035 552-C1
2000 PHME 93041 552-C1
JEWEL CT
- CMRL 93010 493-H7
JILL CT
2000 SIMI 93063 499-C2
JILL PL
2700 PHME 93041 552-D1
JIM BOWIE RD
3900 Ago 91301 558-F7
3900 AGRH 91301 558-F7
JIMILYN ST
6400 SIMI 93063 499-C2
JIMS CANYON RD
23600 VeCo 93040 458-E7
JOAN DR
800 PHME 93041 552-F5
JOAN LN
8300 LA 91304 529-F2
JOAN WY
4700 VeCo 93036 493-A5
N JOANNE AV
- VEN 93003 491-G3
S JOANNE AV
100 VEN 93003 491-G4
JOANNE CT
1500 OXN 93030 522-E4
JOANNE WY
1600 OXN 93030 522-E3
JODY LN
- VeCo 93010 494-D7
100 VEN 93001 491-C1
JOELTON DR
4000 AGRH 91301 558-E7
JOHN WY
6000 SIMI 93063 499-B3
JOHN COX DR
400 VeCo 93015 455-B6
JOHNELL RD
9200 Chat 91311 499-F7
JOHNSON DR
500 VEN 93003 492-D3
3000 VeCo 93003 492-E6
JOHNSON MTWY
- Chat 91311 479-F6
23600 VeCo 93063 479-F6
JOHNSON PL
9300 Chat 91311 499-F6
JOHNSON RD
100 OXN 93033 552-G4
JOIE CT
4700 SIMI 93063 498-H2
JOLIET PL
700 OXN 93030 522-D4
JONATHAN ST
23100 LA 91304 529-F3
JON DODSON DR
5300 AGRH 91301 557-H5
JONES ST
300 VEN 93003 491-F3
JONES WY
2100 OXN 93033 552-J2
23600 SIMI 93065 478-C7
JONESBORO AV
2200 SIMI 93063 499-C1
JONNA CIR
- CMRL 93010 524-C3
JONQUIL FIELD RD
3300 WLKV 91361 557-B7
JONQUILL AV
- VEN 93004 493-A1
JOPLIN WY
10100 VEN 93004 492-J2
JORDAN AV
- VEN 93001 491-F3
JOSE AV
1600 CMRL 93010 524-G1
1700 CMRL 93010 494-G7
JOSE DR
800 VeCo 93023 451-C1
JOSHUA CT
2500 OXN 93036 522-F1
JOSHUA PL
1500 CMRL 93012 525-B1
JOSHUA ST
6400 VeCo 91377 558-B2
JOSHUA TR
5900 CMRL 93012 525-B1
JOSHUA TREE CT
23600 SIMI 93063 499-C3
JOURDAN ST
2800 VeCo 93036 492-H7
2800 VeCo 93036 522-H1
JOYA ST
- OXN 93030 522-G4
JOYCE DR
500 PHME 93041 552-F5
JOYCE PL
2100 OXN 93033 553-A2
JUANITA AV
100 OXN 93030 522-H4
N JUANITA AV
100 OXN 93030 522-H5
JUAREZ AV
4800 MRPK 93021 496-D2
JUBILEE LN
500 SIMI 93065 527-D1
JUDSON AV
200 VEN 93003 492-B2
JUDY CIR
300 THO 91360 526-E4
JUDY LN
1300 VeCo 93023 451-C2
JUEGO ST
- OXN 93030 522-H4
JULIA CT
1400 CMRL 93010 524-G1
JULIAN ST
- VEN 93001 491-A1
100 OXN 93030 523-A5
JULIANA ST
- SIMI 93063 498-H1
JULIE CIR
1700 SIMI 93065 498-A3
JULIE LN
6600 LACo 91307 529-D6
JULLIARD AV
6600 MRPK 93021 476-H6
JUNE CIR
1500 VEN 93004 492-H3
JUNE CT
- THO 91360 526-F5
JUNE ST
1000 SPLA 93060 464-B3
JUNEAU CIR
4300 SIMI 93063 478-F7
JUNEAU PL
200 OXN 93036 492-H7
JUNEBERRY PL
800 OXN 93036 522-E2
JUNEWOOD CT
900 OXN 93030 522-F3
JUNEWOOD WY
1300 OXN 93030 522-E3
JUNIATA CT
5600 VEN 93003 492-B1
JUNIATA ST
5600 VEN 93003 492-B2
JUNIPER CT
- SIMI 93063 499-B3
500 THO 91320 555-G3
JUNIPER LN
- VeCo 93023 441-E6
JUNIPER ST
300 OXN 93033 552-H2
W JUNIPER ST
200 OXN 93033 552-E2
JUNIPERO ST
100 VEN 93001 491-B2
3500 VeCo 93063 499-B4
JUNTO LN
- OXN 93036 522-H3
JUPITER CT
3400 OXN 93030 523-D4
JURYMAST DR
900 OXN 93030 522-F7
JUSTICE ST
23200 LA 91304 529-F3
JUSTICIA LN
- OXN 93030 523-A4
N JUSTIN AV
2000 SIMI 93065 498-B2
JUSTIN CT
4700 MRPK 93021 496-C2
7700 LA 91304 529-G4
JUSTIN WY
4100 OXN 93033 552-H4

K

K ST
- OXN 93030 522-F6
1100 OXN 93033 522-F7
1100 OXN 93033 552-F1
N K ST
- OXN 93030 522-F5
KACHINA WY
2700 SIMI 93063 479-B7
KADOTA ST
2500 SIMI 93063 498-H1
2600 SIMI 93063 478-G6
KAILAS ST
5500 VEN 93003 472-B7
KAITIS ST
- PHME 93043 552-D3
KALINDA PL
400 THO 91320 526-C7
KALMIA CT
- OXN 93030 523-A4
KALORAMA DR
200 VEN 93001 491-D1
N KALORAMA ST
- VEN 93001 491-D2
S KALORAMA ST
- VEN 93001 491-D2
KAMALA ST
300 OXN 93033 552-H2
W KAMALA ST
400 OXN 93033 552-F2
KAMASA RD
3500 VeCo 93060 465-B4
KAMET CT
5500 VEN 93003 492-B1
KANAINA CT
- Chat 91311 499-J1
KANAN RD
- VeCo 91377 558-A1
600 VeCo 91377 557-H1
1000 VeCo 91377 527-E6
1900 THO 91362 527-C6
4600 VeCo 91362 527-E6
5200 AGRH 91301 558-A5
KANAN RD Rt#-N9
4100 Ago 91301 558-A7
4100 AGRH 91301 558-A7
KANE AV
1500 SIMI 93065 498-B3
KAPALUA DR
1600 OXN 93036 522-E2
KAREN AV
10400 VeCo 93022 451-C6
KAREN PL
- THO 91320 556-A1
KARENA CT
3500 CMRL 93010 524-G2
KAROC CT
2700 SIMI 93063 479-A7
KASTEN ST
2000 SIMI 93065 498-A3
KATARI AV
- VEN 93001 471-D5
KATHERINE AV
2100 VeCo 93003 492-D5
2500 VEN 93003 492-D5
E KATHERINE AV
500 VeCo 93022 451-C6
N KATHERINE DR
- VEN 93003 491-G2
S KATHERINE DR
- VEN 93003 491-G3
KATHERINE LN
1500 SIMI 93063 499-B3
KATHERINE RD
600 VeCo 93063 499-B4
6500 SIMI 93063 499-B3
KATHERINE ST
5300 SIMI 93063 498-J3
5500 SIMI 93063 499-A3
KATHERINE WY
5900 SIMI 93063 499-B3
KATHLEEN DR
500 VeCo 91320 556-B3
500 THO 91320 556-B3
KATRINA WY
23600 OXN 93030 522-H4
KATY LN
1100 VeCo 93063 499-B4
KAWAI CT
3100 SIMI 93063 478-J6
KAY AV
1600 SIMI 93063 499-C3
KAYAK CV
2600 PHME 93041 552-C3
KAZUKO CT
200 MRPK 93021 496-D1
KEARNEY AV
1400 SIMI 93065 497-J4
1700 SIMI 93065 498-A4
KEARNY ST
6200 VEN 93003 492-C1
KEATS AV
2400 THO 91360 526-E3
KEATS CIR
100 VEN 93003 492-E3
KEATS PL
1800 OXN 93033 552-J4
1800 OXN 93033 553-A4
KEEL AV
3400 OXN 93035 552-B1
KEEL WY
2900 OXN 93035 552-C1
KEHALA AV
- VEN 93001 471-B5
KEISHA DR
13900 MRPK 93021 496-G4
KEITH RD
2400 VeCo 93015 455-E7
KELLEY AV
400 CMRL 93010 524-F3
KELLOGG ST
- VEN 93001 471-B7
100 FILM 93015 456-B6
KELLWOOD CT
900 VeCo 91377 557-H1
E KELLY RD
- THO 91320 556-A1
W KELLY RD
- THO 91320 555-H2
- VeCo 91320 555-H2
KELLY KNOLL LN
2700 THO 91320 555-H2
2700 VeCo 91320 555-H2
KELMSCOTT CT
2200 THO 91361 557-A6
KELP LN
2800 OXN 93035 522-C7
KELP ST
1100 OXN 93035 522-C7
1300 OXN 93035 552-C1
KELSEY ST
2200 SIMI 93063 498-G2
KELSFORD CT
1100 THO 91361 557-A5
KELTIC LODGE DR
- OXN 93036 522-C3
KELTON CT
23600 SIMI 93065 497-F7
KEMPER LAKES CT
1900 OXN 93036 522-E2
KENDALE LN
600 THO 91360 526-D6
KENDALL AV
1300 CMRL 93010 524-F1
1700 CMRL 93010 494-F7
KENEWA ST
1600 VeCo 93022 451-E5
KENMORE CIR
700 THO 91320 555-F4
KENNEBEC ST
8800 VEN 93004 492-H4
KENNEDY AV
23600 VEN 93003 492-E2
KENNEDY LN
1500 VeCo 93023 442-D4
KENNEDY PL
1800 OXN 93033 552-J2
1800 OXN 93033 553-A2
KENNERICK LN
900 SIMI 93065 497-D6
KENNETH ST
- CMRL 93010 524-D3
KENNY ST
900 VeCo 93036 522-J1

STREET Block City ZIP Pg-Grid

KENROSE CIR
26100 CALB 91302 558-H4
KENS WY
- LA 91304 529-G4
KENSINGTON AV
2400 THO 91362 527-B3
KENSINGTON CT
7400 CanP 91307 529-E4
KENSINGTON DR
500 FILM 93015 456-A6
KENSINGTON LN
1700 OXN 93030 522-E4
KENT CT
1500 OXN 93030 522-E4
KENT DR
1500 VEN 93004 492-H3
KENT PL
1000 THO 91362 527-B7
KENTFIELD CT
31700 WLKV 91361 557-D6
E KENTFIELD ST
2200 SIMI 93065 478-B7
KENTIA ST
2200 OXN 93036 522-F1
KENTLAND AV
6100 WdHl 91367 529-H7
6500 CanP 91307 529-H5
7600 LA 91304 529-H2
9600 Chat 91311 499-H6
KENTON CT
3000 SIMI 93065 498-D5
KENTWOOD DR
500 OXN 93030 522-F3
KENWATER AV
6100 WdHl 91367 529-E7
6400 CanP 91307 529-E7
KENWATER PL
6400 CanP 91307 529-E7
KENWOOD CT
600 THO 91320 556-D2
KENWOOD ST
500 THO 91320 556-D2
KEPLER DR
1800 OXN 93033 553-A2
KERN ST
300 VEN 93003 492-B3
1700 OXN 93033 552-F3
1700 PHME 93033 552-F3
1700 PHME 93041 552-F3
KERNVALE AV
15500 MRPK 93021 477-A6
KERRIA CT
- OXN 93030 523-A4
KERRMOOR DR
6000 WLKV 91362 557-F3
KERRY DR
2700 SIMI 93063 478-E7
KERRYGLEN ST
1500 THO 91361 556-J6
KERRYHILL CT
6300 AGRH 91301 558-A3
KESWICK CT
2400 SIMI 93063 498-D1
KESWICK ST
22200 LA 91304 529-F4
KETCH AV
3300 OXN 93035 552-B1
KETCH PL
2900 OXN 93035 552-C1
KEVIN ST
100 THO 91360 526-F5
KEY LARGO CT
4800 VeCo 91377 557-G2
KEYSER RONDO
700 CMRL 93010 524-F2
KEYSTONE ST
2200 SIMI 93063 499-C1
KEY WEST CT
1100 OXN 93030 522-F6
KHYBER DR
700 VEN 93001 491-C1
KIAWAH RIVER DR
- OXN 93036 492-G6
KICKAPOO DR
600 VEN 93001 471-D6
KILAINE DR
2900 SIMI 93063 478-E7
KILBURN CT
5300 VeCo 91377 527-G6
KILLDALE CT
600 SIMI 93065 497-D7
KILTY AV
7100 CanP 91307 529-F5
KILTY PL
23400 CanP 91307 529-F5
KIMBALL CT
2000 SIMI 93065 498-A2
N KIMBALL RD
- VEN 93004 492-E1
S KIMBALL RD
- VEN 93004 492-E2
KIMBER DR
3300 THO 91320 555-F2
W KIMBER DR
3700 THO 91320 555-F2
KIMBERLY AV
2400 CMRL 93010 524-E1
KIMBERLY DR
- VeCo 93001 471-C2
29600 AGRH 91301 557-H3
KIMBERWICK LN
4300 MRPK 93021 496-F3
KINETIC DR
200 OXN 93030 523-C5
KING CT
400 SPLA 93060 463-H6
KING DR
6000 VEN 93003 492-D6
KING PL
3500 SIMI 93063 498-E3
KING ST
400 FILM 93015 455-H6
900 OXN 93030 522-F7
KING CANYON RD
700 VeCo 93015 465-J3
700 VeCo 93015 466-A3
KINGFISHER PL
6300 VEN 93003 492-D5
KINGFISHER WY
700 OXN 93030 522-F7
KINGHAM CT
5900 AGRH 91301 558-A4
KING JAMES CT
1500 VeCo 91377 527-H6
KINGLET ST
6800 VEN 93003 492-E5
KINGMAN AV
2000 SIMI 93063 498-J2
KING PALM DR
23600 SIMI 93063 498-D4
23600 SIMI 93065 498-D4
KINGS RD
10800 VEN 93004 472-H6
KINGSBORO CT
1400 THO 91362 527-E7
KINGSBRIDGE LN
2200 OXN 93035 552-A2
KINGSBRIDGE WY
2000 OXN 93035 552-A1
KINGS CANYON CT
2200 OXN 93033 553-B5
KINGS CANYON DR
- OXN 93036 492-H6
KINGSGROVE DR
5000 VeCo 93066 495-A1
5200 VeCo 93066 474-J7
5200 VeCo 93066 494-J1
KINGSLEY CIR
400 THO 91360 526-F7
KINGSPARK CT
31900 WLKV 91361 557-C6
KINGSTON CIR
1300 THO 91362 527-D7
KINGSTON LN
1100 VEN 93001 491-E4
KINGSVIEW RD
4100 MRPK 93021 496-B3
KINGSWOOD LN
400 SIMI 93065 497-D5
KINGSWOOD WY
1300 OXN 93030 522-E3
KINO ST
1900 CMRL 93010 524-D3
KINROSS CT
2200 THO 91361 557-A6
KINZIE ST
22000 Chat 91311 499-J5
KIOWA CT
1600 VeCo 93022 451-E4
KIPANA AV
- VEN 93001 471-C5
KIPLING CT
1500 OXN 93033 552-J4
KIPLING LN
500 VEN 93003 492-D1
KIPLING PL
1000 OXN 93033 552-J4
KIRK AV
600 VEN 93003 491-H4
1400 THO 91360 526-F6
KIRKCALDY CIR
24000 CanP 91307 529-E5
KIRKFORD WY
1200 THO 91361 557-C5
KIRKSIDE PL
- SIMI 93065 527-E1
KIRKWOOD CT
2600 SIMI 93063 498-E1
KIRSTEN AV
1600 SIMI 93063 498-J3
KIRSTEN LEE DR
1800 WLKV 91361 586-J1
KIRTLAND CIR
2000 THO 91360 526-D4
KITE DR
2000 OXN 93035 522-D6
KITETAIL ST
100 SIMI 93065 527-E1
KITSY LN
1500 SIMI 93063 499-B3
KITTRIDGE ST
22000 CanP 91303 529-H6
22000 CanP 91307 529-D6
24500 LACo 91307 529-C6
KITTY ST
500 VeCo 91320 525-G7
500 VeCo 91320 555-G1
KIVA CT
29100 AGRH 91301 558-A5
KIWI WY
6900 VEN 93003 492-E4
KLAMATH AV
2800 SIMI 93063 479-B7
KLAMATH DR
1900 CMRL 93010 494-E7
KLEBERG ST
4600 SIMI 93063 478-G7
KNAPP RD
7600 Chat 91311 499-F6
KNAPP WY
9300 Chat 91311 499-F7
KNAPP RANCH RD
- WHil 91304 499-C7
- WHil 91304 529-C1
KNIGHT CT
2200 SIMI 93065 497-H2
KNIGHT DR
28200 AGRH 91301 558-C7
KNIGHT RONDO
2900 CMRL 93010 524-F3
KNIGHTSBRIDGE AV
2600 THO 91362 527-A3
KNIGHTSBRIDGE PL
3100 THO 91362 527-C3
KNIGHTSGATE RD
4500 WLKV 91361 557-D6
N KNIGHTWOOD CIR
2500 SIMI 93063 498-E1
N KNIGHTWOOD PL
2400 SIMI 93063 498-E1
KNOB LN
13500 VeCo 93012 496-F4
KNOLL DR
1800 VEN 93003 492-B5
KNOLL CREST PL
2200 THO 91361 557-A4
E KNOLLHAVEN ST
2200 SIMI 93065 498-B2
KNOLL RIDGE RD
23600 SIMI 93065 497-F7
KNOLLVIEW CT
23600 SIMI 93065 527-F1
KNOLLVIEW LN
400 THO 91360 526-D7
KNOLLWOOD CIR
23600 SIMI 93065 497-F7
KNOLLWOOD CT
- CanP 91307 529-E5
KNOLLWOOD DR
- THO 91320 555-E3
KNOTTINGHAM ST
1100 SIMI 93065 498-C4
KNOTTY PINE ST
12900 MRPK 93021 496-E3
KNOWLES ST
100 THO 91360 526-E6
KNOX AV
- VEN 93003 492-B2
KOALA DR
2000 OXN 93036 522-F3
KOALA WY
2000 VEN 93003 492-F5
KODIAK CIR
2700 SIMI 93063 478-G7
KODIAK ST
7100 VEN 93003 492-F5
KOENIGSTEIN RD
12400 VeCo 93060 366-L7
12400 VeCo 93060 453-D1
KOHALA ST
100 OXN 93030 523-A5
KONA DR
23600 OXN 93033 552-J1
KONA LN
4800 OXN 93033 552-J5
KOREAN WAR VET MEM HWY Rt#-126
2300 VeCo 93015 455-F6
2500 VeCo 93015 455-E7
2700 VeCo 93015 465-B2
17900 VeCo 93060 464-F3
18400 SPLA 93060 464-F3
20100 VeCo 93060 465-B2
KRENWINKLE CT
100 SIMI 93065 527-E1
KROTONA RD
- OJAI 93023 451-E1
KUDU PL
2300 VEN 93003 492-F5
KUEHNER DR
1300 SIMI 93063 499-C1
2500 SIMI 93063 479-D7
KUMQUAT PL
800 OXN 93036 522-E2
KUNKLE ST
- VeCo 93022 451-B7
KYLE CT
7400 CanP 91307 529-G4
KYLE LN
2800 SIMI 93063 478-E7

L

L AV
- VeCo 93042 583-D5
L CT
500 OXN 93030 522-E6
L ST
100 OXN 93030 522-E5
1100 OXN 93033 522-F7
1100 OXN 93033 552-F1
LA BAYA DR
5600 WLKV 91362 557-E4
LA BREA DR
1200 THO 91362 526-H7
LA BREA ST
100 VeCo 93035 552-A3
4500 OXN 93035 552-A3
LA BROCHE CANYON RD
- VeCo - 453-G1
- VeCo 93060 453-G1
23600 VeCo - 366-L7
LA CAM RD
2200 THO 91320 555-H2
2200 VeCo 91320 555-H2
N LA CAMPANA RD
800 VeCo 93015 455-F5
LA CANADA AV
100 OXN 93033 552-G3
LA CASA CT
3100 THO 91362 527-C3
LA CORONA CT
2100 OXN 93030 522-D4
LA COSTA CT
600 VeCo 91377 557-J2
LA COSTA PL
3500 OXN 93033 552-G3
LA CRESCENTA DR
- VeCo 93010 493-J7
LA CRESCENTA ST
- VeCo 93035 552-A3
LA CRESTA DR
800 THO 91362 526-H7
23600 VeCo 93023 451-D2
LA CROSSE DR
- VeCo 93022 451-B6
LA CUESTA CT
6500 VEN 93003 472-D6
LA CULEBRA CIR
1200 CMRL 93012 524-J1
LA CUMBRA ST
- VeCo 93022 451-C4
LA CUMBRE CIR
7200 VEN 93003 472-D7
LA CUMBRE RD
5800 VeCo 93066 495-A3
LADA AV
6300 CMRL 93012 525-C6
LADBROOK WY
2500 VeCo 91361 556-D7
2500 VeCo 91361 586-D1
LADERA RD
1500 VeCo 93023 442-D4
2600 VeCo - 442-D4
LADERA VISTA DR
4900 CMRL 93012 524-J3
LADONIA ST
4800 SIMI 93063 478-H6
LADYCLIFF CIR
2000 THO 91360 526-C4
LADYFACE CT
29800 AGRH 91301 557-H6
LA ENCINA
- THO 91320 525-E6
E LA FALDA WY
23600 VeCo 93040 458-D5
LAFAYETTE CT
6500 MRPK 93021 476-G6
LAFAYETTE DR
200 OXN 93036 522-H2
LAFAYETTE ST
4700 VEN 93003 492-A3
6700 MRPK 93021 476-G6
LAFITTE DR
1500 VeCo 91377 527-H6
LA FONDA CT
7000 VEN 93003 492-D1
LA FONDA DR
400 VEN 93003 492-D1
LA FONDA DR E
400 VEN 93003 472-D7
400 VEN 93003 492-D1
LA FORTUNA
100 THO 91320 525-E7
LAGO LN
- OXN 93036 522-H3
LAGOON LN
- OXN 93035 522-E6
LA GRANADA DR
700 THO 91362 527-A6
1100 THO 91362 526-H6
LA GRANADA ST
100 VeCo 93035 552-A4
LA GRANGE AV
500 THO 91320 555-F4
LAGROSS WY
9400 Chat 91311 499-F6
LAGUNA DR
600 SIMI 93065 497-G5
600 VeCo 93065 497-G5
LAGUNA RD
- VeCo 93042 583-G4
- VeCo 93012 553-F2
- VeCo 93012 554-A2
1600 VeCo 93033 553-F2
LAGUNA TER
300 VeCo 93065 497-F5
LAGUNA WY
300 VeCo 93065 497-G4
LAGUNA PEAK ACCESS RD
- VeCo - 584-C4
23600 VeCo 93033 583-J4
23600 VeCo 93033 584-A4
LAGUNA RIDGE FIRE RD
- VeCo - 366-G8
- VeCo - 450-B6
- VeCo 93001 450-B6
LA JOLLA DR
1100 THO 91362 526-H7
LA JOLLA ST
100 VEN 93004 472-H7
100 VEN 93004 492-H1
LAKE AV
1100 VeCo 93023 451-C3
LAKE CT
300 SIMI 93065 497-F5
LAKE DR
2500 OXN 93036 522-F1
LAKE BREEZE PL
500 SIMI 93065 497-E6
LAKE CANYON
- VeCo 93003 472-C4
LAKE CASITAS FIRE RD
23600 VeCo 93001 460-A3
LAKE CREST CT
3300 WLKV 91361 557-C7
LAKE CREST DR
5300 AGRH 91301 557-F6
LAKEFIELD RD
100 THO 91361 557-B4
LAKEFRONT DR
30600 AGRH 91301 557-G5
LAKE HARBOR LN
3800 WLKV 91361 557-C6
LAKEHURST AV
1700 CMRL 93010 524-G1
1700 CMRL 93010 494-G7
LAKEHURST ST
1400 OXN 93030 522-F4
LAKELAND TER
24000 LA 91304 529-C1
LAKE LINDERO DR
5300 AGRH 91301 557-G3
LAKE MANOR DR
23200 Chat 91311 499-F7
23400 Chat 91311 499-F7
LAKEMEADOW LN
32100 WLKV 91361 557-C6
LAKE NADINE PL
6000 AGRH 91301 557-G3
LAKE PARK DR
500 SIMI 93065 497-D6
LAKE PLEASANT DR
32300 WLKV 91361 557-B7
LAKEPORT DR
3300 WLKV 91361 557-C7
LAKERIDGE LN
1300 THO 91361 557-B5
LAKE SHERWOOD DR
- VeCo 91361 556-F7
900 THO 91361 556-F7
LAKE SHORE DR
200 VeCo 93035 552-B4
200 VeCo 93043 552-B4
200 PHME 93035 552-B4
200 PHME 93043 552-B4
LAKESIDE AV
300 CMRL 93010 524-D2
LAKEVIEW CT
- OXN 93036 492-H6
LAKEVIEW TER
9200 Chat 91311 499-F7
LAKEVIEW CANYON RD
- THO 91362 557-G1
100 THO 91361 557-C5
300 WLKV 91361 557-C5
1100 THO 91362 527-E7
2000 VeCo 91362 557-G1
LAKEVISTA ST
9900 VEN 93004 492-J3
LAKEWOOD AV
1000 VEN 93004 492-G2
LAKEWOOD CIR
8300 VEN 93004 492-F2
LAKEWOOD CT
1300 THO 91361 557-C5
LAKEWOOD PL
2700 THO 91361 557-B5
LAKOTA ST
- SIMI 93065 477-J6
- SIMI 93065 478-A5
LA LOMA AV
500 VeCo 93066 493-H2
500 VeCo 93066 494-A1
600 VeCo 93066 474-B7
LA LOMITA
- THO 91320 525-E6
N LA LUNA AV
200 VeCo 93023 441-D6
S LA LUNA AV
100 VeCo 93023 441-D7
600 VeCo 93023 451-C2
LA MARINA DR
300 CMRL 93010 523-J2
LAMBERT ST
100 VeCo 93036 492-J5
LAMBOURNE PL
7000 VeCo 91377 528-B7
LA MESA AV
3400 SIMI 93063 478-G5
LAMINGTON ST
- VeCo 91361 556-D7
LAMONT AV
1200 THO 91362 527-A6
LAMPLIGHTER ST
2900 SIMI 93065 498-D4
LAMP POST CIR
400 SIMI 93065 497-F6
LANA CT
2200 SIMI 93063 499-C1
LA NARANJA ST E
600 VeCo 93015 455-E5
LANARK ST
22100 LA 91304 529-G3
LANCASTER CIR
1400 THO 91360 526-A4
LANCE PL
24000 CanP 91307 529-E5
E LANDEN ST
2600 CMRL 93010 494-F7
N LANDEN ST
1700 CMRL 93010 494-F7
1700 CMRL 93010 524-F1
LANDER CT
2600 THO 91320 555-H1
LANDING CV
- VeCo 93012 554-E4
LANDINO DR
6100 WLKV 91362 557-F3
LANDSBURN CIR
1100 THO 91361 557-C5
LANG ST
100 VEN 93003 491-H3
LANGDON WY
1700 VEN 93001 491-E2
LANGFORD DR
1500 OXN 93030 522-E4
LANGHALL CT
6300 AGRH 91301 557-J3
LANGLEY ST
- OXN 93033 553-A4
LANG RANCH PKWY
3000 THO 91362 527-C4
LANGSPUR CT
31800 WLKV 91361 557-D6
LANGUID LN
600 SIMI 93065 497-G5
LANIER PL
3200 THO 91360 526-G2
E LANSDALE CT
2200 SIMI 93065 498-B2
E LANSING PL
2300 SIMI 93065 498-B4
LANTANA ST
100 CMRL 93010 524-C2
1400 VeCo 93010 524-C1
1600 VeCo 93010 494-C7
1800 OXN 93010 522-F3
1900 OXN 93036 522-F3
LANTANA WY
100 VEN 93004 473-A7
LANTERN AV
- SIMI 93063 498-H1
LANTERN LN
4300 MRPK 93021 496-F3
LANYARD WY
2000 OXN 93035 522-D6
LA PALMA
100 THO 91320 525-E6
LA PALOMA CIR
2500 THO 91360 526-D3
LA PATERA CT
- VeCo 93010 493-J7
- VeCo 93010 494-A7
LA PATERA DR
- VeCo 93010 494-A7
- VeCo 93010 493-J7
W LA PAZ CT
- SIMI 93065 497-E4
LA PAZ DR
1100 OJAI 93023 451-F1
LA PERESA DR
1200 THO 91362 526-H7
LAPEYRE RD
23600 VeCo 93021 497-A3
LA PLATA DR
- CMRL 93010 493-H7
LA PLAZA
1400 VeCo 93023 451-C2
LA PORTE ST
600 CMRL 93012 525-A2
LA PUENTE DR
23600 FILM 93015 456-C6
LA PUERTA AV
1800 OXN 93030 522-J6
1800 OXN 93030 523-A6
LA PUMA CT
- CMRL 93012 494-J7
- CMRL 93012 524-J1
LAPWORTH DR
5800 AGRH 91301 558-C4
LA QUILLA DR
22300 Chat 91311 479-J7
22400 Chat 91311 499-H1
LA QUINTA LN
1600 OXN 93036 522-E2
LA RAMADA DR
1800 CMRL 93012 495-B7
1800 CMRL 93012 525-C1
LARAMIE CT
700 THO 91320 555-G5
LARAMIE ST
9600 VEN 93004 492-H2
LARBOARD LN
5800 AGRH 91301 557-G4
LARCH ST
1800 SIMI 93065 498-A2
E LARCH ST
2000 SIMI 93065 498-A2
LARCH CREST CT
2700 THO 91320 556-D2
LARCHMONT ST
1200 SIMI 93065 497-D6
LARCHWOOD CIR
6900 CanP 91307 529-F6
LARCOM ST
2700 THO 91360 526-E3
LAREDO LN
2000 OJAI 93023 451-F1
LA REINA
100 THO 91320 525-E6
S LARGO LN
800 VeCo 93015 465-B2
LARIAT LN
23600 SIMI 93065 527-D1
LARK AV
1100 VEN 93003 492-D4
LARK DR
- VeCo 93041 583-G2
LARK ST
100 OXN 93033 552-G3
600 VeCo 93023 451-C4
1600 SIMI 93063 498-F3
LARKDALE CT
600 SIMI 93065 497-G6
LARK ELLEN AV
200 OJAI 93023 442-A6
LARKELLEN CT
6000 VeCo 91377 558-A2
LARKFIELD AV
1300 THO 91362 527-C6
LARKHAVEN CT
3300 THO 91360 526-H2
LARKHAVEN LN
2400 OXN 93036 522-F2
LARKHILL ST
100 THO 91360 526-F2
LARKIN CT
4700 SIMI 93063 498-H1
LARKIN ST
5400 VEN 93003 492-B3
LARKSBERRY LN
23600 SIMI 93065 497-A2
LARKSPUR DR
5000 VeCo 93001 471-C1
5200 VeCo 93001 461-C7
LARKSPUR ST
1200 VeCo 93063 499-B4
1400 SPLA 93060 464-B2
LARMIER AV
100 VeCo 93022 451-A7
600 VeCo 93022 461-A1
LARO DR
28900 AGRH 91301 558-A3
29300 AGRH 91301 557-J4
LA ROSA DR
4800 VeCo 91377 557-G1
LARRY CT
23600 THO 91320 556-C1
LARSON WY
9300 Chat 91311 499-F6
9300 Chat 91311 499-F6
LARWIN AV
10000 Chat 91311 499-H4
LA SALLE AV
300 VEN 93003 492-A1
LAS BRISAS DR
2700 VeCo 93012 496-A6
LAS CRUCES ST
9500 VEN 93004 492-H3
LA SENDA CT
6400 CMRL 93012 495-C7
LAS ESTRELLAS CT
- CMRL 93012 494-J7
LA SIERRA CT
- CMRL 93012 495-A6
LAS LLAJAS CANYON RD
- Nwhl 91382 479-E2
- StvR 91381 479-E2
5100 VeCo 93063 478-J5
5100 VeCo 93063 479-A5
5500 Chat 91311 479-E2
5500 VeCo - 479-E2
LAS PALMAS ST
100 VeCo 93035 552-A4
LAS PALOMAS DR
400 PHME 93041 552-C2
LAS POSAS CIR
2500 VeCo 93012 496-B6
LAS POSAS RD
- CMRL 93010 524-B2
900 VeCo 93010 524-B2
2100 CMRL 93010 494-F7
2400 VeCo 93012 554-A4
3200 VeCo 93010 494-F7
3600 VeCo 93033 554-A7
5400 VeCo 93033 583-J3
5400 VeCo 93033 584-A3
E LAS POSAS RD
10800 VeCo 93012 496-A6
N LAS POSAS RD
300 CMRL 93010 524-B2
S LAS POSAS RD
100 CMRL 93010 524-B6
700 VeCo 93010 524-B6
1100 VeCo 93012 524-B6
1500 VeCo 93012 554-B1
LAS POSAS ST
300 VeCo 93015 465-J3
LASSEN AV
300 MRPK 93021 496-D1
LASSEN CT
10700 VEN 93004 472-H7
23600 MRPK 93021 496-D1
LASSEN DR
600 SPLA 93060 463-H6
LASSEN ST
2200 OXN 93033 552-F2
22000 Chat 91311 499-H5
LAS TUERO CT
300 VeCo 93010 493-J7
300 VeCo 93010 494-A7
LAS TUNAS PL
3500 OXN 93033 552-H3
LA SUEN DR
100 CMRL 93010 494-E7
100 VeCo 93010 494-E7
LAS VEREDAS PL
- CMRL 93012 494-H7
LAS VIRGENES RD
5100 CALB 91302 558-H3
5100 LACo 91302 558-H3
5700 VeCo 91302 558-H3
LAS VIRGENES RD Rt#-N1
3700 CALB 91302 558-H7
4800 LACo 91302 558-H7
E LAS VIRGENES CANYON RD
23600 VeCo 91302 528-J7
23600 VeCo 91302 529-A7
23600 VeCo 91302 558-H2
LATHAM ST
2000 SIMI 93065 478-A7
LATHAN AV
1700 CMRL 93010 494-D7
1700 CMRL 93010 524-D1
LATHROP AV
3300 SIMI 93063 478-F6
LA TIENDA RD
31600 THO 91362 557-D5
31600 WLKV 91362 557-D5
LATIGO AV
2200 OXN 93030 523-B4
LATIMER RD
6300 SIMI 93063 499-C3
LA TUNA LN
- CMRL 93012 494-H6
LAURA ST
1100 VeCo 93023 451-B2
LAURA LA PLANTE DR
28100 AGRH 91301 558-C6
LAUREL CT
200 VeCo 93035 552-B4
LAUREL LN
- MRPK 93021 496-G3
LAUREL RD
900 SPLA 93060 464-B2
LAUREL ST
100 OXN 93033 552-H2
N LAUREL ST
- VEN 93001 491-D2
S LAUREL ST
- VEN 93001 491-D2
W LAUREL ST
100 OXN 93033 552-F2
LAUREL BLUFF PL
5600 AGRH 91301 557-J5
LAUREL FIG DR
23600 SIMI 93063 498-D4
23600 SIMI 93065 498-D4
LAUREL GLEN DR
4200 MRPK 93021 496-E3
LAURELHURST RD
13200 MRPK 93021 496-F3
LAUREL PARK CIR
800 CMRL 93012 524-J2
LAUREL PARK CT
2100 THO 91362 527-B4
LAUREL PARK DR
5000 CMRL 93012 524-J2
5000 CMRL 93012 525-A2
LAUREL RIDGE DR
23600 SIMI 93065 497-F7
E LAUREL RIDGE LN
5600 CMRL 93012 525-A1
LAUREL VALLEY PL
1900 OXN 93036 522-D2
LAURELVIEW DR
4100 MRPK 93021 496-B3
LAURELWOOD AV
- SIMI 93063 499-A2
LAUREL WOOD CT
23600 SIMI 93065 497-G7
LAURELWOOD CT
1800 THO 91362 526-J3
1800 THO 91362 527-A3
LAURELWOOD DR
1900 THO 91362 527-A3
LAUREN LN
- LA 91304 529-G4
LAUREN ST
3300 SIMI 93063 498-D1
LAURIE LN
100 SPLA 93060 463-J7
300 THO 91360 526-F7
300 THO 91360 556-F1
400 SPLA 93060 473-J1
400 SPLA 93060 474-A1
LAUTREC CT
400 THO 91360 526-D5
LAVA PL
8700 LA 91304 529-E1
LAVANDA DR
2200 OXN 93036 522-H2
LA VELLA DR
4800 VeCo 91377 557-G1
LAVENDER AV
1900 SIMI 93065 498-A2
LAVENDER ST
10700 VEN 93004 493-A7
LAVENDER BELL LN
22300 WdHl 91367 529-J7
LA VENTA DR
1200 THO 91361 557-B6
LA VERADA CT
23600 CMRL 93010 524-C4
LA VERNE AV
- VEN 93003 492-C2
LAVERY CT
2600 THO 91320 525-J6
LA VETA DR
5000 CMRL 93012 524-G3
LA VISTA AV
4000 VeCo 93066 493-H3
LA VUELTA PL
900 SPLA 93060 464-B4
LAWNVIEW CT
2300 SIMI 93065 498-B2
LAWNWOOD WY
500 OXN 93030 522-F3
LAWRENCE CIR
1200 SIMI 93065 498-A3
LAWRENCE DR
800 THO 91320 525-J7
800 THO 91320 526-A5
LAWRENCE WY
1100 OXN 93035 522-D7
1200 OXN 93035 552-D1
LAWSON AV
1700 SIMI 93065 498-B3
LAWTON RANCH RD
23600 VeCo 93015 456-G6
LAYTON CIR
1000 SIMI 93065 497-J4
LAYTON ST
100 VeCo 93023 441-G5
2000 THO 91362 526-J5
LAZARO LN
- OXN 93035 522-C6
LAZIO WY
4900 VeCo 91377 557-G2
LAZY BROOK CT
500 SIMI 93065 497-E6
LAZY OAK PL
29600 AGRH 91301 557-J5
LEADWELL ST
22000 CanP 91303 529-J4
22500 CanP 91307 529-H4
LEAFLOCK AV
2400 THO 91361 557-B5
LEAFWOOD DR
2500 CMRL 93010 494-F6
LEAR CIR
100 THO 91360 526-F7
LEAR CT
1600 OXN 93030 522-E4
LEATHERWOOD CT
4300 CMRL 93012 524-H4
LEAVENS CT
400 SPLA 93060 463-H6
E LECONT CT
3500 SIMI 93063 498-F2
LEDERER AV
6100 WdHl 91367 529-F7
6400 CanP 91307 529-F7
LEE PL
2800 OXN 93035 552-C1
LEE ST
1600 SIMI 93065 498-B2
LEEDS ST
4800 SIMI 93063 498-H2
LEEWARD CIR
2300 THO 91361 557-B6
LEEWARD WY
2900 OXN 93035 552-B1
LEGACY DR
- SIMI 93065 477-J7
- SIMI 93065 478-A6
LEGAN
23600 VeCo 93015 456-G6
LEGENDS DR
- SIMI 93065 478-A5
LEHIGH ST
5300 VEN 93003 492-B2
LEHMAN RD
- PHME 93043 552-C4
LEI DR
1000 OXN 93033 552-J5
LEI LN
1800 OXN 93033 552-J1
1800 OXN 93033 553-A1
LEIGHTON DR
- VEN 93001 471-C7
LEIGHTON POINT RD
3800 CALB 91302 558-G7
LEISURE LN
900 SIMI 93065 497-H5
1300 THO 91320 556-B1
LEISURE VILLAGE DR
5600 CMRL 93012 525-B2
LEISURE VILLAGE DR W
5100 CMRL 93012 525-A3
LELAND CIR
5300 SIMI 93063 498-J3
LELAND ST
6000 VEN 93003 492-D6
LE MAR AV
- VeCo 93042 583-F5
LEMAR AV
300 VeCo 93036 492-J7
700 VeCo 93036 493-A7
LEMARSH ST
22000 Chat 91311 499-J4
LEMAY ST
24000 CanP 91307 529-D6
LEMBERT ST
2600 SIMI 93065 498-C4
LEMON AV
3600 OXN 93033 553-B3
LEMON DR
2600 SIMI 93063 498-E1
2700 SIMI 93063 478-E7
2800 VeCo 93010 494-E7
3200 VeCo 93063 478-E7
E LEMON DR
800 VeCo 93010 494-F7
2900 CMRL 93010 494-F7
LEMON WY
600 FILM 93015 455-J5
LEMONBERRY PL
3900 THO 91362 497-A7
3900 THO 91362 527-A1
LEMON GROVE AV
500 VEN 93003 491-H4
LEMONWOOD DR
1700 SPLA 93060 464-D5
10400 VeCo 93021 495-J1
LEMONWOOD ST
700 THO 91320 555-G4
LEMUR CT
6900 VEN 93003 492-E5
LEMUR ST
7000 VEN 93003 492-E4
LENA AV
6200 WdHl 91367 529-G7
6800 CanP 91307 529-G4
7600 LA 91304 529-G3
LENNOX CT
1800 OXN 93030 522-E4
LEON DR
1900 OXN 93036 522-H3
LEONARD ST
500 CMRL 93010 524-F2
LEORA ST
3400 SIMI 93063 478-D6
LEOTA LN
7100 WHil 91304 499-E7
22700 WHil 91304 499-E7
LE SAGE AV
6100 WdHl 91367 529-F7
LESLIE CT
3100 SIMI 93063 478-D6
LESSER DR
3200 VeCo 91320 525-F7
3500 THO 91320 525-F7
LESTER LN
8300 LA 91304 529-F2
LETA YANCY RD
- MRPK 93021 496-D2
LETICIA CT
30100 AGRH 91301 557-H5
LEVEN AV
2000 CMRL 93010 494-H7
LEVI CT
3400 SIMI 93063 478-F6
LEVI WY
1600 OXN 93033 552-J3
LEWIS LN
900 FILM 93015 455-J6
5500 AGRH 91301 558-C5

VENTURA CO.

STREET
Block City ZIP Pg-Grid

LEWIS PL
28400 AGRH 91301 558-C6
LEWIS RD
600 VeCo 93012 524-F5
1800 VeCo 93012 554-D2
4900 AGRH 91301 558-C5
N LEWIS RD Rt#-34
- CMRL 93010 524-G2
1700 CMRL 93010 494-H7
S LEWIS RD Rt#-34
- CMRL 93010 524-F4
200 CMRL 93012 524-F4
E LEWIS ST
- VEN 93001 471-C7
W LEWIS ST
200 VEN 93001 471-B6
LEXINGTON CT
1400 CMRL 93010 524-E1
LEXINGTON DR
2300 VEN 93001 491-G2
2400 VEN 93003 491-G2
LEXINGTON WY
30900 AGRH 91301 557-F6
30900 WLKV 91361 557-F6
LEXINGTON HILLS LN
13000 VeCo 93012 496-F5
LEYTE ST
- PHME 93041 552-E4
LIADA WY
- OXN 93030 522-H4
LIBBEY AV
700 OJAI 93023 441-H6
LIBERTY CV
2600 PHME 93041 552-C3
LIBERTY CANYON RD
3900 AGRH 91301 558-E7
4000 Ago 91301 558-E7
LIBRARY VIEW RD
23600 VeCo 93063 497-B3
LIBRE ST
- OXN 93030 522-G4
LICHO WY
- OXN 93030 522-J4
LICIA PL
2700 SIMI 93065 478-B7
2700 SIMI 93065 498-B1
LIDO BLVD
2500 PHME 93041 552-D2
2700 OXN 93035 552-E2
2700 OXN 93041 552-E2
LIDO CT
300 CMRL 93010 524-D3
LIDO DR
2600 PHME 93041 552-D2
2700 OXN 93035 552-D2
2700 OXN 93041 552-D2
LIGGETT ST
22000 Chat 91311 499-J6
LIGHTHOUSE LN
700 OXN 93030 522-F7
LIGHTHOUSE WY
500 PHME 93041 552-F7
LIGHTNING RIDGE WY
- SIMI 93063 478-E6
LILAC LN
200 SPLA 93060 464-A5
10200 VeCo 93063 499-F3
10200 SIMI 93063 499-F3
LILAC WK
2500 OXN 93030 522-D4
LILAC WY
- VEN 93004 473-A7
LILLA PL
7500 LA 91304 529-E4
LILLIAN DR
400 PHME 93041 552-F5
LILY CT
3400 VeCo 91320 525-F7
LILY PL
200 VEN 93004 473-A7
LILYWOOD LN
1800 OXN 93030 522-H4
LIMCO RD
600 VeCo 93015 457-A6
LIME AV
1600 OXN 93033 553-B5
LIME CANYON RD
23600 VeCo 93040 367-D7
LIMEROCK TR
8600 LA 91304 529-E1
LIMESTONE DR
- THO 91362 527-B3
LIMOGES CT
- LACo 91302 558-G3
LIMONEIRA AV
- VeCo 93003 492-D2
- VEN 93003 492-D2
LIMONERO PL
- OXN 93030 522-H4
LINCOLN CT
- SIMI 93065 497-D5
1800 OXN 93033 553-A4
1900 OXN 93033 552-J5
LINCOLN DR
- VEN 93001 491-E1
LINDA CT
1500 SIMI 93065 497-J3
LINDA FLORA DR
12000 VeCo 93023 451-A2
LINDALE AV
2000 SIMI 93065 498-C2
LINDAMERE CT
- SIMI 93065 497-H5
LINDA VISTA AV
200 VEN 93001 491-E1
LINDAWOOD ST
800 THO 91320 556-C1
LINDBERGH DR
1800 OXN 93033 553-A1
LINDEN CIR
800 THO 91360 526-F7
LINDEN DR
400 OXN 93033 552-F2
N LINDEN DR
- VEN 93004 472-H7
S LINDEN DR
- VEN 93004 472-J7
LINDENGROVE ST
2000 THO 91361 557-A4
LINDERO CANYON RD
100 THO 91362 557-G3
100 WLKV 91362 557-G3
5400 WLKV 91361 557-E5
5500 VeCo 91377 527-G7
5900 VeCo 91362 527-G7
5900 VeCo 91362 557-G3
6000 VeCo 91377 557-G3
W LINDERO CANYON RD
5300 WLKV 91362 557-C7
5400 WLKV 91361 557-C7
LINDSAY CT
- THO 91320 555-E2
LINDSAY LN
100 SPLA 93060 463-H7
100 SPLA 93060 473-H1
LINDSAY PL
1000 OXN 93033 552-J4
LINFIELD DR
300 VEN 93003 492-A3
LINGDOLY RANCH RD
- VeCo 93060 463-E4
LINKS VIEW DR
- SIMI 93065 497-C6
LINLEY LN
7500 LA 91304 529-E4
LINVILLE CT
6400 MRPK 93021 477-A6
LION ST
300 OJAI 93023 441-H6
LION CANYON FIRE RD
23600 VeCo 93023 451-H3
23600 VeCo 93023 452-C3
LIONS CIR
- SIMI 93065 477-C7
LIONS GATE DR
600 OXN 93030 522-D4
LIRIO AV
1400 VeCo 93004 493-B2
LISA CT
700 VeCo 91320 525-G7
LISBON LN
- OXN 93036 492-G6
N LITA PL
2500 SIMI 93063 498-E1
LITTLE CREEK CIR
2300 THO 91320 555-J2
LITTLE FARMS RD
1500 OXN 93030 522-E5
LITTLE FAWN CT
1400 THO 91362 527-F6
LITTLE FEATHER AV
3200 SIMI 93063 479-A6
LITTLEFIELD CT
2500 THO 91362 527-D3
LITTLE HOLLOW PL
4000 MRPK 93021 496-D3
LITTLE OAK LN
6000 WdHl 91367 529-C7
LITTLER CT
- MRPK 93021 476-D5
LITTLE SYCAMORE CANYON RD
100 VeCo 90265 586-D4
200 LACo 90265 586-D4
LIVELY CIR
- VeCo 93023 452-D1
LIVEOAK AV
7300 VeCo 93060 453-B7
7300 VeCo 93060 463-B1
LIVE OAK CT
26800 CALB 91301 558-G7
LIVE OAK DR
- VEN 93001 491-E2
LIVE OAK RD
1500 THO 91320 556-A2
LIVE OAK ST
2500 THO 91362 557-A2
LIVE OAK TER
22600 Chat 91311 499-H5
LIVE OAK TR
6700 VeCo 93063 499-D4
LIVERMORE AV
100 VEN 93004 492-F1
LIVERPOOL CT
5500 VeCo 91377 527-J6
LIVINGSTON AV
- VEN 93003 492-B3
LIVORNO CT
30800 WLKV 91362 557-G6
LIZ CT
7400 LA 91304 529-E4
LLAMA CT
1200 VEN 93003 492-E4
LLANERCH LN
600 SIMI 93065 497-D5
LLEVARANCHO RD
2100 SIMI 93065 497-D2
LLOYD CT
- THO 91320 555-F2
LLOYD BUTLER RD
23600 VeCo 93036 493-D3
23600 VeCo 93066 493-D3
LLOYD TURN-OFF
- VeCo 93001 471-C4
LOBELIA AV
1500 VEN 93004 493-A2
LOBELIA DR
1900 OXN 93030 522-F3
1900 OXN 93036 522-F1
LOCKE AV
- SIMI 93065 497-H4
LOCKFORD CT
3600 THO 91360 526-H1
LOCKHART LN
600 FILM 93015 456-A5
LOCKHURST DR
6000 WdHl 91367 529-E7
6300 CanP 91307 529-E7
LOCKWOOD CT
3400 SIMI 93063 498-D1
LOCKWOOD ST
700 OXN 93036 523-A3
1700 OXN 93036 522-J3
LOCKWOOD VALLEY RD
900 VeCo - 367-A1
15900 VeCo - 366-H2
LOCUST AV
- VeCo 91377 558-A2
LOCUST ST
- SIMI 93063 499-B2
LODESTONE CT
900 THO 91320 555-G5
LODGEWOOD ST
2800 THO 91320 555-G3
LODGEWOOD WY
900 OXN 93030 522-E3
LOEWE LN
900 VEN 93003 492-A4
LOFTUS CANYON RD
- VeCo 93066 465-A7
- VeCo 93066 474-J1
23600 VeCo 93066 464-J5
23600 VeCo 93066 464-J7
LOGAN AV
800 VEN 93004 492-G3
LOGAN LN
- SIMI 93065 497-E2
LOGWOOD RD
5800 WLKV 91362 557-G4
LOIRE CT
30800 WLKV 91362 557-F5
LOIRE VALLEY DR
- SIMI 93065 497-G7
- SIMI 93065 527-G1
N LOIS AV
600 THO 91320 525-G7
600 VeCo 91320 525-G7
LOIS LN
1100 CMRL 93010 524-C4
LOISE ST
300 SPLA 93060 464-A7
LOLA WY
- OXN 93030 522-J4
LOMA DR
- CMRL 93010 494-F7
- VeCo 93010 494-F7
800 VeCo 93023 451-D1
1400 CMRL 93010 524-F1
LOMA LN
1000 VeCo 93063 499-B4
LOMA VERDE MTWY
- Cstc 91384 458-F1
- VeCo 93040 367-E7
- VeCo 93040 458-F1
LOMA VISTA PL
600 SPLA 93060 464-A4
LOMA VISTA RD
2600 VEN 93003 491-G2
4300 VEN 93003 492-C1
7500 VEN 93004 492-E1
10100 VeCo 93004 472-H7
10100 VEN 93004 472-H6
10900 VEN 93060 472-H6
LOMBARD ST
100 OXN 93030 523-A4
200 THO 91360 556-F1
LOMITA AV
600 VeCo 93023 441-C7
N LOMITA AV
100 VeCo 93023 441-E6
S LOMITA AV
100 VeCo 93023 441-E7
LOMITA ST
2300 CMRL 93010 524-E3
LONDELIUS ST
21900 LA 91304 529-J1
LONDON CIR
700 THO 91360 526-G7
LONDON LN
- OXN 93036 492-H6
LONDON GROVE CT
12100 MRPK 93021 496-D3
LONE OAK DR
400 THO 91362 556-J1
400 THO 91362 557-A1
400 THO 91362 526-J7
LONESTAR WY
2000 THO 91362 556-J1
2000 THO 91362 557-A1
LONE TRAIL CT
- MRPK 93021 476-D6
LONE TREE CT
2400 THO 91362 526-J4
LONG CT
- THO 91360 556-G1
LONGBRANCH RD
100 SIMI 93065 497-F5
LONG CANYON DR
100 VeCo 93004 492-G1
100 VEN 93004 492-G1
LONG CANYON RD
1300 VeCo 93003 472-F5
1300 VeCo 93060 472-F5
23600 SIMI 93065 497-G7
23600 SIMI 93065 527-F1
LONG COVE DR
- OXN 93036 522-C3
LONGFELLOW CT
100 THO 91360 526-E3
LONGFELLOW ST
100 THO 91360 526-E3
LONGFELLOW WY
5100 OXN 93033 552-H5
S LONGFORD AV
600 THO 91320 555-F4
LONGHORN LN
100 OJAI 93023 441-H7
100 OJAI 93023 451-H1
LONG RIDGE CT
1500 THO 91360 526-E6
LONGRIDGE CT
6300 VEN 93003 472-D6
LONG SHADOW CT
5000 THO 91362 527-F7
LONGVIEW DR
9200 VEN 93004 492-H3
LONGVIEW PL
300 THO 91360 526-E5
LONGWOOD CT
200 THO 91320 555-E2
LONSDALE ST
2100 CMRL 93010 524-E1
LOOKOUT DR
1100 OXN 93035 522-C7
1500 OXN 93035 552-C1
LOOKOUT ROCK TR
1000 VeCo 93063 499-C4
LOON DR
- VeCo 93041 583-G1
E LOOP DR
300 CMRL 93010 494-F6
300 VeCo 93010 494-F6
N LOOP DR
100 VeCo 93010 494-E6
W LOOP DR
- CMRL 93010 494-E6
- CMRL 93010 524-E1
100 VeCo 93010 494-E6
LOOP LN
18000 VeCo 93060 464-D4
LOOP RD
3000 VEN 93003 492-E6
LOPACO CT
300 VeCo 93010 494-A7
LOPEZ CT
- MRPK 93021 476-B5
LORA LN
100 FILM 93015 456-B6
LORABEL WY
- SIMI 93065 527-E1
LORAINE PL
2700 SIMI 93065 478-B7
2700 SIMI 93065 498-B1
LORD CREEK RD
600 VeCo 93015 455-D4
LORENA DR
- OXN 93030 522-J4
LORENZO DR
500 VeCo 91377 557-G1
LORETA CT
3300 CMRL 93010 524-G2
LORETO CIR
3800 THO 91320 555-E1
N LORETTA CIR
2500 SIMI 93065 498-B1
LORETTA DR
11900 MRPK 93021 496-C2
LORI CIR
3000 SIMI 93063 478-E7
LORI LN
- VeCo 93010 494-E6
LORRAINE LN
- MRPK 93021 496-F2
LOS ALAMOS DR
400 OJAI 93023 442-A6
LOS ALISOS CT
23600 CMRL 93010 524-C4
LOS ALTOS ST
- VeCo 93035 552-A3
LOS AMIGOS AV
- SIMI 93065 497-E3
LOS ANGELES AV
- VeCo 93012 554-D4
- VEN 93004 493-A1
- VeCo 93035 552-C6
1000 VeCo 93004 493-A1
1300 VeCo 93015 465-E3
LOS ANGELES AV Rt#-118
- MRPK 93021 496-F1
900 VeCo 93066 493-H4
900 VeCo 93066 494-A4
1200 VeCo 93004 493-B2
2000 VeCo 93036 493-B2
4500 VeCo 93066 495-A4
8000 VeCo 93021 495-H3
10700 VeCo 93021 496-A2
E LOS ANGELES AV
100 SIMI 93065 497-G2
1700 SIMI 93065 498-A2
3200 SIMI 93063 498-A2
5400 SIMI 93063 499-A2
W LOS ANGELES AV
100 SIMI 93065 477-D7
100 SIMI 93065 497-E1
LOS ARCOS CIR
2500 THO 91360 526-G3
LOS ARCOS DR
5300 VeCo 91377 557-H1
LOS CABOS LN
- VeCo 93001 471-C2
LOS CEDROS CIR
2800 VeCo 93012 496-C6
LOS COYOTES PL
6800 CMRL 93012 495-D6
LOS DAMASCOS PL
- CMRL 93012 494-H6
LOS ENCINOS RD
2000 VeCo 93023 451-A4
LOS FELIZ DR
1600 THO 91362 556-J1
2000 THO 91362 557-A2
LOS FELIZ ST
100 VeCo 93035 552-A3
200 OXN 93035 552-A3
LOS FRESNOS CIR
2800 VeCo 93012 496-C6
LOS NOGALES AV
2700 CMRL 93010 524-F1
LOS NOGALES RD
3300 SIMI 93063 478-F6
LOS OLIVOS
2900 OXN 93036 523-B2
LOS PADRES CT
6600 VEN 93003 472-D6
LOS PADRES DR
- THO 91361 556-F2
LOS PINOS CIR
2700 VeCo 93012 496-C6
LOS PRIETOS CT
1300 OXN 93035 552-E1
LOS PUEBLOS DR
100 CMRL 93012 525-A3
600 CMRL 93012 524-J2
LOS ROBLES DR
1200 SPLA 93060 464-B3
LOS ROBLES RD
2700 THO 91362 557-A2
LOS ROBLES ST
100 VeCo 93035 552-A4
LOS ROSAS ST
23900 LA 91304 529-E2
LOS SANTOS CT
23600 CMRL 93010 524-C4
LOS SERENOS DR
200 FILM 93015 455-H6
LOST CANYONS DR
- SIMI 93063 478-C4
- SIMI 93065 477-J6
- SIMI 93065 478-C4
LOST HILLS RD
4100 CALB 91302 558-G7
4100 CALB 91301 558-G7
4800 Ago 91301 558-F5
5000 LACo 91302 558-G7
LOST OAK CT
26900 CALB 91301 558-G7
LOST POINT LN
1200 OXN 93030 522-E6
LOST SPRINGS DR
3800 CALB 91301 558-G7
N LOS VIENTOS DR
- THO 91320 555-E1
500 THO 91320 525-F7
S LOS VIENTOS DR
- THO 91320 555-E1
LOTA LN
- AGRH 91301 558-C5
LOT DYLAN DR
- OXN 93033 552-H5
LOTUS AV
500 THO 91360 526-D5
LOU DR
4100 SIMI 93063 498-F3
LOUIS DR
400 VeCo 91320 525-F7
400 VeCo 91320 555-G1
LOUISE ST
3200 SIMI 93063 478-D7
LOUISIANA PL
200 OXN 93036 492-H7
LOVE CIR
1700 SIMI 93063 499-B2
LOVEDAY AV
1000 SIMI 93065 498-C4
LOWELL CT
2500 SIMI 93065 497-J1
LOWELL PL
300 OXN 93033 552-H4
LOWER LAKE RD
- VeCo 91361 556-F7
LOWERY ST
1300 SIMI 93065 497-J4
LOYOLA AV
- VEN 93003 492-C2
LOYOLA PL
6600 MRPK 93021 476-H6
LOYOLA ST
14500 MRPK 93021 476-H6
E LOYOLA ST
14300 MRPK 93021 476-G6
LUBBOCK CT
23600 SIMI 93063 478-G7
LUBBOCK DR
4400 SIMI 93063 478-G7
LUCADA ST
100 SPLA 93060 463-J7
400 SPLA 93060 473-J1
400 SPLA 93060 474-A1
LUCAS CT
- THO 91320 555-J1
3800 SIMI 93063 498-E2
LUCERNE CT
1300 VEN 93004 492-H3
LUCERNE ST
9500 VEN 93004 492-H3
LUCERO CT
1100 CMRL 93010 524-C1
LUCERO ST
- OXN 93030 523-A4
- THO 91360 526-F1
1100 CMRL 93010 524-C2
LUCIA CT
3900 MRPK 93021 496-C4
LUCILLE CIR
600 MRPK 93021 476-F7
LUCILLE CT
700 MRPK 93021 476-F7
LUCKY LN
1800 SIMI 93063 498-G3
LUCY CIR
400 SIMI 93065 498-D5
LUDGATE DR
5000 CALB 91301 558-F6
LUFF CT
2900 OXN 93035 552-C1
LUGANO WY
400 VeCo 91377 557-G3
LUIS DR
5400 AGRH 91301 557-H5
LUKENS LN
2500 SIMI 93065 498-B4
LULL ST
7600 LA 91304 529-F4
LUNA CT
- CALB 91302 558-H6
LUNA DR
- CMRL 93010 523-J2
2900 VEN 93003 491-G2
LUNAR CT
3400 OXN 93030 523-D4
LUNDY DR
1100 SIMI 93065 497-G4
LUPE AV
- THO 91320 555-H1
LUPIN ST
2000 SIMI 93065 498-C2
LUPINE LN
4600 VeCo 93023 442-F5
LUPINE WY
300 VEN 93001 491-E1
LUPITA ST
100 OXN 93030 522-H6
LURAY CIR
2500 VeCo 93065 478-C7
LUSTRE DR
- OXN 93030 522-H4
LUTHER AV
3200 THO 91360 526-E2
LUTHER CIR
6800 MRPK 93021 476-H6
LUXENBERG DR
9200 VeCo 93021 475-G5
LYDIA CIR
1700 SIMI 93065 498-A3
LYME BAY
4400 OXN 93035 552-A2
LYNDBROOK CT
31900 WLKV 91361 557-C6
LYNDHURST AV
1700 CMRL 93010 494-D7
1700 CMRL 93010 524-D1
E LYNDHURST AV
1500 CMRL 93010 524-D1
LYNETTE ST
3100 SIMI 93063 498-D1
LYNN CT
3100 VeCo 91320 525-G7
3100 VeCo 91320 555-G1
3400 VEN 93003 491-H2
LYNN DR
200 VEN 93003 491-H2
LYNN RD
400 THO 91360 526-D3
400 THO 91320 556-C2
500 VeCo 91360 526-D7
1500 THO 91320 556-A2
1900 VeCo 91320 556-C2
2500 THO 91320 555-H2
W LYNN RD
3800 THO 91320 555-D4
LYNNBROOK AV
300 VEN 93003 492-B1
LYNNMERE DR
500 THO 91360 526-B4
LYNN OAKS AV
- THO 91320 525-J5
LYNN OAKS CT
100 THO 91320 556-C2
LYNN OAKS ST
200 THO 91320 556-C2
LYNNVIEW ST
2500 THO 91320 555-H3
LYNNWOOD DR
5100 CMRL 93012 525-A1
5200 CMRL 93012 524-J1
LYNWOOD ST
500 THO 91360 526-C5
2300 SIMI 93065 498-B1
LYON CT
- LACo 91302 558-G3
LYON PL
6100 VeCo 93063 499-B4
LYONIA LN
- OXN 93030 523-A4
LYONS CT
700 SIMI 93065 497-G4
LYONS ST
- PHME 93043 552-D3
LYSANDER AV
2000 SIMI 93065 497-F2

M

M CT
900 OXN 93030 522-E7
M ST
- VeCo 93042 583-D4
400 OXN 93030 522-E6
1100 OXN 93033 522-E7
1100 OXN 93033 552-F2
3200 PHME 93041 552-F3
N M ST
300 OXN 93030 522-E4
MAARTEN DR
6000 VeCo 93021 475-J7
6000 VeCo 93021 495-H1
MABREY CT
1400 THO 91360 526-H2
MACADAM CT
6000 AGRH 91301 558-A3
MACADEMIA LN
23600 SIMI 93065 497-E5
MACARTHUR PL
1800 OXN 93033 552-J2
1800 OXN 93033 553-A2
MACAW AV
- VEN 93003 492-E5
MACDONALD LN
2500 PHME 93041 552-D2
MACHADO ST
2700 SIMI 93065 498-C3
MACKAY AV
200 VEN 93004 492-F2
MACMILLAN AV
- VEN 93001 491-E2
MACODA LN
11800 Chat 91311 479-J7
MAD RD
- VeCo 93042 583-D4
MADERA AV
- VEN 93003 492-C2
MADERA CIR
2400 PHME 93041 552-E2
MADERA PL
3000 OXN 93033 553-B3
MADERA RD
900 SIMI 93065 497-F4
900 VeCo 93065 497-F4
2600 SIMI 93065 477-F7
MADISON ST
3900 VEN 93003 491-J3
MADONNA LN
- THO 91320 556-B2
MADRESELVA CT
300 CMRL 93012 525-A2
MADRID AV
100 THO 91320 555-J1
MADRINA PL
500 OXN 93030 522-H5
MADRONE ST
2000 SIMI 93065 498-B2
MAEGAN PL
100 THO 91362 556-H1
MAESTRO AV
7600 LA 91304 529-F3
MAESTRO PL
23400 LA 91304 529-F4
MAGDA CIR
2100 THO 91360 526-E4
MAGELLAN AV
500 OXN 93033 552-G6
MAGELLAN ST
- THO 91360 526-F1
MAGNOLIA AV
100 OXN 93030 522-E5
MAGNOLIA DR
- VeCo 93001 471-C2
1300 SPLA 93060 464-B2
MAGNOLIA ST
600 MRPK 93021 476-E7
600 MRPK 93021 496-E1
2000 SIMI 93065 498-B2
2700 CMRL 93012 524-F4
MAGPIE CT
- THO 91320 525-J5
MAHAN CT
15300 MRPK 93021 476-J5
MAHAN RD
- VeCo 93021 476-G3
MAHOGANY LN
23600 SIMI 93065 497-E5
MAHONEY AV
- VeCo 93022 451-B6
600 VeCo 93001 451-B6
MAIDSTONE LN
400 THO 91320 556-D1
MAIDU CT
5900 SIMI 93063 479-B7
MAIN RD
- VeCo 93041 583-H3
- VeCo 93042 583-G4
MAIN ST
100 FILM 93015 456-A6
100 VeCo 93040 457-F3
700 SPLA 93060 463-J7
E MAIN ST
- VEN 93001 491-C2
100 SPLA 93060 464-B6
1300 VeCo 93060 464-B6
2300 VEN 93003 491-H4
3900 VEN 93003 492-A4
N MAIN ST
100 VeCo 93015 465-E1
100 VeCo 93015 455-E7
S MAIN ST
100 VeCo 93015 465-E1
W MAIN ST
- VEN 93001 491-A1
100 SPLA 93060 463-J6
100 SPLA 93060 464-A6
MAINMAST DR
30500 AGRH 91301 557-G5
MAINMAST PL
5600 AGRH 91301 557-G5
MAINSAIL CIR
3800 WLKV 91361 557-B6
MAINSAIL CT
100 PHME 93041 552-E6
MAINSAIL LN
- OXN 93035 522-E7
MAJESTIC CT
- MRPK 93021 496-E2
MAJORCA CT
800 THO 91360 526-C3
MAJORCA DR
1900 OXN 93035 552-A1
MAKENZIE CT
- THO 91362 557-A1
MALAGA CT
600 THO 91320 525-F7
MALAT DR
600 VeCo 91320 525-G7
MALCOLM ST
1800 SIMI 93065 498-A3
MALDEN ST
22300 LA 91304 529-H1
MALIBU AV
- VeCo 93035 552-B5
200 VEN 93004 492-E1
MALIBU HILLS RD
26700 CALB 91301 558-G7
26700 CALB 91302 558-G7
MALLARD AV
1600 VEN 93003 492-E4
2900 THO 91360 526-F3
MALLARD ST
400 FILM 93015 455-H6
MALLARD WY
100 OXN 93030 522-E5
100 VeCo 93030 522-E5
MALLATT WY
1000 CMRL 93010 524-C3
MALLORY CT
15300 MRPK 93021 477-A4
MALLORY WY
300 OJAI 93023 441-H6
MALO CT
700 SIMI 93065 497-G4
MALONE ST
- PHME 93043 552-D3
E MALTON AV
5800 SIMI 93063 499-A1
N MALTON AV
2100 SIMI 93063 499-B2
MAMMOTH ST
10100 VEN 93004 492-J3
10300 VEN 93004 493-A2
MAMMOTH PEAK DR
- MRPK 93021 476-D6
MANASSAS AV
1400 VEN 93003 492-B4
MANCHESTER CT
2500 THO 91362 527-B3
MANCINI CT
5600 VEN 93003 492-C4
MANDALAY CT
1400 CMRL 93010 524-D1
MANDALAY BEACH RD
500 OXN 93035 521-H6
1200 OXN 93035 551-J1
1900 OXN 93035 552-A2
MANDAN CT
2500 VEN 93001 471-C5
MANDAN PL
400 SIMI 93065 497-D2
MANDELL ST
22300 LA 91304 529-J2
MANDEVILLE PL
23600 VeCo 91377 528-A7
MANDOLIN CIR
- SIMI 93063 478-G5
MANDRILL AV
2000 VEN 93003 492-F5
MANET LN
2400 SIMI 93063 499-B1
MANGO LN
6100 SIMI 93063 499-B3
MANGROVE ST
- MRPK 93021 496-G3
MANLEY CT
25900 LACo 91302 558-J3
MANN CT
- MRPK 93021 476-B5
MANORGATE PL
3200 SIMI 93065 498-D5
MANOR RIDGE RD
600 SPLA 93060 464-A4
MANORVIEW CT
4200 MRPK 93021 496-B3
MANSFIELD LN
100 CMRL 93010 494-E7
100 VeCo 93010 494-E7
MANTON AV
6100 WdHl 91367 529-F7
MANUEL CANYON
23600 VeCo 93001 471-D1
MANZANILLO DR
5200 VeCo 93021 475-G7
5200 VeCo 93021 495-G1
MANZANITA AV
200 VEN 93001 491-E1
MANZANITA CT
400 VEN 93001 491-E1
MANZANITA DR
600 FILM 93015 455-J5
1200 SPLA 93060 464-B3
2200 OXN 93033 552-F2
MANZANITA LN
- THO 91362 557-A3
200 THO 91361 557-A3
200 THO 91361 556-J3
MANZANITA ST
300 CMRL 93012 524-J3
300 CMRL 93012 525-A3
MAPLE CT
200 VEN 93003 491-H3
500 FILM 93015 455-J4
23600 SIMI 93063 499-B3
MAPLE RD
100 THO 91320 556-B2
200 VeCo 91320 556-B2
MAPLE ST
200 OXN 93033 552-G2
1200 SPLA 93060 464-B2
3500 VEN 93003 491-J3
MAPLECREEK WK
- CMRL 93012 524-H2
MAPLECREST ST
11800 MRPK 93021 496-C4
MAPLEGROVE ST
6400 VeCo 91377 558-B2
MAPLEKNOLL PL
3400 THO 91362 527-A1
MAPLELEAF AV
100 THO 91320 555-J2
MAPLERIDGE CT
11400 MRPK 93021 496-B4
MAPLE VIEW CIR
5300 CMRL 93012 525-A2
MAPLEWOOD AV
700 THO 91320 555-G4
MAPLEWOOD CT
700 THO 91320 555-G4
MAPLEWOOD WY
800 PHME 93041 552-F5
MARA AV
- VEN 93004 492-F2
MARBELLA CT
- OXN 93035 522-C6
MARBLEHEAD AV
300 SIMI 93065 497-D7
MARCELLA ST
1700 SIMI 93065 498-C3
MARCELLO AV
100 THO 91320 556-C1
MARCH AV
7500 LA 91304 529-F3
MARCH ST
200 SPLA 93060 463-J6
200 SPLA 93060 464-A6
MARCO DR
1800 CMRL 93010 494-H7
1800 CMRL 93010 524-H1
MARCUS CT
- THO 91320 555-E2
MARCY CT
3300 SIMI 93063 498-D1
MARDIGRAS CT
700 CMRL 93010 524-D2
MARETO WY
700 VeCo 91377 557-H1
MARGARITA AV
400 CMRL 93012 525-A5
MARGATE PL
1500 THO 91361 556-H6
MARGO DR
700 SIMI 93065 497-G3
MARIA DR
6200 VeCo 93021 475-J5
MARIA LN
- VeCo 93010 494-E6
MARIA WY
23600 OXN 93030 522-H4
MARIA HERRERA LN
- OXN 93033 552-H6
MARIAN AV
1500 THO 91360 526-D5
1500 VeCo 91360 526-D5
MARIANO DR
1100 VeCo 93023 451-B1
MARIANO ST
1600 CMRL 93010 493-J5
MARICIO CIR
1900 THO 91360 526-F5
MARICOPA DR
5300 SIMI 93063 478-J7
5400 SIMI 93063 479-A7
MARICOPA HWY Rt#-33
1000 OJAI 93023 441-E6
1000 OJAI 93023 451-F1
1700 VeCo 93023 441-B2
10000 VeCo 93023 366-J6
E MARIE ST
2300 SIMI 93065 498-B1
MARIETTA CIR
2800 THO 91360 526-H3
MARIGOLD AV
1500 VEN 93004 493-A2
MARIGOLD CT
26600 CALB 91302 558-G7
MARIGOLD LN
- SIMI 93065 497-H3
1100 SPLA 93060 464-B3
MARIGOLD PL
1200 THO 91360 526-H2
MARILLA ST
22200 Chat 91311 499-H5
MARILYN CT
3000 THO 91320 555-G2
MARILYN ST
2200 SIMI 93065 498-B1
MARIMAR ST
- THO 91360 526-F5
MARIN LN
7800 VEN 93004 492-E1
MARIN RD
100 SPLA 93060 464-A6
MARIN ST
100 THO 91360 556-E1
MARIN WY
2100 OXN 93033 553-A2
MARINA CIR E
- VeCo 93040 457-F4
MARINA CIR W
300 VeCo 93040 457-F4
MARINA VILLAGE
700 PHME 93041 552-B2
MARINE WY
1400 OXN 93035 551-J1
MARINER CIR
4000 WLKV 91361 557-C6
MARINER CV
2600 PHME 93041 552-C3
MARINER DR
1300 OXN 93033 522-H7
1300 OXN 93033 552-H1
MARINERO PL
- OXN 93030 522-H4
MARINE VIEW DR
- CMRL 93010 494-B7
- VeCo 93010 494-B7
MARINO WY
2000 VEN 93003 492-E5
MARION ST
1000 THO 91320 525-H7
MARIPOSA CT
- LA 91304 529-E2

STREET
Block City ZIP Pg-Grid

MARIPOSA DR
100 CMRL 93012 525-A3
200 THO 91320 555-E1
300 VEN 93001 491-E1
400 CMRL 93012 524-J3
1100 SPLA 93060 464-B2
2200 OXN 93036 522-E2
MARIPOSA PL
5100 CMRL 93012 525-A3
MARIPOSA ST
2000 OXN 93036 522-E3
MARISA PL
2400 SIMI 93065 498-A1
MARISOL DR
1600 VEN 93001 491-E2
MARISSA LN
- VeCo 93010 494-D6
MARJORI AV
100 THO 91320 556-C2
MARK CT
700 SIMI 93065 497-G4
5300 AGRH 91301 557-H5
MARK DR
400 SIMI 93065 497-G4
MARK LN
1500 SIMI 93063 499-B3
MARKER ST
100 CMRL 93010 524-D4
MARKET ST
100 PHME 93041 552-E6
300 FILM 93015 456-B6
3400 VEN 93003 491-H4
3800 VeCo 93040 457-E4
4200 VEN 93003 492-A5
4700 VeCo 93003 492-A5
MARKHAM AV
2100 THO 91360 526-F4
MARKS RD
3800 Ago 91301 558-F7
MARK TWAIN LN
600 VEN 93003 492-D3
MARLA AV
8300 LA 91304 529-E2
N MARLBORO LN
- VeCo 91307 528-J4
- VeCo 91307 529-A3
MARLBOROUGH CT
7600 LA 91304 529-F4
E MARLIES AV
5800 SIMI 93063 499-A1
N MARLIES AV
2100 SIMI 93063 499-A2
MARLIES ST
28900 AGRH 91301 558-A3
MARLIN PL
22200 CanP 91303 529-J5
22400 CanP 91307 529-H5
MARLIN WY
5000 OXN 93035 551-J1
5000 OXN 93035 552-A1
MARLOWE ST
1800 THO 91360 526-E5
MARMON AV
- THO 91362 557-B3
MARMOTA CT
7400 VEN 93003 492-F4
MARMOTA ST
7000 VEN 93003 492-E4
MARQUAND AV
7700 LA 91304 529-E3
MARQUETTE CIR
14800 MRPK 93021 476-H5
MARQUETTE ST
14700 MRPK 93021 476-J6
N MARQUETTE ST
6400 MRPK 93021 476-J6
MARQUIS CT
7000 VeCo 91377 528-B7
MARQUITA ST
100 OXN 93030 522-J6
N MARQUITA ST
100 OXN 93030 522-H5
MARRISA WY
- CMRL 93012 524-H1
MARSALA WY
- CMRL 93012 524-J1
MARSALIS AV
- VEN 93003 492-C3
MARSDEN CT
25900 LACo 91302 558-J3
MARSEILLE WY
30800 WLKV 91362 557-F5
MARSELLA DR
- OXN 93030 522-J4
MARSHA AV
6200 SIMI 93063 499-B3
MARSHALL AV
2100 SIMI 93063 498-G1
MARSHALL ST
3900 VEN 93003 491-J3
MARSH BROOK RD
2100 VeCo 91361 556-E7
MARSH RONDO
700 CMRL 93010 524-F2
MARTER AV
2200 SIMI 93065 498-A2
N MARTER CT
2200 SIMI 93065 498-A2
MARTHA DR
500 VeCo 91320 525-G7
3000 VEN 93003 491-G2
N MARTHA MORRISON DR
- SIMI 93065 497-D7
S MARTHA MORRISON DR
- SIMI 93065 497-D7
100 SIMI 93065 527-D1
MARTHAS VINEYARD CT
1100 VEN 93001 491-E5
MARTIN CT
6300 VEN 93003 492-D5
MARTIN ST
800 VeCo 93023 451-C3
MARTINDALE AV
200 OJAI 93023 442-A6
MARTINIQUE DR
9500 VeCo 93021 475-H6
MARTINIQUE LN
2100 OXN 93035 552-A2
MARTINIQUE PL
400 THO 91320 525-F7
400 THO 91320 555-F1
MARTIN LUTHER KING JR DR
1400 OXN 93030 522-H4
MARTONA DR
4900 VeCo 91377 557-G1
MARTY CT
- THO 91320 555-G2
MARTZ ST
3600 SIMI 93063 478-E6
N MARVEL AV
2000 SIMI 93065 498-A2
MARVELLA CT
12400 VeCo 93012 496-G6
MARVIEW DR
1600 THO 91362 526-J5
1700 THO 91362 527-A5
MARVIN CT
- SIMI 93065 497-E3
MAR VISTA DR
2300 CMRL 93010 494-G6
2300 VeCo 93010 494-G6
MARY CT
2900 THO 91320 555-H2
MARYGOLD AV
2500 OXN 93033 552-H2
MARYMOUNT CT
400 VeCo 93003 492-B1
400 VEN 93003 492-B1
MARYMOUNT ST
14500 MRPK 93021 476-H5
MARYVILLE AV
400 VEN 93003 492-A1
MASADA WY
- SIMI 93063 479-C7
MASCAGNI ST
4900 VEN 93003 492-A4
MASEFIELD CT
8000 LA 91304 529-E3
MASON CT
3400 SIMI 93063 478-F5
MASON RD
- LACo 90265 586-D7
MASSEY ST
300 THO 91360 526-E5
MASTERSON DR
600 THO 91360 526-G7
MASTHEAD DR
1100 OXN 93035 522-C7
1600 OXN 93035 552-C1
MATILIJA RD
200 VeCo - 366-H6
200 VeCo - 441-A1
200 VeCo 93023 366-H6
200 VeCo 93023 441-A1
MATILIJA RD N
200 VeCo - 441-A1
200 VeCo 93023 441-A1
MATILIJA RD S
- VeCo - 441-A2
700 VeCo 93023 441-A2
MATILIJA ST
100 OJAI 93023 441-H6
W MATILIJA ST
100 OJAI 93023 441-H7
MATTEO ST
4800 VeCo 91377 557-G2
MATTHEWS DR
1500 VEN 93004 492-J3
MAUI LN
1800 OXN 93033 552-J5
1800 OXN 93033 553-A1
MAULHARDT AV
500 OXN 93030 523-B4
MAULHARDT RD
4000 OXN 93033 553-B4
4000 VeCo 93033 553-B4
MAUREEN LN
4700 MRPK 93021 496-C1
MAURICE DR
3900 THO 91320 555-E3
MAURY AV
5900 WdHl 91367 529-C7
E MAVERICK LN
- VeCo 91307 528-G3
MAX CT
23600 SIMI 93065 498-A6
MAXANA DR
400 VeCo 93023 451-D1
MAXINE AV
- VeCo 93022 451-B7
800 OXN 93033 552-F5
800 PHME 93041 552-F5
MAXINE DR
- VeCo 93010 494-E7
MAY CT
2100 SIMI 93063 499-C2
MAYA CIR
- MRPK 93021 496-G3
MAYA LINDA
3300 CMRL 93012 524-G2
MAYALL ST
21900 Chat 91311 499-J4
MAYANS LN
200 VEN 93001 471-C5
MAYA PRADERA LN
- THO 93021 497-A6
MAYBROOK AV
2200 CMRL 93010 494-E7
MAYBROOK WY
1700 SIMI 93065 497-F2
MAYENNE CT
30800 WLKV 91362 557-F5
E MAYFAIR ST
1300 SIMI 93065 497-J1
MAYFIELD CT
200 THO 91320 555-E2
MAYFIELD ST
3500 THO 91320 555-E2
MAYFLOWER ST
- THO 91360 526-F6
E MAYLAND PL
1900 SIMI 93065 498-A5
MAYNARD AV
- THO 91320 555-F2
6800 CanP 91307 529-H4
7600 LA 91304 529-H2
MAYSVILLE CIR
1700 THO 91360 526-C5
MAYWIND LN
23600 SIMI 93065 497-A1
MAYWOOD CT
300 THO 91362 557-G2
MAYWOOD WY
2500 OXN 93033 552-G2
MCAFEE CT
- THO 91360 526-F2
MCANDREW RD
100 VeCo 93023 442-F6
MCBEAN RD
5800 VeCo 93066 495-B2
MCBETH CT
4500 MRPK 93021 496-F2
MCCAMPBELL ST
200 FILM 93015 455-J6
MCCLOUD AV
400 THO 91360 526-E7
MCCLOUD RD
8900 VEN 93004 492-H4
MCCOY PL
- SIMI 93065 497-F3
MCCREA RD
2600 THO 91362 527-A1
3500 THO 91362 526-J1
MCCULLOCH ST
2600 CMRL 93010 524-F2
MCDONALD DR
11900 VeCo 93023 451-A1
MC DONALD ST
2200 SIMI 93065 498-A2
MCEDDON PL
100 VEN 93001 491-D1
MCFADDEN AV
300 MRPK 93021 496-E1
W MCFARLANE DR
- VEN 93001 471-B6
E MCFARLANE ST
- VEN 93001 471-C6
MCGILL AV
300 VEN 93003 491-J2
MCGRATH ST
4400 VEN 93003 492-A5
MCGREGER RD
- VeCo 93015 466-J1
- VeCo 93021 466-J1
MCHUGH CT
900 VEN 93003 492-C4
MCKEE ST
- VeCo 93001 471-C2
200 OJAI 93023 441-H6
MCKEEHAN DR
700 PHME 93041 552-F4
MCKENZIE ST
- FILM 93015 456-B6
MCKEVETT HTS
400 SPLA 93060 464-B5
MCKEVETT RD
800 SPLA 93060 464-B5
MCKINLEY AV
100 OXN 93030 522-H6
N MCKINLEY AV
100 OXN 93030 522-H5
MCKINLEY DR
2300 VEN 93003 491-G2
MCKNIGHT RD
1200 VeCo 91320 556-B2
1200 THO 91320 556-B2
S MCKNIGHT RD
100 VeCo 91320 556-B2
MCLAREN AV
6200 WdHl 91367 529-H7
6800 CanP 91307 529-H5
7500 LA 91304 529-H3
MCLEOD RONDO
700 CMRL 93010 524-F2
MCLOUGHLIN AV
1300 OXN 93035 552-D1
MCMILLAN AV
100 OXN 93033 552-G3
MCNAB CT
200 FILM 93015 455-H6
MCNELL RD
100 VeCo 93023 442-E5
MCPHERSON WY
10900 VeCo 93001 450-H5
MCWANE BLVD
400 OXN 93033 552-H7
W MCWANE BLVD
500 OXN 93033 552-G7
MEAD AV
1000 SIMI 93065 497-J4
1200 VEN 93004 492-J2
MEADOW CT
11600 MRPK 93021 496-B2
MEADOW ST
4600 MRPK 93021 496-B2
MEADOW TR
2500 OXN 93036 522-E1
MEADOWBLUFF CT
5300 CMRL 93012 525-A1
MEADOW BROOK CT
1900 THO 91362 526-J3
1900 THO 91362 527-A3
MEADOWBROOK RD
1100 OJAI 93023 441-J5
MEADOWCREST ST
700 THO 91320 555-F4
MEADOW GATE ST
3900 THO 91362 557-C3
MEADOWGLADE DR
6000 VeCo 93021 475-G7
MEADOWGLEN CT
1500 THO 91320 556-A1
MEADOW GROVE LN
200 THO 91362 557-E3
MEADOW HAVEN DR
6300 AGRH 91301 558-A3
MEADOWLAND CT
2300 THO 91361 557-B5
MEADOWLARK DR
- FILM 93015 455-J6
MEADOW LARK LN
1200 OXN 93036 522-E2
MEADOWLARK LN
100 VeCo 91377 557-J3
MEADOWLARK ST
6800 VEN 93003 492-E4
MEADOW MIST CT
200 SIMI 93065 498-A6
MEADOWMIST WY
29500 AGRH 91301 557-J4
MEADOW OAK DR
3200 WLKV 91361 557-C7
MEADOWRIDGE CT
5200 CMRL 93012 524-J1
5200 CMRL 93012 525-A1
MEADOWRUN ST
500 THO 91360 526-G1
MEADOWSIDE DR
2500 THO 91362 527-A3
MEADOWSTONE DR
2900 SIMI 93063 478-C7
MEADOW VIEW CT
1900 THO 91362 526-J5
MEADOWVIEW CT
6700 VEN 93003 472-D6
MEADOW VIEW DR
5100 CMRL 93012 524-J2
5200 CMRL 93012 525-A2
MEADOW VISTA WY
5400 AGRH 91301 557-J5
MEADOWWOOD AV
2900 THO 91360 526-F3
MEANDER DR
1400 SIMI 93065 497-J7
MEDEA LN
- AGRH 91301 558-A5
MEDEABROOK PL
5600 AGRH 91301 557-J5
MEDEA CREEK LN
- VeCo 91377 558-A1
MEDEA VALLEY DR
5500 AGRH 91301 558-A5
MEDFIELD ST
28500 AGRH 91301 558-B5
MEDFORD PL
800 VEN 93004 492-G3
MEDFORD ST
8300 VEN 93004 492-F3
MEDICAL CENTER DR
7100 CanP 91307 529-G5
N MEDICINE BOW CT
200 THO 91362 557-B3
S MEDICINE BOW CT
100 THO 91362 557-B3
N MEDINA AV
2000 SIMI 93063 498-C2
MEEHAM WY
13800 MRPK 93021 496-F3
MEG CT
3300 SIMI 93063 478-D7
MEINERS RD
1800 VeCo 93023 441-E6
MELBA AV
6200 WdHl 91367 529-G7
6600 CanP 91307 529-F4
7500 LA 91304 529-F2
MELBOURNE CT
3600 THO 91320 555-F3
MELFORD CT
2200 VeCo 91361 556-E7
MELIA ST
500 VeCo 93010 524-C1
6200 SIMI 93063 499-B3
MELITO DR
- OXN 93030 522-H4
MELLISA CT
3900 SIMI 93063 478-E6
MELLOW LN
800 SIMI 93065 497-H6
MELODY LN
3000 SIMI 93063 478-E7
MELRAY ST
6400 MRPK 93021 477-A6
MELROSE DR
200 VeCo 93035 552-B4
MELVILLE LN
500 VEN 93003 492-D1
MELVIN CT
3400 VeCo 91320 525-F7
E MELVINA PL
800 SIMI 93065 498-A5
MEMORIAL PKWY
- THO 91360 526-E2
MEMPHIS CT
600 VEN 93004 492-H1
MENCKEN AV
7900 LA 91304 529-E3
MENDOCINO CT
10100 VEN 93004 472-H7
MENDOCINO LN
1500 THO 91360 526-A7
MENDOCINO PL
3000 OXN 93033 553-B3
MENLO ST
6300 SIMI 93063 499-C2
MENLO PARK AV
- VEN 93004 492-G2
MENOTTI LN
4700 VEN 93003 492-B7
MENTA LN
1500 CMRL 93010 524-A1
MERALDA AV
2400 SIMI 93063 499-A1
MERCANTILE ST
700 OXN 93030 522-H7
MERCED DR
800 CMRL 93010 494-F7
MERCED PL
3000 OXN 93033 553-B3
MERCED ST
10500 VEN 93004 472-H7
MERCER AV
600 OJAI 93023 442-A6
600 VEN 93004 492-J1
MERCURY PL
3800 SIMI 93063 498-E2
MEREDITH AV
- SIMI 93063 477-J7
300 VEN 93003 491-J1
MEREDITH CT
23900 LA 91304 529-E3
MERIDIAN AV
4200 OXN 93035 552-A2
MERIDIAN HILLS DR
- MRPK 93021 476-E6
MERION WY
- OXN 93036 522-C3
MERLIN ST
- VEN 93003 492-D5
E MERRILL CT
3800 SIMI 93063 498-E2
MERRITT AV
300 CMRL 93010 524-F3
MESA AV
- THO 91320 556-A2
MESA CIR
7200 VEN 93003 472-D7
MESA DR
- VeCo 93010 494-E6
100 VeCo 93023 441-D7
200 CMRL 93010 494-E6
800 FILM 93015 456-A5
7800 VeCo 93063 499-F4
MESA RD
100 WHil 91304 499-D6
MESA MINT CT
- SIMI 93063 498-J3
MESA RIDGE AV
1600 THO 91362 527-G6
MESA SCHOOL RD
- VeCo 93066 493-H4
MESA VERDE AV
1400 VEN 93003 492-C5
MESA VERDE DR
12800 MRPK 93021 496-E2
MESCALLERO PL
6100 SIMI 93063 479-B6
MESQUITE ST
500 CMRL 93012 524-J3
MESSINA PL
600 VeCo 91377 557-G1
META ST
400 OXN 93030 522-G6
1000 VEN 93001 491-D2
METZ CT
1900 SIMI 93065 498-A4
MEYER RD
1100 VeCo 93023 441-C5
MIAMI LN
800 VEN 93004 492-J2
MICAELA DR
5400 AGRH 91301 557-H5
MICHAEL DR
2200 THO 91320 555-H1
2900 VeCo 91320 555-G1
MICHALE ST
22100 LA 91304 529-H1
MICHELLE CT
3300 SIMI 93063 478-D6
MICHELLE DR
28800 AGRH 91301 558-B4
MICOMA CT
5500 SIMI 93063 479-A7
MIDBURY HILL RD
- VeCo 91320 556-B2
MIDDLE CREST DR
5600 AGRH 91301 557-H4
MIDDLE FORK CIR
4700 THO 91362 557-D1
MIDDLEGATE RD
3900 WLKV 91361 557-D6
MIDDLE RANCH RD
- VeCo 93021 476-G3
MIDDLE RANGE FIRE RD
23600 VeCo - 467-D7
23600 VeCo - 477-E1
23600 VeCo - 478-A1
23600 VeCo 93021 466-J7
23600 VeCo 93021 467-A7
23600 VeCo 93021 476-G1
23600 VeCo 93021 477-E1
23600 VeCo 93063 478-D2
23600 VeCo 93065 478-D2
MIDDLESBURY RIDGE CIR
7000 CanP 91307 529-E5
MIDNIGHT MOON LN
23600 SIMI 93065 497-A1
MIDWAY DR
4500 PHME 93041 552-E5
MIGUEL LN
400 OXN 93030 522-H4
MIKA WY
- OXN 93030 522-H4
MILAGRO PL
- OXN 93030 523-A4
MILAN DR
1400 SIMI 93065 497-G3
MILANO PL
4000 MRPK 93021 496-C4
MILBURN ST
1900 CMRL 93010 524-E3
MILDRED ST
5200 SIMI 93063 498-J3
MILESTONE AV
- SIMI 93065 477-J7
MILL CT
23600 SIMI 93065 497-F7
MILL DR
- VeCo 93001 471-C3
MILL PL
1000 SPLA 93060 464-B4
N MILL ST
100 SPLA 93060 464-B4
S MILL ST
100 SPLA 93060 464-B6
MILLARD ST
- MRPK 93021 496-E1
MILLBRAE CT
200 VEN 93004 492-G2
MILL CANYON RD
23600 VeCo 93001 460-G7
23600 VeCo 93001 470-H1
23600 VeCo 93001 471-A1
MILL CREEK CT
3500 THO 91360 526-H2
MILLCROFT CT
700 SIMI 93065 498-D5
MILLER CT
800 VEN 93003 492-C3
MILLER PKWY
100 MRPK 93021 496-F2
MILLER PL
- THO 91362 527-C3
100 SPLA 93060 464-C5
E MILLERTON RD
13100 MRPK 93021 496-E2
N MILLERTON RD
4400 MRPK 93021 496-E2
MILLIGAN DR
1000 CMRL 93010 524-G2
MILLIGAN BARRANCA RD
4000 VeCo 93066 494-C2
4600 VeCo 93066 474-C7
MILLPARK LN
23600 SIMI 93065 497-A2
MILLS RD
- PHME 93043 552-C3
N MILLS RD
- VEN 93003 491-H2
S MILLS RD
- VEN 93003 491-H3
MILLTRACE WY
- SIMI 93065 497-F3
MILL VALLEY RD
4300 MRPK 93021 496-F2
MILLVILLE CT
1900 THO 91360 526-D5
MILLWOOD CIR
9900 VEN 93004 492-J3
MILLWOOD ST
9800 VEN 93004 492-J3
MILNE CT
15800 MRPK 93021 477-A5
MILPAS ST
4200 CMRL 93012 524-H4
MILTON AV
700 VEN 93003 491-H4
MILTON ST
- VeCo 93022 451-B7
MIMOSA CT
5600 VeCo 91377 557-J2
MINDENVALE CT
400 SIMI 93065 527-D1
MINE RD
- VeCo - 478-G2
MINERAL WELLS DR
3000 SIMI 93063 478-G7
MINERS CANDLE CT
- SIMI 93063 498-J2
MINGUS DR
30800 WLKV 91362 557-F3
MINNA ST
3300 VeCo 93036 492-J7
MINNECOTA DR
4100 THO 91360 496-J7
MINOR ST
300 MRPK 93021 496-F1
MINSTREL AV
6900 CanP 91307 529-G4
7600 LA 91304 529-G3
MINT LN
400 VEN 93001 491-E1
MINT WY
2400 OXN 93036 522-F2
MINUET PL
400 VeCo 93022 451-B7
MINUTEMAN WY
30900 AGRH 91301 557-F6
30900 WLKV 91361 557-F6
MIPOLOMOL RD
8100 VeCo 90265 585-F5
MIRABELLA ST
23600 MRPK 93021 496-C4
MIRADA LN
- OXN 93033 553-C4
MIRA FLORES CT
300 CMRL 93012 525-A2
MIRAGE CT
700 THO 91320 555-G6
MIRA LOMA CIR
500 OXN 93030 522-E6
500 OXN 93035 522-E6
MIRAMAR CT
2900 OXN 93035 522-C7
MIRAMAR DR
1700 VEN 93001 491-E1
MIRAMAR PL
2400 OXN 93035 522-D7
MIRAMAR ST
- CMRL 93010 524-D4
MIRAMAR WK
2000 OXN 93035 552-D1
2100 OXN 93035 522-D7
MIRAMAR WY
3300 OXN 93035 522-B7
MIRAMONTE DR
200 OXN 93036 522-J2
MIRA MONTES
7800 VeCo 93063 499-F3
MIRA SOL DR
4700 MRPK 93021 496-B2
MIRASOL LN
- OXN 93036 522-H3
MIRROR LAKE AV
1900 VeCo 93023 451-C3
MISSILE WY
- PHME 93043 552-C5
W MISSION AV
- VEN 93001 491-B1
MISSION CIR
11300 Chat 91311 499-H1
MISSION DR
- CMRL 93010 494-D7
- CMRL 93010 524-D1
100 VeCo 93010 494-D6
MISSION PZ
- VEN 93001 491-B2
MISSION TER
900 VeCo 93010 494-D6
MISSION HILLS DR
- OXN 93036 522-C3
MISSION OAKS BLVD
3000 CMRL 93012 524-F3
5100 CMRL 93012 525-A2
6200 CMRL 93012 495-B7
MISSION ROCK RD
100 VeCo 93060 473-F3
MISSION VERDE DR
5400 CMRL 93012 525-A1
MISTLETOE RD
8000 VeCo 93060 453-J5
MISTRAL PL
2000 OXN 93035 522-D6
MISTY CT
5900 AGRH 91301 558-B4
MISTY CANYON AV
600 THO 91362 557-G1
MISTY CREEK RD
1600 THO 91362 527-G6
MISTY FALLS CT
300 SIMI 93065 497-E6
MISTY GROVE ST
12400 MRPK 93021 496-D4
MISTY HOLLOW CT
4100 MRPK 93021 496-D3
MISTY LAKE CT
500 SIMI 93065 497-E6
MISTYMEADOW ST
4300 MRPK 93021 496-D3
MISTY TRAILS PL
400 SIMI 93065 497-E6
MITCHELL RD
800 THO 91320 525-J7
MOBERLY CT
2300 THO 91360 526-B4
MOBIL AV
- CMRL 93010 524-E2
MOBIL LN
100 VeCo 93001 461-A3
MOBILE ST
22300 CanP 91303 529-J7
22600 CanP 91307 529-E7
MOBIL PIER RD
23600 VeCo 93001 459-E6
MOBY DICK LN
700 OXN 93030 522-E7
MOCKINGBIRD CT
- VeCo 91377 557-J2
MOCKINGBIRD LN
400 FILM 93015 455-H6
2100 OXN 93033 553-A4
MOCKINGBIRD ST
6200 VEN 93003 492-D4
MODELLO CANYON RD
23600 VeCo 93040 367-D7
23600 VeCo 93040 457-G1
MODENA PL
5500 AGRH 91301 557-G5
MODESTO AV
200 VEN 93004 492-E1
1000 CMRL 93010 524-D2
MODOC CT
- VEN 93004 472-J7
MODOC DR
3300 OXN 93033 553-B3
MODOC ST
10500 VEN 93004 472-J7
MOFFATT CIR
700 SIMI 93065 497-J5
MOHAVE DR
5100 SIMI 93063 478-J7
MOHAWK AV
- THO 91362 557-A2
2800 VEN 93001 471-C5
MOHICAN LN
2300 VEN 93001 471-C6
MOHICAN ST
6100 SIMI 93063 479-B6
MOJAVE DR
1600 VEN 93004 492-H4
E MOLINE ST
4100 SIMI 93063 478-F6
MOLLISON DR
300 SIMI 93065 497-F6
MOLLY CT
2900 VeCo 91320 555-G1
MONACO CT
30800 WLKV 91362 557-G6
MONACO DR
2300 OXN 93035 552-B2
MONARCH CT
2400 SIMI 93063 498-H1
MONDEGO PL
700 THO 91360 526-C3
MONDOVI CT
3900 MRPK 93021 496-C4
MONET CT
1500 OXN 93033 552-J4
MONET DR
9900 VeCo 93021 475-J6
MONET PL
1000 OXN 93033 552-J4
MONICA CIR
100 THO 91320 555-G2
MONITA DR
1700 VEN 93001 491-E1
MONMOUTH DR
2100 VEN 93001 491-E4
MONMOUTH WY
600 VEN 93001 491-E4
MONO CT
4900 VEN 93003 492-A1
MONO ST
1900 OXN 93036 522-J3
MONROE AV
15300 MRPK 93021 476-J5
MONROE ST
3900 VEN 93003 491-J3
MONTAGNE WY
3100 THO 91362 526-J2
MONTAIR DR
23600 MRPK 93021 496-A1
MONTALVO DR
6000 VeCo 93003 492-D6
6000 VEN 93003 492-D6
MONTANA CIR
300 VeCo 93023 441-F6
MONTANA DR
1900 VEN 93003 492-C5
MONTANA RD
100 OJAI 93023 441-E7
100 VeCo 93023 441-E7
MONTAUK LN
1000 VEN 93001 491-E4
MONT BLANC DR
700 VEN 93001 491-D1
MONT CALABASAS DR
- Ago 91301 558-G3
- LACo 91302 558-G3
MONTCLAIR DR
700 SPLA 93060 464-A4
6200 VEN 93003 472-C7
MONTE CT
500 VeCo 93022 451-A6
MONTEBELLO AV
200 VEN 93004 492-F2
MONTEBELLO ST
1100 SPLA 93060 464-C6
MONTE CARLO DR
3000 THO 91362 527-A2
3100 THO 91362 526-J2
MONTE CARLO ST
600 OXN 93035 522-B6
MONTECITO AV
23600 THO 91362 527-B5
MONTELEONE AV
800 VeCo 91377 557-H1
MONTENEGRO CIR
- THO 91320 555-F1
MONTEREY CT
3900 THO 91320 555-E1
MONTEREY DR
- VeCo 93022 451-D4
MONTEREY PL
23600 SPLA 93060 464-B4
MONTEREY ST
3000 OXN 93033 552-F3
MONTE SERENO DR
900 THO 91360 526-D6
MONTESSA DR
5800 CMRL 93012 525-B1
MONTE VIA
- VeCo 93022 451-A6
MONTEVINA CIR
- OXN 93030 523-B4
MONTE VISTA
- THO 91320 525-E6
MONTE VISTA AV
500 VEN 93003 472-D7
MONTE VISTA CT
6900 VEN 93003 472-D7
MONTE VISTA DR
800 SPLA 93060 464-B4
1700 CMRL 93010 524-D3
MONTE VISTA PL
400 SPLA 93060 464-A4
MONTGOMERY AV
100 VeCo 93036 492-J5
500 VEN 93004 492-G2
1300 VeCo 93004 492-G4
MONTGOMERY CT
900 THO 91360 526-G5
8300 VEN 93004 492-G3
MONTGOMERY PL
700 VEN 93004 492-G3
MONTGOMERY RD
1400 THO 91360 526-G5
9200 Chat 91311 499-F7
MONTGOMERY ST
100 OJAI 93023 441-J5
S MONTGOMERY ST
100 OJAI 93023 441-H7
MONTGOMERY FIRE RD
23600 SIMI 93065 498-A7
23600 SIMI 93065 528-B1
MONTICELLO AV
3300 SIMI 93063 478-F6
MONTILLA CIR
800 THO 91360 526-C3
MONTROSE DR
2000 THO 91362 527-A6
MONTROSE ST
1700 OXN 93033 552-H1
MONTSALAS CT
- CMRL 93012 524-H1
MONTVIEW CT
2700 WLKV 91361 557-A7
MONUMENT ST
- SIMI 93063 498-H1
MOODY CT
- THO 91360 556-G1
MOON DR
5700 VEN 93003 492-C5
5900 VeCo 93003 492-C5
MOONCREST CT
3300 THO 91320 555-G2
MOONDANCE ST
400 THO 91360 526-D2
MOONFLOWER CIR
2800 THO 91360 526-H3
MOONLIGHT CT
3500 THO 91362 527-D3
MOONLIGHT PARK AV
- OXN 93036 492-G7
MOONRIDGE AV
300 THO 91320 555-J2
400 VeCo 91320 555-J2
MOONSEED LN
23600 SIMI 93065 497-A2
MOONSHADOW CIR
1700 CMRL 93012 495-B7
1700 CMRL 93012 525-A1
MOONSHADOW ST
5300 SIMI 93063 478-J6
5500 SIMI 93063 479-A6
MOONSONG CT
- MRPK 93021 496-E1
MOONSTONE AV
- SIMI 93065 478-A7
MOONSTONE WY
5000 OXN 93035 521-J7
MOORCROFT AV
6500 CanP 91303 529-J4
7600 LA 91304 529-J1
8800 LA 91304 499-J7
MOORCROFT PL
8700 LA 91304 529-J1
MOORE ST
1700 SIMI 93065 497-J4
1700 SIMI 93065 498-A4
MOORE CANYON RD
- CanP 91307 529-C7
23600 VeCo 91302 529-C7
23600 VeCo 91307 529-C7
MOORING WK
1100 OXN 93030 522-F7
MOORPARK AV
100 MRPK 93021 496-E2
100 VeCo 93035 552-B5
100 VeCo 93043 552-B5
MOORPARK AV Rt#-23
- MRPK 93021 476-E7
500 MRPK 93021 496-E1
N MOORPARK AV Rt#-23
- MRPK 93021 496-E1
MOORPARK RD
- VeCo 93012 496-G4
- VeCo 93021 496-G4
N MOORPARK RD
200 THO 91360 556-F1
500 THO 91360 526-F1
3100 THO 91360 496-G6
3100 THO 93012 496-G6
3100 VeCo 93012 496-G6
S MOORPARK RD
- THO 91360 556-E2
- THO 91361 556-E2
MORADO PL
- OXN 93030 522-H4
MORAGA CT
2400 SIMI 93065 498-A1
MORAINE WY
2500 OXN 93030 522-D4
MORANDA PKWY
100 PHME 93041 552-F6
MORELAND RD
- SIMI 93065 497-E2
MORELIA CT
600 VeCo 91360 526-C6
MORENA LN
4100 OXN 93033 553-C4
MORENO DR
800 VeCo 93023 451-B1
1400 SIMI 93063 498-D3
2800 CMRL 93010 494-E7
E MORGAN RD
- VeCo 91307 528-H4
MORGAN ST
1700 VeCo 93023 451-C3
MORGAN CANYON RD
- VeCo 93066 464-D7
MORGAN HILL ST
200 SIMI 93065 527-E1
MORLEY ST
1600 SIMI 93065 498-A3
MORNING ARBOR WY
1600 SIMI 93065 497-F2
MORNING GLORY ST
2000 SIMI 93065 498-A2
MORNING RIDGE AV
- THO 91362 527-D2

STREET Block City ZIP Pg-Grid

MORNINGSIDE DR
2800 THO 91362 526-J3
2800 THO 91362 527-A2
MORNINGSTAR AV
23600 THO 91360 526-E2
MORNING VIEW CT
1900 THO 91362 526-J1
MORNINGWOOD WY
23600 SIMI 93065 497-A1
MOROCCO LN
9300 WHil 91304 499-E7
MORONGO DR
1600 CMRL 93012 525-D1
1700 CMRL 93012 495-D7
MORRIS DR
500 FILM 93015 456-A4
MORRIS ST
1300 OXN 93030 522-J5
MORRISON LN
400 SPLA 93060 463-H6
MORRISON RANCH RD
\- Ago 91301 558-F4
26400 CALB 91302 558-F4
26400 LACo 91302 558-F4
MORRO WY
700 OXN 93033 552-H3
MORRO BAY LN
5600 VEN 93003 492-C4
MORROW CIR
1300 THO 91362 527-A6
MORSE AV
800 VEN 93003 491-J5
MORVALE DR
2900 VeCo 91361 586-D2
MOSER RD
1300 VeCo 91320 555-J3
2100 THO 91320 555-J3
MOSES LN
500 VEN 93003 492-D1
MOSS CT
2100 THO 91362 526-J4
MOSS LANDING BLVD
\- OXN 93036 492-H7
MOTT CT
11000 VeCo 93012 526-B1
MOTT PL
23600 VeCo 93060 453-G2
MOULTRIE PL
200 SPLA 93060 464-A7
200 SPLA 93060 463-J7
MOUND AV
3500 VEN 93003 491-H2
MOUNTAIN CREEK DR
3900 THO 91320 555-E3
MOUNTAIN CREST CIR
\- THO 91362 557-A1
MOUNTAIN LION RD
11900 VeCo 93023 452-H1
MOUNTAIN LOOKOUT RD
\- VeCo 93066 474-C1
S MOUNTAIN LOOKOUT RD
23600 VeCo 93066 474-H2
23600 VeCo 93066 475-A2
MOUNTAIN MEADOW DR
4200 MRPK 93021 496-C3
MOUNTAIN OAK PL
1000 THO 91320 556-C1
MOUNTAIN PARK CT
4100 MRPK 93021 496-B2
MOUNTAIN SHADOW CT
2900 THO 91360 526-B2
MOUNTAIN TRAIL AV
3300 THO 91320 555-G4
MOUNTAIN TRAIL ST
11200 MRPK 93021 496-B3
MOUNTAIN VIEW AV
500 OXN 93030 522-H6
800 OJAI 93023 441-J5
900 OJAI 93023 442-A5
MOUNTAIN VIEW DR
\- LACo 91302 558-J3
5500 CMRL 93012 525-A3
MOUNTAIN VIEW RD
1200 VeCo 91320 556-B3
MOUNTAIN VIEW ST
\- VeCo 93022 451-B7
100 FILM 93015 456-B5
MOUNTAIN VISTA LN
\- SIMI 93065 498-A6
MOUNTCLEF BLVD
2800 THO 91360 526-F3
MOUNT PINOS RD
23600 VeCo - 367-A1
MOUNT SINAI DR
23600 SIMI 93063 479-B7
23600 SIMI 93063 499-C1
MOUNT WHITNEY CT
100 VEN 93003 492-C2
MOWER CT
900 THO 91362 526-J7
MOZART LN
5000 VEN 93003 492-B4
MUD CREEK RD
\- VeCo 93060 453-J5
\- VeCo 93060 454-A5
MUGU RD
1300 VeCo 93041 583-G2
1300 VeCo 93042 583-F4

MUIR ST
1200 VeCo 93015 455-G4
5800 SIMI 93063 499-A2
N MUIRFIELD AV
800 SIMI 93065 498-A5
MUIRFIELD DR
1600 OXN 93036 522-E2
E MUIRWOOD CT
2800 SIMI 93063 478-H7
N MUIRWOOD CT
2700 SIMI 93063 478-H7
MULBERRY CIR
3000 THO 91360 526-H2
MULBERRY DR
\- VeCo 93001 471-C3
MULBERRY LN
\- VeCo 93023 441-E6
MULBERRY PL
23600 SIMI 93063 499-B3
MULBERRY RIDGE DR
5600 CMRL 93012 525-B2
MULCAHEY DR
\- VeCo 93033 553-F7
MULHOLLAND HWY
32400 LACo 90265 586-J5
35500 LACo 90265 625-J3
MULHOLLAND HWY Rt#-23
33000 LACo 90265 586-G6
MUNDA DR
1100 PHME 93041 552-E4
MUNGER DR
500 SPLA 93060 463-H6
MUNNINGS WY
2700 VeCo 91361 586-C1
MUNSON ST
1800 CMRL 93010 524-F1
1800 CMRL 93010 494-F7
MUPU AV
100 SPLA 93060 464-A5
MUPU RD
\- VeCo 93060 453-J4
MURDOCH LN
700 VEN 93003 492-D3
MUREAU RD
25400 CALB 91302 558-J5
25400 LACo 91302 558-J5
MURPHY LN
1800 OXN 93033 553-B4
MURRAY AV
\- CMRL 93010 524-D3
MURRE WY
3800 OXN 93035 552-B4
MURRIETA ST
5400 VEN 93003 492-B3
MUSTANG CT
1700 VeCo 93023 451-C3
MUSTANG DR
5700 SIMI 93063 479-A6
N MUSTANG LN
\- VeCo 91307 528-H4
MUTAU CIR
200 FILM 93015 455-J6
MUTAU FLAT RD
\- VeCo - 366-L2
MYRNA DR
500 PHME 93041 552-F6
MYRNA-JOYCE DR
800 OXN 93033 552-F5
800 PHME 93033 552-F5
800 PHME 93041 552-F5
MYRTLE CT
\- SIMI 93063 499-B2
5100 VeCo 91377 557-H1
MYRTLE ST
\- OXN 93036 522-H1
MYSTIC LN
7300 CanP 91307 529-E5

N

N ST
400 OXN 93030 522-E5
1100 OXN 93033 522-E7
1100 OXN 93033 552-E1
NACIMIENTO AV
\- VEN 93004 492-J3
NADADOR PL
\- OXN 93030 522-J4
NADINE CT
\- THO 91320 555-G2
NADIR ST
23600 LA 91304 529-E2
NAHUA LN
2300 VEN 93001 471-D6
NANCHARO RD
2100 VeCo 93012 496-A7
2100 VeCo 93012 526-A1
NANCY CIR
1800 THO 91362 526-J6
NANCY ST
\- VeCo 93010 494-D7
NANDINA CIR
2400 OXN 93036 522-G2
NANDINA CT
2300 OXN 93036 522-F2
NANDINA PL
300 OXN 93036 522-F2

NANNYBERRY CT
\- MRPK 93021 496-F2
NANTUCKET PKWY
3600 OXN 93035 522-B6
NAPA CT
23600 SIMI 93065 497-G7
NAPA ST
3000 OXN 93033 552-E3
22100 LA 91304 529-H1
NAPLES CT
1300 SIMI 93065 497-F3
NAPLES DR
2900 OXN 93035 522-C6
NAPOLEON AV
1800 OXN 93033 552-J2
1800 OXN 93033 553-A2
5500 VeCo 91377 527-H6
NAPOLI DR
2000 OXN 93035 552-B2
NAPOLI PL
4000 MRPK 93021 496-C4
NARANJA
700 VeCo 93015 455-D5
NARANJA LN
\- OXN 93036 522-J3
NARDO ST
10900 VeCo 93004 493-A2
NARROWS CT
1700 OXN 93035 552-C1
NASH LN
1800 OXN 93033 553-B4
NASHVILLE PL
1900 OXN 93033 553-A5
NASSAU DR
2100 OXN 93036 522-E2
NATALIE LN
8300 LA 91304 529-F2
NATALIE PL
1600 OXN 93030 522-D4
NATALIE WY
\- VeCo 93010 494-E7
NATASHA CT
5300 AGRH 91301 557-H5
NATHAN LN
1300 VEN 93001 491-F5
NAUMAN RD
5600 VeCo 93033 553-E5
NAUTICAL WY
1200 OXN 93030 522-E7
NAUTILUS ST
4900 OXN 93035 521-J7
4900 OXN 93035 551-J1
NAVAJO AV
2700 THO 91362 557-A2
NAVAL AIR RD
7800 VeCo 93041 583-G1
15100 VeCo 93041 553-F6
15100 VeCo 93042 553-F6
18500 VeCo 93033 553-F6
NAVARRO ST
100 OXN 93030 522-J6
NAVIGATOR DR
1100 VEN 93001 491-G6
NAVIGATOR WY
\- OXN 93035 522-E7
NAVITO WY
\- OXN 93030 522-H4
NAVY LN
1000 OXN 93035 522-C7
NEAL CT
1100 SIMI 93065 497-H4
NEAP CT
3100 OXN 93035 522-C7
NEAP PL
3000 OXN 93035 522-C7
NEATH ST
8400 VEN 93004 492-G4
NEBULA ST
2800 OXN 93030 522-D4
NECTARINE ST
200 OXN 93033 552-G2
NEDDY AV
6100 WdHl 91367 529-D7
6400 CanP 91307 529-D7
NEEDLES ST
22100 Chat 91311 499-J5
NEISH ST
100 VeCo 93010 494-D7
E NELDA ST
5900 SIMI 93063 499-B2
NELLIE CT
200 THO 91320 555-H1
NELLORA ST
\- CMRL 93010 524-F3
NELSON PL
1000 OXN 93033 552-J4
NELSON RD
\- MRPK 93021 476-C5
NEMESIS CT
\- PHME 93043 552-C5
NEPTUNE PL
2500 PHME 93041 552-E2
NEPTUNE SQ
5100 OXN 93035 521-J6
5100 OXN 93035 551-J1
NET CT
2900 OXN 93035 522-C7
NET PL
3100 OXN 93035 522-C7

NETTLEBROOK ST
1900 THO 91361 557-A4
NEVA CIR
3400 THO 91320 555-G1
NEVADA AV
\- VEN 93004 472-H6
3000 OXN 93033 553-A3
6100 WdHl 91367 529-J7
6500 CanP 91303 529-J6
7700 LA 91304 529-J1
8900 LA 91304 499-J7
9600 Chat 91311 499-J3
NEVELSON LN
5900 SIMI 93063 499-B1
NEVIN AV
1400 VEN 93004 492-G4
NEW ST
1000 SPLA 93060 464-C5
NEWARK WY
10000 VEN 93004 492-J2
NEW BEDFORD CT
1100 VEN 93001 491-F5
NEWBOLT LN
500 VEN 93003 492-D1
NEWBURY LN
\- VeCo 91320 556-B2
NEWBURY RD
800 THO 91320 556-A1
1900 THO 91320 555-J1
NEWCASTLE DR
\- OXN 93036 522-C3
NEWCASTLE ST
400 THO 91361 556-F2
NEWCOMB DR
300 VEN 93003 492-A3
NEWGATE RD
6900 CanP 91307 529-E5
NEW HAVEN PL
2200 OXN 93035 522-D7
NEW HAVEN ST
\- VEN 93004 492-J1
NEWHAVEN ST
4900 VeCo 91377 557-G1
NEWMAN ST
\- VEN 93003 492-C3
1200 SIMI 93065 497-H4
NEWMAN RANCH RD
23600 VeCo 93001 450-H7
23600 VeCo 93001 460-J1
NEWPORT AV
200 VEN 93004 492-G2
NEWPORT CIR
1300 THO 91360 526-F6
7000 CanP 91307 529-E5
NEWPORT WEIGH
23600 OXN 93035 552-B1
NEWQUIST CT
2200 CMRL 93010 494-D7
NEWTOWN ST
8400 VEN 93004 492-G4
NEY CT
1000 SIMI 93065 497-J4
NICE CT
4000 OXN 93035 552-B2
NICHOLAS ST
2500 SIMI 93065 478-B7
NICOLE DR
500 THO 91320 525-H7
NICOLLE ST
5700 VEN 93003 492-C6
NIDIA WY
\- OXN 93030 522-J4
NIELSEN ST
\- VEN 93003 492-A3
NIGHTFALL PL
3200 SIMI 93063 479-B6
NIGHTINGALE PL
800 OXN 93036 522-F2
NIGHTINGALE ST
6300 VEN 93003 492-D6
11800 MRPK 93021 496-C2
NIGHT JASMINE DR
\- SIMI 93065 478-C7
\- SIMI 93065 498-C1
NIGHT RAIN LN
23600 SIMI 93065 497-A1
NIGHTSKY DR
13200 VeCo 93012 496-F4
NIGHTWIND LN
23600 SIMI 93065 497-A1
NIKE ZEUS RD
\- VeCo 93042 583-D5
NILE RIVER DR
\- OXN 93036 492-G6
NILES ST
2700 SIMI 93065 498-C2
NILGAI PL
7200 VEN 93003 492-F4
NIMES LN
\- OXN 93036 492-H7
NIMITZ DR
4200 OXN 93033 552-H4
NINA DR
23600 OXN 93030 522-J4
NITA AV
6200 WdHl 91367 529-J7
6800 CanP 91303 529-J4
7600 LA 91304 529-J3
9600 Chat 91311 499-J5

NIVEO LN
400 OXN 93030 522-H4
NIXON CT
7300 VEN 93003 492-E1
NOB HILL LN
6200 VEN 93003 472-C7
NOBLE RD
23600 SIMI 93065 497-F5
NOBLETREE CT
700 VeCo 91377 557-H1
NOCHE DR
\- OXN 93030 522-H4
NOCUMI ST
\- VEN 93001 471-D5
NOEL CIR
1500 SIMI 93065 498-B3
NOGALES AV
5600 MRPK 93021 476-G7
NOGUERA AV
11500 VeCo 93001 450-E3
NOLAN CT
2300 THO 91362 527-A6
NOLANA WY
\- OXN 93030 522-G4
NOME CIR
4200 SIMI 93063 478-F7
NONCHALANT DR
900 SIMI 93065 497-H6
NOONTIDE WY
\- OXN 93035 522-E7
NOPAL WK
300 OXN 93030 522-J5
NOPALITO ST
10500 VEN 93004 492-J1
NORDHOFF RD
3800 VeCo 93023 442-E7
3800 VeCo 93023 452-E1
NORDHOFF ST
22000 Chat 91311 499-J7
NORDMAN DR
1000 CMRL 93010 524-C2
NORFIELD CT
2200 VeCo 91361 556-E7
NORFLEET LN
200 SIMI 93065 497-D6
NORFOLK CT
\- MRPK 93021 496-E2
NORITE PL
2600 OXN 93030 522-D4
NORMA CT
\- VeCo 93010 494-E7
2100 OXN 93036 522-E2
NORMA ST
1900 OXN 93036 522-E3
NORMA WY
6000 SIMI 93063 499-B3
NORMAN AV
1300 THO 91360 526-F6
W NORMAN AV
\- THO 91360 526-F6
NORMANDY DR
\- LACo 91302 558-G3
NORMANDY TER
6800 VeCo 91377 528-B7
NORSEMAN CT
500 OXN 93030 522-E6
NORTH ST
4500 VeCo 93066 494-J4
5000 VeCo 93066 495-A4
NORTHAM AV
\- THO 91320 555-J1
NORTH AMERICAN CUT OFF
23600 VeCo 93063 499-C5
NORTH BANK DR
6700 VEN 93003 492-E6
8400 VEN 93004 492-J3
10300 VeCo 93004 493-A2
10300 VEN 93004 493-A2
NORTHBROOK DR
2400 OXN 93036 522-E1
NORTHCREST CT
3600 SIMI 93063 478-E7
NORTHDALE DR
11600 MRPK 93021 496-C3
NORTHLAKE CIR
2400 THO 91361 557-B5
NORTHLAND ST
3800 THO 91320 555-E2
NORTHPARK ST
2200 THO 91362 527-A4
NORTHPORT LN
3600 OXN 93035 522-C6
NORTHRIDGE DR
4400 VeCo 93066 493-F3
NORTHSHORE LN
1100 THO 91361 557-B5
NORTHSTAR CV
2600 PHME 93041 552-C3
NORTHSTAR LN
2400 OXN 93036 522-E1
NORTH VALLEY DR
500 THO 91362 557-C2
NORTH VIEW DR
1400 THO 91362 527-D6
NORTHWIND CT
\- VEN 93003 492-B4
NORTHWOOD PKWY
2900 THO 91360 526-H2

NORTHWOODS VIEW RD
23800 CanP 91307 529-E5
NORTON AV
6800 VEN 93003 492-E5
NORTON ST
\- OXN 93033 552-J2
NORWALK ST
10000 VEN 93004 492-H2
NORWAY DR
4000 VeCo 93001 471-C1
4900 VeCo 93001 461-C7
NORWICH AV
1400 THO 91360 526-F6
NORWICH LN
1100 VEN 93001 491-E5
NORWOOD CT
1100 VEN 93004 492-J2
NOTRE DAME AV
9200 Chat 91311 499-F7
9200 Chat 91311 499-F7
9200 Chat 91311 499-F6
NOTTINGHAM DR
700 OXN 93030 522-E4
NOTTINGWOOD CIR
1200 THO 91361 557-B5
NOVA CT
4900 VEN 93003 492-A1
NOVA LN
1300 VeCo 93023 451-E2
NOVARA WY
500 VeCo 91377 557-G1
NOVATO DR
600 OXN 93035 522-D7
1300 OXN 93035 552-D1
NOVINA PL
500 CMRL 93012 524-J3
N NOWAK AV
1800 THO 91360 526-E5
NUEVE CT
300 CMRL 93012 525-A3
NUEVO CANYON RD
\- VeCo 93040 367-E7
\- VeCo 93040 458-C1
NO 2 CANYON FIRE RD
23600 MRPK 93021 477-B3
23600 VeCo - 477-B3
23600 VeCo 93021 477-B3
23600 VeCo 93065 477-B3
NUMBER TEN CANYON RD
\- VeCo - 367-E9
23600 VeCo 93040 367-E9
23600 VeCo 93040 458-D7
NUTCRACKER CT
\- THO 91320 526-A5
NUTMEG CIR
2600 SIMI 93065 498-C1
NUTWOOD CIR
5700 SIMI 93063 499-A2
NYE RD
8600 VeCo 93001 461-A3
NYELAND AV
3200 VeCo 93036 523-C2
NYE RANCH FIRE RD
23600 VeCo 93001 460-J2

O

OAHU LN
4900 OXN 93033 552-J5
OAK
2000 VeCo 93023 451-C3
OAK AV
700 VeCo 93015 455-G4
OAK BEND
\- VeCo 91377 527-J7
\- VeCo 91377 528-A7
OAK CT
800 PHME 93041 552-F5
OAK DR
\- VeCo 93022 451-B6
\- VeCo 93023 451-G1
5100 OXN 93033 552-J5
OAK LN
100 THO 91362 556-H1
OAK RD
1400 SIMI 93063 499-B3
OAK ST
\- CMRL 93010 524-E3
100 OJAI 93023 441-J6
100 VeCo 93015 465-E1
600 VeCo 93022 451-B7
600 VeCo 93022 461-B1
N OAK ST
\- VEN 93001 491-C2
100 SPLA 93060 464-B4
S OAK ST
\- VEN 93001 491-C2
100 SPLA 93060 464-C5
W OAK ST
100 OJAI 93023 441-H6
OAK BANK
\- VeCo 91377 557-J1
OAK BLUFF DR
900 MRPK 93021 476-E7
OAK BRANCH DR
700 VeCo 91377 558-B1
OAK BROOK DR
2400 THO 91362 526-J4

OAKBURY CT
2700 THO 91360 526-D3
OAK CANYON RD
900 CMRL 93012 525-B1
OAKCLIFF DR
4100 MRPK 93021 496-G3
OAKCOTTAGE CT
23600 VeCo 91361 556-F6
OAK CREEK DR
400 THO 91361 556-E2
OAK CREEK LN
\- AGRH 91301 558-A5
200 OJAI 93023 441-H7
N OAKCREST AV
10900 VeCo 93022 451-C4
10900 VeCo 93023 451-B4
OAK CREST DR
31200 WLKV 91361 557-E6
OAKDALE CIR
2100 SIMI 93063 498-J2
OAKDALE LN
100 FILM 93015 455-J7
OAKDALE PL
1000 SPLA 93060 464-B3
OAKFEN CT
5500 AGRH 91301 557-G5
OAK FERN CT
\- SIMI 93063 499-A3
OAK FOREST DR
6500 VeCo 91377 558-A1
OAK GLEN AV
100 OJAI 93023 442-A7
OAK GLEN CT
4000 MRPK 93021 496-E3
OAK GLEN DR
200 THO 91320 555-E1
OAK GLEN ST
4300 CALB 91302 558-H7
OAK GROVE CT
700 VeCo 93023 451-A3
OAK GROVE PL
1200 THO 91362 527-C7
OAK GROVE FIRE RD
7400 VeCo 93012 525-D5
OAKHAMPTON ST
400 THO 91361 556-F3
OAK HAVEN AV
2200 SIMI 93063 498-J1
OAK HAVEN CT
400 VeCo 91377 558-B1
OAKHILL CIR
2100 OXN 93036 522-E2
OAK HILLS DR
300 VeCo 91377 558-A2
500 VeCo 91377 557-J1
OAK HOLLOW CIR
900 THO 91362 557-C1
OAKHURST CT
1300 CMRL 93010 524-E1
OAK KNOLL RD
10700 VeCo 93022 451-D6
OAK KNOLLS RD
5800 VeCo 93063 499-A3
OAKLAWN DR
100 VeCo 93022 461-A1
OAKLEAF AV
\- VeCo 91377 558-B2
OAK LEAF DR
100 THO 91360 526-E7
9400 Chat 91311 499-J6
OAK MEADOW PL
5900 VeCo 91377 558-A2
OAK MIRAGE PL
1000 THO 91362 527-D7
1000 THO 91362 557-D1
OAKMONT CT
800 SIMI 93065 497-G5
OAKMONT PL
23900 LA 91304 529-E1
OAKMORE ST
1200 OJAI 93023 441-F7
OAKMOUND AV
800 THO 91320 555-E4
OAK PARK LN
4900 VeCo 91377 557-G1
4900 VeCo 91377 527-G7
OAK PATH CT
700 VeCo 91377 558-B1
OAKPATH DR
28800 AGRH 91301 558-A4
OAK PLACE DR
4100 THO 91362 527-C6
OAK POINT DR
600 VeCo 91377 558-A1
OAK RANCH CT
31800 WLKV 91361 557-D7
OAKRIDGE CT
1600 THO 91362 526-J6
OAKRIDGE PL
9500 Chat 91311 499-H6
OAKRIDGE RD
\- LA 91304 529-C1
23600 VeCo - 367-E9
OAKRIM DR
30800 WLKV 91362 557-F4
OAK RUN TR
\- VeCo 91377 527-J7
\- VeCo 91377 557-J1

OAK SHADOW VIEW PL
600 THO 91320 556-D1
OAKSHORE DR
2400 THO 91361 557-B6
2600 WLKV 91361 557-B6
OAK SPRINGS DR
6500 VeCo 91377 558-B1
OAKSTAFF CT
2000 THO 91361 557-A6
OAK TERRACE LN
1800 THO 91320 526-A7
OAK TRAIL RD
23600 SIMI 93065 527-F1
OAK TRAIL ST
\- THO 91320 526-A6
OAK TREE CT
23600 SIMI 93065 527-F1
OAK TREE LN
400 THO 91360 526-F7
400 THO 91360 556-F1
OAK VALLEY LN
2500 THO 91362 527-C3
OAK VIEW AV
\- VeCo 93022 451-A7
E OAK VIEW AV
\- VeCo 93022 451-B7
OAK VIEW CT
23600 SIMI 93065 527-F1
OAK VIEW DR
\- THO 91362 557-A2
OAK VILLAGE RD
300 VeCo 93015 455-E7
OAKVISTA CT
29900 AGRH 91301 557-H4
OAKWOOD DR
1600 THO 91362 556-J2
OAKWOOD ST
200 VEN 93001 471-B7
700 VeCo 93023 451-C1
OARFISH CT
800 OXN 93035 522-D7
OARFISH LN
1000 OXN 93035 522-B7
OATFIELD WY
10300 VeCo 93012 495-J6
OAT MOUNTAIN MTWY
\- Nor 91326 479-J2
\- StvR 91381 479-J2
OBERLIN AV
200 VEN 93003 491-J2
1300 THO 91360 526-E6
OBERS PL
2500 PHME 93041 552-C2
OBRIEN CIR
2500 CMRL 93010 524-F3
OBSIDIAN CT
\- SIMI 93063 479-A7
OCASO PL
\- OXN 93030 523-A4
OCATILLO AV
\- THO 91320 555-J2
OCATILLO CT
\- THO 91320 555-J2
\- THO 91320 556-A2
OCCIDENTAL DR
200 OXN 93036 522-H2
OCEAN AV
1500 VEN 93001 491-E3
2200 VEN 93003 491-F3
23600 VeCo 93001 459-D6
OCEAN DR
\- PHME 93043 552-B5
100 VeCo 93035 552-A2
2900 OXN 93035 552-B5
OCEANAIRE LN
11900 VeCo 90265 625-F5
OCEANAIRE ST
5000 OXN 93035 551-J1
5000 OXN 93035 552-A1
OCEAN BLUFF AV
23600 THO 91362 527-B2
OCEANMIST CT
2500 PHME 93041 552-C2
OCEAN VIEW DR
400 PHME 93041 552-F7
600 VeCo 93010 494-F6
E OCEAN VIEW DR
1200 VeCo 93010 494-F6
OCEAN VIEW RD
8000 VeCo 93001 459-C3
23600 VeCo 93001 366-G9
OCEAN WALK CT
\- PHME 93041 552-D6
OCHO RIOS WY
300 VeCo 91377 557-G2
OCIE AV
2700 SIMI 93065 478-B7
OCOTLAN WY
\- OXN 93030 522-H4
ODEBOLT DR
100 THO 91360 526-E3
OFELIA WY
\- OXN 93030 522-J4
OFFSHORE ST
900 OXN 93035 522-C7
1300 OXN 93035 552-C1
OGDEN ST
8800 VEN 93004 492-G3

OHARA CANYON RD
1900 VeCo 93060 463-E4
OJAI AV
100 VeCo 93035 552-B5
6700 VeCo 93001 459-C5
E OJAI AV Rt#-150
200 OJAI 93023 441-H7
1100 OJAI 93023 442-B7
1600 VeCo 93023 442-B7
W OJAI AV Rt#-150
100 OJAI 93023 441-G7
1000 OJAI 93023 451-G1
OJAI DR
\- VeCo 93022 451-B6
OJAI FRWY Rt#-33
\- VeCo - 461-B6
\- VeCo - 471-C3
\- VEN - 471-B7
\- VEN - 491-A1
N OJAI RD Rt#-150
100 SPLA 93060 464-B3
300 VeCo 93060 464-B3
OJAI ST
600 VeCo 93015 465-J3
N OJAI ST
100 SPLA 93060 464-B5
S OJAI ST
100 SPLA 93060 464-C6
OJAI SANTA PAULA RD Rt#-150
3100 VeCo 93023 442-D7
7000 VeCo 93023 452-E1
11900 VeCo 93023 453-A1
OJAI VALLEY SCHOOL
23600 VeCo 93023 442-J7
23600 VeCo 93023 453-A1
OKAPI LN
1100 VEN 93003 492-E4
OLD BALCOM CANYON RD
6200 VeCo 93066 475-D7
OLD BALDWIN RD
1200 VeCo 93023 451-B3
OLD BURY PL
1300 THO 91361 556-J6
OLD BUTTERFIELD RD
\- VeCo 93012 496-F7
OLD CARRIAGE CT
29000 AGRH 91301 558-A3
OLDCASTLE PL
1500 THO 91361 556-H6
OLD COACH DR
3000 VeCo 93010 494-C6
3300 VeCo 93066 494-C6
OLD COLONY WY
30900 AGRH 91301 557-F6
30900 WLKV 91361 557-F6
OLD CONEJO RD
3000 THO 91320 525-E6
3000 VeCo 91320 525-F7
E OLD CREEK RD
200 VeCo 93001 461-B2
200 VeCo 93022 461-B2
W OLD CREEK RD
9500 VeCo 93001 461-A2
OLD DAIRY RD
\- VeCo 93012 554-E1
OLD DUMP RD
2400 THO 91361 556-J3
OLDENBERG WY
6000 SIMI 93063 499-B1
OLD FARM CT
\- THO 91360 526-G5
OLD FARM RD
600 THO 91360 526-G5
OLD GRADE RD
200 VeCo 93022 451-B7
1800 VeCo 93023 451-C3
OLDHAM CIR
2400 OXN 93035 552-A2
OLD HWY 150
9100 VeCo 93023 452-G1
OLD OAK AV
1200 THO 91320 526-A6
OLD ORCHARD RD
2100 VeCo 93015 455-E5
OLD PACIFIC COAST HWY
6200 VeCo 93001 459-D5
OLD RANCH CIR
11300 Chat 91311 499-J1
OLD RANCH RD
1100 CMRL 93012 525-B1
1700 CMRL 93012 495-B7
OLD RINCON HWY Rt#-1
2900 VeCo 93001 470-F6
4200 VeCo 93001 366-G9
4200 VeCo 93001 459-F7
4200 VeCo 93001 469-H1
23600 VeCo 93001 490-G1
OLDS RD
3000 OXN 93033 553-A3
4200 VeCo 93033 553-B6
OLD SALT LN
5500 AGRH 91301 557-G5
OLDSTONE CT
300 SIMI 93065 497-G6

OLDSTONE PL
400 SIMI 93065 497-F5
OLD TELEGRAPH RD
700 FILM 93015 456-A6
700 FILM 93015 455-H5
1100 VeCo 93015 455-H5
OLD TELEGRAPH RD Rt#-126
2500 VeCo 93015 455-E7
2700 VeCo 93015 465-E1
OLD VENTURA AV
300 VeCo 93022 451-B7
OLD WALNUT RD
23600 VeCo 93023 452-G1
OLEANDER CT
100 THO 91320 555-J2
600 OXN 93033 552-G2
OLEANDER DR
500 OXN 93033 552-F2
OLEANDER WY
\- SIMI 93065 497-H3
OLEARY CT
1700 THO 91320 556-A1
OLGA ST
1900 OXN 93036 522-E3
OLIN DR
9200 Chat 91311 499-F7
OLIVAS PARK DR
1100 VEN 93001 491-H7
3300 VeCo 93001 491-H7
4500 VeCo 93001 492-B7
4500 VeCo 93003 492-B7
4500 VeCo 93003 491-H7
4800 VEN 93003 492-D7
5800 VEN 93001 492-B7
OLIVE RD
300 VeCo 93060 473-C3
OLIVE ST
\- MRPK 93021 496-G2
\- OXN 93036 522-H1
\- VeCo 93022 451-B7
200 FILM 93015 456-A6
200 OXN 93033 552-G2
700 OJAI 93023 441-H6
800 VeCo 93040 457-F3
1700 VeCo 93023 442-B5
N OLIVE ST
\- VeCo 93022 451-B6
\- VEN 93001 491-B1
100 SPLA 93060 464-A5
600 VEN 93001 471-B7
S OLIVE ST
\- VEN 93001 491-B2
100 SPLA 93060 464-B6
W OLIVE ST
800 OXN 93033 552-F2
OLIVEBROOK WK
\- CMRL 93012 524-H2
OLIVEGROVE PL
2500 THO 91362 527-D3
N OLIVE HILL RD
5100 VeCo 93066 495-B1
5600 VeCo 93066 475-C7
OLIVE MILL LN
\- OJAI 93023 441-J7
OLIVER ST
800 FILM 93015 455-J6
OLIVEWOOD CT
1900 THO 91362 526-J4
1900 THO 91362 527-A4
OLIVEWOOD DR
2200 THO 91362 527-A4
OLIVIA DR
23600 OXN 93030 522-J4
OLIVO CT
3800 CMRL 93010 524-H1
OLOROSO CIR
4200 MRPK 93021 496-E3
OLSEN RD
\- THO 91360 526-G1
1100 THO 91360 496-H7
1900 SIMI 93065 497-A6
2000 THO 91360 497-A6
2500 THO 93021 497-A6
2500 THO 93065 497-A6
2500 VeCo 91360 497-A6
2500 VeCo 93021 497-A6
2500 VeCo 93065 497-A6
W OLSEN RD
\- THO 91360 526-E2
OLYMPIA AV
800 VEN 93004 492-G3
OLYMPIC ST
1300 SIMI 93063 498-D3
OLYMPUS LN
23600 OXN 93035 522-C6
OLYMPUS ST
\- MRPK 93021 496-D1
OMAHA AV
2800 VEN 93001 471-C4
OMAHA CT
300 VEN 93001 471-D5
OMEGA AV
3000 SIMI 93063 478-E7
3100 VeCo 93063 478-E7
ONA CIR
1600 SIMI 93063 498-J3
ONDA DR
1700 CMRL 93010 524-D2

STREET Block	City	ZIP	Pg-Grid
ONEIDA CT			
-	MRPK	93021	496-G3
1000	OXN	93030	522-E4
ONEIDA PL			
1500	OXN	93030	522-D4
ONEIDA ST			
9500	VEN	93004	492-H3
ONEIDA WY			
2300	OXN	93030	522-D4
ONEILL PL			
1800	OXN	93033	552-J2
1800	OXN	93033	553-A2
ONE OAK LN			
2400	SIMI	93063	499-A1
ONONDAGA LN			
100	VEN	93001	471-C5
ONTARIO AV			
1200	VEN	93004	492-G3
ONTARIO ST			
900	OXN	93035	522-E7
1400	OXN	93035	552-E1
ONYX CIR			
3300	SIMI	93063	478-D7
ONYX ST			
-	VEN	93004	492-F3
OPAL AV			
500	VEN	93004	492-F3
OPAL CT			
2800	SIMI	93063	478-C7
8000	VEN	93004	492-F3
OPALO DR			
-	OXN	93030	522-J4
OPEN CIR			
4700	SIMI	93063	478-H5
OPHELIA CT			
2600	SIMI	93063	478-J7
OPTAR LN			
400	OXN	93030	522-H4
W ORACLE CT			
1900	THO	91320	555-J2
1900	THO	91320	556-A2
ORANGE CIR			
10600	VEN	93004	472-H7
ORANGE CT			
3600	SIMI	93063	478-E7
ORANGE DR			
-	VeCo	93036	492-J7
300	VeCo	93036	522-J1
900	VeCo	93036	523-A1
3200	OXN	93036	523-C2
ORANGE LN			
1200	VeCo	93010	494-F7
ORANGE MALL			
5100	OXN	93033	552-H5
ORANGE RD			
600	OJAI	93023	442-B6
600	VeCo	93023	442-B6
ORANGE ST			
200	VeCo	93015	465-E1
ORANGE BLOSSOM LN			
100	FILM	93015	455-J6
ORANGE GROVE AV			
200	FILM	93015	456-A6
3600	OXN	93033	553-B4
ORANGEWOOD AV			
600	THO	91320	555-G3
N ORANGEWOOD PL			
2400	SIMI	93065	498-A1
ORCHARD DR			
-	VeCo	93001	471-C3
1300	VeCo	93023	451-D2
ORCHARD LN			
700	VeCo	93060	473-C2
ORCHARD PL			
100	OXN	93036	522-F1
ORCHARD ST			
400	FILM	93015	456-A6
600	VeCo	93040	457-F3
1000	SPLA	93060	464-B4
1500	VeCo	93060	464-B4
ORCHARD FARM RD			
23600	VeCo	93060	473-D4
ORCHARD VIEW CIR			
-	CMRL	93010	524-D4
ORCHARDVIEW CT			
4200	WLKV	91361	557-D6
ORCHID AV			
1900	SIMI	93065	498-B2
ORCHID DR			
1700	OXN	93033	553-A2
ORCHID PL			
200	VEN	93004	473-C7
ORCUTT RD			
200	VeCo	93060	464-E3
ORCUTT CANYON RD			
200	VeCo	93060	454-E7
1000	VeCo	93060	464-E2
OREGON DR			
2100	VEN	93003	492-C5
ORENA CT			
400	CMRL	93010	524-B1
ORIENT ST			
-	FILM	93015	455-J7
ORILLA WK			
300	OXN	93030	522-H4
ORINDA CT			
1600	THO	91362	526-J4
ORIOLE CIR			
1100	FILM	93015	455-H6
ORIOLE DR			
-	VeCo	93041	583-H2
ORIOLE LN			
4000	OXN	93033	553-B4
ORIOLE ST			
200	OJAI	93023	442-A6
6200	VEN	93003	492-D4
ORION WY			
900	OXN	93036	522-F1
ORIONS FLIGHT WY			
-	VeCo	93012	496-F6
ORLEANS CT			
30800	WLKV	91362	557-F4
ORLEANS LN			
-	OXN	93036	492-H7
ORLOP PL			
2000	OXN	93035	522-E6
ORO ST			
400	VeCo	93022	451-A7
ORR AV			
1600	SIMI	93065	498-C3
ORR RD			
100	VeCo	93060	473-G3
ORTEGA DR			
-	THO	91320	556-B1
ORTEGA ST			
-	OXN	93030	523-B4
900	FILM	93015	455-J6
4600	VEN	93003	492-A6
ORWELL LN			
-	OXN	93033	552-J2
500	VEN	93003	492-D1
OSA CT			
1100	OXN	93035	522-E7
OSAGE CIR			
800	CMRL	93012	525-A2
OSAGE LN			
1100	VEN	93004	492-H3
OSBORN RD			
23600	VeCo	93060	453-D1
OSO RD			
700	VeCo	93023	441-C5
OSPREY AV			
-	THO	91320	526-A5
N OSPREY LN			
1100	VEN	93003	492-F4
S OSPREY LN			
1300	VEN	93003	492-F4
OSTRICH HILL RD			
1100	OXN	93036	522-E1
OTANO WY			
-	OXN	93030	522-H4
OTERO CT			
500	VeCo	93010	494-B7
E OTONO CIR			
2200	THO	91362	527-A2
OTONO CT			
300	CMRL	93012	525-A2
OTTAWA DR			
100	VEN	93001	471-C4
OTTER CREEK LN			
2400	OXN	93036	522-E1
OUTER DR			
-	SPLA	93060	464-A7
OUTLET CENTER DR			
2000	OXN	93036	523-B3
21400	OXN	93030	523-B3
OUTLOOK CIR			
1300	THO	91362	527-C7
OUTLOOK CV			
2600	PHME	93041	552-C3
OUTRIGGER AV			
3100	VEN	93001	491-G5
OUTRIGGER WY			
5100	OXN	93035	521-J7
OUTSAIL LN			
2000	OXN	93035	522-D7
OVERFALL DR			
30800	WLKV	91362	557-F4
OVERLAND DR			
24500	LA	91304	529-C4
OVERLOOK DR			
700	VEN	93001	491-C1
OVERLOOK RD			
600	SIMI	93065	497-E6
OVERLY ST			
6400	MRPK	93021	477-A6
OWEN ST			
1000	VeCo	93015	465-H3
OWENS AV			
1200	VEN	93004	492-G3
OWENS RIVER DR			
-	OXN	93036	492-G6
OWL CT			
6900	VEN	93003	492-E4
OWLS COVE LN			
23600	SIMI	93065	497-G2
E OXFORD CIR			
14400	MRPK	93021	476-G6
OXFORD DR			
600	OXN	93030	522-E4
OXFORD ST			
10400	VEN	93004	492-J1
11900	VeCo	93021	476-D3
OXLEY PL			
4900	THO	91362	527-E6
OXNARD AV			
100	VeCo	93035	552-B5
7000	VeCo	93001	459-C4
OXNARD BLVD			
600	OXN	93036	492-H6
1000	OXN	93030	522-G3
2000	OXN	93036	522-G3
OXNARD BLVD Rt#-1			
-	OXN	93033	553-A2
-	VeCo	93033	553-B3
100	OXN	93030	522-G7
1200	OXN	93030	552-H1
1200	OXN	93033	522-G7
1200	OXN	93033	552-H1
1500	OXN	93036	522-G1
19200	OXN	93036	492-G7
N OXNARD BLVD			
-	OXN	93036	492-H6
OXNARD CIR			
-	OXN	93036	492-H6
OXNARD SHORES DR			
5100	OXN	93035	521-J6
OYSTER PL			
1100	OXN	93030	522-E7
OYSTER ST			
900	VeCo	93001	491-F5
900	VEN	93001	491-F5
P			
PACIFIC AV			
100	VeCo	93015	457-D5
500	OXN	93030	522-J7
700	SIMI	93065	497-G3
1100	OXN	93033	522-J7
1300	OXN	93033	552-J1
3500	VeCo	93040	457-D5
N PACIFIC AV			
-	VEN	93001	491-E2
S PACIFIC AV			
-	VEN	93001	491-E2
PACIFIC CIR			
400	THO	91320	555-G3
PACIFIC RD			
-	PHME	93041	552-D4
-	PHME	93043	552-D4
2800	VeCo	93041	583-H4
3400	VeCo	93042	583-H4
18600	VeCo	93033	583-H4
PACIFICA DR			
100	OXN	93033	553-C4
PACIFIC BREEZE DR			
-	VeCo	93012	496-F6
PACIFIC COAST FRWY Rt#-1			
-	OXN	-	553-C4
-	VeCo	-	553-C4
-	VeCo	-	583-H1
PACIFIC COAST HWY Rt#-1			
2900	VeCo	93001	470-B3
4200	VeCo	93001	366-G9
4200	VeCo	93001	459-F6
4200	VeCo	93001	469-H1
9000	VeCo	90265	387-F4
9000	VeCo	90265	625-A3
9400	VeCo	-	584-A6
12300	LACo	90265	625-F5
19900	VeCo	93033	583-J5
19900	VeCo	93033	584-A6
23600	VeCo	93001	490-G1
34100	MAL	90265	625-F5
PACIFIC COVE DR			
500	PHME	93041	552-C2
N PACIFIC MILLING RD			
6400	VeCo	93066	493-D2
13600	VeCo	93066	473-E7
S PACIFIC MILLING RD			
100	OXN	93036	492-H6
PACIFIC OAK DR			
22400	Chat	91311	499-H5
PACIFIC RIDGE RD			
6300	VeCo	93063	499-C4
PACIFIC STRAND CT			
-	VEN	93003	492-B4
PACIFIC STRAND PL			
-	VEN	93003	492-B4
PACIFIC VIEW LN			
900	VEN	93001	491-D1
PACIFIC VIEW RD			
10300	VeCo	90265	585-A7
10700	VeCo	90265	387-A4
10700	VeCo	90265	625-A1
PACKARD CIR			
100	THO	91362	557-C4
PACKARD ST			
23600	OXN	93033	553-B4
PACOS ST			
-	VEN	93001	471-B5
PADDINGTON PL			
800	OXN	93030	522-E4
PADELFORD RD			
900	FILM	93015	456-B4
PADOVA CT			
30800	WLKV	91362	557-F5
PADRE LN			
-	CMRL	93012	524-H1
200	VeCo	93060	464-D3
N PADRE JUAN AV			
100	VeCo	93023	441-D6
S PADRE JUAN AV			
100	VeCo	93023	441-D7
PADRE JUAN CANYON RD			
4000	VeCo	93001	470-A3
23600	VeCo	93001	460-C7
PADUA CIR			
100	THO	91320	555-E1
PADUA LN			
3700	THO	91320	555-E1
PAGENT CT			
3200	THO	91360	526-F2
PAGENT ST			
-	THO	91360	526-F2
PAIGE AV			
3000	SIMI	93063	478-E7
3100	VeCo	93063	478-E7
PAIGE LN			
600	THO	91360	526-G7
900	THO	91362	526-H6
PAINE AV			
300	VEN	93003	492-B3
PAINTED PONY CIR			
5800	SIMI	93063	479-A6
PAINTED SKY ST			
3800	MRPK	93021	496-E4
PAIUTE AV			
11200	Chat	91311	499-J2
PAIUTE LN			
200	VEN	93001	471-C5
PAJARO AV			
-	VEN	93004	472-J6
-	VEN	93004	473-A7
PAJARO ST			
-	OXN	93030	523-B4
PALA DR			
400	VeCo	93023	441-D7
PALA MESA DR			
6800	VeCo	91377	528-B7
PALA VISTA			
-	CMRL	93012	494-J7
PALERMO CT			
23600	SIMI	93063	478-G6
PALI DR			
1000	OXN	93033	552-J5
PALISADES PARK DR			
-	OXN	93036	492-H7
N PALM AV			
100	SPLA	93060	464-A6
S PALM AV			
100	SPLA	93060	464-A6
PALM CT			
1400	THO	91360	526-H2
E PALM CT			
300	SPLA	93060	464-A5
N PALM CT			
300	SPLA	93060	464-A5
PALM DR			
-	CMRL	93010	524-E4
23600	FILM	93015	456-C6
W PALM DR			
100	OXN	93030	522-E5
PALM LN			
5100	OXN	93033	552-H5
PALM ST			
200	FILM	93015	456-A6
N PALM ST			
-	VEN	93001	491-C2
S PALM ST			
-	VEN	93001	491-C2
PALMA DR			
1400	VEN	93003	492-A6
2900	VeCo	93003	492-A6
PALMER AV			
900	CMRL	93010	524-E2
PALMER DR			
-	MRPK	93021	476-D4
-	VeCo	93021	476-D4
PALMETTO LN			
400	THO	91320	556-D1
PALMGROVE AV			
-	THO	91320	556-C2
PALMWOOD CIR			
2500	THO	91362	527-D3
PALO ALTO			
2100	VeCo	93023	451-C3
PALO COMADO DR			
5900	AGRH	91301	558-D4
PALO COMADO CANYON RD			
5000	AGRH	91301	558-D6
PALO COMADO FIRE RD			
-	VeCo	91377	527-J4
-	VeCo	91377	528-A4
-	VeCo	93065	528-A4
23600	SIMI	93065	527-J4
23600	VeCo	93065	527-J4
PALOMA CT			
30800	WLKV	91362	557-F5
PALOMA DR			
3600	VEN	93003	491-H2
PALOMAR AV			
600	MRPK	93021	496-D1
2100	VEN	93001	491-F2
PALOMAR CIR			
5800	CMRL	93012	495-B7
PALOMAR RD			
200	OJAI	93023	441-G5
500	VeCo	93023	441-G6
PALOMAR WY			
800	OXN	93033	552-F3
PALOMARES AV			
-	VEN	93003	491-H2
PALOMINO CIR			
4100	THO	91362	527-C7
6000	VeCo	93066	495-B3
PALOMINO DR			
4300	VeCo	93066	495-B3
PALOMITAS CIR			
4200	MRPK	93021	496-D2
PALOS CT W			
2100	THO	91320	555-J2
PALO VERDE CIR			
11200	VeCo	93012	496-B6
PAMELA CT			
100	SPLA	93060	463-J7
1800	SIMI	93065	497-J2
1800	SIMI	93065	498-A2
PAMELA LN			
100	SPLA	93060	463-H6
PAMELA ST			
1900	OXN	93036	522-E3
PAMELA WOOD ST			
700	THO	91320	556-C1
PAMPAS LN			
-	VEN	93001	491-B1
PAN CT			
23600	THO	91320	556-B1
PANAL CT			
1200	OXN	93030	522-H4
PANAMA DR			
2200	PHME	93035	552-B4
2200	PHME	93043	552-B4
2200	VeCo	93035	552-B4
2600	VeCo	93043	552-B4
E PANAMINT CT			
2800	THO	91362	557-C3
W PANAMINT CT			
2700	THO	91362	557-B3
PANCHO RD			
100	VeCo	93012	524-H7
400	CMRL	93012	524-H7
1600	VeCo	93012	554-H1
S PANCHO RD			
400	CMRL	93012	524-H4
PANDA PL			
2300	VEN	93003	492-E5
PANORAMA CT			
1300	THO	91360	526-H2
PANSY ST			
-	SIMI	93063	499-A2
PANSY WY			
-	VEN	93004	473-C7
PAPAGO TER			
8400	LA	91304	529-D1
PAQUITA ST			
1000	CMRL	93012	525-C6
PARADE AV			
-	SIMI	93063	498-H1
PARADISE CIR			
300	VeCo	93010	494-F6
PARAKEET CT			
1600	VEN	93003	492-F4
PAR FIVE CT			
1900	THO	91362	527-D5
PAR FIVE DR			
1800	THO	91362	527-C6
PARIS CT			
30800	WLKV	91362	557-F5
PARK AV			
-	VeCo	93022	451-B7
400	PHME	93041	552-F4
PARK DR			
1400	VeCo	93023	451-B2
2000	VEN	93003	492-C5
PARK LN			
-	MRPK	93021	496-E2
PARK PL			
2200	THO	91362	527-A4
PARK RD			
100	OJAI	93023	441-J5
PARK ST			
-	PHME	93041	552-E4
200	OJAI	93023	441-H6
700	VeCo	93040	457-F3
1000	SPLA	93060	464-B4
1600	SIMI	93063	498-G3
PARK AND RIDE DR			
-	CMRL	93010	524-B3
PARK CENTER DR			
2600	SIMI	93065	477-F7
2600	SIMI	93065	497-F1
PARK COTTAGE PL			
-	CMRL	93012	524-G5
PARK CREST LN			
-	MRPK	93021	496-E2
N PARKDALE AV			
2400	SIMI	93063	498-E1
PARKER AV			
-	THO	91360	556-F1
PARKER CT			
2000	SIMI	93065	498-A2
N PARKER CT			
2100	SIMI	93065	498-A2
PARKER LN			
8400	VEN	93004	492-G4
PARKFRONT PL			
400	SIMI	93065	497-E6
PARKHAVEN CT			
200	FILM	93015	455-H7
PARKHEATH DR			
28900	AGRH	91301	558-B5
PARKHILL CIR			
6000	VEN	93003	472-C6
PARKHILL CT			
1300	CMRL	93010	524-E1
PARK HILL RD			
23600	SIMI	93065	497-F7
23600	SIMI	93065	527-F1
PARKHURST ST			
1200	SIMI	93065	497-H4
PARKING LOT RD			
23600	VeCo	93063	498-H7
PARK MEADOW CT			
2500	SIMI	93065	497-H1
PARKMOR RD			
5300	CALB	91302	558-H3
E PARK ROW AV			
-	VEN	93001	491-B1
W PARK ROW AV			
-	VEN	93001	491-B1
PARKSIDE CT			
-	VeCo	91377	527-J7
-	VeCo	91377	528-A7
PARKSIDE DR			
23600	SIMI	93065	527-F1
PARK SPRINGS CT			
400	VeCo	91377	558-B1
PARK TERRACE DR			
4300	WLKV	91361	557-E6
PARKVIEW AV			
2300	THO	91362	527-A4
PARKVIEW CT			
23600	SIMI	93065	527-F1
PARK VIEW DR			
100	VeCo	91377	558-A2
PARKVIEW DR			
2400	THO	91362	527-A3
8000	VeCo	93001	461-A4
PARKVILLE RD			
5000	CALB	91301	558-G6
5100	Ago	91301	558-G6
PARKWAY DR			
2300	CMRL	93010	494-E7
PARKWOOD CT			
1900	THO	91362	526-J3
PARMA DR			
4800	VeCo	91377	557-G1
PARMENTER CT			
700	THO	91362	527-A7
PARRISH ST			
-	VEN	93003	492-A3
PARRON ST			
3900	CMRL	93010	494-H7
PARROT CT			
1600	VEN	93003	492-E4
PARSONS AV			
300	VEN	93003	492-A2
PARSONS DR			
900	PHME	93041	552-E4
PARTHENIA ST			
22000	LA	91304	529-J1
PARTRIDGE CT			
5100	THO	91362	527-F6
PARTRIDGE DR			
800	OXN	93036	522-F1
1000	VEN	93003	492-D3
PARTRIDGE PL			
1600	VEN	93003	492-D4
PASADENA AV			
100	VeCo	93035	552-C6
100	VeCo	93043	552-C6
700	VeCo	93015	465-F2
700	VeCo	93015	466-A2
PASEO ARROYO			
800	CMRL	93010	524-B2
PASEO BARONA			
1300	CMRL	93010	524-C1
PASEO BRISAS LINDAS			
23600	OXN	93030	523-C6
PASEO CAMARILLO			
200	CMRL	93010	524-C3
PASEO CASTILLE			
1000	CMRL	93010	524-C1
PASEO DE CORTAGA			
600	CMRL	93010	524-B3
PASEO DE INVIERNO			
3500	THO	91360	526-B1
PASEO DE LA PAZ			
23600	THO	91320	555-D4
PASEO DEL CAMPO			
5200	CMRL	93012	524-J1
5300	CMRL	93012	525-A1
PASEO DE LEON			
500	THO	91320	555-F3
PASEO DEL ROBLEDO			
800	VeCo	91360	526-C6
PASEO DEL ROBLES CT			
1100	OJAI	93023	442-A6
PASEO DEL VALLE			
200	CMRL	93010	524-B3
PASEO DE NUBLADO			
3500	THO	91360	526-D1
PASEO DE PETALOS			
23600	CMRL	93010	523-G2
PASEO DE PLAYA			
300	VEN	93001	491-C2
PASEO ELEGANTE			
-	OXN	93030	523-A5
PASEO ENCANTADA			
5900	CMRL	93012	525-B5
PASEO ESMERALDA			
500	THO	91320	526-A7
PASEO ESPLENDIDO			
-	CMRL	93010	524-A2
PASEO GIRASOL			
23600	CMRL	93012	494-H7
PASEO GRANDE			
400	THO	91320	526-C7
PASEO HACIENDA			
-	OXN	93030	523-A5
PASEO ISLA			
-	OXN	93030	523-A4
PASEO LA PERLA			
500	THO	91320	526-A7
PASEO LAS NUBES			
23600	OXN	93030	523-B4
PASEO LA VIDA			
23600	OXN	93030	523-C7
PASEO LA VISTA			
6100	WdHl	91367	529-C7
PASEO LINDO			
-	OXN	93030	523-A4
PASEO LOMA			
23600	CMRL	93010	524-D4
PASEO LUNAR			
4400	CMRL	93010	524-B3
PASEO MARAVILLA			
23600	CMRL	93012	494-H7
23600	CMRL	93012	524-H1
PASEO MARGARITA			
-	OXN	93030	523-A5
5400	CMRL	93012	525-A5
PASEO MERCADO			
2800	OXN	93036	523-B2
PASEO MONTECITO			
600	THO	91320	525-F7
PASEO MONTELENA			
4600	CMRL	93012	524-J2
PASEO NOCHE			
1800	CMRL	93012	495-C7
PASEO NOGALES			
-	OXN	93030	523-A5
PASEO ORTEGA			
-	OXN	93030	523-B5
PASEO RICOSO			
5200	CMRL	93012	525-A2
PASEO SABANERO			
100	CMRL	93012	524-H3
PASEO SANTA BARBARA			
23600	THO	91320	555-D4
PASEO SANTA CATARINA			
23600	THO	91320	555-D4
PASEO SANTA CRUZ			
23600	THO	91320	555-D4
PASEO SANTA FE			
23600	THO	91320	555-D4
PASEO SANTA MONICA			
23600	THO	91320	555-D4
PASEO SANTA ROSA			
23600	THO	91320	555-D4
PASEO SERENATA			
800	CMRL	93012	525-C5
PASEO TESORO			
23600	OXN	93030	523-C7
PASEO TOSAMAR			
800	CMRL	93012	525-B5
PASEO VERDE			
500	VeCo	93010	494-A6
PASEO VISTA			
500	THO	91320	526-C7
PASEO YOLO			
2600	CMRL	93010	494-F7
N PASO FLORES RD			
5500	VeCo	93066	475-C7
5500	VeCo	93066	495-B1
PASO ROBLES			
7700	VEN	93004	492-E1
PASO ROBLES CT			
1500	CMRL	93012	524-J1
PASQUAL AV			
100	VEN	93004	472-J7
100	VEN	93004	473-A7
PASSAGEWAY PL			
30300	AGRH	91301	557-G5
PASTEUR DR			
5800	VEN	93003	492-C6
PAT AV			
5900	WdHl	91367	529-D7
6200	CanP	91307	529-D7
PATHELEN AV			
-	VeCo	93022	451-B7
PATHFINDER AV			
1300	THO	91362	527-G6
4700	VeCo	91362	527-G6
4700	VeCo	91377	527-G6
PATHWAY AV			
-	SIMI	93063	498-H1
PATINA CT			
-	CMRL	93010	493-H6
PATRICIA AV			
1200	SIMI	93065	497-H2
1700	SIMI	93065	498-A3
PATRICIA CT			
900	OJAI	93023	441-J5
PATRICIA ST			
1000	OXN	93030	522-E4
1800	SIMI	93065	497-H3
1800	OXN	93036	522-E3
PATRICK ST			
3100	SIMI	93065	498-D3
PATRICK HENRY PL			
3800	AGRH	91301	558-E7
PATRIOT PL			
-	VeCo	93041	583-H2
-	VeCo	93042	583-H2
PATTERSON RD			
2400	PHME	93043	552-D5
2500	PHME	93041	552-D5
2700	PHME	93035	552-D5
N PATTERSON RD			
100	VeCo	93030	522-D4
500	OXN	93030	522-D4
1900	OXN	93036	522-C2
S PATTERSON RD			
500	OXN	93030	522-D7
500	OXN	93035	522-D7
1200	OXN	93035	552-D1
PATTON CT			
1600	OXN	93030	522-J7
PATTY CT			
3100	SIMI	93063	478-E6
PAUL DR			
800	PHME	93041	552-F5
PAUL ST			
1400	SIMI	93065	497-G3
PAULA CIR			
2900	OXN	93033	552-H3
PAULA ST			
2900	OXN	93033	552-H3
PAULINE ST			
100	OJAI	93023	441-H6
PAULING DR			
600	THO	91320	526-A7
PAVAROTTI DR			
500	VeCo	91377	557-G2
PAVIN DR			
-	OXN	93036	522-C3
PAVO CT			
2000	THO	91362	556-H2
PAWNEE CT			
2500	VEN	93001	471-C5
3100	SIMI	93063	478-J6
PAZ MORADA			
1000	VEN	93003	472-D6
PEACEFUL CT			
400	SIMI	93065	497-J6
PEACE PIPE CT			
5700	SIMI	93063	479-A7
PEACH AV			
200	VEN	93004	473-A7
300	VeCo	93004	473-A7
PEACH LN			
1400	OXN	93033	553-B5
PEACH HILL RD			
13000	MRPK	93021	496-F2
PEACH SLOPE RD			
4200	MRPK	93021	496-E3
PEACHSPRING CT			
4200	MRPK	93021	496-B2
PEACHWOOD PL			
32700	WLKV	91361	586-J1
PEACOCK AV			
2300	VEN	93003	492-D5
PEACOCK CT			
3900	THO	91362	527-C6
PEACOCK RIDGE RD			
3700	CALB	91301	558-F7
PEAK PL			
2100	THO	91362	527-A2
PEAR AV			
1200	OXN	93033	553-B4
PEARL CIR			
3300	SIMI	93063	478-D6
PEARL CT			
200	PHME	93043	552-E4
PEARL ST			
100	PHME	93041	552-E6
600	OJAI	93023	441-J7
7900	VEN	93004	492-F3
PEARL WY			
1600	OXN	93035	552-B1
PEARSON RD			
400	PHME	93041	552-F3
PEBBLE PL			
3500	THO	91320	555-F2
PEBBLE BEACH DR			
100	THO	91320	556-D1
PEBBLE BEACH TR			
2100	OXN	93036	522-D2
PEBBLESTONE PL			
3100	SIMI	93063	478-D7
PECAN AV			
6600	MRPK	93021	476-J5
PECAN VALLEY PL			
2000	SIMI	93065	497-C6
PECIOLO CT			
1600	THO	91362	556-J1
PECK PL			
100	SPLA	93060	463-H7
PECK RD			
400	SPLA	93060	473-J1
500	VeCo	93060	473-J1
N PECK RD			
200	SPLA	93060	463-H6
200	VeCo	93060	463-H6
S PECK RD			
200	SPLA	93060	463-J7
200	SPLA	93060	473-J1
PEDERSON RD			
600	THO	91360	526-G2
1500	THO	91362	526-J3
19400	THO	91362	527-A3
PEGASUS ST			
800	VeCo	93023	451-C3
PEGGY CT			
3100	SIMI	93063	478-E6
PEKING ST			
-	VEN	93001	491-B1
PELICAN AV			
1600	VEN	93003	492-D4
PELICAN WY			
3700	OXN	93035	552-B4
PELLBURNE CT			
200	SIMI	93065	527-E1
PEMBRIDGE ST			
3300	THO	91360	526-G2
PEMBROKE CT			
1700	THO	91362	527-E6
PEMBROKE ST			
5600	VEN	93003	492-B1
E PENA CT			
3400	SIMI	93063	498-D2
PENA RANCH RD			
23600	Cstc	91384	458-H1
23600	VeCo	93040	458-G4
PENELOPE PL			
2300	VeCo	93012	496-B7
PENGUIN ST			
6800	VEN	93003	492-E6
PENINSULA RD			
2000	OXN	93035	552-B2
PENINSULA ST			
800	VEN	93001	491-F5
N PENLAN AV			
2100	SIMI	93063	499-B2
PENN ST			
6400	MRPK	93021	476-J6
PENNEY DR			
3000	SIMI	93063	478-D7
PENNGROVE ST			
1900	SIMI	93065	498-A1
PENNSFIELD PL			
400	THO	91360	526-F7
400	THO	91360	556-F1
PENNY WY			
-	OXN	93030	522-E4
PENOBSCOT DR			
-	LA	91304	529-D4
PENROD DR			
30400	AGRH	91301	557-G5
PENROSE AV			
4700	MRPK	93021	496-C2
PENROSE CT			
2000	THO	91362	527-A5
PENTLAND WY			
23900	CanP	91307	529-E5
PENZANCE AV			
-	CMRL	93012	524-F4
PEONY ST			
10500	VEN	93004	493-A2
PEOPLES AV			
200	CMRL	93010	524-F3
PEORIA AV			
1800	OXN	93033	553-A5
E PEORIA AV			
4000	SIMI	93063	478-F6
N PEORIA AV			
3000	SIMI	93063	478-F7
PEORIA PL			
1900	OXN	93033	553-A5
PEPPER			
2100	VeCo	93023	451-C3
PEPPER LN			
-	VEN	93001	491-B1
PEPPER RD			
-	THO	91320	556-B2
N PEPPERDINE CIR			
6400	MRPK	93021	476-H6
PEPPER MILL ST			
4600	MRPK	93021	496-B2
PEPPERMINT PL			
3100	THO	91320	555-G3
PEPPERMINT ST			
3200	THO	91320	555-G3
PEPPER TREE CT			
1800	THO	91362	526-J4
PEPPER TREE LN			
400	VeCo	93022	451-B7
PEPPERTREE LN			
900	VeCo	93064	498-F4
1200	SIMI	93063	498-F4
1200	VeCo	93063	498-F4
6000	VeCo	93063	499-B3
6400	VeCo	93066	495-B3
PEPPERTREE CANYON RD			
700	VeCo	93060	472-J3
700	VeCo	93060	473-A4
PEPPERWOOD CT			
300	THO	91360	526-F2
PEPPERWOOD DR			
2800	CMRL	93010	494-E6
PERALTA DR			
300	SPLA	93060	463-J7
300	SPLA	93060	464-A7
PERCY ST			
400	OXN	93033	552-H4
PEREGRINE CIR			
-	VeCo	91377	558-B3
PEREGRINE CT			
-	SIMI	93065	477-J6
-	SIMI	93065	478-A6
PERELLO RANCH RD			
-	VeCo	93036	493-B4
PERES LN			
300	VeCo	93060	464-E3
PERICLES PL			
1800	OXN	93033	553-A2
PERIMETER RD			
-	OXN	93033	583-A2
-	OXN	93042	583-A2
-	VeCo	93041	583-G1
-	VeCo	93042	553-G7
-	VeCo	93042	583-G1
PERIWINKLE CT			
400	THO	91360	526-D3
PERIWINKLE WY			
-	WdHl	91367	529-J7
PERKIN AV			
3100	VEN	93003	492-D7
23600	VEN	93001	492-D7
PERKINS RD			
5100	OXN	93033	552-G7
PERRY DR			
-	PHME	93041	552-D4
PERRY WY			
4700	VeCo	93036	493-A5
PERSIMMON LN			
1400	OXN	93033	553-B5
PERSIMMON ST			
-	MRPK	93021	496-G3
PERTH PL			
600	OXN	93035	522-D6
PERTHSHIRE CIR			
6900	CanP	91307	529-E6
PESARO ST			
400	VeCo	91377	557-G1
PESCADOR WY			
-	OXN	93030	522-J3
PESTO WY			
5300	VeCo	91377	557-H2
PETER PL			
500	SIMI	93065	498-A5
PETERSON AV			
6100	WdHl	91367	529-E7
6500	CanP	91307	529-E6
N PETIT AV			
-	VEN	93004	492-F1
300	VEN	93004	472-F7
S PETIT AV			
-	VEN	93004	492-G2
PETIT CIR			
9500	VEN	93004	492-H3
PETIT CT			
9400	VEN	93004	492-H2
PETIT DR			
3700	OXN	93033	552-H4
PETIT RD			
1800	VeCo	93060	465-C5
PETIT ST			
2600	CMRL	93012	524-G3
PETIT RANCH RD			
1700	VeCo	93060	465-D5
PETREL PL			
1800	VEN	93003	492-D4
PETTICOAT LN			
500	OXN	93036	522-F1
PETUNIA ST			
-	VEN	93004	493-A2
PETUNIA WY			
-	OXN	93030	522-G4
PHEASANT LN			
6700	VeCo	91377	528-A7
N PHEASANT LN			
1100	VEN	93003	492-F4
S PHEASANT LN			
1300	VEN	93003	492-F4
PHEASANT HILL			
2600	CMRL	93010	524-F2
PHEASANT RUN ST			
3900	MRPK	93021	496-E4
PHELPS AV			
1100	VEN	93004	492-J2
1200	VEN	93004	493-A2
PHELPS CT			
1000	VEN	93004	492-J2
PHILRICH CIR			
2600	CALB	91302	558-J4
E PHIPPS AV			
2500	SIMI	93065	498-C3
PHLEGER RD			
4900	VeCo	93066	495-B1
PHLOX CT			
400	THO	91360	526-D3
PHOENIX AV			
700	VEN	93004	492-G3
PHOENIX CIR			
-	VeCo	93042	583-H2

STREET
Block City ZIP Pg-Grid

PHOENIX DR
4400 OXN 93033 553-A5
PHYLLIS CT
- THO 91320 556-B1
E PHYLLIS ST
2400 SIMI 93065 498-B1
N PHYLLIS ST
2500 SIMI 93065 498-B1
PICADO DR
5000 CMRL 93012 524-G3
PICASO LN
2400 SIMI 93063 499-B1
PICASSO LN
- OXN 93033 552-J2
PICCADILLY CIR
2800 THO 91362 527-B3
PICKET AV
- CMRL 93012 524-G4
PICKFORD CT
700 THO 91320 555-G3
PICKWICK CT
900 THO 91360 526-G5
PICKWICK DR
2100 CMRL 93010 524-E2
PICO AV
1300 SIMI 93065 497-H3
PICO PL
3000 OXN 93033 552-J3
PIDDUCK RD
2600 VeCo 93033 553-C4
PIEDMONT DR
4800 VeCo 91377 557-G2
PIEDMONT ST
900 OXN 93035 522-E7
1400 OXN 93035 552-E1
PIEDRA WY
- OXN 93030 522-H4
PIER WK
3400 OXN 93035 522-C7
PIERCE CT
600 THO 91360 556-G1
2400 SIMI 93065 498-B4
PIERCE ST
7300 VEN 93003 492-E1
PIERCE ARROW AV
- THO 91362 557-B4
PIERPONT BLVD
2000 VEN 93001 491-E3
PIERSIDE LN
1500 CMRL 93010 524-D3
PILOT WY
900 OXN 93035 522-C7
PIMA LN
2300 VEN 93001 471-C6
PIMLICO DR
10600 MRPK 93021 476-A6
PINATA DR
- OXN 93030 522-J4
PINE LN
- VEN 93001 491-B1
PINE RD
7400 VeCo 93060 473-B3
PINE ST
1200 VeCo 93063 499-C4
1400 OXN 93030 552-H1
PINEBLUFF PL
32500 WLKV 91361 557-B7
PINECLIFF PL
400 SIMI 93065 497-G5
PINECONE CT
100 SIMI 93065 497-F6
PINE CREEK CT
- THO 91320 526-A6
PINECREST DR
- THO 91361 556-E3
PINECREST ST
2200 SIMI 93065 498-B2
PINEDALE RD
11600 MRPK 93021 496-C3
PINEFIELD CT
- MRPK 93021 476-F5
PINEGROVE RD
5600 VeCo 93060 454-A6
5800 VeCo 93060 453-J4
PINEHILL LN
400 SPLA 93060 464-A5
PINEHILL RD
- VeCo 91320 555-D5
PINEHILL ST
1000 THO 91320 555-E4
PINE HOLLOW PL
4000 MRPK 93021 496-D3
PINEHURST DR
2200 OXN 93036 522-E2
PINEHURST PL
1000 CMRL 93010 524-C2
PINELAKE DR
8400 LA 91304 529-F2
PINEPLANK LN
23600 SIMI 93065 497-A1
PINE RIDGE CT
4400 MRPK 93021 496-E3
PINE ROSE CT
- SIMI 93063 498-J2
PINESONG LN
23600 SIMI 93065 497-A1
PINE TERRACE DR
2000 THO 91362 527-A4

PINETREE CIR
500 THO 91360 526-E7
PINE VALLEY PL
4500 THO 91362 527-D6
PINE VIEW DR
23600 SIMI 93063 498-D5
23600 SIMI 93065 498-D5
PINEWOOD AV
- AGRH 91301 558-B2
- VeCo 91377 558-B2
N PINEWOOD PL
2000 SIMI 93065 498-A1
PINION ST
6300 VeCo 91377 558-B2
PINK CEDAR CT
3200 SIMI 93065 498-D4
PINKERTON RD
13300 VeCo 93060 473-F4
PINKERTON RANCH RD
500 VeCo 93060 472-G5
PINNACLE CT
- MRPK 93021 476-F6
PINNACLE WY
- MRPK 93021 476-F6
PINO CT
1400 CMRL 93010 524-A1
PINTO ST
1400 SIMI 93065 497-J3
PIONEER AV
3200 THO 91360 526-E2
PIRATE CV
2600 PHME 93041 552-C3
PIRIE RD
200 OJAI 93023 441-F7
PIROPO CT
600 VeCo 93010 494-B6
PIRU AV
2200 VeCo 93035 552-B5
PIRU SQ
600 VeCo 93040 457-F4
PIRU CANYON RD
- VeCo - 367-D7
- VeCo 93040 367-D7
23600 VeCo 93040 457-G3
23600 VeCo 93040 458-A1
PISCES ST
28700 AGRH 91301 558-B3
PISCO LN
1000 OXN 93035 522-E7
PISTACHIO AV
- VEN 93004 473-A6
E PITTMAN ST
5600 SIMI 93063 499-A1
PITTSFIELD LN
1000 VEN 93001 491-E4
PIUMA CT
5900 SIMI 93063 479-B7
PIUTE AV
2700 THO 91362 557-A2
PIVOT POINT WY
- OXN 93035 522-E7
PIXTON ST
23600 VeCo 91361 556-F6
PLACER AV
100 VEN 93004 472-H7
PLACER CT
100 VEN 93004 472-H7
PLACERITA DR
5200 SIMI 93063 478-J7
5400 SIMI 93063 498-J1
PLACERVILLE CT
2600 SIMI 93063 478-J7
2600 SIMI 93063 498-J1
PLACID AV
1100 VEN 93004 492-G3
PLACID CT
1500 SIMI 93065 497-J6
PLACITA BUENA ROSA
23600 CMRL 93012 524-H3
PLACITA SAN DIMAS
2200 CMRL 93010 494-H6
PLACITA SAN LEANDRO
2200 CMRL 93010 494-H6
PLACITA SAN RUFINO
2200 CMRL 93010 494-H6
PLAINFIELD PL
2100 OXN 93036 522-E2
PLAINVIEW ST
5600 VEN 93003 472-C7
N PLANETREE AV
700 SIMI 93065 498-B5
PLATA LN
26300 CALB 91302 558-H4
PLATA ROSA CT
- CMRL 93012 495-A7
PLATFORM PL
2000 OXN 93035 522-D7
PLATINUM ST
- VEN 93004 492-F3
PLATO CT
2000 SIMI 93065 497-G2
PLATT AV
6100 WdHl 91367 529-F7
6400 CanP 91307 529-F5
7300 LA 91304 529-F3
PLATTE AV
1200 VEN 93004 492-G3
PLATTE WY
- OXN 93036 492-H5

PLATTS HARBOR
- VeCo 93012 554-F3
PLAYA CT
3200 OXN 93035 552-B4
3200 VeCo 93035 552-B4
N PLAZA
- VeCo 93035 552-A3
S PLAZA
- VeCo 93035 552-A3
PLAZA MALL
300 OXN 93030 522-G6
PLAZA LA VISTA
100 CMRL 93010 524-C4
PLEASANT AV
500 OJAI 93023 441-J5
800 OJAI 93023 442-A5
1000 VeCo 93023 442-A5
PLEASANT PL
- VEN 93001 471-B6
PLEASANT ST
100 SPLA 93060 464-A5
PLEASANT WY
2400 THO 91362 557-A2
PLEASANT DALE PL
400 THO 91362 557-G1
PLEASANT GROVE CIR
2400 THO 91362 526-J4
PLEASANT OAKS PL
1500 THO 91362 526-J6
PLEASANTON PL
- SIMI 93065 497-G6
PLEASANT VALLEY RD
- PHME 93043 552-D5
- CMRL 93010 524-A5
- VeCo 93010 524-A5
100 PHME 93041 552-D5
400 VeCo 93010 523-J5
400 CMRL 93010 523-J5
800 OXN 93033 552-D5
1200 VeCo 93033 523-F7
1200 VeCo 93033 553-C3
2200 VeCo 93012 524-F5
2200 CMRL 93012 524-H5
2300 OXN 93033 553-C3
23600 VeCo 93030 523-J5
PLEASANT VALLEY RD Rt#-34
2200 VeCo 93012 524-F5
2200 CMRL 93012 524-F5
E PLEASANT VALLEY RD
100 OXN 93033 552-J5
800 VeCo 93033 552-J5
1800 OXN 93033 553-A4
W PLEASANT VALLEY RD
- OXN 93033 552-G5
PLEASANT VALLEY CANAL RD
- PHME 93043 552-C5
PLUM AV
1200 SIMI 93065 498-B4
PLUM PL
200 OXN 93036 522-G1
PLUM ST
11300 VEN 93004 473-A7
PLUMAS AV
300 VEN 93004 472-H7
400 VeCo 93004 472-H7
PLUMBAGO ST
500 VeCo 93010 524-C1
PLUMERIA CIR
1500 THO 91360 526-H3
PLUM HOLLOW CIR
1600 THO 91362 527-D6
PLUMMER ST
22000 Chat 91311 499-H6
PLUM TREE CT
24400 CanP 91307 529-D5
PLYMOUTH CIR
1400 THO 91360 526-G6
POCANO CT
2900 THO 91362 527-A2
POCATELLO CT
2400 SIMI 93065 497-J1
POCOMOKE CT
2400 SIMI 93065 497-J1
POE LN
500 VEN 93003 492-D1
POEMA PL
11400 Chat 91311 479-J7
14100 Chat 91311 499-J1
POGGI ST
600 CMRL 93010 524-C2
POINDEXTER AV
100 MRPK 93021 496-C1
POINSETTIA AV
900 THO 91362 557-F1
POINSETTIA PL
700 VEN 93001 491-C2
POINSETTIA GARDENS DR
- VEN 93004 473-B7
- VEN 93004 493-A1
POINTED OAK PL
5500 AGRH 91301 558-A5
POKE LN
2000 SIMI 93065 498-A1

POL RD
- VeCo 93033 553-F6
POLARIS DR
- VeCo 93041 583-H2
POLARIS WY
700 PHME 93041 552-F3
800 OXN 93033 552-F3
800 PHME 93033 552-F3
POLE CREEK ST
- FILM 93015 456-C4
- VeCo 93015 456-C4
N POLI AV
100 VeCo 93023 441-D6
S POLI AV
100 VeCo 93023 441-D7
POLI ST
100 VEN 93001 491-C1
2400 VEN 93001 491-E2
POLK ST
23600 VEN 93003 492-E2
POLLOCK LN
6800 VEN 93003 492-D3
POMELO DR
6900 CanP 91307 529-E5
7400 LA 91304 529-E4
POMO DR
200 VEN 93001 471-C5
POMONA ST
4000 VEN 93003 491-J2
4400 VEN 93003 492-A2
PONCE AV
6300 WdHl 91367 529-H7
6400 CanP 91307 529-H4
7600 LA 91304 529-H2
PONDERA CIR
7200 CanP 91307 529-E5
PONDEROSA CIR
2900 THO 91360 526-H3
PONDEROSA DR
- CMRL 93010 524-C2
3400 CMRL 93010 494-G7
W PONDEROSA DR
100 CMRL 93010 524-A2
300 CMRL 93010 523-G2
PONDEROSA DR N
3600 CMRL 93010 494-G7
3600 VeCo 93010 494-G7
PONDEROSA LP
2200 OXN 93033 553-B5
PONDEROSA RD
- VeCo 93066 494-H4
PONOMA ST
100 PHME 93041 552-E6
PONS CT
900 THO 91320 555-F4
PONTOON WY
- OXN 93035 522-E7
POPE AV
1700 SIMI 93065 498-C3
POPE LN
600 OJAI 93023 441-J7
POPLAR CT
1000 SIMI 93063 498-D4
POPLAR ST
200 OXN 93033 552-G2
W POPLAR ST
800 OXN 93033 552-F2
POPLAR CREST AV
- THO 91320 556-C2
POPPY CT
2900 THO 91360 526-D2
POPPY LN
1100 SPLA 93060 464-B3
POPPY ST
1500 VEN 93004 493-A2
POPPYGLEN CT
11500 MRPK 93021 496-B2
POPPYSEED PL
3900 CALB 91302 558-H7
POPPY TREE PL
23600 SIMI 93063 498-D4
POPPYVIEW DR
6600 VeCo 91377 528-B7
6600 VeCo 91377 558-A1
PORPOISE WY
4100 OXN 93035 552-B2
PORT CIR
1100 OXN 93035 522-C7
PORT DR
1300 OXN 93035 522-C7
1300 OXN 93035 552-C1
PORTAL ST
- VeCo 93022 451-B7
PORTER LN
2800 VEN 93003 491-G3
PORTHOLE CT
1100 OXN 93030 522-F7
E PORT HUENEME RD
800 PHME 93033 552-E6
800 PHME 93041 552-E6
PORTIA ST
5100 SIMI 93063 478-J7
PORTOFINO PL
- OXN 93030 522-C6
- OXN 93035 522-C6
500 THO 91360 526-D6
PORTOLA CT
- SPLA 93060 464-B4
5700 WLKV 91362 557-G6

PORTOLA LN
300 FILM 93015 456-C6
2100 THO 91361 557-A5
PORTOLA RD
700 VEN 93003 492-B4
1800 VeCo 93003 492-B5
PORTOLA WY
800 OXN 93033 552-F3
PORTSIDE PL
30500 AGRH 91301 557-G5
PORTSMOUTH CT
700 VeCo 91377 557-H1
PORTULACA PL
3900 THO 91362 557-C1
POSADA DR
- OXN 93030 523-A4
POSADA LILLIA PETALOS
23600 CMRL 93010 523-F2
POSEY LN
23600 LA 91304 529-E4
POSITA RD
8000 VeCo 93066 475-E6
POST ST
400 CMRL 93010 523-J4
400 CMRL 93010 524-A4
POTAWATOMI ST
- VEN 93001 471-B5
POTEAU DR
- VeCo 93001 471-C3
POTOMAC AV
1700 VEN 93004 492-H4
POTRERO RD
- VeCo 91361 556-A5
1000 THO 91320 555-G5
1000 VeCo 91320 555-G5
1000 THO 91361 556-H6
1500 VeCo 91361 555-G5
W POTRERO RD
1600 VeCo 93012 554-C4
3100 VeCo 93012 555-B5
3900 VeCo 91320 555-B5
3900 THO 91320 555-D4
POTTER AV
1900 SIMI 93065 498-A2
2800 THO 91360 526-H2
N POTTER AV
2000 SIMI 93065 498-A2
POWDERHORN CT
1000 VeCo 91377 528-B7
POWELL DR
1700 VEN 93004 492-H4
POWELL RD
100 VeCo 93015 457-C6
E PRADERA RD
11500 VeCo 93012 496-C7
PRADO WY
- OXN 93030 523-A4
PRAIRIE CT
3300 THO 91320 555-G6
PRAIRIE ST
22000 Chat 91311 499-J7
PRAIRIE DOG PL
1300 VEN 93003 492-F4
PRAIRIE RIDGE CT
- SIMI 93063 478-H5
PRAIRIEVIEW ST
5100 CMRL 93012 524-J2
PRANCE CT
1800 SIMI 93065 498-A6
N PRATHER ST
2500 SIMI 93065 498-B3
PRATO CT
3900 MRPK 93021 496-C5
PREAKNESS PL
700 THO 91320 555-E4
PREBLE AV
2400 VEN 93003 491-F3
PRENTISS ST
- THO 91360 526-E4
PRESIDENTIAL DR
700 SIMI 93065 497-D5
700 VeCo 93065 497-D5
PRESIDIO DR
3400 SIMI 93063 478-F5
PRESILLA PL
2100 VeCo 93010 494-D7
PRESILLA RD
7500 VeCo 93012 495-G5
10600 VeCo 93012 496-A5
PRESTBURY LN
- VeCo 91361 586-E2
PRESTON WY
300 SIMI 93065 497-D6
PRICE RD
4000 VeCo 93066 494-D3
5100 VeCo 93066 474-D7
PRICE ST
400 FILM 93015 455-J6
PRIDE ST
1200 SIMI 93065 497-H4
PRIETO ST
1400 SPLA 93060 464-C4
PRIMA CT
1400 CMRL 93010 524-D1
PRIMPTON CT
300 SIMI 93065 497-D7
PRIMROSE DR
5000 VeCo 93001 471-C1

PRIMROSE DR
5200 VeCo 93001 461-C7
PRIMROSE ST
600 THO 91360 526-D3
PRINCE AL
1900 VEN 93001 491-E3
PRINCE RD
6000 VeCo 93063 499-B3
PRINCESSA DR
23600 OXN 93030 522-J5
PRINCETON AV
- OXN 93036 522-H2
200 VEN 93003 492-A3
500 MRPK 93021 476-H6
500 MRPK 93021 496-F1
PRINCETON RD
1000 THO 91360 526-H5
PRINCETON ST
300 SPLA 93060 463-J7
PRINCEVILLE LN
2200 OXN 93036 522-E2
PRINCIPE PL
10400 VeCo 93012 495-J7
PRINGLE CT
- THO 91320 556-B1
PROMENADE
- VEN 93001 491-B3
PROMENADE ST
- SIMI 93063 498-H1
PROMONTORY PL
29400 AGRH 91301 557-J5
PROPANE RD
23600 VeCo 93015 456-F7
PROSPECT ST
- VeCo 93022 451-A7
E PROSPECT ST
- VEN 93001 491-B1
W PROSPECT ST
- VEN 93001 491-B1
PROSPECTOR PL
900 THO 91320 555-G4
PROVENCE DR
- Ago 91301 558-G3
- LACo 91302 558-G3
PROVENCE PL
3100 THO 91362 526-J2
PROVIDENCE AV
600 VEN 93004 492-H2
PROVIDENT RD
27300 AGRH 91301 558-E7
PROVO LN
800 VEN 93004 492-J2
PUCCINI RD
4900 VEN 93003 492-B7
N PUEBLO AV
100 VeCo 93023 441-E6
S PUEBLO AV
100 VeCo 93023 441-D7
PUEBLO DR
500 THO 91362 526-H7
PUEBLO ST
9500 VEN 93004 492-H2
22100 Chat 91311 499-J2
PUEBLO VISTA
6900 CMRL 93012 525-C1
PUESTA DEL SOL
600 VeCo 91360 526-C7
10500 VeCo 93022 451-B4
10900 VeCo 93023 451-B4
PULLMAN AV
2000 SIMI 93063 499-A2
PURCELL LN
1000 VEN 93003 492-A7
PURDUE AV
300 VEN 93003 492-A2
PURDUE ST
100 OXN 93036 522-H2
E PURDUE ST
14300 MRPK 93021 476-G6
PYRAMID AV
1500 VEN 93004 492-J3
PYRITE PL
2500 OXN 93030 522-D4

Q

Q ST
1500 VEN 93004 493-A2
QUAIL CT
300 SPLA 93060 464-D5
1200 FILM 93015 455-H6
QUAIL ST
700 VeCo 93023 451-C1
6400 VEN 93003 492-D5
N QUAIL CANYON RD
6000 VeCo 93066 495-C1
6200 VeCo 93066 475-D7
QUAILCREEK CT
11600 MRPK 93021 496-C3
QUAIL OAKS DR
400 OJAI 93023 441-G6
QUAIL PASS RD
300 SIMI 93065 527-D1
QUAILRIDGE DR
5300 CMRL 93012 525-A1
QUAIL RUN DR
29100 AGRH 91301 558-A5
29400 AGRH 91301 557-H5

QUAIL RUN WY
900 OXN 93036 522-F1
QUAILS TR
100 THO 91361 556-F2
QUAILSPRING CT
4200 MRPK 93021 496-B2
QUAIL SUMMIT
13200 MRPK 93021 496-E3
QUAIL VIEW CT
700 VeCo 91377 558-B1
QUAILWOOD ST
3900 MRPK 93021 496-C4
QUAINT ST
28600 AGRH 91301 558-B3
QUARTER HORSE LN
900 VeCo 91377 558-A1
QUARTERS A DR
- PHME 93041 552-E5
QUARTZ ST
- VEN 93004 492-F3
N QUARZO CIR
3200 THO 91362 527-A2
QUASAR CT
23600 SIMI 93065 497-H4
QUEENS CT
6800 MRPK 93021 476-H6
QUEENS ST
5300 VEN 93003 492-B3
QUEENS WY
2700 THO 91362 527-B3
29300 AGRH 91301 557-J4
29300 AGRH 91301 558-A4
QUEENSBURY ST
300 THO 91360 526-E5
QUEENS GARDEN CT
23600 VeCo 91361 586-F1
QUEENS GARDEN DR
- VeCo 91361 556-G7
23600 VeCo 91361 586-E1
QUEENSLAND CT
2100 THO 91360 526-B4
QUIET CT
200 SIMI 93065 497-J6
QUIET HILLS CT
8200 LA 91304 529-E3
QUILAN CT
- OXN 93035 522-C6
QUIMBY AV
7400 CanP 91307 529-G4
7600 LA 91304 529-G4
QUIMISA DR
23600 SIMI 93065 477-C7
QUINCY AV
3400 SIMI 93063 478-F6
QUINCY ST
- OXN 93033 552-J2
8100 VEN 93004 492-F2
QUINN ST
- VEN 93003 492-C3
QUINTA VISTA DR
- THO 91362 557-A2
QUITO CT
6900 CMRL 93012 525-D1
6900 CMRL 93012 495-D7

R

R ST
1500 VEN 93004 493-A2
RABBIT CREEK LN
4200 THO 91320 555-E3
RACCOON CT
7200 VEN 93003 492-F4
RACHAEL AV
3400 SIMI 93063 478-F6
RACHEL DR
1100 OXN 93030 522-E4
RACINE ST
2700 SIMI 93065 498-C1
RACQUET CLUB LN
500 THO 91360 526-D7
RADCLIFF ST
5100 VEN 93003 492-B2
RADCLIFFE RD
800 THO 91360 526-G2
RADFORD CT
2500 SIMI 93063 498-D1
RADNOR AV
1500 VEN 93004 492-G4
RAEMERE ST
2100 CMRL 93010 524-E3
RAFFERTY RD
4800 VeCo 93060 454-A7
RAFT LN
500 OXN 93035 522-D7
RAIDERS WY
1200 OXN 93033 552-J3
RAILROAD AV
800 SPLA 93060 464-B5
RAINBOW DR
10 OXN 93033 553-C3
RAINBOW CREEK CIR
3300 THO 91360 526-C2
N RAINBOW CREST DR
5500 AGRH 91301 557-G5
W RAINBOW CREST DR
29800 AGRH 91301 557-H5
RAINBOW HILL RD
5700 AGRH 91301 557-G3

RAINBOW VIEW DR
30300 AGRH 91301 557-G4
RAINCLOUD CT
3500 THO 91362 526-J1
RAINDANCE ST
300 THO 91360 526-D2
RAINEY RD
1200 VeCo 93063 499-A3
RAINFIELD AV
23600 THO 91362 527-B5
RAINIER ST
- MRPK 93021 496-D1
5400 VEN 93003 492-B1
RAINS CT
1000 OJAI 93023 441-J5
15300 MRPK 93021 476-J5
RAINTREE CT
800 THO 91361 557-A4
RAIN WOOD ST
5200 SIMI 93063 498-J2
RALEIGH PL
800 THO 91360 526-G2
RALLEY CT
2100 THO 91362 527-A2
RALPH WY
700 SPLA 93060 464-C3
RALSTON AV
2000 SIMI 93063 498-H1
RALSTON ST
4700 VEN 93003 492-D4
7300 VeCo 93003 492-E4
RAMA PL
5000 CMRL 93012 524-G3
RAMBLE RIDGE DR
100 THO 91360 526-F2
RAMBLING RD
1000 SIMI 93065 497-H6
1600 SIMI 93065 498-A6
RAMBLING ROSE DR
- CMRL 93012 495-A7
RAMELLI AV
1100 VeCo 93003 492-E4
1100 VEN 93003 492-F5
RAMELLI RANCH RD
- VeCo - 366-G8
- VeCo 93001 366-G8
23600 VeCo 93001 459-H1
RAMONA DR
1100 THO 91320 556-A1
1300 CMRL 93010 494-A6
1400 CMRL 93010 493-J6
1400 VeCo 93010 494-A6
RAMONA PL
- VeCo 93010 493-J7
- VeCo 93010 523-J1
RAMONA ST
1600 CMRL 93010 493-J7
1600 VeCo 93010 493-J7
E RAMONA ST
- VEN 93001 471-B7
- VEN 93001 491-C1
W RAMONA ST
- VEN 93001 471-B7
RAMONA CANYON RD
- VeCo 93040 458-D1
RAMROD CT
3500 THO 91320 555-F4
RAMSGATE CIR
1800 THO 91360 526-C5
N RAMUDA LN
- VeCo 91307 529-A5
RANCH RD
- VeCo 93001 461-A4
12400 VeCo 93060 473-C2
23600 VeCo 93001 366-G9
23600 VeCo 93001 459-D4
23600 VeCo 93023 450-J2
RANCH CREEK CT
23600 SIMI 93065 497-G7
RANCHERO PL
- OXN 93030 522-J3
E RANCHERO RD
- VeCo 91307 528-J4
RANCHGROVE DR
2400 WLKV 91361 586-J1
RANCH HOUSE RD
900 THO 91361 557-A5
RANCHITA LN
4100 OXN 93033 553-C4
RANCHO CT
1100 VeCo 93023 441-F6
RANCHO DR
100 OJAI 93023 441-E7
100 OJAI 93023 441-F6
200 VEN 93003 491-G4
S RANCHO DR
100 OJAI 93023 441-E7
100 VeCo 93023 441-E7
300 OJAI 93023 451-E1
300 VeCo 93023 451-E1
RANCHO LN
- THO 91362 526-J7
1300 THO 91362 556-H1
RANCHO RD
- THO 91362 556-H1
300 THO 91362 526-H7
23600 THO 91361 556-H1
23600 VeCo 93012 524-H7

S RANCHO RD
- THO 91361 556-H2
RANCHO ADOLFO CT
100 CMRL 93012 524-H2
RANCHO ADOLFO DR
- CMRL 93012 524-H2
RANCHO CALLEGUAS DR
100 CMRL 93012 524-H3
RANCHO CONEJO BLVD
600 THO 91320 525-H5
1000 THO 91320 526-A6
23600 THO 91320 555-H1
RANCHO DOS RIOS
23600 VeCo 93023 451-F3
RANCHO DOS VIENTOS DR
1000 THO 91320 555-A3
RANCHO FILOSO
400 VeCo 93060 463-H5
RANCHO LA VISTA RD
1500 VeCo 93023 451-E2
RANCHO VISTA CT
13300 VeCo 93012 496-E6
RANCHO VISTA LN
500 VeCo 93060 472-J5
RANCH VIEW PL
600 THO 91362 557-A1
700 THO 91362 527-A7
RANCHWOOD ST
3200 THO 91320 555-G4
RAND ST
6400 MRPK 93021 476-J6
RANDI AV
6200 WdHl 91367 529-J7
6400 CanP 91303 529-J7
RANDIWOOD LN
6600 LACo 91307 529-C6
RANDY DR
500 VeCo 91320 525-G7
500 VeCo 91320 555-G1
RANGELY CT
200 SIMI 93065 497-F6
RANGER CT
3000 THO 91360 526-D2
RANGE VIEW CIR
- MRPK 93021 476-F5
RANGEWOOD CT
- MRPK 93021 476-E6
RANSOM RD
13800 MRPK 93021 496-F4
RASPBERRY PL
100 OXN 93036 522-G1
RATEL PL
7000 VEN 93003 492-E4
RATTLESNAKE RD
- LACo 90265 586-G7
RAVELLO CT
- THO 91362 527-C3
RAVEN AV
1300 VEN 93003 492-C4
RAVEN LN
4000 OXN 93033 553-B5
RAVENCREST CT
200 THO 91320 555-G2
RAVENNA ST
2100 SIMI 93065 498-C2
RAVENSBURY ST
500 VeCo 91361 556-G6
RAVENS POINT CT
23600 SIMI 93065 498-C5
RAVENWOOD AV
800 THO 91320 555-E4
RAVOLI DR
2000 OXN 93035 552-B1
RAWHIDE PL
900 THO 91320 555-G5
RAWLS RD
- MRPK 93021 476-B5
RAYBURN ST
1800 THO 91362 527-D5
RAYEN ST
22000 LA 91304 529-J1
23900 WHil 91304 529-E1
RAYLENE CT
6200 SIMI 93063 499-C2
RAYMOND ST
200 OJAI 93023 441-G6
23200 Chat 91311 499-F7
E RAYMOND ST
500 VeCo 93022 451-C6
RAYSHIRE ST
1900 THO 91362 526-J7
1900 THO 91362 527-A7
RAYTHEON RD
4100 VeCo 93033 553-F6
REA WY
200 VEN 93001 491-A1
READ RD
4900 THO 93021 496-J6
4900 THO 93021 497-A6
4900 VeCo 93021 496-J6
4900 VeCo 93021 497-A5
13100 VeCo 93012 496-G5
13100 THO 93012 496-G5
READING DR
4400 OXN 93033 553-A5
READING ST
- FILM 93015 455-J7

REAGAN CT
100 VEN 93003 492-E1
REAL CANYON RD
700 VeCo 93040 457-E3
REATA AV
- VEN 93004 473-A6
REBECCA RD
- SIMI 93063 479-C7
REBECCA ST
2000 SIMI 93063 498-F2
REBURTA LN
3500 SIMI 93063 478-E7
RECODO WY
5800 CMRL 93012 525-B1
RED BARN RD
11000 VeCo 93012 496-A7
RED BIRD CT
- MRPK 93021 476-E6
RED BLUFF CT
3400 SIMI 93063 479-A6
RED BLUFF DR
26000 CALB 91302 558-J4
REDCOAT LN
4200 WLKV 91361 557-F6
REDDINGTON CT
100 CMRL 93010 524-D1
100 CMRL 93010 494-D7
REDFIELD AV
- THO 91320 555-H1
RED HAWK CT
- SIMI 93063 478-G5
RED HILL RD
500 OJAI 93023 441-J5
RED LAKES PL
600 SIMI 93065 497-C5
REDMAN CT
2000 SIMI 93063 498-J2
REDMESA DR
10900 Chat 91311 499-J2
RED MOUNTAIN EAST FIRE RD
23600 VeCo 93001 460-G6
RED MOUNTAIN FIRE RD
23600 VeCo 93001 460-B2
RED OAK AV
100 THO 91320 556-D2
RED OAK PL
1000 CMRL 93010 524-C2
REDONDO AV
2700 VeCo 93012 496-C6
REDONDO CIR
2700 VeCo 93012 496-C7
REDONDO ST
7600 VEN 93004 492-E1
RED PINE DR
23600 SIMI 93065 498-D4
RED ROBIN PL
- THO 91320 526-A5
RED ROCK AV
- VEN 93004 492-J3
RED ROCK CT
5100 THO 91362 527-F6
RED SAIL CIR
1300 THO 91361 557-B6
REDWING LN
1200 OXN 93036 522-E1
REDWOOD AV
- VEN 93003 491-J3
REDWOOD CIR
- VEN 93003 491-J3
1500 THO 91360 526-H3
REDWOOD DR
1000 VeCo 93063 499-C4
REDWOOD LN
100 SPLA 93060 464-A5
REDWOOD ST
200 OXN 93033 552-E2
1500 OXN 93043 552-E2
REED WY
400 PHME 93041 552-D2
REEDER AV
4100 OXN 93033 553-B5
REEDLEY ST
14700 MRPK 93021 476-H6
REEF CIR
600 PHME 93041 552-F7
REEF ST
2900 VEN 93001 491-F5
REEF WY
5100 OXN 93035 521-J7
11800 VeCo 90265 625-F5
REEVES RD
3200 VeCo 93023 442-G6
REFLECTIONS LN
- SIMI 93065 478-B4
REFSING DR
3800 OXN 93033 552-G4
REFSING PL
4700 OXN 93033 552-G5
REGAL AV
100 THO 91320 555-J2
REGAL OAK CT
100 THO 91320 556-A2
REGAN CIR
1700 SIMI 93065 498-A3
REGATTA PL
3300 OXN 93035 522-C7

STREET Block City ZIP Pg-Grid

REGENT AV
3200 THO 91360 526-F2
REGENT CT
700 SPLA 93060 464-A4
REGENT ST
1500 CMRL 93010 524-D2
REGENTS CT
4400 WLKV 91361 557-D6
REGINA AV
2700 THO 91360 526-E3
REGIS AV
200 VEN 93003 492-C1
REGULUS DR
- VeCo 93041 583-G1
REIMER PETIT RD
1600 VeCo 93060 465-C5
REINA CIR
- OXN 93030 523-B4
REINHARDT AV
- VEN 93003 492-C3
N REINO RD
- THO 91320 555-F1
400 THO 91320 525-F7
S REINO RD
- THO 91320 555-F3
REMINGTON AV
600 VEN 93003 492-D3
REMINGTON PL
800 THO 91320 555-G4
REMONT CIR
1600 VeCo 91377 527-H6
RENAISSANCE PL
- WLKV 91362 557-G6
RENATA CT
2500 THO 91362 527-C4
RENE ST
3400 VeCo 93036 493-A7
RENEE CT
- SIMI 93065 478-B6
RENEE DR
28100 AGRH 91301 558-C7
REPOSO DR
- VeCo 93022 451-C4
RESEDA CT
3500 CMRL 93010 494-G7
RESERVOIR DR
2600 SIMI 93065 478-C7
2600 SIMI 93065 498-C1
2800 SIMI 93063 478-C7
3000 VeCo 93063 478-C7
3000 VeCo 93065 478-C7
RESPLANDOR WY
- OXN 93030 522-H4
RESTFUL CT
1700 SIMI 93065 497-J6
1700 SIMI 93065 498-A6
RETIRO CT
900 VeCo 93010 494-B5
REVELLO ST
4000 MRPK 93021 496-C3
REVERE AV
- VEN 93004 472-H6
REX ST
200 VEN 93001 491-B1
REXFORD PL
1100 THO 91360 526-F6
REXFORD ST
3400 VEN 93003 491-H4
REYES ST
- MRPK 93021 496-D1
REYES ADOBE RD
4900 AGRH 91301 557-G3
REYNOLDS CT
1300 THO 91362 526-H7
RHAME TER
100 SPLA 93060 464-A5
RHAPSODY DR
4800 VeCo 91377 557-G2
RHEINLAND CT
23600 SIMI 93065 498-A5
RHODA ST
2000 SIMI 93065 498-A3
RHODES CT
200 FILM 93015 455-H6
RHONA CT
5300 AGRH 91301 557-H5
RHONDA AV
1900 OXN 93036 522-E3
RHONDA ST
2000 OXN 93036 522-E3
RHONE ST
- VEN 93004 492-J3
RIALTO ST
700 OXN 93035 522-E7
1400 OXN 93035 552-E1
RIATA CT
2400 VeCo 93012 496-D6
RIAVE CT
2400 CMRL 93012 495-B6
RIBERA DR
- OXN 93030 522-J4
- OXN 93030 523-A4
RIBERA WY
- OXN 93030 523-A4
N RICE AV
200 OXN 93030 523-B5
1900 OXN 93036 523-B5
23600 OXN 93033 523-B5

S RICE AV
- OXN 93033 553-B3
100 OXN 93030 523-B7
900 VeCo 93030 523-B7
900 VeCo 93033 523-B7
1500 VeCo 93033 553-B3
RICE CT
100 THO 91362 556-J1
4500 VEN 93003 492-A2
RICE RD
- VeCo 93023 441-C2
N RICE RD
100 VeCo 93023 441-D5
S RICE RD
100 VeCo 93023 441-C7
600 VeCo 93023 451-C2
RICE ST
5300 VeCo 93066 495-A5
RICE CANYON RD
- VeCo 93023 441-B5
RICHARD RD
400 SPLA 93060 463-H6
RICHARDS AV
1000 VEN 93004 492-J2
RICHARDSON AV
900 SIMI 93065 497-G5
RICHARDSON CANYON RD
- VeCo 93066 464-D7
- VeCo 93066 474-E1
RICHFORD LN
400 VeCo 93022 451-A7
RICHGROVE CT
31900 WLKV 91361 557-C6
RICHMOND AV
500 OXN 93030 522-H7
RICHMOND CT
600 SPLA 93060 464-C4
25900 LACo 91302 558-J3
RICHMOND RD
1100 SPLA 93060 464-B4
RICKEY CT
3100 THO 91362 527-A2
RIDDEN ST
3400 CMRL 93010 494-G7
RIDGE DR
12200 VeCo 93012 496-D6
RIDGEBROOK DR
5700 AGRH 91301 557-H4
RIDGEBROOK PL
2100 THO 91362 527-A3
RIDGECREST CT
6900 VEN 93003 472-D7
RIDGE CREST DR
500 SPLA 93060 463-H6
RIDGECREST DR
- MRPK 93021 476-F6
RIDGECREST LN
6500 VeCo 93066 475-A6
RIDGECREST PL
900 THO 91362 527-C7
RIDGEFORD DR
3200 WLKV 91361 557-D7
RIDGEGATE LN
1700 SIMI 93065 497-E2
RIDGE LINE DR
400 VeCo 93022 451-C6
RIDGEMARK CT
- MRPK 93021 476-D6
RIDGEMARK DR
- MRPK 93021 476-D6
RIDGEMONT CT
300 THO 91320 555-E2
RIDGEMOOR DR
5200 VeCo 93021 475-H7
5200 VeCo 93021 495-J1
RIDGETON LN
900 SIMI 93065 497-E6
RIDGE VIEW CT
2400 SIMI 93065 497-H1
RIDGE VIEW DR
2200 SIMI 93065 497-E2
RIDGE VIEW ST
4200 CMRL 93012 524-H4
5200 CMRL 93012 525-A5
RIDGEWAY CT
4800 THO 91362 557-F1
RIDGEWAY DR
29500 AGRH 91301 557-J3
RIDGEWAY PL
- VEN 93004 472-H6
RIDGEWOOD DR
1600 CMRL 93012 525-A1
1700 CMRL 93012 495-A7
RIDLEY CIR
900 SIMI 93065 498-C5
RIENTE ST
900 VeCo 93010 494-B5
RIESS RD
900 VeCo 93063 499-B4
RIFLEMAN RD
- VeCo 93021 475-J4
RIGEL DR
- VeCo 93041 583-H2
RIGGER RD
30500 AGRH 91301 557-G5
RIGGING PL
1100 OXN 93030 522-F7

RIKKARD DR
2400 THO 91362 527-A2
RILEY LN
500 VEN 93003 492-D1
RIM CREST CIR
2300 THO 91361 557-B4
RIM CREST DR
2200 THO 91361 557-B4
RIMROCK RD
200 VeCo 91361 556-G2
RINCON CT
300 SPLA 93060 463-J6
RINCON DR
- VeCo 93012 554-E3
RINCON RD Rt#-150
6600 StBC 93013 459-A1
23600 VeCo 93001 366-G9
23600 VeCo 93001 459-A1
RINCON ST
100 OJAI 93023 441-H6
100 VEN 93001 491-E2
1200 SIMI 93065 498-B4
RINCON WY
400 OXN 93033 552-G3
RINCON BEACH PARK DR
- VeCo 93001 459-G7
- VeCo 93001 469-G1
RING CIR
3200 SIMI 93063 478-D7
RINGO AV
- VEN 93003 492-C3
RINGWOOD ST
2700 SIMI 93063 478-H7
E RINGWOOD ST
4900 SIMI 93063 478-H7
RIO BRAVO CT
- MRPK 93021 496-G2
RIODOSA TR
5500 VeCo 91377 557-J1
RIO GRANDE CIR
500 THO 91360 526-D3
RIO GRANDE ST
- FILM 93015 455-J7
- VEN 93004 492-J4
RIO GRANDE WY
- OXN 93036 492-H5
RIO HATO CT
3500 CMRL 93010 494-G7
RIO LINDO ST
400 OXN 93036 522-H2
S RIOPELLE CT
900 THO 91320 555-F4
RIO SCHOOL LN
- VeCo 93036 522-H1
RIO VIA
200 VeCo 93022 451-B6
RIO VISTA CT
1300 SIMI 93065 497-H1
RIPLEY ST
- CMRL 93010 524-A2
RIPLEY WY
1700 OXN 93033 552-J3
RIPPLE DR
900 OXN 93035 522-C7
RIPPLE CREEK LN
13000 VeCo 93012 496-F5
RISING STAR AV
- SIMI 93063 479-A6
RISTA DR
5700 AGRH 91301 557-J4
RIVA CT
3900 MRPK 93021 496-C4
RIVAS LN
1100 OXN 93035 522-E7
RIVENDELL CIR
1800 THO 91320 556-A2
RIVER DR
2700 SIMI 93065 498-C3
RIVER ST
200 FILM 93015 456-A6
500 VeCo 93040 457-F4
700 FILM 93015 455-G7
RIVERA ST
800 SIMI 93065 497-G4
RIVERBIRCH DR
2000 SIMI 93063 498-J2
RIVERDALE CT
- CMRL 93012 524-G4
RIVER FARM DR
3700 WLKV 91361 557-C7
RIVERFIELD CT
200 SIMI 93065 497-F6
RIVERGLEN ST
4200 MRPK 93021 496-D3
RIVERGROVE CT
11900 MRPK 93021 496-C3
RIVERGROVE ST
12100 MRPK 93021 496-D3
RIVER HILLS CT
500 SIMI 93065 497-G6
RIVERMORE ST
3400 CMRL 93010 494-G7
RIVERPARK BLVD
- OXN 93036 492-H7
- OXN 93036 522-G1
RIVER RIDGE RD
2200 OXN 93036 522-E2

RIVERROCK CIR
400 THO 91362 557-G1
RIVERRUN LN
13200 VeCo 93012 496-E4
RIVERSIDE AV
700 VeCo 93015 465-H2
700 VeCo 93015 466-A2
RIVERSIDE RD
- VeCo 93022 451-A6
RIVERSIDE ST
700 VEN 93001 471-B7
RIVERSTONE LN
600 VeCo 91377 527-G7
RIVER WOOD CT
23600 SIMI 93063 499-B3
RIVIERA CT
- OXN 93035 522-C6
RIVOL RD
7000 CanP 91307 529-D5
ROADRUNNER AV
- THO 91320 525-J5
- THO 91320 526-A5
ROADRUNNER DR
6800 VEN 93003 492-E4
ROADRUNNER PL
- THO 91320 525-J5
ROADSIDE DR
28300 AGRH 91301 558-A6
29300 AGRH 91301 557-J6
ROAN ST
1400 SIMI 93065 497-J3
ROB CT
2800 THO 91362 527-A3
ROBBINS CT
- SIMI 93065 497-E3
ROBERT AV
100 OXN 93033 552-G3
W ROBERT AV
200 OXN 93030 522-F4
ROBERTA CT
- SIMI 93065 498-C4
ROBERTS AV
200 MRPK 93021 496-E1
ROBERT S HOLLAND DR
- THO 91361 556-G2
ROBERTSON RD
23600 VeCo 93063 499-D4
ROBERTSON WY
- THO 91320 556-B1
ROBIN AV
1100 VEN 93003 492-D4
1100 VEN 93009 492-D4
2100 OXN 93033 553-A4
ROBIN CT
400 FILM 93015 455-H6
ROBIN ST
1100 OJAI 93023 442-A6
ROBIN HILL ST
3500 THO 91360 526-G2
ROBINWOOD LN
4300 MRPK 93021 496-F3
ROBLE LN
23600 OXN 93036 522-H3
ROBLES LN
5300 AGRH 91301 557-H5
ROBYN WY
1100 CMRL 93010 524-C3
ROCA AV
2600 THO 91360 526-C3
ROCA RD
23600 VeCo 93063 528-H2
ROCHELLE PL
2600 SIMI 93063 478-D7
2600 SIMI 93063 498-D1
ROCHESTER CT
600 VEN 93004 492-H1
ROCK ST
2700 SIMI 93065 498-C3
ROCKAWAY RD
3900 VeCo 93001 471-C3
ROCK CASTLE CT
5300 VeCo 91377 527-G6
ROCK CREEK RD
5600 AGRH 91301 558-A4
N ROCKDALE AV
2000 SIMI 93063 499-B1
ROCKEDGE DR
300 VeCo 91377 558-A1
ROCKET ST
- VeCo 93042 583-D4
ROCKETDYNE RD
23700 LA 91304 499-D7
23900 WHil 91304 499-D7
24900 VeCo 93063 499-B7
ROCKFIELD ST
4800 THO 91362 557-G1
4900 VeCo 91362 557-G1
5000 VeCo 91377 557-H1
ROCKFORD CT
4700 VEN 93003 492-A2
ROCKGATE PL
3000 SIMI 93063 478-E7
ROCKHILL DR
23500 Chat 91311 499-F7
ROCKINGHAM DR
1300 SIMI 93063 499-C4
ROCKING HORSE DR
1700 SIMI 93065 497-J6
1700 SIMI 93065 498-A7

ROCKLITE RD
- VEN 93001 471-C6
- VeCo 93001 471-C6
ROCKLYN ST
2000 CMRL 93010 524-E1
ROCKMAN WY
400 PHME 93041 552-D2
ROCKRIDGE PL
2800 THO 91360 526-E3
ROCKRIDGE TER
7100 CanP 91307 529-E5
ROCKROSE LN
100 VeCo 91377 557-J2
ROCK SPRING ST
- THO 91320 526-A6
ROCK TREE DR
5500 AGRH 91301 558-A5
ROCK VISTA DR
29000 AGRH 91301 558-A5
ROCKY RD
1200 VeCo 93063 499-D4
ROCKY HIGH RD
- VeCo 93012 526-A1
ROCKY MESA PL
9200 WHil 91304 499-D7
ROCKY MOUNTAIN
- VeCo 93001 461-B6
ROCKY MOUNTAIN DR
- OXN 93036 492-H7
ROCKY PEAK FIRE RD
- Chat 91311 479-E3
- StvR 91381 479-E3
15900 SIMI 93063 499-F1
23600 VeCo 93063 479-D4
23600 VeCo 93063 499-F1
ROCKY POINT CT
2600 THO 91362 527-D3
ROCKYRIVER CT
1600 SIMI 93063 498-E3
ROCKYRIVER ST
3700 SIMI 93063 498-E3
ROCKY TOP CIR
- MRPK 93021 476-F5
ROD AV
6000 WdHl 91367 529-C7
RODAX ST
22700 LA 91304 529-H2
RODENE ST
- THO 91320 555-E3
RODEO CT
2000 THO 91362 556-H2
RODEO DR
200 VeCo 93022 451-C5
W RODERICK AV
- OXN 93030 522-F4
RODGERS ST
200 VEN 93003 492-B3
RODNEY ST
2600 THO 91320 525-H7
ROGER RD
800 SPLA 93060 464-C3
12400 VeCo 93060 473-E6
ROGUE RIVER CIR
1800 VEN 93004 492-G4
ROHDEA WY
- OXN 93030 523-A4
ROHNER AV
2000 SIMI 93063 499-C2
ROHNER CT
2200 SIMI 93063 499-C1
ROIA LN
- OXN 93036 492-H7
ROLAND WY
5400 OXN 93033 552-F6
ROLDAN AV
1100 SIMI 93065 498-A4
ROLLING KNOLL RD
4400 MRPK 93021 496-F3
ROLLING MEADOWS CT
- THO 91320 526-B7
ROLLING OAKS DR
100 THO 91361 556-F2
500 VeCo 91361 556-G2
ROLLING RIDGE DR
29900 AGRH 91301 557-H4
ROLLING RIVER LN
- SIMI 93063 498-G2
ROLLINGS AV
2800 THO 91360 526-H2
ROLLINS RD
9300 Chat 91311 499-F6
ROMAN AV
1700 CMRL 93010 494-G7
1700 CMRL 93010 524-G1
ROMANO DR
800 VeCo 93023 451-C1
ROMANY DR
4000 OXN 93035 552-B2
ROMAR ST
22000 Chat 91311 499-J4
ROMBERG LN
800 VEN 93003 492-B7
ROMERO PL
- CMRL 93012 494-H7
RONALD REAGAN FRWY Rt#-118
- Chat - 499-E2
- MRPK - 476-H7
- MRPK - 477-B6

RONALD REAGAN FRWY Rt#-118
- MRPK - 496-G1
- SIMI - 477-B6
- SIMI - 497-G1
- SIMI - 498-F1
- SIMI - 499-E2
- VeCo - 477-B6
RONDELL ST
4100 AGRH 91301 558-E7
RONEL CT
400 THO 91320 556-C1
ROOSEVELT AV
100 OXN 93030 522-H6
200 VEN 93003 492-E1
N ROOSEVELT AV
100 OXN 93030 522-H5
ROOSEVELT BLVD
2300 VeCo 93035 552-B5
ROOSEVELT CT
- SIMI 93065 497-D5
- VEN 93003 492-E1
RORY LN
1600 SIMI 93063 499-B2
RORY WY
5900 SIMI 93063 499-B3
ROSA LN
100 THO 91320 555-H2
W ROSA ST
200 OXN 93033 552-G5
ROSADA CT
900 VeCo 93010 494-B5
ROSAL LN
10900 VeCo 93004 493-B1
ROSALIE ST
3500 SIMI 93063 498-D2
ROSALINDA DR
23600 OXN 93030 522-J5
ROSARIO CT
500 THO 91362 526-H7
ROSARIO DR
400 THO 91362 526-H7
ROSCOE BLVD
22000 LA 91304 529-D2
24000 WHil 91304 529-D2
ROSE AV
2900 VeCo 93036 523-A1
3300 VeCo 93036 493-C5
N ROSE AV
100 OXN 93030 522-J4
1900 OXN 93036 522-J4
2600 OXN 93036 523-A2
2600 VeCo 93036 523-A2
S ROSE AV
100 OXN 93030 522-J7
500 VeCo 93030 522-J7
1100 OXN 93033 522-J7
1100 VeCo 93033 522-J7
ROSE CIR
- VEN 93004 493-A2
ROSE LN
2300 VeCo 93012 496-B7
ROSE ST
1200 VeCo 93063 499-B4
E ROSE ST
200 OXN 93033 552-G5
ROSE ARBOR LN
- SIMI 93065 497-H3
ROSEBAY ST
2000 THO 91361 557-A5
ROSEBUD DR
500 OXN 93036 522-F1
ROSECRANS ST
2100 SIMI 93065 498-A4
ROSECREEK DR
11400 MRPK 93021 496-B3
ROSEDALE CT
13100 VeCo 93012 496-E6
ROSE GARDEN CIR
- THO 91361 556-H5
ROSEHEDGE LN
200 VeCo 91377 557-J2
ROSEHILL CIR
3200 THO 91360 526-F2
ROSELAND AV
8200 VeCo 93021 476-E2
ROSELAWN AV
1300 THO 91362 527-A6
ROSEMARY ST
2100 SIMI 93065 498-A4
ROSEMONT CT
- VeCo 91361 556-F6
4700 VEN 93003 492-A2
ROSETTA WY
- CMRL 93012 524-H1
ROSETTE ST
2700 SIMI 93065 498-C5
ROSETTI LN
500 VEN 93003 492-D1
ROSE VALLEY RD
- VeCo - 366-K5
ROSE VISTA TER
- CMRL 93012 495-A7
ROSEWATER PL
23600 OXN 93035 522-C7
ROSEWOOD AV
100 CMRL 93010 524-C3
ROSEWOOD CT
1800 OXN 93030 522-F3

ROSEWOOD CT
1900 THO 91362 526-J3
1900 THO 91362 527-A3
ROSEWOOD DR
900 OXN 93030 522-F3
ROSEWOOD ST
200 VEN 93001 471-B7
ROSITA DR
1500 SIMI 93065 497-F3
ROSITA RD
8900 VeCo 93012 495-G7
10600 VeCo 93012 496-A7
ROSS CIR
1700 SIMI 93065 498-C3
ROSSINI LN
4600 VEN 93003 492-A4
ROSSMORE DR
200 VeCo 93035 552-B5
ROSWELL CT
700 VEN 93004 492-G2
ROSWELL ST
8300 VEN 93004 492-G3
ROTELLA ST
1000 THO 91320 555-F4
ROTH CT
2600 THO 91320 525-H6
ROTHKO LN
6000 SIMI 93063 499-B1
ROULETTE CIR
1700 THO 91362 526-J2
ROUNDHOUSE RD
- PHME 93043 552-D2
ROUND MOUNTAIN RD
- VeCo 93012 554-D4
ROUNDTREE PL
4800 THO 91362 557-F1
ROUNDUP CIR
3000 THO 91360 526-C2
N ROUNDUP RD
- VeCo 91307 528-J5
- VeCo 91307 529-A5
ROUSSEAU ST
- PHME 93041 552-E4
ROWELL AV
9200 Chat 91311 499-F6
9200 Chat 91311 499-F7
ROWLAND AV
2100 SIMI 93063 498-G1
E ROWLAND AV
1600 CMRL 93010 524-D1
N ROWLAND AV
300 CMRL 93010 524-E2
ROXBURY PL
1100 THO 91360 526-F6
ROXBURY ST
4100 SIMI 93063 478-F5
ROXY ST
2400 SIMI 93065 478-B7
ROYAL AV
- SIMI 93065 497-G3
1600 SIMI 93065 498-D3
3200 SIMI 93063 498-E3
ROYAL GLEN RD
3900 WLKV 91361 557-C6
ROYAL HILLS CT
23600 SIMI 93065 478-B7
ROYAL LONDON CT
23600 VeCo 91361 556-F5
ROYAL OAK PL
1100 SPLA 93060 464-B3
ROYAL OAKS DR
3000 THO 91362 557-A3
ROYAL RIDGE CT
5000 THO 91362 527-F6
ROYAL SAINT GEORGE DR
1600 THO 91362 527-D6
ROYAL VISTA CT
5000 THO 91362 557-E1
ROYCE CT
1400 CMRL 93010 524-D1
ROYCETON CT
32000 WLKV 91361 557-C6
ROYER AV
6200 WdHl 91367 529-G7
6400 CanP 91307 529-G5
7500 LA 91304 529-G2
ROYMOR DR
26100 CALB 91302 558-H4
RUBENS PL
600 OXN 93033 552-H4
RUBICON AV
1100 VEN 93004 492-J2
RUBICON CT
10000 VEN 93004 492-J2
RUBIO AV
100 CMRL 93010 524-D4
RUBIO CIR
- OXN 93030 522-J4
RUBY AV
800 VEN 93004 492-F3
RUBY DR
200 THO 91320 525-H6
2500 OXN 93030 522-D4
RUDDER AV
2500 PHME 93041 552-C2
RUDMAN DR
600 VeCo 91320 525-G7

RUDNICK AV
6600 CanP 91303 529-J6
7600 LA 91304 529-J1
9500 Chat 91311 499-J5
RUDOLPH DR
300 VeCo 91320 556-B3
23600 SIMI 93065 498-B5
RUGBY AV
1100 VEN 93004 492-G3
RUGBY CIR
1500 THO 91360 526-F5
RUGBY RD
1100 VeCo 93023 442-F5
RUNKLE FIRE RD
23600 SIMI 93063 528-E1
23600 VeCo 93063 528-E1
RUNKLE HAUL RD
- SIMI 93063 498-D7
RUNNING CREEK CT
- SIMI 93065 497-G6
RUNNING TRAILS AV
3200 SIMI 93063 478-J6
RUNNYMEDE ST
22000 CanP 91303 529-J4
22700 CanP 91307 529-G4
RUNWAY ST
4400 SIMI 93063 498-G3
RUSCHIA WY
- OXN 93030 523-A4
RUSH CIR
2000 THO 91362 526-J6
2000 THO 91362 527-A6
RUSH HAVEN WY
1700 SIMI 93065 497-F3
RUSHING CREEK PL
500 THO 91360 526-G1
RUSHMORE ST
5400 VEN 93003 472-B7
RUSKIN AV
2100 THO 91360 526-G4
RUSS CT
3800 SIMI 93063 478-E6
RUSSELL CT
6800 VEN 93003 492-E3
RUSSELL RANCH RD
31300 WLKV 91362 557-E5
RUSSEL TEMPLE RD
300 VeCo 93060 455-B6
RUSSETWOOD LN
23600 SIMI 93065 497-A2
RUSTIC GLEN DR
2700 THO 91362 526-J3
RUSTIC HILLS DR
23600 SIMI 93065 527-F1
RUSTIC OAK DR
31500 WLKV 91361 557-D6
RUSTIC PARK CT
2100 THO 91362 527-A4
RUSTIC VIEW CT
4200 MRPK 93021 496-B2
RUSTLING HEIGHTS CT
- SIMI 93065 497-G7
RUSTLING OAKS DR
5900 AGRH 91301 558-A3
E RUTGER CIR
14400 MRPK 93021 476-G6
RUTGERS CT
700 THO 91360 526-G5
RUTGERS DR
1800 THO 91360 526-G5
RUTH AV
200 MRPK 93021 496-E1
RUTH DR
600 VeCo 91320 525-G7
RUTHERFORD HILL DR
- LA 91304 529-D4
RUTHWOOD DR
5400 CALB 91302 558-H3
RUTLAND PL
2300 THO 91362 527-A2
RYDER CUP DR
1600 THO 91362 527-D6
RYE CT
- THO 91362 557-A1
RYNERSON CT
2600 SIMI 93065 478-B7

S

S ST
1500 VEN 93004 493-A2
S & D RD
- VeCo 93015 455-G5
S S & J RD
23600 VeCo 93015 456-J7
S & J RANCH RD
23600 VeCo 93015 456-J5
23600 VeCo 93015 457-A5
SABET CT
1800 CMRL 93010 494-G7
SABINA CIR
1500 SIMI 93063 499-A3
SABINA ST
8900 VEN 93004 492-H4
SABLE ST
7500 VEN 93003 492-F5
SABLE RIDGE CT
- SIMI 93063 478-H5

SABRA AV
- VeCo 91377 558-A2
SABRINA ST
1300 OXN 93036 522-J3
SACRAMENTO DR
300 VEN 93004 472-H6
SACRAMENTO ST
- VeCo 93040 457-F4
SADDLE AV
2600 OXN 93036 522-G1
2600 OXN 93036 492-G7
SADDLE LN
200 OJAI 93023 441-J7
200 OJAI 93023 451-H1
SADDLE TR
200 VeCo 91361 556-G2
SADDLEBACK CIR
1100 CMRL 93012 525-B2
SADDLEBACK CT
3000 THO 91360 526-C2
SADDLEBACK DR
- MRPK 93021 476-F5
SADDLEBACK TR
1100 CMRL 93012 525-B1
SADDLEBACK WY
2500 CMRL 93012 525-B1
N SADDLEBOW RD
- VeCo 91307 528-G3
SADDLEBROOK DR
29000 AGRH 91301 558-A4
SADDLE CREST LN
4200 WLKV 91361 557-E6
SADDLEHORN PL
900 THO 91320 555-G5
SADDLE MOUNTAIN DR
32300 WLKV 91361 557-C7
SADDLERIDGE CT
12600 VeCo 93012 496-D6
SADDLERIDGE LN
- CALB 91302 558-H4
SADDLE TREE DR
31500 WLKV 91361 557-D7
SADRING AV
7800 LA 91304 529-F3
SAFED RD
- SIMI 93063 479-B7
- SIMI 93063 499-B1
SAFFRON CIR
3000 THO 91360 526-H2
SAGAMORE LN
1200 VEN 93001 491-E5
E SAGE LN
- VeCo 91307 528-J3
- VeCo 91307 529-A4
SAGE ST
11300 VEN 93004 473-A6
23600 SIMI 93065 497-F7
SAGEBROOK RD
- Chat 91311 499-J3
SAGEBRUSH AV
- Chat 91311 499-H6
SAGEBRUSH PL
800 THO 91320 555-G5
SAGEWOOD DR
11500 MRPK 93021 496-C3
SAILBOAT CIR
5300 AGRH 91301 557-G6
SAILFISH WY
2600 OXN 93035 552-A2
SAILOR AV
2700 VEN 93001 491-F5
SAILVIEW LN
32100 WLKV 91361 557-C6
SAILWIND CT
- SIMI 93065 497-E6
SAINT ANDREWS CT
1900 OXN 93036 522-D3
SAINT ANDREWS PL
1700 THO 91362 527-E5
SAINT CHARLES CT
- THO 91320 556-B1
SAINT CHARLES DR
200 THO 91360 526-E7
SAINT CHARLES PL
2100 THO 91360 526-E7
SAINT CLAIR AV
2100 SIMI 93063 499-B2
E SAINT CLAIR CT
2200 SIMI 93063 499-B2
SAINT CLAIR ST
10100 VEN 93004 493-A2
SAINT CROIX AV
1800 VEN 93004 492-G4
SAINT CROIX CT
4800 VeCo 91377 557-G2
SAINT EDENS CIR
24200 CanP 91307 529-D5
SAINT JAMES CT
- THO 91320 556-B1
SAINT JEAN CT
30800 WLKV 91362 557-F5
SAINT JOHN CT
- THO 91320 556-B1
SAINT LAURENT DR
5800 AGRH 91301 557-G3
SAINT MARYS DR
100 OXN 93036 522-H2
SAINT PAULS DR
- VEN 93003 491-H2

SAINT STEPHEN CT
- THO 91320 556-B1
SAINT THOMAS DR
100 VeCo 93023 441-E7
4800 VeCo 91377 557-G2
SAINT VINCENT DR
300 VeCo 91377 557-G2
SAIPAN
- PHME 93041 552-E5
SALAS ST
500 SPLA 93060 463-J6
SALE AV
6100 WdHl 91367 529-H7
6400 CanP 91307 529-H4
7600 LA 91304 529-H2
SALEM AV
300 VeCo 93036 492-J7
700 VeCo 93036 493-A7
700 VeCo 93036 523-A1
SALERNO DR
5500 WLKV 91362 557-F5
SALINAS CT
5400 SIMI 93063 498-J1
5400 SIMI 93063 499-A1
SALISBURY RD
7000 CanP 91307 529-D5
SALLY ST
2300 SIMI 93065 478-B7
SALMON RIVER CIR
3400 THO 91362 557-C2
SALSA ST
- PHME 93043 552-D3
SALT CANYON RD
- Nwhl 91382 458-J7
SALT CREEK AV
- SIMI 93063 478-H5
SALT CREEK RD
23600 Nwhl 91382 458-J6
23600 VeCo 93040 458-J6
SALTINO WY
4800 VeCo 91377 557-G2
SALT MARSH RD
- VeCo 93060 453-E5
SALT RIVER AV
- VEN 93004 492-J3
SALVADOR DR
- OXN 93033 552-H6
SAMANTHA CT
2600 SIMI 93063 498-D1
SAMRA DR
8300 LA 91304 529-G2
N SAMSON AV
2000 SIMI 93063 498-E2
SAMUEL AV
2900 OXN 93033 552-G3
SAMUEL DR
3800 OXN 93033 552-G4
SAN ANDRES CIR
600 THO 91360 526-C3
SAN ANGELO AV
2900 SIMI 93063 478-H6
SAN ANTONIO ST
- THO 91320 555-E2
400 OJAI 93023 441-H7
SAN ARDO CT
6100 CMRL 93012 495-B7
SAN BENITO AV
- VEN 93004 492-F1
SAN BENITO ST
1900 OXN 93033 553-A2
SAN BERNARDINO AV
- VEN 93004 492-F1
SAN CARLOS DR
600 THO 91320 526-A7
SAN CAYETANO RD
1000 VeCo 455-E1
1000 VeCo 93015 455-E1
SAN CAYETANO ST
900 VeCo 93015 465-F4
SANCHEZ DR
2100 CMRL 93010 494-H7
SAN CLEMENTE AV
100 VeCo 93035 552-B4
SAN CLEMENTE CT
3700 THO 91320 555-F1
SAN CLEMENTE ST
- VEN 93001 491-F3
300 SPLA 93060 463-J6
SAN CLEMENTE WY
900 VeCo 93010 494-D6
SAN COMO CT
1000 CMRL 93012 525-C6
SAN COMO LN
6300 CMRL 93012 525-C6
SAND CT
900 VEN 93001 491-F4
SANDALWOOD DR
6400 SIMI 93063 499-C3
SANDALWOOD PL
100 FILM 93015 456-B6
1700 THO 91362 526-J3
SANDALWOOD ST
23300 CanP 91307 529-E4
SANDBERG AV
2100 OXN 93033 553-A3
SANDBERG LN
800 VEN 93003 492-D3
SANDBERG ST
- THO 91360 526-E3

STREET — Block City ZIP Pg-Grid

SAND CANYON RD
4200 VeCo 93066 495-C1
4700 VeCo 93066 475-D7
SANDCROFT ST
23600 VeCo 91361 556-G6
SANDDOLLAR LN
- PHME 93041 552-E5
SANDERLING ST
2000 VEN 93003 492-D5
SANDHURST AV
2700 THO 91362 527-A3
SAN DIEGO AV
300 VEN 93004 492-F1
SANDIMAN ST
5400 SIMI 93063 498-J2
5500 SIMI 93063 499-A2
SAN DIMAS AV
5900 CMRL 93012 525-B5
SAN DOVAL PL
600 THO 91360 526-C3
SANDPIPER CIR
800 THO 91361 557-A5
SANDPIPER CT
900 VEN 93001 491-F5
3600 WLKV 91361 557-B7
SANDPIPER WY
5100 OXN 93035 521-J7
SANDPOINT LN
1100 VEN 93004 492-H3
SANDRA CT
- THO 91320 555-G2
SANDSTONE
2900 SIMI 93063 478-D7
SANDTRAP DR
30400 AGRH 91301 557-G4
SANDY AV
600 SIMI 93065 498-C5
SANDY CIR
500 VeCo 93036 492-J5
SANDY HOLLOW CT
4100 MRPK 93021 496-D3
SAN FELICE CT
11800 MRPK 93021 496-C5
SAN FELIPE AV
3700 THO 91320 555-E1
SAN FERNANDO AV
100 VeCo 93035 552-C6
6800 VeCo 93001 459-C4
SANFORD ST
1800 OXN 93033 553-A5
1800 OXN 93033 552-J5
2000 VeCo 93033 553-A5
SAN FRANCESCA DR
5200 CMRL 93012 525-A2
SAN FRANCISCO AV
300 VEN 93004 472-F7
300 VEN 93004 492-F1
SAN GABRIEL AV
1700 VEN 93004 492-H4
SAN GABRIEL ST
1400 OJAI 93023 442-A6
3700 SIMI 93063 498-E1
SAN GORGONIO AV
1800 OXN 93030 522-J5
1800 OXN 93030 523-A5
SAN GUILLERMO RD
- VeCo - 366-L3
SANITATION RD
4900 CMRL 93012 524-J6
4900 CMRL 93012 525-A6
SAN JACINTO AV
2600 SIMI 93063 498-E1
SAN JACINTO ST
100 OXN 93030 523-A5
SAN JOAQUIN AV
1700 VEN 93004 492-H4
SAN JOAQUIN ST
5400 SIMI 93063 478-J7
5400 SIMI 93063 479-A7
SANJON RD
300 VEN 93001 491-D3
SAN JON BARRANCA RD
500 VeCo 93001 471-F5
500 VEN 93001 471-F7
500 VEN 93001 491-F1
SAN JOSE ST
2000 OXN 93030 523-A5
22000 Chat 91311 499-J4
SAN JUAN AV
3500 OXN 93033 552-H4
SAN JUAN DR
100 FILM 93015 456-C6
SAN JUAN ST
500 SPLA 93060 463-H6
SAN LUCAS AV
- THO 91320 555-E2
SAN LUIS ST
2000 OXN 93030 523-A5
3200 VEN 93003 491-H3
4000 THO 91320 555-E1
SAN MARCOS CT
3700 THO 91320 555-E1
SAN MARCOS ST
2200 VEN 93001 491-F3
2200 VEN 93003 491-F3
SAN MARINO AV
- VEN 93003 491-H2
SAN MARINO ST
1700 OXN 93033 552-G2
SAN MARINO OIL COMPANY RD
1300 VeCo 93015 465-J4
1300 VeCo 93015 466-A4
SAN MARTIN PL
600 THO 91360 526-C3
SAN MARTINEZ GRANDE CYN RD
28500 Cstc 91384 458-G1
N SAN MATEO AV
- VEN 93004 492-F1
300 VEN 93004 472-F7
S SAN MATEO AV
- VEN 93004 492-F2
SAN MATEO PL
1800 OXN 93033 553-A2
SAN MIGUEL AL
- VEN 93001 491-E2
SAN MIGUEL AV
- VeCo 93035 552-B4
SAN MIGUEL CIR
400 PHME 93041 552-E6
2600 THO 91360 526-C3
SAN MIGUEL DR
- VeCo 93010 494-D7
SAN MIGUEL WY
400 SPLA 93060 463-H5
SAN MIGUEL ISLAND DR
- VeCo 93012 554-F3
SAN NICHOLAS ST
1600 VEN 93001 491-E2
2300 VEN 93003 491-E2
SAN NICOLAS AV
- VeCo 93035 552-B5
300 SPLA 93060 463-J5
SAN NICOLAS CIR
100 PHME 93041 552-E6
SAN NICOLAS CT
3700 THO 91320 555-E1
SAN ONOFRE DR
1700 CMRL 93012 495-B7
1700 CMRL 93012 525-C1
SAN PABLO ST
3300 VEN 93003 491-H2
SAN PEDRO ST
400 PHME 93041 552-E5
600 VEN 93001 491-E3
SAN RAFAEL AV
6200 CMRL 93012 525-C1
SAN RAFAEL ST
1400 OJAI 93023 442-A6
SAN RAFAEL WY
1200 CMRL 93012 525-C1
SAN RAMON WY
1200 OJAI 93023 442-A6
SAN REMO DR
1300 SIMI 93063 499-C3
SAN ROQUE AV
- VEN 93003 491-H2
SAN SEBASTIAN CT
- VeCo 93012 496-D7
SAN SEBASTIAN DR
1900 OXN 93035 552-A1
SAN SIMEON AV
3500 OXN 93033 552-J4
SAN SIMEON CT
1300 VEN 93003 492-C4
SAN SIMEON DR
800 THO 91320 526-A7
4200 OXN 93033 552-J4
SANTA ANA AV
100 VeCo 93035 552-A4
SANTA ANA BLVD
- VeCo 93022 451-A6
800 VeCo 93001 450-J6
800 VeCo 93022 450-J6
SANTA ANA RD
7700 VeCo 93001 460-J1
8300 VeCo 93001 461-A2
10400 VeCo 93001 450-E3
11000 VeCo 93001 451-A6
SANTA ANA ST
100 OJAI 93023 441-H7
SANTA ANA WY
- VeCo 93022 451-B6
SANTA ANITA CT
2100 CMRL 93010 494-D7
SANTA ANNA ST
100 SPLA 93060 464-A7
W SANTA ANNA ST
200 SPLA 93060 463-J7
200 SPLA 93060 464-A7
SANTA BARBARA AV
- VeCo 93012 554-D3
6700 VeCo 93001 459-C5
SANTA BARBARA CIR
400 THO 91320 555-F1
SANTA BARBARA ST
1600 VEN 93001 491-E2
E SANTA BARBARA ST
100 SPLA 93060 464-A6
W SANTA BARBARA ST
100 SPLA 93060 463-H7
100 SPLA 93060 464-A6
SANTA BELLA PL
23600 THO 91362 527-B4
SANTA CLARA AV
3000 OXN 93030 523-C2
SANTA CLARA AV
3000 OXN 93036 523-C2
3300 VeCo 93036 523-C2
3800 VeCo 93036 493-D7
4600 VeCo 93010 493-D7
4600 VeCo 93066 493-D7
SANTA CLARA ST
100 FILM 93015 456-A6
700 FILM 93015 455-J6
1200 SPLA 93060 464-C6
E SANTA CLARA ST
- VEN 93001 491-C2
W SANTA CLARA ST
- VEN 93001 491-B2
SANTA CREG LP
23600 SPLA 93060 473-J2
SANTA CRUZ AV
- VeCo 93035 552-B4
SANTA CRUZ CIR
400 PHME 93041 552-E6
SANTA CRUZ CT
3700 SIMI 93063 478-E7
SANTA CRUZ ST
500 SPLA 93060 464-A7
600 SPLA 93060 463-J7
700 SPLA 93060 473-J1
N SANTA CRUZ ST
- VEN 93001 491-E2
S SANTA CRUZ ST
- VEN 93001 491-E3
SANTA CRUZ WY
900 VeCo 93010 494-D6
SANTA CRUZ ISLAND DR
- VeCo 93012 554-E3
SANTA FE AV
900 VEN 93004 492-H2
SANTA FE ST
- FILM 93015 455-J7
- FILM 93015 456-A7
SANTA FELICIA CANYON FIRE RD
23600 VeCo 93040 367-E7
SANTA LUCIA AV
1800 OXN 93030 522-J5
1800 OXN 93030 523-A5
SANTA LUCIA CT
- VEN 93003 492-C1
SANTA LUCIA ST
3700 SIMI 93063 478-E7
SANTA MARGARITA RD
8900 VEN 93004 492-H4
SANTA MARIA ST
6200 VeCo 93063 499-B4
9300 VEN 93004 492-G2
E SANTA MARIA ST
100 SPLA 93060 464-C6
W SANTA MARIA ST
100 SPLA 93060 463-J7
100 SPLA 93060 464-A7
600 SPLA 93060 473-J1
SANTA MONICA AV
100 VeCo 93035 552-C6
SANTA MONICA CT
3800 THO 91320 555-E1
SANTA MONICA DR
200 VeCo 93035 552-B4
SANTA PAULA AV
- VeCo 93012 554-E4
100 VeCo 93035 552-B5
100 VeCo 93043 552-B5
7000 VeCo 93001 459-C4
SANTA PAULA FRWY Rt#-126
- SPLA - 463-J7
- SPLA - 464-D5
- SPLA - 473-F4
- VeCo - 473-B6
- VeCo - 492-D3
- VEN - 472-J7
- VEN - 473-B6
- VEN - 491-J4
- VEN - 492-D3
SANTA PAULA ST
700 VeCo 93015 465-G3
14600 VeCo 93060 463-G7
14900 VeCo 93060 473-E2
E SANTA PAULA ST
100 SPLA 93060 464-A5
W SANTA PAULA ST
100 SPLA 93060 463-J6
100 SPLA 93060 464-A6
SANTA PAULA CANYON RD
23600 VeCo 93040 458-A3
SANTA PAULA OJAI RD Rt#-150
4300 VeCo 93060 464-A1
4400 VeCo 93060 454-A7
4600 VeCo 93060 453-H4
12400 VeCo 93023 453-H4
SANTA ROSA AV
100 VeCo 93035 552-B5
SANTA ROSA DR
4100 VeCo 93021 496-A3
SANTA ROSA LP
400 SPLA 93060 473-J2
SANTA ROSA RD
4600 CMRL 93012 524-J3
SANTA ROSA RD
5000 CMRL 93012 525-B2
6900 VeCo 93012 525-G1
7200 CMRL 93012 495-E7
7200 VeCo 93012 495-E7
10600 VeCo 93012 496-D7
N SANTA ROSA ST
- VEN 93001 491-E2
S SANTA ROSA ST
- VEN 93001 491-E2
SANTA ROSA ISLAND DR
- VeCo 93012 554-F2
SANTA SUSANA CT
- VEN 93003 492-C1
SANTA SUSANA TR
8600 VeCo 93063 499-C4
SANTA SUSANA FIRE RD
23600 VeCo 93063 499-E4
SANTA SUSANA PASS RD
6600 SIMI 93063 499-G2
6700 VeCo 93063 499-D4
7600 Chat 91311 499-G2
SANTA TOMAS PL
3900 THO 91320 555-E1
SANTA YNEZ AV
2200 SIMI 93063 478-E7
2300 SIMI 93063 498-F1
SANTA YNEZ ST
1600 VEN 93001 491-E2
SANTEE CT
10000 VEN 93004 492-J3
SAN TELMO CIR
500 THO 91320 525-E7
500 THO 91320 555-E1
SANTI ST
23600 THO 91320 556-C1
SANTIAGO CT
2300 OXN 93030 523-B4
SANTIAGO ST
2900 THO 91362 557-C3
SANTINA ST
23600 Chat 91311 499-F7
SANTO DR
4900 VeCo 91377 557-G1
SANTO DOMINGO
- CMRL 93012 494-H7
- CMRL 93012 524-H1
SAN TROPEZ CIR
1700 OXN 93035 552-A1
SAN TROPEZ PL
23600 MRPK 93021 496-C4
SAN VINCENT CT
3600 THO 91320 555-F1
SAN VINCENT PL
3600 THO 91320 555-F1
SAN VINCENTE CIR
200 THO 91320 555-F1
SAN VITO LN
- CMRL 93012 524-J1
SAN YSIDRO CT
1200 VEN 93003 472-D6
SAN YSIDRO ST
2200 CMRL 93010 494-G7
2300 VeCo 93010 494-G7
SAPPANWOOD AV
1400 THO 91320 526-A6
SAPPHIRE AV
500 VEN 93004 492-F3
2800 SIMI 93063 478-D7
SAPPHIRE CIR
900 VEN 93004 492-F3
SAPPHIRE DRAGON ST
1300 THO 91320 525-J5
1300 THO 91320 526-A5
SAPRA ST
1800 THO 91362 526-J5
1800 THO 91362 527-A5
SARA DR
23600 OXN 93030 522-J5
SARAH AV
200 MRPK 93021 496-E1
SARAH CT
2900 VeCo 91320 555-G1
SARALYNN DR
9100 Chat 91311 499-F7
SARALYNN LN
100 Chat 91311 499-E6
SARANAC ST
10200 VEN 93004 492-J2
SARATOGA AV
1100 VEN 93003 492-B4
SARATOGA ST
- FILM 93015 456-A5
700 OXN 93035 522-E7
1600 OXN 93035 552-E1
SARAZEN DR
- MRPK 93021 476-E5
SARELDA RD
23800 WHil 91304 499-E7
SARGENT AV
2000 SIMI 93063 498-D2
SARGENT LN
6600 VEN 93003 492-D3
SARITA DR
100 OXN 93030 522-J6
SARNO CT
3900 MRPK 93021 496-C4
SASHA CT
2600 SIMI 93063 498-D1
2700 SIMI 93063 478-D7
SASPARILLA ST
6600 SIMI 93063 499-D2
SASSAFRAS WY
1300 VeCo 91377 527-H7
SATICOY AV
200 VeCo 93004 492-J1
200 VEN 93004 492-J1
1200 VEN 93004 493-A2
N SATICOY AV
100 VEN 93004 472-H7
100 VeCo 93004 472-H7
S SATICOY AV
- VeCo 93004 472-H7
- VEN 93004 472-H7
- VeCo 93004 492-J1
SATICOY ST
1000 SPLA 93060 464-C4
22000 CanP 91303 529-G4
22200 CanP 91307 529-G4
22800 LA 91304 529-F4
SATINWOOD AV
100 VeCo 91377 558-B2
SATURN AV
1200 CMRL 93010 524-F1
SAUL PL
300 VEN 93004 472-H6
SAUSALITO AV
6500 CanP 91307 529-J5
7600 LA 91304 529-J2
SAUSALITO DR
700 CMRL 93010 524-C1
SAVANNAH AV
1700 VEN 93004 492-H4
SAVIERS RD
1100 OXN 93033 522-G7
1100 OXN 93033 552-G3
SAVONA WY
500 VeCo 91377 557-G1
SAVOY CT
400 VeCo 91377 557-H2
SAWMILL WY
- MRPK 93021 476-F6
SAWTELLE AV
100 VeCo 93035 552-C6
100 PHME 93043 552-C6
SAWTELLE CT
23600 SIMI 93065 497-F7
S SAWTOOTH CT
100 THO 91362 557-B2
SAWYER AV
1200 SIMI 93065 498-B4
SAXE CT
2100 THO 91360 526-F4
SAXON PL
1000 THO 91360 526-F6
SAY RD
1100 SPLA 93060 464-B3
SCANDIA AV
900 VEN 93004 492-J2
SCANNO DR
400 VeCo 91377 557-G2
SCARAB FIRE RD
23600 VeCo - 477-H3
23600 VeCo - 478-A2
23600 VeCo 93065 477-H3
SCARBOROUGH ST
200 THO 91361 556-F3
SCARBOROUGH PEAK DR
6900 CanP 91307 529-D5
SCARLET OAK AV
1200 THO 91360 526-H2
SCATTERWOOD LN
23600 SIMI 93065 497-G3
SCENIC DR
2200 SIMI 93065 497-E2
SCENICPARK ST
2200 THO 91362 527-A4
SCENIC WAY DR
800 VEN 93003 472-D6
SCHOENBORN ST
22200 LA 91304 529-E2
SCHOLARTREE CT
- MRPK 93021 496-H3
SCHOOL ST
2800 SIMI 93065 498-C2
SCHOOL CANYON RD
- VeCo 93001 471-C5
- VEN 93001 471-C5
SCHOOLCRAFT ST
22000 CanP 91303 529-J5
22300 CanP 91307 529-F6
SCHOOLHOUSE CIR
1600 THO 91362 527-C6
SCHOONER DR
1000 VeCo 93001 491-G6
1000 VEN 93001 491-G6
SCHOONER WK
3400 OXN 93035 522-B7
SCHUMAN PL
23600 VEN 93003 492-B7
SCHUMANN RD
23100 Chat 91311 499-G7
SCIENCE DR
- MRPK 93021 496-F1
SCIOTO CIR
1000 SIMI 93065 497-C5
SCOFIELD AV
3400 SIMI 93063 478-F6
SCOTER AV
2300 VEN 93003 492-E5
SCOTT AV
1800 VEN 93004 492-H4
SCOTT DR
3100 SIMI 93063 478-F6
SCOTT PL
2500 THO 91360 526-E4
SCOTT ST
100 PHME 93041 552-E6
SCOTTSDALE ST
9800 VEN 93004 492-H2
SCOTTYS TER
3100 SIMI 93063 478-F6
SCRIPPS CT
4700 VEN 93003 492-A1
SEABISCUIT PL
6000 MRPK 93021 476-A7
SEABORG AV
2800 VEN 93001 492-C7
2800 VEN 93003 492-C7
SEABREEZE CT
1700 THO 91320 526-A5
SEABREEZE ST
- THO 91320 525-J5
- THO 91320 526-A5
SEABREEZE TER
- VeCo 90265 585-G7
SEABREEZE WY
5100 OXN 93035 521-J7
SEABRIDGE LN
- OXN 93035 522-B7
- OXN 93035 552-B1
SEABURY CT
- THO 91320 555-J1
SEACLIFF CT
5700 VEN 93003 492-C4
SEACOVE CT
2500 PHME 93041 552-C2
SEACREST CT
23600 THO 91362 527-B2
SEADRIFT CT
2500 PHME 93041 552-C2
SEA ESTA PL
500 VEN 93003 491-J4
SEAFARER ST
1200 VEN 93001 491-F5
SEAFOAM CT
2500 PHME 93041 552-C2
SEAFOAM WY
2600 OXN 93035 552-A2
SEAGULL AV
2300 VEN 93003 492-E5
SEAHAWK ST
5900 VEN 93003 492-D5
6000 VeCo 93003 492-D5
SEAHORSE AV
2400 VEN 93001 491-F4
SEAHORSE CT
900 VEN 93001 491-F4
SEAHORSE WY
1000 OXN 93035 521-J7
SEAL CT
1100 VEN 93001 491-G5
SEALANE WY
4900 OXN 93035 521-J7
5100 OXN 93035 551-J1
SEAMIST CT
2500 PHME 93041 552-C2
SEAMIST PL
- VEN 93003 492-B4
SEAPORT DR
1100 OXN 93030 522-E7
SEASHELL AV
3100 VEN 93001 491-G5
SEASHORE CT
2500 PHME 93041 552-B2
SEASIDE CT
900 VEN 93001 491-F5
SEASIDE DR
2500 PHME 93041 552-C2
2700 OXN 93035 552-C2
2700 PHME 93035 552-C2
SEASONS ST
- SIMI 93065 478-A6
SEASPRAY WY
100 PHME 93041 552-E6
SEAVIEW AV
2900 VEN 93001 491-G5
SEAVIEW DR
5300 OXN 93035 521-H6
SEAVIEW ST
100 PHME 93041 552-E6
N SEAWARD AV
- VEN 93001 491-F2
- VEN 93003 491-F2
S SEAWARD AV
- VEN 93001 491-F3
- VEN 93003 491-F3
SEAWIND WY
600 PHME 93041 552-F7
SEBRING AV
2000 SIMI 93065 498-C2
SEBRING CT
2000 SIMI 93065 498-C2
SECKER DR
23600 WHil 91304 499-D6
SECO CT
2000 THO 91362 556-H2
SEDAN AV
6600 CanP 91307 529-G4
7600 LA 91304 529-G2
SEDGEWICK CT
7500 LA 91304 529-D4
SEDGEWORTH CT
600 SIMI 93065 527-C1
SEDGEWORTH PL
200 SIMI 93065 527-D1
SEEGER AV
- VEN 93003 492-B3
SEELY PL
1100 SIMI 93065 497-H5
SEINE CT
5400 WLKV 91362 557-F5
SEINE RIVER WY
- OXN 93036 492-H5
SEITZ CT
15300 MRPK 93021 476-J5
15300 MRPK 93021 477-A5
SELBY CIR
1800 CMRL 93010 494-H7
SELF DEFENSE RD
- PHME 93043 552-C5
SEMINARY RD
4700 CMRL 93012 494-J7
SEMINOLE CIR
4800 SIMI 93063 478-H6
SEMINOLE LN
2300 VEN 93001 471-C6
SEMPLE ST
3500 SIMI 93063 498-E2
SEMRAD RD
6900 CanP 91307 529-E5
SENAN ST
3700 CMRL 93010 494-G7
SENECA PL
5100 SIMI 93063 478-J7
5400 SIMI 93063 479-A6
SENECA ST
- VEN 93001 471-C5
SENNA WY
- OXN 93030 523-A4
SENTINEL CIR
900 VEN 93003 472-C7
SENTINEL CT
- SIMI 93065 478-B6
SEPTO ST
22000 Chat 91311 499-J5
SEQUAN CT
1400 CMRL 93010 524-D2
SEQUOIA AV
- VeCo 93003 492-D2
1400 SIMI 93063 498-D2
1400 SIMI 93065 498-D4
2400 SIMI 93063 478-D7
SEQUOIA CT
200 THO 91360 526-E7
SEQUOIA DR
1200 OXN 93033 553-B5
SEQUOIA ST
700 OXN 93033 552-H3
SERAPE PL
- CMRL 93010 494-F7
SERENA LN
- OXN 93033 553-C4
SERENA ST
5800 SIMI 93063 499-B1
SERENIDAD PL
- VeCo 93022 451-C5
SERENO AV
2600 VEN 93003 491-F4
SERENO PL
- CMRL 93010 523-J2
SERENTO CIR
400 THO 91360 526-D3
SERRA DR
- FILM 93015 456-C6
SERRANO RD
11600 VeCo 90265 585-D6
SERRANO CANYON RD
- VeCo - 584-H7
- VeCo - 585-A6
SERVICE RD
3600 OXN 93035 552-A2
SERVICE AREA RD
23600 VeCo 93063 498-J7
23600 VeCo 93063 499-A7
SESPE AV
- FILM 93015 456-A6
700 FILM 93015 455-H6
SESPE DR
1800 VEN 93004 492-H4
SESPE PL
700 FILM 93015 455-J6
700 FILM 93015 456-A6
SESPE ST
800 VeCo 93015 465-G2
S SESPE ST
1700 VeCo 93015 465-G4
SESPE LAND & WATER
100 FILM 93015 456-C6
100 VeCo 93015 456-C6
SESPE RIVER RD
- VeCo - 366-K6
SESPE RIVER RD
- VeCo - 367-A5
SETON HALL AV
200 VEN 93003 492-A1
500 VeCo 93003 492-A1
SEVENOAKS CT
4400 WLKV 91361 557-D6
SEVILLA ST
1300 CMRL 93010 524-C4
SEVILLE CT
3500 THO 91320 525-F7
SEXTANT AV
2500 PHME 93041 552-C2
SEXTON CANYON RD
2900 VeCo 93003 472-A4
2900 VeCo 93003 492-C1
2900 VEN 93003 472-B6
2900 VEN 93003 492-C1
SEYBOLT AV
1000 CMRL 93010 524-C2
SEYMOUR CREEK RD
- VeCo - 366-L1
- VeCo - 367-A1
SHAD CT
3100 SIMI 93063 478-E6
SHADE TREE LN
7000 CanP 91307 529-D5
SHADOW LN
23600 SIMI 93065 527-E1
SHADOWBEND WY
23600 SIMI 93065 497-F3
SHADOW BROOK LN
2900 THO 91361 557-C5
SHADOW CANYON PL
4800 THO 91362 557-F1
SHADOW CREEK DR
- OXN 93036 522-B3
SHADOWGLEN CT
1400 THO 91361 556-J5
SHADOW HILL CIR
2900 THO 91360 526-B2
SHADOW HILLS RD
- CALB 91301 558-G7
SHADOW LAKE DR
500 THO 91360 526-D7
SHADOW MESA CIR
2900 THO 91360 526-B2
SHADOW OAK DR
10400 Chat 91311 499-J4
SHADOW OAKS PL
1400 THO 91362 526-J5
SHADOW RIDGE CT
7100 CanP 91307 529-D5
SHADOW SPRING PL
2200 THO 91361 557-B4
SHADOW VALLEY CIR
22200 Chat 91311 499-J1
SHADOW WOOD DR
- MRPK 93021 476-D6
SHADOW WOOD PL
- MRPK 93021 476-E5
SHADY LN
1100 FILM 93015 455-J4
N SHADY LN
100 OJAI 93023 442-A6
S SHADY LN
100 OJAI 93023 442-A7
SHADY BROOK CT
2400 THO 91362 527-A4
SHADY BROOK DR
1600 THO 91362 526-J4
1900 THO 91362 527-A4
SHADYCREEK DR
6000 AGRH 91301 558-A3
SHADY GROVE LN
100 THO 91361 556-F2
SHADY GROVE PL
25800 LACo 91302 558-J3
SHADY HILLS CT
200 SIMI 93065 497-E6
SHADY KNOLL CT
- MRPK 93021 496-F4
SHADY OAK LN
5500 SIMI 93063 499-A1
SHADY OAKS DR
400 THO 91320 526-A7
SHADY POINT DR
4100 MRPK 93021 496-F3
SHADYRIDGE DR
11100 MRPK 93021 496-B4
SHADY TRAIL ST
- SIMI 93063 478-H5
SHAKESPEARE DR
- OXN 93033 553-B3
SHAKESPEARE PL
6900 MRPK 93021 477-A5
SHAKESPEARE WY
6500 VEN 93003 492-D1
SHALIMAR ST
2500 CMRL 93010 524-F1
SHALLOWS DR
800 OXN 93035 522-B7
SHAMROCK CT
100 THO 91320 556-A1
SHAMROCK DR
- VEN 93003 491-H2
400 VeCo 93003 491-H2
SHANNON AV
1700 VEN 93004 492-H4
SHANNON DR
2800 SIMI 93063 478-E7
SHARON DR
600 CMRL 93010 524-F2
SHARON LN
200 PHME 93041 552-D2
900 VEN 93001 491-E4
SHARP RD
2700 SIMI 93065 478-C6
2700 VeCo 93065 478-C6
SHASTA AV
- MRPK 93021 496-D1
400 OXN 93033 552-G4
SHASTA DR
100 OXN 93033 553-B5
600 SPLA 93060 463-H6
SHASTA PL
6000 CMRL 93012 525-B1
SHASTA ST
8100 VEN 93004 492-F3
SHASTA WY
2200 SIMI 93065 497-G2
SHAVER CT
900 SIMI 93065 497-F5
900 VeCo 93065 497-F5
SHAVER ST
8100 VEN 93004 492-F3
SHAW CT
1900 THO 91362 527-A6
SHAW WY
6500 VEN 93003 492-D3
SHAWNEE CT
- MRPK 93021 496-G4
SHAWNEE DR
- Chat 91311 499-J1
SHAWNEE LN
2300 VEN 93001 471-C6
SHAWNEE ST
- MRPK 93021 496-G3
SHAWNESS CT
1700 THO 91362 527-E6
SHEARWATER ST
6300 VEN 93003 492-D5
SHEFFIELD LN
200 FILM 93015 455-J6
SHEFFIELD PL
800 THO 91360 526-F7
SHEFFIELD ST
700 SPLA 93060 463-H6
SHEKELL RD
8000 VeCo 93021 476-A2
SHELBURN LN
1100 VEN 93001 491-E4
SHELBURNE LN
1000 SIMI 93065 497-D6
SHELBY LN
2000 SIMI 93065 498-A2
SHELDON DR
3600 VEN 93003 491-H2
SHELL RD
200 VeCo 93001 471-B4
600 VeCo 93060 473-J2
E SHELL RD
- VeCo 93001 471-C4
W SHELL RD
- VeCo 93001 471-C4
SHELLCREEK PL
2800 WLKV 91361 557-A7
SHELLEY CIR
6900 VEN 93003 492-E3
SHELL HARBOR LN
- PHME 93041 552-E6
SHELL HARTMAN RD
- VeCo 93001 471-D3
SHELLY PL
- OXN 93033 553-B4
SHELTER WOOD CT
2800 THO 91362 526-J3
SHELTONDALE AV
6200 WdHl 91367 529-D6
6300 CanP 91307 529-D6
SHENANDOAH AV
3200 SIMI 93063 498-D3
SHENANDOAH DR
- OXN 93036 492-H7
SHENANDOAH ST
400 THO 91360 526-D3
4700 VEN 93003 492-B4
SHENANDOAH WY
- MRPK 93021 476-F6
SHEPHERD DR E
3100 CMRL 93010 524-F1
SHEPPARD RD
100 SPLA 93060 463-H7
SHERBORNE ST
2100 CMRL 93010 524-E1
SHERGRA PL
3300 SIMI 93063 498-D1
SHERI DR
3100 SIMI 93063 478-E6
SHERIDAN CT
2000 SIMI 93065 498-A2
SHERIDAN WY
400 VEN 93001 491-B1
500 VEN 93001 471-B7
SHERMAN AV
200 MRPK 93021 496-E1
SHERMAN PL
23100 CanP 91307 529-G5
SHERMAN ST
2000 SIMI 93065 498-A2
SHERMAN WY
22000 CanP 91303 529-G5
22300 CanP 91307 529-F5
SHERWIN AV
2600 VEN 93003 492-E6
SHERWOOD CT
300 THO 91361 556-F2
SHERWOOD DR
2400 VEN 93001 491-F2
SHERWOOD RD NW
800 VeCo 93023 451-C3
SHERWOOD WY
500 OXN 93033 552-G5
SHETLAND PL
1500 THO 91362 527-D6
SHIELDS CT
2700 THO 91360 526-E3
SHIELLS DR
600 FILM 93015 456-A5
SHIELLS CANYON
- VeCo 93015 466-E2
- VeCo 93021 466-E2
SHILOH WY
5200 VEN 93003 492-B4
SHIPPEE LN
1100 VeCo 93023 442-D5
SHIPSIDE RD
- PHME 93043 552-D5
SHIRLEY DR
2800 THO 91320 525-H7
2900 VeCo 91320 525-H7
SHIRLEY ST
1700 CMRL 93010 524-D4
SHOAL CREEK CT
2100 SIMI 93065 497-C6
SHOEMAKER LN
1900 THO 91320 525-J7
1900 THO 91320 526-A7
SHOKAT DR
700 VeCo 93023 450-J2
700 VeCo 93023 451-A2
SHOOTINGSTAR LN
23600 SIMI 93065 497-A1
SHOPPING LN
4200 SIMI 93063 498-F2
SHORE DR
1000 VEN 93001 491-E4
SHORELINE DR
- VEN 93001 491-B3
SHORELINE ST
1500 CMRL 93010 524-D2
SHORELINE WY
5000 OXN 93035 551-J1
5000 OXN 93035 552-A1
SHOREVIEW CIR
2800 THO 91361 557-C6
SHOREVIEW DR
400 PHME 93041 552-E6
3300 WLKV 91361 557-C7
SHORT ST
- VeCo 93042 583-E4
- VeCo 93022 451-B7
SHOSHONE AV
11300 Chat 91311 499-J1
SHOSHONE ST
- VEN 93001 471-C6
5500 SIMI 93063 479-A7
W SHOSHONE ST
- VEN 93001 471-C6
SHOUP AV
6100 WdHl 91367 529-J7
6400 CanP 91307 529-J4
7600 LA 91304 529-J4
9300 Chat 91311 499-J6
SHREVE AV
2200 SIMI 93063 499-C1
SHREWSBURY CIR
24300 CanP 91307 529-D5
SHROPSHIRE CT
4100 WLKV 91361 557-D6
SHRUBWOOD CIR
2600 SIMI 93065 498-C1
2700 SIMI 93065 478-C7
SHUNK RD
1700 SIMI 93063 499-B2
E SIBLEY ST
6400 SIMI 93063 499-C2
SIDEWINDER DR
- VeCo 93041 583-H3
SIDLEE ST
- THO 91360 526-F5
E SIDLEE ST
- THO 91360 526-F4
W SIDLEE ST
- THO 91360 526-E4
SIDNEY LN
500 VEN 93003 492-D1
SIDONIA AV
700 VEN 93003 491-H4
SIENA CT
11800 MRPK 93021 496-C5
SIENNA LN
1000 SIMI 93065 478-A7
1000 SIMI 93065 498-A1
SIENNA WY
5500 WLKV 91362 557-F5

STREET Block City ZIP Pg-Grid

SIERRA AV
100 MRPK 93021 496-D1
SIERRA CT
1200 VeCo 93023 451-B1
SIERRA DR
300 VEN 93003 491-H2
E SIERRA DR
3300 THO 91362 557-C3
W SIERRA DR
2700 THO 91362 557-B2
SIERRA PL
1900 OXN 93033 553-A3
SIERRA RD
100 OJAI 93023 441-G7
200 VeCo 93023 441-G7
SIERRA WY
2100 OXN 93033 553-B2
SIERRA HEIGHTS CT
400 THO 91320 555-G3
SIERRA MADRE CT
3700 SIMI 93063 478-E7
SIERRA MADRE DR
1500 CMRL 93010 524-F1
SIERRA MESA DR
1800 CMRL 93010 494-C7
1800 CMRL 93010 524-C1
SIERRA PASS PL
11200 Chat 91311 499-J2
SIERRA VISTA AV
200 FILM 93015 455-H6
SIESTA AV
100 THO 91360 526-E4
SIESTA CIR
2300 THO 91360 526-E4
SIESTA WY
3400 VeCo 93033 553-D5
SIGNAL ST
100 OJAI 93023 441-H6
S SIGNAL ST
100 OJAI 93023 441-H7
SILAS AV
100 THO 91320 555-H2
100 VeCo 91320 555-H2
SILAS LN
200 THO 91320 555-H2
23600 THO 91320 555-H2
SILENTBROOK WY
1600 SIMI 93065 497-G3
SILKFIELD CT
- VeCo 91361 556-D7
SILK OAK AV
2800 THO 91362 527-C3
SILVER CIR
- VEN 93004 492-F3
SILVERADO DR
1700 THO 91360 496-J7
SILVERBELL CIR
- MRPK 93021 496-G2
SILVER CLOUD ST
700 THO 91360 526-C2
SILVER CREEK RD
28900 Ago 91301 558-B7
SILVER CREEK ST
12900 MRPK 93021 496-E3
SILVERCREST ST
11800 MRPK 93021 496-C4
SILVER FERN CT
400 SIMI 93065 497-E6
SILVER LAKE CT
400 SIMI 93065 497-E6
SILVER MAPLE CIR
3100 THO 91360 526-H2
SILVER MOSS CT
400 SIMI 93065 497-E6
SILVER OAK LN
- MRPK 93021 496-F2
SILVER SPRING DR
2100 THO 91361 557-A4
SILVER SPUR CT
1000 VeCo 93023 451-C3
3200 THO 91360 526-C2
SILVER SPUR LN
- VeCo 91307 529-A5
SILVER SPUR ST
1700 VeCo 93023 451-C3
SILVERSTAR AV
- SIMI 93065 478-A6
SILVERSTONE CT
- SIMI 93065 478-A5
SILVERSTONE ST
- SIMI 93065 478-A6
SILVERSTREAM CT
- SIMI 93063 499-A1
SILVER TREE LN
- SIMI 93065 497-H3
SILVER VALLEY AV
5600 AGRH 91301 557-J5
SILVERWHEEL PL
500 THO 91320 555-H3
SILVERWOOD ST
1300 SIMI 93065 497-H5
SIMI AV
100 VeCo 93035 552-B5
SIMI ST
1200 VeCo 93015 465-H3
SIMI HILLS LN
2600 SIMI 93063 478-H7
SIMI TOWN CENTER WY
- SIMI 93065 497-H1
- SIMI 93065 498-A1
SIMI VILLAGE DR
100 SIMI 93065 497-F3
SIMON WY
- VeCo 93036 492-J7
500 VeCo 93036 493-A7
700 VeCo 93036 523-A1
SIMPSON DR
4300 OXN 93033 553-A4
SIMPSON ST
200 VEN 93001 491-C1
E SIMPSON ST
- VEN 93001 491-B1
W SIMPSON ST
- VEN 93001 491-B1
200 VEN 93001 471-B7
SIMSBURY CT
1900 THO 91360 526-C5
SINALOA RD
300 SIMI 93065 497-G6
600 VeCo 93065 497-G5
SINALOA VILLA
400 SIMI 93065 497-G3
SINGLETREE LN
6700 VeCo 91377 528-A7
SIOUX AV
2800 VEN 93001 471-C5
SIOUX CT
3000 SIMI 93063 478-J7
SIOUX DR
22000 Chat 91311 499-J1
SIR GEORGE CT
700 MRPK 93021 476-F7
SIRIUS CIR
2600 THO 91360 526-F3
SIRIUS ST
2100 THO 91360 526-E3
SISAR RD
- VeCo - 366-L7
13000 VeCo 93023 453-C1
SI SE PUEDE ST
10200 VEN 93004 492-J3
10200 VEN 93004 493-A3
SISKIN CT
2000 SIMI 93065 497-D2
SISKIN PL
400 SIMI 93065 497-D2
SISKIYOU ST
8100 VEN 93004 472-F7
8100 VEN 93004 492-F1
SITKA AV
1500 SIMI 93063 498-D3
SITTING BULL PL
6000 SIMI 93063 479-A7
SIX OAK CT
2400 SIMI 93063 499-A1
SKAGWAY ST
3400 SIMI 93063 498-D2
SKEEL DR
800 CMRL 93010 524-C2
SKELTON CANYON CIR
3800 THO 91362 557-C1
SKIDMORE CT
4500 MRPK 93021 496-F2
SKINNER CT
2100 THO 91362 556-H2
SKUNK RANCH RD
23600 OJAI 93023 451-H1
23600 VeCo 93023 451-H1
SKY CT
3100 SIMI 93063 478-E6
SKYBROOK CT
4200 MRPK 93021 496-B2
SKYCREST CT
800 VEN 93003 472-C7
SKYFLOWER LN
23600 SIMI 93065 497-A1
SKYGLEN CT
4400 MRPK 93021 496-D2
SKY HIGH DR
300 VeCo 93001 460-J4
N SKYLARK CT
4300 MRPK 93021 496-E3
SKYLINE DR
700 SPLA 93060 463-H6
23600 VeCo 93063 498-J7
23600 VeCo 93063 528-H1
N SKYLINE DR
100 THO 91362 557-A2
S SKYLINE DR
- THO 91362 557-A3
100 THO 91361 557-A3
100 THO 91361 556-J3
SKYLINE RD
500 VEN 93003 492-B1
600 VEN 93003 472-B7
8900 VeCo 93021 476-C1
SKYRIDGE CT
1600 THO 91320 556-A2
SKY RIDGE LN
5300 VeCo 91377 527-G7
SKYVIEW TER
6200 VEN 93003 472-C7
SKYVIEW WY
5700 AGRH 91301 558-A4
SKYWALKER DR
4000 VeCo 93066 493-F3
SKYWAY DR
200 CMRL 93010 523-J5
200 CMRL 93010 524-A5
SLATE PL
- THO 91362 527-C3
SLATER TER
9200 Chat 91311 499-F7
SLEEPY HOLLOW ST
2900 SIMI 93065 498-D4
SLEEPY WIND ST
12900 MRPK 93021 496-E3
SLICERS CIR
5600 AGRH 91301 557-G5
SMETANA CT
600 VEN 93003 492-B7
SMETANA ST
600 VEN 93003 492-B7
SMITH RD
6500 SIMI 93063 499-C3
23100 Chat 91311 499-F7
SMITH ST
200 OXN 93033 552-G5
5100 VEN 93003 492-B1
SMITH CANYON RD
900 VeCo 93015 457-F7
900 VeCo 93040 457-F7
SMOKETREE AV
- VeCo 91377 558-A2
SMOKETREE WY
23600 SIMI 93065 527-E1
SMOKEWOOD CT
1900 THO 91362 526-J3
1900 THO 91362 527-A3
SMOKEY RIDGE AV
1800 THO 91362 527-G6
SMOKY MOUNTAIN DR
- OXN 93036 492-H7
- OXN 93036 522-H1
SMUGGLERS CV
- VeCo 93012 554-E3
SNAPDRAGON ST
- VEN 93004 493-A1
SNEAD DR
- MRPK 93021 476-D4
SNIPE AV
1200 VEN 93003 492-C4
SNIPE WK
600 OXN 93035 522-E6
SNOW AV
- OXN 93030 522-J3
1900 OXN 93036 522-J3
SNOW CT
1000 VEN 93001 471-B7
SNOWBERRY CT
2000 SIMI 93063 498-J2
SNOW CREEK AV
5200 SIMI 93063 498-J2
SNOWGOOSE ST
- SIMI 93065 478-A5
SNOWPEAK DR
32400 WLKV 91361 557-B7
SOBRE COLINAS PL
400 CMRL 93012 524-J3
SOCORRO WY
1700 OXN 93030 522-J4
1700 OXN 93030 523-A4
SOCRATES AV
2000 SIMI 93065 497-F2
SOFT WHISPER CT
- SIMI 93065 478-A6
SOFTWIND WY
5400 AGRH 91301 557-J5
5400 AGRH 91301 558-A5
SOJKA DR
2800 SIMI 93065 498-C1
3000 SIMI 93063 498-C1
SOLANO DR
2000 CMRL 93012 495-D7
SOLANO ST
7800 VEN 93004 492-F1
SOLANO WY
2200 OXN 93033 553-B3
SOLANO VERDE DR
7000 VeCo 93066 475-A3
SOLAR DR
1800 OXN 93030 523-B3
1900 OXN 93036 523-B3
SOLIMAR BEACH RD
2800 VeCo 93001 470-D4
SOLWAY CT
2300 THO 91362 527-A3
SOMBRA WY
- OXN 93030 522-J4
SOMERA CT
- SIMI 93065 497-H5
SOMERSET CIR
200 THO 91360 526-E6
SOMIS RD Rt#-34
2400 CMRL 93010 494-J6
2400 VeCo 93010 494-J6
2400 VeCo 93066 494-J6
2600 VeCo 93066 495-A5
SONATA DR
- OXN 93030 522-J4
SONATA WY
23600 SIMI 93065 527-D1
SONIA DR
- OXN 93030 522-J4
SONOMA CT
400 VEN 93004 492-E1
2100 THO 91362 526-J4
SONOMA LN
100 SPLA 93060 464-A6
SONOMA PL
22000 Chat 91311 499-J6
SONOMA ST
7800 VEN 93004 492-E1
SONOMA WY
500 OXN 93033 552-F5
SONORA CT
6700 VEN 93003 472-D6
SONORA DR
300 CMRL 93010 524-D3
SOPHIA CT
1500 OXN 93030 522-E4
SOPHIA DR
1600 OXN 93030 522-E3
SOPHOMORE CT
15700 MRPK 93021 477-A5
SORA ST
6500 VEN 93003 492-D4
SORORITY LN
23800 WHil 91304 499-E7
SORREL ST
1400 SIMI 93065 497-H3
1800 CMRL 93010 524-D1
SORRELWOOD CT
800 THO 91361 557-A4
SORTINO CT
11800 MRPK 93021 496-C4
SOSNA CT
15300 MRPK 93021 476-J5
SOULE PARK DR
1100 OJAI 93023 442-A7
1100 OJAI 93023 452-A1
SOUSA RD
5100 VEN 93003 492-B3
SOUTH DR
6400 VEN 93003 492-D4
N SOUTH BANK RD
3800 VeCo 93036 492-J5
SOUTHBY DR
7500 LA 91304 529-D4
SOUTHCREST PL
- SIMI 93065 497-E2
SOUTHERN CROSS CT
- VeCo 93012 496-F5
SOUTHERN HILLS DR
2200 OXN 93036 522-E2
SOUTHERN HILLS PL
1700 THO 91362 527-E6
SOUTHERN OAK AV
- SIMI 93063 499-A3
SOUTHERN PACIFIC ST
- FILM 93015 455-J7
SOUTHFIELD RD
500 CMRL 93010 524-D4
SOUTHFORK RD
- MRPK 93021 496-F2
SOUTHHAMPTON RD
3800 MRPK 93021 496-F3
SOUTH MOUNTAIN RD
400 SPLA 93060 464-D6
2100 VeCo 93015 465-A5
2400 VeCo 93060 465-A5
16500 VeCo 93066 474-A1
16500 VeCo 93060 474-A1
21000 VeCo 93066 464-G5
21000 VeCo 93060 464-G5
21700 VeCo 93066 465-A5
SOUTHPORT DR
1100 THO 91361 557-A5
SOUTHRIDGE DR
300 VeCo 91377 558-A1
SOUTH RIM ST
5000 THO 91362 527-F7
SOUTHSHORE PL
32500 WLKV 91361 557-B7
SOUTHVIEW CIR
6100 VEN 93003 472-C5
SOUTHWICK ST
600 SPLA 93060 463-H6
SOUTHWIND CIR
1300 THO 91361 557-B6
SOUTHWIND CT
- VEN 93003 492-B4
SPALDING DR
100 VeCo 93015 465-D1
SPALDING ST
600 THO 91360 526-G6
SPANISH GATE DR
3700 THO 91320 525-F7
SPANISH MOSS PL
- CMRL 93010 524-A2
SPANISH OAK LN
5400 VeCo 91377 557-J1
SPARKMAN AV
1200 CMRL 93010 524-D1
SPARKS CT
1900 SIMI 93065 498-A4
SPARROW DR
- VeCo 93041 583-G2
SPARROW ST
6000 VEN 93003 492-C4
SPARROWHAWK LN
100 VeCo 91377 557-J3
SPARTA CT
2100 SIMI 93065 497-F2
SPECK LN
2100 THO 91320 555-J2
2100 THO 91320 556-A2
SPECTRUM CIR
500 OXN 93030 523-D5
SPENCE ST
1600 SIMI 93065 497-J2
SPENCER CT
25900 LACo 91302 558-J3
SPENSER LN
700 VEN 93003 492-D2
SPERRY AV
1700 VEN 93003 492-C6
SPICEWOOD CT
23600 SIMI 93063 498-E4
SPINDLEWOOD AV
200 CMRL 93012 524-H4
SPINDLEWOOD CT
4300 CMRL 93012 524-H4
SPINDRIFT CT
5300 CMRL 93012 525-A1
SPINNAKER AV
2400 PHME 93041 552-C2
SPINNAKER DR
1100 VEN 93001 491-F7
SPINWOOD LN
23600 SIMI 93065 497-A2
SPIRES ST
23200 LA 91304 529-F3
SPIRITLAKE CT
5800 SIMI 93063 479-B6
SPLIT ROCK LN
5300 VeCo 91377 527-G7
S P MILLING RD
500 VeCo 93001 471-A7
500 VEN 93001 471-A7
500 VEN 93001 491-A1
SPRING CT
7200 CanP 91307 529-F5
SPRING RD
- MRPK 93021 476-F5
100 MRPK 93021 496-F2
SPRING ST
100 VeCo 93001 461-C7
500 VeCo 93022 451-B7
600 VeCo 93022 461-B1
7600 VeCo 93021 476-D4
SPRING BREEZE CT
700 SIMI 93065 497-E6
SPRINGBROOK CT
23600 THO 91362 527-B2
SPRINGBROOK ST
23600 THO 91362 527-B2
SPRING CANYON PL
3000 THO 91320 555-G4
SPRING CREEK CT
12500 MRPK 93021 496-D3
SPRING CREEK RD
12300 MRPK 93021 496-D3
SPRINGDALE CT
- THO 91360 526-F2
SPRINGFIELD AV
600 VEN 93004 492-G2
E SPRINGFIELD ST
4200 SIMI 93063 478-F6
N SPRINGFIELD ST
3000 SIMI 93063 478-F7
SPRING FOREST LN
4000 THO 91362 557-D1
SPRINGGATE LN
1700 SIMI 93065 497-F3
SPRINGHAVEN AV
- THO 91320 556-A1
SPRING HILL CT
4800 THO 91362 557-F1
SPRING MEADOW AV
3200 THO 91360 526-F2
SPRINGMIST LN
23600 SIMI 93065 497-A1
SPRING PARK RD
- CMRL 93012 524-G5
SPRINGTIME LN
3900 MRPK 93021 496-E4
SPRINGVILLE RD
3200 OXN 93030 523-E3
3200 VeCo 93030 523-E3
SPRING WOOD ST
600 THO 91320 556-C2
SPRUCE CIR
23600 SIMI 93065 497-F7
SPRUCE DR
100 OXN 93033 552-H5
SPRUCE ST
200 OXN 93033 552-F3
SPRUCE HILL CT
800 THO 91320 556-C2
SPRUCE MEADOW PL
400 THO 91362 557-D2
SPRUCEWOOD AV
300 VeCo 91377 558-A1
SPUR DR
100 OXN 93036 522-G1
SPURWOOD LN
23600 SIMI 93065 497-A2
SPYGLASS LN
500 THO 91320 556-D1
SPYGLASS TR
1800 OXN 93036 522-D3
SPYGLASS TR W
2400 OXN 93036 522-D2
SPYGLASS WY
1400 CMRL 93012 525-A1
SQUAW FLAT RD
- VeCo - 367-C5
SQUIRES DR
4500 OXN 93033 552-H5
SQUIRREL LN
1600 VEN 93003 492-E4
STABEN CT
100 SPLA 93060 464-A6
STABER RD
23600 VeCo 91361 555-J7
STACEY LN
- CMRL 93012 495-A7
STACY DR
2800 SIMI 93063 478-E7
STACY LN
- CMRL 93012 495-A7
STADIUM AV
- VEN 93003 492-A2
STADIUM WY
600 FILM 93015 456-A5
STAFFORD RD
2200 VeCo 91361 556-F7
W STAFFORD RD
2200 VeCo 91361 556-D7
2200 VeCo 91361 586-D1
STAGECOACH CT
- MRPK 93021 496-F2
STAGECOACH RD
- VeCo 90265 585-G7
- VeCo 90265 625-G1
E STAGECOACH RD
- VeCo 91307 528-J3
- VeCo 91307 529-A4
STAGECOACH TR
- MRPK 93021 496-F2
STAGG ST
22100 LA 91304 529-D3
STALLION CT
1000 VeCo 93010 494-C6
N STALLION RD
- VeCo 91307 528-J4
STANFORD AV
- OXN 93036 522-G2
STANFORD DR
900 SIMI 93065 498-A4
STANFORD ST
200 SPLA 93060 464-B6
5500 VEN 93003 492-B2
23600 OXN 93036 522-G2
E STANFORD ST
14600 MRPK 93021 476-H6
STANHOPE CT
23600 VeCo 91361 556-F6
STANISLAUS AV
- VEN 93004 492-F1
2700 SIMI 93063 478-J7
2700 SIMI 93063 498-J1
STANLEY AV
- VEN 93001 471-B6
STANLEY AV E
- VeCo 93001 471-C6
- VEN 93001 471-C6
STANLEY CT
15300 MRPK 93021 476-J5
STANTON CT
3600 SIMI 93063 478-E7
STANWOOD RD
23600 SIMI 93065 497-G7
STARBOARD LN
- PHME 93041 552-E5
STARBRIGHT CT
600 SIMI 93065 527-C2
STARDUST DR
100 SIMI 93065 497-E2
STARFIRE AV
3100 THO 91360 526-D2
STARFISH DR
4500 OXN 93035 552-A2
STARFISH LN
11800 VeCo 90265 625-F4
STARGAZE PL
400 SIMI 93065 497-E2
STARKLAND AV
8300 LA 91304 529-E2
STARLIGHT LN
24500 CanP 91307 529-D4
STARLING AV
2900 THO 91360 526-F3
STARPINE WY
1600 SIMI 93065 497-A2
STARR LN
2600 SIMI 93063 478-J7
2600 SIMI 93063 498-J1
STARSHINE ST
3500 THO 91360 526-H2
STARSTONE CT
100 SIMI 93065 497-J6
STARWOOD CT
1200 THO 91362 527-G7
STATHAM BLVD
1700 OXN 93033 552-J1
STATHAM PKWY
900 OXN 93033 552-H2
STAUNTON ST
400 CMRL 93010 524-F2
STEARMAN ST
500 CMRL 93010 524-A5
STEARNS ST
1700 SIMI 93063 498-J1
2600 SIMI 93063 478-J7
N STECKEL DR
100 SPLA 93060 463-J6
400 VeCo 93060 463-J6
S STECKEL DR
100 SPLA 93060 463-J6
200 SPLA 93060 464-A7
STEFFEN LN
800 VeCo 93063 499-B4
STEINBECK ST
6800 VEN 93003 492-D1
STELL DR
3800 SIMI 93063 478-F6
STELLAR DR
1100 OXN 93033 522-J7
1100 OXN 93033 552-J1
STEPHANIE WY
6000 SIMI 93063 499-B3
STEPHEN LN
8300 LA 91304 529-F2
STEPHENS ST
500 FILM 93015 456-A5
STEPHLY RD
1300 VeCo 93015 367-B7
1300 VeCo 93015 455-H1
STERLING AV
800 VEN 93004 492-F3
STERLING DR
1200 THO 91360 526-F6
STERLING CENTER DR
5300 WLKV 91361 557-E6
STERLING HILLS DR
- CMRL 93010 493-H6
STERLING OAKS CT
1300 VeCo 91377 527-G7
STERLINGVIEW DR
4100 MRPK 93021 496-B3
STERN CT
1000 OXN 93035 522-D7
STERN LN
900 OXN 93035 522-D7
STETSON CT
600 THO 91360 526-D4
STEVENS CIR
6900 VEN 93003 492-E3
STEVENS WY
9000 LA 91304 499-E7
9000 WHil 91304 499-E7
STILES AV
3100 CMRL 93010 524-F1
STILLWATER CT
10300 VEN 93004 492-J2
STILMAN CT
2100 SIMI 93063 498-J2
STINSON ST
500 CMRL 93010 524-A5
2100 SIMI 93065 498-A4
N STIRRUP LN
- VeCo 91307 529-B3
STOCK AV
1500 VEN 93004 493-A2
STOCKBRIDGE LN
100 VeCo 93023 441-E7
STOCKTON AV
- VEN 93004 492-F1
STOCKTON RD
7900 VeCo 93021 475-H3
7900 VeCo 93066 475-E7
STODDARD AV
1400 THO 91360 526-D5
E STOKE CT
6100 SIMI 93063 499-B1
STONE PL
8000 VEN 93004 492-F3
STONE ST
900 VeCo 93015 455-G4
7800 VEN 93004 492-F3
STONEBROOK ST
100 SIMI 93065 497-F6
STONECREEK CT
- VeCo 91361 556-F6
STONE CREEK DR
1200 OXN 93036 522-E1
STONECREST DR
5700 AGRH 91301 557-H4
STONECROFT CT
2000 THO 91361 557-A5
STONECUTTER ST
- THO 91362 527-B3
STONEGATE DR
24500 LA 91304 529-D4
STONEGATE RD
1000 SPLA 93060 464-A2
STONEHAVEN LN
300 VeCo 91377 557-J2
STONEHEDGE DR
500 FILM 93015 456-A5
STONEHILL CIR
1900 THO 91360 526-C4
STONEMAN ST
1800 SIMI 93065 478-A7
STONE MEADOW DR
1300 CMRL 93010 524-E1
STONE MOUNTAIN LN
5200 THO 91362 527-G6
STONEPINE CT
1400 THO 91360 526-H2
STONERIVER CT
3400 THO 91362 557-C2
STONESGATE ST
1700 THO 91361 556-J5
1800 THO 91361 557-A5
STONESHEAD CT
1000 THO 91361 556-J5
STONETREE ST
4200 CMRL 93012 524-H4
STONEWALL CIR
1200 THO 91361 557-B5
STONEWOOD ST
2900 SIMI 93063 478-C7
STONEYBROOK LN
1100 THO 91361 557-C5
STONEYGLEN CT
4400 MRPK 93021 496-D3
STONEY PEAK CT
500 SIMI 93065 497-D2
STONEY RUN LN
23600 SIMI 93065 497-A2
STONEYVIEW LN
6400 SIMI 93063 499-C3
STORAGE RD
- VeCo 93042 583-F5
STORK ST
6400 VEN 93003 492-D5
STORM CLOUD ST
3200 THO 91360 526-C2
STORMCROFT CT
2300 THO 91361 557-B5
STOW ST
1500 SIMI 93063 499-A1
STOWE DR
- OXN 93033 552-J2
STRANDWAY CT
1600 THO 91361 556-J6
STRATFORD AV
200 VEN 93003 492-B2
STRATFORD ST
- THO 91360 526-F5
STRATHEARN PL
- SIMI 93065 497-E2
STRATHERN ST
22000 LA 91304 529-E3
STRATHMORE DR
3100 VEN 93003 491-H4
STRAUSS DR
500 THO 91320 525-H7
500 THO 91320 555-H1
800 VEN 93003 492-B7
STRAVINSKY LN
1000 VEN 93003 492-A7
STRAWBERRY LN
500 OXN 93036 522-F1
STRAWBERRY HILL DR
29600 AGRH 91301 557-J5
STRAWBERRY HILL RD
1300 THO 91360 526-G6
STRICKLAND DR
4700 VeCo 93036 493-A4
STRONG CT
400 VeCo 93003 491-J1
400 VEN 93003 491-J1
STROUBE ST
- VeCo 93036 522-H1
100 OXN 93036 492-H7
100 OXN 93036 522-H1
1000 VeCo 93036 523-A2
STUART CIR
900 THO 91362 526-J6
STUART CT
400 OJAI 93023 451-F1
STUART LN
600 VEN 93003 492-D2
STUDENT ST
4600 VEN 93003 492-A3
STUDIO RD
7100 VeCo 93063 499-E5
STUMP RD
100 VeCo 93015 466-B2
STURGIS RD
2200 OXN 93030 523-B5
3400 VeCo 93030 523-E5
STYLES ST
22500 WdHl 91367 529-F7
SUBIDA CIR
3100 VeCo 93012 496-D6
SUBROCK CIR
- VeCo 93041 583-H3
SUDARIO CT
1000 VeCo 93010 494-C6
SUE WY
200 VeCo 93036 493-A4
N SUEDE AV
2000 SIMI 93063 499-B2
SUENO CT
1000 VeCo 93010 494-B5
SUE SUE LN
200 CMRL 93010 524-C4
SUFFOLK AV
1200 THO 91360 526-F6
SUFFOLK CT
4700 VEN 93003 492-A1
SUGAR MAPLE CT
4400 MRPK 93021 496-E3
SUGARPINE CT
500 THO 91320 556-D2
SULLIVAN ST
4500 VEN 93003 492-A4
SULPHUR CANYON
23600 VeCo 93001 451-H7
23600 VeCo 93001 461-J1
SULPHUR CASCADE
23600 VeCo 93060 453-G2
SULPHUR MOUNTAIN RD
- VeCo 93001 461-B2
6000 VeCo 93060 453-D3
6700 VeCo 93023 452-J2
6700 VeCo 93023 453-A4
6700 VeCo 93060 452-J3
9300 VeCo 93023 451-H6
9300 VeCo 93060 451-H6
10700 VeCo 93001 451-H6
10700 VeCo 93022 451-E7
12200 VeCo 93022 461-C2
SULPHUR SPRINGS ST
4600 SIMI 93063 478-G7
SUMAC DR
2000 VeCo 93023 451-C4
SUMAC LN
11000 VeCo 93012 526-A1
11300 VeCo 93012 496-B7
SUMMER CT
- Chat 91311 499-J3
SUMMER ST
100 OJAI 93023 441-H6
12600 MRPK 93021 496-D3
SUMMER CLOUD DR
1700 THO 91362 526-J2
1700 THO 91362 527-A2
SUMMERFIELD ST
- THO 91360 526-F3
1400 CMRL 93012 525-A1
3000 CMRL 93012 495-A7
SUMMERGLEN CT
4400 MRPK 93021 496-C2
SUMMERHILL CT
6600 VeCo 91377 528-A7
SUMMER PARK CT
2200 THO 91362 527-A4
SUMMERSHADE LN
4000 MRPK 93021 496-F3
SUMMERSHORE LN
3600 WLKV 91361 557-C7
SUMMERTIME AV
23600 SIMI 93065 497-E3
SUMMERTON CT
- CMRL 93012 524-F4
SUMMER TREE CT
23600 SIMI 93065 498-A5
SUMMER VIEW CIR
10600 VeCo 93012 495-J7
10600 VeCo 93012 496-A7
SUMMERWOOD AV
- SIMI 93063 498-H1
SUMMIT AV
4700 SIMI 93063 478-H5
SUMMIT CIR
2900 VeCo 93012 496-E6
SUMMIT DR
400 VEN 93001 491-C1
23500 WHil 91304 499-E6
N SUMMIT DR
23500 WHil 91304 499-E6
SUMMIT TR
100 VeCo 93060 453-C1
SUMMIT KNOLL CT
400 VeCo 91377 558-B1
N SUMMIT RIDGE CIR
22300 Chat 91311 499-H6
S SUMMIT RIDGE CIR
22300 Chat 91311 499-H6
SUMMIT RIDGE CT
3900 THO 91362 557-C1
SUMMIT VIEW DR
4900 THO 91362 557-E1
SUMMIT VUE DR
- WdHl 91367 529-J7
SUMMIT VUE DR E
- WdHl 91367 529-J7
SUMMIT VUE DR N
- WdHl 91367 529-J7
SUMTER CT
1800 THO 91360 526-D5
SUNBEAM LN
23600 SIMI 93065 497-A2
SUN BONNET ST
300 SIMI 93065 527-D2
SUNBURST PL
3000 THO 91360 526-H2
SUN CIRCLE CT
300 SIMI 93065 497-E7
SUNDANCE ST
300 THO 91360 526-D2
SUNDANCE WY
1400 CMRL 93012 525-A1
SUNDOWN RD
100 VeCo 91361 556-G2
SUNER CIR
2000 CMRL 93010 494-H7
SUNFIELD CT
300 THO 91362 557-F2
SUNFISH WY
500 PHME 93041 552-F7
SUNFLOWER ST
- SIMI 93063 499-A1
2900 THO 91360 526-D3
10500 VEN 93004 493-A2
SUNGLOW AV
3200 SIMI 93063 478-F6
SUNGROVE DR
700 CMRL 93010 524-C2
SUNKIST CIR
1800 OXN 93033 552-H1
SUNKIST DR
1900 OXN 93033 552-H1
SUNKIST ST
400 PHME 93041 552-E3
N SUNLAND AV
7000 VeCo 93001 459-C4
SUNLIGHT ST
5400 SIMI 93063 478-J6
SUNLOFT LN
23600 SIMI 93065 497-A1
SUNNY LN
13300 VeCo 93012 496-E6
SUNNY ST
300 SPLA 93060 464-A7
SUNNY BROOK CT
400 VeCo 91377 558-B1
SUNNYCREST AV
1000 VEN 93003 472-C6
SUNNYCREST DR
6000 VeCo 91377 558-A1
SUNNYDALE AV
1500 SIMI 93065 497-J5
1700 SIMI 93065 498-A6
SUNNYDALE CT
1600 SIMI 93065 497-J5
SUNNYGLEN AV
1100 OJAI 93023 442-A6
SUNNYGLEN DR
12300 MRPK 93021 496-D3
SUNNYHILL CT
6300 VEN 93003 472-C7
SUNNYHILL ST
4400 THO 91362 527-D7
SUNNY POINT ST
23600 THO 91362 527-A2
SUNNYRIDGE DR
30000 AGRH 91301 557-H4
SUNNYSLOPE PL
13300 MRPK 93021 496-E4
SUNNYVISTA AV
- VeCo 91377 558-A3
SUNNYWAY DR
- VEN 93001 471-B7
SUNOAK PL
300 THO 91320 556-A2
SUN RANCH CT
22100 Chat 91311 499-J2
SUNRIDGE DR
1500 VEN 93003 492-D4
SUNRISE CT
1400 CMRL 93010 524-D1
7000 VEN 93003 472-D7
SUNRISE DR
2100 SIMI 93065 497-E2
SUNRISEMEADOW CIR
12800 MRPK 93021 496-E2
SUNROCK CT
200 SIMI 93065 527-E1
SUNSET
10800 VeCo 93021 496-A4
SUNSET AV
100 VeCo 93022 461-B1
300 VeCo 93022 451-A7
3400 SIMI 93063 478-J6
SUNSET CT
100 VeCo 93022 451-C6
SUNSET DR
- THO 91362 557-A3
100 THO 91361 557-A3
200 VeCo 93035 552-B4
1700 VEN 93001 491-F1
5200 OXN 93035 521-H6
SUNSET LN
3300 OXN 93035 552-A3
3300 VeCo 93035 552-A2
SUNSET PL
800 OJAI 93023 441-J6
3400 SIMI 93063 479-B6
SUNSET ST
- VeCo 93022 451-B6
SUNSET HILLS BLVD
1000 THO 91360 526-H1
1700 THO 91362 526-H1
1900 THO 91362 527-A2
SUNSET KNOLLS DR
3500 THO 91362 526-J1
SUNSETMEADOW CT
4400 MRPK 93021 496-D3
SUNSET OAK CIR
1000 THO 91320 556-C2
SUNSET RIDGE CT
6800 CanP 91307 529-D6
SUNSETRIDGE RD
3800 MRPK 93021 496-B4
SUNSET VALLEY RD
3200 VeCo 93021 496-H4

STREET Block City ZIP Pg-Grid

SUNSET VIEW CT
6100 VEN 93003 472-C7
SUNSHINE CT
1800 THO 91362 526-J2
SUNSHINE VALLEY CT
- SIMI 93063 479-B7
- SIMI 93063 499-B1
SUNSTONE ST
- VEN 93004 492-F3
4800 THO 91362 557-G1
SUNTREE LN
1600 SIMI 93063 498-J2
SUNVALE AV
500 VEN 93003 491-H4
SUN VALLEY CT
5400 AGRH 91301 557-J5
SUNWOOD LN
1000 VeCo 91377 528-A7
SUPERIOR AV
1100 VEN 93004 492-F3
SURFRIDER AV
2600 VEN 93001 491-F5
SURFRIDER WY
5100 OXN 93035 521-J7
SURFSIDE DR
500 OXN 93035 521-H6
600 PHME 93041 552-E6
W SURFSIDE ST
6900 VeCo 93001 459-C4
SURREY CIR
- OXN 93036 492-F7
- OXN 93036 522-F1
SURREY CT
2000 THO 91360 526-D4
SURREY WY
100 FILM 93015 456-A7
SURVEYOR AV
1600 SIMI 93063 498-F3
SUSAN AV
200 MRPK 93021 496-E1
10500 VeCo 93022 451-C6
SUSAN DR
1500 THO 91320 556-A2
SUSSEX CIR
800 THO 91360 526-G6
SUTTER AV
1100 SIMI 93065 497-H3
1700 SIMI 93065 498-A3
SUTTER DR
3300 OXN 93033 553-B3
SUTTER PL
1900 OXN 93033 553-A3
SUTTER ST
6000 VEN 93003 492-C1
SUTTON CREST TR
- VeCo 91377 527-J7
SUZANNE CT
100 THO 91320 556-B1
SWALLOW ST
6300 VEN 93003 492-D4
SWAN ST
6500 VEN 93003 492-D5
SWANFIELD CT
- VeCo 91361 556-E7
SWANSEA AV
1100 VEN 93004 492-H3
SWANSEA PL
1600 THO 91361 556-J6
SWEET BRIAR PL
1500 THO 91362 526-J3
SWEET BRIAR ST
4300 VEN 93003 491-J2
4300 VEN 93003 492-A2
SWEET CLOVER ST
3200 THO 91362 527-D3
SWEETGRASS AV
- SIMI 93065 478-A6
SWEETLAND ST
2000 OXN 93033 553-A5
SWEETLEAF LN
23600 SIMI 93065 497-A2
SWEETSHADE WY
- SIMI 93065 478-C7
SWEETWATER AV
1100 CMRL 93010 524-F1
SWEETWATER LN
9800 VEN 93004 492-H3
SWEETWOOD ST
3500 SIMI 93063 498-D1
N SWEETWOOD ST
2400 SIMI 93063 498-D1
SWIFT AV
1500 VEN 93003 492-D4
SWIFT PL
15800 MRPK 93021 477-A5
SWIFT FOX CT
- SIMI 93065 478-A5
SWIFT RUN CT
- MRPK 93021 476-G6
SWIFT RUN ST
- MRPK 93021 476-F6
N SWINDON AV
2000 SIMI 93063 499-C2
SWISS PINE PL
23600 SIMI 93063 498-D4
SWITZAR LN
600 THO 91360 526-G7
SYCAMORE
2100 VeCo 93023 451-C4
SYCAMORE DR
- VeCo 93001 461-A4
600 PHME 93041 552-F5
700 OXN 93033 552-F5
1000 SIMI 93065 498-C2
2600 SIMI 93065 478-C7
SYCAMORE LN
- VeCo 93023 441-E6
SYCAMORE RD
600 VeCo 93022 451-A5
1400 VeCo 93015 455-F4
3600 VeCo 93015 465-B2
3800 VeCo 93060 465-B2
SYCAMORE ST
- OXN 93036 522-H1
300 SPLA 93060 464-C4
3200 OXN 93033 552-H3
SYCAMORE CANYON DR
1600 THO 91361 586-H1
1600 WLKV 91361 586-H1
SYCAMORE CANYON RD
- VeCo - 555-C7
- VeCo - 584-H7
- VeCo - 585-A2
- VeCo 91320 555-C7
SYCAMORE COTTAGE CT
- CMRL 93012 524-G4
SYCAMORE GROVE ST
100 SIMI 93065 527-E1
100 SIMI 93065 497-E7
SYCAMORE RIDGE ST
100 SIMI 93065 497-D7
200 SIMI 93065 527-D1
SYLVAN DR
6100 VeCo 93063 499-B3
SYLVAN ST
22200 WdHI 91367 529-E7
SYMPHONY LN
4800 VeCo 91377 557-G2
SYRACUSE DR
4300 OXN 93033 553-A5
SYRINGA ST
400 THO 91360 526-D3

T

T ST
1500 VEN 93004 493-A3
TABOR CIR
800 VeCo 93010 494-F6
TACKABERRY CT
29000 AGRH 91301 558-A3
TACOMA ST
8700 VEN 93004 492-G3
TAFFRAIL CT
900 OXN 93035 522-B7
TAFFRAIL DR
1000 OXN 93035 522-C7
TAFFRAIL LN
2400 OXN 93035 522-B7
TAFT AV
100 VEN 93003 492-E2
TAHOE DR
8600 VEN 93004 492-G4
TAHOE LN
2200 OXN 93033 553-B5
TAHOE PL
6000 CMRL 93012 525-B1
TAHQUITZ CT
- CMRL 93012 524-H2
TAHQUITZ DR
- CMRL 93012 524-H2
TALAL CT
1800 VeCo 93012 526-B1
TALBERT AV
400 SIMI 93065 498-C4
TALLOWBERRY LN
23600 SIMI 93065 497-A1
TALMADGE RD
4700 MRPK 93021 496-C2
TALOS AV
- VeCo 93041 583-H3
TALOS RD
- PHME 93043 552-C5
TALUD TER
200 CMRL 93012 524-H2
TALUS ST
2800 OXN 93030 522-D3
TAM CT
2000 SIMI 93063 499-B2
TAMARAC ST
600 OXN 93033 552-H3
TAMARACK ST
1900 THO 91361 556-J4
1900 THO 91361 557-A4
TAMARIN AV
1700 VEN 93003 492-F4
TAMARIND ST
6000 VeCo 91377 558-A3
TAMARIX ST
1300 VeCo 93010 524-C1
1400 CMRL 93010 524-C1
TAMLEI AV
800 THO 91362 526-J7
TAM O SHANTER DR
4500 THO 91362 527-D6
TAMPA WY
10100 VEN 93004 492-J2
TANAGER ST
- VEN 93003 492-D5
TANBARK CT
1500 THO 91361 557-A6
TANGELO PL
6000 SIMI 93063 499-B3
TANGERINE PL
400 OXN 93033 552-G3
TANGLBRUSH LN
23600 SIMI 93065 497-A2
TANGLEWOOD CT
100 THO 91360 526-F2
TANGLEWOOD DR
2600 CMRL 93010 494-F6
TANISHA CT
23600 SIMI 93065 478-C7
TANNER RIDGE AV
400 THO 91362 557-G1
TANOAK LN
900 VeCo 91377 557-G1
TAORMINA LN
200 OJAI 93023 451-E1
TAOS AV
- VEN 93001 471-C5
TAPIES CT
900 THO 91320 555-F4
TAPIR CIR
1600 VEN 93003 492-E4
TAPLEY CT
1900 SIMI 93063 499-C2
TAPLEY ST
6500 SIMI 93063 499-C2
TAPO ST
3500 SIMI 93063 478-G7
13500 SIMI 93063 498-G2
TAPO CANYON RD
1400 SIMI 93063 498-F2
2600 SIMI 93063 478-F7
3400 VeCo 93063 478-F3
4800 VeCo - 478-F3
23600 VeCo 93040 367-E9
23600 VeCo 93040 458-E6
TARA ST
600 THO 91320 525-H7
TARANTO WY
4800 VeCo 91377 557-G2
TARKIO ST
100 THO 91360 526-E4
TARLOW AV
- VEN 93003 492-A3
TARRYTOWN LN
3900 AGRH 91301 558-E7
TARSIER LN
7200 VEN 93003 492-F4
TARTAR DR
- VeCo 93041 583-H3
TARTAR RD
- PHME 93043 552-C5
TASCOSA CT
- VeCo 91377 527-J7
TATU ST
3200 SIMI 93063 479-A6
TAXCO CT
1600 CMRL 93010 524-D2
W TAXCO CT
- SIMI 93065 497-F4
TAYLOR CT
- THO 91360 556-G1
- THO 91362 556-G1
TAYLOR LN
- FILM 93015 455-J4
TAYLOR ST
3800 VEN 93003 491-H2
TAYLOR RANCH RD
500 VeCo 93001 470-J4
500 VeCo 93001 471-A5
500 VeCo 93001 490-J1
500 VeCo 93001 491-A1
500 VEN 93001 490-J1
TEAGUE DR
600 SPLA 93060 464-B4
TEAGUE PL
23600 VeCo 93060 453-G2
TEAKWOOD CT
800 THO 91320 556-C2
TEAKWOOD ST
200 OXN 93033 552-F3
800 PHME 93041 552-F3
TEAL AV
1200 VEN 93003 492-D4
TEAL CT
2900 THO 91360 526-F3
TEAL CLUB RD
1500 OXN 93030 522-B5
1500 VeCo 93030 522-B5
TEARDROP CT
- THO 91320 555-F2
TEASDALE ST
- THO 91360 526-F4
TECH CIR
5400 MRPK 93021 496-D1
TECOLOTE CT
4200 MRPK 93021 496-E3
TECOPA SPRINGS LN
- SIMI 93063 479-A6
TEHAMA ST
1400 OXN 93035 552-E1
TEITSORT DR
- FILM 93015 456-A4
- VeCo 93015 456-A4
TEJEDA AV
12100 MRPK 93021 496-D1
TEJON CT
1600 CMRL 93010 524-D1
2800 SIMI 93063 479-A7
TELEGRAPH PL
- VEN 93003 491-J2
TELEGRAPH RD
6200 VEN 93003 492-D2
6400 VeCo 93003 492-D2
7500 VEN 93004 492-G1
9900 VEN 93004 472-H7
10600 VeCo 93004 472-H7
11000 VEN 93060 472-H7
11200 VEN 93004 473-A6
11200 VEN 93060 473-A6
11200 VeCo 93060 473-A6
15900 VEN 93003 491-H3
TELEGRAPH RD Rt#-126
- FILM 93015 456-E6
- VeCo 93015 456-E6
900 VeCo 93015 457-E5
1400 VeCo 93040 457-G4
2200 VeCo 93040 458-B5
2700 VeCo 93015 465-C1
17900 VeCo 93060 464-F3
18400 SPLA 93060 464-F3
20100 VeCo 93060 465-A2
E TELEGRAPH RD
17000 VeCo 93060 464-D5
17200 SPLA 93060 464-D5
E TELEGRAPH RD Rt#-126
100 FILM 93015 456-C6
300 VeCo 93015 456-C6
W TELEGRAPH RD
800 SPLA 93060 463-H6
800 SPLA 93060 463-H7
11000 VeCo 93004 473-B5
11000 VeCo 93060 473-C1
11000 VEN 93004 473-B5
TELEPHONE RD
4500 VeCo 93003 492-A5
4700 VEN 93003 492-B4
6800 VEN 93009 492-B4
7300 VEN 93004 492-B4
10500 VEN 93004 493-A1
23600 VeCo 93004 493-A1
TELEPHONE RELAY RD
23600 VeCo 93001 471-E7
TELLER RD
2200 THO 91320 525-J7
TELOMA DR
100 VEN 93003 492-B1
TELON CT
100 SIMI 93065 497-F6
TELSA ST
600 VeCo 93023 451-C3
TELSTAR DR
1100 OXN 93030 522-J7
1100 OXN 93033 522-J7
TEMESCAL ST
300 VeCo 93040 457-F4
TEMPE CT
4000 SIMI 93063 478-F6
TEMPE WY
32300 WLKV 91361 557-C7
TEMPLE AV
500 CMRL 93010 524-F1
700 VEN 93004 492-J1
1800 CMRL 93010 494-E6
TEMPLETON ST
- VEN 93003 492-A4
TENNEYSON DR
5700 AGRH 91301 557-J4
TENNYSON CT
2500 THO 91360 526-D3
TENNYSON LN
700 VEN 93003 492-D3
TENNYSON ST
100 THO 91360 526-D3
TERAZZA WY
- OXN 93030 523-A3
TERESA ST
23600 OXN 93030 522-J4
TERI CT
- LA 91304 529-J2
TERN CT
1500 VEN 93003 492-E4
TERNEZ DR
3800 VeCo 93021 496-A4
10400 VeCo 93021 495-J4
TERRA BELLA CT
5700 CMRL 93012 495-B7
TERRA BELLA LN
2200 CMRL 93012 495-A7
TERRACE AV
4200 OXN 93033 552-J5
TERRACE DR
200 SIMI 93065 497-E2
1800 VEN 93001 491-E1
3500 OXN 93033 552-J4
TERRACE HILL CIR
4900 THO 91362 557-G1
TERRACEMEADOW CT
4400 MRPK 93021 496-E3
TERRACERIDGE RD
3900 MRPK 93021 496-B4
TERRACE VIEW PL
400 PHME 93041 552-E6
TERRACINA DR
900 SPLA 93060 464-B4
TERRA GLEN WY
23600 SIMI 93065 497-A1
TERRAMAR WY
5000 OXN 93035 521-J7
TERRIER DR
- PHME 93043 552-C5
TERRIER ST
- VeCo 93041 583-H3
TERRONEZ PL
- OXN 93030 522-J4
TERRY DR
4900 VEN 93003 492-A1
TERRY RD
- VeCo 93012 554-C5
TEST AREA RD
23600 VeCo 93063 498-H7
23600 VeCo 93063 528-G1
TETLOW AV
1700 SIMI 93063 499-C2
TETON LN
4700 VEN 93003 492-B4
TEWA CT
1600 VeCo 93022 451-E4
TEXANIA TER
- LA 91304 529-D2
TEXAS AV
2700 SIMI 93063 478-H7
23600 FILM 93015 456-B6
23600 VeCo 93015 456-B6
TEXAS LN
800 VeCo 93060 464-D4
THACHER RD
3000 VeCo 93023 442-E4
THACHER SCHOOL RD
5000 VeCo 93023 442-G4
THACKERY CT
6800 VEN 93003 492-E3
THAMES ST
100 THO 91360 526-E5
THAMES RIVER DR
100 OXN 93036 492-H7
THAYER LN
700 PHME 93041 552-F3
THELMA LN
11000 VeCo 93012 496-A7
THERESA DR
2900 THO 91320 555-G1
2900 VeCo 91320 555-G1
THERESA ST
2600 THO 91320 555-H1
THICKET PL
2700 SIMI 93065 478-C7
THILLE ST
4600 VEN 93003 492-B3
7800 VEN 93004 492-F3
THIONNET PL
15300 MRPK 93021 476-J5
THISTLEGATE RD
900 VeCo 91377 528-A7
900 VeCo 91377 558-A1
THISTLEWOOD ST
3000 THO 91360 526-F2
THOMAS AV
100 OXN 93033 552-G3
THOMAS CT
4200 SIMI 93063 478-F5
THOMAS DR
300 SPLA 93060 464-A7
THOMAS LN
1000 VEN 93003 492-A7
E THOMAS ST
500 VeCo 93022 451-C6
THOMASVILLE CT
13000 MRPK 93021 496-E4
THOMPSON AV
9400 Chat 91311 499-F6
E THOMPSON BLVD
- VEN 93001 491-C2
2300 VEN 93001 491-E2
W THOMPSON BLVD
- VEN 93001 491-B2
THOMPSON LN
200 Chat 91311 499-F6
500 VeCo 93063 499-F6
1400 SIMI 93065 497-J3
9200 Chat 91311 499-F7
THOMPSON RD
300 Chat 91311 499-F6
9200 Chat 91311 499-F6
9200 Chat 91311 499-F6
THOREAU CIR
100 THO 91360 526-F6
THOREAU LN
500 VEN 93003 492-D1
THORNCROFT CT
1300 THO 91361 556-J5
THORNHILL AV
1400 THO 91361 556-J5
THORN RIDGE CT
- SIMI 93063 478-H4
N THORNWOOD ST
800 SIMI 93065 498-A5
THORPE CIR
300 THO 91360 526-E5
THORSBY RD
2100 VeCo 91361 556-F7
THOUSAND OAKS BLVD
25800 LACo 91302 558-H4
26000 CALB 91302 558-H4
28700 AGRH 91301 558-A4
29400 AGRH 91301 557-G4
30700 WLKV 91301 557-G4
E THOUSAND OAKS BLVD
- THO 91360 556-F1
800 THO 91362 556-F1
2400 THO 91362 557-A3
30700 WLKV 91362 557-E4
W THOUSAND OAKS BLVD
- THO 91360 556-E1
THRASHER CT
1500 VEN 93003 492-F4
THREE OAK CT
2400 SIMI 93063 499-A1
THREE SPRINGS DR
2600 WLKV 91361 557-A7
THRUSH AV
1500 VEN 93003 492-E4
2200 OXN 93033 553-A4
THUNDERBIRD DR
2300 THO 91362 556-J2
2300 THO 91362 557-A2
THUNDERHEAD ST
300 THO 91360 526-D2
THURGOOD MARSHALL DR
- OXN 93030 522-D3
- OXN 93036 522-D3
TIARA DR
1800 VeCo 93023 451-D3
TIARA ST
8100 VEN 93004 492-F3
TIBER ST
8800 VEN 93004 492-H4
TIBERIAS WY
- SIMI 93063 479-C7
TIBER RIVER DR
- OXN 93036 492-H5
TIBURON CT
1600 THO 91362 526-J4
TICO AV
200 OJAI 93023 441-H6
TICO RD
400 VeCo 93023 441-D7
600 VeCo 93023 451-D2
N TICO RD
100 OJAI 93023 441-G6
TIERNEY AV
- VEN 93003 492-C3
TIERRA DR
1200 THO 91362 526-H7
TIERRA BUENA CT
23600 CMRL 93010 524-C4
TIERRA LINDA CT
700 CMRL 93010 524-C1
TIERRA REJADA RD
- SIMI 93065 497-A3
900 VeCo 93021 497-A3
900 VeCo 93065 497-A3
2000 MRPK 93021 496-C2
9900 VeCo 93021 496-G4
TIESA DR
- OXN 93030 522-J3
TIFFANEY LN
2700 SIMI 93063 478-D7
TIFFANY CT
1600 CMRL 93010 494-D7
1600 CMRL 93010 524-D1
TIGHE LN
700 FILM 93015 456-A5
TIKI DR
1300 OXN 93033 552-J5
TIKI WK
1800 OXN 93033 552-J2
1800 OXN 93033 553-A1
TILBURY CT
2000 THO 91360 526-D4
TILDEN CT
- SIMI 93065 527-E1
TILLER AV
2500 PHME 93041 552-C2
2600 OXN 93035 552-C2
2600 PHME 93035 552-C2
TILLER DR
3600 OXN 93035 522-B7
TIMBER RD
- THO 91320 556-B2
- VeCo 91320 556-B2
TIMBER CANYON RD
1900 VeCo 93060 454-H4
3400 VeCo 93060 464-H2
TIMBERCREEK TR
800 OXN 93036 522-F1
TIMBERDALE RD
4200 MRPK 93021 496-C3
TIMBERHILL CT
1800 SIMI 93063 498-E2
TIMBER HOLLOW AV
- MRPK 93021 476-F6
TIMBERLANE AV
2100 SIMI 93063 499-A2
TIMBERLANE CT
2200 OXN 93036 522-E2
TIMBERLANE ST
6200 AGRH 91301 558-A3
TIMBERRIDGE CT
32400 WLKV 91361 557-B7
TIMBERRIDGE RD
3800 MRPK 93021 496-B4
TIMBERVIEW CT
3800 MRPK 93021 496-C4
TIMBERWOOD AV
400 THO 91360 526-D3
TINIAN
- PHME 93041 552-E5
TINKERMAN ST
5500 SIMI 93063 499-A2
TINSLEY MOUNTAIN RD
23600 VeCo 93060 453-F3
TIOGA DR
300 VEN 93001 491-C1
TIOGA PL
700 THO 91320 526-B7
22200 LA 91304 529-J1
TIPPERARY LN
1800 THO 91320 556-A1
TIRRE CT
300 SPLA 93060 464-A7
TITAN PL
1300 OXN 93033 522-J7
TITANIA PL
2600 SIMI 93063 478-J7
TIVERTON DR
- CMRL 93012 524-G4
TIVOLI LN
1100 SIMI 93065 497-H1
TOBAGA WY
300 VeCo 91377 557-G2
N TOBY PL
2300 SIMI 93065 498-B1
TODD CT
300 OXN 93030 523-B5
TODD LN
100 SPLA 93060 473-H1
400 VeCo 93060 473-H2
TODD RD
100 VeCo 93060 473-E3
900 SPLA 93060 473-E3
TODD VIEW CT
8600 LA 91304 529-C1
TOLAND RD
100 VeCo 93060 454-J7
100 VeCo 93060 455-A6
100 VeCo 93060 464-J1
TOLAND PARK RD
- VeCo 93060 454-J7
- VeCo 93060 464-J1
TOLEDO CT
3500 THO 91320 525-F7
TOLSTOY PL
- OXN 93033 552-J2
TOLTECS CT
2500 VEN 93001 471-C5
TOMAHAWK DR
- PHME 93043 552-C5
- VeCo 93042 583-H2
TOMAHAWK TER
8400 LA 91304 529-D1
TONALE WY
400 VeCo 91377 557-G1
TONGA ST
11500 VeCo 90265 625-F5
TONGAREVA ST
11400 VeCo 90265 625-F5
TONOPAH CT
23600 SIMI 93063 479-A6
TONY AV
6100 WdHI 91367 529-E7
6400 CanP 91307 529-E6
TOP CIR
4800 SIMI 93063 478-H5
TOPA LN
100 VeCo 93060 453-C1
TOPANGA CANYON BLVD Rt#-27
9500 Chat 91311 499-J6
TOPANGA CANYON PL
9500 Chat 91311 499-J6
TOPA TOPA CT
700 VEN 93003 472-B7
TOPA TOPA DR
100 OJAI 93023 441-H7
5400 VEN 93003 472-B7
E TOPA TOPA ST
100 OJAI 93023 441-H7
W TOPA TOPA ST
100 OJAI 93023 441-H7
TOPA VIEW TR
1400 VeCo 91320 556-B3
TOPAZ AV
1700 VEN 93004 492-H4
2800 SIMI 93063 478-D7
TOPAZ CT
900 OJAI 93023 441-J5
2400 OXN 93030 522-D3
TOPEKA AV
600 VEN 93004 492-H2
TOPSAIL CIR
2300 THO 91361 557-B6
TOPSAIL CT
900 OXN 93035 522-B7
TORENA WY
- OXN 93030 523-A4
TORERO DR
- OXN 93030 522-H4
TORINO ST
23600 MRPK 93021 496-C3
E TORRANCE ST
2100 SIMI 93065 498-A4
TORREPINES PL
30000 AGRH 91301 557-H5
TORREY RD
100 VeCo 93015 457-F5
100 VeCo 93040 457-F5
TORREY CANYON RD
- VeCo - 467-F1
- VeCo 93040 467-F1
900 VeCo 93015 457-F7
900 VeCo 93015 467-F1
TORREY PINE CT
1500 THO 91360 526-H2
TORREY PINES CT
2200 OXN 93033 553-B5
TORRIDON CT
- MRPK 93021 496-E2
TORY WY
10100 VEN 93004 492-J2
TOTH PL
5700 AGRH 91301 558-C5
TOTTENHAM CT
1500 VeCo 91377 527-H6
TOUCAN WY
6900 VEN 93003 492-E4
TOULOUSE CIR
3100 THO 91362 526-J2
TOURMALINE DR
1000 THO 91320 525-H7
TOWER CT
- CMRL 93010 493-H7
TOWER DR
2500 VeCo 93023 442-C7
TOWER SQ
1300 VEN 93003 491-J4
TOWHEE CT
1400 VEN 93003 492-E4
TOWN CENTER DR
1000 OXN 93036 492-G7
TOWN FOREST CT
- CMRL 93012 524-G4
TOWNLEY CIR
1700 SIMI 93063 499-A3
TOWNS CT
300 SPLA 93060 463-H6
TOWNSGATE RD
2100 THO 91361 557-B4
TOWNSHIP AV
2900 SIMI 93063 478-D6
2900 VeCo 93063 478-D6
TRABAJO DR
1000 OXN 93030 523-E3
TRABUCO OAK DR
23600 SIMI 93063 498-D4
TRACT 13 RD
- PHME 93043 552-C6
TRACT 14 RD
- PHME 93043 552-C3
N TRACY AV
2000 SIMI 93063 498-E2
TRACY CT
100 THO 91320 555-G2
TRADEWINDS DR
3900 OXN 93035 522-A7
TRAFALGER PL
1500 THO 91361 556-H6
TRAIL CREEK DR
29900 AGRH 91301 557-H5
TRAILCREST DR
4000 MRPK 93021 496-F4
TRAILROCK CT
700 SIMI 93065 527-C1
TRAILS END DR
23600 Chat 91311 499-F6
TRAILSIDE CT
200 THO 91320 556-C1
TRAILVIEW CT
3400 THO 91360 526-H2
TRAILWAY LN
29200 AGRH 91301 558-A5
29400 AGRH 91301 557-J5
TRANA CIR
26000 CALB 91302 558-J3
TRANCAS LAKES DR
- LACo 90265 586-H6
TRANQUIL LN
300 VeCo 91377 558-A1
600 SIMI 93065 497-G5
TRANQUILA CIR
100 CMRL 93012 524-H2
TRANQUILA DR
- CMRL 93012 524-H2
TRANSOM WY
600 OXN 93035 522-E6
TRANSPORT ST
3700 VEN 93003 491-J5
4100 VEN 93003 492-A5
TRAPANI CT
11800 MRPK 93021 496-C5
TRAVIS AV
2900 SIMI 93063 478-H6
TREADWELL AV
1000 SIMI 93065 498-B4
TREE FERN CT
- CMRL 93010 524-A2
TREE HOLLOW CT
400 SIMI 93065 527-E1
TREE HOLLOW GN
29300 AGRH 91301 558-A5
TREELINE RD
- PHME 93043 552-C3
TREE RANCH RD
12300 VeCo 93023 453-B1
TREE TOP LN
500 THO 91360 526-D6
TREEVIEW CT
11500 MRPK 93021 496-B2
TREFOIL AV
6400 VeCo 91377 558-B1
TREGO CT
- SIMI 93065 477-J6
TRELLIS PL
- CMRL 93012 524-G4
N TREMONT AV
2000 SIMI 93063 499-C2
E TREMONT CIR
6600 SIMI 93063 499-C2
TRENLEY CT
2600 SIMI 93063 498-E1
TRENT LN
300 SPLA 93060 463-H6
TRENTHAM RD
1900 VeCo 91361 556-H7
TRENTON LN
9700 VEN 93004 492-H2
TRENTWOOD DR
23600 VeCo 91361 556-E7
TREVI PL
400 VeCo 91377 557-G2
TREVINO DR
- MRPK 93021 476-B5
TREVINO TER
800 OXN 93033 552-H5
TRIANGLE ST
- THO 91360 526-F5
TRICKLNG BROOK CT
200 SIMI 93065 498-A6
TRIGGER PL
9700 Chat 91311 499-H5
E TRIGGER RD
- VeCo 91307 528-H4
TRIGGER ST
22700 Chat 91311 499-G6
TRILLIUM ST
2800 THO 91360 526-D3
TRINIDAD WY
800 OXN 93033 552-H3
TRINITY DR
3100 VEN 93003 491-G4
TRINITY PL
2400 OXN 93033 553-A2
TRINWAY AV
2100 SIMI 93065 498-C2
TRITON ST
2500 PHME 93041 552-D2
2800 OXN 93041 552-D2
TRIUNFO CANYON RD
100 THO 91361 557-B4
1100 WLKV 91361 557-A5
TRIUNFO RIDGE FIRE TR
- LACo 90265 586-D4
- VeCo 90265 586-D4
TROJAN CT
6700 MRPK 93021 476-H6
TROLLOPE CT
15700 MRPK 93021 477-A5
TROUSDALE ST
5300 VeCo 91377 527-H7
TROWBRIDGE CT
3900 WLKV 91361 557-D6
TRUCKEE DR
8300 VEN 93004 492-G4
TRUCK HAUL RD
100 OXN 93036 492-H6
TRUENO AV
600 VeCo 93010 494-B5
TRUETT CIR
2000 THO 91360 526-D5
TRUMAN AV
- VEN 93004 492-E1
TRUMAN ST
2500 CMRL 93010 524-F1
TRUSTY LN
1300 VeCo 93023 451-B2
TUBA ST
22100 Chat 91311 499-J4
TUBBS ST
1600 THO 91362 526-J7
TUCKER ST
11900 VeCo 93021 476-D3
TUCSON ST
4100 SIMI 93063 478-F6
TUCSON WY
10100 VEN 93004 492-J2
TUDOR CIR
700 THO 91360 526-G6
TUDOR LN
1000 FILM 93015 455-J6
TUGBOAT WY
- PHME 93041 552-E5
TUJUNGA AV
100 VeCo 93035 552-B5
TULANE AV
200 VEN 93003 491-J2
N TULANE AV
6700 MRPK 93021 476-G6
TULARE LN
28400 AGRH 91301 558-C6
TULARE PL
2400 OXN 93033 553-A2
TULARE ST
10100 VEN 93004 492-J2
TULE LAKE ST
- VEN 93004 492-J3
TULIP AV
- SIMI 93063 499-A2
TULIP CT
200 VEN 93004 473-A7
TULIPAN CIR
- OXN 93030 523-A4
TULIPAN DR
- OXN 93030 523-A4
TULIP WOOD CT
- SIMI 93063 479-B7
- SIMI 93063 499-B1
TULL ST
- VEN 93003 492-C3
TULSA CIR
10400 VEN 93004 492-J1
TULSA DR
4700 OXN 93033 553-A5
4700 VeCo 93033 553-A5
TULSA ST
22000 Chat 91311 499-J3
TUMBLEWEED AV
2600 SIMI 93065 478-C7
2600 SIMI 93065 498-C1
TUOLUMNE AV
100 VEN 93004 472-H7
N TUOLUMNE AV
500 THO 91360 526-D7
TUPELO WOOD CT
800 THO 91320 556-C2
TURFWAY RD
6100 MRPK 93021 476-A6
TURIN ST
400 VeCo 91377 557-G1
TURLOCK AV
1300 VEN 93004 492-H3
TURNBERRY DR
- OXN 93036 522-B3
TURNBURY ST
1200 SIMI 93065 497-D7
TURNOUT PARK CRES
3300 OXN 93036 492-J7
TURNSTONE CIR
- MRPK 93021 476-E6
TURNSTONE CT
- VEN 93003 492-D5
TURQUOISE AV
- VEN 93004 492-F3
TURQUOISE CIR
2500 THO 91320 525-H6
TURTLE CREEK LN
100 THO 91320 526-B6
TUSCANA CT
11800 MRPK 93021 496-C4
TUSCAN GROVE PL
- CMRL 93012 495-D7
TUSCANY DR
- VeCo 91377 557-G2
TUSCARORA AV
2300 VEN 93001 471-D6
TUTTLE AV
900 SIMI 93065 497-G5
TUXEDO RW
- OXN 93036 492-F7
TUXFORD PL
3300 THO 91360 526-G2
TWILIGHT CT
- CMRL 93012 524-F4
TWILIGHT CANYON TR
- SIMI 93063 499-E3
TWILIGHT GLEN LN
23600 SIMI 93065 497-A1
TWILIGHT RIDGE CIR
1600 THO 91362 527-F6
TWILLIN CT
700 SIMI 93065 497-D6
TWIN CIRCLE LN
6400 SIMI 93063 499-C3
TWIN FALLS CT
200 THO 91320 556-A1
TWINFOOT CT
1000 THO 91361 557-B5
TWIN HARBOR
- VeCo 93012 554-F3
TWINING LN
200 SIMI 93065 497-E6
TWIN LAKE RDG
3400 WLKV 91361 557-B7
TWIN OAK DR
1200 OXN 93036 522-E1

STREET
Block City ZIP Pg-Grid

TWIN OAKS CT
400 THO 91362 557-A1
TWIN PEAKS ST
1300 SIMI 93065 497-D7
TWIN RIVER CIR
1800 VEN 93004 492-G4
TWIN SPRINGS AV
6300 VeCo 91377 558-A1
TWIN TIDES PL
- OXN 93035 522-A7
- OXN 93035 552-A1
TWISTED OAK DR
- CanP 91307 529-C7
23600 SIMI 93065 527-F1
TWO OAK CT
2400 SIMI 93063 499-A1
TYLER AV
200 VEN 93003 492-E1
TYLER CT
- VEN 93003 492-E1
2900 SIMI 93063 478-G7
TYNEBOURNE CT
31800 WLKV 91361 557-D6

U

U ST
1500 VEN 93004 493-A3
UKIAH ST
200 PHME 93041 552-E2
1300 OXN 93035 552-E1
2000 OXN 93041 552-E1
ULVERSTON ST
4900 VeCo 91377 557-H1
ULYSSES ST
100 SIMI 93065 497-F2
UNDERPASS ST
2600 OXN 93036 522-G1
UNICORN CIR
7200 VEN 93003 492-E4
UNIDAD WY
- OXN 93030 522-H3
UNIDOS AV
12400 MRPK 93021 496-D2
UNION PL
2100 SIMI 93065 497-F2
UNION PACIFIC ST
- FILM 93015 455-J7
- FILM 93015 456-A7
UNITED RD
3900 AGRH 91301 558-F7
UNIVERSE CIR
1500 OXN 93033 552-J1
UNIVERSITY AV
- VEN 93003 492-A2
UNIVERSITY DR
1900 VeCo 93012 554-E2
6900 MRPK 93021 477-A5
UNIVERSITY PL
200 SPLA 93060 464-B6
UPLAND RD
4500 CMRL 93010 494-J7
4500 VeCo 93010 494-J7
4600 CMRL 93012 494-J7
5100 CMRL 93012 495-A7
6600 CMRL 93012 525-D1
UPPER BAY DR
700 OXN 93036 522-F1
UPPER LAKE RD
- VeCo 91361 586-F1
- VeCo 91361 556-F7
UPPER RANCH RD
1400 THO 91362 527-C5
UPPINGHAM DR
700 THO 91360 526-G2
UPTON SINCLAIR DR
- OXN 93033 552-J2
URANIUM DR
2400 OXN 93030 522-D3
URBANA AV
100 THO 91320 555-H1
URBANA LN
- OXN 93030 522-J3
URSULA DR
23600 OXN 93030 522-J4
UTE LN
200 VEN 93001 471-C6
UTICA AV
700 VEN 93004 492-H2
UTIL CIR
- OXN 93030 522-J3

V

V ST
1500 VEN 93004 492-J2
1500 VEN 93004 493-A3
VALARIE AV
3200 SIMI 93063 478-E6
VALDEZ AL
- VEN 93001 491-B2
VALE PL
4000 THO 91362 527-C7
VALECROFT AV
900 THO 91361 556-J5
VALENCIA AV
2700 SIMI 93063 478-E7
2700 SIMI 93063 498-E1
VALENCIA CIR
2600 THO 91360 526-B3
VALENCIA CT
2600 SIMI 93063 498-E1
VALENCIA DR
1000 VeCo 93010 494-F6
VALENCIA PL
1400 OXN 93035 522-E7
VALENTINA DR
23600 OXN 93030 522-J5
VALENTINE RD
4400 VEN 93003 492-B4
VALERIO ST
22000 CanP 91303 529-H4
22300 CanP 91307 529-F4
23200 LA 91304 529-F4
VALERIO WY
- CMRL 93012 524-H1
VALERO CIR
4900 VeCo 91377 557-G2
VALEROSA WY
- OXN 93030 522-J3
VALEWOOD CIR
3200 THO 91360 526-F2
VALJEAN AV
1200 SIMI 93065 498-C4
VALLECITO DR
800 VEN 93001 491-D1
VALLEJO AV
800 SIMI 93065 498-A4
VALLE LINDO DR
700 CMRL 93010 524-C2
VALLERIO AV
100 OJAI 93023 441-F7
200 OJAI 93023 451-F1
VALLEY CIR
8300 LA 91304 529-E2
VALLEY RD
- VeCo 93022 451-A7
700 MRPK 93021 476-F7
23600 VeCo 91361 556-A6
VALLEY CIRCLE BLVD
6000 WdHl 91367 529-D6
6300 CanP 91307 529-D5
6900 LACo 91307 529-D5
7100 LA 91304 529-E2
8600 LA 91304 499-G7
9000 Chat 91311 499-H5
9200 Chat 91311 499-G7
VALLEY CIRCLE TER
6300 CanP 91307 529-D7
VALLEY CREST
3600 VeCo 93021 495-H3
VALLEY CREST RD
300 SIMI 93065 497-E5
VALLEY FAIR ST
4000 SIMI 93063 498-F2
VALLEYFIELD AV
2100 THO 91360 526-A4
VALLEY FLORES DR
7800 LA 91304 529-E1
VALLEY GATE RD
- SIMI 93065 497-F6
VALLEY HEIGHTS DR
28900 AGRH 91301 558-A5
VALLEY HIGH AV
800 THO 91362 526-J7
1200 THO 91362 527-A6
VALLEY MEADOW CT
2300 VeCo 93022 451-C4
2300 VeCo 93023 451-C4
VALLEY MEADOW DR
2100 VeCo 93022 451-C4
2100 VeCo 93023 451-C4
VALLEY OAK LN
- THO 91362 527-B3
VALLEY PARK DR
1400 OXN 93033 552-G1
W VALLEY RIDGE ST
- VeCo 93023 451-B4
VALLEY SPRING DR
4000 THO 91362 527-C7
VALLEY TERRACE DR
23600 SIMI 93065 478-B7
VALLEY VIEW DR
- VeCo 93022 451-B6
VALLEY VIEW RD
1400 OJAI 93023 441-H4
1400 VeCo 93023 441-H4
1400 VeCo 93023 442-A4
VALLEYVIEW WY
500 VEN 93003 492-B1
VALLEY VISTA
800 FILM 93015 456-A5
VALLEY VISTA DR
100 CMRL 93010 524-A1
100 VeCo 93010 524-A1
200 CMRL 93010 494-A7
200 VeCo 93010 494-B6
VALMORE AV
300 VEN 93003 491-G4
VAL VERDE DR
8400 LA 91304 529-D1
8500 WHIL 91304 529-D1
VAN BUREN ST
7300 VEN 93003 492-E2
7400 VEN 93004 492-E2
VANCOUVER AV
2600 VEN 93003 491-G3
VANDA LN
- OXN 93036 522-B2
VANDERBILT CT
4500 VEN 93003 492-A1
VANDERBILT DR
200 OXN 93036 522-H2
VAN DYKE ST
- THO 91360 526-E4
VANESSA ST
2000 SIMI 93063 498-F2
VANETTA ST
2000 OXN 93033 553-A5
VAN GOUGH DR
- OXN 93033 552-J2
VANGUARD DR
1100 OXN 93033 522-J7
1100 OXN 93033 552-J1
2300 CMRL 93010 494-E7
VANILLA LN
- SIMI 93065 498-C1
VANITA PL
2100 VeCo 93010 494-E7
VAN NESS AV
300 OXN 93033 552-F5
VAN NUYS AV
100 VeCo 93035 552-C6
VANOWEN ST
21900 CanP 91303 529-G6
22200 CanP 91307 529-D6
24400 LACo 91307 529-D6
VAQUERO CIR
- OXN 93030 522-H3
VAQUERO DR
- OXN 93030 522-H3
1400 SIMI 93065 497-F3
VARE CT
- MRPK 93021 476-B5
VARSITY CT
- VEN 93003 492-A2
VARSITY ST
4200 VEN 93003 491-J3
4300 VEN 93003 492-A2
15000 MRPK 93021 476-J6
N VASSAR CIR
6400 MRPK 93021 476-H6
VASSAR ST
4300 VEN 93003 491-J1
4300 VEN 93003 492-A1
VAUGHN ST
23600 Chat 91311 499-G6
VEDDER MTWY
- VeCo 90265 586-C3
- VeCo 91361 586-C3
VEGA WY
800 VeCo 93023 451-C2
VEGAS DR
200 OXN 93030 522-J6
VEJAR DR
4900 AGRH 91301 558-B6
VELA CT
100 SPLA 93060 463-J6
VELARDE DR
600 THO 91360 526-C3
VELMA CT
2600 SIMI 93065 478-C7
VELVET OAK CT
- SIMI 93063 499-A4
VENADO AV E
100 THO 91320 556-C1
VENDELL RD
27400 AGRH 91301 558-E7
VENETIAN DR
5200 OXN 93035 521-J6
VENEZIA LN
- THO 91362 527-B3
VENICE RD
- PHME 93043 552-C6
VENICE ST
1300 SIMI 93065 497-G3
VENTANA CT
100 THO 91360 526-F1
VENTAVO DR
9400 VeCo 93012 495-J3
9400 VeCo 93021 495-J3
VENTOSO AV
6200 CMRL 93012 525-C1
N VENTU PARK RD
100 THO 91320 556-B1
400 THO 91320 526-A6
S VENTU PARK RD
- THO 91320 556-B1
- THO 91320 556-B2
VENTU PARK FIRE RD
1100 VeCo 91320 556-A3
1900 THO 91320 555-H3
1900 VeCo 91320 555-H3
2100 THO 91320 556-A3
23600 VeCo 91361 556-A3
VENTURA AV
100 VeCo 93035 552-C6
700 SIMI 93065 497-G3
2800 VeCo 93001 471-C1
2800 VEN 93001 471-C4
5500 VeCo 93001 461-B6
5900 VEN 93001 461-B6
VENTURA AV Rt#-33
- VeCo 93022 451-B5
4400 VeCo 93001 461-A2
4400 VeCo 93022 461-A2
VENTURA AV Rt#-33
11200 VeCo 93023 451-D2
11800 OJAI 93023 451-F1
N VENTURA AV
- VEN 93001 491-B1
600 VEN 93001 471-C6
2500 VeCo 93001 471-C6
S VENTURA AV
- VEN 93001 491-B2
VENTURA BLVD
- OXN 93036 522-H1
100 VeCo 93036 522-H1
800 CMRL 93010 523-F3
1000 VeCo 93010 523-F3
1100 OXN 93036 523-A2
1200 VeCo 93030 523-F3
1200 CMRL 93030 523-F3
1500 CMRL 93010 524-D3
2300 VEN 93003 492-D6
2300 VeCo 93003 492-D6
2500 VeCo 93036 523-C3
2900 OXN 93010 523-C3
E VENTURA BLVD
- CMRL 93010 524-B3
W VENTURA BLVD
- CMRL 93010 524-A3
100 CMRL 93010 523-J3
VENTURA FRWY
U.S.-101
- Ago - 558-D6
- AGRH - 557-G6
- AGRH - 558-D6
- CALB - 558-D6
- CMRL - 523-A3
- CMRL - 524-A3
- CMRL - 525-C5
- LACo - 558-D6
- OXN - 492-F7
- OXN - 522-H2
- OXN - 523-A3
- THO - 525-C5
- THO - 526-D7
- THO - 555-J1
- THO - 556-E1
- THO - 557-B4
- VeCo - 366-F6
- VeCo - 459-A3
- VeCo - 469-J1
- VeCo - 470-B3
- VeCo - 490-H1
- VeCo - 491-A2
- VeCo - 492-F7
- VeCo - 523-A3
- VeCo - 525-C5
- VEN - 490-H1
- VEN - 491-A2
- VEN - 492-F7
- WLKV - 557-B4
VENTURA RD
100 OXN 93030 522-E4
100 PHME 93041 552-E2
900 OXN 93035 522-E7
1100 OXN 93033 522-E7
1100 OXN 93033 552-E2
1200 OXN 93035 552-E2
2000 OXN 93041 552-E2
3300 VEN 93003 492-E7
N VENTURA RD
100 OXN 93030 522-E1
100 PHME 93041 552-E5
1900 OXN 93036 522-E1
2100 PHME 93043 552-E5
2400 OXN 93033 552-E5
2500 VeCo 93036 492-F7
2500 VeCo 93036 522-E1
2700 OXN 93043 552-E5
2800 OXN 93036 492-G6
2800 PHME 93033 552-E5
S VENTURA RD
- OXN 93030 522-E6
1300 OXN 93033 552-E1
2300 PHME 93033 552-E1
13900 OXN 93033 522-E6
VENTURA ST
- VeCo 93012 554-D3
100 OJAI 93023 441-H6
100 SPLA 93060 464-A6
800 VeCo 93015 465-H3
VENTURA ST Rt#-126
100 FILM 93015 456-A6
400 FILM 93015 455-F7
800 VeCo 93015 455-F7
E VENTURA ST
Rt#-126
- FILM 93015 456-B6
S VENTURA ST
100 OJAI 93023 441-H7
100 OJAI 93023 451-H1
200 VeCo 93023 451-H1
VENTURA WY
100 Chat 91311 499-F7
9200 Chat 91311 499-F7
VENUS AV
600 SPLA 93060 463-J6
VENUS CT
2700 THO 91360 526-F3
VENUS ST
- THO 91360 526-F3
VENWOOD AV
800 VEN 93001 471-B7
N VERA CT
2000 SIMI 93063 499-B2
E VERA ST
6000 SIMI 93063 499-B2
VERACRUZ LN
2000 OXN 93036 522-G3
VERA CRUZ ST
- SIMI 93065 497-E3
VERANO DR
300 VeCo 93023 441-F7
VERBENA ST
10500 VEN 93004 493-A2
VERCELLY CT
5600 WLKV 91362 557-G6
N VERDA CT
2400 SIMI 93065 498-B1
VERDEMONT CIR
1200 SIMI 93065 497-H5
VERDE OAK DR
100 VeCo 93022 461-A1
VERDE RIDGE LN
1000 THO 91361 556-H6
VERDE VISTA DR
- THO 91360 526-F1
VERDI RD
100 VEN 93003 492-B4
VERDUGO WY
4900 CMRL 93012 524-J3
5100 CMRL 93012 525-A4
W VERDULERA ST
600 CMRL 93010 523-H3
N VERNA AV
600 VeCo 91320 525-G7
VERNON PL
300 SPLA 93060 464-A7
VERNON ST
- VEN 93003 492-B3
VERNON WY
300 SPLA 93060 464-A7
VERONA CT
5500 WLKV 91362 557-G6
VERONICA LN
- VEN 93004 493-A2
VERSAILLE CT
3100 THO 91362 526-J2
VESSEL WY
- OXN 93035 522-D7
VETS CT
30600 AGRH 91301 557-G3
VEVA WY
26100 CALB 91302 558-H4
VIA ACIANDO
23600 CMRL 93012 494-H7
VIA ACORDE
1400 CMRL 93010 494-D7
VIA ACOSTA
1100 THO 91320 555-B4
VIA ADORNA
1000 THO 91320 555-D4
VIA ALAMITOS
- THO 91320 555-C2
VIA ALBA
6900 CMRL 93012 495-D7
6900 CMRL 93012 525-D1
VIA ALCAZAR
1100 CMRL 93010 494-C7
E VIA ALEGRE
5900 SIMI 93063 499-B2
VIA ALISTA
1000 THO 91320 555-C4
VIA ALLEGRA
23600 CMRL 93010 523-F2
VIA ALONDRA
500 CMRL 93012 524-G2
VIA AMISTOSA
27800 AGRH 91301 558-D6
VIA ANDREA
4800 THO 91320 555-C4
VIA ANITA
900 THO 91320 555-C4
VIA ARABELLA
- THO 91320 555-B4
VIA ARACENA
1400 CMRL 93010 523-J1
VIA ARANDANA
23600 CMRL 93012 494-H7
VIA ARROYO
200 VEN 93003 472-C5
500 VEN 93003 492-D1
VIA ARROYO CIR
6400 VEN 93003 472-C6
VIA AURORA
4800 THO 91320 555-C2
VIA AZUL
- THO 91320 555-D2
VIA BAJA
100 VEN 93003 492-D1
200 VEN 93003 472-D7
VIA BAJADA
1500 THO 91360 526-J1
VIA BARON
900 THO 91320 555-C4
VIA BELLA
- THO 91320 555-C2
VIA BENSA
4800 VeCo 91377 557-G1
VIA BONITA
100 THO 91320 555-A3
VIA BONITO
- CMRL 93012 524-H1
VIA BRAVA
- THO 91320 555-C2
E VIA BREVE
5900 SIMI 93063 499-B2
VIA BRISAS
23600 OXN 93030 523-B4
VIA CALDERON
5000 CMRL 93012 524-J3
5100 CMRL 93012 525-A3
VIA CAMINO
- THO 91320 555-D2
VIA CANADA
4500 THO 91320 555-D4
VIA CANDELLA
4700 THO 91320 555-B4
VIA CANTILENA
100 CMRL 93012 524-H3
VIA CAPOTE
23600 THO 91320 555-B3
VIA CARILLO
1100 THO 91320 555-D4
VIA CARRANZA
1100 CMRL 93012 524-J2
1100 CMRL 93012 525-A2
VIA CARRO
600 THO 91320 555-C3
VIA CERRITOS
- THO 91320 555-D2
VIA CIELITO
500 VEN 93003 472-C6
500 VEN 93003 492-C1
VIA COLINAS
- THO 91362 557-E4
- WLKV 91362 557-E5
VIA CON DIOS
900 VeCo 93010 494-B6
VIA CORONADO
- THO 91320 555-C2
VIA CORZA
2600 CMRL 93010 494-F7
VIA COZUMEL
6200 CMRL 93012 525-C5
VIA CRESTA
- THO 91320 555-C2
VIA CRISTAL
100 CMRL 93012 524-J3
100 CMRL 93012 525-A3
VIA CRISTINA
23600 THO 91320 555-B3
VIA CUPERTINO
4600 CMRL 93012 524-J2
VIA DE CANTO
- CMRL 93012 524-J1
VIA DE CERRO
800 VeCo 93010 494-A6
VIA DE COSTA
3500 THO 91360 526-D1
VIA DE LA LUZ
- THO 91320 555-C3
VIA DE LA MESA
- THO 91320 555-C2
VIA DEL CABALLO
200 VeCo 91377 558-A1
200 VeCo 91377 557-J2
VIA DEL LAGO
- THO 91320 555-C2
VIA DEL NOGAL
2700 CMRL 93010 494-F7
VIA DEL PRADO
200 SPLA 93060 473-F1
VIA DEL RANCHO
4500 THO 91320 555-D3
VIA DEL REY
- THO 91320 555-D2
VIA DEL SOL
- CMRL 93012 524-H1
VIA DEL SUELO
2500 CMRL 93010 494-F7
VIA DE TIERRA
600 THO 91320 555-D3
VIA DOLORES
23600 THO 91320 555-B2
VIA DON LUIS
4600 THO 91320 555-D4
VIA DONTE
- THO 91320 555-A3
VIA DULCE
- CMRL 93012 524-H1
VIA EL CERRO
- THO 91320 555-B3
VIA EL MOLINO
23600 THO 91320 555-B1
VIA EL TORO
23600 THO 91320 555-C2
VIA ENCANTO
- THO 91320 555-D2
VIA ENTRADA
- THO 91320 555-E2
VIA ESCONDIDO
- THO 91320 555-C2
VIA ESPINOSA
23600 THO 91320 555-B2
VIA ESTRADA
23600 OXN 93036 523-A2
VIA ESTRELLA
- THO 91320 555-C2
VIA FELICIA
- THO 91320 555-C2
VIA FIESTA
- THO 91320 555-E2
VIA FRESCO
- CMRL 93012 524-J1
VIA FUSTERO
400 VeCo 93040 457-F4
VIA GABILAN
3900 CMRL 93012 524-H4
VIA GABRIELLA
- THO 91320 555-D2
VIA GALO
23600 THO 91320 555-B3
VIA GOLETA
1000 THO 91320 555-D4
VIA GRANDE
4500 THO 91320 555-D3
VIA GREGORIO
- THO 91320 555-C3
VIA HACIENDA
- THO 91320 555-D2
VIA HELENA
23600 THO 91320 555-B3
VIA HERALDO
900 THO 91320 555-C4
VIA HISPANO
23600 THO 91320 555-C4
VIA IMPRESSO
900 THO 91320 555-C4
VIA INEZ
- THO 91320 555-D2
VIA JACARA
23600 CMRL 93012 524-H2
VIA JACINTO
23600 THO 91320 555-B3
VIA JUANITA
- THO 91320 555-D2
VIA JUAREZ
23600 THO 91320 555-B2
VIA LA CIMA
23600 THO 91320 555-B1
VIA LAGUNA
- THO 91320 555-D2
VIA LA JOLLA
- THO 91320 555-C3
VIA LA PAZ
500 VEN 93003 492-D1
VIA LA PRIMAVERA
3500 THO 91360 526-C1
VIA LARA
- THO 91320 555-D2
VIA LAS BRISAS
23600 THO 91320 555-D3
VIA LA SILVA
1500 CMRL 93010 524-C1
VIA LATINA DR
900 CMRL 93012 525-B1
VIA LEAL
2500 CMRL 93010 494-F7
VIA LINDA
23600 THO 91320 555-C3
VIA LISBOA
3900 CMRL 93012 524-H4
VIA LOMA
2000 CMRL 93012 495-B7
VIA LORENTE
800 CMRL 93012 525-B5
VIA LOS ALTOS
23600 THO 91320 555-B1
VIA MADERA
600 THO 91320 555-D3
VIA MAGNOLIA
- THO 91320 555-D2
VIA MANTILLA
2400 CMRL 93010 494-H6
VIA MARIANO
- THO 91320 555-D1
VIA MARINA AV
3100 OXN 93035 522-C7
VIA MARINA CT
2900 OXN 93035 522-D7
VIA MARIPOSA
- THO 91320 555-D1
VIA MARISMA
3900 CMRL 93012 524-H4
VIA MARQUESA
500 CMRL 93012 524-H2
VIA MEDANOS
4200 CMRL 93012 524-H3
VIA MERIDA
- THO 91362 557-D4
VIA MERLA
23600 THO 91320 555-B2
VIA MESITA
23600 THO 91320 555-C2
VIA MIRABELLA
- THO 91320 555-C2
VIA MIRA FLORES
23600 THO 91320 555-A3
VIA MONTANEZ
500 CMRL 93012 525-C5
VIA MONTE
- THO 91320 555-D1
VIA MONTECITO
1700 CMRL 93012 525-D1
1700 CMRL 93012 495-C7
VIA MONTEREY
- THO 91320 555-D2
VIA MONTOYA
1100 CMRL 93010 524-F2
VIA NICOLA
23600 THO 91320 555-B3
VIA NOVELLA
500 VeCo 91377 557-J1
VIA OLAS
23600 THO 91320 555-B2
VIA OLIVERA
23600 CMRL 93012 524-H3
VIA ONDULANDO
500 VEN 93003 472-D7
VIA OVIEDO
- THO 91320 555-A3
VIA PACHECO
600 CMRL 93012 524-J2
VIA PACIFICA
1000 SPLA 93060 463-H7
23600 THO 91320 555-B2
VIA PACIFICA WK
3500 OXN 93035 522-B7
VIA PAJARO
- CMRL 93012 524-H1
VIA PALERMO
900 THO 91320 555-C4
VIA PALOMA
3900 CMRL 93012 524-H3
VIA PARQUE
1500 THO 91360 526-J1
VIA PASADA
1000 SPLA 93060 473-F1
VIA PASITO
6100 VEN 93003 472-D7
VIA PATRICIA
23600 THO 91320 555-B2
VIA PESCADOR
3500 CMRL 93012 524-G2
VIA PETIRROJO
23600 THO 91320 525-J5
VIA PISA
23600 THO 91320 555-B2
VIA PLAZA
500 VEN 93003 492-D1
VIA PLUMA
- THO 91320 555-D2
VIA PRESIDIO
- CMRL 93012 524-H1
VIA QUINTO
23600 THO 91320 555-B2
VIA RAFAEL
1100 THO 91320 555-C4
VIA REAL
- CMRL 93012 524-H1
VIA REBECCA
- THO 91320 555-D2
VIA RICARDO
23600 THO 91320 555-B3
VIA RINCON
23600 THO 91320 555-B2
VIA RIO
23500 THO 91320 555-D2
VIA RIVERA
900 THO 91320 555-D4
VIA ROBLE EXT
23600 VeCo 93040 458-F6
VIA ROCAS
5400 WLKV 91362 557-E5
VIA RODEO
500 FILM 93015 455-J5
4500 THO 91320 555-D3
VIA ROSAL
- CMRL 93012 524-H4
VIA ROTA
900 CMRL 93012 525-B5
VIA SANDRA
23600 THO 91320 555-B2
VIA SAN JOSE
1000 THO 91320 555-C4
VIA SAN LUCAS
23600 THO 91320 555-B1
VIA SAN MARTIN
23600 THO 91320 555-C2
VIA SANTANA
23600 THO 91320 555-C1
VIA SECOYA
23600 CMRL 93012 494-J7
VIA SEDONA
- THO 91320 555-A3
VIA SERENA
- CMRL 93012 524-H1
VIA SIENA
- THO 91320 555-H2
VIA SILVESTRE
23600 CMRL 93012 525-A2
VIA SINTRA
3900 CMRL 93012 524-H4
VIA SOLANA
100 SPLA 93060 463-H7
VIA SORRENTO
1000 THO 91320 555-B4
VIA TECA
23600 THO 91320 555-B2
VIA TERRADO
500 CMRL 93010 523-H1
VIA TERRASOL
2000 CMRL 93010 494-B7
2000 VeCo 93010 494-B7
VIA TOMAS
2300 CMRL 93010 494-F7
VIA VELA
2700 CMRL 93010 494-F7
VIA VENETO
1900 VeCo 93010 493-J7
1900 VeCo 93010 494-A7
VIA VERDE
3800 THO 91360 526-J1
VIA VISTA
23600 THO 91320 555-C3
VIA VISTOSA
23600 THO 91320 555-C1
VIA ZAMORA
400 CMRL 93010 523-J2
VIA ZURITA CT
2400 VeCo 93012 496-D6
VICKI CT
3400 SIMI 93063 478-D6
VICKIVIEW DR
6600 LACo 91307 529-C6
VICKSBURG LN
1400 VEN 93003 492-B4
VICKY AV
6500 CanP 91307 529-H5
7600 LA 91304 529-H4
VICTOR HERBERT DR
- VEN 93003 492-A7
VICTORIA AV
- VeCo 93003 492-C7
- VEN 93003 492-C7
100 OXN 93035 522-B3
300 VeCo 93030 522-B3
500 OXN 93035 522-B7
1000 VeCo 93001 492-C7
1200 OXN 93036 522-B3
1200 VeCo 93036 522-B3
1400 OXN 93035 552-B3
1800 PHME 93035 552-B3
1800 VeCo 93001 522-B3
2100 PHME 93041 552-B3
4000 VeCo 93035 552-B3
N VICTORIA AV
- VEN 93003 492-C1
600 VeCo 93003 472-C7
600 VeCo 93003 492-C1
600 VEN 93003 472-C7
S VICTORIA AV
- VEN 93003 492-C2
700 VEN 93009 492-C3
2000 VeCo 93003 492-C3
VICTORIA ST
2400 SIMI 93065 498-B3
VICTORY BLVD
22000 WdHl 91367 529-C7
22000 CanP 91303 529-F7
22200 CanP 91307 529-C7
23600 VeCo 91302 529-C7
VIDA DR
- OXN 93030 522-J4
VIEJO DR
300 CMRL 93010 524-D3
VIENTOS RD
400 VeCo 93010 494-B7
VIEW DR
100 SPLA 93060 464-A5
2100 SIMI 93065 497-E2
VIEWCREST CT
5900 VEN 93003 472-C7
VIEWCREST DR
600 VeCo 93003 472-C7
600 VEN 93003 472-C7
VIEWLAKE LN
32000 WLKV 91361 557-C7
VIEW LINE DR
- SIMI 93065 477-F7
VIEW MESA ST
12900 MRPK 93021 496-E4
VIEW PARK CT
400 VeCo 91377 558-B1
VIEW POINT CIR
6100 VEN 93003 472-C5
VIEWPOINT DR
- OXN 93035 522-A7
- OXN 93035 552-A1
VIEW POINTE DR
3200 WLKV 91361 557-C7
VIKING DR
1900 CMRL 93010 494-E7
VILLA ADOBE
600 CMRL 93012 524-G3
VILLA CAMPESINA AV
12400 MRPK 93021 496-D2
VILLAGE CT
1200 SIMI 93065 497-H4
1700 THO 91362 527-A5
VILLAGE GN
900 THO 91361 557-C5
VILLAGE PKWY
2100 SIMI 93065 497-E2
VILLAGE RD
200 PHME 93041 552-E6
VILLAGE SQ
200 FILM 93015 455-J6
VILLAGE 1
- CMRL 93012 525-A3
VILLAGE 11
500 CMRL 93012 525-B2
VILLAGE 13
5800 CMRL 93012 525-B2
VILLAGE 14
400 CMRL 93012 525-B2
VILLAGE 15
500 CMRL 93012 525-B2
VILLAGE 16
- CMRL 93012 525-A3
VILLAGE 17
5600 CMRL 93012 525-B3
VILLAGE 18
- CMRL 93012 525-A3
VILLAGE 19
- CMRL 93012 525-B3
VILLAGE 2
100 CMRL 93012 525-A3
VILLAGE 20
- CMRL 93012 525-B3
VILLAGE 22
5700 CMRL 93012 525-B3
VILLAGE 23
- CMRL 93012 525-B3
VILLAGE 24
5700 CMRL 93012 525-B3
VILLAGE 25
- CMRL 93012 525-B2
VILLAGE 26
5800 CMRL 93012 525-B3
VILLAGE 28
- CMRL 93012 525-B3
VILLAGE 29
6000 CMRL 93012 525-B2
VILLAGE 3
200 CMRL 93012 525-A3
VILLAGE 30
6000 CMRL 93012 525-C2
VILLAGE 31
6100 CMRL 93012 525-C2
VILLAGE 32
6000 CMRL 93012 525-C2
VILLAGE 33
6200 CMRL 93012 525-C2
VILLAGE 34
6200 CMRL 93012 525-C2
VILLAGE 35
6300 CMRL 93012 525-C2
VILLAGE 37
900 CMRL 93012 525-C1
VILLAGE 38
- CMRL 93012 525-C2
VILLAGE 39
900 CMRL 93012 525-C1
VILLAGE 4
100 CMRL 93012 525-A3
VILLAGE 40
6500 CMRL 93012 525-C2
VILLAGE 41
100 CMRL 93012 525-C1
VILLAGE 42
- CMRL 93012 525-D1
VILLAGE 44
1000 CMRL 93012 525-D1
VILLAGE 5
300 CMRL 93012 525-A2
VILLAGE 6
- CMRL 93012 525-A3
VILLAGE 7
5600 CMRL 93012 525-A2
VILLAGE 8
- CMRL 93012 525-B2
VILLAGE 9
5700 CMRL 93012 525-B2
VILLAGE AT THE PARK DR
- CMRL 93012 524-F4
VILLAGE BROOK RD
31800 WLKV 91361 557-D6
VILLAGE CENTER RD
31600 WLKV 91361 557-D6
VILLAGE COMMONS BLVD
- CMRL 93012 524-G5
VILLAGE SCHOOL RD
31600 WLKV 91361 557-D6
VILLAGEVIEW CT
11700 MRPK 93021 496-B2
VILLA MALLORCA PL
5200 CMRL 93012 525-A2
VILLAMONTE CT
4300 CMRL 93010 494-G7
VILLANOVA AV
- OXN 93036 522-H2
300 VEN 93003 492-B1
VILLANOVA RD
100 VeCo 93023 451-D3
E VILLANOVA RD
100 VeCo 93023 451-E2
800 OJAI 93023 451-E2
VINA DEL MAR
2100 OXN 93035 552-A2
VINCA LN
- VEN 93004 493-A2
VINCA ST
- SIMI 93063 499-A2
VINCA WY
- OXN 93030 523-A3
E VINCE ST
- VEN 93001 471-C7
W VINCE ST
- VEN 93001 471-B7

STREET
Block City ZIP Pg-Grid

VINCENNES ST
22000 Chat 91311 499-J6
VINCENTE AV
3800 CMRL 93010 494-G7
VINE PL
400 OXN 93033 552-G3
VINE ST
500 VeCo 93022 451-B7
500 VeCo 93022 461-B1
VINEWOOD
13300 MRPK 93021 496-F3
E VINEYARD AV
Rt#-232
500 OXN 93036 522-G2
2600 VeCo 93036 522-G2
2800 OXN 93036 492-H7
2800 VeCo 93036 492-H7
4100 VeCo 93036 493-A4
5100 VeCo 93066 493-A4
W VINEYARD AV
100 OXN 93036 522-D2
VINEYARD DR
- SIMI 93065 497-G7
VINTAGE ST
22000 Chat 91311 499-J5
VINTAGE OAK ST
- SIMI 93063 499-A3
VINTON CT
700 THO 91360 556-G1
VIOLA WY
- OXN 93030 523-A4
VIOLET LN
- SIMI 93065 497-H3
VIOLET WY
500 OXN 93036 522-F1
VIOLETA ST
11000 VeCo 93004 493-A1
VIRGINIA DR
- VeCo 91320 555-H1
- VEN 93003 491-G2
VIRGINIA TER
100 SPLA 93060 464-A5
VIRGINIA COLONY PL
5500 MRPK 93021 476-H7
VIRGO CT
200 THO 91360 526-E2
VISALIA CT
100 VEN 93004 492-F2
VISALIA ST
1300 OXN 93035 552-E1
8200 VEN 93004 492-F2
VISTA CIR
2600 CMRL 93010 524-F1
VISTA CT
1300 CMRL 93010 524-F1
VISTA LP
2600 OXN 93036 492-F7
2600 OXN 93036 522-F1
VISTA RD
5900 VeCo 93063 499-B4
VISTA ST
2600 CMRL 93010 524-F1
VISTA ALCEDO
1800 CMRL 93012 495-D7
1800 CMRL 93012 525-D1
VISTA ANACAPA RD
9000 VeCo 93021 475-F5
VISTA ARRIAGO
800 CMRL 93012 525-C5
VISTA ARROYO DR
2500 VeCo 93012 496-E6
VISTA BONITA
100 THO 91320 525-E6
VISTA CONEJO
- THO 91320 525-E6
VISTA COTO VERDE
1100 CMRL 93010 494-C7
VISTA CREEK CIR
23600 SIMI 93065 497-D7
VISTA DEL CAMPO
800 VeCo 93010 494-A6
VISTA DEL CIMA
1100 VeCo 93010 494-B6
VISTA DEL MAR AV
1100 CMRL 93010 494-B7
1100 VeCo 93010 494-B7
VISTA DEL MAR DR
900 VEN 93001 491-E3
VISTA DEL MAR PL
1000 VEN 93001 491-D3
VISTA DEL MONTE
23600 FILM 93015 456-C6
VISTA DEL RINCON DR
6800 VeCo 93001 459-D5
VISTA DEL SOL
300 CMRL 93010 524-B3
VISTA DEL VALLE RD
4400 MRPK 93021 496-F2
VISTA DE VENTURA
500 VEN 93003 492-B1
VISTA DORADO LN
400 VeCo 91377 557-J2
VISTA GRANDE
2600 VeCo 93012 496-E6
VISTA GRANDE DR
23600 SPLA 93060 464-B4
VISTA HERMOSA DR
400 OJAI 93023 441-G5

VISTA HERMOSA ST
1100 SIMI 93065 497-E4
VISTA LAGO DR
- SIMI 93065 497-F4
- VeCo 93065 497-F4
VISTA LEVANA DR
13300 MRPK 93021 496-F2
VISTAMEADOW CT
4400 MRPK 93021 496-D3
VISTA MERCADO
3300 CMRL 93012 524-G2
VISTA MONTANA
400 VeCo 93010 494-A6
VISTA OAKS WY
1400 THO 91361 556-H6
VISTA PALACIO
700 CMRL 93012 524-H2
E VISTAPARK DR
12900 MRPK 93021 496-E2
VISTA POINTE PL
23600 SPLA 93060 464-B4
VISTA RIDGE LN
900 THO 91362 557-D1
VISTA WOOD CIR
2400 THO 91362 527-B4
VIVIAN CIR
800 THO 91320 526-C7
VIVIANA DR
- OXN 93030 522-J4
VOLCANO CT
2600 OXN 93030 522-D3
VOLTAIRE DR
3000 OXN 93033 552-J3
VOLTAIRE WY
10400 VeCo 93012 495-J6
10400 VeCo 93012 496-A6
VORALE AV
400 SIMI 93065 497-G3
VOSE ST
22500 CanP 91307 529-G5
VOYAGER AV
1600 SIMI 93063 498-E3
VOYAGER PL
1000 OXN 93033 522-H7

W

W ST
1500 VEN 93004 492-J3
1500 VEN 93004 493-A3
WABASH ST
8200 VEN 93004 492-G3
WACO DR
2900 SIMI 93063 478-G6
WACO ST
8700 VEN 93004 492-G2
WADE CIR
1600 SIMI 93065 497-J5
WADES RD
600 VeCo 93015 455-J1
600 VeCo 93015 456-A1
WAGNER RD
5100 VEN 93003 492-B4
WAGNER WY
5300 VeCo 91377 527-H6
N WAGON LN
- VeCo 91307 528-J3
WAGON WHEEL RD
900 OXN 93036 492-F7
2000 OXN 93036 522-G1
WAITE ST
100 OJAI 93023 441-J6
WAKE LN
- OXN 93035 522-D7
WAKEFIELD AV
1500 THO 91360 526-F5
E WAKEFORD AV
100 SPLA 93060 464-A6
W WAKEFORD AV
100 SPLA 93060 463-J6
100 SPLA 93060 464-A6
WAKE FOREST AV
- VEN 93003 492-C2
N WAKE FOREST AV
- VEN 93003 492-B2
WALCOTT AV
- VEN 93003 492-B3
WALDEMAR DR
23600 VeCo 91361 556-D7
WALDEN ST
100 SPLA 93060 463-H6
1900 OXN 93030 553-A5
WALDO AV
2100 SIMI 93065 498-C2
WALES DR
900 OXN 93035 522-E7
WALES ST
- THO 91360 526-F6
WALFORD CT
30200 AGRH 91301 557-H4
WALKER AV
400 CMRL 93010 524-F2
WALKER LN
- FILM 93015 456-A5
WALKER ST
4700 VEN 93003 492-B5
WALKER CUP CIR
1700 THO 91362 527-D6

WALKING HORSE LN
31500 WLKV 91361 557-E6
WALL ST
100 VEN 93001 491-B1
WALLABY CT
7400 VEN 93003 492-F4
WALLABY ST
7100 VEN 93003 492-E4
WALLACE ST
7800 VeCo 93021 475-G3
WALLBRIDGE WY
400 VeCo 93023 441-D7
WALLINGTON CT
31900 WLKV 91361 557-C6
WALNUT AV
4000 VeCo 93066 494-A3
WALNUT CT
700 THO 91320 556-C2
WALNUT DR
- VeCo 93036 492-J7
300 VEN 93003 492-A1
500 VeCo 93036 522-J1
700 VeCo 93036 523-A1
WALNUT ST
300 SPLA 93060 464-B5
600 MRPK 93021 476-E7
600 MRPK 93021 496-E1
3400 VeCo 93063 478-E6
3400 SIMI 93063 478-E6
WALNUT CANYON RD
Rt#-23
800 MRPK 93021 476-E7
1100 VeCo 93021 476-E4
WALNUT CREEK RD
3900 MRPK 93021 496-D3
WALNUT GROVE LN
- SIMI 93065 497-H3
WALNUT RIDGE DR
5600 AGRH 91301 557-J5
WALSH RD
1100 VeCo 93063 499-G4
WALTER AV
100 THO 91320 555-F2
WALTER CIR
3600 THO 91320 555-F2
WALTER ST
600 VEN 93001 491-J5
WALTHAM CIR
1100 SIMI 93065 497-H4
WALTHAM RD
1000 SIMI 93065 497-H4
WALWORTH CT
1500 VeCo 91377 527-H6
WANDA AV
2600 SIMI 93065 498-B1
2600 SIMI 93065 478-B7
WANKEL WY
2300 OXN 93030 523-A3
WARBLE CT
- THO 91320 525-J5
- THO 91320 526-A5
WARBLER AV
2300 VEN 93003 492-E5
WARD AV
2100 SIMI 93065 497-G2
WARD WY
1700 VeCo 93023 451-A3
WAREHOUSE AV
500 OXN 93030 522-H7
WARFIELD CIR
1700 SIMI 93063 499-A3
WARING PL
28400 AGRH 91301 558-C6
WARMSPRINGS AV
1300 THO 91320 526-A6
E WARNER ST
- VEN 93001 471-C7
W WARNER ST
- VEN 93001 471-B7
WARREN AV
100 SPLA 93060 464-A6
WARREN CIR
700 MRPK 93021 476-F7
WARRENDALE ST
1400 SIMI 93065 497-D7
WARRING CANYON RD
700 VeCo 93040 457-E2
WARRINGTON WY
1000 OJAI 93023 451-F1
WARWICK AV
400 THO 91360 526-F6
400 THO 91360 556-F1
W WASATCH CT
2700 THO 91362 557-C3
WASHBURN ST
- SIMI 93065 497-E3
WASHINGTON DR
1900 VEN 93003 492-C5
WATCH WY
- OXN 93035 522-D7
WATERBURY LN
900 VEN 93001 491-E4
WATERBY ST
2100 THO 91361 557-A5
WATERFALL LN
23600 SIMI 93065 478-C7
WATERFORD LN
900 FILM 93015 455-H7

WATERGATE CT
31900 WLKV 91361 557-C6
WATERGATE RD
2700 THO 91361 557-B5
32000 WLKV 91361 557-C6
WATEROAK LN
500 VeCo 91377 557-J1
WATERS RD
7800 VeCo 93021 475-G3
WATERSIDE CIR
23600 THO 91362 527-B4
WATERSIDE LN
- OXN 93035 522-A7
32000 WLKV 91361 557-C7
WATERTOWN CT
2100 THO 91360 526-B4
WATERTREE CT
6200 AGRH 91301 558-A3
WATERWHEEL PL
- THO 91361 556-H5
WATKINS WY
- VeCo 93022 451-B6
WATSON AV
600 SIMI 93065 498-C5
WATSON DR
- MRPK 93021 476-B5
WATT DR
700 OXN 93030 552-H1
WATTS TREE FARM RD
100 VeCo 93023 453-B1
N WAUKEGAN AV
3000 SIMI 93063 478-F7
WAUNETA ST
3000 THO 91320 555-G2
WAVECREST WY
5000 OXN 93035 521-J7
WAVERLY AV
2600 CMRL 93010 524-F2
WAVERLY CT
500 OXN 93030 522-D4
2700 CMRL 93010 524-F2
WAVERLY DR
200 SIMI 93065 497-E2
WAVERLY HEIGHTS DR
600 THO 91360 526-G5
WAXWING AV
2300 VEN 93003 492-E5
WAYNE CIR
2300 SIMI 93065 498-A1
WAYSIDE CIR
1000 VeCo 93010 494-F6
WAYVIEW CT
6300 VEN 93003 472-D7
WEATHERFORD CT
3200 SIMI 93063 478-G6
WEATHERLY CIR
3800 WLKV 91361 557-B7
E WEAVER ST
600 SIMI 93065 497-G5
WEBB RD
23700 Chat 91311 499-E6
WEBER CIR
800 VEN 93003 492-A4
WEBER CT
4500 VEN 93003 492-A4
WEBSTER DR
4700 OXN 93033 553-A5
WEBSTER ST
5900 VEN 93003 492-C3
WEDGEWOOD CIR
100 THO 91360 526-F3
WEEPING WILLOW DR
3900 MRPK 93021 496-F4
29400 AGRH 91301 557-J4
WEINBERG ST
22400 Chat 91311 499-H4
WELAND
23600 VeCo 93015 456-F6
WELBY WY
2400 CanP 91307 529-D6
22100 CanP 91303 529-H6
24500 LACo 91307 529-C6
WELCOME CT
2300 SIMI 93063 499-B1
WELDON CANYON
23600 VeCo 93001 461-C5
WELLBROOK DR
32700 WLKV 91361 557-A7
32700 WLKV 91361 556-J7
WELLER CT
600 SIMI 93065 497-G4
WELLESLEY CT
700 THO 91360 526-G5
WELLESLEY DR
1700 THO 91360 526-G5
WELLINGTON CT
25900 LACo 91302 558-J3
WELLINGTON PL
1500 THO 91361 556-J6
WELLINGTON ST
8500 VEN 93004 492-G4
WELLS LN
200 WHil 91304 499-D6
WELLS RD
- VeCo 90265 585-G7
- VeCo 90265 625-G1
N WELLS RD
- VEN 93004 472-J6
- VeCo 93004 472-J6

N WELLS RD
- VEN 93060 472-J6
200 VeCo 93060 472-J6
S WELLS RD
- VEN 93004 472-J7
S WELLS RD Rt#-118
300 VEN 93004 472-J7
700 VEN 93004 473-A7
800 VEN 93004 493-A1
900 VeCo 93004 493-A1
WELLSTON CT
3500 SIMI 93063 478-F5
WELSH CT
1400 SIMI 93065 497-E3
WEMBLY AV
5500 VeCo 91377 527-H6
WENDELL ST
2700 CMRL 93010 524-F1
N WENDY DR
- VeCo 91320 555-G1
400 VeCo 91320 525-G7
600 THO 91320 525-G7
S WENDY DR
- THO 91320 555-G3
WENDY LN
400 SPLA 93060 464-A5
WENDY PL
2000 PHME 93041 552-D1
WESHAM ST
8400 VEN 93004 492-G4
WESLEY AV
200 VEN 93003 491-J3
WESLEYAN AV
300 VEN 93003 491-J1
WEST DR
1200 VEN 93003 492-D4
WEST RD
- PHME 93043 552-B4
WEST ST
3500 VeCo 93066 495-A5
WESTAR DR
1100 OXN 93033 552-J1
WESTBEND RD
600 THO 91362 557-D1
800 THO 91362 527-D7
WESTBLUFF PL
23600 SIMI 93065 497-E4
WESTBURY CT
- THO 91360 526-F6
WESTBURY ST
100 THO 91360 526-F6
WESTCHESTER CT
1900 OXN 93036 522-D3
WESTCHESTER LN
600 THO 91320 556-D1
WESTCLIFF DR
7300 LA 91304 529-D4
WESTCOTT CT
- MRPK 93021 496-E2
WESTCREEK LN
900 THO 91362 557-G1
900 VeCo 91362 557-G1
1000 THO 91362 527-G7
WESTDALE RD
4200 MRPK 93021 496-B3
WESTFIELD CT
600 VEN 93004 492-H2
WEST FORK HALL
CANYON RD
2800 VeCo 93001 471-G4
WESTGATE RD
13200 MRPK 93021 496-E3
WESTHAM CIR
2700 THO 91362 527-A3
WESTHILLS CT
2600 SIMI 93065 477-E7
2600 SIMI 93065 497-E1
WESTINGHOUSE ST
4400 VEN 93003 492-A5
WESTLAKE BLVD
700 THO 91361 556-J6
WESTLAKE BLVD
Rt#-23
100 LACo 90265 586-H4
400 WLKV 90265 586-H4
400 WLKV 91361 586-H4
800 LACo 91361 586-H4
800 THO 91361 586-H4
N WESTLAKE BLVD
- THO 91362 557-C3
1000 THO 91362 527-B4
S WESTLAKE BLVD
- THO 91362 557-B5
S WESTLAKE BLVD
Rt#-23
100 THO 91362 557-C4
100 THO 91361 557-C4
600 THO 91361 556-J7
800 THO 91361 586-H1
WESTLAKE EDISON RD
100 THO 91361 556-G4
100 VeCo 91361 556-G4
WESTLAKE VISTA LN
- THO 91362 557-A2
WESTLAND AV
23600 THO 91362 527-A1
WESTMINSTER AV
100 VEN 93003 492-B3

WESTMINSTER ST
500 THO 91360 526-G7
WESTMONT DR
12500 MRPK 93021 496-D3
WESTMONT ST
4400 VEN 93003 492-A3
WEST MOUNTAIN RD
20000 VeCo 93066 473-E7
20000 VeCo 93066 493-E1
WESTON CIR
1700 CMRL 93010 494-F7
1700 CMRL 93010 524-F1
WESTON CT
300 SPLA 93060 463-J6
WESTOVER PL
700 THO 91320 555-G3
WESTPARK CT
- CMRL 93012 524-F4
WEST POINT ST
5000 VEN 93003 492-B1
WESTPORT ST
12900 MRPK 93021 496-E4
WESTRANCH PL
23600 SIMI 93065 497-E4
WESTRIDGE CIR
2900 THO 91360 526-C3
WESTRIDGE DR
1000 VEN 93003 472-D6
WEST SHORE LN
1300 THO 91361 557-A6
WEST VAIL DR
23100 CanP 91307 529-F5
WESTVIEW CT
4800 THO 91362 557-F1
WESTWIND CIR
1300 THO 91361 557-B6
WESTWOOD DR
2100 CMRL 93010 494-E7
WESTWOOD ST
- SIMI 93063 478-G5
E WESTWOOD ST
6300 MRPK 93021 476-G6
N WESTWOOD ST
700 MRPK 93021 476-G6
WETHERBY ST
- SIMI 93065 497-H4
WETSTONE CT
2000 THO 91362 527-A4
WETSTONE DR
2100 THO 91362 527-A4
E WEXFORD CIR
1700 SIMI 93065 497-J5
1700 SIMI 93065 498-A5
WEYLAND CT
2600 SIMI 93065 478-B7
WEYMOUTH LN
1200 VEN 93001 491-F5
WHALEBOAT PL
30700 AGRH 91301 557-G5
WHALEN WY
- OXN 93036 492-H5
WHALERS LN
11900 VeCo 90265 625-F5
WHARF WY
- PHME 93041 552-E5
WHEATFIELD CIR
2600 SIMI 93063 498-D1
2600 SIMI 93063 478-D7
WHEATON CT
14600 MRPK 93021 476-H6
WHEATON DR
4500 VEN 93003 492-A3
WHEELER CANYON RD
2500 VeCo 93060 473-B1
2600 VeCo 93060 463-A3
7300 VeCo 93060 453-B6
WHEELHOUSE AV
2400 PHME 93041 552-C2
WHEELHOUSE LN
5800 AGRH 91301 557-G4
WHEELWRIGHT LN
1900 THO 91320 525-J7
1900 THO 91320 526-A7
WHIM DR
30800 WLKV 91362 557-F4
WHIPPLE RD
100 VeCo 93060 464-D5
WHIPPOORWILL ST
6300 VEN 93003 492-D6
WHISPERING GATES CT
- SIMI 93065 497-G7
WHISPERING GLEN CT
- SIMI 93065 478-B6
WHISPERING HILLS AV
23600 THO 91320 555-E4
WHISPERING OAKS PL
600 THO 91320 556-D1
WHISPERING PINES
4900 THO 91362 557-G1
WHISTLER WY
6500 VEN 93003 492-D1
WHITCOMB AV
1000 SIMI 93065 498-B4
WHITE ST
6300 SIMI 93063 499-C2
WHITE BIRCH CIR
3100 THO 91360 526-H2
WHITECAP CT
200 PHME 93041 552-E6

WHITE CAP DR
400 VEN 93003 491-H1
WHITECAP ST
5000 OXN 93035 521-J7
WHITE CEDAR PL
3100 THO 91362 527-C3
WHITECHAPEL PL
2400 THO 91362 527-B2
WHITECLIFF RD
900 THO 91360 526-G7
WHITE CLOUD CIR
5100 THO 91362 527-G7
WHITE DOVE CIR
1300 THO 91362 527-G7
WHITE FEATHER CT
1300 THO 91320 526-A6
WHITEGATE RD
400 THO 91320 555-H3
400 VeCo 91320 555-H3
E WHITEHALL CT
1900 SIMI 93065 498-A5
WHITEHALL LN
- CanP 91307 529-D5
WHITEHALL PL
1500 THO 91361 556-J6
WHITE HAWK LN
- SIMI 93065 478-B4
WHITEHEAD PL
23600 VEN 93003 492-C6
WHITE OAK CIR
500 OJAI 93023 441-J5
WHITE OAK LN
600 THO 91320 556-D2
WHITE PINE CT
1300 VeCo 91377 527-G7
WHITE RIDGE PL
2700 THO 91362 527-B3
WHITE RIVER PL
3400 WLKV 91361 557-B7
WHITE ROCK RD
- CMRL 93012 524-F4
WHITE SAGE RD
23600 MRPK 93021 496-G1
WHITESAIL CIR
4000 WLKV 91361 557-B6
WHITESIDE PL
200 THO 91362 557-A2
WHITE STALLION RD
- VeCo 91320 555-H4
- VeCo 91361 555-H4
WHITE SWAN CT
500 SIMI 93065 497-E6
WHITETAIL AV
3400 SIMI 93063 479-A6
WHITEWATER LN
11800 VeCo 90265 625-F5
WHITE WING CT
2600 VeCo 93012 496-A7
E WHITEWOOD ST
6500 SIMI 93063 499-C2
WHITFORD AV
23600 VeCo 91361 556-G6
WHITINGHAM CT
29300 AGRH 91301 558-A3
WHITMAN CT
500 THO 91360 526-G2
6800 VEN 93003 492-E3
WHITNEY AV
100 MRPK 93021 496-D1
WHITNEY CIR
100 OXN 93033 553-C3
WHITTIER CT
4300 VEN 93003 492-A3
WHITTIER ST
4400 VEN 93003 492-A3
WHITWORTH ST
100 THO 91360 526-E4
WICHITA FALLS AV
3200 SIMI 93063 478-H6
WICKFORD PL
- CMRL 93012 524-G4
WICKLOW CT
1600 THO 91361 556-J5
WICKS RD
- MRPK 93021 476-E7
WIGGIN ST
4800 VeCo 91377 557-G1
WILBUR CT
500 THO 91360 526-G7
WILBUR RD
- THO 91360 556-E1
E WILBUR RD
- THO 91360 526-F7
W WILBUR RD
- THO 91360 526-F7
100 THO 91360 556-F1
WILCOX ST
2100 CMRL 93010 524-E2
WILDCAT AV
2300 VEN 93003 492-E5
WILDCAT CT
- MRPK 93021 476-F5
WILD CLOVER WY
300 SIMI 93065 527-D1
WILDCREEK CIR
700 THO 91360 526-C2
WILDER ST
1200 THO 91362 527-A6

WILDFLOWER CT
11500 MRPK 93021 496-B2
WILD HORSE CT
3000 THO 91360 526-C2
WILDLIFE DR
- SIMI 93065 497-E5
W WILDOAK ST
- VeCo 93023 451-B4
WILDON RD
23600 CMRL 93010 524-C4
WILDRIDGE CT
- MRPK 93021 476-D5
WILD ROSE CT
- SIMI 93065 497-G7
WILD ROSE ST
2500 THO 91361 557-B5
WILDROSE WK
- OXN 93036 522-B3
WILD SAGE CT
3900 THO 91362 527-C6
WILDWEST CIR
13800 MRPK 93021 496-F3
WILDWOOD AV
300 THO 91360 526-B1
WILDWOOD LN
- FILM 93015 456-B6
WILDWOOD PL
22200 Chat 91311 499-J2
WILEMAN ST
300 FILM 93015 455-J6
WILEY CANYON RD
23600 VeCo - 467-B1
23600 VeCo 93015 467-B1
23600 VeCo 93021 467-B6
WILL AV
300 VeCo 93036 492-J7
700 VeCo 93036 493-A7
WILLAMETTE ST
10000 VEN 93004 492-J3
WILLARD RD
- VeCo 93060 464-F4
WILLDEN DR
- VeCo 93010 494-D7
W WILLEY ST
- VeCo 93023 451-B4
WILLIAM CT
600 SIMI 93065 497-G4
WILLIAM DR
3300 VeCo 91320 555-F1
WILLIAMS DR
1900 OXN 93030 523-A3
1900 OXN 93036 523-A3
WILLIAMS LN
1600 SIMI 93063 499-B3
WILLIAMS PL
700 OJAI 93023 441-J6
WILLIAMS ST
1800 SIMI 93065 497-H3
WILLIAMS WY
5900 SIMI 93063 499-B3
WILLIAMSBURG CT
- VeCo 91361 586-G1
WILLIAMSBURG WY
- VeCo 91361 586-F1
WILLIAMS CANYON RD
500 VeCo 93060 472-H5
500 VEN 93060 472-H5
WILLIAMS RANCH RD
12600 MRPK 93021 496-D3
WILLIS AV
200 CMRL 93010 523-J4
200 CMRL 93010 524-A4
WILLIS CANYON RD
- VeCo 93023 366-H7
- VeCo 93023 441-A6
WILLOUGHBY RD
- VeCo 93060 453-A6
- VeCo 93060 452-J6
23600 VeCo 93060 452-H7
WILLOW CT
- AGRH 91301 558-A5
2600 SIMI 93063 498-E1
WILLOW LN
100 SPLA 93060 464-A5
2400 THO 91361 556-J2
2400 THO 91361 557-A3
WILLOW ST
400 OXN 93033 552-G3
E WILLOW ST
400 OJAI 93023 441-J7
WILLOWBROOK DR
100 PHME 93041 552-F6
WILLOWBROOK LN
1400 SIMI 93065 497-H3
WILLOW CANYON ST
- THO 91362 527-C2
WILLOW CREEK CT
2200 OXN 93036 522-D1
WILLOW CREEK LN
3900 MRPK 93021 496-G3
WILLOW FOREST DR
12300 MRPK 93021 496-C3
WILLOW GLEN CIR
23600 SIMI 93065 527-F1
WILLOW GLEN CT
- CMRL 93012 524-G5
WILLOW GLEN ST
4300 CALB 91302 558-H7
WILLOWGREEN CT
1900 THO 91361 557-A5

WILLOW GROVE CT
12400 MRPK 93021 496-D3
WILLOW HAVEN CT
- THO 91362 527-C2
WILLOW HILL DR
12200 MRPK 93021 496-C3
WILLOWICK DR
3500 VEN 93003 491-H2
WILLOW OAK ST
- SIMI 93063 498-J3
WILLOWOOD CT
11500 MRPK 93021 496-B2
WILLOWPARK CT
2200 THO 91362 527-A4
WILLOW SPRINGS DR
12200 MRPK 93021 496-C3
WILLOW TREE CT
1900 THO 91362 526-J4
1900 THO 91362 527-A4
WILLOWTREE DR
5700 AGRH 91301 557-H4
WILLOW VIEW DR
5300 CMRL 93012 525-A2
WILLSBROOK CT
1200 THO 91361 556-J5
1200 THO 91361 557-A5
E WILMOT ST
3200 SIMI 93063 498-D2
WILSHIRE PL
400 THO 91320 555-H3
WILSON AV
100 OXN 93030 522-H6
WILSON DR
800 VeCo 93015 455-D5
1000 SIMI 93065 498-C4
WILSON ST
2500 VeCo 93015 465-E1
23600 VEN 93003 492-E2
WILTON ST
1600 SIMI 93065 497-J2
WIMBLEDON CIR
1300 THO 91361 557-A5
WINCHESTER DR
300 OXN 93036 522-G1
6200 VeCo 93021 475-J6
WINCHESTER WY
5400 CMRL 93012 525-A1
WINDBREEZE AV
23600 THO 91362 527-B2
WINDBROOK CT
1900 THO 91361 557-A7
WINDCREST CT
2700 OXN 93036 492-F7
2700 OXN 93036 522-F1
WINDFLOWER CIR
3200 THO 91360 526-H2
WINDHARP LN
23600 SIMI 93065 497-A2
WINDHAVEN DR
4800 THO 91362 557-E2
WINDING LN
3000 THO 91361 557-C5
WINDINGWAY DR
800 VEN 93001 491-D1
WINDMILL LN
1000 VeCo 91377 528-B7
1000 VeCo 91377 558-A1
WINDMILL WY
- SIMI 93065 497-H3
WINDMIST AV
23600 THO 91362 527-B2
WINDOM ST
22800 CanP 91307 529-G4
23200 LA 91304 529-F4
WINDOVER RD
8400 VeCo 93021 476-D3
WINDRIDGE AV
- THO 91362 527-C2
WINDRIFT CT
3000 THO 91360 526-F2
WIND RIVER CIR
400 THO 91362 557-B2
WINDROSE CT
23600 THO 91320 556-C1
WINDROSE DR
100 THO 91320 556-C1
WINDSHORE WY
- OXN 93035 522-B7
- OXN 93035 552-B1
WINDSONG LN
29600 AGRH 91301 557-J5
WINDSONG ST
2900 THO 91360 526-F2
WINDSOR CT
2200 CMRL 93010 494-D7
WINDSOR DR
1000 THO 91360 526-G6
WINDSWEPT PL
500 SIMI 93065 497-D7
500 SIMI 93065 527-D1
WINDTREE AV
100 THO 91320 556-C1
WINDWARD CIR
2300 THO 91361 557-B6
WINDWARD WY
1000 OXN 93035 522-D7
WINDWILLOW WY
1500 SIMI 93065 497-D6

WINDY MOUNTAIN AV
5000 THO 91362 527-F7
WINFIELD ST
900 THO 91320 555-E4
WINFORD AV
1100 VEN 93004 492-G3
WING RD
200 Chat 91311 499-F6
WINGED FOOT CT
2200 OXN 93036 522-D2
WINIFRED ST
2000 SIMI 93063 498-G2
WINNCASTLE ST
500 SIMI 93065 527-D2
WINONA CT
6400 VeCo 91377 558-A1
WINROCK WY
23600 SIMI 93065 497-A1
WINSIDE ST
4800 THO 91362 557-G2
WINSTON CT
1000 THO 91361 557-B5
WINTER AV
12600 MRPK 93021 496-E4
WINTERBERRY AV
5200 SIMI 93063 498-J2
WINTERBROOK CT
3100 THO 91360 526-F2
WINTERDEW AV
23600 SIMI 93065 497-D2
WINTERGREEN LN
13200 MRPK 93021 496-E4
WINTERSET PL
1800 SIMI 93065 497-D2
WINTERWOOD CT
4000 MRPK 93021 496-C3
WINTHROP CT
2500 SIMI 93065 497-J1
WINTHROP LN
1000 VEN 93001 491-E4
WINTON CT
- SIMI 93065 497-E2
WISCASSET DR
- CanP 91307 529-C4
- LA 91304 529-D4
WISDOM CT
3200 SIMI 93063 478-D6
WISHARD AV
600 SIMI 93065 497-J5
WISTERIA LN
900 SPLA 93060 473-J1
WISTERIA ST
2000 SIMI 93065 498-B2
WISTERIA WY
- VEN 93004 473-C7
WITHERSPOON DR
700 THO 91360 526-G2
WOLF CREEK CT
3300 SIMI 93063 479-A6
WOLFF RD
100 VeCo 93030 523-E7
500 VeCo 93033 523-E7
500 VeCo 93033 553-E1
WOLFF ST
100 OXN 93033 522-F7
WOLSEY CT
4500 WLKV 91361 557-C5
WOLVERINE ST
7000 VEN 93003 492-E5
WOLVERTON AV
1300 CMRL 93010 524-F1
1700 CMRL 93010 494-F7
WOLVERTON ST
9000 VEN 93004 492-H3
WOOD PL
1900 VEN 93003 492-A5
WOOD RD
- CMRL 93010 523-H3
400 VeCo 93010 523-H5
1000 VeCo 93012 523-H5
1100 VeCo 93012 553-H3
1100 VeCo 93033 523-H7
1100 VeCo 93033 553-H3
6400 VeCo 93033 583-G1
6800 VeCo 93041 583-G1
WOODBINE CT
3000 THO 91360 526-D3
WOODBLUFF CT
23600 THO 91362 527-A2
WOODBRIAR PL
30100 AGRH 91301 557-H4
WOODBRIDGE LN
- SIMI 93063 498-H1
WOODBROOK DR
29500 AGRH 91301 557-J4
WOODBURN AV
2000 THO 91361 557-A7
2600 WLKV 91361 557-A7
WOODBURY ST
5300 VEN 93003 492-B3
WOODCREEK CT
29000 AGRH 91301 558-A3
WOODCREEK RD
600 CMRL 93012 525-A1
1700 CMRL 93012 495-A7
N WOODCREEK RD
- CMRL 93012 495-A7
WOODCREST PL
6500 VeCo 91377 558-B2

STREET Block City ZIP Pg-Grid

WOODCUTTER LN
1900 THO 91320 525-J7
1900 THO 91320 526-A7
WOODED VISTA
24600 CanP 91307 529-C7
WOODFERN CIR
3100 THO 91360 526-H2
WOODFLOWER ST
- THO 91362 527-B2
WOODGATE CT
1000 CMRL 93010 524-C2
WOODGLADE LN
24500 CanP 91307 529-C5
WOODGLEN DR
4300 MRPK 93021 496-E3
5800 AGRH 91301 557-H4
WOODGLEN ST
1800 SIMI 93065 478-A7
WOODGREEN CT
2900 THO 91362 527-B2
WOODGROVE RD
800 FILM 93015 456-A5
WOODHALL AV
7600 LA 91304 529-F3
WOODHAVEN ST
3500 SIMI 93063 498-D1
N WOODHAVEN ST
2400 SIMI 93063 498-E1
WOODHILL DR
11200 MRPK 93021 496-B3
WOODLAKE AV
6100 WdHl 91367 529-G7
6400 CanP 91307 529-G5
7500 LA 91304 529-G2
WOODLAKE MNR
3900 MRPK 93021 496-F4
WOODLAND AV
700 VeCo 93023 451-B3
WOODLAND DR
1000 SPLA 93060 464-B3
WOODLAND RD
23600 SIMI 93065 497-G7
WOODLAND ST
1400 OXN 93035 552-E1
5900 VEN 93003 492-C2
6200 VeCo 93003 492-C2
WOODLAND GROVE CT
1300 THO 91362 527-E7
WOODLAND OAK PL
- THO 91320 555-F3
WOODLAND VIEW DR
6000 WdHl 91367 529-C7
WOODLANE CT
4100 THO 91362 527-C6
WOODLAWN DR
500 THO 91360 526-D7
WOODLET WY
- THO 91361 556-F2
WOODLEY AV
- THO 91362 527-C2
WOODLOCH LN
23600 SIMI 93065 497-A2
WOODLOW CT
1300 THO 91361 557-A6
WOOD OPAL WY
2400 OXN 93030 522-D3
WOODPECKER AV
2300 VEN 93003 492-E5
N WOOD RANCH PKWY
300 SIMI 93065 497-D5
S WOOD RANCH PKWY
- SIMI 93065 527-E1
200 SIMI 93065 497-E7
WOODRIDGE AV
1100 THO 91362 527-A6
WOODROW AV
2300 SIMI 93065 498-B1
2600 SIMI 93065 478-C7
WOODROW CT
2600 SIMI 93065 498-B1
WOODSCENT LN
23600 SIMI 93065 497-A2
WOODSIDE DR
1600 THO 91362 526-J3
WOODSIDE PL
1100 OXN 93036 522-F1
WOODSTEAD WY
100 SIMI 93065 497-F3
WOODSTOCK LN
900 VEN 93001 491-E4
WOODSTONE CT
3100 THO 91360 526-C2
WOODSTONE PL
7100 CanP 91307 529-C5
WOODVALE CT
7000 CanP 91307 529-F5
WOODVIEW CT
3200 THO 91362 527-C3
WOODWIND CT
2000 SIMI 93063 498-J2
WOODWORTH AV
- THO 91362 527-C2
WOOLEY RD
100 OXN 93030 522-C7
100 OXN 93033 522-C7
1000 OXN 93035 521-J7
1600 OXN 93035 522-C7
1800 VeCo 93030 522-C7
1800 VeCo 93030 523-A7
WOOLEY RD
1800 VeCo 93033 522-C7
1800 VeCo 93033 523-A7
3800 VeCo 93035 522-A7
E WOOLEY RD
- OXN 93030 522-H7
1000 OXN 93033 522-G7
WOOLSEY CANYON RD
23700 LA 91304 499-D7
23900 WHil 91304 499-D7
24900 VeCo 93063 499-B7
WOOSTER ST
4300 VEN 93003 491-J2
4300 VEN 93003 492-A2
WORDSWORTH CT
2600 THO 91362 527-B3
WORDSWORTH WY
6500 VEN 93003 492-D3
WORKMAN AV
2100 SIMI 93063 498-G2
WORMWOOD ST
- VeCo 93023 451-B4
WORTH WY
5200 CMRL 93012 495-A7
5200 VeCo 93012 495-B5
N WRANGLER LN
- VeCo 91307 529-B3
WRANGLER RD
- SIMI 93065 497-J7
WREN CT
6900 VEN 93003 492-E4
WRIGHT RD
200 VeCo 93036 522-H1
2500 VeCo 93066 493-F6
3200 VeCo 93010 493-F6
WYANDOTTE ST
22000 CanP 91303 529-J5
22700 CanP 91307 529-G5
WYCHOFF AV
1600 SIMI 93063 499-A3
WYETH LN
500 VEN 93003 492-D1
WYNN CT
300 THO 91362 557-A1
WYNNEFIELD AV
1300 THO 91362 527-C6
WYSTERIA DR
6100 VeCo 93063 499-B4

X

XANADU WY
- OXN 93036 492-H5
300 SIMI 93065 527-D1
XAVIER AV
100 VEN 93003 492-B2

Y

YACHT WY
- OXN 93035 522-D7
YAGER WY
3300 WLKV 91361 557-B7
YALE AV
100 VEN 93003 492-B3
N YALE AV
6400 MRPK 93021 476-H6
YALE CT
100 SPLA 93060 464-A6
400 OXN 93036 522-H2
YALE PL
500 OXN 93033 552-H4
YALE ST
200 SPLA 93060 464-A6
1100 OXN 93033 552-J4
YANA CT
5900 SIMI 93063 479-B7
YANKEE DR
4000 AGRH 91301 558-E7
YARDARM AV
2500 PHME 93041 552-B2
YARDLEY PL
3200 SIMI 93063 478-D6
YARNELL AV
3200 SIMI 93063 478-F6
YARNELL PL
800 OXN 93033 552-H1
YARNTON CT
23600 VeCo 91361 556-F6
YARROW DR
- SIMI 93065 527-E1
YEARLING CT
800 CMRL 93010 524-C2
YEARLING PL
2600 OXN 93036 492-F7
2600 OXN 93036 522-F1
YEATS LN
600 VEN 93003 492-D1
YELLOW HILL RD
12000 VeCo 90265 625-G1
YELLOWSTONE AV
200 THO 91320 556-D2
YELLOWSTONE DR
100 OXN 93033 553-C3
YELLOW THROAT PL
- THO 91320 525-J5
- THO 91320 526-A5
YELLOWWOOD DR
2600 WLKV 91361 557-A7
YERBA BUENA RD
8400 VeCo 90265 586-A3
9800 VeCo 90265 585-H4
12600 VeCo 90265 625-F2
YERBA SECA AV
6200 AGRH 91301 558-B3
YEW DR
2300 THO 91320 555-J1
YOKUTS CT
2700 SIMI 93063 479-A7
YOLANDA ST
1900 CMRL 93010 524-D2
YOLO ST
10600 VEN 93004 472-H7
YORBA LINDA PL
400 CMRL 93012 524-G3
YORK PL
1000 THO 91362 527-A7
YORK ST
1100 OXN 93033 552-J4
YORKFIELD CT
4400 WLKV 91361 557-D6
YORKSHIRE AV
800 THO 91360 526-G7
YOSEMITE
100 OXN 93033 553-C3
YOSEMITE AV
- SIMI 93063 478-J6
1500 SIMI 93063 499-A2
2600 SIMI 93063 479-A6
YOSEMITE CT
- VEN 93003 492-C2
YOSEMITE DR
100 OXN 93033 553-B5
YOUMANS DR
200 VEN 93003 492-B3
YOUNAN DR
- Chat 91311 479-H7
- Chat 91311 499-H1
YOUNG AV
1900 THO 91360 526-E4
YOUNG RD
2100 VeCo 93015 455-D5
YOUNG WOLF DR
- SIMI 93065 478-A5
YSRELLA AV
1500 SIMI 93065 498-A3
YUBA CT
8100 VEN 93004 492-F1
YUBA DR
2800 SIMI 93063 479-A7
YUCCA CT
3700 OXN 93033 552-H4
YUCCA DR
500 FILM 93015 455-J5
1800 VeCo 93012 495-J7
1800 VeCo 93012 525-J1
YUCCA LN
- THO 91362 557-A3
YUCCA ST
- OXN 93033 552-H4
800 PHME 93041 552-H4
W YUCCA ST
100 OXN 93033 552-G3
YUCCA WY
2300 VeCo 93012 495-J7
YUKON AV
4200 SIMI 93063 478-F7
YUKON TR
8400 LA 91304 529-C2
YUKONITE PL
1000 OXN 93030 522-D4
YUMA CT
2400 VEN 93001 471-C5
YUMA ST
4100 SIMI 93063 478-F6
YUROK CT
2800 SIMI 93063 479-A7

Z

ZACHARY ST
300 MRPK 93021 496-F1
ZAHARIAS CT
- MRPK 93021 476-D5
ZALTANA ST
22500 Chat 91311 499-H1
N ZANJA LN
- VeCo 91307 528-H5
ZAPATA CT
2800 SIMI 93063 478-G7
ZELDA WY
9200 Chat 91311 499-G7
ZELZAH AV
6800 VeCo 93001 459-C4
ZENITH AV
3600 THO 91360 526-G1
ZENO DR
400 VeCo 91377 557-G3
ZEPHYR CT
2300 VEN 93001 491-E4
ZIEGLER DR
- SIMI 93063 479-B7
ZIMMAN LN
2600 SIMI 93063 478-J7
2600 SIMI 93063 498-J1
ZINNIA CT
600 THO 91360 526-D2
ZINNIA WY
- VEN 93004 493-A2
ZION AV
400 OXN 93033 552-G4
ZION WY
1300 VEN 93003 492-B4
ZIRCON AV
1600 OXN 93030 522-D3
ZIRON AV
- SIMI 93065 478-A7
ZOCALO CIR
4400 THO 91360 496-J7
ZOLA AV
500 VEN 93003 492-D1
ZUNI CT
2400 VEN 93001 471-C5
ZUNIGA RIDGE PL
1700 THO 91362 556-J2

#

1ST AV
- PHME 93043 552-C2
1ST ST
- MRPK 93021 496-E1
100 SIMI 93065 497-H2
200 THO 91320 556-B2
300 FILM 93015 456-A6
700 FILM 93015 455-J6
E 1ST ST
200 OXN 93030 522-H5
W 1ST ST
100 OXN 93030 522-F5
2ND ST
- MRPK 93021 496-E1
100 FILM 93015 456-A5
100 PHME 93041 552-E5
200 THO 91320 556-B2
700 FILM 93015 455-J5
1400 SIMI 93065 497-H3
E 2ND ST
200 OXN 93030 522-H5
W 2ND ST
100 OXN 93030 522-F5
3RD ST
- VeCo 93042 583-G2
- MRPK 93021 496-E1
100 FILM 93015 456-A5
100 OXN 93030 522-E6
100 PHME 93041 552-E5
200 THO 91320 556-B1
700 FILM 93015 455-J5
1400 SIMI 93065 497-G3
23600 VeCo 93063 498-G7
E 3RD ST
100 OXN 93030 522-H6
W 3RD ST
100 OXN 93030 522-F6
4TH AV
- PHME 93043 552-D2
4TH PL
400 PHME 93041 552-E5
4TH ST
- VeCo 93042 583-G2
- FILM 93015 456-A5
- OXN 93030 522-F6
600 FILM 93015 455-J5
1000 SIMI 93065 497-G3
N 4TH ST
100 SPLA 93060 464-A6
S 4TH ST
100 SPLA 93060 464-B6
5TH PL
1000 PHME 93041 552-E4
5TH ST
- VeCo 93042 583-G2
100 PHME 93041 552-E4
700 FILM 93015 455-J5
1600 SIMI 93065 497-G3
1700 VeCo 93015 455-E6
5TH ST Rt#-34
100 OXN 93030 522-H6
1800 VeCo 93030 522-H6
1800 VeCo 93030 523-A6
1800 OXN 93030 523-A6
2600 OXN 93033 523-A6
2600 VeCo 93033 523-D6
E 5TH ST Rt#-34
- VeCo 93012 523-H6
- VeCo 93012 524-C6
N 5TH ST
200 SPLA 93060 464-A5
S 5TH ST
300 SPLA 93060 464-B6
W 5TH ST
100 OXN 93030 522-F6
3800 OXN 93030 521-J6
3800 OXN 93035 521-J6
3800 VeCo 93030 522-A6
6TH PL
1000 PHME 93041 552-F4
6TH ST
- VeCo 93042 583-G2
100 OXN 93030 522-F6
600 FILM 93015 455-J4
600 FILM 93015 456-A4
600 VeCo 93015 456-A4
1000 PHME 93041 552-F4
E 6TH ST
- OXN 93030 522-G6
N 6TH ST
200 SPLA 93060 464-A5
7TH PL
1200 PHME 93041 552-F4
7TH ST
- VeCo 93042 583-F2
100 OXN 93030 522-F6
600 FILM 93015 455-J4
600 FILM 93015 456-A4
1000 PHME 93041 552-F4
1600 OXN 93035 522-E6
1700 VeCo 93015 455-F6
N 7TH ST
100 SPLA 93060 464-B5
S 7TH ST
100 SPLA 93060 464-B6
8TH AV
- PHME 93043 552-D2
8TH CIR
1600 PHME 93041 552-F3
8TH PL
1400 PHME 93041 552-F4
8TH ST
- OXN 93035 522-E6
- VeCo 93042 583-G3
100 OXN 93030 522-G7
1400 PHME 93041 552-F4
5900 VEN 93003 492-C5
5900 VeCo 93003 492-C5
N 8TH ST
100 SPLA 93060 464-B5
S 8TH ST
100 SPLA 93060 464-B6
9TH AV NW
1100 VeCo 93023 451-C2
9TH ST
- VeCo 93042 583-G2
100 OXN 93030 522-G7
200 SPLA 93060 464-B5
1500 OXN 93035 522-E7
10TH AV
- PHME 93043 552-D3
10TH ST
- VeCo 93042 583-F3
23600 VeCo 93063 498-G7
23600 VeCo 93063 528-G1
N 10TH ST
300 SPLA 93060 464-B4
N 10TH ST Rt#-150
100 SPLA 93060 464-B5
S 10TH ST Rt#-150
100 SPLA 93060 464-C6
11TH AV
- PHME 93043 552-D3
11TH ST
600 VeCo 93042 583-F3
700 VeCo 93041 583-F3
23600 VeCo 93063 528-G1
N 11TH ST
100 SPLA 93060 464-C5
S 11TH ST
100 SPLA 93060 464-C5
12TH ST
- VeCo 93042 583-G4
23600 VeCo 93063 528-G1
N 12TH ST
100 SPLA 93060 464-C4
S 12TH ST
100 SPLA 93060 464-C5
13TH ST
- VeCo 93042 583-F4
N 13TH ST
100 SPLA 93060 464-C4
S 13TH ST
200 SPLA 93060 464-C5
14TH ST
- VeCo 93042 583-E3
300 SPLA 93060 464-C4
15TH AV
- PHME 93043 552-E3
15TH ST
- VeCo 93042 583-E4
16 DE SEPTIEMBRE
1500 VEN 93004 492-J3
1500 VEN 93004 493-A3
16TH ST
- VeCo 93042 583-D4
17TH ST
- VeCo 93042 583-D4
23600 VeCo 93063 528-F1
18TH ST
- VeCo 93042 583-D5
23600 VeCo 93063 528-G1
19TH AV
- PHME 93043 552-E3
19TH ST
- VeCo 93042 583-E6
20TH AV
- PHME 93043 552-E3
20TH ST
- VeCo 93042 583-F6
23600 VeCo 93063 528-F1
21ST AV
- PHME 93043 552-D3
22ND ST
23600 VeCo 93063 528-F1
24TH AV
- PHME 93043 552-E3
24TH ST
23600 VeCo 93063 528-F1
25TH AV
- PHME 93043 552-E3
27TH AV
- PHME 93043 552-E3
28TH AV
- PHME 93043 552-D3
29TH AV
- PHME 93043 552-E4
32ND AV
- PHME 93041 552-D4
- PHME 93043 552-C4
33RD AV
- PHME 93041 552-E4
34TH AV
- PHME 93041 552-D4
35TH AV
- PHME 93043 552-D4
36TH AV
- PHME 93041 552-E4
41ST ST
- PHME 93041 552-E5
- PHME 93043 552-E5
NW 144TH ST
400 OJAI 93023 451-G1
NW 171ST ST
1300 VeCo 93023 451-D2
N 188TH ST
700 OJAI 93023 451-H1
N 201ST ST
2000 VeCo 93023 451-C3
Rt#-N1 LAS VIRGENES RD
3700 CALB 91302 558-H7
4800 LACo 91302 558-H7
Rt#-N9 KANAN RD
4100 Ago 91301 558-A7
4100 AGRH 91301 558-A7
Rt#-1 OLD RINCON HWY
2900 VeCo 93001 470-F6
4200 VeCo 93001 366-G9
4200 VeCo 93001 459-F7
4200 VeCo 93001 469-H1
23600 VeCo 93001 490-G1
Rt#-1 OXNARD BLVD
- OXN 93033 553-A2
- VeCo 93033 553-B3
100 OXN 93030 522-G7
1200 OXN 93030 552-H1
1200 OXN 93033 522-G7
1200 OXN 93033 552-H1
1500 OXN 93036 522-G1
19200 OXN 93036 492-G7
Rt#-1 PACIFIC COAST FRWY
- OXN - 553-C4
- VeCo - 553-C4
- VeCo - 583-H1
Rt#-1 PACIFIC COAST HWY
2900 VeCo 93001 470-B3
4200 VeCo 93001 366-G9
4200 VeCo 93001 459-F6
4200 VeCo 93001 469-H1
9000 VeCo 90265 387-F4
9000 VeCo 90265 625-A3
9400 VeCo - 584-A6
12300 LACo 90265 625-F5
19900 VeCo 93033 583-J5
19900 VeCo 93033 584-A6
23600 VeCo 93001 490-G1
34100 MAL 90265 625-F5
Rt#-23 A ST
- FILM 93015 456-A6
- FILM 93015 466-A1
Rt#-23 BELLEVUE AV
700 VeCo 93015 465-J3
700 VeCo 93015 466-A3
Rt#-23 BROADWAY
14900 VeCo 93021 476-D4
Rt#-23 CHAMBERSBURG RD
300 FILM 93015 466-A2
300 VeCo 93015 466-A2
Rt#-23 DECKER CANYON RD
1400 LACo 90265 586-F7
Rt#-23 FRWY
- MRPK - 496-G1
- THO - 496-J7
- THO - 497-A7
- THO - 526-J1
- THO - 556-H1
- VeCo - 496-H3
- VeCo - 497-A4
Rt#-23 GRIMES CANYON RD
1300 VeCo 93015 465-J4
4800 VeCo 93015 466-A5
4800 VeCo 93021 466-A5
8000 VeCo 93021 476-B2
Rt#-23 MOORPARK AV
- MRPK 93021 476-E7
500 MRPK 93021 496-E1
Rt#-23 N MOORPARK AV
- MRPK 93021 496-E1
Rt#-23 MULHOLLAND HWY
33000 LACo 90265 586-G6
Rt#-23 WALNUT CANYON RD
800 MRPK 93021 476-E7
1100 VeCo 93021 476-E4
Rt#-23 WESTLAKE BLVD
100 LACo 90265 586-H4
400 WLKV 90265 586-H4
400 WLKV 91361 586-H4
800 LACo 91361 586-H4
800 THO 91361 586-H4
Rt#-23 S WESTLAKE BLVD
100 THO 91362 557-C4
100 THO 91361 557-C4
600 THO 91361 556-J7
800 THO 91361 586-H1
Rt#-27 TOPANGA CANYON BLVD
9500 Chat 91311 499-J6
Rt#-33 HIGHWAY
- VeCo 93023 366-J6
- VeCo 93252 366-G1
Rt#-33 MARICOPA HWY
1000 OJAI 93023 441-E6
1000 OJAI 93023 451-F1
1700 VeCo 93023 441-B2
10000 VeCo 93023 366-J6
Rt#-33 OJAI FRWY
- VeCo - 461-B6
- VeCo - 471-C3
- VEN - 471-B7
- VEN - 491-A1
Rt#-33 VENTURA AV
- VeCo 93022 451-B5
4400 VeCo 93001 461-A2
4400 VeCo 93022 461-A2
11200 VeCo 93023 451-D2
11800 OJAI 93023 451-F1
Rt#-34 5TH ST
100 OXN 93030 522-H6
1800 VeCo 93030 522-H6
1800 VeCo 93030 523-A6
1800 OXN 93030 523-A6
2600 OXN 93033 523-A6
2600 VeCo 93033 523-D6
Rt#-34 E 5TH ST
- VeCo 93012 523-H6
- VeCo 93012 524-C6
Rt#-34 N LEWIS RD
- CMRL 93010 524-G2
1700 CMRL 93010 494-H7
Rt#-34 S LEWIS RD
- CMRL 93010 524-F4
200 CMRL 93012 524-F4
Rt#-34 PLEASANT VALLEY RD
2200 VeCo 93012 524-F5
2200 CMRL 93012 524-F5
Rt#-34 SOMIS RD
2400 CMRL 93010 494-J6
2400 VeCo 93010 494-J6
2400 VeCo 93066 494-J6
2600 VeCo 93066 495-A5
Rt#-118 LOS ANGELES AV
- MRPK 93021 496-F1
900 VeCo 93066 493-H4
900 VeCo 93066 494-A4
1200 VeCo 93004 493-B2
2000 VeCo 93036 493-B2
4500 VeCo 93066 495-A4
8000 VeCo 93021 495-H3
10700 VeCo 93021 496-A2
Rt#-118 RONALD REAGAN FRWY
- Chat - 499-E2
- MRPK - 476-H7
- MRPK - 477-B6
- MRPK - 496-G1
- SIMI - 477-B6
- SIMI - 497-G1
- SIMI - 498-F1
- SIMI - 499-E2
- VeCo - 477-B6
Rt#-118 S WELLS RD
300 VEN 93004 472-J7
700 VEN 93004 473-A7
800 VEN 93004 493-A1
900 VeCo 93004 493-A1
Rt#-126 HENRY MAYO DR
31100 Cstc 91384 458-H5
31800 VeCo 93040 458-H5
Rt#-126 KOREAN WAR VET MEM HY
2500 VeCo 93015 455-E7
2700 VeCo 93015 465-B2
17900 VeCo 93060 464-F3
18400 SPLA 93060 464-F3
20100 VeCo 93060 465-B2
Rt#-126 OLD TELEGRAPH RD
2500 VeCo 93015 455-E7
2700 VeCo 93015 465-E1
Rt#-126 SANTA PAULA FRWY
- SPLA - 463-J7
- SPLA - 464-D5
- SPLA - 473-F4
- VeCo - 473-B6
- VeCo - 492-D3
- VEN - 472-J7
- VEN - 473-B6
- VEN - 491-J4
- VEN - 492-D3
Rt#-126 TELEGRAPH RD
- FILM 93015 456-E6
- VeCo 93015 456-E6
900 VeCo 93015 457-E5
1400 VeCo 93040 457-G4
2200 VeCo 93040 458-B5
2700 VeCo 93015 465-C1
17900 VeCo 93060 464-F3
18400 SPLA 93060 464-F3
20100 VeCo 93060 465-A2
Rt#-126 E TELEGRAPH RD
100 FILM 93015 456-C6
300 VeCo 93015 456-C6
Rt#-126 VENTURA ST
100 FILM 93015 456-A6
400 FILM 93015 455-F7
800 VeCo 93015 455-F7
Rt#-126 E VENTURA ST
- FILM 93015 456-B6
Rt#-150 N 10TH ST
100 SPLA 93060 464-B5
Rt#-150 S 10TH ST
100 SPLA 93060 464-C6
Rt#-150 BALDWIN RD
- VeCo 93001 450-H3
- VeCo 93023 450-H3
600 VeCo 93023 451-A3
Rt#-150 CASITAS PASS RD
2000 VeCo 93001 450-D5
3500 VeCo 93001 460-B1
4000 VeCo 93001 366-G8
4000 VeCo 93001 459-G1
7100 StBC 93013 459-G1
Rt#-150 E OJAI AV
200 OJAI 93023 441-H7
1100 OJAI 93023 442-B7
1600 VeCo 93023 442-B7
Rt#-150 N OJAI RD
100 SPLA 93060 464-B3
300 VeCo 93060 464-B3
Rt#-150 W OJAI AV
100 OJAI 93023 441-G7
1000 OJAI 93023 451-G1
Rt#-150 OJAI SANTA PAULA RD
3100 VeCo 93023 442-D7
7000 VeCo 93023 452-E1
11900 VeCo 93023 453-A1
Rt#-150 RINCON RD
6600 StBC 93013 459-A1
23600 VeCo 93001 366-G9
23600 VeCo 93001 459-A1
Rt#-150 SANTA PAULA OJAI RD
4300 VeCo 93060 464-A1
4400 VeCo 93060 454-A7
4600 VeCo 93060 453-H4
12400 VeCo 93023 453-H4
Rt#-192 CASITAS PASS RD
6800 StBC 93013 459-A1
Rt#-232 E VINEYARD AV
500 OXN 93036 522-G2
2600 VeCo 93036 522-G2
2800 OXN 93036 492-H7
2800 VeCo 93036 492-H7
4100 VeCo 93036 493-A4
5100 VeCo 93066 493-A4
U.S.-101 EL CAMINO REAL
- VeCo - 366-E8
- VeCo - 459-C5
- VeCo - 469-H1
- VeCo - 470-E5
- VeCo - 490-H1
- VEN - 490-H1
- VEN - 491-G4
U.S.-101 VENTURA FRWY
- Ago - 558-D6
- AGRH - 557-G6
- AGRH - 558-D6
- CALB - 558-D6
- CMRL - 523-A3
- CMRL - 524-A3
- CMRL - 525-C5
- LACo - 558-D6
- OXN - 492-F7
- OXN - 522-H2
U.S.-101 VENTURA FRWY
- OXN - 523-A3
- THO - 525-C5
- THO - 526-D7
- THO - 555-J1
- THO - 556-E1
- THO - 557-B4
- VeCo - 366-F9
- VeCo - 459-A3
- VeCo - 469-J1
- VeCo - 470-B3
- VeCo - 490-H1
- VeCo - 492-F7
- VeCo - 523-A3
- VeCo - 525-C5
- VEN - 490-H1
- VEN - 491-A2
- VEN - 492-F7
- WLKV - 557-B4

AIRPORTS

FEATURE NAME	Address City, ZIP Code	PAGE-GRID
CAMARILLO, CMRL		523 - G4
HELIPORT, VEN		491 - F7
OXNARD, OXN		522 - D5
SANTA PAULA, SPLA		464 - B6

BEACHES, HARBORS & WATER REC

FEATURE NAME	Address City, ZIP Code	PAGE-GRID
CARRILLO, LEO ST BCH, VeCo		625 - G5
CHANNEL ISLANDS BEACH PK, OXN		552 - B4
COUNTY LINE BEACH, VeCo		625 - E5
HOLLYWOOD BEACH, VeCo		552 - A4
WESTLAKE YACHT CLUB, WLKV		557 - C7
MANDALAY STATE BEACH, OXN		521 - G4
MARINA COVE BEACH, VEN		491 - F7
MCGRATH STATE BEACH, OXN		521 - G2
MUSSEL SHOAL BEACH, VeCo		459 - D6
NICHOLAS CANYON CO BEACH, MAL		625 - J6
OIL PIERS BEACH, VeCo		459 - E6
OXNARD BEACH PK, OXN		551 - J1
SAN BUENAVENTURA STATE BEACH, VEN		491 - D3
SILVER STRAND BEACH, VeCo		552 - C6
VENTURA YACHT CLUB, VEN		491 - F7
WOOD, EMMA STATE BEACH, VeCo		470 - G7

BUILDINGS

FEATURE NAME	Address City, ZIP Code	PAGE-GRID
FOR DOWNTOWN BLDGS SEE PAGE E		-
ASSOC FOR RETARDED CITIZENS-VENTURA CO	1183 CL SUERTE, CMRL, 93012	524 - H1
BOY SCOUTS COUNTY HEADQUARTERS	509 E DAILY DR, CMRL, 93010	524 - B3

BUILDINGS - GOVERNMENTAL

FEATURE NAME	Address City, ZIP Code	PAGE-GRID
AGOURA HILLS CITY HALL	30001 LADYFACE CT, AGRH, 91301	557 - H6
BRANDEIS-BARDIN INSTITUTE	1101 PEPPERTREE LN, VeCo, 93064	498 - F4
CALABASAS CITY HALL	26135 MUREAU RD, CALB, 91302	558 - H5
CAMARILLO CITY HALL	601 CARMEN DR, CMRL, 93010	524 - D2
COUNTY ADMIN BLDG	800 S VICTORIA AV, VEN, 93009	492 - C3
CRIMINAL JUSTICE COMPLEX	800 S VICTORIA AV, VEN, 93009	492 - C3
EAST COUNTY COURTHOUSE	3855 ALAMO ST, SIMI, 93063	478 - E7
FILLMORE CITY HALL	250 CENTRAL AV, FILM, 93015	456 - A6
JUVENILE COURTHOUSE	4353 E VINEYARD AV, VeCo, 93036	492 - J5
MOORPARK CITY HALL	799 MOORPARK AV, MRPK, 93021	476 - E7
OJAI CITY HALL	401 S VENTURA ST, OJAI, 93023	441 - H7
OXNARD CITY HALL	300 W 3RD ST, OXN, 93030	522 - G6
PORT HUENEME CITY HALL	250 N VENTURA RD, PHME, 93041	552 - E6
SANTA PAULA CITY HALL	970 VENTURA ST, SPLA, 93060	464 - C6
SIMI VALLEY CITY HALL	2929 TAPO CANYON RD, SIMI, 93063	478 - F7
THOUSAND OAKS CITY HALL	2100 E THOUSAND OAKS BLVD, THO, 91362	556 - J2
VENTURA CITY HALL	501 POLI ST, VEN, 93001	491 - C1
VENTURA COUNTY COURTHOUSE	800 S VICTORIA AV, VEN, 93009	492 - C3
VENTURA COUNTY HONOR FARM	370 BALDWIN RD, VeCo, 93023	451 - B3
VENTURA COUNTY JAIL	600 TODD RD, VeCo, 93060	473 - F5
VENTURA CALIFORNIA YOUTH AUTHORITY	3100 WRIGHT RD, VeCo, 93010	493 - F7
WESTLAKE VILLAGE CITY HALL	31200 OAK CREST DR, WLKV, 91361	557 - F6

CEMETERIES

FEATURE NAME	Address City, ZIP Code	PAGE-GRID
ASSUMPTION CEM, SIMI		497 - H4
BARDSDALE CEM, VeCo		465 - G4
CONEJO MTN MEM PK, VeCo		554 - J1
F & AM CEM, OXN		553 - B4
IVY LAWN CEM, VEN		492 - C6
JAPANESE CEM, OXN		553 - A4
MOUNT SINAI MEM PK, SIMI		479 - B7
NORDHOFF CEM, OJAI		441 - F7
OAKWOOD MEM PK, Chat		499 - H5
PIRU CEM, VeCo		457 - D4
SANTA CLARA CEM, OXN		522 - F2
SANTA PAULA CEM, SPLA		463 - J5
SIMI CEM, SIMI		497 - J3
VALLEY OAKS MEM PK, WLKV		557 - F5

COLLEGES & UNIVERSITIES

FEATURE NAME	Address City, ZIP Code	PAGE-GRID
AQUINAS, THOMAS COLLEGE	10000 N SANTA PAULA OJAI RD, VeCo, 93060	453 - H2
CALIFORNIA LUTHERAN UNIV	60 W OLSEN RD, THO, 91360	526 - E2
CSU CHANNEL ISLANDS	1 UNIVERSITY DR, VeCo, 93012	554 - E3
ITT TECHNICAL INSTITUTE	2051 SOLAR DR, OXN, 93036	523 - B3
MOORPARK COLLEGE	7075 CAMPUS RD, MRPK, 93021	476 - J6
OXNARD COLLEGE	4000 ROSE AV, OXN, 93033	552 - J3
SAINT JOHNS SEMINARY COLLEGE	5012 SEMINARY RD, CMRL, 93012	494 - J7
VENTURA COLLEGE	4667 TELEGRAPH RD, VEN, 93003	491 - J2
VENTURA COLLEGE EAST CAMPUS	115 DEAN DR, SPLA, 93060	464 - A6

ENTERTAINMENT & SPORTS

FEATURE NAME	Address City, ZIP Code	PAGE-GRID
CAMARILLO SKATEPARK	1030 TEMPLE AV, CMRL, 93010	524 - F1
CIVIC ARTS PLAZA	2100 E THOUSAND OAKS BLVD, THO, 91362	556 - J2
KAVLI, FRED THEATRE FOR THE PERF-ARTS	2100 E THOUSAND OAKS BLVD, THO, 91362	556 - J2
NEWBURY PARK SKATEPARK	190 N REINO RD, THO, 91320	555 - F1
OJAI SKATEPARK	414 E OJAI AV, OJAI, 93023	441 - H7
OXNARD SKATEPARK	3250 S ROSE AV, OXN, 93033	552 - J3
PERF ARTS & CONV CTR	800 HOBSON WY, OXN, 93030	522 - F7
SANTA PAULA SKATEPARK	S 10TH ST & VENTURA ST, SPLA, 93060	464 - C6
SEASIDE PARK & VENTURA CO-FAIRGROUND	10 W HARBOR BLVD, VEN, 93001	491 - B2
SIMI VALLEY CULTURAL ARTS CTR	3050 LOS ANGELES AV, SIMI, 93065	498 - C2
SKATELAB SKATEPARK	4226 VALLEY FAIR ST, SIMI, 93063	498 - F2

GOLF COURSES

FEATURE NAME	Address City, ZIP Code	PAGE-GRID
BUENAVENTURA GC, VEN		492 - C7
CAMARILLO SPRINGS GC, CMRL		525 - A5
CLARK, JOHN E GC, VeCo		583 - G2
ELKINS RANCH GC, VeCo		466 - A3
LAKE LINDERO CC, AGRH		557 - G4
LAS POSAS CC, VeCo		493 - J6
LOS ROBLES GREENS GC, THO		556 - D1
LOST CANYONS GC, SIMI		478 - D3
MALIBU CC, LACo		586 - J6
MOORPARK CC, MRPK		476 - C5
MOUNTAIN VIEW GC, VeCo		474 - B1
NORTH RANCH CC, THO		527 - D7
OJAI VALLEY INN AND SPA, OJAI		441 - G7
OLIVAS PK GC, VEN		491 - H7
RIVER RIDGE GC, OXN		522 - D1
RUSTIC CANYON GC, VeCo		476 - G4
SATICOY CC, VeCo		493 - F3
SATICOY REGL GC, VEN		492 - J1
SEABEE GC, PHME		552 - D2
SHERWOOD CC, VeCo		556 - F7
SHERWOOD CC, VeCo		586 - E1
SIMI HILLS GC, SIMI		478 - H6
SINALOA GC, SIMI		497 - F4
SOULE PK GC, OJAI		442 - A7
SPANISH HILLS GOLF & CC, CMRL		523 - H1
STERLING HILLS GC, CMRL		493 - H6
SUNSET HILLS CC, THO		496 - J7
TIERRA REJADA GC, VeCo		496 - J2
WESTLAKE VILLAGE GC, THO		557 - D5
WOOD RANCH GC, SIMI		497 - D6

HISTORIC SITES

FEATURE NAME	Address City, ZIP Code	PAGE-GRID
CAMARILLO RANCH	201 CAMARILLO RANCH RD, CMRL, 93012	524 - H3
FATHER SERRA CROSS	GRANT PARK, VEN, 93001	491 - B1
MISSION SAN BUENAVENTURA	211 E MAIN ST, VEN, 93001	491 - B1
OLIVAS ADOBE	4200 OLIVAS PARK DR, VEN, 93001	491 - J7
ORTEGA ADOBE	215 W MAIN ST, VEN, 93001	491 - B2
REYES ADOBE HIST SITE	5464 REYES ADOBE RD, AGRH, 91301	557 - H5
SANTA SUSANA PASS STATE HIST PK	DEVONSHIRE ST, Chat, 91311	499 - G3
STAGECOACH INN MUS	51 S VENTU PARK RD, THO, 91320	556 - B2
STRATHEARN, ROBERT P HIST PK & MUS	137 STRATHEARN PL, SIMI, 93065	497 - E2
VENTURA COUNTY COURTHOUSE	501 POLI ST, VEN, 93001	491 - C1

HOSPITALS

FEATURE NAME	Address City, ZIP Code	PAGE-GRID
COMMUNITY MEM HOSP	147 N BRENT ST, VEN, 93003	491 - G2
LOS ROBLES REGL MED CTR	215 W JANSS RD, THO, 91360	526 - E4
OJAI VALLEY COMM HOSP	1306 MARICOPA HWY, OJAI, 93023	441 - F7
SAINT JOHNS PLEASANT VALLEY HOSP	2309 ANTONIO AV, CMRL, 93010	494 - G7
SAINT JOHNS REGL MED CTR	1600 N ROSE AV, OXN, 93030	523 - A3
SANTA PAULA HOSP	825 N 10TH ST, SPLA, 93060	464 - B4
SIMI VALLEY HOSP & HEALTH CARE SERV	2975 SYCAMORE DR, SIMI, 93065	478 - B7
VENTURA COUNTY MED CTR	3291 LOMA VISTA RD, VEN, 93003	491 - H2
WEST HILLS HOSP & MED CTR	7300 MEDICAL CENTER DR, CanP, 91307	529 - G4

HOTELS

FEATURE NAME	Address City, ZIP Code	PAGE-GRID
CASA SIRENA MARINA RESORT	3605 PENINSULA RD, OXN, 93035	552 - B3
CLOCKTOWER INN, THE	181 E SANTA CLARA ST, VEN, 93001	491 - B2
COUNTRY INN & SUITES BY CARLSON	298 CHESTNUT ST, VEN, 93001	491 - C1
COUNTRY INN AT PORT HUENEME	350 E PORT HUENEME RD, PHME, 93041	552 - E6
COURTYARD BY MARRIOTT	600 ESPLANADE DR, OXN, 93036	522 - H2
COURTYARD MARRIOTT	4994 VERDUGO WY, CMRL, 93012	524 - J3
CROWNE PLAZA VENTURA BEACH	450 E HARBOR BLVD, VEN, 93001	491 - C2
EMBASSY SUITES MANDALAY BEACH-RESORT	2101 MANDALAY BEACH RD, OXN, 93035	552 - A2
FOUR POINTS VEN HARBORTOWN BY-SHERATON	1050 SCHOONER DR, VEN, 93001	491 - G6
GRAND VISTA HOTEL	999 ENCHANTED WY, SIMI, 93065	497 - G1
HAMPTON INN	30255 AGOURA RD, AGRH, 91301	557 - G6
HOLIDAY INN SIMI VALLEY	2550 ERRINGER RD, SIMI, 93065	498 - A1
HYATT WESTLAKE PLAZA	880 S WESTLAKE BLVD, THO, 91361	557 - C4
LA QUINTA INN	5818 VALENTINE RD, VEN, 93003	492 - C6
LA QUINTA INN & SUITES	1320 NEWBURY RD, THO, 91320	556 - B1
MARRIOTT VENTURA BEACH	2055 E HARBOR BLVD, VEN, 93001	491 - E3
OJAI VALLEY INN	905 COUNTRY CLUB RD, OJAI, 93023	451 - G1
PALM GARDEN HOTEL	495 N VENTU PARK RD, THO, 91320	556 - A1
POSADA ROYALE HOTEL	1775 MADERA RD, SIMI, 93065	497 - E3
RENAISSANCE AGOURA HILLS HOTEL	30100 AGOURA RD, AGRH, 91301	557 - H6
RESIDENCE INN BY MARRIOTT	2101 W VINEYARD AV, OXN, 93036	522 - E1

LAW ENFORCEMENT

FEATURE NAME	Address City, ZIP Code	PAGE-GRID
CALIFORNIA HIGHWAY PATROL-VENTURA	4656 VALENTINE RD, VEN, 93003	492 - A4
CAMARILLO POLICE STA	3701 LAS POSAS RD, CMRL, 93010	494 - G7
FILLMORE POLICE STA	524 SESPE AV, FILM, 93015	456 - A6
MALIBU/LOST HILLS POLICE STA	27050 AGOURA RD, CALB, 91301	558 - F7
MOORPARK POLICE DEPARTMENT	610 SPRING RD, MRPK, 93021	496 - F1
OJAI POLICE DEPARTMENT	402 S VENTURA ST, OJAI, 93023	441 - H7
OXNARD POLICE DEPARTMENT	251 C ST, OXN, 93030	522 - G6
PORT HUENEME POLICE DEPARTMENT	250 N VENTURA RD, PHME, 93041	552 - E6
SANTA PAULA POLICE DEPARTMENT	214 S 10TH ST, SPLA, 93060	464 - C6
SHERIFFS STA	2101 OLSEN RD, THO, 91360	497 - A6
SIMI VALLEY POLICE STA	3901 ALAMO ST, SIMI, 93063	478 - F7
VENTURA POLICE STA	1425 DOWELL DR, VEN, 93003	492 - B4

LIBRARIES

FEATURE NAME	Address City, ZIP Code	PAGE-GRID
AGOURA HILLS	29901 LADYFACE CT, AGRH, 91301	557 - H6
AVENUE	606 N VENTURA AV, VEN, 93001	491 - B1
BLANCHARD	119 N 8TH ST, SPLA, 93060	464 - B5
CAMARILLO	3100 PONDEROSA DR, CMRL, 93010	524 - F1
CAMARILLO	4101 LAS POSAS RD, CMRL, 93010	494 - H7
COLONIA CTR	1500 CM DL SOL, OXN, 93030	522 - J5
DOHENY, CARRIE ESTELLE MEM	5118 SEMINARY RD, CMRL, 93012	494 - J6
DOHENY, EDWARD LAURENCE MEM	5012 SEMINARY RD, CMRL, 93012	494 - J7
FILLMORE	502 2ND ST, FILM, 93015	456 - A5
FOSTER, E P	651 E MAIN ST, VEN, 93001	491 - C2
MEINERS OAKS	114 N PADRE JUAN AV, VeCo, 93023	441 - E6
MOORPARK	699 MOORPARK AV, MRPK, 93021	476 - E7
NEWBURY PARK	2331 BORCHARD RD, THO, 91320	555 - J1
OAK PARK	899 KANAN RD, VeCo, 91377	558 - A1
OAK VIEW	555 MAHONEY AV, VeCo, 93022	451 - A6
OJAI	111 E OJAI AV, OJAI, 93023	441 - H7
OXNARD	251 S A ST, OXN, 93030	522 - G6
PIRU	3811 CENTER ST, VeCo, 93040	457 - F4
PLATT BRANCH	23600 VICTORY BLVD, WdHl, 91367	529 - F7
PRUETER, RAY D	510 PARK AV, PHME, 93041	552 - E5
SATICOY	11426 VIOLETA ST, VeCo, 93004	493 - B1
SIMI VALLEY	2969 TAPO CANYON RD, SIMI, 93063	478 - F7
SOLIZ, ALBERT H	2820 JOURDAN ST, VeCo, 93036	522 - H1
SOUTH OXNARD	200 E BARD RD, OXN, 93033	552 - G4
THOUSAND OAKS	1401 E JANSS RD, THO, 91362	526 - H5
VENTURA CO MUS HIST RESEARCH	100 E MAIN ST, VEN, 93001	491 - B2
WESTLAKE VILLAGE	31220 OAK CREST DR, WLKV, 91361	557 - F6
WRIGHT, H P	57 DAY RD, VEN, 93003	492 - B2

MILITARY INSTALLATIONS

FEATURE NAME	Address City, ZIP Code	PAGE-GRID
CALIFORNIA AIR NATL GUARD	4146 NAVAL AIR RD, VeCo, 93033	553 - F7
NATL GUARD ARMORY	1270 ARUNDELL AV, VEN, 93003	491 - J4
NAVAL BASE VENTURA COUNTY	311 MAIN RD, VeCo, 93033	583 - E4
US COAST GUARD STA	4201 VICTORIA AV, OXN, 93035	552 - B4
US NAVAL CONSTRUCTION BATTALION CTR	N VENTURA RD & PLEASANT VLY RD, PHME, 93043	552 - D4

MUSEUMS

FEATURE NAME	Address City, ZIP Code	PAGE-GRID
ALBINGER ARCHAEOLOGICAL MUS	113 E MAIN ST, VEN, 93001	491 - B2
CALIFORNIA OIL MUS	1001 E MAIN ST, SPLA, 93060	464 - C5
CARNEGIE ART MUS	424 S C ST, OXN, 93030	522 - G6

FEATURE NAME Address City, ZIP Code	PAGE-GRID
CBC SEABEE MUS CUTTING RD & DODSON ST, PHME, 93043	552 - E3
COMSTOCK, A J FIRE MUS FIGUEROA ST & E SANTA CLARA ST, VEN, 93001	491 - B2
FILLMORE HIST MUS 350 MAIN ST, FILM, 93015	456 - B6
GULL WINGS CHILDRENS MUS 418 W 4TH ST, OXN, 93030	522 - G6
MUSEUM OF VENTURA COUNTY 100 E MAIN ST, VEN, 93001	491 - B2
OJAI VALLEY HIST SOCIETY AND MUS 130 W OJAI AV, OJAI, 93023	441 - H7
SAN BUENAVENTURA MISSION MUS 225 E MAIN ST, VEN, 93001	491 - C2
SANTA MONICA MTNS NRA MUS 401 W HILLCREST DR, THO, 91360	526 - E7
STRATHEARN MUS 137 STRATHEARN PL, SIMI, 93065	497 - E2
VENTURA COUNTY MARITIME MUS 2731 S VICTORIA AV, OXN, 93035	552 - B2

OPEN SPACE

FEATURE NAME Address City, ZIP Code	PAGE-GRID
BELL CANYON OPEN SPACE, LA	529 - C3
CHATSWORTH RESERVOIR NATURE-PRESERVE, LA	499 - E7
CONEJO OPEN SPACE, THO	526 - D6
MCCREA, JOEL WILDLIFE PRESERVE, -THO	496 - H7
POINT MUGU GAME RESERVE, VeCo	583 - D1
POTRERO OPEN SPACE, THO	555 - D1
SANTA CLARA RIV ESTUARY NATURAL-RESRV, OXN	521 - F2
SESPE CONDOR PRESERVE, VeCo	367 - B6
VENTURA COUNTY GAME RESERVE, VeCo	583 - B3

OTHER

FEATURE NAME Address City, ZIP Code	PAGE-GRID
CABRILLO RACQUET CLUB 3945 N CLUBHOUSE DR, VeCo, 93066	493 - F4
CAMP BLOOMFIELD MULHOLLAND HWY, LACo, 90265	625 - J2
CHANNEL ISLANDS NATL PK HDQTRS 1901 SPINNAKER DR, VEN, 93001	491 - F6
CHUMASH INDIAN INTERPRETIVE CTR 3290 LANG RANCH PKWY, THO, 91362	527 - D4
CONEJO VALLEY BOTANIC GARDEN 350 W GAINSBOROUGH RD, THO, 91360	526 - E6
DRY GULCH RANCH 12420 YELLOW HILL RD, VeCo, 90265	625 - G1
LIGHTHOUSE HUENEME RD, PHME, 93043	552 - D6
MATILIJA HOT SPRINGS MATILIJA RD S, VeCo, 93023	441 - A2
REAGAN, RONALD PRESIDENTIAL LIBRARY 40 PRESIDENTIAL DR, VeCo, 93065	497 - C4
STATE FISH HATCHERY TELEGRAPH & FISH HATCHERY RD, VeCo, 93015	456 - D7
TWO WINDS EQUESTRIAN CTR 4790 W LYNN RD, VeCo, 91320	555 - C5
WALNUT GROVE EQUESTRIAN CTR 401 RONEL CT, THO, 91320	556 - C1

PARK & RIDE

FEATURE NAME Address City, ZIP Code	PAGE-GRID
ARMY NATL GUARD, VEN	491 - J4
CAMARILLO METROLINK, CMRL	524 - F3
COCHRAN ST, SIMI	498 - D1
ERRINGER, SIMI	498 - A1
HIGH ST & SPRING RD, MRPK	496 - E1
JANSS, THO	526 - H5
KANAN RD (NW LOT), AGRH	558 - A5
KANAN RD (SE LOT), AGRH	558 - A6
KANAN RD (SW LOT), AGRH	558 - A6
KMART, SPLA	473 - J1
LAS POSAS RD, CMRL	524 - B3
MONTALVO METROLINK, VEN	492 - D6
MOORPARK, MRPK	476 - J6
OAKS MALL, THE, THO	526 - E7
OAK VIEW COMM CTR, VeCo	451 - B6
OJAI, OJAI	441 - J7
OXNARD METROLINK, OXN	522 - G6
PALMS, THE, OXN	523 - B3
PLEASANT VALLEY RD, CMRL	524 - J4
RANCHO CONEJO BLVD, THO	525 - J7
RANCHO RD, THO	556 - H2
ROUTE 118, SIMI	498 - C1
SAINT PETER CLAVER, SIMI	499 - A1
SIMI VALLEY, SIMI	498 - J1
SIMI VALLEY METROLINK, SIMI	498 - H2
TAPO CANYON, SIMI	498 - F1

PARKS & RECREATION

FEATURE NAME Address City, ZIP Code	PAGE-GRID
ADOLFO PK, CMRL	524 - G1
ANTONOVICH, MICHAEL D REGL PK --LACo, Nor	479 - G3
ARNEILL RANCH PK, CMRL	524 - E1
ARROYO PK, SIMI	497 - F2
ARROYO SEQUIT, LACo	586 - D7
ARROYO SIMI EQUESTRIAN CTR, SIMI	498 - E3
ARROYOSTOW PK, SIMI	499 - A3
ARROYO VERDE PK, VEN	472 - A7
ARROYO VISTA COMM PK, MRPK	496 - D2
ARUNDELL LINEAR PK, VEN	491 - H4
ATHERWOOD PK, SIMI	478 - B7
BANYAN PK, THO	555 - F4
BARD, RICHARD BUBBLING SPRINGS PK,-PHME	552 - F4
BARRANCA VISTA PK, VEN	492 - E4
BECK PK, OXN	552 - G2
BELAIRE LINEAR PK, VEN	492 - H3
BELL CANYON PK, CanP	529 - C5
BENNETT, BERNIECE PK, WLKV	557 - D6
BERYLWOOD PK, SIMI	498 - B2
BEYER PK, THO	557 - A1
BIG SKY PK, SIMI	478 - B4
BIRCH VIEW PK, CMRL	525 - A2
BOAT LAUNCH RAMP & PK, OXN	552 - B2
BOLKER PK, PHME	552 - D2
BORCHARD OAK PK, OXN	522 - H3
BORCHARD PK, THO	555 - F1
BOYAR, MAE REC CTR, CanP	529 - E6
BOYER, MAE PK, VeCo	558 - A2
BRISTOL BAY LINEAR PK, VEN	492 - E6
BROCK LINEAR PK, VEN	471 - D6
BUBBLING SPRINGS LINEAR PK, PHME	552 - F6
CABRILLO PK, OXN	522 - D4
CALABASAS PK LAND, CALB	558 - F7
CALLEGUAS CREEK PK, CMRL	524 - H2
CAMARILLO GROVE PK, VeCo	525 - D5
CAMINO REAL PK, VEN	491 - J3
CAMP COMFORT PK, VeCo	451 - G3
CAMPUS CANYON PK, MRPK	476 - J5
CAMPUS PK, MRPK	476 - H6
CAMPUS PK, OXN	522 - F6
CANADA PK, THO	496 - J7
CANNON, MARION PK, VEN	492 - B4
CANYON OAKS PK, WLKV	557 - F3
CARMENITA PK, CMRL	524 - D4
CARRILLO, LEO STATE PK, LACo	625 - J4
CARTY PK, OXN	552 - G4
CASTAIC LAKE STATE REC AREA, LACo	367 - F5
CASTLE PEAK PK, LA	529 - D4
CENTRAL PK, FILM	456 - A6
CHALLENGER PK, SIMI	497 - H7
CHANNEL ISLANDS NATL PK, VeCo	386 - F6
CHANNEL VIEW PK, OXN	552 - B4
CHAPARRAL PK, VeCo	558 - A2
CHARTER OAK PK, CMRL	494 - E7
CHASE PK, LA	529 - H2
CHATSWORTH OAKS PK, Chat	499 - G6
CHATSWORTH PK NORTH, Chat	499 - J3
CHEESEBORO CANYON, VeCo	528 - D5
CHUMASH PK, AGRH	558 - B5
CHUMASH PK, SIMI	479 - B7
CHUMASH PK, VEN	492 - G2
CIRCLE X RANCH, VeCo	585 - H3
CITRUS GROVE PK, SIMI	498 - A2
COHASSET MELBA PK, CanP	529 - F4
COLLEGE ESTATES PK, OXN	552 - J3
COLLEGE PK, OXN	552 - J3
COLLEGE VIEW PK, MRPK	477 - A6
COLONIA PK, OXN	522 - H5
COMM CTR PK, CMRL	524 - D2
COMM CTR PK EAST, OXN	522 - F6
COMM CTR PK WEST, OXN	522 - F6
CONEJO CANYONS PK, THO	525 - H3
CONEJO COMM PK, THO	526 - E6
CONEJO CREEK EQUESTRIAN PK, THO	526 - H5
CONEJO CREEK PK, THO	526 - H6
CONNELLY PK, OXN	522 - E2
CONSTITUTION PK, CMRL	524 - C3
CORRIGANVILLE PK, SIMI	499 - E3
COUNTRY TRAIL PK, MRPK	496 - B4
COUNTY OWNED LAND, Chat	499 - J2
COUNTY SQUARE LINEAR PK, VEN	492 - C3
COYOTE HILLS PK, SIMI	497 - F6
CRESTVIEW PK, CMRL	524 - A2
CYPRESS PK, THO	555 - E3
DALY PK, OJAI	441 - J5
DARRAH VOLUNTEER PK, SIMI	498 - E3
DEERHILL PK, VeCo	528 - A7
DEER RIDGE PK, THO	555 - G4
DELORES PK, FILM	455 - J5
DEL SOL PK, OXN	522 - J5
DENNISON PK, VeCo	452 - E1
DEWAR PK, PHME	552 - E6
DIZDAR PK, CMRL	524 - E3
DOS CAMINOS PK, CMRL	494 - G7
DOS VIENTOS COMM PK, THO	555 - C2
DOS VIENTOS NEIGHBORHOOD PK, THO	555 - C4
DURLEY PK, OXN	552 - F1
EAGLE VIEW PK, VeCo	527 - H6
EASTWOOD MEM PK, OXN	522 - F4
EASTWOOD PK, VEN	491 - B2
EBELL PK, SPLA	464 - B6
EL ESCORPION PK, CanP	529 - C5
EL PARQUE DE LA PAZ, THO	557 - A2
ENCANTO PK, CMRL	525 - A3
ESTELLA PK, THO	556 - J1
EVENSTAR PK, THO	557 - A5
FARIA COUNTY PK, VeCo	469 - J3
FIORE, ALEX PLAYFIELD, THO	526 - J4
FOOTHILL PK, SIMI	499 - D2
FOOTHILL PK, CMRL	494 - D7
FOREST COVE PK, AGRH	557 - H5
FORT WILDWOOD PK, THO	526 - D3
FOSTER PK, VeCo	460 - J6
FOXFIELD PK, WLKV	557 - C7
FREEDOM PK, CMRL	523 - J5
FREMONT PK, OXN	522 - F4
FRONTIER PK, SIMI	498 - A3
GATES CANYON PK, LACo	558 - J3
GLEN WOOD PK, THO	526 - G6
GLENWOOD PK, MRPK	496 - C2
GRANT PK, VEN	471 - C7
GRAPE ARBOR PK, CALB	558 - G6
HAPPY CAMP CANYON REGL PK, VeCo	466 - H7
HARDING PK, SPLA	464 - D5
HERITAGE PK, CMRL	525 - B1
HERTEL LINEAR PK, VEN	492 - F3
HICKORY PK, THO	555 - E4
HOBERT PK, VEN	492 - G1
HOBSON COUNTY PK, VeCo	469 - G1
HUNGRY VALLEY STATE VEH REC AREA, -LACo	367 - C1
HUNTSINGER, FRITZ YOUTH SPORTS, -VEN	492 - J1
INDIAN SPRINGS PK, VeCo	557 - H1
JOHNSON CREEK PK, OXN	552 - H4
JUANAMARIA PK, VEN	492 - E1
KENNEY GROVE PK, VeCo	455 - F5
KIMBER PK, THO	555 G2
KNAPP RANCH PK, CanP	529 - C7
KNOLL PK, THO	525 - F7
KNOLLS PK, VeCo	499 - B3
LA JANELLE PK, PHME	552 - C6
LAKE CACHUMA REC AREA, StBC	366 - A5
LAKE CASITAS REC AREA, VeCo	450 - E5
LANG RANCH PK, THO	527 - C3
LAS PIEDRAS PK, SPLA	464 - C4
LAS POSAS EQUESTRIAN PK, VeCo	494 - A7
LAS VIRGENES CANYON, VeCo	528 - F5
LATHROP PK, OXN	552 - H1
LAURELWOOD PK, CMRL	524 - E2
LAZY J RANCH PK, LA	529 - E3
LEMONWOOD PK, OXN	553 - A2
LIBBEY PK, OJAI	441 - H7
LINCOLN PK, SIMI	497 - H4
LINEAR PK, VEN	492 - J3
LINEAR PK, VEN	492 - H2
LINEAR PK, VEN	492 - E1
LOKKER, ELDRED PK, CMRL	494 - C7
LOS PADRES NATL FOREST, VeCo	441 - D2
LYNN OAKS PK, THO	556 - C2
LYON, HARRY PK, VEN	471 - C6
MAHOOD SENIOR CTR, WLA	387 - J4
MALIBU CREEK STATE PK, LACo	387 - E3
MARINA PK, VEN	491 - F5
MARINA WEST PK, OXN	552 - D1
MASONIC PK, FILM	456 - A6
MAYFAIR PK, SIMI	497 - J1
MEDEA CREEK PK, VeCo	528 - A7
MEM PK, VEN	491 - D2
MILLER PK, MRPK	496 - G2
MILL PK, SPLA	464 - B4
MISSION OAKS COMM PK, CMRL	525 - B1
MISSION PK, VEN	491 - B2
MISSION VERDE PK, CMRL	525 - A1
MONTALVO NEIGHBORHOOD PK, VEN	492 - D4
MONTE VISTA NATURE PK, MRPK	496 - G3
MORANDA, WALTER B PK, PHME	552 - F6
MORRISON PK, AGRH	557 - J4
MOUNTAIN MEADOWS PK, MRPK	496 - D3
NEPTUNE SQUARE PK, OXN	551 - J1
NEWBURY PK, THO	555 - J1
NORTHBANK LINEAR PK, VEN	492 - J4
NORTH RANCH PK, THO	527 - C6
NORTH RANCH PLAYFIELD, THO	557 - G1
OAKBROOK NEIGHBORHOOD PK, THO	526 - J3
OAKBROOK PK, THO	527 - B4
OAKBROOK REGL PK, THO	527 - E4
OAK CANYON COMM PK, VeCo	527 - J7
OAK PK, SIMI	477 - C7
OBREGON PK, SPLA	463 - J6
OCEAN AVENUE PK, VEN	491 E2
OLD AGOURA PK, AGRH	558 - D5
OLD MEADOWS PK, THO	526 - J5
OLD WINDMILL PK, SIMI	497 - F7
ORCHARD PK, OXN	522 - G2
ORCUTT RANCH HORTICULTURAL CTR PK,-LA	529 - F2
PALO COMADO CANYON, VeCo	527 - J5
PARK AT WESTPORT, OXN	522 - A7
PEACH HILL PK, MRPK	496 - E3
PENINSULA PK, OXN	552 - B3
PEPPER TREE PLAYFIELD, THO	525 - E7
PITTS RANCH PK, CMRL	524 - H1
PLAZA PK, VEN	491 - C2
PLAZA PK, OXN	522 - G6
PLEASANT VALLEY PK, CMRL	524 - F2
PLEASANT VALLEY PK, OXN	552 - H4
POINDEXTER PK, MRPK	496 - D1
POINT MUGU STATE PK, VeCo	554 - G7
PORT HUENEME BEACH PK, PHME	552 - E7
PROMENADE PK, VEN	491 - B2
QUITO PK, CMRL	495 - D7
RALSTON VILLAGE LINEAR PK, VEN	492 - C4
RANCHO CONEJO PLAY FIELD, THO	526 - B6
RANCHO MADERA COMM PK, SIMI	497 - D6
RANCHO SANTA SUSANA COMM PK, SIMI	498 - H2
RANCHO SIERRA VISTA / SATWIWA PK, -VeCo	555 - F5
RANCHO SIMI COMM PK, SIMI	497 - J3
RANCHO SIMI REC AREA, SIMI	497 - F7
RANCHO SIMI REC AREA, VeCo	528 - B7
RANCHO TAPO COMM CTR & VETERANS, -SIMI	478 - E7
RANCHO VENTURA LINEAR PK, VEN	492 - E4
REYES ADOBE PK, AGRH	557 - H5
REYNOLDS, BLANCHE PK, VEN	491 - G4
RIO LINDO PK, OXN	522 - H2
RIVERVIEW LINEAR PK, VEN	492 G4
ROCKY PEAK PK, VeCo	479 - D4
ROCKY POINTE NATURAL PK, SIMI	499 - C3
ROSCOE-VALLEY CIRCLE PK, LA	529 D3
ROTARY COMM PK, OJAI	441 - G7
RUSSELL PK, THO	557 - B2
RUSSELL RANCH PK, WLKV	557 - F5
SAGE RANCH PK, VeCo	499 - A6
SANTA SUSANA PK, VeCo	499 - C4
SARZOTTI PK, OJAI	441 - J6
SATICOY PK, VeCo	493 - B1
SCHREIBER, HOUGHTON PK, SIMI	478 - F6
SEA AIR PK, OXN	522 - D7
SEASIDE WILDERNESS PK, VEN	490 - J2
SEAVIEW PK, OXN	522 - C7
SEQUOIA PK, SIMI	498 - E2
SERRA, JUNIPERO PK, VEN	492 - H4
SHADOW RANCH PK, CanP	529 - H6
SHIELLS PK, FILM	455 - H5
SIERRA LINDA PK, OXN	522 - F2
SIMI HILLS NEIGHBORHOOD PK, SIMI	478 - H7
SOULE PK, OJAI	442 - A7
SOUTHBANK PK, OXN	522 - F1
SOUTH SHORE HILLS PK, THO	557 - A6
SOUTHWEST COMM PK, OXN	522 - D6
SOUTH WINDS PK, OXN	552 - G6
SPRING MEADOW PK, THO	526 - F2
SPRINGVILLE PK, CMRL	523 - H2
STAGECOACH INN PK, THO	556 - B1
STARGAZE PK, SIMI	497 - D2
STECKEL PK, VeCo	453 - J5
STRAUSS, PETER RANCH, Ago	387 - D3
SUBURBIA PK, THO	526 - E3
SUMAC PK, AGRH	558 - B4
SUNSET HILLS PK, THO	526 - J2
SYCAMORE CANYON PK, SIMI	527 - D1
SYCAMORE DRIVE COMM CTR, SIMI	498 - C3
SYCAMORE PK, SIMI	498 - B5
TAPO CANYON PK, VeCo	478 - F2
TAXCO TRAILS PK, LA	529 - F3
TEAGUE PK, SPLA	463 - J7
THILLE PK, VEN	492 - B4
THOMPSON PK, OXN	523 - A5
THOUSAND OAKS COMM PK, THO	526 - F3
THREE SPRINGS PK, WLKV	557 B7
TIERRA REJADA PK, SIMI	497 - D1
TIERRA REJADA PK, MRPK	496 - C3
TOLAND PK, VeCo	454 - J7
TOPANGA STATE PK, PacP	387 - G3
TRAILSIDE PK, CMRL	525 - A2
TRIUNFO COMM PK, THO	556 - J4
VALLE LINDO PK, CMRL	524 - C2
VALLEY VIEW PK, VeCo	557 - H1

FEATURE NAME Address City, ZIP Code	PAGE-GRID
VENTU PK, THO	556 - A2
VENTURA COMM PK, VEN	492 - E3
VERDE PK, SIMI	499 - B2
VETERANS MEM PK, SPLA	464 - B6
VIA MARINA PK, OXN	552 - C1
VIRGINIA COLONY PK, MRPK	476 - H7
VISTA DEL ARROYO PK, SIMI	498 - D3
WALNUT GROVE PK, THO	556 - C1
WARRING PK, VeCo	457 - F3
WAVERLY PK, THO	526 - H5
WENDY PK, THO	555 - G4
WEST HILLS REC CTR, CanP	529 - D5
WEST PK, VEN	491 - B1
WEST VILLAGE PK, OXN	522 - J4
WILDFLOWER PLAYFIELD, THO	526 - C3
WILDWOOD REGL PK, THO	496 - D7
WILLOWBROOK PK, SIMI	497 - H3
WILSON PK, OXN	522 - G5
WOOD CREEK PK, CMRL	525 - A1
WOODSIDE LINEAR PK, VEN	472 - J7
WOODSIDE PK, CMRL	524 - H4
ZUMA TRANCAS CANYONS, LACo	387 - D4

POST OFFICES

FEATURE NAME Address City, ZIP Code	PAGE-GRID
AGOURA HILLS 5158 CLARETON DR, AGRH, 91301	558 - B5
CAMARILLO 2150 PICKWICK DR, CMRL, 93010	524 - E3
CONEJO VALLEY 235 N MOORPARK RD, THO, 91360	556 - F1
EAST VENTURA 41 S WAKE FOREST AV, VEN, 93003	492 - B2
FEDERAL BLDG 350 S A ST, OXN, 93030	522 - G6
FILLMORE 333 CENTRAL AV, FILM, 93015	456 - A6
LAS POSAS 528 LAS POSAS RD, CMRL, 93010	524 - B2
MONTALVO 2481 GRAND AV, VEN, 93003	492 - D6
MOORPARK 215 W LOS ANGELES AV, MRPK, 93021	496 - E1
MOUNT MCCOY STA 225 SIMI VILLAGE DR, SIMI, 93065	497 - F2
NEWBURY PARK 1602 NEWBURY RD, THO, 91320	556 - A1
OAK VIEW 360 VENTURA AV, VeCo, 93022	451 - B7
OJAI 201 E OJAI AV, OJAI, 93023	441 - H7
OXNARD MAIN 1961 N C ST, OXN, 93036	522 - G3
PIRU 652 N MAIN ST, VeCo, 93040	457 - F4
PORT HUENEME 560 E PLEASANT VALLEY RD, PHME, 93041	552 - F5
SANTA PAULA 111 S MILL ST, SPLA, 93060	464 - B5
SATICOY 11043 CITRUS DR, VEN, 93004	473 - A7
SAVIERS 2532 SAVIERS RD, OXN, 93033	552 - G2
SIMI VALLEY 2551 GALENA AV, SIMI, 93065	498 - D1
SOMIS 3349 SOMIS RD, VeCo, 93066	495 - A5
THOUSAND OAKS 3435 E THOUSAND OAKS BLVD, THO, 91362	557 - B3
VENTURA MAIN 675 E SANTA CLARA ST, VEN, 93001	491 - C2
WEST HILLS 23055 SHERMAN WY, CanP, 91307	529 - G5

SCHOOLS

FEATURE NAME Address City, ZIP Code	PAGE-GRID
ACACIA ELEM 55 W NORMAN AV, THO, 91360	526 - F6
AGOURA HIGH 28545 W DRIVER AV, AGRH, 91301	558 - B5
ANACAPA MID 100 S MILLS RD, VEN, 93003	491 - H3
APOLLO HIGH 3150 SCHOOL ST, SIMI, 93065	498 - D2
ARROYO ELEM 225 ULYSSES ST, SIMI, 93065	497 - F2
ARROYO MONTESSORI ELEM 9 W BONITA DR, SIMI, 93065	497 - F3
ARROYO WEST ELEM 4117 COUNTRY HILL RD, MRPK, 93021	496 - B3
ASCENSION LUTHERAN ELEM 1600 E HILLCREST DR, THO, 91362	556 - J1
ASPEN ELEM 1870 OBERLIN AV, THO, 91360	526 - E5
ATHERWOOD ELEM 2350 GREENSWARD ST, SIMI, 93065	498 - B1
BALBOA MID 247 S HILL RD, VEN, 93003	492 - D2
BANYAN ELEM 1120 KNOLLWOOD DR, THO, 91320	555 - F4
BARD, RICHARD ELEM 622 PLEASANT VALLEY RD, PHME, 93041	552 - F5
BEDELL, THELMA B ELEM 1305 LAUREL RD, SPLA, 93060	464 - B2
BERYLWOOD ELEM 2300 HEYWOOD ST, SIMI, 93065	498 - B3
BETHANY CHRISTIAN ELEM 200 BETHANY CT, THO, 91360	526 - E5
BIG SPRINGS ELEM 3401 BIG SPRINGS AV, SIMI, 93063	478 - G5
BLACKSTOCK, CHARLES JR HIGH 701 E BARD RD, OXN, 93033	552 - H4
BLANCHARD ELEM 115 N PECK RD, SPLA, 93060	463 - J7
BREKKE ELEM 1400 MARTIN LUTHER KING JR DR, OXN, 93030	522 - J4
BRIGGS ELEM 14438 W TELEGRAPH RD, VeCo, 93060	473 - F2
BROOKSIDE ELEM 165 SATINWOOD AV, VeCo, 91377	558 - B2
BUENA HIGH 5670 TELEGRAPH RD, VEN, 93003	492 - C2
CABRILLO MID 1426 E SANTA CLARA ST, VEN, 93001	491 - E2
CAMARILLO, ADOLFO HIGH 4660 MISSION OAKS BLVD, CMRL, 93012	524 - H3
CAMARILLO CHRISTIAN 579 ANACAPA DR, VeCo, 93010	494 - D7
CAMARILLO HEIGHTS ELEM 35 W CATALINA DR, VeCo, 93010	494 - D7
CAMPUS CANYON ELEM 15300 MONROE AV, MRPK, 93021	476 - J5
CAPISTRANO AVENUE ELEM 8118 CAPISTRANO AV, LA, 91304	529 - J3
CARDEN CONEJO 975 EVENSTAR AV, THO, 91361	557 - B5
CARDEN OF CAMARILLO 1915 LAS POSAS RD, CMRL, 93010	524 - D1
CHAMINADE COLLEGE PREP HIGH 7500 CHAMINADE AV, LA, 91304	529 - F4
CHANNEL ISLANDS HIGH 1400 RAIDERS WY, OXN, 93033	552 - J3
CHAPARRAL MID 280 POINDEXTER AV, MRPK, 93021	496 - D1
CHATSWORTH PK ELEM 22005 DEVONSHIRE ST, Chat, 91311	499 - J4
CHAVEZ, CESAR ELEM 301 N MARQUITA ST, OXN, 93030	522 - H5
CHIME CHARTER MID 22280 DEVONSHIRE ST, Chat, 91311	499 - J4
CITRUS GLEN ELEM 9655 DARLING RD, VEN, 93004	492 - H2
COLINA MID 1500 E HILLCREST DR, THO, 91362	556 - J1
COLLEGE HEIGHTS CHRISTIAN 6360 TELEPHONE RD, VEN, 93003	492 - D4
COLUMBUS MID 22250 ELKWOOD ST, LA, 91304	529 - J3
COMM HIGH 5700 CONDOR DR, MRPK, 93021	476 - H7
CONEJO ADVENTIST ELEM 2645 W HILLCREST DR, THO, 91320	525 - J7
CONEJO ELEM 280 CONEJO SCHOOL RD, THO, 91362	557 - A1
CONEJO VALLEY HIGH 1872 NEWBURY RD, THO, 91320	556 - A1
CORNERSTONE CHRISTIAN HIGH 1777 ARNEILL RD, CMRL, 93010	524 - E1
CORNERSTONE CHRISTIAN 1777 ARNEILL RD, CMRL, 93010	524 - E1
CRESTVIEW ELEM 900 CROSBY AV, SIMI, 93065	498 - B5
CURREN, BERNICE ELEM 1101 N F ST, OXN, 93030	522 - F4
CYPRESS ELEM 4200 W KIMBER DR, THO, 91320	555 - E3
DE ANZA MID 2060 CAMERON ST, VEN, 93001	471 - C6
DOS CAMINOS ELEM 3635 APPIAN WY, CMRL, 93010	494 - G7
DRIFFILL ELEM 910 S E ST, OXN, 93030	522 - G7
EL CAMINO HIGH 3777 DEAN DR, VEN, 93003	491 - J3
EL DESCANSO ELEM 1099 BEDFORD DR, CMRL, 93010	524 - D2
ELMHURST ELEM 5080 ELMHURST ST, VEN, 93003	492 - B3
ELM STREET ELEM 450 E ELM ST, OXN, 93033	552 - H1
EL RIO ELEM 2714 E VINEYARD AV, VeCo, 93036	522 - H1
FAITH BAPTIST 7644 FARRALONE AV, LA, 91304	529 - J4
FILLMORE HIGH 555 CENTRAL AV, FILM, 93015	456 - A5
FILLMORE MID 543 A ST, FILM, 93015	456 - A6
FIRST BAPTIST ACADEMY 1250 ERBES RD, THO, 91362	527 - A6
FLORY ELEM 240 FLORY AV, MRPK, 93021	496 - E1
FOOTHILL TECHNOLOGY HIGH 100 DAY RD, VEN, 93003	492 - B2
FOSTER, E P ELEM 20 PLEASANT PL, VEN, 93001	471 - B7
FRANK, ROBERT J INTERMED 701 N JUANITA AV, OXN, 93030	522 - H4
FREMONT, JOHN CHARLES INTERMED 1130 N M ST, OXN, 93030	522 - F4
FRIENDS ELEM 3503 ARUNDELL CIR, VEN, 93003	491 - H5
FRONTIER HIGH 545 AIRPORT WY, CMRL, 93010	524 - A5
GARDEN GROVE ELEM 2250 N TRACY AV, SIMI, 93063	498 - E2
GLEN CITY ELEM 141 S STECKEL DR, SPLA, 93060	463 - J6
GLENWOOD ELEM 1135 WINDSOR DR, THO, 91360	526 - G6
GOOD SHEPHERD LUTHERAN ELEM 2949 ALAMO ST, SIMI, 93063	478 - C7
GRACE BRETHREN ELEM 1717 ARCANE ST, SIMI, 93065	497 - J4
GRACE BRETHREN JR/SR HIGH 1350 CHERRY AV, SIMI, 93065	498 - B3
GRACE LUTHERAN CHRISTIAN DAY 6190 TELEPHONE RD, VEN, 93003	492 - D4
GREEN, E O JR HIGH 3739 C ST, OXN, 93033	552 - G4
HAMLIN STREET ELEM 22627 HAMLIN ST, CanP, 91307	529 - H6
HARRINGTON, NORMA ELEM 2501 GISLER AV, OXN, 93033	552 - H2
HATHAWAY, JULIEN ELEM 405 DOLLIE ST, OXN, 93033	552 - H5
HAYCOX, ART ELEM 5400 PERKINS RD, OXN, 93033	552 - G6
HAYDOCK, RICHARD B INTERMED 647 HILL ST, OXN, 93033	522 - F7
HAYNES ELEM 6624 LOCKHURST DR, CanP, 91307	529 - E6
HERCHEL DAY WEST 27400 CANWOOD ST, Ago, 91301	558 - F6
HILLCREST CHRISTIAN ELEM 384 ERBES RD, THO, 91362	556 - J1
HILLCREST CHRISTIAN HIGH 384 ERBES RD, THO, 91362	556 - J1
HILLSIDE MID 2222 FITZGERALD RD, SIMI, 93065	498 - A4
HOLLOW HILLS ELEM 828 GIBSON AV, SIMI, 93065	497 - J5
HOLLYWOOD BEACH ELEM 4000 SUNSET LN, VeCo, 93035	552 - A2
HOLY CROSS ELEM 211 E MAIN ST, VEN, 93001	491 - B2
HUENEME CHRISTIAN ELEM 312 N VENTURA RD, PHME, 93041	552 - E5
HUENEME ELEM 354 3RD ST, PHME, 93041	552 - E6
HUENEME HIGH 500 W BARD RD, OXN, 93033	552 - G4
INDIAN HILLS HIGH 4345 N LAS VIRGENES RD, CALB, 91302	558 - H7
ISBELL MID 221 S 4TH ST, SPLA, 93060	464 - B6
IVY ACADEMIA CHARTER 6221 FALLBROOK AV, WdHl, 91367	529 - H7
JORDAN, JAMES CHARTER MID 22250 ELKWOOD ST, LA, 91304	529 - J3
JUANAMARIA ELEM 100 S CROCKER AV, VEN, 93004	492 - F2
JUSTICE STREET ELEM 23350 JUSTICE ST, LA, 91304	529 - F3
JUSTIN ELEM 2245 N JUSTIN AV, SIMI, 93065	498 - A2
KAMALA ELEM 634 W KAMALA ST, OXN, 93033	552 - F2
KATHERINE ELEM 5455 KATHERINE ST, SIMI, 93063	499 - A3
KNOLLS ELEM 6334 KATHERINE RD, SIMI, 93063	499 - C3
LADERA ELEM 1211 CL ALMENDRO, THO, 91360	526 - H3
LAGUNA VISTA ELEM 5084 ETTING RD, VeCo, 93012	553 - H4
LA MARIPOSA ELEM 4800 CTE OLIVAS, CMRL, 93012	524 - J1
LANG RANCH ELEM 2450 WHITECHAPEL PL, THO, 91362	527 - B3
LA REINA HIGH 106 W JANSS RD, THO, 91360	526 - F5
LARSEN, ANSGAR ELEM 550 THOMAS AV, OXN, 93033	552 - H3
LAS COLINAS MID 5750 FIELDCREST DR, CMRL, 93012	525 - B1
LAS POSAS ELEM 75 E CL LA GUERRA, CMRL, 93010	524 - B2
LAUREL SPRINGS ELEM 302 EL PASEO RD, OJAI, 93023	441 - H7
LAUREL SPRINGS HIGH 302 EL PASEO RD, OJAI, 93023	441 - H7
LAW, MARY PRIVATE ELEM 2929 ALBANY DR, OXN, 93033	552 - H3
LEMONWOOD ELEM 2200 CARNEGIE CT, OXN, 93033	553 - A2
LINCOLN ELEM 1107 E SANTA CLARA ST, VEN, 93001	491 - D2
LINCOLN, ABRAHAM ELEM 1220 4TH ST, SIMI, 93065	497 - G4
LINDA VISTA JR ACADEMY 5050 PERRY WY, VeCo, 93036	493 - B4
LINDERO CANYON MID 5844 LARBOARD LN, AGRH, 91301	557 - G4
LOCKHURST DRIVE ELEM 6170 LOCKHURST DR, WdHl, 91367	529 - E7
LOMA VISTA ELEM 300 LYNN DR, VEN, 93003	491 - H2
LOS ALTOS MID 700 TEMPLE AV, CMRL, 93010	524 - F2
LOS CERRITOS MID 2100 AVD DE LAS FLORES, THO, 91362	527 - A4
LOS PRIMEROS STRUCTURED ELEM 2222 E VENTURA BLVD, CMRL, 93010	524 - E3
LOS SENDEROS ELEM 1555 KENDALL AV, CMRL, 93010	524 - F1
LUPIN HILL ELEM 26210 ADAMOR RD, CALB, 91302	558 - H3
MADERA ELEM 250 ROYAL AV, SIMI, 93065	497 - F4
MADRONA ELEM 612 CM MANZANAS, VeCo, 91360	526 - D6
MANZANITA ELEM 2626 MICHAEL DR, THO, 91320	555 - H1
MAPLE ELEM 3501 KIMBER DR, THO, 91320	555 - F2
MARINA WEST ELEM 2501 CAROB ST, OXN, 93035	552 - D1
MARSHALL, THURGOOD 2900 THURGOOD MARSHALL DR, OXN, 93036	522 - D3
MAR VISTA ELEM 2382 ETTING RD, OXN, 93033	553 - B4
MATILIJA JR HIGH 703 EL PASEO RD, OJAI, 93023	441 - G7
MCAULIFFE, CHRISTA ELEM 3300 W VIA MARINA AV, OXN, 93035	522 - C7
MCKEVETT ELEM 955 PLEASANT ST, SPLA, 93060	464 - B5
MCKINNA, DENNIS ELEM 1611 J ST, OXN, 93033	552 - F1
MEADOWS ELEM 2000 LA GRANADA DR, THO, 91362	527 - A6
MEDEA CREEK MID 1002 DOUBLETREE RD, VeCo, 91377	558 - A1
MEINERS OAKS ELEM 400 S LOMITA AV, VeCo, 93023	441 - E7
MESA ELEM 3901 MESA SCHOOL RD, VeCo, 93066	493 - H4
MESA VERDE MID 14000 PEACH HILL RD, MRPK, 93021	496 - G3
MIRA MONTE ELEM 1216 LOMA DR, VeCo, 93023	451 - D2
MONICA ROS ELEM 783 MCNELL RD, VeCo, 93023	442 - E5
MONTALVO ELEM 2050 GRAND AV, VEN, 93003	492 - D5
MONTESSORI OF OJAI, THE 806 BALDWIN RD, VeCo, 93001	451 - A3
MONTE VISTA HIGH 1755 BLACKSTOCK AV, SIMI, 93065	498 - D3
MONTE VISTA MID 888 LANTANA ST, CMRL, 93010	524 - C2
MOORPARK HIGH 4500 TIERRA REJADA RD, MRPK, 93021	496 - C3
MORGAN CREEK CHRISTIAN ELEM 723 S D ST, OXN, 93030	522 - G7

VENTURA CO.

FEATURE NAME	Address City, ZIP Code	PAGE-GRID
MOUND ELEM	455 S HILL RD, VEN, 93003	492 - D3
MOUNTAIN MEADOWS ELEM	4200 MOUNTAIN MEADOW DR, MRPK, 93021	496 - D3
MOUNTAIN VIEW ELEM	2925 FLETCHER ST, SIMI, 93065	498 - C4
MUPU ELEM	4410 SANTA PAULA-OJAI RD, VeCo, 93060	464 - A1
NEVADA AVENUE ELEM	22120 CHASE ST, LA, 91304	529 - J2
NEWBURY PARK ADVENTIST ACADEMY HIGH	180 ACADEMY DR, THO, 91320	525 - H6
NEWBURY PARK HIGH	456 N REINO RD, THO, 91320	525 - F7
NEW COMM JEWISH HIGH	7353 VALLEY CIRCLE BLVD, CanP, 91307	529 - D5
NORDHOFF HIGH	1401 MARICOPA HWY, OJAI, 93023	441 - E7
OAK GROVE-KRISHNAMURTI ELEM	220 W LOMITA AV, VeCo, 93023	441 - D7
OAK GROVE-KRISHNAMURTI HIGH	220 W LOMITA AV, VeCo, 93023	441 - D7
OAK HILLS ELEM	1010 KANAN RD, VeCo, 91377	557 - H1
OAK PARK HIGH	899 KANAN RD, VeCo, 91377	558 - A1
OAKS CHRISTIAN HIGH	31749 LA TIENDA RD, WLKV, 91362	557 - D5
OAKS CHRISTIAN MID	31749 LE TIENDA RD, WLKV, 91362	557 - E5
OAK VIEW HIGH	5701 CONIFER ST, VeCo, 91377	558 - A2
OCEAN VIEW JR HIGH	4300 OLDS RD, OXN, 93033	553 - B4
OJAI VALLEY ELEM	723 EL PASEO RD, OJAI, 93023	441 - G7
OJAI VALLEY HIGH	723 EL PASEO RD, OJAI, 93023	441 - G7
OLIVELANDS ELEM	12465 FOOTHILL RD, VeCo, 93060	473 - B2
OUR LADY OF GUADALUPE ELEM	530 N JUANITA AV, OXN, 93030	522 - H5
OUR LADY OF THE ASSUMPTION ELEM	3169 TELEGRAPH RD, VEN, 93003	491 - G3
OXNARD HIGH	3400 GONZALES RD, VeCo, 93030	522 - C3
PACIFIC HIGH	501 COLLEGE DR, VEN, 93003	491 - J3
PACIFIC VIEW HIGH	1701 GARY DR, OXN, 93033	552 - J3
PACIFICA HIGH	600 E GONZALES RD, OXN, 93030	522 - H3
PARK OAKS ELEM	1335 CL BOUGANVILLA, THO, 91360	526 - H4
PARKVIEW ELEM	1416 6TH PL, PHME, 93041	552 - F4
PARK VIEW ELEM	1500 ALEXANDER ST, SIMI, 93065	497 - J2
PEACH HILL ELEM	13400 CHRISTIAN BARRETT DR, MRPK, 93021	496 - F3
PHOENIX RANCH	1845 OAK RD, SIMI, 93063	499 - A2
PIERPONT ELEM	1254 MARTHAS VINEYARD CT, VEN, 93001	491 - F5
PINECREST ELEM	449 WILBUR RD, THO, 91360	526 - G7
PINECREST ELEM	4974 COCHRAN ST, SIMI, 93063	498 - H1
PINECREST - MOORPARK PRIVATE ELEM	14100 PEACH HILL RD, MRPK, 93021	496 - G3
PIRU ELEM	3811 E CENTER ST, VeCo, 93040	457 - E4
PLEASANT VALLEY CHRISTIAN	1101 PONDEROSA DR, CMRL, 93010	524 - C2
POINSETTIA ELEM	350 N VICTORIA AV, VEN, 93003	492 - C1
POMELO DRIVE ELEM	7633 MARCH AV, LA, 91304	529 - E4
PORTOLA ELEM	6700 EAGLE ST, VEN, 93003	492 - D4
PUENTE HIGH	545 CENTRAL AV, VeCo, 93036	493 - B5
RAMONA ELEM	804 COOPER RD, OXN, 93030	522 - H5
RED OAK ELEM	4857 ROCKFIELD ST, VeCo, 91377	557 - H1
REDWOOD MID	233 W GAINSBOROUGH RD, THO, 91360	526 - E6
RENAISSANCE HIGH	325 N PALM AV, SPLA, 93060	464 - A5
REYNOLDS, BLANCHE ELEM	450 VALMORE AV, VEN, 93003	491 G4
RIO DEL NORTE ELEM	2500 LOBELIA DR, OXN, 93036	522 - F1
RIO DEL VALLE JR HIGH	3100 ROSE AV, VeCo, 93036	523 - A1
RIO LINDO ELEM	2131 SNOW AV, OXN, 93036	522 - J3
RIO MESA HIGH	545 CENTRAL AV, VeCo, 93036	493 - B5
RIO PLAZA ELEM	600 SIMON WY, VeCo, 93036	492 - J7
RIO REAL ELEM	1140 KENNY ST, VeCo, 93036	522 - J2
RIO ROSALES ELEM	2001 JACINTO DR, OXN, 93030	523 - A4
RITCHEN, EMILIE ELEM	2200 CABRILLO WY, OXN, 93030	522 - E4
ROGERS, WILL ELEM	316 HOWARD ST, VEN, 93003	491 F3
ROSE AVENUE ELEM	220 DRISKILL ST, OXN, 93030	523 - A6
ROYAL HIGH	1402 ROYAL AV, SIMI, 93065	497 - J3
SACRED HEART ELEM	10770 HENDERSON RD, VEN, 93004	492 - J1
SAINT ANTHONY ELEM	2421 C ST, OXN, 93033	552 - G2
SAINT BERNARDINE OF SIENA ELEM	6061 VALLEY CIRCLE BLVD, WdHl, 91367	529 - D7
SAINT BONAVENTURE HIGH	3167 TELEGRAPH RD, VEN, 93003	491 - G3
SAINT JOHNS LUTHERAN ELEM	1500 N C ST, OXN, 93030	522 - G3
SAINT JUDE THE APOSTLE	32036 W LINDERO CANYON RD, WLKV, 91361	557 - C7
SAINT MARY MAGDALEN ELEM	2534 VENTURA BLVD, CMRL, 93010	524 - F3
SAINT PASCHAL BAYLON ELEM	154 E JANSS RD, THO, 91360	526 - G5
SAINT PATRICKS ELEM	1 CHURCH RD, THO, 91362	526 - J5
SAINT PAULS ELEM	3290 LOMA VISTA RD, VEN, 93003	491 - H2
SAINT ROSE OF LIMA ELEM	1325 ROYAL AV, SIMI, 93065	497 - H3
SAINT SEBASTIAN ELEM	325 E SANTA BARBARA ST, SPLA, 93060	464 - A5
SAN ANTONIO ELEM	650 CARNE RD, VeCo, 93023	442 - D6
SAN CAYETANO ELEM	514 MOUNTAIN VIEW ST, FILM, 93015	456 B5
SANTA CLARA ELEM	20030 TELEGRAPH RD, VeCo, 93060	464 - J2
SANTA CLARA ELEM	324 S E ST, OXN, 93030	522 - F6
SANTA CLARA HIGH	2121 SAVIERS RD, OXN, 93033	552 - G2
SANTA PAULA HIGH	404 N 6TH ST, SPLA, 93060	464 - A5
SANTA ROSA ELEM	13282 SANTA ROSA RD, VeCo, 93012	496 - F6
SANTA SUSANA ELEM	4300 APRICOT RD, SIMI, 93063	498 - G1
SANTA SUSANA HIGH	3570 E COCHRAN ST, SIMI, 93063	498 - E1
SATICOY ELEM	760 JAZMIN AV, VEN, 93004	492 J1
SEQUOIA MID	2855 BORCHARD RD, THO, 91320	555 - H1
SERRA, JUNIPERO ELEM	8880 HALIFAX ST, VEN, 93004	492 - H3
SESPE ELEM	425 ORCHARD ST, FILM, 93015	456 - A6
SHEPHERD OF THE VALLEY LUTHERAN-ELEM	23838 KITTRIDGE ST, CanP, 91307	529 - E6
SHERIDAN WAY ELEM	573 SHERIDAN WY, VEN, 93001	491 - B1
SIERRA LINDA ELEM	2201 JASMINE ST, OXN, 93036	522 - F2
SIMI ELEM	2956 SCHOOL ST, SIMI, 93065	498 - C3
SIMI VALLEY HIGH	5400 COCHRAN ST, SIMI, 93063	499 - A1
SINALOA MID	601 ROYAL AV, SIMI, 93065	497 - G3
SOMIS ELEM	5268 NORTH ST, VeCo, 93066	495 - A5
SUMAC ELEM	6050 CALMFIELD AV, AGRH, 91301	558 - B3
SUMMIT ELEM	12525 SANTA PAULA OJAI RD, VeCo, 93023	453 - C1
SUNKIST ELEM	1400 TEAKWOOD ST, PHME, 93041	552 - E3
SUNSET ELEM	400 SUNSET AV, VeCo, 93022	461 - A1
SYCAMORE ELEM	2100 RAVENNA ST, SIMI, 93065	498 - C2
SYCAMORE CANYON ELEM	4601 VIA RIO, THO, 91320	555 - D2
TEMPLE CHRISTIAN ELEM	5415 RALSTON ST, VEN, 93003	492 - C4
THACHER HIGH	5025 THACHER RD, VeCo, 93023	442 - F4
THILLE, GRACE S ELEM	1144 VENTURA ST, SPLA, 93060	464 - C6
THOUSAND OAKS BAPTIST	2685 CL ABEDUL, THO, 91360	526 G3
THOUSAND OAKS HIGH	2323 MOORPARK RD, THO, 91360	526 - F4
TIERRA LINDA ELEM	1201 WOODCREEK RD, CMRL, 93012	525 - A1
TIERRA VISTA ELEM	2001 SANFORD ST, OXN, 93033	553 - A5
TOPA TOPA ELEM	916 MOUNTAIN VIEW AV, OJAI, 93023	441 - J5
TOWNSHIP ELEM	4101 TOWNSHIP AV, SIMI, 93063	478 - F6
UNIVERSITY ELEM	2801 ATLAS AV, THO, 91360	526 - F3
UNIVERSITY PREP	550 TEMPLE AV, CMRL, 93010	524 - F2
VALLEY VIEW MID	3347 TAPO ST, SIMI, 93063	478 G6
VENTURA COUNTY CHRISTIAN ELEM	96 MACMILLAN AV, VEN, 93001	491 - E2
VENTURA COUNTY CHRISTIAN HIGH	96 MACMILLAN AV, VEN, 93001	491 - E2
VENTURA HIGH	2 N CATALINA ST, VEN, 93001	491 - F2
VENTURA MISSIONARY CHRISTIAN ELEM	500 HIGH POINT DR, VEN, 93003	472 - E7
VILLANOVA PREP HIGH	12096 VENTURA AV, VeCo, 93023	451 - F2
VISTA FUNDAMENTAL ELEM	2175 WISTERIA ST, SIMI, 93065	498 - B2
WALNUT ELEM	581 DENA DR, VeCo, 91320	555 - G1
WALNUT CANYON ELEM	280 CASEY RD, MRPK, 93021	476 - D7
WEATHERSFIELD ELEM	3151 DARLINGTON DR, THO, 91360	526 - G2
WEBSTER, BARBARA ELEM	1150 SATICOY ST, SPLA, 93060	464 - C5
WELBY WAY ELEM	23456 WELBY WY, CanP, 91307	529 F6
WESTLAKE ELEM	1571 POTRERO RD, THO, 91361	556 - J6
WESTLAKE HIGH	100 N LAKEVIEW CANYON RD, THO, 91362	557 - D3
WESTLAKE HILLS ELEM	3333 S MEDICINE BOW CT, THO, 91362	557 - B3
WEST VALLEY CHRISTIAN	22450 SHERMAN WY, CanP, 91307	529 - J5
WHITE OAK ELEM	2201 ALSCOT AV, SIMI, 93063	499 C2
WHITE OAK ELEM	31761 W VILLAGE SCHOOL RD, WLKV, 91361	557 - D6
WILDWOOD ELEM	620 VELARDE DR, THO, 91360	526 - D3
WILLIAMS, FRED ELEM	4300 ANCHORAGE ST, OXN, 93033	552 - J4
WILLOW ELEM	29026 LARO DR, AGRH, 91301	558 - A4
WOOD RANCH ELEM	455 CIRCLE KNOLL DR, SIMI, 93065	527 - D1
WRIGHT, ARTHUR E MID	4029 N LAS VIRGENES RD, CALB, 91302	558 - H7
YERBA BUENA ELEM	5844 LARBOARD LN, AGRH, 91301	557 - G4

SHOPPING CENTERS

FEATURE NAME	Address City, ZIP Code	PAGE-GRID
CAMARILLO PREMIUM OUTLETS	740 E VENTURA BLVD, CMRL, 93010	524 - C3
CENTERPOINT MALL	2655 SAVIERS RD, OXN, 93033	552 - G2
ESPLANADE, THE	195 ESPLANADE DR, OXN, 93036	492 - G7
FALLBROOK MALL	6633 FALLBROOK AV, CanP, 91307	529 - G6
JANSS MARKETPLACE	275 N MOORPARK RD, THO, 91360	526 - E7
LINCOLN OAKS VILLAGE	W HILLCREST DR & WILBUR RD, THO, 91360	556 - E1
OAKS, THE	222 W HILLCREST DR, THO, 91360	526 - D7
PACIFIC VIEW MALL	3301 E MAIN ST, VEN, 93003	491 - H4
SHOPPING AT THE ROSE	ROSE AVE & VENTURA FRWY, OXN, 93036	522 - J3
SIMI VALLEY TOWN CTR	1555 SIMI TOWN CENTER WY, SIMI, 93065	497 - J1
SYCAMORE SQUARE	2845 COCHRAN ST, SIMI, 93065	498 - C1
TELEPHONE ROAD PLAZA	TELEPHONE RD & VALENTINE RD, VEN, 93003	492 - A4

TRANSPORTATION

FEATURE NAME	PAGE-GRID
AMTRAK/METROLINK STA, SIMI	498 - H2
AMTRAK STA-VENTURA, VEN	491 - B2
GREYHOUND BUS TERMINAL, OXN	522 - G6
GREYHOUND STA-VENTURA, VEN	491 - C2
METROLINK CAMARILLO STA, CMRL	524 - F3
METROLINK MONTALVO STA, VEN	492 - D6
METROLINK-MOORPARK STA, MRPK	496 - F1
METROLINK OXNARD STA, OXN	522 - G6

VISITOR INFORMATION

FEATURE NAME	Address City, ZIP Code	PAGE-GRID
SANTA MONICA MTNS NRA PK VISTOR CTR	401 W HILLCREST DR, THO, 91360	526 - E7
VENTURA VISITORS BUREAU	89 S CALIFORNIA ST, VEN, 93001	491 - C2

CUT ALONG DOTTED LINE

The Thomas Guide®

Thank you for purchasing this Rand McNally Thomas Guide! We value your comments and suggestions.

Please help us serve you better by completing this postage-paid reply card.
This information is for internal use ONLY and will not be distributed or sold to any external third party.

Missing pages? Maybe not... Please refer to the "Using Your Street Guide" page for further explanation.

Thomas Guide Title: Ventura County **MKT: LAO**

Today's Date: ____________ Gender: ☐M ☐F Age Group: ☐18-24 ☐25-31 ☐32-40 ☐41-50 ☐51-64 ☐65+

1. What type of industry do you work in?
   ☐Real Estate ☐Trucking ☐Delivery ☐Construction ☐Utilities ☐Government
   ☐Retail ☐Sales ☐Transportation ☐Landscape ☐Service & Repair
   ☐Courier ☐Automotive ☐Insurance ☐Medical ☐Police/Fire/First Response
   ☐Other, please specify: ____________
2. What type of job do you have in this industry? ____________
3. Where did you purchase this Thomas Guide? (store name & city) ____________
4. Why did you purchase this Thomas Guide? ____________
5. How often do you purchase an updated Thomas Guide? ☐Annually ☐2 yrs. ☐3-5 yrs. ☐Other: ____________
6. Where do you use it? ☐Primarily in the car ☐Primarily in the office ☐Primarily at home ☐Other: ____________
7. How do you use it? ☐Exclusively for business ☐Primarily for business but also for personal or leisure use
   ☐Both work and personal evenly ☐Primarily for personal use ☐Exclusively for personal use
8. What do you use your Thomas Guide for?
   ☐Find Addresses ☐In-route navigation ☐Planning routes ☐Other: ____________
   Find points of interest: ☐Schools ☐Parks ☐Buildings ☐Shopping Centers ☐Other: ____________
9. How often do you use it? ☐Daily ☐Weekly ☐Monthly ☐Other: ____________
10. Do you use the internet for maps and/or directions? ☐Yes ☐No
11. How often do you use the internet for directions? ☐Daily ☐Weekly ☐Monthly ☐Other: ____________
12. Do you use any of the following mapping products in addition to your Thomas Guide?
    ☐Folded paper maps ☐Folded laminated maps ☐Wall maps ☐GPS ☐PDA ☐In-car navigation ☐Phone maps
13. What features, if any, would you like to see added to your Thomas Guide? ____________
14. What features or information do you find most useful in your Rand McNally Thomas Guide? (please specify) ____________
15. Please provide any additional comments or suggestions you have. ____________

We strive to provide you with the most current updated information available if you know of a map correction, please notify us here.

Where is the correction? Map Page #: ______ Grid #: ______ Index Page #: ______

Nature of the correction: ☐Street name missing ☐Street name misspelled ☐Street information incorrect
☐Incorrect location for point of interest ☐Index error ☐Other: ____________

Detail: ____________

I would like to receive information about updated editions and special offers from Rand McNally
☐via e-mail E-mail address: ____________
☐via postal mail
Your Name: ____________ Company (if used for work): ____________
Address: ____________ City/State/ZIP: ____________

Thank you for your time and help. We are working to serve you better.
This information is for internal use ONLY and will not be distributed or sold to any external third party.

CUT ALONG DOTTED LINE

TG-noCD.06

TAPE SHUT

TAPE SHUT

get directions at

randmcnally.com

CUT ALONG DOTTED LINE

2ND FOLD LINE

NO POSTAGE
NECESSARY
IF MAILED
IN THE
UNITED STATES

BUSINESS REPLY MAIL

FIRST-CLASS MAIL   PERMIT NO. 388   CHICAGO IL

POSTAGE WILL BE PAID BY ADDRESSEE

RAND MCNALLY
CONSUMER AFFAIRS
PO BOX 7600
CHICAGO IL 60680-9915

1ST FOLD LINE

RAND McNALLY

The most trusted name on the map.

You'll never need to ask for directions again with these Rand McNally products!

- EasyFinder® Laminated Maps
- Folded Maps
- Street Guides
- Wall Maps
- CustomView Wall Maps
- Road Atlases
- Motor Carriers' Road Atlases

CUT ALONG DOTTED LINE

SGTG_07